CODE OF FEDERAL REGULATIONS

Title 9
Animals and Animal Products

Parts 1 to 199

Revised as of January 1, 2018

Containing a codification of documents
of general applicability and future effect

As of January 1, 2018

Published by the Office of the Federal Register
National Archives and Records Administration
as a Special Edition of the Federal Register

Table of Contents

Cite this Code: CFR

To cite the regulations in this volume use title, part and section number. Thus, 9 CFR 1.1 *refers to title 9, part 1, section 1.*

Explanation

The Code of Federal Regulations is a codification of the general and permanent rules published in the Federal Register by the Executive departments and agencies of the Federal Government. The Code is divided into 50 titles which represent broad areas subject to Federal regulation. Each title is divided into chapters which usually bear the name of the issuing agency. Each chapter is further subdivided into parts covering specific regulatory areas.

Each volume of the Code is revised at least once each calendar year and issued on a quarterly basis approximately as follows:

Title 1 through Title 16 .... as of January 1
Title 17 through Title 27 .... as of April 1
Title 28 through Title 41 .... as of July 1
Title 42 through Title 50 .... as of October 1

The appropriate revision date is printed on the cover of each volume.

LEGAL STATUS

The contents of the Federal Register are required to be judicially noticed (44 U.S.C. 1507). The Code of Federal Regulations is prima facie evidence of the text of the original documents (44 U.S.C. 1510).

HOW TO USE THE CODE OF FEDERAL REGULATIONS

The Code of Federal Regulations is kept up to date by the individual issues of the Federal Register. These two publications must be used together to determine the latest version of any given rule.

To determine whether a Code volume has been amended since its revision date (in this case, January 1, 2018), consult the "List of CFR Sections Affected (LSA)," which is issued monthly, and the "Cumulative List of Parts Affected," which appears in the Reader Aids section of the daily Federal Register. These two lists will identify the Federal Register page number of the latest amendment of any given rule.

EFFECTIVE AND EXPIRATION DATES

Each volume of the Code contains amendments published in the Federal Register since the last revision of that volume of the Code. Source citations for the regulations are referred to by volume number and page number of the Federal Register and date of publication. Publication dates and effective dates are usually not the same and care must be exercised by the user in determining the actual effective date. In instances where the effective date is beyond the cut-off date for the Code a note has been inserted to reflect the future effective date. In those instances where a regulation published in the Federal Register states a date certain for expiration, an appropriate note will be inserted following the text.

OMB CONTROL NUMBERS

The Paperwork Reduction Act of 1980 (Pub. L. 96–511) requires Federal agencies to display an OMB control number with their information collection request.

Many agencies have begun publishing numerous OMB control numbers as amendments to existing regulations in the CFR. These OMB numbers are placed as close as possible to the applicable recordkeeping or reporting requirements.

PAST PROVISIONS OF THE CODE

Provisions of the Code that are no longer in force and effect as of the revision date stated on the cover of each volume are not carried. Code users may find the text of provisions in effect on any given date in the past by using the appropriate List of CFR Sections Affected (LSA). For the convenience of the reader, a "List of CFR Sections Affected" is published at the end of each CFR volume. For changes to the Code prior to the LSA listings at the end of the volume, consult previous annual editions of the LSA. For changes to the Code prior to 2001, consult the List of CFR Sections Affected compilations, published for 1949-1963, 1964-1972, 1973-1985, and 1986-2000.

"[RESERVED]" TERMINOLOGY

The term "[Reserved]" is used as a place holder within the Code of Federal Regulations. An agency may add regulatory information at a "[Reserved]" location at any time. Occasionally "[Reserved]" is used editorially to indicate that a portion of the CFR was left vacant and not accidentally dropped due to a printing or computer error.

INCORPORATION BY REFERENCE

What is incorporation by reference? Incorporation by reference was established by statute and allows Federal agencies to meet the requirement to publish regulations in the Federal Register by referring to materials already published elsewhere. For an incorporation to be valid, the Director of the Federal Register must approve it. The legal effect of incorporation by reference is that the material is treated as if it were published in full in the Federal Register (5 U.S.C. 552(a)). This material, like any other properly issued regulation, has the force of law.

What is a proper incorporation by reference? The Director of the Federal Register will approve an incorporation by reference only when the requirements of 1 CFR part 51 are met. Some of the elements on which approval is based are:

(a) The incorporation will substantially reduce the volume of material published in the Federal Register.

(b) The matter incorporated is in fact available to the extent necessary to afford fairness and uniformity in the administrative process.

(c) The incorporating document is drafted and submitted for publication in accordance with 1 CFR part 51.

What if the material incorporated by reference cannot be found? If you have any problem locating or obtaining a copy of material listed as an approved incorporation by reference, please contact the agency that issued the regulation containing that incorporation. If, after contacting the agency, you find the material is not available, please notify the Director of the Federal Register, National Archives and Records Administration, 8601 Adelphi Road, College Park, MD 20740-6001, or call 202-741-6010.

CFR INDEXES AND TABULAR GUIDES

A subject index to the Code of Federal Regulations is contained in a separate volume, revised annually as of January 1, entitled CFR INDEX AND FINDING AIDS. This volume contains the Parallel Table of Authorities and Rules. A list of CFR titles, chapters, subchapters, and parts and an alphabetical list of agencies publishing in the CFR are also included in this volume.

An index to the text of "Title 3—The President" is carried within that volume.

The Federal Register Index is issued monthly in cumulative form. This index is based on a consolidation of the "Contents" entries in the daily Federal Register.

A List of CFR Sections Affected (LSA) is published monthly, keyed to the revision dates of the 50 CFR titles.

REPUBLICATION OF MATERIAL

There are no restrictions on the republication of material appearing in the Code of Federal Regulations.

INQUIRIES

For a legal interpretation or explanation of any regulation in this volume, contact the issuing agency. The issuing agency's name appears at the top of odd-numbered pages.

For inquiries concerning CFR reference assistance, call 202–741–6000 or write to the Director, Office of the Federal Register, National Archives and Records Administration, 8601 Adelphi Road, College Park, MD 20740-6001 or e-mail *fedreg.info@nara.gov.*

SALES

The Government Publishing Office (GPO) processes all sales and distribution of the CFR. For payment by credit card, call toll-free, 866-512-1800, or DC area, 202-512-1800, M-F 8 a.m. to 4 p.m. e.s.t. or fax your order to 202-512-2104, 24 hours a day. For payment by check, write to: US Government Publishing Office – New Orders, P.O. Box 979050, St. Louis, MO 63197-9000.

ELECTRONIC SERVICES

The full text of the Code of Federal Regulations, the LSA (List of CFR Sections Affected), The United States Government Manual, the Federal Register, Public Laws, Public Papers of the Presidents of the United States, Compilation of Presidential Documents and the Privacy Act Compilation are available in electronic format via *www.ofr.gov.* For more information, contact the GPO Customer Contact Center, U.S. Government Publishing Office. Phone 202-512-1800, or 866-512-1800 (toll-free). E-mail, *ContactCenter@gpo.gov.*

The Office of the Federal Register also offers a free service on the National Archives and Records Administration's (NARA) World Wide Web site for public law numbers, Federal Register finding aids, and related information. Connect to NARA's web site at *www.archives.gov/federal-register.*

The e-CFR is a regularly updated, unofficial editorial compilation of CFR material and Federal Register amendments, produced by the Office of the Federal Register and the Government Publishing Office. It is available at *www.ecfr.gov.*

OLIVER A. POTTS,
Director,
Office of the Federal Register
January 1, 2018

THIS TITLE

Title 9—ANIMALS AND ANIMAL PRODUCTS is composed of two volumes. The first volume contains chapter I—Animal and Plant Health Inspection Service, Department of Agriculture (parts 1–199). The second volume contains chapter II—Packers and Stockyards Administration, Department of Agriculture and chapter III—Food Safety and Inspection Service, Department of Agriculture (part 200–End). The contents of these volumes represent all current regulations codified under this title of the CFR as of January 1, 2018.

For this volume, Gabrielle E. Burns was Chief Editor. The Code of Federal Regulations publication program is under the direction of John Hyrum Martinez, assisted by Stephen J. Frattini.

Title 9—Animals and Animal Products

(This book contains parts 1 to 199)

EDITORIAL NOTE: Other regulations issued by the Department of Agriculture appear in title 7, title 36, chapter II, and title 41, chapter 4.

CHAPTER I—ANIMAL AND PLANT HEALTH INSPECTION SERVICE, DEPARTMENT OF AGRICULTURE

SUBCHAPTER A—ANIMAL WELFARE

SUBCHAPTER B—COOPERATIVE CONTROL AND ERADICATION OF LIVESTOCK OR POULTRY DISEASES

SUBCHAPTER C—INTERSTATE TRANSPORTATION OF ANIMALS (INCLUDING POULTRY) AND ANIMAL PRODUCTS

SUBCHAPTER A—ANIMAL WELFARE

PART 1—DEFINITION OF TERMS

AUTHORITY: 7 U.S.C. 2131–2159; 7 CFR 2.22, 2.80, and 371.7.

§ 1.1 Definitions.

For the purposes of this subchapter, unless the context otherwise requires, the following terms shall have the meanings assigned to them in this section. The singular form shall also signify the plural and the masculine form shall also signify the feminine. Words undefined in the following paragraphs shall have the meaning attributed to them in general usage as reflected by definitions in a standard dictionary.

AC Regional Director means a veterinarian or his designee, employed by APHIS, who is assigned by the Administrator to supervise and perform the official work of APHIS in a given State or States. As used in part 2 of this subchapter, the AC Regional Director shall be deemed to be the person in charge of the official work of APHIS in the State in which the dealer, exhibitor, research facility, intermediate handler, carrier, or operator of an auction sale has his principal place of business.

Act means the Act of August 24, 1966 (Pub. L. 89–544), (commonly known as the Laboratory Animal Welfare Act), as amended by the Act of December 24, 1970 (Pub. L. 91–579), (the Animal Welfare Act of 1970), the Act of April 22, 1976 (Pub. L. 94–279), (the Animal Welfare Act of 1976), and the Act of December 23, 1985 (Pub. L. 99–198), (the Food Security Act of 1985), and as it may be subsequently amended.

Activity means, for purposes of part 2, subpart C of this subchapter, those elements of research, testing, or teaching procedures that involve the care and use of animals.

Administrative unit means the organizational or management unit at the departmental level of a research facility.

Administrator. The Administrator, Animal and Plant Health Inspection Service, or any person authorized to act for the Administrator.

Ambient temperature means the air temperature surrounding the animal.

Animal means any live or dead dog, cat, nonhuman primate, guinea pig, hamster, rabbit, or any other warm-blooded animal, which is being used, or is intended for use for research, teaching, testing, experimentation, or exhibition purposes, or as a pet. This term excludes birds, rats of the genus *Rattus*, and mice of the genus *Mus*, bred for use in research; horses not used for research purposes; and other farm animals, such as, but not limited to, livestock or poultry used or intended for use as food or fiber, or livestock or poultry used or intended for use for improving animal nutrition, breeding, management, or production efficiency, or for improving the quality of food or fiber. With respect to a dog, the term means all dogs, including those used for hunting, security, or breeding purposes.

Animal act means any performance of animals where such animals are trained to perform some behavior or action or are part of a show, performance, or exhibition.

APHIS official means any person employed by the Department who is authorized to perform a function under the Act and the regulations in 9 CFR parts 1, 2, and 3.

Attending veterinarian means a person who has graduated from a veterinary school accredited by the American Veterinary Medical Association's Council on Education, or has a certificate issued by the American Veterinary Medical Association's Education Commission for Foreign Veterinary Graduates, or has received equivalent formal education as determined by the Administrator; has received training and/or experience in the care and management of the species being attended; and who has direct or delegated authority for activities involving animals at a facility subject to the jurisdiction of the Secretary.

Buffer area means that area in a primary enclosure for a swim-with-the-dolphin program that is off-limits to members of the public and that directly abuts the interactive area.

Business hours means a reasonable number of hours between 7 a.m. and 7 p.m., Monday through Friday, except for legal Federal holidays, each week of the year, during which inspections by APHIS may be made.

Business year means the 12-month period during which business is conducted, and may be either on a calendar or fiscal-year basis.

Carrier means the operator of any airline, railroad, motor carrier, shipping line, or other enterprise which is engaged in the business of transporting any animals for hire.

Cat means any live or dead cat (Felis catus) or any cat-hybrid cross.

Class "A" licensee (breeder) means a person subject to the licensing requirements under part 2 and meeting the definition of a "dealer" (§ 1.1), and whose business involving animals consists only of animals that are bred and raised on the premises in a closed or stable colony and those animals acquired for the sole purpose of maintaining or enhancing the breeding colony.

Class "B" licensee means a person subject to the licensing requirements under part 2 and meeting the definition of a "dealer" (§ 1.1), and whose business includes the purchase and/or resale of any animal. This term includes brokers, and operators of an auction sale, as such individuals negotiate or arrange for the purchase, sale, or transport of animals in commerce. Such individuals do not usually take actual physical possession or control of the animals, and do not usually hold animals in any facilities. A class "B" licensee may also exhibit animals as a minor part of the business.

Class "C" licensee (exhibitor) means a person subject to the licensing requirements under part 2 and meeting the definition of an "exhibitor" (§ 1.1), and whose business involves the showing or displaying of animals to the public. A class "C" licensee may buy and sell animals as a minor part of the business in order to maintain or add to his animal collection.

Commerce means trade, traffic, transportation, or other commerce:

(1) Between a place in a State and any place outside of such State, including any foreign country, or between points within the same State but through any place outside thereof, or within any territory, possession, or the District of Columbia; or

(2) Which affects the commerce described in this part.

Committee means the Institutional Animal Care and Use Committee (IACUC) established under section 13(b) of the Act. It shall consist of at least three (3) members, one of whom is the attending veterinarian of the research facility and one of whom is not affiliated in any way with the facility other than as a member of the committee, however, if the research facility has more than one Doctor of Veterinary Medicine (DVM), another DVM with delegated program responsibility may serve. The research facility shall establish the Committee for the purpose of evaluating the care, treatment, housing, and use of animals, and for certifying compliance with the Act by the research facility.

Dealer means any person who, in commerce, for compensation or profit, delivers for transportation, or transports, except as a carrier, buys, or sells, or negotiates the purchase or sale of: Any dog or other animal whether alive or dead (including unborn animals, organs, limbs, blood, serum, or other parts) for research, teaching, testing, experimentation, exhibition, or for use as a pet; or any dog at the wholesale level for hunting, security, or breeding purposes. This term does not include: A retail pet store, as defined in this section; any retail outlet where dogs are sold for hunting, breeding, or security purposes; or any person who does not sell or negotiate the purchase or sale of any wild or exotic animal, dog, or cat and who derives no more than $500 gross income from the sale of animals other than wild or exotic animals, dogs, or cats during any calendar year.

Department means the U.S. Department of Agriculture.

Deputy Administrator means the Deputy Administrator for Animal Care (AC) or any other official of AC to whom authority has been delegated to act in his stead.

Dog means any live or dead dog (*Canis familiaris*) or any dog-hybrid cross.

Dwarf hamster means any species of hamster such as the Chinese and Armenian species whose adult body size is substantially less than that attained by the Syrian or Golden species of hamsters.

Endangered species means those species defined in the Endangered Species Act (16 U.S.C. 1531 *et seq.*) and as it may be subsequently amended.

Euthanasia means the humane destruction of an animal accomplished by a method that produces rapid unconsciousness and subsequent death without evidence of pain or distress, or a method that utilizes anesthesia produced by an agent that causes painless loss of consciousness and subsequent death

Exhibitor means any person (public or private) exhibiting any animals, which were purchased in commerce or the intended distribution of which affects commerce, or will affect commerce, to the public for compensation, as determined by the Secretary. This term includes carnivals, circuses, animal acts, zoos, and educational exhibits, exhibiting such animals whether operated for profit or not. This term excludes retail pet stores, horse and dog races, organizations sponsoring and all persons participating in State and county fairs, livestock shows, rodeos, field trials, coursing events, purebred dog and cat shows and any other fairs or exhibitions intended to advance agricultural arts and sciences as may be determined by the Secretary.

Exotic animal means any animal not identified in the definition of "animal" provided in this part that is native to a foreign country or of foreign origin or character, is not native to the United States, or was introduced from abroad. This term specifically includes animals such as, but not limited to, lions, tigers, leopards, elephants, camels, antelope, anteaters, kangaroos, and water buffalo, and species of foreign domestic cattle, such as Ankole, Gayal, and Yak.

Farm animal means any domestic species of cattle, sheep, swine, goats, llamas, or horses, which are normally and have historically, been kept and raised on farms in the United States, and used or intended for use as food or fiber, or for improving animal nutrition, breeding, management, or production efficiency, or for improving the quality of food or fiber. This term also includes animals such as rabbits, mink, and chinchilla, when they are used solely for purposes of meat or fur, and animals such as horses and llamas when used solely as work and pack animals.

Federal agency means an Executive agency as such term is defined in section 105 of title 5, United States Code, and with respect to any research facility means the agency from which the research facility receives a Federal award for the conduct of research, experimentation, or testing involving the use of animals.

Federal award means any mechanism (including a grant, award, loan, contract, or cooperative agreement) under which Federal funds are used to support the conduct of research, experimentation, or testing, involving the use of animals. The permit system established under the authorities of the Endangered Species Act, the Marine Mammal Protection Act, and the Migratory Bird Treaty Act, are not considered to be Federal awards under the Animal Welfare Act.

Federal research facility means each department, agency, or instrumentality of the United States which uses live animals for research or experimentation.

Field study means a study conducted on free-living wild animals in their natural habitat. However, this term excludes any study that involves an invasive procedure, harms, or materially alters the behavior of an animal under study.

Handling means petting, feeding, watering, cleaning, manipulating, loading, crating, shifting, transferring, immobilizing, restraining, treating, training, working and moving, or any similar activity with respect to any animal.

Housing facility means any land, premises, shed, barn, building, trailer, or other structure or area housing or intended to house animals.

Hybrid cross means an animal resulting from the crossbreeding between two different species or types of animals. Crosses between wild animal species, such as lions and tigers, are considered to be wild animals. Crosses between wild animal species and domestic animals, such as dogs and wolves or buffalo and domestic cattle, are considered to be domestic animals.

Impervious surface means a surface that does not permit the absorption of fluids. Such surfaces are those that can be thoroughly and repeatedly cleaned and disinfected, will not retain odors, and from which fluids bead up and run off or can be removed without their being absorbed into the surface material.

Indoor housing facility means any structure or building with environmental controls housing or intended to house animals and meeting the following three requirements:

(1) It must be capable of controlling the temperature within the building or structure within the limits set forth for that species of animal, of maintaining humidity levels of 30 to 70 percent and of rapidly eliminating odors from within the building; and

(2) It must be an enclosure created by the continuous connection of a roof, floor, and walls (a shed or barn set on top of the ground does not have a continuous connection between the walls and the ground unless a foundation and floor are provided); and

(3) It must have at least one door for entry and exit that can be opened and closed (any windows or openings which provide natural light must be covered with a transparent material such as glass or hard plastic).

Interactive area means that area in a primary enclosure for a swim-with-the-dolphin program where an interactive session takes place.

Interactive session means a swim-with-the-dolphin program session where members of the public enter a primary enclosure to interact with cetaceans.

Intermediate handler means any person, including a department, agency, or instrumentality of the United States or of any State or local government (other than a dealer, research facility, exhibitor, any person excluded from the definition of a dealer, research facility, or exhibitor, an operator of an auction sale, or a carrier), who is engaged in any business in which he receives custody of animals in connection with their transportation in commerce.

Inspector means any person employed by the Department who is authorized to perform a function under the Act and the regulations in 9 CFR parts 1, 2, and 3.

Institutional official means the individual at a research facility who is authorized to legally commit on behalf of the research facility that the requirements of 9 CFR parts 1, 2, and 3 will be met.

Isolation in regard to marine mammals means the physical separation of animals to prevent contact and a separate, noncommon, water circulation and filtration system for the isolated animals.

Licensed veterinarian means a person who has graduated from an accredited school of veterinary medicine or has received equivalent formal education as determined by the Administrator, and who has a valid license to practice veterinary medicine in some State.

Licensee means any person licensed according to the provisions of the Act and the regulations in part 2 of this subchapter.

Major operative procedure means any surgical intervention that penetrates and exposes a body cavity or any procedure which produces permanent impairment of physical or physiological functions.

Minimum horizontal dimension (MHD) means the diameter of a circular pool of water, or in the case of a square, rectangle, oblong, or other shape pool, the diameter of the largest circle that can be inserted within the confines of such a pool of water.

Mobile or traveling housing facility means a transporting vehicle such as a truck, trailer, or railway car, used to house animals while traveling for exhibition or public education purposes.

Nonconditioned animals means animals which have not been subjected to special care and treatment for sufficient time to stabilize, and where necessary, to improve their health.

Nonhuman primate means any nonhuman member of the highest order of mammals including prosimians, monkeys, and apes.

Operator of an auction sale means any person who is engaged in operating an auction at which animals are purchased or sold in commerce.

Outdoor housing facility means any structure, building, land, or premise, housing or intended to house animals, which does not meet the definition of any other type of housing facility provided in the regulations, and in which temperatures cannot be controlled within set limits.

Painful procedure as applied to any animal means any procedure that would reasonably be expected to cause more than slight or momentary pain or distress in a human being to which that procedure was applied, that is, pain in excess of that caused by injections or other minor procedures.

Paralytic drug means a drug which causes partial or complete loss of muscle contraction and which has no anesthetic or analgesic properties, so that the animal cannot move, but is completely aware of its surroundings and can feel pain.

Person means any individual, partnership, firm, joint stock company, corporation, association, trust, estate, or other legal entity.

Pet animal means any animal that has commonly been kept as a pet in family households in the United States, such as dogs, cats, guinea pigs, rabbits, and hamsters. This term excludes exotic animals and wild animals.

Positive physical contact means petting, stroking, or other touching, which is beneficial to the well-being of the animal.

Pound or shelter means a facility that accepts and/or seizes animals for the purpose of caring for them, placing them through adoption, or carrying out law enforcement, whether or not the facility is operated for profit.

Primary conveyance means the main method of transportation used to convey an animal from origin to destination, such as a motor vehicle, plane, ship, or train.

Primary enclosure means any structure or device used to restrict an animal or animals to a limited amount of space, such as a room, pen, run, cage, compartment, pool, or hutch.

Principal investigator means an employee of a research facility, or other person associated with a research facility, responsible for a proposal to conduct research and for the design and implementation of research involving animals.

Quorum means a majority of the Committee members.

Random source means dogs and cats obtained from animal pounds or shelters, auction sales, or from any person who did not breed and raise them on his or her premises.

Registrant means any research facility, carrier, intermediate handler, or exhibitor not required to be licensed under section 3 of the Act, registered pursuant to the provisions of the Act and the regulations in part 2 of this subchapter.

Research facility means any school (except an elementary or secondary school), institution, organization, or person that uses or intends to use live animals in research, tests, or experiments, and that (1) purchases or transports live animals in commerce, or (2) receives funds under a grant, award, loan, or contract from a department, agency, or instrumentality of the United States for the purpose of carrying out research, tests, or experiments: *Provided*, That the Administrator may exempt, by regulation, any such school, institution, organization, or person that does not use or intend to use live dogs or cats, except those schools, institutions, organizations, or persons, which use substantial numbers (as determined by the Administrator) of live animals the principal function of which schools, institutions, organizations, or persons, is biomedical research or testing, when in the judgment of the Administrator, any such exemption does not vitiate the purpose of the Act.

Retail pet store means a place of business or residence at which the seller, buyer, and the animal available for sale are physically present so that every buyer may personally observe the animal prior to purchasing and/or taking custody of that animal after purchase, and where only the following animals are sold or offered for sale, at retail, for use as pets: Dogs, cats, rabbits, guinea pigs, hamsters, gerbils, rats, mice, gophers, chinchillas, domestic ferrets, domestic farm animals, birds, and coldblooded species. In addition to persons that meet these criteria, *retail pet store* also includes any person who meets the criteria in § 2.1(a)(3)(vii) of this subchapter. Such definition excludes—

(1) Establishments or persons who deal in dogs used for hunting, security, or breeding purposes;

(2) Establishments or persons, except those that meet the criteria in § 2.1(a)(3)(vii), exhibiting, selling, or offering to exhibit or sell any wild or exotic or other nonpet species of warmblooded animals (except birds), such as skunks, raccoons, nonhuman primates, squirrels, ocelots, foxes, coyotes, etc.;

(3) Any establishment or person selling warmblooded animals (except birds, and laboratory rats and mice) for research or exhibition purposes;

(4) Any establishment wholesaling any animals (except birds, rats, and mice); and

(5) Any establishment exhibiting pet animals in a room that is separate from or adjacent to the retail pet store, or in an outside area, or anywhere off the retail pet store premises.

Sanctuary area means that area in a primary enclosure for a swim-with-the-dolphin program that is off-limits to the public and that directly abuts the buffer area.

Sanitize means to make physically clean and to remove and destroy, to the maximum degree that is practical, agents injurious to health.

Secretary means the Secretary of Agriculture of the United States or his representative who shall be an employee of the Department.

Sheltered housing facility means a housing facility which provides the animals with shelter; protection from the elements; and protection from temperature extremes at all times. A sheltered housing facility may consist of runs or pens totally enclosed in a barn or building, or of connecting inside/outside runs or pens with the inside pens in a totally enclosed building.

Standards means the requirements with respect to the humane housing, exhibition, handling, care, treatment, temperature, and transportation of animals by dealers, exhibitors research facilities, carriers, intermediate handlers, and operators of auction sales as set forth in part 3 of this subchapter.

State means a State of the United States, the District of Columbia, Commonwealth of Puerto Rico, the Virgin Islands, Guam, American Samoa, or any other territory or possession of the United States.

Study area means any building room, area, enclosure, or other containment outside of a core facility or centrally designated or managed area in which animals are housed for more than 12 hours.

Swim-with-the-dolphin (SWTD) program means any human-cetacean interactive program in which a member of the public enters the primary enclosure in which an SWTD designated cetacean is housed to interact with the animal. This interaction includes, but such inclusions are not limited to, wading, swimming, snorkeling, or scuba diving in the enclosure. This interaction excludes, but such exclusions are not limited to, feeding and petting pools, and the participation of any member(s) of the public audience as a minor segment of an educational presentation or performance of a show.

Transporting device means an interim vehicle or device, other than man, used to transport an animal between the primary conveyance and the terminal facility or in and around the terminal facility of a carrier or intermediate handler.

Transporting vehicle means any truck, car, trailer, airplane, ship, or railroad car used for transporting animals.

Weaned means that an animal has become accustomed to take solid food and has so done, without nursing, for a period of at least 5 days.

Wild animal means any animal which is now or historically has been found in the wild, or in the wild state, within the boundaries of the United States, its territories, or possessions. This term includes, but is not limited to, animals such as: Deer, skunk, opossum, raccoon, mink, armadillo, coyote, squirrel, fox, wolf.

Wild state means living in its original, natural condition; not domesticated.

Zoo means any park, building, cage, enclosure, or other structure or premise in which a live animal or animals are kept for public exhibition or viewing, regardless of compensation.

[54 FR 36119, Aug. 31, 1989, as amended at 55 FR 12631, Apr. 5, 1990; 58 FR 39129, July 22, 1993; 62 FR 43275, Aug. 13, 1997; 63 FR 47148, Sept. 4, 1998; 63 FR 62926, Nov. 10, 1998; 65 FR 6314, Feb. 9, 2000; 68 FR 12285, Mar. 14, 2003; 69 FR 31514, June 4, 2004; 69 FR 42099, July 14, 2004; 78 FR 57249, Sept. 18, 2013]

EFFECTIVE DATE NOTE: At 64 FR 15920, Apr. 2, 1999, the definitions of *buffer area, interactive area, interactive session, sanctuary area,* and *swim-with-the-dolphin (SWTD) program* were suspended, effective Apr. 2, 1999.

PART 2—REGULATIONS

Subpart A—Licensing

Subpart B—Registration

Subpart C—Research Facilities

Subpart D—Attending Veterinarian and Adequate Veterinary Care

Subpart E—Identification of Animals

Subpart F—Stolen Animals

Subpart G—Records

Subpart H—Compliance With Standards and Holding Period

Subpart I—Miscellaneous

Subpart J—Importation of Live Dogs

AUTHORITY: 7 U.S.C. 2131–2159; 7 CFR 2.22, 2.80, and 371.7.

SOURCE: 54 FR 36147, Aug. 31, 1989, unless otherwise noted.

Subpart A—Licensing

§ 2.1 Requirements and application.

(a)(1) Any person operating or intending to operate as a dealer, exhibitor, or operator of an auction sale, except persons who are exempted from the licensing requirements under paragraph (a)(3) of this section, must have a valid license. A person must be 18 years of age or older to obtain a license. A person seeking a license shall apply on a form which will be furnished by the AC Regional Director in the State in which that person operates or intends to operate. The applicant shall provide the information requested on the application form, including a valid mailing address through which the licensee or applicant can be reached at all times, and a valid premises address where animals, animal facilities, equipment, and records may be inspected for compliance. The applicant shall file the completed application form with the AC Regional Director.

(2) If an applicant for a license or license renewal operates in more than one State, he or she shall apply in the State in which he or she has his or her principal place of business. All premises, facilities, or sites where such person operates or keeps animals shall be indicated on the application form or on a separate sheet attached to it. The completed application form, along with the application fee indicated in paragraph (c) of this section, and the annual license fee indicated in table 1 or 2 of § 2.6 shall be filed with the AC Regional Director.

(3) The following persons are exempt from the licensing requirements under section 2 or section 3 of the Act:

(i) Retail pet stores as defined in part 1 of this subchapter;

(ii) Any person who sells or negotiates the sale or purchase of any animal except wild or exotic animals, dogs, or cats, and who derives no more than $500 gross income from the sale of such animals during any calendar year and is not otherwise required to obtain a license;

(iii) Any person who maintains a total of four or fewer breeding female dogs, cats, and/or small exotic or wild mammals, such as hedgehogs, degus, spiny mice, prairie dogs, flying squirrels, and jerboas, and who sells, at wholesale, only the offspring of these dogs, cats, and/or small exotic or wild mammals, which were born and raised on his or her premises, for pets or exhibition, and is not otherwise required to obtain a license. This exemption does not extend to any person residing in a household that collectively maintains a total of more than four breeding female dogs, cats, and/or small exotic or wild mammals, regardless of ownership, nor to any person maintaining breeding female dogs, cats, and/or small exotic or wild mammals on premises on which more than four breeding female dogs, cats, and/or small exotic or wild mammals are maintained, nor to any person acting in concert with others where they collectively maintain a total of more than four breeding female dogs, cats, and/or small exotic or wild mammals regardless of ownership;

(iv) Any person who sells fewer than 25 dogs and/or cats per year, which were born and raised on his or her premises, for research, teaching, or testing purposes or to any research facility and is not otherwise required to obtain a license. This exemption does not extend to any person residing in a household that collectively sells 25 or more dogs and/or cats, regardless of ownership, nor to any person acting in concert with others where they collectively sell 25 or more dogs and/or cats, regardless of ownership. The sale of any dog or cat not born and raised on the premises for research purposes requires a license;

(v) Any person who arranges for transportation or transports animals solely for the purpose of breeding, exhibiting in purebred shows, boarding (not in association with commercial transportation), grooming, or medical treatment, and is not otherwise required to obtain a license;

(vi) Any person who buys, sells, transports, or negotiates the sale, purchase, or transportation of any animals used only for the purposes of food or fiber (including fur);

(vii) Any person including, but not limited to, purebred dog or cat fanciers, who maintains a total of four or fewer breeding female dogs, cats, and/or small exotic or wild mammals, such as hedgehogs, degus, spiny mice, prairie dogs, flying squirrels, and jerboas, and who sells, at retail, only the offspring of these dogs, cats, and/or small exotic or wild mammals, which were born and raised on his or her premises, for pets or exhibition, and is not otherwise required to obtain a license. This exemption does not extend to any person residing in a household that collectively maintains a total of more than four breeding female dogs, cats, and/or small exotic or wild mammals, regardless of ownership, nor to any person maintaining breeding female dogs, cats, and/or small exotic or wild mammals on premises on which more than four breeding female dogs, cats, and/or small exotic or wild mammals are maintained, nor to any person acting in concert with others where they collectively maintain a total of more than four breeding female dogs, cats, and/or small exotic or wild mammals regardless of ownership.

(viii) Any person who buys animals solely for his or her own use or enjoyment and does not sell or exhibit animals, or is not otherwise required to obtain a license;

(b) No person shall have more than one license.

(c) A license will be issued to any applicant, except as provided in §§ 2.10 and 2.11, when:

(1) The applicant has met the requirements of this section and §§ 2.2 and 2.3; and

(2) The applicant has paid the application fee of $10 and the annual license fee indicated in § 2.6 to the appropriate Animal Care regional office for an initial license, and, in the case of a license renewal, the annual license fee has been received by the appropriate Animal Care regional office on or before the expiration date of the license.

(d)(1) A licensee who wishes a renewal must submit to the appropriate Animal Care regional office a completed application form and the annual license fee indicated in § 2.6 by certified check, cashier's check, personal check, money order, or credit card. The application form and the annual license fee must be received by the appropriate Animal Care regional office on or before the expiration date of the license. An applicant whose check is returned by the bank will be charged a fee of $20 for each returned check. A returned check will be deemed nonpayment of fee and will result in the denial of the license. If an applicant's check is returned, subsequent fees must be paid by certified check, cashier's check, or money order.

(2) A license fee indicated in § 2.6 must also be paid if an applicant is applying for a changed class of license. The applicant may pay the fee by certified check, cashier's check, personal check, money order, or credit card. An applicant whose check is returned by a bank will be charged a fee of $20 for each returned check. If an applicant's check is returned, subsequent fees must be paid by certified check, cashier's check, or money order.

(e) The failure of any person to comply with any provision of the Act, or any of the provisions of the regulations or standards in this subchapter, shall constitute grounds for denial of a license; or for its suspension or revocation by the Secretary, as provided in the Act.

(Approved by the Office of Management and Budget under control numbers 0579–0254 and 0579–0392)

[54 FR 36147, Aug. 31, 1989, as amended at 63 FR 62926, Nov. 10, 1998; 69 FR 42099, July 14, 2004; 78 FR 57249, Sept. 18, 2013]

§ 2.2 Acknowledgement of regulations and standards.

(a) *Application for initial license.* APHIS will supply a copy of the applicable regulations and standards to the applicant with each request for a license application. The applicant shall acknowledge receipt of the regulations and standards and agree to comply with them by signing the application form before a license will be issued.

(b) *Application for license renewal.* APHIS will renew a license after the applicant certifies by signing the application form that, to the best of the applicant's knowledge and belief, he or she is in compliance with the regulations and standards and agrees to continue to comply with the regulations and standards. APHIS will supply a copy of the applicable regulations and standards to the applicant upon request.

(Approved by the Office of Management and Budget under control number 0579–0254)

[60 FR 13895, Mar. 15, 1995, as amended at 69 FR 42100, July 14, 2004]

§ 2.3 Demonstration of compliance with standards and regulations.

(a) Each applicant must demonstrate that his or her premises and any animals, facilities, vehicles, equipment, or other premises used or intended for use in the business comply with the regulations and standards set forth in parts 2 and 3 of this subchapter. Each applicant for an initial license or license renewal must make his or her animals, premises, facilities, vehicles, equipment, other premises, and records available for inspection during business hours and at other times mutually agreeable to the applicant and APHIS, to ascertain the applicant's compliance with the standards and regulations.

(b) Each applicant for an initial license must be inspected by APHIS and demonstrate compliance with the regulations and standards, as required in paragraph (a) of this section, before APHIS will issue a license. If the first inspection reveals that the applicant's animals, premises, facilities, vehicles, equipment, other premises, or records do not meet the requirements of this subchapter, APHIS will advise the applicant of existing deficiencies and the corrective measures that must be completed to come into compliance with the regulations and standards. An applicant who fails the first inspection will have two additional chances to demonstrate his or her compliance with the regulations and standards through a second inspection by APHIS. The applicant must request the second inspection, and if applicable, the third inspection, within 90 days following the first inspection. If the applicant fails inspection or fails to request reinspections within the 90-day period, he or she will forfeit the application fee and cannot reapply for a license for a period of 6 months from the date of the failed third inspection or the expiration of the time to request a third inspection. Issuance of a license will be denied until the applicant demonstrates upon inspection that the animals, premises, facilities, vehicles, equipment, other premises, and records are in compliance with all regulations and standards in this subchapter.

(Approved by the Office of Management and Budget under control number 0579–0254)

[54 FR 36147, Aug. 31, 1989, as amended at 69 FR 42100, July 14, 2004]

§ 2.4 Non-interference with APHIS officials.

A licensee or applicant for an initial license shall not interfere with, threaten, abuse (including verbally abuse), or harass any APHIS official in the course of carrying out his or her duties.

§ 2.5 Duration of license and termination of license.

(a) A license issued under this part shall be valid and effective unless:

(1) The license has been revoked or suspended pursuant to section 19 of the Act.

(2) The license is voluntarily terminated upon request of the licensee, in writing, to the AC Regional Director.

(3) The license has expired or been terminated under this part.

(4) The annual license fee has not been paid to the appropriate Animal Care regional office as required. There will not be a refund of the annual license fee if a license is terminated prior to its expiration date.

(b) Any person who is licensed must file an application for a license renewal and an annual report form (APHIS Form 7003), as required by § 2.7 of this part, and pay the required annual license fee. The required annual license fee must be received in the appropriate Animal Care regional office on or before the expiration date of the license or the license will expire and automatically terminate. Failure to comply with the annual reporting requirements or pay the required annual license fee on or before the expiration date of the license will result in automatic termination of the license.

(c) Any person who seeks the reinstatement of a license that has been automatically terminated must follow the procedure applicable to new applicants for a license set forth in § 2.1.

(d) Licenses are issued to specific persons for specific premises and do not transfer upon change of ownership, nor are they valid at a different location.

(e) A license which is invalid under this part shall be surrendered to the AC Regional Director. If the license cannot be found, the licensee shall provide a written statement so stating to the AC Regional Director.

[54 FR 36147, Aug. 31, 1989, as amended at 60 FR 13895, Mar. 15, 1995; 63 FR 62926, Nov. 10, 1998; 69 FR 42100, July 14, 2004]

§2.6 Annual license fees.

(a) For an initial license, the applicant must submit a $10 application fee in addition to the initial license fee prescribed in this section. Licensees applying for license renewal or changed class of license must submit only the license fee prescribed in this section. The license fee for an initial license, license renewal, or changed class of license is determined from table 1 or 2 in paragraph (c) of this section. Paragraph (b) of this section indicates the method used to calculate the license fee. All initial license and changed class of license fees must be submitted to the appropriate Animal Care regional office, and, in the case of license renewals, all fees must be received by the appropriate Animal Care regional office on or before the expiration date of the license.

(b)(1) Class "A" license. The annual license renewal fee for a Class "A" dealer shall be based on 50 percent of the total gross amount, expressed in dollars, derived from the sale of animals to research facilities, dealers, exhibitors, retail pet stores, and persons for use as pets, directly or through an auction sale, by the dealer or applicant during his or her preceding business year (calendar or fiscal) in the case of a person who operated during such a year. If animals are leased, the lessor shall pay a fee based on 50 percent of any compensation received from the leased animals and the lessee shall pay a fee based upon the net compensation received from the leased animals, as indicated for dealers in Table 1 in paragraph (c) of this section.

(2) Class "B" license. The annual license renewal fee for a Class "B" dealer shall be established by calculating the total amount received from the sale of animals to research facilities, dealers, exhibitors, retail pet stores, and persons for use as pets, directly or through an auction sale, during the preceding business year (calendar or fiscal) less the amount paid for the animals by the dealer or applicant. This net difference, exclusive of other costs, shall be the figure used to determine the license fee of a Class "B" dealer. If animals are leased, the lessor and lessee shall each pay a fee based on the net compensation received from the leased animals calculated from Table 1 in paragraph (c) of this section.

(3) The annual license renewal fee for a broker or operator of an auction sale shall be that of a class "B" dealer and shall be based on the total gross amount, expressed in dollars, derived from commissions or fees charged for the sale of animals, or for negotiating the sale of animals, by brokers or by the operator of an auction sale, to research facilities, dealers, exhibitors, retail pet stores, and persons for use as pets, during the preceding business year (calendar or fiscal).

(4) In the case of a new applicant for a license as a dealer, broker or operator of an auction sale who did not operate during a preceding business year, the annual license fee will be based on the anticipated yearly dollar amount of business, as provided in paragraphs (b)(1), (2), and (3) of this section, derived from the sale of animals to research facilities, dealers, exhibitors, retail pet stores, and persons for use as pets, directly or through an auction sale.

(5) The amount of the annual fee to be paid upon application for a class "C" license as an exhibitor under this section shall be based on the number of animals which the exhibitor owned, held, or exhibited at the time the application is signed and dated or during the previous year, whichever is greater, and will be the amount listed in Table 2 in paragraph (c) of this section. Animals which are leased shall be included in the number of animals being held by both the lessor and the lessee when calculating the annual fee. An exhibitor shall pay his or her annual license fee on or before the expiration date of the license and the fee shall be based on

the number of animals which the exhibitor is holding or has held during the year (both owned and leased).

(c) The license fee shall be computed in accordance with the following tables:

TABLE 1—DEALERS, BROKERS, AND OPERATORS OF AN AUCTION SALE—CLASS "A" AND "B" LICENSE

Over	But not over	Initial license fee	Annual or changed class of license fee
$0	$500	$30	$40
500	2,000	60	70
2,000	10,000	120	130
10,000	25,000	225	235
25,000	50,000	350	360
50,000	100,000	475	485
100,000		750	760

TABLE 2—EXHIBITORS—CLASS "C" LICENSE

Number of animals	Initial license fee	Annual or changed class of license fee
1 to 5	$30	$40
6 to 25	75	85
26 to 50	175	185
51 to 500	225	235
501 and up	300	310

(d) If a person meets the licensing requirements for more than one class of license, he shall be required to obtain a license and pay the fee for the type business which is predominant for his operation, as determined by the Secretary.

(e) In any situation in which a licensee shall have demonstrated in writing to the satisfaction of the Secretary that he or she has good reason to believe that the dollar amount of his or her business for the forthcoming business year will be less than the previous business year, then his or her estimated dollar amount of business shall be used for computing the license fee for the forthcoming business year: *Provided, however*, That if the dollar amount upon which the license fee is based for that year does in fact exceed the amount estimated, the difference in amount of the fee paid and that which was due under paragraphs (b) and (c) of this section based upon the actual dollar business upon which the license fee is based, shall be payable in addition to the required annual license fee for the next subsequent year, on the anniversary date of his or her license as prescribed in this section.

[54 FR 36147, Aug. 31, 1989, as amended at 63 FR 62926, Nov. 10, 1998; 69 FR 42101, July 14, 2004]

§ 2.7 Annual report by licensees.

(a) Each year, within 30 days prior to the expiration date of his or her license, a licensee shall file with the AC Regional Director an application for license renewal and annual report upon a form which the AC Regional Director will furnish to him or her upon request.

(b) A person licensed as a dealer shall set forth in his or her license renewal application and annual report the dollar amount of business, from the sale of animals, upon which the license fee is based, directly or through an auction sale, to research facilities, dealers, exhibitors, retail pet stores, and persons for use as pets, by the licensee during the preceding business year (calendar or fiscal), and any other information as may be required thereon.

(c) A licensed dealer who operates as a broker or an operator of an auction sale shall set forth in his or her license renewal application and annual report the total gross amount, expressed in dollars, derived from commissions or fees charged for the sale of animals by the licensee to research facilities, dealers, exhibitors, retail pet stores, and persons for use as pets, during the preceding business year (calendar or fiscal), and any other information as may be required thereon.

(d) A person licensed as an exhibitor shall set forth in his or her license renewal application and annual report the number of animals owned, held, or exhibited by him or her, including those which are leased, during the previous year or at the time he signs and dates the report, whichever is greater.

[54 FR 36147, Aug. 31, 1989, as amended at 63 FR 62926, Nov. 10, 1998]

§ 2.8 Notification of change of name, address, control, or ownership of business.

A licensee shall promptly notify the AC Regional Director by certified mail of any change in the name, address, management, or substantial control or ownership of his business or operation, or of any additional sites, within 10 days of any change.

[54 FR 36147, Aug. 31, 1989, as amended at 63 FR 62926, Nov. 10, 1998]

§2.9 Officers, agents, and employees of licensees whose licenses have been suspended or revoked.

Any person who has been or is an officer, agent, or employee of a licensee whose license has been suspended or revoked and who was responsible for or participated in the violation upon which the order of suspension or revocation was based will not be licensed within the period during which the order of suspension or revocation is in effect.

§2.10 Licensees whose licenses have been suspended or revoked.

(a) Any person whose license has been suspended for any reason shall not be licensed in his or her own name or in any other manner within the period during which the order of suspension is in effect. No partnership, firm, corporation, or other legal entity in which any such person has a substantial interest, financial or otherwise, will be licensed during that period. Any person whose license has been suspended for any reason may apply to the AC Regional Director, in writing, for reinstatement of his or her license. No license will be renewed during the period that it is suspended. Renewal of the license may be initiated during the suspension in accordance with §§2.2(b) and 2.12.

(b) Any person whose license has been revoked shall not be licensed in his or her own name or in any other manner; nor will any partnership, firm, corporation, or other legal entity in which any such person has a substantial interest, financial or otherwise, be licensed.

(c) Any person whose license has been suspended or revoked shall not buy, sell, transport, exhibit, or deliver for transportation, any animal during the period of suspension or revocation.

[54 FR 36147, Aug. 31, 1989, as amended at 63 FR 62926, Nov. 10, 1998; 69 FR 42101, July 14, 2004]

§2.11 Denial of initial license application.

(a) A license will not be issued to any applicant who:

(1) Has not complied with the requirements of §§2.1, 2.2, 2.3, and 2.4 and has not paid the fees indicated in §2.6;

(2) Is not in compliance with any of the regulations or standards in this subchapter;

(3) Has had a license revoked or whose license is suspended, as set forth in §2.10;

(4) Has pled *nolo contendere* (no contest) or has been found to have violated any Federal, State, or local laws or regulations pertaining to animal cruelty within 1 year of application, or after 1 year if the Administrator determines that the circumstances render the applicant unfit to be licensed;

(5) Is or would be operating in violation or circumvention of any Federal, State, or local laws; or

(6) Has made any false or fraudulent statements or provided any false or fraudulent records to the Department or other government agencies, or has pled *nolo contendere* (no contest) or has been found to have violated any Federal, State, or local laws or regulations pertaining to the transportation, ownership, neglect, or welfare of animals, or is otherwise unfit to be licensed and the Administrator determines that the issuance of a license would be contrary to the purposes of the Act.

(b) An applicant whose license application has been denied may request a hearing in accordance with the applicable rules of practice for the purpose of showing why the application for license should not be denied. The license denial shall remain in effect until the final legal decision has been rendered. Should the license denial be upheld, the applicant may again apply for a license 1 year from the date of the final order denying the application, unless the order provides otherwise.

(c) No partnership, firm, corporation, or other legal entity in which a person whose license application has been denied has a substantial interest, financial or otherwise, will be licensed within 1 year of the license denial.

(d) No license will be issued under circumstances that the Administrator determines would circumvent any order suspending, revoking, terminating, or denying a license under the Act.

[54 FR 36147, Aug. 31, 1989, as amended at 69 FR 42101, July 14, 2004]

§ 2.12 Termination of a license.

A license may be terminated during the license renewal process or at any other time for any reason that an initial license application may be denied pursuant to § 2.11 after a hearing in accordance with the applicable rules of practice.

[69 FR 42101, July 14, 2004]

Subpart B—Registration

§ 2.25 Requirements and procedures.

(a) Each carrier and intermediate handler, and each exhibitor not required to be licensed under section 3 of the Act and the regulations of this subchapter, shall register with the Secretary by completing and filing a properly executed form which will be furnished, upon request, by the AC Regional Director. The registration form shall be filed with the AC Regional Director for the State in which the registrant has his or her principal place of business, and shall be updated every 3 years by the completion and filing of a new registration form which will be provided by the AC Regional Director.

(b) A subsidiary of a business corporation, rather than the parent corporation, will be registered as an exhibitor unless the subsidiary is under such direct control of the parent corporation that the Secretary determines that it is necessary that the parent corporation be registered to effectuate the purposes of the Act.

(c) No registrant or person required to be registered shall interfere with, threaten, abuse (including verbally abuse), or harass any APHIS official who is in the course of carrying out his or her duties.

[54 FR 36147, Aug. 31, 1989, as amended at 63 FR 62926, Nov. 10, 1998; 69 FR 42101, July 14, 2004]

§ 2.26 Acknowledgment of regulations and standards.

APHIS will supply a copy of the regulations and standards in this subchapter with each registration form. The registrant shall acknowledge receipt of and shall agree to comply with the regulations and standards by signing a form provided for this purpose by APHIS, and by filing it with the AC Regional Director.

[54 FR 36147, Aug. 31, 1989, as amended at 63 FR 62926, Nov. 10, 1998]

§ 2.27 Notification of change of operation.

(a) A registrant shall notify the AC Regional Director by certified mail of any change in the name, address, or ownership, or other change in operations affecting its status as an exhibitor, carrier, or intermediate handler, within 10 days after making such change.

(b)(1) A registrant which has not used, handled, or transported animals for a period of at least 2 years may be placed in an inactive status by making a written request to the AC Regional Director a registrant shall notify the AC Regional Director in writing at least 10 days before using, handling, or transporting animals again after being in an inactive status.

(2) A registrant which goes out of business or which ceases to function as a carrier, intermediate handler, or exhibitor, or which changes its method of operation so that it no longer uses, handles, or transports animals, and which does not plan to use, handle, or transport animals again at any time in the future, may have its registration canceled by making a written request to the AC Regional Director. The former registrant is responsible for re-registering and demonstrating its compliance with the Act and regulations should it start using, handling, or transporting animals at any time after its registration is canceled.

[54 FR 36147, Aug. 31, 1989, as amended at 63 FR 62926, Nov. 10, 1998]

Subpart C—Research Facilities

§ 2.30 Registration.

(a) *Requirements and procedures.* (1) Each research facility other than a Federal research facility, shall register with the Secretary by completing and filing a properly executed form which will be furnished, upon request, by the AC Regional Director. The registration form shall be filed with the AC Regional Director for the State in which the research facility has its principal place of business, and shall be updated every 3 years by the completion and filing of a new registration form which will be provided by the AC Regional Director. Except as provided in paragraph (a)(2) of this section, where a school or department of a university or college uses or intends to use live animals for research, tests, experiments, or teaching, the university or college rather than the school or department will be considered the research facility and will be required to register with the Secretary. An official who has the legal authority to bind the parent organization shall sign the registration form.

(2) In any situation in which a school or department of a university or college demonstrates to the Secretary that it is a separate legal entity and its operations and administration are independent of those of the university or college, the school or department will be registered rather than the university or college.

(3) A subsidiary of a business corporation, rather than the parent corporation, will be registered as a research facility unless the subsidiary is under such direct control of the parent corporation that the Secretary determines that it is necessary that the parent corporation be registered to effectuate the purposes of the Act.

(b) *Acknowledgment of regulations and standards.* APHIS will supply a copy of the regulations and standards in this subchapter with each registration form. The research facility shall acknowledge receipt of and shall agree to comply with the regulations and standards by signing a form provided for this purpose by APHIS, and by filing it with the AC Regional Director.

(c) *Notification of change of operation.* (1) A research facility shall notify the AC Regional Director by certified mail of any change in the name, address, or ownership, or other change in operations affecting its status as a research facility, within 10 days after making such change.

(2) A research facility which has not used, handled, or transported animals for a period of at least 2 years may be placed in an inactive status by making a written request to the AC Regional Director. A research facility shall file an annual report of its status (active or inactive). A research facility shall notify the AC Regional Director in writing at least 10 days before using, handling, or transporting animals again after being in an inactive status.

(3) A research facility which goes out of business or which ceases to function as a research facility, or which changes its method of operation so that it no longer uses, handles, or transports animals, and which does not plan to use, handle, or transport animals at any time in the future, may have its registration canceled by making a written request to the AC Regional Director. The research facility is responsible for reregistering and demonstrating its compliance with the Act and regulations should it start using, handling, or transporting animals at any time after its registration is canceled.

(d) No research facility shall interfere with, threaten, abuse (including verbally abuse), or harass any APHIS official who is in the course of carrying out his or her duties.

[54 FR 36147, Aug. 31, 1989, as amended at 63 FR 62926, Nov. 10, 1998; 69 FR 42101, July 14, 2004]

§2.31 Institutional Animal Care and Use Committee (IACUC).

(a) The Chief Executive Officer of the research facility shall appoint an Institutional Animal Care and Use Committee (IACUC), qualified through the experience and expertise of its members to assess the research facility's animal program, facilities, and procedures. Except as specifically authorized by law or these regulations, nothing in this part shall be deemed to permit the Committee or IACUC to prescribe methods or set standards for the design, performance, or conduct of actual research or experimentation by a research facility.

(b) *IACUC membership.* (1) The members of each Committee shall be appointed by the Chief Executive Officer of the research facility;

(2) The Committee shall be composed of a Chairman and at least two additional members;

(3) Of the members of the Committee:

(i) At least one shall be a Doctor of Veterinary Medicine, with training or experience in laboratory animal science and medicine, who has direct or delegated program responsibility for activities involving animals at the research facility;

(ii) At least one shall not be affiliated in any way with the facility other than as a member of the Committee, and shall not be a member of the immediate family of a person who is affiliated with the facility. The Secretary intends that such person will provide representation for general community interests in the proper care and treatment of animals;

(4) If the Committee consists of more than three members, not more than three members shall be from the same administrative unit of the facility.

(c) *IACUC functions.* With respect to activities involving animals, the IACUC, as an agent of the research facility, shall:

(1) Review, at least once every six months, the research facility's program for humane care and use of animals, using title 9, chapter I, subchapter A—Animal Welfare, as a basis for evaluation;

(2) Inspect, at least once every six months, all of the research facility's animal facilities, including animal study areas, using title 9, chapter I, subchapter A-Animal Welfare, as a basis for evaluation; *Provided, however,* That animal areas containing free-living wild animals in their natural habitat need not be included in such inspection;

(3) Prepare reports of its evaluations conducted as required by paragraphs (c)(1) and (2) of this section, and submit the reports to the Institutional Official of the research facility; *Provided, however,* That the IACUC may determine the best means of conducting evaluations of the research facility's programs and facilities; and *Provided, further,* That no Committee member wishing to participate in any evaluation conducted under this subpart may be excluded. The IACUC may use subcommittees composed of at least two Committee members and may invite *ad hoc* consultants to assist in conducting the evaluations, however, the IACUC remains responsible for the evaluations and reports as required by the Act and regulations. The reports shall be reviewed and signed by a majority of the IACUC members and must include any minority views. The reports shall be updated at least once every six months upon completion of the required semiannual evaluations and shall be maintained by the research facility and made available to APHIS and to officials of funding Federal agencies for inspection and copying upon request. The reports must contain a description of the nature and extent of the research facility's adherence to this subchapter, must identify specifically any departures from the provisions of title 9, chapter I, subchapter A—Animal Welfare, and must state the reasons for each departure. The reports must distinguish significant deficiencies from minor deficiencies. A significant deficiency is one which, with reference to Subchapter A, and, in the judgment of the IACUC and the Institutional Official, is or may be a threat to the health or safety of the animals. If program or facility deficiencies are noted, the reports must contain a reasonable and specific plan and schedule with dates for correcting each deficiency. Any failure to adhere to the plan and schedule that results in a significant deficiency remaining uncorrected shall be reported in writing within 15 business days by the IACUC, through the Institutional Official, to APHIS and any Federal agency funding that activity;

(4) Review, and, if warranted, investigate concerns involving the care and use of animals at the research facility resulting from public complaints received and from reports of noncompliance received from laboratory or research facility personnel or employees;

(5) Make recommendations to the Institutional Official regarding any aspect of the research facility's animal program, facilities, or personnel training;

(6) Review and approve, require modifications in (to secure approval), or withhold approval of those components of proposed activities related to the care and use of animals, as specified in paragraph (d) of this section;

(7) Review and approve, require modifications in (to secure approval), or

withhold approval of proposed significant changes regarding the care and use of animals in ongoing activities; and

(8) Be authorized to suspend an activity involving animals in accordance with the specifications set forth in paragraph (d)(6) of this section.

(d) IACUC review of activities involving animals. (1) In order to approve proposed activities or proposed significant changes in ongoing activities, the IACUC shall conduct a review of those components of the activities related to the care and use of animals and determine that the proposed activities are in accordance with this subchapter unless acceptable justification for a departure is presented in writing; *Provided, however,* That field studies as defined in part 1 of this subchapter are exempt from this requirement. Further, the IACUC shall determine that the proposed activities or significant changes in ongoing activities meet the following requirements:

(i) Procedures involving animals will avoid or minimize discomfort, distress, and pain to the animals;

(ii) The principal investigator has considered alternatives to procedures that may cause more than momentary or slight pain or distress to the animals, and has provided a written narrative description of the methods and sources, *e. g.*, the Animal Welfare Information Center, used to determine that alternatives were not available;

(iii) The principal investigator has provided written assurance that the activities do not unnecessarily duplicate previous experiments;

(iv) Procedures that may cause more than momentary or slight pain or distress to the animals will:

(A) Be performed with appropriate sedatives, analgesics or anesthetics, unless withholding such agents is justified for scientific reasons, in writing, by the principal investigator and will continue for only the necessary period of time;

(B) Involve, in their planning, consultation with the attending veterinarian or his or her designee;

(C) Not include the use of paralytics without anesthesia;

(v) Animals that would otherwise experience severe or chronic pain or distress that cannot be relieved will be painlessly euthanized at the end of the procedure or, if appropriate, during the procedure;

(vi) The animals' living conditions will be appropriate for their species in accordance with part 3 of this subchapter, and contribute to their health and comfort. The housing, feeding, and nonmedical care of the animals will be directed by the attending veterinarian or other scientist trained and experienced in the proper care, handling, and use of the species being maintained or studied;

(vii) Medical care for animals will be available and provided as necessary by a qualified veterinarian;

(viii) Personnel conducting procedures on the species being maintained or studied will be appropriately qualified and trained in those procedures;

(ix) Activities that involve surgery include appropriate provision for pre-operative and post-operative care of the animals in accordance with established veterinary medical and nursing practices. All survival surgery will be performed using aseptic procedures, including surgical gloves, masks, sterile instruments, and aseptic techniques. Major operative procedures on non-rodents will be conducted only in facilities intended for that purpose which shall be operated and maintained under aseptic conditions. Non-major operative procedures and all surgery on rodents do not require a dedicated facility, but must be performed using aseptic procedures. Operative procedures conducted at field sites need not be performed in dedicated facilities, but must be performed using aseptic procedures;

(x) No animal will be used in more than one major operative procedure from which it is allowed to recover, unless:

(A) Justified for scientific reasons by the principal investigator, in writing;

(B) Required as routine veterinary procedure or to protect the health or well-being of the animal as determined by the attending veterinarian; or

(C) In other special circumstances as determined by the Administrator on an individual basis. Written requests and supporting data should be sent to the Animal and Plant Health Inspection

Service, Animal Care, 4700 River Road, Unit 84, Riverdale, Maryland 20737–1234;

(xi) Methods of euthanasia used must be in accordance with the definition of the term set forth in 9 CFR part 1, § 1.1 of this subchapter, unless a deviation is justified for scientific reasons, in writing, by the investigator.

(2) Prior to IACUC review, each member of the Committee shall be provided with a list of proposed activities to be reviewed. Written descriptions of all proposed activities that involve the care and use of animals shall be available to all IACUC members, and any member of the IACUC may obtain, upon request, full Committee review of those activities. If full Committee review is not requested, at least one member of the IACUC, designated by the chairman and qualified to conduct the review, shall review those activities, and shall have the authority to approve, require modifications in (to secure approval), or request full Committee review of any of those activities. If full Committee review is requested for a proposed activity, approval of that activity may be granted only after review, at a convened meeting of a quorum of the IACUC, and with the approval vote of a majority of the quorum present. No member may participate in the IACUC review or approval of an activity in which that member has a conflicting interest (e.g., is personally involved in the activity), except to provide information requested by the IACUC, nor may a member who has a conflicting interest contribute to the constitution of a quorum;

(3) The IACUC may invite consultants to assist in the review of complex issues arising out of its review of proposed activities. Consultants may not approve or withhold approval of an activity, and may not vote with the IACUC unless they are also members of the IACUC;

(4) The IACUC shall notify principal investigators and the research facility in writing of its decision to approve or withhold approval of those activities related to the care and use of animals, or of modifications required to secure IACUC approval. If the IACUC decides to withhold approval of an activity, it shall include in its written notification a statement of the reasons for its decision and give the principal investigator an opportunity to respond in person or in writing. The IACUC may reconsider its decision, with documentation in Committee minutes, in light of the information provided by the principal investigator;

(5) The IACUC shall conduct continuing reviews of activities covered by this subchapter at appropriate intervals as determined by the IACUC, but not less than annually;

(6) The IACUC may suspend an activity that it previously approved if it determines that the activity is not being conducted in accordance with the description of that activity provided by the principal investigator and approved by the Committee. The IACUC may suspend an activity only after review of the matter at a convened meeting of a quorum of the IACUC and with the suspension vote of a majority of the quorum present;

(7) If the IACUC suspends an activity involving animals, the Institutional Official, in consultation with the IACUC, shall review the reasons for suspension, take appropriate corrective action, and report that action with a full explanation to APHIS and any Federal agency funding that activity; and

(8) Proposed activities and proposed significant changes in ongoing activities that have been approved by the IACUC may be subject to further appropriate review and approval by officials of the research facility. However, those officials may not approve an activity involving the care and use of animals if it has not been approved by the IACUC.

(e) A proposal to conduct an activity involving animals, or to make a significant change in an ongoing activity involving animals, must contain the following:

(1) Identification of the species and the approximate number of animals to be used;

(2) A rationale for involving animals, and for the appropriateness of the species and numbers of animals to be used;

(3) A complete description of the proposed use of the animals;

(4) A description of procedures designed to assure that discomfort and pain to animals will be limited to that

which is unavoidable for the conduct of scientifically valuable research, including provision for the use of analgesic, anesthetic, and tranquilizing drugs where indicated and appropriate to minimize discomfort and pain to animals; and

(5) A description of any euthanasia method to be used.

[54 FR 36147, Aug. 31, 1989, as amended at 59 FR 67611, Dec. 30, 1994; 63 FR 62926, Nov. 10, 1998]

§2.32 Personnel qualifications.

(a) It shall be the responsibility of the research facility to ensure that all scientists, research technicians, animal technicians, and other personnel involved in animal care, treatment, and use are qualified to perform their duties. This responsibility shall be fulfilled in part through the provision of training and instruction to those personnel.

(b) Training and instruction shall be made available, and the qualifications of personnel reviewed, with sufficient frequency to fulfill the research facility's responsibilities under this section and §2.31.

(c) Training and instruction of personnel must include guidance in at least the following areas:

(1) Humane methods of animal maintenance and experimentation, including:

(i) The basic needs of each species of animal;

(ii) Proper handling and care for the various species of animals used by the facility;

(iii) Proper pre-procedural and post-procedural care of animals; and

(iv) Aseptic surgical methods and procedures;

(2) The concept, availability, and use of research or testing methods that limit the use of animals or minimize animal distress;

(3) Proper use of anesthetics, analgesics, and tranquilizers for any species of animals used by the facility;

(4) Methods whereby deficiencies in animal care and treatment are reported, including deficiencies in animal care and treatment reported by any employee of the facility. No facility employee, Committee member, or laboratory personnel shall be discriminated against or be subject to any reprisal for reporting violations of any regulation or standards under the Act;

(5) Utilization of services (e.g., National Agricultural Library, National Library of Medicine) available to provide information:

(i) On appropriate methods of animal care and use;

(ii) On alternatives to the use of live animals in research;

(iii) That could prevent unintended and unnecessary duplication of research involving animals; and

(iv) Regarding the intent and requirements of the Act.

§2.33 Attending veterinarian and adequate veterinary care.

(a) Each research facility shall have an attending veterinarian who shall provide adequate veterinary care to its animals in compliance with this section:

(1) Each research facility shall employ an attending veterinarian under formal arrangements. In the case of a part-time attending veterinarian or consultant arrangements, the formal arrangements shall include a written program of veterinary care and regularly scheduled visits to the research facility;

(2) Each research facility shall assure that the attending veterinarian has appropriate authority to ensure the provision of adequate veterinary care and to oversee the adequacy of other aspects of animal care and use; and

(3) The attending veterinarian shall be a voting member of the IACUC; *Provided, however*, That a research facility with more than one Doctor of Veterinary Medicine (DVM) may appoint to the IACUC another DVM with delegated program responsibility for activities involving animals at the research facility.

(b) Each research facility shall establish and maintain programs of adequate veterinary care that include:

(1) The availability of appropriate facilities, personnel, equipment, and services to comply with the provisions of this subchapter;

(2) The use of appropriate methods to prevent, control, diagnose, and treat

diseases and injuries, and the availability of emergency, weekend, and holiday care;

(3) Daily observation of all animals to assess their health and well-being; *Provided, however,* That daily observation of animals may be accomplished by someone other than the attending veterinarian; and *Provided, further,* That a mechanism of direct and frequent communication is required so that timely and accurate information on problems of animal health, behavior, and well-being is conveyed to the attending veterinarian;

(4) Guidance to principal investigators and other personnel involved in the care and use of animals regarding handling, immobilization, anesthesia, analgesia, tranquilization, and euthanasia; and

(5) Adequate pre-procedural and post-procedural care in accordance with current established veterinary medical and nursing procedures.

§ 2.34 [Reserved]

§ 2.35 Recordkeeping requirements.

(a) The research facility shall maintain the following IACUC records:

(1) Minutes of IACUC meetings, including records of attendance, activities of the Committee, and Committee deliberations;

(2) Records of proposed activities involving animals and proposed significant changes in activities involving animals, and whether IACUC approval was given or withheld; and

(3) Records of semiannual IACUC reports and recommendations (including minority views), prepared in accordance with the requirements of § 2.31(c)(3) of this subpart, and forwarded to the Institutional Official.

(b) Every research facility shall make, keep, and maintain records or forms which fully and correctly disclose the following information concerning each live dog or cat purchased or otherwise acquired, owned, held, or otherwise in their possession or under their control, transported, euthanized, sold, or otherwise disposed of by the research facility. The records shall include any offspring born of any animal while in the research facility's possession or under its control:

(1) The name and address of the person from whom a dog or cat was purchased or otherwise acquired, whether or not the person is required to be licensed or registered under the Act;

(2) The USDA license or registration number of the person if he or she is licensed or registered under the Act;

(3) The vehicle license number and State, and the driver's license number (or photographic identification card for nondrivers issued by a State) and State of the person, if he or she is not licensed or registered under the Act;

(4) The date of acquisition of each dog or cat;

(5) The official USDA tag number or tattoo assigned to each dog or cat under § 2.38(g) of this subpart;

(6) A description of each dog or cat which shall include:

(i) The species and breed or type of animal;

(ii) The sex;

(iii) The date of birth or approximate age; and

(iv) The color and any distinctive markings;

(7) Any identification number or mark assigned to each dog or cat by the research facility;

(8) If dogs or cats are acquired from any person not licensed or registered under the Act and not a pound or shelter, the research facility must obtain a certification that the animals were born and raised on the person's premises and that the person has sold fewer than 25 dogs and/or cats that year.

(c) In addition to the information required to be kept and maintained by every research facility concerning each live dog or cat under paragraph (a) of this section, every research facility transporting, selling, or otherwise disposing of any live dog or cat to another person, shall make and maintain records or forms which fully and correctly disclose the following information:

(1) The name and address of the person to whom a live dog or cat is transported, sold, or otherwise disposed of;

(2) The date of transportation, sale, euthanasia, or other disposition of the animal; and

(3) The method of transportation, including the name of the initial carrier

or intermediate handler, or if a privately owned vehicle is used to transport the dog or cat, the name of the owner of the privately owned vehicle.

(d)(1) The USDA Interstate and International Certificate of Health Examination for Small Animals (APHIS Form 7001) and Record of Aquisition and Dogs and Cats on Hand (APHIS Form 7005) are forms which may be used by research facilities to keep and maintain the information required by paragraph (b) of this section.

(2) The USDA Interstate and International Certificate of Health Examination for Small Animals (APHIS Form 7001) and Record of Disposition of Dogs and Cats (APHIS Form 7006) are forms which may be used by research facilities to keep and maintain the information required by paragraph (c) of this section.

(e) One copy of the record containing the information required by paragraphs (b) and (c) of this section shall accompany each shipment of any live dog or cat sold or otherwise disposed of by a research facility; *Provided, however*, That, except as provided in §2.133 of this part, information that indicates the source and date of acquisition of any dog or cat need not appear on the copy of the record accompanying the shipment. One copy of the record containing the information required by paragraphs (b) and (c) of this section shall be retained by the research facility.

(f) All records and reports shall be maintained for at least three years. Records that relate directly to proposed activities and proposed significant changes in ongoing activities reviewed and approved by the IACUC shall be maintained for the duration of the activity and for an additional three years after completion of the activity. All records shall be available for inspection and copying by authorized APHIS or funding Federal agency representatives at reasonable times. APHIS inspectors will maintain the confidentiality of the information and will not remove the materials from the research facilities' premises unless there has been an alleged violation, they are needed to investigate a possible violation, or for other enforcement purposes. Release of any such materials, including reports, summaries, and photographs that contain trade secrets or commercial or financial information that is privileged or confidential will be governed by applicable sections of the Freedom of Information Act. Whenever the Administrator notifies a research facility in writing that specified records shall be retained pending completion of an investigation or proceeding under the Act, the research facility shall hold those records until their disposition is authorized in writing by the Administrator.

(Approved by the Office of Management and Budget under control number 0579–0254)

[54 FR 36147, Aug. 31, 1989, as amended at 58 FR 39129, July 22, 1993; 60 FR 13895, Mar. 15, 1995; 69 FR 42101, July 14, 2004]

§2.36 Annual report.

(a) The reporting facility shall be that segment of the research facility, or that department, agency, or instrumentality of the United States, that uses or intends to use live animals in research, tests, experiments, or for teaching. Each reporting facility shall submit an annual report to the AC Regional Director for the State where the facility is located on or before December 1 of each calendar year. The report shall be signed and certified by the CEO or Institutional Official, and shall cover the previous Federal fiscal year.

(b) The annual report shall:

(1) Assure that professionally acceptable standards governing the care, treatment, and use of animals, including appropriate use of anesthetic, analgesic, and tranquilizing drugs, prior to, during, and following actual research, teaching, testing, surgery, or experimentation were followed by the research facility;

(2) Assure that each principal investigator has considered alternatives to painful procedures;

(3) Assure that the facility is adhering to the standards and regulations under the Act, and that it has required that exceptions to the standards and regulations be specified and explained by the principal investigator and approved by the IACUC. A summary of all such exceptions must be attached to the facility's annual report. In addition

to identifying the IACUC-approved exceptions, this summary must include a brief explanation of the exceptions, as well as the species and number of animals affected;

(4) State the location of all facilities where animals were housed or used in actual research, testing, teaching, or experimentation, or held for these purposes;

(5) State the common names and the numbers of animals upon which teaching, research, experiments, or tests were conducted involving no pain, distress, or use of pain-relieving drugs. Routine procedures (e.g., injections, tattooing, blood sampling) should be reported with this group;

(6) State the common names and the numbers of animals upon which experiments, teaching, research, surgery, or tests were conducted involving accompanying pain or distress to the animals and for which appropriate anesthetic, analgesic, or tranquilizing drugs were used;

(7) State the common names and the numbers of animals upon which teaching, experiments, research, surgery, or tests were conducted involving accompanying pain or distress to the animals and for which the use of appropriate anesthetic, analgesic, or tranquilizing drugs would have adversely affected the procedures, results, or interpretation of the teaching, research, experiments, surgery, or tests. An explanation of the procedures producing pain or distress in these animals and the reasons such drugs were not used shall be attached to the annual report;

(8) State the common names and the numbers of animals being bred, conditioned, or held for use in teaching, testing, experiments, research, or surgery but not yet used for such purposes.

[54 FR 36147, Aug. 31, 1989, as amended at 63 FR 62926, Nov. 10, 1998]

§ 2.37 Federal research facilities.

Each Federal research facility shall establish an Institutional Animal Care and Use Committee which shall have the same composition, duties, and responsibilities required of nonfederal research facilities by § 2.31 with the following exceptions:

(a) The Committee shall report deficiencies to the head of the Federal agency conducting the research rather than to APHIS; and

(b) The head of the Federal agency conducting the research shall be responsible for all corrective action to be taken at the facility and for the granting of all exceptions to inspection protocol.

§ 2.38 Miscellaneous.

(a) *Information as to business: furnishing of same by research facilities.* Each research facility shall furnish to any APHIS official any information concerning the business of the research facility which the APHIS official may request in connection with the enforcement of the provisions of the Act, the regulations, and the standards in this subchapter. The information shall be furnished within a reasonable time and as may be specified in the request for information.

(b) *Access and inspection of records and property.* (1) Each research facility shall, during business hours, allow APHIS officials:

(i) To enter its place of business;

(ii) To examine records required to be kept by the Act and the regulations in this part;

(iii) To make copies of the records;

(iv) To inspect the facilities, property, and animals, as the APHIS officials consider necessary to enforce the provisions of the Act, the regulations, and the standards in this subchapter; and

(v) To document, by the taking of photographs and other means, conditions and areas of noncompliance.

(2) The use of a room, table or other facilities necessary for the proper examination of the records and for inspection of the property or animals shall be extended to APHIS officials by the research facility.

(c) *Publication of names of research facilities subject to the provisions of this part.* APHIS will publish lists of research facilities registered in accordance with the provisions of this subpart in the FEDERAL REGISTER. The lists may be obtained upon request from the AC Regional Director.

(d) *Inspection for missing animals.* Each research facility shall allow, upon request and during business hours, police or officers of other law enforcement agencies with general law enforcement authority (not those agencies whose duties are limited to enforcement of local animal regulations) to enter its place of business to inspect animals and records for the purpose of seeking animals that are missing, under the following conditions:

(1) The police or other law officer shall furnish to the research facility a written description of the missing animal and the name and address of its owner before making a search;

(2) The police or other law officer shall abide by all security measures required by the research facility to prevent the spread of disease, including the use of sterile clothing, footwear, and masks where required, or to prevent the escape of an animal.

(e) *Confiscation and destruction of animals.* (1) If an animal being held by a research facility is not being used to carry out research, testing, or experimentation, and is found by an APHIS official to be suffering as a result of the failure of the research facility to comply with any provision of the regulations or the standards set forth in this subchapter, the APHIS official shall make a reasonable effort to notify the research facility of the condition of the animal(s) and request that the condition be corrected and that adequate care be given to alleviate the animal's suffering or distress, or that the animal(s) be destroyed by euthanasia. In the event that the research facility refuses to comply with this request, the APHIS official may confiscate the animal(s) for care, treatment, or disposal as indicated in paragraph (e)(2) of this section, if, in the opinion of the Administrator, the circumstances indicate the animal's health is in danger.

(2) In the event that the APHIS official is unable to locate or notify the research facility as required in this section, the APHIS official shall contact a local police or other law officer to accompany him or her to the premises and shall provide for adequate care when necessary to alleviate the animal's suffering. If, in the opinion of the Administrator, the condition of the animal(s) cannot be corrected by this temporary care, the APHIS official shall confiscate the animal(s).

(3) Confiscated animals may be placed, by sale or donation, with other registrants or licensees that comply with the standards and regulations and can provide proper care, or they may be euthanized. The research facility from which the animals were confiscated shall bear all costs incurred in performing the placement or euthanasia activities authorized by this section.

(f) *Handling.* (1) Handling of all animals shall be done as expeditiously and carefully as possible in a manner that does not cause trauma, overheating, excessive cooling, behavioral stress, physical harm, or unnecessary discomfort.

(2)(i) Physical abuse shall not be used to train, work, or otherwise handle animals.

(ii) Deprivation of food or water shall not be used to train, work, or otherwise handle animals; *Provided, however:* That the short-term withholding of food or water from animals, when specified in an IACUC-approved activity that includes a description of monitoring procedures, is allowed by these regulations.

(g) *Identification of dogs and cats.* (1) All live dogs or cats, including those from any exempt source, delivered for transportation, transported, purchased or otherwise acquired. sold, or disposed of by a research facility, shall be identified at the time of such delivery for transportation, purchase, sale, disposal, or acquisition in one of the following ways:

(i) By the official tag or tattoo which was affixed to the animal at the time it was acquired by the research facility, as required by this section; or

(ii) By a tag, tattoo, or collar, applied to the live dog or cat by the research facility and which individually identifies the dog or cat by number.

(2) All official tag or tattoo numbers shall be correctly listed in the records of purchase, acquisition, disposal, or sale which shall be maintained in accordance with §2.35.

(3) Unweaned puppies or kittens need not be individually identified while they are maintained as a litter with

their dam in the same primary enclosure, provided the dam has been individually identified.

(4) The official tag shall be made of a durable alloy such as brass, bronze, or steel, or of a durable plastic. Aluminum of a sufficient thickness to assure the tag is durable and legible may also be used. The tag may be circular in shape and not less than 1¼ inches in diameter, or oblong and flat in shape and not less than 2 inches by ¾ inch, and riveted to an acceptable collar.

(5) Each tag shall have the following information embossed or stamped on so that it is easily readable:

(i) The letters "USDA";

(ii) Numbers identifying the State and dealer, exhibitor, or research facility (e.g., 39–AB); and

(iii) Numbers identifying the animal (e.g., 82488).

(6) Official tags shall be serially numbered and shall be applied to dogs or cats in the manner set forth in this section in as close to consecutive numerical order as possible. No tag number shall be used to identify more than one animal or shall be reused within a 5-year period.

(7) Research facilities may obtain, at their own expense, official tags from commercial tag manufacturers.[1] At the time the research facility is registered, the Department will assign identification letters and numbers to be used on the official tags.

(8) Each research facility shall be held accountable for all official tags acquired. In the event an official tag is lost from a dog or cat while in the possession of a research facility, the facility shall make a diligent effort to locate and reapply the tag to the proper animal. If the lost tag is not located, the research facility shall affix another official tag to the animal in the manner prescribed in this section and record the tag number on the official records.

(9) When a dog or cat wearing or identified by an official tag arrives at a research facility, the facility may continue to use that tag to identify the dog or cat or the tag may be replaced as indicated in paragraph (g)(1) of this section. All tags removed by a research facility shall be retained and disposed of as indicated in this section.

(10) Where a dog or cat to which is affixed or which is identified by an official tag is euthanized, or dies from other causes, the research facility shall remove and retain the tag for the required period, as set forth in paragraph (g)(11) of this section.

(11) All official tags removed and retained by a research facility shall be held until called for by an APHIS official or for a period of 1 year.

(12) When official tags are removed from animals for disposal, the tags must be disposed of so as to preclude their reuse for animal identification. No animal identification number shall be used within any 5-year period following its previous use.

(h) *Health certification.* (1) No research facility, including a Federal research facility, shall deliver to any intermediate handler or carrier for transportation, in commerce, or shall transport in commerce any dog, cat, or nonhuman primate unless the dog, cat, or nonhuman primate is accompanied by a health certificate executed and issued by a licensed veterinarian. The health certificate shall state that:

(i) The licensed veterinarian inspected the dog, cat, or nonhuman primate on a specified date which shall not be more than 10 days prior to the delivery of the dog, cat, or nonhuman primate for transportation; and

(ii) When so inspected, the dog, cat, or nonhuman primate appeared to the licensed veterinarian to be free of any infectious disease or physical abnormality which would endanger the animal(s) or other animals or endanger public health.

(2) The Secretary may provide exceptions to the health certification requirement on an individual basis for animals shipped to a research facility for purposes of research, testing, or experimentation when the research facility requires animals not eligible for certification. Requests should be addressed to the Animal and Plant Health Inspection Service, Animal

[1] A list of the commercial manufacturers who produce these tags and are known to the Department may be obtained from the AC Regional Director. Any manufacturer who desires to be included in the list should notify the Administrator.

Care, 4700 River Road, Unit 84, Riverdale, Maryland 20737–1234.

(3) The U.S. Interstate and International Certificate of Health Examination for Small Animals (APHIS Form 7001) may be used for health certification by a licensed veterinarian as required by this section.

(i) *Holding of animals.* If any research facility obtains prior approval of the AC Regional Director, it may arrange to have another person hold animals: *Provided,* That:

(1) The other person agrees, in writing, to comply with the regulations in this part and the standards in part 3 of this subchapter, and to allow inspection of the premises by an APHIS official during business hours;

(2) The animals remain under the total control and responsibility of the research facility; and

(3) The Institutional Official agrees, in writing, that the other person or premises is a recognized animal site under its research facility registration. APHIS Form 7009 shall be used for approval.

(4) The other person or premises must either be directly included in the research facility's contingency plan required under paragraph (l) of this section or must develop its own contingency plan in accordance with paragraph (l) of this section.

(j) *Holding period.* Research facilities that obtain dogs and cats from sources other than dealers, exhibitors, and exempt persons shall hold the animals for 5 full days, not including the day of acquisition, after acquiring the animal, excluding time in transit, before they may be used by the facility. Research facilities shall comply with the identification of animals requirements set forth in §2.38(g) during this period.

(k) *Compliance with standards and prohibitions.* (1) Each research facility shall comply in all respects with the regulations set forth in subpart C of this part and the standards set forth in part 3 of this subchapter for the humane handling, care, treatment, housing, and transportation of animals; *Provided, however,* That exceptions to the standards in part 3 and the provisions of subpart C of this part may be made only when such exceptions are specified and justified in the proposal to conduct the activity and are approved by the IACUC.

(2) No person shall obtain live dogs or cats by use of false pretenses, misrepresentation, or deception.

(3) No person shall acquire, buy, sell, exhibit, use for research, transport, or offer for transportation, any stolen animal.

(4) Each research facility shall comply with the regulations set forth in §2.133 of subpart I of this part.

(l) *Contingency planning.* (1) Research facilities must develop, document, and follow an appropriate plan to provide for the humane handling, treatment, transportation, housing, and care of their animals in the event of an emergency or disaster (one which could reasonably be anticipated and expected to be detrimental to the good health and well-being of the animals in their possession). Such contingency plans must:

(i) Identify situations the facility might experience that would trigger the need for the measures identified in a contingency plan to be put into action including, but not limited to, emergencies such as electrical outages, faulty HVAC systems, fires, and animal escapes, as well as natural disasters the facility is most likely to experience.

(ii) Outline specific tasks required to be carried out in response to the identified emergencies or disasters including, but not limited to, detailed animal evacuation instructions or shelter-in-place instructions and provisions for providing backup sources of food and water as well as sanitation, ventilation, bedding, veterinary care, etc.;

(iii) Identify a chain of command and who (by name or by position title) will be responsible for fulfilling these tasks; and

(iv) Address how response and recovery will be handled in terms of materials, resources, and training needed.

(2) For current registrants, the contingency plan must be in place by July 29, 2013. For research facilities registered after this date, the contingency plan must be in place prior to conducting regulated activities. The plan must be reviewed by the research facility on at least an annual basis to ensure that it adequately addresses the criteria listed in paragraph (l)(1) of this

section. Each registrant must maintain documentation of their annual reviews, including documenting any amendments or changes made to their plan since the previous year's review, such as changes made as a result of recently predicted, but historically unforeseen, circumstances (e.g., weather extremes). Contingency plans, as well as all annual review documentation and training records, must be made available to APHIS and any funding Federal agency representatives upon request. Facilities maintaining or otherwise handling marine mammals in captivity must also comply with the requirements of § 3.101(b) of this subchapter.

(3) The facility must provide and document participation in and successful completion of training for its personnel regarding their roles and responsibilities as outlined in the plan. For current registrants, training of facility personnel must be completed by September 27, 2013; for research facilities registered after July 29, 2013, training of facility personnel must be completed within 60 days of the facility putting its contingency plan in place. Employees hired 30 days or more before the contingency plan is put in place must also be trained by that date. For employees hired less than 30 days before that date or after that date, training must be conducted within 30 days of their start date. Any changes to the plan as a result of the annual review must be communicated to employees through training which must be conducted within 30 days of making the changes.

[54 FR 36147, Aug. 31, 1989, as amended at 58 FR 39129, July 22, 1993; 59 FR 67612, Dec. 30, 1994; 60 FR 13895, Mar. 15, 1995; 63 FR 62926, Nov. 10, 1998; 69 FR 42101, July 14, 2004; 77 FR 76823, Dec. 31, 2012]

EFFECTIVE DATE NOTE: At 78 FR 46255, July 31, 2013, in § 2.38, paragraph (l) was stayed indefinitely, effective July 31, 2013.

Subpart D—Attending Veterinarian and Adequate Veterinary Care

§ 2.40 Attending veterinarian and adequate veterinary care (dealers and exhibitors).

(a) Each dealer or exhibitor shall have an attending veterinarian who shall provide adequate veterinary care to its animals in compliance with this section.

(1) Each dealer and exhibitor shall employ an attending veterinarian under formal arrangements. In the case of a part-time attending veterinarian or consultant arrangements, the formal arrangements shall include a written program of veterinary care and regularly scheduled visits to the premises of the dealer or exhibitor; and

(2) Each dealer and exhibitor shall assure that the attending veterinarian has appropriate authority to ensure the provision of adequate veterinary care and to oversee the adequacy of other aspects of animal care and use.

(b) Each dealer or exhibitor shall establish and maintain programs of adequate veterinary care that include:

(1) The availability of appropriate facilities, personnel, equipment, and services to comply with the provisions of this subchapter;

(2) The use of appropriate methods to prevent, control, diagnose, and treat diseases and injuries, and the availability of emergency, weekend, and holiday care;

(3) Daily observation of all animals to assess their health and well-being; *Provided, however*, That daily observation of animals may be accomplished by someone other than the attending veterinarian; and *Provided, further*, That a mechanism of direct and frequent communication is required so that timely and accurate information on problems of animal health, behavior, and well-being is conveyed to the attending veterinarian;

(4) Adequate guidance to personnel involved in the care and use of animals regarding handling, immobilization, anesthesia, analgesia, tranquilization, and euthanasia; and

(5) Adequate pre-procedural and post-procedural care in accordance with established veterinary medical and nursing procedures.

Subpart E—Identification of Animals

§ 2.50 Time and method of identification.

(a) A class "A" dealer (breeder) shall identify all live dogs and cats on the premises as follows:

(1) All live dogs and cats held on the premises, purchased, or otherwise acquired, sold or otherwise disposed of, or removed from the premises for delivery to a research facility or exhibitor or to another dealer, or for sale, through an auction sale or to any person for use as a pet, shall be identified by an official tag of the type described in § 2.51 affixed to the animal's neck by means of a collar made of material generally considered acceptable to pet owners as a means of identifying their pet dogs or cats[2], or shall be identified by a distinctive and legible tattoo marking acceptable to and approved by the Administrator.

(2) Live puppies or kittens, less than 16 weeks of age, shall be identified by:

(i) An official tag as described in § 2.51;

(ii) A distinctive and legible tattoo marking approved by the Administrator; or

(iii) A plastic-type collar acceptable to the Administrator which has legibly placed thereon the information required for an official tag pursuant to § 2.51.

(b) A class "B" dealer shall identify all live dogs and cats under his or her control or on his or her premises as follows:

(1) When live dogs or cats are held, purchased, or otherwise acquired, they shall be immediately identified:

(i) By affixing to the animal's neck an official tag as set forth in § 2.51 by means of a collar made of material generally acceptable to pet owners as a means of identifying their pet dogs or cats[3]; or

(ii) By a distinctive and legible tattoo marking approved by the Administrator.

(2) If any live dog or cat is already identified by an official tag or tattoo which has been applied by another dealer or exhibitor, the dealer or exhibitor who purchases or otherwise acquires the animal may continue identifying the dog or cat by the previous identification number, or may replace the previous tag with his own official tag or approved tattoo. In either case, the class B dealer or class C exhibitor shall correctly list all old and new official tag numbers or tattoos in his or her records of purchase which shall be maintained in accordance with §§ 2.75 and 2.77. Any new official tag or tattoo number shall be used on all records of any subsequent sales by the dealer or exhibitor, of any dog or cat.

(3) Live puppies or kittens less than 16 weeks of age, shall be identified by:

(i) An official tag as described in § 2.51;

(ii) A distinctive and legible tattoo marking approved by the Administrator; or

(iii) A plastic-type collar acceptable to the Administrator which has legibly placed thereon the information required for an official tag pursuant to § 2.51.

(4) When any dealer has made a reasonable effort to affix an official tag to a cat, as set forth in paragraphs (a) and (b) of this section, and has been unable to do so, or when the cat exhibits serious distress from the attachment of a collar and tag, the dealer shall attach the collar and tag to the door of the primary enclosure containing the cat and take measures adequate to maintain the identity of the cat in relation to the tag. Each primary enclosure shall contain no more than one weaned cat without an affixed collar and official tag, unless the cats are identified by a distinctive and legible tattoo or plastic-type collar approved by the Administrator.

(c) A class "C" exhibitor shall identify all live dogs and cats under his or her control or on his or her premises, whether held, purchased, or otherwise acquired:

(1) As set forth in paragraph (b)(1) or (b)(3) of this section, or

(2) By identifying each dog or cat with:

[2] In general, well fitted collars made of leather or plastic will be acceptable under this provision. The use of certain types of chains presently used by some dealers may also be deemed acceptable. APHIS will determine the acceptability of a material proposed for usage as collars from the standpoint of humane considerations on an individual basis in consultation with the dealer or exhibitor involved. The use of materials such as wire, elastic, or sharp metal that might cause discomfort or injury to the dogs or cats is not acceptable.

[3] See footnote 2 in § 2.50(a)(1).

(i) An official USDA sequentially numbered tag that is kept on the door of the animal's cage or run;

(ii) A record book containing each animal's tag number, a written description of each animal, the data required by § 2.75(a), and a clear photograph of each animal; and

(iii) A duplicate tag that accompanies each dog or cat whenever it leaves the compound or premises.

(d) Unweaned puppies or kittens need not be individually identified as required by paragraphs (a) and (b) of this section while they are maintained as a litter with their dam in the same primary enclosure, provided the dam has been individually identified.

(e)(1) All animals, except dogs and cats, delivered for transportation, transported, purchased, sold, or otherwise acquired or disposed of by any dealer or exhibitor shall be identified by the dealer or exhibitor at the time of delivery for transportation, purchase, sale, acquisition or disposal, as provided for in this paragraph and in records maintained as required in §§ 2.75 and 2.77.

(2) When one or more animals, other than dogs or cats, are confined in a primary enclosure, the animal(s) shall be identified by:

(i) A label attached to the primary enclosure which shall bear a description of the animals in the primary enclosure, including:

(A) The number of animals;

(B) The species of the animals;

(C) Any distinctive physical features of the animals; and

(D) Any identifying marks, tattoos, or tags attached to the animals;

(ii) Marking the primary enclosure with a painted or stenciled number which shall be recorded in the records of the dealer or exhibitor together with:

(A) A description of the animal(s);

(B) The species of the animal(s); and

(C) Any distinctive physical features of the animal(s); or

(iii) A tag or tattoo applied to each animal in the primary enclosure by the dealer or exhibitor which individually identifies each animal by description or number.

(3) When any animal, other than a dog or cat, is not confined in a primary enclosure, it shall be identified on a record, as required by § 2.75, which shall accompany the animal at the time it is delivered for transportation, transported, purchased, or sold, and shall be kept and maintained by the dealer or exhibitor as part of his or her records.

§ 2.51 Form of official tag.

(a) The official tag shall be made of a durable alloy such as brass, bronze, or steel, or of a durable plastic. Aluminum of a sufficient thickness to assure the tag is durable and legible may also be used. The tag shall be one of the following shapes:

(1) Circular in shape and not less than 1¼ inches in diameter, or

(2) Oblong and flat in shape, not less than 2 inches by ¾ inch and riveted to an acceptable collar.

(b) Each tag shall have the following information embossed or stamped on so that it is easily readable:

(1) The letters "USDA";

(2) Numbers identifying the State and dealer, exhibitor, or research facility (e.g., 39–AB); and

(3) Numbers identifying the animal (e.g., 82488).

(c) Official tags shall be serially numbered. No individual dealer or exhibitor shall use any identification tag number more than once within a 5-year period.

§ 2.52 How to obtain tags.

Dealers or exhibitors may obtain, at their own expense, official tags from commercial tag manufacturers.[4] At the time the dealer or exhibitor is issued a license or is registered, the Department will assign identification letters and numbers and inform them of the identification letters and numbers to be used on the official tags.

[54 FR 36147, Aug. 31, 1989, as amended at 63 FR 62927, Nov. 10, 1998]

§ 2.53 Use of tags.

Official tags obtained by a dealer, exhibitor, or research facility, shall be

[4] A list of the commercial manufacturers who produce these tags and are known to the Department may be obtained from the AC Regional Director. Any manufacturer who desires to be included in the list should notify the Administrator.

applied to dogs or cats in the manner set forth in § 2.50 and in as close to consecutive numerical order as possible. No tag number shall be used to identify more than one animal. No number shall be repeated within a 5-year period.

§ 2.54 Lost tags.

Each dealer or exhibitor shall be held accountable for all official tags acquired. In the event an official tag is lost from a dog or cat while in the possession of a dealer or exhibitor, the dealer or exhibitor shall make a diligent effort to locate and reapply the tag to the proper animal. If the lost tag is not located, the dealer or exhibitor shall affix another official tag to the animal in the manner prescribed in § 2.50, and record the tag number on the official records.

§ 2.55 Removal and disposal of tags.

(a) Where a dog or cat to which is affixed or which is identified by an official tag is euthanized, or dies from other causes, the dealer or exhibitor shall remove and retain the tag for the required period, as set forth in paragraph (b) of this section.

(b) All official tags removed and retained by a dealer or exhibitor shall be held until called for by an APHIS official or for a period of 1 year.

(c) When official tags are removed from animals for disposal, the tags must be disposed of so as to preclude their reuse for animal identification. No animal identification number shall be used within any 5-year period following its previous use.

Subpart F—Stolen Animals

§ 2.60 Prohibition on the purchase, sale, use, or transportation of stolen animals.

No person shall buy, sell, exhibit, use for research, transport, or offer for transportation, any stolen animal.

Subpart G—Records

§ 2.75 Records: Dealers and exhibitors.

(a)(1) Each dealer, other than operators of auction sales and brokers to whom animals are consigned, and each exhibitor shall make, keep, and maintain records or forms which fully and correctly disclose the following information concerning each dog or cat purchased or otherwise acquired, owned, held, or otherwise in his or her possession or under his or her control, or which is transported, euthanized, sold, or otherwise disposed of by that dealer or exhibitor. The records shall include any offspring born of any animal while in his or her possession or under his or her control.

(i) The name and address of the person from whom a dog or cat was purchased or otherwise acquired whether or not the person is required to be licensed or registered under the Act;

(ii) The USDA license or registration number of the person if he or she is licensed or registered under the Act;

(iii) The vehicle license number and State, and the driver's license number (or photographic identification card for nondrivers issued by a State) and State of the person, if he or she is not licensed or registered under the Act;

(iv) The name and address of the person to whom a dog or cat was sold or given and that person's license or registration number if he or she is licensed or registered under the Act;

(v) The date a dog or cat was acquired or disposed of, including by euthanasia;

(vi) The official USDA tag number or tattoo assigned to a dog or cat under §§ 2.50 and 2.54;

(vii) A description of each dog or cat which shall include:

(A) The species and breed or type;

(B) The sex;

(C) The date of birth or approximate age; and

(D) The color and any distinctive markings;

(viii) The method of transportation including the name of the initial carrier or intermediate handler or, if a privately owned vehicle is used to transport a dog or cat, the name of the owner of the privately owned vehicle;

(ix) The date and method of disposition of a dog or cat, e.g., sale, death, euthanasia, or donation.

(2) Each dealer and exhibitor shall use Record of Aquisition and Dogs and Cats on Hand (APHIS Form 7005) and Record of Disposition of Dogs and Cats (APHIS Form 7006) to make, keep, and

maintain the information required by paragraph (a)(1) of this section: *Provided*, that if a dealer or exhibitor who uses a computerized recordkeeping system believes that APHIS Form 7005 and APHIS Form 7006 are unsuitable for him or her to make, keep, and maintain the information required by paragraph (a)(1) of this section, the dealer or exhibitor may request a variance from the requirement to use APHIS Form 7005 and APHIS Form 7006.

(i) The request for a variance must consist of a written statement describing why APHIS Form 7005 and APHIS Form 7006 are unsuitable for the dealer or exhibitor to make, keep, and maintain the information required by paragraph (a)(1) of this section, and a description of the computerized recordkeeping system the person would use in lieu of APHIS Form 7005 and APHIS Form 7006 to make, keep, and maintain the information required by paragraph (a)(1) of this section. APHIS will advise the person as to the disposition of his or her request for a variance from the requirement to use APHIS Form 7005 and APHIS Form 7006.

(ii) A dealer or exhibitor whose request for a variance has been denied may request a hearing in accordance with the applicable rules of practice for the purpose of showing why the request for a variance should not be denied. The denial of the variance shall remain in effect until the final legal decision has been rendered.

(3) The USDA Interstate and International Certificate of Health Examination for Small Animals (APHIS Form 7001) may be used by dealers and exhibitors to make, keep, and maintain the information required by § 2.79.

(4) One copy of the record containing the information required by paragraph (a)(1) of this section shall accompany each shipment of any dog or cat purchased or otherwise acquired by a dealer or exhibitor. One copy of the record containing the information required by paragraph (a)(1) of this section shall accompany each shipment of any dog or cat sold or otherwise disposed of by a dealer or exhibitor: *Provided, however*, that, except as provided in § 2.133(b) of this part for dealers, information that indicates the source and date of acquisition of a dog or cat need not appear on the copy of the record accompanying the shipment. One copy of the record containing the information required by paragraph (a)(1) of this section shall be retained by the dealer or exhibitor.

(b)(1) Every dealer other than operators of auction sales and brokers to whom animals are consigned, and exhibitor shall make, keep, and maintain records or forms which fully and correctly disclose the following information concerning animals other than dogs and cats, purchased or otherwise acquired, owned, held, leased, or otherwise in his or her possession or under his or her control, or which is transported, sold, euthanized, or otherwise disposed of by that dealer or exhibitor. The records shall include any offspring born of any animal while in his or her possession or under his or her control.

(i) The name and address of the person from whom the animals were purchased or otherwise acquired;

(ii) The USDA license or registration number of the person if he or she is licensed or registered under the Act;

(iii) The vehicle license number and State, and the driver's license number (or photographic identification card for nondrivers issued by a State) and State of the person, if he or she is not licensed or registered under the Act;

(iv) The name and address of the person to whom an animal was sold or given;

(v) The date of purchase, acquisition, sale, or disposal of the animal(s);

(vi) The species of the animal(s); and

(vii) The number of animals in the shipment.

(2) Record of Animals on Hand (other than dogs and cats) (APHIS Form 7019) and Record of Acquisition, Disposition, or Transport of Animals (other than dogs and cats) (APHIS Form 7020) are forms which may be used by dealers and exhibitors to keep and maintain the information required by paragraph (b)(1) of this section concerning animals other than dogs and cats except as provided in § 2.79.

(3) One copy of the record containing the information required by paragraph (b)(1) of this section shall accompany each shipment of any animal(s) other than a dog or cat purchased or otherwise acquired by a dealer or exhibitor.

One copy of the record containing the information required by paragraph (b)(1) of this section shall accompany each shipment of any animal other than a dog or cat sold or otherwise disposed of by a dealer or exhibitor; *Provided, however,* That information which indicates the source and date of acquisition of any animal other than a dog or cat need not appear on the copy of the record accompanying the shipment. The dealer or exhibitor shall retain one copy of the record containing the information required by paragraph (b)(1) of this section.

[54 FR 36147, Aug. 31, 1989, as amended at 58 FR 39129, July 22, 1993; 58 FR 45041, Aug. 26, 1993; 60 FR 13895, Mar. 15, 1995; 69 FR 42102, July 14, 2004]

§2.76 Records: Operators of auction sales and brokers.

(a) Every operator of an auction sale or broker shall make, keep, and maintain records or forms which fully and correctly disclose the following information concerning each animal consigned for auction or sold, whether or not a fee or commission is charged:

(1) The name and address of the person who owned or consigned the animal(s) for sale;

(2) The name and address of the buyer or consignee who received the animal;

(3) The USDA license or registration number of the person(s) selling, consigning, buying, or receiving the animals if he or she is licensed or registered under the Act;

(4) The vehicle license number and State, and the driver's license number (or photographic identification card for nondrivers issued by a State) and State of the person, if he or she is not licensed or registered under the Act;

(5) The date of the consignment;

(6) The official USDA tag number or tattoo assigned to the animal under §§2.50 and 2.54;

(7) A description of the animal which shall include:

(i) The species and breed or type of animal;

(ii) The sex of the animal; and

(iii) The date of birth or approximate age; and

(iv) The color and any distinctive markings;

(8) The auction sales number or records number assigned to the animal.

(b) One copy of the record containing the information required by paragraph (a) of this section shall be given to the consignor of each animal, one copy of the record shall be given to the purchaser of each animal: *Provided, however,* That information which indicates the source and date of consignment of any animal need not appear on the copy of the record given the purchaser of any animal. One copy of the record containing the information required by paragraph (a) of this section shall be retained by the operator of such auction sale, or broker, for each animal sold by the auction sale or broker.

[54 FR 36147, Aug. 31, 1989, as amended at 69 FR 42102, July 14, 2004]

§2.77 Records: Carriers and intermediate handlers.

(a) In connection with all live animals accepted for shipment on a C.O.D. basis or other arrangement or practice under which the cost of an animal or the transportation of an animal is to be paid and collected upon delivery of the animal to the consignee, the accepting carrier or intermediate handler, if any, shall keep and maintain a copy of the consignor's written guarantee for the payment of transportation charged for any animal not claimed as provided in §2.80, including, where necessary, both the return transportation charges and an amount sufficient to reimburse the carrier for out-of-pocket expenses incurred for the care, feeding, and storage of the animal. The carrier or intermediate handler at destination shall also keep and maintain a copy of the shipping document containing the time, date, and method of each attempted notification and the final notification to the consignee and the name of the person notifying the consignee, as provided in §2.80.

(b) In connection with all live dogs, cats, or nonhuman primates delivered for transportation, in commerce, to any carrier or intermediate handler, by any dealer, research facility, exhibitor, operator of an auction sale, broker, or department, agency or instrumentality of the United States or of any state or local government, the accepting carrier or intermediate handler shall keep and maintain a copy of the health certification completed as required by § 2.79, tendered with each live dog, cat, or nonhuman primate.

§ 2.78 Health certification and identification.

(a) No dealer, exhibitor, operator of an auction sale, broker, or department, agency, or instrumentality of the United States or of any State or local government shall deliver to any intermediate handler or carrier for transportation, in commerce, or shall transport in commerce any dog, cat, or nonhuman primate unless the dog, cat, or nonhuman primate is accompanied by a health certificate executed and issued by a licensed veterinarian. The health certificate shall state that:

(1) The licensed veterinarian inspected the dog, cat, or nonhuman primate on a specified date which shall not be more than 10 days prior to the delivery of the dog, cat, or nonhuman primate for transportation; and

(2) when so inspected, the dog, cat, or nonhuman primate appeared to the licensed veterinarian to be free of any infectious disease or physical abnormality which would endanger the animal(s) or other animals or endanger public health.

(b) The Secretary may provide exceptions to the health certification requirement on an individual basis for animals shipped to a research facility for purposes of research, testing, or experimentation when the research facility requires animals not eligible for certification. Requests should be addressed to the Animal and Plant Health Inspection Service, Animal Care, 4700 River Road, Unit 84, Riverdale, Maryland 20737–1234.

(c) No intermediate handler or carrier to whom any live dog, cat, or nonhuman primate is delivered for transportation by any dealer, research facility, exhibitor, broker, operator of an auction sale, or department, agency, or instrumentality of the United States or any State or local government shall receive a live dog, cat, or nonhuman primate for transportation, in commerce, unless and until it is accompanied by a health certificate issued by a licensed veterinarian in accordance with paragraph (a) of this section, or an exemption issued by the Secretary in accordance with paragraph (b) of this section.

(d) The U.S. Interstate and International Certificate of Health Examination for Small Animals (APHIS Form 7001) may be used for health certification by a licensed veterinarian as required by this section.

[54 FR 36147, Aug. 31, 1989, as amended at 59 FR 67612, Dec. 30, 1994; 60 FR 13896, Mar. 15, 1995; 63 FR 62927, Nov. 10, 1998; 69 FR 42102, July 14, 2004]

§ 2.79 C.O.D. shipments.

(a) No carrier or intermediate handler shall accept any animal for transportation, in commerce, upon any C.O.D. or other basis where any money is to be paid and collected upon delivery of the animal to the consignee, unless the consignor guarantees in writing the payment of all transportation, including any return transportation, if the shipment is unclaimed or the consignee cannot be notified in accordance with paragraphs (b) and (c) of this section, including reimbursing the carrier or intermediate handler for all out-of-pocket expenses incurred for the care, feeding, and storage or housing of the animal.

(b) Any carrier or intermediate handler receiving an animal at a destination on a C.O.D. or other basis any money is to be paid and collected upon delivery of the animal to the consignee shall attempt to notify the consignee at least once every 6 hours for a period of 24 hours after arrival of the animal at the animal holding area of the terminal cargo facility. The carrier or intermediate handler shall record the time, date, and method of each attempted notification and the final notification to the consignee, and the name of the person notifying the consignee, on the shipping document and on the copy of the shipping document accompanying the C.O.D. shipment. If the consignee cannot be notified of the C.O.D. shipment within 24 hours after its arrival, the carrier or intermediate handler shall return the animal to the consignor, or to whomever the consignor has designated, on the next practical available transportation, in accordance with the written agreement required in paragraph (a) of this section and shall notify the consignor. Any carrier or intermediate handler which has notified a consignee of the arrival of a C.O.D. or other shipment of an animal, where any money is to be paid and collected upon delivery of the animal to the consignee, which is not claimed by the consignee within 48 hours from the time of notification, shall return the animal to the consignor, or to whomever the consignor has designated, on the next practical available transportation, in accordance with the written agreement required in paragraph (a) of this section and shall notify the consignor.

(c) It is the responsibility of any carrier or intermediate handler to hold, feed, and care for any animal accepted for transportation, in commerce, under a C.O.D. or other arrangement where any money is to be paid and collected upon delivery of the animal until the consignee accepts shipment at destination or until returned to the consignor or his or her designee should the consignee fail to accept delivery of the animal or if the consignee could not be notified as prescribed in paragraph (b) of this section.

(d) Nothing in this section shall be construed as prohibiting any carrier or intermediate handler from requiring any guarantee in addition to that required in paragraph (a) of this section for the payment of the cost of any transportation or out-of-pocket or other incidental expenses incurred in the transportation of any animal.

§2.80 Records, disposition.

(a) No dealer, exhibitor, broker, operator of an auction sale, carrier, or intermediate handler shall, for a period of 1 year, destroy or dispose of, without the consent in writing of the Administrator, any books, records, documents, or other papers required to be kept and maintained under this part.

(b) Unless otherwise specified, the records required to be kept and maintained under this part shall be held for 1 year after an animal is euthanized or disposed of and for any period in excess of one year as necessary to comply with any applicable Federal, State, or local law. Whenever the Administrator notifies a dealer, exhibitor, broker, operator of an auction sale, carrier, or intermediate handler in writing that specified records shall be retained pending completion of an investigation or proceeding under the Act, the dealer, exhibitor, broker, operator of an auction sale, carrier, or intermediate handler shall hold those records until their disposition is authorized by the Administrator.

Subpart H—Compliance With Standards and Holding Period

§2.100 Compliance with standards.

(a) Each dealer, exhibitor, operator of an auction sale, and intermediate handler shall comply in all respects with the regulations set forth in part 2 and the standards set forth in part 3 of this subchapter for the humane handling, care, treatment, housing, and transportation of animals.

(b) Each carrier shall comply in all respects with the regulations in part 2 and the standards in part 3 of this subchapter setting forth the conditions and requirements for the humane transportation of animals in commerce and their handling, care, and treatment in connection therewith.

§2.101 Holding period.

(a) Any live dog or cat acquired by a dealer[5] or exhibitor shall be held by him or her, under his or her supervision and control, for a period of not less than 5 full days, not including the day of acquisition, after acquiring the animal, excluding time in transit: *Provided, however:*

(1) That any live dog or cat acquired by a dealer or exhibitor from any private or contract animal pound or shelter shall be held by that dealer or exhibitor under his or her supervision and control for a period of not less than 10 full days, not including the day of acquisition, after acquiring the animal, excluding time in transit;

(2) Live dogs or cats which have completed a 5-day holding period with another dealer or exhibitor, or a 10-day holding period with another dealer or

[5] An operator of an auction sale is not considered to have acquired a dog or cat which is sold through the auction sale.

exhibitor if obtained from a private or contract shelter or pound, may be sold or otherwise disposed of by subsequent dealers or exhibitors after a minimum holding period of 24 hours by each subsequent dealer or exhibitor excluding time in transit;

(3) Any dog or cat suffering from disease, emaciation, or injury may be destroyed by euthanasia prior to the completion of the holding period required by this section; and

(4) Any live dog or cat, 120 days of age or less, that was obtained from the person that bred and raised such dog or cat, may be exempted from the 5-day holding requirement and may be disposed of by dealers or exhibitors after a minimum holding period of 24 hours, excluding time in transit. Each subsequent dealer or exhibitor must also hold each such dog or cat for a 24-hour period excluding time in transit.

(b) During the period in which any dog or cat is being held as required by this section, the dog or cat shall be unloaded from any means of conveyance in which it was received, for food, water, and rest, and shall be handled, cared for, and treated in accordance with the standards set forth in part 3, subpart A, of this subchapter and § 2.131.

§ 2.102 Holding facility.

(a) If any dealer or exhibitor obtains the prior approval of the AC Regional Director, he may arrange to have another person hold animals for the required period provided for in paragraph (a) of § 2.101: *Provided*, That:

(1) The other person agrees in writing to comply with the regulations in part 2 and the standards in part 3 of this subchapter and to allow inspection of his premises by an APHIS official during business hours; and

(2) The animals remain under the total control and responsibility of the dealer or exhibitor.

(3) Approval will not be given for a dealer or exhibitor holding a license as set forth in § 2.1 to have animals held for purposes of this section by another licensed dealer or exhibitor. APHIS Form 7009 shall be used for approval.

(4) The other person or premises must either be directly included in the dealer's or exhibitor's contingency plan required under § 2.134 or must develop its own contingency plan in accordance with § 2.134.

(b) If any intermediate handler obtains prior approval of the AC Regional Director, it may arrange to have another person hold animals: *Provided*, That:

(1) The other person agrees in writing to comply with the regulations in part 2 and the standards in part 3 of this subchapter and to allow inspection of the premises by an APHIS official during business hours; and

(2) The animals remain under the total control and responsibility of the research facility or intermediate handler.

(3) The other person or premises must either be directly included in the intermediate handler's contingency plan required under § 2.134 or must develop its own contingency plan in accordance with § 2.134.

[54 FR 36147, Aug. 31, 1989, as amended at 60 FR 13896, Mar. 15, 1995; 63 FR 62927, Nov. 10, 1998; 69 FR 42102, July 14, 2004; 77 FR 76823, Dec. 31, 2012]

Subpart I—Miscellaneous

§ 2.125 Information as to business; furnishing of same by dealers, exhibitors, operators of auction sales, intermediate handlers, and carriers.

Each dealer, exhibitor, operator of an auction sale, intermediate handler, and carrier shall furnish to any APHIS official any information concerning the business of the dealer, exhibitor, operator of an auction sale, intermediate handler or carrier which the APHIS official may request in connection with the enforcement of the provisions of the Act, the regulations and the standards in this subchapter. The information shall be furnished within a reasonable time and as may be specified in the request for information.

§ 2.126 Access and inspection of records and property; submission of itineraries.

(a) Each dealer, exhibitor, intermediate handler, or carrier, shall, during business hours, allow APHIS officials:

(1) To enter its place of business;

(2) To examine records required to be kept by the Act and the regulations in this part;

(3) To make copies of the records;

(4) To inspect and photograph the facilities, property and animals, as the APHIS officials consider necessary to enforce the provisions of the Act, the regulations and the standards in this subchapter; and

(5) To document, by the taking of photographs and other means, conditions and areas of noncompliance.

(b) The use of a room, table, or other facilities necessary for the proper examination of the records and inspection of the property or animals must be extended to APHIS officials by the dealer, exhibitor, intermediate handler or carrier, and a responsible adult shall be made available to accompany APHIS officials during the inspection process.

(c) Any person who is subject to the Animal Welfare regulations and who intends to exhibit any animal at any location other than the person's approved site (including, but not limited to, circuses, traveling educational exhibits, animal acts, and petting zoos), except for travel that does not extend overnight, shall submit a written itinerary to the AC Regional Director. The itinerary shall be received by the AC Regional Director no fewer than 2 days in advance of any travel and shall contain complete and accurate information concerning the whereabouts of any animal intended for exhibition at any location other than the person's approved site. If the exhibitor accepts an engagement for which travel will begin with less than 48 hours' notice, the exhibitor shall immediately contact the AC Regional Director in writing with the required information. APHIS expects such situations to occur infrequently, and exhibitors who repeatedly provide less than 48 hours' notice will, after notice by APHIS, be subject to increased scrutiny under the Act.

(1) The itinerary shall include the following:

(i) The name of the person who intends to exhibit the animal and transport the animal for exhibition purposes, including any business name and current Act license or registration number and, in the event that any animal is leased, borrowed, loaned, or under some similar arrangement, the name of the person who owns such animal;

(ii) The name, identification number or identifying characteristics, species (common or scientific name), sex and age of each animal; and

(iii) The names, dates, and locations (with addresses) where the animals will travel, be housed, and be exhibited, including all anticipated dates and locations (with addresses) for any stops and layovers that allow or require removal of the animals from the transport enclosures. Unanticipated delays of such length shall be reported to the AC Regional Director the next APHIS business day. APHIS Regional offices are available each weekday, except on Federal holidays, from 8 a.m. to 5 p.m.

(2) The itinerary shall be revised as necessary, and the AC Regional Director shall be notified of any changes. If initial notification of a change due to an emergency is made by a means other than email or facsimile, it shall be followed by written documentation at the earliest possible time. For changes that occur after normal APHIS business hours, the change shall be conveyed to the AC Regional Director no later than the following APHIS business day. APHIS Regional offices are available each weekday, except on Federal holidays, from 8 a.m. to 5 p.m.

(Approved by the Office of Management and Budget under control number 0579–0361)

[54 FR 36147, Aug. 31, 1989, as amended at 69 FR 42102, July 14, 2004; 77 FR 76814, Dec. 31, 2012]

§2.127 Publication of names of persons subject to the provisions of this part.

APHIS will publish lists of persons licensed or registered in accordance with the provisions of this part in the FEDERAL REGISTER. The lists may be obtained upon request from the AC Regional Director.

[54 FR 36147, Aug. 31, 1989, as amended at 63 FR 62927, Nov. 10, 1998]

§2.128 Inspection for missing animals.

Each dealer, exhibitor, intermediate handler and carrier shall allow, upon request and during business hours, police or officers of other law enforcement agencies with general law enforcement authority (not those agencies whose duties are limited to enforcement of local animal regulations) to enter his or her place of business to inspect animals and records for the purpose of seeking animals that are missing, under the following conditions:

(a) The police or other law officer shall furnish to the dealer, exhibitor, intermediate handler or carrier a written description of the missing animal and the name and address of its owner before making a search.

(b) The police or other law officer shall abide by all security measures required by the dealer, exhibitor, intermediate handler or carrier to prevent the spread of disease, including the use of sterile clothing, footwear, and masks where required, or to prevent the escape of an animal.

§ 2.129 Confiscation and destruction of animals.

(a) If an animal being held by a dealer, exhibitor, intermediate handler, or by a carrier is found by an APHIS official to be suffering as a result of the failure of the dealer, exhibitor, intermediate handler, or carrier to comply with any provision of the regulations or the standards set forth in this subchapter, the APHIS official shall make a reasonable effort to notify the dealer, exhibitor, intermediate handler, or carrier of the condition of the animal(s) and request that the condition be corrected and that adequate care be given to alleviate the animal's suffering or distress, or that the animal(s) be destroyed by euthanasia. In the event that the dealer, exhibitor, intermediate handler, or carrier refuses to comply with this request, the APHIS official may confiscate the animal(s) for care, treatment, or disposal as indicated in paragraph (b) of this section, if, in the opinion of the Administrator, the circumstances indicate the animal's health is in danger.

(b) In the event that the APHIS official is unable to locate or notify the dealer, exhibitor, intermediate handler, or carrier as required in this section, the APHIS official shall contact a local police or other law officer to accompany him to the premises and shall provide for adequate care when necessary to alleviate the animal's suffering. If in the opinion of the Administrator, the condition of the animal(s) cannot be corrected by this temporary care, the APHIS official shall confiscate the animals.

(c) Confiscated animals may be:

(1) Placed, by sale or donation, with other licensees or registrants that comply with the standards and regulations and can provide proper care; or

(2) Placed with persons or facilities that can offer a level of care equal to or exceeding the standards and regulations, as determined by APHIS, even if the persons or facilities are not licensed by or registered with APHIS; or

(3) Euthanized.

(d) The dealer, exhibitor, intermediate handler, or carrier from whom the animals were confiscated must bear all costs incurred in performing the placement or euthanasia activities authorized by this section.

[54 FR 36147, Aug. 31, 1989, as amended at 66 FR 239, Jan. 3, 2001]

§ 2.130 Minimum age requirements.

No dog or cat shall be delivered by any person to any carrier or intermediate handler for transportation, in commerce, or shall be transported in commerce by any person, except to a registered research facility, unless such dog or cat is at least eight (8) weeks of age and has been weaned.

§ 2.131 Handling of animals.

(a) All licensees who maintain wild or exotic animals must demonstrate adequate experience and knowledge of the species they maintain.

(b)(1) Handling of all animals shall be done as expeditiously and carefully as possible in a manner that does not cause trauma, overheating, excessive cooling, behavioral stress, physical harm, or unnecessary discomfort.

(2)(i) Physical abuse shall not be used to train, work, or otherwise handle animals.

(ii) Deprivation of food or water shall not be used to train, work, or otherwise handle animals; *Provided, however,* That the short-term withholding of food or water from animals by exhibitors is allowed by these regulations as long as each of the animals affected receives its full dietary and nutrition requirements each day.

(c)(1) During public exhibition, any animal must be handled so there is minimal risk of harm to the animal and to the public, with sufficient distance and/or barriers between the animal and the general viewing public so as to assure the safety of animals and the public.

(2) Performing animals shall be allowed a rest period between performances at least equal to the time for one performance.

(3) Young or immature animals shall not be exposed to rough or excessive public handling or exhibited for periods of time which would be detrimental to their health or well-being.

(4) Drugs, such as tranquilizers, shall not be used to facilitate, allow, or provide for public handling of the animals.

(d)(1) Animals shall be exhibited only for periods of time and under conditions consistent with their good health and well-being.

(2) A responsible, knowledgeable, and readily identifiable employee or attendant must be present at all times during periods of public contact.

(3) During public exhibition, dangerous animals such as lions, tigers, wolves, bears, or elephants must be under the direct control and supervision of a knowledgeable and experienced animal handler.

(4) If public feeding of animals is allowed, the food must be provided by the animal facility and shall be appropriate to the type of animal and its nutritional needs and diet.

(e) When climatic conditions present a threat to an animal's health or well-being, appropriate measures must be taken to alleviate the impact of those conditions. An animal may never be subjected to any combination of temperature, humidity, and time that is detrimental to the animal's health or well-being, taking into consideration such factors as the animal's age, species, breed, overall health status, and acclimation.

[54 FR 36147, Aug. 31, 1989, as amended at 63 FR 10498, Mar. 4, 1998; 69 FR 42102, July 14, 2004]

§2.132 Procurement of dogs, cats, and other animals; dealers.

(a) A class "B" dealer may obtain live random source dogs and cats only from:

(1) Other dealers who are licensed under the Act and in accordance with the regulations in part 2;

(2) State, county, or city owned and operated animal pounds or shelters; and

(3) A legal entity organized and operated under the laws of the State in which it is located as an animal pound or shelter, such as a humane shelter or contract pound.

(b) No person shall obtain live dogs, cats, or other animals by use of false pretenses, misrepresentation, or deception.

(c) Any dealer, exhibitor, research facility, carrier, or intermediate handler who also operates a private or contract animal pound or shelter shall comply with the following:

(1) The animal pound or shelter shall be located on premises that are physically separated from the licensed or registered facility. The animal housing facility of the pound or shelter shall not be adjacent to the licensed or registered facility.

(2) Accurate and complete records shall be separately maintained by the licensee or registrant and by the pound or shelter. The records shall be in accordance with §§2.75 and 2.76, unless the animals are lost or stray. If the animals are lost or stray, the pound or shelter records shall provide:

(i) An accurate description of the animal;

(ii) How, where, from whom, and when the dog or cat was obtained;

(iii) How long the dog or cat was held by the pound or shelter before being transferred to the dealer; and

(iv) The date the dog or cat was transferred to the dealer.

(3) Any dealer who obtains or acquires a live dog or cat from a private or contract pound or shelter, including a pound or shelter he or she operates, shall hold the dog or cat for a period of at least 10 full days, not including the day of acquisition, excluding time in transit, after acquiring the animal, and otherwise in accordance with §2.101.

(d) No dealer or exhibitor shall knowingly obtain any dog, cat, or other animal from any person who is required to be licensed but who does not hold a current, valid, and unsuspended license. No dealer or exhibitor shall knowingly obtain any dog or cat from any person who is not licensed, other than a pound or shelter, without obtaining a certification that the animals were born and raised on that person's premises and, if the animals are for research purposes, that the person has sold fewer than 25 dogs and/or cats that year, or, if the animals are for use as pets, that the person does not maintain more than four breeding female dogs and/or cats.

(Approved by the Office of Management and Budget under control number 0579–0254)

[54 FR 36147, Aug. 31, 1989, as amended at 69 FR 42102, July 14, 2004; 80 FR 3463, Jan. 23, 2015]

§ 2.133 Certification for random source dogs and cats.

(a) Each of the entities listed in paragraphs (a)(1) through (a)(3) of this section that acquire any live dog or cat shall, before selling or providing the live dog or cat to a dealer, hold and care for the dog or cat for a period of not less than 5 full days after acquiring the animal, not including the date of acquisition and excluding time in transit. This holding period shall include at least one Saturday. The provisions of this paragraph apply to:

(1) Each pound or shelter owned and operated by a State, county, or city;

(2) Each private pound or shelter established for the purpose of caring for animals, such as a humane society, or other organization that is under contract with a State, county, or city, that operates as a pound or shelter, and that releases animals on a voluntary basis; and

(3) Each research facility licensed by USDA as a dealer.

(b) A dealer shall not sell, provide, or make available to any person a live random source dog or cat unless the dealer provides the recipient of the dog or cat with certification that contains the following information:

(1) The name, address, USDA license number, and signature of the dealer;

(2) The name, address, USDA license or registration number, if such number exists, and signature of the recipient of the dog or cat;

(3) A description of each dog or cat being sold, provided, or made available that shall include:

(i) The species and breed or type (for mixed breeds, estimate the two dominant breeds or types);

(ii) The sex;

(iii) The date of birth or, if unknown, then the approximate age;

(iv) The color and any distinctive markings; and

(v) The Official USDA-approved identification number of the animal. However, if the certification is attached to a certificate provided by a prior dealer which contains the required description, then only the official identification numbers are required;

(4) The name and address of the person, pound, or shelter from which the dog or cat was acquired by the dealer, and an assurance that the person, pound, or shelter was notified that the cat or dog might be used for research or educational purposes;

(5) The date the dealer acquired the dog or cat from the person, pound, or shelter referred to in paragraph (b)(4) of this section; and

(6) If the dealer acquired the dog or cat from a pound or shelter, a signed statement by the pound or shelter that it met the requirements of paragraph (a) of this section. This statement must at least describe the animals by their official USDA identification numbers. It may be incorporated within the certification if the dealer makes the certification at the time that the animals are acquired from the pound or shelter or it may be made separately and attached to the certification later. If made separately, it must include the same information describing each animal as is required in the certification. A photocopy of the statement will be regarded as a duplicate original.

(c) The original certification required under paragraph (b) of this section shall accompany the shipment of a live dog or cat to be sold, provided, or otherwise made available by the dealer.

(d) A dealer who acquires a live dog or cat from another dealer must obtain from that dealer the certification required by paragraph (b) of this section and must attach that certification (including any previously attached certification) to the certification which he or she provides pursuant to paragraph (b) of this section (a photocopy of the original certification will be deemed a duplicate original if the dealer does not dispose of all of the dogs or cats in a single transaction).

(e) A dealer who completes, provides, or receives a certification required under paragraph (b) of this section shall keep, maintain, and make available for APHIS inspection a copy of the certification for at least 1 year following disposition.

(f) A research facility which acquires any live random source dog or cat from a dealer must obtain the certification required under paragraph (b) of this section and shall keep, maintain, and make available for APHIS inspection the original for at least 3 years following disposition.

(g) In instances where a research facility transfers ownership of a live random source dog or cat acquired from a dealer to another research facility, a copy of the certification required by paragraph (b) of this section must accompany the dog or cat transferred. The research facility to which the dog or cat is transferred shall keep, maintain, and make available for APHIS inspection the copy of the certification for at least 3 years following disposition.

[58 FR 39129, July 22, 1993]

§2.134 Contingency planning.

(a) Dealers, exhibitors, intermediate handlers, and carriers must develop, document, and follow an appropriate plan to provide for the humane handling, treatment, transportation, housing, and care of their animals in the event of an emergency or disaster (one which could reasonably be anticipated and expected to be detrimental to the good health and well-being of the animals in their possession). Such contingency plans must:

(1) Identify situations the licensee or registrant might experience that would trigger the need for the measures identified in a contingency plan to be put into action including, but not limited to, emergencies such as electrical outages, faulty HVAC systems, fires, mechanical breakdowns, and animal escapes, as well as natural disasters most likely to be experienced;

(2) Outline specific tasks required to be carried out in response to the identified emergencies or disasters including, but not limited to, detailed animal evacuation instructions or shelter-in-place instructions and provisions for providing backup sources of food and water as well as sanitation, ventilation, bedding, veterinary care, etc.;

(3) Identify a chain of command and who (by name or by position title) will be responsible for fulfilling these tasks; and

(4) Address how response and recovery will be handled in terms of materials, resources, and training needed.

(b) For current licensees and registrants, the contingency plan must be in place by July 29, 2013. For new dealers, exhibitors, intermediate handlers, and carriers licensed or registered after this date, the contingency plan must be in place prior to conducting regulated activities. The plan must be reviewed by the dealer, exhibitor, intermediate handler, or carrier on at least an annual basis to ensure that it adequately addresses the criteria listed in paragraph (a) of this section. Each licensee and registrant must maintain documentation of their annual reviews, including documenting any amendments or changes made to their plan since the previous year's review, such as changes made as a result of recently predicted, but historically unforeseen, circumstances (e.g., weather extremes). Contingency plans, as well as all annual review documentation and training records, must be made available to APHIS upon request. Traveling entities must carry a copy of their contingency plan with them at all times and make it available for APHIS inspection while in travel status. Dealers, exhibitors, intermediate handlers, and carriers maintaining or otherwise handling marine mammals in captivity must also comply with the requirements of §3.101(b) of this subchapter.

(c) Dealers, exhibitors, intermediate handlers, and carriers must provide and document participation in and successful completion of training for personnel regarding their roles and responsibilities as outlined in the plan. For current licensees and registrants, training of dealer, exhibitor, intermediate handler, and carrier personnel must be completed by September 27, 2013. For new dealers, exhibitors, intermediate handlers, or carriers licensed or registered after July 29, 2013, training of personnel must be completed within 60 days of the dealer, exhibitor, intermediate handler, or carrier putting their contingency plan in place. Employees hired 30 days or more before their contingency plan is put in place must also be trained by that date. For employees hired less than 30 days before that date or after that date, training must be conducted within 30 days of their start date. Any changes to the plan as a result of the annual review must be communicated to employees through training which must be conducted within 30 days of making the changes.

[77 FR 76823, Dec. 31, 2012]

EFFECTIVE DATE NOTE: At 78 FR 46255, July 31, 2013, § 2.134 was stayed indefinitely, effective July 31, 2013.

Subpart J—Importation of Live Dogs

SOURCE: 79 FR 48659, Aug. 18, 2014, unless otherwise noted.

§ 2.150 Import permit.

(a) No person shall import a live dog from any part of the world into the continental United States or Hawaii for purposes of resale, research, or veterinary treatment unless the dog is accompanied by an import permit issued by APHIS and is imported into the continental United States or Hawaii within 30 days after the proposed date of arrival stated in the import permit.

(b) An application for an import permit must be submitted to the Animal and Plant Health Inspection Service, Animal Care, 4700 River Road Unit 84, Riverdale, MD 20737–1234 or though Animal Care's Web site (*http://www.aphis.usda.gov/animal_welfare/*). Application forms for import permits may be obtained from Animal Care at the address listed above.

(c) The completed application must include the following information:

(1) The name and address of the person intending to export the dog(s) to the continental United States or Hawaii;

(2) The name and address of the person intending to import the dog(s) into the continental United States or Hawaii;

(3) The number of dogs to be imported and the breed, sex, age, color, markings, and other identifying information of each dog;

(4) The purpose of the importation;

(5) The port of embarkation and the mode of transportation;

(6) The port of entry in the United States;

(7) The proposed date of arrival in the continental United States or Hawaii; and

(8) The name and address of the person to whom the dog(s) will be delivered in the continental United States or Hawaii and, if the dog(s) is or are imported for research purposes, the USDA registration number of the research facility where the dog will be used for research, tests, or experiments.

(d) After receipt and review of the application by APHIS, an import permit indicating the applicable conditions for importation under this subpart may be issued for the importation of the dog(s) described in the application if such dog(s) appears to be eligible to be imported. Even though an import permit has been issued for the importation of a dog, the dog may only be imported if all applicable requirements of this subpart and any other applicable regulations of this subchapter and any other statute or regulation of any State or of the United States are met.

(Approved by the Office of Management and Budget under control number 0579–0379)

§ 2.151 Certifications.

(a) *Required certificates.* Except as provided in paragraph (b) of this section, no person shall import a live dog from any part of the world into the continental United States or Hawaii for purposes of resale, research, or veterinary treatment unless the following conditions are met:

(1) *Health certificate.* Each dog is accompanied by an original health certificate issued in English by a licensed veterinarian with a valid license to practice veterinary medicine in the country of export that:

(i) Specifies the name and address of the person intending to import the dog into the continental United States or Hawaii;

(ii) Identifies the dog on the basis of breed, sex, age, color, markings, and other identifying information;

(iii) States that the dog is at least 6 months of age;

(iv) States that the dog was vaccinated, not more than 12 months before the date of arrival at the U.S. port, for distemper, hepatitis, leptospirosis, parvovirus, and parainfluenza virus (DHLPP) at a frequency that provides continuous protection of the dog from those diseases and is in accordance with currently accepted practices as cited in veterinary medicine reference guides;

(v) States that the dog is in good health (*i.e.*, free of any infectious disease or physical abnormality which would endanger the dog or other animals or endanger public health, including, but not limited to, parasitic infection, emaciation, lesions of the skin, nervous system disturbances, jaundice, or diarrhea); and

(vi) Bears the signature and the license number of the veterinarian issuing the certificate.

(2) *Rabies vaccination certificate.* Each dog is accompanied by a valid rabies vaccination certificate[6] that was issued in English by a licensed veterinarian with a valid license to practice veterinary medicine in the country of export for the dog not less than 3 months of age at the time of vaccination that:

(i) Specifies the name and address of the person intending to import the dog into the continental United States or Hawaii;

(ii) Identifies the dog on the basis of breed, sex, age, color, markings, and other identifying information;

(iii) Specifies a date of rabies vaccination at least 30 days before the date of arrival of the dog at a U.S. port;

(iv) Specifies a date of expiration of the vaccination which is after the date of arrival of the dog at a U.S. port. If no date of expiration is specified, then the date of vaccination shall be no more than 12 months before the date of arrival at a U.S. port; and

(v) Bears the signature and the license number of the veterinarian issuing the certificate.

(b) *Exceptions.* (1) *Research.* The provisions of paragraphs (a)(1)(iii), (a)(1)(iv), (a)(1)(v), and/or (a)(2) of this section do not apply to any person who imports a live dog from any part of the world into the continental United States or Hawaii for use in research, tests, or experiments at a research facility, provided that: Such person submits satisfactory evidence to Animal Care at the time of his or her application for an import permit that the specific provision(s) would interfere with the dog's use in such research, tests, or experiments in accordance with a research proposal and the proposal has been approved by the research facility IACUC.

(2) *Veterinary care.* The provisions of paragraphs (a)(1)(iii) through (a)(1)(v) and (a)(2) of this section do not apply to any person who imports a live dog from any part of the world into the continental United States or Hawaii for veterinary treatment by a licensed veterinarian, provided that:

(i) The original health certificate required in paragraph (a)(1) of this section states that the dog is in need of veterinary treatment that cannot be obtained in the country of export and states the name and address of the licensed veterinarian in the United States who intends to provide the dog such veterinary treatment; and

(ii) The person who imports the dog completes a veterinary treatment agreement with Animal Care at the time of application for an import permit and confines the animal until the conditions specified in the agreement are met. Such conditions may include

[6] Alternatively, this requirement can be met by providing an exact copy of the rabies vaccination certificate if so required under the Public Health Service regulations in 42 CFR 71.51.

determinations by the licensed veterinarian in the United States that the dog is in good health, has been adequately vaccinated against DHLPP and rabies, and is at least 6 months of age. The person importing the dog shall bear the expense of veterinary treatment and confinement.

(3) *Dogs imported into Hawaii from the British Isles, Australia, Guam, or New Zealand.* The provisions of paragraph (a)(1)(iii) of this section do not apply to any person who lawfully imports a live dog into the State of Hawaii from the British Isles, Australia, Guam, or New Zealand in compliance with the applicable regulations of the State of Hawaii, provided that the dog is not transported out of the State of Hawaii for purposes of resale at less than 6 months of age.

(Approved by the Office of Management and Budget under control number 0579–0379)

§ 2.152 Notification of arrival.

Upon the arrival of a dog at the port of first arrival in the continental United States or Hawaii, the person intending to import the dog, or his or her agent, must present the import permit and any applicable certifications and veterinary treatment agreement required by this subpart to the collector of customs for use at that port.

§ 2.153 Dogs refused entry.

Any dog refused entry into the continental United States or Hawaii for noncompliance with the requirements of this subpart may be removed from the continental United States or Hawaii or may be seized and the person intending to import the dog shall provide for the care (including appropriate veterinary care), forfeiture, and adoption of the dog, at his or her expense.

PART 3—STANDARDS

Subpart A—Specifications for the Humane Handling, Care, Treatment, and Transportation of Dogs and Cats

Subpart B—Specifications for the Humane Handling, Care, Treatment, and Transportation of Guinea Pigs and Hamsters

Subpart C—Specifications for the Humane Handling, Care, Treatment and Transportation of Rabbits

Subpart D—Specifications for the Humane Handling, Care, Treatment, and Transportation of Nonhuman Primates

Subpart E—Specifications for the Humane Handling, Care, Treatment, and Transportation of Marine Mammals

Subpart F—Specifications for the Humane Handling, Care, Treatment, and Transportation of Warmblooded Animals Other Than Dogs, Cats, Rabbits, Hamsters, Guinea Pigs, Nonhuman Primates, and Marine Mammals

AUTHORITY: 7 U.S.C. 2131–2159; 7 CFR 2.22, 2.80, and 371.7.

SOURCE: 32 FR 3273, Feb. 24, 1967, unless otherwise noted.

Subpart A—Specifications for the Humane Handling, Care, Treatment, and Transportation of Dogs and Cats [1]

SOURCE: 56 FR 6486, Feb. 15, 1991, unless otherwise noted.

FACILITIES AND OPERATING STANDARDS

§ 3.1 Housing facilities, general.

(a) *Structure; construction.* Housing facilities for dogs and cats must be designed and constructed so that they are structurally sound. They must be kept in good repair, and they must protect the animals from injury, contain the animals securely, and restrict other animals from entering.

(b) *Condition and site.* Housing facilities and areas used for storing animal food or bedding must be free of any accumulation of trash, waste material, junk, weeds, and other discarded materials. Animal areas inside of housing facilities must be kept neat and free of clutter, including equipment, furniture, and stored material, but may contain materials actually used and necessary for cleaning the area, and fixtures or equipment necessary for proper husbandry practices and research needs. Housing facilities other than those maintained by research facilities and Federal research facilities must be physically separated from any other business. If a housing facility is located on the same premises as another business, it must be physically separated from the other business so that animals the size of dogs, skunks, and raccoons are prevented from entering it.

(c) *Surfaces*—(1) *General requirements.* The surfaces of housing facilities—including houses, dens, and other furniture-type fixtures and objects within the facility—must be constructed in a manner and made of materials that allow them to be readily cleaned and sanitized, or removed or replaced when worn or soiled. Interior surfaces and any surfaces that come in contact with dogs or cats must:

(i) Be free of excessive rust that prevents the required cleaning and sanitization, or that affects the structural strength of the surface; and

(ii) Be free of jagged edges or sharp points that might injure the animals.

(2) *Maintenance and replacement of surfaces.* All surfaces must be maintained on a regular basis. Surfaces of housing facilities—including houses, dens, and other furniture-type fixtures and objects within the facility—that cannot be readily cleaned and sanitized, must be replaced when worn or soiled.

(3) *Cleaning.* Hard surfaces with which the dogs or cats come in contact must be spot-cleaned daily and sanitized in accordance with § 3.11(b) of this subpart to prevent accumulation of excreta and reduce disease hazards. Floors made of dirt, absorbent bedding, sand, gravel, grass, or other similar material must be raked or spot-cleaned with sufficient frequency to ensure all animals the freedom to avoid contact with excreta. Contaminated material must be replaced whenever this raking and spot-cleaning is not sufficient to prevent or eliminate odors, insects, pests, or vermin infestation. All other surfaces of housing facilities must be cleaned and sanitized when necessary to satisfy generally accepted husbandry standards and practices. Sanitization may be done using any of the methods provided in § 3.11(b)(3) for primary enclosures.

(d) *Water and electric power.* The housing facility must have reliable electric power adequate for heating, cooling, ventilation, and lighting, and for carrying out other husbandry requirements in accordance with the regulations in this subpart. The housing facility must provide adequate running potable water for the dogs' and cats' drinking needs, for cleaning, and for carrying out other husbandry requirements.

(e) *Storage.* Supplies of food and bedding must be stored in a manner that protects the supplies from spoilage, contamination, and vermin infestation. The supplies must be stored off the floor and away from the walls, to allow cleaning underneath and around the supplies. Foods requiring refrigeration must be stored accordingly, and all food must be stored in a manner that

[1] These minimum standards apply only to live dogs and cats, unless stated otherwise.

prevents contamination and deterioration of its nutritive value. All open supplies of food and bedding must be kept in leakproof containers with tightly fitting lids to prevent contamination and spoilage. Only food and bedding that is currently being used may be kept in the animal areas. Substances that are toxic to the dogs or cats but are required for normal husbandry practices must not be stored in food storage and preparation areas, but may be stored in cabinets in the animal areas.

(f) *Drainage and waste disposal.* Housing facility operators must provide for regular and frequent collection, removal, and disposal of animal and food wastes, bedding, debris, garbage, water, other fluids and wastes, and dead animals, in a manner that minimizes contamination and disease risks. Housing facilities must be equipped with disposal facilities and drainage systems that are constructed and operated so that animal waste and water are rapidly eliminated and animals stay dry. Disposal and drainage systems must minimize vermin and pest infestation, insects, odors, and disease hazards. All drains must be properly constructed, installed, and maintained. If closed drainage systems are used, they must be equipped with traps and prevent the backflow of gases and the backup of sewage onto the floor. If the facility uses sump or settlement ponds, or other similar systems for drainage and animal waste disposal, the system must be located far enough away from the animal area of the housing facility to prevent odors, diseases, pests, and vermin infestation. Standing puddles of water in animal enclosures must be drained or mopped up so that the animals stay dry. Trash containers in housing facilities and in food storage and food preparation areas must be leakproof and must have tightly fitted lids on them at all times. Dead animals, animal parts, and animal waste must not be kept in food storage or food preparation areas, food freezers, food refrigerators, or animal areas.

(g) *Washrooms and sinks.* Washing facilities such as washrooms, basins, sinks, or showers must be provided for animal caretakers and must be readily accessible.

§3.2 Indoor housing facilities.

(a) *Heating, cooling, and temperature.* Indoor housing facilities for dogs and cats must be sufficiently heated and cooled when necessary to protect the dogs and cats from temperature or humidity extremes and to provide for their health and well-being. When dogs or cats are present, the ambient temperature in the facility must not fall below 50 °F (10 °C) for dogs and cats not acclimated to lower temperatures, for those breeds that cannot tolerate lower temperatures without stress or discomfort (such as short-haired breeds), and for sick, aged, young, or infirm dogs and cats, except as approved by the attending veterinarian. Dry bedding, solid resting boards, or other methods of conserving body heat must be provided when temperatures are below 50 °F (10 °C). The ambient temperature must not fall below 45 °F (7.2 °C) for more than 4 consecutive hours when dogs or cats are present, and must not rise above 85 °F (29.5 °C) for more than 4 consecutive hours when dogs or cats are present. The preceding requirements are in addition to, not in place of, all other requirements pertaining to climatic conditions in parts 2 and 3 of this chapter.

(b) *Ventilation.* Indoor housing facilities for dogs and cats must be sufficiently ventilated at all times when dogs or cats are present to provide for their health and well-being, and to minimize odors, drafts, ammonia levels, and moisture condensation. Ventilation must be provided by windows, vents, fans, or air conditioning. Auxiliary ventilation, such as fans, blowers, or air conditioning must be provided when the ambient temperature is 85 °F (29.5 °C) or higher. The relative humidity must be maintained at a level that ensures the health and well-being of the dogs or cats housed therein, in accordance with the directions of the attending veterinarian and generally accepted professional and husbandry practices.

(c) *Lighting.* Indoor housing facilities for dogs and cats must be lighted well enough to permit routine inspection and cleaning of the facility, and observation of the dogs and cats. Animal areas must be provided a regular diurnal lighting cycle of either natural or artificial light. Lighting must be uniformly diffused throughout animal facilities and provide sufficient illumination to aid in maintaining good housekeeping practices, adequate cleaning, adequate inspection of animals, and for the well-being of the animals. Primary enclosures must be placed so as to protect the dogs and cats from excessive light.

(d) *Interior surfaces.* The floors and walls of indoor housing facilities, and any other surfaces in contact with the animals, must be impervious to moisture. The ceilings of indoor housing facilities must be impervious to moisture or be replaceable (e.g., a suspended ceiling with replaceable panels).

[56 FR 6486, Feb. 15, 1991, as amended at 63 FR 10498, Mar. 4, 1998]

§ 3.3 Sheltered housing facilities.

(a) *Heating, cooling, and temperature.* The sheltered part of sheltered housing facilities for dogs and cats must be sufficiently heated and cooled when necessary to protect the dogs and cats from temperature or humidity extremes and to provide for their health and well-being. The ambient temperature in the sheltered part of the facility must not fall below 50 °F (10 °C) for dogs and cats not acclimated to lower temperatures, for those breeds that cannot tolerate lower temperatures without stress and discomfort (such as short-haired breeds), and for sick, aged, young, or infirm dogs or cats, except as approved by the attending veterinarian. Dry bedding, solid resting boards, or other methods of conserving body heat must be provided when temperatures are below 50 °F (10 °C). The ambient temperature must not fall below 45 °F (7.2 °C) for more than 4 consecutive hours when dogs or cats are present, and must not rise above 85 °F (29.5 °C) for more than 4 consecutive hours when dogs or cats are present. The preceding requirements are in addition to, not in place of, all other requirements pertaining to climatic conditions in parts 2 and 3 of this chapter.

(b) *Ventilation.* The enclosed or sheltered part of sheltered housing facilities for dogs and cats must be sufficiently ventilated when dogs or cats are present to provide for their health and well-being, and to minimize odors, drafts, ammonia levels, and moisture condensation. Ventilation must be provided by windows, doors, vents, fans, or air conditioning. Auxiliary ventilation, such as fans, blowers, or air-conditioning, must be provided when the ambient temperature is 85 °F (29.5 °C) or higher.

(c) *Lighting.* Sheltered housing facilities for dogs and cats must be lighted well enough to permit routine inspection and cleaning of the facility, and observation of the dogs and cats. Animal areas must be provided a regular diurnal lighting cycle of either natural or artificial light. Lighting must be uniformly diffused throughout animal facilities and provide sufficient illumination to aid in maintaining good housekeeping practices, adequate cleaning, adequate inspection of animals, and for the well-being of the animals. Primary enclosures must be placed so as to protect the dogs and cats from excessive light.

(d) *Shelter from the elements.* Dogs and cats must be provided with adequate shelter from the elements at all times to protect their health and well-being. The shelter structures must be large enough to allow each animal to sit, stand, and lie in a normal manner and to turn about freely.

(e) *Surfaces.* (1) The following areas in sheltered housing facilities must be impervious to moisture:

(i) Indoor floor areas in contact with the animals;

(ii) Outdoor floor areas in contact with the animals, when the floor areas are not exposed to the direct sun, or are made of a hard material such as wire, wood, metal, or concrete; and

(iii) All walls, boxes, houses, dens, and other surfaces in contact with the animals.

(2) Outside floor areas in contact with the animals and exposed to the direct sun may consist of compacted earth, absorbent bedding, sand, gravel, or grass.

[56 FR 6486, Feb. 15, 1991, as amended at 63 FR 10498, Mar. 4, 1998]

§ 3.4 Outdoor housing facilities.

(a) *Restrictions.* (1) The following categories of dogs or cats must not be kept in outdoor facilities, unless that practice is specifically approved by the attending veterinarian:

(i) Dogs or cats that are not acclimated to the temperatures prevalent in the area or region where they are maintained;

(ii) Breeds of dogs or cats that cannot tolerate the prevalent temperatures of the area without stress or discomfort (such as short-haired breeds in cold climates); and

(iii) Sick, infirm, aged or young dogs or cats.

(2) When their acclimation status is unknown, dogs and cats must not be kept in outdoor facilities when the ambient temperature is less than 50 °F (10 °C).

(b) *Shelter from the elements.* Outdoor facilities for dogs or cats must include one or more shelter structures that are accessible to each animal in each outdoor facility, and that are large enough to allow each animal in the shelter structure to sit, stand, and lie in a normal manner, and to turn about freely. In addition to the shelter structures, one or more separate outside areas of shade must be provided, large enough to contain all the animals at one time and protect them from the direct rays of the sun. Shelters in outdoor facilities for dogs or cats must contain a roof, four sides, and a floor, and must:

(1) Provide the dogs and cats with adequate protection and shelter from the cold and heat;

(2) Provide the dogs and cats with protection from the direct rays of the sun and the direct effect of wind, rain, or snow;

(3) Be provided with a wind break and rain break at the entrance; and

(4) Contain clean, dry, bedding material if the ambient temperature is below 50 °F (10 °C). Additional clean, dry bedding is required when the temperature is 35 °F (1.7 °C) or lower.

(c) *Construction.* Building surfaces in contact with animals in outdoor housing facilities must be impervious to moisture. Metal barrels, cars, refrigerators or freezers, and the like must not be used as shelter structures. The floors of outdoor housing facilities may be of compacted earth, absorbent bedding, sand, gravel, or grass, and must be replaced if there are any prevalent odors, diseases, insects, pests, or vermin. All surfaces must be maintained on a regular basis. Surfaces of outdoor housing facilities—including houses, dens, etc.—that cannot be readily cleaned and sanitized, must be replaced when worn or soiled.

§ 3.5 Mobile or traveling housing facilities.

(a) *Heating, cooling, and temperature.* Mobile or traveling housing facilities for dogs and cats must be sufficiently heated and cooled when necessary to protect the dogs and cats from temperature or humidity extremes and to provide for their health and well-being. The ambient temperature in the mobile or traveling housing facility must not fall below 50 °F (10 °C) for dogs and cats not acclimated to lower temperatures, for those breeds that cannot tolerate lower temperatures without stress or discomfort (such as short-haired breeds), and for sick, aged, young, or infirm dogs and cats. Dry bedding, solid resting boards, or other methods of conserving body heat must be provided when temperatures are below 50 °F (10 °C). The ambient temperature must not fall below 45 °F (7.2 °C) for more than 4 consecutive hours when dogs or cats are present, and must not exceed 85 °F (29.5 °C) for more than 4 consecutive hours when dogs or cats are present. The preceding requirements are in addition to, not in place of, all other requirements pertaining to climatic conditions in parts 2 and 3 of this chapter.

(b) *Ventilation.* Mobile or traveling housing facilities for dogs and cats must be sufficiently ventilated at all times when dogs or cats are present to provide for the health and well-being of the animals, and to minimize odors, drafts, ammonia levels, moisture condensation, and exhaust fumes. Ventilation must be provided by means of windows, doors, vents, fans, or air conditioning. Auxiliary ventilation, such as fans, blowers, or air conditioning, must be provided when the ambient temperature within the animal housing area is 85 °F (29.5 °C) or higher.

(c) *Lighting.* Mobile or traveling housing facilities for dogs and cats must be lighted well enough to permit proper cleaning and inspection of the facility, and observation of the dogs and cats. Animal areas must be provided a regular diurnal lighting cycle of either natural or artificial light. Lighting must be uniformly diffused throughout animal facilities and provide sufficient illumination to aid in maintaining good housekeeping practices, adequate cleaning, adequate inspection of animals, and for the well-being of the animals.

[32 FR 3273, Feb. 24, 1967, as amended at 63 FR 10498, Mar. 4, 1998]

§ 3.6 Primary enclosures.

Primary enclosures for dogs and cats must meet the following minimum requirements:

(a) *General requirements.* (1) Primary enclosures must be designed and constructed of suitable materials so that they are structurally sound. The primary enclosures must be kept in good repair.

(2) Primary enclosures must be constructed and maintained so that they:

(i) Have no sharp points or edges that could injure the dogs and cats;

(ii) Protect the dogs and cats from injury;

(iii) Contain the dogs and cats securely;

(iv) Keep other animals from entering the enclosure;

(v) Enable the dogs and cats to remain dry and clean;

(vi) Provide shelter and protection from extreme temperatures and weather conditions that may be uncomfortable or hazardous to all the dogs and cats;

(vii) Provide sufficient shade to shelter all the dogs and cats housed in the primary enclosure at one time;

(viii) Provide all the dogs and cats with easy and convenient access to clean food and water;

(ix) Enable all surfaces in contact with the dogs and cats to be readily cleaned and sanitized in accordance with § 3.11(b) of this subpart, or be replaceable when worn or soiled;

(x) Have floors that are constructed in a manner that protects the dogs' and cats' feet and legs from injury, and that, if of mesh or slatted construction, do not allow the dogs' and cats' feet to pass through any openings in the floor;

(xi) Provide sufficient space to allow each dog and cat to turn about freely, to stand, sit, and lie in a comfortable, normal position, and to walk in a normal manner; and

(xii) Primary enclosures constructed on or after February 20, 1998 and floors replaced on or after that date, must comply with the requirements in this paragraph (a)(2). On or after January 21, 2000, all primary enclosures must be in compliance with the requirements in this paragraph (a)(2). If the suspended floor of a primary enclosure is constructed of metal strands, the strands must either be greater than 1/8 of an inch in diameter (9 gauge) or coated with a material such as plastic or fiberglass. The suspended floor of any primary enclosure must be strong enough so that the floor does not sag or bend between the structural supports.

(b) *Additional requirements for cats*—(1)*Space.* Each cat, including weaned kittens, that is housed in any primary enclosure must be provided minimum vertical space and floor space as follows:

(i) Prior to February 15, 1994 each cat housed in any primary enclosure shall be provided a minimum of 2½ square feet of floor space;

(ii) On and after February 15, 1994:

(A) Each primary enclosure housing cats must be at least 24 in. high (60.96 cm);

(B) Cats up to and including 8.8 lbs (4 kg) must be provided with at least 3.0 ft^2 (0.28 m^2);

(C) Cats over 8.8 lbs (4 kg) must be provided with at least 4.0 ft^2 (0.37 m^2);

(iii) Each queen with nursing kittens must be provided with an additional amount of floor space, based on her breed and behavioral characteristics, and in accordance with generally accepted husbandry practices. If the additional amount of floor space for each nursing kitten is equivalent to less than 5 percent of the minimum requirement for the queen, such housing must be approved by the attending veterinarian in the case of a research facility, and, in the case of dealers and exhibitors, such housing must be approved by the Administrator; and

(iv) The minimum floor space required by this section is exclusive of any food or water pans. The litter pan may be considered part of the floor space if properly cleaned and sanitized.

(2) *Compatibility.* All cats housed in the same primary enclosure must be compatible, as determined by observation. Not more than 12 adult nonconditioned cats may be housed in the same primary enclosure. Queens in heat may not be housed in the same primary enclosure with sexually mature males, except for breeding. Except when maintained in breeding colonies, queens with litters may not be housed in the same primary enclosure with other adult cats, and kittens under 4 months of age may not be housed in the same primary enclosure with adult cats, other than the dam or foster dam. Cats with a vicious or aggressive disposition must be housed separately.

(3) *Litter.* In all primary enclosures, a receptacle containing sufficient clean litter must be provided to contain excreta and body wastes.

(4) *Resting surfaces.* Each primary enclosure housing cats must contain a resting surface or surfaces that, in the aggregate, are large enough to hold all the occupants of the primary enclosure at the same time comfortably. The resting surfaces must be elevated, impervious to moisture, and be able to be easily cleaned and sanitized, or easily replaced when soiled or worn. Low resting surfaces that do not allow the space under them to be comfortably occupied by the animal will be counted as part of the floor space.

(5) *Cats in mobile or traveling shows or acts.* Cats that are part of a mobile or traveling show or act may be kept, while the show or act is traveling from one temporary location to another, in transport containers that comply with all requirements of §3.14 of this subpart other than the marking requirements in §3.14(a)(6) of this subpart. When the show or act is not traveling, the cats must be placed in primary enclosures that meet the minimum requirements of this section.

(c) *Additional requirements for dogs*—(1) *Space.* (i) Each dog housed in a primary enclosure (including weaned puppies) must be provided a minimum amount of floor space, calculated as follows: Find the mathematical square of the sum of the length of the dog in inches (measured from the tip of its nose to the base of its tail) plus 6 inches; then divide the product by 144. The calculation is: (length of dog in inches + 6) × (length of dog in inches + 6) = required floor space in square inches. Required floor space in inches/144 = required floor space in square feet.

(ii) Each bitch with nursing puppies must be provided with an additional amount of floor space, based on her breed and behavioral characteristics, and in accordance with generally accepted husbandry practices as determined by the attending veterinarian. If the additional amount of floor space for each nursing puppy is less than 5 percent of the minimum requirement for the bitch, such housing must be approved by the attending veterinarian in the case of a research facility, and, in the case of dealers and exhibitors, such housing must be approved by the Administrator.

(iii) The interior height of a primary enclosure must be at least 6 inches higher than the head of the tallest dog in the enclosure when it is in a normal standing position: *Provided* That, prior to February 15, 1994, each dog must be able to stand in a comfortable normal position.

(2) *Compatibility.* All dogs housed in the same primary enclosure must be compatible, as determined by observation. Not more than 12 adult nonconditioned dogs may be housed in the same primary enclosure. Bitches in heat may not be housed in the same primary enclosure with sexually mature males, except for breeding. Except when maintained in breeding colonies, bitches with litters may not be housed in the same primary enclosure with other adult dogs, and puppies under 4 months of age may not be housed in the same primary enclosure with adult dogs, other than the dam or foster dam. Dogs with a vicious or aggressive disposition must be housed separately.

(3) *Dogs in mobile or traveling shows or acts.* Dogs that are part of a mobile or traveling show or act may be kept, while the show or act is traveling from one temporary location to another, in transport containers that comply with all requirements of §3.14 of this subpart other than the marking requirements in §3.14(a)(6) of this subpart. When the

show or act is not traveling, the dogs must be placed in primary enclosures that meet the minimum requirements of this section.

(4) *Prohibited means of primary enclosure.* Permanent tethering of dogs is prohibited for use as primary enclosure. Temporary tethering of dogs is prohibited for use as primary enclosure unless approval is obtained from APHIS.

(d) Innovative primary enclosures not precisely meeting the floor area and height requirements provided in paragraphs (b)(1) and (c)(1) of this section, but that provide the dogs or cats with a sufficient volume of space and the opportunity to express species-typical behavior, may be used at research facilities when approved by the Committee, and by dealers and exhibitors when approved by the Administrator.

(Approved by the Office of Management and Budget under control number 0579–0093)

[56 FR 6486, Feb. 15, 1991, as amended at 62 FR 43275, Aug. 13, 1997; 63 FR 3023, Jan. 21, 1998; 63 FR 37482, July 13, 1998]

ANIMAL HEALTH AND HUSBANDRY STANDARDS

§ 3.7 Compatible grouping.

Dogs and cats that are housed in the same primary enclosure must be compatible, with the following restrictions:

(a) Females in heat (estrus) may not be housed in the same primary enclosure with males, except for breeding purposes;

(b) Any dog or cat exhibiting a vicious or overly aggressive disposition must be housed separately;

(c) Puppies or kittens 4 months of age or less may not be housed in the same primary enclosure with adult dogs or cats other than their dams or foster dams, except when permanently maintained in breeding colonies;

(d) Dogs or cats may not be housed in the same primary enclosure with any other species of animals, unless they are compatible; and

(e) Dogs and cats that have or are suspected of having a contagious disease must be isolated from healthy animals in the colony, as directed by the attending veterinarian. When an entire group or room of dogs and cats is known to have or believed to be exposed to an infectious agent, the group may be kept intact during the process of diagnosis, treatment, and control.

§ 3.8 Exercise for dogs.

Dealers, exhibitors, and research facilities must develop, document, and follow an appropriate plan to provide dogs with the opportunity for exercise. In addition, the plan must be approved by the attending veterinarian. The plan must include written standard procedures to be followed in providing the opportunity for exercise. The plan must be made available to APHIS upon request, and, in the case of research facilities, to officials of any pertinent funding Federal agency. The plan, at a minimum, must comply with each of the following:

(a) *Dogs housed individually.* Dogs over 12 weeks of age, except bitches with litters, housed, held, or maintained by any dealer, exhibitor, or research facility, including Federal research facilities, must be provided the opportunity for exercise regularly if they are kept individually in cages, pens, or runs that provide less than two times the required floor space for that dog, as indicated by § 3.6(c)(1) of this subpart.

(b) *Dogs housed in groups.* Dogs over 12 weeks of age housed, held, or maintained in groups by any dealer, exhibitor, or research facility, including Federal research facilities, do not require additional opportunity for exercise regularly if they are maintained in cages, pens, or runs that provide in total at least 100 percent of the required space for each dog if maintained separately. Such animals may be maintained in compatible groups, unless:

(1) Housing in compatible groups is not in accordance with a research proposal and the proposal has been approved by the research facility Committee;

(2) In the opinion of the attending veterinarian, such housing would adversely affect the health or well-being of the dog(s); or

(3) Any dog exhibits aggressive or vicious behavior.

(c) *Methods and period of providing exercise opportunity.* (1) The frequency, method, and duration of the opportunity for exercise shall be determined by the attending veterinarian and, at research facilities, in consultation with and approval by the Committee.

(2) Dealers, exhibitors, and research facilities, in developing their plan, should consider providing positive physical contact with humans that encourages exercise through play or other similar activities. If a dog is housed, held, or maintained at a facility without sensory contact with another dog, it must be provided with positive physical contact with humans at least daily.

(3) The opportunity for exercise may be provided in a number of ways, such as:

(i) Group housing in cages, pens or runs that provide at least 100 percent of the required space for each dog if maintained separately under the minimum floor space requirements of §3.6(c)(1) of this subpart;

(ii) Maintaining individually housed dogs in cages, pens, or runs that provide at least twice the minimum floor space required by §3.6(c)(1) of this subpart;

(iii) Providing access to a run or open area at the frequency and duration prescribed by the attending veterinarian; or

(iv) Other similar activities.

(4) Forced exercise methods or devices such as swimming, treadmills, or carousel-type devices are unacceptable for meeting the exercise requirements of this section.

(d) *Exemptions.* (1) If, in the opinion of the attending veterinarian, it is inappropriate for certain dogs to exercise because of their health, condition, or well-being, the dealer, exhibitor, or research facility may be exempted from meeting the requirements of this section for those dogs. Such exemption must be documented by the attending veterinarian and, unless the basis for exemption is a permanent condition, must be reviewed at least every 30 days by the attending veterinarian.

(2) A research facility may be exempted from the requirements of this section if the principal investigator determines for scientific reasons set forth in the research proposal that it is inappropriate for certain dogs to exercise. Such exemption must be documented in the Committee-approved proposal and must be reviewed at appropriate intervals as determined by the Committee, but not less than annually.

(3) Records of any exemptions must be maintained and made available to USDA officials or any pertinent funding Federal agency upon request.

(Approved by the Office of Management and Budget under control number 0579–0093)

§3.9 Feeding.

(a) Dogs and cats must be fed at least once each day, except as otherwise might be required to provide adequate veterinary care. The food must be uncontaminated, wholesome, palatable, and of sufficient quantity and nutritive value to maintain the normal condition and weight of the animal. The diet must be appropriate for the individual animal's age and condition.

(b) Food receptacles must be used for dogs and cats, must be readily accessible to all dogs and cats, and must be located so as to minimize contamination by excreta and pests, and be protected from rain and snow. Feeding pans must either be made of a durable material that can be easily cleaned and sanitized or be disposable. If the food receptacles are not disposable, they must be kept clean and must be sanitized in accordance with §3.11(b) of this subpart. Sanitization is achieved by using one of the methods described in §3.11(b)(3) of this subpart. If the food receptacles are disposable, they must be discarded after one use. Self-feeders may be used for the feeding of dry food. If self-feeders are used, they must be kept clean and must be sanitized in accordance with §3.11(b) of this subpart. Measures must be taken to ensure that there is no molding, deterioration, and caking of feed.

§3.10 Watering.

If potable water is not continually available to the dogs and cats, it must be offered to the dogs and cats as often as necessary to ensure their health and well-being, but not less than twice daily for at least 1 hour each time, unless restricted by the attending veterinarian. Water receptacles must be kept clean and sanitized in accordance with §3.11(b) of this subpart, and before being used to water a different dog or cat or social grouping of dogs or cats.

§ 3.11 Cleaning, sanitization, housekeeping, and pest control.

(a) *Cleaning of primary enclosures.* Excreta and food waste must be removed from primary enclosures daily, and from under primary enclosures as often as necessary to prevent an excessive accumulation of feces and food waste, to prevent soiling of the dogs or cats contained in the primary enclosures, and to reduce disease hazards, insects, pests and odors. When steam or water is used to clean the primary enclosure, whether by hosing, flushing, or other methods, dogs and cats must be removed, unless the enclosure is large enough to ensure the animals would not be harmed, wetted, or distressed in the process. Standing water must be removed from the primary enclosure and animals in other primary enclosures must be protected from being contaminated with water and other wastes during the cleaning. The pans under primary enclosures with grill-type floors and the ground areas under raised runs with mesh or slatted floors must be cleaned as often as necessary to prevent accumulation of feces and food waste and to reduce disease hazards pests, insects and odors.

(b) *Sanitization of primary enclosures and food and water receptacles.* (1) Used primary enclosures and food and water receptacles must be cleaned and sanitized in accordance with this section before they can be used to house, feed, or water another dog or cat, or social grouping of dogs or cats.

(2) Used primary enclosures and food and water receptacles for dogs and cats must be sanitized at least once every 2 weeks using one of the methods prescribed in paragraph (b)(3) of this section, and more often if necessary to prevent an accumulation of dirt, debris, food waste, excreta, and other disease hazards.

(3) Hard surfaces of primary enclosures and food and water receptacles must be sanitized using one of the following methods:

(i) Live steam under pressure;

(ii) Washing with hot water (at least 180 °F (82.2 °C)) and soap or detergent, as with a mechanical cage washer; or

(iii) Washing all soiled surfaces with appropriate detergent solutions and disinfectants, or by using a combination detergent/disinfectant product that accomplishes the same purpose, with a thorough cleaning of the surfaces to remove organic material, so as to remove all organic material and mineral buildup, and to provide sanitization followed by a clean water rinse.

(4) Pens, runs, and outdoor housing areas using material that cannot be sanitized using the methods provided in paragraph (b)(3) of this section, such as gravel, sand, grass, earth, or absorbent bedding, must be sanitized by removing the contaminated material as necessary to prevent odors, diseases, pests, insects, and vermin infestation.

(c) *Housekeeping for premises.* Premises where housing facilities are located, including buildings and surrounding grounds, must be kept clean and in good repair to protect the animals from injury, to facilitate the husbandry practices required in this subpart, and to reduce or eliminate breeding and living areas for rodents and other pests and vermin. Premises must be kept free of accumulations of trash, junk, waste products, and discarded matter. Weeds, grasses, and bushes must be controlled so as to facilitate cleaning of the premises and pest control, and to protect the health and well-being of the animals.

(d) *Pest control.* An effective program for the control of insects, external parasites affecting dogs and cats, and birds and mammals that are pests, must be established and maintained so as to promote the health and well-being of the animals and reduce contamination by pests in animal areas.

[56 FR 6486, Feb. 15, 1991, as amended at 63 FR 3023, Jan. 21, 1998]

§ 3.12 Employees.

Each person subject to the Animal Welfare regulations (9 CFR parts 1, 2, and 3) maintaining dogs and cats must have enough employees to carry out the level of husbandry practices and care required in this subpart. The employees who provide for husbandry and care, or handle animals, must be supervised by an individual who has the knowledge, background, and experience in proper husbandry and care of dogs and cats to supervise others. The employer must be certain that the supervisor and other employees can perform to these standards.

TRANSPORTATION STANDARDS

§ 3.13 Consignments to carriers and intermediate handlers.

(a) Carriers and intermediate handlers must not accept a dog or cat for transport in commerce more than 4 hours before the scheduled departure time of the primary conveyance on which the animal is to be transported. However, a carrier or intermediate handler may agree with anyone consigning a dog or cat to extend this time by up to 2 hours.

(b) Carriers and intermediate handlers must not accept a dog or cat for transport in commerce unless they are provided with the name, address, and telephone number of the consignee.

(c) Carriers and intermediate handlers must not accept a dog or cat for transport in commerce unless the consignor certifies in writing to the carrier or intermediate handler that the dog or cat was offered food and water during the 4 hours before delivery to the carrier or intermediate handler. The certification must be securely attached to the outside of the primary enclosure in a manner that makes it easily noticed and read. Instructions for no food or water are not acceptable unless directed by the attending veterinarian. Instructions must be in compliance with § 3.16 of this subpart. The certification must include the following information for each dog and cat:

(1) The consignor's name and address;

(2) The tag number or tattoo assigned to each dog or cat under §§ 2.38 and 2.50 of this chapter;

(3) The time and date the animal was last fed and watered and the specific instructions for the next feeding(s) and watering(s) for a 24-hour period; and

(4) The consignor's signature and the date and time the certification was signed.

(d) Carriers and intermediate handlers must not accept a dog or cat for transport in commerce in a primary enclosure unless the primary enclosure meets the requirements of § 3.14 of this subpart. A carrier or intermediate handler must not accept a dog or cat for transport if the primary enclosure is obviously defective or damaged and cannot reasonably be expected to safely and comfortably contain the dog or cat without causing suffering or injury.

(e) Carriers and intermediate handlers must not accept a dog or cat for transport in commerce unless their animal holding area meets the minimum temperature requirements provided in §§ 3.18 and 3.19 of this subpart, or unless the consignor provides them with a certificate signed by a veterinarian and dated no more than 10 days before delivery of the animal to the carrier or intermediate handler for transport in commerce, certifying that the animal is acclimated to temperatures lower than those required in §§ 3.18 and 3.19 of this subpart. Even if the carrier or intermediate handler receives this certification, the temperatures the dog or cat is exposed to while in a terminal facility must not be lower than 45 °F (2.2 °C) for more than 4 consecutive hours when dogs or cats are present, as set forth in § 3.18, nor lower than 45 °F (2.2 °C) for more than 45 minutes, as set forth in § 3.19, when moving dogs or cats to or from terminal facilities or primary conveyances. A copy of the certification must accompany the dog or cat to its destination and must include the following information:

(1) The consignor's name and address;

(2) The tag number or tattoo assigned to each dog or cat under §§ 2.38 and 2.50 of this chapter;

(3) A statement by a veterinarian, dated no more than 10 days before delivery, that to the best of his or her knowledge, each of the dogs or cats contained in the primary enclosure is acclimated to air temperatures lower than 50 °F (10 °C); but not lower than a minimum temperature, specified on a certificate, that the attending veterinarian has determined is based on generally accepted temperature standards for the age, condition, and breed of the dog or cat; and

(4) The signature of the veterinarian and the date the certification was signed.

(f) When a primary enclosure containing a dog or cat has arrived at the animal holding area at a terminal facility after transport, the carrier or intermediate handler must attempt to notify the consignee upon arrival and at least once in every 6-hour period thereafter. The time, date, and method of all attempted notifications and the actual notification of the consignee, and the name of the person who notifies or attempts to notify the consignee must be written either on the carrier's or intermediate handler's copy of the shipping document or on the copy that accompanies the primary enclosure. If the consignee cannot be notified within 24 hours after the dog or cat has arrived at the terminal facility, the carrier or intermediate handler must return the animal to the consignor or to whomever the consignor designates. If the consignee is notified of the arrival and does not accept delivery of the dog or cat within 48 hours after arrival of the dog or cat, the carrier or intermediate handler must return the animal to the consignor or to whomever the consignor designates. The carrier or intermediate handler must continue to provide proper care, feeding, and housing to the dog or cat, and maintain the dog or cat in accordance with generally accepted professional and husbandry practices until the consignee accepts delivery of the dog or cat or until it is returned to the consignor or to whomever the consignor designates. The carrier or intermediate handler must obligate the consignor to reimburse the carrier or intermediate handler for the cost of return transportation and care.

(Approved by the Office of Management and Budget under control number 0579–0093)

§ 3.14 Primary enclosures used to transport live dogs and cats.

Any person subject to the Animal Welfare regulations (9 CFR parts 1, 2, and 3) must not transport or deliver for transport in commerce a dog or cat unless the following requirements are met:

(a) *Construction of primary enclosures.* The dog or cat must be contained in a primary enclosure such as a compartment, transport cage, carton, or crate. Primary enclosures used to transport dogs and cats must be constructed so that:

(1) The primary enclosure is strong enough to contain the dogs and cats securely and comfortably and to withstand the normal rigors of transportation;

(2) The interior of the primary enclosure has no sharp points or edges and no protrusions that could injure the animal contained in it;

(3) The dog or cat is at all times securely contained within the enclosure and cannot put any part of its body outside the enclosure in a way that could result in injury to itself, to handlers, or to persons or animals nearby;

(4) The dog or cat can be easily and quickly removed from the enclosure in an emergency;

(5) Unless the enclosure is permanently affixed to the conveyance, adequate devices such as handles or handholds are provided on its exterior, and enable the enclosure to be lifted without tilting it, and ensure that anyone handling the enclosure will not come into physical contact with the animal contained inside;

(6) Unless the enclosure is permanently affixed to the conveyance, it is clearly marked on top and on one or more sides with the words "Live Animals," in letters at least 1 inch (2.5 cm.) high, and with arrows or other markings to indicate the correct upright position of the primary enclosure;

(7) Any material, treatment, paint, preservative, or other chemical used in or on the enclosure is nontoxic to the animal and not harmful to the health or well-being of the animal;

(8) Proper ventilation is provided to the animal in accordance with paragraph (c) of this section; and

(9) The primary enclosure has a solid, leak-proof bottom or a removable, leak-proof collection tray under a slatted or mesh floor that prevents seepage of waste products, such as excreta and body fluids, outside of the enclosure. If a slatted or mesh floor is used in the enclosure, it must be designed and constructed so that the animal cannot put any part of its body between the slats or through the holes in the mesh. Unless the dogs and cats are on raised slatted floors or raised floors made of mesh, the primary enclosure must contain enough previously unused litter to

absorb and cover excreta. The litter must be of a suitably absorbent material that is safe and nontoxic to the dogs and cats.

(b) *Cleaning of primary enclosures.* A primary enclosure used to hold or transport dogs or cats in commerce must be cleaned and sanitized before each use in accordance with the methods provided in §3.11(b)(3) of this subpart. If the dogs or cats are in transit for more than 24 hours, the enclosures must be cleaned and any litter replaced, or other methods, such as moving the animals to another enclosure, must be utilized to prevent the soiling of the dogs or cats by body wastes. If it becomes necessary to remove the dog or cat from the enclosure in order to clean, or to move the dog or cat to another enclosure, this procedure must be completed in a way that safeguards the dog or cat from injury and prevents escape.

(c) *Ventilation.* (1) Unless the primary enclosure is permanently affixed to the conveyance, there must be:

(i) Ventilation openings located on two opposing walls of the primary enclosure and the openings must be at least 16 percent of the surface area of each such wall, and the total combined surface area of the ventilation openings must be at least 14 percent of the total combined surface area of all the walls of the primary enclosure; or

(ii) Ventilation openings on three walls of the primary enclosure, and the openings on each of the two opposing walls must be at least 8 percent of the total surface area of the two walls, and the ventilation openings on the third wall of the primary enclosure must be at least 50 percent of the total surface area of that wall, and the total combined surface area of the ventilation openings must be at least 14 percent of the total combined surface area of all the walls of the primary enclosure; or

(iii) Ventilation openings located on all four walls of the primary enclosure and the ventilation openings on each of the four walls must be at least 8 percent of the total surface area of each such wall, and the total combined surface area of the openings must be at least 14 percent of total combined surface area of all the walls of the primary enclosure; and

(iv) At least one-third of the ventilation area must be located on the upper half of the primary enclosure.

(2) Unless the primary enclosure is permanently affixed to the conveyance, projecting rims or similar devices must be located on the exterior of each enclosure wall having a ventilation opening, in order to prevent obstruction of the openings. The projecting rims or similar devices must be large enough to provide a minimum air circulation space of 0.75 in. (1.9 cm) between the primary enclosure and anything the enclosure is placed against.

(3) If a primary enclosure is permanently affixed to the primary conveyance so that there is only a front ventilation opening for the enclosure, the primary enclosure must be affixed to the primary conveyance in such a way that the front ventilation opening cannot be blocked, and the front ventilation opening must open directly to an unobstructed aisle or passageway inside the conveyance. The ventilation opening must be at least 90 percent of the total area of the front wall of the enclosure, and must be covered with bars, wire mesh, or smooth expanded metal having air spaces.

(d) *Compatibility.* (1) Live dogs or cats transported in the same primary enclosure must be of the same species and be maintained in compatible groups, except that dogs and cats that are private pets, are of comparable size, and are compatible, may be transported in the same primary enclosure.

(2) Puppies or kittens 4 months of age or less may not be transported in the same primary enclosure with adult dogs or cats other than their dams.

(3) Dogs or cats that are overly aggressive or exhibit a vicious disposition must be transported individually in a primary enclosure.

(4) Any female dog or cat in heat (estrus) may not be transported in the same primary enclosure with any male dog or cat.

(e) *Space and placement.* (1) Primary enclosures used to transport live dogs and cats must be large enough to ensure that each animal contained in the primary enclosure has enough space to turn about normally while standing, to stand and sit erect, and to lie in a natural position.

(2) Primary enclosures used to transport dogs and cats must be positioned in the primary conveyance so as to provide protection from the elements.

(f) *Transportation by air.* (1) No more than one live dog or cat, 6 months of age or older, may be transported in the same primary enclosure when shipped via air carrier.

(2) No more than one live puppy, 8 weeks to 6 months of age, and weighing over 20 lbs (9 kg), may be transported in a primary enclosure when shipped via air carrier.

(3) No more than two live puppies or kittens, 8 weeks to 6 months of age, that are of comparable size, and weighing 20 lbs (9 kg) or less each, may be transported in the same primary enclosure when shipped via air carrier.

(4) Weaned live puppies or kittens less than 8 weeks of age and of comparable size, or puppies or kittens that are less than 8 weeks of age that are littermates and are accompanied by their dam, may be transported in the same primary enclosure when shipped to research facilities, including Federal research facilities.

(g) *Transportation by surface vehicle or privately owned aircraft.* (1) No more than four live dogs or cats, 8 weeks of age or older, that are of comparable size, may be transported in the same primary enclosure when shipped by surface vehicle (including ground and water transportation) or privately owned aircraft, and only if all other requirements of this section are met.

(2) Weaned live puppies or kittens less than 8 weeks of age and of comparable size, or puppies or kittens that are less than 8 weeks of age that are littermates and are accompanied by their dam, may be transported in the same primary enclosure when shipped to research facilities, including Federal research facilities, and only if all other requirements in this section are met.

(h) *Accompanying documents and records.* Shipping documents that must accompany shipments of dogs and cats may be held by the operator of the primary conveyance, for surface transportation only, or must be securely attached in a readily accessible manner to the outside of any primary enclosure that is part of the shipment, in a manner that allows them to be detached for examination and securely reattached, such as in a pocket or sleeve. Instructions for administration of drugs, medication, and other special care must be attached to each primary enclosure in a manner that makes them easy to notice, to detach for examination, and to reattach securely. Food and water instructions must be attached in accordance with § 3.13(c).

(Approved by the Office of Management and Budget under control number 0579–0093)

[56 FR 6486, Feb. 15, 1991, as amended at 63 FR 3023, Jan. 21, 1998]

§ 3.15 Primary conveyances (motor vehicle, rail, air, and marine).

(a) The animal cargo space of primary conveyances used to transport dogs and cats must be designed, constructed, and maintained in a manner that at all times protects the health and well-being of the animals transported in them, ensures their safety and comfort, and prevents the entry of engine exhaust from the primary conveyance during transportation.

(b) The animal cargo space must have a supply of air that is sufficient for the normal breathing of all the animals being transported in it.

(c) Each primary enclosure containing dogs or cats must be positioned in the animal cargo space in a manner that provides protection from the elements and that allows each dog or cat enough air for normal breathing.

(d) During air transportation, dogs and cats must be held in cargo areas that are heated or cooled as necessary to maintain an ambient temperature and humidity that ensures the health and well-being of the dogs or cats. The cargo areas must be pressurized when the primary conveyance used for air transportation is not on the ground, unless flying under 8,000 ft. Dogs and cats must have adequate air for breathing at all times when being transported.

(e) During surface transportation, auxiliary ventilation, such as fans, blowers or air conditioning, must be used in any animal cargo space containing live dogs or cats when the ambient temperature within the animal cargo space reaches 85 °F (29.5 °C). Moreover, the ambient temperature may not exceed 85 °F (29.5 °C) for a period of more than 4 hours; nor fall below 45 °F (7.2 °C) for a period of more than 4 hours. The preceding requirements are in addition to, not in place of, all other requirements pertaining to climatic conditions in parts 2 and 3 of this chapter.

(f) Primary enclosures must be positioned in the primary conveyance in a manner that allows the dogs and cats to be quickly and easily removed from the primary conveyance in an emergency.

(g) The interior of the animal cargo space must be kept clean.

(h) Live dogs and cats may not be transported with any material, substance (e.g., dry ice) or device in a manner that may reasonably be expected to harm the dogs and cats or cause inhumane conditions.

[56 FR 6486, Feb. 15, 1991, as amended at 63 FR 10498, 10499, Mar. 4, 1998]

§3.16 Food and water requirements.

(a) Each dog and cat that is 16 weeks of age or more must be offered food at least once every 24 hours. Puppies and kittens less than 16 weeks of age must be offered food at least once every 12 hours. Each dog and cat must be offered potable water at least once every 12 hours. These time periods apply to dealers, exhibitors, research facilities. including Federal research facilities, who transport dogs and cats in their own primary conveyance, starting from the time the dog or cat was last offered food and potable water before transportation was begun. These time periods apply to carriers and intermediate handlers starting from the date and time stated on the certificate provided under §3.13(c) of this subpart. Each dog and cat must be offered food and potable water within 4 hours before being transported in commerce. Consignors who are subject to the Animal Welfare regulations (9 CFR parts 1, 2, and 3) must certify that each dog and cat was offered food and potable water within the 4 hours preceding delivery of the dog or cat to a carrier or intermediate handler for transportation in commerce, and must certify the date and time the food and potable water was offered, in accordance with §3.13(c) of this subpart.

(b) Any dealer, research facility, including a Federal research facility, or exhibitor offering any dog or cat to a carrier or intermediate handler for transportation in commerce must securely attach to the outside of the primary enclosure used for transporting the dog or cat, written instructions for the in-transit food and water requirements for a 24-hour period for the dogs and cats contained in the enclosure. The instructions must be attached in a manner that makes them easily noticed and read.

(c) Food and water receptacles must be securely attached inside the primary enclosure and placed so that the receptacles can be filled from outside the enclosure without opening the door. Food and water containers must be designed, constructed, and installed so that a dog or cat cannot leave the primary enclosure through the food or water opening.

(Approved by the Office of Management and Budget under control number 0579–0093)

§3.17 Care in transit.

(a) *Surface transportation (ground and water).* Any person subject to the Animal Welfare regulations transporting dogs or cats in commerce must ensure that the operator of the conveyance, or a person accompanying the operator, observes the dogs or cats as often as circumstances allow, but not less than once every 4 hours, to make sure they have sufficient air for normal breathing, that the ambient temperature is within the limits provided in §3.15(e), and that all applicable standards of this subpart are being complied with. The regulated person must ensure that the operator or person accompanying the operator determines whether any of the dogs or cats are in obvious physical distress and obtains any veterinary care needed for the dogs or cats at the closest available veterinary facility.

(b) *Air transportation.* During air transportation of dogs or cats, it is the responsibility of the carrier to observe the dogs or cats as frequently as circumstances allow, but not less than once every 4 hours if the animal cargo area is accessible during flight. If the animal cargo area is not accessible during flight, the carrier must observe the dogs or cats whenever they are loaded and unloaded and whenever the animal cargo space is otherwise accessible to make sure they have sufficient air for normal breathing, that the animal cargo area meets the heating and cooling requirements of §3.15(d), and that all other applicable standards of this subpart are being complied with. The carrier must determine whether any of the dogs or cats are in obvious physical distress, and arrange for any needed veterinary care as soon as possible.

(c) If a dog or cat is obviously ill, injured, or in physical distress, it must not be transported in commerce, except to receive veterinary care for the condition.

(d) Except during the cleaning of primary enclosures, as required in §3.14(b) of this subpart, during transportation in commerce a dog or cat must not be removed from its primary enclosure, unless it is placed in another primary enclosure or facility that meets the requirements of §3.6 or §3.14 of this subpart.

(e) The transportation regulations contained in this subpart must be complied with until a consignee takes physical delivery of the dog or cat if the animal is consigned for transportation, or until the animal is returned to the consignor.

§3.18 Terminal facilities.

(a) *Placement.* Any person subject to the Animal Welfare regulations (9 CFR parts 1, 2, and 3) must not commingle shipments of dogs or cats with inanimate cargo in animal holding areas of terminal facilities.

(b) *Cleaning, sanitization, and pest control.* All animal holding areas of terminal facilities must be cleaned and sanitized in a manner prescribed in §3.11(b)(3) of this subpart, as often as necessary to prevent an accumulation of debris or excreta and to minimize vermin infestation and disease hazards. Terminal facilities must follow an effective program in all animal holding areas for the control of insects, ectoparasites, and birds and mammals that are pests to dogs and cats.

(c) *Ventilation.* Ventilation must be provided in any animal holding area in a terminal facility containing dogs or cats, by means of windows, doors, vents, or air conditioning. The air must be circulated by fans, blowers, or air conditioning so as to minimize drafts, odors, and moisture condensation. Auxiliary ventilation, such as exhaust fans, vents, fans, blowers, or air conditioning must be used in any animal holding area containing dogs and cats, when the ambient temperature is 85 °F (29.5 °C) or higher

(d) *Temperature.* The ambient temperature in an animal holding area containing dogs or cats must not fall below 45 °F (7.2 °C) or rise above 85 °F (29.5 °C) for more than four consecutive hours at any time dogs or cats are present. The ambient temperature must be measured in the animal holding area by the carrier, intermediate handler, or a person transporting dogs or cats who is subject to the Animal Welfare regulations (9 CFR parts 1, 2, and 3), outside any primary enclosure containing a dog or cat at a point not more than 3 feet (0.91 m) away from an outside wall of the primary enclosure, and approximately midway up the side of the enclosure. The preceding requirements are in addition to, not in place of, all other requirements pertaining to climatic conditions in parts 2 and 3 of this chapter.

(e) *Shelter.* Any person subject to the Animal Welfare regulations (9 CFR parts 1, 2, and 3) holding a live dog or cat in an animal holding area of a terminal facility must provide the following:

(1) *Shelter from sunlight and extreme heat.* Shade must be provided that is sufficient to protect the dog or cat from the direct rays of the sun.

(2) *Shelter from rain or snow.* Sufficient protection must be provided to allow the dogs and cats to remain dry during rain, snow, and other precipitation.

(f) *Duration.* The length of time any person subject to the Animal Welfare regulations (9 CFR parts 1, 2, and 3) can hold dogs and cats in animal holding areas of terminal facilities upon arrival is the same as that provided in §3.13(f) of this subpart.

[56 FR 6486, Feb. 15, 1991, as amended at 63 FR 10499, Mar. 4, 1998]

§ 3.19 Handling.

(a) Any person subject to the Animal Welfare regulations (9 CFR parts 1, 2, and 3) who moves (including loading and unloading) dogs or cats within, to, or from the animal holding area of a terminal facility or a primary conveyance must do so as quickly and efficiently as possible and must provide the following during movement of the dog or cat:

(1) Shelter from sunlight and extreme heat. Sufficient shade must be provided to protect the dog or cat from the direct rays of the sun. The dog or cat must not be exposed to an ambient air temperature above 85 °F (29.5 °C) for a period of more than 45 minutes while being moved to or from a primary conveyance or a terminal facility. The temperature must be measured in the manner provided in § 3.18(d) of this subpart. The preceding requirements are in addition to, not in place of, all other requirements pertaining to climatic conditions in parts 2 and 3 of this chapter.

(2) *Shelter from rain and snow.* Sufficient protection must be provided to allow the dogs and cats to remain dry during rain, snow, and other precipitation.

(3) *Shelter from cold temperatures.* Transporting devices on which live dogs or cats are placed to move them must be covered to protect the animals when the outdoor temperature falls below 50 °F (10 °C). The dogs or cats must not be exposed to an ambient temperature below 45 °F (7.2 °C) for a period of more than 45 minutes, unless they are accompanied by a certificate of acclimation to lower temperatures as provided in § 3.13(e). The temperature must be measured in the manner provided in § 3.18(d) of this subpart. The preceding requirements are in addition to, not in place of, all other requirements pertaining to climatic conditions in parts 2 and 3 of this chapter.

(b) Any person handling a primary enclosure containing a dog or cat must use care and must avoid causing physical harm or distress to the dog or cat.

(1) A primary enclosure containing a live dog or cat must not be placed on unattended conveyor belts, or on elevated conveyor belts, such as baggage claim conveyor belts and inclined conveyor ramps that lead to baggage claim areas, at any time; except that a primary enclosure may be placed on inclined conveyor ramps used to load and unload aircraft if an attendant is present at each end of the conveyor belt.

(2) A primary enclosure containing a dog or cat must not be tossed, dropped, or needlessly tilted, and must not be stacked in a manner that may reasonably be expected to result in its falling. It must be handled and positioned in the manner that written instructions and arrows on the outside of the primary enclosure indicate.

(c) This section applies to movement of a dog or cat from primary conveyance to primary conveyance, within a primary conveyance or terminal facility, and to or from a terminal facility or a primary conveyance.

(Approved by the Office of Management and Budget under control number 0579–0093)

[56 FR 6486, Feb. 15, 1991, as amended at 63 FR 10499, Mar. 4, 1998]

Subpart B—Specifications for the Humane Handling, Care, Treatment, and Transportation of Guinea Pigs and Hamsters

FACILITIES AND OPERATING STANDARDS

§ 3.25 Facilities, general.

(a) *Structural strength.* Indoor and outdoor housing facilities for guinea pigs or hamsters shall be structurally sound and shall be maintained in good repair, to protect the animals from injury, to contain the animals, and to restrict the entrance of other animals.

(b) *Water and electric power.* Reliable and adequate electric power, if required to comply with other provisions of this subpart, and adequate potable water shall be available.

(c) *Storage.* Supplies of food and bedding shall be stored in facilities which adequately protect such supplies against spoilage or deterioration and infestation or contamination by vermin. Food supplies shall be stored in containers with tightly fitting lids or covers or in the original containers as received from the commercial sources of supply. Refrigeration shall be provided for supplies of perishable food.

(d) *Waste disposal.* Provisions shall be made for the removal and disposal of animal and food wastes, bedding, dead animals, and debris. Disposal facilities shall be so provided and operated as to minimize vermin infestation, odors, and disease hazards.

(e) *Washroom and sinks.* Facilities, such as washrooms, basins, or sinks, shall be provided to maintain cleanliness among animal caretakers.

[32 FR 3273, Feb. 24, 1967, as amended at 44 FR 63492, Nov. 2, 1979]

§ 3.26 Facilities, indoor.

(a) *Heating.* Indoor housing facilities for guinea pigs or hamsters shall be sufficiently heated when necessary to protect the animals from the cold, and to provide for their health and comfort. The ambient temperature shall not be allowed to fall below 60 °F. nor to exceed 85 °F.

(b) *Ventilation.* Indoor housing facilities for guinea pigs or hamsters shall be adequately ventilated to provide for the health and comfort of the animals at all times. Such facilities shall be provided with fresh air either by means of windows, doors, vents, or air conditioning, and shall be ventilated so as to minimize drafts, odors, and moisture condensation. The ambient temperature shall not be allowed to rise above 85 °F.

(c) *Lighting.* Indoor housing facilities for guinea pigs or hamsters shall have ample light, by natural or artificial means, or both, of good quality and well distributed. Such lighting shall provide uniformly distributed illumination of sufficient light intensity to permit routine inspection and cleaning during the entire working period. Primary enclosures shall be so placed as to protect the guinea pigs or hamsters from excessive illumination.

(d) *Interior surfaces.* The interior building surfaces of indoor housing facilities shall be constructed and maintained so that they are substantially impervious to moisture and may be readily sanitized.

§ 3.27 Facilities, outdoor.

(a) Hamsters shall not be housed in outdoor facilities.

(b) Guinea pigs shall not be housed in outdoor facilities unless such facilities are located in an appropriate climate and prior approval for such outdoor housing is obtained from the Deputy Administrator.

§ 3.28 Primary enclosures.

All primary enclosures for guinea pigs and hamsters shall conform to the following requirements:

(a) *General.* (1) Primary enclosures shall be structurally sound and maintained in good repair to protect the guinea pigs and hamsters from injury. Such enclosures, including their racks, shelving and other accessories, shall be constructed of smooth material substantially impervious to liquids and moisture.

(2) Primary enclosures shall be constructed and maintained so that the guinea pigs or hamsters contained therein have convenient access to clean food and water as required in this subpart.

(3) Primary enclosures having a solid floor shall be provided with clean bedding material.

(4) Primary enclosures equipped with mesh or wire floors shall be so constructed as to allow feces to pass through the spaces of the mesh or wire: *Provided, however,* That such floors shall be constructed so as to protect the animals' feet and legs from injury.

(b) *Space requirements for primary enclosures acquired before August 15, 1990*—(1) *Guinea pigs and hamsters.* Primary enclosures shall be constructed and maintained so as to provide sufficient space for each animal contained therein to make normal postural adjustments with adequate freedom of movement.

(2) *Guinea pigs.* In addition to the provisions of paragraph (b)(1) of this section, the following space requirements are applicable to primary enclosures for guinea pigs:

(i) The interior height of any primary enclosure used to confine guinea pigs shall be at least 6½ inches.

(ii) Each guinea pig housed in a primary enclosure shall be provided a minimum amount of floor space in accordance with the following table:

Weight or stage of maturity	Minimum space per guinea pig (square inches)
Weaning to 350 grams	60
350 grams or more	90
Breeders	180

(3) *Hamsters.* In addition to the provisions of paragraph (b)(1) of this section, the following space requirements are applicable to primary enclosures for hamsters:

(i) The interior height of any primary enclosure used to confine hamsters shall be at least 5½ inches, except that in the case of dwarf hamsters, such interior height shall be at least 5 inches.

(ii) A nursing female hamster, together with her litter, shall be housed in a primary enclosure which contains no other hamsters and which provides at least 121 square inches of floor space: *Provided, however,* That in the case of dwarf hamsters such floor space shall be at least 25 square inches.

(iii) The minimum amount of floor space per individual hamster and the maximum number of hamsters allowed in a single primary enclosure, except as provided for nursing females in paragraph (b)(3)(ii) of this section, shall be in accordance with the following table:

Age	Minimum space per hamster (square inches)		Maximum population per enclosure
	Dwarf	*Other*	
Weaning to 5 wks	5.0	10.0	20
5 to 10 wks	7.5	12.5	16
10 wks. or more	9	15.0	13

(c) *Space requirements for primary enclosures acquired on or after August 15, 1990*—(1) *Guinea pigs.* (i) Primary enclosures shall be constructed and maintained so as to provide sufficient space for each guinea pig contained therein to make normal postural adjustments with adequte freedom of movement.

(ii) The interior height of any primary enclosure used to confine guinea pigs shall be at least 7 inches (17.78 cm).

(iii) Each guinea pig shall be provided a minimum amount of floor space in any primary enclosure as follows:

Weight or stage of maturity	Minimum floor space	
	in ^{2}	cm ^{2}
Weaning to 350 grams	60	387.12
>350 grams	101	651.65
Nursing females with their litters	101	651.65

(2) *Hamsters.* (i) Primary enclosures shall be constructed and maintained so as to provide sufficient space for each hamster contained therein to make normal postural adjustments with adequate freedom of movement.

(ii) The interior height of any primary enclosure used to confine hamsters shall be at least 6 inches (15.24 cm).

(iii) Except as provided in paragraph (c)(2)(iv) of this section, each hamster shall be provided a minimum amount of floor space in any primary enclosure as follows:

Weight		Minimum floor space per hamster	
g	ozs	in ^{2}	cm ^{2}
<60	<2.1	10	64.52
60 to 80	2.1–2.8	13	83.88
80 to 100	2.8–3.5	16	103.23
>100	>3.5	19	122.59

(iv) A nursing female hamster, together with her litter, shall be housed in a primary enclosure that contains no other hamsters and that provides at least 121 square inches of floor space: *Provided, however,* That in the case of nursing female dwarf hamsters such floor space shall be at least 25 square inches.

(3) Innovative primary enclosures that do not precisely meet the space requirements of paragraph (c)(1) or (c)(2) of this section, but that do provide guinea pigs or hamsters with a sufficient volume of space and the opportunity to express species-typical behavior, may be used at research facilities when approved by the Institutional Animal Care and Use Committee, and by dealers and exhibitors when approved by the Administrator.

[32 FR 3273, Feb. 24, 1967, as amended at 55 FR 28882, July 16, 1990]

ANIMAL HEALTH AND HUSBANDRY STANDARDS

§ 3.29 Feeding.

(a) Guinea pigs and hamsters shall be fed each day except as otherwise might be required to provide adequate veterinary care. The food shall be free from contamination, wholesome, palatable and of sufficient quantity and nutritive value to meet the normal daily requirements for the condition and size of the guinea pig or hamster.

(b) Food comprising the basic diet shall be at least equivalent in quality and content to pelleted rations produced commercially and commonly available from feed suppliers.

(c) The basic diet of guinea pigs and hamsters may be supplemented with good quality fruits or vegetables consistent with their individual dietary requirements.

(d) Food receptacles, if used, shall be accessible to all guinea pigs or hamsters in a primary enclosure and shall be located so as to minimize contamination by excreta. All food receptacles shall be kept clean and shall be sanitized at least once every 2 weeks. If self-feeders are used for the feeding of pelleted feed, measures must be taken to prevent molding, deterioration or caking of the feed. Hamsters may be fed pelleted feed on the floor of a primary enclosure.

(e) Fruit or vegetable food supplements may be placed upon the bedding within the primary enclosure: *Provided, however,* That the uneaten portion of such supplements and any bedding soiled as a result of such feeding practices shall be removed from the primary enclosure when such uneaten supplements accumulate or such bedding becomes soiled to a degree that might be harmful or uncomfortable to animals therein.

§ 3.30 Watering.

Unless food supplements consumed by guinea pigs or hamsters supply them with their normal water requirements, potable water shall be provided daily except as might otherwise be required to provide adequate veterinary care. Open containers used for dispensing water to guinea pigs or hamsters shall be so placed in or attached to the primary enclosure as to minimize contamination from excreta. All watering receptacles shall be sanitized when dirty: *Provided, however,* That such receptacles shall be sanitized at least once every 2 weeks.

§ 3.31 Sanitation.

(a) *Cleaning and sanitation of primary enclosures.* (1) Primary enclosures shall be cleaned and sanitized often enough to prevent an accumulation of excreta or debris: *Provided, however,* That such enclosures shall be sanitized at least once every 2 weeks in the manner provided in paragraph (a)(4) of this section.

(2) In the event a primary enclosure becomes soiled or wet to a degree that might be harmful or uncomfortable to the animals therein due to leakage of the watering system, discharges from dead or dying animals, spoiled perishable foods, or moisture condensation, the guinea pigs or hamsters shall be transferred to clean primary enclosures.

(3) Prior to the introduction of guinea pigs or hamsters into empty primary enclosures previously occupied, such enclosures shall be sanitized in the manner provided in paragraph (a)(4) of this section.

(4) Primary enclosures for guinea pigs or hamsters shall be sanitized by washing them with hot water (180 °F.) and soap or detergent as in a mechanical cage washer, or by washing all soiled surfaces with a detergent solution followed by a safe and effective disinfectant, or by cleaning all soiled surfaces with live steam.

(b) *Housekeeping.* Premises (buildings and grounds) shall be kept clean and in good repair in order to protect the animals from injury and to facilitate the prescribed husbandry practices set forth in this subpart. Premises shall remain free of accumulations of trash.

(c) *Pest control.* An effective program for the control of insects, ectoparasites, and avian and mammalian pests shall be established and maintained.

§ 3.32 Employees.

A sufficient number of employees shall be utilized to maintain the prescribed level of husbandry practices set forth in this subpart. Such practices shall be under the supervision of an animal caretaker who has a background in animal husbandry or care.

§3.33 Classification and separation.

Animals housed in the same primary enclosure shall be maintained in compatible groups, with the following additional restrictions:

(a) Except where harem breeding is practiced, preweanling guinea pigs shall not be housed in the same primary enclosure with adults other than their parents.

(b) Guinea pigs shall not be housed in the same primary enclosure with hamsters, nor shall guinea pigs or hamsters be housed in the same primary enclosure with any other species of animals.

(c) Guinea pigs or hamsters under quarantine or treatment for a communicable disease shall be separated from other guinea pigs or hamsters and other susceptible species of animals in such a manner as to minimize dissemination of such disease.

§3.34 [Reserved]

TRANSPORTATION STANDARDS

AUTHORITY: Sections 3.35 through 3.41 issued under secs. 3, 5, 6, 10, 11, 14, 16, 17, 21; 80 Stat. 353; 84 Stat. 1561, 1562, 1563, 1564; 90 Stat. 418, 419, 420, 423; (7 U.S.C. 2133, 2135, 2136, 2140, 2141, 2144, 2146, 2147, 2151); 37 FR 28464, 28477, 38 FR 19141.

§3.35 Consignments to carriers and intermediate handlers.

(a) Carriers and intermediate handlers shall not accept any live guinea pig or hamster presented by any dealer, research facility, exhibitor, operator of an auction sale, or other person, or any department, agency, or instrumentality of the United States or any State or local government for shipment, in commerce, more than 4 hours prior to the scheduled departure of the primary conveyance on which it is to be transported: *Provided, however*, That the carrier or intermediate handler and any dealer, research facility, exhibitor, operator of an auction sale, or other person, or any department, agency, or instrumentality of the United States or any State or local government may mutually agree to extend the time of acceptance to not more than 6 hours if specific prior scheduling of the animal shipment to destination has been made.

(b) Any carrier or intermediate handler shall only accept for transportation or transport, in commerce any live guinea pig or hamster in a primary enclosure which conforms to the requirements set forth in §3.36 of the standards: *Provided, however*, That any carrier or intermediate handler may accept for transportation or transport, in commerce, any live guinea pig or hamster consigned by any department, agency, or instrumentality of the United States having laboratory animal facilities or exhibiting animals, or any licensed or registered dealer, research facility, exhibitor, or operator of an auction sale, if such consignor furnishes to the carrier or intermediate handler a certificate, signed by the consignor, stating that the primary enclosure complies with §3.36 of the standards, unless such primary enclosure is obviously defective or damaged and it is apparent that it cannot reasonably be expected to contain the live guinea pig or hamster without causing suffering or injury to such live guinea pig or hamster. A copy of such certificate shall accompany the shipment to destination. The certificate of compliance shall include at least the following information:

(1) Name and address of the consignor;

(2) The number of guinea pigs or hamsters in the primary enclosure(s);

(3) A certifying statement (e.g., "I hereby certify that the ____ (number) primary enclosure(s) which are used to transport the animal(s) in this shipment complies (comply) with USDA standards for primary enclosures (9 CFR part 3)."); and

(4) The signature of the consignor, and date.

(c) Carriers or intermediate handlers whose facilities fail to meet the minimum temperature allowed by the standards may accept for transportation or transport, in commerce, any live hamster consigned by any department, agency, or instrumentality of the United States or of any State or local government, or by any person (including any licensee or registrant under the Act, as well as any private individual) if the consignor furnishes to the carrier or intermediate handler a certificate executed by a veterinarian accredited by this Department pursuant to part 160 of this title on a specified date which shall not be more than 10 days prior to delivery of such hamster for transportation in commerce, stating that such live hamster is acclimated to air temperatures lower than those prescribed in §§ 3.40 and 3.41. A copy of such certificate shall accompany the shipment to destination. The certificate shall include the following information:

(1) Name and address of the consignor;

(2) The number of hamsters in the shipment;

(3) A certifying statement (e.g., "I hereby certify that the animal(s) in this shipment is (are), to the best of my knowledge, acclimated to air temperatures lower than 7.2 °C. (45 °F.)."); and

(4) The signature of the USDA accredited veterinarian, assigned accreditation number, and date.

(d) Carriers and intermediate handlers shall attempt to notify the consignee at least once in every 6 hour period following the arrival of any live guinea pig or hamster at the animal holding area of the terminal cargo facility. The time, date, and method of each attempted notification and the final notification to the consignee and the name of the person notifying the consignee shall be recorded on the copy of the shipping document retained by the carrier or intermediate handler and on a copy of the shipping document accompanying the animal shipment.

[42 FR 31563, June 21, 1977, as amended at 43 FR 22163, May 16, 1978; 44 FR 63492, Nov. 2, 1979]

§ 3.36 Primary enclosures used to transport live guinea pigs and hamsters.

No person subject to the Animal Welfare regulations shall offer for transportation, or transport, in commerce any live guinea pig or hamster in a primary enclosure that does not conform to the following requirements:

(a) Primary enclosures, such as compartments, transport cages, cartons, or crates, used to transport live guinea pigs or hamsters shall be constructed in such a manner that (1) the structural strength of the enclosure shall be sufficient to contain the live guinea pigs or hamsters and to withstand the normal rigors of transportation; (2) the interior of the enclosure shall be free from any protrusions that could be injurious to the live guinea pigs or hamsters contained therein; (3) the inner surfaces of corrugated fiberboard, cardboard, or plastic containers shall be covered or laminated with wire mesh or screen where necessary to prevent escape of the animals; (4) the openings of such enclosures are easily accessible at all times for emergency removal of the live guinea pigs or hamsters; (5) except as provided in paragraph (i) of this section, there are ventilation openings located on two opposite walls of the primary enclosure and the ventilation openings on each such wall shall be at least 16 percent of the total surface area of each such wall, or there are ventilation openings located on all four walls of the primary enclosure and the ventilation openings on each such wall shall be at least 8 percent of the total surface area of each such wall: *Provided, however*, That at least one-third of the total minimum area required for ventilation of the primary enclosure shall be located on the lower one-half of the primary enclosure and at least one-third of the total minimum area required for ventilation of the primary enclosure shall be located on the upper one-half of the primary enclosure; (6) except as provided in paragraph (i) of this section, projecting rims or other devices shall be on the exterior of the outside walls with any ventilation openings to prevent obstruction of the ventilation openings and to provide a minimum air circulation space of 1.9 centimeters (.75 inches) between the primary enclosure and any adjacent cargo or conveyance wall; and (7) except as provided in paragraph (i) of this section, adequate handholds or other devices for lifting shall be provided on the exterior of the primary enclosure to enable the primary enclosure to be lifted without tilting and to ensure that the person handling the primary enclosure will not be in contact with the guinea pigs or hamsters.

(b) Live guinea pigs or hamsters tranported in the same primary enclosure shall be of the same species and maintained in compatible groups.

(c) Primary enclosures used to transport live guinea pigs or hamsters shall be large enough to ensure that each animal contained therein has sufficient space to turn about freely and to make normal postural adjustments.

(d) Not more than 15 live guinea pigs shall be transported in the same primary enclosure. No more than 50 live hamsters shall be transported in the same primary enclosure.

(e) In addition to the other provisions of this section, the following requirements shall also apply to primary enclosures used to transport live guinea pigs or hamsters:

(1) *Guinea pigs.* (i) The interior height of primary enclosures used to tranport live guinea pigs weighing up to 500 grams shall be at least 15.2 centimeters (6 inches) and the interior height of primary enclosures used to transport live guinea pigs weighing over 500 grams shall be at least 17.8 centimeters (7 inches).

(ii) Each live guinea pig transported in a primary enclosure shall be provided a minimum amount of floor space in accordance with the following table:

MINIMUM SPACE PER LIVE GUINEA PIG

Weight (grams)	Square centimeters	Square inches
Up to 350	193.6	30
350 to 600	290.3	45
Over 600	354.8	55

(2) *Hamsters.* (i) The interior height of primary enclosures used to transport live hamsters shall be at least 15.2 centimeters (6 inches) except that in the case of dwarf hamsters such interior height shall be at least 12.7 centimeters (5 inches).

(ii) Each live hamster transported in a primary enclosure shall be provided a minimum amount of floor space in accordance with the following table:

MINIMUM SPACE PER LIVE HAMSTER

Age	Dwarf		Other	
	Square centimeters	Square inches	Square centimeters	Square inches
Weaning to 5 wks	32.2	5.0	45.2	7
5 to 10 wks	48.3	7.5	71.0	11
Over 10 wks	58.1	9.0	96.8	15

(f) Primary enclosures used to transport live guinea pigs or hamsters as provided in this section shall have solid bottoms to prevent leakage in shipment and shall be cleaned and sanitized in a manner prescribed in §3.31 of the standards, if previously used. Such primary enclosures shall contain clean litter of a suitable absorbent material, which is safe and nontoxic to the guinea pigs or hamsters, in sufficient quantity to absorb and cover excreta, unless the guinea pigs or hamsters are on wire or other nonsolid floors.

(g) Primary enclosures used to transport live guinea pigs or hamsters, except where such primary enclosures are permanently affixed in the animal cargo space of the primary conveyance, shall be clearly marked on top and on one or more sides with the words "Live Animals" in letters not less than 2.5 centimeters (1 inch) in height, and with arrows or other markings, to indicate the correct upright position of the container.

(h) Documents accompanying the shipment shall be attached in an easily accessible manner to the outside of a primary enclosure which is part of such shipment.

(i) When a primary enclosure is permanently affixed within the animal cargo space of the primary conveyance so that the front opening is the only source of ventilation for such primary enclosure, the front opening shall open directly to the outside or to an unobstructed aisle or passageway within the primary conveyance. Such front ventilation opening shall be at least 90 percent of the total surface area of the front wall of the primary enclosure and covered with bars, wire mesh or smooth expanded metal.

[42 FR 31563, June 21, 1977, as amended at 43 FR 21163, May 16, 1978; 55 FR 28882, July 16, 1990]

§ 3.37 Primary conveyances (motor vehicle, rail, air, and marine).

(a) The animal cargo space of primary conveyances used in transporting live guinea pigs and hamsters shall be designed and constructed to protect the health, and ensure the safety and comfort of the live guinea pigs and hamsters at all times.

(b) The animal cargo space shall be constructed and maintained in a manner to prevent the ingress of engine exhaust fumes and gases from the primary conveyance during transportation in commerce.

(c) No live guinea pig or hamster shall be placed in an animal cargo space that does not have a supply of air sufficient for normal breathing for each live animal contained therein, and the primary enclosures shall be positioned in the animal cargo space in such a manner that each live guinea pig or hamster has access to sufficient air for normal breathing.

(d) Primary enclosures shall be positioned in the primary conveyance in such a manner that in an emergency the live guinea pigs or hamsters can be removed from the primary conveyance as soon as possible.

(e) The interior of the animal cargo space shall be kept clean.

(f) Live guinea pigs and hamsters shall not be transported with any material, substance (e.g., dry ice) or device which may reasonably be expected to be injurious to the health and well-being of the guinea pigs and hamsters unless proper precaution is taken to prevent such injury.

(g) The animal cargo space of primary conveyances used to transport guinea pigs or hamsters shall be mechanically sound and provide fresh air by means of windows, doors, vents, or air conditioning so as to minimize drafts, odors, and moisture condensation. Auxiliary ventilation, such as fans, blowers, or air conditioners, shall be used in any cargo space containing live guinea pigs or hamsters when the ambient temperature in the animal cargo space is 75 °F (23.9 °C) or higher. The ambient temperature within the animal cargo space shall not exceed 85 °F (29.5 °C) or fall below 45 °F (7.2 °C), except that the ambient temperature in the cargo space may be below 45 °F (7.2 °C) for hamsters if the hamsters are accompanied by a certificate of acclimation to lower temperatures, as provided in § 3.35(c) of this part.

[42 FR 31563, June 21, 1977, as amended at 55 FR 28882, July 16, 1990]

§ 3.38 Food and water requirements.

(a) If live guinea pigs or hamsters are to be transported for a period of more than 6 hours, the animals shall have access to food and water or a type of food, which provides the requirements for food and water in quantity and quality sufficient to satisfy their food and water needs, during transit.

(b) Any dealer, research facility, exhibitor or operator of an auction sale offering any live guinea pig or hamster to any carrier or intermediate handler for transportation, in commerce, shall provide an adequate supply of food or type of food, which provides the requirements for food and water, within the primary enclosure to meet the requirements of this section.

(c) No carrier or intermediate handler shall accept for transportation, in commerce, any live guinea pig or hamster without an adequate supply of food or type of food, which provides the requirements for food and water, within the primary enclosure to meet the requirements of this section.

[42 FR 31563, June 21, 1977]

§ 3.39 Care in transit.

(a) During surface transportation, it shall be the responsibility of the driver or other employee to visually observe the live guinea pigs or hamsters as frequently as circumstances may dictate, but not less than once every 4 hours, to assure that they are receiving sufficient air for normal breathing, their ambient temperatures are within the prescribed limits, all other applicable standards are being complied with and to determine whether any of the live guinea pigs or hamsters are in obvious physical distress and to provide any needed veterinary care as soon as possible. When transported by air, live guinea pigs and hamsters shall be visually observed by the carrier as frequently as circumstances may dictate, but not less than once every 4 hours, if the animal cargo space is accessible during flight. If the animal cargo space is not accessible during flight, the carrier shall visually observe the live guinea pigs or hamsters whenever loaded and unloaded and whenever the animal cargo space is otherwise accessible to assure that they are receiving sufficient air for normal breathing, their ambient temperatures are within the prescribed limits, all other applicable standards are being complied with and to determine whether any such live guinea pigs or hamsters are in obvious physical distress. The carrier shall provide any needed veterinary care as soon as possible. No guinea pig or hamster in obvious physical distress shall be transported in commerce.

(b) During the course of transportation, in commerce, live guinea pigs or hamsters shall not be removed from their primary enclosures unless placed in other primary enclosures or facilities conforming to the requirements provided in this subpart.

[42 FR 31563, June 21, 1977]

§ 3.40 Terminal facilities.

No person subject to the Animal Welfare regulations shall commingle shipments of live guinea pigs or hamsters with inanimate cargo. All animal holding areas of a terminal facility where shipments of live guinea pigs or hamsters are maintained shall be cleaned and sanitized as prescribed in § 3.31 of the standards often enough to prevent an accumulation of debris or excreta, to minimize vermin infestation, and to prevent a disease hazard. An effective program for the control of insects, ectoparasites, and avian and mammalian pests shall be established and maintained for all animal holding areas. Any animal holding area containing live guinea pigs or hamsters shall be provided with fresh air by means of windows, doors, vents, or air conditioning and may be ventilated or air circulated by means of fans, blowers, or an air conditioning system so as to minimize drafts, odors, and moisture condensation. Auxiliary ventilation, such as exhaust fans and vents or fans or blowers or air conditioning shall be used for any animal holding area containing live guinea pigs and hamsters when the air temperature within such animal holding area is 23.9 °C. (75. °F.) or higher. The air temperature around any live guinea pig or hamster in any animal holding area shall not be allowed to fall below 7.2 °C. (45 °F.) nor be allowed to exceed 29.5 °C. (85 °F.) at any time. To ascertain compliance with the provisions of this paragraph, the air temperature around any live guinea pig or hamster shall be measured and read outside the primary enclosure which contains such guinea pig or hamster at a distance not to exceed .91 meters (3 feet) from any one of the external walls of the primary enclosure and measured on a level parallel to the bottom of such primary enclosure at a point which approximates half the distance between the top and bottom of such primary enclosure.

[43 FR 56215, Dec. 1, 1978, as amended at 55 FR 28883, July 16, 1990]

§ 3.41 Handling.

(a) Any person who is subject to the Animal Welfare regulations and who moves live guinea pigs or hamsters from an animal holding area of a terminal facility to a primary conveyance or vice versa shall do so as quickly and efficiently as possible. Any person subject to the Animal Welfare Act and holding any live guinea pig or hamster in an animal holding area of a terminal facility or transporting any live guinea pig or hamster to or from a terminal facility shall provide the following:

(1) *Shelter from sunlight.* When sunlight is likely to cause overheating or discomfort, sufficient shade shall be provided to protect the live guinea pigs and hamsters from the direct rays of the sun and such live guinea pigs or hamsters shall not be subjected to surrounding air temperatures which exceed 29.5 °C. (85 °F.), and which shall be measured and read in the manner prescribed § 3.40 of this part, for a period of more than 45 minutes.

(2) *Shelter from rain or snow.* Live guinea pigs and hamsters shall be provided protection to allow them to remain dry during rain or snow.

(3) *Shelter from cold weather.* Transporting devices shall be covered to provide protection for live guinea pigs and hamsters when the outdoor air temperature falls below 10 °C. (50 °F.), and such live guinea pigs and hamsters shall not be subjected to surrounding air temperatures which fall below 7.2 °C. (45 °F.), and which shall be measured and read in the manner prescribed in §3.40 of this part, for a period of more than 45 minutes.

(b) Care shall be exercised to avoid handling of the primary enclosure in such a manner that may cause physical or emotional trauma to the live guinea pig or hamster contained therein.

(c) Primary enclosures used to transport any live guinea pig or hamster shall not be tossed, dropped, or needlessly tilted and shall not be stacked in a manner which may reasonably be expected to result in their falling.

[43 FR 21163, May 16, 1978, as amended at 43 FR 56216, Dec. 1, 1978; 55 FR 28883, July 16, 1990]

Subpart C—Specifications for the Humane Handling, Care, Treatment and Transportation of Rabbits

FACILITIES AND OPERATING STANDARDS

§3.50 Facilities, general.

(a) *Structural strength.* Indoor and outdoor housing facilities for rabbits shall be structurally sound and shall be maintained in good repair, to protect the animals from injury, to contain the animals, and to restrict the entrance of other animals.

(b) *Water and electric power.* Reliable and adequate electric power, if required to comply with other provisions of this subpart, and adequate potable water shall be available.

(c) *Storage.* Supplies of food and bedding shall be stored in facilities which adequately protect such supplies against infestation or contamination by vermin. Refrigeration shall be provided for supplies of perishable food.

(d) *Waste disposal.* Provision shall be made for the removal and disposal of animal and food wastes, bedding, dead animals, and debris. Disposal facilities shall be so provided and operated as to minimize vermin infestation, odors, and disease hazards.

(e) *Washroom and sinks.* Facilities, such as washrooms, basins, or sinks, shall be provided to maintain cleanliness among animal caretakers.

[32 FR 3273, Feb. 24, 1967, as amended at 44 FR 63492, Nov. 2, 1979]

§3.51 Facilities, indoor.

(a) *Heating.* Indoor housing facilities for rabbits need not be heated.

(b) *Ventilation.* Indoor housing facilities for rabbits shall be adequately ventilated to provide for the health and comfort of the animals at all times. Such facilities shall be provided with fresh air either by means of windows, doors, vents, or air conditioning and shall be ventilated so as to minimize drafts, odors, and moisture condensation. Auxiliary ventilation, such as exhaust fans and vents or air conditioning, shall be provided when the ambient temperature is 85 °F. or higher.

(c) *Lighting.* Indoor housing facilities for rabbits shall have ample light, by natural or artificial means, or both, of good quality and well distributed. Such lighting shall provide uniformly distributed illumination of sufficient light intensity to permit routine inspection and cleaning during the entire working period. Primary enclosures shall be so placed as to protect the rabbits from excessive illumination.

(d) *Interior surfaces.* The interior building surfaces of indoor housing facilities shall be constructed and maintained so that they are substantially impervious to moisture and may be readily sanitized.

§3.52 Facilities, outdoor.

(a) *Shelter from sunlight.* When sunlight is likely to cause overheating or discomfort, sufficient shade shall be provided to allow all rabbits kept outdoors to protect themselves from the direct rays of the sun. When the atmospheric temperature exceeds 90 °F. artificial cooling shall be provided by a sprinkler system or other means.

(b) *Shelter from rain or snow.* Rabbits kept outdoors shall be provided with access to shelter to allow them to remain dry during rain or snow.

(c) *Shelter from cold weather.* Shelter shall be provided for all rabbits kept outdoors when the atmospheric temperature falls below 40 °F.

(d) *Protection from predators.* Outdoor housing facilities for rabbits shall be fenced or otherwise enclosed to minimize the entrance of predators.

(e) *Drainage.* A suitable method shall be provided to rapidly eliminate excess water.

§ 3.53 Primary enclosures.

All primary enclosures for rabbits shall conform to the following requirements:

(a) *General.* (1) Primary enclosures shall be structurally sound and maintained in good repair to protect the rabbits from injury, to contain them, and to keep predators out.

(2) Primary enclosures shall be constructed and maintained so as to enable the rabbits to remain dry and clean.

(3) Primary enclosures shall be constructed and maintained so that the rabbits contained therein have convenient access to clean food and water as required in this subpart.

(4) The floors of the primary enclosures shall be constructed so as to protect the rabbits' feet and legs from injury. Litter shall be provided in all primary enclosures having solid floors.

(5) A suitable nest box containing clean nesting material shall be provided in each primary enclosure housing a female with a litter less than one month of age.

(b) *Space requirements for primary enclosures acquired before August 15, 1990.* Primary enclosures shall be constructed and maintained so as to provide sufficient space for the animal to make normal postural adjustments with adequate freedom of movement. Each rabbit housed in a primary enclosure shall be provided a minimum amount of floor space, exclusive of the space taken up by food and water receptacles, in accordance with the following table:

Category	Individual weights (pounds)	Minimum space per rabbit (square inches)
Groups	3 through 5	144
	6 through 8	288
	9 or more	432
Individual adults	3 through 5	180
	6 through 8	360
	9 through 11	540
	12 or more	720
Nursing females	3 through 5	576
	6 through 8	720
	9 through 11	864
	12 or more	1080

(c) *Space requirements for primary enclosures acquired on or after August 15, 1990.* (1) Primary enclosures shall be constructed and maintained so as to provide sufficient space for the animal to make normal postural adjustments with adequate freedom of movement.

(2) Each rabbit housed in a primary enclosure shall be provided a minimum amount of floor space, exclusive of the space taken up by food and water receptacles, in accordance with the following table:

	Individual weights		Minimum floor space		Minimum interior height	
	kg	lbs	m²	ft²	cm	in
Individual rabbits (weaned)	<2	<4.4	0.14	1.5	35.56	14
	2–4	4.4–8.8	0.28	3.0	35.56	14
	4–5.4	8.8–11.9	0.37	4.0	35.56	14
	>5.4	>11.9	0.46	5.0	35.56	14

	Weight of nursing female		Minimum floor space/female & litter		Minimum interior height	
	kg	lbs	m²	ft²	cm	in
Females with litters	<2	<4.4	0.37	4.0	35.56	14
	2–4	4.4–8.8	0.46	5.0	35.56	14
	4–5.4	8.8–11.9	0.56	6.0	35.56	14
	>5.4	>11.9	0.70	7.5	35.56	14

(3) Innovative primary enclosures that do not precisely meet the space requirements of paragraph (c)(2) of this section, but that do provide rabbits with a sufficient volume of space and the opportunity to express species-typical behavior, may be used at research facilities when approved by the Institutional Animal Care and Use Committee, and by dealers and exhibitors when approved by the Administrator.

[32 FR 3273, Feb. 24, 1967, as amended at 55 FR 28883, July 16, 1990]

ANIMAL HEALTH AND HUSBANDRY STANDARDS

§ 3.54 Feeding.

(a) Rabbits shall be fed at least once each day except as otherwise might be required to provide adequate veterinary care. The food shall be free from contamination, wholesome, palatable and of sufficient quantity and nutritive value to meet the normal daily requirements for the condition and size of the rabbit.

(b) Food receptacles shall be accessible to all rabbits in a primary enclosure and shall be located so as to minimize contamination by excreta. All food receptacles shall be kept clean and sanitized at least once every 2 weeks. If self feeders are used for the feeding of dry feed, measures must be taken to prevent molding, deterioration or caking of the feed.

§ 3.55 Watering.

Sufficient potable water shall be provided daily except as might otherwise be required to provide adequate veterinary care. All watering receptacles shall be sanitized when dirty: *Provided, however,* That such receptacles shall be sanitized at least once every 2 weeks.

§ 3.56 Sanitation.

(a) *Cleaning of primary enclosures.* (1) Primary enclosures shall be kept reasonably free of excreta, hair, cobwebs and other debris by periodic cleaning. Measures shall be taken to prevent the wetting of rabbits in such enclosures if a washing process is used.

(2) In primary enclosures equipped with solid floors, soiled litter shall be removed and replaced with clean litter at least once each week.

(3) If primary enclosures are equipped with wire or mesh floors, the troughs or pans under such enclosures shall be cleaned at least once each week. If worm bins are used under such enclosures they shall be maintained in a sanitary condition.

(b) *Sanitization of primary enclosures.* (1) Primary enclosures for rabbits shall be sanitized at least once every 30 days in the manner provided in paragraph (b)(3) of this section.

(2) Prior to the introduction of rabbits into empty primary enclosures previously occupied, such enclosures shall be sanitized in the manner provided in paragraph (b)(3) of this section.

(3) Primary enclosures for rabbits shall be sanitized by washing them with hot water (180 °F.) and soap or detergent as in a mechanical cage washer, or by washing all soiled surfaces with a detergent solution followed by a safe and effective disinfectant, or by cleaning all soiled surfaces with live steam or flame.

(c) *Housekeeping.* Premises (buildings and grounds) shall be kept clean and in good repair in order to protect the animals from injury and to facilitate the prescribed husbandry practices set forth in this subpart. Premises shall remain free of accumulations of trash.

(d) *Pest control.* An effective program for the control of insects, ectoparasites, and avian and mammalian pests shall be established and maintained.

§ 3.57 Employees.

A sufficient number of employees shall be utilized to maintain the prescribed level of husbandry practices set forth in this subpart. Such practices shall be under the supervision of an animal caretaker who has a background in animal husbandry or care.

§ 3.58 Classification and separation.

Animals housed in the same primary enclosure shall be maintained in compatible groups, with the following additional restrictions:

(a) Rabbits shall not be housed in the same primary enclosure with any other species of animals unless required for scientific reasons.

(b) Rabbits under quarantine or treatment for a communicable disease shall be separated from other rabbits and other susceptible species of animals in such a manner as to minimize dissemination of such disease.

§ 3.59 [Reserved]

TRANSPORTATION STANDARDS

AUTHORITY: Sections 3.60 through 3.66 issued under secs. 3, 5, 6, 10, 11, 14, 16, 17, 21; 80 Stat. 353; 84 Stat. 1561, 1562, 1563, 1564; 90 Stat. 418, 420, 423 (7 U.S.C. 2133, 2135, 2136, 2140, 2141, 2144, 2146, 2147, 2151); 37 FR 28464, 28477, 38 FR 19141.

SOURCE: Sections 3.60 through 3.66 appear at 42 FR 31565, June 21, 1977, unless otherwise noted.

§ 3.60 Consignments to carriers and intermediate handlers.

(a) Carriers and intermediate handlers shall not accept any live rabbit presented by any dealer, research facility, exhibitor, operator of an auction sale, or other person, or any department, agency, or instrumentality of the United States or any State or local government for shipment, in commerce, more than 4 hours prior to the scheduled departure of the primary conveyance on which it is to be transported: *Provided, however,* That the carrier or intermediate handler and any dealer, research facility, exhibitor, operator of an auction sale, or other person, or any department, agency, or instrumentality of the United States or any State or local government may mutually agree to extend the time of acceptance to not more than 6 hours if specific prior scheduling of the animal shipment to destination has been made.

(b) Any carrier or intermediate handler shall only accept for transportation or transport, in commerce, any live rabbit in a primary enclosure which conforms to the requirements set forth in § 3.61 of the standards: *Provided, however,* That any carrier or intermediate handler may accept for transportation or transport, in commerce, any live rabbit consigned by any department, agency, or instrumentality of the United States having laboratory animal facilities or exhibiting animals or any licensed or registered dealer, research facility, exhibitor, or operator of any auction sale, if such consignor furnishes to the carrier or intermediate handler a certificate, signed by the consignor, stating that the primary enclosure complies with § 3.61 of the standards, unless such primary enclosure is obviously defective or damaged and it is apparent that it cannot reasonably be expected to contain the live rabbit without causing suffering or injury to such live rabbit. A copy of such certificate shall accompany the shipment to destination. The certificate shall include at least the following information:

(1) Name and address of the consignor;

(2) The number of rabbits in the primary enclosure(s);

(3) A certifying statement (e.g., "I hereby certify that the ___ (number) primary enclosure(s) which are used to transport the animal(s) in this shipment complies (comply) with USDA standards for primary enclosures (9 CFR part 3)."); and

(4) The signature of the consignor, and date.

(c) Carriers or intermediate handlers whose facilities fail to meet the minimum temperature allowed by the standards may accept for transportation or transport, in commerce, any live rabbit consigned by any department, agency, or instrumentality of the United States or of any State or local government, or by any person (including any licensee or registrant under the Act, as well as any private individual) if the consignor furnishes to the carrier or intermediate handler a certificate executed by a veterinarian accredited by this Department pursuant to part 160 of this title on a specified date which shall not be more than 10 days prior to delivery of such rabbit for transportation in commerce, stating that such live rabbit is acclimated to air temperatures lower than those prescribed in §§ 3.65 and 3.66. A copy of such certificate shall accompany the shipment to destination. The certificate shall include at least the following information:

(1) Name and address of the consignor;

(2) The number of rabbits in the shipment;

(3) A certifying statement (e.g., "I hereby certify that the animal(s) in this shipment is (are), to the best of my knowledge, acclimated to air temperatures lower than 7.2 °C. (45 °F.)."; and

(4) The signature of the USDA accredited veterinarian, assigned accreditation number, and date.

(d) Carriers and intermediate handlers shall attempt to notify the consignee at least once in every 6 hour period following the arrival of any live rabbit at the animal holding area of the terminal cargo facility. The time, date, and method of each attempted notification and the final notification to the consignee and the name of the person notifying the consignee shall be recorded on the copy of the shipping document retained by the carrier or intermediate handler and on a copy of the shipping document accompanying the animal shipment.

[42 FR 31565, June 21, 1977, as amended at 43 FR 21164, May 16, 1978; 44 FR 63493, Nov. 2, 1979]

§ 3.61 Primary enclosures used to transport live rabbits.

No person subject to the Animal Welfare regulations shall offer for transportation or transport in commerce any live rabbit in a primary enclosure that does not conform to the following requirements:

(a) Primary enclosures, such as compartments, transport cages, cartons, or crates, used to transport live rabbits shall be constructed in such a manner that:

(1) The stuctural strength of the enclosure shall be sufficient to contain the live rabbits and to withstand the normal rigors of transportation;

(2) The interior of the enclosure shall be free from any protrusions that could be injurious to the live rabbits contained therein;

(3) The openings of such enclosures are easily accessible at all times for emergency removal of the live rabbits;

(4) Except as provided in paragraph (h) of this section, there are ventilation openings located on two opposite walls of the primary enclosure and the ventilation openings on each such wall shall be at least 16 percent of the total surface area of each such wall, or there are ventilation openings located on all four walls of the primary enclosure and the ventilation openings on each such wall shall be at least 8 percent of the total surface area of each such wall: *Provided, however,* That at least one-third of the total minimum area required for ventilation of the primary enclosure shall be located on the lower one-half of the primary enclosure and at least one-third of the total minimum area required for ventilation of the primary enclosure shall be located on the upper one-half of the primary enclosure;

(5) Except as provided in paragraph (h) of this section, projecting rims or other devices shall be on the exterior of the outside walls with any ventilation openings to prevent obstruction of the ventilation openings and to provide a minimum air circulation space 1.9 centimeters (.75 inch) between the primary enclosure and any adjacent cargo or conveyance wall; and

(6) Except as provided in paragraph (h) of this section, adequate handholds or other devices for lifting shall be provided on the exterior of the primary enclosure to enable the primary enclosure to be lifted without tilting and to ensure that the person handling the primary enclosure will not be in contact with the rabbit.

(b) Live rabbits transported in the same primary enclosure shall be maintained in compatible groups and shall not be transported in the same primary enclosure with other specie of animals.

(c) Primary enclosures used to transport live rabbits shall be large enough to ensure that each rabbit contained therein has sufficient space to turn about freely and to make normal postural adjustments.

(d) Not more than 15 live rabbits shall be transported in the same primary enclosure.

(e) Primary enclosures used to transport live rabbits as provided in this section shall have solid bottoms to prevent leakage in shipment and shall be cleaned and sanitized in a manner prescribed in § 3.56 of the standards, if previously used. Such primary enclosures shall contain clean litter of a suitable absorbent material which is safe and nontoxic to the rabbits, in sufficient quantity to absorb and cover excreta, unless the rabbits are on wire or other nonsolid floors.

(f) Primary enclosures used to transport live rabbits, except where such primary enclosures are permanently affixed in the animal cargo space of the primary conveyance, shall be clearly marked on top and on one or more sides with the works "Live Animal" in letters not less than 2.5 centimeters (1 inch) in height, and with arrows or other markings, to indicate the correct upright position of the container.

(g) Documents accompanying the shipment shall be attached in an easily accessible manner to the outside of a primary enclosure which is part of such shipment.

(h) When a primary enclosure is permanently affixed within the animal cargo space of the primary conveyance so that the front opening is the only source of ventilation for such primary enclosure, the front opening shall open directly to the outside or to an unobstructed aisle or passageway within the primary conveyance. Such front ventilation opening shall be at least 90 percent of the total surface area of the front wall of the primary enclosure and covered with bars, wire mesh or smooth expanded metal.

[42 FR 31565, June 21, 1977, as amended at 43 FR 21164, May 16, 1978; 55 FR 28883, July 16, 1990]

§ 3.62 Primary conveyances (motor vehicle, rail, air, and marine).

(a) The animal cargo space of primary conveyances used in transporting live rabbits shall be designed and constructed to protect the health, and ensure the safety and comfort of the rabbits contained therein at all times.

(b) The animal cargo space shall be constructed and maintained in a manner to prevent the ingress of engine exhaust fumes and gases from the primary conveyance during transportation in commerce.

(c) No live rabbit shall be placed in an animal cargo space that does not have a supply of air sufficient for normal breathing for each live animal contained therein, and the primary enclosures shall be positioned in the animal cargo space in such a manner that each rabbit has access to sufficient air for normal breathing.

(d) Primary enclosures shall be positioned in the primary conveyance in such a manner that in an emergency the live rabbits can be removed from the primary conveyance as soon as possible.

(e) The interior of the animal cargo space shall be kept clean.

(f) Live rabbits shall not be transported with any material, substance (e.g., dry ice) or device which may reasonably be expected to be injurious to the health and well-being of the rabbits unless proper precaution is taken to prevent such injury.

(g) The animal cargo space of primary conveyances used to transport rabbits shall be mechanically sound and provide fresh air by means of windows, doors, vents, or air conditioning so as to minimize drafts, odors, and moisture condensation. Auxiliary ventilation, such as fans, blowers, or air conditioners, shall be used in any cargo space containing live rabbits when the ambient temperature in the animal cargo space is 75 °F (23.9 °C) or higher. The ambient temperature within the animal cargo space shall not exceed 85 °F (29.5 °C) or fall below 45 °F (7.2 °C), except that the ambient temperature in the cargo space may be below 45 °F (7.2 °C) if the rabbits are accompanied by a certificate of acclimation to lower temperatures, as provided in § 3.60(c) of this part.

[42 FR 31565, June 21, 1977, as amended at 55 FR 28883, July 16, 1990]

§ 3.63 Food and water requirements.

(a) If live rabbits are to be transported for a period of more than 6 hours, they shall have access to food and water or a type of food, which provides the requirements for food and water in quantity and quality sufficient to satisfy their food and water needs, during transit.

(b) Any dealer, research facility, exhibitor or operator of an auction sale offering any live rabbit to any carrier or intermediate handler for transportation, in commerce, shall provide an adequate supply of food or type of food, which provides the requirements for food and water, within the primary enclosure to meet the requirements of this section.

(c) No carrier or intermediate handler shall accept for transportation, in commerce, any live rabbit without an adequate supply of food or type of food, which provides the requirements for food and water, within the primary enclosure to meet the requirements of this section.

§ 3.64 Care in transit.

(a) During surface transportation, it shall be the responsibility of the driver or other employee to visually observe the live rabbits as frequently as circumstances may dictate, but not less than once every 4 hours, to assure that they are receiving sufficient air for normal breathing, their ambient temperatures are within the prescribed limits, all other applicable standards are being complied with and to determine whether any of the live rabbits are in obvious physical disress and to provide any needed veterinary care as soon as possible. When transported by air, live rabbits shall be visually observed by the carrier as frequently as circumstances may dictate, but not less than once every 4 hours, if the cargo space is accessible during flight. If the animal cargo space is not accessible during flight, the carrier shall visually observe the live rabbits whenever loaded and unloaded and whenever the animal cargo space is otherwise accessible to assure that they are receiving sufficient air for normal breathing, their ambient temperatures are within the prescribed limits, all other applicable standards are being complied with and to determine whether any such live rabbits are in obvious physical distress. The carrier shall provide any needed veterinary care as soon as possible. No rabbit in obvious physical distress shall be transported in commerce.

(b) During the course of transportation, in commerce, live rabbits shall not be removed from their primary enclosures unless placed in other primary enclosures or facilities conforming to the requirements provided in this subpart.

§ 3.65 Terminal facilities.

No person subject to the Animal Welfare regulations shall commingle shipments of live rabbits with inanimate cargo. All animal holding areas of a terminal facility where shipments of rabbits are maintained shall be cleaned and sanitized as prescribed in § 3.56 of the standards often enough to prevent an accumulation of debris or excreta, to minimize vermin infestation, and to prevent a disease hazard. An effective program for the control of insects, ectoparasites, and avian and mammalian pests shall be established and maintained for all animal holding areas. Any animal holding area containing live rabbits shall be provided with fresh air by means of windows, doors, vents, or air conditioning and may be ventilated or air circulated by means of fans, blowers, or an air conditioning system so as to minimize drafts, odors, and moisture condensation. Auxiliary ventilation, such as exhaust fans and vents or fans or blowers or air conditioning shall be used for any animal holding area containing live rabbits when the air temperature within such animal holding area is 23.9 °C. (75 °F.) or higher. The air temperature around any live rabbit in any animal holding area shall not be allowed to fall below 7.2 °C. (45 °F.) nor be allowed to exceed 29.5 °C. (85 °F.) at any time. To ascertain compliance with the provisions of this paragraph, the air temperature around any live rabbit shall be measured and read outside the primary enclosure which contains such rabbit at a distance not to exceed .91 meters (3 feet) from any one of the external walls of the primary enclosure and on a level parallel to the bottom of such primary enclosure at a point which approximates half the distance between the top and bottom of such primary enclosure.

[43 FR 56216, Dec. 1, 1978, as amended at 55 FR 28883, July 16, 1990]]

§ 3.66 Handling.

(a) Any person who is subject to the Animal Welfare regulations and who moves live rabbits from an animal holding area of a terminal facility to a primary conveyance or vice versa shall do so as quickly and efficiently as possible. Any person subject to the Animal Welfare regulations and holding any live rabbit in an animal holding area of a terminal facility or transporting any live rabbit to or from a terminal facility shall provide the following:

(1) *Shelter from sunlight.* When sunlight is likely to cause overheating or discomfort, sufficient shade shall be provided to protect the live rabbits from the direct rays of the sun and such live rabbits shall not be subjected to surrounding air temperatures which exceed 29.5 °C. (85 °F.), and which shall be measured and read in the manner prescribed in §3.65 of this part, for a period of more than 45 minutes.

(2) *Shelter from rain or snow.* Live rabbits shall be provided protection to allow them to remain dry during rain or snow.

(3) *Shelter from cold weather.* Transporting devices shall be covered to provide protection for live rabbits when the outdoor air temperature falls below 10 °C. (50 °F.), and such live rabbits shall not be subjected to surrounding air temperatures which fall below 7.2 °C. (45 °F.), and which shall be measured and read in the manner prescribed in §3.65 of this part, for a period of more than 45 minutes unless such rabbits are accompanied by a certificate of acclimation to lower temperatures as prescribed in §3.60(c).

(b) Care shall be exercised to avoid handling of the primary enclosure in such a manner that may cause physical or emotional trauma to the live rabbit contained therein.

(c) Primary enclosures used to transport any live rabbit shall not be tossed, dropped, or needlessly tilted and shall not be stacked in a manner which may reasonably be expected to result in their falling.

[43 FR 21164, May 16, 1978, as amended at 43 FR 56216, Dec. 1, 1978; 55 FR 28883, July 16, 1990]

Subpart D—Specifications for the Humane Handling, Care, Treatment, and Transportation of Nonhuman Primates [2]

SOURCE: 56 FR 6495, Feb. 15, 1991, unless otherwise noted.

FACILITIES AND OPERATING STANDARDS

§3.75 Housing facilities, general.

(a) *Structure:* construction. Housing facilities for nonhuman primates must be designed and constructed so that they are structurally sound for the species of nonhuman primates housed in them. They must be kept in good repair, and they must protect the animals from injury, contain the animals securely, and restrict other animals from entering.

(b) *Condition and site.* Housing facilities and areas used for storing animal food or bedding must be free of any accumulation of trash, waste material, junk, weeds, and other discarded materials. Animal areas inside of housing facilities must be kept neat and free of clutter, including equipment, furniture, or stored material, but may contain materials actually used and necessary for cleaning the area, and fixtures and equipment necessary for proper husbandry practices and research needs. Housing facilities other than those maintained by research facilities and Federal research facilities must be physically separated from any other businesses. If a housing facility is located on the same premises as any other businesses, it must be physically separated from the other businesses so that animals the size of dogs, skunks, and raccoons, are prevented from entering it.

[2] Nonhuman primates include a great diversity of forms, ranging from the marmoset weighing only a few ounces, to the adult gorilla weighing hundreds of pounds, and include more than 240 species. They come from Asia, Africa, and Central and South America, and they live in different habitats in nature. Some have been transported to the United States from their natural habitats and some have been raised in captivity in the United States. Their nutritional and activity requirements differ, as do their social and environmental requirements. As a result, the conditions appropriate for one species do not necessarily apply to another. Accordingly, these minimum specifications must be applied in accordance with the customary and generally accepted professional and husbandry practices considered appropriate for each species, and necessary to promote their psychological well-being.

These minimum standards apply only to live nonhuman primates, unless stated otherwise.

(c) *Surfaces*—(1) *General requirements.* The surfaces of housing facilities—including perches, shelves, swings, boxes, houses, dens, and other furniture-type fixtures or objects within the facility—must be constructed in a manner and made of materials that allow them to be readily cleaned and sanitized, or removed or replaced when worn or soiled. Furniture-type fixtures or objects must be sturdily constructed and must be strong enough to provide for the safe activity and welfare of nonhuman primates. Floors may be made of dirt, absorbent bedding, sand, gravel, grass, or other similar material that can be readily cleaned, or can be removed or replaced whenever cleaning does not eliminate odors, diseases, pests, insects, or vermin. Any surfaces that come in contact with nonhuman primates must:

(i) Be free of excessive rust that prevents the required cleaning and sanitization, or that affects the structural strength of the surface; and

(ii) Be free of jagged edges or sharp points that might injure the animals.

(2) *Maintenance and replacement of surfaces.* All surfaces must be maintained on a regular basis. Surfaces of housing facilities—including houses, dens, and other furniture-type fixtures and objects within the facility—that cannot be readily cleaned and sanitized, must be replaced when worn or soiled.

(3) *Cleaning.* Hard surfaces with which nonhuman primates come in contact must be spot-cleaned daily and sanitized in accordance with § 3.84 of this subpart to prevent accumulation of excreta or disease hazards. If the species scent mark, the surfaces must be sanitized or replaced at regular intervals as determined by the attending veterinarian in accordance with generally accepted professional and husbandry practices. Floors made of dirt, absorbent bedding, sand, gravel, grass, or other similar material, and planted enclosures must be raked or spot-cleaned with sufficient frequency to ensure all animals the freedom to avoid contact with excreta. Contaminated material must be removed or replaced whenever raking and spot cleaning does not eliminate odors, diseases, insects, pests, or vermin infestation. All other surfaces of housing facilities must be cleaned and sanitized when necessary to satisfy generally accepted husbandry standards and practices. Sanitization may be done by any of the methods provided in § 3.84(b)(3) of this subpart for primary enclosures.

(d) *Water and electric power.* The housing facility must have reliable electric power adequate for heating, cooling, ventilation, and lighting, and for carrying out other husbandry requirements in accordance with the regulations in this subpart. The housing facility must provide running potable water for the nonhuman primates' drinking needs. It must be adequate for cleaning and for carrying out other husbandry requirements.

(e) *Storage.* Supplies of food and bedding must be stored in a manner that protects the supplies from spoilage, contamination, and vermin infestation. The supplies must be stored off the floor and away from the walls, to allow cleaning underneath and around the supplies. Food requiring refrigeration must be stored accordingly, and all food must be stored in a manner that prevents contamination and deterioration of its nutritive value. Only the food and bedding currently being used may be kept in animal areas, and when not in actual use, open food and bedding supplies must be kept in leakproof containers with tightly fitting lids to prevent spoilage and contamination. Substances that are toxic to the nonhuman primates but that are required for normal husbandry practices must not be stored in food storage and preparation areas, but may be stored in cabinets in the animal areas.

(f) *Drainage and waste disposal.* Housing facility operators must provide for regular and frequent collection, removal, and disposal of animal and food wastes, bedding, dead animals, debris, garbage, water, and any other fluids and wastes, in a manner that minimizes contamination and disease risk. Housing facilities must be equipped with disposal facilities and drainage systems that are constructed and operated so that animal wastes and water are rapidly eliminated and the animals stay dry. Disposal and drainage systems must minimize vermin and pest infestation, insects, odors, and disease hazards. All drains must be properly constructed, installed, and maintained. If closed drainage systems are used, they must be equipped with traps and prevent the backflow of gases and the backup of sewage onto the floor. If the facility uses sump ponds, settlement ponds, or other similar systems for drainage and animal waste disposal, the system must be located far enough away from the animal area of the housing facility to prevent odors, diseases, insects, pests, and vermin infestation. If drip or constant flow watering devices are used to provide water to the animals, excess water must be rapidly drained out of the animal areas by gutters or pipes so that the animals stay dry. Standing puddles of water in animal areas must be mopped up or drained so that the animals remain dry. Trash containers in housing facilities and in food storage and food preparation areas must be leakproof and must have tightly fitted lids on them at all times. Dead animals, animal parts, and animal waste must not be kept in food storage or food preparation areas, food freezers, food refrigerators, and animal areas.

(g) *Washrooms and sinks.* Washing facilities, such as washrooms, basins, sinks, or showers must be provided for animal caretakers and must be readily accessible.

§3.76 Indoor housing facilities.

(a) *Heating, cooling, and temperature.* Indoor housing facilities must be sufficiently heated and cooled when necessary to protect nonhuman primates from temperature extremes and to provide for their health and well-being. The ambient temperature in the facility must not fall below 45 °F (7.2 °C) for more than 4 consecutive hours when nonhuman primates are present, and must not rise above 85 °F (29.5 °C) for more than 4 consecutive hours when nonhuman primates are present. The ambient temperature must be maintained at a level that ensures the health and well-being of the species housed, as directed by the attending veterinarian, in accordance with generally accepted professional and husbandry practices.

(b) *Ventilation.* Indoor housing facilities must be sufficiently ventilated at all times when nonhuman primates are present to provide for their health and well-being and to minimize odors, drafts, ammonia levels, and moisture condensation. Ventilation must be provided by windows, doors, vents, fans, or air conditioning. Auxiliary ventilation, such as fans, blowers, or air conditioning, must be provided when the ambient temperature is 85 °F (29.5 °C) or higher. The relative humidity maintained must be at a level that ensures the health and well-being of the animals housed, as directed by the attending veterinarian, in accordance with generally accepted professional and husbandry practices.

(c) *Lighting.* Indoor housing facilities must be lighted well enough to permit routine inspection and cleaning of the facility, and observation of the nonhuman primates. Animal areas must be provided a regular diurnal lighting cycle of either natural or artificial light. Lighting must be uniformly diffused throughout animal facilities and provide sufficient illumination to aid in maintaining good housekeeping practices, adequate cleaning, adequate inspection of animals, and for the well-being of the animals. Primary enclosures must be placed in the housing facility so as to protect the nonhuman primates from excessive light.

§3.77 Sheltered housing facilities.

(a) *Heating, cooling, and temperature.* The sheltered part of sheltered housing facilities must be sufficiently heated and cooled when necessary to protect the nonhuman primates from temperature extremes, and to provide for their health and well-being. The ambient temperature in the sheltered part of the facility must not fall below 45 °F (7.2 °C) for more than 4 consecutive hours when nonhuman primates are present, and must not rise above 85 °F (29.5 °C) for more than 4 consecutive hours when nonhuman primates are present, unless temperatures above 85 °F (29.5 °C) are approved by the attending veterinarian, in accordance with generally accepted husbandry practices. The ambient temperature must be maintained at a level that ensures the health and well-being of the species housed, as directed by the attending veterinarian, in accordance with generally accepted professional and husbandry practices.

(b) *Ventilation.* The sheltered part of sheltered animal facilities must be sufficiently ventilated at all times to provide for the health and well-being of nonhuman primates and to minimize odors, drafts, ammonia levels, and moisture condensation. Ventilation must be provided by windows, doors, vents, fans, or air conditioning. Auxiliary ventilation, such as fans, blowers, or air conditioning, must be provided when the ambient temperature is 85 °F (29.5 °C) or higher. The relative humidity maintained must be at a level that ensures the health and well-being of the species housed, as directed by the attending veterinarian, in accordance with generally accepted professional and husbandry practices.

(c) *Lighting.* The sheltered part of sheltered housing facilities must be lighted well enough to permit routine inspection and cleaning of the facility, and observation of the nonhuman primates. Animal areas must be provided a regular diurnal lighting cycle of either natural or artificial light. Lighting must be uniformly diffused throughout animal facilities and provide sufficient illumination to aid in maintaining good housekeeping practices, adequate cleaning, adequate inspection of animals, and for the well-being of the animals. Primary enclosures must be placed in the housing facility so as to protect the nonhuman primates from excessive light.

(d) *Shelter from the elements.* Sheltered housing facilities for nonhuman primates must provide adequate shelter from the elements at all times. They must provide protection from the sun, rain, snow, wind, and cold, and from any weather conditions that may occur.

(e) *Capacity: multiple shelters.* Both the sheltered part of sheltered housing facilities and any other necessary shelter from the elements must be sufficiently large to provide protection comfortably to each nonhuman primate housed in the facility. If aggressive or dominant animals are housed in the facility with other animals, there must be multiple shelters or other means to ensure that each nonhuman primate has access to shelter.

(f) *Perimeter fence.* On and after February 15, 1994, the outdoor area of a sheltered housing facility must be enclosed by a fence that is of sufficient height to keep unwanted species out. Fences less than 6 feet high must be approved by the Administrator. The fence must be constructed so that it protects nonhuman primates by restricting unauthorized humans, and animals the size of dogs, skunks, and raccoons from going through it or under it and having contact with the nonhuman primates. It must be of sufficient distance from the outside wall or fence of the primary enclosure to prevent physical contact between animals inside the enclosure and outside the perimeter fence. Such fences less than 3 feet in distance from the primary enclosure must be approved by the Administrator. A perimeter fence is not required if:

(1) The outside walls of the primary enclosure are made of a sturdy, durable material such as concrete, wood, plastic, metal, or glass, and are high enough and constructed in a manner that restricts contact with or entry by humans and animals that are outside the sheltered housing facility; or

(2) The housing facility is surrounded by a natural barrier that restricts the nonhuman primates to the housing facility and protects them from contact with unauthorized humans and animals that are outside the sheltered housing facility, and the Administrator gives written permission

(g) *Public barriers.* Fixed public exhibits housing nonhuman primates, such as zoos, must have a barrier between the primary enclosure and the public at any time the public is present, that restricts physical contact between the public and the nonhuman primates. Nonhuman primates used in trained animal acts or in uncaged public exhibits must be under the direct control and supervision of an experienced handler or trainer at all times when the public is present. Trained nonhuman primates may be permitted physical contact with the public, as allowed under § 2.131, but only if they are under the direct control and supervision of an experienced handler or trainer at all times during the contact.

(Approved by the Office of Management and Budget under control number 0579–0093)

§ 3.78 Outdoor housing facilities.

(a) *Acclimation.* Only nonhuman primates that are acclimated, as determined by the attending veterinarian, to the prevailing temperature and humidity at the outdoor housing facility during the time of year they are at the facility, and that can tolerate the range of temperatures and climatic conditions known to occur at the facility at that time of year without stress or discomfort, may be kept in outdoor facilities.

(b) *Shelter from the elements.* Outdoor housing facilities for nonhuman primates must provide adequate shelter from the elements at all times. It must provide protection from the sun, rain, snow, wind, and cold, and from any weather conditions that may occur. The shelter must safely provide heat to the nonhuman primates to prevent the ambient temperature from falling below 45 °F (7.2 °C), except as directed by the attending veterinarian and in accordance with generally accepted professional and husbandry practices.

(c) *Capacity: multiple shelters.* The shelter must be sufficiently large to comfortably provide protection for each nonhuman primate housed in the facility. If aggressive or dominant animals are housed in the facility with other animals there must be multiple shelters, or other means to ensure protection for each nonhuman primate housed in the facility.

(d) *Perimeter fence.* On and after February 15, 1994, an outdoor housing facility must be enclosed by a fence that is of sufficient height to keep unwanted species out. Fences less than 6 feet high must be approved by the Administrator. The fence must be constructed so that it protects nonhuman primates by restricting unauthorized humans, and animals the size of dogs, skunks, and raccoons from going through it or under it and having contact with the nonhuman primates. It must be of sufficient distance from the outside wall or fence of the primary enclosure to prevent physical contact between animals inside the enclosure and outside the perimeter fence. Such fences less than 3 feet in distance from the primary enclosure must be approved by the Administrator. A perimeter fence is not required if:

(1) The outside walls of the primary enclosure are made of a sturdy, durable material such as concrete, wood, plastic, metal, or glass, and are high enough and constructed in a manner that restricts contact with or entry by humans and animals that are outside the housing facility; or

(2) The housing facility is surrounded by a natural barrier that restricts the nonhuman primates to the housing facility and protects them from contact with unauthorized humans and animals that are outside the housing facility, and the Administrator gives written permission.

(e) *Public barriers.* Fixed public exhibits housing nonhuman primates, such as zoos, must have a barrier between the primary enclosure and the public at any time the public is present, in order to restrict physical contact between the public and the nonhuman primates. Nonhuman primates used in trained animal acts or in uncaged public exhibits must be under the direct control and supervision of an experienced handler or trainer at all times when the public is present. Trained nonhuman primates may be allowed physical contact with the public, but only if they are under the direct control and supervision of an experienced handler or trainer at all times during the contact.

(Approved by the Office of Management and Budget under control number 0579–0093)

§ 3.79 Mobile or traveling housing facilities.

(a) *Heating, cooling, and temperature.* Mobile or traveling housing facilities must be sufficiently heated and cooled when necessary to protect nonhuman primates from temperature extremes and to provide for their health and well-being. The ambient temperature in the traveling housing facility must not fall below 45 °F (7.2 °C) for more than 4 consecutive hours when nonhuman primates are present, and must not rise above 85 °F (29.5 °C) for more than 4 consecutive hours when nonhuman primates are present. The ambient temperature must be maintained at a level that ensures the health and well-being of the species housed, as directed by the attending veterinarian, and in accordance with generally accepted professional and husbandry practices.

(b) *Ventilation.* Traveling housing facilities must be sufficiently ventilated at all times when nonhuman primates are present to provide for the health and well-being of nonhuman primates and to minimize odors, drafts, ammonia levels, moisture condensation, and exhaust fumes. Ventilation must be provided by means of windows, doors, vents, fans, or air conditioning. Auxiliary ventilation, such as fans, blowers, or air conditioning, must be provided when the ambient temperature in the traveling housing facility is 85 °F (29.5 °C) or higher.

(c) *Lighting.* Mobile or traveling housing facilities must be lighted well enough to permit routine inspection and cleaning of the facility, and observation of the nonhuman primates. Animal areas must be provided a regular diurnal lighting cycle of either natural or artificial light. Lighting must be uniformly diffused throughout animal facilities and provide sufficient illumination to aid in maintaining good housekeeping practices, adequate cleaning, adequate inspection of animals, and for the well-being of the animals. Primary enclosures must be placed in the housing facility so as to protect the nonhuman primates from excessive light.

(d) *Public barriers.* There must be a barrier between a mobile or traveling housing facility and the public at any time the public is present, in order to restrict physical contact between the nonhuman primates and the public. Nonhuman primates used in traveling exhibits, trained animal acts, or in uncaged public exhibits must be under the direct control and supervision of an experienced handler or trainer at all times when the public is present. Trained nonhuman primates may be allowed physical contact with the public, but only if they are under the direct control and supervision of an experienced handler or trainer at all times during the contact.

§ 3.80 Primary enclosures.

Primary enclosures for nonhuman primates must meet the following minimum requirements:

(a) *General requirements.* (1) Primary enclosures must be designed and constructed of suitable materials so that they are structurally sound for the species of nonhuman primates contained in them. They must be kept in good repair.

(2) Primary enclosures must be constructed and maintained so that they:

(i) Have no sharp points or edges that could injure the nonhuman primates;

(ii) Protect the nonhuman primates from injury;

(iii) Contain the nonhuman primates securely and prevent accidental opening of the enclosure, including opening by the animal;

(iv) Keep other unwanted animals from entering the enclosure or having physical contact with the nonhuman primates;

(v) Enable the nonhuman primates to remain dry and clean;

(vi) Provide shelter and protection from extreme temperatures and weather conditions that may be uncomfortable or hazardous to the species of nonhuman primate contained;

(vii) Provide sufficient shade to shelter all the nonhuman primates housed in the primary enclosure at one time;

(viii) Provide the nonhuman primates with easy and convenient access to clean food and water;

(ix) Enable all surfaces in contact with nonhuman primates to be readily cleaned and sanitized in accordance with § 3.84(b)(3) of this subpart, or replaced when worn or soiled;

(x) Have floors that are constructed in a manner that protects the nonhuman primates from injuring themselves; and

(xi) Provide sufficient space for the nonhuman primates to make normal postural adjustments with freedom of movement.

(b) *Minimum space requirements.* Primary enclosures must meet the minimum space requirements provided in this subpart. These minimum space requirements must be met even if perches, ledges, swings, or other suspended fixtures are placed in the enclosure. Low perches and ledges that do not allow the space underneath them to be comfortably occupied by the animal will be counted as part of the floor space.

(1) Prior to February 15, 1994:

(i) Primary enclosures must be constructed and maintained so as to provide sufficient space to allow each nonhuman primate to make normal postural adjustments with adequate freedom of movement; and

(ii) Each nonhuman primate housed in a primary enclosure must be provided with a minimum floor space equal to an area at least three times the area occupied by the primate when standing on four feet.

(2) On and after February 15, 1994:

(i) The minimum space that must be provided to *each* nonhuman primate, whether housed individually or with other nonhuman primates, will be determined by the typical weight of animals of its species, except for brachiating species and great apes[3] and will be calculated by using the following table:[4]

Group	Weight		Floor area/animal		Height	
	lbs.	(kg.)	ft.[2]	(m[2])	in.	(cm.)
1	under 2.2	(under 1)	1.6	(0.15)	20	(50.8)
2	2.2–6.6	(1–3)	3.0	(0.28)	30	(76.2)
3	6.6–22.0	(3–10)	4.3	(0.40)	30	(76.2)
4	22.0–33.0	(10–15)	6.0	(0.56)	32	(81.28)
5	33.0–55.0	(15–25)	8.0	(0.74)	36	(91.44)
6	over 55.0	(over 25)	25.1	(2.33)	84	(213.36)

(ii) Dealers. exhibitors, and research facilities, including Federal research facilities, must provide great apes weighing over 110 lbs. (50 kg) an additional volume of space in excess of that required for Group 6 animals as set forth in paragraph (b)(2)(i) of this section, to allow for normal postural adjustments.

(iii) In the case of research facilities, any exemption from these standards must be required by a research proposal or in the judgment of the attending veterinarian and must be approved by the Committee. In the case of dealers and exhibitors, any exemption from these standards must be required in the judgment of the attending veterinarian and approved by the Administrator.

(iv) When more than one nonhuman primate is housed in a primary enclosure, the minimum space requirement for the enclosure is the sum of the minimum floor area space required for each individual nonhuman primate in the table in paragraph (b)(2)(i) of this

[3]The different species of nonhuman primates are divided into six weight groups for determining minimum space requirements, except that all brachiating species of any weight are grouped together since they require additional space to engage in species-typical behavior. The grouping provided is based upon the typical weight for various species and not on changes associated with obesity, aging, or pregnancy. These conditions will not be considered in determining a nonhuman primate's weight group unless the animal is obviously unable to make normal postural adjustments and movements within the primary enclosure. Different species of prosimians vary in weight and should be grouped with their appropriate weight group. They have not been included in the weight table since different species typically fall into different weight groups. Infants and juveniles of certain species are substantially lower in weight than adults of those species and require the minimum space requirements of lighter weight species, unless the animal is obviously unable to make normal postural adjustments and movements within the primary enclosure.

[4]Examples of the kinds of nonhuman primates typically included in each age group are:

Group 1—marmosets, tamarins, and infants (less than 6 months of age) of various species.

Group 2—capuchins, squirrel monkeys and similar size species, and juveniles (6 months to 3 years of age) of various species.

Group 3—macaques and African species.

Group 4—male macaques and large African species.

Group 5—baboons and nonbrachiating species larger than 33.0 lbs. (15 kg.).

Group 6—great apes over 55.0 lbs. (25 kg.), except as provided in paragraph (b)(2)(ii) of this section, and brachiating species.

section, and the minimum height requirement for the largest nonhuman primate housed in the enclosure. Provided however, that mothers with infants less than 6 months of age may be maintained together in primary enclosures that meet the floor area space and height requirements of the mother.

(c) Innovative primary enclosures not precisely meeting the floor area and height requirements provided in paragraphs (b)(1) and (b)(2) of this section, but that do provide nonhuman primates with a sufficient volume of space and the opportunity to express species-typical behavior, may be used at research facilities when approved by the Committee, and by dealers and exhibitors when approved by the Administrator.

(Approved by the Office of Management and Budget under control number 0579–0093)

§ 3.81 Environment enhancement to promote psychological well-being.

Dealers, exhibitors, and research facilities must develop, document, and follow an appropriate plan for environment enhancement adequate to promote the psychological well-being of nonhuman primates. The plan must be in accordance with the currently accepted professional standards as cited in appropriate professional journals or reference guides, and as directed by the attending veterinarian. This plan must be made available to APHIS upon request, and, in the case of research facilities, to officials of any pertinent funding agency. The plan, at a minimum, must address each of the following:

(a) *Social grouping.* The environment enhancement plan must include specific provisions to address the social needs of nonhuman primates of species known to exist in social groups in nature. Such specific provisions must be in accordance with currently accepted professional standards, as cited in appropriate professional journals or reference guides, and as directed by the attending veterinarian. The plan may provide for the following exceptions:

(1) If a nonhuman primate exhibits vicious or overly aggressive behavior, or is debilitated as a result of age or other conditions (e.g., arthritis), it should be housed separately;

(2) Nonhuman primates that have or are suspected of having a contagious disease must be isolated from healthy animals in the colony as directed by the attending veterinarian. When an entire group or room of nonhuman primates is known to have or believed to be exposed to an infectious agent, the group may be kept intact during the process of diagnosis, treatment, and control.

(3) Nonhuman primates may not be housed with other species of primates or animals unless they are compatible, do not prevent access to food, water, or shelter by individual animals. and are not known to be hazardous to the health and well-being of each other. Compatibility of nonhuman primates must be determined in accordance with generally accepted professional practices and actual observations, as directed by the attending veterinarian, to ensure that the nonhuman primates are in fact compatible. Individually housed nonhuman primates must be able to see and hear nonhuman primates of their own or compatible species unless the attending veterinarian determines that it would endanger their health, safety, or well-being.

(b) *Environmental enrichment.* The physical environment in the primary enclosures must be enriched by providing means of expressing noninjurious species-typical activities. Species differences should be considered when determining the type or methods of enrichment. Examples of environmental enrichments include providing perches, swings, mirrors, and other increased cage complexities; providing objects to manipulate; varied food items; using foraging or task-oriented feeding methods; and providing interaction with the care giver or other familiar and knowledgeable person consistent with personnel safety precautions.

(c) *Special considerations.* Certain nonhuman primates must be provided special attention regarding enhancement of their environment, based on the needs of the individual species and in accordance with the instructions of the attending veterinarian. Nonhuman primates requiring special attention are the following:

(1) Infants and young juveniles;

(2) Those that show signs of being in psychological distress through behavior or appearance;

(3) Those used in research for which the Committee-approved protocol requires restricted activity;

(4) Individually housed nonhuman primates that are unable to see and hear nonhuman primates of their own or compatible species; and

(5) Great apes weighing over 110 lbs. (50 kg). Dealers, exhibitors, and research facilities must include in the environment enhancement plan special provisions for great apes weighing over 110 lbs. (50 kg), including additional opportunities to express species-typical behavior.

(d) *Restraint devices.* Nonhuman primates must not be maintained in restraint devices unless required for health reasons as determined by the attending veterinarian or by a research proposal approved by the Committee at research facilities. Maintenance under such restraint must be for the shortest period possible. In instances where long-term (more than 12 hours) restraint is required, the nonhuman primate must be provided the opportunity daily for unrestrained activity for at least one continuous hour during the period of restraint, unless continuous restraint is required by the research proposal approved by the Committee at research facilities.

(e) *Exemptions.* (1) The attending veterinarian may exempt an individual nonhuman primate from participation in the environment enhancement plan because of its health or condition, or in consideration of its well-being. The basis of the exemption must be recorded by the attending veterinarian for each exempted nonhuman primate. Unless the basis for the exemption is a permanent condition, the exemption must be reviewed at least every 30 days by the attending veterinarian.

(2) For a research facility, the Committee may exempt an individual nonhuman primate from participation in some or all of the otherwise required environment enhancement plans for scientific reasons set forth in the research proposal. The basis of the exemption shall be documented in the approved proposal and must be reviewed at appropriate intervals as determined by the Committee, but not less than annually.

(3) Records of any exemptions must be maintained by the dealer, exhibitor, or research facility and must be made available to USDA officials or officials of any pertinent funding Federal agency upon request.

(Approved by the Office of Management and Budget under control number 0579–0093)

ANIMAL HEALTH AND HUSBANDRY STANDARDS

§3.82 Feeding.

(a) The diet for nonhuman primates must be appropriate for the species, size, age, and condition of the animal, and for the conditions in which the nonhuman primate is maintained, according to generally accepted professional and husbandry practices and nutritional standards. The food must be clean, wholesome, and palatable to the animals. It must be of sufficient quantity and have sufficient nutritive value to maintain a healthful condition and weight range of the animal and to meet its normal daily nutritional requirements.

(b) Nonhuman primates must be fed at least once each day except as otherwise might be required to provide adequate veterinary care. Infant and juvenile nonhuman primates must be fed as often as necessary in accordance with generally accepted professional and husbandry practices and nutritional standards, based upon the animals' age and condition.

(c) Food and food receptacles, if used, must be readily accessible to all the nonhuman primates being fed. If members of dominant nonhuman primate or other species are fed together with other nonhuman primates, multiple feeding sites must be provided. The animals must be observed to determine that all receive a sufficient quantity of food.

(d) Food and food receptacles, if used, must be located so as to minimize any risk of contamination by excreta and pests. Food receptacles must be kept clean and must be sanitized in accordance with the procedures listed in §3.84(b)(3) of this subpart at least once every 2 weeks. Used food receptacles must be sanitized before they can be used to provide food to a different nonhuman primate or social grouping of nonhuman primates. Measures must be taken to ensure there is no molding, deterioration, contamination, or caking or wetting of food placed in self-feeders.

§ 3.83 Watering.

Potable water must be provided in sufficient quantity to every nonhuman primate housed at the facility. If potable water is not continually available to the nonhuman primates, it must be offered to them as often as necessary to ensure their health and well-being, but no less than twice daily for at least 1 hour each time, unless otherwise required by the attending veterinarian, or as required by the research proposal approved by the Committee at research facilities. Water receptacles must be kept clean and sanitized in accordance with methods provided in § 3.84(b)(3) of this subpart at least once every 2 weeks or as often as necessary to keep them clean and free from contamination. Used water receptacles must be sanitized before they can be used to provide water to a different nonhuman primate or social grouping of nonhuman primates.

(Approved by the Office of Management and Budget under control number 0579–0093)

§ 3.84 Cleaning, sanitization, housekeeping, and pest control.

(a) *Cleaning of primary enclosures.* Excreta and food waste must be removed from inside each indoor primary enclosure daily and from underneath them as often as necessary to prevent an excessive accumulation of feces and food waste, to prevent the nonhuman primates from becoming soiled, and to reduce disease hazards, insects, pests, and odors. Dirt floors, floors with absorbent bedding, and planted areas in primary enclosures must be spot-cleaned with sufficient frequency to ensure all animals the freedom to avoid contact with excreta, or as often as necessary to reduce disease hazards, insects, pests, and odors. When steam or water is used to clean the primary enclosure, whether by hosing, flushing, or other methods, nonhuman primates must be removed, unless the enclosure is large enough to ensure the animals will not be harmed, wetted, or distressed in the process. Perches, bars, and shelves must be kept clean and replaced when worn. If the species of the nonhuman primates housed in the primary enclosure engages in scent marking, hard surfaces in the primary enclosure must be spot-cleaned daily.

(b) *Sanitization of primary enclosures and food and water receptacles.* (1) A used primary enclosure must be sanitized in accordance with this section before it can be used to house another nonhuman primate or group of nonhuman primates.

(2) Indoor primary enclosures must be sanitized at least once every 2 weeks and as often as necessary to prevent an excessive accumulation of dirt, debris, waste, food waste, excreta, or disease hazard, using one of the methods prescribed in paragraph (b)(3) of this section. However, if the species of nonhuman primates housed in the primary enclosure engages in scent marking, the primary enclosure must be sanitized at regular intervals determined in accordance with generally accepted professional and husbandry practices.

(3) Hard surfaces of primary enclosures and food and water receptacles must be sanitized using one of the following methods:

(i) Live steam under pressure;

(ii) Washing with hot water (at least 180 °F (82.2 °C)) and soap or detergent, such as in a mechanical cage washer;

(iii) Washing all soiled surfaces with appropriate detergent solutions or disinfectants, or by using a combination detergent/disinfectant product that accomplishes the same purpose, with a thorough cleaning of the surfaces to remove organic material, so as to remove all organic material and mineral buildup, and to provide sanitization followed by a clean water rinse.

(4) Primary enclosures containing material that cannot be sanitized using the methods provided in paragraph (b)(3) of this section, such as sand, gravel, dirt, absorbent bedding, grass, or planted areas, must be sanitized by removing the contaminated material as necessary to prevent odors, diseases, pests, insects, and vermin infestation.

(c) *Housekeeping for premises.* Premises where housing facilities are located, including buildings and surrounding grounds, must be kept clean and in good repair in order to protect the nonhuman primates from injury, to facilitate the husbandry practices required in this subpart, and to reduce or eliminate breeding and living areas for rodents, pests, and vermin. Premises must be kept free of accumulations of trash, junk, waste, and discarded matter. Weeds, grass, and bushes must be controlled so as to facilitate cleaning of the premises and pest control.

(d) *Pest control.* An effective program for control of insects, external parasites affecting nonhuman primates, and birds and mammals that are pests, must be established and maintained so as to promote the health and well-being of the animals and reduce contamination by pests in animal areas.

§ 3.85 Employees.

Every person subject to the Animal Welfare regulations (9 CFR parts 1, 2, and 3) maintaining nonhuman primates must have enough employees to carry out the level of husbandry practices and care required in this subpart. The employees who provide husbandry practices and care, or handle nonhuman primates, must be trained and supervised by an individual who has the knowledge, background, and experience in proper husbandry and care of nonhuman primates to supervise others. The employer must be certain that the supervisor can perform to these standards.

TRANSPORTATION STANDARDS

§ 3.86 Consignments to carriers and intermediate handlers.

(a) Carriers and intermediate handlers must not accept a nonhuman primate for transport in commerce more than 4 hours before the scheduled departure time of the primary conveyance on which the animal is to be transported. However, a carrier or intermediate handler may agree with anyone consigning a nonhuman primate to extend this time by up to 2 hours.

(b) Carriers and intermediate handlers must not accept a nonhuman primate for transport in commerce unless they are provided with the name, address, telephone number, and telex number, if applicable, of the consignee.

(c) Carriers and intermediate handlers must not accept a nonhuman primate for transport in commerce unless the consignor certifies in writing to the carrier or intermediate handler that the nonhuman primate was offered food and water during the 4 hours before delivery to the carrier or intermediate handler. The certification must be securely attached to the outside of the primary enclosure in a manner that makes it easily noticed and read. Instructions for no food or water are not acceptable unless directed by the attending veterinarian. Instructions must be in compliance with § 3.89 of this subpart. The certification must include the following information for each nonhuman primate:

(1) The consignor's name and address;

(2) The species of nonhuman primate;

(3) The time and date the animal was last fed and watered and the specific instructions for the next feeding(s) and watering(s) for a 24-hour period; and

(4) The consignor's signature and the date and time the certification was signed.

(d) Carriers and intermediate handlers must not accept a nonhuman primate for transport in commerce unless the primary enclosure meets the requirements of § 3.87 of this subpart. A carrier or intermediate handler must not accept a nonhuman primate for transport if the primary enclosure is obviously defective or damaged and cannot reasonably be expected to safely and comfortably contain the nonhuman primate without suffering or injury.

(e) Carriers and intermediate handlers must not accept a nonhuman primate for transport in commerce unless their animal holding area facilities meet the minimum temperature requirements provided in §§ 3.91 and 3.92 of this subpart, or unless the consignor provides them with a certificate signed by a veterinarian and dated no more than 10 days before delivery of the animal to the carrier or intermediate handler for transport in commerce, certifying that the animal is acclimated to temperatures lower than those that are required in §§ 3.91 and 3.92 of this subpart. Even if the carrier or intermediate handler receives this certification, the temperatures the nonhuman primate is exposed to while in the carrier's or intermediate handler's custody must not be lower than the minimum temperature specified by the veterinarian in accordance with paragraph (e)(4) of this section, and must be reasonably within the generally and professionally accepted temperature range for the nonhuman primate, as determined by the veterinarian, considering its age, condition, and species. A copy of the certification must accompany the nonhuman primate to its destination and must include the following information for each primary enclosure:

(1) The consignor's name and address;

(2) The number of nonhuman primates contained in the primary enclosure;

(3) The species of nonhuman primate contained in the primary enclosure;

(4) A statement by a veterinarian that to the best of his or her knowledge, each of the nonhuman primates contained in the primary enclosure is acclimated to air temperatures lower than 50 °F (10 °C), but not lower than a minimum temperature specified on the certificate based on the generally and professionally accepted temperature range for the nonhuman primate, considering its age, condition, and species; and

(5) The veterinarian's signature and the date the certification was signed.

(f) When a primary enclosure containing a nonhuman primate has arrived at the animal holding area of a terminal facility after transport, the carrier or intermediate handler must attempt to notify the consignee upon arrival and at least once in every 6-hour period after arrival. The time, date, and method of all attempted notifications and the actual notification of the consignee, and the name of the person who notifies or attempts to notify the consignee must be written either on the carrier's or intermediate handler's copy of the shipping document or on the copy that accompanies the primary enclosure. If the consignee cannot be notified within 24 hours after the nonhuman primate has arrived at the terminal facility, the carrier or intermediate handler must return the animal to the consignor or to whomever the consignor designates. If the consignee is notified of the arrival and does not take physical delivery of the nonhuman primate within 48 hours after arrival of the nonhuman primate, the carrier or intermediate handler must return the animal to the consignor or to whomever the consignor designates. The carrier or intermediate handler must continue to provide proper care, feeding, and housing to the nonhuman primate, and maintain the nonhuman primate in accordance with generally accepted professional and husbandry practices until the consignee accepts delivery of the nonhuman primate or until it is returned to the consignor or to whomever the consignor designates. The carrier or intermediate handler must obligate the consignor to reimburse the carrier or intermediate handler for the cost of return transportation and care.

(Approved by the Office of Management and Budget under control number 0579–0093)

§ 3.87 Primary enclosures used to transport nonhuman primates.

Any person subject to the Animal Welfare regulations (9 CFR parts 1, 2, and 3) must not transport or deliver for transport in commerce a nonhuman primate unless it is contained in a primary enclosure, such as a compartment, transport cage, carton, or crate, and the following requirements are met:

(a) *Construction of primary enclosures.* Primary enclosures used to transport nonhuman primates may be connected or attached to each other and must be constructed so that:

(1) The primary enclosure is strong enough to contain the nonhuman primate securely and comfortably and to withstand the normal rigors of transportation;

(2) The interior of the enclosure has no sharp points or edges and no protrusions that could injure the animal contained in it;

(3) The nonhuman primate is at all times securely contained within the enclosure and cannot put any part of its body outside the enclosure in a way that could result in injury to the animal, or to persons or animals nearby;

(4) The nonhuman primate can be easily and quickly removed from the enclosure in an emergency;

(5) The doors or other closures that provide access into the enclosure are secured with animal-proof devices that prevent accidental opening of the enclosure, including opening by the nonhuman primate;

(6) Unless the enclosure is permanently affixed to the conveyance, adequate devices such as handles or handholds are provided on its exterior, and enable the enclosure to be lifted without tilting it, and ensure that anyone handling the enclosure will not come into physical contact with the animal contained inside;

(7) Any material, treatment, paint, preservative, or other chemical used in or on the enclosure is nontoxic to the animal and not harmful to the health or well-being of the animal;

(8) Proper ventilation is provided to the nonhuman primate in accordance with paragraph (c) of this section;

(9) Ventilation openings are covered with bars, wire mesh, or smooth expanded metal having air spaces; and

(10) The primary enclosure has a solid, leak-proof bottom, or a removable, leak-proof collection tray under a slatted or wire mesh floor that prevents seepage of waste products, such as excreta and body fluids, outside of the enclosure. If a slatted or wire mesh floor is used in the enclosure, it must be designed and constructed so that the animal cannot put any part of its body between the slats or through the holes in the mesh. It must contain enough previously unused litter to absorb and cover excreta. The litter must be of a suitably absorbent material that is safe and nontoxic to the nonhuman primate and is appropriate for the species transported in the primary enclosure.

(b) *Cleaning of primary enclosures.* A primary enclosure used to hold or transport nonhuman primates in commerce must be cleaned and sanitized before each use in accordance with the methods provided in §3.84(b)(3) of this subpart.

(c) *Ventilation.* (1) If the primary enclosure is movable, ventilation openings must be constructed in one of the following ways:

(i) If ventilation openings are located on two opposite walls of the primary enclosure, the openings on each wall must be at least 16 percent of the total surface area of each such wall and be located above the midline of the enclosure; or

(ii) If ventilation openings are located on all four walls of the primary enclosure, the openings on every wall must be at least 8 percent of the total surface area of each such wall and be located above the midline of the enclosure.

(2) Unless the primary enclosure is permanently affixed to the conveyance, projecting rims or similar devices must be located on the exterior of each enclosure wall having a ventilation opening, in order to prevent obstruction of the openings. The projecting rims or similar devices must be large enough to provide a minimum air circulation space of 0.75 inches (1.9 centimeters) between the primary enclosure and anything the enclosure is placed against.

(3) If a primary enclosure is permanently affixed to the primary conveyance so that there is only a front ventilation opening for the enclosure, the primary enclosure must be affixed to the primary conveyance in such a way that the front ventilation opening cannot be blocked, and the front ventilation opening must open directly to an unobstructed aisle or passageway inside of the conveyance. The ventilation opening must be at least 90 percent of the total area of the front wall of the enclosure, and must be covered with bars, wire mesh, or smooth expanded metal having air spaces.

(d) *Compatibility.* (1) Only one live nonhuman primate may be transported in a primary enclosure, except as follows:

(i) A mother and her nursing infant may be transported together;

(ii) An established male-female pair or family group may be transported together, except that a female in estrus must not be transported with a male nonhuman primate;

(iii) A compatible pair of juveniles of the same species that have not reached puberty may be transported together.

(2) Nonhuman primates of different species must not be transported in adjacent or connecting primary enclosures.

(e) *Space requirements.* Primary enclosures used to transport nonhuman primates must be large enough so that each animal contained in the primary enclosure has enough space to turn around freely in a normal manner and to sit in an upright, hands down position without its head touching the top of the enclosure. However, certain larger species may be restricted in their movements, in accordance with professionally accepted standards of care, when greater freedom of movement would be dangerous to the animal, its handler, or to other persons.

(f) *Marking and labeling.* Primary enclosures, other than those that are permanently affixed to a conveyance, must be clearly marked in English on the top and on one or more sides with the words "Wild Animals," or "Live Animals," in letters at least 1 inch (2.5 cm.) high, and with arrows or other markings to indicate the correct upright position of the primary enclosure. Permanently affixed primary enclosures must be clearly marked in English with the words "Wild Animals" or "Live Animals," in the same manner.

(g) *Accompanying documents and records.* Shipping documents that must accompany shipments of nonhuman primates may be held by the operator of the primary conveyance, for surface transportation only, or must be securely attached in a readily accessible manner to the outside of any primary enclosure that is part of the shipment, in a manner that allows them to be detached for examination and securely reattached, such as in a pocket or sleeve. Instructions for administration of drugs, medication, and other special care must be attached to each primary enclosure in a manner that makes them easy to notice, to detach for examination, and to reattach securely. Food and water instructions must be attached in accordance with § 3.86(c) of this subpart.

(Approved by the Office of Management and Budget under control number 0579–0093)

§ 3.88 Primary conveyances (motor vehicle, rail, air, and marine).

(a) The animal cargo space of primary conveyances used to transport nonhuman primates must be designed, constructed, and maintained in a manner that at all times protects the health and well-being of the animals transported in it, ensures their safety and comfort, and prevents the entry of engine exhaust from the primary conveyance during transportation.

(b) The animal cargo space must have a supply of air that is sufficient for the normal breathing of all the animals being transported in it.

(c) Each primary enclosure containing nonhuman primates must be positioned in the animal cargo space in a manner that provides protection from the elements and that allows each nonhuman primate enough air for normal breathing.

(d) During air transportation, the ambient temperature inside a primary conveyance used to transport nonhuman primates must be maintained at a level that ensures the health and well-being of the species housed, in accordance with generally accepted professional and husbandry practices, at all times a nonhuman primate is present.

(e) During surface transportation, the ambient temperature inside a primary conveyance used to transport nonhuman primates must be maintained between 45 °F (7.2 °C) and 85 °F (30 °C) at all times a nonhuman primate is present.

(f) A primary enclosure containing a nonhuman primate must be placed far enough away from animals that are predators or natural enemies of nonhuman primates, whether the other animals are in primary enclosures or not, so that the nonhuman primate cannot touch or see the other animals.

(g) Primary enclosures must be positioned in the primary conveyance in a manner that allows the nonhuman primates to be quickly and easily removed from the primary conveyance in an emergency.

(h) The interior of the animal cargo space must be kept clean

(i) Nonhuman primates must not be transported with any material, substance (e.g., dry ice), or device in a manner that may reasonably be expected to harm the nonhuman primates or cause inhumane conditions.

§ 3.89 Food and water requirements.

(a) Each nonhuman primate that is 1 year of age or more must be offered food[5] at least once every 24 hours. Each nonhuman primate that is less than 1 year of age must be offered food at least once every 12 hours. Each nonhuman primate must be offered potable water at least once every 12 hours. These time periods apply to dealers, exhibitors, and research facilities, including Federal research facilities, who transport nonhuman primates in their own primary conveyances, starting from the time the nonhuman primate was last offered food and potable water before transportation was begun. These time periods apply to carriers and intermediate handlers starting from the date and time stated on the certification provided under § 3.86(c) of this subpart. Each nonhuman primate must be offered food and potable water within 4 hours before being transported in commerce. Consignors who are subject to the Animal Welfare regulations (9 CFR parts 1, 2, and 3) must certify that each nonhuman primate was offered food and potable water within the 4 hours preceding delivery of the nonhuman primate to a carrier or intermediate handler for transportation in commerce, and must certify the date and time the food and potable water was offered, in accordance with § 3.86(c) of this subpart.

(b) Any dealer, exhibitor, or research facility, including a Federal research facility, offering a nonhuman primate to a carrier or intermediate handler for transportation in commerce must securely attach to the outside of the primary enclosure used for transporting the nonhuman primate, written instructions for a 24-hour period for the in-transit food and water requirements of the nonhuman primate(s) contained in the enclosure. The instructions must be attached in a manner that makes them easily noticed and read.

(c) Food and water receptacles must be securely attached inside the primary enclosure and placed so that the receptacles can be filled from outside of the enclosure without opening the door. Food and water receptacles must be designed, constructed, and installed so that a nonhuman primate cannot leave the primary enclosure through the food or water opening.

(Approved by the Office of Management and Budget under control number 0579–0093)

§ 3.90 Care in transit.

(a) *Surface transportation (ground and water).* Any person subject to the Animal Welfare regulations (9 CFR parts 1, 2, and 3) transporting nonhuman primates in commerce must ensure that the operator of the conveyance or a person accompanying the operator of the conveyance observes the nonhuman primates as often as circumstances allow, but not less than once every 4 hours, to make sure that they have sufficient air for normal breathing, that the ambient temperature is within the limits provided in § 3.88(d) of this subpart, and that all other applicable standards of this subpart are being complied with. The regulated person transporting the nonhuman primates must ensure that the operator or the person accompanying the operator determines whether any of the nonhuman primates are in obvious physical distress, and obtains any veterinary care needed for the nonhuman primates at the closest available veterinary facility.

(b) *Air transportation.* During air transportation of nonhuman primates, it is the responsibility of the carrier to observe the nonhuman primates as frequently as circumstances allow, but not less than once every 4 hours if the animal cargo area is accessible during flight. If the animal cargo area is not accessible during flight, the carrier must observe the nonhuman primates whenever they are loaded and unloaded and whenever the animal cargo space is otherwise accessible to make sure that

[5] Proper food for purposes of this section is described in § 3.82 of this subpart, with the necessities and circumstances of the mode of travel taken into account.

the nonhuman primates have sufficient air for normal breathing, that the ambient temperature is within the limits provided in § 3.88(d) of this subpart, and that all other applicable standards of this subpart are being complied with. The carrier must determine whether any of the nonhuman primates is in obvious physical distress, and arrange for any needed veterinary care for the nonhuman primates as soon as possible.

(c) If a nonhuman primate is obviously ill, injured, or in physical distress, it must not be transported in commerce, except to receive veterinary care for the condition.

(d) During transportation in commerce, a nonhuman primate must not be removed from its primary enclosure unless it is placed in another primary enclosure or a facility that meets the requirements of § 3.80 or § 3.87 of this subpart. Only persons who are experienced and authorized by the shipper, or authorized by the consignor or the consignee upon delivery, if the animal is consigned for transportation, may remove nonhuman primates from their primary enclosure during transportation in commerce, unless required for the health or well-being of the animal.

(e) The transportation regulations contained in this subpart must be complied with until a consignee takes physical delivery of the animal if the animal is consigned for transportation, or until the animal is returned to the consignor.

§ 3.91 Terminal facilities.

(a) *Placement.* Any persons subject to the Animal Welfare regulations (9 CFR parts 1, 2, and 3) must not commingle shipments of nonhuman primates with inanimate cargo or with other animals in animal holding areas of terminal facilities. Nonhuman primates must not be placed near any other animals, including other species of nonhuman primates, and must not be able to touch or see any other animals, including other species of nonhuman primates.

(b) *Cleaning, sanitization, and pest control.* All animal holding areas of terminal facilities must be cleaned and sanitized in a manner prescribed in § 3.84(b)(3) of this subpart, as often as necessary to prevent an accumulation of debris or excreta and to minimize vermin infestation and disease hazards. Terminal facilities must follow an effective program in all animal holding areas for the control of insects, ectoparasites, and birds and mammals that are pests of nonhuman primates.

(c) *Ventilation.* Ventilation must be provided in any animal holding area in a terminal facility containing nonhuman primates by means of windows, doors, vents, or air conditioning. The air must be circulated by fans, blowers, or air conditioning so as to minimize drafts, odors, and moisture condensation. Auxiliary ventilation, such as exhaust fans, vents, fans, blowers, or air conditioning, must be used in any animal holding area containing nonhuman primates when the ambient temperature is 85 °F (29.5 °C) or higher.

(d) *Temperature.* The ambient temperature in an animal holding area containing nonhuman primates must not fall below 45 °F (7.2 °C) or rise above 85 °F (29.5 °C) for more than four consecutive hours at any time nonhuman primates are present. The ambient temperature must be measured in the animal holding area by the carrier, intermediate handler, or a person transporting nonhuman primates who is subject to the Animal Welfare regulations (9 CFR parts 1, 2, and 3), outside any primary enclosure containing a nonhuman primate at a point not more than 3 feet (0.91 m.) away from an outside wall of the primary enclosure, on a level that is even with the enclosure and approximately midway up the side of the enclosure.

(e) *Shelter.* Any person subject to the Animal Welfare regulations (9 CFR parts 1, 2, and 3) holding a nonhuman primate in an animal holding area of a terminal facility must provide the following:

(1) *Shelter from sunlight and extreme heat.* Shade must be provided that is sufficient to protect the nonhuman primate from the direct rays of the sun.

(2) *Shelter from rain or snow.* Sufficient protection must be provided to allow nonhuman primates to remain dry during rain, snow, and other precipitation.

(f) *Duration.* The length of time any person subject to the Animal Welfare regulations (9 CFR parts 1, 2, and 3) can hold a nonhuman primate in an animal holding area of a terminal facility upon arrival is the same as that provided in §3.86(f) of this subpart.

§3.92 Handling.

(a) Any person subject to the Animal Welfare regulations (9 CFR parts 1, 2, and 3) who moves (including loading and unloading) nonhuman primates within, to, or from the animal holding area of a terminal facility or a primary conveyance must do so as quickly and efficiently as possible, and must provide the following during movement of the nonhuman primate:

(1) *Shelter from sunlight and extreme heat.* Sufficient shade must be provided to protect the nonhuman primate from the direct rays of the sun. A nonhuman primate must not be exposed to an ambient temperature above 85 °F (29.5 °C) for a period of more than 45 minutes while being moved to or from a primary conveyance or a terminal facility, The ambient temperature must be measured in the manner provided in §3.91(d) of this subpart.

(2) *Shelter from rain or snow.* Sufficient protection must be provided to allow nonhuman primates to remain dry during rain, snow, and other precipitation.

(3) *Shelter from cold temperatures.* Transporting devices on which nonhuman primates are placed to move them must be covered to protect the animals when the outdoor temperature falls below 45 °F (7.2 °C). A nonhuman primate must not be exposed to an ambient air temperature below 45 °F (7.2 °C) for a period of more than 45 minutes, unless it is accompanied by a certificate of acclimation to lower temperatures as provided in §3.86(e) of this subpart. The ambient temperature must be measured in the manner provided in §3.91(d) of this subpart.

(b) Any person handling a primary enclosure containing a nonhuman primate must use care and must avoid causing physical harm or distress to the nonhuman primate.

(1) A primary enclosure containing a nonhuman primate must not be placed on unattended conveyor belts or on elevated conveyor belts, such as baggage claim conveyor belts and inclined conveyor ramps that lead to baggage claim areas, at any time; except that a primary enclosure may be placed on inclined conveyor ramps used to load and unload aircraft if an attendant is present at each end of the conveyor belt.

(2) A primary enclosure containing a nonhuman primate must not be tossed, dropped, or needlessly tilted, and must not be stacked in a manner that may reasonably be expected to result in its falling. It must be handled and positioned in the manner that written instructions and arrows on the outside of the primary enclosure indicate.

(c) This section applies to movement of a nonhuman primate from primary conveyance to primary conveyance, within a primary conveyance or terminal facility, and to or from a terminal facility or a primary conveyance.

(Approved by the Office of Management and Budget under control number 0579–0093)

Subpart E—Specifications for the Humane Handling, Care, Treatment, and Transportation of Marine Mammals

SOURCE: 44 FR 36874, June 22, 1979, unless otherwise noted.

FACILITIES AND OPERATING STANDARDS

§3.100 Special considerations regarding compliance and/or variance.

(a) All persons subject to the Animal Welfare Act who maintain or otherwise handle marine mammals in captivity must comply with the provisions of this subpart, except that they may apply for and be granted a variance,[6] by the Deputy Administrator, from one or more specified provisions of §3.104. The provisions of this subpart shall not apply, however, in emergency circumstances where compliance with one or more requirements would not serve the best interest of the marine mammals concerned.

[6] Written permission from the Deputy Administrator to operate as a licensee or registrant under the Act without being in full compliance with one or more specified provisions of §3.104.

(b) An application for a variance must be made to the Deputy Administrator in writing. The request must include:

(1) The species and number of animals involved,

(2) A statement from the attending veterinarian concerning the age and health status of the animals involved, and concerning whether the granting of a variance would be detrimental to the marine mammals involved,

(3) Each provision of the regulations that is not met,

(4) The time period requested for a variance,

(5) The specific reasons why a variance is requested, and

(6) The estimated cost of coming into compliance, if construction is involved.

(c) After receipt of an application for a variance, the Deputy Administrator may require the submission in writing of a report by two experts recommended by the American Association of Zoological Parks and Aquariums and approved by the Deputy Administrator concerning potential adverse impacts on the animals involved or on other matters relating to the effects of the requested variance on the health and well-being of such marine mammals. Such a report will be required only in those cases when the Deputy Administrator determines that such expertise is necessary to determine whether the granting of a variance would cause a situation detrimental to the health and well-being of the marine mammals involved. The cost of such report is to be paid by the applicant.

(d) Variances granted for facilities because of ill or infirm marine mammals that cannot be moved without placing their well-being in jeopardy, or for facilities within 0.3048 meters (1 foot) of compliance with any space requirement may be granted for up to the life of the marine mammals involved. Otherwise, variances shall be granted for a period not exceeding July 30, 1986, *Provided, however,* That under circumstances deemed justified by the Deputy Administrator, a maximum extension of 1 year may be granted to attain full compliance. A written request for the extension must be received by the Deputy Administrator by May 30, 1986. Consideration for extension by the Deputy Administrator will be limited to unforeseen or unusual situations such as when necessary public funds cannot be allocated in an appropriate time frame for a facility to attain full compliance by July 30, 1986.

(e) The Deputy Administrator shall deny any application for a variance if he determines that it is not justified under the circumstances or that allowing it will be detrimental to the health and well-being of the marine mammals involved.

(f) Any facility housing marine mammals that does not meet all of the space requirements as of July 30, 1984, must meet all of the requirements by September 28, 1984, or may operate without meeting such requirements until action is taken on an application for a variance if the application is submitted to the Deputy Administrator on or before September 28, 1984.

(g) A research facility may be granted a variance from specified requirements of this subpart when such variance is necessary for research purposes and is fully explained in the experimental design. Any time limitation stated in this section shall not be applicable in such case.

[49 FR 26681, June 28, 1984; 63 FR 2, Jan. 2, 1998]

§ 3.101 Facilities, general.

(a) *Construction requirements.* (1) Indoor and outdoor housing facilities for marine mammals must be structurally sound and must be maintained in good repair to protect the animals from injury, to contain the animals within the facility, and to restrict the entrance of unwanted animals. Lagoon and similar natural seawater facilities must maintain effective barrier fences extending above the high tide water level, or other appropriate measures, on all sides of the enclosure not contained by dry land to fulfill the requirements of this section.

(2) All marine mammals must be provided with protection from abuse and harassment by the viewing public by the use of a sufficient number of uniformed or readily identifiable employees or attendants to supervise the viewing public, or by physical barriers, such as fences, walls, glass partitions,

or distance, or any combination of these.

(3) All surfaces in a primary enclosure must be constructed of durable, nontoxic materials that facilitate cleaning, and disinfection as appropriate, sufficient to maintain water quality parameters as designated in §3.106. All surfaces must be maintained in good repair as part of a regular, ongoing maintenance program. All facilities must implement a written protocol on cleaning so that surfaces do not constitute a health hazard to animals.

(4) Facilities that utilize natural water areas, such as tidal basins, bays, or estuaries (subject to natural tidewater action), for housing marine mammals are exempt from the drainage requirements of paragraph (c)(1) of this section.

(b) *Water and power supply.* Reliable and adequate sources of water and electric power must be provided by the facility housing marine mammals. Written contingency plans must be submitted to and approved by the Deputy Administrator regarding emergency sources of water and electric power in the event of failure of the primary sources, when such failure could reasonably be expected to be detrimental to the good health and well-being of the marine mammals housed in the facility. Contingency plans must include, but not be limited to, specific animal evacuation plans in the event of a disaster and should describe back-up systems and/or arrangements for relocating marine mammals requiring artificially cooled or heated water. If the emergency contingency plan includes release of marine mammals, the plan must include provision for recall training and retrieval of such animals. Facilities handling marine mammals must also comply with the requirements of §2.134 of this subchapter.

(c) *Drainage.* (1) Adequate drainage must be provided for all primary enclosure pools and must be located so that all of the water contained in such pools may be effectively eliminated when necessary for cleaning the pool or for other purposes. Drainage effluent from primary enclosure pools must be disposed of in a manner that complies with all applicable Federal, State, and local pollution control laws.

(2) Drainage must be provided for primary enclosures and areas immediately surrounding pools. All drain covers and strainers must be securely fastened in order to minimize the potential risk of animal entrapment. Drains must be located so as to rapidly eliminate excess water (except in pools). Drainage effluent must be disposed of in a manner that complies with all applicable Federal, State, and local pollution control laws.

(d) *Storage.* Supplies of food must be stored in facilities that adequately protect such supplies from deterioration, spoilage (harmful microbial growth), and vermin or other contamination. Refrigerators and freezers (or chilled and/or iced coolers for under 12 hours) must be used for perishable food. No substances that are known to be or may be toxic or harmful to marine mammals may be stored or maintained in the marine mammal food storage or preparation areas, except that cleaning agents may be kept in secured cabinets designed and located to prevent food contamination. Food, supplements, and medications may not be used beyond commonly accepted shelf life or date listed on the label.

(e) *Waste disposal.* Provision must be made for the removal and disposal of animal and food wastes, dead animals, trash, and debris. Disposal facilities must be provided and operated in a manner that will minimize odors and the risk of vermin infestation and disease hazards. All waste disposal procedures must comply with all applicable Federal, State, and local laws pertaining to pollution control, protection of the environment, and public health.

(f) *Employee washroom facilities.* Washroom facilities containing basins, sinks, and, as appropriate, showers, must be provided and conveniently located to maintain cleanliness among employees, attendants, and volunteers. These facilities must be cleaned and sanitized daily.

(g) *Enclosure or pool environmental enhancements.* Any nonfood objects provided for the entertainment or stimulation of marine mammals must be of sufficient size and strength to not be ingestible, readily breakable, or likely to cause injury to marine mammals, and be able to be cleaned, sanitized, and/or replaced effectively.

[66 FR 251, Jan. 3, 2001, as amended at 77 FR 76824, Dec. 31, 2012]

§ 3.102 Facilities, indoor.

(a) *Ambient temperature.* The air and water temperatures in indoor facilities shall be sufficiently regulated by heating or cooling to protect the marine mammals from extremes of temperature, to provide for their good health and well-being and to prevent discomfort, in accordance with the currently accepted practices as cited in appropriate professional journals or reference guides, depending upon the species housed therein. Rapid changes in air and water temperatures shall be avoided.

(b) *Ventilation.* Indoor housing facilities shall be ventilated by natural or artificial means to provide a flow of fresh air for the marine mammals and to minimize the accumulation of chlorine fumes, other gases, and objectionable odors. A vertical air space averaging at least 1.83 meters (6 feet) shall be maintained in all primary enclosures housing marine mammals, including pools of water.

(c) *Lighting.* Indoor housing facilities for marine mammals shall have ample lighting, by natural or artificial means, or both, of a quality, distribution, and duration which is appropriate for the species involved. Sufficient lighting must be available to provide uniformly distributed illumination which is adequate to permit routine inspections, observations, and cleaning of all parts of the primary enclosure including any den areas. The lighting shall be designed so as to prevent overexposure of the marine mammals contained therein to excessive illumination.[7]

[44 FR 36874, June 22, 1979; 63 FR 2, Jan. 2, 1998]

§ 3.103 Facilities, outdoor.

(a) *Environmental temperatures.* Marine mammals shall not be housed in outdoor facilities unless the air and water temperature ranges which they may encounter during the period they are so housed do not adversely affect their health and comfort. A marine mammal shall not be introduced to an outdoor housing facility until it is acclimated to the air and water temperature ranges which it will encounter therein. The following requirements shall be applicable to all outdoor pools.

(1) The water surface of pools in outdoor primary enclosures housing polar bears and ice or cold water dwelling species of pinnipeds shall be kept sufficiently free of solid ice to allow for entry and exit of the animals.

(2) The water surface of pools in outdoor primary enclosures housing cetaceans and sea otters shall be kept free of ice.

(3) No sirenian or warm water dwelling species of pinnipeds or cetaceans shall be housed in outdoor pools where water temperature cannot be maintained within the temperature range to meet their needs.

(b) *Shelter.* Natural or artificial shelter which is appropriate for the species concerned, when the local climatic conditions are taken into consideration, shall be provided for all marine mammals kept outdoors to afford them protection from the weather or from direct sunlight.

(c) *Perimeter fence.* On and after May 17, 2000, all outdoor housing facilities (*i.e.*, facilities not entirely indoors) must be enclosed by a perimeter fence that is of sufficient height to keep animals and unauthorized persons out. Fences less than 8 feet high for polar bears or less than 6 feet high for other marine mammals must be approved in writing by the Administrator. The fence must be constructed so that it protects marine mammals by restricting animals and unauthorized persons from going through it or under it and having contact with the marine mammals, and so that it can function as a secondary containment system for the animals in the facility when appropriate. The fence must be of sufficient distance from the outside of the primary enclosure to prevent physical

[7] Lighting intensity and duration must be consistent with the general well-being and comfort of the animal involved. When possible, it should approximate the lighting conditions encountered by the animal in its natural environment. At no time shall the lighting be such that it will cause the animal discomfort or trauma.

contact between animals inside the enclosure and animals or persons outside the perimeter fence. Such fences less than 3 feet in distance from the primary enclosure must be approved in writing by the Administrator. For natural seawater facilities, such as lagoons, the perimeter fence must prevent access by animals and unauthorized persons to the natural seawater facility from the abutting land, and must encompass the land portion of the facility from one end of the natural seawater facility shoreline as defined by low tide to the other end of the natural seawater facility shoreline defined by low tide. A perimeter fence is not required:

(1) Where the outside walls of the primary enclosure are made of sturdy, durable material, which may include certain types of concrete, wood, plastic, metal, or glass, and are high enough and constructed in a manner that restricts entry by animals and unauthorized persons and the Administrator gives written approval; or

(2) Where the outdoor housing facility is protected by an effective natural barrier that restricts the marine mammals to the facility and restricts entry by animals and unauthorized persons and the Administrator gives written approval; or

(3) Where appropriate alternative security measures are employed and the Administrator gives written approval; or

(4) For traveling facilities where appropriate alternative security measures are employed.

[44 FR 36874, June 22, 1979, as amended at 64 FR 56147, Oct. 18, 1999]

§ 3.104 Space requirements.

(a) *General.* Marine mammals must be housed in primary enclosures that comply with the minimum space requirements prescribed by this part. These enclosures must be constructed and maintained so that the animals contained within are provided sufficient space, both horizontally and vertically, to be able to make normal postural and social adjustments with adequate freedom of movement, in or out of the water. (An exception to these requirements is provided in § 3.110(b) for isolation or separation for medical treatment and/or medical training.) Enclosures smaller than required by the standards may be temporarily used for nonmedical training, breeding, holding, and transfer purposes. If maintenance in such enclosures for nonmedical training, breeding, or holding is to last longer than 2 weeks, such extension must be justified in writing by the attending veterinarian on a weekly basis. If maintenance in such enclosures for transfer is to last longer than 1 week, such extension must be justified in writing by the attending veterinarian on a weekly basis. Any enclosure that does not meet the minimum space requirement for primary enclosures (including, but not limited to, medical pools or enclosures, holding pools or enclosures, and gated side pools smaller than the minimum space requirements) may not be used for permanent housing purposes. Rotating animals between enclosures that meet the minimum space requirements and enclosures that do not is not an acceptable means of complying with the minimum space requirements for primary enclosures.

(b) *Cetaceans.* Primary enclosures housing cetaceans shall contain a pool of water and may consist entirely of a pool of water. In determining the minimum space required in a pool holding cetaceans, four factors must be satisfied. These are MHD, depth, volume, and surface area. For the purposes of this subpart, cetaceans are divided into Group I cetaceans and Group II cetaceans as shown in Table III in this section.

(1)(i) *The required minimum horizontal dimension* (MHD) of a pool for Group I cetaceans shall be 7.32 meters (24.0 feet) or two times the average adult length of the longest species of Group I cetacean housed therein (as measured in a parallel or horizontal line, from the tip of its upper jaw, or from the most anterior portion of the head in bulbous headed animals, to the notch in the tail fluke[8]), whichever is greater; except that such MHD measurement may be reduced from the greater number by up to 20 percent if the amount of the reduction is added to the MHD at the 90-degree angle and if the minimum volume and surface area requirements are met based on an MHD of 7.32 meters (24.0 feet) or two times the average adult length of the longest species of Group I cetacean housed therein, whichever is greater.

(ii) The MHD of a pool for Group II cetaceans shall be 7.32 meters (24.0 feet) or four times the average adult length of the longest species of cetacean to be housed therein (as measured in a parallel or horizontal line from the tip of its upper jaw, or from the most anterior portion of the head in bulbous headed animals, to the notch in the tail fluke), whichever is greater; except that such MHD measurement may be reduced from the greater number by up to 20 percent if the amount of the reduction is added to the MHD at the 90-degree angle and if the minimum volume and surface area requirements are met based on an MHD of 7.32 meters (24.0 feet) or four times the average adult length of the longest species of Group II cetacean housed therein, whichever is greater.

(iii) In a pool housing a mixture of Group I and Group II cetaceans, the MHD shall be the largest required for any cetacean housed therein.

(iv) Once the required MHD has been satisfied, the pool size may be required to be adjusted to increase the surface area and volume when cetaceans are added. Examples of MHD and volume requirements for Group I cetaceans are shown in Table I, and for Group II cetaceans in Table II.

TABLE I—GROUP I CETACEANS [1]

Representative average adult lengths		Minimum horizontal dimension (MHD)		Minimum required depth		Volume of water required for each additional cetacean in excess of two	
Meters	Feet	Meters	Feet	Meters	Feet	Cubic meters	feet
1.68	5.5	7.32	24	1.83	6	8.11	284.95
2.29	7.5	7.32	24	1.83	6	15.07	529.87
2.74	9.0	7.32	24	1.83	6	21.57	763.02
3.05	10.0	7.32	24	1.83	6	26.73	942.00
3.51	11.5	7.32	24	1.83	6	35.40	1,245.79
3.66	12.0	7.32	24	1.83	6	38.49	1,356.48
4.27	14.0	8.53	28	2.13	7	60.97	2,154.04
5.49	18.0	10.97	36	2.74	9	129.65	4,578.12
5.64	18.5	11.28	37	2.82	9.25	140.83	4,970.33
5.79	19.0	11.58	38	2.90	9.50	152.64	5,384.32
6.71	22.0	13.41	44	3.36	11	237.50	8,358.68
6.86	22.5	13.72	45	3.43	11.25	253.42	8,941.64
7.32	24.0	14.63	48	3.66	12	307.89	10,851.84
8.53	28.0	17.07	56	4.27	14	487.78	17,232.32

[1] All calculations are rounded off to the nearest hundredth. In converting the length of cetaceans from feet to meters, 1 foot equals .3048 meter. Due to rounding of meter figures as to the length of the cetacean, the correlation of meters to feet in subsequent calculations of MHD and additional volume of water required per cetacean, over two, may vary slightly from a strict feet to meters ratio. Cubic meters is based on: 1 cubic foot = 0.0283 cubic meter.

TABLE II—GROUP II CETACEANS [1]

Representative average adult length		Minimum horizontal dimension (MHD)		Minimum required depth		Volume of water required for each additional cetacean in excess of four	
Meters	Feet	Meters	Feet	Meters	Feet	Cubic meters [1]	Cubic feet
1.52	5.0	7.32	24	1.83	6	13.28	471.00
1.68	5.5	7.32	24	1.83	6	16.22	569.91
1.83	6.0	7.32	24	1.83	6	19.24	678.24
2.13	7.0	8.53	28	1.83	6	26.07	923.16
2.29	7.5	9.14	30	1.83	6	30.13	1,059.75
2.44	8.0	9.75	32	1.83	6	34.21	1,205.76
2.59	8.5	10.36	34	1.83	6	38.55	1,361.19

[8] The body length of a *Monodon monoceros* (narwhale) is measured from the tip of the upper incisor tooth to the notch in the tail fluke. If the upper incisor is absent or does not extend beyond the front of the head, then it is measured like other cetaceans, from the tip of the upper jaw to the notch in the tail fluke. Immature males should be anticipated to develop the "tusk" (usually left incisor tooth) beginning at sexual maturity.

TABLE II—GROUP II CETACEANS [1]—Continued

Representative average adult length		Minimum horizontal dimension (MHD)		Minimum required depth		Volume of water required for each additional cetacean in excess of four	
Meters	Feet	Meters	Feet	Meters	Feet	Cubic meters [1]	Cubic feet
2.74	9.0	10.97	36	1.83	6	43.14	1,526.04

[1] Converting cubic feet to cubic meters is based on: 1 cubic foot = 0.0283 of a cubic meter.

TABLE III—AVERAGE ADULT LENGTHS OF MARINE MAMMALS MAINTAINED IN CAPTIVITY [1]

Species	Common name	Average adult length	
		In meters	In feet
Group I Cetaceans:			
Balaenoptera acutorostrata	Minke whale	8.50	27.9
Cephalorhynchus commersonii	Commerson's dolphin	1.52	5.0
Delphinapterus leucas	Beluga whale	4.27	14.0
Monodon monoceros	Narwhale	3.96	13.0
Globicephala melaena	Long-finned pilot whale	5.79	19.0
Globicephala macrorhynchus	Short-finned pilot whale	5.49	18.0
Grampus griseus	Risso's dolphin	3.66	12.0
Orcinus orca	Killer whale	7.32	24.0
Pseudorca carassidens	False killer whale	4.35	14.3
Tursiops truncatus (Atlantic)	Bottlenose dolphin	2.74	9.0
Tursiops truncatus (Pacific)	Bottlenose dolphin	3.05	10.0
Inia geoffrensis	Amazon porpoise	2.44	8.0
Phocoena phocoena	Harbor porpoise	1.68	5.5
Pontoporia blainvillei	Franciscana	1.52	5.0
Sotalia fluviatilis	Tucuxi	1.68	5.5
Platanista, all species	River dolphin	2.44	8.0
Group II Cetaceans:			
Delphinus delphis	Common dolphin	2.59	8.5
Feresa attenuata	Pygmy killer whale	2.44	8.0
Kogia breviceps	Pygmy sperm whale	3.96	13.0
Kogia simus	Dwarf sperm whale	2.90	9.5
Lagenorhynchus acutus	Atlantic white-sided dolphin	2.90	9.5
Lagenorhynchus cruciger	Hourglass dolphin	1.70	5.6
Lagenorhynchus obliquidens	Pacific white-sided dolphin	2.29	7.5
Lagenorhynchus albirostris	White-beaked dolphin	2.74	9.0
Lagenorhynchus obscurus	Duskey dolphin	2.13	7.0
Lissodelphis borealis	Northern right whale dolphin	2.74	9.0
Neophocaena phocaenoides	Finless porpoise	1.83	6.0
Peponocephala electra	Melon-headed whale	2.74	9.0
Phocoenoides dalli	Dall's porpoise	2.00	6.5
Stenella longirostris	Spinner dolphin	2.13	7.0
Stenella coeruleoalba	Striped dolphin	2.29	7.5
Stenella attenuata	Spotted dolphin	2.29	7.5
Stenella plagiodon	Spotted dolphin	2.29	7.5
Steno bredanensis	Rough-toothed dolphin	2.44	8.0

[1] This table contains the species of marine mammals known by the Department to be presently in captivity or that are likely to become captive in the future. Anyone who is subject to the Animal Welfare Act having species of marine mammals in captivity which are not included in this table should consult the Deputy Administrator with regard to the average adult length of such animals.

Species	Common name	Average adult length			
		In meters		In feet	
		Male	Female	Male	Female
Group I Pinnipeds:					
*Arctocephalus gazella***	Antarctic Fur Seal	1.80	1.20	5.9	3.9
*Arctocephalus tropicalis***	Amsterdam Island Fur Seal	1.80	1.45	5.9	4.75
*Arctocephalus australis***	South American Fur Seal	1.88	1.42	6.2	4.7
*Arctocephalus pusillis***	Cape Fur Seal	2.73	1.83	8.96	6.0
*Callorhinus ursinus***	Northern Fur Seal	2.20	1.45	7.2	4.75
*Eumetopias jubatus***	Steller's Sea Lion	2.86	2.40	9.4	7.9
Hydrurga leptonyx	Leopard Seal	2.90	3.30	9.5	10.8
*Mirounga angustirostris***	Northern Elephant Seal	3.96	2.49	13.0	8.2
*Mirounga leonina***	Southern Elephant Seal	4.67	2.50	15.3	8.2

Species	Common name	Average adult length			
		In meters		In feet	
		Male	Female	Male	Female
*Odobenus rosmarus***	Walrus	3.15	2.60	10.3	8.5
*Otaria flavescens***	South American Sea Lion	2.40	2.00	7.9	6.6
Phoca caspica	Caspian Seal	1.45	1.40	4.75	4.6
Phoca fasciata	Ribbon Seal	1.75	1.68	5.7	5.5
Phoca larga	Harbor Seal	1.70	1.50	5.6	4.9
Phoca vitulina	Habor Seal	1.70	1.50	5.6	4.9
Zalophus californianus	California Sea Lion	2.24	1.75	7.3	5.7
*Halichoerus grypus***	Grar Seal	2.30	1.95	7.5	6.4
Phoca sibirica	Baikal Seal	1.70	1.85	5.6	6.1
Phoca groenlandica	Harp Seal	1.85	1.85	6.1	6.1
*Leptonychotes weddelli***	Weddell Seal	2.90	3.15	9.5	10.3
*Lobodon carcinophagus***	Crabeater Seal	2.21	2.21	7.3	7.3
*Ommatophoca rossi***	Ross Seal	1.99	2.13	6.5	7.0
Group II Pinnipeds:					
Erignathus barbatus	Bearded Seal	2.33	2.33	7.6	7.6
Phoca hispida	Ringed Seal	1.35	1.30	4.4	4.3
Cystophora cristata	Hooded Seal	2.60	2.00	8.5	6.6

NOTE. **Any Group I animals maintained together will be considered as Group II when the animals maintained together include two or more sexually mature males from species marked with a double asterisk (**) regardless of whether the sexually mature males from the same species.

Species	Common name	Average adult length	
		In meters	In feet
Sirenia:			
Dugong dugong	Dugong	3.35	11.0
Trichechus manatus	West Indian Manatee	3.51	11.5
Trichechus inunguis	Amazon Manatee	2.44	8.0
Mustelidae:			
Enhydra lutris	Sea Otter	1.25	4.1

(2) *The minimum depth requirement* for primary enclosure pools for all cetaceans shall be one-half the average adult length of the longest species to be housed therein, regardless of Group I or Group II classification, or 1.83 meters (6.0 feet), whichever is greater, and can be expressed as d = L/2 or 6 feet, whichever is greater. Those parts of the primary enclosure pool which do not meet the minimum depth requirement cannot be included when calculating space requirements for cetaceans.

(3) *Pool volume.* A pool of water housing cetaceans which satisfies the MHD and which meets the minimum depth requirement, will have sufficient volume and surface area to hold up to two Group I cetaceans or up to four Group II cetaceans. If additional cetaceans are to be added to the pool, the volume as well as the surface area may have to be adjusted to allow for additional space necessary for such cetaceans. See Tables I, II, and IV for volumes and surface area requirements. The additional volume needed shall be based on the number and kind of cetaceans housed therein and shall be determined in the following manner.

(i) The minimum volume of water required for up to two Group I cetaceans is based upon the following formula:

$$\text{Volume} = \left(\frac{\text{MHD}}{2}\right)^2 \times 3.14 \times \text{depth}$$

When there are more than two Group I cetaceans housed in a primary enclosure pool, the additional volume of water required for each additional Group I cetacean in excess of two is based on the following formula:

$$\text{Volume} = \left(\frac{\text{Average Adult Length}}{2}\right)^2 \times 3.14 \times \text{depth}$$

See Table I for required volumes.

(ii) The minimum volume of water required for up to four Group II cetaceans is based upon the following formula:

$$\text{Volume} = \left(\frac{\text{MHD}}{2}\right)^2 \times 3.14 \times \text{depth}$$

When there are more than four Group II cetaceans housed in a primary enclosure pool, the additional volume of water required for each additional Group II cetacean in excess of four is based on the following formula:

Volume = $(\text{Average Adult Length})^2 \times 3.14 \times$ depth

See Table II for required volumes.

(iii) When a mixture of both Group I and Group II cetaceans are housed together, the MHD must be satisfied as stated in §3.104(b)(1), and the minimum depth must be satisfied as stated in §3.104(b)(2). Based on these figures, the resulting volume must then be calculated

$$\text{Volume} = \left(\frac{\text{MHD}}{2}\right)^2 \times 3.14 \times \text{depth}$$

Then the volume necessary for the cetaceans to be housed in the pool must be calculated (by obtaining the sum of the volumes required for each animal). If this volume is greater than that obtained by using the MHD and depth figures, then the additional volume required may be added by enlarging the pool in its lateral dimensions or by increasing its depth, or both. The minimum surface area requirements discussed next must also be satisfied.

(4)(i) *The minimum surface area* requirements for each cetacean housed in a pool, regardless of Group I or Group II classification, are calculated as follows:

$$\text{Surface Area} = \left(\frac{\text{average adult body length}}{2}\right)^2 \times 3.14 \times 1.5, \text{ or: } SA = (L/2)^2 \times 3.14 \times 1.5$$

In a pool containing more than two Group I cetaceans or more than four Group II cetaceans,[9] the additional surface area which may be required when animals are added must be calculated for each such animal.

(ii) When a mixture of Group I and Group II cetaceans are to be housed in a pool, the required MHD, depth, and volume must be met. Then the required surface area must be determined for each animal in the pool. The sum of these surface areas must then be compared to the surface area which is obtained by a computation based on the required MHD of the pool.[10] The larger of the two figures represents the surface area which is required for a pool housing a mixture of Group I and Group II cetaceans. Pool surfaces where the depth does not meet the minimum requirements cannot be used in determining the required surface area.

(iii) Surface area requirements are given in Table IV.

[9] A pool containing up to two Group I cetaceans or up to four Group II cetaceans which meets the required MHD and depth will have the necessary surface area and volume required for the animals contained therein.

[10] Since the MHD represents the diameter of a circle, the surface area based on the MHD is calculated by use of the following formula:

$SA = \pi \times (\text{MHD} / 2).^2$

TABLE IV—MINIMUM SURFACE AREA REQUIRED FOR EACH CETACEAN

Average adult length of each cetacean		Surface area required for each cetacean	
Meters	Feet	Sq. meters [1]	Sq. feet
1.68	5.5	3.31	33.62
2.13	7.0	5.36	57.70
2.29	7.5	6.15	66.23
2.59	8.5	7.90	85.07
2.74	9.0	8.86	95.38
3.05	10.0	10.94	117.75
3.51	11.5	14.47	155.72
3.66	12.0	15.75	169.56
4.27	14.0	21.44	230.79
5.49	18.0	35.44	381.51
5.64	18.5	37.43	403.00
5.79	19.0	39.49	425.08
6.71	22.0	52.94	569.91
6.86	22.5	55.38	596.11
7.32	24.0	63.01	678.24
8.53	28.0	85.76	923.16

[1] Square meter = square feet/9 × 0.8361.

(c) *Sirenians.* Primary enclosures housing sirenians shall contain a pool of water and may consist entirely of a pool of water.

(1) The required MHD of a primary enclosure pool for sirenians shall be two times the average adult length of the longest species of sirenian to be housed therein. Calculations shall be based on the average adult length of such sirenians as measured in a horizontal line from the tip of the muzzle to the notch in the tail fluke of dugongs and from the tip of the muzzle to the most distal point in the rounded tail of the manatee.

(2) The minimum depth requirements for primary enclosure pools for all sirenians shall be one-half the average adult length of the longest species to be housed therein, or 1.52 meters (5.0 feet), whichever is greater. Those parts of the primary enclosure pool which do not meet the minimum depth requirements cannot be included when calculating space requirements for sirenians.

(3) A pool which satisfies the required MHD and depth shall be adequate for one or two sirenians. Volume and surface area requirements for additional animals shall be calculated using the same formula as for Group I cetaceans, except that the figure for depth requirement for sirenians shall be one-half the average adult length or 1.52 meters (5.0 feet), whichever is greater.

(d) *Pinnipeds.* (1) Primary enclosures housing pinnipeds shall contain a pool of water and a dry resting or social activity area that must be close enough to the surface of the water to allow easy access for entering or leaving the pool. For the purposes of this subpart, pinnipeds have been divided into Group I pinnipeds and Group II pinnipeds as shown in Table III in this section. In certain instances some Group I pinnipeds shall be considered as Group II pinnipeds. (See Table III).

(2) The minimum size of the dry resting or social activity area of the primary enclosure for pinnipeds (exclusive of the pool of water) shall be based on the average adult length of each pinniped contained therein, as measured in a horizontal or extended position in a straight line from the tip of its nose to the tip of its tail. The minimum size of the dry resting or social activity area shall be computed using the following methods:

(i) *Group I pinnipeds.* Square the average adult length of each pinniped to be contained in the primary enclosure. Add the figures obtained for each of the pinnipeds in the primary enclosure to determine the dry resting or social activity area required for such pinnipeds. If only a single Group I pinniped is maintained in the primary enclosure, the minimum dry resting or social activity area shall be twice the square of the average adult length of that single Group I pinniped. Examples:

(average adult length)^2 of 1st Group I pinniped + (average adult length)^2 of 2nd Group I pinniped = Total DRA for two pinnipeds

DRA for one pinniped = 2 × (average adult length of Group I pinniped)^2

(ii) *Group II pinnipeds.* List all pinnipeds contained in a primary enclosure by average adult length in descending order from the longest species of pinniped to the shortest species of pinniped. Square the average adult length of each pinniped. Multiply the average adult length squared of the longest pinniped by 1.5, the second longest by 1.4, the third longest by 1.3, the fourth longest by 1.2, and the fifth longest by 1.1, as indicated in the following example. Square the average adult length of the sixth pinniped and each additional pinniped. Add the figures obtained for all the pinnipeds in the primary enclosure to determine the required minimum dry resting or social activity area required for such pinnipeds. If only a single Group II pinniped is maintained in the primary enclosure, the minimum dry resting or social activity area must be computed for a minimum of two pinnipeds.

Examples: DRA for 1 Group II Pinniped = [(Average adult length)^2 × 1.5] + [(Average adult length)^2 × 1.4]

1st pinniped (avg. adult length)^2 × 1.5 = social and DRA required
2nd pinniped (avg. adult length)^2 × 1.4 = social and DRA required
3rd pinniped (avg. adult length)^1 × 1.3 = social and DRA required
4th pinniped (avg. adult length)^2 × 1.2 = social and DRA required
5th pinniped (avg. adult length)^2 × 1.1 = social and DRA required
Each pinniped over 5 (avg. adult length)^2 = social and DRA required

---

Total minimum social activity and dry resting area required for all pinnipeds housed in a primary enclosure.

If all the pinnipeds in the primary enclosure are of the same species, the same descending order of calculation shall apply. Example: Hooded seal—average adult length of male = 8.5 feet and female = 6.6 feet. In a primary enclosure containing 2 males and 2 females, the social or DRA required would be the sum of [(8.5)^2 × 1.5] + [(8.5)^2 × 1.4] + [(6.6)^2 × 1.3] + [(6.6)^2 × 1.2].

If two or more sexually mature males are maintained together in a primary enclosure, the dry resting or social activity area shall be divided into two or more separate areas with sufficient visual barriers (such as fences, rocks, or foliage) to provide relief from aggressive animals.

(iii) *Mixture of Group I and Group II pinnipeds.* In a primary enclosure where a mixture of Group I and Group II pinnipeds is to be housed, the dry resting or social activity area shall be calculated as for Group II pinnipeds. The dry resting or social activity area shall be divided into two or more separate areas with sufficient visual barriers (such as fences, rocks, or foliage) to provide relief from aggressive animals.

(3)(i) The minimum surface area of a pool of water for pinnipeds shall be at least equal to the dry resting or social activity area required.

(ii) The MHD of the pool shall be at least one and one-half (1.5) times the average adult length of the largest species of pinniped to be housed in the enclosure; except that such MHD measurement may be reduced by up to 20 percent if the amount of the reduction is added to the MHD at the 90-degree angle.

(iii) The pool of water shall be at least 0.91 meters (3.0 feet) deep or one-half the average adult length of the longest species of pinniped contained therein, whichever is greater. Parts of the pool that do not meet the minimum depth requirement cannot be used in the calculation of the dry resting and social activity area, or as part of the MHD or required surface area of the pool.

(e) *Polar bears.* Primary enclosures housing polar bears shall consist of a pool of water, a dry resting and social activity area, and a den. A minimum of 37.16 square meters (400 square feet) of dry resting and social activity area shall be provided for up to two polar bears, with an additional 3.72 square meters (40 square feet) of dry resting and social activity area for each additional polar bear. The dry resting and social activity area shall be provided with enough shade to accommodate all of the polar bears housed in such primary enclosure at the same time. The pool of water shall have an MHD of not less than 2.44 meters (8.0 feet) and a surface area of at least 8.93 square meters (96.0 square feet) with a minimum depth of 1.52 meters (5.0 feet) with the exception of any entry and exit area. This size pool shall be adequate for two polar bears. For each additional bear, the surface area of the pool must be increased by 3.72 square meters (40 square feet). In measuring this additional surface area, parts of the pool which do not meet minimum depth cannot be considered. The den shall be at least 1.83 meters (6 feet) in width and depth and not less than 1.52 meters (5 feet) in height. It will be so positioned that the viewing public shall not be visible from the interior of the den. A separate den shall be provided for each adult female of breeding age which is permanently housed in the same primary enclosure with an adult male of breeding age. Female polar bears in traveling acts or shows must be provided a den when pregnancy has been determined.

(f) *Sea otters.* (1) Primary enclosures for sea otters shall consist of a pool of water and a dry resting area. The MHD of the pool of water for sea otters shall be at least three times the average adult length of the sea otter contained therein (measured in a horizontal line from the tip of its nose to the tip of its tail) and the pool shall be not less than .91 meters (3.0 feet) deep. When more than two sea otters are housed in the same primary enclosure, additional dry resting area as well as pool volume is required to accommodate the additional sea otters. (See Table V).

(2) The minimum volume of water required for a primary enclosure pool for sea otters shall be based on the sea otter's average adult length. The minimum volume of water required in the pool shall be computed using the following method: Multiply the square of the sea otter's average adult length by 3.14 and then multiply the total by 0.91 meters (3.0 feet). This volume is satisfactory for one or two otters. To calculate the additional volume of water for each additional sea otter above two in a primary enclosure, multiply one-half of the square of the sea otter's average adult length by 3.14, then multiply by 0.91 meters (3.0 feet). (See Table V).

(3) The minimum dry resting area required for one or two sea otters shall be based on the sea otter's average adult length. The minimum dry resting area for one or two sea otters shall be computed using the following method: Square the average adult length of the sea otter and multiply the total by 3.14. When the enclosure is to contain more than two sea otters, the dry resting area for each additional animal shall be computed by multiplying one-half of the sea otter's average adult length by 3.14. Using 1.25 meters or 4.1 feet (the average adult length of a sea otter), the calculations for additional space will result in the following figures:

TABLE V—ADDITIONAL SPACE REQUIRED FOR EACH SEA OTTER WHEN MORE THAN TWO IN A PRIMARY ENCLOSURE

Average adult length of sea otter		Resting area		Pool Volume	
Meters	Feet	Square meters	Square Feet	Cubic meters	Cubic feet
1.25	4.1	1.96	6.44	2.23	79.17

[44 FR 36874, June 22, 1979, as amended at 45 FR 63261, Sept. 24, 1980; 49 FR 26682, 26685, June 28, 1984; 49 FR 27922, July 9, 1984; 63 FR 2, Jan. 2, 1998; 63 FR 47148, Sept. 4, 1998; 66 FR 252, Jan. 3, 2001]

ANIMAL HEALTH AND HUSBANDRY STANDARDS

§ 3.105 Feeding.

(a) The food for marine mammals must be wholesome, palatable, and free from contamination and must be of sufficient quantity and nutritive value to maintain marine mammals in a state of good health. The diet must be prepared with consideration for factors such as age, species, condition, and size of the marine mammal being fed. Marine mammals must be offered food at least once a day, except as directed by the attending veterinarian.

(b) Food receptacles, if used, must be located so as to be accessible to all marine mammals in the same primary enclosure and must be placed so as to minimize contamination of the food they contain. Such food receptacles must be cleaned and sanitized after each use.

(c) Food, when given to each marine mammal individually, must be given by an employee or attendant responsible to management who has the necessary knowledge to assure that each marine mammal receives an adequate quantity of food to maintain it in good health. Such employee or attendant is required to have the ability to recognize deviations from a normal state of good health in each marine mammal so that the food intake can be adjusted accordingly. Inappetence exceeding 24 hours must be reported immediately to the attending veterinarian. Public feeding may be permitted only in the presence and under the supervision of a sufficient number of knowledgeable, uniformed employees or attendants.

Such employees or attendants must assure that the marine mammals are receiving the proper amount and type of food. Only food supplied by the facility where the marine mammals are kept may be fed to the marine mammals by the public. Marine mammal feeding records noting the estimated individual daily consumption must be maintained at the facility for a period of 1 year and must be made available for APHIS inspection. For marine mammals that are individually fed and not subject to public feeding, the feeding records should reflect an accurate account of food intake; for animals fed, in part, by the public, and for large, group-fed colonies of marine mammals where individual rations are not practical or feasible to maintain, the daily food consumption should be estimated as precisely as possible.

(d) Food preparation and handling must be conducted so as to assure the wholesomeness and nutritive value of the food. Frozen fish or other frozen food must be stored in freezers that are maintained at a maximum temperature of −18 °C (0 °F). The length of time food is stored and the method of storage, the thawing of frozen food, and the maintenance of thawed food must be conducted in a manner that will minimize contamination and that will assure that the food retains nutritive value and wholesome quality until the time of feeding. When food is thawed in standing or running water, cold water must be used. All foods must be fed to the marine mammals within 24 hours following the removal of such foods from the freezers for thawing, or if the food has been thawed under refrigeration, it must be fed to the marine mammals within 24 hours of thawing.

[66 FR 252, Jan. 3, 2001]

§ 3.106 Water quality.

(a) *General.* The primary enclosure shall not contain water which would be detrimental to the health of the marine mammal contained therein.

(b) *Bacterial standards.* (1) The coliform bacteria count of the primary enclosure pool shall not exceed 1,000 MPN (most probable number) per 100 ml. of water. Should a coliform bacterial count exceed 1,000 MPN, two subsequent samples may be taken at 48-hour intervals and averaged with the first sample. If such average count does not fall below 1,000 MPN, then the water in the pool shall be deemed unsatisfactory, and the condition must be corrected immediately.

(2) When the water is chemically treated, the chemicals shall be added so as not to cause harm or discomfort to the marine mammals.

(3) Water samples shall be taken and tested at least weekly for coliform count and at least daily for pH and any chemical additives (e.g. chlorine and copper) that are added to the water to maintain water quality standards. Facilities using natural seawater shall be exempt from pH and chemical testing unless chemicals are added to maintain water quality. However, they are required to test for coliforms. Records must be kept documenting the time when all such samples were taken and the results of the sampling. Records of all such test results shall be maintained by management for a 1-year period and must be made available for inspection purposes on request.

(c) *Salinity.* Primary enclosure pools of water shall be salinized for marine cetaceans as well as for those other marine mammals which require salinized water for their good health and well-being. The salinity of the water in such pools shall be maintained within a range of 15–36 parts per thousand.

(d) *Filtration and water flow.* Water quality must be maintained by filtration, chemical treatment, or other means so as to comply with the water quality standards specified in this section.

§ 3.107 Sanitation.

(a) *Primary enclosures.* (1) Animal and food waste in areas other than the pool of water must be removed from the primary enclosures at least daily, and more often when necessary, in order to provide a clean environment and minimize health and disease hazards.

(2) Particulate animal and food waste, trash, or debris that enters the primary enclosure pools of water must be removed at least daily, or as often as necessary, to maintain the required water quality and to minimize health

and disease hazards to the marine mammals.

(3) The wall and bottom surfaces of the primary enclosure pools of water must be cleaned as often as necessary to maintain proper water quality. Natural organisms (such as algae, coelenterates, or molluscs, for example) that do not degrade water quality as defined in § 3.106, prevent proper maintenance, or pose a health or disease hazard to the animals are not considered contaminants.

(b) *Food preparation.* Equipment and utensils used in food preparation must be cleaned and sanitized after each use. Kitchens and other food handling areas where animal food is prepared must be cleaned at least once daily and sanitized at least once every week. Sanitizing must be accomplished by washing with hot water (8 °C, 180 °F, or higher) and soap or detergent in a mechanical dishwasher, or by washing all soiled surfaces with a detergent solution followed by a safe and effective disinfectant, or by cleaning all soiled surfaces with live steam. Substances such as cleansing and sanitizing agents, pesticides, and other potentially toxic agents must be stored in properly labeled containers in secured cabinets designed and located to prevent contamination of food storage preparation surfaces.

(c) *Housekeeping.* Buildings and grounds, as well as exhibit areas, must be kept clean and in good repair. Fences must be maintained in good repair. Primary enclosures housing marine mammals must not have any loose objects or sharp projections and/or edges which may cause injury or trauma to the marine mammals contained therein.

(d) *Pest control.* A safe and effective program for the control of insects, ectoparasites, and avian and mammalian pests must be established and maintained. Insecticides or other such chemical agents must not be applied in primary enclosures housing marine mammals except when deemed essential by an attending veterinarian.

[66 FR 253, Jan. 3, 2001]

§ 3.108 Employees or attendants.

(a) A sufficient number of adequately trained employees or attendants, responsible to management and working in concert with the attending veterinarian, must be utilized to maintain the prescribed level of husbandry practices set forth in this subpart. Such practices must be conducted under the supervision of a marine mammal caretaker who has demonstrable experience in marine mammal husbandry and care.

(b) The facility will provide and document participation in and successful completion of a facility training course for such employees. This training course will include, but is not limited to, species appropriate husbandry techniques, animal handling techniques, and information on proper reporting protocols, such as recordkeeping and notification of veterinary staff for medical concerns.

(c) Any training of marine mammals must be done by or under the direct supervision of experienced trainers.

(d) Trainers and handlers must meet professionally recognized standards for experience and training.

[66 FR 253, Jan. 3, 2001]

§ 3.109 Separation.

Marine mammals, whenever known to be primarily social in the wild, must be housed in their primary enclosure with at least one compatible animal of the same or biologically related species, except when the attending veterinarian, in consultation with the husbandry/training staff, determines that such housing is not in the best interest of the marine mammal's health or well-being. However, marine mammals that are not compatible must not be housed in the same enclosure. Marine mammals must not be housed near other animals that cause them unreasonable stress or discomfort or interfere with their good health. Animals housed separately must have a written plan, approved by the attending veterinarian, developed in consultation with the husbandry/training staff, that includes the justification for the length of time the animal will be kept separated or isolated, information on the type and frequency of enrichment and interaction, if appropriate, and provisions for periodic review of the plan by the attending veterinarian. Marine mammals that are separated for nonmedical purposes must be held in facilities that meet minimum space requirements as outlined in §3.104.

[66 FR 253, Jan. 3, 2001]

§3.110 Veterinary care.

(a) Newly acquired marine mammals must be isolated from resident marine mammals. Animals with a known medical history must be isolated unless or until the newly acquired animals can be reasonably determined to be in good health by the attending veterinarian. Animals without a known medical history must be isolated until it is determined that the newly acquired animals are determined to be in good health by the attending veterinarian. Any communicable disease condition in a newly acquired marine mammal must be remedied before it is placed with resident marine mammals, unless, in the judgment of the attending veterinarian, the potential benefits of a resident animal as a companion to the newly acquired animal outweigh the risks to the resident animal.

(b) Holding facilities must be in place and available to meet the needs for isolation, separation, medical treatment, and medical training of marine mammals. Marine mammals that are isolated or separated for nonmedical purposes must be held in facilities that meet minimum space requirements as outlined in §3.104. Holding facilities used only for medical treatment and medical training need not meet the minimum space requirements as outlined in §3.104. Holding of a marine mammal in a medical treatment or medical training enclosure that does not meet minimum space requirements for periods longer than 2 weeks must be noted in the animal's medical record and the attending veterinarian must provide a justification in the animal's medical record. If holding in such enclosures for medical treatment and/or medical training is to last longer than 2 weeks, such extension must be justified in writing by the attending veterinarian on a weekly basis. In natural lagoon or coastal enclosures where isolation cannot be accomplished, since water circulation cannot be controlled or isolated, separation of newly acquired marine mammals must be accomplished using separate enclosures situated within the facility to prevent direct contact and to minimize the risk of potential airborne and water cross-contamination between newly acquired and resident animals.

(c) Any holding facility used for medical purposes that has contained a marine mammal with an infectious or contagious disease must be cleaned and/or sanitized in a manner prescribed by the attending veterinarian. No healthy animals may be introduced into this holding facility prior to such cleaning and/or sanitizing procedures. Any marine mammal exposed to a contagious animal must be evaluated by the attending veterinarian and monitored and/or isolated for an appropriate period of time as determined by the attending veterinarian.

(d) Individual animal medical records must be kept and made available for APHIS inspection. These medical records must include at least the following information:

(1) Animal identification/name, a physical description, including any identifying markings, scars, etc., age, and sex; and

(2) Physical examination information, including but not limited to length, weight, physical examination results by body system, identification of all medical and physical problems with proposed plan of action, all diagnostic test results, and documentation of treatment.

(e) A copy of the individual animal medical record must accompany any marine mammal upon its transfer to another facility, including contract or satellite facilities.

(f) All marine mammals must be visually examined by the attending veterinarian at least semiannually and must be physically examined under the supervision of and when determined to be necessary by the attending veterinarian. All cetaceans and sirenians must be physically examined by the attending veterinarian at least annually, unless APHIS grants an exception from this requirement based on considerations related to the health and safety of the cetacean or sirenian. These examinations must include, but are not limited to, a hands-on physical examination, hematology and blood chemistry, and other diagnostic tests as determined by the attending veterinarian.

(g)(1) A complete necropsy, including histopathology samples, microbiological cultures, and other testing as appropriate, must be conducted by or under the supervision of the attending veterinarian on all marine mammals that die in captivity. A preliminary necropsy report must be prepared by the veterinarian listing all pathologic lesions observed. The final necropsy report must include all gross and histopathological findings, the results of all laboratory tests performed, and a pathological diagnosis.

(2) Necropsy records will be maintained at the marine mammal's home facility and at the facility at which it died, if different, for a period of 3 years and must be presented to APHIS inspectors when requested.

[66 FR 253, Jan. 3, 2001]

§3.111 Swim-with-the-dolphin programs.

Swim-with-the-dolphin programs shall comply with the requirements in this section, as well as with all other applicable requirements of the regulations pertaining to marine mammals.

(a) *Space requirements.* The primary enclosure for SWTD cetaceans shall contain an interactive area, a buffer area, and a sanctuary area. None of these areas shall be made uninviting to the animals. Movement of cetaceans into the buffer or sanctuary area shall not be restricted in any way. Notwithstanding the space requirements set forth in §3.104, each of the three areas required for SWTD programs shall meet the following space requirements:

(1) The horizontal dimension for each area must be at least three times the average adult body length of the species of cetacean used in the program;

(2) The minimum surface area required for each area is calculated as follows:

(i) *Up to two cetaceans:*

$$\text{Surface Area (SA)} = \left(\frac{3 \times \text{average adult body length (L)}}{2}\right)^2 \times 3.14$$

(ii) *Three cetaceans:*

$$\text{SA} = \left(\frac{3 \times \text{L}}{2}\right)^2 \times 3.14 \times 2$$

(iii) *Additional SA for each animal in excess of three:*

$$\text{SA} = \left(\frac{2 \times \text{L}}{2}\right)^2 \times 3.14$$

(3) The average depth for sea pens, lagoons, and similar natural enclosures at low tide shall be at least 9 feet. The average depth for any manmade enclosure or other structure not subject to tidal action shall be at least 9 feet. A portion of each area may be excluded when calculating the average depth, but the excluded portion may not be used in calculating whether the interactive, buffer, and sanctuary area meet the requirements of paragraphs (a)(1), (a)(2), and (a)(4) of this section.

(4) The minimum volume required for each animal is calculated as follows:

$$\text{Volume} = \text{SA} \times 9$$

(b) *Water clarity.* Sufficient water clarity shall be maintained so that attendants are able to observe cetaceans and humans at all times while within the interactive area. If water clarity does not allow these observations, the interactive sessions shall be canceled until the required clarity is provided.

(c) *Employees and attendants.* Each SWTD program shall have, at the minimum, the following personnel, with the following minimum backgrounds (each position shall be held by a separate individual, with a sufficient number of attendants to comply with §3.111(e)(4)):

(1) Licensee or manager—at least one full-time staff member with at least 6

years experience in a professional or managerial position dealing with captive cetaceans;

(2) Head trainer/behaviorist—at least one full-time staff member with at least 6 years experience in training cetaceans for SWTD behaviors in the past 10 years, or an equivalent amount of experience involving in-water training of cetaceans, who serves as the head trainer for the SWTD program;

(3) Trainer/supervising attendant—at least one full-time staff member with at least 3 years training and/or handling experience involving human/cetacean interaction programs;

(4) Attendant—an adequate number of staff members who are adequately trained in the care, behavior, and training of the program animals. Attendants shall be designated by the trainer, in consultation with the head trainer/behaviorist and licensee/manager, to conduct and monitor interactive sessions in accordance with §3.111(e); and

(5) Attending veterinarian—at least one staff or consultant veterinarian who has at least the equivalent of 2 years full-time experience (4,160 or more hours) with cetacean medicine within the past 10 years, and who is licensed to practice veterinary medicine.

(d) *Program animals.* Only cetaceans that meet the requirements of §3.111(e)(2) and (3) may be used in SWTD programs.

(e) *Handling.* (1) Interaction time (*i.e.*, designated interactive swim sessions) for each cetacean shall not exceed 2 hours per day. Each program cetacean shall have at least one period in each 24 hours of at least 10 continuous hours without public interaction.

(2) All cetaceans used in an interactive session shall be adequately trained and conditioned in human interaction so that they respond in the session to the attendants with appropriate behavior for safe interaction. The head trainer/behaviorist, trainer/supervising attendant, or attendant shall, at all times, control the nature and extent of the cetacean interaction with the public during a session, using the trained responses of the program animal.

(3) All cetaceans used in interactive sessions shall be in good health, including, but not limited to, not being infectious. Cetaceans undergoing veterinary treatment may be used in interactive sessions only with the approval of the attending veterinarian.

(4) The ratio of human participants to cetaceans shall not exceed 3:1. The ratio of human participants to attendants or other authorized SWTD personnel (*i.e.*, head trainer/behaviorist or trainer/supervising attendant) shall not exceed 3:1.

(5) Prior to participating in an SWTD interactive session, members of the public shall be provided with oral and written rules and instructions for the session, to include the telephone and FAX numbers for APHIS, Animal Care, for reporting injuries or complaints. Members of the public shall agree, in writing, to abide by the rules and instructions before being allowed to participate in the session. Any participant who fails to follow the rules or instructions shall be removed from the session by the facility.

(6) All interactive sessions shall have at least two attendants or other authorized SWTD personnel (*i.e.*, head trainer/behaviorist or trainer/supervising attendant). At least one attendant shall be positioned out of the water. One or more attendants or other authorized SWTD personnel may be positioned in the water. If a facility has more than two incidents during interactive sessions within a year's time span that have been dangerous or harmful to either a cetacean or a human, APHIS, in consultation with the head trainer/behaviorist, will determine if changes in attendant positions are needed.

(7) All SWTD programs shall limit interaction between cetaceans and humans so that the interaction does not harm the cetaceans, does not remove the element of choice from the cetaceans by actions such as, but not limited to, recalling the animal from the sanctuary area, and does not elicit unsatisfactory, undesirable, or unsafe behaviors from the cetaceans. All SWTD programs shall prohibit grasping or holding of the cetacean's body, unless under the direct and explicit instruction of an attendant eliciting a specific cetacean behavior, and shall

prevent the chasing or other harassment of the cetaceans.

(8) In cases where cetaceans used in an interactive session exhibit unsatisfactory, undesirable, or unsafe behaviors, including, but not limited to, charging, biting, mouthing, or sexual contact with humans, such cetaceans shall either be removed from the interactive area or the session shall be terminated. Written criteria shall be developed by each SWTD program, and shall be submitted to and approved by APHIS[11] regarding conditions and procedures for maintaining compliance with paragraph (e)(4) of this section; for the termination of a session when removal of a cetacean is not possible; and regarding criteria and protocols for handling program animal(s) exhibiting unsatisfactory, undesirable, or unsafe behaviors, including retraining time and techniques, and removal from the program and/or facility, if appropriate. The head trainer/behaviorist shall determine when operations will be terminated, and when they may resume. In the absence of the head trainer/behaviorist, the determination to terminate a session shall be made by the trainer/supervising attendant. Only the head trainer/behaviorist may determine when a session may be resumed.

(f) *Recordkeeping.* (1) Each facility shall provide APHIS[12] with a description of its program at least 30 days prior to initiation of the program, or in the case of any program in place before September 4, 1998, not later than October 5, 1998. The description shall include at least the following:

(i) Identification of each cetacean in the program, by means of name and/or number, sex, age, and any other means the Administrator determines to be necessary to adequately identify the cetacean;

(ii) A description of the educational content and agenda of planned interactive sessions, and the anticipated average and maximum frequency and duration of encounters per cetacean per day;

(iii) The content and method of pre-encounter orientation, rules, and instructions, including restrictions on types of physical contact with the cetaceans;

(iv) A description of the SWTD facility, including the primary enclosure and other SWTD animal housing or holding enclosures at the facility;

(v) A description of the training, including actual or expected number of hours each cetacean has undergone or will undergo prior to participation in the program;

(vi) The resume of the licensee and/or manager, the head trainer/behaviorist, the trainer/supervising attendant, any other attendants, and the attending veterinarian;

(vii) The current behavior patterns and health of each cetacean, to be assessed and submitted by the attending veterinarian;

(viii) For facilities that employ a part-time attending veterinarian or consultant arrangements, a written program of veterinary care (APHIS form 7002), including protocols and schedules of professional visits; and

(ix) A detailed description of the monitoring program to be used to detect and identify changes in the behavior and health of the cetaceans.

(2) All SWTD programs shall comply in all respects with the regulations and standards set forth in parts 2 and 3 of this subchapter.

(3) Individual animal veterinary records, including all examinations, laboratory reports, treatments, and necropsy reports shall be kept at the SWTD site for at least 3 years and shall be made available to an APHIS official upon request during inspection.

(4) The following records shall be kept at the SWTD site for at least 3 years and shall be made available to an APHIS official upon request during inspection:

(i) Individual cetacean feeding records; and

(ii) Individual cetacean behavioral records.

(5) The following reports shall be kept at the SWTD site for at least 3 years and shall be made available to an APHIS official upon request during inspection:

[11] Send to Administrator, c/o Animal and Plant Health Inspection Service, Animal Care, 4700 River Road Unit 84, Riverdale, Maryland 20737–1234.

[12] See footnote 11 in §3.111(e)(8).

(i) Statistical summaries of the number of minutes per day that each animal participated in an interactive session;

(ii) A statistical summary of the number of human participants per month in the SWTD program; and

(6) A description of any changes made in the SWTD program, which shall be submitted to APHIS[13] on a semi-annual basis.

(7) All incidents resulting in injury to either cetaceans or humans participating in an interactive session, which shall be reported to APHIS within 24 hours of the incident.[14] Within 7 days of any such incident, a written report shall be submitted to the Administrator.[15] The report shall provide a detailed description of the incident and shall establish a plan of action for the prevention of further occurrences.

(g) *Veterinary care.* (1) The attending veterinarian shall conduct on-site evaluations of each cetacean at least once a month. The evaluation shall include a visual inspection of the animal; examination of the behavioral, feeding, and medical records of the animal; and a discussion of each animal with an animal care staff member familiar with the animal.

(2) The attending veterinarian shall observe an interactive swim session at the SWTD site at least once each month.

(3) The attending veterinarian shall conduct a complete physical examination of each cetacean at least once every 6 months. The examination shall include a profile of the cetacean, including the cetacean's identification (name and/or number, sex, and age), weight,[16] length, axillary girth, appetite, and behavior. The attending veterinarian shall also conduct a general examination to evaluate body condition, skin, eyes, mouth, blow hole and cardio-respiratory system, genitalia, and feces (gastrointestinal status). The examination shall also include a complete blood count and serum chemistry analysis. Fecal and blow hole smears shall be obtained for cytology and parasite evaluation.

(4) The attending veterinarian, during the monthly site visit, shall record the nutritional and reproductive status of each cetacean (*i.e.*, whether in an active breeding program, pregnant, or nursing).

(5) The attending veterinarian shall examine water quality records and provide a written assessment, to remain at the SWTD site for at least 3 years, of the overall water quality during the preceding month. Such records shall be made available to an APHIS official upon request during inspection.

(6) In the event that a cetacean dies, complete necropsy results, including all appropriate histopathology, shall be recorded in the cetacean's individual file and shall be made available to APHIS officials during facility inspections, or as requested by APHIS. The necropsy shall be performed within 48 hours of the cetacean's death, by a veterinarian experienced in marine mammal necropsies. If the necropsy is not to be performed within 3 hours of the discovery of the cetacean's death, the cetacean shall be refrigerated until necropsy. Written results of the necropsy shall be available in the cetacean's individual file within 7 days after death for gross pathology and within 45 days after death for histopathology.

(Approved by the Office of Management and Budget under control numbers 0579–0036 and 0579–0115)

[63 FR 47148, Sept. 4, 1998]

EFFECTIVE DATE NOTE: At 64 FR 15920, Apr. 2, 1999, § 3.111 was suspended, effective Apr. 2, 1999.

TRANSPORTATION STANDARDS

§ 3.112 Consignments to carriers and intermediate handlers.

(a) Carriers and intermediate handlers shall not accept any marine

[13] See footnote 11 in § 3.111(e)(8).

[14] Telephone numbers for APHIS, Animal Care, regional offices can be found in local telephone books.

[15] See footnote 11 in § 3.111(e)(8).

[16] Weight may be measured either by scale or calculated using the following formulae:

Females: Natural log of body mass = −8.44 + 1.34(natural log of girth) + 1.28(natural log of standard length).

Males: Natural log of body mass= −10.3 + 1.62(natural log of girth) + 1.38(natural log of standard length).

mammal that is presented by any dealer, research facility, exhibitor, operator of an auction sale, or other person, or any department, agency, or instrumentality of the United States or any State or local government for shipment, in commerce, more than 4 hours prior to the scheduled departure of the primary conveyance on which it is to be transported, and that is not accompanied by a health certificate signed by the attending veterinarian stating that the animal was examined within the prior 10 days and found to be in acceptable health for transport: *Provided, however,* That the carrier or intermediate handler and any dealer, research facility, exhibitor, operator of an auction sale, or other person, or any department, agency, or instrumentality of the United States or any State or local government may mutually agree to extend the time of acceptance to not more than 6 hours if specific prior scheduling of the animal shipment to destination has been made.

(b) Any carrier or intermediate handler shall only accept for transportation or transport, in commerce, any marine mammal in a primary transport enclosure that conforms to the requirements in §3.113 of this subpart: *Provided, however,* That any carrier or intermediate handler may accept for transportation or transport, in commerce, any marine mammal consigned by any department, agency, or instrumentality of the United States having laboratory animal facilities or exhibiting animals or any licensed or registered dealer, research facility, exhibitor, or operator of an auction sale if the consignor furnishes to the carrier or intermediate handler a certificate, signed by the consignor, stating that the primary transport enclosure complies with §3.113 of this subpart, unless such primary transport enclosure is obviously defective or damaged and it is apparent that it cannot reasonably be expected to contain the marine mammal without causing suffering or injury to the marine mammal. A copy of any such certificate must accompany the shipment to destination. The certificate must include at least the following information:

(1) Name and address of the consignor;

(2) The number, age, and sex of animals in the primary transport enclosure(s);

(3) A certifying statement (e.g., "I hereby certify that the—(number) primary transport enclosure(s) that are used to transport the animal(s) in this shipment complies (comply) with USDA standards for primary transport enclosures (9 CFR part 3)."); and

(4) The signature of the consignor, and date.

(c) Carriers or intermediate handlers whose facilities fail to maintain a temperature within the range of 7.2 °C (45 °F) to 23.9 °C (75 °F) allowed by §3.117 of this subpart may accept for transportation or transport, in commerce, any marine mammal consigned by any department, agency, or instrumentality of the United States or of any State or local government, or by any person (including any licensee or registrant under the Act, as well as any private individual) if the consignor furnishes to the carrier or intermediate handler a certificate executed by the attending veterinarian on a specified date that is not more than 10 days prior to delivery of the animal for transportation in commerce, stating that the marine mammal is acclimated to a specific air temperature range lower or higher than those prescribed in §§3.117 and 3.118. A copy of the certificate must accompany the shipment to destination. The certificate must include at least the following information:

(1) Name and address of the consignor;

(2) The number, age, and sex of animals in the shipment;

(3) A certifying statement (e.g., "I hereby certify that the animal(s) in this shipment is (are), to the best of my knowledge, acclimated to an air temperature range of ________"); and

(4) The signature of the attending veterinarian and the date.

(d) Carriers and intermediate handlers must attempt to notify the consignee (receiving party) at least once in every 6-hour period following the arrival of any marine mammals at the animal holding area of the terminal cargo facility. The time, date, and method of each attempted notification and the final notification to the consignee and the name of the person notifying the consignee must be recorded on the copy of the shipping document retained by the carrier or intermediate handler and on a copy of the shipping document accompanying the animal shipment.

[66 FR 254, Jan. 3, 2001]

§3.113 Primary enclosures used to transport marine mammals.

No dealer, research facility, exhibitor, or operator of an auction sale shall offer for transportation or transport, in commerce, any marine mammal in a primary enclosure that does not conform to the following requirements:

(a) Primary enclosures that are used to transport marine mammals other than cetaceans and sirenians must:

(1) Be constructed from materials of sufficient structural strength to contain the marine mammals;

(2) Be constructed from material that is durable, nontoxic, and cannot be chewed and/or swallowed;

(3) Be able to withstand the normal rigors of transportation;

(4) Have interiors that are free from any protrusions or hazardous openings that could be injurious to the marine mammals contained within;

(5) Be constructed so that no parts of the contained marine mammals are exposed to the outside of the enclosures in any way that may cause injury to the animals or to persons who are nearby or who handle the enclosures;

(6) Have openings that provide access into the enclosures and are secured with locking devices of a type that cannot be accidentally opened;

(7) Have such openings located in a manner that makes them easily accessible at all times for emergency removal and potential treatment of any live marine mammal contained within;

(8) Have air inlets at heights that will provide cross ventilation at all levels (particularly when the marine mammals are in a prone position), are located on all four sides of the enclosures, and cover not less than 20 percent of the total surface area of each side of the enclosures;

(9) Have projecting rims or other devices placed on any ends and sides of the enclosures that have ventilation openings so that there is a minimum air circulation space of 7.6 centimeters (3.0 inches) between the enclosures and any adjacent cargo or conveyance wall;

(10) Be constructed so as to provide sufficient air circulation space to maintain the temperature limits set forth in this subpart; and

(11) Be equipped with adequate handholds or other devices on the exterior of the enclosures to enable them to be lifted without unnecessary tilting and to ensure that the persons handling the enclosures will not come in contact with any marine mammal contained inside.

(b) Straps, slings, harnesses, or other devices used for body support or restraint, when transporting marine mammals such as cetaceans and sirenians must:

(1) Be designed so as not to prevent access to the marine mammals by attendants for the purpose of administering in-transit care;

(2) Be equipped with special padding to prevent trauma or injury at critical weight pressure points on the body of the marine mammals; and

(3) Be capable of keeping the animals from thrashing about and causing injury to themselves or their attendants, and yet be adequately designed so as not to cause injury to the animals.

(c) Primary enclosures used to transport marine mammals must be large enough to assure that:

(1) In the case of pinnipeds, polar bears, and sea otters, each animal has sufficient space to turn about freely in a stance whereby all four feet or flippers are on the floor and the animal can sit in an upright position and lie in a natural position;

(2) In the case of cetaceans and sirenians, each animal has sufficient space for support of its body in slings, harnesses, or other supporting devices, if used (as prescribed in paragraph (b) of this section), without causing injury to such cetaceans or sirenians due to contact with the primary transport enclosure: *Provided, however,* That animals may be restricted in their movements according to professionally accepted standards when such freedom of movement would constitute a danger to the animals, their handlers, or other persons.

(d) Marine mammals transported in the same primary enclosure must be of the same species and maintained in compatible groups. Marine mammals that have not reached puberty may not be transported in the same primary enclosure with adult marine mammals other than their dams. Socially dependent animals (e.g., sibling, dam, and other members of a family group) must be allowed visual and olfactory contact whenever reasonable. Female marine mammals may not be transported in the same primary enclosure with any mature male marine mammals.

(e) Primary enclosures used to transport marine mammals as provided in this section must have solid bottoms to prevent leakage in shipment and must be cleaned and sanitized in a manner prescribed in §3.107 of this subpart, if previously used. Within the primary enclosures used to transport marine mammals, the animals will be maintained on sturdy, rigid, solid floors with adequate drainage.

(f) Primary enclosures used to transport marine mammals, except where such primary enclosures are permanently affixed in the animal cargo space of the primary conveyance, must be clearly marked on top (when present) and on at least one side, or on all sides whenever possible, with the words "Live Animal" or "Wild Animal" in letters not less than 2.5 centimeters (1 inch) in height, and with arrows or other markings to indicate the correct upright position of the container.

(g) Documents accompanying the shipment must be attached in an easily accessible manner to the outside of a primary enclosure that is part of such shipment or be in the possession of the shipping attendant.

(h) When a primary transport enclosure is permanently affixed within the animal cargo space of the primary conveyance so that the front opening is the only source of ventilation for such primary enclosure, the front opening must open directly to the outside or to an unobstructed aisle or passageway within the primary conveyance. Such front ventilation opening must be at least 90 percent of the total surface area of the front wall of the primary enclosure and covered with bars, wire mesh, or smooth expanded metal.

[66 FR 255, Jan. 3, 2001]

§3.114 Primary conveyances (motor vehicle, rail, air and marine).

(a) The animal cargo space of primary conveyances used in transporting live marine mammals must be constructed in a manner that will protect the health and assure the safety and comfort of the marine mammals contained within at all times. All primary conveyances used must be sufficiently temperature-controlled to provide an appropriate environmental temperature for the species involved and to provide for the safety and comfort of the marine mammal, or other appropriate safeguards (such as, but not limited to, cooling the animal with cold water, adding ice to water-filled enclosures, and use of fans) must be employed to maintain the animal at an appropriate temperature.

(b) The animal cargo space must be constructed and maintained in a manner that will prevent the ingress of engine exhaust fumes and gases in excess of that ordinarily contained in the passenger compartments.

(c) Marine mammals must only be placed in animal cargo spaces that have a supply of air sufficient for each live animal contained within. Primary transport enclosures must be positioned in the animal cargo spaces of primary conveyances in such a manner that each marine mammal contained within will have access to sufficient air.

(d) Primary transport enclosures must be positioned in primary conveyances in such a manner that, in an emergency, the live marine mammals can be removed from the conveyances as soon as possible.

(e) The interiors of animal cargo spaces in primary conveyances must be kept clean.

(f) Live marine mammals must not knowingly be transported with any material, substance, or device that may be injurious to the health and well-being of the marine mammals unless proper precaution is taken to prevent such injury.

(g) Adequate lighting must be available for marine mammal attendants to properly inspect the animals at any time. If such lighting is not provided by the carrier, provisions must be made by the shipper to supply such lighting.

[66 FR 255, Jan. 3, 2001]

§3.115 Food and drinking water requirements.

(a) Those marine mammals that require drinking water must be offered potable water within 4 hours of being placed in the primary transport enclosure for transport in commerce. Marine mammals must be provided water as often as necessary and appropriate for the species involved to prevent dehydration, which would jeopardize the good health and well-being of the animals.

(b) Marine mammals being transported in commerce must be offered food as often as necessary and appropriate for the species involved or as determined by the attending veterinarian.

[66 FR 256, Jan. 3, 2001]

§3.116 Care in transit.

(a) A licensed veterinarian, employee, and/or attendant of the shipper or receiver of any marine mammal being transported, in commerce, knowledgeable and experienced in the area of marine mammal care and transport, must accompany all marine mammals during periods of transportation to provide for their good health and well-being, to observe such marine mammals to determine whether they need veterinary care, and to obtain any needed veterinary care as soon as possible. Any transport of greater than 2 hours duration requires a transport plan approved by the attending veterinarian that will include the specification of the necessity of the presence of a veterinarian during the transport. If the attending veterinarian does not accompany the animal, communication with the veterinarian must be maintained in accordance with §§2.33(b)(3) and 2.40(b)(3) of this chapter.

(b) The following marine mammals may be transported in commerce only when the transport of such marine mammals has been determined to be appropriate by the attending veterinarian:

(1) A pregnant animal in the last half of pregnancy;

(2) A dependent unweaned young animal;

(3) A nursing mother with young; or

(4) An animal with a medical condition requiring veterinary care, that would be compromised by transport. The attending veterinarian must note on the accompanying health certificate the existence of any of the above conditions. The attending veterinarian must also determine whether a veterinarian should accompany such marine mammals during transport.

(c) Carriers must inform the crew as to the presence of the marine mammals on board the craft, inform the individual accompanying the marine mammals of any unexpected delays as soon as they become known, and accommodate, except as precluded by safety considerations, requests by the shipper or his agent to provide access to the animals or take other necessary actions for the welfare of the animals if a delay occurs.

(d) A sufficient number of employees or attendants of the shipper or receiver of cetaceans or sirenians being transported, in commerce, must provide for such cetaceans and sirenians during periods of transport by:

(1) Keeping the skin moist or preventing the drying of the skin by such methods as intermittent spraying of water or application of a nontoxic emollient;

(2) Assuring that the pectoral flippers are allowed freedom of movement at all times;

(3) Making adjustments in the position of the marine mammals when necessary to prevent necrosis of the skin at weight pressure points;

(4) Keeping the animal cooled and/or warmed sufficiently to prevent overheating, hypothermia, or temperature related stress; and

(5) Calming the marine mammals to avoid struggling, thrashing, and other unnecessary activity that may cause overheating or physical trauma.

(e) A sufficient number of employees or attendants of the shipper or receiver of pinnipeds or polar bears being transported, in commerce, must provide for such pinnipeds and polar bears during periods of transport by:

(1) Keeping the animal cooled and/or warmed sufficiently to prevent overheating, hypothermia, or temperature related stress; and

(2) Calming the marine mammals to avoid struggling, thrashing, and other unnecessary activity that may cause overheating or physical trauma.

(f) Sea otters must be transported in primary enclosures that contain false floors through which water and waste freely pass to keep the interior of the transport unit free from waste materials. Moisture must be provided by water sprayers or ice during transport.

(g) Marine mammals may be removed from their primary transport enclosures only by the attendants or other persons capable of handling such mammals safely.

[66 FR 256, Jan. 3, 2001]

§ 3.117 Terminal facilities.

Carriers and intermediate handlers must not commingle marine mammal shipments with inanimate cargo. All animal holding areas of a terminal facility of any carrier or intermediate handler where marine mammal shipments are maintained must be cleaned and sanitized in a manner prescribed in § 3.107 of this subpart to minimize health and disease hazards. An effective program for the control of insects, ectoparasites, and avian and mammalian pests must be established and maintained for all animal holding areas. Any animal holding area containing marine mammals must be ventilated with fresh air or air circulated by means of fans, blowers, or an air conditioning system so as to minimize drafts, odors, and moisture condensation. Auxiliary ventilation, such as exhaust fans and vents or fans or blowers or air conditioning must be used for any animal holding area containing marine mammals when the air temperature within such animal holding area is 23.9 °C (75 °F) or higher. The air temperature around any marine mammal in any animal holding area must not be allowed to fall below 7.2 °C (45 °F). The air temperature around any polar bear must not be allowed to exceed 29.5 °C (85 °F) at any time and no polar bear may be subjected to surrounding air temperatures that exceed 23.9 °C (75 °F) for more than 4 hours at any time. The ambient temperature must be measured in the animal holding area upon arrival of the shipment by the attendant, carrier, or intermediate handler. The ambient temperature must be measured halfway up the outside of the primary transport enclosure at a distance from the external wall of the primary transport enclosure not to exceed 0.91 meters (3 feet).

[66 FR 256, Jan. 3, 2001]

§ 3.118 Handling.

(a) Carriers and intermediate handlers moving marine mammals from the animal holding area of the terminal facility to the primary conveyance or from the primary conveyance to the animal holding area of the terminal facility must provide the following:

(1) *Movement of animals as expeditiously as possible.*

(2) *Shelter from overheating and direct sunlight.* When sunlight is likely to cause overheating, sunburn, or discomfort, sufficient shade must be provided to protect the marine mammals. Marine mammals must not be subjected to surrounding air temperatures that exceed 23.9 °C (75 °F) unless accompanied by an acclimation certificate in accordance with § 3.112 of this subpart. The temperature must be measured and read within or immediately adjacent to the primary transport enclosure.

(3) *Shelter from cold weather.* Marine mammals must be provided with species appropriate protection against cold weather, and such marine mammals must not be subjected to surrounding air temperatures that fall below 7.2 °C (45 °F) unless accompanied by an acclimation certificate in accordance with § 3.112 of this subpart. The temperature must be measured and read within or immediately adjacent to the primary transport enclosure.

(b) Care must be exercised to avoid handling of the primary transport enclosure in a manner that may cause physical harm or distress to the marine mammal contained within.

(c) Enclosures used to transport any marine mammal must not be tossed, dropped, or needlessly tilted and must not be stacked unless properly secured.

[66 FR 257, Jan. 3, 2001]

Subpart F—Specifications for the Humane Handling, Care, Treatment, and Transportation of Warmblooded Animals Other Than Dogs, Cats, Rabbits, Hamsters, Guinea Pigs, Nonhuman Primates, and Marine Mammals

SOURCE: 36 FR 24925, Dec. 24, 1971, unless otherwise noted. Redesignated at 44 FR 36874, July 22, 1979.

FACILITIES AND OPERATING STANDARDS

§ 3.125 Facilities, general.

(a) *Structural strength.* The facility must be constructed of such material and of such strength as appropriate for the animals involved. The indoor and outdoor housing facilities shall be structurally sound and shall be maintained in good repair to protect the animals from injury and to contain the animals.

(b) *Water and power.* Reliable and adequate electric power, if required to comply with other provisions of this subpart, and adequate potable water shall be available on the premises.

(c) *Storage.* Supplies of food and bedding shall be stored in facilities which adequately protect such supplies against deterioration, molding, or contamination by vermin. Refrigeration shall be provided for supplies of perishable food.

(d) *Waste disposal.* Provision shall be made for the removal and disposal of animal and food wastes, bedding, dead animals, trash and debris. Disposal facilities shall be so provided and operated as to minimize vermin infestation, odors, and disease hazards. The disposal facilities and any disposal of animal and food wastes, bedding, dead animals, trash, and debris shall comply with applicable Federal, State, and local laws and regulations relating to pollution control or the protection of the environment.

(e) *Washroom and sinks.* Facilities, such as washrooms, basins, showers, or sinks, shall be provided to maintain cleanliness among animal caretakers.

[36 FR 24925, Dec. 24, 1971. Redesignated at 44 FR 36874, June 22, 1979, and amended at 44 FR 63492, Nov. 2, 1979]

§ 3.126 Facilities, indoor.

(a) *Ambient temperatures.* Temperature in indoor housing facilities shall be sufficiently regulated by heating or cooling to protect the animals from the extremes of temperature, to provide for their health and to prevent their discomfort. The ambient temperature shall not be allowed to fall below nor rise above temperatures compatible with the health and comfort of the animal.

(b) *Ventilation.* Indoor housing facilities shall be adequately ventilated by natural or mechanical means to provide for the health and to prevent discomfort of the animals at all times. Such facilities shall be provided with fresh air either by means of windows, doors, vents, fans, or air-conditioning and shall be ventilated so as to minimize drafts, odors, and moisture condensation.

(c) *Lighting.* Indoor housing facilities shall have ample lighting, by natural or artificial means, or both, of good quality, distribution, and duration as appropriate for the species involved. Such lighting shall be uniformly distributed and of sufficient intensity to permit routine inspection and cleaning. Lighting of primary enclosures shall be designed to protect the animals from excessive illumination.

(d) *Drainage.* A suitable sanitary method shall be provided to eliminate rapidly, excess water from indoor housing facilities. If drains are used, they shall be properly constructed and kept in good repair to avoid foul odors and installed so as to prevent any backup of sewage. The method of drainage shall comply with applicable Federal, State, and local laws and regulations relating to pollution control or the protection of the environment.

§ 3.127 Facilities, outdoor.

(a) *Shelter from sunlight.* When sunlight is likely to cause overheating or discomfort of the animals, sufficient shade by natural or artificial means shall be provided to allow all animals kept outdoors to protect themselves from direct sunlight.

(b) *Shelter from inclement weather.* Natural or artificial shelter appropriate to the local climatic conditions for the species concerned shall be provided for all animals kept outdoors to afford them protection and to prevent discomfort to such animals. Individual animals shall be acclimated before they are exposed to the extremes of the individual climate.

(c) *Drainage.* A suitable method shall be provided to rapidly eliminate excess water. The method of drainage shall comply with applicable Federal, State, and local laws and regulations relating to pollution control or the protection of the environment.

(d) *Perimeter fence.* On or after May 17, 2000, all outdoor housing facilities (*i.e.*, facilities not entirely indoors) must be enclosed by a perimeter fence that is of sufficient height to keep animals and unauthorized persons out. Fences less than 8 feet high for potentially dangerous animals, such as, but not limited to, large felines (e.g., lions, tigers, leopards, cougars, etc.), bears, wolves, rhinoceros, and elephants, or less than 6 feet high for other animals must be approved in writing by the Administrator. The fence must be constructed so that it protects the animals in the facility by restricting animals and unauthorized persons from going through it or under it and having contact with the animals in the facility, and so that it can function as a secondary containment system for the animals in the facility. It must be of sufficient distance from the outside of the primary enclosure to prevent physical contact between animals inside the enclosure and animals or persons outside the perimeter fence. Such fences less than 3 feet in distance from the primary enclosure must be approved in writing by the Administrator. A perimeter fence is not required:

(1) Where the outside walls of the primary enclosure are made of sturdy, durable material, which may include certain types of concrete, wood, plastic, metal, or glass, and are high enough and constructed in a manner that restricts entry by animals and unauthorized persons and the Administrator gives written approval; or

(2) Where the outdoor housing facility is protected by an effective natural barrier that restricts the animals to the facility and restricts entry by animals and unauthorized persons and the Administrator gives written approval; or

(3) Where appropriate alternative security measures are employed and the Administrator gives written approval; or

(4) For traveling facilities where appropriate alternative security measures are employed; or

(5) Where the outdoor housing facility houses only farm animals, such as, but not limited to, cows, sheep, goats, pigs, horses (for regulated purposes), or donkeys, and the facility has in place effective and customary containment and security measures.

[36 FR 24925, Dec. 24, 1971. Redesignated at 44 FR 36874, July 22, 1979, as amended at 64 FR 56147, Oct. 18, 1999; 65 FR 70770, Nov. 28, 2000]

§ 3.128 Space requirements.

Enclosures shall be constructed and maintained so as to provide sufficient space to allow each animal to make normal postural and social adjustments with adequate freedom of movement. Inadequate space may be indicated by evidence of malnutrition, poor condition, debility, stress, or abnormal behavior patterns.

Animal Health and Husbandry Standards

§ 3.129 Feeding.

(a) The food shall be wholesome, palatable, and free from contamination and of sufficient quantity and nutritive value to maintain all animals in good health. The diet shall be prepared with consideration for the age, species, condition, size, and type of the animal. Animals shall be fed at least once a day except as dictated by hibernation, veterinary treatment, normal fasts, or other professionally accepted practices.

(b) Food, and food receptacles, if used, shall be sufficient in quantity and located so as to be accessible to all animals in the enclosure and shall be placed so as to minimize contamination. Food receptacles shall be kept clean and sanitary at all times. If self-feeders are used, adequate measures shall be taken to prevent molding, contamination, and deterioration or caking of food.

§3.130 Watering.

If potable water is not accessible to the animals at all times, it must be provided as often as necessary for the health and comfort of the animal. Frequency of watering shall consider age, species, condition, size, and type of the animal. All water receptacles shall be kept clean and sanitary.

§3.131 Sanitation.

(a) *Cleaning of enclosures.* Excreta shall be removed from primary enclosures as often as necessary to prevent contamination of the animals contained therein and to minimize disease hazards and to reduce odors. When enclosures are cleaned by hosing or flushing, adequate measures shall be taken to protect the animals confined in such enclosures from being directly sprayed with the stream of water or wetted involuntarily.

(b) *Sanitation of enclosures.* Subsequent to the presence of an animal with an infectious or transmissible disease, cages, rooms, and hard-surfaced pens or runs shall be sanitized either by washing them with hot water (180 F. at source) and soap or detergent, as in a mechanical washer, or by washing all soiled surfaces with a detergent solution followed by a safe and effective disinfectant, or by cleaning all soiled surfaces with saturated live steam under pressure. Pens or runs using gravel, sand, or dirt, shall be sanitized when necessary as directed by the attending veterinarian.

(c) *Housekeeping.* Premises (buildings and grounds) shall be kept clean and in good repair in order to protect the animals from injury and to facilitate the prescribed husbandry practices set forth in this subpart. Accumulations of trash shall be placed in designated areas and cleared as necessary to protect the health of the animals.

(d) *Pest control.* A safe and effective program for the control of insects, ectoparasites, and avian and mammalian pests shall be established and maintained.

§3.132 Employees.

A sufficient number of adequately trained employees shall be utilized to maintain the professionally acceptable level of husbandry practices set forth in this subpart. Such practices shall be under a supervisor who has a background in animal care.

§3.133 Separation.

Animals housed in the same primary enclosure must be compatible. Animals shall not be housed near animals that interfere with their health or cause them discomfort.

§§3.134–3.135 [Reserved]

TRANSPORTATION STANDARDS

SOURCE: Sections 3.136 through 3.142 appear at 42 FR 31569, June 21, 1977, unless otherwise noted. Redesignated at 44 FR 36874, July 22, 1979.

§3.136 Consignments to carriers and intermediate handlers.

(a) Carriers and intermediate handlers shall not accept any live animals presented by any dealer, research facility, exhibitor, operator of an auction sale, or other person, or any department, agency, or instrumentality of the United States or any State or local government for shipment, in commerce, more than 4 hours prior to the scheduled departure of the primary conveyance on which it is to be transported: *Provided, however,* That the carrier or intermediate handler and any dealer, research facility, exhibitor, operator of an auction sale, or other person, or any department, agency, or instrumentality of the United States or any State or local government may mutually agree to extend the time of acceptance to not more than 6 hours if specific prior scheduling of the animal shipment to destination has been made.

(b) Any carrier or intermediate handler shall only accept for transportation or transport, in commerce, any live animal in a primary enclosure which conforms to the requirements set forth in § 3.137 of the standards: *Provided, however,* That any carrier or intermediate handler may accept for transportation or transport, in commerce, any live animal consigned by any department, agency, or instrumentality of the United States having laboratory animal facilities or exhibiting animals or any licensed or registered dealer, research facility, exhibitor, or operator of an auction sale if the consignor furnishes to the carrier or intermediate handler a certificate, signed by the consignor, stating that the primary enclosure complies with § 3.137 of the standards, unless such primary enclosure is obviously defective or damaged and it is apparent that it cannot reasonably be expected to contain the live animal without causing suffering or injury to such live animal. A copy of such certificate shall accompany the shipment to destination. The certificate shall include at least the following information:

(1) Name and address of the consignor;

(2) The number of animals in the primary enclosure(s);

(3) A certifying statement (e.g., "I hereby certify that the ___ (number) primary enclosure(s) which are used to transport the animal(s) in this shipment complies (comply) with USDA standards for primary enclosures (9 CFR part 3)."); and

(4) The signature of the consignor, and date.

(c) Carriers or intermediate handlers whose facilities fail to meet the minimum temperature allowed by the standards may accept for transportation or transport, in commerce, any live animal consigned by any department, agency, or instrumentality of the United States or of any State or local government, or by any person (including any licensee or registrant under the Act, as well as any private individual) if the consignor furnishes to the carrier or intermediate handler a certificate executed by a veterinarian accredited by this Department pursuant to part 160 of this title on a specified date which shall not be more than 10 days prior to delivery of such animal for transportation in commerce, stating that such live animal is acclimated to air temperatures lower than those prescribed in §§ 3.141 and 3.142. A copy of such certificate shall accompany the shipment to destination. The certificate shall include at least the following information:

(1) Name and address of the consignor;

(2) The number of animals in the shipment;

(3) A certifying statement (e.g., "I hereby certify that the animal(s) in this shipment is (are), to the best of my knowledge, acclimated to air temperatures lower than 7.2 °C. (45 °F.)"); and

(4) The signature of the USDA accredited veterinarian, assigned accrediation number, and date.

(d) Carriers and intermediate handlers shall attempt to notify the consignee at least once in every 6 hour period following the arrival of any live animals at the animal holding area of the terminal cargo facility. The time, date, and method of each attempted notification and the final notification to the consignee and the name of the person notifying the consignee shall be recorded on the copy of the shipping document retained by the carrier or intermediate handler and on a copy of the shipping document accompanying the animal shipment.

[42 FR 31569, June 21, 1977, as amended at 43 FR 21166, May 16, 1978. Redesignated at 44 FR 36874, July 22, 1979, and amended at 44 FR 63493, Nov. 2, 1979]

§ 3.137 Primary enclosures used to transport live animals.

No dealer, research facility, exhibitor, or operator of an auction sale shall offer for transportation or transport, in commerce, any live animal in a primary enclosure which does not conform to the following requirements:

(a) Primary enclosures, such as compartments, transport cages, cartons, or crates, used to transport live animals shall be constructed in such a manner that (1) the structural strength of the enclosure shall be sufficient to contain the live animals and to withstand the normal rigors of transportation; (2) the interior of the enclosure shall be free from any protrusions that could be injurious to the live animals contained therein; (3) the opernings of such enclosures are easily accessible at all times for emergency removal of the live animals; (4) except as provided in paragraph (g) of this section, there are ventilation openings located on two opposite walls of the primary enclosure and the ventilation openings on each such wall shall be at least 16 percent of the total surface area of each such wall, or there are ventilation openings located on all four walls of the primary enclosure and the ventilation openings on each such wall shall be at least 8 percent of the total surface area of each such wall: *Provided, however,* That at least one-third of the total minimum area required for ventilation of the primary enclosure shall be located on the lower one-half of the primary enclosure and at least one-third of the total minimum area required for ventilation of the primary enclosure shall be located on the upper one-half of the primary enclosure; (5) except as provided in paragraph (g) of this section, projecting rims or other devices shall be on the exterior of the outside walls with any ventilation openings to prevent obstruction of the ventilation openings and to provide a minimum air circulation space of 1.9 centimeters (.75 inch) between the primary enclosure and any adjacent cargo or conveyance wall; and (6) except as provided in paragraph (g) of this section, adequate handholds or other devices for lifting shall be provided on the exterior of the primary enclosure to enable the primary enclosure to be lifted without tilting and to ensure that the person handling the primary enclosure will not be in contact with the animal.

(b) Live animals transported in the same primary enclosure shall be of the same species and maintained in compatible groups. Live animals that have not reached puberty shall not be transported in the same primary enclosure with adult animals other than their dams. Socially dependent animals (e.g., sibling, dam, and other members of a family group) must be allowed visual and olfactory contact. Any female animal in season (estrus) shall not be transported in the same primary enclosure with any male animal.

(c) Primary enclosures used to transport live animals shall be large enough to ensure that each animal contained therein has sufficient space to turn about freely and to make normal postural adjustments: *Provided, however,* That certain species may be restricted in their movements according to professionally acceptable standards when such freedom of movement would constitute a danger to the animals, their handlers, or other persons.

(d) Primary enclosures used to transport live animals as provided in this section shall have solid bottoms to prevent leakage in shipment and still be cleaned and sanitized in a manner prescribed in §3.131 of the standards, if previously used. Such primary enclosures shall contain clean litter of a suitable absorbant material, which is safe and nontoxic to the live animals contained therein, in sufficient quantity to absorb and cover excreta, unless the animals are on wire or other nonsolid floors.

(e) Primary enclosures used to transport live animals, except where such primary enclosures are permanently affixed in the animal cargo space of the primary conveyance, shall be clearly marked on top and on one or more sides with the words "Live Animal" or "Wild Animal", whichever is appropriate, in letters not less than 2.5 centimeters (1 inch) in height, and with arrows or other markings to indicate the correct upright position of the container.

(f) Documents accompanying the shipment shall be attached in an easily accessible manner to the outside of a primary enclosure which is part of such shipment.

(g) When a primary enclosure is permanently affixed within the animal cargo space of the primary conveyance so that the front opening is the only source of ventilation for such primary enclosure, the front opening shall open directly to the outside or to an unobstructed aisle or passageway within the primary conveyance. Such front ventilation opening shall be at least 90 percent of the total surface area of the front wall of the primary enclosure and covered with bars, wire mesh or smooth expanded metal.

[42 FR 31569, June 21, 1977, as amended at 43 FR 21166, May 16, 1978. Redesignated at 44 FR 36874, July 22, 1979]

§ 3.138 Primary conveyances (motor vehicle, rail, air, and marine).

(a) The animal cargo space of primary conveyances used in transporting live animals shall be designed and constructed to protect the health, and ensure the safety and comfort of the live animals contained therein at all times.

(b) The animal cargo space shall be constructed and maintained in a manner to prevent the ingress of engine exhaust fumes and gases from the primary conveyance during transportation in commerce.

(c) No live animal shall be placed in an animal cargo space that does not have a supply of air sufficient for normal breathing for each live animal contained therein, and the primary enclosures shall be positioned in the animal cargo space in such a manner that each live animal has access to sufficient air for normal breathing.

(d) Primary enclosures shall be positioned in the primary conveyance in such a manner that in an emergency the live animals can be removed from the primary conveyance as soon as possible.

(e) The interior of the animal cargo space shall be kept clean.

(f) Live animals shall not be transported with any material, substance (e.g., dry ice) or device which may reasonably be expected to be injurious to the health and well-being of the animals unless proper precaution is taken to prevent such injury.

§ 3.139 Food and water requirements.

(a) All live animals shall be offered potable water within 4 hours prior to being transported in commerce. Dealers, exhibitors, research facilities and operators of auction sales shall provide potable water to all live animals transported in their own primary conveyance at least every 12 hours after such transportation is initiated, and carriers and intermediate handlers shall provide potable water to all live animals at least every 12 hours after acceptance for transportation in commerce: *Provided, however,* That except as directed by hibernation, veterinary treatment or other professionally accepted practices, those live animals which, by common accepted practices, require watering more frequently shall be so watered.

(b) Each live animal shall be fed at least once in each 24 hour period, except as directed by hibernation, veterinary treatment, normal fasts, or other professionally accepted practices. Those live animals which, by common accepted practice, require feeding more frequently shall be so fed.

(c) A sufficient quantity of food and water shall accompany the live animal to provide food and water for such animals for a period of at least 24 hours, except as directed by hibernation, veterinary treatment, normal fasts, and other professionally accepted practices.

(d) Any dealer, research facility, exhibitor or operator of an auction sale offering any live animal to any carrier or intermediate handler for transportation in commerce shall affix to the outside of the primary enclosure used for transporting such live animal, written instructions concerning the food and water requirements of such animal while being so transported.

(e) No carrier or intermediate handler shall accept any live animals for transportation in commerce unless written instructions concerning the food and water requirements of such animal while being so transported is affixed to the outside of its primary enclosure.

§ 3.140 Care in transit.

(a) During surface transportation, it shall be the responsibility of the driver or other employee to visually observe the live animals as frequently as circumstances may dictate, but not less than once every 4 hours, to assure that they are receiving sufficient air for normal breathing, their ambient temperatures are within the prescribed limits, all other applicable standards are being complied with and to determine whether any of the live animals are in obvious physical distress and to provide any needed veterinary care as soon as possible. When transported by air, live animals shall be visually observed by the carrier as frequently as circumstances may dictate, but not less than once every 4 hours, if the animal cargo space is accessible during flight. If the animal cargo space is not accessible during flight, the carrier shall visually observe the live animals whenever loaded and unloaded and whenever the animal cargo space is otherwise accessible to assure that they are receiving sufficient air for normal breathing, their ambient temperatures are within the prescribed limits, all other applicable standards are being complied with and to determine whether any such live animals are in obvious physical distress. The carrier shall provide any needed veterinary care as soon as possible. No animal in obvious physical distress shall be transported in commerce.

(b) Wild or otherwise dangerous animals shall not be taken from their primary enclosure except under extreme emergency conditions: *Provided, however,* That a temporary primary enclosure may be used, if available, and such temporary primary enclosure is structurally strong enough to prevent the escape of the animal. During the course of transportation, in commerce, live animals shall not be removed from their primary enclosures unless placed in other primary enclosures or facilities conforming to the requirements provided in this subpart.

§3.141 Terminal facilities.

Carriers and intermediate handlers shall not commingle live animal shipments with inanimate cargo. All animal holding areas of a terminal facility of any carrier or intermediate handler wherein live animal shipments are maintained shall be cleaned and sanitized in a manner prescribed in §3.141 of the standards often enough to prevent an accumulation of debris or excreta, to minimize vermin infestation and to prevent a disease hazard. An effective program for the control of insects, ectoparasites, and avian and mammalian pests shall be established and maintained for all animal holding areas. Any animal holding area containing live animals shall be provided with fresh air by means of windows, doors vents, or air conditioning and may be ventilated or air circulated by means of fans, blowers, or an air conditioning system so as to minimize drafts, odors, and moisture condensation. Auxiliary ventilation, such as exhaust fans and vents or fans or blowers or air conditioning shall be used for any animal holding area containing live animals when the air temperature within such animal holding area is 23.9 °C. (75.°F.) or higher. The air temperature around any live animal in any animal holding area shall not be allowed to fall below 7.2 °C. (45 °F.) nor be allowed to exceed 29.5 °C. (85 °F.) at any time: *Provided, however,* That no live animal shall be subjected to surrounding air temperatures which exceed 23.9 °C. (75 °F.) for more than 4 hours at any time. To ascertain compliance with the provisions of this paragraph, the air temperature around any live animal shall be measured and read outside the primary enclosure which contains such animal at a distance not to exceed .91 meters (3 feet) from any one of the external walls of the primary enclosure and on a level parallel to the bottom of such primary enclosure at a point which approximates half the distance between the top and bottom of such primary enclosure.

[43 FR 56217, Dec. 1, 1978. Redesignated at 44 FR 36874, July 22, 1979]

§3.142 Handling.

(a) Carriers and intermediate handlers shall move live animals from the animal holding area of the terminal facility to the primary conveyance and from the primary conveyance to the animal holding area of the terminal facility as expeditiously as possible. Carriers and intermediate handlers holding any live animal in an animal holding area of a terminal facility or in transporting any live animal from the animal holding area of the terminal facility to the primary conveyance and from the primary conveyance to the animal holding area of the terminal facility, including loading and unloading procedures, shall provide the following:

(1) *Shelter from sunlight.* When sunlight is likely to cause overheating or discomfort, sufficient shade shall be provided to protect the live animals from the direct rays of the sun and such live animals shall not be subjected to surrounding air temperatures which exceed 29.5 °C. (85 °F), and which shall be measured and read in the manner prescribed in §3.141 of this part, for a period of more than 45 minutes.

(2) *Shelter from rain or snow.* Live animals shall be provided protection to allow them to remain dry during rain or snow.

(3) *Shelter from cold weather.* Transporting devices shall be covered to provide protection for live animals when the outdoor air temperature falls below 10 °C. (50 °F) and such live animals shall not be subjected to surrounding air temperatures which fall below 7.2 °C. (45 °F.), and which shall be measured and read in the manner prescribed in §3.141 of this part, for a period of more than 45 minutes unless such animals are accompanied by a certificate of acclimation to lower temperatures as prescribed in §3.136(c).

(b) Care shall be exercised to avoid handling of the primary enclosure in such a manner that may cause physical or emotional trauma to the live animal contained therein.

(c) Primary enclosures used to transport any live animal shall not be tossed, dropped, or needlessly tilted and shall not be stacked in a manner which may reasonably be expected to result in their falling.

[43 FR 21167, May 16, 1978, as amended at 43 FR 56217, Dec. 1, 1978. Redesignated at 44 FR 36874, July 22, 1979]

PART 4—RULES OF PRACTICE GOVERNING PROCEEDINGS UNDER THE ANIMAL WELFARE ACT

Subpart A—General

Subpart B—Supplemental Rules of Practice

AUTHORITY: 7 U.S.C. 2149 and 2151; 7 CFR 2.22, 2.80, and 371.7.

SOURCE: 42 FR 10959, Feb. 25, 1977, unless otherwise noted.

Subpart A—General

§4.1 Scope and applicability of rules of practice.

The Uniform Rules of Practice for the Department of Agriculture promulgated in subpart H of part 1, subtitle A, title 7, Code of Federal Regulations, are the Rules of Practice applicable to adjudicatory, administrative proceedings under section 19 of the Animal Welfare Act (7 U.S.C. 2149). In addition, the Supplemental Rules of Practice set forth in subpart B of this part shall be applicable to such proceedings.

Subpart B—Supplemental Rules of Practice

§4.10 Summary action.

(a) In any situation where the Administrator has reason to believe that any person licensed under the Act has violated or is violating any provision of the Act, or the regulations or standards issued thereunder, and he deems it warranted under the circumstances, the Administrator may suspend such person's license temporarily, for a period not to exceed 21 days, effective, except as provided in §4.10(b), upon written notification given to such person of the suspension of his license pursuant to §1.147(b) of the Uniform Rules of Practice (7 CFR 1.147(b)).

(b) In any case of actual or threatened physical harm to animals in violation of the Act, or the regulations or standards issued thereunder, by a person licensed under the Act, the Administrator may suspend such person's license temporarily, for a period not to exceed 21 days, effective upon oral or written notification, whichever is earlier. In the event of oral notification, a written confirmation thereof shall be given to such person pursuant to §1.147(b) of the Uniform Rules of Practice (7 CFR 1.147(b)) as promptly as circumstances permit.

(c) The temporary suspension of a license shall be in addition to any sanction which may be imposed against said person by the Secretary pursuant to the Act after notice and opportunity for hearing.

§4.11 Stipulations.

(a) At any time prior to the issuance of a complaint seeking a civil penalty under the Act, the Administrator, in his discretion, may enter into a stipulation with any person in which:

(1) The Administrator gives notice of an apparent violation of the Act, or the

regulations or standards issued thereunder, by such person and affords such person an opportunity for a hearing regarding the matter as provided by the Act;

(2) Such person expressly waives hearing and agrees to pay a specified penalty within a designated time; and

(3) The Administrator agrees to accept the specified penalty in settlement of the particular matter involved if it is paid within the designated time.

(b) If the specified penalty is not paid within the time designated in such a stipulation, the amount of the stipulated penalty shall not be relevant in any respect to the penalty which may be assessed after issuance of a complaint.

PART 11—HORSE PROTECTION REGULATIONS

Sec.

AUTHORITY: 15 U.S.C. 1823–1825 and 1828; 7 CFR 2.22, 2.80, and 371.7.

SOURCE: 44 FR 25179, Apr. 27, 1979, unless otherwise noted.

§ 11.1 Definitions.

For the purpose of this part, unless the context otherwise requires, the following terms shall have the meanings assigned to them in this section. The singular form shall also impart the plural and the masculine form shall also impart the feminine. Words of art undefined in the following paragraphs shall have the meaning attributed to them by trade usage or general usage as reflected by definition in a standard dictionary, such as "Webster's."

Act means the Horse Protection Act of 1970 (Pub. L. 91–540) as amended by the Horse Protection Act Amendments of 1976 (Pub. L. 94–360), 15 U.S.C. 1821 *et seq.*, and any legislation amendatory thereof.

Action device means any boot, collar, chain, roller, or other device which encircles or is placed upon the lower extremity of the leg of a horse in such a manner that it can either rotate around the leg, or slide up and down the leg so as to cause friction, or which can strike the hoof, coronet band or fetlock joint.

Administrator means the Administrator, Animal and Plant Health Inspection Service, or any person authorized to act for the Administrator.

Animal and Plant Health Inspection Service (APHIS) means the Animal and Plant Health Inspection Service of the United States Department of Agriculture.

APHIS representative means any employee of APHIS, or any officer or employee of any State agency who is authorized by the Administrator to perform inspections or any other functions authorized by the Act, including the inspection of the records of any horse show, horse exhibition, horse sale or horse auction.

APHIS Show Veterinarian means the APHIS Doctor of Veterinary Medicine responsible for the immediate supervision and conduct of the Department's activities under the Act at any horse show, horse exhibition, horse sale or horse auction.

Department means the United States Department of Agriculture.

Designated Qualified Person or *DQP* means a person meeting the requirements specified in § 11.7 of this part who has been licensed as a DQP by a horse industry organization or association having a DQP program certified by the Department and who may be appointed and delegated authority by the management of any horse show, horse exhibition, horse sale or horse auction under section 4 of the Act to detect or diagnose horses which are sore or to otherwise inspect horses and any records pertaining to such horses for the purposes of enforcing the Act.

Exhibitor means (1) any person who enters any horse, any person who allows his horse to be entered, or any person who directs or allows any horse in his custody or under his direction, control or supervision to be entered in any horse show or horse exhibition; (2) any person who shows or exhibits any horse, any person who allows his horse to be shown or exhibited, or any person who directs or allows any horse in his custody or under his direction, control, or supervision to be shown or exhibited in any horse show or horse exhibition; (3) any person who enters or presents any horse for sale or auction, any person who allows his horse to be entered or presented for sale or auction, or any person who allows any horse in his custody or under his direction, control, or supervision to be entered or presented for sale or auction in any horse sale or horse auction; or (4) any person who sells or auctions any horse, any person who allows his horse to be sold or auctioned, or any person who directs or allows any horse in his custody or under his direction, control, or supervision to be sold or auctioned.

Horse means any member of the species *Equus caballus.*

Horse exhibition means a public display of any horses, singly or in groups, but not in competition, except events where speed is the prime factor, rodeo events, parades, or trail rides.

Horse industry organization or association means an organized group of people, having a formal structure, who are engaged in the promotion of horses through the showing, exhibiting, sale, auction, registry, or any activity which contributes to the advancement of the horse.

Horse sale or horse auction means any event, public or private, at which horses are sold or auctioned, regardless of whether or not said horses are exhibited prior to or during the sale or auction.

Horse show means a public display of any horses, in competition, except events where speed is the prime factor, rodeo events, parades, or trail rides.

Inspection means the examination of any horse and any records pertaining to any horse by use of whatever means are deemed appropriate and necessary for the purpose of determining compliance with the Act and regulations. Such inspection may include, but is not limited to, visual examination of a horse and records, actual physical examination of a horse including touching, rubbing, palpating and observation of vital signs, and the use of any diagnostic device or instrument, and may require the removal of any shoe, pad, action device, or any other equipment, substance or paraphernalia from the horse when deemed necessary by the person conducting such inspection.

Lubricant means mineral oil, glycerine or petrolatum, or mixtures exclusively thereof, that is applied to the limbs of a horse solely for protective and lubricating purposes while the horse is being shown or exhibited at a horse show, horse exhibition, horse sale or horse auction.

Management means any person or persons who organize, exercise control over, or administer or are responsible for organizing, directing, or administering any horse show, horse exhibition, horse sale or horse auction and specifically includes, but is not limited to, the sponsoring organization and show manager.

Person means any individual, corporation, company, association, firm, partnership, society, organization, joint stock company, or other legal entity.

Regional Director means the APHIS veterinarian who is assigned by the Administrator to supervise and perform official duties of APHIS under the Act in a specified State or States.[1]

Secretary means the Secretary of Agriculture or anyone who has heretofore or may hereafter be delegated authority to act in his stead.

Show manager means the person who has been delegated primary authority by a sponsoring organization for managing a horse show, horse exhibition, horse sale or horse auction.

[1] Information as to the name and address of the Regional Director for the State or States concerned can be obtained by writing to the Animal and Plant Health Inspection Service, Animal Care, 4700 River Road Unit 84, Riverdale, MD 20737–1234.

Sore when used to describe a horse means:

(1) An irritating or blistering agent has been applied, internally or externally by a person to any limb of a horse,

(2) Any burn, cut, or laceration has been inflicted by a person on any limb of a horse,

(3) Any tack, nail, screw, or chemical agent has been injected by a person into or used by a person on any limb of a horse, or

(4) Any other substance or device has been used by a person on any limb of a horse or a person has engaged in a practice involving a horse, and, as a result of such application, infliction, injection, use, or practice, such horse suffers, or can reasonably be expected to suffer, physical pain or distress, inflammation, or lameness when walking, trotting, or otherwise moving, except that such term does not include such an application, infliction, injection, use, or practice in connection with the therapeutic treatment of a horse by or under the supervision of a person licensed to practice veterinary medicine in the State in which such treatment was given.

Sponsoring organization means any person under whose immediate auspices and responsibility a horse show, horse exhibition, horse sale, or horse auction is conducted.

State means any of the several States, the District of Columbia, the Commonwealth of Puerto Rico, the Virgin Islands, Guam, American Samoa, or the Trust Territory of the Pacific Islands.

[44 FR 1561, Jan. 5, 1979, as amended at 53 FR 14782, Apr. 26, 1988; 53 FR 28372, July 28, 1988; 56 FR 13749, Apr. 4, 1991; 59 FR 67612, Dec. 30, 1994; 63 FR 62927, Nov. 10, 1998]

§ 11.2 Prohibitions concerning exhibitors.

(a) *General prohibitions.* Notwithstanding the provisions of paragraph (b) of this section, no chain, boot, roller, collar, action device, nor any other device, method, practice, or substance shall be used with respect to any horse at any horse show, horse exhibition, or horse sale or auction if such use causes or can reasonably be expected to cause such horse to be sore.

(b) *Specific prohibitions.* The use of any of the following devices, equipment, or practices on any horse at any horse show, horse exhibition, or horse sale or auction is prohibited:

(1) All beads, bangles, rollers, and similar devices, with the exception of rollers made of lignum vitae (hardwood), aluminum, or stainless steel, with individual rollers of uniform size, weight and configuration, provided each such device may not weigh more than 6 ounces, including the weight of the fastener.

(2) Chains weighing more than 6 ounces each, including the weight of the fastener.

(3) Chains with links that are not of uniform size, weight and configuration; and, chains that have twisted links or double links.

(4) Chains that have drop links on any horse that is being ridden, worked on a lead, or otherwise worked out or moved about.

(5) More than one action device on any one limb of a horse.

(6) Chains or lignum vitae, stainless steel, or aluminum rollers which are not smooth and free of protrusions, projections, rust, corrosion, or rough or sharp edges.

(7)(i) Boots, collars, or any other devices, with protrusions or swellings, or rigid, rough, or sharp edges, seams or any other abrasive or abusive surface that may contact a horse's leg; and

(ii) Boots, collars, or any other devices that weigh more than 6 ounces, except for soft rubber or soft leather bell boots and quarter boots that are used as protective devices.

(8) Pads or other devices on yearling horses (horses up to 2 years old) that elevate or change the angle of such horses' hooves in excess of 1 inch at the heel.

(9) Any weight on yearling horses, except a keg or similar conventional horseshoe, and any horseshoe on yearling horses that weighs more than 16 ounces.

(10) Artificial extension of the toe length, whether accomplsihed with pads, acrylics or any other material or combinations thereof, that exceeds 50 percent of the natural hoof length, as measured from the coronet band, at the center of the front pastern along the

front of the hoof wall, to the distal portion of the hoof wall at the tip of the toe. The artificial extension shall be measured from the distal portion of the hoof wall at the tip of the toe at a 90 degree angle to the proximal (foot/ hoof) surface of the shoe.

(11) Toe length that does not exceed the height of the heel by 1 inch or more. The length of the toe shall be measured from the coronet band, at the center of the front pastern along the front of the hoof wall to the ground. The heel shall be measured from the coronet band, at the most lateral portion of the rear pastern, at a 90 degree angle to the ground, not including normal caulks at the rear of a horseshoe that do not exceed ¾ inch in length. That portion of caulk at the rear of a horseshoe in excess of ¾ of an inch shall be added to the height of the heel in determining the heel/toe ratio.

(12) Pads that are not made of leather, plastic, or a similar pliant material.

(13) Any object or material inserted between the pad and the hoof other than acceptable hoof packing, which includes pine tar, oakum, live rubber, sponge rubber, silicone, commercial hoof packing or other substances used to maintain adequate frog pressure or sole consistency.

(14) Single or double rocker-bars on the bottom surface of horseshoes which extend more than 1½ inches back from the point of the toe, or which would cause, or could reasonably be expected to cause, an unsteadiness of stance in the horse with resulting muscle and tendon strain due to the horse's weight and balance being focused upon a small fulcrum point. [2]

(15) Metal hoof bands, such as used to anchor or strengthen pads and shoes, placed less than ½ inch below the coronet band.

(16) Metal hoof bands that can be easily and quickly loosened or tightened by hand, by means such as, but not limited to, a wing-nut or similar fastener.

(17) Any action device or any other device that strikes the coronet band of the foot of a horse except for soft rubber or soft leather bell boots that are used as protective devices.

(18) Shoeing a horse, or trimming a horse's hoof in a manner that will cause such horse to suffer, or can reasonably be expected to cause such horse to suffer pain or distress, inflammation, or lameness when walking, trotting, or otherwise moving.

(19) Lead or other weights attached to the outside of the hoof wall, the outside surface of the horseshoe, or any portion of the pad except the bottom surface within the horseshoe. Pads may not be hollowed out for the purpose of inserting or affixing weights, and weights may not extend below the bearing surface of the shoe. Hollow shoes or artificial extensions filled with mercury or similar substances are prohibited.

(c) *Substances.* All substances are prohibited on the extremities above the hoof of any Tennessee Walking Horse or racking horse while being shown, exhibited, or offered for sale at any horse show, horse exhibition, or horse sale or auction, except lubricants such as glycerine, petrolatum, and mineral oil, or mixtures thereof: *Provided,* That:

(1) The horse show, horse exhibition, or horse sale or auction management agrees to furnish all such lubricants and to maintain control over them when used at the horse show, horse exhibition, or horse sale or auction.

(2) Any such lubricants shall be applied only after the horse has been inspected by management or by a DQP and shall only be applied under the supervision of the horse show, horse exhibition, or horse sale, or auction management.

(3) Horse show, horse exhibition, or horse sale or auction management makes such lubricants available to Department personnel for inspection and sampling as they deem necessary.

(d) *Competition restrictions—2 Year-Old Horses.* Horse show or horse exhibition workouts or performances of 2-year-old

[2] This prohibition is not intended to disallow corrective devices, such as Memphis bars which consist of a metal bar(s) crossing from the ground surface of one side of the horseshoe to the ground surface of the other side of the horseshoe, and the purpose of which is to correct a lameness or pathological condition of the foot: *Provided,* That such metal bar(s) do not act as a single fulcrum point so as to affect the balance of the horse.

Tennessee Walking Horses and racking horses and working exhibitions of 2-year-old Tennessee Walking Horses and racking horses (horses eligible to be shown or exhibited in 2-year-old classes) at horse sales or horse auctions that exceed a total of 10 minutes continuous workout or performance without a minimum 5-minute rest period between the first such 10-minute period and the second such 10-minute period, and, more than two such 10-minute periods per performance, class, or workout are prohibited.

(e) *Information requirements—horse related.* Failing to provide information or providing any false or misleading information required by the Act or regulations or requested by Department representatives, by any person that owns, trains, shows, exhibits, or sells or has custody of, or direction or control over any horse shown, exhibited, sold, or auctioned or entered for the purpose of being shown, exhibited, sold, or auctioned at any horse show, horse exhibition, or horse sale or auction is prohibited. Such information shall include, but is not limited to: Information concerning the registered name, markings, sex, age, and legal ownership of the horse; the name and address of the horse's training and/or stabling facilities; the name and address of the owner, trainer, rider, any other exhibitor, or other legal entity bearing responsibility for the horse; the class in which the horse is entered or shown; the exhibitor identification number; and, any other information reasonably related to the identification, ownership, control, direction, or supervision of any such horse.

[44 FR 25179, Apr. 27, 1979, as amended at 53 FR 14782, Apr. 26, 1988, 53 FR 15641, May 2, 1988, 53 FR 28372, July 28, 1988, 53 FR 41562, Oct. 24, 1988, 53 FR 45854, Nov. 14, 1988; 54 FR 7178, Feb. 17, 1989]

§ 11.3 Scar rule.

The scar rule applies to all horses born on or after October 1, 1975. Horses subject to this rule that do not meet the following scar rule criteria shall be considered to be "sore" and are subject to all prohibitions of section 5 of the Act. The scar rule criteria are as follows:

(a) The anterior and anterior-lateral surfaces of the fore pasterns (extensor surface) must be free of bilateral granulomas,[5] other bilateral pathological evidence of inflammation, and, other bilateral evidence of abuse indicative of soring including, but not limited to, excessive loss of hair.

(b) The posterior surfaces of the pasterns (flexor surface), including the sulcus or "pocket" may show bilateral areas of uniformly thickened epithelial tissue if such areas are free of proliferating granuloma tissue, irritation, moisture, edema, or other evidence of inflammation.

[44 FR 25179, Apr. 27, 1979, as amended at 53 FR 14782, Apr. 26, 1988, 53 FR 28373, July 28, 1988]

§ 11.4 Inspection and detention of horses.

For the purpose of effective enforcement of the Act:

(a) Each horse owner, exhibitor, trainer, or other person having custody of, or responsibility for, any horse at any horse show, horse exhibition, or horse sale or auction, shall allow any APHIS representative to reasonably inspect such horse at all reasonable times and places the APHIS representative may designate. Such inspections may be required of any horse which is stabled, loaded on a trailer, being prepared for show, exhibition, or sale or auction, being exercised or otherwise on the grounds of, or present at, any horse show, horse exhibition, or horse sale or auction, whether or not such horse has or has not been shown, exhibited, or sold or auctioned, or has or has not been entered for the purpose of being shown or exhibited or offered for sale or auction at any such horse show, horse exhibition, or horse sale or auction. APHIS representatives will not generally or routinely delay or interrupt actual individual classes or performances at horse shows, horse exhibitions, or horse sales or auctions for the purpose of examining horses, but they

---

[3] [4] [Reserved]

[5] Granuloma is defined as any one of a rather large group of fairly distinctive focal lesions that are formed as a result of inflammatory reactions caused by biological, chemical, or physical agents.

may do so in extraordinary situations, such as but not limited to, lack of proper facilities for inspection, refusal of management to cooperate with Department inspection efforts, reason to believe that failure to immediately perform inspection may result in the loss, removal, or masking of any evidence of a violation of the Act or the regulations, or a request by management that such inspections be performed by an APHIS representative.

(b) When any APHIS representative notifies the owner, exhibitor, trainer, or other person having custody of or responsibility for a horse at any horse show, horse exhibition, or horse sale or auction that APHIS desires to inspect such horse, it shall not be moved from the horse show, horse exhibition, or horse sale or auction until such inspection has been completed and the horse has been released by an APHIS representative.

(c) For the purpose of examination, testing, or taking of evidence, APHIS representatives may detain for a period not to exceed 24 hours any horse, at any horse show, horse exhibition, or horse sale or auction, which is sore or which an APHIS veterinarian has probable cause to believe is sore. Such detained horse may be marked for identification and any such identifying markings shall not be removed by any person other than an APHIS representative.

(d) Detained horses shall be kept under the supervision of an APHIS representative or secured under an official USDA seal or seals in a horse stall, horse trailer, or other facility to which access shall be limited. It shall be the policy of APHIS to have at least one representative present in the immediate detention area when a horse is being held in detention. The official USDA seal or seals may not be broken or removed by any person other than an APHIS representative, unless:

(1) The life or well-being of the detained horse is immediately endangered by fire, flood, windstorm, or other dire circumstances that are beyond human control.

(2) The detained horse is in need of such immediate veterinary attention that its life may be in peril before an APHIS representative can be located.

(3) The horse has been detained for a maximum 24-hour detention period, and an APHIS representative is not available to release the horse.

(e) The owner, exhibitor, trainer, or other person having custody of or responsibility for any horse detained by APHIS for further examination, testing, or the taking of evidence shall be allowed to feed, water, and provide other normal custodial and maintenance care, such as walking, grooming, etc., for such detained horse: *Provided*, That:

(1) Such feeding, watering, and other normal custodial and maintenance care of the detained horse is rendered under the direct supervision of an APHIS representative.

(2) Any non-emergency veterinary care of the detained horse requiring the use, application, or injection of any drugs or other medication for therapeutic or other purposes is rendered by a Doctor of Veterinary Medicine in the presence of an APHIS representative and, the identity and dosage of the drug or other medication used, applied, or injected and its purpose is furnished in writing to the APHIS representative prior to such use, application, or injection by the Doctor of Veterinary Medicine attending the horse. The use, application, or injection of such drug or other medication must be approved by the APHIS Show Veterinarian or his appointed representative.

(f) It shall be the policy of APHIS to inform the owner, trainer, exhibitor, or other person having immediate custody of or responsibility for any horse allegedly found to be in violation of the Act or the regulations of such alleged violation or violations before the horse is released by an APHIS representative.

(g) The owner, trainer, exhibitor, or other person having immediate custody of or responsibility for any horse or horses that an APHIS representative determines shall be detained for examination, testing, or taking of evidence pursuant to paragraph (e) of this section shall be informed after such determination is made and shall allow said horse to be immediately put under the supervisory custody of APHIS or secured under official USDA seal as provided in paragraph (d) of this section until the completion of such examination, testing, or gathering of evidence, or until the 24-hour detention period expires.

(h) The owner, trainer, exhibitor, or other person having custody of or responsibility for any horse allegedly found to be in violation of the Act or regulations, and who has been notified of such alleged violation by an APHIS representative as stated in paragraph (f) of this section, may request reexamination and testing of said horse within a 24-hour period: *Provided*, That:

(1) Such request is made to the APHIS Show Veterinarian immediately after the horse has been examined by APHIS representatives and before such horse has been removed from the APHIS inspection facilities; and

(2) The APHIS Show Veterinarian determines that sufficient cause for reexamination and testing exists; and

(3) The horse is maintained under APHIS supervisory custody as prescribed in paragraph (d) of this section until such reexamination and testing has been completed.

(i) The owner, exhibitor, trainer, or other person having custody of, or responsibility for any horse being inspected shall render such assistance as the APHIS representative may request for purposes of such inspection.

(ii) [Reserved]

[44 FR 25179, Apr. 27, 1979, as amended at 56 FR 13750, Apr. 4, 1991]

§ 11.5 Access to premises and records.

Requirements regarding access to premises for inspection of horses and records are as follows:

(a) *Management*. (1) The management of any horse show, horse exhibition, or horse sale or auction shall, without fee, charge, assessment, or other compensation, provide APHIS representatives with unlimited access to the grandstands, sale ring, barns, stables, grounds, offices, and all other areas of any horse show, horse exhibition, or horse sale or auction, including any adjacent areas under their direction, control, or supervision for the purpose of inspecting any horses, or any records required to be kept by regulation or otherwise maintained.

(2) The management of any horse show, horse exhibition, or horse sale or auction shall, without fee, charge, assessment, or other compensation, provide APHIS representatives with an adequate, safe, and accessible area for the visual inspection and observation of horses while such horses are competitively or otherwise performing at any horse show or horse exhibition, or while such horses are being sold or auctioned or offered for sale or auction at any horse sale or horse auction.

(b) *Exhibitors*. (1) Each horse owner, exhibitor, or other person having custody of or responsibility for any horse at any horse show, horse exhibition, or horse sale or auction shall, without fee, charge, assessment, or other compensation, admit any APHIS representative or Designated Qualified Person appointed by management, to all areas of barns, compounds, horse vans, horse trailers, stables, stalls, paddocks, or other show, exhibition, or sale or auction grounds or related areas at any horse show, horse exhibition, or horse sale or auction, for the purpose of inspecting any such horse at any and all reasonable times.

(2) Each owner, trainer, exhibitor, or other person having custody of or responsibility for, any horse at any horse show, horse exhibition, or horse sale or auction shall promptly present his horse for inspection upon notification, orally or in writing, by any APHIS representative or Designated Qualified Person appointed by management, that said horse has been selected for examination for the purpose of determining whether such horse is in compliance with the Act and regulations.

[44 FR 25179, Apr. 27, 1979, as amended at 56 FR 13750, Apr. 4, 1991]

§ 11.6 Inspection space and facility requirements.

The management of every horse show, horse exhibition, or horse sale or auction, containing Tennessee Walking Horses or racking horses, shall provide, without fee, sufficient space and facilities for APHIS representatives to carry out their duties under the Act and regulations at every horse show, horse exhibition, or horse sale or auction, containing Tennessee Walking Horses or racking horses, whether or not management has received prior notification or otherwise knows that such show may be inspected by APHIS. The management of every horse show, horse exhibition, horse sale or auction which does not contain Tennessee Walking Horses or racking horses shall provide, without fee, such sufficient space and facilities when requested to do so by APHIS representatives. With respect to such space and facilities, it shall be the responsibility of management to provide at least the following:

(a) Sufficient space in a convenient location to the horse show, horse exhibition, or horse sale or auction arena, acceptable to the APHIS Show Veterinarian, in which horses may be physically, thermographically, or otherwise inspected.

(b) Protection from the elements of nature, such as rain, snow, sleet, hail, windstorm, etc., if required by the APHIS Show Veterinarian.

(c) A means to control crowds or onlookers in order that APHIS personnel may carry out their duties without interference and with a reasonable measure of safety, if requested by the APHIS Show Veterinarian.

(d) An accessible, reliable, and convenient 110-volt electrical power source, if electrical service is available at the show, exhibition, or sale or auction site and is requested by the APHIS Show Veterinarian.

(e) An appropriate area adjacent to the inspection area for designated horses to wait for inspection, and an area to be used for detention of horses.

[44 FR 25181, Apr. 27, 1979, as amended at 56 FR 13750, Apr. 4, 1991]

§ 11.7 Certification and licensing of designated qualified persons (DQP's).

(a) *Basic qualifications of DQP applicants.* DQP's holding a valid, current DQP license issued in accordance with this part may be appointed by the management of any horse show, horse exhibition, horse sale, or horse auction, as qualified persons in accordance with section 4(c) of the Act, to inspect horses to detect or diagnose soring and to otherwise inspect horses, or any records pertaining to any horse for the purpose of enforcing the Act. Individuals who may be licensed as DQP's under this part shall be:

(1) Doctors of Veterinary Medicine who are accredited in any State by the United States Department of Agriculture under part 161 of chapter I, title 9 of the Code of Federal Regulations, and who are:

(i) Members of the American Association of Equine Practitioners, or

(ii) Large animal practitioners with substantial equine experience, or

(iii) Knowledgeable in the area of equine lameness as related to soring and soring practices (such as Doctors of Veterinary Medicine with a small animal practice who own, train, judge, or show horses, or Doctors of Veterinary Medicine who teach equine related subjects in an accredited college or school of veterinary medicine). Accredited Doctors of Veterinary Medicine who meet these criteria may be licensed as DQP's by a horse industry organization or association whose DQP program has been certified by the Department under this part without undergoing the formal training requirements set forth in this section.

(2) Farriers, horse trainers, and other knowledgeable horsemen whose past experience and training would qualify them for positions as horse industry organization or association stewards or judges (or their equivalent) and who have been formally trained and licensed as DQP's by a horse industry organization or association whose DQP program has been certified by the Department in accordance with this section.

(b) *Certification requirements for DQP programs.* The Department will not license DQP's on an individual basis. Licensing of DQP's will be accomplished only through DQP programs certified by the Department and initiated and maintained by horse industry organizations or associations. Any horse industry organization or association desiring Department certification to train and license DQP's under the Act shall submit to the Administrator[6] a formal request in writing for certification of its DQP program and a detailed outline of such program for Department approval. Such outline shall include the

[6] Animal and Plant Health Inspection Service, Animal Care, 4700 River Road, Unit 84, Riverdale, Maryland 20737–1234.

organizational structure of such organization or association and the names of the officers or persons charged with the management of the organization or association. The outline shall also contain at least the following:

(1) The criteria to be used in selecting DQP candidates and the minimum qualifications and knowledge regarding horses each candidate must have in order to be admitted to the program.

(2) A copy of the formal training program, classroom and practical, required to be completed by each DQP candidate before being licensed by such horse industry organization or association, including the minimum number of hours, classroom and practical, and the subject matter of the training program. Such training program must meet the following minimum standards in order to be certified by the Department under the Act.

(i) Two hours of classroom instruction on the anatomy and physiology of the limbs of a horse. The instructor teaching the course must be specified, and a resume of said instructor's background, experience, and qualifications to teach such course shall be provided to the Administrator.[6]

(ii) Two hours of classroom instruction on the Horse Protection Act and regulations and their interpretation. Instructors for this course must be furnished or recommended by the Department. Requests for instructors to be furnished or recommended must be made to the Administrator[6] in writing at least 30 days prior to such course.

(iii) Four hours of classroom instruction on the history of soring, the physical examination procedures necessary to detect soring, the detection and diagnosis of soring, and related subjects. The instructor teaching the course must be specified and a summary of said instructor's background, experience, and qualifications to teach such course must be provided to the Administrator.[6]

(iv) Four hours of practical instruction in clinics and seminars utilizing live horses with actual application of the knowledge gained in the classroom subjects covered in paragraphs (b)(2)(i), (ii), and (iii) of this section. Methods and procedures required to perform a thorough and uniform examination of a horse shall be included. The names of the instructors and a resume of their background, academic and practical experience, and qualifications to present such instruction shall be provided to the Administrator.[6] Notification of the actual date, time, duration, subject matter, and geographic location of such clinics or seminars must be sent to the Administrator[6] at least 10 days prior to each such clinic or seminar.

(v) One hour of classroom instruction regarding the DQP standards of conduct promulgated by the licensing organization or association pursuant to paragraph (d)(7) of this section.

(vi) One hour of classroom instruction on recordkeeping and reporting requirements and procedures.

(3) A sample of a written examination which must be passed by DQP candidates for successful completion of the program along with sample answers and the scoring thereof, and proposed passing and failing standards.

(4) The criteria to be used to determine the qualifications and performance abilities of DQP candidates selected for the training program and the criteria used to indicate successful completion of the training program, in addition to the written examination required in paragraph (b)(3) of this section.

(5) The criteria and schedule for a continuing education program and the criteria and methods of monitoring and appraising performance for continued licensing of DQP's by such organization or association. A continuing education program for DQP's shall consist of not less than 4 hours of instruction per year.

(6) Procedures for monitoring horses in the unloading, preparation, warmup, and barn areas, or other such areas. Such monitoring may include any horse that is stabled, loaded on a trailer, being prepared for show, exhibition, sale, or auction, or exercised, or that is otherwise on the grounds of, or present at, any horse show, horse exhibition, or horse sale or auction.

(7) The methods to be used to insure uniform interpretation and enforcement of the Horse Protection Act and

regulations by DQP's and uniform procedures for inspecting horses for compliance with the Act and regulations;

(8) Standards of conduct for DQP's promulgated by the organization or association in accordance with paragraph (d)(7) of this section; and

(9) A formal request for Department certification of the DQP program.

The horse industry organizations or associations that have formally requested Department certification of their DQP training, enforcement, and maintenance program will receive a formal notice of certification from the Department, or the reasons, in writing, why certification of such program cannot be approved. A current list of certified DQP programs and licensed DQP's will be published in the FEDERAL REGISTER at least once each year, and as may be further required for the purpose of deleting programs and names of DQP's that are no longer certified or licensed, and of adding the names of programs and DQP's that have been certified or licensed subsequent to the publication of the previous list.

(c) *Licensing of DQP's.* Each horse industry organization or association receiving Department certification for the training and licensing of DQP's under the Act shall:

(1) Issue each DQP licensed by such horse industry organization or association a numbered identification card bearing the name and personal signature of the DQP, a picture of the DQP, and the name and address, including the street address or post office box and zip code, of the licensing organization or association;

(2) Submit a list to the Administrator[6] of names and addresses including street address or post office box and zip code, of all DQP's that have successfully completed the certified DQP program and have been licensed under the Act and regulations by such horse industry organization or association;

(3) Notify the Department of any additions or deletions of names of licensed DQP's from the licensed DQP list submitted to the Department or of any change in the address of any licensed DQP or any warnings and license revocations issued to any DQP licensed by such horse industry organization or association within 10 days of such change;

(4) Not license any person as a DQP if such person has been convicted of any violation of the Act or regulations occurring after July 13, 1976, or paid any fine or civil penalty in settlement of any proceeding regarding a violation of the Act or regulations occurring after July 13, 1976, for a period of at least 2 years following the first such violation, and for a period of at least 5 years following the second such violation and any subsequent violation;

(5) Not license any person as a DQP until such person has attended and worked two recognized or affiliated horse shows, horse exhibitions, horse sales, or horse auctions as an apprentice DQP and has demonstrated the ability, qualifications, knowledge and integrity required to satisfactorily execute the duties and responsibilities of a DQP;

(6) Not license any person as a DQP if such person has been disqualified by the Secretary from making detection, diagnosis, or inspection for the purpose of enforcing the Act, or if such person's DQP license is canceled by another horse industry organization or association.

(d) *Requirements to be met by DQP's and Licensing Organizations or Associations.* (1) Any licensed DQP appointed by the management of any horse show, horse exhibition, horse sale or auction to inspect horses for the purpose of detecting and determining or diagnosing horses which are sore and to otherwise inspect horses for the purpose of enforcing the Act and regulations, shall keep and maintain the following information and records concerning any horse which said DQP recommends be disqualified or excused for any reason at such horse show, horse exhibition, horse sale or auction, from being shown, exhibited, sold or auctioned, in a uniform format required by the horse industry organization or association that has licensed said DQP:

(i) The name and address, including street address or post office box and zip code, of the show and the show manager.

[6] See footnote 6 to this section.

(ii) The name and address, including street address or post office box and zip code, of the horse owner.

(iii) The name and address, including street address or post office box and zip code, of the horse trainer.

(iv) The name and address, including street address or post office box and zip code, of the horse exhibitor.

(v) The exhibitors number and class number, or the sale or auction tag number of said horse.

(vi) The date and time of the inspection.

(vii) A detailed description of all of the DQP's findings and the nature of the alleged violation, or other reason for disqualifying or excusing the horse, including said DQP's statement regarding the evidence or facts upon which the decision to disqualify or excuse said horse was based.

(viii) The name, age, sex, color, and markings of the horse; and

(ix) The name or names of the show manager or other management representative notified by the DQP that such horse should be excused or disqualified and whether or not such manager or management representative excused or disqualified such horse.

Copies of the above records shall be submitted by the involved DQP to the horse industry organization or association that has licensed said DQP within 72 hours after the horse show, horse exhibition, horse sale, or horse auction is over.

(2) The DQP shall inform the custodian of each horse allegedly found in violation of the Act or its regulations, or disqualified or excused for any other reason, of such action and the specific reasons for such action.

(3) Each horse industry organization or association having a Department certified DQP program shall submit a report to the Department containing the following information, from records required in paragraph (d)(1) of this section and other available sources, to the Department on a monthly basis:

(i) The identity of all horse shows, horse exhibitions, horse sales, or horse auctions that have retained the services of DQP's licensed by said organization or association during the month covered by the report. Information concerning the identity of such horse shows, horse exhibitions, horse sales, or horse auctions shall include:

(A) The name and location of the show, exhibition, sale, or auction.

(B) The name and address of the manager.

(C) The date or dates of the show, exhibition, sale, or auction.

(ii) The identity of all horses at each horse show, horse exhibition, horse sale, or horse auction that the licensed DQP recommended be disqualified or excused for any reason. The information concerning the identity of such horses shall include:

(A) The registered name of each horse.

(B) The name and address of the owner, trainer, exhibitor, or other person having custody of or responsibility for the care of each such horse disqualified or excused.

(4) Each horse industry organization or association having a Department certified DQP program shall provide, by certified mail if personal service is not possible, to the trainer and owner of each horse allegedly found in violation of the Act or its regulations or otherwise disqualified or excused for any reason, the following information;

(i) The name and date of the show, exhibition, sale, or auction.

(ii) The name of the horse and the reason why said horse was excused, disqualified, or alleged to be in violation of the Act or its regulations.

(5) Each horse industry organization or association having a Department certified DQP program shall provide each of its licensed DQP's with a current list of all persons that have been disqualified by order of the Secretary from showing or exhibiting any horse, or judging or managing any horse show, horse exhibition, horse sale, or horse auction. The Department will make such list available, on a current basis, to organizations and associations maintaining a certified DQP program.

(6) Each horse industry organization or association having a Department certified DQP program shall develop and provide a continuing education program for licensed DQP's which provides not less than 4 hours of instruction per year to each licensed DQP.

(7) Each horse industry organization or association having a Department certified DQP program shall promulgate standards of conduct for its DQP's, and shall provide administrative procedures within the organization or association for initiating, maintaining, and enforcing such standards. The procedures shall include the causes for and methods to be utilized for canceling the license of any DQP who fails to properly and adequately carry out his duties. Minimum standards of conduct for DQP's shall include the following;

(i) A DQP shall not exhibit any horse at any horse show or horse exhibition, or sell, auction, or pruchase any horse sold at a horse sale or horse auction at which he or she has been appointed to inspect horses;

(ii) A DQP shall not inspect horses at any horse show, horse exhibition, horse sale or horse auction in which a horse or horses owned by a member of the DQP's immediate family or the DQP's employer are competing or are being offered for sale;

(iii) A DQP shall follow the uniform inspection procedures of his certified organization or association when inspecting horses; and

(iv) The DQP shall immediately inform management of each case regarding any horse which, in his opinion, is in violation of the Act or regulations.

(e) *Prohibition of appointment of certain persons to perform duties under the Act.* The management of any horse show, horse exhibition, horse sale, or horse auction shall not appoint any person to detect and diagnose horses which are sore or to otherwise inspect horses for the purpose of enforcing the Act, if that person:

(1) Does not hold a valid, current DQP license issued by a horse industry organization or association having a DQP program certified by the Department.

(2) Has had his DQP license canceled by the licensing organization or association.

(3) Is disqualified by the Secretary from performing diagnosis, detection, and inspection under the Act, after notice and opportunity for a hearing,[7] when the Secretary finds that such person is unfit to perform such diagnosis, detection, or inspection because he has failed to perform his duties in accordance with the Act or regulations, or because he has been convicted of a violation of any provision of the Act or regulations occurring after July 13, 1976, or has paid any fine or civil penalty in settlement of any proceeding regarding a violation of the Act or regulations occurring after July 13, 1976.

(f) *Cancellation of DQP license.* (1) Each horse industry organization or association having a DQP program certified by the Department shall issue a written warning to any DQP whom it has licensed who violates the rules, regulations, by-laws, or standards of conduct promulgated by such horse industry organization or association pursuant to this section, who fails to follow the procedures set forth in § 11.21 of this part, or who otherwise carries out his duties and responsibilities in a less than satisfactory manner, and shall cancel the license of any DQP after a second violation. Upon cancellation of his DQP license, the DQP may, within 30 days thereafter, request a hearing before a review committee of not less than three persons appointed by the licensing horse industry organization or association. If the review committee sustains the cancellation of the license, the DQP may appeal the decision of such committee to the Administrator within 30 days from the date of such decision, and the Administrator shall make a final determination in the matter. If the Administrator finds, after providing the DQP whose license has been canceled with a notice and an opportunity for a hearing,[7] that there is sufficient cause for the committee's determination regarding license cancellation, he shall issue a decision sustaining such determination. If he does not find that there was sufficient cause to cancel the license, the licensing organization or association shall reinstate the license.

[7] Hearing would be in accordance with the Uniform Rules of Practice for the Department of Agriculture in subpart H of part 1, subtitle A, title 7, Code of Federal Regulations (7 CFR 1.130 *et seq.*)

(2) Each horse industry organization or association having a Department certified DQP program shall cancel the license of any DQP licensed under its program who has been convicted of any violation of the Act or regulations or of any DQP who has paid a fine or civil penalty in settlement of any alleged violation of the Act or regulations if such alleged violation occurred after July 13, 1976.

(g) *Revocation of DQP program certification of horse industry organizations or associations.* Any horse industry organization or association having a Department certified DQP program that has not received Department approval of the inspection procedures provided for in paragraph (b)(6) of this section, or that otherwise fails to comply with the requirements contained in this part, may have such certification of its DQP program revoked, unless, upon written notification from the Department of such failure to comply with the requirements in this section, such organization or association takes immediate action to rectify such failure and takes appropriate steps to prevent a recurrence of such noncompliance within the time period specified in the Department notification, or otherwise adequately explains such failure to comply to the satisfaction of the Department. Any horse industry organization or association whose DQP program certification has been revoked may appeal such revocation to the Administrator[6] in writing within 30 days after the date of such revocation and, if requested, shall be afforded an opportunity for a hearing.[7] All DQP licenses issued by a horse industry organization or association whose DQP program certification has been revoked shall expire 30 days after the date of such revocation, or 15 days after the date the revocation becomes final after appeal, unless they are transferred to a horse industry organization or association having a program currently certified by the Department.

(Approved by the Office of Management and Budget under control number 0579–0056)

[44 FR 1563, Jan. 5, 1979, as amended at 44 FR 25182, Apr. 27, 1979; 48 FR 57471, Dec. 30, 1983; 55 FR 41993, Oct. 17, 1990; 56 FR 13750, Apr. 4, 1991; 59 FR 67612, Dec. 30, 1994; 63 FR 62927, Nov. 10, 1998; 77 FR 33618, June 7, 2012]

§ 11.20 Responsibilities and liabilities of management.

(a) The management of any horse show, horse exhibition, or horse sale or auction which does not appoint and retain a DQP shall be responsible for identifying all horses that are sore or otherwise in violation of the Act or regulations, and shall disqualify or disallow any horses which are sore or otherwise in violation of the Act or regulations from participating or competing in any horse show, horse exhibition, horse sale, or horse auction. Horses entered for sale or auction at a horse sale or horse auction must be identified as sore or otherwise in violation of the Act or regulations prior to the sale or auction and prohibited from entering the sale or auction ring. Sore horses or horses otherwise in violation of the Act or regulations that have been entered in a horse show or horse exhibition for the purpose of show or exhibition must be identified and excused prior to the show or exhibition. Any horses found to be sore or otherwise in violation of the Act or regulations during actual participation in the show or exhibition, must be removed from further participation prior to the tyeing of the class or the completion of the exhibition. All horses tyed first in each Tennessee Walking Horse or racking horse class or event at any horse show or horse exhibition shall be inspected after being shown or exhibited to determine if such horses are sore or otherwise in violation of the Act or regulations.

(b)(1) The management of any horse show, horse exhibition, horse sale or auction which designates and appoints a Designated Qualified Person (or persons) to inspect horses shall accord said DQP access to all records and areas of the grounds of such show, exhibition, sale, or auction and the same right to inspect horses and records as

[6] [7] See previous footnotes 6 and 7.

is accorded to any APHIS representative. Further, management shall not take any action which would interfere with or influence said DQP in carrying out his duties or making decisions concerning whether or not any horse is sore or otherwise in violation of the Act or regulations. In the event management is dissatisfied with the performance of a particular DQP, including disagreement with decisions concerning violations, management shall not dismiss or otherwise interfere with said DQP during the DQP's appointed tour of duty.[8] However, management should immediately notify, in writing, the Department[6] and the organization or association that licensed the DQP, as to why the performance of said DQP was inadequate or otherwise unsatisfactory. Management which designates and appoints a DQP shall immediately disqualify or disallow from being shown, exhibited, sold, or auctioned any horse identified by the DQP to be sore or otherwise in violation of the Act or regulations or any horse otherwise known by management to be sore or in violation of the Act or regulations. Should management fail to disqualify or disallow from being shown, exhibited, sold or auctioned any such horse, said management shall assume full responsibility for and liabilities arising from the showing, exhibition, sale, or auction of said horses.

(2) The DQP shall physically inspect: (i) All Tennessee Walking Horses and racking horses entered for sale or auction, (ii) all Tennessee Walking Horses and racking horses entered in any animated gait class (whether under saddle, horse to cart, or otherwise), (iii) all Tennessee Walking Horses and racking horses entered for exhibition before they are admitted to be shown, exhibited, sold, or auctioned, and (iv) all Tennessee Walking Horses and racking horses tyed first in their class or event at any horse show, horse exhibition, horse sale, or horse auction. Such inspection shall be for the purpose of determining whether any such horses are in violation of the Act or regulations. Such physical examination shall be conducted in accordance with the inspection procedures provided for in §11.21 of this part. The DQP shall observe horses in the warmup ring and during actual performances whenever possible, and shall inspect any Tennessee Walking Horse or racking horse at any time he deems necessary to determine whether any such horse shown, exhibited, sold, or auctioned is in violation of the Act or regulations. If present at other shows, he shall examine any horse which he determines should be examined for compliance with the Act and regulations.

(3) The DQP shall immediately report, to the management of any horse show, horse exhibition, or horse sale or auction, any horse which, in his opinion, is sore or otherwise in violation of the Act or regulations. Such report shall be made, whenever possible, before the show class or exhibition involving said horse has begun or before said horse is offered for sale or auction.

(c) The management of any horse show, exhibition, sale, or auction that designates and appoints a DQP to inspect horses shall appoint and designate at least two DQP's when more than 150 horses are entered.

(Approved by the Office of Management and Budget under control number 0579–0056)

[44 FR 25182, Apr. 27, 1979, as amended at 48 FR 57471, Dec. 30, 1983; 55 FR 41993, Oct. 17, 1990; 56 FR 13750, Apr. 4, 1991; 57 FR 62175, Dec. 30, 1992]

§ 11.21 Inspection procedures for designated qualified persons (DQPs).

(a)(1) During the preshow inspection, the DQP shall direct the custodian of the horse to walk and turn the horse in a manner that allows the DQP to determine whether the horse exhibits signs of soreness. The DQP shall determine whether the horse moves in a free and easy manner and is free of any signs of soreness.

(2) The DQP shall digitally palpate the front limbs of the horse from knee to hoof, with particular emphasis on the pasterns and fetlocks. The DQP shall examine the posterior surface of the pastern by picking up the foot and examining the posterior (flexor) surface. The DQP shall apply digital pressure to the pocket (sulcus), including the bulbs of the heel, and continue the

[8] The duration of the show, exhibition, or sale or auction.

[6] See footnote 6 to §11.7.

palpation to the medial and lateral surfaces of the pastern, being careful to observe for responses to pain in the horse. While continuing to hold onto the pastern, the DQP shall extend the foot and leg of the horse to examine the front (extensor) surfaces, including the coronary band. The DQP may examine the rear limbs of all horses inspected after showing, and may examine the rear limbs of any horse examined preshow or on the showgrounds when he deems it necessary, except that the DQP shall examine the rear limbs of all horses exhibiting lesions on, or unusual movement of, the rear legs. While carrying out the procedures set forth in this paragraph, the DQP shall also inspect the horse to determine whether the provisions of § 11.3 of this part are being complied with, and particularly whether there is any evidence of inflammation, edema, or proliferating granuloma tissue.

(3) The DQP shall observe and inspect all horses for compliance with the provisions set forth in § 11.2(a) through § 11.2(c) of this part. All action devices, pads, and other equipment shall be observed and/or examined to assure that they are in compliance with the regulations. All such equipment on horses examined postshow, and on horses examined preshow that are not clearly in compliance, shall be weighed and/or measured.

(4) The DQP shall instruct the custodian of the horse to control it by holding the reins approximately 18 inches from the bit shank. The DQP shall not be required to examine a horse if it is presented in a manner that might cause the horse not to react to a DQP's examination, or if whips, cigarette smoke, or other actions or paraphernalia are used to distract a horse during examination. All such incidents shall be reported to the show management and the DQP licensing organization.

(b) The DQP shall inspect horses no more than three classes ahead of the time the inspected horses are to be shown, except that, in shows with fewer than 150 horses, the DQP shall inspect horses no more than 2 classes ahead of the time the inspected horses are to be shown. Inspected horses shall be held in a designated area that is under observation by the DQP or APHIS representative. Horses shall not be permitted to leave the designated area before showing. Only the horse, the rider, the groom, the trainer, the DQP(s) and APHIS representatives shall be allowed in the designated area.

(c) The DQP may carry out additional inspection procedures as he deems necessary to determine whether the horse is sore.

(d) The HIO that licensed the DQP shall assess and enforce penalties for violations in accordance with § 11.25 and shall report all violations in accordance with § 11.20(b)(3).

[55 FR 41993, Oct. 17, 1990, as amended at 56 FR 13750, Apr. 4, 1991; 57 FR 62175, Dec. 30, 1992; 77 FR 33618, June 7, 2012; 78 FR 27001, May 9, 2013]

§ 11.22 Records required and disposition thereof.

(a) The management of any horse show, horse exhibition, or horse sale or auction, that contains Tennessee Walking Horses or racking horses, shall maintain for a period of at least 90 days following the closing date of said show, exhibition, or sale or auction, all pertinent records containing:

(1) The dates and place of the horse show, horse exhibition, horse sale, or horse auction.

(2) The name and address (including street address or post office box number and ZIP code) of the sponsoring organization.

(3) The name and address of the horse show, exhibition, horse sale or horse auction management.

(4) The name and address (including street address or post office box number and ZIP code) of the DQP, if any, employed to conduct inspections under § 11.20; and, the name of the horse industry organization or association certifying the DQP.

(5) The name and address (including street address or post office box number, and ZIP code) of each show judge.

(6) A copy of each class or sale sheet containing the names of horses, the names and addresses (including street address, post office box and ZIP code) of horse owners, the exhibitor number and class number, or sale number assigned to each horse, the show class or

sale lot number, and the name and address (including street address, post office box, and ZIP code) of the person paying the entry fee and entering the horse in a horse show, horse exhibition, or horse sale or auction.

(7) A copy of the official horse show, horse exhibition, horse sale, or horse auction program, if any such program has been prepared.

(8) The identification of each horse, including the name of the horse, the name and address (including street address, post office box, and ZIP code) of the owner, the trainer, the rider or other exhibitor, and the location (including street address, post office box, and ZIP code) of the home barn or other facility where the horse is stabled.

(b) The management of any horse show, horse exhibition, or horse sale or auction containing Tennessee Walking Horses or racking horses shall designate a person to maintain the records required in this section.

(c) The management of any horse show, horse exhibition, or horse sale or auction containing Tennessee Walking Horses or racking horses shall furnish to any APHIS representative, upon request, the name and address (including street address, or post office box, and ZIP code) of the person designated by the sponsoring organization or manager to maintain the records required by this section.

(d) The Administrator may, in specific cases, require that a horse show, horse exhibition, or horse sale or auction records be maintained by management for a period in excess of 90 days.

(Approved by the Office of Management and Budget under control numbers 0579–0056, and 0579–0058)

(44 U.S.C. 3506)

[44 FR 25179, Apr. 27, 1979, as amended at 48 FR 57471, Dec. 30, 1983. Redesignated at 55 FR 41993, Oct. 17, 1990; 56 FR 13750, Apr. 4, 1991]

§ 11.23 Inspection of records.

(a) The management of any horse show, horse exhibition, or horse sale or auction shall permit any APHIS representative, upon request, to examine and make copies of any and all records pertaining to any horse, either required in any part of the regulations, or otherwise maintained, during ordinary business hours or such other times as may be mutually agreed upon. A room, table, or other facilities necessary for proper examination of such records shall be made available to the APHIS representative.

(b) Horse industry organizations or associations who train, maintain, and license DQP's under a certified DQP program shall permit any APHIS representative, upon request, to examine and copy any and all records relating to the DQP program which are required by any part of the regulations. Such requests shall be made during ordinary business hours or such other times as mutually agreed upon. A room, table or other facilities necessary for proper examination shall be made available upon the request of the APHIS representative.

[44 FR 25179, Apr. 27, 1979. Redesignated at 55 FR 41993, Oct. 17, 1990, as amended at 56 FR 13750, Apr. 4, 1991]

§ 11.24 Reporting by management.

(a) Within 5 days following the conclusion of any horse show, horse exhibition, or horse sale or auction, containing Tennessee Walking Horses or racking horses, the managements of such show, exhibition, sale or auction shall submit to the Regional Director[1] for the State in which the show, exhibition, sale or auction was held, the information required by § 11.22(a)(1) through (6) for each horse excused or disqualified by management or its representatives from being shown, exhibited, sold or auctioned, and the reasons for such action. If no horses are excused or disqualified, the management shall submit a report so stating.

(b) Within 5 days following the conclusion of any horse show, horse exhibition, or horse sale or auction which does not contain Tennessee Walking Horses or racking horses, the management of such show, exhibition, sale or auction shall inform the Regional Director for the State in which the show, exhibition, sale or auction was held, of any case where a horse was excused or

[1] See footnote 1 to § 11.1.

disqualified by management or its representatives from being shown, exhibited, sold or auctioned because it was found to be sore.

(Approved by the Office of Management and Budget under control number 0579–0056)

[44 FR 25179, Apr. 27, 1979, as amended at 48 FR 57471, Dec. 30, 1983; 55 FR 41994, Oct. 17, 1990; 56 FR 13750, Apr. 4, 1991; 63 FR 62927, Nov. 10, 1998]

§ 11.25 Minimum penalties to be assessed and enforced by HIOs that license DQPs.

(a) *Rulebook.* Each HIO that licenses DQPs in accordance with § 11.7 must include in its rulebook, and enforce, penalties for the violations listed in this section that equal or exceed the penalties listed in paragraph (c) of this section and must also enforce the requirement in paragraph (d) of this section.

(b) *Suspensions.* (1) For the violations listed in paragraph (c) of this section that require a suspension, any individuals who are responsible for showing the horse, exhibiting the horse, entering or allowing the entry of the horse in a show or exhibition, selling the horse, auctioning the horse, or offering the horse for sale or auction must be suspended. This may include, but may not be limited to, the manager, trainer, rider, custodian, or seller, as applicable. In addition, if the owner allowed any activity listed in this paragraph, the owner must be suspended as well.

(2) Any person who is responsible for the shipping, moving, delivering, or receiving of any horse that is found to be bilaterally sore or unilaterally sore as defined in paragraph (c) of this section, in violation of the scar rule in § 11.3, or in violation of the prohibition against the use of foreign substances in § 11.2(c), with reason to believe that such horse was to be shown, exhibited, entered for the purpose of being shown or exhibited, sold, auctioned, or offered for sale in any horse show, horse exhibition, or horse sale or auction, must be suspended; *Provided,* that this requirement does not apply if the horse was transported by a common or contract carrier or an employee thereof in the usual course of the carrier's business or the employee's employment, unless the carrier or employee had reason to believe that the horse was sore.

(3) A person who is suspended must not be permitted to show or exhibit any horse or judge or manage any horse show, horse exhibition, or horse sale or auction for the duration of the suspension.

(4) Any person with multiple suspensions must serve them consecutively, not concurrently.

(c) *Minimum penalties*—(1) *Bilateral sore.* A horse is found to be sore in both its forelimbs or hindlimbs. The horse must be dismissed from the remainder of the horse show, exhibition, sale, or auction. First offense: Suspension for 1 year. Second offense: Suspension for 2 years. Third offense and any subsequent offenses: Suspension for 4 years.

(2) *Unilateral sore.* A horse is found to be sore in one of its forelimbs or hindlimbs. The horse must be dismissed from the remainder of the horse show, exhibition, sale, or auction. First offense: Suspension for 60 days. Second offense: Suspension for 120 days. Third offense and any subsequent offenses: Suspension for 1 year.

(3) *Scar rule violation.* A horse is found to be in violation of the scar rule in § 11.3. The horse must be dismissed from the remainder of the horse show, exhibition, sale, or auction. First offense: Suspension for 2 weeks (14 days). Second offense: Suspension for 60 days. Third offense and any subsequent offenses: Suspension for 1 year.

(4) *Foreign substance violations.* Violations of the prohibition against the use of foreign substances in § 11.2(c).

(i) *Before or during the show, exhibition, sale, or auction.* The horse must be dismissed from the remainder of the horse show, exhibition, sale, or auction.

(ii) *After the show, exhibition, sale, or auction.* Suspension for 2 weeks (14 days). The horse must be dismissed from the remainder of the horse show, exhibition, sale, or auction.

(5) *Equipment violation.* Violations of the equipment-related prohibitions in § 11.2(b)(1) through (b)(10) and (b)(12) through (b)(17).

(i) *Before or during the show, exhibition, sale, or auction.* The horse must be dismissed from the remainder of the horse show, exhibition, sale, or auction.

(ii) *After the show, exhibition, sale, or auction.* Suspension for 2 weeks (14 days). The horse must be dismissed from the remainder of the horse show, exhibition, sale, or auction.

(6) *Shoeing violation.* Violation of the shoeing-related prohibitions in § 11.2(b)(18) and (b)(19). The horse must be dismissed from the remainder of the horse show, exhibition, sale, or auction.

(7) *Heel-toe ratio.* Violation of the heel-toe ratio requirement in § 11.2(b)(11). The horse must be dismissed from the remainder of the horse show, exhibition, sale, or auction.

(8) *Suspension violation.* A violation of any suspension penalty previously issued. Suspension for an additional 6 months (180 days) for each occurrence.

(d) *Unruly or fractious horse.* A horse that cannot be inspected in accordance with § 11.21. The horse must be dismissed from the individual class for which it was to be inspected.

(e) *Appeals.* The HIO must provide a process in its rulebook for alleged violators to appeal penalties. The process must be approved by the Department. For all appeals, the appeal must be granted and the case heard and decided by the HIO or the violator must begin serving the penalty within 60 days of the date of the violation. The HIO must submit to the Department all decisions on penalty appeals within 30 days of the completion of the appeal. When a penalty is overturned on appeal, the HIO must also submit evidence composing the record of the HIO's decision on the appeal.

(f) *Departmental prosecution.* The Department retains the authority to initiate enforcement proceedings with respect to any violation of the Act, including violations for which penalties are assessed in accordance with this section, and to impose the penalties authorized by the Act if the Department determines that such actions are necessary to fulfill the purpose of the Act and this part. In addition, the Department reserves the right to inform the Attorney General of any violation of the Act or of this part, including violations for which penalties are assessed in accordance with this section.

[77 FR 33618, June 7, 2012, as amended at 79 FR 3071, Jan. 17, 2014]

§ 11.40 Prohibitions and requirements concerning persons involved in transportation of certain horses.

(a) Each person who ships, transports, or otherwise moves, or delivers or receives for movement, any horse with reason to believe such horse may be shown, exhibited, sold or auctioned at any horse show, horse exhibition, or horse sale or auction, shall allow and assist in the inspection of such horse at any such show, exhibition, sale, or auction to determine compliance with the Act as provided in § 11.4 of the regulations and shall furnish to any APHIS representatives upon his request the following information:

(1) Name and address (including street address, post office box, and ZIP code) of the horse owner and of the shipper, if different from the owner or trainer.

(2) Name and address (including street address, post office box, and ZIP code) of the horse trainer.

(3) Name and address (including street address, post office box, and ZIP code) of the carrier transporting the horse, and of the driver of the means of conveyance used.

(4) Origin of the shipment and date thereof, and,

(5) Destination of shipment.

(b) [Reserved]

(Approved by the Office of Management and Budget under control number 0579–0056)

[44 FR 25179, Apr. 27, 1979, as amended at 48 FR 57471, Dec. 30, 1983; 56 FR 13750, Apr. 4, 1991]

§ 11.41 Reporting required of horse industry organizations or associations.

Each horse industry organization or association which sponsors, or which sanctions any horse show, horse exhibition, or horse sale or auction, shall furnish the Department[6] by March 1 of each year with all such organization or association rulebooks, and disciplinary

[6] See footnote 6 to § 11.7.

procedures for the previous year pertaining to violations of the Horse Protection Act or regulations, applicable to such horse show, horse exhibition, or horse sale or auction. Rulebooks and information relating to disciplinary procedures for violations of the Horse Protection Act or regulations should be readily available to all exhibitors, trainers, and owners of horses at such show, exhibition, sale, or auction. Each horse industry organization or association shall furnish the Department[6] with a quarterly report of all disciplinary actions taken against the management or any horse show, horse exhibition, horse sale, or horse auction, any exhibitor, or any licensed DQP, for violation of the Horse Protection Act or regulations, and the results thereof.

(Approved by the Office of Management and Budget under control number 0579–0056)

[44 FR 25179, Apr. 27, 1979, as amended at 48 FR 57471, Dec. 30, 1983]

PART 12—RULES OF PRACTICE GOVERNING PROCEEDINGS UNDER THE HORSE PROTECTION ACT

AUTHORITY: 15 U.S.C. 1825 and 1828; 7 CFR 2.22, 2.80, and 371.7.

Subpart A—General

§ 12.1 Scope and applicability of rules of practice.

The Uniform Rules of Practice for the Department of Agriculture promulgated in subpart H of part 1, subtitle A, title 7, Code of Federal Regulations, are the Rules of Practice applicable to adjudicatory, administrative proceedings under section 6(a) of the Horse Protection Act of 1970 (15 U.S.C. 1825(a)) and sections 6 (b) and (c) of the Horse Protection Act (15 U.S.C. 1825 (b) and (c)). In addition, the Supplemental Rules of Practice set forth in subpart B of this part shall be applicable to such proceedings.

[42 FR 10959, Feb. 25, 1977, as amended at 68 FR 6342, Feb. 7, 2003]

Subpart B—Supplemental Rules of Practice

§ 12.10 Stipulations.

(a) At any time prior to the issuance of a complaint seeking a civil penalty under the Act, the Administrator, in his discretion, may enter into a stipulation with any person in which:

(1) The Administration gives notice of an apparent violation of the Act or the regulations issued thereunder by such person and affords such person an opportunity for a hearing regarding the matter as provided by the Act;

(2) Such person expressly waives hearing and agrees to a specified order including an agreement to pay a specified civil penalty within a designated time; and

(3) The Administrator agrees to accept the specified order including a civil penalty in settlement of the particular matter involved if it is paid within the designated time.

(b) If the specified penalty is not paid within the time designated in such a stipulation, the amount of the stipulated penalty shall not be relevant in any respect to the penalty which may be assessed after issuance of a complaint.

[42 FR 10960, Feb. 25, 1977, as amended at 68 FR 6342, Feb. 7, 2003]

SUBCHAPTER B—COOPERATIVE CONTROL AND ERADICATION OF LIVESTOCK OR POULTRY DISEASES

PART 49—RULES OF PRACTICE GOVERNING PROCEEDINGS UNDER CERTAIN ACTS

AUTHORITY: 7 U.S.C. 8301–8317; 7 CFR 2.22, 2.80, and 371.4.

SOURCE: 48 FR 30094, June 30, 1983, unless otherwise noted.

Subpart A—General

§ 49.1 Scope and applicability of rules of practice.

The Uniform Rules of Practice for the Department of Agriculture promulgated in subpart H of part 1, subtitle A, title 7, Code of Federal Regulations, are the Rules of Practice applicable to adjudicatory, administrative proceedings under the following statutory provisions:

Act of May 29, 1884, commonly known as the Animal Industry Act, section 7, as amended (21 U.S.C. 117),

Act of February 2, 1903, commonly known as the Cattle Contagious Diseases Act of 1903, section 3, as amended (21 U.S.C. 122),

Act of March 3, 1905, Section 6, as amended (21 U.S.C. 127),

Act of July 2, 1962, section 6(a), as amended (21 U.S.C. 134e).

The Animal Health Protection Act (7 U.S.C. 8301 *et seq.*)

In addition, the Supplemental Rules of Practice set forth in subpart B of this part shall be applicable to such proceedings.

[48 FR 30094, June 30, 1983, as amended at 68 FR 6342, Feb. 7, 2003]

Subpart B—Supplemental Rules of Practice

§ 49.10 Stipulations.

(a) At any time prior to the issuance of a complaint seeking a civil penalty under any of the Acts listed in § 49.1, the Administrator, in his discretion, may enter into a stipulation with any person in which:

(1) The Administrator or the Administrator's delegate gives notice of an apparent violation of the applicable Act, or the regulations issued thereunder, by such person and affords such person an opportunity for a hearing regarding the matter as provided by such Act;

(2) Such person expressly waives hearing and agrees to pay a specified penalty within a designated time; and

(3) The Administrator agrees to accept the penalty in settlement of the particular matter involved if the penalty is paid within the designated time.

(b) If the penalty is not paid within the time designated in such a stipulation, the amount of the stipulated penalty shall not be relevant in any respect to the penalty which may be assessed after issuance of a complaint.

PART 50—ANIMALS DESTROYED BECAUSE OF TUBERCULOSIS

Subpart B—Dairy Cattle and Facilities in the El Paso, Texas, Region

AUTHORITY: 7 U.S.C. 8301–8317; 7 CFR 2.22, 2.80, and 371.4.

SOURCE: 40 FR 27009, June 26, 1975, unless otherwise noted.

§50.1 Definitions.

For the purposes of this part, the following terms mean:

Accredited veterinarian. A veterinarian approved by the Administrator in accordance with the provisions of part 161 of this title to perform functions specified in parts 1, 2, 3, and 11 of subchapter A, and subchapters B, C, and D of this chapter, and to perform functions required by cooperative State-Federal disease control and eradication programs.

Administrator. The Administrator, Animal and Plant Health Inspection Service, or any person authorized to act for the Administrator.

Animal and Plant Health Inspection Service. The Animal and Plant Health Inspection Service of the United States Department of Agriculture (APHIS).

APHIS representative. A veterinarian or other person employed by APHIS in animal health activities, who is authorized to perform the function involved.

Approved herd plan. A herd management and testing plan based on the disease history and movement patterns of an individual herd, designed by the herd owner and a State representative or APHIS representative to determine the disease status of livestock in the herd and to eradicate tuberculosis within the herd. The plan must be jointly approved by the State animal health official and the Veterinarian in Charge.

Captive cervid. All species of deer, elk, moose, and all other members of the family Cervidae raised or maintained in captivity for the production of meat and other agricultural products, for sport, or for exhibition, including time such animals are moved interstate; or any wild cervid that is moved interstate, during the period of time from capture until release into the wild. A captive cervid that escapes will continue to be considered a captive cervid as long as it bears an official eartag or other identification approved by the Administrator as unique and traceable with which to trace the animal back to its herd of origin.

Department. The United States Department of Agriculture.

Designated tuberculosis epidemiologist (DTE). A State or Federal epidemiologist designated by the Administrator to make decisions concerning the use and interpretation of diagnostic tests for tuberculosis and the management of tuberculosis affected herds. A DTE has the responsibility to determine the scope of epidemiologic investigations, determine the status of animals and herds, assist in the development of individual herd plans, and coordinate disease surveillance and eradication programs within the geographic area of the DTE's responsibility.

Destroyed. Condemned under State authority and destroyed by slaughter or by death otherwise.

Heifer. A female dairy cow that has not given birth.

Herd. Except for livestock assembled at feedlots, any group of livestock maintained for at least 4 months on common ground for any purpose, or two or more groups of livestock under common ownership or supervision, geographically separated but that have an interchange or movement of livestock without regard to health status, as determined by the Administrator.

Herd depopulation. Removal by slaughter or other means of destruction of all cattle, bison, and captive cervids in a herd, as well as any other exposed livestock in the herd, prior to restocking with new livestock.

Livestock. Cattle, bison, captive cervids, swine, dairy goats, and other hoofed animals (such as llamas, alpacas, and antelope) raised or maintained in captivity for the production of meat and other products, for sport, or for exhibition.

Milking cow. A female dairy cow that has given birth and is being used for milk production.

Mortgage. Any mortgage, lien or other security or interest that is recorded under State law or identified in the indemnity claim form filed under §50.12 and held by any person other than the one claiming indemnity.

Net salvage. The amount received for animals destroyed because of tuberculosis, after deducting freight, trucking, yardage, commission, slaughtering charges, and similar costs to the owner.

Owner. Any person who has a legal or rightful title to livestock whether or not they are subject to a mortgage.

Permit. A permit for movement of livestock directly to slaughter, listing the disease status and identification of the animal, where consigned, cleaning and disinfection requirements, and proof of slaughter certification.

Person. Any individual, corporation, company, association, firm, partnership, society, or joint stock company, or any organized group of any of the foregoing.

Quarantined feedlot. A confined area under the direct supervision and control of a State livestock official who shall establish procedures for the accounting of all livestock entering or leaving the area. The quarantined feedlot shall be maintained for finish feeding of livestock in drylot with no provision for pasturing and grazing. All livestock leaving such feedlot must only move directly to slaughter in accordance with established procedures for handling quarantined livestock.

Reactor cattle, bison, and captive cervids. Cattle, bison, and captive cervids are classified as reactors for tuberculosis in accordance with the "Uniform Methods and Rules Bovine Tuberculosis Eradication," based on a positive response to an official tuberculin test.

Registered livestock. Livestock for which individual records of ancestry are maintained, and for which individual registration certificates are issued and recorded by a recognized breed association whose purpose is the improvement of the breed.

State. Any State, territory, the District of Columbia, or Puerto Rico.

State animal health official. The individual employed by a State who is responsible for livestock and poultry disease control and eradication programs in that State.

State representative. A veterinarian or other person who is employed in livestock sanitary work of a State or a political subdivision of a State and who is authorized by the State or political subdivision to perform the function involved under a memorandum of understanding with the Department.

Tuberculosis. The contagious, infectious, and communicable disease caused by *Mycobacterium bovis.*

Veterinarian in Charge. The veterinary official of APHIS who is assigned by the Administrator to supervise and perform official animal health work of APHIS in the State concerned.

[40 FR 27009, June 26, 1975, as amended at 45 FR 32287, May 16, 1980; 51 FR 33735, Sept. 23, 1986; 52 FR 1317, Jan. 13, 1987; 52 FR 39614, Oct. 23, 1987; 56 FR 36998, Aug. 2, 1991; 58 FR 34698, June 29, 1993; 60 FR 37808, July 24, 1995; 63 FR 34263, June 24, 1998; 63 FR 72122, Dec. 31, 1998; 67 FR 7590, Feb. 20, 2002; 67 FR 48750, July 26, 2002]

Subpart A—General Indemnity

§50.2 Applicability of this subpart; cooperation with States.

(a) The provisions of this subpart apply to all payments made by the Department for the destruction of animals because of tuberculosis, except as specifically provided in subpart B of this part.

(b) The Administrator cooperates with the proper State authorities in the eradication of tuberculosis and pays Federal indemnities for the destruction of cattle, bison, captive cervids, or swine affected with or exposed to tuberculosis.

[67 FR 48751, July 26, 2002]

§50.3 Payment to owners for animals destroyed.

(a) The Administrator is authorized to agree on the part of the Department to pay indemnity to owners of the following animals:

(1) Cattle, bison, or captive cervids destroyed because the animals are infected with or exposed to tuberculosis;

(2) Cattle, bison, or captive cervids that have been classified as suspect for tuberculosis, except that the payment of indemnity for the destruction of suspect cattle, bison, and captive cervids will be withheld until the tuberculosis status of the suspect animal has been determined and, if the cattle, bison, or captive cervid is found to be infected with tuberculosis, until all cattle, bison, and captive cervids 12 months of age or older in the claimant's herd have been tested for tuberculosis under APHIS or State supervision; and

(3) Other livestock destroyed because they are classified as exposed to tuberculosis by the designated tuberculosis epidemiologist by reason of an association with an affected herd of cattle, bison, or captive cervids.

(b) In each case, the joint State-Federal indemnity paid, together with the amount for net salvage the owner receives, may not exceed the appraised value of the animal, as determined in accordance with § 50.9. Additionally, the Department will in no case pay more than $3,000 for an animal that is destroyed.

[67 FR 7591, Feb. 20, 2002]

§ 50.4 Classification of cattle, bison, captive cervids, and other livestock as infected, exposed, or suspect.

(a) Cattle, bison, and captive cervids are classified as infected with tuberculosis on the basis of an intradermal tuberculin test applied by a Federal, State, or an accredited veterinarian or by other diagnostic procedure approved in advance by the Administrator.

(b) Cattle, bison, and captive cervids are classified as exposed to tuberculosis when such cattle, bison, and captive cervids (1) are part of a known infected herd, or (2) are found to have moved from an infected herd before the time infection was disclosed in such herd and after the time such herd had apparently become infected, or (3) are found to have been exposed by virtue of nursing a reactor dam: *Provided*, That cattle, bison, and captive cervids classified as exposed to tuberculosis shall be removed direct to slaughter.

(c) Cattle and bison are classified as suspects for tuberculosis based on a positive response to an official tuberculin test, in accordance with the "Uniform Methods and Rules—Bovine Tuberculosis Eradication" (incorporated into the regulations by reference in part 77). Captive cervids are classified as suspects for tuberculosis in the same manner as cattle and bison.

(d) The designated tuberculosis epidemiologist will determine whether livestock other than cattle, bison, or captive cervids are classified as exposed to tuberculosis by reason of association with an affected herd of cattle, bison, or captive cervids.

[40 FR 27009, June 26, 1975, as amended at 52 FR 39614, Oct. 23, 1987; 56 FR 36998, Aug. 2, 1991; 60 FR 37809, July 24, 1995; 63 FR 34264, June 24, 1998; 67 FR 7591, Feb. 20, 2002]

§ 50.5 Record of tests.

When any cattle, bison, or captive cervid in a herd is classified by an APHIS or State representative or accredited veterinarian as a reactor to a test for tuberculosis, a complete test record shall be made for such herd, including the reactor tag number of each reacting animal and the registration name and number of each reacting registered animal. VS Form 6–22 or an equivalent State form shall be used for the record of any herd having any reactor to a tuberculin test. A copy of the applicable test record shall be given to the owner of any such herd, and one copy of each such record shall be furnished to the appropriate State veterinarian's office.

[40 FR 27009, June 26, 1975, as amended at 52 FR 39614, Oct. 23, 1987; 56 FR 36998, Aug. 2, 1991; 60 FR 37809, July 24, 1995; 63 FR 34264, June 24, 1998]

§ 50.6 Identification of animals to be destroyed because of tuberculosis.

(a) Livestock to be destroyed because of tuberculosis must be identified as follows:

(1) Livestock classified as reactors for tuberculosis must be identified within 15 days after being classified as reactors, except that the veterinarian in charge may extend the time limit for identification to 30 days when he or

she receives a request for such an extension prior to the expiration date of the original 15-day period allowed and circumstances beyond the control of the owner warrant such an extension, and the Administrator may extend the time limit for identification beyond 30 days upon request in specific cases when circumstances beyond the control of the owner warrant such an extension.

(2) Livestock other than reactors for tuberculosis that are to be destroyed because of tuberculosis must be identified prior to movement from the premises of origin to the place of destruction.

(b) *Reactor cattle, bison, and captive cervids.* Reactor cattle, bison, and captive cervids must be identified by branding the letter "T," at least 5 by 5 centimeters (2 by 2 inches) in size, high on the left hip near the tailhead and by attaching to the left ear an approved metal eartag bearing a serial number and the inscription "U.S. Reactor," or a similar State reactor tag. Reactor cattle, bison, and captive cervids may be moved interstate to slaughter without branding if they are permanently identified by the letters "TB" tattooed legibly in the left ear, they are sprayed on the left ear with yellow paint, and they are either accompanied by an APHIS or State representative or moved directly to slaughter in vehicles closed with official seals. The official seals must be applied and removed by an APHIS representative, State representative, accredited veterinarian, or an individual authorized for this purpose by an APHIS representative.

(c) *Exposed cattle, bison, and captive cervids.* Exposed cattle, bison, and captive cervids must be identified by branding the letter "S," at least 5 by 5 centimeters (2 by 2 inches) in size, high on the left hip near the tailhead and by attaching to either ear an approved metal eartag bearing a serial number. Exposed cattle, bison, and captive cervids may be moved interstate to slaughter without branding if they are either accompanied by an APHIS or State representative or moved directly to slaughter in vehicles closed with official seals. The official seals must be applied and removed by an APHIS representative, State representative, accredited veterinarian, or an individual authorized for this purpose by an APHIS representative.

(d) *Other exposed livestock.* Livestock other than cattle, bison, or captive cervids that are destroyed under the provisions of § 50.3 must be identified by tagging with a serially numbered metal eartag attached to either ear. All such animals to be destroyed must be transported to the place of destruction in vehicles closed with seals provided by APHIS or shall be accompanied to the place of destruction by an APHIS or State representative: *Provided, however,* that animals destroyed and disposed of under the direct supervision of an APHIS or State representative on the premises where they were exposed do not require individual identification.

[67 FR 7591, Feb. 20, 2002]

§ 50.7 Destruction of animals.

(a) *Slaughter or disposal.* Livestock to be destroyed because of tuberculosis must be shipped direct to slaughter under permit to a Federal or State inspected slaughtering establishment or be disposed of by rendering, burial, or incinerating in an approved manner under supervision of an APHIS or State employee.

(b) *Time limit for destruction of animals.* Livestock for which Federal indemnity may be paid because of tuberculosis must be destroyed and carcass disposal completed within 15 days after the date of appraisal, except that the appropriate Veterinarian in Charge, for reasons satisfactory to him, may extend the time limit for slaughter to 30 days when request for such extension is received by him prior to the expiration of the original 15-day period allowed, and the Administrator may extend the time limit for slaughter beyond 30 days, upon request in specific cases and for reasons satisfactory to him.

(Approved by the Office of Management and Budget under control number 0579–0051)

[40 FR 27009, June 26, 1975, as amended at 45 FR 32287, May 16, 1980; 52 FR 39614, Oct. 23, 1987; 56 FR 36998, Aug. 2, 1991; 60 FR 37809, July 24, 1995; 63 FR 34264, June 24, 1998; 67 FR 7591, Feb. 20, 2002]

§ 50.8 Payment of expenses for transporting and disposing of infected, exposed, and suspect animals.

The Department may pay, when approved in advance in writing by the Veterinarian in Charge, one half the expenses of transporting infected, exposed, or suspect livestock to slaughter or to the point where disposal will take place, and one half the expenses of destroying, burying, incinerating, rendering, or otherwise disposing of infected, exposed, or suspect livestock; *Provided that,* the Department may pay more than one-half of the expenses when the Administrator determines that doing so will contribute to the tuberculosis eradication program. For reimbursement to be made, the owner of the animals must present the Veterinarian in Charge with a copy of either a receipt for expenses paid or a bill for services rendered. Any bill for services rendered by the owner must not be greater than the normal fee for similar services provided by a commercial hauler or renderer.

[62 FR 49592, Sept. 23, 1997, as amended at 63 FR 34264, June 24, 1998; 67 FR 7591, Feb. 20, 2002]

§ 50.9 Appraisals.

(a) Livestock to be destroyed because of tuberculosis under § 50.3 must be appraised within 15 days after being classified as infected with tuberculosis, except that the veterinarian in charge may extend the time limit for appraisal to 30 days when he or she receives a request for such an extension before the end of the expiration date of the original 15-day period allowed and circumstances beyond the control of the owner warrant such an extension, and the Administrator may extend the time limit for appraisal beyond 30 days upon request in specific cases when circumstances beyond the control of the owner warrant such an extension.

(b) Animals for which indemnity is to be paid under this part must be appraised at their fair market value by an appraiser selected by APHIS. APHIS may decline to accept any appraisal that appears to it to be unreasonable or out of proportion to the value of like animals of a like quality. Should the appraisal made by the appraiser selected by APHIS be deemed inadequate by the owner of the animals, the owner will have 15 days from the receipt of the appraisal to submit to the Administrator a request for a review of the appraisal, along with the reasons why the animals should be appraised at a higher value. The decision by the Administrator regarding the value of the animals is final.

(c) When livestock to be destroyed because of tuberculosis are appraised, due consideration will be given to their breeding value as well as to their dairy or meat value. Livestock presented for payment as registered must be accompanied by their registration papers. If the registration papers are temporarily not available, or if the livestock are less than 3 years old and unregistered, the veterinarian in charge may grant a reasonable time for the presentation of their registration papers.

[67 FR 7591, Feb. 20, 2002]

§ 50.10 Report of appraisals.

Appraisals of livestock made in accordance with § 50.9 shall be recorded on forms furnished by APHIS. The appraisal form shall be signed by the appraiser and by the owner certifying his acceptance of the appraisal. The "date of appraisal" shall be the date that the owner signs the appraisal form. The original of the appraisal form and as many copies thereof as may be required for APHIS, the State, and the owner of the animals shall be sent to the appropriate Veterinarian in Charge.

[40 FR 27009, June 26, 1975, as amended at 52 FR 39614, Oct. 23, 1987; 56 FR 36998, Aug. 2, 1991; 60 FR 37809, July 24, 1995; 63 FR 34264, June 24, 1998; 67 FR 7592, Feb. 20, 2002]

§ 50.11 Report of salvage proceeds.

A report of the salvage derived from the sale of each animal on which a claim for indemnity may be made under the provisions of § 50.3 shall be made on a salvage form acceptable to APHIS which shall be signed by the purchaser or his agent or by the selling agent handling the animals. If the livestock are sold by the pound, the salvage form shall show the weight, price per pound, gross receipts, expenses if any, and net proceeds. If the livestock are not sold on a per pound basis, the net purchase price of each animal must be stated on the salvage form and an explanation showing how the amount was arrived at must be submitted. In the event the animals are not disposed of through regular slaughterers or through selling agents, the owner shall furnish, in lieu of the salvage form, an affidavit showing the amount of salvage obtained by him and shall certify that such amount is all that he has received or will receive as salvage for said animals. In an emergency, a certificate executed by the appropriate Veterinarian in Charge will be acceptable in lieu of the owner's affidavit. The salvage shall be considered to be the net amount received for an animal after deducting freight, truckage, yardage, commission, slaughtering charges, and similar costs. The original of the salvage form or the affidavit of the owner or certificate of the appropriate Veterinarian in Charge, furnished in lieu thereof, shall be furnished to the Veterinarian in charge if it is not already in his possession. Additional copies may be furnished to the State officials, if required. Destruction of livestock by burial, incineration or other disposal of carcasses shall be supervised by an APHIS or State representative who shall prepare and transmit to the Veterinarian in Charge a report identifying the animals and showing the disposition thereof.

(Approved by the Office of Management and Budget under control number 0579–0001)

[40 FR 27009, June 26, 1975, as amended at 48 FR FR 57471, Dec. 30, 1983; 52 FR 39614, Oct. 23, 1987; 56 FR 36998, Aug. 2, 1991; 60 FR 37809, July 24, 1995; 63 FR 34264, June 24, 1998; 67 FR 7592, Feb. 20, 2002]

§ 50.12 Claims for indemnity.

Claims for Federal indemnity for livestock destroyed because of tuberculosis shall be presented on indemnity claim forms furnished by APHIS on which the owner of the animals covered thereby shall certify that the animals are or are not, subject to any mortgage as defined in this Part. If the owner states there is a mortgage, the APHIS indemnity claim form shall be signed by the owner and by each person holding a mortgage on the animals consenting to the payment of any indemnity allowed to the person specified thereon. Payment will be made only if the APHIS indemnity claim form has been approved by a proper State official and if payment of the claim has been recommended by the appropriate Veterinarian in Charge or an official designated by him. On claims for indemnity made under the provisions of § 50.3, the Veterinarian in Charge or official designated by him shall record on the APHIS indemnity claim form the amount of Federal and State indemnity payments that appear to be due to the owner of the animals. The owner of the animals shall be furnished a copy of the APHIS indemnity claim form. The Veterinarian in Charge or official designated by him shall then forward the APHIS indemnity claim form to the appropriate official for further action on the claim. No charges for holding the livestock on the farm pending slaughter or for trucking by the owner shall be so deducted or otherwise paid by the Department.

[40 FR 27009, June 26, 1975, as amended at 52 FR 39614, Oct. 23, 1987; 56 FR 36998, Aug. 2, 1991; 60 FR 37809, July 24, 1995; 63 FR 34264, June 24, 1998; 67 FR 7592, Feb. 20, 2002]

§ 50.13 Disinfection of premises, conveyances, and materials.

All premises, including all structures, holding facilities, conveyances, or materials which are determined by the appropriate Veterinarian in Charge to constitute a health hazard to humans or animals because of tuberculosis shall be properly cleaned and disinfected, in accordance with procedures approved by the Department, within 15 days after the removal of tuberculosis infected or exposed livestock except that the Veterinarian in Charge, for reasons satisfactory to him, may extend the time limit for disinfection to 30 days when request for such extension is received by him prior to the expiration date of the original 15-day period allowed.

[40 FR 27009, June 26, 1975, as amended at 52 FR 39614, Oct. 23, 1987; 60 FR 37809, July 24, 1995; 67 FR 7592, Feb. 20, 2002]

§ 50.14 Claims not allowed.

Claims for compensation for livestock destroyed because of tuberculosis will not be allowed in any of the following cases:

(a) The claimant has failed to comply with any of the requirements of this part:

(b) All cattle, bison, and captive cervids 12 months of age or over in the claimant's herd have not been tested for tuberculosis under APHIS or State supervision: *Provided, however,* that cattle, bison, and captive cervids destroyed because of tuberculosis are exempt from this testing requirement if the cattle, bison, and captive cervids are subjected to a postmortem examination for tuberculosis by a Federal or State veterinarian.

(c) There is substantial evidence that the owner of the animals or the agent of the owner has in any way been responsible for any attempt to obtain indemnity funds for the animals unlawfully or improperly.

(d) At the time the cattle, bison, or captive cervids in the claimant's herd were tested for tuberculosis, the cattle, bison, captive cervids, or other livestock in the herd belonged to or were on the premises of any person to whom they had been sold, shipped, or delivered for slaughter unless or until all of the cattle, bison, captive cervids, and other livestock remaining on the premises or in the herd from which the tested cattle, bison, or captive cervids originated are tested or otherwise examined for tuberculosis in a manner satisfactory to the Administrator or his or her designated representative.

(e) If the cattle, bison, or captive cervids were added to a herd while the herd was quarantined for tuberculosis, unless an approved herd plan was in effect at the time the claim was filed. As part of the approved herd plan, cattle, bison, or captive cervids added to a herd quarantined for tuberculosis must:

(1) Be from an accredited herd, as defined in §77.1 of this chapter; or

(2)(i) Be from a herd that tested negative to an official tuberculin test, as defined in §77.1 of this chapter, during the 60 days before the cattle, bison, or captive cervids were added to the claimant's herd; and

(ii) Have been found negative to an official tuberculin test, as defined in §77.1 of this chapter, during the 60 days before the cattle, bison, or captive cervids were added to the claimant's herd.

(f) For exposed cattle, bison, or captive cervids destroyed during herd depopulation, if a designated tuberculosis epidemiologist has determined that other livestock in the herd have been exposed to tuberculosis by reason of association with tuberculous livestock, and those other livestock determined to have been exposed to tuberculosis have not been destroyed.

(g) For livestock other than cattle, bison, and captive cervids that are destroyed because of association with herds of affected cattle, bison, or captive cervids:

(1) If the livestock did not reside among the herd for a period of 4 months or more;

(2) If the livestock have not received a postmortem examination for tuberculosis; or

(3) If the livestock were added to a herd that was under quarantine for tuberculosis at the time the livestock were added to the herd, unless an approved herd plan was in effect at that time.

[67 FR 7592, Feb. 20, 2002]

§§50.15–50.16 [Reserved]

Subpart B—Dairy Cattle and Facilities in the El Paso, Texas, Region

SOURCE: 67 FR 48751, July 26, 2002, unless otherwise noted.

§50.17 Payment.

(a) *Eligibility for payment.* Owners of dairy operations, including owners of dairy cattle and other property used in connection with a dairy business or fluid milk processing plant, are eligible to receive payment from the Department under this subpart in connection with a buffer zone depopulation program due to tuberculosis, provided the owners meet all applicable requirements of this subpart and the dairy cattle herd is within the area circumscribed by the following boundaries: Beginning at the point where the Hudspeth-El Paso County line intersects U.S. Highway 62; then west along U.S. Highway 62 to the El Paso Toll

Bridge; then southeast along the Rio Grande River to the Fort Hancock-El Porvenir Bridge; then northeast along spur 148 to Interstate 10; then northwest along Interstate 10 to the Hudspeth-El Paso County line; then north along the Hudspeth-El Paso County line to the point of beginning.

(b) To be eligible for payment, each of the owners of dairy cattle and other property within the area described in paragraph (a) of this section must sign and adhere to an agreement with APHIS to do the following:

(1) Cease all dairy cattle operations within the described area and dispose of all sexually intact cattle on the dairy operation premises no later than 3 years after all eligible owners have signed their respective agreements;

(2) Conduct no dairy farming or other dairy activity, including the rearing of breeding cattle, but not including the grazing or feeding of steers and spayed heifers intended for terminal market, within the area described in paragraph (a) of this section until the described area and the adjoining area of Mexico have been declared free of bovine tuberculosis, as determined epidemiologically by APHIS, but in any event for a period of not less than 20 years after all eligible owners have signed their respective agreements.

(3) Allow a covenant to be placed on their properties where dairy operations have been conducted that will prevent the establishment of any breeding cattle operations (not including the grazing or feeding of steers and spayed heifers intended for terminal market) on the premises until the described area and the adjoining area of Mexico have been declared free of bovine tuberculosis, as determined epidemiologically by APHIS, but in any event for a period of not less than 20 years after all eligible owners have signed their respective agreements.

(4) Maintain responsibility for all cattle on the premises used in the dairy operation until those animals are removed from the premises;

(5) Make all arrangements for the removal of sexually intact cattle from the premises;

(6) Notify APHIS officials of the intended removal of all sexually intact cattle from the premises and provide APHIS officials with the opportunity to monitor and evaluate the removal operations; and

(7) Such other terms, provisions, and conditions as agreed by each owner and APHIS.

(c) *Amount of payment for cattle and other property.* Upon approval of a claim submitted in accordance with § 50.20 of this subpart, owners eligible for payments under paragraph (a) of this section will receive payments for cattle and other property, the amount of which is determined by the following rates:

(1) For milking cows, an amount not to exceed $2,922 per animal; and

(2) For heifers, an amount not to exceed $834 per animal.

(d) Any dairy cattle added to a premises after the date an owner has signed the agreement required under paragraph (b) of this section will not be included in the rate calculation in paragraph (c) of this section and must be disposed of within 3 years after all eligible owners have signed their respective agreements.

(e) *Amount of payment for certain other property.* In addition to the amounts paid under paragraph (c) of this section, amounts will be paid as follows:

(1) For expenses in relocating equipment of a reverse osmosis plant in El Paso County, TX, an amount equal to the costs of relocating the plant's equipment, not to exceed $675,000.

(2) In conjunction with the permanent closure of a fluid milk processing plant in El Paso County, TX, an amount not to exceed $950,000, with payment to be made in the same manner and at the same times, on a pro rata basis, as payments are made to such owners for their dairy cattle and other property.

(Approved by the Office of Management and Budget under control number 0579–0193)

[67 FR 48751, July 26, 2002, as amended at 68 FR 10361, Apr. 4, 2003]

§ 50.18 Identification and disposal of cattle.

(a) All dairy cattle disposed of under this subpart must travel from the premises of origin to their final destination with an approved metal eartag, supplied by APHIS or the State representative, bearing a serial number and attached to each animal's left ear.

(b) Dairy cattle disposed of under this subpart must be shipped under permit either:

(1) Directly to slaughter at a Federal or State inspected slaughtering establishment; or

(2) Under permit directly to a livestock market and, under the supervision of an APHIS representative or State representative, through a livestock market pen that is dedicated to and marked exclusively for use for animals moved to slaughter, and then directly to slaughter at a Federal or State inspected slaughtering establishment.

(Approved by the Office of Management and Budget under control number 0579–0193)

§ 50.19 Report of salvage proceeds.

A report of the salvage derived from the sale of each animal for which a claim for payment is made under this subpart must be made on a salvage form acceptable to APHIS that must be signed by the purchaser or by the selling agent handling the animals. If the cattle are sold by the pound, the salvage form must show the weight, price per pound, gross receipts, expenses if any, and net proceeds. If the cattle are not sold on a per-pound basis, the net purchase price of each animal must be stated on the salvage form and an explanation showing how the amount was arrived at must be submitted. In the event the animals are not disposed of through regular slaughterers or through selling agents, the owner must furnish, in lieu of the salvage form, an affidavit showing the amount of salvage obtained by him or her and must certify that such amount is all he or she has received or will receive as salvage for the animals. The original of the salvage form or the affidavit of the owner must be furnished to the veterinarian in charge within 3 months of destruction of the animals, if such document is not already in his or her possession. Disposal of cattle by burial, incineration, or other means must be supervised by an APHIS or State representative, who will prepare and transmit to the veterinarian in charge a report identifying the animals and showing their disposition, or be documented by an affidavit of the owner that identifies the animals and describes their disposition. The owner must provide a copy of the affidavit to the veterinarian in charge within 3 months of destruction of the animals. The salvage form, disposal certificate, or affidavit will be for information purposes only and will have no effect on the amount of any payment due.

(Approved by the Office of Management and Budget under control number 0579–0193)

§ 50.20 Claims for payment.

Claims for payment, other than for reimbursement of relocation expenses of the reverse osmosis dairy plant, must be presented on payment claim forms furnished by APHIS.[3] On the claim form, the owner must certify that the animals or other property are, or are not, subject to any mortgage. If the owner states that there is a mortgage, the claim form must be signed by the owner and by each person holding a mortgage on the cattle or other property, who must agree that the person specified on the claim form may receive any payment due. The APHIS veterinarian in charge or the official designated by him or her will record on the claim form the amount of payment that appears to be due to the owner, and the owner will be furnished a copy of the APHIS payment claim form. The veterinarian in charge or official designated by him or her will then forward the APHIS payment claim form to the appropriate APHIS official for further action on the claim. The Department will not pay any costs arising from the holding of the cattle pending slaughter, or for trucking and other transportation costs, yardage, commission, slaughtering charges, or for any other costs related to having the cattle slaughtered. The owner of the reverse osmosis plant must submit copies of

---

[1] [2] [Reserved]

[3] Claim forms may obtained from the veterinarian in charge. The location of the veterinarian in charge may be obtained by writing to National Animal Health Program VS, APHIS, 4700 River Road Unit 43, Riverdale, MD 20737, or by referring to the local telephone book.

the relevant documentation for relocation of equipment to the veterinarian in charge.

(Approved by the Office of Management and Budget under control number 0579–0193)

§ 50.21 Schedule of payments.

(a) The Department will make payment, other than for reimbursement of relocation expenses of the equipment of the reverse osmosis plant, at 90-day intervals. The first payment will be made no earlier than 30 days after all owners eligible for payment have signed their agreements required under § 50.17(b). The Department will determine the amount to be paid to each owner in each payment by multiplying the total agreement amount for that owner by a fraction that is arrived at by dividing the initial census number of dairy cattle for the respective owner into the number of dairy cattle that have been removed from the owner's herd during that payment period. From this amount, 10 percent will be withheld until all animals in the herd have been disposed of and the requirements of this subpart have been met. The payments to other property owners will be determined by multiplying the total agreement amount for that other property times the same ratio as for the herd related to that other property, minus 10 percent. The Department will make payment for reimbursement of relocation expenses of the reverse osmosis plant within 30 days after the relocation of the plant is completed and the owner of the plant has submitted to APHIS all documentation of the costs of the relocation.

(b) The Department will not make final payments until the premises used for dairy operations have been without sexually intact cattle for at least 30 days and until APHIS has inspected the premises and has found them to be free of manure, except for non-solid areas such as lagoons, and free of all feedstuffs that are not in barns, containers or feeders.

§ 50.22 Claims not allowed.

The Department will not allow claims for payment if the claimant has failed to comply with any of the requirements of this subpart, or there is substantial evidence, as determined by the Administrator, that the claimant has been responsible for any attempt to obtain payment funds for such cattle or other dairy property unlawfully or improperly.

PART 51—ANIMALS DESTROYED BECAUSE OF BRUCELLOSIS

Subpart A—Indemnity for Cattle, Bison, and Swine

Subpart B—Indemnity for Sheep, Goats, and Horses

AUTHORITY: 7 U.S.C. 8301–8317; 7 CFR 2.22, 2.80, and 371.4.

Subpart A—Indemnity for Cattle, Bison, and Swine

§ 51.1 Definitions.

For the purposes of this part, the following terms shall be construed, respectively, to mean:

Accredited veterinarian. A veterinarian approved by the Administrator in accordance with the provisions of part 161 of this title to perform functions specified in parts 1, 2, 3, and 11 of subchapter A, and subchapters B, C, and D of this chapter, and to perform functions required by cooperative state-federal disease control and eradication programs.

Administrator. The Administrator, Animal and Plant Health Inspection Service, or any person authorized to act for the Administrator.

Animal and Plant Health Inspection Service. The Animal and Plant Health Inspection Service of the United States Department of Agriculture (APHIS or Service).

Animals. Cattle, bison, and breeding swine.

APHIS representative. An individual employed by APHIS who is authorized to perform the function involved.

Appraisal. An estimate of the fair market value of an animal to be destroyed because of brucellosis. The estimate shall be based upon the meat, dairy, or breeding value of the animal.

Brucellosis exposed animal. Except for a brucellosis reactor animal, any animal that: (1) Is part of or has been in contact with a herd known to be affected; or (2) has been in contact with a brucellosis reactor animal for a period of 24 hours or longer; or (3) has been in contact with a brucellosis reactor animal which has aborted, calved or farrowed within the past 30 days, or has a vaginal or uterine discharge.

Brucellosis reactor animal. Any animal classified as a brucellosis reactor as provided in the definition of official test in §78.1 of this chapter.

Claimant. A person who files a claim for indemnity under §51.7 for animals destroyed under this part.

Complete herd test. An official test for brucellosis (as defined in 9 CFR 78.1) performed under APHIS supervision in a cattle or bison herd on all cattle or bison that are (1) 6 months of age or more and not official vaccinates, except steers and spayed heifers; or (2) Official calfhood vaccinates of any age that are parturient or postparturient; or (3) Official calfhood vaccinates of beef breeds or bison with the first pair of permanent incisors fully erupted (2 years of age or more); or (4) Official calfhood vaccinates of dairy breeds with partial eruption of the first pair of permanent incisors (20 months of age or more).

Condemn. The determination made by an APHIS representative, State representative, or accredited veterinarian that animals for which indemnity is sought under this Part shall be destroyed.

Dairy cattle. A female bovine of a recognized dairy breed over 20 months of age, which has calved or is within 90 days of parturition and which is a member of a dairy herd used to produce milk for commercial use.

Destroyed. Condemned under State authority and slaughtered or otherwise dies.

Herd. Any group of animals of the same species maintained on common ground for any purpose, or two or more groups of animals (of the same species) under common ownership or supervision, geographically separated but which have an interchange or movement of animals without regard to health status.

Herd Depopulation. Removal by slaughter or other means of destruction of all cattle, bison, or swine in a herd or from a specific premises or under common ownership prior to restocking such premises with new animals, except that steers and spayed heifers or barrows and gilts maintained for feeding purposes may be retained on the premises if the Veterinarian in Charge finds such retention to be compatible with eradication efforts. The Veterinarian in Charge may also permit removal of nonpregnant heifers, without payment of indemnity, to Quarantined Feedlots in lieu of immediate slaughter.

Herd known to be affected. Any herd in which any animal has been classified as a brucellosis reactor and which has not been released from quarantine.

Inbred or hybrid swine. Any breeding swine which are the progeny of two or more breeds of registered swine and which are maintained to produce inbred or hybrid swine, and for which records of ancestry exist through which such swine can be individually identified as progeny of said registered swine.

Mortgage. Any mortgage, lien, or other security or interest that is recorded under State law or identified in the indemnity claim form filed under § 51.7 and held by any person other than the one claiming indemnity.

Official seal. A serially numbered metal strip consisting of a self-locking device on one end and a slot on the other end, which forms a loop when the ends are engaged, which cannot be reused if opened, and is applied by a representative of the Veterinarian in Charge or the State animal health official.

Owner. Any person who has a legal or rightful title to animals whether or not they are subject to a mortgage.

Permit. An official document for movement of animals under this subpart issued by an APHIS representative, state representative, or accredited veterinarian listing the disease status and identification of the animal, where consigned, cleaning and disinfecting requirements, and proof of slaughter certification.

Person. Any individual, corporation, company, association, firm, partnership, society, or joint stock company, or other legal entity.

Recognized slaughtering establishment. Any slaughtering establishment operating under the Federal Meat Inspection Act (21 U.S.C. 601 *et seq.*)or a State meat inspection act.[1]

Registered breed association. An association formed and perpetuated for the maintenance of records of purebreeding of animal species for a specific breed whose characteristics are set forth in Constitutions, By-Laws, and other rules of the association. The records maintained by such an association shall include an Official Herd Book or other recordkeeping format and Certificates of Registration or Recordation which identify an animal as a registered animal of that registered breed association. Known registered breed associations are: American Angus Association, American Beefalo Association, Inc., The American Black Maine-Anjou Association, American Blonde d'Aquitaine Association, American Brahman Breeders Association, American Brahmental Association, American Breed Association, Inc., American Chianina Association, American Dexter Cattle Association, American Galloway Breeders Association, American Gelbvieh Association, American Guernsey Cattle Club, American Hereford Association, American International Charolais Association, American (International Marchigiana Society, American Jersey Cattle Club, American Maine-Anjou Association, American Milking Shorthorn Society, American Murray Grey Association, American Normande Association, American Pinzgauer Association, American Polled Hereford Association, American Red Brangus Association, American Red Poll Association, American Salers Association, American Scotch Highland Breeders Association, American Shorthorn Association, American Simmental Association, Inc., American Tarentaise Association, Ankina Breeders, Inc., Ayrshire Breeders Association, Barzona Breed Association of America, Beefmaster Breeders Universal, Belted Galloway Society, Brahmanstein Breeders Association, Brown Swiss Beef International, Inc., Brown Swiss Cattle Breeders Association of U.S.A., Char-Swiss Breeders Association, Devon Cattle Association, Inc., Dutch Belted Cattle Association of America, Inc., Foundation Beefmaster Association, Galloway Cattle Society of America, Inc., Galloway Performance International, Holstein-Friesian Association of America, International Braford Association, International Brangus Breeders Association, Inc., International Maine-Anjou Association, Marky Cattle Association, Mid America RX[3] Cattle Company, National Beefmaster Association, North American Limousin Foundation, Pan American Zebu Association, Red and White Dairy Cattle Association, Red Angus Association of America, Red Poll Beef Breeders International, Red Poll Cattle Club of America, Santa Gertrudis Breeders International, Simbrah Association, South Devon Breed Society, Sussex Cattle Association of America, Texas Longhorn Breeders Association of America, and White Park Cattle Association of America.

[1] A list of recognized slaughtering establishments is available upon request from the Animal and Plant Health Inspection Service, 4700 River Road Unit 37, Riverdale, MD 20737–1231.

Registered cattle. Cattle for which individual records of ancestry are recorded and maintained by a breed association whose purpose is the improvement of the bovine species, and for which individual registration certificates are issued and recorded by such breed association.

Registered swine. Any breeding swine for which a certificate of pure breeding has been issued by a purebred swine association.

Sexually intact exposed female calf. A female bovine less than 6 months of age that is nursed by a brucellosis reactor at the time such reactor is condemned, and that has not been altered to make it incapable of reproduction.

Specifically approved stockyard. Premises approved by the Administrator, in accordance with §71.20 of this chapter, for assembling cattle or bison for sale.[2]

State. Any State, the District of Columbia, Puerto Rico, the Virgin Islands of the United States, Guam, the Northern Mariana Islands, or any other territory or possession of the United States.

State animal health official. The individual employed by a State who is responsible for livestock and poultry disease control and eradication programs in that State.

State representative. An individual employed in animal health activities by a State or a political subdivision thereof, and who is authorized by such State or political subdivision to perform the function involved under a cooperative agreement with the United States Department of Agriculture.

Unofficial vaccinate. Any cattle or bison which have been vaccinated for brucellosis other than in accordance with the provisions for official vaccinates set forth in §78.1 of this chapter.

Veterinarian in Charge. The veterinary official of the Animal and Plant Health Inspection Service, United States Department of Agriculture, who is assigned by the Administrator to supervise and perform offical animal health work of the Animal and Plant Health Inspection Service, in the State concerned.

[42 FR 64336, Dec. 23, 1977]

EDITORIAL NOTE: For FEDERAL REGISTER citations affecting §51.1, see the List of CFR Sections Affected, which appears in the Finding Aids section of the printed volume and at *www.fdsys.gov.*

§51.2 Cooperation with States.

The Administrator has been delegated the authority to cooperate with the proper State authorities in the eradication of brucellosis and to pay indemnities for the destruction of brucellosis-reactor animals or brucellosis-exposed animals.

[42 FR 64336, Dec. 23, 1977, as amended at 54 FR 32435, Aug. 8, 1989]

§51.3 Payment to owners for animals destroyed.

(a) *Cattle and bison.* The Administrator may authorize the payment of Federal indemnity by the U.S. Department of Agriculture to any owner whose cattle or bison are destroyed after having been approved for destruction by APHIS under the brucellosis eradication program.[3] In all cases, the amount of Federal indemnity will be determined in accordance with the regulations in this part that were in effect on the date that reactors were found or the date that whole-herd depopulation or destruction of individual animals was approved. Prior to payment of indemnity, proof of destruction[4] must be

---

[2] Notices containing lists of specifically approved stockyards are published in the FEDERAL REGISTER. Lists of specifically approved stockyards also may be obtained from the State animal health official, State representatives, or APHIS representatives.

[3] The Administrator shall authorize payment of Federal indemnity by the U.S. Department of Agriculture at the maximum per-head rates in §51.3: (a) As long as sufficient funds appropriated by Congress appear to be available for this purpose for the remainder of the fiscal year; (b) in States or areas not under Federal quarantine; (c) in States requesting payment of Federal indemnity; and (d) in States not requesting a lower rate.

[4] The Veterinarian in Charge shall accept any of the following documents as proof of destruction: (a) A postmortem report; (b) a meat inspection certification of slaughter; (c) a written statement by a State representative, APHIS representative, or accredited veterinarian attesting to the destruction of the animal; (d) a written, sworn statement by the owner or caretaker of the animal attesting to the destruction of the animal; (e)

Continued

furnished to the Veterinarian in Charge.

(1) *Eligibility for indemnity.* Owners of the following types of animals destroyed because of brucellosis are eligible to receive Federal indemnity for their animals:

(i) Cattle and bison identified as reactors as a result of a complete herd test and any sexually intact exposed female calves;

(ii) Cattle and bison in a herd that has been approved for depopulation; and

(iii) Brucellosis-exposed cattle and brucellosis-exposed bison that were previously sold or traded from any herd that was, subsequent to the sale or trade, found to be affected with brucellosis. Epidemiological information such as test results, herd history, and related evidence will be used to establish a probable date when the herd was first affected with brucellosis. Animals sold after that date will be considered to be exposed; those sold before that date will not.

(2) *Maximum per-head indemnity amounts.* Owners of the types of animals described in §51.3(a)(1) are eligible to receive Federal indemnity for their animals in the following amounts:

(i) *Brucellosis reactors and sexually intact exposed female calves.* Except for brucellosis reactors and sexually intact exposed female calves destroyed as part of a whole-herd depopulation, the indemnity for cattle and bison that are brucellosis reactors shall not exceed $250 for any registered cattle and nonregistered dairy cattle or $50 for any bison or nonregistered cattle other than dairy cattle, and the indemnity for sexually intact exposed female calves shall not exceed $50.

(ii) *Herd depopulations and individual exposed animals.* Owners of herds that have been approved for depopulation and owners of brucellosis-exposed cattle and brucellosis-exposed bison that meet the conditions of §51.3 (a)(1)(iii) may choose either of the two methods described in paragraphs (a)(2)(ii)(A) and (a)(2)(ii)(B) of this section, involving fair market value of the animal to be destroyed or a fixed rate, for determining the maximum amounts of indemnity they may receive.[3] The method chosen must be used for all animals to be destroyed. Owners have the option of having an appraisal done prior to choosing the method used. Appraisals will be conducted by an independent appraiser selected by the Administrator. The cost of the appraisals will be borne by APHIS.

(A) *Appraisal method.* Each eligible animal will be appraised to determine its fair market value. The indemnity shall be the appraised value, minus the salvage value.

(B) *Fixed-rate method.* The indemnity shall not exceed $250 per animal for bison and nonregistered cattle other than dairy cattle and $750 per animal for registered cattle and nonregistered dairy cattle.

(b) *Swine*—(1) *Brucellosis reactor swine.* The Administrator may authorize[3] the payment of Federal indemnity by the United States Department of Agriculture to an owner whose breeding swine are destroyed as brucellosis reactors. The indemnity shall not exceed $25 per head for registered, inbred, or hybrid swine, or $10 per head for all other breeding swine. Prior to payment of indemnity, proof of destruction[4] shall be furnished to the Veterinarian in Charge.

(2) *Herd depopulation.* The Administrator may authorize[3] the payment of Federal indemnity by the United States Department of Agriculture to an owner whose herd of breeding swine or whose whole herd is destroyed because of brucellosis. The indemnity shall not exceed $150 per head for registered, inbred, or hybrid breeding swine, and $65 per head for all other breeding swine, except that in the case of whole herd depopulation, indemnity payments shall be paid on all swine in the herd at fair market value, as determined by the Administrator, based on an appraisal conducted by an independent appraiser assigned by the Administrator. In cases where indemnity is paid for whole herd depopulation, indemnity payments, plus any salvage, must not exceed the appraised value of

---

a permit (VS Form 1–27) consigning the animal from a farm or livestock market directly to a recognized slaughtering establishment; or (f) in unique situations where the documents listed above are not available, other similarly reliable forms of proof of destruction.

each animal. Indemnity payment shall be made only for brucellosis exposed swine or for swine from a herd known to be affected and only when the Administrator determines that the destruction of all swine in the herd will contribute to the Brucellosis Eradication Program. Prior to payment of indemnity, proof of destruction[4] shall be furnished to the Veterinarian in Charge.

(3) *Exposed swine.* The Administrator may authorize[3] the payment of Federal indemnity by the United States Department of Agriculture to an owner whose breeding swine are destroyed because of brucellosis. The indemnity shall not exceed $150 per head for registered, inbred, or hybrid swine, or $65 per head for all other breeding swine. Indemnity payment shall be made only for such brucellosis exposed swine and only when the Administrator determines that the destruction of such swine will contribute to the Brucellosis Eradication Program. Prior to payment of indemnity, proof of destruction[4] shall be furnished to the Veterinarian in Charge.

(Approved by the Office of Management and Budget under control number 0579–0047)

[42 FR 64336, Dec. 23, 1977]

EDITORIAL NOTE: For FEDERAL REGISTER citations affecting §51.3, see the List of CFR Sections Affected, which appears in the Finding Aids section of the printed volume and at *www.fdsys.gov.*

§51.4 Record of tests.

The claimant shall be responsible for providing information to an APHIS representative, State representative, or accredited veterinarian so that a complete test record may be made by such person on an APHIS approved form for each herd known to be affected, including the reactor tag number of each brucellosis reactor animal and the registration name and number of each brucellosis reactor registered animal. A copy of the applicable test record shall be given to the owner of any such herd, and one copy of each such record shall be furnished to the appropriate State veterinarian's office by such person who completes the test record.

(Approved by the Office of Management and Budget under control number 0579–0047)

[42 FR 64336, Dec. 23, 1977, as amended at 48 FR 57472, Dec. 30, 1983; 54 FR 32435, Aug. 8, 1989; 56 FR 18506, Apr. 23, 1991]

§51.5 Identification of animals to be destroyed because of brucellosis.

(a) The claimant shall be responsible for insuring that any animal for which indemnity is claimed shall be identified in accordance with the provisions of this section within 15 days after having been classified as a reactor or for any other animal subject to this part within 15 days after having been condemned. The veterinarian in charge may extend the time limit to 30 days when a request for such extension is received by him prior to the expiration date of the original 15 day period allowed, and when he determines that the extension will not adversely affect the brucellosis eradication program; and except further, that the Administrator shall upon request in specific cases, extend the time limit beyond the 30-day period when unusual or unforeseen circumstances occur which prevent or hinder the identification of the animals within the 30-day period, such as, but not limited to, floods, storms, or other Acts of God which are beyond the control of the owner, or when identification is delayed due to requirements of another Federal Agency.

(b) Except as provided in paragraph (b)(4) of this section, cattle and bison to be destroyed because of brucellosis shall be individually identified prior to moving interstate by attaching to the left ear a metal tag bearing a serial number and the inscription "U.S. Reactor," or a similar State reactor tag, and must be:

(1) "B" branded (as defined in §78.1); or

(2) Accompanied directly to slaughter by an APHIS or State representative; or

(3) Moved in vehicles closed with official seals applied and removed by an APHIS representative, State representative, accredited veterinarian, or an individual authorized for this purpose by an APHIS representative. The official

seal numbers must be recorded on the accompanying permit.

(4) Reactor and exposed cattle and bison in herds scheduled for herd depopulation may be moved interstate without eartagging or branding if they are identified by USDA approved backtags and either accompanied directly to slaughter by an APHIS or State representative or moved directly to slaughter in vehicles closed with official seals. Such official seals must be applied and removed by an APHIS representative, State representative, accredited veterinarian, or an individual authorized for this purpose by an APHIS representative.

(c) Swine shall be individually identified by tagging with a metal tag bearing a serial number and inscription "U.S. Reactor" or a similar State reactor tag or other identification approved by the Administrator, upon request in specific cases, attached to the left ear of each animal.

(Approved by the Office of Management and Budget under control number 0579–0047)

[42 FR 64336, Dec. 23, 1977, as amended at 47 FR 53324, Nov. 26, 1982; 48 FR 57472, Dec. 30, 1983; 50 FR 11993, Mar. 27, 1985; 54 FR 32435, Aug. 8, 1989; 56 FR 18506, Apr. 23, 1991; 60 FR 48367, Sept. 19, 1995]

§51.6 Destruction of animals; time limit for destruction of animals.

(a) *Cattle.* The claimant shall be responsible for ensuring that cattle subject to this part shall be sold under permit to a recognized slaughtering establishment or to a specifically approved stockyard for sale to a recognized slaughtering establishment.

(b) *Bison.* The claimant shall be responsible for insuring that bison subject to this part shall be sold under permit to a State or Federal slaughtering establishment approved by the Administrator for this purpose or to a stockyard approved by the Administrator for sale to such a slaughtering establishment, *Provided, However*, That the Administrator may approve such other bison slaughtering establishments as may be deemed necessary to accomplish destruction of bison subject to this part.

(c) *Swine.* The claimant shall be responsible for insuring that swine subject to this part shall be sold under permit to a slaughtering establishment where State or Federal Meat inspection is available, or to a market approved by the State Animal Health Official, or to a market approved by the Administrator, for sale to such slaughtering establishment;[5] except that in the case of indemnity for whole herd depopulation, as provided for in §51.3, swine shall be destroyed, if possible, on the premises where the animals are held or penned at the time the indemnity is approved, or may be moved for destruction to another location when movement to the location is approved in advance by an APHIS representative. In cases where the swine are destroyed other than at a slaughtering establishment, the carcasses of the swine shall be disposed of by burial, incineration, or other disposal means authorized by applicable State law. The destruction and disposition of animals destroyed in accordance with this section other than at a slaughtering establishment shall be performed in the presence of an APHIS representative.

(d) *Time limit for destruction of animals.* Payment of indemnity shall be made under this part only if the animals are destroyed within 15 days after the date of identification, pursuant to §51.5 of the regulations in this part, except that the appropriate Veterinarian in Charge may extend the time limit to 30 days when request for such extension is received from the owner prior to the expiration date of the original 15–day period allowed, or when the animals were sold for slaughter prior to the expiration date of the original 15–day period, and when the Veterinarian in Charge determines that such extension will not adversely affect the Brucellosis Eradication Program; and except further, that the Administrator shall, upon request in specific cases, extend the time limit beyond the 30-day period when unusual and unforeseen circumstances occur which prevent or hinder the destruction of the animals within the 30-day period, such as, but not limited to, floods, storms, or other Acts of God which are beyond

[5] Markets are approved by the Administrator in accordance with §76.18 of this chapter.

the control of the owner, or when destruction is delayed due to requirements of another Federal Agency.

(Approved by the Office of Management and Budget under control number 0579–0047)

[42 FR 64336, Dec. 23, 1977, as amended at 45 FR 43680, June 27, 1980; 45 FR 86410, Dec. 31, 1980; 46 FR 5861, Jan. 21, 1981; 47 FR 53324, Nov. 26, 1982; 48 FR 57472, Dec. 30, 1983; 50 FR 11993, Mar. 27, 1985; 51 FR 11300, Apr. 2, 1986; 51 FR 32599, Sept. 12, 1986; 54 FR 32435, Aug. 8, 1989; 56 FR 18506, Apr. 23, 1991; 59 FR 12533, Mar. 17, 1994]

§51.7 Claims for indemnity.

(a) Claims for indemnity for animals destroyed because of brucellosis shall be presented on indemnity claim forms furnished by APHIS on which the owner of the animals covered thereby shall certify that the animals are or are not subject to any mortgage as defined in this part. If the owner states there is a mortgage, the APHIS indemnity claim form shall be signed by the owner and by each person holding a mortgage on the animals, consenting to the payment of any indemnity allowed to the person specified thereon. Payment will be made only if the claimant has submitted a complete indemnity claim form to, and such claim has been approved by the Veterinarian in Charge or by an APHIS representative designated by him. On claims for indemnity made under the provisions of §51.3, the Veterinarian in Charge or an APHIS representative designated by him shall record on the APHIS indemnity claim form the amount of Federal and State indemnity payments that appear to be due to the owner of the animals. The owner of the animals shall be furnished a copy of the completed APHIS indemnity claim form. The Veterinarian in Charge or an APHIS representative designated by him shall then forward the completed APHIS indemnity claim form to the Administrator for further action on the claim. No charges for holding the animals on the farm pending slaughter or for trucking by the owner shall be so deducted or otherwise paid by the United States Department of Agriculture.

(b) Claims for indemnity for registered cattle shall be accompanied by the cattle's registration papers issued in the name of the owner. If the registration papers are unavailable or if the cattle are less than 1 year old and are not registered at the time the claim for indemnity is submitted, the Veterinarian in Charge may grant a 60-day extension or the Administrator may grant an extension longer than 60 days for the presentation of registration papers.

(Approved by the Office of Management and Budget under control number 0579–0047)

[42 FR 64336, Dec. 23, 1977. Redesignated at 46 FR 13674, Feb. 23, 1981, and 47 FR 53324, Nov. 26, 1982, and amended at 47 FR 53324, Nov. 26, 1982; 48 FR 57472, Dec. 30, 1983; 50 FR 11993, Mar. 27, 1985; 54 FR 32435, Aug. 8, 1989; 56 FR 18506, Apr. 23, 1991]

§51.8 Disinfection of premises, conveyances, and materials.

All premises, including all structures, holding facilities, conveyances, and materials, contaminated because of occupation or use by brucellosis reactor or exposed animals shall be properly cleaned and disinfected with a disinfectant permitted by APHIS in accordance with recommendations of the APHIS or State representative within 15 days from the date reactors were removed from the premises, except that the appropriate Veterinarian in Charge may extend the time limit for disinfection to 30 days when request for such extension is received by him prior to the expiration date of the original 15-day period allowed, and when he determines that such extension will not adversely affect the Brucellosis Eradication Program; and except further, that the Administrator may, upon request in specific cases, extend the time limit beyond the 30-day period when unusual and unforeseen circumstances occur, such as but not limited to floods, storms, or other Acts of God, which are beyond the control of the owner, preventing or hindering the disinfection of premises, conveyances, and materials. Certain premises may be exempted from such cleaning and disinfecting requirements by approval of the appropriate Veterinarian in Charge on written recommendations by the APHIS or State representative or when a written report by the APHIS or State representative determines that there are no buildings, holding facilities, conveyances, or other materials on the premises that would require such cleaning and disinfection.

(Approved by the Office of Management and Budget under control number 0579–0047)

[42 FR 64336, Dec. 23, 1977. Redesignated at 46 FR 13674, Feb. 23, 1981, and 47 FR 53324, Nov. 26, 1982; 48 FR 57472, Dec. 30, 1983; 50 FR 11993, Mar. 27, 1985; 54 FR 32435, Aug. 8, 1989; 56 FR 18506, Apr. 23, 1991]

§ 51.9 Claims not allowed.

Claims for compensation for animals destroyed because of brucellosis shall not be allowed if any of the following circumstances exist:

(a) If the claimant has failed to comply with any of the requirements of this part.

(b) If the existence of brucellosis in the animal was determined based on the results of an official test, as defined in § 78.1 of this chapter, and specific instructions for the administration of the official test had not previously been issued to the individual performing the test by APHIS and the State animal health official.

(c) If all cattle, bison, and swine eligible for testing in the claimant's herd have not been tested for brucellosis under APHIS or State supervision.

(d) If the animals are:

(1) Barrows or gilts maintained for feeding purposes; or

(2) Spayed heifers or steers, unless the steers are work oxen, or unless the spayed heifers or steers are unweaned animals in a herd approved for depopulation in accordance with § 51.3 of this part.

(e) If the animals are classified as reactors and are unofficial vaccinates, unless there is either a record of a negative official test made not less than 30 days following the date of unofficial vaccination or unless other APHIS approved tests show the unofficial vaccinates are affected with virulent Brucella.

(f) If there is substantial evidence that the owner or his agent has in any way been responsible for any unlawful or improper attempt to obtain indemnity funds for such animal.

(g) If, at the time of test or condemnation, the animals belonged to or were upon the premises of any person to whom they had been sold for slaughter; shipped for slaugher, or delivered for slaughter.

(h) If any known brucellosis reactor animal remains in the herd, unless, in the opinion of the Veterinarian in Charge, a reasonable search has been made for the brucellosis reactor animal and the brucellosis reactor animal could not be found and removed.

(i) If the animals are brucellosis reactor animals which are slaughtered other than as part of a herd depopulation, and which are from a herd: (1) That was already classified as a "herd known to be affected" at the time the animals were identified as brucellosis reactor animals and (2) for which an approved action plan or approved individual herd plan (as defined in § 78.1 of this chapter) was not in effect at the time the claim was filed.

(Approved by the Office of Management and Budget under control number 0579–0047)

[42 FR 64336, Dec. 23, 1977. Redesignated at 46 FR 13674, Feb. 23, 1981, and 47 FR 53324, Nov. 26, 1982, and amended at 47 FR 53324, Nov. 26, 1982; 48 FR 57472, Dec. 30, 1983; 50 FR 11993, Mar. 27, 1985; 50 FR 47036, Nov. 14, 1985; 51 FR 11300, Apr. 2, 1986; 54 FR 32435, Aug. 8, 1989; 56 FR 18506, Apr. 23, 1991; 63 FR 47423, Sept. 8, 1998]

§ 51.10 Part 53 of this chapter not applicable.

No claim for indemnity for animals destroyed because of brucellosis shall hereafter be paid under the regulations contained in part 53 of this chapter, but all such claims shall be presented and paid pursuant to and in compliance with regulations contained in this part.

[42 FR 64336, Dec. 23, 1977. Redesignated at 46 FR 13674, Feb. 23, 1981, and 47 FR 53324, Nov. 26, 1982; 50 FR 11993, Mar. 27, 1985]

Subpart B—Indemnity for Sheep, Goats, and Horses

SOURCE: 69 FR 41912, July 13, 2004, unless otherwise noted.

§ 51.20 Definitions.

Accredited veterinarian. A veterinarian approved by the Administrator in accordance with the provisions of part 161 of this title to perform functions specified in parts 1, 2, 3, and 11 of subchapter A, and subchapters B, C, and D of this chapter, and to perform functions required by cooperative State-Federal disease control and eradication programs.

Administrator. The Administrator, Animal and Plant Health Inspection Service, or any person authorized to act for the Administrator.

Affected herd/flock. Any herd or flock in which any cattle, bison, breeding swine, sheep, or goat has been classified as a brucellosis reactor and which has not been released from quarantine.

Animal. Sheep, goats, and horses.

Animal and Plant Health Inspection Service (APHIS). The Animal and Plant Health Inspection Service of the United States Department of Agriculture.

APHIS representative. An individual employed by APHIS who is authorized to perform the function involved.

Appraisal. An estimate of the fair market value of an animal to be destroyed because of brucellosis.

Brucellosis exposed. Except for brucellosis reactors, animals that are part of a herd known to be affected, or are in a quarantined feedlot or a quarantined pasture, or are brucellosis suspects, or that have been in contact with a brucellosis reactor for a period of 24 hours or more, or for a period of less than 24 hours if the brucellosis reactor has aborted, calved, or farrowed within the past 30 days or has a vaginal or uterine discharge.

Brucellosis reactor animal. (1) Any sheep or goat that has been determined by a designated brucellosis epidemiologist[1] to be affected with brucellosis, based on test results, herd/flock history, and/or culture results. Any test used for cattle and bison under the APHIS official brucellosis eradication program (*see* part 78 of this chapter) may be used, but test results must be interpreted by a designated brucellosis epidemiologist.

(2) Any horse that has been determined by a designated brucellosis epidemiologist to be affected with brucellosis, based on epidemiological information or culture results, or positive results for brucellosis in accordance with one of the following tests:

Test	Positive results
Standard plate test (SPT)	If antibody titer positive at 1:100 dilution or higher.
Standard tube test (STT)	If antibody titer positive at 1:100 dilution or higher.
Rivanol test	If antibody titer positive at 1:50 dilution or higher.
Particle concentration fluorescence immunoassay (PCFIA).	If reading is 0.3 or lower.
Complement fixation test (CF)	If reading is 2 + :20 dilution.

(3) Any cattle, bison, or swine classified as a brucellosis reactor as provided in the definition of official test in §78.1 of this chapter.

Condemn. The determination made by an APHIS representative, State representative, or accredited veterinarian that animals for which indemnity is sought under this subpart will be destroyed.

Designated brucellosis epidemiologist. An epidemiologist selected by the State animal health official and the Veterinarian in Charge to perform the functions required. The regional epidemiologist and the APHIS brucellosis staff must concur in the selection and appointment of the designated epidemiologist.

Destroyed. Condemned under State authority and slaughtered or otherwise dies.

Flock. Any group of sheep maintained on common ground for any purpose, or two or more groups of sheep under common ownership or supervision, geographically separated but which have an interchange or movement of animals without regard to health status.

Herd. Any group of goats, or mixed sheep and goats, maintained on common ground for any purpose, or two or more groups of goats, or two or more groups of mixed sheep and goats, under common ownership or supervision, geographically separated but which have an interchange or movement of animals without regard to health status.

Herd/flock depopulation. Removal by slaughter or other means of destruction of all sheep or goats in a flock or herd, or from a specific premises or under common ownership prior to restocking such premises with new animals.

[1] Requirements for designated brucellosis epidemiologists are contained in Veterinary Services Memorandum No. 551.10. A copy of this memorandum may be obtained from an APHIS representative, the State animal health official, or a State representative.

Mortgage. Any mortgage, lien, or interest that is recorded under State law or identified in the indemnity claim form filed in accordance with this subpart, and held by any person other than the one claiming indemnity.

Official seal. A serially numbered metal strip consisting of a self-locking device on one end and a slot on the other end, which forms a loop when the ends are engaged and which cannot be reused if opened, and is applied by a representative of the Veterinarian in Charge or the State animal health official.

Owner. Any person who has legal or rightful title to sheep, goats, and horses, whether or not the animals are subject to a mortgage.

Permit. An official document for movement of animals under this subpart issued by an APHIS representative, State representative, or accredited veterinarian listing the disease status and identification of the animal, where consigned, cleaning and disinfecting requirements, and proof of slaughter certification.

Person. Any individual, corporation, company, association, firm, partnership, society, or joint stock company, or other legal entity.

Registered sheep and goats. Sheep and goats for which individual records of ancestry are recorded and maintained by a breed association whose purpose is the improvement of the species, and for which individual registration certificates are issued and recorded by such breed association.

State. Any State, the District of Columbia, Puerto Rico, the Virgin Islands of the United States, Guam, the Northern Mariana Islands, or any other territory or possession of the United States.

State representative. An individual employed in animal health activities by a State or a political subdivision thereof, and who is authorized by such State or political subdivision to perform the function involved under a cooperative agreement with the United States Department of Agriculture.

Veterinarian in Charge. The APHIS veterinary official who is assigned by the Administrator to supervise and perform the official animal health work of APHIS in the State or area concerned, or any person authorized to act for the Veterinarian in Charge.

§ 51.21 Cooperation with States.

The Administrator has been delegated the authority to cooperate with the proper State authorities in the eradication of brucellosis and to pay indemnities for the destruction of brucellosis-reactor animals or brucellosis-exposed animals.

§ 51.22 Payment to owners for goats, sheep, and horses destroyed.

(a) The Administrator may authorize the payment of Federal indemnity by the U.S. Department of Agriculture to any owner whose goats, sheep, or horses are destroyed after having been approved for destruction by APHIS.[1] Goats or sheep must be destroyed as part of a whole herd/flock depopulation to be eligible for Federal indemnity.

(b) The amount of Federal indemnity will be determined in accordance with the regulations in this part that were in effect on the date infected animals were found, or the date that the whole-herd/flock depopulation or destruction of individual animals was approved.

(c) Prior to payment of indemnity, proof of destruction must be furnished to the Veterinarian in Charge.

§ 51.23 Eligibility for indemnity.

Owners of animals destroyed because of brucellosis are eligible to receive Federal indemnity for their animals if the animals are:

(a) Sheep and goats in an affected herd or flock;

(b) Sheep and goats that were obtained from a herd or flock that was subsequently found to be an affected herd or flock. Epidemiological information such as test results, herd/flock history, and related evidence will be used to establish a probable date when the herd or flock was first affected with

[1] The Administrator will authorize payment of Federal indemnity by the U.S. Department of Agriculture as provided in § 51.24: (a) As long as sufficient funds appropriated by Congress appear to be available for this purpose for the remainder of the fiscal year; (b) in States or areas not under Federal quarantine; (c) in States requesting payment of Federal indemnity; and (d) in States not requesting a lower rate.

brucellosis. Animals removed from the herd or flock after that date will be considered exposed to the disease and eligible for indemnity; those removed before that date will not;

(c) Individual horses that have been found to be brucellosis reactor animals.

§51.24 Maximum per-head indemnity amounts.

Owners of the types of animals listed in §51.22 of this subpart are eligible to receive Federal indemnity for their animals. All animals must be individually appraised to determine their fair market value. The indemnity amount will be the appraised value minus the salvage value of the animal, up to a maximum of $20,000 per animal in the case of horses. An independent appraiser selected by the Administrator will conduct appraisals. APHIS will pay the cost of appraisals.

§51.25 Proof of destruction.

The Veterinarian in Charge will accept any of the following documents as proof of destruction:

(a) A postmortem report;

(b) A meat inspection certification of slaughter;

(c) A written statement by a State representative, APHIS representative, or accredited veterinarian attesting to the destruction of the animals;

(d) A written, sworn statement by the owner or caretaker of the animal attesting to the destruction of the animals;

(e) A permit (VS Form 1–27) consigning the animal from a farm or livestock market directly to a slaughter establishment; or

(f) In unique situations where none of the documents listed above are available, other similarly reliable forms of proof of destruction.

(Approved by the Office of Management and Budget under control number 0579–0185)

§51.26 Record of tests.

An APHIS representative, State representative, or accredited veterinarian will compile, on an APHIS-approved form, a complete test record for each animal. The claimant must provide any information necessary to complete the form. The test record must include the type of test and the test results for each animal. It must also include the individual identification of each tested animal. Any unique, individually numbered identification is acceptable. The animal's owner and the appropriate State veterinarian's office will each receive a copy of the test record.

(Approved by the Office of Management and Budget under control number 0579–0185)

§51.27 Identification of goats, sheep, and horses to be destroyed.

The claimant must ensure that any goats, sheep, and horses for which indemnity is claimed are marked with unique, individually numbered identification showing they are to be destroyed. This must be done within 15 days after the animals are condemned. The Veterinarian in Charge may extend the time limit to 30 days when the Veterinarian in Charge receives a request for extension prior to the expiration date of the original 15-day period, and when the Veterinarian in Charge determines that the extension will not adversely affect the brucellosis eradication program. However, the Administrator may extend the time limit beyond 30 days when unusual or unforeseen circumstances occur that prevent or hinder the identification of the animal within 30 days, such as, but not limited to, floods, storms, or other Acts of God, which are beyond the control of the owner, or when identification is delayed due to requirements of another Federal agency.

(Approved by the Office of Management and Budget under control number 0579–0185)

§51.28 Moving goats, sheep, and horses to be destroyed.

Goats, sheep, and horses to be destroyed because of brucellosis must be accompanied by a permit and either:

(a) Accompanied directly to slaughter by an APHIS or State representative; or

(b) Moved in vehicles closed with official seals applied and removed by an APHIS representative, State representative, accredited veterinarian, or an individual authorized for this purpose by an APHIS representative. The official seal numbers must be recorded on the accompanying permit.

(Approved by the Office of Management and Budget under control number 0579–0185)

§ 51.29 Destruction of animals; time limit.

(a) The claimant must ensure that goats, sheep, and horses infected with or exposed to *B. abortus* are either:

(1) Sold under permit to a recognized slaughtering establishment;

(2) Moved to an approved stockyard for sale to a recognized slaughtering establishment; or

(3) Destroyed and buried, incinerated, or rendered in accordance with applicable State law.

(b) The claimant must ensure that goats and sheep destroyed because of *B. melitensis* are destroyed and buried, incinerated, or rendered in accordance with applicable State law.

(c) Indemnity will be paid under this part only if the animals are destroyed within 15 days after the date they are marked with identification showing they are to be destroyed. However, the Veterinarian in Charge may extend the time limit to 30 days if:

(1) The animals' owner asks the Veterinarian in Charge for an extension before the initial 15-day period expires, or the animals were sold for slaughter before the original 15-day period expires; and

(2) The Veterinarian in Charge determines that extending the time limit will not adversely affect the Brucellosis Eradication Program.

(d) The Administrator may extend the time limit beyond 30 days when unusual and unforeseen circumstances occur that prevent or hinder the destruction of the animals within 30 days, such as, but not limited to, floods, storms, or other Acts of God, which are beyond the control of the owner, or when destruction is delayed due to requirements of another Federal agency.

(Approved by the Office of Management and Budget under control number 0579–0185)

§ 51.30 Claims for indemnity.

(a) Claims for indemnity for goats, sheep, and horses destroyed because of brucellosis must be made using an indemnity claim form furnished by APHIS. On the form, the owner of the animals must certify whether the animals are subject to a mortgage. If the owner states there is a mortgage, the claim form must be signed by the owner and by each mortgage holder, consenting to the payment of any indemnity allowed to the owner. Payment will be made only if the claimant has submitted a complete indemnity claim form to the Veterinarian in Charge and the claim has been approved by the Veterinarian in Charge or by an APHIS representative designated by him or her. The Veterinarian in Charge or an APHIS representative designated by the Veterinarian in Charge will record on the APHIS indemnity claim form the amount of Federal and State indemnity payments that appear to be due to the owner of the animals. The owner of the animals will receive a copy of the completed APHIS indemnity claim form. The owner is responsible for paying all fees for holding the animals on the farm pending disposal and for all trucking fees.

(b) Claims for indemnity for registered sheep and registered goats must be accompanied by the animal's registration papers, issued in the name of the owner. If the registration papers are unavailable or if the animal is less than 1 year old and not registered at the time the claim for indemnity is submitted, the Veterinarian in Charge may grant a 60-day extension or the Administrator may grant an extension longer than 60 days for the presentation of registration papers. Any animal that is not registered but is eligible for registration at the time the claim is submitted will be considered unregistered unless the animal has been in the flock for less than 12 months.

(Approved by the Office of Management and Budget under control number 0579–0185)

§ 51.31 Disinfecting premises, conveyances, and materials.

All premises, including all structures, holding facilities, conveyances, and materials contaminated because they have been used by animals destroyed because of brucellosis, must be properly cleaned and disinfected in accordance with recommendations of the

APHIS or State representative. Cleaning and disinfecting must be completed within 15 days from the date the animals were removed from the premises, except that the Veterinarian in Charge may extend the time limit for disinfection to 30 days when he or she receives a request prior the expiration date of the original 15 days, and when the Veterinarian in Charge determines that an extension will not adversely affect the Brucellosis Eradication Program. The Administrator may extend the time limit beyond 30 days when unusual and unforeseen circumstances occur that prevent or hinder disinfection of the premises, conveyances, and materials within 30 days, such as, but not limited to floods, storms, or other Acts of God, which are beyond the control of the owner. A premises may be exempted from such cleaning and disinfecting requirements if the APHIS or State representative recommends it in writing and the Veterinarian in Charge approves.

(Approved by the Office of Management and Budget under control number 0579–0185)

§51.32 Claims not allowed.

Claims for indemnity for goats, sheep, and horses destroyed because of brucellosis will not be allowed if any of the following circumstances exist:

(a) The claimant has failed to comply with any of the requirements of this part;

(b) The claim is based on a brucellosis test, and the person who administered the test was not properly trained, authorized, or certified at the time of the test;

(c) Testing of goats, sheep, and horses in the herd or flock for brucellosis was not done under APHIS or State supervision, or by an accredited veterinarian;

(d) There is substantial evidence that the claim is an unlawful or improper attempt to obtain indemnity; or

(e) If, at the time of test or condemnation, the animals belonged to or were upon the premises of any person to whom they had been sold for slaughter, shipped for slaughter, or delivered for slaughter.

§51.33 Multiple indemnity payments.

APHIS has indemnity programs for several other livestock diseases. However, if a claim is paid for indemnity for animals destroyed because of brucellosis, no other claims for indemnity will be paid for the same animals.

PART 52—SWINE DESTROYED BECAUSE OF PSEUDORABIES

AUTHORITY: 7 U.S.C. 8301–8317; 7 CFR 2.22, 2.80, and 371.4.

SOURCE: 64 FR 2549, Jan. 15, 1999, unless otherwise noted.

§52.1 Definitions.

Accredited veterinarian. A veterinarian approved by the Administrator in accordance with the provisions of part 161 of this chapter to perform functions specified in subchapters B, C, and D of this chapter.

Administrator. The Administrator, Animal and Plant Health Inspection Service, or any other employee of the Animal and Plant Health Inspection Service, United States Department of Agriculture, delegated to act in the Administrator's stead.

Animal and Plant Health Inspection Service (APHIS). The Animal and Plant Health Inspection Service of the United States Department of Agriculture.

APHIS employee. Any individual employed by the Animal and Plant Health Inspection Service who is authorized by the Administrator to do any work or perform any duty in connection with the control and eradication of disease.

Approved differential pseudorabies test. Any test for the diagnosis of pseudorabies that can distinguish vaccinated swine from infected swine; is produced under license from the Secretary of Agriculture under the Virus-Serum-Toxin Act of March 4, 1913, and subsequent amendments (21 U.S.C. 151 *et seq.*) with indications for use in the Cooperative State-Federal

Pseudorabies Eradication Program; and is conducted in a laboratory approved by the Administrator.[1]

Department. The United States Department of Agriculture.

Herd. Any group of swine maintained on common ground for any purpose, or two or more groups of swine under common ownership or supervision that are geographically separated but that are determined by an official pseudorabies epidemiologist to have an interchange or movement of animals that could cause the transmission of pseudorabies from one group to another.

Inspector in charge. An APHIS employee who is designated by the Administrator to take charge of work in connection with the control and eradication of disease.

Known infected breeding sow. Any breeding sow that has been determined to be infected with pseudorabies based on an official pseudorabies test or an approved differential pseudorabies test, or as diagnosed by an official pseudorabies epidemiologist as having pseudorabies.

Known infected herd. Any herd in which swine have been determined to be infected with pseudorabies based on an official pseudorabies test or an approved differential pseudorabies test, or based on a diagnosis by an official pseudorabies epidemiologist.

Materials. Parts of barns or other structures, straw, hay, and other feed for animals, farm products or equipment, clothing, and articles stored in or adjacent to barns or other structures.

Mortgage. Any mortgage, lien, or other security or beneficial interest held by any person other than the one claiming indemnity.

Net salvage. The amount received for swine destroyed because of pseudorabies, after deducting freight, trucking, yardage, commission, slaughtering charges, and similar costs to the owner.

Official pseudorabies epidemiologist. A State or Federally employed veterinarian designated by the State animal health official and the veterinarian in charge to investigate and diagnose pseudorabies in livestock.

Official pseudorabies test. Any test for the diagnosis of pseudorabies approved by the Administrator and conducted in a laboratory approved by the Administrator. The following tests for the diagnosis of pseudorabies have been approved by the Administrator: Microtitration Serum-Virus Neutralization Test; Virus Isolation and Identification Test; Fluorescent Antibody Tissue Section Test; Enzyme-Linked Immunosorbent Assay (ELISA) Test, except for approved differential pseudorabies tests other than the glycoprotein I (gpI) ELISA test; Latex Agglutination Test (LAT); and Particle Concentration Fluorescence Immunoassay (PCFIA) Test.[2] State, Federal, and university laboratories will be approved by the Administrator following his determination that the laboratory: has personnel trained at the Veterinary Services Diagnostic Laboratory at Ames, Iowa, assigned to supervise the test; follows standard test protocol; meets check test proficiency requirements; and will report

[1] The names and addresses of laboratories approved by the Administrator to conduct approved differential pseudorabies tests are published in the Notices Section of the FEDERAL REGISTER. A list of approved laboratories is also available upon request from the Animal and Plant Health Inspection Service, 4700 River Road Unit 37, Riverdale, Maryland 20737–1231. State, Federal, and university laboratories will be approved by the Administrator when he or she determines that the laboratory: employs personnel trained at the National Veterinary Services Laboratories assigned to supervise the testing; follows standard test protocols; meets check test proficiency requirements; and will report all test results to State and Federal animal health officials. Before the Administrator may withdraw approval of any laboratory for failure to meet any of these conditions, the Administrator must give written notice of the proposed withdrawal to the director of the laboratory, and must give the director an opportunity to respond. If there are conflicts as to any material fact, a hearing will be held to resolve the conflict.

[2] Copies of the test protocols (Recommended Minimum Standards for Diagnostic Tests Employed in the Diagnosis of Pseudorabies (Aujeszky's Disease) are available upon request from the Animal and Plant Health Inspection Service, Veterinary Services, Operational Support, 4700 River Road Unit 33, Riverdale, MD 20737–1231.

all test results to State and Federal animal health officials.[3]

Official seal. A serially numbered metal or plastic strip, consisting of a self-locking device on one end and a slot on the other end, that forms a loop when the ends are engaged and that cannot be reused if opened, or a serially numbered, self-locking button that can be used for this purpose.

Permit. An official document for movement of swine under this part that is issued by an APHIS employee, State representative, or accredited veterinarian and that lists the disease status and individual identification of the animal, where consigned, cleaning and disinfection requirements, and proof of slaughter certification by a recognized slaughtering establishment.

Person. Any individual, corporation, company, association, firm, partnership, society, joint stock company, or other legal entity.

Pseudorabies. The contagious, infectious, and communicable disease of livestock and other animals, also known as Aujeszky's disease, mad itch, or infectious bulbar paralysis.

Recognized slaughtering establishment. A slaughtering establishment operating under the Federal Meat Inspection Act (21 U.S.C. 601 *et seq.*) or a State meat inspection act.[4]

Secretary. The Secretary of Agriculture of the United States, or any officer or employee of the Department delegated to act in the Secretary's stead.

State. Each of the States of the United States, the District of Columbia, Puerto Rico, the Northern Mariana Islands, Guam, the Virgin Islands of the United States, or any other territory or possession of the United States.

State representative. A person regularly employed in the animal health work of a State and who is authorized by that State to perform the function involved under a cooperative agreement with the United States Department of Agriculture.

Veterinarian in charge. The veterinary official of Veterinary Services, APHIS, who is assigned by the Administrator to supervise and perform official animal health work for APHIS in the State concerned.

[64 FR 2549, Jan. 15, 1999, as amended at 65 FR 20711, Apr. 18, 2000; 68 FR 6342, Feb. 7, 2003]

§52.2 Payment of indemnity.

(a) Except as provided in paragraph (b) of this section, the Administrator is authorized to agree on the part of the Department to pay indemnity to the owner of herds of swine destroyed because the herds are known to be infected with pseudorabies, or individual breeding sows destroyed because they are known to be infected with pseudorabies. The amount of indemnity paid, together with the amount for net salvage the owner receives when the animals are slaughtered, shall not exceed the fair market value of the swine. Such swine must be sent directly to slaughter under permit in a conveyance closed with an official seal applied and removed by either an APHIS employee, a State representative, an accredited veterinarian, or an individual authorized for this purpose by an APHIS employee. The swine must be sent to a recognized slaughtering establishment.

(b) If swine from herds that are destroyed because the herds are known to be infected with pseudorabies are not accepted at a recognized slaughtering establishment, or the owner and an APHIS employee or State representative agree they will not be accepted by a recognized slaughtering establishment, the Administrator is authorized to pay 100 percent of the expenses of the purchase, destruction, and disposition of such swine.

(Approved by the Office of Management and Budget under control number 0579–0151)

[65 FR 20711, Apr. 18, 2000]

[3] Before the Administrator withdraws the approval of any laboratory, the Director of the laboratory will be given a notice by the Administrator of the proposed disapproval and the reasons for it, and the Director will have the opportunity to respond. In those instances where there are conflicts as to the facts, a hearing will be held to resolve such conflicts.

[4] A list of recognized slaughtering establishments is available upon request from the Animal and Plant Health Inspection Service, 4700 River Road Unit 37, Riverdale, Maryland 20737–1231.

§ 52.3 Appraisal of swine.

(a) Herds of swine and individual breeding sows to be destroyed because they are known to be infected with pseudorabies will be appraised by an APHIS employee and a representative of the State jointly, a representative of the State alone, or, if the State authorities approve, by an APHIS employee alone.

(b) The appraisal of swine will be based on the fair market value as determined by the meat or breeding value of the animals. Animals may be appraised in groups, provided that where appraisal is by the head, each animal in the group is the same value per head, and where appraisal is by the pound, each animal in the group is the same value per pound.

(c) Appraisals of swine must be reported on forms furnished by APHIS and signed by the owner of the swine. Reports of appraisals must show the number of swine and the value per head or the weight and value by pound.

(Approved by the Office of Management and Budget under control number 0579–0137)

[64 FR 2549, Jan. 15, 1999, as amended at 65 FR 20711, Apr. 18, 2000]

§ 52.4 Presentation of claims.

(a) When swine have been destroyed under § 52.2(a), any claim for indemnity must be presented, along with the report of net salvage proceeds required under § 52.5, to the veterinarian in charge on a form furnished by APHIS.

(b) When swine have been destroyed under § 52.2(b), any claim for indemnity must be presented, through the inspector in charge, to APHIS on a form furnished by APHIS.

(c) For all claims for indemnity, the owner of the swine must certify on the claim form that the swine covered are, or are not, subject to any mortgage as defined in this part. If the owner states there is a mortgage, the owner and each person holding a mortgage on the swine must sign, consenting to the payment of indemnity to the person specified on the form.

(Approved by the Office of Management and Budget under control number 0579–0137)

[65 FR 20711, Apr. 18, 2000]

§ 52.5 Report of net salvage proceeds.

A report of the amount for net salvage derived from the sale of each animal for which a claim for indemnity is made under § 52.2(a) must be made on a salvage form that shows the gross receipts, expenses if any, and net proceeds. The original or a copy of the salvage form must be furnished by the owner to the veterinarian in charge.

(Approved by the Office of Management and Budget under control number 0579–0151)

[65 FR 20712, Apr. 18, 2000]

§ 52.6 Claims not allowed.

(a) The Department will not allow claims arising out of the destruction of swine unless the swine have been appraised as prescribed in this part and the owners have signed a written agreement to the appraisals.

(b) The Department will not allow claims arising out of the destruction of swine that have been moved or handled by the owner or a representative of the owner in violation of a law or regulation administered by the Secretary regarding animal disease, or in violation of a law or regulation for which the Secretary has entered into a cooperative agreement.

(Approved by the Office of Management and Budget under control number 0579–0137)

[64 FR 2549, Jan. 15, 1999. Redesignated at 65 FR 20711, Apr. 18, 2000]

§ 52.7 Disinfection of premises, conveyances, and materials.

All premises, including barns, stockyards and pens, and all cars and other conveyances, and the materials on any premises or conveyances used to house or transport swine for which indemnity is paid under this part must be cleaned and disinfected under the supervision of an APHIS employee after removal of the swine from the known infected herd. Premises may be restocked with swine 30 days following an approved cleaning and disinfection, unless an official pseudorabies epidemiologist determines that a shorter or longer period of time is adequate or necessary to protect new animals against infection. The owner to whom the indemnity is paid will be responsible for expenses incurred in connection with the cleaning and disinfection, except for cleaning and disinfection of the conveyances used to transport the swine to the location of disposal.

[64 FR 13065, Mar. 17, 1999. Redesignated at 65 FR 20711, Apr. 18, 2000]

PART 53—FOOT-AND-MOUTH DISEASE, PLEUROPNEUMONIA, RINDERPEST, AND CERTAIN OTHER COMMUNICABLE DISEASES OF LIVESTOCK OR POULTRY

AUTHORITY: 7 U.S.C. 8301–8317; 7 CFR 2.22, 2.80, and 371.4.

CROSS REFERENCE: For non-applicability of part 53 with respect to certain claims for indemnity, see §51.10 of this chapter.

§53.1 Definitions.

Accredited veterinarian. A veterinarian approved by the Administrator in accordance with part 161 of this chapter to perform functions specified in parts 1, 2, 3, and 11 of subchapter A of this chapter and subchapters B, C, and D of this chapter, and to perform functions required by cooperative State-Federal disease control and eradication programs.

Administrator. The Administrator, Animal and Plant Health Inspection Service, or any person authorized to act for the Administrator.

Animal and Plant Health Inspection Service. The Animal and Plant Health Inspection Service of the United States Department of Agriculture (APHIS).

Animals. Livestock, poultry, and all other members of the animal kingdom, including birds whether domesticated or wild, but not including man.

APHIS employee. Any individual employed by the Animal and Plant Health Inspection Service who is authorized by the Administrator to do any work or perform any duty in connection with the control and eradication of disease.

Bird. Any member of the class *aves* other than poultry.

Department. The United States Department of Agriculture.

Disease. Foot-and-mouth disease, rinderpest, contagious pleuropneumonia, Newcastle disease, highly pathogenic avian influenza, infectious salmon anemia, spring viremia of carp, or any other communicable disease of livestock or poultry that in the opinion of the Secretary constitutes an emergency and threatens the livestock or poultry of the United States.

Highly pathogenic avian influenza. (1) Any influenza virus that kills at least 75 percent of eight 4- to 6-week-old susceptible chickens within 10 days following intravenous inoculation with 0.2 ml of a 1:10 dilution of a bacteria-free, infectious allantoic fluid;

(2) Any H5 or H7 virus that does not meet the criteria in paragraph (1) of this definition, but has an amino acid sequence at the hemagglutinin cleavage site that is compatible with highly pathogenic avian influenza viruses; or

(3) Any influenza virus that is not an H5 or H7 subtype and that kills one to five chickens and grows in cell culture in the absence of trypsin.

Inspector in charge. An APHIS employee who is designated by the Administrator to take charge of work in connection with the control and eradication of disease.

ISA Program veterinarian. The APHIS veterinarian assigned to manage the infectious salmon anemia program for APHIS in the State of Maine and who reports to the Area Veterinarian in Charge.

Materials. Parts of barns or other structures, straw, hay, and other feed for animals, farm products or equipment, clothing, and articles stored in or adjacent to barns or other structures.

Mortgage. Any mortgage, lien, or other security or beneficial interest held by any person other than the one claiming indemnity.

Newcastle disease. Newcastle disease is an acute, rapidly spreading, and usually fatal viral infection of poultry caused by an avian paramyxovirus serotype 1 that meets one of the following criteria for virulence: The virus has an intracerebral pathogenicity index (ICPI) in day-old chicks (*Gallus gallus*) of 0.7 or greater; or multiple basic amino acids have been demonstrated in the virus (either directly or by deduction) at the C-terminus of the F2 protein and phenylalanine at residue 117, which is the N-terminus of the F1 protein. The term "multiple basic amino acids" refers to at least three arginine or lysine residues between residues 113 and 116. In this definition, amino acid residues are numbered from the N-terminus of the amino acid sequence deduced from the nucleotide sequence of the F0 gene; 113–116 corresponds to residues −4 to −1 from the cleavage site. Failure to demonstrate the characteristic pattern of amino acid residues as described above may require characterization of the isolated virus by an ICPI test. A failure to detect a cleavage site that is consistent with virulent strains does not confirm the absence of a virulent virus.

Person. Any individual, corporation, company, association, firm, partnership, society, joint stock company, or other legal entity.

Pet bird. Any bird that is kept for personal pleasure and is not for sale.

Poultry. Chickens, ducks, geese, swans, turkeys, pigeons, doves, pheasants, grouse, partridges, quail, guinea fowl, and pea fowl.

Secretary. The Secretary of Agriculture of the United States, or any officer or employee of the Department to whom authority has been or may be delegated to act in the Secretary's stead.

State. Each of the States of the United States, the District of Columbia, Puerto Rico, the Northern Mariana Islands, Guam, the Virgin Islands of the United States, or any other territory or possession of the United States.

[61 FR 56882, Nov. 5, 1996, as amended at 67 FR 17610, Apr. 11, 2002; 69 FR 27827, May 17, 2004; 74 FR 18287, Apr. 22, 2009; 78 FR 19082, Mar. 29, 2013]

§ 53.2 Determination of existence of disease; agreements with States.

(a) The Administrator is hereby authorized to invite the proper State authorities to cooperate with the Department in the control and eradication of any disease within the meaning of § 53.1.

(b) Upon agreement of the authorities of the State to enforce quarantine restrictions and orders and directives properly issued in the control and eradication of such a disease, the Administrator is hereby authorized to agree, on the part of the Department, to cooperate with the State in the control and eradication of the disease, and to pay 50 percent (and in the case of Newcastle disease or highly pathogenic avian influenza, up to 100 percent, and in the case of infectious salmon anemia, up to 60 percent) of the expenses of purchase, destruction and disposition of animals, eggs, and materials required to be destroyed because of being contaminated by or exposed to such disease: *Provided, however, that* if the animals or eggs were exposed to such disease prior to or during interstate movement and the owners or parties contracting with the owners to raise or care for the animals or eggs are not eligible to receive indemnity from any State, the Department may pay up to 100 percent of the purchase, destruction, and disposition of animals, eggs, and materials required to be destroyed; *Provided further*, that the cooperative program for the purchase, destruction, and disposition of birds shall be limited to birds which are identified in documentation pursuant to Agreements between the Department and the particular State involved relating to cooperative animal (including poultry) disease prevention, control, and eradication, as constituting a threat to the poultry industry of the United States; *And provided further*, that the Secretary may authorize other arrangements for the payment of such expenses upon finding that an extraordinary emergency exists.

[37 FR 5689, Mar. 18, 1972, as amended at 49 FR 3448, Jan. 27, 1984; 49 FR 26712, June 29, 1984; 61 FR 56883, Nov. 5, 1996; 67 FR 17610, Apr. 11, 2002; 67 FR 67095, Nov. 4, 2002; 78 FR 19082, Mar. 29, 2013; 81 FR 6750, Feb. 9, 2016]

§53.3 Appraisal of animals, eggs, or materials.

(a) Animals or eggs affected by or exposed to disease, and materials required to be destroyed because of being contaminated by or exposed to disease shall be appraised by an APHIS employee and a representative of the State jointly, or, if the State authorities approve, by an APHIS employee alone.

(b) The appraisal of animals shall be based on the fair market value and shall be determined by the meat, egg production, dairy or breeding value of such animals. Animals may be appraised in groups providing they are the same species and type and providing that where appraisal is by the head each animal in the group is the same value per head or where appraisal is by the pound each animal in the group is the same value per pound.

(c) Appraisals of animals shall be reported on forms furnished by APHIS. Reports of appraisals shall show the number of animals of each species and the value per head or the weight and value by pound.

(d) Appraisals of materials shall be reported on forms furnished by APHIS. Reports of appraisals of materials shall, when practicable, show the number, size or quantity, unit price, and total value of each kind of material appraised.

(e) Indemnity for eggs required to be destroyed due to an outbreak of highly pathogenic avian influenza will be based on the fair market value of the eggs, as determined by an appraisal. Appraisals of eggs shall be reported on forms furnished by APHIS. The amount of indemnity paid, together with the amount for net salvage the owner or contractor received, if any, shall not exceed the appraised fair market value of the eggs.

[28 FR 5935, June 13, 1963, as amended at 35 FR 13981, Sept. 3, 1970; 36 FR 25217, Dec. 30, 1971; 56 FR 51974, Oct. 17, 1991; 68 FR 6343, Feb. 7, 2003; 81 FR 6750, Feb. 9, 2016]

§53.4 Destruction of animals or eggs.

(a) Except as provided in paragraph (b) of this section, animals infected with or exposed to disease shall be killed promptly after appraisal and disposed of by burial or burning, unless otherwise specifically provided by the Administrator, at his or her discretion. In the case of animals depopulated due to spring viremia of carp or infectious salmon anemia, salvageable fish may be sold for rendering, processing, or any other purpose approved by the Administrator. The proceeds gained from the sale of the fish will be subtracted from any payment from APHIS for which the producer or owner is eligible under §53.2(b) or §53.11.

(b) Eggs infected with, exposed to, or contaminated by highly pathogenic avian influenza shall be disposed of pursuant to the regulations in this part under the supervision of an APHIS employee who shall prepare and transmit to the Administrator a report identifying all eggs disposed thereof.

(c) The killing of animals and the burial, burning, or other disposal of carcasses of animals pursuant to the regulations in this part shall be supervised by an APHIS employee who shall prepare and transmit to the Administrator a report identifying the animals and showing the disposition thereof.

[28 FR 5935, June 13, 1963, as amended at 56 FR 51974, Oct. 17, 1991; 67 FR 67095, Nov. 4, 2002; 68 FR 42569, July 18, 2003; 69 FR 27827, May 17, 2004; 71 FR 56323, Sept. 26, 2006; 81 FR 6750, Feb. 9, 2016]

§53.5 Disinfection or destruction of materials.

(a) In order to prevent the spread of disease, materials contaminated by or exposed to disease shall be disinfected: *Provided, however*, That in all cases in which the cost of disinfection would exceed the value of the materials or disinfection would be impracticable for any reason, the materials shall be destroyed, after appraisal as provided in §53.3.

(b) The disinfection or destruction of materials under this section shall be under the supervision of an APHIS employee who shall prepare and transmit to the Administrator a certificate identifying all materials which are destroyed, showing the disposition thereof.

[28 FR 5935, June 13, 1963, as amended at 56 FR 51974, Oct. 17, 1991]

§ 53.6 Disinfection of animals.

Animals of species not susceptible to the disease for which a quarantine has been established, but which have been exposed to the disease, shall be disinfected when necessary by such methods as the Administrator shall prescribe from time to time.

[28 FR 5935, June 13, 1963, as amended at 56 FR 51974, Oct. 17, 1991]

§ 53.7 Disinfection of premises, conveyances, and materials.

All premises, including barns, corrals, stockyards and pens, and all cars, vessels, aircraft, and other conveyances, and the materials thereon, shall be cleaned and disinfected under supervision of an APHIS employee whenever necessary for the control and eradication of disease. Expenses incurred in connection with such cleaning and disinfection shall be shared according to the agreement reached under § 53.2 with the State in which the work is done. In the case of low pathogenic avian influenza related to the 2002 disease situations in Virginia and Texas associated with the H5 or H7 virus, premises may not be restocked with poultry until at least 7 days following such cleaning and disinfection, unless the Administrator determines that a shorter or longer period of time is adequate or necessary to protect new poultry against infection.

[68 FR 42569, July 18, 2003]

§ 53.8 Presentation of claims.

(a) Claims for the following must be presented to APHIS, through the inspector in charge, on a form approved by the Administrator:

(1) Compensation for the value of animals;

(2) The cost of burial, burning, or other disposition of animals;

(3) The value of material destroyed; and

(4) The expenses of destruction.

(b) [Reserved]

(Approved by the Office of Management and Budget under control number 0579–0208)

[67 FR 67095, Nov. 4, 2002, as amended at 68 FR 42570, July 18, 2003; 71 FR 56323, Sept. 26, 2006]

§ 53.9 Mortgage against animals, eggs, or materials.

When animals, eggs, or materials have been destroyed pursuant to the requirements contained in this part, any claim for indemnity shall be presented on forms furnished by APHIS on which the owner of the animals, eggs, or materials shall certify that the animals, eggs, or materials covered thereby, are, or are not, subject to any mortgage as defined in this part. If the owner states there is a mortgage, forms furnished by APHIS shall be signed by the owner and by each person holding a mortgage on the animals, eggs, or materials, consenting to the payment of any indemnity allowed to the person specified thereon.

[28 FR 5935, June 13, 1963, as amended at 56 FR 51974, Oct. 17, 1991; 81 FR 6750, Feb. 9, 2016]

§ 53.10 Claims not allowed.

(a) The Department will not allow claims arising under the terms of this part if the payee has not complied with all quarantine requirements.

(b) Expenses for the care and feeding of animals held for destruction will not be paid by the Department, unless the payment of such expense is specifically authorized or approved by the Administrator.

(c) The Department will not allow claims arising out of the destruction of animals, eggs, or materials unless they shall have been appraised as prescribed in this part and the owners thereof shall have executed a written agreement to the appraisals.

(d) The Department will not allow claims arising out of the destruction of animals, eggs, or materials which have been moved or handled by the owner thereof or its officer, employee, or agent, acting within the scope of his or its office, employment or agency, in violation of a law or regulation administered by the Secretary for the prevention of the introduction into or the dissemination within the United States of any communicable disease of livestock or poultry for which the animal or material was destroyed, or in violation of a law or regulation for the enforcement of which the Secretary enters or has entered into a cooperative agreement for the control and eradication of such disease.

(e) The Department will not allow claims arising out of the destruction of fish due to infectious salmon anemia (ISA) unless the claimants have agreed in writing to participate fully in the cooperative ISA control program administered by APHIS and the State of Maine. Participants in the ISA control program must:

(1) Establish and maintain a veterinary client-patient relationship with an APHIS accredited veterinarian and inform the ISA Program Veterinarian in writing of the name of their accredited veterinarian at the time the participant enrolls in the ISA program and within 15 days of any change in accredited veterinarians.

(2) Cooperate with and assist in periodic on-site disease surveillance, testing, and reporting activities for ISA, which will be conducted by their APHIS accredited veterinarian or a State or Federal official as directed by the ISA Program Veterinarian.

(3) Develop and implement biosecurity protocols for use at all participant-leased finfish sites and participant-operated vessels engaged in aquaculture operations throughout Maine. A copy of these protocols shall be submitted to the ISA Program Veterinarian at the time the participant enrolls in the ISA program and within 15 days of any change in the protocols.

(4) Develop, with the involvement of the participant's accredited veterinarian and the fish site health manager, a site-specific ISA action plan for the control and management of ISA. A copy of the action plan shall be submitted to APHIS for review at the time the participant enrolls in the ISA program and within 15 days of any change in the action plan.

(5) Participate in the State of Maine's integrated pest management (IPM) program for the control of sea lice on salmonids. A copy of the management plan developed by the participant for the State IPM program shall be submitted to APHIS for review at the time the participant enrolls in the ISA program and within 15 days of any change in the management plan.

(6) Submit to the ISA Program Veterinarian at the time the participant enrolls in the ISA program a complete and current fish inventory information for each participant-leased finfish site with site and cage identifiers. Fish inventory information must include the numbers, age, date of saltwater transfer, vaccination status, and previous therapeutant history for all fish in each participant-leased finfish site.

(7) Maintain, and make available to the ISA Program Veterinarian upon request, mortality data for each participant-leased finfish site and pen in production.

(8) Cooperate with and assist APHIS in the completion of biosecurity audits at all participant-leased finfish sites and participant-operated vessels involved in salmonid aquaculture.

(f) The Department will not allow claims arising out of the destruction of fish due to spring viremia of carp (SVC) unless the claimants have done the following:

(1) Depopulated all SVC-infected and SVC-exposed fish on their property under the supervision of USDA or State officials;

(2) Thoroughly cleaned and disinfected all affected sites and all affected equipment under the supervision of USDA or State officials;

(3) If an affected site is to be restocked after cleaning and disinfection, the claimant must have done the following:

(i) Restocked with fish certified free of SVC by an APHIS-approved laboratory or in accordance with the diagnostic procedures described in the Office of International des Epizooties Manual of Diagnostic Tests For Aquatic Animals;

(ii) Demonstrated that their water sources are from first-use spring water, spring water without fish, well water, ozone or ultraviolet treated surface water, or bore-hole water and are free of wild carp and any other SVC-susceptible species; and

(iii) Prevented the migration of wild carp and any other wild SVC-susceptible species into their farming establishment.

(Approved by the Office of Management and Budget under control number 0579–0192)

(g) The Department will not allow claims arising out of the destruction of animals or eggs destroyed due to an outbreak of highly pathogenic avian influenza unless the owner of the animals or eggs and any party that enters into a contract with the owners to grow or care for the poultry or eggs, unless exempted under paragraph (g)(2) of this section, provide to APHIS a statement that at the time of detection of highly pathogenic avian influenza in the facility, the owner and contractor (if applicable), had in place and was following a biosecurity plan.

(1) The biosecurity plan should include the following:

(i) A biosecurity training program for premises/farm personnel;

(ii) Biosecurity protocols for personnel;

(iii) Procedures to control wild birds, rodents, and insects to reduce the risk of introduction or spread of HPAI;

(iv) Measures taken to prevent HPAI introduction via vehicles and equipment;

(v) Maintenance of a line of separation; and

(vi) A clean water source for the facility.

(2) Owners and contractors are exempted from the requirements of paragraph (g)(1) of this section if the facilities where the animals or eggs are raised or cared for falls under one of the following categories:

(i) Premises meeting the criteria of the National Poultry Improvement Plan regulations in §§ 146.22(b) or 146.52(c) of this chapter;

(ii) Premises on which fewer than 100,000 broilers are raised annually; and

(iii) Premises on which fewer than 30,000 meat turkeys are raised annually.

[28 FR 5935, June 13, 1963, as amended at 45 FR 86411, Dec. 31, 1980; 56 FR 51974; 67 FR 17611, Apr. 11, 2002; 69 FR 27827, May 17, 2004; 81 FR 6750, Feb. 9, 2016]

§ 53.11 Highly pathogenic avian influenza; conditions for payment.

(a) When poultry or eggs have been destroyed pursuant to this part, the Administrator may pay claims to any party with whom the owner of the poultry or eggs has entered into a contract for the growing or care of the poultry or eggs. The indemnity the Administrator may pay to such a party or parties shall be determined as by the following method:

(1) Divide the value in dollars of the contract the owner entered into with the contractor by the duration in days of the contract as it was signed prior to the highly pathogenic avian influenza outbreak;

(2) Multiply this figure by the time in days between the date the contractor began to provide services relating to the destroyed poultry or eggs under the contract and the date the poultry or eggs were destroyed due to highly pathogenic avian influenza.

(b) If a contractor receiving indemnity under this section has received any payment under his or her contract from the owner of the poultry or eggs at the time the poultry or eggs are destroyed, the amount of indemnity for which the contractor is eligible will be reduced by the amount of the payment the contractor has already received.

(c) If indemnity is paid to a contractor under this section, the owner of the poultry or eggs will be eligible to receive the difference between the indemnity paid to the contractors and the total amount of indemnity that may be paid for the poultry or eggs.

(d) In the event that determination of indemnity due a contractor using the method described in paragraph (a) of this section is determined to be impractical or inappropriate, APHIS may use any other method that the Administrator deems appropriate to make that determination.

[81 FR 6750, Feb. 9, 2016]

PART 54—CONTROL OF SCRAPIE

Subpart A—Scrapie Indemnification Program

Subpart B—Scrapie Flock Certification Program

AUTHORITY: 7 U.S.C. 8301–8317; 7 CFR 2.22, 2.80, and 371.4.

SOURCE: 66 FR 43982, Aug. 21, 2001, unless otherwise noted.

§ 54.1 Definitions.

Accredited veterinarian. A veterinarian approved by the Administrator in accordance with part 161 of this chapter to perform functions specified in subchapters B, C, and D of this chapter.

Administrator. The Administrator of the Animal and Plant Health Inspection Service or any employee of the United States Department of Agriculture authorized to act for the Administrator.

Animal. A sheep or goat.

Animal and Plant Health Inspection Service (APHIS). The Animal and Plant Health Inspection Service of the United States Department of Agriculture.

APHIS representative. An individual employed by APHIS in animal health activities who is authorized by the Administrator to perform the function involved.

Approved laboratory. A laboratory approved by the Administrator in accordance with § 54.11 to conduct one or more scrapie tests, or genotype tests, on one or more tissues.

Approved test. A test for the diagnosis of scrapie approved by the Administrator for use in the scrapie eradication or certification program in accordance with § 54.10.

Area veterinarian in charge. The veterinary official of APHIS who is assigned by the Administrator to supervise and perform the official animal health work of APHIS in the State concerned.

Breed association and registries. Organizations listed in § 151.9 of this chapter that maintain the permanent records of ancestry or pedigrees of animals (including the animal's sire and dam), individual identification of animals, and ownership of animals.

Certificate. An official document issued in accordance with § 79.5 of this chapter by an APHIS representative, State representative, or accredited veterinarian at the point of origin of an interstate movement of animals.

Commingle, commingled, commingling. Animals grouped together and having physical contact with each other, including contact through a fence, but not limited contacts. Commingling also includes sharing the same section in a transportation unit where there is physical contact.

Designated scrapie epidemiologist. An epidemiologist who has demonstrated the knowledge and ability to perform the functions required and who has been selected by the State animal health official and the area veterinarian in charge. The regional epidemiologist and the APHIS National Scrapie Program Coordinator must concur in the selection and appointment of the designated scrapie epidemiologist. The designated scrapie epidemiologist must satisfactorily complete training designated by APHIS.

Destroyed. (1) Euthanized by means other than slaughter, and the carcass disposed of, by means authorized by the Administrator; or

(2) In the case of exposed or high-risk animals that are not known to be infected, either euthanized or disposed of by slaughter; or

(3) Moved to a quarantined research facility if the movement has been approved by the Administrator.

Electronic implant. Any radio frequency identification implant device approved for use in the scrapie program by the Administrator. The Administrator will approve an electronic implant after determining that it is tamper resistant, not harmful to the animal, and readable by equipment available to APHIS and State representatives.

Exposed animal. (1) Any animal that has been in the same flock at the same time as a scrapie-positive female animal, excluding limited contacts; or

(2) Any animal born in a flock after a scrapie-positive animal was born into

that flock or lambed in that flock, if born before that flock completes the requirements of a flock plan; or

(3) Any animal that was commingled with a scrapie-positive female animal during or up to 30 days after she lambed, kidded, or aborted, or while a visible vaginal discharge was present, or that was commingled with any other scrapie-positive female animal for 24 hours or more, including during activities such as shows and sales or while in marketing channels; or

(4) Any animal in a noncompliant flock.

Exposed flock. Any flock in which a scrapie-positive animal was born or lambed. Any flock that currently contains a female high-risk, exposed, or suspect animal, or that once contained a female high-risk, exposed, or suspect animal that lambed in the flock and from which tissues were not submitted for official testing and found negative. A flock that has completed a post-exposure management and monitoring plan following the exposure will no longer be an exposed flock.

Flock. All animals that are maintained on a single premises and all animals under common ownership or supervision on two or more premises with animal interchange between the premises. Changes in ownership of part or all of a flock do not change the identity of the flock or the regulatory requirements applicable to the flock. Animals maintained temporarily on a premises for activities such as shows and sales or while in marketing channels are not a flock. More than one flock may be maintained on a single premises if:

(1) The flocks are enrolled as separate flocks in the SFCP; or

(2) A State or APHIS representative determines, based upon examination of flock records, that:

(i) There is no interchange of animals between the flocks;

(ii) The flocks never commingle and are kept at least 30 feet apart at all times or are separated by a solid wall through, over, or under which fluids cannot pass and through which contact cannot occur;

(iii) The flocks have separate flock records and identification;

(iv) The flocks have separate lambing facilities, including buildings and pastures, and a pasture or building used for lambing by one flock is not used by the other flock at any time; and

(v) The flocks do not share equipment without cleaning and disinfection in accordance with § 54.7(e). Additional guidance on acceptable means of cleaning and disinfection is also available in the Scrapie Flock Certification Program standards and the Scrapie Eradication Uniform Methods and Rules.

Flock of origin. The flock in which an animal most recently resided in which it either was born, gave birth, or was used for breeding purposes. The determination of an animal's flock of origin may be based either on the physical presence of the animal in the flock, the presence of official identification on the animal traceable to the flock, the presence of other identification on the animal that is listed on the bill of sale, or other evidence, such as registry records.

Flock plan. A written flock management agreement signed by the owner of a flock, the accredited veterinarian, if one is employed by the owner, and a State or APHIS representative in which each participant agrees to undertake actions specified in the flock plan to control the spread of scrapie from, and eradicate scrapie in, an infected flock or source flock or to reduce the risk of the occurrence of scrapie in a flock that contains a high-risk or an exposed animal. As part of a flock plan, the flock owner must provide the facilities and personnel needed to carry out the requirements of the flock plan. The flock plan must include the requirements in § 54.8(a) through (f).

Flock sire. A sexually intact male animal that has ever been used for breeding in a flock.

High-risk animal. A sexually intact animal, excluding male sheep that have tested RR at codon 171 and AA at codon 136 using an official genotype test, that is:

(1) The progeny of a scrapie-positive dam; or

(2) Born in the same flock during the same lambing season as progeny of a scrapie-positive dam, unless the progeny of the scrapie-positive dam are

from separate contemporary lambing groups; or

(3) Born in the same flock during the same lambing season that a scrapie-positive animal was born, or during any subsequent lambing season, if born before that flock completes the requirements of a flock plan; or

(4) An exposed female sheep that has not tested QR, HR, or RR at codon 171 using an official genotype test.

Infected flock. The flock of origin of a female animal that a State or APHIS representative has determined to be a scrapie-positive animal; or any flock in which a State or APHIS representative has determined that a scrapie-positive female animal has resided unless an epidemiologic investigation conducted by a State or APHIS representative shows that the animal did not lamb or abort in the flock. A flock will no longer be considered an infected flock after it has completed the requirements of a flock plan.

Limited contacts. Incidental contacts between animals from different flocks off the flock's premises such as at fairs, shows, exhibitions and sales; between ewes being inseminated, flushed, or implanted; or between rams at ram test or collection stations. Embryo transfer and artificial insemination equipment and surgical tools must be sterilized between animals for these contacts to be considered limited contacts. Limited contacts do not include any contact, incidental or otherwise, with animals in the same flock or with a female animal during or up to 30 days after she lambed, kidded or aborted or when there is any visible vaginal discharge. Limited contacts do not include any activity where uninhibited contact occurs, such as sharing an enclosure, sharing a section of a transport vehicle, or residing in other flocks for breeding or other purposes. Examples of limited contacts may be found in the Scrapie Flock Certification Program standards.

Live-animal screening test. Any test for the diagnosis of scrapie in a live animal that is approved by the Administrator as usually reliable but not definitive for diagnosing scrapie, and that is conducted in a laboratory approved by the Administrator.[1]

Mortgage. Any mortgage, lien, or other security or interest held by any person other than the one claiming indemnity.

National Scrapie Database. A database designated by the Administrator in which APHIS and State animal health agencies cooperatively enter data concerning scrapie outbreaks, flocks and premises affected by scrapie, individual animal identification and premises identification data, and other data to support the Scrapie Eradication Program and the Scrapie Flock Certification Program.

National Veterinary Services Laboratories (NVSL). The National Veterinary Services Laboratories, APHIS, U.S. Department of Agriculture, or an NVSL cooperating or contract laboratory.

Noncompliant flock. (1) Any source or infected flock whose owner declines to enter into a flock plan or post-exposure management and monitoring plan agreement within 30 days of being so designated, or whose owner is not in compliance with either agreement;

(2) Any exposed flock whose owner fails to make animals available for testing within 60 days of notification, or as mutually agreed, or whose owner

---

[1] The names and addresses of laboratories approved by the Administrator to conduct live-animal screening tests will be published in the Notices Section of the FEDERAL REGISTER. A list of approved laboratories is also available upon request from the Animal and Plant Health Inspection Service, Veterinary Services, National Animal Health Programs Staff, 4700 River Road Unit 43, Riverdale, MD 20737–1235. State, Federal, and university laboratories will be approved by the Administrator when he or she determines that the laboratory: (a) Employs personnel trained by the National Veterinary Services Laboratories assigned to supervise the testing; (b) follows standard test protocols; (c) meets check test proficiency requirements; and (d) will report all test results to State and Federal animal health officials. Before the Administrator may withdraw approval of any laboratory for failure to meet any of these conditions, the Administrator must give written notice of the proposed withdrawal to the director of the laboratory and must give the director an opportunity to respond. If there are conflicts as to any material fact, a hearing will be held to resolve the conflicts.

fails to submit required postmortem samples;

(3) Any flock whose owner has misrepresented, or who employs a person who has misrepresented, the scrapie status of an animal or any other information on a certificate, permit, owner statement, or other official document within the last 5 years; or

(4) Any flock whose owner or manager has moved, or who employs a person who has moved, an animal in violation of this chapter within the last 5 years.

Official genotype test. Any test to determine the genotype of a live or dead animal that is conducted at either an approved laboratory or at the National Veterinary Services Laboratories, when the animal is officially identified and the samples used for the test are collected and shipped to the laboratory by either an accredited veterinarian or a State or APHIS representative

Official test. Any test for the diagnosis of scrapie in a live or dead animal that is approved by the Administrator for that use and conducted either at an approved laboratory or at the National Veterinary Services Laboratories.

Owner. A person, partnership, company, corporation, or any other legal entity who has legal or rightful title to animals, whether or not they are subject to a mortgage.

Post-exposure management and monitoring plan. A written agreement signed by the owner of a flock, any accredited veterinarian employed by the owner, and a State or APHIS representative in which each participant agrees to undertake actions specified in the agreement to monitor for the occurrence of scrapie in the flock for at least 5 years after the last high-risk or scrapie-positive animal is removed from the flock or after the last exposure of the flock to a scrapie-positive animal, unless otherwise specified by a State or APHIS representative. As part of a post-exposure management and monitoring plan, the flock owner must provide the facilities and personnel needed to carry out the requirements of the plan. The plan must include the requirements in § 54.8.

Scrapie control pilot project. A pilot project authorized by the Administrator in writing, designed to test or improve program procedures or to facilitate research, in order to control and eradicate scrapie. In addition to APHIS, participants may include State animal health agencies, flock owners, and other parties as necessary.

Scrapie Eradication Program. The cooperative State-Federal program administered by APHIS and Consistent States to control and eradicate scrapie.

Scrapie Eradication Uniform Methods and Rules (UM&R). Cooperative procedures and standards adopted by APHIS and Consistent States for controlling and eradicating scrapie. The UM&R will be reviewed at least annually by representatives of the livestock industry and appropriate State and Federal agencies and the public and will be revised, and published as needed by APHIS.

Scrapie Flock Certification Program (SFCP). The cooperative Federal-State-industry voluntary program for the control of scrapie conducted in accordance with this subpart.

Scrapie Flock Certification Program standards. Cooperative procedures and standards adopted by APHIS and State scrapie certification boards for reducing the incidence and controlling the spread of scrapie through flock certification.[2]

Scrapie-positive animal. An animal for which a diagnosis of scrapie has been made by the National Veterinary Services Laboratories or another laboratory authorized by the Administrator to conduct scrapie tests in accordance with this part, through:

(1) Histopathological examination of central nervous system (CNS) tissues from the animal for characteristic microscopic lesions of scrapie;

(2) The use of proteinase-resistant protein analysis methods including but not limited to immunohistochemistry and/or western blotting on CNS and/or peripheral tissue samples from a live or a dead animal for which a given method has been approved by the Administrator for use on that tissue;

[2] Individual copies of the Scrapie Flock Certification Program standards may be obtained on the World Wide Web at URL *http://www.aphis.usda.gov/vs/scrapie,* or from the Animal and Plant Health Inspection Service, National Animal Health Programs Staff, 4700 River Road Unit 43, Riverdale, MD 20737–1235.

(3) Bioassay;

(4) Scrapie associated fibrils (SAF) detected by electron microscopy; or

(5) Any other test method approved by the Administrator in accordance with § 54.10. [3]

Separate contemporary lambing groups. To be a separate contemporary lambing group, the group must be maintained separately such that the animals cannot come into physical contact with other lambs, kids, ewes or does or birth fluids or placenta from other ewes or does. This separate maintenance must preclude contact through a fence, during lambing and for 60 days following the date the last lamb or kid is born in a lambing season, and must preclude using the same lambing facility as other ewes or does, unless the lambing facility is cleaned and disinfected under supervision by an APHIS representative, State representative, or an accredited veterinarian between lambings in accordance with § 54.7(e). Additional guidance on acceptable means of cleaning and disinfection is also available in the Scrapie Flock Certification Program standards and the Scrapie Eradication Uniform Methods and Rules. The flock owner must maintain adequate records to document which animals were maintained in each contemporary lambing group and to document when cleaning and disinfection was performed and who supervised it.

Slaughter channels. Animals in slaughter channels include any animal that is sold, transferred, or moved either directly to a slaughter facility, to an individual for custom slaughter, or for feeding for the express purpose of improving the animals' condition for movement to slaughter. Any sexually intact animal that is commingled with breeding animals or that has been bred is not in slaughter channels. When selling animals for slaughter, owners should note on the bill of sale that the animals are sold only for slaughter.

Source flock. A flock in which a State or APHIS representative has determined that at least one animal was born that was diagnosed as a scrapie-positive animal at an age of 72 months or less. The determination that an animal was born in a flock will be based on such information as the presence of official identification on the animal traceable to the flock, the presence of other identification on the animal that is listed on the bill of sale, or other evidence, such as registry records, to show that a scrapie-positive animal was born in the flock, combined with the absence of records indicating that the animal was purchased from outside and added to the flock. If DNA from the animal was previously collected by an accredited veterinarian and stored at an approved genotyping laboratory, or if DNA collection and storage are required for breed registration and the breed registration has appropriate safeguards in place to ensure the integrity of the banking process, the owner may request verification of the animal's identity based on DNA comparison if adequate records and identification have been maintained by the owner and the repository to show that the archived DNA is that of the animal that has been traced to the flock. The owner will be responsible for all costs for the DNA comparison. A flock will no longer be a source flock after it has completed the requirements of a flock plan.

[3] The names and addresses of laboratories approved by the Administrator to conduct tests are published in the Notices Section of the FEDERAL REGISTER. A list of approved laboratories is also available upon request from the Animal and Plant Health Inspection Service, Veterinary Services, National Animal Health Programs Staff, 4700 River Road Unit 43, Riverdale, MD 20737–1235. State, Federal, and university laboratories will be approved by the Administrator when he or she determines that the laboratory: (a) Employs personnel trained by the National Veterinary Services Laboratories assigned to supervise the testing; (b) follows standard test protocols; (c) meets check test proficiency requirements; and (d) will report all test results to State and Federal animal health officials. Before the Administrator may withdraw approval of any laboratory for failure to meet any of these conditions, the Administratr must give written notice of the proposed withdrawal to the director of the laboratory and must give the director an opportunity to respond. If there are conflicts as to any material fact, a hearing will be held to resolve the conflict.

State. Each of the 50 States, the District of Columbia, the Northern Mariana Islands, Puerto Rico, and all territories or possessions of the United States.

State representative. An individual employed in animal health activities by a State or a political subdivision of a State and who is authorized by the State or political subdivision to perform the function involved.

Suspect animal. An animal will be designated a suspect animal in accordance with § 79.4 of this chapter if it is:

(1) A sheep or goat that exhibits any of the following possible signs of scrapie and that has been determined to be suspicious for scrapie by an accredited veterinarian or a State or APHIS representative: Weight loss despite retention of appetite; behavioral abnormalities; pruritus (itching); wool pulling; biting at legs or side; lip smacking; motor abnormalities such as incoordination, high stepping gait of forelimbs, bunny hop movement of rear legs, or swaying of back end; increased sensitivity to noise and sudden movement; tremor, "star gazing," head pressing, recumbency, or other signs of neurological disease or chronic wasting.

(2) A sheep or goat that has tested positive for scrapie or for the proteinase resistant protein associated with scrapie on a live-animal screening test or any other test, unless the animal is designated a scrapie-positive animal.

(3) A sheep or goat that has tested inconclusive or suggestive on an official test for scrapie.

Unofficial test. Any test for the diagnosis of scrapie or for the detection of the proteinase resistant protein associated with scrapie in a live or dead animal that either has not been approved by the Administrator or that was not conducted at an approved laboratory or at the National Veterinary Services Laboratories.

§ 54.2 Cooperative agreements and memoranda of understanding with States.

APHIS will execute cooperative agreements and/or memoranda of understanding with the animal health agency of any State in order to cooperatively administer the Scrapie Eradication Program and the Scrapie Flock Certification Program within that State. These agreements will describe the respective roles of APHIS and State personnel in implementing the Scrapie Eradication Program and the Scrapie Flock Certification Program. Each agreement may specify the financial, material, and personnel resources to be committed to these programs and other scrapie control measures by APHIS and the State; assign specific activities related to the control of scrapie within a State to APHIS or State personnel; establish schedules for APHIS representatives or State representatives to visit flocks; establish procedures for maintaining and sharing program records specified in this part, and specify other responsibilities of State representatives and APHIS representatives in support of the Scrapie Eradication Program and the Scrapie Flock Certification Program.

(Approved by the Office of Management and Budget under control number 0579–0101)

Subpart A—Scrapie Indemnification Program

§ 54.3 Animals eligible for indemnity payments.

(a) Indemnity may be paid for an animal only after the owner of the animal has applied for indemnification and been approved in accordance with § 54.4. Indemnity may be paid only for the following:

(1) Destruction of high-risk animals;

(2) Destruction of animals based on an epidemiologic investigation, when the Administrator determines that the destruction of these animals will contribute to the eradication of scrapie;

(3) Destruction of live scrapie-positive animals;

(4) Destruction of animals that test positive on a live-animal screening test; and

(5) Destruction of suspect animals that are destroyed at the request of an APHIS representative.

(b) No indemnity will be paid for an animal if the owner of the animal fails to provide APHIS, within 30 days of request, animal registration certificates, sale and movement records, or other records requested in accordance with

§54.5. No indemnity will be paid until the premises, including all structures, holding facilities, conveyances, and materials contaminated because of occupation or use by the depopulated animals, have been properly cleaned and disinfected in accordance with §54.7(e). Additional guidance on acceptable means of cleaning and disinfection is also available in the Scrapie Flock Certification Program standards and the Scrapie Eradication Uniform Methods and Rules. Premises or portions of premises may be exempted from the cleaning and disinfecting requirements if a designated scrapie epidemiologist determines, based on epidemiologic investigation, that cleaning and disinfection of such buildings, holding facilities, conveyances, or other materials on the premises will not significantly reduce the risk of the spread of scrapie, either because effective disinfection is not possible or because the normal operations on the premises prevent transmission of scrapie. No indemnity will be paid to an owner if the owner assembled or increased his flock for the purpose of collecting or increasing indemnity.

§54.4 Application by owners for indemnity payments.

(a) Normally, an application for indemnification will be initiated by a State or APHIS representative who is working with the owner of a flock that has already been determined to be an infected flock or source flock, or that is already under a State movement restriction. In such cases, the flock owner will confirm information about the flock's eligibility for indemnity that is contained in the application submitted by the State or APHIS representative. However, the owner of any flock may apply directly to receive indemnification by submitting to the Administrator a written request containing the following information:

(1) Name, address, and social security number of the flock owner;

(2) Number and breed(s) of animals in the flock, including a current inventory;

(3) Location of flock premises;

(4) Reasons the owner believes animals in his or her flock may be eligible for indemnification, including any diagnosis of scrapie made for animals in the flock; any signs of scrapie observed in the flock by the owner; and any movement of animals into the flock from flocks infected with or exposed to scrapie;

(5) A copy of the registration papers issued in the name of the owner for any registered animals in the flock (registration papers are not required for the payment of indemnity for animals that are not registered). If the registration papers are unavailable, the owner may choose to accept a lesser indemnity in accordance with §54.6(b)(2) or the area veterinarian in charge may grant a 60-day extension or the Administrator may grant an extension longer than 60 days for the presentation of registration papers; and

(6) Signed release letters addressed to any sheep or goat registry associations that maintain records of the owner's sheep or goats requesting the associations to release to APHIS all records maintained by the association on sheep or goats currently or formerly owned by the applicant.

(b) APHIS will evaluate each application to determine whether the owner's flock contains animals eligible for indemnity in accordance with §54.3.

§54.5 Certification by owners.

Before any indemnity is paid to an owner, the owner must sign a written agreement with APHIS, certifying the following:

(a) The owner will make available for review upon request by a State or APHIS representative all bills of sale, pedigree registration certificates, and other records regarding movement of animals into and from the flock;

(b) If the owner maintains any flock after the payment of indemnity or acquires a new flock that is housed on the same premises within 5 years after the last high-risk or scrapie-positive animal is removed, the owner will maintain the flock in accordance with a post-exposure management and monitoring plan for 5 years;

(c) If the animal for which indemnity is paid is subject to any mortgage, the owner consents to the payment of the indemnity, up to the value of the mortgage, to the person(s) holding the mortgage;

(d) That the animal may be removed to a U.S. Department of Agriculture facility or a quarantined research facility, slaughtered, or euthanized and necropsied and tissues removed for diagnostic or other purposes.

§ 54.6 Amount of indemnity payments.

(a) Indemnity paid for sheep in accordance with § 54.3 will be set based on the following price reports published by the Agricultural Marketing Service (AMS). If pricing information is unavailable from these markets during a given week or month or if the numbers of animals sold are too low to give an accurate market value, the preceding week or month's value will be used. The AMS reports from the most recent week or month prior to the date APHIS offers to pay an owner indemnity shall be used to calculate the indemnity for that owner's sheep:

(1) The weekly weighted average Choice/Prime slaughter lamb price per pound at Greeley, CO;

(2) The weekly weighted average Utility slaughter ewe price per pound at San Angelo, TX;

(3) The monthly weighted average commercial western ewe lamb replacement price per head;

(4) The monthly weighted average commercial western yearling ewe replacement price per head;

(5) The monthly weighted average commercial western running age ewe price per head.

(6) The monthly weighted average commercial western aged ewe price per head.

(b) For animals under 1 year of age, the basic indemnity shall equal the price per pound from paragraph (a)(1) of this section times the greater of 50 lbs or the actual weight of the animal; except that, for ewe lambs under 1 year of age, the indemnity shall equal the per-head price from paragraph (a)(3) of this section if that price is higher. For sexually intact sheep 8 years of age or older and castrated animals 1 year of age or older, the basic indemnity shall equal the price per pound from paragraph (a)(2) of this section times 150, based on an average weight of 150 lbs. For sexually intact sheep at least 1 year of age and under 2 years of age, the indemnity shall equal the greater of the price per head from paragraph (a)(4) of this section, or the price per pound from paragraph (a)(2) of this section times 150, based on an average weight of 150 lbs. For sexually intact sheep at least 2 years of age and under 6 years of age, the basic indemnity shall equal the greater of the price per head from paragraph (a)(5) of this section or the price per pound from paragraph (a)(2) of this section times 150, based on an average weight of 150 lbs. For sexually intact sheep at least 6 years of age and under 8 years of age, the basic indemnity will equal the greater of the price per head from paragraph (a)(6) of this section or the price per pound from paragraph (a)(2) of this section times 150, based on an average weight of 150 lbs. A premium shall be added to the basic indemnity for each registered animal, equal to $100 for each registered animal under 1 year of age, $200 for each registered animal at least 1 year of age and under 4 years of age, and $100 for each registered animal at least 4 years of age and under 8 years of age. An additional premium of $50 will be added to the basic indemnity for each flock sire. The owner must provide adequate records to qualify for these premiums. When the animals to be indemnified are goats, or are sheep that fall outside the classes covered previously in this paragraph, the Administrator may take into consideration the producer's purchase records and sales records for the preceding 12 to 24 months in determining the indemnity amount, but the indemnity shall not exceed the maximum indemnity calculated for registered sheep in accordance with this section.

(1) If records and identification are inadequate to determine the actual age of animals, an APHIS or State representative will count all sexually intact animals that are apparently under 1 year of age, and those that are apparently at least 1 and under 2 years of age, based on examination of their teeth, and the indemnity for these animals will be calculated. The total number of these animals will be subtracted from the total number of sexually intact animals in the group to be indemnified, and indemnity for the remainder will be calculated based on the assumption that the remainder of the

flock is 80 percent aged 2 to 6 years and 20 percent aged 6 to 8 years.

(2) Any animal that is not registered at the time indemnity is first offered, but is eligible to be registered, will receive the registered animal premium reduced by $50.

(c) For animals destroyed by slaughter, the owner will retain the salvage value (the amount paid by a slaughter plant for the animal) of the animals in lieu of receiving the base indemnity. If the salvage value, less transport costs, is less than the base indemnity, APHIS will pay the owner the difference. APHIS will also indemnify the owner in the amount of any registered animal or flock sire premiums for which the animal qualifies.

(d) If the owner disagrees with the average weight estimate, he may have the sheep weighed at a public scale at his own expense, provided that the sheep may not come in contact with other sheep or goats during movement to the public scales, and will be paid based on the actual weight times the AMS weekly average price.

(e) Indemnity will be paid to an owner only for animals actually in a flock at the time indemnity is first offered. Animals removed from the flock as part of a post-exposure management and monitoring plan will be paid indemnity based on the AMS average prices at the time an APHIS representative designates the animals for removal.

§54.7 Procedures for destruction of animals.

(a) Scrapie-positive and suspect animals for which indemnification is sought must be destroyed on the premises where they are held, pastured, or penned at the time indemnity is approved or moved to an approved research facility, unless the APHIS representative involved approves in advance of destruction moving the animals to another location for destruction. Animals that are not scrapie-positive or suspect animals for which indemnification is sought may be:

(1) Slaughtered when moved in accordance with part 79 of this chapter and with the prior written approval of the APHIS representative involved;

(2) Destroyed on the premises where they are held, pastured, or penned at the time indemnity is approved;

(3) Moved to an approved research facility; or

(4) Moved to another location for destruction if an APHIS representative approves the movement in advance.

(b) The carcasses of animals destroyed in accordance with this section are authorized by the Administrator to be buried, incinerated, or disposed of by other methods in accordance with local, State, and Federal laws. The carcasses of scrapie-positive and suspect animals may not be processed for human or animal food.

(c) The destruction of animals and disposition of their carcasses in accordance with this part must be monitored by an APHIS representative who will prepare and transmit to the Administrator a report identifying the animals and showing their disposition.

(d) APHIS may pay the reasonable costs of disposal for scrapie-positive and suspect animals that are indemnified. To obtain reimbursement for disposal costs, animal owners must obtain written approval of the disposal costs from APHIS, prior to disposal. The Administrator may also authorize payment of up to half the reasonable disposal costs for animals that are eligible to be destroyed by slaughter under this section but for which slaughter is not a practical or cost efficient means of disposal; *Provided that,* APHIS may pay more than one-half of the expenses when the Administrator determines that doing so will contribute to scrapie eradication. For reimbursement to be made, the owner of the animals must present the area veterinarian in charge with a copy of either a receipt for expenses paid or a bill for services rendered. Any bill for services rendered by the owner must not be greater than the normal fee for similar services provided by a commercial hauler or disposal facility.

(e) *Cleaning and disinfection of premises and equipment.* When required, cleaning and disinfection shall be conducted under the supervision of a State or APHIS representative as follows. Additional guidance on acceptable means of cleaning and disinfection is also available in the Scrapie Flock Certification Program standards and the Scrapie Eradication Uniform Methods and Rules:

(1) *Drylot areas.* When required, remove the manure and top 1–2 inches of soil to reduce contamination. Bury, till under, or compost the removed material in areas not accessed by domestic animals or wildlife.

(2) *Cement, wood, metal, and other non-earth surfaces, tools, equipment, instruments, feed, hay, bedding, and other materials.* Remove all organic material and compost or incinerate. Clean and wash all surfaces, tools, equipment, and instruments using hot water and detergent. Allow all surfaces, tools, equipment, and instruments to dry completely before disinfecting and sanitizing using the following methods:

(i) Incinerate items by high-temperature incineration methods;

(ii) Autoclave instruments, small tools, and other items at 136 °C for 1 hour;

(iii) To clean dry surfaces, apply a 2-percent chlorine bleach solution at room temperature (at least 18.3 °C for 1 hour, or apply a 1-molar solution of sodium hydroxide (approximately 5 oz. of sodium hydroxide dissolved in 1 gallon water) at room temperature for at least 1 hour. Note: A 2-molar solution is more effective than a 1-molar solution and should be used when circumstances permit.

§ 54.8 Requirements for flock plans and post-exposure management and monitoring plans.

(a) The owner of the flock or his or her agent must identify all animals 1 year of age or over within the flock. All animals less than 1 year of age must be identified when a change of ownership occurs, with the exception of those animals under 1 year of age moving within slaughter channels that must be identified in accordance with §§ 79.2 and 79.3 of this chapter. The form of identification must be an electronic implant, flank tattoo, ear tattoo, or tamper-resistant ear tag approved for this use by APHIS. In the case of goats, the form of identification may alternatively be a tail fold tattoo. The official identification must provide a unique identification number that is applied by the owner of the flock or his or her agent and must be linked to that flock in the National Scrapie Database.

(b) Upon request by a State or APHIS representative, the owner of the flock or his or her agent must have an accredited veterinarian collect tissues from animals for scrapie diagnostic purposes and submit them to a laboratory designated by a State or APHIS representative.

(c) Upon request by a State or APHIS representative, the owner of the flock or his or her agent must make animals in the flock and the records required to be kept as a part of these plans available for inspection.

(d) The owner of the flock or his or her agent must meet requirements found necessary by a State or APHIS representative to monitor for scrapie and to prevent the recurrence of scrapie in the flock and to prevent the spread of scrapie from the flock. These other requirements may include, but are not limited to: Utilization of a live-animal screening test; restrictions on the animals that may be moved from the flock; segregated lambing; cleaning and disinfection of lambing facilities; and/or education of the owner of the flock and personnel working with the flock in techniques to recognize clinical signs of scrapie and to control the spread of scrapie.

(e) The owner of the flock or his or her agent must immediately report the following animals to a State representative, APHIS representative, or an accredited veterinarian, and not remove them from a flock without written permission of a State or APHIS representative:

(1) Any sheep or goat exhibiting weight loss despite retention of appetite; behavioral abnormalities; pruritus (itching); wool pulling; biting at legs or side; lip smacking; motor abnormalities such as incoordination, high stepping gait of forelimbs, bunny hop movement of rear legs, swaying of back end; increased sensitivity to noise and sudden movement; tremor, "star gazing," head pressing, recumbency, or other signs of neurological disease or chronic wasting illness; and

(2) Any sheep or goat in the flock that has tested positive for scrapie or

for the proteinase resistant protein associated with scrapie on a live-animal screening test or any other test.

(f) *Requirements for flock plans only.* (1) An epidemiologic investigation must be conducted to identify high-risk and exposed animals that currently reside in the flock or that previously resided in the flock, and all high-risk animals, scrapie-positive animals, and suspect animals must be removed from the flock. The animals must be removed either by movement to an approved research facility or by euthanization and disposal of the carcasses by burial, incineration, or other methods in accordance with local, State, and Federal laws, or, in the case of high-risk animals, by movement to slaughter in accordance with the provisions of part 79 of this chapter, or upon request in individual cases by another means determined by the Administrator to be sufficient to prevent the spread of scrapie;

(2) The premises of a flock under a flock plan must be cleaned and disinfected in accordance with §54.7(e). Additional guidance on acceptable means of cleaning and disinfection is also available in the Scrapie Flock Certification Program standards and the Scrapie Eradication Uniform Methods and Rules. Premises or portions of premises may be exempted from the cleaning and disinfecting requirements if a designated scrapie epidemiologist determines, based on epidemiologic investigation, that cleaning and disinfection of such buildings, holding facilities, conveyances, or other materials on the premises will not significantly reduce the risk of the spread of scrapie, either because effective disinfection is not possible or because the normal operations on the premises prevent transmission of scrapie. No area where a scrapie-positive animal lambed or aborted may be exempted;

(3) The owner of the flock, or his or her agent, must request breed associations and registries, livestock markets, and packers to disclose records to APHIS representatives or State representatives, to be used to identify source flocks and trace exposed animals, including high-risk animals; and

(4) The flock owner must agree to conduct post-exposure management and monitoring.

(g) *Requirements for post-exposure management and monitoring plans only:* The plan must require that a State or APHIS representative inspect the flock and flock records at least once every 12 months. The owner of the flock or his or her agent must maintain, and keep for a minimum of 5 years after an animal dies or is otherwise removed from a flock, the following records for each animal in the flock:

(1) Any identifying marks or tags present on the animal, including the animal's individual official identification number from its electronic implant, flank tattoo, ear tattoo, tamper resistant ear tag, or, in the case of goats, tail fold tattoo, and any secondary form of identification the owner of the flock may choose to maintain;

(2) Sex, year of birth, breed, and when possible to determine, the following: sire, dam, and offspring of the animal;

(3) Date of acquisition and previous flock, if the animal was not born in the flock; and

(4) Disposition of the animal, including the date and cause of death, if known, or date of removal from the flock and name and address of the person to whom the animal was transferred.

(h) *Modification of flock plans and post-exposure management and monitoring plans.* A designated scrapie epidemiologist may modify the requirements of a flock plan or post-exposure management and monitoring plan to accommodate the situation of a particular flock if the modified plan requires:

(1) That a State or APHIS representative inspect the flock and flock records at least once every 12 months;

(2) The testing of animals at a level that will result in 99 percent confidence of detecting a 1 percent prevalence in the flock (for flock plans only);

(3) The official identification of all animals upon leaving the premises of the flock for purposes other than slaughter and of all animals over 18 months of age (as evidenced by the

eruption of the second incisor) in slaughter channels; and

(4) Recordkeeping including:

(i) For acquired animals, the date of acquisition, name and address of the person from whom the animal was acquired, any identifying marks or tags present on the animal including the animal's individual official identification number from its electronic implant, flank tattoo, ear tattoo, tamper resistant ear tag, or, in the case of goats, tail fold tattoo, and any secondary form of identification the owner of the flock may choose to maintain.

(ii) For animals leaving the premises of the flock, the disposition of the animal, including, for those animals that are required to be identified, any identifying marks or tags present on the animal, including the animal's individual official identification number from its electronic implant, flank tattoo, ear tattoo, tamper resistant ear tag, or, in the case of goats, a tail fold tattoo, and any secondary form of identification the owner of the flock may choose to maintain, the date and cause of death, if known, or date of removal from the flock and name and address of the person to whom the animal was transferred.

(iii) Maintenance of these records for 5 years.

(5) Requirements equivalent to those contained in paragraphs (b), (c), (d), and (e) of this section.

(i) *Post-exposure management and monitoring plans for exposed flocks that were not source flocks and in which a scrapie infected animal did not lamb.* A designated scrapie epidemiologist shall determine the testing and monitoring requirements for these flocks based on the exposure risk of the individual flock.

§ 54.9 Waiver of requirements for scrapie control pilot projects.

The Administrator may waive the following requirements of this part for participants in a scrapie control pilot project by recording the requirements waived in the scrapie control pilot project plan:

(a) The determination that an animal is a high-risk animal, if the scrapie control pilot project plan contains testing or other procedures that indicate that an animal, despite meeting the definition of high-risk animal, is unlikely to spread scrapie; and

(b) The requirement that high-risk animals must be removed from a flock if the scrapie control pilot project plan contains alternative procedures to prevent the further spread of scrapie without removing high-risk animals from the flock.

§ 54.10 Tests for scrapie.

(a) The Administrator may approve new tests for the diagnosis of scrapie conducted on live or dead animals for use in the Scrapie Eradication Program. The Administrator will base the approval or disapproval of a test on the evaluation by APHIS and, when appropriate, outside scientists, of:

(1) A standardized test protocol that must include a description of the test, a description of the reagents, materials, and equipment used for the test, the test methodology, and any control or quality assurance procedures;

(2) Data to support reproducibility, that is, the ability to reproduce the same result repeatedly on a given sample;

(3) Data to support suitability, that is, data to show that similar results can be produced when the test is run at other laboratories;

(4) Data to support the sensitivity and specificity of the test; and

(5) Any other data requested by the Administrator to determine the suitability of the test for program use.

(b) To be approved, a scrapie test must be able to be replicated at the National Veterinary Services Laboratories, or another reliable, timely, and cost effective method of check testing must be available to APHIS.

(c) A test or combination of tests may be approved for the identification of suspect animals, for the identification of scrapie-positive animals, or for other purposes such as flock certification. For a test to be approved for the identification of scrapie-positive animals, the test must have a specificity comparable to the specificity of the currently approved tests. For a test to be approved as a live animal screening test for the identification of suspect animals, the test must be usually reliable but need not be definitive for diagnosing scrapie.

(d) Specific guidelines for use of approved scrapie tests within the Scrapie Eradication Program or Scrapie Flock Certification Program will be added to this part as tests are approved and will also be contained in the Scrapie Eradication UM&R and the Scrapie Flock Certification Program standards based on the characteristics of the test, including specificity, sensitivity, and predictive value.

(e) If an owner elects to have an unofficial test conducted on an animal for scrapie, or for the proteinase resistant protein associated with scrapie, and that animal tests positive to such a test, the animal will be designated a suspect animal, unless:

(1) The test was run as part of a bona fide research protocol designed to evaluate an unapproved test in which the owner is not informed of the test result; or

(2) The test protocol includes appropriate measures to prevent the spread of scrapie.

§54.11 Approval of laboratories to run official scrapie tests and official genotype tests.

(a) State, Federal, and university laboratories, or in the case of genotype tests, private laboratories will be approved by the Administrator when he or she determines that the laboratory:

(1) Employs personnel assigned to supervise the testing who are qualified to conduct the test based on education, training, and experience and who have been trained by the National Veterinary Services Laboratories (NVSL) or who have completed equivalent training approved by NVSL;

(2) Has adequate facilities and equipment to conduct the test;

(3) Follows standard test protocols;

(4) Meets check test proficiency requirements;

(5) Meets recordkeeping requirements;

(6) Will retain records, slides, blocks, and other specimens from all cases for at least 1 year and from positive cases for 5 years;

(7) Will allow APHIS to inspect the laboratory without notice during normal business hours; and

(8) Will report all test results to State and Federal animal health officials within agreed timeframes. An inspection may include, but is not limited to, review and copying of records, examination of slides, observation of the test being conducted, and interviewing of personnel.

(b) A laboratory may request approval to conduct one or more types of scrapie test or genotype test on one or more types of tissue. To be approved, a laboratory must meet the requirements in paragraph (a) of this section for each type of test and for each type of tissue for which they request approval.

(c) The Administrator may withdraw approval of any laboratory for failure to meet any of the conditions required by paragraph (a) of this section. The Administrator shall give written notice of the proposed withdrawal to the director of the laboratory and shall give the director an opportunity to respond. If there are conflicts as to any material fact concerning the reason for withdrawal, a hearing will be held to resolve the conflicts.

Subpart B—Scrapie Flock Certification Program

§54.20 Administration.

The Scrapie Flock Certification Program is a cooperative effort between APHIS; members of the sheep and goat industry, including owners of flocks, slaughtering and rendering establishments, and breed associations and registries; accredited veterinarians; and State governments. APHIS coordinates with State scrapie certification boards and State animal health agencies to encourage flock owners to certify their flocks as free of scrapie by being in continuous compliance with the Scrapie Flock Certification Program standards.

§54.21 Participation.

Any owner of a sheep or goat flock may apply to enter the Scrapie Flock Certification Program by sending a written request to a State scrapie certification board or to the area veterinarian in charge. A notice containing a current list of flocks participating in the Scrapie Flock Certification Program, and the certification status of each flock, may be obtained from the APHIS web site at URL *http:// www.aphis.usda.gov/vs/scrapie*. A list of noncompliant flocks may also be obtained from this site, and either list may be obtained by writing to the Animal and Plant Health Inspection Service, National Animal Health Programs Staff, VS, APHIS, 4700 River Road Unit 43, Riverdale, MD 20737–1235.

(Approved by the Office of Management and Budget under control number 0579–0101)

§ 54.22 State scrapie certification boards.

An area veterinarian in charge, after consulting with a State representative and industry representatives, may appoint a State scrapie certification board for the purpose of coordinating activities for the Scrapie Flock Certification Program, including making decisions to admit flocks to the Scrapie Flock Certification Program and to change flock status in accordance with the Scrapie Flock Certification Program standards. These boards are not appointed for the purpose of providing APHIS with consensus advice or policy recommendations. No more than one State scrapie certification board may be formed in each State. Each State scrapie certification board shall include as members the area veterinarian in charge, one or more State representatives, one or more accredited veterinarians, when possible, and one or more owners of flocks, and, at the discretion of the area veterinarian in charge, may include other members.

PART 55—CONTROL OF CHRONIC WASTING DISEASE

Subpart A—Chronic Wasting Disease Indemnification Program

Subpart B—Chronic Wasting Disease Herd Certification Program

AUTHORITY: 7 U.S.C. 8301–8317; 7 CFR 2.22, 2.80, and 371.4.

SOURCE: 67 FR 5931, Feb. 8, 2002, unless otherwise noted.

§ 55.1 Definitions.

Accredited veterinarian. A veterinarian approved by the Administrator in accordance with part 161 of this chapter to perform functions specified in subchapters B, C, and D of this chapter.

Administrator. The Administrator, Animal and Plant Health Inspection Service, or any person authorized to act for the Administrator.

Animal. Any farmed or captive deer, elk, or moose.

Animal identification. A device or means of animal identification approved for use under this part by APHIS. Examples of animal identification devices that APHIS has approved are listed in § 55.25.

Animal identification number (AIN). A numbering system for the official identification of individual animals in the United States. The AIN contains 15 digits, with the first 3 being the country code (840 for the United States), the alpha characters USA, or the numeric code assigned to the manufacturer of the identification device by the International Committee on Animal Recording.

Animal and Plant Health Inspection Service (APHIS). The Animal and Plant Health Inspection Service of the United States Department of Agriculture.

APHIS employee. Any individual employed by the Animal and Plant Health Inspection Service who is authorized by the Administrator to do any work or perform any duty in connection with the control and eradication of disease.

Approved State CWD Herd Certification Program. A program operated by a State government for certification of cervid herds with respect to CWD that the Administrator has determined to meet the requirements of §55.23(a).

Cervid. All members of the family Cervidae and hybrids, including deer, elk, moose, caribou, reindeer, and related species. For the purposes of this part, the term "cervid" refers specifically to cervids susceptible to CWD. These are animals in the genera Odocoileus, Cervus, and Alces and their hybrids, *i.e.*, deer, elk, and moose.

Commingled, commingling. Animals are commingled if they have direct contact with each other, have less than 10 feet of physical separation, or share equipment, pasture, or water sources/watershed. Animals are considered to have commingled if they have had such contact with a positive animal or contaminated premises within the last 5 years.

CWD-exposed animal. An animal that is part of a CWD-positive herd, or that has been exposed to a CWD-positive animal or contaminated premises within the previous 5 years.

CWD-exposed herd. A herd in which a CWD-positive animal has resided within 5 years prior to that animal's diagnosis as CWD-positive, as determined by an APHIS employee or State representative.

CWD Herd Certification Program. The Chronic Wasting Disease Herd Certification Program established by this part. This program includes both herds that are directly enrolled in the CWD Herd Certification Program and herds that are included based on their participation in Approved State CWD Herd Certification Programs.

CWD-positive animal. An animal that has had a diagnosis of CWD established through official confirmatory testing conducted by the National Veterinary Services Laboratories.

CWD positive herd. A herd in which a CWD positive animal resided at the time it was diagnosed and which has not been released from quarantine.

CWD-source herd. A herd that is identified through testing, tracebacks, and/or epidemiological evaluations to be the source of CWD-positive animals identified in other herds.

CWD-suspect animal. An animal for which an APHIS employee or State representative has determined that unofficial CWD test results, laboratory evidence or clinical signs suggest a diagnosis of CWD, but for which official laboratory results have been inconclusive or not yet conducted.

CWD-suspect herd. A herd for which unofficial CWD test results, laboratory evidence, or clinical signs suggest a diagnosis of CWD, as determined by an APHIS employee or State representative, but for which official laboratory results have been inconclusive or not yet conducted.

Deer, elk, and moose. All animals in the genera Odocoileus, Cervus, and Alces and their hybrids.

Department. The United States Department of Agriculture.

Farmed or captive. Privately or publicly maintained or held for economic or other purposes within a perimeter fence or confined area, or captured from a free-ranging population for interstate movement and release.

Herd. One or more animals that are:

(1) Under common ownership or supervision and are grouped on one or more parts of any single premises (lot, farm, or ranch) or

(2) All animals under common ownership or supervision on two or more premises which are geographically separated but on which animals have been interchanged or had direct or indirect contact with one another.

Herd plan. A written herd and/or premises management agreement developed by APHIS in collaboration with the herd owner, State representatives, and other affected parties. The herd plan will not be valid until it has been reviewed and signed by the Administrator, the State representative, and the herd owner. A herd plan sets out the steps to be taken to control the spread of CWD from a CWD-positive herd, to control the risk of CWD in a CWD-exposed or CWD-suspect herd, or to prevent introduction of CWD into that herd or any other herd. A herd plan will require specified means of identification for each animal in the herd; regular examination of animals in the herd by a veterinarian for clinical signs of disease; reporting to a State or APHIS representative of any clinical signs of a central nervous system disease or chronic wasting condition in the herd; maintaining records of the acquisition and disposition of all animals entering or leaving the herd, including the date of acquisition or removal, name and address of the person from whom the animal was acquired or to whom it was disposed; and the cause of death, if the animal died while in the herd. A herd plan may also contain additional requirements to prevent or control the possible spread of CWD, depending on the particular circumstances of the herd and its premises, including but not limited to depopulation of the herd, specifying the time for which a premises must not contain cervids after CWD-positive, -exposed, or -suspect animals are removed from the premises; fencing requirements; selective culling of animals; restrictions on sharing and movement of possibly contaminated livestock equipment; premises cleaning and disinfection requirements; or other requirements. A herd plan may be reviewed and changes to it suggested at any time by any party signatory to it, in response to changes in the situation of the herd or premises or improvements in understanding of the nature of CWD epidemiology or techniques to prevent its spread. The revised herd plan will become effective after it is reviewed by the Administrator and signed by the Administrator, the State representative, and the herd owner.

Herd status. The status of a herd assigned under the CWD Herd Certification Program in accordance with § 55.24, indicating a herd's relative risk for CWD. Herd status is based on the number of years of monitoring without evidence of the disease and any specific determinations that the herd has contained or has been exposed to a CWD-positive, -exposed or -suspect animal.

Materials. Parts of barns or other structures, straw, hay, and other feed for animals, farm products or equipment, clothing, and any other articles on the premises that have been in contact with captive cervids.

Mortgage. Any mortgage, lien, or other security or beneficial interest held by any person other than the one claiming indemnity.

National Uniform Eartagging System. A numbering system for the official identification of individual animals in the United States providing a nationally unique identification number for each animal. The National Uniform Eartagging System employs an eight- or nine-character alphanumeric format, consisting of a two-number State or territory code, followed by two or three letters and four additional numbers. Official APHIS disease control programs may specify which format to employ.

Official animal identification. A device or means of animal identification approved for use under this part by APHIS to uniquely identify individual animals. Examples of approved official animal identification devices are listed in § 55.25. The official animal identification must include a nationally unique animal identification number that adheres to one of the following numbering systems:

(1) National Uniform Eartagging System. The CWD program allows the use of either the eight-character or nine-character format for cervids.

(2) Animal identification number (AIN).

(3) Premises-based number system. The premises-based number system combines an official premises identification number (PIN), as defined in this section, with a producer's livestock production numbering system to provide a unique identification number. The PIN and the production number must both appear on the official tag.

(4) Any other numbering system approved by the Administrator for the identification of animals in commerce.

Official appraiser (APHIS official appraiser, State official appraiser). A person authorized by APHIS (an APHIS official appraiser) or a State (a State official appraiser) to appraise animals for the purposes of this part. An official appraiser may be an APHIS employee, a State employee, or a professional livestock appraiser working under contract to APHIS or a State.

Official CWD test. Any test for the diagnosis of CWD approved by the Administrator and conducted in a laboratory approved by the Administrator in accordance with § 55.8 of this part.

Person. Any individual, corporation, company, association, firm, partnership, society, joint stock company, or other legal entity.

Premises identification number (PIN). A nationally unique number assigned by a State, Tribal, and/or Federal animal health authority to a premises that is, in the judgment of the State, Tribal, and/or Federal animal health authority, a geographically distinct location from other premises. The premises identification number is associated with an address, geospatial coordinates, and/or location descriptors which provide a verifiably unique location. The premises identification number may be used in conjunction with a producer's own livestock production numbering system to provide a unique identification number for an animal. It may also be used as a component of a group/lot identification number. The premises identification number may consist of:

(1) The State's two-letter postal abbreviation followed by the premises' assigned number; or

(2) A seven-character alphanumeric code, with the right-most character being a check digit. The check digit number is based upon the ISO 7064 Mod 36/37 check digit algorithm.

Secretary. The Secretary of Agriculture of the United States, or any officer or employee of the Department delegated to act in the Secretary's stead.

State. Each of the States of the United States, the District of Columbia, Puerto Rico, the Northern Mariana Islands, Guam, the Virgin Islands of the United States, or any other territory or possession of the United States.

State representative. A person regularly employed in the animal health work of a State and who is authorized by that State to perform the function involved.

Trace back herd. A herd in which a CWD-positive animal formerly resided.

Trace forward herd. A herd that has received exposed animals from a CWD-positive herd within 5 years prior to the diagnosis of CWD in the positive herd or from the identified date of entry of CWD into the positive herd.

Veterinarian in charge. The veterinary official of Veterinary Services, APHIS, who is assigned by the Administrator to supervise and perform official animal health work for APHIS in the State concerned.

[67 FR 5931, Feb. 8, 2002, as amended at 71 FR 41701, July 21, 2006; 77 FR 35565, June 13, 2012; 79 FR 23891, Apr. 29, 2014]

Subpart A—Chronic Wasting Disease Indemnification Program

§ 55.2 Payment of indemnity.

The Administrator is authorized to pay for the purchase and destruction of CWD positive animals, CWD exposed animals, and CWD suspect animals. Subject to available funding, the amount of the Federal payment for any such animals will be 95 percent of the appraised value established in accordance with § 55.3 of this part, but the Federal payment shall not exceed $3,000 per animal. If a non-Federal source makes a payment for an animal for which a Federal indemnity is paid, and the non-Federal payment exceeds 5 percent of the appraised value established in accordance with § 55.3 of this part, the amount of the Federal payment for any such animals will be reduced by the amount by which the non-Federal payment exceeds 5 percent of the appraised value. The Administrator is also authorized to reimburse State governments or State animal health agencies for payments they make for the purchase and destruction, on or after October 1, 2001, of CWD positive animals, CWD exposed animals, and CWD suspect animals, and for State expenditures for associated carcass disposal and cleaning and disinfection costs resulting from such purchase and destruction, in accordance with cooperative agreements signed by the Administrator and the duly authorized agent of the State.

§ 55.3 Appraisal and destruction of captive cervids.

(a) CWD positive herds, or individual CWD suspect animals or exposed animals removed by APHIS from a herd for testing, will be appraised by an APHIS official appraiser and a State official appraiser jointly, or, if APHIS and State authorities agree, by either a State official appraiser or an APHIS official appraiser alone.

(b) The appraisal of cervids will be the fair market value as determined by the meat or breeding value of the animals. Animals may be appraised in groups, provided that where appraisal is by the head, each animal in the group is the same value per head, and where appraisal is by the pound, each animal in the group is the same value per pound.

(c) Appraisals of cervids must be reported on forms furnished by APHIS and signed by the appraisers, and signed by the owner of the cervids to indicate agreement with the appraisal amount. Reports of appraisals must show the number of cervids and the value per head or the weight and value by pound.

(d) In accordance with instructions from an APHIS employee, cervids for which indemnification is sought must be:

(1) Destroyed on the premises where they are held, pastured, or penned at the time indemnity is approved;

(2) Moved to another location for destruction under conditions specified by the APHIS employee; or

(3) Moved to an approved research facility under conditions specified by the APHIS employee.

(e) The carcasses of any cervids destroyed in accordance with this part are authorized by the Administrator to be incinerated, destroyed in an alkaline hydrolysis tissue digestor, or disposed of by any other method authorized by an APHIS employee and in accordance with local, State, and Federal laws. APHIS will pay the reasonable costs of destruction and carcass disposal for animals that are indemnified. To obtain reimbursement for disposal costs, animal owners must obtain written approval of the disposal costs from APHIS, prior to disposal. Except in cases where APHIS or a State directly arranges for disposal, the owner of the animals must present an APHIS employee with a written contract or estimate of disposal costs. Prior to receiving reimbursement, the owner must also present an APHIS employee with a copy of either a receipt for expenses paid by the owner or a bill for services rendered to the owner. Any bill for services rendered presented by the owner must not be greater than the normal fee for similar services provided by commercial entities. The carcasses of cervids destroyed in accordance with this section may not be sold to be processed for human or animal food, including dietary supplements.

(Approved by the Office of Management and Budget under control number 0579–0189)

§ 55.4 Disinfection of premises, conveyances, and materials.

After cervids are destroyed in accordance with this part, all premises, including barns, stockyards and pens, all cars and other conveyances, and all other materials on any premises or conveyances used to house or transport such cervids must be cleaned and disinfected under the supervision of an APHIS employee or a State representative, using methods specified by the APHIS employee or a State representative. Premises may not be restocked with cervids until after the date specified in the herd plan required by § 55.7(b) of this part. The owner to whom the indemnity is paid will be responsible for expenses incurred in connection with the cleaning and disinfection, except that APHIS or a State will pay for cleaning and disinfection of the conveyances used to transport the cervids to the location of disposal. However, APHIS may also decide to pay the cost of cleaning and disinfecting premises when the procedures needed to conduct effective cleaning and disinfection are unusually extensive and require methods that are not normally available on a premises. For example, normal procedures would include washing surfaces with high-pressure hoses and disinfectants and burying or burning contaminated materials. Unusually extensive procedures would include disposing of contaminated materials by digestive disposal or high-temperature incineration.

§ 55.5 Presentation of claims for indemnity.

Claims for indemnity for the value of animals destroyed must be documented on a form furnished by APHIS and presented to an APHIS employee or a State representative authorized to accept the claims.

(Approved by the Office of Management and Budget under control number 0579–0189)

§55.6 Mortgage against animals.

When cervids have been destroyed under this part, any claim for indemnity must be presented on forms furnished by APHIS. The owner of the cervids must certify on the forms that the cervids covered are, or are not, subject to any mortgage as defined in this part. If the owner states there is a mortgage, the owner and each person holding a mortgage on the cervids must sign, consenting to the payment of indemnity to the person specified on the form.

(Approved by the Office of Management and Budget under control number 0579–0189)

§55.7 Claims not allowed.

(a) The Department will not allow claims arising out of the destruction of cervids unless the cervids have been appraised as prescribed in this part and the owners have signed the appraisal form indicating agreement with the appraisal amount as required by §55.3(c) of this part.

(b) The Department will not allow claims arising out of the destruction of cervids unless the owners have signed a written agreement with APHIS in which they agree that if they maintain cervids in the future on the premises used for cervids for which indemnity is paid, they will maintain the cervids in accordance with a herd plan and will not introduce cervids onto the premises until after the date specified in that herd plan. Persons who violate this written agreement may be subject to civil and criminal penalties.

(c) The Department will not allow claims arising out of the destruction of cervids that have been moved or handled by the owner or a representative of the owner in violation of a law or regulation administered by the Secretary regarding animal disease, or in violation of a law or regulation for which the Secretary has entered into a cooperative agreement.

(Approved by the Office of Management and Budget under control number 0579–0189)

§55.8 Official CWD tests and approval of laboratories to conduct official CWD tests.

(a) An official CWD test is:

(1) Histopathological examination of central nervous system (CNS) tissues from the animal for characteristic microscopic lesions of CWD, using test protocols provided by the National Veterinary Services Laboratories (NVSL);

(2) The use of proteinase-resistant protein analysis methods including but not limited to immunohistochemistry and/or western blotting on CNS and/or peripheral tissue samples from a live or a dead animal, using test protocols provided by NVSL; or

(3) Any other test method approved by the Administrator in accordance with this section.

(b) The Administrator may approve new tests for the diagnosis of CWD conducted on live or dead animals, and will base the approval or disapproval of a test on the evaluation by APHIS and, when appropriate, outside scientists, of:

(1) A standardized test protocol that must include a description of the test, a description of the reagents, materials, and equipment used for the test, the test methodology, and any control or quality assurance procedures;

(2) Data to support reproducibility, that is, the ability to reproduce the same result repeatedly on a given sample;

(3) Data to support suitability, that is, data to show that similar results can be produced when the test is run at other laboratories;

(4) Data to support the sensitivity and specificity of the test; and

(5) Any other data requested by the Administrator to determine the suitability of the test for program use.

(c) Specific protocols for official CWD tests are available upon request to NVSL.

(d) State, Federal, and university laboratories will be approved by the Administrator to conduct official CWD tests when he or she determines that the laboratory:

(1) Employs personnel assigned to supervise the testing who are qualified to conduct the test based on education, training, and experience and who have been trained by NVSL or who have completed equivalent training approved by NVSL;

(2) Has adequate facilities and equipment to conduct the test;

(3) Follows standard test protocols;

(4) Meets check test proficiency requirements;

(5) Meets recordkeeping requirements;

(6) Will retain records, slides, blocks, and other specimens from all cases for at least 1 year and from positive cases for 5 years;

(7) Will allow APHIS to inspect[1] the laboratory without notice during normal business hours; and

(8) Will report all test results to State and Federal animal health officials within agreed timeframes.

(e) The Administrator may withdraw approval of any laboratory for failure to meet any of the conditions required by paragraph (d) of this section. The Administrator shall give written notice of the proposed withdrawal to the director of the laboratory and shall give the director an opportunity to respond. If there are conflicts as to any material fact concerning the reason for withdrawal, a hearing will be held to resolve the conflicts. The hearing will be conducted in accordance with rules of practice that will be adopted by the Administrator for the proceeding.

Subpart B—Chronic Wasting Disease Herd Certification Program

SOURCE: 77 FR 35566, June 13, 2012, unless otherwise noted.

§ 55.21 Administration.

The CWD Herd Certification Program is a cooperative effort between APHIS, State animal health and wildlife agencies, and deer, elk, and moose owners. APHIS coordinates with these State agencies to encourage deer, elk, and moose owners to certify their herds as low risk for CWD by being in continuous compliance with the CWD Herd Certification Program standards.

[1] An inspection may include, but is not limited to, review and copying of records, examination of slides, observation of the test being conducted, and interviewing of personnel.

§ 55.22 Participation and enrollment.

(a) *Participation by States.* Any State that operates a State program to certify the CWD status of deer, elk, or moose may request the Administrator to designate the State program as an Approved State CWD Herd Certification Program. The Administrator will approve or disapprove a State program in accordance with § 55.23(a). In States with an Approved State CWD Herd Certification Program, program activities will be conducted in accordance with the guidelines of that program as long as the State program meets the minimum requirements of this part. A list of Approved State CWD Herd Certification Programs may be obtained by writing to the National Center for Animal Health Program, VS, APHIS, 4700 River Road Unit 43, Riverdale, MD 20737–1235.

(b) *Participation by owners.* Any owner of a farmed or captive deer, elk, or moose herd may apply to enroll in an Approved State CWD Herd Certification Program by sending a written request to the appropriate State agency. Subject to the availability of appropriated funds for a Federal CWD Herd Certification Program, the owner may apply to the APHIS veterinarian in charge if no Approved State CWD Herd Certification Program exists in the herd's State. APHIS or the State will determine the herd's eligibility, and if needed will require the owner to submit more details about the herd animals and operations. An application for participation may be denied if APHIS or the State determines that the applicant has previously violated State or Federal laws or regulations for livestock, and that the nature of the violation indicates that the applicant may not faithfully comply with the requirements of the CWD Herd Certification Program. If the enrolling herd is a CWD-positive herd or CWD-exposed herd, immediately after enrollment it must begin complying with a herd plan developed in accordance with § 55.24. After determining that the herd is eligible to participate in accordance with this paragraph, APHIS or the appropriate State agency will send the herd owner a notice of enrollment that includes the herd's enrollment date. Inquiries regarding which herds are participating in the CWD Herd Certification Program and their certification should be directed to the State representative of the relevant State.

(1) *Enrollment date.* With the exceptions listed in this paragraph, the enrollment date for any herd that joins the CWD Herd Certification Program after August 13, 2012 will be the date the herd is approved for participation.

(i) For herds already participating in State CWD programs, the enrollment date will be the first day that the herd participated in a State program that APHIS subsequently determines qualifies as an Approved State CWD Herd Certification Program in accordance with §55.23(a) of this part.

(ii) For herds that enroll directly in the Federal CWD Herd Certification Program, which is allowed only when there is no Approved State CWD Herd Certification Program in their State and which is subject to the availability of appropriated funds, the enrollment date will be the earlier of:

(A) The date APHIS approves enrollment; or

(B) If APHIS determines that the herd owner has maintained the herd in a manner that substantially meets the conditions specified in §55.23(b) for herd owners, the first day that the herd participated in such a program. However, in such cases the enrollment date may not be set at a date more than 3 years prior to the date that APHIS approved enrollment of the herd.

(iii) For new herds that were formed from and contain only animals from herds enrolled in the CWD Herd Certification Program, the enrollment date will be the latest enrollment date for any source herd for the animals.

(2) [Reserved]

(Approved by the Office of Management and Budget under control number 0579–0237)

§55.23 Responsibilities of States and enrolled herd owners.

(a) *Approval of State programs and responsibilities of States.* In reviewing a State program's eligibility to be designated an Approved State CWD Herd Certification Program, the Administrator will evaluate a written statement from the State that describes the State's CWD control and deer, elk, and moose herd certification activities and that cites relevant State statutes, regulations, and directives pertaining to animal health activities and reports and publications of the State. In determining whether the State program qualifies, the Administrator will determine whether the State:

(1) Has the authority, based on State law or regulation, to restrict the intrastate movement of all CWD-positive, CWD-suspect, and CWD-exposed animals.

(2) Has the authority, based on State law or regulation, to require the prompt reporting of any animal suspected of having CWD and test results for any animals tested for CWD to State or Federal animal health authorities.

(3) Has, in cooperation with APHIS personnel, drafted and signed a memorandum of understanding with APHIS that delineates the respective roles of the State and APHIS in CWD Herd Certification Program implementation.

(4) Has placed all known CWD-positive, CWD-exposed, and CWD-suspect animals and herds under movement restrictions, with movement of animals from them only for destruction or under permit.

(5) Has effectively implemented policies to:

(i) Promptly investigate all animals reported as CWD-suspect animals;

(ii) Designate herds as CWD-positive, CWD-exposed, or CWD-suspect and promptly restrict movement of animals from the herd after an APHIS employee or State representative determines that the herd contains or has contained a CWD-positive animal;

(iii) Remove herd movement restrictions only after completion of a herd plan agreed upon by the State representative, APHIS, and the owner;

(iv) Conduct an epidemiologic investigation of CWD-positive, CWD-exposed, and CWD-suspect herds that includes the designation of suspect and exposed animals and that identifies animals to be traced;

(v) Conduct tracebacks of CWD-positive animals and traceouts of CWD-exposed animals and report any out-of-State traces to the appropriate State promptly after receipt of notification of a CWD-positive animal; and

(vi) Conduct tracebacks based on slaughter or other sampling promptly after receipt of notification of a CWD-positive animal at slaughter.

(6) Effectively monitors and enforces State quarantines and State reporting laws and regulations for CWD.

(7) Has designated at least one State animal health official, or has worked with APHIS to designate an APHIS official, to coordinate CWD Herd Certification Program activities in the State.

(8) Has programs to educate those engaged in the interstate movement of deer, elk, and moose regarding the identification and recordkeeping requirements of this part.

(9) Requires, based on State law or regulation, and effectively enforces identification of all animals in herds participating in the CWD Herd Certification Program;

(10) Maintains in the CWD National Database administered by APHIS, or in a State database approved by the Administrator as compatible with the CWD National Database, the State's:

(i) Premises information and assigned premises numbers;

(ii) Individual animal information on all deer, elk, and moose in herds participating in the CWD Herd Certification Program in the State;

(iii) Individual animal information on all out-of-State deer, elk, and moose to be traced; and

(iv) Accurate herd status data.

(11) Requires that tissues from all CWD-exposed or CWD-suspect animals that die or are depopulated or otherwise killed be submitted to a laboratory authorized by the Administrator to conduct official CWD tests and requires appropriate disposal of the carcasses of CWD-positive, CWD-exposed, and CWD-suspect animals.

(b) *Responsibilities of enrolled herd owners.* Herd owners who enroll in the CWD Herd Certification Program agree to maintain their herds in accordance with the following conditions:

(1) Each animal in the herd must be identified using means of animal identification specified in §55.25. All animals in an enrolled herd must be identified before reaching 12 months of age. In addition, all animals of any age in an enrolled herd must be identified before being moved from the herd premises. In addition, all animals in an enrolled herd must be identified before the inventory required under paragraph (b)(4) of this section, and animals found to be in violation of this requirement during the inventory must be identified during or after the inventory on a schedule specified by the APHIS employee or State representative conducting the inventory;

(2) The herd premises must have perimeter fencing adequate to prevent ingress or egress of cervids. This fencing must also comply with any applicable State regulations;

(3) The owner must immediately report to an APHIS employee or State representative all animals that escape or disappear, and all deaths (including animals killed on premises maintained for hunting and animals sent to slaughter) of deer, elk, and moose in the herd aged 12 months or older; Except that, APHIS employees or State representatives may approve reporting schedules other than immediate notification when herd conditions warrant it in the opinion of both APHIS and the State. The report must include the identification numbers of the animals involved and the estimated time and date of the death, escape, or disappearance. For animals that die (including animals killed on premises maintained for hunting and animals sent to slaughter), the owner must inform an APHIS or State representative and must make the carcasses of the animals available for tissue sampling and testing in accordance with instructions from the APHIS or State representative. In cases where animals escape or disappear and thus are not available for tissue sampling and testing, or when the owner provides samples that are of such poor quality that they cannot be tested for CWD, an APHIS representative will investigate whether the unavailability of animals or usable samples for testing constitutes a failure to comply with program requirements and will affect the herd's status in the CWD Herd Certification Program;

(4) The owner must maintain herd records that include a complete inventory of animals that states the species, age, and sex of each animal, the date of

acquisition and source of each animal that was not born into the herd, the date of disposal and destination of any animal removed from the herd, and all individual identification numbers (from tags, tattoos, electronic implants, etc.) associated with each animal. Upon request by an APHIS employee or State representative, the owner must allow either of these officials or a designated accredited veterinarian access to the premises and herd to conduct an inventory. The owner will be responsible for assembling, handling, and restraining the animals and for all costs incurred to present the animals for inspection. The APHIS employee or State representative may order either an inventory that consists of review of herd records with visual examination of an enclosed group of animals, or a complete physical herd inventory with verification to reconcile all animals and identifications with the records maintained by the owner. In the latter case, the owner must present the entire herd for inspection under conditions where the APHIS employee, State representative, or accredited veterinarian can safely read all identification on the animals. During inventories, the owner must cooperate with the inspector to resolve any discrepancies to the satisfaction of the person performing the inventory. Inventory of a herd will be conducted no more frequently than once per year, unless an APHIS employee, State representative, or accredited veterinarian determines that more frequent inventories are needed based on indications that the herd may not be in compliance with CWD Herd Certification Program requirements. A complete physical herd inventory must be performed on a herd in accordance with this paragraph at the time a herd is enrolled in the CWD Herd Certification Program; Except that, APHIS may accept a complete physical herd inventory performed by an APHIS employee, State representative, or accredited veterinarian not more than 1 year before the herd's date of enrollment in the CWD Herd Certification Program as fulfilling the requirement for an initial inventory. In addition, a complete physical herd inventory must be performed for all herds enrolled in the CWD Herd Certification Program no more than 3 years after the last complete physical herd inventory for the herd;

(5) If an owner wishes to maintain separate herds, he or she must maintain separate herd inventories, records, working facilities, water sources, equipment, and land use. There must be a buffer zone of at least 30 feet between the perimeter fencing around separate herds, and no commingling of animals may occur. Movement of animals between herds must be recorded as if they were separately owned herds;

(6) New animals may be introduced into the herd only from other herds enrolled in the CWD Herd Certification Program. If animals are received from an enrolled herd with a lower program status, the receiving herd will revert to that lower program status. If animals are obtained from a herd not participating in the program, then the receiving herd will be required to start over in the program.

(Approved by the Office of Management and Budget under control number 0579–0237)

§ 55.24 Herd status.

(a) *Initial and subsequent status.* When a herd is first enrolled in the CWD Herd Certification Program, it will be placed in First Year status; except that, if the herd is composed solely of animals obtained from herds already enrolled in the Program, the newly enrolled herd will have the same status as the lowest status of any herd that provided animals for the new herd. If the herd continues to meet the requirements of the CWD Herd Certification Program, each year, on the anniversary of the enrollment date the herd status will be upgraded by 1 year; *i.e.*, Second Year status, Third Year status, Fourth Year status, and Fifth Year status. One year from the date a herd is placed in Fifth Year status, the herd status will be changed to Certified, and the herd will remain in Certified status as long as it is enrolled in the program, provided its status is not lost or suspended in accordance with this section.

(b) *Loss or suspension of herd status.* (1) If a herd is designated a CWD-positive herd or a CWD-exposed herd, it will immediately lose its program status and may only reenroll after entering into a herd plan.

(2) If a herd is designated a CWD-suspect herd, a trace back herd, or a trace forward herd, it will immediately be placed in Suspended status pending an epidemiologic investigation by APHIS or a State animal health agency. If the epidemiologic investigation determines that the herd was not commingled with a CWD-positive animal, the herd will be reinstated to its former program status, and the time spent in Suspended status will count toward its promotion to the next herd status level.

(i) If the epidemiologic investigation determines that the herd was commingled with a CWD-positive animal, the herd will lose its program status and will be designated a CWD-exposed herd.

(ii) If the epidemiological investigation is unable to make a determination regarding the exposure of the herd, because the necessary animal or animals are no longer available for testing (*i.e.*, a trace animal from a known positive herd died and was not tested) or for other reasons, the herd status will continue as Suspended unless and until a herd plan is developed for the herd. If a herd plan is developed and implemented, the herd will be reinstated to its former program status, and the time spent in Suspended status will count toward its promotion to the next herd status level; *Except that*, if the epidemiological investigation finds that the owner of the herd has not fully complied with program requirements for animal identification, animal testing, and recordkeeping, the herd will be reinstated into the CWD Herd Certification Program at the First Year status level, with a new enrollment date set at the date the herd entered into Suspended status. Any herd reinstated after being placed in Suspended status must then comply with the requirements of the herd plan as well as the requirements of the CWD Herd Certification Program. The herd plan will require testing of all animals that die in the herd for any reason, regardless of the age of the animal, may require movement restrictions for animals in the herd based on epidemiologic evidence regarding the risk posed by the animals in question, and may include other requirements found necessary to control the risk of spreading CWD.

(3) If an APHIS or State representative determines that animals from a herd enrolled in the program have commingled with animals from a herd with a lower program status, the herd with the higher program status will be reduced to the status of the herd with which its animals commingled.

(c) *Cancellation of enrollment by Administrator.* The Administrator may cancel the enrollment of an enrolled herd by giving written notice to the herd owner. In the event of such cancellation, any herd enrolled in the CWD Herd Certification Program by that herd owner may not reach Certified status until 5 years after the herd owner's new application for enrollment is approved by APHIS, regardless of the status of the animals of which the herd is composed. The Administrator may cancel enrollment after determining that the herd owner failed to comply with any requirements of this subpart. Before enrollment is canceled, an APHIS representative will inform the herd owner of the reasons for the proposed cancellation.

(1) Herd owners may appeal designation of an animal as CWD-positive, cancellation of enrollment of a herd, or loss or suspension of herd status by writing to the Administrator within 10 days after being informed of the reasons for the action. The appeal must include all of the facts and reasons upon which the herd owner relies to show that the reasons for the action are incorrect or do not support the action. Specifically, to appeal designation of an animal as CWD-positive, the owner may present as evidence the results of a DNA test requested and paid for by the owner to determine whether previous official CWD test results were correctly associated with an animal that belonged to the owner. If the owner intends to present such test results as evidence, he or she shall request the tests and state this in the written notice sent to the Administrator. In such cases the Administrator may postpone a decision on the appeal for a reasonable period pending receipt

of such test results. To this end, laboratories approved under §55.8 are authorized to conduct DNA tests to compare tissue samples tested for CWD to samples from tissues that were collected at the same time from the same animal and are attached to an official identification device. Such DNA tests are available only if the animal owner arranged to submit animal tissue attached to an official identification device along with the other tissues that were collected for the official CWD test. The Administrator will grant or deny the appeal in writing as promptly as circumstances permit, stating the reason for his or her decision. If the Administrator grants an appeal of the status of a CWD-positive animal, the animal shall be redesignated as CWD-suspect pending further investigation to establish the final status of the animal and its herd. If there is a conflict as to any material fact, a hearing will be held to resolve the conflict. Rules of practice concerning the hearing will be adopted by the Administrator.

(2) [Reserved]

(d) *Herd status of animals added to herds.* A herd may add animals from herds with the same or a higher herd status in the CWD Herd Certification Program with no negative impact on the certification status of the receiving herd.[5] If animals are acquired from a herd with a lower herd status, the receiving herd reverts to the program status of the sending herd. If a herd participating in the CWD Herd Certification Program acquires animals from a nonparticipating herd, the receiving herd reverts to First Year status with a new enrollment date of the date of acquisition of the animal.

(Approved by the Office of Management and Budget under control number 0579–0237)

§55.25 Animal identification.

Each animal required to be identified by this subpart must have at least two forms of animal identification attached to the animal. One of the animal identifications must be official animal identification as defined in this part, with a nationally unique animal identification number that is linked to that animal in the CWD National Database or in an approved State database. The second animal identification must be unique for the individual animal within the herd and also must be linked to that animal and herd in the CWD National Database or in an approved State database. The means of animal identification must be approved for this use by APHIS, and must be an electronic implant, flank tattoo, ear tattoo, tamper-resistant ear tag, or other device approved by APHIS.

(Approved by the Office of Management and Budget under control number 0579–0237)

[5] Note that in addition to this requirement, §81.3 of this chapter restricts the interstate movement of farmed and captive deer, elk, and moose based on their status in the CWD Herd Certification Program.

PART 56—CONTROL OF H5/H7 LOW PATHOGENIC AVIAN INFLUENZA

Sec.

AUTHORITY: 7 U.S.C. 8301–8317; 7 CFR 2.22, 2.80, and 371.4.

SOURCE: 71 FR 56323, Sept. 26, 2006, unless otherwise noted.

§56.1 Definitions.

Administrator. The Administrator, Animal and Plant Health Inspection Service, or any other employee of the Animal and Plant Health Inspection Service delegated to act in the Administrator's stead.

Animal and Plant Health Inspection Service (APHIS). The Animal and Plant Health Inspection Service of the U.S. Department of Agriculture.

Breeding flock. A flock that is composed of stock that has been developed for commercial egg or meat production and is maintained for the principal purpose of producing progeny for the ultimate production of eggs or meat for human consumption.

Classification. A designation earned by participation in a Plan program.

Commercial flock or slaughter plant. A commercial poultry flock or slaughter plant that is required because of its size to participate in the special provisions in part 146 of this chapter in order to participate in the Plan.

Cooperating State Agency. Any State authority recognized by the Department to cooperate in the administration of the provisions of this part 56. This may include the State animal health authority or the Official State Agency.

Department. The U.S. Department of Agriculture.

Domesticated. Propagated and maintained under the control of a person.

Flock plan. A written flock management agreement developed by APHIS and the Official State Agency with input from the flock owner and other affected parties. A flock plan sets out the steps to be taken to eradicate H5/H7 LPAI from a positive flock, or to prevent introduction of H5/H7 LPAI into another flock. A flock plan shall include, but is not necessarily limited to, poultry and poultry product movement and geographically appropriate infected and control/monitoring zones. Control measures in the flock plan should include detailed plans for safe handling of conveyances, containers, and other associated materials that could serve as fomites; disposal of flocks; cleaning and disinfection; downtime; and repopulation.

H5/H7 low pathogenic avian influenza (LPAI). An infection of poultry caused by an influenza A virus of H5 or H7 subtype that has an intravenous pathogenicity index in 6-week-old chickens less than or equal to 1.2 or causes less than 75 percent mortality in 4- to 8-week-old chickens infected intravenously, or an infection with influenza A viruses of H5 or H7 subtype with a cleavage site that is not consistent with a previously identified highly pathogenic avian influenza virus.

H5/H7 LPAI exposed. At risk of developing H5/H7 LPAI because of association with birds or poultry infected with H5/H7 LPAI, excrement from birds or poultry infected with H5/H7 LPAI, or other material touched by birds or poultry infected with H5/H7 LPAI, or because there is reason to believe that association has occurred with H5/H7 LPAI or vectors of H5/H7 LPAI, as determined by the Cooperating State Agency and confirmed by APHIS.

H5/H7 LPAI virus infection (infected). (1) Poultry will be considered to be infected with H5/H7 LPAI for the purposes of this part if:

(i) H5/H7 LPAI virus has been isolated and identified as such from poultry; or

(ii) Viral antigen or viral RNA specific to the H5 or H7 subtype of AI virus has been detected in poultry; or

(iii) Antibodies to the H5 or H7 subtype of the AI virus that are not a consequence of vaccination have been detected in poultry. If vaccine is used, methods should be used to distinguish vaccinated birds from birds that are both vaccinated and infected. In the case of isolated serological positive results, H5/H7 LPAI infection may be ruled out on the basis of a thorough epidemiological investigation that does not demonstrate further evidence of H5/H7 LPAI infection, as determined by the Cooperating State Agency, the Official State Agency, and APHIS.

(2) The official determination that H5/H7 LPAI virus has been isolated and identified, viral antigen or viral RNA specific to the H5 or H7 subtype of AI virus has been detected, or antibodies to the H5 or H7 subtype of AI virus have been detected may only be made by the National Veterinary Services Laboratories.

Mortgage. Any mortgage, lien, or other security or beneficial interest held by any person other than the one claiming indemnity for the destruction of poultry or eggs due to H5/H7 LPAI.

Official appraiser (APHIS official appraiser, State official appraiser). A person authorized by APHIS to appraise poultry for the purposes of this part. A State official appraiser is selected by a State and authorized by APHIS.

Official State Agency. The State authority recognized by the Department to cooperate in the administration of the Plan.

Plan. The provisions of the National Poultry Improvement Plan contained in parts 145, 146, and 147 of this chapter.

Poultry. Domesticated fowl, including chickens, turkeys, ostriches, emus, rheas, cassowaries, waterfowl, and game birds, except doves and pigeons, which are bred for the primary purpose of producing eggs or meat.

Secretary. The Secretary of the United States Department of Agriculture, or any officer or employee of the Department delegated to act in the Secretary's stead.

State. Any of the States, the District of Columbia, the Commonwealth of Puerto Rico, Guam, the Commonwealth of the Northern Mariana Islands, the Virgin Islands of the United States, or any territory or possession of the United States.

Table-egg layer. A domesticated chicken grown for the primary purpose of producing eggs for human consumption.

United States. All of the States.

[71 FR 56323, Sept. 26, 2006, as amended at 75 FR 10656, Mar. 9, 2010; 76 FR 15792, Mar. 22, 2011; 79 FR 38753, July 9, 2014; 81 FR 53249, Aug. 12, 2016]

§56.2 Cooperation with States.

(a) The Administrator has been delegated the authority to cooperate with Cooperating State Agencies in the eradication of H5/H7 LPAI. This cooperation may include, but is not necessarily limited to, the following activities:

(1) Payment to Cooperating State Agencies for surveillance and monitoring associated with poultry that have been infected with or exposed to H5/H7 LPAI;

(2) Transfer of vaccine for H5/H7 LPAI to Cooperating State Agencies if provided for in the initial State response and containment plan approved by APHIS under §56.10; and

(3) Payment for vaccine administration by Cooperating State Agencies, if provided for in the initial State response and containment plan approved by APHIS under §56.10.

(b)(1) Any payment made to a State or an Official State Agency for the activities listed in paragraphs (a)(1) and (a)(3) of this section must be made through a cooperative agreement between the Cooperating State Agency and APHIS. The payment for which the Cooperating State Agency is eligible will be determined in the cooperative agreement.

(i) For any Cooperating State Agency that participates in the National Poultry Improvement Plan diagnostic surveillance program for H5/H7 LPAI, as described in §146.14 of this chapter, and has an initial State response and containment plan for H5/H7 LPAI that is approved by APHIS, as described in §56.10 of this part, the cooperative agreement will provide that the Cooperating State Agency is eligible for payment of 100 percent of the costs of surveillance and monitoring and 100 percent of the costs of vaccine administration, as determined in the cooperative agreement.

(ii) For any Cooperating State Agency that does not meet the criteria in paragraph (b)(1)(i) of this section, the cooperative agreement will provide that the Cooperating State Agency is eligible for payment of 25 percent of the costs of surveillance and monitoring and 25 percent of the costs of vaccine administration, as determined in the cooperative agreement.

(2) Transfer of vaccine under paragraph (a)(2) of this section must be accomplished through a cooperative agreement between the Cooperating State Agency and APHIS.

(c) Cooperating State Agencies will be responsible for making the determination to request Federal assistance under this part in the event of an outbreak of H5/H7 LPAI.

[71 FR 56323, Sept. 26, 2006, as amended at 75 FR 10656, Mar. 9, 2010]

§56.3 Payment of indemnity.

(a) *Activities eligible for indemnity.* The Administrator may pay indemnity for the activities listed in paragraphs (a)(1) through (a)(3) of this section, as provided in paragraph (b) of this section:

(1) Destruction and disposal of poultry that were infected with or exposed to H5/H7 LPAI;

(2) Destruction of any eggs destroyed during testing of poultry for H5/H7 LPAI during an outbreak of H5/H7 LPAI; and

(3) Cleaning and disinfection of premises, conveyances, and materials that came into contact with poultry that were infected with or exposed to H5/H7 LPAI; or, in the case of materials, if the cost of cleaning and disinfection would exceed the value of the materials or cleaning and disinfection would be impracticable for any reason, the destruction and disposal of the materials.

(b) *Percentage of costs eligible for indemnity.* Except for poultry that are described by the categories in paragraphs (b)(1) through (b)(3) of this section, the Administrator is authorized to pay 100 percent of the costs, as determined in accordance with § 56.4, of the activities described in paragraphs (a)(1) through (a)(3) of this section, regardless of whether the infected or exposed poultry participate in the Plan. For infected or exposed poultry that are described by the categories in paragraphs (b)(1) through (b)(3) of this section, the Administrator is authorized to pay 25 percent of the costs of the activities described in paragraphs (a)(1) through (a)(3) of this section:

(1) The poultry are from a breeding flock that participates in any Plan program in part 145 of this chapter but that does not participate in the U.S. Avian Influenza Clean or the U.S. H5/H7 Avian Influenza Clean program of the Plan available to the flock in part 145 of this chapter; or

(2) The poultry are from a commercial flock or slaughter plant, but the flock or slaughter plant does not participate in the U.S. Avian Influenza Monitored program available to the commercial flock or slaughter plant in part 146 of this chapter; or

(3) The poultry are located in a State that does not participate in the diagnostic surveillance program for H5/H7 LPAI, as described in § 146.14 of this chapter, or that does not have an initial State response and containment plan for H5/H7 LPAI that is approved by APHIS under § 56.10, unless such poultry participate in the Plan with another State that does participate in the diagnostic surveillance program for H5/H7 LPAI, as described in § 146.14 of this chapter, and has an initial State response and containment plan for H5/H7 LPAI that is approved by APHIS under § 56.10.

(c) *Other sources of payment.* If the recipient of indemnity for any of the activities listed in paragraphs (a)(1) through (a)(3) of this section also receives payment for any of those activities from a State or from other sources, the indemnity provided under this part will be reduced by the total amount of payment received from the State or other sources.

[71 FR 56323, Sept. 26, 2006, as amended at 75 FR 10657, Mar. 9, 2010; 76 FR 15792, Mar. 22, 2011; 76 FR 65935, Oct. 25, 2011]

§ 56.4 Determination of indemnity amounts.

(a) *Destruction and disposal of poultry.* (1) Indemnity for the destruction of poultry infected with or exposed to H5/H7 LPAI will be based on the fair market value of the poultry, as determined by an appraisal. Poultry infected with or exposed to H5/H7 LPAI that are removed by APHIS or a Cooperating State Agency from a flock will be appraised by an APHIS official appraiser and a State official appraiser jointly, or, if APHIS and State authorities agree, by either an APHIS official appraiser or a State official appraiser alone. For laying hens, the appraised value should include the hen's projected future egg production. Appraisals of poultry must be reported on forms furnished by APHIS and signed by the appraisers and must be signed by the owners of the poultry to indicate agreement with the appraisal amount. Appraisals of poultry must be signed by the owners of the poultry prior to the destruction of the poultry, unless the owners, APHIS, and the Cooperating State Agency agree that the poultry may be destroyed immediately. Reports of appraisals must show the number of birds and the value per head.

(2) Indemnity for disposal of poultry infected with or exposed to H5/H7 LPAI will be based on receipts or other documentation maintained by the claimant verifying expenditures for disposal activities authorized by this part. Any disposal of poultry infected with or exposed to H5/H7 LPAI for which indemnity is requested must be performed under a compliance agreement between the claimant, the Cooperating State

Agency, and APHIS. APHIS will review claims for indemnity for disposal to ensure that all expenditures relate directly to activities described in §56.5 and in the initial State response and containment plan described in §56.10. If disposal is performed by the Cooperating State Agency, APHIS will indemnify the Cooperating State Agency for disposal under a cooperative agreement.

(3) The destruction and disposal of the indemnified poultry must be conducted in accordance with the initial State response and containment plan for H5/H7 LPAI, as described in §56.10.

(b) *Destruction of eggs.* Indemnity for eggs destroyed during an outbreak for testing for H5/H7 LPAI will be based on the fair market value of the eggs, as determined by an appraisal. Eggs destroyed for testing for H5/H7 LPAI will be appraised by an APHIS official appraiser and a State official appraiser jointly, or, if APHIS and State authorities agree, by either an APHIS official appraiser or a State official appraiser alone. Appraisals of eggs must be reported on forms furnished by APHIS and signed by the appraisers and must be signed by the owners of the eggs to indicate agreement with the appraisal amount. Appraisals of eggs must be signed by the owners of the eggs prior to the destruction of the poultry, unless the owners, APHIS, and the Cooperating State Agency agree that the eggs may be destroyed immediately. Reports of appraisals must show the number of eggs and the value per egg.

(c) *Cleaning and disinfection.* (1) Indemnity for cleaning and disinfection of premises, conveyances, and materials that came into contact with poultry that are infected with or exposed to H5/H7 LPAI will be based on receipts or other documentation maintained by the claimant verifying expenditures for cleaning and disinfection activities authorized by this part. Any cleaning and disinfection of premises, conveyances, and materials for which indemnity is requested must be performed under a compliance agreement between the claimant, the Cooperating State Agency, and APHIS. APHIS will review claims for indemnity for cleaning and disinfection to ensure that all expenditures relate directly to activities described in §56.5 and in the initial State response and containment plan described in §56.10.

(2) In the case of materials, if the cost of cleaning and disinfection would exceed the value of the materials or cleaning and disinfection would be impracticable for any reason, indemnity for the destruction of the materials will be based on the fair market value of those materials, as determined by an appraisal. Materials will be appraised by an APHIS official appraiser and a State official appraiser jointly, or, if APHIS and State authorities agree, by either an APHIS official appraiser or a State official appraiser alone. Indemnity for disposal of the materials will be based on receipts or other documentation maintained by the claimant verifying expenditures for disposal activities authorized by this part. Appraisals of materials must be reported on forms furnished by APHIS and signed by the appraisers and must be signed by the owners of the materials to indicate agreement with the appraisal amount. Appraisals of materials must be signed prior to the destruction of the materials, unless the owners, APHIS, and the Cooperating State Agency agree that the materials may be destroyed immediately. Any disposal of materials for which indemnity is requested must be performed under a compliance agreement between the claimant, the Cooperating State Agency, and APHIS. APHIS will review claims for compensation for disposal to ensure that all expenditures relate directly to activities described in §56.5 and in the initial State response and containment plan described in §56.10.

(d) *Requirements for compliance agreements.* The compliance agreement is a comprehensive document that describes the depopulation, disposal, and cleaning and disinfection plans for poultry that were infected with or exposed to H5/H7 LPAI, or a premises that contained such poultry. The compliance agreement sets out APHIS responsibilities, owner responsibilities, and Cooperating State Agency responsibilities. The compliance agreement must include the owner's name and the name and address of the affected premises. The compliance agreement must have signatories that include, but are not necessarily limited to, the owner, the grower (if applicable), the Cooperating State Agency representative, the State veterinarian, and the APHIS area supervisor. In addition, the compliance agreement must contain a flock plan with estimated cost breakdowns that include labor, materials, personal protective equipment, travel expenses for personnel involved, and any additional information deemed necessary by the Service. A signed compliance agreement is required before beginning any work for which indemnity funds will be requested. Once work associated with the compliance agreement is completed, receipts and documentation detailing the activities specified in the agreement should be forwarded to APHIS for review, approval, and final payment. This documentation should be submitted to APHIS no later than 30 days after the quarantine release of the affected or exposed premises.

(Approved by the Office of Management and Budget under control number 0579–0007)

[71 FR 56323, Sept. 26, 2006, as amended at 75 FR 10657, Mar. 9, 2010; 79 FR 38753, July 9, 2014]

§ 56.5 Destruction and disposal of poultry and cleaning and disinfection of premises, conveyances, and materials.

(a) *Destruction of poultry.* Poultry that are infected with or exposed to H5/H7 LPAI may be required to be destroyed at the discretion of the Cooperating State Agency and APHIS and in accordance with the initial State response and containment plan described in § 56.10. The Cooperating State Agency and APHIS will select a method to use for the destruction of such poultry based on the following factors:

(1) The species, size, and number of the poultry to be destroyed;

(2) The environment in which the poultry are maintained;

(3) The risk to human health or safety of the method used;

(4) Whether the method requires specialized equipment or training;

(5) The risk that the method poses of spreading the H5/H7 LPAI virus;

(6) Any hazard the method could pose to the environment;

(7) The degree of bird control and restraint required to administer the destruction method;

(8) The speed with which destruction must be conducted; and

(9) Consistency of the method with humane euthanasia guidelines.

(b) *Disposal of poultry.* Carcasses of poultry that have died from H5/H7 LPAI infection or poultry that have been humanely slaughtered to fulfill depopulation requirements must be disposed of promptly and efficiently in accordance with the initial State response and containment plan described in § 56.10 to prevent the spread of H5/H7 LPAI infection. Disposal methods will be selected by the Cooperating State Agency and APHIS and may include one or more of the following: Burial, incineration, composting, or rendering. Regardless of the method used, strict biosecurity procedures must be implemented and enforced for all personnel and vehicular movement into and out of the area in accordance with the initial State response and containment plan to prevent dissemination of the H5/H7 LPAI virus.

(c) *Controlled marketing.* (1) At the discretion of the Cooperating State Agency and APHIS, poultry that has been infected with or exposed to H5/H7 LPAI may be allowed to move for controlled marketing in accordance with the initial State response and containment plan described in § 56.10 and in accordance with the following requirements:

(i) Poultry infected with or exposed to H5/H7 LPAI must not be transported to a market for controlled marketing until approved by the Cooperating State Agency in accordance with the initial State response and containment plan described in § 56.10.

(ii) Within 7 days prior to slaughter, each flock to be moved for controlled marketing must be tested for H5/H7 LPAI using a test approved by the Cooperating State Agency and found to be free of the virus.

(iii) Routes to slaughter must avoid other commercial poultry operations whenever possible. All load-out equipment, trailers, and trucks used on premises that have housed poultry that were infected with or exposed to H5/H7 LPAI must be cleaned and disinfected and not enter other poultry premises or facilities for 48 hours after removing such poultry from their premises.

(iv) Flocks moved for controlled marketing must be the last poultry marketed during the week they are marketed.

(2) Poultry moved for controlled marketing will not be eligible for indemnity under § 56.3. However, any costs related to cleaning and disinfection of premises, conveyances, and materials that came into contact with poultry that are moved for controlled marketing will be eligible for indemnity under § 56.3.

(d) *Cleaning and disinfection of premises, conveyances, and materials.* Premises, conveyances, and materials that came into contact with poultry infected with or exposed to H5/H7 LPAI must be cleaned and disinfected; *Provided*, that materials for which the cost of cleaning and disinfection would exceed the value of the materials or for which cleaning and disinfection would be impracticable for any reason may be destroyed and disposed. Cleaning and disinfection must be performed in accordance with the initial State response and containment plan described in § 56.10, which must be approved by APHIS. Cleaning and disinfection must also be performed in accordance with any applicable State and local environmental regulations. This paragraph (d) provides guidelines for the development of a cleaning and disinfection plan for a premises and for the materials and conveyances on that premises.

(1) *Preparation for cleaning and disinfection.* Following the depopulation or controlled marketing of all poultry infected with or exposed to H5/H7 LPAI on a premises, the following procedures should be completed prior to cleaning and disinfection:

(i) Secure all feathers and debris that might blow around outside the house in which the infected or exposed poultry were held by gathering and pushing the material into the house;

(ii) Apply insecticides and rodenticides immediately after the removal of the birds, before the house cools;

(iii) Close the house in which the poultry were held, maintaining just enough ventilation to remove moisture. Leave the house undisturbed for a minimum of 72 hours.

(2) *Cleaning and disinfection.* All premises, conveyances, and materials that came into contact with poultry that were infected with or exposed to H5/H7 LPAI must be cleaned and disinfected. Cleaning and disinfection must be performed on all buildings that came into contact with poultry that were infected with or exposed to H5/H7 LPAI within a premises, including pumphouses and service areas. To accomplish cleaning and disinfection, the following procedures should be completed:

(i) *Disposal of manure, debris, and feed.* Clean up all manure, debris, and feed. Compost manure, debris, and feed by windrowing in the house if possible. If this is not possible, set up a system for hauling manure, debris, and feed to an approved site for burial, piling, or composting. Manure, debris, and feed may be removed from the house or premises and disposed of by composting it on site, leaving it in a undisturbed pile on site, or removing it from the site in covered vehicles. Land application of manure, debris, and feed should only be performed in accordance with the initial State response and containment plan described in § 56.10. Clean out the house or move or spread litter as determined by the Cooperating State Agency and in accordance with the initial State response and containment plan. If composting is used as a disposal method, manure and litter should be composted in accordance with State and local regulations. If litter is piled, the litter pile must be covered and allowed to sit undisturbed for an amount of time approved by the Cooperating State Agency and APHIS and in accordance the initial State response and containment plan described in § 56.10. Drying and heat *in situ* over time are effective and may be used in place of composting if weather conditions or conditions in the building are favorable. After use, equipment used to clean out manure, debris, and feed must be cleaned, disinfected, and inspected at the site to which the manure and litter was transported. In the case of inclement weather, the equipment may be cleaned, disinfected, and inspected at off-site wash stations at the discretion of the Cooperating State Agency and APHIS.

(ii) *Cleaning of premises and materials.* Cleaning and washing should be thorough to ensure that all materials or substances contaminated with H5/H7 LPAI virus, especially manure, dried blood, and other organic materials, are removed from all surfaces. Spray all contaminated surfaces above the floor with detergent and water to knock dust down to the floor, using no more water than necessary. Wash equipment and houses with detergent and water. Disassemble equipment as required to clean all contaminated surfaces. Special attention should be given to automatic feeders and other closed areas to ensure adequate cleaning. Inspect houses and equipment to ensure that cleaning has removed all contaminated materials or substances. Rinse with fresh water and let houses and equipment dry completely before applying disinfectant.

(iii) *Disinfection of premises and materials.* When cleaning has been completed and all surfaces are dry, all interior surfaces of the structure should be saturated with a disinfectant registered with the U.S. Environmental Protection Agency (EPA) for AI virus per label instructions or a disinfectant approved by the EPA for use under a Federal Insecticide, Rodenticide, and Fungicide Act section 18 exemption. A power spray unit should be used to spray the disinfectant on all surfaces that may be treated with the disinfectant according to its EPA label, making sure that the disinfectant gets into cracks and crevices. Special attention should be given to automatic feeders and other closed areas to ensure adequate disinfection.

(vi) *Cleaning and disinfection of conveyances.* Clean and disinfect all trucks and vehicles used in transporting affected poultry or materials before soil dries in place. Both exterior, including the undercarriage, and interior surfaces, including truck cabs, must be cleaned. The interior of the truck cabs should be washed with clean water and sponged with a disinfectant authorized in §71.10(a) of this chapter. Manure and litter removed from these vehicles should be handled in a manner similar to that described in paragraph (d)(2)(i) of this section.

(3) *Activities after cleaning and disinfection.* Premises should remain empty until testing provides negative virus detection results and checked by the Cooperating State Agency in accordance with the initial State response and containment plan described in §56.10. The premises may not be restocked with poultry until after the date specified in the initial State response and containment plan described in §56.10.

(4) *Destruction and disposal of materials.* In the case of materials for which the cost of cleaning and disinfection would exceed the value of the materials or for which cleaning and disinfection would be impracticable for any reason, the destruction and disposal of the materials must be conducted in accordance with the initial State response and containment plan described in §56.10.

[71 FR 56323, Sept. 26, 2006, as amended at 75 FR 10657, Mar. 9, 2010; 79 FR 38753, July 9, 2014]

§ 56.6 Presentation of claims for indemnity.

Claims for the following must be documented on a form furnished by APHIS and presented to an APHIS employee or the State representative authorized to accept the claims:

(a) Compensation for the value of poultry to be destroyed due to infection with or exposure to H5/H7 LPAI;

(b) Compensation for the value of eggs to be destroyed during testing for H5/H7 LPAI; and

(c) Compensation for the cost of cleaning and disinfection of premises, conveyances, and materials that came into contact with poultry infected with or exposed to H5/H7 LPAI, or, in the case of materials, if the cost of cleaning and disinfection would exceed the value of the materials or cleaning and disinfection would be impracticable for any reason, the cost of destruction and disposal for the materials.

(Approved by the Office of Management and Budget under control number 0579–0007)

[71 FR 56323, Sept. 26, 2006, as amended at 75 FR 10657, Mar. 9, 2010]

§56.7 Mortgage against poultry or eggs.

When poultry or eggs have been destroyed under this part, any claim for indemnity must be presented on forms furnished by APHIS. The owner of the poultry or eggs must certify on the forms that the poultry or eggs covered are, or are not, subject to any mortgage as defined in this part. If the owner states there is a mortgage, the owner and each person holding a mortgage on the poultry or eggs must sign the APHIS-furnished form, consenting to the payment of indemnity to the person specified on the form.

(Approved by the Office of Management and Budget under control number 0579–0007)

[71 FR 56323, Sept. 26, 2006, as amended at 75 FR 10657, Mar. 9, 2010]

§56.8 Conditions for payment.

(a) When poultry or eggs have been destroyed pursuant to this part, the Administrator may pay claims to any party with which the owner of the poultry or eggs has entered into a contract for the growing or care of the poultry or eggs. The indemnity the Administrator may pay to such a party or parties shall be determined as follows:

(1) Divide the value of the contract the owner of the poultry or eggs entered into with another party for the growing and care of the poultry or eggs in dollars by the duration of the contract as it was signed prior to the H5/H7 LPAI outbreak in days;

(2) Multiply this figure by the time in days between the date the other party began to provide services relating to the destroyed poultry or eggs under the contract and the date the poultry or eggs were destroyed due to H5/H7 LPAI.

(b)(1) If indemnity for the destroyed poultry or eggs is being provided for 100 percent of eligible costs under §56.3(b), the Administrator may pay contractors eligible for compensation under this section 100 percent of the indemnity determined in paragraph (a) of this section.

(2) If indemnity for the destroyed poultry or eggs is being provided for 25 percent of eligible costs under §56.3(b), the Administrator may pay contractors eligible for compensation under this section 25 percent of the indemnity determined in paragraph (a) of this section.

(c) If a contractor receiving indemnity under this section has received any payment under his or her contract from the owner of the poultry or eggs at the time the poultry or eggs are destroyed, the amount of indemnity for which the contract grower is eligible will be reduced by the amount of the payment the contract grower has already received.

(d) If indemnity is paid to a contractor under this section, the owner of the poultry or eggs will be eligible to receive the difference between the indemnity paid to the growers and the total amount of indemnity that may be paid for the poultry or eggs.

(e) In the event that determination of indemnity to a party with which the owner of destroyed poultry or eggs has entered into a contract for the growing or care of the poultry or eggs using the method described in paragraph (a) of this section is determined to be impractical or inappropriate, APHIS may use any other method that the Administrator deems appropriate to make that determination.

[71 FR 56323, Sept. 26, 2006, as amended at 75 FR 10657, Mar. 9, 2010]

§56.9 Claims not allowed.

(a) The Department will not allow claims arising out of the destruction of poultry unless the poultry have been appraised as prescribed in this part and the owners have signed the appraisal form indicating agreement with the appraisal amount as required by §56.4(a)(1).

(b) The Department will not allow claims arising out of the destruction of poultry unless the owners have signed a written agreement with APHIS in which they agree that if they maintain poultry in the future on the premises used for poultry for which indemnity is paid, they will maintain the poultry in accordance with a plan set forth by the Cooperating State Agency and will not introduce poultry onto the premises until after the date specified by the Cooperating State Agency. Persons who do not maintain their poultry and premises in accordance with this written agreement will not be eligible to receive indemnity under this part.

(c) The Department will not allow claims arising out of the destruction of poultry unless the poultry have been moved or handled by the owner in accordance with an agreement for the control and eradication of H5/H7 LPAI and in accordance with part 56, for any progeny of any poultry unless the poultry have been moved or handled by the owner in accordance with an agreement for the control and eradication of H5/H7 LPAI and in accordance with part 56, or for any poultry that become or have become infected with or exposed to H5/H7 LPAI because of actions not in accordance with an agreement for the control and eradication of H5/H7 LPAI or a violation of this part.

(Approved by the Office of Management and Budget under control number 0579–0007)

[71 FR 56323, Sept. 26, 2006, as amended at 75 FR 10657, Mar. 9, 2010]

§ 56.10 Initial State response and containment plan.

(a) In order for poultry owners within a State to be eligible for indemnity for 100 percent of eligible costs under § 56.3(b), the State in which the poultry participate in the Plan must have in place an initial State response and containment plan that has been approved by APHIS. The initial State response and containment plan must be developed by the Official State Agency. In States where the Official State Agency is different than the Cooperating State Agency, the Cooperating State Agency must also participate in the development of the plan. The plan must be administered by the Cooperating State Agency of the relevant State. This plan must include:

(1) Provisions for a standing emergency disease management committee, regular meetings, and exercises, including coordination with any tribal governments that may be affected;

(2) A minimum biosecurity plan followed by all poultry producers;

(3) Provisions for adequate diagnostic resources;

(4) Detailed, specific procedures for initial handling and investigation of suspected cases of H5/H7 LPAI;

(5) Detailed, specific procedures for reporting test results to APHIS. These procedures must be developed after appropriate consultation with poultry producers in the State and must provide for the reporting only of confirmed cases of H5/H7 LPAI in accordance with § 146.13 of this chapter;

(6) Detailed, strict quarantine measures for presumptive and confirmed index cases;

(7) Provisions for developing flock plans for infected and exposed flocks;

(8) Detailed plans for disposal of infected flocks, including preexisting agreements with regulatory agencies and detailed plans for carcass disposal, disposal sites, and resources for conducting disposal, and detailed plans for disposal of materials that come into contact with poultry infected with or exposed to H5/H7 LPAI;

(9) Detailed plans for cleaning and disinfection of premises, repopulation, and monitoring after repopulation;

(10) Provisions for appropriate control/monitoring zones, contact surveys, and movement restrictions;

(11) Provisions for monitoring activities in control zones;

(12) If vaccination is considered as an option, a written plan for use in place with proper controls and provisions for APHIS approval of any use of vaccine;

(13) Plans for H5/H7 LPAI-negative flocks that provide for quarantine, testing, and controlled marketing; and

(14) Public awareness and education programs regarding avian influenza.

(b) If a State is designated a U.S. Avian Influenza Monitored State, Layers under § 146.24(a) of this chapter or a U.S. Avian Influenza Monitored State, Turkeys under § 146.44(a) of this chapter, it will lose that status during any outbreak of H5/H7 LPAI and for 90 days after the destruction and disposal of all infected or exposed birds and cleaning and disinfection of all affected premises are completed.

[71 FR 56323, Sept. 26, 2006, as amended at 75 FR 10658, Mar. 9, 2010]

SUBCHAPTER C—INTERSTATE TRANSPORTATION OF ANIMALS (INCLUDING POULTRY) AND ANIMAL PRODUCTS

PART 70—RULES OF PRACTICE GOVERNING PROCEEDINGS UNDER CERTAIN ACTS

AUTHORITY: 7 U.S.C. 8301–8317; 7 CFR 2.22, 2.80, and 371.4.

SOURCE: 48 FR 30094, June 30, 1983, unless otherwise noted.

Subpart A—General

§ 70.1 Scope and applicability of rules of practice.

The Uniform Rules of Practice for the Department of Agriculture promulgated in subpart H of part 1, subtitle A, title 7, Code of Federal Regulations, are the Rules of Practice applicable to adjudicatory, administrative proceedings under the following statutory provisions:

Act of May 29, 1884, commonly known as the Animal Industry Act, section 7, as amended (21 U.S.C. 117),

Act of February 2, 1903, commonly known as the Cattle Contagious Diseases Act of 1903, Section 3, as amended (21 U.S.C. 122),

Act of March 3, 1905, Section 6, as amended (21 U.S.C. 127),

Act of July 2, 1962, Section 6(a), as amended (21 U.S.C. 134e).

The Animal Health Protection Act (7 U.S.C. 8301 *et seq.*).

Sections 901–905 of the Federal Agriculture Improvement and Reform Act of 1996 (7 U.S.C. 1901 note).

In addition, the Supplemental Rules of Practice set forth in subpart B of this part shall be applicable to such proceedings.

[48 FR 30094, June 30, 1983, as amended at 66 FR 63615, Dec. 7, 2001; 68 FR 6343, Feb. 7, 2003]

Subpart B—Supplemental Rules of Practice

§ 70.10 Stipulations.

(a) At any time prior to the issuance of a complaint seeking a civil penalty under any of the Acts listed in § 70.1, the Administrator, in his discretion, may enter into a stipulation with any person in which:

(1) The Administrator or the Administrator's delegate gives notice of an apparent violation of the Act, or the regulations issued thereunder, by such person and affords such person an opportunity for a hearing regarding the matter as provided by the Act;

(2) Such person expressly waives hearing and agrees to pay a specified penalty within a designated time; and

(3) The Administrator agrees to accept the penalty in settlement of the particular matter involved if the penalty is paid within the designated time.

(b) If the penalty is not paid within the time designated in such a stipulation, the amount of the stipulated penalty shall not be relevant in any respect to the penalty which may be assessed after issuance of a complaint.

PART 71—GENERAL PROVISIONS

AUTHORITY: 7 U.S.C. 8301–8317; 7 CFR 2.22, 2.80, and 371.4.

SOURCE: 28 FR 5937, June 13, 1963, unless otherwise noted.

§ 71.1 Definitions.

As used in this part, the following terms shall have the meanings set forth in this section.

Accredited veterinarian. A veterinarian who is approved by the Administrator, in accordance with part 161 of this chapter, to perform official animal health work of the Animal and Plant Health Inspection Service specified in subchapters A, B, C, and D of this chapter and to perform work required by cooperative State-Federal disease control and eradication programs.

Administrator. The Administrator, Animal and Plant Health Inspection Service, or any person authorized to act for the Administrator.

Animal and Plant Health Inspection Service. The Animal and Plant Health Inspection Service of the United States Department of Agriculture (APHIS).

Animal identification number (AIN). A numbering system for the official identification of individual animals in the United States that provides a nationally unique identification number for each animal. The AIN consists of 15 digits, with the first 3 being the country code (840 for the United States or a unique country code for any U.S. territory that has such a code and elects to use it in place of the 840 code). The alpha characters USA or the numeric code assigned to the manufacturer of the identification device by the International Committee on Animal Recording may be used as an alternative to the 840 or other prefix representing a U.S territory; however, only the AIN beginning with the 840 or other prefix representing a U.S. territory will be recognized as official for use on AIN tags applied to animals on or after March 11, 2015. The AIN beginning with the 840 prefix may not be applied to animals known to have been born outside the United States.

APHIS representative. An individual employed by APHIS who is authorized to perform the function involved.

Approved livestock facility. A stockyard, livestock market, buying station, concentration point, or any other premises under State or Federal veterinary supervision where livestock are assembled and that has been approved under § 71.20.

Area veterinarian in charge. The veterinary official of APHIS who is assigned by the Administrator to supervise and perform the official animal health work of the Animal and Plant Health Inspection Service in the State concerned.

Breeding sheep and goats. Any sexually intact sheep or goat that is not moving either directly to slaughter or through one or more restricted sales and/or terminal feedlots and then directly to slaughter.

Breeder swine. Sexually intact swine over 6 months of age.

Commingling. The mixing or assembling of swine from one premises with swine from any other premises, including, but not limited to, loading swine from more than one premises on the same truck, trailer, vessel, or railroad car, unless swine from different premises are kept separate on the means of conveyance by dividers.

Consistent States. Those States listed as consistent States in § 79.1 of this subchapter because they meet certain standards, as provided in § 79.6 of this subchapter, for conducting an active State scrapie program involving the identification of scrapie in sheep and goats for the purpose of controlling the spread of scrapie.

Department. The United States Department of Agriculture.

Feeder swine. Swine under 6 months of age that are not slaughter swine.

Flock-based number system. The flock-based number system combines a flock identification number (FIN) with a producer's unique livestock production numbering system to provide a nationally unique identification number for an animal.

Flock identification number (FIN). A nationally unique number assigned by a State, Tribal, or Federal animal health authority to a group of animals that are managed as a unit on one or more premises and are under the same ownership.

Food Safety and Inspection Service (FSIS). The Food Safety and Inspection Service, United States Department of Agriculture.

Free area. The States, Territories, or the District of Columbia or portions thereof not quarantined by the Secretary of Agriculture for the specific contagious, infectious, or communicable animal disease mentioned in each part.

Group/lot identification number (GIN). The identification number used to uniquely identify a "unit of animals" of the same species that is managed together as one group throughout the preharvest production chain. When a GIN is used, it is recorded on documents accompanying the animals moving interstate; it is not necessary to have the GIN attached to each animal.

Horses. Horses, asses, mules, ponies, and zebras.

Inconsistent States. Those States not included in the list of consistent States appearing in §79.1 of this subchapter.

Interstate. From one State into or through any other State.

Interstate commerce. Trade, traffic, transportation, or other commerce between a place in a State and any place outside of that State, or between points within a State but through any place outside of that State.

Interstate swine movement report. A paper or electronic document signed by a producer moving swine giving notice that a group of animals is being moved across State lines in a swine production system. This document must contain the name of the swine production system; the name, location, and premises identification number of the premises from which the swine are to be moved; the name, location, and premises identification number of the premises to which the swine are to be moved; the date of movement; and the number, age, and type of swine to be moved. This document must also contain a description of any individual or group identification associated with the swine, the name of the swine production system accredited veterinarian(s), the health status of the herd from which the swine are to be moved, including any disease of regulatory concern to APHIS or to the States involved, and an accurate statement that swine on the premises from which the swine are to be moved have been inspected by the swine production system accredited veterinarian(s) within 30 days prior to the interstate movement and consistent with the dates specified by the premises' swine production health plan and found free from signs of communicable disease.

Livestock. All farm-raised animals.

Livestock market. A stockyard, buying station, concentration point, or any other premises where livestock are assembled for sale or sale purposes.

Move. To carry, enter, import, mail, ship, or transport; to aid, abet, cause, or induce carrying, entering, importing, mailing, shipping, or transporting; to offer to carry, enter, import, mail, ship, or transport; to receive in order to carry, enter, import, mail, ship, or transport; or to allow any of these activities.

National Uniform Eartagging System (NUES). A numbering system for the official identification of individual animals in the United States that provides a nationally unique identification number for each animal.

Official Brand Inspection Agency. The duly constituted body elected, appointed, or delegated or granted authority by a State or governmental subdivision thereof, to administer laws, regulations, ordinances or rules pertaining to the brand identification of livestock.

Official brand inspection certificate. A certificate issued by an official brand inspection agency in any State in which such certificates are required for movement of livestock.

Official eartag. An identification tag approved by APHIS that bears an official identification number for individual animals. Beginning March 11, 2014, all official eartags manufactured must bear an official eartag shield. Beginning March 11, 2015, all official eartags applied to animals must bear an official eartag shield. The design, size, shape, color, and other characteristics of the official eartag will depend on the needs of the users, subject to the approval of the Administrator. The official eartag must be tamper-resistant and have a high retention rate in the animal.

Official eartag shield. The shield-shaped graphic of the U.S. Route Shield with "U.S." or the State postal abbreviation or Tribal alpha code imprinted within the shield.

Official identification device or method. A means approved by the Administrator of applying an official identification number to an animal of a specific species or associating an official identification number with an animal or group of animals of a specific species.

Official identification number. A nationally unique number that is permanently associated with an animal or group of animals and that adheres to one of the following systems:

(1) National Uniform Eartagging System (NUES).

(2) Animal identification number (AIN).

(3) Location-based number system.

(4) Flock-based number system.

(5) Any other numbering system approved by the Administrator for the official identification of animals.

Official swine tattoo. A tattoo, conforming to the six-character alpha-numeric National Tattoo System, that provides a unique identification for each herd or lot of swine.

Person. Any individual, corporation, company, association, firm, partnership, society, or joint stock company, or other legal entity.

Premises. A location where livestock or poultry are housed or kept.

Premises identification number (PIN). A nationally unique number assigned by a State, Tribal, and/or Federal animal health authority to a premises that is, in the judgment of the State, Tribal, and/or Federal animal health authority a geographically distinct location from other premises. The PIN may be used in conjunction with a producer's own unique livestock production numbering system to provide a nationally unique and herd-unique identification number for an animal. It may be used as a component of a group/lot identification number (GIN).

Purebred registry association. A swine breed association formed and perpetuated for the maintenance of records of purebreeding of swine species for a specific breed whose characteristics are set forth in constitutions, by-laws, and other rules of the association.

Quarantined area. The States, Territories, or the District of Columbia or portions thereof quarantined by the Secretary of Agriculture for the specific contagious, infectious, or communicable animal disease mentioned in each part.

Slaughter swine. Swine being sold or moved for slaughter purposes only.

State. Any of the 50 States, the Commonwealth of Puerto Rico, the Commonwealth of the Northern Mariana Islands, the District of Columbia, and any territories and possessions of the United States.

State animal health official. The State official responsible for livestock and poultry disease control and eradication programs.

State representative. An individual employed in animal health work by a State or a political subdivision thereof and authorized by such State or political subdivision to perform the function involved.

Swine production health plan. A written agreement developed for a swine production system designed to maintain the health of the swine and detect signs of communicable disease.

The plan must identify all premises that are part of the swine production system and that receive or send swine in interstate commerce and must provide for health monitoring of all swine within the system. Such health monitoring must include inspections by the swine production system accredited veterinarian(s). Inspections of all identified premises that contain swine that are or will be in the process of moving interstate within the swine production system and of all swine on those premises must be conducted by the accredited veterinarian(s) at intervals of no greater than 30 days. Inspections of all identified receiving premises that contain only swine that have completed their interstate movement within a single swine production system and of all swine on those premises must be conducted in accordance with State regulations. The plan must also describe the recordkeeping system of the swine production system. The plan will not be valid unless it is signed by an official of each swine production system identified in the plan, the swine production system accredited veterinarian(s), an APHIS representative, and the State animal health official from each State in which the swine production system has premises. In the plan, the swine production system must acknowledge that it has been informed of and has notified the managers of all its premises listed in the plan that any failure of the participants in the swine production system to abide by the provisions of the plan and the applicable provisions of this part and part 85 of this chapter constitutes a basis for the cancellation of the swine production health plan, as well as other administrative or criminal sanctions, as appropriate.

Swine production system. A swine production enterprise that consists of multiple sites of production; *i.e.*, sow herds, nursery herds, and growing or finishing herds, but not including slaughter plants or livestock markets, that are connected by ownership or contractual relationships, between which swine move while remaining under the control of a single owner or a group of contractually connected owners.

Swine production system accredited veterinarian. An accredited veterinarian who is named in a swine production health plan for a premises within a swine production system and who performs inspection of such premises and animals and other duties related to the movement of swine in a swine production system.

Tick infested. Infested with the ticks Boophilus annulatus (Margaropus annulatus), Boophilus microplus, or Rhipicephalus evertsi evertsi.

United States. All of the States.

United States Department of Agriculture (USDA) approved backtag. A backtag issued by APHIS that provides a temporary unique identification for each animal.

[28 FR 5937, June 13, 1963]

EDITORIAL NOTE: For FEDERAL REGISTER citations affecting §71.1, see the List of CFR Sections Affected, which appears in the Finding Aids section of the printed volume and at *www.fdsys.gov*.

§71.2 Secretary to issue rule governing quarantine and interstate movement of diseased animals, including poultry.

When the Secretary of Agriculture shall determine the fact that poultry or other animals in any State, Territory, or the District of Columbia are affected with any contagious, infectious, or communicable disease of livestock or poultry for which, in his opinion, a quarantine should be established or that other basis for a quarantine exists, notice will be given of that fact, and a rule will be issued accordingly, placing in quarantine such State, Territory, or the District of Columbia, or specified portion thereof. This rule will either absolutely forbid the interstate movement of the quarantined animals from the quarantined area or will indicate the regulations under which interstate movements may be made.

[34 FR 15641, Oct. 9, 1969]

§71.3 Interstate movement of diseased animals and poultry generally prohibited.

(a) Animals or poultry affected with any of the following diseases, which are endemic to the United States: Equine piroplasmosis, bovine piroplasmosis or splenetic fever, scabies in cattle, pseudorabies, acute swine erysipelas, tuberculosis, Johne's disease, brucellosis, scrapie, bluetongue, anthrax, chlamydiosis, and Newcastle disease, or any other communicable disease which is endemic to the United States, or which are cattle fever tick infested, shall not be moved interstate.

(b) Animals or poultry affected with any of the following diseases, not known to exist in the United States:

foot-and-mouth disease, rinderpest, African swine fever, classical swine fever, Teschen disease, contagious bovine pleuropneumonia, highly pathogenic avian influenza, dourine, contagious equine metritis, vesicular exanthema, screwworms and glanders, scabies in sheep or any other communicable foreign disease not known to exist in the United States, shall not be moved interstate.

(c) Notwithstanding the provisions of paragraphs (a) and (b) of this section:

(1) Domestic animals that have reacted to an official test for brucellosis, are not affected with any other disease referred to in this section, and are not tick infested may be moved interstate in accordance with part 78 of this chapter.

(2) Domestic animals that are positive to an official Johne's disease test, are not affected with any other disease referred to in this section, and are not tick infested may be moved interstate in accordance with part 80 of this chapter.

(3) Cattle which have reacted to the tuberculin test, which are not affected with any other disease referred to in this section and are not tick infested, may be moved interstate in accordance with the provisions of §77.17 of this subchapter.

(4) Swine infected with or exposed to pseudorabies may be moved interstate in accordance with part 85 of this chapter.

(5) [Reserved]

(6) Sheep or goats designated, with regard to scrapie, as exposed animals, high-risk animals, suspect animals, or scrapie-positive animals, as those terms are defined in part 79 of this subchapter, may be moved interstate only in accordance with part 79 of this subchapter.

(d) Notwithstanding the provisions of paragraphs (a) and (b) of this section, livestock which is found to be diseased may be moved interstate in accordance with paragraphs (d)(1) through (6) of this section: *Provided*, That such livestock is not tick infested or affected with any disease referred to in this section other than the diseases named in this paragraph: *And provided further*, That such livestock is accompanied by a certificate, issued by an APHIS or State representative or accredited veterinarian stating the destination of the animals; the purpose for which they are to be moved; the number of animals covered by the certificate; the point from which the animals are moved interstate; and the name and address of the owner or shipper.

(1) Livestock affected with one or more of the following diseases may be moved interstate for immediate slaughter to a slaughtering establishment where State or Federal meat inspection is maintained; Actinomycosis, actinobacillosis, anaplasmosis, atrophic rhinitis, contagious ecthyma, foot rot, infectious keratitis, ram epididymitis, ringworm, swine influenza, arthritis (simple lesions only), and shipping fever.

(2) Cattle with slight unopened cases of actinomycosis or actinobacillosis (or both) may be moved interstate to a feed lot in the State of destination: *Provided*, That such cattle are not affected with any other disease named in this paragraph.

(3) Sheep affected with or exposed to contagious ecthyma may be moved interstate to a feed lot located in a State the laws, rules, or regulations of which require that such sheep be segregated or quarantined under a permit from an official of such State: *Provided*, That such sheep are not affected with any other disease named in this paragraph.

(4) Livestock affected with one or more of the following diseases may be moved interstate for any purpose to a State the laws, rules, or regulations of which require that such livestock be segregated or quarantined under a permit from the appropriate livestock sanitary official of such State: actinomycosis, actinobacillosis, contagious ecthyma, foot rot, and shipping fever: *Provided*, That such livestock is not affected with any other disease named in this paragraph.

(5) Livestock affected with infectious keratitis or ringworm (or both) may be moved interstate for any purpose if treated under the supervision of an APHIS or State representative or an accredited veterinarian prior to movement: *Provided*, That such livestock is not affected with any other disease

named in this paragraph. Livestock affected with infectious keratitis or ringworm (or both) and also with another disease named in this paragraph may be moved interstate only under the applicable provisions of paragraphs (d)(1) through (4) of this section after being so treated for infectious keratitis or ringworm (or both). Such livestock will be subject to further treatment at destination, if required.

(6) Fish affected with spring viremia of carp may be moved interstate only if they are being moved directly to a facility to be processed into food for human consumption.

(7) *Other movements.* The Administrator may provide for the movement, not otherwise provided for in this paragraph, of animals affected with the diseases named in paragraph (d)(1) of this section, under such conditions as he may prescribe to prevent the spread of disease. The Administrator will promptly notify the appropriate livestock sanitary officials of the States involved of any such action.

(e) Notwithstanding the provisions of paragraphs (a) and (b) of this section, the Administrator in specific cases and under such conditions as he may prescribe to prevent the dissemination of disease may provide for the interstate movement of individual animals affected with contagious, infectious, or communicable disease to a designated diagnostic or research facility when accompanied by a permit from the appropriate livestock sanitary official in the State of destination: *Provided,* That animals so moved shall be maintained in quarantine at such designated facility until freed of disease as determined by tests recognized by the Department, until natural death, or until disposal by euthanasia.

(f) Before offering cattle or other livestock or poultry for interstate transportation, transporting them interstate, or introducing them into any stockyards or upon routes of traffic for interstate transportation, all persons, companies, or corporations are required to exercise reasonable diligence to ascertain whether such animals or poultry are affected with any contagious, infectious, or communicable disease, or have been exposed to the contagion or infection of any such disease by contact with other animals or poultry so diseased or by location in pens, cars, or other vehicles, or upon premises that have contained animals or poultry so diseased.

[28 FR 5937, June 13, 1963]

EDITORIAL NOTE: For FEDERAL REGISTER citations affecting §71.3, see the List of CFR Sections Affected, which appears in the Finding Aids section of the printed volume and at *www.fdsys.gov.*

§71.4 Maintenance of certain facilities and premises in a sanitary condition required; cleaning and disinfection, when required; animals classed as "exposed."

(a) Yards, pens, chutes, alleys, and other facilities and premises which are used in connection with the interstate movement of livestock or poultry shall be maintained by the person in possession of the facilities and premises in a clean and sanitary condition, in accordance with good animal husbandry practices, and shall be subject to inspection by an APHIS or State representative. When an APHIS or State representative determines that such facilities or premises are not in such clean and sanitary condition and gives written notice of his determination to such person, the facilities and premises shall be cleaned and disinfected in accordance with §§71.7 and 71.10 through 71.12 by such person under the supervision of an APHIS or State representative or an accredited veterinarian before such premises are again used for livestock or poultry.

(b) Yards, pens, chutes, alleys, and other facilities and premises which have contained interstate shipments of cattle, sheep, swine, poultry, or other animals affected with, or carrying the infection of, any contagious, infectious, or communicable disease of livestock or poultry other than slight unopened cases of actinomycosis or actinobacillosis (or both), bovine foot rot, atrophic rhinitis, ram epididymitis, ringworm, infectious keratitis, and arthritis (simple lesions only), shall be cleaned and disinfected under the supervision of an APHIS or State representative or an accredited veterinarian in accordance with §§71.7 and 71.10 through 71.12 before such premises are again used for animals, and any poultry or other animals unloaded into such yards or premises before they have been so cleaned and disinfected shall thereafter be classed as "exposed" within the meaning of the regulations in this subchapter and shall not be moved interstate except in compliance with the provisions of such regulations applicable to "exposed" animals.

[34 FR 15641, Oct. 9, 1969, as amended at 55 FR 11156, Mar. 27, 1990; 55 FR 15320, Apr. 23, 1990; 62 FR 27933, May 22, 1997]

§ 71.5 Unsanitary railroad cars, trucks, boats, aircraft or other means of conveyance; interstate movement restricted.

No person who receives notice from an APHIS representative that a railroad car, truck, boat, aircraft or other means of conveyance owned or operated by such person is not in a clean and sanitary condition in accordance with good animal husbandry practices, shall thereafter use such means of conveyance in connection with the interstate movement of livestock or poultry, or move said means of conveyance interstate, until it has been cleaned and disinfected under the supervision of an APHIS or State representative or an accredited veterinarian in accordance with §§ 71.7 and 71.10 through 71.12.

[34 FR 15641, Oct. 9, 1969, as amended at 55 FR 11156, Mar. 27, 1990; 55 FR 15320, Apr. 23, 1990; 62 FR 27933, May 22, 1997]

§ 71.6 Carrier responsible for cleaning and disinfecting of railroad cars, trucks, boats, aircraft or other means of conveyance.

(a) Railroad cars, trucks, boats, aircraft, and other means of conveyance which have been used in the interstate transportation of cattle, sheep, goats, swine, poultry, or other animals affected with, or carrying the infection of, any contagious, infectious, or communicable disease of livestock or poultry, other than slight unopened cases of actinomycosis or actinobacillosis (or both), atrophic rhinitis, bovine foot rot, brucellosis, ram epididymitis, ringworm, infectious keratitis, and arthritis (simple lesions only), shall be cleaned and disinfected under APHIS supervision in accordance with §§ 71.7 and 71.10 through 71.12 at the point where the animals are unloaded and the final carrier shall be responsible for such cleaning and disinfecting: *Provided*, That when APHIS supervision is not available at such point, the means of conveyance may be cleaned and disinfected under the supervision of a State representative or an accredited veterinarian.

(b) No railroad car, truck, boat, aircraft or other means of conveyance from which poultry or other animals affected with an infectious, contagious or communicable disease of livestock or poultry, other than those specified in § 71.4(b), have been unloaded shall thereafter be used in connection with the interstate movement of animals, including poultry, or be moved interstate until it has been cleaned and disinfected by the final carrier under the supervision of an APHIS or State representative or an accredited veterinarian in accordance with §§ 71.7 and 71.10 through 71.12.

(c) If APHIS supervision or other supervision as required by paragraph (a) or (b) of this section or proper cleaning and disinfecting facilities are not available at the point where the animals are unloaded, upon permission first received from the Animal and Plant Health Inspection Service, the means of conveyance may be forwarded empty to a point at which such supervision and facilities are available, and there be cleaned and disinfected under supervision in accordance with §§ 71.7 and 71.10 through 71.12.

[34 FR 15641, Oct. 9, 1969, as amended at 37 FR 25337, Nov. 30, 1972; 39 FR 4465, Feb. 4, 1974; 55 FR 11156, Mar. 27, 1990; 55 FR 15320, Apr. 23, 1990; 62 FR 27934, May 22, 1997; 74 FR 14709, Apr. 1, 2009]

§ 71.7 Means of conveyance, facilities, premises, and cages and other equipment; methods of cleaning and disinfecting.

(a) Railroad cars, trucks, aircraft, or other means of conveyance, except boats, required by the regulations in this subchapter to be cleaned and disinfected shall be treated in the following manner: Remove all litter and manure from all portions of the conveyance, including any external ledges and framework; clean the exterior and interior of the conveyance; and saturate the entire interior surface, including the inner surface of the doors of the conveyance, with a permitted disinfectant specified in §§71.10 through 71.12.

(b) Boats required by the regulations in this subchapter to be cleaned and disinfected shall be treated in the following manner: Remove all litter and manure from the decks and stalls, and all other parts of the boat occupied or traversed by any poultry or other animals and from the portable chutes or other appliances or fixtures used in loading and unloading the animals, and saturate with a permitted disinfectant the entire surface of the deck, stalls, or other parts of the boat occupied or traversed by any animals or with which they may come in contact or which have contained litter or manure.

(c) Yards, pens, chutes, alleys, cages, and other equipment required by the regulations in this subchapter to be disinfected shall be treated in the following manner: Empty all troughs, racks, or other feeding or watering appliances; remove all litter and manure from the floors, posts, or other parts; and saturate the entire surface of the fencing, troughs, chutes, floors, walls, and other parts with a permitted disinfectant specified in §§71.10 through 71.12.

[34 FR 15642, Oct. 9, 1969, as amended at 61 FR 56883, Nov. 5, 1996]

§71.10 Permitted disinfectants.

(a) Disinfectants permitted for use on cars, boats, and other vehicles, premises, and cages and other equipment are as follows:

(1) "Cresylic disinfectant" in the proportion of at least 4 fluid ounces to 1 gallon of water.

(2) Liquefied phenol (U.S.P. strength 87 percent phenol) in the proportion of at least 6 fluid ounces to 1 gallon of water.

(3) Chlorinated lime (U.S.P. strength, 30 percent available chlorine) in the proportion of 1 pound to 3 gallons of water.

(4) Sodium hydroxide (Lye) prepared in a fresh solution in the proportion of not less than 1 pound avoirdupois of sodium hydroxide of not less than 95 percent purity to 6 gallons of water, or one 13½ ounce can to 5 gallons of water. Due to the extreme caustic nature of sodium hydroxide solution, precautionary measures such as the wearing of rubber gloves, boots, raincoat, and goggles should be observed. An acid solution such as vinegar shall be kept readily available in case any of the sodium hydroxide solution should come in contact with the body.

(5) Disinfectants which are registered under the Federal Insecticide, Fungicide, and Rodenticide Act (7 U.S.C. 135 *et seq.*), with tuberculocidal claims, as disinfectants for general use, may be used for the purpose of this part in accordance with directions on the labels accepted in connection with their registration. However, disinfectants which fall in this category are not permitted for use in outbreaks of foreign animal diseases unless in specific cases such use is approved in advance by the Administrator.

(b) The use of "cresylic disinfectant" is permitted subject to the following conditions:

(1) The manufacturer thereof shall have obtained specific permission from APHIS for the use of his products in official disinfection. To obtain such permission manufacturers shall first submit a sample of at least 8 ounces for examination, together with a statement of the formula employed and a guaranty that the product will be maintained of a quality uniform with the sample submitted.

(2) To prevent confusion, the product of each manufacturer and distributor shall bear a distinctive trade name or brand, together with the name of the manufacturer or distributor.

(3) The product shall at all times conform to specifications for composition and performance issued by the Administrator.

[28 FR 5937, June 13, 1963, as amended at 32 FR 19157, Dec. 20, 1967; 37 FR 8864, May 2, 1972; 37 FR 9460, May 11, 1972; 55 FR 11156, Mar. 27, 1990; 55 FR 15320, Apr. 23, 1990; 61 FR 56883, Nov. 5, 1996]

§71.11 Cresylic disinfectant as permitted disinfectant; specifications.

The following specifications will be employed for determining the suitability of cresylic disinfectant for use under the provisions of §71.10(b)(3):

(a) The product shall remain a uniform liquid when held at 0 °C. (32 °F.) for 3 hours (chill test).

(b) The product shall dissolve completely in 30 parts of distilled water at 25 °C. (77 °F.) within 2 minutes (solution-rate test), producing a solution entirely free from globules and not more than faintly opalescent (solubility-degree test).

(c) The product shall contain not more than 25 percent of inert ingredients (water and glycerin), not more excess alkali than the equivalent of 0.5 percent of sodium hydroxide, and not less than 21 percent of soap exclusive of water, glycerin, and excess alkali.

(d) The product shall contain not less than 50 percent and not more than 53 percent of total phenols. It shall contain less than 5 percent of benzophenol (C^6H^5OH).

(e) The methods of determining compliance with the specifications in paragraphs (a) to (d) of this section will be those described in United States Department of Agriculture Bulletin 1308, Chemical and Physical Methods for the Control of Saponified Cresol Solutions, so far as they are applicable.

(f) Any suitable glyceride, fat acid, or resin acid may be used in preparing the soap, but not all are suitable nor are all grades of a single product equally suitable, Also various grades of commercial cresylic acid differ in suitability. Therefore, manufacturers are cautioned to prepare a trial laboratory batch from every set of ingredients and to prove its conformity with paragraphs (a) and (b) of this section, before proceeding with manufacture on a factory scale.

§ 71.12 Sodium orthophenylphenate as permitted disinfectant for premises infected with tuberculosis.

(a) A permitted brand of sodium orthophenylphenate in a proportion of at least one pound to 12 gallons of water is permitted in tuberculosis eradication work for disinfecting infected premises following the removal of cattle that reacted to the tuberculin test.

(b) It is absolutely necessary that the solution be applied at a temperature of 60 °F. or over. Whenever the temperature of the building to be disinfected is below 60 °F., as indicated by a wall thermometer, the solution shall be heated to 120 °F. and higher in very cold weather, to insure effective disinfection.

§ 71.13 Inspection of shipments in transit by APHIS representative.

All persons and corporations having control of the interstate transportation of livestock or poultry shall, when directed by an APHIS inspector so to do, stop the same in transit for inspection, and if any of such poultry or other animals are found upon such inspection to be infected with any contagious, infectious, or communicable disease or to have been exposed to such infection, the person or corporation having control of the transportation of such poultry or other animals shall, upon receipt of an order from an APHIS representative so to do, cease the carriage, transportation, or moving of such poultry or other animals unless such carriage, transportation, or moving can be accomplished in accordance with the regulations in this subchapter governing the interstate movement of poultry or other animals infected with or which have been exposed to the infection of such disease, and in all cases after the discovery of such infection or exposure thereto such poultry or other animals shall be handled in accordance with such regulations.

[28 FR 5937, June 13, 1963, as amended at 34 FR 15642, Oct. 9, 1969; 55 FR 11156, Mar. 27, 1990; 55 FR 15320, Apr. 23, 1990; 62 FR 27934, May 22, 1997]

§ 71.14 Slaughter of poultry or other animals to prevent spread of disease; ascertainment of value and compensation.

When, in order to prevent the spread of any contagious, infectious, or communicable disease, it becomes necessary to slaughter any diseased or exposed animals, including poultry, and the purchase of such animals, including poultry, by the United States is authorized by law and an appropriation is available therefor, the value of the animals, including poultry shall be ascertained and compensation made therefor in accordance with the orders or regulations of the Secretary of Agriculture.

[28 FR 5937, June 13, 1963, as amended at 34 FR 15642, Oct. 9, 1969]

§71.15 Movement from quarantined to free area and shipment therefrom; conditions under which permitted.

No livestock or poultry shall be shipped, trailed, driven, or hauled in private conveyance from the quarantined area in any State, Territory, or the District of Columbia to the free area in the same State, Territory, or the District of Columbia and subsequently delivered to a transportation company for shipment or moved to any other State, Territory, or the District of Columbia without complying with all Federal and State regulations pertaining to such movements.

[28 FR 5937, June 13, 1963, as amended at 34 FR 15642, Oct. 9, 1969]

§71.16 Inspection and certification of poultry or other animals for interstate movement.

(a) *Assistance and facilities.* When poultry or other animals are to be inspected and certified by an APHIS representative, assistance and proper facilities for restraining them shall be provided in order that a careful inspection may be made, and the representative while making the inspection shall not be interfered with in any manner; otherwise inspection will be immediately discontinued.

(b) *Certificates and other statements to accompany shipments.* Whenever inspection or treatment and the issuance of a certificate, statement, test chart, or other writing showing the performance of such inspection or treatment and the result thereof is required by any of the regulations in this subchapter as a condition precedent to the movement interstate of any poultry or other animal or class of poultry or other animals, or any poultry or other animal or class of poultry or other animals is so required to be accompanied in interstate movement by such certificate, statement, test chart, or other writing, no such poultry or other animal or poultry or other animals shall be moved interstate unless and until the following requirements are also complied with:

(1) In the case of such movement by a common carrier issuing waybills or other form or forms of billing covering the movement, the said certificate, statement, test chart, or other writing shall be delivered to such carrier at the time the poultry or other animal or poultry or other animals are delivered for shipment, and shall become the property of the carrier, and be by such carrier attached to the billing covering the transportation of such poultry or other animal or poultry or other animals, and accompany such billing to destination, and be filed with such billing for future reference.

(2) In case of such movement otherwise than by common carrier issuing waybills or other form or forms of billing, the said certificate, statement, test chart, or other writing shall accompany the poultry or other animal or poultry or other animals to destination and be delivered to the consignees, or, in case the consignor and consignee is the same person, to the first purchaser purchasing during or after such movement in interstate commerce, or to the person to whom the poultry or other animal or poultry or other animals are delivered.

[28 FR 5937, June 13, 1963, as amended at 34 FR 15642, Oct. 9, 1969; 55 FR 11156, Mar. 27, 1990; 55 FR 15320, Apr. 23, 1990; 62 FR 27934, May 22, 1997]

§71.17 Interstate movement of dead poultry or other animals prohibited in same car with live poultry or other animals.

No dead poultry or other animals shall be offered or accepted for transportation or transported in the same car with live poultry or other animals from the original point of shipment in any State or Territory or the District of Columbia to or through any other State, Territory, or the District of Columbia.

[28 FR 5937, June 13, 1963, as amended at 34 FR 15642, Oct. 9, 1969]

§71.18 [Reserved]

§71.19 Identification of swine in interstate commerce.

(a)(1) Except as provided in paragraphs (c) and (g) of this section, no swine may be sold, transported, received for transportation, or offered for sale or transportation, in interstate commerce, unless each swine is identified at whichever of the following comes first:

(i) The point of first commingling of the swine in interstate commerce with swine from any other source;

(ii) Upon unloading of the swine in interstate commerce at any livestock market;

(iii) Upon transfer of ownership of the swine in interstate commerce; or

(iv) Upon arrival of the swine in interstate commerce at their final destination.

(2) The identification shall be by means of identification approved by the Administrator and listed in paragraph (b) of this section. All swine shall remain so identified while they are in interstate commerce.

(3) Each person who buys or sells, for his or her own account or as the agent of the buyer or seller, transports, receives for transportation, offers for sale or transportation, or otherwise handles swine in interstate commerce, is responsible for the identification of the swine as provided by this section.

(b) Means of swine identification approved by the Administrator are:

(1) Official eartags, when used on any swine;

(2) United States Department of Agriculture (USDA) approved backtag, when used on swine moving to slaughter;

(3) Official swine tattoos, when used on swine moving to slaughter, when the use of the official swine tattoo has been requested by a user or the State animal health official, and the Administrator authorizes its use in writing based on a determination that the tattoo will be retained and visible on the carcass of the swine after slaughter, so as to provide identification of the swine;

(4) Tattoos of at least 4-characters when used on swine moving to slaughter, except sows and boars as provided in § 78.33 of this chapter;

(5) Ear notching when used on any swine, if the ear notching has been recorded in the book of record of a purebred registry association;

(6) Tattoos on the ear or inner flank of any swine, if the tattoos have been recorded in the book of record of a swine registry association;

(7) For slaughter swine and feeder swine, an eartag or tattoo bearing the premises identification number assigned by the State animal health official to the premises on which the swine originated; and

(8) Any other official identification device or method that is approved by the Administrator.

(c) Swine that are kept as a group are not required to be individually identified when in interstate commerce if:

(1) They were born on the same premises;

(2) They were raised on the same premises where they were born;

(3) They are moved in a group directly to a slaughtering establishment from the place where they were raised;

(4) They are not mixed with swine from any other premises, between the time they are born and the time they arrive at the slaughtering establishment; and

(5) They are slaughtered one after another, as a group, and not mixed with other swine at slaughter; or approved identification is applied to the swine after entry into the slaughtering establishment.

(d) Serial numbers of United States Department of Agriculture (USDA) approved backtag and official swine tattoos will be assigned to each person who applies to the State animal health official or the area veterinarian in charge for the State in which that person maintains his/her or its place of business. Serial numbers of official eartags will be assigned to each accredited veterinarian or State or Federal representative who requests official eartags from the State animal health official or the area veterinarian in charge, whoever is responsible for issuing official eartags in that State. Persons assigned serial numbers of United States Department of Agriculture (USDA) approved backtag, official swine tattoos, and official eartags must:

(1) Record the following information on a document:

(i) All serial numbers applied to the swine;

(ii) Any other serial numbers and approved identification appearing on the swine that are needed to identify the swine to its previous owner and location;

(iii) The street address, including the city and state, or the township, county, and state, of the premises where the approved means of identification were applied; and

(iv) The telephone number, if available, of the person who owns or possesses the swine.

(2) Maintain these records at the person's place of business for 2 years; and

(3) Make these records available for inspection and copying during ordinary business hours (8 a.m. to 5:30 p.m., Monday through Friday) upon request by any authorized employee of the United States Department of Agriculture, upon that employee's request and presentation of his or her official credentials.

(e)(1) Each person who buys or sells, for his or her own account or as the agent of the buyer or seller, transports, receives for transportation, offers for sale or transportation, or otherwise handles swine in interstate commerce, must keep records relating to the transfer of ownership, shipment, or handling of the swine, such as yarding receipts, sale tickets, invoices, and waybills upon which is recorded:

(i) All serial numbers and other approved means of identification appearing on the swine that are necessary to identify it to the person from whom it was purchased or otherwise obtained; and

(ii) The street address, including city and state, or the township, county, and state, and the telephone number, if available, of the person from whom the swine were purchased or otherwise obtained.

(2) Each person required to keep records under this paragraph must maintain the records at his/her or its place of business for at least 2 years after the person has sold or otherwise disposed of the swine to another person, and for such further period as the Administrator may require by written notice to the person, for purposes of any investigation or action involving the swine identified in the records. The person shall make the records available for inspection and copying during ordinary business hours (8 a.m. to 5:30 p.m., Monday through Friday) by any authorized employee of the United States Department of Agriculture, upon that employee's request and presentation of his or her official credentials.

(f) No person may remove or tamper with any approved means of identification required to be on swine pursuant to this section while it is in interstate commerce, except at the time of slaughter as provided in 9 CFR 309.16(e).

(g) *Swine moving interstate within a swine production system.* Swine moving within a swine production system to other than slaughter or a livestock market are not required to be individually identified when moved in interstate commerce under the following conditions:

(1) The swine may be moved interstate only to another premises identified in a valid swine production health plan for that swine production system.

(2) The swine production system must operate under a valid swine production health plan, in which both the sending and receiving States have agreed to allow the movement.

(3) The swine must have been found free from signs of any communicable disease during the most recent inspection of the premises by the swine production system accredited veterinarian(s) within 30 days prior to movement.

(4) Prior to the movement of any swine, the producer(s) moving swine must deliver the required interstate swine movement report to the following individuals identified in the swine production health plan:

(i) The swine production system accredited veterinarian for the premises from which the swine are to be moved, and

(ii) The State animal health officials for the sending and receiving States, and any other State employees designated by the State animal health officials.

(5) The receiving premises must not commingle swine received from different premises in a manner that prevents identification of the premises that sent the swine or groups of swine.

This may be achieved by use of permanent premises or individual identification marks on animals, by keeping groups of animals received from one premises physically separate from animals received from other premises, or by any other effective means.

(6) Each premises must maintain, for 3 years after their date of creation, records that will allow an APHIS representative or State animal health official to trace any animal on the premises back to its previous premises, and must maintain copies of each swine production health plan signed by the producer, all interstate swine movement reports issued by the producer, and all reports the swine production system accredited veterinarian(s) issue documenting the health status of the swine on the premises.

(7) Each premises must allow APHIS representatives and State animal health officials access to the premises upon request to inspect animals and review records.

(8) Once a month, each swine production system must send APHIS a written summary based on the interstate swine movement report data that shows how many animals were moved in the past month, the premises from which they were moved, and the premises to which they were moved.

(h) *Cancellation of and withdrawal from a swine production health plan.* The following procedures apply to cancellation of, or withdrawal from, a swine production health plan:

(1) A State animal health official may cancel his or her State's participation in a swine production health plan by giving written notice to all swine producers, APHIS representatives, accredited veterinarians, and other State animal health officials listed in the plan. Withdrawal shall be effective upon the date specified by the State animal health official in the notice, but for shipments in transit, withdrawal shall become effective 7 days after the date of such notice. Upon withdrawal of a State, the swine production health plan may continue to operate among the other States and parties signatory to the plan.

(2) A swine production system may withdraw one or more of its premises from participation in the plan upon giving written notice to the Administrator, the accredited veterinarian(s), all swine producers listed in the plan, and State animal health officials listed in the plan. Withdrawal shall be effective upon the date specified by the swine production system in the written notice, but for shipments in transit, withdrawal shall become effective 7 days after the date of such notice.

(3) The Administrator may cancel a swine production health plan by giving written notice to all swine producers, accredited veterinarians, and State animal health officials listed in the plan. The Administrator shall cancel a swine production health plan after determining that swine movements within the swine production system have occurred that were not in compliance with the swine production health plan or with other requirements of this chapter. Before a swine health production plan is canceled, an APHIS representative will inform a representative of the swine production system of the reasons for the proposed cancellation. The swine production system may appeal the proposed cancellation in writing to the Administrator within 10 days after being informed of the reasons for the proposed cancellation. The appeal must include all of the facts and reasons upon which the swine production system relies to show that the reasons for the proposed cancellation are incorrect or do not support the cancellation. The Administrator will grant or deny the appeal in writing as promptly as circumstances permit, stating the reason for his or her decision. If there is a conflict as to any material fact, a hearing will be held to resolve the conflict. Rules of practice concerning the hearing will be adopted by the Administrator. However, cancellation of the disputed swine production health plan shall become effective pending final determination in the proceeding if the Administrator determines that such action is necessary to protect the public's health, interest, or safety. Such cancellation shall become effective upon oral or written notification, whichever is earlier, to the swine production system representative. In the event of oral notification, written

confirmation shall be given as promptly as circumstances allow. This cancellation shall continue in effect pending the completion of the proceeding, and any judicial review thereof, unless otherwise ordered by the Administrator.

[53 FR 40385, Oct. 14, 1988, as amended at 55 FR 11156, Mar. 27, 1990; 55 FR 15320, Apr. 23, 1990; 59 FR 67612, Dec. 30, 1994; 62 FR 27934, May 22, 1997; 62 FR 54758, Oct. 22, 1997; 66 FR 65603, Dec. 20, 2001; 69 FR 64649, Nov. 8, 2004; 74 FR 14709, Apr. 1, 2009; 78 FR 2064, Jan. 9, 2013]

§ 71.20 Approval of livestock facilities.

(a) To qualify for approval by the Administrator as an approved livestock facility[7] and to retain such designation, the individual legally responsible for the day-to-day operations of the livestock facility shall execute the following agreement:

AGREEMENT—APPROVED LIVESTOCK FACILITY FOR HANDLING LIVESTOCK PURSUANT TO TITLE 9 OF THE CODE OF FEDERAL REGULATIONS

[*Name of facility*]

[*Address and telephone number of facility*]

I, [*name of the individual legally responsible for the day-to-day operations of the livestock facility*], operator of [*name of facility*], hereby agree to maintain and operate the livestock facility located at [*address of premises*] in accordance with the applicable provisions of this agreement and Chapter I, Title 9, of the Code of Federal Regulations (9 CFR).

Cooperation

(1) The State animal health official and the area veterinarian in charge shall be provided with a schedule of the facility's sale days, which shall indicate the types of animals that will be handled at the facility on each sale day, and shall be apprised of any changes to that schedule prior to the implementation of the changes.

(2) An accredited veterinarian, State representative, or APHIS representative shall be on the facility premises on all sale days to perform duties in accordance with State and Federal regulations.

(3) State representatives and APHIS representatives shall be granted access to the facility during normal business hours to evaluate whether the facility and its operations are in compliance with the applicable provisions of this agreement and 9 CFR parts 71, 75, 78, 79, and 85.

(4) An APHIS representative, State representative, or accredited veterinarian shall be immediately notified of the presence at the facility of any livestock that are known to be infected, exposed, high-risk and scrapie-positive or suspect, or that show signs of possibly being infected, with any infectious, contagious, or communicable disease.

(5) Any reactor, suspect, exposed, high-risk, or scrapie positive livestock shall be held in quarantined pens apart from all other livestock at the facility. This requirement shall not apply to scrapie-exposed sheep that are not also designated high-risk animals or to sheep or goats designated under 9 CFR part 79 as scrapie-exposed or high-risk animals that either are not pregnant based on the animal being male, an owner certification that any female animals have not been exposed to a male in the preceding 6 months, or a certificate issued by an accredited veterinarian stating the animals are open; or that the animals are under 12 months of age and are not visibly pregnant and are maintained in the same pen only with other animals that will be moved directly to slaughter or to a terminal feedlot in accordance with 9 CFR parts 71 and 79.

(6) No reactor, suspect, exposed, high-risk, or scrapie-positive livestock, nor any livestock that show signs of being infected with any infectious, contagious, or communicable disease, may be sold at or moved from the facility, except in accordance with 9 CFR parts 71, 75, 78, 79, and 85.

Records

(7) Documents such as weight tickets, sales slips, and records of origin, identification, and destination that related to livestock that are in, or that have been in, the facility shall be maintained by the facility. For poultry and swine, such documents must be kept for at least 2 years, and for cattle and bison, sheep and goats, cervids, and equines, for at least 5 years. APHIS representatives and State representatives shall be permitted to review and copy those documents during normal business hours.

Identification

(8) All livestock must be officially identified in accordance with the applicable regulations in 9 CFR parts 71, 75, 78, 79, 85, and 86 at the time of, or prior to, entry into the facility.

Cleaning and Disinfection

(9) The facility, including all yards, docks, pens, alleys, sale rings, chutes, scales, means of conveyance, and their associated equipment, shall be maintained in a clean and

[7] A list of approved livestock facilities may be obtained by writing to National Animal Health Programs, VS, APHIS, 4700 River Road Unit 36, Riverdale, MD 20737–1231.

sanitary condition. The operator of the facility shall be responsible for the cleaning and disinfection of the facility in accordance with 9 CFR part 71 and for maintaining an adequate supply of disinfectant and serviceable equipment for cleaning and disinfection.

General Facilities and Equipment Standards

(10) All facilities and equipment shall be maintained in a state of good repair. The facility shall contain well-constructed and well-lighted livestock handling chutes, pens, alleys, and sales rings for the inspection, identification, vaccination, testing, and branding of livestock.

(11) Quarantined pens shall be clearly labeled with paint or placarded with the word "Quarantined" or the name of the disease of concern, and shall be cleaned and disinfected in accordance with 9 CFR part 71 as well as 9 CFR 54.7(e)(2) if the disease of concern is scrapie and the quarantined animal gave birth or aborted at the facility, before being used to pen livestock that are not reactor, suspect, exposed, high-risk, or scrapie-positive animals.

(12) Quarantined pens shall have adequate drainage, and the floors and those parts of the walls of the quarantined pens with which reactor, suspect, exposed, high-risk, or scrapie-positive livestock, their excrement, or discharges may have contact shall be constructed of materials that are substantially impervious to moisture and able to withstand continued cleaning and disinfection.

(13) Electrical outlets shall be provided at the chute area for branding purposes.

Standards for Handling Different Classes of Livestock

(By his or her initials, the operator of the facility shall signify the class or classes of livestock that the facility will handle.)

(14) Cattle and bison:

—This facility will handle cattle and bison: [*Initials of operator, date*]

—This facility will handle cattle and bison known to be brucellosis reactors, suspects, or exposed: [*Initials of operator, date*]

—This facility will not handle cattle and bison known to be brucellosis reactors, suspects, or exposed and such cattle and bison will not be permitted to enter the facility: [*Initials of operator, date*]

(i) Cattle and bison shall be received, handled, and released by the facility only in accordance with 9 CFR parts 71 and 78.

(ii) All brucellosis reactor, brucellosis suspect, and brucellosis exposed cattle or bison arriving at the facility shall be placed in quarantined pens and consigned from the facility only in accordance with 9 CFR part 78.

(iii) Any cattle or bison classified as brucellosis reactors at the facility shall be identified in accordance with 9 CFR part 78, placed in quarantined pens, and consigned from the facility only to a recognized slaughtering establishment or an approved intermediate handling facility in accordance with 9 CFR part 78.

(iv) Any cattle or bison classified as brucellosis exposed at the facility shall be identified in accordance with 9 CFR part 78, placed in quarantined pens, and consigned from the facility only to a recognized slaughtering establishment, approved intermediate handling facility, quarantined feedlot, or farm of origin in accordance with 9 CFR part 78.

(v) The identity of cattle from Class Free States or areas and Class A States or areas shall be maintained.

(vi) The identity of cattle from Class B States or areas shall be maintained, and test-eligible cattle from Class B States or areas shall not be placed in pens with cattle from any other area until they have fulfilled the requirements of 9 CFR part 78 for release from the facility.

(vii) The identity of cattle from Class C States or areas shall be maintained, and test-eligible cattle from Class C States or areas shall not be placed in pens with cattle from any other area until they have fulfilled the requirements of 9 CFR part 78 for release from the facility.

(viii) The identity of cattle from quarantined areas shall be maintained, and test-eligible cattle from quarantined areas shall not be placed in pens with cattle from any other area until they have fulfilled the requirements of 9 CFR part 78 for release from the facility.

(ix) Test-eligible cattle that are penned with test-eligible cattle from a lower class State or area, in violation of this agreement, shall have the status of the State or area of lower class for any subsequent movement.

(x) Laboratory space shall be furnished and maintained for conducting diagnostic tests. All test reagents, testing equipment, and documents relating to the State-Federal cooperative eradication programs on the facility's premises shall be secured to prevent misuse and theft. Adequate heat, cooling, electricity, water piped to a properly drained sink, and sanitation shall be provided for properly conducting diagnostic tests.

(15) Swine:

—This facility will handle breeding swine: [*Initials of operator, date*]

—This facility will handle slaughter swine: [*Initials of operator, date*]

—This facility will handle feeder swine: [*Initials of operator, date*]

—This facility will handle pseudorabies reactor, suspect, or exposed swine: [*Initials of operator, date*].

—This facility will not handle swine known to be pseudorabies reactor, suspect, or exposed swine and such swine will not be permitted to enter the facility: [*Initials of operator, date*].

(i) Swine shall be received, handled, and released by the livestock facility only in accordance with 9 CFR parts 71, 78, and 85.

(ii) Pens, alleys, and sales rings for holding, inspecting, and otherwise handling swine shall be imperviously surfaced.

(iii) Slaughter swine may be handled only on days when no feeder swine or breeder swine are present at the facility, unless the facility has provisions to keep slaughter swine physically separated from feeder swine and breeder swine or unless those areas of the facility used by slaughter swine have been cleaned and disinfected before being used by feeder swine or breeder swine.

(iv) No feeder swine or breeder swine may remain in the livestock facility for more than 72 hours, and no slaughter swine may remain in the livestock market for more than 120 hours.

(v) Feeder swine shall be kept separate and apart from other swine while in the livestock facility.

(vi) No release shall be issued for the removal of slaughter swine from the livestock facility unless the slaughter swine are consigned for immediate slaughter or to another slaughter market and the consignee is identified on the release document.

(16) Horses:

—This facility will handle horses: [*Initials of operator, date*]

—This facility will handle equine infectious anemia (EIA) reactors: [*Initials of operator, date*]

—This facility will not handle horses known to be EIA reactors and will not permit EIA reactors to enter the facility: [*Initials of operator, date*]

(i) Horses shall be received, handled, and released by the livestock facility only in accordance with 9 CFR parts 71 and 75.

(ii) Any horses classified as EIA reactors and accepted by the facility for sale shall be placed in quarantined pens at least 200 yards from all non-EIA-reactor horses.

(iii) Any horses classified as EIA reactors and accepted by the facility for sale shall be consigned from the facility only to a slaughtering establishment or to the home farm of the reactor in accordance with 9 CFR part 75.

(iv) Fly Control Program: The livestock facility shall have in effect a fly control program utilizing at least one of the following: Baits, fly strips, electric bug killers ("Fly Zappers," "Fly Snappers," or similar equipment), or the application of a pesticide effective against flies, applied according to the schedule and dosage recommended by the manufacturer for fly control.

(17) Sheep and goats:

—This facility will handle breeding sheep or goats: [*Initials of operator, date*]

—This facility will handle slaughter sheep or goats: [*Initials of operator, date*]

—This facility will handle scrapie-exposed goats or high-risk sheep or goats: [*Initials of operator, date*]

—This facility will not handle goats known to be scrapie-exposed or sheep or goats known to be high-risk animals, nor permit such animals to enter the facility: [*Initials of operator, date*]

(i) All sheep and goats must be received, handled, and released by the facility only in accordance with 9 CFR parts 71 and 79.

(ii) All sheep and goats at the facility must be officially identified and relevant records related to those identified animals must be maintained by the facility operator, as required under 9 CFR part 79.

(iii) The identity of sheep and goats from consistent States and inconsistent States must be maintained by the facility operator.

(iv) Sexually intact animals that do not meet the requirements of part 79 to be sold as breeding animals must be maintained in separated enclosures at all times from animals that may be offered for sale as breeding animals unless all animals maintained in an enclosure arrived at the facility as part of the same consignment and are separated prior to sale.

(v) Any sheep or goats that are designated, with regard to scrapie, as high-risk, suspect or scrapie-positive animals, and goats designated with regard to scrapie as exposed animals, excluding slaughter sheep or goats that are designated as exposed or high-risk animals and are not pregnant, must be held in quarantined pens while at the facility.

Approvals

(18) Request for approval:

I hereby request approval for this facility to operate as an approved livestock facility for the classes of livestock indicated in paragraphs (14) through (17) of this agreement. I acknowledge that I have received a copy of 9 CFR parts 71, 75, 78, 79, and 85, and acknowledge that I have been informed and understand that failure to abide by the provisions of this agreement and the applicable provisions of 9 CFR parts 71, 75, 78, 79, and 85 constitutes a basis for the withdrawal of this approval. [*Printed name and signature of operator, date of signature*]

(19) Pre-approval inspection of livestock facility conducted by [*printed name and title of APHIS representative*] on [*date of inspection*].

(20) Recommend approval:

[*Printed name and signature of State animal health official, date of signature*]

[*Printed name and signature of area veterinarian in charge, date of signature*]

(21) Approval granted:

[*Printed name and signature of the Administrator, Animal and Plant Health Inspection Service, date of signature*]

(b) *Denial and withdrawal of approval.* The Administrator may deny or withdraw the approval of a livestock facility to receive livestock moved interstate under this subchapter upon a determination that the livestock facility is not or has not been maintained and operated in accordance with the agreement set forth in paragraph (a) of this section.

(1) In the case of a denial, the operator of the facility will be informed of the reasons for the denial and may appeal the decision in writing to the Administrator within 10 days after receiving notification of the denial. The appeal must include all of the facts and reasons upon which the person relies to show that the livestock facility was wrongfully denied approval to receive livestock moved interstate under this subchapter. The Administrator will grant or deny the appeal in writing as promptly as circumstances permit, stating the reason for his or her decision. If there is a conflict as to any material fact, a hearing will be held to resolve the conflict. Rules of practice concerning the hearing will be adopted by the Administrator.

(2) In the case of withdrawal, before such action is taken, the operator of the facility will be informed of the reasons for the proposed withdrawal. The operator of the facility may appeal the proposed withdrawal in writing to the Administrator within 10 days after being informed of the reasons for the proposed withdrawal. The appeal must include all of the facts and reasons upon which the person relies to show that the reasons for the proposed withdrawal are incorrect or do not support the withdrawal of the approval of the livestock facility to receive livestock moved interstate under this subchapter. The Administrator will grant or deny the appeal in writing as promptly as circumstances permit, stating the reason for his or her decision. If there is a conflict as to any material fact, a hearing will be held to resolve the conflict. Rules of practice concerning the hearing will be adopted by the Administrator. However, withdrawal shall become effective pending final determination in the proceeding when the Administrator determines that such action is necessary to protect the public health, interest, or safety. Such withdrawal shall be effective upon oral or written notification, whichever is earlier, to the operator of the facility. In the event of oral notification, written confirmation shall be given as promptly as circumstances allow. This withdrawal shall continue in effect pending the completion of the proceeding, and any judicial review thereof, unless otherwise ordered by the Administrator.

(3) Approval for a livestock facility to handle livestock under this subchapter will be automatically withdrawn by the Administrator when:

(i) The operator of the facility notifies the Administrator, in writing, that the facility no longer handles livestock moved interstate under this subchapter; or

(ii) The person who signed the agreement executed in accordance with paragraph (a) of this section is no longer responsible for the day-to-day operations of the facility.

(Approved by the Office of Management and Budget under control numbers 0579–0258 and 0579–0342)

[62 FR 27934, May 22, 1997, as amended at 62 FR 54758, Oct. 22, 1997; 63 FR 32119, June 12, 1998; 68 FR 62226, Nov. 3, 2003; 74 FR 14709, Apr. 1, 2009; 78 FR 26489, May 7, 2013]

§71.21 Tissue and blood testing at slaughter.

(a) Any person moving livestock or poultry interstate for slaughter or rendering may only move the animals to a slaughtering establishment or a rendering establishment that has been listed by the Administrator[8] for the purposes of this part. Livestock or poultry may not be removed from the premises of a slaughtering establishment or a rendering establishment listed by the Administrator except under a permit issued by APHIS, and in accordance with applicable FSIS regulations in this title. A slaughtering establishment or rendering establishment may

[8] A list of these slaughtering or rendering establishments may be obtained by writing to National Center for Animal Health Programs, VS, APHIS, 4700 River Road Unit 43, Riverdale, MD 20737–1231.

receive livestock or poultry in interstate commerce only if the establishment has been listed by the Administrator. The Administrator may list a slaughtering establishment or a rendering establishment after determining that collecting samples for testing from the establishment is not currently necessary for the purposes of APHIS disease surveillance programs and the establishment has agreed to allow testing and to provide the access and facilities required by this section upon future APHIS notification that testing is required at the establishment. The Administrator will list a slaughtering or rendering establishment after determining that it meets the following facility and access requirements:

(1) The owner or operator of the establishment must agree, in writing, to meet the requirements for a listed facility under this section by signing a listing agreement.

(2) The establishment provides space and equipment in accordance with paragraph (b) of this section[9] within their facility for blood and tissue sample collection;

(3) The establishment allows APHIS, FSIS, or APHIS contractors to take blood and tissue samples from all livestock or poultry at the facility without cost to the United States, and specifically allows these personnel access to the processing line to collect samples; and

(4) The establishment allows APHIS, FSIS, or APHIS contractors to record the identification of individual animals and retain any external or internal identification devices.

(5) The management of the slaughtering or rendering establishment agrees that weight tickets, sales slips, and records of origin, identification, and destination that relate to livestock that are in, or have been in, the establishment will be maintained by the establishment. For poultry and swine, such documents must be kept for at least 2 years, and for cattle and bison, sheep and goats, cervids, and equines, for at least 5 years. APHIS, APHIS contractors, and State animal health representatives will be permitted to review and copy or scan these documents during normal business hours.

(b) The establishment must provide office and sample collection space, including necessary furnishings, light, heat, and janitor service, rent free, for the use by APHIS, FSIS, or APHIS contractors collecting samples for blood and tissue testing under this section. The Administrator will inform each establishment of the exact amount and type of space required, taking into account whether APHIS will be conducting complete tests at the facility, or only collecting samples and sending them elsewhere for testing. At the discretion of the Administrator, small plants need not furnish facilities as prescribed in this section if adequate facilities exist in a nearby convenient location. In granting or denying listing of an establishment, the Administrator will consider whether the space at the facility:

(1) Is conveniently located, properly ventilated, and provided with lockers suitable for the protection and storage of supplies;

(2) Has sufficient light to be adequate for proper conduct of sample collection and processing;

(3) Includes racks, receptacles, or other suitable devices for retaining such parts as the head, glands, and viscera, and all parts and blood to be collected, until after the post-mortem examination is completed;

(4) Includes tables, benches, and other equipment on which sample collection and processing are to be performed, of such design, material, and construction as to enable sample collection and processing in a safe, ready, efficient, and clean manner;

(5) Has adequate arrangements, including liquid soap and cleansers, for cleansing and disinfecting hands, dissection tools, floors, and other articles and places that may be contaminated by diseased carcasses or otherwise; and

(6) Has adequate facilities, including denaturing materials, for the proper disposal in accordance with this chapter of tissue, blood, and other waste generated during test sample collection.

[9] FSIS also has equipment and space requirements for official establishments at § 307.2(c) of this title.

(c) The Administrator will give the operator of the establishment actual notice that APHIS, FSIS, or an APHIS contractor will be taking blood and/or tissue samples at the establishment. The Administrator may give the operator of the establishment notice in any form or by any means that the Administrator reasonably believes will reach the operator of the establishment prior to the start of sample collection.

(1) The notice will include the anticipated date and time sample collection will begin. The notice will also include the anticipated ending date and time.

(2) The Administrator will give the operator of the establishment as much advance notice as possible. However, the actual amount of notice will depend on the specific situation.

(d) *Denial and withdrawal of listing.* The Administrator may deny or withdraw the listing of an establishment upon a determination that the establishment is not in compliance with the requirements of this section.

(1) In the case of a denial, the operator of the establishment will be informed of the reasons for the denial and may appeal the decision in writing to the Administrator within 10 days after receiving notification of the denial. The appeal must include all of the facts and reasons upon which the person relies to show that the establishment was wrongfully denied listing. The Administrator will grant or deny the appeal in writing as promptly as circumstances permit, stating the reason for his or her decision. If there is a conflict as to any material fact, a hearing will be held to resolve the conflict. Rules of practice concerning the hearing will be adopted by the Administrator.

(2) In the case of withdrawal, before such action is taken, the operator of the establishment will be informed of the reasons for the proposed withdrawal. The operator of the establishment may appeal the proposed withdrawal in writing to the Administrator within 10 days after being informed of the reasons for the proposed withdrawal. The appeal must include all of the facts and reasons upon which the person relies to show that the reasons for the proposed withdrawal are incorrect or do not support the withdrawal of the listing. The Administrator will grant or deny the appeal in writing as promptly as circumstances permit, stating the reason for his or her decision. If there is a conflict as to any material fact, a hearing will be held to resolve the conflict. Rules of practice concerning the hearing will be adopted by the Administrator. However, withdrawal shall become effective pending final determination in the proceeding when the Administrator determines that such action is necessary to protect the public health, interest, or safety. Such withdrawal shall be effective upon oral or written notification, whichever is earlier, to the operator of the establishment. In the event of oral notification, written confirmation shall be given as promptly as circumstances allow. This withdrawal shall continue in effect pending the completion of the proceeding, and any judicial review thereof, unless otherwise ordered by the Administrator.

(Approved by the Office of Management and Budget under control numbers 0579–0212 and 0579–0342)

[69 FR 10150, Mar. 4, 2004, as amended at 78 FR 26489, May 7, 2013]

§ 71.22 [Reserved]

PART 72—BOVINE BABESIOSIS

Sec.

AUTHORITY: 7 U.S.C. 8301–8317; 7 CFR 2.22, 2.80, and 371.4.

SOURCE: 28 FR 5940, June 13, 1963, unless otherwise noted.

§ 72.1 Interstate movement of infested or exposed animals prohibited.

No animals infested with ticks [*Boophilus annulatus* or *Rhipicephalus* (*Boophilus*) *annulatus*, *Margaropus annulatus*, *Boophilus microplus* or *Rhipicephalus* (*Boophilus*) *microplus*, or Babesiasis (Babesiosis) species vectors of *Margaropus*, *Rhipicephalus*, *Amblyomma*, *Demacentor*, or *Ixodes*] or exposed to tick infestation may be moved interstate, except as provided in this part.

[78 FR 8960, Feb. 7, 2013]

§ 72.2 Restrictions on movement of cattle.

Notice is hereby given that the contagious, infectious, and communicable disease known as bovine piroplasmosis, bovine babesiosis, redwater, or splenetic, southern, cattle, Texas or tick fever exists in cattle in portions of the State of Texas and the Virgin Islands of the United States. Notice is also hereby given that ticks which are vectors of said disease exist in the Northern Mariana Islands, the Commonwealth of Puerto Rico, and the Island of Guam. Therefore, portions of the State of Texas, the Virgin Islands of the United States, the Northern Mariana Islands, the Commonwealth of Puerto Rico and the Island of Guam are hereby quarantined as provided in §§ 72.3 and 72.5, and the movement of cattle therefrom into any other State or Territory or the District of Columbia shall be made only in accordance with the provisions of this part and part 71 of this chapter.

[43 FR 60864, Dec. 29, 1978, as amended at 78 FR 8960, Feb. 7, 2013]

§ 72.3 Areas quarantined in the Virgin Islands of the United States, the Northern Mariana Islands, the Commonwealth of Puerto Rico, and the Island of Guam.

The entire Territories of the Virgin Islands of the United States and the Island of Guam, the Northern Mariana Islands, and the Commonwealth of Puerto Rico are quarantined.

[43 FR 60864, Dec. 29, 1978]

§ 72.4 [Reserved]

§ 72.5 Area quarantined in Texas.

The area quarantined in Texas is the quarantined area described in the regulations of the Texas Animal Health Commission (TAHC) contained in §§ 41.14 through 41.22 of title 4, part II, of the Texas Administrative Code (4 TAC 41.14 through 41.22), effective June 23, 2002, which is incorporated by reference. This incorporation by reference was approved by the Director of the Federal Register in accordance with 5 U.S.C. 552(a) and 1 CFR part 51. Copies of 4 TAC 41.14 through 41.22 may be obtained from the TAHC at 2105 Kramer Lane, Austin, TX 78758, and from area offices of the TAHC, which are listed in local Texas telephone directories. The TAHC also maintains a copy of its regulations on its Internet homepage at *http://www.tahc.state.tx.us/*. Copies may be inspected at the Animal and Plant Health Inspection Service, Veterinary Services, suite 3B08, 4700 River Road, Riverdale, MD, or at the National Archives and Records Administration (NARA). For information on the availability of this material at NARA, call 202–741–6030, or go to: *http://www.archives.gov/federal_register/code_of_federal_regulations/ibr_locations.html.*

[69 FR 8329, Feb. 24, 2004, as amended at 69 FR 18803, Apr. 9, 2004]

§ 72.6 Interstate movement of cattle from quarantined areas not eradicating ticks.

Cattle in quarantined areas where tick eradication is not being conducted[3] may be shipped or transported interstate in accordance with §§ 72.9 through 72.15 under the following conditions: The cattle must have been dipped twice with a permitted dip as provided in § 72.13, with an interval of 7 to 12 days between dippings immediately preceding shipment, at a designated dipping station approved under § 72.16 and located in the State of origin of the shipment or, in specific cases, after having been otherwise treated at a designated dipping station under the supervision of an APHIS inspector and in a manner approved by the Administrator. In all cases, the cattle must be inspected by an APHIS inspector just prior to final dipping, found to be apparently free of ticks, and be certified as such by APHIS before the cattle may be released for interstate movement.

[66 FR 21061, Apr. 27, 2001]

§ 72.7 Interstate movement of cattle from cooperating States.

Cattle in areas where tick eradication is being conducted in cooperation with State authorities,[3] which on inspection by an APHIS inspector are found to be apparently free from ticks, may, after one dipping, with a permitted dip as provided in § 72.13, under the supervision of an APHIS inspector and certification by the inspector, be shipped or transported interstate for dip as provided in § 72.13, under the supervision of an APHIS inspector and certification by the inspector, be shipped or transported interstate for any purpose upon compliance with the requirements set forth in §§ 72.9 through 72.15.

[36 FR 20358, Oct. 21, 1971, as amended at 56 FR 51975, Oct. 17, 1991]

§ 72.8 Interstate movement of cattle from free premises upon inspection and certification by APHIS inspector.

Cattle located in areas where tick eradication is being conducted in cooperation with the State authorities, and which are on premises shown by the official records of tick eradication to be free from ticks, may, upon inspection and certification by an APHIS inspector, be shipped or transported interstate for any purpose without dipping upon compliance with the requirements set forth under §§ 72.9, 72.10, 72.12.

[28 FR 5940, June 13, 1963, as amended at 56 FR 51975, Oct. 17, 1991]

§ 72.9 Interstate movements of cattle; inspection and certification by APHIS inspector required.

All interstate movements of inspected and certified and dipped and certified cattle shall be accompanied to final destination by a certificate of an APHIS inspector (which certificate shall show that the cattle so being moved have been dipped as required by § 72.6 or by § 72.7 and are free of ticks, or have been inspected as required by § 72.8 and are free of ticks); all such certificates shall be handled, delivered, kept, and preserved in accordance with the provisions of § 72.16; and all such cattle shall be handled through noninfectious pens, alleys, and chutes, and when shipped shall be loaded into clean and disinfected cars or trucks, and shall not be unloaded in the quarantined area except at such points reserved for noninfested cattle as may from time to time be authorized by APHIS.

[28 FR 5940, June 13, 1963, as amended at 56 FR 51975, Oct. 17, 1991]

[3] Information regarding the identities of such areas may be obtained from the Animal and Plant Health Inspection Service, Veterinary Services, National Animal Health Programs, 4700 River Road Unit 43, Riverdale, Maryland 20737–1231.

§72.10 Inspected or dipped and certified cattle subject to restrictions of State of destination.

All such interstate movements of inspected or dipped and certified cattle are subject to such restrictions, which are not inconsistent with the regulations in this subchapter, as may be imposed at destination by the officials of the State, Territory, or the District of Columbia.

§72.11 Quarantined area; cattle considered infested; requirements for placing in noninfectious pens or premises.

Cattle of the quarantined area shall be considered infested and shall not be placed in noninfectious pens or premises until after the final inspection or dipping.

§72.12 Cattle; exposure to tick infestation after treatment or inspection prohibited.

The cattle shall not be exposed to tick infestation after treatment and/or inspection.

§72.13 Permitted dips and procedures.

(a) *Dipping requirements; facilities; handling.* The dipping of cattle for interstate movement shall be done only with a permitted dip and at places where proper equipment is provided for dipping and for handling the cattle in a manner to prevent exposure to infection after the final dipping. Cattle which are to be dipped shall be given an opportunity to drink sufficient water to quench their thirst prior to dipping, be carefully handled, and not dipped while they are in a heated or exhausted condition. Dipped cattle shall not be loaded for shipment until dry.[4]

(b) *Permitted dips.* The dips at present permitted by the U.S. Department of Agriculture in official dipping for interstate movement are:

(1) Approved proprietary brands of coumaphos (Co-Ral®), 25 percent wettable powder or flowable form labeled for use as a 0.25 percent dip and used at a concentration of 0.125 to 0.250.[4]

(2) [Reserved]

(c) *Approval of dips.* Proprietary brands of dips are permitted to be used for purposes of this part only when approved by the Administrator, APHIS. Before a dip will be specifically approved as a permitted dip for the eradication of ticks, APHIS will require that the product be registered under the provisions of the Federal Insecticide, Fungicide and Rodenticide Act, as amended (7 U.S.C. 135 *et seq.*); that its efficacy and stability have been demonstrated; that trials have been conducted to determine that its concentration can be maintained and that under actual field conditions the dipping of cattle with a solution of definite strength will effectually eradicate ticks without injury to the animals dipped.

(d) *Tissue residues; restriction on slaughter.* Tissue residues are created following use of certain dips. Animals treated with such dips should not be slaughtered for food purposes until the expiration of such period as may be required under the Federal Meat Inspection Act (21 U.S.C. 601 *et seq.*). The length of this period shall be specified on each certificate issued by the inspector who supervises the dipping.

[33 FR 18089, Dec. 5, 1968, as amended at 34 FR 12214, July 24, 1969; 36 FR 19157, Sept. 30, 1971; 36 FR 19972, Oct. 14, 1971; 37 FR 13529, July 11, 1972; 38 FR 19012, July 17, 1973; 40 FR 12768, Mar. 21, 1975; 42 FR 19854, Apr. 15, 1977; 47 FR 11002, Mar. 15, 1982; 49 FR 19799, May 10, 1984; 49 FR 32540, Aug. 15, 1984; 50 FR 430, 431, Jan. 4, 1985; 56 FR 51974, Oct. 17, 1991; 66 FR 21062, Apr. 27, 2001; 78 FR 8961, Feb. 7, 2013]

§72.14 [Reserved]

§72.15 Owners assume responsibility; must execute agreement prior to dipping or treatment waiving all claims against United States.

When the cattle are to be dipped under APHIS supervision the owner of the cattle, offered for shipment, or his agent duly authorized thereto, shall first execute and deliver to an APHIS

[4] Care is required when treating animals and in maintaining the required concentration of chemicals in dipping baths. Detailed information concerning the use of, criteria for, and names of proprietary brands of permitted dips—as well the use of compressed air, vat management techniques, and other information—is available from the Animal and Plant Health Inspection Service, Veterinary Services, National Animal Health Programs, 4700 River Road Unit 43, Riverdale, MD 20737-1231.

inspector an application for inspection and supervised dipping wherein he shall agree to waive all claims against the United States for any loss or damage to said cattle occasioned by or resulting from dipping or other treatment under this part, or resulting from any subsequent treatment prior to their interstate shipment, or resulting from the fact that they are later found to be still tick infested, and also for all subsequent loss or damage to any other cattle in the possession or control of such owner which may come into contact with the cattle so dipped or treated.

[28 FR 5940, June 13, 1963, as amended at 56 FR 51975, Oct. 17, 1991]

§ 72.16 Designated dipping stations to be approved by the Administrator, APHIS on recommendations of State authorities; facilities.

When deemed advisable and upon recommendation by the proper livestock sanitary authorities, designated dipping stations may be approved by the Administrator, APHIS as points at which cattle of the quarantined area of the State in which said station is located may be inspected, dipped, and certified for interstate movement. The facilities furnished shall include proper dipping equipment, noninfectious pens constructed in accordance with § 72.17 and a roofed or covered section of pens of sufficient size to protect all dipped animals from exposure to rain or hot sun. All alleys, chutes, and pens shall be paved or properly floored.

[28 FR 5940, June 13, 1963, as amended at 50 FR 430, Jan. 4, 1985; 56 FR 51974, Oct. 17, 1991]

§ 72.17 Unloading noninfected cattle for rest, feed, and water only, permitted in authorized pens for such purpose.

(a) *Specifications for construction and maintenance.* Cattle of the free area, and cattle of the quarantined area when properly dipped, inspected, and certified in accordance with this part, which are transported interstate by rail through the quarantined area shall not be unloaded therein for rest, feed, and water unless they are unloaded into the properly equipped, noninfectious pens set apart for such cattle at such points as may from time to time be authorized by APHIS. Such noninfectious pens and the platforms, chutes, and alleys leading thereto shall be constructed and maintained in accordance with the specifications set out in paragraphs (a)(1) to (6) of this section.

(1) The outside fences enclosing such pens, and the fences on either side of the alleys, chutes, and platforms leading thereto, shall be tight board fences not less than 6 feet high on the inside.

(2) If such pens, alleys, chutes, and platforms are adjacent to pens, alleys, chutes, and platforms used by cattle of the quarantined area, there shall be between them a space not less than 10 feet wide, which shall be inaccessible to livestock. This space shall be limited on each side by the 6–foot fence required by paragraph (a)(1) of this section. The remaining space around such yards shall be limited as in paragraph (a)(3) of this section.

(3) If such pens, alleys, chutes, and platforms are isolated from other pens, alleys, chutes, or platforms, there shall be built and maintained outside thereof on all sides to which cattle of the vicinity might otherwise approach a cattle-proof fence not less than 5 feet high and not less than 15 feet from the 6–foot fence required by paragraph (a)(1) of this section.

(4) The only means of egress from such pens shall be by way of the alleys, chutes, and platforms inclosed by 6–foot fences as required by paragraph (a)(1) of this section, to cars for reforwarding; and under no circumstances shall there exist any connection between such pens and other adjacent premises.

(5) Such noninfectious premises shall be so located, or such drainage facilities shall be provided therefor, that water from the surrounding area will not flow on to or through them.

(6) Such pens shall be marked by a conspicuous sign bearing the words "Noninfectious Pens" in letters not less than 10 inches in height.

(b) *Materials for use in noninfectious pens; source, shipment, handling.* The hay, straw, or similar materials required for feed and bedding in such noninfectious pens shall be shipped in noninfectious cars from points outside of the quarantined area so handled that they may not become infectious.

[28 FR 5940, June 13, 1963, as amended at 56 FR 51975, Oct. 17, 1991]

§ 72.18 Movement interstate; specification by the Deputy Administrator, Veterinary Services of treatment required when dipping facilities unavailable.

(a) *Tick-infested cattle.* Cattle of the free area which are tick-infested may be moved interstate for any purpose after they have been treated in the same manner as cattle under § 72.6: *Provided, however,* That when dipping equipment is not available at the place where the cattle are, said treatment shall be given at a place and in the manner specified by the Administrator, APHIS.

(b) *Tick-exposed cattle.* Cattle of the free area which have been exposed to tick infestation may be moved interstate for any purpose after they have been treated in the same manner as cattle under § 72.7: *Provided, however,* That when dipping equipment is not available at the place where the cattle are, said treatment shall be given at a place and in the manner specified by the Administrator, APHIS.

(c) *Cattle moved contrary to regulations.* Cattle which have been moved from the quarantined area to the free area without first having been treated in the manner provided in either § 72.6 or § 72.7 or inspected in the manner provided in § 72.8 shall not be shipped or moved interstate until they have been treated in the same manner as cattle under § 72.6: *Provided, however,* That when dipping equipment is not available at the place where the cattle are, said treatment shall be given at a place and in the manner specified by the Administrator, APHIS.

[28 FR 5940, June 13, 1963, as amended at 50 FR 430, Jan. 4, 1985; 56 FR 51974, Oct. 17, 1991]

§ 72.19 Interstate shipments and use of pine straw, grass, litter from quarantined area; prohibited until disinfected.

Pine straw, grass, or similar litter collected from tick-infested pastures, ranges, or premises may disseminate the contagion of splenetic, southern, or Texas fever; therefore pine straw, grass, or similar litter originating in the quarantined area shall not be transported or moved interstate therefrom or used as packing material or car bedding for commodities or livestock to be transported or moved from the quarantined area of any State, Territory, or the District of Columbia, to or through the free area of any other State, Territory, or the District of Columbia, unless such material is first disinfected in accordance with the provisions of § 72.24.

§ 72.20 Exhibition of noninfected cattle in the quarantined area; restrictions under which permitted.

The exhibition of noninfected cattle at fairs or exhibitions in the quarantined area and their reshipment to the free area without dipping may, by written order of the Administrator, APHIS be permitted: *Provided,* That the cattle shall be handled under such conditions as may be prescribed in each case to preclude any danger of the spread of infection.

[28 FR 5940, June 13, 1963, as amended at 56 FR 51974, Oct. 17, 1991]

§ 72.21 Animals infested with or exposed to ticks subject to same restrictions as cattle.

Animals other than cattle which are infested with ticks [Boophilus annulatus (Margaropus annulatus), Boophilus microplus, or Rhipicephalus evertsi evertsi] or exposed to tick infestation shall not be moved interstate unless they are treated, handled, and moved in accordance with the requirements specified in §§ 72.9 through 72.15 and § 72.18 of this part governing the interstate movement of cattle.

§ 72.22 Cars, vehicles, and premises; cleaning and treatment after containing infested or exposed animals.

Cars and other vehicles, and yards, pens, chutes, or other premises or facilities, which have contained interstate shipments of animals infested with or exposed to ticks, shall be cleaned and treated within 72 hours of use and prior to further use in the required concentration with a permitted dip listed in § 72.13 under supervision of a State or Federal inspector or an accredited veterinarian.

[38 FR 21996, Aug. 15, 1973]

§ 72.23 Cars or other vehicles having carried infested or exposed cattle in quarantined area shall be cleaned and treated.

Cars or others vehicles which have carried cattle exposed to or infested with ticks within the quarantined area of any State shall be cleaned and treated in the required concentration with a permitted dip listed in § 72.13 before being moved interstate under supervision of a State or Federal inspector or an accredited veterinarian.

[38 FR 21996, Aug. 15, 1973]

§ 72.24 Litter and manure from carriers and premises of tick-infested animals; destruction or treating required.

The litter and manure removed from cars, boats, or other vehicles and from pens, chutes, alleys, or other premises or inclosures which have contained interstate shipments of tick-infested animals, shall be destroyed or treated by the transportation or yard company, or other owner thereof, under APHIS supervision, by saturating it in the required concentration with a permitted dip listed in § 72.13, or shall be otherwise disposed of under prior permission received from the Administrator, APHIS.

[38 FR 21996, Aug. 15, 1973, as amended at 56 FR 51974, 51975, Oct. 17, 1991]

§ 72.25 Dipping methods.

Dipping is accomplished by thoroughly wetting the entire skin by either immersion in a chemical solution in a dip vat, or by spraying with a chemical solution using a spray-dip machine or a hand-held sprayer.

[50 FR 430, Jan. 4, 1985]

PART 73—SCABIES IN CATTLE

Sec.

AUTHORITY: 7 U.S.C. 8301–8317; 7 CFR 2.22, 2.80, and 371.4.

§ 73.1 Interstate movement prohibited.

(a) *Cattle affected with scabies.* No cattle affected with scabies shall be shipped, trailed, driven, or otherwise moved interstate for any purpose except as provided in this part.

(b) *Cattle affected with or exposed to scabies.* No cattle which, just prior to movement, were affected with or exposed to scabies shall be shipped, trailed, driven, or otherwise moved interstate for any purpose except as provided in this part.

(c) *Cattle from area quarantined for scabies.* No cattle shall be shipped, trailed, driven, or otherwise moved interstate from the area quarantined for the disease of scabies in cattle except as provided in this part.

[28 FR 5945, June 13, 1963, as amended at 41 FR 5384, Feb. 6, 1976]

§ 73.1a [Reserved]

§ 73.1b Quarantine policy.

Under the Animal Health Protection Act (7 U.S.C. 8301 *et seq.*), the Secretary may promulgate regulations and may prohibit or restrict the movement in interstate commerce of any animal, article, or means of conveyance as the Secretary determines necessary to prevent the introduction or dissemination of any pest or disease of livestock. Pursuant to this authority, the Department has quarantined various areas because of cattle scabies and has issued the regulations in this part governing the interstate movement of cattle from such areas. It is the policy of the Department to quarantine those portions of any State that are clearly identifiable, and in which exist animals affected with cattle scabies, or mites which are the contagion of said disease and not to quarantine an entire State for cattle scabies if the State adopts and enforces requirements for the intrastate movement of cattle that are at least as stringent as the requirements in the regulations in this part for interstate movements of cattle. Further, it is the policy of the Department to remove the quarantine from any quarantined area when it is determined that scabies-affected animals and the mites which are the contagion of scabies no longer exist in such areas.

[38 FR 31671, Nov. 16, 1973, as amended at 68 FR 6343, Feb. 7, 2003]

§ 73.1c Definitions.

For purposes of this part the following terms shall have the meaning set forth in this section.

Administrator. The Administrator, Animal and Plant Health Inspection Service, or any person authorized to act for the Administrator.

Animal and Plant Health Inspection Service. The Animal and Plant Health Inspection Service of the United States Department of Agriculture (APHIS or Service).

APHIS Inspector. A veterinarian or livestock inspector employed by the Animal and Plant Health Inspection Service, U.S. Department of Agriculture, in animal health activities, who is authorized to perform the function involved.

State Inspector. A veterinarian or livestock inspector regularly employed in animal health activities by a State or a political subdivision thereof, authorized by such State or political subdivision to perform the function involved under a cooperative agreement with the U.S. Department of Agriculture.

[41 FR 5384, Feb. 6, 1976, as amended at 56 FR 52463, Oct. 21, 1991]

§ 73.2 Interstate shipment for immediate slaughter from quarantined or nonquarantined areas; conditions under which permitted.

(a) *Conditions under which permitted after one dipping.* Cattle which, just prior to shipment, were affected with scabies but have been dipped once in a permitted dip (other than a toxaphene dip), under the supervision of an APHIS inspector or State inspector, within 10 days prior to the date of shipment may be shipped or transported interstate for immediate slaughter to a recognized slaughtering center, upon compliance with the following conditions:

(1) They shall not be diverted en route.

(2) The means of conveyance shall be placarded and the billing shall be marked "Treated Scabby Cattle," in accordance with § 73.6.

(b) *After one dipping; to be slaughtered within 14 days or redipped by owner.* Cattle shipped interstate subject to the provisions of paragraph (a) of this section shall be slaughtered within 14 days from the date of the dipping or shall be again dipped by the owner.

(c) *When part of diseased herd not visibly affected.* Cattle of the free area not visibly diseased with scabies, but which may be part of a diseased herd, may be shipped or transported interstate for immediate slaughter to any recognized slaughtering center where separate pens are provided for yarding exposed cattle: *Provided,* That means of conveyance in which the cattle are transported shall be placarded and the billing accompanying the shipment shall be marked "Cattle Exposed to Scabies" in accordance with § 73.6.

(d) *Undiseased herds in quarantined area; conditions under which permitted.* Cattle of herds of the quarantined area which are not diseased with scabies may be shipped, transported, or otherwise moved interstate for immediate slaughter, upon inspection by an APHIS or State inspector within 10 days prior to the date of shipment and when accompanied by a certificate from such inspector showing the cattle to be free from disease.

[31 FR 8907, June 28, 1966, as amended at 36 FR 23996, Dec. 17, 1971; 38 FR 18011, July 6, 1973; 41 FR 5384, Feb. 6, 1976; 49 FR 10530, Mar. 20, 1984; 49 FR 33120, Aug. 21, 1984; 56 FR 52463, Oct. 21, 1991; 66 FR 21062, Apr. 27, 2001]

§ 73.3 Shipment for purposes other than slaughter; conditions under which permitted.

Cattle affected with scabies may be shipped interstate for any purpose if dipped twice in a permitted dip, 10 to 14 days apart, under the supervision of an APHIS inspector or State inspector, and so certified by such inspector, or such cattle may be so shipped if dipped once in a permitted dip under APHIS supervision or State supervision at the point of origin, provided arrangements have been made for the second dipping, under APHIS supervision, en route or at destination within 10 to 14 days after the first dipping. If shipped in the latter manner the means of conveyance containing the cattle shall be placarded and the billing shall be marked "Treated Scabby Cattle," in accordance with § 73.6.

[28 FR 5945, June 13, 1963, as amended at 41 FR 5384, Feb. 6, 1976; 49 FR 10530, Mar. 20, 1984; 49 FR 33120, Aug. 21, 1984; 56 FR 52463, Oct. 21, 1991; 66 FR 21062, Apr. 27, 2001]

§ 73.4 Interstate shipment of exposed but not visibly diseased cattle from a quarantined or nonquarantined area; conditions under which permitted.

Cattle not visibly diseased with scabies, but which are known to be part of a diseased herd or to have come in contact with diseased cattle or infectious means of conveyance or premises, may be shipped interstate for any purpose if dipped at the point of origin, under the supervision of an APHIS inspector or State inspector, in a permitted dip, or the cattle may be dipped en route by special permission first had and obtained from the Administrator; but in such event the means of conveyance shall be placarded and the billing shall be marked "Cattle Exposed to Scabies," in accordance with § 73.6, and the cattle shall not be permitted to mingle with other cattle until disposed of in accordance with the regulations in this part.

[28 FR 5945, June 13, 1963, as amended at 41 FR 5384, Feb. 6, 1976; 56 FR 52463, Oct. 21, 1991]

§ 73.5 Interstate shipment of undiseased cattle from quarantined area; when permitted.

Cattle of any herd in any quarantined area, which herd is not diseased with scabies, may be shipped, transported, or otherwise moved interstate for any purpose upon inspection by an APHIS or State inspector within 10 days prior to the date of shipment and when accompanied by a certificate from such inspector showing the cattle to be free from such disease or exposure thereto. When it is determined by the Administrator that all cattle of all herds in any quarantined area have been inspected for scabies by an APHIS or State inspector, that all the infected or exposed herds have been identified, and that all the infected herds have been dipped twice, and all the exposed herds have been dipped in a permitted dip as prescribed in § 73.10, under supervision of an APHIS or APHIS-approved inspector, cattle of herds in such area which are not diseased with or exposed to scabies may be moved interstate in accordance with this section, without further APHIS inspection or certification, directly to a slaughtering plant where Federal Meat Inspection is maintained: *Provided further*, that treatment with ivermectin may be used in lieu of dipping for a herd of cattle treated together if the herd is physically separated for 14 days following treatment from all cattle not a part of the herd treated together with ivermectin. Information may be obtained from an APHIS inspector whether a determination as required by this section is currently applicable to authorize such movement. Cattle moved interstate under this section shall not be diverted en route and must be accompanied by a waybill or similar document, or a statement signed by the owner or shipper of the cattle, stating: (a) That the cattle are not known to be infected with scabies or exposed thereto; (b) [Reserved]; (c) the purpose for which the cattle are to be moved; (d) the number of the cattle; (e) the point from which the cattle are to be moved interstate; (f) that the cattle shall not be diverted en route; and (g) the name and address of the owner or shipper of the cattle.

(Approved by the Office of Management and Budget under control number 0579–0051)

[31 FR 8907, June 28, 1966, as amended at 36 FR 23996, Dec. 17, 1971; 38 FR 10252, Apr. 26, 1973; 38 FR 18011, July 6, 1973; 41 FR 5384, Feb. 6, 1976; 48 FR 57472, Dec. 30, 1983; 49 FR 10530, Mar. 20, 1984; 49 FR 33120, Aug. 21, 1984; 56 FR 52463, Oct. 21, 1991; 66 FR 21062, Apr. 27, 2001]

§ 73.6 Placarding means of conveyance and marking billing of shipments of treated scabby cattle or cattle exposed to scabies.

When cattle are shipped as "Treated Scabby Cattle," or "Cattle Exposed to Scabies," the transportation companies shall securely affix to and maintain upon both sides of each means of conveyance carrying such cattle a durable, conspicuous placard, not less than 5½ by 8 inches in size, on which shall be printed with permanent black ink in boldfaced letters, not less than 1½ inches in height, the words, "Treated Scabby Cattle," or "Cattle Exposed to Scabies," as the case may be. These placards shall also show the name of the place from which the shipment was made, the date of the shipment (which must correspond to the date of the waybills and other papers), the name of the transportation company, and the name of the place of destination. The carrier issuing the waybills, conductors' manifests, memoranda, and bills of lading pertaining to such shipments shall plainly write or stamp upon the face of each such paper the words, "Treated Scabby Cattle," or "Cattle Exposed to Scabies," as the case may be. If for any reason the placards required by this part have not been affixed to the means of conveyance as aforesaid, or the placards have been removed, destroyed, or rendered illegible, or the cattle are rebilled or are transferred to other means of conveyance, the placards shall be immediately affixed or replaced by the carrier, and the new waybills shall be marked as aforesaid by the carrier issuing them, the intention being that the billing accompanying the shipment shall be marked and the means of conveyance containing the cattle shall be placarded "Treated Scabby Cattle," or "Cattle Exposed to Scabies," as the case may be, from the time of shipment until the cattle arrive at destination or point of dipping and the disposition of the means of conveyance is indicated by an APHIS inspector or State inspector.

[28 FR 5945, June 13, 1963, as amended at 41 FR 5384, Feb. 6, 1976; 49 FR 10530, Mar. 20, 1984; 49 FR 33120, Aug. 21, 1984; 56 FR 52463, Oct. 21, 1991; 66 FR 21062, Apr. 27, 2001]

§ 73.7 Movement from quarantined to free area and shipment therefrom; restrictions under which permitted.

No person, firm, or corporation shall deliver for transportation, transport, drive on foot, or otherwise move interstate from the free area of any State, Territory, or the District of Columbia any cattle which have been moved from the quarantined area of the same State, Territory, or the District of Columbia into such free area: *Provided, however*, That such cattle may be delivered for transportation, transported, driven on foot, or otherwise moved interstate for the purposes for which the shipment, transportation, or other movement interstate of cattle of the quarantined area is permitted by this part, *Provided*, That in such shipment and transportation or other movement the requirements of this part governing the shipment and transportation or other movement of cattle of the quarantined area are strictly complied with: *And provided further*, That this section shall not apply to cattle of the quarantined area which, before being moved into the free area, are certified by an APHIS inspector or State inspector as free from disease and are accompanied by such certificate in their shipment by transportation or other movement interstate.

(Approved by the Office of Management and Budget under control number 0579–0051)

(44 U.S.C. 3506)

[28 FR 5945, June 13, 1963, as amended at 41 FR 5384, Feb. 6, 1976; 48 FR 57472, Dec. 30, 1983; 56 FR 52463, Oct. 21, 1991]

§ 73.8 Cattle infected or exposed during transit.

(a) *Healthy cattle from unquarantined State exposed en route.* Should healthy cattle in transit from a State not quarantined by the Secretary of Agriculture for scabies in cattle be unloaded en route and placed in infectious premises, they shall be treated as exposed cattle, and their further movement shall be subject to the provisions of this part with respect to the movement of exposed cattle.

(b) *Interstate shipments of cattle under APHIS or State certificate found affected or exposed en route.* Cattle shipped interstate under a certificate from an APHIS inspector or State inspector or other cattle which are found en route to be affected with scabies or to have been exposed thereto, shall thereafter be handled in the same manner as diseased or exposed cattle are required by this part to be handled, and the means of conveyance and the chutes, alleys, and pens which have been occupied by diseased animals shall be cleaned and disinfected as provided in §§ 71.4 through 71.11 of this subchapter.

[28 FR 5945, June 13, 1963, as amended at 41 FR 5384, Feb. 6, 1976; 56 FR 52463, Oct. 21, 1991]

§ 73.9 Owners assume responsibility; must execute agreement prior to dipping or treatment waiving all claims against United States.

When the cattle are to be dipped under APHIS supervision or control, the owner of the cattle offered for shipment, or his agent duly authorized thereto, shall first execute and deliver to an APHIS inspector an application for inspection and supervised dipping wherein he shall agree to waive all claims against the United States for any loss or damage to said cattle occasioned by or resulting from dipping or other treatment under this part, or resulting from any subsequent treatment prior to their interstate shipment, or resulting from the fact that they are later found to be still scabies infested, and also for all subsequent loss or damage to any other cattle in the possession or control of such owner which may come into contact with the cattle so dipped or treated.

[41 FR 4012, Jan. 28, 1976, as amended at 56 FR 52463, Oct. 21, 1991]

§ 73.10 Permitted dips; substances allowed.

(a) The dips at present permitted by the Department for the treatment, as required in this part, of cattle affected with or exposed to scabies, are as follows:

(1) Lime-sulphur dip, other than proprietary brands thereof, made in the proportion of 12 pounds of unslaked lime (or 16 pounds of commercial hydrated lime, not airslaked lime) and 24 pounds of flowers of sulphur or sulphur flour to 100 gallons of water; or a specifically permitted proprietary brand of lime-sulphur dip.

(2) Dips made from specifically permitted proprietary brand emulsions of toxaphene and maintained throughout the dipping operation at a concentration between 0.50 and 0.60 percent toxaphene. Animals treated by such dips should not be slaughtered for food purposes until the expiration of such period as may be required under the Federal Meat Inspection Act (21 U.S.C., Supp. III, 601 *et seq.*). The length of this required period shall be specified on each certificate issued by the APHIS inspector or State inspector who supervises the dipping with such dips.

(3) Approved proprietary brands of coumaphos (Co-Ral®), 25 percent wettable powder or flowable form used at a concentration of 0.30 percent.

(4) Approved proprietary brands of organophosphorous insecticides (Prolate®) used at a concentration of 0.15 percent to 0.25 percent.

(b) The dipping bath for lime-sulphur dip must be used at a temperature of 95° to 105 °F., and must be maintained through the dipping operation at a concentration of not less than 2 percent of "sulphide sulphur", as indicated by the field test for lime-sulphur dipping baths approved by the APHIS.[1] The

[1] The field test for lime-sulphur dipping baths is described in U.S. Department of Agriculture Bulletin 163, for sale by the Superintendent of Documents, Government Printing Office, Washington, D.C. 20402, at 5 cents a copy.

dipping bath for toxaphene emulsions must be kept within a temperature range of 40–80 °F., and at a concentration between 0.50 and 0.60 percent throughout the dipping operations.[2]

(c) Proprietary brands of lime-sulphur or toxaphene dips may be used in official dipping only after specific permission therefor has been granted by the Administrator. Before a dip will be specifically approved as a permitted dip for the eradication of scabies in cattle, the APHIS[3] will require that the product be registered under the provisions of the Federal Insecticide, Fungicide and Rodenticide Act, as amended (7 U.S.C. 135 *et seq.*); that is efficacy and stability have been demonstrated; that trials have been conducted to determine that its concentration can be maintained and that under actual filed conditions the dipping of cattle in a bath of definite strength will effectually eradicate scabies infection without injury to the animals dipped.

[34 FR 7443, May 8, 1969, as amended at 39 FR 39715, Nov. 11, 1974; 40 FR 12768, Mar. 21, 1975; 40 FR 42179, Sept. 11, 1975; 41 FR 5384, Feb. 6, 1976; 41 FR 37307, Sept. 3, 1976; 50 FR 431, Jan. 4, 1985; 56 FR 52463, Oct. 21, 1991]

§ 73.11 Treatment of means of conveyance and premises having contained scabby cattle.

Means of conveyance, yards, pens, sheds, chutes, or other premises or facilities which have contained cattle of a consignment in which scabies is found shall be treated within 72 hours of use and prior to further use in the required concentration with a permitted dip listed in § 73.10 under supervision of a State or Federal inspector or an accredited veterinarian.

[38 FR 21996, Aug. 15, 1973, as amended at 41 FR 5384, Feb. 6, 1976]

[2] Care must be exercised in dipping animals and in maintaining the bath at the standard concentration. Detailed instructions will be issued for the guidance of employees who may be called upon to use them in the scabies eradication program.

[3] Information as to the names of such dips may be obtained from the APHIS or a APHIS inspector.

§ 73.12 Ivermectin.[1]

(a) Cattle affected with scabies or which just prior to movement were affected with or exposed to scabies may be moved interstate from a nonquarantined area after being treated with ivermectin under the supervision of an APHIS inspector or State inspector in accordance with the directions on the label of the drug if the following conditions are met:

(1) Such cattle are kept physically separated for 14 days following treatment from all cattle not part of the group treated together with ivermectin (regardless of whether the cattle are moved interstate before the end of the 14-day period); and

(2) If such cattle are moved interstate before the end of the 14th day following treatment, at the time of interstate movement they are accompanied by a certificate issued and signed by an APHIS inspector or State inspector identifying the group of cattle treated with ivermectin and stating the date on which the cattle were treated with ivermectin; and

(3) If such cattle are moved interstate before the end of the 14th day following treatment, at the time of interstate movement the means of conveyance carrying them is placarded and the billing marked in accordance with § 73.6.

NOTE: Cattle from nonquarantined areas which are not affected with scabies or which just prior to movement were not affected with or exposed to scabies may be moved

[1] Tissue residues remain following treatment with ivermectin. Cattle treated with ivermectin are not allowed to be slaughtered for food purposes until the expiration of such period as may be required under the Federal Meat Inspection Act (21 U.S.C. 601 *et seq.*). Further, the animal drug regulations in 21 CFR parts 522 and 556 promulgated under the Federal Food, Drug, and Cosmetic Act (21 U.S.C. 301 *et seq.*) contain limitations on the use of ivermectin and contain tolerances for ivermectin in edible cattle tissue. With respect to the limitations 21 CFR part 522 provides the following: "For subcutaneous use only. Not for intramuscular use. Do not treat cattle within 35 days of slaughter. Because a withdrawal time in milk has not been established, do not use in female dairy cattle of breeding age. Federal law restricts this drug to use by or on the order of a licensed veterinarian."

interstate without restrictions under this part. Accordingly, cattle from nonquarantined areas which had been treated with ivermectin more than 14 days before movement interstate may be moved interstate without restriction under this part unless following treatment they become affected with scabies or just prior to movement become affected with or exposed to scabies.

(b) Cattle may be moved interstate from a quarantined area after being treated with ivermectin under the supervision of an APHIS inspector or State inspector in accordance with the directions on the label of the drug if the following conditions are met:

(1) Such cattle are moved interstate within 21 days following treatment with ivermectin; and

(2) Such cattle are kept physically separated for 14 days following treatment from all cattle not part of the group treated together with ivermectin (regardless of whether the cattle are moved interstate before the end of the 14 day period); and, if such cattle are moved within the 15- to 21-day period following treatment, they remain kept physically separated from all cattle not a part of the group treated together with ivermectin until after they are moved interstate; and

(3) Such cattle are accompanied at the time of interstate movement by a certificate issued and signed by an APHIS inspector or State inspector identifying the group of cattle treated with ivermectin and stating the date on which the cattle were treated with ivermectin; and

(4) If such cattle are moved interstate before the end of the 14 day period following treatment, at the time of interstate movement the means of conveyance carrying them is placarded and the billing marked in accordance with §73.6.

[49 FR 10530, Mar. 20, 1984 and 49 FR 33120, Aug. 21, 1984; 56 FR 52463, Oct. 21, 1991; 66 FR 21062, Apr. 27, 2001]

PART 74—PROHIBITION OF INTERSTATE MOVEMENT OF LAND TORTOISES

AUTHORITY: 7 U.S.C. 8301–8317; 7 CFR 2.22, 2.80, and 371.4.

§74.1 General prohibition.

The interstate movement of leopard tortoise (*Geochelone pardalis*), African spurred tortoise (*Geochelone sulcata*), and Bell's hingeback tortoise (*Kinixys belliana*) is prohibited except when tortoises are accompanied by either a health certificate or a certificate of veterinary inspection. The health certificate or certificate of veterinary inspection must be signed by an accredited veterinarian within 30 days prior to the interstate movement and must state that the tortoises have been examined by that veterinarian and found free of ticks.

[66 FR 37128, July 17, 2001]

PART 75—COMMUNICABLE DISEASES IN HORSES, ASSES, PONIES, MULES, AND ZEBRAS

AUTHORITY: 7 U.S.C. 8301–8317; 7 CFR 2.22, 2.80, and 371.4.

SOURCE: 28 FR 5950, June 13, 1963, unless otherwise noted.

DOURINE IN HORSES AND ASSES

§§75.1–75.3 [Reserved]

EQUINE INFECTIOUS ANEMIA (SWAMP FEVER)

§75.4 Interstate movement of equine infectious anemia reactors and approval of laboratories, diagnostic facilities, and research facilities.

(a) *Definitions*. For the purpose of this section, the following terms have the meanings set forth in this paragraph.

Accredited veterinarian. A veterinarian approved by the Administrator in accordance with the provisions of part 161 of this title to perform functions specified in parts 1, 2, 3, and 11 of subchapter A, and subchapters B, C and

D of this chapter, and to perform functions required by cooperative State-Federal disease control and eradication programs.

Administrator. The Administrator, Animal and Plant Health Inspection Service, or any person authorized to act for the Administrator.

Animal and Plant Health Inspection Service. The Animal and Plant Health Inspection Service of the United States Department of Agriculture (APHIS or Service).

Animals. Cattle, sheep, goats, other ruminants, swine, horses, asses, mules, zebras, dogs, and poultry.

APHIS representative. An individual employed by APHIS who is authorized to perform the functions involved.

Approved stockyard. A stockyard, livestock market, or other premises, under state or federal veterinary supervision where horses or other equines are assembled for sale purposes, and which has been approved by the Administrator under § 71.20 of this chapter.

Certificate. An official document issued by a State representative, APHIS representative, or an accredited veterinarian at the point of origin of the interstate movement on which are listed: (1) The description, including age, breed, color, sex, and distinctive markings when present (such as brands, tattoos, scars or blemishes), of each reactor to be moved; (2) the number of reactors covered by the document; (3) the purpose for which the reactors are to be moved; (4) the points of origin and destination; (5) consignor; and (6) the consignee; and which states that each reactor identified on the certificate meets the requirements of § 75.4(b).

Interstate. From any State into or through any other State.

Official seal. A serially numbered metal or plastic strip, or a serially numbered button, consisting of a self-locking device on one end and a slot on the other end, which forms a loop when the ends are engaged and which cannot be reused if opened. It is applied by an APHIS representative or State representative.

Official test. Any test for the laboratory diagnosis of equine infectious anemia that utilizes a diagnostic product that is: (1) Produced under license from the Secretary of Agriculture, and found to be efficacious for that diagnosis, under the Virus-Serum-Toxin Act of March 4, 1913, and subsequent amendments (21 U.S.C. 151 *et seq.*); and (2) conducted in a laboratory approved by the Administrator.

Officially identified. The permanent identification of a reactor using the National Uniform Tag code number assigned by the United States Department of Agriculture to the State in which the reactor was tested, followed by the letter "A",[1] which markings shall be permanently applied to the reactor by an APHIS representative, State representative or accredited veterinarian who shall use for the purpose a hot iron or chemical brand, freezemarking or a lip tattoo. If hot iron or chemical branding or freezemarking is used, the markings shall be not less than two inches high and shall be applied to the left shoulder or left side of the neck of the reactor. If a lip tattoo is used, each character of the tattoo shall be not less than one inch high and three-fourths of an inch wide and shall be applied to the inside surface of the upper lip of the reactor.

Operator. The individual responsible for the day-to-day operations of the specifically approved stockyard.

Permit. An official document (VS Form 1–27 or a State form which contains the same information, but not a "permit for entry") issued by an APHIS representative, State representative, or accredited veterinarian which lists the owner's name and address, points of origin and destination, number of animals covered, purpose of the movement, and one of the following: The individual animal registered breed association registration tattoo, individual animal registered breed association registration number, or similar individual identification, including name, age, sex, breed, color, and markings.

Reactor. Any horse, ass, mule, pony or zebra which is subjected to an official test and found positive.

---

[1] Information as to the National Uniform Tag code number system can be obtained from the Animal and Plant Health Inspection Service, Veterinary Services, National Animal Health Programs, 4700 River Road Unit 43, Riverdale, Maryland 20737–1231.

State. Any State, the District of Columbia, Puerto Rico, the Virgin Islands of the United States, Guam, the Northern Mariana Islands, or any other territory or possession of the United States.

State animal health official. The individial employed by a State who is responsible for livestock and poultry disease control and eradication programs.

State representative. An individual employed in animal health activities of a State or a State's political subdivision, who is authorized by that State to perform the function involved under a cooperative agreement with the United States Department of Agriculture.

Veterinarian in Charge. The veterinary official of APHIS who is assigned by the Administrator to supervise and perform the animal health activities of APHIS in the State concerned.

(b) *Interstate movement*. No reactor may be moved interstate unless the reactor is officially identified, is accompanied by a certificate, and meets the conditions of either paragraph (b)(1), (b)(2), (b)(3), or (b)(4) of this section: *Provided*, That official identification is not necessary if the reactor is moved directly to slaughter under a permit and in a conveyance sealed with an official seal:

(1) The reactor is moved interstate for immediate slaughter, either to a Federally inspected slaughtering establishment operating under the provisions of the Federal Meat Inspection Act (21 U.S.C. 601 *et seq.*) or to a State-inspected slaughtering establishment that has inspection by a State representative at time of slaughter; or

(2) The reactor is moved interstate to a diagnostic or research facility after the individual issuing the certificate has consulted with the State animal health official in the State of destination and has determined that the reactor to be moved interstate will be maintained in isolation sufficient to prevent the transmission of equine infectious anemia to other horses, asses, ponies, mules, or zebras, and will remain quarantined under State authority at the diagnostic or research facility until natural death, slaughter, or until disposed of by euthanasia; or

(3) The reactor is moved interstate to its home farm after the individual issuing the certificate has consulted with the State animal health official in the State of destination and has determined that the reactor to be moved interstate will be maintained in isolation sufficient to prevent the transmission of equine infectious anemia to other horses, asses, ponies, mules, or zebras, and will remain quarantined under State authority on the reactor's home farm until natural death, slaughter, or until disposed of by euthanasia; and

(4) The reactor is moved interstate through no more than one approved stockyard for sale for immediate slaughter, and is moved within five days of its arrival at the approved stockyard directly to:

(i) Slaughter at a federally inspected slaughtering establishment operating under the provisions of the Federal Meat Inspection Act (21 U.S.C. 601 *et seq.*), or,

(ii) Slaughter at a state-inspected slaughtering establishment that has inspection by a state representative at the time of slaughter, or,

(iii) The home farm of the reactor in accordance with paragraph (b)(3) of this section.

(c) *Approval of Laboratories, and Diagnostic or Research Facilities*. (1) The Administrator will approve laboratories to conduct the official test only after consulting with the State animal health official in the State in which the laboratory is located and after determining that the laboratory:

(i) Has technical personnel assigned to conduct the official test who have received training prescribed by the National Veterinary Services Laboratories;

(ii) Uses United States Department of Agriculture licensed antigen;

(iii) Follows standard test protocol prescribed by the National Veterinary Services Laboratories;

(iv) Meets check test proficiency requirements prescribed by the National Veterinary Services Laboratories; and

(v) Reports all official test results to the State animal health official and the Veterinarian in Charge.[2]

[2] Training requirements, standard test protocols, and check test proficiency requirements prescribed by the National Veterinary Services Laboratories, and the names and

(2) The Administrator will approve diagnostic or research facilities to which reactors may be moved interstate under paragraph (b)(2) of this section, after a determination by the Administrator that the facility has facilities and employs procedures which are adequate to prevent the transmission of equine infectious anemia from reactors to other equine animals.[3]

(d) *Denial and withdrawal of approval of laboratories and diagnostic or research facilities.* The Administrator may deny or withdraw approval of any laboratory to conduct the official test, or of any diagnostic or research facility to receive reactors moved interstate, upon a determination that the laboratory or diagnostic or research facility does not meet the criteria for approval under paragraph (c) of this section.

(1) In the case of a denial, the operator of the laboratory or facility will be informed of the reasons for denial and may appeal the decision in writing to the Administrator within 10 days after receiving notification of the denial. The appeal must include all of the facts and reasons upon which the person relies to show that the laboratory or facility was wrongfully denied approval to conduct the official test or receive reactors moved interstate. The Administrator will grant or deny the appeal in writing as promptly as circumstances permit, stating the reason for his or her decision. If there is a conflict as to any material fact, a hearing will be held to resolve the conflict. Rules of practice concerning the hearing will be adopted by the Administrator.

(2) In the case of withdrawal, before such action is taken, the operator of the laboratory or facility will be informed of the reasons for the proposed withdrawal. The operator of the laboratory or facility may appeal the proposed withdrawal in writing to the Administrator within 10 days after being informed of the reasons for the proposed withdrawal. The appeal must include all of the facts and reasons upon which the person relies to show that the reasons for the proposed withdrawal are incorrect or do not support the withdrawal of the approval of the laboratory or facility to conduct the official test or receive reactors moved interstate. The Administrator will grant or deny the appeal in writing as promptly as circumstances permit, stating the reason for his or her decision. If there is a conflict as to any material fact, a hearing will be held to resolve the conflict. Rules of practice concerning the hearing will be adopted by the Administrator. However, the withdrawal shall become effective pending final determination in the proceeding when the Administrator determines that such action is necessary to protect the public health, interest, or safety. Such withdrawal shall be effective upon oral or written notification, whichever is earlier, to the operator of the laboratory or facility. In the event of oral notification, written confirmation shall be given as promptly as circumstances allow. The withdrawal shall continue in effect pending the completion of the proceeding, and any judicial review thereof, unless otherwise ordered by the Administrator.

(3) Approval for a laboratory to conduct the official test will be automatically withdrawn by the Administrator when the operator of the approved laboratory notifies the National Veterinary Services Laboratories in Ames, Iowa, in writing, that the laboratory no longer conducts the official test.

(4) Approval for a diagnostic or research facility to receive reactors moved interstate will be automatically withdrawn by the Administrator when the operator of the approved diagnostic or research facility notifies the Administrator, in writing, that the diagnostic

addresses of approved laboratories can be obtained from the Animal and Plant Health Inspection Service, Veterinary Services, National Animal Health Programs, 4700 River Road Unit 43, Riverdale, Maryland 20737–1231.

[3] Facilities and procedures which are adequate to prevent the transmission of equine infectious anemia, and the names and addresses of approved diagnostic or research facilities, can be obtained from the Animal and Plant Health Inspection Service, Veterinary Services, National Animal Health Programs, 4700 River Road Unit 43, Riverdale, Maryland 20737–1231.

or research facility no longer receives reactors moved interstate.

(Approved by the Office of Management and Budget under control number 0579–0051)

[51 FR 12597, Apr. 14, 1986, as amended at 51 FR 30327, Aug. 26, 1986; 55 FR 13506, 13507, Apr. 11, 1990; 57 FR 2440, Jan. 22, 1992; 57 FR 57337, Dec. 4, 1992; 59 FR 67133, Dec. 29, 1994; 59 FR 67613, Dec. 30, 1994; 60 FR 14619, Mar. 20, 1995; 62 FR 27936, May 22, 1997; 66 FR 21062, Apr. 27, 2001]

CONTAGIOUS EQUINE METRITIS (CEM)

§§ 75.5–75.10 [Reserved]

PART 76 [RESERVED]

PART 77—TUBERCULOSIS

Subpart A—General Provisions

Subpart B—Cattle and Bison

Subpart C—Captive Cervids

AUTHORITY: 7 U.S.C. 8301–8317; 7 CFR 2.22, 2.80, and 371.4.

SOURCE: 65 FR 63517, Oct. 23, 2000, unless otherwise noted.

Subpart A—General Provisions

§ 77.1 Material incorporated by reference.

Uniform Methods and Rules—Bovine Tuberculosis Eradication. The Uniform Methods and Rules—Bovine Tuberculosis Eradication (January 22, 1999, edition) has been approved for incorporation by reference into the Code of Federal Regulations by the Director of the Federal Register in accordance with 5 U.S.C. 552(a) and 1 CFR part 51.

(a) The procedures specified in the Uniform Methods and Rules—Bovine Tuberculosis Eradication (January 22, 1999, edition) must be followed for the interstate movement of certain animals regulated under this part.

(b) *Availability.* Copies of the Uniform Methods and Rules—Bovine Tuberculosis Eradication:

(1) Are available for inspection at the National Archives and Records Administration (NARA). For information on

the availability of this material at NARA, call 202–741–6030, or go to: *http://www.archives.gov/federal_register/code_of_federal_regulations/ibr_locations.html*;

(2) Are available for inspection at the APHIS reading room, room 1141, USDA South Building, 14th Street and Independence Avenue, SW., Washington, DC; or

(3) May be obtained from the National Animal Health Programs, Veterinary Services, APHIS, 4700 River Road Unit 43, Riverdale, MD 20737–1231.

[65 FR 63517, Oct. 23, 2000, as amended at 69 FR 18803, Apr. 9, 2004]

§77.2 Definitions.

As used in this part, the following terms shall have the meanings set forth in this section except as otherwise specified.

Accredited veterinarian. A veterinarian approved by the Administrator in accordance with the provisions of part 161 of subchapter J to perform functions specified in subchapters B, C, and D of this chapter.

Administrator. The Administrator, Animal and Plant Health Inspection Service, or any person authorized to act for the Administrator.

Affected herd. A herd of livestock in which there is strong and substantial evidence that *Mycobacterium bovis* exists. This evidence should include, but is not limited to, any of the following: Histopathology, polymerase chain reaction (PCR) assay, bacterial isolation or detection, testing data, or epidemiologic evidence such as contact with known sources of infection.

Animal. All species of animals except man, birds, or reptiles.

Animal and Plant Health Inspection Service (APHIS). The Animal and Plant Health Inspection Service of the United States Department of Agriculture.

Animal identification number (AIN). A numbering system for the official identification of individual animals in the United States that provides a nationally unique identification number for each animal. The AIN consists of 15 digits, with the first 3 being the country code (840 for the United States or a unique country code for any U.S. territory that has such a code and elects to use it in place of the 840 code). The alpha characters USA or the numeric code assigned to the manufacturer of the identification device by the International Committee on Animal Recording may be used as an alternative to the 840 or other prefix representing a U.S territory; however, only the AIN beginning with the 840 or other prefix representing a U.S. territory will be recognized as official for use on AIN tags applied to animals on or after March 11, 2015. The AIN beginning with the 840 prefix may not be applied to animals known to have been born outside the United States.

APHIS representative. An individual employed by APHIS who is authorized to perform the function involved.

Area veterinarian in charge. The veterinary official of APHIS who is assigned by the Administrator to supervise and perform the official animal health work of APHIS in the State concerned.

Cooperating State and Federal animal health officials. The State and Federal animal health officials responsible for overseeing and implementing the National Cooperative State/Federal Bovine Tuberculosis Eradication Program.

Depopulate. To destroy all livestock in a herd by slaughter or by death otherwise.

Directly. Moved in a means of conveyance, without stopping to unload while en route, except for stops of less than 24 hours to feed, water, or rest the animals being moved, and with no commingling of animals at such stops.

Epidemiologic investigation. An investigation that is conducted by a State in conjunction with APHIS representatives, in which an official test for tuberculosis is conducted on all livestock in any tuberculosis-affected herd in a State or zone, all livestock in any herd into which livestock from the affected herd have been moved, all potential tuberculosis source herds, and all livestock herds and animals that are likely to have been exposed to the affected herd.

Herd. Except for livestock assembled at feedlots, any group of livestock maintained for at least 4 months on common ground for any purpose, or two or more groups of livestock under common ownership or supervision, geographically separated but that have an interchange or movement of livestock without regard to health status, as determined by the Administrator.

Interstate. From one State into or through any other State.

Interstate certificate of veterinary inspection (ICVI). An official document issued by a Federal, State, Tribal, or accredited veterinarian certifying the inspection of animals in preparation for interstate movement.

(a) The ICVI must show the species of animals covered by the ICVI; the number of animals covered by the ICVI; the purpose for which the animals are to be moved; the address at which the animals were loaded for interstate movement; the address to which the animals are destined; and the names of the consignor and the consignee and their addresses if different from the address at which the animals were loaded or the address to which the animals are destined. Additionally, unless the species-specific requirements for ICVIs provide an exception, the ICVI must list the official identification number of each animal, except as provided in paragraph (b) of this definition, or group of animals moved that is required to be officially identified, or, if an alternative form of identification has been agreed upon by the sending and receiving States, the ICVI must include a record of that identification. If animals moving under a GIN also have individual official identification, only the GIN must be listed on the ICVI. An ICVI may not be issued for any animal that is not officially identified if official identification is required. If the animals are not required by the regulations to be officially identified, the ICVI must state the exemption that applies (e.g., the cattle and bison do not belong to one of the classes of cattle and bison to which the official identification requirements of 9 CFR part 86 apply). If the animals are required to be officially identified but the identification number does not have to be recorded on the ICVI, the ICVI must state that all animals to be moved under the ICVI are officially identified.

(b) As an alternative to typing or writing individual animal identification on an ICVI, if agreed to by the receiving State or Tribe, another document may be used to provide this information, but only under the following conditions:

(1) The document must be a State form or APHIS form that requires individual identification of animals or a printout of official identification numbers generated by computer or other means;

(2) A legible copy of the document must be stapled to the original and each copy of the ICVI;

(3) Each copy of the document must identify each animal to be moved with the ICVI, but any information pertaining to other animals, and any unused space on the document for recording animal identification, must be crossed out in ink; and

(4) The following information must be written in ink in the identification column on the original and each copy of the ICVI and must be circled or boxed, also in ink, so that no additional information can be added:

(i) The name of the document; and

(ii) Either the unique serial number on the document or, if the document is not imprinted with a serial number, both the name of the person who prepared the document and the date the document was signed.

Livestock. All farm-raised animals.

Location-based numbering system. The location-based number system combines a State or Tribal issued location identification (LID) number or a premises identification number (PIN) with a producer's unique livestock production numbering system to provide a nationally unique and herd-unique identification number for an animal.

Location identification (LID) number. A nationally unique number issued by a State, Tribal, and/or Federal animal health authority to a location as determined by the State or Tribe in which it is issued. The LID number may be used in conjunction with a producer's own unique livestock production numbering system to provide a nationally unique and herd-unique identification number for an animal. It may also be used as a component of a group/lot identification number (GIN).

Move. To carry, enter, import, mail, ship, or transport; to aid, abet, cause, or induce carrying, entering, importing, mailing, shipping, or transporting; to offer to carry, enter, import, mail, ship, or transport; to receive in order to carry, enter, import, mail, ship, or transport; or to allow any of these activities.

National Uniform Eartagging System (NUES). A numbering system for the official identification of individual animals in the United States that provides a nationally unique identification number for each animal.

Official eartag. An identification tag approved by APHIS that bears an official identification number for individual animals. Beginning March 11, 2014, all official eartags manufactured must bear an official eartag shield. Beginning March 11, 2015, all official eartags applied to animals must bear an official eartag shield. The design, size, shape, color, and other characteristics of the official eartag will depend on the needs of the users, subject to the approval of the Administrator. The official eartag must be tamper-resistant and have a high retention rate in the animal.

Official eartag shield. The shield-shaped graphic of the U.S. Route Shield with "U.S." or the State postal abbreviation or Tribal alpha code imprinted within the shield.

Official identification number. A nationally unique number that is permanently associated with an animal or group of animals and that adheres to one of the following systems:

(1) National Uniform Eartagging System (NUES).

(2) Animal identification number (AIN).

(3) Flock-based number system.

(4) Location-based number system.

(5) Any other numbering system approved by the Administrator for the official identification of animals.

Official seal. A seal issued by a State or APHIS representative, consisting of a serially numbered, metal or plastic strip, with a self-locking device on one end and a slot on the other end, which forms a loop when the ends are engaged and that cannot be reused if opened, or a serially numbered, self-locking button that can be used for this purpose.

Officially identified. Identified by means of an official eartag or by means of an individual tattoo or hot brand that provides unique identification for each animal.

Person. Any individual, corporation, company, association, firm, partnership, society, joint stock company, or other legal entity.

Premises identification number (PIN). A nationally unique number assigned by a State, Tribal, and/or Federal animal health authority to a premises that is, in the judgment of the State, Tribal, and/or Federal animal health authority a geographically distinct location from other premises. The PIN may be used in conjunction with a producer's own livestock production numbering system to provide a nationally unique and herd-unique identification number for an animal. It may be used as a component of a group/lot identification number (GIN).

Recognized slaughtering establishment. Any slaughtering facility operating under the Federal Meat Inspection Act (21 U.S.C. 601 *et seq.*), the Poultry Products Inspection Act (21 U.S.C. 451 *et seq.*), or State meat or poultry inspection acts that is approved in accordance with 9 CFR 71.21.

State. Any State, the District of Columbia, Puerto Rico, or any territory of the United States.

State animal health official. The State official responsible for livestock and poultry disease control and eradication programs.

State representative. A veterinarian or other person employed in livestock sanitary work of a State or a political subdivision of a State and who is authorized by such State or political subdivision of a State to perform the function involved under a memorandum of understanding with APHIS.

Transportation document. Any document accompanying the interstate movement of livestock, such as an owner's statement, manifest, switch order, or vehicle record, on which is stated the point from which the animals are moved interstate, the destination of the animals, the number of animals covered by the document, and the name and address of the owner or shipper.

Tuberculosis. The contagious, infectious, and communicable disease caused by *Mycobacterium bovis*. (Also referred to as bovine tuberculosis.)

United States. All of the States.

United States Department of Agriculture (USDA) approved backtag. A backtag issued by APHIS that provides a temporary unique identification for each animal.

Zone. A defined geographic land area identifiable by geological, political, manmade, or surveyed boundaries, with mechanisms of disease spread, epidemiological characteristics, and the ability to control the movement of animals across the boundaries of the zone taken into account.

[65 FR 63517, Oct. 23, 2000, as amended at 66 FR 7592, Feb. 20, 2002; 69 FR 64649, Nov. 8, 2004; 70 FR 61026, Oct. 20, 2005; 72 FR 39305, July 18, 2007; 73 FR 54062, Sept. 18, 2008; 78 FR 2064, Jan. 9, 2013; 79 FR 43926, July 29, 2014]

§ 77.3 Tuberculosis classifications of States and zones.

The Administrator shall classify each State for tuberculosis in accordance with this part. A zone comprising less than an entire State will be given a particular classification upon request of the State only if the Administrator determines that:

(a) The State meets the requirements of this part for establishment of zones;

(b) The State has adopted and is enforcing regulations that impose restrictions on the intrastate movement of cattle, bison, and captive cervids that are substantially the same as those in place under this part for the interstate movement of cattle, bison, and captive cervids; and

(c) The designation of part of a State as a zone will otherwise be adequate to prevent the interstate spread of tuberculosis.

§ 77.4 Application for and retention of zones.

(a) A State animal health official may request at any time that the Administrator designate part of a State as having a different tuberculosis classification under this part than the rest of the State. The requested zones must be delineated by the State animal health authorities, subject to approval by the Administrator. The request from the State must demonstrate that the State complies with the following requirements:

(1) The State must have the legal and financial resources to implement and enforce a tuberculosis eradication program and must have in place an infrastructure, laws, and regulations that require and ensure that State and Federal animal health authorities are notified of tuberculosis cases in domestic livestock or outbreaks in wildlife;

(2) The State in which the intended zones are located must maintain, in each intended zone, clinical and epidemiologic surveillance of animal species at risk of tuberculosis at a rate that allows detection of tuberculosis in the overall population of livestock at a 2 percent prevalence rate with 95 percent confidence. The designated tuberculosis epidemiologist must review reports of all testing for each zone within the State within 30 days of the testing; and

(3) The State must enter into a memorandum of understanding with APHIS in which the State agrees to adhere to any conditions for zone recognition particular to that request.

(b) Retention of APHIS recognition of a zone is subject to annual review by the Administrator. To retain recognition of a zone, a State must continue to comply with the requirements of paragraphs (a)(1), (a)(2), and (a)(3) of this section, as well as the requirements for maintaining or improving the tuberculosis risk classification of each zone in the State, and must retain for at least 2 years all certificates required under this part for the movement of cattle, bison, and captive cervids.

(Approved by the Office of Management and Budget under control number 0579–0146)

Subpart B—Cattle and Bison

§ 77.5 Definitions.

As used in subpart B, the following terms shall have the meanings set forth in this section except as otherwise specified.

Accreditation preparatory State or zone. A State or zone that is or is part of a State that has the authority to enforce and complies with the provisions of the "Uniform Methods and Rules—Bovine Tuberculosis Eradication" and in which tuberculosis is prevalent in less than 0.5 percent of the total number of herds of cattle and bison in the State or zone.

Accredited-free State or zone. A State or zone that is or is part of a State that has the authority to enforce and complies with the provisions of the "Uniform Methods and Rules—Bovine Tuberculosis Eradication," has zero percent prevalence of affected cattle and bison herds, and has had no findings of tuberculosis in any cattle or bison herds in the State or zone for the previous 5 years. *Except that:* The requirement of freedom from tuberculosis in herds is 2 years from the depopulation of the last affected herd in States or zones that were previously accredited free and in which all herds affected with tuberculosis were depopulated, 3 years in all other States or zones that have depopulated all affected herds, and 3 years in States or zones that have conducted surveillance that demonstrates that other livestock herds and wildlife are not at risk of being infected with tuberculosis, as determined by the Administrator based on a risk assessment conducted by APHIS.

Accredited herd. To establish or maintain accredited herd status, the herd owner must comply with all of the provisions of the "Uniform Methods and Rules—Bovine Tuberculosis Eradication" regarding accredited herds. All cattle and bison in a herd must be free from tuberculosis.

Approved feedlot. A confined area approved jointly by the State animal health official and the Administrator for feeding cattle and bison for slaughter, with no provisions for pasturing or grazing.

Cattle and bison not known to be affected. All cattle and bison except those originating from tuberculosis affected herds or from herds containing tuberculosis suspect cattle or bison.

Department. The U.S. Department of Agriculture (USDA).

Exposed cattle and bison. Cattle and bison, except reactor cattle and bison, that are part of an affected herd.

Feedlot. A facility for congregating finished fed cattle prior to their being shipped to slaughter.

Finished fed cattle. Cattle fattened on a ration of feed concentrates to reach a slaughter condition equivalent to that which would be attained on full feed with a high concentrate grain ration for 90 days.

Modified accredited advanced State or zone. A State or zone that is or is part of a State that has the authority to enforce and complies with the provisions of the "Uniform Methods and Rules—Bovine Tuberculosis Eradication" and in which tuberculosis has been prevalent in less than 0.01 percent of the total number of herds of cattle and bison in the State or zone for each of the most recent 2 years. *Except that:* The Administrator, upon his or her review, may allow a State or zone with fewer than 30,000 herds to have up to 3 affected herds for each of the most recent 2 years, depending on the veterinary infrastructure, livestock demographics, and tuberculosis control and eradication measures in the State or zone.

Modified accredited State or zone. A State or zone that is or is part of a State that has the authority to enforce and complies with the provisions of the "Uniform Methods and Rules—Bovine Tuberculosis Eradication" and in which tuberculosis has been prevalent in less than 0.1 percent of the total number of herds of cattle and bison in the State or zone for the most recent year. *Except that:* The Administrator, upon his or her review, may allow a State or zone with fewer than 10,000 herds to have up to 10 affected herds for the most recent year, depending on the veterinary infrastructure, livestock demographics, and tuberculosis control and eradication measures in the State or zone.

Negative cattle and bison. Cattle and bison that are classified negative for tuberculosis in accordance with the "Uniform Methods and Rules—Bovine Tuberculosis Eradication," based on the results of an official tuberculin test.

Nonaccredited State or zone. A State or zone that is or is part of a State that does not meet the standards of the "Uniform Methods and Rules—Bovine Tuberculosis Eradication" or in which tuberculosis is prevalent in 0.5 percent or more of the total number of herds of cattle and bison in the State or zone.

Official tuberculin test. Any test for tuberculosis conducted on cattle or bison in accordance with the "Uniform Methods and Rules—Bovine Tuberculosis Eradication."

Permit. An official document issued for movement of cattle or bison under this part by an APHIS representative, State representative, or an accredited veterinarian at the point of origin of a shipment of cattle or bison to be moved directly to slaughter, that shows the tuberculosis status of each animal (reactor, suspect, or exposed), the eartag number of each animal and the name of the owner of such animal, the establishment to which the animals are to be moved, the purpose for which the animals are to be moved, and that they are eligible for such movement under the applicable provisions of §§ 77.17 and 77.18.

Quarantined feedlot. A confined area under the direct supervision and control of a State livestock official who shall establish procedures for the accounting of all livestock entering or leaving the area. The quarantined feedlot shall be maintained for finish feeding of livestock in drylot with no provision for pasturing and grazing. All livestock leaving such feedlot must only move directly to slaughter in accordance with established procedures for handling quarantined livestock.

Reactor cattle and bison. Cattle and bison that are classified as reactors for tuberculosis in accordance with the "Uniform Methods and Rules—Bovine Tuberculosis Eradication."

Recognized slaughtering establishment. Any slaughtering facility operating under the Federal Meat Inspection Act (21 U.S.C. 601 *et seq.*), the Poultry Products Inspection Act (21 U.S.C. 451 *et seq.*), or State meat or poultry inspection acts that is approved in accordance with 9 CFR 71.21.

Suspect cattle and bison. Cattle and bison that are classified as suspects for tuberculosis in accordance with the "Uniform Methods and Rules—Bovine Tuberculosis Eradication."

Uniform Methods and Rules—Bovine Tuberculosis Eradication. Uniform methods and rules for eradicating bovine tuberculosis in the United States, approved by APHIS on January 22, 1999, which is incorporated by reference at § 77.1.

Whole herd test. An official tuberculin test of all cattle and bison in a herd that are 12 months of age or older, and of all cattle and bison in the herd that are less than 12 months of age and were not born into the herd, except those cattle and bison that are less than 12 months of age and were born in and originated from an accredited herd.

Zero percent prevalence. No finding of tuberculosis in any cattle, bison, or goat herd in a State or zone.

[65 FR 63517, Oct. 23, 2000, as amended at 70 FR 61026, Oct. 20, 2005; 78 FR 2065, Jan. 9, 2013]

§ 77.6 Applicability of this subpart.

All references in this subpart to the tuberculosis status of States and zones pertain to such status for cattle and bison only.

§ 77.7 Accredited-free States or zones.

(a) The following are accredited-free States: Alabama, Alaska, Arizona, Arkansas, California, Colorado, Connecticut, Delaware, Florida, Georgia, Hawaii, Idaho, Illinois, Indiana, Iowa, Kansas, Kentucky, Louisiana, Maine, Maryland, Massachusetts, Minnesota, Mississippi, Missouri, Montana, Nebraska, Nevada, New Hampshire, New Jersey, New Mexico, New York, North Carolina, North Dakota, Ohio, Oklahoma, Oregon, Pennsylvania, Puerto Rico, Rhode Island, South Carolina, South Dakota, Tennessee, Texas, Utah, Vermont, Virginia, the Virgin Islands of the United States, Washington, West Virginia, Wisconsin, and Wyoming.

(b) The following are accredited-free zones:

(1) All of the State of Michigan except for the zone that comprises those counties in Michigan described in § 77.11(b)(1).

(2) [Reserved]

(c) If an affected herd is detected in a State or zone classified as accredited-free, and the herd is depopulated and an epidemiologic investigation is completed within 90 days of the detection of the affected herd with no evidence of the spread of tuberculosis, the State or zone may retain its accredited-free status. If two or more affected herds are detected in an accredited-free State or zone within a 48-month period, the State or zone will be removed from the list of accredited-free States or zones and will be reclassified as modified accredited advanced.

(d) If any livestock other than cattle or bison are included in a newly assembled herd on a premises where a tuberculous herd has been depopulated, the State or zone must apply the herd test requirements contained in the "Uniform Methods and Rules—Bovine Tuberculosis Eradication" (January 22, 1999, edition), which is incorporated by reference at §77.1, to those other livestock in the same manner as to cattle and bison. Failure to do so will result in reclassification of the State or zone as modified accredited advanced.

(e) If tuberculosis is diagnosed within an accredited-free State or zone in an animal not specifically regulated by this part and a risk assessment conducted by APHIS determines that the outbreak poses a tuberculosis risk to livestock within the State or zone, the State or zone must implement a tuberculosis management plan, approved jointly by the State animal health official and the Administrator, within 6 months of the diagnosis. The management plan must include provisions for immediate investigation of tuberculosis in animals held for exhibition and in livestock and wildlife; the prevention of the spread of the disease to other animals held for exhibition and to livestock and wildlife; increased surveillance for tuberculosis in animals held for exhibition and wildlife; eradication of tuberculosis from individual herds; a timeline for tuberculosis eradication; and performance standards by which to measure yearly progress toward eradication. If a State or zone does not implement such a plan within the required 6 months, the State or zone will lose its accredited-free status and will be reclassified as modified accredited advanced.

(f) Accredited-free State or zone status must be renewed annually. To qualify for renewal of accredited-free State or zone status, a State must submit an annual report to APHIS certifying that the State or zone within the State complies with the provisions of the "Uniform Methods and Rules—Bovine Tuberculosis Eradication." The report must be submitted to APHIS each year between October 1 and November 30.

(Approved by the Office of Management and Budget under control number 0579–0146)

[65 FR 63517, Oct. 23, 2000]

EDITORIAL NOTE: For FEDERAL REGISTER citations affecting §77.7, see the List of CFR Sections Affected, which appears in the Finding Aids section of the printed volume and at *www.fdsys.gov*.

§77.8 Interstate movement from accredited-free States and zones.

Cattle or bison that originate in an accredited-free State or zone may be moved interstate in accordance with 9 CFR part 86 without further restriction under this part.

[78 FR 2065, Jan. 9, 2013]

§77.9 Modified accredited advanced States or zones.

(a) The following are modified accredited advanced States: None.

(b) The following are modified accredited advanced zones: None.

(c) If any livestock other than cattle or bison are included in a newly assembled herd on a premises where a tuberculous herd has been depopulated, the State or zone must apply the herd test requirements contained in the "Uniform Methods and Rules—Bovine Tuberculosis Eradication" (January 22, 1999), which is incorporated by reference at §77.1, for such newly assembled herds to those other livestock in the same manner as to cattle and bison. Failure to do so will result in the removal of the State or zone from the list of modified accredited advanced States or zones and its being reclassified as modified accredited.

(d) If tuberculosis is diagnosed within a modified accredited advanced State or zone in an animal not specifically regulated by this part and a risk assessment conducted by APHIS determines that the outbreak poses a tuberculosis risk to livestock within the State or zone, the State or zone must implement a tuberculosis management plan, approved jointly by the State animal health official and the Administrator, within 6 months of the diagnosis. The management plan must include provisions for immediate investigation of tuberculosis in animals held for exhibition and in livestock and wildlife; the prevention of the spread of the disease to other animals held for exhibition and to livestock and wildlife; increased surveillance for tuberculosis in animals held for exhibition and wildlife; eradication of tuberculosis from individual herds; a timeline for tuberculosis eradication; and performance standards by which to measure yearly progress toward eradication. If a State or zone does not implement such a plan within the required 6 months, the State or zone will be reclassified as modified accredited.

(e) Modified accredited advanced State or zone status must be renewed annually. To qualify for renewal of a modified accredited advanced State or zone status, a State must submit an annual report to APHIS certifying that the State or zone complies with the provisions of the "Uniform Methods and Rules—Bovine Tuberculosis Eradication." The report must be submitted to APHIS each year between October 1 and November 30.

(f) To qualify for accredited-free status, a modified accredited advanced State or zone must demonstrate to the Administrator that it complies with the provisions of the "Uniform Methods and Rules—Bovine Tuberculosis Eradication," has zero percent prevalence of affected cattle and bison herds, and has had no findings of tuberculosis in any cattle or bison in the State or zone for the previous 5 years. *Except that:* The requirement of freedom from tuberculosis is 2 years from the depopulation of the last affected herd in States or zones that were previously accredited free and in which all herds affected with tuberculosis were depopulated, 3 years in all other States or zones that have depopulated all affected herds, and 3 years in States or zones that have conducted surveillance that demonstrates that other livestock herds and wildlife are not at risk of being infected with tuberculosis, as determined by the Administrator based on a risk assessment conducted by APHIS.

(Approved by the Office of Management and Budget under control number 0579–0146)

[65 FR 63517, Oct. 23, 2000]

EDITORIAL NOTE: For FEDERAL REGISTER citations affecting § 77.9, see the List of CFR Sections Affected, which appears in the Finding Aids section of the printed volume and at *www.fdsys.gov*.

§ 77.10 Interstate movement from modified accredited advanced States and zones.

Cattle or bison that originate in a modified accredited advanced State or zone, and that are not known to be infected with or exposed to tuberculosis, may be moved interstate only in accordance with 9 CFR part 86 and, if moved anywhere other than directly to slaughter at a recognized slaughtering establishment, under one of the following additional conditions:

(a) The cattle or bison are sexually intact heifers moved to an approved feedlot, or are steers or spayed heifers, and are officially identified.

(b) The cattle or bison are from an accredited herd, are officially identified, and are accompanied by an ICVI stating that the accredited herd completed the testing necessary for accredited status with negative results within 1 year prior to the date of movement.

(c) The cattle or bison are sexually intact animals; are not from an accredited herd; are officially identified; and are accompanied by an ICVI stating that they were negative to an official tuberculin test conducted within 60 days prior to the date of movement.

(Approved by the Office of Management and Budget under control numbers 0579–0146, 0579–0220, and 0579–0229)

[78 FR 2065, Jan. 9, 2013]

§ 77.11 Modified accredited States or zones.

(a) The following are modified accredited States: None.

(b) The following are modified accredited zones:

(1) A zone in Michigan that comprises Alcona, Alpena, Montmorency, and Oscoda Counties.

(2) [Reserved]

(c) If any livestock other than cattle or bison are included in a newly assembled herd on a premises where a tuberculous herd has been depopulated, the State or zone must apply the herd test requirements contained in the "Uniform Methods and Rules—Bovine Tuberculosis Eradication" (January 22, 1999, edition), which is incorporated by reference at §77.1, for such newly assembled herds to those other livestock in the same manner as to cattle and bison. Failure to do so will result in the removal of the State or zone from the list of modified accredited States or zones and its being reclassified as accreditation preparatory.

(d) If tuberculosis is diagnosed within a modified accredited State or zone in an animal not specifically regulated by this part and a risk assessment conducted by APHIS determines that the outbreak poses a tuberculosis risk to livestock within the State or zone, the State or zone must implement a tuberculosis management plan, approved jointly by the State animal health official and the Administrator, within 6 months of the diagnosis. The management plan must include provisions for immediate investigation of tuberculosis in animals held for exhibition and in livestock and wildlife; the prevention of the spread of the disease to other animals held for exhibition and to livestock and wildlife; increased surveillance for tuberculosis in animals held for exhibition and wildlife; eradication of tuberculosis from individual herds; a timeline for tuberculosis eradication; and performance standards by which to measure yearly progress toward eradication. If a State or zone does not implement such a plan within the required 6 months, the State or zone will be reclassified as accreditation preparatory.

(e) Modified accredited State or zone status must be renewed annually. To qualify for renewal of a modified accredited State or zone status, a State must submit an annual report to APHIS certifying that the State or zone complies with the provisions of the "Uniform Methods and Rules—Bovine Tuberculosis Eradication." The report must be submitted to APHIS each year between October 1 and November 30.

(f) To qualify for modified accredited advanced status, a modified accredited State or zone must demonstrate to the Administrator that it complies with the provisions of the "Uniform Methods and Rules—Bovine Tuberculosis Eradication" and that tuberculosis has been prevalent in less than 0.01 percent of the total number of herds of cattle and bison in the State or zone for the most recent 2 years. *Except that:* The Administrator, upon his or her review, may allow a State or zone with fewer than 30,000 herds to have up to 3 affected herds for each of the most recent 2 years, depending on the veterinary infrastructure, livestock demographics, and tuberculosis control and eradication measures in the State or zone.

(Approved by the Office of Management and Budget under control number 0579–0146)

[65 FR 63517, Oct. 23, 2000; 65 FR 64479, Oct. 27, 2000, as amended at 69 FR 20809, Apr. 19, 2004; 73 FR 19142, Apr. 9, 2008; 73 FR 60102, Oct. 10, 2008; 74 FR 67053, Dec. 18, 2009; 75 FR 60588, Oct. 1, 2010; 76 FR 56636, Sept. 14, 2011]

§77.12 Interstate movement from modified accredited States and zones.

Cattle or bison that originate in a modified accredited State or zone, and that are not known to be infected with or exposed to tuberculosis, may be moved interstate only in accordance with 9 CFR part 86 and, if moved anywhere other than directly to slaughter at a recognized slaughtering establishment, under one of the following additional conditions:

(a) The cattle or bison are sexually intact heifers moved to an approved feedlot, or are steers or spayed heifers; are officially identified, and are accompanied by an ICVI stating that they were classified negative to an official tuberculin test conducted within 60 days prior to the date of movement.

(b) The cattle or bison are from an accredited herd, are officially identified, and are accompanied by an ICVI stating that the accredited herd completed the testing necessary for accredited status with negative results within 1 year prior to the date of movement.

(c) The cattle or bison are sexually intact animals; are not from an accredited herd; are officially identified; and are accompanied by an ICVI stating that the herd from which they originated was negative to a whole herd test conducted within 1 year prior to the date of movement and that the individual animals to be moved were negative to an additional official tuberculin test conducted within 60 days prior to the date of movement, except that the additional test is not required if the animals are moved interstate within 60 days following the whole herd test.

(Approved by the Office of Management and Budget under control number 0579–0146)

[78 FR 2066, Jan. 9, 2013]

§ 77.13 Accreditation preparatory States or zones.

(a) The following are accreditation preparatory States: None.

(b) The following are accreditation preparatory zones: None.

(c) If any livestock other than cattle or bison are included in a newly assembled herd on a premises where a tuberculous herd has been depopulated, the State or zone must apply the herd test requirements contained in the "Uniform Methods and Rules—Bovine Tuberculosis Eradication" (January 22, 1999 edition), which is incorporated by reference at § 77.1, for such newly assembled herds to those other livestock in the same manner as to cattle and bison. Failure to do so will result in the removal of the State or zone from the list of accreditation preparatory States or zones and its being reclassified as nonaccredited.

(d) If tuberculosis is diagnosed within an accreditation preparatory State or zone in an animal not specifically regulated by this part and a risk assessment conducted by APHIS determines that the outbreak poses a tuberculosis risk to livestock within the State or zone, the State or zone must implement a tuberculosis management plan, approved jointly by the State animal health official and the Administrator, within 6 months of the diagnosis. The management plan must include provisions for immediate investigation of tuberculosis in animals held for exhibition and in livestock and wildlife; the prevention of the spread of the disease to other animals held for exhibition and to livestock and wildlife; increased surveillance for tuberculosis in animals held for exhibition and wildlife; eradication of tuberculosis from individual herds; a timeline for tuberculosis eradication; and performance standards by which to measure yearly progress toward eradication. If a State or zone does not implement such a plan within the required 6 months, the State or zone will be reclassified as nonaccredited.

(e) Accreditation preparatory State or zone status must be renewed annually. To qualify for renewal of accreditation preparatory State or zone status, a State must submit an annual report to APHIS certifying that the State or zone complies with the provisions of the "Uniform Methods and Rules—Bovine Tuberculosis Eradication." The report must be submitted to APHIS each year between October 1 and November 30.

(f) To qualify for modified accredited status, an accreditation preparatory State or zone must demonstrate to the Administrator that it complies with the provisions of the "Uniform Methods and Rules—Bovine Tuberculosis Eradication" and that tuberculosis has been prevalent in less than 0.1 percent of the total number of herds of cattle and bison in the State or zone for the most recent year. *Except that:* The Administrator, upon his or her review, may allow a State or zone with fewer than 10,000 herds to have up to 10 affected herds for the most recent year, depending on the veterinary infrastructure, livestock demographics, and tuberculosis control and eradication measures in the State or zone.

(Approved by the Office of Management and Budget under control number 0579–0146)

§ 77.14 Interstate movement from accreditation preparatory States and zones.

Cattle or bison that originate in an accreditation preparatory State or zone, and that are not known to be infected with or exposed to tuberculosis, may be moved interstate only in accordance with 9 CFR part 86 and, if moved anywhere other than directly to slaughter at a recognized slaughtering establishment, under one of the following additional conditions:

(a) The cattle or bison are sexually intact heifers moved to an approved feedlot, or are steers or spayed heifers; are officially identified; and are accompanied by an ICVI stating that the herd from which they originated was negative to a whole herd test conducted within 1 year prior to the date of movement and that the individual animals to be moved were negative to an additional official tuberculin test conducted within 60 days prior to the date of movement; *Except that:* The additional test is not required if the animals are moved interstate within 6 months following the whole herd test.

(b) The cattle or bison are from an accredited herd; are officially identified; and are accompanied by an ICVI stating that the accredited herd completed the testing necessary for accredited status with negative results within 1 year prior to the date of movement and that the animals to be moved were negative to an official tuberculin test conducted within 60 days prior to the date of movement.

(c) The cattle or bison are sexually intact animals; are not from an accredited herd; are officially identified; and are accompanied by an ICVI stating that the herd from which they originated was negative to a whole herd test conducted within 1 year prior to the date of movement and that the individual animals to be moved were negative to two additional official tuberculin tests conducted at least 60 days apart and no more than 6 months apart, with the second test conducted within 60 days prior to the date of movement; *Except that:* The second additional test is not required if the animals are moved interstate within 60 days following the whole herd test.

(Approved by the Office of Management and Budget under control number 0579–0146)

[78 FR 2066, Jan. 9, 2013]

§77.15 Nonaccredited States or zones.

(a) The following are nonaccredited States: None.

(b) The following are nonaccredited zones: None.

(c) To qualify for accreditation preparatory status, a nonaccredited State or zone must demonstrate to the Administrator that it complies with the provisions of the "Uniform Methods and Rules—Bovine Tuberculosis Eradication" and that tuberculosis is prevalent in less than 0.5 percent of the total number of herds of cattle and bison in the State or zone.

§77.16 Interstate movement from nonaccredited States and zones.

Cattle or bison that originate in a nonaccredited State or zone, and that are not known to be infected with or exposed to tuberculosis, may be moved interstate only if the cattle or bison are accompanied by VS Form 1–27 and are moved interstate for slaughter in an officially sealed means of conveyance directly to a recognized slaughtering establishment.

[65 FR 63517, Oct. 23, 2000, as amended at 78 FR 2066, Jan. 9, 2013]

§77.17 Interstate movement of cattle and bison that are exposed, reactors, or suspects, or from herds containing suspects.

(a) *Reactor cattle and bison.* Cattle or bison that have been classified as reactor cattle or bison may be moved interstate only if they are moved directly to slaughter at a recognized slaughtering establishment and only in accordance with the following conditions:

(1) Reactor cattle and bison must be individually identified by attaching to the left ear an approved metal eartag bearing a serial number and the inscription "U.S. Reactor," or a similar State reactor tag, and must be:

(i) Branded with the letter "T," at least 5 by 5 centimeters (2 by 2 inches) in size, high on the left hip near the tailhead; or

(ii) Permanently identified with the letters "TB" tattooed legibly in the left ear and sprayed with yellow paint on the left ear and either accompanied directly to slaughter by an APHIS or State representative or moved directly to slaughter in vehicles closed with official seals. Such official seals must be applied and removed by an APHIS representative, State representative, accredited veterinarian, or an individual authorized for this purpose by an APHIS representative.

(2) The reactor cattle or bison must be accompanied by a permit; and

(3) The reactor cattle or bison may not be moved interstate in a means of conveyance containing any animals susceptible to tuberculosis unless all of

the animals are being moved directly to slaughter; and

(4) Any person who moves reactor cattle or bison interstate under this paragraph must plainly write or stamp upon the face of the VS Form 1–27 the words "Tuberculin Reactor" and the following statement: "This conveyance must be cleaned and disinfected in accordance with 9 CFR 77.17(a)(5)."; and

(5) Each means of conveyance in which reactor cattle or bison have been transported interstate under this paragraph must be cleaned and disinfected by the carrier, in accordance with the provisions of §§ 71.6, 71.7, and 71.10 of this subchapter, under the supervision of an APHIS representative or State representative or an accredited veterinarian or other person designated by the Administrator. If, at the point where the cattle or bison are unloaded, such supervision or proper cleaning and disinfecting facilities are not available, and permission is obtained from an APHIS representative or State representative, the empty means of conveyance may be moved to a location where such supervision and facilities are available for cleaning and disinfecting. Permission will be granted if such movement does not present a risk of disseminating tuberculosis.

(b) *Exposed cattle and bison.* Except for the movement of exposed cattle to a quarantined feedlot in accordance with § 50.16 of this chapter, exposed cattle or bison may be moved interstate only if they are moved directly to slaughter to a recognized slaughtering establishment and only in accordance with the following conditions:

(1) Exposed cattle and bison must be individually identified by attaching to either ear an approved metal eartag bearing a serial number and must be:

(i) Branded with the letter "S," at least 5 by 5 centimeters (2 by 2 inches) in size, high on the left hip near the tailhead; or

(ii) Accompanied directly to slaughter by an APHIS or State representative; or

(iii) Moved directly to slaughter in vehicles closed with official seals. Such official seals must be applied and removed by an APHIS representative, State representative, accredited veterinarian, or an individual authorized for this purpose by an APHIS representative.

(2) The exposed cattle and bison must be moved in accordance with paragraphs (a)(2), (a)(3), and (a)(5) of this section.

(c) *Suspect cattle and bison.* Suspect cattle or bison from herds in which no reactor cattle or bison have been disclosed on an official tuberculin test, as well as negative cattle or bison from such herds, may be moved interstate only if they are moved directly to slaughter to a recognized slaughtering establishment in accordance with 9 CFR part 86.

(Approved by the Office of Management and Budget under control number 0579–0051)

[65 FR 63517, Oct. 23, 2000, as amended at 78 FR 2066, Jan. 9, 2013]

§ 77.18 Other movements.

The Administrator may, with the concurrence of the State animal health official of the State of destination, upon request in specific cases, allow the interstate movement of cattle or bison not otherwise provided for in this part that have not been classified as reactor cattle or bison and are not otherwise known to be affected with tuberculosis, under such conditions as the Administrator may prescribe in each specific case to prevent the spread of tuberculosis. The Administrator shall promptly notify the appropriate State animal health official of the State of destination of any such action.

§ 77.19 Cleaning and disinfection of premises, conveyances, and materials.

All conveyances and associated equipment, premises, and structures that are used for receiving, holding, shipping, loading, unloading, and delivering cattle or bison in connection with their interstate movement and that are determined by cooperating State and Federal animal health officials to be contaminated because of occupation or use by tuberculous or reactor livestock must be cleaned and disinfected under the supervision of the cooperating State or Federal animal health officials. Such cleaning and disinfecting must be done in accordance with procedures approved by the cooperating State or Federal animal health officials. Cleaning and disinfection must be completed before the premises, conveyances, or materials may again be used to convey, hold, or in any way come in contact with any livestock.

Subpart C—Captive Cervids

§77.20 Definitions.

As used in subpart C, the following terms shall have the meanings set forth in this section except as otherwise specified.

Accreditation preparatory State or zone. A State or zone that is or is part of a State that has the authority to enforce and complies with the provisions of the "Uniform Methods and Rules—Bovine Tuberculosis Eradication" and in which tuberculosis is prevalent in less than 0.5 percent of the total number of herds of captive cervids in the State or zone.

Accredited herd. A herd of captive cervids that has tested negative to at least two consecutive official tuberculosis tests of all eligible captive cervids in accordance with §77.33(f) and that meets the standards set forth in §77.35. The tests must be conducted at 9–15 month intervals.

Accredited-free State or zone. A State or zone that is or is part of a State that has the authority to enforce and complies with the provisions of the "Uniform Methods and Rules—Bovine Tuberculosis Eradication," has zero percent prevalence of affected captive cervid herds, and has had no findings of tuberculosis in any captive cervid herds in the State or zone for the previous 5 years. *Except that:* The requirement of freedom from tuberculosis in herds is 2 years from the depopulation of the last affected herd in States or zones that were previously accredited free and in which all herds affected with tuberculosis were depopulated, 3 years in all other States or zones that have depopulated all affected herds, and 3 years in States or zones that have conducted surveillance that demonstrates that other livestock herds and wildlife are not at risk of being infected with tuberculosis, as determined by the Administrator based on a risk assessment conducted by APHIS.

Captive cervid. All species of deer, elk, moose, and all other members of the family Cervidae raised or maintained in captivity for the production of meat and other agricultural products, for sport, or for exhibition, including time such animals are moved interstate; or any wild cervid that is moved interstate, during the period of time from capture until release into the wild. A captive cervid that escapes will continue to be considered a captive cervid as long as it bears an official eartag or other identification approved by the Administrator as unique and traceable with which to trace the animal back to its herd of origin.

Comparative cervical tuberculin (CCT) test. The intradermal injection of biologically balanced USDA bovine PPD tuberculin and avian PPD tuberculin at separate sites in the mid-cervical area to determine the probable presence of bovine tuberculosis (*M. bovis*) by comparing the response of the two tuberculins at 72 hours (plus or minus 6 hours) following injection.

Designated accredited veterinarian. An accredited veterinarian who is trained and approved by cooperating State and Federal animal health officials to conduct the single cervical tuberculin (SCT) test or draw blood for the DPP® test on captive cervids.

Dual Path Platform (DPP®) test. A serological assay to determine the presence of antibodies to bovine tuberculosis (*M. bovis*) in elk, red deer, white-tailed deer, fallow deer, and reindeer, in which a blood sample taken from a captive cervid and a buffer solution are placed on a strip. The diluted sample then migrates to another strip, which contains an antibody-detecting reagent. This latter strip indicates if antibodies are present in the sample.

Exposed captive cervid. Any captive cervid that has been exposed to tuberculosis by reason of associating with captive cervids, cattle, bison, or other livestock from which *M. bovis* has been isolated.

Modified accredited State or zone. A State or zone that is or is part of a State that has the authority to enforce and complies with the provisions of the "Uniform Methods and Rules—Bovine Tuberculosis Eradication" and in which tuberculosis has been prevalent in less than 0.1 percent of the total number of herds of captive cervids in the State or zone for the most recent year. *Except that:* The Administrator, upon his or her review, may allow a State or zone with fewer than 10,000 herds to have up to 10 affected herds for the most recent year, depending on the veterinary infrastructure, livestock demographics, and tuberculosis control and eradication measures in the State or zone.

Modified accredited advanced State or zone. A State or zone that is or is part of a State that has the authority to enforce and complies with the provisions of the "Uniform Methods and Rules—Bovine Tuberculosis Eradication" and in which tuberculosis has been prevalent in less than 0.01 percent of the total number of herds of captive cervids in the State or zone for the most recent 2 years. *Except that:* The Administrator, upon his or her review, may allow a State or zone with fewer than 30,000 herds to have up to 3 affected herds for each of the most recent 2 years, depending on the veterinary infrastructure, livestock demographics, and tuberculosis control and eradication measures in the State or zone.

Monitored herd. A herd on which identification records are maintained on captive cervids inspected for tuberculosis at an approved slaughtering establishment or an approved diagnostic laboratory and on captive cervids tested for tuberculosis in accordance with interstate movement requirements, and which meets the standards set forth in § 77.37.

Negative. Showing no response to an official tuberculosis test or classified negative for tuberculosis by the testing veterinarian based upon history, supplemental tests, examination of the carcass, and histopathology and culture of selected tissues.

No gross lesions (NGL). Having no visible lesions indicative of bovine tuberculosis detected upon necropsy or slaughter inspection.

Nonaccredited State or zone. A State or zone that is or is part of a State or zone that does not meet the standards of the "Uniform Methods and Rules—Bovine Tuberculosis Eradication" or in which tuberculosis is prevalent in 0.5 percent or more of the total number of herds of captive cervids in the State or zone.

Official tuberculosis test. Any of the following tests for bovine tuberculosis in captive cervids, applied and reported in accordance with this part:

(1) The single cervical tuberculin (SCT) test.

(2) The comparative cervical tuberculin test (CCT) test.

(3) The Dual Path Platform (DPP®) test.

Permit. An official document issued by a representative of APHIS, a State representative, or an accredited veterinarian that must accompany any reactor, suspect, or exposed captive cervid moved interstate.

Purified protein derivative (PPD). Protein extract from an *M. bovis* culture that is resuspended in solution at a standard concentration of 1 mg protein per 1 mL of solution.

Qualified herd. A herd of captive cervids that has tested negative to at least one official tuberculosis test of all eligible captive cervids (see § 77.33(f)) within the past 12 months and that is not classified as an accredited herd.

Quarantine. Prohibition from interstate movement, except for slaughter or necropsy.

Reactor. Any captive cervid that shows a response to an official tuberculosis test and is classified a reactor by the testing veterinarian; or any suspect captive cervid that is classified a reactor upon slaughter inspection or necropsy after histopathology and/or culture of selected tissues by the USDA or State veterinarian performing or supervising the slaughter inspection or necropsy.

Regular-kill slaughter animal. An animal that is slaughtered for food or any reason other than because of a disease regulated under 9 CFR chapter I (such as tuberculosis, brucellosis, or any other livestock disease for which movement of animals is restricted under 9 CFR chapter I).

Single cervical tuberculin (SCT) test. The intradermal injection of 0.1 mL (5,000 tuberculin units) of USDA PPD bovis tuberculin in the mid-cervical area with a reading by visual observation and palpation at 72 hours (plus or minus 6 hours) following injection.

Suspect. Any captive cervid that is not negative to an official tuberculosis test and that is not classified as a reactor by the testing veterinarian.

Tuberculin. A product that is approved by and produced under USDA license for injection into cervids and other animals for the purpose of detecting bovine tuberculosis.

Tuberculous. Having lesions indicative of tuberculosis, infected with tuberculosis based on isolation of *M. bovis*, or being from a herd in which *M. bovis* has been isolated.

USDA. The United States Department of Agriculture.

Whole herd test. An official tuberculosis test of all captive cervids in a herd that are 12 months of age or older, and of all captive cervids in the herd that are less than 12 months of age and were not born into the herd, except those captive cervids that are less than 12 months of age and were born in and originated from an accredited herd.

Zero percent prevalence. No finding of tuberculosis in any herd of captive cervids in a State or zone.

[65 FR 63517, Oct. 23, 2000, as amended at 70 FR 61026, Oct. 20, 2005; 71 FR 24805, Apr. 27, 2006; 78 FR 1721, Jan. 9, 2013; 79 FR 43926, July 29, 2014]

§ 77.21 Applicability of this subpart.

All references in this subpart to the tuberculosis status of States and zones pertain to such status for captive cervids.

§ 77.22 Accredited-free States or zones.

(a) The following are accredited-free States: None.

(b) The following are accredited-free zones: None.

(c) If an affected herd is detected in a State or zone classified as accredited-free, and the herd is depopulated and a complete epidemiologic investigation is completed within 120 days of the detection of the affected herd with no evidence of the spread of tuberculosis, the State or zone may retain its accredited-free status. If two or more affected herds are detected in an accredited-free State or zone within a 48-month period, the State or zone will be removed from the list of accredited-free States or zones and will be reclassified as modified accredited advanced.

(d) If any livestock other than captive cervids are included in a newly assembled herd on a premises where a tuberculous herd has been depopulated, the State or zone must apply the herd test requirements contained in the "Uniform Methods and Rules—Bovine Tuberculosis Eradication" (January 22, 1999 edition), which is incorporated by reference at § 77.1, to those other livestock in the same manner as to captive cervids. Failure to do so will result in reclassification of the State or zone as modified accredited advanced.

(e) If tuberculosis is diagnosed within an accredited-free State or zone in an animal not specifically regulated by this part and a risk assessment conducted by APHIS determines that the outbreak poses a tuberculosis risk to livestock within the State or zone, the State or zone must implement a tuberculosis management plan, approved jointly by the State animal health official and the Administrator, within 6 months of the diagnosis. The management plan must include provisions for immediate investigation of tuberculosis in animals held for exhibition and in livestock and wildlife; the prevention of the spread of the disease to other animals held for exhibition and to livestock and wildlife; increased surveillance for tuberculosis in animals held for exhibition and wildlife; eradication of tuberculosis from individual herds; a timeline for tuberculosis eradication; and performance standards by which to measure yearly progress toward eradication. If a State or zone does not implement such a plan within the required 6 months, the State or zone will lose its accredited-free status and will be reclassified as modified accredited advanced.

(f) Accredited-free State or zone status must be renewed annually. To qualify for renewal of accredited-free State or zone status, a State must submit an annual report to APHIS certifying that the State or zone within the State complies with the provisions of the "Uniform Methods and Rules—Bovine Tuberculosis Eradication." The report must be submitted to APHIS each year between October 1 and November 30.

(Approved by the Office of Management and Budget under control number 0579–0146)

§ 77.23 Interstate movement from accredited-free States and zones.

Notwithstanding any other provisions of this part, captive cervids that originate in an accredited-free State or zone may be moved interstate in accordance with 9 CFR part 86 and without further restriction under this part.

[78 FR 2066, Jan. 9, 2013]

§ 77.24 Modified accredited advanced States or zones.

(a) The following are modified accredited advanced States: None.

(b) The following are modified accredited advanced zones: None.

(c) If any livestock other than captive cervids are included in a newly assembled herd on a premises where a tuberculous herd has been depopulated, the State or zone must apply the herd test requirements contained in the "Uniform Methods and Rules—Bovine Tuberculosis Eradication" (January 22, 1999 edition), which is incorporated by reference at § 77.1, for such newly assembled herds to those other livestock in the same manner as to captive cervids. Failure to do so will result in the removal of the State or zone from the list of modified accredited advanced States or zones and its being reclassified as modified accredited.

(d) If tuberculosis is diagnosed within a modified accredited advanced State or zone in an animal not specifically regulated by this part and a risk assessment conducted by APHIS determines that the outbreak poses a tuberculosis risk to livestock within the State or zone, the State or zone must implement a tuberculosis management plan, approved jointly by the State animal health official and the Administrator, within 6 months of the diagnosis. The management plan must include provisions for immediate investigation of tuberculosis in animals held for exhibition and in livestock and wildlife; the prevention of the spread of the disease to other animals held for exhibition and to livestock and wildlife; increased surveillance for tuberculosis in animals held for exhibition and wildlife; eradication of tuberculosis from individual herds; a timeline for tuberculosis eradication; and performance standards by which to measure yearly progress toward eradication. If a State or zone does not implement such a plan within the required 6 months, the State or zone will be reclassified as modified accredited.

(e) Modified accredited advanced State or zone status must be renewed annually. To qualify for renewal of a modified accredited advanced State or zone status, a State must submit an annual report to APHIS certifying that the State or zone complies with all the provisions of the "Uniform Methods and Rules—Bovine Tuberculosis Eradication" regarding modified accredited advanced States. The report must be submitted to APHIS each year between October 1 and November 30.

(f) To qualify for accredited-free status, a modified accredited advanced State or zone must demonstrate to the Administrator that it complies with the provisions of the "Uniform Methods and Rules—Bovine Tuberculosis Eradication," has zero percent prevalence of affected captive cervid herds, and has had no findings of tuberculosis in any captive cervids in the State or zone for the previous 5 years. *Except that:* The requirement of freedom from tuberculosis is 2 years from the depopulation of the last affected herd in States or zones that were previously accredited-free and in which all herds affected with tuberculosis were depopulated, 3 years in all other States or zones that have depopulated all affected herds, and 3 years in States or zones that have conducted surveillance that demonstrates that other livestock herds and wildlife are not at risk of being infected with tuberculosis, as determined by the Administrator based on a risk assessment conducted by APHIS.

(Approved by the Office of Management and Budget under control number 0579–0146)

§ 77.25 Interstate movement from modified accredited advanced States and zones.

Captive cervids that originate in a modified accredited advanced State or zone, and that are not known to be infected with or exposed to tuberculosis, may be moved interstate only in accordance with 9 CFR part 86 and, if moved anywhere other than directly to slaughter at a recognized slaughtering establishment, under one of the following additional conditions:

(a) The captive cervids are from an accredited herd, qualified herd, or monitored herd; are officially identified; and are accompanied by an ICVI stating that the herd completed the requirements for accredited herd, qualified herd, or monitored herd status within 24 months prior to the date of movement.

(b) The captive cervids are officially identified and are accompanied by an ICVI stating that they were negative to an official tuberculin test conducted within 90 days prior to the date of movement.

(Approved by the Office of Management and Budget under control number 0579–0146)

[78 FR 2066, Jan. 9, 2013]

§77.26 Modified accredited States or zones.

(a) States listed in paragraph (b) of this section must submit to APHIS[1] by October 23, 2001 data demonstrating that the State complies with the UMR or the State will be redesignated as nonaccredited. If a State does submit surveillance data by October 23, 2001 that meets the UMR standards, and that APHIS believes qualifies the State for a classification other than modified accredited, APHIS will initiate rulemaking to change the State's classification.

(b) The following are modified accredited States: Alabama, Alaska, Arizona, Arkansas, California, Colorado, Connecticut, Delaware, Florida, Georgia, Hawaii, Idaho, Illinois, Indiana, Iowa, Kansas, Kentucky, Louisiana, Maine, Maryland, Massachusetts, Michigan, Minnesota, Mississippi, Missouri, Montana, Nebraska, Nevada, New Hampshire, New Jersey, New Mexico, New York, North Carolina, North Dakota, Ohio, Oklahoma, Oregon, Pennsylvania, Puerto Rico, Rhode Island, South Carolina, South Dakota, Tennessee, Texas, Utah, Vermont, the Virgin Islands of the United States, Virginia, Washington, West Virginia, Wisconsin, and Wyoming.

(c) The following are modified accredited zones: None.

(d) If any livestock other than captive cervids are included in a newly assembled herd on a premises where a tuberculous herd has been depopulated, the State or zone must apply the herd test requirements contained in the "Uniform Methods and Rules—Bovine Tuberculosis Eradication" (January 22, 1999, edition), which is incorporated by reference at §77.1, for such newly assembled herds to those other livestock in the same manner as to captive cervids. Failure to do so will result in the removal of the State or zone from the list of modified accredited States or zones and its being reclassified as accreditation preparatory.

(e) If tuberculosis is diagnosed within a modified accredited State or zone in an animal not specifically regulated by this part and a risk assessment conducted by APHIS determines that the outbreak poses a tuberculosis risk to livestock within the State or zone, the State or zone must implement a tuberculosis management plan, approved jointly by the State animal health official and the Administrator, within 6 months of the diagnosis. The management plan must include provisions for immediate investigation of tuberculosis in animals held for exhibition and in livestock and wildlife; the prevention of the spread of the disease to other animals held for exhibition and to livestock and wildlife; increased surveillance for tuberculosis in animals held for exhibition and wildlife; eradication of tuberculosis from individual herds; a timeline for tuberculosis eradication; and performance standards by which to measure yearly progress toward eradication. If a State or zone does not implement such a plan within the required 6 months, the State or zone will be reclassified as accreditation preparatory.

(f) Modified accredited State or zone status must be renewed annually. To qualify for renewal of a modified accredited State or zone status, a State

[1] Send the information to National Animal Health Programs, Veterinary Services, APHIS, 4700 River Road, Unit 42, Riverdale, Maryland 20737–1231.

must submit an annual report to APHIS certifying that the State or zone complies with the provisions of the "Uniform Methods and Rules—Bovine Tuberculosis Eradication." The report must be submitted to APHIS each year between October 1 and November 30.

(g) To qualify for modified accredited advanced status, a modified accredited State or zone must demonstrate to the Administrator that it complies with the provisions of the "Uniform Methods and Rules—Bovine Tuberculosis Eradication" and that tuberculosis has been prevalent in less than 0.01 percent of the total number of captive cervids in the State or zone for the most recent 2 years. *Except that:* The Administrator, upon his or her review, may allow a State or zone with fewer than 30,000 herds to have up to 3 affected herds for each of the most recent 2 years, depending on the veterinary infrastructure, livestock demographics, and tuberculosis control and eradication measures in the State or zone.

(Approved by the Office of Management and Budget under control number 0579–0146)

§ 77.27 Interstate movement from modified accredited States and zones.

Except for captive cervids from a qualified herd or monitored herd, as provided in §§ 77.36 and 77.37, respectively, captive cervids that originate in a modified accredited State or zone, and that are not known to be infected with or exposed to tuberculosis, may be moved interstate only in accordance with 9 CFR part 86 and, if moved anywhere other than directly to slaughter at a recognized slaughtering establishment, under one of the following additional conditions:

(a) The captive cervids are from an accredited herd, are officially identified, and are accompanied by an ICVI stating that the accredited herd completed the testing necessary for accredited status with negative results within 24 months prior to the date of movement.

(b) The captive cervids are sexually intact animals; are not from an accredited herd; are officially identified; and are accompanied by an ICVI stating that the herd from which they originated was negative to a whole herd test conducted within 1 year prior to the date of movement and that the individual animals to be moved were negative to an additional official tuberculin test conducted within 90 days prior to the date of movement; *Except that:* The additional test is not required if the animals are moved interstate within 6 months following the whole herd test.

(Approved by the Office of Management and Budget under control number 0579–0146)

[78 FR 2066, Jan. 9, 2013]

§ 77.28 Accreditation preparatory States or zones.

(a) The following are accreditation preparatory States: None.

(b) The following are accreditation preparatory zones: None.

(c) If any livestock other than captive cervids are included in a newly assembled herd on a premises where a tuberculous herd has been depopulated, the State or zone must apply the herd test requirements contained in the "Uniform Methods and Rules—Bovine Tuberculosis Eradication" (January 22, 1999, edition), which is incorporated by reference at § 77.1, for such newly assembled herds to those other livestock in the same manner as to captive cervids. Failure to do so will result in the removal of the State or zone from the list of accreditation preparatory States or zones and its being reclassified as nonaccredited.

(d) If tuberculosis is diagnosed within an accreditation preparatory State or zone in an animal not specifically regulated by this part and a risk assessment conducted by APHIS determines that the outbreak poses a tuberculosis risk to livestock within the State or zone, the State or zone must implement a tuberculosis management plan, approved jointly by the State animal health official and the Administrator, within 6 months of the diagnosis. The management plan must include provisions for immediate investigation of tuberculosis in animals held for exhibition and in livestock and wildlife; the prevention of the spread of the disease to other animals held for exhibition and to livestock and wildlife; increased surveillance for tuberculosis in animals held for exhibition and wildlife;

eradication of tuberculosis from individual herds; a timeline for tuberculosis eradication; and performance standards by which to measure yearly progress toward eradication. If a State or zone does not implement such a plan within the required 6 months, the State or zone will be reclassified as nonaccredited.

(e) Accreditation preparatory State or zone status must be renewed annually. To qualify for renewal of accreditation preparatory State or zone status, a State must submit an annual report to APHIS certifying that the State or zone complies with the provisions of the "Uniform Methods and Rules—Bovine Tuberculosis Eradication." The report must be submitted to APHIS each year between October 1 and November 30.

(f) To qualify for modified accredited status, an accreditation preparatory State or zone must demonstrate to the Administrator that it complies with the provisions of the "Uniform Methods and Rules—Bovine Tuberculosis Eradication" and that tuberculosis has been prevalent in less than 0.1 percent of the total number of herds of captive cervids in the State or zone for the most recent year. *Except that:* The Administrator, upon his or her review, may allow a State or zone with fewer than 10,000 herds to have up to 10 affected herds for the most recent year, depending on the veterinary infrastructure, livestock demographics, and tuberculosis control and eradication measures in the State or zone.

(Approved by the Office of Management and Budget under control number 0579–0146)

§ 77.29 Interstate movement from accreditation preparatory States and zones.

Except for captive cervids from a qualified herd or monitored herd, as provided in §§ 77.36 and 77.37, respectively, captive cervids that originate in an accreditation preparatory State or zone, and that are not known to be infected with or exposed to tuberculosis, may be moved interstate only in accordance with 9 CFR part 86 and, if moved anywhere other than directly to slaughter at a recognized slaughtering establishment, under one of the following additional conditions:

(a) The captive cervids are from an accredited herd; are officially identified; and are accompanied by an ICVI stating that the accredited herd completed the testing necessary for accredited status with negative results within 24 months prior to the date of movement and that the individual animals to be moved were negative to an official tuberculin test conducted within 90 days prior to the date of movement.

(b) The captive cervids are sexually intact animals; are not from an accredited herd; are officially identified; and are accompanied by an ICVI stating that the herd from which they originated was negative to a whole herd test conducted within 1 year prior to the date of movement and that the individual animals to be moved were negative to two additional official tuberculin tests conducted at least 90 days apart and no more than 6 months apart, with the second test conducted within 90 days prior to the date of movement; *Except that:* The second additional test is not required if the animals are moved interstate within 6 months following the whole herd test.

(Approved by the Office of Management and Budget under control number 0579–0146)

[78 FR 2067, Jan. 9, 2013]

§ 77.30 Nonaccredited States or zones.

(a) The following are nonaccredited States: None.

(b) The following are nonaccredited zones: None.

(c) To qualify for accreditation preparatory status, a nonaccredited State or zone must demonstrate to the Administrator that it complies with the provisions of the "Uniform Methods and Rules—Bovine Tuberculosis Eradication" and that tuberculosis is prevalent in less than 0.5 percent of the total number of herds of captive cervids in the State or zone.

§ 77.31 Interstate movement from nonaccredited States and zones.

Captive cervids that originate in a nonaccredited State or zone and that are not known to be infected with or exposed to tuberculosis may not be moved interstate only if they are accompanied by VS Form 1–27 and are moved interstate in an officially sealed means of conveyance directly to slaughter at a recognized slaughtering establishment.

[65 FR 63517, Oct. 23, 2000, as amended at 78 FR 2067, Jan. 9, 2013]

§ 77.32 General restrictions.

(a) Except for movement from accredited-free States and zones in accordance with § 77.23, movement from accredited herds in accordance with § 77.35, and movement to slaughter in accordance with 9 CFR part 86, no captive cervid may be moved interstate unless it has been tested using an official tuberculosis test, and it is moved in compliance with this part.

(b) No captive cervid with a response to any official tuberculosis test is eligible for interstate movement unless the captive cervid subsequently tests negative to a supplemental official tuberculosis test or is moved interstate directly to slaughter or necropsy in accordance with § 7.40.

(c) Except for captive cervids moving interstate under permit directly to slaughter or necropsy under § 77.40, each captive cervid or shipment of captive cervids to be moved interstate must be officially identified and accompanied by an ICVI issued within 30 days of the movement by a State or Federal animal health official or an accredited veterinarian.

(d) Captive cervids in zoological parks that have been accredited by the American Zoo and Aquarium Association (AZA) are exempt from the regulations in this part when the captive cervids are moved directly interstate between AZA member facilities. Any captive cervids moved interstate that are not moved directly from an AZA member facility to another AZA member facility must be moved in accordance with the regulations in this subpart.

[65 FR 63517, Oct. 23, 2000, as amended at 78 FR 2067, Jan. 9, 2013]

§ 77.33 Testing procedures for tuberculosis in captive cervids.

(a) *Approved testers.* Except as explained in paragraphs (a)(1) or (a)(2) of this section, official tuberculosis tests may only be given by a veterinarian employed by the State in which the test is administered or by a veterinarian employed by USDA.

(1) A designated accredited veterinarian may conduct the SCT test, except as provided in § 77.34(a)(1)(ii) and § 77.39(e) and (f).

(2) A designated accredited veterinarian may draw blood for the DPP® test.

(b) *Approved diagnostic laboratories.* (1) With one exception, histopathology and culture results for all tuberculosis diagnoses will be accepted only from the National Veterinary Services Laboratories (NVSL) in Ames, IA. The exception is that results will be accepted from a laboratory of the Food Safety and Inspection Service, USDA, for tissue examination of regular-kill slaughter animals in those cases where no submission is made to NVSL.

(2) [Reserved]

(c) *Identification.* Any captive cervid tested with an official tuberculosis test must bear official identification in the form of an official eartag, or another identification device or method approved by the Administrator as unique and traceable, at the time of the official tuberculosis test. Use of any identification device or method other than an official eartag must first be approved by the Administrator as unique and traceable. Written requests for approval must be sent to National Animal Health Programs, VS, APHIS, 4700 River Road Unit 43, Riverdale, MD 20737–1231.

(d) *Reporting of tests*—(1) *SCT and CCT tests.* For the SCT and CCT tests, the testing veterinarian must submit a report to cooperating State and Federal animal health officials of the State in which the captive cervid is tested. The report must include the following information for all SCT and CCT tests administered: The number of the individual eartag or other identification approved by the Administrator; the age, sex, and breed of each captive cervid tested; a record of all responses; the size of each response for the CCT test; and the test interpretation.

(2) *DPP® test.* The veterinarian who draws blood from the captive cervid must submit a form specified by APHIS for such requests to NVSL to perform the DPP® test on the blood sample. The form is available at the following

Web site: *http://www.aphis.usda.gov/wps/portal/footer/resources/forms;* click on the "VS forms" link on that Web page. The veterinarian must also fill out the relevant portions of a test record. This form may be obtained by contacting the local district VS office, information regarding which is available at: *http://www.aphis.usda.gov/wps/portal/aphis/ourfocus/animalhealth? 1dmy&urile = wcm%3apath%3a %2Faphis_content_library%2Fsa_ our_focus %2Fsa_ animal_health %2Fsa_contact_ us%2Fsa_map%2Fct_ state_contacts_map.* This record must be sent to the offices of the State and Federal animal health officials in the State.

(e) *Test interpretation.* (1) Interpretation of an SCT test will be based upon the judgment of the testing veterinarian after observation and palpation of the injection site, in accordance with the classification requirements described in § 77.34(a).

(2) Interpretation of a CCT test will be in accordance with the classification requirements described in § 77.34(b).

(3) Interpretation of DPP® test results will be in accordance with the classification requirements described in § 77.34.

(f) *Captive cervids eligible for testing.* Except as provided in § 77.35(a)(1) and § 77.36(a)(1), testing of herds for individual herd classification must include all captive cervids 1 year of age or over and any captive cervids other than natural additions (captive cervids born into the herd) under 1 year of age.

(Approved by the Office of Management and Budget under control number 0579–0412)

[65 FR 63517, Oct. 23, 2000, as amended at 71 FR 24806, Apr. 27, 2006; 78 FR 1722, Jan. 9, 2013; 79 FR 43926, July 29, 2014]

§ 77.34 Official tuberculosis tests.

(a) *Primary tests.* (1) *Single cervical tuberculin (SCT) test.* (i) The SCT test is a primary test that may be used in individual captive cervids and in herds of unknown tuberculous status. Each captive cervid that responds to the SCT test must be classified as a suspect until it is retested with the CCT test and is either found negative for tuberculosis or is classified as a reactor, unless, with exception of a designated accredited veterinarian, the testing veterinarian determines that the captive cervid should be classified as a reactor based on its response to the SCT test. A designated accredited veterinarian must classify a responding captive cervid as a suspect, unless APHIS determines, based on epidemiological evidence, that the captive cervid should be classified as a reactor. A captive cervid that responds to the SCT test must not be retested using the DPP® test.

(ii) The SCT test is a primary test that may be used in affected herds and in herds that have received captive cervids from an affected herd. When used with affected herds or in herds that have received a captive cervid from an affected herd, the SCT test may only be administered by a veterinarian employed by the State in which the test is administered or employed by USDA. In affected herds or herds that have received captive cervids from an affected herd, each captive cervid that responds to the SCT test must be classified as a reactor, unless APHIS determines, based on epidemiological evidence, that the cervid should be classified as a suspect because of possible exposure to a tuberculous animal.

(2) *DPP® test.* (i) The DPP® test is a primary test that may be used in individual captive elk, red deer, white-tailed deer, fallow deer, and reindeer, and in herds of these species that are of unknown tuberculous status. Except as specified in paragraph (a)(2)(ii) of this section, each captive cervid that has non-negative test results to this initial DPP® test will be classified as a suspect and retested with the DPP® test. A captive cervid that has non-negative test results to the DPP® test must not be retested using the SCT or CCT test.

(ii) The DPP® test is a primary test that may be used in affected herds of captive elk, red deer, white-tailed deer, fallow deer, and reindeer, and in herds of these species that have received captive cervids from an affected herd. In such herds, each captive cervid that has non-negative test results to the DPP® test will be classified as a reactor, unless APHIS determines that the captive cervid should be classified as a suspect because of possible exposure to a tuberculous animal.

(b) *Supplemental tests.* (1) *Comparative cervical tuberculin (CCT) test.*

(i) The CCT test is a supplemental test that may only be used in order to retest captive cervids that have been classified as suspects after being tested with the SCT test. The CCT test may be used in affected herds only after the herd has tested negative to at least two whole herd SCT tests and only with the prior written consent of APHIS. The CCT test may not be used as a primary test.

(ii) A captive cervid tested with the CCT test must be classified as negative if it has a response to the bovine PPD tuberculin that is less than 1 mm.

(iii) Unless the testing veterinarian determines that the captive cervid should be classified as a reactor because of possible exposure to a tuberculous animal, a captive cervid tested with the CCT test must be classified as a suspect if:

(A) It has a response to the bovine PPD tuberculin that is greater than 2 mm and that is equal to the response to the avian PPD tuberculin; or

(B) It has a response to the bovine PPD tuberculin that is equal to or greater than 1 mm and equal to or less than 2 mm and that is equal to or greater than the response to the avian PPD tuberculin.

(iv) A captive cervid tested with the CCT test must be classified as a reactor if:

(A) It has a response to the bovine PPD tuberculin that is greater than 2 mm and that is at least 0.5 mm greater than the response to the avian PPD tuberculin; or

(B) It has been classified as a suspect on two successive CCT tests.

(C) Any exceptions to the reactor classification under the conditions in paragraph (b)(1)(iv) of this section must be justified by the testing veterinarian in writing and have the concurrence of APHIS.

(2) *DPP® test.* The DPP® test may be used as a supplemental test in order to retest captive cervids that have been classified as suspects based on an initial DPP® test. In such instances, the supplemental DPP® test must evaluate a new serum sample drawn from the cervid no sooner than 30 days after the initial DPP® test. A captive cervid that has non-negative test results on two successive DPP® tests will be classified as a reactor, unless APHIS determines that another disease classification is warranted.

[78 FR 1722, Jan. 9, 2013, as amended at 79 FR 43926, July 29, 2014]

§ 77.35 Interstate movement from accredited herds.

(a) *Qualifications.* To be recognized as an accredited herd:

(1) All captive cervids in the herd eligible for testing in accordance with § 77.33(f) must have tested negative to at least two consecutive official tuberculosis tests, conducted at 9–15 month intervals. However, captive cervids under 1 year of age that are not natural additions to the herd do not have to be tested if they were born in and originate from an accredited herd.

(2) The owner of the herd must have a document issued by cooperating State or Federal animal health officials stating that the herd has met the requirements in paragraph (a)(1) of this section and is classified as an accredited herd.

(b) *Movement allowed.* Except as provided in § 77.23 with regard to captive cervids that originate in an accredited-free State or zone, and except as provided in § 77.31 with regard to captive cervids that originate in a nonaccredited State or zone, a captive cervid from an accredited herd may be moved interstate without further tuberculosis testing only if it is officially identified and is accompanied by an ICVI, as provided in § 77.32(c), that includes a statement that the captive cervid is from an accredited herd. If a group of captive cervids from an accredited herd is being moved interstate together to the same destination, all captive cervids in the group may be moved under one ICVI.

(c) *Herd additions allowed.* No captive cervid may be added to an accredited herd except in accordance with paragraphs (c)(4) and (c)(5), and either paragraph (c)(1), (c)(2), or (c)(3) of this section, as follows:

(1) The captive cervid to be added must be moved directly from an accredited herd;

(2) The captive cervid to be added must be moved directly from a qualified or monitored herd and must have tested negative to an official tuberculosis test conducted within 90 days prior to movement to the premises of the accredited herd. Any captive cervid moved from a qualified or monitored herd must also be isolated from all members of the accredited herd until it tests negative to an official tuberculosis test conducted at least 90 days following the date of arrival at the premises of the accredited herd. If a group of captive cervids is being moved together, the entire group must be isolated from all other livestock during the testing period, but captive cervids in the group need not be isolated from each other during that period. Such herd additions will not receive status as members of the accredited herd for purposes of interstate movement until they have tested negative to an official tuberculosis test and have been released from isolation; or

(3) If the captive cervid to be added is not being moved directly from a classified herd, the captive cervid must be isolated from all other members of the herd of origin and must test negative to two official tuberculosis tests. The isolation must begin at the time of the first official tuberculosis test. The tests must be conducted at least 90 days apart, and the second test must be conducted within 90 days prior to movement to the premises of the accredited herd. The captive cervid must also be isolated from all members of the accredited herd until it tests negative to an official tuberculosis test conducted at least 90 days following the date of arrival at the premises of the accredited herd. If a group of captive cervids is being moved together, the entire group must be isolated from all other animals during the testing period, but captive cervids in the group need not be isolated from each other during that period. Such herd additions will not receive status as members of the accredited herd for purposes of interstate movement until they have tested negative to an official tuberculosis test and have been released from isolation.

(4) A captive cervid to be added must not have been exposed during the 90 days prior to its movement to either:

(i) A captive cervid from a herd with a lower classification status than its own; or

(ii) Any tuberculous livestock.

(d) *Maintenance of accredited herd status.* To maintain status as an accredited herd, the herd must test negative to an official tuberculosis test within 33–39 months from the anniversary date of the second consecutive test with no evidence of tuberculosis disclosed (that is, the test on which the herd was recognized as accredited or the accrediting test). Each time the herd is tested for reaccreditation, it must be tested 33–39 months from the anniversary date of the accrediting test, not from the last date of reaccreditation (for example, if a herd is accredited on January 1 of a given year, the anniversary date will be January 1 of every third year). Accredited herd status is valid for 36 months (1,095 days) from the anniversary date of the accrediting test. If the herd is tested between 36 and 39 months after the anniversary date, its accredited herd status will be suspended for the interim between the anniversary date and the reaccreditation test. During the suspension period, the herd will be considered "unclassified" and captive cervids may be moved interstate from the herd only in accordance with the movement requirements for the State or zone in which the herd is located.

[65 FR 63517, Oct. 23, 2000, as amended at 71 FR 24806, Apr. 27, 2006; 78 FR 2067, Jan. 9, 2013]

§ 77.36 Interstate movement from qualified herds.

(a) *Qualifications.* To be recognized as a qualified herd:

(1) All captive cervids in the herd eligible for testing in accordance with § 77.33(f) must have tested negative to one official tuberculosis test that was administered to the herd within a 7-month period. However, captive cervids under 1 year of age that are not natural additions do not have to be tested if they were born in and originate from an accredited, qualified, or monitored herd.

(2) The owner of the herd must have a document issued by cooperating State and Federal animal health officials stating that the herd has met the requirement in paragraph (a)(1) of this section and is classified as a qualified herd.

(b) *Movement allowed.* Except as provided in § 77.23 with regard to captive cervids that originate in an accredited-free State or zone, and except as provided in § 77.31 with regard to captive cervids that originate in a nonaccredited State or zone, a captive cervid from a qualified herd may be moved interstate only if:

(1) The captive cervid is not known to be infected with or exposed to tuberculosis; and

(2) The captive cervid is officially identified and is accompanied by an ICVI, as provided in § 77.32(c), that includes a statement that the captive cervid is from a qualified herd. Except as provided in paragraphs (b)(3) and (b)(4) of this section, the ICVI must also state that the captive cervid has tested negative to an official tuberculosis test conducted within 90 days prior to the date of movement. If a group of captive cervids from a qualified herd is being moved interstate together to the same destination, all captive cervids in the group may be moved under one ICVI.

(3) Captive cervids under 1 year of age that are natural additions to the qualified herd or that were born in and originate from a classified herd may move without testing, provided that they are officially identified and that the ICVI accompanying them states that the captive cervids are natural additions to the qualified herd or were born in and originated from a classified herd and have not been exposed to captive cervids from an unclassified herd.

(4) Captive cervids being moved interstate for the purpose of exhibition only may be moved without testing, provided they are returned to the premises of origin no more than 90 days after leaving the premises, have no contact with other livestock during movement and exhibition, are officially identified, and are accompanied by an ICVI that includes a statement that the captive cervid is from a qualified herd and will otherwise meet the requirements of this paragraph.

(c) *Herd additions allowed.* No captive cervid may be added to a qualified herd except in accordance with paragraph (c)(4) and either paragraph (c)(1), (c)(2), or (c)(3) of this section, as follows:

(1) The captive cervid to be added must be moved directly from an accredited herd;

(2) The captive cervid to be added must be moved directly from a qualified or monitored herd and must have tested negative to an official tuberculosis test conducted within 90 days prior to movement to the premises of the accredited herd;

(3) If the captive cervid to be added is not being moved directly from a classified herd, the captive cervid must be isolated from all other animals in its herd of origin and must test negative to two official tuberculosis tests prior to movement. The isolation must begin at the time of the first official tuberculosis test. The tests must be conducted at least 90 days apart, and the second test must be conducted within 90 days prior to movement to the premises of the qualified herd. The captive cervid must then be kept in isolation from all animals until it tests negative to an official tuberculosis test conducted at least 90 days following the date of arrival at the premises of the qualified herd. If a group of captive cervids is being moved together, the entire group must be isolated from all other livestock during the testing period, but captive cervids in the group need not be isolated from each other during that period. Such herd additions will not receive status as members of the qualified herd for purposes of interstate movement until they have tested negative to an official tuberculosis test and been released from isolation.

(4) A captive cervid to be added must not have been exposed during the 90 days prior to its movement to either:

(i) A captive cervid from a herd with a lower classification status than its own; or

(ii) Any tuberculous livestock.

(d) *Maintenance of qualified herd status.* To maintain status as a qualified herd, the herd must test negative to an official tuberculosis test within 9–15 months from the anniversary date of the first test with no evidence of tuberculosis disclosed (this is the qualifying test). Each time the herd is retested for qualified status, it must be tested 9–15 months from the anniversary date of the qualifying test, not from the last date of requalification (for example, if a herd is qualified on January 1 of a given year, the anniversary date will be January 1 of each consecutive year). Qualified herd status remains in effect for 12 months (365 days) following the anniversary date of the qualifying test. Qualified herd status will be suspended between the anniversary date and the requalifying test, if the herd is not tested within 12 months. During the suspension period, the herd will be considered "unclassified" and captive cervids may be moved interstate from the herd only in accordance with the movement requirements for the State or zone in which the herd is located.

[65 FR 63517, Oct. 23, 2000, as amended at 78 FR 2067, Jan. 9, 2013]

§ 77.37 Interstate movement from monitored herds.

(a) *Qualifications.* To be recognized as a monitored herd:

(1) Identification records must be maintained by the person, firm, or corporation responsible for the management of the herd for as long as status as a monitored herd is desired. Such records must be maintained on all captive cervids in the herd that are slaughtered, inspected, and found negative for tuberculosis at an approved slaughtering establishment or necropsied at an approved diagnostic laboratory. Identification records may also include captive cervids from the herd that tested negative for tuberculosis in accordance with requirements for interstate movement. No less than one-half of the captive cervids on which records are kept must be slaughter inspected; and

(2) A sufficient number of captive cervids in the herd must be slaughter inspected or tested for interstate movement to ensure that tuberculosis infection at a prevalence level of 2 percent or more will be detected with a confidence level of 95 percent.[2] A maximum number of 178 captive cervids must be slaughter inspected or tested for interstate movement over a 3-year period to meet this requirement.

(b) *Movement allowed.* Except as provided in § 77.23 with regard to captive cervids that originate in an accredited-free State or zone, and except as provided in § 77.31 with regard to captive cervids that originate in a nonaccredited State or zone, a captive cervid from a monitored herd may be moved interstate only if:

(1) The captive cervid is not known to be infected with or exposed to tuberculosis; and

(2) The captive cervid is officially identified and is accompanied by an ICVI, as provided in § 77.32(c), that includes a statement that the captive cervid is from a monitored herd. Except as provided in paragraph (b)(3) of this section, the ICVI must also state that the captive cervid has tested negative to an official tuberculosis test conducted within 90 days prior to the date of movement. If a group of captive cervids from a monitored herd is being moved interstate together to the same destination, all captive cervids in the group may be moved under one ICVI.

(3) Captive cervids under 1 year of age that are natural additions to the monitored herd or that were born in and originate from a classified herd may move without testing, provided that they are officially identified and that the ICVI accompanying them states that the captive cervids are natural additions to the monitored herd or were born in and originated from a classified herd and have not been exposed to captive cervids from an unclassified herd.

(c) *Herd additions allowed.* No captive cervid may be added to a monitored herd except in accordance with paragraph (c)(4) and either paragraph (c)(1), (c)(2), or (c)(3) of this section, as follows:

(1) The captive cervid to be added must be moved directly from an accredited herd;

[2] A chart showing the number of captive cervids that must be slaughter inspected or tested for interstate movement, depending on the size of a herd, to meet this requirement may be obtained from the National Animal Health Programs staff, Veterinary Services, APHIS, 4700 River Road Unit 43, Riverdale, MD 20737–1231.

(2) The captive cervid to be added must be moved directly from a qualified or monitored herd and must have tested negative to an official tuberculosis test conducted within 90 days prior to movement to the premises of the monitored herd; or

(3) If the captive cervid to be added is not being moved directly from a classified herd, the captive cervid must be isolated from all other animals and must test negative to two official tuberculosis tests. The isolation must begin at the time of the first official tuberculosis test. The tests must be conducted at least 90 days apart, and the second test must be conducted within 90 days prior to movement to the premises of the monitored herd. The captive cervid must then be kept in isolation from all animals until it tests negative to an official tuberculosis test conducted at least 90 days following the date it arrives at the premises of the monitored herd. If a group of captive cervids is being moved together, the entire group must be isolated from all other animals during the testing period, but captive cervids in the group need not be isolated from each other during that period. Such herd additions will not receive status as members of the monitored herd for purposes of interstate movement until they have tested negative to an official tuberculosis test and been released from isolation.

(4) A captive cervid to be added must not have been exposed during the 90 days prior to its movement to either:

(i) A captive cervid from a herd with a lower classification status than its own; or

(ii) Any tuberculous livestock.

(d) *Maintenance of monitored herd status.* The person, firm, or corporation responsible for the management of the herd must submit an annual report to cooperating State or Federal animal health officials prior to the anniversary date of classification. This report must give the number of captive cervids currently in the herd; the number of captive cervids from the herd 1 year of age and older identified, slaughtered, and inspected at an approved slaughtering establishment or necropsied at an approved diagnostic laboratory during the preceding year; and the number of captive cervids that have tested negative for tuberculosis in accordance with interstate movement requirements. The number of slaughter inspections or negative testing captive cervids reported in any given year must be at least 25 percent of the total number required over a 3-year period to qualify a herd for monitored herd status. During each consecutive 3-year period, 100 percent of the qualifying total must be reported.

[65 FR 63517, Oct. 23, 2000, as amended at 71 FR 24806, Apr. 27, 2006; 78 FR 2067, Jan. 9, 2013]

§ 77.38 Interstate movement from herds that are not accredited, qualified, or monitored.

The Administrator may, with the concurrence of the cooperating State animal health officials of the State of destination, and upon request in specific cases, permit the movement of captive cervids not otherwise provided for in this part which have not been classified as reactors and are not otherwise known to be affected with tuberculosis, under such conditions as the Administrator may prescribe in each specific case to prevent the spread of tuberculosis. The Administrator shall promptly notify the appropriate cooperating State animal health officials of the State of destination of any such action.

§ 77.39 Other interstate movements.

(a) *Herds containing a suspect*—(1) *The suspect.* (i) A captive cervid classified as a suspect on the SCT test must be quarantined until it is slaughtered or retested by the CCT test and found negative for tuberculosis. Retesting must be as follows:

(A) The first CCT test must be administered within the first 10 days following the SCT test or, if not, must be administered at least 90 days after the SCT test. If the CCT test is administered within 10 days of the SCT test, the injection must be on the side of the neck opposite the injection for the SCT test.

(B) [Reserved]

(ii) A captive cervid classified as a suspect on the first CCT test must be quarantined until the following has occurred:

(A) A suspect on the first CCT test is tested with a second CCT test at least 90 days after the first CCT test and is found negative for tuberculosis.

(B) [Reserved]

(iii) A captive cervid classified as a suspect on an initial DPP® test must be slaughtered or otherwise must be quarantined until it is retested using the DPP® test. A captive cervid that has negative test results to this second DPP® test may be released from quarantine. A captive cervid that has non-negative test results to this second DPP® test must be classified as a reactor and may only be moved in accordance with paragraph (b) of this section.

(2) *The remainder of the herd.* Any herd containing a suspect to an official tuberculosis test must be quarantined until the suspect is retested by the CCT test, DPP® test, or the BTB test and found negative for tuberculosis, or the suspect is inspected at slaughter or necropsied and found negative for tuberculosis after histopathology and culture of selected tissues. If the suspect is found negative for tuberculosis upon testing, or after slaughter inspection or necropsy and histopathology and culture of selected tissues, the herd may be released from quarantine and will return to the herd classification status in effect before the herd was quarantined. If the suspect is classified as a reactor upon testing, or after slaughter inspection or necropsy and histopathology and/or culture of selected tissues, the herd may be released from quarantine only in accordance with paragraph (b) of this section for herds containing a reactor.

(b) *Herds containing a reactor.* The following requirements apply to herds containing a reactor, except for herds that have received captive cervids from an affected herd. Herds that have received captive cervids from an affected herd must be quarantined and tested in accordance with paragraph (e) of this section.

(1) *The reactor.* Captive cervids classified as reactors must be quarantined.

(2) *The remainder of the herd.* Any herd containing reactors must be quarantined until the reactors are slaughtered or necropsied in accordance with § 77.40 and:

(i) If, upon slaughter inspection or necropsy, any reactors exhibit lesions compatible with or suggestive of tuberculosis, found by histopathology, without the isolation of *M. bovis*, the remainder of the herd may be released from quarantine in accordance with the provisions of paragraph (c) of this section.

(ii) If *M. bovis* is isolated from any reactors, the remainder of the herd will be considered an affected herd, and will be subject to the provisions for affected herds in paragraph (d) of this section.

(iii) If upon slaughter inspection or necropsy all reactors exhibit no gross lesions (NGL) of tuberculosis and no evidence of tuberculosis infection is found by histopathology and culture of *M. bovis* on specimens taken from the NGL animals, the remainder of the herd may be released from quarantine, and captive cervids from the herd may be moved interstate in accordance with the herd classification status in effect before the herd was quarantined if one of the following conditions is met:

(A) The remainder of the herd is given a whole herd test and is found negative for tuberculosis.

(B) The remainder of the herd is given a whole herd test, and all reactors to the whole herd test exhibit no gross lesions (NGL) of tuberculosis upon slaughter inspection or necropsy and no evidence of tuberculosis infection is found by histopathology or culture of *M. bovis* on specimens taken from the NGL animals.

(iv) If no evidence of tuberculosis is found in any reactor upon slaughter inspection or necropsy, but it is not possible to conduct a whole herd test on the remainder of the herd, the herd will be evaluated, based on criteria such as the testing history of the herd and the State history of tuberculosis infection, by APHIS to determine whether the herd may be released from quarantine.

(c) *Herds found to have only lesions of tuberculosis.* A herd in which captive cervids with lesions compatible with or suggestive of tuberculosis are found by histopathology without the isolation of *M. bovis* may be released from quarantine and return to the herd classification status in effect before the herd was quarantined, with the concurrence of APHIS, if the herd tests negative to tuberculosis on a whole herd test conducted 90 days following the removal of the lesioned captive cervid, provided the herd has not been exposed to *M. bovis* during the 90 days. To maintain its herd classification status, the herd must test negative to two annual whole herd tests beginning 10–12 months after the herd is released from quarantine. If any captive cervids in the herd respond to one of the tests, the herd will be subject to the provisions of paragraph (a) or (b) of this section. If the herd is not given the two annual whole herd tests, it will become an unclassified herd.

(d) *Affected herds.* A herd determined to be an affected herd must be quarantined until the herd has tested negative to three whole herd tests in succession, with the first test given 90 days or more after the last test yielding a reactor and the last two tests given at intervals of not less than 180 days. If the herd tests negative to the three whole herd tests, it will be released from quarantine, but will be considered an unclassified herd, and captive cervids may only be moved interstate from the herd in accordance with the movement requirements for the State or zone in which the herd is located. In addition, the herd must be given five consecutive annual whole herd tests after release from quarantine. (These five tests will count toward qualifying the herd for herd classification.) As an alternative to testing, the herd may be depopulated.

(e) *Herds that have received captive cervids from an affected herd.* If a herd has received captive cervids from an affected herd, the captive cervids from the affected herd of origin will be considered exposed to tuberculosis. The exposed captive cervids and the receiving herd must be quarantined. The exposed captive cervids must be slaughtered, necropsied, or tested with the SCT test by a veterinarian employed by the State in which the test is administered or employed by USDA, or tested with the DPP® test. Any exposed captive cervid that responds to the SCT test must be classified as a reactor and must be inspected at slaughter or necropsied. Any exposed captive cervid that has non-negative test results to the DPP® test must be classified as a reactor and must be inspected at slaughter or necropsied. Any exposed captive cervid that tests negative to the SCT or DPP® test will be considered as part of the affected herd of origin for purposes of testing, quarantine, and the five annual whole herd tests required for affected herds in paragraph (d) of this section.

(1) If bovine tuberculosis is confirmed in any of the exposed captive cervids by bacterial isolation of *M. bovis*, the receiving herd will be classified as an affected herd and will be subject to the provisions for affected herds in paragraph (d) of this section.

(2) If any of the exposed captive cervids are found to exhibit lesions compatible with or suggestive of tuberculosis, found by histopathology, without the isolation of *M. bovis*, the receiving herd will be subject to appropriate testing as determined by APHIS.

(3) If all the exposed captive cervids test negative for tuberculosis, the receiving herd will be released from quarantine if it is given a whole herd test and is found negative for tuberculosis and will return to the herd classification in effect before the herd was quarantined. In addition, the receiving herd will must be retested with the SCT or DPP® test 1 year after release from quarantine in order for captive cervids from the herd to continue to be moved interstate. Supplemental diagnostic tests may be used if any captive cervids in the herd show a response to the SCT test or have non-negative test results to the DPP® test.

(f) *Source herds.* A herd suspected of being the source of tuberculous captive cervids based on a slaughter traceback investigation must be quarantined upon notification (by the person conducting the investigation) to the USDA area veterinarian in charge for the State in which the herd resides, and a herd test must be scheduled. If the herd is suspected of being the source of slaughter captive cervids having lesions of tuberculosis, the herd test must be done by a veterinarian employed by the State in which the test is administered or employed by USDA.

(1) If the herd is identified as the source of captive cervids having lesions of tuberculosis and *M. bovis* has been confirmed by bacterial isolation from

the slaughter animal, all captive cervids in the herd that respond to the SCT must be classified as reactors. All captive cervids in the herd that respond to the DPP® test must be classified as reactors. If none respond to the SCT test or have non-negative test results to the DPP® test, the herd may be released from quarantine and will return to the herd classification status in effect before the herd was quarantined, unless APHIS determines that additional testing is appropriate to ensure the herd's freedom from tuberculosis.

(2) If the herd is identified as the source of captive cervids that exhibit lesions compatible with or suggestive of tuberculosis, found by histopathology, without the isolation of *M. bovis*, all captive cervids in the herd that respond to the SCT test or the DPP® test must be classified as suspects, and supplemental tests must be applied.

(3) If the herd is not identified as the source herd, the herd will be released from quarantine if the herd is given a whole herd test and is found negative for tuberculosis. The herd will then return to the herd classification status in effect before the herd was quarantined.

(g) *Newly assembled herds.* (1) A newly assembled herd will be classified as having the herd status of the herd from which the captive cervids originated. If the herd is assembled from captive cervids from more than one herd, it will be classified as having the herd status of the originating herd with the lowest status. A newly assembled herd will also assume the testing schedule of the herd status it is given. Captive cervids in the herd must have no exposure to captive cervids from a herd of lesser status than the herd of origin determining the status of the newly assembled herd or to any tuberculous livestock.

(2) A herd newly assembled on premises where a tuberculous herd has been depopulated must be given two consecutive annual whole herd tests. The first test must be administered at least 6 months after the assembly of the new herd. If the whole herd tests are not conducted within the indicated timeframe, the herd will be quarantined. If the herd tests negative to the two whole herd tests, there are no further requirements. If any captive cervid in the herd responds on one of the whole herd tests, the herd will be subject to the provisions of paragraph (a) or (b) of this section. If the premises has been vacant for more than 1 year preceding the assembly of the new herd on the premises, these requirements may be waived if the risk of tuberculosis transmission to the newly assembled herd is deemed negligible by cooperating State and Federal animal health officials.

[65 FR 63517, Oct. 23, 2000, as amended at 71 FR 24806, Apr. 27, 2006; 78 FR 1723, Jan. 9, 2013; 79 FR 43926, July 29, 2014]

§ 77.40 Procedures for and interstate movement to necropsy and slaughter.

(a) *Procedures for necropsy and slaughter.* (1) A necropsy must be performed by or under the supervision of a veterinarian who is employed by USDA or employed by the State in which the captive cervid was classified, and who is trained in tuberculosis necropsy procedures.

(2) If, upon necropsy, a captive cervid is found without evidence of *M. bovis* infection by histopathology and culture, the captive cervid will be considered negative for tuberculosis.

(3) Reactors, suspects, and exposed captive cervids may be slaughtered only at a recognized slaughtering establishment, as defined in § 77.20.

(b) *Interstate movement to necropsy or slaughter*—(1) *Permit.* Any reactor, suspect, or exposed captive cervid to be moved interstate to necropsy or slaughter must be accompanied by a permit issued by a representative of APHIS, a State representative, or an accredited veterinarian. The captive cervid must remain on the premises where it was identified as a reactor, suspect, or exposed captive cervid until a permit for its movement is obtained. No stopover or diversion from the destination listed on the permit is allowed. If a change in destination becomes necessary, a new permit must be obtained from a cooperating State or Federal animal health official or an accredited veterinarian before the interstate movement begins. The permit must list:

(i) The classification of the captive cervid (reactor, suspect, or exposed);

(ii) The reactor eartag number or, for suspects and exposed captive cervids, the official eartag or other approved identification number;

(iii) The owner's name and address;

(iv) The origin and destination of the captive cervids;

(v) The number of captive cervids covered by the permit; and

(vi) The purpose of the movement.

(2) *Identification of reactors.* Reactors must be tagged with an official eartag attached to the left ear and bearing a serial number and the inscription "U.S. Reactor," and either:

(i) Branded with the letter "T" high on the left hip near the tailhead and at least 5 by 5 centimeters (2 by 2 inches) in size; or

(ii) Permanently identified by the letters "TB" tattooed legibly in the left ear, sprayed on the left ear with yellow paint, and either accompanied directly to necropsy or slaughter by an APHIS or State representative or moved directly to necropsy or slaughter in a vehicle closed with official seals. Such official seals must be applied and removed by an APHIS representative, State representative, accredited veterinarian, or an individual authorized for this purpose by an APHIS representative.

(3) *Identification of exposed captive cervids.* Exposed captive cervids must be identified by an official eartag or other approved identification and either:

(i) Branded with the letter "S" high on the left hip near the tailhead and at least 5 by 5 centimeters (2 by 2 inches) in size; or

(ii) Either accompanied directly to necropsy or slaughter by an APHIS or State representative or moved directly to necropsy or slaughter in a vehicle closed with official seals. Such official seals must be applied and removed by an APHIS representative, State representative, accredited veterinarian, or an individual authorized for this purpose by an APHIS representative.

[65 FR 63517, Oct. 23, 2000, as amended at 78 FR 2068, Jan. 9, 2013]

§ 77.41 Cleaning and disinfection of premises, conveyances, and materials.

All conveyances and associated equipment, premises, and structures that are used for receiving, holding, shipping, loading, unloading, and delivering captive cervids in connection with their interstate movement and that are determined by cooperating State and Federal animal health officials to be contaminated because of occupation or use by tuberculous or reactor livestock must be cleaned and disinfected under the supervision of the cooperating State or Federal animal health officials. Such cleaning and disinfecting must be done in accordance with the procedures approved by the cooperating State or Federal animal health officials. Cleaning and disinfection must be completed before the premises, conveyances, or materials may again be used to convey, hold, or in any way come in contact with any livestock.

PART 78—BRUCELLOSIS

Subpart A—General Provisions

Sec.

Subpart B—Restrictions on Interstate Movement of Cattle Because of Brucellosis

Subpart C—Restrictions on Interstate Movement of Bison Because of Brucellosis

Subpart D—Restrictions on Interstate Movement of Swine Because of Brucellosis

Subpart E—Designation of Brucellosis Areas

AUTHORITY: 7 U.S.C. 8301–8317; 7 CFR 2.22, 2.80, and 371.4.

SOURCE: 51 FR 32580, Sept. 12, 1986, unless otherwise noted.

Subpart A—General Provisions

§ 78.1 Definitions.

The following terms are defined in this section:

Accredited veterinarian
Administrator
Animals
Animal and Plant Health Inspection Service
Animal identification number
APHIS representative
Approved brucella vaccine
Approved individual herd plan
Approved intermediate handling facility
Area
"B" branded
Boar
Brucellosis
Brucellosis exposed
Brucellosis negative
Brucellosis reactor
Brucellosis ring test
Brucellosis suspect
Certificate
Certified brucellosis-free herd
Class A State or area
Class B State or area
Class C State or area
Class Free State or area
Complete herd test (CHT)
Confirmatory test
Dairy cattle
Designated epidemiologist
Directly
Epidemiologist
Epidemiology
Farm of origin
Feral swine
Finished fed cattle
Herd
Herd blood test
Herd known to be affected
Herd not known to be affected
Herd of origin of swine
Interstate
Market cattle identification test cattle
Market swine test (MST) reactor
Market swine test swine
Monitored-negative feral swine population
Moved
Moved (movement) in interstate commerce
Official adult vaccinate
Official brand inspection certificate
Official brand recording agency
Official calfhood vaccinate
Official eartag
Official seal
Official swine tattoo
Official test
Official vaccinate
Official vaccination eartag
Originate
Parturient
Permit
Permit for entry
Person
Postparturient
Purebred registry association
Qualified herd
Quarantined area
Quarantined feedlot
Quarantined pasture
Recognized slaughtering establishment
"S" branded
"S" brand permit
Sow
Specifically approved stockyard
State
State animal health official
State representative
Successfully closed case
Swine brucellosis
Test-eligible cattle and bison
United States
United States Department of Agriculture backtag
Validated brucellosis-free herd
Validated brucellosis-free State
Veterinarian in Charge
Whole herd vaccination

As used in this part, the following terms shall have the meanings set forth in this section.

Accredited veterinarian. A veterinarian approved by the Administrator in accordance with the provisions of part 161 of this title to perform functions specified in parts 1, 2, 3, and 11 of subchapter A, and subchapters B, C, and D of this chapter, and to perform functions required by cooperative State-Federal disease control and eradication programs.

Administrator. The Administrator, Animal and Plant Health Inspection Service, or any person authorized to act for the Administrator.

Animals. Cattle, bison, and swine.

Animal and Plant Health Inspection Service (APHIS). The Animal and Plant Health Inspection Service of the United States Department of Agriculture.

Animal identification number (AIN). A numbering system for the official identification of individual animals in the United States that provides a nationally unique identification number for each animal. The AIN consists of 15 digits, with the first 3 being the country code (840 for the United States or a unique country code for any U.S. territory that has such a code and elects to use it in place of the 840 code). The alpha characters USA or the numeric code assigned to the manufacturer of the identification device by the International Committee on Animal Recording may be used as an alternative to the 840 or other prefix representing a U.S territory; however, only the AIN beginning with the 840 or other prefix representing a U.S. territory will be recognized as official for use on AIN tags applied to animals on or after March 11, 2015. The AIN beginning with the 840 prefix may not be applied to animals known to have been born outside the United States.

APHIS representative. An individual employed by APHIS who is authorized to perform the function involved.

Approved brucella vaccine. A *Brucella* product approved by and produced under license of the United States Department of Agriculture for injection into cattle or bison to enhance their resistance to brucellosis.

Approved individual herd plan. A herd management and testing plan designed by the herd owner, the owner's veterinarian if so requested, and a State representative or APHIS representative to determine the disease status of animals in the herd and to control and eradicate brucellosis within the herd. The plan must be jointly approved by the State animal health official and the Veterinarian in Charge.

Approved intermediate handling facility. Premises approved by the Administrator and the State animal health official for receiving and handling cattle and bison for release only to recognized slaughtering establishments and quarantined feedlots. Cattle and bison may be held at an approved intermediate handling facility for a maximum of 7 days and may not change ownership during this time. No cattle or bison, except cattle or bison moved directly from a farm of origin, shall be permitted to enter an approved intermediate handling facility unless they are accompanied by a permit or "S" brand permit. Cattle or bison transported in vehicles closed with official seals are prohibited from entering the approved intermediate handling facility. No cattle or bison shall be permitted to leave an approved intermediate handling facility unless they are accompanied by a permit or "S" brand permit which lists a recognized slaughtering establishment or a quarantined feedlot as the point of destination. To qualify for and retain approval, the following conditions must be met: (a) The facility must be separate and apart from other livestock handling facilities for breeding cattle and breeding bison; (b) Serviceable equipment for cleaning and disinfection shall be furnished and maintained with adequate disinfectant on hand; (c) The facility must be cleaned and disinfected in accordance with § 71.4(a) of this chapter; (d) Any document relating to cattle or bison which are or have been in the facility shall be maintained by the facility for a period of 2 years; (e) State representatives and APHIS representatives shall be granted, at reasonable hours, access to all documents required to be maintained by the facility and authority to reproduce the documents; and (f) Each entrance and exit to the facility must prominently display a sign bearing the following words: "All cattle and bison entering this facility must go directly to slaughter or a quarantined feedlot". The Administrator may withdraw or deny approval of any intermediate handling facility in accordance with § 71.20 of this chapter.

Area. That portion of any State which has a separate brucellosis classification under this part.

"B" branded. Branding with a hot iron the letter "B" high on the left hip near the tailhead and at least 5 by 5 centimeters (2 by 2 inches) in size.

Boar. An uncastrated male swine 6 months of age or over which is or has been capable of being used for breeding purposes.

Brucellosis. The contagious, infectious, and communicable disease caused by bacteria of the genus *Brucella.* It is also known as Bangs disease, undulant fever, and contagious abortion.

Brucellosis exposed. Except for brucellosis reactors, animals that are part of a herd known to be affected, or are in a quarantined feedlot or a quarantined pasture, or are brucellosis suspects, or that have been in contact with a brucellosis reactor for a period of 24 hours or more, or for a period of less than 24 hours if the brucellosis reactor has aborted, calved, or farrowed within the past 30 days or has a vaginal or uterine discharge.

Brucellosis negative. An animal subjected to one or more official tests resulting in a brucellosis negative classification or reclassified as brucellosis negative by a designated epidemiologist as provided for in the definition of official test.

Brucellosis reactor. An animal subjected to an official test resulting in a brucellosis reactor classification or subjected to a bacteriological examination for field strain *Brucella abortus* and found positive or reclassified as a brucellosis reactor by a designated epidemiologist as provided for in the definition of official test.

Brucellosis ring test. The brucellosis ring test is conducted on composite milk or cream samples from dairy herds and is interpreted as either negative or suspicious (positive). Herds which are negative to the brucellosis ring test and which are not quarantined as brucellosis affected are classified as brucellosis negative for public health ordinances and surveillance purposes. Herds classified as suspicious require a herd blood test to determine animal and herd status.

Brucellosis suspect. An animal subjected to an official test resulting in a brucellosis suspect classification or reclassified as a brucellosis suspect by a designated epidemiologist as provided for in the definition of official test.

Certified brucellosis-free herd. A herd of cattle or bison which has qualified for and whose owner has been issued a certified brucellosis-free herd certificate signed by the appropriate State animal health official and the Veterinarian in Charge.

(a) *Certification.* The following methods may be used to qualify a herd:

(1) By conducting at least two consecutive negative herd blood tests not less than 10 months nor more than 14 months apart; or

(2) As an alternative for dairy cattle, by conducting a minimum of four consecutive negative brucellosis ring tests, or other official brucellosis milk test approved by the Administrator, at not less than 90-day intervals, followed by a negative herd blood test within 90 days after the last negative brucellosis ring test or other official brucellosis milk test approved by the Administrator.

(b) *Maintaining certification.* Certified brucellosis-free herd status will remain in effect for 1 year beginning with the date of issuance of the certified brucellosis-free herd certificate. The following methods may be used to maintain herd certification:

(1) A negative herd blood test must be conducted within 10 to 12 months of the last certification date for continuous status. Lapsed certification may be reinstated if a herd blood test is conducted within 14 months of the last certification date. A new recertification test date may be established if requested by the owner and if the herd is negative to a herd blood test on that date, provided that date is within 1 year of the previous certification date.

(2) As an alternative for dairy cattle, a minimum of four consecutive negative brucellosis ring tests, or other official brucellosis milk test approved by the Administrator, must be conducted at approximately 90-day intervals, with the fourth test conducted within 60

days before the 1-year anniversary of the previous certification date.

(3) The Administrator may allow another testing protocol to be used if the Administrator determines that such a protocol is adequate to determine there is no evidence of brucellosis in the herd.

(c) *Loss of certification.* A herd which loses certified brucellosis-free herd status because a brucellosis reactor is found in the herd may be recertified only by repeating the certification process, except that certified brucellosis-free herd status may be reinstated without repeating the certification process if epidemiological studies and bacteriological cultures conducted by an APHIS representative or State representative show that the herd was not affected with *Brucella abortus.*

Class A State or area. A State or area which meets standards for classification as a Class A State or area and is certified as such on initial classification or on reclassification by the State animal health official, the Veterinarian in Charge, and the Administrator. Any reclassification will be made in accordance with § 78.40 of this part. The following are the standards to attain and maintain Class A status.

(a) *Surveillance*—(1) *Brucellosis ring test.* The brucellosis ring test shall be conducted in the State or area at least four times per year at approximately 90-day intervals. All herds producing milk for sale shall be included in at least three of the four brucellosis ring tests per year.

(2) *Market Cattle Identification (MCI) program*—(i) *Coverage.* All recognized slaughtering establishments in the State or area must participate in the MCI program. Blood samples shall be collected from at least 95 percent of all cows and bulls 2 years of age or over at each recognized slaughtering establishment and subjected to an official test;

(ii) *Brucellosis reactors*—(A) *Tracebacks.* At least 90 percent of all brucellosis reactors found in the course of MCI testing must be traced to the farm of origin.

(B) *Successfully closed cases.* The State or area must successfully close at least 95 percent of the MCI reactor cases traced to the farm of origin during the 12-consecutive-month period immediately prior to the most recent anniversary of the date the State or area was classified Class A. To successfully close an MCI reactor case, State representatives or APHIS representatives must conduct an epidemiologic investigation at the farm of origin within 15 days after notification by the cooperative State-Federal laboratory that brucellosis reactors were found on the MCI test. Herd blood tests must be conducted or the herd must be confined to the premises under quarantine within 30 days after notification that brucellosis reactors were found on the MCI test, unless a designated epidemiologist determines that:

(*1*) The brucellosis reactor is located in a herd in a different State than the State where the MCI blood sample was collected. In such cases a State representative or APHIS representative must give written notice of the MCI test results to the State animal health official in the State where the brucellosis reactor is located; or

(*2*) Evidence indicates that the brucellosis reactor is from a herd that no longer presents a risk of spreading brucellosis, or is from a herd that is unlikely to be infected with brucellosis. Such evidence could include, but is not limited to, situations where:

(*i*) The brucellosis reactor is traced back to a herd that has been sold for slaughter in entirety;

(*ii*) The brucellosis reactor is traced back to a herd that is certified brucellosis free and is 100-percent vaccinated; or

(*iii*) The brucellosis reactor showed a low titer in the MCI test and is traced back to a dairy herd that is 100 percent vaccinated and has tested negative to the most recent brucellosis ring test required by this section for herds producing milk for sale.

(3) *Epidemiologic surveillance*—(i) *Adjacent herds.* All adjacent herds or other herds having contact with cattle or bison in a herd known to be affected shall have an approved individual herd plan in effect within 15 days of notification of brucellosis in the herd known to be affected;

(ii) *Epidemiologically traced herds.* All herds from which cattle or bison are moved into a herd known to be affected and all herds which have received cattle or bison from a herd known to be affected shall have an approved individual herd plan in effect within 15 days of locating the source herd or recipient herd.

(iii) Each State shall ensure that such approved individual herd plans are effectively complied with, as determined by the Administrator.

(b) *Herd infection rate*—(1) *Percentage of herds affected.* States or areas must not exceed a cattle or bison herd infection rate, based on the number of herds found to have brucellosis reactors within the State or area during any 12 consecutive months due to field strain *Brucella abortus*, of 0.25 percent or 2.5 herds per 1,000, except in States with 10,000 or fewer herds. A special review by the Administrator will be made to determine if such small herd population States would qualify for Class A status. Locations of herds, sources of brucellosis, and brucellosis control measures taken by the State will be considered.

(2) *Epidemiologic investigation.* Within 15 days after notification by the cooperative State-Federal laboratory that brucellosis reactors have been found in any herd, State representatives or APHIS representatives shall investigate that herd to identify possible sources of brucellosis. All possible sources of brucellosis identified shall be contacted within an additional 15 days to determine appropriate action.

(3) All herds known to be affected shall have approved individual herd plans in effect within 15 days after notification by a State representative or APHIS representative of a brucellosis reactor in the herd. Each State shall ensure that such approved individual herd plans are effectively complied with, as determined by the Administrator.

Class B State or area. A State or area which meets standards for classification as a Class B State or area and is certified as such on initial classification or on reclassification by the State animal health official, the Veterinarian in Charge, and the Administrator. Any reclassification will be made in accordance with § 78.40 of this part. The following are the standards to attain and maintain Class B status.

(a) *Surveillance*—(1) *Brucellosis ring test.* The brucellosis ring test shall be conducted in the State or area at least four times per year at approximately 90-day intervals. All herds producing milk for sale shall be included in at least three of the four brucellosis ring tests per year.

(2) *Market Cattle Identification (MCI) program*—(i) *Coverage.* All recognized slaughtering establishments in the State or area must participate in the MCI program. Blood samples shall be collected from at least 95 percent of all cows and bulls 2 years of age or over at each recognized slaughtering establishment and subjected to an official test;

(ii) *Brucellosis reactors*—(A) *Tracebacks.* At least 80 percent of all brucellosis reactors found in the course of MCI testing must be traced to the farm of origin.

(B) *Successfully closed cases.* The State or area must successfully close at least 90 percent of the MCI reactor cases traced to the farm of origin during the 12-consecutive-month period immediately prior to the most recent anniversary of the date the State or area was classified Class B. To successfully close an MCI reactor case, State representatives or APHIS representatives must conduct an epidemiologic investigation at the farm of origin within 30 days after notification by the cooperative State-Federal laboratory that brucellosis reactors were found on the MCI test. Herd blood tests must be conducted or the herd must be confined to the premises under quarantine within 30 days after notification that brucellosis reactors were found on the MCI test, unless a designated epidemiologist determines that:

(*1*) The brucellosis reactor is located in a herd in a different State than the State where the MCI blood sample was collected. In such cases a State representative or APHIS representative must give written notice of the MCI test results to the State animal health official in the State where the brucellosis reactor is located; or

(*2*) Evidence indicates that the brucellosis reactor is from a herd that no longer presents a risk of spreading brucellosis, or is from a herd that is unlikely to be infected with brucellosis.

Such evidence could include, but is not limited to, situations where:

(*i*) The brucellosis reactor is traced back to a herd that has been sold for slaughter in entirety;

(*ii*) The brucellosis reactor is traced back to a herd that is certified brucellosis free and is 100-percent vaccinated; or

(*iii*) The brucellosis reactor showed a low titer in the MCI test and is traced back to a dairy herd that is 100 percent vaccinated and has tested negative to the most recent brucellosis ring test required by this section for herds producing milk for sale.

(3) *Epidemiologic surveillance*—(i) *Adjacent herds.* All adjacent herds or other herds having contact with cattle or bison in a herd known to be affected shall have an approved individual herd plan in effect within 45 days of notification of brucellosis in the herd known to be affected;

(ii) *Epidemiologically traced herds.* All herds from which cattle or bison are moved into a herd known to be affected and all herds which have received cattle or bison from a herd known to be affected shall have an approved individual herd plan in effect within 45 days of locating the source herd or recipient herd.

(iii) Each State shall ensure that such approved individual herd plans are effectively complied with, as determined by the Administrator.

(b) *Herd infection rate*—(1) *Percentage of herds affected.* States or areas must not exceed a cattle or bison herd infection rate, based on the number of herds found to have brucellosis reactors within the State or area during any 12 consecutive months due to field strain *Brucella abortus*, of 1.5 percent or 15 herds per 1,000, except in States with 1,000 or fewer herds. A special review by the Administrator will be made to determine if such small herd population States would qualify for Class B status. Locations of herds, sources of brucellosis, and brucellosis control measures taken by the State will be considered.

(2) *Epidemiologic investigation.* Within 45 days after notification by the cooperative State-Federal laboratory that brucellosis reactors have been found in any herd, State representatives or APHIS representatives shall investigate that herd to identify possible sources of brucellosis. All possible sources of brucellosis identified shall be contacted within an additional 30 days to determine appropriate action.

(3) All herds known to be affected shall have approved individual herd plans in effect within 45 days after notification by a State representative or APHIS representative of a brucellosis reactor in the herd. Each State shall ensure that such approved individual herd plans are effectively complied with, as determined by the Administrator.

Class C State or area. A State or area which meets standards for classification as a Class C State or area and is certified as such on initial classification or on reclassification by the State animal health official, the Veterinarian in Charge, and the Administrator. Any reclassification will be made in accordance with § 78.40 of this part. The following are the standards to attain and maintain Class C status.

(a) *Surveillance*—(1) *Brucellosis ring test.* The brucellosis ring test shall be conducted in the State or area at least four times per year at approximately 90-day intervals. All herds producing milk for sale shall be included in at least three of the four brucellosis ring tests per year.

(2) *Market Cattle Identification (MCI) program*—(i) *Coverage.* All recognized slaughtering establishments in the State or area must participate in the MCI program. Blood samples shall be collected from at least 95 percent of all cows and bulls 2 years of age or over at each recognized slaughtering establishment and subjected to an official test;

(ii) *Brucellosis reactors*—(A) *Tracebacks.* At least 80 percent of all brucellosis reactors found in the course of MCI testing must be traced to the farm of origin.

(B) *Successfully closed cases.* The State or area must successfully close at least 90 percent of the MCI reactor cases traced to the farm of origin during the 12-consecutive-month period immediately prior to the most recent anniversary of the date the State or area was classified Class C. To successfully close an MCI reactor case, State representatives or APHIS representatives must conduct an epidemiologic investigation at the farm of origin within 30 days after notification by the cooperative State-Federal laboratory that brucellosis reactors were found on the MCI test. Herd blood tests must be conducted or the herd must be confined to the premises under quarantine within 30 days after notification that brucellosis reactors were found on the MCI test, unless a designated epidemiologist determines that:

(*1*) The brucellosis reactor is located in a herd in a different State than the State where the MCI blood sample was collected. In such cases a State representative or APHIS representative must give written notice of the MCI test results to the State animal health official in the State where the brucellosis reactor is located; or

(*2*) Evidence indicates that the brucellosis reactor is from a herd that no longer presents a risk of spreading brucellosis, or is from a herd that is unlikely to be infected with brucellosis. Such evidence could include, but is not limited to, situations where:

(*i*) The brucellosis reactor is traced back to a herd that has been sold for slaughter in entirety;

(*ii*) The brucellosis reactor is traced back to a herd that is certified brucellosis free and is 100-percent vaccinated; or

(*iii*) The brucellosis reactor showed a low titer in the MCI test and is traced back to a dairy herd that is 100 percent vaccinated and has tested negative to the most recent brucellosis ring test required by this section for herds producing milk for sale.

(3) *Epidemiologic surveillance*—(i) *Adjacent herds.* All adjacent herds or other herds having contact with cattle or bison in a herd known to be affected shall have an approved individual herd plan in effect within 45 days of notification of brucellosis in the herd known to be affected;

(ii) *Epidemiologically traced herds.* All herds from which cattle or bison are moved into a herd known to be affected and all herds which have received cattle or bison from a herd known to be affected shall have an approved individual herd plan in effect within 45 days of locating the source herd or recipient herd.

(iii) Each State shall ensure that such approved individual herd plans are effectively complied with, as determined by the Administrator.

(b) *Herd infection rate*—(1) *Percentage of herds affected.* States or areas exceed a cattle or bison herd infection rate, based on the number of herds found to have brucellosis reactors within the State or area during any 12 consecutive months due to field strain *Brucella abortus*, of 1.5 percent or 15 herds per 1,000, except in States with 1,000 or fewer herds. A special review by the Administrator will be made to determine if such small herd population States should be classified as a Class C State. Locations of herds, sources of brucellosis, and brucellosis control measures taken by the State will be considered.

(2) *Epidemiologic investigation.* Within 45 days after notification by the cooperative State-Federal laboratory that brucellosis reactors have been found in any herd, State representatives or APHIS representatives shall investigate that herd to identify possible sources of brucellosis. All possible sources of brucellosis identified shall be contacted within an additional 30 days to determine appropriate action.

(3) All herds known to be affected shall have approved individual herd plans in effect within 45 days after notification by a State representative or APHIS representative of a brucellosis reactor in the herd. Each State shall ensure that such approved individual herd plans are effectively complied with, as determined by the Administrator.

(c) *Compliance with minimum procedural standards.* (1) A State must implement and maintain minimum procedural standards.

(2) A State or area must make continued progress over a 2-year period in reducing the prevalence of brucellosis as determined by epidemiologic evaluation or it will be placed under Federal quarantine.

Class Free State or area. A State or area which meets standards for classification as a Class Free State or area and is certified as such on initial classification or on reclassification by the

State animal health official, the Veterinarian in Charge, and the Administrator. For initial classification or reclassification, all cattle herds in the State or area must have remained free of *Brucella abortus* for 12 consecutive months, based on surveillance and epidemiologic investigations as required for Class A States or areas, and the State or area must have a cattle herd infection rate, based on the number of herds found to have brucellosis reactors within the State or area during any 12 consecutive months due to *Brucella abortus*, of 0.0 percent or 0 herds per 1,000. The Administrator may reclassify a State or area to a lower status upon finding that continued detection of brucellosis presents a risk that the disease will spread. Any reclassification will be made in accordance with § 78.40 of this part. All cattle herds in the State or area in which brucellosis has been known to exist must be released from any State or Federal brucellosis quarantine prior to classification. In addition, if any herds of other species of domestic livestock have been found to be affected with brucellosis, they must be subjected to an official test and found negative, slaughtered, or quarantined so that no foci of brucellosis in any species of domestic livestock are left uncontrolled. The following are the standards to maintain Class Free status.

(a) *Surveillance*—(1) *Testing requirements*—(i) *States or areas that have been Class Free for 5 consecutive years or longer and that do not have B. abortus in wildlife.* All recognized slaughtering establishments in the State or area, upon request by APHIS, must agree to participate in market cattle identification (MCI) testing as part of the national brucellosis surveillance plan.

(ii) *States or areas that have not been Class Free for 5 consecutive years or longer or that have B. abortus in wildlife.* The State or area must carry out testing as provided in paragraphs (a)(1)(ii)(A) and (a)(1)(ii)(B) or (a)(1)(ii)(C) of this definition:

(A) *Brucellosis ring test.* The State or area shall conduct as many brucellosis ring tests per year as are necessary to ensure that all herds producing milk for sale are tested at least twice per year at approximately 6-month intervals. Another official brucellosis milk test may be used as approved by the Administrator.

(B) *Market Cattle Identification (MCI) program.* All recognized slaughtering establishments in the State or area must participate in the MCI program. Blood samples shall be collected from at least 95 percent of all cows and bulls 2 years of age or over at each recognized slaughtering establishment and subjected to an official test.

(C) *Alternative surveillance plan.* As an alternative to the testing described in paragraphs (a)(1)(ii)(A) and (a)(1)(ii)(B) of this definition, the State or area may develop an alternative surveillance plan that would have to meet or exceed the level of disease detection provided by combined brucellosis ring testing and collection of blood samples from at least 95 percent of test eligible slaughter cattle slaughtered within the State. The alternative surveillance plan must be developed in conjunction with the State animal health official and the area veterinarian in charge.

(2) *Brucellosis reactors.* All Class Free States or areas must comply with the following requirements upon detection of a brucellosis reactor:

(i) *Tracebacks.* The State or area must trace at least 90 percent of all brucellosis reactors found in the course of MCI testing to the farm of origin.

(ii) *Successfully closed cases.* The State or area must successfully close at least 95 percent of the MCI reactor cases traced to the farm of origin during the 12-consecutive-month period immediately prior to the most recent anniversary of the date the State or area was classified Class Free. To successfully close an MCI reactor case, State representatives or APHIS representatives must conduct an epidemiologic investigation at the farm of origin within 15 days after notification by the cooperative State-Federal laboratory that brucellosis reactors were found on the MCI test. Herd blood tests must be conducted or the herd must be confined to the premises under quarantine within 30 days after notification that brucellosis reactors were found on the MCI test, unless a designated epidemiologist determines that:

(A) The brucellosis reactor is located in a herd in a different State than the

State where the MCI blood sample was collected. In such cases a State representative or APHIS representative must give written notice of the MCI test results to the State animal health official in the State where the brucellosis reactor is located; or

(B) Evidence indicates that the brucellosis reactor is from a herd that no longer presents a risk of spreading brucellosis, or is from a herd that is unlikely to be infected with brucellosis. Such evidence could include, but is not limited to, situations where:

(*1*) The brucellosis reactor is traced back to a herd that has been sold for slaughter in entirety;

(*2*) The brucellosis reactor is traced back to a herd that is certified brucellosis free and is 100-percent vaccinated; or

(*3*) The brucellosis reactor showed a low titer in the MCI test and is traced back to a dairy herd that is 100 percent vaccinated and has tested negative to the most recent brucellosis ring test required by this section for herds producing milk for sale.

(iii) *Epidemiologic surveillance*—(A) *Adjacent herds.* All adjacent herds or other herds having contact with cattle or bison in a herd known to be affected shall be placed under quarantine and have an approved individual herd plan in effect within 15 days after notification of brucellosis in the herd known to be affected;

(B) *Epidemiologically traced herds.* All herds from which cattle or bison are moved into a herd known to be affected and all herds which have received cattle or bison from a herd known to be affected shall be placed under quarantine and have an approved individual herd plan in effect within 15 days of locating the source herd or recipient herd. Each State shall ensure that such approved individual herd plans are effectively complied with, as determined by the Administrator.

(b) *Herd infection rate*—(1) *Affected herds.* Except as provided in paragraph (b)(4) of this definition, all cattle and bison herds in the State or area must remain free of *Brucella abortus*.

(2) *Epidemiologic investigation.* Within 15 days after notification by the cooperative State-Federal laboratory that brucellosis reactors have been found in any herd, State representatives or APHIS representatives shall investigate that herd to identify possible sources of brucellosis. All possible sources of brucellosis identified shall be contacted within an additional 15 days to determine appropriate action.

(3) *Approved herd plans.* All herds known to be affected shall have approved individual herd plans in effect within 15 days after notification by a State representative or APHIS representative of a brucellosis reactor in the herd. Each State shall ensure that such approved individual herd plans are effectively complied with, as determined by the Administrator.

(4) *Affected herd.* If any herd in a Class Free State or area is found to be affected with brucellosis, the State or area may retain its Class Free status if it meets the conditions of this paragraph.

(i) *The affected herd.* (A) The affected herd must be quarantined immediately, and, within 60 days, tested for brucellosis and depopulated; or

(B) The affected herd must be quarantined immediately and tested for brucellosis as required by the Administrator until there is no evidence of brucellosis in the herd; and

(ii) *Other herds.* An epidemiological investigation must be performed within 60 days of the detection of an infected animal in a herd. All herds on premises adjacent to the affected herd (adjacent herds), all herds from which animals may have been brought into the affected herd (source herds), and all herds that may have had contact with or accepted animals from the affected herd (contact herds) must be epidemiologically investigated, and each of those herds must be placed under an approved individual herd plan. If the investigating epidemiologist determines that a herd blood test for a particular adjacent herd, source herd, or contact herd is not warranted, the epidemiologist must include that determination, and the reasons supporting it, in the individual herd plan.

(iii) *APHIS review.* After the close of the 60-day period following the date an animal in the herd is determined to be infected, APHIS will conduct a review to confirm that the requirements of paragraphs (b)(4)(i) and (b)(4)(ii) of this definition have been satisfied and that the State or area is in compliance with all other applicable provisions.

(c) *Brucellosis management plans.* (1) Any State in which the Administrator has determined wildlife are infected with *B. abortus* must develop and implement a brucellosis management plan approved by the Administrator. The existence of *B. abortus* in wildlife will be determined by the Administrator, based on, but not limited to, histopathology, testing data, or epidemiology. The Administrator may also require a Class Free State or area to develop and implement a brucellosis management plan under any other circumstances if the Administrator determines it is necessary to prevent the spread of brucellosis. The State must sign a memorandum of understanding (MOU) with the Administrator that describes its brucellosis management plan. The MOU must be updated annually. The Administrator may reclassify to a lower status any State or area that has not implemented an approved brucellosis management plan within 6 months of being required to develop one.

(2) The brucellosis management plan reflected in the MOU must:

(i) Define and explain the basis for the geographic area in which a disease risk exists from *B. abortus* and to which the brucellosis management plan activities apply;

(ii) Describe epidemiologic assessment and surveillance activities to identify occurrence of *B. abortus* in domestic livestock and wildlife and potential risks for spread of disease; and

(iii) Describe mitigation activities to prevent the spread of *B. abortus* from domestic livestock and/or wildlife, as applicable, within or from the brucellosis management area.

Commuter herd. A herd of cattle or bison moved interstate during the course of normal livestock management operations and without change of ownership directly between two premises, as provided in a commuter herd agreement.

Commuter herd agreement. A written agreement between the owner(s) of a herd of cattle or bison and the animal health officials for the States or Tribes of origin and destination specifying the conditions required for the interstate movement from one premises to another in the course of normal livestock management operations and specifying the time period, up to 1 year, that the agreement is effective. A commuter herd agreement may be renewed annually.

Complete herd test (CHT). An official swine brucellosis test of all swine on a premises that are 6 months of age or older and maintained for breeding purposes.

Confirmatory test. A follow-up test to verify any official test results. Confirmatory tests include the standard tube test, the Rivanol test, the complement fixation test (CF), the fluorescence polarization assay (FP assay), the particle concentration fluorescence immunoassay (PCFIA), the semen plasma test, and the standard plate test.

Dairy cattle. All cattle, regardless of age or sex or current use, that are of a breed(s) used to produce milk or other dairy products for human consumption, including, but not limited to, Ayrshire, Brown Swiss, Holstein, Jersey, Guernsey, Milking Shorthorn, and Red and Whites.

Designated epidemiologist. An epidemiologist selected by the State animal health official and the Veterinarian in Charge to perform the functions required. The regional epidemiologist and the APHIS brucellosis staff must concur in the selection and appointment of the designated epidemiologist.

Directly. Moved in a means of conveyance, without stopping to unload while en route, except for stops of less than 24 hours to feed, water or rest the animals being moved, and with no commingling of animals at such stops.

Epidemiologist. A veterinarian who has received a master's degree in epidemiology or completed a course of study in epidemiology sponsored by the Animal and Plant Health Inspection Service, United States Department of Agriculture.

Epidemiology. A branch of medical science that deals with the incidence, distribution, and control of disease in the animal population.

Farm of origin. (a) Premises where cattle or bison are born and remain prior to movement from the premises but which are not used to assemble cattle or bison from any other premises for 4 months before such movement; or

(b) Premises where cattle or bison remain for not less than 4 months immediately before movement from the premises but which are not used to assemble cattle or bison from any other premises for 4 months before such movement.

Feral swine. Free-roaming swine. Formerly free-roaming swine could qualify for reclassification as domestic swine upon testing negative to an official swine brucellosis test after a period of at least 60 days' confinement in isolation from other feral swine.

Finished fed cattle. Cattle fattened on a ration of feed concentrates to reach a slaughter condition equivalent to that which would be attained on full feed with a high concentrate grain ration for 90 days.

Herd. (a) All animals under common ownership or supervision that are grouped on one or more parts of any single premises (lot, farm, or ranch); or

(b) All animals under common ownership or supervision on two or more premises which are geographically separated but on which animals from the different premises have been interchanged or had contact with each other.

(c) For the purposes of this part, the term *herd* does not include animals that are contained within a federally approved research facility.

Herd blood test. A blood test for brucellosis conducted in a herd on all cattle and bison 18 months of age or older, except for steers and spayed heifers, and except when conducting herd blood tests as part of affected herd investigations or other epidemiological investigations or when the Administrator determines testing at a younger age is necessary to prevent the spread of brucellosis.

Herd known to be affected. Any herd in which any animal has been classified as a brucellosis reactor and which has not been released from quarantine.

Herd not known to be affected. Any herd in which no animal has been classified as a brucellosis reactor or any herd in which one or more animals have been classified as brucellosis reactors but which has been released from quarantine.

Herd of origin of swine. Any herd in which swine are farrowed and remain until movement or any herd in which swine remain for 30 days immediately prior to movement.

Interstate. From any State into or through any other State.

Interstate certificate of veterinary inspection (ICVI). An official document issued by a Federal, State, Tribal, or accredited veterinarian certifying the inspection of animals in preparation for interstate movement.

(1) The ICVI must show the species of animals covered by the ICVI; the number of animals covered by the ICVI; the purpose for which the animals are to be moved; the address at which the animals were loaded for interstate movement; the address to which the animals are destined; and the names of the consignor and the consignee and their addresses if different from the address at which the animals were loaded or the address to which the animals are destined. Additionally, unless the species-specific requirements for ICVIs provide an exception, the ICVI must list the official identification number of each animal, except as provided in paragraph (2) of this definition, or group of animals moved that is required to be officially identified, or, if an alternative form of identification has been agreed upon by the sending and receiving States, the ICVI must include a record of that identification. If animals moving under a GIN also have individual official identification, only the GIN must be listed on the ICVI. An ICVI may not be issued for any animal that is not officially identified if official identification is required. If the animals are not required by the regulations to be officially identified, the ICVI must state the exemption that applies (e.g., the cattle and bison do not belong to one of the classes of cattle and bison to which the official identification requirements of 9 CFR part 86 apply). If the animals are required to be officially identified but the identification number does not have to be recorded on the ICVI, the ICVI must state that all animals to be moved under the ICVI are officially identified.

(2) As an alternative to typing or writing individual animal identification on an ICVI, if agreed to by the receiving State or Tribe, another document may be used to provide this information, but only under the following conditions:

(i) The document must be a State form or APHIS form that requires individual identification of animals or a printout of official identification numbers generated by computer or other means;

(ii) A legible copy of the document must be stapled to the original and each copy of the ICVI;

(iii) Each copy of the document must identify each animal to be moved with the ICVI, but any information pertaining to other animals, and any unused space on the document for recording animal identification, must be crossed out in ink; and

(iv) The following information must be written in ink in the identification column on the original and each copy of the ICVI and must be circled or boxed, also in ink, so that no additional information can be added:

(A) The name of the document; and

(B) Either the unique serial number on the document or, if the document is not imprinted with a serial number, both the name of the person who prepared the document and the date the document was signed.

Location-based number system. The location-based number system combines a State or Tribal issued location identification (LID) number or a premises identification number (PIN) with a producer's unique livestock production numbering system to provide a nationally unique and herd-unique identification number for an animal.

Location identification (LID) number. A nationally unique number issued by a State, Tribal, and/or Federal animal health authority to a location as determined by the State or Tribe in which it is issued. The LID number may be used in conjunction with a producer's own unique livestock production numbering system to provide a nationally unique and herd-unique identification number for an animal. It may also be used as a component of a group/lot identification number (GIN).

Market cattle identification test cattle. Cows and bulls 18 months of age or over which have been moved to recognized slaughtering establishments, and test-eligible cattle which are subjected to an official test for the purposes of movement at farms, ranches, auction markets, stockyards, quarantined feedlots, or other assembly points. Such cattle must be identified with an official identification device as specified in § 86.4(a) of this chapter prior to or at the first market, stockyard, quarantined feedlot, or slaughtering establishment they reach.

Market swine test (MST) reactor. Market swine test swine with a positive reaction to a swine brucellosis confirmatory test or other official test, if no confirmatory test is performed.

Market swine test swine. Sows and boars which have been moved to slaughtering establishments and sows and boars which are subjected to an official test for the purposes of movement at farms, ranches, auction markets, stockyards, or other assembly points.

Monitored-negative feral swine population. Feral swine indicating no evidence of infection (indicators would include positive blood tests or clinical signs, such as abortion) and originating from a specified, geographically isolated area (a forest area, hunting preserve, or swamp, for example) may be classified by the designated epidemiologist as a monitored-negative feral swine population.

Moved. Shipped, transported, delivered, or received for movement, or otherwise aided, induced, or caused to be moved.

Moved (movement) in interstate commerce. Moved from the point of origin of the interstate movement to the animals' final destination, such as a slaughtering establishment or a farm for breeding or raising, and including any temporary stops for any purpose along the way, such as at a stockyard or dealer premises for feed, water, rest, or sale.

National Uniform Eartagging System (NUES). A numbering system for the official identification of individual animals in the United States that provides a nationally unique identification number for each animal.

Official adult vaccinate. (a) Female cattle or female bison older than the specified ages defined for official calfhood vaccinate and vaccinated by an APHIS representative, State representative, or accredited veterinarian with a reduced dose approved brucella vaccine, diluted so as to contain at least 300 million and not more than 1 billion live cells per 2 mL dose of *Brucella abortus* Strain 19 vaccine or at the dosage indicated on the label instructions for other approved brucella vaccines, as part of a whole herd vaccination plan authorized jointly by the State animal health official and the Veterinarian in Charge; and

(b)(1) Permanently identified by a "V" hot brand high on the hip near the tailhead at least 5 by 5 centimeters (2 by 2 inches) in size, or by an official AV (adult vaccination) tattoo in the right ear preceded by the quarter of the year and followed by the last digit of the year; and

(2) Identified with an official eartag or individual animal registered breed association registration brand or individual animal registered breed association tattoo.

Official brand inspection certificate. A document issued by an official brand inspection agency in any State which requires such documents for movement of cattle or bison.

Official brand recording agency. The duly constituted body authorized by a State or governmental subdivision thereof to administer laws, regulations, ordinances or rules pertaining to the brand identification of cattle or bison.

Official calfhood vaccinate. (a) Female cattle or female bison vaccinated while from 4 through 12 months of age by an APHIS representative, State representative, or accredited veterinarian with a reduced dose approved brucella vaccine containing at least 2.7 billion and not more than 10 billion live cells per 2 mL dose of *Brucella abortus* Strain 19 vaccine or at the dosage indicated on the label instructions for other approved brucella vaccines; and

(b) Permanently identified by a tattoo and by an official vaccination eartag in the right ear. However, if already identified with an official eartag prior to vaccination, an additional tag is not required. The tattoo must include the U.S. Registered Shield and "V," preceded by the quarter of the year and followed by the last digit of the year of vaccination. Individual animal registered breed association registration brands or individual animal registered breed association registration tattoos may be substituted for official eartags.

Official eartag. An identification tag approved by APHIS that bears an official identification number for individual animals. Beginning March 11, 2014, all official eartags manufactured must bear an official eartag shield. Beginning March 11, 2015, all official eartags applied to animals must bear an official eartag shield. The design, size, shape, color, and other characteristics of the official eartag will depend on the needs of the users, subject to the approval of the Administrator. The official eartag must be tamper-resistant and have a high retention rate in the animal.

Official eartag shield. The shield-shaped graphic of the U.S. Route Shield with "U.S." or the State postal abbreviation or Tribal alpha code imprinted within the shield.

Official identification number. A nationally unique number that is permanently associated with an animal or group of animals and that adheres to one of the following systems:

(1) National Uniform Eartagging System.

(2) Animal identification number (AIN).

(3) Location-based number system.

(4) Flock-based number system.

(5) Any other numbering system approved by the Administrator for the official identification of animals.

Officially identified. Identified by means of an official identification device or method approved by the Administrator.

Official seal. A serially numbered, metal or plastic strip, consisting of a self-locking device on one end and a slot on the other end, which forms a loop when the ends are engaged and which cannot be reused if opened, or a serially numbered, self-locking button which can be used for this purpose.

Official swine tattoo. A tattoo, conforming to the six-character alpha-numeric National Tattoo System, that provides a unique identification for each herd or lot of swine.

Official test—(a) *Classification of cattle and bison*—(1) *Standard card test.* (i) A test to determine the brucellosis disease status of test-eligible cattle and bison when conducted according to instructions approved by APHIS and the State in which the test is to be conducted and when conducted under the following circumstances:

(A) When conditions and time are such that no other test is available; or

(B) When the owner or the owner's agent requests it because of time or situation constraints; or

(C) In specifically approved stockyards when the State animal health official either:

(*1*) Designates the standard card test as the official test for determining the brucellosis disease status of cattle and bison in all specifically approved stockyards in the State. In these States, no other official test except the Buffered Acidified Plate Antigen test shall be used in specifically approved stockyards; or

(*2*) Designates the standard card test as the official test for determining the brucellosis disease status of non-vaccinated cattle or bison (the CITE® test may be designated as a supplemental test for non-vaccinated cattle or bison that test positive to the standard card test); and designates the standard card test as the official test for determining the brucellosis disease status of official vaccinates and the CITE® test, the standard plate test, or the Rivanol test as supplemental tests for official vaccinates that test positive to the standard card test. If supplemental tests are conducted, cattle or bison that are positive to the standard card test shall be classified as brucellosis suspects if all of the supplemental tests conducted disclose a negative or suspect reaction, and shall be classified as brucellosis reactors if any one of the supplemental tests conducted has a positive reaction; or

(D) To test market cattle identification (MCI) program test samples. Cattle and bison which test positive to the BAPA test or RST under the MCI program must be retested using the standard card test or the standard plate or tube agglutination test.

(ii) Results of the standard card test also may be used to supplement the results of other official tests conducted in the cooperative State-Federal laboratory to give the designated epidemiologist additional information when classifying cattle and bison.

(iii) *Standard card test results are interpreted as either negative or positive.* A moderate to marked clumping agglutination reaction is a positive result. Test-eligible cattle and bison positive to the standard card test are classified as brucellosis reactors. Test-eligible cattle and bison negative to the standard card test are classified as brucellosis negative.

(2) *Standard tube test (STT) or standard plate test (SPT).* A test to determine the brucellosis disease status of test-eligible cattle and bison when conducted according to instructions approved by APHIS and the State in which the test is to be conducted. Cattle and bison are classified according to the following agglutination reactions:

SPT OR STT CLASSIFICATION—OFFICIAL VACCINATES VACCINATED WITH A BRUCELLA ABORTUS STRAIN 19 APPROVED BRUCELLA VACCINE

Titer			Classification
1:50	1:100	1:200	
–	–	–	Negative.
I	–	–	Do.
+	–	–	Do.
+	I	–	Suspect.
+	+	–	Do.
+	+	I	Do.
+	+	+	Reactor.

– No agglutination.
I Incomplete agglutination.
+ Complete agglutination.

OFFICIAL VACCINATES VACCINATED WITH AN APPROVED BRUCELLA VACCINE OTHER THAN A BRUCELLA ABORTUS STRAIN 19 APPROVED BRUCELLA VACCINE

Titer			Classification
1:50	1:100	1:200	
–	–	–	Negative.
I	–	–	Suspect.
+	–	–	Do.
+	I	–	Do.
+	+	–	Reactor.
+	+	I	Do.

OFFICIAL VACCINATES VACCINATED WITH AN APPROVED BRUCELLA VACCINE OTHER THAN A BRUCELLA ABORTUS STRAIN 19 APPROVED BRUCELLA VACCINE—Continued

Titer			Classification
1:50	1:100	1:200	
+	+	+	Do.

− No agglutination.
I Incomplete agglutination.
+ Complete agglutination.

ALL CATTLE AND BISON WHICH ARE NOT OFFICIAL VACCINATES

Titer			Classification
1:50	1:100	1:200	
−	−	−	Negative.
I	−	−	Suspect.
+	−	−	Do.
+	I	−	Do.
+	+	−	Reactor.
+	+	I	Do.
+	+	+	Do.

− No agglutination.
I Incomplete agglutination.
+ Complete agglutination.

(3) *Manual complement-fixation (CF) test.* A test to determine the brucellosis disease status of test-eligible cattle and bison when conducted according to instructions approved by APHIS and the State in which the test is to be conducted. Cattle and bison are classified according to the following reactions:

(i) Cattle and bison which are not official vaccinates:

(A) Fifty percent fixation (2 plus) in a dilution of 1:20 or higher—brucellosis reactor;

(B) Fifty percent fixation (2 plus) in a dilution of 1:10 but less than 50 percent fixation (2 plus) in a dilution of 1:20—brucellosis suspect;

(C) Less than 50 percent fixation (2 plus) in a dilution of 1:10—brucellosis negative;

(ii) Official vaccinates vaccinated with a *Brucella abortus* Strain 19 approved brucella vaccine:

(A) Twenty-five percent fixation (1 plus) in a dilution of 1:40 or higher—brucellosis reactor;

(B) Fifty percent fixation (2 plus) in a dilution of 1:10 but less than 25 percent fixation (1 plus) in a dilution of 1:40—brucellosis suspect;

(C) Less than 50 percent fixation (2 plus) in a dilution of 1:10—brucellosis negative.

(iii) Official vaccinates vaccinated with an approved brucella vaccine other than a *Brucella abortus* Strain 19 approved brucella vaccine:

(A) Fifty percent fixation (2 plus) in a dilution of 1:20 or higher—brucellosis reactor;

(B) Fifty percent fixation (2 plus) in a dilution of 1:10 but less than 50 percent fixation (2 plus) in a dilution of 1:20—brucellosis suspect;

(C) Less than 50 percent fixation (2 plus) in a dilution of 1:10—brucellosis negative.

(4) *Technicon automated complement-fixation test.* A test to determine the brucellosis disease status of test-eligible cattle and bison when conducted according to instructions approved by APHIS and the State in which the test is to be conducted. Cattle and bison are classified according to the following reactions:

(i) Cattle and bison which are not official vaccinates:

(A) Fixation in a dilution of 1:10 or higher—brucellosis reactor;

(B) Fixation in a dilution of 1:5 but no fixation in a dilution of 1:10—brucellosis suspect;

(C) No fixation in a dilution of 1:5 or lower—brucellosis negative;

(ii) Official vaccinates vaccinated with a *Brucella abortus* Strain 19 approved brucella vaccine:

(A) Fixation in a dilution of 1:20 or higher—brucellosis reactor;

(B) Fixation in a dilution of 1:10 but no fixation in a dilution of 1:20—brucellosis suspect;

(C) Fixation in a dilution of 1:5 or less but no fixation in a dilution of 1:10—brucellosis negative.

(iii) Official vaccinates vaccinated with an approved brucella vaccine other than a *Brucella abortus* Strain 19 approved brucella vaccine:

(A) Fixation in a dilution of 1:10 or higher—brucellosis reactor;

(B) Fixation in a dilution of 1:5 but no fixation in a dilution of 1:10—brucellosis suspect;

(C) No fixation in a dilution of 1:5 or lower—brucellosis negative.

(5) *Rivanol test.* A test to determine the brucellosis disease status of test-eligible cattle and bison when conducted according to instructions approved by APHIS and the State in which the test is to be conducted. Cattle and bison are classified according to the following agglutination reactions:

(i) Cattle and bison which are not official vaccinates:

(A) Complete agglutination at a titer of 1:25 or higher—brucellosis reactor;

(B) Less than complete agglutination at a titer of 1:25—brucellosis negative;

(ii) Official adult vaccinates more than 5 months after vaccination with a *Brucella abortus* Strain 19 approved brucella vaccine and official calfhood vaccinates vaccinated with a *Brucella abortus* Strain 19 approved brucella vaccine:

(A) Incomplete agglutination at a titer of 1:100 or higher—brucellosis reactor;

(B) Complete agglutination at a titer of 1:25 or higher when the manual or technicon automated complement-fixation test is not conducted—brucellosis reactor;

(C) Complete agglutination at a titer of 1:50 or less when the manual complement-fixation test or the technicon automated complement-fixation test is conducted and results in a classification of brucellosis suspect or brucellosis negative—brucellosis suspect;

(D) Less than complete agglutination at a titer of 1:25—brucellosis negative;

(iii) Official adult vaccinates less than 5 months after vaccination with a *Brucella abortus* Strain 19 approved brucella vaccine: Less than complete agglutination at the 1:50 titer—brucellosis negative.

(iv) Official vaccinates vaccinated with an approved brucella vaccine other than a *Brucella abortus* Strain 19 approved brucella vaccine:

(A) Complete agglutination at a titer of 1:25 or higher—brucellosis reactor;

(B) Less than complete agglutination at a titer of 1:25—brucellosis negative.

(6) *Semen plasma test.* A test to determine the brucellosis disease status of bulls used for artificial insemination when conducted in conjunction with an official serological test and according to instructions approved by APHIS and the State in which the test is to be conducted. The classification of such bulls shall be based on the maximum agglutination titer of either the official serological test or the semen plasma test.

(7) *Buffered acidified plate antigen (BAPA) test.* A test to determine the brucellosis disease status of test-eligible cattle and bison at recognized slaughtering establishments and specifically approved stockyards when conducted according to instructions approved by APHIS and the State in which the test is to be conducted. BAPA test results are interpreted as either negative or positive. Cattle and bison negative to the BAPA test are classified as brucellosis negative. Cattle and bison positive to the BAPA test shall be subjected to other official tests to determine their brucellosis classification.

(8) *Rapid screening test (RST).* A test to determine the brucellosis disease status of test-eligible cattle and bison in cooperative State-Federal laboratories when conducted according to instructions approved by APHIS and the State in which the test is to be conducted. RST results are interpreted as either negative or positive. Cattle and bison negative to the RST are classified as brucellosis negative. Cattle and bison positive to the RST shall be subjected to other official tests to determine their brucellosis classification.

(9) *Concentration immunoassay technology (CITE®) test.* An enzyme immunoassay that may be used as a diagnostic supplement to the standard card test by designated epidemiologists determining the brucellosis disease status of cattle and bison. The test must be done in accordance with the CITE® *Brucella abortus* Antibody Test Kit instructions, licensed by the United States Department of Agriculture and approved as of December 31, 1987, and incorporated by reference. This incorporation by reference was approved by the Director of the Federal Register in accordance with 5 U.S.C. 552(a) and 1 CFR part 51. Copies may be obtained from AgriTech Systems, Inc., 100 Fore Street, Portland, ME 04101. Copies may be inspected at the Animal and Plant Health Inspection Service,

Veterinary Services, Operational Support, 4700 River Road Unit 33, Riverdale, Maryland 20737–1231, or at the National Archives and Records Administration (NARA). For information on the availability of this material at NARA, call 202–741–6030, or go to: *http://www.archives.gov/federal_register/code_of_federal_regulations/ibr_locations.html.*

(10) *Particle concentration fluorescence immunoassay (PCFIA) test.* An automated serologic test to determine the brucellosis disease status of test-eligible cattle and bison when conducted according to instructions approved by APHIS. Cattle and bison are classified according to the following ratio between the test sample and a known negative sample (S/N ratio):

S/N ratio	Classification
Greater than .60	Negative.
Greater than .30 but less than or equal to .60.	Suspect.
.30 or less	Positive.

(11) *D-Tec® Brucella A test.* An automated serologic test to determine the brucellosis disease status of test-eligible cattle and bison when conducted according to instructions approved by APHIS. The degree of reactivity is measured by the ratio of the average optical density of the sample to that of the Negative Control (S/N) and is expressed as Percent Inhibition (1–S/N) × 100. The brucellosis disease status of the animals is classified according to the following established criteria:

Percent inhibition	Classification
Less than or equal to 40 percent	Negative.
Greater than 40 percent and less than or equal to 70 percent.	Suspect.
Greater than 70 percent	Reactor.

(12) *Rapid Automated Presumptive (RAP) test.* An automated serologic test to detect the presence of *Brucella* antibodies in test-eligible cattle and bison. RAP test results are interpreted as either positive or negative; the results are interpreted and reported by a scanning autoreader that measures alterations in light transmission through each test well and the degree of agglutination present. Cattle and bison negative to the RAP test are classified as brucellosis negative; cattle and bison positive to the RAP test shall be subjected to other official tests to determine their brucellosis disease classification.

(13) *Fluorescence polarization assay (FP assay).* An automated serologic test to determine the brucellosis status of test-eligible cattle and bison when conducted according to instructions approved by APHIS. FP assays are interpreted as either positive, negative, or suspect. A 10-microliter sample is used. If a sample reads <10 millipolarization units (mP) above the mean negative control, the sample is considered negative. If a sample reads >20 mP above the mean negative control, the sample is considered positive. Samples that read between 10 and 20 mP above the negative control mean should be retested using 20 microliters of sample. If the 20-microliter sample is >20 mP above the mean negative control, the sample is considered positive. If the 20-microliter sample is still in the 10 to 20 mP range above the mean negative control, the sample is considered suspect. If the 20-microliter sample is <10 mP above the mean negative control, the sample is considered negative. Cattle and bison negative to the FP assay are classified as brucellosis negative. Cattle and bison with positive FP assay results are classified as brucellosis reactors, while cattle and bison with suspect FP assay results are classified as brucellosis suspects.

(14) The evaluation of test results for all cattle and bison shall be the responsibility of a designated epidemiologist in each State. The designated epidemiologist shall consider the animal and herd history and other epidemiologic factors when determining the brucellosis classification of cattle and bison. Deviations from the brucellosis classification criteria as provided in this definition of official test are acceptable when made by the designated epidemiologist.

(i) The designated epidemiologist may consider the results of CITE® tests when evaluating the results of standard card tests of cattle and bison.

(b) *Classification of swine*—(1) *Standard card test.* A test to determine the brucellosis disease status of swine. Standard card test results are interpreted as either negative or positive. A moderate to marked clumping agglutination reaction is a positive result. Swine negative to the standard card test are classified as brucellosis negative. Swine positive to the standard card test in a herd not known to be affected but negative to any other official test or bacteriological culture for *brucella* are classified as brucellosis suspects. Other swine positive to the standard card test are classified as brucellosis reactors.

(2) *Standard tube test.* A test to determine the brucellosis disease status of swine.

(i) If all of the following apply: (A) The swine are part of a herd not known to be affected; (B) No swine tested, individually or as part of a group, has a complete agglutination reaction at a dilution of 1:100 or higher; and (C) the swine are tested as part of a herd blood test or are part of a validated brucellosis-free herd, then the swine are classified according to the following agglutination reactions:

Titer		Classification	
1:25	1:50	1:100	
I	]—	–	Negative.
+	–	–	Do.
+	I	–	Do.
+	+	–	Do.
+	+	I	Do.

– No agglutination.
I Incomplete agglutination.
+ Complete agglutination.

(ii) If any of the following apply: (A) The swine are part of a herd known to be affected; (B) Any swine tested, individually or as part of a group, has a complete agglutination reaction at a dilution of 1:100 or higher or; (C) The swine are not part of a validated brucellosis-free herd and are not being tested as part of a herd blood test, then the swine are classified according to the following agglutination reactions:

Titer		Classification	
1:25	1:50	1:100	
I	–	–	Negative.
+	–	–	Reactor.
+	I	–	Do.
+	+	–	Do.
+	+	I	Do.
+	+	+	Do.

– No agglutination.
I Incomplete agglutination.
+ Complete agglutination.

(3) *Particle concentration fluoresence immunoassay (PCFIA).* An automated serologic test to determine the brucellosis disease status of test-eligible swine when conducted according to instructions approved by the Animal and Plant Health Inspection Service. Swine are classified according to the following ratios between the test sample and a known negative sample (S/N ratio):

S/N Ratio	Classification
0.71 or greater	Negative.
0.51 to 0.70	Suspect.
0.50 or less	Reactor.

(4) *Rapid Automated Presumptive (RAP) test.* An automated serologic test to detect the presence of *Brucella* antibodies in test-eligible swine. RAP test results are interpreted as either positive or negative; the results are interpreted and reported by a scanning autoreader that measures agglutination based on alterations in light transmission through each test well. Swine negative to the RAP test are classified as brucellosis negative; swine positive to the RAP test shall be subjected to other official tests to determine their brucellosis disease classification.

(5) *Fluorescence polarization assay (FP assay).* An automated serologic test to determine the brucellosis status of test-eligible swine when conducted according to instructions approved by APHIS. FP assays are interpreted as either positive, negative, or suspect. A 40-microliter sample is used. If a sample reads <10 millipolarization units (mP) above the mean negative control, the sample is considered negative. If a sample reads >20 mP above the mean negative control, the sample is considered positive. Samples that read between 10 and 20 mP above the negative control mean must be retested using 40 microliters of sample. If the 40-microliter sample is >20 mP above the mean negative control, the sample is considered positive. If the 40-microliter sample is still in the 10 to 20 mP range above the mean negative control, the sample is considered suspect. If the 40-microliter sample is <10 mP above the mean negative control, the sample is considered negative. Swine with negative FP assay results are classified as

brucellosis negative. Swine with positive FP assay results are classified as brucellosis reactors, while swine with suspect FP assay results are classified as brucellosis suspects.

(6) The evaluation of test results for all swine shall be the responsibility of a designated epidemiologist in each State. The designated epidemiologist shall consider the animal and herd history and other epidemiologic factors when determining the brucellosis classification of swine. Deviations from the brucellosis classification criteria as provided in this definition of official test are acceptable when made by the designated epidemiologist.

Official vaccinate. An official calfhood vaccinate or an official adult vaccinate. The accredited veterinarian, State representative or APHIS representative who performs the vaccination must forward a completed official vaccination certificate for each animal vaccinated to the State animal health official of the State in which the animal was vaccinated.

Official vaccination eartag. An APHIS approved identification eartag conforming to the alpha-numeric National Uniform Eartagging System which provides unique identification for each animal. The eartag shall have a "V" followed by 2 letters and 4 numbers. States which require more official vaccination eartags than the number of combinations available in the "V" series of tags shall use a "T" or "S" followed by 2 letters and 4 numbers. Duplicate reissue of official vaccination eartags shall not be made more often than once each 15 years.

Originate. (a) Animals will have the status of the herd from which they are moved if:

(1) They were born and maintained in the herd since birth; or

(2) They have been in the herd for at least 120 days.

(b) Animals will have the status of the State or area from which they are moved if:

(1) They were born and maintained in the State or area since birth; or

(2) They were previously moved from a State or area of equal or higher class to the State or area; or

(3) They were previously moved from a State or area of lower class to the State or area where they are now located and have been in the new State or area for at least 120 days.

(c) Cattle or bison penned in a specifically approved stockyard with cattle or bison from a lower class State or area, in violation of the requirements set forth in §71.20 of this chapter, shall have the status of the State or area of lower class for any subsequent movement.

Parturient. Visibly prepared to give birth or within 2 weeks of giving birth (springers).

Permit. An official document (VS Form 1–27 or a State form which contains the same information but not a "permit for entry" or "'S' brand permit") issued by an APHIS representative, State representative, or accredited veterinarian which lists the owner's name and address, points of origin and destination, number of animals covered, purpose of the movement, any reactor tag number, and one of the following: The official eartag number, individual animal registered breed association registration tattoo, individual animal registered breed association registration brand, United States Department of Agriculture backtag (when applied serially, only the beginning and the ending numbers need be recorded), individual animal registered breed association registration number, or similar individual identification. (A new permit is required for each change in destination. However, permits accompanying cattle or bison to an approved intermediate handling facility may list either the approved intermediate handling facility, a quarantined feedlot or a recognized slaughtering establishment as the point of destination. If the permit lists a quarantined feedlot or a recognized slaughtering establishment as the point of destination, then the permit must list the approved intermediate handling facility as a temporary stopping point, and no additional permit is required for the subsequent movement of the cattle or bison to the quarantined feedlot or to the recognized slaughtering establishment.)

Permit for entry. A premovement authorization for entry of cattle into a

State from the State animal health official of the State of destination. It may be oral or written.

Person. Any individual, corporation, company, association, firm, partnership, society, or joint stock company or other legal entity.

Postparturient. Having given birth.

Purebred registry association. A swine breed association formed and perpetuated for the maintenance of records of purebreeding of swine species for a specific breed whose characteristics are set forth in Constitutions, By-Laws, and other rules of the association.

Qualified herd. (a) *Qualification.* (1) Any herd of cattle or bison which is in a quarantined area, not known to be affected, and negative to two consecutive herd blood tests. The first of these two herd blood tests shall be conducted not more than 240 days nor less than 120 days prior to the date of classification as a qualified herd. The second herd blood test may not be conducted less than 90 days nor more than 150 days after the first test. Additionally, the second herd blood test must be within 120 days of the date of classification as a qualified herd; or

(2) Any certified brucellosis-free herd in a quarantined area which is negative to a herd blood test 120 days before or after designation of the area as a quarantined area.

(b) *Requalification.* In order to remain a qualified herd, a herd must be negative to successive requalifying herd blood tests. Each requalifying test shall be conducted not more than 120 days from the date of the preceding herd blood test. All cattle or bison added to a qualified herd must be included in two successive herd blood tests of the qualified herd to qualify as cattle or bison from the qualified herd.

Quarantined area. An area that does not meet the criteria for classification as Class Free, Class A, Class B, or Class C.

Quarantined feedlot.[1] A confined area under State quarantine approved jointly by the State animal health official and the Veterinarian in Charge. Approval will be granted only after a State representative or APHIS representative inspects the confined area and determines that all cattle and bison are secure and isolated from contact with all other cattle and bison, that there are facilities for identifying cattle and bison, and that there is no possibility of brucellosis being mechanically transmitted from the confined area. The quarantined feedlot shall be maintained for feeding cattle and bison for slaughter, with no provisions for pasturing or grazing. All cattle and bison in a quarantined feedlot, except steers and spayed heifers, shall be treated as brucellosis exposed.

(a) All cattle and bison, except steers and spayed heifers, leaving the quarantined feedlot must (1) Be accompanied by a permit and move directly to a recognized slaughtering establishment; or (2) Be "S" branded and accompanied by an "S" brand permit and move directly to an approved intermediate handling facility and then directly to another quarantined feedlot or a recognized slaughtering establishment; or (3) Be accompanied by a permit issued by the State animal health official and move directly to another quarantined feedlot; or (4) After being "S" branded at the quarantined feedlot, be accompanied by an "S" brand permit and move directly to a specifically approved stockyard approved to receive brucellosis exposed cattle and bison and then directly to a recognized slaughtering establishment or another quarantined feedlot; or (5) After being "S" branded at the quarantined feedlot, be accompanied by an "S" brand permit and move directly to a specifically approved stockyard approved to receive brucellosis exposed cattle and bison and then directly to an approved intermediate handling facility and then directly to another quarantined feedlot or a recognized slaughtering establishment. However, finished fed cattle moving directly to a recognized slaughtering establishment are exempt from the permit/"S" brand permit requirement.

(b) The State animal health official and the Veterinarian in Charge shall establish procedures for accounting for all cattle and bison entering or leaving quarantined feedlots.

[1] A list of quarantined feedlots in any State may be obtained from the State animal health official, a State representative, or an APHIS representative.

Quarantined pasture. A confined grazing area under State quarantine approved by the State animal health official, Veterinarian in Charge and the Administrator. A justification of the need for the quarantined pasture must be prepared by the State animal health official and/or Veterinarian in Charge and submitted to the Administrator. An intensified brucellosis eradication effort which produces large numbers of brucellosis exposed cattle or bison or official adult vaccinates needing the grazing period to reach slaughter condition would be an acceptable justification. Approval will be granted only after a State representative or APHIS representative inspects the confined grazing area and determines that all cattle and bison are secure and isolated from contact with all other cattle and bison, that there are facilities for identifying the cattle and bison, and that there is no possibility of brucellosis being mechanically transmitted from the confined grazing area. The quarantined pasture shall be for utilizing available forage for growth or to improve flesh condition of cattle or bison. No cattle or bison may be moved interstate into these quarantined pastures, which shall be restricted for use by cattle or bison originating within the State. All cattle or bison shall be of the same sex, except that neutered cattle and bison may share the quarantined pasture. All cattle and bison, except steers and spayed heifers, must be "S" branded upon entering the quarantined pasture. All cattle and bison, except steers and spayed heifers, leaving the quarantined pasture must move directly to a recognized slaughtering establishment or quarantined feedlot, or directly to an approved intermediate handling facility and then directly to a recognized slaughtering establishment, or directly to an approved intermediate handling facility and then directly to a quarantined feedlot and then directly to a recognized slaughtering establishment. The movement shall be in accordance with established procedures for handling brucellosis exposed cattle and bison, including issuance of "S" brand permits prior to movement. The State animal health official and Veterinarian in Charge shall establish procedures for accounting for all cattle and bison entering and leaving the quarantined pasture. All brucellosis exposed cattle and bison must vacate the premises on or before the expiration of approval, which may not last longer than 10 months.

Recognized slaughtering establishment. Any slaughtering facility operating under the Federal Meat Inspection Act (21 U.S.C. 601 *et seq.*), the Poultry Products Inspection Act (21 U.S.C. 451 *et seq.*), or State meat or poultry inspection acts that is approved in accordance with 9 CFR 71.21.

Rodeo cattle. Cattle used at rodeos or competitive events.

"S" branded. Branding with a hot iron the letter "S" high on the left hip near the tailhead and at least 5 by 5 centimeters (2 by 2 inches) in size.

"S" brand permit. A document prepared at the point of origin which lists the points of origin and destination, the number of animals covered, the purpose of movement, and one of the following: The official eartag number, individual animal registered breed association registration tattoo, individual animal registered breed association registration brand, individual animal registered breed association registration number, United States Department of Agriculture backtag (when applied serially, only the beginning and the ending numbers need be recorded), or similar individual identification. If the document is prepared at a quarantined feedlot, it shall be prepared by an accredited veterinarian, a State representative, or an individual designated for that purpose by the State animal health official. If the document is prepared at any other point of origin, it shall be prepared by an accredited veterinarian, State representative, or APHIS representative. (A new "S" brand permit is required for each change in destination. However, "S" brand permits accompanying cattle or bison to approved intermediate handling facilities may list either the approved intermediate handling facility, a quarantined feedlot, or a recognized slaughtering establishment as the point of destination. If the "S" brand permit lists a quarantined feedlot or a recognized slaughtering establishment as the point of destination, the "S"

brand permit must list the approved intermediate handling facility as a temporary stopping point, and no additional "S" brand permit is required for the subsequent movement of the cattle or bison from the approved intermediate handling facility to the quarantined feedlot or to the recognized slaughtering establishment. Subsequent movements from the quarantined feedlot shall be subject to requirements set forth in the definition of "quarantined feedlot" in this section.)

Sow. A female swine which is parturient or postparturient.

Specifically approved stockyard.[3] Premises where cattle or bison are assembled for sale or sale purposes and which meet the standards set forth in § 71.20 of this chapter and are approved by the Administrator.

State. Any State, the District of Columbia, Puerto Rico, the Virgin Islands of the United States, Guam, the Northern Mariana Islands or any other territory or possession of the United States.

State animal health official. The State official responsible for livestock and poultry disease control and eradication programs.

State representative. An individual employed in animal health work by a State or a political subdivision thereof and authorized by such State or political subdivision to perform the function involved under a memorandum of understanding with the United States Department of Agriculture.

Successfully closed case. Follow up of an MCI reactor traceback with an epidemiologic investigation which results in brucellosis testing or quarantine of the herd of origin, or a determination by a designated brucellosis epidemiologist that justification exists for not testing or quarantining the herd of origin.

Swine brucellosis. The communicable disease of swine caused by *Brucella suis* (*B. suis*) biovar 1 or 3.

[3] Notices containing lists of specifically approved stockyards are published in the FEDERAL REGISTER. Lists of specifically approved stockyards also may be obtained from the State animal health official, State representatives, or APHIS representatives.

Test-eligible cattle and bison. For purposes of interstate movement, test-eligible cattle and bison are:

(a) Cattle and bison which are not official vaccinates and which have lost their first pair of temporary incisors (18 months of age or over), except steers and spayed heifers;

(b) Official calfhood vaccinates 18 months of age or over which are parturient or postparturient;

(c) Official calfhood vaccinates of beef breeds or bison with the first pair of permanent incisors fully erupted (2 years of age or over); and

(d) Official calfhood vaccinates of dairy breeds with partial eruption of the first pair of permanent incisors (20 months of age or over).

United States. All of the States.

United States Department of Agriculture backtag. A backtag issued by APHIS that provides unique identification for each animal.

Validated brucellosis-free herd. (a) A swine herd not known to be infected with swine brucellosis, located in a validated brucellosis-free State; or

(b) A swine herd in a State that has not been validated as brucellosis-free, provided the herd meets the conditions for validation, as follows:

(1) *Validation.* A swine herd may be validated as brucellosis-free if it has been found brucellosis negative after either a complete-herd test (CHT) or an incremental CHT. The incremental CHT may be conducted by testing all breeding swine 6 months of age or older with negative results within 365 days, either in four 25-percent increments, with those tests being conducted on the 90th, 180th, 270th, and 360th days of the testing cycle, or in 10-percent increments every 25–35 days until 100 percent of those swine have been tested. In cases where unforseen circumstances warrant such action, the Administrator may approve an extension of up to 15 days of the date on which a test under the 25-percent incremental herd test is to be conducted, thus allowing a test to be conducted no later than the 105th, 195th, 285th, or 375th day of the testing cycle. No swine may be tested twice during the testing cycle to comply with either the 25 percent requirement or the 10 percent requirement. No

further testing is required once 100 percent of the breeding swine have been tested. After all breeding swine have tested brucellosis negative, a herd may be validated as brucellosis-free. Unless the Administrator has approved an alternative testing schedule, which might extend the testing cycle, a herd retains validated brucellosis-free status for a maximum of 365 days.

(2) *Maintaining validation.* Validation may be continuously maintained if a complete herd test (CHT) is performed once every 365 days, with negative results, or an incremental CHT is performed. The incremental CHT may be conducted by testing all breeding swine 6 months of age or older, with negative results, within 365 days in either four 25-percent increments, with those tests being conducted on the 90th, 180th, 270th, and 360th days of the testing cycle, or in 10-percent increments every 25–35 days until 100 percent of those swine have been tested. In cases where unforeseen circumstances warrant such action, the Administrator may approve an alternative testing schedule under which the 25 percent or 10 percent incremental CHT would be completed, with negative results, within 420 days, during which time the herd's validated brucellosis-free status would be continued. No swine may be tested twice during the testing cycle to comply with these requirements. No further testing is required once 100 percent of the breeding swine have been tested.

Validated brucellosis-free State. A State may apply for validated-free status when:

(a) Any herd found to have swine brucellosis during the 2-year qualification period preceding the application has been depopulated. More than one finding of a swine brucellosis-infected herd during the qualification period disqualifies the State from validation as brucellosis-free; and

(b) During the 2-year qualification period, the State has completed surveillance, annually, as follows:

(1) *Complete herd testing.* Subjecting all swine in the State that are 6 months of age or older and maintained for breeding purposes to an official swine brucellosis test; or

(2) *Market swine testing.* Subjecting 20 percent of the State's swine 6 months of age or older and maintained for breeding purposes to an official swine brucellosis test, and demonstrating successful traceback of at least 80 percent of market swine test (MST) reactors to the herd of origin. Blood samples may be collected from MST swine if the swine can be identified to their herd of origin, in accordance with § 71.19(b) of this subchapter. All MST reactor herds are subject to a CHT within 30 days of the MST laboratory report date, as determined by a designated epidemiologist; or

(3) *Statistical analysis.* Demonstrating, by a statistical analysis of all official swine brucellosis test results (including herd validation, MST, change-of-ownership, diagnostic) during the 2-year qualification period, a surveillance level equivalent or superior to CHT and MST testing programs discussed in this paragraph.

(c) To maintain validation, a State must annually survey at least 5 percent of its breeding swine, and demonstrate traceback to herd of origin of at least 80 percent of all MST reactors. A State must demonstrate its continuing ability to meet the criteria set forth in paragraph (c) of this definition within 36–40 months of receiving validated brucellosis-free State status to retain that status.

Veterinarian in Charge. The veterinary official of the Animal and Plant Health Inspection Service, United States Department of Agriculture, who is assigned by the Administrator to supervise and perform the official animal health work of the Animal and Plant Health Inspection Service in the State concerned.

Whole herd vaccination. The vaccination of all female cattle and female bison 4 months of age or over in a herd when authorized by the State animal health official and the Veterinarian in Charge, and conducted in accordance with the definitions of official adult vaccinate and official calfhood vaccinate.

(Approved by the Office of Management and Budget under control number 0579–0047)

[51 FR 32580, Sept. 12, 1986]

EDITORIAL NOTE: For FEDERAL REGISTER citations affecting § 78.1, see the List of CFR Sections Affected, which appears in the Finding Aids section of the printed volume and at *www.fdsys.gov*.

§ 78.2 Handling of certificates, permits, and "S" brand permits for interstate movement of animals.

(a) Any ICVI, other interstate movement document used in lieu of an ICVI, permit, or "S" brand permit required by this part for the interstate movement of animals shall be delivered to the person moving the animals by the shipper or shipper's agent at the time the animals are delivered for movement and shall accompany the animals to their destination and be delivered to the consignee or the person receiving the animals.

(b) The APHIS representative, State representative, Tribal representative, or accredited veterinarian issuing an ICVI or other interstate movement document used in lieu of an ICVI or a permit, except for permits for entry and "S" brand permits, that is required for the interstate movement of animals under this part shall forward a copy of the ICVI, other interstate movement document used in lieu of an ICVI, or permit to the State animal health official of the State of origin within 5 working days. The State animal health official of the State of origin shall forward a copy of the ICVI, other interstate movement document used in lieu of an ICVI, or permit to the State animal health official of the State of destination within 5 working days.

(Approved by the Office of Management and Budget under control number 0579–0047)

[78 FR 2069, Jan. 9, 2013]

§ 78.3 Handling in transit of cattle and bison moved interstate.

Cattle and bison moving interstate, except cattle and bison moved directly to a recognized slaughtering establishment, approved intermediate handling facility, or quarantined feedlot, shall be moved only in a means of conveyance which has been cleaned in accordance with §§ 71.5, 71.7, 71.10, and 71.11 of this chapter and, if unloaded in the course of such movement, shall be handled only in pens cleaned in accordance with the provisions of §§ 71.4, 71.7, 71.10, and 71.11 of this chapter.

§ 78.4 [Reserved]

Subpart B—Restrictions on Interstate Movement of Cattle Because of Brucellosis

§ 78.5 General restrictions.

Cattle may not be moved interstate except in compliance with this subpart and with 9 CFR part 86. Cattle moved interstate under permit in accordance with this subpart are not required to be accompanied by an interstate certificate of veterinary inspection or owner-shipper statement.

[78 FR 2069, Jan. 9, 2013]

§ 78.6 Steers and spayed heifers.

Steers and spayed heifers may be moved interstate in accordance with 9 CFR part 86 and without further restriction under this subpart.

[78 FR 2069, Jan. 9, 2013]

§ 78.7 Brucellosis reactor cattle.

(a) *Destination*. Brucellosis reactor cattle may be moved interstate only for immediate slaughter as follows:

(1) Directly to a recognized slaughtering establishment;

(2) Directly to an approved intermediate handling facility and then directly to a recognized slaughtering establishment; or

(3) From a farm of origin directly to a specifically approved stockyard approved to receive brucellosis reactors and then

(i) Directly to a recognized slaughtering establishment; or

(ii) Directly to an approved intermediate handling facility and then directly to a recognized slaughtering establishment.

(b) *Identification*. Brucellosis reactor cattle must be individually identified prior to moving interstate by attaching to the left ear a metal tag bearing a serial number and the inscription "U.S. Reactor," or a metal tag bearing a serial number designated by the State animal health official for identifying brucellosis reactors, and must be:

(1) "B" branded (as defined in § 78.1); or

(2) Accompanied directly to slaughter by an APHIS or State representative; or

(3) Moved in vehicles closed with official seals applied and removed by an APHIS representative, State representative, accredited veterinarian, or an individual authorized for this purpose by an APHIS representative. The official seal numbers must be recorded on the accompanying permit.

(c) *Permit.* Brucellosis reactor cattle moving interstate shall be accompanied to destination by a permit.

(d) *Marking of records.* Each person moving brucellosis reactor cattle interstate shall, in the course of interstate movement, plainly write or stamp the words "Brucellosis Reactor" upon the face of any document that person prepares in connection with such movement.

(e) *Segregation en route.* Brucellosis reactor cattle shall not be moved interstate in any means of conveyance containing animals which are not brucellosis reactors unless all the animals are for immediate slaughter or unless the brucellosis reactor cattle are kept separate from the other animals by a partition securely affixed to the sides of the means of conveyance.

(Approved by the Office of Management and Budget under control number 0579–0051)

[51 FR 32580, Sept. 12, 1986, as amended at 59 FR 67133, Dec. 29, 1994; 60 FR 48367, Sept. 19, 1995]

§ 78.8 Brucellosis exposed cattle.

Brucellosis exposed cattle may be moved interstate only as follows:

(a) *Movement to recognized slaughtering establishments.* (1) Finished fed cattle from a quarantined feedlot may be moved interstate

(i) Directly to a recognized slaughtering establishment without further restriction under this part; or

(ii) Directly to an approved intermediate handling facility and then directly to a recognized slaughtering establishment if accompanied by a permit or "S" brand permit.

(2) Brucellosis exposed cattle may be moved interstate directly to a recognized slaughtering establishment if such cattle are:

(i) Individually identified by an official eartag or a United States Department of Agriculture backtag;

(ii) Accompanied by a permit or "S" brand permit; and

(iii)(A) "S" branded before leaving the premises from which they are to be moved interstate; or

(B) "B" branded when a claim for indemnity is made under part 51 of this chapter; or

(C) Official adult vaccinates; or

(D) Accompanied directly to slaughter by an APHIS or State representative; or

(E) Moved in vehicles closed with official seals applied and removed by an APHIS representative, State representative, accredited veterinarian, or an individual authorized for this purpose by an APHIS representative.

The official seal numbers must be recorded on the accompanying permit or "S" brand permit.

(3) Brucellosis exposed cattle may be moved interstate directly to an approved intermediate handling facility and then directly to a recognized slaughtering establishment if such cattle are:

(i) Individually identified by an official eartag or a United States Department of Agriculture backtag;

(ii) Accompanied by a permit or "S" brand permit; and

(iii)(A) "S" branded before leaving the premises from which they are to be moved interstate; or

(B) "B" branded when a claim for indemnity is made under part 51 of this chapter; or

(C) Official adult vaccinates; or

(D) Moved in vehicles closed with official seals applied and removed by an APHIS representative, State representative, accredited veterinarian, or an individual authorized for this purpose by an APHIS representative. The official seal numbers must be recorded on the accompanying permit or "S" brand permit.

(4) Brucellosis exposed cattle moving to slaughter from a farm of origin may be moved directly to a specifically approved stockyard approved to receive brucellosis exposed cattle and then directly to a recognized slaughtering establishment if such cattle are:

(i) Individually identified by an official eartag or United States Department of Agriculture backtag;

(ii) Accompanied by a permit or "S" brand permit; and

(iii)(A) "S" branded before leaving the premises from which they are to be moved interstate; or

(B) "B" branded when a claim for indemnity is made under part 51 of this chapter; or

(C) Official adult vaccinates; or

(D) Moved in vehicles closed with official seals applied and removed by an APHIS representative, State representative, accredited veterinarian, or an individual authorized for this purpose by an APHIS representative.

The official seal numbers must be recorded on the accompanying permit or "S" brand permit.

(5) Brucellosis exposed cattle moving to slaughter from a farm of origin may be moved directly to a specifically approved stockyard approved to receive brucellosis exposed cattle and then directly to an approved intermediate handling facility and then directly to a recognized slaughtering establishment if such cattle are:

(i) Individually identified by an official eartag or United States Department of Agriculture backtag;

(ii) Accompanied by a permit or "S" brand permit; and

(iii)(A) "S" branded before leaving the premises from which they are to be moved interstate; or

(B) "B" branded when a claim for indemnity is made under part 51 of this chapter; or

(C) Official adult vaccinates; or

(D) Moved in vehicles closed with official seals applied and removed by an APHIS representative, State representative, accredited veterinarian, or an individual authorized for this purpose by an APHIS representative. The official seal numbers must be recorded on the accompanying permit or "S" brand permit.

(b) *Movement to quarantined feedlots.* Brucellosis exposed cattle for which no claim for indemnity is being made by the owner under part 51 of this chapter may be moved interstate directly to a quarantined feedlot, or from a farm of origin directly to a specifically approved stockyard approved to receive brucellosis exposed cattle and then directly to a quarantined feedlot, or from a farm of origin directly to an approved intermediate handling facility and then directly to a quarantined feedlot, or from a farm of origin directly to a specifically approved stockyard approved to receive brucellosis exposed cattle and then directly to an approved intermediate handling facility and then directly to a quarantined feedlot, if the cattle are:

(1) Individually identified by an official eartag or a United States Department of Agriculture backtag;

(2) Accompanied by a permit or "S" brand permit; and

(3)(i) "S" branded before leaving the premises from which they are to be moved interstate; or

(ii) Official adult vaccinates; or

(iii) Moved in vehicles closed with official seals applied and removed by an APHIS representative, State representative, accredited veterinarian, or an individual authorized for this purpose by an APHIS representative. The official seal numbers must be recorded on the accompanying permit or "S" brand permit.

(c) *Movement other than in accordance with paragraphs (a) and (b) of this section.* Brucellosis exposed cattle for which no claim for indemnity is being made by the owner under part 51 of this chapter also may be moved interstate in accordance with § 78.10 and as follows:

(1) Such brucellosis exposed cattle from herds known to be affected other than female cattle which originate in Class B States or areas or Class C States or areas may be moved interstate if the cattle are:

(i) Under 6 months of age and weaned from brucellosis reactors or brucellosis exposed cows not less than 30 days immediately preceding interstate movement; or

(ii) Under 6 months of age and nursing brucellosis exposed cows in a herd subjected to a herd blood test within 10 days prior to interstate movement; or

(iii) Official vaccinates under 1 year of age from a herd following an approved individual herd plan.

(2) Cattle moved interstate from a farm of origin directly to a specifically approved stockyard in accordance with

§ 78.9(b)(3)(iii), 78.9(c)(3)(iii), or 78.9(d)(3) of this part and subsequently determined to be brucellosis exposed may be moved interstate directly back to the farm of origin under the following conditions:

(i) Prior to interstate movement, State representatives of the State in which the cattle are located and the State of destination advise APHIS that such movement would not be contrary to the laws and regulations of their respective States;

(ii) Prior to interstate movement, the State representative of the State of destination agrees to quarantine the cattle on arrival and to require that all test-eligible cattle on the farm of origin be subjected to an official test; and

(iii) The cattle are accompanied to the farm of origin by a permit.

(Approved by the Office of Management and Budget under control number 0579–0051)

[51 FR 32580, Sept. 12, 1986, as amended at 54 FR 1925, Jan. 18, 1989; 56 FR 54533, 54534, Oct. 22, 1991; 56 FR 65782, Dec. 18, 1991; 59 FR 67133, Dec. 29, 1994; 60 FR 48367, Sept. 19, 1995]

§ 78.9 Cattle from herds not known to be affected.

Male cattle which are not test eligible and are from herds not known to be affected may be moved interstate without further restriction under this subpart. Female cattle which are not test eligible and are from herds not known to be affected may be moved interstate only in accordance with § 78.10 of this part and this section. Test-eligible cattle which are not brucellosis exposed and are from herds not known to be affected may be moved interstate only in accordance with § 78.10 and as follows:

(a) *Class Free States/areas.* Test-eligible cattle which originate in Class Free States or areas, are not brucellosis exposed, and are from a herd not known to be affected may be moved interstate from Class Free States or areas only as specified below:

(1) *Movement to recognized slaughtering establishments.* (i) Such cattle may be moved interstate directly to a recognized slaughtering establishment or directly to a specifically approved stockyard and then directly to a recognized slaughtering establishment without restriction under this subpart.

(ii) Such cattle may be moved interstate from a farm of origin directly to an approved intermediate handling facility and then directly to a recognized slaughtering establishment if accompanied by a permit.

(iii) Such cattle may be moved interstate from other than a farm of origin directly to an approved intermediate handling facility and then directly to a recognized slaughtering establishment if such cattle are accompanied by a permit.

(2) *Movement to quarantined feedlots.* Such cattle may be moved interstate without restriction under this subpart directly to a quarantined feedlot, or directly to a specifically approved stockyard and then directly to a quarantined feedlot, or directly to a specifically approved stockyard and then directly to an approved intermediate handling facility and then directly to a quarantined feedlot, or directly to an approved intermediate handling facility and then directly to a quarantined feedlot.

(3) *Movement other than in accordance with paragraphs* (a)(1) *and* (2) *of this section.* Such cattle may be moved interstate other than in accordance with paragraphs (a)(1) and (2) of this section only if:

(i) Such cattle are moved interstate from a farm of origin directly to a specifically approved stockyard; or

(ii) Such cattle are moved interstate as part of a commuter herd in accordance with a commuter herd agreement or other documents as agreed to by the shipping and receiving States or Tribes.

(iii) Such cattle are moved interstate accompanied by an ICVI which states, in addition to the items specified in § 78.1, that the cattle originated in a Class Free State or area.

(b) *Class A States/areas.* Test-eligible cattle which originate in Class A States or areas, are not brucellosis exposed, and are from a herd not known to be affected may be moved interstate from Class A States or areas only as specified below:

(1) *Movement to recognized slaughtering establishments.* (i) Such cattle may be moved interstate from a farm of origin or nonquarantined feedlot directly to a recognized slaughtering establishment

or directly to a specifically approved stockyard and then directly to a recognized slaughtering establishment without restriction under this subpart.

(ii) Such cattle may be moved interstate from a farm of origin directly to an approved intermediate handling facility without restriction under this subpart.

(iii) Such cattle from other than a farm of origin or nonquarantined feedlot may be moved interstate directly to a recognized slaughtering establishment or directly to a specifically approved stockyard and then directly to a recognized slaughtering establishment if identity to the Class A State or area is maintained by means of identification tag numbers appearing on sale records showing the consignor or by penning cattle from the farm or State or area apart from other animals.

(iv) Such cattle from other than a farm of origin may be moved interstate accompanied by a permit.

(A) Directly to an approved intermediate handling facility and then directly to a recognized slaughtering establishment; or

(B) Directly to a specifically approved stockyard and then directly to an approved intermediate handling facility and then directly to a recognized slaughtering establishment.

(2) *Movement to quarantined feedlots.* (i) Such cattle may be moved interstate from a farm of origin directly to a quarantined feedlot, or directly to a specifically approved stockyard and then directly to a quarantined feedlot, or directly to a specifically approved stockyard and then directly to an approved intermediate handling facility and then directly to a quarantined feedlot, or directly to an approved intermediate handling facility and then directly to a quarantined feedlot, if the identity of the farm of origin of the cattle is maintained by means of identification tag numbers appearing on sale records showing the consignor or by penning cattle from the farm of origin apart from other animals.

(ii) Such cattle from other than a farm of origin may be moved interstate directly to a quarantined feedlot or directly to a specifically approved stockyard and then directly to a quarantined feedlot if identity to the Class A State or area is maintained by means of identification tag numbers appearing on sale records showing the consignor or by penning cattle from one farm or State or area apart from other animals.

(3) *Movement other than in accordance with paragraphs* (b)(1) *and* (2) *of this section.* Such cattle may be moved interstate other than in accordance with paragraphs (b)(1) and (2) of this section only if:

(i) Such cattle originate in a certified brucellosis-free herd and are accompanied interstate by an ICVI which states, in addition to the items specified in § 78.1, that the cattle originated in a certified brucellosis-free herd; or

(ii) Such cattle are negative to an official test within 30 days prior to such interstate movement and are accompanied interstate by an ICVI which states, in addition to the items specified in § 78.1, the test dates and results of the official tests; or

(iii) Such cattle are moved interstate from a farm of origin directly to a specifically approved stockyard and are subjected to an official test upon arrival at the specifically approved stockyard prior to losing their identity with the farm of origin; or

(iv) Such cattle are moved as part of a commuter herd in accordance with a commuter herd agreement or other documents as agreed to by the shipping and receiving States or Tribes..

(c) *Class B States/areas.* Test-eligible cattle which originate in Class B States or areas, are not brucellosis exposed, and are from a herd not known to be affected may be moved interstate from Class B States or areas only under the conditions specified below:

(1) *Movement to recognized slaughtering establishments.* (i) Such cattle may be moved interstate from a farm of origin or a nonquarantined feedlot directly to a recognized slaughtering establishment without further restriction under this subpart.

(ii) Such cattle may be moved interstate from a farm of origin directly to an approved intermediate handling facility without further restriction under this subpart.

(iii) Such cattle may be moved interstate from a nonquarantined feedlot directly to an approved intermediate handling facility and then directly to a recognized slaughtering establishment if they are accompanied by a permit or "S" brand permit.

(iv) Such cattle may be moved interstate from a farm of origin or a nonquarantined feedlot directly to a specifically approved stockyard and then to a recognized slaughtering establishment if:

(A) They are negative to an official test conducted at the specifically approved stockyard and are accompanied to slaughter by an ICVI or "S" brand permit which states, in addition to the items specified in §78.1, the test dates and results of the official tests; or

(B) They originate from a certified brucellosis-free herd and identity to the certified brucellosis-free herd is maintained; or

(C) They are "S" branded at the specifically approved stockyard, accompanied by an "S" brand permit, and moved directly to a recognized slaughtering establishment; or

(D) They are moved from the specifically approved stockyard accompanied by an "S" brand permit and in vehicles closed with official seals applied and removed by an APHIS representative, a State representative, an accredited veterinarian, or an individual authorized for this purpose by an APHIS representative.

The official seal numbers must be recorded on the accompanying "S" brand permit.

(v) Such cattle may be moved interstate from a farm of origin or a nonquarantined feedlot directly to a specifically approved stockyard and then to an approved intermediate handling facility and then directly to a recognized slaughtering establishment if:

(A) They are negative to an official test conducted at the specifically approved stockyard and are accompanied by an "S" brand permit which states, in addition to the items specified in §78.1, the test dates and results of the official tests; or

(B) They originate from a certified brucellosis-free herd, identity to the certified brucellosis-free herd is maintained, and they are accompanied by an "S" brand permit; or

(C) They are "S" branded at the specifically approved stockyard, accompanied by an "S" brand permit, and moved directly to an approved intermediate handling facility; or

(D) They are accompanied by an "S" brand permit and moved in vehicles closed with official seals applied and removed by an APHIS representative, State representative, accredited veterinarian, or an individual authorized for this purpose by an APHIS representative. The official seal numbers must be recorded on the accompanying "S" brand permit.

(vi) Such cattle from other than a farm of origin or a nonquarantined feedlot may be moved interstate to a recognized slaughtering establishment only if:

(A) They are negative to an official test within 30 days prior to such interstate movement and are accompanied by an ICVI or "S" brand permit which states, in addition to the items specified in §78.1, the test dates and results of the official tests; or

(B) They originate from a certified brucellosis-free herd and identity to the certified brucellosis-free herd is maintained; or

(C) They are "S" branded, accompanied by an "S" brand permit, and moved directly to a recognized slaughtering establishment; or

(D) They are accompanied by an "S" brand permit and moved in vehicles closed with official seals applied and removed by an APHIS representative, a State representative, an accredited veterinarian, or by an individual authorized for this purpose by an APHIS representative.

The official seal numbers must be recorded on the accompanying "S" brand permit.

(vii) Such cattle from other than a farm of origin or a nonquarantined feedlot may be moved interstate to an approved intermediate handling facility and then directly to a recognized slaughtering establishment only if:

(A) They are negative to an official test within 30 days prior to such interstate movement and are accompanied by a permit or "S" brand permit which states, in addition to the items specified in §78.1, the test dates and results of the official tests; or

(B) They originate from a certified brucellosis-free herd, identity to the certified brucellosis-free herd is maintained, and they are accompanied by an "S" brand permit; or

(C) They are "S" branded, accompanied by an "S" brand permit, and moved directly to an approved intermediate handling facility; or

(D) They are accompanied by an "S" brand permit and moved in vehicles closed with official seals applied and removed by an APHIS representative, State representative, accredited veterinarian, or an individual authorized for this purpose by an APHIS representative. The official seal numbers must be recorded on the accompanying "S" brand permit.

(2) *Movement to quarantined feedlots.* (i) Such cattle may be moved interstate from a farm of origin directly to:

(A) A quarantined feedlot if such cattle are "S" branded upon arrival at the quarantined feedlot; or

(B) A specifically approved stockyard and then directly to a quarantined feedlot or directly to an approved intermediate handling facility and then directly to a quarantined feedlot, if the cattle are "S" branded upon arrival at the specifically approved stockyard and are accompanied to the quarantined feedlot by an "S" brand permit; or

(C) An approved intermediate handling facility and then directly to a quarantined feedlot, if the cattle are "S" branded upon arrival at the approved intermediate handling facility and are accompanied to the quarantined feedlot by an "S" brand permit; or

(D) A quarantined feedlot, a specifically approved stockyard and then directly to a quarantined feedlot, or an approved intermediate handling facility and then directly to a quarantined feedlot if the cattle are accompanied by an "S" brand permit and moved in vehicles closed with official seals applied and removed by an APHIS representative, State representative, accredited veterinarian, or an individual authorized for this purpose by an APHIS representative. The official seal numbers must be recorded on the accompanying "S" brand permit.

(ii) Such cattle from other than a farm of origin may be moved interstate to a quarantined feedlot if:

(A) They are negative to an official test within 30 days prior to such movement and are accompanied by an ICVI which states, in addition to the items specified in § 78.1, the test dates and results of the official tests; or

(B) They are "S" branded, accompanied by an "S" brand permit, and moved directly to a quarantined feedlot; or

(C) They are accompanied by an "S" brand permit and moved in vehicles closed with official seals applied and removed by an APHIS representative, State representative, accredited veterinarian, or an individual authorized for this purpose by an APHIS representative. The official seal numbers must be recorded on the accompanying "S" brand permit.

(3) *Movement other than in accordance with paragraphs* (c)(1) *and* (2) *of this section.* Such cattle may be moved interstate other than in accordance with paragraphs (c)(1) and (2) of this section only if:

(i) Such cattle originate in a certified brucellosis-free herd and are accompanied interstate by an ICVI which states, in addition to the items specified in § 78.1, that the cattle originated in a certified brucellosis-free herd; or

(ii) Such cattle are negative to an official test within 30 days prior to interstate movement, have been issued a permit for entry, and are accompanied interstate by an ICVI which states, in addition to the items specified in § 78.1, the test dates and results of the official tests; or

(iii) Such cattle are moved interstate from a farm of origin directly to a specifically approved stockyard and are subjected to an official test upon arrival at the specifically approved stockyard prior to losing their identity with the farm of origin; or

(iv) Such cattle are moved interstate as part of a commuter herd in accordance with a commuter herd agreement or other documents as agreed to by the shipping and receiving States or Tribes, and

(A) The cattle being moved originate from a herd in which:

(*1*) All the cattle were negative to a herd blood test within 1 year prior to the interstate movement;

(*2*) Any cattle added to the herd after such herd blood test were negative to an official test within 30 days prior to the date the cattle were added to the herd;

(*3*) None of the cattle in the herd have come in contact with any other cattle; and

(B) The cattle are accompanied interstate by a document which states the dates and results of the herd blood test and the name of the laboratory in which the official tests were conducted.

(v) The State animal health officials of the State of origin and State of destination may waive the requirements of paragraph (c)(3)(iv) of this section in writing.

(d) *Class C States/areas.* All female cattle and test-eligible male cattle which originate in Class C States or areas, are not brucellosis exposed, and are from a herd not known to be affected may be moved interstate from Class C States or areas only under the conditions specified below:

(1) *Movement to recognized slaughtering establishments.* (i) Such cattle may be moved interstate from a farm of origin or a nonquarantined feedlot directly to a recognized slaughtering establishment without further restriction under this subpart.

(ii) Such cattle may be moved interstate from a farm of origin directly to an approved intermediate handling facility without further restriction under this subpart.

(iii) Such cattle may be moved interstate from a nonquarantined feedlot directly to an approved intermediate handling facility and then directly to a recognized slaughtering establishment if they are accompanied by a permit or "S" brand permit.

(iv) Such cattle may be moved interstate from a farm of origin or a nonquarantined feedlot directly to a specifically approved stockyard and then to a recognized slaughtering establishment if:

(A) They are negative to an official test conducted at the specifically approved stockyard and are accompanied by an ICVI or "S" brand permit which states, in addition to the items specified in §78.1, the test dates and results of the official tests; or

(B) They originate from a certified brucellosis-free herd and identity to the certified brucellosis-free herd is maintained; or

(C) They are "S" branded at the specifically approved stockyard, accompanied by an "S" brand permit, and moved directly to a recognized slaughtering establishment; or

(D) They are moved from the specifically approved stockyard accompanied by an "S" brand permit and in vehicles closed with official seals applied and removed by an APHIS representative, a State representative, an accredited veterinarian, or an individual authorized for this purpose by an APHIS representative.

The official seal numbers must be recorded on the accompanying "S" brand permit.

(v) Such cattle may be moved interstate from a farm of origin or a nonquarantined feedlot directly to a specifically approved stockyard and then to an approved intermediate handling facility and then directly to a recognized slaughtering establishment if:

(A) They are negative to an official test conducted at the specifically approved stockyard and are accompanied by an "S" brand permit which states, in addition to the items specified in §78.1, the test dates and results of the official tests; or

(B) They originate from a certified brucellosis-free herd, identity to the certified brucellosis-free herd is maintained, and they are accompanied by an "S" brand permit; or

(C) They are "S" branded at the specifically approved stockyard, accompanied by an "S" brand permit, and moved directly to an approved intermediate handling facility; or

(D) They are accompanied by an "S" brand permit and moved in vehicles closed with official seals applied and removed by an APHIS representative, State representative, accredited veterinarian, or an individual authorized for this purpose by an APHIS representative. The official seal numbers must be recorded on the accompanying "S" brand permit.

(vi) Such cattle from other than a farm of origin or a nonquarantined feedlot may be moved interstate to a recognized slaughtering establishment only if:

(A) They are negative to an official test within 30 days prior to such interstate movement and are accompanied by an ICVI or "S" brand permit which states, in addition to the items specified in § 78.1, the test dates and results of the official tests; or

(B) They originate from a certified brucellosis-free herd and identity to the certified brucellosis-free herd is maintained; or

(C) They are "S" branded, accompanied by an "S" brand permit, and moved directly to a recognized slaughtering establishment; or

(D) They are accompanied by an "S" brand permit and moved in vehicles closed with official seals applied and removed by an APHIS representative, a State representative, an accredited veterinarian, or by an individual authorized for this purpose by the APHIS representative.

The official seal numbers must be recorded on the accompanying "S" brand permit.

(vii) Such cattle from other than a farm of origin or a nonquarantined feedlot may be moved interstate to an approved intermediate handling facility and then directly to a recognized slaughtering establishment only if:

(A) They are negative to an official test within 30 days prior to such interstate movement and are accompanied by a permit or "S" brand permit which states, in addition to the items specified in § 78.1, the test dates and results of the official tests; or

(B) They originate from a certified brucellosis-free herd, identity to the certified brucellosis-free herd is maintained, and they are accompanied by an "S" brand permit; or

(C) They are "S" branded, accompanied by an "S" brand permit, and moved directly to an approved intermediate handling facility; or

(D) They are accompanied by an "S" brand permit and moved in vehicles closed with official seals applied and removed by an APHIS representative, State representative, accredited veterinarian, or an individual authorized for this purpose by an APHIS representative. The official seal numbers must be recorded on the accompanying "S" brand permit.

(2) *Movement to quarantined feedlots.* (i) Such cattle may be moved interstate from a farm of origin directly to:

(A) A quarantined feedlot if such cattle are "S" branded upon arrival at the quarantined feedlot; or

(B) A specifically approved stockyard and then directly to a quarantined feedlot, or directly to an approved intermediate handling facility and then directly to a quarantined feedlot, if the cattle are "S" branded upon arrival at the specifically approved stockyard and are accompanied to the quarantined feedlot by an "S" brand permit; or

(C) An approved intermediate handling facility and then directly to a quarantined feedlot, if the cattle are "S" branded upon arrival at the approved intermediate handling facility and are accompanied to the quarantined feedlot by an "S" brand permit; or

(D) A quarantined feedlot, a specifically approved stockyard and then directly to a quarantined feedlot, or an approved intermediate handling facility and then directly to a quarantined feedlot if the cattle are accompanied by an "S" brand permit and moved in vehicles closed with official seals applied and removed by an APHIS representative, State representative, accredited veterinarian, or an individual authorized for this purpose by an APHIS representative. The official seal numbers must be recorded on the accompanying "S" brand permit.

(ii) Such cattle from other than a farm of origin may be moved interstate to a quarantined feedlot if:

(A) They are negative to an official test within 30 days prior to such movement and are accompanied by an ICVI which states, in addition to the items specified in § 78.1, the test dates and results of the official tests; or

(B) They are "S" branded, accompanied by an "S" brand permit, and moved directly to a quarantined feedlot; or

(C) They are accompanied by an "S" brand permit and moved in vehicles closed with official seals applied and removed by an APHIS representative,

State representative, accredited veterinarian, or an individual authorized for this purpose by an APHIS representative. The official seal numbers must be recorded on the accompanying "S" brand permit.

(3) *Movement other than in accordance with paragraphs (d)(1) or (2) of this section.* Such cattle may be moved interstate other than in accordance with paragraphs (d)(1) or (2) of this section only if such cattle originate in a certified brucellosis-free herd and are accompanied interstate by an ICVI which states, in addition to the items specified in § 78.1, that the cattle originated in a certified brucellosis-free herd.

(Approved by the Office of Management and Budget under control number 0579–0051)

[51 FR 32580, Sept. 12, 1986, as amended at 54 FR 1925, Jan. 18, 1989; 56 FR 54533, 54534, Oct. 22, 1991; 56 FR 58638, Nov. 21, 1991; 59 FR 67133, Dec. 29, 1994; 60 FR 48368, Sept. 19, 1995; 78 FR 2069, Jan. 9, 2013]

§ 78.10 Official vaccination of cattle moving into and out of Class B and Class C States or areas.

(a) Female dairy cattle born after January 1, 1984, which are 4 months of age or over must be official vaccinates to move interstate into or out of a Class B State or area[4] unless they are moved interstate directly to a recognized slaughtering establishment or quarantined feedlot, or directly to an approved intermediate handling facility and then directly to a recognized slaughtering establishment, or directly to an approved intermediate handling facility and then directly to a quarantined feedlot and then directly to a recognized slaughtering establishment, or directly to an approved intermediate handling facility and then directly to a quarantined feedlot and then directly to a recognized slaughtering establishment. Female cattle eligible for official calfhood vaccination and required by this paragraph to be officially vaccinated may be moved interstate from a farm of origin directly to a specifically approved stockyard and be officially vaccinated upon arrival at the specifically approved stockyard.

(b) Female cattle born after January 1, 1984, which are 4 months of age or over must be official vaccinates to move into a Class C State or area[4] unless they are moved interstate directly to a recognized slaughtering establishiment, or directly to an approved intermediate handling facility and then directly to a recognized slaughtering establishment, or directly to an approved intermediate handling facility and then directly to a quarantined feedlot and then directly to a recognized slaughtering establishment. Female cattle eligible for official calfhood vaccination and required by this paragraph to be officially vaccinated may be moved interstate from a farm of origin directly to a specifically approved stockyard and be officially vaccinated upon arrival at the specifically approved stockyard.

(c) Female cattle born after January 1, 1984, which are 4 months of age or over must be official vaccinates to move interstate out of a Class C State or area[4] inder § 78.9(d)(3) of this part. Female cattle from a certified brucellosis-free herd that are eligible for official calfhood vaccination and required by this paragraph to be officially vaccinated may be moved interstate from a farm of origin directly to a specifically approved stockyard and be officially vaccinated upon arrival at the specifically approved stockyard.

[51 FR 32580, Sept. 12, 1986, as amended at 54 FR 1926, Jan. 18, 1989; 56 FR 58638, Nov. 21, 1991]

§ 78.11 Cattle moved to a specifically approved stockyard not in accordance with this part.

Cattle, except brucellosis reactors and brucellosis exposed cattle, which are moved interstate to a specifically approved stockyard but fail to comply with the requirements of this part for release from the specifically approved stockyard may be moved from the specifically approved stockyard only as follows:

(a) With the concurrence of the State animal health officials of the State of

[4] Female cattle imported into the United States may be exempted from the vaccination requirements of this paragraph with the concurrence of the State animal health official of the State of destination. This concurrence is required prior to the importation of the cattle into the United States.

origin and State of destination, directly back to the farm of origin accompanied by a permit; or

(b) Directly to an approved intermediate handling facility and then directly to a recognized slaughtering establishment or directly to an approved intermediate handling facility and then directly to a quarantined feedlot and then directly to a recognized slaughtering establishment if such cattle are "S" branded and accompanied by an "S" brand permit; or

(c) Directly to a recognized slaughtering establishment if such cattle are

(1) "S" branded and accompanied by an "S" brand permit; or

(2) Accompanied by an "S" brand permit and moved in vehicles closed with official seals applied and removed by an APHIS representative, State representative, an accredited veterinarian, or an individual authorized for this purpose by an APHIS representative.

The official seal numbers must be recorded on the "S" brand permit; or

(d) Directly to a quarantined feedlot if such cattle are "S" branded and accompanied by an "S" brand permit.

(Approved by the Office of Management and Budget under control number 0579–0047)

[51 FR 32580, Sept. 12, 1986, as amended at 56 FR 54534, Oct. 22, 1991; 56 FR 58638, 58639, Nov. 21, 1991]

§ 78.12 Cattle from quarantined areas.

Not withstanding any provisions in the regulations to the contrary, cattle may be moved interstate from a quarantined area only in accordance with § 78.10, 9 CFR part 86, and this section.

(a) *Steers and spayed heifers.* Steers and spayed heifers may be moved interstate without further restriction under this section.

(b) *Brucellosis reactor cattle.* Brucellosis reactor cattle may be moved interstate in accordance with § 78.7.

(c) *Brucellosis exposed cattle.* Brucellosis exposed cattle may be moved interstate in accordance with § 78.8(a) or (b).

(d) *Movement from qualified herds.* Cattle from qualified herds in any quarantined area may be moved interstate only as follows:

(1) *Movement to recognized slaughtering establishments.* (i) Cattle from qualified herds in a quarantined area may be moved interstate from a farm of origin directly to a recognized slaughtering establishment or directly to a specifically approved stockyard and then directly to a recognized slaughtering establishment if they are negative to an official test within 30 days prior to such interstate movement and are accompanied by an ICVI or "S" brand permit which states, in addition to the items specified in § 78.1, the test dates and results of the official tests; or

(ii) Cattle from qualified herds in a quarantined area may be moved interstate from a farm of origin directly to an approved intermediate handling facility and then directly to a recognized slaughtering establishment or directly to an approved intermediate handling facility and then directly to a quarantined feedlot and then directly to a recognized slaughtering establishment if they are negative to an official test within 30 days prior to such interstate movement and are accompanied by an "S" brand permit which states, in addition to the items specified in § 78.1, the test dates and results of the official tests; or

(iii) Cattle from qualified herds in a quarantined area may be moved interstate from a farm of origin directly to a specifically approved stockyard and then directly to an approved intermediate handling facility and then directly to a recognized slaughtering establishment or directly to an approved intermediate handling facility and then directly to a quarantined feedlot and then directly to a recognized slaughtering establishment if they are negative to an official test within 30 days prior to such interstate movement and are accompanied by a permit or "S" brand permit which states, in addition to the items specified in § 78.1, the test dates and results of the official tests; or

(iv) Cattle from qualified herds in a quarantined area may be moved interstate in accordance with § 78.8(a).

(2) *Movement to quarantined feedlots.* (i) Cattle from qualified herds in a quarantined area may be moved interstate from a farm of origin directly to a quarantined feedlot, or directly to a specifically approved stockyard and then directly to a quarantined feedlot,

or directly to an approved intermediate handling facility and then directly to a quarantined feedlot if the cattle are negative to an official test within 30 days prior to such interstate movement and are accompanied by an ICVI which states, in addition to the items specified in § 78.1 of this part, the test dates and results of the official tests; or

(ii) Cattle from qualified herds in a quarantined area may be moved in accordance with § 78.8(b).

(3) *Movement other than in accordance with paragraph* (d)(1) *or* (2) *of this section.* Cattle from qualified herds in a quarantined area may be moved interstate other than in accordance with paragraph (d)(1) or (2) of this section, either directly from a farm of origin or from a farm of origin through no more than one specifically approved stockyard if

(i) The cattle, except official vaccinates less than 1 year of age and cattle less than 6 months of age, are negative to an official test within 30 days prior to such interstate movement; and

(ii) The cattle are accompanied interstate by an ICVI which states, in addition to the items specified in § 78.1, the test dates and results of the official tests when such tests are required.

(e) *Movement from herds which are not qualified.* Cattle from herds known to be affected or from herds which are not qualified in any quarantined area may be moved interstate only in accordance with § 78.8(a) or (b).[5]

(Approved by the Office of Management and Budget under control number 0579–0051)

[51 FR 32580, Sept. 12, 1986, as amended at 56 FR 58638, Nov. 21, 1991; 59 FR 67133, Dec. 29, 1994; 78 FR 2070, Jan. 9, 2013]

§ 78.13 Other movements.

The Administrator may, upon request in specific cases, permit the interstate movement of cattle not otherwise provided for in this subpart, under such conditions as the Administrator may prescribe in each case to prevent the spread of brucellosis. The Administrator shall promptly notify the State animal health officials of the States involved of any such action.

[51 FR 32580, Sept. 12, 1986, as amended at 56 FR 54534, Oct. 22, 1991]

§ 78.14 Rodeo cattle.

(a) Rodeo cattle that are test-eligible and that are from a herd not known to be affected may be moved interstate if:

(1) They are classified as brucellosis negative based upon an official test conducted less than 365 days before the date of interstate movement: *Provided, however, That:* The official test is not required for rodeo cattle that are moved only between Class Free States;

(2) The cattle are identified with an official eartag or any other official identification device or method approved by the Administrator in accordance with § 78.5;

(3) There is no change of ownership since the date of the last official test;

(4) An ICVI accompanies each interstate movement of the cattle; and

(5) A permit for entry is issued for each interstate movement of the cattle.

(b) Cattle that would qualify as rodeo cattle, but that are used for breeding purposes during the 365 days following the date of being tested, may be moved interstate only if they meet the requirements for cattle in this subpart and in 9 CFR part 86.

(Approved by the Office of Management and Budget under control number 0579–0047)

[78 FR 2070, Jan. 9, 2013]

§§ 78.15–78.19 [Reserved]

Subpart C—Restrictions on Interstate Movement of Bison Because of Brucellosis

§ 78.20 General restrictions.

Bison may not be moved interstate except in compliance with this subpart and with 9 CFR part 86.

[51 FR 32580, Sept. 12, 1986, as amended at 78 FR 2070, Jan. 9, 2013]

[5] A herd which is not qualified in a quarantined area may become a qualified herd upon compliance with the provisions set forth in § 78.1 in the definition of "qualified herd."

§ 78.21 Bison steers and spayed heifers.

Bison steers and spayed heifers may be moved interstate without further restriction under this subpart.

[51 FR 32580, Sept. 12, 1986, as amended at 78 FR 2070, Jan. 9, 2013]

§ 78.22 Brucellosis reactor bison.

(a) *Destination.* Brucellosis reactor bison may be moved interstate only for immediate slaughter as follows:

(1) Directly to a recognized slaughtering establishment;

(2) Directly to an approved intermediate handling facility and then directly to a recognized slaughtering establishment; or

(3) From a farm of origin directly to a specifically approved stockyard approved to receive brucellosis reactors and then

(i) Directly to a recognized slaughtering establishment; or

(ii) Directly to an approved intermediate handling facility and then directly to a recognized slaughtering establishment.

(b) *Identification.* Brucellosis reactor bison must be individually identified prior to moving interstate by attaching to the left ear a metal tag bearing a serial number and the inscription "U.S. Reactor," or a metal tag bearing a serial number designated by the State animal health official for identifying brucellosis reactors, and must be:

(1) "B" branded (as defined in § 78.1); or

(2) Accompanied directly to slaughter by an APHIS or State representative; or

(3) Moved in vehicles closed with official seals applied and removed by an APHIS representative, State representative, accredited veterinarian, or an individual authorized for this purpose by an APHIS representative. The official seal numbers must be recorded on the accompanying permit.

(c) *Permit.* Brucellosis reactor bison moving interstate shall be accompanied to destination by a permit.

(d) *Marking of records.* Each person moving brucellosis reactor bison interstate shall, in the course of interstate movement, plainly write or stamp the words "Brucellosis Reactor" upon the face of any document that person prepares in connection with such movement.

(e) *Segregation en route.* Brucellosis reactor bison shall not be moved interstate in any means of conveyance containing animals which are not brucellosis reactors unless all of the animals are for immediate slaughter or unless the brucellosis reactor bison are kept separate from the other animals by a partition securely affixed to the sides of the means of conveyance.

(Approved by the Office of Management and Budget under control number 0579–0051)

[51 FR 32580, Sept. 12, 1986, as amended at 59 FR 67133, Dec. 29, 1994; 60 FR 48368, Sept. 19, 1995]

§ 78.23 Brucellosis exposed bison.

Brucellosis exposed bison may be moved interstate only as follows:

(a) *Movement to recognized slaughtering establishments.* Brucellosis exposed bison may be moved interstate for slaughter accompanied by a permit or "S" brand permit and as follows:

(1) Directly to a recognized slaughtering establishment or directly to an approved intermediate handling facility and then directly to a recognized slaughtering establishment; or

(2) From a farm of origin directly to a specifically approved stockyard approved to receive brucellosis exposed bison and then

(i) Directly to a recognized slaughtering establishment; or

(ii) Directly to an approved intermediate handling facility and then directly to a recognized slaughtering establishment.

(b) *Movement to quarantined feedlots.* Brucellosis exposed bison may be moved directly to a quarantined feedlot or, from a farm of origin, directly to a specifically approved stockyard approved to receive brucellosis exposed bison and then directly to a quarantined feedlot. Such bison shall be accompanied by a permit or "S" brand permit.

(c) *Movement other than in accordance with paragraphs (a) or (b) of this section.* Brucellosis exposed bison which are from herds known to be affected, but which are not part of a herd being depopulated under part 51 of this chapter, may move without further restriction under this subpart if the bison:

(1) Are under 6 months of age and were weaned from brucellosis reactor or brucellosis exposed bison not less than 30 days immediately preceding interstate movement; or

(2) Are under 6 months of age and nursing brucellosis exposed bison in a herd subjected to a herd blood test within 10 days prior to interstate movement; or

(3) Are official vaccinates under 1 year of age from a herd following an approved individual herd plan.

(Approved by the Office of Management and Budget under control number 0579–0051)

[51 FR 32580, Sept. 12, 1986, as amended at 59 FR 67133, Dec. 29, 1994; 78 FR 2070, Jan. 9, 2013]

§ 78.24 Bison from herds not known to be affected.

Bison from herds not known to be affected may be moved interstate only as follows:

(a) *Movement to recognized slaughtering establishments.* Bison from herds not known to be affected may be moved directly to a recognized slaughtering establishment without further restriction under this subpart.

(b) *Movement to quarantined feedlots.* Bison from herds not known to be affected may be moved directly to a quarantined feedlot without further restriction under this subpart.

(c) *Movement from public zoo to public zoo.* Bison from herds not known to be affected may be moved from a zoo owned by a governmental agency to another such zoo if handled in accordance with § 78.3.

(d) *Movement other than in accordance with paragraphs (a), (b), or (c) of this section.* Bison from herds not known to be affected may be moved interstate other than in accordance with paragraphs (a), (b), or (c) of this section only as follows:

(1) Such bison under 6 months of age may be moved interstate when accompanied by an ICVI.

(2) Such bison which are official vaccinates under 2 years of age and are not parturient or postparturient may be moved interstate when accompanied by an ICVI.

(3) Such bison may be moved interstate if they are negative to an official test within 30 days prior to such movement and are accompanied by an ICVI which states, in addition to the items specified in § 78.1, the dates and results of the official tests.

(4) Such bison may be moved interstate if they originate in a certified brucellosis-free herd and are accompanied by an ICVI which states, in addition to the items specified in § 78.1, that the bison originated in a certified brucellosis-free herd.

(Approved by the Office of Management and Budget under control number 0579–0047)

[51 FR 32580, Sept. 12, 1986, as amended at 56 FR 58639, Nov. 21, 1991; 78 FR 2070, Jan. 9, 2013]

§ 78.25 Other movements.

The Administrator may, upon request in specific cases, permit the interstate movement of bison not otherwise provided for in this subpart, under such conditions as the Administrator may prescribe in each case to prevent the spread of brucellosis. The Administrator shall promptly notify the State animal health officials of the States involved of any such action.

[51 FR 32580, Sept. 12, 1986, as amended at 56 FR 54534, Oct. 22, 1991]

§§ 78.26–78.29 [Reserved]

Subpart D—Restrictions on Interstate Movement of Swine Because of Brucellosis

§ 78.30 General restrictions.

(a) Brucellosis reactor swine, brucellosis exposed swine, feral swine, sows, and boars may not be moved interstate or in interstate commerce except in compliance with this subpart.

(b) Each person who causes the movement of swine in interstate commerce is responsible for the identification of the swine as required by this subpart. No such person shall remove or tamper with or cause the removal of or tampering with an identification tattoo or approved swine identification tag required in this subpart except at the time of slaughter, or as may be authorized by the Administrator upon request in specific cases and under such conditions as the Administrator may impose to ensure continuing identification.

(c)(1) Feral swine may be moved interstate directly to slaughter if they do not come into physical contact with any domestic swine or other livestock.

(2) Feral swine from monitored-negative populations may be moved interstate other than directly to slaughter if accompanied by a permit issued by the APHIS representative or the State animal health official in the State of origin.

(3) Feral swine found negative to an official test within the 30 days prior to the interstate movement may be moved interstate other than directly to slaughter if accompanied by a permit issued by the APHIS representative or the State animal health official in the State of origin.

[51 FR 32580, Sept. 12, 1986, as amended at 56 FR 54534, Oct. 22, 1991; 59 FR 18952, Apr. 21, 1994]

§ 78.31 Brucellosis reactor swine.

(a) *Destination.* Brucellosis reactor swine may be moved interstate only for immediate slaughter as follows:

(1) Directly to a recognized slaughtering establishment; or

(2) Directly to a stockyard posted under the Packers and Stockyards Act, as amended (7 U.S.C. 181 *et seq.*), or directly to a market agency or dealer registered under the Packers and Stockyards Act, for sale to a recognized slaughtering eatablishment in accordance with the following requirements:

(b) *Identification.* Brucellosis reactor swine shall be individually identified by attaching to the left ear a metal tag bearing a serial number and the inscription, "U.S. Reactor," or a metal tag bearing a serial number designated by the State animal health official for identifying brucellosis reactors.

(c) *Permit.* Brucellosis reactor swine shall be accompanied to destination by a permit.

(d) *Marking of records.* Each person moving brucellosis reactor swine interstate shall, in the course of interstate movement, plainly write or stamp the words "Brucellosis Reactor" upon the face of any document that person prepares in connection with such movement.

(e) *Segregation en route.* Brucellosis reactor swine shall not be moved interstate in any means of conveyance containing animals which are not brucellosis reactors unless all of the animals in the shipment are for immediate slaughter, or unless the brucellosis reactor swine are kept separate from other animals by a partition securely affixed to the sides of the means of conveyance.

(Approved by the Office of Management and Budget under control number 0579–0051)

[51 FR 32580, Sept. 12, 1986, as amended at 59 FR 67133, Dec. 29, 1994]

§ 78.32 Brucellosis exposed swine.

(a) Brucellosis exposed swine may be moved interstate only if accompanied by a permit and only for immediate slaughter as follows:

(1) Directly to a recognized slaughtering establishment; or

(2) Directly to a stockyard posted under the Packers and Stockyards Act, as amended (7 U.S.C. 181 *et seq.*), or directly to a market agency or dealer registered under the Packers and Stockyards Act, for sale to a recognized slaughtering establishment.

(b) Brucellosis exposed swine from a herd known to be affected with brucellosis may be moved interstate from the herd known to be affected only if such swine are individually identified by attaching to the left ear a metal tag bearing a serial number and the inscription, "U.S. Reactor," or a metal tag bearing a serial number designated by the State animal health official for identifying brucellosis reactors.

(Approved by the Office of Management and Budget under control number 0579-0051)

[59 FR 12533, Mar. 17, 1994, as amended at 59 FR 67133, Dec. 29, 1994]

§ 78.33 Sows and boars.

(a) Sows and boars may be moved in interstate commerce for slaughter or for sale for slaughter if they are identified in accordance with § 71.19 of this chapter either:

(1) Before being moved in interstate commerce and before being mixed with swine from any other source; or

(2) After being moved in interstate commerce but before being mixed with swine from any other source only if they have been moved directly from their herd of origin to:

(i) A recognized slaughtering establishment; or

(ii) A stockyard, market agency, or dealer operating under the Packers and Stockyards Act, as amended (7 U.S.C. 181 *et seq.*).

(b) Sows and boars may be moved in interstate commerce for breeding only if they are identified in accordance with § 71.19 of this chapter before being moved in interstate commerce and before being mixed with swine from any other source, and the sows and boars either:

(1) Are from a validated brucellosis-free herd or a validated brucellosis-free State and are accompanied by a certificate that states, in addition to the items specified in § 78.1, that the swine originated in a validated brucellosis-free herd or a validated brucellosis-free State; or

(2) Have tested negative to an official test conducted within 30 days prior to interstate movement and are accompanied by a certificate that states, in addition to the items specified in § 78.1, the dates and results of the official tests.

(c) Sows and boars may be moved in interstate commerce for purposes other than slaughter or breeding without restriction under this subpart if they are identified in accordance with § 71.19 of this chapter.

[62 FR 27936, May 22, 1997]

§ 78.34 Other movements.

The Administrator may, upon request in specific cases, permit the movement in interstate commerce of swine not otherwise provided for in this subpart under such conditions as the Administrator may prescribe in each case to prevent the spread of brucellosis. The Administrator shall promptly notify the State animal health officials of the States involved of any such action.

[51 FR 32580, Sept. 12, 1986, as amended at 56 FR 54534, Oct. 22, 1991]

§§ 78.35–78.39 [Reserved]

Subpart E—Designation of Brucellosis Areas

§ 78.40 Designation of States/areas.

The Administrator may amend §§ 78.41 and 78.42 to reclassify States and areas as Class Free, Class A, Class B, Class C, or quarantined when the Administrator determines that the States or areas meet the appropriate definitions in § 78.1. The Administrator may approve the division of a State into two brucellosis classification areas upon finding that: (a) The State has legislative and regulatory authority for maintaining separate areas; (b) The State has committed resources to enforcing the different requirements in each area; (c) The State has an effective method for monitoring and controlling movement of cattle across the intrastate boundary; (d) The State has defined the intrastate boundary by county lines or by recognizable geographic features, such as rivers and highways; and (e) Each area of the State meets the standards for the brucellosis classification requested. The Administrator may amend § 78.43 to reclassify States as validated brucellosis-free States or remove such status when the Administrator determines that such States meet or do not meet the standards of a validated brucellosis-free State as defined in § 78.1. In the case of any reclassification to a lower class, reclassification as a quarantined State or area, or removal of validated brucellosis-free status, the State animal health official of the State involved will be notified of such reclassification or removal, and will be given an opportunity to present objections and arguments to the Administrator prior to the reclassification or removal taking place.

[51 FR 32580, Sept. 12, 1986, as amended at 53 FR 2222, Jan. 27, 1988; 56 FR 54533, Oct. 22, 1991; 56 FR 55803, Oct. 30, 1991]

§ 78.41 State/area classification.

(a) *Class Free.* Alabama, Alaska, Arizona, Arkansas, California, Colorado, Connecticut, Delaware, Florida, Georgia, Hawaii, Idaho, Illinois, Indiana, Iowa, Kansas, Kentucky, Louisiana,

Maine, Maryland, Massachusetts, Michigan, Minnesota, Mississippi, Missouri, Montana, Nebraska, Nevada, New Hampshire, New Jersey, New Mexico, New York, North Carolina, North Dakota, Ohio, Oklahoma, Oregon, Pennsylvania, Puerto Rico, Rhode Island, South Carolina, South Dakota, Tennessee, Texas, Utah, Vermont, Virgin Islands, Virginia, Washington, West Virginia, Wisconsin, and Wyoming.

(b) *Class A.* None.

(c) *Class B.* None.

[51 FR 32580, Sept. 12, 1986]

EDITORIAL NOTE: For FEDERAL REGISTER citations affecting § 78.41, see the List of CFR Sections Affected, which appears in the Finding Aids section of the printed volume and at *www.fdsys.gov.*

§ 78.42 Quarantined areas.

None.

§ 78.43 Validated brucellosis-free States.

Alabama, Alaska, Arizona, Arkansas, California, Colorado, Connecticut, Delaware, Florida, Georgia, Hawaii, Idaho, Illinois, Indiana, Iowa, Kansas, Kentucky, Louisiana, Maine, Maryland, Massachusetts, Michigan, Minnesota, Mississippi, Missouri, Montana, Nebraska, Nevada, New Hampshire, New Jersey, New Mexico, New York, North Carolina, North Dakota, Ohio, Oklahoma, Oregon, Pennsylvania, Puerto Rico, Rhode Island, South Carolina, South Dakota, Tennessee, Texas, Utah, Vermont, Virgin Islands, Virginia, Washington, West Virginia, Wisconsin, Wyoming.

[53 FR 4382, Feb. 16, 1988; 53 FR 21979, June 13, 1988]

EDITORIAL NOTE: For FEDERAL REGISTER citations affecting § 78.43, see the List of CFR Sections Affected, which appears in the Finding Aids section of the printed volume and at *www.fdsys.gov.*

PART 79—SCRAPIE IN SHEEP AND GOATS

Sec.

AUTHORITY: 7 U.S.C. 8301–8317; 7 CFR 2.22, 2.80, and 371.4.

SOURCE: 66 FR 43990, Aug. 21, 2001, unless otherwise noted.

§ 79.1 Definitions.

Accredited veterinarian. A veterinarian approved by the Administrator in accordance with part 161 of this chapter to perform functions specified in subchapters B, C, and D of this chapter.

Administrator. The Administrator of the Animal and Plant Health Inspection Service or any employee of the United States Department of Agriculture authorized to act for the Administrator.

Animal. A sheep or goat.

Animal and Plant Health Inspection Service (APHIS). The Animal and Plant Health Inspection Service of the United States Department of Agriculture.

Animal identification number (AIN). A numbering system for the official identification of individual animals in the United States providing a nationally unique identification number for each animal. The AIN contains 15 digits, with the first 3 being the country code (840 for the United States), the alpha characters USA, or the numeric code assigned to the manufacturer of the identification device by the International Committee on Animal Recording. The AIN beginning with the 840 prefix may be used only on animals born in the United States.

APHIS representative. An individual employed by APHIS in animal health activities who is authorized by the Administrator to perform the function involved.

Approved laboratory. A laboratory approved by the Administrator in accordance with § 54.11 of this chapter to conduct one or more scrapie tests, or genotype tests, on one or more tissues.

Area veterinarian in charge. The veterinary official of APHIS who is assigned by the Administrator to supervise and perform the official animal health work of APHIS in the State concerned.

Blackfaced sheep. Any purebred suffolk, hampshire, shropshire or cross thereof, any non-purebred sheep known to have suffolk, hampshire, or shropshire ancestors, and any non-purebred sheep of unknown ancestry with a black face, except commercial hair sheep.

Breed association and registries. Organizations listed in § 151.9 of this chapter that maintain the permanent records of ancestry or pedigrees of animals (including the animal's sire and dam), individual identification of animals, and ownership of animals.

Certificate. An official document issued in accordance with § 79.5 by an APHIS representative, State representative, or accredited veterinarian at the point of origin of an interstate movement of animals.

Commercial hair sheep. Any commercial sheep with hair rather than wool that is either a full-blooded hair sheep or that resulted from the cross of a hair sheep with a whitefaced wool sheep.

Commercial sheep or goat. Any animal from a flock from which animals are moved only either directly to slaughter or through slaughter channels to slaughter or any animal that is raised only for meat or fiber production and that is not registered with a sheep or goat registry or used for exhibition.

Commingle, commingled, commingling. Animals grouped together and having physical contact with each other, including contact through a fence, but not limited contacts. Commingling also includes sharing the same section in a transportation unit where there is physical contact.

Consistent State. (1) A State that the Administrator has determined conducts an active State scrapie control program that either:

(i) Meets the requirements of § 79.6; or

(ii) Effectively enforces a State designed plan that the Administrator determines is at least as effective in controlling scrapie as the requirements of § 79.6.

(2) The Administrator has determined the following States to be Consistent States: Alabama, Alaska, Arizona, Arkansas, California, Colorado, Connecticut, Delaware, Florida, Georgia, Hawaii, Idaho, Illinois, Indiana, Iowa, Kansas, Kentucky, Louisiana, Maine, Maryland, Massachusetts, Michigan, Minnesota, Mississippi, Missouri, Montana, Nebraska, Nevada, New Hampshire, New Jersey, New Mexico, New York, North Carolina, North Dakota, Ohio, Oklahoma, Oregon, Pennsylvania, Rhode Island, South Carolina, South Dakota, Tennessee, Texas, Utah, Vermont, Virginia, Washington, West Virginia, Wisconsin, and Wyoming.

Designated scrapie epidemiologist. An epidemiologist who has demonstrated the knowledge and ability to perform the functions required and who has been selected by the State animal health official and the area veterinarian in charge. The regional epidemiologist and the APHIS National Scrapie Program Coordinator must concur in the selection and appointment of the designated scrapie epidemiologist. The designated scrapie epidemiologist must satisfactorily complete training designated by APHIS.

Direct movement to slaughter. Transported to a facility for slaughter, without stops or unloading except for feeding and watering during which the animals are not commingled with any other animals.

Electronic implant. Any radio frequency identification implant device approved for use in the scrapie program by the Administrator. The Administrator will approve an electronic implant after determining that it is tamper resistant, not harmful to the animal, and readable by equipment available to APHIS and State representatives.

Exposed animal. (1) Any animal that has been in the same flock at the same time as a scrapie-positive female animal, excluding limited contacts; or

(2) Any animal born in a flock after a scrapie-positive animal was born into that flock or lambed in that flock, if born before that flock completes the requirements of a flock plan; or

(3) Any animal that was commingled with a scrapie-positive female animal during or up to 30 days after she lambed, kidded, or aborted, or while a visible vaginal discharge was present,

or that was commingled with any other scrapie-positive female animal for 24 hours or more, including during activities such as shows and sales or while in marketing channels; or

(4) Any animal in a noncompliant flock.

Exposed flock. Any flock in which a scrapie-positive animal was born or lambed. Any flock that currently contains a female high-risk, exposed, or suspect animal, or that once contained a female high-risk, exposed, or suspect animal that lambed in the flock and from which tissues were not submitted for official testing and found negative. A flock that has completed a post-exposure management and monitoring plan following the exposure will no longer be an exposed flock.

Flock. All animals that are maintained on a single premises and all animals under common ownership or supervision on two or more premises with animal interchange between the premises. Changes in ownership of part or all of a flock do not change the identity of the flock or the regulatory requirements applicable to the flock. Animals maintained temporarily on a premises for activities such as shows and sales or while in marketing channels are not a flock. More than one flock may be maintained on a single premises if:

(1) The flocks are enrolled as separate flocks in the SFCP; or

(2) A State or APHIS representative determines, based upon examination of flock records, that:

(i) There is no interchange of animals between the flocks;

(ii) The flocks never commingle and are kept at least 30 feet apart at all times or are separated by a solid wall through, over, or under which fluids cannot pass and through which contact cannot occur;

(iii) The flocks have separate flock records and identification;

(iv) The flocks have separate lambing facilities, including buildings and pastures, and a pasture or building used for lambing by one flock is not used by the other flock at any time; and

(v) The flocks do not share equipment without cleaning and disinfection in accordance with § 54.7(e) of this chapter. Additional guidance on acceptable means of cleaning and disinfection is also available in the Scrapie Flock Certification Program standards and the Scrapie Eradication Uniform Methods and Rules.

Flock of origin. The flock in which an animal most recently resided in which it either was born, gave birth, or was used for breeding purposes. The determination of an animal's flock of origin may be based either on the physical presence of the animal in the flock, the presence of official identification on the animal traceable to the flock, the presence of other identification on the animal that is listed on the bill of sale, or other evidence, such as registry records.

Flock plan. A written flock management agreement signed by the owner of a flock, the accredited veterinarian, if one is employed by the owner, and a State or APHIS representative in which each participant agrees to undertake actions specified in the flock plan to control the spread of scrapie from, and eradicate scrapie in, an infected flock or source flock or to reduce the risk of the occurrence of scrapie in a flock that contains a high-risk or an exposed animal. As part of a flock plan, the flock owner must provide the facilities and personnel needed to carry out the requirements of the flock plan. The flock plan must include the requirements in § 54.8(a)(f) of this chapter.

High-risk animal. A sexually intact animal, excluding male sheep that have tested RR at codon 171 and AA at codon 136 using an official genotype test, that is:

(1) The progeny of a scrapie-positive dam; or

(2) Born in the same flock during the same lambing season as progeny of a scrapie-positive dam, unless the progeny of the scrapie-positive dam are from separate contemporary lambing groups; or

(3) Born in the same flock during the same lambing season that a scrapie-positive animal was born, or during any subsequent lambing season, if born before that flock completes the requirements of a flock plan; or

(4) An exposed female sheep that has not tested QR, HR, or RR at codon 171 using an official genotype test.

Inconsistent State. Any State other than a Consistent State.

Infected flock. The flock of origin of a female animal that a State or APHIS representative has determined to be a scrapie-positive animal; or any flock in which a State or APHIS representative has determined that a scrapie-positive female animal has resided unless an epidemiologic investigation conducted by a State or APHIS representative shows that the animal did not lamb or abort in the flock. A flock will no longer be considered an infected flock after it has completed the requirements of a flock plan.

Interstate commerce. Trade, traffic, transportation, or other commerce between a place in a State and any place outside of that State, or between points within a State but through any place outside that State.

Limited contacts. Incidental contacts between animals from different flocks off the flock's premises such as at fairs, shows, exhibitions and sales; between ewes being inseminated, flushed, or implanted; or between rams at ram test or collection stations. Embryo transfer and artificial insemination equipment and surgical tools must be sterilized between animals for these contacts to be considered limited contacts. Limited contacts do not include any contact, incidental or otherwise, with animals in the same flock or with an animal during or up to 30 days after she lambed, kidded or aborted or when there is any visible vaginal discharge. Limited contacts do not include any activity where uninhibited contact occurs, such as sharing an enclosure, sharing a section of a transport vehicle, or residing in other flocks for breeding or other purposes. Examples of limited contacts may be found in the Scrapie Flock Certification Program standards.

Live-animal screening test. Any test for the diagnosis of scrapie in a live animal that is approved by the Administrator as usually reliable but not definitive for diagnosing scrapie, and that is conducted in a laboratory approved by the Administrator.[1]

Low-risk commercial sheep. Commercial whitefaced, whitefaced cross, or commercial hair sheep from a flock with no known risk factors for scrapie, including any exposure to female blackfaced sheep, that are identified with a legible permanent brand or earnotch pattern registered with an official brand registry and that are not scrapie-positive, suspect, high-risk, or exposed animals and are not animals from an infected, source, or exposed flock. The term brand includes official brand registry brands on eartags in those States whose brand law or regulation recognizes brands placed on eartags as official brands. Low-risk commercial sheep may only exist in a State where scrapie has not been diagnosed in the previous 10 years in commercial whitefaced, whitefaced cross, or commercial hair sheep that were not commingled with female blackfaced sheep.

Low-risk goat. A goat that is not a scrapie-positive, suspect, high-risk, or exposed animal, that has not been commingled with sheep, and that is from:

(1) A State in which scrapie has not been identified in a goat during the previous 10 years;

(2) A State in which scrapie has been identified in a goat during the previous 10 years, but the scrapie-positive goat was not born in the State and resided in the State for less than 54 months and did not kid while in the State; or,

---

[1] The names and addresses of laboratories approved by the Administrator to conduct live-animal screening tests will be published in the Notices Section of the FEDERAL REGISTER. A list of approved laboratories is also available upon request from the Animal and Plant Health Inspection Service, Veterinary Services, National Animal Health Programs Staff, 4700 River Road Unit 43, Riverdale, MD 20737–1235. State, Federal, and university laboratories will be approved by the Administrator when he or she determines that the laboratory: (a) Employs personnel trained by the National Veterinary Services Laboratories assigned to supervise the testing; (b) follows standard test protocols; (c) meets check test proficiency requirements; and (d) will report all test results to State and Federal animal health officials. Before the Administrator may withdraw approval of any laboratory for failure to meet any of these conditions, the Administrator will give written notice of the proposed withdrawal to the director of the laboratory, and will give the director an opportunity to respond. If there are conflicts as to any material fact, a hearing will be held to resolve the conflicts.

(3) A State in which scrapie has been identified in a goat during the previous 10 years, and the scrapie-positive goat was commingled with sheep, but flock records allowed a complete epidemiologic investigation to be completed and all resulting infected, source, and exposed goat herds have completed flock plans and are in compliance with post-exposure monitoring plans.

National Scrapie Database. A database designated by the Administrator in which APHIS and State animal health agencies cooperatively enter data concerning scrapie outbreaks, flocks and premises affected by scrapie, individual animal identification and premises identification data, and other data to support the Scrapie Eradication Program and the Scrapie Flock Certification Program.

Noncompliant flock. (1) Any source or infected flock whose owner declines to enter into a flock plan or post-exposure management and monitoring plan agreement within 30 days of being so designated, or whose owner is not in compliance with either agreement;

(2) Any exposed flock whose owner fails to make animals available for testing within 60 days of notification, or as mutually agreed, or whose owner fails to submit required postmortem samples;

(3) Any flock whose owner has misrepresented, or who employs a person who has misrepresented, the scrapie status of an animal or any other information on a certificate, permit, owner statement, or other official document within the last 5 years; or

(4) Any flock whose owner or manager has moved, or who employs a person who has moved, an animal in violation of this chapter within the last 5 years.

Official eartag. An identification tag providing unique identification for individual animals. An official eartag which contains or displays an AIN with an 840 prefix must bear the U.S. shield. The design, size, shape, color, and other characteristics of the official eartag will depend on the needs of the users, subject to the approval of the Administrator. The official eartag must be tamper-resistant and have a high retention rate in the animal. Official eartags must adhere to one of the following numbering systems:

(1) National Uniform Eartagging System.

(2) Animal identification number (AIN).

(3) Premises-based number system. The premises-based number system combines an official premises identification number (PIN), as defined in this section, with a producer's livestock production numbering system to provide a unique identification number. The PIN and the production number must both appear on the official tag.

(4) Any other numbering system approved by the Administrator for the identification of animals in commerce.

Official genotype test. Any test to determine the genotype of a live or dead animal that is conducted at either an approved laboratory or at the National Veterinary Services Laboratories, when the animal is officially identified and the samples used for the test are collected and shipped to the laboratory by either an accredited veterinarian or a State or APHIS representative.

Official identification. Identification mark or device approved by APHIS for use in the Scrapie Eradication Program. Examples are listed in § 79.2(a)(2).

Official identification device or method. A means of officially identifying an animal or group of animals using devices or methods approved by the Administrator, including, but not limited to, official tags, tattoos, and registered brands when accompanied by a certificate of inspection from a recognized brand inspection authority.

Official test. Any test for the diagnosis of scrapie in a live or dead animal that is approved by the Administrator for that use and conducted either at an approved laboratory or at the National Veterinary Services Laboratories.

Owner. A person, partnership, company, corporation, or any other legal entity who has legal or rightful title to animals, whether or not they are subject to a mortgage.

Owner statement. A written statement by the owner that includes the owner's name, signature, address, and phone number, date the animals left the flock of origin, the premises identification number assigned to the premises, the number of animals, the premises portion of the premises identification if premises identification is used, and a statement that the animals were either born or were used for breeding purposes on the premises to which the premises identification is assigned.

Ownership brand. A unique permanent legible brand or earnotch pattern applied to an animal that indicates ownership by a particular person when the brand pattern is registered with a State's official brand recording agency.

Permit. An official document issued in connection with the interstate movement of animals (VS Form 1–27 or a State form that contains the same information) that is issued by an APHIS representative, State representative, or an accredited veterinarian authorized to sign such permits. A new permit is required for each change in destination for an animal. A permit lists the owner's name and address; points of origin and destination; number of animals covered; purpose of the movement; whether the animals are from an exposed, noncompliant, infected, or source flock; whether the animal is a high-risk, exposed, scrapie-positive, or scrapie suspect animal; transportation vehicle license number or other identification number; and seal number (if a seal is required). A permit also lists all official identification on the animals covered, including the official eartag number, individual animal registered breed association registration tattoo, individual animal registered breed association registration brand, United States Department of Agriculture backtag (when applied serially, only the beginning and the ending numbers need be recorded), individual animal registered breed association registration number, or any other form of official identification present on the animal.

Premises identification. An APHIS approved eartag, backtag, or legible tattoo bearing the premises identification number (PIN), as defined in this section, or a flock identification number, or a legible permanent brand or ear notch pattern registered with an official brand registry. Premises identification may be used when official individual animal identification is required, if the premises identification method either includes a unique animal number or is used in conjunction with the producer's livestock production numbering system to provide a unique identification number and where, if brands or ear notches are used, the animals are accompanied by an official brand inspection certificate. Clearly visible and/or legible paint brands may be used on animals moving directly to slaughter and on animals moving for grazing or other management purposes without change in ownership.

Premises identification number (PIN). A nationally unique number assigned by a State, Tribal, and/or Federal animal health authority to a premises that is, in the judgment of the State, Tribal, and/or Federal animal health authority, a geographically distinct location from other premises. The premises identification number is associated with an address, geospatial coordinates, and/or other location descriptors which provide a verifiably unique location. The premises identification number may be used in conjunction with a producer's own livestock production numbering system to provide a unique identification number for an animal. The premises identification number may consist of:

(1) The State's two-letter postal abbreviation followed by the premises' assigned number; or

(2) A seven-character alphanumeric code, with the right-most character being a check digit. The check digit number is based upon the ISO 7064 Mod 36/37 check digit algorithm.

Scrapie Eradication Program. The cooperative State-Federal program administered by APHIS and Consistent States to control and eradicate scrapie.

Scrapie Eradication Uniform Methods and Rules (UM&R). Cooperative procedures and standards adopted by APHIS and Consistent States for controlling and eradicating scrapie. The UM&R will be reviewed at least annually by representatives of the livestock industry, appropriate State and Federal agencies, and the public and will be drafted, revised, and published as needed by APHIS.

Scrapie Flock Certification Program (SFCP). The cooperative Federal-State-industry voluntary program for the control of scrapie conducted in accordance with subpart B of part 54 of this chapter.

Scrapie Flock Certification Program standards. Cooperative procedures and standards adopted by APHIS and State Scrapie Certification Boards for reducing the incidence and controlling the spread of scrapie through flock certification.[2]

Scrapie-positive animal. An animal for which a diagnosis of scrapie has been made by the National Veterinary Services Laboratories or another laboratory authorized by the Administrator to conduct scrapie tests in accordance with this chapter, through:

(1) Histopathological examination of central nervous system (CNS) tissues from the animal for characteristic microscopic lesions of scrapie;

(2) The use of proteinase-resistant protein analysis methods including but not limited to immunohistochemistry and/or western blotting on CNS and/or peripheral tissue samples from a live or a dead animal for which a given method has been approved by the Administrator for use on that tissue;

(3) Bioassay;

(4) Scrapie associated fibrils (SAF) detected by electron microscopy; or

(5) Any other test method approved by the Administrator in accordance with § 54.10 of this chapter.[3]

Separate contemporary lambing groups. To be a separate contemporary lambing group, the group must be maintained separately such that the animals cannot come into physical contact with other lambs, kids, ewes or does or birth fluids or placenta from other ewes or does. This separate maintenance must preclude contact through a fence, during lambing and for 60 days following the date the last lamb or kid is born in a lambing season, and must preclude using the same lambing facility as other ewes or does, unless the lambing facility is cleaned and disinfected under supervision by an APHIS representative, State representative, or an accredited veterinarian between lambings in accordance with § 54.7(e) of this chapter. Additional guidance on acceptable means of cleaning and disinfection is also available in the Scrapie Flock Certification Program standards and the Scrapie Eradication Uniform Methods and Rules. The flock owner must maintain adequate records to document which animals were maintained in each contemporary lambing group and to document when cleaning and disinfection was performed and who supervised it.

Slaughter channels. Animals in slaughter channels include any animal that is sold, transferred, or moved either directly to a slaughter facility, to an individual for custom slaughter, or for feeding for the express purpose of improving the animals' condition for movement to slaughter. Any sexually intact animal that is commingled with breeding animals or that has been bred is not in slaughter channels. When selling animals for slaughter, owners should note on the bill of sale that the animals are sold only for slaughter.

Source flock. A flock in which a State or APHIS representative has determined that at least one animal was born that was diagnosed as a scrapie-positive animal at an age of 72 months

[2] Individual copies of the SFCP standards may be obtained on the World Wide Web at URL *http://www.aphis.usda.gov/vs*, or from the Animal and Plant Health Inspection Service, National Animal Health Programs Staff, 4700 River Road Unit 43, Riverdale, MD 20737–1235.

[3] The names and addresses of laboratories approved by the Administrator to conduct tests are published in the Notices Section of the FEDERAL REGISTER. A list of approved laboratories is also available upon request from the Animal and Plant Health Inspection Service, Veterinary Services, National Animal Health Programs Staff, 4700 River Road Unit 43, Riverdale, MD 20737–1235. State, Federal, and university laboratories will be approved by the Administrator when he or she determines that the laboratory: (a) Employs personnel trained by the National Veterinary Services Laboratories assigned to supervise the testing; (b) follows standard test protocols; (c) meets check test proficiency requirements; and (d) will report all test results to State and Federal animal health officials. Before the Administrator may withdraw approval of any laboratory for failure to meet any of these conditions, the Administrator must give written notice of the proposed withdrawal to the director of the laboratory and must give the director an opportunity to respond. If there are conflicts as to any material fact, a hearing will be held to resolve the conflict.

or less. The determination that an animal was born in a flock will be based on such information as the presence of official identification on the animal traceable to the flock, the presence of other identification on the animal that is listed on the bill of sale, or other evidence, such as registry records, to show that a scrapie-positive animal was born in the flock, combined with the absence of records indicating that the animal was purchased from outside and added to the flock. If DNA from the animal was previously collected by an accredited veterinarian and stored at an approved genotyping laboratory, or if DNA collection and storage are required for breed registration and the breed registration has appropriate safeguards in place to ensure the integrity of the banking process, the owner may request verification of the animal's identity based on DNA comparison if adequate records and identification have been maintained by the owner and the repository to show that the archived DNA is that of the animal that has been traced to the flock. The owner will be responsible for all costs for the DNA comparison. A flock will no longer be a source flock after it has completed the requirements of a flock plan.

State. Each of the 50 States, the District of Columbia, the Northern Mariana Islands, Puerto Rico, and all territories or possessions of the United States.

State representative. An individual employed in animal health activities by a State or a political subdivision of a State and who is authorized by the State or political subdivision to perform the function involved.

Suspect animal. An animal will be designated a suspect animal in accordance with § 79.4 if it is:

(1) A sheep or goat that exhibits any of the following possible signs of scrapie and that has been determined to be suspicious for scrapie by an accredited veterinarian or a State or APHIS representative: Weight loss despite retention of appetite; behavioral abnormalities; pruritus (itching); wool pulling; biting at legs or side; lip smacking; motor abnormalities such as incoordination, high stepping gait of forelimbs, bunny hop movement of rear legs, or swaying of back end; increased sensitivity to noise and sudden movement; tremor, "star gazing," head pressing, recumbency, or other signs of neurological disease or chronic wasting.

(2) A sheep or goat that has tested positive for scrapie or for the proteinase resistant protein associated with scrapie on a live-animal screening test or any other test, unless the animal is designated a scrapie-positive animal.

(3) A sheep or goat that has tested inconclusive or suggestive on an official test for scrapie.

Terminal feedlot. (1) A dry lot approved by a State or APHIS representative or an accredited veterinarian authorized to perform this function where animals are separated from all other animals by at least 30 feet at all times or are separated by a solid wall through, over, or under which fluids cannot pass and contact cannot occur and from which animals are moved only to another terminal feedlot or directly to slaughter; or

(2) A pasture when approved by and maintained under the supervision of the State and in which only nonpregnant animals are permitted, where there is no direct fence-to-fence contact with another flock, and from which animals are moved only to another terminal feedlot or directly to slaughter.

(3) Records of all animals entering and leaving a terminal feedlot must be maintained for 1 year after the animal leaves the feedlot and must include the person from whom the animals were acquired and the slaughtering facility in which they were slaughtered. Records must be made available for inspection by an APHIS or State representative upon request.

United States. All of the States.

Unofficial test. Any test for the diagnosis of scrapie or for the detection of the proteinase resistant protein associated with scrapie in a live or dead animal that either has not been approved by the Administrator or that was not conducted at an approved laboratory or at the National Veterinary Services Laboratories.

[66 FR 43990, Aug. 21, 2001, as amended at 69 FR 64650, Nov. 8, 2004; 72 FR 39306, July 18, 2007; 73 FR 54062, Sept. 18, 2008]

§ 79.2 Identification of sheep and goats in interstate commerce.

(a) No sheep or goat that is required to be individually identified or premises identified by § 79.3 may be sold, transported, received for transportation, or offered for sale or transportation in interstate commerce unless each sheep or goat is identified in accordance with this section.

(1) The sheep or goat must be identified to its flock of origin and, for an animal born after January 1, 2002, to its flock of birth, by the owner of the flock or his or her agent; at whichever of the following points in commerce comes first, *Except that;* animals born after January 1, 2002, may be moved interstate direct to slaughter without identification to flock of birth until June 1, 2003, and animals that cannot be identified to their flock of origin because Consistent States have exempted them from flock of origin identification in intrastate commerce in accordance with § 79.6(a)(10)(i) may be moved interstate with only individual animal identification traceable to the State of origin and to the owner of the animals at the time they were so identified:

(i) The point of first commingling of the sheep or goats in interstate commerce with sheep or goats from any other flock of origin;

(ii) Upon unloading of the sheep or goats in interstate commerce at any livestock market, except a market described in paragraph (a)(1)(iii) of this section;

(iii) Upon leaving a livestock market that has been approved in accordance with this chapter to handle sheep and goats in interstate commerce and that has agreed to act as an agent for the owner to apply official identification to the animals. In such cases the animals must be:

(A) Moved to the market and maintained until officially identified in distinguishable groups identifiable to their flocks of origin and when required their flock of birth by means of partitions or other such maintenance; and,

(B) Accompanied by an owner statement that contains the information needed to officially identify the animals to their flock of origin and, when required, their flock of birth;

(iv) Upon transfer of ownership of the sheep or goats in interstate commerce;

(v) In the case of animals shipped directly to slaughter at a slaughter plant that has agreed to act as an agent for the owner to apply official identification to the animals, upon arrival of the sheep or goats in interstate commerce at the slaughter plant. In such cases the animals must be:

(A) Moved to the slaughter plant and maintained until officially identified in distinguishable groups identifiable to their flocks of origin and when required their flock of birth by means of partitions or other such maintenance; and,

(B) Accompanied by an owner statement that contains the information needed to officially identify the animals to their flock of origin and, when required, their flock of birth. If the slaughter plant has agreed to allow APHIS to conduct slaughter sampling, animals need not be identified if they arrive at the plant on days that an APHIS designated sampler is not available at the plant to collect samples; or

(vi) Prior to moving a sheep or goat across a State line, unless the animals are moving to an approved livestock market in accordance with paragraph (a)(1)(iii) of this section or to an approved slaughter plant in accordance with paragraph (a)(1)(v) of this section.

(2) The sheep or goats must be identified by one of the following means of identification, and must remain so identified until they reach their final destination:

(i) Electronic implants for animals required to be identified by the SFCP, when used in a flock participating in the SFCP and when accompanied by a certificate or owner statement that includes the electronic implant numbers and the name of the chip manufacturer;

(ii) Official eartags, including tags approved for use in the SFCP or APHIS-approved premises identification number eartags when combined with a unique animal identification number;

(iii) United States Department of Agriculture backtags or official premises identification backtags that include a unique animal identification number, when used on sheep or goats moving directly to slaughter and when applied within 3 inches of the poll on the dorsal surface of the head or neck;

(iv) Legible official registry tattoos that have been recorded in the book of record of a sheep or goat registry association when the animal is accompanied by either a registration certificate or a certificate of veterinary inspection. These tattoos may also be used as premises identification if they contain a unique premises prefix that has been linked in the National Scrapie Database with the assigned premises identification number of the flock of origin;

(v) Premises identification eartags or tattoos, if the premises identification method includes a unique animal number or is combined with a flock eartag that has a unique animal number and the animal is accompanied by an owner statement;

(vi) Premises identification when premises identification is allowed by § 79.3 and the animal is accompanied by an owner statement; or

(vii) Any other official identification method or device approved by the Administrator.

(3) The owner of the flock of origin is responsible for the identification of animals required to be identified by this section. No person who buys or sells, for his or her own account or as the agent of the buyer or seller, transports, receives for transportation, offers for sale or transportation, or otherwise handles sheep or goats in interstate commerce shall receive or otherwise handle any animal in interstate commerce that has not been identified as required by this section. If an animal loses its identification to its flock of origin while in interstate commerce it is the responsibility of the person who has control or possession of the animal to identify the animal prior to commingling it with any other animals. This shall be done by applying individual animal identification to the animal as required in paragraph (a)(2) of this section and recording the means of identification and the corresponding animal identification number. If the flock of origin cannot be determined, all possible flocks of origin shall be listed on the record.

(b) Serial numbers for use in official identification will be assigned to each person who applies to the State animal health official or the area veterinarian in charge for the State in which that person maintains his or her place of business. Serial numbers of official eartags will be assigned to each accredited veterinarian or State or APHIS representative who requests official eartags from the State animal health official or the area veterinarian in charge, whoever is responsible for issuing official eartags in that State. The official responsible for issuing eartags in a State may assign serial numbers of official eartags to other responsible persons, such as 4–H leaders, if the State animal health official and the area veterinarian in charge agree that such assignments will improve scrapie control and eradication within the State. Persons assigned serial numbers may either directly apply eartags to animals, or may reassign eartag numbers to producers. If these persons reassign eartag numbers, they must maintain appropriate records that permit traceback of animals to their flock of origin, or flock of birth when required. Premises identification eartag, backtag, and tattoo numbers (series of alphanumeric USDA tags and backtags may be assigned as premises identification if they are linked to the premises in the National Scrapie Database) will be assigned to animal owners by the State animal health official or the area veterinarian in charge, whoever is responsible for assigning premises codes in that State. Persons assigned serial numbers of United States Department of Agriculture backtags, official sheep and goat tattoos, official eartags, and premises identification numbers must:

(1) If the person assigned the numbers is a flock owner, so that the assigned numbers are directly linked to the flock of origin in the national scrapie database, record the following information on a document:

(i) The premises identification number or serial numbers;

(ii) The number of animals so identified;

(iii) The date the animals were identified;

(iv) For animals born after January 1, 2002, that were not born in the flock of origin and that are not identified to the previous flock of origin, the individual identification number applied and the name, street address, including the city and State, or the township, county, and State, and the telephone number, if the telephone number is available, of the flock of birth if known.

(2) If the person assigned the numbers is a veterinarian, extension agent, auction market operator, dealer, or any person other than the owner of the flock of origin, record the following information on a document:

(i) All serial numbers applied to a sheep or goat;

(ii) Any other serial numbers and approved identification appearing on the sheep or goat;

(iii) The street address, including the city and State, or the township, county, and State, of the premises where the approved means of identification was applied;

(iv) The date the identification was applied;

(v) The name, street address, including the city and State, or the township, county, and State, and the telephone number if the telephone number is available, of the owner of the flock of origin and, if different, the person who owns or possesses the sheep or goat, and

(vi) For animals born after January 1, 2002, that were not born in the flock of origin and that are not identified to the previous flock of origin, the individual identification number applied and the name, street address, including the city and State, or the township, county, and State, and the telephone number if the telephone number is available, of the flock of birth if known.

(vii) The serial numbers, the manufacturer, and the type and color of all official tags received. Usually maintaining the tag invoice will meet this requirement.

(3) Maintain these records for 5 years; and

(4) Make these records available for inspection and copying during ordinary business hours (8 a.m. to 5:30 p.m., Monday through Friday) upon request by any authorized employee of the United States Department of Agriculture or the State, and presentation of his or her official credentials.

(5) Any person who fails to comply with these requirements shall not be assigned serial numbers of United States Department of Agriculture backtags, official sheep and goat tattoos, official eartags, or premises identification numbers. If a person who is not in compliance with these requirements has already been assigned such serial numbers, the Administrator may withdraw the assignment by giving notice to such person. After such notice the person shall be subject to criminal and civil penalties if he continues to use those assigned serial numbers.

(c) No person shall apply a premises identification number or a brand or earnotch pattern to an animal that did not originate on the premises to which the number was assigned by a State or APHIS representative or to which the brand or earnotch pattern has been assigned by an official brand registry. This includes individual identification such as USDA tags and backtags that have been assigned to a premises for use as premises identification and registration tattoos that contain prefixes that have been assigned to a premises for use as premises identification. This does not preclude the owner of a flock from using a premises identification number tag assigned to that flock on an animal owned by him that resides in that flock but that was born or previously resided on a different premises as long as the records required in paragraph (b)(1)(iv) of this section are maintained.

(d) Each person who buys or sells, for his or her own account or as the agent of the buyer or seller, transports, receives for transportation, offers for sale or transportation, or otherwise handles sheep or goats in interstate commerce must ensure that the animals are identified as required in this part and must keep records relating to the transfer of ownership, shipment, or handling of the sheep or goats, such as yarding receipts, sale tickets, invoices, and waybills.

(1) If official individual animal identification is required, the records must include the number of sheep and/or goats; the breed or cross if known; the name, street address, including city and State, or the township, county, and State, and the telephone number if the telephone number is available, of the owner of the flock of origin and, if different, the person from whom the sheep or goats were purchased or otherwise obtained; and a copy of any documents required to accompany the animal including any certificate, owner statement, letter, or permit; and

(i) For animals not in slaughter channels the records must include all serial numbers and other approved means of identification appearing on the sheep or goat. This requirement may usually be met by maintaining a copy of the certificate that accompanied the animals. The premises number may be recorded instead of the individual numbers in the case of animals identified with premises identification if:

(A) The premises identification meets the requirements of paragraph (a)(2)(v) of this section for individual animal identification; or

(B) The animals are allowed to move interstate with only premises identification in accordance with § 79.3.

(ii) For animals in slaughter channels that are identified with individual animal identification traceable to the flock of origin or that are identified to the flock of origin with official premises identification that meets the requirements for individual animal identification, no additional records are required;

(iii) For animals in slaughter channels that are identified with individual animal identification traceable to a previous flock but not to the flock of origin, or that are identified with official premises identification that meets the requirements for individual animal identification that is traceable to a previous flock but not to the flock of origin, the records must include all serial numbers and other approved means of identification appearing on the sheep or goat;

(iv) For animals that are not required to be identified until they reach their final destination, the records must include the final destination.

(2) If official premises identification is required or allowed, the records must include:

(i) The premises identification number(s) and the number of animals identified with each premises number;

(ii) Copies of any required documents such as the brand inspection certificate, an owner's statement, an accredited veterinarian's statement, or a health certificate;

(iii) The name, street address, including city and State, or the township, county, and State, and the telephone number if the telephone number is available, of the owner of the flock of origin and, if different, the person from whom the sheep or goats were purchased or otherwise obtained.

(3) Each person required to keep records under this paragraph must maintain the records for at least 5 years after the person has sold or otherwise disposed of the sheep or goat to another person, and for such further period as the Administrator may require by written notice to the person, for purposes of any investigation or action involving the sheep or goat identified in the records. The person must make the records available for inspection and copying during ordinary business hours (8 a.m. to 5:30 p.m., Monday through Friday) by any authorized employee of the United States Department of Agriculture or the State, upon that employee's request and presentation of his or her official credentials.

(e) No person may remove or tamper with any means of identification required to be on sheep or goats pursuant to this section while the animals are in interstate commerce, and, at the time of slaughter, animal identification must be maintained throughout postmortem inspection in accordance with regulations of the Food Safety and Inspection Service, U.S. Department of Agriculture, in chapter III of this title.

(f) *Requirements for approval of official premises and individual identification tags.* (1) The Administrator may approve tag companies to produce official premises and/or individual identification tags for use on sheep or goats.

Tags may be plastic or metal and must be an appropriate size for use in sheep and goats. Tags must be able to legibly accommodate the required alphanumeric sequences. Tags must resist removal and be difficult to place on another animal once removed, but need not be tamper-proof. Tags must be readily distinguishable as USDA official sheep and goat tags, must carry the alphanumeric sequences, symbols, or logos specified by APHIS, and must have a means of discouraging counterfeiting, such as use of a unique copywrited logo or trade mark. Tags for use only on animals in slaughter channels must be marked with the words "Meat" or "For Slaughter Only," or else must be used in conjunction with an ear tattoo of the word "Meat."

(2) Written requests for approval of official premises identification tags for sheep and goats should be sent to the Animal and Plant Health Inspection Service, Veterinary Services, National Animal Health Programs Staff, Attention: National Scrapie Program Coordinator, 4700 River Road Unit 43, Riverdale, MD 20737–1235. The request must include:

(i) Data supporting the durability of the tag and durability and legibility of the identification numbers and high retention rates of the tags in animals, preferably sheep and/or goats. Preference will be given to tags with high legibility and retention rates in sheep and goats that minimize injury to the ear.

(ii) A signed statement agreeing to:

(A) Send official eartags only to a State or APHIS representative, to a flock owner at the address to which the premises number or tag sequence was assigned by a State or APHIS representative, or as directed by APHIS;

(B) Provide a monthly report by State of all tags produced, including the tag sequences produced and the person's and address to which the tags were shipped; and

(C) When required by APHIS, enter the sequences of tags shipped into the National Scrapie Database through a web page interface or other means specified by APHIS.

(iii) Twenty-five sample tags. Additional tags must be submitted if requested by APHIS.

(3) Approval to produce official premises and/or individual identification tags will be valid for 1 year and must be renewed annually. The Administrator may also grant approval to produce tags for periods of less than 1 year in cases where all of the submissions required by this section have not been received or evaluated but there is substantial evidence that the tags meet the requirements of this section. The Administrator may decline to renew a company's approval if the tags do not show adequate retention and durability in field use or if any of the requirements of this section are not met by the tag company. If a company's tags do not show adequate retention and durability in field use or if any of the requirements of this section are not met by the tag company, the approval may be withdrawn with 60 days written notice. Any person who is approved to produce official premises or individual identification tags in accordance with this section and who knowingly produces tags that are not in compliance with the requirements of this section, and any person who is not approved to produce such tags but does so, shall be subject to such civil penalties and such criminal liabilities as are provided by 18 U.S.C. 1001, 7 U.S.C. 8313, or other applicable Federal statutes. Such action may be in addition to, or in lieu of, withdrawal of approval to produce tags.

(g) *New types of identification.* Written requests for approval of sheep or goat identification devices and markings not listed in paragraph (a)(2) of this section should be sent to the Animal and Plant Health Inspection Service, Veterinary Services, National Animal Health Programs Staff, 4700 River Road Unit 43, Riverdale, MD 20737–1235. If the Administrator determines that the devices and markings will provide a means of tracing sheep and goats in interstate commerce, a proposal will be published in the FEDERAL REGISTER to add the devices and markings to the list of approved means of sheep and goat identification.

[66 FR 43990, Aug. 21, 2001, as amended at 68 FR 6343, Feb. 7, 2003; 69 FR 64650, Nov. 8, 2004]

§ 79.3 General restrictions.

The following prohibitions and movement conditions apply to the interstate movement of sheep and goats, and no sheep or goat may move interstate except in compliance with them.

INTERSTATE MOVEMENT GENERAL RESTRICTIONS FOR SHEEP AND GOATS

Note: A CONSISTENT STATE is one whose intrastate identification, reporting, and movement restrictions for infected and source flocks and high-risk animals are consistent with the APHIS standards for State scrapie programs.

Type of interstate movement	Moved from INCONSISTENT state	Moved from CONSISTENT state
(a) Sale or other movement of breeding animals, show animals or any other animal not specifically addressed in this chart. General Condition: No animal may be removed from slaughter channels in interstate commerce if it was sold at a slaughter-only auction, is identified with a tag or ear tattoo marked "meat" or "slaughter only," or was sold with a bill of sale marked for slaughter only, and other animals may be removed from slaughter channels in interstate commerce only if they are identified to their flock of birth.—		
(1) High-risk, scrapie-positive, or suspect animals, or animals from a noncompliant flock.	Prohibited [1]	Prohibited [1]
(2) Non-high-risk animals from an infected or source flock that are not scrapie-positive or suspect animals.	Prohibited [1]	Prohibited, [1] except as allowed in an approved scrapie control pilot project flock plan and must meet the requirements for exposed animals.
(3) Sexually intact exposed animals that are not scrapie-positive, suspect, or high-risk animals and are not animals from an infected or source flock.	Flock must be enrolled in the Complete Monitored category of the Scrapie Flock Certification Program or equivalent APHIS recognized program, have official individual animal identification, and a permit. [2] For any female exposed sheep the results of an official genotype test must be included on or attached to the permit and must be QR or RR at codon 171. For any female animal moving for exhibition, the permit must include a statement by both the owner and the accredited veterinarian that the animal has not lambed or aborted within 30 days of being exhibited and is not due to lamb within 30 days of being exhibited and that there is no visible vaginal discharge. For any animal born after 1–1–2002, the certificate must include the flock of birth and the flock of origin, if different.	Official individual animal identification and a permit. [2] For any female exposed sheep the results of an official genotype test must be included on or attached to the permit and must be QR or RR at codon 171. For any female animal moving for exhibition, the permit must include a statement by both the owner and an accredited veterinarian that the animal has not lambed or aborted within 30 days of being exhibited and is not due to lamb within 30 days of being exhibited and that there is no visible vaginal discharge. For any animal born after 1–1–2002, the permit must include the flock of birth and the flock of origin, if different.
(4)(i) Sexually intact sheep except as allowed in (a)(7).		
(ii) Sexually intact goats, except for low-risk goats.	Flock must be enrolled in the Complete Monitored category of the Scrapie Flock Certification Program or equivalent APHIS-recognized program, have official individual animal identification, and a certificate. For any animal born after 1–1–2002, the certificate must include the flock of birth and the flock of origin, if different.	Official individual animal identification and a certificate. For any animal born after 1–1–2002, the certificate must include the flock of birth and the flock of origin, if different.
(5) Sexually intact low-risk goats	Official individual animal identification and a certificate. For any animal born after 1–1–2002, the certificate must include the flock of birth and the flock of origin, if different.	Official individual animal identification and a certificate. For any animal born after 1–1–2002, the certificate must include the flock of birth and the flock of origin, if different.
(6) Castrated animals that are not scrapie-positive or suspect animals.	Official individual animal identification and a certificate.	None, except for exposed animals that must have official individual animal identification.

INTERSTATE MOVEMENT GENERAL RESTRICTIONS FOR SHEEP AND GOATS—Continued

Note: A CONSISTENT STATE is one whose intrastate identification, reporting, and movement restrictions for infected and source flocks and high-risk animals are consistent with the APHIS standards for State scrapie programs.

Type of interstate movement	Moved from INCONSISTENT state	Moved from CONSISTENT state
(7) Low-risk commercial sheep ..	Official individual animal identification and a certificate, and the flock must be enrolled in the Complete Monitored category of the Scrapie Flock Certification Program or an equivalent APHIS-recognized program. For any animal born after 1–1–2002, the certificate must include the flock of birth and the flock of origin, if different.	(i) Official premises identification that is a permanent brand or ear notch pattern registered with an official brand registry; (ii) A brand inspection certificate; (iii) An owner statement dated within 30 days stating that the animals were born in the flock, that the flock does not contain any animal exhibiting signs of scrapie, that to the best of his or her knowledge the flock has no risk factors for or exposure to scrapie, and that the flock has never contained: (A) Any animal diagnosed as having scrapie; (B) any female blackfaced sheep; or (C) any female blackfaced cross sheep that were not born in the flock; and (iv) An accredited veterinarian's statement issued within 12 months of the date of movement indicating that, to the best of his or her knowledge, the flock has no known risk factors for or exposure to scrapie, and that he or she has inspected the flock and it does not contain: (A) Any animal exhibiting signs of scrapie; (B) any female blackfaced sheep; or (C) any female blackfaced cross sheep that were not born in the flock. The statements must include the owner's name, address, and the premises identification number and a drawing of the owner's registered brand or ear notch pattern.
(8) Commercial low-risk goats. ...	Official individual animal identification and a certificate. For any animal born after 1–1–2002, the certificate must include the flock of birth and the flock of origin, if different.	None.
(b) Sale or other movement directly to slaughter, through slaughter channels to slaughter, or to feedlots for later movement to slaughter of animals that are under 18 months of age as evidenced by eruption of the second incisor, not pregnant, and have not lambed or kidded. General Condition: No animal may be removed from slaughter channels in interstate slaughter channels in interstate commerce if it was sold at a slaughter-only auction, is identified with a tag or ear tattoo marked "meat" or "slaughter only," or was sold with a bill of sale marked for slaughter only, and other animals may be removed from slaughter channels in interstate commerce only if they are identified to their flock of birth.—		
(1) Scrapie-positive or suspect animal.	Prohibited [1]	Prohibited. [1]
(2) Sexually intact high-risk animals and sexually intact animals from infected or source flocks that are not scrapie-positive or suspect animals.	Official individual animal identification and a permit, or a permit and an indelible "S" mark on the left jaw, or sealed conveyance and a permit. (Note: these animals may only be permitted to slaughter or to terminal feedlots. [3])	Official individual animal identification and a permit, or a permit and an indelible "S" mark on the left jaw, or sealed conveyance and a permit. (Note: these animals may only be permitted to slaughter or to terminal feedlots. [3])

INTERSTATE MOVEMENT GENERAL RESTRICTIONS FOR SHEEP AND GOATS—Continued

Note: A CONSISTENT STATE is one whose intrastate identification, reporting, and movement restrictions for infected and source flocks and high-risk animals are consistent with the APHIS standards for State scrapie programs.

Type of interstate movement	Moved from INCONSISTENT state	Moved from CONSISTENT state
(3) Exposed sexually intact animals that are not scrapie-positive, suspect, or high-risk. animals and that are not animals from an infected or source flock.	Official individual animal identification for any animal that is not moving directly to slaughter or to a terminal feedlot. [3 4] (Note: pregnant animals and animals with a visible vaginal discharge may only be permitted to slaughter or to terminal feedlots.).	Official individual animal identification for any animal that is not moving direct to slaughter or to a terminal feedlot. [3 4] (Note: Pregnant animals and animals with a visible vaginal discharge may only be permitted to slaughter or to terminal feedlots.)
(4) Sexually intact sheep that are not scrapie-positive, suspect, high-risk, or exposed animals and are not animals from an infected or source flock.	Official premises identification or official individual animal identification for any animal that is not moving direct to slaughter or to a terminal feedlot. [3]	None.
(5) Sheep enrolled in the selective monitored or complete monitored category of the SFCP that are not scrapie-positive, suspect, high-risk, or exposed animals.	None	None.
(6) Castrated animals that are not scrapie-positive, or suspect animals.	None	None.
(7) Sexually intact goats that are not scrapie-positive, suspect, high-risk, or exposed animals and are not animals from an infected or source flock.	None	None.
(c) Sale or other movement directly to slaughter, through slaughter channels to slaughter, or to feedlots for later movement to slaughter of animals that are over 18 months of age, as evidenced by eruption of the second incisor, or that are pregnant or that have lambed or kidded. General Condition: No animal may be removed from slaughter channels in interstate commerce if it was sold at a slaughter-only auction, is identified with a tag or ear tattoo marked "meat" or "slaughter only," or was sold with a bill of sale marked for slaughter only, and other animals may be removed from slaughter channels in interstate commerce only if they are identified to their flock of birth.—		
(1) Scrapie-positive or suspect animal.	Prohibited [1]	Prohibited. [1]
(2) Sexually intact high-risk animals and sexually intact animals from an infected or source flock that are not scrapie-positive, or suspect animals.	Official individual animal identification and a permit, or a permit and an indelible "S" mark on the left jaw, or sealed conveyance and a permit. (Note: these animals may only be permitted to slaughter or to terminal feedlots. [3]	Official individual animal identification and a permit, or a permit and an indelible "S" mark on the left jaw, or sealed conveyance and a permit. (Note: These animals may only be permitted to slaughter or to terminal feedlots. [3]
(3) Sexually intact exposed animals that are not scrapie-positive, suspect, or high-risk animals and are not animals from an infected or source flock.	Official individual animal identification and a permit, or a permit and an indelible "S" mark on the left jaw, or sealed conveyance and a permit when moving directly to slaughter. (Note: pregnant animals and animals with a visible vaginal discharge may only be permitted to slaughter or to terminal feedlots. [3 4]	Official individual animal identification. (Note: pregnant animals and animals with a visible vaginal discharge may only be moved directly to slaughter or to terminal feedlots. [3 4]

INTERSTATE MOVEMENT GENERAL RESTRICTIONS FOR SHEEP AND GOATS—Continued

Note: A CONSISTENT STATE is one whose intrastate identification, reporting, and movement restrictions for infected and source flocks and high-risk animals are consistent with the APHIS standards for State scrapie programs.

Type of interstate movement	Moved from INCONSISTENT state	Moved from CONSISTENT state
(4) Sheep over 18 months of age that are not scrapie-positive, suspect, sexually intact high-risk, or sexually intact exposed animals and that are not sexually intact animals from an infected or source flock.	Official individual animal identification and a certificate. [4].	Official individual animal identification. [4]
(5) Low-risk commercial sheep ..	Official individual animal identification and a certificate [4].	(i) Official premises identification that is a permanent legible brand or ear notch pattern registered with an official brand registry or, in the case of animals moving directly to slaughter, may be a legible paint brand registered with an official brand registry; (ii) A brand inspection certificate; (iii) An owner statement dated within 30 days of the movement stating that the flock does not contain any animal exhibiting signs of scrapie, and that, to the best of his or her knowledge, the flock has no risk factors for or exposure to scrapie and has never contained: (A) Any animal diagnosed as having scrapie; (B) any female blackfaced sheep; or (C) any female blackfaced cross sheep that was not born in the flock; (iv) An accredited veterinarian's statement issued within 12 months of the date of movement indicating that, to the best of his or her knowledge, the flock has no known risk factors for or exposure to scrapie, and that he or she has inspected the flock and it does not contain: (A) Any animal exhibiting signs of scrapie; (B) any female blackfaced sheep; or (C) any female blackfaced cross sheep that was not born in the flock. The statements must include the owner's name, address, and the premises identification number and a drawing of the owner's registered brand or ear notch pattern. [4]
(6) Goats that are not scrapie-positive, suspect, sexually intact high-risk, or sexually intact exposed animals and that are not sexually intact animals from an infected or source flock.	None	None.
(d) Movement of animals for grazing or other management purposes without change of ownership.—		
(1) Scrapie-positive, suspect, or sexually intact high-risk animals.	Prohibited [1]	Prohibited. [1]
(2) Non-high-risk animals from an infected or source flock.	Prohibited [1]	Prohibited, [1] except as allowed in an approved scrapie control pilot project flock plan and must meet the requirements for exposed animals.
(3) Sexually intact exposed animals that are not scrapie-positive, suspect, or high-risk animals and that are not animals from an infected or source flock.	Official individual animal identification and a permit. [2] For any female exposed sheep the results of an official genotype test must be included on or attached to the permit and must be QR or RR at codon 171.	Official individual animal identification and a permit. [2] For any female exposed sheep the results of an official genotype test must be included on or attached to the permit and must be QR or RR at codon 171.

INTERSTATE MOVEMENT GENERAL RESTRICTIONS FOR SHEEP AND GOATS—Continued

Note: A CONSISTENT STATE is one whose intrastate identification, reporting, and movement restrictions for infected and source flocks and high-risk animals are consistent with the APHIS standards for State scrapie programs.

Type of interstate movement	Moved from INCONSISTENT state	Moved from CONSISTENT state
(4) Sexually intact sheep or sexually intact goats that have been commingled with sheep and that are not scrapie-positive, suspect, high-risk, or exposed animals and are not animals from an infected or source flock.	Official premises identification and a certificate..	None.
(5) Sexually intact goats that have not been commingled with sheep and that are not scrapie-positive, suspect, high-risk, or exposed animals and are not animals from an infected or source flock.	None	None.
(6) Castrated animals that are not scrapie-positive or suspect animals and are not an animal from an infected or source flock.	None	None.

[1] Animals prohibited movement may be moved interstate only if they are moving interstate for destruction or research as approved by the Administrator.

[2] A copy of the permit must be sent to the State veterinarian and the AVIC of the receiving State prior to movement of animals.

[3] No exposed or high-risk animal from any State or any animal from an Inconsistent State shall be removed from slaughter channels once it has entered interstate commerce.

[4] Official individual animal identification or official premises identification is not required for these slaughter animals if the animals are kept as a group on the same premises on which they were born or used for breeding purposes and are not commingled with animals from another premises at any time, including throughout the feeding, marketing, and slaughter process.

§ 79.4 Designation of scrapie-positive animals, high-risk animals, exposed animals, suspect animals, exposed flocks, infected flocks, noncompliant flocks, and source flocks; notice to owners.

(a) *Designation.* A designated scrapie epidemiologist will designate an animal to be a scrapie-positive animal, high-risk animal, exposed animal, or suspect animal after determining that the animal meets the criteria of the relevant definition in § 79.1.

(1) A State or APHIS veterinarian will designate an animal to be a suspect animal after determining that the animal meets the criteria of the relevant definition in § 79.1.

(2) A designated scrapie epidemiologist will designate a flock to be a source, infected, or exposed flock after reviewing sale, movement, and breeding records that indicate the flock meets the criteria of the relevant definition in § 79.1.

(i) A designated scrapie epidemiologist may conduct testing of animals if he or she determines such testing is needed to properly designate a flock to be a source, infected, or exposed flock. The designated scrapie epidemiologist will select animals for testing in a manner that will provide a 95 percent confidence of detecting scrapie at a prevalence of 1 percent or, when flock records are adequate and all exposed animals that lambed in the flock are available for testing, may limit the testing to all exposed and suspect animals. Flocks meeting the definition of infected or source flocks that are designated as exposed flocks must complete a post exposure monitoring and management plan. Testing may include live-animal testing using a live-animal official test, an official genotype test, the culling and postmortem examination and testing of genetically susceptible animals in the flock that cannot be evaluated by a live animal test, and postmortem examination and testing of animals found dead or cull animals at slaughter.

(ii) If an owner does not make his or her animals available for testing within 60 days of notification or as mutually agreed or fails to submit required postmortem samples, the flock will be designated a source, infected, or exposed flock, whichever definition applies. Any flock that is pending designation must comply with the movement restrictions for infected flocks.

(3) A designated scrapie epidemiologist will designate a flock to be a noncompliant flock after determining that the flock meets the definition of a noncompliant flock in § 79.1.

(b) *Redesignation.* (1) A designated scrapie epidemiologist may reclassify an animal designated a high-risk animal as an exposed animal after receiving negative results from an official test or in accordance with an approved Scrapie Control Pilot Project.

(2) A State or APHIS veterinarian may remove the suspect animal designation from an animal that had clinical signs of scrapie and that did not test positive for scrapie or for the proteinase resistant protein associated with scrapie upon determination that it is alive and no longer exhibits such signs, or that the signs are not caused by scrapie.

(3) A designated scrapie epidemiologist may remove the suspect animal designation from an animal that has tested positive for scrapie or for the proteinase resistant protein associated with scrapie on an unofficial test based on knowledge of the test used or based on an epidemiologic investigation which may include additional testing of the suspect animal and or animals that have been commingled with the suspect animal.

(4) A designated scrapie epidemiologist may remove the suspect animal designation from an animal that tested positive on a live-animal screening test based on an epidemiologic investigation which includes additional official testing of the suspect animal and when appropriate, animals that have been commingled with the suspect animal.

(5) A designated scrapie epidemiologist may remove the exposed flock designation after completing an epidemiologic investigation or upon completion of a post-exposure management and monitoring plan. As part of the epidemiologic investigation the designated scrapie epidemiologist may conduct testing of animals if he or she determines such testing is needed to properly redesignate the flock. The designated scrapie epidemiologist will select animals for testing in a manner that will provide a 95 percent confidence of detecting scrapie at a prevalence of 1 percent or, when flock records are adequate and all exposed animals that lambed in the flock are available for testing, may limit the testing to all exposed and suspect animals. Testing may include live-animal testing using a live-animal official test, an official genotype test, the culling and postmortem examination and testing of genetically susceptible animals in the flock that cannot be evaluated by a live animal test, and postmortem examination and testing of animals found dead or cull animals at slaughter. A designated scrapie epidemiologist shall redesignate an exposed flock as a noncompliant flock if the owner fails to make his animals available for testing within 60 days of notification or as mutually agreed or fails to submit required postmortem samples.

(6) Based on an epidemiologic investigation and testing, a designated scrapie epidemiologist may redesignate an infected flock or source flock as an exposed flock. The designated scrapie epidemiologist may only use this option when the epidemiologic investigation reveals that the scrapie exposure was minor or could not be confirmed due to inadequate records. The designated scrapie epidemiologist will select animals for testing in a manner that will provide a 95 percent confidence of detecting scrapie at a prevalence of 1 percent or, when flock records are adequate and all exposed animals that lambed in the flock are available for testing, may limit the testing to all exposed and suspect animals. Testing may include live-animal testing using a live-animal official test, an official genotype test, the culling and postmortem examination and testing of genetically susceptible animals in the flock that cannot be evaluated by a live animal test, and postmortem examination and testing of animals found dead or cull animals at slaughter. Infected or source flocks that are redesignated as exposed flocks must complete a post exposure monitoring and management plan. If an

owner does not make his or her animals available for testing within 60 days of notification or as mutually agreed or fails to submit required post-mortem samples, the flock designation will remain unchanged.

(7) A designated scrapie epidemiologist may remove the noncompliant flock designation after reviewing any required testing of the flock and determining that the flock has complied with the required testing or no longer meets the definition of a noncompliant flock.

(8) A designated scrapie epidemiologist may redesignate an exposed animal, exposed flock, or infected flock by removing that designation after completing an epidemiologic investigation and determining that the exposure was limited to a scrapie-positive male animal that was not born in the flock (the owner must have adequate records and animal identification to show that the scrapie-positive male animal was purchased).

(c) *Notice to owner.* As soon as possible after making such a determination, a State or APHIS representative will attempt to notify the owner(s) of the flock(s) in writing that their flock contained or contains a scrapie-positive animal, a suspect animal, a high-risk animal or an exposed animal, or that the flock is an infected, source, exposed, or noncompliant flock or that the flock is pending designation as an infected, source, exposed, or noncompliant flock. The notice will include:

(1) A description of the interstate movement restrictions and identification requirements;

(2) Reporting requirements;

(3) Sample submission requirements for suspect and high-risk animals contained in this part;

(4) Options for controlling the spread of scrapie from, and eradicating scrapie in, an infected flock or source flock or to reduce the risk of the occurrence of scrapie in a flock that contains a high-risk or an exposed animal; and

(5) In the case of flocks that are pending designation the notification shall include the testing options available to them and the designation their flock will receive if they decline to test.

§ 79.5 Issuance of certificates.

(a) Certificates are required as specified by § 79.3 for certain interstate movements of animals. A certificate must show the official ear tag number, individual animal registered breed association registration tattoo, individual animal registered breed association registration brand, individual animal registered breed association registration number, and any other official individual identification of each animal to be moved; *provided that,* in the case of animals identified with premises identification[4] that is assigned to the flock of origin and that meets the requirements for individual animal identification, the premises number may be recorded instead of the individual identification numbers. A certificate must also show the number of animals covered by the certificate; the purpose for which the animals are to be moved; the points of origin and destination; the consignor, and the consignee. Certificates must indicate the flock of birth for any breeding sheep born after January 1, 2002, that are covered by the certificate. The certificate must include a statement by the issuing accredited or State or Federal veterinarian that the animals were not exhibiting clinical signs associated with scrapie at the time of examination and an owner statement indicating whether the animal is or is not a scrapie-positive, suspect, high-risk or exposed animal and whether it originated in an infected, source, exposed, or noncompliant flock. Except as provided in paragraphs (b) and (c) of this section, all of the information required by this paragraph must be typed or written on the certificate. Note that in accordance with § 79.3(a), (b), and (c), scrapie-positive, suspect, and high-risk animals, some exposed animals, and animals that originated in an infected or source flock require permits rather than certificates.

[4] Ownership brands may be used on certificates for sheep and goats moved interstate when premises identification is required under this part, provided the ownership brands are legible and are registered with the official brand recording agency and the animals are accompanied by a brand inspection certificate.

(b) *Animal identification documents attached to certificates.* As an alternative to typing or writing individual animal identification on a certificate, another document may be used to provide this information, but only under the following conditions:

(1) The document must be a State form or APHIS form that requires individual identification of animals;

(2) A legible copy of the document must be stapled to the original and each copy of the certificate;

(3) Each copy of the document must identify each animal to be moved with the certificate, but any information pertaining to other animals, and any unused space on the document for recording animal identification, must be crossed out in ink; and

(4) The following information must be typed or written in ink in the identification column on the original and each copy of the certificate and must be circled or boxed, also in ink, so that no additional information can be added:

(i) The name of the document; and

(ii) Either the serial number on the document or, if the document is not imprinted with a serial number, both the name of the person who prepared the document and the date the document was signed.

(c) *Ownership brands documents attached to certificates.* As an alternative to typing or writing ownership brands on a certificate, an official brand inspection certificate may be used to provide this information, but only under the following conditions:

(1) A legible copy of the official brand inspection certificate must be stapled to the original and each copy of the certificate;

(2) Each copy of the official brand inspection certificate must show the ownership brand of each animal to be moved with the certificate, but any other ownership brands, and any unused space for recording ownership brands, must be crossed out in ink; and

(3) The following information must be typed or written in ink in the official identification column on the original and each copy of the certificate and must be circled or boxed, also in ink, so that no additional information can be added:

(i) The name of the attached document; and

(ii) Either the serial number on the official brand inspection certificate or, if the official brand inspection certificate is not imprinted with a serial number, both the name of the person who prepared the official brand inspection certificate and the date it was signed.

§ 79.6 Standards for States to qualify as Consistent States.

(a) In reviewing a State for Consistent State status, the Administrator will evaluate the State statutes, regulations, and directives pertaining to animal health activities; reports and publications of the State animal health agency; and a written statement from the State animal health agency describing State scrapie control activities and certifying that these activities meet the requirements of this section. In determining whether a State is a Consistent State, the Administrator will determine whether the State:

(1) Has the authority, based on State law or regulation, to restrict the movement of all scrapie-infected and source flocks.

(2) Has the authority, based on State law or regulation, to require the reporting of any animal suspected of having scrapie and test results for any animals tested for scrapie to State or Federal animal health authorities.

(3) Has, in cooperation with APHIS personnel, drafted and signed a memorandum of understanding between APHIS and the State that delineates the respective roles of each in the National Scrapie Program implementation.

(4) Has placed all known scrapie-infected and source flocks under movement restrictions, with movement of animals only to slaughter, to feedlots under permit and movement restrictions that ensure later movement to slaughter, for destruction, or for research. Scrapie-positive and suspect animals may be moved only for transport to an approved research facility or for purposes of destruction.

(5) Has effectively implemented policies to:

(i) Investigate all animals reported as scrapie suspect animals within 7 days of notification;

(ii) Designate a flock's status, within 15 days of notification that the flock contains a scrapie-positive animal, based on an investigation by State or Federal animal health authorities and in accordance with this part;

(iii) Restrict the movement, in accordance with paragraph (a)(4) of this section, of newly designated scrapie-infected and source flocks within 7 days after they are designated in accordance with § 79.4;

(iv) Relieve infected and source flock movement restrictions only after completion of a flock plan created in accordance with § 54.14 of this chapter or a flock plan created in accordance with an approved scrapie control pilot project, or as permitted by the conditions of such a flock plan, and after agreement by the owner to comply with a 5-year post-exposure management and monitoring plan;

(v) Conduct an epidemiologic investigation of source and infected flocks that includes the designation of high-risk and exposed animals and that identifies animals to be traced;

(vi) Conduct tracebacks of scrapie-positive animals and traceouts of high-risk and exposed animals and report any out-of-State traces to the appropriate State within 45 days of receipt of notification of a scrapie-positive animal; and

(vii) Conduct tracebacks based on slaughter sampling within 15 days of receipt of notification of a scrapie-positive animal at slaughter.

(6) Effectively monitors and enforces quarantines.

(7) Effectively enforces State reporting laws and regulations for scrapie.

(8) Has designated at least one APHIS or State animal health official to coordinate scrapie program activities in the State and to serve as the designated scrapie epidemiologist in the State.

(9) Has educated those engaged in the interstate movement of sheep and goats regarding the identification and recordkeeping requirements of this part.

(10) Has provided APHIS with a plan and timeline for complying with the following additional requirements, which must be met within 2 years of designation of the State as a Consistent State[5]:

(i) Requires, based on State law or regulation, and effectively enforces official identification upon change of ownership of all animals of any age not in slaughter channels and any sheep over 18 months of age as evidenced by eruption of the second incisor such that the animal may be traced to its flock of birth; provided that:

(A) A State may exempt commercial goats in intrastate commerce that have not been in contact with sheep from this identification requirement if there has been in that State no case of scrapie in a commercial goat in the past 10 years that originated in that State and cannot be attributed to exposure to infected sheep, and there are no exposed commercial goat herds in that State; and

(B) A State may exempt commercial whitefaced sheep or commercial hair sheep under 18 months of age in intrastate commerce from this identification requirement if there has been in that State no case of scrapie in the exempted class that originated from that State, and there are no exposed commercial whitefaced or hair sheep flocks in that State that have been exposed by a female animal.

(C) States that exempt these types of commercial animals must put in place the regulations necessary to require identification of these animals within 90 days of these conditions no longer existing.

(ii) Maintains in the National Scrapie Database administered by APHIS, or in a State database approved by the Administrator as compatible with the National Scrapie Database, the State's:

(A) Premises information and assigned premises numbers and individual identification number sequences assigned for use as premises identification;

[5] This provision would apply until January 1, 2003. Any State designated as a Consistent State after that date would have to meet all requirements prior to designation.

(B) Individual animal information on all scrapie-positive, suspect, high-risk, and exposed animals in the State;

(C) Individual animal information on all out-of-State animals to be traced; and

(D) Accurate flock status data.

(iii) Requires official individual identification of any live scrapie-positive, suspect, or high-risk animal of any age and of any sexually intact exposed animal of more than 1 year of age or any sexually intact exposed animal of less than 1 year of age upon change of ownership (except for exposed animals moving in slaughter channels at less than 1 year of age), whether or not the animal resides in a source or infected flock.

(iv) Effectively enforces movement restrictions on all scrapie-positive, suspect, and high-risk animals throughout their lives unless they are moved in accordance with § 79.3.

(v) Requires that tissues from all scrapie-positive or suspect animals and female high-risk animals that have lambed (when they have died or have been destroyed) be submitted to a laboratory authorized by the Administrator to conduct scrapie tests and requires complete destruction of the carcasses of scrapie-positive and suspect animals.

(vi) Prohibits any animal from being removed from slaughter channels unless it is identified to the flock of birth, is not from an Inconsistent State, and is not scrapie-exposed or from an infected or source flock.

(b) If the Administrator determines that statutory changes are needed to bring a State into full compliance, the Administrator may grant up to a 2-year extension to allow a State to acquire additional authorities before removing a State's Consistent Status. The decision to grant an extension will be based on the State's ability to prevent the movement of scrapie-infected animals out of the State and on the progress being made in making the needed statutory changes.

§ 79.7 Waiver of requirements for scrapie control pilot projects.

(a) The Administrator may waive the following requirements of this part for participants in a scrapie control pilot project by recording the requirements waived in the scrapie control pilot project plan:

(1) The determination that an animal is a high-risk animal, if the scrapie control pilot project plan contains testing or other procedures that indicate that an animal, despite meeting the definition of high-risk animal, is unlikely to spread scrapie; and

(2) The requirement that high-risk animals must be removed from a flock, if the scrapie control pilot project plan contains alternative procedures to prevent the further spread of scrapie without removing high-risk animals from the flock.

(b) [Reserved]

PART 80—JOHNE'S DISEASE IN DOMESTIC ANIMALS

Sec.

AUTHORITY: 7 U.S.C. 8301–8317; 7 CFR 2.22, 2.80, and 371.4.

SOURCE: 65 FR 18878, Apr. 10, 2000, unless otherwise noted.

§ 80.1 Definitions.

The following definitions apply to this part:

Administrator. The Administrator, Animal and Plant Health Inspection Service, or any person authorized to act for the Administrator.

Animal identification number (AIN). A numbering system for the official identification of individual animals in the United States providing a nationally unique identification number for each animal. The AIN contains 15 digits, with the first 3 being the country code (840 for the United States), the alpha characters USA, or the numeric code assigned to the manufacturer of the identification device by the International Committee on Animal Recording. The AIN beginning with the 840 prefix may be used only on animals born in the United States.

APHIS. The Animal and Plant Health Inspection Service of the United States Department of Agriculture.

APHIS representative. An individual employed by APHIS who is authorized to perform the function involved.

Approved livestock facility. A stockyard, livestock market, buying station, concentration point, or any other premises that has been approved under § 71.20 of this chapter.

Area veterinarian in charge. An APHIS veterinarian authorized by the Administrator to supervise and manage the animal health work of APHIS in a specified area of the United States.

Interstate. From one State into or through any other State.

Johne's disease. An infectious and communicable disease that primarily affects cattle, sheep, goats, and other domestic, exotic, and wild ruminants, also known as paratuberculosis, caused by *Mycobacterium paratuberculosis.*

Moved. Shipped, transported, delivered, or received for movement, or otherwise aided, induced, or caused to be moved.

Official eartag. An identification tag providing unique identification for individual animals. An official eartag which contains or displays an AIN with an 840 prefix must bear the U.S. shield. The design, size, shape, color, and other characteristics of the official eartag will depend on the needs of the users, subject to the approval of the Administrator. The official eartag must be tamper-resistant and have a high retention rate in the animal. Official eartags must adhere to one of the following numbering systems:

(1) National Uniform Eartagging System.

(2) Animal identification number (AIN).

(3) Premises-based number system. The premises-based number system combines an official premises identification number (PIN), as defined in this section, with a producer's livestock production numbering system to provide a unique identification number. The PIN and the production number must both appear on the official tag.

(4) Any other numbering system approved by the Administrator for the identification of animals in commerce.

Official Johne's disease test. An organism detection test approved by the Administrator and conducted in a laboratory approved by the Administrator.[1]

Owner-shipper statement. A statement signed by the owner or shipper of animals, which states: The number of animals to be moved, the official eartag number of each animal, the species of the animals, points of origin and destination, the consignor and consignee, a statement that the animals are positive to an official Johne's disease test, and any additional information required by this part.

Premises identification number (PIN). A nationally unique number assigned by a State, Tribal, and/or Federal animal health authority to a premises that is, in the judgment of the State, Tribal, and/or Federal animal health authority, a geographically distinct location from other premises. The premises identification number is associated with an address, geospatial coordinates, and/or other location descriptors which provide a verifiably unique location. The premises identification number may be used in conjunction with a producer's own livestock production numbering system to provide a unique identification number for an animal. The premises identification number may consist of:

(1) The State's two-letter postal abbreviation followed by the premises' assigned number; or

(2) A seven-character alphanumeric code, with the right-most character being a check digit. The check digit number is based upon the ISO 7064 Mod 36/37 check digit algorithm.

[1] A list of currently approved laboratories and the requirements for obtaining approval are available from the Diagnostic Bacteriology Laboratory, National Veterinary Services Laboratories, P.O. Box 844, Ames, Iowa 50010. the Administrator will approve laboratories to conduct an official Johne's disease test only after determining that the laboratory meets the check test proficiency requirements prescribed by the National Veterinary Services Laboratories. Approval will continue as long as such check test proficiency requirements are met on an annual basis.

Recognized slaughtering establishment. A slaughtering establishment[2] operating under the Federal Meat Inspection Act (21 U.S.C. 601 *et seq.*) or a State inspected slaughtering establishment.

State. Any of the 50 States, the Commonwealth of Puerto Rico, the Commonwealth of the Northern Mariana Islands, the District of Columbia, and any territories and possessions of the United States.

State animal health official. The State official responsible for livestock and poultry disease control and eradication programs.

State representative. An individual employed in animal health work by a State or political subdivision of a State, and who is authorized by the State or political subdivision to perform tasks required by this part.

United States. All of the States.

[65 FR 18878, Apr. 10, 2000, as amended at 69 FR 64650, Nov. 8, 2004; 72 FR 39306, July 18, 2007; 73 FR 54062, Sept. 18, 2008]

§ 80.2 General restrictions.

Domestic animals that are positive to an official Johne's disease test may not be moved interstate except in compliance with this part.

§ 80.3 Movement of domestic animals that are positive to an official Johne's disease test.

(a) *Movement of domestic animals for slaughter*. Domestic animals that are positive to an official Johne's disease test may be moved interstate for slaughter if:

(1) The animals are moved directly to a recognized slaughtering establishment or to an approved livestock facility for sale to a recognized slaughtering establishment;

(2) An owner-shipper statement that identifies the animals as positive to an official Johne's disease test accompanies the animals during the movement and is delivered to the consignee;

(3) Each animal bears an official eartag; and

(4) The animals are moved to the destination in one continuous movement without unloading.

(b) *Other movements*. The Administrator may, upon request in specific cases, allow domestic animals that are positive to an official Johne's disease test to be moved interstate other than as provided in paragraph (a) of this section, under such conditions as the Administrator may prescribe in each case to prevent the spread of Johne's disease. The Administrator will promptly notify the State animal health officials of the States involved of any such action.

(c) *Cleaning and disinfecting*. Each means of conveyance used to transport the animals must be cleaned and disinfected in accordance with § 71.6 of this chapter. The facilities in which the animals were maintained must be cleaned and disinfected in accordance with § 71.7 of this chapter.

§ 80.4 Segregation of animals positive to an official Johne's disease test during interstate movement.

Animals that are positive to an official Johne's disease test may not be moved interstate in a railroad car, boat, truck, or other vehicle containing healthy animals susceptible to Johne's disease unless all of the animals are for immediate slaughter, or unless the positive animals are kept separate from the other animals by a partition that is securely affixed to the sides of the vehicle and prevents the transfer of fecal matter from the animals positive to an official Johne's disease test to the healthy animals in the vehicle.

PART 81—CHRONIC WASTING DISEASE IN DEER, ELK, AND MOOSE

Sec.

AUTHORITY: 7 U.S.C. 8301–8317; 7 CFR 2.22, 2.80, and 371.4.

[2] A list of recognized slaughtering establishments in any State may be obtained from an APHIS representative, the State animal health official, or a State representative.

SOURCE: 77 FR 35569, June 13, 2012, unless otherwise noted.

§81.1 Definitions.

These definitions are applicable to this part:

Accredited veterinarian. A veterinarian approved by the Administrator in accordance with part 161 of this chapter to perform functions specified in subchapters B, C, and D of this chapter.

Administrator. The Administrator, Animal and Plant Health Inspection Service, or any person authorized to act for the Administrator.

Animal. Any farmed or captive deer, elk, or moose.

Animal and Plant Health Inspection Service (APHIS). The Animal and Plant Health Inspection Service of the United States Department of Agriculture.

Animal identification. A device or means of animal identification approved for use under this part by APHIS. Examples of animal identification devices that APHIS has approved are listed in §55.25 of this chapter.

Animal identification number (AIN). A numbering system for the official identification of individual animals in the United States. The AIN contains 15 digits, with the first 3 being the country code (840 for the United States), the alpha characters USA, or the numeric code assigned to the manufacturer of the identification device by the International Committee on Animal Recording.

APHIS employee. Any individual employed by the Animal and Plant Health Inspection Service who is authorized by the Administrator to do any work or perform any duty in connection with the control and eradication of disease.

Cervid. All members of the family Cervidae and hybrids, including deer, elk, moose, caribou, reindeer, and related species. For the purposes of this part, the term "cervid" refers specifically to cervids susceptible to CWD. These are animals in the genera Odocoileus, Cervus, and Alces and their hybrids, *i.e.*, deer, elk, and moose.

Chronic wasting disease (CWD). A transmissible spongiform encephalopathy of cervids. Clinical signs in affected animals include, but are not limited to, loss of body condition, behavioral changes, excessive salivation, increased drinking and urination, depression, and eventual death.

CWD Herd Certification Program. The Chronic Wasting Disease Herd Certification Program established in part 55 of this chapter.

Deer, elk, and moose. All animals in the genera Odocoileus, Cervus, and Alces and their hybrids.

Farmed or captive. Privately or publicly maintained or held for economic or other purposes within a perimeter fence or confined area, or captured from a wild population for interstate movement and release.

National Uniform Eartagging System. A numbering system for the official identification of individual animals in the United States providing a nationally unique identification number for each animal. The National Uniform Eartagging System employs an eight- or nine-character alphanumeric format, consisting of a two-number State or territory code, followed by two or three letters and four additional numbers. Official APHIS disease control programs may specify which format to employ.

Official animal identification. A device or means of animal identification approved for use under this part by APHIS to uniquely identify individual animals. Examples of approved official animal identification devices are listed in §55.25 of this chapter. The official animal identification must include a nationally unique animal identification number that adheres to one of the following numbering systems:

(1) National Uniform Eartagging System. The CWD program allows the use of either the eight-character or nine-character format for cervids.

(2) Animal identification number (AIN).

(3) Premises-based number system. The premises-based number system combines an official premises identification number (PIN), as defined in this section, with a producer's livestock production numbering system to provide a unique identification number. The PIN and the production number must both appear on the official tag.

(4) Any other numbering system approved by the Administrator for the identification of animals in commerce.

Premises identification number (PIN). A nationally unique number assigned by a State, Tribal, and/or Federal animal health authority to a premises that is, in the judgment of the State, Tribal, and/or Federal animal health authority, a geographically distinct location from other premises. The premises identification number is associated with an address, geospatial coordinates, and/or location descriptors which provide a verifiably unique location. The premises identification number may be used in conjunction with a producer's own livestock production numbering system to provide a unique identification number for an animal. It may also be used as a component of a group/lot identification number. The premises identification number may consist of:

(1) The State's two-letter postal abbreviation followed by the premises' assigned number; or

(2) A seven-character alphanumeric code, with the right-most character being a check digit. The check digit number is based upon the ISO 7064 Mod 36/37 check digit algorithm.

Recognized slaughtering establishment. An establishment where slaughtering operations are regularly carried out under Federal or State inspection and which has been approved by the Animal and Plant Health Inspection Service to receive animals for slaughter.

[77 FR 35569, June 13, 2012, as amended at 79 FR 23891, Apr. 29, 2014]

§ 81.2 Identification of deer, elk, and moose in interstate commerce.

Each animal required to be identified by this part must have at least two forms of animal identification attached to the animal. The means of animal identification must be approved for this use by APHIS, and must be an electronic implant, flank tattoo, ear tattoo, tamper-resistant ear tag, or other device approved by APHIS. One of the animal identifications must be an official animal identification as defined in this part, with a nationally unique animal identification number that is linked to that animal in the CWD National Database or in an approved State database. The second animal identification must be unique for the individual animal within the herd and also must be linked to that animal and herd in the CWD National Database or in an approved State database.

(Approved by the Office of Management and Budget under control number 0579–0237)

§ 81.3 General restrictions.

No farmed or captive deer, elk, or moose may be moved interstate unless it meets the requirements of this section.

(a) *Animals in the CWD Herd Certification Program.* The captive deer, elk, or moose is:

(1) Enrolled in the CWD Herd Certification Program and the herd has achieved Certified status in accordance with § 55.24 of this chapter; and

(2) Is accompanied by a certificate issued in accordance with § 81.4 that identifies its herd of origin and that states that the animal's herd has achieved Certified status and that the animal does not show clinical signs associated with CWD.

(b) *Animals captured for interstate movement and release.* If the captive deer, elk, or moose was captured from a wild population for interstate movement and release, each animal must have two forms of animal identification, one of which is official animal identification, and the certificate issued in accordance with § 81.4 that accompanies the animal must state that the source population has been documented to be low risk for CWD, based on a CWD surveillance program in wild cervid populations that is approved by the State Government of the receiving State and by APHIS.

(c) *Animals moved to slaughter.* The farmed or captive deer, elk, or moose must be moved directly to a recognized slaughtering establishment for slaughter, must have two forms of animal identification, one of which is official animal identification, and must be accompanied by a certificate issued in accordance with § 81.4.

(d) *Research animal movements and permits.* A research animal permit is required for the interstate movement of cervids for research purposes. The permit will specify any special conditions of the movement determined by the

Administrator to be necessary to prevent the dissemination of CWD. The Administrator may, at his or her discretion, issue the permit if he or she determines that the destination facility has adequate biosecurity and that the movement authorized will not result in the interstate dissemination of CWD.

(1) To apply for a research animal permit, contact an APHIS employee or State representative and provide the following information:

(i) The name and address of the person to whom the special permit is issued, the address at which the research cervids to be moved interstate are being held, and the name and address of the person receiving the cervids to be moved interstate;

(ii) The number and type of cervids to be moved interstate;

(iii) The reason for the interstate movement;

(iv) Any safeguards in place to prevent transmission of CWD during movement or at the receiving location; and

(v) The date on which movement will occur.

(2) A copy of the research animal permit must accompany the cervids moved, and copies must be submitted so that a copy is received by the State animal health official and the veterinarian in charge for the State of destination at least 72 hours prior to the arrival of the cervids at the destination listed on the research animal permit.

(e) *Interstate movements approved by the Administrator.* Notwithstanding any other provision of this part, interstate movement of farmed or captive deer, elk, and moose may be allowed on a case-by-case basis when the Administrator determines that adequate survey and mitigation procedures are in place to prevent dissemination of CWD and issues a permit for the movement.

§81.4 Issuance of certificates.

(a) *Information required on certificates.* A certificate must show any official animal identification numbers of each animal to be moved. A certificate must also show the number of animals covered by the certificate; the purpose for which the animals are to be moved; the points of origin and destination; the consignor; and the consignee. The certificate must include a statement by the issuing accredited veterinarian, State veterinarian, or Federal veterinarian that the animals were not exhibiting clinical signs associated with CWD at the time of examination. The certificate must also include a statement that the animals are from a herd that has achieved Certified status in the CWD Herd Certification Program, and must provide the herd's program status, with the following exceptions:

(1) Certificates issued for animals captured from a wild population for interstate movement and release do not need to state that the animals are from a herd that has achieved Certified status in the CWD Herd Certification Program but must include the statement required in §81.3(b); and

(2) Certificates issued for animals moved directly to slaughter do not need to state that the animals are from a herd that has achieved Certified status in the CWD Herd Certification Program and must state that an APHIS employee or State representative has been notified in advance of the date the animals are being moved to slaughter.

(b) *Animal identification documents attached to certificates.* As an alternative to typing or writing individual animal identification on a certificate, another document may be used to provide this information, but only under the following conditions:

(1) The document must be a State form or APHIS form that requires individual identification of animals;

(2) A legible copy of the document must be stapled to the original and each copy of the certificate;

(3) Each copy of the document must identify each animal to be moved with the certificate, but any information pertaining to other animals, and any unused space on the document for recording animal identification, must be crossed out in ink; and

(4) The following information must be typed or written in ink in the identification column on the original and each copy of the certificate and must be circled or boxed, also in ink, so that no additional information can be added:

(i) The name of the document; and

(ii) Either the serial number on the document or, if the document is not imprinted with a serial number, both the name of the person who issued the document and the date the document was issued.

(Approved by the Office of Management and Budget under control number 0579–0237)

§81.5 Movement of deer, elk, or moose through a State to another State.

Farmed or captive deer, elk, or moose may be moved through a State or locality whose laws or regulations on the movement of those animals are more restrictive than this part to another State under the following conditions:

(a) The farmed or captive deer, elk, or moose must be eligible to move interstate under §81.3.

(b) The farmed or captive deer, elk, or moose must meet the entry requirements of the destination State listed on the certificate or permit accompanying the animal.

(c) Except in emergencies, the farmed or captive deer, elk, or moose must not be unloaded until their arrival at their destination.

§81.6 Federal preemption of State and local laws and regulations with respect to CWD.

State and local laws and regulations on farmed or captive deer, elk, or moose with respect to CWD that are more restrictive than the regulations in this part are not preempted by this part, except as described in §81.5.

PART 82—NEWCASTLE DISEASE AND CHLAMYDIOSIS

Subpart A—Newcastle Disease

Sec.

Subpart B—Chlamydiosis in Poultry

AUTHORITY: 7 U.S.C. 8301–8317; 7 CFR 2.22, 2.80, and 371.4.

SOURCE: 61 FR 56883, Nov. 5, 1996, unless otherwise noted.

Subpart A—Newcastle Disease

EDITORIAL NOTE: Nomenclature changes to subpart A of part 82 appear at 78 FR 19083, Mar. 29, 2013.

§82.1 Definitions.

As used in connection with this subpart, the following terms shall have the meaning set forth in this section.

Administrator. The Administrator of the Animal and Plant Health Inspection Service or any individual authorized to act for the Administrator.

Animal and Plant Health Inspection Service. The Animal and Plant Health Inspection Service of the United States Department of Agriculture.

Bird. Any member of the class *aves* other than poultry.

Commercial birds. Birds that are moved or kept for resale, breeding, public display, or any other purpose, except pet birds.

Dressed carcasses. Carcasses of birds or poultry that have been eviscerated, with heads and feet removed, or parts or products of such carcasses.

Exposed. At risk of developing Newcastle disease because of association with birds or poultry infected with Newcastle disease, excrement from birds or poultry infected with Newcastle disease, or other material touched by birds or poultry infected with Newcastle disease, or because there is reason to believe that association has occurred with Newcastle disease or vectors of Newcastle disease, as determined by either a Federal veterinarian or a State veterinarian.

Federal representative. An individual employed and authorized by the Federal government to perform the tasks required by this subpart.

Federal veterinarian. A veterinarian employed and authorized by the Federal government to perform the tasks required by this subpart.

Hatching eggs. Eggs in which birds or poultry are allowed to develop.

Infected. Affected by the virus or bacterium that causes the specified disease.

Interstate. From one State into or through any other State.

Known to be exposed. Determined by either a Federal veterinarian or a State veterinarian to be at risk of developing Newcastle disease because of association with birds or poultry infected with Newcastle disease, excrement from birds or poultry infected with Newcastle disease, or other material touched by birds or poultry infected with Newcastle disease, or because there is reason to believe that association has occurred with Newcastle disease or vectors of Newcastle disease, as determined by either a Federal veterinarian or a State veterinarian.

Known to be infected. Determined by either a Federal veterinarian or a State veterinarian to be affected by the virus or bacterium that causes the specified disease.

Litter. Material that is used to collect and absorb bodily wastes from birds or poultry.

Moved. Shipped, transported or otherwise moved, or delivered or received for movement, by any person.

Newcastle disease. Newcastle disease is an acute, rapidly spreading, and usually fatal viral infection of poultry caused by an avian paramyxovirus serotype 1 that meets one of the following criteria for virulence: The virus has an intracerebral pathogenicity index (ICPI) in day-old chicks (*Gallus gallus*) of 0.7 or greater; or multiple basic amino acids have been demonstrated in the virus (either directly or by deduction) at the C-terminus of the F2 protein and phenylalanine at residue 117, which is the N-terminus of the F1 protein. The term "multiple basic amino acids" refers to at least three arginine or lysine residues between residues 113 and 116. In this definition, amino acid residues are numbered from the N-terminus of the amino acid sequence deduced from the nucleotide sequence of the F0 gene; 113–116 corresponds to residues −4 to −1 from the cleavage site. Failure to demonstrate the characteristic pattern of amino acid residues as described above may require characterization of the isolated virus by an ICPI test. A failure to detect a cleavage site that is consistent with virulent strains does not confirm the absence of a virulent virus.

Official seal. A serially numbered metal or plastic strip, consisting of a self-locking device on one end and a slot on the other end, that forms a loop when the ends are engaged and that cannot be reused if opened, or a serially numbered, self-locking button that can be used for this purpose.

Person. Any individual, corporation, company, association, firm, partnership, society, joint stock company, or other legal entity.

Pet birds. Birds, except ratites, that are kept for the personal pleasure of their individual owners and are not intended for resale.

Poultry. Chickens, doves, ducks, geese, grouse, guinea fowl, partridges, pea fowl, pheasants, pigeons, quail, swans, and turkeys.

Ratites. Cassowaries, emus, kiwis, ostriches, and rheas.

Recognized slaughtering establishment. Any slaughtering facility operating under the Federal Meat Inspection Act (21 U.S.C. 601 *et seq.*), the Poultry Products Inspection Act (21 U.S.C. 451 *et seq.*), or State meat or poultry inspection acts.

Render. Reduce, convert, or melt down by heating to a temperature of at least 230 °F so that oil is removed.

State. Each of the States of the United States, the District of Columbia, Puerto Rico, the Northern Mariana Islands, Guam, the Virgin Islands of the United States, or any other territory or possession of the United States.

State animal health official. The State official responsible for livestock- and poultry-disease control and eradication programs.

State representative. An individual employed in animal health work and authorized by a State or political subdivision of a State to perform the tasks required by this subpart.

State veterinarian. A veterinarian employed and authorized by a State or political subdivision of a State to perform the tasks required by this subpart.

Veterinarian in charge. A Federal veterinarian employed by the Animal and Plant Health Inspection Service and authorized by the Administrator to supervise and manage the animal health work of the Animal and Plant Health Inspection Service in a specified area of the United States.

[61 FR 56883, Nov. 5, 1996, as amended at 73 FR 30297, May 27, 2008; 74 FR 18287, Apr. 22, 2009; 78 FR 19083, Mar. 29, 2013]

§ 82.2 Criteria for determining birds or poultry to be infected with, exposed to, or free from Newcastle disease.

(a) The determination that birds or poultry are infected with Newcastle disease must be made by either a Federal veterinarian or a State veterinarian.[1] They will base that determination on one or more of the following factors: clinical evidence (signs, post-mortem lesions, and history of the occurrence of Newcastle disease); diagnostic tests;[2] or epidemiological evidence (evaluation of clinical evidence and the degree of risk posed by the potential spread of Newcastle disease based on population and exposure factors, including evaluation of whether the birds and poultry have had the opportunity to be in contact with birds or poultry infected with Newcastle disease or with excrement from birds or poultry infected with Newcastle disease, or if the birds and poultry have shared feed or water with birds or poultry infected with Newcastle disease).

(b) The determination that birds or poultry are exposed to Newcastle disease must be made by either a Federal veterinarian or a State veterinarian. They will base that determination on an evaluation of all related circumstances, including: the proximity of the birds or poultry to birds or poultry infected with Newcastle disease, to excrement from birds or poultry infected with Newcastle disease, and to other material touched by birds or poultry infected with Newcastle disease; the number of birds or poultry infected with Newcastle disease to which the birds or poultry were exposed; the species involved; the virulence of the Newcastle disease to which the birds or poultry were exposed; and the length of time the birds or poultry were in contact with birds or poultry infected with Newcastle disease, and to material touched by birds or poultry infected with Newcastle disease. Birds or poultry determined to be exposed to Newcastle disease will continue to be treated as exposed unless they are subsequently determined to be infected with Newcastle disease or until either a Federal veterinarian or a State veterinarian finds them to be free of Newcastle disease based on one or more of the factors listed in paragraph (a) of this section.

(Approved by the Office of Management and Budget under control number 0579–0116)

---

[1] The location of Federal veterinarians and State veterinarians may be obtained by writing to Emergency Programs, Veterinary Services, Animal and Plant Health Inspection Service, 4700 River Road, Unit 41, Riverdale, MD 20737–1231, or by referring to the local telephone book.

[2] A copy of the protocols for Newcastle disease diagnostic tests may be obtained by writing to Emergency Programs, Veterinary Services, Animal and Plant Health Inspection Service, 4700 River Road Unit 41, Riverdale, MD 20737–1231. The protocols are also found in "Recommended Uniform Diagnostic Procedures," published by the Committee of the American Association of Veterinary Laboratory Diagnosticians.

§ 82.3 Quarantined areas.

(a) Any area where birds or poultry infected with Newcastle disease are located will be designated as a quarantined area. A quarantined area is any geographical area, which may be a premises or all or part of a State, deemed by epidemiological evaluation to be sufficient to contain all birds or poultry known to be infected with or exposed to Newcastle disease. Less than an entire State will be designated as a quarantined area only if the State enforces restrictions on intrastate movements from the quarantined area that are at least as stringent as this subpart.

(b) Any area designated as a quarantined area because of Newcastle disease will remain designated as a quarantined area until all of the requirements of § 82.14 have been met.

(c) The following areas are quarantined because of Newcastle disease: There are no areas in the United States quarantined because of Newcastle disease.

[61 FR 56883, Nov. 5, 1996, as amended at 67 FR 70675, Nov. 26, 2002; 68 FR 1517, Jan. 13, 2003; 68 FR 3376, Jan. 24, 2003; 68 FR 7413, Feb. 14, 2003; 68 FR 18532, Apr. 16, 2003; 68 FR 26987, 26989, May 19, 2003; 68 FR 34781, June 11, 2003; 68 FR 45744, Aug. 4, 2003; 68 FR 54800, Sept. 19, 2003]

§ 82.4 General provisions.

(a) *Prohibitions.* The following articles may not be moved interstate from a quarantined area:

(1) Dead birds and dead poultry, including any parts of the birds or poultry, that are infected with Newcastle disease, or are from a flock of birds or poultry infected with Newcastle disease;

(2) Litter used by or manure generated by birds or poultry, or a flock of birds or poultry, infected with Newcastle disease, except as provided in § 82.7(b);

(3) Any eggs from birds or poultry, or a flock of birds or poultry, infected with Newcastle disease;

(4) Hatching eggs from flocks of birds or poultry exposed to Newcastle disease; and

(5) Live birds or live poultry from flocks infected with or exposed to Newcastle disease.

(b) *Restrictions.* The following articles may be moved interstate from a quarantined area only in accordance with this subpart:

(1) Live birds or live poultry not known to be infected with or exposed to Newcastle disease;

(2) Dressed carcasses of birds and poultry, and other dead birds and dead poultry, including any parts of the birds or poultry, that are not known to be infected with Newcastle disease;

(3) Litter used by or manure generated by birds or poultry not known to be infected with Newcastle disease;

(4) Eggs, other than hatching eggs, from birds or poultry from flocks not known to be infected with Newcastle disease;

(5) Hatching eggs from birds or poultry not known to be infected with or exposed to Newcastle disease; and

(6) Cages, coops, containers, troughs, vehicles, or other equipment used for birds, poultry, eggs, manure, or litter.

(c) *Exceptions.* This subpart does not apply to the interstate movement of birds, poultry, or other articles from a quarantined area if the interstate movement is made by the United States Department of Agriculture for purposes of research or diagnosis.

[61 FR 56883, Nov. 5, 1996, as amended at 73 FR 30297, May 27, 2008]

§ 82.5 Interstate movement of live birds and live poultry from a quarantined area.

(a) *Pet birds.* An individual may move his or her pet birds interstate from a quarantined area only if the birds are not known to be infected with or exposed to Newcastle disease and the following requirements are fulfilled:

(1) *Epidemiological and testing requirements.* For all pet birds moved interstate, epidemiological evidence must indicate that the birds are not infected with any communicable disease.

(i) *Pet birds that have been under the control and ownership of the owner for at least 90 days.* Pet birds that have been under the ownership and control of the individual to whom the permit is issued for the 90 days before interstate movement, show no clinical signs of sickness (such as diarrhea, nasal discharge, ocular discharge, ruffled feathers, or lack of appetite) during the 90 days before interstate movement, and have been maintained apart from other birds and poultry in the quarantined area during the 90 days before interstate movement may be moved to a location outside the quarantined area for subsequent examination. The individual to whom the permit is issued must maintain ownership and control of the birds and maintain them apart from other birds and poultry from the time they arrive at the place to which the individual is taking them until a Federal representative or State representative[3] examines the birds and determines that the birds show no clinical signs of Newcastle disease. The examination will not be less than 30 days after the interstate movement. The individual to whom the permit is issued must allow Federal representatives and State representatives to examine the birds at any time until they are declared free of Newcastle disease by either a Federal veterinarian or a State veterinarian.

(ii) *All other pet birds.* Pet birds that do not meet the criteria in paragraph (a)(2)(i) of this section may only be moved to a USDA-approved quarantine facility outside the quarantined area for a 30-day quarantine before being released. The individual to whom the permit is issued must maintain ownership and control of the birds and maintain them isolated from other birds or poultry until the time they arrive at the USDA-approved quarantine facility. The pet bird owner is responsible for all costs associated for keeping his or her pet birds at the USDA-approved quarantine facility for the 30-day quarantine period.

(2) *Movement restrictions.* All pet birds must be moved interstate from a quarantined area under the following conditions:

(i) The birds are accompanied by a permit obtained in accordance with § 82.11.

(ii) The birds are moved interstate by the individual to whom the permit is issued.

(iii) The birds are caged while being moved interstate.

(iv) Within 24 hours of a bird's dying or showing clinical signs of sickness (such as diarrhea, nasal discharge, ocular discharge, ruffled feathers, or lack of appetite), the individual to whom the permit is issued notifies the veterinarian in charge or the State animal health official[4] in the State to which the birds are moved.

(v) The individual to whom the permit is issued submits copies of the permit so that a copy is received by the State animal health official and the veterinarian in charge for the State of destination within 72 hours of the arrival of the birds at the destination listed on the permit.

(b) *Other birds (including commercial birds) and poultry.* Except as provided for pet birds in paragraph (a) of this section, a person may move live birds (including commercial birds) and live poultry that are not known to be infected with or exposed to Newcastle disease interstate from a quarantined area only if:

(1) The birds and poultry are accompanied by a permit obtained in accordance with § 82.11;

(2) The birds or poultry are covered in such a way as to prevent feathers and other debris from blowing or falling off the means of conveyance;

(3) The birds or poultry are moved in a means of conveyance either under official seal or are accompanied by a Federal representative;

(4) Except for emergencies, the birds or poultry are not unloaded until their arrival at the destination listed on the permit required by paragraph (b)(1) of this section;

(5) If poultry or ratites, the poultry or ratites are moved interstate to a recognized slaughtering establishment[5] and are slaughtered within 24

[3] The location of Federal representatives and State representatives may be obtained by writing to Emergency Programs, Veterinary Services, Animal and Plant Health Inspection Service, 4700 River Road, Unit 41, Riverdale, MD 20737–1231.

[4] The location of the veterinarian in charge or the State animal health official may be obtained by writing to Emergency Programs, Veterinary Services, Animal and Plant Health Inspection Service, 4700 River Road, Unit 41, Riverdale, MD 20737–1231, or by referring to the local telephone book.

[5] A list of recognized slaughtering establishments in any State may be obtained from a Federal representative, the State animal health official, or a State representative.

hours of arrival at the recognized slaughtering establishment;

(6) If birds other than poultry, the birds are moved to a site approved by the Administrator; and

(7) The permit required by paragraph (b)(1) of this section is presented upon arrival at the recognized slaughtering establishment or approved site to a State representative or Federal representative. Copies of the permit must also be submitted so that a copy is received by the State animal health official and the veterinarian in charge for the State of destination within 72 hours of arrival at the recognized slaughtering establishment.

(Approved by the Office of Management and Budget under control number 0579–0116)

[61 FR 56883, Nov. 5, 1996, as amended at 73 FR 30297, May 27, 2008]

§ 82.6 Interstate movement of dead birds and dead poultry from a quarantined area.

(a) Except as provided in paragraph (b) of this section for dressed carcasses, dead birds and dead poultry, including any parts of the birds and poultry, that are not known to be infected with Newcastle disease may be moved interstate from a quarantined area only if:

(1) The dead birds and dead poultry are accompanied by a permit obtained in accordance with § 82.11;

(2) The dead birds and dead poultry are covered in such a way as to prevent feathers and other debris from blowing or falling off the means of conveyance;

(3) The dead birds and dead poultry are moved in a means of conveyance either under official seal or accompanied by a Federal representative;

(4) The dead birds and dead poultry are not unloaded until their arrival at the destination listed on the permit required by paragraph (a)(1) of this section;

(5) The dead birds and dead poultry are moved, without stopping, to the destination listed on the permit required by paragraph (a)(1) of this section, except for normal traffic conditions, such as traffic lights and stop signs;

(6) The dead birds and dead poultry are disposed of, within 24 hours after being loaded for interstate movement, by burial or composting in accordance with the procedures set forth in § 82.14(c)(1) and (c)(2), or by rendering, incineration, or other means approved by the Administrator as being adequate to prevent the dissemination of Newcastle disease; and

(7) Copies of the permit accompanying the dead birds and dead poultry interstate are submitted so that a copy is received by the State animal health official and the veterinarian in charge for the State of destination within 72 hours of the arrival of the dead birds and dead poultry at the destination listed on the permit required by paragraph (a)(1) of this section.

(b) Dressed carcasses from birds and poultry that are not known to be infected with Newcastle disease may be moved interstate from a quarantined area only if:

(1) The dressed carcasses are from birds or poultry that were slaughtered in a recognized slaughtering establishment;[6]

(2) The dressed carcasses have been processed in one of the following ways:

(i) They are packed in hermetically sealed containers and cooked by a commercial method after such packing to produce articles which are shelf-stable without refrigeration; or

(ii) They have been thoroughly cooked and have a thoroughly cooked appearance throughout;

(3) If the dressed carcasses are from poultry, the processing establishment that treats the dressed carcasses in accordance with paragraph (b)(2) of this section employs the following safeguards:

(i) If receiving or handling any live poultry, there must be complete separation between the slaughter portion of the establishment and the portions of the establishment in which further processing takes place;

(ii) If the plant processes dressed carcasses from both quarantined and nonquarantined areas, all areas, utensils, and equipment likely to contact the poultry carcasses to be processed, including skimming, deboning, cutting, and packing areas, are cleaned and disinfected in accordance with part 71 of this chapter between the processing of dressed poultry carcasses from the

[6] See footnote 5 to § 82.5.

quarantined area and the processing of dressed poultry carcasses from non-quarantined areas;

(iii) The dressed carcasses are stored in a manner that ensures that no cross-contamination with potentially infectious materials, such as raw or unprocessed products, occurs;

(4) The dressed carcasses are accompanied by a permit obtained in accordance with § 82.11;

(5) The dressed carcasses are moved in a means of conveyance either under official seal or accompanied by a Federal representative;

(6) The dressed carcasses are not unloaded until their arrival at the destination listed on the permit required by paragraph (b)(4) of this section;

(7) The dressed carcasses are moved, without stopping, to the destination listed on the permit required by paragraph (b)(4) of this section, except for normal traffic conditions, such as traffic lights and stop signs; and

(8) Copies of the permit accompanying the dressed carcasses are submitted so that a copy is received by the State animal health official and the veterinarian in charge for the State of destination within 72 hours of the arrival of the dressed carcasses at the destination listed on the permit required by paragraph (b)(4) of this section.

(Approved by the Office of Management and Budget under control number 0579–0116)

[61 FR 56883, Nov. 5, 1996, as amended at 73 FR 30298, May 27, 2008]

§ 82.7 Interstate movement of manure and litter from a quarantined area.

(a) Manure generated by and litter used by birds or poultry not known to be infected with Newcastle disease may be moved interstate from a quarantined area only if:

(1) The manure and litter is accompanied by a permit obtained in accordance with § 82.11;

(2) The manure and litter has been heated throughout, in the quarantined area, to a temperature of not less than 175 °F (79.4 °C) or subjected to any other treatment approved by the Administrator as being adequate to prevent the dissemination of Newcastle disease, and then placed either in a previously unused container or in a container that has been cleaned and disinfected, since last being used, in accordance with part 71 of this chapter;

(3) The declaration or affidavit required by § 82.11(b) lists the location of the poultry or birds that generated the manure or used the litter, and the name and address of the owner of the poultry or birds that generated the manure or used the litter; and

(4) Copies of the permit accompanying the manure and litter interstate are submitted so that a copy is received by the State animal health official and the veterinarian in charge for the State of destination within 72 hours of the arrival of the manure and litter at the destination listed on the permit.

(b) Compost derived from manure generated by and litter used by birds or poultry known to be infected with Newcastle disease may be moved interstate from a quarantined area only if:

(1) The manure and litter is accompanied by a permit obtained in accordance with § 82.11;

(2) All birds and poultry have been removed from the premises where the manure or litter is held;

(3) After all birds are removed from the premises where the manure or litter is held, all manure and litter inside and outside the bird or poultry house remains undisturbed for at least 28 days before being moved from the infected premises for composting;

(4) Composting is done at a site approved by the Administrator and under a protocol approved by the Administrator as being adequate to prevent the dissemination of Newcastle disease. All manure and litter from the infected premises must be moved to the composting site at the same time;

(5) Following the composting process, the composted manure or litter remains undisturbed for an additional 15 days before movement;

(6) After this 15-day period, all of the composted manure or litter from the infected site is removed at the same time;

(7) The resulting compost must be transported either in a previously unused container or in a container that has been cleaned and disinfected, since last being used, in accordance with part 71 of this chapter;

(8) The vehicle in which the resulting compost is to be transported has been cleaned and disinfected, since last being used, in accordance with part 71 of this chapter; and

(9) Copies of the permit accompanying the compost derived from the manure and the litter are submitted so that a copy is received by the State animal health official and the veterinarian in charge for the State of destination within 72 hours of arrival of the compost at the destination listed on the permit.

[61 FR 56883, Nov. 5, 1996, as amended at 73 FR 30298, May 27, 2008]

§82.8 Interstate movement of eggs, other than hatching eggs, from a quarantined area.

(a) Eggs, other than hatching eggs, from birds or poultry from flocks not known to be infected with Newcastle disease may be moved interstate from a quarantined area only if:

(1) The eggs are accompanied by a permit obtained in accordance with §82.11;

(2) The eggs have been cleaned and sanitized in accordance with 9 CFR part 590;

(3) The establishment that processes the eggs, other than hatching eggs, for sale establishes procedures adequate to ensure that the eggs are free of Newcastle disease, including:

(i) The establishment separates processing and layer facilities, the incoming and outgoing eggs at the establishment, and any flocks that may reside at the establishment;

(ii) The establishment implements controls to ensure that trucks, shipping companies, or other visitors do not expose the processing plant to Newcastle disease;

(iii) Equipment used in the establishment is cleaned and disinfected in accordance with part 71 of this chapter at intervals determined by the Administrator to ensure that the equipment cannot transmit Newcastle disease to the eggs, other than hatching eggs, being processed; and

(iv) The eggs are packed either in previously unused flats or cases, or in used plastic flats that were cleaned or disinfected since last being used, in accordance with part 71 of this chapter;

(4) The eggs are moved to a facility where they are examined to ensure they have been cleaned and sanitized in accordance with paragraph (a)(2) of this section; and

(5) Copies of the permit accompanying the eggs interstate are submitted so that a copy is received by both the State animal health official and the veterinarian in charge for the State of destination within 72 hours of the arrival of the eggs at the facility.

(b) Any flats or cases intended for reuse after being used to move eggs interstate to a facility under this section must be cleaned and disinfected in accordance with part 71 of this chapter before being moved to a premises where birds or poultry are kept.

[61 FR 56883, Nov. 5, 1996, as amended at 73 FR 30299, May 27, 2008]

§82.9 Interstate movement of hatching eggs from a quarantined area.

Hatching eggs from birds or poultry not known to be infected with or exposed to Newcastle disease may be moved interstate from a quarantined area only if:

(a) The hatching eggs are accompanied by a permit obtained in accordance with §82.11;

(b) Copies of the permit accompanying the hatching eggs are submitted so that a copy is received by both the State animal health official and the veterinarian in charge for the State of destination within 72 hours of the arrival of the hatching eggs at the premises described in paragraph (c) of this section;

(c) The hatching eggs have been kept in accordance with the sanitation practices specified in §§147.22 and 147.25 of the National Poultry Improvement Plan; and

(d) The hatching eggs are held in the State of destination at a premises designated jointly by the veterinarian in charge and the State animal health official from the time of arrival until hatch and the birds and poultry hatched from the eggs are held at the designated premises for not less than 30 days following hatch. During this holding period, the eggs and any birds or poultry hatched from the eggs are subject to any inspections, disinfections, and tests as may be required by the Administrator to determine their freedom from Newcastle disease.

[61 FR 56883, Nov. 5, 1996, as amended at 73 FR 30299, May 27, 2008]

§ 82.10 Interstate movement of vehicles, cages, coops, containers, troughs, and other equipment from a quarantined area.

(a) This section does not apply to cages, coops, or other containers or equipment used by or to move pet birds moved interstate in accordance with § 82.5(a).

(b) Vehicles, cages, coops, containers, troughs, and other equipment that have held or that have otherwise been used in a quarantined area in the handling of birds or poultry or their eggs, or for manure generated by or litter used by the birds or poultry, may be moved interstate from a quarantined area only in accordance with the following conditions:

(1) They are made of hard plastic or metal, and the other conditions of this section are met; or

(2) They are made of a disposable material, such as cardboard, fiber, or waxed cardboard, are previously unused, and are disposed of by incineration without being reused after being moved interstate.

(c) Before moving interstate any vehicles, cages, coops, containers, troughs, or other equipment described in paragraph (b)(1) of this section, and after using these items to move birds, poultry, eggs, manure, or litter interstate from a quarantined area, the vehicles, cages, coops, containers, troughs, and other equipment must be cleaned and disinfected in accordance with paragraphs (c)(1) through (c)(5) of this section:

(1) Clean and disinfect the vehicles, cages, coops, containers, troughs, and other equipment at the place where the birds, poultry, eggs, manure, and litter are unloaded or where the equipment is used, no more than 2 hours after the birds, poultry, eggs, manure, and litter are unloaded or the equipment is used;

(2) Clean the items in accordance with part 71 of this chapter;

(3) Have a Federal representative or State representative[7] inspect the items after they have been cleaned;

(4) Disinfect the items in the presence of a Federal representative or State representative; and

(5) Disinfect the items in accordance with part 71 of this chapter and by using a disinfectant as specified in part 71 of this chapter.

(d) If the place where the cleaning and disinfection would otherwise be required has no facilities for cleaning and disinfecting, the items may be moved to a place where facilities are available for cleaning and disinfecting, provided a Federal representative or State representative has determined that such movement will not cause a risk of the spread of Newcastle disease.

(e) Vehicles, cages, coops, containers, troughs, and other equipment that are moved interstate under this section must be accompanied by a permit obtained in accordance with § 82.11, and copies of the permit accompanying the vehicles, cages, coops, containers, troughs, and other equipment interstate must be submitted so that a copy is received by the State animal health official and the veterinarian in charge[8] for the State of destination within 72 hours of the arrival of the vehicles, cages, coops, containers, troughs, and other equipment at the destination listed on the permit.

(Approved by the Office of Management and Budget under control number 0579–0116)

§ 82.11 Issuance of permits.

(a) Application for the permits required by this subpart to move interstate from a quarantined area birds, eggs, poultry, or other items requiring a permit under this part must be in writing. The application must be submitted to a Federal representative or State representative and must include the following:

(1) The applicant's name and mailing address;

(2) The name and mailing address of the person who will receive the birds, eggs, poultry, or other items;

---

[7] See footnote 3 to § 82.5.

[8] See footnote 4 of § 82.5.

(3) The addresses of both the origin and destination of the birds, eggs, poultry, or other items;

(4) The number and types of birds, poultry, eggs, and other items intended for interstate movement; and

(5) The reason for the interstate movement.

(b) In addition to the information required by paragraph (a) of this section, to obtain permits to move birds, poultry, eggs, manure, litter, cages, coops, containers, troughs, vehicles or other equipment interstate from a quarantined area, an applicant for a permit must submit to a Federal representative or State representative a declaration or affidavit listing the requirements of §82.5 for live birds or live poultry, §82.6 for dead birds and dead poultry, §82.7 for litter or manure, §82.8 for eggs other than hatching eggs, §82.9 for hatching eggs, or §82.10 for cages, coops, containers, troughs, vehicles, and other equipment, and stating that the applicant will move the items interstate only if all of the listed requirements are met.

(Approved by the Office of Management and Budget under control number 0579–0116)

§82.12 Other interstate movements and special permits.

(a) A special permit is required for the interstate movement of birds, poultry, or other items whose movement is restricted under this subpart, from a quarantined area in a manner or to a destination other than is specifically prescribed by this subpart, under special conditions determined by the Administrator to be necessary to prevent the dissemination of Newcastle disease. A special permit is required for the disposal of dead birds or dead poultry that are infected with Newcastle disease, or dead birds or dead poultry from flocks infected with Newcastle disease, or manure generated by or eggs from birds or poultry infected with Newcastle disease, in a manner other than is specifically prescribed in this subpart, and for cleaning and disinfection carried out in a manner other than is specifically prescribed in this subpart, under special conditions determined by the Administrator to be necessary to prevent the dissemination of Newcastle disease. To apply for a special permit, contact the veterinarian in charge[9] for the State in which the birds, poultry, or other items are located. The Administrator may, at his or her discretion, issue special permits if he or she determines that the activity authorized will not result in the interstate dissemination of Newcastle disease.

(b) The special permit will list the name and address of the person to whom the special permit is issued, and the special conditions under which the interstate movement, disposal, or cleaning and disinfection may be carried out.

(1) For an interstate movement, the special permit will also include the following:

(i) The name and mailing address of the person who will receive the birds, poultry, or other items;

(ii) The addresses of both the origin and destination of the birds, poultry, or other items;

(iii) The number and type of birds, poultry, or other items to be moved interstate; and

(iv) The reason for the interstate movement.

(2) For destruction or cleaning and disinfection, the special permit will also include the following:

(i) The address of the place where the dead birds, dead poultry, manure, or eggs are located; and

(ii) The number and type of birds, poultry, or other items involved.

(c) For an interstate movement, a copy of the special permit must accompany the items moved, and copies must be submitted so that a copy is received by the State animal health official and the veterinarian in charge for the State of destination within 72 hours of the arrival of the birds, poultry, or other items at the destination listed on the special permit.

(Approved by the Office of Management and Budget under control number 0579–0116)

§82.13 Denial and withdrawal of permits and special permits.

(a) *Denial.* If the Administrator determines that the applicant for a permit or special permit is not complying with or could not comply with this subpart or any special conditions needed

[9] See footnote 4 to §82.5.

to prevent the dissemination of Newcastle disease, or, in the case of a special permit, that the special permit is not required under this subpart, the Administrator may deny the request for a permit or special permit. If the request is denied, the Administrator will send the applicant a written notice explaining why the permit or special permit was denied.

(b) *Withdrawal.* The Administrator may withdraw a permit or special permit, orally or in writing, if he or she determines the person to whom the permit or special permit has been issued is violating either this subpart or some condition specified in the permit or special permit. The Administrator may withdraw the permit or special permit without advance notice if he or she determines that the person to whom the permit or special permit has been issued is violating either this subpart or some condition specified in the permit or special permit in a way that threatens the public health, interest, or safety. The Administrator will send the person to whom the permit or special permit has been issued a written explanation of why the permit or special permit is to be or was withdrawn.

(c) *Appeals.* Denial or withdrawal of a permit or special permit may be appealed to the Administrator within 10 days after receipt of the written notice of denial or withdrawal. The appeal must be in writing [10] and must state all of the facts and reasons upon which the person relies to show that the permit or special permit was wrongfully denied or withdrawn. The Administrator will grant or deny the appeal, in writing, explaining all of the reasons for the decision, as promptly as circumstances allow. In cases where there is a conflict as to any material fact, the person denied a permit or special permit, or from whom a permit or special permit is withdrawn, shall be given an opportunity for a hearing with respect to the merits of the validity of the denial or withdrawal in accordance with rules of practice adopted for the proceeding.

(Approved by the Office of Management and Budget under control number 0579–0116)

§ 82.14 Removal of quarantine.

An area will be removed from quarantine only when all of the following requirements have been met:

(a) All birds and poultry exposed to Newcastle disease in the quarantined area have been found to be free of Newcastle disease;

(b) All birds and poultry infected with Newcastle disease in the quarantined area have been euthanized;

(c) All birds and poultry, including any parts of the birds and poultry, euthanized in accordance with paragraph (b) of this section, and all birds and poultry in the quarantined area, including any parts of the birds and poultry, that died from any cause other than slaughter, have been buried, reduced to ashes by incineration, rendered, or reduced to dust by composting:

(1) If the birds and poultry are buried, all birds and poultry infected with Newcastle disease must be buried in the quarantined area. The birds and poultry must be buried in a location that meets all United States Environmental Protection Agency, State, and local requirements for landfills. They must be buried at least 6 feet deep and be covered at the time of burial with soil; and

(2) If the birds and poultry are composted, all birds and poultry infected with Newcastle disease must be composted in the quarantined area. The birds and poultry must be composted according to the following instructions or according to another procedure approved by the Administrator as being adequate to prevent the dissemination of Newcastle disease:

(i) Place a 1-foot layer of litter and manure in a free-standing composter bin, unless the compost pile will be covered in accordance with paragraph (c)(2)(ii) of this section. Add a 6-inch layer of straw, peanut hulls, or wood chips. Add a layer of dead birds or dead poultry, leaving 6 inches between the carcasses and the bin walls. Add water sparingly and cover with 6 inches of a

[10] Written appeals should be sent to the Administrator, c/o Emergency Programs, Veterinary Services, Animal and Plant Health Inspection Service, 4700 River Road, Riverdale, MD 20737–1231.

dry mixture of litter and manure. Repeat the layering process two more times and cap with a double layer of dry manure cake. After the bin is capped off and covered, monitor the temperature in the compost pile daily, using a 36-inch probe-type thermometer. The temperature of the compost pile must reach at least 140 °F. After 30 days from the date the compost pile is created, turn over to aerate the entire mixture. Allow mixture to reach at least 140 °F once again. After completion of the second cycle, the mixture must remain covered with any material that prevents penetration of air and moisture until spread or otherwise utilized. The composted material may not be spread or otherwise utilized until at least 30 days following completion of the second heating cycle.

(ii) Composting of birds and poultry may be accomplished outside of covered bins by following the layering and temperature requirements set forth in paragraph (c)(2)(i) of this section, then covering the compost pile with tarpaulins or 6-mm polyethylene sheets anchored with tires or straw bales. The mixture must be kept moist. The final product may not be spread or otherwise utilized until at least 30 days following completion of the second heating cycle.

(iii) Composting of birds and poultry must be carried out at least 50 yards from any building or pen where poultry and birds are housed and be inaccessible to birds and poultry. Composted material may not be commingled with, or otherwise be brought into contact with, non-composted manure cake;

(d) All eggs produced by birds or poultry infected with or exposed to Newcastle disease in the quarantined area have been buried, reduced to ashes by incineration, or rendered. If the eggs are buried, the eggs must be buried in the quarantined area in a location that meets all United States Environmental Protection Agency requirements and all State and local requirements for landfills. The eggs must be buried at least 6 feet deep and be covered at the time of burial with soil;

(e) All manure generated by or litter used by birds or poultry infected with or exposed to Newcastle disease in the quarantined area has been reduced to ashes by incineration, or has been buried, composted, or spread on a field and turned under, as follows:

(1) *Burial*. If the manure or litter is buried, the manure and litter must be buried at least 6 feet deep and covered at the time of burial with soil. The manure and litter must be buried in the quarantined area in a location that meets all United States Environmental Protection Agency and State and local requirements for landfills;

(2) *Composting*. If the manure and litter is composted, the manure and litter must be composted in the quarantined area. The manure and litter must be composted according to the following method, or according to another procedure approved by the Administrator as being adequate to prevent the dissemination of Newcastle disease: Place the manure and litter in rows 3 to 5 feet high and 5 to 10 feet at the base. The area where the manure, litter, and other material used in composting are placed must be such that there is no runoff from the composted material out of the area, no saturation into the ground, and no moisture, except for that required by this paragraph, onto the composted material from above. The composting area must be at least 50 yards from any building or pen where birds or poultry are housed and be inaccessible to birds and poultry. The manure and litter must be mixed so as to attain a carbon to nitrogen ratio of approximately 30:1, a moisture content of between 40 to 50 percent, and a supply of oxygen to the composted material. If a carbon source other than manure or litter is needed, wood chips, straw, or peanut hulls may be used. The manure and litter must be covered with tarpaulin or 6-mm polyethylene sheets, be anchored with tires or straw bales, and be mixed to ensure adequate ventilation every 10 to 15 days. The composted material must rise to a temperature of 140 °F, as determined by use of a 36-inch probe-type thermometer. The composted material may not be spread or otherwise utilized for at least 30 days from the time the 140 °F temperature is reached; and

(3) *Spreading and turning under*. Spreading and turning under of manure

or litter may be used as a means of disposal only if carried out under the direct supervision of a Federal representative or a State representative. If the manure or litter is spread on a field and turned under, the field must be in the quarantined area, at least 50 yards away from any building or pen where poultry or birds are housed, and inaccessible to birds and poultry. The manure or litter must be turned under within 24 hours of being spread on the field, and the field must be left undisturbed for at least 30 days;

(f) All vehicles with which the birds or poultry infected with or exposed to Newcastle disease or their excrement or litter have had physical contact have been cleaned and disinfected in accordance with part 71 of this chapter. The vehicles have been inspected after cleaning, and before disinfection, by a Federal representative or State representative, and then have been disinfected in the presence of a Federal representative or State representative with a disinfectant listed in part 71 of this chapter;

(g) All cages, coops, containers, troughs, and other equipment used for birds or poultry infected with or exposed to Newcastle disease, or their excrement or litter have been reduced to ashes by incineration, or have been cleaned and disinfected in accordance with part 71 of this chapter. The items must be inspected after cleaning, and before disinfection, by a Federal representative or State representative, and then must be disinfected in the presence of a Federal representative or State representative, with a disinfectant listed in part 71 of this chapter; and

(h) The premises where birds or poultry infected with or exposed to Newcastle disease were located have been cleaned and disinfected in accordance with part 71 of this chapter. The premises have been inspected after cleaning, and before disinfection, by a Federal representative or State representative, and then have been disinfected in the presence of a Federal representative or State representative with a disinfectant listed in part 71 of this chapter.

(i) After the other conditions of this section are fulfilled, an area will not be released from quarantine until followup surveillance over a period of time determined by the Administrator indicates Newcastle disease is not present in the quarantined area.

(Approved by the Office of Management and Budget under control number 0579–0116)

[61 FR 56883, Nov. 5, 1996, as amended at 73 FR 30299, May 27, 2008]

§ 82.15 Replacement birds and poultry.

Birds and poultry that have been destroyed because of a quarantine for Newcastle disease may not be replaced by birds or poultry moved interstate into the quarantined area until the Administrator decides that Newcastle disease has been eradicated and that replacement birds or poultry will not become infected with Newcastle disease.

§ 82.16 Extraordinary emergencies; applicability of regulations.

When, in accordance with sec. 10407 of the Animal Health Protection Act (7 U.S.C. 8306), the Secretary of Agriculture determines that an extraordinary emergency exists because of Newcastle disease, the regulations in this subpart regarding interstate movement shall be applicable to intrastate movement within any State or portion of a State subject to the Secretary's declaration of extraordinary emergency until such time as the Secretary terminates that declaration.

[68 FR 1517, Jan. 13, 2003]

Subpart B—Chlamydiosis in Poultry

§ 82.19 Definitions.

As used in connection with this subpart, the following terms shall have the meaning set forth in this section.

Accredited veterinarian. A veterinarian approved by the Administrator in accordance with part 161 of this chapter to perform functions specified in subchapters B, C, and D of this chapter.

Administrator. The Administrator of the Animal and Plant Health Inspection Service or any individual authorized to act for the Administrator.

Animal and Plant Health Inspection Service. The Animal and Plant Health Inspection Service of the United States Department of Agriculture.

Bird. Any member of the class *aves* other than poultry.

Chlamydiosis. A contagious bacterial disease of birds and poultry, characterized by respiratory and systemic infection. The disease is also known as psittacosis in psittacine birds and as ornithosis in poultry.

Federal representative. An individual employed and authorized by the Federal government to perform the tasks required by this subpart.

Federal veterinarian. A veterinarian employed and authorized by the Federal government to perform the tasks required by this subpart.

Infected. Affected by the virus or bacterium that causes the specified disease.

Interstate. From one State into or through any other State.

Moved. Shipped, transported or otherwise moved, or delivered or received for movement, by any person.

Person. Any individual, corporation, company, association, firm, partnership, society, joint stock company, or other legal entity.

Poultry. Chickens, doves, ducks, geese, grouse, guinea fowl, partridges, pea fowl, pheasants, pigeons, quail, swans, and turkeys.

State. Each of the States of the United States, the District of Columbia, Puerto Rico, the Northern Mariana Islands, Guam, the Virgin Islands of the United States, or any other territory or possession of the United States.

State animal health official. The State official responsible for livestock- and poultry-disease control and eradication programs.

State representative. An individual employed in animal health work and authorized by a State or political subdivision of a State to perform the tasks required by this subpart.

Veterinarian in charge. A Federal veterinarian employed by the Animal and Plant Health Inspection Service and authorized by the Administrator to supervise and manage the animal health work of the Animal and Plant Health Inspection Service in a specified area of the United States.

§82.20 General restrictions.

The following items may not be moved interstate:

(a) Live poultry infected with chlamydiosis;

(b) Dead poultry that were infected with chlamydiosis when they died, and parts of dead poultry that were infected with chlamydiosis when they died; and

(c) Offal from poultry infected with chlamydiosis.

§82.21 Vehicles, cages, coops, containers, troughs, and other equipment used for infected poultry.

(a) Before moving vehicles, cages, coops, containers, troughs, and other equipment interstate that have held or have otherwise been used in the handling of poultry infected with chlamydiosis, and after using these items to move poultry infected with chlamydiosis interstate, the vehicles, cages, coops, containers, troughs, and other equipment must be cleaned and disinfected in accordance with paragraphs (a)(1) through (a)(5) of this section:

(1) Clean and disinfect the vehicles, cages, coops, containers, troughs, and other equipment at the place where the poultry are unloaded or where the equipment is used, no more than 2 hours after the poultry infected with chlamydiosis are unloaded or the equipment is used;

(2) Clean the items in accordance with part 71 of this chapter;

(3) Have a Federal representative, State representative,[1] or an accredited veterinarian, inspect the items after they have been cleaned;

(4) Disinfect the items in the presence of a Federal representative, State representative, or an accredited veterinarian; and

(5) Disinfect the items in accordance with part 71 of this chapter and by using a disinfectant as specified in part 71 of this chapter.

(b) If the place where the cleaning and disinfection would otherwise be required has no facilities for cleaning and disinfecting, the items may be moved to a place where facilities are available for cleaning and disinfecting, provided a Federal representative or State representative has determined that such

[1] See footnote 3 to §82.5.

movement will not cause a risk of the spread of chlamydiosis.

(c) Vehicles, cages, coops, containers, troughs, and other equipment moved interstate under this section must be accompanied by a permit obtained in accordance with § 82.23, and copies of the permit accompanying the vehicles, cages, coops, containers, troughs, and other equipment interstate must be submitted so that a copy is received by both the State animal health official and the veterinarian in charge[2] for the State of destination within 72 hours of the arrival of the vehicles, cages, coops, containers, troughs, and other equipment at the destination listed on the permit.

(Approved by the Office of Management and Budget under control numbers 0579–0116 and 0579–0032)

§ 82.22 Cleaning and disinfecting premises.

Premises that contained poultry that were infected with chlamydiosis must be cleaned and disinfected in accordance with this section before any poultry are moved interstate onto the premises.

(a) The premises must be cleaned in accordance with part 71 of this chapter;

(b) After being cleaned, the premises must be inspected by a Federal representative, State representative, or an accredited veterinarian; and

(c) After being inspected, the premises must be disinfected in the presence of a Federal representative, State representative, or an accredited veterinarian, in accordance with part 71 of this chapter, using a disinfectant listed in part 71 of this chapter.

(Approved by the Office of Management and Budget under control numbers 0579–0116 and 0579–0032)

§ 82.23 Issuance of permits.

(a) Application for the permit required by this subpart to move vehicles, cages, coops, containers, troughs, or other equipment interstate must be in writing, and must be submitted to a Federal representative or State representative. The application must include the following:

(1) The applicant's name and mailing address;

(2) The name and mailing address of the person who will receive the items;

(3) The addresses of both the origin and destination of the items;

(4) The number and types of items intended for interstate movement; and

(5) The reason for the interstate movement.

(b) *Exceptions.* This subpart does not apply to the interstate movement of poultry, vehicles, cages, coops, containers, troughs, or other equipment or material if the interstate movement is made by the United States Department of Agriculture for the purposes of research or diagnosis.

(Approved by the Office of Management and Budget under control number 0579–0116)

§ 82.24 Other interstate movements and special permits.

(a) A special permit is required for the interstate movement of items whose movement interstate is restricted under this subpart in a manner or to a destination other than is specifically prescribed by this subpart. A special permit is required for the disinfection of vehicles, premises, cages, coops, containers, troughs, and other equipment by a method other than is specifically prescribed by this subpart. To apply for a special permit, contact the veterinarian in charge for the State in which the items are located. The Administrator may, at his or her discretion, issue special permits if he or she determines the activity authorized will not increase the risk of spreading chlamydiosis interstate.

(b) The special permit will list the name and address of the person to whom the special permit is issued, and the special conditions under which the interstate movement, or cleaning and disinfection, may be carried out.

(1) For an interstate movement, the special permit will also include the following:

(i) The name and mailing address of the person who will receive the items;

(ii) The addresses of both the origin and destination of the items;

(iii) The number and type of items to be moved interstate; and

(iv) The reason for the interstate movement.

[2] See footnote 4 to § 82.5.

(2) For cleaning and disinfection, the special permit will also include the following:

(i) The address of the place where the items are located; and

(ii) The number and type of items involved.

(c) For an interstate movement, a copy of the special permit must accompany the items moved, and copies must be submitted so that a copy is received by both the State animal health official and the veterinarian in charge for the State of destination within 72 hours of the arrival of the items at the destination listed on the special permit.

(Approved by the Office of Management and Budget under control number 0579–0116)

§ 82.25 Denial and withdrawal of permits and special permits.

(a) *Denial.* If the Administrator determines that the applicant for a permit or special permit is not complying with or could not comply with this subpart or any special conditions needed to prevent the spread of chlamydiosis, or, in the case of a special permit, that the special permit is not required under this subpart, the Administrator may deny the request for a permit or special permit. If the request is denied, the Administrator will send the applicant a written notice explaining why the permit or special permit was denied.

(b) *Withdrawal.* The Administrator may withdraw a permit or special permit, orally or in writing, if he or she determines the person to whom the permit or special permit has been issued is violating either this subpart or some condition specified in the permit or special permit. The Administrator may withdraw the permit or special permit without advance notice if he or she determines that the person to whom the permit or special permit has been issued is violating either this subpart or some condition specified in the permit or special permit in a way that threatens the public health, interest, or safety. The Administrator will send the person to whom the permit or special permit has been issued a written explanation of why the permit or special permit is to be or was withdrawn.

(c) *Appeals.* Denial or withdrawal of a permit or special permit may be appealed to the Administrator within 10 days after receipt of the written notice of denial or withdrawal. The appeal must be in writing[3] and must state all of the facts and reasons upon which the person relies to show that the permit or special permit was wrongfully denied or withdrawn. The Administrator will grant or deny the appeal, in writing, explaining all of the reasons for the decision, as promptly as circumstances allow. In cases where there is a conflict as to any material fact, the person denied a permit or special permit, or from whom a permit or special permit is withdrawn, shall be given an opportunity for a hearing with respect to the merits or validity of the denial or withdrawal in accordance with rules of practice adopted for the proceeding.

(Approved by the Office of Management and Budget under control number 0579–0116)

PART 85—PSEUDORABIES

Sec.

AUTHORITY: 7 U.S.C. 8301–8317; 7 CFR 2.22, 2.80, and 371.4.

[3] See footnote 10 to § 82.13.

SOURCE: 44 FR 10309, Feb. 16, 1979, unless otherwise noted.

§85.1 Definitions.

For purposes of this part, the following terms mean:

Accredited veterinarian. A veterinarian approved by the Administrator in accordance with the provisions of part 161 of this title to perform functions specified in parts 1, 2, 3, and 11 of subchapter A, and subchapters B, C, and D of this chapter, and to perform functions required by cooperative state-federal disease control and eradication programs.

Administrator. The Administrator, Animal and Plant Health Inspection Service, or any person authorized to act for the Administrator.

Animal and Plant Health Inspection Sevice. The Animal and Plant Health Inspection Service of the United States Department of Agriculture (APHIS or Service).

Approved differential pseudorabies test. Any test for the diagnosis of pseudorabies that: (a) Can distinguish vaccinated swine from infected swine; (b) Is produced under license from the Secretary of Agriculture under the Virus-Serum-Toxin Act of March 4, 1913, and subsequent amendments (21 U.S.C. 151 *et seq.*) with indications for use in the Cooperative State-Federal Pseudorabies Eradication Program; and (c) Is conducted in a laboratory approved by the Administrator.[1]

Approved livestock market. A stockyard, livestock market, buying station, concentration point or any other premises under State or Federal veterinary supervision where swine are assembled for sale or sale purposes, and which has been approved by the Administrator under §71.20 of this chapter.[2, 3]

Certificate. An official document issued by an Animal and Plant Health Inspection Service representative, State representative, or accredited veterinarian for and prior to the interstate movement of swine that are not known to be infected with or exposed to pseudorabies, and are not pseudorabies vaccinates, except for official gene-altered pseudorabies vaccinates vaccinated with a glycoprotein I (gpI) deleted gene-altered pseudorabies vaccine or from a qualified negative gene-altered vaccinated herd. The document must state: (a) The number and description of the swine to be moved; (b) That the swine to be moved are not known to be infected with or exposed to pseudorabies; (c) The purpose for which the swine are to be moved; (d) The points of origin and destination; (e) The consignor and consignee; and (f) Any additional information required by this part.

Common ground. The ground, areas, buildings or equipment communally shared by any specific group or groups of livestock.

[1] The names and addresses of laboratories approved by the Administrator to conduct approved differential pseudorabies tests are published in the Notices Section of the FEDERAL REGISTER. A list of approved laboratories is also available upon request from the Animal and Plant Health Inspection Service, Veterinary Services, Operational Support, 4700 River Road Unit 33, Riverdale, Maryland 20737–1231. State, Federal, and university laboratories will be approved by the Administrator when he or she determines that the laboratory: (a) Employs personnel trained at the National Veterinary Services Laboratories assigned to supervise the testing; (b) follows standard test protocols; (c) meets check test proficiency requirements; and (d) will report all test results to State and Federal animal health officials. Before the Administrator may withdraw approval of any laboratory for failure to meet any of these conditions, the Administrator must give written notice of the proposed withdrawal to the director of the laboratory, and must give the director an opportunity to respond. If there are conflicts as to any material fact, a hearing will be held to resolve the conflict.

[2] Notices containing lists of such approved livestock markets are published in the FEDERAL REGISTER. Information concerning livestock markets can be obtained from the Veterinarian in Charge, Veterinary Services, Animal and Plant Health Inspection Service, United States Department of Agriculture for the State in question.

[3] Before the Administrator withdraws approval of any livestock market, the owner of such livestock market shall be given notice by the Administrator of the proposed withdrawal of approval and the reasons therefor and such owner shall have an opportunity to present his views thereon. In those instances where there are conflicts as to the facts, a hearing shall be held to resolve such conflicts.

Contact. Direct access to other swine, their excrement, or discharges; or sharing a building with a common ventilation system with other swine, or being within ten feet of other swine if not sharing a building with a common ventilation system.

Exposed livestock. Any livestock that has been in contact with an animal infected with pseudorabies, including all livestock in a known infected herd; except that livestock, other than swine, that have not been exposed to a clinical case of the disease for a period of 10 consecutive days shall no longer be considered to be exposed livestock.

Exposed swine. Any swine that has been in contact with an animal infected with pseudorabies, including all swine in a known infected herd.

Farm of origin. A farm where the swine were born, or on which they have resided for at least 90 consecutive days immediately prior to the interstate shipment.

Feedlot. A premises where swine are fed physically separated from swine kept for breeding or other purposes and from which such swine are moved directly to a recognized slaughtering establishment or directly through one or more slaughter markets and then directly to a recognized slaughtering establishment, quarantined herd, or quarantined feedlot.

Herd. Any group of livestock maintained on common ground for any purpose, or two or more groups of livestock under common ownership or supervision, geographically separated, but which have an interchange or movement of animals without regard to whether the animals are infected with or exposed to pseudorabies.

Infected livestock. Any livestock determined to be infected with pseudorabies by an official pseudorabies test, or diagnosed by an official pseudorabies epidemiologist as having pseudorabies.

Interstate. From any State into or through any other State.

Isolation. Separation of swine by a physical barrier in such a manner that other swine do not have access to the isolated swine's body, excrement, or discharges; not allowing the isolated swine to share a building with a common ventilation system with other swine; and not allowing the isolated swine to be within ten feet of other swine if not sharing a building with a common ventilation system.

Known infected herd. Any herd in which any livestock has been determined to be infected with pseudorabies by an official pseudorabies test, an approved differential pseudorabies test, or diagnosed by an official pseudorabies epidemiologist as having pseudorabies.

(a) A herd of livestock, other than swine, shall no longer be classified as a known infected herd after 10 days since the last clinical case of pseudorabies in the herd.

(b) A herd of swine which has been released from pseudorabies quarantine in accordance with the following provisions shall no longer be classified as a known infected herd if:

(1) All swine positive to an official pseudorabies test have been removed from the premises; all swine which remain in the herd, except swine nursing from their mothers, are subjected to an official pseudorabies serologic test and found negative 30 days or more after removal of swine positive to an official pseudorabies test; and no livestock on the permises have shown clinical signs of pseudorabies after removal of the postive swine; or

(2) All swine have been depopulated for 30 days and the herd premises have been cleaned and disinfected in accordance with § 85.13; or

(3) In a herd of swine in which swine are positive to an official pseudorabies serologic test but no swine are postive at titers greater than 1:8, all titered swine are subjected to another official pseudorabies serologic test and found negative; and all other swine in the herd which an epidemiologist, approved by the State animal health official and the Veterinarian in Charge, requires to be subjected to an official pseudorabies serologic test are tested and found negative.[4]

[4] The epidemiologist shall consider the following epidemiologic evidence to determine which swine in the herd, in addition to the titered swine, must be subjected to an official pseudorbies serologic test and found negative: (a) the percentage and number of titered swine in the herd; (b) the number of

Continued

(4) In a herd of swine containing official gene-altered pseudorabies vaccinates:

(i) All vaccinates have been vaccinated with the same official gene-altered pseudorabies vaccine; and

(ii) All swine positive to an approved differential pseudorabies test have been gone from the herd for at least 60 days; and

(iii) No livestock on the same premises as the herd have shown clinical signs of pseudorabies since removal of the positive swine; and

(iv) The herd has been tested for pseudorabies and found negative in accordance with one of the following two provisions:

(A) All swine in the herd, except suckling swine, are tested with an approved differential pseudorabies test. If all tested swine are found negative, no further testing is required. If any swine test positive, they may be retested with an approved differential pseudorabies test within 30 days of the first test if they are isolated from the remainder of the herd until the retest shows them to be negative.

(B) All swine in the herd over 6 months of age and a random sample of 30 or more swine in each segregated group of swine in the herd between 2 and 6 months of age are tested with an approved differential pseudorabies test. Not less than 30 days nor more than 60 days after this first test, another random sample of 30 or more swine in each segregated group of swine in the herd between 2 and 6 months of age is tested with an approved differential pseudorabies test. If all swine are negative on these tests, no further testing is required. If any swine test positive on either of these tests, the positive swine may be retested with an approved differential test within 30 days of the initial test if they are isolated from the remainder of the herd until the retest shows them to be negative.

Livestock. Swine, cattle, sheep or goats.

Moved. Shipped, transported, or otherwise moved, or delivered or received for movement by land, water, or air.

Official gene-altered pseudorabies vaccinate. Swine vaccinated with an official gene-altered pseudorabies vaccine, in accordance with directions on the label.

Official gene-altered pseudorabies vaccine. Any official pseudorabies vaccine for which there is an approved differential pseudorabies test.

Official pseudorabies epidemiologist. A state or federally employed veterinarian designated by the State animal health official and the veterinarian in charge to investigate and diagnose pseudorabies in livestock.

Official pseudorabies serologic test. An official pseudorabies test, as defined in this section, conducted on swine serum to detect the presence or absence of pseudorabies antibodies.

Official pseudorabies test. Any test for the diagnosis of pseudorabies approved by the Administrator conducted in a laboratory approved by the Administrator as listed in a Veterinary Services Notice listing such laboratories.[5] The following tests for the diagnosis of pseudorabies have been approved by the Administrator: 1. Microtitration Serum-Virus Neutralization Test; 2. Virus Isolation and Identification Test; 3. Fluorescent Antibody Tissue Section Test; 4. Enzyme-Linked Immunosorbent Assay (ELISA) Test, except for approved differential pseudorabies tests other than the glycoprotein I (gpI) ELISA test; 5. Latex Agglutination Test (LAT); and 6. Particle Concentration Fluorescence Immunoassay (PCFIA) Test, including the gpI PCFIA test.[6] State, Federal,

titered swine as compared to the number of swine tested; (c) the extent of the contact of members of the herd with the titered swine; (d) the prevalence of pseudorabies in the area; (e) the herd management practices; and (f) any other reliable epidemiologic evidence.

[5] Notices containing lists of laboratories approved for the purposes of the regulations in this part are published in the FEDERAL REGISTER Notices Section. The lists are also available upon request from the Animal and Plant Health Inspection Service, Veterinary Services, Operational Support, 4700 River Road Unit 33, Riverdale, Maryland 20737–1231.

[6] Copies of the test protocols (Recommended Minimum Standards for Diagnostic Tests Employed in the Diagnosis of Pseudorabies (Aujeszky's Disease)) published as a Veterinary Services Notice, May 17, 1978, are available upon request from the Animal and Plant Health Inspection Service, Veterinary Services, Operational Support,

and University laboratories will be approved by the Administrator following the determination by him that the laboratory: (a) Has personnel trained at the Veterinary Services Diagnostic Laboratory, Ames, Iowa, assigned to supervise the test, (b) follows standard test protocol, (c) meets check test proficiency requirements, and (d) will report all test results to State and Federal animal health officials.[7]

Official pseudorabies vaccine. Any pseudorabies virus vaccine produced under license from the Secretary of Agriculture under the Virus, Serum and Toxin Act of March 4, 1913, and any legislation amendatory thereof (21 U.S.C. 151 *et seq.*).

Official vaccinate. Any swine which have been: (a) Vaccinated with an official pseudorabies vaccine by an accredited veterinarian or a State or Federal veterinarian in accordance with recommendations on the vaccine label and the laws and regulations of the State in which the swine are vaccinated; (b) identified by a numbered pink eartag approved by the State in which such swine are vaccinated;[8] and (c) reported as official vaccinates at the time of vaccination to the State animal health official.

Owner-shipper statement. A statement signed by the owner or shipper of swine which states: (a) The number of swine to be moved; (b) the points of origin and destination; (c) the consignor and consignee; and (d) any additional information required by this part.

Permit. An official document issued for and prior to the interstate movement of pseudorabies infected, exposed or vaccinated swine under this part by an Animal and Plant Health Inspection Service representative, State representative, or an accredited veterinarian which states: (a) The number of swine to be moved; (b) the purpose for which the swine are to be moved; (c) the points of origin and destination; (d) the consignor and the consignee; and (e) any additional information required by this part.

Pseudorabies. The contagious, infectious, and communicable disease of livestock and other animals also known as Aujeszky's disease, mad itch, or infectious bulbar paralysis.

Pseudorabies controlled vaccinated herd. (a) Pseudorabies controlled vaccinated herd status is attained by subjecting all swine over 6 months of age to an official pseudorabies serologic test and finding all swine so tested negative. The herd must not have been a known infected herd within the past 30 days. Any swine in the herd over 6 months of age may be vaccinated for pseudorabies within 15 days after being subjected to an official pseudorabies serologic test and found negative.[1]

(b) If on the qualifying official pseudorabies serologic test or any subsequent official pseudorabies test, any swine so tested are positive, pseudorabies controlled vaccinated herd status is attained or regained by: removing all positive swine; cleaning and disinfecting the herd premises in accordance with §85.13; subjecting all swine in the herd, except swine nursing from their mothers, to an official pseudorabies serologic test 30 days or more after removal of the positive swine and finding all swine so tested negative; and, after an interval of 30 to 60 days after the first such negative official pseudorabies serologic herd test, subjecting all swine in the herd over 6 months of age to another official pseudorabies serologic test and finding all swine so tested negative.

(c)(1) Pseudorabies controlled vaccinated herd status is maintained by: subjecting 25 percent of all the offspring to an official pseudorabies serologic test when they are between 16 and 20 weeks of age and finding all swine so tested negative, or by leaving 10 percent of the swine over 6 months of age in the herd unvaccinated and subjecting all such unvaccinated swine to

4700 River Road, Unit 33, Riverdale, Maryland 20737-1231.

[7] Before the Administrator withdraws the approval of any laboratory, the Director of such laboratory shall be given a notice by the Administrator of the proposed disapproval and the reasons therefore and such Director shall have an opportunity to present his views thereon. In those instances where there are conflicts as to the facts, a hearing shall be held to resolve such conflicts.

[8] The numbered pink eartags are available commercially. Should any problem arise regarding the availability of such eartags, contact the appropriate State animal health official.

an official pseudorabies serologic test every 80–105 days and finding all swine so tested negative.

(2) Any swine in the herd over 6 months of age may be vaccinated for pseudorabies within 15 days after being subjected to an official pseudorabies serologic test and found negative; *Provided* That, if pseudorabies controlled vaccinated herd status is to be maintained by testing unvaccinated swine over 6 months of age, at least 10 percent of the swine in the herd over 6 months of age shall remain unvaccinated.

(3) All swine intended to be added to a pseudorabies controlled vaccinated herd shall be isolated until the swine have been found negative to an official pseudorabies serologic test conducted 30 days or more after the swine have been placed in isolation. Not more than 90 percent of the swine over 6 months of age added to the herd may be vaccinated for pseudorabies. All additions to the herd which are to be vaccinated for pseudorabies shall be vaccinated within 15 days after being subjected to such official pseudorabies serologic test. All additions to the herd shall be added to the herd within 30 days after such official pseudorabies serologic test.

(4) Swine which have not been vaccinated for pseudorabies and which are to be tested to maintain pseudorabies controlled vaccinated herd status shall be maintained in the herd so that the pseudorabies vaccinates can physically touch nonvaccinates or so that the pseudorabies vaccinates are within 10 feet of nonvaccinates while sharing a direct common ventilation system with such nonvaccinates.

Pseudorabies vaccinate. Any swine that have been vaccinated with any product containing antigens for pseudorabies.

Qualified negative gene-altered vaccinated herd. (a) Any herd in which no swine are known to be infected with or exposed to pseudorabies, and in which no swine are vaccinated for pseudorabies, may achieve status as a qualified negative gene-altered vaccinated herd under the following conditions:

(1) All swine in the herd over 6 months of age must be tested with an official pseudorabies serologic test. For a minimum of 30 days before the test, the herd must not have been a known infected herd. During the 90 days before the test, at least 90 percent of the swine in the herd either must have been on the premises and a part of the herd, or must have entered the herd directly from a qualified pseudorabies negative herd. If any of the tested swine are found positive on this or any other official pseudorabies test prior to vaccination with the official gene-altered pseudorabies vaccine, the requirements in paragraph (a)(2) must be met.

(2) All swine that are positive on an official pseudorabies test must be removed from the herd, or must be isolated until another official pseudorabies test conducted within 30 days of the first test shows them to be negative. If the results of the second test are negative, no additional testing is required before the herd may be vaccinated in accordance with paragraph (a)(3). If the results of the second test are positive, all swine that tested positive must be removed from the herd. Not less than 30 days after any positive swine are removed from the herd, all remaining swine in the herd, except suckling swine, must be tested with an official pseudorabies serologic test and found negative. Not less than 30 days after this negative test, the herd must be tested again in accordance with paragraph (a)(1).

(3) Not more than 30 days after test results show the herd to be negative for pseudorabies in accordance with paragraph (a)(1), all swine in the herd over 6 months of age must be vaccinated with an official gene-altered pseudorabies vaccine. Only one official gene-altered pseudorabies vaccine may be used in the herd.

(b) Any herd designated as a qualified pseudorabies negative herd may achieve new status as a qualified negative gene-altered vaccinated herd if all swine in the herd over 6 months of age are vaccinated with an official gene-altered pseudorabies vaccine. Only one official gene-altered pseudorabies vaccine may be used in the herd.

(c) Any herd in which no swine are known to be infected with or exposed to pseudorabies, and in which the only swine vaccinated for pseudorabies are official gene-altered pseudorabies vaccinates, may achieve status as a qualified negative gene-altered vaccinated herd under the following conditions:

(1) Only one official gene-altered pseudorabies vaccine may be used in the herd.

(2) All swine in the herd over 6 months of age must be tested with an approved differential pseudorabies test. For a minimum of 60 days before the test, the herd must not have been a known infected herd. During the 90 days before the test, at least 90 percent of the swine in the herd either must have been on the premises and a part of the herd or must have entered the herd directly from a qualified pseudorabies negative herd or a qualified negative gene-altered vaccinated herd. If any of the tested swine are found positive on this test, the requirements in paragraph (c)(3) must be met.

(3) All swine positive on an approved differential pseudorabies test must be removed from the herd, or must be isolated until another approved differential pseudorabies test conducted within 30 days of the first test shows them to be negative. If the results of the second test are negative, no additional testing is required before the herd may be vaccinated in accordance with paragraph (c)(4). If the results of the second test are positive, all swine that tested positive must be removed from the herd. No less than 30 days after any negative swine are removed from the herd, all remaining swine in the herd, except suckling swine, must be tested with an approved differential pseudorabies test and found negative. No less than 30 days after this negative test, the herd must be tested again in accordance with paragraph (c)(2).

(4) No more than 30 days after test results show the herd to be negative for pseudorabies in accordance with paragraph (c)(2), all swine in the herd over 6 months of age that are not already official gene-altered pseudorabies vaccinates must be vaccinated with an official gene-altered pseudorabies vaccine. Only one official gene-altered pseudorabies vaccine may be used in the herd.

(d) Qualified negative gene-altered vaccinated herd status is maintained under the following conditions:

(1) All swine over 6 months of age in the herd must be official gene-altered pseudorabies vaccinates, and only one official gene-altered pseudorabies vaccine may be used in the herd.

(2) All swine over 6 months of age in the herd must be tested at least once a year with an approved differential pseudorabies test and found negative; except that, if any swine are positive, the herd may maintain its status if the positive swine are isolated from the rest of the herd until they are found negative to a second approved differential pseudorabies test conducted within 30 days of the first. The requirement for annual testing of all swine in the herd over 6 months of age may be met by testing 25 percent of the swine over 6 months of age every 80–105 days, or by testing 10 percent of the swine over 6 months of age each month. No swine may be tested twice in 1 year to comply with the 25 percent requirement, or twice in 10 months to comply with the 10 percent requirement.

(3) Swine may be added to a qualified negative gene-altered vaccinated herd only under one of the following conditions:

(i) The swine are moved to the qualified negative gene-altered vaccinated herd from another qualified negative gene-altered vaccinated herd, or from a qualified pseudorabies negative herd, without having any contact en route with swine other than those from a qualified negative gene-altered vaccinated herd or a qualified pseudorabies negative herd.

(ii) The swine are moved to the qualified negative gene-altered vaccinated herd from a qualified pseudorabies negative herd, have contact en route with swine other than those from a qualified negative gene-altered vaccinated herd or a qualified pseudorabies negative herd, and, before being added, are isolated until they are found negative to an official pseudorabies serologic test conducted 30 days or more after the swine are isolated.

(iii) The swine are moved to the qualified negative gene-altered vaccinated herd from another qualified negative gene-altered vaccinated herd, have contact en route with swine other than those from a qualified negative gene-altered vaccinated herd or a qualified pseudorabies negative herd, and, before being added, are isolated until they are found negative to an approved differential pseudorabies test conducted 30 days or more after the swine are isolated.

(iv) The swine are removed to the qualified negative gene-altered vaccinated herd from a herd other than a qualified negative gene-altered vaccinated herd or a qualified pseudorabies negative herd, and, before being added, are isolated until they are found negative to two official pseudorabies serologic tests, one conducted at the time the swine are isolated, and the second conducted 30 days or more after the swine are isolated.

Qualified pseudorabies negative herd. (a) Qualified pseudorabies negative herd status is attained by subjecting all swine over 6 months of age to an official pseudorabies serologic test and finding all swine so tested negative. The herd must not have been a known infected herd within the past 30 days. A minimum of 90 percent of the swine in the herd must have been on the premises and a part of the herd for at least 90 days prior to the qualifying official pseudorabies serologic test or have entered directly from another qualified pseudorabies negative herd.

(b)(1) If on a qualifying official pseudorabies serologic test or any subsequent official pseudorabies test, any swine so tested are positive, qualified pseudorabies negative herd status is attained or regained by: Removing all positive swine and cleaning and disinfecting the herd premises in accordance with § 85.13; subjecting all swine in the herd, except swine nursing from their mothers, to an official pseudorabies serologic test 30 days or more after removal of the positive swine and finding all swine so tested negative; and, after an interval of 30 to 60 days after the first such negative official pseudorabies serologic herd test, subjecting all swine in the herd over 6 months of age to another official pseudorabies serologic test and finding all swine so tested negative; or

(2) If on any qualifying official pseudorabies serologic test or any subsequent official pseudorabies serologic test, any swine so tested are positive, but no swine are positive at titers greater than 1:8, qualified pseudorabies negative herd status is attained or regained by: Subjecting all titered swine and all other swine required to be tested by an epidemiologist, approved by the State animal health official and the Veterinarian in Charge, to an official pseudorabies serologic test and finding all such swine negative.[1]

(c) Qualified pseudorabies negative herd status is maintained by subjecting all swine over 6 months of age in the herd to an official pseudorabies serologic test at least once each year (this must be accomplished by testing 25 percent of swine over 6 months of age every 80–105 days and finding all swine so tested negative, or by testing 10 percent of the swine over 6 months of age each month and finding all swine so tested negative; no swine shall be tested twice in 1 year to comply with the 25 percent requirement or twice in 10 months to comply with the 10 percent requirement). All swine intended to be added to a qualified pseudorabies negative herd shall be isolated until the swine have been found negative to two official pseudorabies serologic tests, one conducted 30 days or more after the swine have been placed in isolation, the second test being conducted 30 days or more after the first test; except (1) swine intended to be added to a qualified pseudorabies negative herd directly from another qualified pseudorabies negative herd may be added without isolation or testing; (2) swine intended to be added to a qualified pseudorabies negative herd from another qualified pseudorabies negative herd, but with interim contact with swine other than those from a single qualified pseudorabies negative herd, shall be isolated until the swine have been found negative to an official pseudorabies serologic test, conducted 30 days or more after the swine have been placed in isolation; (3) swine returned to the herd after contact with swine other than those from a single qualified pseudorabies negative herd shall be isolated until the swine have been found negative to an official pseudorabies serologic test conducted

30 days or more after the swine have been placed in isolation.

Quarantined feedlot. A premises where pseudorabies infected or exposed swine are fed under the supervision and control of the State animal health official, and from which such swine are moved directly to a recognized slaughtering establishment or directly through one or more slaughter markets and then directly to a recognized slaughtering establishment in accordance with the provisions of this part.

Quarantined herd. A herd in which pseudorabies infected or exposed swine are bred, reared, and fed under the supervision and control of the State animal health official, and from which such swine are moved interstate directly to a recognized slaughtering establishment or directly through one or more slaughter markets and then directly to a recognized slaughtering establishment, or from which exposed officially vaccinated swine which were negative to an official pseudorabies serologic test may be moved only to a quarantined herd or quarantined feedlot.

Recognized slaughtering establishment. A slaughtering establishment operated under the provisions of the Federal Meat Inspection Act (21 U.S.C. 601 *et seq.*) or a State inspected slaughtering establishment.

Slaughter market. A livestock market approved in accordance with §71.20 of this chapter, at which swine for sale and shipment for slaughter are handled only on days when no swine are handled for sale and shipment for feeding or breeding purposes unless facilities are provided to keep slaughter swine physically separated from feeder and breeder swine, and feeder and breeder swine use no facilities previously used by slaughter swine on the day these classes of swine are at the market. The facilities used by slaughter swine shall be cleaned and disinfected in accordance with the requirements of this part before being used for feeding or breeding swine.[9, 10]

State. Any State or Territory of the United States, the District of Columbia, Puerto Rico, Guam or the Northern Mariana Islands.

State animal health official. The State animal health official who is responsible for the livestock and poultry disease control and eradication programs in the official's State or his designated representative.

State representative. A person regularly employed in animal health work of a State and who is authorized by such State to perform the function involved under a Cooperative Agreement with the United States Department of Agriculture.

Swine not known to be infected with or exposed to pseudorabies. Any swine from a herd of swine in which no animal has been classified as a reactor to an official pseudorabies test, or has been diagnosed as having pseudorabies or suspected of having pseudorabies by a veterinarian; or any swine from a herd of swine which has been released from quarantine or has met the requirements of release from quarantine in accordance with the definition of known infected herd in §85.1.

Veterinarian in charge. The veterinary official of Veterinary Services, Animal and Plant Health Inspection Service, United States Department of Agriculture, who is assigned by the Administrator to supervise and perform official animal health work of the Animal and Plant Health Inspection Service in the State concerned.

Veterinary Services. Veterinary Services, Animal and Plant Health Inspection Service, United States Department of Agriculture.

[9] Notices containing lists of slaughter markets approved for the purposes of the regulations in this part are published in the FEDERAL REGISTER. Information concerning slaughter markets can be obtained from the Veterinarian in Charge, Veterinary Services, Animal and Plant Health Inspection Service, U.S. Department of Agriculture, for the State in question.

[10] Before the Administrator withdraws approval of any slaughter market, the owner of such slaughter market shall be given notice by the Administrator of the proposed withdrawal of approval and the reasons therefore and such owner shall have an opportunity to present his views thereon. In those instances where there are conflicts as to the facts, a hearing shall be held to resolve such conflicts.

Veterinary Services representative. A person employed by Veterinary Services, Animal and Plant Health Inspection Service, United States Department of Agriculture, who is authorized to perform the function involved.

(Approved by the Office of Management and Budget under control number 0579–0069)

[44 FR 10309, Feb. 16, 1979]

EDITORIAL NOTE: For FEDERAL REGISTER citations affecting § 85.1, see the List of CFR Sections Affected, which appears in the Finding Aids section of the printed volume and at *www.fdsys.gov.*

§ 85.2 Notice relating to the existence of the contagion of pseudorabies.

Notice is hereby given that there is reason to believe that the contagion of pseudorabies may exist in each State and that to prevent the spread and dissemination of the contagion thereof, and to protect the livestock of the United States, the regulations in this part are promulgated.

§ 85.3 General restriction.

Livestock shall not be moved interstate except in compliance with the regulations in this part.

§ 85.4 Interstate movement of livestock.

(a) Livestock showing clinical evidence of pseudorabies shall not be moved interstate.

(b) Livestock that have been exposed to an animal showing clinical evidence of pseudorabies shall not be moved interstate within 10 days of such exposure.

(c) Except as provided in paragraphs (a) and (b) of this section, livestock other than swine may be moved interstate without restriction under this part.

(d) Except as provided in paragraphs (a) and (b) of this section, swine, swine semen, and swine embryos shall be moved interstate only in compliance with the regulations in this part.

[44 FR 10309, Feb. 16, 1979, as amended at 50 FR 47352, Nov. 15, 1985]

§ 85.5 Interstate movement of infected swine or exposed swine.

Infected swine or exposed swine, other than swine described in § 85.4 (a) or (b), shall only be moved interstate in accordance with the following provisions:

(a) *Movement of infected or exposed swine for slaughter.* Infected or exposed swine shall be moved interstate for slaughter only if:

(1) The swine are moved directly to a recognized slaughtering establishment or directly through one or more slaughter markets and then directly to a recognized slaughtering establishment;

(2) The swine are accompanied by a permit or owner-shipper statement and such permit or owner-shipper statement is delivered to the consignee;

(3) The permit, in addition to the information in § 85.1, or the owner-shipper statement, in addition to the information in § 85.1, lists the identification of the swine as required by § 71.19 of this chapter; *except* if the swine are moved interstate and the indentity of the farm of origin of each swine is maintained, the permit or the owner-shipper statement need not list the identification required by § 71.19 of this chapter, if such swine are identified to the farm of orgin at the recognized slaughtering establishment or the first slaughter market; and

(4) The swine are moved to destination in one continuous movement without unloading enroute.

(b) *Movement of exposed swine to a quarantined herd or a quarantined feedlot.* Exposed swine shall be moved interstate directly to a quarantined herd or quarantined feedlot only if:

(1) The swine are negative to an official pseudorabies serologic test 21 days or more after last being exposed to any livestock showing clinical evidence of pseudorabies;

(2) The swine are officially vaccinated for pseudorabies within 15 days after the negative test;

(3) The swine are moved interstate within 30 days after the negative test;

(4) The swine are accompanied by a permit and such permit is delivered to the consignee; and

(5) The permit, in addition to the information described in § 85.1, states: (i) The present pseudorabies quarantine status of the farm of origin; (ii) the identification of the swine as required by § 71.19 of this chapter; (iii) the date

of the official pseudorabies serologic test and the name of the laboratory where the test was conducted; (iv) the date of the official vaccination for pseudorabies; and (v) that approval for the interstate movement has been issued by the State animal health official of the State of destination prior to the interstate movement of the swine.

(Approved by the Office of Management and Budget under control number 0579–0051)

[44 FR 10309, Feb. 16, 1979, as amended at 48 FR 57472, Dec. 30, 1983; 50 FR 47352, Nov. 15, 1985; 53 FR 40387, Oct. 14, 1988; 59 FR 67133, Dec. 29, 1994]

§ 85.6 Interstate movement of pseudorabies vaccinate swine, except swine from qualified negative gene-altered vaccinated herds, not known to be infected with or exposed to pseudorabies.

Pseudorabies vaccinate swine, except swine from qualified negative gene-altered vaccinated herds, not known to be infected with or exposed to pseudorabies shall only be moved interstate in accordance with the following provisions:

(a) *Movement of pseudorabies vaccinate swine, except swine from qualified negative gene-altered vaccinated herds, for slaughter.* Pseudorabies vaccinate swine, except swine from qualified negative gene-altered vaccinated herds, not known to be infected with or exposed to pseudorabies shall be moved interstate for slaughter only if:

(1) The swine are moved directly to a recognized slaughtering establishment or directly through one or more slaughter markets and then directly to a recognized slaughtering establishment;

(2) The swine are accompanied by a permit or owner-shipper statement and such permit or owner-shipper statement is delivered to the consignee; and

(3) The swine are moved to destination in one continuous movement without unloading enroute.

(b) *Movement of pseudorabies vaccinate swine, except swine from qualified negative gene-altered vaccinated herds, to a quarantined herd or quarantined feedlot.* Pseudorabies vaccinate swine, except swine from qualified negative gene-altered vaccinated herds, not known to be infected with or exposed to pseudorabies shall be moved interstate directly to a quarantined herd or quarantined feedlot only if:

(1) The swine are accompanied by a permit and such permit is delivered to the consignee; and

(2) The permit in addition to information described in § 85.1 states: (i) The pseudorabies status of the herd; (ii) the identification of the swine required by § 71.19 of this chapter; (iii) the date of the vaccination for pseudorabies; and (iv) that approval for the interstate movement has been issued by the State animal health official of the State of destination prior to the interstate movement of the swine.

(c) *General movements.* Swine vaccinated for pseudorabies with a glycoprotein I (gpI) deleted gene-altered pseudorabies vaccine and not known to be infected with or exposed to pseudorabies, but that are not from a qualified negative gene-altered vaccinated herd, may be moved interstate to destinations other than those set forth in paragraphs (a) and (b) of this section only if:

(1) The swine are accompanied by a certificate and such certificate is delivered to the consignee; and

(2) The certificate, in addition to the information described in § 85.1, states:

(i) The identification required by § 71.19 of this chapter;

(ii) That each animal to be moved was vaccinated for pseudorabies with a gpI-deleted gene-altered pseudorabies vaccine;

(iii) That each animal to be moved was subjected to a gpI enzyme-linked immunosorbent assay (ELISA) or a gpI Particle Concentration Fluorescence Immunoassay (PCFIA) approved differential pseudorabies test no more than 30 days prior to the interstate movement and was found negative;

(iv) The date of the gpI ELISA or the gpI PCFIA approved differential pseudorabies test; and

(v) The name of the laboratory that conducted the gpI ELISA or the gpI

PCFIA approved differential pseudorabies test.

(Approved by the Office of Management and Budget under control number 0579–0051)

[44 FR 10309, Feb. 16, 1979, as amended at 48 FR 57472, Dec. 30, 1983; 50 FR 47352, Nov. 15, 1985; 53 FR 40387, Oct. 14, 1988; 55 FR 19253, May 9, 1990; 59 FR 67133, Dec. 29, 1994; 60 FR 26355, May 17, 1995; 63 FR 17316, Apr. 9, 1998]

§ 85.7 Interstate movement of swine not vaccinated for pseudorabies and not known to be infected with or exposed to pseudorabies.

Swine not vaccinated for/ pseudorabies and not known to be infected with or exposed to pseudorabies shall only be moved interstate in accordance with the following provisions:

(a) *Movement for slaughter.* Swine not vaccinated for pseudorabies and not known to be infected with or exposed to pseudorabies may be moved interstate for slaughter without further restriction under this part directly to a recognized slaughtering establishment or directly through one or more slaughter markets and then directly to a recognized slaughtering establishment.

(b) *Movement to a feedlot, quarantined feedlot, quarantined herd, or approved livestock market.* Swine not vaccinated for pseudorabies and not known to be infected with or exposed to pseudorabies may be moved interstate only if:

(1) The swine are moved from a qualified pseudorabies negative herd directly to a feedlot, quarantined feedlot, quarantined herd, or approved livestock market; or

(2) The swine are moved directly to a feedlot, quarantined feedlot, quarantined herd, or to an approved livestock market for subsequent movement to a feedlot or quarantined feedlot, quarantined herd in accordance with paragraph (c) of this section; or

(3) The swine are moved from a State which requires the State animal health official of that State to be immediately notified of any suspected or confirmed case of pseudorabies in that State and which requires that exposed or infected livestock be quarantined, such quarantine to be released only after having met quarantine release standards no less restrictive than those in the definition of known infected herd in § 85.1, and

(i) Unless the swine are moving interstate in a swine production system in compliance with § 71.19(g) of this chapter, the swine are accompanied by an owner-shipper statement and are moved from a farm of origin directly to an approved livestock market; and

(A) The owner-shipper statement is delivered to the consignee, and

(B) The swine are identified at the approved livestock market to the farm of origin by the identification required by § 71.19 of this chapter.

(ii) Unless the swine are moving interstate in a swine production system in compliance with § 71.19(g) of this chapter, the swine are accompanied by a certificate and such certificate is delivered to the consignee; the certificate, in addition to the information in § 85.1, states the identification of the farm of origin of each swine being moved by a means of identification required by § 71.19 of this chapter, and approval for the interstate movement has been issued by the State animal health official of the State of destination prior to the interstate movement of the swine, and

(A) The swine are moved directly to a feedlot, quarantined feedlot, quarantined herd or approved livestock market from a farm of origin; or

(B) The swine are moved directly to a feedlot, quarantined feedlot, quarantined herd or approved livestock market from an approved livestock market which received the swine directly from a farm of origin, or

(C) The swine are moved directly to a feedlot, quarantined feedlot, or quarantined herd from an approved livestock market, which received the swine from another approved livestock market, which received the swine directly from a farm of origin.

(c) *General movements.* Swine not vaccinated for pseudorabies and not known to be infected with or exposed to pseudorabies may be moved interstate only if:

(1) Unless the swine are moving interstate in a swine production system in compliance with § 71.19(g) of this chapter, the swine are accompanied by a certificate and such certificate is delivered to the consignee; and

(2) The certificate, in addition to the information described in § 85.1, states: (i) The identification required by § 71.19 of this chapter; and (ii) that each animal to be moved: (A) Was subjected to an official pseudorabies serologic test within 30 days prior to the interstate movement and was found negative, the test date and the name of the laboratory conducting the test; or (B) is part of a currently recognized qualified pseudorabies negative herd and the date of the last qualifying test; or, (C) is part of a pseudorabies controlled vaccinated herd and is one of the offspring that was subjected to the official pseudorabies serologic test to achieve or maintain the status of the herd as a pseudorabies controlled vaccinated herd, and the date of the last test to maintain said status.

(Approved by the Office of Management and Budget under control number 0579–0069)

[44 FR 10309, Feb. 16, 1979, as amended at 48 FR 57472, Dec. 30, 1983; 50 FR 47352, Nov. 15, 1985; 53 FR 40387, Oct. 14, 1988; 66 FR 65604, Dec. 20, 2001; 69 FR 64651, Nov. 8, 2004]

§ 85.8 Interstate movement of swine from a qualified negative gene-altered vaccinated herd.

Swine from a qualified negative gene-altered vaccinated herd, and not known to be infected with or exposed to pseudorabies, may be moved interstate only in accordance with the following provisions:

(a) Without further restriction under this part if:

(1) The swine are moved directly to a recognized slaughtering establishment, or directly through one or more slaughter markets and then directly to a recognized slaughtering establishment; or

(2) The swine are moved directly to a feedlot, quarantined feedlot, or approved livestock market; or

(3) The swine are moved from an approved livestock market to a feedlot, quarantined feedlot, or other approved livestock market; or

(4) The swine are moved interstate in a swine production system in compliance with § 71.19(g) of this chapter.

(b) For all interstate movements other than those set forth in paragraph (a) of this section, the swine must be accompanied by a certificate, and the certificate must be delivered to the consignee. In addition to the information required by § 85.1 of this part, the certificate must state: (1) That the swine are from a qualified negative gene-altered vaccinated herd; (2) The date of the herd's last qualifying test; (3) The identification for the swine to be moved interstate, in accordance with § 71.19 of this chapter; and (4) If the swine to be moved are official gene-altered pseudorabies vaccinates, the official gene-altered pseudorabies vaccine used in the herd.

[55 FR 19253, May 9, 1990, as amended at 66 FR 65604, Dec. 20, 2001; 69 FR 64651, Nov. 8, 2004]

§ 85.9 Other interstate movements.

The Administrator may, upon request in specific cases, permit the interstate movement of livestock not otherwise provided for in this part under such conditions as he may prescribe to prevent the spread of pseudorabies. The Animal and Plant Health Inspection Service intends that such authority be used only in situations and under circumstances presenting problems that could not have been reasonably anticipated in advance and in unique situations. The Animal and Plant Health Inspection Service does not intend that such authority be used repeatedly to cover the same problem, but that the regulation be amended to conform with needed changes as they come to light.

[44 FR 10309, Feb. 16, 1979, as amended at 54 FR 21049, May 16, 1989. Redesignated at 55 FR 19253, May 9, 1990]

§ 85.10 Interstate movement of swine semen and swine embryos for insemination of or implantation into swine.

Swine semen and swine embryos moved interstate for insemination of swine or implantation into swine shall be accompanied by a document issued by an accredited veterinarian stating that the donor swine are not known to be infected with or exposed to pseudorabies, were negative to an official pseudorabies serologic test within 30 days prior to the collection of the semen or embryos or were members of a qualified pseudorabies negative herd, and had not been exposed to pseudorabies within 30 days prior to the collection of the semen or embryos.

(Approved by the Office of Management and Budget under control number 0579–0032)

[44 FR 10309, Feb. 16, 1979, as amended at 50 FR 47353, Nov. 15, 1985. Redesignated at 55 FR 19253, May 9, 1990; 59 FR 67133, Dec. 29, 1994]

§ 85.11 Permits and certificates.

(a) Each permit, certificate or owner-shipper statement required under this part to accompany swine interstate shall be delivered with the swine to the consignee by the person delivering the swine.

(b) A copy of each permit or certificate required under this part to accompany swine interstate shall be mailed or delivered to the State animal health official of the State of destination by the person issuing the document within 3 days of the interstate movement of the swine covered by said document.

(Approved by the Office of Management and Budget under control number 0579–0069)

[44 FR 10309, Feb. 16, 1979, as amended at 48 FR 57472, Dec. 30, 1983. Redesignated at 55 FR 19253, May 9, 1990]

§ 85.12 Cleaning and disinfecting means of conveyance.

All means of conveyance used in connection with the interstate movement of pseudorabies infected or exposed livestock shall be cleaned and disinfected in accordance with § 71.7 of this chapter using one of the disinfectants registered under the Federal Insecticide, Fungicide and Rodenticide Act, as amended (7 U.S.C. 135 *et seq.*) with herpes virucidal claims. These disinfectants shall be used in accordance with directions on their labels accepted in connection with their registration.

[44 FR 10309, Feb. 16, 1979, as amended at 62 FR 27937, May 22, 1997]

§ 85.13 Cleaning and disinfecting livestock markets and other facilities.

Livestock markets and other facilities used in connection with the interstate movement of pseudorabies infected or exposed livestock shall be cleaned and disinfected in compliance with § 71.7 of this chapter using one of the disinfectants registered under the Federal Insecticide, Fungicide and Rodenticide Act, as amended (7 U.S.C. 135 *et seq.*) with herpes virucidal claims. These disinfectants shall be used in accordance with directions on their labels accepted in connection with their registration.

[44 FR 10309, Feb. 16, 1979, as amended at 62 FR 27937, May 22, 1997]

PART 86—ANIMAL DISEASE TRACEABILITY

Sec.

AUTHORITY: 7 U.S.C. 8301–8317; 7 CFR 2.22, 2.80, and 371.4.

SOURCE: 78 FR 2071, Jan. 9, 2013, unless otherwise noted.

§ 86.1 Definitions.

Animal identification number (AIN). A numbering system for the official identification of individual animals in the United States that provides a nationally unique identification number for each animal. The AIN consists of 15 digits, with the first 3 being the country code (840 for the United States or a unique country code for any U.S. territory that has such a code and elects to use it in place of the 840 code). The alpha characters USA or the numeric code assigned to the manufacturer of the identification device by the International Committee on Animal Recording may be used as an alternative to the 840 or other prefix representing a U.S. territory; however, only the AIN beginning with the 840 or other prefix representing a U.S. territory will be recognized as official for use on AIN tags applied to animals on or after March 11, 2015. The AIN beginning with the 840 prefix may not be applied to animals known to have been born outside the United States.

Approved livestock facility. A stockyard, livestock market, buying station, concentration point, or any other premises under State or Federal veterinary inspection where livestock are assembled and that has been approved under §71.20 of this chapter.

Approved tagging site. A premises, authorized by APHIS, State, or Tribal animal health officials, where livestock may be officially identified on behalf of their owner or the person in possession, care, or control of the animals when they are brought to the premises.

Commuter herd. A herd of cattle or bison moved interstate during the course of normal livestock management operations and without change of ownership directly between two premises, as provided in a commuter herd agreement.

Commuter herd agreement. A written agreement between the owner(s) of a herd of cattle or bison and the animal health officials for the States or Tribes of origin and destination specifying the conditions required for the interstate movement from one premises to another in the course of normal livestock management operations and specifying the time period, up to 1 year, that the agreement is effective. A commuter herd agreement may be renewed annually.

Covered livestock. Cattle and bison, horses and other equine species, poultry, sheep and goats, swine, and captive cervids.

Dairy cattle. All cattle, regardless of age or sex or current use, that are of a breed(s) used to produce milk or other dairy products for human consumption, including, but not limited to, Ayrshire, Brown Swiss, Holstein, Jersey, Guernsey, Milking Shorthorn, and Red and Whites.

Directly. Moved in a means of conveyance, without stopping to unload while en route, except for stops of less than 24 hours to feed, water, or rest the animals being moved, and with no commingling of animals at such stops.

Flock-based number system. The flock-based number system combines a flock identification number (FIN) with a producer's unique livestock production numbering system to provide a nationally unique identification number for an animal.

Flock identification number (FIN). A nationally unique number assigned by a State, Tribal, or Federal animal health authority to a group of animals that are managed as a unit on one or more premises and are under the same ownership.

Group/lot identification number (GIN). The identification number used to uniquely identify a "unit of animals" of the same species that is managed together as one group throughout the preharvest production chain. When a GIN is used, it is recorded on documents accompanying the animals moving interstate; it is not necessary to have the GIN attached to each animal.

Interstate certificate of veterinary inspection (ICVI). An official document issued by a Federal, State, Tribal, or accredited veterinarian certifying the inspection of animals in preparation for interstate movement.

(a) The ICVI must show the species of animals covered by the ICVI; the number of animals covered by the ICVI; the purpose for which the animals are to be moved; the address at which the animals were loaded for interstate movement; the address to which the animals are destined; and the names of the consignor and the consignee and their addresses if different from the address at which the animals were loaded or the address to which the animals are destined. Additionally, unless the species-specific requirements for ICVIs provide an exception, the ICVI must list the official identification number of each animal, except as provided in paragraph (b) of this definition, or group of animals moved that is required to be officially identified, or, if an alternative form of identification has been agreed upon by the sending and receiving States, the ICVI must include a record of that identification. If animals moving under a GIN also have individual official identification, only the GIN must be listed on the ICVI. An ICVI may not be issued for any animal that is not officially identified if official identification is required. If the animals are not required by the regulations to be officially identified, the ICVI must state the exemption that applies (e.g., the cattle and bison do not belong to one of the classes of cattle and bison to which the official identification requirements of this part apply). If the animals are required to be officially identified but the identification number does not have to be recorded on the ICVI, the ICVI must state that all animals to be moved under the ICVI are officially identified.

(b) As an alternative to typing or writing individual animal identification on an ICVI, if agreed to by the receiving State or Tribe, another document may be used to provide this information, but only under the following conditions:

(1) The document must be a State form or APHIS form that requires individual identification of animals or a printout of official identification numbers generated by computer or other means;

(2) A legible copy of the document must be stapled to the original and each copy of the ICVI;

(3) Each copy of the document must identify each animal to be moved with the ICVI, but any information pertaining to other animals, and any unused space on the document for recording animal identification, must be crossed out in ink; and

(4) The following information must be written in ink in the identification column on the original and each copy of the ICVI and must be circled or boxed, also in ink, so that no additional information can be added:

(i) The name of the document; and

(ii) Either the unique serial number on the document or, if the document is not imprinted with a serial number, both the name of the person who prepared the document and the date the document was signed.

Interstate movement. From one State into or through any other State.

Livestock. All farm-raised animals.

Location-based numbering system. The location-based number system combines a State or Tribal issued location identification (LID) number or a premises identification number (PIN) with a producer's unique livestock production numbering system to provide a nationally unique and herd-unique identification number for an animal.

Location identification (LID) number. A nationally unique number issued by a State, Tribal, and/or Federal animal health authority to a location as determined by the State or Tribe in which it is issued. The LID number may be used in conjunction with a producer's own unique livestock production numbering system to provide a nationally unique and herd-unique identification number for an animal. It may also be used as a component of a group/lot identification number (GIN).

Move. To carry, enter, import, mail, ship, or transport; to aid, abet, cause, or induce carrying, entering, importing, mailing, shipping, or transporting; to offer to carry, enter, import, mail, ship, or transport; to receive in order to carry, enter, import, mail, ship, or transport; or to allow any of these activities.

National Uniform Eartagging System (NUES). A numbering system for the official identification of individual animals in the United States that provides a nationally unique identification number for each animal.

Official eartag. An identification tag approved by APHIS that bears an official identification number for individual animals. Beginning March 11, 2014, all official eartags manufactured must bear an official eartag shield. Beginning March 11, 2015, all official eartags applied to animals must bear an official eartag shield. The design, size, shape, color, and other characteristics of the official eartag will depend on the needs of the users, subject to the approval of the Administrator. The official eartag must be tamper-resistant and have a high retention rate in the animal.

Official eartag shield. The shield-shaped graphic of the U.S. Route Shield with "U.S." or the State postal abbreviation or Tribal alpha code imprinted within the shield.

Official identification device or method. A means approved by the Administrator of applying an official identification number to an animal of a specific species or associating an official identification number with an animal or group of animals of a specific species or otherwise officially identifying an animal or group of animals.

Official identification number. A nationally unique number that is permanently associated with an animal or group of animals and that adheres to one of the following systems:

(1) National Uniform Eartagging System (NUES).

(2) Animal identification number (AIN).

(3) Location-based number system.

(4) Flock-based number system.

(5) Any other numbering system approved by the Administrator for the official identification of animals.

Officially identified. Identified by means of an official identification device or method approved by the Administrator.

Owner-shipper statement. A statement signed by the owner or shipper of the livestock being moved stating the location from which the animals are moved interstate; the destination of the animals; the number of animals covered by the statement; the species of animal covered; the name and address of the owner at the time of the movement; the name and address of the shipper; and the identification of each animal, as required by the regulations, unless the regulations specifically provide that the identification does not have to be recorded.

Person. Any individual, corporation, company, association, firm, partnership, society, or joint stock company, or other legal entity.

Premises identification number (PIN). A nationally unique number assigned by a State, Tribal, and/or Federal animal health authority to a premises that is, in the judgment of the State, Tribal, and/or Federal animal health authority a geographically distinct location from other premises. The PIN may be used in conjunction with a producer's own livestock production numbering system to provide a nationally unique and herd-unique identification number for an animal. It may be used as a component of a group/lot identification number (GIN).

Recognized slaughtering establishment. Any slaughtering facility operating under the Federal Meat Inspection Act (21 U.S.C. 601 *et seq.*), the Poultry Products Inspection Act

(21 U.S.C. 451 *et seq.*), or State meat or poultry inspection acts that is approved in accordance with 9 CFR 71.21.

United States Department of Agriculture (USDA) approved backtag. A backtag issued by APHIS that provides a temporary unique identification for each animal.

§ 86.2 General requirements for traceability.

(a) The regulations in this part apply only to covered livestock, as defined in § 86.1.

(b) No person may move covered livestock interstate or receive such livestock moved interstate unless the livestock meet all applicable requirements of this part.

(c) The regulations in this part will apply to the movement of covered livestock onto and from Tribal lands only when the movement is an interstate movement; *i.e.*, when the movement is across a State line.

(d) In addition to meeting all applicable requirements of this part, all covered livestock moved interstate must be moved in compliance with all applicable provisions of APHIS program disease regulations (subchapter C of this chapter).

(e) The interstate movement requirements in this part do not apply to the movement of covered livestock if:

(1) The movement occurs entirely within Tribal land that straddles a State line and the Tribe has a separate traceability system from the States in which its lands are located; or

(2) The movement is to a custom slaughter facility in accordance with Federal and State regulations for preparation of meat.

§ 86.3 Recordkeeping requirements.

(a) *Official identification device distribution records.* Any State, Tribe, accredited veterinarian, or other person or entity who distributes official identification devices must maintain for 5 years a record of the names and addresses of anyone to whom the devices were distributed.

(b) *Interstate movement records.* Approved livestock facilities must keep any ICVIs or alternate documentation that is required by this part for the interstate movement of covered livestock that enter the facility on or after March 11, 2013. For poultry and swine, such documents must be kept for at least 2 years, and for cattle and bison, sheep and goats, cervids, and equines, 5 years.

§ 86.4 Official identification.

(a) *Official identification devices and methods.* The Administrator has approved the following official identification devices or methods for the species listed. The Administrator may authorize the use of additional devices or methods for a specific species if he or she determines that such additional devices or methods will provide for adequate traceability.

(1) *Cattle and bison.* Cattle and bison that are required to be officially identified for interstate movement under this part must be identified by means of:

(i) An official eartag; or

(ii) Brands registered with a recognized brand inspection authority and accompanied by an official brand inspection certificate, when agreed to by the shipping and receiving State or Tribal animal health authorities; or

(iii) Tattoos and other identification methods acceptable to a breed association for registration purposes, accompanied by a breed registration certificate, when agreed to by the shipping and receiving State or/Tribal animal health authorities; or

(iv) Group/lot identification when a group/lot identification number (GIN) may be used.

(2) *Horses and other equine species.* Horses and other equine species that are required to be officially identified for interstate movement under this part must be identified by one of the following methods:

(i) A description sufficient to identify the individual equine including, but not limited to, name, age, breed, color, gender, distinctive markings, and unique and permanent forms of identification when present (e.g., brands, tattoos, scars, cowlicks, blemishes or biometric measurements). When the identity of the equine is in question at the receiving destination, the State or Tribal animal health official in the State or Tribe of destination or APHIS representative may determine if the description provided is sufficient; or

(ii) Electronic identification that complies with ISO 11784/11785; or

(iii) Non-ISO electronic identification injected to the equine on or before March 11, 2014; or

(iv) Digital photographs sufficient to identify the individual equine; or

(v) For equines being commercially transported to slaughter, a device or method authorized by 88 of this chapter.

(3) *Poultry.* Poultry that are required to be officially identified for interstate movement under this part must be identified by one of the following methods:

(i) Sealed and numbered leg bands in the manner referenced in the National Poultry Improvement Plan regulations (parts 145 through 147 of this chapter); or

(ii) Group/lot identification when a group/lot identification number (GIN) may be used.

(4) *Sheep and goats.* Sheep and goats that are required to be officially identified for interstate movement under this part must be identified by a device or method authorized by part 79 of this chapter.

(5) *Swine.* Swine that are required to be officially identified for interstate movement under this part must be identified by a device or method authorized by § 71.19 of this chapter.

(6) *Captive cervids.* Captive cervids that are required to be officially identified for interstate movement under this part must be identified by a device or method authorized by part 77 of this chapter.

(b) *Official identification requirements for interstate movement*—(1) *Cattle and bison.* (i) All cattle and bison listed in paragraphs (b)(1)(iii)(A) through (b)(1)(iii)(D) of this section must be officially identified prior to the interstate movement, using an official identification device or method listed in paragraph (a)(1) of this section unless:

(A) The cattle and bison are moved as a commuter herd with a copy of the commuter herd agreement or other documents as agreed to by the shipping and receiving States or Tribes. If any of the cattle or bison are shipped to a State or Tribe not included in the commuter herd agreement or other documentation, then these cattle or bison must be officially identified and documented to the original State of origin.

(B) The cattle and bison are moved directly from a location in one State through another State to a second location in the original State.

(C) The cattle and bison are moved interstate directly to an approved tagging site and are officially identified before commingling with cattle and bison from other premises or identified by the use of backtags or other methods that will ensure that the identity of the animal is accurately maintained until tagging so that the official eartag can be correlated to the person responsible for shipping the animal to the approved tagging site.

(D) The cattle and bison are moved between shipping and receiving States or Tribes with another form of identification, as agreed upon by animal health officials in the shipping and receiving States or Tribes.

(ii) Cattle and bison may also be moved interstate without official identification if they are moved directly to a recognized slaughtering establishment or directly to no more than one approved livestock facility and then directly to a recognized slaughtering establishment, where they are harvested within 3 days of arrival; and

(A) They are moved interstate with a USDA-approved backtag; or

(B) A USDA-approved backtag is applied to the cattle or bison at the recognized slaughtering establishment or federally approved livestock facility.

(C) If a determination to hold the cattle or bison for more than 3 days is made after the animals arrive at the slaughter establishment, the animals must be officially identified in accordance with § 86.4(d)(4)(ii).

(iii) Beginning on March 11, 2013, all cattle and bison listed below are subject to the official identification requirements of this section:

(A) All sexually intact cattle and bison 18 months of age or over;

(B) All female dairy cattle of any age and all dairy males born after March 11, 2013;

(C) Cattle and bison of any age used for rodeo or recreational events; and

(D) Cattle and bison of any age used for shows or exhibitions.

(2) *Sheep and goats.* Sheep and goats moved interstate must be officially identified prior to the interstate movement unless they are exempt from official identification requirements under 9 CFR part 79 or are officially identified after the interstate movement, as provided in 9 CFR part 79.

(3) *Swine.* Swine moving interstate must be officially identified in accordance with § 71.19 of this chapter.

(4) *Horses and other equines.* Horses and other equines moving interstate moved interstate must be officially identified prior to the interstate movement, using an official identification device or method listed in paragraph (a)(2) of this section unless:

(i) They are used as the mode of transportation (horseback, horse and buggy) for travel to another location and then return direct to the original location.

(ii) They are moved from the farm or stable for veterinary medical examination or treatment and returned to the same location without change in ownership.

(iii) They are moved directly from a location in one State through another State to a second location in the original State.

(iv) They are moved between shipping and receiving States or Tribes with another form of identification as agreed upon by animal health officials in the shipping and receiving States or Tribes.

(5) *Poultry.* Poultry moving interstate must be officially identified prior to interstate movement unless:

(i) The shipment of poultry is from a hatchery to a redistributor or poultry grower and the person responsible for receiving the shipment maintains a record of the supplier; or

(ii) The shipment is from a redistributor to a poultry grower and the person responsible for receiving the chicks maintains a record of the supplier of the chicks; or

(iii) The poultry are identified as agreed upon by the States or Tribes involved in the movement.

(6) *Captive cervids.* Captive cervids moving interstate must be officially identified prior to interstate movement in accordance with part 77 of this chapter.

(c) *Use of more than one official eartag.* Beginning on March 13, 2013, no more than one official eartag may be applied to an animal, except that:

(1) Another official eartag may be applied providing it bears the same official identification number as an existing one.

(2) In specific cases when the need to maintain the identity of an animal is intensified (e.g., such as for export shipments, quarantined herds, field trials, experiments, or disease surveys), a State or Tribal animal health official or an area veterinarian in charge may approve the application of an additional official eartag to an animal that already has one or more. The person applying the additional official eartag must record the following information about the event and maintain the record for 5 years: The date the additional official eartag is added; the reason for the additional official eartag device; and the official identification numbers of both the new official eartag and the one(s) already attached to the animal.

(3) An eartag with an animal identification number (AIN) beginning with the 840 prefix (either radio frequency identification or visual-only tag) may be applied to an animal that is already officially identified with one or more National Uniform Eartagging System tags and/or an official vaccination eartag used for brucellosis. The person applying the AIN eartag must record the date the AIN tag is added and the official identification numbers of both official eartags and must maintain those records for 5 years.

(4) A brucellosis vaccination eartag with a National Uniform Eartagging System number may be applied in accordance with part 78 of this chapter to an animal that is already officially identified with one or more official eartags under this part. The person applying the vaccination eartag must record the date the tag is added and the official identification numbers of both the existing official eartag(s) and the vaccination eartag and must maintain those records for 5 years.

(d) *Removal or loss of official identification devices.* (1) Official identification devices are intended to provide permanent identification of livestock and to ensure the ability to find the source of animal disease outbreaks. Removal of these devices, including devices applied to imported animals in their countries of origin and recognized by the Administrator as official, is prohibited except at the time of slaughter, at any other location upon the death of the animal, or as otherwise approved by the State or Tribal animal health official or an area veterinarian in charge when a device needs to be replaced.

(2) All man-made identification devices affixed to covered livestock unloaded at slaughter plants after moving interstate must be removed at the slaughter facility by slaughter-facility personnel with the devices correlated with the animal and its carcass through final inspection or condemnation by means approved by the Food Safety Inspection Service (FSIS). If diagnostic samples are taken, the identification devices must be packaged with the samples and be correlated with the carcasses through final inspection or condemnation by means approved by FSIS. Devices collected at slaughter must be made available to APHIS and FSIS by the slaughter plant.

(3) All official identification devices affixed to covered livestock carcasses moved interstate for rendering must be removed at the rendering facility and made available to APHIS.

(4) If an animal loses an official identification device and needs a new one: (i) A replacement tag with a different official identification number may be applied. The person applying a new official identification device with a different official identification number must record the following information about the event and maintain the record for 5 years: The date the new official identification device was added; the official identification number on the device; and the official identification number on the old device if known.

(ii) Replacement of a temporary identification device with a new official identification device is considered to be a retagging event, and all applicable information must be maintained in accordance with paragraph (d)(4)(i) of this section.

(iii) A duplicate replacement eartag with the official number of the lost tag may be applied in accordance with APHIS' protocol for the administration of such tags.

(e) *Replacement of official identification devices for reasons other than loss.* (1) Circumstances under which a State or Tribal animal health official or an area veterinarian in charge may authorize replacement of an official identification device include, but are not limited to:

(i) Deterioration of the device such that loss of the device appears likely or the number can no longer be read;

(ii) Infection at the site where the device is attached, necessitating application of a device at another location (e.g., a slightly different location of an eartag in the ear);

(iii) Malfunction of the electronic component of a radio frequency identification (RFID) device; or

(iv) Incompatibility or inoperability of the electronic component of an RFID device with the management system or unacceptable functionality of the management system due to use of an RFID device.

(2) Any time an official identification device is replaced, as authorized by the State or Tribal animal health official or area veterinarian in charge, the person replacing the device must record the following information about the event and maintain the record for 5 years:

(i) The date on which the device was removed;

(ii) Contact information for the location where the device was removed;

(iii) The official identification number (to the extent possible) on the device removed;

(iv) The type of device removed (e.g., metal eartag, RFID eartag);

(v) The reason for the removal of the device;

(vi) The new official identification number on the replacement device; and

(vii) The type of replacement device applied.

(f) *Sale or transfer of official identification devices.* Official identification devices are not to be sold or otherwise transferred from the premises to which they were originally issued to another premises without authorization by the Administrator or a State or Tribal animal health official.

§ 86.5 Documentation requirements for interstate movement of covered livestock.

(a) The persons responsible for animals leaving a premises for interstate movement must ensure that the animals are accompanied by an interstate certificate of veterinary inspection (ICVI) or other document required by this part for the interstate movement of animals.

(b)(1) The APHIS representative, State or Tribal representative, or accredited veterinarian issuing an ICVI or other document required for the interstate movement of animals under this part must forward a copy of the ICVI or other document to the State or Tribal animal health official of the State or Tribe of origin within 7 calendar days from the date on which the ICVI or other document is issued. The State or Tribal animal health official in the State or Tribe of origin must forward a copy of the ICVI or other document to the State or Tribal animal health official the State or Tribe of destination within 7 calendar days from date on which the ICVI or other document is received.

(2) The animal health official or accredited veterinarian issuing or receiving an ICVI or other interstate movement document in accordance with paragraph (b)(1) of this section must keep a copy of the ICVI or alternate documentation. For poultry and swine, such documents must be kept for at least 2 years, and for cattle and bison, sheep and goats, cervids, and equines, 5 years.

(c) *Cattle and bison.* Cattle and bison moved interstate must be accompanied by an ICVI unless:

(1) They are moved directly to a recognized slaughtering establishment, or directly to an approved livestock facility and then directly to a recognized slaughtering establishment, and they are accompanied by an owner-shipper statement.

(2) They are moved directly to an approved livestock facility with an owner-shipper statement and do not move interstate from the facility unless accompanied by an ICVI.

(3) They are moved from the farm of origin for veterinary medical examination or treatment and returned to the

farm of origin without change in ownership.

(4) They are moved directly from one State through another State and back to the original State.

(5) They are moved as a commuter herd with a copy of the commuter herd agreement or other document as agreed to by the States or Tribes involved in the movement.

(6) Additionally, cattle and bison may be moved between shipping and receiving States or Tribes with documentation other than an ICVI, e.g., a brand inspection certificate, as agreed upon by animal health officials in the shipping and receiving States or Tribes.

(7) The official identification number of cattle or bison must be recorded on the ICVI or alternate documentation unless:

(i) The cattle or bison are moved from an approved livestock facility directly to a recognized slaughtering establishment; or

(ii) The cattle and bison are sexually intact cattle or bison under 18 months of age or steers or spayed heifers; *Except that:* This exception does not apply to sexually intact dairy cattle of any age or to cattle or bison used for rodeo, exhibition, or recreational purposes.

(d) *Sheep and goats.* Sheep and goats moved interstate must be accompanied by documentation as required by part 79 of this chapter.

(e) *Swine.* Swine moved interstate must be accompanied by documentation in accordance with § 71.19 of this chapter or, if applicable, with part 85.

(f) *Horses and other equines.* Horses and other equines moved interstate must be accompanied by an ICVI unless:

(1) They are used as the mode of transportation (horseback, horse and buggy) for travel to another location and then return direct to the original location.

(2) They are moved from the farm or stable for veterinary medical examination or treatment and returned to the same location without change in ownership.

(3) They are moved directly from a location in one State through another State to a second location in the original State.

(4) Additionally, equines may be moved between shipping and receiving States or Tribes with documentation other than an ICVI, e.g., an equine infectious anemia test chart, as agreed to by the shipping and receiving States or Tribes involved in the movement.

(5) Equines moving commercially to slaughter must be accompanied by documentation in accordance with part 88 of this chapter. Equine infectious anemia reactors moving interstate must be accompanied by documentation as required by part 75 of this chapter.

(g) *Poultry.* Poultry moved interstate must be accompanied by an ICVI unless:

(1) They are from a flock participating in the National Poultry Improvement Plan (NPIP) and are accompanied by the documentation required under the NPIP regulations (parts 145 through 147 of this chapter) for participation in that program; or

(2) They are moved directly to a recognized slaughtering or rendering establishment; or

(3) They are moved from the farm of origin for veterinary medical examination, treatment, or diagnostic purposes and either returned to the farm of origin without change in ownership or euthanized and disposed of at the veterinary facility; or

(4) They are moved directly from one State through another State and back to the original State; or

(5) They are moved between shipping and receiving States or Tribes with a VS Form 9–3 or documentation other than an ICVI, as agreed upon by animal health officials in the shipping and receiving States or Tribes.

(6) They are moved under permit in accordance with part 82 of this chapter.

(h) *Captive cervids.* Captive cervids moved interstate must be accompanied by documentation as required by part 77 of this chapter.

§§ 86.6–86.7 [Reserved]

§ 86.8 Preemption.

State, Tribal, and local laws and regulations may not specify an official identification device or method that would have to be used if multiple devices or methods may be used under this part for a particular species, nor may the State or Tribe of destination impose requirements that would otherwise cause the State or Tribe from which the shipments originate to have to develop a particular kind of traceability system or change its existing system in order to meet the requirements of the State or Tribe of destination.

PART 88—COMMERCIAL TRANSPORTATION OF EQUINES FOR SLAUGHTER

Sec.

AUTHORITY: 7 U.S.C. 1901, 7 CFR 2.22, 2.80, 371.4.

SOURCE: 66 FR 63615, Dec. 7, 2001, unless otherwise noted.

§88.1 Definitions.

The following definitions apply to this part:

APHIS. The Animal and Plant Health Inspection Service of the U.S. Department of Agriculture.

Assembly point. Any facility, including auction markets, ranches, feedlots, and stockyards, in which equines are gathered in commerce.

Commercial transportation. Movement for profit via conveyance on any highway or public road.

Conveyance. Trucks, tractors, trailers, or semitrailers, or any combination of these, propelled or drawn by mechanical power.

Equine. Any member of the *Equidae* family, which includes horses, asses, mules, ponies, and zebras.

Equine for slaughter. Any member of the Equidae family being transferred to a slaughter facility, including an assembly point, feedlot, or stockyard.

Euthanasia. The humane destruction of an animal by the use of an anesthetic agent or other means that causes painless loss of consciousness and subsequent death.

Feedlot. Any facility which consolidates livestock for preconditioning, feeding, fattening, or holding before being sent to slaughter.

Owner/shipper. Any individual, partnership, corporation, or cooperative association that engages in the commercial transportation of more than 20 equines per year to slaughtering facilities, except any individual or other entity who transports equines to slaughtering facilities incidental to his or her principal activity of production agriculture (production of food or fiber).

Owner-shipper certificate. VS Form 10–13,[1] which requires the information specified by §88.4(a)(3) of this part.

Secretary. The Secretary of Agriculture.

Slaughtering facility. A commercial establishment that slaughters equines for any purpose.

Stallion. Any uncastrated male equine that is 1 year of age or older.

Stockyard. Any place, establishment, or facility commonly known as stockyards, conducted, operated, or managed for profit or nonprofit as a public market for livestock producers, feeders, market agencies, and buyers, consisting of pens, or other enclosures, and their appurtenances, in which live cattle, sheep, swine, horses, mules, or goats are received, held, or kept for sale or shipment in commerce.

USDA. The U.S. Department of Agriculture.

USDA backtag. A backtag issued by APHIS that conforms to the eight-character alpha-numeric National Backtagging System and that provides unique identification for each animal.

USDA representative. Any employee of the USDA who is authorized by the Deputy Administrator for Veterinary Services of APHIS, USDA, to enforce this part.

[66 FR 63615, Dec. 7, 2001, as amended at 76 FR 55216, Sept. 7, 2011]

§88.2 General information.

(a) State governments may enact and enforce regulations that are consistent with or that are more stringent than the regulations in this part.

[1] Forms may be obtained from the National Animal Health Programs Staff, Veterinary Services, APHIS, 4700 River Road Unit 43, Riverdale, MD 20737–1231.

(b) To determine whether an individual or other entity found to transport equines for slaughter is subject to the regulations in this part, a USDA representative may request from any individual or other entity who transported the equines information regarding the business of that individual or other entity. When such information is requested, the individual or other entity who transported the equines must provide the information within 30 days and in a format as may be specified by the USDA representative.

[66 FR 63615, Dec. 7, 2001, as amended at 76 FR 55216, Sept. 7, 2011]

§ 88.3 Standards for conveyances.

(a) The animal cargo space of conveyances used for the commercial transportation of equines for slaughter must:

(1) Be designed, constructed, and maintained in a manner that at all times protects the health and well-being of the equines being transported (e.g., provides adequate ventilation, contains no sharp protrusions, etc.);

(2) Include means of completely segregating each stallion and each aggressive equine on the conveyance so that no stallion or aggressive equine can come into contact with any of the other equines on the conveyance;

(3) Have sufficient interior height to allow each equine on the conveyance to stand with its head extended to the fullest normal postural height; and

(4) Be equipped with doors and ramps of sufficient size and location to provide for safe loading and unloading.

(b) Equines for slaughter must not be transported in any conveyance that has the animal cargo space divided into two or more stacked levels, except that conveyances lacking the capability to convert from two or more stacked levels to one level may be used until December 7, 2006. Conveyances with collapsible floors (also known as "floating decks") must be configured to transport equines on one level only.

[66 FR 63615, Dec. 7, 2001, as amended at 76 FR 55216, Sept. 7, 2011]

§ 88.4 Requirements for transport.

(a) Prior to the commercial transportation of equines for slaughter, the owner/shipper must:

(1) For a period of not less than 6 consecutive hours immediately prior to the equines being loaded on the conveyance, provide each equine appropriate food (*i.e.*, hay, grass, or other food that would allow an equine in transit to maintain well-being), potable water, and the opportunity to rest;

(2) Apply a USDA backtag[2] to each equine in the shipment;

(3) Complete and sign an owner-shipper certificate for each equine being transported. The owner-shipper certificate for each equine must accompany the equine throughout transit to slaughter and must include the following information, which must be typed or legibly completed in ink:

(i) The owner/shipper's name, address, and telephone number;

(ii) The receiver's (destination) name, address, and telephone number;

(iii) The name of the auction/market, if applicable;

(iv) A description of the conveyance, including the license plate number;

(v) A description of the equine's physical characteristics, including such information as sex, breed, coloring, distinguishing markings, permanent brands, tattoos, and electronic devices that could be used to identify the equine;

(vi) The number of the USDA backtag applied to the equine in accordance with paragraph (a)(2) of this section;

(vii) A statement of fitness to travel at the time of loading, which will indicate that the equine is able to bear weight on all four limbs, able to walk unassisted, not blind in both eyes, older than 6 months of age, and not likely to give birth during the trip;

[2] USDA backtags are available at recognized slaughtering establishments and specifically approved stockyards and from State representatives and APHIS representatives. A list of recognized slaughtering establishments and specifically approved stockyards may be obtained as indicated in § 78.1 of this chapter. The terms "State representative" and "APHIS representative" are defined in § 78.1 of this chapter.

(viii) A description of any preexisting injuries or other unusual condition of the equine, such as a wound or blindness in one eye, that may cause the equine to have special handling needs;

(ix) The date, time, and place the equine was loaded on the conveyance; and

(x) A statement that the equine was provided access to food, water, and rest prior to transport in accordance with paragraph (a)(1) of this section; and

(4) Load the equines on the conveyance so that:

(i) Each equine has enough floor space to ensure that no equine is crowded in a way likely to cause injury or discomfort; and

(ii) Each stallion and any aggressive equines are completely segregated so that no stallion or aggressive equine can come into contact with any other equine on the conveyance.

(b) During commercial transportation of equines for slaughter, the owner/shipper must:

(1) Drive in a manner to avoid causing injury to the equines;

(2) Observe the equines as frequently as circumstances allow, but not less than once every 6 hours, to check the physical condition of the equines and ensure that all requirements of this part are being followed. The owner/shipper must obtain veterinary assistance as soon as possible from an equine veterinarian for any equines in obvious physical distress. Equines that become nonambulatory en route must be euthanized by an equine veterinarian. If an equine dies en route, the owner/shipper must contact the nearest APHIS office as soon as possible and allow an APHIS veterinarian to examine the equine. If an APHIS veterinarian is not available, the owner/shipper must contact an equine veterinarian;

(3) Offload from the conveyance any equine that has been on the conveyance for 28 consecutive hours and provide the equine appropriate food, potable water, and the opportunity to rest for at least 6 consecutive hours; and

(4) If offloading is required en route to the slaughtering facility, the owner/shipper must prepare another owner-shipper certificate as required by paragraph (a)(2) of this section and record the date, time, and location where the offloading occurred. In this situation, both owner-shipper certificates would need to accompany the equines for slaughter.

(c) Handling of all equines for slaughter shall be done as expeditiously and carefully as possible in a manner that does not cause unnecessary discomfort, stress, physical harm, or trauma. Electric prods may not be used on equines for slaughter for any purpose, including loading or offloading on the conveyance, except when human safety is threatened.

(d) At any point during the commercial transportation of equines for slaughter, a USDA representative may examine the equines, inspect the conveyance, or review the owner-shipper certificates required by paragraph (a)(3) of this section.

(e) At any time during the commercial transportation of equines for slaughter, a USDA representative may direct the owner/shipper to take appropriate actions to alleviate the suffering of any equine. If deemed necessary by the USDA representative, such actions could include securing the services of an equine veterinarian to treat an equine, including performing euthanasia if necessary.

(f) The individual or other entity who signs the owner-shipper certificate must maintain a copy of the owner-shipper certificate for 1 year following the date of signature.

(Approved by the Office of Management and Budget under control numbers 0579–0160 and 0579–0332)

[66 FR 63615, Dec. 7, 2001, as amended at 76 FR 55216, Sept. 7, 2011]

§ 88.5 Requirements at a slaughtering facility.

(a) Upon arrival at a slaughtering facility, the owner/shipper must:

(1) Ensure that each equine has access to appropriate food and potable water after being offloaded;

(2) Present the owner-shipper certificates to a USDA representative;

(3) Allow a USDA representative access to the equines for the purpose of examination; and

(4) Allow a USDA representative access to the animal cargo area of the

conveyance for the purpose of inspection.

(b) If the owner/shipper arrives during normal business hours, the owner/shipper must not leave the premises of a slaughtering facility until the equines have been examined by a USDA representative. However, if the owner/shipper arrives outside of normal business hours, the owner/shipper may leave the premises but must return to the premises of the slaughtering facility to meet the USDA representative upon his or her arrival.

(c) Any owner/shipper transporting equines to slaughtering facilities outside of the United States must present the owner-shipper certificates to USDA representatives at the border.

§ 88.6 Violations and penalties.

(a) The Secretary is authorized to assess civil penalties of up to $5,000 per violation of any of the regulations in this part.

(b) Each equine transported in violation of the regulations of this part will be considered a separate violation.

(Approved by the Office of Management and Budget under control number 0579–0160)

PART 89—STATEMENT OF POLICY UNDER THE TWENTY-EIGHT HOUR LAW

AUTHORITY: 49 U.S.C. 80502; 7 CFR 2.22, 2.80, and 371.4.

SOURCE: 28 FR 5967, June 13, 1963, unless otherwise noted.

§ 89.1 Amount of feed.

(a) Under normal conditions, the amount of feed designated in the following schedule will be considered as sustaining rations for livestock in transit when fed at the intervals required by the Twenty-Eight Hour Law:

Species and quantity of livestock	At first feeding station	At second and subsequent feeding stations
Cattle and beef type or range calves (for each car [1])	200 lbs. of hay [1,2]	300 lbs. of hay. [1,2]
Dairy calves (for each car deck [1])	100 lbs. of hay [1,2]	150 lbs. of hay. [1,2]
Horses and mules (for each car [1])	400 lbs. of hay [1,2]	400 lbs. of hay. [1,2]
Sheep and goats (for each car deck [1])	200 lbs. of hay [1,2]	300 lbs. of hay. [1,2]
Lambs and kids (for each car deck [1])	100 lbs. of hay [1,2]	150 lbs. of hay. [1,2]
Swine (for each carload lot, in single or double deck car, the amount of shelled corn [2] indicated):		
Lots of not more than 18,000 lbs	2 bushels	2 bushels.
More than 18,000 lbs. but not more than 21,000 lbs	2½ bushels	2½ bushels.
More than 21,000 lbs. but not more than 24,000 lbs	3 bushels	3 bushels.
More than 24,000 lbs. but not more than 27,000 lbs	3½ bushels	3½ bushels.
More than 27,000 lbs. but not more than 30,000 lbs	4 bushels	4 bushels.
More than 30,000 lbs.—proportionately larger amounts.		

[1] The requirements set forth the sustaining rations for a full load of livestock in a railroad car 40 feet in length. The requirements for a full load of livestock in railroad cars of different sizes should be modified proportionately, *i.e.*, a load of livestock transported in a car 50 feet in length would require an additional 25 percent of feed or 2.5 percent for each additional foot of car over 40 feet.

[2] Or the equivalent in other suitable feed. Dairy calves too young to eat hay or grain, or shipped without their dams, should be given a sufficient amount of prepared calf feed, milk, raw eggs, or other suitable feed. All feed should be of good quality.

(b) When the owner of a consignment of livestock desires that they be fed larger amounts of feed than those designated in paragraph (a) of this section for the particular kind and quantity of livestock, or the carrier believes that they should be fed larger amounts, the amounts to be fed should be agreed upon, if practicable, by the owner and the carrier at the time the animals are offered for shipment.

(c) When emergency conditions arise, such as severe changes in the weather, which increase the rigors of transportation, the livestock should receive amounts of feed, additional to those designated in paragraph (a) of this section, sufficient to sustain them until they arrive at the next feeding station or destination.

(d) When the movement of livestock is delayed en route so that the period of their confinement in the cars materially exceeds that specified by the Twenty-Eight Hour Law, the livestock should receive additional feed in proportion to such excess time.

§89.2 Two or more feedings at same station.

When livestock are held at a feeding station 12 hours after the last previous feed has been substantially consumed, they should again be fed the ration prescribed by §89.1(a) for that station: *Provided, however,* That they may be held without such feeding for a period longer than 12 hours if the time they are so held, added to the time required to reach the next feeding station or destination, whichever is closer, would not ordinarily exceed 40 hours.

§89.3 Feeding, watering, and resting livestock in the car.

(a) Livestock should be unloaded into pens of the character described in §89.5(a) for feeding, watering, and resting, unless there is ample room in the car for all of the animals to lie down at the same time.

(b) If livestock are watered in the car, adequate facilities should be provided and ample water furnished to insure all the animals an opportunity to drink their fill. In the case of hogs, water should be available for not less than 1 hour.

(c) Livestock unloaded for feed and water and returned to the car for rest should be allowed to remain in the pens not less than 2 hours.

(d) Livestock unloaded for water and returned to the car for feed and rest should be allowed to remain in the pens not less than 1 hour.

(e) When livestock are fed in the car, the feed should be evenly distributed throughout the car.

§89.4 Watering.

Livestock should be furnished an ample supply of potable water. Water treated with chemicals for industrial or boiler use, or taken from streams or ponds containing sewage, mud, or other objectionable matter should not be used. Troughs and other receptacles should be clean. In cold weather, the water should be free from ice.

§89.5 Feeding pens.

(a) Stock pens and other enclosures for feeding, watering, and resting livestock in transit should have (1) sufficient space for all of the livestock to lie down at the same time, (2) properly designed facilities for feeding and watering the livestock, (3) reasonably well-drained, clean, and safe floors of concrete, cinders, gravel, hard-packed earth, or other suitable material, and (4) suitable protection from weather reasonably to be expected in the region in which the pens are located.

(b) Care should be taken to protect livestock unloaded en route at a point having marked difference in temperature from that at the point from which they were shipped.

SUBCHAPTER D—EXPORTATION AND IMPORTATION OF ANIMALS (INCLUDING POULTRY) AND ANIMAL PRODUCTS

PART 91—EXPORTATION OF LIVE ANIMALS, HATCHING EGGS OR OTHER EMBRYONATED EGGS, ANIMAL SEMEN, ANIMAL EMBRYOS, AND GAMETES FROM THE UNITED STATES

AUTHORITY: 7 U.S.C. 8301–8317; 19 U.S.C. 1644a(c); 21 U.S.C. 136, 136a, and 618; 46 U.S.C. 3901 and 3902; 7 CFR 2.22, 2.80, and 371.4.

SOURCE: 81 FR 2980, Jan. 20, 2016, unless otherwise noted.

Subpart A—General Provisions

§ 91.1 Definitions.

As used in this part, the following terms will have the meanings set forth in this section:

Accredited veterinarian. A veterinarian approved by the Administrator in accordance with part 161 of this chapter to perform functions specified in parts 1, 2, 3, and 11 of subchapter A, and subchapters B, C, and D of this chapter, and to perform functions required by cooperative State-Federal disease control and eradication programs.

Administrator. The Administrator, Animal and Plant Health Inspection Service, or any person authorized to act for the Administrator.

Animal. Any member of the animal kingdom (except a human).

Animal and Plant Health Inspection Service (APHIS). The Animal and Plant Health Inspection Service of the United States Department of Agriculture.

APHIS representative. An individual who is authorized by APHIS to perform the function involved.

Date of export. The date animals intended for export are loaded onto an ocean vessel or aircraft or, if moved by land to Canada or Mexico, the date the animals cross the border.

Export health certificate. An official document issued in the United States that certifies that animals or other commodities listed on the certificate meet the export requirements of this part and the importing country.

Export inspection facility. A facility that is affiliated with a port of embarkation and that has been approved by the Administrator as the location where APHIS will conduct health inspections of livestock before they are loaded onto ocean vessels or aircraft for export from the United States.

Export isolation facility. A facility where animals intended for export are isolated from other animals for a period of time immediately before being moved for export.

Horses. Horses, mules, and asses.

Inspector. An individual authorized by APHIS to inspect animals and/or animal products intended for export from the United States.

Livestock. Horses, cattle (including American bison), captive cervids, sheep, swine, and goats, regardless of intended use.

Premises of export. The premises where the animals intended for export are isolated as required by the importing country prior to export or, if the importing country does not require pre-export isolation, the farm or other premises where the animals are assembled for pre-export inspection and/or testing, or the germplasm is collected or stored, before being moved to a port of embarkation or land border port.

Program diseases. Diseases for which there are cooperative State-Federal programs and domestic regulations in subchapter C of this chapter.

Program Handbook. A document that contains guidance and other information related to the regulations in this part. The Program Handbook is available on APHIS' import-export Web site (*http://www.aphis.usda.gov/import_export/index.shtml*).

State of origin. The State in which the premises of export is located.

§ 91.2 Applicability.

You may not export any animal or animal germplasm from the United States except in compliance with this part.

§ 91.3 General requirements.

(a) *Issuance of export health certificates.* (1) Livestock must have an endorsed export health certificate in order to be eligible for export from the United States.

(2) If APHIS knows that an importing country requires an export health certificate endorsed by the competent veterinary authority of the United States for any animal other than livestock or for any animal semen, animal embryos, hatching eggs, other embryonated eggs, or gametes intended for export to that country, the animal or other commodity must have an export health certificate endorsed by APHIS in order to be eligible for export from the United States.

(b) *Content of export health certificates*—(1) *Livestock; minimum requirements.* Regardless of the requirements of the importing country, at a minimum, the following information must be contained on an export health certificate for livestock:

(i) The species of each animal.

(ii) The breed of each animal.

(iii) The sex of each animal.

(iv) The age of each animal.

(v) The individual identification of the animals as required by § 91.5.

(vi) The importing country.

(vii) The consignor.

(viii) The consignee.

(ix) A certification that an accredited veterinarian inspected the livestock and found them to be fit for export.

(x) A signature and date by an accredited veterinarian.

(xi) An endorsement by the APHIS veterinarian responsible for the State of origin.

(2) *Livestock; additional requirements.* In addition to the minimum requirements in paragraph (b)(1) of this section, the export health certificate must meet any other information or issuance requirements specified by the importing country.

(3) *Animals other than livestock, animal semen, animal embryos, hatching eggs, other embryonated eggs, and gametes.* Export health certificates for animals other than livestock, animal semen, animal embryos, hatching eggs, other embryonated eggs, and gametes must meet any information requirements specified by the importing country.

(c) *Inspection requirements for livestock.* In order to be eligible for export, livestock must be inspected within the timeframe required by the importing country. If the importing country does not specify a timeframe, the livestock must be inspected within 30 days prior to the date of export.

(d) *Testing requirements for livestock.* All samples for tests of livestock that are required by the importing country must be taken by an APHIS representative or accredited veterinarian. The samples must be taken and tests made within the timeframe allowed by the importing country and, if specified, at the location required by the importing country. If the importing country does not specify a timeframe, the samples must be taken and tests made within 30 days prior to the date of export, except that tuberculin tests may be conducted within 90 days prior to the date of export. All tests for program diseases must be made in laboratories and using methods approved by the Administrator for those diseases. The Program Handbook contains a link to an APHIS Web site that lists laboratories approved to conduct tests for specific diseases. Approved methods are those specified or otherwise incorporated within the domestic regulations in subchapter C of this chapter.

(e) *Movement of livestock, animals other than livestock, animal semen, animal embryos, hatching eggs, other embryonated eggs, or gametes with an export health certificate*—(1) *Livestock.* An export health certificate for livestock must be issued and endorsed before the livestock move from the premises of export.

(2) *Animals other than livestock, animal semen, animal embryos, hatching eggs, other embryonated eggs, and gametes.* When an export health certificate is required by the importing country for any animal other than livestock or for animal semen, animal embryos, hatching eggs, other embryonated eggs, or gametes, it must be issued and, if required by the importing country, endorsed by an APHIS representative prior to departure of the animal or other commodity from the port of embarkation or the crossing of the land border port. When presented for endorsement, the health certificate must be accompanied by reports for all laboratory tests specifically identified on the certificate. The laboratory reports must either be the originals prepared by the laboratory that performed the tests or must be annotated by the laboratory that performed the test to indicate how the reports may be verified.

(f) *Validity of export health certificate*—(1) *Livestock.* Unless specified by the importing country, the export health certificate is valid for 30 days from the date of issuance, provided that the inspection and test results under paragraphs (c) and (d) of this section are still valid.

(2) *Animals other than livestock, animal semen, animal embryos, hatching eggs, other embryonated eggs, and gametes.* Unless specified by the importing country, the export health certificate is valid for 30 days from the date of issuance.

(Approved by the Office of Management and Budget under control number 0579–0432)

[81 FR 2980, Jan. 20, 2016, as amended at 81 FR 74279, Oct. 26, 2016]

§ 91.4 Prohibited exports.

No animal, animal semen, animal embryos, hatching eggs, other embryonated eggs, or gametes under Federal, State, or local government quarantine or movement restrictions for animal health reasons may be exported from the United States unless the importing country issues an import permit or other written instruction allowing entry of the animal, animal semen, animal embryos, hatching eggs, other embryonated eggs, or gametes, and APHIS concurs with the export of the animal, animal semen, animal embryos, hatching eggs, other embryonated eggs, or gametes.

Subpart B—Livestock

§ 91.5 Identification of livestock intended for export.

Livestock that are intended for export must be identified in a manner that allows individual animals to be correlated to the animals listed in the export health certificate. If the importing country requires a specific or an additional form of identification, the livestock must also bear that form of identification.

(Approved by the Office of Management and Budget under control number 0579–0432)

§ 91.6 Cleaning and disinfection of means of conveyance, containers, and facilities used during movement; approved disinfectants.

(a) All export health certificates for livestock must be accompanied by a statement issued by an APHIS representative and/or accredited veterinarian that the means of conveyance or container in which the livestock will be transported from the premises of export has been cleaned and disinfected prior to loading the livestock with a disinfectant approved by the Administrator for purposes of this section or by a statement that the means of conveyance or container was not previously used to transport animals.

(b) Livestock moved for export may be unloaded only into a facility which has been cleaned and disinfected prior to such unloading with a disinfectant approved by the Administrator for purposes of this section, and has subsequently been inspected by an APHIS representative or accredited veterinarian. A statement certifying to such action must be attached to the export health certificate by the APHIS representative or accredited veterinarian.

(c) *Approved disinfectants.* The Administrator will approve a disinfectant for purposes of this section upon determining that the disinfectant is effective against pathogens that may be spread by the animals intended for export and, if the disinfectant is a chemical disinfectant, that it is registered or exempted for the specified use by the U.S. Environmental Protection Agency. The Program Handbook provides access to a list of disinfectants approved by the Administrator for use as required by this section. Other disinfectants may also be approved by the Administrator in accordance with this paragraph. The Administrator will withdraw approval of a disinfectant, and remove it from the list of approved disinfectants, if the disinfectant no longer meets the conditions for approval in this section.

(Approved by the Office of Management and Budget under control number 0579–0432)

§91.7 Pre-export inspection.

(a) All livestock intended for export by air or sea must receive a visual health inspection from an APHIS veterinarian within 48 hours prior to embarkation, unless the importing country specifies otherwise. The purpose of the inspection is to determine whether the livestock are sound, healthy, and fit to travel. The APHIS veterinarian will reject for export any livestock that he or she finds unfit to travel. The owner of the animals or the owner's agent must make arrangements for any livestock found unfit to travel. Livestock that are unfit to travel include, but are not limited to:

(1) Livestock that are sick, injured, weak, disabled, or fatigued;

(2) Livestock that are unable to stand unaided or bear weight on each leg;

(3) Livestock that are blind in both eyes;

(4) Livestock that cannot be moved without causing additional suffering;

(5) Newborn livestock with an unhealed navel;

(6) Livestock that have given birth within the previous 48 hours and are traveling without their offspring;

(7) Pregnant livestock that would be in the final 10 percent of their gestation period at the planned time of unloading in the importing country; and

(8) Livestock with unhealed wounds from recent surgical procedures, such as dehorning.

(b) The APHIS veterinarian must conduct the inspection at the export inspection facility associated with the port of embarkation of the livestock; at an export isolation facility, when authorized by the Administrator in accordance with paragraph (c) of this section; or at an export inspection facility other than the facility associated with the port of embarkation, when authorized by the Administrator in accordance with paragraph (d) of this section. Unless APHIS has authorized otherwise, any sorting, grouping, identification, or other handling of the livestock by the exporter must be done before this inspection. The APHIS veterinarian may also conduct clinical examination, including testing, of any livestock during or after this inspection if he or she deems it necessary in order to determine the animal's health. Any treatment related to this clinical examination performed on the animal must be performed by a licensed veterinarian. Finally, if the facility used to conduct the inspection is a facility other than the export inspection facility associated with the port of embarkation, it must be located within 28 hours driving distance under normal driving conditions from the port of embarkation; livestock must be afforded at least 48 hours rest, with sufficient feed and water during that time period, prior to the pre-export inspection; and the exporter must maintain contact information for a veterinarian licensed in the State of embarkation to perform emergency medical services, as needed, on the animals intended for export.

(c) *Conditions for approval of pre-export inspection at an export isolation facility.* (1) The Administrator may allow pre-export inspection of livestock to be conducted at an export isolation facility, rather than at an export inspection facility, when the exporter can show to the satisfaction of the Administrator that the livestock would suffer undue hardship if they had to be inspected at the export inspection facility, when the distance from the export isolation facility to the port of embarkation is significantly less than the distance from the export isolation facility to the export inspection facility associated with the port of embarkation, when inspection at the export isolation facility would be a more efficient use of APHIS resources, or for other reasons acceptable to the Administrator.

(2) The Administrator's approval is contingent upon APHIS having personnel available to provide services at that location. Approval is also contingent upon the Administrator determining that the facility has space, lighting, and humane means of handling livestock sufficient for the APHIS personnel to safely conduct required inspections. The Program Handbook contains guidance on ways to meet these requirements. Owners and operators may submit alternative plans for meeting the requirements to APHIS for evaluation and approval. Alternatives must be at least as effective in meeting the requirements as those described in the Program Handbook in order to be approved. Alternate plans must be approved by APHIS before the facility may be used for purposes of this section.

(d) The Administrator may allow pre-export inspection of livestock to be conducted at an export inspection facility other than the export inspection facility associated with the port of embarkation when the exporter can show to the satisfaction of the Administrator that the livestock would suffer undue hardship if they had to be inspected at the export inspection facility associated with the port of embarkation, when inspection at this different export inspection facility would be a more efficient use of APHIS resources, or for other reasons acceptable to the Administrator.

(e) The APHIS veterinarian will maintain an inspection record that includes the date and place of the pre-export inspection, species and number of animals inspected, the number of animals rejected, a description of those animals, and the reasons for rejection.

(f) If requested by the importing country or an exporter, the APHIS veterinarian who inspects the livestock will issue a certificate of inspection for livestock he or she finds to be sound, healthy, and fit to travel.

§91.8 Rest, feed, and water at an export inspection facility associated with the port of embarkation prior to export.

All livestock that are intended for export by air or sea and that will be inspected for export at an export inspection facility associated with the port of embarkation must be allowed a period of at least 2 hours rest at an export inspection facility prior to being loaded onto an ocean vessel or aircraft for export. Adequate food and water must be available to the livestock during the rest period. An inspector may extend the required rest period up to 5 hours, at his or her discretion and based on a determination that more rest is needed in order to have assurances that the animals are fit to travel prior to loading. Pre-export inspection of the animals must take place at the conclusion of this rest period.

§91.9 Ports.

(a) Except as provided in paragraph (b) of this section, livestock exported by air or sea may be exported only through ports designated as ports of embarkation by the Administrator. Any port that has an export inspection facility that meets the requirements of §91.10 permanently associated with it is designated as a port of embarkation. The Program Handbook contains a list of designated ports of embarkation. A list may also be obtained from a Veterinary Services area office. Information on area offices is available on APHIS' import-export Web site (*http://www.aphis.usda.gov/import_export/index.shtml*).

(b) The Administrator may approve other ports for the exportation of livestock on a temporary basis with the concurrence of the port director. The Administrator will grant such temporary approvals only for a specific shipment of livestock, and only if pre-export inspection of that shipment has occurred at an export isolation facility or an export inspection facility not associated with the port of embarkation, as provided in §91.7.

(c) Temporarily approved ports of embarkation will not be added to the list of designated ports of embarkation and are only approved for the time period and shipment conditions specified by APHIS at the time of approval.

(Approved by the Office of Management and Budget under control number 0579–0432)

§91.10 Export inspection facilities.

(a) Export inspection facilities must be approved by the Administrator before they may be used for any livestock intended for export. The Administrator will approve an export inspection facility upon determining that it meets the requirements in paragraph (b) of this section. This approval remains in effect unless it is revoked in accordance with paragraph (c) of this section, or unless any of the following occur, in which case reapproval must be sought:

(1) The owner of the facility changes.

(2) Significant damage to the facility occurs or significant structural changes are made to the facility.

(b)(1) Export inspection facilities must be constructed, equipped, and managed in a manner that prevents transmission of disease to and from livestock in the facilities, provides for the safe and humane handling and restraint of livestock, and provides sufficient offices, space, and lighting for APHIS veterinarians to safely conduct required health inspections of livestock and related business. The Program Handbook contains guidance on ways to meet these requirements. Owners and operators may submit alternative plans for meeting the requirements to APHIS for evaluation and approval; the address to which to submit such alternatives is contained in the Program Handbook. Alternatives must be at least as effective in meeting the requirements as the methods described in the Program Handbook in order to be approved. Alternatives must be approved by APHIS before being used for purposes of this section.

(2) For the purposes of approval or a subsequent audit, APHIS representatives must have access to all areas of the facility during the facility's business hours to evaluate compliance with the requirements of this section.

(3) The application for approval of an export inspection facility must be accompanied by a certification from the authorities having jurisdiction over environmental affairs in the locality of the facility. The certification must state that the facility complies with any applicable requirements of the State and local governments, and the U.S. Environmental Protection Agency regarding disposal of animal wastes.

(c) The Administrator will deny or revoke approval of an export inspection facility for failure to meet the requirements in paragraph (b) of this section.

(1) APHIS will conduct site inspections of approved export inspection facilities at least once a year for continued compliance with the standards. If a facility fails to pass the inspection, the Administrator may revoke its approval. If the Administrator revokes approval for a facility that serves a designated port of embarkation, the Administrator may also remove that port from the list of designated ports of embarkation.

(2) APHIS will provide written notice of any proposed denial or revocation to the operator of the facility, who will be given an opportunity to present his or her views on the issues before a final decision is made. The notice will list any deficiencies in detail. APHIS will provide notice of pending revocations at least 60 days before the revocation is scheduled to take effect, but may suspend facility operations before that date and before any consideration of objections by the facility operator if the Administrator determines the suspension is necessary to protect animal health or public health, interest, or safety. The operator of any facility whose approval is denied or revoked may request another inspection after remedying the deficiencies.

§91.11 Export isolation.

If an importing country requires export isolation for livestock, such isolation must occur before the animals may be moved to a port of embarkation, and both the manner in which this isolation occurs and the facility at which it occurs must meet the requirements specified by the importing country.

§91.12 Ocean vessels.

(a) *Inspection of the ocean vessel*—(1) *Certification to carry livestock.* Ocean vessels must be certified by APHIS prior to initial use to transport any livestock from the United States. The owner or the operator of the ocean vessel must make arrangements prior to the vessel's arrival at a designated port of embarkation in the United States for an APHIS representative to inspect the vessel while it is at that port of embarkation. Alternatively, at the discretion of the Administrator and upon request of the exporter, transporting company, or their agent, the inspection may be done at a foreign port. If APHIS determines that the ocean vessel meets the requirements of paragraph (d) of this section, APHIS will certify the vessel to transport livestock from the United States. APHIS may certify a vessel that does not meet all of the requirements in paragraph (d), provided that an exemption from the requirements the vessel does not meet has been granted to the vessel pursuant to paragraph (e) of this section. The certification will specify the species of livestock for which the vessel is approved. The certification will be valid for up to 3 years; however, the ocean vessel must be recertified prior to transporting livestock any time significant changes are made to the vessel, including to livestock transport spaces or life support systems; any time a major life support system fails; any time species of livestock not covered by the existing certification are to be transported; and any time the owner or operator of the ocean vessel changes. The owner or operator of the vessel must present the following documentation to APHIS prior to its initial inspection for certification and when requested by APHIS prior to subsequent inspections for recertification:

(i) General information about the vessel, including year built, length and breadth, vessel name history, port of registry, call sign, maximum and average speed, fresh water tank capacity and fresh water generation rate, and feed silo capacity (if the vessel has a silo);

(ii) A notarized statement from an engineer concerning the rate of air exchange in each compartment of the vessel;

(iii) The species of livestock that the vessel would transport;

(iv) Scale drawings that provide details of the design, materials, and methods of construction and arrangement of fittings for the containment and movement of livestock; provisions for the storage and distribution of feed and water; drainage arrangements; primary and secondary sources of power; and lighting;

(v) A photograph of the rails and gates of any pens;

(vi) A description of the flooring surface on the livestock decks; and

(vii) The following measurements: Width of the ramps; the clear height from the ramps to the lowest overhead structures; the incline between the ramps and the horizontal plane; the distance between footlocks on the ramps; the height of side fencing on the ramps; the height of the vessel's side doors through which livestock are loaded; the width of alleyways running fore and aft between livestock pens; and the distance from the floor of the livestock pens to the beams or lowest structures overhead.

(2) *Prior to each voyage.* Prior to loading any livestock intended for export from the United States, an APHIS representative must inspect the vessel to confirm that the ocean vessel has been adequately cleaned and disinfected as required by paragraph (b) of this section, has sufficient food and water for the voyage as required by paragraph (c) of this section, and continues to meet the requirements of paragraph (d) of this section. APHIS will schedule the inspection after the owner or operator of the ocean vessel provides the following information:

(i) The name of the ocean vessel;

(ii) The port, date, and time the ocean vessel will be available for inspection, and estimated time that loading will begin;

(iii) A description of the livestock to be transported, including the type, number, and estimated average weight of the livestock;

(iv) Stability data for the ocean vessel with livestock on board;

(v) The port of discharge; and

(vi) The route and expected length of the voyage.

(3) The information in paragraphs (a)(2)(i) through (a)(2)(vi) must be provided at least 72 hours before the vessel will be available for inspection.

(b) *Cleaning and disinfection.* (1) Any ocean vessel intended for use in exporting livestock, and all fittings, utensils, containers, and equipment (unless new) used for loading, stowing, or other handling of livestock aboard the vessel must be thoroughly cleaned and disinfected to the satisfaction of an APHIS representative prior to any livestock being loaded. The disinfectant must be approved by the Administrator. Guidance on cleaning and disinfecting ocean vessels may be found in the Program Handbook.

(2) The Administrator will approve a disinfectant for the purposes of this paragraph upon determining that the disinfectant is effective against pathogens that may be spread by the animals and, if the disinfectant is a chemical disinfectant, that it is registered or exempted for the specified use by the U.S. Environmental Protection Agency. The Program Handbook provides access to a list of disinfectants approved by the Administrator. Other disinfectants may also be approved by the Administrator in accordance with this paragraph. The Administrator will withdraw approval of a disinfectant, and remove it from the list of approved disinfectants in the Program Handbook, if the disinfectant no longer meets the conditions for approval in this section.

(3) All ocean vessels, upon docking at a U.S. port to load livestock, must have disinfectant foot baths at entryways where persons board and exit the ocean vessel, and require such baths before allowing any person to disembark.

(c) *Feed and water.* Sufficient feed and water must be provided to livestock aboard the ocean vessel, taking into consideration the livestock's species, body weight, the expected duration of the voyage, and the likelihood of adverse climatic conditions during transport. Guidance on this requirement may be found in the Program Handbook. Livestock aboard the vessel must be provided feed and water within 28 hours of the time they were last fed and watered within the United States.

(d) *Accommodations for the humane transport of livestock; general requirements.* Ocean vessels used to transport livestock intended for export must be designed, constructed, and managed to reasonably assure the livestock are protected from injury and remain healthy during loading and transport to the importing country. Except as provided below in paragraph (e) of this section, no livestock may be loaded onto an ocean vessel unless, in the opinion of an APHIS representative, the ocean vessel meets the requirements of this section. The Program Handbook contains guidance on ways to meet the requirements. Owners and operators may submit alternative means and methods for meeting the requirements to APHIS for evaluation and approval. Alternatives must be at least as effective in meeting the requirements as those described in the Program Handbook in order to be approved. Alternatives must be approved by APHIS before being used for purposes of this section.

(1) *Pens.* All pens, including gates and portable rails used to close access ways, must be designed and constructed of material of sufficient strength to securely contain the livestock. They must be properly formed, closely fitted, and rigidly secured in place. They must have smooth finished surfaces free from sharp protrusions. They must not have worn, decayed, unsound, or otherwise defective parts. Flooring must be strong enough to support the livestock to be transported and provide a satisfactory non-slip foothold. Pens on exposed upper decks must protect the livestock from the weather. Pens next to engine or boiler rooms or similar sources of heat must be fitted to protect the livestock from injury due to transfer of heat to the livestock or livestock transport spaces. Any fittings or protrusions from the vessel's sides that abut pens must be covered to protect the livestock from injury. Pens must be of appropriate size for the species, size, weight, and condition of the livestock being transported and take into consideration the vessel's route. Animals that may be hostile to each other may not be housed in the same pen.

(2) *Positioning.* Livestock must be positioned during transport so that an animal handler or other responsible person can observe each animal regularly and clearly to ensure the livestock's safety and welfare.

(3) *Resources for sick or injured animals.* The vessel must have an adequate number of appropriately sized and located pens set aside to segregate livestock that become sick or injured from other animals. It must also have adequate veterinary medical supplies, including medicines, for the species, condition, and number of livestock transported.

(4) *Ramps, doors, and passageways.* Ramps, doors, and passageways used for livestock must be of sufficient width and height for their use and allow the safe passage of the species transported. They must have secure, smooth fittings free from sharp protrusions and non-slip flooring, and must not have worn, decayed, unsound, or otherwise defective parts. Ramps must not have an incline that is excessive for the species of livestock transported and must be fitted with foot battens to prevent slippage at intervals suitable for the species. The sides of ramps must be of sufficient height and strength to prevent escape of the species of livestock transported.

(5) *Feed and water.* The feeding and watering system must be designed to permit all livestock in each pen adequate access to feed and water. The system must also be designed to minimize soiling of pens and to prevent animal waste from contaminating feed and water. Similarly, feed must be loaded and stored aboard the vessel in a manner that protects it from weather and sea water and, if kept under animal transport spaces, protects it from spillage from animal watering and feeding and from animal waste. If the normal means of tending, feeding, and watering of livestock on board the ocean vessel is wholly or partially by automatic means, the vessel must have alternative arrangements for the satisfactory tending, feeding, and watering of the animals in the event of a malfunction of the automatic means.

(6) *Ventilation.* Ventilation during loading, unloading, and transport must provide fresh air and remove excessive heat, humidity, and noxious fumes (such as ammonia and carbon dioxide). Ventilation must be adequate for variations in climate and weather and to meet the needs of the livestock being transported. Ventilation must be effective both when the vessel is stationary and when it is moving and must be turned on when the first animal is loaded. The vessel must have on board a back-up ventilation system (including emergency power supply) in good working order or replacement parts and the means, including qualified personnel, to make the repairs or replacements.

(7) *Waste management.* The vessel must have a system or arrangements, including a backup system in working order or alternate arrangements, for managing waste to prevent excessive buildup in livestock transport spaces during the voyage.

(8) *Lighting.* The vessel must have adequate illumination to allow clear observation of livestock during loading, unloading, and transport.

(9) *Bedding.* Bedding must be loaded and stored aboard the vessel in a manner that protects it from weather and sea water and, if kept under animal transport spaces, protects it from spillage from animal watering and feeding and from animal waste.

(10) *Cleaning.* The vessel must be designed and constructed to allow thorough cleaning and disinfection and to prevent feces and urine from livestock on upper levels from soiling livestock or their feed or water on lower levels.

(11) *Halters and ropes.* Halters, ropes, or other equipment provided for the handling and tying of horses or other livestock must be satisfactory to ensure the humane treatment of the livestock.

(12) *Personnel.* The owner or operator of the ocean vessel must have on board during loading, transport, and unloading at least 3 persons (or at least 1 person if fewer than 800 head of livestock will be transported) with previous experience with ocean vessels that have handled the kind(s) of livestock to be carried, as well as a sufficient number of personnel with the appropriate experience to be able to ensure proper care

of the livestock. The APHIS representative assigned to inspect the ocean vessel prior to loading will determine whether the personnel aboard the vessel are sufficient and possess adequate experience, including, if necessary, veterinary experience, to ensure proper care of the livestock.

(13) *Vessel stability*. The vessel must have adequate stability, taking into consideration the weight and distribution of livestock and fodder, as well as effects of high winds and seas. If requested by APHIS, the owner or operator of the vessel must present stability calculations for the voyage that have been independently verified for accuracy.

(14) *Means of humane euthanasia*. Ocean vessels must maintain a means of humanely euthanizing sick or injured livestock aboard the vessel. One of the personnel aboard the vessel must be trained in humanely euthanizing livestock by using the means of euthanasia carried by the vessel.

(15) *Life support systems*. The ocean vessel must maintain replacement parts for major life support systems aboard the vessel, and the means, including qualified personnel, to make the repairs or replacements.

(16) *Additional conditions*. The vessel must meet any other condition the Administrator determines is necessary for approval, as dictated by specific circumstances and communicated to the owner and operator of the vessel, to protect the livestock and keep them healthy during loading, unloading, and transport to the importing country.

(e) *Accommodations for the humane transport of livestock; vessels using shipping containers*. An inspector may exempt an ocean vessel that uses shipping containers to transport livestock to an importing country from requirements in paragraph (d) of this section that he or she specifies, if the inspector determines that the containers themselves are designed, constructed, and managed in a manner to reasonably assure the livestock are protected from injury and remain healthy during loading, unloading, and transport to the importing country. During such inspections, particular attention will be paid to the manner in which containers are constructed, the space the containers afford to livestock transported within them, the manner in which the vessel would provide feed and water to the animals in the containers, and the manner in which air and effluent are managed within the containers. The Program Handbook contains exemption guidance.

(f) *Operator's report*. (1) The owner or operator of any ocean vessel used to export livestock (including vessels that use shipping containers) from the United States must submit a written report to APHIS within 5 business days after completing a voyage. The report must include the name of the ocean vessel; the name and address of all exporters of livestock transported on the vessel; the port of embarkation; dates of the voyage; the port where the livestock were discharged; the number of each species of livestock loaded; the number of each species that died and an explanation for those mortalities; and the number of animals that sustained injuries or sustained illnesses that were significant enough to require medical attention from the personnel entrusted with the care of the animals, as well as the nature of these injuries or illnesses. The report must also document any failure of any major life support system for the livestock, including, but not limited to, systems for providing feed and water, ventilation systems, and livestock waste management systems. Any such failure must be documented, regardless of the duration or whether the failure resulted in any harm to the livestock. The report must include the name, telephone number, and email address of the person who prepared the report and the date of the report. The report must be submitted to APHIS by facsimile or email. Contact numbers and addresses, as well as an optional template for the report, are provided in the Program Handbook.

(2) If an ocean vessel used to export livestock experiences any failure of a major life support system for livestock during the voyage, the owner or operator of the ocean vessel must notify APHIS immediately by telephone, facsimile, or other electronic means. Contact numbers and addresses are provided in the Program Handbook.

(3) Failure to provide timely reports as required by this section may result

in APHIS disapproving future livestock shipments by the responsible owner or operator or revoking the vessel's certification under paragraph (a) of this section to carry livestock.

(Approved by the Office of Management and Budget under control number 0579–0432)

§91.13 Aircraft.

(a) Prior to loading livestock aboard aircraft, the stowage area of the aircraft and any loading ramps, fittings, and equipment to be used in loading the animals must be cleaned and then disinfected with a disinfectant approved by the Administrator, to the satisfaction of an APHIS representative, unless the representative determines that the aircraft has already been cleaned and disinfected to his or her satisfaction.

(1) The Administrator will approve a disinfectant for purposes of this section upon determining that the disinfectant is effective against pathogens that may be spread by the animals and, if the disinfectant is a chemical disinfectant, that it is registered or exempted for the specified use by the U.S. Environmental Protection Agency.

(2) The Program Handbook provides access to a list of disinfectants approved by the Administrator for use as required by this section. Other disinfectants may also be approved by the Administrator in accordance with paragraph (a)(1) of this section.

(3) The Administrator will withdraw approval of a disinfectant, and remove it from the list of approved disinfectants in the Program Handbook, if the disinfectant no longer meets the conditions for approval in this section.

(b) The time at which the cleaning and disinfection are to be performed must be approved by the APHIS representative, who will give approval only if he or she determines that the cleaning and disinfection will be effective up to the projected time the livestock will be loaded. If the livestock are not loaded by the projected time, the APHIS representative will determine whether further cleaning and disinfection are necessary.

(c) The cleaning must remove all garbage, soil, manure, plant materials, insects, paper, and other debris from the stowage area. The disinfectant solution must be applied with a device that creates an aerosol or mist that covers 100 percent of the surfaces in the stowage area, except for any loaded cargo and deck surface under it that, in the opinion of the APHIS representative, do not contain material, such as garbage, soil, manure, plant materials, insects, waste paper, or debris, that may harbor animal disease pathogens.

(d) After cleaning and disinfection is performed, the APHIS representative will sign and deliver to the captain of the aircraft or other responsible official of the airline involved a document stating that the aircraft has been properly cleaned and disinfected, and stating further the date, the carrier, the flight number, and the name of the airport and the city and state in which it is located. If an aircraft is cleaned and disinfected at one airport, then flies to a subsequent airport, with or without stops en route, to load animals for export, an APHIS representative at the subsequent airport will determine, based on examination of the cleaning and disinfection documents, whether the previous cleaning and disinfection is adequate or whether to order a new cleaning and disinfection. If the aircraft has loaded any cargo in addition to animals, the APHIS representative at the subsequent airport will determine whether to order a new cleaning and disinfection, based on both examination of the cleaning and disinfection documents and on the inspection of the stowage area for materials, such as garbage, soil, manure, plant materials, insects, waste paper, or debris, that may harbor animal disease pathogens.

(e) Cargo containers used to ship livestock must be designed and constructed of a material of sufficient strength to securely contain the animals and must provide sufficient space for the species being transported given the duration of the trip, as determined by APHIS.

§91.14 Other movements and conditions.

The Administrator may, upon request in specific cases, permit the exportation of livestock not otherwise provided for in this part under such conditions as he or she may prescribe in each specific case to prevent the spread of livestock diseases and to ensure the humane treatment of the animals during transport to the importing country.

PART 92—IMPORTATION OF ANIMALS AND ANIMAL PRODUCTS: PROCEDURES FOR REQUESTING RECOGNITION OF REGIONS

AUTHORITY: 7 U.S.C. 1622 and 8301–8317; 21 U.S.C. 136 and 136a; 31 U.S.C. 9701; 7 CFR 2.22, 2.80, and 371.4.

SOURCE: 62 FR 56012, Oct. 28, 1997, unless otherwise noted.

§92.1 Definitions.

Active surveillance. Sample collection using a systematic or statistically designed survey methodology to actively seek out and find cases of animals with a restricted disease agent, or to determine the prevalence of the restricted disease agent in the population.

Adjacent region. Any geographic land area, whether or not identifiable by geological, political or surveyed boundaries, that shares common boundaries with any region.

Administrator. The Administrator of the Animal and Plant Health Inspection Service or any other employee of the Animal and Plant Health Inspection Service, United States Department of Agriculture, delegated to act in the Administrator's stead.

Animal and Plant Health Inspection Service (APHIS). The Animal and Plant Health Inspection Service of the United States Department of Agriculture.

Animals. All species of the animal kingdom, except man, including: Cattle, sheep, goats, other ruminants, swine, horses, asses, mules, zebras, dogs, poultry, and birds that are susceptible to communicable diseases of livestock and poultry or capable of being carriers of those diseases or their arthropod vectors.

Approved laboratory. A properly equipped institution in the exporting region, approved by the official authority who is responsible for animal health matters in that region, that is staffed by technically competent personnel under the control of a specialist in veterinary diagnostic methods who is responsible for the results.

Bovine. Bos taurus, Bos indicus, and *Bison bison.*

Communicable disease. Any contagious or infectious disease of animals. It can be transmitted either directly or indirectly to a susceptible animal from an infected animal, vector, inanimate source, or other sources.

Contagious disease. Any communicable disease transmitted from one animal to another by direct contact or by feed, water, aerosol, or contaminated objects.

Disease agent. A virus, bacterium, or other organism that causes disease in animals.

Exporting region. A region from which shipments are sent to the United States.

European Union. The organization of Member States consisting of Austria, Belgium, Bulgaria, Cyprus, the Czech Republic, Denmark, Estonia, Finland, France, Germany, Greece, Hungary, Italy, Latvia, Lithuania, Luxembourg, Malta, the Netherlands, Poland, Portugal, Romania, Slovakia, Slovenia, Republic of Ireland, Spain, Sweden, and the United Kingdom (England, Scotland, Wales, the Isle of Man, and Northern Ireland).

Import (imported, importation) into the United States. To bring into the territorial limits of the United States.

OIE. The World Organization for Animal Health.

OIE Code. The Terrestrial Animal Health Code of the World Organization for Animal Health.

OIE Terrestrial Manual. The Manual of Diagnostic Tests and Vaccines for Terrestrial Animals of the World Organization for Animal Health.

Passive surveillance. A surveillance system that does not depend on active participation by the responsible agency to seek out and monitor a restricted disease agent. The system relies on mandatory reporting, a pool of trained investigators, diagnostic submission procedures and laboratory support, and periodic public information and continuing education programs on diseases.

Prevalence. The number of cases of a disease in existence at a given time in a designated area.

Processed animal protein. Meat meal, bone meal, meat-and-bone meal, blood meal, dried plasma and other blood products, hydrolyzed protein, hoof meal, horn meal, poultry meal, feather meal, fish meal, and any other similar products.

Region. Any defined geographic land region identifiable by geological, political or surveyed boundaries. A region may consist of any of the following:

(1) A national entity (country);

(2) Part of a national entity (zone, county, department, municipality, parish, Province, State, etc.);

(3) Parts of several national entities combined into an area; or

(4) A group of national entities (countries) combined into a single area.

Region of controlled risk for bovine spongiform encephalopathy (BSE).[1] A region for which a risk assessment has been conducted sufficient to identify the historical and existing BSE risk factors in the region and that:

(1) Has demonstrated that appropriate mitigations are being taken to manage all identified risks, but may not have been taken for the periods of time necessary to be classified as a region of negligible risk for BSE.

(2) Is a region in which it can be demonstrated through an appropriate control and audit that neither meat-and-bone meal nor greaves derived from ruminants has been fed to ruminants.

(3) Has demonstrated that Type A surveillance in accordance with Article 11.5.22 of the OIE Code, incorporated by reference in §92.7, or with equivalent guidelines recognized by the Administrator is in place and the relevant points target, in accordance with Table 1 of Article 11.5.22 of the OIE Code, or with equivalent guidelines recognized by the Administrator has been met. Type B surveillance in accordance with Article 11.5.22 of the OIE Code, or with equivalent guidelines recognized by the Administrator, is sufficient in place of Type A surveillance or its equivalent once the relevant points target for Type A surveillance or its equivalent has been met.

(4) Meets one of the following conditions:

(i) Has had no case of BSE in the region or every case has been demonstrated to have been imported and has been completely destroyed; or

(ii) Has had at least one indigenous case, and all bovines described in either paragraph (4)(ii)(A) or (4)(ii)(B) of this definition, if still alive, are officially identified with unique individual identification that is traceable to the premises of origin of the animal, have their movements controlled, and, when slaughtered or at death, are completely destroyed:

(A) All bovines that, during their first year of life, were reared with a bovine determined to be infected with BSE during its first year of life, and that investigation showed consumed the same potentially contaminated feed as the infected animal during that period; or

(B) If the investigation was unable to determine whether the feed source that was used to feed the bovine known to be infected was also used to feed other bovines in the herd of the infected animal, all bovines born in the same herd as a BSE-infected bovine either within 12 months before or 12 months after the birth of the infected animal.

(5) Meets the conditions in one of or both paragraphs (5)(i) or (5)(ii) of this definition:

(i) Has met the following conditions, but not for at least the past 7 years:

(A) Conducted an ongoing awareness program for veterinarians, farmers,

[1] A list of regions classified by APHIS as regions of controlled risk for BSEs is available at *http://www.aphis.usda.gov/import_export/animals/animal_disease_status.shtml.*

and workers involved in transportation, marketing, and slaughter of bovines to encourage reporting of bovines showing clinical signs that could be indicative of BSE;

(B) Required notification and investigation of all bovines showing clinical signs consistent with BSE; and

(C) Has carried out the examination, in accordance with internationally accepted diagnostic tests and procedures and in approved laboratories, of brain or other tissues collected as part of the surveillance and monitoring described in paragraphs (3) and (5)(i)(A) and (5)(i)(B) of this definition; or

(ii) Has prohibited the feeding to ruminants in the region of meat-and-bone meal and greaves derived from ruminants, but it cannot be demonstrated through an appropriate level of control and audit that the prohibited materials have not been fed to ruminants in the region for at least the past 8 years.

Region of negligible risk for bovine spongiform encephalopathy (BSE).[2] A region for which a risk assessment has been conducted sufficient to identify the historical and existing BSE risk factors in the region and that:

(1) Has demonstrated that appropriate mitigations to manage all identified risks have been taken for each relevant period of time to meet each identified risk, as set forth in this definition.

(2) Has demonstrated that Type B surveillance in accordance with Article 11.5.22 of the OIE Code, incorporated by reference in §92.7, or with equivalent guidelines recognized by the Administrator is in place and the relevant points target, in accordance with Table 1 of Article 11.5.22 of the OIE Code, or with equivalent guidelines recognized by the Administrator has been met.

(3) Meets one of the following conditions:

(i) Has had no case of BSE in the region or every case has been demonstrated to have been imported and has been completely destroyed; or

(ii) Has had at least one indigenous case, but every indigenous case was born more than 11 years ago, and all bovines described in either paragraph (3)(ii)(A) or (3)(ii)(B) of this definition, if still alive, are officially identified with unique individual identification that is traceable to the premises of origin of the animal, have their movements controlled, and, when slaughtered or at death, are completely destroyed:

(A) All bovines that, during their first year of life, were reared with a bovine determined to be infected with BSE during its first year of life, and that investigation showed consumed the same potentially contaminated feed as the infected animal during that period; or

(B) If the investigation was unable to determine whether the feed source that was used to feed the bovine known to be infected was also used to feed other bovines in the herd of the infected animal, all bovines born in the same herd as a BSE-infected bovine either within 12 months before or 12 months after the birth of the infected animal.

(4) Has, for at least the past 7 years:

(i) Conducted an ongoing awareness program for veterinarians, farmers, and workers involved in transportation, marketing, and slaughter of bovines to encourage reporting of bovines showing clinical signs that could be indicative of BSE;

(ii) Required notification and investigation of all bovines showing clinical signs consistent with BSE; and

(iii) Carried out the examination, in accordance with internationally accepted diagnostic tests and procedures and in approved laboratories, of brain or other tissues collected as part of the required surveillance and monitoring described in paragraphs (2) and (4)(i) and (4)(ii) of this definition.

(5) Has demonstrated through an appropriate level of control and audit that, for at least the past 8 years, neither meat-and-bone meal nor greaves derived from ruminants have been fed to ruminants in the region.

Region of undetermined risk for bovine spongiform encephalopathy (BSE). Any region that is not classified as either a region of negligible risk for BSE or a region of controlled risk for BSE.

[2] A list of regions classified by APHIS as regions of negligible risk for BSEs is available at *http://www.aphis.usda.gov/import_export/animals/animal_disease_status.shtml.*

Restricted disease agent. Any communicable disease agent or its vector not known to exist in the United States or that is subject to a Federal or cooperative Federal/State control or eradication program within the United States.

Specified risk materials (SRMs) from regions of controlled risk for BSE. Those bovine parts considered to be at particular risk of containing the BSE agent in infected animals, as listed in the FSIS regulations at 9 CFR 310.22(a).

Specified risk materials (SRMs) from regions of undetermined risk for BSE. Those bovine parts considered to be at particular risk of containing the BSE agent in infected animals, as listed in the FSIS regulations at 9 CFR 310.22(a), except that the following bovine parts from regions of undetermined risk for BSE are considered SRMs if they are derived from bovines over 12 months of age: Brain, skull, eyes, trigeminal ganglia, spinal cord, vertebral column (excluding the vertebrae of the tail, the transverse processes of the thoracic and lumbar vertebrae, and the wings of the sacrum), and the dorsal root ganglia.

Surveillance. Systems to find, monitor, and confirm the existence or absence of a restricted disease agent or agents in livestock, poultry and other animals. Surveillance may be passive or active.

United States. All of the States of the United States, the District of Columbia, Guam, the Northern Mariana Islands, Puerto Rico, the Virgin Islands of the United States, and all other territories and possessions of the United States.

Vector-borne disease. A disease transmitted to an animal through an intermediate arthropod vector, including ticks or insects.

[62 FR 56012, Oct. 28, 1997, as amended at 68 FR 16938, Apr. 7, 2003; 72 FR 67232, Nov. 28, 2007; 78 FR 72993, Dec. 4, 2013]

Subpart A—Procedures for Requesting Recognition of Regions Other Than for BSE

SOURCE: 78 FR 72994, Dec. 4, 2013, unless otherwise noted.

§ 92.2 Application for recognition of the animal health status of a region.

(a) The representative of the national government(s) of any country or countries who has the authority to make such a request may request that APHIS recognize the animal health status of a region.[1] Such requests must be made in English and must be sent to the Administrator, c/o National Center for Import and Export, VS, APHIS, 4700 River Road Unit 38, Riverdale, MD 20737–1231. (Where possible, include a copy of the request and accompanying information in electronic format.)

(b) Requests for recognition of the animal health status of a region, other than requests submitted in accordance with paragraph (c) of this section, must include, in English, the following information about the region. More detailed information regarding the specific types of information that will enable APHIS to most expeditiously conduct an evaluation of the request is available at *http://www.aphis.usda.gov/import_export/animals/reg_request.shtml* or by contacting the Director, Sanitary Trade Issues Team, National Center for Import and Export, VS, APHIS, 4700 River Road Unit 38, Riverdale, MD 20737.

(1) Scope of the evaluation being requested.

(2) Veterinary control and oversight.

(3) Disease history and vaccination practices.

(4) Livestock demographics and traceability.

(5) Epidemiological separation from potential sources of infection.

(6) Surveillance.

(7) Diagnostic laboratory capabilities.

(8) Emergency preparedness and response.

(c) Requests for recognition that a region is historically free of a disease based on the amount of time that has elapsed since the disease last occurred in a region, if it has ever occurred, must include, in English, the following

[1] Additionally, APHIS may choose to initiate an evaluation of the animal health status of a foreign region on its own initiative. In such cases, APHIS will follow the same evaluation and notification procedures set forth in this section.

information about the region. More detailed information regarding the specific types of information that will enable APHIS to most expeditiously conduct an evaluation of the request is available at *http://www.aphis.usda.gov/import_export/animals/reg_request.shtml* or by contacting the Director, Sanitary Trade Issues Team, National Center for Import and Export, VS, APHIS, 4700 River Road Unit 38, Riverdale, MD 20737. For a region to be considered historically free of a disease, the disease must not have been reported in domestic livestock for at least the past 25 years and must not have been reported in wildlife for at least the past 10 years.

(1) Scope of the evaluation being requested.

(2) Veterinary control and oversight.

(3) Disease history and vaccination practices

(4) Disease notification.

(5) Disease detection.

(6) Barriers to disease introduction.

(d) A list of those regions that have requested APHIS' recognition of their animal health status, the disease(s) under evaluation, and, if available, the animal(s) or product(s) the region wishes to export, is available at *http://www.aphis.usda.gov/import_export/animals/reg_request.shtml.*

(e) If, after review and evaluation of the information submitted in accordance with paragraph (b) or (c) of this section, APHIS believes the request can be safely granted, APHIS will indicate its intent and make its evaluation available for public comment through a document published in the FEDERAL REGISTER.

(f) APHIS will provide a period of time during which the public may comment on its evaluation. During the comment period, the public will have access to the information upon which APHIS based its evaluation, as well as the evaluation itself. Once APHIS has reviewed all comments received, it will make a final determination regarding the request and will publish that determination in the FEDERAL REGISTER.

(g) If a region is granted animal health status under the provisions of this section, that region may be required to submit additional information pertaining to animal health status or allow APHIS to conduct additional information collection activities in order for that region to maintain its animal health status.

(Approved by the Office of Management and Budget under control number 0579–0219)

[62 FR 56012, Oct. 28, 1997, as amended at 68 FR 50054, Aug. 20, 2003; 77 FR 1389, Jan. 10, 2012; 77 FR 44109, July 27, 2012]

§92.3 Movement restrictions.

Whenever the European Commission (EC) establishes a quarantine for a disease in the European Union in a region the Animal and Plant Health Inspection Service recognizes as one in which the disease is not known to exist and the EC imposes prohibitions or other restrictions on the movement of animals or animal products from the quarantined area in the European Union, such animals and animal products are prohibited importation into the United States.

[68 FR 16938, Apr. 7, 2003]

§92.4 Reestablishment of a region's disease-free status.

This section applies to regions that are designated under this subchapter as free of a specific animal disease and then experience an outbreak of that disease.

(a) *Interim designation.* If a region recognized as free of a specified animal disease in this subchapter experiences an outbreak of that disease, APHIS will take immediate action to prohibit or restrict imports of animals and animal products from that region. The prohibitions or restrictions may be imposed on only a portion of the region previously recognized as free of a disease. In these cases, APHIS will inform the public as soon as possible through notice in the FEDERAL REGISTER of the basis for its decision to prohibit or restrict imports from the smaller area of that region previously recognized as free.

(b) *Reassessment of the disease situation.* (1) Following removal of disease-free status from all or part of a region, APHIS may reassess the disease situation in that region to determine whether it is necessary to continue the interim prohibitions or restrictions. In reassessing a region's disease status,

APHIS will take into consideration the standards of the World Organization for Animal Health (OIE) for reinstatement of disease-free status, as well as all relevant information obtained through public comments or collected by or submitted to APHIS through other means.

(2) Prior to taking any action to relieve prohibitions or restrictions, APHIS will make information regarding its reassessment of the region's disease status available to the public for comment. APHIS will announce the availability of this information in the FEDERAL REGISTER.

(c) *Determination.* Based on the reassessment conducted in accordance with paragraph (b) of this section, including comments regarding the reassessment information, APHIS will take one of the following actions:

(1) Publish a notice of its decision to reinstate the disease-free status of the region, or a portion of the region;

(2) Publish a notice of its decision to continue the prohibitions or restrictions on the imports of animals and animal products from that region; or

(3) Publish another document in the FEDERAL REGISTER for comment.

[77 FR 1389, Jan. 10, 2012]

Subpart B—Procedures for Requesting BSE Risk Status Classification With Regard to Bovines

SOURCE: 78 FR 72994, Dec. 4, 2013, unless otherwise noted.

§ 92.5 Determination of the BSE risk classification of a region.

All countries of the world are considered by APHIS to be in one of three BSE risk categories—negligible risk, controlled risk, or undetermined risk. These risk categories are defined in § 92.1. Any region that is not classified by APHIS as presenting either negligible risk or controlled risk for BSE is considered to present an undetermined risk. The listing of those regions classified by APHIS as having either negligible risk or controlled risk can be accessed on the APHIS Web site at *http://www.aphis.usda.gov/import_export/animals/ animal_disease_status.shtml.* The listing can also be obtained by writing to APHIS at National Import Export Services, 4700 River Road Unit 38, Riverdale, MD 20737. APHIS may classify a region for BSE according to either paragraph (a) or paragraph (b) of this section.

(a) *BSE risk classification based on OIE classification.* If the OIE has classified a country as either BSE negligible risk or BSE controlled risk, APHIS will seek information to support concurrence with the OIE classification. This information could be publicly available information, or APHIS could request that countries supply the same information given to the OIE. APHIS will announce in the FEDERAL REGISTER, subject to public comment, each intent to concur with an OIE classification. APHIS will also post the summary of the BSE OIE ad hoc group conclusions for review during the comment period. The summaries would be available for review on the APHIS Web site at *http://www.aphis.usda.gov/import_export/ animals/reg_request.shtml.* Following review of any comments received, the Administrator will announce his or her final determination regarding classification of the country in the FEDERAL REGISTER, along with a discussion of and response to pertinent issues raised by commenters. If APHIS recognizes a country as either negligible risk or controlled risk for BSE, the Agency will include that country in a list of regions of negligible risk or controlled risk for BSE, as applicable, that APHIS will make available to the public on the Agency's Web site at *http://www.aphis.usda.gov/import_export/ animals/animal_disease_status.shtml.*

(b) *Regions seeking classification as negligible or controlled risk that have not been classified by the OIE.* A region that has not received classification by OIE as either negligible risk or controlled risk for BSE and that wishes to be classified by APHIS as negligible risk or controlled risk must submit to the Administrator a request for classification, along with documentation sufficient to allow APHIS to conduct an evaluation of whether the region meets the criteria for classification. A list of the documentation required can be accessed on the APHIS Web site at *http://www.aphis.usda.gov/import_export/*

animals/reg_request.shtml. If, following evaluation of the information submitted, the Administrator determines that the region meets the criteria for classification as negligible risk or controlled risk, APHIS will announce that determination in the FEDERAL REGISTER and will make available to the public on the APHIS Web site the evaluation conducted by APHIS, as well as the information provided by the requesting region. APHIS will accept public comment on its intent. Following review of any comments received, the Administrator will announce his or her final determination regarding classification of the region in the FEDERAL REGISTER, along with a discussion of and response to pertinent issues raised by commenters.

(c) *Retention of classification as either negligible risk or controlled risk.* (1) As required by the OIE for countries classified as either negligible risk or controlled risk by the OIE, regions evaluated by APHIS and classified as negligible or controlled risk would need to submit updated information to APHIS each year. The required information includes documentation of the following:

(i) Relevant changes in BSE legislation, compared to the previous year;

(ii) The importation into the region during the year of cattle, processed animal protein, and products containing processed animal protein;

(iii) Audit findings in rendering plants and feed mills that process ruminant material or material from mixed species that contains ruminant material, related to the prohibition of the feeding to ruminants of processed animal protein;

(iv) Audit findings in rendering plants and feed mills that process nonruminant material, related to the prohibition of the feeding to ruminants of processed animal protein;

(v) Infractions at the types of facilities listed above;

(vi) If and why, in light of the audit findings, there has been no significant exposure of cattle to the BSE agent through consumption of processed animal protein of bovine origin;

(vii) Surveillance efforts;

(viii) All clinical BSE suspects; and

(ix) Any new cases of BSE.

(2) If APHIS at any time determines that a region no longer meets the criteria for the risk classification it had previously received, APHIS will remove the region from its list of regions so classified. If the OIE determines the region no longer meets the criteria for the risk classification it had previously received, APHIS may concur with the OIE determination or may request updated information from the region and determine whether to concur with the OIE decision APHIS will announce its intent in the FEDERAL REGISTER and accept public comment regarding that intent. Following review of any comments received, the Administrator will announce in the FEDERAL REGISTER his or her final determination regarding classification of the region, along with a discussion of and response to pertinent issues raised by commenters.

(Approved by the Office of Management and Budget under control number 0579–0393)

§92.6 Determination of the date of effective enforcement of a ruminant-to-ruminant feed ban.

(a) In order for APHIS to determine the eligibility of live bovines for importation from a region classified as BSE negligible risk or BSE controlled risk, APHIS must determine the date from which a ban on the feeding of ruminant material to ruminants has been effectively enforced in the region. APHIS will base its determination of the date of effective enforcement on the information included in the dossier the region submitted when it requested to be classified regarding BSE risk. The information APHIS will consider will include, but not be limited to:

(1) Policies and infrastructure for feed ban enforcement, including an awareness program for producers and farmers;

(2) Livestock husbandry practices;

(3) Disposition of processed animal protein produced from domestic bovines, including the feeding of such material to any animal species;

(4) Measures taken to control cross-contamination and mislabeling of feed; and

(5) Monitoring and enforcement of the ruminant-to-ruminant feed ban, including audit findings in rendering

plants and feed mills that process ruminant material.

(b) After conducting its evaluation, APHIS will announce in the FEDERAL REGISTER for public comment the date APHIS considers to be the date of effective enforcement of a ruminant-to-ruminant feed ban in the requesting region, and will make available to the public the evaluation conducted by APHIS, as well as the supporting documentation. Following review of any comments received, the Administrator will announce his or her final determination in the FEDERAL REGISTER, along with a discussion of and response to pertinent issues raised by commenters.

§ 92.7 Incorporation by reference.

(a) Certain material is incorporated by reference into this part with the approval of the Director of the Federal Register under 5 U.S.C. 552(a) and 1 CFR part 51. To enforce any edition other than that specified in this section, USDA must publish notice of change in the FEDERAL REGISTER and the material must be available to the public. All approved material is available for inspection at the Animal and Plant Health Inspection Service (APHIS), and is available from the sources listed below. For information about the availability of this material at APHIS, call 301–851–3300 or write to National Import Export Services, 4700 River Road Unit 38, Riverdale, MD 20737. It is also available for inspection at the National Archives and Records Administration (NARA). For information on the availability of this material at NARA, call 202-741-6030 or go to *http://www.archives.gov/federal_register/code_of_federal_regulations/ibr_locations.html.*

(b) World Organization for Animal Health (OIE), 12, rue de Prony 75017 Paris, France, or email oie@oie.int, *http://www.oie.int/eng/normes/Mcode/en_sommaire.htm.*

(1) Terrestrial Animal Health Code, Chapter 11.5–Bovine Spongiform Encephalopathy, Article 11.5.22 (Surveillance activities), 22nd Edition, 2013.

(2) [Reserved]

(Approved by the Office of Management and Budget under control number 0579–0393)

PART 93—IMPORTATION OF CERTAIN ANIMALS, BIRDS, FISH, AND POULTRY, AND CERTAIN ANIMAL, BIRD, AND POULTRY PRODUCTS; REQUIREMENTS FOR MEANS OF CONVEYANCE AND SHIPPING CONTAINERS

Subpart A—Birds

Subpart B—Poultry

Subpart C—Horses

Subpart D—Ruminants

AUTHORITY: 7 U.S.C. 1622 and 8301–8317; 21 U.S.C. 136 and 136a; 31 U.S.C. 9701; 7 CFR 2.22, 2.80, and 371.4.

SOURCE: 55 FR 31495, Aug. 2, 1990, unless otherwise noted. Redesignated at 62 FR 56012, Oct. 28, 1997.

Subpart A—Birds

§ 93.100 Definitions.

Wherever in this subpart the following terms are used, unless the context otherwise requires, they shall be construed, respectively, to mean:

Administrator. The Administrator of the Animal and Plant Health Inspection Service or any other employee of the Animal and Plant Health Inspection Service, United States Department of Agriculture, to whom authority has been or may be delegated to act in the Administrator's stead.

Animal and Plant Health Inspection Service. The Animal and Plant Health Inspection Service of the United States Department of Agriculture (APHIS or Service.)

Animals. Cattle, sheep, goats, other ruminants, swine, horses, asses, mules, zebras, dogs, and poultry.

APHIS representative. A veterinarian or other individual employed by the Animal and Plant Health Inspection Service, United States Department of Agriculture, who is authorized to perform the services required by this part.

Birds. All members of the class aves (including eggs for hatching), other than poultry.

Commercial birds. Birds which are imported for resale, breeding, public display, or any other purpose, except pet birds, zoological birds, research birds, or performing or theatrical birds.

Communicable disease. Any contagious, infectious, or communicable disease of domestic livestock, poultry or other animals.

Department. The United States Department of Agriculture (USDA).

Highly pathogenic avian influenza (HPAI). Highly pathogenic avian influenza is defined as follows:

(1) Any influenza virus that kills at least 75 percent of eight 4- to 6-week-old susceptible chickens within 10 days following intravenous inoculation with 0.2 mL of a 1:10 dilution of a bacteria-free, infectious allantoic fluid or inoculation of 10 susceptible 4- to 8-week-old chickens resulting in an intravenous pathogenicity index (IVPI) of greater than 1.2;

(2) Any H5 or H7 virus that does not meet the criteria in paragraph (1) of this definition, but has an amino acid sequence at the haemagglutinin cleavage site that is compatible with highly pathogenic avian influenza viruses; or

(3) Any influenza virus that is not an H5 or H7 subtype and that kills one to five out of eight inoculated chickens and grows in cell culture in the absence of trypsin within 10 days.

Inspector. An employee of the Animal and Plant Health Inspection Service authorized to perform duties required under this subpart.

Licensed veterinarian. Any person licensed by any region or political subdivision thereof to practice veterinary medicine.

Pen-raised. Cared for in a fenced enclosure, such that the ratites are kept apart from wild ratites, poultry, and other animals; can be readily observed, and be restrained for inspection and treatment. A flock is not considered to be pen-raised if ratites captured in the wild have been added to it after March 8, 1994.

Performing or theatrical birds. Birds, except ratites, which are to be used in shows, theatrical acts or performances only.

Persons. Any individual, corporation, company, association, firm, partnership, society or joint stock company.

Pet birds. Birds, except ratites, which are imported for the personal pleasure of their individual owners and are not intended for resale.

Port Veterinarian. A veterinarian employed by the Animal and Plant Health Inspection Service to perform duties required under this part at a port of entry.

Poultry. Chickens, doves, ducks, geese, grouse, guinea fowl, partridges, pea fowl, pheasants, pigeons, quail, swans, and turkeys (including eggs for hatching).

Production season. That period of time, usually approximately 9 months each year, from the time ratites in a flock begin laying eggs until the ratites cease laying eggs.

Quarantine facility. A USDA facility, or a private facility approved by APHIS, for the secure housing of imported birds, poultry, or other animals for specified periods.

Ratites. Cassowaries, emus, kiwis, ostriches, and rheas.

Region. Any defined geographic land area identifiable by geological, political, or surveyed boundaries. A region may consist of any of the following:

(1) A national entity (country);

(2) Part of a national entity (zone, county, department, municipality, parish, Province, State, etc.);

(3) Parts of several national entities combined into an area; or

(4) A group of national entities (countries) combined into a single area.

Research birds. Birds which are to be used for research purposes only.

Smuggled birds. Any bird which has been brought into the United States contrary to any Federal law or regulation and which has been seized by any official of any Department of the United States Government or which has been abandoned to the United States.

United States. All of the States of the United States, the District of Columbia, Guam, Northern Mariana Islands, Puerto Rico, the Virgin Islands of the United States, and all other Territories and Possessions of the United States.

Veterinary Services. The Veterinary Services unit of the Department.

Zoological birds. Birds intended for breeding or public display, for recreational or educational purposes, at a zoological park.

Zoological park. A professionally operated zoo, park, garden or other place, maintained under the constant surveillance of a Doctor of Veterinary Medicine, for the exhibition of live animals, pigeons or birds, for the purpose of public recreation or education.

[55 FR 31495, Aug. 2, 1990, as amended at 56 FR 31865, July 12, 1991; 59 FR 10732, Mar. 8, 1994; 59 FR 47068, Sept. 14, 1994. Redesignated and amended at 62 FR 56012, 56013, Oct. 28, 1997; 79 FR 71004, Dec. 1, 2014]

§ 93.101 General prohibitions; exceptions.

(a) No product or bird subject to the provisions of this part shall be brought into the United States except in accordance with the regulations in this part and part 94 of this subchapter;[1] nor shall any such product or bird be handled or moved after physical entry into the United States before final release from quarantine orany other form of governmental detention except in compliance with such regulations; *Provided,* That the Administrator may upon request in specific cases permit products or birds to be brought into or through the United States under such conditions as he or she may prescribe, when he or she determines in the specific case that such action will not endanger the livestock or poultry of the United States. Unless otherwise indicated in the regulations, no live birds, and no hatching eggs from birds, shall be imported into the United States if the birds have originated from a region referenced in § 94.6(a) of this subchapter where highly pathogenic avian influenza or Newcastle disease is known to exist in commercial poultry populations, have transited highly pathogenic avian influenza- or Newcastle disease-affected regions, or have been vaccinated for the H5 or H7 subtype of avian influenza.

(b)(1) Birds from Canada may be imported in accordance with this section or, except for ratites in accordance with the provisions applicable to importation of poultry from Canada as specified in §§ 93.205, 93.214, and 93.216 of this part.

(2) Ratites and hatching eggs of ratites may be imported into the United States only in accordance with the provisions in this part that apply to commercial and zoological birds, and, where specified, with the provisions that apply to ratites or hatching eggs of ratites.

(3) Except for ratites imported as zoological birds, and ratites and ratite hatching eggs imported from Canada in accordance with § 93.107, ratites and hatching eggs of ratites may not be imported into the United States unless the following conditions are met:

(i) The ratites or hatching eggs are produced by a pen-raised flock, and, in the case of ratites, maintained in a pen-raised flock;

(ii) Each ratite produced in the flock is identified with an identification number by means of a microchip implanted at 1-day of age in the pipping muscle of ostriches and in the upper neck of other ratites, each ratite added from outside the flock is identified in like manner upon arrival in the flock, except that the microchip need not be implanted in the pipping muscle or the upper neck, and each ratite already in the flock as of March 8, 1994 is identified in like manner, prior to the next visit to the flock premises by an APHIS representative under § 93.103(a)(2)(iv), except that the microchip need not be implanted in the pipping muscle or the upper neck;

(iii) On the date it is produced, each hatching egg produced in the flock is marked in indelible ink with the date of the production, and with identification, assigned by the national government of the region of export, of the premises and region from which the ratites or hatching eggs are intended for exportation;

(iv) The owner or manager of the premises from which the ratites or hatching eggs are intended for importation into the United States maintains on a daily basis a register listing the following:

(A) Number of live ratites hatched in the flock or added to the flock, and number of live ratites removed from the flock, and the microchip number for each of these ratites;

[1] Importations of certain animals from various regions are absolutely prohibited under part 94 because of specified diseases.

(B) Number of eggs produced in the flock and date of production, and number of eggs removed from the flock and date of production; and

(C) Number of eggs in incubator/hatcher and date of production;

(v) The owner or manager of the premises submits a copy of the registers to the National Veterinary Service of the region of export on a quarterly basis. The region of export in turn submits a copy of the registers to the Administrator upon his or her request;[2]

(vi) The region from which the ratites or hatching eggs are exported to the United States maintains a registry of premises that wish to export ratites or hatching eggs of ratites to the United States, that lists each ratite according to the microchip number required under paragraph (b)(3)(iv) of this section, and also maintains a count of hatching eggs of ratites produced on or added to the premises;

(vii) Before a premises is added to the registry, either a veterinary officer of the national government of the region of export, or an employee of that government responsible for the protection of fish and wildlife, visits the premises and determines that all ratites and hatching eggs of ratites are identified as required under paragraphs (b)(3)(ii) and (b)(3)(iii) of this section.

(viii) The region from which the ratites or hatching eggs of ratites are exported to the United States requires each premises from which ratites or hatching eggs of ratites are exported to the United States to receive approval from the National Veterinary Service of that region before ratites are added to the premises from outside the premises, and also prohibits the addition of ratites to a flock during production seasons;

(ix) The region from which ratites or hatching eggs of ratites are exported to the United States establishes a maximum number of hatching eggs of ratites that may be produced on each premises over a set production season. The ceiling for each premises is calculated jointly by a full-time salaried veterinary officer of the national government of the region of export and the APHIS representative who conducts the site visit required under §93.103(a)(2)(iv), and is adjusted jointly by an APHIS representative and a full-time salaried veterinary officer of the national government of the region of export according to changes in the number of laying hens in the flock;

(x) The region of export conducts random inspections of each premises intending to export ratites or hatching eggs of ratites to the United States, at least twice during each production season, to ensure that all ratites and hatching eggs of ratites on the premises are identified as required under paragraphs (b)(3)(ii) and (b)(3)(iii) of this section. These inspections must be conducted by either a veterinary officer of the national government of the region of export or an employee of that government responsible for the protection of fish and wildlife. If any ratites or hatching eggs are not identified as required, the region of export must not issue the export certificate required under §93.104(a). The region of export must record, on the copy of the report required to be sent to the Administrator under paragraph (b)(3)(v) of this section, whether all ratites and hatching eggs are identified as required;

(xi) The region of export requires each premises on which ratites or hatching eggs of ratites intended for export to the United States are kept to submit to the National Veterinary Service of that region a copy of the certificate required under §93.104(a);

(xii) The person intending to import ratites into the United States provides the APHIS veterinary inspector at the intended port of entry with a reader capable of reading the microchip implanted in each of the ratites.

(4) Ratites and hatching eggs of ratites may not be imported into the United States in any container that holds hay, straw, grasses, wood chips, sawdust, or other materials likely to harbor ectoparasites. Ratites and hatching eggs of ratites that are imported into the United States in containers holding such materials will be refused entry.

[2] Copies should be mailed to the Animal and Plant Health Inspection Service, Veterinary Services, National Center for Import-Export, 4700 River Road Unit 38, Riverdale, Maryland 20737–1231.

(c)(1) Pet birds offered for entry from Canada and which are not known to be affected with or exposed to any communicable disease of poultry, which are caged (prior to release from the port of entry) and which are personal pets, may be imported by the owner thereof at any port of entry designated in §§93.103 or 93.203: *Provided*, That, such birds are found upon port of entry veterinary inspection under §93.105 to be free of poultry diseases and at the time of entry the owner signs and furnishes to the Administrator, a statement stating that the bird or birds have been in his or her possession for a minimum of 90 days preceding the date of importation and that during such time such birds have not been in contact with poultry or other birds (for example, association with other avian species at exhibitions or in aviaries.)

(2)(i) Except for pet birds that have been in any region where highly pathogenic avian influenza exists, which are subject to the provisions of paragraph (c)(3) of this section, pet birds of United States origin that have not been outside the country for more than 60 days may be offered for entry under the provisions of paragraph (c)(1) of this section if:

(A) The pet birds are accompanied by an import permit issued by APHIS: *Provided*, that an import permit will not be required for pet birds returning from Canada or Mexico through a land border port; and

(B) The birds are also accompanied by a United States veterinary health certificate issued prior to the departure of the birds from the United States and the certificate shows the number from the leg band, tattoo, or microchip affixed to the birds prior to departure; and

(C) During port of entry veterinary inspection it is determined that the number from the leg band, tattoo, or microchip on the bird is the same as the one listed on the health certificate.

(ii) Except for pet birds that have been in any region where highly pathogenic avian influenza exists, which are subject to the provisions of paragraph (c)(3) of this section, pet birds of United States origin that have been outside the country for more than 60 days may be imported by their owner if:

(A) The pet birds are accompanied by an import permit issued by APHIS: *Provided*, that an import permit will not be required for pet birds returning from Canada or Mexico through a land border port; and

(B) The pet birds are found upon port of entry veterinary inspection to be free of poultry diseases; and

(C) The pet birds are accompanied by a United States veterinary health certificate issued prior to the departure of the birds from the United States and the certificate shows the number from the leg band, tattoo, or microchip affixed to the birds prior to departure; and

(D) During port of entry veterinary inspection it is determined that the number from the leg band, tattoo, or microchip on the bird is the same as the one listed on the health certificate; and

(E) The owner importing the pet birds signs and furnishes to the Administrator the following:

(*1*) A notarized declaration under oath or affirmation (or a statement signed by the owner and witnessed by a Department inspector) stating that the bird or birds have not been in contact with poultry or other birds while out of the region (for example, association with other avian species at exhibitions or at aviaries); and

(*2*) An agreement on VS Form 17–8, obtainable from a Federal inspector at the port of entry, stating:

(*i*) That the birds will be maintained in confinement in his or her personal possession separate and apart from all poultry and other birds for a minimum of 30 days following importation at the address where the birds are to be held and made available for health inspection and testing by Department inspectors upon request until released at the end of such period by such an inspector; and

(*ii*) That appropriate Federal officials in the State of destination will be immediately notified if any signs of disease are noted in any of the birds or any bird dies during that period. The owner importing such birds must comply with the provisions of the aforementioned agreement before the birds may be released from confinement. Except for pet birds that have been in any region where highly pathogenic avian influenza exists, lots of pet birds of United States origin which do not otherwise meet the requirements of paragraphs (c)(1) or (2) of this section may be offered for entry under the provisions of paragraph (c)(4) of this section.

(3) Any pet birds of United States origin that have been in any region identified in accordance with §94.6(a)(2) of this subchapter as a region where highly pathogenic avian influenza exists, regardless of the length of time such birds have been outside of the United States, may only be imported through the port of Los Angeles, CA, Miami, FL, or New York, NY, and only under the following conditions:

(i) The birds meet the requirements of paragraphs (c)(2)(ii)(A) through (D) of this section; and

(ii) The birds are quarantined for a minimum of 30 days, and for such longer period as may be required by the Administrator in any specific case, at a USDA quarantine facility in accordance with §93.106.

(4) Pet birds which are not known to be affected with or exposed to communicable diseases of poultry may be offered for entry at one of the ports of entry designated in §93.102(a) under the following conditions:

(i) The pet birds shall be accompanied by a veterinary health certificate issued by a national government veterinary officer of the region of export stating that he or she personally inspected the birds listed on the health certificate and found them to be free of evidence of highly pathogenic avian influenza, Newcastle disease, chlamydiosis, and other communicable diseases of poultry, and that the birds were being exported in compliance with the laws and regulations of the region of export, or if exported from Mexico, shall be accompanied either by such a certificate or by a certificate issued by a veterinarian accredited by the National Government of Mexico and endorsed by a full-time salaried veterinary officer of the National Government of Mexico, thereby representing that the veterinarian issuing the certificate was authorized to do so. Certificates in a foreign language must be translated into English at the expense of the importer.

(ii) An advanced reservation fee as required by §93.103(a)(3) and a request for space which has been confirmed in writing, at a USDA-operated quarantine facility shall be made with the port veterinarian[3] at the port where the birds are to be held for a minimum 30-day isolation in a biologically secure unit separate and apart from all other avian species, except, that birds arriving without an advanced reservation may be handled if an isolation unit is available, provided the reservation fee as required in §93.103(a)(3) is paid. Pet birds offered for entry at a port of entry that has not been designated in §93.102(a), or pet birds arriving without an advanced reservation at a port of entry designated in §93.102(a) but at which isolation units are not available, shall be refused entry at such port. However, such pet birds may be transported at the owner's expense to another port of entry designated in §93.102(a) if available quarantine space exists, if the reservation fee is paid and the birds are shipped to such other port under conditions deemed sufficient by the Administrator to prevent the spread of communicable diseases of poultry: *Provided,* That pet birds arriving with or without an advance reservation at the port of Hidalgo, Texas, will be transported at Department expense to the quarantine facility at Mission, Texas, if available quarantine space exists at that facility, until quarantine facilities are available at Hidalgo, Texas; and pet birds arriving with or without an approved reservation entered at the port of New York, New York, will be transported at Department expense to the quarantine facility at Newburgh, New York, if available quarantine space exists at the facility, until quarantine facilities are available at New York, New York. Following the isolation period, if such birds are found to be free from communicable diseases of poultry, the birds

[3] The names and addresses of the port veterinarians, as well as a fee schedule for quarantine charges, are available from the Animal and Plant Health Inspection Service, Veterinary Services, Operational Support, 4700 River Road Unit 33, Riverdale, Maryland 20737–1231.

shall be returned at Department expense to the respective ports of Hidalgo, Texas, or New York, New York, as appropriate, for Agriculture release for entry through U.S. Customs.

(iii) During the isolation period, the birds shall be subjected to such tests and procedures as required by the Administrator to determine whether the birds are free from communicable diseases of poultry.

(iv) Following the isolation period, if the birds are found to be free of communicable disease of poultry, the port veterinarian shall issue an agriculture release for entry through U.S. Customs. If the birds are found during port of entry inspection or during quarantine to be infected with or exposed to a communicable disease of poultry, such birds shall be refused entry and handled in accordance with § 93.106(a) of this part.

(v) The owner of the birds is responsible for all costs which result from these procedures and shall reimburse APHIS for governmental expenses in accordance with § 93.210 (b) and (c) of this part.

(d) The provisions in this subpart relating to birds shall not apply to healthy birds, except ratites, not known to be infected with or exposed, within the 90 days preceding the date of export from the region of origin, to communicable diseases of poultry, if an import permit[4] has been obtained under § 93.103 of this chapter and all conditions therein are observed; and if such birds are handled as follows:

(1)(i) They are maintained under continuous confinement in transit through the United States aboard an aircraft, ocean vessel, or other means of conveyance; or

(ii) Except for birds in transit through Anchorage, Alaska, under § 93.103(c) of this part, which are not allowed to be unloaded, they are unloaded, in the course of such transit, into a bird holding facility which is provided by the carrier or its agent and has been approved[5] in advance by the Administrator in accordance with paragraph (d)(3) of this section as adequate to prevent the spread within the United States of any livestock or poultry disease, and they are maintained there under continuous confinement until loaded aboard a means of conveyance for transportation from the United States and are maintained under continuous confinement aboard such means of conveyance until it leaves the United States; the import permit will specify any additional conditions necessary to assure that the transit of the poultry or birds through the United States can be made without endangering the livestock or poultry of the United States, and that Department inspectors may inspect the poultry or birds on board such means of conveyance or in such holding facility to ascertain whether the requirements of this paragraph are met, and dispose of them in accordance with the Animal Health Protection Act (7 U.S.C. 8301 *et seq.*) if such conditions are not met; and

(2) The carrier or its agent executes and furnishes to the collector of Customs at the first port of arrival a declaration stating that the poultry or birds will be retained aboard such means of conveyance or in an approved holding facility during transhipment as required by this paragraph.

(3) Provisions for the approval of facilities required in this paragraph are:

(i) They must be sufficiently isolated to prevent direct or indirect contact with all other animals and birds while in the United States.

(ii) They must be so constructed that they provide adequate protection against environmental conditions and can be adequately cleaned, washed and disinfected.

(iii) They must provide for disposal of animal and bird carcasses, manure, bedding, waste and any related shipping materials in a manner that will prevent dissemination of disease.

(iv) They must have provisions for adequate sources of feed and water and

[4] Such permit may be obtained from the Animal and Plant Health Inspection Service, Veterinary Services, Operational Support, 4700 River Road Unit 33, Riverdale, Maryland 20737–1231 or by visiting *http://www.aphis.usda.gov/animal_health/permits/*". Requests for approval of such facilities should also be made to the Deputy Administrator.

[5] See footnote 4 in subpart A.

for attendants for the care and feeding of birds in the facility.

(v) They must comply with additional requirements as may be imposed by the Administrator if deemed applicable for a particular shipment.

(vi) They must also comply with all applicable local, State and Federal requirements for environmental quality and with the provisions of the Animal Welfare Regulations in chapter I of this title, as applicable.

(e) Commercial birds, zoological birds, research birds, or pet birds may be imported into the United States if they meet the requirements of §§93.102(a), 93.103, 93.104, 93.105(a), and 93.106(a) which specifically apply to such birds and the requirements of all other sections in this part that are applicable to poultry generally.

(f) *Performing or theatrical birds returning to the United States.* (1) Performing or theatrical birds of United States origin that are returning to the United States from Canada or Mexico may be imported if:

(i) The birds are found upon port of entry veterinary inspection to be free of avian diseases; and

(ii) The birds are accompanied by a United States veterinary health certificate issued prior to the departure of the birds from the United States and the certificate shows the number from the leg band, tattoo, or microchip affixed to the birds prior to departure; and

(iii) During port of entry veterinary inspection it is determined that the number from the leg band, tattoo, or microchip on the birds is the same as the one listed on the health certificate.

(2) Except for performing or theatrical birds that have been in any region where highly pathogenic avian influenza exists, which are subject to the provisions of paragraph (f)(3) of this section, performing or theatrical poultry of United States origin that have been outside the United States in a region other than Canada or Mexico may be imported if:

(i) The birds meet the requirements of paragraphs (f)(1)(i) through (iii) of this section; and

(ii) The birds are accompanied by an import permit issued by APHIS; and

(iii) The owner importing the birds signs and furnishes to the Administrator the following:

(A) A notarized declaration under oath or affirmation (or a statement signed by the owner and witnessed by a Department inspector) stating that the birds have not been in contact with other birds while out of the region (for example, association with other avian species at exhibitions or at aviaries); and

(B) An agreement on VS Form 17–8, available electronically or through other authorized method, obtainable from a Federal inspector at the port of entry, stating:

(*1*) That the birds will be maintained in confinement in his or her personal possession separate and apart from all birds and other birds for a minimum of 30 days following importation at the address where the birds are to be held and made available for health inspection and testing by Department inspectors upon request until released at the end of such period by such an inspector; and

(*2*) That appropriate Federal officials in the State of destination will be immediately notified if any signs of disease are noted in any of the birds or any birds die during that period. The owner importing such poultry must comply with the provisions of the aforementioned agreement before the birds may be released from confinement. Except for performing or theatrical birds that have been in any region where highly pathogenic avian influenza exists, performing or theatrical birds of United States origin which do not otherwise meet the requirements of paragraphs (f)(1) or (2) of this section may be offered for entry under the provisions of §93.101(c).

(3) Any performing or theatrical birds of United States origin that have been in any region identified in accordance with §94.6(a)(2) of this subchapter as a region where highly pathogenic avian influenza exists may only be imported through the port of Los Angeles, CA, Miami, FL, or New York, NY, and only under the following conditions:

(i) The birds meet the requirements of paragraphs (f)(1)(i) through (iii) of this section; and

(ii) The birds are accompanied by an import permit issued by APHIS; and

(iii) The birds are quarantined for a minimum of 30 days, and for such longer period as may be required by the Administrator in any specific case, at a quarantine facility maintained by APHIS in accordance with paragraphs (c)(3)(ii) through (c)(3)(iv) of this section.

(g) Any smuggled bird shall:

(1) Be refused entry into the United States and be removed from the United States,[6] or

(2) Be quarantined in a USDA-operated quarantine facility pending negative results to two consecutive tests for highly pathogenic avian influenza and Newcastle disease[7] administered not less than 30 days apart, with the first test administered within seven days after the bird enters the facility.

(3) Tissue samples from any smuggled bird which has died prior to release from quarantine shall be submitted for highly pathogenic avian influenza and Newcastle disease isolation. Smuggled birds shall also be subject to such other tests and procedures to determine whether the birds are free from communicable diseases of poultry other than highly pathogenic avian influenza and Newcastle disease when the port veterinarian determine that the bird in question has shown physical symptoms of being affected with or exposed to communicable diseases of poultry. A lot of smuggled birds placed into the quarantine facility shall be handled on an "all-in, all-out" basis: *Provided*, That birds of endangered and threatened species, as determined by the Department of the Interior (16 U.S.C. 1533, as amended) shall be separated for quarantine and testing as separate lots. If highly pathogenic avian influenza or Newcastle disease or any other communicable disease of poultry is diagnosed in any smuggled bird at any point or if it is determined that any smuggled bird has been exposed to highly pathogenic avian influenza or Newcastle disease or any other such communicable disease, such birds shall not be released from quarantine and shall be disposed of in accordance with procedures established by the Administrator to prevent the entry of communicable diseases of livestock or poultry into the United States. However, if endangered or threatened species are determined to be exposed such birds shall be held in permanent quarantine in accordance with such conditions as the Deputy Administrator may prescribe to protect poultry of the United States. At the time any smuggled bird enters the quarantine facility, it shall be identified in a manner approved by the Administrator.

(4) If the laboratory tests for highly pathogenic avian influenza and Newcastle disease are negative and as determined by the port veterinarian the birds are free of clinical evidence of diseases of poultry at the end of the quarantine period, the port veterinarian shall issue an agricultural release for entry of the birds through the United States Customs Service at the termination of the quarantine period. Providing that the sale of the smuggled birds is not contrary to any Federal law or regulation, expenses incurred by the Department for the handling of the smuggled birds under this paragraph shall be reimbursed from funds derived from the sale or disposition of the smuggled birds after their release from quarantine. Any smuggled bird which by law may not be sold, or so disposed, shall be quarantined in accordance with such procedures as the Deputy Administrator may establish to prevent the introduction of communicable diseases of livestock or poultry into the United States, in accordance with the law.

(Approved by the Office of Management and Budget under control numbers 0579–0220 and 0579–0245)

[55 FR 31495, Aug. 2, 1990. Redesignated at 62 FR 56012, Oct. 28, 1997]

EDITORIAL NOTE: For FEDERAL REGISTER citations affecting §93.101, see the List of CFR Sections Affected, which appears in the Finding Aids section of the printed volume and at *www.fdsys.gov*.

[6] Birds that would require handfeeding will be refused entry.

[7] Such tests are conducted according to protocols for highly pathogenic avian influenza and Newcastle disease which are available upon request from the Administrator.

§93.102 Ports designated for the importation of birds.

(a) *Special ports for pet birds.* The following ports are designated as ports of entry for pet birds imported under the provisions of §93.101(c) and performing or theatrical birds imported under the provisions of §93.101(f): Los Angeles and San Ysidro, CA; Miami, FL; New York, NY; Baudette, MN; and Hidalgo, TX.

(b) *Designation of other ports.* The Secretary of the Treasury has approved the designation as quarantine stations of the ports specified in this section. In special cases other ports may be designated as quarantine stations under this section by the Administrator, with the concurrence of the Secretary of the Treasury.

(c) Notwithstanding any other provisions of this section, all commercial birds, zoological birds, or research birds shall be imported only at a port of entry specified in §93.105.

(d) *Limited ports.* The following ports are designated as ports of entry for pet birds imported under the provisions of §93.101(c)(1) or (2) and performing or theatrical birds imported under the provisions of §93.101(f): Anchorage and Fairbanks, AK; San Diego, CA; Jacksonville, Port Canaveral, St. Petersburg-Clearwater, and Tampa, FL; Atlanta, GA; Honolulu, HI; Chicago, IL; New Orleans, LA; Baltimore, MD; Portland, ME; Minneapolis, MN; Great Falls, MT; Covington, KY (Greater Cincinnati International Airport); Portland, OR; San Juan, PR; Galveston and Houston, TX; and Seattle, Spokane, and Tacoma, WA.

[55 FR 31495, Aug. 2, 1990, as amended at 59 FR 36026, July 15, 1994; 60 FR 16045, Mar. 29, 1995; 60 FR 25120, May 11, 1995; 61 FR 68125, Dec. 27, 1996. Redesignated and amended at 62 FR 56012, 56014, Oct. 28, 1997; 65 FR 38178, June 20, 2000; 67 FR 6370, Feb. 12, 2002]

§93.103 Import permits for birds; and reservation fees for space at quarantine facilities maintained by APHIS.

(a) *Application for permit; reservation required.* Before any permit application is submitted, all construction at the quarantine facility must be completed.

(1) For pet birds, commercial birds, research birds, zoological birds, and performing or theatrical birds, intended for importation into the United States, except as otherwise provided in §§93.101(b) and (c), 93.103(c), and 93.107(b), the importer shall first apply for and obtain an import permit. The importer (permit applicant) shall submit a completed VS form 17–128 for ratites or hatching eggs of ratites; or, for other birds, a completed VS form 17–20; or shall submit a document that states that it is an application for a permit to import ratites, hatching eggs of ratites, or birds other than ratites or hatching eggs of ratites. The application[8] must include the following information:

(i) The name, address, and telephone number of the importer;

(ii) The status of the importer, such as individual, partnership, or corporation (if incorporated, include State where incorporated and date of incorporation);

(iii) Name and address of the quarantine facility;

(iv) Date of intended quarantine;

(v) The purpose of the importation;

(vi) The region of origin;

(vii) The name and address of the exporter;

(viii) The port of embarkation in the foreign region;

(ix) The mode of transportation, route of travel, and port of entry in the United States;

(x) The name and location of the quarantine facility in the United States to which delivery will be made from the port of entry, in accordance with §93.106(c)(5);

(xi) A drawing of the floor plan for the facility showing the location of the bird holding area; equipment storage areas; office areas; clothes storage and change areas; feed storage areas; necropsy areas (showing entry and refrigeration); washing areas for equipment;

[8] VS import permit application forms are available from local offices of Veterinary Services, which are listed in telephone directories, or from the Animal and Plant Health Inspection Service, Veterinary Services, National Center for Import-Export, 4700 River Road Unit 38, Riverdale, Maryland 20737–1231 or by visiting *http://www.aphis.usda.gov/animal_health/permits/*. For other permit requirements for birds, the regulations issued by the U.S. Department of the Interior (title 50, Code of Federal Regulations, parts 14 and 17) should be consulted.

shower areas; ventilation arrangements; and entries and exits; and, for a facility for hatching eggs of ratites in which the hatching eggs of one lot may be quarantined at the same time as the hatched chicks from a previously quarantined lot, the incubation/hatcher and bird (chick) holding areas; and

(xii) Date and certification, by signature of the importer (permit applicant), after the following language:

I certify that the information provided herein is true and correct to the best of my knowledge and belief, and agree to comply with the applicable regulations in title 9, Code of Federal Regulations, §§ 93.100 through 93.107;

(xiii) In addition, the application for a permit to import ratites or hatching eggs of ratites, except for ratites and hatching eggs of ratites imported from Canada in accordance with § 93.107, shall specify the number of ratites or hatching eggs intended for importation, the size of the flock of origin, and the location of the premises where the flock of origin is kept; and shall state that, from the date of application through the date of export, APHIS representatives shall be granted access to the premises where the flock of origin is kept. (For ratites intended for importation as zoological birds, the flock of origin shall be the ratites intended for importation.)

(2)(i) An import permit will be issued only after an APHIS representative has inspected the quarantine facility identified on the permit application, and has determined that it meets the standards set forth in § 93.106(c) of this part.

(ii) An application for a permit to import pet birds, commercial birds, research birds, zoological birds, and performing or theatrical birds, may be denied or withdrawn because of: Communicable disease conditions in the area or region of origin, or in a region where the shipment has been or will be held or through which the shipment has been or will be transported; deficiencies in the regulatory programs for the control or eradication of animal diseases and the unavailability of veterinary services in the above mentioned countries; the importer's failure to provide satisfactory evidence concerning the origin, history, and health status of the animals; the lack of satisfactory information necessary to determine that the importation will not be likely to transmit any communicable disease to livestock or poultry of the United States; the lack of APHIS personnel; any outstanding debts to APHIS the permit applicant has not paid when due; or any other circumstances which the Administrator believes require such denial or withdrawal to prevent the dissemination of any communicable disease of livestock or poultry into the United States, such as if:

(A) Any requirement of this subpart is not complied with;

(B) The importer (permit applicant) or any person responsibly connected with the importer's business, any person responsibly connected with the privately owned bird quarantine facility through which the importation is intended, or, in the case of the importation of ratites or ratite hatching eggs, the operator of the flock of origin or a person responsibly connected with the owner of the flock of origin, has been convicted of any crime under any law regarding the import or export of goods, regarding the quarantine of any animal or bird, or the illegal movement of goods within a region, or involving fraud, bribery, extortion, or of any other crime involving lack of the integrity needed for the conduct of operations affecting the importation of birds;

(C) The importer (permit applicant) or any person responsibly connected with the importer's business, any person responsibly connected with the privately owned bird quarantine facility intended for use for the importation, or, in the case of the importation of ratites or ratite hatching eggs, the operator of the flock of origin or a person responsibly connected with the owner of the flock of origin, threatens to forcibly assault or forcibly assaults, intimidates, or interferes with any APHIS representative or employee in or on account of the performance of his or her official duties, unless, promptly upon the incident being brought to the importer's attention by the authorized supervisor of the APHIS representative or employee, and to the satisfaction of that supervisor, the importer justifies the incident, takes effective steps to prevent a recurrence, or provides acceptable assurance that there will not be any recurrences; or

(D) For any violation of the regulations in this subpart.

(iii) In addition, a permit to import ratites or hatching eggs of ratites, except for ratites or hatching eggs of ratites imported from Canada in accordance with §93.107, will be denied or withdrawn unless APHIS representatives are granted access to the premises where the flock of origin is kept (or, in the case of zoological birds, to the premises where the birds are kept), from the date of the application for the permit through the date of export.

(iv) Except for ratites intended for importation as zoological birds and ratites and hatching eggs of ratites imported from Canada in accordance with §93.107, a permit to import ratites or hatching eggs of ratites will be denied or withdrawn unless an APHIS representative has visited the premises where the flock of origin is kept within the 12-month period before the intended importation and has determined that the flock is pen-raised and contains sufficient breeding pairs to produce the number of ratites or hatching eggs intended for importation.

(v) A permit to import ratites or hatching eggs of ratites will be denied or withdrawn if an inspection of the premises of the flock or origin, carried out by the national government of the region of export under §93.101(b)(3), indicates that the ratites and hatching eggs are not identified and marked as required under §93.101(b)(3).

(vi) For the purposes of this section, a person shall be deemed to be responsibly connected with an importer's business, a privately owned bird quarantine facility, or an owner of a flock of origin, if such person has an ownership, mortgage, or lease interest in the physical plant of the importer's business, the privately owned bird quarantine facility, or the farm of the flock of origin, or if such person is a partner, officer, director, holder or owner of 10 per centum or more of the voting stock of the importer's business, the privately owned bird quarantine facility, or the farm of the flock of origin, or is an employee of the importer's business, the privately owned bird quarantine facility, or the owner of the flock of origin.

(vii) A permit may be denied or withdrawn at any time by the Administrator, for any of the reasons provided in paragraphs (a)(2)(ii), (iii), (iv), or (v) of this section. Before such action is taken, the importer will be informed of the reasons for the proposed action and, upon request in case of a dispute of material facts, shall be afforded an opportunity for a hearing with respect to the merits or validity of such action, in accordance with rules of practice which shall be adopted for the proceeding. However, withdrawal of a permit shall become effective pending final determination in the proceeding, when the Administrator determines that such action is necessary to protect the public health, interest, or safety. Such withdrawal shall be effective upon oral or written notification, whichever is earlier, to the importer. In the event of oral notification, written confirmation shall be given to the importer as promptly as circumstances permit. This withdrawal shall continue in effect pending the completion of the proceeding and any judicial review thereof, unless otherwise ordered by the Administrator.

(viii) If APHIS receives more than one application for a permit to import birds through a specified port of entry at approximately the same time, such that APHIS personnel could provide services to only one importer (permit applicant) who requests them, APHIS will issue the permit to the first importer who meets the requirements of this subpart to deposit, with the Administrator, the completed cooperative and trust fund agreement, accompanied by the required deposit.

(3)(i) The importer or importer's agent shall pay or ensure payment of a reservation fee for each lot of birds to be quarantined in a facility maintained by USDA. For birds the reservation fee shall be 100 percent of the cost of providing care, feed, and handling during quarantine, as estimated by the quarantine facility's veterinarian in charge.

(ii) At the time the importer or the importer's agent requests a reservation of quarantine space, the importer or importer's agent shall pay the reservation fee by check or U.S. money order or ensure payment of the reservation fee by an irrevocable letter of credit from a commercial bank (the effective date on such letter of credit shall run to 30 days after the date the birds are scheduled to be released from quarantine); except that anyone who issues a check to the Department for a reservation fee which is returned because of insufficient funds shall be denied any further request for reservation of a quarantine space until the outstanding amount is paid.

(iii) Any reservation fee paid by check or U.S. money order shall be applied against the expenses incurred for services received by the importer or importer's agent in connection with the quarantine for which the reservation was made. Any part of the reservation fee which remains unused after being applied against the expenses incurred for services received by the importer or the importer's agent in connection with the quarantine for which the reservation was made, shall be returned to the individual who paid the reservation fee. If the reservation fee is ensured by a letter of credit, the Department will draw against the letter of credit unless payment for services received by the importer or importer's agent in connection with the quarantine is otherwise made at least 3 days prior to the expiration date of the letter of credit.

(iv) Any reservation fee shall be forfeited if the importer or the importer's agent fails to present for entry, within 24 hours following the designated time of arrival, the lot of birds for which the reservation was made: *Except* that a reservation fee shall not be forfeited if:

(A) Written notice of cancellation from the importer or the importer's agent is received by the office of the veterinarian in charge of the quarantine facility[9] during regular business hours (8:00 a.m. to 4:30 p.m. Monday through Friday, excluding holidays) no later than 15 days for birds prior to the beginning of the time of importation as specified in the import permit or as arranged with the veterinarian in charge of the quarantine facility if no import permit is required (the 15 day period shall not include Saturdays, Sundays, or holidays), or

(B) The Administrator determines that services, other than provided by carriers, necessary for the importation of the poultry or birds within the requested period are unavailable because of unforeseen circumstances as determined by the Administrator, (such as the closing of an airport due to inclement weather or the unavailability of the reserved space due to the extension of another quarantine.)

(v) If the reservation fee was ensured by a letter of credit and the fee is to be forfeited under paragraph (a)(3)(iv) of this section, the Department will draw against the letter of credit unless the reservation fee is otherwise paid at least 3 days prior to the expiration date of the letter of credit.

(vi) When a reservation is cancelled in accordance with paragraph (a)(3)(iv)(A) of this section and the provisions of paragraph (a)(3)(iv)(B) of this section do not apply, a $40.00 cancellation fee shall be charged. If a reservation fee was paid, the cancellation fee shall be deducted from any reservation fee returned to the importer or the importer's agent. If the reservation fee was ensured by a letter of credit, the Department will draw the amount of the cancellation fee against the letter of credit unless the cancellation fee is otherwise paid at least 3 days prior to the expiration date of the letter of credit.

(4) *Permit applications for ratites.* (i) If quarantine space for ratites is desired at either the New York Animal Import Center or the Miami Animal Import Center, permit applications must be submitted to the New York Animal Import Center, USDA, APHIS, Veterinary Services, 200 Drury Lane, Rock Tavern, NY, 12575, or to the port veterinarian in charge of the New York Animal Import Center.

(ii) Quarantine space for ratites will be offered in the order that permit applications are or have been received,

[9] The addresses of USDA quarantine facilities may be found in telephone directories listing the facilities or by contacting the Animal and Plant Health Inspection Service, Veterinary Services, National Center for Import-Export, 4700 River Road Unit 38, Riverdale, Maryland 20737–1231.

beginning with those permit applications received on August 12, 1991. Reservations for quarantine space at the Miami Animal Import Center will be limited to a maximum of 100 ratites per permit application. There will be a single waiting list for quarantine space at the Miami Animal Import Center and the New York Animal Import Center. Importers who prefer one of these two facilities over the other may remain on the waiting list until space opens up at the facility of their choice.

(b) *Permit.* Except as provided in paragraph (c) of this section, when a permit is issued, the original and two copies will be sent to the importer. It shall be the responsibility of the importer to forward the original permit and one copy to the shipper in the region of origin, and it shall also be the responsibility of the importer to insure that the shipper presents the copy of the permit to the carrier and makes proper arrangements for the original permit to accompany the shipment to the specified U.S. port of entry for presentation to the collector of customs. The time prescribed in permits from the importation of pet birds, commercial birds, zoological birds, or research birds, shall not exceed 30 days, and for performing or theatrical birds shall not exceed 90 days. Birds for which a permit is required by these regulations will not be eligible for entry if a permit has not been issued; if unaccompanied by such a permit; if shipment is from any port other than the one designated in the permit; if arrival in the United States is at any port other than the one designated in the permit; if the birds offered for entry differ from those described in the permit.

(c) Notwithstanding any other provisions in this part, importers are not required to obtain an import permit and provide the shipper with an original import permit for each individual shipment of birds other than ratites transiting the port of Anchorage, Alaska, if the following conditions are met:

(1) The importer applies for and obtains an import permit for multiple shipments of birds transiting the port of Anchorage, Alaska, in accordance with the provisions of this section and related requirements concerning application for the permit. However, the following information is not required on the application:

(i) The species, breed, and number of birds to be imported;

(ii) The region of origin;

(iii) The name and address of the exporter;

(iv) The port of embarkation in the foreign region;

(v) The mode of transportation and the route of travel;

(vi) The proposed date of arrival of the birds; and

(vii) The name and address of the person to whom the birds or poultry will be delivered.

(2) The importer completes a copy of the import permit obtained under paragraph (c)(1) of this section for each separate shipment of birds intended to transit the port of Anchorage, Alaska, by inserting the following information on a copy of the permit:

(i) The species, breed, and number of birds to be imported;

(ii) The region of origin;

(iii) The name and address of the exporter;

(iv) The port of embarkation in the foreign region;

(v) The mode of transportation and the route of travel;

(vi) The proposed date of arrival of the birds; and

(vii) The name and address of the person to whom the birds will be delivered.

(3) The importer, not less than 2 weeks prior to the anticipated date of arrival of each separate intransit shipment of birds at the port of Anchorage, Alaska, provides the port veterinarian with a copy of the completed import permit;

(4) A copy of the completed import permit accompanies each separate intransit shipment of birds or poultry to the port of Anchorage, Alaska;

(5) Import permits issued for multiple shipments of birds transiting the port of Anchorage, Alaska, will be

valid only during the calendar year in which they are issued.

(Approved by the Office of Management and Budget under control number 0579–0040)

[55 FR 31495, Aug. 2, 1990, as amended at 56 FR 31866, July 12, 1991; 57 FR 21725, May 22, 1992; 59 FR 10733, Mar. 8, 1994; 59 FR 47068, Sept. 14, 1994; 59 FR 47235, Sept. 15, 1994; 59 FR 67614, Dec. 30, 1994; 61 FR 68125, Dec. 27, 1996. Redesignated and amended at 56012, 56014, Oct. 28, 1997; 65 FR 38178, June 20, 2000; 81 FR 40151, June 21, 2016]

§ 93.104 Certificate for pet birds, commercial birds, zoological birds, and research birds.

(a) *General.* All pet birds, except as provided for in § 93.101 (b) and (c) of this part; all research birds; and all commercial birds and zoological birds, including ratites and hatching eggs of ratites, offered for importation from any part of the world, shall be accompanied by a certificate issued by a full-time salaried veterinary officer of the national government of the exporting region, or issued by a veterinarian authorized or accredited by the national government of the exporting region and endorsed by a full-time salaried veterinary officer of the national government of that region.

(b) *Birds other than ratites.* The certificate for birds other than ratites must state:

(1) That all birds covered by the certificate have been inspected by the veterinarian issuing the certificate;

(2) That no evidence of Newcastle disease, highly pathogenic avian influenza, chlamydiosis, or other communicable disease of poultry was found among the birds;

(3) That insofar as has been possible to determine, the birds were not exposed to Newcastle disease, highly pathogenic avian influenza, chlamydiosis, or other communicable disease of poultry during the 90 days immediately preceding their exportation;

(4) That the birds have not been vaccinated with a vaccine for the H5 or H7 subtype of avian influenza; however, zoological birds that have been vaccinated for avian influenza subtypes H5 or H7 as part of an official program, using vaccine products approved and used under supervision by the veterinary authorities of the exporting country, may be imported under specific conditions as determined by the Administrator and specified in an import permit. Such birds must be exported with permanent individual identification and meet the other requirements for entry under this part, and will be subject to official testing and quarantine on arrival to the United States.

(5) That highly pathogenic avian influenza or Newcastle disease did not occur anywhere on the premises from which the birds were to be exported or on adjacent premises during the 90 days immediately preceding the exportation of the birds;

(6) That neither the premises from which the birds were to be exported nor any adjacent premises were located in any area under quarantine for poultry diseases at any time during the 90 days immediately preceding the exportation of the birds, and that the birds have not originated from or been moved through a region identified in accordance with § 94.6(a) of this subchapter as a region where highly pathogenic avian influenza exists; and

(7) That the birds were placed into new or appropriately sanitized packaging materials at the premises from which the birds were to be exported.

(c) *Ratites other than hatching eggs.* The certificate for ratites other than hatching eggs must state:

(1) That, except as provided in paragraph (c)(13) of this section, all ratites covered by the certificate, and their flock of origin, have been inspected by the veterinarian issuing the certificate;

(2) That, except when the certificate is for zoological birds or ratites imported from Canada in accordance with § 93.107, the flock of origin is pen-raised and the ratites covered by the certificate were produced and maintained in that flock;

(3) That no evidence of Newcastle disease, highly pathogenic avian influenza, chlamydiosis, or other communicable disease of poultry was found in the flock of origin;

(4) That insofar as has been possible to determine, the flock of origin was not exposed to Newcastle disease, highly pathogenic avian influenza, chlamydiosis, or other communicable

disease of pountry during the 90 days immediately preceding the exportation;

(5) That none of the ratites intended for shipment to the United States have been vaccinated with Newcastle disease vaccine or with a vaccine for the H5 or H7 subtype of avian influenza;

(6) That highly pathogenic avian influenza or Newcastle disease did not occur anywhere on the premises where the flock of origin was kept or on adjacent premises during the 90 days immediately preceding the exportation;

(7) That neither the premises where the flock of origin was kept nor any adjacent premises was located in any area under quarantine for poultry diseases at any time during the 90 days immediately preceding the exportation, and that the ratites have not originated from or been moved through a region identified in accordance with § 94.6(a) of this subchapter as a region where highly pathogenic avian influenza exists;

(8) That, except as provided in § 93.107 for ratites imported from Canada for immediate slaughter, the ratites were treated at least 3 days but not more than 14 days before being loaded for shipment to the United States with a pesticide of a type and concentration sufficient to kill ectoparasites on the ratites;

(9) That the pesticide was applied to all body surfaces of the ratites under the supervision of the veterinarian issuing the certificate;

(10) That the ratites, after being treated for ectoparasites, did not have physical contact with, or share a pen or bedding materials with, any ratite not in the same shipment to the United States; and

(11) That the ratites were placed in new or appropriately sanitized packaging materials for shipment to the United States at the premises where the flock of origin was kept.

(12) The number of ratites contained in the shipment;

(13) That the number of ratites and hatching eggs of ratites exported from the flock of origin has not exceeded the ceiling required to be established under § 93.101(b)(3)(ix);

(14) That all the ratites and hatching eggs of ratites in the flock from which the ratites come were identified in accordance with § 93.101(b)(3);

(15) Except for ratites imported from Canada in accordance with § 93.107, the number of ratite laying hens in the flock from which the ratites come;

(16) For ratites required to be treated prior to shipment with a pesticide for ectoparasites, the certificate must also state the name, concentration, and date of administration of the pesticide used to treat the ratites;

(17) When ratites intended for importation are zoological birds, only the ratites to be imported must be inspected, and the provisions in paragraphs (c)(3), (c)(4), (c)(5), (c)(6), (c)(7), and (c)(11) that apply to the flock of origin shall apply only to the ratites intended for importation.

(d) *Hatching eggs of ratites.* The certificate for hatching eggs of ratites must state:

(1) That the flock of origin of the hatching eggs has been inspected by the veterinarian issuing the certificate;

(2) That, except when the certificate is for hatching eggs of ratites imported from Canada in accordance with § 93.107, the flock of origin is pen-raised, and the hatching eggs covered by the certificate were produced by that flock;

(3) That no evidence of Newcastle disease, highly pathogenic avian influenza, chlamydiosis, or other communicable disease of poultry was found in the flock of origin;

(4) That insofar as has been possible to determine, the flock of origin was not exposed to Newcastle disease, highly pathogenic avian influenza, chlamydiosis, or other communicable disease of poultry during the 90 days immediately preceding the exportation of the hatching eggs;

(5) That highly pathogenic avian influenza or Newcastle disease did not occur anywhere on the premises where the flock of origin was kept or on adjacent premises during the 90 days immediately preceding the exportation of the hatching eggs;

(6) That neither the premises where the flock of origin was kept nor any adjacent premises were located in any area under quarantine for poultry diseases at any time during the 90 days

immediately preceding the exportation of the hatching eggs; and

(7) That the hatching eggs were placed into new or appropriately sanitized packaging materials for shipment to the United States at the premises where the flock of origin was kept.

(8) The number of hatching eggs contained in the shipment;

(9) That the number of ratites and hatching eggs of ratites exported from the flock of origin has not exceeded the ceiling required to be established under § 93.101(b)(3)(ix);

(10) That all the ratites and hatching eggs of ratites in the flock from which the hatching eggs come were identified in accordance with § 93.101(b)(3);

(11) Except for hatching eggs of ratites imported from Canada in accordance with § 93.107, the number of ratite laying hens in the flock from which the hatching eggs come.

(Approved by the Office of Management and Budget under control number 0579–0040)

[56 FR 31866, July 12, 1991; 56 FR 41726, Aug. 22, 1991, as amended at 57 FR 28080, June 24, 1992; 59 FR 10733, Mar. 8, 1994; 59 FR 47235, Sept. 15, 1994; 61 FR 56891, Nov. 5, 1996; 61 FR 68126, Dec. 27, 1996. Redesignated and amended at 62 FR 56012, 56014, Oct. 28, 1997; 76 FR 4053, Jan. 24, 2011; 79 FR 71005, Dec. 1, 2014]

§ 93.105 Inspection at the port of entry.

(a) All commercial birds, zoological birds, and research birds, including hatching eggs of ratites, but excluding other ratites, imported into the United States, must be inspected by the port veterinarian at the Customs port of entry, which may be any international airport, or any land-border port within 20 miles of an international airport, serviced by Customs, as well as, for Canadian-origin hatching eggs of ratites, ports listed in § 93.107 (c). However, hatching eggs of ratites may be shipped, in bond, from the port of first arrival to the Customs port of entry at which they will be quarantined, for inspection, at that port.

(b) All pet birds imported from any part of the world, except pet birds from Canada and pet birds meeting the provisions of § 93.101(c)(2), shall be subjected to inspection at the Customs port of entry by a veterinary inspector of APHIS and such birds shall be permitted entry only at the ports listed in § 93.102(a). Pet birds of Canadian origin and those birds meeting the provisions of § 93.101(c)(2) shall be subject to veterinary inspection at any of the ports of entry listed in § 93.102 and 93.203.

(c) Ratites, other than hatching eggs of ratites, imported from any part of the world must be inspected at the Customs port of entry by a veterinary inspector of APHIS and, except as provided in § 93.107(b) for ratites imported from Canada, shall be permitted entry only at one of the following ports of entry:

(1) Ostriches:

(i) Up to 36 inches in height (as measured from the top of the head to the base of the feet) or 30 pounds in weight: New York, NY; Stewart Airport, Newburgh, NY; and Miami, FL.

(ii) Exceeding 36 inches in height or 30 pounds in weight: New York, NY, and Stewart Airport, Newburgh, NY.

(2) Ratites other than ostriches: New York, NY; Stewart Airport, Newburgh, NY; and Miami, FL.

[55 FR 31495, Aug. 2, 1990, as amended at 56 FR 31867, July 12, 1991; 57 FR 21726, May 22, 1992; 59 FR 36026, July 15, 1994; 59 FR 47069, Sept. 14, 1994; 61 FR 68126, Dec. 27, 1996. Redesignated and amended at 62 FR 56012, 56014, Oct. 28, 1997; 65 FR 38178, June 20, 2000]

§ 93.106 Quarantine requirements.

(a) *Birds other than ratites and hatching eggs of ratites.* Each lot of pet birds, except as provided for in § 93.101(c) of this part; research birds; and commercial birds and zoological birds, except ratites and hatching eggs of ratites, imported into the United States shall be quarantined for a minimum of 30 days, and for such longer period as may be required by the Administrator, in any specific case, on an "all-in, all-out" basis, at a Customs port of entry, at a USDA quarantine facility when arrangements have been made in advance by the importer and approval is granted in the permit described in § 93.103, or in facilities that meet the requirements of paragraph (c) of this section. At a USDA quarantine facility each psittacine bird shall be individually identified by the Department within 7 days of the entry of the bird into the bird quarantine facility with a serially numbered legband which has been coded to the quarantine facility or by other suitable means of identification. The identification device must be approved by the Administrator, before it shall be used to identify birds under this section. Such means of identification shall be supplied by the Department at cost to the importer. The Department shall make an identification record at the time such bird is so identified containing the species of the bird, including the common and scientific name, and the number of the identification device placed on the bird. The daily log and the identification record shall be maintained for 12 months following the date of the release of the bird from quarantine. Prior to use of a privately owned quarantine facility, a Cooperative and Trust Fund Agreement as set forth in paragraph (c)(5) of this section shall be executed by the importer and the Department and appropriate funds shall be deposited with the Administrator pursuant to the Cooperative and Trust Fund Agreement. If the birds are found free of evidence of communicable diseases of poultry during quarantine, then the port veterinarian shall issue an agriculture release for entry through U.S. Customs. If the birds are found during port of entry inspection or during quarantine, to be infected with or exposed to a communicable disease of poultry, such birds shall be refused entry or shall be held for an additional period in quarantine until determined to be free of evidence of any communicable disease, or shall be otherwise disposed of as directed by the Administrator. See also paragraph (c)(3)(ii)(E) of this section.

(b) *Ratites and hatching eggs of ratites.* (1) Each lot of ratites imported from any part of the world except as provided in §93.107, shall be quarantined upon arrival for a minimum of 30 days, and for such longer period as may be required by the Administrator to determine the ratites' freedom from ectoparasites and communicable diseases. Quarantine shall be on an "all-in, all-out" basis, as described in paragraph (c)(3)(ii)(A) of this section, at the New York Animal Import Center at Newburgh, NY, when the port of entry is either New York, NY, or Stewart Airport, Newburgh, NY; or at the Miami Animal Import Center, Miami, FL, when the port of entry is Miami, FL. Reservations for space in these quarantine facilities must be made in advance of arrival and in accordance with §93.103 of this part.

(2) Each lot of hatching eggs of ratites imported from any part of the world except as provided in §93.107, shall be quarantined upon arrival, incubated for the full incubation period (approximately 42 days), and held in quarantine for a minimum of 30 days following the hatch of the last chick in the lot, and for such longer period as may be required by the Administrator to determine the ratites' freedom from communicable diseases. Quarantine shall be conducted at a facility that meets the requirements of paragraph (c) of this section, and in the manner prescribed by paragraph (c) of this section.

(3) During the quarantine period, the ratites, including chicks hatched in quarantine, shall be tested for viral diseases of poultry, including highly pathogenic avian influenza and Newcastle disease. If any of the ratites exhibit evidence of other communicable diseases, they will be subjected to such additional tests as may be required by the Administrator to determine their freedom from communicable diseases. Ratites other than those imported as hatching eggs also shall be treated for ectoparasites[10] by an inspector until the inspector determines that the ratites are free of ectoparasites.

(4) If the ratites, including chicks hatched during quarantine, are determined to be free of communicable diseases, the port veterinarian shall issue an agricultural release for entry through U.S. Customs. If the port veterinarian finds evidence of communicable disease, or exposure to communicable disease, during port of entry inspection or quarantine of the ratites, the ratites shall be refused entry, or shall be held in quarantine until they

[10] APHIS will use an EPA registered dust formulation that contains 5 percent carbaryl as the only active ingredient. The dust formulation will be used in accordance with all applicable directions, restrictions, and precautions on the label. Treated birds may not be slaughtered for food purposes.

are determined to be free of communicable disease, or shall be otherwise disposed of as directed by the Administrator.

(c) *Standards for privately owned bird quarantine facilities and handling procedures for importation of birds.* Before the Administrator will issue an import permit for a lot of birds, the Administrator must determine that the privately owned bird quarantine facility to be used to quarantine birds imported into the United States (the facility) and its maintenance and operation meet the minimum requirements of paragraphs (c)(1) through (c)(5) of this section, that adequate APHIS personnel are available to provide services required by the facility, and that a Cooperative and Trust Fund Agreement between the importer and the Department has been executed, and the required funds have been deposited, in accordance with that agreement. The cost of the facility and all costs associated with its maintenance and operation must be borne by the importer, in accordance with the provisions of paragraph (e) of this section.

(1) *Supervision of the facility.* The facility shall be maintained under the supervision of the port veterinarian at the Customs port of entry.

(2) *Physical plant requirements.* The facility shall comply with the following requirements:

(i) *Location.* Each privately owned bird quarantine facility shall be located:

(A) Within the immediate metropolitan area of the port of entry to prevent the imported birds, while in transit to the quarantine facility, from introducing or disseminating disease to domestic poultry or livestock.

(B) At least one-half mile from any concentration of avian species, such as, but not limited to, poultry processing plants, poultry or bird farms, pigeon lofts, or other bird quarantine facilities. Factors such as prevailing winds, the efficiency of the air filtration system of the quarantine facility, possible exposure to poultry or birds moving in local traffic, etc., shall be taken into consideration.

(ii) *Construction.* Each quarantine facility shall consist of a single, self-contained building, which shall:

(A) Be constructed only with material that can withstand continued cleaning and disinfection. All solid walls, floors, and ceilings must be constructed of impervious material. All openings to the outside must be double-screened, with an interior screen of metal or nylon mesh that is impervious to biting insects such as gnats or mosquitos, and an exterior metal screen that is rodent-proof and is made of wire, such as rabbit wire, hardware cloth, or smooth welded wire, with mesh size no larger than 1 inch × 1.5 inches (2.54 cm × 3.81 cm). The interior and exterior screens must be separated by at least 3 inches (7.62 cm);

(B) Have a bird holding area of sufficient size to prevent overcrowding of the birds in quarantine. (All access into this holding area shall be from within the building and each entryway into such area shall be equipped with self-closing, double doors: *Provided,* That emergency exits to the outside may exist in the bird holding area if required by local fire ordinances. Such emergency exits shall be constructed so as to permit their opening from the inside of the facility only.);

(C) Have a ventilation capacity sufficient to control moisture and odor at levels that are not injurious to the health of the birds in quarantine;

(D) Have a vermin-proof feed storage area;

(E) Have office space for recordkeeping;

(F) Have a separate necropsy room which shall have refrigerated storage space for carcasses retained for laboratory examination and facilities adequate for specimen preparation and carcass disposal;

(G) Have a separate area for washing facility equipment;

(H) Have a shower at the entrance into the area comprised of the bird holding and necropsy rooms and a clothes storage and change area at each end of the shower area;

(I) Have a storage area for equipment necessary for quarantine operations;

(J) Have equipment necessary to maintain the facility in clean and sanitary condition, including insect and pest control equipment;

(K) Have a receptacle for soiled and contaminated clothing in the clothes change area located nearest the entrance to the bird holding area;

(L) All construction must be completed before any permit application is submitted in accordance with §93.103.

(M) An APHIS representative shall inspect the facility to determine whether the facility complies with the standards set forth in this section before any permit is issued in accordance with §93.103. Inspections shall take place at least once each year.

(N) In addition, a facility for hatching eggs of ratites, in which the hatching eggs of one lot may be quarantined at the same time as the hatched chicks from the previously quarantined lot, shall:

(*1*) Have a wall or a wall with a lockable door separating the incubator/hatcher area from the bird (chick) holding area, and this wall or wall-with-door shall provide an airtight seal between the two areas, shall be impervious to water, and shall be able to withstand continued cleaning and disinfection;

(*2*) Have a necropsy or sample collection area in both the incubator/hatcher area and the bird (chick) holding area; and

(*3*) Have separate entrances, showers, toilets, and dressing room facilities for the exclusive use of personnel working in the incubator/hatcher area and the bird (chick) holding area.

(O) The bird (chick) holding area in any facility for hatching eggs of ratites shall be of a size large enough to accommodate 75 percent of the incubator capacity, with a minimum of 10 square feet per egg.

(P) If a facility for hatching eggs of ratites has a sun room, the sun room shall be connected to the chick holding area by a wall with a lockable door. This wall; the other walls, if any; and the flooring, must be impervious to water and able to withstand continued cleaning and disinfection. All walls of the sun room must be at least 8 feet high.

(*1*) Any of the exterior walls may be replaced by a double-screened wall set in a concrete or concrete-block curb. The double screening shall be of wire mesh or wire mesh and nylon mesh, as provided in paragraph (c)(2)(ii)(A) of this section, with the interior and exterior screens of the sun room wall separated by at least 3 inches (7.62 cm); the concrete or concrete block curb must be at least 12 inches high, impermeable to water, and able to prevent the escape of water, manure, and debris.

(*2*) The sun room shall have a roof, such as a double-mesh-screened roof or a glass roof, that is both impervious to free-flying birds and biting insects (such as gnats or mosquitoes) and capable of preventing contact between chicks and free-flying birds.

(*3*) Be attended by personnel working in the bird (chick) holding area whenever chicks are in the sun room.

(iii) *Sanitation and security.* Arrangements shall exist for:

(A) A supply of water adequate to meet all watering and cleaning needs.

(B) Disposal of wastes by incineration or a public sewer system which meets all applicable environmental quality control standards;

(C) Control of surface drainage onto or from the facility to prevent any disease agent from entering or escaping;

(D) Protective clothing and footwear adequate to insure that workers at the facility have clean clothing and footwear at the start of each workday and at any time such articles become soiled or contaminated;

(E) Power cleaning and disinfecting equipment with adequate capacity to disinfect the facility and equipment;

(F) Sufficient stocks of a disinfectant authorized in §71.10(a)(5) of this chapter;

(G) A security system which prevents contact of birds in quarantine with persons not authorized entry to the facility and with other birds and animals. Such a system shall include a daily log to record the entry and exit of all persons entering the facility and controls at all doorways and other openings to the facility to prevent escape or accidental entry of birds.

(3) *Operational procedures.* The following procedures shall be observed at the facility at all times.

(i) *Personnel.* Access to the facility shall be granted only to persons working at the facility or to persons specifically granted such access by the port veterinarian.

(A) All personnel granted access to the bird holding area or the incubator/hatcher area shall:

(*1*) Wear clean protective clothing and footwear upon entering the bird holding area or the incubator/hatcher area;

(*2*) Change protective clothing and footwear when they become soiled or contaminated;

(*3*) Shower when entering and leaving any bird holding area, any incubator/hatcher area, and any necropsy area. Showering when moving between the incubator/hatcher area and the bird holding area is not required when the eggs in the hatching area and the chicks in the holding area are part of the same lot;

(*4*) Work exclusively with one lot of birds until the lot's release from quarantine, and have no contact with other birds or poultry until the release date.

(B) The importer shall handle soiled clothing worn within the quarantine unit in a manner approved by the port veterinarian as adequate to preclude transmission of a poultry disease agent from the facility.

(ii) *Handling of the birds in quarantine.* The birds shall be kept in the quarantine facility for a minimum of 30 days and while in quarantine shall be handled in compliance with the following requirements:

(A) Each lot of birds to be quarantined shall be placed in the facility on an "all-in, all-out" basis. No birds shall be taken out of the lot while it is in quarantine except for diagnostic purposes and if additional birds are added to a lot, the total quarantine period for that lot shall be extended so that all birds will have completed at least 30 consecutive days of quarantine before release for entry into the commerce of the United States. The quarantine period may be extended as provided in paragraph (a) of this section.

(*1*) Hatching eggs of ratites comprising a single lot may be added to the facility in stages, provided the entire lot has been placed in the facility no later than 15 days after the arrival of the first shipment.

(*2*) If hatching eggs of ratites begin to hatch in the incubator/hatcher area while ratite chicks from the previously quarantined lot remain in the bird (chick) holding area, then the separate lots assume the status of a single lot, and will be released from quarantine in accordance with paragraph (c)(3)(ii)(A) of this section.

(B) The birds may be vaccinated during quarantine only with a vaccine that has been approved by the Administrator, and is administered by a licensed veterinarian under the direct supervision of a veterinarian employed by the Animal and Plant Health Inspection Service. The Administrator will approve a vaccine if:

(*1*) The vaccine is licensed by the Animal and Plant Health Inspection Service in accordance with §102.5 of this chapter; and

(*2*) The vaccine is not one that is used to prevent Newcastle disease, avian influenza, or any other hemagglutinating virus of poultry.[11]

(C) Birds of the psittacine family shall receive a balanced, medicated feed ration treatment containing not less than 1% CTC with not more than 0.7% calcium for the entire quarantine period as a precautionary measure against chlamydiosis (psittacosis).

(D) The importer shall immediately collect all birds which die in quarantine and hold them under refrigeration, within the facility, shall account for all birds in the shipment, and shall not dispose of any carcass or parts thereof unless authorized to do so by a Veterinary Medical Officer of APHIS of the Department. Birds that die enroute to the United States or while in quarantine shall be made available at the port of entry for necropsy by a Department poultry disease diagnostician who may submit specimens from such birds for laboratory examination.

(E) During the period of quarantine, the birds shall be subjected to such tests and procedures as are required in specific cases by the port veterinarian, to determine whether the birds are free from communicable diseases of poultry and it shall be the responsibility of the importer to identify individually each psittacine bird within 7 days of the entry of the bird into the quarantine

[11] A list of approved vaccines is available from the Animal and Plant Health Inspection Service, Veterinary Services, National Center for Import-Export, 4700 River Road Unit 38, Riverdale, Maryland 20737–1231.

facility with a serially numbered legband which has been coded to the quarantine facility or by other suitable means of identification. Any identification device must be approved by the Administrator, upon written request to him, before it shall be used to identify birds under this section. Such means of identification shall be supplied by the importer, and the importer shall insure that each bird is so identified at the time the bird is released from the facility. If Newcastle disease or highly pathogenic avian influenza is found or detected among any birds in quarantine, all birds in the facility shall be destroyed or refused entry and the entire facility shall be thoroughly cleaned and then disinfected as directed under the supervision of an inspector.

(F) The quarantine facility from which a lot of birds has been released shall be thoroughly cleaned and disinfected with a disinfectant authorized in § 71.10(a)(5) of this chapter, under supervision of an inspector before a new lot is placed in the facility.

(iii) *Records.* It shall be the responsibility of the importer to maintain a current daily log for each lot of birds, recording such information as the general condition of the birds each day, source of origin of the birds in the lot, total number of birds in the lot when imported, number of dead birds when lot arrived, date lot was placed into the facility, number of deaths each day in the lot during the quarantine period, necropsy results, and laboratory findings on birds that died during the quarantine date of prescribed tests and results, Department import permit numbers of each lot, date lot was removed from the facility, and any other observations pertinent to the general health of the birds in the lot. The importer shall also make an identification record, at the time each psittacine bird is identified, containing the species of the bird, including the common and scientific name and the number of the identification device placed on each psittacine bird. The daily log and the identification record shall be maintained for 12 months following the date of release of the bird from quarantine and shall be made available to APHIS personnel upon request.

(4) Additional requirements as to location, security, physical plant and facilities, sanitation, and other items may be imposed by the Administrator, in each specific case in order to assure that the quarantine of the birds in such facility will be adequate to enable determination of their health status, prevent spread of disease among birds in quarantine, and prevent escape of poultry disease agents from the facility.

(5) Cooperative and Trust Fund Agreement for services required by importer at a privately owned bird quarantine facility.

(i) When the Administrator determines that a privately owned bird quarantine facility meets the requirements set forth in paragraph (c) of this section, the Department and the importer shall execute a Cooperative and Trust Fund Agreement, as specified in paragraph (c)(5)(iii) of this section. In conjunction with the Cooperative and Trust Fund Agreement, the importer shall deposit with the Administrator a money order or cashier's check in an amount determined by the Administrator to cover all costs incurred by the Department in providing services in accordance with the provisions of the Cooperative and Trust Fund Agreement. Any unobligated funds will, upon request, be returned to the importer, after the birds' release from quarantine.

(ii) The Administrator may provide services required by the importer at a privately owned quarantine facility for the importation of birds on a first come, first served basis, if adequate APHIS personnel are available to provide those services, upon determining that the importer has executed a Cooperative and Trust Fund Agreement, and has deposited funds in an amount determined by the Administrator to be sufficient to cover all costs incurred by the Department in providing services in accordance with that agreement, as specified in paragraph (c)(5)(iii) of this section.

(iii) Cooperative and Trust Fund Agreement.

COOPERATIVE AND TRUST FUND AGREEMENT BETWEEN _____ (NAME OF IMPORTER) AND THE UNITED STATES DEPARTMENT OF AGRICULTURE, ANIMAL AND PLANT HEALTH INSPECTION SERVICE.

This agreement is made and entered into by and between _____ (name of importer), hereinafter referred to as the Importer, and the U.S. Department of Agriculture, Animal and Plant Health Inspection Service, hereinafter referred to as the Service, with respect to _____ (quarantine facility and address of facility). Whereas, the Service is authorized pursuant to the Animal Health Protection Act (7 U.S.C. 8301 *et seq.*) to regulate the introduction of animals into the United States in order to prevent the introduction of animal and poultry diseases into the United States; and

Whereas, the Importer is interested in the importation of certain birds from regions presently under restrictions for such importation; and

Whereas, the Importer is equipped with a bird quarantine facility that meets the requirements of paragraph (c) of this section; and

Whereas, the Importer has requested the Service to conduct inspections, perform laboratory procedures, complete examinations, and supervise the isolation, quarantine, and care and handling of birds to insure that they meet the Department's quarantine requirements before release into the United States; and

Whereas, it is the intention of the parties hereto that such cooperation shall be for their mutual benefit and the benefit of the people of the United States;

Now therefore, for and in consideration of the promises and mutual covenants herein contained, the parties hereto do hereby mutually agree with each other as follows:

(A) The Importer Agrees:

(1) To operate the quarantine facility in accordance with all Federal Laws and regulations.

(2) To provide a current list of designated personnel employed by the Importer who will be used to handle and care for birds during the quarantine period. The list will include the legal names, current residential addresses, and social security numbers of the designated personnel. The list will be furnished to the port veterinarian at the time an application for an import permit to import birds into the quarantine facility is submitted to the Service. The list will be updated for any changes in or additions to the designated personnel in advance of such personnel working in the quarantine facility.

(3) To furnish to the Service a signed statement from each of the designated personnel employed by the Importer which provides that such personnel agree that for a period of 3 days from their most recent contact with birds in the quarantine facility, such personnel will refrain from having contact with other birds and poultry. This restriction ceases to apply on the date the birds are released from quarantine.

(4) To not permit any designated personnel which the Service determines to be unfit to be employed at a quarantine facility upon written notice from the Service. Such determination shall be based upon such employee's committing or aiding and abetting in the commission of any violation of title 9, Code of Federal Regulations, part 93. The Importer further agrees to suspend any designated employee from working at a quarantine facility when the Service has reason to believe that such employee has violated any provision of title 9, Code of Federal Regulations, part 93, and the Administrator has determined that the actions of such employee constitute a severe threat to introduce or disseminate a communicable disease of poultry into the United States. Such action shall be made upon receipt of notice from the Service requiring such action by the Importer.

(5) To allow the unannounced entry into the quarantine facility of Service personnel or other persons authorized by the Service for the purpose of inspecting birds in quarantine, the operations at the quarantine facility and to ascertain compliance with the Standards for quarantine facilities and handling procedures for importation of birds contained in title 9, Code of Federal Regulations, §93.106(c).

(6) To provide permanent restrooms in both the clean and the quarantine areas of the quarantine facility.

(7) To provide a T.V. monitoring system or a window or windows sufficient to provide a full view of the quarantine area excluding the clothes changing area.

(8) To install a communication system between the clean and quarantine areas of the quarantine facility. Such communication system shall not interfere with the maintenance of the biological security of the quarantine area.

(9) To secure all windows and any openings in the quarantine facility in a manner satisfactory to the Department which will insure the biological security of the quarantine facility and prevent the unauthorized removal of birds.

(10) To install tamperproof hasps and to install hinges on doors from which the pins cannot be removed.

(11) To install a hood with a viewing window over the necropsy table.

(12) To bag waste material in leakproof bags. Such material shall be handled in a manner that spoilage is kept to a minimum and control of pests is maintained. Such material shall be disposed of by incineration or by public sewer or other method authorized by the Administrator to prevent the spread

of disease. The disposition of such material shall only be under the direction and supervision of the Service.

(13) To feed chlortetracycline to psittacine birds, upon their arrival in the facility as prescribed in §93.106(c)(3)(ii)(C).

(14) To install an electronic security system which is coordinated through or with the local police so that monitoring of the quarantine facility is maintained whenever Service personnel are not at the facility or, in lieu of such electronic monitoring system to arrange for continuous guarding of the facility with personnel from a bonded, security company. *Provided,* That, if highly pathogenic avian influenza or Newcastle disease is diagnosed in any of the birds in the quarantine facility, continuous guarding of the facility with personnel from a bonded security company shall be maintained by the Importer. The electronic security system if installed shall be of the "silent type" and shall be triggered to ring at the monitoring site and not at the facility. The electronic system shall be approved by Underwriter's Laboratories.

Written instructions shall be provided to the monitoring agency which shall require that upon activation of the alarm, the police and a representative of the Service designated by the Service shall be notified by the monitoring agency. Such instructions, as well as any changes in such instructions, shall be filed in writing with the Administrator. The Importer shall notify the Service whenever a break in security occurs or is suspected of occurring.

(15) To not have non-Service personnel in the quarantine area when birds are in the quarantine facility unless Service personnel are present.

(16) To have seals of the Service placed on all entrances and exits of the facility when determined necessary by the Service and to take all necessary steps to ensure that such seals are only broken in the presence of Service personnel.

(17) To decide what the disposition of a lot of birds will be within 48 hours following official notification that such a lot is infected with or exposed to highly pathogenic avian influenza or Newcastle disease. Final disposition of the infected or exposed lot is to be accomplished within 4 working days following official notification. Disposition of the birds will be under the supervision of the Service.

(18) To furnish a telephone number or numbers to the Service at which the Importer can be reached on a daily basis or furnish the same for an agent or representative that can act and make decisions on the Importer's behalf.

(19) To deposit with the Service, upon execution of this agreement, a money order or cashier's check, in an amount determined by the Administrator to be sufficient to defray all costs incurred by the Service in providing services required. If such costs exceed the deposited amount, the importer will pay for additional costs incurred, based on official accounting records, within 14 days of receipt of the bill showing the balance due.

(20) To provide for the maintenance and operation of the quarantine facility in accordance with standards for quarantine facilities and handling procedures for importation of birds contained in title 9, Code of Federal Regulations, §93.106(c).

(B) The Service agrees:

(1) To furnish the services of technical and/or professional personnel needed to conduct inspections, perform laboratory procedures, complete examinations, and supervise the isolation, quarantine, and care and handling of birds being imported to ensure that they meet the Department's quarantine requirements before release into the United States.

(2) To issue permits 3 working days following receipt of the permit application, depending upon the availability of personnel to provide the services required for quarantine and the results of an APHIS representative's inspection of the quarantine facility.

(3) To provide the Importer within 30 days following receipt of a written request from the Importer, with an accounting of funds expended in providing services under paragraph (B)(1) of this agreement. Any unobligated balance upon termination or expiration of this agreement shall be returned to the Importer.

(4) To inform the Importer when a diagnosis of highly pathogenic avian influenza or Newcastle disease has been made in any facility.

(5) To promptly inform the Embassy or Consulate of the foreign region to which lots of birds, refused entry into the United States due to a diagnosis of highly pathogenic avian influenza or Newcastle disease, are to be shipped.

(6) To notify in writing the Importer of any designated employee which the Service believes should be suspended from work at the quarantine facility and the basis for such action. Similar notice shall be afforded to the designated employee. Subsequent to such suspension, the designated employee shall have the right to request an immediate review of such action by the Administrator, including presenting his or her views to the Administrator in an informal conference. If the Administrator makes a final determination that grounds existed to suspend such employee, he or she shall notify the Importer and the suspended employee of his or her decision and such employee shall be discharged by the Importer.

(7) Prior to any final determination being made by the Service concerning the discharge of any designated personnel employed by the Importer, the Service will inform, in writing, the Importer and the designated personnel of the basis for such action. If such

person contests such action he or she shall be permitted to present his or her views to the Administrator, provided such request is made within 30 days of the receipt of the aforementioned written notice. If a final determination is made by the Administrator that such personnel should be discharged, he or she shall notify such personnel and the Importer of such determination.

(C) It is mutually understood and agreed:

(*1*) That a maximum capacity will be established for each quarantine lot. This will be based upon the capacity of the quarantine facility to handle the birds. The number of birds on the permits will not exceed this capacity.

(*2*) If the seals referred to in paragraph (c)(5)(iii)(A)(*16*) of this section are broken by other than Service personnel, it will be considered a breach in security and an immediate accounting of all birds in the facility shall be made by the Service. If any birds are determined to be missing from the facility, the quarantine period will be extended for an additional 30-day period.

(*3*) During the performance of this cooperative work, the Importer agrees to be bound by the equal opportunity and nondiscrimination provisions as set forth in exhibit B and nonsegregation of facilities provisions as set forth in exhibit C,[12] which are attached hereto and made a part thereof.

(*4*) No member of or delegate to Congress or resident commissioner, shall be admitted to any share or part of this agreement or to any benefit to arise therefrom; but this provision shall not be construed to extend to this agreement if made with a corporation of its general benefit.

(*5*) This agreement shall become effective upon date of final signature and shall continue until the permitted lot of birds is released from quarantine. This agreement may be amended by agreement of the parties in writing. It may be terminated by either party upon 30 days written notice to the other party.

Date ____________________

____

Importer
Date ____________________

____

Administrator, Animal and Plant Health Inspection Service, United States Department of Agriculture

(d) *Charges for services.* The charges to be borne by the importer for services provided for quarantine facilities approved in accordance with paragraph (c) of this section shall be:

(1) The appropriate GS hourly rate (including appropriate premium pay in accordance with 5 U.S.C. 5541–5549) of the employee who actually performs the service, including his or her travel time and his or her travel expenses: *Provided, however,* Such time and travel expense shall not exceed the time and travel expense to and from his or her official duty station;

(2) All applicable user fees, as listed in part 130 of this chapter; and

(3) A surcharge for overhead based on the most current historical data available showing the percentage of APHIS funds expended for administrative support.

(e) Requirements of other Federal laws and regulations, such as the Department's Animal Welfare Regulations in subchapter A of this chapter shall also apply as applicable to the quarantine facilities.

[55 FR 31495, Aug. 2, 1990. Redesignated at 62 FR 56012, Oct. 28, 1997]

EDITORIAL NOTE: For FEDERAL REGISTER citations affecting § 93.106, see the List of CFR Sections Affected, which appears in the Finding Aids section of the printed volume and at *www.fdsys.gov.*

CANADA[13]

§ 93.107 Special provisions.

(a) *In-bond shipments from Canada.* Birds from Canada transported in-bond through the United States for immediate export shall be inspected at the border port of entry and, when accompanied by an import permit obtained under § 93.103 of this part and all conditions therein are observed, shall be allowed entry into the United States and shall be otherwise handled as provided in paragraph (d) of § 93.101.

(b) *Ratites from Canada.* Ratites that were hatched and raised in Canada or ratites that were legally imported into Canada and, upon arrival in Canada, were quarantined for a minimum of 28 days at a Canadian quarantine facility

[12] Import-Export Animals Staff, Veterinary Services, APHIS, USDA, will furnish each importer with copies of exhibits B and C prior to their signing the Cooperative and Trust Fund Agreement.

[13] Importations from Canada shall be subject to § 93.107, in addition to other sections in this part which are in terms applicable to such importations.

and remained in Canada for an additional 60 days following completion of quarantine may be imported into the United States:

(1) Without being quarantined upon arrival in the United States; and

(2) At any of the following ports of entry: Anchorage, AK; Fairbanks, AK; Los Angeles, CA; San Diego, CA; Denver, CO; Miami, FL; Tampa, FL; Atlanta, GA; Eastport, ID; Chicago, IL; New Orleans, LA; Boston, MA; Baltimore, MD; Houlton, ME; Jackman, ME; Detroit, MI; Port Huron, MI; Sault Ste. Marie, MI; Minneapolis, MN; Raymond, MT; Sweetgrass, MT; Buffalo, NY; Champlain, NY; New York, NY; Stewart Airport, Newburgh, NY; Dunseith, ND; Pembina, ND; Portal, ND; Portland, OR; San Juan, PR; Houston, TX; Highgate Springs, VT; Seattle, WA; and Sumas, WA; and

(3) If offered for entry at a Canadian land border port listed in § 93.203(b), without an import permit; and

(4) If consigned directly to slaughter from the port of entry, without being treated for ectoparasites within 3 to 14 days before shipment to the United States, as otherwise required by § 93.104(c)(8); and

(5) If in compliance with all of the applicable regulations of the U.S. Fish and Wildlife Service contained in Title 50, subchapter B, of the Code of Federal Regulations.

(c) *Ratite eggs from Canada.* Hatching eggs of ratites that were laid in Canada may be imported into the United States:

(1) Without being quarantined upon arrival in the United States; and

(2) At any of the ports of entry listed in paragraph (b)(2) of this section or authorized by § 93.105(a); and

(3) If offered for entry at a Canadian land border port listed in § 93.203(b), without an import permit; and

(4) If in compliance with all of the applicable regulations of the U.S. Fish and Wildlife Service contained in Title 50, subchapter B, of the Code of Federal Regulations.

[55 FR 31495, Aug. 2, 1990, as amended at 61 FR 68126, Dec. 27, 1996. Redesignated and amended at 56012, 56015, Oct. 28, 1997; 65 FR 38178, June 20, 2000; 67 FR 68022, Nov. 8, 2002]

Subpart B—Poultry

§ 93.200 Definitions.

Wherever in this subpart the following terms are used, unless the context otherwise requires, they shall be construed, respectively, to mean:

Accredited veterinarian. A veterinarian approved by the Administrator in accordance with the provisions of part 161 of this title to perform functions specified in parts 1, 2, 3, and 11 of subchapter A, and subchapters B, C, and D of this chapter, and to perform functions required by cooperative state-federal disease control and eradication programs.

Administrator. The Administrator of the Animal and Plant Health Inspection Service or any other employee of the Animal and Plant Health Inspection Service, United States Department of Agriculture, to whom authority has been or may be delegated to act in the Administrator's stead.

Animal and Plant Health Inspection Service. The Animal and Plant Health Inspection Service of the United States Department of Agriculture (APHIS or Service).

Animals. Cattle, sheep, goats, other ruminants, swine, horses, asses, mules, zebras, dogs, and poultry.

Commercial poultry. Chickens, doves, ducks, geese, grouse, guinea fowl, partridges, pea fowl, pheasants, pigeons, quail, swans, and turkeys (including eggs for hatching) which are imported for resale, breeding, public display, or any other commercial purpose.

Communicable disease. Any contagious, infectious, or communicable disease of domestic livestock, poultry or other animals.

Department. The United States Department of Agriculture (USDA).

Fever tick. Boophilus annulatus, including, but not limited to, the varieties Americana and Australia.

Highly pathogenic avian influenza (HPAI). Highly pathogenic avian influenza is defined as follows:

(1) Any influenza virus that kills at least 75 percent of eight 4- to 6-week-old susceptible chickens within 10 days following intravenous inoculation with 0.2 mL of a 1:10 dilution of a bacteria-free, infectious allantoic fluid or inoculation of 10 susceptible 4- to 8-week-old

chickens resulting in an intravenous pathogenicity index (IVPI) of greater than 1.2;

(2) Any H5 or H7 virus that does not meet the criteria in paragraph (1) of this definition, but has an amino acid sequence at the haemagglutinin cleavage site that is compatible with highly pathogenic avian influenza viruses; or

(3) Any influenza virus that is not an H5 or H7 subtype and that kills one to five out of eight inoculated chickens and grows in cell culture in the absence of trypsin within 10 days.

Immediate slaughter. Consignment directly from the port of entry to a recognized slaughtering establishment[1] and slaughter thereat within two weeks from the date of entry.

Inspector. An employee of the Animal and Plant Health Inspection Service authorized to perform duties required under this subpart.

Operator. For the purpose of § 93.209, any person operating an approved quarantine facility.

Performing or theatrical poultry. Poultry which are to be used in shows, theatrical acts or performances only.

Port veterinarian. A veterinarian employed by the Animal and Plant Health Inspection Service to perform duties required under this part at a port of entry.

Poultry. Chickens, doves, ducks, geese, grouse, guinea fowl, partridges, pea fowl, pheasants, pigeons, quail, swans, and turkeys (including eggs for hatching).

Quarantine facility. A USDA facility, or a private facility approved by APHIS, for the secure housing of imported birds, poultry, or other animals for specified periods.

Region. Any defined geographic land area identifiable by geological, political, or surveyed boundaries. A region may consist of any of the following:

(1) A national entity (country);

(2) Part of a national entity (zone, county, department, municipality, parish, Province, State, etc.)

(3) Parts of several national entities combined into an area; or

(4) A group of national entities (countries) combined into a single area.

Swine. The domestic hog and all varieties of wild hogs.

United States. All of the States of the United States, the District of Columbia, Guam, Northern Mariana Islands, Puerto Rico, the Virgin Islands of the United States, and all other Territories and Possessions of the United States.

Veterinary services. The Veterinary Services unit of the Department.

[55 FR 31495, Aug. 2, 1990. Redesignated and amended at 62 FR 56012, 56015, Oct. 28, 1997; 79 FR 71005, Dec. 1, 2014]

§ 93.201 General prohibitions; exceptions.

(a) No poultry or product subject to the provisions of this part shall be brought into the United States except in accordance with the regulations in this part and part 94 of this subchapter;[2] nor shall any such poultry or product be handled or moved after physical entry into the United States before final release from quarantine or any other form of governmental detention except in compliance with such regulations; *Provided,* That, the Administrator may upon request in specific cases permit poultry or products to be brought into or through the United States under such conditions as he or she may prescribe, when he or she determines in the specific case that such action will not endanger the livestock or poultry of the United States. Unless otherwise indicated in the regulations, no live poultry, and no hatching eggs from poultry, shall be imported into the United States if the poultry have originated from a region referenced in § 94.6(a) of this subchapter where highly pathogenic avian influenza or Newcastle disease is known to exist in commercial poultry populations, have transited highly pathogenic avian influenza- or Newcastle disease-affected regions, or have been vaccinated for the H5 or H7 subtype of avian influenza.

(b) The provisions in this part 93 relating to poultry shall not apply to

[1] The name of recognized slaughtering establishments approved under this part may be obtained from the Area Veterinarian in Charge, Veterinary Services, for the State of destination of the shipment.

[2] Importations of certain animals from various regions are absolutely prohibited under part 94 because of specific diseases.

healthy poultry not known to be infected with or exposed, within the 90 days preceding the date of export from the region of origin, to communicable diseases of poultry, if an import permit[3] has been obtained under §93.204 of this chapter and all conditions therein are observed; and if such poultry are handled as follows:

(1)(i) They are maintained under continuous confinement in transit through the United States aboard an aircraft, ocean vessel, or other means of conveyance; or

(ii) Except for poultry in transit through Anchorage, Alaska, under §93.204(c) of this part, which are not allowed to be unloaded, they are unloaded, in the course of such transit, into an animal or bird holding facility which is provided by the carrier or its agent and has been approved[4] in advance by the Administrator in accordance with paragraph (b)(3) of this section as adequate to prevent the spread within the United States of any livestock or poultry disease, and they are maintained there under continuous confinement until loaded aboard a means of conveyance for transportation from the United States and are maintained under continuous confinement aboard such means of conveyance until it leaves the United States; the import permit will specify any additional conditions necessary to assure that the transit of the poultry through the United States can be made without endangering the livestock or poultry of the United States, and that Department inspectors may inspect the poultry on board such means of conveyance or in such holding facility to ascertain whether the requirements of this paragraph are met, and dispose of them in accordance with the Animal Health Protection Act (7 U.S.C. 8301 *et seq.*) if such conditions are not met; and

(2) The carrier or its agent executes and furnishes to the collector of Customs at the first port of arrival a declaration stating that the poultry will be retained aboard such means of conveyance or in an approved holding facility during transshipment as required by this paragraph.

(3) Provisions for the approval of facilities required in this paragraph are:

(i) They must be sufficiently isolated to prevent direct or indirect contact with all other animals and birds while in the United States.

(ii) They must be so constructed that they provide adequate protection against environmental conditions and can be adequately cleaned, washed and disinfected.

(iii) They must provide for disposal of animal and bird carcasses, manure, bedding, waste and any related shipping materials in a manner that will prevent dissemination of disease.

(iv) They must have provisions for adequate sources of feed and water and for attendants for the care and feeding of poultry in the facility.

(v) They must comply with additional requirements as may be imposed by the Administrator if deemed applicable for a particular shipment.

(vi) They must also comply with all applicable local, State and Federal requirements for environmental quality and with the provisions of the Animal Welfare Regulations in chapter I of this title, as applicable.

(c) *Performing or theatrical poultry returning to the United States.* (1) Performing or theatrical poultry of United States origin that are returning to the United States from Canada or Mexico may be imported if:

(i) The poultry are found upon port of entry veterinary inspection to be free of poultry diseases; and

(ii) The poultry are accompanied by a United States veterinary health certificate issued prior to the departure of the poultry from the United States and the certificate shows the number from the leg band, tattoo, or microchip affixed to the poultry prior to departure; and

(iii) During port of entry veterinary inspection it is determined that the number from the leg band, tattoo, or microchip on the poultry is the same as the one listed on the health certificate.

[3] Such permit may be obtained from the Animal and Plant Health Inspection Service, Veterinary Services, National Center for Import-Export, 4700 River Road Unit 38, Riverdale, Maryland 20737–1231. Requests for approval of such facilities should also be made to the Deputy Administrator.

[4] See footnote 3 in subpart B.

(2) Except for performing or theatrical poultry that have been in any region where highly pathogenic avian influenza exists, which are subject to the provisions of paragraph (c)(3) of this section, performing or theatrical poultry of United States origin that have been outside the United States in a region other than Canada or Mexico may be imported if:

(i) The poultry meet the requirements of paragraphs (c)(1)(i) through (iii) of this section; and

(ii) The poultry are accompanied by an import permit issued by APHIS; and

(iii) The owner importing the poultry signs and furnishes to the Administrator the following:

(A) A notarized declaration under oath or affirmation (or a statement signed by the owner and witnessed by a Department inspector) stating that the poultry have not been in contact with poultry or other birds while out of the region (for example, association with other avian species at exhibitions or at aviaries); and

(B) An agreement on VS Form 17–8, obtainable from a Federal inspector at the port of entry, stating:

(*1*) That the poultry will be maintained in confinement in his or her personal possession separate and apart from all poultry and other birds for a minimum of 30 days following importation at the address where the poultry are to be held and made available for health inspection and testing by Department inspectors upon request until released at the end of such period by such an inspector; and

(*2*) That appropriate Federal officials in the State of destination will be immediately notified if any signs of disease are noted in any of the poultry or any poultry die during that period. The owner importing such poultry must comply with the provisions of the aforementioned agreement before the poultry may be released from confinement.

(3) Any performing or theatrical poultry of United States origin that have been in any region listed in § 94.6(d) of this subchapter as a region where highly pathogenic avian influenza exists may only be imported through the port of Los Angeles, CA, Miami, FL, or New York, NY, and only under the following conditions:

(i) The poultry meet the requirements of paragraphs (c)(1)(i) through (iii) of this section; and

(ii) The poultry are accompanied by an import permit issued by APHIS; and

(iii) The poultry are quarantined for a minimum of 30 days, and for such longer period as may be required by the Administrator in any specific case, at a quarantine facility maintained by APHIS in accordance with §§ 93.209 and 93.210.

(d) The provisions in this part relating to poultry shall not be applicable to performing or theatrical poultry.

(e) Pigeons, doves, and other Columbiform species that have originated from or transited regions where highly pathogenic avian influenza is considered to exist may be imported into the United States under permit and controlled conditions to approved establishments subject to all applicable requirements in this part.

(Approved by the Office of Management and Budget under control number 0579–0245)

[55 FR 31495, Aug. 2, 1990. Redesignated and amended at 56012, 56015, Oct. 28, 1997; 68 FR 6344, Feb. 7, 2003; 69 FR 25825, May 10, 2004; 76 FR 4053, Jan. 24, 2011; 79 FR 71005, Dec. 1, 2014]

§ 93.202 Inspection of certain aircraft and other means of conveyance and shipping containers thereon; unloading, cleaning, and disinfection requirements.

(a) *Inspection:* All aircraft and other means of conveyance (including shipping containers thereon) moving into the United States from any foreign region are subject to inspection without a warrant by properly identified and designated inspectors to determine whether they are carrying any animal, carcass, product or article regulated or subject to disposal under any law or regulation administered by the Secretary of Agriculture for prevention of the introduction or dissemination of any communicable animal disease.

(b) *Unloading requirements:* Whenever in the course of any such inspection at any port in the United States the inspector has reason to believe that the means of conveyance or container is contaminated with material of animal (including poultry) origin, such as, but not limited to, meat, organs, glands, extracts, secretions, fat, bones, blood, lymph, urine, or manure, so as to present a danger of the spread of any communicable animal disease, the inspector may require the unloading of the means of conveyance and the emptying of the container if he or she deems it necessary to enable him or her to determine whether the means of conveyance or container is in fact so contaminated. The principal operator of the means of conveyance and his or her agent in charge of the means of conveyance shall comply with any such requirement under the immediate supervision of, and in the time and manner prescribed by, the inspector.

(c) *Cleaning and disinfection:* Whenever, upon inspection under this section, an inspector determines that a means of conveyance or shipping container is contaminated with material of animal origin so as to present a danger of the spread of any communicable animal disease, he or she shall notify the principal operator of the means of conveyance or his or her agent in charge, of such determination and the requirements under this section. The person so notified shall cause the cleaning and disinfection of such means of conveyance and container under the immediate supervision of, and in the time and manner prescribed by, the inspector.

(d) For purposes of this section, the term "shipping container" means any container of a type specially adapted for use in transporting any article on the means of conveyance involved.

[55 FR 31495, Aug. 2, 1990, as amended at 59 FR 67614, Dec. 30, 1994. Redesignated and amended at 62 FR 56012, 56015, Oct. 28, 1997; 68 FR 6344, Feb. 7, 2003]

§93.203 Ports designated for the importation of poultry.

(a) *Air and ocean ports.* The following ports have APHIS inspection and quarantine facilities necessary for quarantine stations and all poultry shall be entered into the United States through these stations, except as provided in paragraphs (b), (c), (d) and (e) of this section: Los Angeles, California; Miami, Florida; and Newburgh, New York.

(b) *Canadian border ports.* The following land border ports are designated as having the necessary inspection facilities for the entry of poultry from Canada: Eastport, Idaho; Houlton and Jackman, Maine; Detroit, Port Huron, and Sault Ste. Marie, Michigan; Baudette, Minnesota; Opheim, Raymond, and Sweetgrass, Montana; Alexandria Bay, Buffalo, and Champlain, New York; Dunseith, Pembina, and Portal, North Dakota; Derby Line and Highgate Springs, Vermont; Oroville and Sumas, Washington.

(c) *Mexican border ports.* The following land border ports are designated as having the necessary inspection facilities for the entry of poultry from Mexico: Brownsville, Hidalgo, Laredo, Eagle Pass, Del Rio, Presidio, and El Paso, Texas; Douglas, Naco, Nogales, Sasabe, and San Luis, Arizona; Calexico and San Ysidro, California; and Antelope Wells, and Columbus, New Mexico.

(d) *Limited ports.* The following ports are designated as having inspection facilities for the entry of poultry and poultry products such as poultry test specimens, or hatching eggs and day old chicks which do not appear to require restraint and holding inspection facilities: Anchorage and Fairbanks, Alaska; San Diego, California; Jacksonville, Port Canaveral, St. Petersburg-Clearwater, and Tampa, Florida; Atlanta, Georgia; Honolulu, Hawaii; Chicago, Illinois; New Orleans, Louisiana; Portland, Maine; Baltimore, Maryland; Minneapolis, Minnesota; Great Falls, Montana; Portland, Oregon; San Juan, Puerto Rico; Galveston and Houston, Texas; and Seattle, Spokane, and Tacoma, Washington.

(e) *Designation of other ports.* The Secretary of the Treasury has approved the designation as quarantine stations of the ports specified in this section. In special cases other ports may be designated as quarantine stations under this section by the Administrator, with the concurrence of the Secretary of the Treasury.

[55 FR 31495, Aug. 2, 1990, as amended at 58 FR 37642, July 13, 1993; 60 FR 16045, Mar. 29, 1995; 60 FR 25120, May 11, 1995. Redesignated at 56012, Oct. 28, 1997, as amended at 65 FR 38178, June 20, 2000; 67 FR 6370, Feb. 12, 2002; 67 FR 68022, Nov. 8, 2002]

§ 93.204 Import permits for poultry and for poultry test specimens for diagnostic purposes; and reservation fees for space at quarantine facilities maintained by APHIS.

(a) *Application for permit; reservation required.* (1) For poultry and poultry test specimens for diagnostic screening purposes, intended for importation from any part of the world, except as otherwise provided for in §§ 93.204(c), 93.214, 93.217, and 93.218, the importer shall first apply for and obtain from APHIS an import permit. The application shall specify the name and address of the importer; the species, breed, number or quantity of poultry or poultry test specimens to be imported; the purpose of the importation; the region of origin; the name and address of the exporter; the port of embarkation in the foreign region; the mode of transportation, route of travel, and the port of entry in the United States; the proposed date of arrival of the poultry or poultry test specimens to be imported; and the name of the person to whom the poultry or poultry test specimens will be delivered and the location of the place in the United States to which delivery will be made from the port of entry. Additional information may be required in the form of certificates concerning specific diseases to which the poultry are susceptible, as well as vaccinations or other precautionary treatments to which the poultry or poultry test specimens have been subjected. Notice of any such requirement will be given to the applicant in each case.

(2) An application for permit to import poultry may also be denied because of: Communicable disease conditions in the area or region of origin, or in a region where the shipment has been or will be held or through which the shipment has been or will be transported; deficiencies in the regulatory programs for the control or eradication of animal diseases and the unavailability of veterinary services in the above mentioned regions; the importer's failure to provide satisfactory evidence concerning the origin, history, and health status of the poultry; the lack of satisfactory information necessary to determine that the importation will not be likely to transmit any communicable disease to livestock or poultry of the United States; or any other circumstances which the Administrator believes require such denial to prevent the dissemination of any communicable disease of livestock or poultry into the United States.

(3)(i) The importer or importer's agent shall pay or ensure payment of a reservation fee for each lot of poultry to be quarantined in a facility maintained by USDA. For poultry, the reservation fee shall be 100 percent of the cost of providing care, feed, and handling during quarantine, as estimated by the quarantine facility's veterinarian in charge.

(ii) At the time the importer or the importer's agent requests a reservation of quarantine space, the importer or importer's agent shall pay the reservation fee by check or U.S. money order or ensure payment of the reservation fee by an irrevocable letter of credit from a commercial bank (the effective date on such letter of credit shall run to 30 days after the date the poultry are scheduled to be released from quarantine); except that anyone who issues a check to the Department for a reservation fee which is returned because of insufficient funds shall be denied any further request for reservation of a quarantine space until the outstanding amount is paid.

(iii) Any reservation fee paid by check or U.S. money order shall be applied against the expenses incurred for services received by the importer or importer's agent in connection with the quarantine for which the reservation was made. Any part of the reservation fee which remains unused after being applied against the expenses incurred for services received by the importer or the importer's agent in connection with the quarantine for which the reservation was made, shall be returned to the individual who paid the reservation fee. If the reservation fee is ensured by a letter of credit, the Department will draw against the letter of credit unless payment for services received by the importer or importer's agent in connection with the quarantine is otherwise made at least 3 days prior to the expiration date of the letter of credit.

(iv) Any reservation fee shall be forfeited if the importer or the importer's agent fails to present for entry, within 24 hours following the designated time of arrival, the lot of poultry for which the reservation was made: *Except* that a reservation fee shall not be forfeited if:

(A) Written notice of cancellation from the importer or the importer's agent is received by the office of the veterinarian in charge of the quarantine facility[5] during regular business hours (8:00 a.m. to 4:30 p.m., Monday through Friday, excluding holidays) no later than 15 days prior to the beginning of the time of importation as specified in the import permit or as arranged with the veterinarian in charge of the quarantine facility if no import permit is required (the 15 day period shall not include Saturdays, Sundays, or holidays), or

(B) The Administrator determines that services, other than provided by carriers, necessary for the importation of the poultry within the requested period are unavailable because of unforeseen circumstances as determined by the Administrator, (such as the closing of an airport due to inclement weather or the unavailability of the reserved space due to the extension of another quarantine).

(v) If the reservation fee was ensured by a letter of credit and the fee is to be forfeited under paragraph (a)(3)(iv) of this section, the Department will draw against the letter of credit unless the reservation fee is otherwise paid at least 3 days prior to the expiration date of the letter of credit.

(vi) When a reservation is cancelled in accordance with paragraph (a)(3)(iv)(A) of this section and the provisions of paragraph (a)(3)(iv)(B) of this section do not apply, a $40.00 cancellation fee shall be charged. If a reservation fee was paid, the cancellation fee shall be deducted from any reservation fee returned to the importer or the importer's agent. If the reservation fee was ensured by a letter of credit, the Department will draw the amount of the cancellation fee against the letter of credit unless the cancellation fee is otherwise paid at least 3 days prior to the expiration date of the letter of credit.

(b) *Permit.* Except as provided in paragraph (c) of this section, when a permit is issued, the original and two copies will be sent to the importer. It shall be the responsibility of the importer to forward the original permit and one copy to the shipper in the region of origin, and it shall also be the responsibility of the importer to insure that the shipper presents the copy of the permit to the carrier and makes proper arrangements for the original permit to accompany the shipment to the specified U.S. port of entry for presentation to the collector of customs. Poultry and poultry test specimens for diagnostic screening purposes for poultry intended for importation into the United States for which a permit has been issued, will be received at the specified port of entry within the time prescribed in the permit which shall not exceed 14 days from the first day that the permit is effective for all permits, except that the time prescribed in permits from the importation of poultry shall not exceed 30 days, and for performing or theatrical poultry shall not exceed 90 days. Poultry and poultry test specimens for which a permit is required by these regulations will not be eligible for entry if a permit has not been issued; if unaccompanied by such a permit; if shipment is from any port other than the one designated in the permit; if arrival in the United States is at any port other than the one designated in the permit; if the poultry or poultry test specimens offered for entry differ from those described in the permit; or if the poultry or poultry test specimens

[5] The addresses of USDA quarantine facilities may be found in telephone directories listing the facilities or by contacting the Animal and Plant Health Inspection Service, Veterinary Services, National Center for Import-Export, 4700 River Road Unit 38, Riverdale, Maryland 20737–1231.

are not handled as outlined in the application for the permit and as specified in the permit issued.

(c) Notwithstanding any other provisions in this part, importers are not required to obtain an import permit and provide the shipper with an original import permit for each individual shipment of poultry or pigeons transiting the port of Anchorage, Alaska, if the following conditions are met:

(1) The importer applies for and obtains an import permit for multiple shipments of poultry or pigeons transiting the port of Anchorage, Alaska, in accordance with the provisions of this section and related requirements concerning application for the permit. However, the following information is not required on the application:

(i) The species, breed, and number of poultry or pigeons to be imported;

(ii) The individual poultry identification;

(iii) The region of origin;

(iv) The name and address of the exporter;

(v) The port of embarkation in the foreign region;

(vi) The mode of transportation and the route of travel;

(vii) The proposed date of arrival of the poultry or pigeons; and

(viii) The name and address of the person to whom the poultry or pigeons will be delivered.

(2) The importer completes a copy of the import permit obtained under paragraph (c)(1) of this section for each separate shipment of poultry or pigeons intended to transit the port of Anchorage, Alaska, by inserting the following information on a copy of the permit:

(i) The species, breed, and number of poultry or pigeons to be imported;

(ii) The region of origin;

(iii) The name and address of the exporter;

(iv) The port of embarkation in the foreign region;

(v) The mode of transportation and the route of travel;

(vi) The proposed date of arrival of the poultry or pigeons; and

(vii) The name and address of the person to whom the poultry or pigeons will be delivered.

(3) The importer, not less than 2 weeks prior to the anticipated date of arrival of each separate intransit shipment of poultry or pigeons at the port of Anchorage, Alaska, provides the port veterinarian with a copy of the completed import permit;

(4) A copy of the completed import permit accompanies each separate intransit shipment of poultry or pigeons to the port of Anchorage, Alaska;

(5) Import permits issued for multiple shipments of poultry or pigeons transiting the port of Anchorage, Alaska, will be valid only during the calendar year in which they are issued.

[55 FR 31495, Aug. 2, 1990, as amended at 59 FR 67614, Dec. 30, 1994. Redesignated and amended at 56012, 56015, Oct. 28, 1997]

§ 93.205 Certificate for live poultry and hatching eggs.

(a) *Live poultry*. (1) All live poultry, except eggs for hatching, offered for importation from any region of the world shall be accompanied by a certificate stating that such poultry and their flock or flocks of origin were inspected on the premises of origin immediately before the date of movement from such region and that they were then found to be free of evidence of communicable diseases of poultry. The certificate shall also state that, as far as it has been possible to determine, during the 90 days prior to movement, the poultry were not exposed to communicable diseases of poultry and the premises were not in any area under quarantine. The certificate shall also state that the poultry have not been vaccinated with a vaccine for the H5 or H7 subtype of avian influenza. The certificate shall also state that the poultry have been kept in the region from which they are offered for importation since they were hatched, or for at least 90 days immediately preceding the date of movement, that the poultry have not originated from or have been moved through a region referenced in § 94.6(a) of this subchapter as a region where any form of highly pathogenic influenza exists, and that, as far as it has been possible to determine, no case of highly pathogenic avian influenza or Newcastle disease occurred on the premises where such poultry were kept, or on adjoining premises, during that 90-day period. The certificate must also state that the birds were placed into new or appropriately sanitized packaging materials at the premises from which the birds were to be exported.

(2) Live poultry certificates accompanying pigeons, doves, and other Columbiform species that have originated from or been moved through regions where highly pathogenic avian influenza is considered to exist must additionally state that the Columbiform species have been moved and handled under conditions specified on the import permit ensuring that their movement and handling involved no direct or indirect exposure to other animals, birds, and poultry.

(b) *Hatching eggs.* All eggs for hatching offered for importation from any part of the world shall be accompanied by a certificate stating that the flock or flocks of origin were found upon inspection to be free from evidence of communicable diseases of poultry, the hatching eggs are from poultry that have not been vaccinated with a vaccine for the H5 or H7 subtype of avian influenza, that during the 90 days prior to movement, the flock or flocks of origin were not exposed to communicable diseases of poultry and the premises were not in any area under quarantine, and that the hatching eggs and the flock or flocks of origin have not originated in or been moved through a region referenced in accordance with § 94.6(a) of this subchapter as a region where any form of highly pathogenic avian influenza exists. The certificate must also state that the hatching eggs were placed into new or appropriately sanitized packaging materials at the premises from which the hatching eggs were to be exported.

(c) *Nature of certificate.* The certificate required by this section shall be issued by a salaried veterinary officer of the national government of the region of origin, or if the articles are exported from Mexico, may alternatively be issued by a veterinarian accredited by the National Government of Mexico and endorsed by a full-time salaried veterinary officer of the National Government of Mexico, thereby representing that the veterinarian issuing the certificate was authorized to do so.

[76 FR 4053, Jan. 24, 2011, as amended at 78 FR 19083, Mar. 29, 2013; 79 FR 71006, Dec. 1, 2014]

§ 93.206 Declaration and other documents for poultry.

(a) The certificates, declarations, and affidavits required by the regulations in this part shall be presented by the importer or his or her agent to the collector of customs at the port of entry, upon arrival of poultry at such port, for the use of the veterinary inspector at the port of entry.

(b) For all poultry offered for importation, the importer or his or her agent shall first present two copies of a declaration which shall list the port of entry, the name and address of the importer, the name and address of the broker, the origin of the poultry, the number, breed, species, and purpose of the importation, the name of the person to whom the poultry will be delivered, and the location of the place to which such delivery will be made.

(c) Any declaration, permit, or other document for poultry required under this subpart may be issued and presented using a U.S. Government electronic information exchange system or other authorized method.

[55 FR 31495, Aug. 2, 1990, as amended at 81 FR 40151, June 21, 2016]

§ 93.207 Inspection at the port of entry.

Inspection shall be made at the port of entry of all poultry imported from any part of the world except as provided in §§ 93.215 and 93.220. All poultry found to be free from communicable disease and not to have been exposed thereto within 90 days prior to their exportation to the United States shall be admitted subject to the other provisions in this part; all other poultry shall be refused entry. Poultry refused entry, unless exported within a time fixed in each case by the Administrator, and in accordance with other provisions he or she may require in each case for their handling shall be disposed of as the Administrator may direct. Such portions of the transporting vessel, and of its cargo, which have been exposed to any such poultry or their emanations shall be disinfected in such manner as may be considered necessary by the inspector in charge at the port of entry, to prevent the introduction or spread of livestock or poultry disease, before the cargo is allowed to land.

[55 FR 31495, Aug. 2, 1990. Redesignated and amended at 56012, 56015, Oct. 28, 1997; 68 FR 6344, Feb. 7, 2003]

§ 93.208 Articles accompanying poultry.

No litter or manure, fodder or other aliment, nor any equipment such as boxes, buckets, ropes, chains, blankets, or other things used for or about poultry governed by the regulations this part, shall be landed from any conveyance except under such restrictions as the inspector in charge at the port of entry shall direct.

§ 93.209 Quarantine requirements.

(a) Poultry, other than eggs for hatching, imported, except as provided in § 93.216 of this part, shall be quarantined for not less than 30 days, counting from the date of arrival at the port of entry. During their quarantine, such poultry shall be subject to any inspections, disinfections, and tests as may be required by the Administrator, to determine their freedom from communicable diseases of poultry, and their freedom from exposure to such diseases.

(b) Poultry eggs for hatching imported, except from regions designated in § 94.6(a) of this subchapter as free of Newcastle disease and highly pathogenic avian influenza, shall be quarantined from time of arrival at the port of entry until hatched and the poultry from such eggs shall remain quarantined for not less than 30 days following hatch. During their quarantine, such eggs for hatching and poultry from such eggs shall be subject to any inspections, disinfections, and tests as may be required by the Administrator, to determine their freedom from communicable diseases of poultry.

[55 FR 31495, Aug. 2, 1990, as amended at 61 FR 56891, Nov. 5, 1996. Redesignated and amended at 62 FR 56012, 56015, Oct. 28, 1997; 76 FR 4054, Jan. 24, 2011; 78 FR 19083, Mar. 29, 2013]

§ 93.210 Poultry quarantine facilities.

(a) *Privately operated quarantine facilities.* The importer, or his or her agent, of poultry subject to quarantine under the regulations in this part shall arrange for acceptable transportation to the privately operated quarantine facility and for the care, feed, and handling of the poultry from the time of unloading at the quarantine port to the time of release from quarantine. Such arrangements shall be agreed to in advance by the Administrator. All expenses resulting therefrom or incident thereto shall be the responsibility of the importer; APHIS assumes no responsibility with respect thereto. The quarantine facility must be suitable for the quarantine of such poultry and must be approved by the Administrator prior to the issuance of any import permit. The facilities occupied by poultry should be kept clean and sanitary to the satisfaction of the inspector assigned to supervise the quarantine. If for any cause the care, feed, or handling of poultry, or the sanitation of the facilities, is neglected, in the opinion of the inspector assigned to supervise the quarantine, such services may be furnished by APHIS in the same manner as though arrangements had been made for such services as provided by paragraph (b) of this section, and/or the poultry may be disposed of as the Administrator, may direct, including sale in accordance with the procedure described in paragraph (b) of this section. The importer, or his or her agent, shall request in writing such inspection and other services as may be required, and shall waive all claim against the United States and APHIS or any employee of APHIS for damages which may arise from such services. The Administrator may prescribe reasonable rates for the services provided under this paragraph. When it is found necessary to extend the usual minimum quarantine period, the importer, or his or her agent, shall be so advised in writing and shall pay for such additional quarantine and other services required. Payment for all services received by the importer, or his or her agent, in connection with each separate lot of poultry shall be made by certified check or U.S. money order prior to release of the poultry. If such payment is not made, the poultry may be sold in accordance with the procedure described in paragraph (b) of this section, or otherwise disposed of as directed by the Administrator.

(b) *Quarantine facilities maintained by APHIS.* The importer, or his or her agent, of poultry subject to quarantine under the regulations in this part shall arrange for acceptable transportation to the quarantine facility, and for the care, feed, and handling of the poultry from the time they arrive at the quarantine port to the time of release from quarantine. Such arrangements shall be agreed to in advance by the Administrator. The importer or his or her agent shall request in writing such inspection and other services as may be required, and shall waive all claim against the United States and APHIS or any employee of APHIS, for damages which may arise from such services. All expenses resulting therefrom or incident thereto shall be the responsibility of the importer; APHIS assumes no responsibility with respect thereto. The Administrator may prescribe reasonable rates for the services provided under this paragraph. When it is found necessary to extend the usual minimum quarantine period, the importer, or his or her agent, shall be so advised in writing and shall pay for such additional quarantine and other services required. Payment for services received by the importer, or his or her agent, in connection with each separate lot of poultry shall be made by certified check or U.S. money order prior to release of the poultry. If such payment is not made, the poultry may be sold in accordance with the procedure described in this paragraph or otherwise disposed of as directed by the Administrator. When payment is not made and the poultry are to be sold to recover payment for services received, the importer, or his or her agent, will be notified by the inspector that if said charges are not immediately paid or satisfactory arrangements made for payment, the poultry will be sold at public sale to pay the expense of care, feed, and handling during that period. The sale will be held after the expiration of the quarantine period, at such time and place as may be designated by the General Services Administration or other designated selling agent. The proceeds of the sale, after deducting the charges for care, feed, and handling of the poultry and other expenses, including the expense of the sale, shall be held in a Special Deposit Account in the United States Treasury for 6 months from the date of sale. If not claimed by the importer, or his or her agent, within 6 months from the date of sale, the amount so held shall be transferred from the Special Deposit Account to the General Fund Account in the United States Treasury.

(c) Amounts collected from the importer, or his or her agent, for service rendered shall be deposited so as to be available for defraying the expenses involved in this service.

§93.211 Quarantine stations, visiting restricted; sales prohibited.

Visitors shall not be admitted to the quarantine enclosure during any time that poultry are in quarantine except that an importer (or his or her accredited agent or veterinarian) may be admitted to the yards and buildings containing his or her quarantined poultry at such intervals as may be deemed necessary, and under such conditions and restrictions as may be imposed, by the inspector in charge of the quarantine station. On the last day of the quarantine period, owners, officers or registry societies, and others having official business or whose services may be necessary in the removal of the poultry may be admitted upon written permission from the said inspector. No exhibition or sale shall be allowed within the quarantine grounds.

§93.212 Manure from quarantined poultry.

No manure shall be removed from the quarantine premises until the release of the poultry producing same.

§93.213 Appearance of disease among poultry in quarantine.

If any contagious disease appears among poultry during the quarantine period special precautions shall be taken to prevent spread of the infection to other poultry in the quarantine station or to those outside the grounds. The affected poultry shall be disposed of as the Administrator may direct, depending upon the nature of the disease.

CANADA[6]

§ 93.214 Import permit and declaration for poultry.

(a) For poultry intended for importation from Canada, the importer shall first apply for and obtain from APHIS an import permit as provided in § 93.204: *Provided,* That an import permit is not required for poultry if offered for entry at a land border port designated in § 93.203(b).

(b) For all poultry offered for importation from Canada, the importer or his or her agent shall present two copies of a declaration as provided in § 93.206.

[55 FR 31495, Aug. 2, 1990. Redesignated and amended at 62 FR 56012, 56015, Oct. 28, 1997]

§ 93.215 Special provisions.

(a) *In-bond shipments from Canada.* (1) Poultry from Canada transported in-bond through the United States for immediate export shall be inspected at the border port of entry and, when accompanied by an import permit obtained under § 93.204 of this part and all conditions therein are observed, shall be allowed entry into the United States and shall be otherwise handled as provided in paragraph (b) of § 93.201. Poultry not accompanied by a permit shall meet the requirements of this part in the same manner as poultry destined for importation into the United States, except that the Administrator may permit their inspection at some other point when he or she finds that such action will not increase the risk that communicable disease of livestock and poultry will be disseminated to the livestock or poultry of the United States.

(2) *In-transit shipments through Canada.* Poultry originating in the United States and transported directly through Canada may re-enter the United States without Canadian health or test certificates when accompanied by copies of the United States export health certificates properly issued and endorsed in accordance with regulations in part 91 of this chapter: *Provided,* That, to qualify for entry, the date, time, port of entry, and signature of the Canadian Port Veterinarian that inspected the poultry for entry into Canada shall be recorded on the United States health certificate, or a document containing the information shall be included with the certificate that accompanies the poultry. In all cases it shall be determined by the veterinary inspector at the United States port of entry that the poultry are the identical poultry covered by said certificate.

(b) *Exhibition poultry.* Poultry from the United States which have been exhibited at the Royal Agricultural Winter Fair at Toronto or other publicly recognized expositions in Canada, including racing, rodeo, circus, or stage exhibitions in Canada, and have not been in that region for more than 90 days are eligible for return to the United States without Canadian health or test certificates, if they are accompanied by copies of the United States health certificate, issued and endorsed in accordance with the export regulations contained in part 91 of this chapter for entry into Canada: *Provided,* That all poultry offered for re-entry upon examination by the veterinary inspector at the U.S. port of entry, are found by the inspector to be free of communicable diseases and exposure thereto and are determined to be the identical poultry covered by said certificates or that they otherwise qualified for entry into Canada under the Canadian regulations.

(Approved by the Office of Management and Budget under control number 0579–0020)

[55 FR 31495, Aug. 2, 1990, as amended at 59 FR 67133, Dec. 29, 1994. Redesignated and amended at 62 FR 56012, 56015, Oct. 28, 1997; 81 FR 40151, June 21, 2016]

§ 93.216 Poultry from Canada.

Poultry imported from Canada is not required to meet the requirements of § 93.209 but shall meet all other requirements of this part applicable to poultry or to animals generally.

[55 FR 31495, Aug. 2, 1990. Redesignated and amended at 62 FR 56012, 56015, Oct. 28, 1997]

[6] Importations from Canada shall be subject to §§ 93.214 to 93.216, inclusive, in addition to other sections in this part which are in terms applicable to such importations.

CENTRAL AMERICA AND THE WEST INDIES [7]

§ 93.217 Import permit and declaration for poultry.

(a) For poultry intended for importation from regions of Central America or of the West Indies, the importer shall first apply for and obtain from APHIS an import permit as provided in § 93.204: *Provided*, That the Administrator, when he or she finds that such action may be taken without endangering the livestock or poultry industry of the United States, may, upon request by any person, authorize the importation by such person, without such application or permit, from the British Virgin Islands into the Virgin Islands of the United States, of poultry consigned for immediate slaughter, and such authorization may be limited to a particular shipment or extend to all shipments under this paragraph by such person during a specified period of time.

(b) For all poultry offered for importation from regions of Central America or of the West Indies, the importer or his or her agent shall present two copies of a declaration as provided in § 93.206.

(c) All poultry offered for importation from regions of Central America and the West Indies shall also meet the additional requirements in §§ 93.205, 93.207, 93.209, and 93.210 to qualify for entry. All poultry which fail to meet these requirements shall be rejected entry and shall be disposed of as directed by the Administrator in accordance with applicable laws.

[55 FR 31495, Aug. 2, 1990. Redesignated and amended at 62 FR 56012, 56015, Oct. 28, 1997]

MEXICO [8]

§ 93.218 Import permits and applications for inspection for poultry.

(a) For poultry intended for importation from Mexico, the importer shall first apply for and obtain from APHIS an import permit as provided in § 93.204.

(b) For poultry intended for importation into the United States from Mexico, the importer or his or her agent shall deliver to the veterinary inspector at the port of entry an application, in writing, for inspection, so that the veterinary inspector and customs representatives may make mutually satisfactory arrangements for the orderly inspection of the poultry.

[55 FR 31495, Aug. 2, 1990. Redesignated and amended at 62 FR 56012, 56016, Oct. 28, 1997]

§ 93.219 Declaration for poultry.

For all poultry offered for importation from Mexico, the importer or his or her agent shall present two copies of a declaration as provided in § 93.206.

[55 FR 31495, Aug. 2, 1990. Redesignated and amended at 62 FR 56012, 56016, Oct. 28, 1997]

§ 93.220 Inspection at port of entry.

(a) All poultry offered for entry from Mexico, including such poultry intended for movement through the United States in bond for immediate return to Mexico, shall be inspected at the port of entry, and all such poultry found to be free from communicable disease and fever tick infestation and not to have been exposed thereto, shall be admitted into the United States subject to the other applicable provisions of this part. Poultry found to be affected with or to have been exposed to a communicable disease, or infested with fever ticks, shall be refused entry. Poultry refused entry, unless exported within a time fixed in each case by the Administrator, shall be disposed of as said Administrator may direct.

(b) Poultry covered by paragraph (a) of this section shall be imported through ports designated in § 93.203.

[55 FR 31495, Aug. 2, 1990, as amended at 57 FR 12190, Apr. 9, 1992. Redesignated and amended at 62 FR 56012, 56016, Oct. 28, 1997]

[7] Importations from regions of Central America and the West Indies shall be subject to § 93.217, in addition to other sections in this part, which are in terms applicable to such importations.

[8] Importations from Mexico shall be subject to §§ 93.218 to 93.220 inclusive, in addition to other sections in this part which are in terms applicable for such importations.

Subpart C—Horses

§ 93.300 Definitions.

Wherever in this subpart the following terms are used, unless the context otherwise requires, they shall be construed, respectively, to mean:

Accredited veterinarian. A veterinarian approved by the Administrator in accordance with the provisions of part 161 of this title to perform functions specified in parts 1, 2, 3, and 11 of subchapter A, and subchapters B, C, and D of this chapter, and to perform functions required by cooperative State-Federal disease control and eradication programs.

Administrator. The Administrator of the Animal and Plant Health Inspection Service or any other employee of the Animal and Plant Health Inspection Service, United States Department of Agriculture, to whom authority has been or may be delegated to act in the Administrator's stead.

Animals. Cattle, sheep, goats, other ruminants, swine, horses, asses, mules, zebras, dogs, and poultry.

Animal and Plant Health Inspection Service. The Animal and Plant Health Inspection Service of the United States Department of Agriculture (APHIS or Service).

APHIS representative. A veterinarian or other individual employed by the Animal and Plant Health Inspection Service, United States Department of Agriculture, who is authorized to perform the services required by this part.

Code of practice. A voluntary system of procedures designed to reduce disease spread, that is established by the veterinarians and horse industry in a region and that includes procedures for the following: Testing for and treatment of the diseases, quarantine of horses that are affected with or are suspected of being affected with the disease, certification of whether horses have been affected with or exposed to the disease, and hygiene for personnel conducting treatments and specimen collections.

Communicable disease. Any contagious, infectious, or communicable disease of domestic livestock, poultry or other animals.

Department. The United States Department of Agriculture (USDA).

Fever tick. Boophilus annulatus, including, but not limited to, the varieties Americana and Australia.

Horses. Horses, asses, mules, and zebras.

Immediate slaughter. Consignment directly from the port of entry to a recognized slaughtering establishment[1] and slaughter thereat within two weeks from the date of entry.

Inspector. An employee of the Animal and Plant Health Inspection Service authorized to perform duties required under this subpart.

Licensed Veterinarian. Any person licensed by any country or political subdivision thereof to practice veterinary medicine.

Lot. A group of horses that, while held on a premises or conveyance, have had opportunity for physical contact with other horses in the group or with their excrement or discharges at any time during their shipment to the United States.

Lot-holding area. That area in a permanent, privately owned quarantine facility in which a single lot of horses is held at one time.

Nonquarantine area. That area in a permanent, privately owned quarantine facility that includes offices, storage areas, and other areas outside the quarantine area, and that is off limits to horses, samples taken from horses, and any other objects or substances that have been in the quarantine area during the quarantine of horses.

Operator. A person other than the Federal Government who owns or manages and has responsibility for the services provided by a temporary, privately owned quarantine facility or a permanent, privately owned quarantine facility.

Permanent, privately owned quarantine facility. A facility that offers quarantine services for horses to the general public on a continuing basis and that is owned and operated by an entity other than the Federal Government (also permanent facility).

[1] The name of recognized slaughtering establishments approved under this part may be obtained from the Area Veterinarian in Charge, Veterinary Services, for the State of destination of the shipment.

Persons. Any individual, corporation, company, association, firm, partnership, society or joint stock company.

Port Veterinarian. A veterinarian employed by the Animal and Plant Health Inspection Service to perform duties required under this part at a port of entry.

Quarantine area. That area in a permanent, privately owned quarantine facility that comprises all of the lot-holding areas in the facility, and any other areas in the facility that horses have access to, including loading docks for receiving and releasing horses, and any areas used to conduct examinations of horses and take samples and where samples are processed or examined.

Recognized slaughtering establishment.[2] An establishment where slaughtering operations are regularly carried on under federal or state inspection and which has been approved by the Animal and Plant Health Inspection Service to receive animals for slaughter under this part.

Region. Any defined geographic land area identifiable by geological, political, or surveyed boundaries. A region may consist of any of the following:

(1) A national entity (country);

(2) Part of a national entity (zone, county, department, municipality, parish, Province, State, etc.)

(3) Parts of several national entities combined into an area; or

(4) A group of national entities (countries) combined into a single area.

State animal health official. The State official responsible for livestock and poultry disease control and eradication programs.

Temporary, privately owned quarantine facility. A facility that offers quarantine services for horses imported for a specific event and that is owned and operated by an entity other than the Federal Government (also temporary facility).

United States. All of the States of the United States, the District of Columbia, Guam, Northern Mariana Islands, Puerto Rico, the Virgin Islands of the United States, and all other Territories and Possessions of the United States.

[2] See footnote 1 to subpart C.

Veterinarian in Charge. The veterinary official of the Animal and Plant Health Inspection Service, United States Department of Agriculture, who is assigned by the Administrator to supervise and perform the official animal health work of the Animal and Plant Health Inspection Service in the State concerned.

Veterinary Services. The Veterinary Services unit of the Department.

Weanling or yearling. Any horse, weaned from its dam, that was foaled not more than 731 days prior to its being offered for entry into the United States. A horse will not be considered to be a weanling or yearling if its first permanent incisors have erupted.

[55 FR 31495, Aug. 2, 1990, as amended at 56 FR 15489, Apr. 17, 1991; 61 FR 52239, Oct. 7, 1996. Redesignated and amended at 62 FR 56012, 56016, Oct. 28, 1997; 74 FR 31595, July 2, 2009]

§93.301 General prohibitions; exceptions.

(a) No horse or product subject to the provisions of this part shall be brought into the United States except in accordance with the regulations in this part and part 94 of this subchapter;[3] nor shall any such horse or product be handled or moved after physical entry into the United States before final release from quarantine or any other form of governmental detention except in compliance with such regulations; *Provided*, That, the Administrator may upon request in specific cases permit horses to be brought into or through the United States under such conditions as he or she may prescribe, when he or she determines in the specific case that such action will not endanger the livestock or poultry of the United States.

(b) The provisions in this part 93 relating to horses shall not apply to healthy horses in transit through the United States if they are not known to be infected with or exposed, within 60 days preceding the date of export from the region of origin, to communicable

[3] Importations of certain animals from various regions are absolutely prohibited under part 94 because of specific diseases.

diseases of horses if an import permit[4] has been obtained under § 93.304 of this chapter and all conditions therein are observed; and if such horses are handled as follows:

(1)(i) They are maintained under continuous confinement in transit through the United States aboard an aircraft, ocean vessel, or other means of conveyance; or

(ii) They are unloaded, in the course of such transit, into a horse holding facility which is provided by the carrier or its agent and has been approved[5] in advance by the Administrator in accordance with paragraph (b)(3) of this section as adequate to prevent the spread within the United States of any livestock or poultry disease, and they are maintained there under continuous confinement until loaded aboard a means of conveyance for transportation from the United States and are maintained under continuous confinement aboard such means of conveyance until it leaves the United States; the import permit will specify any additional conditions necessary to assure that the transit of the horses through the United States can be made without endangering the livestock or poultry of the United States, and that Department inspectors may inspect the horses on board such means of conveyance or in such holding facility to ascertain whether the requirements of this paragraph are met, and dispose of them in accordance with the Animal Health Protection Act (7 U.S.C. 8301 *et seq.*) if such conditions are not met; and

(2) The carrier or its agent executes and furnishes to the collector of Customs at the first port of arrival a declaration stating that the horses will be retained aboard such means of conveyance or in an approved holding facility during transshipment as required by this paragraph.

(3) Provisions for the approval of facilities required in this paragraph are:

(i) They must be sufficiently isolated to prevent direct or indirect contact with all other animals and birds while in the United States.

(ii) They must be so constructed that they provide adequate protection against environmental conditions and can be adequately cleaned, washed and disinfected.

(iii) They must provide for disposal of horse carcasses, manure, bedding, waste and any related shipping materials in a manner that will prevent dissemination of disease.

(iv) They must have provisions for adequate sources of feed and water and for attendants for the care and feeding of horses in the facility.

(v) They must comply with additional requirements as may be imposed by the Administrator if deemed applicable for a particular shipment.

(vi) They must also comply with all applicable local, State and Federal requirements for environmental quality and with the provisions of the Animal Welfare Regulations in chapter I of this title, as applicable.

(c) *Specific prohibitions regarding contagious equine metritis; exceptions*—(1) *Importation prohibited.* Except as provided in paragraph (c)(2) of this section, notwithstanding the other provisions of this part concerning the importation of horses into the United States, the importation of all horses from any region that APHIS considers to be affected with contagious equine metritis (CEM) and the importation of all horses that have been in any such region within the 12 months immediately preceding their being offered for entry into the United States is prohibited.

(i) A list of regions that APHIS considers to be affected with CEM is maintained on the APHIS Web site at *http://www.aphis.usda.gov/import_export/animals/animal_disease_status.shtml.* Copies of the list will also be available via postal mail, fax, or email upon request to the Sanitary Trade Issues Team, National Center for Import and Export, Veterinary Services, Animal and Plant Health Inspection Service, 4700 River Road Unit 38, Riverdale, Maryland 20737.

(ii) APHIS will add a region to the list upon determining that the disease exists in the region based on reports

[4] Such permit may be obtained from the Animal and Plant Health Inspection Service, Veterinary Services, National Center for Import-Export, 4700 River Road Unit 38, Riverdale, Maryland 20737–1231.

[5] See footnote 4 to subpart C.

APHIS receives of outbreaks of the disease from veterinary officials of the exporting country, from the World Organization for Animal Health (OIE), or from other sources the Administrator determines to be reliable, or upon determining that the region trades horses freely with a region in which CEM exists without testing for CEM. APHIS will remove a region from the list after conducting an evaluation of the region in accordance with § 92.2 of this subchapter and finding that the disease is not present in the region. In the case of a region formerly not on this list that is added due to an outbreak, the region may be removed from the list in accordance with the procedures for reestablishment of a region's disease-free status in § 92.4 of this subchapter.

(2) *Exceptions*. The provisions of paragraph (c)(1) of this section shall not apply to the following:

(i) Wild (non-domesticated) species of equidae if captured in the wild or imported from a zoo or other facility where it would be unlikely that the animal would come in contact with domesticated horses used for breeding;

(ii) Geldings;

(iii) Weanlings or yearlings that have never been used for breeding, and whose age and breeding status are certified on the import health certificate required under § 93.314(a);

(iv) Horses imported in accordance with conditions prescribed by the Administrator as provided in § 93.301(a);

(v) Spanish Pure Breed horses imported for permanent entry from Spain or thoroughbred horses imported for permanent entry from France, Germany, Ireland, or the United Kingdom if the horses meet the requirements of paragraph (d) of this section;

(vi) Stallions or mares over 731 days of age imported for permanent entry if the horses meet the requirements of paragraph (e) of this section;

(vii) Horses over 731 days of age imported into the United States for no more than 90 days to compete in specified events if the horses meet the requirements of paragraph (f)(1) of this section;

(viii) Horses over 731 days of age imported into the United States for noncompetitive public exhibition and entertainment purposes if the horses meet the requirements of paragraph (f)(2) of this section; and

(ix) Horses temporarily exported from the United States or from another region not known to be affected with CEM to a region listed under paragraph (c)(1) of this section within the 12 months immediately preceding their being offered for entry into the United States if the horses meet the requirements of paragraph (g) of this section.

(d) *Spanish Pure Breed horses from Spain and thoroughbred horses from France, Germany, Ireland, and the United Kingdom*. (1) Spanish Pure Breed horses from Spain and thoroughbred horses from France, Germany, Ireland, and the United Kingdom may be imported for permanent entry if the horses meet the following requirements:

(i) Each horse is accompanied at the time of importation by an import permit in accordance with § 93.304;

(ii) Each horse is accompanied at the time of importation by an import health certificate issued in accordance with § 93.314(a). In addition to the information required by § 93.314(a), the veterinarian signing and issuing the certificate must certify that:

(A) He or she has examined the daily records of the horse's activities maintained by the trainer and certified to be current, true, and factual by the veterinarian in charge of the training or racing stable;

(B) He or she has examined the records of the horse's activities maintained by a breed association specifically approved by the Department[6] and certified by the breed association to be current, true, and factual for the following information:

(*1*) Identification of the horse by name, sex, age, breed, and all identifying marks;

(*2*) Identification of all premises where the horse has been since reaching 731 days of age and the dates that the horse was at such premises;

[6] The following breed associations and their record systems have been approved by the Department: Asociacion National de Criadores de Caballos de Pura Raza Espanola for Spain; Weatherby's Ltd. for the United Kingdom and Ireland; Haras du Pain for France; and Direktorium für Vollblutzucht und Rennen e.v. for Germany.

(*3*) For thoroughbred horses, that none of the premises where the horse has been since reaching 731 days of age are breeding premises; and

(*4*) For Spanish Pure Breed horses from Spain, that since reaching 731 days of age:

(*i*) The horse has never been on a premises that is exclusively a breeding premises;

(*ii*) The horse has never been bred;

(*iii*) Breeding of the horse has never been attempted; and

(*iv*) The horse has never been commingled and left unattended with adult horses of the opposite sex;

(C) He or she has compared the records maintained by the approved breed association with the records kept by the trainer and has found the information in those two sets of records to be consistent and current;

(D) For Spanish Pure Breed horses and thoroughbred horses over 731 days of age, cultures negative for CEM were obtained from three sets of specimens collected within a 12-day period from the mucosal surfaces of the clitoral fossa and the clitoral sinuses, with one set of specimens including a specimen from the surfaces of the distal cervix or endometrium, of any female horses and from the surfaces of the prepuce, the urethral sinus, the distal urethra, and the fossa glandis, including the diverticulum of the fossa glandis, of any male horses. For both male and female horses, the sets of specimens must be taken within a 12-day period with no less than 72 hours between each set, and the last of these sets of specimens must be collected within 30 days prior to exportation. All specimens required by this paragraph must be collected by a licensed veterinarian who either is, or is acting in the presence of, the veterinarian signing the certificate; and

(E) All specimens required by paragraph (d)(1)(ii)(D) of this section were received within 48 hours of collection by a laboratory approved to culture for CEM by the national veterinary service of the region of export and were accompanied by a statement indicating the date and time of their collection.

(2) If any specimen collected in accordance with paragraph (d)(1)(ii)(D) of this section is found to be positive for CEM, the horse must be treated for CEM in a manner approved by the national veterinary service of the region of export. After the treatment is completed, at least 21 days must pass before the horse will be eligible to be tested again in accordance with paragraph (d)(1)(ii)(D) of this section. All treatments performed, and the dates of the treatments, must be recorded on the health certificate.

(3) Spanish Pure Breed horses and thoroughbred horses imported under paragraph (d)(1) of this section may be released upon completion of the Federal quarantine required under § 93.308. Spanish Pure Breed horses and thoroughbred horses found positive for CEM that have been treated and retested as provided in paragraph (d)(2) of this section shall, upon completion of the Federal quarantine required under § 93.308, be consigned to an approved State listed under paragraph (h)(6) or (h)(7) of this section, where they shall be quarantined under State or Federal supervision until the stallions have met the testing and treatment requirements of paragraph (e)(3) of this section and the mares have met the testing and treatment requirements of paragraph (e)(5) of this section.

(e) *Stallions and mares over 731 days of age from CEM-affected regions.* (1) Stallions or mares over 731 days of age may be imported for permanent entry from a region listed under paragraph (c)(1) of this section if the horses meet the following requirements:

(i) Each horse is accompanied at the time of importation by an import permit issued in accordance with § 93.304. The import permit must indicate that, after completion of the Federal quarantine required in § 93.308, the stallion or mare will be consigned to a State that the Administrator has approved to receive such horses in accordance with paragraph (h) of this section;

(ii) The horses are accompanied at the time of importation by an import health certificate issued in accordance with § 93.314(a);

(iii) A set of specimens must be collected from each horse within 30 days prior to the date of export by a licensed veterinarian who either is, or is acting in the presence of, the veterinarian signing the certificate. For stallions, the set of specimens consists of one culture swab from each location shall be taken from the prepuce, the urethral sinus, the distal urethra, and the fossa glandis, including the diverticulum of the fossa glandis; for mares, the specimens must be collected from the mucosal surfaces of the clitoral fossa, clitoral sinuses, and the distal cervix or endometrium in nonpregnant mares. All of the specimens collected must be cultured for CEM with negative results in a laboratory approved to culture for CEM by the national veterinary service of the region of origin;

(iv) The horses described on the certificate must not have been used for natural breeding, for the collection of semen for artificial insemination in the case of stallions, or for artificial insemination in the case of mares, from the time the specimens were collected through the date of export;

(v) All specimens required by paragraph (e)(1)(iii) of this section must be received within 48 hours of collection by a laboratory approved to culture for CEM by the national veterinary service of the region of export and must be accompanied by a statement indicating the date and time of their collection; and

(vi) If any specimen collected in accordance with paragraph (e)(1)(iii) of this section is found to be positive for CEM, the stallion or mare must be treated for CEM in a manner approved by the national veterinary service of the region of export. After the treatment is completed, at least 21 days must pass before the horse will be eligible to be tested again in accordance with paragraph (e)(1)(ii) of this section. All treatments performed, and the dates of the treatments, must be recorded on the health certificate.

(2) *Post-entry.* (i) Stallions and mares imported under paragraph (e)(1) of this section must complete the Federal quarantine required under § 93.308. Upon completion of the Federal quarantine, stallions must be sent to an approved State listed under paragraph (h)(6) of this section, and mares must be sent to an approved State listed under paragraph (h)(7) of this section.

(ii) Once in the approved State, the stallions or mares shall be quarantined under State or Federal supervision until the stallions have met the testing and treatment requirements of paragraph (e)(3) of this section and the mares have met the testing and treatment requirements of paragraph (e)(5) of this section.

(iii) All tests and cultures required by paragraphs (e)(3) through (e)(5) of this section shall be conducted at the National Veterinary Services Laboratories, Ames, IA, or at a laboratory approved by the Administrator in accordance with paragraph (i) of this section to conduct CEM cultures and tests.

(iv) To be eligible for CEM culture or testing, all specimens collected in accordance with paragraphs (e)(3) through (e)(5) of this section must be received by the National Veterinary Services Laboratories or the approved laboratory within 48 hours of collection and must be accompanied by a statement indicating the date and time of their collection.

(3) *Testing and treatment requirements for stallions.* (i) Once the stallion is in the approved State, one specimen each shall be taken from the prepuce, the urethral sinus, the distal urethra, and the fossa glandis, including the diverticulum of the fossa glandis, of the stallion and be cultured for CEM. After negative results have been obtained, the stallion must be test bred to two test mares that meet the requirements of paragraph (e)(4) of this section. Upon completion of the test breeding:

(A) The stallion must be treated for 5 consecutive days by thoroughly cleaning and washing (scrubbing) its prepuce, penis, including the fossa glandis, and urethral sinus while the stallion is in full erection with a solution of not less than 2 percent surgical scrub chlorhexidine and then thoroughly coating (packing) the stallion's prepuce, penis, including the fossa glandis, and urethral sinus with an ointment effective against the CEM organism.[7] The treatment shall be performed by an accredited veterinarian and monitored by a State or Federal veterinarian.

(B) Each mare to which the stallion has been test bred shall be cultured for

[7] A list of ointments effective against the CEM organism may be obtained from the National Center for Import and Export, Import/Export Animals, VS, APHIS, 4700 River Road Unit 39, Riverdale, MD 20737–1231.

CEM from three sets of specimens from the mucosal surfaces of the clitoral fossa and clitoral sinuses, with one set of specimens including a specimen from either the distal cervix or endometrium, between the third and fourteenth day after breeding, with negative results. The sets of specimens must be collected on three separate occasions within a 12-day period with no less than 72 hours between each set. A complement fixation test for CEM must be done with negative results between the twenty-first and twenty-eighth day after the breeding.

(ii) If any culture or test required by this paragraph is positive for CEM, the stallion shall be treated as described in paragraph (e)(3)(i)(A) of this section and retested by being test bred to two mares no less than 21 days after the last day of treatment.

(iii) A stallion may be released from State quarantine only if all cultures and tests of specimens from the mares used for test breeding are negative for CEM and all cultures performed on specimens taken from the stallion are negative for CEM.

(4) *Requirements for test mares.* (i) Mares to be used to test stallions for CEM shall be permanently identified before the mares are used for such testing with the letter "T." The marking shall be permanently applied by an inspector, a State inspector, or an accredited veterinarian who shall use a hot iron, freezemarking, or a lip tattoo. If a hot iron or freezemarking is used, the marking shall not be less than 2 inches (5.08 cm) high and shall be applied to the left shoulder or left side of the neck of the mare. If a lip tattoo is used, the marking shall not be less than 1 inch (2.54 cm) high and 0.75 inch (1.9 cm) wide and shall be applied to the inside surface of the upper lip of the test mare.

(ii) The test mares must be qualified prior to breeding as apparently free from CEM and may not be used for breeding from the time specimens are taken to qualify the mares as free from CEM. To qualify, each mare shall be tested with negative results by a complement fixation test for CEM, and specimens taken from each mare shall be cultured negative for CEM. Sets of specimens shall be collected on three separate occasions from the mucosal surfaces of the clitoral fossa and the clitoral sinuses, with one set of specimens including a specimen from either the distal cervix or endometrium, within a 12-day period with no less than 72 hours between each set.

(iii) A test mare that has been used to test stallions for CEM may be released from quarantine only if:

(A) The test mare is found negative for CEM on all cultures and tests required under paragraph (e)(3)(ii) of this section; or

(B) The test mare is subjected to an ovariectomy by an accredited veterinarian under the direct supervision of a State or Federal veterinarian; or

(C) The test mare is treated and handled in accordance with paragraph (e)(5) of this section; or

(D) The test mare is moved directly to slaughter without unloading en route, is euthanized, or dies.

(5) *Testing and treatment requirements for mares.* (i) Once the mare is in the approved State, a complement fixation test for CEM must be done, and three sets of specimens shall be collected from the mucosal surfaces of the clitoral fossa and clitoral sinuses, with one set of specimens including a specimen from the surfaces of the distal cervix or endometrium in nonpregnant mares. The sets of specimens must be collected on three separate occasions within a 12-day period with no less than 72 hours between each set. An accredited veterinarian shall collect specimens and shall submit each set of specimens to the National Veterinary Services Laboratories in Ames, IA, or to a laboratory approved by the Administrator in accordance with paragraph (i) of this section to conduct CEM cultures and tests.

(ii) After the three sets of specimens required by paragraph (e)(5)(i) of this section have been collected, an accredited veterinarian shall manually remove organic debris from the sinuses of each mare and then flush the sinuses with a cerumalytic agent.[8]

[8] Recommended protocols for the flushing of sinuses may be obtained from the National Center for Import and Export, Import/Export Animals, VS, APHIS, 4700 River Road Unit 39, Riverdale, MD 20737–1231.

(iii) For 5 consecutive days after the sinuses have been cleaned, an accredited veterinarian shall aseptically clean and wash (scrub) the external genitalia and vaginal vestibule, including the clitoral fossa, with a solution of not less than 2 percent chlorhexidine in a detergent base and then fill the clitoral fossa and sinuses, and coat the external genitalia and vaginal vestibule with an antibiotic ointment effective against the CEM organism.[9]

(iv) A mare may be released from State quarantine only if all cultures performed on specimens taken from the mare are negative for CEM.

(v) If any culture required by this paragraph is positive for CEM, the mare shall be treated as described in paragraphs (e)(5)(ii) and (e)(5)(iii) of this section. No less than 21 days after the last day of treatment, the mare shall be tested again in accordance with paragraph (e)(5)(i) of this section. If all specimens are negative for CEM, the mare may be released from quarantine.

(f) *Special provisions for temporary importation for competition or entertainment purposes.* (1) Horses over 731 days of age may be imported into the United States for no more than 90 days to compete in specified events provided that the conditions in paragraphs (f)(3) through (f)(12) of this section are met.

(2) Horses over 731 days of age may be temporarily imported into the United States solely for noncompetitive public exhibition and entertainment purposes provided that the conditions in paragraphs (f)(3) through (f)(12) of this section are met.

(3) At the time of importation, each horse must be accompanied by an import permit in accordance with § 93.304 and a health certificate issued in accordance with § 93.314. For horses imported in accordance with paragraph (f)(2) of this section, the health certificate must also certify that cultures negative for CEM were obtained from three sets of specimens collected from the mucosal surfaces of the clitoral fossa and clitoral sinuses, with one set of specimens including a specimen from the surfaces of the distal cervix or endometrium, of any female horses and from the surfaces of the prepuce, the urethral sinus, the distal urethra, and the fossa glandis, including the diverticulum of the fossa glandis, of any male horses. For both female and male horses, the sets of specimens must be collected on three separate occasions within a 12-day period with no less than 72 hours between each set, and the last of these sets of specimens must be collected within 30 days prior to exportation. All specimens required by this paragraph must be collected by a licensed veterinarian who either is, or is acting in the presence of, the veterinarian signing the certificate.

(4) Following the horse's arrival in the United States:

(i) A horse imported in accordance with paragraph (f)(1) of this section may remain in the United States for not more than 90 days, except as provided in paragraph (f)(9) of this section.

(ii) A horse imported in accordance with paragraph (f)(2) of this section may remain in the United States indefinitely, except as provided in paragraph (f)(9) of this section, as long as the conditions of paragraphs (f)(3) through (f)(12) of this section are met and the horse's owner or importer applies for and obtains from APHIS an import permit, as provided for in § 93.304, each year prior to the anniversary date of the horse's arrival in the United States.

(5) While the horse is in the United States, the following conditions must be met:

(i) A horse imported in accordance with paragraph (f)(2) of this section:

(A) Must not be entered in competitions.

(B) Must be regularly used in performances or exhibitions, unless sick or injured. A horse that is no longer performing or being exhibited must be exported or made eligible for permanent entry in accordance with paragraph (f)(9) of this section.

(C) Must be kept with the other horses listed on the import permit, unless otherwise approved by an APHIS representative.

(ii) Except as provided in paragraph (f)(5)(viii) of this section, the horse

[9] A list of ointments effective against the CEM organism may be obtained from the National Center for Import and Export, Import/Export Animals, VS, APHIS, 4700 River Road Unit 39, Riverdale, MD 20737–1231.

must be moved according to the itinerary and methods of transport specified in the import permit provided for in § 93.304.

(iii) The horse must be monitored by an accredited veterinarian or APHIS representative to ensure that the provisions of paragraphs (f)(5)(ii), (f)(5)(vi), and (f)(5)(vii) of this section are met. If the monitoring is performed by an accredited veterinarian, the Veterinarian in Charge will ensure that the accredited veterinarian is familiar with the requirements of this section and spot checks will be conducted by an APHIS representative to ensure that the requirements of this section are being met. If an APHIS representative finds that requirements are not being met, the Administrator may require that all remaining monitoring be conducted by APHIS representatives to ensure compliance.

(iv) Except when in transit, the horse must be kept on a premises that has been approved by an APHIS representative. For horses imported in accordance with paragraph (f)(1) of this section, such approval may be oral or in writing. If the approval is oral, it will be confirmed in writing by the Administrator as soon as circumstances permit. For horses imported in accordance with paragraph (f)(2) of this section, the approval will be in writing. To receive approval, the premises:

(A) Must not be a breeding premises; and

(B) Must be or contain a building or temporary structure in which the horse can be kept in a stall that is separated from other stalls that contain horses that are not listed on the import permit, either by an empty stall, by an open area across which horses cannot touch each other, or by a solid wall that is at least 8 feet (2.4 meters) high.

(v) While in transit, the horse must be moved in either an aircraft or a sealed van or trailer. If the horse is moved in a sealed van or trailer, the seal may be broken only by an APHIS representative at the horse's destination, except in situations where the horse's life is in danger.

(vi) Except when actually competing, performing, or being exhibited or exercised, the horse must be kept in a pasture approved by APHIS or in a stall that is separated from other stalls containing horses that are not listed on the import permit, either by an empty stall, by an open area across which horses cannot touch each other, or by a solid wall that is at least 8 feet (2.4 meters) high.

(vii) The horse may not be used for breeding purposes (including artificial insemination or semen collection) and may not have any other sexual contact with other horses. The horse may not undergo any genital examinations, except that a horse imported in accordance with paragraph (f)(2) of this section may undergo genital examinations for diagnosis or treatment of a medical condition with the prior approval of an APHIS representative.

(viii) The horse may be moved for diagnosis or treatment of a medical condition with the prior approval of an APHIS representative.

(ix) After the horse is transported anywhere in the United States, any vehicle in which the horse was transported must be cleaned and disinfected in the presence of an APHIS representative, according to the procedures specified in §§ 71.7 through 71.12 of this chapter, before any other horse is transported in the vehicle.

(x) The cleaning and disinfection specified in paragraph (f)(5)(ix) of this section must be completed before the vehicle is moved from the place where the horse is unloaded. In those cases where the facilities or equipment for cleaning and disinfection are inadequate at the place where the horse is unloaded, the Administrator may allow the vehicle to be moved to another location for cleaning and disinfection when the move will not pose a disease risk to other horses in the United States.

(xi) The owner or importer of the horse must comply with any other provisions of this part applicable to him or her.

(6) Except as provided in paragraph (f)(7) of this section, if the owner or importer wishes to change the horse's itinerary or the methods by which the horse is transported from that which he or she specified in the application for the import permit, the owner or importer must make the request for

change in writing to the Administrator. Requests for change must be submitted to APHIS no less than 15 days before the proposed date of the change. Requests may be submitted to APHIS by postal mail, commercial delivery service, fax, or e-mail. The change in itinerary or method of transport may not be made without the written approval of the Administrator, who may grant the request for change when he or she determines that granting the request will not endanger other horses in the United States and that sufficient APHIS personnel are available to provide the services required by the owner or importer.

(7) In response to an emergency or other unforeseen circumstances or events (e.g., weather-related transportation delays, vehicle breakdown, medical emergencies, etc.), the horse's itinerary or methods of transportation may be changed, with the prior approval of an APHIS representative, from that which is specified in the application for an import permit. Requests for such a change may be submitted to APHIS by telephone, postal mail, commercial delivery service, fax, or e-mail. Approval may be oral or in writing. If the approval is oral, it will be confirmed in writing by the Administrator as soon as circumstances permit.

(8) The Administrator may cancel, orally or in writing, the import permit provided for under § 93.304 whenever the Administrator finds that the owner or importer of the horse has not complied with the provisions of paragraphs (f)(3) through (f)(7) of this section or any conditions imposed under those provisions. If the cancellation is oral, the Administrator will confirm the cancellation and the reasons for the cancellation in writing as soon as circumstances permit. Any person whose import permit is canceled may appeal the decision in writing to the Administrator within 10 days after receiving oral or written notification of the cancellation, whichever is earlier. If the appeal is sent by mail, it must be postmarked within 10 days after the owner or importer receives oral or written notification of the cancellation, whichever is earlier. The appeal must include all of the facts and reasons upon which the person relies to show that the import permit was wrongfully canceled. The Administrator will grant or deny the appeal in writing as promptly as circumstances permit, stating the reason for his or her decision. If there is a conflict as to any material fact, a hearing will be held to resolve the conflict. Rules of practice concerning the hearing will be adopted by the Administrator.

(9) Except in those cases where an appeal is in process, any person whose import permit is canceled must move the horse identified in the import permit out of the United States within 10 days after receiving oral or written notification of cancellation, whichever is earlier. The horse is not permitted to enter competition, perform, or be exhibited from the date the owner or importer receives the notice of cancellation until the horse is moved out of the United States or until resolution of an appeal in favor of the owner or importer. Except when being exercised, the horse must be kept, at the expense of the owner or importer, in a stall on the premises where the horse is located when the notice of cancellation is received or, if the horse is in transit when the notice of cancellation is received, on the premises where it is next scheduled to compete, perform, or be exhibited according to the import permit. The stall in which the horse is kept must be separated from other stalls containing horses that are not listed on the import permit, either by an empty stall, by an open area across which horses cannot touch each other, or by a solid wall that is at least 8 feet (2.4 meters) high. In cases where the owners of the above specified premises do not permit the horse to be kept on those premises, or when the Administrator determines that keeping the horse on the above specified premises will pose a disease risk to horses in the United States, the horse must be kept, at the expense of the owner or importer, on an alternative premises approved by the Administrator.

(10) Stallions or mares over 731 days of age that are imported in accordance with paragraphs (f)(1) or (f)(2) of this section may be eligible to remain in the United States if the following is completed:

(i) Following completion of the itinerary specified in the import permit provided for in §93.304, the horse's owner or importer applies for and receives a new import permit that specifies that the stallion or mare will be moved to an approved State listed under paragraph (h)(6) or (h)(7) of this section; and

(ii) The stallion or mare is transported in a sealed vehicle that has been cleaned and disinfected to an approved facility in an approved State where it is quarantined under State or Federal supervision until the stallion or mare has met the testing and treatment requirements of paragraph (e)(3) or (e)(5) of this section.

(11) All costs and charges associated with the supervision and maintenance of a horse imported under paragraphs (f)(1) or (f)(2) of this section will be borne by the horse's owner or importer. The costs associated with the supervision and maintenance of the horse by an APHIS representative at his or her usual places of duty will be reimbursed by the horse's owner or importer through user fees payable under part 130 of this chapter.

(12) In the event that an APHIS representative must be temporarily detailed from his or her usual place of duty in connection with the supervision and maintenance of a horse imported under this paragraph (f), the owner or importer of the horse must execute a trust fund agreement with APHIS to reimburse all expenses (including travel costs, salary, per diem or subsistence, administrative expenses, and incidental expenses) incurred by the Department in connection with the temporary detail. Under the trust fund agreement, the horse's owner or importer must deposit with APHIS an amount equal to the estimated cost, as determined by APHIS, for the APHIS representative to inspect the premises at which the horse will compete, perform, or be exhibited; to conduct the monitoring required by paragraph (f)(5)(iii) of this section; and to supervise the cleaning and disinfection required by paragraph (f)(5)(ix) of this section. The estimated costs will be based on the following factors:

(i) Number of hours needed for an APHIS representative to conduct the required inspection and monitoring;

(ii) For services provided during regular business hours (8 a.m. to 4:30 p.m., Monday through Saturday, except holidays), the average salary, per hour, for an APHIS representative;

(iii) For services provided outside regular business hours, the applicable rate for overtime, night differential, or Sunday or holiday pay, based on the average salary, per hour, for an APHIS representative;

(iv) Number of miles from the premises at which the horse competes, performs, or is exhibited to the APHIS office or facility that is monitoring the activities;

(v) Government rate per mile for automobile travel or, if appropriate, cost of other means of transportation between the premises at which the horse competes, performs, or is exhibited and the APHIS office or facility;

(vi) Number of trips between the premises at which the horse competes, performs, or is exhibited and the APHIS office or facility that APHIS representatives are required to make in order to conduct the required inspection and monitoring;

(vii) Number of days the APHIS representative conducting the inspection and monitoring must be in "travel status";

(viii) Applicable Government per diem rate; and

(ix) Cost of related administrative support services.

(13) If a trust fund agreement with APHIS has been executed by the owner or importer of a horse in accordance with paragraph (f)(12) of this section and APHIS determines, during the horse's stay in the United States, that the amount deposited will be insufficient to cover the services APHIS is scheduled to provide during the remainder of the horse's stay, APHIS will issue to the horse's owner or importer a bill to restore the deposited amount to a level sufficient to cover the estimated cost to APHIS for the remainder of the horse's stay in the United States. The horse's owner or importer must pay the amount billed within 14 days after receiving the bill. If the bill is not paid within 14 days

after its receipt, APHIS will cease to perform the services provided for in paragraph (f)(5) of this section until the bill is paid. The Administrator will inform the owner or importer of the cessation of services orally or in writing. If the notice of cessation is oral, the Administrator will confirm, in writing, the notice of cessation and the reason for the cessation of services as soon as circumstances permit. In such a case, the horse must be kept, at the expense of the owner or importer and until the bill is paid, in a stall either on the premises at which the horse is located when the notice of cessation of services is received or, if the horse is in transit when the notice of cessation of services is received, on the premises at which it is next scheduled to compete, perform, or be exhibited according to the import permit. The stall in which the horse is kept must be separated from other stalls containing horses that are not listed on the import permit, either by an empty stall, by an open area across which horses cannot touch each other, or by a solid wall that is at least 8 feet (2.4 meters) high. In cases where the owners of the premises where the horse would be kept following a cessation of services do not permit the horse to be kept on those premises, or when the Administrator determines that keeping the horse on the premises will pose a disease risk to other horses in the United States, the horse must be kept, at the expense of the owner or importer, on an alternative premises approved by the Administrator. Until the bill is paid, the horse is not permitted to enter competition, perform, or be exhibited. Any amount deposited in excess of the costs to APHIS to provide the required services will be refunded to the horse's owner or importer.

(g) *Special provisions for the importation of horses that have been temporarily exported to a CEM-affected region.* If a horse has been temporarily exported for not more than 60 days from the United States to a CEM-affected region listed under paragraph (c)(1) of this section, or if a horse has been temporarily exported for not more than 60 days from another region not known to be affected with CEM to a CEM-affected region during the 12 months preceding its exportation to the United States, the horse may be eligible for return or importation into the United States without meeting the requirements of paragraphs (d) through (f) of this section under the following conditions:

(1) The horse must be accompanied by a certificate that meets the requirements of §93.314(a) of this part issued by each CEM-affected region that the horse has visited during the term of its temporary exportation, and each certificate must contain the following additional declarations:

(i) That the horse was held separate and apart from all other horses except for the time it was actually participating in an event or was being exercised by its trainer;

(ii) That the premises on which the horse was held were not used for any equine breeding purpose;

(iii) That the horse was not bred to or bred by any animal, nor did it have any other sexual contact or genital examination while in such region; and

(iv) That all transport while in such region was carried out in cleaned and disinfected vehicles in which no other horses were transported since such cleaning and disinfection;

(2) The horse is accompanied by an import permit issued in accordance with §93.304 of this part at the time of exportation;

(3) If the horse was temporarily exported from the United States and is being returned to the United States, the horse must be accompanied by a copy of the United States health certificate issued for its exportation from the United States and endorsed in accordance with the export regulations in part 91 of this chapter;

(4) The horse must be examined by an inspector at the U.S. port of entry and found by the inspector to be the identical horse covered by the documents required by paragraphs (a) through (c) of this section and found by the inspector to be free of communicable disease and exposure thereto; and

(5) The horse must be quarantined and tested at the U.S. port of entry as provided in §93.308 of this part prior to release.

(h) *Approval of States.* In order for a State to be approved to receive stallions or mares over 731 days of age from a CEM-affected region listed under paragraph (c)(1) of this section that are imported under paragraph (e) of this section, the State must meet the following conditions:

(1) The State must enter into a written agreement with the Administrator, whereby the State agrees to enforce its laws and regulations to control CEM and to abide by the conditions of approval established by the regulations in this part.

(2) The State must agree to quarantine all stallions and mares over 731 days of age imported under the provisions of paragraph (e) of this section until the stallions have been treated in accordance with paragraph (e)(3) of this section and the mares have been treated in accordance with paragraph (e)(5) of this section.

(3) The State must agree to quarantine all mares used to test stallions for CEM until the mares have been released from quarantine in accordance with paragraph (e)(4) of this section.

(4) The State must have laws or regulations requiring that stallions over 731 days of age imported under paragraph (e) of this section be treated in the manner specified in paragraph (e)(3) of this section, and that mares over 731 days of age imported under paragraph (e) of this section be treated in the manner specified in paragraph (e)(5) of this section.

(5) Approval of any State to receive stallions or mares imported from regions affected with CEM may be suspended by the Administrator upon his or her determination that any requirements of this section are not being met. After such action is taken, the animal health authorities of the approved State will be informed of the reasons for the action and afforded an opportunity to present their views thereon before such suspension is finalized; however, such suspension of approval shall continue in effect unless otherwise ordered by the Administrator. In those instances where there is a conflict as to the facts, a hearing shall be held to resolve such conflict.

(6) A list of States approved by APHIS to receive stallions over 731 days of age imported under paragraph (e) of this section is maintained on the APHIS Web site at *http://www.aphis.usda.gov/import_export/animals/downloads/states_app_conduct_cem_testing.pdf.* Copies of the list will also be available via postal mail, fax, or email upon request to the Sanitary Trade Issues Team, National Center for Import and Export, Veterinary Services, Animal and Plant Health Inspection Service, 4700 River Road Unit 38, Riverdale, Maryland 20737.

(7) A list of States approved by APHIS to receive mares over 731 days of age imported under paragraph (e) of this section is maintained on the APHIS Web site at *http://www.aphis.usda.gov/import_export/animals/downloads/states_app_conduct_cem_testing.pdf.* Copies of the list will also be available via postal mail, fax, or email upon request to the Sanitary Trade Issues Team, National Center for Import and Export, Veterinary Services, Animal and Plant Health Inspection Service, 4700 River Road Unit 38, Riverdale, Maryland 20737.

(i) *Approval of laboratories.* (1) The Administrator will approve a laboratory to conduct CEM cultures and tests only after consulting with the State animal health official in the State in which the laboratory is located and after determining that the laboratory:

(i) Has technical personnel assigned to conduct the CEM culturing and testing who possess the following minimum qualifications:

(A) A bachelor's degree in microbiology;

(B) A minimum of 2 years experience working in a bacteriology laboratory; and

(C) Experience working with the CEM organism, including knowledge of the specific media requirements, atmospheric requirements, and procedures for the isolation and identification of the CEM organism.[10]

---

[10] When training regarding CEM culturing and testing is necessary, it may be obtained at the National Veterinary Services Laboratories, Ames, IA 50010.

(ii) Follows standard test protocols that will reliably and consistently provide for the isolation and identification of the CEM organism;[11] and

(iii) Reports all official test results to the State animal health official and the Veterinarian in Charge.

(2) To retain approval, the laboratory must meet the requirements prescribed in paragraph (i)(1) of this section, and shall test with the CEM organism each lot of media it prepares to ensure that the media will support growth of the laboratory's reference culture. Media that will not support growth of the reference culture must be discarded.

(3) The Administrator may deny or withdraw approval of any laboratory to conduct CEM culturing or testing upon a determination that the laboratory does not meet the criteria for approval or maintenance of approval under paragraphs (i)(1) and (i)(2) of this section.

(i) In the case of a denial of approval, the operator of the laboratory will be informed of the reasons for denial and, upon request, will be afforded an opportunity for a hearing with respect to the merits or validity of the denial in accordance with rules of practice that will be adopted for the hearing.

(ii) In the case of a withdrawal of approval, before such action is taken, the operator of the laboratory will be informed of the reasons for the proposed withdrawal and, upon request, will be afforded an opportunity for a hearing with respect to the merits or validity of the proposed withdrawal in accordance with rules of practice that will be adopted for the hearing. However, the withdrawal will become effective pending a final determination in the hearing when the Administrator determines that such action is necessary to protect the public health, interest, or safety. The withdrawal will be effective upon oral or written notification, whichever is earlier, to the operator of the laboratory. In the event of oral notification, written confirmation will be given as promptly as circumstances allow. The withdrawal will continue in effect pending completion of the hearing and any judicial review of the hearing, unless otherwise ordered by the Administrator.

(iii) Approval for a laboratory to conduct CEM culturing or testing will be automatically withdrawn by the Administrator when the operator of the approved laboratory notifies the National Veterinary Services Laboratories, Ames, IA 50010, in writing, that the laboratory no longer conducts CEM culturing and testing.

(j) *Examination and treatment for screwworm.* Horses from regions where APHIS considers screwworm to exist may be imported into the United States only if they meet the requirements in paragraphs (j)(1) through (7) of this section and all other applicable requirements of this part. APHIS will maintain a list of regions where screwworm is considered to exist on the APHIS Web site at *http://www.aphis.usda.gov/import_export/animals/ animal_disease_status.shtml.* Copies of the list will also be available via postal mail, fax, or email upon request to the Sanitary Trade Issues Team, National Center for Import and Export, Veterinary Services, Animal and Plant Health Inspection Service, 4700 River Road Unit 38, Riverdale, Maryland 20737. APHIS will add a region to the list upon determining that screwworm exists in the region based on reports APHIS receives of detections of the pest from veterinary officials of the exporting country, from the World Organization for Animal Health (OIE), or from other sources the Administrator determines to be reliable. APHIS will remove a region from the list after conducting an evaluation of the region in accordance with § 92.2 of this subchapter and finding that screwworm is not present in the region. In the case of a region formerly not on this list that is added due to a detection, the region may be removed from the list in accordance with the procedures for reestablishment of a region's disease-free status in § 92.4 of this subchapter.

(1) A veterinarian must treat horses with ivermectin 3 to 5 days prior to the date of export to the United States according to the recommended dose prescribed on the product's label.

[11] Standard test protocols recommended by the National Veterinary Services Laboratories and a list of approved laboratories can be obtained from the National Veterinary Services Laboratories, Ames, IA 50010.

(2) Horses must be examined for screwworm by a full-time salaried veterinary official of the exporting country within 24 hours prior to shipment to the United States. The official must fully examine the horses, including their external genitalia. If horses are found to be infested with screwworm, they must be treated until free from infestation.

(3) At the time horses are loaded onto a means of conveyance for export, a veterinarian must treat any visible wounds on the animals with a solution of coumaphos dust at a concentration of 5 percent active ingredient.

(4) Horses must be accompanied to the United States by a certificate signed by a full-time salaried veterinary official of the exporting country. The certificate must state that the horses, including their external genitalia, have been thoroughly examined and found free of screwworm and that the horses have been treated in accordance with paragraphs (j)(1) and (j)(3) of this section.

(5) Horses must be quarantined upon arrival in the United States at an APHIS animal import center for at least 7 days.

(6) Horses must be examined for screwworm by a veterinarian within 24 hours after arrival at an APHIS animal import center in the United States. The examining veterinarian must examine horses, including their external genitalia, to determine whether the horse is infested with screwworm.

(7) Horses must be held at the animal import center for a minimum of 7 days. On day 7, prior to the horses' release, the horses must be examined by a veterinarian at the expense of the owner or broker. For this examination, male horses must be tranquilized or sedated so that the external genitalia of the horses can be thoroughly examined. If screwworm is found during this examination, the horses must be held in quarantine and treated until free of infestation.

(Approved by the Office of Management and Budget under control numbers 0579–0040, 0579–0165, and 0579–0324)

[55 FR 31495, Aug. 2, 1990. Redesignated and amended at 62 FR 56012, 56016, Oct. 28, 1997]

EDITORIAL NOTE: For FEDERAL REGISTER citations affecting § 93.301, see the List of CFR Sections Affected, which appears in the Finding Aids section of the printed volume and at *www.fdsys.gov*.

§ 93.302 Inspection of certain aircraft and other means of conveyance and shipping containers thereon; unloading, cleaning, and disinfection requirements.

(a) *Inspection:* All aircraft and other means of conveyance (including shipping containers thereon) moving into the United States from any foreign region are subject to inspection without a warrant by properly identified and designated inspectors to determine whether they are carrying any animal, carcass, product or article regulated or subject to disposal under any law or regulation administered by the Secretary of Agriculture for prevention of the introduction or dissemination of any communicable animal disease.

(b) *Unloading requirements:* Whenever in the course of any such inspection at any port in the United States the inspector has reason to believe that the means of conveyance or container is contaminated with material of animal (including poultry) origin, such as, but not limited to, meat, organs, glands, extracts, secretions, fat, bones, blood, lymph, urine, or manure, so as to present a danger of the spread of any communicable animal disease, the inspector may require the unloading of the means of conveyance and the emptying of the container if he or she deems it necessary to enable him or her to determine whether the means of conveyance or container is in fact so contaminated. The principal operator of the means of conveyance and his or her agent in charge of the means of conveyance shall comply with any such requirement under the immediate supervision of, and in the time and manner prescribed by, the inspector.

(c) *Cleaning and disinfection:* Whenever, upon inspection under this section, an inspector determines that a means of conveyance or shipping container is contaminated with material of animal origin so as to present a danger of the spread of any communicable animal disease, he or she shall notify the principal operator of the means of conveyance or his or her agent in charge, of such determination and the requirements under this section. The person so notified shall cause the cleaning and disinfection of such means of conveyance and container under the immediate supervision of, and in the time and manner prescribed by, the inspector.

(d) For purposes of this section, the term "shipping container" means any container of a type specially adapted for use in transporting any article on the means of conveyance involved.

[55 FR 31495, Aug. 2, 1990. Redesignated and amended at 62 FR 56012, 56016, Oct. 28, 1997; 68 FR 6344, Feb. 7, 2003]

§ 93.303 Ports designated for the importation of horses.

(a) *Air and ocean ports.* The following ports have APHIS inspection and quarantine facilities necessary for quarantine stations and all horses shall be entered into the United States through these stations, except as provided in paragraphs (b), (c), (d), (e), and (f) of this section, §§ 93.308(a), (b) and (c) and 93.317: Los Angeles, California; Miami, Florida; and Newburgh, New York.

(b) *Canadian border ports.* (1) The following land border ports are designated as having the necessary inspection facilities for the entry of horses from Canada: Eastport, Idaho; Houlton and Jackman, Maine; Detroit, Port Huron, and Sault Ste. Marie, Michigan; Baudette, Minnesota; Opheim, Raymond, and Sweetgrass, Montana; Alexandria Bay, Buffalo, and Champlain, New York; Dunseith, Pembina, and Portal, North Dakota; Derby Line and Highgate Springs, Vermont; Oroville and Sumas, Washington.

(2) International Falls, Minnesota, is designated as a port of entry for horses from Canada.

(c) *Mexican border ports.* The following land border ports are designated for the entry of horses from Mexico: Brownsville, Hidalgo, Laredo, Eagle Pass, Del Rio, Presidio, and El Paso, Texas; Douglas, Naco, Nogales, Sasabe, and San Luis, Arizona; Calexico and San Ysidro, California; and Antelope Wells, Columbus, and Santa Teresa, New Mexico.

(d) *Limited ports.* The following ports are designated as having inspection facilities for the entry of horses and horse products such as horse test specimens which do not appear to require restraint and holding inspection facilities: Anchorage and Fairbanks, Alaska; San Diego, California; Jacksonville, St. Petersburg-Clearwater, and Tampa, Florida; Atlanta, Georgia; Honolulu, Hawaii; Chicago, Illinois; New Orleans, Louisiana; Portland, Maine; Baltimore, Maryland; Boston, Massachusetts; Minneapolis, Minnesota; Great Falls, Montana; Dayton, Ohio; Portland, Oregon; San Juan, Puerto Rico; Memphis, Tennessee (no live animals); Galveston and Houston, Texas; and Seattle, Spokane, and Tacoma, Washington.

(e) *Ports for horses to be quarantined at privately owned quarantine facilities.* Horses, except horses from or which have transited any region in which African horsesickness is declared to exist,[12] may be entered into the United States at any port specified in paragraph (a) of this section, or at any other port designated as an international port or airport by the U.S. Customs Service and quarantined at privately owned quarantine facilities provided that applicable provisions of §§ 93.301(c), 93.304(a), 93.306, 93.308(a), (b) and (c), and 93.314 are met.

(f) *Designation of other ports.* The Secretary of the Treasury has approved the designation as quarantine stations of the ports specified in this section. In special cases other ports may be designated as quarantine stations under this section by the Administrator, with the concurrence of the Secretary of the Treasury.

[55 FR 31495, Aug. 2, 1990. Redesignated at 62 FR 56012, Oct. 28, 1997]

EDITORIAL NOTE: For FEDERAL REGISTER citations affecting § 93.303, see the List of CFR Sections Affected, which appears in the Finding Aids section of the printed volume and at *www.fdsys.gov*.

§ 93.304 Import permits for horses from regions affected with CEM and for horse specimens for diagnostic purposes; reservation fees for space at quarantine facilities maintained by APHIS.

(a) *Application for permit; reservation required.* (1)(i) For horses from regions listed in § 93.301(c)(1) of the regulations,

[12] Information as to the regions where African horsesickness is declared to exist may be obtained from the Administrator.

horses intended for quarantine at a privately owned quarantine facility, and horse test specimens for diagnostic screening purposes, intended for importation from any part of the world, except as otherwise provided for in §§ 93.315, 93.319, and 93.321, the importer shall first apply for and obtain from APHIS an import permit. The application shall specify the name and address of the importer; the species, breed, number or quantity of horses or horse test specimens to be imported; the purpose of the importation; individual horse identification which includes a description of the horse, name, age, markings, if any, registration number, if any, and tattoo or eartag; the region of origin; the name and address of the exporter; the port of embarkation in the foreign region; the mode of transportation, route of travel, and the port of entry in the United States; the proposed date of arrival of the horses or horse test specimens to be imported; and the name of the person to whom the horses or horse test specimens will be delivered and the location of the place in the United States to which delivery will be made from the port of entry. Additional information may be required in the form of certificates concerning specific diseases to which the horses are susceptible, as well as vaccinations or other precautionary treatments to which the horses or horse test specimens have been subjected. Notice of any such requirements will be given to the applicant in each case.

(ii) Horses intended for importation under § 93.301(f)(1) of this part must meet the permit requirements of paragraph (a)(1)(i) of this section. Additionally, for horses intended for importation under § 93.301(f)(1) of this part, the horse's owner or importer must include the following information with the application for permit that is required by paragraph (a)(1)(i) of this section:

(A) That the application is being made for a horse that will remain in the United States for no more than 90 days;

(B) The names, dates, and locations of the events in which the horse will compete while in the United States;

(C) The names and locations of the premises on which the horse will be kept while in the United States, and the dates the horse will be kept on each premises; and

(D) The methods and routes by which the horse will be transported while in the United States.

(iii) Horses intended for importation under § 93.301(f)(2) must meet the permit requirements of paragraph (a)(1)(i) of this section. Additionally, for horses intended for importation under § 93.301(f)(2), the horse's owner or importer must include the following information with the application for permit that is required by paragraph (a)(1)(i) of this section:

(A) The individual identifying information required in paragraph (a)(1)(i) of this section for all horses to be imported.

(B) The permanent electronic identification of each horse to be imported, if applicable. In the event that a horse has permanent electronic identification, the horse must be accompanied by a compatible reader.

(C) Photographs (head and lateral views) that are sufficient to identify each horse on an electronic medium approved by APHIS.

(D) The proposed total length of stay in the United States.

(E) A description of the shows or events in which the horse will perform while in the United States.

(F) The names, dates, and locations of the venues in which the horse will perform while in the United States.

(G) The names and locations of the premises on which the horse will be kept while in the United States, and the dates the horse will be kept on each premises.

(H) The methods and routes by which the horse will be transported while in the United States.

(I) A written plan for handling sick or injured horses that includes:

(*1*) The name, address, and phone number of each accredited veterinarian who will provide veterinary services in the United States;

(*2*) The name, address, and phone number of medical facilities to be used to diagnose or treat sick or injured horses while in the United States; and

(*3*) A plan to return sick or injured horses to performance condition.

(J) An application for a trust fund or escrow account agreement with APHIS in accordance with § 93.301(f)(12).

(iv) Approval of an application for a permit to import a horse under § 93.301(f) of this part is contingent upon a determination by the Administrator that sufficient APHIS personnel are available to provide the services required. If more than one application for an import permit is received, APHIS personnel will be assigned in the order that applications that otherwise meet the requirements of this section are received.

(2) An application for permit to import horses from regions listed in § 93.301(c)(1) or horses intended for quarantine at a privately owned quarantine facility, may also be denied because of: Communicable disease conditions in the area or region of origin, or in a region where the shipment has been or will be held or through which the shipment has been or will be transported; deficiencies in the regulatory programs for the control or eradication of animal diseases and the unavailability of veterinary services in the above mentioned regions; the importer's failure to provide satisfactory evidence concerning the origin, history, and health status of the horses; the lack of satisfactory information necessary to determine that the importation will not be likely to transmit any communicable disease to livestock or poultry of the United States; or any other circumstances which the Administrator believes require such denial to prevent the dissemination of any communicable disease of livestock or poultry into the United States.

(3)(i) The importer or importer's agent shall pay or ensure payment of a reservation fee for each lot of horses to be quarantined in a facility maintained by USDA. For horses, the reservation fee shall be 100 percent of the cost of providing care, feed, and handling during quarantine, as estimated by the quarantine facility's veterinarian in charge.

(ii) At the time the importer or the importer's agent requests a reservation of quarantine space, the importer or importer's agent shall pay the reservation fee by check or U.S. money order or ensure payment of the reservation fee by an irrevocable letter of credit from a commercial bank (the effective date on such letter of credit shall run to 30 days after the date the horses are scheduled to be released from quarantine); except that anyone who issues a check to the Department for a reservation fee which is returned because of insufficient funds shall be denied any further request for reservation of a quarantine space until the outstanding amount is paid.

(iii) Any reservation fee paid by check or U.S. money order shall be applied against the expenses incurred for services received by the importer or importer's agent in connection with the quarantine for which the reservation was made. Any part of the reservation fee which remains unused after being applied against the expenses incurred for services received by the importer or the importer's agent in connection with the quarantine for which the reservation was made, shall be returned to the individual who paid the reservation fee. If the reservation fee is ensured by a letter of credit, the Department will draw against the letter of credit unless payment for services received by the importer or importer's agent in connection with the quarantine is otherwise made at least 3 days prior to the expiration date of the letter of credit.

(iv) Any reservation fee shall be forfeited if the importer or the importer's agent fails to present for entry, within 24 hours following the designated time of arrival, the horse for which the reservation was made: *Except* that a reservation fee shall not be forfeited if the Administrator determines that services, other than provided by carriers, necessary for the importation of the horses within the required period are unavailable because of unforeseen circumstances as determined by the Administrator (such as the closing of an airport due to inclement weather or the unavailability of the reserved space due to the extension of another quarantine).

(v) If the reservation fee was ensured by a letter of credit and the fee is to be forfeited under paragraph (a)(3)(iv) of this section, the Department will draw against the letter of credit unless the reservation fee is otherwise paid at least 3 days prior to the expiration date of the letter of credit.

(vi) If a reservation is canceled, the importer or the importer's agent will be charged a fee according to the following schedule:

Cancellation date	Fee
30 or more days before the scheduled reservation date	25 percent of the reservation fee.
15–29 days before the scheduled reservation date	50 percent of the reservation fee.
Less than 15 days before the scheduled reservation date	100 percent of the reservation fee.

(vii) If the reservation fee was ensured by a letter of credit, the Department will draw the amount of the cancellation fee against the letter of credit unless the cancellation fee is otherwise paid at least 3 days prior to the expiration date of the letter of credit.

(b) *Permit.* (1) When a permit is issued, the original and two copies will be sent to the importer. It shall be the responsibility of the importer to forward the original permit and one copy to the shipper in the region of origin, and it shall also be the responsibility of the importer to ensure that the shipper presents the copy of the permit to the carrier and makes the necessary arrangements for the original permit to accompany the shipment to the specified U.S. port of entry for presentation to the collector of customs.

(2) Horses and horse test specimens for which a permit is required under paragraph (a) of this section will be received at the port of entry specified on the permit within the time prescribed in the permit, which shall not exceed 14 days from the first day that the permit is effective.

(3) Horses and horse test specimens for which a permit is required under paragraph (a) of this section will not be eligible for entry if:

(i) A permit has not been issued for the importation of the horse or horse test specimen;

(ii) If the horse or horse test specimen is unaccompanied by the permit issued for its importation;

(iii) If the horse or horse test specimen is shipped from any port other than the one designated in the permit;

(iv) If the horse or horse test specimen arrives in the United States at any port other than the one designated in the permit;

(v) If the horse or horse test specimen offered for entry differs from that described in the permit; or

(vi) If the horse or horse test specimen is not handled as outlined in the application for the permit and as specified in the permit issued.

(Approved by the Office of Management and Budget under control numbers 0579–0040 and 0579–0324)

[55 FR 31495, Aug. 2, 1990. Redesignated at 62 FR 56012, Oct. 28, 1997]

EDITORIAL NOTE: For FEDERAL REGISTER citations affecting § 93.304, see the List of CFR Sections Affected, which appears in the Finding Aids section of the printed volume and at *www.fdsys.gov.*

§ 93.305 Declaration and other documents for horses.

(a) The certificates, declarations, and affidavits required by the regulations in this part shall be presented by the importer or his or her agent to the collector of customs at the port of entry, upon arrival of horses at such port, for the use of the veterinary inspector at the port of entry.

(b) For all horses offered for importation, the importer or his or her agent shall first present two copies of a declaration which shall list the port of entry, the name and address of the importer, the name and address of the broker, the origin of the horses, the number, breed, species, and purpose of the importation, the name of the person to whom the horses will be delivered, and the location of the place to which such delivery will be made.

(c) Any declaration, permit, or other document for horses required under this subpart may be issued and presented using a U.S. Government electronic information exchange system or other authorized method.

[55 FR 31495, Aug. 2, 1990,as amended at 81 FR 40151, June 21, 2016]

§93.306 Inspection at the port of entry.

Inspection shall be made at the port of entry of all horses imported from any part of the world except as provided in §§93.318 and 93.323. All horses found to be free from communicable disease and not to have been exposed thereto within 60 days prior to their exportation to the United States shall be admitted subject to the other provisions in this part; all other horses shall be refused entry. Horses refused entry, unless exported within a time fixed in each case by the Administrator of Veterinary Service, and in accordance with other provisions he or she may require in each case for their handling shall be disposed of as the Administrator may direct. Such portions of the transporting vessel, and of its cargo, which have been exposed to any such horses or their emanations shall be disinfected in such manner as may be considered necessary by the inspector in charge at the port of entry, to prevent the introduction or spread of livestock or poultry disease, before the cargo is allowed to land.

[55 FR 31495, Aug. 2, 1990. Redesignated and amended at 62 FR 56012, 56016, Oct. 28, 1997; 68 FR 6344, Feb. 7, 2003]

§93.307 Articles accompanying horses.

No litter or manure, fodder or other aliment, nor any equipment such as boxes, buckets, ropes, chains, blankets, or other things used for or about horses governed by the regulations this part, shall be landed from any conveyance except under such restrictions as the inspector in charge at the port of entry shall direct.

§93.308 Quarantine requirements.

(a) Except as provided in this section and in §93.324, horses intended for importation into the United States from any part of the world shall be shipped directly to a port designated in §§93.303 and 92.324 and be quarantined at said port until negative results to port of entry tests are obtained and the horses are certified by the port veterinarian to be free from clinical evidence of disease.

(1) Except as provided in §§93.317 and 93.324 and in paragraph (a)(1)(i) of this section, horses intended for importation from the Western Hemisphere shall be quarantined at a port designated in §93.303 for not less than 7 days to be evaluated for signs of Venezuelan equine encephalomyelitis.

(i) Horses imported from regions of the Western Hemisphere that APHIS considers to be free of Venezuelan equine encephalomyelitis are exempt from the requirements of paragraph (a)(1) of this section. A list of regions that APHIS has declared free of Venezuelan equine encephalomyelitis is maintained on the APHIS Web site at *http://www.aphis.usda.gov/import_export/animals/ animal_import/equine/equine_import_quarantine.shtml*. Copies of the list will also be available via postal mail, fax, or email upon request to the Sanitary Trade Issues Team, National Center for Import and Export, Veterinary Services, Animal and Plant Health Inspection Service, 4700 River Road Unit 38, Riverdale, Maryland 20737.

(ii) APHIS will add a region to the list of those it has declared free of Venezuelan equine encephalomyelitis after it conducts an evaluation of the region in accordance with §92.2 of this subchapter and finds that the disease is not present. In the case of a region formerly on this list that is removed due to an outbreak, the region may be returned to the list in accordance with the procedures for reestablishment of a region's disease-free status in §92.4 of this subchapter. APHIS will remove a region from the list of those it has declared free of Venezuelan equine encephalomyelitis upon determining that the disease exists in the region based on reports APHIS receives of outbreaks of the disease from veterinary officials of the exporting country, from the World Organization for Animal Health (OIE), or from other sources the Administrator determines to be reliable.

(2) Horses intended for importation from regions APHIS considers to be affected with African horse sickness may enter the United States only at the port of New York, and must be quarantined at the New York Animal Import Center in Newburgh, New York, for at least 60 days. This restriction also applies to horses that have stopped in or transited a region considered affected with African horse sickness.

(i) A list of regions that APHIS considers affected with African horse sickness is maintained on the APHIS Web site at *http://www.aphis.usda.gov/import_export/animals/animal_disease_status.shtml.* Copies of the list will also be available via postal mail, fax, or email upon request to the Sanitary Trade Issues Team, National Center for Import and Export, Veterinary Services, Animal and Plant Health Inspection Service, 4700 River Road Unit 38, Riverdale, Maryland 20737.

(ii) APHIS will add a region to the list upon determining that the disease exists in the region based on reports APHIS receives of outbreaks of the disease from veterinary officials of the exporting country, from the World Organization for Animal Health (OIE), or from other sources the Administrator determines to be reliable. APHIS will remove a region from the list after conducting an evaluation of the region in accordance with § 92.2 of this subchapter and finding that the disease is not present in the region. In the case of a region formerly not on this list that is added due to an outbreak, the region may be removed from the list in accordance with the procedures for reestablishment of a region's disease-free status in § 92.4 of this subchapter.

(3) To qualify for release from quarantine, all horses, except horses from Iceland, must test negative to official tests for dourine, glanders, equine piroplasmosis, and equine infectious anemia.[13] However, horses imported from Australia and New Zealand are exempt from testing for dourine and glanders. In addition, all horses must undergo any other tests, inspections, disinfections, and precautionary treatments that may be required by the Administrator to determine their freedom from communicable diseases.

(4) Any quarantine period required for a horse shall be counted using the first day after arrival of the horse at the quarantine facility as the first day of quarantine and may be extended for such additional period as the Administrator may require to determine its freedom from disease. Any horse which is positive to any of the port of entry tests named in this paragraph or any other test required by the Administrator, or which is found by the port veterinarian to exhibit evidence of communicable disease during quarantine shall be refused entry into the United States and removed by the importer to a country other than the United States within 10 days of the date that the importer is notified by APHIS that such horse has been refused entry into the United States. Upon request, the Administrator may grant additional time for the removal of a horse from the United States in any case in which he or she determines that delay is unavoidable due to unforseen circumstances and the additional time for removal of the horse will not present a threat of the spread of communicable disease to other animals in the United States. At the option of the importer, such horse may be disposed of in accordance with such conditions as the Administrator believes necessary to prevent the dissemination of communicable disease into the United States. The importer shall be responsible for all costs of such removal or disposal.

(b) *Temporary, privately owned quarantine facilities.* Horses presented for entry into the United States as provided in § 93.303(e) may be quarantined

[13] Because the official tests for dourine and glanders are performed only at the National Veterinary Services Laboratories in Ames, IA, the protocols for those tests have not been published and are, therefore, not available; however, copies of "Protocol for the Complement-Fixation Test for Equine Piroplasmosis" and "Protocol for the Immunno-Diffusion (Coggins) Test For Equine Infectious Anemia" may be obtained from the Animal and Plant Health Inspection Service, Veterinary Services, National Center for Import-Export, 4700 River Road Unit 38, Riverdale, MD 20737–1231.

in temporary, privately owned quarantine facilities that meet the requirements of paragraphs (b)(1) and (b)(2) of this section and that have been approved by the Administrator for a specific importation.

(1) *Approval.* Requests for approval and plans for proposed temporary facilities must be submitted no less than 15 days before the proposed date of entry of horses into the facility to APHIS, Veterinary Services, National Center for Import and Export, 4700 River Road Unit 39, Riverdale, MD 20737–1231. Before facility approval can be granted, a veterinary medical officer of APHIS must inspect the facility to determine whether it complies with the standards set forth in this section: *Provided, however,* that approval of any temporary facility and use of such facility will be contingent upon a determination made by the Administrator that adequate personnel are available to provide required services at the facility. Approval of any facility may be refused and approval of any quarantine facility may be withdrawn at any time by the Administrator, upon his or her determination that any requirements of this section are not being met. Before such action is taken, the operator of the facility will be informed of the reasons for the proposed action by the Administrator and afforded an opportunity to present his or her views. If there is a conflict as to any material fact, a hearing will be held to resolve the conflict. The cost of the facility and all maintenance and operational costs of the facility will be borne by the operator.

(2) *Standards and handling procedures.* The facility must be maintained and operated in accordance with the following standards:

(i) *Inspection.* Inspection and quarantine services must be arranged by the operator or his or her agent with the APHIS Veterinarian in Charge for the State in which the approved facility is located[14] no less than 7 days before the proposed date of entry of the horses into the quarantine facility.

(ii) *Physical plant requirements.* (A) The facility must be located and constructed to prevent horses from having physical contact with animals outside the facility.

(B) The facility must be constructed only with materials that can withstand repeated cleaning and disinfection. Disinfectants authorized in 9 CFR part 71 must be used. All walls, floors, and ceilings must be constructed of solid material that is impervious to moisture. Doors, windows, and other openings of the facility must be provided with double screens that will prevent insects from entering the facility.

(iii) *Sanitation and security.* (A) The operator of the facility must arrange for a supply of water adequate to clean and disinfect the facility.

(B) All feed and bedding must originate from an area not under quarantine because of splenetic or tick fever (*see* part 72 of this chapter) and must be stored within the facility.

(C) Upon the death of any horse, the operator must arrange for the disposal of the horse's carcass by incineration. Disposal of all other waste removed from the facility during the time the horses are in quarantine or from horses that are refused entry into the United States must be either by incineration or in a public sewer system that meets all applicable environmental quality control standards. Following completion of the quarantine period and the release of the horses into the United States, all waste may be removed from the quarantine facility without further restriction.

(D) The facility must be maintained and operated in accordance with any additional requirements the Administrator deems appropriate to prevent the dissemination of any communicable disease.

(E) The facility must comply with all applicable local, State, and Federal requirements for environmental quality.

(iv) *Personnel.* (A) Access to the facility will be granted only to persons working at the facility or to persons specifically granted such access by an APHIS representative.

[14] The name and the address of the Veterinarian in Charge in any State is available from APHIS, Veterinary Services, National Center for Import and Export, 4700 River Road Unit 39, Riverdale, MD 20737–1231.

(B) The operator must provide attendants for the care and feeding of horses while in the quarantine facility.

(C) Persons working in the quarantine facility may not come in contact with any horses outside the quarantine facility during the quarantine period for any horses in the facility.

(v) *Handling of horses in quarantine.* Horses offered for importation into the United States that are quarantined in an approved temporary facility must be handled in accordance with paragraph (a) of this section while in quarantine.

(c) *Permanent, privately owned quarantine facilities.* Horses presented for entry into the United States as provided in §93.303(e) may be quarantined in permanent, privately owned quarantine facilities approved by the Administrator as meeting the requirements of paragraphs (c)(1) through (c)(6) of this section.

(1) *APHIS approval*—(i) *Approval procedures.* Persons seeking APHIS approval of a permanent, privately owned quarantine facility must write to the Administrator, c/o National Center for Import and Export, Veterinary Services, APHIS, 4700 River Road Unit 39, Riverdale, MD 20737–1231. The application letter must include the full name and mailing address of the applicant; the location and street address of the facility for which approval is sought; blueprints of the facility; a description of the financial resources available for construction, operation, and maintenance of the facility; the anticipated source or origin of horses to be quarantined, as well as the expected size and frequency of shipments; a contingency plan for horses needing emergency veterinary care; and a contingency plan for the disposal of all the horses capable of being housed in the facility.

(A) If APHIS determines that an application is complete and merits further consideration, the person applying for facility approval must enter into a service agreement with APHIS wherein the applicant agrees to pay the cost of all APHIS services associated with APHIS' evaluation of the application and facility. APHIS charges for the evaluation of the application and facility at hourly rates listed in §130.30 of this chapter. This service agreement applies only to fees accrued during the application process. If the facility is approved by APHIS, facility owners must enter into a compliance agreement in accordance with paragraph (c)(2) of this section.

(B) Requests for approval must be submitted to APHIS at least 120 days prior to the date of application for local building permits. Requests for approval will be evaluated on a first-come, first-served basis.

(ii) *Criteria for approval.* Before a facility may operate as a permanent, privately owned quarantine facility for horses, it must be approved by APHIS. To be approved:

(A) The facility must meet all of the requirements of this section;

(B) The facility must meet any additional requirements that may be imposed by the Administrator in each specific case, as specified in the compliance agreement required under paragraph (c)(2) of this section, to ensure that the quarantine of horses in the facility will be adequate to determine their health status, as well as to prevent the transmission of diseases into, within, and from the facility; and

(C) The Administrator must determine that sufficient personnel, including one or more APHIS veterinarians and other professional, technical, and support personnel, are available to serve as APHIS representatives at the facility. If the facility is approved, APHIS representatives will be present at all import quarantine operations in order to monitor them and will be present in order to provide other technical services to ensure the biological security of the facility, including, but not limited to, those specified in paragraph (c)(4)(v)(H) of §93.308. The Administrator's determination will be based on the expected size and frequency of shipments to the facility, as described in the application for approval of a permanent facility, as well as any other pertinent information in the application. APHIS will assign personnel to facilities requesting approval in the order that the facilities are approved. The Administrator has sole discretion on the number of APHIS personnel to be assigned to the facility.

(iii) *Maintaining approval.* To maintain APHIS approval, the operator must continue to comply with all the requirements of paragraph (c) of this section and the terms of the compliance agreement executed in accordance with paragraph (c)(2) of this section.

(iv) *Denial or withdrawal of approval.* Approval for a proposed permanent, privately owned quarantine facility may be denied or approval for a facility already in operation may be withdrawn at any time by the Administrator for any of the reasons provided in paragraph (c)(1)(iv)(C) of this section.

(A) Before facility approval is denied or withdrawn, the operator of the facility will be informed of the reasons for the proposed action by the Administrator and afforded an opportunity to present his or her views. If there is a conflict as to any material fact, APHIS will afford the operator, upon request, the opportunity for a hearing with respect to the merits or validity of such action.

(B) The Administrator may withdraw approval of an existing facility prior to a final determination in the hearing if the Administrator determines that such action is necessary to protect animal health or the public health, interest, or safety. Such withdrawal will be effective upon oral or written notification, whichever is earlier, to the operator of the facility. In the event of oral notification, APHIS will promptly give written confirmation to the operator of the facility. This withdrawal will continue in effect pending the completion of the hearing and any judicial review, unless otherwise ordered by the Administrator. In addition to withdrawal of approval for the reasons provided in paragraph (c)(1)(iv)(C) of this section, the Administrator will also automatically withdraw approval when the operator of any approved facility notifies the APHIS Veterinarian in Charge for the State in which the facility is located, in writing, that the facility is no longer in operation.[15]

(C) The Administrator may deny or withdraw approval of a permanent, privately owned facility if:

(*1*) Any requirement of this section or the compliance agreement is not complied with; or

(*2*) The operator fails to remit any charges for APHIS services rendered; or

(*3*) The operator or a person responsibly connected with the business of the quarantine facility acts as a paid agent (broker) for the importation or subsequent sale of horses; or

(*4*) The operator or a person responsibly connected with the business of the quarantine facility is or has been found by a court of competent jurisdiction to have violated any law or regulation pertaining to the importation or quarantine of any animal; or

(*5*) The operator or a person responsibly connected with the business of the quarantine facility is or has been convicted of any crime involving fraud, bribery, or extortion or any other crime involving a lack of the integrity needed for the conduct of operations affecting the importation of animals; or

(*6*) The approved quarantine facility has not been in use to quarantine horses for a period of at least 1 year.

(D) For the purposes of this section, a person is deemed to be responsibly connected with the business of the quarantine facility if such person has an ownership, mortgage, or lease interest in the facility's physical plant, or if such person is a partner, officer, director, holder, or owner of 10 percent or more of its voting stock, or is an employee in a managerial or executive capacity.

(v) *Approval for existing facilities.* Any permanent, privately owned quarantine facility operating under APHIS authorization on August 3, 2009 must be approved by APHIS to continue quarantine operations by August 3, 2010 or else must cease horse quarantine operations.

(2) *Compliance agreement.* (i) All permanent, privately owned quarantine facilities for horses must operate in accordance with a compliance agreement executed by the operator or his or her agent and the Administrator, which must be renewed on an annual basis.

[15] The name and address of the Veterinarian in Charge in any State is available from APHIS, Veterinary Services, National Center for Import and Export, 4700 River Road Unit 39, Riverdale, MD 20737–1231.

(ii) The compliance agreement must provide that:

(A) The facility must meet all applicable requirements of this section;

(B) The operator agrees to have APHIS representatives present at all import quarantine operations at the facility in order to monitor the import quarantine operations;

(C) The operator agrees to be responsible for the cost of the facility; all costs associated with its maintenance and operation; all costs associated with the hiring of employees and other personnel to attend to the horses as well as to maintain and operate the facility; all costs associated with the care of quarantined horses, such as feed, bedding, medicines, inspections, testing, laboratory procedures, and necropsy examinations; and all APHIS charges for the services of APHIS representatives in accordance with this section and part 130 of this chapter;

(D) The operator agrees to bar from the facility any employee or other personnel at the facility who fails to comply with paragraph (c) of this section or other provisions of this part, any terms of the compliance agreement, or related instructions from APHIS representatives;

(E) The operator agrees to demonstrate, to the satisfaction of the Administrator, that the routine cleaning and maintenance of the facility, the daily care of animals in quarantine, the disposal of wastes at the facility, the cleaning and disinfection procedures employed by the facility, the handling, washing, and disposal of soiled and contaminated clothing worn within the facility, and the disposal of dead horses, whether onsite or offsite, adhere to the best practices of biological security and animal care;

(F) The operator agrees to random spot audits by APHIS representatives to determine whether employees and other personnel are complying with these practices; and

(G) The operator of the facility allows the Administrator to amend the compliance agreement at any time after approval of the facility in order to incorporate related instructions issued by APHIS representatives while the facility is operational

(3) *Physical plant requirements.* The facility must meet the following requirements as determined by an APHIS inspection prior to admitting horses into the facility:

(i) *Location.* The quarantine facility must be located in proximity to a port authorized under §93.303(e). The site and the specific routes for the movement of horses from the port to the site must be approved by the Administrator based on consideration of whether the site or routes would put the horses in a position that could result in the transmission of communicable diseases to domestic horses.

(ii) *Construction.* The facility must be of sound construction, in good repair, and properly designed to prevent the escape of quarantined horses. It must have adequate capacity to receive and house shipments of horses as lots on an "all in, all out" basis, whereby separate lots of horses can be received and housed without contact with any other lots being quarantined at the facility. The facility must include the following:

(A) *Perimeter fencing.* The facility must be surrounded by a security fence of sufficient height and design to prevent the entry of unauthorized people and animals from outside the facility and to prevent the escape of the horses in quarantine.

(B) *Entrances and exits.* All entryways into the nonquarantine area of the facility must be equipped with a secure and lockable door. While horses are in quarantine, all access to the quarantine area for horses must be from within the building, and each such entryway to the quarantine area must be equipped with a series of solid self-closing double doors. Emergency exits to the outside are permitted in the quarantine area. Such emergency exits must be constructed so as to permit their being opened from the inside of the facility only.

(C) *Windows and other openings.* The facility must be constructed so that any windows or other openings in the quarantine area are double-screened with screening of sufficient gauge and mesh to prevent the entry or exit of insects and other vectors of diseases of horses and to provide ventilation sufficient to ensure the comfort and safety of all horses in the facility. The interior and exterior screens must be separated by at least 3 inches (7.62 cm). All screening of windows or other openings must be easily removable for cleaning, but must otherwise remain locked and secure at all times in a manner satisfactory to APHIS representatives in order to ensure the biological security of the facility.

(D) *Lighting*. The entire facility, including its stalls and hallways, must have adequate lighting.

(E) *Loading docks*. The facility must have separate docks for animal receiving and releasing and for general receiving and pickup, unless a single dock used for both purposes is cleaned and disinfected after each use in accordance with paragraph (c)(4)(iv)(F) of this section.

(F) *Surfaces*. The facility must be constructed so that the floor surfaces with which horses have contact are nonslip and wear-resistant. All floor surfaces with which the horses, their excrement, or discharges have contact must provide for adequate drainage. All floor and wall surfaces with which the horses, their excrement, or discharges have contact must be impervious to moisture and be able to withstand frequent cleaning and disinfection without deterioration. Ceilings and wall surfaces with which the horses, their excrement, or discharges do not have contact must be able to withstand cleaning and disinfection between shipments of horses. All floor and wall surfaces must be free of sharp edges that could cause injury to horses.

(G) *Horse stalls*. The stalls in which horses are kept must be large enough to allow each animal to make normal postural and social adjustments with adequate freedom of movement. Exercise equipment for horses may be kept in the stalls, provided that there will still be sufficient space within the stalls for the horses to move freely once the equipment is installed.

(H) *Aisleways*. The aisleways through which horses are moved to and from stalls must be wide enough to provide for safe movement of horses, including allowing horses to turn around in the aisleway, preventing horses in facing stalls from coming into contact with horses in the aisleway, and adequately ventilating the stalls.

(I) *Means of isolation*. Physical barriers must separate different lots of horses in the facility so that horses in one lot cannot have physical contact with horses in another lot or with their excrement or discharges. Stalls must be available that are capable of isolating any horses exhibiting signs of illness.

(J) *Showers*. A shower must be located at each entrance to the quarantine area. If the facility has a necropsy area, a shower must be located at the entrance to the necropsy area. A clothes-storage and clothes-changing area must be provided with each shower area. There must also be one or more receptacles near each shower so that clothing that has been worn into the quarantine area can be deposited in a receptacle prior to entering the shower.

(K) *APHIS space*. The facility must have adequate space for APHIS representatives to conduct examinations and testing of the horses in quarantine, prepare and package samples for mailing, and store the necessary equipment and supplies for duplicate samples. The space provided to conduct examinations and testing must include a refrigerator-freezer in which to store samples. The examination space must include equipment to provide for the safe inspection of horses. The facility must also include a secure, lockable office for APHIS use with enough room for a desk, chair, and filing cabinet.

(L) *Necropsy area*. The facility must either include an area for conducting necropsies onsite or must have designated an alternate facility at which a suitable necropsy area is available. If the facility has a necropsy area, it must be of sufficient size to perform necropsies on horses and be equipped with adequate lighting, hot and cold running water, a drain, a cabinet for storing instruments, a refrigerator-freezer for storing specimens, and an autoclave to sterilize veterinary equipment. If the facility does not have such an area, it must specify an alternate facility at which a suitable necropsy area is available, a route from the quarantine facility to the alternate facility's necropsy area, and the safeguards that will be in place to ensure that communicable diseases of horses are not spread during transit. This alternate facility and transport methodology must be approved by the Administrator under the procedures for requesting variances outlined in paragraph (c)(6) of this section.

(M) *Storage.* The facility must have sufficient storage space for equipment and supplies used in import quarantine operations. Storage space must include separate, secure storage for pesticides and for medical and other biological supplies, as well as a separate vermin-proof storage area for feed and bedding, if feed and bedding are stored at the facility. If the facility has multiple lot-holding areas, then separate storage space for any reusable supplies and equipment that are not disinfected after each use in accordance with part 71 of this chapter must be provided for each lot-holding area.

(N) *Additional space needs.* The facility must have an area for washing and drying clothes, linens, and towels and an area for cleaning and disinfecting equipment used in the facility. The facility must also include a work area for the repair of equipment.

(O) *Restrooms.* The facility must have permanent restrooms in both the quarantine and nonquarantine areas of the facility.

(P) *Ventilation and climate control.* The facility must be constructed with an air handling system capable of controlling and maintaining the ambient temperature, air quality, humidity, and odor at levels that are not injurious or harmful to the health of horses in quarantine. Air supplied to the quarantine area must not be recirculated or reused for other ventilation needs. Air handling systems for lot-holding areas must be separate from air handling systems for other operational and administrative areas of the facility. In addition, if the facility is equipped to handle more than one lot of horses at a time, the air handling system must be adequate to ensure that there is no cross-contamination of air between separate lot-holding areas.

(Q) *Fire protection.* The facility, including the lot-holding areas, must have a fire alarm voice communication system.

(R) *Communication system.* The facility must have a communication system between the nonquarantine and quarantine areas of the facility.

(iii) *Sanitation.* To ensure that proper animal health and biological security measures are observed, the facility must have the following:

(A) Equipment and supplies necessary to maintain the facility in clean and sanitary condition, including pest control equipment and supplies and cleaning and disinfecting equipment with adequate capacity to disinfect the facility and equipment.

(B) Any reusable equipment and supplies that are not disinfected after each use in accordance with part 71 of this chapter maintained separately for each lot of horses.

(C) Equipment and supplies used in the quarantine area maintained separately from equipment and supplies used in the nonquarantine area.

(D) A supply of potable water adequate to meet all watering and cleaning needs, with water faucets for hoses located throughout the facility. An emergency supply of water for horses in quarantine must also be maintained.

(E) A stock of disinfectant authorized in part 71 of this chapter or otherwise approved by the Administrator that is sufficient to disinfect the entire facility.

(F) The capability to dispose of wastes, including manure, urine, and used bedding, by means of burial, incineration, or public sewer. Other waste material must be handled in such a manner that minimizes spoilage and the attraction of pests and must be disposed of by incineration, public sewer, or other preapproved manner that prevents the spread of disease. Disposal of wastes must be carried out in accordance with the terms of the compliance agreement, and is subject to spot audits by APHIS representatives.

(G) The capability to dispose of horse carcasses in a manner approved by the Administrator and under conditions that minimize the risk of disease spread from carcasses.

(H) For incineration to be carried out at the facility, the facility must have incineration equipment that is detached from other facility structures and is capable of burning animal waste and refuse. The incineration site must also include an area sufficient for solid waste holding. Incineration may also take place at a local site away from the facility premises. All incineration activities, whether onsite or offsite, must be carried out in accordance with the terms of the compliance agreement, and are subject to spot audits by APHIS representatives.

(I) The capability to control surface drainage and effluent into, within, and from the facility in a manner that prevents the spread of disease into, within, or from the facility. If the facility is approved to handle more than one lot of horses at the same time, the drainage system must be adequate to ensure that there is no cross-contamination between lot-holding areas.

(iv) *Security.* Facilities must provide the following security measures:

(A) The facility and premises must be kept locked and secure at all times while horses are in quarantine.

(B) The facility and premises must have signs indicating that the facility is a quarantine area and no visitors are allowed.

(C) The facility and premises must be guarded at all times by one or more representatives of a bonded security company, or, alternatively, the facility must have an electronic security system that indicates the entry of unauthorized persons into the facility. Electronic security systems must be coordinated through or with the local police so that monitoring of the quarantine facility is maintained whenever APHIS representatives are not at the facility. The electronic security system must be of the "silent type" and must be triggered to ring at the monitoring site and not at the facility. The electronic security system must be approved by Underwriter's Laboratories. The operator must provide written instructions to the monitoring agency stating that the police and a representative of APHIS designated by APHIS must be notified by the monitoring agency if the alarm is triggered. The operator must also submit a copy of those instructions to the Administrator. The operator must notify the designated APHIS representative whenever a breach of security occurs or is suspected of having occurred. In the event that disease is diagnosed in quarantined horses, the Administrator may require the operator to have the facility guarded by a bonded security company in a manner that the Administrator deems necessary to ensure the biological security of the facility.

(D) The operator must furnish a telephone number or numbers to APHIS at which the operator or his or her agent can be reached at all times.

(E) APHIS is authorized to place APHIS seals on any or all entrances and exits of the facility when determined necessary by APHIS and to take all necessary steps to ensure that such seals are broken only in the presence of an APHIS representative. If someone other than an APHIS representative breaks such seals, APHIS will consider the act a breach in security and APHIS representatives will make an immediate accounting of all horses in the facility. If a breach in security occurs, APHIS may extend the quarantine period as long as necessary to determine that the horses are free of communicable diseases.

(4) *Operating procedures.* The following procedures must be observed at the facility at all times:

(i) *Oversight by APHIS representatives.* (A) Import quarantine operations at a privately owned quarantine facility may only be conducted with the physical presence of and monitoring by APHIS representatives. APHIS representatives are also authorized to perform the services required by this section and by the compliance agreement.

(B) If, as the result of a spot audit, or for any other reason, APHIS determines that the operator has failed to properly care for, feed, or handle quarantined horses as required in this paragraph (c) or in accordance with the terms of the compliance agreement, or has failed to maintain and operate the facility as provided in this paragraph (c) or in accordance with the terms of the compliance agreement, APHIS representatives will furnish such services, will make arrangements for the sale or disposal of quarantined horses at the quarantine facility owner's expense, or will begin the process for withdrawal of approval of the quarantine facility specified in paragraph (c)(1)(iv) of this section.

(ii) *Personnel.* (A) The operator must provide adequate personnel to maintain the facility and care for the horses in quarantine, including attendants to care for and feed horses, and other personnel as needed to maintain, operate, and administer the facility.

(B) The operator must provide APHIS with an up-to-date list of all personnel who have access to the facility. The list must include the names, current residential addresses, and employee identification numbers of each person. When the operator wishes to grant access to the facility to persons who have not previously had access to it, the operator must update the list prior to such persons having access to the quarantine facility.

(C) The operator must provide APHIS with signed statements from each employee and any other personnel hired by the operator and working at the facility in which the person agrees to comply with paragraph (c) of this section and applicable provisions of this part, all terms of the compliance agreement, and any related instructions from APHIS representatives pertaining to import quarantine operations, including contact with animals both inside and outside the facility.

(iii) *Authorized access.* Access to the facility premises as well as inside the quarantine area will be granted only to APHIS representatives, authorized employees, and other personnel of the operator assigned to work at the facility. All other persons are prohibited from the premises unless specifically granted access by an APHIS representative. Any visitors granted access must be accompanied at all times by an APHIS representative while on the premises or in the quarantine area of the facility.

(iv) *Sanitary requirements.* (A) All persons granted access to the quarantine area must:

(*1*) Shower when entering and leaving the quarantine area;

(*2*) Shower when leaving the necropsy area if a necropsy is in the process of being performed or has just been completed, or if all or portions of the examined animal remain exposed;

(*3*) Wear clean protective work clothing and footwear upon entering the quarantine area;

(*4*) Wear disposable gloves when handling sick horses and then wash hands after removing gloves; and

(*5*) Change protective clothing, footwear, and gloves when they become soiled or contaminated.

(B) The operator is responsible for providing a sufficient supply of clothing and footwear to ensure that all persons provided access to the quarantine area at the facility have clean, protective clothing, and footwear when they enter the quarantine area.

(C) The operator is responsible for the handling, washing, and disposal of soiled and contaminated clothing worn within the quarantine facility in accordance with the terms of the compliance agreement. At the end of each workday, work clothing worn into the quarantine area must be collected and kept in a bag until the clothing is washed. Used footwear must either be left in the clothes-changing area or cleaned with hot water (148 °F minimum) and detergent and disinfected in accordance with the terms of the compliance agreement. APHIS representatives may conduct spot audits of all handling, cleaning, and/or disposal of used clothing or used footwear.

(D) All equipment (including tractors) must be cleaned and disinfected prior to being used in the quarantine area of the facility with a disinfectant authorized in part 71 of this chapter or otherwise approved by the Administrator. The equipment must remain dedicated to the facility for the entire quarantine period. Any equipment used with quarantined horses (e.g., halters, floats, feed, water buckets, and exercise equipment) must remain dedicated to that particular lot of quarantined horses for the duration of the quarantine period or be cleaned and disinfected before coming in contact with horses from another lot. Prior to its removal from the quarantine premises, any equipment must be cleaned and disinfected in accordance with the terms of the compliance agreement. APHIS representatives may conduct spot audits of all cleaning and disinfection of equipment.

(E) Any vehicle, before entering or leaving the quarantine area of the facility, must be cleaned and disinfected in accordance with the terms of the compliance agreement within a time period authorized by the APHIS representative and with a disinfectant authorized in part 71 of this chapter or otherwise approved by the Administrator. APHIS representatives may conduct spot audits of all cleaning and disinfection of vehicles.

(F) If the facility has a single loading dock, the loading dock must be cleaned and disinfected after each use in accordance with the terms of the compliance agreement within a time period authorized by the APHIS representative and with a disinfectant authorized in part 71 of this chapter or otherwise approved by the Administrator. APHIS representatives may conduct spot audits of all cleaning and disinfection of the loading dock.

(G) That area of the facility in which a lot of horses has been held or has had access to must be thoroughly cleaned and disinfected, with a disinfectant authorized in part 71 of this chapter or otherwise approved by the Administrator, in accordance with the terms of the compliance agreement, upon release of the horses before a new lot of horses is placed in that area of the facility. APHIS representatives may conduct spot audits of all cleaning and disinfection of lot-holding areas.

(v) *Handling of the horses in quarantine.* (A) All horses must be handled in accordance with paragraph (a) of this section.

(B) Each lot of horses to be quarantined must be placed in the facility on an "all-in, all out" basis. No horse may be taken out of the lot while it is in quarantine, except for diagnostic purposes or as provided in paragraph (a)(4) of this section, and no horse may be added to the lot while the lot is in quarantine. Once import quarantine operations have been completed on a lot, but while the lot is still at the facility, a horse may be removed from that lot.

(C) The facility must provide sufficient feed and bedding for the horses in quarantine, and it must be free of vermin and not spoiled. Feed and bedding must originate from an area that is not listed in part 72 of this chapter as an area quarantined for splenetic or tick fever.

(D) Breeding of horses or collection of germplasm from horses is prohibited during the quarantine period.

(E) Horses in quarantine will be subjected to such tests and procedures as directed by an APHIS representative to determine whether they are free from communicable diseases of horses.

(F) Any death or suspected illness of horses in quarantine must be reported immediately to APHIS. The affected horses must be disposed of as the Administrator may direct, or depending on the nature of the disease, must be cared for as directed by APHIS to prevent the spread of the disease.

(G) Quarantined horses requiring specialized medical attention or additional postmortem testing may be transported off the quarantine site, if authorized by APHIS. A second quarantine site must be established to house the horses at the facility of destination (e.g., veterinary teaching hospital). In such cases, APHIS may extend the quarantine period for that horse and for its lot until the results of any outstanding tests or postmortem results are received.

(H) Should a horse be determined to be infected with or exposed to a Federally regulated disease of horses, arrangements for the final disposition of the infected or exposed horse must be accomplished within 10 days of the date that the importer is notified by the overseeing APHIS representative that the horse has been refused entry into the United States. APHIS representatives must be physically present at and directly monitor the subsequent disposition of the horse. The operator must have a preapproved contingency plan for the disposal of all horses housed at the facility prior to issuance of the import permit.

(I) Vaccination of horses in quarantine is prohibited. However, once import quarantine operations have been completed on a lot, but while the lot is still at the facility, horses in that lot may be vaccinated.

(vi) *Records.* (A) The facility operator must maintain a current daily record to record the entry and exit of all persons entering and leaving the quarantine facility.

(B) The operator must maintain the daily record, along with any records kept by APHIS and deposited with the operator, for at least 2 years following the date of release of the horses from quarantine and must make such records available to APHIS representatives upon request.

(5) *Environmental quality.* If APHIS determines that a privately operated quarantine facility does not meet applicable local, State, or Federal environmental regulations, APHIS may deny or suspend approval of the facility until appropriate remedial measures have been applied.

(6) *Variances.* The Administrator may grant variances to existing requirements relating to location, construction, and other design features of the physical facility, as well as to sanitation, security, operating procedures, recordkeeping, and other provisions of paragraph (c) of this section, but only if the Administrator determines that the variance causes no detrimental impact to the overall biological security of the import quarantine operations. The operator must submit a request for a variance from the requirements for the construction of the facility in paragraph (c)(3) of this section to the Administrator in writing prior to the construction of the facility. The operator must submit a request for a variance from the operational requirements in paragraph (c)(4) of this section to the Administrator in writing at least 30 days in advance of the arrival of horses to the facility. Any variance must also be expressly provided for in the compliance agreement.

(Approved by the Office of Management and Budget under control number 0579–0313)

[55 FR 31495, Aug. 2, 1990]

EDITORIAL NOTE: For FEDERAL REGISTER citations affecting § 93.308, see the List of CFR Sections Affected, which appears in the Finding Aids section of the printed volume and at *www.fdsys.gov*.

§ 93.309 Horse quarantine facilities; payment information.

(a) *Privately operated quarantine facilities.* The importer, or his or her agent, of horses subject to quarantine under the regulations in this part shall arrange for acceptable transportation to the privately operated quarantine facility and for the care, feed, and handling of the horses from the time of unloading at the quarantine port to the time of release from quarantine. Such arrangements shall be agreed to in advance by the Administrator. All expenses resulting therefrom or incident thereto shall be the responsibility of the importer; APHIS assumes no responsibility with respect thereto. The quarantine facility must be suitable for the quarantine of such horses and must be approved by the Administrator prior to the issuance of any import permit. The facilities occupied by horses should be kept clean and sanitary to the satisfaction of the inspector assigned to supervise the quarantine. If for any cause the care, feed, or handling of horses, or the sanitation of the facilities, is neglected, in the opinion of the inspector assigned to supervise the quarantine, such services may be furnished by APHIS in the same manner as though arrangements had been made for such services as provided by paragraph (b) of this section, and/or the horses may be disposed of as the Administrator, may direct, including sale in accordance with the procedure described in paragraph (b) of this section. The importer, or his or her agent, shall request in writing such inspection and other services as may be required, and shall waive all claim against the United States and APHIS or any employee of APHIS for damages which may arise from such services. The Administrator, may prescribe reasonable rates for the services provided under this paragraph. When it is found necessary to extend the usual minimum quarantine period, the importer, or his or her agent, shall be so advised in writing and shall pay for such additional quarantine and other services required. Payment for all services received by the importer, or his or her agent, in connection with each separate lot of horses shall be made by certified check or U.S. money order prior to release of the horses. If such payment is not made, the horses may be sold in accordance with the procedure described in paragraph (b) of this section, or otherwise disposed of as directed by the Administrator.

(b) *Quarantine facilities maintained by APHIS.* The importer, or his or her agent, of horses subject to quarantine under the regulations in this part shall arrange for acceptable transportation to the quarantine facility, and for the care, feed, and handling of the horses from the time they arrive at the quarantine port to the time of release from quarantine. Such arrangements shall be agreed to in advance by the Administrator. The importer or his or her agent shall request in writing such inspection and other services as may be required, and shall waive all claim against the United States and APHIS or any employee of APHIS, for damages which may arise from such services. All expenses resulting therefrom or incident thereto shall be the responsibility of the importer; APHIS assumes no responsibility with respect thereto. The Administrator may prescribe reasonable rates for the services provided under this paragraph. When it is found necessary to extend the usual minimum quarantine period, the importer, or his or her agent, shall be so advised in writing and shall pay for such additional quarantine and other services required. Payment for services received by the importer, or his or her agent, in connection with each separate lot of horses shall be made by certified check or U.S. money order prior to release of the horses. If such payment is not made, the horses may be sold in accordance with the procedure described in this paragraph or otherwise disposed of as directed by the Administrator. When payment is not made and the horses are to be sold to recover payment for services received, the importer, or his or her agent, will be notified by the inspector that if said charges are not immediately paid or satisfactory arrangements made for payment, the horses will be sold at public sale to pay the expense of care, feed, and handling during that period. The sale will be held after the expiration of the quarantine period, at such time and place as may be designated by the General Services Administration or other designated selling agent. The proceeds of the sale, after deducting the charges for care, feed, and handling of the horses and other expenses, including the expense of the sale, shall be held in a Special Deposit Account in the United States Treasury for 6 months from the date of sale. If not claimed by the importer, or his or her agent, within 6 months from the date of sale, the amount so held shall be transferred from the Special Deposit Account to the General Fund Account in the United States Treasury.

(c) Amounts collected from the importer, or his or her agent, for service rendered shall be deposited so as to be available for defraying the expenses involved in this service.

§93.310 Quarantine stations, visiting restricted; sales prohibited.

Visitors are not permitted in the quarantine enclosure during any time that the horses are in quarantine unless an APHIS representative specifically grants access under such conditions and restrictions as may be imposed by APHIS. An importer (or his or her agent or accredited veterinarian) may be admitted to the lot-holding area(s) containing his or her quarantined horses at such intervals as may be deemed necessary, and under such conditions and restrictions as may be imposed, by an APHIS representative. On the last day of the quarantine period, owners, officers or registry societies, and others having official business or whose services may be necessary in the removal of the horses may be admitted upon written permission from an APHIS representative. No exhibition or sale shall be allowed within the quarantine grounds.

[74 FR 31601, July 2, 2009]

§93.311 Milk from quarantined horses.

Milk or cream from horses quarantined under the provisions of this part shall not be used by any person other than those in charge of such horses, nor be fed to any animals other than those within the same enclosure, without permission of the inspector in charge of the quarantine station and subject to such restrictions as he or she may consider necessary to each instance. No milk or cream shall be removed from the quarantine premises except in compliance with all State and local regulations.

§ 93.312 Manure from quarantined horses.

No manure shall be removed from the quarantine premises until the release of the horses producing same.

§ 93.313 Appearance of disease among horses in quarantine.

If any contagious disease appears among horses during the quarantine period special precautions shall be taken to prevent spread of the infection to other animals in the quarantine station or to those outside the grounds. The affected horses shall be disposed of as the Administrator may direct, depending upon the nature of the disease.

§ 93.314 Horses, certification, and accompanying equipment.

(a) Horses offered for importation from any part of the world shall be accompanied by a certificate of a salaried veterinary officer of the national government of the region of origin, or if exported from Mexico, shall be accompanied either by such a certificate or by a certificate issued by a veterinarian accredited by the National Government of Mexico and endorsed by a full-time salaried veterinary officer of the National Government of Mexico, thereby representing that the veterinarian issuing the certificate was authorized to do so, showing that:

(1) The horses described in the certificate have been in said region during the 60 days preceding exportation;

(2) That each horse has been inspected on the premises of origin and found free of evidence of communicable disease and, insofar as can be determined, exposure thereto during the 60 days preceding exportation;

(3) That each horse has not been vaccinated with a live or attenuated or inactivated vaccine during the 14 days preceding exportation: *Provided, however*, that in specific cases the Administrator may authorize horses that have been vaccinated with an inactivated vaccine to enter the United States when he or she determines that in such cases and under such conditions as he or she may prescribe such importation will not endanger the livestock in the United States, and such horses comply with all other applicable requirements of this part;

(4) That, insofar as can be determined, no case of African horse sickness, dourine, glanders, surra, epizootic lymphangitis, ulcerative lymphangitis, equine piroplasmosis, Venezuelan equine encephalomyelitis, vesicular stomatitis, or equine infectious anemia has occurred on the premises of origin or on adjoining premises during the 60 days preceding exportation; and

(5) That, except as provided in § 93.301(g):

(i) The horses have not been in any region listed in § 93.301(c)(1) as affected with CEM during the 12 months immediately prior to their importation into the United States;

(ii) The horses have not been on any premises at any time during which time such premises were found by an official of the veterinary services of the national government of the region where such premises are located, to be affected with CEM;

(iii) The horses have not been bred by or bred to any horses from an affected premises; and

(iv) The horses have had no other contact with horses that have been found to be affected with CEM or with horses that were imported from regions affected with CEM.

(b) If a horse is presented for importation from a region where it has been for less than 60 days, the horse must be accompanied by a certificate that meets the requirements of paragraph (a) of this section that has been issued by a salaried veterinary officer of the national government of each region in which the horse has been during the 60 days immediately preceding its shipment to the United States. The dates during which the horse was in each region during the 60 days immediately preceding its exportation to the United States shall be included as a part of the certification.

(c) Following the port-of-entry inspection required by § 93.306 of this part, and before a horse offered for importation from any part of the world is released from the port of entry, an inspector may require the horse and its accompanying equipment to be disinfected as a precautionary measure against the introduction of foot-and-mouth disease or any other disease dangerous to the livestock of the United States.

[61 FR 52245, Oct. 7, 1996. Redesignated and amended at 62 FR 56012, 56017, Oct. 28, 1997; 63 FR 53783, Oct. 7, 1998]

CANADA [16]

§ 93.315 Import permit and declaration for horses.

For all horses offered for importation from Canada, the importer or his or her agent shall present two copies of a declaration as provided in § 93.305.

[55 FR 31495, Aug. 2, 1990. Redesignated and amended at 62 FR 56012, 56017, Oct. 28, 1997]

§ 93.316 Horses from Canada for immediate slaughter.

Horses imported from Canada for immediate slaughter shall be consigned from the port of entry directly to a recognized slaughtering establishment and there be slaughtered within two weeks from the date of entry. Such horses shall be inspected at the port of entry and otherwise handled in accordance with § 93.306. As used in this section, "directly" means without unloading en route if moved in a means of conveyance, or without stopping if moved in any other manner.

[55 FR 31495, Aug. 2, 1990, as amended at 59 FR 28216, June 1, 1994. Redesignated and amended at 62 FR 56012, 56017, Oct. 28, 1997]

§ 93.317 Horses from Canada.

(a) Except as provided in paragraph (c) of this section, horses from Canada shall be inspected as provided in § 93.306; shall be accompanied by a certificate as required by § 93.314 which shall include evidence of a negative test for equine infectious anemia for which blood samples were drawn during the 180 days preceding exportation to the United States and which test was conducted in a laboratory approved by the Canada Department of Agriculture or the United States Department of Agriculture; *Except*, that horses accompanying their dams which were foaled after their dam was so tested negative need not be so tested; and shall otherwise be handled as provided in § 93.314: *Provided, however*, That certificates required for horses from Canada may be either issued or endorsed by a salaried veterinarian of the Canadian Government: *And provided, further*, That USDA veterinary port inspection is not required for horses imported from Canada under temporary Customs authorization for a period of 30 days from the date of issue of the certificate and the certificate issued is valid for an unlimited number of importations into the United States during the 30-day period.

(b) Horses of United States origin that are imported into Canada under an export health certificate valid for a period of 30 days from the date of issue may re-enter the United States an unlimited number of times during the 30-day period, without USDA veterinary port inspection, at any Custom land border port of entry designated for animals from Canada, if accompanied by the original export health certificate under which they were permitted entry into Canada.

(c) Horses for immediate slaughter may be imported from Canada without the certification prescribed in paragraph (a) of this section, but shall be subject to the other applicable provisions of this part, and shall be accompanied by a certificate issued or endorsed by a salaried veterinarian of the Canadian Government stating that:

(1) The horses were inspected on the premises where assembled for shipment to the United States within the 30 days immediately prior to the date of export and were found free of evidence of communicable disease, and

(2) As far as can be determined, they have not been exposed to any such disease during the 60 days immediately preceding their exportation.

[55 FR 31495, Aug. 2, 1990, as amended at 56 FR 33863, July 24, 1991. Redesignated and amended at 62 FR 56012, 56017, Oct. 28, 1997]

§ 93.318 Special provisions.

(a) *In-bond shipments from Canada.* (1) Horses from Canada transported in-bond through the United States for immediate export shall be inspected at

[16] Importations from Canada shall be subject to §§ 93.315, 93.316, 93.317 and 93.318, in addition to other sections in this part which are in terms applicable to such importations.

the border port of entry and, when accompanied by an import permit obtained under § 93.304 of this part and all conditions therein are observed, shall be allowed entry into the United States and shall be otherwise handled as provided in paragraph (b) of § 93.301. Horses not accompanied by a permit shall meet the requirements of this part in the same manner as horses destined for importation into the United States, except that the Administrator may permit their inspection at some other point when he or she finds that such action will not increase the risk that communicable diseases of livestock and poultry will be disseminated to the livestock or poultry of the United States.

(2) *In-transit shipments through Canada.* Horses originating in the United States and transported directly through Canada may re-enter the United States without Canadian health or test certificates when accompanied by copies of the United States export health certificates properly issued and endorsed in accordance with regulations in part 91 of this chapter: *Provided,* That, to qualify for entry, the date, time, port of entry, and signature of the Canadian Port Veterinarian that inspected the horses for entry into Canada shall be recorded on the United States health certificate, or a paper containing the information shall be attached to the certificate that accompanies the horses. In all cases it shall be determined by the veterinary inspector at the United States port of entry that the horses are the identical horses covered by said certificate.

(b) *Exhibition horses.* Except as provided in § 93.317(b), horses from the United States which have been exhibited at the Royal Agricultural Winter Fair at Toronto or other publicly recognized expositions in Canada, including racing, horse shows, rodeo, circus, or stage exhibitions in Canada, and have not been in that region for more than 90 days are eligible for return to the United States without Canadian health or test certificates, if they are accompanied by copies of the United States health certificate, issued and endorsed in accordance with the export regulations contained in part 91 of this chapter for entry into Canada: *Provided,* That in the case of horses for exhibition, including race horses, the certificates shall certify that negative results were obtained from official tests for equine infectious anemia for which blood samples were drawn within 180 days of the date that the horses are offered for return to the United States: *And, provided further,* That all horses offered for re-entry upon examination by the veterinary inspector at the U.S. port of entry, are found by the inspector to be free of communicable diseases and exposure thereto and are determined to be the identical horses covered by said certificates or are the natural increase of such horses born after official test dates certified on the dam's health certificate.

[55 FR 31495, Aug. 2, 1990. Redesignated and amended at 62 FR 56012, 56017, Oct. 28, 1997]

CENTRAL AMERICA AND THE WEST INDIES [17]

§ 93.319 Import permit and declaration for horses.

For all horses offered for importation from regions of Central America or of the West Indies, the importer or his or her agent shall present two copies of a declaration as provided in § 93.305.

[55 FR 31495, Aug. 2, 1990. Redesignated and amended at 62 FR 56012, 56017, Oct. 28, 1997]

§ 93.320 Horses from Central America and the West Indies.

Horses from Central America and the West Indies shall be inspected as provided in § 93.306; shall be accompanied by a certificate and otherwise handled as provided in § 93.314; and shall be quarantined and tested as provided in § 93.308(a), (b) and (c): *Provided,* That any such horses that are found to be infested with fever ticks, Boophilus annulatus, shall not be permitted entry until they have been freed therefrom by dipping in a permitted arsenical solution or by other treatment approved by the Administrator.

[55 FR 31495, Aug. 2, 1990. Redesignated and amended at 62 FR 56012, 56017, Oct. 28, 1997]

[17] Importations from regions of Central America and the West Indies shall be subject to §§ 93.319 and 93.320, in addition to other sections in this subpart, which are in terms applicable to such importations.

MEXICO[18]

§93.321 Import permits and applications for inspection for horses.

For horses intended for importation into the United States from Mexico, the importer or his or her agent shall deliver to the veterinary inspector at the port of entry an application, in writing, for inspection, so that the veterinary inspector and customs representatives may make mutually satisfactory arrangements for the orderly inspection of the horses. The veterinary inspector at the port of entry will provide the importer or his or her agent with a written statement assigning a date when the horses may be presented for import inspection.

§93.322 Declaration for horses.

For all horses offered for importation from Mexico, the importer or his or her agent shall present two copies of a declaration as provided in §93.305.

[55 FR 31495, Aug. 2, 1990. Redesignated and amended at 62 FR 56012, 56017, Oct. 28, 1997]

§93.323 Inspection.

(a) All horses offered for entry from Mexico, including such horses intended for movement through the United States in bond for immediate return to Mexico, shall be inspected at a facility described in §93.324, and all such horses found to be free from communicable disease and fever tick infestation, and not to have been exposed thereto, shall be admitted into the United States subject to the other applicable provisions of this part. Horses found to be affected with or to have been exposed to a communicable disease, or infested with fever ticks, shall be refused entry. Horses refused entry, unless exported within a time fixed in each case by the Administrator, shall be disposed of as said Administrator may direct.

(b) Horses covered by paragraph (a) of this section shall be imported through facilities described in §93.324, which are equipped with facilities necessary for proper chute inspection, dipping, and testing, as provided in this part.

[55 FR 31495, Aug. 2, 1990, as amended at 58 FR 45238, Aug. 27, 1993. Redesignated at 62 FR 56012, 56017, Oct. 28, 1997]

§93.324 Detention for quarantine.

Horses intended for importation from Mexico shall be quarantined until they qualify for release from such quarantine, either at an APHIS facility designated in §93.303 (a) or at a facility in Mexico. In order to qualify for such release, all horses while so detained shall test negative to an official test for dourine, glanders, equine piroplasmosis, equine infectious anemia,[19] and such other tests that may be required by the Administrator to determine their freedom from other communicable diseases. Such horses shall also be subjected to such other inspections and disinfections deemed necessary by the Administrator, and they shall be released from quarantine only if found to be free from any communicable disease upon inspection.

[55 FR 31495, Aug. 2, 1990, as amended at 56 FR 15489, Apr. 17, 1991; 58 FR 45238, Aug. 27, 1993; 59 FR 67614, Dec. 30, 1994; 60 FR 5128, Jan. 26, 1995; 61 FR 39853, July 31, 1996; 61 FR 52246, Oct. 7, 1996. Redesignated at 62 FR 56012, 56017, Oct. 28, 1997, as amended at 63 FR 3640, Jan. 26, 1998]

§93.325 Horses from Mexico.

Horses offered for entry from Mexico shall be inspected as provided in §§93.306 and 93.323; shall be accompanied by a certificate and otherwise handled as provided in §93.314; and shall be quarantined and tested as provided in §93.324: *Provided*, That horses offered for importation from tick-infected areas of Mexico shall be chute

[18] Importations from Mexico shall be subject to §§93.321 to 93.326 inclusive, in addition to other sections in this subpart which are in terms applicable for such importations.

[19] In view of the fact that official test for dourine and glanders are run exclusively at the National Veterinary Services Laboratory, Ames, Iowa, protocols for these tests have not been published and are therefore not available; copies of "Protocol for the Complement-Fixation Test for Equine Piroplasmosis" and "Protocol for the Immuno-Diffusion (Coggins) Test for Equine Infectious Anemia" may be obtained from the Animal and Plant Health Inspection Service, Veterinary Services, National Center for Import-Export, 4700 River Road Unit 38, Riverdale, Maryland 20737–1231.

inspected, unless in the judgment of the inspector a satisfactory inspection can be made otherwise. If upon inspection they are found to be apparently free from fever ticks, before entering the United States they shall be dipped once in a permitted arsenical solution or be otherwise treated in a manner approved by the Administrator.

[55 FR 31495, Aug. 2, 1990. Redesignated and amended at 62 FR 56012, 56017, Oct. 28, 1997]

§ 93.326 Horses for immediate slaughter.

Horses may be imported from Mexico, subject to the applicable provisions of §§ 93.321, 93.322, and 93.323 for immediate slaughter if accompanied by a certificate of a salaried veterinarian of the Mexican Government, or by a certificate issued by a veterinarian accredited by the Mexican Government and endorsed by a salaried veterinarian of the Mexican Government, thereby representing that the veterinarian issuing the certificate was authorized to do so, stating that he or she has inspected such horses on the premises of origin and found them free of evidence of communicable disease, and that, so far as it has been possible to determine, they have not been exposed to any such disease common to animals of their kind during the preceding 60 days, and if the horses are shipped by rail or truck, the certificate shall further specify that the horses were loaded into cleaned and disinfected cars or trucks for transportation directly to the port of entry. Such horses shall be consigned from a facility described in § 93.324 to a recognized slaughtering establishment and there slaughtered within 2 weeks from the date of entry. Such horses shall be moved from the port of entry in conveyances sealed with seals of the United States Government.

[55 FR 31495, Aug. 2, 1990, as amended at 57 FR 28080, June 24, 1992; 58 FR 45238, Aug. 27, 1993; 60 FR 5128, Jan. 26, 1995; 61 FR 39853, July 31, 1996. Redesignated and amended at 62 FR 56012, 56017, Oct. 28, 1997; 63 FR 3640, Jan. 26, 1998]

Subpart D—Ruminants

SOURCE: 55 FR 31495, Aug. 2, 1990, unless otherwise noted. Redesignated at 62 FR 56012, Oct. 28, 1997.

§ 93.400 Definitions.

Wherever in this subpart the following terms are used, unless the context otherwise requires, they shall be construed, respectively, to mean:

Accredited herd. An accredited herd is one that has passed at least two consecutive annual official tuberculin tests and has no evidence of bovine tuberculosis. All animals in a herd must be free from tuberculosis.

Accredited veterinarian. A veterinarian approved by the Administrator in accordance with the provisions of part 161 of this title to perform functions specified in parts 1, 2, 3, and 11 of subchapter A, and subchapters B, C, and D of this chapter, and to perform functions required by cooperative state-federal disease control and eradication programs.

Administrator. The Administrator of the Animal and Plant Health Inspection Service or any other employee of the Animal and Plant Health Inspection Service, United States Department of Agriculture, to whom authority has been or may be delegated to act in the Administrator's stead.

Animal and Plant Health Inspection Service. Animal and Plant Health Inspection Service of the United States Department of Agriculture (APHIS or Service).

Animals. Cattle, sheep, goats, other ruminants, swine, horses, asses, mules, zebras, dogs, and poultry.

APHIS representative. A veterinarian or other individual employed by the Animal and Plant Health Inspection Service, United States Department of Agriculture, who is authorized to perform the services required by this part.

Area veterinarian in charge (AVIC). The veterinary official of APHIS who is assigned by the Administrator to supervise and perform the official animal health work of APHIS in the State concerned.

As a group. Collectively, in such a manner that the identity of the animals as a unique group is maintained.

Authorized USDA representative. An APHIS Veterinary Services employee, a USDA Food Safety and Inspection Service inspector, a State representative, an accredited veterinarian, or an employee of an accredited veterinarian, slaughtering establishment, or feedlot who is designated by the accredited veterinarian or management of the slaughtering establishment or feedlot to perform the function involved. In order to designate an employee to break official seals, an accredited veterinarian or the management of a slaughtering establishment or feedlot must first supply in writing the name of the designated individual to the APHIS AVIC in the State where the seals will be broken. Additionally, the management of a slaughtering establishment or feedlot must enter into an agreement with Veterinary Services in which the management of the facility agrees that only designated individuals will break the seals, that the facility will contact an APHIS representative or USDA Food Safety and Inspection Service inspector immediately if the seals are not intact when the means of conveyance arrives or if the animals being transported appear to be sick or injured due to transport conditions, and that the facility will cooperate with APHIS representatives, USDA Food Safety and Inspection Service inspectors, and State representatives in maintaining records of sealed shipments received.

Bovine. Bos taurus, Bos indicus, and *Bison bison.*

Bovine spongiform encephalopathy (BSE) minimal risk region. A region listed in §94.18(a)(3) of this subchapter.

Brucellosis certified free herd. A herd in which all eligible cattle in the herd were negative to brucellosis tests under the Canadian requirements and which is officially certified by the Canadian Government as a brucellosis free listed herd.

Brucellosis certified-free province or territory of Canada. A province or territory of Canada in which all herds of cattle are brucellosis certified free. The brucellosis certified free provinces and territories of Canada are Alberta, British Columbia, Manitoba, New Brunswick, Newfoundland (including Labrador), Northwest Territories, Nova Scotia, Ontario, Quebec, Prince Edward Island, Saskatchewan, and Yukon Territory.

Camelid. All species of the family *Camelidae,* including camels, guanacos, llamas, alpacas, and vicunas.

Cattle. Animals of the bovine species.

Cervid. All members of the family *Cervidae* and hybrids, including deer, elk, moose, caribou, reindeer, and related species.

Communicable disease. Any contagious, infectious, or communicable disease of domestic livestock, poultry or other animals.

Department. The United States Department of Agriculture (USDA).

Designated feedlot. A feedlot that has been designated by the Administrator as one that is eligible to receive sheep and goats imported from a BSE minimal-risk region and whose owner or legally responsible representative has signed an agreement in accordance with §93.419(d)(8) of this subpart to adhere to, and is in compliance with, the requirements for a designated feedlot.

Exporting region. A region from which shipments are sent to the United States.

Federal veterinarian. A veterinarian employed and authorized by the Federal Government to perform the tasks required by this subpart.

Fever tick. Rhipicephalus annulatus, Rhipicephalus microplus, and any other species of tick determined by the Administrator to be a vector of bovine babesiosis and specified on the Internet at *http://www.aphis.usda.gov/wps/portal/aphis/ ourfocus/importexport.*

Flock. Any group of one or more sheep maintained on common ground; or two or more groups of sheep under common ownership or supervision on two or more premises that are geographically separated, but among which there is an interchange or movement of animals.

Herd. Any group of one or more animals maintained on common ground; or two or more groups of animals under common ownership or supervision on two or more premises that are geographically separated, but among which there is an interchange or movement of animals.

Herd of origin. The herd within which an individual animal was born and raised and that was maintained on common ground for at least 4 months. For a group of one or more animals to qualify as a herd of origin for the purposes of § 93.406, animals may be added to the herd during or after the 4-month qualifying period only if they:

(1) Originated from a tuberculosis-free herd; or

(2) Originated from an accredited herd or originated from a herd of origin that tested negative to a whole herd test, and the individual cattle to be added to the herd also tested negative to any additional individual tests for tuberculosis required by the Administrator.

Immediate slaughter. Consignment directly from the port of entry to a recognized slaughtering establishment[1] and slaughtered within 2 weeks from the date of entry.

Inspector. Any individual authorized by the Administrator of APHIS or the Commissioner of Customs and Border Protection, Department of Homeland Security, to enforce the regulations in this subpart.

Lot. A group of ruminants that, while held on a conveyance or premises, has opportunity for physical contact with each other or with each other's excrement or discharges at any time between arrival at the quarantine facility and 60 days prior to export to the United States.

Lot-holding area. That area in a privately owned medium or minimum security quarantine facility in which a single lot of ruminants is held at one time.

Moved directly. Moved without unloading and without stopping except for refueling, or for traffic conditions such as traffic lights or stop signs.

Moved directly by land. Moved by rail, truck, or other land vehicle without unloading and without stopping except for refueling, or for traffic conditions such as traffic lights or stop signs.

Nonquarantine area. That area of a privately owned medium or minimum security quarantine facility that includes offices, storage areas, and other areas outside the quarantine area, and that is off limits to ruminants, samples taken from ruminants, and any other objects or substances that have been in the quarantine area during the quarantine of ruminants.

Official identification device or method. A means of officially identifying an animal or group of animals using devices or methods approved by the Administrator, including, but not limited to, official tags, tattoos, and registered brands when accompanied by a certificate of inspection from a recognized brand inspection authority. For animals intended for importation into the United States, the device or method of identification used must have been approved by the Administrator for that type of import before the animal is exported to the United States.

Official tuberculin test. A test for bovine tuberculosis that is approved by the Administrator as equivalent to the international standard test described in the Manual of Standards for Diagnostic Tests and Vaccines, Office International des Episodes, and that is administered and reported by a full-time salaried veterinary officer of the national government of the region of origin, or administered and reported by a veterinarian designated or accredited by the national government of the region of origin and endorsed by a full-time salaried veterinary officer of the national government of the region of origin, representing that the veterinarian issuing the certificate was authorized to do so.

Officially identified. Individually identified by means of an official identification device or method.

Operator. A person other than the Federal Government who owns or operates, subject to APHIS' approval and oversight, a privately owned medium or minimum security quarantine facility.

Permitted dip. A dip permitted by the Administrator to be used in the official dipping of cattle for fever ticks and for dipping cattle and sheep for scabies.

[1] The name of recognized slaughtering establishments approved under this part may be obtained from the area veterinarian in charge for the State of destination of the shipment. The name and address of the area veterinarian in charge in any State is available from the Animal and Plant Health Inspection Service, Veterinary Services, National Center for Import and Export, 4700 River Road Unit 39, Riverdale, MD 20737–1231.

Persons. Any individual, corporation, company, association, firm, partnership, society or joint stock company.

Port Veterinarian. A veterinarian employed by the Animal and Plant Health Inspection Service to perform duties required under this part at a port of entry.

Positive for a transmissible spongiform encephalopathy. A sheep or goat for which a diagnosis of a transmissible spongiform encephalopathy has been made.

Premises of origin. Except as otherwise used in §93.423 of this subpart, the premises where the animal was born.

Privately owned medium security quarantine facility (medium security facility). A facility that:

(1) Is owned, operated, and financed by a person other than the Federal Government;

(2) Is subject to the strict oversight of APHIS representatives;

(3) Is constructed, operated, and maintained in accordance with the requirements for medium security facilities in §93.412(d); and

(4) Provides the necessary level of quarantine services for the holding of ruminants in an indoor, vector-proof environment prior to the animals' entry into the United States. Quarantine services would have to include testing or observation for any OIE listed diseases and other livestock diseases exotic to the United States, as well as any other diseases, as necessary, to be determined by the Administrator.

Privately owned minimum security quarantine facility (minimum security facility). A facility that:

(1) Is owned, operated, and financed by a person other than the Federal Government;

(2) Is subject to the strict oversight of APHIS representatives;

(3) Is constructed, operated, and maintained in accordance with the requirements for minimum security facilities in §93.412(d);

(4) Is used for the quarantine of ruminants that pose no significant risk, as determined by the Administrator, of introducing or transmitting to the U.S. livestock population any livestock disease that is biologically transmissible by vectors; and

(5) Provides the necessary level of quarantine services for the outdoor holding of ruminants, prior to the animals' entry into the United States. Quarantine services would have to include testing or observation for any OIE listed diseases and other livestock diseases exotic to the United States, as well as any other diseases, as necessary, to be determined by the Administrator.

Processed animal protein. Meat meal, bone meal, meat-and-bone meal, blood meal, dried plasma and other blood products, hydrolyzed protein, hoof meal, horn meal, poultry meal, feather meal, fish meal, and any other similar products.

Quarantine area. That area of a privately owned medium or minimum security quarantine facility that comprises all of the lot-holding areas in the facility and any other areas in the facility that ruminants have access to, including loading docks for receiving and releasing ruminants, and any areas used to conduct examinations of ruminants and take samples and any areas where samples are processed or examined.

Recognized slaughtering establishment. Any slaughtering establishment operating under the provisions of the Federal Meat Inspection Act (21 U.S.C. 601 *et seq.*) or a State meat inspection act.[2]

Region. Any defined geographic land area identifiable by geological, political, or surveyed boundaries. A region may consist of any of the following:

(1) A national entity (country);

(2) Part of a national entity (zone, county, department, municipality, parish, Province, State, etc.);

(3) Parts of several national entities combined into an area; or

(4) A group of national entities (countries) combined into a single area.

Ruminants. All animals which chew the cud, such as cattle, buffaloes, sheep, goats, deer, antelopes, camels, llamas and giraffes.

State representative. A veterinarian or other person employed in livestock sanitary work by a State or political subdivision of a State who is authorized by such State or political subdivision of a State to perform the function

[2] See footnote 1.

involved under a memorandum of understanding with APHIS.

State veterinarian. A veterinarian employed and authorized by a State or political subdivision of a State to perform the tasks required by this subpart.

Suspect for a transmissible spongiform encephalopathy. (1) A sheep or goat that has tested positive for a transmissible spongiform encephalopathy or for the proteinase resistant protein associated with a transmissible spongiform encephalopathy, unless the animal is designated as positive for a transmissible spongiform encephalopathy; or

(2) A sheep or goat that exhibits any of the following signs and that has been determined to be suspicious for a transmissible spongiform encephalopathy by a veterinarian: Weight loss despite retention of appetite; behavior abnormalities; pruritus (itching); wool pulling; biting at legs or side; lip smacking; motor abnormalities such as incoordination, high stepping gait of forelimbs, bunny hop movement of rear legs, or swaying of back end; increased sensitivity to noise and sudden movement; tremor, "star gazing," head pressing, recumbency, or other signs of neurological disease or chronic wasting.

Swine. The domestic hog and all varieties of wild hogs.

Temporary inspection facility. A temporary facility that is constructed of metal panels that can be erected and broken down alongside the transportation vessel carrying ruminants that are imported into the United States in accordance with § 93.408 of this subpart and that will be quarantined at a minimum or medium security quarantine facilities located more than 1 mile from the port of entry.

Tuberculosis-free herd. A herd which is not known to be infected with bovine tuberculosis (*M. bovis*) and which is certified by the Canadian Government as a tuberculosis-free herd.

United States. All of the States of the United States, the District of Columbia, Guam, Northern Mariana Islands, Puerto Rico, the Virgin Islands of the United States, and all other Territories and Possessions of the United States.

Veterinary Services. The Veterinary Services unit of the Department.

Wether. A castrated male sheep or goat.

Whole herd test. An official tuberculin test of all cattle in a herd of origin that are 6 months of age or older, and of all cattle in the herd of origin that are less than 6 months of age and were not born into the herd of origin, except those cattle that are less than 6 months of age and:

(1) Were born in and originated from a tuberculosis-free herd; or

(2) Were born in and originated from an accredited herd or originated from a herd of origin that has tested negative to a whole herd test, and the individual cattle have tested negative to any additional individual tests for tuberculosis required by the Administrator.

World Organization for Animal Health (OIE). The international organization recognized by the World Trade Organization for setting animal health standards, reporting global animal situations and disease status, and presenting guidelines and recommendations on sanitary measures related to animal health.

Zoological park. A professionally operated zoo, park, garden or other place, maintained under the constant surveillance of a Doctor of Veterinary Medicine, for the exhibition of live animals, pigeons or birds, for the purpose of public recreation or education.

[55 FR 31495, Aug. 2, 1990. Redesignated at 62 FR 56012, Oct. 28, 1997]

EDITORIAL NOTE: For FEDERAL REGISTER citations affecting § 93.400, see the List of CFR Sections Affected, which appears in the Finding Aids section of the printed volume and at *www.fdsys.gov.*

§ 93.401 General prohibitions; exceptions.

(a) No ruminant or product subject to the provisions of this part shall be brought into the United States except in accordance with the regulations in this part and part 94 of this subchapter;[3] nor shall any such ruminant or product be handled or moved after physical entry into the United States

[3] Importations of certain animals from various regions are absolutely prohibited under part 94 because of specified diseases.

before final release from quarantine or any other form of governmental detention except in compliance with such regulations. Notwithstanding any other provision of this subpart, the importation of any non-bovine ruminant that has been in a region listed in §94.24(a) of this subchapter is prohibited. *Provided, however,* the Administrator may upon request in specific cases permit ruminants or products to be brought into or through the United States under such conditions as he or she may prescribe, when he or she determines in the specific case that such action will not endanger the livestock or poultry of the United States.

(b) Except for ruminants prohibited entry, the provisions in this part relating to ruminants shall not apply to healthy ruminants in transit through the United States if they are not known to be infected with or exposed, within 60 days preceding the date of export from the region of origin, to communicable diseases of such ruminants, if an import permit[4] has been obtained under §93.404 of this chapter and all conditions therein are observed; and if such ruminants are handled as follows:

(1)(i) They are maintained under continuous confinement in transit through the United States aboard an aircraft, ocean vessel, or other means of conveyance; or

(ii) They are unloaded, in the course of such transit, into a ruminant holding facility which is provided by the carrier or its agent and has been approved[5] in advance by the Administrator in accordance with paragraph (b)(3) of this section as adequate to prevent the spread within the United States of any livestock disease, and they are maintained there under continuous confinement until loaded aboard a means of conveyance for transportation from the United States and are maintained under continuous confinement aboard such means of conveyance until it leaves the United States; the import permit will specify any additional conditions necessary to assure that the transit of the ruminants through the United States can be made without endangering the livestock or poultry of the United States, and that Department inspectors may inspect the ruminants on board such means of conveyance or in such holding facility to ascertain whether the requirements of this paragraph are met, and dispose of them in accordance with the Animal Health Protection Act (7 U.S.C. 8301 *et seq.*) if such conditions are not met; and

(2) The carrier or its agent executes and furnishes to the collector of Customs at the first port of arrival a declaration stating that the ruminants will be retained aboard such means of conveyance or in an approved holding facility during transshipment as required by this paragraph.

(3) Provisions for the approval of facilities required in this paragraph are:

(i) They must be sufficiently isolated to prevent direct or indirect contact with all other animals and birds while in the United States.

(ii) They must be so constructed that they provide adequate protection against environmental conditions and can be adequately cleaned, washed and disinfected.

(iii) They must provide for disposal of ruminant carcasses, manure, bedding, waste and any related shipping materials in a manner that will prevent dissemination of disease.

(iv) They must have provisions for adequate sources of feed and water and for attendants for the care and feeding of ruminants in the facility.

(v) They must comply with additional requirements as may be imposed by the Administrator if deemed applicable for a particular shipment.

(vi) They must also comply with all applicable local, State and Federal requirements for environmental quality and with the provisions of the Animal Welfare Regulations in chapter I of this title, as applicable.

(c) *Removal and loss of official identification devices.* Official identification devices are intended to provide permanent identification of livestock and to ensure the ability to find the source of animal disease outbreaks. Removal of

---

[4] Such permit may be obtained from the Animal and Plant Health Inspection Service, Veterinary Services, National Center for Import-Export, 4700 River Road Unit 38, Riverdale, Maryland 20737–1231. Requests for approval of such facilities should also be made to the Administrator.

[5] See footnote 4 to subpart D.

these devices is prohibited except at the time of slaughter. If an official identification device is lost, and it is necessary to retag an animal with a new official number, every effort should be made to correlate the new official number with the previous official number of the animal.

[55 FR 31495, Aug. 2, 1990, as amended at 59 FR 67614, Dec. 30, 1994. Redesignated and amended at 62 FR 56012, 56017, Oct. 28, 1997; 68 FR 6344, Feb. 7, 2003; 68 FR 31940, May 29, 2003; 69 FR 64651, Nov. 8, 2004; 78 FR 72996, Dec. 4, 2013]

§ 93.402 Inspection of certain aircraft and other means of conveyance and shipping containers thereon; unloading, cleaning, and disinfection requirements.

(a) *Inspection:* All aircraft and other means of conveyance (including shipping containers thereon) moving into the United States from any foreign region are subject to inspection without a warrant by properly identified and designated inspectors to determine whether they are carrying any animal, carcass, product or article regulated or subject to disposal under any law or regulation administered by the Secretary of Agriculture for prevention of the introduction or dissemination of any communicable animal disease.

(b) *Unloading requirements:* Whenever in the course of any such inspection at any port in the United States the inspector has reason to believe that the means of conveyance or container is contaminated with material of animal (including poultry) origin, such as, but not limited to, meat, organs, glands, extracts, secretions, fat, bones, blood, lymph, urine, or manure, so as to present a danger of the spread of any communicable animal disease, the inspector may require the unloading of the means of conveyance and the emptying of the container if he or she deems it necessary to enable him or her to determine whether the means of conveyance or container is in fact so contaminated. The principal operator of the means of conveyance and his or her agent in charge of the means of conveyance shall comply with any such requirement under the immediate supervision of, and in the time and manner prescribed by, the inspector.

(c) *Cleaning and disinfection:* Whenever, upon inspection under this section, an inspector determines that a means of conveyance or shipping container is contaminated with material of animal origin so as to present a danger of the spread of any communicable animal disease, he or she shall notify the principal operator of the means of conveyance or his or her agent in charge, of such determination and the requirements under this section. The person so notified shall cause the cleaning and disinfection of such means of conveyance and container under the immediate supervision of, and in the time and manner prescribed by, the inspector.

(d) For purposes of this section, the term "shipping container" means any container of a type specially adapted for use in transporting any article on the means of conveyance involved.

[55 FR 31495, Aug. 2, 1990. Redesignated and amended at 62 FR 56012, 56017, Oct. 28, 1997; 68 FR 6344, Feb. 7, 2003]

§ 93.403 Ports designated for the importation of ruminants.

(a) *Air and ocean ports.* The following ports have APHIS inspection and quarantine facilities necessary for quarantine stations and all ruminants shall be entered into the United States through these stations, except as provided in paragraphs (b), (c), (d), (e), and (f) of this section; Miami, Florida; and Newburgh, New York.

(b) *Canadian border ports.* The following land border ports are designated as having the necessary inspection facilities for the entry of ruminants from Canada: Eastport, Idaho; Houlton and Jackman, Maine; Detroit, Port Huron, and Sault Ste. Marie, Michigan; Baudette, Minnesota; Opheim, Raymond, and Sweetgrass, Montana; Alexandria Bay, Buffalo, and Champlain, New York; Dunseith, Pembina, and Portal, North Dakota; Derby Line and Highgate Springs, Vermont; Oroville and Sumas, Washington.

(c) *Mexican border ports.* The following land border ports are designated as having the necessary inspection facilities for the entry of ruminants from Mexico: Brownsville, Hidalgo, Laredo, Eagle Pass, Del Rio, and Presidio, Texas: Douglas, Naco, Nogales, Sasabe, and San Luis, Arizona; Calexico and San Ysidro, California; and Antelope Wells, Columbus, and Santa Teresa, New Mexico.

(d) *Special ports*. Charlotte Amalie, St. Thomas, and Christiansted, St. Croix, in the United States Virgin Islands, are hereby designated as quarantine stations for the entry of ruminants from the British Virgin Islands into the United States Virgin Islands for immediate slaughter.

(e) *Limited ports*. The following ports are designated as having inspection facilities for the entry of ruminants and ruminant products such as ruminant test specimens which do not appear to require restraint and holding inspection facilities: Anchorage and Fairbanks, Alaska; San Diego, California; Jacksonville, St. Petersburg-Clearwater, and Tampa, Florida; Atlanta, Georgia; Honolulu, Hawaii, Chicago, Illinois; New Orleans, Louisiana; Portland, Maine; Baltimore, Maryland; Boston, Massachusetts; Minneapolis, Minnesota; Great Falls, Montana; Portland, Oregon; San Juan, Puerto Rico; Memphis, Tennessee (no live animals); El Paso, Galveston, and Houston, Texas; and Seattle, Spokane, and Tacoma, Washington.

(f) *Designation of other ports*. The Secretary of the Treasury has approved the designation as quarantine stations of the ports specified in this section. In special cases other ports may be designated as quarantine stations under this section by the Administrator, with the concurrence of the Secretary of the Treasury.

(g) *Ports and privately owned quarantine facilities*. Ruminants may be imported into the United States at any port specified in paragraph (a) of this section, or at any other port designated as an international port or airport by the Bureau of Customs and Border Protection, and quarantined at an APHIS-approved privately owned quarantine facility, provided the applicable provisions of §§ 93.401, 93.404(a), 93.407, 93.408, and 93.412 are met.

[55 FR 31495, Aug. 2, 1990, as amended at 57 FR 2010, Jan. 17, 1992; 58 FR 38283, July 16, 1993; 60 FR 16045, Mar. 29, 1995; 60 FR 25120, May 11, 1995. Redesignated and amended at 62 FR 56012, 56017, Oct. 28, 1997; 64 FR 23179, Apr. 30, 1999; 65 FR 38178, June 20, 2000; 67 FR 68022, Nov. 8, 2002; 71 FR 29773, May 24, 2006]

§ 93.404 Import permits for ruminants and for ruminant test specimens for diagnostic purposes; and reservation fees for space at quarantine facilities maintained by APHIS.

(a) *Application for permit; reservation required*. (1) For ruminants and ruminant test specimens for diagnostic screening purposes intended for importation from any part of the world, except as otherwise provided for in §§ 93.417, 93.422, and 93.424, the importer shall first apply for and obtain from APHIS an import permit. The application shall specify the name and address of the importer; the species, breed, number or quantity of ruminants or ruminant test specimens to be imported; the purpose of the importation; individual ruminant identification, which includes a description of the ruminant, name, age, markings, if any, registration number, if any, and tattoo or eartag; the region of origin; for cattle, the address of or other means of identifying the premises of the herd of origin and any other premises where the cattle resided prior to export, including the State or its equivalent, the municipality or nearest city, and the specific location of the premises, or an equivalent method, approved by the Administrator, of identifying the location of the premises; the name and address of the exporter; the port of embarkation in the foreign region; the mode of transportation, route of travel, and the port of entry in the United States; the name and address of the quarantine facility, if the ruminants are to be quarantined at a privately owned quarantine facility; the proposed date of arrival of the ruminants or ruminant test specimens to be imported; and the name of the person to whom the ruminants or ruminant test specimens will be delivered and the location of the place in the United States to which delivery will be made from the port of entry. Additional information may be required in the form of certificates concerning specific diseases to which the ruminants are susceptible, as well as vaccinations or other precautionary treatments to which the ruminants or ruminant test specimens have been subjected. Notice of any such requirement will be given to the applicant in each case.

(2) An application for permit to import will be denied for domestic ruminants from any region designated in § 94.1 of this chapter as a region where rinderpest or foot-and-mouth disease exists.

(3) An application for permit to import ruminants may also be denied because of: Communicable disease conditions in the area or region of origin, or in a region where the shipment has been or will be held or through which the shipment has been or will be transported; deficiencies in the regulatory programs for the control or eradication of animal diseases and the unavailability of veterinary services in the above mentioned regions; the importer's failure to provide satisfactory evidence concerning the origin, history, and health status of the ruminants; the lack of satisfactory information necessary to determine that the importation will not be likely to transmit any communicable disease to livestock or poultry of the United States; or any other circumstances which the Administrator believes require such denial to prevent the dissemination of any communicable disease of livestock or poultry into the United States.

(4)(i) The importer or importer's agent shall pay or ensure payment of a reservation fee for each lot of ruminants to be quarantined in a facility maintained by USDA. For ruminants, the reservation fee shall be 100 percent of the cost of providing care, feed, and handling during quarantine, as estimated by the quarantine facility's veterinarian in charge.

(ii) At the time the importer or the importer's agent requests a reservation of quarantine space, the importer or importer's agent shall pay the reservation fee by check or U.S. money order or ensure payment of the reservation fee by an irrevocable letter of credit from a commercial bank (the effective date on such letter of credit shall run to 30 days after the date the ruminants are scheduled to be released from quarantine); except that anyone who issues a check to the Department for a reservation fee which is returned because of insufficient funds shall be denied any further request for reservation of a quarantine space until the outstanding amount is paid.

(iii) Any reservation fee paid by check or U.S. money order shall be applied against the expenses incurred for services received by the importer or importer's agent in connection with the quarantine for which the reservation was made. Any part of the reservation fee which remains unused after being applied against the expenses incurred for services received by the importer or the importer's agent in connection with the quarantine for which the reservation was made, shall be returned to the individual who paid the reservation fee. If the reservation fee is ensured by a letter of credit, the Department will draw against the letter of credit unless payment for services received by the importer or importer's agent in connection with the quarantine is otherwise made at least 3 days prior to the expiration date of the letter of credit.

(iv) Any reservation fee shall be forfeited if the importer or the importer's agent fails to present for entry, within 24 hours following the designated time of arrival, the lot of ruminants for which the reservation was made: *Except* that a reservation fee shall not be forfeited if:

(A) Written notice of cancellation from the importer or the importer's agent is received by the office of the veterinarian in charge of the quarantine facility[6] during regular business hours (8:00 a.m. to 4:30 p.m. Monday through Friday, excluding holidays) no later than 15 days for ruminants prior

[6] The addresses of USDA quarantine facilities may be found in telephone directories listing the facilities or by contacting the Animal and Plant Health Inspection Service, Veterinary Services, National Center for Import-Export, 4700 River Road Unit 38, Riverdale, Maryland 20737–1231.

to the beginning of the time of importation as specified in the import permit or as arranged with the veterinarian in charge of the quarantine facility if no import permit is required (the 15 days period shall not include Saturdays, Sundays, or holidays), or

(B) The Administrator determines that services, other than provided by carriers, necessary for the importation of the ruminants within the requested period are unavailable because of unforeseen circumstances as determined by the Administrator, (such as the closing of an airport due to inclement weather or the unavailability of the reserved space due to the extension of another quarantine).

(v) If the reservation fee was ensured by a letter of credit and the fee is to be forfeited under paragraph (a)(4)(iv) of this section, the Department will draw against the letter of credit unless the reservation fee is otherwise paid at least 3 days prior to the expiration date of the letter of credit.

(vi) When a reservation is cancelled in accordance with paragraph (a)(4)(iv)(A) of this section and the provisions of paragraph (a)(4)(iv)(B) of this section do not apply, a $40.00 cancellation fee shall be charged. If a reservation fee was paid, the cancellation fee shall be deducted from any reservation fee returned to the importer or the importer's agent. If the reservation fee was ensured by a letter of credit, the Department will draw the amount of the cancellation fee against the letter of credit unless the cancellation fee is otherwise paid at least 3 days prior to the expiration date of the letter of credit.

(b) *Permit.* When a permit is issued, the original and two copies will be sent to the importer. It shall be the responsibility of the importer to forward the original permit and one copy to the shipper in the region of origin, and it shall also be the responsibility of the importer to insure that the shipper presents the copy of the permit to the carrier and makes proper arrangements for the original permit to accompany the shipment to the specified U.S. port of entry for presentation to the collector of customs. Ruminants and ruminant test specimens for diagnostic screening purposes for ruminants intended for importation into the United States for which a permit has been issued, will be received at the specified port of entry within the time prescribed in the permit which shall not exceed 14 days from the first day that the permit is effective for all permits. Ruminants and ruminant test specimens for which a permit is required by these regulations will not be eligible for entry if a permit has not been issued; if unaccompanied by such a permit; if shipment is from any port other than the one designated in the permit; if arrival in the United States is at any port other than the one designated in the permit; if the ruminants or ruminant test specimens offered for entry differ from those described in the permit; if the ruminants or ruminant test specimens are not handled as outlined in the application for the permit and as specified in the permit issued; or if ruminants or swine other than those covered by import permits are aboard the transporting carrier.

(c) *Wild ruminants from regions where foot-and-mouth disease or rinderpest exists.* This paragraph (c) applies to the importation of wild ruminants, such as, but not limited to, giraffes, deer and antelopes, from regions designated in part 94 of this subchapter as countries in which foot-and-mouth disease or rinderpest exist.

(1) Permits for the importation of wild ruminants will be issued only for importations through the Port of New York, and only if the animals are imported for exhibition in a PEQ Zoo. A PEQ Zoo is a zoological park or other place maintained for the exhibition of live animals for recreational or educational purposes that:

(i) Has been approved by the Administrator in accordance with paragraph (c)(2) of this section to receive and maintain imported wild ruminants; and

(ii) Has entered into the agreement with APHIS set forth in paragraph (c)(4) of this section for the maintenance and handling of imported wild ruminants.

(2) Approval of a PEQ Zoo shall be on the basis of an inspection, by an authorized representative of the Department, of the physical facilities of the

establishment and its methods of operation. Standards for acceptable physical facilities shall include satisfactory pens, cages, or enclosures in which the imported ruminants can be maintained so as not to be in contact with the general public and free from contact with domestic livestock; natural or established drainage from the PEQ Zoo which will avoid contamination of land areas where domestic livestock are kept or with which domestic livestock may otherwise come in contact; provision for the disposition of manure, other wastes, and dead ruminants within the PEQ Zoo; and other reasonable facilities considered necessary to prevent the dissemination of diseases from the PEQ Zoo. The operator of the PEQ Zoo shall have available the services of a full-time or part-time veterinarian, or a veterinarian on a retainer basis, who shall make periodic examinations of all animals maintained at the PEQ Zoo for evidence of disease; who shall make a post-mortem examination of each animal that dies; and who shall make a prompt report of suspected cases of contagious or communicable diseases to an APHIS representative or the State agency responsible for livestock disease control programs.

(3) Manure and other animal wastes must be disposed of within the PEQ Zoo park for a minimum of one year following the date an imported wild ruminant enters the zoo. If an APHIS veterinarian determines that an imported ruminant shows no signs of any communicable disease or exposure to any such disease during this 1-year period, its manure and other wastes need not be disposed of within the zoo after the 1-year period. If, however, an APHIS veterinarian determines that an imported ruminant does show signs of any communicable disease during this 1-year period, an APHIS veterinarian will investigate the disease and determine whether the ruminant's manure and other wastes may safely be disposed of outside the zoo after the 1-year period has ended.

(4) Prior to the issuance of an import permit under this section, the operator of the approved PEQ Zoo to which the imported ruminants are to be consigned, and the importer of the ruminants, if such operator and importer are different parties, shall execute an agreement covering each ruminant or group of ruminants for which the import permit is requested. The agreement shall be in the following form:

AGREEMENT FOR THE IMPORTATION, QUARANTINE AND EXHIBITION OF CERTAIN WILD RUMINANTS AND WILD SWINE

_______, operator(s) of the zoological park known as _______ (Name) located at _______ (City and state), and _______ (Importer) hereby request a permit for the importation of _______ (Number and kinds of animals) for exhibition purposes at the said zoological park, said animals originating in a region where foot-and-mouth disease or rinderpest exists and being subject to restrictions under regulations contained in part 93, title 9, Code of Federal Regulations.

In making this request, it is understood and agreed that:

1. The animals for which an import permit is requested will be held in isolation at a port of embarkation in the region of origin, approved by the Administrator as a port having facilities which are adequate for maintaining wild animals in isolation from all other animals and having veterinary supervision by officials of the region of origin of the animals. Such animals will be held in such isolation for not less than 60 days under the supervision of the veterinary service of that region to determine whether the animals show any clinical evidence of foot-and-mouth disease, rinderpest, or other communicable disease that is exotic to the United States or for which APHIS has an eradication or control program in 9 CFR chapter I, and to assure that the animals will not have been exposed to such a disease within the 60 days next before their exportation from that region.

2. Shipment will be made direct from such port of embarkation to the port of New York as the sole port of entry in the United States. If shipment is made by ocean vessel the animals will not be unloaded in any foreign port en route. If shipment is made by air, the animals will not be unloaded at any port or other place of landing, except at a port approved by the Administrator as a port not located in a region where rinderpest or foot-and-mouth disease exists or as a port in such a region having facilities and inspection adequate for maintaining wild animals in isolation from all other animals.

3. No ruminants or swine will be aboard the transporting vehicle, vessel or aircraft, except those for which an import permit has been issued.

4. The animals will be quarantined for not less than 30 days in the Department's Animal Import Center in Newburgh, New York.

5. Upon release from quarantine the animals will be delivered to the zoological park named in this agreement to become the property of the park and they will not be sold, exchanged or removed from the premises without the prior consent of APHIS. If moved to another zoological park in the United States, the receiving zoological park must be approved by the Administrator in accordance with paragraph 6 of this agreement.

6. The Administrator will approve the movement of an imported animal subject to this agreement if the Administrator determines that the animal has spent at least one year in quarantine in a PEQ Zoo following importation without showing clinical evidence of foot-and-foot mouth disease, rinderpest, or other communicable disease that is exotic to the United States or for which APHIS has an eradication or control program in 9 CFR chapter I, and determines that the receiving zoological park is accredited by the American Zoo and Aquarium Association (AZA), or the receiving zoological park has facilities and procedures in place related to preventing the spread of communicable animal diseases (including but not limited to procedures for animal identification, record keeping, and veterinary care) that are equivalent to those required for AZA accreditation. The Administrator will approve the movement of a carcass, body part, or biological specimen derived from an imported animal subject to this agreement if the Administrator determines that the animal has spent at least one year in quarantine in a PEQ Zoo following importation without showing clinical evidence of foot-and-foot mouth disease, rinderpest, or other communicable disease that is exotic to the United States or for which APHIS has an eradication or control program in 9 CFR chapter I, and determines that the carcass, body part, or biological specimen will be moved only for scientific research or museum display purposes.

____

(Signature of importer)

Subscribed and sworn to before me this ____ day of ____, ____.

____

(Title or designation)

____

(Name of zoological park)

By ____________________________

(Signature of officer of zoological park)

____

(Title of officer)

Subscribed and sworn to before me this ____ day of ____, ____

____

(Title or designation)

(Approved by the Office of Management and Budget under control numbers 0579–0040 and 0579–0224)

[55 FR 31495, Aug. 2, 1990, as amended at 59 FR 28216, June 1, 1994; 59 FR 31924, June 21, 1994; 59 FR 67615, Dec. 30, 1994; 62 FR 23637, May 1, 1997. Redesignated and amended at 62 FR 56012, 56018, Oct. 28, 1997; 65 FR 38178, June 20, 2000; 68 FR 6344, Feb. 7, 2003; 68 FR 35533, June 16, 2003; 71 FR 29773, May 24, 2006]

§93.405 Health certificate for ruminants.

(a) All ruminants intended for importation from any part of the world, except as provided in §§93.423(c) and 93.428(d), shall be accompanied by a certificate issued by a full-time salaried veterinary officer of the national government of the region of origin, or issued by a veterinarian designated or accredited by the national government of the region of origin and endorsed by a full-time salaried veterinary officer of the national government of the region of origin, representing that the veterinarian issuing the certificate was authorized to do so. The certificate shall state:

(1) That the ruminants have been kept in that region during the last 60 days immediately preceding the date of shipment to the United States, and that during this time the region has been entirely free from foot-and-mouth disease, rinderpest, contagious pleuropneumonia, and surra; *provided, however*, that for wild ruminants for exhibition purposes, the certificate need specify only that the district of origin has been free from the listed diseases; *and provided further*, that for sheep and goats, with respect to contagious pleuropneumonia, the certificate may specify only that the district of origin has been free from this disease;

(2) That the ruminants are not in quarantine in the region of origin; and

(3) If the ruminants are from any region where screwworm is considered to exist, the ruminants may be imported into the United States only if they meet the requirements of paragraphs (a)(3)(i) through (iv) of this section and all other applicable requirements of this part. APHIS will maintain a list of regions where screwworm is considered to exist on the APHIS Web site at

http://www.aphis.usda.gov/import_export/animals/ animal_disease_status.shtml. Copies of the list will also be available via postal mail, fax, or email upon request to the Sanitary Trade Issues Team, National Center for Import and Export, Veterinary Services, Animal and Plant Health Inspection Service, 4700 River Road Unit 38, Riverdale, Maryland 20737. APHIS will add a region to the list upon determining that screwworm exists in the region based on reports APHIS receives of detections of the pest from veterinary officials of the exporting country, from the World Organization for Animal Health (OIE), or from other sources the Administrator determines to be reliable. APHIS will remove a region from the list after conducting an evaluation of the region in accordance with § 92.2 of this subchapter and finding that screwworm is not present in the region. In the case of a region formerly not on this list that is added due to a detection, the region may be removed from the list in accordance with the procedures for reestablishment of a region's disease-free status in § 92.4 of this subchapter.

(i) A veterinarian must treat the ruminants with ivermectin 3 to 5 days prior to the date of export to the United States according to the recommended dose prescribed on the product's label.

(ii) The ruminants must be fully examined for screwworm by a full-time salaried veterinary official of the exporting country within 24 hours prior to shipment to the United States. If ruminants are found to be infested with screwworm, they must be treated until free from infestation.

(iii) At the time ruminants are loaded onto a means of conveyance for export, a veterinarian must treat any visible wounds on the animals with a solution of coumaphos dust at a concentration of 5 percent active ingredient.

(iv) The ruminants must be accompanied to the United States by a certificate signed by a full-time salaried veterinary official of the exporting country. The certificate must state that the ruminants have been thoroughly examined and found free of screwworm and that the ruminants have been treated in accordance with paragraphs (a)(3)(i) and (a)(3)(iii) of this section.

(4) If the ruminants are sheep or goats from Canada, the certificate must also include the name and address of the importer; the species, breed, number or quantity of ruminants to be imported; the purpose of the importation; individual ruminant identification, which includes the official identification required under § 93.419(c) of this subchapter, and any other identification present on the animal, including registration number, if any; a description of the ruminant, including age, color, and markings, if any; region of origin; the address of or other means of identifying the premises of origin and any other premises where the ruminants resided immediately prior to export, including the State or its equivalent, the municipality or nearest city, or an equivalent method, approved by the Administrator, of identifying the location of the premises, and the specific physical location of the destination where the ruminants are to be moved after importation; the name and address of the exporter; the port of embarkation in the foreign region; and the mode of transportation, route of travel, and port of entry in the United States.

(b) *Goats.* (1) In addition to the statements required by paragraph (a) of this section, the certificate accompanying goats from any part of the world, except for goats imported from Canada for immediate slaughter, must state:

(i) That none of the goats in the herd from which the goats will be imported is the progeny of a sire or dam that has been affected with scrapie or that has produced offspring that have been affected with scrapie;

(ii) That none of the female goats in the herd from which the goats will be imported has been impregnated, during the 5 years immediately preceding shipment of the goats to the United States, with germ plasm from a herd known to be infected with scrapie;

(iii) That the veterinarian issuing the certificate has inspected the goats in the herd from which the animals will be imported and found the herd to be free of any evidence of infectious or contagious disease; and

(iv) That as far as it is possible for the veterinarian who inspects the animals to determine, none of the goats in the herd from which the animals will be imported has been exposed to any infectious or contagious disease during the 60 days immediately preceding shipment to the United States.

(2) In addition, the certificate accompanying goats intended for importation from any part of the world except Australia and New Zealand must state:

(i) That the goats have not been in any herd nor had contact with sheep or goats that have been in any flock or herd where scrapie has been diagnosed or suspected during the 5 years immediately prior to shipment; and

(ii) That the goats have not had any contact with sheep during the 5 years immediately prior to shipment; *provided that*, this statement is not required if the goats are imported in accordance with § 93.435(a) into a herd in the United States that participates in the Voluntary Scrapie Flock Certification Program.

(c) *Sheep*. (1) In addition to the statements required by paragraph (a) of this section, the certificate accompanying sheep intended for importation from any part of the world must state:

(i) That none of the sheep in the flock from which the sheep will be imported is the progeny of a sire or dam that has been affected with scrapie or that has produced offspring that have been affected with scrapie;

(ii) That none of the female sheep in the flock from which the sheep will be imported has been impregnated, during the 5 years immediately preceding shipment of the sheep to the United States, with germ plasm from a flock known to be infected with scrapie;

(iii) That the veterinarian issuing the certificate has inspected the sheep in the flock from which the animals will be imported and found the flock to be free of any evidence of infectious or contagious disease; and

(iv) That as far as it is possible for the veterinarian who inspects the animals to determine, none of the sheep in the flock from which the animals will be imported has been exposed to any infectious or contagious disease during the 60 days immediately preceding shipment to the United States.

(2) In addition, except for sheep imported from Canada for immediate slaughter, the certificate accompanying sheep intended for importation from any part of the world except Australia and New Zealand must state that the sheep have not been in any flock nor had contact with sheep or goats that have been in any flock or herd where scrapie has been diagnosed or suspected during the 5 years immediately prior to shipment.

(3) In addition, the certificate accompanying sheep intended for importation from Australia and New Zealand must state that none of the female sheep in the flock from which the sheep will be imported has been impregnated, during the 5 years immediately preceding shipment of the sheep to the United States, with germ plasm from a region other than Australia, New Zealand, or the United States, or from a flock of unknown scrapie status; *provided that*, this statement is not required if the sheep are imported in accordance with § 93.435(a) into a flock in the United States that participates in the Voluntary Scrapie Flock Certification Program.

(d) If ruminants are unaccompanied by the certificate as required by paragraphs (a), (b), and (c) of this section, or if such ruminants are found upon inspection at the port of entry to be affected with a communicable disease or to have been exposed thereto, they shall be refused entry and shall be handled or quarantined, or otherwise disposed of as the Administrator may direct.

(Approved by the Office of Management and Budget under control numbers 0579–0040, 0579–0165, 0579–0234, and 0579–0393)

[55 FR 31495, Aug. 2, 1990. Redesignated and amended at 62 FR 56012, 56018, Oct. 28, 1997]

EDITORIAL NOTE: For FEDERAL REGISTER citations affecting § 93.405, see the List of CFR Sections Affected, which appears in the Finding Aids section of the printed volume and at *www.fdsys.gov*.

§ 93.406 Diagnostic tests.

(a) *Tuberculosis and brucellosis tests of cattle*. Except as provided in paragraph (d) of this section and in §§ 93.418, 93.427(d), and 93.432, all cattle imported from any part of the world, except for immediate slaughter, must be accompanied by a certificate of a salaried veterinary officer of the national government of the region of origin, or if exported from Mexico, must be accompanied either by such a certificate or by a certificate issued by a veterinarian accredited by the National Government of Mexico and endorsed by a full-time salaried veterinary officer of the National Government of Mexico, thereby representing that the veterinarian issuing the certificate was authorized to do so, stating that:

(1) *Brucellosis.* The cattle have been tested for brucellosis with negative results within 30 days prior to the date of their exportation to the United States; Provided, that the brucellosis test will not be required for steers, spayed heifers, or any cattle less than 6 months old. The certificate must give the dates and places of testing, names of the consignor and consignee, and a description of the cattle, with breed, ages, and markings; and

(2) *Tuberculosis.* (i) For steers and spayed heifers, the cattle originated from a herd of origin that tested negative to a whole herd test for tuberculosis within 1 year prior to the date of exportation to the United States, and the animals each tested negative to an additional official tuberculin test conducted within 60 days prior to the date of exportation to the United States, and any individual cattle that had been added to the herd tested negative to any individual tests for tuberculosis required by the Administrator; or

(ii) For sexually intact cattle that are from an accredited herd, the herd was certified as an accredited herd for tuberculosis within 1 year prior to the date of exportation to the United States; or

(iii) For sexually intact cattle that are not from an accredited herd, the cattle originated from a herd of origin that tested negative to a whole herd test for tuberculosis within 1 year prior to the date of exportation to the United States, and the animals each tested negative to one additional official tuberculin test conducted no more than 6 months and no less than 60 days prior to the date of exportation to the United States, and any individual cattle that had been added to the herd tested negative to any individual tests for tuberculosis required by the Administrator, except that the additional test is not required if the animals are exported within 6 months of when the herd of origin tested negative to a whole herd test.

(b) *Tuberculosis and brucellosis tests of goats.* Except as provided in §§ 93.419 and 93.428(b), all goats offered for importation, except for immediate slaughter, shall be accompanied by a satisfactory certificate of a salaried veterinary officer of the national government of the region of origin, or if exported from Mexico, shall be accompanied either by such a certificate or by a certificate issued by a veterinarian accredited by the National Government of Mexico and endorsed by a full-time salaried veterinary officer of the National Government of Mexico, thereby representing that the veterinarian issuing the certificate was authorized to do so, showing that the goats have been tested for tuberculosis and brucellosis with negative results within 30 days of the date of their exportation. The said certificate shall give the dates and places of testing, method of testing, names of consignor and consignee, and a description of the goats, including breed, ages, markings, and tattoo and eartag numbers.

(c) *Further tests during quarantine.* Ruminants that have been tested as prescribed in paragraphs (a) and (b) of this section and that are subject to quarantine at the port of entry, as provided in § 93.411 or § 93.427, must be retested during the last 10 days of the quarantine period under the supervision of a veterinary inspector by one or more of the methods approved by the Administrator, except that cattle tested in accordance with paragraph (a)(2)(i) of this section are not required to be retested for tuberculosis.

(d) *Testing exemptions.* Cattle from Australia and New Zealand are exempt from the brucellosis testing requirements of paragraph (a)(1) of this section.

[55 FR 31495, Aug. 2, 1990, as amended at 57 FR 28080, June 24, 1992; 58 FR 68509, Dec. 28, 1993. Redesignated and amended at 62 FR 56012, 56018, Oct. 28, 1997; 66 FR 20190, Apr. 20, 2001; 68 FR 35533, June 16, 2003; 69 FR 21042, Apr. 20, 2004]

§93.407 Declaration and other documents for ruminants.

(a) The certificates, declarations, and affidavits required by the regulations in this part shall be presented by the importer or his or her agent to the collector of customs at the port of entry, upon arrival of ruminants at such port, for the use of the veterinary inspector at the port of entry.

(b) For all ruminants offered for importation, the importer or his or her agent shall first present two copies of a declaration which shall list the port of entry, the name and address of the importer, the name and address of the broker, the origin of the ruminants, the number, breed, species, and purpose of the importation, the name of the person to whom the ruminants will be delivered, and the location of the place to which such delivery will be made.

(c) Any declaration, permit, or other document for ruminants required under this subpart may be issued and presented using a U.S. Government electronic information exchange system or other authorized method.

[55 FR 31495, Aug. 2, 1990, as amended at 81 FR 40151, June 21, 2016]

§93.408 Inspection at the port of entry.

Inspection shall be made at the port of entry of all ruminants imported from any part of the world except as provided in §§93.421 and 93.426. All ruminants found to be free from communicable disease and not to have been exposed thereto within 60 days prior to their exportation to the United States shall be admitted subject to the other provisions in this part; all other ruminants except as provided in §§93.423(c) and 93.427(a) shall be refused entry. Ruminants refused entry, unless exported within a time fixed in each case by the Administrator, and in accordance with other provisions he or she may require in each case for their handling shall be disposed of as the Administrator may direct in accordance with the Animal Health Protection Act (7 U.S.C. 8301 *et seq.*). Such portions of the transporting vessel, and of its cargo, which have been exposed to any such ruminants or their emanations shall be disinfected in such manner as may be considered necessary by the inspector in charge at the port of entry, to prevent the introduction or spread of livestock or poultry disease, before the cargo is allowed to land.

[55 FR 31495, Aug. 2, 1990. Redesignated and amended at 62 FR 56012, 56018, Oct. 28, 1997; 68 FR 6344, Feb. 7, 2003]

§93.409 Articles accompanying ruminants.

No litter or manure, fodder or other aliment, nor any equipment such as boxes, buckets, ropes, chains, blankets, or other things used for or about ruminants governed by the regulations in this part, shall be landed from any conveyance except under such restrictions as the inspector in charge at the port of entry shall direct.

§93.410 Movement from conveyances to quarantine station.

Platforms and chutes used for handling imported ruminants shall be cleaned and disinfected under APHIS supervision after being so used. The said ruminants shall not be unnecessarily moved over any highways nor allowed to come in contact with other animals, but shall be transferred from the conveyance to the quarantine grounds in boats, cars, or vehicles approved by the inspector in charge at the port of entry. Such cars, boats, or vehicles shall be cleaned and disinfected under APHIS supervision immediately after such use, by the carrier moving the same. The railway cars so used shall be either cars reserved for this exclusive use or box cars not otherwise employed in the transportation of animals or their fresh products. When movement of the aforesaid ruminants upon or across a public highway is unavoidable, it shall be under such careful supervision and restrictions as the inspector in charge at the port of entry and the local authorities may direct.

§ 93.411 Quarantine requirements.

(a) Except for cattle from Central America and the West Indies, and except for ruminants from Canada and Mexico, all ruminants imported into the United States shall be quarantined for not less than 30 days counting from the date of arrival at the port of entry.

(b) Wild ruminants shall be subject, during their quarantine, to such inspections, disinfection, blood tests, or other tests as may be required by the Administrator to determine their freedom from disease.

[61 FR 17238, Apr. 19, 1996. Redesignated at 62 FR 56012, Oct. 28, 1997]

§ 93.412 Ruminant quarantine facilities.

(a) *Privately owned quarantine facilities.* The operator of a privately owned medium or minimum security quarantine facility subject to the regulations in this subpart shall arrange for acceptable transportation from the port to the privately owned quarantine facility and for the care, feeding, and handling of the ruminants from the time of unloading at the port to the time of release from the quarantine facility. Such arrangements shall be agreed to in advance by the Administrator. All expenses related to these activities shall be the responsibility of the operator. The privately owned quarantine facility must be suitable for the quarantine of the ruminants and must be approved by the Administrator prior to the issuance of any import permit. The facilities occupied by the ruminants should be kept clean and sanitary to the satisfaction of the APHIS representatives. If for any cause, the care, feeding, or handling of ruminants, or the sanitation of the facilities is neglected, in the opinion of the overseeing APHIS representative, such services may be furnished by APHIS in the same manner as though arrangements had been made for such services as provided by paragraph (b) of this section. The operator must request in writing inspection and other services as may be required, and shall waive all claims against the United States and APHIS or any employee of APHIS for damages which may arise from such services. The Administrator may prescribe reasonable rates for the services provided under this paragraph. When APHIS finds it necessary to extend the usual minimum quarantine period, APHIS shall advise the operator in writing, and the operator must pay for such additional quarantine and other services required. The operator must pay for all services received in connection with each separate lot of ruminants as specified in the compliance agreement required under paragraph (d)(2) of this section.

(b) *Quarantine facilities maintained by APHIS.* The importer, or his or her agent, of ruminants subject to quarantine under the regulations in this part shall arrange for acceptable transportation to the quarantine facility, and for the care, feed, and handling of the ruminants from the time they arrive at the quarantine port to the time of release from quarantine. Such arrangements shall be agreed to in advance by the Administrator. The importer or his or her agent shall request in writing such inspection and other services as may be required, and shall waive all claim against the United States and APHIS or any employee of APHIS, for damages which may arise from such services. All expenses resulting therefrom or incident thereto shall be the responsibility of the importer; APHIS assumes no responsibility with respect thereto. The Administrator may prescribe reasonable rates for the services provided under this paragraph. When it is found necessary to extend the usual minimum quarantine period, the importer, or his or her agent, shall be so advised in writing and shall pay for such additional quarantine and other services required. Payment for services received by the importer, or his or her agent, in connection with each separate lot of ruminants shall be made by certified check or U.S. money order prior to release of the ruminants. If such payment is not made, the ruminants may be sold in accordance with the procedure described in this paragraph or otherwise disposed of as directed by the Administrator. When payment is not made and the ruminants are to be sold to recover payment for services received, the importer, or his or her agent, will be notified by the inspector that if said charges are not immediately paid or satisfactory arrangements made for payment, the ruminants will be sold at public sale to pay the expense of care, feed, and handling during that period. The sale will be held after the expiration of the quarantine period, at such time and place as may be designated by the General Services Administration or other designated selling agent. The proceeds of the sale, after deducting the charges for care, feed, and handling of the ruminants and other expenses, including the expense of the sale, shall be held in a Special Deposit Account in the United States Treasury for 6 months from the date of sale. If not claimed by the importer, or his or her agent, within 6 months from the date of sale, the amount so held shall be transferred from the Special Deposit Account to the General Fund Account in the United States Treasury.

(c) APHIS collection of payments from the importer, or his or her agent, or the operator, for service rendered shall be deposited so as to be available for defraying the expenses involved in this service.

(d) *Standards for privately owned quarantine facilities for ruminants*—(1) *APHIS approval of facilities*—(i) *Approval procedures.* Persons seeking APHIS approval of a privately owned medium or minimum security quarantine facility for ruminants must make written application to the Administrator, c/o National Center for Import and Export, Veterinary Services, APHIS, 4700 River Road Unit 39, Riverdale, MD 20737–1231. The application must include the full name and mailing address of the applicant; the location and street address of the facility for which approval is sought; blueprints of the facility; a description of the financial resources available for construction, operation and maintenance of the facility; copies of all approved State permits for construction and operation of the facility (but not local building permits), as well as copies of all approved Federal, State, and local environmental permits; the anticipated source(s) or origin(s) of ruminants to be quarantined, as well as the expected size and frequency of shipments, and a contingency plan for the possible destruction and disposal of all ruminants capable of being held in the facility.

(A) If APHIS determines that an application is complete and merits further consideration, the person applying for facility approval must agree to pay the costs of all APHIS services associated with APHIS' evaluation of the application and facility. APHIS charges for evaluation services at hourly rates are listed in §130.30 of this chapter. If the facility is approved by APHIS, the operator must enter into a compliance agreement in accordance with paragraph (d)(2) of this section.

(B) Requests for approval must be submitted at least 120 days prior to the date of application for local building permits. Requests for approval will be evaluated on a first-come, first-served basis.

(ii) *Criteria for approval.* Before a facility may be built to operate as a privately owned medium or minimum security quarantine facility for ruminants, it must be approved by APHIS. To be approved:

(A) APHIS must find, based on an environmental assessment, and based on any required Federal, State, and local environmental permits or evaluations secured by the operator and copies of which are provided to APHIS, that the operation of the facility will not have significant environmental effects;

(B) The facility must meet all the requirements of paragraph (d) of this section;

(C) The facility must meet any additional requirements that may be imposed by the Administrator in each specific case, as specified in the compliance agreement required under paragraph (d)(2) of this section, to ensure that the quarantine of ruminants in the facility will be adequate to enable determination of their health status, as well as to prevent the transmission of livestock diseases into, within, and from the facility; and

(D) The Administrator must determine whether sufficient personnel, including one or more APHIS veterinarians and other professional, technical, and support personnel, are available to serve as APHIS representatives at the facility and provide continuous oversight and other technical services to ensure the biological security of the facility, if approved. APHIS will assign personnel to facilities requesting approval in the order that the facilities meet all of the criteria for approval. The Administrator has sole discretion on the number of APHIS personnel to be assigned to the facility.

(iii) *Maintaining approval.* To maintain APHIS approval, the operator must continue to comply with all the requirements of paragraph (d) of this section as well as the terms of the compliance agreement executed in accordance with paragraph (d)(2) of this section.

(iv) *Withdrawal or denial of approval.* Approval of a proposed privately owned medium or minimum security quarantine facility may be denied or approval of a facility already in operation may be withdrawn at any time by the Administrator for any of the reasons provided in paragraph (d)(1)(iv)(C) of this section.

(A) Before facility approval is denied or withdrawn, APHIS will inform the operator of the proposed or existing facility and include the reasons for the proposed action. If there is a conflict as to any material fact, APHIS will afford the operator, upon request, the opportunity for a hearing with respect to the merits or validity of such action in accordance with rules of practice that APHIS adopts for the proceeding.

(B) Withdrawal of approval of an existing facility will become effective pending final determination in the proceeding when the Administrator determines that such action is necessary to protect the public health, interest, or safety. Such withdrawal will be effective upon oral or written notification, whichever is earlier, to the operator of the facility. In the event of oral notification, APHIS will give written confirmation to the operator of the facility as promptly as circumstances allow. This withdrawal will continue in effect pending the completion of the proceeding and any judicial review, unless otherwise ordered by the Administrator. In addition to withdrawal of approval for the reasons provided in paragraph (d)(1)(iv)(C) of this section, the Administrator will also automatically withdraw approval when the operator of any approved facility notifies the area veterinarian in charge for the State in which the facility is located, in writing, that the facility is no longer in operation.[7]

(C) The Administrator may deny or withdraw the approval of a privately owned medium or minimum security quarantine facility if:

(*1*) Any requirement of paragraph (d) of this section or the compliance agreement is not met; or

(*2*) The facility has not been in use to quarantine ruminants for a period of at least 1 year; or

(*3*) The operator fails to remit any charges for APHIS services rendered; or

(*4*) The operator or a person responsibly connected with the business of the facility is or has been convicted of any crime under any law regarding the importation or quarantine of any animal; or

(*5*) The operator or a person responsibly connected with the business of the facility is or has been convicted of a crime involving fraud, bribery, extortion, or any other crime involving a lack of integrity needed for the conduct of operations affecting the importation of animals; or

(*6*) Any other requirement under the Animal Health Protection Act (7 U.S.C. 8301–8317) or the regulations thereunder are not met.

(D) For the purposes of paragraph (d)(1)(iv) of this section, a person is deemed to be responsibly connected with the business of the facility if such person has an ownership, mortgage, or lease interest in the facility, or if such person is a partner, officer, director, holder, or owner of 10 percent or more of its voting stock, or an employee in a managerial or executive capacity.

(2) *Compliance agreement.* (i) A privately owned medium or minimum security quarantine facility must operate in accordance with a compliance agreement executed by the operator or other designated representative of the facility and by the Administrator. The compliance agreement must be signed

[7] The name and address of the area veterinarian in charge in any State is available from the Animal and Plant Health Inspection Servcie, Veterinary Services, National Center for Import and Export, 4700 River road Unit 39, Riverdale, MD 20737–1231.

by both parties before a facility may commence operations. The compliance agreement must provide that:

(A) The facility must meet all applicable requirements of paragraph (d) of this section;

(B) The facility's quarantine operations are subject to the strict oversight of APHIS representatives;

(C) The operator agrees to be responsible for the cost of building the facility; all costs associated with its maintenance and operation; all costs associated with the hiring of personnel to attend to the ruminants, as well as to maintain and operate the facility; all costs associated with the care of quarantined ruminants, such as feed, bedding, medicines, inspections, testing, laboratory procedures, and necropsy examinations; all costs associated with the death or destruction and disposition of quarantined ruminants; and all APHIS charges for the services of APHIS representatives in accordance with this section and part 130 of this chapter;

(D) The operator obtained, prior to execution of this agreement, a financial instrument (insurance or surety bond) approved by APHIS that financially guarantees the operator's ability to cover all costs and other financial liabilities and obligations of the facility, including a worst case scenario in which all quarantined ruminants must be destroyed and disposed of because of an animal health emergency, as determined by the Administrator.

(E) The operator will deposit with the Administrator, prior to commencing quarantine operations, a certified check or U.S. money order to cover the estimated costs, as determined by the Administrator, of professional, technical, and support services to be provided by APHIS at the facility over the duration of the quarantine. If actual costs incurred by APHIS over the quarantine period exceed the deposited amount, the operator will pay for any additional costs incurred by APHIS, based on official accounting records. Payment for all services received in connection with each lot of ruminants in quarantine shall be made prior to release of the ruminants. The operator must pay for any other costs incurred by APHIS with respect to the quarantine following the release of the ruminants, based on official records, within 14 days of receipt of the bill showing the balance due. APHIS will return to the operator any unobligated funds deposited with APHIS, after the release of the lot of ruminants from the facility and termination or expiration of the compliance agreement, or, if requested, credit to the operator's account such funds to be applied towards payment of APHIS services at a future date.

(ii) Prior to the entry of each subsequent lot of ruminants into the medium or minimum security facility, a new compliance agreement must be executed, and a certified check or U.S. money order to the Administrator must be deposited to cover the estimated costs, as determined by the Administrator, of professional, technical, and support services to be provided by APHIS at the facility over the duration of the quarantine.

(3) *Physical plant requirements.* A privately owned medium or minimum security quarantine facility must meet the following requirements as determined by an APHIS inspection before ruminants may be admitted to it.

(i) *Location.* (A) The medium or minimum security facility must be located at a site approved by the Administrator, and the specific routes for the movement of ruminants from the port must be approved in advance by the Administrator, based on consideration of whether the site or routes would put the animals in a position that could result in their transmitting communicable livestock diseases.

(B) In the case of a medium security facility, the facility must be located at least one-half mile from any premises holding livestock. In the case of a minimum security facility, the Administrator will establish the required minimum distance between the facility and other premises holding livestock on a case-by-case basis.

(C) If the medium or minimum security facility is to be located more than 1 mile from a designated port, the operator must make arrangements for the imported ruminants to be held in a temporary inspection facility to allow for the inspection of the imported ruminants by a Federal or State veterinarian prior to the animals' movement to the medium or minimum security facility.

(*1*) The temporary inspection facility must have adequate space for Federal or State veterinarians to conduct examinations and testing of the imported ruminants.

(*2*) The examination space of the temporary inspection facility must be equipped with appropriate animal restraining devices for the safe inspection of ruminants.

(*3*) The temporary inspection facility may not hold more than one lot of animals at the same time.

(*4*) In seeking APHIS approval of the temporary inspection facility, the operator must provide APHIS with the following information: The port of entry; a description of the temporary inspection facility; and the anticipated source(s) of the materials to be used for the facility.

(*5*) If the ruminants, upon inspection at the temporary inspection facility, are determined to be infected with or exposed to a disease that precludes their entry into the United States, the animals will be refused entry. Ruminants refused entry remain the responsibility of the operator, but subject to further handling or disposition as directed by the Administrator in accordance with § 93.408 of this subpart.

(*6*) APHIS' approval to build and operate a medium or minimum security facility outside the immediate vicinity of a designated port is contingent upon APHIS' approval of the temporary inspection facility at the port, as well as approval of the routes for the movement of ruminants from the port to the medium or minimum security facility.

(ii) *Construction.* The medium or minimum security facility must be of sound construction, in good repair, and properly designed to prevent the escape of quarantined ruminants. It must have adequate capacity to receive and hold a shipment of ruminants as a lot on an "all-in, all-out" basis and must include the following:

(A) *Loading docks.* The facility must include separate docks for animal receiving and releasing and for general receiving and pickup, or, alternatively, a single dock may be used for both purposes if the dock is cleaned and disinfected after each use in accordance with paragraph (d)(4)(iv)(D) of this section.

(B) *Perimeter fencing.* The facility must be surrounded by double-security perimeter fencing separated by at least 30 feet and of sufficient height and design to prevent the entry of unauthorized persons and animals from outside the facility and to prevent the escape of any ruminants in quarantine.

(C) *Means of isolation.* The facility must provide pens, chutes, and other animal restraining devices, as appropriate, for inspection and identification of each animal, as well as for segregation, treatment, or both, of any ruminant exhibiting signs of illness. The medium or minimum security facility must also have lot-holding areas of sufficient size to prevent overcrowding. A medium security facility may hold more than one lot of ruminants as long as the lots are separated by physical barriers such that ruminants in one lot do not have physical contact with ruminants in another lot or with their excrement or discharges. A minimum security facility may not hold more than one lot of animals at the same time.

(D) *APHIS space.* The facility must have adequate space for APHIS representatives to conduct examinations and draw samples for testing of ruminants in quarantine, prepare and package samples for mailing, and store duplicate samples and the necessary equipment and supplies for each lot of ruminants. The examination space must be equipped with appropriate animal restraining devices for the safe inspection of ruminants. The facility must also provide a secure, lockable office for APHIS use with enough room for a desk, chair, and filing cabinet.

(E) *Storage.* The facility must have sufficient storage space for equipment and supplies used in quarantine operations. Storage space must include separate, secure storage for pesticides and for medical and other biological supplies, as well as a separate storage area for feed and bedding, if feed and bedding are stored at the facility.

(F) *Other work areas.* The facility must include work areas for the repair of equipment and for cleaning and disinfecting equipment used in the facility.

(iii) *Additional construction requirements for medium security facilities.* For medium security facilities only, the following requirements must also be met:

(A) *Self-contained building.* The medium security facility must be constructed so that the quarantine area is located in a secure, self-contained building that contains appropriate control measures against the spread of livestock diseases biologically transmissible by vectors. All entryways into the nonquarantine area of the building must be equipped with a secure and lockable door. While ruminants are in quarantine, all access to the quarantine area must be from within the building. Each entryway to the quarantine area must be equipped with a solid self-closing door. Separate access must be provided within the quarantine area to each lot-holding area so that it is not necessary to move through one lot-holding area to gain access to another lot-holding area. Entryways to each lot-holding area within the quarantine area would also have to be equipped with a solid lockable door. Emergency exits to the outside may exist in the quarantine area if required by local fire ordinances. Such emergency exits must be constructed so as to permit their opening from the inside of the facility only.

(B) *Windows and other openings.* Any windows or other openings in the quarantine area must be double-screened with screening of sufficient gauge and mesh to prevent the entry or exit of insects and other vectors of livestock diseases and to provide ventilation sufficient to ensure the comfort and safety of all ruminants in the facility. The interior and exterior screens must be separated by at least 3 inches (7.62 cm). All screening of windows or other openings must be easily removable for cleaning, yet otherwise remain locked and secure at all times in a manner satisfactory to APHIS representatives in order to ensure the biological security of the facility.

(C) *Surfaces.* The medium security facility must be constructed so that the floor surfaces with which ruminants have contact are nonslip and wear-resistant. All floor surfaces with which the ruminants, their excrement, or discharges have contact must slope gradually to the center, where one or more drains of at least 8 inches in diameter are located for adequate drainage, or, alternatively, must be of slatted or other floor design that allows for adequate drainage. All floor and wall surfaces with which the ruminants, their excrement, or discharges have contact must be impervious to moisture and be able to withstand frequent cleaning and disinfection without deterioration. Other ceiling and wall surfaces with which the ruminants, their excrement, or discharges do not have contact must be able to withstand cleaning and disinfection between shipments of ruminants. All floor and wall surfaces must be free of sharp edges that could cause injury to ruminants.

(D) *Ventilation and climate control.* The medium security facility must be constructed with a heating, ventilation, and air conditioning (HVAC) system capable of controlling and maintaining the ambient temperature, air quality, moisture, and odor at levels that are not injurious or harmful to the health of ruminants in quarantine. Air supplied to lot-holding areas must not be recirculated or reused for other ventilation needs. HVAC systems for lot-holding areas must be separate from air handling systems for other operational and administrative areas of the facility. In addition, if the facility is approved to handle more than one lot of ruminants at a time, each lot-holding area must have its own separate HVAC system that is designed to prevent cross-contamination between the separate lot-holding areas.

(E) *Lighting.* The medium security facility must have adequate lighting throughout, including in the lot-holding areas and other areas used to examine ruminants and conduct necropsies.

(F) *Fire protection.* The medium security facility, including the lot-holding areas, must have a fire alarm and voice communication system.

(G) *Monitoring system.* The medium security facility must have a television monitoring system or other arrangement sufficient to provide a full view of the lot-holding areas.

(H) *Communication system.* The medium security facility must have a communication system between the nonquarantine and quarantine areas of the facility.

(I) *Necropsy area.* The medium security facility must have an area that is of sufficient size to perform necropsies on ruminants and that is equipped with adequate lighting, hot and cold running water, a drain, a cabinet for storing instruments, a refrigerator-freezer for storing specimens, and an autoclave to sterilize veterinary equipment.

(J) *Additional storage requirements.* Feed storage areas in the medium security facility must be vermin-proof. Also, if the medium security facility has multiple lot-holding areas, then separate storage space for supplies and equipment must be provided for each lot-holding area.

(K) *Showers.* In a medium security facility, there must be a shower at the entrance to the quarantine area. A shower also must be located at the entrance to the necropsy area. A clothes-storage and clothes-changing area must be provided at each end of each shower area. There also must be one or more receptacles near each shower so that clothing that has been worn in a lot-holding area or elsewhere in the quarantine area can be deposited in the receptacle(s) prior to entering the shower.

(L) *Restrooms.* The medium security facility must have permanent restrooms in both the nonquarantine and quarantine areas of the facility.

(M) *Break room.* The medium security facility must have an area within the quarantine area for breaks and meals.

(N) *Laundry area.* The medium security facility must have an area for washing and drying clothes, linens, and towels.

(iv) *Sanitation.* To ensure that proper animal health and biological security measures are observed, a privately owned medium or minimum security quarantine facility must provide the following:

(A) Equipment and supplies necessary to maintain the facility in a clean and sanitary condition, including pest control equipment and supplies and cleaning and disinfecting equipment with adequate capacity to disinfect the facility and equipment.

(B) Separately maintained sanitation and pest control equipment and supplies for each lot-holding area if the facility will hold more than one lot of ruminants at a time (applicable to medium security facilities only).

(C) A supply of potable water adequate to meet all watering and cleaning needs, with water faucets for hoses located throughout the facility. An emergency supply of water for ruminants in quarantine also must be maintained.

(D) A stock of disinfectant authorized in §71.10(a)(5) of this chapter or otherwise approved by the Administrator that is sufficient to disinfect the entire facility.

(E) The capability to dispose of wastes, including manure, urine, and used bedding, by means of burial, incineration, or public sewer. Other waste material must be handled in such a manner that minimizes spoilage and the attraction of pests and must be disposed of by incineration, public sewer, or other preapproved manner that prevents the spread of disease. Disposal of wastes must be carried out under the direct oversight of APHIS representatives.

(F) The capability to dispose of ruminant carcasses in a manner approved by the Administrator and under conditions that prevent the spread of disease from the carcasses.

(G) For incineration to be carried out at the facility, incineration equipment that is detached from other facility structures and is capable of burning wastes or carcasses as required. The incineration site must include an area sufficient for solid waste holding. Incineration may also take place at a local site away from the facility premises. All incineration activities must be carried out under the direct oversight of an APHIS representative.

(H) The capability to control surface drainage and effluent into, within, and from the facility in a manner that prevents the spread of disease into, within, and from the facility. If the facility is approved to handle more than one lot of ruminants at the same time, there must be separate drainage systems for each lot-holding area in order to prevent cross contamination.

(v) *Security.* (A) A privately owned medium or minimum security quarantine facility must provide the following security measures:

(*1*) The facility and premises must be kept locked and secure at all times while the ruminants are in quarantine.

(*2*) The facility and premises must have signs indicating that the facility is a quarantine area and no visitors are allowed.

(*3*) The operator must furnish a telephone number or numbers to APHIS at which the operator or his or her agent can be reached at all times.

(*4*) APHIS is authorized to place seals on any or all entrances and exits of the facility, when determined necessary by APHIS to ensure security, and to take all necessary steps to ensure that the seals are broken only in the presence of an APHIS representative. If the seals are broken by someone other than an APHIS representative, it will be considered a breach in security, and an immediate accounting of all ruminants in the facility will be made by an APHIS representative. If a breach in security occurs, APHIS may extend the quarantine period as long as necessary to determine that the ruminants are free of communicable livestock diseases.

(*5*) In the event that a communicable livestock disease is diagnosed in quarantined ruminants, the Administrator may require that the operator have the facility guarded by a bonded security company, at the expense of the operator of the facility, in a manner that the Administrator deems necessary to ensure the biological security of the facility.

(B) A privately owned medium security facility also must provide the following security measures:

(*1*) The medium security facility and premises must be guarded at all times by one or more representatives of a bonded security company, or, alternatively, the medium security facility must have an electronic security system that prevents the entry of unauthorized persons into the facility and prevents animals outside the facility from having contact with ruminants in quarantine;

(*2*) If an electronic security system is used, the electronic security system must be coordinated through or with the local police so that monitoring of the facility is maintained whenever APHIS representatives are not at the facility. The electronic security system must be of the "silent type" and must be triggered to ring at the monitoring site and, if the operator chooses, at the facility. The operator must provide written instructions to the monitoring agency stating that the police and an APHIS representative designated by APHIS must be notified by the monitoring agency if the alarm is triggered. The operator also must submit a copy of those instructions to the Administrator. The operator must notify the designated APHIS representative whenever a break in security occurs or is suspected of occurring.

(4) *Operating procedures.* The following procedures must be followed at a privately owned medium or minimum security quarantine facility at all times:

(i) *APHIS oversight.* (A) The quarantine of ruminants at the facility will be subject to the strict oversight of APHIS representatives authorized to perform the services required by this subpart.

(B) If, for any reason, the operator fails to properly care for, feed, or handle the quarantined ruminants as required in paragraph (d) of this section, or in accordance with animal health and husbandry standards provided elsewhere in this chapter, or fails to maintain and operate the facility as provided in paragraph (d) of this section, APHIS representatives are authorized to furnish such neglected services at the operator's expense, as authorized in paragraph (a) of this section.

(ii) *Personnel.* (A) The operator must provide adequate personnel to maintain the facility and care for the ruminants in quarantine, including attendants to care for and feed ruminants, and other personnel as needed to maintain, operate, and administer the facility.

(B) The operator must provide APHIS with an updated list of all personnel who have access to the facility. The list must include the names, current residential addresses, and identification numbers of each person, and must be updated with any changes or additions in advance of such person having access to the quarantine facility.

(C) The operator must provide APHIS with signed statements from all personnel having access to the facility in which the person agrees to comply with paragraph (d) of this section and applicable provisions of this part, all terms of the compliance agreement, and any related instructions from APHIS representatives pertaining to quarantine operations, including contact with animals both inside and outside the facility.

(iii) *Authorized access.* (A) Access to the facility premises as well as inside the quarantine area will be granted only to APHIS representatives and other persons specifically authorized to work at the facility. All other persons are prohibited from the premises unless specifically granted access by an APHIS representative. Any visitors granted access must be accompanied at all times by an APHIS representative while on the premises.

(B) All visitors, except veterinary practitioners who enter the facility to provide emergency care, must sign an affidavit before entering the quarantine area, if determined necessary by the overseeing APHIS representative, declaring that they will not have contact with any susceptible animals outside the facility for at least 5 days after contact with the ruminants in quarantine, or for a period of time determined by the overseeing APHIS representative as necessary to prevent the transmission of communicable livestock diseases of ruminants.

(iv) *Sanitary practices.* (A) All persons granted access to the quarantine area must:

(*1*) Wear clean protective work clothing and footwear upon entering the quarantine area.

(*2*) Wear disposable gloves when handling sick animals and then wash hands after removing gloves.

(*3*) Change protective clothing, footwear, and gloves when they become soiled or contaminated.

(*4*) Be prohibited, if determined necessary by the overseeing APHIS representative, from having contact with any susceptible animals outside the facility for at least 5 days after the last contact with ruminants in quarantine, or for a longer period of time determined necessary by the overseeing APHIS representative to prevent the transmission of livestock diseases.

(B) All equipment (including tractors) must be cleaned and disinfected prior to being used in the quarantine area of the facility with a disinfectant that is authorized in §71.10(a)(5) of this chapter or that is otherwise approved by the Administrator. The equipment must remain dedicated to the facility for the entire quarantine period. Any equipment used with quarantined ruminants must remain dedicated to that particular lot of ruminants for the duration of the quarantine period or be cleaned and disinfected before coming in contact with ruminants from another lot. Prior to its use on another lot of ruminants or its removal from the quarantine area, such equipment must be cleaned and disinfected to the satisfaction of an APHIS representative.

(C) Any vehicle, before entering or leaving the quarantine area of the facility, must be immediately cleaned and disinfected under the oversight of an APHIS representative with a disinfectant that is authorized in §71.10(a)(5) of this chapter or that is otherwise approved by the Administrator.

(D) If the facility has a single loading dock, the loading dock must be immediately cleaned and disinfected after each use under the oversight of an APHIS representative with a disinfectant that is authorized in §71.10(a)(5) of this chapter or that is otherwise approved by the Administrator.

(E) That area of the facility in which a lot of ruminants had been held or had access must be thoroughly cleaned and disinfected under the oversight of an APHIS representative upon release of the ruminants, with a disinfectant that is authorized in §71.10(a)(5) of this chapter or that is otherwise approved by the Administrator, before a new lot of ruminants is placed in that area of the facility.

(F) For medium security facilities only, the following additional sanitary practices also must be followed:

(*1*) All persons granted access to the quarantine area, must:

(*i*) Shower when leaving the quarantine area.

(*ii*) Shower before entering a lot-holding area if previously exposed from access to another lot-holding area.

(*iii*) Shower when leaving the necropsy area if a necropsy is in the process of being performed or has just been completed, or if all or portions of the examined animal remain exposed.

(*iv*) Be prohibited, unless specifically allowed otherwise by the overseeing APHIS representative, from having contact with any ruminants in the facility, other than the lot or lots of ruminants to which the person is assigned or is granted access.

(*2*) The operator is responsible for providing a sufficient supply of clothing and footwear to ensure that workers and others provided access to the quarantine area of the facility have clean, protective clothing and footwear before entering the facility.

(*3*) The operator is responsible for the proper handling, washing, and disposal of soiled and contaminated clothing worn in the quarantine area in a manner approved by an APHIS representative as adequate to preclude the transmission of disease within and from the facility. At the end of each workday, work clothing worn into each lot-holding area and elsewhere in the quarantine area must be collected and kept in bags until the clothing is washed. Used footwear must either be left in the clothes changing area or cleaned with hot water (148 °F minimum) and detergent and disinfected as directed by an APHIS representative.

(v) *Handling of ruminants in quarantine.* (A) Each lot of ruminants to be quarantined must be placed in the facility on an "all-in, all-out" basis. No ruminant may be taken out of a lot while the lot is in quarantine, except for diagnostic purposes, and no ruminant may be added to a lot while in quarantine.

(B) The facility must provide sufficient feed and bedding for the ruminants in quarantine, and it must be free of vermin and not spoiled. Feed and bedding must originate from a region that has been approved by APHIS as a source for feed and bedding.

(C) Breeding of ruminants or collection of germ plasm from ruminants is prohibited during the quarantine period unless necessary for a required import testing procedure.

(D) Ruminants in quarantine will be subjected to such tests and procedures as directed by an APHIS representative to determine whether the ruminants are free of communicable livestock diseases. While in quarantine, ruminants may be vaccinated only with vaccines that have been approved by the APHIS representative and licensed in accordance with § 102.5 of this chapter.[8] Vaccines must be administered either by an APHIS veterinarian or an accredited veterinarian under the direct oversight of an APHIS representative.

(E) Any death or suspected illness of ruminants in quarantine must be reported immediately to the overseeing APHIS representative. The affected ruminants must be disposed of as the Administrator may direct or, depending on the nature of the disease, must be cared for as directed by APHIS to prevent the spread of disease.

(F) Quarantined ruminants requiring specialized medical attention or additional postmortem testing may be transported off the quarantine site, if authorized by APHIS. A second quarantine site must be established to house the ruminants at the facility of destination (e.g., veterinary college hospital). In such cases, APHIS may extend the quarantine period until the results of any outstanding tests or postmortems are received.

(G) Should the Administrator determine that an animal health emergency exists at the facility, arrangements for the final disposition of the infected or exposed lot of ruminants must be accomplished within 4 workdays following disease confirmation. Subsequent disposition of the ruminants must occur under the direct oversight of APHIS representatives.

(vi) *Recordkeeping.* (A) The operator must maintain a current daily log, to record the entry and exit of all persons entering and leaving the facility.

[8] A list of approved vaccines is available from the Center for Veterinary Biologics, USDA, APHIS, VS, 510 south 17th Street6, Suite 104, Ames, IA 50010.

(B) The operator must retain the daily log, along with any logs kept by APHIS and deposited with the operator, for at least 2 years following the date of release of the ruminants from quarantine and must make such logs available to APHIS representatives upon request.

(5) *Environmental quality.* If APHIS determines that a privately owned medium or minimum security quarantine facility does not meet applicable local, State, or Federal environmental regulations, APHIS may deny or suspend approval of the facility until appropriate remedial measures have been applied.

(6) *Other laws.* A privately owned medium or minimum security quarantine facility must comply with other applicable Federal laws and regulations, as well as with all applicable State and local codes and regulations.

(7) *Variances.* The Administrator may grant variances to existing requirements relating to location, construction, and other design features of a privately owned medium security quarantine facility or minimum security quarantine facility as well as to sanitation, security, operating procedures, recordkeeping, and other provisions in paragraph (d) of this section, but only if the Administrator determines that the variance causes no detrimental impact to the health of the ruminants or to the overall biological security of the quarantine operations. The operator must submit a request for a variance to the Administrator in writing at least 30 days in advance of the arrival of the ruminants to the facility. Any variance also must be expressly provided for in the compliance agreement.

(Approved by the Office of Management and Budget under control number 0579–0232)

[55 FR 31495, Aug. 2, 1990. Redesignated at 62 FR 56012, Oct. 28, 1997, as amended at 71 FR 29773, May 24, 2006]

§ 93.413 Quarantine stations, visiting restricted; sales prohibited.

Visitors are not permitted in the quarantine enclosures during any time that ruminants are in quarantine unless the APHIS representative or inspector in charge specifically grants access under such conditions and restrictions as may be imposed by the APHIS representative or inspector in charge. An importer (or his or her accredited agent or veterinarian) may be admitted to the yards and buildings containing his or her quarantined ruminants at such intervals as may be deemed necessary, and under such conditions and restrictions as may be imposed, by the APHIS representative or the inspector in charge of the quarantine facility or station. On the last day of the quarantine period, owners, officers, or registry societies, and others having official business or whose services may be necessary in the removal of the ruminants may be admitted upon written permission from the APHIS representative or inspector in charge. No exhibition or sale shall be allowed within the quarantine grounds.

[71 FR 29779, May 24, 2006]

§ 93.414 Milk from quarantined ruminants.

Milk or cream from ruminants quarantined under the provisions of this part shall not be used by any person other than those in charge of such ruminants, nor be fed to any animals other than those within the same enclosure, without permission of the APHIS representative or inspector in charge of the quarantine station and subject to such restrictions as he or she may consider necessary to each instance. No milk or cream shall be removed from the quarantine premises except in compliance with all State and local regulations.

[55 FR 31495, Aug. 2, 1990. Redesignated at 62 FR 56012, Oct. 28, 1997, as amended at 71 FR 29779, May 24, 2006]

§ 93.415 Manure from quarantined ruminants.

No manure shall be removed from the quarantine premises until the release of the ruminants producing same.

§ 93.416 Appearance of disease among ruminants in quarantine.

If any contagious disease appears among ruminants during the quarantine period special precautions shall be taken to prevent spread of the infection to other animals in the quarantine station or to those outside the grounds.

The affected ruminants shall be disposed of as the Administrator may direct, depending upon the nature of the disease.

CANADA[8]

§93.417 Import permit and declaration for ruminants.

(a) For ruminants intended for importation from Canada, the importer shall first apply for and obtain from APHIS an import permit as provided in §93.404: *Provided*, That an import permit is not required for ruminants offered for entry at a land border port designated in §93.403(b) if such ruminant is:

(1) A wether;

(2) A sheep or goat imported for immediate slaughter; or

(3) A ruminant other than a sheep or goat and that ruminant:

(i) Was born in Canada or the United States, and has been in no region other than Canada or the United States, or

(ii) Has been legally imported into Canada from some other region and unconditionally released in Canada so as to be eligible to move freely within that region without restriction of any kind and has been in Canada after such release for 60 days or longer.

(b) For all ruminants offered for importation from Canada, the importer or his or her agent shall present two copies of a declaration as provided in §93.407.

[55 FR 31495, Aug. 2, 1990, as amended at 60 FR 13900, Mar. 15, 1995. Redesignated and amended at 62 FR 56012, 56018, Oct. 28, 1997]

§93.418 Cattle and other bovines from Canada.

(a) *Health certificates*. Cattle intended for importation from Canada must be accompanied by a certificate issued in accordance with §93.405(a). The certificate must state that the cattle have been inspected and were found to be free from any evidence of communicable disease and that, as far as can be determined, they have not been exposed to any such disease during the preceding 60 days. Cattle found unqualified upon inspection at the port of entry will be refused entry into the United States.

(b) *Tuberculin-test certificates*. (1) Cattle from Canada from a herd in which any cattle have been determined to have tuberculosis shall not be imported into the United States.

(2) Except for cattle prohibited from importation under paragraph (b)(1) of this section, cattle from Canada may be imported into the United States if:

(i) The cattle are imported for immediate slaughter in accordance with §93.420; or

(ii) The cattle are imported for movement to a feedlot and then to slaughter and the certificate accompanying the cattle shows, in addition to the information required under §93.405, the breed of the animal, and:

(A) That the cattle are from a tuberculosis-free herd; or

(B) The date and place the cattle were last tested for tuberculosis; that the cattle were found negative for tuberculosis on such test; and that such test was performed within 60 days preceding the arrival of the cattle at the port of entry; or

(C) That the cattle are at least five days but not more than four weeks of age and, therefore, exempt from the tuberculosis testing requirement; or

(D) For a calf imported with its dam, the date and place the calf's dam was last tested for tuberculosis; that the dam was found negative for tuberculosis on such test; that such test was performed within 60 days preceding the arrival of the calf and dam at the port of entry; and that the calf was born after such test was performed.

(c) *Brucellosis test or vaccination certificates*. (1) Cattle from Canada from a herd in which any cattle have been determined to have brucellosis may not be imported into the United States;

(2) Except for cattle prohibited from importation into the United States under paragraph (c)(1) of this section, cattle 6 months of age or older from Canada may be imported into the United States if the following conditions are met:

(i) The cattle are imported for immediate slaughter in accordance with §93.420;

(ii) The cattle are steers; or

[8] Importations from Canada shall be subject to §§93.417 to 93.421, inclusive, in addition to other sections in this part which are in terms applicable to such importations.

(iii) The cattle are imported for movement to a feedlot and then to slaughter and the certificate accompanying the cattle shows, in addition to the information required under § 93.405, the breed of the animal, and:

(A) That the cattle are from a brucellosis certified-free herd, province, or territory; or

(B) The date and place the cattle were last tested for brucellosis; that the cattle were found negative for brucellosis on such test; and that such test was performed within 30 days preceding the arrival of the cattle at the port of entry; or

(C) That the female cattle under 18 months of age were vaccinated against brucellosis in accordance with Canadian regulations; the date of such vaccination; the dosage of vaccine used; and the age of each animal on the date of vaccination.

(d) In addition to meeting the requirements of paragraphs (a) through (c) of this section, bovines may be imported from Canada only under the following conditions:

(1) The bovines are imported for immediate slaughter under § 93.420; or

(2) The bovines are imported for other than immediate slaughter under the following conditions:

(i) The bovines were born after March 1, 1999, the date determined by APHIS to be the date of effective enforcement of a ruminant-to-ruminant feed ban in Canada;

(ii) The bovines are imported only through a port of entry listed in § 93.403(b) or as provided for in § 93.403(f);

(iii) The bovines were officially identified prior to arriving at the port of entry in the United States with unique individual identification that is traceable to each bovine's premises of origin. No person may alter, deface, remove, or otherwise tamper with the official identification while the animal is in the United States or moving into or through the United States, except that the identification may be removed at slaughter; and

(iv) The bovines are permanently and humanely identified using one of the following additional methods:

(A) A "CΛN" mark properly applied with a freeze brand, hot iron, or other method, and easily visible on the live animal and on the carcass before skinning. Such a mark must be not less than 2 inches nor more than 3 inches high, and must be applied to each animal's right hip, high on the tail-head (over the junction of the sacral and first coccygeal vertebrae); or

(B) A tattoo with the letters "CΛN" applied to the inside of one ear of the animal; or

(C) Other means of permanent identification upon request if deemed adequate by the Administrator to humanely identify the animal in a distinct and legible way as having been imported from Canada.

(3) The bovines are accompanied by a certificate issued in accordance with § 93.405 that states, in addition to the statements required by § 93.405, that the conditions of paragraph (d)(2) of this section, as applicable, have been met.

(Approved by the Office of Management and Budget under control number 0579–0393)

[55 FR 31495, Aug. 2, 1990, as amended at 55 FR 49990, Dec. 4, 1990; 58 FR 37641, July 13, 1993; 59 FR 28216, June 1, 1994; 61 FR 17238, Apr. 19, 1996. Redesignated and amended at 62 FR 56012, 56018, Oct. 28, 1997; 71 FR 12997, Mar. 14, 2006; 78 FR 72996, Dec. 4, 2013; 78 FR 73993, Dec. 10, 2013]

§ 93.419 Sheep and goats from Canada.

(a) Sheep and goats intended for importation from Canada must be accompanied by a certificate issued in accordance with § 93.405.

(b) If the sheep or goats are unaccompanied by the certificate required by paragraph (a) of this section, or if they are found upon inspection at the port of entry to be affected with or exposed to a communicable disease, they shall be refused entry and shall be handled or quarantined, or otherwise disposed of, as the Administrator may direct.

(c) Any sheep or goats imported from Canada must not be pregnant, must be less than 12 months of age when imported into the United States and when slaughtered, must be from a flock or herd subject to a ruminant feed ban equivalent to the requirements established by the U.S. Food and Drug Administration at 21 CFR 589.2000, and, before the animal's arrival at the port of entry into the United States, must be officially identified with unique individual identification that is traceable to the premises of origin of the animal. No person may alter, deface, remove, or otherwise tamper with the official identification while the animal is in the United States or moving into or through the United States, except that the identification may be removed at the time of slaughter. The animals must be accompanied by the certification issued in accordance with §93.405 that states, in addition to the statements required by §93.405, that the conditions of this paragraph have been met. Additionally, for sheep and goats imported for immediate slaughter, the certificate must state that the conditions of paragraphs (d)(1) through (d)(3) of this section have been met, and, for sheep and goats imported for other than immediate slaughter, the certificate must state that the conditions of paragraphs (e)(1) and (e)(2) of this section have been met.

(d) *Sheep and goats imported for immediate slaughter.* Sheep and goats imported from Canada for immediate slaughter must be imported only through a port of entry listed in §93.403(b) or as provided for in §93.403(f) in a means of conveyance sealed in Canada with seals of the Canadian Government, and must be moved directly as a group from the port of entry to a recognized slaughtering establishment for slaughter as a group. The sheep and goats shall be inspected at the port of entry and otherwise handled in accordance with §93.408. The seals on the means of conveyance must be broken only at the port of entry by the APHIS port veterinarian or at the recognized slaughtering establishment by an authorized USDA representative. If the seals are broken by the APHIS port veterinarian at the port of entry, the means of conveyance must be resealed with seals of the U.S. Government before being moved to the recognized slaughtering establishment. The shipment must be accompanied from the port of entry to the recognized slaughtering establishment by APHIS Form VS 17–33, which must include the location of the recognized slaughtering establishment. Additionally, the sheep and goats must meet the following conditions:

(1) The animals have not tested positive for and are not suspect for a transmissible spongiform encephalopathy;

(2) The animals have not resided in a flock or herd that has been diagnosed with BSE; and

(3) The animals' movement is not restricted within Canada as a result of exposure to a transmissible spongiform encephalopathy.

(e) *Imported for feeding.* Any sheep or goats imported from Canada for feeding at a feedlot must be imported only through a port of entry listed in §93.403(b) or as provided for in §93.403(f) in a means of conveyance sealed in the region of origin with seals of the national government of the region of origin, must be moved directly as a group from the port of entry to a designated feedlot, must not be commingled with any sheep or goats that are not being moved directly to slaughter from the designated feedlot at less than 12 months of age, and must meet the following conditions:

(1) The sheep and goats must be permanently and humanely identified before arrival at the port of entry with a distinct and legible "C" mark, properly applied with a freeze brand, hot iron, or other method, and easily visible on the live animal and on the carcass before skinning. The mark must be not less than 1 inch or more than 1¼ inches high. Other means of permanent identification may be used upon request if deemed adequate by the Administrator to humanely identify the animal in a distinct and legible way as having been imported from Canada;

(2) The animals may be moved from the port of entry only to a feedlot designated in accordance with paragraph (e)(7) of this section and must be accompanied from the port of entry to the designated feedlot by APHIS Form VS 17–130 or other movement documentation deemed acceptable by the Administrator, which must identify the physical location of the feedlot, the individual responsible for the movement of the animals, and the individual identification of each animal, which includes the official identification required under paragraph (c) of this section and any other identification present on the animal, including registration number, if any;

(3) The seals of the national government of Canada must be broken only at the port of entry by the APHIS port veterinarian or at the designated feedlot by an authorized USDA representative. If the seals are broken by the APHIS port veterinarian at the port of entry, the means of conveyance must be resealed with seals of the U.S. Government before being moved to the designated feedlot;

(4) The animals must remain at the designated feedlot until transported to a recognized slaughtering establishment. The animals must be moved directly to the recognized slaughtering establishment in a means of conveyance sealed with seals of the U.S. Government by an accredited veterinarian, a State representative, or an APHIS representative. The seals must be broken at the recognized slaughtering establishment only by an authorized USDA representative;

(5) The animals must be accompanied to the recognized slaughtering establishment by APHIS Form VS 1–27 or other documentation deemed acceptable by the Administrator, which must identify the physical location of the recognized slaughtering establishment, the individual responsible for the movement of the animals, and the individual identification of each animal, which includes the official identification required under paragraph (c) of this section and any other identification present on the animal, including registration number, if any;

(6) The animals must be less than 12 months of age when slaughtered;

(7) To be approved to receive sheep or goats imported for feeding, a feedlot must have signed a written agreement with the Administrator stating that the feedlot:

(i) Will not remove official identification from animals unless medically necessary, in which case new official identification will be applied and cross referenced in the records;

(ii) Will monitor all incoming imported feeder animals to ensure that they have the required "C" brand;

(iii) Will maintain records of the acquisition and disposition of all imported sheep and goats entering the feed lot, including the official identification number and all other identifying information, the age of each animal, the date each animal was acquired and the date each animal was shipped to slaughter, and the name and location of the plant where each animal was slaughtered. For Canadian animals that die in the feedlot, the feedlot will remove the official identification device if affixed to the animal, or will record any other official identification on the animal and place the official identification device or record of official identification in a file with a record of the disposition of the carcass;

(iv) Will maintain copies of the APHIS Forms VS 17–130 and VS 1–27 or other movement documentation deemed acceptable by the Administrator that have been issued for incoming animals and for animals moved to slaughter and that list the official identification of each animal;

(v) Will allow State and Federal animal health officials access to inspect its premises and animals and to review inventory records and other required files upon request;

(vi) Will keep required records for at least 5 years;

(vii) Will designate either the entire feedlot or pens within the feedlot as terminal for sheep and goats to be moved only directly to slaughter at less than 12 months of age, and

(viii) Agrees that if inventory cannot be reconciled or if animals are not moved to slaughter as required the approval of the feedlot will be immediately withdrawn.

(Approved by the Office of Management and Budget under control numbers 0579–0040, 0579–0234, and 0579–0277)

[55 FR 31495, Aug. 2, 1990, as amended at 59 FR 28216, June 1, 1994; 61 FR 17239, Apr. 19, 1996. Redesignated and amended at 62 FR 56012, 56018, Oct. 28, 1997; 68 FR 6344, Feb. 7, 2003; 70 FR 547, Jan. 4, 2005; 70 FR 71217, Nov. 28, 2005; 71 FR 12997, Mar. 14, 2006; 72 FR 53376, Sept. 18, 2007; 73 FR 3383, Jan. 18, 2008]

§93.420 Ruminants from Canada for immediate slaughter other than sheep and goats.

(a) *General requirements.* The requirements for the importation of sheep and goats from Canada for immediate slaughter are contained in §93.419. There are no BSE-related restrictions on the importation of cervids or camelids from Canada. All other ruminants imported from Canada for immediate slaughter, in addition to meeting all other applicable requirements of this part, may be imported only under the following conditions:

(1) The ruminants must be imported only through a port of entry listed in § 93.403(b) or as provided for in § 93.403(f) and be inspected at the port of entry and otherwise handled in accordance with § 93.408.

(2) The ruminants must be moved directly from the port of entry to a recognized slaughtering establishment in conveyances that are sealed with seals of the U.S. Government at the port of entry. The seals may be broken only at the recognized slaughtering establishment by an authorized USDA representative.

(3) The ruminants must be accompanied from the port of entry to the recognized slaughtering establishment by APHIS Form VS 17–33, which must include the location of the recognized slaughtering establishment.

(b) *Bovines.* In addition to meeting the requirements of paragraph (a) of this section, bovines may be imported from Canada for immediate slaughter only under the following conditions:

(1) The bovines must have been born after March 1, 1999, the date determined by APHIS to be the date of effective enforcement of a ruminant-to-ruminant feed ban in Canada;

(2) Before the animal's arrival at the port of entry into the United States, each bovine imported into the United States from Canada must be officially identified with unique individual identification that is traceable to the premises of origin of the animal. No person may alter, deface, remove, or otherwise tamper with the official identification while the animal is in the United States or moving into or through the United States, except that the identification may be removed at slaughter; and

(3) The bovines must be accompanied by a certificate issued in accordance with § 93.405 that states, in addition to the statements required by § 93.405, that the conditions of paragraphs (b)(1) and (b)(2) of this section have been met.

(Approved by the Office of Management and Budget under control numbers 0579–0234 and 0579–0393)

[78 FR 72996, Dec. 4, 2013]

§ 93.421 Special provisions.

(a) *In-bond shipments from Canada.* (1) Cattle, sheep, and goats from Canada transported in-bond through the United States for immediate export shall be inspected at the border port of entry and, when accompanied by an import permit obtained under § 93.404 of this part and all conditions therein are observed, shall be allowed entry into the United States and shall be otherwise handled as provided in paragraph (b) of § 93.401. Ruminants not accompanied by a permit shall meet the requirements of this part in the same manner as ruminants destined for importation into the United States, except that the Administrator may permit their inspection at some other point when he or she finds that such action will not increase the risk that communicable diseases of livestock and poultry will be disseminated to the livestock or poultry of the United States.

(2) *In-transit shipments through Canada.* Ruminants originating in the United States and transported directly through Canada may re-enter the United States without Canadian health or test certificates when accompanied by copies of the United States export health certificates properly issued and endorsed in accordance with regulations in part 91 of this chapter: *Provided,* That, to qualify for entry, the date, time, port of entry, and signature of the Canadian Port Veterinarian that inspected the ruminants for entry into Canada shall be recorded on the United States health certificate, or a document containing information shall be included with the certificate that accompanies the ruminants. In all cases it shall be determined by the veterinary inspector at the United States port of entry that the ruminants are the identical ruminants covered by said certificate.

(b) *Exhibition ruminants.* Ruminants from the United States which have been exhibited at the Royal Agricultural Winter Fair at Toronto or other publicly recognized expositions in Canada, including racing, rodeo, circus, or stage exhibitions in Canada, and have not been in that region for more than 90 days are eligible for return to the United States without Canadian health or test certificates, if they are accompanied by copies of the United States health certificate, issued and endorsed in accordance with the export regulations contained in part 91 of this chapter for entry into Canada: *Provided*, That all ruminants offered for re-entry upon examination by the veterinary inspector at the U.S. port of entry, are found by the inspector to be free of communicable diseases and exposure thereto and are determined to be the identical ruminants covered by said certificates or are the natural increase of such ruminants born after official test dates certified on the dam's health certificate.

[55 FR 31495, Aug. 2, 1990. Redesignated and amended at 62 FR 56012, 56018, Oct. 28, 1997; 81 FR 40151, June 21, 2016]

CENTRAL AMERICA AND WEST INDIES [9]

§ 93.422 Import permit and declaration for ruminants.

(a) For ruminants intended for importation from regions of Central America or of the West Indies, the importer shall first apply for and obtain from APHIS an import permit as provided in § 93.404: *Provided*, That the Administrator, when he or she finds that such action may be taken without endangering the livestock or poultry industry of the United States, may, upon request by any person, authorize the importation by such person, without such application or permit, from the British Virgin Islands into the Virgin Islands of the United States, of ruminants consigned for immediate slaughter, and such authorization may be limited to a particular shipment or extend to all shipments under this paragraph by such person during a specified period of time. The importation of cattle from any area infested with cattle fever ticks is prohibited except as provided in paragraph (c) of § 93.423.

(b) For all ruminants offered for importation from countries of Central America or of the West Indies, the importer or his or her agent shall present two copies of a declaration as provided in § 93.407.

[55 FR 31495, Aug. 2, 1990. Redesignated and amended at 62 FR 56012, 56019, Oct. 28, 1997]

§ 93.423 Ruminants from Central America and the West Indies.

(a) Ruminants intended for importation from Central America and the West Indies, except as provided in paragraph (c) of this section, must be accompanied by a certificate issued in accordance with § 93.405(a) stating that the animals have been in that region at least 60 days immediately preceding the date of shipment to the United States; that he or she has inspected the ruminants on the premises of origin and found them free from evidence of any communicable disease; and that, as far as it has been possible to determine, the ruminants have not been exposed to any communicable disease during the preceding 60 days. If no such veterinary officer is available in the region of origin, ruminants, other than sheep and goats, may be accompanied by an affidavit of the owner or importer stating that such ruminants have been in the region from which they were directly shipped to the United States for a period of at least 60 days immediately preceding the date of shipment therefrom, and that during such period no communicable disease has existed among them or among animals of their kind with which they have come in contact. Ruminants for which such affidavit is presented, unless imported for immediate slaughter, shall be quarantined at the port of entry at least seven days and during that time shall be subjected to such dipping, blood tests or other tests, as may be required by the Administrator to determine their freedom from communicable diseases. If imported for immediate slaughter, such animals shall be handled as provided in § 93.420.

[9] Importations from regions of Central America and the West Indies shall be subject to §§ 93.422 and 93.423, in addition to other sections in this part, which are in terms applicable to such importations.

(b) The certificate accompanying sheep and goats intended for importation from Central America and the West Indies must, in addition to the statements required by paragraph (a) of this section, meet all of the requirements of § 93.405.

(c) Cattle, which have been infested with or exposed to fever ticks, may be imported from the British Virgin Islands into the United States Virgin Islands, for immediate slaughter, only, if they are free from fever ticks at the time of such importation; if they are entered through one of the ports designated in § 93.403(d) and are consigned to a recognized slaughtering establishment with facilities approved by the Administrator for holding the animals in isolation until slaughtered, which shall be within 14 days after the date of entry into the United States Virgin Islands; and if they are accompanied by a certificate of a responsible official of the government of the British Virgin Islands certifying that the cattle originated in and are being shipped directly from the British Virgin Islands, that they are free of fever ticks, and that, as far as it has been possible to determine, such cattle are free from evidence of communicable disease and have not been exposed to any such disease common to animals of their kind, other than bovine babesiosis, during the 60 days preceding their movement to the United States Virgin Islands.

(d) If ruminants are unaccompanied by the certificate or affidavit as required by paragraphs (a), (b), or (c) of this section, or if they are found upon inspection at the port of entry to be affected with a communicable disease or to have been exposed thereto, they shall be refused entry, except as provided in paragraph (c) of this section. Ruminants refused entry shall be handled or quarantined, or otherwise disposed of as the Administrator may direct.

(e) In addition to meeting all other applicable requirements of this part, bovines from Central America and the West Indies may be imported only in accordance with § 93.436.

(Approved by the Office of Management and Budget under control number 0579–0040)

[55 FR 31495, Aug. 2, 1990, as amended at 61 FR 17239, Apr. 19, 1996. Redesignated and amended at 62 FR 56012, 56019, Oct. 28, 1997; 68 FR 6344, Feb. 7, 2003; 78 FR 72997, Dec. 4, 2013; 80 FR 10324, Feb. 26, 2015]

MEXICO [10]

§ 93.424 Import permits and applications for inspection of ruminants.

(a) For ruminants intended for importation from Mexico, the importer shall first apply for and obtain from APHIS an import permit as provided in § 93.404: *Provided*, That an import permit is not required for a ruminant offered for entry at a land border port designated in § 93.403(c), if such animal is:

(1) A wether; or

(2) A sheep or goat imported for immediate slaughter.

(b) For ruminants intended for importation into the United States from Mexico, the importer or his or her agent shall deliver to the veterinary inspector at the port of entry an application, in writing, for inspection, so that the veterinary inspector and customs representatives may make mutually satisfactory arrangements for the orderly inspection of the animals. For all cattle, except those entering pursuant to the third proviso in § 93.427(d), and except for steers, an official record of negative brucellosis test conducted on the herd of origin as required in § 93.427(d) shall be presented to the veterinary inspector at the port of entry when application is made for inspection. The veterinary inspector at the port of entry will provide the importer or his or her agent with a written statement assigning a date when the animals may be presented for import inspection.

[55 FR 31495, Aug. 2, 1990, as amended at 60 FR 13898, 13900, Mar. 15, 1995. Redesignated and amended at 56012, 56019, Oct. 28, 1997; 68 FR 35534, June 16, 2003]

[10] Importations from Mexico shall be subject to §§ 93.424 to 93.429, inclusive, in addition to other sections in this part which are in terms applicable for such importations.

§ 93.425 Declaration for ruminants.

For all ruminants offered for importation from Mexico, the importer or his or her agent shall present two copies of a declaration as provided in § 93.407.

[55 FR 31495, Aug. 2, 1990. Redesignated and amended at 62 FR 56012, 56019, Oct. 28, 1997]

§ 93.426 Inspection at port of entry.

(a) All ruminants offered for entry from Mexico, including such ruminants intended for movement through the United States in bond for immediate return to Mexico, shall be inspected at the port of entry, and all such ruminants found to be free from communicable disease and fever tick infestation, and not to have been exposed thereto, shall be admitted into the United States subject to the other applicable provisions of this part. Ruminants found to be affected with or to have been exposed to a communicable disease, or infested with fever ticks, shall be refused entry except as provided in § 93.427(b)(2). Ruminants refused entry shall be handled or quarantined or otherwise disposed of as the Administrator may direct.

(b) Ruminants covered by paragraph (a) of this section shall be imported through ports, designated in § 93.403, which are equipped with facilities necessary for proper chute inspection, dipping, and testing, as provided in this part.

[55 FR 31495, Aug. 2, 1990, as amended at 60 FR 13898, Mar. 15, 1995. Redesignated and amended at 62 FR 56012, 56019, Oct. 28, 1997; 68 FR 6344, Feb. 7, 2003]

§ 93.427 Cattle and other bovines from Mexico.

(a) Cattle and other ruminants imported from Mexico, except animals being transported in bond for immediate return to Mexico or animals imported for immediate slaughter, may be detained at the port of entry, and there subjected to such disinfection, blood tests, other tests, and dipping as required in this part to determine their freedom from any communicable disease or infection of such disease. The importer shall be responsible for the care, feed, and handling of the animals during the period of detention.

(b)(1) *Cattle from regions of Mexico that APHIS has determined to be free from fever ticks.* APHIS has evaluated certain regions of Mexico in accordance with § 92.2 of this chapter, and determined that they are free from fever ticks; a list of all such regions is found on the Internet *http://www.aphis.usda.gov/wps/portal/aphis/ourfocus/importexport*. Copies of the list are also available by contacting APHIS at the following address: Regionalization Evaluation Services, National Import Export Services, Veterinary Services, Animal and Plant Health Inspection Service, 4700 River Road Unit 38, Riverdale, MD 20737. Regions may be removed from the list based on a determination by APHIS that fever ticks exist in the region, on the discovery of tick-infested cattle from the region at a port of entry into the United States, or on information provided by a representative of the government of that region that fever ticks exist in the region. Cattle from regions of Mexico that APHIS has determined to be free from fever ticks may be imported into the United States subject to the following conditions:

(i) The cattle are accompanied by a certificate issued in accordance with § 93.405 that states that the cattle originate from a region of Mexico that APHIS has determined to be free from fever ticks.

(ii) If the cattle will transit to the United States through an area of Mexico that APHIS has not determined to be free from fever ticks, they are moved in a sealed means of conveyance, and that seal remains intact throughout such transit.

(iii) The cattle are presented for entry into the United States at a land border port of entry listed in § 93.403(c).

(iv) The cattle are segregated at the U.S. port of entry from cattle from regions of Mexico that APHIS has not determined to be free from fever ticks.

(v) The importer, or his or her agent, executes and delivers to the inspector at the port of entry an application for inspection or supervised dipping. In this application, the importer, or his or her agent, waive all claims against the United States for any loss or damage to the cattle occasioned by or resulting from inspection or dipping or from the fact that the cattle are later found still to be tick infested, and for any loss or damage to any other cattle in the importer's possession or control that come in contact with the dipped cattle.

(vi) The cattle are either inspected by an APHIS inspector at the port of entry for evidence of tick infestation or are treated with a tickicidal dip that is listed in § 72.13 of this chapter under the supervision of an inspector at the port of entry.

(vii) If any cattle are determined to be infested with fever ticks, the lot of cattle is refused entry and may only be imported into the United States subject to the requirements in paragraph (b)(2) of this section.

(2) *Cattle from regions of Mexico that APHIS has not determined to be free from fever ticks.* Cattle from regions of Mexico that APHIS has not determined to be free from fever ticks may only be imported into the United States subject to the following conditions:

(i) The cattle have been inspected by a veterinarian in Mexico and, in the determination of the veterinarian, are free from fever ticks and all evidence of communicable diseases, and have not been exposed to communicable diseases, other than bovine babesiosis, during the 60 days prior to movement to a port of entry into the United States.

(ii) The cattle have been treated in Mexico with a tickicidal dip that is listed in § 72.13 of this chapter within 7 to 14 days before being offered for entry into the United States.

(iii) The cattle are accompanied by a certificate issued in accordance with § 93.405 that states that this inspection and dipping have occurred.

(iv) The cattle are presented for entry into the United States at the port of entry at Santa Teresa, NM, or a port of entry within Texas that is listed in § 93.403(c).

(v) The importer, or his or her agent, executes and delivers to the inspector at the port of entry an application for inspection and supervised dipping. In this application, the importer, or his or her agent, agrees to waive all claims against the United States for any loss or damage to the cattle occasioned by or resulting from this dipping or from the fact that the cattle are later found to still be infested with ticks, and for any loss or damage to any other cattle in the importer's possession or control that come in contact with the dipped cattle.

(vi) When offered for entry, the cattle receive an inspection by an inspector. If free from fever ticks, the cattle are treated once with a tickicidal dip that is listed in § 72.13 of this chapter 7 to 14 days after the dipping required in paragraph (b)(2)(ii) of this section. If found to be infested with fever ticks, the cattle are refused entry and may not be inspected again at a port of entry until they are again dipped and 7 to 14 days have elapsed.

(vii) The cattle are not imported into an area of Texas that is quarantined in accordance with § 72.5 of this chapter for bovine babesiosis, or for tick infestation.

(c) *Tuberculosis.* (1) Each steer imported into the United States from Mexico shall be identified with a distinct, permanent, and legible "M" mark applied with a freeze brand, hot iron, or other method prior to arrival at a port of entry, unless the steer is imported for slaughter in accordance with § 93.429. Each spayed heifer imported into the United States from Mexico shall be identified with a distinct, permanent, and legible "M_x" mark applied with a freeze brand, hot iron, or other method prior to arrival at a port of entry, unless the spayed heifer is imported for slaughter in accordance with § 93.429. The "M" or "M_x" mark shall be not less than 2 inches nor more than 3 inches high, and shall be applied to each animal's right hip, high on the tailhead (over the junction of the sacral and first coccygeal vertebrae).

(2) Cattle from a herd or herds in which one or more reactors to the tuberculin test have been disclosed shall not be eligible for importation until the herd to which the animals in the lot belong achieve accredited herd status as defined in § 93.400, and provided that the animals offered for entry have met the other applicable requirements of this section.

(3) All sexually intact cattle accompanied by the certificate required by § 93.405(a) will be detained at the port of entry under the supervision of the port

veterinarian until tested for tuberculosis with negative results: Provided, That if any reactor is disclosed in any lot when so tested at the port of entry, the entire lot will be refused entry and the entire lot or any portion of it will not be eligible for importation until the herd to which the animals in the lot belong achieve accredited herd status as defined in § 93.400, and provided that the animals offered for entry have met the other applicable requirements of this section.

(4) The importation of Holstein steers, Holstein spayed heifers, Holstein cross steers, and Holstein cross spayed heifers from Mexico is prohibited.

(d) *Brucellosis.* All cattle offered for importation into the United States from Mexico shall be individually identified with a numbered, blue metal eartag issued by the Mexican Ministry of Agriculture and Water Resources (SARH); and except in the case of steers, shall be eligible for entry into the United States only if, in addition to complying with other applicable provisions of this part, they:

(1) Are accompanied by a certificate issued in accordance with § 93.405(a) stating:

(i) That such cattle originated in a herd in which all cattle (except calves under 6 months of age and steers) were tested for brucellosis not less than 30 days nor more than 90 days prior to the date of certification and were found to be negative;

(ii) The date and place such herd was tested; and

(iii) That the cattle in the herd have been isolated from all other cattle from the time the herd was tested negative for brucellosis to the date of the offer of the cattle for entry into the United States; and

(2) Except for calves under 6 months of age, are subjected to an additional test for brucellosis at the port of entry and found negative to such test: *Provided,* That if any reactor is disclosed in any lot when so tested at the port of entry, the entire lot shall be refused entry and the entire lot or any portion thereof may not be reoffered for entry until retested and recertified in accordance with paragraphs (d)(1) and (2) of this section or any cattle found to be negative to such test and any calves under 6 months of age in such lot may enter if consigned and moved under U.S. Department of Agriculture seal and without diversion to recognized slaughtering establishment as defined in § 78.1 of this chapter for immediate slaughter, or if consigned and moved under U.S. Department of Agriculture seal and without diversion to a quarantined feedlot, as defined in § 78.1 of this chapter and thereafter handled in accordance with the provisions of § 78.12 of this chapter: *Provided, further,* That if any suspect but no reactor is disclosed in any lot when so tested at the port of entry, any cattle found to be negative to such test and any calves under 6 months of age in such lot may enter without further restriction under this paragraph (d): *And provided further,* That any cattle other than cattle which are classified as a reactor or suspect to a test for brucellosis may enter the United States from Mexico without the certificate or any test otherwise required by this paragraph, if they are individually identified with a numbered, blue metal eartag issued by the Mexican Ministry of Agriculture and Water Resources (SARH) and are consigned and moved to a slaughtering establishment for immediate slaughter, or to a quarantined feedlot, in accordance with the first proviso in this paragraph and otherwise comply with the applicable provisions of this part.

(e) *BSE.* In addition to meeting the requirements of paragraphs (a) through (d) of this section and all other applicable requirements of this part, bovines may be imported from Mexico only under the following conditions:

(1) The bovines were born after November 30, 2007, the date determined by APHIS to be the date of effective enforcement of a ruminant-to-ruminant feed ban in Mexico.

(2) The bovines were officially identified prior to arriving at the port of entry in the United States with unique individual identification that is traceable to each bovine's premises of origin. No person may alter, deface, remove, or otherwise tamper with the official identification while the animal is in the United States or moving into or through the United States, except that

the identification may be removed at slaughter.

(3) The bovines, if sexually intact, are permanently and humanely identified using one of the following additional methods:

(i) An "MX" mark properly applied with a freeze brand, hot iron, or other method, and easily visible on the live animal and on the carcass before skinning. Such a mark must be not less than 2 inches nor more than 3 inches high, and must be applied to each animal's right hip, high on the tail-head (over the junction of the sacral and first coccygeal vertebrae); or

(ii) A tattoo with the letters "MX" applied to the inside of one ear of the animal; or

(iii) Other means of permanent identification upon request if deemed adequate by the Administrator to humanely identify the animal in a distinct and legible way as having been imported from Mexico.

(4) The bovines are accompanied by a certificate issued in accordance with §93.405 that states, in addition to the statements required by §93.405, that the conditions of paragraphs (e)(1) through (e)(3) of this section have been met.

(Approved by the Office of Management and Budget under control numbers 0579–0040, 0579–0224, 0579–0393, and 0579–0425)

[55 FR 31495, Aug. 2, 1990, as amended at 57 FR 2010, Jan. 17, 1992; 57 FR 28080, 28081, June 24, 1992; 58 FR 68509, Dec. 28, 1993; 59 FR 24886, May 13, 1994; 59 FR 65897, Dec. 22, 1994; 60 FR 13898, Mar. 15, 1995; 61 FR 17239, Apr. 19, 1996. Redesignated and amended at 62 FR 56012, 56019, Oct. 28, 1997; 62 FR 64266, Dec. 5, 1997; 66 FR 20190, Apr. 20, 2001; 69 FR 9750, Mar. 2, 2004; 74 FR 5, Jan. 2, 2009; 78 FR 72997, Dec. 4, 2013; 80 FR 10324, Feb. 26, 2015]

EFFECTIVE DATE NOTE: At 74 FR 5, Jan. 2, 2009, as corrected at 74 FR 22091, May 12, 2009, §93.427 was amended by revising paragraph (b)(2) introductory text, effective date delayed indefinitely. For the convenience of the user, the revised text is set forth as follows:

§93.427 Cattle from Mexico.

* * * * *

(b) * * *

(2) Cattle that have been exposed to splenetic, southern, or tick fever, or that have been infested with or exposed to fever ticks, may be imported from Mexico for admission into the United States, except into areas of Texas quarantined because of said disease or tick infestation as specified in §72.5 of this chapter, at one of the land border ports in Texas listed in §93.403(c), the port of Santa Teresa, NM, or the port of San Luis, AZ, provided that the following conditions are strictly observed and complied with:

* * * * *

§93.428 Sheep and goats and wild ruminants from Mexico.

(a) Sheep and goats intended for importation from Mexico shall be accompanied by a certificate issued in accordance with §93.405 and stating, if such sheep and goats are shipped by rail or truck, that such animals were loaded into cleaned and disinfected cars or trucks for transportation direct to the port of entry. Notwithstanding such certificate, such sheep and goats shall be detained as provided in §93.427(a) and shall be dipped at least once in a permitted scabies dip under supervision of an inspector.

(b) The certificate accompanying goats offered for importation from Mexico shall, in addition to the statements required by paragraph (a) of this section, state that such goats have been tested for tuberculosis and brucellosis with negative results within 30 days preceding their being offered for entry, and give the date and method of testing, the name of the consignor and of the consignee, and a description of the animals including breed, ages, markings, and tattoo and eartag numbers. Notwithstanding such certification, such goats shall be detained or quarantined as provided in §93.427 and retested for brucellosis.

(c) If sheep or goats are unaccompanied by the certificate as required by paragraphs (a) and (b) of this section, or if they are found upon inspection or retesting, as provided for in this part, to be affected with a communicable disease or to have been exposed thereto, they shall be refused entry and shall be handled or quarantined, or otherwise disposed of as the Administrator may direct.

(d) Certificates will not be required for wild ruminants, other than sheep and goats, originating in and shipped direct from Mexico, but such animals are subject to inspection at the port of entry as provided in § 93.426.

(Approved by the Office of Management and Budget under control number 0579–0040)

[55 FR 31495, Aug. 2, 1990, as amended at 56 FR 367, Jan. 4, 1991; 57 FR 28081, June 24, 1992; 61 FR 17239, Apr. 19, 1996. Redesignated and amended at 62 FR 56012, 56019, Oct. 28, 1997; 68 FR 6344, Feb. 7, 2003]

§ 93.429 Ruminants for immediate slaughter.

Ruminants, other than sheep and goats, may be imported from Mexico, subject to the applicable provisions of §§ 93.424, 93.425, 93.426, and 93.427(b)(2) for immediate slaughter if accompanied by a certificate issued in accordance with § 93.405(a) and stating that the veterinarian who issued the certificate has inspected the animals in the herd from which the ruminants will be imported and found them free of evidence of communicable disease, and that, so far as it has been possible to determine, they have not been exposed to any such disease common to animals of their kind during the preceding 60 days, and if the ruminants are shipped by rail or truck, the certificate shall further specify that the ruminants were loaded into cleaned and disinfected cars or trucks for transportation directly to the port of entry. Such ruminants shall be moved from the port of entry in conveyances sealed with seals of the United States Government. Sheep and goats from any part of Mexico may be imported only in compliance with other applicable sections in this part.

[55 FR 31495, Aug. 2, 1990, as amended at 57 FR 28081, June 24, 1992; 61 FR 17239, Apr. 19, 1996. Redesignated and amended at 62 FR 56012, 56019, Oct. 28, 1997]

Additional General Provisions

§§ 93.430–93.431 [Reserved]

§ 93.432 Cattle and other bovines from the Republic of Ireland.

(a) All cattle to be imported from the Republic of Ireland shall be accompanied by a certificate issued or endorsed by a salaried veterinarian of the Republic of Ireland showing that the cattle originated from a herd which is officially certified by the Republic of Ireland as a brucellosis qualified for export herd and that the cattle meet the requirements in § 93.432(c).

(b) A brucellosis qualified for export herd is a herd in which all of the cattle have been maintained as a herd unit for at least two years prior to importation and all of the test eligible cattle in the herd (*i.e.*, cattle over 6 months of age, except steers and spayed heifers) have been tested annually for brucellosis and found negative in accordance with Republic of Ireland requirements for at least two years prior to importation. The most recent negative herd test must have been conducted within 12 months of the date of importation. In addition:

(1) Such herd unit may include cattle which were born and raised within such herd unit during the two year period, or cattle which were moved directly to the herd from another herd unit of like status; or

(2) Such herd unit may include other cattle (except brucellosis reactors, suspects and animals listed in § 93.432(c)(1)) if:

(i) Such other cattle have been tested for brucellosis and found negative within 30 days prior to entry into the herd unit and all eligible cattle in the herd unit have been tested for brucellosis and found negative not less than 90 days following the date when the last of the other cattle had been added to the herd unit; or

(ii) All eligible cattle in the herd unit have been tested negative for brucellosis no less than 180 days nor more than 12 months (365 days) following the date when the last of the other cattle had been added to the herd unit.

(c) The certificate accompanying cattle offered for importation from the Republic of Ireland shall show that the cattle are from a brucellosis qualified for export herd and that they meet the following requirements:

(1) The cattle to be exported were not born to or nursed by brucellosis reactors and they were not born in a herd at the time the herd was under quarantine due to brucella infection.

(2) The cattle were placed in an isolation facility approved by a full-time, salaried, Government of Ireland veterinary official, on separate premises a

minimum of 500 yards from other livestock not destined for export to the United States for at least 60 days prior to export.

(3) The cattle were negative to the following tests conducted not less than 60 nor more than 120 days from the date of export and a second set of tests conducted within 30 days of the date of export;

(i) Plate or Tube agglutination test conducted in dilutions to detect reactions at 30, 60, 120, and 240 International Units per milliliter (IU/ml);

(ii) Brucellosis card test (Rose Bengal test);

(iii) Complement Fixation (CF) test conducted in dilutions to detect prozone reactions, when present.

(4) Cattle are eligible for entry only if classified as negative at 30 IU to the Plate or Tube agglutination test, negative to the brucellosis card test and negative to the CF test as performed and interpreted by standard methods at the Republic of Ireland Brucellosis Diagnostic Laboratory. Any animal exhibiting a prozone serological reaction is ineligible for export to the United States.

(5) Cattle showing a serological titer more than 60 IU to the Plate or Tube agglutination test, or a reaction to the Brucellosis card test (Rose Bengal) or CF test that would be interpreted to be an infected animal (reactor) under the Republic of Ireland brucellosis control program. Animals from that herd of origin and all other cattle having the opportunity for contact with the reactor animal shall not be eligible for export to the United States. Brucellosis bacteriologically positive animals, if known, regardless of serologic reactions, are not eligible for importation nor are any animals in contact with such animals.

(6) The cattle were moved directly to the port of export from the isolation facility without contact with any other cattle which are not qualified for export to the United States.

(d) The certificate accompanying the cattle offered for importation must also show the dates and places of testing, names of the consignor and consignee, and descriptions of the cattle, including breed, ages, markings, and tattoo and eartag numbers.

(e) In addition to meeting all other applicable requirements of this part, bovines from the Republic of Ireland may be imported only in accordance with § 93.436.

[55 FR 31495, Aug. 2, 1990. Redesignated and amended at 62 FR 56012, 56019, Oct. 28, 1997; 78 FR 72997, Dec. 4, 2013]

§§ 93.433–93.434 [Reserved]

§ 93.435 Sheep and goats.

(a) Except as provided in paragraph (b) of this section, all sheep and goats imported into the United States must be placed in a flock or herd in the United States that participates in the Voluntary Scrapie Flock Certification Program (see 9 CFR part 54, subpart B) and:

(1) The flock or herd qualifies as a "Certified" flock or herd; or

(2) The flock or herd owner has agreed, in writing, to maintain the flock or herd in compliance with all requirements of the Voluntary Scrapie Flock Certification Program until the flock or herd qualifies as a "Certified" flock or herd.

(b) The following sheep and goats are not subject to paragraph (a) of this section:

(1) Goats intended for importation from Australia, Canada, or New Zealand;

(2) Goats intended for importation from any region other than Australia, Canada, or New Zealand, provided that such goats have not had any contact with sheep during the 5 years immediately prior to shipment, in accordance with § 93.405(b)(2)(ii);

(3) Sheep intended for importation from Australia, Canada, or New Zealand, provided that none of the female sheep in the flock from which the sheep will be imported has been impregnated, during the 5 years immediately preceding shipment of the sheep to the United States, with germ plasm from a region other than Australia, Canada, New Zealand, or the United States, in accordance with § 93.405(c)(3);

(4) Wethers;

(5) Sheep or goats imported for immediate slaughter; and

(6) Wild sheep or goats imported for exhibition purposes to an approved zoological park in accordance with § 93.404(c).

(c) Sheep or goats may be imported under paragraph (a) of this section only if the importer provides the Voluntary Scrapie Flock Certification Program identification number of the receiving flock or herd as part of the application for an import permit.

(d) Sheep and goats may be imported under paragraph (a)(1) of this section only if they come from a flock or herd in the region of origin that participates in a program determined by the Administrator to be equivalent to the Voluntary Scrapie Flock Certification Program, and the flock or herd has been determined by the Administrator to be at a level equivalent to "Certified" in the Voluntary Scrapie Flock Certification Program.

(e) Sheep and goats may be imported under paragraph (a)(2) of this section only if they are placed in a Certifiable Class C flock or herd participating in the Voluntary Scrapie Flock Certification Program; *except*, that if the sheep and goats come from a flock or herd in the region of origin that participates in a program determined by the Administrator to be equivalent to the Voluntary Scrapie Flock Certification Program, then the sheep and goats may be placed in a herd or flock in the United States which would be classified at a level equivalent to or lower (*i.e.*, at a greater risk) than the certification level, as determined by the Administrator, of the flock or herd from which the sheep or goats are to be imported.

(f) Sheep and goats imported under paragraph (a)(2) of this section must be monitored for scrapie disease until the flock or herd qualifies as a "Certified" flock or herd.

(g) Except for imported sheep and goats placed in Certifiable Class C flocks or herds, the certificate accompanying sheep or goats imported under paragraph (a) of this section must contain the following statement: "The animals identified on this certificate have been monitored by a salaried veterinary officer of [*name of country of origin*], for [*number of months*], in the same source flock or herd which had been determined by the Administrator, APHIS, prior to the exportation of these animals to the United States, to be equivalent to [*certification level*] of the Voluntary Scrapie Flock Certification Program authorized under 9 CFR part 54, subpart B."

(1) The Administrator will determine, based upon information supplied by the importer, whether the flock or herd from which the animals are to be imported participates in a program in the country of origin that is equivalent to the Voluntary Scrapie Flock Certification Program, and if so, at what level the source flock or herd should be classified.

(2) In order for the Administrator to make a determination, the importer must supply the following information with the application for an import permit no less than 1 month prior to the anticipated date of importation:

(i) The name, title, and address of a knowledgeable official in the veterinary services of the region of origin;

(ii) The details of scrapie control programs in the region of origin, including information on disease surveillance and border control activities and the length of time such activities have been in effect;

(iii) Any available information concerning additions, within the 5 years immediately preceding shipment to the United States, to the flock or herd from which the sheep and goats will be imported;

(iv) Any available data concerning disease incidence, within the 5 years immediately preceding shipment to the United States, in the flock or herd from which the sheep or goats are to be imported, including, but not limited to, the results of diagnostic tests, especially histopathology tests, conducted on any animals in the flock or herd;

(v) Information concerning the health, within the 5 years immediately preceding shipment to the United States, of other ruminants, flocks, and herds with which the imported sheep and goats, and with which animals in the sheep or goats' flock or herd might have had physical contact, and a description of the type and frequency of such physical contact; and

(vi) Any other information requested by the Administrator in specific cases as needed to make a determination.

(Approved by the Office of Management and Budget under control numbers 0579–0040 and 0579–0101)

[61 FR 17240, Apr. 19, 1996. Redesignated and amended at 62 FR 56012, 56019, Oct. 28, 1997]

§ 93.436 Bovines from regions of negligible risk, controlled risk, and undetermined risk for BSE.

The importation of bovines is prohibited, unless the conditions of this section and any other applicable conditions of this part are met. Once the bovines are imported, if they do not meet the conditions of this section, they must be disposed of as the Administrator may direct.

(a) *Bovines from a region of negligible risk for BSE in which there has been no indigenous case of BSE.* Bovines from a region of negligible risk for BSE, as defined in § 92.1 of this subchapter, in which there has been no indigenous case of BSE, may be imported only if the bovines are accompanied by an original certificate issued by a full-time salaried veterinary officer of the national government of the exporting region, or issued by a veterinarian designated or accredited by the national government of the exporting region and endorsed by a full-time salaried veterinary officer of the national government of the exporting region, representing that the veterinarian issuing the certificate was authorized to do so, and the certificate attests that the exporting region of the bovines is classified by APHIS as a negligible-risk region for BSE in which there has been no indigenous case of BSE.

(b) *Bovines from a region of negligible risk for BSE in which there has been an indigenous case of BSE and bovines from a region of controlled risk for BSE.* Bovines from a region of negligible risk for BSE, as defined in § 92.1 of this subchapter, in which there has been an indigenous case of BSE, and bovines from a region of controlled risk for BSE, as defined in § 92.1 of this subchapter, may be imported only under the following conditions:

(1) Prior to importation into the United States, each bovine is officially identified with unique individual identification that is traceable to the premises of origin of the animal. No person may alter, deface, remove, or otherwise tamper with the official identification while the animal is in the United States or moving into or through the United States, except that the identification may be removed at slaughter.

(2) The bovines are permanently and humanely identified before arrival at the port of entry with a distinct and legible mark identifying the exporting country. Acceptable means of permanent identification include the following:

(i) A mark properly applied with a freeze brand, hot iron, or other method, and easily visible on the live animal and on the carcass before skinning. Such a mark must be not less than 2 inches nor more than 3 inches high, and must be applied to each animal's right hip, high on the tail-head (over the junction of the sacral and first coccygeal vertebrae);

(ii) A tattoo with letters identifying the exporting country must be applied to the inside of one ear of the animal; or

(iii) Other means of permanent identification upon request if deemed adequate by the Administrator to humanely identify the animal in a distinct and legible way as having been imported from a region of negligible risk for BSE in which there has been an indigenous case of BSE or from a region of controlled risk for BSE.

(3) The bovines were born after the date from which the ban on the feeding of ruminants meat-and-bone meal or greaves derived from ruminants has been effectively enforced.

(4) The bovines are accompanied by an original certificate issued by a full-time salaried veterinary officer of the national government of the exporting region, or issued by a veterinarian designated or accredited by the national government of the exporting region and endorsed by a full-time salaried veterinary officer of the national government of the exporting region, representing that the veterinarian issuing the certificate was authorized to do so, and the certificate attests to the BSE

risk classification of the exporting region and that the conditions of paragraphs (b)(1) through (b)(3) of this section have been met.

(5) If there has been an indigenous case of BSE in the exporting region, the following restrictions apply:

(i) Bovines that, during their first year of life, were reared with a bovine determined to be infected with BSE during its first year of life, and that an investigation showed consumed the same potentially contaminated feed as the infected animal during that period are not eligible for importation into the United States; and

(ii) If the investigation was unable to determine whether the feed source that was used to feed the bovine known to be infected was also used to feed other bovines in the herd of the infected animal, all bovines born in the same herd as a BSE-infected bovine either within 12 months before or 12 months after the birth of the infected animal are not eligible for importation into the United States.

(c) *Bovines from a region of undetermined risk for BSE.* Importation of bovines from a region of undetermined risk for BSE, as defined in § 92.1 of this subchapter, is prohibited; *Except that:* The Administrator may allow such imports on a case-by-case basis if the live bovines are imported for specific uses, including, but not limited to, show or exhibition, and under conditions determined by the Administrator to be adequate to prevent the spread of BSE.

(Approved by the Office of Management and Budget under control number 0579–0234)

[78 FR 72997, Dec. 4, 2013]

Subpart E—Swine

§ 93.500 Definitions.

Wherever in this subpart the following terms are used, unless the context otherwise requires, they shall be construed, respectively, to mean:

Accredited veterinarian. A veterinarian approved by the Administrator in accordance with the provisions of part 161 of this title to perform functions specified in parts 1, 2, 3, and 11 of subchapter A, and subchapters B, C, and D of this chapter, and to perform functions required by cooperative state-federal disease control and eradication programs.

Administrator. The Administrator of the Animal and Plant Health Inspection Service or any other employee of the Animal and Plant Health Inspection Service, United States Department of Agriculture, to whom authority has been or may be delegated to act in the Administrator's stead.

Animal and Plant Health Inspection Service. The Animal and Plant Health Inspection Service of the United States Department of Agriculture (APHIS or Service).

Animals. Cattle, sheep, goats, other ruminants, swine, horses, asses, mules, zebras, dogs, and poultry.

APHIS representative. A veterinarian or other individual employed by the Animal and Plant Health Inspection Service, United States Department of Agriculture, who is authorized to perform the services required by this part.

Communicable disease. Any contagious, infectious, or communicable disease of domestic livestock, poultry or other animals.

Department. The United States Department of Agriculture (USDA).

Immediate slaughter. Consignment directly from the port of entry to a recognized slaughtering establishment[1] and slaughter thereat within two weeksfrom the date of entry.

Inspector. An employee of the Animal and Plant Health Inspection Service authorized to perform duties required under this subpart.

Official identification device or method. A means of officially identifying an animal or group of animals using devices or methods approved by the Administrator, including, but not limited to, official tags, tattoos, and registered brands when accompanied by a certificate of inspection from a recognized brand inspection authority.

Port veterinarian. A veterinarian employed by the Animal and Plant Health Inspection Service to perform duties required under this part at a port of entry.

---

[1] The name of recognized slaughtering establishments approved under this part may be obtained from the Area Veterinarian in Charge, Veterinary Services, for the State of destination of the shipment.

Recognized slaughtering establishment.[2] An establishment where slaughtering operations are regularly carried on under federal or state inspection and which has been approved by the Animal and Plant Health Inspection Service to receive animals for slaughter under this part.

Region. Any defined geographic land area identifiable by geological, political, or surveyed boundaries. A region may consist of any of the following:

(1) A national entity (country);

(2) Part of a national entity (zone, county, department, municipality, parish, Province, State, etc.);

(3) Parts of several national entities combined into an area; or

(4) A group of national entities (countries) combined into a single area.

Ruminants. All animals which chew the cud, such as cattle, buffaloes, sheep, goats, deer, antelopes, camels, llamas and giraffes.

Swine. The domestic hog and all varieties of wild hogs.

United States. All of the States of the United States, the District of Columbia, Guam, Northern Mariana Islands, Puerto Rico, the Virgin Islands of the United States, and all other Territories and Possessions of the United States.

Veterinary Services. The Veterinary Services unit of the Department.

Zoological park. A professionally operated zoo, park, garden or other place, maintained under the constant surveillance of a Doctor of Veterinary Medicine, for the exhibition of live animals, pigeons or birds, for the purpose of public recreation or education.

[55 FR 31495, Aug. 2, 1990. Redesignated and amended at 62 FR 56012, 56020, Oct. 28, 1997; 69 FR 64651, Nov. 8, 2004; 71 FR 29070, May 19, 2006; 72 FR 67232, Nov. 28, 2007; 76 FR 70039, Nov. 10, 2011; 77 FR 1391, Jan. 10, 2012]

§93.501 General prohibitions; exceptions.

(a) No swine or product subject to the provisions of this part shall be brought into the United States except in accordance with the regulations in this part and part 94 of this subchapter;[3] nor shall any such swine or product be handled or moved after physical entry into the United States before final release from quarantine or any other form of governmental detention except in compliance with such regulations; *Provided,* That, the Administrator may upon request in specific cases permit swine or products to be brought into or through the United States under such conditions as he or she may prescribe, when he or she determines in the specific case that such action will not endanger the livestock or poultry of the United States.

(b) Except for swine prohibited entry, the provisions in this part 93 relating to swine shall not apply to healthy swine in transit through the United States if they are not known to be infected with or exposed, within 60 days preceding the date of export from the region of origin, to communicable diseases of such swine, if an import permit[4] has been obtained under §93.504 of this Chapter and all conditions therein are observed; and if such swine are handled as follows:

(1)(i) They are maintained under continuous confinement in transit through the United States aboard an aircraft, ocean vessel, or other means of conveyance; or

(ii) They are unloaded, in the course of such transit, into a swine holding facility which is provided by the carrier or its agent and has been approved[5] in advance by the Administrator in accordance with paragraph (d)(3) of this section as adequate to prevent the spread within the United States of any livestock or poultry disease, and they are maintained there under continuous confinement until loaded aboard a means of conveyance for transportation from the United States and are maintained under continuous confinement aboard such means of conveyance

[2] The name of recognized slaughtering establishments approved under this part may be obtained from the Area Veterinarian in Charge, Veterinary Services, for the State of destination of the shipment.

[3] Importations of certain animals from various countries are absolutely prohibited under part 94 because of specified diseases.

[4] Such permit may be obtained from the Animal and Plant Health Inspection Service, Veterinary Services, National Center for Import-Export, 4700 River Road Unit 38, Riverdale, Maryland 20737–1231. Requests for approval of such facilities should also be made to the Administrator.

until it leaves the United States; the import permit will specify any additional conditions necessary to assure that the transit of the swine through the United States can be made without endangering the livestock or poultry of the United States, and that Department inspectors may inspect the swine on board such means of conveyance or in such holding facility to ascertain whether the requirements of this paragraph are met, and dispose of them in accordance with the Animal Health Protection Act (7 U.S.C. 8301 *et seq.*) if such conditions are not met; and

(2) The carrier or its agent executes and furnishes to the collector of Customs at the first port of arrival a declaration stating that the swine will be retained aboard such means of conveyance or in an approved holding facility during transshipment as required by this paragraph.

(3) Provisions for the approval of facilities required in this paragraph are:

(i) They must be sufficiently isolated to prevent direct or indirect contact with all other animals and birds while in the United States.

(ii) They must be so constructed that they provide adequate protection against environmental conditions and can be adequately cleaned, washed and disinfected.

(iii) They must provide for disposal of swine carcasses, manure, bedding, waste and any related shipping materials in a manner that will prevent dissemination of disease.

(iv) They must have provisions for adequate sources of feed and water and for attendants for the care and feeding of swine in the facility.

(v) They must comply with additional requirements as may be imposed by the Administrator if deemed applicable for a particular shipment.

(vi) They must also comply with all applicable local, State and Federal requirements for environmental quality and with the provisions of the Animal Welfare Regulations in chapter I of this title, as applicable.

(c) *Removal and loss of official identification devices.* Official identification devices are intended to provide permanent identification of livestock and to ensure the ability to find the source of animal disease outbreaks. Removal of these devices is prohibited except at the time of slaughter. If an official identification device is lost and it is necessary to retag an animal with a new official number, every effort should be made to correlate the new official number with the previous official number of the animal.

[55 FR 31495, Aug. 2, 1990, as amended at 59 FR 67615, Dec. 30, 1994. Redesignated and amended at 62 FR 56012, 56020, Oct. 28, 1997; 68 FR 6344, Feb. 7, 2003; 69 FR 64651, Nov. 8, 2004]

§ 93.502 Inspection of certain aircraft and other means of conveyance and shipping containers thereon; unloading, cleaning, and disinfection requirements.

(a) *Inspection:* All aircraft and other means of conveyance (including shipping containers thereon) moving into the United States from any foreign region are subject to inspection without a warrant by properly identified and designated inspectors to determine whether they are carrying any animal, carcass, product or article regulated or subject to disposal under any law or regulation administered by the Secretary of Agriculture for prevention of the introduction or dissemination of any communicable animal disease.

(b) *Unloading requirements:* Whenever in the course of any such inspection at any port in the United States the inspector has reason to believe that the means of conveyance or container is contaminated with material of animal (including poultry) origin, such as, but not limited to, meat, organs, glands, extracts, secretions, fat, bones, blood, lymph, urine, or manure, so as to present a danger of the spread of any communicable animal disease, the inspector may require the unloading of the means of conveyance and the emptying of the container if he or she deems it necessary to enable him or her to determine whether the means of conveyance or container is in fact so contaminated. The principal operator of the means of conveyance and his or her agent in charge of the means of conveyance shall comply with any such requirement under the immediate supervision of, and in the time and manner prescribed by, the inspector.

[5] See footnote 4 to subpart E.

(c) *Cleaning and disinfection:* Whenever, upon inspection under this section, an inspector determines that a means of conveyance or shipping container is contaminated with material of animal origin so as to present a danger of the spread of any communicable animal disease, he or she shall notify the principal operator of the means of conveyance or his or her agent in charge, of such determination and the requirements under this section. The person so notified shall cause the cleaning and disinfection of such means of conveyance and container under the immediate supervision of, and in the time and manner prescribed by, the inspector.

(d) For purposes of this section, the term "shipping container" means any container of a type specially adapted for use in transporting any article on the means of conveyance involved.

[55 FR 31495, Aug. 2, 1990. Redesignated and amended at 62 FR 56012, 56020, Oct. 28, 1997; 68 FR 6344, Feb. 7, 2003]

§ 93.503 Ports designated for the importation of swine.

(a) *Air and ocean ports.* The following ports have APHIS inspection and quarantine facilities necessary for quarantine stations and all swine shall be entered into the United States through these stations, except as provided in paragraphs (b), (c), (d), (e), and (f) of this section: Los Angeles, California; Miami, Florida; and Newburgh, New York.

(b) *Canadian border ports.* The following land border ports are designated as having the necessary inspection facilities for the entry of swine from Canada: Eastport, Idaho; Houlton and Jackman, Maine; Detroit, Port Huron, and Sault Ste. Marie, Michigan; Baudette, Minnesota; Opheim, Raymond, and Sweetgrass, Montana; Alexandria Bay, Buffalo, and Champlain, New York; Dunseith, Pembina, and Portal, North Dakota; Derby Line and Highgate Springs, Vermont; Oroville and Sumas, Washington.

(c) *Mexican border ports.* The following land border ports are designated as having the necessary inspection facilities for the entry of swine from Mexico: Brownsville, Hidalgo, Laredo, Eagle Pass, Del Rio, Presidio, and El Paso, Texas; Douglas, Naco, Nogales, Sasabe, and San Luis, Arizona; Calexico and San Ysidro, California; and Antelope Wells, and Columbus, New Mexico.

(d) *Special ports.* Charlotte Amalie, St. Thomas, and Christiansted, St. Croix, in the United States Virgin Islands, are hereby designated as quarantine stations for the entry of swine from the British Virgin Islands into the United States Virgin Islands for immediate slaughter.

(e) *Limited ports.* The following ports are designated as having inspection facilities for the entry of swine and swine products such as swine test specimens which do not appear to require restraint and holding inspection facilities: Anchorage and Fairbanks, Alaska; San Diego, California; Jacksonville, St. Petersburg-Clearwater, and Tampa, Florida; Atlanta, Georgia; Honolulu, Hawaii; Chicago, Illinois; New Orleans, Louisiana; Portland, Maine; Baltimore, Maryland; Boston, Massachusetts; Minneapolis, Minnesota; Great Falls, Montana; Portland, Oregon; San Juan, Puerto Rico; Memphis, Tennessee (no live animals); Galveston and Houston, Texas; and Seattle, Spokane, and Tacoma, Washington.

(f) *Designation of other ports.* The Secretary of the Treasury has approved the designation as quarantine stations of the ports specified in this section. In special cases other ports may be designated as quarantine stations under this section by the Administrator, with the concurrence of the Secretary of the Treasury.

[55 FR 31495, Aug. 2, 1990, as amended at 58 FR 38283, July 16, 1993; 60 FR 16045, Mar. 29, 1995; 60 FR 25120, May 11, 1995. Redesignated at 62 FR 56012, Oct. 28, 1997, as amended at 64 FR 23179, Apr. 30, 1999; 65 FR 38178, June 20, 2000; 67 FR 68022, Nov. 8, 2002]

§ 93.504 Import permits for swine and for swine specimens for diagnostic purposes; and reservation fees for space at quarantine facilities maintained by APHIS.

(a) *Application for permit; reservation required.* (1) For swine and swine test specimens for diagnostic screening purposes, intended for importation from any part of the world, except as otherwise provided for in §§ 93.516 and 93.520, the importer shall first apply for and obtain from APHIS an import permit. The application shall specify the name and address of the importer; the species, breed, number or quantity of swine or swine test specimens to be imported; the purpose of the importation; individual swine identification which includes a description of the swine, name, age, markings, if any, registration number, if any, and tattoo or eartag; the region of origin; the name and address of the exporter; the port of embarkation in the foreign region; the mode of transportation, route of travel, and the port of entry in the United States; the proposed date of arrival of the swine or swine test specimens to be imported; and the name of the person to whom the swine or swine test specimens will be delivered and the location of the place in the United States to which delivery will be made from the port of entry. Additional information may be required in the form of certificates concerning specific diseases to which the swine are susceptible, as well as vaccinations or other precautionary treatments to which the swine or swine test specimens have been subjected. Notice of any such requirements will be given to the applicant in each case.

(2) An application for permit to import will be denied for domestic swine from any region designated in § 94.1 of this chapter as a region where rinderpest or foot-and-mouth disease exists.

(3) An application for permit to import swine may also be denied because of: Communicable disease conditions in the area or region of origin, or in a region where the shipment has been or will be held or through which the shipment has been or will be transported; deficiencies in the regulatory programs for the control or eradication of animal diseases and the unavailability of veterinary services in the above mentioned regions; the importer's failure to provide satisfactory evidence concerning the origin, history, and health status of the swine; the lack of satisfactory information necessary to determine that the importation will not be likely to transmit any communicable disease to livestock or poultry of the United States; or any other circumstances which the Administrator believes require such denial to prevent the dissemination of any communicable disease of livestock or poultry into the United States.

(4)(i) The importer or importer's agent shall pay or ensure payment of a reservation fee for each lot of swine to be quarantined in a facility maintained by USDA. For swine the reservation fee shall be 100 percent of the cost of providing care, feed, and handling during quarantine, as estimated by the quarantine facility's veterinarian in charge.

(ii) At the time the importer or the importer's agent requests a reservation of quarantine space, the importer or importer's agent shall pay the reservation fee by check or U.S. money order or ensure payment of the reservation fee by an irrevocable letter of credit from a commercial bank (the effective date on such letter of credit shall run to 30 days after the date the swine are scheduled to be released from quarantine); except that anyone who issues a check to the Department for a reservation fee which is returned because of insufficient funds shall be denied any further request for reservation of a quarantine space until the outstanding amount is paid.

(iii) Any reservation fee paid by check or U.S. money order shall be applied against the expenses incurred for services received by the importer or importer's agent in connection with the quarantine for which the reservation was made. Any part of the reservation fee which remains unused after being applied against the expenses incurred for services received by the importer or the importer's agent in connection with the quarantine for which the reservation was made, shall be returned to the individual who paid the reservation fee. If the reservation fee is ensured by a letter of credit, the Department will draw against the letter of credit unless payment for services received by the importer or importer's agent in connection with the quarantine is otherwise made at least 3 days prior to the expiration date of the letter of credit.

(iv) Any reservation fee shall be forfeited if the importer or the importer's agent fails to present for entry, within 24 hours following the designated time of arrival the lot of swine for which the reservation was made: *Except* that a reservation fee shall not be forfeited if:

(A) Written notice of cancellation from the importer or the importer's agent is received by the office of the veterinarian in charge of the quarantine facility[6] during regular business hours (8:00 a.m. to 4:30 p.m. Monday through Friday, excluding holidays) no later than 15 days prior to the beginning of the time of importation as specified in the import permit or as arranged with the veterinarian in charge of the quarantine facility if no import permit is required (the 15 day period shall not include Saturdays, Sundays, or holidays), or

(B) The Administrator determines that services, other than provided by carriers, necessary for the importation of the swine within the requested period are unavailable because of unforeseen circumstances as determined by the Administrator, (such as the closing of an airport due to inclement weather or the unavailability of the reserved space due to the extension of another quarantined.)

(v) If the reservation fee was ensured by a letter of credit and the fee is to be forfeited under paragraph (a)(4)(iv) of this section, the Department will draw against the letter of credit unless the reservation fee is otherwise paid at least 3 days prior to the expiration date of the letter of credit.

(vi) When a reservation is cancelled in accordance with paragraph (a)(4)(iv)(A) of this section and the provisions of paragraph (a)(4)(iv)(B) of this section do not apply, a $40.00 cancellation fee shall be charged. If a reservation fee was paid, the cancellation fee shall be deducted from any reservation fee returned to the importer or the importer's agent. If the reservation fee was ensured by a letter of credit, the Department will draw the amount of the cancellation fee against the letter of credit unless the cancellation fee is otherwise paid at least 3 days prior to the expiration date of the letter of credit.

[6] The addresses of USDA quarantine facilities may be found in telephone directories listing the facilities or by contacting the Animal and Plant Health Inspection Service, Veterinary Services, National Center for Import-Export, 4700 River Road Unit 38, Riverdale, Maryland 20737–1231.

(b) *Permit.* When a permit is issued, the original and two copies will be sent to the importer. It shall be the responsibility of the importer to forward the original permit and one copy to the shipper in the region of origin, and it shall also be the responsibility of the importer to insure that the shipper presents the copy of the permit to the carrier and makes proper arrangements for the original permit to accompany the shipment to the specified U.S. port of entry for presentation to the collector of customs. Swine and swine test specimens for diagnostic screening purposes for swine intended for importation into the United States for which a permit has been issued, will be received at the specified port of entry within the time prescribed in the permit which shall not exceed 14 days from the first day that the permit is effective for all permits. Swine and swine test specimens for which a permit is required by these regulations will not be eligible for entry if a permit has not been issued; if unaccompanied by such a permit; if shipment is from any port other than the one designated in the permit; if arrival in the United States is at any port other than the one designated in the permit; if the swine or swine test specimens offered for entry differ from those described in the permit; if the swine or swine test specimens are not handled as outlined in the application for the permit and as specified in the permit issued; or if ruminants or swine other than those covered by import permits are aboard the transporting carrier.

(c) *Wild swine from regions where foot-and-mouth disease or rinderpest exists.* This paragraph (c) applies to the importation of wild swine from countries designated in part 94 of this subchapter as regions in which foot-and-mouth disease or rinderpest exist.

(1) Permits for the importation of wild swine will be issued only for importations through the Port of New York, and only if the animals are imported for exhibition in a PEQ Zoo. A PEQ Zoo is a zoological park or other place maintained for the exhibition of live animals for recreational or educational purposes that:

(i) Has been approved by the Administrator in accordance with paragraph (c)(2) of this section to receive and maintain imported wild swine; and

(ii) Has entered into the agreement with APHIS set forth in paragraph (c)(4) of this section for the maintenance and handling of imported wild swine.

(2) Approval of a PEQ Zoo shall be on the basis of an inspection, by an authorized representative of the Department, of the physical facilities of the establishment and its methods of operation. Standards for acceptable physical facilities shall include satisfactory pens, cages, or enclosures in which the imported swine can be maintained so as not to be in contact with the general public and free from contact with domestic livestock; natural or established drainage from the PEQ Zoo which will avoid contamination of land areas where domestic livestock are kept or with which domestic livestock may otherwise come in contact; provision for the disposition of manure, other wastes, and dead swine within the PEQ Zoo; and other reasonable facilities considered necessary to prevent the dissemination of diseases from the PEQ Zoo. The operator of the PEQ Zoo shall have available the services of a full-time or part-time veterinarian, or a veterinarian on a retainer basis, who shall make periodic examinations of all animals maintained at the PEQ Zoo for evidence of disease; who shall make a post-mortem examination of each animal that dies; and who shall make a prompt report of suspected cases of contagious or communicable diseases to appropriate state or federal livestock sanitary officials.

(3) Manure and other animal wastes must be disposed of within the PEQ Zoo park for a minimum of one year following the date an imported wild swine enters the zoo. If an APHIS veterinarian determines that an imported swine shows no signs of any communicable disease during this 1-year period, its manure and other wastes need not be disposed of within the zoo after the 1-year period. If, however, an APHIS veterinarian determines that the swine does show signs of any communicable disease during this 1-year period, an APHIS veterinarian will investigate the disease and determine whether the swine's manure and other wastes may safely be disposed of outside the zoo after the 1-year period has ended.

(4) Prior to the issuance of an import permit under this section, the operator of the approved PEQ Zoo to which the imported swine are to be consigned, and the importer of the swine, if such operator and importer are different parties, shall execute an agreement covering each swine or group of swine for which the import permit is requested. The agreement shall be in the following form:

AGREEMENT FOR THE IMPORTATION, QUARANTINE AND EXHIBITION OF CERTAIN WILD RUMINANTS AND WILD SWINE

_______, operator(s) of the zoological park known as _________ (Name) located at _________ (City and state), and _________ (Importer) hereby request a permit for the importation of _______ (Number and kinds of animals) for exhibition purposes at the said zoological park, said animals originating in a region where foot-and-mouth disease or rinderpest exists and being subject to restrictions under regulations contained in part 93, title 9, Code of Federal Regulations.

In making this request, it is understood and agreed that:

1. The animals for which an import permit is requested will be held in isolation at a port of embarkation in the region of origin, approved by the Administrator as a port having facilities which are adequate for maintaining wild animals in isolation from all other animals and having veterinary supervision by officials of the region of origin of the animals. Such animals will be held in such isolation for not less than 60 days under the supervision of the veterinary service of that region to determine whether the animals show any clinical evidence of foot-and-mouth disease, rinderpest, or other communicable disease that is exotic to the United States or for which APHIS has an eradication or control program in 9 CFR chapter I, and to assure that the animals will not have been exposed to such a disease within the 60 days next before their exportation from that region.

2. Shipment will be made direct from such port of embarkation to the port of New York as the sole port of entry in this region. If shipment is made by ocean vessel, the animals will not be unloaded in any foreign port en route. If shipment is made by air, the animals will not be unloaded at any port or other place of landing, except at a port approved by the Administrator as a port not located in a region where rinderpest or foot-

and-mouth disease exists or as a port in such a region having facilities and inspection adequate for maintaining wild animals in isolation from all other animals.

3. No ruminants or swine will be aboard the transporting vehicle, vessel or aircraft, except those for which an import permit has been issued.

4. The animals will be quarantined for not less than 30 days in the Department's Animal Import Center in Newburgh, New York.

5. Upon release from quarantine the animals will be delivered to the zoological park named in this agreement to become the property of the park and they will not be sold, exchanged or removed from the premises without the prior consent of APHIS. If moved to another zoological park in the United States, the receiving zoological park must be approved by the Administrator in accordance with paragraph 6 of this agreement.

6. The Administrator will approve the movement of an imported animal subject to this agreement if the Administrator determines that the animal has spent at least one year in quarantine in a PEQ Zoo following importation without showing clinical evidence of foot-and-mouth disease, rinderpest, or other communicable disease that is exotic to the United States or for which APHIS has an eradication or control program in 9 CFR chapter I, and determines that the receiving zoological park is accredited by the American Zoo and Aquarium Association (AZA), or the receiving zoological park has facilities and procedures in place related to preventing the spread of communicable animal diseases (including but not limited to procedures for animal identification, record keeping, and veterinary care) that are equivalent to those required for AZA accreditation. The Administrator will approve the movement of a carcass, body part, or biological specimen derived from an imported animal subject to this agreement if the Administrator determines that the animal has spent at least one year in quarantine in a PEQ Zoo following importation without showing clinical evidence of foot-and-foot mouth disease, rinderpest, or other communicable disease that is exotic to the United States or for which APHIS has an eradication or control program in 9 CFR chapter I, and determines that the carcass, body part, or biological specimen will be moved only for scientific research or museum display purposes.

____

(Signature of importer)

Subscribed and sworn to before me this ___ day of ___, ___

____

(Title or designation)

____

(Name of zoological park)

By ______________________________

(Signature of officer of zoological park)

____

(Title of officer)

Subscribed and sworn to before me this ___ day of ___, ___

____

(Title or designation)

(Approved by the Office of Management and Budget under control number 0579–0040)

[55 FR 31495, Aug. 2, 1990, as amended at 59 FR 28216, June 1, 1994; 59 FR 31924, June 21, 1994; 59 FR 67615, Dec. 30, 1994; 62 FR 23638, May 1, 1997. Redesignated and amended at 62 FR 56012, 56020, Oct. 28, 1997; 68 FR 6344, Feb. 7, 2003]

§93.505 Certificate for swine.

(a) All swine offered for importation from any part of the world except as provided in §93.517 shall be accompanied by a certificate of a salaried veterinary officer of the national government of the region of origin, or if exported from Mexico, shall be accompanied either by such a certificate or by a certificate issued by a veterinarian accredited by the National Government of Mexico and endorsed by a full-time salaried veterinary officer of the National Government of Mexico, thereby representing that the veterinarian issuing the certificate was authorized to do so, stating that such swine have been kept in said region at least 60 days immediately preceding the date of movement therefrom and that said region during such period has been entirely free from foot-and-mouth disease, rinderpest, contagious pleuropneumonia, and surra: *Provided, however*, That certificates for wild swine for exhibition purposes need specify freedom from the said diseases of the district of origin only: *And provided further*, That in the case of swine the certificate, as far as it relates to contagious pleuropneumonia, may specify freedom from such disease of the district of origin only. For domestic swine, the certificate shall also show that the entire region of origin is free of African swine fever and swine vesicular disease and that, for 60 days immediately preceding the time of movement from the premises of origin, no swine erysipelas or swine plague has existed on such premises or on adjoining premises. Additionally, except for the APHIS-defined European CSF region, as defined in § 94.0 of this subchapter, for which additional certification is required under § 94.24(b)(6), for domestic swine the certificate shall show that the entire region of origin is free of classical swine fever.

(b) Swine from any region where screwworm is considered to exist may only be imported into the United States if they meet the requirements of paragraphs (b)(1) through (b)(4) of this section and all other applicable requirements of this part. APHIS will maintain a list of regions where screwworm is considered to exist on the APHIS Web site at *http://www.aphis.usda.gov/import_export/animals/ animal_disease_status.shtml.* Copies of the list will also be available via postal mail, fax, or email upon request to the Sanitary Trade Issues Team, National Center for Import and Export, Veterinary Services, Animal and Plant Health Inspection Service, 4700 River Road Unit 38, Riverdale, Maryland 20737. APHIS will add a region to the list upon determining that screwworm exists in the region based on reports APHIS receives of detections of the pest from veterinary officials of the exporting country, from the World Organization for Animal Health (OIE), or from other sources the Administrator determines to be reliable. APHIS will remove a region from the list after conducting an evaluation of the region in accordance with § 92.2 of this subchapter and finding that screwworm is not present in the region. In the case of a region formerly not on this list that is added due to a detection, the region may be removed from the list in accordance with the procedures for reestablishment of a region's disease-free status in § 92.4 of this subchapter.

(1) A veterinarian must treat the swine with ivermectin 3 to 5 days prior to the date of export to the United States according to the recommended dose prescribed on the product's label.

(2) The swine must be fully examined for screwworm by a full-time salaried veterinary official of the exporting country within 24 hours prior to shipment to the United States. If swine are found to be infested with screwworm, they must be treated until free from infestation.

(3) At the time swine are loaded onto a means of conveyance for export, a veterinarian must treat any visible wounds on the animals with a solution of coumaphos dust at a concentration of 5 percent active ingredient.

(4) The swine must be accompanied to the United States by a certificate signed by a full-time salaried veterinary official of the exporting country. The certificate must state that the swine have been thoroughly examined and found free of screwworm and that the swine have been treated in accordance with paragraphs (b)(1) and (b)(3) of this section.

(c) If swine are unaccompanied by the certificate as required by paragraph (a) of this section, or if such swine are found upon inspection at the port of entry to be affected with a communicable disease or to have been exposed thereto, they shall be refused entry and shall be handled or quarantined, or otherwise disposed of as the Administrator may direct.

(Approved by the Office of Management and Budget under control number 0579–0165)

[55 FR 31495, Aug. 2, 1990, as amended at 57 FR 28081, June 24, 1992. Redesignated and amended at 62 FR 56012, 56020, Oct. 28, 1997; 65 FR 67623, Nov. 13, 2000; 67 FR 11565, Mar. 15, 2002; 68 FR 6344, Feb. 7, 2003; 68 FR 16938, Apr. 7, 2003; 71 FR 29070, May 19, 2006; 71 FR 31069, June 1, 2006; 72 FR 67232, Nov. 28, 2007; 73 FR 50878, Aug. 29, 2008; 76 FR 70039, Nov. 10, 2011; 77 FR 1391, Jan. 10, 2012]

§ 93.506 Declaration and other documents for swine.

(a) The certificates, declarations, and affidavits required by the regulations in this part shall be presented by the importer or his or her agent to the collector of customs at the port of entry, upon arrival of swine at such port, for the use of the veterinary inspector at the port of entry.

(b) For all swine offered for importation, the importer or his or her agent shall first present two copies of a declaration which shall list the port of entry, the name and address of the importer, the name and address of the broker, the origin of the swine, the number, breed, species, and purpose of the importation, the name of the person to whom the swine will be delivered, and the location of the place to which such delivery will be made.

(c) Any declaration, permit, or other document for swine required under this subpart may be issued and presented using a U.S. Government electronic information exchange system or other authorized method.

[55 FR 31495, Aug. 2, 1990, as amended at 81 FR 40151, June 21, 2016]

§93.507 Inspection at the port of entry.

Inspection shall be made at the port of entry of all swine imported from any part of the world except as provided in §93.519. All swine found to be free from communicable disease and not to have been exposed thereto within 60 days prior to their exportation to the United States shall be admitted subject to the other provisions in this part; all other swine shall be refused entry. Swine refused entry, unless exported within a time fixed in each case by the Administrator, and in accordance with other provisions he or she may require in each case for their handling shall be disposed of as the Administrator may direct. Such portions of the transporting vessel, and of its cargo, which have been exposed to any such swine or their emanations shall be disinfected in such manner as may be considered necessary by the inspector in charge at the port of entry, to prevent the introduction or spread of livestock or poultry disease, before the cargo is allowed to land.

[55 FR 31495, Aug. 2, 1990. Redesignated and amended at 62 FR 56012, 56020, Oct. 28, 1997; 68 FR 6344, Feb. 7, 2003]

§93.508 Articles accompanying swine.

No litter or manure, fodder or other aliment, nor any equipment such as boxes, buckets, ropes, chains, blankets, or other things used for or about swine governed by the regulations in this part, shall be landed from any conveyance except under such restrictions as the inspector in charge at the port of entry shall direct.

§93.509 Movement from conveyances to quarantine station.

Platforms and chutes used for handling imported swine shall be cleaned and disinfected under APHIS supervision after being so used. The said swine shall not be unnecessarily moved over any highways nor allowed to come in contact with other swine, but shall be transferred from the conveyance to the quarantine grounds in boats, cars, or vehicles approved by the inspector in charge at the port of entry. Such cars, boats, or vehicles shall be cleaned and disinfected under APHIS supervision immediately after such use, by the carrier moving the same. The railway cars so used shall be either cars reserved for this exclusive use or box cars not otherwise employed in the transportation of swine or their fresh products. When movement of the aforesaid swine upon or across a public highway is unavoidable, it shall be under such careful supervision and restrictions as the inspector in charge at the port of entry and the local authorities may direct.

§93.510 Quarantine requirements.

Swine shall be quarantined for not less than 15 days, counting from the date of arrival at the port of entry. During their quarantine, wild swine shall be subject to such inspections, disinfection, blood tests, or other tests as may be required by the Administrator, to determine their freedom from disease and the infection of disease.

§93.511 Swine quarantine facilities.

(a) *Privately operated quarantine facilities.* The importer, or his or her agent, of swine subject to quarantine under the regulations in this part shall arrange for acceptable transportation to the privately operated quarantine facility and for the care, feed, and handling of the swine from the time of unloading at the quarantine port to the time of release from quarantine. Such arrangements shall be agreed to in advance by the Administrator. All expenses resulting therefrom or incident thereto shall be the responsibility of the importer; APHIS assumes no responsibility with respect thereto. The quarantine facility must be suitable for the quarantine of such swine and must be approved by the Administrator prior to the issuance of any import permit. The facilities occupied by swine should be kept clean and sanitary to the satisfaction of the inspector assigned to supervise the quarantine. If for any cause the care, feed, or handling of swine, or the sanitation of the facilities, is neglected, in the opinion of the inspector assigned to supervise the quarantine, such services may be furnished by APHIS in the same manner as though arrangements had been made for such services as provided by paragraph (b) of this section, and/or the swine may be disposed of as the Administrator, may direct, including sale in accordance with the procedure described in paragraph (b) of this section. The importer, or his or her agent, shall request in writing such inspection and other services as may be required, and shall waive all claim against the United States and APHIS or any employee of APHIS for damages which may arise from such services. The Administrator, may prescribe reasonable rates for the services provided under this paragraph. When it is found necessary to extend the usual minimum quarantine period, the importer, or his or her agent, shall be so advised in writing and shall pay for such additional quarantine and other services required. Payment for all services received by the importer, or his or her agent, in connection with each separate lot of swine shall be made by certified check or U.S. money order prior to release of the swine. If such payment is not made, the swine may be sold in accordance with the procedure described in paragraph (b) of this section, or otherwise disposed of as directed by the Administrator.

(b) *Quarantine facilities maintained by APHIS.* The importer, or his or her agent, of swine subject to quarantine under the regulations in this part shall arrange for acceptable transportation to the quarantine facility, and for the care, feed, and handling of the swine from the time they arrive at the quarantine facility, and for the care, feed, and handling of the swine from the time they arrive at the quarantine port to the time of release from quarantine. Such arrangements shall be agreed to in advance by the Administrator. The importer or his or her agent shall request in writing such inspection and other services as may be required, and shall waive all claim against the United States and APHIS or any employee of APHIS, for damages which may arise from such services. All expenses resulting therefrom or incident thereto shall be the responsibility of the importer; APHIS assumes no responsibility with respect thereto. The Administrator may prescribe reasonable rates for the services provided under this paragraph. When it is found necessary to extend the usual minimum quarantine period, the importer, or his or her agent, shall be so advised in writing and shall pay for such additional quarantine and other services required. Payment for services received by the importer, or his or her agent, in connection with each separate lot of swine shall be made by certified check or U.S. money order prior to release of the swine. If such payment is not made, the swine may be sold in accordance with the procedure described in this paragraph or otherwise disposed of as directed by the Administrator. When payment is not made and the swine are to be sold to recover payment for services received, the importer, or his or her agent, will be notified by the inspector that if said charges are not immediately paid or satisfactory arrangements made for payment, the swine will be sold at public sale to pay the expense of care, feed, and handling during that period. The sale will be held after the expiration of the quarantine period, at such time and place as may be designated by the General Services Administration or other designated selling agent. The proceeds of the sale, after deducting the charges for care, feed, and handling of the swine and other expenses, including the expense of the sale, shall be held in a Special Deposit Account in the United States Treasury for 6 months from the date of sale. If not claimed by the importer, or his or her agent, within 6 months from the date of sale, the amount so held shall be transferred from the Special Deposit Account to the General Fund Account in the United States Treasury.

(c) Amounts collected from the importer, or his or her agent, for service rendered shall be deposited so as to be available for defraying the expenses involved in this service.

§93.512 Quarantine stations, visiting restricted; sales prohibited.

Visitors shall not be admitted to the quarantine enclosure during any time that swine are in quarantine except that an importer (or his or her accredited agent or veterinarian) may be admitted to the yards and buildings containing his or her quarantined swine at such intervals as may be deemed necessary, and under such conditions and restrictions as may be imposed, by the inspector in charge of the quarantine station. On the last day of the quarantine period, owners, officers or registry societies, and others having official business or whose services may be necessary in the removal of the swine may be admitted upon written permission from the said inspector. No exhibition or sale shall be allowed within the quarantine grounds.

§93.513 Milk from quarantined swine.

Milk or cream from swine quarantined under the provisions of this part shall not be used by any person other than those in charge of such swine, nor be fed to any animals other than those within the same enclosure, without permission of the inspector in charge of the quarantine station and subject to such restrictions as he or she may consider necessary to each instance. No milk or cream shall be removed from the quarantine premises except in compliance with all State and local regulations.

§93.514 Manure from quarantined swine.

No manure shall be removed from the quarantine premises until the release of the swine producing same.

§93.515 Appearance of disease among swine in quarantine.

If any contagious disease appears among swine during the quarantine period special precautions shall be taken to prevent spread of the infection to other animals in the quarantine station or to those outside the grounds. The affected swine shall be disposed of as the Administrator may direct, depending upon the nature of the disease.

CANADA[7]

§93.516 Import permit and declaration for swine.

(a) For swine intended for importation from Canada, the importer shall first apply for and obtain from APHIS an import permit as provided in §93.504: *Provided*, That an import permit is not required for swine offered for entry at a land border port designated in §93.503(b) if such swine:

(1) Was born in Canada or the United States, and has been in no region other than Canada or the United States, or

(2) Has been legally imported into Canada from some other region and unconditionally released in Canada so as to be eligible to move freely within that region without restriction of any kind and has been in Canada after such release for 60 days or longer.

(b) For all swine offered for importation from Canada, the importer or his or her agent shall present two copies of a declaration as provided in §93.506.

[55 FR 31495, Aug. 2, 1990. Redesignated and amended at 62 FR 56012, 56020, Oct. 28, 1997]

§93.517 Swine from Canada.

(a) *For purposes other than immediate slaughter*. Swine offered for importation from Canada for purposes other than immediate slaughter shall be accompanied by a certificate issued or endorsed by a salaried veterinarian of the Canadian Government showing that said swine have been inspected on the premises of origin immediately before the date of movement therefrom and found to be free of evidence of communicable disease and that, as far as it has been possible to determine, they were not exposed to any such disease during the preceding 60 days; in addition, the certificate shall show that no classical swine fever or swine plague has existed on the premises of origin or on adjoining premises for such 60 days.

(b) *For immediate slaughter*. Swine for immediate slaughter may be imported from Canada without certification as

[7] Importations from Canada shall be subject to §§93.516 to 93.519, inclusive, in addition to other sections in this part which are in terms applicable to such importations.

prescribed in paragraph (a) of this section but shall be subject to the provisions of §§ 93.507, 93.516, and 93.518.

[55 FR 34195, Aug. 2, 1990. Redesignated and amended at 62 FR 56012, 56020, Oct. 28, 1997; 68 FR 16938, Apr. 7, 2003]

§ 93.518 Swine from Canada for immediate slaughter.

Swine imported from Canada for immediate slaughter shall be consigned from the port of entry directly to a recognized slaughtering establishment and there be slaughtered within two weeks from the date of entry. As used in this section, "directly" means without unloading en route if moved in a means of conveyance, or without stopping if moved in any other manner.

[55 FR 31495, Aug. 2, 1990, as amended at 59 FR 28216, June 1, 1994. Redesignated at 62 FR 56012, Oct. 28, 1997]

§ 93.519 Special provisions.

(a) *In-bond shipments from Canada.* (1) Swine from Canada transported in-bond through the United States for immediate export shall be inspected at the border port of entry and, when accompanied by an import permit obtained under § 93.504 of this part and all conditions therein are observed, shall be allowed entry into the United States and shall be otherwise handled as provided in paragraph (b) of § 93.501. Swine not accompanied by a permit shall meet the requirements of this part in the same manner as swine destined for importation into the United States, except that the Administrator may permit their inspection at some other point when he or she finds that such action will not increase the risk that communicable diseases of livestock and poultry will be disseminated to the livestock or poultry of the United States.

(2) *In-transit shipments through Canada.* Swine originating in the United States and transported directly through Canada may re-enter the United States without Canadian health or test certificates when accompanied by copies of the United States export health certificates properly issued and endorsed in accordance with regulations in part 91 of this chapter: *Provided,* That, to qualify for entry, the date, time, port of entry, and signature of the Canadian Port Veterinarian that inspected the swine for entry into Canada shall be recorded on the United States health certificate, or a document containing the information shall be included with the certificate that accompanies the swine. In all cases it shall be determined by the veterinary inspector at the United States port of entry that the swine are the identical swine covered by said certificate.

(b) *Exhibition swine.* Swine from the United States which have been exhibited at the Royal Agricultural Winter Fair at Toronto or other publicly recognized expositions in Canada, including racing, rodeo, circus, or stage exhibitions in Canada, and have not been in that region for more than 90 days are eligible for return to the United States without Canadian health or test certificates, if they are accompanied by copies of the United States health certificate, issued and endorsed in accordance with the export regulations contained in Part 91 of this chapter for entry into Canada: *Provided,* That all swine offered for re-entry upon examination by the veterinary inspector at the U.S. port of entry, are found by the inspector to be free of communicable diseases and exposure thereto and are determined to be the identical swine covered by said certificates or are the natural increase of such swine born after official test dates certified on the dam's health certificate.

(Approved by the Office of Management and Budget under control number 0579–0020)

[55 FR 31495, Aug. 2, 1990, as amended at 59 FR 67133, Dec. 29, 1994. Redesignated and amended at 62 FR 56012, 56020, Oct. 28, 1997; 81 FR 40151, June 21, 2016]

CENTRAL AMERICA AND WEST INDIES [8]

§ 93.520 Import permit and declaration for swine.

For all swine offered for importation from countries of Central America or of the West Indies, the importer or his

[8] Importations from regions of Central America and the West Indies shall be subject to § 93.520, in addition to other sections in this part, which are in terms applicable to such importations.

or her agent shall present two copies of a declaration as provided in §93.506.

[55 FR 34195, Aug. 2, 1990. Redesignated and amended at 62 FR 56012, 56020, Oct. 28, 1997]

MEXICO [9]

§93.521 Declaration for swine.

For all swine offered for importation from Mexico, the importer or his or her agent shall present two copies of a declaration as provided in §93.506.

[55 FR 34195, Aug. 2, 1990. Redesignated and amended at 62 FR 56012, 56020, Oct. 28, 1997]

Subpart F—Dogs

§93.600 Importation of dogs.

(a) *All dogs.* Dogs from any region of the world where screwworm is considered to exist may only be imported into the United States if they meet the requirements of paragraphs (a)(1) and (2) of this section and all other applicable requirements of this part. APHIS will maintain a list of regions where screwworm is considered to exist on the APHIS Web site at *http://www.aphis.usda.gov/import_export/animals/animal_disease_status.shtml.* Copies of the list will also be available via postal mail, fax, or email upon request to the Sanitary Trade Issues Team, National Center for Import and Export, Veterinary Services, Animal and Plant Health Inspection Service, 4700 River Road Unit 38, Riverdale, Maryland 20737. APHIS will add a region to the list upon determining that screwworm exists in the region based on reports APHIS receives of detections of the pest from veterinary officials of the exporting country, from the World Organization for Animal Health (OIE), or from other sources the Administrator determines to be reliable. APHIS will remove a region from the list after conducting an evaluation of the region in accordance with §92.2 of this subchapter and finding that screwworm is not present in the region. In the case of a region formerly not on this list that is added due to a detection, the region may be removed from the list in accordance with the procedures for reestablishment of a region's disease-free status in §92.4 of this subchapter.

(1) Dogs must be accompanied by a certificate signed by a full-time salaried veterinary official of the region of origin stating that the dog has been inspected for screwworm within 5 days preceding its shipment to the United States.

(2) The certificate must state that the dog is either free from screwworm or was found to be infested with screwworm and was held in quarantine and treated until free from screwworm prior to leaving the region of origin.

(b) *Dogs for handling livestock.* Collie, Shepherd, and other dogs that are imported from any part of the world except Canada, Mexico, and regions of Central America and the West Indies and that are to be used in the handling of sheep or other livestock must be inspected and quarantined at the port of entry for a sufficient time to determine their freedom from tapeworm (*Taenia* spp.). If found to be infested with tapeworm, dogs must be treated under the supervision of an inspector at the port of entry until they are free from infestation.

(Approved by the Office of Management and Budget under control number 0579–0165)

[65 FR 67623, Nov. 13, 2000, as amended at 67 FR 11565, Mar. 15, 2002; 73 FR 50878, Aug. 29, 2008; 77 FR 1391, Jan. 10, 2012]

Subpart G—Miscellaneous Animals

SOURCE: 60 FR 55181, unless otherwise noted. Redesignated at 62 FR 56012, Oct. 28, 1997.

§93.700 Definitions.

Wherever in this subpart the following terms are used, unless the context otherwise requires, they shall be construed, respectively, to mean:

Administrator. The Administrator of the Animal and Plant Health Inspection Service or any other employee of the Animal and Plant Health Inspection Service, United States Department of Agriculture, delegated to act in the Administrator's stead.

[9] Importations from Mexico shall be subject to §93.521, in addition to other sections in this subpart, which are in terms applicable to such importations.

Animal and Plant Health Inspection Service. The Animal and Plant Health Inspection Service of the United States Department of Agriculture (APHIS).

Brushtail possum. Vulpine phalangers (*Trichosurus vulpecula*) of the family Phalangeridae.

Delivery. The transfer of goods or interest in goods from one person to another.

Enter (entry). To introduce into the commerce of the United States after release from government detention.

Hedgehog. All members of the family Erinaceidae.

Import (imported, importation). To bring into the territorial limits of the United States.

Inspector. An employee of the Animal and Plant Health Inspection Service authorized to perform duties required under this subpart.

Person. Any individual, corporation, company, association, firm, partnership, society, or joint stock company.

Region. Any defined geographic land area identifiable by geological, political, or surveyed boundaries. A region may consist of any of the following:

(1) A national entity (country);

(2) Part of a national entity (zone, county, department, municipality, parish, Province, State, etc.)

(3) Parts of several national entities combined into an area; or

(4) A group of national entities (countries) combined into a single area.

Tenrec. All members of the family Tenrecidae.

United States. All of the States of the United States, the District of Columbia, Guam, the Northern Mariana Islands, Puerto Rico, the Virgin Islands of the United States, and all other territories and possessions of the United States.

[55 FR 34195, Aug. 2, 1990. Redesignated and amended at 62 FR 56012, 56020, Oct. 28, 1997]

§ 93.701 Prohibitions.

(a) No person may import a hedgehog or tenrec into the United States from any region designated in §94.1 of this chapter as a region where foot-and-mouth disease exists.

(b) No person may import a brushtail possum or hedgehog into the United States from New Zealand.

(c) No person may import leopard tortoise (*Geochelone pardalis*), African spurred tortoise (*Geochelone sulcata*), or Bell's hingeback tortoise (*Kinixys belliana*) into the United States.

[55 FR 31495, Aug. 2, 1990. Redesignated and amended at 56012, 56021, Oct. 28, 1997; 65 FR 15218, Mar. 22, 2000]

§ 93.702 Restrictions.

Hedgehogs and tenrecs not specifically prohibited from being imported under § 93.701 may be imported into the United States only in accordance with the regulations in this subpart.

[55 FR 31495, Aug. 2, 1990. Redesignated and amended at 62 FR 56012, 56021, Oct. 28, 1997]

§ 93.703 Ports designated for importation.

(a) Any person importing a hedgehog or tenrec into the United States may import it, except as provided in paragraph (b) of this section, only through the following ports:

(1) *Air and ocean ports.* Anchorage and Fairbanks, AK; San Diego and Los Angeles, CA; Denver, CO; Jacksonville, Miami, St. Petersburg-Clearwater, and Tampa, FL; Atlanta, GA; Chicago, IL; New Orleans, LA; Portland, ME; Baltimore, MD; Boston, MA; Minneapolis, MN; Great Falls, MT; Newburgh, NY; Portland, OR; San Juan, PR; Galveston and Houston, TX; and Seattle, Spokane, and Tacoma, WA.

(2) *Canadian border ports.* Eastport, ID; Houlton and Jackman, ME; Detroit, Port Huron, and Sault Ste. Marie, MI; Opheim, Raymond, and Sweetgrass, MT; Alexandria Bay, Buffalo, and Champlain, NY; Dunseith, Pembina, and Portal, ND; Derby Line and Highgate Springs, VT; Oroville and Sumas, WA.

(3) *Mexican border ports.* Douglas, Naco, Nogales, Sasabe, and San Luis, AZ; Calexico and San Ysidro, CA; Antelope Wells, and Columbus, NM; and Brownsville, Hidalgo, Laredo, Eagle Pass, Del Rio, Presidio, and El Paso, TX.

(b) The Secretary of the Treasury has approved the designation, as inspection stations, of the ports specified in paragraph (a) of this section. In special cases, the Administrator may designate other ports as inspection stations in accordance with this section, with the concurrence of the Secretary of the Treasury.

[60 FR 55181, Oct. 30, 1995. Redesignated at 62 FR 56012, Oct. 28, 1997, as amended at 65 FR 38178, June 20, 2000; 67 FR 68022, Nov. 8, 2002]

§93.704 Import permit.

(a) *General requirements.* No person may import a hedgehog or tenrec into the United States unless it is accompanied by an import permit issued by APHIS and is imported into the United States within 30 days after the proposed date of arrival stated in the import permit. The importer or his or her agent must notify the inspector at the port of first arrival of the date of arrival at least 72 hours before the hedgehog or tenrec arrives in the United States.

(b) *Import permit required.* Any person who desires to import a hedgehog or tenrec must submit an application (VS Form 17–129) for an import permit. Applications are available from the Import-Export Animals Staff, National Center for Import-Export, Veterinary Services, APHIS, 4700 River Road Unit 39, Riverdale, MD 20737–1231 or by visiting *http://www.aphis.usda.gov/animal_health/permits/*. A separate application must be prepared for each shipment.

(c) *Application for an import permit.* The importer must complete, sign, and date the application for an import permit, which must include the following information:

(1) The name and address of the shipper in the region of origin of the hedgehog or tenrec intended for importation into the United States.

(2) The name, address, and telephone number of the importer.

(3) The port of embarkation.

(4) The region from which the hedgehog or tenrec will be shipped to the United States.

(5) The mode of transportation.

(6) The number, breed, species, and descriptions of the hedgehogs or tenrecs to be imported.

(7) The purpose of the importation.

(8) The route of travel, including all carrier stops en route.

(9) The proposed shipping and arrival dates.

(10) The port of first arrival in the United States.

(11) The name, mailing address, and telephone number of the person to whom the hedgehog or tenrec will be delivered in the United States.

(12) The location of the place where delivery will be made in the United States.

(13) Any remarks regarding the shipment.

(d) *Issuance of an import permit.* Upon receipt of the application, APHIS will review the application. If the hedgehog or tenrec appears to be eligible to be imported into the United States, APHIS will issue an import permit indicating the applicable requirements under this subpart for the importation of the hedgehog or tenrec. Even though an import permit has been issued for the importation of a hedgehog or tenrec, the animal may enter the United States only if all other applicable requirements of this subpart have been met.

(Approved by the Office of Management and Budget under control number 0579–0040)

[55 FR 31495, Aug. 2, 1990. Redesignated and amended at 62 FR 56012, 56021, Oct. 28, 1997; 81 FR 40151, June 21, 2016]

§93.705 Health certificate.

(a) No person may import a hedgehog or tenrec into the United States unless it is accompanied by a health certificate either issued by a full-time salaried veterinary officer of the national government of the exporting region or issued by a veterinarian authorized or accredited by the national government of the exporting region and endorsed by a full-time salaried veterinary officer of the national government of that region. The health certificate must contain the names and street addresses of the consignor and consignee and must state:

(1) That the hedgehog or tenrec originated in a region that has been recognized as free of foot-and-mouth disease by the USDA;

(2) That the hedgehog or tenrec has never been in a region where foot-and-mouth disease exists;

(3) That the hedgehog or tenrec has not been commingled with any other hedgehog or tenrec that originated in or has ever been in a region where foot-and-mouth disease exists;

(4) That the hedgehog or tenrec was inspected by the individual issuing the health certificate and was found free of any ectoparasites not more than 72 hours before being loaded on the means of conveyance which transported the animal to the United States;

(5) That all body surfaces of the hedgehog or tenrec were treated for ectoparasites under the supervision of the veterinarian issuing the health certificate at least 3 days but not more than 14 days before being loaded on the means of conveyance that transported the animal to the United States;

(6) That the pesticide and the concentration used would kill the types of ectoparasites that may infest the animal to be imported;

(7) That the hedgehog or tenrec, after being treated for ectoparasites in accordance with paragraphs (a)(5) and (a)(6) of this section, had physical contact only with, or shared a pen or bedding materials only with, treated hedgehogs or tenrecs in the same shipment to the United States; and

(8) The name and concentration of the pesticide used to treat the hedgehog or tenrec.

(b) [Reserved]

(Approved by the Office of Management and Budget under control number 0579–0040)

[55 FR 31495, Aug. 2, 1990. Redesignated and amended at 62 FR 56012, 56021, Oct. 28, 1997]

§ 93.706 Notification of arrival.

Upon the arrival of a hedgehog or tenrec at the port of first arrival in the United States, the importer or his or her agent must present the import permits and health certificates required by this subpart to the collector of customs for the use of the inspector at that port.

§ 93.707 Inspection at the port of first arrival.

(a) A hedgehog or tenrec from any part of the world must be inspected by an APHIS inspector at the port of first arrival. Subject to the other provisions in this subpart, a shipment of hedgehogs or tenrecs may enter the United States only if each hedgehog or tenrec in the shipment is found free of ectoparasites and any clinical signs of communicable diseases.

(b) If any hedgehog or tenrec in a shipment is found to be infested with ectoparasites or demonstrates any clinical signs of communicable diseases, then the entire shipment will be refused entry. The importer will be given the following options:

(1) Remove the shipment from the United States; or

(2) Release the shipment to the U.S. Department of Agriculture. The Administrator will destroy or otherwise dispose of the shipment as necessary to prevent the possible introduction into the United States of communicable animal diseases.

Subpart H—Elephants, Hippopotami, Rhinoceroses, and Tapirs

§ 93.800 Definitions.

The following terms, when used in this part, shall be construed as defined. Those terms used in the singular form in this part shall be construed as the plural form and vice versa, as the case may demand.

Accredited veterinarian. A veterinarian approved by the Administrator in accordance with part 161 of this chapter to perform functions specified in parts 1, 2, 3, and 11 of this chapter, and subchapters B, C, and D of this chapter; and to perform functions required by cooperative State-Federal disease control and eradication programs.

Administrator. The Administrator, Animal and Plant Health Inspection Service, or any person authorized to act for the Administrator.

Animal and Plant Health Inspection Service. The Animal and Plant Health Inspection Service of the United States Department of Agriculture (APHIS).

APHIS representative. A veterinarian or other person employed by APHIS in animal health activities, who is authorized to perform the function involved.

Enter (entered, entry) into the United States. To introduce into the commerce of the United States after release from government detention.

Import (imported, importation) into the United States. To bring into the territorial limits of the United States.

Incinerate (incinerated). To reduce to ash by burning.

Inspector. An employee of APHIS who is authorized to perform the function involved.

Person. Any individual, corporation, company, association, firm, partnership, society, joint stock company, or any other legal entity.

Region. Any defined geographic land area identifiable by geological, political, or surveyed boundaries. A region may consist of any of the following:

(1) A national entity (country);

(2) Part of a national entity (zone, county, department, municipality, parish, Province, State, etc.)

(3) Parts of several national entities combined into an area; or

(4) A group of national entities (countries) combined into a single area.

United States. All of the several States of the United States, the District of Columbia, Guam, the Northern Mariana Islands, Puerto Rico, the Virgin Islands of the United States, and all other territories and possessions of the United States.

United States health certificate. An official document issued by an APHIS representative or an accredited veterinarian at the point of origin of a movement of animals. It must show the identification tag, tattoo, or registration number of each animal to be moved; the age and sex of each animal to be moved; the number of animals covered by the document; the points of origin and destination; the consignor; and the consignee.

Veterinary Services. The Veterinary Services unit of the Animal and Plant Health Inspection Service of the United States Department of Agriculture.

[52 FR 29502, Aug. 10, 1987, as amended at 57 FR 23048, 23049, June 1, 1992. Redesignated and amended at 62 FR 56012, 56021, Oct. 28, 1997]

§93.801 Prohibitions.

Elephants, hippopotami, rhinoceroses, or tapirs shall not be imported or entered into the United States unless in accordance with this part.

[52 FR 29502, Aug. 10, 1987. Redesignated at 62 FR 56012, Oct. 28, 1997]

§93.802 Import permit.

(a) An elephant, hippopotamus, rhinoceros, or tapir shall not be imported into the United States unless accompanied by an import permit issued by APHIS and unless imported into the United States within 30 days after the proposed date of arrival stated in the import permit. The port veterinarian must be notified of the date of arrival at least 72 hours before the animal arrives in the United States.

(b) An application for an import permit may be obtained from the Import-Export Animals Staff, National Center for Import-Export, Veterinary Services, APHIS, 4700 River Road Unit 38, Riverdale, MD 20737–1231 or by visiting *http://www.aphis.usda.gov/animal_health/permits/*.

(c) The completed application shall include the following information:

(1) The name and address of the person intending to export an elephant, hippopotamus, rhinoceros, or tapir to the United States;

(2) The name and address of the person intending to import an elephant, hippopotamus, rhinoceros, or tapir into the United States;

(3) The species, breed, and number of elephants, hippopotami, rhinoceroses, or tapirs to be imported;

(4) The purpose of the importation;

(5) The port of embarkation;

(6) The name and concentration of the pesticide intended to be used to treat the elephant, hippopotamus, rhinoceros, or tapir for ectoparasites prior to the animal being transported to the United States;

(7) The mode of transportation;

(8) The route of travel;

(9) The port of entry in the United States and, if applicable, the address of the facility to be provided by the importer for inspection, treatment, and incineration pursuant to §93.6 of this part;

(10) The proposed date of arrival in the United States; and

(11) The name and address of the person to whom the elephant, hippopotamus, rhinoceros, or tapir will be delivered in the United States.

(d) After receipt and review of the application by APHIS, an import permit indicating the applicable conditions under this part for importation into the United States shall be issued for the importation of the elephant, hippopotamus, rhinoceros, or tapir described in the application if such animal appears to be eligible to be imported. Even though an import permit has been issued for the importation of an elephant, hippopotamus, rhinoceros, or tapir, the animal may be imported only if all applicable requirements of this part are met.

[52 FR 29502, Aug. 10, 1987, as amended at 57 FR 23049, June 1, 1992; 59 FR 67615, Dec. 30, 1994. Redesignated at 62 FR 56012, Oct. 28, 1997; 81 FR 40151, June 21, 2016]

§ 93.803 Health certificate.

(a) An elephant, hippopotamus, rhinoceros, or tapir shall not be imported into the United States unless accompanied by a health certificate either signed by a salaried veterinarian of the national veterinary services of the region where the inspection and treatment required by this section occurred or signed by a veterinarian authorized by the national veterinary services of such region and endorsed by a salaried veterinarian of the national veterinary services of such region (the endorsement representing that the veterinarian signing the health certificate was authorized to do so), certifying:

(1) That the elephant, hippopotamus, rhinoceros, or tapir was inspected by the individual signing the health certificate and found free of any ectoparasites not more than 72 hours before being loaded on the means of conveyance which transported the animal to the United States; and

(2) That the elephant, hippopotamus, rhinoceros, or tapir was treated for ectoparasites at least 3 days but not more than 14 days before being loaded on the means of conveyance which transported the animal to the United States. The animal shall have been treated, under the supervision of the individual signing the health certificate, by being thoroughly wetted with a pesticide applied with either a sprayer with a hand-held nozzle, a spray-dip machine, or a dip vat; and

(3) That the elephant, hippopotamus, rhinoceros, or tapir, after being treated for ectoparasites in accordance with paragraph (a)(2) of this section, did not have physical contact with or share a pen or bedding materials with any elephant, hippopotamus, rhinoceros, or tapir not in the same shipment to the United States; and

(4) The name and concentration of the pesticide used to treat the animal (such pesticide and the concentration used must be adequate to kill the types of ectoparasites likely to infest the animal to be imported; a list of recommended pesticides and concentrations may be obtained from the Animal and Plant Health Inspection Service, Veterinary Services, National Center for Import-Export, 4700 River Road Unit 38, Riverdale, Maryland 20737–1231; and

(5) The name and address of the consignor and consignee.

[52 FR 29502, Aug. 10, 1987; 52 FR 35350, Sept. 18, 1987, as amended at 57 FR 23049, June 1, 1992; 59 FR 67615, Dec. 30, 1994. Redesignated and amended at 62 FR 56012, 56021, Oct. 28, 1997]

§ 93.804 Declaration upon arrival.

Upon arrival of an elephant, hippopotamus, rhinoceros, or tapir at a port of entry, the importer or the importer's agent shall notify APHIS of the arrival by giving an inspector a completed VS Form 17–29, "Declaration of Importation for Animals, Animal Semen, Birds, Poultry, and Eggs for Hatching." (This form is available from the Animal and Plant Health Inspection Service, Veterinary Services, National Center for Import-Export, 4700 River Road Unit 38, Riverdale, Maryland 20737–1231 or by visiting *http://www.aphis.usda.gov/animal_health/permits/*.) Forms may be provided to the inspector using a U.S. Government electronic information exchange system or other authorized method. The completed form must state:

(a) The port of entry;

(b) The date of arrival;

(c) The import permit number;

(d) The name of the carrier and identification of the means of conveyance;

(e) The name and address of the importer;

(f) The name and address of the broker;

(g) The region from which the elephant, hippopotamus, rhinoceros, or tapir was shipped;

(h) The number, species, and purpose of importation of the elephant, hippopotamus, rhinoceros, or tapir; and

(i) The name and address of the person to whom the elephant, hippopotamus, rhinoceros, or tapir will be delivered.

[52 FR 29502, Aug. 10, 1987; 52 FR 35350, Sept. 18, 1987, as amended at 57 FR 23049, June 1, 1992; 59 FR 67615, Dec. 30, 1994. Redesignated and amended at 62 FR 56012, 56021, Oct. 28, 1997, as amended at 81 FR 40151, June 21, 2016]

§ 93.805 Ports of entry, inspection, and treatment.[1]

(a) An elephant, hippopotamus, rhinoceros, or tapir shall be imported into the United States only:

(1) At Los Angeles, California; Miami, Florida; and Newburgh, New York; or

(2) On a case-by-case basis, at another port of entry if:

(i) The animals will be inspected and treated at a facility provided by the importer;

(ii) The Administrator has determined that the importer's facility is adequate for inspection, treatment, and incineration required under this section;

(iii) The Administrator has determined that an inspector is available to perform at the importer's facility the services that are required under this section; and

(iv) The Administrator has determined that an inspector is available to perform at the port of entry the services that are required under this section if the animals will be inspected and treated at a facility provided by the importer.

(b) An elephant, hippopotamus, rhinoceros, or tapir shall be entered into the United States only under the following conditions:

(1) Any documents accompanying the animal shall be subject to inspection by an inspector at the port of entry;

(2) If the animal is to be moved from the port of entry to a facility provided by the importer:

(i) At the port of entry the animal shall be subject to as much inspection by an inspector as is feasible and shall be sprayed or dipped, as feasible, under the supervision of an inspector and with a permitted dip listed in § 72.13(b) of this chapter;

(ii) At the port of entry, as much hay, straw, feed, bedding, and other material as can feasibly be removed from the shipping crate or vehicle containing the animal shall be removed, sealed in plastic bags, and incinerated by the importer under the supervision of an inspector;

(iii) At the port of entry, the shipping crate or the vehicle containing the animal shall be sealed by an inspector with an official seal of the United States Department of Agriculture:

(iv) If the animal is moved from the port of entry in a shipping crate, plastic must be fastened around the shipping crate so that all animal waste, hay, straw, feed, bedding, and other material accompanying the animal are retained inside the crate, but not so as to interefere with ventilation, feeding, and watering of the animal;

(v) After the arrival of the animal at the facility provided by the importer, the seal shall be broken by an inspector;

(3) The animal shall be inspected by an inspector within 24 hours of being unloaded at the port of entry or at a facility provided by the importer, and shall be treated under the supervision of an inspector, as follows:

(i) The animal shall be removed from its shipping crate or cargo hold, placed on a concrete or other nonporous surface, and physically inspected for ectoparasites by an inspector. If inspection and treatment are not performed upon unloading, the animal must be isolated from all other animals, except those in the same shipment, and kept in a facility with a nonporous floor and where any ectoparasites that may drop off the animal can be contained and destroyed, until the animal has been inspected and treated;

(ii) If the inspector finds no ectoparasites, the animal shall be

[1] Importers must also meet all requirements of the U.S. Department of the Interior regulations relevant to the importation of elephants, hippopotami, rhinoceroses, and tapirs, including regulations concerning ports of entry.

sprayed or dipped one time in accordance with label instructions with a permitted dip listed in § 72.13(b) of this chapter; or

(iii) If the inspector finds ectoparasites, the animal shall be sprayed or dipped in accordance with label instructions with a permitted dip listed in § 72.13(b) of this chapter for as many times as necessary until the inspector finds no ectoparasites; and thereafter the animal shall be sprayed or dipped one additional time in accordance with label instructions with a permitted dip listed in § 72.13(b) of this chapter;

(4) All hay, straw, feed, bedding, and other material that has been placed with the animal at any time prior to the final treatment referred to in paragraph (b)(3) of this section, and any plastic sheet used to wrap any shipping crate, shall be sealed in plastic bags and incinerated under the supervision of an inspector;

(5) Any shipping crate shall be, under the supervision of an inspector, either cleaned and disinfected using a disinfectant listed in § 71.10 of this chapter or incinerated; and if the shipping crate is cleaned and disinfected, it shall then be treated under the supervision of an inspector with a permitted dip listed in § 72.13(b) of this chapter;

(6) Any means of conveyance used to transport an animal not in a shipping crate shall be, under the supervision of an inspector, cleaned and disinfected using a disinfectant listed in § 71.10 of this chapter and then treated with a permitted dip listed in § 72.13(b) of this chapter.

[52 FR 29502, Aug. 10, 1987, as amended at 57 FR 23049, June 1, 1992. Redesignated at 62 FR 56012, Oct. 28, 1997; 65 FR 38178, June 20, 2000]

§ 93.806 Animals refused entry.

Any elephant, hippopotamus, rhinoceros, or tapir refused entry into the United States for noncompliance with the requirements of this part shall be removed from the United States within a time period specified by the Administrator or shall be considered abandoned by the importer, and pending removal or abandonment, the animal shall be subject to such safeguards as the inspector determines necessary to prevent the possible introduction of ectoparasites into the United States. If such animal is not removed from the United States within such time period or is abandoned, it may be seized, destroyed, or otherwise disposed of as the Administrator determines necessary to prevent the possible introduction of ectoparasites into the United States.

[52 FR 29502, Aug. 10, 1987, as amended at 57 FR 23049, June 1, 1992. Redesignated at 62 FR 56012, Oct. 28, 1997]

§ 93.807 Other importations.

(a) Elephants, hippopotami, rhinoceroses, and tapirs are exempt from the regulations in this part under the following circumstances:

(1) They are imported from Canada and are accompanied by a document signed by a salaried veterinarian of the Canadian Government that states:

(i) They were not imported into Canada during the year preceding their importation into the United States; and

(ii) They did not, during the year preceding their importation into the United States, have physical contact with or share a pen or bedding materials with any elephant, hippopotamus, rhinoceros, or tapir imported into Canada during that year; or

(2) They were exported into Canada from the United States and then imported back into the United States accompanied by a United States health certificate.

(b) Notwithstanding other provisions in this part, the Administrator may in specific cases allow the importation and entry of elephants, hippopotami, rhinoceroses, or tapirs into the United States other than as provided for in this part under such conditions as the Administrator may prescribe to prevent the introduction of ectoparasites into the United States.

(Approved by the Office of Management and Budget under control number 0579–0020)

[52 FR 29502, Aug. 10, 1987; 52 FR 35350, Sept. 18, 1987, as amended at 57 FR 23049, June 1, 1992; 59 FR 67133, Dec. 29, 1994. Redesignated at 62 FR 56012, Oct. 28, 1997, as amended at 64 FR 23179, Apr. 30, 1999]

Subpart I—Aquatic Animal Species

SOURCE: 71 FR 51435, Aug. 30, 2006, unless otherwise noted.

§93.900 Definitions.

Wherever in this subpart the following terms are used, unless the context otherwise requires, they shall be construed, respectively, to mean:

Administrator. The Administrator, Animal and Plant Health Inspection Service, or any person authorized to act for the Administrator.

Animal and Plant Health Inspection Service. The Animal and Plant Health Inspection Service of the United States Department of Agriculture (APHIS).

APHIS representative. A veterinarian or other individual employed by the Animal and Plant Health Inspection Service, United States Department of Agriculture, who is authorized to perform the services required by this part.

Certifying official. An individual authorized by the competent authority of a country to sign health certificates for aquatic animals.

Competent authority. The national veterinary services or other authority of a country, having the responsibility and competence for ensuring or supervising the implementation of aquatic animal health measures.

Container. A transport receptacle that is specially constructed to facilitate transportation of aquatic animals or aquatic animal products by one or several means of transport.

Department. The United States Department of Agriculture (USDA).

Fertilized egg. A viable fertilized ovum of an aquatic animal.

Gamete. The sperm or unfertilized egg of aquatic animals that is held or transported separately.

Inspector. An employee of the Animal and Plant Health Inspection Service authorized to perform duties required under this subpart.

Person. Any individual, corporation, company, association, firm, partnership, society or joint stock company.

Port veterinarian. A veterinarian employed by the Animal and Plant Health Inspection Service to perform duties required under this subpart at a port of entry.

Region. Any defined geographic land area identifiable by geological, political, or surveyed boundaries. A region may consist of any of the following:

(1) A national entity (country);

(2) Part of a national entity (zone, county, department, municipality, parish, Province, State, etc.);

(3) Parts of several national entities combined into an area; or

(4) A group of national entities (countries) combined into a single area.

Spring viremia of carp (SVC). A disease caused by infection with spring viremia of carp virus, a rhabodivrus capable of infecting several carp species, in addition to some other cyprinid and ictalurid fish species.

SVC-susceptible species. Common carp (*Cyprinus carpio*), grass carp (*Ctenopharyngodon idellus*), silver carp (*Hypophthalmichthys molitrix*), bighead carp (*Aristichthys nobilis*), Crucian carp (*Carassius carassius*), goldfish (*Carassius auratus*), tench (*Tinca tinca*), and sheatfish (*Silurus glanis*).

United States. All of the States of the United States, the District of Columbia, Guam, Northern Mariana Islands, Puerto Rico, the Virgin Islands of the United States, and all other territories and possessions of the United States.

§93.901 General restrictions; exceptions.

(a) No live fish, fertilized eggs, or gametes of SVC-susceptible species may be imported into the United States except in accordance with this subpart,[11] nor shall any such live fish, fertilized eggs, or gametes be moved from the port of entry after arrival until released by the port veterinarian; provided that the Administrator may, upon request in specific cases, allow the importation of SVC-susceptible live fish, fertilized eggs, or gametes under conditions other than those set

[11] The importation of live cultures of SVC virus, preserved SVC virus viral RNA or DNA, tissue samples containing viable SVC virus, or other specimens intended for diagnostic or research purposes and which contain viable SVC virus may be imported only under permit in accordance with 9 CFR part 122.

forth in this subpart when the Administrator determines that such movement will not result in the introduction of SVC into the United States.

(b) Other provisions of this subpart relating to the importation of live fish, fertilized eggs, and gametes shall not apply to shipments of SVC-susceptible species of live fish, fertilized eggs, or gametes in transit through the United States if an import permit has been obtained under § 93.903 and all conditions of the permit are observed; and if the live fish, fertilized eggs, and gametes are handled as follows:

(1) They are maintained under continuous confinement while in transit through the United States aboard an aircraft, ocean vessel, or other means of conveyance; or

(2) They are unloaded, in the course of such transit, into a holding facility[12] that is provided by the carrier or its agent and has been approved by the Administrator in accordance with paragraph (b)(4) of this section as adequate to prevent the spread within the United States of any finfish disease; they are maintained there under continuous confinement until loaded aboard a means of conveyance for transportation from the United States; and are maintained under continuous confinement aboard such means of conveyance until it leaves the United States.

(3) They are moved in accordance with any additional conditions prescribed in the permit and determined by the Administrator to be necessary to ensure that the live fish, fertilized eggs, or gametes through the United States do not introduce SVC into the United States.

(4) For a holding facility to be approved by the Administrator:

(i) The holding facility must be sufficiently isolated to prevent direct or indirect contact of the live fish, fertilized eggs, or gametes it contains with any other SVC-susceptible species in the United States;

(ii) The holding facility must be constructed to provide adequate protection against environmental conditions and so that it can be adequately cleaned, washed and disinfected;

(iii) Provision must be made for disposal of fish carcasses, shipping water, waste and any associated shipping materials in a manner that will prevent dissemination of disease;

(iv) Provision must be made for adequate sources of feed and water and for attendants for the care and feeding of live fish, fertilized eggs, or gametes in the facility;

(v) The holding facility must comply with all applicable local, State and Federal requirements for environmental quality.

(vi) The holding facility must comply with any additional requirements that may be imposed by the Administrator for a particular shipment if necessary to prevent the dissemination of disease.

(Approved by the Office of Management and Budget under control number 0579–0301)

[71 FR 51435, Aug. 30, 2006; 71 FR 54552, Sept. 15, 2006]

§ 93.902 Ports designated for the importation of live fish, fertilized eggs, and gametes.

(a) The following ports are designated as ports of entry for live fish, fertilized eggs, and gametes of SVC-susceptible species imported under this subpart:

(1) *Air and ocean ports.* Los Angeles and San Francisco, CA; Miami and Tampa, FL; Atlanta, GA; Honolulu, HI; Chicago, IL; Boston, MA; Newark, NJ; New York, NY; Portland, OR; Dallas-Ft. Worth, TX; and San Juan, PR.

(2) *Canadian border ports.* Detroit, MI; Buffalo-Niagara, NY; and Blaine and Seattle, WA.

(3) *Mexican border ports.* Otay Mesa, CA.

(b) *Designation of other ports.* Other ports may be designated by the Administrator in specific cases with the concurrence of the Secretary of the Department of Homeland Security.

§ 93.903 Import permits for live fish, fertilized eggs, and gametes.

(a) Live fish, fertilized eggs, or gametes of SVC-susceptible species imported into the United States must be accompanied by an import permit

[12] Requests for approval of such facilities should be made to the Animal and Plant Health Inspection Service at the address provided in § 93.903 for permit applications.

issued by APHIS and must be imported within 30 days after the proposed date of arrival stated in the import permit.

(b) An application for an import permit must be submitted for each shipment of live fish, fertilized eggs, or gametes of SVC-susceptible species to the Animal and Plant Health Inspection Service, Veterinary Services, National Center for Import and Export, 4700 River Road Unit 38, Riverdale, MD 20737–1231. Application forms for import permits may be obtained from this address.

(c) A completed application shall include the following information:

(1) The name and address of the person intending to export live fish, fertilized eggs, or gametes of SVC-susceptible species to the United States;

(2) The proposed date of shipment to the United States;

(3) The name and address of the person intending to import live fish, fertilized eggs, or gametes of SVC-susceptible species into the United States;

(4) The species and number of live fish, fertilized eggs, or gametes of SVC-susceptible species to be imported into the United States;

(5) The purpose of the importation;

(6) The port of embarkation;

(7) The mode of transportation;

(8) The route of travel, including all carrier stops en route;

(9) The port of entry in the United States;

(10) The proposed date of arrival in the United States; and

(11) The name and address of the person to whom the live fish, fertilized eggs, or gametes of SVC-susceptible species will be delivered in the United States.

(d) If APHIS determines that the live fish, fertilized eggs, or gametes are eligible for importation, APHIS will issue an import permit indicating the applicable conditions for importation. An import permit does not guarantee that any live fish, fertilized eggs, or gametes will be allowed entry into the United States; the fish, fertilized eggs, or gametes will be allowed to enter the United States only if they meet all applicable requirements of the permit and regulations.

(Approved by the Office of Management and Budget under control number 0579–0301)

§93.904 Health certificate for live fish, fertilized eggs, and gametes.

(a) *General.* All live fish, fertilized eggs, and gametes of SVC-susceptible species that are imported from any region of the world must be accompanied by a health certificate issued by a full-time salaried veterinarian of the national government of the exporting region, or issued by a certifying official and endorsed by the competent authority of that country. The health certificate must be written in English or contain an English translation. The health certificate will be valid for 30 days from the date of issuance. The health certificate for the live fish, fertilized eggs, or gametes must state that:

(1) The live fish, fertilized eggs, or gametes were inspected by the veterinarian or certifying official who issued the certificate within 72 hours prior to shipment, and were found to be free of any clinical signs of disease consistent with SVC; and

(2) The live fish, fertilized eggs, or gametes covered by the health certificate meet the requirements of this section.

(b) *Surveillance.* The live fish, fertilized eggs, or gametes must meet the following conditions to be eligible for importation into the United States:

(1) The live fish, fertilized eggs, or gametes must originate in a region or establishment which conducts a surveillance program for SVC under the supervision of the competent authority.

(2) The region or establishment must demonstrate freedom from SVC through a minimum of 2-years' continuous health history, supported by laboratory testing by a pathogen detection facility approved for SVC viral assays by the competent authority.

(3) SVC-susceptible fish populations in the region or establishment must be tested at least twice annually, with at least 3 months between the tests and at times or under environmental conditions that would facilitate the detection of SVCV if it were present. Sampling procedures must utilize an assumed pathogen prevalence of 2 percent, with a corresponding confidence level of 95 percent. Samples must be collected and submitted by a certifying official or veterinarian recognized by

the competent authority. The standard screening method for SVC must include isolation of SVCV in cell culture, using either the epithelioma papulosum cyprini (EPC) or fathead minnow (FHM) cell lines. However, the Administrator may authorize other assays for SVCV detection in lieu of virus isolation through cell culture, if the Administrator determines that such assays provide equivalent assurance of the SVC status of an exporting region or establishment. All viral testing results must be negative.

(c) *Shipping containers*. All live fish, fertilized eggs, and gametes must be shipped to the United States in new containers or in used containers that have been cleaned and disinfected in accordance with this section.

(1) Cleaning and disinfection of shipping containers must take place under the supervision of the veterinarian or certifying official who issues the health certificate.

(2) Cleaning and disinfection must be sufficient to neutralize any SVC virus to which shipping containers may have been exposed. Acceptable disinfection procedures include individual or combination treatments with: Solutions having a pH of 12 or higher or 3 or lower with a contact time of at least 10 minutes; heat at or above 56 °C for at least 15 minutes; chlorine solutions having a concentration of at least 500 ppm with a contact time of at least 10 minutes; iodine solutions having a concentration of at least 100 ppm with a contact time of at least 10 minutes; ultraviolet exposure (254 nm; min exposure of 10,000 microwatt seconds/cm^2); or other disinfectants such as Virkon used according to the manufacturer's directions. The Administrator may authorize other procedures if the Administrator determines they are adequate to neutralize the SVC virus.

(3) Cleaning and disinfection protocols must be referenced in the health certificate or in a separate cleaning and disinfection certificate accompanying the shipment to the U.S. port of entry.

(Approved by the Office of Management and Budget under control number 0579–0301)

§ 93.905 Declaration and other documents for live fish, fertilized eggs, and gametes.

(a) For all live fish, fertilized eggs, and gametes offered for importation under this subpart, the importer or his or her agent must submit the following documents to the collector of customs for use by the port veterinarian:

(1) All permits, certificates, or other documentation required by this subpart; and

(2) Two copies of a declaration that lists the port of entry, the name and address of the importer, the name and address of the broker, the origin of the live fish, fertilized eggs, or gametes, the number, species, and the purpose of the importation, the name of the person to whom the fish will be delivered, and the location of the place to which such delivery will be made.

(b) Any declaration, permit, or other document for live fish, fertilized eggs, and gametes required under this subpart may be issued and presented using a U.S. Government electronic information exchange system or other authorized method.

(Approved by the Office of Management and Budget under control number 0579–0301)

[71 FR 51435, Aug. 30, 2006, as amended at 81 FR 40152, June 21, 2016]

§ 93.906 Inspection at the port of entry.

(a) All live fish, fertilized eggs, and gametes of SVC-susceptible species imported from any part of the world must be presented for inspection at a port of entry designated under § 93.902. The APHIS port veterinarian must be notified at least 72 hours in advance of the arrival in the United States of a shipment of live fish, fertilized eggs, or gametes of SVC-susceptible species. Any shipment of live SVC-susceptible fish species that the port veterinarian determines to exhibit clinical signs consistent with SVCV infection or disease, or any shipments of live fish, fertilized eggs, and gametes of SVC-susceptible species that otherwise do not meet the requirements of this subpart, shall be refused entry.

(b) Shipments refused entry, unless exported within a time fixed in each case by the Administrator, and in accordance with other provisions he or she may require in each case for their handling, shall be disposed of as the Administrator may direct.

(Approved by the Office of Management and Budget under control number 0579–0301)

PART 94—RINDERPEST, FOOT-AND-MOUTH DISEASE, NEWCASTLE DISEASE, HIGHLY PATHOGENIC AVIAN INFLUENZA, AFRICAN SWINE FEVER, CLASSICAL SWINE FEVER, SWINE VESICULAR DISEASE, AND BOVINE SPONGIFORM ENCEPHALOPATHY: PROHIBITED AND RESTRICTED IMPORTATIONS

Sec.

AUTHORITY: 7 U.S.C. 450, 7701–7772, 7781–7786, and 8301–8317; 21 U.S.C. 136 and 136a; 31 U.S.C. 9701; 7 CFR 2.22, 2.80, and 371.4.

§94.0 Definitions.

As used in this part, the following terms shall have the meanings set forth in this section.

Administrator. The Administrator, Animal and Plant Health Inspection Service, or any person authorized to act for the Administrator.

Animal and Plant Health Inspection Service. The Animal and Plant Health Inspection Service, of the United States Department of Agriculture (APHIS.)

APHIS representative. An individual employed by Animal and Plant Health Inspection Service, United States Department of Agriculture, who is authorized to perform the function involved.

APHIS-defined EU Poultry Trade Region. The European Union Member States of Austria, Belgium, Cyprus, the Czech Republic, Denmark, Estonia, Finland, France, Germany, Greece, Hungary, Ireland, Italy, Latvia, Lithuania, Luxembourg, Malta, the Netherlands, Poland, Portugal, Slovakia, Slovenia, Spain, Sweden, and the United Kingdom (England, Scotland, Wales, the Isle of Man, and Northern Ireland).

APHIS-defined European CSF region. A single region of Europe recognized by APHIS as low risk for classical swine fever.

(1) A list of areas included in the region is maintained on the APHIS Web site at *http://www.aphis.usda.gov/import_export/animals/animal_disease_status.shtml.* Copies of the list will also be available via postal mail, fax, or email upon request to the Sanitary Trade Issues Team, National Center for Import and Export, Veterinary Services, Animal and Plant Health Inspection Service, 4700 River Road Unit 38, Riverdale, Maryland 20737.

(2) APHIS will add an area to the region after it conducts an evaluation of the area to be added in accordance with § 92.2 of this subchapter and finds that the risk profile for the area is equivalent with respect to classical swine fever to the risk profile for the region it is joining.

Approved establishment means an establishment authorized by Veterinary Services for the receipt and handling of restricted imported animal carcasses, products, and byproducts.

Authorized inspector. Any individual authorized by the Administrator of APHIS or the Commissioner of Customs and Border Protection, Department of Homeland Security, to enforce the regulations in this part.

Birds. All members of the class Aves (other than poultry or game birds).

Bovine. Bos taurus, Bos indicus, and *Bison bison.*

Bovine spongiform encephalopathy (BSE) minimal-risk region. A region that:

(1) Maintains, and, in the case of regions where BSE was detected, had in place prior to the detection of BSE in an indigenous ruminant, risk mitigation measures adequate to prevent widespread exposure and/or establishment of the disease. Such measures include the following:

(i) Restrictions on the importation of animals sufficient to minimize the possibility of infected ruminants being imported into the region, and on the importation of animal products and animal feed containing ruminant protein sufficient to minimize the possibility of ruminants in the region being exposed to BSE;

(ii) Surveillance for BSE at levels that meet or exceed recommendations of the World Organization for Animal Health (Office International des Epizooties) for surveillance for BSE; and

(iii) A ruminant-to-ruminant feed ban that is in place and is effectively enforced.

(2) In regions where BSE was detected, conducted an epidemiological investigation following detection of BSE sufficient to confirm the adequacy of measures to prevent the further introduction or spread of BSE, and continues to take such measures.

(3) In regions where BSE was detected, took additional risk mitigation measures, as necessary, following the BSE outbreak based on risk analysis of the outbreak, and continues to take such measures.

Cold spot. The area in a flexible plastic cooking tube or other type of container loaded with meat product, or the areas at various points along the belt in an oven chamber, slowest to reach the required temperature during the cooking process. The cold spot(s) for each container is experimentally determined before the cooking process begins, and once identified, remains constant.

Commercial birds. Birds that are imported for resale, breeding, public display, or any other purpose, except pet birds, zoological birds, research birds, or performing or theatrical birds.

Commercial poultry. Chickens, doves, ducks, geese, grouse, guinea fowl, partridges, pea fowl, pheasants, pigeons, quail, swans, and turkeys (including eggs for hatching) which are imported for resale, breeding, public display, or any other commercial purpose.

Contact. Known or potential commingling of products during processing or storage, or while being transported from any point to any other point. Contact includes the simultaneous processing in the same room, locker, or container, but not necessarily the same storage facility or conveyance, as long as adequate security measures are taken to prevent commingling, as determined by an authorized APHIS representative.

Container. For the purposes of § 94.1(c) and § 94.16(c), this term means a receptacle, sometimes refrigerated, which is designed to be filled with cargo, sealed, and then moved, without unsealing or unloading, aboard a variety of different transporting carriers.

Department. The United States Department of Agriculture (USDA, Department).

Direct transloading. The transfer of cargo directly from one means of conveyance to another.

Exporting region. A region from which shipments are sent to the United States.

Farm equipment. Equipment used in the production of livestock or crops, including, but not limited to, mowers, harvesters, loaders, slaughter machinery, agricultural tractors, farm engines, farm trailers, farm carts, and farm wagons, but excluding automobiles and trucks.

Flock of origin. The flock in which the eggs were produced.

Food Safety and Inspection Service. The Food Safety and Inspection Service (FSIS) of the United States Department of Agriculture.

FSIS inspector. An individual authorized by the Administrator, Food Safety and Inspection Service, United States Department of Agriculture, to perform the function involved.

Game birds. Migratory birds, including certain ducks, geese, pigeons, and doves ("migratory" refers to seasonal flight to and from the United States); free-flying quail, wild grouse, wild pheasants (as opposed to those that are commercial, domestic, or pen-raised).

Highly pathogenic avian influenza (HPAI). Highly pathogenic avian influenza is defined as follows:

(1) Any influenza virus that kills at least 75 percent of eight 4- to 6-week-old susceptible chickens within 10 days following intravenous inoculation with 0.2 mL of a 1:10 dilution of a bacteria-free, infectious allantoic fluid or inoculation of 10 susceptible 4- to 8-week-old chickens resulting in an intravenous pathogenicity index (IVPI) of greater than 1.2;

(2) Any H5 or H7 virus that does not meet the criteria in paragraph (1) of this definition, but has an amino acid sequence at the haemagglutinin cleavage site that is compatible with highly pathogenic avian influenza viruses; or

(3) Any influenza virus that is not an H5 or H7 subtype and that kills one to five out of eight inoculated chickens and grows in cell culture in the absence of trypsin within 10 days.

House. A structure, enclosed by walls and a roof, in which poultry are raised.

Immediate export. The period of time determined by APHIS, based on shipping routes and timetables, to be the shortest practicable interval of time between the arrival in the United States of an incoming carrier and the departure from the United States of an outgoing carrier, to transport a consignment of products.

Import (imported, importation) into the United States. To bring into the territorial limits of the United States.

Indicator piece. A cube or slice of meat to be used for the pink juice test, required to meet minimum size specifications.

Mechanically separated meat. A finely comminuted product resulting from the mechanical separation and removal of most of the bone from attached skeletal muscle of bovine carcasses that meets the FSIS specifications contained in 9 CFR 319.5.

Newcastle disease. Newcastle disease is an acute, rapidly spreading, and usually fatal viral infection of poultry caused by an avian paramyxovirus serotype 1 that meets one of the following criteria for virulence: The virus has an intracerebral pathogenicity index (ICPI) in day-old chicks (*Gallus gallus*) of 0.7 or greater; or multiple basic amino acids have been demonstrated in the virus (either directly or by deduction) at the C-terminus of the F2 protein and phenylalanine at residue 117, which is the N-terminus of the F1 protein. The term "multiple basic amino acids" refers to at least three arginine or lysine residues between residues 113 and 116. In this definition, amino acid residues are numbered from the N-terminus of the amino acid sequence deduced from the nucleotide sequence of the F0 gene; 113–116 corresponds to residues −4 to −1 from the cleavage site. Failure to demonstrate the characteristic pattern of amino acid residues as described above may require characterization of the isolated virus by an ICPI test. A failure to detect a cleavage site that is consistent with virulent strains does not confirm the absence of a virulent virus.

Operator. The operator responsible for the day-to-day operations of a facility.

Personal use. Only for personal consumption or display and not distributed further or sold.

Pink juice test. Determination of whether meat has been thoroughly cooked by observation of whether the flesh and juices have lost all red and pink color.

Port of arrival. Any place in the United States at which a product or article arrives, unless the product or article remains on the means of conveyance on which it arrived within the territorial limits of the United States.

Positive for a transmissible spongiform encephalopathy. A sheep or goat for which a diagnosis of a transmissible spongiform encephalopathy has been made.

Poultry. Chickens, turkeys, swans, partridges, guinea fowl, pea fowl; nonmigratory ducks, geese, pigeons, and doves; commercial, domestic, or pen-raised grouse, pheasants, and quail.

Processed animal protein. Meat meal, bone meal, meat-and-bone meal, blood meal, dried plasma and other blood products, hydrolyzed protein, hoof meal, horn meal, poultry meal, feather meal, fish meal, and any other similar products.

Premises of origin. The premises where the flock of origin is kept.

Region. Any defined geographic land area identifiable by geological, political, or surveyed boundaries. A region may consist of any of the following:

(1) A national entity (country);

(2) Part of a national entity (zone, county, department, municipality, parish, Province, State, etc.)

(3) Parts of several national entities combined into an area; or

(4) A group of national entities (countries) combined into a single area.

Region of origin. For meat and meat products, the region in which the animal from which the meat or meat products were derived was born, raised and slaughtered; and for eggs, the region in which the eggs were laid.

Restricted zone for classical swine fever. An area, delineated by the relevant competent veterinary authorities of the region in which the area is located, that surrounds and includes the location of an outbreak of classical swine fever in domestic swine or detection of the disease in wild boar, and from which the movement of domestic swine is prohibited.

Ruminants. All animals that chew the cud, such as cattle, buffaloes, sheep, goats, deer, antelopes, camels, llamas and giraffes.

Sentinel bird. A chicken that has been raised in an environment free of pathogens that cause communicable diseases of poultry and that has not been infected with, exposed to, or immunized with any strain of virus that causes Newcastle disease.

Specified risk materials (SRMs) from regions of controlled risk for BSE. Those bovine parts considered to be at particular risk of containing the BSE agent in infected animals, as listed in the FSIS regulations at 9 CFR 310.22(a).

Specified risk materials (SRMs) from regions of undetermined risk for BSE. Those bovine parts considered to be at particular risk of containing the BSE agent in infected animals, as listed in the FSIS regulations at 9 CFR 310.22(a), except that the following bovine parts from regions of undetermined risk for BSE are considered SRMs if they are derived from bovines over 12 months of age: Brain, skull, eyes, trigeminal ganglia, spinal cord, vertebral column (excluding the vertebrae of the tail, the transverse processes of the thoracic and lumbar vertebrae, and the wings of the sacrum), and the dorsal root ganglia.

State. Any of the several States of the United States, the Commonwealth of the Northern Mariana Islands, the Commonwealth of Puerto Rico, the District of Columbia, Guam, the Virgin Islands of the United States, or any other territory or possession of the United States.

Suspect for a transmissible spongiform encephalopathy. (1) A sheep or goat that has tested positive for a transmissible spongiform encephalopathy or for the proteinase resistant protein associated with a transmissible spongiform encephalopathy, unless the animal is designated as positive for a transmissible spongiform encephalopathy; or

(2) A sheep or goat that exhibits any of the following signs and that has been determined to be suspicious for a transmissible spongiform encephalopathy by a veterinarian: Weight loss despite retention of appetite; behavior abnormalities; pruritus (itching); wool pulling; biting at legs or side; lip smacking; motor abnormalities such as incoordination, high stepping gait of forelimbs, bunny hop movement of rear legs, or swaying of back end; increased sensitivity to noise and sudden movement; tremor, "star gazing," head pressing, recumbency, or other signs of neurological disease or chronic wasting.

Temperature indicator device (TID). A precalibrated temperature-measuring instrument containing a chemical compound activated at a specific temperature (the melting point of the chemical compound) identical to the processing temperature that must be reached by the meat being cooked. The Administrator will approve a TID for use after determining that the chemical compound in the device is activated at the specific temperature required.

Thoroughly cooked. Heated sufficiently to inactivate any pathogen that may be present, as indicated by the required TID or pink juice test.

United States. All of the States.

Veterinarian in Charge. The veterinary official of the Animal and Plant Health Inspection Service, United States Department of Agriculture, who is assigned by the Administrator to supervise and perform the official animal health work of the Animal and Plant Health Inspection Service in the State or area concerned.

Wild swine. Any swine which are allowed to roam outside an enclosure.

[52 FR 33801, Sept. 8, 1987]

EDITORIAL NOTE: For FEDERAL REGISTER citations affecting §94.0, see the List of CFR Sections Affected, which appears in the Finding Aids section of the printed volume and at *www.fdsys.gov.*

§94.1 Regions where rinderpest or foot-and-mouth disease exists; importations prohibited.

(a) APHIS considers rinderpest or foot-and-mouth disease to exist in all regions of the world except those declared free of one or both of these diseases by APHIS.

(1) A list of regions that APHIS has declared free of rinderpest and a list of regions APHIS has declared free of foot and mouth disease are maintained on the APHIS Web site at *http://www.aphis.usda.gov/import_export/animals/ animal_disease_status.shtml.* Copies of the list will also be available via postal mail, fax, or email upon request to the Sanitary Trade Issues Team, National Center for Import and Export, Veterinary Services, Animal and Plant Health Inspection Service, 4700 River Road Unit 38, Riverdale, Maryland 20737.

(2) APHIS will add a region to the list of those it has declared free of rinderpest or foot-and-mouth disease, or both, after it conducts an evaluation of the region in accordance with §92.2 of this subchapter and finds that the disease, or diseases, are not present. In the case of a region formerly on this list that is removed due to an outbreak, the region may be returned to the list in accordance with the procedures for reestablishment of a region's disease-free status in §92.4 of this subchapter. APHIS will remove a region from the list of those it has declared free of rinderpest or foot-and-mouth disease upon determining that the disease exists in the region based on reports APHIS receives of outbreaks of the disease from veterinary officials of

the exporting country, from the World Organization for Animal Health (OIE), or from other sources the Administrator determines to be reliable.

(b) The importation of any ruminant or swine or any fresh (chilled or frozen) meat of any ruminant or swine[1] that originates in any region where rinderpest or foot-and-mouth disease exists, as designated in paragraph (a) of this section, or that enters a port in or otherwise transits a region in which rinderpest or foot-and-mouth disease exists, is prohibited:

(1) Except as provided in part 93 of this chapter for wild ruminants and wild swine;

(2) Except as provided in paragraph (d) of this section for fresh (chilled or frozen) meat of ruminants or swine that is otherwise eligible for importation under this part but that enters a port or otherwise transits a region where rinderpest or foot-and-mouth disease exists; and

(3) Except as provided in § 94.4 of this part for cooked or cured meat from regions where rinderpest or foot-and-mouth disease exists.

(4) Except as provided in § 94.29 for fresh (chilled or frozen) beef and ovine meat.

(c) The importation of any used farm equipment that originates in any region where rinderpest or foot-and-mouth disease exists, as designated in paragraph (a) of this section, is prohibited, unless the equipment is accompanied by an original certificate signed by an authorized official of the national animal health service of the exporting region that states that the equipment, after its last use and prior to export, was steam-cleaned free of all exposed dirt and other particulate matter. Such farm equipment is subject to APHIS inspection at the port of arrival. If it is found during such inspection to contain any exposed dirt or other particulate matter, it will be denied entry into the United States, unless, in the judgment of the APHIS inspector, the amount of exposed soil is minimal enough to allow cleaning at the port of arrival, and there are adequate facilities and personnel at the port to conduct such cleaning without risk of disease contamination.

(d) Except as otherwise provided in this part, fresh (chilled or frozen) meat of ruminants or swine raised and slaughtered in a region free of foot-and-mouth disease and rinderpest, as designated in paragraph (a) of this section, and fresh (chilled or frozen) beef and ovine meat exported in accordance with § 94.29, which during shipment to the United States enters a port or otherwise transits a region where rinderpest or foot-and-mouth disease exists, may be imported provided that all of the following conditions are met:

(1) The meat is accompanied by the foreign meat inspection certificate required by § 327.4 of this title and, upon arrival of the meat in the United States, the foreign meat inspection certificate is presented to an authorized inspector at the port of arrival;

(2) The meat is placed in the transporting carrier in a hold, compartment, or, if the meat is containerized, in a container that which was sealed in the region of origin by an official of such region with serially numbered seals approved by APHIS, so as to prevent contact of the meat with any other cargo, handling of the meat after the hold, compartment, or container is sealed, and the loading of any cargo into and the removal of any cargo from the sealed hold, compartment, or container en route to the United States;

(3) If any foreign official breaks a seal applied in the region of origin in order to inspect the meat, he or she then reseals the hold, compartment, or container with a new serially numbered seal; and, if any member of a ship's crew breaks a seal, the serial number of the seal, the location of the seal, and the reason for breaking the seal are recorded in the ship's log.

(4) The serial numbers of the seals used to seal the hold, compartment, or container are recorded on the foreign meat inspection certificate which accompanies the meat;

(5) Upon arrival of the carrier in the United States port of arrival, the seals are found by an APHIS representative to be intact, and the representative

[1] Importation of animals and meat includes bringing the animals or meat within the territorial limits of the United States on a means of conveyance for use as sea stores or for other purposes.

finds that there is no evidence indicating that any seal has been tampered with; *Provided that,* if the representative finds that any seal has been broken or has a different number than is recorded on the foreign meat inspection certificate, then the meat may remain eligible for entry into the United States only if APHIS personnel are available to inspect the hold, compartment, or container, the packages of meat, and all accompanying documentation; and the importer furnishes additional documentation (either copies of pages from the ship's log signed by the officer-in-charge, or certification from a foreign government that the original seal was removed and the new seal applied by officials of that government) that demonstrates to the satisfaction of the Administrator that the meat was not contaminated or exposed to contamination during movement from the region of origin to the United States; and

(6) The meat is found by an authorized inspector to be as represented on the foreign meat inspection certificate.

(Approved by the Office of Management and Budget under control numbers 0579–0015 and 0579–0195)

[30 FR 12118, Sept. 23, 1965]

EDITORIAL NOTE: For FEDERAL REGISTER citations affecting § 94.1, see the List of CFR Sections Affected, which appears in the Finding Aids section of the printed volume and at *www.fdsys.gov.*

§ 94.2 Fresh (chilled or frozen) products (other than meat), and milk and milk products of ruminants and swine.

(a) The importation of fresh (chilled or frozen) products (other than meat and milk and milk products) derived from ruminants or swine, originating in, shipped from, or transiting any region designated in § 94.1(a) as a region affected with rinderpest or foot-and-mouth disease is prohibited, except as provided in § 94.3 and parts 95 and 96 of this chapter.

(b) The importation of milk and milk products of ruminants and swine originating in, shipped from, or transiting any region designated in § 94.1(a) as a region affected with rinderpest or foot-and-mouth disease is prohibited, except as provided in § 94.16.

[40 FR 44123, Sept. 25, 1975, as amended at 62 FR 56022, Oct. 28, 1997; 77 FR 1392, Jan. 10, 2012]

§ 94.3 Organs, glands, extracts, or secretions of ruminants or swine.

The importation of fresh (chilled or frozen) organs, glands, extracts, or secretions derived from ruminants or swine, originating in any region where rinderpest or foot-and-mouth disease exists, as designated in § 94.1, except for pharmaceutical or biological purposes under conditions prescribed by the Administrator in each instance, is prohibited.

[28 FR 5980, June 13, 1963, as amended at 53 FR 48520, Dec. 1, 1988; 62 FR 56022, Oct. 28, 1997; 63 FR 67574, Dec. 8, 1998]

§ 94.4 Cured or cooked meat from regions where rinderpest or foot-and-mouth disease exists.

(a) The importation of cured meats derived from ruminants or swine, originating in any region where rinderpest or foot-and-mouth disease exists, as designated in § 94.1, is prohibited unless the following conditions have been fulfilled:

(1) All bones shall have been completely removed in the region of origin.

(2) The meat shall have been held in an unfrozen, fresh condition for at least 3 days immediately following the slaughter of the animals from which it was derived.

(3)(i) The meat shall have been thoroughly cured and fully dried in such manner that it may be stored and handled without refrigeration, as in the case of salami and other summer sausages, tasajo, xarque, or jerked beef, bouillon cubes, dried beef, and Westphalia, Italian and similar type hams. The term "fully dried" as used in this paragraph means dried to the extent that the water-protein ratio in the wettest portion of the product does not exceed 2.25 to 1.

(ii) Laboratory analysis of samples to determine the water-protein ratios will not be made in the case of all shipments of cured and dried meats. However, in any case in which the inspector is uncertain whether the meat complies with the requirements of paragraph (a)(3)(i) of this section, he will send a sample of the meat representative of the wettest portion to the Meat Inspection Division for analysis of the water-protein ratio. Pending such analysis the meat shall not be released or removed from the port of arrival.

(4) The cured meat shall be accompanied by a certificate issued by an official of the national government of the region of origin who is authorized to issue the foreign meat inspection certificate required by § 327.4 of this title, stating that such meat has been prepared in accordance with paragraphs (a)(1), (a)(2) and (a)(3)(i) of this section. Upon arrival of the cured meat in the United States, the certificate must be presented to an authorized inspector at the port of arrival.

(b) The importation of cooked meats from ruminants or swine originating in any region where rinderpest or foot-and-mouth disease exists, as designated in § 94.1, is prohibited, except as provided in this section.

(1) The cooked meat must be boneless and must be thoroughly cooked.

(2) The cooked meat must have been prepared in an establishment that is eligible to have its products imported into the United States under the Federal Meat Inspection Act (21 U.S.C. 601 *et seq.*) and the regulations in 9 CFR 327.2; must meet all other applicable requirements of the Federal Meat Inspection Act and regulations thereunder (9 CFR Chapter III); and must have been approved by the Administrator in accordance with paragraph (c) of this section.

(3) Canned product (canned meat), as defined in § 318.300(d) of this chapter, is exempt from the requirements in this section.

(4) *Ground meat cooked in an oven.* Ground meat must be shaped into patties no larger than 5 inches in diameter and 1-inch thick. Each patty must weigh no more than 115 grams, with fat content no greater than 30 percent. These patties must be broiled at 210 °C for at least 133 seconds, then cooked in moist heat (steam heat) in a continuous, belt-fed oven for not less than 20 minutes, to yield an internal exit temperature of at least 99.7 °C, as measured by temperature indicator devices (TID's) placed in temperature monitor patties positioned, before the belt starts moving through the oven, on each of the predetermined cold spots along the oven belt. TID's must be used at the beginning of each processing run.

(5) *Meat cooked in tubes.* Ground meat (which must not include cardiac muscle), cubes of meat, slices of meat, or anatomical cuts of meat (cuts taken from the skeletal muscle tissue) weighing no more than 5 kg (11.05 lbs) must be loaded into a flexible or semiflexible cooking tube constructed of plastic or other material approved by the U.S. Food and Drug Administration. The meat must then be cooked in either boiling water or in a steam-fed oven, in either a batch cooker or a continuous cooker, to reach a minimum internal temperature of 79.4 °C (175 °F) at the cold spot after cooking for at least 1.75 hours. Thoroughness of cooking must be determined by a TID registering the target temperature at the cold spot, or by the pink juice test as follows:

(i) *Cubes of meat and ground meat.* For cubes of meat, at least 50 percent of meat pieces per tube must be 3.8 cm (1.5 in) or larger in each dimension after cooking or, if more than 50 percent of the cubes of meat pieces per tube are smaller than 3.8 cm (1.5 in) in any dimension after cooking, or if the meat is ground meat, an indicator piece consisting of a single piece of meat of sufficient size for a pink juice test to be performed (3.8 cm (1.5 in) or larger in each dimension after cooking) must have been placed at the cold spot of the tube.

(ii) *Slices of meat.* At least 50 percent of the slices of meat must be 3.8 cm (1.5 in) or larger in each dimension after cooking or, if more than 50 percent of meat pieces are smaller than 3.8 cm (1.5 in) in any dimension after cooking, an indicator piece of sufficient size for a pink juice test to be performed (3.8 cm (1.5 in) or larger in each dimension after cooking) must be placed at the cold spot of the tube.

(iii) *Anatomical cuts of meat.* An indicator piece removed from an anatomical cut of meat after cooking must be removed from the center of the cut, farthest from all exterior points and be

3.8 cm (1.5 in) or larger in each dimension for performance of the pink juice test.

(6) *Further processing of meat cooked in tubes.* Cubes of meat, slices of meat, or anatomical cuts of meat (cuts taken from the skeletal muscle tissue) cooked in tubes in accordance with paragraph (b)(5) of this section may be processed further after cooking if the following provisions are met:

(i) For meat that is cooked and is intended for further processing, up to two tubes from each batch per cooker must be randomly selected by the official of the National Government of the region of origin who is authorized to issue the meat inspection certificate required by §327.4 of this title. If a TID is not used, a cylindrical or square piece of at least 3.8 cm (1.5 in) in each dimension must be cut from the cold spot of each tube. The cylindrical or square piece will be the indicator piece for the pink juice test. The indicator piece or piece containing the TID must be sealed in plastic or other material approved by the U.S. Food and Drug Administration, and be accompanied by a certificate issued by the official who selected the tube. The certificate must provide the date the tube was cooked and the cooker and batch number, and the date the tube was selected for sampling. Each batch per cooker must have at least one but no more than two indicator pieces or pieces containing TID's. All indicator pieces and pieces containing TID's must be individually sealed, properly labeled, and enclosed together in one sealed box that accompanies the shipment. Any indicator pieces or pieces containing TID's that are not used to accompany a shipment to the United States must be destroyed following loading of the batch into a container; and

(ii) After removing the indicator piece or piece containing a TID, all remaining meat from the same batch may be cut into smaller cubes and sealed in plastic or other material approved by the U.S. Food and Drug Administration. After being processed into smaller cubes once, the meat may not be further processed before shipment to the United States. The cubes of meat and the indicator piece or piece containing a TID must be accompanied to the United States by a certificate as provided in paragraph (b)(8) of this section.

(7) Any TID used in accordance with paragraph (b)(4) or (b)(5) of this section must remain in the meat, as originally inserted, and must accompany the cooked meat whose temperature it has gauged when that meat is shipped to the United States.

(8) *Pork rind pellets (pork skins).* Pork rind pellets (pork skins) must be cooked in one of the following ways:

(i) *One-step process.* The pork skins must be cooked in oil for at least 80 minutes when oil temperature is consistently maintained at a minimum of 114 °C.

(ii) *Two-step process.* The pork skins must be dry-cooked at 260 °C for approximately 210 minutes after which they must be cooked in hot oil (deep-fried) at 104 °C for an additional 150 minutes.

(9) *Certificate.* (i) The cooked meat must be accompanied by a certificate issued by an official of the National Government of the region of origin who is authorized to issue the foreign meat inspection certificate required under §327.4 of this title, stating: "This cooked meat produced for export to the United States meets the requirements of title 9, Code of Federal Regulations, §94.4(b)." Upon arrival of the cooked meat in the United States, the certificate must be presented to an authorized inspector at the port of arrival.

(ii) For cooked meat that is further processed in accordance with paragraph (b)(6) of this section, the certificate must include the following statement, in addition to the certification required under paragraph (b)(9)(i) of this section: "No more than two tubes were randomly selected per batch per cooker for cutting an indicator piece or obtaining a piece containing a TID. The indicator piece or piece containing a TID represents a shipment of (describe form of processed product—e.g., diced cubes of a particular size). A piece containing a TID or a piece 3.8 cm (1.5 in) or larger in each dimension was cut from the cold spot of the tube, and was sealed and marked with the following cooking date, cooker, and batch: ________ and the following date of selection of the tube________. The total number of indicator pieces or pieces containing TID's enclosed in a sealed box is________.''

(10) The meat is inspected by an FSIS inspector at a port of arrival in a defrost facility approved by the Administrator[2] and the meat is found to be thoroughly cooked.

(i) Request for approval of any defrost facility must be made to the Administrator. The Administrator will approve a defrost facility only under the following conditions:

(A) The defrost facility has equipment and procedures that permit FSIS inspectors to determine whether meat is thoroughly cooked;

(B) The defrost facility is located at a port of arrival; and

(C) The defrost facility is approved by the Food Safety and Inspection Service, United States Department of Agriculture.[3]

(ii) The Administrator may deny approval of any defrost facility if the Administrator determines that the defrost facility does not meet the conditions for approval. If approval is denied, the operator of the defrost facility will be informed of the reasons for denial and be given an opportunity to respond. The operator will be afforded an opportunity for a hearing with respect to any disputed issues of fact. The hearing will be conducted in accordance with rules of practice that will be adopted for the proceeding.

(iii) The Administrator may withdraw approval of any defrost facility as follows: (A) When the operator of the defrost facility notifies the Administrator in writing that the defrost facility no longer performs the required services; or (B) when the Administrator determines that the defrost facility does not meet the conditions for approval. Before the Administrator withdraws approval from any defrost facility, the operator of the defrost facility will be informed of the reasons for the proposed withdrawal and given an opportunity to respond. The operator will be afforded a hearing with respect to any disputed issues of fact. The hearing will be conducted in accordance with rules of practice that will be adopted for the proceeding. If approval of a defrost facility is withdrawn, the Administrator will remove its name from the list of approved defrost facilities.

(c) *Meat processing establishment; standards.* (1) Before the Administrator will approve a meat processing establishment for export shipment of cooked meat to the United States, the Administrator must determine:

(i) That the meat processing establishment has furnished APHIS with a description of the process used to inactivate rinderpest or FMD virus that may be present in meat intended for export to the United States, and with blueprints of the facilities where this meat is cooked and packaged;

(ii) That an APHIS representative has inspected the establishment and found that it meets the standards set forth in paragraph (c)(2) of this section;

(iii) That the operator of the establishment has signed a cooperative service agreement with APHIS, stating: (A) That all cooked meat processed for importation into the United States will be processed in accordance with the requirements of this part; (B) that a full-time, salaried meat inspection official of the National Government of the exporting region will supervise the processing (including certification of the cold spot) and examination of the product, and certify that it has been processed in accordance with this section; and (C) that APHIS personnel or other persons authorized by the Administrator may enter the establishment, unannounced, to inspect the establishment and its records; and

(iv) That the operator of the establishment has entered into a trust fund agreement with APHIS and is current in paying all costs for an APHIS representative to inspect the establishment for initial evaluation, and periodically thereafter, including travel, salary, subsistence, administrative

[2] The names and addresses of approved defrost facilities and conditions for approval may be obtained from the Administrator, Animal and Plant Health Inspection Service, United States Department of Agriculture, Washington, DC 20250.

[3] Conditions for the approval of any defrost facility by the Food Safety and Inspection Service, United States Department of Agriculture, may be obtained from the Import Inspection Division, International Programs, Food Safety and Inspection Service, United States Department of Agriculture, Washington, DC 20250.

overhead, and other incidental expenses (including an excess baggage provision up to 150 pounds). In accordance with the terms of the trust fund agreement, before the APHIS representative's site inspection, the operator of the processing establishment must deposit with the Administrator an amount equal to the approximate cost of one inspection by an APHIS representative, including travel, salary, subsistence, administrative overhead, and other incidental expenses (including an excess baggage provision up to 150 pounds). As funds from that amount are obligated, a bill for costs incurred based on official accounting records will be issued, to restore the deposit to the original level, revised as necessary to allow for inflation or other changes in estimated costs. To be current, bills must be paid within 14 days of receipt.

(2) *Establishment.* An APHIS representative will conduct an on-site evaluation, and subsequent inspections, as provided in § 94.4(c)(1), to determine whether the following conditions are met:

(i) The facilities used for processing cooked meat in the meat processing establishment are separate from the facilities used for processing raw meat (precooking, boning, preparation, and curing), with only the through-the-wall cooking system through which the meat product is delivered at the end of the cooking cycle connecting them; and there is at all times a positive air flow from the cooked to the raw product side;

(ii) The cooking equipment has the capacity to cook all meat pieces in accordance with § 94.4(b)(4) or (b)(5);

(iii) Workers who process cooked meat are at all times kept separate from workers who process raw meat, and have, for their exclusive use: A separate entrance, dining area, toilets, lavatories with cold and hot water, soap, disinfectants, paper towels, clothes hampers and waste baskets for disposal, and changing rooms stocked with the clean clothing and rubber boots into which all persons must change upon entering the establishment. Workers and all other persons entering the establishment must wash their hands and change into the clean clothing and boots provided in the changing rooms before entering the cooking facilities, and must leave this clothing for laundering and disinfecting before exiting from the establishment, regardless of the amount of time spent inside or away from the establishment;

(iv) Original records identifying the slaughtering facility from which the meat was obtained and the date the meat entered the meat processing establishment, and original certification (including temperature recording charts and graphs), must be kept for all cooked meat by the full-time salaried meat inspection official of the National Government of the exporting region assigned to the establishment, and must be retained for 2 years.

(Approved by the Office of Management and Budget under control number 0579–0015)

[28 FR 5980, June 13, 1963]

EDITORIAL NOTE: For FEDERAL REGISTER citations affecting § 94.4, see the List of CFR Sections Affected, which appears in the Finding Aids section of the printed volume and at *www.fdsys.gov.*

§ 94.5 Regulation of certain garbage.

(a) *General restrictions*—(1) *Interstate movements of garbage from Hawaii and U.S. territories and possessions to the continental United States.* Hawaii, Puerto Rico, American Samoa, the Commonwealth of the Northern Mariana Islands, the Federated States of Micronesia, Guam, the U.S. Virgin Islands, Republic of the Marshall Islands, and the Republic of Palau are hereby quarantined, and the movement of garbage therefrom to any other State is hereby prohibited except as provided in this section in order to prevent the introduction and spread of exotic plant pests and diseases.

(2) *Imports of garbage.* In order to protect against the introduction of exotic animal and plant pests, the importation of garbage from all foreign countries except Canada is prohibited except as provided in paragraph (c)(2) of this section.

(b) *Definitions*—*Agricultural waste.* Byproducts generated by the rearing of animals and the production and harvest of crops or trees. Animal waste, a large component of agricultural waste, includes waste (e.g., feed waste, bedding and litter, and feedlot and paddock runoff) from livestock, dairy, and other animal-related agricultural and farming practices.

Approved facility. A facility approved by the Administrator, Animal and Plant Health Inspection Service, upon his determination that it has equipment and uses procedures that are adequate to prevent the dissemination of plant pests and livestock or poultry diseases, and that it is certified by an appropriate Government official as currently complying with the applicable laws for environmental protection.

Approved sewage system. A sewage system approved by the Administrator, Animal and Plant Health Inspection Service, upon his determination that the system is designed and operated in such a way as to preclude the discharge of sewage effluents onto land surfaces or into lagoons or other stationary waters, and otherwise is adequate to prevent the dissemination of plant pests and livestock or poultry diseases, and that is certified by an appropriate Government official as currently complying with the applicable laws for environmental protection.

Carrier. The principal operator of a means of conveyance.

Continental United States. The 49 States located on the continent of North America and the District of Columbia.

Garbage. All waste material that is derived in whole or in part from fruits, vegetables, meats, or other plant or animal (including poultry) material, and other refuse of any character whatsoever that has been associated with any such material.

Incineration. To reduce garbage to ash by burning.

Inspector. A properly identified employee of the U.S. Department of Agriculture or other person authorized by the Department to enforce the provisions of applicable statutes, quarantines, and regulations.

Interstate. From one State into or through any other State.

Person. Any individual, corporation, company, association, firm, partnership, society, or joint stock company.

Shelf-stable. The condition achieved in a product, by application of heat, alone or in combination with other ingredients and/or other treatments, of being rendered free of microorganisms capable of growing in the product under nonrefrigerated conditions (over 50 °F or 10 °C).

Sterilization. Cooking garbage at an internal temperature of 212 °F for 30 minutes.

Stores. The food, supplies, and other provisions carried for the day-to-day operation of a conveyance and the care and feeding of its operators.

Yard waste. Solid waste composed predominantly of grass clippings, leaves, twigs, branches, and other garden refuse.

(c) *Garbage generated onboard a conveyance*—(1) *Applicability.* This section applies to garbage generated onboard any means of conveyance during international or interstate movements as provided in this section and includes food scraps, table refuse, galley refuse, food wrappers or packaging materials, and other waste material from stores, food preparation areas, passengers' or crews' quarters, dining rooms, or any other areas on the means of conveyance. This section also applies to meals and other food that were available for consumption by passengers and crew on an aircraft but were not consumed.

(i) Not all garbage generated onboard a means of conveyance is regulated for the purposes of this section. Garbage regulated for the purposes of this section is defined as "regulated garbage" in paragraphs (c)(2) and (c)(3) of this section.

(ii) Garbage that is commingled with regulated garbage is also regulated garbage.

(2) *Garbage regulated because of movements outside the United States or Canada.* For purposes of this section, garbage on or removed from a means of conveyance is regulated garbage, if, when the garbage is on or removed from the means of conveyance, the means of conveyance has been in any port outside the United States and Canada within the previous 2-year period. There are, however, two exceptions to this provision. These exceptions are as follows:

(i) *Exception 1: Aircraft.* Garbage on or removed from an aircraft is exempt from requirements under paragraph (c)(4) of this section if the following conditions are met when the garbage is on or removed from the aircraft:

(A) The aircraft had previously been cleared of all garbage and of all meats and meat products, whatever the country of origin, except meats that are shelf-stable; all fresh and condensed milk and cream from countries designated in § 94.1 as those in which foot-and-mouth disease exists; all fresh fruits and vegetables; and all eggs; and the items previously cleared from the aircraft as prescribed by this paragraph have been disposed of according to the procedures for disposing of regulated garbage, as specified in paragraphs (c)(4)(ii) and (c)(4)(iii) of this section.

(B) After the garbage and stores referred to in paragraph (c)(2)(i)(A) of this section were removed, the aircraft has not been in a non-Canadian foreign port.

(ii) *Exception 2: Other conveyances.* Garbage on or removed in the United States from a means of conveyance other than an aircraft is exempt from requirements under paragraph (c)(4) of this section if the following conditions are met when the garbage is on or removed from the means of conveyance:

(A) The means of conveyance is accompanied by a certificate from an inspector stating the following:

(*1*) That the means of conveyance had previously been cleared of all garbage and of all meats and meat products, whatever the country of origin, except meats that are shelf-stable; all fresh and condensed milk and cream from countries designated in §94.1 as those in which foot-and-mouth disease exists; all fresh fruits and vegetables; and all eggs; and the items previously cleared from the means of conveyance as prescribed by this paragraph have been disposed of according to the procedures for disposing of regulated garbage, as specified in paragraphs (c)(4)(ii) and (c)(4)(iii) of this section.

(*2*) That the means of conveyance had then been cleaned and disinfected in the presence of the inspector; and

(B) Since being cleaned and disinfected, the means of conveyance has not been in a non-Canadian foreign port.

(3) *Garbage regulated because of certain movements to or from Hawaii, territories, or possessions.* For purposes of this section, garbage on or removed from a means of conveyance is regulated garbage, if at the time the garbage is on or removed from the means of conveyance, the means of conveyance has moved during the previous 1-year period, either directly or indirectly, to the continental United States from any territory or possession or from Hawaii, to any territory or possession from any other territory or possession or from Hawaii, or to Hawaii from any territory or possession. There are, however, two exceptions to this provision. These exceptions are as follows:

(i) *Exception 1: Aircraft.* Garbage on or removed from an aircraft is exempt from requirements under paragraph (c)(4) of this section if the following two conditions are met when the garbage is on or removed from the aircraft:

(A) The aircraft had been previously cleared of all garbage and all fresh fruits and vegetables, and the items previously cleared from the aircraft as prescribed by this paragraph have been disposed of according to the procedures for disposing of regulated garbage, as specified in paragraphs (c)(4)(ii) and (c)(4)(iii) of this section.

(B) After the garbage and stores referred to in paragraph (c)(3)(i)(A) of this section were removed, the aircraft has not moved to the continental United States from any territory or possession or from Hawaii, to any territory or possession from any other territory or possession or from Hawaii, or to Hawaii from any territory or possession.

(ii) *Exception 2: Other conveyances.* Garbage on or removed from a means of conveyance other than an aircraft is exempt from requirements under paragraph (c)(4) of this section if the following two conditions are met when the garbage is on or removed from the means of conveyance:

(A) The means of conveyance is accompanied by a certificate from an inspector stating that the means of conveyance had been cleared of all garbage and all fresh fruits and vegetables, and the items previously cleared from the means of conveyance as prescribed by this paragraph have been disposed of according to the procedures for disposing of regulated garbage, as specified in paragraphs (c)(4)(ii) and (c)(4)(iii) of this section.

(B) After being cleared of the garbage and stores referred to in paragraph (c)(3)(ii)(A) of this section, the means of conveyance has not moved to the continental United States from any territory or possession or from Hawaii; to any territory or possession from any other territory or possession or from Hawaii; or to Hawaii from any territory or possession.

(4) *Restrictions on regulated garbage.* (i) Regulated garbage may not be disposed of, placed on, or removed from a means of conveyance except in accordance with this section.

(ii) Regulated garbage is subject to general surveillance for compliance with this section by inspectors and to disposal measures authorized by the Plant Protection Act and the Animal Health Protection Act to prevent the introduction and dissemination of pests and diseases of plants and livestock.

(iii) All regulated garbage must be contained in tight, covered, leak-proof receptacles during storage on board a means of conveyance while in the territorial waters, or while otherwise within the territory of the United States. All such receptacles shall be contained inside the guard rail if on a watercraft. Such regulated garbage shall not be unloaded from such means of conveyance in the United States unless such regulated garbage is removed in tight, covered, leak-proof receptacles under the direction of an inspector to an approved facility for incineration, sterilization, or grinding into an approved sewage system, under direct supervision by such an inspector, or such regulated garbage is removed for other handling in such manner and under such supervision as may, upon request in specific cases, be approved by the Administrator as adequate to prevent the introduction and dissemination of plant pests and animal diseases and sufficient to ensure compliance with applicable laws for environmental protection. *Provided that,* a cruise ship may dispose of regulated garbage in landfills at Alaskan ports only, if and only if the cruise ship does not have prohibited or restricted meat or animal products on board at the time it enters Alaskan waters for the cruise season, and only if the cruise ship, except for incidental travel through international waters necessary to navigate safely between ports, remains in Canadian and U.S. waters off the west coast of North America, and calls only at continental U.S. and Canadian ports during the entire cruise season.

(A) Application for approval of a facility or sewage system may be made in writing by the authorized representative of any carrier or by the official having jurisdiction over the port or place of arrival of the means of conveyance to the Administrator, Animal and Plant Health Inspection Service, U.S. Department of Agriculture, Washington, DC 20250. The application must be endorsed by the operator of the facility or sewage system.

(B) Approval will be granted if the Administrator determines that the requirements set forth in this section are met. Approval may be denied or withdrawn at any time, if the Administrator determines that such requirements are not met, after notice of the proposed denial or withdrawal of the approval and the reasons therefor, and an opportunity to demonstrate or achieve compliance with such requirements, has been afforded to the operator of the facility or sewage system and to the applicant for approval. However, approval may also be withdrawn without such prior procedure in any case in which the public health, interest, or safety requires immediate action, and in such case, the operator of the facility or sewage system and the applicant for approval shall promptly thereafter be given notice of the withdrawal and the reasons therefore and an opportunity to show cause why the approval should be reinstated.

(iv) The Plant Protection and Quarantine Programs and Veterinary Services, Animal, and Plant Health Inspection Service, will cooperate with other Federal, State, and local agencies responsible for enforcing other statutes and regulations governing disposal of the regulated garbage to the end that such disposal shall be adequate to prevent the dissemination of plant pests and livestock or poultry diseases and comply with applicable laws for environmental protection. The inspectors, in maintaining surveillance over regulated garbage movements and disposal, shall coordinate their activities with the activities of representatives of the U.S. Environmental Protection Agency and other Federal, State, and local agencies also having jurisdiction over such regulated garbage.

(d) *Garbage generated in Hawaii*—(1) *Applicability*. This section applies to garbage generated in households, commercial establishments, institutions, and businesses prior to interstate movement from Hawaii, and includes used paper, discarded cans and bottles, and food scraps. Such garbage includes, and is commonly known as, municipal solid waste.

(i) Industrial process wastes, mining wastes, sewage sludge, incinerator ash, or other wastes from Hawaii that the Administrator determines do not pose risks of introducing animal or plant pests or diseases into the continental United States are not regulated under this section.

(ii) The interstate movement from Hawaii to the continental United States of agricultural wastes and yard waste (other than incidental amounts (less than 3 percent) that may be present in municipal solid waste despite reasonable efforts to maintain source separation) is prohibited.

(iii) Garbage generated onboard any means of conveyance during interstate movement from Hawaii is regulated under paragraph (c) of this section.

(2) *Restrictions on interstate movement of garbage*. The interstate movement of garbage generated in Hawaii to the continental United States is regulated as provided in this section.

(i) The garbage must be processed, packaged, safeguarded, and disposed of using a methodology that the Administrator has determined is adequate to prevent the introduction and dissemination of plant pests into noninfested areas of the United States.

(ii) The garbage must be moved under a compliance agreement in accordance with paragraph (e) of this section. APHIS will only enter into a compliance agreement when the Administrator is satisfied that the Agency has first satisfied all its obligations under the National Environmental Policy Act and all applicable Federal and State statutes to fully assess the impacts associated with the movement of garbage under the compliance agreement.

(iii) All such garbage moved interstate from Hawaii to any of the continental United States must be moved in compliance with all applicable laws for environmental protection.

(e) *Compliance agreement and cancellation*—(1) Any person engaged in the business of handling or disposing of garbage in accordance with this section must first enter into a compliance agreement with the Animal and Plant Health Inspection Service (APHIS). Compliance agreement forms (PPQ Form 519) are available without charge from local USDA/APHIS/Plant Protection and Quarantine offices, which are listed in telephone directories.

(2) A person who enters into a compliance agreement, and employees or agents of that person, must comply with the following conditions and any supplemental conditions which are listed in the compliance agreement, as deemed by the Administrator to be necessary to prevent the introduction and dissemination into or within the United States of plant pests and livestock or poultry diseases:

(i) Comply with all applicable provisions of this section;

(ii) Allow inspectors access to all records maintained by the person regarding handling or disposal of garbage, and to all areas where handling or disposal of garbage occurs;

(iii)(A) If the garbage is regulated under paragraph (c) of this section, remove garbage from a means of conveyance only in tight, covered, leak-proof receptacles;

(B) If the garbage is regulated under paragraph (d) of this section, transport garbage interstate in sealed, leak-proof packaging approved by the Administrator;

(iv) Move the garbage only to a facility approved by the Administrator; and

(v) At the approved facility, dispose of the garbage in a manner approved by the Administrator and described in the compliance agreement.

(3) Approval for a compliance agreement may be denied at any time if the

Administrator determines that the applicant has not met or is unable to meet the requirements set forth in this section. Prior to denying any application for a compliance agreement, APHIS will provide notice to the applicant thereof, and will provide the applicant with an opportunity to demonstrate or achieve compliance with requirements.

(4) Any compliance agreement may be canceled, either orally or in writing, by an inspector whenever the inspector finds that the person who has entered into the compliance agreement has failed to comply with this section. If the cancellation is oral, the cancellation and the reasons for the cancellation will be confirmed in writing as promptly as circumstances allow. Any person whose compliance agreement has been canceled may appeal the decision, in writing, within 10 days after receiving written notification of the cancellation. The appeal must state all of the facts and reasons upon which the person relies to show that the compliance agreement was wrongfully canceled. As promptly as circumstances allow, the Administrator will grant or deny the appeal, in writing, stating the reasons for the decision. A hearing will be held to resolve any conflict as to any material fact. Rules of practice concerning a hearing will be adopted by the Administrator. This administrative remedy must be exhausted before a person can file suit in court challenging the cancellation of a compliance agreement.

(5) Where a compliance agreement is denied or canceled, the person who entered into or applied for the compliance agreement may be prohibited, at the discretion of the Administrator, from handling or disposing of regulated garbage.

(Approved by the Office of Management and Budget under control numbers 0579–0015, 0579–0054, and 0579–0292)

[71 FR 49317, Aug. 23, 2006]

§94.6 Carcasses, meat, parts or products of carcasses, and eggs (other than hatching eggs) of poultry, game birds, or other birds; importations from regions where Newcastle disease or highly pathogenic avian influenza is considered to exist.

(a) *Disease status of regions for Newcastle disease and highly pathogenic avian influenza (HPAI)*—(1) *Regions in which Newcastle disease is not considered to exist.* (i) A list of such regions is maintained on the APHIS National Import Export Services Web site at *http://www.aphis.usda.gov/import_export/animals/animal_disease_status.shtml.* Copies of the list will also be available upon request to Regional Evaluation Services, National Import Export Services, Veterinary Services, Animal and Plant Health Inspection Service, 4700 River Road Unit 38, Riverdale, Maryland 20737; fax: (301) 851–3300; email: *AskNCIE.Products@aphis.usda.gov.*

(ii) APHIS will remove a region from the list referenced in paragraph (a)(1)(i) of this section upon determining that Newcastle disease exists there based on reports APHIS receives of outbreaks of the disease in commercial birds or poultry from veterinary officials of the exporting country, from the World Organization for Animal Health (OIE), or from other sources the Administrator determines to be reliable. APHIS will add a region to this list after it conducts an evaluation of the region and finds that Newcastle disease is not likely to be present in its commercial bird or poultry populations. In the case of a region formerly on this list that is removed due to an outbreak, the region may be returned to the list in accordance with the procedures for reestablishment of a region's disease-free status in §92.4 of this subchapter.

(2) *Regions in which HPAI is considered to exist.* (i) A list of such regions is maintained on the APHIS National Center for Import and Export Web site at *http://www.aphis.usda.gov/import_export/animals/animal_disease_status.shtml.* Copies of the list will also be available via postal mail, fax, or e-mail upon request to Sanitary Trade Issue Team, National Center for Import and Export, Veterinary Services, Animal and Plant Health Inspection Service, 4700 River

Road, Unit 38, Riverdale, Maryland 20737.

(ii) APHIS will consider a region to have HPAI and add it to this list referenced in paragraph (a)(2)(i) of this section upon determining that HPAI exists in commercial birds or poultry in the region based on reports APHIS receives of outbreaks of the disease from veterinary officials of the exporting country, from the OIE, or from other sources the Administrator determines to be reliable. APHIS will remove a region from this list only after it conducts an evaluation of the region and finds that HPAI is not likely to be present in its commercial bird or poultry populations.

(b) *Carcasses, and parts or products of carcasses, including meat, from regions where Newcastle disease or HPAI is considered to exist.* This paragraph applies to carcasses, and parts or products of carcasses,[4] including meat, of poultry, game birds, or other birds that were raised or slaughtered in any region where Newcastle disease or any subtype of HPAI is considered to exist (*see* paragraph (a) of this section); are imported from any such region; or are moved into or through any such region at any time before importation or during shipment to the United States.

(1) Carcasses of game birds, if eviscerated with heads and feet removed, may be imported from regions where Newcastle disease is considered to exist. Carcasses of game birds may not be imported from regions where any subtype of HPAI is considered to exist. Viscera, heads, and feet removed from game birds in any of these regions are ineligible for entry into the United States.

(2) Carcasses, or parts or products of carcasses, of poultry, game birds, and other birds from regions where Newcastle disease or HPAI are considered to exist may be imported for consignment to any museum, educational institution or other establishment which has provided the Administrator with evidence that it has the equipment, facilities, and capabilities to store, handle, process, or disinfect such articles so as to prevent the introduction or dissemination of Newcastle disease or HPAI into the United States, and which is approved by the Administrator.[5]

(3) Carcasses, or parts or products of carcasses, including meat, of poultry, game birds, or other birds, may be imported if packed in hermetically sealed containers and if cooked by a commercial method after such packing to produce articles that are shelf stable without refrigeration.

(4) Carcasses and parts or products of carcasses, including meat, of poultry, game birds, or other birds, may be imported if they are accompanied by a certificate that is signed by a full-time, salaried veterinarian of the government agency responsible for animal health in the region and that specifies that the articles were cooked throughout to reach a minimum internal temperature of 74 °C (165 °F).

(5) Carcasses, and parts or products of carcasses, including meat, of poultry, game birds, or other birds, that originated in a region considered to be free of Newcastle disease and any subtype of HPAI, and that are processed (cut, packaged, or other processing) in a region where Newcastle disease or HPAI is considered to exist, may be imported under the following conditions:

(i) *Shipment to processing establishments.* All poultry, game bird, or other bird products from such regions shall be shipped from the Newcastle disease and HPAI-free region where they originated to a processing establishment[6] in the region where Newcastle disease or HPAI is considered to exist in closed

[4] Animal byproducts are regulated under part 95 of this subchapter.

[5] The names and addresses of approved establishments may be obtained from, and requests for approval may be made to the National Center for Import-Export, Veterinary Services, APHIS, 4700 River Road, Unit 38, Riverdale, Maryland 20737–1231.

[6] As a condition of entry into the United States, poultry species and poultry products addressed by the Poultry Products Inspection Act (PPIA, 21 U.S.C. 451 *et seq.*) and regulations thereunder (9 CFR, chapter III, part 381), must also meet all of the requirements of the PPIA and part 381, including requirements that the poultry or poultry products be prepared only in establishments approved by FSIS. Species subject to these requirements include chickens, turkeys, ducks, geese, guineas, ratites, or squabs.

containers sealed with serially numbered seals applied by an official of the national government of that region. They must be accompanied by a certificate that is signed by a full-time, salaried veterinarian of the government agency responsible for animal health in the region and that specifies the products' region of origin, the processing establishment to which the carcasses or parts or products are consigned, and the numbers of the seals applied to the shipping containers.

(A) The poultry, game bird, or other bird carcasses or parts or products may be removed from containers at the processing establishment in the region where Newcastle disease or HPAI is considered to exist only after an official of the national government has determined that the seals are intact and free of any evidence of tampering. The official must attest to this fact by signing the certificate accompanying the shipment.

(B) [Reserved]

(ii) *Handling of poultry, game bird, or other bird carcasses or parts or products.* Establishments in regions where Newcastle disease or HPAI is considered to exist that process poultry, game bird, or other bird carcasses or parts or products for export to the United States:

(A) May not receive or handle any live poultry or birds.

(B) Must keep any records required by this section on file at the facility for a period of at least 2 years after export of processed products to the United States, and must make those records available to USDA inspectors during inspections.

(C) May process carcasses or parts or products that originate in any region, provided that:

(*1*) All areas, utensils, and equipment likely to contact the carcasses or parts or products to be processed, including skinning, deboning, cutting, and packing areas, are cleaned and disinfected between processing carcasses or parts or products from regions where Newcastle disease or HPAI is considered to exist and processing those from Newcastle disease and HPAI-free regions.

(*2*) Carcasses or parts or products intended for export to the United States are not handled, cut, or otherwise processed at the same time as any carcasses or parts or products not eligible for export to the United States.

(*3*) Carcasses or parts or products intended for export to the United States are packed in clean new packaging that is clearly distinguishable from that containing any carcasses or parts or products not eligible for export to the United States.

(*4*) Carcasses or parts or products are stored in a manner that ensures that no cross-contamination occurs.

(iii) *Cooperative service agreement.* Operators of processing establishments must enter into a cooperative service agreement with APHIS to pay all expenses incurred by APHIS in inspecting the establishment. APHIS anticipates that such inspections will occur once a year. The cooperative service account must always contain a balance that is at least equal to the cost of one inspection. APHIS will charge the cooperative service account for travel, salary, and subsistence of APHIS employees, as well as administrative overhead and other incidental expenses (including excess baggage charges up to 150 pounds).

(iv) *Shipment to the United States.* Poultry, game bird, or other bird carcasses or parts or products to be imported into the United States must be shipped from the region where they were processed in closed containers sealed with serially numbered seals applied by an official of the national government of that region. The shipments must be accompanied by a certificate signed by an official of the national government of the region where articles were processed that lists the numbers of the seals applied and states that all of the conditions of this section have been met. A copy of this certificate must be kept on file at the processing establishment for at least 2 years.

(6) Poultry, game bird, or other bird carcasses or parts or products that do not otherwise qualify for importation under paragraphs (b)(1) through (5) of this section may be imported only if the importer applies to, and is granted a permit by, the Administrator, authorizing such importation. A permit

will be given only when the Administrator determines that such importation will not constitute a risk of introduction or dissemination of Newcastle disease or HPAI into the United States. Application for a permit may be made in accordance with paragraph (d) of this section.

(c) *Eggs (other than hatching eggs) from regions where Newcastle disease or HPAI is considered to exist.* Eggs (other than hatching eggs[7]) from poultry, game birds, or other birds may be imported only in accordance with this section if they: Are laid by poultry, game birds, or other birds that are raised in any region where Newcastle disease or HPAI is considered to exist (*see* paragraph (a) of this section); are imported from any region where Newcastle disease or HPAI is considered to exist; or are moved into or through any region where Newcastle disease or HPAI is considered to exist at any time before importation or during shipment to the United States.

(1) *With a certificate.* The eggs may be imported if they are accompanied by a certificate signed by a salaried veterinary officer of the national government of the region of origin or, if exported from Mexico, accompanied either by such a certificate or by a certificate issued by a veterinarian accredited by the national government of Mexico and endorsed by a full-time salaried veterinary officer of the national government of Mexico, thereby representing that the veterinarian issuing the certificate was authorized to do so, and:

(i) The eggs are imported in cases marked with the identity of the flock of origin and sealed with the seal of the national government of the region of origin.

(ii) The certificate accompanying the eggs is presented to an authorized inspector when the eggs reach the port of arrival in the United States.

(iii) The certificate identifies the flock of origin and shows the region of origin, the port of embarkation, the port of arrival, the name and address of the exporter and importer, the total number of eggs, and cases of eggs, shipped with the certificate, and the date the certificate was signed.

(iv) The certificate states that the eggs qualify for importation in accordance with this section.

(v) The certificate states that no more than 90 days before the certificate was signed, a salaried veterinary officer of the national government of the region of origin or, if exported from Mexico, by a veterinarian accredited by the national government of Mexico, inspected the flock of origin and found no evidence of communicable diseases of poultry.

(vi) The eggs were washed, to remove foreign material from the surface of the shells, and sanitized on the premises of origin with a hypochlorite solution of from 100 ppm to 200 ppm available chlorine.

(vii) The eggs were packed on the premises of origin in previously unused cases.

(viii) Before leaving the premises of origin, the cases in which the eggs were packed were sealed with a seal of the national government of the region of origin by the salaried veterinarian of the national government of the region of origin who signed the certificate or, if exported from Mexico, by the veterinarian accredited by the national government of Mexico who signed the certificate.

(ix) In addition, if the eggs were laid in any region where Newcastle disease or HPAI is considered to exist (see paragraph (a) of this section), the certificate must also state:

(A) No Newcastle disease or HPAI occurred on the premises of origin or on adjoining premises during the 90 days before the certificate was signed.

(B) There is no evidence that the flock of origin was exposed to Newcastle disease or HPAI during the 90 days before the certificate was signed.

(C) The eggs are from a region free of HPAI, or from a flock of origin found free of Newcastle disease as follows: On the seventh and fourteenth days of the 21-day period before the certificate is signed, at least 1 cull bird (a sick or dead bird, not a healthy bird that was killed) for each 10,000 live birds occupying each poultry house certified for exporting table eggs was tested for Newcastle disease virus using

[7] The requirements for importing hatching eggs are contained in part 93 of this chapter.

embryonated egg inoculation technique. The weekly cull rate of birds of every exporting poultry house within the exporting farm does not exceed 0.1 percent. The tests present no clinical or immunological evidence of Newcastle disease by embryonated egg inoculation technique from tissues of birds that were culled and have been collected by a salaried veterinary officer of the national government of the region of origin or by a veterinarian accredited by the national government of Mexico. All examinations and embryonated egg inoculation tests were conducted in a laboratory located in the region of origin, and the laboratory was approved to conduct the examinations and tests by the veterinary services organization of the national government of that region. All results were negative for Newcastle disease.

(D) Egg drop syndrome is notifiable in the region of origin and there have been no reports of egg drop syndrome in the flocks of origin of the eggs, or within a 50 kilometer radius of the flock of origin, for the 90 days prior to the issuance of the certificate.

(2) *To an approved establishment for breaking and pasteurization.* The eggs may be imported if they are moved from the port of arrival in the United States, under seal of the United States Department of Agriculture, to an approved establishment for breaking and pasteurization. Establishments will be approved when the Administrator determines that pasteurization and sanitation procedures for handling the eggs, and for disposing of egg shells, cases, and packing materials, are adequate to prevent the introduction of Newcastle disease and HPAI into the United States.

(3) *For scientific, educational, or research purposes.* The eggs may be imported if they are imported for scientific, educational, or research purposes and the Administrator has determined that the importation can be made under conditions that will prevent the introduction of Newcastle disease and HPAI into the United States. The eggs must be accompanied by a permit obtained from APHIS prior to the importation in accordance with paragraph (d) of this section, and they must be moved and handled as specified on the permit to prevent the introduction of Newcastle disease and HPAI into the United States.

(4) *Other.* The eggs may be imported when the Administrator determines that the eggs have been cooked or processed or will be handled in a manner that will prevent the introduction of Newcastle disease and HPAI into the United States. The eggs must be accompanied by a permit obtained from APHIS prior to the importation in accordance with paragraph (d) of this section, and they must be moved and handled as specified on the permit to prevent the introduction of Newcastle disease and HPAI into the United States.

(d) To apply for a permit, contact the Animal and Plant Health Inspection Service, Veterinary Services, National Center for Import-Export, 4700 River Road Unit 38, Riverdale, Maryland 20737–1231 or visit *http://www.aphis.usda.gov/animal_health/permits/.*

(Approved by the Office of Management and Budget under control numbers 0579–0015, 0579–0245, 0579–0328, and 0579–0367)

[39 FR 39546, Nov. 8, 1974; 39 FR 41242, Nov. 26, 1974]

EDITORIAL NOTE: For FEDERAL REGISTER citations affecting § 94.6, see the List of CFR Sections Affected, which appears in the Finding Aids section of the printed volume and at *www.fdsys.gov.*

§ 94.7 Disposal of animals, meats, and other articles ineligible for importation.

(a) Ruminants and swine, and fresh (chilled or frozen) meats, prohibited importation under §§ 94.1, 94.8, 94.9, 94.10, 94.12, 94.14, or 94.18, which come into the United States by ocean vessel and are offered for entry and refused admission into this country, shall be destroyed or otherwise disposed of as the Administrator may direct, unless they are exported by the consignee within 48 hours, and meanwhile are retained under such isolation and other safeguards as the Administrator may require to prevent the introduction or dissemination of livestock diseases into the United States.

(b) Ruminants and swine, and fresh (chilled or frozen) meats, prohibited importation under §§ 94.1, 94.8, 94.9, 94.10, 94.12, 94.14, or 94.18, which come into the United States aboard an airplane or railroad car and are offered for entry and refused admission into this country, shall be destroyed or otherwise disposed of as the Administrator may direct, unless they are exported by the consignee within 24 hours, and meanwhile are retained under such isolation and other safeguards as the Administrator may require to prevent the introduction or dissemination of livestock diseases into the United States.

(c) Ruminants and swine, and fresh (chilled or frozen) meats, prohibited importation under §§94.1, 94.8, 94.9, 94.10, 94.12, 94.14, or 94.18, which come into the United States by any means other than ocean vessel, airplane, or railroad car and are offered for entry and refused admission into this country, shall be destroyed or otherwise disposed of as the Administrator may direct, unless they are exported by the consignee within 8 hours, and meanwhile are retained under such isolation and other safeguards as the Administrator may require to prevent the introduction or dissemination of livestock diseases into the United States.

(d) Ruminants and swine, and fresh (chilled or frozen) meats, prohibited importation under §§94.1, 94.8, 94.9, 94.10, 94.12, 94.14, or 94.18, which come into the United States by any means but are not offered for entry into this country, and other animals, meats, and other articles prohibited importation under other sections of this part, which come into the United States by any means, whether they are offered for entry into this country or not, shall be immediately destroyed or otherwise disposed of as the Administrator may direct at any time.

[68 FR 6345, Feb. 7, 2003]

§94.8 Pork and pork products from regions where African swine fever exists or is reasonably believed to exist.

(a) African swine fever exists or the Administrator has reason to believe that African swine fever exists in the regions listed under paragraph (a)(2) of this section.

(1) The Administrator bases the reason to believe African swine fever exists in a region on the following factors:

(i) When a region allows the importation of host animals, pork or pork products, or vectors of African swine fever from a region in which African swine fever exists under conditions which the Administrator has determined are less stringent than those prescribed by this chapter for importing host animals, pork or pork products, or vectors of African swine fever into the United States from a region in which African swine fever exists; or

(ii) When a region allows the importation or use of African swine fever virus or cultures under conditions which the Administrator has determined are less stringent than those prescribed by this chapter for the importation or use of African swine fever virus or cultures into or within the United States; or

(iii) When a region has a contiguous border with, or is subject to commercial exchange or natural spread of African swine fever host animals, host materials, or vectors with, another region with known outbreaks of African swine fever; or

(iv) A region's lack of a disease detection, control, or reporting system capable of detecting or controlling African swine fever and reporting it to the United States in time to allow the United States to take appropriate action to prevent the introduction of African swine fever into the United States; or

(v) Any other fact or circumstance found to exist which constitutes a risk of introduction of African swine fever into the United States.

(2) A list of regions where African swine fever exists or the Administrator has reason to believe that African swine fever exists is maintained on the APHIS Web site at *http://www.aphis.usda.gov/import_export/animals/animal_disease_status.shtml*. Copies of the list will also be available via postal mail, fax, or email upon request to the Sanitary Trade Issues Team, National Center for Import and Export, Veterinary Services, Animal and Plant Health Inspection Service, 4700 River Road Unit 38, Riverdale, Maryland 20737.

(3) APHIS will add a region to the list upon determining that the disease exists in the region based on reports

APHIS receives of outbreaks of the disease from veterinary officials of the exporting country, from the World Organization for Animal Health (OIE), or from other sources the Administrator determines to be reliable, or upon determining that there is reason to believe the disease exists in the region. APHIS will remove a region from the list after conducting an evaluation of the region in accordance with § 92.2 of this subchapter and finding that the disease is not present and that there is no reason to believe the disease is present. In the case of a region formerly not on this list that is added due to an outbreak, the region may be removed from the list in accordance with the procedures for reestablishment of a region's disease-free status in § 92.4 of this subchapter.

(b) No pork or pork products may be imported into the United States from any region listed in this section unless:

(1) Such pork or pork product has been fully cooked by a commercial method in a container hermetically sealed promptly after filling but before such cooking, so that such cooking and sealing produced a fully-sterilized product which is shelf-stable without refrigeration; or

(2) Such pork or pork product is not otherwise prohibited importation under this part and is consigned directly from the port of arrival in the United States to a meat processing establishment operating under Federal meat inspection, approved by the Administrator, for further processing of such pork or pork product by heat.

(3) Such pork or pork product:

(i) Was processed in a single establishment that meets the requirements in paragraph (b)(5) of this section.

(ii) Was heated by other than a flash-heating method to an internal temperature of at least 69 °C. (156 °F.) throughout after the bones had been removed.

(iii) Is accompanied to the United States by an original certificate stating that all of the requirements of this section have been met. The certificate must be written in English. The certificate must be issued by an official of the national government of the region in which the processing establishment is located. The official must be authorized to issue the foreign meat inspection certificate required by part 327 of chapter III of this title. Upon arrival of the pork or pork products in the United States, the certificate must be presented to an authorized inspector at the port of arrival.

(4) The pork product is pork rind pellets (pork skins) that were cooked in one of the following ways in an establishment that meets the requirements in paragraph (b)(5) of this section:

(i) *One-step process.* The pork skins must be cooked in oil for at least 80 minutes when oil temperature is consistently maintained at a minimum of 114 °C.

(ii) *Two-step process.* The pork skins must be dry-cooked at a minimum of 260 °C for approximately 210 minutes after which they must be cooked in hot oil (deep-fried) at a minimum of 104 °C for an additional 150 minutes.

(5) The processing establishment[8] in a region listed in this section must comply with the following requirements:

(i) All areas, utensils, and equipment likely to contact the pork or pork products to be processed, including skinning, deboning, cutting, and packing areas, and related utensils and equipment, must be cleaned and disinfected after processing pork or pork products not eligible for export to the United States and before processing any pork or pork products eligible for export to the United States.

(ii) Pork or pork products eligible for export to the United States may not be handled, cut, or otherwise processed at the same time as any pork or pork products not eligible for export to the United States.

(iii) Pork or pork products eligible for export to the United States must be packed in clean new packaging that is clearly distinguishable from that containing any pork or pork products not eligible for export to the United States.

[8] As a condition of entry into the United States, pork or pork products must also meet all of the requirements of the Federal Meat Inspection Act (21 U.S.C. 601 *et seq.*) and regulations thereunder (9 CFR, chapter III, part 327), including requirements that the pork or pork products be prepared only in approved establishments.

(c) Pork or pork products consigned from the port of arrival to an approved establishment under the provisions of paragraph (b)(2) of this section shall be moved from the port of arrival to the approved establishment under Customs seals or seals of the Administrator, and shall be otherwise handled as the Administrator, may direct in order to guard against the introduction and dissemination of the contagion of African swine fever. Seals applied under this section shall not be broken except by persons authorized to do so by the Administrator.

(d) Pork or pork products imported into the United States from a region listed in this section which do not meet the requirements specified in this section shall be seized, quarantined, and disposed of as the Administrator, may direct in order to guard against the introduction and dissemination of the contagion of the disease.

(Approved by the Office of Management and Budget under control number 0579–0015)

[28 FR 5980, June 13, 1963]

EDITORIAL NOTE: For FEDERAL REGISTER citations affecting §94.8, see the List of CFR Sections Affected, which appears in the Finding Aids section of the printed volume and at *www.fdsys.gov*.

§94.9 Pork and pork products from regions where classical swine fever exists.

(a) APHIS considers classical swine fever to exist in all regions of the world except those declared free of the disease by APHIS.

(1) A list of regions that APHIS has declared free of classical swine fever is maintained on the APHIS Web site at *http://www.aphis.usda.gov/import_export/animals/animal_disease_status.shtml*. Copies of the list will also be available via postal mail, fax, or email upon request to the Sanitary Trade Issues Team, National Center for Import and Export, Veterinary Services, Animal and Plant Health Inspection Service, 4700 River Road Unit 38, Riverdale, Maryland 20737.

(2) APHIS will add a region to the list of those it has declared free of classical swine fever after it conducts an evaluation of the region in accordance with §92.2 of this subchapter and finds that the disease is not present. In the case of a region formerly on this list that is removed due to an outbreak, the region may be returned to the list in accordance with the procedures for reestablishment of a region's disease-free status in §92.4 of this subchapter. APHIS will remove a region from the list of those it has declared free of classical swine fever upon determining that the disease exists in the region based on reports APHIS receives of outbreaks of the disease from veterinary officials of the exporting country, from the World Organization for Animal Health (OIE), or from other sources the Administrator determines to be reliable.

(b) The APHIS-defined European CSF region is a single region of low-risk for CSF.

(c) Except as provided in §94.31 for the APHIS-defined European CSF region, no fresh pork or pork product may be imported into the United States from any region where classical swine fever is known to exist unless it complies with the following requirements:[9]

(1) Such pork or pork product has been treated in accordance with one of the following procedures:

(i) Such pork and pork product has been fully cooked by a commercial method in a container hermetically sealed promptly after filling but before such cooking, so that such cooking and sealing produced a fully sterilized product which is shelf-stable without refrigeration;

(ii) Such pork or pork product is in compliance with the following requirements:

(A) All bones were completely removed prior to cooking; and

(B) Such pork or pork product was heated by other than a flash-heating method to an internal temperature of 69 °C. (156 °F.) throughout;

(iii) Such pork or pork product is in compliance with the following requirements:

(A) All bones have been completely removed in the region of origin, and

[9] See also other provisions of this part and parts 93, 95, and 96 of this chapter, and part 327 of this title, for other prohibitions and restrictions upon the importation of swine and swine products.

(B) The meat has been held in an unfrozen, fresh condition for at least 3 days immediately following the slaughter of the animals from which it was derived, and

(C) The meat has been thoroughly cured and fully dried for a period of not less than 90 days so that the product is shelf stable without refrigeration: *Provided*, That the period of curing and drying shall be 45 days if the pork or pork product is accompanied to the processing establishment by a certificate of an official of the national government of a classical swine fever free region which specifies that:

(*1*) The pork involved originated in that region and the pork or pork product was consigned to a processing establishment in __________ (a region not listed under paragraph (a) of this section as free of classical swine fever), in a closed container sealed by the national veterinary authorities of the classical swine fever free region by seals of a serially numbered type; and

(*2*) The numbers of the seals used were entered on the meat inspection certificate of the classical swine fever free region which accompanied the shipment from such free region: *And, provided further*, That the certificate required by paragraph (c)(3) of this section also states that: The container seals specified in paragraph (c)(1)(iii)(C)(*1*) of this section were found intact and free of any evidence of tampering on arrival at the processing establishment by a national veterinary inspector; and the processing establishment from which the pork or pork product is shipped to the United States does not receive or process any live swine, and uses only pork or pork product which originates in regions listed under paragraph (a) of this section as free of classical swine fever and processes all such pork or pork products in accordance with paragraph (c)(1)(i), (ii), or (iii) of this section; or

(iv) Pork rind pellets (pork skins) originating in regions where classical swine fever is known to exist may be imported into the United States provided they have been cooked in one of the following ways:

(A) *One-step process*. The pork skins must be cooked in oil for at least 80 minutes when oil temperature is consistently maintained at a minimum of 114 °C.

(B) *Two-step process*. The pork skins must be dry-cooked at a minimum of 260 °C for approximately 210 minutes after which they must be cooked in hot oil (deep-fried) at a minimum of 104 °C for an additional 150 minutes.

(2) Articles under paragraph (c)(1)(ii), (iii), or (iv) of this section were prepared in an inspected establishment that is eligible to have its products imported into the United States under the Federal Meat Inspection Act and § 327.2 of this title; and,

(3) In addition to the foreign meat inspection certificate required by § 327.4 of this title, pork and pork products prepared under paragraph (c)(1)(ii), (iii), or (iv) of this section shall be accompanied by a certificate that states that the provisions of paragraph (c)(1)(ii), (iii), or (iv) of this section have been met. This certificate shall be issued by an official of the national government of the region of origin who is authorized to issue the foreign meat inspection certificate required by § 327.4 of this title.[10] Upon arrival of the pork or pork products in the United States, the certificate must be presented to an authorized inspector at the port of arrival.

(4) Small amounts of pork or pork product, subject to the restrictions in this section, may in specific cases be imported for purposes of examination, testing, or analysis if the importer applies for and receives written approval for such importation from the Administrator. Approval will be granted only when the Administrator determines that the articles have been processed by heat in a manner so that such importation will not endanger the livestock of the United States.

(d) Thoroughly cured and fully dried pork and pork products from regions where both classical swine fever and swine vesicular disease are known or considered to exist need not comply with paragraph (c)(1)(iii) of this section if they are in compliance with the provisions of § 94.12(b)(1)(iii) of this part.

[10] The certification required may be placed on the foreign meat inspection certificate prescribed by § 327.4 of this title or may be contained in a separate document.

(e) Uncooked pork or pork products that originated in a region considered to be free of classical swine fever (CSF) and are processed in a region where CSF exists may be imported into the United States under the following conditions:

(1) *Shipment to approved establishments.* (i) The uncooked pork or pork products must be shipped from the CSF-free region of origin in closed containers sealed with serially numbered seals applied by an official of the national government of that region. They must be accompanied by a certificate that is signed by an official of that region's national government and that specifies the product's region of origin, the name and number of the establishment of origin, and the processing establishment to which the uncooked pork or pork products are consigned, and the numbers of the seals applied to the shipping containers.

(ii) The uncooked pork or pork products may be removed from containers at the processing establishment in the region where CSF is considered to exist only after an official of that region's national government has determined that the seals are intact and free of any evidence of tampering.

(2) *Handling of uncooked pork and pork products.* Establishments[11] in regions where CSF is considered to exist that process uncooked pork or pork products for export to the United States:

(i) May not receive or handle any live swine;

(ii) May not receive, handle, or process uncooked pork or pork products that originate in regions affected with CSF;

(iii) Must keep the certificate required by paragraph (e)(1)(i) of this section on file at the facility for a period of at least 2 years after export of processed products to the United States, and must make those records available to USDA inspectors during inspections; and

(iv) Must be evaluated and approved by APHIS through a site inspection.

(3) *Compliance agreement.* The operators of the processing establishment must sign a compliance agreement with APHIS, stating that:

(i) All meat processed for importation to the United States will be processed in accordance with the requirements of this part; and

(ii) A full-time, salaried meat inspection official of the national government of the region in which the processing facility is located will supervise the processing and examination of the product, and certify that it has been processed in accordance with this section; and

(iii) APHIS personnel or other persons authorized by the Administrator may enter the establishment, unannounced, to inspect the establishment and its records.

(4) *Cooperative service agreement.* The processing establishment, or a party on its behalf, must enter into a cooperative service agreement with APHIS to pay all expenses incurred by APHIS for the initial evaluation of the processing establishment and periodically thereafter, including travel, salary, subsistence, administrative overhead, and other incidental expenses, including excess baggage up to 150 pounds. In accordance with the terms of the cooperative service agreement, before the APHIS representative's site inspection, the operator of the processing establishment or the party acting on their behalf must deposit with the Administrator an amount equal to the approximate cost of one inspection by an APHIS representative, including travel, salary, subsistence, administrative overhead, and other incidental expenses, including excess baggage up to 150 pounds. As funds from that amount are obligated, a bill for costs incurred based on official accounting records will be issued to restore the deposit to the original level, revised as necessary to allow for inflation or other changes in estimated costs. To be current, bills must be paid within 14 days of receipt.

(5) *Shipment to the United States.* Uncooked pork or pork products to be imported into the United States must be shipped from the region where they were processed in closed containers sealed with serially numbered seals applied by an official of the national government of that region. The shipments must be accompanied by a certificate signed by an official of the national government of the region where the

[11] See footnote 9.

pork or pork products were processed that lists the numbers of the seals applied and states that all of the conditions of this paragraph (e) have been met. The certificate shall also state that the container seals specified in paragraph (e)(1)(i) and (ii) of this section were found by an official of the region's national government to be intact and free of any evidence of tampering on arrival at the processing establishment in the CSF-affected region. A copy of this certificate must be kept on file at the processing establishment for at least 2 years.

(Approved by the Office of Management and Budget under control numbers 0579–0015 and 0579–0333)

[37 FR 21149, Oct. 6, 1972]

EDITORIAL NOTE: For FEDERAL REGISTER citations affecting § 94.9, see the List of CFR Sections Affected, which appears in the Finding Aids section of the printed volume and at *www.fdsys.gov.*

§ 94.10 Swine from regions where classical swine fever exists.

(a) APHIS considers classical swine fever to exist in all regions of the world except those declared free of the disease by APHIS.

(1) A list of regions that APHIS has declared free of classical swine fever is maintained on the APHIS Web site at *http://www.aphis.usda.gov/import_export/animals/animal_disease_status.shtml.* Copies of the list will also be available via postal mail, fax, or email upon request to the Sanitary Trade Issues Team, National Center for Import and Export, Veterinary Services, Animal and Plant Health Inspection Service, 4700 River Road, Unit 38, Riverdale, Maryland 20737.

(2) APHIS will add a region to the list of those it has declared free of classical swine fever after it conducts an evaluation of the region in accordance with § 92.2 of this subchapter and finds that the disease is not present. In the case of a region formerly on this list that is removed due to an outbreak, the region may be returned to the list in accordance with the procedures for reestablishment of a region's disease-free status in § 92.4 of this subchapter. APHIS will remove a region from the list of those it has declared free of classical swine fever upon determining that the disease exists in the region based on reports APHIS receives of outbreaks of the disease from veterinary officials of the exporting country, from the World Organization for Animal Health (OIE), or from other sources the Administrator determines to be reliable.

(b) The APHIS-defined European CSF region is a single region of low-risk for CSF.

(c) Except as provided in § 94.31 for the APHIS-defined European CSF region, no swine that are moved from or transit any region where classical swine fever is known to exist may be imported into the United States, except for wild swine imported into the United States in accordance with paragraph (d) of this section.

(d) Wild swine may be allowed importation into the United States by the Administrator upon request in specific cases under § 93.501 or § 93.504(c) of this chapter.

[71 FR 29070, May 19, 2006, as amended at 71 FR 31070, June 1, 2006; 72 FR 30470, June 1, 2007; 72 FR 67232, Nov. 28, 2007; 75 FR 69857, Nov. 16, 2010; 76 FR 70039, Nov. 10, 2011; 77 FR 1393, Jan. 10, 2012; 78 FR 72998, Dec. 4, 2013]

§ 94.11 Restrictions on importation of meat and other animal products from specified regions.

(a) The meat of ruminants or swine, and other animal products, and ship stores, airplane meals, and baggage containing such meat or animal products originating in any region listed as provided in paragraph (a)(2) of this section may not be imported into the United States unless the requirements in this section, in addition to other applicable requirements of chapter III of this title, are met. However, meat and meat products that meet the requirements of § 94.4 do not have to comply with the requirements of this section. As used in this section, the term "other animal product" means all parts of the carcass of any ruminant or swine, other than meat and articles regulated under part 95 or part 96 of this chapter.

(1) The regions listed under paragraph (a)(2) of this section have been declared free of rinderpest and foot-and-mouth disease by APHIS as provided in § 94.1(a) but supplement their

national meat supply by the importation of fresh (chilled or frozen) meat of ruminants or swine from regions that APHIS considers to be affected with rinderpest or foot-and-mouth disease as provided in § 94.1(a); or have a common land border with regions considered to be affected with rinderpest or foot-and-mouth disease; or import ruminants or swine from regions considered to be affected with rinderpest or foot-and-mouth disease under conditions less restrictive than would be acceptable for importation into the United States. Thus, the meat may be commingled with the fresh (chilled or frozen) meat of animals from an affected region, resulting in an undue risk of introducing rinderpest or foot-and-mouth disease into the United States.

(2) A list of regions whose products are regulated under this section is maintained on the APHIS Web site at *http://www.aphis.usda.gov/import_export/animals/animal_disease_status.shtml.* Copies of the list will also be available via postal mail, fax, or email upon request to the Sanitary Trade Issues Team, National Center for Import and Export, Veterinary Services, Animal and Plant Health Inspection Service, 4700 River Road Unit 38, Riverdale, Maryland 20737.

(3) APHIS will add a region to the list of those whose products are regulated under this section after conducting an evaluation of the region and determining that one or more of the circumstances described in paragraph (a)(1) of this section exists. APHIS will remove a region from the list upon conducting an evaluation of the region and determining that the circumstances in paragraph (a)(1) of this section no longer exist or upon determining that rinderpest or foot-and-mouth disease exists in the region.

(b) All meat or other animal product from such regions, whether in personal-use amounts or commercial lots (except that which has been fully cooked by a commercial method in a container hermetically sealed promptly after filling but before such cooking and sealing produced a fully sterilized product which is shelf-stable without refrigeration) shall have been prepared only in an inspected establishment that is eligible to have its products imported into the United States under the Federal Meat Inspection Act (21 U.S.C. 601 *et seq.*) and the regulations in § 327.2, chapter III of this title, issued thereunder, and shall be accompanied by a Department-approved meat inspection certificate prescribed in § 327.4 in chapter III of this title, or similar certificate approved by the Administrator, as adequate to effectuate the purposes of this section, regardless of the purpose or amount of product in the shipment.

(c) *Additional certification.* Meat of ruminants or swine or other animal products from any region listed under paragraph (a)(2) of this section must be accompanied by additional certification by a full-time salaried veterinary official of the agency in the national government that is responsible for the health of the animals within that region. Upon arrival of the meat of ruminants or swine or other animal product in the United States, the certification must be presented to an authorized inspector at the port of arrival. The certification must give the name and official establishment number of the establishment where the animals were slaughtered, and shall state that:

(1) The slaughtering establishment is not permitted to receive animals that originated in, or have ever been in, or that have been aboard a means of conveyance at the time such means of conveyance called at or landed at a port in, a region designated under § 94.1(a) as a region where rinderpest or foot-and-mouth disease exists;

(2) The slaughtering establishment is not permitted to receive meat or other animal products derived from ruminants or swine which originated in such a rinderpest or foot-and-mouth disease affected region, or meat or other animal products from a rinderpest and foot-and-mouth disease free region transported through a rinderpest or foot-and-mouth disease affected region except in containers sealed with serially numbered seals of the National Government of the noninfected region of origin;

(3) The meat or other animal product covered by the certificate was derived from animals born and raised in a region listed under § 94.1(a) as free of rinderpest and foot-and-mouth disease and

the meat or other animal product has never been in any region in which rinderpest or foot-and-mouth disease existed;

(4) The meat or other animal product has been processed, stored, and transported to the means of conveyance that will bring the article to the United States in a manner to preclude its being commingled or otherwise in contact with meat or other animal products that do not comply with the conditions contained in this certificate.

(Approved by the Office of Management and Budget under control number 0579–0015)

[38 FR 2752, Jan. 30, 1973]

EDITORIAL NOTE: For FEDERAL REGISTER citations affecting § 94.11, see the List of CFR Sections Affected, which appears in the Finding Aids section of the printed volume and at *www.fdsys.gov*.

§ 94.12 Pork and pork products from regions where swine vesicular disease exists.

(a) APHIS considers swine vesicular disease to exist in all regions of the world except those declared free of the disease by APHIS.

(1) A list of regions that APHIS has declared free of swine vesicular disease is maintained on the APHIS Web site at *http://www.aphis.usda.gov/import_export/animals/animal_disease_status.shtml*. Copies of the list will also be available via postal mail, fax, or email upon request to the Sanitary Trade Issues Team, National Center for Import and Export, Veterinary Services, Animal and Plant Health Inspection Service, 4700 River Road Unit 38, Riverdale, Maryland 20737.

(2) APHIS will add a region to the list of those it has declared free of swine vesicular disease after it conducts an evaluation of the region in accordance with § 92.2 of this subchapter and finds that the disease is not present. In the case of a region formerly on this list that is removed due to an outbreak, the region may be returned to the list in accordance with the procedures for reestablishment of a region's disease-free status in § 92.4 of this subchapter. APHIS will remove a region from the list of those it has declared free of swine vesicular disease upon determining that the disease exists in the region based on reports APHIS receives of outbreaks of the disease from veterinary officials of the exporting country, from the World Organization for Animal Health (OIE), or from other sources the Administrator determines to be reliable.

(b) No pork or pork product may be imported into the United States from any region where swine vesicular disease is known to exist unless it complies with the following requirements and it is not otherwise prohibited importation into the United States under this part:

(1) Such pork or pork product has been treated in accordance with one of the following procedures:

(i) Such pork or pork product has been fully cooked by a commercial method in a container hermetically sealed promptly after filling, but before such cooking, so that such cooking and sealing produced a fully sterilized product which is shelf-stable without refrigeration.

(ii) Such pork or pork product is in compliance with the following requirements:

(A) All bones were completely removed prior to cooking; and

(B) Such pork or pork product received heat treatment in a commercially accepted manner used for perishable canned pork products so that it reached an internal temperature of 69 °C. (156 °F.) throughout.

(iii) Such pork or pork product if cured and dried is in compliance with the following requirements:

(A) All bones have been completely removed in the region of origin, and

(B) Such pork or pork products shall be consigned directly from the port of entry in the United States to a meat processing establishment operating under Federal meat inspection and approved by the Administrator,[12] for

[12] The names and addresses of approved establishments may be obtained from, and request for approval of any establishment may be made to, the Animal and Plant Health Inspection Service, Veterinary Services, National Center for Import-Export, 4700 River Road Unit 38, Riverdale, Maryland 20737–1231. Establishments will be approved only if the Administrator determines that the imported

heating to an internal temperature of 166 °F. During movement from the port of entry to the meat processing establishment, the pork or pork products must be moved under Department seals or seals of the U.S. Customs Service, and shall be otherwise handled as the Administrator may direct in order to guard against the introduction and dissemination of swine vesicular disease. Seals applied under this section may not be broken except by persons authorized by the Administrator to do so.

(iv) Such pork or pork product, if it originated in a swine vesicular disease free region, has been cured and dried and is in compliance with the following requirements:

(A) All bones have been completely removed, either in the region of origin or in the region where the pork or pork products are processed; and

(B)(*1*) Such pork or pork product is accompanied from the swine vesicular disease free region of origin to the processing establishment in the swine vesicular disease affected region by a certificate signed by an official of the National Government of the swine vesicular disease free region of origin specifying that the pork or pork product involved originated in that region and the pork or pork product was consigned to a processing establishment in __________ (a region not listed under paragraph (a)(1) of this section as free of swine vesicular disease), in a closed container sealed by the national veterinary authorities of the swine vesicular disease free region of origin by seals of a serially numbered type. The numbers of these seals shall be entered on this certificate; and

(*2*) The certificate required by paragraph (b)(3) of this section shall also state that:

(*i*) The container seals specified in paragraph (b)(1)(iv)(B)(*1*) of this section were found intact and free of any evidence of tampering on arrival at the processing establishment in the swine vesicular disease affected region by a national veterinary inspector of that region,

(*ii*) The processing establishment from which the pork or pork product was shipped to the United States does not receive or process any live swine, and uses only pork or pork products which originate in regions listed under paragraph (a)(1) of this section as free of swine vesicular disease; and

(*iii*) That such establishment processes all such pork or pork products in accordance with paragraph (b)(1)(i), (ii), (iii) or (iv) of this section.

(v) Such pork or pork product is in compliance with the following requirements:

(A) All bones were completely removed prior to cooking; and

(B) Such pork or pork product received continual heat treatment in an oven for a minimum of 10 hours so that it reached an internal temperature of 65 °C. (149 °F.) throughout. The oven temperature started at a minimum of 62 °C. (143.6 °F.) and reached at least 85 °C. (185 °F.).

(vi) Pork rind pellets (pork skins) must be cooked in one of the following ways:

(A) *One-step process*. The pork skins must be cooked in oil for at least 80 minutes when oil temperature is consistently maintained at a minimum of 114 °C.

(B) *Two-step process*. The pork skins must be dry-cooked at a minimum of 260 °C for approximately 210 minutes after which they must be cooked in hot oil (deep-fried) at a minimum of 104 °C for an additional 150 minutes.

(2) Articles under paragraph (b)(1)(ii), (iii) or (iv) of this section were prepared in an inspected establishment that is eligible to have its products imported into the United States under the Federal Meat Inspection Act and the regulations in § 327.2 in chapter III of this title.

(3) In addition to the foreign meat inspection certificate required in § 327.4 of this title, pork or pork products prepared under paragraph (b)(1)(ii), (iii) or (iv) of this section shall be accompanied by certification that paragraph (b)(1)(ii), (b)(1)(iii)(A), or (b)(1)(iv)(B)(2)

---

articles will be so handled at the establishment as to prevent the introduction and dissemination of livestock or poultry diseases into the United States. Approval of any establishment may be refused or withdrawn only after the operator thereof has been given notice of the proposed action and has had an opportunity to present his views thereon.

of this section has been met. The certification shall be issued by an official of the national government of the region of origin who is authorized to issue the foreign meat inspection certificate required by §327.4 of this title.[13] Upon arrival of the pork or pork products in the United States, the certificate must be presented to an authorized inspector at the port of arrival.

(4) Small amounts of pork or pork product subject to the restrictions of this section, may in specific cases be imported for purposes of examination, testing, or analysis, if the importer applies for and receives written approval for such importation from the Administrator, authorizing such importation. Approval will be granted only when the Administrator determines that the articles have been processed by heat in a manner so that such importation will not endanger the livestock of the United States.

(c) *Requirements for pork-filled pasta products from regions affected with swine vesicular disease.* (1) Pork-filled pasta products processed for export to the United States may only be filled with pork or pork products that are otherwise eligible to be exported to the United States and that meet the requirements of paragraph (b)(1)(i), (ii), or (v) of this section or of §94.17.

(2) The operator of the pork-filled pasta processing facility must have signed a cooperative service agreement with APHIS prior to receipt of the pork intended to be used in pork-filled pasta products, stating that all such pork will be processed only in accordance with §94.12 or §94.17. Pursuant to the cooperative service agreement, the establishment must allow the unannounced entry into the establishment of APHIS representatives, or other persons authorized by the Administrator, for the purpose of inspecting the facilities, operations, and records of the establishment. The establishment must be current in paying all costs for such inspections (it is anticipated that such inspections will occur up to four times per year). These costs include travel, salary, subsistence, administrative overhead, and other incidental expenses (including an excess baggage provision up to 150 pounds). In accordance with the terms of the cooperative service agreement, the operator of the processing establishment must deposit with the Administrator an amount equal to the approximate costs for APHIS to inspect the establishment one time, including travel, salary, subsistence, administrative overhead and other incidental expenses (including an excess baggage provision up to 150 pounds), and, as funds from that amount are obligated, bills for costs incurred based on official accounting records will be issued to restore the deposit to its original level. Amounts to restore the deposit to its original level must be paid within 14 days of receipt of such bills.

(3) At the pasta processing establishment, pork intended to be used for pork-filled pasta products for export to the United States must be stored apart from any meat or meat products not eligible for export to the United States, either in a separate storage room or facility or in a separate area of the same storage room. Any storage room area reserved for pork or pork products eligible for export to the United States must be separated by at least 1 meter from any storage room area where meat or meat products ineligible for export to the United States are stored and must be marked by signs and by having its borders outlined on the floor.

(4) Prior to handling pork used for pork-filled pasta products intended for export to the United States, workers at the processing facility who handle pork or pork products in the facility must shower and put on a full set of clean clothes, or wait 24 hours after handling pork or pork products that are not eligible for importation into the United States.

(5) All equipment and machinery that will come in contact with the pork or other ingredients of pork-filled pasta products intended for export to the United States must be cleaned and disinfected before each use.

(6) Processing lines working with pork-filled pasta products for export to the United States must be totally dedicated to the production of such products for the time needed to complete a

[13] See footnote 10.

given lot. When any processing line in a facility is working with pork-filled pasta products intended for export to the United States, no other processing lines in the same facility may work on products using meat that is not eligible for export to the United States.

(7) Processing facilities that are completely dedicated to producing only pork-filled pasta products for export to the United States and do not receive, handle, or process any animal product not intended for export to the United States are exempt from the requirements of paragraphs (c)(3) through (c)(6) of this section.

(8) During processing, the pork-filled pasta must be steam-heated to a minimum internal temperature of 90 °C, then dried, cooled, and packed to make the product shelf stable without refrigeration.

(9) The processing facility must maintain under lock and key, for a minimum of 2 years, an original record of each lot of pork or pork products used for pork-filled pasta products for export to the United States. Each record must include the following:

(i) The date that the cooked or dry-cured pork product was received in the processing facility;

(ii) The number of packages, the number of hams or cooked pork products per package, and the weight of each package;

(iii) A lot number or other identification marks;

(iv) The health certificate that accompanied the cooked or dry-cured pork product from the slaughter/processing facility to the meat-filled pasta product processing facility; and

(v) The date that the pork or pork product used in the pasta started dry curing (if the product used is a dry-cured ham) or the date that the product was cooked (if the product used is a cooked pork product).

(10) The pork-filled pasta must be accompanied by a certificate issued by an official of the National Government of the region in which the pasta product is processed who is authorized to issue the foreign meat inspection certificate required under §327.4 of this title, stating that the pork-filled pasta product has been processed in accordance with the requirements of this section.

Upon arrival of the pork-filled pasta in the United States, the certificate must be presented to an inspector at the port of arrival.

(Approved by the Office of Management and Budget under control numbers 0579–0015 and 0579–0214)

[38 FR 20610, Aug. 2, 1973]

EDITORIAL NOTE: For FEDERAL REGISTER citations affecting §94.12, see the List of CFR Sections Affected, which appears in the Finding Aids section of the printed volume and at *www.fdsys.gov*.

§94.13 Restrictions on importation of pork or pork products from specified regions.

(a) Pork or pork products and ship's stores, airplane meals, and baggage containing pork or pork products, other than those articles regulated under part 95 or part 96 of this chapter, produced in any region listed under paragraph (a)(2) of this section may not be imported into the United States unless the requirements of this section, in addition to other applicable requirements of part 327 of this title, are met.

(1) The regions listed under paragraph (a)(2) of this section have been declared free of swine vesicular disease as provided in §94.12(a) but supplement their national pork supply by the importation of fresh (chilled or frozen) meat of animals from regions where swine vesicular disease is considered to exist, or have a common border with such regions, or have trade practices that are less restrictive than are acceptable to the United States. Thus, the pork or pork products may be commingled with fresh (chilled or frozen) meat of animals from a region where swine vesicular disease is considered to exist, resulting in an undue risk of swine vesicular disease introduction into the United States.

(2) A list of regions whose products are regulated under this section is maintained on the APHIS Web site at *http://www.aphis.usda.gov/import_export/animals/animal_disease_status.shtml*. Copies of the list will also be available via postal mail, fax, or email upon request to the Sanitary Trade Issues Team, National Center for Import and Export, Veterinary Services, Animal and Plant Health Inspection Service,

4700 River Road Unit 38, Riverdale, Maryland 20737.

(3) APHIS will add a region to the list of those whose products are regulated under this section after conducting an evaluation of the region and determining that one or more of the circumstances listed in paragraph (a)(1) of this section exists. APHIS will remove a region from the list upon conducting an evaluation of the region and determining that the circumstances in paragraph (a)(1) of this section no longer exist or upon determining that swine vesicular disease exists in the region.

(b) All such pork or pork products, except those treated in accordance with § 94.12(b)(1)(i) of this part, shall have been prepared only in inspected establishments that are eligible to have their products imported into the United States under the Federal Meat Inspection Act (21 U.S.C. 601 *et seq.*) and under § 327.2 of this title and shall be accompanied by the foreign meat inspection certificate required by § 327.4 of this title. Upon arrival of the pork or pork products in the United States, the foreign meat inspection certificate must be presented to an authorized inspector at the port of arrival.

(c) Unless such pork or pork products are treated according to one of the procedures described in § 94.12(b) of this part, the pork or pork products must be accompanied by an additional certificate issued by a full-time salaried veterinary official of the agency in the national government responsible for the health of the animals within that region. Upon arrival of the pork or pork products in the United States, the certificate must be presented to an authorized inspector at the port of arrival. The certificate shall state the name and official establishment number of the establishment where the swine involved were slaughtered and the pork was processed. The certificate shall also state that:

(1) The slaughtering establishment is not permitted to receive animals that originated in a region considered to have swine vesicular disease or that have ever been in a region in which swine vesicular disease existed.

(2) The slaughtering establishment is not permitted to receive pork derived from swine which originated in such a region or pork from swine from a swine vesicular disease free region which has been transported through a region where swine vesicular disease is considered to exist except pork which was transported in containers sealed with serially numbered seals of the National Government of a region of origin listed under § 94.12(a) as a region considered free of the disease.

(3) The pork has been processed, stored, and transported to the means of conveyance that will bring the article to the United States in a manner that precludes its being commingled or otherwise coming in contact with pork or pork products that have not been handled in accordance with the requirements of this section.

(Approved by the Office of Management and Budget under control number 0579–0015)

[38 FR 20611, Aug. 2, 1973]

EDITORIAL NOTE: For FEDERAL REGISTER citations affecting § 94.13, see the List of CFR Sections Affected, which appears in the Finding Aids section of the printed volume and at *www.fdsys.gov*.

§ 94.14 Swine from regions where swine vesicular disease exists; importations prohibited.

(a) Swine vesicular disease is known to exist in all regions of the world except those listed under § 94.12(a) of this part. No swine which are moved from or transit any region in which swine vesicular disease is known to exist may be imported into the United States except wild swine imported in accordance with paragraph (b) of this section.

(b) Wild swine may be allowed importation into the United States by the Administrator upon request in specific cases under § 93.501 or § 93.504(c) of this chapter.

(Approved by the Office of Management and Budget under control number 0579–0040)

[54 FR 7395, Feb. 21, 1989, as amended at 55 FR 31558, Aug. 2, 1990; 59 FR 67134, Dec. 29, 1994; 62 FR 56023, Oct. 28, 1997; 77 FR 1394, Jan. 10, 2012]

§ 94.15 Animal products and materials; movement and handling.

(a) Any animal product or material which would be eligible for entry into the United States, as specified in the regulations in this part, may transit through the United States for immediate export if the following conditions are met:

(1) Notification of the transiting of such animal product or material must be made by the importer to the Plant Protection and Quarantine Officer at the United States port of arrival prior to such transiting, and

(2) The animal product or material transited shall be contained in a sealed, leakproof carrier or container which shall remain sealed while aboard the transporting carrier or other means of conveyance, or if the container or carrier in which such animal product or material is transported is offloaded in the United States for reshipment, it shall remain sealed at all times.

(b) Pork and pork products from Baja California, Baja California Sur, Campeche, Chihuahua, Coahuila, Nuevo Leon, Quintana Roo, Sinaloa, Sonora, and Yucatan, Mexico, that are not eligible for entry into the United States in accordance with this part may transit the United States via land border ports for immediate export if the following conditions are met:

(1) The person desiring to move the pork and pork products through the United States obtains a United States Veterinary Permit for Importation and Transportation of Controlled Materials and Organisms and Vectors (VS Form 16–6). (An application for the permit may be obtained from the Animal and Plant Health Inspection Service, Veterinary Services, National Center for Import-Export, 4700 River Road Unit 38, Riverdale, Maryland 20737–1231 or by visiting *http://www.aphis.usda.gov/animal_health/permits/*.)

(2) The pork or pork products are packaged at a Tipo Inspección Federal plant in Baja California, Baja California Sur, Campeche, Chihuahua, Coahuila, Nuevo Leon, Quintana Roo, Sinaloa, Sonora, or Yucatan, Mexico, in leakproof containers and sealed with serially numbered seals of the Government of Mexico, and the containers remain sealed during the entire time they are in transit across Mexico and the United States.

(3) The person moving the pork and pork products through the United States notifies, in writing, the Plant Protection and Quarantine Officer at the United States port of arrival prior to such transiting. The notification must include the following information regarding the pork and pork products:

(i) Permit number;

(ii) Times and dates of arrival in the United States;

(iii) Time schedule and route to be followed through the United States; and

(iv) Serial numbers of the seals on the containers.

(4) The pork and pork products transit the United States under Customs bond and are exported from the United States within the time limit specified on the permit. Any pork or pork products that have not been exported within the time limit specified on the permit or that have not been transited in accordance with the permit or applicable requirements of this part will be destroyed or otherwise disposed of as the Administrator may direct pursuant to the Animal Health Protection Act (7 U.S.C. 8301 *et seq.*).

(c) Poultry carcasses, parts, or products (except eggs and egg products) from Baja California, Baja California Sur, Campeche, Chihuahua, Nuevo Leon, Quintana Roo, Sinaloa, Sonora, Tamaulipas, or Yucatan, Mexico, that are not eligible for entry into the United States in accordance with the regulations in this part may transit the United States via land ports for immediate export if the following conditions are met:

(1) The person desiring to move the poultry carcasses, parts, or products through the United States obtains a United States Veterinary Permit for Importation and Transportation of Controlled Materials and Organisms and Vectors (VS Form 16–6). An application for the permit may be obtained from the Animal and Plant Health Inspection Service, Veterinary Services, National Center for Import-Export, 4700 River Road Unit 38, Riverdale, Maryland 20737–1231 or by visiting *http://www.aphis.usda.gov/animal_health/permits/* .

(2) The poultry carcasses, parts, or products are packaged at a Tipo Inspeccioón Federal plant in Baja California, Baja California Sur, Campeche,

Chihuahua, Nuevo Leon, Quintana Roo, Sinaloa, Sonora, Tamaulipas, or Yucatan, Mexico, in leakproof containers with serially numbered seals of the Government of Mexico, and the containers remain sealed during the entire time they are in transit across Mexico and the United States.

(3) The person moving the poultry carcasses, parts, or products through the United States notifies, in writing, the Plant Protection and Quarantine Officer at the U.S. port of arrival prior to such transiting. The notification must include the following information regarding the poultry to transit the United States:

(i) Permit number;

(ii) Times and dates of arrival in the United States;

(iii) Time schedule and route to be followed through the United States; and

(iv) Serial numbers of the seals on the containers.

(4) The poultry carcasses, parts, or products transit the United States under U.S. Customs bond and are exported from the United States within the time limit specified on the permit. Any poultry carcasses, parts, or products that have not been exported within the time limit specified on the permit or that have not transited in accordance with the permit or applicable requirements of this part will be destroyed or otherwise disposed of as the Administrator may direct pursuant to the Animal Health Protection Act (7 U.S.C. 8301 *et seq.*).

(d) Meat and other products of ruminants or swine from regions listed in § 94.11(a) and pork and pork products from regions listed in § 94.13 that do not meet the requirements of § 94.11(b) or § 94.13(a) may transit through the United States for immediate export, provided the provisions of paragraph (a) of this section are met, and provided all other applicable provisions of this part are met.

(e) Any meat or other animal products not otherwise eligible for entry into the United States, as provided in this part and part 95 of this chapter, may transit the United States for immediate export if the following conditions are met:

(1) Notification of the transiting of such meat or other animal product is made by the importer to the Plant Protection and Quarantine officer at the United States port of arrival prior to such transiting;

(2) The meat or other animal product is contained in a sealed, leakproof carrier or container, which remains sealed while aboard the transporting carrier or other means of conveyance, or, if the container or carrier in which the meat or other animal product is transported is offloaded in the United States for reshipment, it remains sealed at all times;

(3) Such transit is limited to the maritime or airport port of arrival only, with no overland movement outside the airport terminal area or dock area of the maritime port; and

(4) The meat or other animal product is not held or stored for more than 72 hours at the maritime or airport port of arrival.

(Approved by the Office of Management and Budget under control numbers 0579–0040 and 0579–0145)

[43 FR 4595, Feb. 3, 1978, as amended at 57 FR 23928, June 5, 1992; 57 FR 43886, Sept. 23, 1992; 59 FR 67616, Dec. 30, 1994; 60 FR 57315, Nov. 15, 1995; 61 FR 32647, June 25, 1996; 62 FR 24804, May 7, 1997; 62 FR 56023, Oct. 28, 1997; 65 FR 37270, June 14, 2000; 65 FR 50605, Aug. 21, 2000; 68 FR 6345, Feb. 7, 2003; 81 FR 40152, June 21, 2016]

§ 94.16 Milk and milk products.

(a) The following milk products are exempt from the provisions of this part:

(1) Cheese, but not including cheese with liquid and not including cheese containing any item that is regulated by other sections of this part, unless such item is independently eligible for importation into the United States under this part;

(2) Butter; and

(3) Butteroil.

(b) Milk and milk products originating in, or shipped from, any region where rinderpest or foot-and-mouth disease is considered to exist under § 94.1(a) may be imported into the United States if they meet the requirements of paragraphs (b)(1), (2), or (3) of this section:

(1) They are in a concentrated liquid form and have been processed by heat by a commercial method in a container hermetically sealed promptly after filling but before such heating, so as to be shelf stable without refrigeration.

(2) They are dry milk or dry milk products, including dry whole milk, nonfat dry milk, dried whey, dried buttermilk, and formulations which contain any such dry milk products, and are consigned directly to an approved establishment[14] for further processing in a manner approved by the Administrator, as adequate to prevent the introduction or dissemination of livestock diseases into the United States. However, in specific cases, upon request by the importer to the Administrator, and approval by the Administrator, they may be stored for a temporary period in an approved warehouse[14] under the supervision of an inspector of the Animal and Plant Health Inspection Service pending movement to an approved establishment. Such products shall be transported from the United States port of first arrival to an approved establishment[14] or an approved warehouse,[14] and from an approved warehouse[14] to an approved establishment[14] only under Department seals or seals of the U.S. Customs Service. Such seals shall be broken only by such an inspector or other person authorized to do so by the Administrator. Such products shall not be removed from the approved warehouse[14] or approved establishment[14] except upon special permission by the Administrator, and upon compliance with all the conditions and requirements specified by him for such movement in each specific case.

(3) Milk and milk products not exempted under paragraph (a) and not of classes included within the provisions of paragraphs (b)(1) or (2) of this section may be imported if the importer first applies to and receives written permission from the Administrator, authorizing such importation. Permission will be granted only when the Administrator determines that such action will not endanger the health of the livestock of the United States. Products subject to this provision include but are not limited to condensed milk, long-life milks such as sterilized milk, casein and caseinates, lactose, and lactalbumin.

(4) Small amounts of milk and milk products subject to the restrictions of this part may in specific cases be imported for purposes of examination, testing, or analysis, if the importer applies to and receives written approval for such importation from the Administrator. Approval will be granted only when the Administrator determines that such action will not endanger the health of the livestock of the United States.

(c) Milk and milk products originating in and shipped from regions listed under §94.1(a) as free of rinderpest and foot-and-mouth disease but which have entered a port or otherwise

[14] The names and addresses of approved establishments or warehouses or information as to approved manner of processing, and request for approval of any such establishment, warehouse, or manner of processing may be made to the Animal and Plant Health Inspection Service, Veterinary Services, National Center for Import-Export, 4700 River Road Unit 38, Riverdale, Maryland 20737–1231. Any establishment or warehouse will be approved for the purpose of this section only if the operator has provided the Administrator, with satisfactory evidence that the establishment or warehouse has the equipment, facilities, and capability to store, handle and process the imported dry milk or dry milk product subject to §94.16(b)(2) in a manner which will prevent the introduction or dissemination of livestock diseases into the United States. Similarly, processing methods will be approved only if the Administrator determines they are adequate to prevent the introduction or dissemination of such diseases into the United States. Approval of any establishment or warehouse or processing method may be refused or withdrawn by the Administrator only after the operator thereof has been given notice of the proposed action and has had an opportunity to present his views thereon, and upon a determination by the Administrator that the conditions for approval are not met. Approval of an establishment or warehouse may also be withdrawn after such notice and opportunity if the Administrator determines that such imported dry milk or milk products have been stored, handled, or processed by the operator thereof other than at an approved establishment or warehouse or other than in an approved manner.

transited a region where APHIS considers either disease to exist may not be imported into the United States unless:

(1) The product was transported under serially numbered official seals applied at the point of origin of the shipment by an authorized representative of the region of such origin; except that, if any seal applied at the point of origin was broken by any foreign official to inspect the shipment, an authorized representative of that region applied a new serially numbered official seal to the hold, compartment, or container in which the milk or milk products were transported; and if any member of a ship's crew broke a seal, the serial number of the seal, the location of the seal, and the reason for breaking the seal were recorded in the ship's log.

(2) The numbers of such seals are listed on, or are on a list attached to, the bill of lading or similar document accompanying the shipment.

(3) Upon arrival of the carrier at the United States port, an inspector of the Animal and Plant Health Inspection Service determines that the seals are intact and that their numbers are in agreement with the numbers appearing on the accompanying document; *Provided*, That, if the representative finds that any seal has been broken or has a different number than is recorded on the accompanying document, then the milk or milk products may remain eligible for entry into the United States only if APHIS personnel are available to inspect the hold, compartment, or container, the cartons or other containers of milk or milk products, and all accompanying documentation; and the importer furnishes additional documentation (either copies of pages from the ship's log signed by the officer-in-charge, or certification from a foreign government that the original seal was removed and the new seal applied by officials of the government) that demonstrates to the satisfaction of the Administrator that the milk or milk products were not contaminated or exposed to contamination during movement from the region of origin to the United States.

(d) Except for milk and milk products imported from Canada, and except as provided in this paragraph, milk or milk products imported from a region listed under § 94.1(a) as free of rinderpest and foot-and-mouth disease must be accompanied by a certificate endorsed by a full-time, salaried veterinarian employed by the region of export. The certificate must state that the milk was produced and processed in a region listed under § 94.1(a) as free of rinderpest and foot-and-mouth disease, or that the milk product was processed in one such region from milk produced in another such region. The certificate must name the region in which the milk was produced and the region in which the milk or milk product was processed. Further, the certificate must state that, except for movement under seal as described in § 94.16(c), the milk or milk product has never been in a region in which rinderpest or foot-and-mouth disease exists. Milk or milk products from a region listed under § 94.1(a) as free of rinderpest and foot-and-mouth disease and that were processed in whole or in part from milk or milk products from a region not listed under § 94.1(a) as free of rinderpest and foot-and-mouth disease may be imported into the United States only in accordance with paragraph (b)(3) of this section.

(Approved by the Office of Management and Budget under control number 0579–0015)

[40 FR 44123, Sept. 25, 1975]

EDITORIAL NOTE: For FEDERAL REGISTER citations affecting § 94.16, see the List of CFR Sections Affected, which appears in the Finding Aids section of the printed volume and at *www.fdsys.gov*.

§ 94.17 Dry-cured pork products from regions where foot-and-mouth disease, rinderpest, African swine fever, classical swine fever, or swine vesicular disease exists.

Notwithstanding any other provisions in this part, dry-cured ham, pork shoulder, or pork loin, whether whole or sliced and packaged, shall not be prohibited from being imported into the United States if it meets the following conditions:

(a) Except for Italian-type hams, Serrano hams, Iberian hams, Iberian pork shoulders, and Iberian pork loins that have been processed in accordance with paragraph (i) of this section, the dry-cured ham, pork shoulder, or pork loin came from a swine that was never out of the region in which the dry-cured ham, pork shoulder, or pork loin was processed;

(b) The ham, pork shoulder, or pork loin came from a region determined by the Administrator, to have and to enforce laws requiring the immediate reporting to the national veterinary services in that region any premises found to have any animal infected with foot-and-mouth disease, rinderpest, African Swine fever, classical swine fever, or swine vesicular disease;

(c) The ham, pork shoulder, or pork loin came from a swine that was not on any premises where foot-and-mouth disease, rinderpest, African swine fever, classical swine fever, or swine vesicular disease exists or had existed within 60 days prior to slaughter;

(d) The whole ham, pork shoulder, or pork loin was accompanied from the slaughtering facility to the processing establishment by a numbered certificate issued by a person authorized by the government of the region of origin stating that the provisions of paragraphs (a) and (c) of this section have been met;

(e) The ham, pork shoulder, or pork loin was processed whole as set forth in paragraph (i) of this section in only one processing establishment;[15]

(f) The ham, pork shoulder, or pork loin was processed whole in a processing establishment that prior to the processing of any hams, pork shoulders, or pork loins in accordance with this section, was inspected by a veterinarian of APHIS and determined by the Administrator, to be capable of meeting the provisions of this section for processing hams, pork shoulders, or pork loins for importation into the United States;

(g) The ham, pork shoulder, or pork loin was processed whole in a processing establishment for which the operator of the establishment has signed an agreement with APHIS prior to receipt of the hams, pork shoulders, or pork loins for processing, stating that all hams, pork shoulders, or pork loins processed for importation into the United States will be processed only in accordance with the provisions of this part;

(h) Workers who handle fresh pork in the processing establishment where the dry-cured ham, pork shoulder, or pork loin was processed whole are required to shower and put on a full set of clean clothes, or to wait 24 hours after handling fresh pork, before handling hams, pork shoulders, or pork loins that have progressed in the aging/curing process as follows:

(1) In the case of Italian-type hams processed in accordance with paragraph (i)(1) of this section, those that have progressed beyond the final wash stage;

(2) In the case of Serrano hams or Iberian hams or pork shoulders processed in accordance with paragraphs (i)(2), (i)(3), or (i)(4) of this section, those that have progressed beyond salting; and

(3) In the case of Iberian pork loins processed in accordance with paragraph (i)(5) of this section, those that have progressed beyond being placed in a casing.

(i) The dry-cured ham, pork shoulder, or pork loin was processed whole in accordance with this paragraph. Except for pork fat treated to at least 76 °C (168.8 °F), which may have been placed over the meat during curing, the dry-cured pork product must have had no contact with any other meat or animal product during processing.

(1) *Italian-type hams.* The ham was processed for a period of not less than 400 days in accordance with the following conditions: after slaughter the ham was held at a temperature of 0–3 °C. (32–34.7 °F) for a minimum of 72 hours during which time the "aitch" bone and the foot was removed and the blood vessels at the end of the femur were massaged to remove any remaining blood; thereafter the ham was covered with an amount of salt equal to 4–6 percent of the weight of the ham, with a sufficient amount of water added to ensure that the salt had adhered to the ham; thereafter the ham

[15] As a condition of entry into the United States, pork and pork products must also meet all of the requirements of the Federal Meat Inspection Act (21 U.S.C. 601 *et seq.*) and regulations thereunder (9 CFR, chapter III), including requirements that the pork or pork products be prepared only in approved establishments.

was placed for 5–7 days on racks in a chamber maintained at a temperature of 0–4 °C. (32–39.2 °F) and at a relative humidity of 70–85 percent; thereafter the ham was covered with an amount of salt equal to 4–6 percent of the weight of the ham, with a sufficient amount of water added to ensure that the salt had adhered to the ham; thereafter the ham was placed for 21 days in a chamber maintained at a temperature of 0–4 °C. (32–39.2 °F.) and at a relative humidity of 70–85 percent; thereafter the salt was brushed off the ham; thereafter the ham was placed in a chamber maintained at a temperature of 1–6 °C. (33.8–42.8 °F.) and at a relative humidity of 65–80 percent for between 52 and 72 days; thereafter the ham was brushed and rinsed with water; thereafter the ham was placed in a chamber for 5–7 days at a temperature of 15–23 °C. (59–73.4 °F.) and a relative humidity of 55–85 percent; thereafter the ham was placed for curing in a chamber maintained for a minimum of 314 days at a temperature of 15–20 °C. (59–68 °F.) and at a relative humidity of 65–80 percent at the beginning and increased by 5 percent every 2½ months until a relative humidity of 85 percent was reached.

(2) *Serrano hams.* Serrano hams were processed as follows (190-day minimum curing process):

(i) If the ham is received frozen, it was thawed in a chamber with relative humidity between 70 and 80 percent, with room temperature maintained at 12 °C to 13 °C (53.6 °F to 55.4 °F) for the first 24 hours, then at 13 °C to 14 °C (55.4 °F to 57.2 °F) until the internal temperature of the ham reached 3 °C to 4 °C (37.4 °F to 39.2 °F), at which point the blood vessels at the end of the femur were massaged to remove any remaining blood.

(ii) The ham was covered in salt and placed in a chamber maintained at a temperature from 0 °C to 4 °C (32 °F to 39.2 °F), with relative humidity between 75 and 95 percent, for a period no less than 0.65 days per kg and no more than 2 days per kg of the weight of the ham.

(iii) The ham was rinsed with water and/or brushed to remove any remaining surface salt.

(iv) The ham was placed in a chamber maintained at a temperature of 0 °C to 6 °C (32 °F to 42.8 °F), with a relative humidity of 70 to 95 percent, for no less than 40 and no more than 60 days;

(v) The ham was placed for curing in a chamber with a relative humidity of 60 to 80 percent and a temperature gradually raised in 3 phases, as follows:

(A) A temperature of 6 °C to 16 °C (42.8 °F to 60.8 °F), maintained for a minimum of 45 days;

(B) A temperature of 16 °C to 24 °C (60.8 °F to 75.2 °F), maintained for a minimum of 35 days;

(C) A temperature of 24 °C to 34 °C (75.2 °F to 93.2 °F), maintained for a minimum of 30 days;

(vi) Finally, with the relative humidity unchanged at 60 to 80 percent, the temperature was lowered to 12 °C to 20 °C (53.6 °F to 68 °F) and maintained at that level for a minimum of 35 days, until at least 190 days after the start of the curing process; *Except that:* In a region where swine vesicular disease exists, the ham must be maintained at that level an additional 370 days, until at least 560 days after the start of the curing process.

(3) *Iberian hams.* Iberian hams were processed as follows (365-day minimum curing process):

(i) If the ham is received frozen, it was thawed in a chamber with relative humidity between 70 and 80 percent, with room temperature maintained at 5.5 °C to 6.5 °C (41.9 °F to 43.7 °F) for the first 24 hours, then at 9.5 °C to 10.5 °C (49.1 °F to 50.9 °F) until the internal temperature of the ham reached 3 °C to 4 °C (37.4 °F to 39.2 °F), at which point the blood vessels at the end of the femur were massaged to remove any remaining blood.

(ii) The ham was covered in salt and placed in a chamber maintained at a temperature from 0 °C to 4 °C (32 °F to 39.2 °F), with relative humidity between 75 and 95 percent, and kept in the chamber for a period no less than 0.65 days per kg and no more than 2 days per kg of the weight of the ham;

(iii) The ham was rinsed with water and/or brushed to remove any remaining surface salt.

(iv) The ham was placed in a chamber maintained at a temperature of 0 °C to

6 °C (32 °F to 42.8 °F), with relative humidity of 70 to 95 percent, for no less than 40 and no more than 60 days.

(v) The ham was placed for curing in a chamber with a temperature of 6 °C to 16 °C (42.8 °F to 60.8 °F) and relative humidity of 60 to 80 percent for a minimum of 90 days.

(vi) The temperature was raised to 16 °C to 26 °C (60.8 °F to 78.8 °F) and the relative humidity reduced to 55 to 85 percent, for a minimum of 90 days.

(vii) Finally, with the relative humidity raised to 60 to 90 percent, the temperature was lowered to 12 °C to 22 °C (53.6 °F to 71.6 °F) and maintained at that level for a minimum of 115 days, until at least 365 days after the start of the curing process; *Except that:* In a region where swine vesicular disease exists, the ham must be maintained at that level an additional 195 days, until at least 560 days after the start of the curing process.

(4) *Iberian pork shoulders.* Iberian pork shoulders were processed as follows (240-day minimum curing process):

(i) If the pork shoulder is received frozen, it was thawed at a room temperature of 12 °C to 13 °C (53.6 °F to 55.4 °F), with the relative humidity between 75 and 85 percent, for approximately 24 hours, until the internal temperature reached 3 °C to 4 °C (37.4 °F to 39.2 °F), at which point the blood vessels in the scapular region were massaged to remove any remaining blood.

(ii) The pork shoulder was covered in salt and placed in a chamber maintained at a temperature of 0 °C to 4 °C (32 °F to 39.2 °F) with the relative humidity between 75 and 95 percent, for a period of no less than 0.65 days per kg and no more than 2 days per kg of the weight of the pork shoulder.

(iii) The pork shoulder was rinsed with water and/or brushed to remove any remaining surface salt.

(iv) The pork shoulder was placed in a chamber maintained at a temperature of 0 °C to 6 °C (32 °F to 42.8 °F) and a relative humidity of 70 to 95 percent for not less than 40 days and not more than 60 days.

(v) The pork shoulder was placed for curing in a chamber at a temperature of 6 °C to 16 °C (42.8 °F to 60.8 °F) and a relative humidity of 60 to 80 percent for a minimum of 90 days.

(vi) The temperature was raised to 16 °C to 26 °C (60.8 °F to 78.8 °F) and the relative humidity was changed to 55 to 85 percent, and those levels were maintained for a minimum of 90 days.

(vii) Finally, the temperature was reduced to 12 °C to 22 °C (53.6 °F to 71.6 °F) and the relative humidity was raised to 60 to 90 percent for a minimum of 45 days, until at least 240 days after the start of the curing process.

(5) *Iberian pork loins.* Iberian pork loins were processed as follows (130-day minimum curing process):

(i) If the pork loin is received frozen, it was thawed at a room temperature maintained at 11 °C to 12 °C (51.8 °F to 53.6 °F), with the relative humidity between 70 and 80 per cent for the first 24 hours, then between 75 and 85 percent, until the loin's internal temperature reached 3 °C to 4 °C (37.4 °F to 39.2 °F), at which point the external fat, aponeurosis, and tendons were cleaned from the loin.

(ii) The pork loin was covered in a pickle preparation (25–30 grams of salt for each kilogram of pork loin) and placed in a chamber where it was maintained at a relative humidity of 75 to 95 percent and a temperature of 3 °C to 4 °C (37.4 °F to 39.2 °F) for 72 hours.

(iii) The pork loin was removed from the pickle preparation (25–30 grams of salt for each kilogram of pork loin), externally cleaned (brushed or rinsed), placed in an artificial casing, and fastened shut with a metal clip.

(iv) The pork loin was placed for curing in a chamber with a relative humidity of 60 to 90 percent and a temperature gradually raised in 3 phases, as follows:

(A) A temperature of 2 °C to 6 °C (35.6 °F to 42.8 °F), maintained for a minimum of 20 days;

(B) A temperature of 6 °C to 15 °C (42.8 °F to 59.0 °F), maintained for a minimum of 20 days;

(C) A temperature of 15 °C to 25 °C (59.0 °F to 77.0 °F), maintained for a minimum of 40 days;

(v) Finally, with the relative humidity unchanged at 60 to 80 percent and the temperature lowered to 0 °C to 5 °C (32.0 °F to 41.0 °F), the pork loin was vacuum-packed and maintained under those conditions for a minimum of 15 days, until at least 130 days after the start of the curing process.

(j)(1) The whole ham, if it is Italian-type ham processed in accordance with paragraph (i)(1) of this section, bears a hot iron brand or an ink seal (with the identifying number of the slaughtering establishment) which was placed thereon at the slaughtering establishment under the direct supervision of a person authorized to supervise such activity by the veterinary services of the national government of the region of origin, bears a button seal (approved by the Administrator, as being tamper-proof) on the hock that states the month and year the ham entered the processing establishment and a hot iron brand (with the identifying number of the processing establishment and the date salting began) which were placed thereon at the processing establishment immediately prior to salting, under the supervision of a person authorized to supervise such activity by the veterinary services of the national government of the region of origin;

(2) The whole dry-cured ham, if it is processed in accordance with paragraphs (i)(2) or (i)(3) of this section, or the whole dry-cured pork shoulder, if it is processed in accordance with paragraph (i)(4) of this section, bears an ink seal (with the identifying number of the slaughtering establishment) which was placed thereon at the slaughtering establishment under the direct supervision of a person authorized to supervise such activity by the veterinary services of the national government of the region of origin, and an ink seal (with the identifying number of the processing establishment and the date the salting began) which was placed thereon at the processing establishment, immediately prior to salting, under the supervision of a person authorized to supervise such activity by the veterinary services of the national government of the region of origin; or

(3) The whole dry-cured pork loin, if it is processed in accordance with paragraph (i)(5) of this section, is packaged with material that bears a seal of the government of the region of origin which was placed thereon at the slaughtering establishment under the direct supervision of a person authorized to supervise such activity by the veterinary services of the national government of the region of origin, and bears a tamper-proof plastic tag, securely attached to the pork loin itself, that states the identifying number of the slaughtering establishment and the date the pork loin was placed in the pickle preparation under the supervision of a person authorized to supervise such activity by the veterinary service of the national government of the region of origin.

(k) The whole dry-cured ham, pork shoulder, or pork loin came from an establishment where a person authorized by the veterinary services of the national government of the region of origin to conduct activities under this paragraph, maintained original records (which shall be kept for a minimum of two years) identifying the dry-cured ham, pork shoulder, or pork loin by the date it entered the processing establishment, by the slaughtering facility from which it came, and by the number of the certificate which accompanied the dry-cured ham, pork shoulder, or pork loin from the slaughtering facility to the processing establishment, and where such original records are maintained under lock and key by such person, with access to such original records restricted to officials of the government of the region of origin, officials of the United States Government, and such person maintaining the records;

(l) The whole dry-cured ham, pork shoulder, or pork loin came from a processing establishment which allows the unannounced entry into the establishment of APHIS personnel, or other persons authorized by the Administrator, for the purpose of inspecting the establishment and records of the establishment;

(m) The dry-cured ham, pork shoulder, or pork loin was processed in accordance with one of the following criteria: (1) The ham, if it is an Italian-type ham processed in accordance with paragraph (i)(1) of this section, was processed in a region which has been determined by the Administrator, to be free of rinderpest, and which has through its veterinary services submitted to the Administrator, a written statement stating that it conducts a program to authorize persons to supervise activities specified under this section;

(2) The Serrano ham, processed in accordance with paragraph (i)(2) of this section, and came from any breed of large, white swine, including but not limited to Landrace, Pietrain, Duroc, Jersey, Hampshire, and Yorkshire breeds, and crosses of such breeds;

(3) The Iberian ham, processed in accordance with paragraph (i)(3) of this section, and came from a swine of the Iberico breed of pigs;

(4) The Iberian pork shoulder, processed in accordance with paragraph (i)(4) of this section, and came from a swine of the Iberico breed of pigs;

(5) The Iberian pork loin, if processed in accordance with paragraph (i)(5) of this section, and came from a swine of the Iberico breed of pigs.

(n) The whole dry-cured ham, pork shoulder, or pork loin came from a processing establishment that has entered into a cooperative service agreement executed by the operator of the establishment or a representative of the establishment and APHIS, and that pursuant to the cooperative service agreement is current in paying all costs for a veterinarian of APHIS to inspect the establishment (it is anticipated that such inspections will occur up to four times per year), including travel, salary, subsistence, administrative overhead, and other incidental expenses (including an excess baggage provision up to 150 pounds). In accordance with the terms of the cooperative service agreement, the operator of the processing establishment shall deposit with the Administrator, an amount equal to the approximate costs for a veterinarian to inspect the establishment one time, including travel, salary, subsistence, administrative overhead and other incidental expenses (including an excess baggage provision up to 150 pounds), and as funds from that amount are obligated, bills for costs incurred based on official accounting records will be issued to restore the deposit to its original level. Amounts to restore the deposit to its original level shall be paid within 14 days of receipt of such bills.

(o) The dry-cured ham, pork shoulder, or pork loin is accompanied at the time of importation into the United States by a certificate issued by a person authorized to issue such certificates by the veterinary services of the national government of the region of origin, stating:

(1) That all the provisions of this section have been complied with, including paragraphs (i) and (m) of this section;

(2) The paragraph of this section under which the dry-cured ham, pork shoulder, or pork loin was processed; and stating further that, if the product covered by the certificate:

(i) Is an Italian-type ham processed under paragraph (i)(1) of this section, it was processed for a minimum of 400 days;

(ii) Is a Serrano ham processed under paragraph (i)(2) of this section, it was:

(A) Processed for a minimum of 190 days in a region free of swine vesicular disease, in a facility authorized by the veterinary services of the national government of that region to process only meat from regions free of swine vesicular disease; or,

(B) Processed for a minimum of 560 days in any region, in a facility that may also process meat from regions where swine vesicular disease exists;

(iii) Is an Iberian ham processed under paragraph (i)(3) of this section, it was:

(A) Processed for a minimum of 365 days in a region free of swine vesicular disease, in a facility authorized by the veterinary services of the national government of that region to process only meat from regions free of swine vesicular disease; or,

(B) Processed for a minimum of 560 days in any region, in a facility that may also process meat from regions where swine vesicular disease exists;

(iv) Is a dry-cured pork shoulder, it was processed in accordance with paragraph (i)(4) of this section for a minimum of 240 days; or

(v) Is a dry-cured pork loin, it was processed in accordance with paragraph (i)(5) of this section for a minimum of 130 days.

(p) Whole hams, pork shoulders, and pork loins that have been dry-cured in accordance with paragraph (i) of this section may be transported to a facility in the same region for slicing and packaging in accordance with this paragraph.

(1) *The slicing/packaging facility.* (i) The slicing/packaging facility[16] must be inspected, prior to slicing and packaging any hams, pork shoulders, or pork loins in accordance with this paragraph, by an APHIS representative and determined by the Administrator to be capable of meeting the provisions of this paragraph.

(ii) The slicing/packaging facility must be either in a separate, physically detached building, or in a separate room in the facility where the whole ham, pork shoulder, or pork loin was dry-cured in accordance with paragraph (i) of this section. If the slicing/packaging facility is in a separate room, the room must have no direct access to areas in the facility where pork is cured and dried and it must be capable of being closed off from the rest of the facility so unauthorized individuals cannot enter.

(iii) The slicing/packaging facility, including all equipment used to handle pork and pork products, such as containers, work surfaces, slicing machines, and packaging equipment, must be cleaned and disinfected after sliced and packaged pork products that are not eligible for export to the United States leave the facility, and before whole dry-cured hams, pork shoulders, or pork intended for importation into the United States enter the facility for slicing and packaging. Cleaning and disinfecting must be adequate to ensure that disease agents of concern are killed or inactivated and that pork products intended for importation into the United States are not contaminated.

(iv) The slicing/packaging facility must maintain under lock and key for a minimum of 2 years, original records on each lot of whole dry-cured hams, pork shoulders, and pork loins entering the facility for slicing and packaging under this section, including:

(A) The approval number of the facility where the whole ham, shoulder, or loin was dry-cured in accordance with paragraph (i) of this section;

(B) The date the whole ham, shoulder, or loin started dry-curing;

(C) The date the whole ham, shoulder, or loin completed dry-curing;

(D) The date the whole ham, shoulder, or loin was sliced and packaged; and

(E) A copy of all certifications required under paragraph (p) of this section.

(v) Access to records required to be maintained under paragraph (p) of this section must be restricted to officials of the national government of the region of origin, representatives of the United States Government, and persons maintaining the records.

(vi) The operator of the slicing/packaging facility must have signed a cooperative service agreement with APHIS prior to receipt of the whole dry-cured hams, pork shoulders, or pork loins for slicing and packaging, stating that all hams, pork shoulders, or pork loins sliced and packaged at the facility for importation into the United States will be sliced and packaged only in accordance with this section.

(vii) The operator of the slicing/packaging facility must be current, in accordance with the terms of the cooperative service agreement signed with APHIS, in paying all costs for an APHIS representative to inspect the establishment, including travel, salary, subsistence, administrative overhead, and other incidental expenses.

(viii) The slicing/packaging facility must allow the unannounced entry into the establishment of APHIS representatives, or other persons authorized by the Administrator, for the purpose of inspecting the establishment and records of the establishment.

(ix) Workers at the slicing/packaging facility who handle pork or pork products in the facility must shower and put on a full set of clean clothes, or wait 24 hours after handling pork or pork products that are not eligible for importation into the United States, before handling dry-cured hams, pork shoulders, or pork loins in the slicing/packaging facility that are intended for importation into the United States.

(x) Pork products intended for importation into the United States may not be in the slicing/packaging facility at the same time as pork products not intended for exportation to the United States.

[16] See footnote 15.

(2) *Slicing and packaging and labeling procedures.* (i) A full-time salaried veterinarian employed by the national government of the region of origin must inspect each lot of whole dry-cured hams, pork shoulders, and pork loins at the slicing/packaging facility, before slicing is begun, and must certify in English that it is eligible for importation into the United States in accordance with this section; and

(ii) Either a full-time salaried veterinarian employed by the national government of the region of origin, or, if the national government of the region of origin recognizes a local consortium as responsible for product quality, a representative of that local consortium, must certify in English that he or she personally supervised the entire process of slicing and packaging each lot of dry-cured hams, pork shoulders, and pork loins at the slicing/packaging facility; that each lot of dry-cured hams, pork shoulders, and pork loins was sliced and packaged in accordance with the requirements of this paragraph; and that the sliced and packaged pork ham, shoulder, or loin is the same dry-cured ham, pork shoulder, or pork loin certified under paragraph (p)(2)(i).

(iii) The sliced and packaged dry-cured pork ham, pork shoulder, or pork loin must be labeled with the date that processing of the meat under paragraph (i) of this section began, and with the date the meat was sliced and packaged.

(Approved by the Office of Management and Budget under control number 0579–0015)

[52 FR 11625, Apr. 10, 1987, as amended at 53 FR 48520, Dec. 1, 1988; 54 FR 7395, Feb. 21, 1989, 59 FR 55024, Nov. 3, 1994; 59 FR 67134, Dec. 29, 1994; 62 FR 46181, Sept. 2, 1997; 62 FR 56023, Oct. 28, 1997; 62 FR 61004, Nov. 14, 1997; 64 FR 38550, July 19, 1999; 68 FR 16939, Apr. 7, 2003; 73 FR 17885, Apr. 2, 2008; 74 FR 18288, Apr. 22, 2009; 76 FR 4054, 4055, Jan. 24, 2011; 77 FR 1395, Jan. 10, 2012]

§94.18 Bovine spongiform encephalopathy; importation of edible products derived from bovines.

(a) The importation of meat, meat products, and other edible products derived from bovines is prohibited with regard to BSE, except as provided in this section and in §§94.19, 94.20, 94.21, 94.22, 94.23, and 94.27.

(b) The following commodities derived from bovines may be imported into the United States without restriction regarding BSE, provided that all other applicable requirements of this part are met:

(1) Milk and milk products;

(2) Boneless skeletal muscle meat (excluding mechanically separated meat) that:

(i) Is derived from bovines that were not, prior to slaughter, subjected to a pithing process or to stunning with a device injecting compressed air or gas into the cranial cavity, and that passed ante-mortem and post-mortem inspection;

(ii) Has been prepared in a manner to prevent contamination with SRMs; and

(iii) Is accompanied to the United States by an original certificate stating that the conditions of paragraphs (b)(2)(i) and (b)(2)(ii) of this section have been met. The certificate must be issued and signed by a full-time salaried veterinary officer of the national government of the exporting region or signed by a person authorized to issue such certificates by the veterinary services of the national government of the exporting region.

(Approved by the Office of Management and Budget under control number 0579–0015)

[78 FR 72998, Dec. 4, 2013]

§94.19 Importation of meat, meat byproducts, and meat food products derived from bovines from regions of negligible risk for BSE.

Meat, meat byproducts, and meat food products, as defined by FSIS in 9 CFR 301.2–except that those terms as applied to bison shall have a meaning comparable to those provided in 9 CFR 301.2 with regard to cattle, and other than boneless skeletal meat that meets the conditions of §94.18(b)(2)—may be imported from a region of negligible risk for BSE, as defined in §92.1 of this subchapter, if the following conditions and all other applicable requirements of this part are met:

(a) The commodities were exported from a region of negligible risk for BSE.

(b) If BSE has been diagnosed in one or more indigenous bovines in the region of negligible risk, the commodities were derived from bovines subject to a ban on the feeding to ruminants of meat-and-bone meal or greaves derived from ruminants.

(c) The commodities were derived from bovines that passed ante-mortem and post-mortem inspections.

(d) The commodities are accompanied by an original certificate stating that the exporting region is classified by APHIS as a region of negligible risk for BSE and that the conditions of paragraphs (a) through (c) of this section, as applicable, have been met. The certificate must be issued and signed by a full-time salaried veterinary officer of the national government of the exporting region, or signed by a person authorized to issue such certificates by the veterinary services of the national government of the exporting region.

NOTE: To be eligible to export meat, meat byproducts, and meat food products under the conditions of this section for human consumption, a region must also be one that has demonstrated to FSIS in accordance with 9 CFR 310.22 that its BSE risk status can reasonably be expected to provide the same level of protection from human exposure to the BSE agent as does prohibiting specified risk materials for use as human food in the United States.

(Approved by the Office of Management and Budget under control number 0579–0393)

[78 FR 72999, Dec. 4, 2013]

§ 94.20 Importation of meat, meat byproducts, and meat food products derived from bovines from regions of controlled risk for BSE.

Meat, meat byproducts, and meat food products, as defined by FSIS in 9 CFR 301.2—except that those terms as applied to bison shall have a meaning comparable to those provided in 9 CFR 301.2 with regard to cattle, and other than boneless skeletal meat that meets the conditions of § 94.18(b)(2)—may be imported from a region of controlled risk for BSE, as defined in § 92.1 of this subchapter, if the following conditions and all other applicable requirements of this part are met:

(a) The commodities were exported from a region of controlled risk for BSE.

(b) The commodities were derived from bovines that passed ante-mortem and post-mortem inspections.

(c) The commodities were derived from bovines that were not subjected to a stunning process, prior to slaughter, with a device injecting compressed air or gas into the cranial cavity, or to a pithing process.

(d) The commodities were produced and handled in a manner that ensured that such commodities do not contain and are not contaminated with either of the following:

(1) SRMs from regions of controlled risk for BSE; or

(2) Mechanically separated meat from the skull and vertebral column from bovines 30 months of age or older.

(e) The commodities are accompanied by an original certificate stating that the exporting region is classified by APHIS as a region of controlled risk for BSE, and that the conditions of this section have been met. The certificate must be issued and signed by a full-time salaried veterinary officer of the national government of the exporting region, or signed by a person authorized to issue such certificates by the veterinary services of the national government of the exporting region.

(Approved by the Office of Management and Budget under control numbers 0579–0015 and 0579–0393)

[78 FR 72999, Dec. 4, 2013]

§ 94.21 Importation of meat, meat byproducts, and meat food products derived from bovines from regions of undetermined risk for BSE.

Meat, meat byproducts, and meat food products, as defined by FSIS in 9 CFR 301.2–except that those terms as applied to bison shall have a meaning comparable to those provided in 9 CFR 301.2 with regard to cattle, and other than boneless skeletal meat that meets the conditions of § 94.18(b)(2)—may be imported from regions of undetermined risk for BSE, as defined in § 92.1 of this subchapter, if the following conditions and all other applicable requirements of this part are met:

(a) The commodities were derived from bovines that have never been fed meat-and-bone meal or greaves derived from ruminants.

(b) The commodities were derived from bovines that passed ante-mortem and post-mortem inspections.

(c) The commodities were derived from bovines that were not subjected to a stunning process, prior to slaughter, with a device injecting compressed air or gas into the cranial cavity, or to a pithing process.

(d) The commodities were produced and handled in a manner that ensured that such commodities do not contain and are not contaminated with any of the following:

(1) SRMs from regions of undetermined risk for BSE; or

(2) Mechanically separated meat from the skull and vertebral column from bovines over 12 months of age.

(e) The commodities are accompanied by an original certificate stating that the exporting region is a region of undetermined risk for BSE and that the conditions of this section have been met. The certificate must be issued and signed by a full-time salaried veterinary officer of the national government of the exporting region, or signed by a person authorized to issue such certificates by the veterinary services of the national government of the exporting region.

(Approved by the Office of Management and Budget under control number 0579–0393)

[78 FR 72999, Dec. 4, 2013]

§ 94.22 Meat or dressed carcasses of hunter-harvested bovines.

The meat or dressed carcass (eviscerated and the head is removed) is derived from a wild bovine that has been legally harvested in the wild, as verified by proof such as a hunting license, tag, or the equivalent that the hunter must show to the authorized inspector.

(Approved by the Office of Management and Budget under control number 0579–0393)

[78 FR 72999, Dec. 4, 2013]

§ 94.23 Importation of gelatin derived from bovines.

(a) The importation of gelatin derived from bovines is prohibited because of BSE, unless:

(1) The gelatin meets the requirements of either paragraph (b), (c), or (d), as well as the requirements of paragraph (e) of this section and all other applicable requirements of this part; or

(2) The gelatin is authorized importation under paragraph (f) of this section and meets all other applicable requirements of this part.

(b) The gelatin is derived from hides and skins, provided the gelatin has not been commingled with materials ineligible for entry into the United States.

(c) The gelatin is derived from the bones of bovines and originates in a region of negligible risk for BSE.

(d) The gelatin is derived from the bones of bovines, originates in a region of controlled risk or undetermined risk for BSE, and meets the requirements of paragraphs (d)(1) through (d)(4) of this section:

(1) The bones from which the gelatin was derived were derived from bovines that passed ante-mortem and post-mortem inspection.

(2) The bones from which the gelatin was derived did not include the skulls of bovines or the vertebral column of bovines 30 months of age or older.

(3) The bones were subjected to a process that includes all of the following steps, or to a process at least as effective in reducing BSE infectivity:

(i) Degreasing;

(ii) Acid demineralization;

(iii) Acid or alkaline treatment;

(iv) Filtration; and

(v) Sterilization at 138 °C (280.4 °F) or greater for a minimum of 4 seconds; and

(4) The gelatin has not been commingled with materials ineligible for entry into the United States.

(e) The gelatin is accompanied to the United States by an original certificate signed by a full-time salaried veterinary officer of the national government of the exporting region, or issued by a veterinarian designated by the national government of the exporting region and endorsed by a full-time salaried veterinary officer of the national government of the exporting region, representing that the veterinarian issuing the certificate was authorized to do so. The certificate must state that the requirements of paragraph (b), (c), or (d) of this section, as applicable, have been met and, for gelatin other than that described in paragraph (b) of this section, must indicate the BSE risk classification of the exporting region.

(f) The Administrator determines that the gelatin will not come into contact with ruminants in the United States and can be imported under conditions that will prevent the introduction of BSE into the United States, and the person importing the gelatin has obtained a United States Veterinary Permit for Importation and Transportation of Controlled Materials and Organisms and Vectors. To apply for a permit, file a permit application on VS Form 16–3 (available from APHIS, Veterinary Services, National Center for Import and Export, 4700 River Road Unit 38, Riverdale, MD 20737–1231, or electronically at *http://www.aphis.usda.gov/animal_health/permits/*). The application for such a permit must state the intended use of the gelatin and name and address of the consignee in the United States.

[78 FR 72999, Dec. 4, 2013]

§ 94.24 Restrictions on importation of meat and edible products from ovines and caprines due to bovine spongiform encephalopathy.

(a) Except as provided in paragraph (b) of this section and in § 94.25, the importation of meat, meat products, and edible products other than meat (excluding milk and milk products) from ovines and caprines that have been in any of the following regions is prohibited: Albania, Andorra, Austria, Belgium, Bosnia-Herzegovina, Bulgaria, Canada, Croatia, the Czech Republic, Denmark, the Federal Republic of Yugoslavia, Finland, France, Germany, Greece, Hungary, the Republic of Ireland, Israel, Italy, Japan, Liechtenstein, Luxembourg, the Former Yugoslav Republic of Macedonia, Monaco, Norway, Oman, the Netherlands, Poland, Portugal, Romania, San Marino, Slovakia, Slovenia, Spain, Sweden, Switzerland, and the United Kingdom.

(b) The importation of gelatin derived from ovines or caprines that have been in any region listed in paragraph (a) of this section is prohibited unless the following conditions have been met:

(1) The gelatin is imported for use in human food, human pharmaceutical products, photography, or some other use that will not result in the gelatin coming in contact with ruminants in the United States.

(2) The person importing the gelatin obtains a United States Veterinary Permit for Importation and Transportation of Controlled Materials and Organisms and Vectors by filing a permit application on VS Form 16–3. Permit applications are available from APHIS, Veterinary Services, National Center for Import and Export, 4700 River Road Unit 38, Riverdale, MD 20737–1231, or at *http://www.aphis.usda.gov/animal_health/permits/*. Forms may be submitted using a U.S. Government electronic information exchange system or other authorized method. The application for such a permit must state the intended use of the gelatin and name and address of the consignee in the United States.

[78 FR 72999, Dec. 4, 2013, as amended at 81 FR 40152, June 21, 2016]

§ 94.25 Restrictions on the importation from Canada of meat and edible products from ovines and caprines other than gelatin.

The commodities listed in paragraphs (a) and (b) of this section may be imported from Canada if the conditions of this section are met.

(a) *Meat, carcasses, meat byproducts, and meat food products from ovines or caprines.* (1) The meat, carcass, meat byproduct, or meat food product, as defined by FSIS in 9 CFR 301.2, is derived from ovines or caprines that are from a flock or herd subject to a ruminant feed ban equivalent to the requirements established by the U.S. Food and Drug Administration at 21 CFR 589.2000, and the ovines or caprines:

(i) Were less than 12 months of age when slaughtered;

(ii) Were slaughtered at a facility that either slaughters only ovines or caprines less than 12 months of age or complies with a segregation process approved by the national veterinary authority of the region of origin and the Administrator as adequate to prevent contamination or commingling of the meat with products not eligible for importation into the United States;

(iii) Did not test positive for and were not suspect for a transmissible spongiform encephalopathy;

(iv) Never resided in a flock or herd that has been diagnosed with BSE; and

(v) Were not subject to any movement restrictions within Canada as a result of exposure to a transmissible spongiform encephalopathy.

(2) The commodities are accompanied by an original certificate of such compliance issued by a full-time salaried veterinary officer of Canada, or issued by a veterinarian designated by the Canadian government and endorsed by a full-time salaried veterinary officer of the Government of Canada, representing that the veterinarian issuing the certificate was authorized to do so; and if all other applicable requirements of this part are met.

(b) *Meat or dressed carcasses of hunter-harvested ovines or caprines.* (1) The meat or dressed carcass (eviscerated and the head is removed) is derived from a wild ovine or caprine that has been legally harvested in the wild, as verified by proof such as a hunting license, tag, or the equivalent that the hunter must show to the United States Customs and Border Protection official; and

(2) The animal from which the meat is derived was harvested within a jurisdiction specified by the Administrator for which the game and wildlife service of the jurisdiction has informed the Administrator either that the jurisdiction conducts no type of game feeding program, or has complied with, and continues to comply with, a ruminant feed ban equivalent to the requirements established by the U.S. Food and Drug Administration at 21 CFR 589.2000.

(c) *Ports.* All products to be brought into the United States under this section must, if arriving at a land border port, arrive at one of the following ports: Eastport, ID; Houlton, ME; Detroit (Ambassador Bridge), Port Huron, and Sault St. Marie, MI; International Falls, MN; Sweetgrass, MT; Alexandria Bay, Buffalo (Lewiston Bridge and Peace Bridge), and Champlain, NY; Pembina and Portal, ND; Derby Line and Highgate Springs, VT; and Blaine (Pacific Highway and Cargo Ops), Lynden, Oroville, and Sumas (Cargo), WA.

[78 FR 72999, Dec. 4, 2013]

§94.26 Gelatin derived from horses or swine or from ovines or caprines that have not been in a region restricted because of BSE.

Gelatin derived from horses or swine, or from ovines or caprines that have not been in any region listed in §94.24(a) must be accompanied at the time of importation into the United States by an official certificate issued by a veterinarian employed by the national government of the region of origin. The official certificate must state the species of animal from which the gelatin is derived and, if the gelatin is derived from ovines or caprines, certify that the gelatin is not derived from ovines or caprines that have been in any region listed in §94.24(a).

[78 FR 72999, Dec. 4, 2013]

§94.27 Transit shipment of articles.

Meat, meat products, and other edible products derived from bovines, ovines, or caprines that are otherwise prohibited importation into the United States in accordance with §94.18 through §94.26 may transit air and ocean ports in the United States for immediate export if the conditions of paragraphs (a) through (c) this section are met. Meat, meat products, and other edible products derived from bovines, ovines, or caprines are eligible to transit the United States by overland transportation if the requirements of paragraphs (a) through (d) of this section are met:

(a) The articles must be sealed in leakproof containers bearing serial numbers during transit. Each container must remain sealed during the entire time that it is in the United States.

(b) The person moving the articles must notify, in writing, the inspector at both the place in the United States where the articles will arrive and the port of export before such transit. Notification may be made using a U.S. Government electronic information exchange system or other authorized method. The notification must include the:

(1) Times and dates of arrival in the United States;

(2) Times and dates of exportation from the United States;

(3) Mode of transportation; and

(4) Serial numbers of the sealed containers.

(c) The articles must transit the United States in Customs bond.

(d) The commodities must be eligible to enter the United States in accordance with the provisions of this part and must be accompanied by the certification required by that section. Additionally, the following conditions must be met:

(1) The shipment must be exported from the United States within 7 days of its entry; and

(2) The commodities may not be transloaded while in the United States, except for direct transloading under the supervision of an authorized inspector, who must break the seals of the national government of the region of origin on the means of conveyance that carried the commodities into the United States and seal the means of conveyance that will carry the commodities out of the United States with seals of the U.S. Government.

(Approved by the Office of Management and Budget under control number 0579–0393)

[78 FR 72999, Dec. 4, 2013, as amended at 81 FR 40152, June 21, 2016]

§ 94.28 Restrictions on the importation of poultry meat and products, and live birds and poultry, from the APHIS-defined EU Poultry Trade Region.

(a) *Poultry meat and products.* In addition to meeting all other applicable provisions of this part, poultry meat and poultry products, including eggs and egg products (other than hatching eggs) imported from the APHIS-defined EU Poultry Trade Region must meet the following conditions:

(1) The poultry meat and products must not have been derived from birds and poultry that were in any of the following regions or zones, unless the birds and poultry were slaughtered after the periods described, or unless the poultry meat and products are accompanied by a certificate specifying that the articles were cooked and processed in accordance with the regulations in § 94.6(b)(3) or (b)(4):

(i) Any region when the region was classified in § 94.6(a)(1)(i) as one in which Newcastle disease is considered to exist, or any region when the region was listed in accordance with § 94.6(a)(2)(i) as one in which HPAI is considered to exist, except for the APHIS-defined EU Poultry Trade Region;

(ii) A restricted zone in the APHIS-defined EU Poultry Trade Region established because of detection of Newcastle disease or HPAI in commercial poultry, from the time of detection until the designation of the zone as a restricted zone is removed by the competent veterinary authority of the Member State or until 3 months (90 days) following depopulation of the poultry on affected premises in the restricted zone and the cleaning and disinfection of the last affected premises in the zone, whichever is later; or

(iii) A restricted zone in the APHIS-defined EU Poultry Trade Region established because of detection of Newcastle disease or HPAI in racing pigeons, backyard flocks, or wild birds, from the time of detection until the designation of the zone as a restricted zone is removed by the competent veterinary authority of the Member State.

(2) The poultry meat and products must not have been commingled with poultry meat and products derived from other birds and poultry that were in any of the regions or zones described in paragraphs (a)(1)(i) through (a)(1)(iii) of this section. Additionally, the poultry meat and products must not have been derived from poultry that were commingled with other poultry that were in any of the regions or zones described in paragraphs (a)(1)(i) through (a)(1)(iii) of this section.

(3) No equipment or materials used in transporting the birds or poultry from which the poultry meat and products were derived from the farm of origin to the slaughtering establishment may have been used previously for transporting live birds or poultry that do not meet the requirements of § 94.28(b), unless the equipment and materials have first been cleaned and disinfected.

(4) The poultry meat and products, including eggs and egg products (other than hatching eggs) must be accompanied by a certificate issued by an official of the competent veterinary authority of the APHIS-defined EU Poultry Trade Region Member State who is

authorized to issue the inspection certificate required by § 93.205 of this subchapter, stating that the applicable provisions of paragraphs (a)(1) through (a)(3) of this section have been met. The certification for poultry meat and products may be placed on the foreign meat inspection certificate required by § 381.196 of this title or may be contained in a separate document.

(b) *Live birds and poultry.* In addition to meeting all other applicable provisions of this title, live birds and poultry, except hatching eggs, imported from the APHIS-defined EU Poultry Trade Region must meet the following conditions:

(1) The birds and poultry must not have been in any of the following regions or zones, unless the birds and poultry are exported to the United States after the periods described.

(i) Any region when the region was classified in § 94.6(a)(1)(i) as one in which Newcastle disease is considered to exist, or any region when the region was listed in accordance with § 94.6(a)(2)(i) as one in which HPAI is considered to exist, except for the APHIS-defined EU Poultry Trade Region;

(ii) A restricted zone in the APHIS-defined EU Poultry Trade Region established because of detection of Newcastle disease or HPAI in commercial poultry, from the time of detection until the designation of the zone as a restricted zone is removed by the competent veterinary authority of the Member State or until 3 months (90 days) following depopulation of the poultry on affected premises in the restricted zone and the cleaning and disinfection of the last affected premises in the zone, whichever is later; or

(iii) A restricted zone in the APHIS-defined EU Poultry Trade Region established because of detection of Newcastle disease or HPAI in racing pigeons, backyard flocks, and wild birds, from the time of detection until the designation of the zone as a restricted zone is removed by the competent veterinary authority of the Member State.

(2) The birds and poultry must not have been commingled with other birds or poultry that have at any time been in any of the regions or zones described in paragraphs (b)(1)(i) through (b)(1)(iii) of this section.

(3) No equipment or materials used in transporting the birds and poultry may have been used previously for transporting birds or poultry that do not meet the requirements of this paragraph, unless the equipment and materials have first been cleaned and disinfected.

(4) The birds and poultry must be accompanied by a certificate issued by an official of the competent veterinary authority of the Member State who is authorized to issue the inspection certificate required by § 93.205 of this subchapter, stating that the applicable provisions of paragraphs (b)(1) through (b)(3) of this section have been met. The certification may be placed on the foreign meat inspection certificate required by § 381.196 of this title or may be contained in a separate document.

(c) *Hatching eggs.* Hatching eggs intended for import from the APHIS-defined EU Poultry Trade Region are subject to all applicable provisions of paragraph (b) of this section, except that such hatching eggs may be moved through zones established because of detection of HPAI within the APHIS-defined EU Poultry Trade Region provided that the hatching eggs are transported under official seal and accompanied by a certificate as indicated in paragraph (b)(4) of this section stating that the applicable provisions of paragraph (b) have been met. The import permit will require the seal number to be listed on the health certificate that accompanies the shipment and the veterinarian who places the seal will be required to sign his or her name under the seal number. Seals must not be broken until the shipment reaches its U.S. port of entry. Hatching egg shipment with seals that are not intact will be rejected upon inspection at the U.S. port of entry.

(d) *Presentation of certificates.* The certificates required by paragraphs (a)(4), (b)(4), and (c) of this section must be presented by the importer to an authorized inspector at the port of arrival, upon arrival of the birds, poultry, hatching eggs, or poultry meat and products at the port.

[78 FR 19084, Mar. 29, 2013, as amended at 79 FR 7568, Feb. 10, 2014]

§ 94.29 Restrictions on importation of fresh (chilled or frozen) beef and ovine meat from specified regions.

Notwithstanding any other provisions of this part, fresh (chilled or frozen) beef from a region in Argentina located north of Patagonia South and Patagonia North B, referred to as Northern Argentina (the region sometimes referred to as Patagonia North A is included in Northern Argentina); fresh (chilled or frozen) beef from a region in Brazil composed of the States of Bahia, Distrito Federal, Espírito Santo, Goiás, Mato Grosso, Mato Grosso do Sul, Minas Gerais, Paraná, Rio Grande do Sul, Rio de Janeiro, Rondônia, São Paulo, Sergipe, and Tocantins; and fresh (chilled or frozen) beef and ovine meat from Uruguay may be exported to the United States under the following conditions:

(a) The meat is:

(1) Beef from animals that have been born, raised, and slaughtered in the exporting regions of Argentina or Brazil; or

(2) Beef or ovine meat from Uruguay derived from animals that have been born, raised, and slaughtered in Uruguay.

(b) Foot-and-mouth disease has not been diagnosed in the exporting region of Argentina (for beef from Argentina), the exporting region of Brazil (for beef from Brazil), or in Uruguay (for beef or ovine meat from Uruguay) within the previous 12 months.

(c) The meat comes from bovines or sheep that originated from premises where foot-and-mouth disease has not been present during the lifetime of any bovines and sheep slaughtered for the export of beef and ovine meat to the United States.

(d) The meat comes from bovines or sheep that were moved directly from the premises of origin to the slaughtering establishment without any contact with other animals.

(e) The meat comes from bovines or sheep that received ante-mortem and post-mortem veterinary inspections, paying particular attention to the head and feet, at the slaughtering establishment, with no evidence found of vesicular disease.

(f) The meat consists only of bovine parts or ovine parts that are, by standard practice, part of the animal's carcass that is placed in a chiller for maturation after slaughter and before removal of any bone, blood clots, or lymphoid tissue. The bovine and ovine parts that may not be imported include all parts of the head, feet, hump, hooves, and internal organs.

(g) All bone and visually identifiable blood clots and lymphoid tissue have been removed from the meat; except that bone-in ovine meat from Uruguay may be exported to the United States under the following conditions:

(1) The meat must be derived from select lambs that have never been vaccinated for FMD;

(2) The select lambs must be maintained in a program approved by the Administrator. Lambs in the program must:

(i) Be segregated from other FMD-susceptible livestock at a select lamb facility operated under the authority of the national veterinary authority of Uruguay;

(ii) Be subjected to an FMD testing scheme approved by the Administrator; and

(iii) Be individually identified with official unique identification that is part of a national traceability system sufficient to ensure that only the products of select lambs meeting all required criteria are exempt from the deboning requirement.

(3) Select lambs and their products must not be commingled with other animals and their products within the slaughter facility.

(h) The meat has not been in contact with meat from regions other than those listed in § 94.1(a).

(i) The meat came from carcasses that were allowed to maturate at 40 to 50 °F (4 to 10 °C) for a minimum of 24 hours after slaughter and that reached a pH below 6.0 in the loin muscle at the end of the maturation period. Measurements for pH must be taken at the middle of both *longissimus dorsi* muscles. Any carcass in which the pH does not reach less than 6.0 may be allowed to maturate an additional 24 hours and be retested, and, if the carcass still has not reached a pH of less than 6.0 after 48 hours, the meat from the carcass may not be exported to the United States.

(j) An authorized veterinary official of the government of the exporting region certifies on the foreign meat inspection certificate that the above conditions have been met.

(k) The establishment in which the bovines and sheep are slaughtered allows periodic on-site evaluation and subsequent inspection of its facilities, records, and operations by an APHIS representative.

(Approved by the Office of Management and Budget under control numbers 0579–0372, 0579–0414, 0579–0428, and 0579–0449)

[80 FR 37952, July 2, 2015; 82 FR 6212, Jan. 19, 2017; 82 FR 42732, Sept. 12, 2017]

§94.30 Importation of poultry meat and other poultry products from Sinaloa and Sonora, Mexico.

Notwithstanding any other provisions of this part, poultry meat and other poultry products from the States of Sinaloa and Sonora, Mexico, may be imported into the United States under the following conditions:

(a) The poultry meat or other poultry products are derived from poultry born and raised in Sinaloa or Sonora and slaughtered in Sinaloa or Sonora at a federally inspected slaughter plant under the direct supervision of a full-time salaried veterinarian of the Government of Mexico, and the slaughter plant must be approved to export poultry meat and other poultry products to the United States in accordance with 9 CFR 381.196.

(b) If processed, the poultry meat or other poultry products were processed in either Sinaloa or Sonora, Mexico, in a federally inspected processing plant that is under the direct supervision of a full-time salaried veterinarian of the Government of Mexico.

(c) The poultry meat or other poultry products have not been in contact with poultry from any State in Mexico other than Sinaloa or Sonora or with poultry from any other region not listed in §94.6 as a region where Newcastle disease is not known to exist.

(d) The foreign meat inspection certificate accompanying the poultry meat or other poultry products (required by 9 CFR 381.197) includes statements certifying that the requirements in paragraphs (a), (b), and (c) of this section have been met and, if applicable, listing the numbers of the seals required by paragraph (e)(1) of this section.

(e) The shipment of poultry meat or other poultry products has not been in any State in Mexico other than Sinaloa or Sonora or in any other region not listed in §94.6 as a region where Newcastle disease is not known to exist, unless:

(1) The poultry meat or other poultry products arrive at the U.S. port of entry in shipping containers bearing intact, serially numbered seals that were applied at the federally inspected slaughter plant by a full-time salaried veterinarian of the Government of Mexico, and the seal numbers correspond with the seal numbers listed on the foreign meat inspection certificate; or

(2) The poultry meat or other poultry products arrive at the U.S. port of entry in shipping containers bearing seals that have different numbers than the seal numbers on the foreign meat inspection certificate, but, upon inspection of the hold, compartment, or container and all accompanying documentation, an APHIS representative is satisfied that the poultry containers were opened and resealed en route by an appropriate official of the Government of Mexico and the poultry meat or other poultry products were not contaminated or exposed to contamination during movement from Sinaloa or Sonora to the United States.

[65 FR 15526, Mar. 23, 2000. Redesignated at 70 FR 550, Jan. 4, 2005, as amended at 78 FR 19084, Mar. 29, 2013. Redesignated at 78 FR 72999, Dec. 4, 2013]

§94.31 Restrictions on the importation of pork, pork products, and swine from the APHIS-defined European CSF region.

(a) *Pork and pork products.* In addition to meeting all other applicable provisions of this part, fresh pork and pork products imported from the APHIS-defined European CSF region must meet the following conditions:

(1) The pork or pork products must not have been derived from swine that were in any of the following regions or zones, unless the swine were slaughtered after the periods described:

(i) Any region when the region was classified under §§ 94.9(a) and 94.10(a) as a region in which classical swine fever is known to exist, except for the APHIS-defined European CSF region;

(ii) A restricted zone in the APHIS-defined European CSF region established because of detection of classical swine fever in domestic swine, from the time of detection until the designation of the zone as a restricted zone is removed by the competent veterinary authority or until 6 months following depopulation of the swine on affected premises in the restricted zone and the cleaning and disinfection of the last affected premises in the zone, whichever is later; or

(iii) A restricted zone in the APHIS-defined European CSF region established because of the detection of classical swine fever in wild boar, from the time of detection until the designation of the zone as a restricted zone is removed by the competent veterinary authority.

(2) The pork and pork products must not have been commingled with pork or pork products derived from other swine that were in any of the regions or zones described in paragraphs (a)(1)(i) through (a)(1)(iii) of this section, unless the other swine were slaughtered after the periods described. Additionally, the pork and pork products must not have been derived from swine that were commingled with other swine that were in any of the regions or zones described in paragraphs (a)(1)(i) through (a)(1)(iii) of this section, unless the swine from which the pork or pork products were derived were slaughtered after the periods described.

(3) The swine from which the pork or pork products were derived must not have transited any region or zone described in paragraphs (a)(1)(i) through (a)(1)(iii) of this section, unless the swine were moved directly through the region or zone in a sealed means of conveyance with the seal determined to be intact upon arrival at the point of destination, or unless the swine were slaughtered after the periods described.

(4) No equipment or materials used in transporting the swine from which the pork or pork products were derived from the farm of origin to the slaughtering establishment may have been used previously for transporting swine that do not meet the requirements of this section, unless the equipment and materials have first been cleaned and disinfected.

(5) The pork and pork products must be accompanied by a certificate issued by an official of the competent veterinary authority who is authorized to issue the foreign meat inspection certificate required by § 327.4 of this title, stating that the applicable provisions of paragraphs (a)(1) through (a)(4) of this section have been met.[19]

(b) *Live swine.* In addition to meeting all other applicable provisions of this title, live swine imported from the APHIS-defined European CSF region must meet the following conditions:

(1) The swine must be breeding swine.

(2) The swine must not have been in any of the following regions or zones, unless the swine are exported to the United States after the periods described:

(i) Any region when the region was classified under §§ 94.9(a) and 94.10(a) as a region in which classical swine fever is known to exist, except for the APHIS-defined European CSF region;

(ii) A restricted zone in the APHIS-defined European CSF region established because of the detection of classical swine fever in domestic swine, from the time of detection until the designation of the zone as a restricted zone is removed by the competent veterinary authority or until 6 months following depopulation of the swine on affected premises in the restricted zone and the cleaning and disinfection of the last affected premises in the zone, whichever is later; or

(iii) A restricted zone in the APHIS-defined European CSF region established because of the detection of classical swine fever in wild boar, from the time of detection until the designation of the zone as a restricted zone is removed by the competent veterinary authority.

(3) The swine must not have been commingled with other swine that

[19] The certification required may be placed on the foreign meat inspection certificate required by § 327.4 of this title or may be contained in a separate document.

have at any time been in any of the regions or zones described in paragraphs (b)(2)(i) through (b)(2)(iii) of this section, unless the swine are exported after the periods described.

(4) The swine must not have transited any region or zone described in paragraphs (b)(2)(i) through (b)(2)(iii) of this section, unless the swine were moved directly through the region or zone in a sealed means of conveyance with the seal determined to be intact upon arrival at the point of destination, or unless the swine are exported after the periods described;

(5) No equipment or materials used in transporting the swine may have been used previously for transporting swine that do not meet the requirements of this section, unless the equipment and materials have first been cleaned and disinfected.

(6) The swine must be accompanied by a certificate issued by a salaried veterinary officer of the competent veterinary authority, stating that the conditions of paragraphs (b)(1) through (b)(5) of this section have been met.[20]

(c) The certificates required by paragraphs (a)(5) and (b)(6) of this section must be presented by the importer to an authorized inspector at the port of arrival, upon arrival of the swine, pork, or pork products at the port.

(Approved by the Office of Management and Budget under control numbers 0579–0218 and 0579–0265)

[71 FR 29071, May 19, 2006. Redesignated at 71 FR 31070, June 1, 2006, as amended at 72 FR 67232, Nov. 28, 2007; 74 FR 18288, Apr. 22, 2009; 76 FR 4054, Jan. 24, 2011; 76 FR 70039, Nov. 10, 2011; 77 FR 1395, Jan. 10, 2012. Redesignated at 78 FR 72999, Dec. 4, 2013]

§ 94.32 Restrictions on the importation of live swine, pork, or pork products from certain regions free of classical swine fever.

(a) Live swine, pork, or pork products and ship stores, airplane meals, and baggage containing pork or pork products, other than those articles regulated under part 95 or part 96 of this chapter, may not be imported into the United States from a region listed under paragraph (a)(2) of this section unless the requirements in this section, in addition to other applicable requirements of part 93 of this chapter and part 327 of this title, are met.

(1) The regions listed under paragraph (a)(2) of this section have been declared free of classical swine fever (CSF) by APHIS in accordance with §§ 94.9(a) and 94.10(a) but either supplement their pork supplies with fresh (chilled or frozen) pork imported from regions considered to be affected by CSF, or supplement their pork supplies with pork from CSF-affected regions that is not processed in accordance with the requirements of this part, or share a common land border with CSF-affected regions, or import live swine from CSF-affected regions under conditions less restrictive than would be acceptable for importation into the United States. Thus, the live swine, pork, or pork products from those regions may be commingled with live swine, pork, or pork products from CSF-affected regions, resulting in a risk of CSF introduction into the United States.

(2) A list of regions whose live swine, pork, and pork products are regulated under this section is maintained on the APHIS Web site at *http://www.aphis.usda.gov/import_export/animals/animal_disease_status.shtml*. Copies of the list will also be available via postal mail, fax, or email upon request to the Sanitary Trade Issues Team, National Center for Import and Export, Veterinary Services, Animal and Plant Health Inspection Service, 4700 River Road Unit 38, Riverdale, Maryland 20737.

(3) APHIS will add a region to the list of those whose live swine, pork, and pork products are regulated under this section after conducting an evaluation of the region and determining that one or more of the circumstances described in paragraph (a)(1) of this section exists. APHIS will remove a region from the list upon conducting an evaluation of the region and determining that the circumstances in paragraph (a)(1) of this section no longer exist or upon determining that classical swine fever exists in the region.

(b) *Live swine.* The swine must be accompanied by a certification issued by

[20] The certification required may be placed on the certificate required by § 93.505(a) of this chapter or may be contained in a separate document

a full-time salaried veterinary officer of the national government of the region of export. Upon arrival of the swine in the United States, the certification must be presented to an authorized inspector at the port of arrival. The certification must identify both the exporting region and the region of origin as a region listed under §§ 94.9 and 94.10 as free of CSF at the time the swine were in the region and must state that:

(1) The swine have not lived in a region classified under §§ 94.9 and 94.10 as a region in which CSF is known to exist;

(2) The swine have never been commingled with swine that have been in a region that is classified under §§ 94.9 and 94.10 as a region in which CSF is known to exist;

(3) The swine have not transited a region classified under §§ 94.9 and 94.10 as a region in which CSF is known to exist unless moved directly through the region to their destination in a sealed means of conveyance with the seal intact upon arrival at the point of destination; and

(4) The conveyances or materials used in transporting the swine, if previously used for transporting swine, have been cleaned and disinfected in accordance with the requirements of § 93.502 of this chapter.

(c) *Pork or pork products.* The pork or pork products must be accompanied by a certification issued by a full-time salaried veterinary officer of the national government of the region of export. Upon arrival of the pork or pork products in the United States, the certification must be presented to an authorized inspector at the port of arrival. The certification must identify both the exporting region and the region of origin of the pork or pork products as a region listed under §§ 94.9 and 94.10 as free of CSF at the time the pork or pork products were in the region and must state that:

(1) The pork or pork products were derived from swine that were born and raised in a region listed under §§ 94.9 and 94.10 as free of CSF and were slaughtered in such a region at a federally inspected slaughter plant that is under the direct supervision of a full-time salaried veterinarian of the national government of that region and that is eligible to have its products imported into the United States under the Federal Meat Inspection Act (21 U.S.C. 601 *et seq.*) and the regulations in § 327.2 of this title;

(2) The pork or pork products were derived from swine that have not lived in a region classified under §§ 94.9 and 94.10 as a region in which CSF is known to exist;

(3) The pork or pork products have never been commingled with pork or pork products that have been in a region that is classified under §§ 94.9 and 94.10 as a region in which CSF is known to exist;

(4) The pork or pork products have not transited through a region classified under §§ 94.9 and 94.10 as a region in which CSF is known to exist unless moved directly through the region to their destination in a sealed means of conveyance with the seal intact upon arrival at the point of destination; and

(5) If processed, the pork or pork products were processed in a region listed under §§ 94.9 and 94.10 as free of CSF in a federally inspected processing plant that is under the direct supervision of a full-time salaried veterinary official of the national government of that region.

(Approved by the Office of Management and Budget under control numbers 0579–0230 and 0579–0235)

[71 FR 31070, June 1, 2006, as amended at 72 FR 30470, June 1, 2007; 76 FR 15211, Mar. 21, 2011; 77 FR 1395, Jan. 10, 2012. Redesignated at 78 FR 72999, Dec. 4, 2013]

§ 94.33 Restrictions on importation of live poultry, poultry meat, and other poultry products from specified regions.

Argentina and the Mexican States of Campeche, Quintana Roo, and Yucatan, which are declared in § 94.6(a)(1) to be free of Newcastle disease, supplement their meat supply by the importation of fresh (chilled or frozen) poultry meat from regions designated in § 94.6(a) as regions where Newcastle disease is considered to exist, have a common land border with regions where Newcastle disease is considered to exist, or import live poultry from regions where Newcastle disease is considered to exist under conditions less restrictive than would be acceptable for importation into the United States. Thus, even though the Department has declared such regions to be free of Newcastle disease, live poultry originating in such free regions may be commingled with live poultry originating in an Newcastle disease-affected region and the meat and other animal products produced in such free regions may be commingled with the fresh (chilled or frozen) meat of animals from an Newcastle disease-affected region, resulting in an undue risk of introducing Newcastle disease into the United States. Therefore, live poultry, poultry meat and other poultry products, and ship stores, airplane meals, and baggage containing such meat or animal products originating in the free regions listed in this section may not be imported into the United States unless the following requirements, in addition to all other applicable requirements of part 93 of this chapter and of chapter III of this title, are met:

(a) *Additional certification.* Live poultry, poultry meat, and other poultry products from any region designated in this section must be accompanied by an additional certification by a full-time salaried veterinary officer of the national Government of the exporting region. Upon arrival of the live poultry, poultry meat, or other poultry product in the United States, the certification must be presented to an authorized inspector at the port of arrival.

(b) *Live poultry.* The certification accompanying live poultry must identify the exporting region of the poultry as a region designated in § 94.6(a) as free of Newcastle disease and highly pathogenic avian influenza at the time the poultry were in the region and must state that:

(1) The poultry have not been in contact with poultry or poultry products from any region where Newcastle disease is considered to exist;

(2) The poultry have not lived in a region where Newcastle disease is considered to exist; and

(3) The poultry have not transited through a region where Newcastle disease is considered to exist unless moved directly through the region in a sealed means of conveyance with the seal intact upon arrival at the point of destination.

(c) *Poultry meat or other poultry products.* The certification accompanying poultry meat or other poultry products must state that:

(1) The poultry meat or other poultry products are derived from poultry that meet all requirements of this section and that have been slaughtered in a region designated in § 94.6(a) as free of Newcastle disease and highly pathogenic avian influenza at a federally inspected slaughter plant that is under the direct supervision of a full-time salaried veterinarian of the national Government of the exporting region and that is approved to export poultry meat and other poultry products to the United States in accordance with § 381.196 of this title;

(2) The poultry meat or other poultry products have not been in contact with poultry meat or other poultry products from any region where Newcastle disease is considered to exist;

(3) The poultry meat or other poultry products have not transited through a region where Newcastle disease is considered to exist unless moved directly through the region in a sealed means of conveyance with the seal intact upon arrival at the point of destination; and

(4) If processed, the poultry meat or other poultry products were processed in a region designated in § 94.6(a) as free of Newcastle disease and highly pathogenic avian influenza in a federally inspected processing plant that is under the direct supervision of a full-time salaried veterinarian of the national Government of the exporting region.

(Approved by the Office of Management and Budget under control number 0579–0228)

[69 FR 3823, Jan. 27, 2004. Redesignated at 70 FR 550, Jan. 4, 2005, as amended at 71 FR 4813, Jan. 30, 2006; 76 FR 4055, Jan. 24, 2011; 78 FR 19084, Mar. 29, 2013. Redesignated at 78 FR 72999, Dec. 4, 2013]

PART 95—SANITARY CONTROL OF ANIMAL BYPRODUCTS (EXCEPT CASINGS), AND HAY AND STRAW, OFFERED FOR ENTRY INTO THE UNITED STATES

Sec.

AUTHORITY: 7 U.S.C. 8301–8317; 21 U.S.C. 136 and 136a; 31 U.S.C. 9701; 7 CFR 2.22, 2.80, and 371.4.

SOURCE: 28 FR 5981, June 13, 1963, unless otherwise noted.

§ 95.1 Definitions.

Whenever in the regulations in this part the following words, names, or terms are used they shall be construed, respectively, to mean:

Administrator means the Administrator, Animal and Plant Health Inspection Service, or any individual authorized to act for the Administrator.

Animal and Plant Health Inspection Service (APHIS) means the Animal and Plant Health Inspection Service of the United States Department of Agriculture.

Animal byproducts means hides, skins, hair, wool, glue stock, bones, hoofs, horns, bone meal, hoof meal, horn meal, blood meal, meat meal, tankage, glands, organs, or other parts or products of ruminants and swine unsuitable for human consumption.

Approved chlorinating equipment means equipment approved by Veterinary Services as efficient for the disinfection of effluents against the contagions of foot-and-mouth disease and rinderpest.

Approved establishment means an establishment approved by Veterinary Services for the receipt and handling of restricted import animal byproducts.

Approved sewerage system means a drainage system equipped and operated so as to carry and dispose of sewage without endangering livestock through the contamination of streams or fields and approved by the Veterinary Services.

Approved warehouse means a warehouse having facilities approved by Veterinary Services for the handling and storage, apart from other merchandise, of restricted import products.

Bird trophy. A carcass or part of a carcass of a wild bird taken as game during a hunting expedition for the purpose of processing into taxidermy mounts for personal exhibition.

Blood meal means dried blood of animals.

Bone meal means ground animal bones and hoof meal and horn meal.

Bovine. Bos taurus, Bos indicus, and *Bison bison.*

Bovine spongiform encephalopathy (BSE) minimal-risk region. A region listed in § 94.18(a)(3) of this subchapter.

Department means the United States Department of Agriculture.

Deputy Administrator of Veterinary Services means the Deputy Administrator of Veterinary Services.

Direct transloading. The transfer of cargo directly from one means of conveyance to another.

Exporting region. A region from which shipments are sent to the United States.

Glue stock means fleshings, hide cuttings and parings, tendons, or other collagenous parts of animal carcasses.

Hay and straw means dried grasses, clovers, legumes, and similar materials or stalks or stems of various grains, such as barley, oats, rice, rye, and wheat.

Highly pathogenic avian influenza (HPAI). Highly pathogenic avian influenza is defined as follows:

(1) Any influenza virus that kills at least 75 percent of eight 4- to 6-week-old susceptible chickens within 10 days following intravenous inoculation with 0.2 mL of a 1:10 dilution of a bacteria-free, infectious allantoic fluid or inoculation of 10 susceptible 4- to 8-week-old chickens resulting in an intravenous pathogenicity index (IVPI) of greater than 1.2;

(2) Any H5 or H7 virus that does not meet the criteria in paragraph (1) of this definition, but has an amino acid sequence at the haemagglutinin cleavage site that is compatible with highly pathogenic avian influenza viruses; or

(3) Any influenza virus that is not an H5 or H7 subtype and that kills one to five out of eight inoculated chickens and grows in cell culture in the absence of trypsin within 10 days.

Inspector. Any individual authorized by the Administrator of APHIS or the Commissioner of Customs and Border Protection, Department of Homeland Security, to enforce the regulations in this part.

Meat meal or tankage means the rendered and dried carcasses or parts of the carcasses of animals.

Offal. The inedible parts of a butchered animal.

Positive for a transmissible spongiform encephalopathy. A sheep or goat for which a diagnosis of a transmissible spongiform encephalopathy has been made.

Processed animal protein means meat meal, bone meal, meat and bone meal, blood meal, dried plasma and other blood products, hydrolyzed proteins, hoof meal, horn meal, poultry meal, feather meal, fish meal, and any other similar products.

Region. Any defined geographic land area identifiable by geological, political, or surveyed boundaries. A region may consist of any of the following:

(1) A national entity (country);

(2) Part of a national entity (zone, county, department, municipality, parish, Province, State, etc.)

(3) Parts of several national entities combined into an area; or

(4) A group of national entities (countries) combined into a single area.

Specified risk materials (SRMs) from regions of controlled risk for BSE. Those bovine parts considered to be at particular risk of containing the BSE agent in infected animals, as listed in the FSIS regulations at 9 CFR 310.22(a).

Specified risk materials (SRMs) from regions of undetermined risk for BSE. Those bovine parts considered to be at particular risk of containing the BSE agent in infected animals, as listed in the FSIS regulations at 9 CFR 310.22(a), except that the following bovine parts from regions of undetermined risk for BSE are considered SRMs if they are derived from bovines over 12 months of age: Brain, skull, eyes, trigeminal ganglia, spinal cord, vertebral column (excluding the vertebrae of the tail, the transverse processes of the thoracic and lumbar vertebrae, and the wings of the sacrum), and the dorsal root ganglia.

Suspect for a transmissible spongiform encephalopathy. (1) A sheep or goat that has tested positive for a transmissible spongiform encephalopathy or for the proteinase resistant protein associated with a transmissible spongiform encephalopathy, unless the animal is designated as positive for a transmissible spongiform encephalopathy; or

(2) A sheep or goat that exhibits any of the following signs and that has been determined to be suspicious for a transmissible spongiform encephalopathy by a veterinarian: Weight loss despite retention of appetite; behavior abnormalities; pruritus (itching); wool pulling; biting at legs or side; lip smacking; motor abnormalities such as incoordination, high stepping gait of forelimbs, bunny hop movement of rear legs, or swaying of back end; increased sensitivity to noise and sudden movement; tremor, "star gazing," head pressing, recumbency, or other signs of neurological disease or chronic wasting.

Tallow derivative. Any chemical obtained through initial hydrolysis, saponification, or transesterification of tallow; chemical conversion of material obtained by hydrolysis, saponification, or transesterification may be applied to obtain the desired product.

United States means the several States, the District of Columbia, Guam, the Northern Mariana Islands, Puerto Rico, the Virgin Islands of the United States, and all other territories and possessions of the United States.

Veterinary Services means the Veterinary Services unit of the Animal and Plant Health Inspection Service, United States Department of Agriculture.

[28 FR 5981, June 13, 1963, as amended at 56 FR 19796, Apr. 30, 1991; 56 FR 63869, Dec. 6, 1991; 62 FR 56024, Oct. 28, 1997; 66 FR 42600, Aug. 14, 2001; 70 FR 551, Jan. 4, 2005; 70 FR 71218, Nov. 28, 2005; 74 FR 66226, Dec. 15, 2009; 78 FR 73001, Dec. 4, 2013; 79 FR 71007, Dec. 1, 2014]

§ 95.2 Region of origin.

No products or materials specified in the regulations in this part shall be imported unless there be shown upon the commercial invoice, or in some other manner satisfactory to the Deputy Administrator, Veterinary Services, the name of the region of origin of such product or material: *Provided,* That the region of origin shall be construed to mean (a) in the case of an animal byproduct, the region in which such product was taken from an animal or animals, and (b) in the case of other materials, the region in which such materials were produced.

[28 FR 5981, June 13, 1963, as amended at 62 FR 56024, Oct. 28, 1997]

§ 95.3 Byproducts from diseased animals prohibited.

The importation of any animal byproduct taken or removed from an animal affected with anthrax, foot-and-mouth disease, highly pathogenic avian influenza, Newcastle disease, or rinderpest is prohibited.

[28 FR 5981, June 13, 1963, as amended at 79 FR 71007, Dec. 1, 2014]

§ 95.4 Restrictions on the importation of processed animal protein, offal, tankage, fat, glands, certain tallow other than tallow derivatives, and serum due to bovine spongiform encephalopathy.

(a) Except as provided in paragraphs (c), (d), (e), (f), or (g) of this section or in § 95.15, any of the materials listed in paragraph (b) of this section derived from animals, or products containing such materials, are prohibited importation into the United States if paragraph (a)(1), (a)(2), or (a)(3) of this section applies:

(1) The animals have been in any region listed in paragraph (a)(4) of this section;

(2) The materials have been stored, rendered, or otherwise processed in a region listed in paragraph (a)(4) of this section; or

(3) The materials have otherwise been associated with a facility in a region listed in paragraph (a)(4) of this section.

(4) Albania, Andorra, Austria, Belgium, Bosnia-Herzegovina, Bulgaria, Canada, Croatia, the Czech Republic, Denmark, the Federal Republic of Yugoslavia, Finland, France, Germany, Greece, Hungary, the Republic of Ireland, Israel, Italy, Japan, Liechtenstein, Luxembourg, the Former Yugoslav Republic of Macedonia, Monaco, Norway, Oman, the Netherlands, Poland, Portugal, Romania, San Marino, Slovakia, Slovenia, Spain, Sweden, Switzerland, and the United Kingdom.

(b) *Restricted materials:* (1) Processed animal protein, tankage, offal, and tallow other than tallow derivatives, unless in the opinion of the Administrator, the tallow cannot be used in feed;

(2) Glands, unprocessed fat tissue, and blood and blood products;

(3) Processed fats and oils, and derivatives of processed animal protein, tankage, and offal; or

(4) Derivatives of glands and blood and blood products.

(c) The import prohibition in paragraph (a) of this section does not apply if the following conditions are met prior to importation:

(1) The material is derived from one of the following:

(i) A nonruminant species and the material is not ineligible for importation under §95.13 or §95.14;

(ii) Cervids or camelids;

(iii) Bovines, and the material is not ineligible for importation under the conditions of §95.5, §95.6, §95.7, §95.8, §95.9, §95.10, or §95.12; or

(iv) Ovines or caprines that have never been in any region listed in paragraph (a)(4) of this section.

(2) In any region other than Canada that is listed in paragraph (a)(4) of this section, all steps of processing and storing the material are carried out in a facility that has not been used for the processing and storage of materials derived from ovines or caprines that have been in any region that is listed in paragraph (a)(4) of this section.

(3) In Canada, all steps of processing and storing the material are carried out in a facility that has not been used for the processing and storage of materials derived from ovines and caprines that have been in any region other than Canada that is listed in paragraph (a)(4) of this section.

(4) The facility demonstrates to APHIS that the materials intended for exportation to the United States were transported to and from the facility in a manner that would prevent cross-contamination by or commingling with prohibited materials.

(5) If the facility processes or handles any material derived from mammals, inspection of the facility for compliance with the provisions of this section is conducted at least annually by a representative of the government agency responsible for animal health in the region, unless the region chooses to have such inspection conducted by APHIS. If APHIS conducts the inspections required by this section, the facility has entered into a cooperative service agreement executed by the operator of the facility and APHIS. In accordance with the cooperative service agreement, the facility must be current in paying all costs for a veterinarian of APHIS to inspect the facility (it is anticipated that such inspections will occur approximately once per year), including travel, salary, subsistence, administrative overhead, and other incidental expenses (including excess baggage provisions up to 150 pounds). In addition, the facility must have on deposit with APHIS an unobligated amount equal to the cost for APHIS personnel to conduct one inspection. As funds from that amount are obligated, a bill for costs incurred based on official accounting records will be issued to restore the deposit to the original level, revised as necessary to allow for inflation or other changes in

estimated costs. To be current, bills must be paid within 14 days of receipt.

(6) The facility allows periodic APHIS inspection of its facilities, records, and operations.

(7) Each shipment to the United States is accompanied by an original certificate signed by a full-time, salaried veterinarian of the government agency responsible for animal health in the exporting region certifying that the conditions of paragraphs (c)(1) through (c)(5) of this section have been met.

(8) The person importing the shipment has applied for and obtained from APHIS a United States Veterinary Permit for Importation and Transportation of Controlled Materials and Organisms and Vectors by filing a permit application on VS Form 16–3. (VS Form 16–3 may be obtained from APHIS, Veterinary Services, National Center for Import and Export, 4700 River Road Unit 38, Riverdale, MD 20737–1231, or electronically at *http://www.aphis.usda.gov/animal_health/permits/.*)

(d) Except as provided in paragraph (e) of this section and in § 95.15, serum from ovines or caprines that have been in any region listed in paragraph (a)(4) of this section is prohibited importation into the United States, except for scientific, educational, or research purposes if the Administrator determines that the importation can be made under conditions that will prevent the introduction of BSE into the United States. Such serum must be accompanied by a permit issued by APHIS in accordance with § 104.4 of this chapter and must be moved and handled as specified on the permit.

(e) The importation of serum albumin, serocolostrum, amniotic liquids or extracts, and placental liquids derived from ovines or caprines that have been in any region listed in paragraph (a)(4) of this section, and collagen and collagen products that are derived from ovines or caprines and that would otherwise be prohibited under paragraphs (a) and (b) of this section, is prohibited unless the following conditions have been met:

(1) The article is imported for use as an ingredient in cosmetics;

(2) The person importing the article has obtained a United States Veterinary Permit for Importation and Transportation of Controlled Materials and Organisms and Vectors by filing a permit application on VS Form 16–3 (VS Form 16–3 may be obtained from APHIS, Veterinary Services, National Center for Import and Export, 4700 River Road Unit 38, Riverdale, MD 20737–1231, or electronically at *http://www.aphis.usda.gov/animal_health/permits/.*); and

(3) The permit application states the intended use of the article and the name and address of the consignee in the United States.

(f) Insulin otherwise prohibited under paragraphs (a) and (b) of this section may be imported if the insulin is for the personal medical use of the person importing it and if the person importing the shipment has applied for and obtained from APHIS a United States Veterinary Permit for Importation and Transportation of Controlled Materials and Organisms and Vectors. To apply for a permit, file a permit application on VS Form 16–3 (available from APHIS, Veterinary Services, National Center for Import and Export, 4700 River Road Unit 38, Riverdale, MD 20737–1231, or electronically at *http://www.aphis.usda.gov/animal_health/permits/*). The application for such a permit must state the intended use of the insulin and the name and address of the consignee in the United States.

NOTE TO PARAGRAPH (f): Insulin that is not prohibited from importation under this paragraph may be prohibited from importation under other Federal laws, including the Federal Food, Drug, and Cosmetic Act, 21 U.S.C. 321 *et seq.*

(g) Offal that is otherwise prohibited under paragraphs (a) and (b) of this section because it is derived from ovines or caprines that have been in a region listed in paragraph (a)(4) of this section may be imported into the United States if the offal is derived from ovines or caprines from Canada that have not been in a region listed in paragraph (a)(4) of this section other than Canada, and the following conditions are met:

(1) The offal:

(i) Is derived from ovines or caprines that were less than 12 months of age when slaughtered and that are from a flock or herd subject to a ruminant feed ban equivalent to the requirements established by the U.S. Food and Drug Administration at 21 CFR 589.2000;

(ii) Is not derived from ovines or caprines that have tested positive for or are suspect for a transmissible spongiform encephalopathy;

(iii) Is not derived from animals that have resided in a flock or herd that has been diagnosed with BSE; and

(iv) Is derived from ovines or caprines whose movement was not restricted in the BSE minimal-risk region as a result of exposure to a transmissible spongiform encephalopathy.

(2) Each shipment to the United States is accompanied by an original certificate signed by a full-time salaried veterinary officer of the national government of the exporting region, or issued by a veterinarian designated by the exporting region and endorsed by a full-time salaried veterinary officer of the national government of the exporting region, representing that the veterinarian issuing the certificate was authorized to do so. The certificate must state that the requirements of paragraph (g)(1) of this section have been met; and

(3) The shipment, if arriving at a U.S. land border port, arrives at a port listed in § 94.25(c) of this subchapter.

(Approved by the Office of Management and Budget under control numbers 0579–0015, 0579–0234, and 0579–0393)

[78 FR 73001, Dec. 4, 2013]

§ 95.5 Processed animal protein derived from ruminants.

The importation of ruminant-derived processed animal protein, or any commodities containing such products, is prohibited unless the conditions of this section are met:

(a) The exporting region is a region of negligible risk for BSE; and

(1) The product has not been commingled or contaminated with ruminant meat-and-bone meal or greaves from a region of controlled or undetermined risk for BSE; and

(2) The product must be derived from ruminants that were subject to a ban on the feeding of ruminants with meat-and-bone meal or greaves derived from ruminants if it is either:

(i) Exported from a region of negligible risk for BSE in which there has been at least one indigenous case of BSE; or

(ii) Derived from ruminants that were in a region of negligible risk for BSE in which there has been at least one indigenous case of BSE.

(b) The exporting region is a region of controlled or undetermined risk, the product is ruminant-derived processed animal protein other than ruminant meat-and-bone meal or greaves, and it has been demonstrated that the product has not been commingled or contaminated with ruminant meat-and-bone meal or greaves from a controlled or undetermined risk region.

(c) Each shipment to the United States is accompanied by an original certificate signed by a full-time salaried veterinary officer of the national government of the exporting region, or issued by a veterinarian designated by the national government of the exporting region and endorsed by a full-time salaried veterinary officer of the national government of the exporting region, representing that the veterinarian issuing the certificate was authorized to do so. The certificate must state the exporting region and that the requirements of this section, as applicable, have been met.

(d) The person importing the processed animal protein obtains a United States Veterinary Permit for Importation and Transportation of Controlled Materials and Organisms and Vectors by filing a permit application on VS Form 16–3. To apply for a permit, file a permit application on VS Form 16–3 (available from APHIS, Veterinary Services, National Center for Import and Export, 4700 River Road Unit 38, Riverdale, MD 20737–1231, or electronically at *http://www.aphis.usda.gov/animal_health/permits/*). The application for such a permit must state the intended use of the processed animal protein and name and address of the consignee in the United States.

(Approved by the Office of Management and Budget under control number 0579–0393)

[78 FR 73003, Dec. 4, 2013]

§95.6 Offal derived from bovines.

Offal derived from bovines is prohibited importation into the United States unless it meets the requirements for the importation of meat, meat products, and meat byproducts in either §94.19, §94.20, or §94.21, with the exception of the requirements in §94.19(c), §94.20(b), and §94.21(b), respectively. The person importing the offal must obtain a United States Veterinary Permit for Importation and Transportation of Controlled Materials and Organisms and Vectors by filing a permit application on VS Form 16–3. To apply for a permit, file a permit application on VS Form 16–3 (available from APHIS, Veterinary Services, National Center for Import and Export, 4700 River Road Unit 38, Riverdale, MD 20737–1231, or electronically at *http://www.aphis.usda.gov/animal_health/permits/*). The application for such a permit must state the intended use of the offal and name and address of the consignee in the United States.

[78 FR 73003, Dec. 4, 2013]

§95.7 Collagen derived from bovines.

(a) The importation of collagen derived from bovines is prohibited because of BSE unless:

(1) The collagen meets the requirements of either paragraph (b), (c), or (d), as well as the requirements of paragraph (e) of this section and all other applicable requirements of this part; or

(2) The collagen is authorized importation under paragraph (f) of this section and meets all other applicable requirements of this part:

(b) The collagen is derived from hides and skins, provided the collagen has not been commingled with materials ineligible for entry into the United States.

(c) The collagen is derived from the bones of bovines that originated from a region of negligible risk for BSE.

(d) The collagen is derived from the bones of bovines that originated from a region of controlled or undetermined risk for BSE and meets the requirements of paragraphs (d)(1) through (d)(4) of this section:

(1) The bones from which the collagen was derived were derived from bovines that passed ante-mortem and post-mortem inspection;

(2) The bones from which the collagen was derived did not include the skulls of bovines or the vertebral column of bovines 30 months of age or older;

(3) The bones were subjected to a process that includes all of the following steps, or to a process at least as effective in reducing BSE infectivity:

(i) Degreasing;

(ii) Acid demineralization;

(iii) Acid or alkaline treatment;

(iv) Filtration; and

(v) Sterilization at 138 °C (280.4 °F) or greater for a minimum of 4 seconds; and

(4) The collagen has not been commingled with materials ineligible for entry into the United States.

(e) The collagen is accompanied to the United States by an original certificate signed by a full-time salaried veterinary officer of the national government of the exporting region, or issued by a veterinarian designated by the national government of the exporting region and endorsed by a full-time salaried veterinary officer of the national government of the exporting region, representing that the veterinarian issuing the certificate was authorized to do so. The certificate must state that the requirements of paragraph (b), (c), or (d) of this section, as applicable, have been met and, for collagen other than that described in paragraph (b) of this section, must indicate the BSE risk classification of the exporting region.

(f) The Administrator determines that the collagen will not come into contact with ruminants in the United States and can be imported under conditions that will prevent the introduction of BSE into the United States, and the person importing the collagen has obtained a United States Veterinary Permit for Importation and Transportation of Controlled Materials and Organisms and Vectors. To apply for a permit, file a permit application on VS Form 16–3 (available from APHIS, Veterinary Services, National Center for Import and Export, 4700 River Road Unit 38, Riverdale, MD 20737–1231, or electronically at *http://*

www.aphis.usda.gov/animal_health/permits/). The application for such a permit must state the intended use of the collagen and the name and address of the consignee in the United States.

(Approved by the Office of Management and Budget under control number 0579–0393)

[78 FR 73003, Dec. 4, 2013]

§ 95.8 Tallow derived from bovines.

(a) The importation of bovine-derived tallow is prohibited unless:

(1) The requirements of either paragraph (b), (c), or (d), as well as the requirements of paragraph (e) of this section are met; or

(2) The requirements of paragraph (f) of this section are met.

(b) The tallow is composed of a maximum level of insoluble impurities of 0.15 percent in weight; or

(c) The tallow originates from a region of negligible risk for BSE; or

(d) The tallow originates from a region of controlled risk for BSE, is derived from bovines that have passed ante-mortem and post-mortem inspections, and has not been prepared using SRMs as defined for regions of controlled risk for BSE in § 92.1 of this subchapter.

(e) The tallow is accompanied to the United States by an original certificate signed by a full-time salaried veterinary officer of the national government of the exporting region, or issued by a veterinarian designated by the national government of the exporting region and endorsed by a full-time salaried veterinary officer of the national government of the exporting region, representing that the veterinarian issuing the certificate was authorized to do so. The certificate must state that the requirements of paragraph (b), (c), or (d) of this section, as applicable, have been met and, for tallow other than that described in paragraph (b) of this section, must indicate the BSE risk classification of the exporting region.

(f) The Administrator determines that the tallow will not come into contact with ruminants in the United States and can be imported under conditions that will prevent the introduction of BSE into the United States, and the person importing the tallow has obtained a United States Veterinary Permit for Importation and Transportation of Controlled Materials and Organisms and Vectors. To apply for a permit, file a permit application on VS Form 16–3 (available from APHIS, Veterinary Services, National Center for Import and Export, 4700 River Road Unit 38, Riverdale, MD 20737–1231, or electronically at *http://www.aphis.usda.gov/animal_health/permits/*). The application for such a permit must state the intended use of the tallow and the name and address of the consignee in the United States.

(Approved by the Office of Management and Budget under control number 0579–0393)

[78 FR 73003, Dec. 4, 2013]

§ 95.9 Derivatives of tallow derived from bovines.

(a) The importation of derivatives of tallow from bovines is prohibited unless the commodity meets the conditions of either paragraph (b), (c), (d), or (e) of this section as well as paragraph (f) of this section, or, alternatively, meets the conditions of paragraph (g) of this section.

(b) The commodity meets the definition of tallow derivative in § 95.1.

(c) The derivative is from tallow composed of a maximum level of insoluble impurities of 0.15 percent in weight.

(d) The derivative is from tallow that originates from a region of negligible risk for BSE.

(e) The derivative is from tallow that originates from a region of controlled risk for BSE, is derived from bovines that have passed ante-mortem and post-mortem inspections, and does not contain SRMs as defined for regions of controlled risk for BSE in § 92.1 of this subchapter.

(f) The tallow derivative is accompanied to the United States by an original certificate signed by a full-time salaried veterinary officer of the national government of the exporting region, or issued by a veterinarian designated by the national government of the exporting region and endorsed by a full-time salaried veterinary officer of the national government of the exporting region, representing that the veterinarian issuing the certificate was authorized to do so. The certificate must state that the requirements of paragraph (b), (c), (d), or (e) of this section, as applicable, have been met and, for tallow derivatives other than those described in paragraph (b) or (c) of this section, must indicate the BSE risk classification of the exporting region.

(g) The Administrator determines that the tallow derivative will not come into contact with ruminants in the United States and can be imported under conditions that will prevent the introduction of BSE into the United States, and the person importing the tallow derivative has obtained a United States Veterinary Permit for Importation and Transportation of Controlled Materials and Organisms and Vectors. To apply for a permit, file a permit application on VS Form 16–3 (available from APHIS, Veterinary Services, National Center for Import and Export, 4700 River Road Unit 38, Riverdale, MD 20737–1231, or electronically at *http://www.aphis.usda.gov/animal_health/permits/*). The application for such a permit must state the intended use of the tallow derivative and the name and address of the consignee in the United States.

(Approved by the Office of Management and Budget under control number 0579–0393)

[78 FR 73003, Dec. 4, 2013]

§ 95.10 Dicalcium phosphate derived from bovines.

(a) The importation of dicalcium phosphate derived from bovines is prohibited unless:

(1) The requirements of either paragraph (b), (c), or (d) and the requirements of paragraph (e) of this section are met; or

(2) The requirements of paragraph (f) of this section are met.

(b) The dicalcium phosphate contains no trace of protein or fat; or

(c) The dicalcium phosphate originates from a region of negligible risk for BSE; or

(d) The dicalcium phosphate originates from a region of controlled risk for BSE, is derived from bovines that have passed ante-mortem and postmortem inspections, and does not contain SRMs as defined for regions of controlled risk for BSE in § 92.1 of this subchapter.

(e) The dicalcium phosphate is accompanied by an original certificate signed by a full-time salaried veterinary officer of the national government of the exporting region, or issued by a veterinarian designated by the national government of the exporting region and endorsed by a full-time salaried veterinary officer of the national government of the exporting region, representing that the veterinarian issuing the certificate was authorized to do so. The certificate must indicate the BSE risk classification of the exporting region and state that the requirements of paragraph (b) (c), or (d) of this section, as applicable, have been met.

(f) The Administrator determines that the dicalcium phosphate will not come into contact with ruminants in the United States and can be imported under conditions that will prevent the introduction of BSE into the United States, and the person importing the dicalcium phosphate has obtained a United States Veterinary Permit for Importation and Transportation of Controlled Materials and Organisms and Vectors. To apply for a permit, file a permit application on VS Form 16–3 (available from APHIS, Veterinary Services, National Center for Import and Export, 4700 River Road Unit 38, Riverdale, MD 20737–1231, or electronically at *http://www.aphis.usda.gov/animal_health/permits/*). The application for such a permit must state the intended use of the dicalcium phosphate and the name and address of the consignee in the United States.

(Approved by the Office of Management and Budget under control number 0579–0393)

[78 FR 73003, Dec. 4, 2013]

§ 95.11 Specified risk materials.

Notwithstanding any other provisions of this part, the importation of specified risk materials from controlled-risk regions or undetermined-risk regions for BSE, and any commodities containing such materials, is prohibited, unless the Administrator determines that the materials or other commodities will not come into contact with ruminants in the United

States and can be imported under conditions that will prevent the introduction of BSE into the United States, and the person importing the materials or other commodities has obtained a United States Veterinary Permit for Importation and Transportation of Controlled Materials and Organisms and Vectors. To apply for a permit, file a permit application on VS Form 16–3 (available from APHIS, Veterinary Services, National Center for Import and Export, 4700 River Road Unit 38, Riverdale, MD 20737–1231, or electronically at *http://www.aphis.usda.gov/animal_health/permits/*). The application for such a permit must state the intended use of the materials and other commodities and the name and address of the consignee in the United States.

[78 FR 73003, Dec. 4, 2013]

§95.12 Blood and blood products derived from bovines.

The importation of bovine blood and products derived from bovine blood is prohibited unless the following conditions and the conditions of all other applicable parts of this chapter are met:

(a) For blood collected at slaughter and for products derived from blood collected at slaughter:

(1) The blood was collected in a hygienic manner, as determined by the Administrator, that prevents contamination of the blood with SRMs; and

(2) The slaughtered animal passed ante-mortem inspection and was not subjected to a pithing process or to a stunning process with a device injecting compressed air or gas into the cranial cavity.

(b) For blood collected from live donor bovines and for products derived from blood collected from live donor bovines:

(1) The blood was collected in a hygienic manner, as determined by the Administrator, that prevents contamination of the blood with SRMs; and

(2) The donor animal was free of clinical signs of disease.

(c) The blood and blood products are accompanied to the United States by an original certificate that states that the conditions of this section have been met. The certificate must be issued by a full-time salaried veterinary officer of the national government of the exporting region, or issued by a veterinarian designated by the national government of the exporting region and endorsed by a full-time salaried veterinary officer of the exporting region, representing that the veterinarian issuing the certificate was authorized to do so.

(Approved by the Office of Management and Budget under control number 0579–0393)

[78 FR 73003, Dec. 4, 2013]

§95.13 Importation from regions of negligible risk for BSE of processed animal protein derived from animals other than ruminants.

The importation from regions of negligible risk for BSE of processed animal protein derived from animals other than ruminants is prohibited importation into the United States unless the following conditions are met:

(a) The processed animal protein is not prohibited importation under §95.4;

(b) The processed animal protein imported into the United States in accordance with this section is accompanied by an original certificate signed by a full-time salaried veterinary officer of the national government of the exporting region, or issued by a veterinarian designated by the national government of the exporting region and endorsed by a full-time salaried veterinary officer of the national government of the exporting region, representing that the veterinarian issuing the certificate was authorized to do so, that indicates that the material is derived from animals other than ruminants.

(c) The person importing the shipment has applied for and obtained from APHIS a United States Veterinary Permit for Importation and Transportation of Controlled Materials and Organisms and Vectors. To apply for a permit, file a permit application on VS Form 16–3 (available from APHIS, Veterinary Services, National Center for Import and Export, 4700 River Road Unit 38, Riverdale, MD 20737–1231, or electronically at *http://*

www.aphis.usda.gov/animal_health/permits/).

(Approved by the Office of Management and Budget under control number 0579–0393)

[78 FR 73003, Dec. 4, 2013]

§ 95.14 Importation from regions of controlled risk or undetermined risk for BSE of processed animal protein derived from animals other than ruminants.

The importation from regions of controlled risk or undetermined risk for BSE of processed animal protein derived from animals other than ruminants is prohibited importation into the United States unless the following conditions are met:

(a) The processed animal protein is not prohibited importation under § 95.4;

(b) Except as provided in paragraph (c) of this section, the processed animal protein does not contain and was not commingled with material derived from ruminants originating in a BSE controlled- or undetermined-risk region;

(c) For blood meal, blood plasma, and other blood products, the material does not contain and was not commingled with ruminant blood or blood products prohibited importation into the United States under this part.

(d) Inspection of the facility for compliance with the provisions of this section is conducted at least annually by a competent authority of the government agency responsible for animal health in the region, unless the region chooses to have such inspections conducted by APHIS. The inspections must verify either that:

(1) All steps of processing and storing the material are carried out in a facility that has not been used for the processing or storage of materials derived from ruminants originating in a BSE controlled- or undetermined-risk region; or

(2) The material is produced in a manner that prevents contamination of the processed animal protein with materials prohibited importation into the United States.

(e) If APHIS conducts the inspections required by paragraph (d) of this section, the facility has entered into a cooperative service agreement executed by the operator of the facility and APHIS. In accordance with the cooperative service agreement, the facility must be current in paying all costs for a veterinarian of APHIS to inspect the facility (it is anticipated that such inspections will occur approximately once per year), including travel, salary, subsistence, administrative overhead, and other incidental expenses (including excess baggage provisions up to 150 pounds). In addition, the facility must have on deposit with APHIS an unobligated amount equal to the cost for APHIS personnel to conduct one inspection. As funds from that amount are obligated, a bill for costs incurred based on official accounting records will be issued to restore the deposit to the original level, revised as necessary to allow for inflation or other changes in estimated costs. To be current, bills must be paid within 14 days of receipt.

(f) The facility allows periodic APHIS inspection of its facilities, records, and operations.

(g) The processed animal protein imported into the United States in accordance with this section is accompanied by an original certificate signed by a full-time, salaried veterinary officer of the national government of the exporting region, or issued by a veterinarian designated by the national government of the exporting region and endorsed by a full-time, salaried veterinary officer of the national government of the exporting region, representing that the veterinarian issuing the certificate was authorized to do so, that states that the processed animal protein is not of ruminant origin and that conditions of this section have been met.

(h) The person importing the shipment has applied for and obtained from APHIS a United States Veterinary Permit for Importation and Transportation of Controlled Materials and Organisms and Vectors. To apply for a permit, file a permit application on VS Form 16–3 (available from APHIS, Veterinary Services, National Center for Import and Export, 4700 River Road Unit 38, Riverdale, MD 20737–1231, or electronically at *http://*

www.aphis.usda.gov/animal_health/permits/).

(Approved by the Office of Management and Budget under control number 0579–0393)

[78 FR 73003, Dec. 4, 2013]

§95.15 Transit shipment of articles.

Articles that are otherwise prohibited importation into the United States in accordance with §§95.4 through 95.14 may transit air and ocean ports in the United States for immediate export if the conditions of paragraphs (a) through (c) of this section are met. Articles are eligible to transit the United States by overland transportation if the requirements of paragraphs (a) through (e) of this section are met.

(a) The articles must be sealed in leakproof containers bearing serial numbers during transit. Each container must remain sealed during the entire time that it is in the United States.

(b) Before such transit, the person moving the articles must notify, in writing, the inspector at both the place in the United States where the articles will arrive and the port of export. The notification must include the:

(1) Times and dates of arrival in the United States;

(2) Times and dates of exportation from the United States; and

(3) Serial numbers of the sealed containers.

(c) The articles must transit the United States under Customs bond.

(d) The person moving the articles must obtain a United States Veterinary Permit for Importation and Transportation of Controlled Materials and Organisms and Vectors. To apply for a permit, file a permit application on VS Form 16–3 (available from APHIS, Veterinary Services, National Center for Import and Export, 4700 River Road Unit 38, Riverdale, MD 20737–1231, or electronically at *http://www.aphis.usda.gov/animal_health/permits/*).

(e) The commodities must be eligible to enter the United States in accordance with §§95.4 through 95.14 and must be accompanied by the certification required by that section. Additionally, the following conditions must be met:

(1) The shipment must be exported from the United States within 7 days of its entry;

(2) The commodities may not be transloaded while in the United States, except for direct transloading under the supervision of an authorized inspector, who must break the seals of the national government of the exporting region on the means of conveyance that carried the commodities into the United States and seal the means of conveyance that will carry the commodities out of the United States with seals of the U.S. Government; and

(3) A copy of the import permit required under paragraph (d) of this section must be presented to the inspector at the port of arrival and the port of export in the United States.

[78 FR 73003, Dec. 4, 2013]

§95.16 Untanned hides and skins and bird trophies; requirements for entry.

Untanned hides and skins and bird trophies[1] may be imported into the United States if they meet the requirements of this section. Except for ruminant hides or skins from Mexico, untanned hides and skins and bird trophies may also be imported if handled at an approved establishment as set forth in §95.17.

(a) *Untanned hides and skins.* (1) Except for ruminant hides or skins from Mexico, any untanned hides or skins of ruminants from regions free of foot-and-mouth disease and rinderpest and any untanned hides or skins of swine from regions free of foot-and-mouth disease, rinderpest, and African swine fever may be imported without further restriction.

(2) Untanned ruminant hides or skins may be imported from any region without other restriction if an inspector determines, based on inspection and upon examination of a shipper or importer certificate, that they are hard dried hides or skins.

(3) Except for ruminant hides or skins from Mexico, untanned abattoir hides or skins of ruminants may be imported from any region without other

[1] The importation of bird trophies is also subject to restrictions under §95.17.

restriction if the following requirements are met:

(i) The ruminants from which the hides or skins were taken have been slaughtered under national government inspection in a region[2] and in an abattoir in which is maintained an inspection service that meets the requirements and has been approved pursuant to part 327 of this title; and

(ii) The hides or skins are accompanied by a certificate bearing the seal of the proper department of that national government and signed by an official veterinary inspector of the region in which the ruminants were slaughtered. The certificate must state that the hides or skins were taken from ruminants slaughtered in an abattoir that meets the requirements of paragraph (a)(3)(i) of this section and that the hides or skins are free from anthrax, foot-and-mouth disease, and rinderpest.

(4) Untanned ruminant hides or skins from any region may be imported without other restriction if an inspector determines, based on inspection and upon examination of a shipper or importer certificate, that they have been pickled in a solution of salt containing mineral acid and packed in barrels, casks, or tight cases while still wet with such solution. The solution must be determined by the inspector to have a pH of less than or equal to 5.

(5) Untanned ruminant hides or skins from any region may be imported without other restriction if an inspector determines, based on inspection and upon examination of a shipper or importer certificate, that they have been treated with lime in such manner and for such period as to have obviously been processed, to have become dehaired, and to have reached the stage of preparation for immediate manufacture into products ordinarily made from rawhide.

(b) *Ruminant hides and skins from Mexico.* Ruminant hides and skins from Mexico may enter the United States without other restriction if:

(1) They are free of ticks and have been subjected to any one of the treatments specified in paragraphs (a)(2), (a)(4), or (a)(5) of this section; or

(2) They are inspected and found to have been frozen solid for 24 hours by an inspector and are accompanied by a certificate attesting to that fact issued by the shipper or importer that is reviewed by the inspector, and are free from ticks; or

(3) They are free from ticks and are accompanied by a certificate issued by a full-time salaried veterinary officer of the Government of Mexico stating that they have been treated with an acaricide; or

(4) They are bovine hides taken from cattle that were subjected to a tickicidal dip in one of the permitted dips listed in § 72.13(b) of this chapter at a Mexican facility 7 to 12 days prior to slaughter, and are free from ticks.

(c) *Bird trophies.* Bird trophies from regions designated in § 94.6 of this subchapter as free of Newcastle disease and free of HPAI may be imported without further restriction if accompanied by a certificate of origin issued by the national government of the region of export.

(Approved by the Office of Management and Budget under control numbers 0579–0015 and 0579–0307)

[74 FR 66226, Dec. 15, 2009, as amended at 76 FR 28887, May 19, 2011; 78 FR 19085, Mar. 29, 2013. Redesignated and amended at 78 FR 73003, 73006, Dec. 4, 2013; 79 FR 71007, Dec. 1, 2014]

§ 95.17 Untanned hides, skins, and bird trophies; importations permitted subject to restrictions.

Except for ruminant hides or skins from Mexico, hides or skins or bird trophies offered for importation which do not meet the conditions or requirements of § 95.16 shall be handled and treated in the following manner after arrival at the port of entry:

(a) They shall be consigned from the coast or border port of arrival to an approved establishment and shall be subject to disinfection by such method or methods as the Deputy Administrator, Veterinary Services may prescribe unless the said establishment discharges drainage into an approved sewerage system or has an approved chlorinating

[2] Names of these regions will be furnished upon request to the Animal and Plant Health Inspection Service, Veterinary Services, National Center for Import and Export, 4700 River Road Unit 38, Riverdale, Maryland 20737-1231.

equipment adequate for the proper disinfection of effluents: *Provided, however*, That upon permission of the Deputy Administrator, Veterinary Services such hides or skins or bird trophies may be stored for a temporary period in approved warehouses under bond, and under the supervision of an inspector: *And provided further*, That I. T. or inbound shipments of hides or skins or bird trophies may go forward under customs seals from a coast or border port of arrival, with the approval of an inspector at said port, to another port in the United States for consumption entry subject to the other provisions of this section.

(b) They shall be moved from the coast or border port of arrival or, in case of I. T. or in-bound shipments, from the interior port to the approved establishment in cars or trucks or in vessel compartments with no other materials contained therein, sealed with seals of the Department, which shall not be broken except by inspectors or other persons authorized by the Deputy Administrator, Veterinary Services so to do, or without sealing as aforesaid and with other freight when packed in tight cases or casks acceptable to the inspector in charge at the port of entry.

(c) They shall be handled at the approved establishment under the direction of an inspector in a manner approved by the Deputy Administrator, Veterinary Services to guard against the dissemination of foot-and-mouth disease, rinderpest, African swine fever, highly pathogenic avian influenza, and Newcastle disease. They shall not be removed therefrom except upon special permission of the Deputy Administrator, Veterinary Services and upon compliance with all the conditions and requirements of this section relative to the movement of the said hides and skins or bird trophies from the port of arrival to the said establishment.

(Approved by the Office of Management and Budget under control number 0579–0015)

[28 FR 5981, June 13, 1963, as amended at 59 FR 67134, Dec. 29, 1994; 74 FR 66227, Dec. 15, 2009; 76 FR 28887, May 19, 2011; 78 FR 19085, Mar. 29, 2013. Redesignated and amended at 78 FR 73003, 73006, Dec. 4, 2013; 79 FR 71007, Dec. 1, 2014]

§ 95.18 Wool, hair, and bristles; requirements for unrestricted entry.

Wool, hair, or bristles derived from ruminants and/or swine which do not meet the conditions or requirements specified in any one of paragraphs (a) to (d) of this section shall not be imported except subject to handling and treatment in accordance with § 95.19 after their arrival at the port of entry: *Provided, however*, That no bloodstained wool, hair, or bristles shall be imported under any condition:

(a) Such wool, hair, or bristles may be imported without other restriction if originating in and shipped directly from a region not declared by the Secretary of Agriculture to be infected with foot-and-mouth disease or rinderpest.

(b) Wool or hair clipped from live animals or pulled wool or hair may be imported without other restriction if the said wool or hair is reasonably free from animal manure in the form of dung locks or otherwise.

(c) Wool, hair, or bristles taken from sheep, goats, cattle, or swine, when such animals have been slaughtered under national government inspection in a region[3] and in an abattoir in which is maintained an inspection service determined by the Secretary of Agriculture to be adequate to assure that such materials have been removed from animals found at time of slaughter to be free from anthrax, foot-and-mouth disease, and rinderpest, and to assure further the identity of such materials until loaded upon the transporting vessel, may be imported without other restriction if accompanied by a certificate bearing the seal of the proper department of said national government and signed by an official veterinary inspector of such region showing that the therein described wool, hair, or bristles were taken from animals slaughtered in such specified abattoir and found free from anthrax, foot-and-mouth disease, and rinderpest.

(d) Wool, hair, or bristles which have been scoured, thoroughly washed, or

[3] See footnote 2 in § 95.16.

dyed may be imported without other restriction.

(Approved by the Office of Management and Budget under control number 0579–0015)

[28 FR 5981, June 13, 1963, as amended at 48 FR 57472, Dec. 30, 1983; 62 FR 56024, Oct. 28, 1997; 74 FR 66226, Dec. 15, 2009. Redesignated and amended at 78 FR 73003, 73006, Dec. 4, 2013]

§ 95.19 Wool, hair, and bristles; importations permitted subject to restrictions.

Wool, hair, or bristles offered for importation which do not meet the conditions or requirements of § 95.18 shall be handled and treated in the following manner after arrival at the port of entry:

(a) Such wool, hair, or bristles shall be consigned from the coast or border port of arrival to an approved establishment: *Provided, however,* That upon permission by the Deputy Administrator, Veterinary Services such wool, hair, or bristles may be stored for a temporary period in approved warehouses under bond and under the supervision of an inspector: *And provided further,* That I. T. on in-bond shipments of wool, hair, or bristles may go forward under customs seals from a coast or border port of arrival, with the approval of an inspector at said port, to another port for consumption entry, subject to the other provisions of this section.

(b) Such wool, hair, or bristles shall be moved from the coast or border port of arrival or, in the case of I. T. or in-bond shipments, from the interior port to the establishment in cars or trucks or in vessel compartments with no other materials contained therein, sealed with seals of the Department, which shall not be broken except by inspectors or other persons authorized by the Deputy Administrator, Veterinary Services so to do, or without sealing as aforesaid and with other freight when packed in tight cases acceptable to an inspector.

(c) Such wool, hair, or bristles shall be handled at the establishment under the direction of an inspector in a manner approved by the Deputy Administrator, Veterinary Services to guard against the dissemination of foot-and-mouth disease and rinderpest. Such products shall not be removed therefrom except upon special permission of the Deputy Administrator, Veterinary Services and upon compliance with all the conditions and requirements of this section relative to the movement of the said wool, hair, or bristles from the port of arrival to the said establishment.

(Approved by the Office of Management and Budget under control number 0579–0015)

[28 FR 5981, June 13, 1963, as amended at 59 FR 67134, Dec. 29, 1994. Redesignated and amended at 78 FR 73003, 73007, Dec. 4, 2013]

§ 95.20 Glue stock; requirements for unrestricted entry.

Glue stock which does not meet the conditions or requirements specified in any one of paragraphs (a) to (c) of this section shall not be imported except subject to handling and treatment in accordance with § 95.21 after arrival at the port of entry:

(a) Glue stock originating in and shipped directly from a region not declared by the Secretary of Agriculture to be infected with foot-and-mouth disease or rinderpest may be imported without other restriction.

(b) Glue stock may be imported without other restriction if found upon inspection by an inspector, or by certificate of the shipper or importer satisfactory to said inspector, to have been properly treated by acidulation or by soaking in milk of lime or a lime paste; or to have been dried so as to render each piece of the hardness of a sun-dried hide.

(c) Glue stock taken from cattle, sheep, goats, or swine slaughtered under national government inspection in a region[4] and in an abattoir in which is maintained an inspection service determined by the Secretary of Agriculture to be adequate to assure that such materials have been removed from animals found at time of slaughter to be free from anthrax, foot-and-mouth disease, and rinderpest, and to assure further the identity of such materials until loaded upon the transporting vessel, may be imported without other restriction if accompanied by a certificate bearing the seal of the proper department of said national

[4] See footnote 2 in § 95.16.

government and signed by an official veterinary inspector of such region showing that the therein described glue stock was taken from animals slaughtered in such specified abattoir and found free from anthrax foot-and-mouth disease, and rinderpest.

(Approved by the Office of Management and Budget under control number 0579–0015)

[28 FR 5981, June 13, 1963, as amended at 48 FR 57472, Dec. 30, 1983; 62 FR 56024, Oct. 28, 1997; 74 FR 66226, Dec. 15, 2009. Redesignated and amended at 78 FR 73003, 73007, Dec. 4, 2013]

§95.21 Glue stock; importations permitted subject to restrictions.

Glue stock offered for importation which does not meet the conditions or requirements of §95.20 shall be handled and treated in the following manner after arrival at the port of entry:

(a) It shall be consigned from the coast or border port of arrival to an approved establishment and shall be subject to disinfection by such method or methods as the Deputy Administrator, Veterinary Services may prescribe unless the said establishment discharges drainage into an approved sewerage system or has an approved chlorinating equipment adequate for the proper disinfection of effluents: *Provided, however*, That upon permission by the Deputy Administrator, Veterinary Services glue stock may be stored for a temporary period in approved warehouses under bond and under the supervision of an inspector: *And provided further*, That I. T. or in-bond shipments of glue stock may go forward under customs seals from a coast or border port of arrival with the approval of an inspector at said port to another port for consumption entry, subject, after arrival at the latter port, to the other provisions of this section.

(b) It shall be moved from the coast or border port of arrival or, in case of I. T. or in-bond shipments, from the interior port to the establishment in cars or trucks or in vessel compartments with no other materials contained therein, sealed with seals of the Department, which shall not be broken except by inspectors or other persons authorized by the Deputy Administrator, Veterinary Services so to do, or without sealing as aforesaid and with other freight when packed in tight cases or casks acceptable to an inspector at port of entry.

(c) It shall be handled at the establishment under the direction of an inspector in a manner approved by the Deputy Administrator, Veterinary Services to guard against the dissemination of foot-and-mouth disease and rinderpest. It shall not be removed therefrom except upon special permission of the Deputy Administrator, Veterinary Services and upon compliance with all the conditions and requirements of this section relative to the movement of the said glue stock from the port of arrival to the said establishment.

(Approved by the Office of Management and Budget under control number 0579–0015)

[28 FR 5981, June 13, 1963, as amended at 59 FR 67134, Dec. 29, 1994. Redesignated and amended at 78 FR 73003, 73007, Dec. 4, 2013]

§95.22 Bones, horns, and hoofs for trophies or museums; disinfected hoofs.

(a) Clean, dry bones, horns, and hoofs, that are free from undried pieces of hide, flesh, and sinew and are offered for entry as trophies or for consignment to museums may be imported without other restrictions.

(b) Clean, dry hoofs disinfected in the region of origin may be imported without other restrictions if the following conditions are met:

(1) The hoofs have been disinfected using one of the following methods:

(i) Dry heat at 180 °F (82.2 °C) for 30 minutes;

(ii) Soaking in boiling water for 20 minutes;

(iii) Soaking in a 0.1 percent chlorine bleach solution for 2 hours;

(iv) Soaking in a 5 percent acetic acid solution for 2 hours; or

(v) Soaking in a 5 percent hydrogen peroxide solution for 2 hours.

(2) The hoofs are accompanied by a certificate issued by the national government of the region of origin and signed by an official veterinary inspector of that region stating that the

hoofs have been disinfected and describing the manner in which the disinfection was accomplished.

[28 FR 5981, June 13, 1963, as amended at 59 FR 9400, Feb. 28, 1994; 62 FR 56024, Oct. 28, 1997. Redesignated at 78 FR 73003, Dec. 4, 2013]

§ 95.23 Bones, horns, and hoofs; importations permitted subject to restrictions.

Bones, horns, and hoofs offered for importation which do not meet the conditions or requirements of § 95.22 shall be handled and treated in the following manner after arrival at the port of entry:

(a) They shall be consigned from the coast or border port of arrival to an approved establishment having facilities for their disinfection or their conversion into products customarily made from bones, horns, or hoofs: *Provided, however*, That I. T. or in-bond shipments of bones, horns, or hoofs may go forward under customs seals from a coast or border port of arrival, with the approval of an inspector at said port, to another port for consumption entry subject to the other provisions of this section.

(b) They shall be moved from the coast or border port of arrival or, in case of I. T. or in-bond shipments, from the interior port to the establishment in cars or trucks with no other materials contained therein, sealed with seals of the Department, which shall not be broken except by inspectors or other persons authorized by the Deputy Administrator, Veterinary Services so to do, or without sealing as aforesaid and with other freight when packed in tight cases or casks acceptable to an inspector at the port of entry.

(c) They shall be handled at the establishment under the direction of an inspector in a manner to guard against the dissemination of anthrax, foot-and-mouth disease, rinderpest, highly pathogenic avian influenza, and Newcastle disease, and the bags, burlap, or other containers thereof, before leaving the establishment, shall be disinfected by heat or otherwise, as directed by the Deputy Administrator, Veterinary Services or burned at the establishment. They shall not be removed therefrom except upon special permission of the Deputy Administrator, Veterinary Services and upon compliance with all the conditions and requirements of this section relative to the movement of the said bones, horns, and hoofs.

(Approved by the Office of Management and Budget under control number 0579–0015)

[28 FR 5981, June 13, 1963, as amended at 59 FR 67134, Dec. 29, 1994. Redesignated at 78 FR 73003, 73007, Dec. 4, 2013; 79 FR 71007, Dec. 1, 2014]

§ 95.24 Bone meal for use as fertilizer or as feed for domestic animals; requirements for entry.

Steamed or degelatinized or special steamed bone meal, which, in the normal process of manufacture, has been prepared by heating bone under a minimum of 20 pounds steam pressure for at least one hour at a temperature of not less than 250 °Fahrenheit (121 °Centigrade), may be imported without further restrictions for use as fertilizer or as feed for domestic animals if such products are free from pieces of bone, hide, flesh, and sinew and contain no more than traces of hair and wool. Bone meal for use as fertilizer or as feed for domestic animals which does not meet these requirements will not be eligible for entry.

[28 FR 5981, June 13, 1963. Redesignated at 78 FR 73003, Dec. 4, 2013]

§ 95.25 Blood meal, tankage, meat meal, and similar products, for use as fertilizer or animal feed; requirements for entry.

Dried blood or blood meal, lungs or other organs, tankage, meat meal, wool waste, wool manure, and similar products, for use as fertilizer or as feed for domestic animals, shall not be imported except subject to handling and treatment in accordance with paragraphs (a), (b), and (c) of § 95.27, unless:

(a) Such products originated in and were shipped directly from a region not declared by the Secretary of Agriculture to be infected with foot-and-mouth disease or rinderpest; or

(b) The inspector at the port of entry finds that such products have been fully processed by tanking under live steam or by dry rendering.

[28 FR 5981, June 13, 1963, as amended at 62 FR 56024, Oct. 28, 1997. Redesignated at 78 FR 73003, 73007, Dec. 4, 2013]

§95.26 Blood meal, blood albumin, intestines, and other animal byproducts for industrial use; requirements for unrestricted entry.

Blood meal, blood albumin, bone meal, intestines, or other animal materials intended for use in the industrial arts shall not be imported except subject to handling and treatment in accordance with §95.27, unless such products originated in and were shipped directly from a region not declared by the Secretary of Agriculture to be infected with foot-and-mouth disease or rinderpest.

(Approved by the Office of Management and Budget under control number 0579–0015)

[28 FR 5981, June 13, 1963, as amended at 59 FR 67134, Dec. 29, 1994; 62 FR 56024, Oct. 28, 1997. Redesignated and amended at 78 FR 73003, 73007, Dec. 4, 2013]

§95.27 Blood meal, blood albumin, intestines, and other animal byproducts for industrial use; importations permitted subject to restrictions.

Blood meal, blood albumin, bone meal, intestines, or other animal materials intended for use in the industrial arts, which do not meet the conditions or requirements of §95.26 shall be handled and treated in the following manner after arrival at the port of entry.

(a) They shall be consigned from the coast or border port of arrival to an approved establishment: *Provided, however,* That upon permission by the Deputy Administrator, Veterinary Services they may be stored for a temporary period in approved warehouses under bond and under the supervision of an inspector: *And provided further,* That I. T. or in-bond shipments of such products may go forward under customs seals from a coast or border port of arrival, with the approval of an inspector at said port, to another port of consumption entry, subject after arrival at the latter port to the other provisions of this section.

(b) They shall be moved from the coast or border port of arrival or, in the case of I. T. or in-bond shipments, from the interior port to the establishment in cars or trucks or in vessel compartments with no other materials contained therein, sealed with seals of the Department, which shall not be broken except by Veterinary Services inspectors or other persons authorized by the Deputy Administrator, Veterinary Services so to do, or without sealing as aforesaid and with other freight when packed in tight cases or casks acceptable to an inspector at the port of entry.

(c) They shall be handled at the establishment under the direction of an inspector in a manner to guard against the dissemination of foot-and-mouth disease and rinderpest. They shall not be removed therefrom except upon special permission of the Deputy Administrator, Veterinary Services and upon compliance with all the conditions and requirements of this section relative to the movement of the said products from the port of arrival to the said establishment.

(Approved by the Office of Management and Budget under control number 0579–0015)

[28 FR 5981, June 13, 1963, as amended at 59 FR 67134, Dec. 29, 1994. Redesignated and amended at 78 FR 73003, 73007, Dec. 4, 2013]

§95.28 Glands, organs, ox gall, and like materials; requirements for unrestricted entry.

Glands, organs, ox gall or bile, bone marrow, and various like materials derived from domestic ruminants or swine, intended for use in the manufacture of pharmaceutical products shall not be imported except subject to handling and treatment in accordance with §95.29, unless such glands, organs, or materials originated in and were shipped directly from a region not declared by the Secretary of Agriculture to be infected with foot-and-mouth disease or rinderpest.

[28 FR 5981, June 13, 1963, as amended at 62 FR 56024, Oct. 28, 1997. Redesignated and amended at 78 FR 73003, 73007, Dec. 4, 2013]

§95.29 Glands, organs, ox gall, and like materials; importations permitted subject to restrictions.

Glands, organs, ox gall or bile, bone marrow, and various like materials derived from domestic ruminants or swine, which do not meet the requirements of §95.28 may be imported for pharmaceutical purposes if in tight containers and consigned to an approved establishment: *Provided, however,* That upon special permission of the Deputy Administrator, Veterinary

Services they may be stored for a temporary period in approved warehouses under bond and under the supervision of an inspector. They shall be handled and processed at the said establishment in a manner approved by the Deputy Administrator, Veterinary Services and the containers shall be destroyed or disinfected as prescribed by him. They shall not be removed therefrom except upon special permission of the Deputy Administrator, Veterinary Services and upon compliance with all the conditions and requirements of this section relative to the movement of the said glands, organs, ox gall, and like materials from the port of arrival to the said establishment.

(Approved by the Office of Management and Budget under control number 0579–0015)

[28 FR 5981, June 13, 1963, as amended at 59 FR 67134, Dec. 29, 1994. Redesignated and amended at 78 FR 73003, 73007, Dec. 4, 2013]

§ 95.30 Animal stomachs.

Stomachs or portions of the stomachs of ruminants or swine, other than those imported for food purposes under the meat-inspection regulations of the Department, shall not be imported without permission from the Deputy Administrator, Veterinary Services. Importations permitted shall be subject to such restrictions as the Deputy Administrator, Veterinary Services may deem necessary in each instance.

(Approved by the Office of Management and Budget under control number 0579–0015)

[28 FR 5981, June 13, 1963, as amended at 59 FR 67134, Dec. 29, 1994. Redesignated at 78 FR 73003, Dec. 4, 2013]

§ 95.31 Animal manure.

Manure of horses, cattle, sheep, other ruminants, and swine shall not be imported except upon permission from the Deputy Administrator, Veterinary Services. Importations permitted shall be subject to such restrictions as he may deem necessary in each instance: *Provided, however,* That manure produced by animals while in transit to the United States shall be subject only to the requirements of the Department regulations governing the importation of domestic livestock and other animals.

(Approved by the Office of Management and Budget under control number 0579–0015)

[28 FR 5981, June 13, 1963, as amended at 59 FR 67134, Dec. 29, 1994. Redesignated at 78 FR 73003, Dec. 4, 2013]

§ 95.32 Hay and straw; requirements for unrestricted entry.

Except as provided in § 95.39, hay or straw shall not be imported except subject to handling and treatment in accordance with § 95.33 after arrival at the port of entry, unless such hay or straw originated in and was shipped directly from a region not declared by the Secretary of Agriculture to be infected with foot-and-mouth disease or rinderpest.

[28 FR 5981, June 13, 1963, as amended at 62 FR 56024, Oct. 28, 1997. Redesignated and amended at 78 FR 73003, 73007, Dec. 4, 2013]

§ 95.33 Hay and straw; importations permitted subject to restrictions.

Except as provided in § 95.39, hay or straw which does not meet the conditions or requirements of § 95.32 shall be handled and treated in the following manner upon arrival at the port of entry:

(a) Hay or straw packing materials shall be burned or disinfected at the expense of the importer or consignee in the manner and at the time directed by the Deputy Administrator, Veterinary Services.

(b) Hay or straw for use as feeding material, bedding, or similar purposes shall be stored and held in quarantine for a period of not less than 90 days in an approved warehouse at the port of entry and shall be otherwise handled as directed by the Deputy Administrator, Veterinary Services.

[28 FR 5981, June 13, 1963. Redesignated and amended at 78 FR 73003, 73007, Dec. 4, 2013]

§ 95.34 Previously used meat covers; importations permitted subject to restrictions.

Cloth or burlap which has been used to cover fresh or frozen meats originating in any region designated in § 94.1 of this subchapter as a region in which rinderpest or foot-and-mouth disease exists, shall not be imported except under the following conditions:

(a) The cloth or burlap shall be consigned from the coast or border port of arrival to an establishment specifically approved for the purpose by the Deputy Administrator, Veterinary Services.

(b) The cloth or burlap shall be immediately moved from the coast or border port of arrival, or in case of I. T. or in-bond shipments from the interior port, to the establishment, in railroad cars or trucks, or in vessel compartments, with no other material contained therein, sealed with seals of the Department, which shall not be broken except by inspectors or other persons authorized by the Deputy Administrator, Veterinary Services: *Provided, however,* That upon permission of the Deputy Administrator, Veterinary Services, such cloth or burlap may be stored for a temporary period in approved warehouses at the port of arrival under bond and under the supervision of an inspector.

(c) The material shall be disinfected and otherwise handled at the establishment under the direction of an inspector in a manner approved by the Deputy Administrator, Veterinary Services to guard against the dissemination of foot-and-mouth disease and rinderpest, and the material shall not be removed therefrom, except upon special permission of the Deputy Administrator, Veterinary Services, until all of the conditions and requirements of this section have been complied with.

(Approved by the Office of Management and Budget under control number 0579–0015)

[28 FR 5981, June 13, 1963, as amended at 59 FR 67134, Dec. 29, 1994; 62 FR 56024, Oct. 28, 1997. Redesignated at 78 FR 73003, Dec. 4, 2013]

§ 95.35 Methods for disinfection of hides, skins, and other materials.

Hides, skins, and other materials required by the regulations in this part to be disinfected shall be subjected to disinfection by methods found satisfactory and approved from time to time by the Deputy Administrator, Veterinary Services.

[28 FR 5981, June 13, 1963. Redesignated at 78 FR 73003, Dec. 4, 2013]

§ 95.36 Transportation of restricted import products; placarding cars and marking billing; unloading enroute.

(a) Transportation companies or other operators of cars, trucks or other vehicles carrying import products or materials moving under restriction, other than those in tight cases or casks, shall affix to and maintain on both sides of all such vehicles durable placards not less than 5½ by 6 inches in size, on which shall be printed with permanent black ink and in boldface letters not less than 1½ inches in height the words "Restricted import product." These placards shall also bear the words "Clean and disinfect this car or truck." Each of the waybills, conductors' manifests, memoranda, and bills of lading pertaining to such shipments shall have the words "Restricted import product, clean and disinfect car or truck," plainly written or stamped upon its face. If for any reason the placards required by this section have not been affixed to each car, or the billing has not been marked by the initial or the connecting carrier, or the placards have been removed, destroyed, or rendered illegible, the placards shall be immediately affixed or replaced and the billing marked by the initial or connecting carrier, the intention being that the billing accompanying the shipment shall be marked and each car, truck or other vehicle placarded as specified in this section from the time such shipment leaves the port of entry until it is unloaded at final destination and the cars, trucks or other vehicles are cleaned and disinfected as required by § 95.37.

(b) If it is necessary to unload enroute any of the materials or products transported in a placarded car, truck or other vehicle as provided in this section, the car, truck or other vehicle from which the transfer is made and any part of the premises in or upon which the product or material may have been placed in the course of unloading or reloading shall be cleaned and disinfected by the carrier, in accordance with the provisions of § 95.37, and the said carrier shall immediately report the matter, by telegraph, to the Deputy Administrator, Veterinary Services, Washington, DC 20251. Such report shall include the following information: Nature of emergency; place where product or material was unloaded; original points of shipment and destination; number and materials of the original car or truck; and number and initials of the car, truck or other vehicle into which the product or material is reloaded in case the original car or truck is not used.

(Approved by the Office of Management and Budget under control number 0579–0015)

[28 FR 5981, June 13, 1963, as amended at 48 FR 57472, Dec. 30, 1983. Redesignated and amended at 78 FR 73003, 73007, Dec. 4, 2013]

§ 95.37 Railroad cars, trucks, boats, aircraft and other means of conveyance, equipment or containers, yards, and premises; cleaning and disinfection.

Railroad cars, trucks, boats, aircraft and other means of conveyance, equipment or containers, yards, and premises which have been used in the transportation, handling, or storing of restricted import products or materials, other than those contained in leak proof cases or casks, shall be cleaned and disinfected with a disinfectant approved for use in this part under the supervision of the division at the time and in the manner provided in this section. Except as provided in paragraph (a) of this section, such railroad cars, trucks, boats, aircraft and other means of conveyance, equipment or containers, shall not be moved in interstate or foreign commerce until they have been so treated.

(a) *Cars to be cleaned and disinfected by final carrier at destination.* Cars required by this part to be cleaned and disinfected shall be so treated by the final carrier at destination as soon as possible after unloading and before the same are moved from such final destination for any purpose: *Provided, however,* That when the products or materials are destined to points at which an inspector or other duly authorized representative of Veterinary Services is not maintained or where proper facilities cannot be provided, the transportation company shall seal, bill, and forward the cars in which the products or materials were transported to a point to be agreed upon between the transportation company and Veterinary Services, and the transportation company shall there clean and disinfect the said cars under the supervision of Veterinary Services.

(b) *Methods of cleaning and disinfecting.* (1) Railroad cars, trucks, aircraft and means of conveyance other than boats, equipment or containers, required by this part to be cleaned and disinfected shall be treated in the following manner: Collect all litter and other refuse therefrom and destroy by burning or other approved method, clean the exterior and interior of the cars or trucks, and the areas of the aircraft or other means of conveyance, equipment or containers that may have been contaminated, and saturate the entire surface with a permitted disinfectant approved for use in this part.

(2) Boats required by this part to be cleaned and disinfected shall be treated in the following manner: Collect all litter and other refuse from the decks, compartments, and all other parts of the boat used for the transportation of the products or materials covered by this part, and from the portable chutes or other appliances, fixtures or areas used in loading and unloading same, and destroy the litter and other refuse by burning or by other approved methods, and saturate the entire surface of the said decks, compartments, and other parts of the boat with a permitted disinfectant approved for use in this part.

(3) Buildings, sheds, and premises required by this part to be disinfected shall be treated in the following manner: Collect all litter and other refuse therefrom and destroy the same by burning or other approved methods, and saturate the entire surface of the fencing, chutes, floors, walls, and other parts with a permitted disinfectant approved for use in this part.

(c) *Permitted disinfectants.* The disinfectants permitted for use in disinfecting railroad cars, trucks, boats, aircraft and other means of conveyance, equipment or containers, yards, and premises against infection of foot-and-mouth disease and rinderpest are freshly prepared solutions of:

(1) Sodium carbonate (4 percent) in the proportion of 1 pound to 3 gallons of water.

(2) Sodium carbonate (4 percent) plus sodium silicate (0.1 percent) in the proportion of 1 pound of sodium carbonate plus sodium silicate to 3 gallons of water.

(3) Sodium hydroxide (Lye) prepared in a fresh solution in the proportion of not less than 1 pound avoirdupois of sodium hydroxide of not less than 95 percent purity to 6 gallons of water, or one 13½-ounce can to 5 gallons of water.[5]

(d) *Permitted disinfectants against ticks.* The disinfectants permitted for use against tick infestation are liquefied phenol (U. S. P. strength 87 percent phenol) in the proportion of at least 6 fluid ounces to one gallon of water; or chlorinated lime (U. S. P. strength 30 percent available chlorine) in the proportion of one pound to three gallons of water; or any one of the cresylic disinfectants permitted by the Animal and Plant Health Inspection Service in the proportion of at least four fluid ounces to one gallon of water; or through application of boiling water if the treatment is against rinder-pest or foot-and-mouth disease and tick infestation; or other disinfectants or treatments approved by the Deputy Administrator, Veterinary Services.

[28 FR 5981, June 13, 1963, as amended at 32 FR 19157, Dec. 20, 1967; 74 FR 66226, Dec. 15, 2009. Redesignated at 78 FR 73003, Dec. 4, 2013]

§ 95.38 Regulations applicable to products from Territorial possessions.

The regulations in this part shall be applicable to all the products and materials specified in this part which are offered for entry into the United States from any place under the jurisdiction of the United States to which the animal-quarantine laws of this country do not apply.

[28 FR 5981, June 13, 1963. Redesignated at 78 FR 73003, Dec. 4, 2013]

§ 95.39 Hay or straw and similar material from tick-infested areas.

Hay or straw, grass, or similar material from tick-infested pastures, ranges, or premises may disseminate the contagion of splenetic, Southern or Texas fever when imported for animal feed or bedding; therefore, such hay or straw, grass, or similar materials shall not be imported unless such material is first disinfected with a disinfectant specified in § 95.26(d).

[28 FR 5981, June 13, 1963. Redesignated at 78 FR 73003, Dec. 4, 2013]

§ 95.40 Certification for certain materials.

(a) In addition to meeting any other certification or permit requirements of this chapter, the following articles, if derived from ovines or caprines, may be imported into the United States from any region not listed in § 95.4(a)(4) only if they are accompanied by a certificate, as described in paragraph (b) of this section:

(1) Processed animal protein, tankage, offal, and tallow other than tallow derivatives, unless, in the opinion of the Administrator, the tallow cannot be used in feed;

(2) Glands and unprocessed fat tissue;

(3) Processed fats and oils, and derivatives of processed animal protein, tankage, and offal;

(4) Derivatives of glands; and

(5) Any product containing any of the materials listed in paragraphs (a)(1) through (a)(4) of this section.

(b) The certificate required by paragraph (a) of this section must be an original official certificate, signed by a full-time, salaried veterinarian of the agency responsible for animal health in the exporting region, that states the following:

(1) The animal species from which the material was derived;

(2) The region in which any facility where the material was processed is located;

(3) That the material was derived only from animals that have never been in any region listed in § 95.4(a)(4), with the regions listed in § 95.4(a)(4) specifically named;

[5] Due to the extreme caustic nature of sodium hydroxide solution, precautionary measures such as the wearing of rubber gloves, boots, raincoat and goggles should be observed. An acid solution such as vinegar shall be kept readily available in case any of the sodium hydroxide solution should come in contact with the body.

(4) That the material did not originate in, and was never stored, rendered, or processed in, or otherwise associated with, a facility in a region listed in § 95.4(a)(4); and

(5) The material was never associated with any of the materials listed in paragraph (a) of this section that have been in a region listed in § 95.4(a)(4).

(c) The certification required by paragraph (a) of this section must clearly correspond to the shipment by means of an invoice number, shipping marks, lot number, or other method of identification.

(Approved by the Office of Management and Budget under control number 0579–0234)

[78 FR 73007, Dec. 4, 2013]

PART 96—RESTRICTION OF IMPORTATIONS OF FOREIGN ANIMAL CASINGS OFFERED FOR ENTRY INTO THE UNITED STATES

Sec.

AUTHORITY: 7 U.S.C. 8301–8317; 21 U.S.C. 136 and 136a; 7 CFR 2.22, 2.80, and 371.4.

SOURCE: 28 FR 5986, June 13, 1963, unless otherwise noted.

§ 96.1 Definitions.

Administrator. The Administrator, Animal and Plant Health Inspector Service, or any person authorized to act for the Administrator.

Animal and Plant Health Inspection Service. The Animal and Plant Health Inspection Service of the United States Department of Agriculture (APHIS or Service).

Animal casings. Intestines, stomachs, esophagi, and urinary bladders from cattle, sheep, swine, or goats that are used to encase processed meats in foods such as sausage.

APHIS representative. An individual employed by APHIS who is authorized to perform the function involved.

Authorized inspector. Any individual authorized by the Administrator of APHIS or the Commissioner of Customs and Border Protection, Department of Homeland Security, to enforce the regulations in this subpart.

Department. The United States Department of Agriculture.

Food and Drug Administration. The Food and Drug Administration of the United States Department of Health and Human Services.

Food Safety and Inspection Service. The Food Safety and Inspection Service of the United States Department of Agriculture.

Import (imported, importation) into the United States. To bring into the territorial limits of the United States.

Region. Any defined geographic land area identifiable by geological, political, or surveyed boundaries. A region may consist of any of the following:

(1) A national entity (country);

(2) Part of a national entity (zone, county, department, municipality, parish, Province, State, etc.)

(3) Parts of several national entities combined into an area; or

(4) A group of national entities (countries) combined into a single area.

United States. All of the States of the United States, the District of Columbia, Guam, the Northern Mariana Islands, Puerto Rico, the Virgin Islands of the United States, American Samoa, and the territories and possessions of the United States.

(Approved by the Office of Management and Budget under control number 0579–0015)

[57 FR 28082, June 24, 1992, as amended at 57 FR 29785, July 7, 1992; 59 FR 67134, Dec. 29, 1994; 62 FR 56024, Oct. 28, 1997; 70 FR 553, Jan. 4, 2005; 72 FR 53379, Sept. 18, 2007]

§96.2 Prohibition of casings due to African swine fever and bovine spongiform encephalopathy.

(a) *Swine casings.* The importation of swine casings that originated in or were processed in a region where African swine fever exists, as listed under §94.8(a) of this subchapter, is prohibited, with the following exception: Swine casings that are processed in a region where African swine fever exists may be imported into the United States under the following conditions:

(1) *Origin of casings.* The swine casings were derived from swine raised and slaughtered in a region not listed under §94.8(a) of this subchapter.

(2) *Shipping requirements.* The casings were shipped from the region of origin to a processing establishment in a region listed under §94.8(a) of this subchapter in a closed container sealed with serially numbered seals applied by an official of the national government of the region of origin.

(3) *Origin certificate.* The casings were accompanied from the region of origin to the processing establishment by a certificate written in English and signed by an official of the national government of the region of origin specifying the region of origin, the processing establishment to which the swine casings were consigned, and the numbers of the seals applied.

(4) *Integrity of seals.* The casings were taken out of the container at the processing establishment only after an official of the national government of the region where the processing establishment is located determined that the seals were intact and free of any evidence of tampering and had so stated on the certificate referred to in paragraph (a)(3) of this section.

(5) *The processing establishment.* The casings were processed at a single processing establishment[1] in a region listed under §94.8(a) of this subchapter. The processing establishment does not receive or process any live swine and uses only pork and pork products that originate in a region not listed under §94.8(a) of this subchapter and that are shipped to the processing establishment in accordance with paragraphs (a)(2) through (a)(4) of this section.

(6) *Compliance agreement.* The processing establishment is operated by persons who have entered into a valid written compliance agreement with APHIS to maintain on file at the processing establishment for at least 2 years copies of the certificates referred to in paragraph (a)(4) of this section, to allow APHIS personnel to make unannounced inspections as necessary to monitor compliance with the provisions of this section, and to otherwise comply with the provisions of this section.

(7) *Cooperative service agreement.* The processing establishment is operated by persons who have entered into a cooperative service agreement with APHIS. The establishment is current in paying for APHIS personnel to inspect the establishment (it is anticipated that such inspections will occur once per year). In addition, the processing establishment has on deposit with APHIS an unobligated amount equal to the cost for APHIS personnel to conduct one inspection, including travel, salary, subsistence, administrative overhead, and other incidental expenses (including excess baggage provisions up to 150 pounds).

(8) *Compliance agreement cancellation.* Any compliance agreement may be canceled orally or in writing by the inspector who is supervising its enforcement whenever the authorized inspector finds that such person has failed to comply with the provisions of this section or any conditions imposed by this section. If the cancellation is oral, the decision and the reasons will be confirmed in writing, as promptly as circumstances allow. Any person whose compliance agreement has been canceled may appeal the decision to the Administrator, in writing, within 10 days after receiving written notification of the cancellation. The appeal should state all of the facts and reasons upon which the person relies to show that the compliance agreement was wrongfully canceled. The Administrator will grant or deny the appeal, in

[1] As a condition of entry into the United States, pork or pork products must also meet all of the requirements of the Federal Meat Inspection Act (21 U.S.C. 601 *et seq.*) and regulations under the Act (9 CFR, chapter III, part 327), including requirements that the pork or pork products be prepared only in approved establishments.

writing, stating the reasons for such decision, as promptly as circumstances allow. If there is a conflict as to any material fact, a hearing will be held to resolve such conflict. Rules of Practice governing such a hearing will be adopted by the Administrator.

(9) *Export certification.* The casings are accompanied to the United States by an original certificate stating that all of the requirements of this section have been met. The certificate must be written in English. The certificate must be issued by an official of the national government of the region in which the processing establishment is located. The official must be authorized to issue the foreign meat inspection certificate required by part 327 in chapter III of this title. Upon arrival of the swine casings in the United States, the certificate must be presented to an authorized inspector at the port of arrival.

(b) *Casings from ovines or caprines.* The importation of casings, except stomachs, derived from ovines or caprines that originated in or were processed in any region listed in § 95.4(a)(4) are prohibited, unless the following conditions are met:

(1) The casings are derived from sheep that were slaughtered in Canada at less than 12 months of age and that were from a flock subject to a ruminant feed ban equivalent to the requirements established by the U.S. Food and Drug Administration at 21 CFR 589.2000; and

(2) The casings are accompanied by an original certificate that meets the requirements of § 96.3 and:

(i) States that the casings meet the conditions of this section;

(ii) Is written in English;

(iii) Is signed by an individual eligible to issue the certificate required under § 96.3; and

(iv) Is presented to an authorized inspector at the port of entry.

(c) *Casings from bovines.* The importation of casings derived from bovines is prohibited, unless the following conditions are met:

(1) If the casings are derived from bovines from a region of negligible risk for BSE, as defined in § 92.1 of this subchapter, the certificate required under § 96.3 indicates the APHIS BSE risk classification of the region in which the bovines were slaughtered and the casings were collected.

(2) If the casings are derived from bovines from a region of controlled risk for BSE or a region of undetermined risk for BSE, as defined in § 92.1 of this subchapter, the casings are not derived from the small intestine or, if the casings are derived from the small intestine, the casings are derived from that part of the small intestine that is eligible for use as human food in accordance with the requirements established by the Food Safety and Inspection Service at 9 CFR 310.22 and the Food and Drug Administration at 21 CFR 189.5.

(3) The casings are accompanied by an original certificate that meets the requirements of § 96.3 and paragraphs (b)(2)(i) through (b)(3)(iv) of this section.

(Approved by the Office of Management and Budget under control number 0579–0015)

[65 FR 1307, Jan. 10, 2000, as amended at 70 FR 553, Jan. 4, 2005; 72 FR 53379, Sept. 18, 2007; 77 FR 1395, Jan. 10, 2012; 78 FR 73007, Dec. 4, 2013]

§ 96.3 Certificate for animal casings.

(a) No animal casings shall be imported into the United States from any foreign region unless they are accompanied by a certificate signed by either (1) a veterinarian salaried by the national government of the region in which the animals were slaughtered and the casings were collected, and who is authorized by the national government to conduct casings inspections and issue certificates, and who has inspected the casings before issuing the certificate and determined that the casings meet the criteria described in the Foreign Official Certificate for Animal Casings; or (2) a non-government veterinarian authorized to issue the certificate by the national government of the region in which the animals were slaughtered and the casings were collected, who has inspected the casings before issuing the certificate and determined that the casings meet the criteria described in the Foreign Official Certificate for Animal Casings. A certificate issued by a non-government veterinarian is valid only if the certificate is endorsed by a veterinarian salaried by the national government of the region in which the animals were slaughtered and the casings were collected.

(b) All signatures on the certificate shall be original.

(c) The certificate shall bear the insignia of the national government of the region in which the animals were slaughtered and the casings were collected, and shall be in the following form:

FOREIGN OFFICIAL CERTIFICATE FOR ANIMAL CASINGS

Place (City) __________ (Region) ______ (Date) ______

I hereby certify that the animal casings herein described were derived from healthy animals (cattle, sheep, swine, or goats), which received, ante mortem and post mortem veterinary inspections at the time of slaughter, are clean and sound, and were prepared and handled only in a sanitary manner and were not subjected to contagion prior to exportation.

Kind of casings __________
Number of packages __________
Weight __________

Identification marks on the packages ______
Consignor __________
(Address)
Consignee __________
(Destination)
Shipping marks __________
Signature: __________
Official issuing the certificate. (Non-government veterinarian authorized to issue the certificate by the national government of the region in which the animals were slaughtered and the casings were collected.)
Official title: __________
Signature: __________
Official issuing the certificate. (Veterinarian salaried by the national government of the region in which the animals were slaughtered and the casings were collected.)
Official title: __________

(d) In addition to meeting the requirements of this section, the certificate accompanying sheep casings from Canada must state that the casings meet the requirements of §96.2(b) and the certificate accompanying bovine casings must state that the casings meet the requirements of either §96.2(c)(1) or (c)(2) as applicable.

(Approved by the Office of Management and Budget under control number 0579–0015)

[28 FR 5986, June 13, 1963, as amended at 48 FR 57472, Dec. 30, 1983. Redesignated and amended at 57 FR 28082, June 24, 1992. Redesignated at 58 FR 47031, Sept. 7, 1993, as amended at 62 FR 56024, Oct. 28, 1997; 70 FR 553, Jan. 4, 2005; 72 FR 53379, Sept. 18, 2007; 78 FR 73008, Dec. 4, 2013]

§96.4 Uncertified animal casings; disposition.

Animal casings which are unaccompanied by the required certificate, those shipped in sheepskins or other skins as containers, and those found upon inspection to be unclean or unsound when offered for importation into the United States shall be kept in customs custody until exported or destroyed, or until disinfected and denaturated as prescribed by the Administrator, Animal and Plant Health Inspection Service (APHIS) in §§96.5 through 96.16.

[28 FR 5986, June 13, 1963. Redesignated and amended at 57 FR 28082, 28083, June 24, 1992; 57 FR 29785, July 7, 1992. Redesignated and amended at 58 FR 47031, Sept. 7, 1993]

§96.5 Instructions regarding handling certified animal casings.

(a) Animal casings are not classed as meat product, therefore the certificate required for foreign meat product is not acceptable for animal casings offered for importation.

(b) Casings offered for importation into the United States shall remain in customs custody at the port until released by an APHIS inspector for admission into the United States or otherwise disposed of as required by this part.

(c) The provision that under certain conditions casings which have been offered for importation shall be exported, shall be construed to mean the removal of the casings from the United States or its possessions.

(1) The provision that under certain conditions casings be destroyed shall be construed to mean the treatment or handling of the casings in a manner to take away completely the usefulness of them as by tanking or incineration.

(2) The provision that under certain conditions casings shall be disinfected and denatured shall be construed to mean such treatment and handling as will be prescribed by the Administrator, Animal and Plant Health Inspection Service (APHIS) to free them from pathogenic substances or organisms, or to render such substances and organisms inert; and that the nature of the casings be changed to make them unfit for eating without destroying other useful properties. For instance, each casing may be split throughout its length and after disinfection, as above indicated, be released for industrial use.

(d) Dried intestines offered for importation into the United States for use as gut strings or similar purpose are not regarded as animal casings within the meaning of this part. Such dried intestines are classed with tendons, sinews, and similar articles and are subject to the provisions of part 95.

[28 FR 5986, June 13, 1963. Redesignated and amended at 57 FR 28082, 28083, June 24, 1992; 57 FR 29785, July 7, 1992. Redesignated at 58 FR 47031, Sept. 7, 1993]

§ 96.6 Certified foreign animal casings arriving at seaboard or border port.

(a) Properly certified foreign animal casings arriving in the United States at a seaboard or border port where an APHIS inspector is stationed shall be released for entry by the inspector at the seaboard or border port.

(b) Properly certified foreign animal casings arriving in the United States at a seaboard or border port where no APHIS inspector is stationed, which are destined to a point in the United States where an APHIS inspector is stationed, shall be shipped in United States Customs custody to destination for release.

(c) Properly certified foreign animal casing arriving in the United States at a seaboard or border port where no APHIS inspector is stationed, which are destined to a point in the United States where no APHIS inspector is stationed, shall be transported in United States Customs custody to the nearest point where an APHIS inspector is stationed for release at that point.

(d) Properly certified foreign animal casings forming a part of a foreign meat consignment routed through a border port to an interior point in the United States shall be transported to destination as though the entire consignment consisted of meat. In such cases the APHIS inspector who inspects the meat at destination shall supervise the release of the casings.

[28 FR 5986, June 13, 1963, as amended at 57 FR 29785, July 7, 1992. Redesignated at 58 FR 47031, Sept. 7, 1993]

§ 96.7 Dried bladders, weasands, and casings.

Dried animal bladders, dried weasands, and all other dried animal casings offered for importation into the United States as food containers unaccompanied by foreign certification which have been retained in the dry state continuously for not less than 90 days from the date of shipment shown on the consular invoice, may be released for entry as food containers without disinfection.

[28 FR 5986, June 13, 1963. Redesignated at 58 FR 47031, Sept. 7, 1993]

§ 96.8 Uncertified casings; disinfection at seaboard port.

Uncertified foreign animal casings arriving at a seaboard port may be imported into the United States for use as food containers after they have been disinfected under the direct supervision of an APHIS inspector at the seaboard port.

[28 FR 5986, June 13, 1963, as amended at 57 FR 29785, July 7, 1992. Redesignated at 58 FR 47031, Sept. 7, 1993]

§ 96.9 Casings admitted on disinfection; sealing; transfer and disinfection.

Foreign animal casings offered for importation into the United States which are admitted upon disinfection shall be handled as follows:

(a) The containers of such casings shall be sealed on the steamship pier or other place of first arrival. Four seals shall be affixed to both ends of each tierce, barrel, and similar container in the space where the ends of the container enter the staves, by means of red sealing wax imprinted with the No. 3 Veterinary Services brass brand from which "INSP'D & P'S'D" and the establishment number have been removed.

(b) Uncertified animal casings sealed as above indicated shall be transferred from the steamship pier or other place of first arrival to the premises of the importer or other designated place, where they shall be disinfected by the importer under the supervision of an APHIS inspector before they are offered for sale. The object of this ruling is to place full responsibility for disinfection of casings on the original importer and to prevent the sale of casings subject to disinfection by the purchaser.

[28 FR 5986, June 13, 1963, as amended at 57 FR 29785, July 7, 1992. Redesignated at 58 FR 47031, Sept. 7, 1993]

§96.10 Uncertified casings; transportation for disinfection; original shipping containers; disposition of salt.

(a) Foreign animal casings imported into the United States without certification may be forwarded in customs custody to a USDA-approved facility for disinfection under APHIS supervision and release by the United States Customs authorities, provided that, before being transported over land in the United States, each and every container of such casings shall be disinfected by the application of a solution of sodium hydroxide prepared as follows:

(1) Sodium hydroxide (Lye) prepared in a fresh solution in the proportion of not less than 1 pound avoirdupois of sodium hydroxide of not less than 95 percent purity to 6 gallons of water, or one 13½-ounce can to 5 gallons of water.[2]

(2) This solution shall be thoroughly applied to all exterior surfaces of the containers and be allowed to remain for at least thirty minutes to accomplish disinfection. The containers should then be washed with water to remove the caustic soda which otherwise might cause injury to the handlers of the packages.

(b) When uncertified foreign casings are removed from the original shipping containers these containers shall be destroyed by burning or promptly and thoroughly disinfected both inside and out with the solution and in the manner above prescribed. If these containers are to be re-used it is important that they be thoroughly washed both inside and out with water after disinfection has been completed, and in order to insure against the injurious effect of caustic soda remaining in the wood it is advisable to allow the containers to stand for not less than six hours filled with water.

(c) The salt removed from all original shipping containers of uncertified foreign animal casings shall be immediately dissolved in water and heated to boiling, or disposed of as provided in paragraph (c)(1) or (2) of this section as follows:

(1) Dissolve the salt in the proportion of 90 pounds of salt to 100 gallons of water. Add 2¾ gallons of C. P. hydrochloric acid containing not less than 35 percent actual HCl; mix thoroughly and allow the solution to stand for at least thirty minutes. The finished solution must contain not less than 1 percent actual hydrochloric acid. (This solution may be utilized in the disinfection of casings as prescribed in §96.13.)

(2) Dissolve the salt in the proportion of 90 pounds of salt to 100 gallons of water. Add 20 pounds of 95 percent to 98 percent sodium hydroxide (commercial "76 percent caustic soda") and stir until solution is complete; and allow it to stand for at least 30 minutes. (This solution may be utilized in the disinfection of casing containers as prescribed in paragraphs (a)(2) and (b) of this section.

(3) It is best to employ flaked caustic soda and not the variety which is very finely powdered. The fine powder is irritating and injurious to workers if it becomes suspended in the air. Containers of caustic soda should be kept

[2] Due to the extreme caustic nature of sodium hydroxide solution, and of sodium carbonate solution to a lesser degree, precautionary measures such as the wearing of rubber gloves, boots, raincoat and goggles should be observed. An acid solution such as vinegar shall be kept readily available in case any of the sodium hydroxide solution should come in contact with the body.

tightly closed as the product deteriorates from contact with the air.

[28 FR 5986, June 13, 1963, as amended at 32 FR 19158, Dec. 20, 1967; 57 FR 29785, July 7, 1992. Redesignated and amended at 58 FR 47031, Sept. 7, 1993; 62 FR 56024, Oct. 28, 1997; 65 FR 1307, Jan. 10, 2000]

§ 96.11 Disinfecting plant and equipment for uncertified casings.

Uncertified foreign animal casings shall be disinfected only at a plant whose sanitation and disinfecting equipment have been approved by an APHIS inspector.

[28 FR 5986, June 13, 1963, as amended at 57 FR 29785, July 7, 1992. Redesignated at 58 FR 47031, Sept. 7, 1993]

§ 96.12 Uncertified casings not disinfected in 30 days; disposition.

Foreign animal casings offered for importation without certification shall be disinfected as prescribed in § 96.13 within a period of 30 days after arrival in the United States, subject to the ability of Division inspectors to cover their respective districts. Otherwise such casings shall be exported or destroyed.

[28 FR 5986, June 13, 1963. Redesignated and amended at 58 FR 47031, Sept. 7, 1993]

§ 96.13 Uncertified casings; disinfection with hydrochloric acid.

Foreign animal casings offered for importation into the United States without certification may be disinfected, as prescribed in this section, under the supervision of an APHIS inspector for use as food containers, as an alternative for foreign certification.

(a) Disinfect the casings in a solution made as follows: Dissolve 90 pounds common salt in 100 gallons water and mix. Add 2¾ gallons (10.35 liters) C. P. hydrochloric acid containing not less than 35 percent actual HCl and mix throughly. The finished solution must contain not less than 1 percent actual hydrochloric acid.

(b) Containers of the disinfectant solution may be either of wood or of metal, but the interior surfaces must be protected by means of an acid resistant coating.

(c) Not more than 175 pounds casings shall be treated with each 100 gallons of the solution. After the treatment of 175 pounds of casings, or at the end of the day if less than 175 pounds of casings are disinfected in any one day, the solution shall be discarded unless means are provided for accurately determining the loss of strength. In event means for accurately determining loss of strength are provided it will be permissible to restore the strength of the solution with fresh acid and use it repeatedly.

(d) Shake as much of the adherent salt as possible from the casings and weigh them. Bundles must be separated but individual hanks need not be untied. Place the casings in the disinfecting solution a few hanks at a time with vigorous agitation to insure the fullest possible contact of the solution with them. Then keep the casings completely submerged in the solution for not less than three-fourths of an hour.

(e) Remove the casings from the solution, rinse them with water, and place them in a solution containing 8½ pounds of sodium bicarbonate in each 100 gallons of water. 100 gallons of this solution is sufficient for 175 pounds of casings. Keep the casings in this solution for 30 minutes, moving them about frequently and vigorously so as to insure complete contact of the solution with the casings. After this neutralization, remove the casings from the sodium bicarbonate solution and wash them to remove the excess of bicarbonate.

(Approved by the Office of Management and Budget under control number 0579–0015)

[28 FR 5986, June 13, 1963, as amended at 57 FR 29785, July 7, 1992. Redesignated at 58 FR 47031, Sept. 7, 1993, as amended at 59 FR 67134, Dec. 29, 1994]

§ 96.14 Uncertified casings; disinfection with saturated brine solution.

Foreign animal casings offered for importation into the United States upon disinfection, may either be disinfected with hydrochloric acid as at present or if preferred may be submerged in a saturated brine solution at a temperature not less than 127 °F. for at least 15 minutes. The time held as well as the temperature of such brine solution must be recorded on a one-hour dial of a recording thermometer and filed in the local APHIS office for official inspection at any time. In order that this required temperature may be more readily maintained, such casings must first be submerged in a brine solution at approximately 127 °F. for about five minutes immediately before the 15-minute recorded submersion period begins. This may be done either in the testing vat or a preliminary vat. By following this procedure the temperature will not vary unduly and thus cause unsatisfactory results. After removing the casings from the testing vat, it will be found advantageous to submerge them in another vat containing cold brine solution or cold water in order to remove the extra heat from the casings as promptly as possible, but of course this is optional with the importer. In order to obtain the most satisfactory results, the hanks, rings, and similar units must be separated as much as possible without untying, but "dolls" will not be permitted to be disinfected by this heating method. In order to keep the temperature of the brine in the testing vat of a uniform degree, it is necessary to agitate the solution occasionally by moving the casings. The tip of the recording thermometer should be located at a point which would be approximately at the bottom of the volume of casings being disinfected.

[28 FR 5986, June 13, 1963, as amended at 57 FR 29785, July 7, 1992. Redesignated at 58 FR 47031, Sept. 7, 1993]

PART 97—OVERTIME SERVICES RELATING TO IMPORTS AND EXPORTS

Sec.

AUTHORITY: 7 U.S.C. 8301–8317; 49 U.S.C. 80503; 7 CFR 2.22, 2.80, and 371.4.

§97.1 Overtime work at laboratories, border ports, ocean ports, and airports.[1]

(a) Any person, firm, or corporation having ownership, custody, or control of animals, animal byproducts, or other commodities or articles subject to inspection, laboratory testing, certification, or quarantine under this subchapter and subchapter G of this chapter, and who requires the services of an employee of the Animal and Plant Health Inspection Service or U.S. Customs and Border Protection on a Sunday or holiday, or at any other time outside the regular tour of duty of the employee, shall sufficiently in advance of the period of Sunday, holiday, or overtime service request the Animal and Plant Health Inspection Service or U.S. Customs and Border Protection inspector in charge to furnish the service and shall pay the Government at the rate listed in the following table, except as provided in paragraphs (a)(1), (a)(2), (a)(3), and (a)(4) of this section:

OVERTIME FOR INSPECTION, LABORATORY TESTING, CERTIFICATION, OR QUARANTINE OF PLANT, PLANT PRODUCTS, ANIMALS, ANIMAL PRODUCTS OR OTHER REGULATED COMMODITIES

Outside the employee's normal tour of duty	Overtime rates (per hour)		
	Nov. 2, 2015–Sept. 30, 2016	Oct. 1, 2016–Sept. 30, 2017	Beginning Oct. 1, 2017
Monday through Saturday and holidays	$75	$75	$75
Sundays	99	99	100

(1) For any services performed on a Sunday or holiday, or at any time after 5 p.m. or before 8 a.m. on a weekday, in connection with the arrival in or departure from the United States of a private aircraft or private vessel, the total amount payable shall not exceed $25 for all inspection services performed by the U.S. Customs and Border Protection , Public Health Service, and the Department of Agriculture;

[1] For designated ports of entry for certain animals, animal semen, poultry, and hatching eggs see 9 CFR §§93.102, 93.203, 93.303, 93.403, 93.503, 93.703, and 93.805 and for designated ports of entry for certain purebred animals see 9 CFR §§151.1 through 151.3.

(2) Owners and operators of aircraft will be provided service without reimbursement during regularly established hours of service on a Sunday or holiday; and

(3) The overtime rate to be charged owners or operators of aircraft at airports of entry or other places of inspection as a consequence of the operation of the aircraft, for work performed outside of the regularly established hours of service is listed in the following table:

OVERTIME FOR COMMERCIAL AIRLINE INSPECTION SERVICES [1]

Outside the employee's normal tour of duty	Overtime rates (per hour)		
	Nov. 2, 2015–Sept. 30, 2016	Oct. 1, 2016–Sept. 30, 2017	Beginning Oct. 1, 2017
Monday through Saturday and holidays	$64	$65	$65
Sundays	85	86	86

[1] These charges exclude administrative overhead costs.

(4) The overtime rate and all other charges, including minimum and commute compensation charges, to be billed for services provided by an employee of U.S. Customs and Border Protection shall be charged according to the provisions of this section, 5 CFR part 551, or 19 CFR 24.16.

(b) A minimum charge of 2 hours shall be made for any Sunday or holiday or unscheduled overtime duty performed by an employee on a day when no work was scheduled for him or her, or which is performed by an employee on his or her regular workday beginning either at least 1 hour before his or her scheduled tour of duty or which is not in direct continuation of the employee's regular tour of duty. In addition, each such period of Sunday or holiday or unscheduled overtime work to which the 2-hour minimum charge applies may include a commuted traveltime period (CTT) the amount of which shall be prescribed in administrative instructions to be issued by the Administrator, Animal and Plant Health Inspection Service or U.S. Customs and Border Protection for the areas in which the Sunday or holiday or overtime work is performed and such period shall be established as nearly as may be practicable to cover the time necessarily spent in reporting to and returning from the place at which the employee performs such Sunday, holiday or overtime duty. With respect to places of duty within the metropolitan area of the employee's headquarters, such CTT period shall not exceed 3 hours. It shall be administratively determined from time to time which days constitute holidays. The circumstances under which such CTT periods shall be charged and the percentage applicable in each circumstance are as reflected in the following table:

	Actual time [1] charge—no minimum	2-hour guarantee charge	Commuted [2] traveltime (CTT) charge
Charges for Inspection Within Metropolitan Area of Employee's Headquarters			
Work beginning before daily tour begins:			
8 to 59 minutes.	Yes	No	None.
60 to 119 minutes.		Yes	½ CTT.
120 minutes or more.		Yes	Full CTT.
Work beginning after daily tour ends:			
Direct continuation.	Yes	No	None.
Break-in-service of:			
2–29 minutes		Yes	None.
30–60 minutes.		Yes	½ CTT.
61 minutes or more.		Yes	Full CTT.
Charges for Inspection Services Performed Outside Metropolitan Area of Employee's Headquarters			
Work beginning before daily tour begins:			
8 to 59 minutes.	Yes	No	½ CTT.
60 minutes or more.		Yes	Full CTT.

	Actual time[1] charge—no minimum	2-hour guarantee charge	Commuted[2] traveltime (CTT) charge
Work beginning after daily tour ends:			
Direct continuations.	Yes	No	½ CTT.
2–59 minutes	No	Yes	½ CTT.
60 minutes or more.	No	Yes	Full CTT.
Charges for Call Out Inspection Service on Holiday or Nonworkday			
Work beginning at any time.	No	Yes	Full CTT.

[1] Actual time charged when work is contiguous with the daily tour will be in quarter hour multiples, with service time of 8 minutes or more rounded up to the next quarter hour and any time of less than 8 minutes will be disregarded.

[2] The full CTT allowance will be the amount of commuted traveltime prescribed for the place at which the inspections are performed. See part 97.2. One-half CTT is ½ of the full CTT period.

(c) As used in this section—

(1) The term *private aircraft* means any civilian aircraft not being used to transport persons or property for compensation or hire, and

(2) The term *private vessel* means any civilian vessel not being used (i) to transport persons or property for compensation or hire, or (ii) in fishing operations or in processing of fish or fish products.

(d)(1) Any principal, or any person, firm, partnership, corporation, or other legal entity acting as an agent or broker by requesting Sunday, holiday, or overtime services of an Animal and Plant Health Inspection Service or U.S. Customs and Border Protection inspector on behalf of any other person, firm, partnership, corporation, or other legal entity (principal), and who has not previously requested such service from an Animal and Plant Health Inspection Service inspector, must pay the inspector before service is provided.

(2) Since the payment must be collected before service can be provided, the Animal and Plant Health Inspection Service or U.S. Customs and Border Protection inspector will estimate the amount to be paid. Any difference between the inspector's estimate and the actual amount owed to the Animal and Plant Health Inspection Service will be resolved as soon as reasonably possible following the delivery of service, with the Animal and Plant Health Inspection Service or U.S. Customs and Border Protection either returning the difference to the agent, broker, or principal, or billing the agent, broker, or principal for the difference.

(3) The prepayment must be in some guaranteed form, such as money order, certified check, or cash. Prepayment in guaranteed form will continue until the Animal and Plant Health Inspection Service or U.S. Customs and Border Protection determines that the agent, broker, or principal has established an acceptable credit history.

(4) For security reasons, cash payments will be accepted only from 7 a.m. to 5 p.m., and only at a location designated by the Animal and Plant Health Inspection Service inspector or U.S. Customs and Border Protection.

(e)(1) Any principal, or any person, firm, partnership, corporation, or other legal entity requesting Sunday, holiday, or overtime services of an Animal and Plant Health Inspection Service inspector, and who has a debt to the Animal and Plant Health Inspection Service or U.S. Customs and Border Protection more than 60 days delinquent, must pay the inspector before service is provided.

(2) Since the payment must be collected before service can be provided, the Animal and Plant Health Inspection Service or U.S. Customs and Border Protection inspector will estimate the amount to be paid. Any difference between the inspector's estimate and the actual amount owed to the Animal and Plant Health Inspection Service or U.S. Customs and Border Protection will be resolved as soon as reasonably possible following the delivery of service, with the Animal and Plant Health Inspection Service or U.S. Customs and Border Protection either returning the difference to the agent, broker, or principal, or billing the agent, broker, or principal for the difference.

(3) The prepayment must be in some guaranteed form, such as money order, certified check, or cash. Prepayment in guaranteed form will continue until the debtor pays the delinquent debt.

(4) For security reasons, cash payments will be accepted only from 7 a.m. to 5 p.m., and only at a location designated by the Animal and Plant

Health Inspection Service or U.S. Customs and Border Protection inspector.

(f) Reimbursable Sunday, holiday, or overtime services will be denied to any principal, or any person, firm, partnership, corporation, or other legal entity who has a debt to the Animal and Plant Health Inspection Service or U.S. Customs and Border Protection more than 90 days delinquent. Services will be denied until the delinquent debt is paid.

[38 FR 28814, Oct. 17, 1973]

EDITORIAL NOTE: For FEDERAL REGISTER citations affecting § 97.1, see the List of CFR Sections Affected, which appears in the Finding Aids section of the printed volume and at *www.fdsys.gov*.

§ 97.2 Administrative instructions prescribing commuted traveltime.

Each period of overtime and holiday duty as prescribed in § 97.1 shall in addition include a commuted traveltime period for the respective ports, stations, and areas in which employees are located. The prescribed computed traveltime periods are as follows:

COMMUTED TRAVELTIME ALLOWANCES

[In hours]

Location covered	Served from	Metropolitan Area	
		Within	Outside
Alaska:			
Anchorage		1	
Do	Palmer		3
Arizona:			
Douglas		1	
Do	Nogales		6
Do	Phoenix		6
Do	Sierra Vista		3
Naco	Douglas		2
Do	Nogales		4
Do	Phoenix		6
Do	Sierra Vista		2
Nogales		1	
Do	Douglas		6
Do	Phoenix		6
Do	Sierra Vista		3
San Luis	Phoenix		6
Do	Yuma		2
Sasabe	Douglas		6
Do	Nogales		4
Do	Phoenix		6
Do	Sierra Vista		6
Do	Tuscon		3
California:			
Calexico	San Ysidro		6
Edwards Air Force Base.	Los Angeles		4
Los Angeles and Los Angeles International Airport.	San Bernardino		5
Do	Los Angeles	2	
Los Angeles Harbor, San Pedro, including Long Beach, Wilmington, and Terminal Island.	Los Angeles		2
March Field	......do		5
Mexicali	Calexico		1
Newport Beach	......do		4
Ontario	......do		3
Ramona	San Ysidro		2
Sacramento		1	
Do	San Francisco		5
San Diego		1	
Do	San Ysidro		2
San Francisco including, Alameda, Richmond, Pittsburg, and other ports in San Francisco and San Pablo Bay areas.		2	
San Louis Obispo.	San Pedro		6
San Ysidro		1	
Stockton	San Francisco		4
Colorado:			
Stapleton International Airport, Denver.	Arvada	1	
Do	Aurora		2
Connecticut:			
Bradley International Airport.	Westerly, RI		5
Do	Willington		1
Bradley International Airport, Windsor Locks.	Ashford		1
Do	Hartford	2	
Do	N. Stonington, CT		4
Do	Waterbury, CT		3
Delaware:			
Wilmington	Dover		3
Florida:			
Jacksonville		2	
Miami		2	
Port Everglades	Miami		2
St. Petersburg	Tampa		2
Do	Miami		6
Tampa		2	
Do	Miami		6
Georgia:			
Atlanta International Airport.	Acworth		3
Do	Carrollton		3
Do	Covington		3
Do	Forsyth		3
Port of Brunswick.	Savannah		4

COMMUTED TRAVELTIME ALLOWANCES—Continued
[In hours]

Location covered	Served from	Metropolitan Area Within	Metropolitan Area Outside
Port of Savannah.	......do	2	
Port of St. Mary's.	......do	....	6
Hawaii:			
Kawaihae	Waimea	....	1
Hilo	......do	....	3
Honolulu, including Aiea, Barber's Point Naval Air Station, Honolulu International Airport, West Loch, Middle Loch, East Loch, Pearl City and Waipahu.	....	2	
Idaho:			
Boise	Caldwell or Middleton.	....	2
Eastport	Bonners Ferry	....	2
Do	Spokane, WA	....	6
Illinois:			
Chicago	....	3	
Do	Geneseo	....	6
Do	Kirkland	....	4
Springfield	....	2	
Indiana:			
Indianapolis	....	1	
Do	Anderson	....	2
Do	West Lafayette	....	3
Iowa:			
Ames	....	1	
Kentucky:			
Standiford Field	Frankfort	....	3
Do	Louisville	1	
Louisiana:			
Acadian Regional Airport, New Iberia.	Abbeville	....	2
Any point below Chalmette and on the East Bank, Belle Chasse, LA, and points to and including Port Sulphur on the west bank.	Baton Rouge	....	4
Any point on the Mississippi River above the St. Charles-Jefferson Parish boundary to and including Gramercy.	......do	....	2
Morgan City	......do	....	5
New Orleans including Orleans Parish and all points on the east bank of the Mississippi River from the St. Charles-Jefferson Parish boundary to and including Chalmette, LA, and all points on the west bank from the St. Charles-Jefferson Parish boundary to but excluding Belle Chasse, LA.	......do	....	4
Undesignated ports.	......do	....	3
Maine:			
Bangor	Augusta	....	3
Do	Newport	....	1
Houlton	....	1	
Jackman	Augusta	....	6
Do	Bangor	....	5
Do	Newport	....	5
Port of Portland	Augusta	....	3
Do	Bangor	....	6
Do	Concord, NH	....	4
Maryland:			
Baltimore:	....	3	
Largo	Bowie	2	
Do	Owings Mills	3	
Do	Easton	....	4
Laurel	Bowie	2	
Do	Owings Mills	3	
Do	Easton	....	4
Massachusetts:			
Boston	....	3	
Do	Grafton	....	4
Do	Loudon, NH	....	5
Do	N. Attleboro	....	4
Do	Westerly, RI	....	4
Mexico:			
Ciudad Acuna	Del Rio, TX	....	1½
Do	Eagle Pass, TX	....	3
Do	Laredo, TX	....	6
Do	Pleasanton, TX	....	6
Juarez	El Paso, TX	....	1
Nuevo Laredo	Del Rio, TX	....	4
Do	Eagle Pass, TX	....	5
Do	Laredo, TX	....	1½
Do	Pharr, TX	....	6
Do	Pleasanton, TX	....	5
Ojinaga	El Paso, TX	....	6
Do	Presidio, TX	....	1
Piedras Negras	Eagle Pass, TX	....	1
Do	Laredo, TX	....	5
Do	Pharr, TX	....	10
Do	Pleasanton, TX	....	5

COMMUTED TRAVELTIME ALLOWANCES—Continued

[In hours]

Location covered	Served from	Metropolitan Area	
		Within	Outside
Reynosa (Pharr International Bridge).	Eagle Pass, TX		12
Do	Hidalgo, TX		1
Do	Laredo, TX		5
Do	Mission, TX		1
Do	Pharr, TX		1
San Jeronimo	El Paso, TX		2
Do	Presidio, TX		6
Do	Santa Theresa, NM.		1
Michigan:			
Detroit		3	
Do	Beaverton		6
Do	Chelsea		3
Do	Clara		6
Do	Kalamazoo		5
Do	Lansing		4
Do	Port Huran		4
Port Huron		1	
Do	Beaverton		6
Do	Chelsea		6
Do	Clara		6
Do	Detroit		3
Do	Lansing		5
Do	Kalamazoo		6
Minnesota:			
Minneapolis/St. Paul International Airport.		2	
Do	Rochester		3
Do	Princeton		3
Noyes	Pembina		1
Missouri:			
Kansas City International Airport.	Jefferson		6
St. Louis Airport	Beaufort		3
St. Louis Zoological Park.	......do		3
Montana:			
Bozeman		1	
Bozeman Laboratory.	Bozeman	1	
Great Falls Airport.	Great Falls	1	
Do	Helena		5
Helena		1	
Port of Opheim	Plentywood		5
Do	Opheim		1
Port of Raymond.	Plentywood	1	
Do	Raymond		1
Port of Sweetgrass.	Great Falls		5
Do	Shelby		2
Do	Sunburst/ Sweetgrass.	1	
Sweetgrass		1	
Nebraska:			
Lincoln Airport		1	
New Jersey:			
Newark International Airport.	Hightstown	2	
Do	Mount Holly	3	
Do	Princeton	2	
Port of Salem	Hightstown	3½	
Do	Mount Holly	3	
Do	Princeton	4	
New Mexico:			
Columbus		1	
Do	Las Cruces		4
Port of Columbus.	Deming		2
New York:			
Alexandria Bay		1	
Buffalo		2	
Do	Akron		2
Champlain		1	
Do	Highgate Springs, VT.		2
Do	Milton, VT		3
Do	Calais, VT		5
Malone	Champlain		3
Newburgh		1	
Do	New York, NY		4
New York		3	
Niagara Falls	Akron		2
Odgensburg		1	
Port of Albany		1	
Rochester	Buffalo		4
Rooseveltown	Odgensburg		2
Rouses Point	Champlain		1
Stewart Airport, Newburgh.	Albany		4
North Carolina:			
Iredell	Franklin		6
Do	Lumberton		6
Do	Raleigh		6
North Dakota:			
Dunseith	Minot		4
Do	Pembina		6
Minot		1	
Peace Gardens	Bottineau		1
Pembina		1	
Do	Fargo		6
Do	Valley City		6
Portal		1	
Do	Bismarck		6
Do	Dickinson		6
Do	Minot		4
Ohio:			
Vandalia Dayton International Airport.	Greenville		2
Do	Pickerington		3
Wilmington	Greenville		4
Do	Pickerington		3
Oregon:			
Hermiston	Troutdale		6
Portland	Salem		3
Do	Sunny Valley		6
Do	Tigard	2	
Do	Troutdale	2	
Pennsylvania:			
Harrisburg	Camp Hill	1	
Do	Morgantown		3
Do	Northumberland		2
Do	Shippensburg		3
Philadelphia		3	
Puerto Rico:			
Aquadilla	Aquadilla		2
Salinas	San Juan		4
San Juan		2	

COMMUTED TRAVELTIME ALLOWANCES—Continued

[In hours]

Location covered	Served from	Metropolitan Area	
		Within	Outside
Tennessee:			
Fort Campbell, Clarkesville.	Nashville		2
Memphis		2	
Memphis	Gadsden		4
Memphis	Jackson		4
Nashville		2	
Texas:			
Brownsville		1	
Do	Laredo or San Antonio.		6
Brownsville and Brownsville International Airport.	Harlingen and San Benito.		1
Do	McAllen or Edinburg.		3
Do	Weslaco		2
Dallas-Fort Worth International Airport.	Decatur		2
Do	Ft. Worth or Dallas.	2	
Del Rio		1	
Do	Eagle Pass		3
Do	Edinburg, McAllen or Mission.		6
Do	Laredo or San Antonio.		5
Eagle Pass		1	
Do	Del Rio		3
Do	Edinburgh, McAllen or Mission.		6
Do	Laredo or San Antonio.		5
El Paso		1	
Do	Hatchita or Deming, NM.		6
Do	Las Cruces, NM		3
Forney	Corsicana		3
Do	Ft. Worth		3
Do	Tyler		3
Harlingen	Edinburg, McAllen or Mission.		2
Do	Weslaco		1
Hidalgo	Brownsville		3
Do	Edinburg, Mission and McAllen.		1
Do	Harlingen		2
Do	Lyford		2
Do	Rio Grande City		2
Houston (including Houston Intercontinental Airport).		2	
Do	Bellville, TX		4
Do	Bryan, TX		4
Do	Georgetown, TX		8
Do	Pleasanton, TX		8
Laredo		1	
Do	Brownsville or San Antonio.		6
Do	Eagle Pass		5
Do	McAllen, Edinburg or Mission.		6
Presidio		1	
Do	El Paso		6
Utah:			
Salt Lake City	Murray and Ogden.	2	
Vermont:			
Burlington International Airport.	Burlington	1	
Do	Milton		1
Do	Calais		3
Derby Line	Milton		4
Do	Calais		4
Highgate		1	
Do	Milton		2
Do	Calais		4
Highgate Springs.	......do		1
Virginia:			
Dulles International Airport.	Annapolis, MD	3	
Do	Richmond		5
Do	Warrenton		3
Port of Richmond.		2	
Washington:			
Blaine		1	
Do	Seattle		6
Lynden	Blaine		2
Do	Seattle		6
Moses Lake	Oroville, WA		6
Do	Spokane		5
Do	Wenatchee		3
Do	Yakima		4
Oroville		1	
Sea-Tac Airport	Olympia		3
Seattle		2	
Sumas	Blaine		2
Do	Olympia		6
Do	Seattle		6
Tacoma	......do		3
Yelm	Olympia		2
Do	Seattle		3
Wisconsin:			
Barron	Ripon		6
Madison		1	
Monroe	Madison		3

[39 FR 41356, Nov. 27, 1974]

EDITORIAL NOTE: For FEDERAL REGISTER citations affecting §97.2, see the List of CFR Sections Affected, which appears in the Finding Aids section of the printed volume and at *www.fdsys.gov*.

PART 98—IMPORTATION OF CERTAIN ANIMAL EMBRYOS AND ANIMAL SEMEN

AUTHORITY: 7 U.S.C. 1622 and 8301–8317; 21 U.S.C. 136 and 136a; 31 U.S.C. 9701; 7 CFR 2.22, 2.80, and 371.4.

§ 98.1 Prohibition.

An embryo shall not be imported or entered into the United States unless in accordance with the provisions of this part.

[50 FR 43563, Oct. 25, 1985. Redesignated at 56 FR 58808, Oct. 30, 1991]

Subpart A—Ruminant and Swine Embryos from Regions Free of Rinderpest and Foot-and-Mouth Disease; and Embryos of Horses and Asses

§ 98.2 Definitions.

The following terms, when used in this subpart, shall be construed as defined. Those terms used in the singular form in this subpart shall be construed as the plural form and vice versa, as the case may demand.

Administrator. The Administrator, Animal and Plant Health Inspection Service, or any person authorized to act for the Administrator.

Animal. Any cattle, sheep, goats, other ruminants, swine, horses, or asses.

Animal and Plant Health Inspection Service. The Animal and Plant Health Inspection Service of the United States Department of Agriculture (APHIS).

Approved artificial insemination center. A facility approved or licensed by the national government of the region in which the facility is located to collect and process semen under the general supervision of such government.

Approved embryo transfer unit. A facility approved or licensed by the national government of the region in which the facility is located for the artificial insemination of donor dams or for conception as a result of artificial breeding by a donor sire and for collecting and processing embryos for export under the general supervision of such government.

Department. The United States Department of Agriculture.

Embryo. The initial stage of an animal's development after collection from the natural mother, while it is capable of being transferred to a recipient dam, but not including an embryo that has been transferred to a recipient dam.

Enter (entered, entry) into the United States. To introduce into the commerce of the United States after release from governmental detention at the port of entry.

Flock. A herd.

Herd. All animals maintained on any single premises; and all animals under common ownership or supervision on two or more premises which are geographically separated, but among which there is an interchange or movement of animals.

Import (imported, importation) into the United States. To bring into the territorial limits of the United States.

Inspector. An employee of APHIS who is authorized to perform the function involved.

Person. Any individual, corporation, company, association, firm, partnership, society, joint stock company, or any other legal entity.

Region. Any defined geographic land area identifiable by geological, political, or surveyed boundaries. A region may consist of any of the following:

(1) A national entity (country);

(2) Part of a national entity (zone, county, department, municipality, parish, Province, State, etc.)

(3) Parts of several national entities combined into an area; or

(4) A group of national entities (countries) combined into a single area.

United States. All of the several States of the United States, the District of Columbia, Guam, the Northern Mariana Islands, Puerto Rico, the Virgin Islands of the United States and all other territories and possessions of the United States.

[50 FR 43563, Oct. 25, 1985. Redesignated and amended at 56 FR 55808, Oct. 30, 1991; 57 FR 29194, July 1, 1992; 61 FR 17241, Apr. 19, 1996; 62 FR 56025, Oct. 28, 1997]

§98.3 General conditions.

Except as provided in subpart B of this part, an animal embryo shall not be imported into the United States unless it is from a region listed under §94.1(a) of this chapter as being free of rinderpest and foot-and-mouth disease, and:

(a) The embryo is exported to the United States from the region in which it was conceived;

(b) The embryo was conceived as a result of artificial insemination with semen collected from a donor sire at an approved artificial insemination center, or the embryo as conceived as a result of natural breeding by a donor sire at an approved embryo transfer unit;

(c) If artificially inseminated, the donor dam conceived the embryo after being inseminated in an approved embryo transfer unit with semen collected at an approved artificial insemination center;

(d) At the time of collection of the semen used to conceive the embryo or at the time of natural breeding, the donor sire met all requirements the donor sire would have to meet under part 93 of this chapter for a health certificate required as a condition of importation into the United States;

(e) At the time of collection of the embryo from the donor dam, the donor dam met all requirements the donor dam would have to meet under part 92 of this chapter for a health certificate required as a condition of importation into the United States;

(f) There is no basis for denying an import permit for the donor sire or donor dam under §93.304(a)(2) for horses, §93.404(a)(2) or (3) for ruminants, and §93.504(a)(2) or (3) for swine of this chapter;

(g) The embryo is collected and maintained under conditions determined by the Administrator to be adequate to protect against contamination of the embryo with infectious animal disease organisms; and

(h) The embryo was determined, based on microscopic examination, to have an intact zona pellucida at the time the embryo was placed into its immediate container (straw or ampule) for shipping.

(i) The embryo is contained in a shipping container which at the time of offer for entry is sealed with an official seal which was affixed to the shipping container by a full-time salaried veterinarian of the national animal health service of the region of origin or by a veterinarian authorized to do so by the national animal health service of the region of origin.

[50 FR 43563, Oct. 25, 1985, as amended at 55 FR 31558, Aug. 2, 1990; 56 FR 55809, Oct. 30, 1991; 57 FR 29194, July 1, 1992; 62 FR 56025, Oct. 28, 1997; 77 FR 1396, Jan. 10, 2012]

§ 98.4 Import permit.

(a) Except as provided in subpart B of this part, an animal embryo shall not be imported into the United States unless accompanied by an import permit issued by APHIS and unless imported into the United States within 14 days after the proposed date of arrival stated in the import permit.

(b) An application for an import permit must be submitted to the Animal and Plant Health Inspection Service, Veterinary Services, National Center for Import-Export, 4700 River Road Unit 38, Riverdale, Maryland 20737–1231. An application form for an import permit may be obtained from this staff.

(c) The completed application shall include the following information:

(1) The name and address of the person intending to export an embryo from the region of origin,

(2) The name and address of the person intending to import an embryo,

(3) The species, breed, and number of embryos to be imported,

(4) The purpose of the importation,

(5) The region in which the embryo is conceived,

(6) The port of embarkation,

(7) The mode of transportation,

(8) The route of travel,

(9) The port of entry in the United States,

(10) The proposed date of arrival in the United States,

(11) The name and address of the person to whom the embryo will be delivered in the United States, and

(12) The measures to be taken to ensure that the embryo is collected and maintained under conditions adequate to protect against contamination of the embryo with infectious animal disease organisms.

(d) After receipt and review of the application by APHIS, an import permit indicating the applicable conditions under this subpart for importation into the United States shall be issued for the importation of embryos described in the application if such embryos appear to be eligible to be imported. Even though an import permit has been issued for the importation of an embryo, the embryo may be imported only if all applicable requirements of this subpart are met.

[50 FR 43563, Oct. 25, 1985, as amended at 56 FR 55809, Oct. 30, 1991; 57 FR 29194, July 1, 1992; 59 FR 67616, Dec. 30, 1994; 62 FR 56025, Oct. 28, 1997]

§ 98.5 Health certificate.

(a) Except as provided in subpart B of this part, an animal embryo shall not be imported into the United States unless it is accompanied by a certificate issued by a full-time salaried veterinary officer of the national government of the region of origin, or issued by a veterinarian designated or accredited by the national government of the region of origin and endorsed by a full-time salaried veterinary officer of the national government of the region of origin, representing that the veterinarian issuing the certificate was authorized to do so. The certificate shall state:

(1) The dates, places, types, and results of all examinations and tests performed on the donor sire and donor dam as a condition for importation of the embryo, and the names and addresses of persons or laboratories conducting the examinations or tests, and a statement that any other requirements established by § 98.3 have been complied with,

(2) The name and address of the consignor and consignee,

(3) The name and address of the approved artificial insemination center where the semen for the embryo was collected, if applicable,

(4) The name and address of the approved embryo transfer unit where the donor dam was inseminated or bred and the embryo was collected, and

(5) The measures taken to ensure that the embryo was collected and maintained under conditions adequate to protect against contamination of the embryo with infectious animal disease organisms.

(b) The certificate accompanying sheep or goat embryos intended for importation from any part of the world shall, in addition to the statements required by paragraph (a) of this section, state that:

(1) The embryos' sire and dam have not been in any flock or herd nor had contact with sheep or goats which have been in any flock or herd where scrapie has been diagnosed or suspected during the 5 years prior to the date of collection of the embryos;

(2) The embryos' sire and dam showed no evidence of scrapie at the time the embryos were collected;

(3) Scrapie has not been suspected nor confirmed in any progeny of the embryos' donor dam; and

(4) The parents of the embryos' sire and dam are not, nor were not, affected with scrapie.

(Approved by the Office of Management and Budget under control number 0579–0040)

[50 FR 43563, Oct. 25, 1985, as amended at 56 FR 55809, Oct. 30, 1991; 61 FR 15183, Apr. 5, 1996; 61 FR 17241, Apr. 19, 1996; 62 FR 56025, Oct. 28, 1997]

§98.6 Ports of entry.

An embryo shall not be imported into the United States unless at a port of entry listed in §93.303 for horses, §93.403 for ruminants, or §93.503 for swine of this chapter.

[50 FR 43563, Oct. 25, 1985, as amended at 55 FR 31558, Aug. 2, 1990; 62 FR 56025, Oct. 28, 1997]

§98.7 Declaration upon arrival.

Upon arrival of an embryo at a port of entry, the importer or the importer's agent shall notify APHIS of the arrival by giving an inspector a document stating:

(a) The port of entry,

(b) The date of arrival,

(c) Import permit number,

(d) Carrier, and identification of the means of conveyance,

(e) The name and address of the importer,

(f) The name and address of the broker,

(g) The region of origin of the embryo,

(h) The number, species, and purpose of importation of the embryo, and

(i) The name and address of the person to whom the embryo will be delivered.

[50 FR 43563, Oct. 25, 1985, as amended at 57 FR 29194, July 1, 1992; 62 FR 56025, Oct. 28, 1997]

§98.8 Inspection.

Any embryo offered for entry into the United States in accordance with this subpart and documents accompanying the embryo shall be subject to inspection by an inspector at the time the embryo is offered for entry in order to determine whether the embryo is eligible for entry. The import permit and the health certificate shall be given to the inspector.

[50 FR 43563, Oct. 25, 1985, as amended at 56 FR 55809, Oct. 30, 1991]

§98.9 Embryos refused entry.

Any embryo refused entry into the United States for noncompliance with the requirements of this subpart shall be removed from the United States within a time period specified by the Administrator or abandoned by the importer for destruction, and pending such action shall be subject to such safeguards as the inspector determines necessary to prevent the possible introduction into the United States of infectious animal diseases. If such embryo is not removed from the United States within such time period, or abandoned for destruction, it may be seized, destroyed, or otherwise disposed of as the inspector determines necessary to prevent the possible introduction into the United States of infectious animal diseases.

[50 FR 43563, Oct. 25, 1985, as amended at 56 FR 55809, Oct. 30, 1991; 57 FR 29194, July 1, 1992]

§98.10 Other importations.

Notwithstanding other provisions in this part, the Administrator may in specific cases allow the importation and entry into the United States of embryos other than as provided for in this part under such conditions as the Administrator may prescribe to prevent the introduction into the United States of infectious animal diseases.

[50 FR 43563, Oct. 25, 1985, as amended at 57 FR 29194, July 1, 1992]

§ 98.10a Embryos from sheep in regions other than Australia, Canada, and New Zealand.

(a) Except for embryos from sheep in Australia, Canada, or New Zealand, embryos from sheep may only be imported into the United States if they comply with all applicable provisions of this subpart and one of the following conditions:

(1) The embryos are transferred to females in a flock in the United States that participates in the Voluntary Scrapie Flock Certification Program (see 9 CFR part 54, subpart B) and qualifies as a "Certified" flock; or

(2) The embryos are transferred to females in a flock in the United States that participates in the Voluntary Scrapie Flock Certification Program (see 9 CFR part 54, subpart B) and the flock owner has agreed, in writing, to maintain the flock, and all first generation progeny resulting from embryos imported in accordance with this section, in compliance with all requirements of the Voluntary Scrapie Flock Certification Program until the flock, including all first generation progeny resulting from embryos imported in accordance with this section, qualifies as a "Certified" flock.

(b) Sheep embryos may be imported under paragraph (a) of this section only if the importer provides the Voluntary Scrapie Flock Certification Program identification number of the receiving flock as part of the application for an import permit.

(c) Sheep embryos may be imported under paragraph (a)(1) of this section only if they are the progeny of a dam and sire that are part of flocks in the region of origin that participate in a program determined by the Administrator to be equivalent to the Voluntary Scrapie Flock Certification Program, and the flocks have been determined by the Administrator to be at a level equivalent to "Certified" in the Voluntary Scrapie Flock Certification Program.

(d) Sheep embryos may be imported under paragraph (a)(2) of this section only if they are transferred to animals in a Certifiable Class C flock participating in the Voluntary Scrapie Flock Certification Program; *except*, that if the embryos are the progeny of a dam and sire whose flock in the region of origin participates in a program determined by the Administrator to be equivalent to the Voluntary Scrapie Flock Certification Program, then the embryos may be placed in a flock in the United States which would be classified at a level equivalent to or lower (*i.e.*, at a greater risk) than the certification level, as determined by the Administrator, of either the flock of the dam or the flock of the sire, whichever one presents the greater risk.

(e) The flock to which the sheep embryos are transferred pursuant to paragraph (a)(2) of this section must be monitored for scrapie disease until the flock, and all first generation progeny resulting from the embryos imported in accordance with this section, qualifies as a "Certified" flock.

(f) Except for sheep embryos being placed in Certifiable Class C flocks, the certificate accompanying sheep embryos imported under paragraph (a) of this section must contain the following statement: "The embryos identified on this certificate are the progeny of a dam and sire that have been monitored by a salaried veterinary officer of [*name of region of origin*], for [*number of months*], in the same source flock which had been determined by the Administrator, APHIS, prior to the exportation of these embryos to the United States, to be equivalent to [*certification level (of dam or sire) presenting greater risk*] of the Voluntary Scrapie Flock Certification Program authorized under 9 CFR part 54, subpart B."

(1) The Administrator will determine, based upon information supplied by the importer, whether the flock of the embryos' dam and sire participates in a program in the region of origin that is equivalent to the Voluntary Scrapie Flock Certification Program, and if so, at what level the source flock would be classified.

(2) In order for the Administrator to make a determination, the importer must supply the following information with the application for an import permit, no less than 1 month prior to the anticipated date of importation:

(i) The name, title, and address of a knowledgeable official in the veterinary services of the region of origin;

(ii) The details of scrapie control programs in the region of origin, including information on disease surveillance and border control activities and the length of time such activities have been in effect;

(iii) Any available information concerning additions, within the 5 years immediately preceding collection of the embryos, to the flock of the embryos' sire and dam;

(iv) Any available data concerning disease incidence, within the 5 years immediately preceding collection of the embryos, in the flock of the embryos' sire and dam, including, but not limited to, the results of diagnostic tests, especially histopathology tests, conducted on any animals in the flock;

(v) Information concerning the health, within the 5 years immediately preceding collection of the embryos, of other ruminants, flocks, and herds with which the embryos' sire and dam and the flock of the embryos' sire and dam might have had physical contact, and a description of the type and frequency of the physical contact; and

(vi) Any other information requested by the Administrator in specific cases as needed to make a determination.

(g) All first generation progeny resulting from embryos imported under this section are subject to the requirements of 9 CFR part 54 and all other applicable regulations.

(Approved by the Office of Management and Budget under control numbers 0579–0040 and 0579–0101)

[61 FR 17241, Apr. 19, 1996, as amended at 62 FR 56025, Oct. 28, 1997]

Subpart B—Ruminant and Swine Embryos From Regions Where Rinderpest or Foot-and-Mouth Disease Exists

SOURCE: 56 FR 55809, Oct. 30, 1991, unless otherwise noted.

§98.11 Definitions.

Animal and Plant Health Inspection Service. The Animal and Plant Health Inspection Service of the United States Department of Agriculture.

Camelid. All species of the family *Camelidae*, including camels, guanacos, llamas, alpacas, and vicunas.

Cervid. All members of the family *Cervidae* and hybrids, including deer, elk, moose, caribou, reindeer, and related species.

Collection of embryos. Embryos removed from a single donor dam in one operation.

Embryo. The initial stages of development of an animal, after collection from the natural mother and while it is capable of being transferred to a recipient dam, but not after it has been transferred to a recipient dam.

Embryo collection unit. Area or areas where the donor dam will be bred to produce embryos for importation into the United States, and where the embryos will be collected, processed, and stored pending shipment to the United States.

Foreign Animal Disease Diagnostic Laboratory. The Foreign Animal Disease Diagnostic Laboratory of the Animal and Plant Health Inspection Service.

Herd of origin. The herd in which the donor dam is kept during the 60 days before the donor dam is required to be housed in an embryo collection unit, in accordance with §98.17(a) of this subpart.

Import. To bring into the territorial limits of the United States.

Inspector. An employee of the Animal and Plant Health Inspection Service who is authorized to perform the function involved.

Official veterinarian. A full-time salaried veterinarian of the national government of the country of origin or a veterinarian employed by the Animal and Plant Health Inspection Service (APHIS), and designated by APHIS to supervise or conduct procedures required by this subpart, and to certify that requirements of this subpart have been met.

Person. Any individual, corporation, company, association, firm, partnership, society, joint stock company, or other legal entity.

Region. Any defined geographic land area identifiable by geological, political, or surveyed boundaries. A region may consist of any of the following:

(1) A national entity (country);

(2) Part of a national entity (zone, county, department, municipality, parish, Province, State, etc.);

(3) Parts of several national entities combined into an area; or

(4) A group of national entities (countries) combined into a single area.

Region of origin. The region in which the embryo is conceived and collected and from which the embryo is imported into the United States.

Ruminant. All animals which chew the cud, including cattle, buffaloes, camelids, cervids (deer, elk, moose, and antelope), sheep, goats, and giraffes.

Swine. The domestic hog and all varieties of wild hogs.

United States. All of the States of the United States, the District of Columbia, Guam, the Northern Mariana Islands, Puerto Rico, the Virgin Islands of the United States, and all other territories and possessions of the United States.

[56 FR 55809, Oct. 30, 1991, as amended at 61 FR 15183, Apr. 5, 1996; 62 FR 56025, Oct. 28, 1997; 78 FR 73008, Dec. 4, 2013]

§ 98.12 General prohibitions.

(a) Ruminant and swine embryos may not be imported from regions where rinderpest or foot-and-mouth disease exists except in accordance with this subpart.

(b) Ruminant and swine embryos may not be imported into the United States from any region other than the region in which they were conceived and collected.

[56 FR 55809, Oct. 30, 1991, as amended at 61 FR 15183, Apr. 5, 1996; 62 FR 56025, Oct. 28, 1997]

§ 98.13 Import permit.

(a) Ruminant and swine embryos and all test samples required by this subpart may be imported into the United States from regions where foot-and-mouth disease or rinderpest exists only if accompanied by import permits issued by the Animal and Plant Health Inspection Service (APHIS).

(b) An application for the import permits must be submitted to the Animal and Plant Health Inspection Service, Veterinary Services, National Center for Import-Export, 4700 River Road Unit 38, Riverdale, Maryland 20737–1231. Application forms also may be obtained at this same address. The application for a permit to import embryos will also serve as the application for a permit to import test samples for those embryos; separate applications are not required. The application must include the following information:

(1) The name and address of the exporter;

(2) The name and address of the importer;

(3) The name and address of the place where the donor dam will be bred and where the embryo(s) will be collected;

(4) The species, breed, and number of embryos to be imported;

(5) The purpose of the importation;

(6) The port of embarkation;

(7) The mode of transportation;

(8) The route of travel;

(9) The port of entry in the United States;

(10) The proposed date of arrival in the United States; and

(11) The name and address of the person to whom the embryos will be delivered in the United States.

(Approved by the Office of Management and Budget under control number 0579–0040)

[56 FR 55809, Oct. 30, 1991, as amended at 59 FR 67616, Dec. 30, 1994; 61 FR 15183, Apr. 5, 1996; 62 FR 56025, Oct. 28, 1997]

§ 98.14 Health certificate.

(a) Ruminant and swine embryos shall not be imported into the United States unless they are accompanied by a certificate issued by a full-time salaried veterinary officer of the national government of the region of origin, or issued by a veterinarian designated or accredited by the national government of the region of origin and endorsed by a full-time salaried veterinary officer of the national government of the region of origin, representing that the veterinarian issuing the certificate was authorized to do so.

(b) The health certificate must state:

(1) The name and address of the place where the embryos were collected;

(2) The name and address of the vetrinarian who collected the embryos;

(3) The date of embryo collection;

(4) The identification and breed of the donor dam and donor sire;

(5) The number of ampules or straws covered by the health certificate and the identification number or code on each ampule or straw;

(6) The dates, types, and results of all examinations and tests performed on

the donor dam and donor sire as a condition for importing the embryos;

(7) The dates and results of all tests performed on unfertilized eggs, nontransferrable embryos, and embryo collection and wash fluids;

(8) The names and addresses of the consignor and consignee;

(9) That the embryos are being imported into the United States in accordance with subpart B of 9 CFR part 98.

(c) If any of the information required by paragraph (b) of this section is provided in code, deciphering information must be attached to the health certificate.

(d) The health certificate accompanying sheep or goat embryos intended for importation from any part of the world shall, in addition to the statements required by paragraph (b) of this section, state that:

(1) The embryos' sire and dam have not been in any flock or herd nor had contact with sheep or goats which have been in any flock or herd where scrapie has been diagnosed or suspected during the 5 years prior to the date of collection of the embryos;

(2) The embryos' sire and dam showed no evidence of scrapie at the time the embryos were collected;

(3) Scrapie has not been suspected nor confirmed in any progeny of the embryos' donor dam; and

(4) The parents of the embryos' sire and dam are not, nor were not, affected with scrapie.

(e) There must be a separate health certificate for each collection of embryos.

(Approved by the Office of Management and Budget under control number 0579–0040)

[56 FR 55809, Oct. 30, 1991, as amended at 61 FR 15183, Apr. 5, 1996; 61 FR 17242, Apr. 19, 1996; 62 FR 56025, Oct. 28, 1997]

§98.15 Health requirements.

Ruminant and swine embryos may be imported from a region where rinderpest or foot-and-mouth disease exists only if all of the following conditions are met:

(a) The donor dam is determined to be free of communicable diseases based on tests, examinations, and other requirements, as follows, except that, with regard to bovine spongiform encephalopathy, the following does not apply to bovines, cervids, or camelids.

(1) During the year before embryo collection, no case of the following diseases occurred in the embryo collection unit or in any herd in which the donor dam was present:

(i) Ruminant: Bovine spongiform encephalopathy, contagious bovine pleuropneumonia, foot-and-mouth disease, Rift Valley fever, rinderpest, or vesicular stomatitis; or

(ii) Swine: African swine fever, foot-and-mouth disease, classical swine fever, pseudorabies, rinderpest, swine vesicular disease, or vesicular stomatitis.

(2) During the year before embryo collection, no case of the following diseases occurred within 5 kilometers of the embryo collection unit or in any herd in which the donor dam was present:

(i) Ruminant: Bovine spongiform encephalopathy, contagious bovine pleuropneumonia, foot-and-mouth disease, Rift Valley fever, rinderpest, or vesicular stomatitis; or

(ii) Swine: African swine fever, foot-and-mouth disease, classical swine fever, pseudorabies, rinderpest, swine vesicular disease, or vesicular stomatitis.

(3) During the 60 days before embryo collection, the donor dam did not receive a vaccination for either rinderpest or foot-and-mouth disease.

(4) During the 60 days before the donor dam was required to be in the embryo collection unit, in accordance with §98.17(a) of this subpart, the donor dam remained in the same herd, and no ruminants or swine were added to that herd.

(5)(i) On the day of embryo collection, and again not less than 30 days nor more than 120 days afterward, one sample of at least 10 ml of serum was collected from the donor dam, frozen, and sent to the Foreign Animal Disease Diagnostic Laboratory for testing.

(ii) The donor dam was determined to be free of foot-and-mouth disease based upon tests of the pair of serum samples. In addition, if any of the following diseases exist in the region of origin, the donor dam was determined to be free of these diseases based upon additional tests of the serum samples:

(A) Ruminant: Contagious bovine pleuropneumonia, Rift Valley fever, rinderpest, or vesicular stomatitis; or

(B) Swine: African swine fever, classical swine fever, pseudorabies, rinderpest, swine vesicular disease, or vesicular stomatitis.

(iii) If the donor dam was in any herd during the year before embryo collection that was not certified free of brucellosis by the national government of the region of origin, the donor dam was determined to be free of brucellosis based on tests of the serum samples.

(iv) The only official test results will be those provided by the Foreign Animal Disease Diagnostic Laboratory.

(6) If the donor dam was in any herd during the year before embryo collection that was not certified free of tuberculosis by the national government of the region of origin, the donor dam was determined to be free of tuberculosis by an official veterinarian based on an intradermal tuberculin test. The test must have been administered to the donor dam by an official veterinarian not less than 30 days nor more than 120 days after embryo collection, and not less than 60 days after any previously administered intradermal test for tuberculosis.

(7)(i) Not less than 30 days nor more than 120 days after embryo collection, the donor dam was examined by an official veterinarian and found free of clinical evidence of the following diseases:

(A) Ruminant: Bovine spongiform encephalopathy, brucellosis, contagious bovine pleuropneumonia, foot-and-mouth disease, Rift Valley fever, rinderpest, tuberculosis, and vesicular stomatitis; or

(B) Swine: African swine fever, brucellosis, foot-and-mouth disease, classical swine fever, pseudorabies, rinderpest, swine vesicular disease, tuberculosis, and vesicular stomatitis.

(ii) All signs of any other communicable disease must be listed on the health certificate that accompanies the embryos to the United States.

(8)(i) Between the time the embryos were collected and all examinations and tests required by this subpart were completed, no animals in the embryo collection unit with the donor dam, or in the donor dam's herd of origin, exhibited any clinical evidence of:

(A) Ruminant: Bovine spongiform encephalopathy, brucellosis, contagious bovine pleuropneumonia, foot-and-mouth disease, Rift Valley fever, rinderpest, tuberculosis, and vesicular stomatitis; or

(B) Swine: African swine fever, brucellosis, foot-and-mouth disease, classical swine fever, pseudorabies, rinderpest, swine vesicular disease, tuberculosis, and vesicular stomatitis.

(ii) All signs of any other communicable disease must be listed on the health certificate that accompanies the embryos to the United States.

(b) The donor dam or donor sire is determined to be free of communicable diseases based on other testing or certifications if required by the Administrator. The Administrator may require additional testing or certifications if he or she determines that they are necessary to determine either the donor dam's or the donor sire's freedom from communicable diseases. Circumstances that may result in additional testing or certifications include, but are not limited to:

(1) The existence of communicable diseases of livestock, other than those diseases specifically listed, in the region of origin;

(2) A high prevalence or an increase in the incidence of a communicable disease in the region of origin;

(3) The use of natural breeding, rather than artificial insemination to conceive the embryos;

(4) The use of fresh, rather than frozen semen, for artificial insemination; and

(5) The use of semen collected at a site other than an artificial insemination center approved by the national government of the region of origin.

(c) Embryos produced by any donor dam or sire that dies before being examined and tested as required under this subpart will not be eligible for importation into the United States.

[56 FR 55809, Oct. 30, 1991, as amended at 61 FR 15183, Apr. 5, 1996; 62 FR 56025, Oct. 28, 1997; 68 FR 16940, Apr. 7, 2003; 78 FR 73008, Dec. 4, 2013]

§98.16 The embryo collection unit.

Ruminant and swine embryos may be imported into the United States from a region where rinderpest or foot-and-mouth disease exists only if they were conceived, collected, processed, and stored prior to importation at an embryo collection unit. The embryo collection unit may be located on the premises where the donor dam's herd of origin is kept, or at any other location, provided that the embryo collection unit has been inspected and approved by an APHIS veterinarian and that the following requirements are met:

(a) *Animal holding and breeding area(s).* The embryo collection unit must have an area or areas for holding the donor dams and for breeding them (either natural breeding or artificial insemination).

(b) *Embryo collection area.* The embryo collection must have a room or outdoor area for collection of embryos that contains a device or devices for restraining embryo donors during embryo collection. If a room, the floor, walls, and ceiling must be impervious to moisture and constructed of materials that can withstand repeated cleaning and disinfection. If an outdoor area, the area must have a floor that is impervious to moisture and is constructed of materials that can withstand repeated cleaning and disinfection. If the outdoor area also has walls or a roof, the walls or roof also must be impervious to moisture and be constructed of materials that can withstand repeated cleaning and disinfection.

(c) *Embryo processing area.* The embryo collection unit must have an enclosed room, which may be mobile, that is used *only* for processing embryos. The walls, floor, and ceiling of the room must be impervious to moisture and constructed of materials that can withstand repeated cleaning and disinfection. The room must contain a work surface for handling the embryos, such as a table or countertop that is impervious to moisture. The room also must contain a microscope with a minimum of 50x magnification, and equipment for freezing the embryos.

(d) *Embryo storage area.* The embryo collection unit must have one lockable area that is used only for storing frozen embryos intended for importation into the United States.

(e) *Area for cleaning and disinfecting or sterilizing equipment.* The embryo collection unit must have an enclosed room used for cleaning and disinfecting or sterilizing equipment used for artificial insemination or for collection, processing, or storage of embryos. The walls, floor, and ceiling of the room must be impervious to moisture and constructed of materials that can withstand repeated cleaning and disinfection.

[56 FR 55809, Oct. 30, 1991, as amended at 61 FR 15184, Apr. 5, 1996; 62 FR 56025, Oct. 28, 1997]

§98.17 Procedures.

(a) *Housing of the donor dam.* (1) Beginning at least 24 hours before a donor dam is bred to produce embryos for importation to the United States, the donor dam must be housed at an embryo collection unit.

(2) The donor dam must remain at the embryo collection unit until the embryos for importation into the United States have been collected.

(3) After collection of embryos, the donor dam must either remain at the embryo collection unit or be returned to the herd of origin and remain there until all examinations and tests required by this subpart have been completed.

(4) During the time the donor dam is in the embryo collection unit, in accordance with paragraphs (a)(1) through (a)(3) of this section, no animals may be in the embryo collection unit with the donor dam unless:

(i) They meet the requirements of §98.15 of this subpart that are applicable to the donor dam at that time;

(ii) They are part of the donor dam's herd of origin; or

(iii) They are serving as donor sires for the production of embryos to be imported into the United States.

(b) *Oversight and supervision.* (1) All procedures associated with the production of embryos for importation into the United States, including artificial insemination, natural breeding, and cleaning and disinfection, must be performed under the oversight of an APHIS veterinarian. Collecting test samples, and collecting, processing, and storing embryos, must be supervised in person by an APHIS veterinarian.

(2) Officials from the Animal and Plant Health Inspection Service must be given access to all areas of the embryo collection unit and the donor dam's herd of origin during the time the donor dam is housed there, in accordance with paragraphs (a)(1) through (a)(3) of this section.

(c) *Personnel.* All personnel must put on clean outer garments, including disinfected boots, and must scrub their hands with soap and water each time they enter the embryo collection unit and before entering any room or area listed in § 98.16 of this subpart.

(d) *Cleaning, disinfection, and sterilization.* (1) All equipment that comes in contact with embryos or with media used for their collection or processing must be sterile. Equipment used for embryos from one donor dam, or with associated media, may not be used for embryos or associated media from any other donor dam until it has been resterilized.

(2) All equipment that comes in contact with a donor dam's secretions or excretions must be sterile and may not be used with any other donor dam until it has been resterilized.

(3) Containers used for storing embryos or for shipping embryos to the United States must be examined and found free of any organic matter and then disinfected before the ampules or straws are placed inside.

(4) The floor, ceiling, and walls of any room or outdoor area used for embryo collection, and the restraining device(s) used for this procedure, must be cleaned with soap and water and disinfected before the room or area is used to collect embryos intended for importation to the United States, and at least daily while in use for this purpose.

(5) The room and work surface used for processing embryos must be kept free of insects, rodents, trash, manure, and other animal matter and must be cleaned with soap and water and disinfected before the room is used for embryos intended for importation to the United States, and the work surface must be cleaned and disinfected at least daily while in use for this purpose.

(6) The area of the embryo collection unit used to store embryos intended for importation to the United States must be kept free of insects, rodents, trash, manure, and other animal matter and must be cleaned with soap and water and disinfected before being used to store the embryos.

(7) The room used for cleaning and disinfecting or sterilizing equipment used for artificial insemination or for collection, processing, or storage of embryos must be kept free of insects, rodents, trash, manure, and other animal matter and must be cleaned with soap and water and disinfected before being used to prepare equipment for donors of embryos intended for importation into the United States, and at least daily while in use for this purpose.

(e) *Media; cryogenic agent.* (1) All media containing products of animal origin and used for embryo collection and processing must be from sources in the United States or Canada.

(2) The liquid nitrogen used to freeze embryos may not have been used previously for any other products of animal origin.

(f) *Collection and processing of embryos.* (1) If embryos are collected in an outdoor area, they must be collected by using a closed collection system so that the embryos are not exposed to open air until they are inside the embryo processing room.

(2) Embryos from donors that do not meet the requirements of § 98.15 of this subpart that are applicable at the time of embryo collection may not be in the processing room at the same time as embryos intended for importation into the United States.

(3) Each embryo must be washed at least 10 times. Each wash must be accomplished by transferring the embryo into an aliquot of fresh medium that is 100 times the volume of the embryo plus any fluid transferred from the previous wash. No more than 10 embryos from the same flush may be washed together. A sterile micropipette must be used for each transfer, and the embryos must be well agitated throughout the entire volume of the wash before the

next transfer. Embryos from different donors may not be washed together.

(4) After the last wash, each embryo must be microscopically examined over its entire surface at not less than 50 × magnification. An embryo may not be imported into the United States unless its zona pellucida is found to be intact and free from any adherent material.

(5) After washing and examination of the zona pellucida, embryos must be individually packaged in sterile ampules or straws and frozen in liquid nitrogen. The donor dam's and sire's identifications and breed, the date of embryo collection, the name and address of the place where the embryos were collected, and an identification number for the straw or ampule must be recorded with indelible markings on each ampule or straw. If any of this information is provided in code, deciphering information must be attached to the health certificate for the embryos.

(6) The Administrator may require additional measures to be taken in processing embryos after collection (for example, adding trypsin to the washes) if he or she determines that such measures are necessary to ensure the embryos freedom from infectious agents that may cause communicable diseases. Circumstances that may result in such additional measures being required include, but are not limited to:

(i) The existence of communicable diseases of livestock, other than those diseases specifically listed, in the region of origin; and

(ii) A high prevalence or an increase in the incidence of a communicable disease in the region of origin.

(g) *Preparation of test samples; tests.* (1) All nontransferrable embryos and unfertilized eggs from each collection of embryos intended for importation into the United States must be pooled, frozen in liquid nitrogen, and sent to the Foreign Animal Disease Diagnostic Laboratory for testing under the personal supervision of an APHIS veterinarian. The collection and last two wash fluids from the collection of embryos must be frozen and sent to the Foreign Animal Disease Diagnostic Laboratory for testing under the personal supervision of an APHIS veterinarian. Samples from different collections may not be mixed.

(2) All samples collected in accordance with paragraph (g)(1) of this section must be tested and found negative for viral contamination. The wash fluids also must be found negative for bacterial contamination. The only official results for these tests will be those provided by the Foreign Animal Disease Diagnostic Laboratory.

(h) *Storage of embryos.* (1) Frozen embryos to be imported into the United States must be stored in a locked area or must remain in the custody of an official veterinarian until they are sealed in accordance with paragraph (h)(2) of this section and released for shipment to the United States in accordance with §98.18(a) of this subpart; except that, the embryos may be moved to a U.S. Department of Agriculture-operated animal import center in either New York, Hawaii, or Florida, under seal and in the custody of that individual, and remain in quarantine there until all tests and examinations required by this subpart have been completed and all test results have been provided by the Foreign Animal Disease Diagnostic Laboratory.

(2) Containers in which embryos will be imported into the United States must be sealed by an official veterinarian with the official seal of the region of origin or, if the official veterinarian is an employee of the Animal and Plant Health Inspection Service, with an official seal of the United States Department of Agriculture. The seal number must be recorded on the health certificate that accompanies the embryos to the United States.

(Approved by the Office of Management and Budget under control number 0579–0040)

[56 FR 55809, Oct. 30, 1991, as amended at 61 FR 15184, Apr. 5, 1996; 62 FR 56026, Oct. 28, 1997]

§98.18 Shipment of embryos to the United States.

(a) *Release from the embryo collection unit.* Except as provided in §98.17(h)(1) of this subpart, embryos may not be moved from the embryo collection unit until all tests and examinations required by this subpart have been completed and the Import-Export Animals Staff, Veterinary Services, APHIS, has received written notification of all test results from the Foreign Animal Disease Diagnostic Laboratory.

(b) *Route.* The sealed shipping containers must be routed directly to the U.S. port of entry designated on the import permit.

(c) *Ports of entry.* The embryos may be imported into the United States only through a port of entry listed in § 93.203(a) of this chapter.

(d) *Date of arrival in the United States.* Embryos that arrive at the port of entry more than 14 days after the proposed date of arrival stated in the import permit will not be eligible for importation into the United States.

[56 FR 55809, Oct. 30, 1991, as amended at 62 FR 56026, Oct. 28, 1997]

§ 98.19 Arrival and inspection at the port of entry.

(a) Upon arrival at the port of entry, the importer or the importer's agent must present an inspector at the port with the original health certificate and the original import permit for the embryos.

(b) The shipping container and all straws or ampules containing embryos must be made available to an inspector at the port of entry for inspection, and may not be removed from the port of entry until an inspector determines that the embryos are eligible for entry in accordance with this subpart and releases them.

§ 98.20 Embryos refused entry.

If any embryos are determined to be ineligible for importation into the United States upon arrival at the port of entry, the importer must remove the embryos from the United States within 30 days, or the embryos will be destroyed.

§ 98.21 Embryos from sheep in regions other than Australia, Canada, and New Zealand.

Except for embryos from sheep in Australia, Canada, or New Zealand, embryos from sheep may only be imported into the United States if they comply with all applicable provisions of this subpart and with § 98.10a.

(Approved by the Office of Management and Budget under control numbers 0579–0040 and 0579–0101)

[61 FR 17242, Apr. 19, 1996]

Subpart C—Certain Animal Semen

SOURCE: 55 FR 31558, Aug. 2, 1990, unless otherwise noted.

§ 98.30 Definitions.

Whenever in this subpart of the following terms are used, unless the context otherwise requires, they shall be construed, respectively, to mean:

Administrator. The Administrator of the Animal and Plant Health Inspection Service or any other employee of the Animal and Plant Health Inspection Service, United States Department of Agriculture, to whom authority has been or may be delegated to act in the Administrator's stead.

Animal and Plant Health Inspection Service. The Animal and Plant Health Inspection Service of the United States Department of Agriculture (APHIS or Service.)

Animals. Cattle, sheep, goats, other ruminants, swine, horses, asses, zebras, and poultry.

Cattle. Animals of the bovine species.

Communicable disease. Any contagious, infectious, or communicable disease of domestic livestock, poultry or other animals.

Department. The United States Department of Agriculture (USDA).

Flock. A herd.

Herd. All animals maintained on any single premises; and all animals under common ownership or supervision on two or more premises which are geographically separated, but among which there is an interchange or movement of animals.

Horses. Horses, asses, mules, and zebras.

Inspector. An employee of the Animal and Plant Health Inspection Service authorized to perform duties required under this subpart.

Port veterinarian. A veterinarian employed by the Animal and Plant Health Inspection Service to perform duties required under this part at a port of entry.

Poultry. Chickens, doves, ducks, geese, grouse, guinea fowl, partridges, pea fowl, pheasants, pigeons, quail, swans, and turkeys (including eggs for hatching).

Region. Any defined geographic land area identifiable by geological, political, or surveyed boundaries. A region may consist of any of the following:

(1) A national entity (country);

(2) Part of a national entity (zone, county, department, municipality, parish, Province, State, etc.)

(3) Parts of several national entities combined into an area; or

(4) A group of national entities (countries) combined into a single area.

Restricted zone for classical swine fever. An area, delineated by the relevant competent veterinary authorities of the region in which the area is located, that surrounds and includes the location of an outbreak of classical swine fever in domestic swine or detection of the disease in wild boar, and from which the movement of domestic swine is prohibited.

Ruminants. All animals which chew the cud, such as cattle, buffaloes, sheep, goats, deer, antelopes, camels, llamas and giraffes.

Swine. The domestic hog and all varieties of wild hogs.

United States. All of the States of the United States, the District of Columbia, Guam, Northern Mariana Islands, Puerto Rico, the Virgin Islands of the United States, and all other Territories and Possessions of the United States.

[55 FR 31558, Aug. 2, 1990. Redesignated at 56 FR 55809, Oct. 30, 1991; 61 FR 17242, Apr. 19, 1996; 62 FR 56026, Oct. 28, 1997; 65 FR 56777, Sept. 20, 2000; 71 FR 29071, May 19, 2006; 72 FR 67233, Nov. 28, 2007; 76 FR 70039, Nov. 10, 2011; 77 FR 1396, Jan. 10, 2012]

§ 98.31 General prohibitions; exceptions.

(a) No product subject to the provisions of this subpart shall be brought into the United States except in accordance with the regulations in this subpart and part 94 of this subchapter; nor shall any such product be handled or moved after physical entry into the United States before final release from quarantine or any other form of governmental detention except in compliance with such regulations; *Provided*, That, except as prohibited by section 306 of the Act of June 17, 1930, as amended (19 U.S.C. 1306), the Administrator may upon request in specific cases permit products to be brought into or through the United States under such conditions as he or she may prescribe, when he or she determines in the specific case that such action will not endanger the livestock or poultry of the United States.

(b) Animal semen may not be imported into the United States from any region other than the region in which it was collected.

[55 FR 31558, Aug. 2, 1990. Redesignated at 56 FR 55809, Oct. 30, 1991, and amended at 58 FR 37643, July 13, 1993; 59 FR 26596, May 23, 1994; 62 FR 56026, Oct. 28, 1997]

§ 98.32 Inspection of certain aircraft and other means of conveyance and shipping containers thereon; unloading, cleaning, and disinfection requirements.

(a) *Inspection:* All aircraft and other means of conveyance (including shipping containers thereon) moving into the United States from any foreign region are subject to inspection without a warrant by properly identified and designated inspectors to determine whether they are carrying any animal, carcass, product or article regulated or subject to disposal under any law or regulation administered by the Secretary of Agriculture for prevention of the introduction or dissemination of any communicable animal disease.

(b) *Unloading requirements:* Whenever in the course of any such inspection at any port in the United States the inspector has reason to believe that the means of conveyance or container is contaminated with material of animal (including poultry) origin, such as, but not limited to, meat, organs, glands, extracts, secretions, fat, bones, blood, lymph, urine, or manure, so as to present a danger of the spread of any communicable animal disease, the inspector may require the unloading of the means of conveyance and the emptying of the container if he or she deems it necessary to enable him or her to determine whether the means of conveyance or container is in fact so contaminated. The principal operator of the means of conveyance and his or her agent in charge of the means of conveyance shall comply with any such requirement under the immediate supervision of, and in the time and manner prescribed by, the inspector.

(c) *Cleaning and disinfection:* Whenever, upon inspection under this section, an inspector determines that a means of conveyance or shipping container is contaminated with material of animal origin so as to present a danger of the spread of any communicable animal disease, he or she shall notify the principal operator of the means of conveyance or his or her agent in charge, of such determination and the requirements under this section. The person so notified shall cause the cleaning and disinfection of such means of conveyance and container under the immediate supervision of, and in the time and manner prescribed by, the inspector.

(d) For purposes of this section, the term "shipping container" means any container of a type specially adapted for use in transporting any article on the means of conveyance involved.

[55 FR 31558, Aug. 2, 1990. Redesignated at 56 FR 55809, Oct. 30, 1991; 62 FR 56026, Oct. 28, 1997; 68 FR 6345, Feb. 7, 2003]

§98.33 Ports designated for the importation of certain animal semen.

(a) *Air and ocean ports.* The following air and ocean ports are designated as having inspection facilities for the entry of animal semen: Los Angeles, California; Miami, Florida; and Newburgh, New York.

(b) *Canadian border ports.* The following land border ports are designated as having inspection facilities for the entry of animal semen from Canada: Eastport, Idaho; Houlton and Jackman, Maine; Detroit, Port Huron, and Sault Ste. Marie, Michigan; Baudette, Minnesota; Opheim, Raymond, and Sweetgrass, Montana; Alexandria Bay, Buffalo, and Champlain, New York; Dunseith, Pembina, and Portal, North Dakota; Derby Line and Highgate Springs, Vermont; Oroville and Sumas, Washington.

(c) *Mexican border ports.* The following land border ports are designated as having inspection facilities for the entry of animal semen from Mexico: Douglas, Naco, Nogales, San Luis, and Sasabe, Arizona; Calexico and San Ysidro, California; Antelope Wells, Columbus, and Santa Teresa, New Mexico; Brownsville, Del Rio, Eagle Pass, El Paso, Hidalgo, Laredo, and Presidio, Texas.

(d) *Limited ports.* The following limited ports are designated as having inspection facilities for the entry of animal semen: Anchorage and Fairbanks, Alaska; San Diego, California; Jacksonville, St. Petersburg-Clearwater, and Tampa, Florida; Atlanta, Georgia; Honolulu, Hawaii; Chicago, Illinois; New Orleans, Louisiana; Portland, Maine; Baltimore, Maryland; Boston, Massachusetts; International Falls and Minneapolis, Minnesota; Great Falls, Montana; Portland, Oregon; San Juan, Puerto Rico; Memphis, Tennessee; Galveston and Houston, Texas; Seattle, Spokane, and Tacoma, Washington.

(e) *Designation of other ports.* The Secretary of the Treasury has approved the designation as quarantine stations of the ports specified in this section. In special cases other ports may be designated as quarantine stations under this section by the Administrator, with the concurrence of the Secretary of the Treasury.

[55 FR 31558, Aug. 2, 1990. Redesignated at 56 FR 55809, Oct. 30, 1991, and amended at 58 FR 37643, July 13, 1993; 60 FR 16045, Mar. 29, 1995; 60 FR 25120, May 11, 1995; 64 FR 23179, Apr. 30, 1999; 65 FR 38178, June 20, 2000; 67 FR 68022, Nov. 8, 2002]

§98.34 Import permits for poultry semen and animal semen.

(a) *Application for permit; reservation required.* (1) For poultry semen and animal semen, intended for importation from any part of the world, except as otherwise provided for in §98.36, the importer shall first apply for and obtain from APHIS an import permit. The application shall specify the name and address of the importer; the species, breed, quantity of animal semen to be imported; the purpose of the importation; individual animal identification (except poultry) which includes a description of the animal, name, age, markings, if any, registration number, if any, and tattoo or eartag; the region of origin; the name and address of the exporter; the port of embarkation in the foreign region; the mode of transportation, route of travel, and the port of entry in the United States; the proposed date of arrival of the animal semen to be imported; and the name of the person to whom the animal semen will be delivered and the location of the place in the United States to which delivery will be made from the port of entry. Additional information may be required in the form of certificates concerning specific diseases to which the animals are susceptible, as well as vaccinations or other precautionary treatments to which the animals or animal semen have been subjected. Notice of any such requirements will be given to the applicant in each case.

(2) An application for permit to import will be denied for semen from ruminants or swine from any region where it has been declared, under section 306 of the Act of June 17, 1930, that foot-and-mouth disease or rinderpest has been determined to exist, except as provided in paragraph (c) of this section.

(3) An application for permit to import poultry semen or animal semen may also be denied because of: Communicable disease conditions in the area or region of origin, or in a region through which the shipment has been or will be transported; deficiencies in the regulatory programs for the control or eradication of animal diseases and the unavailability of veterinary services in the above mentioned regions; the importer's failure to provide satisfactory evidence concerning the origin, history, and health status of the animals or animal semen; the lack of satisfactory information necessary to determine that the importation will not be likely to transmit any communicable disease to livestock or poultry of the United States; or any other circumstances which the Administrator believes require such denial to prevent the dissemination of any communicable disease of livestock or poultry into the United States.

(b) *Permit.* When a permit is issued, the original and two copies will be sent to the importer. It shall be the responsibility of the importer to forward the original permit and one copy to the shipper in the region of origin, and it shall also be the responsibility of the importer to insure that the shipper presents the copy of the permit to the carrier and makes proper arrangements for the original permit to accompany the shipment to the specified U.S. port of entry for presentation to the collector of customs. Animal semen intended for importation into the United States for which a permit has been issued, will be received at the specified port of entry within the time prescribed in the permit which shall not exceed 14 days from the first day that the permit is effective for all permits. Poultry semen and animal semen for which a permit is required by these regulations will not be eligible for entry if a permit has not been issued; if unaccompanied by such a permit; if shipment is from any port other than the one designated in the permit; if arrival in the United States is at any port other than the one designated in the permit; if the animal semen offered for entry differs from that described in the permit; or if the animal semen is not handled as outlined in the application for the permit and as specified in the permit issued.

(c) *Animal semen from regions where rinderpest or foot-and-mouth disease exists.* Importation of semen of ruminants or swine, originating in any region designated in paragraph (a) of § 94.1 of this subchapter as a region where rinderpest or foot-and-mouth disease is determined to exist, is prohibited, except that semen from ruminants or swine originating in such a region may be offered for entry into the United States at the port of New York and later released from such port provided the following conditions have been fulfilled:

(1) The importer has applied for and obtained an import permit for the semen in accordance with the provisions of this section and related requirements concerning application therefor, which permit is in effect at the time of importation, and has deposited with the Department prior to the issuance of the permit sufficient funds so as to be available for defraying estimated expenses to be incurred in connection with the proposed semen importation and following the issuance of the permit has deposited such other amounts as may be required from time

to time to defray unanticipated costs or increased expenses. Such an import permit may be denied for the reasons specified in paragraph (a)(3) of this section. Furthermore, an import permit will be revoked unless the following conditions have been complied with:

(i) The donor animal shall have been inspected on the farm of origin or on another premises (the inspection may be on another premises only if a veterinarian of the Department has traced the donor animal back to its farm of origin) by a veterinarian of the United States Department of Agriculture who, in cooperation with the veterinary service of the region of origin of the donor animal, shall have determined, insofar as possible, that the donor animal was never infected with rinderpest or foot-and-mouth disease; that the donor animal was never on a farm or other premise where rinderpest or foot-and-mouth disease then existed; that the donor animal has not been on a premise that had an animal that was susceptible to the virus of rinderpest or foot-and-mouth disease and that was exposed to either disease during the 12 months immediately prior to the date of inspection of the donor animal; that the donor animal, if a ruminant, has never been vaccinated against rinderpest; that the donor animal, if a swine, has never been vaccinated against rinderpest or foot-and-mouth disease; and that the donor animal was free from evidence of other communicable disease;

(ii) The donor animal shall have been permanently identified in a manner satisfactory to a veterinarian of this Department; a blood sample and an oesophageal-pharyngeal tissue sample (O-P sample) from such a donor ruminant and a blood sample from such a donor swine for tests as specified in paragraph (c)(1)(iv) of this section or other tests shall have been collected by a veterinarian of the United States Department of Agriculture and transported by air to the New York Port Veterinarian for delivery to the Foreign Animal Disease Diagnostic Laboratory, Greenport, New York, in containers approved by a veterinarian of this Department, sealed in the region of origin by a veterinarian of this Department; and pending the results of the tests, the donor animal shall have been kept in isolation on the farm of origin or other acceptable location under the supervision of a veterinarian of this Department, and during such isolation period no animal susceptible to rinderpest or foot-and-mouth disease shall have been permitted to enter such farm or location and no other source of exposure to rinderpest or foot-and-mouth disease shall have been present;

(iii) The blood samples from the donor animal shall have been negative to the tests specified in paragraph (c)(1)(iv) of this section made at the Foreign Animal Disease Diagnostic Laboratory, Greenport, New York, and to any other test for rinderpest, foot-and-mouth disease or other communicable disease prescribed by the Administrator.

(iv) In the case of a ruminant, each blood sample collected pursuant to paragraph (c)(1)(ii) or (vi) of this section shall have been tested for foot-and-mouth disease using the virus infection associated (VIA) test and each O-P sample collected pursuant to paragraph (c)(1)(ii) or (iv) of this section shall have been tested for foot-and-mouth disease using the virus isolation test. In the case of a swine, each blood sample collected pursuant to paragraph (c)(1)(ii) or (vi) of this section shall have been tested for foot-and-mouth disease using the virus infection associated (VIA) test and the virus neutralization test.''[1]

(v) Following isolation, preliminary veterinary inspection, and testing while the donor animal was on the farm of origin or other acceptable location, the donor animal shall have been transported, under such conditions as the Department veterinarian prescribed to prevent exposure of the animal to the virus of rinderpest or foot-and-mouth disease, to an isolation facility properly equipped for the necessary care and maintenance of the donor animal and for the proper collection and handling of semen, approved

[1] The test procedures for the virus infection associated (VIA) test, the virus isolation test, and the virus neutralization test are available from the Chief, Foreign Animal Disease Diagnostic Laboratory, National Veterinary Services Laboratories, P.O. Box 848, Greenport, NY 11944.

by a veterinarian of this Department and under the direct supervision of such veterinarian;

(vi) The semen of the donor animal shall have been collected at the approved isolation facility under the direct supervision of a veterinarian of this Department (any number of collections may be made); such veterinarian shall take a 0.5 ml sample of semen from each semen collection; and all handling procedures, such as examination, dilution, refrigeration, and preparation of the semen for shipment, shall have been under the direct supervision of a veterinarian of this Department. In the case of a ruminant, a blood sample and an O-P sample shall have been taken from the donor animal by a veterinarian of the Department within 7 days after the final semen collection, and between 21 to 28 days after the taking of these samples another blood sample shall have been taken from the donor animal by a veterinarian of the Department. In the case of a swine, a blood sample shall have been taken from the donor animal by a veterinarian of the Department within 7 days after the final semen collection, and between 21 to 28 days after the taking of the sample, another blood sample shall have been taken from the donor animal by a veterinarian of the Department.

(2) The semen collected at the approved isolation facility shall have been at all times, except during air transportation to New York, in the custody of a veterinarian of this Department.

(3) The semen for which an import permit has been issued shall have been transported by air to the port of New York in liquid nitrogen containers approved by a veterinarian of this Department; sealed in the region of origin by a veterinarian of this Department; and accompanied by a statement by such veterinarian showing the identification of the donor animal and the dates the semen was collected, along with a certificate regarding the health status of the donor animal as of the date of shipment of the semen to the port of New York. All semen received at the port of New York shall be held under quarantine in liquid nitrogen storage at such port in the custody of APHIS until released or otherwise disposed of as provided in this section.

(4) The donor animal shall have been retained at the approved isolation facility in the region where the semen was collected until all of the applicable samples referred to in paragraph (c)(1)(vi) of this section have been collected by a veterinarian of the Department for tests as specified in paragraph (c)(1)(iv) of this section at the Foreign Animal Disease Diagnostic Laboratory, Greenport, New York, and any other tests as required by the Administrator.

(5) The semen sample from each collection shall have consisted of unprocessed semen without any added substances, and shall have been tested at the Foreign Animal Disease Diagnostic Laboratory, Greenport, New York. Such tests shall have been performed by injecting the semen samples into test animals which are susceptible to rinderpest or foot-and-mouth disease. The semen collected at the approved isolation facility, other than the semen samples, may be held in the region of origin or at the port of New York, at the option of the importer, until all of the testing required to be conducted under this section is completed.

(6) If it is determined that the requirements set forth in this paragraph have been complied with and there are no indications that the donor animal or the semen from the donor animal harbors the virus of rinderpest or foot-and-mouth disease or any other communicable disease and if the donor animal, blood samples from the donor animal, O-P samples (if applicable) from the donor animal, and semen samples from the donor animal are negative to all other tests required, the semen shall be released for shipment to the consignee listed by the importer; otherwise the semen shall be destroyed or disposed of as the Administrator, may direct.

(7) *Porcine semen from the People's Republic of China.* In addition to the other requirements of this part, porcine semen may be imported into the United States from the People's Republic of China (PRC) only after the official veterinary organization (OVO) of the PRC has certified that the PRC is free of African swine fever, rinderpest, and Teschen's disease, and after the

following conditions have been fulfilled:

(i) The donor boars must pass a 60-day isolation/collection period in a facility jointly approved by the OVO of the PRC and the USDA as adequate to prevent exposure of the donor boars to infectious diseases. Any other swine at the isolation facility, such as teaser animals, must also meet the requirements of this paragraph. No animals may be added to the group after the start of the 60-day isolation/collection period. The Department will permit collection of semen to be initiated at the beginning of the isolation/collection period. The facility shall be cleaned and disinfected with a 4 percent sodium carbonate solution used in accordance with applicable label instructions in the presence of OVO quarantine personnel prior to the start of the isolation. During the isolation/collection period, personnel handling the animals shall not have contact with other domestic farm livestock (this term does not include pets such as dogs and cats). Raw animal food wastes (garbage) shall not be fed to the donor boars while in isolation. At the start of the isolation/collection period, and again after 14 days of isolation, all animals offered for collection of semen must be given an intramuscular injection of dihydrostreptomycin at a rate of 25 mg/kg dosage as a precautionary treatment for leptospirosis. Feed and bedding used during the isolation/collection period shall not originate from areas infected with epizootic diseases and must meet veterinary hygienic requirements established by the OVO of the PRC concerning freedom of the feed and bedding from contamination that could transmit diseases. During the isolation/collection period the swine at the collection center shall not have direct contact with, or exposure to, any other animals not included in the group at the isolation facility. Exposure consists of contact with yards, pens, or other facilities or vehicles that have been in contact with animals and have not been cleaned and disinfected.

(ii) Donor boars shall be selected from premises which are solely swine breeding operations. These premises must be located at the center of an area with a 16 km radius that was free of foot-and-mouth disease (FMD), swine vesicular disease (SVD), and classical swine fever for three years prior to semen collection. Donor boars shall not have been vaccinated against these diseases. There shall have been no cases of these diseases on these premises for five years prior to the collection of semen. There shall have been no animal introduced into these premises from farms affected with these diseases for three years prior to the collection of semen. There shall have been no evidence of brucellosis, tuberculosis, or pseudorabies on these premises or on premises adjacent to these premises for one year prior to the collection of semen.

(iii) During the 60-day isolation/collection period, the boars offered for collection of semen shall be subjected to the following tests,[2] in lieu of the tests required by paragraphs (c)(1)(iv) and (vi) of this section. If test samples from any donor boars are lost, damaged, or destroyed prior to testing, or if test results are inconclusive, the donor boars involved shall be subjected to retesting:

(A) Foot-and-mouth disease:

(*1*) Microtiter virus neutralization (VN) test for types, A, O, C, and Asia. (The PRC will test for types A and O, and the United States will test for types C and Asia at the USDA Foreign Animal Disease Diagnostic Laboratory (FADDL)).

(*2*) Agar gel immunodiffusion (AGID) test using virus infection associated antigen (VIAA) in serum. (Animals having responses to the AGID test or reacting to the VN test at 1:10 dilution or greater shall be eliminated as semen donors, and all other swine in contact with them shall be retested within 30 days. If the whole group does not have the above responses and there is no clinical evidence of FMD, the group shall be eligible for collection of semen with respect to FMD. Otherwise, none of the group shall qualify as donors of semen for export.)

(B) Brucellosis: Standard tube test (STT) at less than 30 IU/ml, and card

[2] Technical information on laboratory methods and procedures for these tests may be obtained from the Administrator, c/o Director, National Veterinary Services Laboratories, P.O. Box 844, Ames, IA 50010.

test (antigen and protocol to be supplied by USDA).

(C) Swine vesicular disease: Virus neutralization test at 1:40 dilution (serums to be tested at FADDL).

(D) Classical swine fever: Fluorescent antibody neutralization (FAN) test at 1:16 dilution.

(E) Japanese B encephalitis: Hemagglutination inhibition (HI) test, negative according to PRC standards.

(F) Pseudorabies: Virus neutralization at 1:4 dilution.

(G) Tuberculosis: Intradermal test using bovine PPD tuberculin (Positive animals will be necropsied. If there are lesions of TB in the test positive pigs, the whole group will be ineligible as semen donors. If no lesions are found, the rest of the pigs will be eligible as semen donors with respect to tuberculosis.

All samples of the above tests, except as noted for FMD, SVD, and TB, will be submitted to laboratories designated by the OVO of the PRC. At least 21 days after the final collection of semen for exportation, the donor animals will be retested for the diseases listed above, with the exception of tuberculosis and Japanese encephalitis. In addition, aliquots of each ejaculate of semen collected shall be submitted to FADDL for pathogen isolation tests for FMD, brucellosis, swine vesicular disease, classical swine fever, Japanese encephalitis, and pseudorabies.

(iv) The semen will not be eligible for release in the United States until all tests in paragraph (c)(7)(iii) of this section have been completed with negative results.

(v) Each semen straw or ampule for export must be identified with the name or identification number of the donor boar and with the date of collection. A USDA veterinarian shall certify that he or she has supervised the collection and processing of the semen and its storage until the time it is shipped to the United States. Each shipment will be accompanied by a USDA veterinarian unless the semen is shipped directly to the port of New York, with no stops en route. Shipment to the United States will be in accordance with the terms of a USDA import permit. Semen imported in accordance with this section shall be released by USDA to the importer only after all requirements of this section have been met.

(d) *Sheep and goat semen from regions where scrapie exists.* Importation of semen of sheep and goats is subject to the requirements in §98.35(e). Applications for a permit to import sheep and goat semen must include statements that:

(1) All first generation (F1) progeny resulting from imported semen will be identified with a permanent official identification consistent with the provisions of §79.2 of this chapter; and

(2) Records of any sale of F1 progeny, including the name and address of the buyer, will be kept for a period of 5 years. APHIS may view and copy these records during normal business hours.

[55 FR 31558, Aug. 2, 1990. Redesignated at 56 FR 55809, Oct. 30, 1991, as amended at 58 FR 37644, July 13, 1993; 59 FR 26596, May 23, 1994; 62 FR 56026, Oct. 28, 1997; 68 FR 16940, Apr. 7, 2003; 72 FR 64128, Nov. 15, 2007]

§98.35 Declaration, health certificate, and other documents for animal semen.

(a) The certificates, declarations, and affidavits required by the regulations in this subpart shall be presented by the importer or his or her agent to the collector of customs at the port of entry, upon arrival of animal semen at such port, for the use of the veterinary inspector at the port of entry.

(b) For all animal semen offered for importation, the importer or his or her agent shall first present two copies of a declaration which shall list the port of entry, the name and address of the importer, the name and address of the broker, the origin of the animal semen, the number, breed, species, and purpose of the importation, the name of the person to whom the animal semen will be delivered, and the location of the place to which such delivery will be made.

(c) All animal semen intended for importation into the United States shall be accompanied by a health certificate issued by a full-time salaried veterinary officer of the national government of the region of origin, or issued by a veterinarian designated or accredited by the national government of the region of origin and endorsed by a full-time salaried veterinary officer of the national government of the region of origin, representing that the veterinarian issuing the certificate was authorized to do so.

(d) The health certificate must state:

(1) The name and address of the place where the semen was collected;

(2) The name and address of the veterinarian who supervised the collection of the semen;

(3) The date of semen collection;

(4) The identification and breed of the donor animal;

(5) The number of ampules or straws covered by the health certificate and the identification number or code on each ampule or straw;

(6) The dates, types, and results of all examinations and tests performed on the donor animal as a condition for importing the semen;

(7) The seal number on the shipping container;

(8) The names and addresses of the consignor and consignee; and

(9) That the semen is being imported into the United States in accordance with subpart C of 9 CFR part 98.

(e) The certificate accompanying sheep or goat semen intended for importation from any part of the world shall, in addition to the statements required by paragraph (d) of this section, state that:

(1) The donor animals:

(i) Are permanently identified, to enable traceback to their establishment of origin; and

(ii) Have been kept since birth in establishments in which no case of scrapie had been confirmed during their residency; and

(iii) Neither showed clinical signs of scrapie at the time of semen collection nor developed scrapie between the time of semen collection and the export of semen to the United States; and

(iv) The dam of the semen donor is not, nor was not, affected with scrapie.

(2) In the region where the semen originates:

(i) Scrapie is a compulsorily notifiable disease; and

(ii) An effective surveillance and monitoring system for scrapie is in place; and

(iii) Affected sheep and goats are slaughtered and completely destroyed; and

(iv) The feeding of sheep and goats with meat-and-bone meal or greaves derived from ruminants has been banned and the ban effectively enforced in the whole region; and

(3) Semen originating in regions other than Australia and New Zealand is to be transferred to females in a flock that is listed in the Scrapie National Database as part of the Scrapie Program in the United States. Imported semen may be further distributed to any other listed flock with written notification to the APHIS Veterinary Services area office.

(f) All shipping containers carrying animal semen for importation into the United States must be sealed with an official seal of the national veterinary service of the region of origin. The health certificate must show the seal number on the shipping container. The semen must remain in the sealed container until arrival in the United States and, at the U.S. port of entry, an inspector determines that either:

(1) The seal numbers on the health certificate and shipping container match; or

(2) The seal numbers on the health certificate and shipping container do not match, but an APHIS representative at the port of entry is satisfied that the shipping container contains the semen described on the health certificate, import permit, declaration, and any other accompanying documents.

(Approved by the Office of Management and Budget under control number 0579–0040)

[55 FR 31558, Aug. 2, 1990. Redesignated at 56 FR 55809, Oct. 30, 1991, as amended at 58 FR 37644, July 13, 1993; 61 FR 15184, Apr. 5, 1996; 61 FR 17242, Apr. 19, 1996; 62 FR 56026, Oct. 28, 1997; 65 FR 56777, Sept. 20, 2000; 72 FR 64128, Nov. 15, 2007]

§ 98.36 Animal semen from Canada.

(a) *General importation requirements for animal semen from Canada.*

If the product is . . .	Then . . .
(1) Equine semen	There are no importation requirements under this part.
(2) Sheep or goat semen	The importer or his agent, in accordance with §§98.34 and 98.35 of this part, must present: (i) An import permit; (ii) Two copies of a declaration; and (iii) A health certificate.
(3) Animal semen other than equine, sheep, or goat semen.	See paragraph (b) of this section.

(b) *Importation requirements for animal semen other than equine, sheep, or goat semen from Canada.*

If the product is offered for entry at a . . .	And . . .	Or . . .	Then . . .
(1) Canadian land border port listed in §98.33(b) of this part.	The donor animal was born in Canada or the United States and has never been in a region other than Canada or the United States.	The donor animal was legally imported into Canada, released to move freely in Canada, and has been released in Canada for no less than 60 days.	The importer or his agent, in accordance with §98.35 of this part, must present: (i) Two copies of a declaration; and (ii) A health certificate.
(2) Canadian land border port listed in §98.33(b) of this part.	The donor animal does not meet the special conditions listed above in paragraph (b)(1) of this table.		The importer or his agent, in accordance with §§98.34 and 98.35 of this part, must present: (i) An import permit; (ii) Two copies of a declaration; and (iii) A health certificate.

If the product is offered for entry at a . . .	And . . .	Or . . .	Then . . .
(3) Port not listed in § 98.33(b) of this part.			The importer or his agent, in accordance with §§ 98.34 and 98.35 of this part, must present: (i) An import permit; (ii) Two copies of a declaration; and (iii) A health certificate.

[65 FR 56778, Sept. 20, 2000]

§ 98.37 [Reserved]

§ 98.38 Restrictions on the importation of swine semen from the APHIS-defined European CSF region.

In addition to meeting all other applicable provisions of this part, swine semen imported from the APHIS-defined European CSF region, as defined in § 94.0 of this subchapter, must meet the following conditions:

(a) The semen must come from a semen collection center approved for export by the competent veterinary authority.

(b) The semen must not have been collected from a donor boar that was in any of the following regions or zones, unless the semen was collected after the periods described:

(1) Any region when the region was classified under §§ 94.9(a) and 94.10(a) of this chapter as a region in which classical swine fever is known to exist, except for the APHIS-defined European CSF region;

(2) A restricted zone in the APHIS-defined European CSF region established because of the detection of classical swine fever in domestic swine, from the time of detection until the designation of the zone as a restricted zone is removed by the competent veterinary authority or until 6 months following depopulation of the swine on affected premises in the restricted zone and the cleaning and disinfection of the last affected premises in the zone, whichever is later; or

(3) A restricted zone in the APHIS-defined European CSF region established because of the detection of classical swine fever in wild boar, from the time of detection until the designation of the zone as a restricted zone is removed by the competent veterinary authority.

(c) The semen must not have been collected from a donor boar that was commingled with swine that at any time were in any of the regions or zones described in paragraphs (b)(1) through (b)(3) of this section, unless the semen was collected after the periods described.

(d) The semen must not have been collected from a donor boar that transited any region or zone described in paragraphs (b)(1) through (b)(3) of this section during the periods described, unless the donor boar was moved directly through the region or zone in a sealed means of conveyance with the seal determined to be intact upon arrival at the point of destination, or unless the semen was collected after the periods described;

(e) The donor boar must be held in isolation for at least 30 days prior to entering the semen collection center.

(f) No more than 30 days prior to being held in isolation as required by paragraph (e) of this section, the donor boar must be tested with negative results with a classical swine fever test approved by the World Organization for Animal Health.

(g) No equipment or materials used in transporting the donor boar from the farm of origin to the semen collection center may have been used previously for transporting swine that do not meet the requirements of this section, unless such equipment or materials have first been cleaned and disinfected.

(h) The semen must be accompanied by a certificate issued by a salaried veterinary officer of the competent veterinary authority, stating that the provisions of paragraphs (a) through (g) of this section have been met.[3]

(Approved by the Office of Management and Budget under control numbers 0579–0218 and 0579–0265)

[71 FR 29072, May 19, 2006, as amended at 72 FR 67233, Nov. 28, 2007; 76 FR 70040, Nov. 10, 2011; 77 FR 1396, Jan. 10, 2012; 77 FR 74558, Dec. 17, 2012]

PART 99—RULES OF PRACTICE GOVERNING PROCEEDINGS UNDER CERTAIN ACTS

Subpart A—General

Subpart B—Supplemental Rules of Practice

AUTHORITY: 7 U.S.C. 8301–8317; 7 CFR 2.22, 2.80, and 371.4.

SOURCE: 48 FR 30095, June 30, 1983, unless otherwise noted. Redesignated at 52 FR 29502, Aug. 10, 1987.

Subpart A—General

§99.1 Scope and applicability of rules of practice.

The Uniform Rules of Practice for the Department of Agriculture promulgated in subpart H of part 1, subtitle A, title 7, Code of Federal Regulations, are the Rules of Practice applicable to adjudicatory, administrative proceedings under the following statutory provisions:

Act of May 29, 1884, commonly known as the Animal Industry Act, section 7, as amended (21 U.S.C. 117),
Act of August 30, 1890, section 6, as amended (21 U.S.C. 104),
Act of February 2, 1903, commonly known as the Cattle Contagious Diseases Act of 1903, section 3, as amended (21 U.S.C. 122),
Act of July 2, 1962, section 6(a), as amended (21 U.S.C. 134e),
Act of May 6, 1970, section 2, as amended (21 U.S.C. 135a).
The Animal Health Protection Act, section 10414 (7 U.S.C. 8313)

In addition, the Supplemental Rules of Practice set forth in subpart B of this part shall be applicable to such proceedings.

[48 FR 30095, June 30, 1983. Redesignated at 52 FR 29502, Aug. 10, 1987, as amended at 68 FR 6345, Feb. 7, 2003]

Subpart B—Supplemental Rules of Practice

§99.10 Stipulations.

(a) At any time prior to the issuance of a complaint seeking a civil penalty under any of the Acts listed in §99.1, the Administrator, in his discretion, may enter into a stipulation with any person in which:

(1) The Administrator or the Administrator's delegate gives notice of an apparent violation of the applicable Act, or the regulations issued thereunder, by such person and affords such person an opportunity for a hearing regarding the matter as provided by such Act;

(2) Such person expressly waives hearing and agrees to pay a specified penalty within a designated time; and

(3) The Administrator agrees to accept the penalty in settlement of the particular matter involved if the penalty is paid within the designated time.

(b) If the penalty is not paid within the time designated in such a stipulation, the amount of the stipulated penalty shall not be relevant in any respect to the penalty which may be assessed after issuance of a complaint.

[48 FR 30095, June 30, 1983. Redesignated and amended at 52 FR 29502, Aug. 10, 1987]

[3] The certification required may be placed on the certificate required under §98.35(c) or may be contained in a separate document.

SUBCHAPTER E—VIRUSES, SERUMS, TOXINS, AND ANALOGOUS PRODUCTS; ORGANISMS AND VECTORS

PART 101—DEFINITIONS

AUTHORITY: 21 U.S.C. 151–159; 7 CFR 2.22, 2.80, and 371.4.

SOURCE: 38 FR 8426, Apr. 2, 1973, unless otherwise noted.

§ 101.1 Applicability.

When used in parts 101 through 117 of this subchapter, the meaning of the words and phrases listed shall be as defined in this part.

§ 101.2 Administrative terminology.

The following administrative words and phrases shall mean:

Adjacent herd. Adjacent herds are herds physically contiguous to the herd of origin; there are no herds between an adjacent herd and the herd of origin.

Administrator. The Administrator, Animal and Plant Health Inspection Service, or any person authorized to act for the Administrator.

Animal and Plant Health Inspection Service. The agency in the Department of Agriculture responsible for administering the Virus-Serum-Toxin Act.

Biological products. The term *biological products,* also referred to in this subchapter as biologics, biologicals, or products, shall mean all viruses, serums, toxins (excluding substances that are selectively toxic to microorganisms, e.g., antibiotics), or analogous products at any stage of production, shipment, distribution, or sale, which are intended for use in the treatment of animals and which act primarily through the direct stimulation, supplementation, enhancement, or modulation of the immune system or immune response. The term "biological products" includes but is not limited to vaccines, bacterins, allergens, antibodies, antitoxins, toxoids, immunostimulants, certain cytokines, antigenic or immunizing components of live organisms, and diagnostic components, that are of natural or synthetic origin, or that are derived from synthesizing or altering various substances or components of substances such as microorganisms, genes or genetic sequences, carbohydrates, proteins, antigens, allergens, or antibodies.

(1) A product's intended use shall be determined through an objective standard and not a subjective one, and would be dependent on factors such as representations, claims (either oral or written), packaging, labeling, or appearance.

(2) The term *analogous products* shall include:

(i) Substances, at any stage of production, shipment, distribution, or sale, which are intended for use in the treatment of animals and which are similar in function to biological products in that they act, or are intended to act, through the stimulation, supplementation, enhancement, or modulation of the immune system or immune response; or

(ii) Substances, at any stage of production, shipment, distribution, or sale, which are intended for use in the treatment of animals through the detection or measurement of antigens, antibodies, nucleic acids, or immunity; or

(iii) Substances, at any stage of production, shipment, distribution, or sale, which resemble or are represented as biological products intended for use in the treatment of animals through appearance, packaging, labeling, claims (either oral or written), representations, or through any other means.

(3) The term *treatment* shall mean the prevention, diagnosis, management, or cure of diseases of animals.

Department. The U.S. Department of Agriculture.

Distributor. A person who sells, distributes, or otherwise places in channels of trade, one or more biological products he does not produce or import.

Division. A marketing unit established by the licensee which may be named on labels, advertisements and promotional material in addition to the name and address of the producer.

Domestic animals. All animals, other than man, including poultry.

Establishment. One or more premises designated on the establishment license.

Guidelines. Guidelines establish principles or practices related to test procedures, manufacturing practices, product standards, scientific protocols, labeling, and other technical or policy considerations. Guidelines contain procedures or standards of general applicability that are usually not regulatory in nature, but that are related to matters that fall under the Virus-Serum-Toxin Act. Guidelines issued by the agency include Veterinary Biologics Licensing Considerations, Memoranda, Notices, and Supplemental Assay Methods.

Herd. Any group of animals, including birds, fish, and reptiles, maintained at a common location (e.g. lot, farm or ranch) for any purpose. The herd (or flock) includes all animals subsequently housed at the common location. If the principal animals of a group are moved to a different location, the group is still considered the same herd.

Herd of origin. The herd from which the microorganism used as seed for production of an autogenous biologic is isolated. Offspring and excess breeding stock (not the principal animals) moved or sold from one group of animals to another have changed herds and are no longer considered part of the herd they originated from. Groups of animals under the same ownership but at different locations are separate herds.

Inspection. An examination made by an inspector to determine the fitness of animals, establishments, facilities, and procedures used in connection with the preparation, testing, and distribution of biological products and the examination or testing of biological products.

Inspector. Any officer or employee of Animal and Plant Health Inspection Service who is authorized by the Administrator to do inspection work.

Licensed establishment. An establishment operated by a person holding an unexpired, unsuspended, and unrevoked U.S. Veterinary Biologics Establishment License.

Licensee. A person to whom an establishment license and at least one product license has been issued.

Microorganisms. Microscopic or submicroscopic organisms, which are sometimes referred to as organisms, which may introduce or disseminate disease of animals.

Nonadjacent herd. Nonadjacent herds are all herds other than the herd of origin and other than herds adjacent to the herd of origin. Herds adjacent to the herd of origin but in a different State from the herd of origin are also considered nonadjacent herds.

Permittee. A person who resides in the United States or operates a business establishment within the United States, to whom a permit to import biological products has been issued.

Person. Any individual, firm, partnership, corporation, company, association, educational institution, State or local governmental agency, or other organized group of any of the foregoing, or any agent, officer, or employee of any thereof.

Premises. All buildings, appurtenances, and equipment used to produce and store biological products located within a particular land area shown on building plans or drawings furnished by the applicant or the licensee and designated by an address adequate for identification.

Prepare or preparation. Sometimes referred to as manufacture or produce, means the steps and procedures used in the processing, testing, packaging, labeling, and storing of a biological product.

Regulations. The provisions in parts 101 through 118 of this subchapter.

Research investigator or research sponsor. A person who has requested authorization to ship an experimental biological product for the purpose of evaluating such product, or has been granted such authorization.

Secretary. The Secretary of Agriculture of the United States or any officer or employee of the Department to whom authority has heretofore been delegated, or to whom authority may hereafter be delegated, to act in his stead.

Subsidiary. A corporation in which a corporate licensee owns in excess of 50 percent of the voting stock.

Veterinary Services. Veterinary Services unit of Animal and Plant Health Inspection Service of the Department.

Virus-Serum-Toxin Act. The Act of March 4, 1913, 37 Stat. 832–833; as amended December 23, 1985, Public Law 99–198, 99 Stat. 1654–1655; and as further amended September 28, 1988, Public Law 100–449, 102 Stat. 1868; 21 U.S.C. 151–159.

U.S. Veterinary Biological Product License. A document, sometimes referred to as a product license, which is issued pursuant to part 102 of this subchapter to the holder of an establishment license, as a part of and ancillary to the establishment license, and which authorizes production of a specified biological product in the designated licensed establishment.

U.S. Veterinary Biological Product Permit. A document, sometimes referred to as a permit, issued to a person authorizing the importation of specified biological products subject to restrictions and controls as provided in the regulations.

U.S. Veterinary Biologics Establishment License. A document referred to as an establishment license, which is issued pursuant to part 102 of this subchapter, authorizing the use of designated premises for production of biological products specified in one or more unexpired, unsuspended, and unrevoked product license(s).

[38 FR 8426, Apr. 2, 1973; 38 FR 9221, Apr. 12, 1973, as amended at 40 FR 46093, Oct. 6, 1975; 41 FR 44358, Oct. 8, 1976; 49 FR 22624, May 31, 1984; 52 FR 30131, Aug. 13, 1987; 56 FR 66782, 66783, Dec. 26, 1991; 57 FR 38756, Aug. 27, 1992; 62 FR 31328, June 9, 1997; 64 FR 43044, Aug. 9, 1999]

§ 101.3 Biological products and related terms.

When used in conjunction with or in reference to a biological product, the following terms shall mean:

(a) *Licensed biological product.* A biological product prepared within a licensed establishment by a person holding an unexpired, unsuspended, and unrevoked product license for such product.

(b) *Experimental biological product.* A biological product which is being evaluated to substantiate an application for a product license or permit.

(c) *Completed product.* A biological product in bulk or final container produced in compliance with the regulations to final form and composition.

(d) *Finished product.* A completed product which has been bottled, sealed, packaged, and labeled as required by the regulations.

(e) *Released product.* A finished product released for marketing after all requirements have been satisfactorily complied with.

(f) *Fraction.* A specific antigen, its antibodies, or its antitoxin which constitutes a component of a biological product.

(g) *Diluent.* A liquid used to rehydrate a desiccated product or a liquid used to dilute another substance.

(h) *Serial.* The total quantity of completed product which has been thoroughly mixed in a single container and identified by a serial number: *Provided,* That, when all or part of a serial of liquid biological product is packaged as diluent for all or part of a serial of desiccated product, the resulting combination packages shall be considered a serial of the multiple fraction product.

(i) *Subserial.* Each of two or more properly identified portions of a serial which are further processed at different times or under different conditions such as, but not limited to, being desiccated in different size final containers and/or at different times.

(j) *Outline of production.* A detailed protocol of methods of manufacture to be followed in the preparation of a biological product and which may sometimes be referred to as an outline.

(k) *Product Code Number.* A number assigned by Animal and Plant Health Inspection Service to each type of licensed biological product.

(l) *Harvest date.* Unless otherwise specified in a filed Outline of Production, the harvest date shall be the date blood or tissues are collected for production or the date cultures of living microorganisms are removed from production incubators.

(m) *Bacterin.* An inactivated bacterial product consisting of an antigenic suspension of organisms or particulate parts of organisms, representing a whole culture or a concentrate thereof, with or without the unevaluated growth products, which has been inactivated as demonstrated by acceptable tests written into the filed Outline of Production for the product.

(n) *Toxoid.* An inactivated bacterial product which consists of a sterile, antigenic toxin or toxic growth product, which has resulted from the growth of bacterial organisms in a culture medium from which the bacterial cells have been removed, which has been inactivated without appreciable loss of antigenicity as measured by suitable tests, and which is nontoxic as demonstrated by acceptable tests written into the filed Outline of Production.

(o) *Bacterin-toxoid.* An inactivated bacterial product which is either:

(1) A suspension of organisms, representing a whole culture or a concentrate thereof, with the toxic growth products from the culture which has been inactivated without appreciable loss of antigenicity as measured by suitable tests, the inactivation of organisms and toxins being demonstrated by acceptable tests written into the filed Outline of Production: *Provided,* That it shall contain cellular antigens and shall stimulate the development of antitoxin; or

(2) A combination product in which one or more toxoids or bacterin-toxoids is combined with one or more bacterins or one or more bacterin-toxoids.

(p) *Bacterial extract.* An inactivated bacterial product which consists of the sterile, nontoxic, antigenic derivatives extracted from bacterial organisms or from culture medium in which bacterial organisms have grown.

(q) *Combination package.* Biological product consisting of two or more licensed biological products. Each completed product in final container is packaged together and mixed prior to administration. A combination package is issued a separate U.S. Veterinary Biological Product License and assigned a product code number to distinguish it from its component products, which also may be marketed individually unless otherwise restricted.

[38 FR 8426, Apr. 2, 1973, as amended at 42 FR 63770, Dec. 20, 1977; 50 FR 24903, June 14, 1985; 56 FR 66782, Dec. 26, 1991; 60 FR 14354, Mar. 17, 1995; 81 FR 59433, Aug. 30, 2016]

§ 101.4 Labeling terminology.

Terms pertaining to identification and packaging of biological products shall mean:

(a) *Label.* All written, graphic, or printed matter:

(1) Upon or attached to a final container of a biological product;

(2) Appearing upon any immediate carton or box used to package such final container; and

(3) Appearing on any accompanying enclosures (leaflets, inserts, or circulars) on which required information or directions as to the use of the biological product shall be found.

(b) *Labeling.* All labels and other written, printed, or graphic matter accompanying the final container.

(c) *Final container.* The unit, bottle, vial, ampule, tube, or other receptacle into which any biological product is filled for distribution and sale.

(d) *True name.* The name entered on the product license or permit at the time of issuance to differentiate the biological product from others: *Provided,* That, the principal part of such name shall be emphasized on such license or permit by being more prominently lettered than descriptive terms which may be necessary to complete the differentiation.

(e) *Serial number.* Numbers or numbers and letters used to identify and distinguish one serial from others.

(f) *Expiration date.* A date designating the end of the period during which a biological product, when properly stored and handled, can be expected with reasonable certainty, to be efficacious.

(g) *Label number.* A number assigned by Animal and Plant Health Inspection Service to each label or sketch submitted for review.

(h) *Master label.* The finished carton, container, or enclosure label for the smallest size final container that is authorized for a biological product, that serves as the Master template label applicable to all other size containers or cartons of the same product that is marketed by a licensee, subsidiary, division, or distributor.

[38 FR 8426, Apr. 2, 1973, as amended at 42 FR 63770, Dec. 20, 1977; 56 FR 66782, Dec. 26, 1991; 61 FR 29464, June 11, 1996]

§ 101.5 Testing terminology.

Terms used when evaluating biological products shall mean:

(a) *Standard Requirement.* Test methods, procedures, and criteria established by Animal and Plant Health Inspection Service for evaluating biological products to be pure, safe, potent, and efficacious, and not to be worthless, contaminated, dangerous, or harmful under the Act.

(b) *Log.* Logarithm computed to the base 10.

(c) *Pure or purity.* Quality of a biological product prepared to a final form relatively free of extraneous micro-organisms and extraneous material (organic or inorganic) as determined by test methods or procedures established by Animal and Plant Health Inspection Service in Standard Requirements or in the approved Outline of Production for such product, but free of extraneous microorganisms or material which in the opinion of the Administrator adversely affects the safety, potency, or efficacy of such product.

(d) *Safe or safety.* Freedom from properties causing undue local or systemic reactions when used as recommended or suggested by the manufacturer.

(e) *Sterile or sterility.* Freedom from viable contaminating microorganisms as demonstrated by procedures prescribed in part 113 of this subchapter, Standard Requirements, and approved Outlines of Production.

(f) *Potent or potency.* Relative strength of a biological product as determined by test methods or procedures as established by Animal and Plant Health Inspection Service in Standard Requirements or in the approved Outline of Production for such product.

(g) *Efficacious or efficacy.* Specific ability or capacity of the biological product to effect the result for which it is offered when used under the conditions recommended by the manufacturer.

(h) *Dose.* The amount of a biological product recommended on the label to be given to one animal at one time.

(i) *Vaccinate.* An animal which has been inoculated, injected, or otherwise administered a biological product being evaluated.

(j) *Control animal.* An animal, which may be referred to as a control, used in a test procedure for purposes of comparison or to add validity to the results.

(k) *Day.* Time elapsing between any regular working hour of one day and any regular working hour of the following day.

(l) *Test results.* Terms used to designate testing results are as follows:

(1) *No Test.* Designation used when a deficiency in the test system has rendered a test unsuitable for drawing a valid conclusion.

(2) *Satisfactory.* Designation is a final conclusion given to a valid test with results that meet the release criteria stated in the filed Outline of Production or Standard Requirement.

(3) *Unsatisfactory.* Designation is a final conclusion given to a valid test with results that do not meet the release criteria stated in the filed Outline of Production or Standard Requirement.

(4) *Inconclusive.* Designation used for an initial test when a sequential test design established in the filed Outline of Production or Standard Requirement allows further testing if a valid initial test is not satisfactory.

(m) *Healthy.* Apparently normal in all vital functions and free of signs of disease.

(n) *Unfavorable reactions.* Overt adverse changes which occur in healthy test animals subsequent to initiation of a test and manifested during the observation period prescribed in the test protocol which are attributable either to the biological product being tested or to factors unrelated to such product as determined by the responsible individual conducting the test.

(o) *Master reference.* A Master Reference is a reference whose potency is correlated, directly or indirectly, to host animal immunogenicity. The Master Reference may be used as the working reference in in vitro tests for relative potency. The Master Reference may also be used to establish the relative potency of a serial of product used in requalification studies and to establish the relative potency of working references. The preparation of a Master Reference as described in a filed Outline of Production may be:

(1) A completed serial of vaccine or bacterin prepared in accordance with a filed Outline of Production;

(2) A purified preparation of a protective immunogen or antigen; or

(3) A nonadjuvanted harvested culture of microorganisms.

(p) *Working reference.* A Working Reference is the reference preparation that is used in the in vitro test for the release of serials of product. Working References may be:

(1) Master References; or

(2) Serials of product that have been prepared and qualified, in a manner acceptable to Animal and Plant Health Inspection Service for use as reference preparations.

(q) *Qualifying serial.* (1) A serial of biological product used to test for immunogenicity when the Master or Working Reference is a purified antigen or nonadjuvanted harvest material. Qualifying serials shall be produced in accordance with the filed Outline of Production, tested for immunogenicity in accordance with methods deemed appropriate by the Animal and Plant Health Inspection Service, and have a geometric mean relative potency, when compared to the Master Reference, of not greater than 1.0 as established by: independent parallel line assays with five or more replicates; or other valid assay methods for determining relative antigen content which demonstrate linearity, specificity, and reproducibility at least equivalent to the parallel line assay and are acceptable to the Animal and Plant Health Inspection Service.

(2) Qualifying serials used to requalify or extend the dating period of a Master Reference shall be determined to be immunogenic in accordance with methods deemed appropriate by the Animal and Plant Health Inspection Service as provided in paragraph (a)(1) of this section, and, in addition, shall be within their permitted dating period and have been prepared in accordance with the production method described in the currently filed Outline of Production.

(r) *Immunogenicity.* The ability of a biological product to elicit an immune response in animals as determined by test methods or procedures acceptable to the Animal and Plant Health Inspection Service.

[38 FR 8426, Apr. 2, 1973, as amended at 40 FR 45419, Oct. 2, 1975; 41 FR 6751, Feb. 13, 1976; 43 FR 3701, Jan. 27, 1978; 56 FR 66782, 66783 Dec. 26, 1991; 62 FR 19037, Apr. 18, 1997; 79 FR 55969, Sept. 18, 2014]

§ 101.6 Cell cultures.

When used in conjunction with or in reference to cell cultures, which may be referred to as tissue cultures, the following terms shall mean:

(a) *Batches of primary cells.* A pool of original cells derived from normal tissue up to and including the 10th subculture.

(b) *Cell line.* A pool of cells which are 11 or more subcultures from the tissue of origin.

(c) *Subculture.* Each flask to flask transfer or passage regardless of the number of cell replications.

(d) *Master Cell Stock (MCS).* The supply of cells of a specific passage level from which cells for production of biologics originate.

[38 FR 8426, Apr. 2, 1973, as amended at 40 FR 45419, Oct. 2, 1975; 49 FR 22624, May 31, 1984]

§ 101.7 Seed organisms.

When used in conjunction with or in reference to seed organisms, the following shall mean:

(a) *Master Seed.* An organism at a specific passage level which has been selected and permanently stored by the producer from which all other seed passages are derived within permitted levels.

(b) *Working Seed.* An organism at a passage level between Master Seed and Production Seed.

(c) *Production Seed.* An organism at a specified passage level which is used without further propagation for initiating preparation of a fraction.

[49 FR 22625, May 31, 1984]

PART 102—LICENSES FOR BIOLOGICAL PRODUCTS

AUTHORITY: 21 U.S.C. 151–159; 7 CFR 2.22, 2.80, and 371.4.

§ 102.1 Licenses issued by the Administrator.

Each establishment qualified to prepare biological products under the Virus-Serum-Toxin Act shall hold an unexpired and unrevoked U.S. Veterinary Biologics Establishment License issued by the Administrator and a U.S. Veterinary Biological Product License for each product prepared in such establishment unless the product is subject to the provisions of 9 CFR parts 103 or 106 of this subchapter.

[60 FR 48021, Sept. 18, 1995]

§ 102.2 Licenses required.

(a) Every person who prepares biological products subject to the Virus-Serum-Toxin Act shall hold an unexpired, unsuspended, and unrevoked U.S. Veterinary Biologics Establishment License and at least one unexpired, unsuspended, and unrevoked U.S. Veterinary Biological Product License issued by the Administrator to prepare a biological product.

(b) An applicant who applies for an establishment license must also apply for at least one product license. An establishment license will not be issued without a license authorizing the production of a biological product in the establishment.

[52 FR 11026, Apr. 7, 1987, as amended at 56 FR 66783, Dec. 26, 1991; 61 FR 52873, Oct. 9, 1996]

§ 102.3 License applications.

(a) *U.S. Veterinary Biologics Establishment License.* (1) The operator of each establishment of the kind specified in § 102.2 shall make written application to the Administrator for a license. Blank forms of application will be furnished upon request to Animal and Plant Health Inspection Service.

(2) When a person conducts more than one establishment, a separate application shall be made for each establishment.

(3) Whenever subsidiaries are to operate in an establishment for which license application is made, the applicant shall apply for permission for such subsidiaries to operate in the establishment and furnish therewith a complete statement regarding the relationship between the applicant and the subsidiaries.

(4) Facilities documents, prepared as prescribed in part 108 of this subchapter, shall accompany the application for license unless previously filed with Animal and Plant Health Inspection Service.

(5) Each application for a U.S. Veterinary Biologics Establishment License shall be accompanied by an application for one or more U.S. Veterinary Biological Product Licenses and the supporting documents required by paragraph (b)(2) of this section.

(6) A new application shall be made when a change of ownership, operation, or location of an establishment occurs; or prior to the expiration of a U.S. Veterinary Biologics Establishment License issued for an interim period of time.

(b) *U.S. Veterinary Biological Product License.* (1) The licensee of each establishment or applicant for an establishment license shall make written application to the Administrator for a U.S. Veterinary Biological Product License for each biological product to be prepared in the licensed establishment.

(2) Each application for a U.S. Veterinary Biological Product License shall be supported by:

(i) At least two copies of an Outline of Production prepared in accordance with §§ 114.8 and 114.9 of this subchapter; and

(ii) At least three copies of test reports and research data sufficient to establish purity, safety, potency, and efficacy of the product; and

(iii) Legends prepared as prescribed in § 108.5 of this subchapter designating which facilities are to be used in the preparation of each fraction; and

(iv) Labels in finished form or sketches prepared as prescribed in §112.5 of this subchapter, together with information regarding all claims to be made on labels and in advertising matter to be used in connection with or related to the biological product.

(Approved by the Office of Management and Budget under control number 0579–0013)

[39 FR 37763, Oct. 24, 1974, as amended at 48 FR 57472, Dec. 30, 1983; 49 FR 21043, May 18, 1984; 50 FR 50763, Dec. 12, 1985; 56 FR 66783, Dec. 26, 1991; 75 FR 20772, Apr. 21, 2010]

§ 102.4 U.S. Veterinary Biologics Establishment License.

(a) Before a U.S. Veterinary Biologics Establishment License will be issued by the Administrator for any establishment, an inspection shall be made to determine whether the condition, equipment, facilities, and the like, of the establishment, and the methods used to prepare biological products are in conformity with the requirements in the regulations.

(b) A license shall not be issued unless:

(1) In the opinion of the Administrator, the condition of the establishment, including its facilities, and the methods of preparation of biological products are such as reasonably to assure that the products shall accomplish the purpose for which they are intended; and

(2) The Administrator is satisfied on the basis of information before him that:

(i) The establishment shall be operated in compliance with the Act and applicable regulations and be under the supervision of person(s) competent in the preparation of biological products; and

(ii) The applicant, or the person having the responsibility for producing biological products in the establishment, or both, is qualified by education and experience, and has demonstrated fitness to produce such products in compliance with the Act and regulations issued pursuant thereto; *Provided*, That, previous violations of the Act, or such regulations or both shall be relevant to the Administrator's determination of fitness.

(3) Written assurance is filed with Animal and Plant Health Inspection Service that the biological products which are licensed to be prepared therein shall not be so advertised as to mislead or deceive the purchasers and that the packages or containers in which the same are to be marketed shall not bear any statement, design, or device which is false or misleading in any particular.

(c) U.S. Veterinary Biologics Establishment Licenses shall be numbered.

(d) Two or more licenses may bear the same number when they are issued for establishments under the same ownership or control, provided a serial letter is added to one or more to identify each license and the product produced thereunder.

(e) When a U.S. Veterinary Biologics Establishment License is issued for an establishment, it shall not apply to more than one person at the same location, except that subsidiaries of the licensee, when named in the license, may operate thereunder at the establishment named. The licensee with its subsidiaries will be held responsible for all operations conducted in the licensed establishment.

(f) When a licensee no longer holds at least one unexpired, unsuspended, or unrevoked product license authorizing the preparation of a biological product, or is in the process of obtaining a product license, the establishment license shall no longer be valid and shall be returned to the Administrator. In the case where an establishment license expires or is suspended or revoked, any product license authorizing preparation of a product at such establishment shall be invalid indefinitely or for as long as the suspension is in effect.

(g) Any license issued under this part to establishments in which biological products are prepared shall be issued on condition that the licensee permit the inspection of such establishments, products, product preparation, and all relevant records as provided in part 115 of this subchapter. Failure to permit inspection may result in the license being suspended or revoked.

(h) The provisions of paragraph (b) of this section shall also be applicable to, and be considered by, the Administrator in connection with each application for an additional product license.

(Approved by the Office of Management and Budget under control number 0579–0013)

[39 FR 37762, Oct. 24, 1974; 39 FR 38364, Nov. 1, 1974, as amended at 41 FR 44359, Oct. 8, 1976; 48 FR 57472, Dec. 30, 1983; 52 FR 11026, Apr. 7, 1987; 52 FR 30131, Aug. 13, 1987; 56 FR 66783, Dec. 26, 1991; 60 FR 48021, Sept. 18, 1995; 61 FR 52873, Oct. 9, 1996; 62 FR 13294, Mar. 20, 1997]

§ 102.5 U.S. Veterinary Biological Product License.

(a) Authorization to produce each biological product shall be specified on a U.S. Veterinary Biological Product License, issued by the Administrator, and supplementary to the U.S. Veterinary Biologics Establishment License named therein.

(b) The following shall appear on the U.S. Veterinary Biological Product License:

(1) The U.S. Veterinary Biologics Establishment License Number for the establishment from which the product is released for marketing.

(2) The true name of the product.

(3) The product code number for the product.

(4) The date of issuance.

(5) Any restrictions designated by the Administrator under paragraph (e) of this section.

(6) When necessary to comply with § 102.6 of this part, a termination date and a brief description of requirements to be met for reissuance.

(c) The following provisions shall apply to all licensed biological products:

(1) Licensed biological products shall be prepared as required by the regulations and in accordance with a filed Outline of Production as prescribed in §§ 114.8 and 114.9 of this subchapter. No change shall be made in the preparation of a biological product without prior approval of the Administrator.

(2) In addition to restrictions imposed by the Administrator pursuant to paragraph (e) of this section, biological products may be subject to restrictions which are imposed by any State or other jurisdiction pertaining to the distribution and use of such products, based on local disease conditions.

(3) When requested by the Administrator, a licensee shall submit a list of licensed biological products prepared in the licensed establishment.

(d) Where the Administrator determines that the protection of domestic animals or the public health, interest, or safety, or both, necessitates restrictions on the use of a product, the product shall be subject to such additional restrictions as are prescribed on the license. Such restrictions may include, but are not limited to, limits on distribution of the product or provisions that the biological product is restricted to use by veterinarians, or under the supervision of veterinarians, or both.

(e) Any person may request that the distribution and use of a veterinary biological product be restricted if the restriction pertains to the protection of domestic animals or the public health, interest, or safety, or both. All requests must be sent, in writing, to the Director, Center for Veterinary Biologics, Policy, Evaluation, and Licensing, 1920 Dayton Avenue, P.O. Box 844, Ames, IA 50010. Requests must specify the restriction(s) being requested and must explain why the restrictions are needed. Copies of any supporting documents, such as scientific literature, published or unpublished articles, or data from tests, should be attached to the request. When a decision is reached regarding the request, the person submitting the request will be sent written notification of such decision.

(Approved by the Office of Management and Budget under control number 0579–0013)

[39 FR 37763, Oct. 24, 1974, as amended at 48 FR 57472, Dec. 30, 1983; 50 FR 50764, Dec. 12, 1985; 52 FR 11026, Apr. 7, 1987; 56 FR 66783, Dec. 26, 1991; 57 FR 38760, Aug. 27, 1992; 59 FR 67616, Dec. 30, 1994; 62 FR 13294, Mar. 20, 1997; 64 FR 43044, Aug. 9, 1999; 75 FR 20772, Apr. 21, 2010]

§ 102.6 Conditional licenses.

In order to meet an emergency condition, limited market, local situation, or other special circumstance, including production solely for intrastate use under a State-operated program, the Administrator may, in response to an application submitted as specified in

§102.3(b) of this part, issue a conditional U.S. Veterinary Biological Product License to an establishment under an expedited procedure which assures purity and safety, and a reasonable expectation of efficacy. Preparation of products under a conditional license shall be in compliance with all applicable regulations and standards and may be restricted as follows:

(a) The preparation may be limited to a predetermined time period which shall be established at the time of issuance and specified on the license. Prior to termination of the license, the licensee may request reissuance. Such requests shall be substantiated with data and information obtained since the license was issued. After considering all data and information available, the Administrator shall either reissue the U.S. Veterinary Biological Product License or allow it to terminate.

(b) Distribution may be limited to the extent necessary to assure that the product will meet the basic criteria for issuance of the conditional license.

(c) Labeling for the product may be required to contain information on the conditional status of the license.

[52 FR 11026, Apr. 7, 1987, as amended at 60 FR 48021; Sept. 18, 1995]

PART 103—EXPERIMENTAL PRODUCTION, DISTRIBUTION, AND EVALUATION OF BIOLOGICAL PRODUCTS PRIOR TO LICENSING

Sec.

AUTHORITY: 21 U.S.C. 151–159; 7 CFR 2.22, 2.80, and 371.4.

§103.1 Preparation of experimental biological products.

Except as otherwise provided in this section, experimental biological products which are neither composed of nor prepared with organisms or antigens used in biologicals already licensed, shall not be prepared in the production facilities of a licensed establishment. Upon application therefor, the Administrator may authorize the preparation of experimental products on the premises of a licensed establishment if he determines that such preparation will not result in contamination of the licensed products. Each request for permission to prepare an experimental biological product on licensed premises shall indicate the nature of the unlicensed product, designate facilities to be used, and specify precautions which will be taken to prevent contamination of licensed products. Such requests shall be submitted to the Administrator. Research facilities that are entirely separate and apart from facilities used for the preparation of licensed biological products will not be considered a part of the licensed premises for purposes of this section.

(Approved by the Office of Management and Budget under control number 0579–0013)

[30 FR 11848, Sept. 16, 1965, as amended at 48 FR 57473, Dec. 30, 1983; 56 FR 66783, Dec. 26, 1991]

§103.2 Disposition of animals administered experimental biological products or live organisms.

Safeguards as herein provided shall be established by the research investigator or research sponsor to control disposition of all animals administered experimental biological products or live organisms.

(a) Surviving test animals (including challenged control animals) shall not be removed from the premises on which the tests are conducted for at least 14 days after administration of an experimental biological product or live organisms: *Provided, however,* That this holding period may be increased or decreased as permitted or requested by the Administrator following review of all relevant information or data available.

(b) All animals administered experimental biological products which are to be slaughtered at establishments subject to the Federal Meat Inspection Act, as amended and extended (21 U.S.C. 601 *et. seq.*) are subject to the applicable requirements of §309.16 of this title (Meat Inspection Regulations).

(c) Except as otherwise provided in this paragraph, the research investigator or research sponsor shall maintain adequate records relative to the disposition of each animal administered experimental biological products. These records shall be maintained for a minimum period of two years from the date that an experimental product was administered to such animal, and shall show the name and address of the owner; number, species, class and location of the animals; and if sold, the name and address of the consignee, buyer, commission, firm or abattoir: *Provided, however,* That a research investigator or research sponsor may be exempted from these recordkeeping requirements by the Administrator on the basis of acceptable data demonstrating that use of the experimental biological product will not result in the presence of any unwholesome condition in the edible parts of animals subsequently presented for slaughter.

(Approved by the Office of Management and Budget under control number 0579–0059)

[30 FR 11848, Sept. 16, 1965, as amended at 48 FR 57473, Dec. 30, 1983; 56 FR 66783, Dec. 26, 1991; 66 FR 21063, Apr. 27, 2001]

§ 103.3 Shipment of experimental biological products.

Except as provided in this section, no person shall ship or deliver for shipment in or from the United States, the District of Columbia, or any Territory of the United States any unlicensed biological product for experimental use in animals. For the benefit of license applicants and to permit and encourage research, a person may be authorized by the Administrator to ship unlicensed biological products for the purpose of evaluating such experimental products by treating limited numbers of animals, *Provided,* that, the Administrator determines that the conditions under which the experiment is to be conducted are adequate to prevent the spread of disease and approves the procedures set forth in the request for such authorization. Special restrictions or tests may be imposed, especially in the case of products containing live organisms, when they are deemed necessary or advisable by the Administrator. A request for authorization to ship an unlicensed biological product for experimental study and evaluation shall be accompanied by the following:

(a) One copy of a permit or letter of permission from the proper State or foreign animal health authorities of each State or foreign country involved.

(b) Two copies of a tentative list of the names of the proposed recipients and quantity of experimental product that is to be shipped to each individual. In the event of subsequent changes, additional information shall be furnished when such facts are known;

(c) Two copies of a description of the product, recommendations for use, and results of preliminary research work;

(d) A copy of the labels or label sketches which show the name or identification of the product and bear the statement "Notice! For experimental use only-Not For Sale" or equivalent. Such statement shall appear on final container labels, except that it may appear on the carton in the case of very small final container labels and labeling for diagnostic test kits. The U.S. Veterinary License legend shall not appear on such labels; and

(e) Two copies of a proposed general plan covering the methods and procedures for evaluating the product and for maintaining records of the quantities of experimental product prepared, shipped and used. At the conclusion of field studies, results shall be obtained, summarized, and submitted to the Animal and Plant Health Inspection Service.

(f) Data acceptable to the Administrator demonstrating that use of the experimental biological product in meat animals is not likely to result in the presence of any unwholesome condition in the edible parts of animals subsequently presented for slaughter.

(g) A statement from the research investigator or research sponsor agreeing to furnish, upon the Administrator's request, additional information concerning each group of meat animals involved prior to movement of these animals from the premises where the test is to be conducted. Such information shall include the owner's name and address; number, species, class and location of animals involved; date shipment is anticipated; along with name and address of consignee, buyer, commission firm or abattoir.

(h) Any information the Administrator may require in order to assess the product's impact on the environment.

[26 FR 7726, Aug. 18, 1961, as amended at 30 FR 11848, Sept. 16, 1965; 52 FR 30131, Aug. 13, 1987; 56 FR 66783, Dec. 26, 1991; 75 FR 20772, Apr. 21, 2010; 81 FR 59433, Aug. 30, 2016]

PART 104—PERMITS FOR BIOLOGICAL PRODUCTS

Sec.

AUTHORITY: 21 U.S.C. 151–159; 7 CFR 2.22, 2.80, and 371.4.

SOURCE: 38 FR 32916, Nov. 29, 1973, unless otherwise noted.

§ 104.1 Permit required.

Unless otherwise authorized or directed by the Administrator, each permit to import a biological product into the United States shall be issued in accordance with the regulations in this part.

(a) No biological product shall be brought into the United States unless a permit has been issued for such product. A separate U.S. Veterinary Biological Product Permit shall be required for each shipment of biological product to be imported: *Provided*, That, a permit shall also be required for each transit shipment of biological products moved through the United States.

(b) Each person importing biological products shall hold an unexpired, unsuspended, and unrevoked permit issued by Animal and Plant Health Inspection Service. Such person shall reside within the United States, or operate a business establishment within the United States, or both.

[38 FR 32916, Nov. 29, 1973, as amended at 56 FR 66783, Dec. 26, 1991; 56 FR 66783, Dec. 26, 1991]

§ 104.2 Permit authorized.

(a) Animal and Plant Health Inspection Service is authorized to issue three types of permits for importing biological products. They shall be:

(1) U.S. Veterinary Biological Product Permit for Research and Evaluation;

(2) U.S. Veterinary Biological Product Permit for Distribution and Sale; or

(3) U.S. Veterinary Biological Product Permit for Transit Shipment Only.

(b) A permit shall not be issued for a biological product from countries known to have exotic diseases, including but not limited to foot-and-mouth disease, rinderpest, highly pathogenic avian influenzaswine vesicular disease, Newcastle disease, and African swine fever, if in the opinion of the Administrator, such products may endanger the livestock or poultry of this country.

(c) A permit shall not be issued until an inspector has determined the condition of the equipment and facilities of the producer, of the applicant, or of both if such a determination is considered necessary by the Administrator.

(d) A permit shall not be issued for a biological product prepared in the United States, exported, and presented for reentry except as provided in § 104.4(d).

[38 FR 32916, Nov. 29, 1973, as amended at 56 FR 66783, Dec. 26, 1991; 56 FR 66783, Dec. 26, 1991; 78 FR 19085, Mar. 29, 2013]

§ 104.3 Permit application.

(a) Each person desiring to import a biological product shall make written application to Animal and Plant Health Inspection Service for a permit. Application forms are available on the Internet at (*http://www.aphis.usda.gov/animal_health/ vet_biologics/vb_forms.shtml*) and application for a permit to import a veterinary biologic for research and evaluation or transit shipment may be made on the Internet at (*http://www.aphis.usda.gov/animal_health/permits/vet_bio_permits.shtml*).

(b) The application shall specify the type of permit required, the port of entry at which the product shall be cleared through Customs, the estimated quantity involved, and the anticipated date on which the importation shall be made.

(Approved by the Office of Management and Budget under control number 0579–0013)

[38 FR 32916, Nov. 29, 1973, as amended at 48 FR 57473, Dec. 30, 1983; 56 FR 66783, Dec. 26, 1991; 75 FR 20772, Apr. 21, 2010]

§ 104.4 Products for research and evaluation.

(a) An application for a U.S. Veterinary Biological Product Permit to import a biological product for research and evaluation shall be accompanied by a brief description of such product, methods of propagating antigens including composition of medium, species of animals or cell cultures involved, degree of inactivation or attenuation, recommendations for use, and the proposed plan of evaluation. The applicant shall also provide any information the Administrator may require in order to assess the product's impact on the environment.

(b)(1) A permit to import a biological product for research and evaluation shall not be issued unless the scientific capabilities of the investigator are determined to be adequate to safeguard domestic animals and protect public health, interest, or safety from any deleterious effects which might result from use of such product. Special restrictions or tests may be specified as part of the permit when they are deemed necessary or advisable by the Administrator.

(2) No person shall ship a product imported under this section for research and evaluation anywhere in or from the United States unless authorized by the Administrator in accordance with the provisions of § 103.3 of this subchapter.

(c) A biological product shall not be imported for Research and Evaluation which is not packaged and labeled in accordance with § 112.9 of this subchapter.

(d) When a licensed product has been exported from the United States, a permit may be issued to the producer for a small quantity of such product for in vitro Research and Evaluation tests: *Provided*, That, the importation of such product will not endanger the livestock or poultry of this country.

(Approved by the Office of Management and Budget under control number 0579–0013)

[38 FR 32916, Nov. 29, 1973, as amended at 48 FR 57473, Dec. 30, 1983; 52 FR 30131, Aug. 13, 1987; 56 FR 66783, Dec. 26, 1991]

§ 104.5 Products for distribution and sale.

An application for a U.S. Veterinary Biological Product Permit to import a biological product for Distribution and Sale shall be accompanied by supporting material necessary to satisfy the requirements provided in this section.

(a) A permit shall not be issued unless the conditions under which the biological product is to be prepared or the methods to be used are such as to reasonably insure that the product is pure, safe, potent, and efficacious.

(1) Two copies of blueprints of the producing foreign establishment shall be submitted with the application unless satisfactory plans are on file with Animal and Plant Health Inspection Service from a previous application. The production facilities to be used for each product prepared at the establishment shall be designated.

(2) The manufacturer shall submit written authorization for properly accredited inspectors to inspect without previous notification, and at such times as may be demanded by the aforesaid inspectors, all parts of the establishment in which biological products shall be prepared, all processes of preparation, and all records relative to such preparation.

(3) The manufacturer shall furnish written assurance that a biological product to be imported for Distribution and Sale shall be prepared under the supervision of a person competent by education and experience to handle all matters pertaining to the preparation of such product and that each biological product shall be prepared in accordance with the regulations applicable to the product or in a manner acceptable to the Administrator so as to carry out the purposes of the Act.

(4) The methods to be used in the preparation of each biological product

shall be written into an approved Outline of Production prepared in accordance with the applicable provisions of part 114 of this subchapter. Two copies of such Outlines of Production shall be submitted to Animal and Plant Health Inspection Service and be approved before the permit is issued.

(5) Data shall be furnished by the applicant which establishes that the product involved complies with the provisions of the Act and the regulations issued pursuant thereto. When deemed necessary to obtain required information, Animal and Plant Health Inspection Service may require that the product be tested under field conditions within or outside the United States as the occasion demands.

(b) The permittee shall furnish the following:

(1) Adequate facilities for storing all imported biological products. An inspection of such facilities shall be made by inspectors before a permit is issued and additional inspections shall be made at any time subsequent to the importation of the biological products if deemed necessary by the Administrator;

(2) Information regarding all claims to be made on labels and advertising matter used in connection with or related to the biological product to be imported;

(3) Mounted copies of final container labels, carton labels, and enclosures to be used with the imported product as provided in part 112 of this subchapter; and

(4) Samples of each serial from each shipment of biological products imported or offered for importation. Such samples shall be collected, examined, and tested in a manner specified by the Administrator. The biological products being sampled shall not be further distributed by the permittee until released by Animal and Plant Health Inspection Service.

(Approved by the Office of Management and Budget under control number 0579–0013)

[38 FR 32916, Nov. 29, 1973, as amended at 48 FR 57473, Dec. 30, 1983; 49 FR 21044, May 18, 1984; 56 FR 66783, Dec. 26, 1991; 75 FR 20772, Apr. 21, 2010]

§ 104.6 Products for transit shipment only.

An application for a permit for Transit Shipment Only shall be required when a biological product is being shipped from one foreign country to another foreign country by way of the United States. The shipment shall move under a permit subject to the following restrictions:

(a) The shipment shall be confined to the carrier at all times when such shipment is to transit the United States on the same carrier on which it arrived. If the shipment is to be transferred to a carrier other than the one on which it shall arrive into the United States, a schedule of arrival and departure of each shipment shall be furnished by the permittee to Animal and Plant Health Inspection Service prior to arrival in the United States.

(b) The permittee shall be responsible to Animal and Plant Health Inspection Service for handling, storing, and forwarding of the biological product. Animal and Plant Health Inspection Service shall be notified of all shipments received and forwarded by the permittee and an accurate accounting shall be made.

(Approved by the Office of Management and Budget under control number 0579–0013)

[38 FR 32916, Nov. 29, 1973, as amended at 48 FR 57473, Dec. 30, 1983; 56 FR 66784, Dec. 26, 1991; 61 FR 52873, Oct. 9, 1996]

§ 104.7 Product permit.

(a) A permit shall be numbered and dated.

(b) The purpose for which the product is imported shall be specified on the permit as for Research and Evaluation, Distribution and Sale, or Transit Shipment Only.

(c) A permit shall not be used after the date specified.

[38 FR 32916, Nov. 29, 1973, as amended at 56 FR 66783, Dec. 26, 1991; 62 FR 13294, Mar. 20, 1997]

§ 104.8 Illegal shipments.

(a) Biological products which are presented for importation without a permit having been issued shall be returned to the country of origin at the expense of the importer or in lieu thereof, destroyed by Department personnel.

(b) Biological products for Distribution and Sale presented for importation under a permit and found to be worthless, contaminated, dangerous, or harmful shall, within a period of 30 days after such finding, be returned to the country of origin at the expense of the importer or in lieu thereof, destroyed by Department personnel: *Provided*, That such product shall not be returned to the country of origin while bearing a U.S. permit number on the label.

PART 105—SUSPENSION, REVOCATION, OR TERMINATION OF BIOLOGICAL LICENSES OR PERMITS

Sec.

AUTHORITY: 21 U.S.C. 151–159; 7 CFR 2.22, 2.80, and 371.4.

§ 105.1 Suspension or revocation.

(a) An establishment license, product license, or permit issued under the Virus-Serum-Toxin Act may be formally suspended or revoked after opportunity for hearing has been accorded the licensee or permittee as provided in part 123 of this subchapter if the Secretary is satisfied that the license or permit is being used to facilitate or effect the preparation, sale, barter, exchange, shipment, or importation contrary to said Act of any worthless, contaminated, dangerous, or harmful biological product. Such use may be found to exist if:

(1) The construction of the establishment in which the biological product is prepared is defective, or the establishment is not conducted as required by the regulations in parts 101 through 118 of this subchapter;

(2) The methods of preparation of the product are faulty, or the product contains impurities or lacks potency;

(3) The product is so labeled or advertised as to mislead or deceive the purchaser in any particular;

(4) The licensee, permittee, or the foreign manufacturer has failed to maintain and make available for inspection records in connection with the development and preparation of product, has failed to provide complete and accurate information when requested, or has failed to provide complete and accurate information in the Outline of Production or in reports and records;

(5) The licensee or permittee has violated or failed to comply with any provision of the Virus-Serum-Toxin Act or the regulations in this subchapter;

(6) The license or permit is otherwise used to facilitate or effect the preparation, sale, barter, exchange, shipment, or importation, contrary to the Virus-Serum-Toxin Act, of any worthless, contaminated, dangerous, or harmful biological product.

(b) In case of willfulness or where the public health, interest, or safety so required the Secretary may, without hearing, informally suspend such establishment license, product license, or permit upon the grounds set forth in paragraph (a) of this section pending determination of formal proceedings under part 123 of this subchapter for suspension or revocation of the license or permit.

[38 FR 23512, Aug. 31, 1973, as amended at 41 FR 44359, Oct. 8, 1976; 61 FR 52874, Oct. 9, 1996; 64 FR 43044, Aug. 9, 1999]

§ 105.2 Notification of infractions.

If an infraction of a requirement of a product license is brought to the attention of the licensee by written notification thereof by Animal and Plant Health Inspection Service, a subsequent violation of similar nature occurring with the same licensed biological product within 6 months of the said written notification shall be primafacie evidence of willful violation and the license for the product shall be subject to suspension or revocation under the provisions of § 105.1(b).

[42 FR 31430, June 21, 1977, as amended at 56 FR 66783, Dec. 26, 1991]

§ 105.3 Notices re: worthless, contaminated, dangerous, or harmful biological products.

(a) If at any time it appears that the preparation, sale, barter, exchange, shipment, or importation, as provided in the Virus-Serum-Toxin Act, of any biological product by any person holding a license or permit may be dangerous in the treatment of domestic animals, the Secretary may without hearing notify the licensee or permittee, and pending determination of formal proceedings instituted under part 123 of this subchapter for suspension or revocation of the license or permit insofar as it authorizes the manufacture or importation of the particular product, no person so notified shall thereafter so prepare, sell, barter, exchange, ship, deliver for shipment, or import such product.

(b) If a serial of biological product is found to be unsatisfactory according to applicable Standard Requirements, the Administrator may notify the licensee to stop distribution and sale of the serial.

(c) When notified to stop distribution and sale of a serial or subserial of a veterinary biological product under the provisions of paragraph (a) or (b) of this section, veterinary biologics licensees or permittees shall:

(1) Stop the preparation, distribution, sale, barter, exchange, shipment, or importation of the affected serial(s) or subserial(s) of any veterinary biological product pending further instructions from APHIS.

(2) Immediately, but no later than 2 days, send stop distribution and sale notifications to any wholesalers, jobbers, dealers, foreign consignees, or other persons known to have any such veterinary biological product in their possession, which instruct them to stop the preparation, distribution, sale, barter, exchange, shipment, or importation of any such veterinary biological product. All notifications shall be documented in writing by the licensee or permittee.

(3) Account for the remaining quantity of each serial(s) or subserial(s) of any such veterinary biological product at each location in the distribution channel known to the manufacturer (licensee) or importer (permittee).

(4) When required by the Administrator, submit complete and accurate reports of all notifications concerning stop distribution and sale actions to the Animal and Plant Health Inspection Service pursuant to § 116.5 of this subchapter.

(Approved by the Office of Management and Budget under control number 0579–0318)

[38 FR 23512, Aug. 31, 1973, as amended at 56 FR 66783, Dec. 26, 1991; 72 FR 17798, Apr. 10, 2007]

§ 105.4 Termination of licenses and permits for inactivity.

(a) If a biological product has not been prepared by a licensee, or imported by a permittee for a period of 5 years or more, the Administrator may require the licensee to show intent to resume production, or the permittee to show intent to resume importation, within 6 months of notification. If the licensee does not resume preparation, or the permittee does not resume importation, within 6 months of notification, or within a mutually agreeable period, the product license, or permit, may be terminated by the Administrator.

(b) When a license or permit is terminated, the licensee or permittee shall continue to be subject to the applicable records provisions of § 116.8.

[61 FR 52874, Oct. 9, 1996]

PART 106—EXEMPTION FOR BIOLOGICAL PRODUCTS USED IN DEPARTMENT PROGRAMS OR UNDER DEPARTMENT CONTROL OR SUPERVISION

AUTHORITY: 21 U.S.C. 151–159; 7 CFR 2.22, 2.80, and 371.4.

§ 106.1 Biological products; exemption.

The Administrator may exempt any biological product from one or more of the requirements of this subchapter if he determines that such product will be used by the Department or under the supervision or control of the Department in the prevention, control or eradication of animal diseases in connection with (a) an official USDA program; or (b) an emergency animal disease situation, or (c) a USDA experimental use of the product.

[45 FR 65184, Oct. 2, 1980, as amended at 56 FR 66783, Dec. 26, 1991]

PART 107—EXEMPTIONS FROM PREPARATION PURSUANT TO AN UNSUSPENDED AND UNREVOKED LICENSE

AUTHORITY: 21 U.S.C. 151–159; 7 CFR 2.22, 2.80, and 371.4.

§ 107.1 Veterinary practitioners and animal owners.

Products prepared as provided in paragraphs (a) and (b) of this section and facilities in which such products are prepared, shall be exempt from preparation pursuant to unsuspended and unrevoked establishment and product licenses. Persons exempt from licensure under this part shipping products which contain live organisms shall provide any information the Administrator may require prior to shipment, or at any other time deemed necessary, in order to assess the products' safety and effect on the environment. The shipment or delivery for shipment anywhere in or from the United States of any exempted product which is worthless, contaminated, dangerous, or harmful is prohibited, and any person shipping such product, or delivering such product for shipment, shall be subject to sanctions under the Act.

(a)(1) Products prepared by a veterinary practitioner (veterinarian) solely for administration to animals in the course of a State licensed professional practice of veterinary medicine by such veterinarian under a veterinarian-client-patient relationship and facilities in which such products are prepared shall be exempt from licensing under the Act and regulations. Such a relationship is considered to exist when:

(i) The veterinarian has assumed the responsibility for making medical judgments regarding the health of the animal(s) and the need for medical treatment, and the client (owner or other caretaker) has agreed to follow the instructions of the veterinarian; and when

(ii) There is sufficient knowledge of the animal(s) by the veterinarian to initiate at least a general or preliminary diagnosis of the medical condition of the animal(s). This means that the veterinarian has recently seen and is personally acquainted with the keeping and care of the animal(s), and/or by medically appropriate and timely visits to the premises where the animal(s) are kept; and when

(iii) The practicing veterinarian is readily available for followup in case of adverse reactions or failure of the regimen.

(2) All steps in the preparation of product being prepared under the exemption in paragraph (a)(1) of this section must be performed at the facilities that the veterinarian utilizes for the day-to-day activities associated with the treatment of animals in the course of his/her State-licensed professional practice of veterinary medicine. A veterinary assistant employed by the veterinary practitioner and working at the veterinary practice's facility under the veterinarian's direct supervision may perform the steps in the preparation of product. Such preparation may not be consigned to any other party or sub-contracted to a commercial laboratory/manufacturing facility.

(3) Veterinarians preparing products subject to the exemption for products under this section shall maintain and make available for inspection by Animal and Plant Health Inspection Service representatives or other Federal employees designated by the Secretary such records as are necessary to establish that a valid veterinarian-client-patient relationship exists and that there is a valid basis for the exemption under this section.

(b) Products prepared by a person solely for administration to animals owned by that person shall be exempt from the requirement that preparation be pursuant to an unsuspended and unrevoked license.

[52 FR 30131, Aug. 13, 1987, as amended at 56 FR 66783, Dec. 26, 1991; 80 FR 26821, May 11, 2015]

§ 107.2 Products under State license.

(a) The Administrator shall exempt from the requirement of preparation pursuant to an unsuspended and unrevoked USDA establishment and product license, any biological product prepared solely for distribution within the State of production pursuant to a license granted by such State under a program determined by the Administrator to be consistent with the intent of the Act to prohibit the preparation, sale, barter, exchange, or shipment of worthless, contaminated, dangerous, or harmful biological products.

(b) A request for exemption under this section must be made by the appropriate State authority and shall include information demonstrating that:

(1) The State has the authority to license viruses, serums, toxins, and analogous products and establishments that produce such products; and

(2) The State has the authority to review the purity, safety, potency, and efficacy of such products prior to release to the market; and

(3) The State has the authority to review product test results to assure compliance with applicable standards of purity, safety, and potency prior to release to the market; and

(4) The State has the authority to deal effectively with violations of State law regulating viruses, serums, toxins, and analogous products; and

(5) The State effectively exercises the authority specified in paragraphs (b)(1) through (4) of this section consistent with the intent of the Act prohibiting the preparation, sale, barter, exchange, or shipment of worthless, contaminated, dangerous, or harmful viruses, serums, toxins, or analogous products.

(c) Each product to be exempted and each establishment preparing such product shall be identified by the State and the State shall give written notification to the Administrator of each such product and establishment. The State shall also give written notice to the Administrator of each new license issued and of each license terminated.

(d) In order to determine whether a State exercises its authority with respect to biological products and establishments and whether its laws and regulations are being achieved, the Administrator, in cooperation with proper State authorities, may conduct an onsite evaluation of the State's program which may include inspection of establishments and/or products to be included under the exemptions in this section.

[52 FR 30131, Aug. 13, 1987, as amended at 56 FR 66783, Dec. 26, 1991]

PART 108—FACILITY REQUIREMENTS FOR LICENSED ESTABLISHMENTS

Sec.

AUTHORITY: 21 U.S.C. 151–159; 7 CFR 2.22, 2.80, and 371.4.

SOURCE: 39 FR 16854, May 10, 1974, unless otherwise noted.

§ 108.1 Applicability.

Unless otherwise authorized by the Administrator, all buildings, appurtenances, and equipment used in the preparation of biological products shall be in compliance with the regulations in this part. Each land area on which such buildings and appurtenances are located shall be identified by an address which shall appear on the establishment license.

[39 FR 16854, May 10, 1974, as amended at 56 FR 66783, Dec. 26, 1991]

§ 108.2 Plot plans, blueprints, and legends required.

Each applicant for an establishment license shall prepare a plot plan showing all buildings for each particular land area, blueprints for each building used in the preparation of biological products and legends containing a brief description of all activities in each room or area.

§ 108.3 Preparation of plot plans.

Plot plans shall show all of the buildings on a particular land area, whether or not they are all used for the preparation and initial shipping of biological products: *Provided*, That, when a great number of buildings are on the same premises, only those surrounding the buildings used for preparation and initial shipping of biological products shall be shown. The presence of the remainder of the buildings may be accounted for by a single statement denoting the total number of such buildings not used for the preparation or shipping of biological products.

(a) Reduce the entire premises to any standard scale on one sheet of paper which meets any of the American standard trimmed sizes. Indicate the scale used.

(b) Clearly mark the boundaries of the licensed premises and indicate what marking denotes the boundaries. Such boundaries shall coincide with some readily apparent perimeter line. Identify all fences, walls, or streets.

(c) Show buildings as reduced dimensional drawings in the proper scale distance relationship with each other.

(d) Number, letter, or otherwise identify all buildings so that they may be correlated with the respective blueprints and legends.

(e) Describe on the plot plan the use of immediate adjacent properties such as, residential area, pasture, box factory, or the like.

(f) Show compass points.

(g) Show date of preparation.

(h) Apply signature of responsible official of the firm.

§ 108.4 Preparation of blueprints.

(a) Blueprints, drawn to any suitable scale, on regular blueprint paper or a good grade of white paper of any one of the American standard trimmed sizes shall be acceptable: *Provided*, That the same scale shall be used for future revisions unless the entire blueprint is revised. Indicate the scale used.

(b) Use a single sheet of paper for each floor of all buildings in which biological products are prepared. Illustrate in detail the areas in each building utilized for such preparation.

(c) If only a portion of a floor is used in the preparation of a biological product, the blueprint shall illustrate the entire floor in essentially the same detail throughout. All functions or activities performed in the remainder of the floor shall be indicated.

(d) Identify the floors if the drawing is not for all floors in a multiple-story building and identify activities on each floor.

(e) Identify all rooms by letters or numbers.

(f) Show the location of important stationary equipment by a suitable code which will be further identified on legends.

(g) Explain on the blueprint or on the legend, by a statement or listing, which rooms are equipped with water outlets, drains, and lighting. Show the location of doors and windows.

(h) Show compass points.

(i) Show building number.

(j) Show date of preparation.

(k) Apply signature of responsible official of firm.

§ 108.5 Preparation of legends.

A brief description of the activities performed in each room or area shall be prepared as provided in this section and shall be referred to as a legend. Legends shall be provided for each plot plan and each blueprint or drawing. All pages of the legends shall be numbered, identified with corresponding plot plan or blueprint, and submitted in booklet form either stapled together or clipped into a suitable folder.

(a) Plot plan legends shall show the following:

(1) Number of each building and the functions performed in each: *Provided*, That if it is a multiple-story building in which biological products are prepared or handled, briefly describe functions performed on each floor.

(2) A practical and nontechnical description of construction materials used throughout those buildings used entirely or partially for production and handling of biological products.

(b) Blueprint legends shall show the following:

(1) A listing of all rooms by identifying letters or numbers and the fractions prepared in each. Exceptions may be listed for general purpose areas or rooms. Functions performed in each area and room shall be described, whether the licensed or unlicensed products. In rooms where products are exposed to the surroundings, a description of decontamination procedures

and other precautions against cross contamination shall be included.

(2) A listing of the coded stationary equipment.

(3) A general listing of other essential biological equipment such as mills, centrifuges, mixing tanks, bottling and sealing equipment, and the like, which are not regarded as stationary but are maintained in certain rooms.

[39 FR 16854, May 10, 1974, as amended at 40 FR 51413, Nov. 5, 1975; 50 FR 50764, Dec. 12, 1985]

§ 108.6 Revision of plot plans, blueprints, and legends.

Preliminary drawings may be submitted to Animal and Plant Health Inspection Service for comment prior to construction of new facilities or when remodeling is anticipated, old facilities are to be torn down, or other changes affecting the workflow are to be made. The licensee shall:

(a) Prepare revised plot plans, blueprints, or legends and submit to Animal and Plant Health Inspection Service for review and filing when changes have been completed. Also prepare a statement to accompany each revision to identify, by date of the superseded item, what is being superseded.

(b) Prepare a drawing of the revised rooms, unit, or section to the same scale as the blueprint on file which shall be stamped and applied to the existing blueprint. If changes are numerous, prepare a new blueprint.

(c) Drawings of new buildings may be added to existing plot plans. Indicate the distance from surrounding buildings and boundary lines.

(d) Any change prescribed in this section shall necessitate a change in one or more pages of the respective legends. The revised pages shall carry the same numbers as superseded pages.

[39 FR 16854, May 10, 1974, as amended at 56 FR 66783, Dec. 26, 1991]

§ 108.7 Filing of plot plans, blueprints, and legends.

Two copies of all plot plans, blueprints, and legends, including revisions, shall be submitted to Animal and Plant Health Inspection Service for review and filing. When the reviewer takes exception to a submitted item, such item shall be returned with appropriate comments for correction and resubmission. Acceptable submissions shall be stamped as filed and the date noted. One stamped copy shall be returned and two copies retained for Animal and Plant Health Inspection Service files.

[39 FR 16854, May 10, 1974, as amended at 56 FR 66783, Dec. 26, 1991; 75 FR 20772, Apr. 21, 2010]

§ 108.8 Construction of buildings.

(a) The floors, walls, ceilings, partitions, posts, doors, and all other parts of all structures, rooms, or facilities used for the preparation of biological products or ingredients of biological products at licensed establishments shall be of such material, construction, and finish as may be readily and thoroughly cleaned.

(b) All rooms used in connection with the preparation of biological products shall be so constructed and arranged as to prevent cross-contamination of such biological products. Halls or walkways shall be provided for the movement of personnel or materials to each biological products preparation area without going through another such area.

(c) Rooms or compartments separate from the remainder of the establishment shall be provided at licensed establishments for preparing, handling, and storing virulent or dangerous microorganisms and products.

(d) All rooms and compartments at licensed establishments shall have an adequate air handling system to supply proper ventilation sufficient to insure sanitary and hygienic conditions for the protection of the products and personnel.

(e) The supply of hot and cold water at licensed establishments shall be ample and clean. Adequate facilities shall be provided for the distribution of water in each establishment and for the washing of all containers, machinery, instruments, other equipment, and animals used in the preparation of a biological product.

(f) There shall be an efficient drainage and plumbing system for each licensed establishment and premises thereof, and all drains and gutters shall be properly installed with approved traps and vents.

§ 108.9 Dressing rooms and other facilities.

Each licensed establishment shall have dressing rooms, toilet facilities, and lavatory accommodations, including hot and cold running water, soap, towels, and the like. They shall be in sufficient number, ample in size, conveniently located, properly ventilated, and meeting all requirements as to sanitary construction and equipment.

(a) These rooms and facilities shall be separate from rooms or compartments in which biological products are prepared, handled, or stored.

(b) These rooms and facilities shall be so located in the establishment as to be readily accessible to all persons without having to enter or pass through biological products preparation areas.

§ 108.10 Outer premises and stables.

(a) The outer premises of licensed establishments, embracing docks, driveways, approaches, yards, pens, chutes, and alleys shall be drained properly and kept in a clean and orderly condition. No nuisance shall be allowed in any licensed establishment or on its premises.

(b) Stables or other premises for animals used in the production or testing of biological products at licensed establishments shall be properly ventilated and lighted, appropriately drained and guttered, and kept in sanitary condition.

(c) Every practical precaution shall be taken to keep licensed establishments free of flies, rats, mice, and other vermin. The accumulation, on the premises of an establishment, of any material in which flies or other vermin may breed is forbidden. Suitable arrangements, in keeping with the local health practices, shall be made for the disposal of all refuse.

§ 108.11 Water quality requirements.

A certification from the appropriate water pollution control agency, that the establishment is in compliance with applicable water quality control standards, pursuant to section 401 of the Federal Water Pollution Control Act, as amended (86 Stat. 877; 33 U.S.C. 1341), shall be filed with Animal and Plant Health Inspection Service for each licensed establishment.

[39 FR 16854, May 10, 1974, as amended at 56 FR 66783, Dec. 26, 1991]

PART 109—STERILIZATION AND PASTEURIZATION AT LICENSED ESTABLISHMENTS

Sec.

AUTHORITY: 21 U.S.C. 151–159; 7 CFR 2.22, 2.80, and 371.4.

§ 109.1 Equipment and the like.

(a) All containers, instruments, and other apparatus and equipment, before being used in preparing, handling, or storing biological products, at a licensed establishment, except as otherwise prescribed herein, shall be thoroughly sterilized by live steam at a temperature of at least 120 °C. for not less than one-half hour, or by dry heat at a temperature of at least 160 °C. for not less than one hour. If for any reason such methods of sterilization are impracticable, then a process known to be equally efficacious in destroying microorganisms and their spores may be substituted after approval by the Administrator.

(b) Instruments which are found to be damaged by exposure to the degree of heat prescribed in this section, after having been thoroughly cleaned, may be sterilized by boiling for not less than 15 minutes.

[23 FR 10051, Dec. 23, 1958, as amended at 34 FR 18119, Nov. 11, 1969; 56 FR 66783, Dec. 26, 1991]

§ 109.2 Sterilizers.

Steam and dry-heat sterilizers used in connection with the processing of biological products at licensed establishments shall be equipped with automatic temperature recording gauges: *Provided*, That other record keeping systems may be used when approved by the Administrator. When gauges are used, they shall be periodically standardized to assure accuracy. Charts and other temperature records made during production shall be available at all times charts and records shall be kept in accordance with part 116 of this chapter.

[35 FR 16039, Oct. 13, 1970, as amended at 56 FR 66783, Dec. 26, 1991]

§ 109.3 Pasteurizers.

All pasteurizing equipment shall meet the requirements in paragraphs (a), (b), and (c) of this section and be acceptable to Animal and Plant Health Inspection Service.

(a) Metal serum containers shall be used in licensed establishments. During the heating process, each container shall be surrounded by a separate water jacket or equivalent so that the entire container, including its lid, is heated to the required temperature. Each serum container shall be equipped with a motor-driven agitator and a separate automatic recording thermometer.

(b) Each water bath shall have an automatic temperature control to limit the temperature of the water to a maximum of 62 °C., an automatic recording thermometer, an indicating thermometer set in a fixed position, and circulating mechanism adequate to insure equal temperatures throughout the bath. The heating unit for the bath shall be separated from the serum container and the water jacket.

(c) Accurate thermometers at licensed establishments shall be used at frequent intervals to check temperatures of the serum as registered by recording thermometers.

[35 FR 16039, Oct. 13, 1970, as amended at 56 FR 66783, Dec. 26, 1991]

PART 112—PACKAGING AND LABELING

Sec.

AUTHORITY: 21 U.S.C. 151–159; 7 CFR 2.22, 2.80, and 371.4.

SOURCE: 38 FR 12094, May 9, 1973, unless otherwise noted.

§ 112.1 General.

(a) Unless otherwise authorized or directed by the Administrator, each biological product prepared at a licensed establishment, or imported, shall be packaged and labeled as prescribed in this part before it is removed from the licensed establishment or presented for importation: *Provided*, That biological products to be imported for research and evaluation shall be subject to packaging and labeling requirements in § 112.9. *Provided further*, That, unless otherwise exempted, all preparation, including packaging and labeling, of biological products shall only be performed in a licensed establishment under an approved Outline of Production.

(b) No person shall apply or affix to or include with, or cause to be applied or affixed to or included with, any carton or final container of a biological product, any label, stamp, mark or statement that is false or misleading in any particular, is not in compliance with the regulations, or is not approved by APHIS.

(c) No person shall alter, mark or remove any approved labeling affixed to or included with any biological product prior to selling or otherwise distributing such product. In addition, no person shall mark any carton, other container, or final container of a biological product so as to falsify the labeling, make it misleading, or cause it to be illegible.

(d) Labels that are stamped, printed or glued directly on cartons, other containers, or final containers shall be legible throughout the dating period. Biological products bearing labels, which have been altered, mutilated, destroyed, obliterated or removed, shall be withheld from the market.

[38 FR 12094, May 9, 1973, as amended at 59 FR 43445, Aug. 24, 1994]

§ 112.2 Final container label, carton label, and enclosure.

(a) Unless otherwise provided, final container labels, carton labels, and enclosures (inserts, circulars, or leaflets) shall include the information specified in this section.

(1) The complete true name of the biological product which name shall be identical with that shown in the product license under which such product is prepared or the permit under which it is imported, shall be prominently lettered and placed giving equal emphasis to each word composing it. Descriptive terms used in the true name on the product license or permit shall also appear. Abbreviations of the descriptive terms may be used on the final container label if complete descriptive terms appear on the carton label and enclosure. The following exceptions are applicable to small final containers, and containers of interchangeable reagents included in diagnostic test kits:

(i) For small final containers, an abbreviated true name of the biological product, which shall be identical with that shown in the product license under which the product is prepared or the permit under which it is imported, may be used: *Provided*, That the complete true name of the product must appear on the carton label and enclosures;

(ii) In addition to the true name of the kit, the functional and/or chemical name of the reagent must appear on labeling for small final containers of reagents included in diagnostic kits: *Provided*, That the true name is not required on labeling for small final containers of interchangeable (non-critical) components of diagnostic kits.

(2) For biological product prepared in the United States or in a foreign country, the name and address of the producer (licensee, or subsidiary) or permittee and of the foreign producer, and an appropriate consumer contact telephone number: *Provided*, That in the case of a biological product exported from the United States in labeled final containers, a consumer contact telephone number is not required; however, small single dose containers marketed in the United States must include contact telephone information on carton and enclosures.

(3) The United States Veterinary Biologics Establishment License Number (VLN) or the United States Veterinary Biological Product Permit Number (VPN), and the Product Code Number (PCN) assigned by the Department, which shall be shown only as "VLN/PCN" and "VPN/PCN," respectively, except that:

(i) Only the VLN or VPN is required on container labels of interchangeable (non-critical) components of diagnostic kits and container labels for individual products packaged together for co-administration.

(ii) The PCN may be used in lieu of the true name of the kit on small container labels for critical components of diagnostic kits.

(iii) Container labels for individually licensed biological products, when marketed as components of combination packages, must include a statement referring the consumer to the carton or enclosure for the PCN of the combination package.

(4) Storage temperature recommendation for the biological product stated as 2 to 8 °C or 35 to 46 °F, or both.

(5) Full instructions for the proper use of the product, including indications for use, target species, minimum age of administration, route of administration, vaccination schedule, product license restriction(s) that bear on product use, warnings, cautions, and any other vital information for the product's use; except that in the case of limited space on final container labels, a statement as to where such information is to be found, such as "See enclosure for complete directions," "Full directions on carton," or comparable statement.

(6) In the case of a multiple-dose final container, a warning to use entire contents when first opened: *Provided*, That a diagnostic or a desensitizing antigen packaged in a multiple-dose final container is exempt.

(7) The following warning statements, or equivalent statements, shall appear on the labeling as applicable:

(i) Products other than diagnostic kits: "Do not mix with other products, except as specified on this label."

(ii) Injectable products and other products containing hazardous components: "In case of human exposure, contact a physician."

(iii) Products containing viable organisms: "Inactivate unused contents before disposal."

(8) In the case of a biological product recommended for use in domestic animals, the edible portion of which may be used for food purposes, a withholding statement of not less than 21 days to read: "Do not vaccinate within (insert number) days before slaughter" or "Do not vaccinate food-producing animals within (insert number) days before slaughter": *Provided*, That longer periods shall be stated when deemed necessary by the Administrator. Very small final container labels are exempted from this requirement.

(9) The following information shall appear on the final container label and carton label, if any, but need not appear on the enclosure:

(i) A permitted expiration date;

(ii) The number of doses where applicable;

(iii) The recoverable quantity of the content of each final container stated in cubic centimeters (cc.) or milliliters (ml.) or units.

(iv) A serial number by which the product can be identified with the manufacturer's records of preparation: *Provided*, That when a liquid antigenic fraction is to be used instead of a water diluent for one or more desiccated antigenic fractions in a combination package, a hyphenated serial number composed of a serial number for the desiccated fraction and the serial number for the liquid fraction shall be used on the carton.

(v) A statement similar to "For more information regarding efficacy and safety data, go to *productdata.aphis.usda.gov*.

(10) In the case of a product that contains a preservative that is added during the production process and is not reduced to undetectable levels in the completed product through the production process, the statement "Contains [name of preservative] as a preservative" or an equivalent statement must appear on cartons and enclosures, if used. If cartons are not used, such information must appear on the final container label.

(11) The number of final containers of biological product and the number of doses in each final container shall be stated on each carton label for all cartons containing more than one final container of biological product. The number of final containers of diluent, if any, and the quantity in each shall also be stated on each carton label.

(12) An indications statement to read, "This product has been shown to be effective for the vaccination of healthy (insert name of species) ___ weeks of age or older against ___." *Provided*, That in the case of very small final container labels or carton, a statement as to where such information is to be found, such as "See enclosure for complete directions," "Full directions on carton," or comparable statement.

(b) Labels may also include any other statement which is not false or misleading and may include factual statements regarding variable response of different animals when vaccinated as directed but may not include disclaimers of merchantability, fitness for the purpose offered, or responsibility for the product.

(c) Labels of biological products prepared at licensed establishments or imported shall not include any statement, design, or device, which overshadows the true name of the product as licensed or which is false or misleading in any particular or which may otherwise deceive the purchaser.

(d) Carton labels and enclosures shall be subject to paragraph (d)(1), (d)(2), and (d)(3) of this section.

(1) The statement, "Restricted to use by or under the direction of a veterinarian" or "Restricted to use by a veterinarian," shall be used on all carton labels and enclosures when such restriction is prescribed on the product license.

(2) If the licensee states on the carton labels and enclosures of a product that its sales are restricted to veterinarians, then the entire production of that particular product in the licensed establishment shall be so restricted by the licensee.

(3) The statement "For use in animals only" may appear on the labeling as appropriate for a product to indicate that the product is recommended specifically for animals and not for humans.

(e) When label requirements of a foreign country differ from the requirements as prescribed in this part, special labels may be approved by APHIS for use on biological products to be exported to such country upon receipt of written authorization, acceptable to APHIS, from regulatory officials of the importing country, provided that:

(1) If the labeling contains claims or indications for use not supported by data on file with APHIS, the special labels for export shall not bear the VLN.

(2) All other labels for export shall bear the VLN unless the importing country provides documentation that the VLN is specifically prohibited. When laws, regulations, or other requirements of foreign countries require exporters of biological products prepared in a licensed establishment to furnish official certification that such products have been prepared in accordance with the Virus-Serum-Toxin Act and regulations issued pursuant to the Act, such certification may be made by APHIS.

(f) Multiple-dose final containers of liquid biological product and carton tray covers showing required labeling information are subject to the requirements in this paragraphs.

(1) If a carton label or an enclosure is required to complete the labeling for a multiple-dose final container of liquid biological product, only one final container, with a container of diluent if applicable, shall be packaged in each carton: *Provided*, That if the multiple-dose final container is fully labeled without a carton label or enclosure, two or more final containers, and a corresponding number of diluent containers, may be packaged in a single carton which shall be considered a shipping box. Labels or stickers for shipping boxes shall not contain false or misleading information, but need not be submitted to APHIS for approval.

(2) When required labeling information is shown on a carton tray cover, it must be printed on the outside face of such tray cover where it may be read without opening the carton. The inside face of the tray cover may contain information suitable for an enclosure.

(Approved by the Office of Management and Budget under control number 0579–0013)

[38 FR 12094, May 9, 1973, as amended at 39 FR 16856, May 10, 1974; 41 FR 44359, Oct. 8, 1976; 42 FR 11825, Mar. 1, 1977; 42 FR 29854, June 10, 1977; 42 FR 41850, Aug. 19, 1977; 48 FR 57473, Dec. 30, 1983; 56 FR 66784, Dec. 26, 1991; 80 FR 39674, July 10, 2015; 81 FR 59433, Aug. 30, 2016; 81 FR 78500, Nov. 8, 2016]

§ 112.3 Diluent labels.

Each final container of diluent, other than a liquid biological product, packaged with desiccated biological products shall bear a label that includes the following:

(a) The name—Sterile Diluent.

(b) True name of the biological product with which the diluent is packaged, except that when the firm packages all desiccated biological products with the same diluent, or two or more types of diluent are used, and the licensees' methods of identification and storage insure that all products are packaged with the correct type of diluent, labels affixed to the containers of diluent are exempt from this provision.

(c) The recoverable quantity of contents in cubic centimeters (cc) or milliliters (ml).

(d) A serial number by which the diluent can be identified with the manufacturer's records of preparation;

(e) Name and address of the licensee or the permittee;

(f) In the case of a diluent with which a desiccated biological product is to come in contact while the diluent is in its original container; and,

(1) Is in a multiple-dose container, a positive warning that all of the biological product shall be used at the time the container is first opened; and/or

(2) The biological product is composed of viable or dangerous organisms or viruses, the notice, "Inactivate unused contents before disposal."

(g) The establishment license number or the permit number, as the case may be, in one of the forms provided in § 112.2(a)(3).

[38 FR 12094, May 9, 1973; 38 FR 13476, May 22, 1973, and amended at 39 FR 16856, May 10, 1974; 81 FR 59434, Aug. 30, 2016]

§ 112.4 Subsidiaries, divisions, distributors, and permittees.

Labels used by subsidiaries, divisions, distributors, and permittees shall be affixed by the licensee in a licensed establishment where the product is produced. Such labels shall comply with requirements for their review, approval, and filing as provided in the regulations.

(a) *Subsidiaries.* Labels to be used on a licensed biological product prepared by a subsidiary operating in a licensed establishment shall be submitted in accordance with § 112.5. Only labels approved for use on such product shall be used by the subsidiary.

(b) *Divisions.* Labels to be used on a licensed biological product prepared in a licensed establishment for distribution by a division or marketing unit of the licensee shall be submitted in accordance with § 112.5. The name, address, and license number of the licensee shall be prominently placed on such labels. The relationship of the division or marketing unit to the licensee shall appear prominently on the label by use of the term "division of" or equivalent.

(c) *Distributors.* The name and address of the distributor or any statement, design, or device shall not be placed on the labels or containers of a licensed biological product in a manner which could be false or misleading or which could indicate that the distributor is the manufacturer of such product or operating under the license number shown on the label. The manufacturer shall be identified by name, address, and license number with the term "manufactured by," "produced by," or an equivalent term prominently placed in connection therewith. The name and address of the distributor may be placed on labels or containers if the term "distributor," or "distributed by," or an equivalent term is prominently placed in connection therewith.

(d) *Permittees.* The name and address of the permittee and any statement, design, or device shall not be placed on the labels or containers of a biological product imported for sale and distribution in accordance with § 104.5 in a manner which could be false or misleading or which could falsely indicate that the permittee is the manufacturer of such product. The manufacturer shall be identified by name and address with the term "manufactured by," "produced by," or an equivalent term prominently placed in connection therewith. Reference to the permittee shall be made by name, address, and permit number with the term "imported by," "produced for," or an equivalent term prominently placed in connection therewith.

[50 FR 46417, Nov. 8, 1985, as amended at 59 FR 43445, Aug. 24, 1994]

§ 112.5 Review and approval of labeling.

Labels used with biological products prepared at licensed establishments or imported for general distribution and sale must be submitted to the Animal and Plant Health Inspection Service for review for compliance with the regulations and approval in writing prior to use, except as provided in paragraph (d) of this section and under the master label system provided in paragraph (e) of this section.

(a) Transmittal forms, available on the APHIS Web page at *http://www.aphis.usda.gov/animalhealth/cvb/forms*, shall be used with each submission of sketches (including proofs) and labels. Separate forms shall be used for each biological product but only one copy of the form shall be used for all sketches and labels submitted at the same time for the same biological product.

(b) A data summary, available on the Internet at *productdata.aphis.usda.gov*, shall be used with each submission of efficacy and safety data in support of a label claim. Manufacturers will submit the efficacy and safety data information with either the efficacy and safety studies or at the time of label submission. This information will be posted at *productdata.aphis.usda.gov* to allow public disclosure of product performance.

(c) Sketches may be submitted for comment to Animal and Plant Health Inspection Service by the licensee or permittee before preparing the finished label. Such sketches shall be returned to the licensee or permittee with comments, if any. Failure of the reviewer to take exception to a sketch shall not constitute approval of a finished label subsequently prepared.

(d)(1) Labels must be submitted to the Animal and Plant Health Inspection Service for review and written approval. Only labels which are approved as provided in paragraph (e) of this section may be used. When changes are made in approved labels, the new labels shall be subject to review and approval before use: *Provided*, That certain minor changes may be made in labels for products with approved labels or master labels, and the revised labels may be used prior to review by APHIS, with the provision that a new label or master label bearing these changes is submitted to APHIS for review and written approval within 60 days of label use, and that such minor changes do not render the product mislabeled or the label false and misleading in any particular.

(2) Minor label changes that may be made under the provision for products with approved labels or master labels are:

(i) Changes in the physical dimensions of the label provided that such change does not affect the legibility of the label;

(ii) Changes in the color of label print or background, provided that such changes do not affect the legibility of the label;

(iii) The addition or deletion of a Trade Mark (TM) or Registered (R) symbol;

(iv) The correction of typographical errors;

(v) Adding, changing, deleting, or repositioning label control numbers, universal product codes, or other inventory control numbers;

(vi) Revising or updating logos;

(vii) Changing the telephone contact number;

(viii) Adding, changing, or deleting an email and/or Web site address;

(ix) Changing the establishment license or permit number assigned by APHIS, and/or changing the name and/or address of the manufacturer or permittee, provided that such changes are identical to information on the current establishment license or permit; and

(x) Adding or changing the name and/or address of a distributor.

(e) Labels and sketches submitted shall be prepared in the number and manner prescribed in this paragraph.

(1) Copies required:

(i) For label sketches, submit two copies of each sketch of a final container label, carton label, and enclosure. Sketches must be legible, and must include all information specified in § 112.2. One copy of each sketch will be returned with applicable comments, and one copy will be held on file by APHIS for no more than one year after processing, until replaced by a finished label: *Provided*, That sketches submitted in support of an application for a license or permit shall be held as long as the application is considered active.

(ii) For master label sketches, submit for each product two copies of each sketch of an enclosure, label for the smallest size final container, and carton label; *Provided*, That labels for larger size containers and/or cartons that are identical, except for physical dimensions, need not be submitted. One copy of each master label sketch will be returned with applicable comments, and one copy will be held on file by APHIS for one year after processing, until replaced by a finished master label that is submitted according to paragraph (e)(1)(iii) of this section: *Provided*, That master label sketches submitted in support of an application for license or permit shall be held as long as the application is considered active.

(iii) For finished labels, submit two copies of each finished final container label, carton label, and enclosure: *Provided*, That when an enclosure is to be used with more than one product, one extra copy shall be submitted for each additional product. One copy of each finished label will be retained by APHIS. One copy will be stamped and returned to the licensee or permittee. Labels to which exceptions are taken shall be marked as sketches and handled under paragraph (e)(1)(i) of this section.

(iv) For finished master labels, submit for each product two copies each of the enclosure and the labels for the smallest size final container and carton. Labels for larger sizes of containers or cartons of the same product that are identical, except for physical dimensions, need not be submitted.

Such labels become eligible for use concurrent with the approval of the appropriate finished master label, provided that the marketing of larger size final containers is approved in the filed Outline of Production, and the appropriate larger sizes of containers or cartons are identified on the label mounting sheet. When a master label enclosure is to be used with more than one product, one extra copy for each additional product shall be submitted. One copy of each finished master label will be retained by APHIS. One copy will be stamped and returned to the licensee or permittee. Master labels to which exception are taken will be marked as sketches and handled under paragraph (e)(1)(ii) of this section.

(2) Mounting:

(i) Each label or sketch shall be securely fastened to a separate sheet of heavy bond paper (8½″ × 11″) in such a manner that all information is available for review.

(ii) Two-or three-part cartons, including "sleeves," shall be considered as one label. All parts shall be submitted together.

(iii)(A) When two final containers are packaged together in a combination package, the labels for each shall be mounted on the same sheet of paper and shall be treated as one label. For diagnostic test kits, the labels for use on the individual reagent containers to be included in the kit shall be mounted together on a single sheet of paper, if possible; if necessary, a second sheet of paper may be used. The carton label and enclosure shall be mounted on separate individual sheets.

(B) If either final container label is also used alone or in another combination package, sets of separate labels for each biological product with which it is used shall be submitted for review.

(iv) When the same final container label is applied by different methods such as paper or screen printing, one of each shall be mounted on the same sheet of paper as one submission.

(3) To appear on the top of each page:

(i)(A) Name and product code number of the biological product as it appears on the product license or permit.

(B) Extra copies of enclosures to be used with another product shall bear the name and code number of the product affected.

(ii)(A) Designation of the specimen as a label or master label: sketch, final container label, carton label, or enclosure.

(B) If two final container labels or multiple parts are on one sheet, each shall be named, and the label or part being revised shall be designated.

(iii) Size of package (dose, ml., cc., or units) for which the labels or enclosures are to be used.

(4) To appear on the bottom of each page in the lower left hand corner, if applicable:

(i) The dose size(s) to which the master label applies.

(ii) The APHIS assigned number for the label or sketch to be replaced.

(iii) The APHIS assigned number for the label to be used as a reference for reviewing the submitted label.

(f) Special requirements for foreign language labels:

(1) An accurate English translation must accompany each foreign language label submitted for approval. A statement affirming the accuracy of the translation must also be included.

(2) Foreign language portion of a bilingual label shall be a true translation of the English portion. Reference to additional information on the enclosure shall not be made unless that enclosure is also bilingual.

(g) When a request is received from Animal and Plant Health Inspection Service, the licensee or permittee shall submit a list of all approved labels currently being used. Each label listed shall be identified as to:

(1) Name and product code number as it appears on the product license or permit for the product; and

(2) Where applicable, the size of the package (doses, ml., cc., or units) on which the label shall be used; and

(3) Label number and date assigned; and

(4) Name of licensee or subsidiary appearing on the label as the producer.

(h) At the time of an inspection, or when requested by APHIS, licensees or permittees shall make all labels and master labels, including labels approved for use but exempted from filing under the master label system, available for review by authorized inspectors. Such labels shall be identical to the approved label or master label except for physical dimensions, reference to recoverable volume or doses and/or certain minor differences permitted in accordance with paragraph (d) of this section.

(Approved by the Office of Management and Budget under control number 0579–0013)

[38 FR 12094, May 9, 1973, as amended at 48 FR 57473, Dec. 30, 1983; 49 FR 21044, May 18, 1984; 56 FR 66783, Dec. 26, 1991; 59 FR 43445, Aug. 24, 1994; 61 FR 29464, June 11, 1996; 61 FR 33175, June 26, 1996; 64 FR 43044, Aug. 9, 1999; 75 FR 20772, Apr. 21, 2010; 80 FR 39675, July 10, 2015; 81 FR 47005, July 20, 2016; 81 FR 59435, Aug. 30, 2016]

§ 112.6 Packaging biological products.

(a) Multiple-dose final containers of a biological product with final container labeling including all information required under the regulations may be packaged one or more per carton with a container(s) of the proper volume of diluent, if required, for that dose as specified in the filed Outline of Production: *Provided*, That cartons containing more than one final container of product must comply with the conditions set forth in paragraphs (c)(1) through (4) of this section. Multiple-dose final containers of a product that require a carton or enclosure in order to provide all information required under the regulations shall be packaged one container per carton with the proper volume of diluent, if required, for that dose as specified in the filed Outline of Production.

(b) Single-dose final containers of a product need not be packaged one per carton. For single-dose products which require a diluent for administration, the number of containers of the proper amount of diluent specified in the filed Outline of Production for the number of doses contained in the carton shall be included in each carton.

(c) Poultry products for mass administration (including but not limited to administration through drinking water and spray) and products used in automatic vaccinating systems (including but not limited to pneumatic beak injectors and automated needle injectors) may be packaged in multiple-dose final containers as specified in the filed Outline of Production. Poultry products for manual administration to individual birds shall not exceed 1,000 doses in each final container. Diluent need not be packaged with the final container(s) of the product, but the licensee shall provide the required number of containers of diluent as specified in the filed Outline of Production. The following requirements apply to cartons containing more than one final container of poultry product:

(1) They shall be sealed prior to leaving the licensed establishment.

(2) The contents may not be repackaged.

(3) The contents of such cartons may not be sold in fractional units.

(4) The following statement must appear in a prominent place on the carton label: "Federal regulations prohibit the repackaging or sale of the contents of this carton in fractional units. Do not accept if seal is broken."

(d) Diluent for the following products need not be packaged with the final container(s) of the product, but the licensee shall provide the consumer with the required number of containers of the proper amount of diluent as specified in the filed Outline of Production:

(1) Marek's Disease Vaccine.

(2) Poultry vaccines administered to individual birds using automatic vaccinating equipment.

(e) Final containers of biological product prepared at a licensed establishment, or imported, in cartons or other containers shall not be removed from such cartons or containers for sale or distribution, unless each final container bears, or is packaged in a carton with, complete and approved labeling which is affixed to or included with each container by the licensed establishment producing the product or by the producer in the case of imported product: *Provided*, That this paragraph is not intended to apply to licensed veterinary practitioners administering or dispensing biological products in the course of their practice under a veterinary-client-patient-relationship as that term is used in § 107.1.

(f) Labels which are affixed to or included with a biological product shall not be removed or altered in any manner.

[47 FR 8761, Mar. 2, 1982, as amended at 48 FR 12691, Mar. 28, 1983; 59 FR 43445, Aug. 24, 1994; 64 FR 43044, Aug. 9, 1999; 81 FR 59435, Aug. 30, 2016]

§112.7 Special additional requirements.

The label requirements in this section are additional to those prescribed elsewhere in this part.

(a) In the case of biological products containing live Newcastle Disease virus, a caution statement indicating that Newcastle Disease can cause inflammation of the eyelids of humans, and a warning to the user to avoid infecting his eyes shall be included on the enclosure.

(b) In the case of a biological product containing infectious bronchitis virus, all labels shall show the infectious bronchitis virus type or types used in the product. Abbreviation is permitted.

(c) In the case of a biological product containing inactivated rabies virus, carton labels, enclosures, and all but very small final container labels shall include a warning against freezing and the recommendations provided in this paragraph.

(1) That vaccine be administered to animals at 3 months of age or older, with a repeat dose 1 year later.

(2) Subsequent revaccination as determined from the results of duration of immunity studies conducted as prescribed in §113.209, paragraph (b) or (c), or both.

(d) In the case of a biological product containing modified live rabies virus, the carton labels, enclosures, and all but very small final container labels shall include the recommendations provided in this paragraph.

(1) For low egg-passage (below the 180th egg-passage level) the statement "For Use in Dogs Only! Not For Use in Any Other Animal!"

(2) For other vaccines containing modified live rabies virus, the statement "For Use In (designate animal(s)) Only! Not For Use In Any Other Animal!"

(3) Intramuscular injection at one site in the thigh shall be recommended.

(4) The statement "In event of accidental exposure to the vaccine virus, the possible hazard to human health should be considered and State Public Health Officials should be consulted for specific recommendations" shall be prominently placed on all carton labels and on enclosures, if used.

(5) That vaccine be administered to animals at 3 months of age or older, with a repeat dose 1 year later.

(6) Subsequent revaccination as determined from the results of duration of immunity studies conducted as prescribed in §113.312, paragraph (b) or (c), or both.

(e) Labeling for all products for use in mammals must bear an appropriate statement concerning use in pregnant animals.

(1) For bovine rhinotracheitis vaccine or bovine virus diarrhea vaccine containing modified live virus, all labeling except small final container labels shall bear the following statement: "Do not use in pregnant cows or in calves nursing pregnant cows.": *Provided*, That such vaccines which have been shown to be safe for use in pregnant cows may be excepted from this label requirement by the Administrator.

(2) For other modified live and inactivated vaccine, labeling shall bear a statement appropriate to the level of safety that has been demonstrated in pregnant animals.

(i) Products known to be unsafe in pregnant animals shall include statements such as "Do not use in pregnant animals," or "Unsafe for use in pregnant animals," or an equivalent statement acceptable to APHIS.

(ii) Products without safety documentation acceptable to APHIS, but not known to be unsafe, labeling shall include the statement "This product has not been tested in pregnant animals" or an equivalent statement acceptable to APHIS.

(3) For modified live vaccines containing agents with potential reproductive effects but having acceptable pregnant animal safety data on file with APHIS, labeling still must bear the following statement concerning residual risk: "Fetal health risks associated with the vaccination of pregnant animals with this vaccine cannot be unequivocally determined during clinical

trials conducted for licensure. Appropriate strategies to address the risks associated with vaccine use in pregnant animals should be discussed with a veterinarian."

(f) For biological products recommending annual booster vaccinations, such recommendations must be supported by data acceptable to APHIS. In the absence of data that establish the need for booster vaccination, labeling must bear the following statement: "The need for annual booster vaccinations has not been established for this product; consultation with a veterinarian is recommended."

(g) In the case of a liquid product authorized in a filed Outline of Production to be used as a diluent in a combination package, the carton labels and enclosures used for serials which are either not tested for bactericidal or viricidal activity or have been found unsatisfactory by such test shall contain the statement: "CAUTION: DO NOT USE AS DILUENT FOR LIVE VACCINES."

(h) In the case of wart vaccine, recommendations shall be limited to use in cattle. Indications for use shall be for prophylactic use only, as an aid in the control of viral papillomas (warts). All labels shall include a dosage recommendation of at least 10 ml to be given subcutaneously and the dose repeated in 3 to 5 weeks.

(i) All but very small final container labels for feline panleukopenia vaccines shall contain the following recommendations for use:

(1) *Killed virus vaccines.* Vaccinate healthy cats with one dose, except that if the animal is less than 12 weeks of age, a second dose should be given no earlier than 16 weeks of age.

(2) *Modified live virus vaccines.* Vaccinate healthy cats with one dose, except that if the animal is less than 12 weeks of age, a second dose should be given no earlier than16 weeks of age.

(j) In the case of normal serum, antiserum, or antiserum derivatives, the type of preservative used shall be indicated on all labels.

(k) Unless acceptable data has been filed with Animal and Plant Health Inspection Service, to show that development of corneal opacity is not associated with the product, carton labels and enclosures used with biological products containing modified live canine hepatitis virus or modified live canine adenovirus Type 2 shall bear the following statement: "Occasionally, transient corneal opacity may occur following the administration of this product."

(l) All labels for autogenous biologics must specify the name of the microorganism(s) or antigen(s) that they contain, and shall bear the following statement: "Potency and efficacy of autogenous biologics have not been established. This product is prepared for use only by or under the direction of a veterinarian or approved specialist."

(m) In the case of biological products containing Marek's disease virus, all labels shall specify the Marek's disease virus serotype(s) used in the product.

(n) All labels for conditionally licensed products shall bear the following statement: "This product license is conditional; efficacy and potency have not been fully demonstrated."

(Approved by the Office of Management and Budget under control number 0579–0013)

[38 FR 12094, May 9, 1973]

EDITORIAL NOTE: For FEDERAL REGISTER citations affecting § 112.7, see the List of CFR Sections Affected, which appears in the Finding Aids section of the printed volume and at *www.fdsys.gov*.

§ 112.8 For export only.

The applicable regulations for packaging and labeling a biological product produced in the United States shall apply to such biological product if exported from the United States except as otherwise provided in this section. Only labels approved as provided in § 112.5 shall be used.

(a) Biological products which have been packaged and labeled for export or which have been exported, shall be subject to the applicable provisions in this paragraph.

(1) After leaving the licensed establishment, a biological product shall not be bottled, repackaged, relabeled, or otherwise altered in any way while in the United States; and

(2) An exported biological product shall not be returned to the United States: *Provided*, That, in the case of a biological product exported in labeled

final containers, the Administrator may authorize by permit the importation of a limited number for research and evaluation by the producing licensee; and

(3) An exported biological product which is bottled, rebottled, or altered in any way in a foreign country shall not bear a label which indicates by establishment license number that it has been prepared in the United States.

(b) Desiccated and frozen liquid products, packaged and labeled as for domestic use, may be exported without the diluent required for rehydration or dilution, as the case may be, if the labeling includes adequate instructions for preparing the product for use and the words "For Export Only".

(c) Final containers of products, labeled or unlabeled, may be exported in sealed shipping boxes, adequately identified as to contents with an approved label, and plainly marked "For Export Only": *Provided*, That such products shall not be diverted to domestic use.

(d) Completed inactivated liquid products, antiserums, and antitoxins, may be exported in large multiple-dose containers identified with an approved label that contains the words "For Export Only" prominently displayed.

(e) Concentrated inactivated liquid product, completed except for dilution to the proper strength for use, may be exported in large multiple-dose containers identified with an approved label that contains the words "For Export Only" prominently displayed.

[38 FR 12094, May 9, 1973, as amended at 39 FR 19202, May 31, 1974; 40 FR 46093, Oct. 6, 1975; 43 FR 11145, Mar. 17, 1978; 56 FR 66784, Dec. 26, 1991]

§ 112.9 Biological products imported for research and evaluation.

A biological product imported for research and evaluation under a permit issued in accordance with § 104.4, with the exception of products imported under § 104.4(d), shall be labeled as provided in this section.

(a) The label shall identify the product and the name and address of the manufacturer and shall provide instructions for proper use of the product, including all warnings and cautions needed by the permittee to safely use the product.

(b) Labels on each product to be further distributed in accordance with § 103.3 shall bear the statement "Notice! For Experimental Use Only—Not for Sale!"

(c) The labeling shall contain any other information deemed necessary by the Administrator and specified on the permit.

[50 FR 46417, Nov. 8, 1985, as amended at 56 FR 66784, Dec. 26, 1991]

§ 112.10 Special packaging and labeling.

A biological product, which requires special packaging and/or labeling not provided for in this part, shall be packaged and/or labeled in accordance with requirements written into the approved outline for such product.

PART 113—STANDARD REQUIREMENTS

APPLICABILITY

AUTHORITY: 21 U.S.C. 151–159; 7 CFR 2.22, 2.80, and 371.4.

SOURCE: 34 FR 18004, Nov. 7, 1969, unless otherwise noted.

EDITORIAL NOTE: Nomenclature changes to part 113 appear at 79 FR 55969, Sept. 18, 2014.

APPLICABILITY

§ 113.1 Compliance.

The regulations in this part apply to each serial or subserial of a licensed biological product manufactured in a licensed establishment and to each serial or subserial of a biological product in each shipment imported for distribution and sale.

§ 113.2 Testing aids.

To better ensure consistent and reproducible test results when Standard Requirement tests prescribed in the regulations are conducted, National Veterinary Services Laboratories, U.S. Department of Agriculture, may provide testing aids, when available, to licensees, permittees, and applicants for licenses and permits. Such aids shall be as follows:

(a) Supplemental Assay Method (SAM) is a technical bulletin containing detailed instructions for conducting a test. Such instructions shall be in accordance with the procedures currently being followed at National Veterinary Services Laboratories and as improved, proven procedures are developed, shall be revised and reissued prior to application.

(b) Standard Reference Preparation is a serum, virus, bacterial culture, or antigen to be used in test systems for direct comparison with serials of biological products under test.

(c) Standard Test Reagent is a serum, antitoxin, fluorescent antibody conjugate, toxin, virus, bacterial cultural, or antigen to be used in test systems but not for direct comparison with serials of biological products under test.

(d) Seed cultures are small quantities of standard organisms to be propagated by the recipient to establish a supply for use.

(e) Test Code Number is a number assigned by Animal and Plant Health Inspection Service to each test procedure specified in the Standard Requirements and in each filed Outline of Production where such test is conducted to support a request for release of a serial or subserial.

[39 FR 21041, June 18, 1974, as amended at 40 FR 758, Jan. 3, 1975; 50 FR 21799, May 29, 1985; 56 FR 66784, Dec. 26, 1991]

§ 113.3 Sampling of biological products.

Each licensee and permittee shall furnish representative samples of each serial or subserial of a biological product manufactured in the United States or imported into the United States as prescribed in this section. Additional samples may be purchased in the open market by a Animal and Plant Health Inspection Service representative.

(a) Either an employee of the Department of Agriculture, of the licensee, or of the permittee, as designated by the Administrator shall select prerelease samples of biological product in the number prescribed in paragraph (b) of this section. Each sample shall be marked for identification by the person making the selection after which they shall be packaged by the licensee or permittee, as the case may be, and forwarded to National Veterinary Services Laboratories; except that an employee of the Department may forward or deliver the samples to National Veterinary Services Laboratories if such action deemed advisable by the Administrator.

(1) Selection shall be made as follows:

(i) Nonviable liquid biological products—either bulk or final container samples of completed product shall be selected for purity, safety, or potency tests. Biological product in final container shall be selected to test for viable bacteria and fungi.

(ii) Viable liquid biological products; samples shall be in final containers and shall be randomly selected at the end of the filling operation. Bulk containers of completed product may be sampled when authorized by the Administrator.

(iii) Desiccated biological products; samples shall be in final containers and shall be randomly selected if desiccated in the final container. Biological products desiccated in bulk shall be sampled at the end of the filling operation.

(iv) Representative samples of each serial or subserial in each shipment of imported biological products shall be selected.

(2) Comparable samples shall be used by Animal and Plant Health Inspection Service, the licensee, and the permittee for similar tests.

(3) When bulk samples of completed product in liquid form are to be tested as prescribed in paragraph (a)(1) of this section, the number of such samples from each serial and the minimum quantity of product to be provided in each sample shall be stated in the filed Outline of Production.

(b) Unless otherwise prescribed by the Administrator, the number of final container samples to be selected from each serial and subserial shall be:

(1) *Vaccines:*

(i) Six multiple-dose samples of Brucella Abortus Vaccine;

(ii) Twelve samples of all other live bacterial vaccines;

(iii) Two samples of Coccidiosis Vaccine;

(iv) Eighteen samples of Rabies Vaccine, Modified Live Virus;

(v) Sixteen samples of all other vaccines consisting of live microorganisms;

(vi) Thirty single-dose or 14 multiple-dose samples of Equine Encephalomyelitis Vaccine, Killed Virus;

(vii) Twenty-two single-dose or 14 multiple-dose samples of Rabies Vaccine, Killed Virus;

(viii) Sixteen single-dose or 12 multiple-dose samples of all other vaccines consisting of killed microorganisms.

(2) *Bacterins and bacterin-toxoids:*

(i) Twelve samples of single-fraction products;

(ii) Thirteen samples of two-fraction products;

(iii) Fourteen samples of products consisting of 3 or more fractions.

(3) *Antiserums:* Twelve samples of antiserum recommended for large animals or 14 samples of antiserum recommended for small animals or the number of reagent serum samples prescribed in the filed Outline of Production for the product.

(4) *Antitoxins:*

(i) Fourteen single-dose or 12 multiple dose samples of Tetanus Antitoxin;

(ii) Twelve samples of all other antitoxins.

(5) *Toxoids:*

(i) Eighteen single-dose or 12 multiple dose samples of all toxoids.

(6) *Antigens:* Twelve samples of poultry antigens or 20 samples of tuberculin or four samples of all other diagnostic antigens.

(7) *Diagnostic test kits:* Two samples of diagnostic test kits. The licensee or permittee will hold one of these selected samples at the storage temperature recommended on the label while awaiting a request by the animal and Plant Health Inspection Service to submit the additional sample. If submission is not requested by the Animal and Plant Health Inspection Service, the additional sample may be returned to the serial inventory after the serial is released. In the case of diagnostic test kits in which final packaging consists of multiple microtiter test plates or strips, the licensee or permittee may submit a specified number of test plates or strips along with all other test reagents as prescribed in a filed Outline of Production and retain a similar amount as a second sample for

submission upon request. When the initial sample is not representative of final packaging by the licensee of permittee, e.g., does not consist of all the microtiter test plates or strips, the second sample is not eligible to be returned to serial inventory after the serial is released.

(8) *Autogenous biologics:* With the exception of the first serial or subserial, 10 samples must be selected and submitted to the Animal and Plant Health Inspection Service from each serial or subserial of an autogenous biologic eligible to be shipped that consists of more than 50 containers. For first serials or subserials eligible for shipment consisting of more than 50 containers, 10 samples from each serial or subserial must be selected and held for submission to the Animal and Plant Health Inspection Service upon request in accordance with paragraph (e)(4) of this section. For serials or subserials of autogenous biologic with 50 or fewer containers, no samples, other than those required by paragraph (e) of this section, are required.

(9) *Miscellaneous:* The number of samples from products not in the categories provided for in paragraphs (b)(1) through (b)(8) of this section shall be prescribed in the filed Outline of Production for the product.

(c) Prelicensing and Outline of Production changes: Samples needed to support a license application or a change in the Outline of Production for a licensed product shall be submitted only upon request from the animal and Plant Health Inspection Service. Except for miscellaneous products specified in paragraph (b)(9) of this section, the number of such samples shall be at least one and one-half times the number prescribed for such product in paragraph (b) of this section. Samples of Master Seeds and Master Cell Stocks with a minimum individual volume of 1 ml shall be submitted as follows:

(1) Ten samples of Bacterial Master Seeds.

(2) Thirteen samples of viral Master Seeds or nonviral Master Seeds requiring cell culture propagation. For Master Seeds isolated or passed in a cell line different from the species of intended use, an additional 2 samples are required for each additional species. For Master Seeds grown in cell culture and intended for use in more than one species, an additional 2 samples are required for each additional species.

(3) Thirty-six samples of at least 1 ml each or six samples of at least 1 ml each, one sample of at least 20 ml, and one sample of at least 10 ml of Master Cell Stocks. In the case of Master Cell Stocks which are persistently infected with a virus, an additional four samples of at least 1 ml each are required. If these persistently infected cell stocks are intended for use in more than one species, an additional two samples of at least 1 ml each are required for each additional species.

(4) Four samples of the Master Cell Stock + n (highest passage) cells.

(d) Sterile diluent: A sample of Sterile Diluent shall accompany each sample of product, other than Marek's Disease Vaccine, if such diluent is required to rehydrate or dilute the product before use. The volume of diluent shall be an appropriate amount to rehydrate or dilute the product. Samples of Sterile Diluent prepared for use with Marek's Disease Vaccine shall be submitted upon request from the Animal and Plant Health Inspection Service.

(e) Reserve samples shall be selected from each serial and subserial of biological product. Such samples shall be selected at random from final containers of completed product by an employee of the Department, of the licensee, or of the permittee, as designated by the administrator. Each sample shall:

(1) Consist of 5 single-dose packages, 2 multiple-dose packages, or 2 diagnostic test kits, except that, in the case of diagnostic test kits in which final packaging consists of multiple microtiter test plates or strips, a sample may consist of a specified number of test plates or strips along with all other test reagents as prescribed in a filed Outline of Production;

(2) Be adequate in quantity for appropriate examination and testing;

(3) Be truly representative and in final containers;

(4) Be held in a special compartment set aside by the licensee or permittee for holding these samples under refrigeration at the storage temperature recommended on the labels for 6 months

after the expiration date stated on the labels. The samples that are stored in this manner shall be delivered to the Animal and Plant Health Inspection Service upon request.

(Approved by the Office of Management and Budget under control number 0579–0013)

[38 FR 29886, Oct. 30, 1973, as amended at 40 FR 758, Jan. 3, 1975; 40 FR 49768, Oct. 24, 1975; 41 FR 56627, Dec. 29, 1976; 48 FR 9506, Mar. 7, 1983; 48 FR 57473, Dec. 30, 1983; 50 FR 21799, May 29, 1985; 56 FR 66784, Dec. 26, 1991; 60 FR 14356, Mar. 17, 1995; 67 FR 15713, Apr. 3, 2002]

§ 113.4 Exemptions to tests.

(a) The test methods and procedures contained in all applicable Standard Requirements shall be complied with unless otherwise exempted by the Administrator and provided that such exemption is noted in the filed Outline of Production for the product.

(b) Test methods and procedures by which the biological products shall be evaluated shall be designated in the Outline of Production for such products.

[38 FR 29887, Oct. 30, 1973, as amended at 56 FR 66784, Dec. 26, 1991]

§ 113.5 General testing.

(a) No biological product shall be released prior to the completion of tests prescribed in a filed Outline of Production or Standard Requirements for the product to establish the product to be pure, safe, potent, and efficacious.

(b) Tests of biological products shall be observed by a competent employee of the manufacturer during all critical periods. A critical period shall be the time when certain specified reactions must occur in required tests to properly evaluate the results.

(c) Records of all tests shall be kept in accordance with part 116 of this chapter. Results of all required tests prescribed in the filed Outline of Production or the Standard Requirements for the product shall be submitted to Animal and Plant Health Inspection Service. Blank forms shall be furnished upon request to Animal and Plant Health Inspection Service.

(d) When the initial or any subsequent test is declared a No Test, the reasons shall be reported in the test records, the results shall not be considered as final, and the test may be repeated. When a test is declared satisfactory, the test designation is considered to be a final conclusion. When a test is declared unsatisfactory, the test designation is considered to be a final conclusion. When the initial or any subsequent test is declared inconclusive, the reasons shall be reported in the test records, the result shall not be considered as final, and the test may be repeated as established in the filed Outline of Production or Standard Requirement. If a test is designated inconclusive or No Test and the biological product is not further tested, the test designation of unsatisfactory is the final conclusion.

(e) When new test methods are developed and approved by Animal and Plant Health Inspection Service, biological products tested thereafter shall be evaluated by such methods, and if not found to be satisfactory when so tested shall not be released.

(Approved by the Office of Management and Budget under control number 0579–0059)

[34 FR 18004, Nov. 4, 1969, as amended at 39 FR 25463, July 11, 1974; 40 FR 45420, Oct. 2, 1975; 40 FR 46093, Oct. 6, 1975; 41 FR 6751, Feb. 13, 1976; 48 FR 57473, Dec. 30, 1983; 56 FR 66784, Dec. 26, 1991; 79 FR 55969, Sept. 18, 2014]

§ 113.6 Animal and Plant Health Inspection Service testing.

A biological product shall with reasonable certainty yield the results intended when used as recommended or suggested in its labeling or proposed labeling prior to the expiration date.

(a) The Administrator is authorized to cause a biological product, manufactured in the United States or imported into the United States, to be examined and tested for purity, safety, potency, or efficacy; in which case, the licensee or permittee shall withhold such product from the market until a determination has been made.

(b) The final results of each test conducted by the licensee and Animal and Plant Health Inspection Service shall be considered in evaluating a biological product. A serial or subserial which has been found unsatisfactory by a required test prescribed in a filed Outline of Production or Standard Requirement is not in compliance with the regulations and shall not be released for market.

[34 FR 18004, Nov. 7, 1969, as amended at 40 FR 45420, Oct. 2, 1975; 40 FR 53378, Nov. 18, 1975; 41 FR 6751, Feb. 13, 1976; 56 FR 66784, Dec. 26, 1991]

§ 113.7 Multiple fractions.

(a) When a biological product contains more than one immunogenic fraction, the completed product shall be evaluated by tests applicable to each fraction.

(b) When similar potency tests are required for more than one fraction of a combination biological product, different animals must be used to evaluate each fraction except when written Standard Requirements or outlines of production make provisions and set forth conditions for use of the same animals for testing different fractions.

(c) When the same safety test is required for more than one fraction, requirements are fulfilled by satisfactory results from one test of the completed product.

(d) When an inactivated fraction(s) is used as a diluent for a live virus fraction(s), the inactivated fraction(s) may be tested separately and the live virus fraction(s) may be tested separately: *Provided*, That, the viricidal test requirements prescribed in § 113.100 are complied with.

(e) Virus titrations for a multivirus product shall be conducted by methods which will quantitate each virus.

[34 FR 18004, Nov. 7, 1969, as amended at 40 FR 46093, Oct. 6, 1975; 56 FR 66785, Dec. 26, 1991]

§ 113.8 In vitro tests for serial release.

(a) Master Seed which has been established as pure, safe, and immunogenic shall be used for preparing seed for production as specified in the Standard Requirements or in the filed Outline of Production. The Administrator may exempt a product from a required animal potency test for release when an evaluation can, with reasonable certainty, be made by:

(1) Subjecting the master seed to the applicable requirements prescribed in §§ 113.64, 113.100, 113.200, and 113.300;

(2) Testing the Master Seed for immunogenicity in a manner acceptable to the Animal and Plant Health Inspection Service (APHIS);

(3) Establishing satisfactory potency for the product in accordance with the following provisions:

(i) Potency for live products may be determined by $\log_{10}$ virus titer or determining the live bacterial count based on the protective dose used in the Master Seed immunogenicity test plus an adequate overage for adverse conditions and test error; and

(ii) Potency for inactivated products may be determined using tests for relative antigen content by comparing the antigen content of the test serial to a reference preparation using a parallel line immunoassay or equivalent method which measures linearity, specificity, and reproducibility in a manner acceptable to APHIS.

(b) In the case of live products, each serial and subserial of desiccated product derived from an approved Master Seed and bulk or final container samples of each serial of completed liquid product derived from an approved Master Seed shall be evaluated by a test procedure acceptable to APHIS. On the basis of the results of the test, as compared with the required minimum potency, each serial and subserial shall either be released to the firm for marketing or withheld from the market. The evaluation of such products shall be made in accordance with the following criteria:

(1) If the initial test shows the count or titer to equal or exceed the required minimum, the serial or subserial is satisfactory without additional testing.

(2) If the initial test shows the count or titer to be lower than the required minimum, the serial or subserial may be retested, using double the number of samples. The average counts or titers obtained in the retests shall be determined. If the average is less than the required minimum, the serial or subserial is unsatisfactory without further consideration.

(3) If the average is equal to or greater than the required minimum, the following shall apply to live virus vaccines:

(i) If the difference between the average titer obtained in the retests and the titer obtained in the initial test is $10^{0.7}$ or greater, the initial titer may be considered a result of test system error and the serial or subserial considered satisfactory for virus titer.

(ii) If the difference between the average titer obtained in the retests and the titer obtained in the initial test is less than $10^{0.7}$, a new average shall be determined using the titers obtained in all tests. If the new average is below the required minimum, the serial or subserial is unsatisfactory.

(4) If the average is equal to or greater than the required minimum, the following shall apply to bacterial vaccines:

(i) If the average count obtained in the retests is at least three times the count obtained in the initial test, the initial count may be considered a result of test system error and the serial or subserial considered satisfactory for bacterial count.

(ii) If the average count obtained in the retests is less than three times the count obtained in the initial test, a new average shall be determined using the counts obtained in all tests. If the new average count is below the required minimum, the serial or subserial is unsatisfactory.

(5) *Exceptions.* When a product is evaluated in terms other than $\log_{10}$ virus titer or organism count, an appropriate difference between the average potency value obtained in the retests and the potency value obtained in the initial test shall be established for use in paragraphs (b)(3) and (b)(4) of this section to evaluate such products and shall be specified in the product Standard Requirement or filed Outline of Production.

(c) In the case of inactivated products, bulk or final container samples of completed product from each serial derived from an approved Master Seed, shall be evaluated for relative antigen content (potency) as compared with an unexpired reference by a parallel line immunoassay or other procedure acceptable to APHIS. Firms currently using immunoassays which do not satisfy this requirement shall have 2 years from the effective date of the final rule to update their filed Outlines of Production to be in compliance with this requirement unless granted an extension by the Administrator based on a showing by the firm seeking the extension that they have made a good faith effort with due diligence to achieve compliance. On the basis of the results of such test procedures, each serial that meets the required minimum potency shall be released to the firm for marketing; each serial not meeting the required minimum potency shall be withheld from the market. The evaluation of such products shall be made in accordance with the following criteria:

(1) A test that results in no valid lines is considered a "no test" and may be repeated.

(2) An initial test (test 1) that results in valid lines that are not parallel is considered a valid equivocal test. Release of the serial may not be based on such test since the result cannot be termed "satisfactory" or "unsatisfactory."

(3) If the initial test (test 1) shows that potency equals or exceeds the required minimum potency, the serial is satisfactory without additional testing.

(4) If the initial test (test 1) is an equivocal test due to lack of parallelism, the serial may be retested up to three times (tests 2, 3, and 4) with disposition to be as specified in paragraphs (c)(4)(i) and (ii) of this section; *Provided,* That, if the serial is not retested or the other provisions of this section are not satisfied, the serial shall be deemed unsatisfactory.

(i) If: The first retest (test 2) following an initial equivocal test; the second retest (test 3) following two consecutive equivocal tests (tests 1 and 2); or the third retest (test 4) following three consecutive equivocal tests (tests 1, 2, and 3) shows that the potency equals or exceeds the required minimum potency, the serial is satisfactory.

(ii) If the first retest (test 2) following an initial equivocal test shows that potency is less than the required minimum potency, disposition of the serial will be based on the outcome of retests 2 and 3 (tests 3 and 4) as follows: if either retest (test 3 or 4) shows that potency is less than the required minimum potency, the serial is unsatisfactory. If either retest 2 or retest 3 (tests 3 or 4) is an equivocal test, or in the event that each retest (tests 2, 3, and 4) following an initial equivocal test is also an equivocal test, the accumulated test results shall be considered indicative of a lack of potency and release of the serial withheld. In which case, the licensee may submit data confirming the continued validity of the test system to APHIS for review and approval. If the data are acceptable to APHIS, the potency test may be repeated by the firm, subject to the provisions specified in paragraphs (i) and (ii) and confirmatory testing by APHIS.

(5) If the initial test (test 1) shows that potency is less than the required minimum potency, the serial may be retested a minimum of two times (tests 2 and 3) but not more than three times (tests 2, 3, and 4) with disposition as specified in paragraphs (c)(5) (i) and (ii) of this section; *Provided,* That, if the serial is not retested or the other provisions of this section are not satisfied, the serial shall be deemed unsatisfactory.

(i) If two consecutive retests (tests 2 and 3) show that potency of the serial equals or exceeds the required minimum potency, the serial is satisfactory. If one of the two retests (test 2 or 3) shows that the potency is less than the required minimum potency, the serial is unsatisfactory.

(ii) If one of the retests (tests 2 or 3) shows that the potency equals or exceeds the required minimum potency and the other retest (test 2 or 3) is an equivocal test, a third retest (test 4) may be performed. If the third retest (test 4) shows that the potency of the serial equals or exceeds the required minimum potency, the serial is deemed satisfactory. If both retests (tests 2 and 3) or if the third retest (test 4) is an equivocal test, the accumulated test results shall be considered indicative of a lack of potency and release of the serial withheld, in which case the licensee may submit data confirming the continued validity of the test system to APHIS for review and approval. If the data are acceptable to APHIS, the potency test may be repeated by the firm, subject to the provisions specified in paragraphs (c)(4) (i) and (ii) and (c)(5) (i) and (ii) of this section, and confirmatory testing by APHIS.

(d) *Extending the dating of a reference.* All determinations of relative antigen content using parallel line immunoassays or equivalent methods shall be conducted with an unexpired reference. The lot of reference used to determine antigenic content shall have an initial dating period equal to the dating of the product or as supported by data acceptable to APHIS, except that frozen references may have an initial dating of up to 5 years, *Provided,* That the request for dating of the frozen references beyond the dating of the product is supported by preliminary data acceptable to APHIS and includes provisions for monitoring the stability of the reference to determine when the potency starts to decline and for taking the appropriate steps to requalify a reference with declining potency either by testing a Qualifying Serial in host animals or by providing other evidence of immunogenicity, e.g., antibody titers or laboratory animal test data previously correlated to host animal protection in a manner acceptable to APHIS. Prior to the expiration date, such reference may be granted an extension of dating, *Provided,* That its immunogenicity has been confirmed using a Qualifying Serial of product in a manner acceptable to APHIS. The dating period of the Master Reference and Working Reference may be extended by data acceptable to APHIS if the minimum potency of the Master Reference is determined to be adequately above the minimum level needed to provide protection in the host animal. If a new Master Reference is established, it shall be allowed an initial dating period equal to the dating of the product or as supported by data acceptable to APHIS, except that frozen references may have an initial dating period of 5 years, or as supported by data acceptable to APHIS. Prior to the expiration date, such reference may be granted an extension of dating by confirming its immunogenicity using a Qualifying Serial of product.

(e) Final container samples of completed product derived from Master Seed found immunogenic in accordance with paragraph (a) of this section and found satisfactory in accordance with paragraphs (b) and (c) of this section may also be subjected to an animal potency test by Animal and Plant Health Inspection Service as provided in this paragraph. Products shall be used according to label directions including dose(s) and route of administration.

(1) A one stage test using 20 vaccinates and 5 controls or a two stage test using 10 vaccinates and 5 controls for each stage shall be used. The criteria used for judging the specific response in the controls and vaccinates shall be in accordance with the test protocol used in the Master Seed immunogenicity test.

(2) If at least 80 percent of the controls do not show specific responses to challenge, the test is inconclusive and may be repeated. If a vaccinate shows the specific responses to challenge expected in the controls, the vaccinate shall be listed as a failure.

(3) The results of the testing shall be evaluated according to the following table:

CUMULATIVE TOTALS

Stage	Number of animals	Failures for satisfactory serials	Failures for unsatisfactory serials
1	10	1 or less	3 or more.
2 (or 1)	20	4 or less	5 or more.

(4) When a serial has been found unsatisfactory for potency by the test provided in paragraphs (e)(1), (2), and (3) of this section, the serial shall be withheld from the market and the following actions taken:

(i) The Administrator shall require that at least two additional serials prepared with the same Master Seed be subjected to similar animal potency tests by Animal and Plant Health Inspection Service or the licensee or both.

(ii) If another serial is found unsatisfactory for potency, the product shall be removed from the market while a reevaluation of the product is made and the problem is resolved.

[49 FR 22625, May 31, 1984, as amended at 56 FR 66784, 66786, Dec. 26, 1991; 62 FR 19038, Apr. 18, 1997; 72 FR 72564, Dec. 21, 2007; 79 FR 31021, May 30, 2014]

§ 113.9 New potency test.

A potency test written into the filed Outline of Production for a product shall be considered confidential information by Animal and Plant Health Inspection Service until at least two additional product licenses are issued for the product or unless use of the test is authorized by the licensee, in which case, such potency test may be published as part of the Standard Requirement for the product.

(a) Until a potency test is published as part of the Standard Requirement for the product, reference to such a test shall be made in the filed Outline of Production and the test shall be conducted.

(b) When a potency test has been published as part of the Standard Requirement, such test shall be conducted unless the product is specifically exempted as provided in § 113.4.

[40 FR 14084, Mar. 28, 1975, as amended at 56 FR 66784, Dec. 26, 1991]

§ 113.10 Testing of bulk material for export or for further manufacture.

When a product is prepared in a licensed establishment for export in large multiple-dose containers as provided in § 112.8(d) or (e) of this subchapter or for further manufacturing purposes as provided in § 114.3(d) of this subchapter, samples of the bulk material shall be subjected to all required tests prescribed in the filed Outline of Production or Standard Requirements for the product. Samples of concentrated liquid product shall be diluted to a volume equal to the contents of the sample times the concentration factor prior to initiating potency tests.

[49 FR 45846, Nov. 21, 1984]

STANDARD PROCEDURES

§ 113.25 Culture media for detection of bacteria and fungi.

(a) Ingredients for which standards are prescribed in the United States Pharmacopeia, or elsewhere in this part, shall conform to such standards. In lieu of preparing the media from the individual ingredients, they may be made from dehydrated mixtures which, when rehydrated with purified water, have the same or equivalent composition as such media and have growth-promoting buffering, and oxygen tension-controlling properties equal to or better than such media. The formulas for the composition of the culture media prescribed in §§ 113.26 and 113.27 are set forth in the United States Pharmacopeia, 19th Edition.

(b) The licensee shall test each quantity of medium prepared at one time from individual ingredients and the first quantity prepared from each lot of commercial dehydrated medium for growth-promoting qualities. If any portion of a lot of commercial dehydrated medium is held for 90 days or longer after being so tested, it shall be retested before use. Two or more strains of micro-organisms that are exacting in their nutritive requirements shall be used. More than one dilution shall be used to demonstrate the adequacy of the medium to support the growth of a minimum number of micro-organisms.

(c) The sterility of the medium shall be confirmed by incubating an adequate number of test vessels and examining each for growth. Additional control may be used by incubation of representative uninoculated test vessels for the required incubation period during each test.

(d) A determination shall be made by the licensee for each biological product of the ratio of inoculum to medium which shall result in sufficient dilution of such product to prevent bacteriostatic and fungistatic activity. The determination may be made by tests on a representative biological product for each group of comparable products containing identical preservatives at equal or lower concentrations. Inhibitors or neutralizers of preservatives, approved by the Administrator, may be considered in determining the proper ratio.

[35 FR 16039, Oct. 13, 1970, as amended at 37 FR 2430, Feb. 1, 1972; 41 FR 27715, July 6, 1976; 56 FR 66784, Dec. 26, 1991]

§ 113.26 Detection of viable bacteria and fungi except in live vaccine.

Each serial and subserial of biological product except live vaccines shall be tested as prescribed in this section unless otherwise specified by the Administrator. When cell lines, primary cells, or ingredients of animal origin used in the preparation of a biological product are required to be free of viable bacteria and fungi, they shall also be tested as prescribed in this section.

(a) The media to be used shall be as follows:

(1) Fluid Thioglycollate Medium with 0.5 percent beef extract shall be used to test for bacteria in biological products containing clostridial toxoids, bacterins, and bacterin-toxoids.

(2) Fluid Thioglycollate Medium with or without 0.5 percent beef extract shall be used to test for bacteria in biological products other than clostridial toxoids, bacterins, and bacterin-toxoids.

(3) Soybean-Casein Digest Medium shall be used to test biological products for fungi; provided, that Fluid Thioglycollate Medium without beef extract shall be substituted when testing biological products containing mercurial preservatives.

(b) Test procedure:

(1) Ten test vessels shall be used for each of two media selected in accordance with paragraph (a)(1), (a)(2), or (a)(3) of this section. Each test vessel shall contain sufficient medium to negate the bacteriostatic or fungistatic activity in the inoculum as determined in § 113.25(d).

(2) Inoculum:

(i) When completed product is tested, 10 final container samples from each serial and each subserial shall be tested. One ml from each sample shall be inoculated into a corresponding individual test vessel of culture medium: *Provided*, That, if each final container sample contains less than 2 ml, one-half of the contents shall be used as inoculum for each test vessel.

(ii) When cell lines, primary cells, or ingredients of animal origin are tested, at least a 20 ml test sample from each lot shall be tested. One ml shall be inoculated into each test vessel of medium.

(3) Incubation shall be for an observation period of 14 days at 30 °to 35 °C. to test for bacteria and 14 days at 20 °to 25 °C. to test for fungi.

(4) If the inoculum renders the medium turbid so that the absence of growth cannot be determined by visual examination, subcultures shall be made

on the seventh to eleventh day from biological products prepared from clostridial toxoids, bacterins, and bacterin-toxoids and the third to seventh day for other biological products. Portions of the turbid medium in amounts of not less than 1.0 ml. shall be transferred to 20 to 25 ml. of fresh medium, and incubated the balance of the 14-day period.

(c) Examine the contents of all test vessels for macroscopic microbial growth during the incubation period. When demonstrated by adequate controls to be invalid, the test may be repeated. For each set of test vessels representing a serial or subserial in a valid test, the following rules shall apply:

(1) If no growth is found in any test vessel, the serial or subserial meets the requirements of the test.

(2) If growth is found in any test vessel, one retest to rule out faulty technique may be conducted using 20 unopened final container samples.

(3) If growth is found in any test vessel of the final test, the serial, subserial, or ingredients to be used in the preparation of a biological product, as the case may be, is unsatisfactory.

[35 FR 16039, Oct. 13, 1970, as amended at 37 FR 2430, Feb. 1, 1972; 39 FR 21042, June 18, 1974; 40 FR 758, Jan. 3, 1975; 40 FR 14084, Mar. 28, 1975; 56 FR 66784, Dec. 26, 1991]

§ 113.27 Detection of extraneous viable bacteria and fungi in live vaccines.

Unless otherwise specified by the Administrator or elsewhere exempted in this part, each serial and subserial of live vaccine and each lot of Master Seed Virus and Master Seed Bacteria shall be tested for extraneous viable bacteria and fungi as prescribed in this section. A Master Seed found unsatisfactory shall not be used in vaccine production and a serial found unsatisfactory shall not be released.

(a) *Live viral vaccines.* Each serial and subserial of live viral vaccine shall be tested for purity as prescribed in this paragraph. However, products of chicken embryo origin recommended for administration other than by parenteral injection may be tested as provided in paragraph (e) of this section.

(1) Soybean Casein Digest Medium shall be used.

(2) Ten final container samples from each serial and subserial shall be tested.

(3) Immediately prior to starting the test, frozen liquid vaccine shall be thawed, and desiccated vaccine shall be rehydrated as recommended on the label with accompanying diluent or with sterile purified water.

(4) To test for bacteria, place 0.2 ml of vaccine from each final container into a corresponding individual vessel containing at least 120 ml of Soybean Casein Digest Medium. Additional medium shall be used if the determination required in § 113.25(d) indicates the need for a greater dilution of the product. Incubation shall be at 30 °to 35 °C for 14 days.

(5) To test for fungi, place 0.2 ml of vaccine from each final container sample into a corresponding individual vessel containing at least 40 ml of Soybean Casein Digest Medium. Additional medium shall be used if the determination required in § 113.25(d) indicates the need for a greater dilution of the product. Incubation shall be at 20 °to 25 °C for 14 days.

(6) Examine the contents of all test vessels macroscopically for microbial growth at the end of the incubation period. If growth in a vessel cannot be reliably determined by visual examination, judgment shall be confirmed by subcultures, microscopic examination, or both.

(7) For each set of test vessels representing a serial or subserial tested according to these procedures, the following rules shall apply:

(i) If growth is found in 2 or 3 test vessels of the initial test, 1 retest to rule out faulty technique may be conducted using 20 unopened final container samples.

(ii) If no growth is found in 9 or 10 of the test vessels in the initial test, or 19 or 20 vessels in the retest, the serial or subserial meets the requirements of the test.

(iii) If growth is found in four or more test vessels in the initial test, or two or more in a retest, the serial or subserial is unsatisfactory.

(b) *Live bacterial vaccines.* Each serial or subserial of live bacterial vaccine shall be tested for purity as prescribed in this paragraph.

(1) Soybean Casein Digest Medium and Fluid Thioglycollate Medium shall be used.

(2) Ten final container samples from each serial and subserial shall be tested.

(3) Immediately prior to starting the test, frozen liquid vaccine shall be thawed, and desiccated vaccine shall be rehydrated as recommended on the label with accompanying diluent or with sterile purified water. Product recommended for mass vaccination shall be rehydrated at the rate of 30 ml sterile purified water per 1,000 doses.

(4) To test for extraneous bacteria, place 0.2 ml of vaccine from each final container into a corresponding individual vessel containing at least 40 ml of Fluid Thioglycollate Medium. Additional medium shall be used if the determination required in § 113.25(d) indicates the need for a greater dilution of the product. Incubation shall be at 30 °to 35 °C for 14 days.

(5) To test for extraneous fungi, place 0.2 ml of vaccine from each final container into a corresponding individual vessel containing at least 40 ml of Soybean Casein Digest Medium. Additional medium shall be used if the determination required in § 113.25(d) indicates the need for a greater dilution of the product. Incubation shall be at 20 °to 25 °C for 14 days.

(6) Examine the contents of all test vessels macroscopically for atypical microbial growth at the end of the incubation period. If growth of extraneous microorganisms cannot be reliably determined by visual examination, judgment shall be confirmed by subculturing, microscopic examination, or both.

(7) For each set of test vessels representing a serial or subserial tested according to these procedures, the following rules shall apply:

(i) If extraneous growth is found in 2 or 3 test vessels of the initial test, 1 retest to rule out faulty technique may be conducted using 20 unopened final container samples.

(ii) If no extraneous growth is found in 9 or 10 test vessels in the initial test, or 19 or 20 vessels in the retest, the serial or subserial meets the requirements of the test.

(iii) If extraneous growth is found in 4 or more test vessels in the initial test, or 2 or more in a retest, the serial or subserial is unsatisfactory.

(c) *Master Seed Virus.* Not less than 4 ml of each lot of Master Seed Virus shall be tested. Frozen liquid Master Seed Virus shall be thawed, and desiccated Master Seed Virus shall be rehydrated with Soybean Casein Digest Medium immediately prior to starting the test.

(1) To test for bacteria, place 0.2 ml of the sample of Master Seed Virus into 10 individual vessels each containing at least 120 ml of Soybean Casein Digest Medium. Incubation shall be at 30 °to 35 °C for 14 days.

(2) To test for fungi, place 0.2 ml of the sample of Master Seed Virus into 10 individual vessels each containing at least 40 ml of Soybean Casein Digest Medium. Incubation shall be at 20 °to 25 °C for 14 days.

(3) Examine the contents of all test vessels macroscopically for microbial growth at the end of the incubation period. If growth in a vessel cannot be reliably determined by visual examination, judgment shall be confirmed by subcultures, microscopic examination, or both.

(4) For each set of test vessels representing a lot of Master Seed Virus tested according to these procedures, the following rules shall apply:

(i) If growth is found in any test vessel of the initial test, one retest to rule out faulty technique may be conducted using a new sample of Master Seed Virus.

(ii) If growth is found in any test vessel of the final test, the lot of Master Seed Virus is unsatisfactory.

(d) *Master Seed Bacteria.* Not less than 4 ml of each lot of Master Seed Bacteria shall be tested. Frozen liquid Master Seed Bacteria shall be thawed, and desiccated Master Seed Bacteria shall be rehydrated with sterile purified water immediately prior to starting the test.

(1) To test for extraneous bacteria, place 0.2 ml of the sample of Master Seed Bacteria into 10 individual vessels each containing at least 40 ml of Fluid Thioglycollate Medium. Incubation shall be at 30 °to 35 °C for 14 days.

(2) To test for extraneous fungi, place 0.2 ml of the sample of Master Seed Bacteria into 10 individual vessels each containing at least 40 ml of Soybean Casein Digest Medium. Incubation shall be at 20 °to 25 °C for 14 days.

(3) Examine the contents of all test vessels macroscopically for atypical microbial growth at the end of the incubation period. If growth of extraneous microorganisms cannot be reliably determined by visual examination, judgment shall be confirmed by subcultures, microscopic examination, or both.

(4) For each set of test vessels representing a lot of Master Seed Bacteria tested according to these procedures, the following rules shall apply:

(i) If extraneous growth is found in any test vessel of the initial test, one retest to rule out faulty technique may be conducted using a new sample of Master Seed Bacteria.

(ii) If extraneous growth is found in any test vessel of the final test, the lot of Master Seed Bacteria is unsatisfactory.

(e) Live viral vaccines of chicken embryo origin recommended for administration other than by parenteral injection, which were not tested or have not been found free of bacteria and fungi by the procedures prescribed in paragraph (a) of this section, may be tested according to the procedures prescribed in this paragraph.

(1) Brain Heart Infusion Agar shall be used with 500 Kinetic (Kersey) units of penicillinase per ml of medium added just prior to pouring the plates.

(2) Ten final containers from each serial and each subserial shall be tested.

(3) Immediately prior to starting the test, frozen liquid vaccine shall be thawed, and lyophilized vaccine shall be rehydrated to the quantity recommended on the label using the accompanying sterile diluent or sterile purified water. Product recommended for mass vaccination shall be rehydrated at the rate of 30 ml sterile purified water per 1,000 doses.

(4) From each container sample, each of 2 plates shall be inoculated with vaccine equal to 10 doses if the vaccine is recommended for poultry or 1 dose if the vaccine is recommended for other animals. Twenty ml of medium shall be added to each plate. One plate shall be incubated at 30 °to 35 °for 7 days and the other plate shall be incubated at 20 °to 25 °C for 14 days.

(5) Colony counts shall be made for each plate at the end of the incubation period. An average colony count for the 10 samples representing the serial or subserial shall be made for each incubation condition.

(6) For each set of test vessels representing a serial or subserial tested according to these procedures, the following rules shall apply:

(i) If the average count at either incubation condition exceeds 1 colony per dose for vaccines recommended for poultry, or 10 colonies per dose for vaccines recommended for other animals in the initial test, 1 retest to rule out faulty technique may be conducted using 20 unopened final containers.

(ii) If the average count at either incubation condition of the final test for a serial or subserial exceeds 1 colony per dose for vaccines recommended for poultry, or 10 colonies per dose for vaccines recommended for other animals, the serial or subserial is unsatisfactory.

[48 FR 28430, June 22, 1983, as amended at 56 FR 66784, Dec. 26, 1991]

§ 113.28 Detection of mycoplasma contamination.

The heart infusion test, using heart infusion broth and heart infusion agar, provided in this section shall be conducted when a test for mycoplasma contamination is prescribed in an applicable Standard Requirement or in the filed Outline of Production for the product.

(a) Media additives provided in this paragraph shall be prepared as follows:

(1) DPN-Cysteine Solution:

(i) Use Nicotinamide adenine dinucleotide (oxidized) and L-Cysteine hydrochloride.

(ii) Prepare 1 gram/100 milliliters (ml) purified water (1 percent solution) of each. Mix the solutions together; the cysteine reduces the DPN. Filter sterilize, dispense in appropriate amounts and store frozen at −20 degrees centigrade.

(2) Inactivated horse serum—horse serum which has been inactivated at 56 °C for 30 minutes.

(b) Heart infusion broth shall be prepared as provided in this paragraph.

(1) Dissolve in 970 ml of purified water, 25 grams of heart infusion broth, 10 grams of proteose peptone No. 3, and either 5 grams of yeast autolysate or 5 ml of fresh yeast extract.

(2) Add the following:

1 percent tetrazolium chloride (ml)	5.5
1 percent thallium acetate (ml)	25
Penicillin (units)	500,000
Inactivated horse serum (ml)	100

(3) Adjust pH to 7.9 with NaOH, filter sterilize, and dispense 100 ml aliquots into 125 ml flasks and store until needed.

(4) Add 2 ml of DPN-Cysteine solution to each 100 ml of broth on day of use.

(c) Heart Infusion Agar shall be prepared as provided in this paragraph.

(1) Dissolve in 900 ml of purified water by boiling the following:

Heart infusion agar (g)	25
Heart-infusion broth (g)	10
Proteose peptone No. 3 (g)	10
1 pct thallium acetate (ml)	25

(2) Cool the medium and adjust pH to 7.9 with NaOH.

(3) Autoclave the medium.

(4) Cool the medium 30 minutes in a 56 °C waterbath.

(5) Dissolve 5 grams of yeast autolysate in 100 ml of distilled water, filter sterilize, and add to the medium.

(6) Add to the medium:

126 ml of inactivated horse serum
21 ml of DPN-Cysteine solution
525,000 units of Penicillin.
Dispense 10 ml aliquots into 60 × 15 mm disposable culture dishes or petri dishes.

(d) The test procedure provided in this paragraph shall be followed when conducting the mycoplasma detection test.

(1) Preparation of inoculum. Immediately prior to starting the test, frozen liquid vaccine shall be thawed, and lyophilized vaccine shall be rehydrated to the volume recommended on the label with mycoplasma medium. In the case of a lyophilized biological product, e.g., 1,000 dose vial of poultry vaccine to be administered via the drinking water, the vaccine shall be rehydrated to 30 ml with mycoplasma medium. In the case of a cell line or a sample of primary cells, the inoculum shall consist of the resuspended cells. Control tests shall be established as provided in paragraph (d)(4) of this section.

(2) Inoculation of plate. Plate 0.1 ml of inoculum on an agar plate and make a short, continuous streak across the plate with a pipet. Tilt the plate to allow the inoculum to flow over the surface.

(3) Inoculation of flask of medium. Transfer 1 ml of the inoculum into a flask containing 100 ml mycoplasma medium and mix thoroughly. Incubate the flask at 33 to 37 °C for 14 days during which time, one of four agar plates shall be streaked with 0.1 ml of material from the incubating flask of inoculated medium on the 3d day, one on the 7th day, one on the 10th day, and one on the 14th day post-inoculation.

(4) Control tests shall be conducted simultaneously with the detection test using techniques provided in paragraphs (d)(2) and (3) of this section, except the inoculum for the positive control test shall be selected mycoplasma cultures and the negative control test shall be uninoculated medium from the same lot used in the detection test.

(5) All plates shall be incubated in a high humidity, 4–6 percent CO_2 atmosphere at 33 °to 37 °C for 10–14 days and examined with a stereoscopic microscope at 35x to 100x or with a regular microscope at 100x.

(e) Interpretation of test results.

(1) If growth appears on at least one of the plates in the positive control test and does not appear on any of the plates in the negative control test, the test is valid.

(2) If mycoplasma colonies are found on any of the plates inoculated with material being tested, the results are positive for mycoplasma contamination.

[38 FR 29887, Oct. 30, 1973, as amended at 41 FR 6752, Feb. 13, 1976; 41 FR 32882, Aug. 6, 1976]

§113.29 Determination of moisture content in desiccated biological products.

Methods provided in this section must be used when a determination of moisture content in desiccated biological products is prescribed in an applicable Standard Requirement or in the filed Outline of Production for the product. Firms currently using methods other than those provided in this section for determining the moisture content in desiccated biological products have until November 5, 2004 to update their Outlines of Production to be in compliance with this requirement.

(a) Final container samples of completed product shall be tested. The weight loss of the sample due to drying in a vacuum oven shall be determined. All procedures should be performed in an environment with a relative humidity less than 45 percent. The equipment necessary to perform the test is as follows:

(1) Cylindrical weighing bottles with airtight glass stoppers.

(2) Vacuum oven equipped with validated thermometer and thermostat. A suitable air-drying device should be attached to the inlet valve.

(3) Balance, accurate to 0.1 mg (rated precision ±0.01mg).

(4) Desiccator jar equipped with phosphorous pentoxide, silica gel, or equivalent.

(5) Desiccated vaccine in original sealed vial. Sample and control should be kept at room temperature in their original airtight containers until use.

(b) Test procedure:

(1) Thoroughly cleaned and labeled sample-weighing bottles with stoppers should be allowed to dry at 60 ±3 °C under vacuum at less than 2.5 kPa.

(i) Transfer hot bottles and stoppers into the desiccator and allow to cool to room temperature.

(ii) After bottles have cooled, insert stoppers and weigh and record the weights of the bottles as "A."

(iii) Return weighing bottles to the desiccator.

(2) Remove the sample container seal.

(i) Using a spatula, break up the sample plug and transfer the required amount of sample to the previously tared weighing bottle.

(ii) Insert the stopper and weigh and record the weights of the weighing bottles as "B."

(3) Place the weighing bottle with the stopper at an angle in the vacuum oven. Set the vacuum to <2.5 kPa and the temperature to 60 ±3 °C.

(4) After a minimum of 3 hours of drying time, turn off the vacuum pump and allow dry air to bleed into the oven until the pressure inside the oven is equalized with the prevailing atmospheric pressure.

(5) While the bottle is still warm, replace the stopper in its normal position and transfer the weighing bottle to the desiccator.

(i) Allow a minimum of 2 hours for the weighing bottle to cool to room temperature or for its weight to reach equilibrium.

(ii) Weigh, and record the weight as "C."

(6) Calculate the percentage of moisture in the original sample as follows:

$(B - C)/(B - A) \times (100)$ = Percentage of residual moisture, where:

A = tare weight of weighing bottle

B − A = weight of sample before drying

B − C = weight of sample after drying

(7) The results are considered satisfactory if the percentage of residual moisture is less than or equal to the manufacturer's specification.

[68 FR 57608, Oct. 6, 2003]

§ 113.30 Detection of Salmonella contamination.

The test for detection of Salmonella contamination provided in this section shall be conducted when such a test is prescribed in an applicable Standard Requirement or in the filed Outline of Production for the product.

(a) Samples shall be collected from the bulk suspension before bacteriostatic or bactericidal agents have been added. When tissue culture products are to be tested, 1 ml of tissue extract used as the source of cells or 1 ml of the minced tissue per se shall be tested.

(b) Five ml of the liquid vaccine suspension shall be used to inoculate each 100 ml of liquid broth medium (tryptose and either selenite F or tetrathionate). The inoculated media shall be incubated 18–24 hours at 35–37 °C.

(c) Transfers shall be made to either MacConkey agar or Salmonella-Shigella agar, incubated for 18–24 hours and examined.

(d) If no growth typical of Salmonella is noted, the plates shall be incubated an additional 18–24 hours and again examined.

(e) If suspicious colonies are observed, further subculture on suitable media shall be made for positive identification. If Salmonella is found, the bulk suspension is unsatisfactory.

[38 FR 29888, Oct. 30, 1973]

§113.31 Detection of avian lymphoid leukosis.

The complement-fixation test for detection of avian lymphoid leukosis provided in this section shall be conducted on all biological products containing virus which has been propagated in substrates of chicken origin: *Provided,* An inactivated viral product shall be exempt from this requirement if the licensee can demonstrate to Animal and Plant Health Inspection Service that the agent used to inactivate the vaccine virus would also inactivate lymphoid leukosis virus.

(a) Propagation of contaminating lymphoid leukosis viruses, if present, shall be done in chick embryo cell cultures.

(1) Each vaccine virus, cytopathic to chick embryo fibroblast cells, shall be effectively neutralized, inactivated, or separated so that minimal amounts of lymphoid leukosis virus can be propagated on cell culture during the 21-day growth period. If a vaccine virus cannot be effectively neutralized, inactivated, or separated, a sample of another vaccine prepared the same week from material harvested from each source flock (or other sampling procedure acceptable to Animal and Plant Health Inspection Service) used for the preparation of the questionable vaccine virus that cannot be neutralized, inactivated, or separated shall be tested each week during the preparation of such questionable vaccine.

(2) When cell cultures are tested, 5 ml of the final cell suspension as prepared for seeding of production cell cultures shall be used as inoculum. When vaccines are tested, the equivalent of 200 doses of Newcastle disease vaccine or 500 doses of other vaccines for use in poultry, or one dose of vaccine for use in other animals shall be used as inoculum. Control cultures shall be prepared from the same cell suspension as the cultures for testing the vaccine.

(3) Uninoculated chick embryo fibroblast cell cultures shall act as negative controls. One set of chick fibroblast cultures inoculated with subgroup A virus and another set inoculated with subgroup B virus shall act as positive controls, A and B respectively.

(4) The cell cultures shall be propagated at 35–37 °C for at least 21 days. They shall be passed when necessary to maintain viability and samples harvested from each passage shall be tested for group specific antigen.

(b) The microtiter complement-fixation test shall be performed using either the 50 percent or the 100 percent hemolytic end point technique to determine complement unitage. Five 50 percent hemolytic units or two 100 percent hemolytic units of complement shall be used for each test.

(1) All test materials, including positive and negative controls, shall be stored at −60 °C or colder until used in the test. Before use, each sample shall be thawed and frozen three times to disrupt intact cells and release the group specific antigen.

(2) The antiserum used in the microtiter complement-fixation test shall be a standard reagent supplied or approved by the Animal and Plant Health Inspection Service. Four units of antiserum shall be used for each test.

(3) Presence of complement-fixing activity in the harvested samples (from passages) at the 1:4 or higher dilution, in the absence of anticomplementary activity, shall be considered a positive test unless the activity can definitely be established to be caused by something other than lymphoid leukosis virus, subgroups A and/or B. Activity at the 1:2 dilution shall be considered suspicious and the sample further subcultured to determine presence or absence of the group specific antigen.

(4) Biological products or primary cells which are found contaminated with lymphoid leukosis viruses are unsatisfactory. Source flocks from which contaminated material was obtained are also unsatisfactory.

[38 FR 29888, Oct. 30, 1973, as amended at 38 FR 32917, Nov. 29, 1973; 39 FR 21042, June 18, 1974; 56 FR 66784, Dec. 26, 1991]

§ 113.32 Detection of Brucella contamination.

The test for detection of Brucella contamination provided in this section shall be conducted when such a test is prescribed in an applicable Standard Requirement or in a filed Outline of Production for the product.

(a) One ml of the minced tissue used as the source of cells or 1 ml of the extract of the tissue prior to the addition of antibiotics, diluent and stabilizer, shall be inoculated onto each of three tryptose agar plates and incubated in a 10 percent CO_2 atmosphere at a temperature of 35–37 °C for at least 7 days.

(b) If colonies are identified as Brucella, the biological product is unsatisfactory.

(c) If colonies suspicious of Brucella are observed but cannot be identified as a Brucella species, either

(1) The biological product shall be regarded as unsatisfactory and destroyed; or

(2) Further subculture or other procedures shall be carried out until a positive identification can be made.

[38 FR 29888, Oct. 30, 1973]

§ 113.33 Mouse safety tests.

One of the mouse safety tests provided in this section shall be conducted when such test is prescribed in a Standard Requirement or in the filed Outline of Production for a biological product recommended for animals other than poultry: *Provided*, That if the inherent nature of one or more ingredients makes the biological product lethal or toxic for mice but not lethal or toxic for the animals for which it is recommended, the licensee shall demonstrate the safety of such product by an acceptable test written into such Outline of Production.

(a) Final container samples of completed product from live virus vaccines shall be tested for safety using young adult mice in accordance with the test provided in this paragraph.

(1) Vaccine prepared for use as recommended on the label shall be tested by inoculating eight mice intraperitoneally or subcutaneously with 0.5 mL (the inoculation volume may be divided among more than one injection site), and the animals observed for 7 days.

(2) If unfavorable reactions attributable to the product occur in any of the mice during the observation period, the serial or subserial is unsatisfactory. If unfavorable reactions which are not attributable to the product occur, the test shall be declared a No Test and may be repeated: *Provided*, That, if the test is not repeated, the serial or subserial shall be declared unsatisfactory.

(b) Bulk or final container samples of completed product from liquid products, such as but not limited to antiserums and bacterins, shall be tested for safety in accordance with the test provided in this paragraph.

(1) Unless otherwise prescribed in the Standard Requirement or approved in a filed Outline of Production for the product, a 0.5 ml dose shall be injected intraperitoneally or subcutaneously into eight mice and the animals observed for 7 days.

(2) If unfavorable reactions attributable to the product occur in any of the mice during the observation period, the serial or subserial is unsatisfactory. If unfavorable reactions which are not attributable to the product occur, the test shall be declared a No Test and may be repeated: *Provided*, That, if the test is not repeated, the serial or subserial shall be declared unsatisfactory.

[38 FR 34727, Dec. 18, 1973, as amended at 39 FR 16857, May 10, 1974; 72 FR 72564, Dec. 21, 2007]

§ 113.34 Detection of hemagglutinating viruses.

The test for detection of hemagglutinating viruses provided in this section shall be conducted when such a test is prescribed in an applicable Standard Requirement or in the filed Outline of Production for the product.

(a) Final container samples of completed product rehydrated as recommended on the label shall be used as inoculum: *Provided*, That poultry vaccines distributed without diluent shall be rehydrated with 30 ml of sterile distilled water per 1,000 doses and used as inoculum. When one or more fractions are to be used in combination with

Newcastle Disease Vaccine, test samples shall be collected from bulk suspensions of each prior to mixing with the Newcastle Disease Vaccine.

(b) Each of ten 9- to 10-day-old embryonating eggs from Newcastle disease susceptible flocks shall be inoculated into the allantoic cavity with 0.2 ml of the undiluted inoculum.

(1) Test five uninoculated embryos of the same age and from the same flock as those used for the test as negative controls.

(2) Test an allantoic fluid sample of Newcastle disease virus as a positive control.

(c) Three to five days post-inoculation, a sample of allantoic fluid from each egg shall be tested separately by a rapid plate test for hemagglutinating activity using a 0.5 percent suspension of fresh chicken red blood cells.

(d) If the results are inconclusive, one or two blind passages shall be made using fluids from each of the original test eggs. Fluids from dead and live embryos may be pooled separately for inoculum in these passages.

(e) If hemagglutinating activity attributable to the product is observed, the serial is unsatisfactory.

[38 FR 29889, Oct. 30, 1973]

§ 113.35 Detection of viricidal activity.

The test for detection of viricidal activity provided in this section shall be conducted when such a test is prescribed in an applicable standard requirement or in the filed Outline of Production for each inactivated liquid biological product used as diluent for a desiccated live virus vaccine in a combination package.

(a) Bulk or final container samples of completed product from each serial shall be tested.

(b) The product shall be tested with each virus fraction for which it is to be used as a diluent. If the vaccine to be rehydrated contains more than one virus fraction, the test shall be conducted with each fraction after neutralization of the other fraction(s), and/or dilution of the vaccine beyond the titer range of the other fraction(s), or the test shall be conducted using representative single-fraction desiccated vaccines which are prepared by the licensee and which are licensed. *Provided*, That the Administrator may authorize licensees to prepare and use unlicensed single-fraction vaccines for this purpose.

(c) Test procedure: (1) Rehydrate at least two vials of the vaccine with the liquid product under test according to label recommendations and pool the contents.

(2) Rehydrate at least two vials of the vaccine with the same volume of sterile purified water and pool the contents.

(3) Neutralize to remove other fractions, if necessary.

(4) Hold the two pools of vaccine at room temperature (20 °to 25 °C) for 2 hours. The holding period shall begin when rehydration is completed.

(5) Titrate the virus(es) in each pool of vaccine as provided in the filed Outline of Production or an applicable standard requirement.

(6) Compare respective titers.

(d) If the titer of the vaccine virus(es) rehydrated with the product under test is more than 0.7 $\log_{10}$ below the titer of the vaccine virus(es) rehydrated with sterile purified water, the product is unsatisfactory for use as diluent.

(e) If the product is unsatisfactory in the first test, one retest to rule out faulty techniques may be conducted using four vials of the vaccine for each pool and the acceptability of the product judged by the results of the second test.

(f) Liquid products found to be unsatisfactory for use as diluent by this test are not prohibited from release as separate licensed products if labeled as prescribed in § 112.7(g).

[44 FR 25412, May 1, 1979, as amended at 56 FR 66784, Dec. 26, 1991; 64 FR 43044, Aug. 9, 1999]

§ 113.36 Detection of pathogens by the chicken inoculation test.

The test for detection of extraneous pathogens provided in this section shall be conducted when such a test is prescribed in an applicable Standard Requirement or in the filed Outline of Production for the product.

(a) The biological product to be tested shall be prepared for use as recommended on the label, or in the case of desiccated vaccine to be used in poultry, rehydrated with sterile distilled water at the rate of 30 ml per 1,000 doses.

(b) At least 25 healthy susceptible young chickens, properly identified and obtained from the same source and hatch, shall be immunized at least 14 days prior to being put on test. The immunizing agent shall be the same as the product to be tested but from a serial previously tested and found satisfactory.

(c) At least 20 of the previously immunized birds shall be inoculated with 10 label doses of the vaccine being tested by each of the following routes: Subcutaneous, intratracheal, eye-drop, and comb scarification (1 cm^2). Twenty birds may be used for each route or combination of routes.

(d) At least five birds shall be isolated as control birds.

(e) All birds shall be observed for 21 days for signs of septicemic diseases, respiratory diseases, or other pathologic conditions.

(f) If the controls remain healthy and unfavorable reactions attributable to the product occur in the vaccinates, the serial or subserial tested is unsatisfactory. If the controls do not remain healthy or if unfavorable reactions not attributable to the product occur in the vaccinates, or both, the test shall be declared a No Test and may be repeated: *Provided*, That, if the test is not repeated, the serial of subserial tested shall be considered unsatisfactory.

[38 FR 29889, Oct. 30, 1973, as amended at 39 FR 21042, June 18, 1974; 43 FR 7610, Feb. 24, 1978]

§ 113.37 Detection of pathogens by the chicken embryo inoculation test.

The test for detection of extraneous pathogens provided in this section shall be conducted when such a test is prescribed in an applicable Standard Requirement or in the filed Outline of Production for the product.

(a) The biological product to be tested shall be prepared for use as recommended on the label, or in the case of desiccated vaccine to be used in poultry, rehydrated with sterile distilled water at the rate of 30 ml per 1,000 doses.

(b) One volume of the prepared vaccine shall be mixed with up to nine volumes of sterile heat-inactivated specific antiserum to neutralize the vaccine virus in the product. Each lot of antiserum shall be demonstrated by virus neutralization tests not to inhibit other viruses known to be possible contaminants.

(c) After neutralization, 0.2 ml of the vaccine-serum mixture shall be inoculated into each of at least 20 fully susceptible chicken embryos.

(1) Twenty embryos, 9 to 11 days old, shall be inoculated on the chorioallantoic membrane (CAM) with 0.1 ml, and in the allantoic sac with 0.1 ml.

(2) Eggs shall be candled daily for 7 days. Deaths occurring during the first 24 hours shall be disregarded but at least 18 viable embryos shall survive 24 hours post-inoculation for a valid test. Examine all embryos and CAM's from embryos which die after the first day. When necessary, embryo subcultures shall be made to determine the cause of a death. The test shall be concluded on the seventh day post-inoculation and the surviving embryos (including CAM's) examined.

(d) If death and/or abnormality attributable to the inoculum occur, the serial is unsatisfactory: *Provided*, That, if there is a vaccine virus override, the test may be repeated, using a higher titered antiserum.

[38 FR 29889, Oct. 30, 1973, as amended at 39 FR 21042, June 18, 1974]

§ 113.38 Guinea pig safety test.

The guinea pig safety test provided in this section shall be conducted when prescribed in a Standard Requirement or approved Outline of Production for a biological product. When desiccated products are tested, final container samples of completed product prepared for administration in the manner recommended on the label shall be used. When liquid products are tested, either bulk or final container samples of completed product shall be used.

(a) Unless otherwise specified in the Standard Requirement or approved Outline of Production for the product, a 2 ml dose shall be injected either intramuscularly or subcutaneously into each of two guinea pigs and the animals observed for 7 days.

(b) If unfavorable reactions attributable to the product occur in either of the guinea pigs during the observation period, the serial or subserial is unsatisfactory. If unfavorable reactions which are not attributable to the product occur, the test shall be declared a No Test and may be repeated: *Provided*, That, if the test is not repeated, the serial or subserial shall be declared unsatisfactory.

[39 FR 16857, May 10, 1974; 39 FR 20368, June 10, 1974]

§ 113.39 Cat safety tests.

The safety tests provided in this section shall be conducted when prescribed in a standard requirement or in the filed Outline of Production for a biological product recommended for use in cats.

(a) The cat safety test provided in this paragraph shall be used when the Master Seed Virus is tested for safety.

(1) The test animals shall be determined to be susceptible to the virus under test as follows:

(i) Throat swabs shall be collected from each cat and individually tested on susceptible cell cultures for the presence of the virus. Blood samples shall also be drawn and individual serum samples tested for antibody to the virus.

(ii) The cats shall be considered susceptible if swabs are negative for virus isolation and the serums are free of virus antibody at the 1:2 final dilution in a 50 percent plaque reduction test or other serum-neutralization test of equal sensitivity.

(iii) When determining susceptibility to a virus which does not lend itself to the methods in paragraphs (a)(1)(i) and (ii) of this section, a method acceptable to Animal and Plant Health Inspection Service shall be used.

(2) Each of at least 10 susceptible cats shall be administered a sample of the Master Seed Virus equivalent to the amount of virus to be used in one cat dose of the vaccine, by the method to be recommended on the label, and the cats observed each day for 14 days.

(3) If unfavorable reactions attributable to the virus occur in any of the cats during the observation period, the Master Seed Virus is unsatisfactory. If unfavorable reactions occur which are not attributable to the Master Seed Virus, the test shall be declared a No Test and repeated: *Provided*, That, if not repeated, the Master Seed Virus shall be unsatisfactory.

(b) The cat safety test provided in this paragraph shall be used when a serial of vaccine is tested for safety before release.

(1) Each of two healthy cats shall be administered 10 cat doses by the method recommended on the label and the cats observed each day for 14 days.

(2) If unfavorable reactions attributable to the biological product occur during the observation period, the serial is unsatisfactory. If unfavorable reactions occur which are not attributable to the product, the test shall be declared a No Test and repeated: *Provided*, That, if not repeated, the serial shall be unsatisfactory.

[44 FR 58898, Oct. 12, 1979, as amended at 56 FR 66784, Dec. 26, 1991]

§ 113.40 Dog safety tests.

The safety tests provided in this section shall be conducted when prescribed in a Standard Requirement or in the filed Outline of Production for a biological product recommended for use in dogs. Serials which are not found to be satisfactory when tested pursuant to the procedures in this section may not be released for shipment.

(a) The dog safety test provided in this paragraph shall be used when the Master Seed Virus is tested for safety.

(1) The test animals shall be determined to be susceptible to the virus under test by a method acceptable to the Animal and Plant Health Inspection Service.

(2) Each of at least 10 susceptible dogs shall be administered a sample of the Master Seed Virus equivalent to the amount of virus to be used in one dog dose of the vaccine, by the method recommended on the label, and the dog shall be observed each day for 14 days.

(3) If unfavorable reactions attributable to the virus occur in any of the dogs during the observation period, the Master Seed Virus is unsatisfactory. If unfavorable reactions occur which are not attributable to the Master Seed Virus, the test shall be declared a No Test and may be repeated: *Provided:* That, if the test is not repeated, the Master Seed Virus shall be considered unsatisfactory.

(b) The dog safety test provided in this paragraph shall be used when a serial of vaccine is tested for safety before release.

(1) Each of two healthy dogs shall be administered 10 dog doses by the method recommended on the label and the dogs shall be observed each day for 14 days.

(2) If unfavorable reactions attributable to the biological product occur during the observation period, the serial is unsatisfactory. If unfavorable reactions occur which are not attributable to the biological product, the test shall be declared a No Test and may be repeated: *Provided,* That, if the test is not repeated, the serial shall be considered unsatisfactory.

[60 FR 14358, Mar. 17, 1995]

§ 113.41 Calf safety test.

The calf safety test provided in this section shall be conducted when prescribed in a Standard Requirement or in the filed Outline of Production for a product.

(a) *Test procedure.* Each of two calves shall be injected with the equivalent of 10 doses of vaccine administered in the manner recommended on the label and observed each day for 21 days.

(b) *Interpretation.* If unfavorable reactions attributable to the product occur in either of the calves during the observation period, the serial or subserial is unsatisfactory. If unfavorable reactions which are not attributable to the product occur, the test shall be declared a No Test and may be repeated: *Provided,* That, if the test is not repeated, the serial or subserial shall be declared unsatisfactory.

[39 FR 27428, July 29, 1974]

§ 113.42 Detection of lymphocytic choriomeningitis contamination.

The test for detection of lymphocytic choriomeningitis (LCM) virus provided in this section shall be conducted when such a test is prescribed in an applicable Standard Requirement or in a filed Outline of Production. Vaccine virus may be neutralized with specific antiserum when necessary.

(a) Each of at least 10 mice obtained from a source free of LCM shall be injected in the footpad of a hindfoot with 0.02 ml of the material being tested and observed each day for 21 days.

(b) If any of the mice show swelling in the injected footpad or if more than one becomes systemically abnormal, the material being tested is unsatisfactory.

[42 FR 6794, Feb. 4, 1977]

§ 113.43 Detection of chlamydial agents.

The test for chlamydial agents provided in this section shall be conducted when such a test is prescribed in an applicable standard requirement or in a filed Outline of Production.

(a) The yolk sac of 6-day-old chicken embryos shall be injected. Three groups of 10 embryos shall be used sequentially.

(1) The inoculum for each embryo in the first group shall consist of 0.5 ml of a mixture of equal parts of the seed virus with phosphate buffered saline that may contain Streptomycin, Vancomycin, Kanamycin, or a combination thereof. Not more than 2 mg/ml of each antibiotic shall be used.

(2) On the 10th day postinoculation, the yolk sac of viable embryos shall be harvested, pooled, homogenized as a 20 percent suspension in phosphate buffered saline antibiotic diluent, and 0.5 ml of the mixture injected into the second group of chicken embryos. This process shall be repeated for the injection of the third group of embryos using the yolk sacs of viable embryos from the second group.

(3) For each of the three passages, embryo deaths occurring within 48 hours of injection shall be disregarded, except that if more than three such deaths occur at any passage, that passage shall be repeated.

(b) If one or more embryo deaths occur at any passage after 48 hours postinjection, the yolk sacs from each of the dead embryos shall be subcultured into 10 additional embryos. If one or more embryo deaths again occur due to chlamydial agents, the Master Seed Virus is unsatisfactory for use to produce vaccine.

[44 FR 58899, Oct. 12, 1979]

§ 113.44 Swine safety test.

The swine safety test provided in this section shall be conducted when prescribed in a Standard Requirement or in the filed Outline of Production for a product.

(a) *Test procedure.* (1) Inject each of two swine of the minimum age for which the product is recommended with the equivalent of two doses of bacterial vaccine or 10 doses of viral vaccine.

(2) Administer vaccine in the manner recommended on the label.

(3) Observe swine each day for 21 days.

(b) *Interpretation.* If unfavorable reactions attributable to the product occur in either of the swine during the observation period, the serial or subserial is unsatisfactory. If unfavorable reactions which are not attributable to the product occur, the test shall be declared a No Test and may be repeated; *Provided,* That, if the test is not repeated, the serial or subserial shall be declared unsatisfactory.

[48 FR 33476, July 22, 1983]

§ 113.45 Sheep safety test.

The sheep safety test provided in this section shall be conducted when prescribed in a Standard Requirement or in the filed Outline of Production for a product.

(a) *Test procedure.* (1) Inject each of two sheep of the minimum age for which the product is recommended with the equivalent of two doses of bacterial vaccine or 10 doses of viral vaccine.

(2) Administer vaccine in the manner recommended on the label.

(3) Observe sheep each day for 21 days.

(b) *Interpretation.* If unfavorable reactions attributable to the product occur in either of the sheep during the observation period, the serial or subserial is unsatisfactory. If unfavorable reactions which are not attributable to the product occur, the test shall be declared a No Test and may be repeated; *Provided,* That, if the test is not repeated, the serial or subserial shall be declared unsatisfactory.

[48 FR 33476, July 22, 1983]

§ 113.46 Detection of cytopathogenic and/or hemadsorbing agents.

The tests for detection of cytopathogenic and/or hemadsorbing agents provided in this section shall be conducted when prescribed in an applicable Standard Requirement or in the filed Outline of Production for a product.

(a) *Test for cytopathogenic agents.* One or more monolayers that are at least 6 cm^2 and at least 7 days from the last subculture shall be tested as provided in this paragraph.

(1) Stain each monolayer with a suitable cytological stain.

(2) Examine the entire area of each stained monolayer for evidence of inclusion bodies, abnormal number of giant cells, or other cytopathology indicative of cell abnormalities attributable to an extraneous agent.

(b) *Test for hemadsorbing agents.* One or more monolayers that are at least 6 cm^2 and at least 7 days from the last subculture shall be tested as provided in this paragraph.

(1) Wash the monolayer with several changes of phosphate buffered saline.

(2) Add an appropriate volume of a 0.2 percent red blood cell suspension to uniformly cover the surface of the monolayer of cultured cells. Suspensions of washed guinea pig and chicken red blood cells shall be used. These suspensions may be mixed before addition to the monolayer or they may be added separately to individual monolayers.

(3) Incubate the monolayer at 4 °C for 30 minutes, wash with phosphate buffered saline, and examine for hemadsorption.

(4) If no hemadsorption is apparent, repeat step (b)(2) of this section and incubate the monolayers at 20–25 °C for 30 minutes, wash with phosphate buffered saline, and examine again for hemadsorption. If desired, separate monolayers may be used for each incubation temperature.

(c) If specific cytopathology or hemadsorption attributable to an extraneous agent is found, the material under test is unsatisfactory and shall not be used to prepare biological products. If an extraneous agent is suspected because of cytopathology or hemadsorption and cannot be eliminated as a possibility by additional testing, the material under test is unsatisfactory.

[50 FR 441, Jan. 4, 1985, as amended at 58 FR 50252, Sept. 27, 1993]

§ 113.47 Detection of extraneous viruses by the fluorescent antibody technique.

The test for detection of extraneous viruses by the fluorescent antibody technique provided in this section shall be conducted when prescribed in an applicable Standard Requirement or in a filed Outline of Production for a product.

(a) Monolayer cultures of cells (monolayers), at least 7 days after the last subculturing, shall be processed and stained with the appropriate antiviral fluorochrome-conjugated antibody as specified in paragraph (b) of this section.

(1) Three groups of one or more monolayers shall be required for each specific virus prescribed in paragraph (b) of this section.

(i) At the time of the last subculturing, one group of test monolayers shall be inoculated with approximately 100–300 $FAID_{50}$ of the specific virus being tested for as positive controls.

(ii) One group of monolayers shall be the "material under test."

(iii) One group of monolayers, that are of the same type of cells as the test monolayers and that have been tested as prescribed in §§ 113.51 or 113.52 (whichever is applicable), shall be prepared as negative controls.

(2) Each group of monolayers shall have a total area of at least 6 cm^2.

(3) Positive control monolayers may be fixed (processed so as to arrest growth and assure attachment of the monolayer to the surface of the vessel in which they are grown) before 7 days after subculturing if fluorescence is enhanced by doing so, *Provided*, That a monolayer of the material under test is also fixed at the same time as the positive control and a monolayer of the material under test is also fixed at least seven days after subculturing. Monolayers that are fixed before 7 days after subculturing shall be stained at the same time as the test monolayers and negative controls fixed at least 7 days after subculturing.

(b) The antiviral fluorochrome-conjugated antibodies to be used shall depend on the type of cells required to be tested for extraneous viruses as specified in an applicable Standard Requirement or in a filed Outline of Production. Antiviral fluorochrome-conjugated antibodies specific for the extraneous viruses shall be applied to each respective type of cell in accordance with the following list. Under certain circumstances, additional tests may need to be conducted, as determined by the Administrator. When a specific antiviral fluorochrome-conjugated antibody is used in testing for the listed extraneous viruses specified in more than one cell type, it need only be applied to the most susceptible cell type.

(1) All cells shall be tested for:

(i) Bovine virus diarrhea virus;

(ii) Reovirus; and

(iii) Rabies virus.

(2) Bovine, caprine, and ovine cells shall, in addition, be tested for:

(i) Bluetongue virus;

(ii) Bovine adenoviruses;

(iii) Bovine parvovirus; and

(iv) Bovine respiratory syncytial virus.

(3) Canine cells shall, in addition, be tested for:

(i) Canine coronavirus;

(ii) Canine distemper virus; and

(iii) Canine parvovirus.

(4) Equine cells shall, in addition, be tested for:

(i) Equine herpesvirus; and

(ii) Equine viral arteritis virus.

(5) Feline cells shall, in addition, be tested for:

(i) Feline infectious peritonitis virus; and

(ii) Feline panleukopenia virus.

(6) Porcine cells shall, in addition, be tested for:

(i) Porcine adenovirus;

(ii) Porcine parvovirus;

(iii) transmissible gastroenteritis virus; and

(iv) Porcine hemagglutinating encephalitis virus.

(7) Firms that do not have rabies virus on premises either for research or production purposes are exempt from having to produce positive rabies virus control monolayers. Fixed positive rabies virus control monolayers will be

provided by the National Veterinary Services Laboratories.

(c) After staining, each group of monolayers shall be examined for the presence of specific fluorescence attributable to the presence of extraneous viruses.

(1) If the material under test shows any evidence of specific viral fluorescence, it is unsatisfactory and may not be used; *Provided*, That, if specific fluorescence attributable to the virus being tested for is absent in the positive control monolayers, the test is a No Test and may be repeated.

(2) If the fluorescence of the monolayers inoculated with the specific virus as positive controls is equivocal, or if the negative monolayers show equivocal fluorescence indicating possible viral contamination, or both, the test shall be declared a No Test, and may be repeated; *Provided*, That, if the test is not repeated, the material under test shall be regarded as unsatisfactory for use in the production of biologics.

[60 FR 24548, May 9, 1995]

INGREDIENT REQUIREMENTS

§ 113.50 Ingredients of biological products.

All ingredients used in a licensed biological product shall meet accepted standards of purity and quality; shall be sufficiently nontoxic so that the amount present in the recommended dose of the product shall not be toxic to the recipient; and in the combinations used shall not denature the specific substances in the product below the minimum acceptable potency within the dating period when stored at the recommended temperature.

[38 FR 29889, Oct. 30, 1973]

§ 113.51 Requirements for primary cells used for production of biologics.

Primary cells used to prepare biological products shall be derived from normal tissue of healthy animals. When prescribed in an applicable Standard Requirement or in the filed Outline of Production, each batch of primary cells used to prepare a biological product shall be tested as prescribed in this section. A batch of primary cells found unsatisfactory by any prescribed test shall not be used. A serial of biological product shall not be released if produced from primary cells that are found unsatisfactory by any prescribed test.

(a) Final container samples of completed product or samples of the final pool of harvested material or samples of each subculture of cells used to prepare the biological product shall be shown free of mycoplasma as prescribed in § 113.28. The sample for testing shall consist of at least 75 cm^2 of actively growing cells or the equivalent in harvest fluids; *Provided*, That all sources of cells in the batch of primary cells are represented.

(b) Final container samples of completed product or samples of the final pool of harvested material or samples of each subculture of cells used to prepare the biological product shall be shown free of bacteria and fungi as prescribed in § 113.26 or § 113.27 (whichever is applicable).

(c) A monolayer at least 75 cm^2 from each batch of primary cells or each subculture of primary cells used to prepare a biological product shall be shown free of extraneous agents as prescribed in this paragraph.

(1) The test monolayer shall be maintained using the medium (with additives) and under conditions similar to those used to prepare biological products.

(i) Monolayers of avian origin shall be maintained for at least 14 days and shall be subcultured at least once during the maintenance period. All but the last subculture shall result in a new monolayer of at least 75 cm^2. The last subculture shall meet the minimum area requirement specified in §§ 113.46 and 113.47.

(ii) Monolayers not of avian origin shall be maintained for at least 28 days and shall be subcultured at least twice during the maintenance period. All but the last subculture shall result in a new monolayer of at least 75 cm^2. The last subculture shall meet the minimum area requirement specified in §§ 113.46 and 113.47.

(2) Monolayers shall be examined regularly throughout the required maintenance period for evidence of the presence of cytopathogenic agents. If evidence of a cytopathogenic agent is found, the batch of primary cells is unsatisfactory.

(3) At the conclusion of the required maintenance period, monolayers shall be tested for:

(i) Cytopathogenic and/or hemadsorbing agents as prescribed in § 113.46;

(ii) Extraneous viruses by the fluorescent antibody technique as prescribed in § 113.47.

[50 FR 442, Jan. 4, 1985, as amended at 60 FR 24549, May 9, 1995]

§ 113.52 Requirements for cell lines used for production of biologics.

When prescribed in an applicable Standard Requirement or in a filed Outline of Production each cell line used to prepare a biological product shall be tested as prescribed in this section. A cell line found unsatisfactory by any prescribed test shall not be used. A serial of biological product shall not be released if produced from a cell line that is found unsatisfactory by any prescribed test.

(a) *General requirements.* (1) A complete record of the cell line shall be kept, such as, but not limited to, the source, passage history, and medium used for propagation.

(2) A Master Cell Stock (MCS) shall be established at a specified passage level for each cell line. The passage level and identity of the MCS and the highest passage level (MCS + n) intended for use in the preparation of a biological product shall be specified in the Outline of Production for the product.

(3) Sufficient 1.0 ml or larger aliquots of MCS and MCS + n shall be prepared, kept in a frozen state, and made available to Animal and Plant Health Inspection Service (APHIS) upon request for performing the tests prescribed in this section.

(4) Each lot of cells shall be monitored for the characteristics determined to be normal for the cell line, such as, but not limited to, microscopic appearance, growth rate, acid production, or other observable features.

(b) The MCS shall be shown to be of the same species of origin as that reported in paragraph (a)(1) of this section by the following method:

(1) At least four monolayers with a total area of at least 6 cm^2 shall be grown to at least 80 percent confluency.

(2) The monolayers shall be removed from their media, processed, stained, and examined.

(i) At least two monolayers shall be stained with an antispecies fluorchrome-conjugated antibody unrelated to the species of origin of the MCS.

(ii) At least two monolayers shall be stained with an antispecies fluorochrome-conjugated antibody specific to the species of origin of the MCS.

(iii) All monolayers shall be examined for evidence of specific fluorescence.

(3) If specific fluorescence is not found in the monolayers stained with the conjugate specific to the species of origin of the MCS, the cell line is unsatisfactory and shall not be used for vaccine production.

(4) If nonspecific fluorescence is found in the monolayers stained with conjugate from an unrelated species of origin or other results make the test results equivocal, the procedure shall be repeated until either specific fluorescence is found only in the monolayers stained with conjugate specific to the species of origin of the MCS and not in the control monolayers or specific fluorescence cannot be identified and the MCS is declared unsatisfactory.

(5) Alternate tests to determine the species of origin of the MCS may be used if approved by APHIS.

(c) The MCS and either each subculture of cells used to prepare a biological product or the final pool of harvested material (with or without the stabilizer) or final container samples of completed product for each serial of such product shall be shown to be free of mycoplasma as prescribed in § 113.28. The sample for testing shall consist of at least 75 cm^2 of actively growing cells or the equivalent, in harvest fluids. The cells shall represent all sources of cells in the batch.

(d) The MCS and either each subculture used to prepare a biological product or the final pool of harvested material for each serial of such product or final container samples of completed product for each serial of such product shall be tested for bacteria and fungi as prescribed in § 113.26 or § 113.27 (whichever is applicable). If bacteria or fungi are found in the MCS, the MCS shall not be used. If bacteria or fungi are found in a subculture, the subculture shall not be used.

(e) A monolayer at least 75 cm^2 from each MCS shall be shown free of extraneous agents as prescribed in this paragraph.

(1) The test monolayer shall be maintained for at least 21 days using the medium (with additives) intended for growth and maintenance and under conditions similar to those used to prepare biological products.

(2) Cells shall be subcultured at least two times during the maintenance period. All but the last subculture shall result in at least one new monolayer of at least 75 cm^2. The last subculture shall meet the minimum area requirement specified in §§ 113.46 and 113.47 and paragraph (f) of this section.

(3) Monolayers shall be examined regularly throughout the 21-day maintenance period for evidence of the presence of cytopathogenic agents. If evidence of a cytopathogenic agent is found, the MCS is unsatisfactory.

(4) At the conclusion of the 21-day maintenance period, monolayers shall be tested for:

(i) Cytopathogenic and/or hemadsorbing agents as prescribed in § 113.46; and

(ii) Extraneous agents by the fluorescent antibody technique as prescribed in § 113.47.

(f) At the conclusion of the 21-day maintenance period provided in paragraph (e) of this section, at least one monolayer of at least 75 cm^2 shall also be shown free of extraneous agents as prescribed in this paragraph.

(1) Alternately freeze and thaw the monolayer(s) three times. Centrifuge the disrupted cells at no greater than 2,000 × g for no more than 15 minutes to remove cellular debris. Divide the supernatant into equal aliquots and dispense 1.0 ml onto each of at least one monolayer (at least 75 cm^2) of:

(i) Vero (African green monkey kidney) cell line;

(ii) Embryonic cells, neonatal cells, or a cell line of the same species of origin as the MCS if different than provided in paragraph (f)(1)(i) of this section;

(iii) Embryonic cells, neonatal cells, or a cell line of the species for which the vaccine is recommended if different than provided in paragraph (f)(1)(ii) of this section; and

(iv) Embryonic cells, neonatal cells, or a cell line of bovine origin if not specified in paragraphs (f)(1)(ii), and (iii) of this section.

(2) The monolayers of cells specified in paragraphs (f)(1)(i), (ii), (iii), and (iv) of this section shall be maintained for at least 14 days after inoculation with the aliquot of disrupted MCS. Monolayers shall be subcultured at least once during the maintenance period. All but the last subculture shall result in a new monolayer of at least 75 cm^2. The last subculture shall meet the minimum area requirement specified in §§ 113.46 and 113.47.

(3) Monolayers shall be examined regularly throughout the 14-day maintenance period for evidence of the presence of cytopathogenic agents. If evidence of a cytopathogenic agent is found, the MCS is unsatisfactory.

(4) At the conclusion of the 14-day maintenance period, monolayers shall be tested for:

(i) Cytopathogenic and/or hemadsorbing agents as prescribed in § 113.46; and

(ii) Extraneous viruses by the fluorescent antibody technique as prescribed in § 113.47.

(g) The karyology of cells lines used in the production of biologics shall be examined as follows. A minimum of 50 mitotic cells shall be examined at both the MCS and MCS + n. The modal number in the MCS + n shall not exceed plus or minus 15 percent of the modal number of the MCS. Any marker chromosomes present in the MCS shall persist at the MCS + n. If the modal number exceeds the limits and/or the marker chromosomes do not persist (through the MCS + n passage level), the cell line shall not be used for vaccine production.

(h) If direct or indirect evidence exists that a cell line which is intended for use in the preparation of a vaccine may induce malignancies in the species for which the product is intended, that cell line shall be tested for tumorigenicity/oncogenicity by a method acceptable to APHIS.

[50 FR 442, Jan. 4, 1985; 50 FR 3316, Jan. 24, 1985, as amended at 56 FR 66784, Dec. 26, 1991; 60 FR 24549, May 9, 1995]

§ 113.53 Requirements for ingredients of animal origin used for production of biologics.

Each lot of ingredient of animal origin which is not subjected to heat sterilization or other sterilization methods acceptable to Animal and Plant Health Inspection Service (APHIS), such as, but not limited to serum and albumin, used to prepare a biological product shall be tested as prescribed in this section by the licensee or a laboratory acceptable to VS. Results of all tests shall be recorded by the testing laboratory and made a part of the licensee's records. A lot of ingredient found unsatisfactory by any prescribed test shall not be used to prepare a biological product. A serial of biological product shall not be released if produced using an ingredient that is found unsatisfactory by any prescribed test.

(a) Samples of each lot of ingredient of animal origin which is not subjected to heat sterilization, used to prepare a biological product shall be shown free of mycoplasma by the method prescribed in § 113.28.

(b) Samples of each lot of ingredient or animal origin which is not subjected to heat sterilization of other sterilization methods acceptable to APHIS used to prepare a biological product shall be shown free of bacteria and fungi as prescribed in § 113.26.

(c) Samples of each lot of ingredient of animal origin, except porcine trypsin, which is not subjected to heat sterilization or other viricidal procedure acceptable to APHIS used in the preparation of biological products shall be tested as prescribed in this paragraph;

(1) Monolayers at least 75 cm^2 of Vero (African green monkey kidney) cell line and of primary cells or a cell line of the same species of origin as the ingredient shall be used in the test. Cell lines used shall have been found satisfactory when tested as prescribed in § 113.52 and primary cells used shall have been found satisfactory when tested as prescribed in § 113.51.

(2) At least 3.75 ml or 15 percent of the ingredient shall be used in the growth medium for the preparation of at least 75 cm^2 test monolayers. The ingredient shall also be used in the growth medium when monolayers are subcultured. If the ingredient being tested is cytotoxic when tested in this manner, other procedures may be used if approved by APHIS.

(3) The test monolayers shall be maintained for at least 21 days.

(4) Cells shall be subcultured at least two times during the maintenance period. All but the last subculture shall result in at least one new monolayer of at least 75 cm^2. The last subculture shall meet the minimum area requirements specified in §§ 113.46 and 113.47.

(5) Monolayers shall be examined regularly throughout the 21-day maintenance period for evidence of cytopathogenic agents. If evidence of a cytopathogenic agent is found, the ingredient is unsatisfactory.

(6) At the conclusion of the 21-day maintenance period, monolayers shall be tested for:

(i) Cytopathogenic and/or hemadsorbing agents as prescribed in § 113.46; and

(ii) Extraneous viruses by the fluorescent antibody technique as prescribed in § 113.47.

(d) Each lot of porcine trypsin which has not been treated to inactivate porcine parvovirus (PPV) in a manner acceptable to VS shall be tested for PPV as prescribed in this paragraph.

(1) Not less than 5.0 grams of trypsin shall be dissolved in a volume of suitable diluent sufficient to fill a centrifuge angle head. After centrifuging for 1 hour at 80,000 × g, the pellet material shall be reconstituted in distilled water and inoculated into a flask containing 75 cm^2 of a 30 to 50 percent confluent monolayer culture of primary porcine cells or a porcine cell line of proven equal PPV susceptibility. An

additional flask of cells shall be held as a negative control.

(2) The test and control monolayers shall be maintained for at least 14 days and subcultured at least once during the maintenance period.

(3) At the end of the 14-day maintenance period, and 4 to 7 days after the last subculturing, monolayers shall be tested for the presence of porcine parvovirus by the fluorescent antibody technique as prescribed in §113.47(c).

(e) A sample of serum from each donor horse used to produce a lot of equine serum used in the preparation of biological products recommended for use in horses shall be tested at a laboratory approved by Animal and Plant Health Inspection Service using the Coggins test for equine infectious anemia antibodies. If antibodies to equine infectious anemia are found, the lot of serum is unsatisfactory.

[50 FR 442, Jan. 4, 1985; 50 FR 3316, Jan. 24, 1985, as amended at 56 FR 66784, Dec. 26, 1991; 60 FR 24549, May 9, 1995]

§ 113.54 Sterile diluent.

Sterile Diluent shall be supplied in a final container by the licensee when such diluent is required for rehydration or dilution of the vaccine.

(a) Sterile Diluent may be distilled or deionized water or it may be a special liquid solution formulated in accordance with an acceptable outline on file with Animal and Plant Health Inspection Service.

(b) Each quantity prepared at one time in a single container and bottled into final containers shall be designated as a serial. Each serial shall be given a number which shall be used in records, test reports, and on the final container label.

(c) Final container samples from each serial shall be tested for bacteria and fungi in accordance with the test provided in §113.26. Any serial found to be unsatisfactory shall not be released.

[39 FR 27428, July 29, 1974, as amended at 56 FR 66784, Dec. 26, 1991]

§ 113.55 Detection of extraneous agents in Master Seed Virus.

Unless otherwise prescribed in a Standard Requirement or in a filed Outline of Production, each Master Seed Virus (MSV) shall be tested as prescribed in this section. A MSV found unsatisfactory by any prescribed test shall not be used. A serial of biological product shall not be released if produced from a MSV that is found unsatisfactory by any prescribed test.

(a) At least a 1.0 ml aliquot per cell culture of MSV shall be dispensed onto monolayers (at least 75 cm^2 in area) of:

(1) Vero (African green monkey kidney) cell line;

(2) Embryonic cells, neonatal cells, or a cell line of the species for which the vaccine is recommended; and

(3) Embryonic cells, neonatal cells, or a cell line of the species of cells in which the MSV is presently being propagated if different than prescribed in paragraphs (a)(1) and (a)(2) of this section. Cell lines used shall have been found satisfactory when tested as prescribed in §113.52 and primary cells used shall have been found satisfactory when tested as prescribed in §113.51. If the MSV is cytopathic for or causes hemadsorption in the cells in which it is to be tested, the MSV shall be neutralized with monospecific antiserum supplied or approved by Animal and Plant Health Inspection Service (APHIS) or counteracted by a method approved by APHIS.

(b) At least one monolayer of each cell type used in the test shall be maintained as an uninoculated control.

(c) Each monolayer shall be maintained at least 14 days.

(d) Cells shall be subcultured at least once during the maintenance period. All but the last subculture shall result in at least one new monolayer at least 75 cm^2. The last subculture shall meet the minimum area requirement specified in §§113.46 and 113.47.

(e) Monolayers shall be examined regularly throughout the 14-day maintenance period for evidence of cytopathogenic agents. If evidence of a cytopathogenic agent is found, the MSV is unsatisfactory.

(f) At the conclusion of the 14-day maintenance period, monolayers shall be tested for:

(1) Cytopathogenic and/or hemadsorbing agents as prescribed in §113.46;

(2) Extraneous agents by the fluorescent antibody technique as prescribed in § 113.47.

[50 FR 444, Jan. 4, 1985, as amended at 56 FR 66784, Dec. 26, 1991]

LIVE BACTERIAL VACCINES

§ 113.64 General requirements for live bacterial vaccines.

When prescribed in an applicable Standard Requirement or in the filed Outline of Production, a live bacterial vaccine shall meet the requirements in this section.

(a) *Purity test.* Final container samples of completed product from each serial and subserial, and samples of each lot of Master Seed Bacteria shall be tested for the presence of extraneous viable bacteria and fungi in accordance with the test provided in § 113.27(b).

(b) *Safety tests.* (1) Samples of completed product from each serial or first subserial and samples of each lot of Master Seed Bacteria shall be tested for safety in young adult mice in accordance with the test provided in § 113.33(b) unless:

(i) The bacteria or agents in the vaccine are inherently lethal for mice.

(ii) The vaccine is recommended for poultry.

(2) Samples of completed product from each serial or first subserial of live bacterial vaccine shall be tested for safety in one of the species for which the product is recommended as follows:

(i) Live bacterial vaccine recommended for use in dogs shall be tested as provided in § 113.40, except that dogs shall be injected with the equivalent of two doses of vaccine administered as recommended on the label.

(ii) Live bacterial vaccine recommended for use in cattle shall be tested as provided in § 113.41, except that calves shall be injected with the equivalent of two doses of vaccine administered as recommended on the label.

(iii) Live bacterial vaccine recommended for use in sheep shall be tested as provided in § 113.45.

(iv) Live bacterial vaccine recommended for use in swine shall be tested as provided in § 113.44.

(c) *Identity test.* At least one of the identity tests provided in this paragraph shall be conducted for the Master Seed Bacteria and final container samples from each serial or first subserial of completed biological product. A known positive control (reference) provided or approved by Animal and Plant Health Inspection Service shall be included in such tests.

(1) *Fluorescent antibody test.* The direct fluorescent antibody staining technique shall be conducted using suitable smears of the vaccine bacteria. Fluorescence typical for the bacteria concerned shall be demonstrated. Fluorescence shall not occur in control smears treated with specific antiserum.

(2) *Tube agglutination test.* A tube agglutination test shall be conducted with a suitable suspension of the vaccine bacteria using the constant antigen decreasing serum method with specific antiserum. Agglutination typical for the bacteria shall be demonstrated. Agglutination shall not occur with negative serum used as a control in this test.

(3) *Slide agglutination test.* The rapid plate (slide) agglutination test shall be conducted with suitable suspensions of the vaccine bacteria using the hanging drop, slide or plate method, with specific antiserum. Agglutination typical for the bacteria shall be demonstrated by microscopic or macroscopic observation. Agglutination shall not occur with negative serum used as a control in this test.

(4) *Characterization tests.* Applicable biochemical and cultural characteristics shall be demonstrated as specified in the filed Outline of Production.

(d) *Ingredient requirements.* Ingredients used for the growth and preparation of Master Seed Bacteria and of live bacterial vaccine shall meet the requirements provided in § 113.50. Ingredients of animal origin shall meet the applicable requirements provided in § 113.53.

(e) *Moisture content.* The maximum percent moisture in desiccated vaccines shall be stated in the filed Outline of Production and shall be established by the licensee as follows:

(1) *Prelicensing.* Data obtained by conducting accelerated stability tests and

bacterial counts shall be acceptable on a temporary basis.

(2) *Licensed products.* Data shall be obtained by determining the percent moisture and bacterial count at release and expiration on a minimum of 10 consecutive released serials.

(3) Final container samples of completed product from each serial and subserial must be tested for moisture content in accordance with the test provided in §113.29.

[48 FR 33476, July 22, 1983, as amended at 54 FR 19352, May 5, 1989; 56 FR 66784, Dec. 26, 1991; 68 FR 57608, Oct. 6, 2003]

§113.65 Brucella Abortus Vaccine.

Brucella Abortus Vaccine shall be prepared as a desiccated live culture bacterial vaccine from smooth colonial forms of the *Brucella abortus* organism, identified as Strain 19. Each serial and subserial shall be tested for purity, potency, and moisture content. A serial or subserial found unsatisfactory by a prescribed test shall not be released.

(a) *Purity tests.* Each serial and subserial shall be tested for purity as provided in this paragraph.

(1) Macroscopic and microscopic examination shall be made on bulk samples from production containers. If organisms not typical of *Brucella abortus* organisms are evident, the serial or subserial is unsatisfactory.

(2) Two final container vials of completed product shall be tested by inoculating one tube of Dextrose Andrades broth with gas tube and one tube of thioglycollate broth from each vial. The inoculated media shall be incubated at 35 to 37 °C for 96 hours. If growth not typical of *Brucella abortus* organisms is evident, the serial or subserial is unsatisfactory.

(3) Bacterial dissociation test. Final container samples of completed product from each serial and subserial shall be tested for bacterial dissociation. Smooth colonies are the desired form. Rough colonies are undesirable terminal dissociation forms. Intermediate and intermediate-to-rough are also undesirable.

(i) The sample container shall be rehydrated and streaked on one potato agar plate in such a manner as to produce confluent colonies. Artificial reflected light shall be used so that the rays pass through the plate at a 45 °angle.

(ii) If the vaccine contains more than 5 percent rough colonies or more than 15 percent total undesirable colonies, the serial or subserial is unsatisfactory. If organisms or growth not characteristic of *Brucella abortus* are found, the serial or subserial is unsatisfactory. The test may be repeated one time using double the number of samples: *Provided,* That, if the test is not repeated, the serial or subserial is unsatisfactory.

(b) *Bacterial count requirements for reduced dose vaccine.* Each serial and each subserial shall be tested for potency.

(1) Two final container vials of completed product shall be tested for the number of viable organisms per dose of rehydrated vaccine. A bacterial count per vial shall be made on tryptose agar plates from suitable dilutions using 1 percent peptone as a diluent. The inoculated media shall be incubated at 35 to 37 °C for 96 hours.

(2) If the average count of the two final container samples of freshly prepared vaccine contains less than 3.0 or more than 10.0 billion organisms per dose, the serial or subserial is unsatisfactory.

(3) If the average count on the initial test is less than the minimum or greater than the maximum required in paragraph (b)(2) of this section, the serial or subserial may be retested one time using four additional final container vials. The average count of the retest is determined. If the average count of the four vials retested is less than the required minimum or greater than the required maximum, the serial or subserial is unsatisfactory. If the average count of the four vials retested is within the required limits described in paragraph (b)(2) of this section, the following shall apply:

(i) If the average count obtained in the initial test is less than one-third or more than three times the average count obtained on the retest, the average count of the initial test shall be considered the result of test system error and the serial or subserial is satisfactory.

(ii) If the average count obtained in the initial test is one-third or more than the average retest count or three times or less than the average retest count, a new average count shall be determined from the counts of all six vials. If the new average is less than the minimum or greater than the maximum required in paragraph (b)(2) of this section, the serial or subserial is unsatisfactory.

(4) If tested at any time within the expiration period, each dose of rehydrated vaccine must contain at least 3.0 billion viable organisms per dose.

(c) *Bacterial count requirements for standard vaccine.* Each serial and subserial shall be tested for potency.

(1) Two final container samples shall be tested for the number of viable organisms per milliliter of rehydrated vaccine. One bacterial count per vial shall be made on tryptose agar plates from suitable dilutions using 1 percent peptone as a diluent. The inoculated media shall be incubated at 35 to 37 °C for 96 hours.

(2) If the average count of the two final container samples of freshly prepared vaccine does not contain at least 10 billion viable organisms per milliliter, the serial or subserial is unsatisfactory.

(3) If the initial bacterial count is less than 10 billion organisms per milliliter, the serial or subserial may be retested one time using four samples. If the average count of the four vials retested is less than the required minimum, the serial or subserial is unsatisfactory.

(4) If tested at any time within the expiration period, each milliliter of rehydrated vaccine does not contain at least 5 billion viable organisms per milliliter, the serial or subserial is unsatisfactory.

[39 FR 16857, May 10, 1974. Redesignated at 39 FR 25463, July 11, 1974, and amended at 40 FR 758, Jan. 3, 1975; 50 FR 23794, Jan. 6, 1985]

§ 113.66 Anthrax Spore Vaccine—Nonencapsulated.

Anthrax Spore Vaccine—Nonencapsulated shall be a live spore suspension prepared from nonencapsulated variants of *Bacillus anthracis*. Only Master Seed which has been established as pure, safe, and immunogenic shall be used for production. All serials of vaccine shall be prepared from the first through the fifth passage from the Master Seed.

(a) The Master Seed shall meet the applicable general requirements prescribed in § 113.64 and the requirements in this section.

(b) Each lot of Master Seed shall be tested for immunogenicity as follows:

(1) Forty-two susceptible guinea pigs from the same source each weighing 400 to 500 grams, shall be used as test animals (30 vaccinates and 12 controls).

(2) An arithmetic mean spore count of vaccine produced from the highest passage of the Master Seed shall be established before the immunogenicity test is conducted. The guinea pigs used as vaccinates shall be injected as recommended on the label with a predetermined number of vaccine spores. To confirm the dosage, five replicate spore counts shall be conducted on a sample of the vaccine dilution used.

(3) Fourteen to fifteen days postvaccination the vaccinates and controls shall each be challenged with not less than 4,500 guinea pig LD_{50} of a virulent suspension of *Bacillus anthracis* furnished or approved by Animal and Plant Health Inspection Service and observed for 10 days.

(4) If at least 10 of the 12 controls do not die from *Bacillus anthracis* within the 10-day postchallenge observation period the test is invalid and may be repeated.

(5) If at least 27 of 30 of the vaccinates do not survive the 10-day postchallenge observation period, the Master Seed is unsatisfactory.

(6) An Outline of Production change shall be made before authority for use of a new lot of Master Seed shall be granted by Animal and Plant Health Inspection Service.

(c) *Test Requirements for Release.* Each serial and subserial shall meet the applicable general requirements prescribed in 9 CFR 113.64 and the requirements in this paragraph. Any serial or subserial found unsatisfactory by a prescribed test shall not be released.

(1) *Safety test.* Samples of completed product from each serial or first subserial shall be tested for safety in sheep or goats by the methods described in 9 CFR 113.45(a).

(2) *Spore Count Requirements.* Final container samples of completed product shall be tested for spore count. Samples shall be diluted in tenfold steps. Each dilution expected to yield 30 to 300 colonies per plate shall be plated in triplicate on tryptose agar, inverted, and incubated at 35 to 70 °C for 24 hours to 28 hours. Each plate having uniformly distributed colonies shall be counted and an average count determined. To be eligible for release, each serial and each subserial shall have a spore count sufficiently greater than that of the vaccine used in the immunogenicity test to assure that when tested at any time within the expiration period, each serial and subserial shall have a spore count of at least twice that used in the immunogenicity test but not less than 2,000,000 spores per dose.

[50 FR 23794, June 6, 1985, as amended at 56 FR 66784, Dec. 26, 1991; 72 FR 72564, Dec. 21, 2007]

§ 113.67 Erysipelothrix Rhusiopathiae Vaccine.

Erysipelothrix Rhusiopathiae Vaccine shall be prepared as a desiccated live culture of an avirulent or modified strain of *Erysipelothrix rhusiopathiae.* Only Master Seed which has been established as pure, safe, and immunogenic shall be used for vaccine production.

(a) The Master Seed shall meet the applicable requirements prescribed in § 113.64 and the requirements in this section.

(b) Each lot of Master Seed used for vaccine production shall be tested for immunogenicity. The selected bacterial count from the lot of Master Seed shall be established as follows:

(1) Thirty *Erysipelothrix rhusiopathiae* susceptible swine shall be used as test animals (20 vaccinates and 10 controls) for each route of administration recommended on the label.

(2) An arithmetic mean count of the colony forming units from vaccine produced from the highest passage of the Master Seed shall be established before the immunogenicity test is conducted. The 20 swine to be used as vaccinates shall be injected as recommended on the label with a predetermined quantity of vaccine bacteria. The 10 control swine shall be held separately from the vaccinates. To confirm the dosage calculation, an arithmetic mean count shall be established by conducting five replicate titrations on a sample of the bacterial vaccine dilution used. Only plates containing between 30 and 300 colonies shall be considered in a valid test.

(3) The vaccinates and controls shall be examined and their average body temperature determined prior to challenge. Fourteen to twenty-one days postvaccination, the vaccinates and controls shall be challenged with a virulent *Erysipelothrix rhusiopathiae* culture and observed for 7 days. The challenge culture and instructions for preparation and use shall be obtained from Animal and Plant Health Inspection Service.

(4) A satisfactory challenge shall be evidenced in the controls by a high body temperature or clinical signs including, but not limited to acute illness with hyperemia of the abdomen and ears, possibly terminating in sudden death; moribundity, with or without metastatic skin lesions; depression with anorexia, stiffness, and/or joint involvement; or any combination of these symptoms and lesions.

(5) If at least 80 percent of the controls do not show characteristic signs during the observation period including, but not limited to a body temperature of 105.6 °F or higher on at least 2 consecutive days, the test shall be considered a No Test: *Provided,* That control pigs which meet the criteria requirements for susceptibility except for high body temperature shall be considered susceptible if sacrificed and organisms identified as *Erysipelothrix rhusiopathiae* can be isolated from the blood, spleen, or other organs.

(6) To demonstrate immunity after challenge, the vaccinates shall remain free of clinical signs and the body temperature shall not exceed 104.6 °F on 2 or more consecutive days. If at least 90 percent of the vaccinates do not remain free from clinical signs and high body temperature throughout the observation period, the Master Seed is unsatisfactory.

(7) An Outline of Production change shall be made before authority for use of a new Master Seed shall be granted

by Animal and Plant Health Inspection Service.

(c) *Test requirements for release.* Each serial and subserial shall meet the applicable requirements in § 113.64 and the requirements in this paragraph. Any serial or subserial found unsatisfactory by a prescribed test shall not be released.

(1) *Safety test.* Samples of completed product from each serial or first subserial shall be tested for safety in young adult mice as prescribed in § 113.33(b) and in swine as prescribed in § 113.44.

(2) *Bacterial count requirements.* Final container samples of completed product from each serial and each subserial shall be tested for bacterial count using the method used in paragraph (b)(2) of this section. Two replicate titrations shall be conducted on each sample. To be eligible for release, each serial and subserial shall have a bacterial count sufficiently greater than that of the vaccine used in the immunogenicity test to assure that, when tested at any time within the expiration period, each serial and subserial shall have a bacterial count two times greater than that used in such immunogenicity test.

[50 FR 23795, June 6, 1985, as amended at 56 FR 66784, Dec. 26, 1991; 72 FR 72564, Dec. 21, 2007]

§ 113.68 Pasteurella Haemolytica Vaccine, Bovine.

Pasteurella Haemolytica Vaccine, Bovine, shall be prepared as a desiccated live culture bacterial vaccine of an avirulent or modified strain of *Pasteurella haemolytica*, identified as serotype 1. Only Master Seed which has been established as pure, safe, and immunogenic shall be used for vaccine production. All serials of vaccine shall be prepared from the first through the fifth passage from the Master Seed.

(a) The Master Seed shall meet the applicable general requirements prescribed in § 113.64 and the requirements in this section.

(b) Each lot of Master Seed used for vaccine production shall be tested for immunogenicity. The immunogenicity of a selected bacterial count from the lot of Master Seed shall be established as follows:

(1) Fifteen *Pasteurella haemolytica* susceptible calves shall be used as test animals (10 vaccinates and 5 controls) for each route of administration recommended on the label.

(2) An arithmetic mean count of the colony forming units from vaccine produced from the highest passage of the Master Seed shall be established before the immunogenicity test is conducted. The 10 calves to be used as vaccinates shall be injected as recommended on the label with a predetermined quantity of vaccine bacteria. The five control calves shall be held separately from the vaccinates. To confirm the dosage calculation, five replicate titrations on a sample of the bacterial vaccine used. Only plates containing between 30 and 300 colonies shall be considered a valid test.

(3) The vaccinates and controls shall be examined and their average body temperature determined prior to challenge. Fourteen to twenty-one days post vaccination, the vaccinates and controls shall each be challenged by the respiratory route with a (virulent) pneumonia producing *Pasteurella haemolytica* culture and observed for 4 to 7 days. The challenge culture and instructions for preparation for use shall be furnished or approved by the Animal and Plant Health Inspection Service.

(4) A satisfactory challenge shall be evidenced in the controls by progression of clinical signs consistent with respiratory system infection following challenge, including but not limited to lacrimation, mucoid nasal exudates, expiratory dyspnea, tachypnea, pulmonary rales, and cough possibly terminating in death; moribundity, depression with anorexia, diarrhea with substantial weight loss; or any combination of these symptoms.

(5) Lung lesion response to challenge will be assessed in all calves. Lung lesions will be assessed at necropsy in calves that succumb to challenge. Surviving calves will be euthanized on day 4 to 7 following challenge and lung lesions assessed at necropsy. Lung lesion scores will be used in the assessment of the response to challenge exposure. If a significant difference in lung lesion scores cannot be demonstrated between vaccinates and controls using a scoring system approved by the Animal and

Plant Health Inspection Service, the Master Seed is unsatisfactory.

(6) An Outline of Production change must be made before authority for use of a new lot of Master Seed is granted by the Animal and Plant Health Inspection Service.

(c) *Test requirements for release.* Each serial and subserial shall meet the applicable general requirements prescribed in §§ 113.8 and 113.64 and the requirements in this paragraph. Any serial or subserial found unsatisfactory by a prescribed test shall not be released.

(1) *Safety test.* Samples of completed product from each serial or first subserial shall be tested for safety in calves as provided in §§ 113.41(a) and 113.41(b) except, that the equivalent of two doses of vaccine shall be used and administered in the manner recommended on the label.

(2) *Bacterial count requirements.* Final container samples of completed product shall be tested for bacterial count using the method used in paragraph (b)(2) of this section. Two replicate titrations shall be conducted on each serial and subserial. Each sample shall be rehydrated with accompanying sterile diluent to the volume indicated on the label. To be eligible for release, each serial and subserial shall have a bacterial count sufficiently greater than that of the vaccine used in the immunogenicity test to assure that, when tested at any time within the expiration period, each serial and subserial shall have a bacterial count at least two times greater than that used in the immunogenicity test.

[55 FR 35559, Aug. 31, 1990, as amended at 72 FR 72564, Dec. 21, 2007]

§ 113.69 Pasteurella Multocida Vaccine, Bovine.

Pasteurella Multocida Vaccine, Bovine, shall be prepared as a desiccated live culture bacterial vaccine of an avirulent or modified strain of *Pasteurella multocida*, of bovine origin. Only Master Seed which has been established as pure, safe, and immunogenic shall be used for vaccine production. All serials of vaccine shall be prepared from the first through the fifth passage from the Master Seed.

(a) The Master Seed shall meet the applicable general requirements prescribed in § 113.64 and the requirements in this section.

(b) Each lot of Master Seed used for vaccine production shall be tested for immunogenicity. The immunogenicity of a selected bacterial count from the lot of Master Seed shall be established as follows:

(1) Fifteen *Pasteurella multocida* susceptible calves shall be used as test animals (10 vaccinates and 5 controls) for each route of administration recommended on the label.

(2) An arithmetic mean count of the colony forming units from vaccine produced from the highest passage of the Master Seed shall be established before the immunogenicity test is conducted. The 10 calves to be used as vaccinates shall be injected as recommended on the label with a predetermined quantity of vaccine bacteria. The five control calves shall be held separately from the vaccinates. To confirm the dosage calculation, arithmetic mean count shall be established by conducting five replicate titrations on a sample of the bacterial vaccine used. Only plates containing between 30 and 300 colonies shall be considered a valid test.

(3) The vaccinates and controls shall be examined and their average body temperature determined prior to challenge. Fourteen to twenty-one days post vaccination, the vaccinates and controls shall each be challenged by the respiratory route with a (virulent) pneumonia producing *Pasteurella multocida* culture and observed for 4 to 10 days. The challenge culture and instructions for preparation for use shall be furnished or approved by the Animal and Plant Health Inspection Service.

(4) A satisfactory challenge shall be evidenced in the controls by progression of clinical signs consistent with respiratory system infection following challenge, including but not limited to acute illness with higher body temperature and respiration rate, lacrimation, mucoid nasal exudate, expiratory dyspnea, tachypnea, pulmonary rales, and cough, possibly terminating in death; moribundity, depression with anorexia; diarrhea with

substantial weight loss; or any combination of these symptoms.

(5) Lung lesion response to challenge will be assessed in all calves. Lung lesions will be assessed at necropsy in calves that succumb to challenge. Surviving calves will be euthanized on day 4 to 10 following challenge and lung lesions assessed at necropsy. Lung lesion scores will be used in the assessment of the response to challenge exposure. If a significant difference in lung lesion scores cannot be demonstrated between vaccinates and controls using a scoring system approved by the Animal and Plant Health Inspection Service, the Master Seed is unsatisfactory.

(6) An Outline of Production change must be made before authority for use of a new lot of Master Seed is granted by the Animal and Plant Health Inspection Service.

(c) *Test requirements for release.* Each serial and subserial shall meet the applicable general requirements prescribed in §§ 113.8 and 113.64 and the requirements in this paragraph. Any serial or subserial found unsatisfactory by a prescribed test shall not be released.

(1) *Safety Test.* Samples of completed product from each serial or first subserial shall be tested for safety in calves as provided in §§ 113.41(a) and 113.41(b), except that the equivalent of two doses of vaccine shall be used and administered in the manner recommended on the label.

(2) *Bacterial count requirements.* Final container samples of completed product shall be tested for bacterial count using the method used in paragraph (b)(2) of this section. Two replicate titrations shall be conducted on each serial and subserial. Each sample shall be rehydrated with accompanying sterile diluent to the volume indicated on the label. To be eligible for release, each serial and subserial shall have a bacterial count sufficiently greater than that of the vaccine used in the immunogenicity test count per dose established to assure that, when tested at any time within the expiration period, each serial and subserial shall have a bacterial count at least two times greater than that used in the immunogenicity test.

[55 FR 35560, Aug. 31, 1990, as amended at 72 FR 72564, Dec. 21, 2007]

§ 113.70 Pasteurella Multocida Vaccine, Avian Isolate.

Pasteurella Multocida Vaccine, Avian Isolate, shall be prepared as a desiccated live culture of an avirulent or modified strain of *Pasteurella multocida.* Only Master Seed which has been established as pure, safe, and immunogenic shall be used for vaccine production.

(a) The Master Seed shall meet the applicable general requirements prescribed in § 113.64 and the requirements in this section.

(b) Each lot of Master Seed used for vaccine production shall be tested for immunogenicity in each species and for each serotype for which the Master Seed is claimed to give protection.

(1) Thirty *Pasteurella multocida* susceptible birds shall be used as test animals (20 vaccinates and 10 controls) for each bird species, route of administration, and serotype for which protection is claimed on the label.

(2) An arithmetic mean count of colony forming units from vaccine produced from the highest passage of Master Seed shall be established before the immunogenicity test is conducted. The 20 birds to be used as vaccinates shall be inoculated, as recommended on the label with a predetermined quantity of vaccine bacteria. The 10 control birds shall be held separately from the vaccinates. To confirm the dosage calculation, an arithmetic mean count shall be established by conducting five replicate titrations on a sample of the bacterial vaccine used. Only plates containing between 30 and 300 colonies shall be considered in a valid test.

(3) Not less than 14 days after vaccination, each of 20 vaccinates and each of 10 unvaccinated controls shall be challenged intramuscularly or by other methods acceptable to the Animal and Plant Health Inspection Service with a virulent *Pasteurella multocida* strain, for which protection is claimed, and observed daily for a 14 day post-challenge period.

(4) Eight or more of the unvaccinated controls must die for the test to be

valid. If at least 16 of 20 of the vaccinates do not survive the 14-day postchallenge period, the Master Seed is unsatisfactory at the selected bacterial count.

(c) *Test requirements for release.* Each serial and subserial shall meet the applicable requirements in §§ 113.8 and 113.64 and the requirements in this paragraph. Any serial or subserial found unsatisfactory by a prescribed test shall not be released.

(1) *Safety test.* Samples of completed product from each serial or first subserial shall be tested for safety.

(i) Ten birds of a species for which the vaccine is recommended shall be given the equivalent of 10 doses each of the vaccine and observed for 10 days. If the vaccine is recommended for more than one species, only one species needs to be tested.

(ii) If unfavorable reactions attributable to the vaccine occur during the observation period in two or more of the test birds, the serial is unsatisfactory.

(iii) If unfavorable reactions occur which are not attributable to the test vaccine, the test is a No Test and may be repeated. If the results of the next test are not satisfactory, or if the test is not repeated, the serial shall be considered unsatisfactory.

(2) *Bacterial count requirements.* Final container samples of completed product shall be tested for bacterial count using the method used in paragraph (b)(2) of this section. Two replicate titrations shall be conducted on each serial and subserial. Each sample shall be rehydrated with accompanying sterile diluent to the volume indicated on the label. To be eligible for release, each serial and subserial shall have a bacterial count sufficiently greater than that of the vaccine used in the immunogenicity test count per dose established to assure that, when tested at any time within the expiration period, each serial and subserial shall have a bacterial count at least two times greater than that used in the immunogenicity test.

[55 FR 35560, Aug. 31, 1990, as amended at 59 FR 19633, Apr. 25, 1994; 64 FR 43044, Aug. 9, 1999; 72 FR 72564, Dec. 21, 2007]

§ 113.71 Chlamydia Psittaci Vaccine (Feline Pneumonitis), Live Chlamydia.

Chlamydia Psittaci Vaccine (Feline Pneumonitis), Live Chlamydia, shall be prepared from chlamydia-bearing cell culture fluids or embryonated chicken eggs. Only Master Seed which has been established as pure, safe, and immunogenic shall be used for vaccine production. All serials of vaccine shall be prepared from the first through the fifth passage from the Master Seed.

(a) The Master Seed shall meet the applicable requirements prescribed in § 113.300 and the requirements in this section. Master Seed propagated in chicken embryos shall be tested for pathogens by the chicken embryo test prescribed in § 113.37. If found unsatisfactory by any prescribed test, the Master Seed shall not be used.

(b) Each lot of Master Seed used for vaccine production shall be tested for immunogenicity. The immunogenicity of a selected dose from the lot of Master Seed shall be established as follows:

(1) Thirty feline pneumonitis susceptible cats shall be used as test animals (20 vaccinates and 10 controls). Blood samples shall be drawn and individual serum samples tested. The cats shall be considered suitable for use if all serums are negative for pneumonitis antibody in a complement fixation test or other test of equal sensitivity.

(2) A geometric mean titer of the dried vaccine produced from the highest passage of the Master Seed shall be established before the immunogenicity test is conducted. The 20 cats used as vaccinates shall be administered a predetermined quantity of vaccine by the method to be recommended on the label and the remaining 10 cats shall be held as controls. To confirm the dosage calculations, five replicate titrations shall be conducted on a sample of the vaccine dilution used. If two doses are used, five replicate confirming titrations shall be conducted on each dose.

(3) Fourteen or more days after the final dose of vaccine, the vaccinates and controls shall each be challenged intranasally with a minimum of 10,000 yolk sac LD50 of virulent feline pneumonitis furnished or approved by the Animal and Plant Health Inspection Service and observed each day for 28

days postchallenge. The rectal temperature of each animal shall be taken and the presence or absence of clinical signs noted and recorded each day.

(i) If less than 8 of 10 controls show clinical signs of feline pneumonitis infection other than fever, the test is a No Test and may be repeated.

(ii) If a significant difference in clinical signs other than fever or chlamydia shedding cannot be demonstrated between vaccinates and controls using a scoring system approved by the Animal and Plant Health Inspection Service, the Master Seed is unsatisfactory.

(4) An Outline of Production change must be made before authority for use of a new lot of Master Seed is granted by the Animal and Plant Health Inspection Service.

(c) *Test requirements for release:* Except for § 113.300(a)(3)(ii), each serial and subserial shall meet the requirements prescribed in § 113.300 and in this paragraph. Final container samples of completed product shall be tested. Any serial or subserial found unsatisfactory by a prescribed test shall not be released.

(1) The test for pathogens prescribed in § 113.37 shall be conducted on each serial or one subserial of avian origin vaccine.

(2) *Chlamydia titer requirements.* Final container samples of completed product shall be tested for chlamydia titer using the titration method used in paragraph (b)(2) of this section. To be eligible for release, each serial and each subserial shall have a titer sufficiently greater than the titer of vaccine used in the immunogenicity test prescribed in paragraph (b) of this section to assure that when tested at any time within the expiration period, each serial and subserial shall have a titer 0.7 greater than that used in such immunogenicity test but not less than 2.5 ID50 per dose.

[55 FR 35561, Aug. 31, 1990, as amended at 56 FR 66786, Dec. 26, 1991; 72 FR 72564, Dec. 21, 2007]

INACTIVATED BACTERIAL PRODUCTS

§ 113.100 General requirements for inactivated bacterial products.

Unless otherwise prescribed in an applicable Standard Requirement or in the filed Outline of Production, an inactivated bacterial product shall meet the applicable requirements in this section.

(a) *Purity tests.* (1) Final container samples of completed product from each serial and each subserial shall be tested for viable bacteria and fungi as provided in § 113.26.

(2) Each lot of Master Seed Bacteria shall be tested for the presence of extraneous viable bacteria and fungi in accordance with the test provided in § 113.27(d).

(b) *Safety tests.* Bulk or final container samples of completed product from each serial shall be tested for safety in young adult mice in accordance with the test provided in § 113.33(b) unless:

(1) The product contains material which is inherently lethal for mice. In such instances, the guinea pig safety test provided in § 113.38 shall be conducted in place of the mouse safety test.

(2) The product is recommended for poultry. In such instances, the product shall be safety tested in poultry as defined in the specific Standard Requirement or Outline of Production for the product.

(3) The product is recommended for fish, other aquatic species, or reptiles. In such instances, the product shall be safety tested in fish, other aquatic species, or reptiles as required by specific Standard Requirement or Outline of Production for the product.

(c) *Identity test.* Methods of identification of Master Seed Bacteria to the genus and species level by laboratory tests shall be sufficient to distinguish the bacteria from other similar bacteria according to criteria described in the most recent edition of "Bergey's Manual of Systematic Bacteriology" or the American Society for Microbiology "Manual of Clinical Microbiology". If Master Seed Bacteria are referred to by serotype, serovar, subtype, pilus type, strain or other taxonomic subdivision below the species level, adequate testing must be used to identify the bacteria to that level. Tests which may be used to identify Master Seed Bacteria include, but are not limited to:

(1) Cultural characteristics,

(2) Staining reaction,

(3) Biochemical reactivity,

(4) Fluorescent antibody tests,

(5) Serologic tests,

(6) Toxin typing,

(7) Somatic or flagellar antigen characterization, and

(8) Restriction endonuclease analysis.

(d) *Ingredient requirements.* Ingredients used for the growth and preparation of Master Seed Bacteria and of final product shall meet the requirements provided in §113.50. Ingredients of animal origin shall meet the applicable requirements provided in §113.53.

(e) Only serials tested for viricidal activity in accordance with the test provided in §113.35 and found satisfactory by such test shall be packaged as diluent for desiccated fractions in combination packages.

(f) If formaldehyde is used as the inactivating agent, and the serial has not been found satisfactory by the viricidal activity test, bulk or final container samples of completed product from each serial must be tested for residual free formaldehyde content using the ferric chloride test.[1] Firms currently using tests for residual free formaldehyde content other than the ferric chloride test have until July 14, 2004 to update their Outline of Production to be in compliance with this requirement.

(1) The residual free formaldehyde content of biological products containing clostridial antigens must not exceed 1.85 grams per liter (g/L).

(2) The residual free formaldehyde content of bacterins, bacterin-toxoids, and toxoids, other than those containing clostridial antigens, must not exceed 0.74 grams per liter (g/L).

[39 FR 16862, May 10, 1974. Redesignated at 55 FR 35562, Aug. 31, 1990, as amended at 60 FR 14355, Mar. 17, 1995; 68 FR 35283, June 13, 2003; 79 FR 31021, May 30, 2014]

[1] The procedures for performing the ferric chloride test for residual free formaldehyde may be obtained from USDA, APHIS, Center for Veterinary Biologics-Laboratory, 1800 Dayton Road, P.O. Box 844, Ames, IA 50010.

§ 113.101 Leptospira Pomona Bacterin.

Leptospira Pomona Bacterin shall be produced from a culture of *Leptospira pomona* which has been inactivated and is nontoxic. Each serial of biological product containing *Leptospira pomona* fraction shall meet the applicable requirements in §113.100 and shall be tested for purity, safety, and potency as prescribed in this section. A serial found unsatisfactory by any prescribed test shall not be released.

(a) *Purity test.* Final container samples of completed product from each serial and each subserial shall be tested for viable bacteria and fungi as provided in §113.26.

(b) *Safety test.* Bulk or final container samples of completed product from each serial shall be tested for safety as provided in §113.38.

(c) *Potency test.* Bulk or final container samples of completed product shall be diluted with physiological saline so that each 0.25 ml contains not more than 1/800th of the dose recommended on the label and shall be tested for potency, using the two-stage test provided in this paragraph.

(1) *Vaccinates.* Inject each of at least 10 but not more than 12 young adult hamsters, each weighing 50 to 90 grams, with 0.25 ml of the diluted bacterin either subcutaneously or intramuscularly, in accordance with the label recommendations for use.

(2) *Controls.* Retain at least 10 but not more than 12 additional hamsters from the same group as unvaccinated controls.

(3) *Challenge.* From 14 to 18 days postvaccination, challenge each of 10 vaccinates and each of 10 controls intraperitoneally with a suspension of virulent *Leptospira pomona* organisms, using a dose of 10–10,000 hamster LD_{50} as determined by titration.

(4) *Post-challenge period.* Observe the vaccinates and controls for 14 days post-challenge and record all deaths. If eight or more controls die of leptospirosis, the test is valid and the results shall be evaluated according to the following table:

Stage	Number of vaccinates	Cumulative number of vaccinates	Cumulative total dead hamsters for satisfactory serial	Cumulative total dead hamsters for unsatisfactory serial
1	10	10	2 or less	5 or more.
2	10	20	5 or less	6 or more.

(5) If three or four vaccinates die in the first stage, the second stage shall be conducted in a manner identical to the first stage.

(6) If the second stage is used, each serial shall be evaluated according to the second part of the table. On the basis of cumulative results, each serial shall either pass or fail.

[39 FR 16862, May 10, 1974, as amended at 40 FR 20067, May 8, 1975; 45 FR 40100, June 13, 1980. Redesignated at 55 FR 35562, Aug. 31, 1990, as amended at 56 FR 66785, Dec. 26, 1991]

§ 113.102 Leptospira Icterohaemorrhagiae Bacterin.

Leptospira Icterohaemorrhagiae Bacterin shall be produced from a culture of *Leptospira icterohaemorrhagiae* which has been inactivated and is nontoxic. Each serial of biological product containing *Leptospira icterohaemorrhagiae* fraction shall meet the applicable requirements in § 113.100 and be tested for purity, safety, and potency as prescribed in this section. A serial found unsatisfactory by any prescribed test shall not be released.

(a) *Purity test.* Final container samples of completed product from each serial and each subserial shall be tested for viable bacteria and fungi as provided in § 113.26.

(b) *Safety test.* Bulk or final container samples of completed product from each serial shall be tested for safety as provided in § 113.38.

(c) *Potency test.* Bulk or final container samples of completed product shall be diluted with physiological saline so that each 0.25 ml contains not more than 1/80th of the dose recommended on the label and shall be tested for potency, using the two-stage test provided in this paragraph.

(1) *Vaccinates.* Inject each of at least 10 but not more than 12 young adult hamsters, each weighing 50 to 90 grams, with 0.25 ml of the diluted bacterin either subcutaneously or intramuscularly, in accordance with the label recommendations for use.

(2) *Controls.* Retain at least 10 but not more than 12 additional hamsters from the same group as unvaccinated controls.

(3) *Challenge.* From 14 to 18 days postvaccination, challenge each of 10 vaccinates and each of 10 controls intraperitoneally with a suspension of virulent *Leptospira icterohaemorrhagiae* organisms, using a dose of 10–10,000 hamster LD_{50} as determined by titration.

(4) *Post-challenge period.* Observe the vaccinates and controls for 14 days post-challenge and record all deaths. If eight or more controls die from leptospirosis, the test is valid and the results shall be evaluated according to the following table:

Stage	Number of vaccinates	Cumulative number of vaccinates	Cumulative total dead hamsters for satisfactory serial	Cumulative total dead hamsters for unsatisfactory serial
1	10	10	2 or less	5 or more.
2	10	20	5 or less	6 or more.

(5) If three or four vaccinates die in the first stage, the second stage shall be used. The second stage shall be conducted in a manner identical to the first stage.

(6) If the second stage is used, each serial shall be evaluated according to the second part of the table. On the basis of cumulative results, each serial shall either pass or fail.

[39 FR 16862, May 10, 1974, as amended at 45 FR 40100, June 13, 1980. Redesignated at 55 FR 35562, Aug. 31, 1990, as amended at 56 FR 66785, Dec. 26, 1991]

§ 113.103 Leptospira Canicola Bacterin.

Leptospira Canicola Bacterin shall be produced from a culture of *Leptospira canicola* which has been inactivated and is nontoxic. Each serial of biological product containing *Leptospira canicola* fraction shall meet the applicable requirements in § 113.100 and shall be tested for purity, safety, and potency as prescribed in this section. Serials found unsatisfactory by any prescribed test shall not be released.

(a) *Purity test.* Final container samples of completed product from each serial and each subserial shall be tested for viable bacteria and fungi as provided in § 113.26.

(b) *Safety test.* Bulk or final container samples of completed product from each serial shall be tested for safety as provided in § 113.38.

(c) *Potency test.* Bulk or final container samples of completed product shall be diluted with physiological saline so that each 0.25 ml contains not more than 1/80th of the dose recommended on the label and shall be tested for potency, using the two-stage test provided in this paragraph.

(1) *Vaccinates.* Inject each of at least 10 but not more than 12 young adult hamsters, each weighing 50 to 90 grams, with 0.25 ml of the diluted bacterin either subcutaneously or intramuscularly, in accordance with the label recommendations for use.

(2) *Controls.* Retain at least 10 but not more than 12 additional hamsters from the same group as unvaccinated controls.

(3) *Challenge.* From 14 to 18 days postvaccination, challenge each of 10 vaccinates and each of 10 controls intraperitoneally with a suspension of virulent *Leptospira canicola* organisms, using a dose of 10–10,000 hamster LD_{50} as determined by titration.

(4) *Post-challenge period.* Observe the vaccinates and controls for 14 days post-challenge and record all deaths. If eight or more controls die from leptospirosis, test is valid and the results shall be evaluated according to the following table:

Stage	Number of vaccinates	Cumulative number of vaccinates	Cumulative total dead hamsters for satisfactory serial	Cumulative total dead hamsters for unsatisfactory serial
1	10	10	2 or less	5 or more.
2	10	20	5 or less	6 or more.

(5) If three or four vaccinates die in the first stage, the second stage shall be used. The second stage shall be conducted in a manner identical to the first stage.

(6) If the second stage is used, each serial shall be evaluated according to the second part of the table. On the basis of cumulative results, each serial shall either pass or fail.

[39 FR 16862, May 10, 1974, as amended at 45 FR 40100, June 13, 1980. Redesignated at 55 FR 35562, Aug. 31, 1990, as amended at 56 FR 66785, Dec. 26, 1991]

§ 113.104 Leptospira Grippotyphosa Bacterin.

Leptospira Grippotyphosa Bacterin shall be produced from a culture of *Leptospira grippotyphosa* which has been inactivated and is nontoxic. Each serial of biological product containing *Leptospira grippotyphosa* fraction shall meet the applicable requirements in § 113.100 and shall be tested for purity, safety, and potency as prescribed in this section. A serial found unsatisfactory by any prescribed test shall not be released.

(a) *Purity test.* Final container samples of completed product from each serial and each subserial shall be tested for viable bacteria and fungi as provided in § 113.26.

(b) *Safety test.* Bulk or final container samples of completed product from each serial shall be tested for safety as provided in § 113.38.

(c) *Potency test.* Bulk or final container samples of completed product shall be diluted with physiological saline so that each 0.25 ml contains not more than 1/800th of the dose recommended on the label and shall be tested for potency, using the two-stage test provided in this paragraph.

(1) *Vaccinates.* Inject each of at least 10 but not more than 12 young adult hamsters, each weighing 50 to 90 grams, with 0.25 ml of the diluted bacterin either subcutaneously or intramuscularly, in accordance with the label recommendations for use.

(2) *Controls.* Retain at least 10 but not more than 12 additional hamsters from the same group as unvaccinated controls.

(3) *Challenge.* From 14 to 18 days postvaccination, challenge each of 10 vaccinates and each of 10 controls intraperitoneally with a suspension of virulent *Leptospira grippotyphosa* organisms, using a dose of 10–10,000 hamster LD_{50} as determined by titration.

(4) *Post-challenge period.* Observe the vaccinates and controls for 14 days post-challenge and record all deaths. If eight or more controls die of leptospirosis, the test is valid and the results shall be evaluated according to the following table:

CUMULATIVE TOTALS

Stage	Number of vaccinates	Dead hamsters for acceptance	Dead hamsters for rejection
1	10	2 or less	5 or more.
2	20	5 or less	6 or more.

(5) If three or four vaccinates die in the first stage, the second stage shall be conducted in a manner identical to the first stage.

(6) If the second stage is used, each serial shall be evaluated according to the second part of the table. On the basis of cumulative results, each serial shall either pass or fail.

[40 FR 17003, Apr. 16, 1975, as amended at 40 FR 23989, June 4, 1975; 45 FR 40100, June 13, 1980. Redesignated at 55 FR 35562, Aug. 31, 1990, as amended at 56 FR 66785, Dec. 26, 1991]

§ 113.105 Leptospira Hardjo Bacterin.

Leptospira Hardjo Bacterin shall be produced from a culture of *Leptospira hardjo* which has been inactivated and is nontoxic. Each serial of biological product containing *Leptospira hardjo* fraction shall meet the applicable requirements in § 113.100 and shall be tested for purity, safety, and potency as prescribed in this section. A serial found unsatisfactory by any prescribed test shall not be released.

(a) *Purity test.* Final container samples of completed product from each serial and each subserial shall be tested for viable bacteria and fungi as provided in § 113.26.

(b) *Safety test.* Bulk or final container samples of completed product from each serial shall be tested for safety as provided in § 113.38.

(c) *Potency test.* Bulk or final container samples of completed product from each serial shall be tested for potency using the test written into the filed Outline of Production.

[40 FR 17003, Apr. 16, 1975, as amended at 40 FR 20067, May 8, 1975. Redesignated at 55 FR 35562, Aug. 31, 1990, as amended at 56 FR 66785, Dec. 26, 1991]

§ 113.106 Clostridium Chauvoei Bacterin.

Clostridium Chauvoei Bacterin shall be produced from a culture of *Clostridium chauvoei* which has been inactivated and is nontoxic. Each serial of biological product containing *Clostridium chauvoei* fraction shall meet the applicable requirements in § 113.100 and shall be tested for purity, safety, and potency as prescribed in this section. Serials found unsatisfactory by any prescribed test shall not be released.

(a) *Purity test.* Final container samples of completed product from each serial and each subserial shall be tested for viable bacteria and fungi as provided in § 113.26.

(b) *Safety test.* Bulk or final container samples of completed product from each serial shall be tested for safety as provided in § 113.38.

(c) *Potency test.* Bulk or final container samples of completed product from each serial shall be tested for potency using the two-stage test provided in this paragraph.

(1) Each of at least 8 but not more than 10 guinea pigs, each weighing 300 to 500 grams, shall be injected subcutaneously with a guinea pig dose. A second guinea pig dose shall be injected 21 to 23 days after the first dose. Each guinea pig dose shall be one-fifth of the dose recommended on the label for a calf.

(2) *Clostridium chauvoei* challenge material, available upon request from Animal and Plant Health Inspection Service, shall be used for challenge 14 to 15 days following the last injection of the product. Each of eight vaccinates and each of five additional nonvaccinated guinea pigs for controls shall be injected intramuscularly with approximately 100 LD_{50} of challenge material. This dose shall be determined by statistical analysis of results of titrations of the challenge material. The vaccinates and controls shall be observed for 3 days postchallenge and all deaths recorded.

(3) For a valid test, at least 80 percent of the controls shall die within the 3 day post-challenge observation period. If this requirement is met, the results of the potency test shall be evaluated according to the following table:

Stage	Number of vaccinates	Cumulative number of vaccinates	Cumulative total number of deaths for a satisfactory test	Cumulative total number of deaths for an unsatisfactory test
1	8	8	1 or less	3 or more.
2	8	16	4 or less	5 or more.

The second stage shall be required only when exactly two animals die in the first stage. The second stage shall be conducted in a manner identical to the first stage.

[39 FR 16862, May 10, 1974, as amended at 45 FR 40100, June 13, 1980. Redesignated at 55 FR 35562, Aug. 31, 1990 and amended at 56 FR 66784, 66785, Dec. 26, 1991]

§ 113.107 Clostridium Haemolyticum Bacterin.

Clostridium Haemolyticum Bacterin shall be produced from a culture of *Clostridium haemolyticum* which has been inactivated and is nontoxic. Each serial of biological product containing *Clostridium haemolyticum* fraction shall meet the applicable requirements in § 113.100 and shall be tested for purity, safety, and potency as prescribed in this section. A serial found unsatisfactory by any prescribed test shall not be released.

(a) *Purity test.* Final container samples of completed product from each serial and each subserial shall be tested for viable bacteria and fungi as provided in § 113.26.

(b) *Safety test.* Bulk or final container samples of completed product from each serial shall be tested for safety as provided in § 113.38.

(c) *Potency test.* Bulk or final container samples of completed product from each serial shall be tested for potency using the two-stage test provided in this paragraph.

(1) Each of at least 8 but not more than 10 guinea pigs, each weighing 300 to 500 grams, shall be injected subcutaneously with a guinea pig dose. A second guinea pig dose shall be injected 21 to 23 days after the first dose. Each guinea pig dose shall be one-fifth of the dose recommended on the label for a calf.

(2) *Clostridium haemolyticum* challenge material, available upon request from Animal and Plant Health Inspection Service, shall be used for challenge 14 to 15 days following the last injection of the product. Each of eight vaccinates and each of five additional nonvaccinated guinea pigs for controls shall be injected intramuscularly with approximately 100 LD_{50} of challenge material. This dose shall be determined by statistical analysis of results of titrations of the challenge material. The vaccinates and controls shall be observed for 3 days postchallenge and all deaths recorded.

(3) For a valid test, at least 80 percent of the controls shall die within the 3 day post-challenge observation period. If this requirement is met, the results of the potency test shall be evaluated according to the following table:

Stage	Number of vaccinates	Cumulative number of vaccinates	Cumulative total number of deaths for a satisfactory test	Cumulative total number of deaths for an unsatisfactory test
1	8	8	1 or less	3 or more.
2	8	16	4 or less	5 or more.

The second stage shall be required only when exactly two animals die in the first stage. The second stage shall be conducted in a manner identical to the first stage.

[39 FR 16862, May 10, 1974, as amended at 40 FR 20067, May 8, 1975; 45 FR 40100, June 13, 1980. Redesignated at 55 FR 35562, Aug. 31, 1990, as amended at 56 FR 66784, 66785, Dec. 26, 1991]

§ 113.108 Clostridium Novyi Bacterin-Toxoid.

Clostridium Novyi Bacterin-Toxoid shall be produced from a culture of *Clostridium novyi* which has been inactivated and is nontoxic. Each serial of biological product containing *Clostridium novyi* fraction shall meet the applicable requirements in § 113.100 and shall be tested for purity, safety, and potency as prescribed in this section. A serial found unsatisfactory by any prescribed test shall not be released.

(a) *Purity test.* Final container samples of completed product from each serial and each subserial shall be tested for viable bacteria and fungi as provided in § 113.26.

(b) *Safety test.* Bulk or final container samples of completed product from each serial shall be tested for safety as provided in § 113.38.

(c) *Potency test.* Bulk or final container samples of completed product from each serial shall be tested for potency using the Alpha toxin-neutralization test provided in this paragraph.

(1) When used in this test, the following words and terms shall mean:

(i) *International antitoxin unit.* (I.U.) That quantity of Alpha Antitoxin which reacts with Lo and L + doses of Standard Toxin according to their definitions.

(ii) *Lo dose.* The largest quantity of toxin which can be mixed with one unit of Standard Antitoxin and not cause sickness or death in injected mice.

(iii) *L + dose.* The smallest quantity of toxin which can be mixed with one unit of Standard Antitoxin and cause death in at least 80 percent of injected mice.

(iv) *Standard antitoxin.* The Alpha Antitoxin preparation which has been standardized as to antitoxin unitage on the basis of the International *Clostridium novyi* Alpha Antitoxin Standard and which is either supplied by or acceptable to the Animal and Plant Health Inspection Service. The antitoxin unit value shall be stated on the label.

(v) *Standard toxin.* The Alpha toxin preparation which is supplied by or is acceptable to the Animal and Plant Health Inspection Service.

(vi) *Diluent.* The solution used to make proper dilutions prescribed in this test. Such solutions shall be made by dissolving 1 gram of peptone and 0.25 gram of sodium chloride in each 100 ml of distilled water; adjusting the pH to 7.2; autoclaving at 121 °C for 25 minutes; and storing at 4 °C until used.

(2) Each of at least eight rabbits of a strain acceptable to the Animal and Plant Health Inspection Service, each weighing 4–8 pounds, shall be injected subcutaneously with not more than half of the recommended cattle dose. *Provided,* That, if the product is recommended only for sheep, half of the recommended sheep dose shall be used. A second dose shall be given not less than 20 days nor more than 23 days after the first dose.

(3) Fourteen to seventeen days after the second dose, all surviving rabbits shall be bled, and the serum tested for antitoxin content.

(i) At least seven rabbits are required to make an acceptable serum pool.

(ii) Equal quantities of serum from each rabbit shall be combined and tested as a single pooled serum.

(iii) If less than seven rabbits are available, the test is invalid and shall be repeated: *Provided,* That, if the test is not repeated, the serial shall be declared unsatisfactory.

(4) The antitoxin content of the rabbit serums shall be determined by the serum neutralization test as follows:

(i) Make a dilution of Standard Antitoxin to contain 0.1 International Unit of antitoxin per ml.

(ii) Make a dilution of Standard Toxin in which 0.1 Lo dose is contained in a volume of 1 ml or less. Make a second dilution of Standard Toxin in which 0.1 L + dose is contained in a volume of 1 ml or less.

(iii) Combine 0.1 International Unit of Standard Antitoxin with 0.1 Lo dose of diluted Standard Toxin and combine 0.1 International Unit of Standard Antitoxin with 0.1 L + dose of diluted Standard Toxin. Each mixture is adjusted to a final volume of 2.0 ml with diluent.

(iv) Combine 0.1 Lo dose of diluted Standard Toxin with a 0.2 ml volume of undiluted serum. The mixture is adjusted to a final volume of 2.0 ml with diluent.

(v) Neutralize all toxin-antitoxin mixtures at room temperature for 1 hour and hold in ice water until injections of mice can be made.

(vi) Five Swiss white mice, each weighing 16–20 grams, shall be used for each toxin-antitoxin mixture. A dose of 0.2 ml shall be injected intravenously into each mouse. Conclude the test 72 hours post injection and record all deaths.

(5) Test Interpretation shall be as follows:

(i) If any mice inoculated with the mixture of 0.1 International Unit of Standard Antitoxin and 0.1 Lo doses of Standard Toxin die, the results of the serum neutralization test are a No Test and shall be repeated: *Provided,* That, if the test is not repeated, the serial shall be declared unsatisfactory.

(ii) If less than 80 percent of the mice inoculated with the mixture of 0.1 International Unit of Standard Antitoxin and 0.1 L + doses of Standard Toxin die, the results of the serum neutralization test are a No Test and shall be repeated: *Provided,* That, if the test is not repeated, the serial shall be declared unsatisfactory.

(iii) If any mice inoculated with the mixture of 0.2 ml undiluted serum with 0.1 Lo dose of Standard Toxin die, the serum is considered to contain less than 0.50 International Units per ml.

(iv) If the single pooled serum from seven or more rabbits contains less than 0.5 International Unit per ml, the serial is unsatisfactory.

[39 FR 16862, May 10, 1974, as amended at 45 FR 40101, June 13, 1980. Redesignated at 55 FR 35562, Aug. 31, 1990; 56 FR 37825, Aug. 9, 1991, as amended at 56 FR 66784, 66785, Dec. 26, 1991]

§ 113.109 Clostridium Sordellii Bacterin-Toxoid.

Clostridium Sordellii Bacterin-Toxoid shall be produced from a culture of *Clostridium sordellii* which has been inactivated and is nontoxic. Each serial of biological product containing *Clostridium sordellii* fraction shall meet the applicable requirements in § 113.100 and shall be tested for purity, safety, and potency as prescribed in this section. A serial found unsatisfactory by any prescribed test shall not be released.

(a) *Purity test.* Final container samples of completed product from each serial and each subserial shall be tested for viable bacteria and fungi as provided in § 113.26.

(b) *Safety test.* Bulk or final container samples of completed product from each serial shall be tested for safety as provided in § 113.38.

(c) *Potency test.* Bulk or final container samples of completed product from each serial shall be tested for potency using the toxin-neutralization test provided in this paragraph.

(1) When used in this test, the following words and terms shall mean:

(i) *International antitoxin unit.* (I.U.) That quantity of antitoxin which reacts with Lo and L + doses of Standard Toxin according to their definitions.

(ii) *Lo dose.* The largest quantity of toxin which can be mixed with one unit of Standard Antitoxin and not cause sickness or death in injected mice.

(iii) *L + dose.* The smallest quantity of toxin which can be mixed with one unit of Standard Antitoxin and cause death in at least 80 percent of injected mice.

(iv) *Standard antitoxin.* The antitoxin preparation which has been standardized as to antitoxin unitage on the basis of the International *Clostridium sordellii* Antitoxin Standard and which is either supplied by or acceptable to the Animal and Plant Health Inspection Service. The antitoxin unit value shall be stated on the label.

(v) *Standard toxin.* The toxin preparation which is supplied by or is acceptable to the Animal and Plant Health Inspection Service.

(vi) *Diluent.* The solution used to make proper dilutions prescribed in this test. Such solutions shall be made by dissolving 1 gram of peptone and 0.25 gram of sodium chloride in each 100 ml of distilled water; adjusting the pH to 7.2; autoclaving at 121 °C for 25 minutes; and storing at 4 °C until used.

(2) Each of at least eight rabbits of a strain acceptable to the Animal and Plant Health Inspection Service, each weighing 4–8 pounds, shall be injected subcutaneously with not more than half of the recommended cattle dose: *Provided,* That, if the product is recommended only for sheep, half of the recommended sheep dose shall be used. A second dose shall be given not less than 20 days nor more than 23 days after the first dose.

(3) Fourteen to seventeen days after the second dose, all surviving rabbits shall be bled, and the serum tested for antitoxin content.

(i) At least seven rabbits are required to make an acceptable serum pool.

(ii) Equal quantities of serum from each rabbit shall be combined and tested as a single pooled serum.

(iii) If less than seven rabbits are available, the test is a No Test and shall be repeated: *Provided,* That, if the test is not repeated, the serial shall be declared unsatisfactory.

(4) The antitoxin content of the rabbit serums shall be determined by the serum neutralization test as follows:

(i) Make a dilution of Standard Antitoxin to contain 1.0 international unit of antitoxin per ml.

(ii) Make a dilution of Standard Toxin in which 1.0 Lo dose is contained in a volume of 1 ml or less. Make a second dilution of Standard Toxin in which 1.0 L + dose is contained in a volume of 1 ml or less.

(iii) Combine 1.0 International Unit Standard Antitoxin with 1.0 Lo dose of diluted Standard Toxin and combine 1.0 International Unit of Standard Antitoxin with 1.0 L + dose of diluted Standard Toxin. Each mixture is adjusted to a final volume of 2.0 ml with diluent.

(iv) Combine 1.0 Lo dose of diluted Standard Toxin with a 1.0 ml volume of undiluted serum. This mixture is adjusted to a final volume of 2.0 ml with diluent.

(v) Neutralize all toxin-antitoxin mixtures at room temperature for 1 hour and hold in ice water until injections of mice can be made.

(vi) Five Swiss white mice, each weighing 16–20 grams, shall be used for each toxin-antitoxin mixture. A dose of 0.2 ml shall be injected intravenously into each mouse. Conclude the test 72 hours post injection and record all deaths.

(5) Test Interpretation shall be as follows:

(i) If any mice inoculated with the mixture of 1.0 International Unit of Standard Antitoxin and 1.0 Lo doses of Standard Toxin die, the results of the serum neutralization test are a No Test and shall be repeated: *Provided*, That, if the test is not repeated, the serial shall be declared unsatisfactory.

(ii) If less than 80 percent of the mice inoculated with the mixture of 1.0 International Unit of Standard Antitoxin and 1.0 L + doses of Standard Toxin die, the results of the serum neutralization test are a No Test and shall be repeated: *Provided*, That, if the test is not repeated, the serial shall be declared unsatisfactory.

(iii) If any mice inoculated with the mixture of 1.0 ml undiluted serum with 1.0 Lo dose of Standard Toxin die, the serum is considered to contain less than 1.0 International Units per ml.

(iv) If the single pooled serum from seven or more rabbits contains less than 1.0 International Unit per ml, the serial is unsatisfactory.

[39 FR 16862, May 10, 1974, as amended at 42 FR 61247, Dec. 2, 1977; 45 FR 40101, June 13, 1980. Redesignated at 55 FR 35562, Aug. 31, 1990; 56 FR 37826, Aug. 9, 1991; 56 FR 66784, 66785, Dec. 26, 1991; 79 FR 55969, Sept. 18, 2014]

§ 113.110 Clostridium Botulinum Type C Bacterin-Toxoid.

Clostridium Botulinum Type C Bacterin-Toxoid shall be produced from a culture of *Clostridium botulinum* Type C which has been inactivated and is nontoxic. Each serial of biological product containing *Clostridium botulinum* Type C fraction shall meet the applicable requirements in § 113.100 and shall be tested for purity, safety, and potency as prescribed in this section. A serial found unsatisfactory by any prescribed test shall not be released.

(a) *Purity test.* Final container samples of completed product from each serial and each subserial shall be tested for viable bacteria and fungi as provided in § 113.26.

(b) *Safety test.* Bulk or final container samples of completed product from each serial shall be tested for safety as provided in § 113.33(b).

(c) *Potency test.* Bulk or final container samples of completed product from each serial shall be tested for potency, using susceptible mink as test animals. At least five vaccinates and three unvaccinated controls of the same source and approximately the same age shall be used.

(1) Each of the vaccinates shall be injected subcutaneously with the dose recommended on the label for mink. Twenty-one to twenty-eight days post-injection, the vaccinates and the controls shall be challenged intraperitoneally with botulinum Type C toxin which has been titrated in mice to provide for a $10^{4.0}$ mouse MLD dose. The titration technique shall include inoculation of the mice intraperitoneally.

(2) The vaccinates and controls shall be observed for 7 days post-challenge and signs of botulism and deaths noted. For a valid test, the controls shall die of botulism. If the test is valid and 80 percent of the vaccinates do not remain free of botulism, the serial is unsatisfactory.

[39 FR 16862, May 10, 1974, as amended at 40 FR 759, Jan. 3, 1975. Redesignated at 55 FR 35562, Aug. 31, 1990, as amended at 56 FR 66785, Dec. 26, 1991]

§ 113.111 Clostridium Perfringens Type C Toxoid and Bacterin-Toxoid.

Clostridium Perfringens Type C Toxoid and Clostridium Perfringens Type C Bacterin-Toxoid shall be produced from a culture of *Clostridium perfringens* Type C which has been inactivated and is nontoxic. Each serial shall meet the applicable requirements in § 113.100 and shall be tested for purity, safety, and potency as prescribed in this section. Any serial found unsatisfactory by a prescribed test shall not be released.

(a) *Purity test.* Final container samples of completed product from each serial and each subserial shall be tested for viable bacteria and fungi as provided in § 113.26.

(b) *Safety test.* Bulk or final container samples of completed product from each serial shall be tested for safety as provided in § 113.33(b).

(c) *Potency test.* Bulk or final container samples of completed product from each serial shall be tested for potency using the Beta toxin-neutralization test provided in this paragraph.

(1) When used in this test, the following words and terms shall mean:

(i) *International antitoxin unit.* (I.U.) That quantity of Beta Antitoxin which reacts with L_0 and L^+ doses of Standard Toxin according to their definitions.

(ii) L_0 dose. The largest quantity of toxin which can be mixed with one unit of Standard Antitoxin and not cause sickness or death in injected mice.

(iii) L^+ *dose.* The smallest quantity of toxin which can be mixed with one unit of Standard Antitoxin and cause death in at least 80 percent of injected mice.

(iv) *Standard antitoxin.* The Beta Antitoxin preparation which has been standardized as to antitoxin unitage on the basis of the International *Clostridium perfringens* Beta Antitoxin Standard and which is either supplied by or acceptable to Animal and Plant Health Inspection Service. The antitoxin unit value shall be stated on the label.

(v) *Standard toxin.* The Beta toxin preparation which is supplied by or is acceptable to Animal and Plant Health Inspection Service.

(vi) *Diluent.* The solution used to make proper dilutions prescribed in this test. Such solutions shall be made by dissolving 1 gram of peptone and 0.25 grams of sodium chloride in each 100 ml of distilled water; adjusting the pH to 7.2; autoclaving at 250 °F for 25 minutes; and storing at 4 °C until used.

(2) Each of at least eight rabbits of a strain acceptable to APHIS, each weighing 4–8 pounds, shall be injected subcutaneously with not more than half of the largest recommended dose for any species indicated on the product label. A second equivalent dose shall be given not less than 20 days nor more than 23 days after the first does.

(3) Fourteen to seventeen days after the second dose, all surviving rabbits shall be bled and the serum tested for antitoxin content.

(i) At least seven rabbits are required to make an acceptable serum pool.

(ii) Equal quantities of serum from each rabbit shall be combined and tested as a single pooled serum.

(iii) If less than seven rabbits are available, the test is a No Test and shall be repeated: *Provided,* That, if the test is not repeated, the serial shall be declared unsatisfactory.

(4) The antitoxin content of the rabbit serums shall be determined as follows:

(i) Make a dilution of Standard Antitoxin to contain 10 International Units of antitoxin per ml.

(ii) Make one dilution of Standard Toxin to contain 10 L_0 doses per ml and make a second dilution of Standard Toxin to contain 10 L_+ doses per ml.

(iii) Combine 10 International Units of Standard Antitoxin with 10 L_0 doses of diluted Standard Toxin and combine 10 International Units of Standard Antitoxin with 10 L_+ doses of diluted Standard Toxin.

(iv) Combine 1 ml of undiluted serum with 10 L_0 doses of diluted Standard Toxin.

(v) Neutralize all toxin-antitoxin mixtures at room temperature for 1 hour and hold in ice water until injections of mice can be made.

(vi) Five Swiss white mice, each weighing 16–20 grams, shall be used for each toxin-antitoxin mixture. A dose of 0.2 ml shall be injected intravenously into each mouse. Conclude the test 24 hours post-injection and record all deaths.

(5) Test Interpretation shall be as follows:

(i) If any mice inoculated with the mixture of 10 International Units of Standard Antitoxin and 10 L_0 doses of Standard Toxin die, the results of the test are a No Test and shall be repeated: *Provided*, That, if the test is not repeated, the serial shall be declared unsatisfactory.

(ii) If less than 80 percent of the mice inoculated with mixture of 10 International Units of Standard Antitoxin and 10 L_+ doses of Standard Toxin die, the results of the test are a No Test and shall be repeated: *Provided*, That, if the test is not repeated, the serial shall be declared unsatisfactory.

(iii) If any mice inoculated with the mixture of serum with 10 L_0 doses of Standard Toxin die, the serum is considered to contain less than 10 International Units per ml. and the serial is unsatisfactory

[39 FR 16862, May 10, 1974, as amended at 40 FR 759, Jan. 3, 1975; 40 FR 41088, Sept. 5, 1975. Redesignated at 55 FR 35562, Aug. 31, 1990, as amended at 56 FR 66784, 66785, Dec. 26, 1991; 62 FR 31330, June 9, 1997; 79 FR 55969, Sept. 18, 2014]

§ 113.112 Clostridium Perfringens Type D Toxoid and Bacterin-Toxoid.

Clostridium Perfringens Type D Toxoid and Clostridium Perfringens Type D Bacterin-Toxoid shall be produced from a culture of *Clostridium perfringens* Type D which has been inactivated and is nontoxic. Each serial shall meet the applicable requirements in § 113.100 and shall be tested for purity, safety, and potency as prescribed in this section. Any serial found unsatisfactory by a prescribed test shall not be released.

(a) *Purity test.* Final container samples of completed product from each serial and each subserial shall be tested for viable bacteria and fungi as provided in § 113.26.

(b) *Safety test.* Bulk or final container samples of completed product from each serial shall be tested for safety as provided in § 113.33(b).

(c) *Potency test.* Bulk or final container samples of completed product from each serial shall be tested for potency using the Epsilon toxin-neutralization test provided in this paragraph.

(1) When used in this test, the following words and terms shall mean:

(i) *International antitoxin unit.* (I.U.) That quantity of Epsilon Antitoxin which reacts with L_0 and L_+ doses of Standard Toxin according to their definitions.

(ii) *L_0 dose.* The largest quantity of toxin which can be mixed with one-tenth unit of Standard Antitoxin and not cause sickness or death in injected mice.

(iii) *L_+ dose.* The smallest quantity of toxin which can be mixed with one-tenth unit of Standard Antitoxin and cause death in at least 80 percent of injected mice.

(iv) *Standard antitoxin.* The Epsilon Antitoxin preparation which has been standardized as to antitoxin unitage on the basis of the International *Clostridium perfringens* Epsilon Antitoxin Standard and which is either supplied by or acceptable to Animal and Plant Health Inspection Service. The antitoxin unit value shall be stated on the label.

(v) *Standard toxin.* The Epsilon toxin preparation which is supplied by or is acceptable to Animal and Plant Health Inspection Service.

(vi) *Diluent.* The solution used to make proper dilutions prescribed in this test. Such solutions shall be made by dissolving 1 gram of peptone and 0.25 gram of sodium chloride in each 100 ml of distilled water; adjusting the pH to 7.2; autoclaving at 250 °F for 25 minutes; and storing at 4 °C until used.

(2) Each of at least eight rabbits of a strain acceptable to APHIS, each weighing 4–8 pounds, shall be injected subcutaneously with not more than half of the largest recommended dose for any species indicated on the product label. A second equivalent dose shall be given not less than 20 days nor more than 23 days after the first dose.

(3) Fourteen to seventeen days after the second dose, all surviving rabbits shall be bled, and the serum tested for antitoxin content.

(i) At least seven rabbits are required to make an acceptable serum pool.

(ii) Equal quantities of serum from each rabbit shall be combined and tested as a single pooled serum.

(iii) If less than seven rabbits are available, the test is a No Test and shall be repeated: *Provided,* That, if the test is not repeated, the serial shall be declared unsatisfactory.

(4) The antitoxin content of the rabbit serums shall be determined as follows:

(i) Make a dilution of Standard Antitoxin to contain 1 International Unit of antitoxin per ml.

(ii) Make one dilution of Standard Toxin to contain 10 L_o doses per ml and make a second dilution of Standard Toxin to contain 10 L_+ doses per ml.

(iii) Combine 1 International Unit of Standard Antitoxin with 10 L_o doses of diluted Standard Toxin and Combine 1 International Unit of Standard Antitoxin with 10 L_+ doses of diluted Standard Toxin.

(iv) Dilute 1 ml of serum with 1 ml of diluent (1:2) and combine 1 ml of this solution with 10 L_o doses of diluted Standard Toxin.

(v) Neutralize all toxin-antitoxin mixtures at room temperature for 1 hour and hold in ice water until injections of mice can be made.

(vi) Five Swiss white mice, each weighing 16–20 grams, shall be used for each toxin-antitoxin mixture. A dose of 0.2 ml shall be injected intravenously into each mouse. Conclude the test 24 hours post-injection and record all deaths.

(5) Test Interpretation shall be as follows:

(i) If any mice inoculated with the mixture of 1 International Unit of Standard Antitoxin and 10 L_o doses of Standard Toxin die, the results of the test are a No Test and shall be repeated: *Provided,* That, if the test is not repeated, the serial shall be declared unsatisfactory.

(ii) If less than 80 percent of the mice inoculated with mixture of 1 International Unit of Standard Antitoxin and 10 L_+ doses of Standard Toxin die, the results of the test area No Test and shall be repeated: *Provided,* That, if the test is not repeated, the serial shall be declared unsatisfactory.

(iii) If any mice inoculated with the mixture of serum with 10 L_o doses of Standard Toxin die, the serum is considered to contain less than 2 International Units per ml, and the serial is unsatisfactory.

[39 FR 16865, May 10, 1974; 39 FR 20783, June 14, 1974. Redesignated at 39 FR 25463, July 11, 1974, and amended at 40 FR 759, Jan. 3, 1975; 40 FR 41088, Sept. 5, 1975. Redesignated at 55 FR 35562, Aug. 31, 1990, as amended at 56 FR 66784, 66785, Dec. 26, 1991; 62 FR 31331, June 9, 1997; 79 FR 55969, Sept. 18, 2014]

§ 113.113 Autogenous biologics.

Autogenous biologics shall be prepared from cultures of microorganisms which have been inactivated and are nontoxic. Such products shall be prepared only for use by or under the direction of a veterinarian under a veterinarian-client-patient relationship, *Provided,* That, such products may be prepared for use under the direction of a person of appropriate expertise in specialized situations such as aquaculture, if approved by the Administrator.

Each serial of an autogenous biologic shall meet the requirements in this section, and if found unsatisfactory by any prescribed test shall not be used.

(a) *Seed requirements.* The microorganisms used as seed to prepare autogenous biologics shall be microorganisms which are isolated from sick or dead animals in the herd of origin and which there is reason to believe are the causative agent(s) of the current disease affecting such animals.

(1) More than one microorganism isolated from the same herd may be used as seed.

(2) Under normal circumstances, microorganisms from one herd must not be used to prepare an autogenous biologic for another herd. The Administrator, however, may authorize preparation of an autogenous biologic for use in herds adjacent to the herd of origin, when adjacent herds are considered to be at risk. To request authorization to prepare a product for use in herds adjacent to the herd of origin, the establishment seeking authorization must submit to the Administrator (in c/o the Director, Center for Veterinary Biologics, Inspection and Compliance, 1920 Dayton Avenue, P.O. Box 844, Ames, IA 50010) the following information. (If any of the data are unavailable, the applicant for authorization

should indicate that such data are unavailable and why.)

(i) Name, address, and phone number of the owner of the herd of origin.

(ii) Attending veterinarian's name, address, and phone number.

(iii) Animal species and number in herd of origin.

(iv) Identification of microorganism(s), at least to genus.

(v) Diagnosis or clinical signs of the disease observed.

(vi) Name and address of the person who isolated the microorganism(s) and the date of isolation.

(vii) Number of doses of autogenous biologic requested and vaccination schedule.

(viii) Each adjacent herd owner's name, address, and phone number.

(ix) Number of animals and species in each adjacent herd.

(x) The attending veterinarian's or approved specialist's assessment of the involvement of the adjacent herd(s) with the disease observed.

The applicant shall give notice to the State Veterinarian or other appropriate State Official in writing when an autogenous biologic is to be used in adjacent herds.

(3) The Administrator may authorize preparation of an autogenous biologic for use in herds which are not adjacent to the herd of origin, but which he or she considers to be at risk of infection with the same microorganism(s). Except as provided below, the same information which is required for preparation of such product for use in herds adjacent to the herd of origin must be submitted to the Administrator (in c/o the Director, Center for Veterinary Biologics, Inspection and Compliance, 1920 Dayton Avenue, P.O. Box 844, Ames, IA 50010) for authorization to prepare a product for use in herds not adjacent to the herd of origin. Because the recipient herd involved may not be known when autogenous biologics are to be used in other geographic areas, the following data may be used in place of the data required in paragraphs (a)(2)(viii) and (a)(2)(ix) of this section.

(i) Names and addresses of practitioners in the area in place of the name, address, and phone number of the adjacent herd owner.

(ii) The geographic designations of the area involved.

(iii) A summary of the epidemiology of the disease situation that links the designated geographic areas with the herd of origin.

In addition, an applicant for authorization under this paragraph (a)(3) shall provide written approval from the State Veterinarian or other appropriate State Official in the State in which the autogenous biologic is to be used in nonadjacent herds.

(4) Under normal circumstances, microorganism(s) used for the production of autogenous biologics may not be older than 15 months from the date of isolation, or 12 months from the date of harvest of the first serial of product produced from the microorganism(s), whichever comes first. The Administrator, however, may authorize production of additional serials from microorganism(s) older than the above stated time periods, *Provided*, That, the person requesting such authorization submits the following supporting information to the address listed in paragraph (a)(3):

(i) The attending veterinarian's or approved specialist's current assessment of the continued involvement of a herd with the originally isolated microorganism(s), including a summary of the diagnostic work that has been done to support this assessment.

(ii) Evidence of satisfactory protection from the previous use of the autogenous biologic produced from the microorganisms involved.

(iii) Any other information the Administrator may require in order to determine the need to use the microorganism to make additional serials.

(b) *Restrictions*. Unless otherwise authorized by the Administrator, each serial of an autogenous biologic shall be subject to the following restrictions:

(1) Microorganisms used to prepare autogenous biologics shall not be maintained in the licensed establishment beyond the time authorized for use in production.

(2) The expiration date of the autogenous biologic shall not exceed 18 months from the date of harvest.

(c) *Testing requirements for autogenous biologics*. (1) Final container samples of completed product from the first serial or subserial of an autogenous biologic produced from an isolate shall be tested for purity as prescribed in § 113.26, and for safety as prescribed in § 113.33(b) or § 113.38 except that:

(i) When the number of final containers in a serial or subserial is 50 or less, two final container samples from each serial and subserial shall be tested as prescribed in § 113.26(b): *Provided*, That, 1 ml aliquots from each sample may be inoculated into five corresponding individual test vessels of each of the test media required.

(ii) Serials which are satisfactory after the third day of observation of purity test cultures and of safety test animals may be released for shipment to the customer and the tests continued throughout the required period; and

(iii) Serials released on the basis of satisfactory results of third day observations shall be immediately recalled if evidence of contamination occurs in test cultures or if any of the test animals used to demonstrate product safety, sicken, or die during the observation period.

(iv) Test summaries must be submitted to the Administrator (in c/o the Director, Center for Veterinary Biologics, Inspection and Compliance, 1920 Dayton Avenue, P.O. Box 844, Ames, IA 50010) on a quarterly basis by the 21st day of January, April, July, and October or more often as required by the Administrator.

(2) Each serial or subserial of autogenous bacterial product other than the first serial or subserial produced from an isolate shall meet the applicable general requirements prescribed in § 113.100 and the special requirements prescribed in this section. Each serial or subserial of autogenous viral product other than the first serial or subserial produced from an isolate shall meet the applicable general requirements prescribed in § 113.200 and the special requirements prescribed in this section. A serial or subserial found unsatisfactory by any prescribed test shall not be released.

(i) *Purity test.* Final container samples of completed product from each serial and subserial shall be tested for viable bacteria and fungi as provided in § 113.26. When the number of final containers in a serial or subserial is 50 or less, two final container samples from each serial and subserial shall be tested as prescribed in § 113.26(b): *Provided*, That, 1 ml aliquots from each sample may be inoculated into five corresponding individual test vessels of each of the test media required.

(ii) *Safety test.* Bulk of final container samples of completed product from each serial shall be tested for safety as provided in § 113.33 (b) or § 113.38.

(iii) *Identification.* All microorganisms used for the production of autogenous biologics shall be identified as follows: Bacteria, fungi, and mycoplasma shall be identified at least to genus and species. Viruses shall be identified at least to family. After 15 months from the date of isolation, or 12 months from the harvest date of the first serial of autogenous product produced from a microorganism, whichever comes first, characterization and identification shall be completed to strain and/or serotype before such microorganism may be used for production.

(iv) *Antigenicity, or immunogenicity, and potency.* Persons seeking authorization to prepare additional serials of autogenous biologics from microorganisms that are older than 24 months from the date of isolation, shall be required to conduct the following additional tests:

(A) Completed product shall be tested for antigenicity or immunogenicity in the species for which the product is recommended or in another animal species whose immunological response has been shown in the scientific literature to correlate with the response of the species for which the product is recommended. Such tests shall be conducted in accordance with a protocol developed by the licensee and approved by the Administrator and the results submitted to the Director, Center for Veterinary Biologics, Policy, Evaluation, and Licensing, 1920 Dayton Avenue, P.O. Box 844, Ames, IA 50010 for review. Microorganisms not shown to be antigenic (that is, not shown to induce a significant serological response) or immunogenic by such approved tests shall not be used for the preparation of such product.

(B) Bulk or final container samples of completed product from each serial of such autogenous biologics containing fractions for which standard requirement potency test procedures have been established shall be tested for potency in accordance with applicable standard requirement potency tests provided in 9 CFR part 113. If the culture of microorganisms used to produce such fractions is shown to be of a different strain or serotype than the reagent or challenge microorganisms used in the standard requirement potency test, reagents or challenges of the same strain or serotype as the microorganism used for production may be used.

(C) If no standard requirement potency test procedures have been established for a fraction(s) in the autogenous biologic, such fraction(s) of each serial of product shall be tested for potency using a developmental potency test described in the filed outline of production or shall at least be standardized to contain an antigenic mass for such fraction(s) that has been shown to be antigenic or immunogenic in accordance with paragraph (c)(2)(iv)(A) of this section.

[57 FR 38756, Aug. 27, 1992, as amended at 59 FR 67616, Dec. 30, 1994; 64 FR 43044, Aug. 9, 1999; 67 FR 15714, Apr. 3, 2002; 75 FR 20773, Apr. 21, 2010]

§ 113.114 Tetanus Toxoid.

Tetanus Toxoid shall be produced from a culture of *Clostridium tetani* which has been inactivated and is nontoxic. The toxoid may be either absorbed, precipitated, or purified and concentrated. Each serial of biological product containing *tetanus toxoid* fraction shall meet the applicable requirements in § 113.100 and shall be tested for purity, safety, and potency as prescribed in this section. A serial or subserial found unsatisfactory by any prescribed test shall not be released.

(a) *Purity test.* Final container samples of completed product from each serial and subserial shall be tested for viable bacteria and fungi as provided in § 113.26.

(b) *Safety test.* Bulk or final container samples of completed product from each serial shall be tested for safety as provided in § 113.33(b).

(c) *Potency test.* Bulk or final container samples of completed product from each serial shall be tested for potency. A group of 10 guinea pigs consisting of an equal number of males and females weighing 450 to 550 grams shall each be injected subcutaneously with 0.4 of the largest dose recommended on the product labels.

(1) Six weeks after injection, all surviving guinea pigs shall be bled and equal portions of serum, but not less than 0.5 ml from each, shall be pooled. For a valid test, the pool shall contain the serum from at least eight animals.

(2) The antitoxin titer of the pooled serum shall be determined in antitoxin units (A.U.) per ml using an enzyme-linked immunosorbent assay method acceptable to the Animal and Plant Health Inspection Service.

(3) If the antitoxin titer of the serum pool is at least 2.0 A.U. per ml, the serial is satisfactory. If the antitoxin titer of the serum pool is less than 2.0 A.U. per ml, the serial may be retested by the following procedure: *Provided,* That, if the serial is not retested, it shall be declared unsatisfactory.

(4) For serials in which the serum pool contains less than 2.0 A.U. per ml, the individual serum that constituted the pool may be tested by the enzyme-linked immunosorbent assay. If at least 80 percent of the individual serums have an antitoxin titer of at least 2.0 A.U. per ml, the serial is satisfactory. If less than 80 percent of the individual serums have an antitoxin titer of at least 2.0 A.U. per ml, the serial may be retested in 10 guinea pigs using the procedure described in (c)(1) and (2) above. The antitoxin titer of the pooled serum from the guinea pigs used in the retest shall be averaged with the antitoxin level of the pooled serum from the initial test. If the average of the two pools is at least 2.0 A.U. per ml, the serial is satisfactory. If the average of the two pools is less than 2.0 A.U. per ml, the serial is unsatisfactory and shall not be retested further.

[39 FR 16862, May 10, 1974, as amended at 46 FR 23224, Apr. 24, 1981; 50 FR 24905, June 14, 1985. Redesignated at 55 FR 35562, Aug. 31, 1990, as amended at 56 FR 37827, Aug. 9, 1991; 56 FR 66785, Dec. 26, 1991]

§ 113.115 Staphylococcus Aureus Bacterin-Toxoid.

Staphylococcus Aureus Bacterin-Toxoid shall be prepared from toxoided broth cultures of selected toxogenic strains of *Staphylococcus aureus* which has been inactivated and is nontoxic. Each serial of biological product containing Staphylococcus Aureus Bacterin-Toxoid shall meet the applicable requirements in § 113.100 and shall be tested for purity, safety, and potency as prescribed in this section. A serial found unsatisfactory by any prescribed test shall not be released.

(a) *Purity test.* Final container samples of completed product from each serial shall be tested for viable bacteria and fungi as provided in § 113.26.

(b) *Safety test.* Bulk or final container samples of completed product shall be tested for safety as provided in § 113.33(b). Also, the rabbits used in the potency test provided in paragraph (c) of this section shall constitute an additional safety test. If unfavorable reactions attributable to the product occur in any of the rabbits during the observation period, the serial is unsatisfactory.

(c) *Potency test.* Rabbits, each weighing 2000–3000 grams, shall be used as test animals. Either a five rabbit individual serum test or an eight rabbit pooled serum test shall be conducted. At the start of the test, individual serums from the five rabbits or pooled serums from the eight rabbits shall contain less than 0.2 alpha antitoxin units per ml.

(1) Each rabbit shall be given a series of not more than three intramuscular injections at 7 day intervals (1.0 ml, 2.0 ml, 3.0 ml) and observed from 7–14 days following the third injection. At the end of the observation period, a blood sample shall be taken from each rabbit.

(2) The sample of serum from each rabbit, if the five rabbit individual test is conducted or a pooled sample of equal quantities of serum from the rabbits if the eight rabbit pooled serum test is conducted, shall be tested to determine the staphylococcus alpha antitoxin units per ml as provided in paragraphs (c)(3), (4), (5), (6), (7), and (8) of this section.

(3) Inactivate rabbit serum 56 °C for 30 minutes.

(4) Make serial twofold dilutions of the serum samples and conduct the test, using 1 ml of the serial dilutions. Appropriate controls should be included for accurate interpretations.

(5) Add 1 ml of the standardized toxin containing the established "Lh" dose. The "Lh" dose is the amount of toxin which when mixed with one unit of standard antitoxin produces a 50 percent hemolysis of rabbit red blood cells.

(6) Incubate toxin-antitoxin mixture at room temperature for 30 minutes and add 1 ml of a 1.5 percent suspension of washed freshly drawn rabbit red blood cells suspended in normal saline to each tube. Mix and incubate the combined product in a 37 °C water bath for 1 hour. Refrigerate at 5 °C overnight.

(7) Read the hemolysis produced and establish the 50 percent end point. The 50 percent end point of hemolysis should be established by determining the size of the button produced by the unlysed red blood cells.

(8) Determine the units of antitoxin per 1 ml of serum.

(9) If the individual samples from four of the five rabbits in the individual serum test or the pooled samples from the eight rabbits in the pooled serum test do not contain three alpha antitoxin units per ml, the serial is unsatisfactory.

[39 FR 16862, May 10, 1974. Redesignated at 55 FR 35562, Aug. 31, 1990, as amended at 56 FR 66785, Dec. 26, 1991]

§ 113.116 Pasteurella Multocida Bacterin, Avian Isolate, Type 4.

Pasteurella Multocida Bacterin, Avian Isolate, Type 4 shall be prepared from cultures of *Pasteurella multocida*, avian isolate, Type 4 (Little and Lyons classification), which have been inactivated, and are nontoxic. Each serial of biological product containing Pasteurella Multocida Bacterin, Avian Isolate, Type 4, shall meet the applicable requirements in § 113.100 and shall be tested for purity, safety, and potency, as prescribed in this section. A serial found unsatisfactory by any prescribed test shall not be released.

(a) *Purity test.* Final container samples of completed product shall be tested for viable bacteria and fungi as provided in 9 CFR 113.26.

(b) *Safety test.* Observation of the vaccinated turkeys during the prechallenge period of the potency test provided in paragraph (c) of this section shall constitute the safety test. If unfavorable reactions that are attributable to the product occur, the serial is unsatisfactory. If unfavorable reactions that are not attributable to the product occur in one turkey, test results shall be determined by observing the remaining 20 turkeys. The test is a No Test and may be repeated if unfavorable reactions that are not attributable to the product occur in two or more turkeys, but the serial is unsatisfactory if the test is not repeated.

(c) *Potency test.* Bulk or final container samples of completed product shall be tested for potency of the Type 4 strain, using the two-stage test provided in this paragraph. Turkeys at least 6 weeks old obtained from the same source and hatch shall be properly identified and used as provided in this paragraph.

(1) *Vaccinates.* Each of not more than 21 turkeys shall be vaccinated with the dose and by the route recommended on the label. A second dose shall be given after 3 weeks and the turkeys observed for an additional 2-week prechallenge period.

(2) *Unvaccinated controls.* Each of not more than 11 turkeys shall be held as controls.

(3) *Challenge.* Not less than 14 days after the second dose, each of 20 vaccinates, and each of 10 unvaccinated controls shall be challenged intramuscularly with virulent *Pasteurella multocida,* Strain P–1662, Type 4 (Little and Lyons classification) and observed daily for a 14-day postchallenge period. Only dead birds shall be considered in evaluating the product.

(4) *Validity requirements.* Eight or more unvaccinated controls must die for the test to be valid. If this requirement is met, the potency test results are evaluated according to stage one of the following table. The test is a No Test and may be repeated if the validity requirement is not met, but the serial is unsatisfactory if the test is not repeated.

Stage	Number of vaccinates	Cumulative number of vaccinates	Cummulative total number of dead vaccinates for_____	
			Satisfactory serial	Unsatisfactory serial
1	20	20	6 or less	9 or more.
2	20	40	15 or less	16 or more.

(5) The serial shall pass or fail based on the stage one results of the potency test. However, the second stage may be conducted if seven or eight vaccinates die in stage one, but the serial is unsatisfactory if the second stage is not conducted.

(6) The second stage shall be conducted in a manner identical to the first stage. The serial shall be evaluated according to stage two of the table. On the basis of accumulated results from the data of both stage tests, a serial shall either pass or fail the second stage.

[47 FR 5795, Feb. 4, 1982; 47 FR 6817, Feb. 17, 1982, as amended at 52 FR 9117, Mar. 23, 1987. Redesignated at 55 FR 35562, Aug. 31, 1990, as amended at 56 FR 66785, Dec. 26, 1991]

§ 113.117 Pasteurella Multocida Bacterin, Avian Isolate, Type 1.

Pasteurella Multocida Bacterin, Avian Isolate, Type 1, shall be prepared from cultures of *Pasteurella multocida,* avian isolate, Type 1 (Little and Lyons classification), which have been inactivated and are nontoxic. Each serial of biological product containing Pasteurella Multocida Bacterin, Avian Isolate, Type 1, shall meet the applicable requirements in § 113.100 and shall be tested for purity, safety, and potency as prescribed in this section. A serial found unsatisfactory by any prescribed test shall not be released.

(a) *Purity test.* Final container samples of completed product shall be tested for viable bacteria and fungi as provided in § 113.26.

(b) *Safety test.* Observation of the vaccinated chickens during the prechallenged period of the potency test provided in paragraph (c) of this section shall constitute the safety test. If unfavorable reactions that are attributable to the product occur, the serial is unsatisfactory. If unfavorable reactions that are not attributable to the product occur in one chicken, test results shall be determined by observing the remaining 20 chickens. The test is a No Test and may be repeated if unfavorable reactions that are not attributable to the product occur in two or more chickens, but the serial is unsatisfactory if the test is not repeated.

(c) *Potency test.* Bulk or final container samples of completed product shall be tested for potency of the Type 1 strain, using the two-stage test provided in this paragraph. Chickens, at least 12 weeks of age, obtained from the same source and hatch, shall be properly identified and used as provided in this paragraph.

(1) *Vaccinates.* Each of not more than 21 chickens shall be injected with the dose and by the route recommended on the label. A second dose shall be injected after 3 weeks and the chickens observed for an additional 2 week prechallenge period.

(2) *Unvaccinated controls.* Each of not more than 11 chickens shall be held as controls.

(3) *Challenge.* Not less than 14 days after the second injection, each of 20 vaccinates, and each of 10 unvaccinated controls shall be challenged intramuscularly with a minimum of 250 colony-forming units of virulent *Pasteurella multocida*, Strain X–73, Type 1 (Little and Lyons classification) and observed daily for a 14-day postchallenge period. Only dead birds shall be considered in evaluating the product.

(4) *Validity requirements.* Eight or more unvaccinated controls must die for the test to be valid. If these requirement are met, the potency test results are evaluated according to stage one of the following table. The test is a No Test and may be repeated if the validity requirements are not met, but the serial is unsatisfactory if the test is not repeated.

Stage	Number of vaccinates	Cumulative number of vaccinates	Cummulative total number of dead vaccinates for_____	
			Satisfactory serial	Unsatisfactory serial
1	20	20	6 or less	9 or more.
2	20	40	15 or less	16 or more.

(5) The serial shall pass or fail based on the stage one results of the potency test. However, the second stage may be conducted if seven or eight vaccinates die in stage one, but the serial is unsatisfactory if the second stage is not conducted.

(6) The second stage shall be conducted in a manner identical to the first stage. The serial shall be evaluated according to stage two of the table. On the basis of accumulated results from the data of both stage tests, a serial shall either pass or fail the second stage.

[39 FR 16866, May 10, 1974; 39 FR 20368, June 10, 1974, as amended at 40 FR 759, Jan. 3, 1975; 40 FR 23989, June 4, 1975; 47 FR 5195, Feb. 4, 1982; 52 FR 9118, Mar. 23, 1987. Redesignated at 55 FR 35562, Aug. 31, 1990, as amended at 56 FR 66785, Dec. 26, 1991]

§ 113.118 Pasteurella Multocida Bacterin, Avian Isolate, Type 3.

Pasteurella Multocida Bacterin, Avian Isolate, Type 3, shall be prepared from culture of *Pasteurella multocida*, avian isolate, Type 3 (Little and Lyons classification), which have been inactivated and are nontoxic. Each serial of biological product containing Pasteurella Multocida Bacterin, Avian Isolate, Type 3, shall meet the applicable requirements in § 113.100 and shall be tested for purity, safety, and potency, as prescribed in this section. A serial found unsatisfactory by any prescribed test shall not be released.

(a) *Purity test.* Final container samples of completed product shall be tested for viable bacteria and fungi as provided in § 113.26.

(b) *Safety test.* Observation of the vaccinated turkeys during the prechallenge period of the potency test provided in paragraph (c) of this section shall constitute the safety test. If unfavorable reactions that are attributable to the product occur, the serial is unsatisfactory. If unfavorable reactions that are not attributable to the product occur in one turkey, test results shall be determined by observing the remaining 20 turkeys. The test is a No Test and may be repeated if unfavorable reactions that are not attributable to the product occur in two or more turkeys, but the serial is unsatisfactory if the test is not repeated.

(c) *Potency test.* Bulk or final container samples of completed product shall be tested for potency of the Type 3 strain, using the two-stage test provided in this paragraph. Turkeys, at least 6 weeks of age, obtained from the same source and hatch, shall be properly identified and used as provided in this paragraph.

(1) *Vaccinates.* Each of not more than 21 turkeys shall be injected with the dose and by the route recommended on the label. A second dose shall be injected after 3 weeks and the turkeys observed for an additional 2 week prechallenge period.

(2) *Unvaccinated controls.* Each of not more than 11 turkeys shall be held as controls.

(3) *Challenge.* Not less than 14 days after the second injection, each of 20 vaccinates, and each of 10 unvaccinated controls shall be challenged intramuscularly with a minimum of 150 colony-forming units of virulent *Pasteurella multocida,* Strain P–1059, Type 3 (Little and Lyons Classification) and observed daily for a 14-day postchallenge period. Only dead birds shall be considered in evaluating the product.

(4) *Validity requirements.* Eight or more unvaccinated controls must die for the test to be valid. If these requirements are met, the potency test results are evaluated according to stage one of the following table. The test is a No Test and may be repeated if the validity requirements are not met, but the serial is unsatisfactory if the test is not repeated.

Stage	Number of vaccinates	Cumulative number of vaccinates	Cummulative total number of dead vaccinates for______	
			Satisfactory serial	Unsatisfactory serial
1	20	20	6 or less	9 or more.
2	20	40	15 or less ...	16 or more.

(5) The serial shall pass or fail based on the stage one results of the potency test. However, the second stage may be conducted if seven or eight vaccinates die in stage one, but the serial is unsatisfactory if the second stage is not conducted.

(6) The second stage shall be conducted in a manner identical to the first stage. The serial shall be evaluated according to stage two of the table. On the basis of accumulated results from the data of both stage tests, a serial shall either pass or fail the second stage.

[39 FR 16862, May 10, 1974, as amended at 40 FR 759, Jan. 3, 1975; 47 FR 5196, Feb. 4, 1982; 52 FR 9118, Mar. 23, 1987. Redesignated at 55 FR 35562, Aug. 31, 1990, as amended at 56 FR 66785, Dec. 26, 1991]

§ 113.119 Erysipelothrix Rhusiopathiae Bacterin.

Erysipelothrix Rhusiopathiae Bacterin shall be produced from a culture of *Erysipelothrix rhusiopathiae* which has been inactivated and is nontoxic. Each serial of biological product containing *Erysipelothrix rhusiopathiae* shall meet the applicable requirements in § 113.100 and shall be tested for purity, safety, and potency as prescribed in this section. A serial found unsatisfactory by any prescribed test shall not be released.

(a) *Purity test.* Final container samples of completed product from each serial and each subserial shall be tested for viable bacteria and fungi as provided in § 113.26.

(b) *Safety test.* Bulk or final container samples of completed product from each serial shall be tested for safety as provided in § 113.38.

(c) *Potency test.* Bulk or final container samples of completed product from each serial shall be tested for potency using the mouse protection test provided in this paragraph. A mouse dose shall be 1⁄10 of the least dose recommended on the label for swine. Such swine dose shall not be less than 1 ml.

(1) The ability of the bacterin being tested (Unknown) to protect mice shall be compared with a Standard Reference Bacterin (Standard) which is either supplied by or acceptable to Animal and Plant Health Inspection Service.

(2) At least three threefold dilutions shall be made with the Standard and the same threefold dilutions shall be made for each Unknown. Dilutions shall be made with physiological saline solution.

(3) For each dilution of the Standard and each dilution of an Unknown, a group of at least 20 mice, each weighing 16 to 22 grams, shall be used. Each mouse in each group shall be injected subcutaneously with one mouse dose of the appropriate dilution.

(4) Each of 20 injected mice from each group shall be challenged subcutaneously 14 to 21 days after being injected. A dose containing at least 100 mouse LD_{50} of a suitable culture of *Erysipelothrix rhusiopathiae* shall be used. All survivors in each group of mice shall be recorded 10 days postchallenge.

(5) Test for valid assay: At least two dilutions of the Standard shall protect more than 0 percent and two dilutions shall protect less than 100 percent of the mice injected. The lowest dilution of the Standard shall protect more than 50 percent of the mice. The highest dilution of the Standard shall protect less than 50 percent of the mice.

(6) The relative potency (RP) of the Unknown is determined by comparing the 50 percent endpoint dilution (highest bacterin dilution protecting 50 percent of the mice) of the Unknown with that of the standard by the following formula:

$$RP = \frac{\text{reciprocal of 50 percent endpoint dilution of Unknown}}{\text{reciprocal of 50 percent endpoint dilution of Standard}}$$

(7) If the RP of the Unknown is less than 0.6, the serial being tested is unsatisfactory.

(8) If the 50 percent endpoint of an Unknown in a valid test cannot be calculated because the lowest dilution does not exceed 50 percent protection, that serial may be retested in a manner identical to the initial test: *Provided*, That, if the Unknown is not retested or if the protection provided by the lowest dilution of the Standard exceeds the protection provided by the lowest dilution of the Unknown by six mice or more; or, if the total number of mice protected by the Standard exceeds the total number of mice protected by the Unknown by eight mice or more, the serial is unsatisfactory.

(9) If the 50 percent endpoint of an Unknown in a valid test cannot be calculated because the highest dilution exceeds 50 percent protection, the Unknown is satisfactory without additional testing.

(10) If the RP is less than 0.6, the serial may be retested by conducting two independent replicate tests in a manner identical to the initial test. The average of the RP values obtained in the retests shall be determined. If the average RP is less than 0.6, the serial is unsatisfactory without further testing. If the average RP obtained in the retests is equal to or greater than 0.6, the following shall apply:

(i) If the RP obtained in the original test is one-third or less than the average RP obtained in the retests, the initial RP may be considered a result of test system error and the serial is satisfactory for potency.

(ii) If the RP value obtained in the original test is more than one-third the average RP obtained in the retests, a new average shall be determined using the RP values obtained in all tests. If the new average is less than 0.6, the serial is unsatisfactory.

[39 FR 16862, May 10, 1974, as amended at 40 FR 759, Jan. 3, 1975; 40 FR 20067, May 8, 1975; 40 FR 51414, Nov. 5, 1975; 44 FR 71408, Dec. 11, 1979; 50 FR 23795, June 6, 1985; 51 FR 23731, July 1, 1986. Redesignated at 55 FR 35562, Aug. 31, 1990; 56 FR 66558, Dec. 24, 1991; 56 FR 66784, 66785, Dec. 26, 1991]

§ 113.120 Salmonella Typhimurium Bacterin.

Salmonella Typhimurium Bacterin shall be prepared from a culture of *Salmonella typhimurium* which has been inactivated and is nontoxic. Each serial of biological product containing *Salmonella typhimurium* fraction shall meet the applicable requirements in § 113.100 and shall be tested for purity, safety, and potency as prescribed in this section. A serial found unsatisfactory by any prescribed test shall not be released.

(a) *Purity test.* Final container samples of completed product shall be tested for viable bacteria and fungi as provided in § 113.26.

(b) *Safety test.* Bulk or final container samples of completed product from each serial shall be tested for safety as provided in § 113.33(b).

(c) *Potency test.* Bulk or final container samples of completed product from each serial shall be tested for potency using the mouse test provided in this paragraph. A mouse dose shall be 1/20 of the least dose recommended on the label for other animals which shall not be less than 2 ml.

(1) The ability of the bacterin being tested (Unknown) to protect mice shall be compared with a Standard Reference Bacterin (Standard) which is either supplied by or acceptable to Animal and Plant Health Inspection Service.

(2) At least three tenfold dilutions shall be made with the Standard and the same tenfold dilutions shall be made for each Unknown. The dilutions shall be made in Phosphate Buffered Saline.

(3) For each dilution of the Standard and each dilution of an Unknown, a group of at least 20 mice, each weighing 16-22 grams, shall be used. Each mouse in a group shall be injected intraperitoneally with one mouse dose of the appropriate dilution. Each mouse shall be revaccinated on day 14, using the same schedule.

(4) Each of 20 vaccinated mice per group shall be challenged intraperitoneally 7–10 days after the second vaccination with a 0.25 ml dose containing 100-10,000 mouse LD_{50} as determined by titration, of a suitable culture of *Salmonella typhimurium.* All survivors in each group of mice shall be recorded 14 days postchallenge.

(5) Test for valid assay: At least two dilutions of the Standard shall protect more than 0 percent and two dilutions shall protect less than 100 percent of the mice injected. The lowest dilution of the Standard shall protect more than 50 percent of the mice. The highest dilution of the Standard shall protect less than 50 percent of the mice.

(6) The relative potency (RP) of the Unknown is determined by comparing the 50 percent endpoint dilution (highest bacterin dilution protecting 50 percent of the mice) of the Unknown with that of the Standard by the following formula:

$$RP = \frac{\text{reciprocal of 50 percent endpoint dilution of Unknown}}{\text{reciprocal of 50 percent endpoint dilution of Standard}}$$

(7) If the RP of the Unknown is less than 0.30, the serial being tested is unsatisfactory.

(8) If the 50 percent endpoint of an Unknown cannot be calculated because the lowest dilution does not exceed 50 percent protection, that serial may be retested in a manner identical to the initial test; *Provided,* That, if the Unknown is not retested or if the protection provided by the lowest dilution of the Unknown by six mice or more; or, if the total number of mice protected by the Standard exceeds the total number of mice protected by the Unknown by eight mice or more, the serial being tested is unsatisfactory.

(9) If the 50 percent endpoint of an Unknown in a valid test cannot be calculated because the highest dilution exceeds 50 percent protection, the Unknown is satisfactory without additional testing.

(10) If the RP is less than the minimum required in paragraph (c)(7) of this section, the serial may be retested by conducting two independent replicate tests in a manner identical to the initial test. The average of the RP values obtained in the retests shall be determined. If the average RP is less than the required minimum, the serial is unsatisfactory. If the average RP obtained in the retests is equal to or greater than the required minimum, the following shall apply:

(i) If the RP obtained in the original test is one-third or less than the average RP obtained in the retests, the initial RP may be considered a result of test system error and the serial is satisfactory.

(ii) If the RP value obtained in the original test is more than one-third the average RP obtained in the retests, a new average shall be determined using the RP values obtained in all tests. If the new average is less than the minimum required in paragraph (c)(7) of this section, the serial is unsatisfactory.

[40 FR 17003, Apr. 16, 1975, as amended at 42 FR 59487, Nov. 18, 1977; 48 FR 31008, July 6, 1983. Redesignated at 55 FR 35562, Aug. 31, 1990, as amended at 56 FR 66784, 66785, Dec. 26, 1991]

§ 113.121 Pasteurella Multocida Bacterin.

Pasteurella Multocida Bacterin shall be prepared from a culture of *Pasteurella multocida* strains other than avian which have been inactivated and are nontoxic. Each serial of biological product containing *Pasteurella multocida* fraction shall meet the applicable requirements in § 113.100 and shall be tested for purity, safety, and potency as prescribed in this section. A serial found unsatisfactory by any prescribed test shall not be released.

(a) *Purity test.* Final container samples of completed product from each serial and each subserial shall be tested for viable bacteria and fungi as provided in § 113.26.

(b) *Safety test.* Bulk or final container samples of completed product from each serial shall be tested for safety as provided in § 113.33(b). The subcutaneous route is to be used.

(c) *Potency test.* Bulk or final container samples of completed product from each serial shall be tested for potency using the mouse test provided in this paragraph. A mouse dose shall be 1/20 of the least dose recommended on the label for other animals which shall not be less than 2 ml.

(1) The ability of the bacterin being tested (Unknown) to protect mice shall be compared with a Standard Reference Bacterin (Standard) which is either supplied by or acceptable to Animal and Plant Health Inspection Service.

(2) At least three fivefold dilutions shall be made with the Standard and the same fivefold dilutions shall be made for each Unknown. The dilutions will be made in Phosphate Buffered Saline.

(3) For each dilution of the Standard and each dilution of each Unknown, a group of at least 20 mice, each weighing 16–22 grams, shall be used. Each mouse in a group shall be injected intraperitoneally with one mouse dose of the appropriate dilution. Each mouse shall be revaccinated on day 14, using the same schedule.

(4) Each of 20 injected mice per group shall be challenged intraperitoneally 10–12 days after the second vaccination with a 0.2 ml dose containing 100–10,000 mouse LD_{50}, as determined by titration, of a suitable culture of *Pasteurella multocida*. All survivors in each group of mice shall be recorded 10 days postchallenge.

(5) Test for valid assay: At least two dilutions of the Standard shall protect more than 0 percent and two dilutions shall protect less than 100 percent of the mice injected. The lowest dilution of the Standard shall protect more than 50 percent of the mice. The highest dilution of the Standard shall protect less than 50 percent of the mice.

(6) The relative potency (RP) of the Unknown is determined by comparing the 50 percent endpoint dilution (highest bacterin dilution protecting 50 percent of the mice) of the Unknown with that of the Standard by the following formula:

$$RP = \frac{\text{reciprocal of 50 percent endpoint dilution of Unknown}}{\text{reciprocal of 50 percent endpoint dilution of Standard}}$$

(7) If the RP of the Unknown is less than 0.50, the serial being tested is unsatisfactory.

(8) If the 50 percent endpoint of an Unknown cannot be calculated because the lowest dilution does not exceed 50 percent protection, that serial may be retested in a manner identical to the initial test: *Provided,* That, if the Unknown is not retested or if the protection provided by the lowest dilution of the Standard exceeds the protection provided by the lowest dilution of the Unknown by six mice or more; or, if the total number of mice protected by the Standard exceeds the total number of mice protected by the Unknown by eight mice or more, the serial being tested is unsatisfactory.

(9) If the 50 percent endpoint of an Unknown in a valid test cannot be calculated because the highest dilution exceeds 50 percent protection, the Unknown is satisfactory without additional testing.

(10) If the RP is less than the minimum required in paragraph (c)(7) of this section, the serial may be retested by conducting two independent replicate tests in a manner identical to the initial test. The average of the RP values obtained in the retests shall be determined. If the average RP is less than the required minimum, the serial is unsatisfactory. If the average RP obtained in the retests is equal to or greater than the required minimum, the following shall apply:

(i) If the RP obtained in the original test is one-third or less than the average RP obtained in the retests, the initial RP may be considered a result of test system error and the serial is satisfactory.

(ii) If the RP value obtained in the original test is more than one-third the average RP obtained in the retests, a new average shall be determined using the RP values obtained in all tests. If the new average is less than the minimum required in paragraph (c)(7) of this section, the serial is unsatisfactory.

[40 FR 17004, Apr. 16, 1975, as amended at 42 FR 59487, Nov. 18, 1977; 48 FR 31008, July 6, 1983. Redesignated at 55 FR 35562, Aug. 31, 1990, as amended at 56 FR 66784, 66785, Dec. 26, 1991]

§ 113.122 Salmonella Choleraesuis Bacterin.

Salmonella Choleraesuis Bacterin shall be prepared from a culture of *Salmonella choleraesuis* which has been inactivated and is nontoxic. Each serial of biological product containing *Salmonella choleraesuis* fraction shall meet the applicable requirements in 9 CFR 113.100 and shall be tested for purity, safety, and potency as prescribed in this section. A serial found unsatisfactory by any prescribed test shall not be released.

(a) *Purity test.* Final container samples of completed product shall be tested for viable bacteria and fungi as provided in 9 CFR 113.26.

(b) *Safety test.* Bulk or final container samples of completed product from each serial shall be tested for safety as provided in 9 CFR 113.33(b).

The subcutaneous route shall be used when the product is in combination with Pasteurella Multocida Bacterin.

(c) *Potency test.* Bulk or final container samples of completed product from each serial shall be tested for potency using the mouse test provided in this paragraph. A mouse dose shall be $\frac{1}{20}$ of the least dose recommended on the label for other animals which shall not be less than 2 ml.

(1) The ability of the bacterin being tested (Unknown) to protect mice shall be compared with a Standard Reference Bacterin (Standard) which is either supplied by or acceptable to Veterinary Services.

(2) At least three fivefold dilutions shall be made with the Standard and the same fivefold dilution shall be made for each Unknown. The dilutions shall be made in Phosphate-Buffered Saline.

(3) For each dilution of the Standard and each dilution of an Unknown, a group of at least 20 mice, each weighing 16 to 22 grams, shall be used. Each mouse in a group shall be injected intraperitoneally with one mouse dose of the appropriate dilution. Each mouse shall be revaccinated on day 14, using the same schedule.

(4) Each of 20 vaccinated mice per group shall be challenged intraperitoneally 7 to 10 days after the second vaccination with a 0.25 ml dose containing 10–1,000 mouse LD_{50} as determined by titration of a suitable culture of *Salmonella choleraesuis.* All survivors in each group of mice shall be recorded 14 days postchallenge.

(5) Test for valid assay: At least two dilutions of the Standard shall protect more than 0 percent and two dilutions shall protect less than 100 percent of the mice injected. The lowest dilution of the Standard shall protect more than 50 percent of the mice. The highest dilution of the Standard shall protect less than 50 percent of the mice.

(6) The relative potency (RP) of the Unknown is determined by comparing the 50 percent endpoint dilution (highest bacterin dilution protecting 50 percent of the mice) of the Unknown with that of the Standard by the following formula:

$$RP = \frac{\text{reciprocal of 50 percent endpoint dilution of Unknown}}{\text{reciprocal of 50 percent endpoint dilution of Standard}}$$

(7) If the RP of the Unknown is less than 0.50, the serial being tested is unsatisfactory.

(8) If the 50 percent endpoint of an Unknown cannot be calculated because the lowest dilution does not exceed 50 percent protection, that serial may be retested in a manner identical to the initial test; *Provided,* That, if the Unknown is not retested or if the protection provided by the lowest dilution of the Standard exceeds the protection provided by the lowest dilution of the Unknown by six mice or more; or, if the total number of mice protected by the Standard exceeds the total number

of mice protected by the Unknown by eight mice or more, the serial being tested is unsatisfactory.

(9) If the 50 percent endpoint of an Unknown in a valid test cannot be calculated because the highest dilution exceeds 50 percent protection, the Unknown is satisfactory without additional testing.

(10) If the RP is less than the minimum required in paragraph (c)(7) of this section, the serial may be retested by conducting two independent replicate tests in a manner identical to the initial test. The average of the RP values obtained in the retests shall be determined. If the average RP is less than the required minimum, the serial is unsatisfactory. If the average RP obtained in the retests is equal to or greater than the required minimum, the following shall apply:

(i) If the RP obtained in the original test is one-third or less than the average RP obtained in the retests, the initial RP may be considered a result of test system error and the serial is satisfactory.

(ii) If the RP value obtained in the original test is more than one-third the average RP obtained in the retests, a new average shall be determined using the RP values obtained in all tests. If the new average is less than the minimum required in paragraph (c)(7) of this section, the serial is unsatisfactory.

[43 FR 25077, June 9, 1978, as amended at 48 FR 31008, July 6, 1983. Redesignated at 55 FR 35562, Aug. 31, 1990, as amended at 56 FR 66785, Dec. 26, 1991]

§ 113.123 Salmonella Dublin Bacterin.

Salmonella Dublin Bacterin shall be prepared from a culture of *Salmonella dublin* which has been inactivated and is nontoxic. Each serial of biological product containing *Salmonella dublin* fraction shall meet the applicable requirements in 9 CFR 113.100 and shall be tested for purity, safety, and potency as prescribed in this section. A serial found unsatisfactory by any prescribed test shall not be released.

(a) *Purity test.* Final container samples of completed product shall be tested for viable bacteria and fungi as provided in 9 CFR 113.26.

(b) *Safety test.* Bulk or final container samples of completed product from each serial shall be tested for safety as provided in 9 CFR 113.33(b).

(c) *Potency test.* Bulk or final container samples of completed product from each serial shall be tested for potency using the mouse test provided in this paragraph. A mouse dose shall be 1/20 of the least dose recommended on the label for other animals which shall not be less than 2 ml.

(1) The ability of the bacterin being tested (Unknown) to protect mice shall be compared with a Standard Reference Bacterin (Standard) which is either supplied by or acceptable to Veterinary Services.

(2) At least three tenfold dilutions shall be made with the Standard and the same tenfold dilutions shall be made for each Unknown. The dilutions shall be made in Phosphate-Buffered Saline.

(3) For each dilution of the Standard and each dilution of an Unknown, a group of at least 20 mice, each weighing 16 to 22 grams, shall be used. Each mouse in a group shall be injected intraperitoneally with one mouse dose of the appropriate dilution. Each mouse shall be revaccinated on day 14, using the same schedule.

(4) Each of 20 vaccinated mice per group shall be challenged intraperitoneally 7 to 10 days after the second vaccination with a 0.25 ml dose containing 1,000–100,000 mouse LD_{50} as determined by titration of a suitable culture of *Salmonella dublin*. All survivors in each group of mice shall be recorded 14 days postchallenge.

(5) Test for valid assay: At least two dilutions of the Standard shall protect more than 0 percent and two dilutions shall protect less than 100 percent of the mice injected. The lowest dilution of the Standard shall protect more than 50 percent of the mice. The highest dilution of the Standard shall protect less than 50 percent of the mice.

(6) The relative potency (RP) of the Unknown is determined by comparing the 50 percent endpoint dilution (highest bacterin dilution protecting 50 percent of the mice) of the Unknown with that of the Standard by the following formula:

$$RP = \frac{\text{reciprocal of 50 percent endpoint dilution of Unknown}}{\text{reciprocal of 50 percent endpoint dilution of Standard}}$$

(7) If the RP of the Unknown is less than 0.30, the serial being tested is unsatisfactory.

(8) If the 50 percent endpoint of an Unknown cannot be calculated because the lowest dilution does not exceed 50 percent protection, that serial may be retested in a manner identical to the initial test; *Provided*, That, if the Unknown is not retested or if the protection provided by the lowest dilution of the Standard exceeds the protection provided by the lowest dilution of the Unknown by six mice or more; or, if the total number of mice protected by the Standard exceeds the total number of mice protected by the Unknown by eight mice or more, the serial being tested is unsatisfactory.

(9) If the 50 percent endpoint of an Unknown in a valid test cannot be calculated because the highest dilution exceeds 50 percent protection, the Unknown is satisfactory without additional testing.

(10) If the RP is less than the minimum required in paragraph (c)(7) of this section, the serial may be retested by conducting two independent replicate tests in a manner identical to the initial test. The average of the RP values obtained in the retests shall be determined. If the average RP is less than the required minimum, the serial is unsatisfactory. If the average RP obtained in the retests is equal to or greater than the required minimum, the following shall apply:

(i) If the RP obtained in the original test is one-third or less than the average RP obtained in the retests, the initial RP may be considered a result of test system error and the serial is satisfactory.

(ii) If the RP value obtained in the original test is more than one-third the average RP obtained in the retests, a new average shall be determined using the RP values obtained in all tests. If the new average is less than the minimum required in paragraph (c)(7) of this section, the serial is unsatisfactory.

[43 FR 25077, June 9, 1978, as amended at 48 FR 31009, July 6, 1983. Redesignated at 55 FR 35562, Aug. 31, 1990, as amended at 56 FR 66785, Dec. 26, 1991]

KILLED VIRUS VACCINES

§ 113.200 General requirements for killed virus vaccines.

When prescribed in an applicable Standard Requirement or in the filed Outline of Production, a killed virus vaccine shall meet the applicable requirements in this section.

(a) *Killing agent.* The vaccine virus shall be killed (inactivated) by an appropriate agent. The procedure involved may be referred to as inactivation. Suitable tests to assure complete inactivation shall be written into the filed Outline of Production.

(b) *Cell culture requirements.* If cell cultures are used in the preparation of the vaccine, primary cells shall meet the requirements in § 113.51 and cell lines shall meet the requirements in § 113.52.

(c) *Purity tests*—(1) *Bacteria and fungi.* Final container samples of completed product from each serial shall be tested as prescribed in § 113.26.

(2) *Avian origin vaccine.* Bulk pooled material or final container samples from each serial shall also be tested for:

(i) *Salmonella* contamination as prescribed in § 113.30; and

(ii) *Lymphoid leukosis virus* contamination as prescribed in § 113.31; and

(iii) *Hemagglutinating viruses* as prescribed in § 113.34.

(3) *Mycoplasma.* If the licensee cannot demonstrate that the agent used to kill the vaccine virus would also kill mycoplasma, each serial of the vaccine shall be tested for mycoplasma as prescribed in § 113.28, prior to adding the killing agent. Material found to contain mycoplasma is unsatisfactory for use.

(4) *Extraneous viruses.* Each lot of Master Seed Virus used to prepare killed virus vaccine recommended for animals other than poultry shall meet the requirements for extraneous viruses as prescribed in § 113.55.

(d) *Safety tests.* Final container samples of completed product from each serial shall be tested for safety in guinea pigs as prescribed in §113.38 and for safety in mice as prescribed in §113.33: *Provided*, That, vaccines recommended for use only in poultry are exempt from this requirement.

(e) *Viricidal activity test.* Only serials tested for viricidal activity in accordance with the test provided in §113.35 and found satisfactory by such test shall be packaged as diluent for desiccated fractions in combination packages.

(f) *Formaldehyde content.* If formaldehyde is used as the killing agent, the residual free formaldehyde content must not exceed 0.74 grams per liter (g/L) as determined using the ferric chloride test.[2] Firms currently using tests for residual free formaldehyde content other than the ferric chloride test have until July 14, 2004 to update their Outline of Production to be in compliance with this requirement.

[39 FR 27428, July 29, 1974, as amended at 40 FR 23989, June 4, 1975; 43 FR 49528, Oct. 24, 1978. Redesignated at 55 FR 35562, Aug. 31, 1990; 68 FR 35283, June 13, 2003; 79 FR 31021, May 30, 2014]

§§ 113.201–113.203 [Reserved]

§ 113.204 Mink Enteritis Vaccine, Killed Virus.

Mink Enteritis Vaccine, Killed Virus, shall be prepared from virus-bearing cell culture fluids or tissues obtained from mink that have developed mink enteritis following inoculation with virulent mink enteritis virus. Each serial shall meet the applicable requirements prescribed in §113.200 and special requirements prescribed in this section. Any serial found unsatisfactory by a prescribed test shall not be released.

(a) *Safety test.* Vaccinates used in the potency test in paragraph (b) of this section shall be observed each day prior to challenge. If unfavorable reactions attributable to the vaccine occur, the serial is unsatisfactory. If unfavorable reactions not attributable to the vaccine occur, the test shall be declared a No Test and may be repeated: *Provided*, That, if the test is not repeated, the serial is unsatisfactory.

(b) *Potency test.* Bulk or final container samples of completed product shall be tested for potency using 10 mink enteritis susceptible mink (five vaccinates and five controls) as follows:

(1) *Vaccination.* Each of the five vaccinates shall be injected with one dose of vaccine as recommended on the label and observed each day for 14 days.

(2) *Challenge.* At least 2 weeks after the last inoculation, the five vaccinates and the five controls shall be challenged with virulent mink enteritis virus and observed each day for 12 days. Fecal material shall be collected on one day between days 4–8 (inclusive) postchallenge from each test animal that remains free of enteric signs and tested for the presence of mink enteritis virus by cell culture with fluorescent antibody examination.

(3) *Interpretation.* A serial is satisfactory if at least 80 percent of the vaccinates remain free of enteric signs and do not shed virus in the feces, while at least 80 percent of the controls develop clinical signs of mink enteritis or shed virus in the feces. If at least 80 percent of the vaccinates remain free of enteric signs and do not shed virus in the feces, while less than 80 percent of the controls develop clinical signs of mink enteritis or shed virus in the feces, the test is considered a No Test and may be repeated: *Provided*, That, if at least 80 percent of the vaccinates do not remain well and free of detectable virus in the feces, the serial is unsatisfactory.

[39 FR 27428, July 29, 1974. Redesignated at 55 FR 35562, Aug. 31, 1990, as amended at 56 FR 66786, Dec. 26, 1991; 60 FR 14361, Mar. 17, 1995]

§ 113.205 Newcastle Disease Vaccine, Killed Virus.

Newcastle Disease Vaccine (Killed Virus) shall be prepared from virus-bearing tissues or fluids obtained from embryonated chicken eggs or cell cultures. With the exception of §113.200(c)(2)(iii), each serial shall meet the applicable general requirements

[2] The procedures for performing the ferric chloride test for residual free formaldehyde may be obtained from USDA, APHIS, Center for Veterinary Biologics-Laboratory, 1800 Dayton Road, P.O. Box 844, Ames, IA 50010.

prescribed in § 113.200 and special requirements prescribed in this section. A serial found unsatisfactory by a prescribed test shall not be released.

(a) *Safety test.* The prechallenge part of the potency test in paragraph (b) of this section shall constitute a safety test. If unfavorable reactions attributable to the product occur in any of the vaccinates, the serial is unsatisfactory. If unfavorable reactions which are not attributable to the product occur, the test shall be declared a No Test and may be repeated: *Provided,* That, if the test is not repeated, the serial shall be declared unsatisfactory.

(b) *Potency test.* A vaccination-challenge test shall be conducted using susceptible chickens 2 to 6 weeks of age at time of vaccination, properly identified and obtained from the same source and hatch.

(1) Ten or more chickens shall be vaccinated as recommended on the label and kept isolated under observation for at least 14 days.

(2) After at least 14 days post-vaccination, the vaccinates and at least 10 unvaccinated chickens that have been kept isolated as controls shall be challenged with a virulent strain of Newcastle disease virus supplied by or approved by Veterinary Services and the vaccinates observed each day for 14 days.

(3) If at least 90 percent of the controls do not show typical signs of Newcastle disease or die, the test is a No Test and may be repeated. If at least 90 percent of the vaccinates do not remain normal, the serial is unsatisfactory.

[39 FR 27428, July 29, 1974. Redesignated at 55 FR 35562, Aug. 31, 1990, as amended at 56 FR 66786, Dec. 26, 1991]

§ 113.206 Wart Vaccine, Killed Virus.

Wart Vaccine, Killed Virus, shall be prepared from virus-bearing epidermal tumors (warts) obtained from a bovine. Each serial shall meet the requirements prescribed in this section and any serial found unsatisfactory by a prescribed test shall not be released.

(a) *Purity.* Final container samples of completed product shall meet the requirements for purity as prescribed in § 113.200 (c)(1) and (3).

(b) *Safety.* Bulk or final container samples of completed product shall meet the requirements for safety as prescribed in §§ 113.33(b) and 113.38.

(c) *Formaldehyde content.* Bulk or final container samples of completed product shall meet the requirements for formaldehyde content as prescribed in § 113.200(f).

(d) *Potency and efficacy.* The efficacy of wart vaccine has been demonstrated to the satisfaction of Veterinary Services as being a valuable biological product. The inherent nature of the product precludes the possible development of serial to serial potency tests and none is required: *Provided,* That,

(1) The vaccine shall be a tissue extract representing at least 10 percent weight to volume suspension of wart tissue; and

(2) The vaccine shall be limited to use in the prevention of warts in cattle. Labeling recommendations shall be in accordance with § 112.7(h).

[40 FR 14084, Mar. 28, 1975, as amended at 40 FR 23989, June 4, 1975; 40 FR 30803, July 23, 1975. Redesignated at 55 FR 35562, Aug. 31, 1990, as amended at 56 FR 66786, Dec. 26, 1991; 81 FR 59436, Aug. 30, 2016]

§ 113.207 Encephalomyelitis Vaccine, Eastern, Western, and Venezuelan, Killed Virus.

Encephalomyelitis Vaccine, Eastern, Western, and Venezuelan, Killed Virus, shall be prepared from virus-bearing cell culture fluids. Each serial or subserial shall meet the requirements prescribed in this section and the general requirements prescribed in § 113.200, except those in § 113.200(d). Any serial or subserial found unsatisfactory by a prescribed test shall not be released.

(a) *Safety test.* Bulk samples of completed product from each serial shall be tested for encephalomyelitis virus inactivation.

(1) Each of at least ten 6 to 12 hour old chickens shall be injected subcutaneously with 0.5 ml of the product and the chickens observed each day for 10 days.

(2) If unfavorable reactions attributable to the product occur in the chickens during the observation period, the serial is unsatisfactory. If unfavorable reactions not attributable to the product occur, the test is a No Test and

may be repeated: *Provided*, That, if the test is not repeated, the serial is unsatisfactory.

(b) *Potency test.* Bulk or final container samples of completed product from each serial shall be tested for potency in accordance with the two-stage test provided in this paragraph. For each fraction contained in the product—Eastern type, Western type, or Venezuelan type—the serological interpretations required in this test shall be made independently. A serial or subserial found unsatisfactory for any of the fractions shall not be released.

(1) For this test, a guinea pig dose shall be one-half the amount recommended on the label for a horse and shall be administered as recommended for a horse. Each of 10 healthy guinea pigs (vaccinates) shall be injected with two guinea pig doses with an interval of 14 to 21 days between doses. Two additional guinea pigs from the same source shall be held as controls.

(2) Fourteen to 21 days after the second injection, serum samples from each vaccinate and each control shall be tested by a plaque reduction, serum neutralization test using Vero 76 cells.

(3) If the control serum samples show a titer of 1:4 or greater for any fraction, the test is a No Test for that fraction and may be repeated: *Provided*, That, if four or more of the vaccinate serum samples show a titer of less than 1:40 for the Eastern type fraction, less than 1:40 for the Western type fraction, or less than 1:4 for the Venezuelan type fraction, the serial or subserial is unsatisfactory without further testing.

(4) If two or three of the vaccinate serum samples show a titer of less than 1:40 for the Eastern type fraction, less than 1:40 for the Western type fraction, or less than 1:4 for the Venezuelan type fraction, the second stage of the test may be used for the relevant fraction(s): *Provided*, That, if a fraction is found acceptable by the first stage of the test, the second stage need not be conducted for that fraction.

(5) If the second stage is used and four or more of the vaccinate serum samples show a titer of less than 1:40 for the Eastern type fraction or the Western type fraction, or less than 1:4 for the Venezuelan type fraction, the serial or subserial is unsatisfactory.

(6) The results shall be evaluated according to the following table:

CUMULATIVE TOTALS

Stage	Vaccinates	Failures for acceptance	Failures for rejection
1	10	1 or less	4 or more.
2	20	3 or less	Do.

[39 FR 44714, Dec. 27, 1974, as amended at 40 FR 14084, Mar. 28, 1975; 42 FR 45284, Sept. 9, 1977. Redesignated at 55 FR 35562, Aug. 31, 1990, as amended at 56 FR 66786, Dec. 26, 1991; 61 FR 67930, Dec. 26, 1996]

§ 113.208 Avian Encephalomyelitis Vaccine, Killed Virus.

Avian Encephalomyelitis Vaccine (Killed Virus) shall be prepared from virus-bearing tissues or fluids obtained from embryonated chicken eggs. Each serial shall meet the general requirements prescribed in § 113.200 and the requirements prescribed in this section. Any serial found unsatisfactory by a prescribed test shall not be released.

(a) *Safety tests.* (1) The prechallenge part of the potency test prescribed in paragraph (b) of this section shall constitute a safety test. If any of the vaccinates develop clinical signs of disease or die due to causes attributable to the product, the serial is unsatisfactory.

(2) An inactivation test for viable avian encephalomyelitis (AE) virus shall be conducted on each serial. The test shall be conducted using susceptible chicken embryos: *Provided*, That, if a non-embryo adapted virus is used for vaccine production, the test shall be conducted in susceptible chickens.

(i) *Chicken Embryo Test.* Each of 15 or more AE susceptible 5 or 6 day old embryos shall be injected in the yolk sac with 0.2 ml of the vaccine. For a valid test, at least 80 percent of the embryos shall survive for 48 hours post-inoculation (PI). Eleven to 13 days PI, all embryos surviving the 48 hour PI period shall be examined for gross lesions of AE; all these embryos shall be normal or the serial is unsatisfactory. Concurrently, five additional embryos from the same source shall be injected with live AE virus of the production strain to serve as positive controls. At least 4 of the 5 embryos shall show evidence of AE virus infection during the 11 to 13 day PI period or the test shall be considered a No Test and repeated: *Provided*, That, if the test is not repeated, the serial shall be declared unsatisfactory.

(ii) *Chicken test*. Each of 10 or more AE susceptible 7 day old chickens shall be injected intracerebrally with 0.1 ml vaccine each. The chickens shall be observed each day for 28 days. If any chickens show clinical signs of AE, the serial is unsatisfactory. Concurrently, 5 additional chickens from the same source shall be injected intracerebrally with live AE virus of the production strain to serve as positive controls. At least 4 of the 5 controls shall show evidence of AE virus infection during the observation period or the test shall be a No Test and may be repeated: *Provided*, That, if the test is not repeated, the serial shall be unsatisfactory.

(b) *Potency test*. Bulk or final container samples of completed product from each serial or one subserial shall be tested. Ten or more AE-susceptible chickens (vaccinates), 4 weeks or older, properly identified and obtained from the same source and hatch, shall be injected as recommended on the label. At least 10 additional AE-susceptible chickens, properly identified and obtained from the same source and hatch shall be kept in isolation as controls.

(1) At least 28 days post-injection, the vaccinates and the controls shall be challenged intramuscularly with a virulent AE virus and the chickens observed each day for 21 days.

(2) If at least 80 percent of the controls do not show clinical signs of or die from AE infection, the test is a No Test and may be repeated.

(3) If at least 80 percent of the vaccinates do not remain normal, the serial is unsatisfactory.

[39 FR 12958, Dec. 27, 1974, as amended at 40 FR 41088, Sept. 5, 1975. Redesignated at 55 FR 35562, Aug. 31, 1990, as amended at 56 FR 66786, Dec. 26, 1991]

§ 113.209 Rabies Vaccine, Killed Virus.

Rabies Vaccine (Killed Virus) shall be prepared from virus-bearing cell cultures or nerve tissues obtained from animals that have developed rabies infection following injection with rabies virus. Only Master Seed Virus which has been established as pure, safe, and immunogenic shall be used for preparing the production seed virus for vaccine production. All serials of vaccine shall be prepared from the first through the fifth passage from the Master Seed Virus.

(a) The Master Seed Virus shall meet the applicable requirements prescribed in § 113.200 and the requirements prescribed in this section.

(1) Each lot of Master Seed Virus propagated in tissue or cells of avian origin shall also be tested for extraneous pathogens by procedures prescribed in § 113.37.

(2) Each lot of Master Seed Virus propagated in primary cell cultures of mouse or hamster origin or brain tissues of mouse origin shall be tested for lymphocytic choriomeningitis (LCM) virus by the procedure prescribed in § 113.42. If LCM virus is detected, the Master Seed Virus is unsatisfactory.

(b) The immunogenicity of vaccine prepared with virus at the highest passage from the Master Seed shall be established in each species for which the vaccine is recommended. Tests shall be conducted in accordance with a protocol filed with Animal and Plant Health Inspection Service before initiation of the tests. The vaccine shall be prepared using methods prescribed in the Outline of Production. If Rabies Vaccine is to be in combination with other fractions, the product to be tested shall include all fractions to be tested.

(1) The preinactivation virus titer must be established as soon as possible after harvest by at least five separate virus titrations. A mean relative potency value of the vaccine to be used in the host animal potency test must be established by at least five replicate potency tests conducted in accordance with the standard NIH test for potency in chapter 37 of "Laboratory Techniques in Rabies," Fourth Edition (1996), edited by F.X. Meslin, M.M. Kaplan, and H. Koprowski, World Health Organization, Geneva, Switzerland (ISBN 92 4 154479 1). The provisions of chapter 37 of "Laboratory Techniques in Rabies," Fourth Edition (1996), are the minimum standards for achieving compliance with this section and are incorporated by reference.

These provisions state that the challenge virus standard to be used as the challenge in the NIH test and the reference vaccine for the test are available from the national control authority. In the United States, that authority is the Animal and Plant Health Inspection Service's Center for Veterinary Biologics Laboratory, located at 1920 Dayton Avenue, P.O. Box 844, Ames, IA 50010; phone (515) 337-6100; fax (515) 337-6120. This incorporation by reference was approved by the Director of the Federal Register in accordance with 5 U.S.C. 552(a) and 1 CFR part 51. Copies may be obtained from the World Health Organization Publications Center USA, 49 Sheridan Avenue, Albany, NY 12210. Copies may be inspected at the Animal and Plant Health Inspection Service, Center for Veterinary Biologics, Policy, Evaluation, and Licensing, 1920 Dayton Avenue, P.O. Box 844, Ames, IA 50010, or at the National Archives and Records Administration (NARA). For information on the availability of this material at NARA, call 202–741–6030, or go to: *http://www.archives.gov/federal_register/code_of_federal_regulations/ibr_locations.html.*

(2) The dose of vaccine to be used in the immunogenicity test shall be no more than the amount which, on the basis of The NIH Test For Potency, has been diluted to the proposed minimum acceptable potency value. [1]

(3) Test animals shall be uniform and have no neutralizing antibodies to rabies as determined by serum-neutralization (SN) tests.

(i) Twenty-five or more animals shall be used as vaccinates. Each shall be administered a dose of vaccine at the proposed minimum potency level and by the method specified in the Outline of Production.

(ii) Ten or more additional animals shall be held as controls.

(iii) On or about 30, 90, 180, 270, and 365 days postvaccination, all test animals shall be bled and individual serum samples tested for neutralizing antibodies to rabies virus.

(iv) All surviving test animals shall be challenged intramuscularly with virulent rabies virus furnished or approved by Animal and Plant Health Inspection Service 1 year after vaccinations, except as provided in (b)(4) of this section. The challenged animals shall be observed each day for 90 days as prescribed in § 113.5(b). The brain of each test animal that dies following challenges shall be examined for rabies by the fluorescent antibody test or other method acceptable to Animal and Plant Health Inspection Service.

(v) Requirements for acceptance in challenge tests shall be death due to rabies in at least 80 percent of the controls while at least 22 of 25 or 26 of 30 or a statistically equivalent number of the vaccinates remain well for a period of 90 days.

(4) An alternative to challenging all surviving test animals in accordance with paragraph (b)(3)(iv) of this section may be used when the test animals are of species other than carnivores. Vaccinates shall be challenged at 1 year postvaccination. These shall include five vaccinates with the lowest SN titers at the 270th-day bleeding, five vaccinates with the lowest SN titers at the 365th-day bleeding, and all vaccinates with SN titers below 1:10 by the mouse SN test or below 1:16 by the rapid-fluorescent-focus-inhibition test at any bleeding. At least five SN-negative controls of each species shall be challenged at the same time as the vaccinates. All SN titers shall be titrated to an endpoint. All of the challenged vaccinates must remain well for a period of 90 days, and at least 80 percent of the controls must die of rabies for a satisfactory test without further challenge. If one or more of the vaccinates die from rabies, all the remaining vaccines, regardless of titer, along with the five controls shall be challenged. The cumulative results from the two challenges shall be evaluated for acceptance as specified in paragraph (b)(3)(v) of this section.

(5) An Outline of Production change shall be made before authority for use a new lot of Master Seed Virus shall be granted by Animal and Plant Health Inspection Service.

(c) If more than 1 year duration of immunity is to be claimed, a duration of immunity test for the additional time shall be conducted and interpreted as prescribed in paragraph (b) of this section for the 1 year test. The test animals shall be monitored serologically at least every 180 days. The time of challenge may be adjusted accordingly.

(d) Test requirements for release: Each serial and each subserial shall meet the general requirements prescribed in § 113.200 and special requirements in this paragraph.

(1) *Purity test.* Primary cell cultures of hamster origin or brain tissues of mouse origin used in vaccine production shall be tested for LCM virus as prescribed in § 113.42. Hamster origin cells shall be disrupted and undiluted cell fluids from each lot shall be tested. Where mouse brains are used in production, at least five mice which have not been injected with rabies virus shall be sacrificed and a 10 percent suspension of brain material shall be prepared and tested.

(2) *Safety tests.* Bulk samples from each serial shall be tested for virus inactivation and safety as follows:

(i) At the end of the inactivation period, each of 20 12 to 16 gram mice shall be injected intracerebrally with 0.03 ml and two rabbits shall be injected into each cerebral hemisphere with 0.25 ml and observed each day for 21 days. The brains of animals dying between the fourth and 21st day post-injection shall be checked for rabies virus. Material from each brain recovered shall be injected into each of five mice and the mice observed each day for 14 days. The fluorescent antibody test or serum neutralization test shall be used to confirm the presence or absence or live rabies virus. If live rabies virus is confirmed, the serial is unsatisfactory unless reprocessed in accordance with § 114.18.

(ii) A test for safety in three young seronegative animals of the most susceptible species for which the vaccine is recommended shall be conducted. Each shall in injected intramuscularly with one recommended dose of vaccine. If unfavorable reactions attributable to the product occur during a 28 day observation period, the serial is unsatisfactory.

(3) *Potency test.* Bulk or final container samples of completed product from each serial must be tested for potency by tests conducted in accordance with the standard NIH test for potency in Chapter 37 of "Laboratory Techniques in Rabies," Fourth Edition (1996), which is incorporated by reference at paragraph (b)(1) of this section. The relative potency of each serial must be at least equal to that used in an approved host animal immunogenicity test.

[39 FR 44715, Dec. 27, 1974, as amended at 42 FR 6794, Feb. 4, 1977; 43 FR 49528, Oct. 24, 1978; 50 FR 20090, May 14, 1985. Redesignated at 55 FR 35562, Aug. 31, 1990; 56 FR 66784, 66786, Dec. 26, 1991; 61 FR 31823, June 21, 1996; 64 FR 45420, Aug. 20, 1999; 69 FR 18803, Apr. 9, 2004; 75 FR 20773, Apr. 21, 2010]

§ 113.210 Feline Calicivirus Vaccine, Killed Virus.

Feline Calicivirus Vaccine, Killed Virus, shall be prepared from virus-bearing cell culture fluids. Only Master Seed which has been established as pure, safe, and immunogenic shall be used for preparing seeds for vaccine production. All serials of vaccine shall be prepared from the first through the fifth passage from the Master Seed.

(a) The Master Seed shall meet the applicable general requirements prescribed in § 113.200.

(b) The Master Seed shall be tested for chlamydial agents as prescribed in § 113.43.

(c) The immunogenicity of vaccine prepared from the Master Seed in accordance with the Outline of Production shall be established by a method acceptable to Animal and Plant Health Inspection Service. Vaccine used for this test shall be at the highest passage from the Master Seed and prepared at the minimum preinactivation titer specified in the Outline of Production.

(d) *Test requirements for release.* Each serial and subserial shall meet the applicable general requirements prescribed in § 113.200 and the special requirements provided in this paragraph. Any serial or subserial found unsatisfactory by a prescribed test shall not be released.

(1) *Safety.* Vaccinates used in the potency test in paragraph (d)(2) of this section shall be observed each day during the prechallenge period. If unfavorable reactions occur, including oral lesions, which are attributable to the vaccine, the serial is unsatisfactory. If unfavorable reactions occur which are

not attributable to the vaccine, the test is inconclusive and may be repeated. If the test is not repeated, the serial is unsatisfactory.

(2) *Potency.* Bulk or final container samples of completed product shall be treated for potency as follows:

(i) Eight feline calicivirus susceptible cats (five vaccinates and three controls) shall be used as test animals. Throat and nasal swabs shall be collected from each cat and individually tested on susceptible cell cultures for the presence of feline calicivirus. Blood samples shall be drawn and individual serum samples tested for neutralizing antibody. The cats shall be considered suitable for use if all swabs are negative for virus isolation and all serums are negative for calicivirus antibody at the 1:2 final dilution in a 50 percent plaque reduction test or other test of equal sensitivity.

(ii) The five cats used as vaccinates shall be administered one dose of vaccine by the method recommended on the label. If two doses are recommended, the second dose shall be given after the interval recommended on the label.

(iii) Fourteen or more days after the final dose of vaccine, the vaccinates and controls shall each be challenged intranasally with virulent feline calicivirus furnished or approved by Animal and Plant Health Inspection Service and observed each day for 14 days postchallenge. The rectal temperature of each animal shall be taken and the presence or absence of clinical signs, particularly lesions on the oral mucosa, noted and recorded each day.

(iv) If three of three controls do not show clinical signs of feline calicivirus infection other than fever, the test is inconclusive and may be repeated.

(v) If a significant difference in clinical signs cannot be demonstrated between vaccinates and controls using a scoring system approved by Animal and Plant Health Inspection Service and prescribed in the Outline of Production, the serial is unsatisfactory.

[50 FR 433, Jan. 4, 1985. Redesignated at 55 FR 35562, Aug. 31, 1990, as amended at 56 FR 66784, 66786, Dec. 26, 1991]

§ 113.211 [Reserved]

§ 113.212 Bursal Disease Vaccine, Killed Virus.

Bursal Disease Vaccine, Killed Virus, shall be prepared from virus-bearing cell culture fluids or embryonated chicken eggs. Only Master Seed which has been established as pure, safe, and immunogenic shall be used for preparing seeds for vaccine production. All serials shall be prepared from the first through the fifth passage from the Master Seed.

(a) The Master Seed shall meet the applicable requirements prescribed in § 113.200.

(b) Each lot of Master Seed shall be tested for pathogens by the chicken embryo inoculation test prescribed in § 113.37, except that, if the test is a No Test because of a vaccine virus override, the chicken inoculation test prescribed in § 113.36 may be conducted and the virus judged accordingly.

(c) The immunogenicity of vaccine prepared in accordance with the Outline of Production shall be established by a method acceptable to Animal and Plant Health Inspection Service. Vaccine used for this test shall be at the highest passage from the Master Seed and prepared at the minimum preinactivation titer specified in the Outline of Production. The test shall establish that the vaccine, when used as recommended on the label, is capable of inducing an immune response in dams of sufficient magnitude to provide significant protection to offspring.

(d) *Test requirements for release.* Each serial and subserial shall meet the applicable general requirements prescribed in § 113.200 and the special requirements in this paragraph. Any serial or subserial found unsatisfactory by a prescribed test shall not be released.

(1) *Safety.* Vaccinates used in the potency test in paragraph (d)(2) of this section shall be observed each day during the prechallenge period. If unfavorable reactions attributable to the vaccine occur, the serial is unsatisfactory. If unfavorable reactions which are not attributable to the vaccine occur, the test is a No Test and may be repeated. If the test is not repeated, the serial is unsatisfactory.

(2) *Potency.* Bulk or final container samples of completed product from each serial shall be tested for potency using the two-stage potency test provided in this paragraph.

(i) *Vaccinates.* Inject each of 21 susceptible chickens 14 to 28 days of age, properly identified and obtained from the same source and hatch, with one dose of vaccine by the route recommended on the label and observe for at least 21 days.

(ii) *Controls.* Retain at least 10 additional chickens from the same source and hatch as unvaccinated controls.

(iii) *Challenge.* Twenty-one to 28 days postvaccination, challenge 20 vaccinates and 10 controls by eyedrop with a virulent infectious bursal disease virus furnished or approved by Animal and Plant Health Inspection Service.

(iv) *Postchallenge period.* Four days postchallenge, necropsy all chickens and examine each for gross lesions of bursal disease. For purposes of this test, gross lesions shall include peribursal edema and/or edema and/or macroscopic hemorrhage in the bursal tissue. Vaccinated chickens showing gross lesions shall be counted as failures. If at least 80 percent of the controls do not have gross lesions of bursal disease in a stage of the test, that stage is considered inconclusive and may be repeated. In a valid test, the results shall be evaluated according to the following table:

Stage	Number of vaccinates	Cumulative number of vaccinates	Cumulative total number of failures for—	
			Satisfactory serial	Unsatisfactory serial
1	20	20	3 or less	6 or more.
2	20	40	8 or less	9 or more.

(v) If four or five vaccinates show lesions of bursal disease in the first stage, the second stage may be conducted in a manner identical to the first stage. If the second stage is not conducted, the serial is unsatisfactory.

(vi) If the second stage is used, each serial shall be evaluated according to the second part of the table on the basis of cumulative results.

[50 FR 434, Jan. 4, 1985. Redesignated at 55 FR 35562, Aug. 31, 1990, as amended at 56 FR 66784, 66786, Dec. 26, 1991; 79 FR 55969, Sept. 18, 2014]

§§ 113.213–113.214 [Reserved]

§ 113.215 Bovine Virus Diarrhea Vaccine, Killed Virus.

Bovine Virus Diarrhea Vaccine, Killed Virus, shall be prepared from virus-bearing cell culture fluids. Only Master Seed virus which has been established as pure, safe, and immunogenic shall be used for preparing seed cultures for vaccine production. All serials of vaccine shall be prepared from the first through the fifth passage from the Master Seed.

(a) The Master Seed shall meet the applicable general requirements prescribed in § 113.200 and the requirements of this section.

(b) The immunogenicity of vaccine prepared from the Master Seed in accordance with the Outline of Production shall be established by a method acceptable to the Animal and Plant Health Inspection Service. Vaccine used for this test shall be at the highest passage from the Master Seed and at the minimum preinactivation titer provided in the Outline of Production.

(c) *Test requirements for release.* Each serial and subserial shall meet the applicable general requirements prescribed in § 113.200 and the special requirements provided in this paragraph. Any serial or subserial found unsatisfactory by a prescribed test shall not be released.

(1) *Safety.* Vaccinates used in the potency test in paragraph (c)(2) of this section shall be observed each day during the prechallenge period. If unfavorable reactions occur, including respiratory signs, which are attributable to the vaccine, the serial is unsatisfactory. If unfavorable reactions occur which are not attributable to the vaccine, the test is a No Test and may be

repeated one time. If results of the second test are not satisfactory, or if the test is not repeated, the serial is unsatisfactory.

(2) *Potency*. Bulk or final container samples of completed product shall be tested for potency using the method described in this paragraph.

(i) Eight bovine virus diarrhea susceptible calves (five vaccinates and three controls) shall be used as test animals. Individual serum samples shall be collected, inactivated, and individually tested for neutralizing antibody.

(ii) A constant virus decreasing serum neutralization test in cell culture using 50–300 TCID50 of virus shall be used. Calves shall be considered susceptible if there is no neutralization at 1:2 final serum dilution. Other tests of equal sensitivity approved by the Animal and Plant Health Inspection Service may be used.

(iii) The five calves used as vaccinates shall be administered one dose of vaccine as recommended on the label. If two doses are recommended, the second dose shall be given according to the interval recommended on the label.

(iv) Fourteen days or more after the last vaccination, blood samples shall be drawn and the individual serum samples inactivated and tested for bovine virus diarrhea virus neutralizing antibody by the same method used to determine susceptibility.

(v) *Test interpretation*. If the controls have not remained seronegative at 1:2, the test is a No Test (NT) and may be repeated. If at least four of the five vaccinates in a valid test have not developed 50 percent endpoint titers of 1:8 or greater, the serial is unsatisfactory, except as provided in paragraph (c)(2)(vi) of this section.

(vi) *Virus Challenge Test*. If the results of a valid serum neutralization test are unsatisfactory, the vaccinates and controls may be challenged with virulent bovine virus diarrhea virus furnished or approved by the Animal and Plant Health Inspection Service. The animals shall be observed for 14 days post-challenge. If two of the three control calves do not show a temperature rise to 104.5 °F and develop respiratory or clinical signs of bovine virus diarrhea, the test is a No Test and may be repeated one time. If two or more vaccinates show a temperature of 104.0 °F for 2 or more days and develop respiratory or clinical or other signs, the serial is unsatisfactory.

(vii) The prevaccination and postvaccination sera from a satisfactory potency test shall be submitted to the National Veterinary Services Laboratories for confirmatory testing.

[55 FR 35562, Aug. 31, 1990]

§ 113.216 Bovine Rhinotracheitis Vaccine, Killed Virus.

Infectious Bovine Rhinotracheitis Vaccine, Killed Virus, shall be prepared from virus-bearing cell culture fluids. Only Master Seed virus which has been established as pure, safe, and immunogenic shall be used for preparing seed cultures for vaccine production. All serials of vaccine shall be prepared from the first through the fifth passage from the Master Seed.

(a) The Master Seed shall meet the applicable general requirements prescribed in § 113.200 and the requirements of this section.

(b) The immunogenicity of vaccine prepared in accordance with the Outline of Production shall be established by a method acceptable to the Animal and Plant Health Inspection Service. Vaccine used for this test shall be at the highest passage from the Master Seed and at the minimum preinactivation titer provided in the Outline of Production.

(c) *Test requirements for release*. Each serial and subserial shall meet the requirements prescribed in § 113.200 and the special requirements provided in this paragraph. Any serial or subserial found unsatisfactory by a prescribed test shall not be released.

(1) *Safety*. Vaccinates used in the potency test in paragraph (c)(2) of this section shall be observed each day during the prechallenge period. If unfavorable reactions occur, which are attributable to the vaccine, the serial is unsatisfactory. If unfavorable reactions occur which are not attributable to the vaccine, the test is a No Test and may be repeated one time. If the results of the second test are not satisfactory, or if the test is not repeated, the serial is unsatisfactory.

(2) *Potency*. Bulk or final container samples of completed product shall be tested for potency using the method described in this paragraph.

(i) Eight infectious bovine rhinotracheitis susceptible calves (five vaccinates, three controls) shall be used as test animals. Individual serum samples shall be collected, inactivated, and individually tested for neutralizing antibody.

(ii) A constant virus decreasing serum neutralization test in cell culture using 50–300 TCID50 of virus shall be used. Calves shall be considered susceptible if there is no neutralization at 1:2 final serum dilution. Other tests of equal sensitivity acceptable to the Animal and Plant Health Inspection Service may be used.

(iii) The five calves used as vaccinates shall be administered one dose of vaccine as recommended on the label. If two doses are recommended, the second dose shall be given according to the interval recommended on the label.

(iv) Fourteen or more days after the last vaccination, blood samples shall be drawn and the individual serum samples inactivated and tested for infectious bovine rhinotracheitis virus neutralizing antibody by the same method used to determine susceptibility.

(v) *Test interpretation*. If the three controls have not remained seronegative at 1:2, the test is a No Test (NT) and may be repeated. If at least four of the five vaccinates in a valid test have not developed 50 percent endpoint titers of 1:8, the serial is unsatisfactory, except as provided in paragraph (c)(2)(vi) of this section.

(vi) *Virus Challenge Test*. If the results of a valid serum neutralization test are unsatisfactory, the vaccinates and controls may be challenged with virulent infectious bovine rhinotracheitis virus furnished or approved by the Animal and Plant Health Inspection Service. The animals shall be observed each day for 14 days post-challenge. If two of the three control calves do not show a temperature rise to 104.5 °F and develop respiratory or other clinical signs of infectious bovine rhinotracheitis, the test is a No Test (NT) and may be repeated one time. If more than one of the vaccinates shows a temperature of 104.0 °F for 2 or more days or if more than one of the vaccinates develops respiratory or clinical or other signs, the serial is unsatisfactory.

(vii) The prevaccination and postvaccination sera from a satisfactory potency test shall be submitted to the National Veterinary Services Laboratories for testing by the Animal and Plant Health Inspection Service.

[55 FR 35562, Aug. 31, 1990, as amended at 56 FR 66786, Dec. 26, 1991]

LIVE VIRUS VACCINES

§ 113.300 General requirements for live virus vaccines.

When prescribed in an applicable Standard Requirement or in the filed Outline of Production, a live virus vaccine shall meet the applicable requirements in this section.

(a) *Purity tests*—(1) *Bacteria and fungi*. Final container samples of completed product and comparable samples of each lot of Master Seed Virus shall be tested for bacteria and fungi in accordance with the test provided in § 113.27.

(2) *Mycoplasma*. Final container samples of completed product and comparable samples of each lot of Master Seed Virus shall be tested for mycoplasma in accordance with the test provided in § 113.28.

(3) *Avian Origin Vaccine*. Samples of each lot of Master Seed Virus and bulk pooled material or final container samples from each serial shall also be tested for:

(i) Salmonella contamination as prescribed in § 113.30; and

(ii) Lymphoid leukosis virus contamination as prescribed in § 113.31; and

(iii) Hemagglutinating viruses as prescribed in § 113.34.

(4) *Extraneous viruses*. Each lot of Master Seed Virus used to prepare live virus vaccine recommended for animals other than poultry shall meet the requirements for extraneous viruses as prescribed in § 113.55

(b) *Safety tests*. Samples of each lot of Master Seed Virus and final container samples of completed product from each serial or first subserial of live virus vaccine recommended for animals other than poultry shall be tested for safety in at least one species for which the vaccine is intended using methods prescribed in §§ 113.39, 113.40, 113.41, 113.44, and 113.45 or in a filed Outline of Production. The mouse safety test prescribed in § 113.33(a) shall also be conducted unless the virus or agent in the vaccine is inherently lethal for mice.

(c) *Virus identity test.* At least one of the virus identity tests provided in this paragraph or a suitable identity test prescribed in the filed Outline of Production shall be conducted on the Master Seed Virus and final container samples from each serial or first subserial of biological product.

(1) *Fluorescent antibody test.* The fluorescent antibody test shall be conducted using virus inoculated cells and uninoculated control cells. Cells shall be stained with fluorochrome conjugated specific antiserum. Fluorescence typical of the virus concerned shall be demonstrated in the inoculated cells. The control cells shall remain free of such fluorescence.

(2) *Serum neutralization test.* The serum neutralization test shall be conducted using the constant serum-decreasing virus method with specific antiserum. For positive identification, at least 100 ID_{50} of vaccine virus shall be neutralized by the antiserum.

(d) *Cell Culture Requirements.* If cell cultures are used in the preparation of Master Seed Virus or of the vaccine, primary cells shall meet the requirements prescribed in § 113.51, cell lines shall meet the requirements prescribed in § 113.52, and ingredients of animal origin shall meet the applicable requirements in § 113.53.

(e) *Moisture content.* (1) The maximum moisture content in desiccated vaccines must be stated in the filed Outline of Production.

(2) Final container samples of completed product from each serial or subserial must be tested for moisture content in accordance with the test prescribed in § 113.29.

[39 FR 27430, July 29, 1974, as amended at 43 FR 49528, Oct. 24, 1978; 50 FR 1042, Jan. 9, 1985; 54 FR 19352, May 5, 1989. Redesignated at 55 FR 35562, Aug. 31, 1990; 60 FR 24549, May 9, 1995; 68 FR 57608, Oct. 6, 2003]

§ 113.301 Ovine Ecthyma Vaccine.

Ovine Ecthyma Vaccine shall be prepared from tissue culture fluids or virus-bearing tissues obtained from sheep that have developed ovine ecthyma following inoculation with virulent ovine ecthyma virus. Ovine Ecthyma Vaccine is exempt from the requirements prescribed in §§ 113.27 and 113.300(a), (b), and (c). Each serial shall meet the moisture requirements in § 113.300(e) and the special requirements prescribed in this section. Any serial found unsatisfactory by a prescribed test shall not be released.

(a) *Safety tests.* (1) Bulk or final container samples of completed product from each serial shall be tested for safety as prescribed in § 113.38.

(2) The prechallenge period of the potency test shall constitute a safety test. If unfavorable reactions attributable to the vaccine occur in either of the vaccinates during the observation period, the serial is unsatisfactory.

(b) *Potency test.* Final container samples of completed product from each serial and each subserial shall be tested for potency using susceptible lambs. The vaccine shall be prepared as recommended for use on the label.

(1) Each of two lambs (vaccinates) shall be vaccinated by application of the vaccine to a scarified area on the medial surface of the thigh and observed each day for 14 days.

(2) The immunity of the two vaccinates and one or more unvaccinated lambs (controls) shall be challenged in the same manner as for vaccination, using the opposite thigh.

(3) If typical signs of ovine ecthyma, such as hyperemia, vesicles, and pustules do not develop on the controls during the first 2 weeks following challenge and persist for approximately 30 days, the test is a No Test and may be repeated.

(4) If the vaccinates do not show a typical immune reaction, the serial is unsatisfactory: *Provided,* That, an initial active reaction with hyperemia which resolves progressively and disappears within 2 weeks, may be characterized as a typical immune reaction.

[39 FR 27430, July 29, 1974. Redesignated at 55 FR 35562, Aug. 31, 1990, as amended at 56 FR 66786, Dec. 26, 1991]

§ 113.302 Distemper Vaccine—Mink.

Distemper Vaccine—Mink shall be prepared from virus-bearing cell culture fluids. Only Master Seed Virus which has been established as pure, safe, and immunogenic shall be used for preparing the production seed virus for vaccine production. All serials of vaccine shall be prepared from the first through the fifth passage from the Master Seed Virus.

(a) The Master Seed Virus shall meet the applicable requirements prescribed in § 113.300 and the requirements prescribed in this section.

(b) The lot of Master Seed Virus shall be tested for extraneous viruses as follows:

(1) To detect virulent canine distemper virus, each of two distemper susceptible mink or ferrets shall be inoculated with 1 ml of the Master Seed Virus and observed each day for 21 days. If undesirable reactions occur in either test animal, the lot of Master Seed Virus is unsatisfactory.

(2) Master Seed Virus propagated in chicken embryos shall be tested for pathogens by the chicken embryo test prescribed in § 113.37 except lesions typical of distemper virus may be disregarded. If found unsatisfactory, the Master Seed Virus shall not be used.

(c) Each lot of Master Seed Virus used for vaccine production shall be tested for immunogenicity. The selected virus dose from the lot of Master Seed Virus shall be established as follows:

(1) At least 25 distemper susceptible mink shall be used as test animals. Blood samples shall be drawn from these animals and individual serum samples tested. The mink shall be considered susceptible if the results are negative at a 1:2 final serum dilution in a varying serum-constant virus neutralization test with less than 500 ID_{50} of canine distemper virus. Other means of insuring susceptibility may be used if prior approval from Animal and Plant Health Inspection Service is received.

(2) A geometric mean titer of the dried vaccine produced from the highest passage of the Master Seed Virus shall be established before the immunogenicity test is conducted. At least 20 mink shall be vaccinated with a predetermined quantity of vaccine virus and at least 5 additional mink shall be held as unvaccinated controls. To confirm the dosage calculations, five replicate virus titrations shall be conducted on a sample of the vaccine virus dilution used.

(3) At least twenty-one days post-injection, the immunity of each of the vaccinates and the controls shall be challenged with the same size dose of virulent distemper virus and observed each day for 21 days.

(i) If at least 80 percent of the controls do not die or show severe signs of distemper, the test is a No Test and may be repeated.

(ii) If at least 19 of 20, 27 of 30, or 36 of 40 of the vaccinates do not survive without showing clinical signs of distemper during the observation period, the Master Seed Virus is unsatisfactory.

(4) An Outline of Production change shall be made before authority for use of a new lot of Master Seed Virus shall be authorized by Animal and Plant Health Inspection Service.

(d) Test requirements for release: Each serial and subserial shall meet the general requirements prescribed in § 113.300 and the requirements in this paragraph. Final container samples of completed product shall be tested. Any serial or subserial found unsatisfactory by a prescribed test shall not be released.

(1) *Mink safety test.* Each of 2 mink shall be vaccinated with the equivalent of 10 doses of vaccine rehydrated with sterile diluent and administered in the manner recommended on the label. The mink shall be observed each day for 21 days. If unfavorable reactions attributable to the product occur in either of the mink during the observation period, the serial or subserial is unsatisfactory. If unfavorable reactions which are not attributable to the product occur, the test shall be declared a No Test and may be repeated: *Provided,* That if the test is not repeated, the serial or subserial shall be declared unsatisfactory.

(2) *Potency Test.* An in vitro potency test shall be conducted. To be eligible for release, each serial and subserial shall have a virus titer sufficiently greater than the titer of vaccine virus

used in the immunogenicity test prescribed in paragraph (c) of this section to assure that, when tested at any time within the expiration period, each serial and subserial shall have a virus titer $10^{0.7}$ greater than that used in such immunogenicity test when tested by the method used in paragraph (c)(2) of this section.

[40 FR 53000, Nov. 14, 1975, as amended at 48 FR 33471, July 22, 1983. Redesignated at 55 FR 35562, Aug. 31, 1990, as amended at 56 FR 66784, 66786, Dec. 26, 1991; 72 FR 72564, Dec. 21, 2007]

§ 113.303 Bluetongue Vaccine.

Bluetongue Vaccine shall be prepared from virus-bearing cell culture fluids. Only Master Seed which has been established as pure, safe, and immunogenic shall be used for preparing the seeds for vaccine production. All serials of vaccine shall be prepared from the first through the tenth passage from the Master Seed.

(a) The Master Seed shall meet the applicable general requirements prescribed in § 113.300 and the requirements in this section.

(b) Each lot of Master Seed shall be tested for transmissibility and reversion to virulence in sheep using a method acceptable to Animal and Plant Health Inspection Service. If reversion to virulence is demonstrated, the Master Seed is unsatisfactory.

(c) Each lot of Master Seed used for vaccine production shall be tested for immunogenicity. The selected virus dose from the lot of Master Seed shall be established as follows:

(1) Twenty-five lambs, susceptible to the bluetongue virus serotype contained in the vaccine, shall be used as test animals (20 vaccinates and 5 controls). Blood samples shall be drawn from these animals and individual serums tested. A lamb shall be considered susceptible if there is no neutralization at a 1:2 final serum dilution in a constant virus varying serum neutralization test with 60 to 300 $TCID_{50}$ of bluetongue virus or another method acceptable to Animal and Plant Health Inspection Service.

(2) A geometric mean titer of the vaccine produced from the highest passage from the Master Seed shall be established before the immunogenicity test is conducted. The 20 lambs to be used as vaccinates shall be administered a predetermined quantity of vaccine virus by the method recommended on the label. To confirm the virus dosage administered, five replicate virus titrations shall be conducted on a sample of the vaccine used.

(3) At least once during the period of 14 to 18 days postvaccination, individual serum samples shall be collected from each of the vaccinates and tested for virus neutralizing antibody using the 60 to 300 $TCID_{50}$ of bluetongue virus.

(4) Twenty-one to twenty-eight days postvaccination the vaccinates and the controls shall each be challenged with virulent bluetongue virus and observed for 14 days. The rectal temperature of each animal shall be taken and recorded for 17 consecutive days beginning 3 days prechallenge. The presence or absence of lesions or other clinical signs of bluetongue noted and recorded on each of 14 consecutive days postchallenge.

(i) If at least four of the five controls do not show clinical signs of bluetongue and a temperature rise of 3 °F or higher over the prechallenge mean temperature, the test shall be considered a No Test and may be repeated.

(ii) If at least 19 of the 20 vaccinates tested as prescribed in paragraph (c)(3) of this section do not have bluetongue neutralizing antibody titers of 1:4 final serum dilution or higher, or if more than one of the vaccinates shows a temperature rise of 3 °F or higher than its prechallenge mean temperature for 2 or more days, or if more than one of the vaccinates exhibits clinical signs of bluetongue, the Master Seed is unsatisfactory.

(5) An Outline of Production change shall be made before authority for use of a new lot of Master Seed shall be granted by Animal and Plant Health Inspection Service.

(d) *Test requirements for release.* Each serial and subserial shall meet the applicable general requirements prescribed in § 113.300 and the requirements in this paragraph. Final container samples of completed product shall be tested. Any serial or subserial found unsatisfactory by a prescribed test shall not be released.

(1) *Safety test.* The mouse safety test prescribed in § 113.33(a) and the lamb safety test prescribed in § 113.45 shall be conducted.

(2) *Virus titer requirements.* Final container samples of completed product shall be tested for virus titer using the titration method used in paragraph (c)(2) of this section. To be eligible for release, each serial and subserial shall have a virus titer sufficiently greater than the titer of vaccine virus used in the immunogenicity test prescribed in paragraph (c) of this section to assure that when tested at any time within the expiration period, each serial and subserial shall have a virus titer of $10^{0.7}$ greater than that used in such immunogenicity test.

[50 FR 23796, June 6, 1985. Redesignated at 55 FR 35562, Aug. 31, 1990, as amended at 56 FR 66784, 66786, Dec. 26, 1991; 72 FR 72564, Dec. 21, 2007]

§ 113.304 Feline Panleukopenia Vaccine.

Feline Panleukopenia Vaccine shall be prepared from virus-bearing cell culture fluids. Only Master Seed Virus which has been established as pure, safe, and immunogenic shall be used for preparing the production seed virus for vaccine production. All serials of vaccine shall be prepared from the first through the fifth passage from the Master Seed Virus.

(a) The Master Seed Virus shall meet the applicable general requirements prescribed in § 113.300 and the requirements prescribed in this section.

(b) The lot of Master Seed Virus shall be tested for other agents as follows:

(1) To detect virulent feline panleukopenia virus or virulent mink enteritis virus, each of two feline panleukopenia susceptible cats, as determined by the criteria prescribed in paragraph (c)(1) of this section, shall be injected subcutaneously with the equivalent of one cat dose each and the cats observed each day for 21 days. If either or both cats show signs of disease or reduced white blood cell counts below 50 percent of the normal level established by an average of three or more counts taken prior to injection, the Master Seed Virus is unsatisfactory.

(2) To detect chlamydial agents, the Master Seed Virus shall be tested as prescribed in § 113.43.

(c) Each lot of Master Seed Virus used for vaccine production shall be tested for immunogenicity. The selected virus dose from the lot of Master Seed Virus shall be established as follows:

(1) Twenty-five feline panleukopenia susceptible cats shall be used as test animals (20 vaccinates and 5 controls). Blood samples drawn from each cat shall be individually tested for neutralizing antibody against feline panleukopenia virus to determine susceptibility.

(i) A constant virus-carrying serum neutralization test in tissue culture using 100 to 300 $TCID_{50}$ of virus shall be used.

(ii) Cats shall be considered susceptible if there is no neutralization at a 1:2 final serum dilution.

(2) A geometric mean titer of the dried vaccine produced from the highest passage of the Master Seed Virus shall be established before the immunogenicity test is conducted. The 20 cats used as vaccinates shall be injected with a predetermined quantity of vaccine virus and the remaining five cats held as uninjected controls. To confirm the dosage calculations, five replicate virus titrations shall be conducted on a sample of the vaccine virus dilution used.

(3) Fourteen days post-injection, the vaccinates and the controls shall be challenged with virulent feline panleukopenia virus furnished by Animal and Plant Health Inspection Service and the cats observed each day for 14 days.

(i) If at least 80 percent of the controls do not show clinical signs of feline panleukopenia during the observation period, the test is a No Test and may be repeated. Clinical signs of feline panleukopenia shall include a pronounced leukopenia wherein the white cell count drops to 4,000 or less per cubic mm, or the white cell count drops to less than 25 percent of the normal level established by an average of three or more counts taken prior to challenge.

(ii) If at least 19 of the 20 vaccinates do not survive the observation period without showing clinical signs of feline panleukopenia as described in paragraph (c)(3)(i) of this section, the Master Seed Virus is unsatisfactory.

(4) An Outline of Production change shall be made before authority for use of a new lot of Master Seed Virus shall be granted by Animal and Plant Health Inspection Service.

(d) *Test requirements for release.* Each serial and subserial shall meet the requirements prescribed in § 113.300 and in this paragraph. Final container samples of completed product shall be tested. Any serial or subserial found unsatisfactory by a prescribed test shall not be released.

(1) *Safety test.* The mouse safety test prescribed in § 113.33(a) and the cat safety test prescribed in § 113.39 shall be conducted.

(i) Each of two healthy cats shall be injected with 10 cat doses by the method recommended on the label and the cats observed each day for 14 days.

(ii) If unfavorable reactions attributable to the biological product occur during the observation period, the serial is unsatisfactory. If unfavorable reactions occur which are not attributable to the product, the test shall be declared a No Test and repeated: *Provided,* That, if not repeated, the serial shall be unsatisfactory.

(2) *Virus titer requirements.* Final container samples of completed product shall be tested for virus titer using the titration method used in paragraph (c)(2) of this section. To be eligible for release, each serial and each subserial shall have a virus titer sufficiently greater than the titer of vaccine virus used in the immunogenicity test prescribed in paragraph (c) of this section to assure that when tested at any time within the expiration period, each serial and subserial shall have a virus titer of $10^{0.7}$ greater than that used in such immunogenicity test but not less than $10^{2.5}$ $TCID_{50}$ per dose.

[39 FR 44716, Dec. 27, 1974, as amended at 40 FR 53378, Nov. 18, 1975; 43 FR 25078, June 9, 1978; 43 FR 41186, Sept. 15, 1978; 44 FR 58900, Oct. 12, 1979; 48 FR 33471, July 22, 1983. Redesignated at 55 FR 35562, Aug. 31, 1990, as amended at 56 FR 66784, 66786, Dec. 26, 1991; 72 FR 72564, Dec. 21, 2007]

§ 113.305 Canine Hepatitis and Canine Adenovirus Type 2 Vaccine.

Canine Hepatitis Vaccine and Canine Adenovirus Type 2 Vaccine shall be prepared from virus-bearing cell culture fluids. Only Master Seed Virus which has been established as pure, safe, and immunogenic shall be used in preparing the production seed virus for vaccine production. All serials shall be prepared from the first through the fifth passage from the Master Seed Virus.

(a) The Master Seed Virus shall meet the applicable requirements prescribed in § 113.300 except that the dog safety test prescribed in § 113.40(a) shall be conducted by the intravenous route.

(b) Each lot of Master Seed Virus used for vaccine production shall be tested for immunogenicity by one or both of the following methods:

(1) *Immunogenicity for canine hepatitis.* Twenty-five canine hepatitis susceptible dogs shall be used as test animals (20 vaccinates and 5 controls). Blood samples shall be drawn from these animals and individual serum samples tested. The dogs shall be considered susceptible if the results are negative at a 1:2 final serum dilution in a varying serum-constant virus neutralization test using 50 to 300 $TCID_{50}$ of canine adenovirus.

(i) A geometric mean titer of the dried vaccine produced from the highest passage of the Master Seed Virus shall be established before the immunogenicity test is conducted. The 20 dogs to be used as vaccinates shall be injected with a predetermined quantity of vaccine virus and the remaining five dogs held as uninjected controls. To confirm the dosage calculations, five replicate virus titrations shall be conducted on a sample of the vaccine virus dilution used.

(ii) Not less than 14 days postinjection, the vaccinates and the controls shall each be challenged intravenously with virulent infectious canine hepatitis virus furnished or approved by the Animal and Plant Health Inspection Service and observed each day for 14 days.

(A) If at least four of the five controls do not show severe clinical signs of canine hepatitis, the test is a No Test and may be repeated.

(B) If at least 19 of the 20 vaccinates do not survive without showing clinical signs of infectious canine hepatitis during the observation period, the Master Seed Virus is unsatisfactory.

(2) *Immunogenicity for canine adenovirus Type 2.* Thirty canine adenovirus type 2 susceptible dogs shall be used as test animals (20 vaccinates and 10 controls). Blood samples shall be drawn from these animals and individual serum samples tested. The dogs shall be considered susceptible if the results are negative at a 1:2 final serum dilution in a varying serum-constant virus neutralization test using 50 to 300 $TCID_{50}$ of canine adenovirus.

(i) A geometric mean titer of the dried vaccine produced from the highest passage of the Master Seed Virus shall be established before the immunogenicity test is conducted. The 20 dogs to be used as vaccinates shall be injected with a predetermined quantity of vaccine virus and the remaining 10 dogs held as uninjected controls. To confirm the dosage calculations, five replicate virus titrations shall be conducted on a sample of the vaccine virus dilution used.

(ii) Not less than 14 days postinjection, the vaccinates and the controls shall be challenged by exposure to a nebulized aerosol of virulent canine adenovirus type 2 furnished or approved by the Animal and Plant Health Inspection Service and observed each day for 14 days postchallenge. The rectal temperature of each animal shall be taken and the presence of respiratory or other clinical signs of canine adenovirus type 2 noted and recorded each day.

(A) If at least 6 of 10 controls do not show clinical signs of canine adenovirus type 2 infection other than fever, the test is a No Test and may be repeated.

(B) If a significant difference in clinical signs in a valid test cannot be demonstrated between vaccinates and controls using a scoring system approved by the Animal and Plant Health Inspection Service, the Master Seed Virus is unsatisfactory.

(iii) An Outline of Production change shall be made before authorization for use of a new lot of Master Seed Virus shall be granted by the Animal and Plant Health Inspection Service.

(c) *Test requirements for release.* Each serial and subserial shall meet the requirements prescribed in § 113.300 and in this paragraph. Final container samples of completed product shall be tested. Any serial or subserial found unsatisfactory by a prescribed test shall not be released.

(1) *Virus titer requirements.* Final container samples of completed product shall be tested for virus titer using the titration method used in paragraph (b)(1)(i) and/or (b)(2)(i) of this section. To be eligible for release, each serial and each subserial shall have a virus titer sufficiently greater than the titer of vaccine virus used in the immunogenicity test(s) prescribed in paragraph (b) of this section to assure that when tested at any time within the expiration period, each serial and subserial shall have a virus titer of $10^{0.7}$ greater than that used in such immunogenicity test(s) but not less than $10^{2.5}$ $TCID_{50}$ dose. If both immunogenicity tests in paragraph (b) of this section are conducted and a different amount of virus is used in each test, the virus titer requirements shall be based on the higher of the two amounts.

(2) [Reserved]

[60 FR 14361, Mar. 17, 1995, as amended at 72 FR 72564, Dec. 21, 2007]

§ 113.306 Canine Distemper Vaccine.

Canine Distemper Vaccine shall be prepared from virus-bearing cell culture fluids or embryonated chicken eggs. Only Master Seed Virus which has been established as pure, safe, and immunogenic shall be used for preparing the production seed virus for vaccine production. All serials of vaccine shall be prepared from the first through the fifth passage from the Master Seed Virus.

(a) *Master Seed Virus.* The Master Seed Virus shall meet the applicable requirements prescribed in § 113.300 and the requirements prescribed in this section.

(1) To detect ferret virulent canine distemper virus, each of five canine distemper susceptible ferrets shall be injected with a sample of the Master Seed Virus equivalent to the amount of

virus to be used in one dog dose and observed each day for 21 days. If undesirable reactions are observed during the observation period, the lot of Master Seed is unsatisfactory.

(2) Master Seed Virus propagated in tissues or cells of avian origin shall be tested for pathogens by the chicken embryo test prescribed in § 113.37. If found unsatisfactory, the Master Seed Virus shall not be used.

(b) Each lot of Master Seed Virus used for vaccine production shall be tested for immunogenicity. The selected virus dose from the lot of Master Seed Virus shall be established as follows:

(1) Twenty-five canine distemper susceptible dogs shall be used as test animals (20 vaccinates and 5 controls). Blood samples shall be drawn from these animals and individual serum samples tested. The dogs shall be considered susceptible if the results are negative at a 1:2 final serum dilution in a varying serum-constant virus neutralization test using 50 to 300 $TCID_{50}$ of canine distemper virus.

(2) A geometric mean titer of the dried vaccine produced from the highest passage of the Master Seed Virus shall be established before the immunogenicity test is conducted. The 20 dogs used as vaccinates shall be injected with a predetermined quantity of vaccine virus and the remaining five dogs held as uninjected controls. To confirm the dosage calculations, five replicate virus titrations shall be conducted on a sample of the vaccine virus dilution used.

(3) At least 14 days post-injection, the vaccinates and the controls shall each be challenged intracerebrally with virulent canine distemper virus furnished or approved by the Animal and Plant Health Inspection Service and observed each day for 21 days.

(i) If at least four of the five controls do not die and the survivor, if any, does not show clinical signs of canine distemper the test is a No Test and may be repeated.

(ii) If at least 19 of the 20 vaccinates do not survive without showing clinical signs of canine distemper during the observation period, the Master Seed Virus is unsatisfactory.

(4) An Outline of Production change shall be made before authorization for use of a new lot of Master Seed Virus shall be granted by the Animal and Plant Health Inspection Service.

(c) *Test requirements for release.* Except for § 113.300(a)(3)(ii), each serial and subserial shall meet the requirements prescribed in § 113.300 and in this paragraph. Final container samples of completed product shall be tested. Any serial or subserial found unsatisfactory by a prescribed test shall not be released.

(1) The test for pathogens prescribed in § 113.37 shall be conducted on each serial or one subserial of avian origin vaccine.

(2) *Virus titer requirements.* Final container samples of completed product shall be tested for virus titer using the titration method used in paragraph (b)(2) of this section. To be eligible for release, each serial and subserial shall have a virus titer sufficiently greater than the titer of vaccine virus used in the immunogenicity test prescribed in paragraph (b) of this section to assure that when tested at any time within the expiration period, each serial and subserial shall have a virus titer of $10^{0.7}$ greater than that used in such immunogenicity test but not less than $10^{2.5}$ $TCID_{50}$ per dose.

[60 FR 14362, Mar. 17, 1995, as amended at 72 FR 72564, Dec. 21, 2007]

§ 113.308 Encephalomyelitis Vaccine, Venezuelan.

Encephalomyelitis Vaccine, Venezuelan, shall be prepared from virus-bearing cell culture fluids. Only Master Seed which has been established as pure, safe, and immunogenic shall be used for preparing seeds for vaccine production. All serials of vaccine shall be prepared from the first through the fifth passage from the Master Seed.

(a) The Master Seed shall meet the applicable general requirements prescribed in § 113.300 except (b), and the requirements prescribed in this section.

(b) Each lot of Master Seed shall be tested for immunogenicity. The selected virus dose from the lot of Master Seed shall be established as follows:

(1) Tests conducted by the Department have established that horses having Venezuelan equine encephalomyelitis antibody titers of 1:20 by the hemagglutination-inhibition (HI) method or 1:40 by the serum neutralization (SN) method were immune to challenge with virulent virus. The immunogenicity test is based on the demonstration of a serological response of at least that magnitude following vaccination of serologically negative horses.

(2) At least 22 horses (20 vaccinates and 2 controls), susceptible to Venezuelan equine encephalomyelitis, shall be used as test animals. Blood samples shall be taken from each horse and the serums individually tested for neutralizing antibody. Horses shall be considered susceptible if there is no neutralization at a 1:2 final serum dilution in a constant virus-varying serum neutralization test using 60 to 300 $TCID_{50}$ of Venezuelan equine encephalomyelitis virus.

(3) A geometric mean titer of the vaccine produced from the highest passage of the Master Seed shall be established using a method acceptable to Veterinary Services before the immunogenicity test is conducted. The 20 horses used as vaccinates shall be injected with a predetermined quantity of vaccine virus by the method to be recommended on the label. To confirm the dosage administered, five replicate virus titrations shall be conducted on a sample of the vaccine virus dilution used.

(4) Twenty-one to twenty-eight days postvaccination, blood samples shall be drawn from all test animals. For a valid test, the controls shall remain seronegative at 1:2 final serum dilution. In a valid test, if at least 19 of 20 vaccinates do not have antibody titers of at least 1:20 in a hemagglutination-inhibition test or at least 1:40 in a serum neutralization test, the Master Seed is unsatisfactory.

(5) An Outline of Production change shall be made before authority for use of a new lot of Master Seed shall be granted by Animal and Plant Health Inspection Service.

(c) *Test requirements for release.* Each serial and subserial shall meet the applicable general requirements prescribed in § 113.300 and special requirements in this paragraph. Any serial or subserial found unsatisfactory by a prescribed test shall not be released.

(1) *Safety test.* The mouse safety test prescribed in § 113.33(b) shall be conducted.

(2) *Virus titer requirements.* Final container samples of completed product shall be tested for virus titer using the method in paragraph (b)(3) of this section. To be eligible for release, each serial and subserial shall have a virus titer sufficiently greater than the titer of the vaccine used in the immunogenicity test prescribed in paragraph (b) of this section to assure that, when tested at any time within the expiration period, each serial and subserial shall have a virus titer of $10^{0.7}$ greater than that used in the immunogenicity test, but not less than $10^{2.5}$ $TCID_{50}$ per dose.

[50 FR 23797, June 6, 1985. Redesignated at 55 FR 35562, Aug. 31, 1990, as amended at 56 FR 66784, 66786, Dec. 26, 1991; 72 FR 72564, Dec. 21, 2007]

§ 113.309 Bovine Parainfluenza$_3$ Vaccine.

Bovine Parainfluenza$_3$ Vaccine shall be produced from virus-bearing cell culture fluids. Only Master Seed Virus which has been established as pure, safe, and immunogenic shall be used for preparing the production seed virus for vaccine production. All serials of vaccine shall be prepared from the first through the tenth passage from the Master Seed Virus.

(a) The Master Seed Virus shall meet the applicable general requirements prescribed in § 113.300.

(b) Each lot of Master Seed Virus shall meet the special requirements prescribed in this section.

(c) Each lot of Master Seed Virus used for vaccine production shall be tested for immunogenicity. The selected virus dose from the lot of Master Seed Virus shall be established as follows:

(1) Twenty-five bovine parainfluenza$_3$ susceptible calves shall be used as test animals (20 vaccinates and five controls). Blood samples shall be drawn from these animals and individual serums tested. Also, nasal specimens

shall be collected for virus isolation attempts. The calves shall be considered susceptible if:

(i) The results are negative at a 1:2 final serum dilution in a varying serum constant virus neutralization test with less than 500 $TCID_{50}$ of bovine $parainfluenza_3$ virus; and

(ii) Shall be negative to bovine $parainfluenza_3$ virus isolation attempts from the nasal specimens on the day of injection.

(2) A geometric mean titer of the dried vaccine produced from the highest passage of the Master Seed Virus shall be established before the immunogenicity test is conducted. The 20 calves to be used as vaccinates shall be injected with a predetermined quantity of vaccine virus and the remaining five calves held as uninjected controls. To confirm the dosage calculation, five replicate virus titrations shall be conducted on a sample of the vaccine virus dilution used.

(3) The vaccinates and controls shall be examined for clinical signs of respiratory disease and the body temperature taken and recorded on each of the first 14 consecutive days post-injection. The vaccinates shall be bled on day 6 ±2 days post-injection.

(4) Three to four weeks post-vaccination, all calves shall be bled for serum antibodies and nasal specimens shall be collected for PI_3 virus isolation. On the same day, all vaccinates and controls shall be given acceptable challenge PI_3 virus titrating at least $10^{7.0}$ $TCID_{50}$ per ml and the animals observed for 14 days. Two ml of the challenge virus shall be instilled in each nostril or shall be inhaled as an aerosol suspension. Upon request, challenge virus and instructions shall be furnished by Animal and Plant Health Inspection Service.

(5) Each animal shall be examined for clinical signs of respiratory disease and the body temperature recorded on each of the 14 consecutive days of the post-challenge observation period. Each day for at least the first 10 days post-challenge, nasal specimens for virus isolation attempts shall be taken. All animals shall be bled on day 6 ±2 days post-challenge, and all animals shall be bled at least once 14 to 28 days post-challenge for serum antibody studies.

(6) Satisfactory Test Criteria:

(i) All virus isolations attempts shall be by culture and at least one subculture in PI_3 susceptible cells for a total of at least 14 days.

(ii) Two to four weeks post-vaccination, at least 19 of the 20 vaccinates shall have PI_3 neutralizing antibody titers of at least 1:4 and all five controls shall be negative at 1:2 dilution. None of the post-vaccination serums collected from the vaccinates on day 6 ±2 days shall reveal serum neutralization antibody titers of 1:32 or greater based upon final dilution.

(iii) Satisfactory resistance to challenge by vaccinates shall be determined by a significant difference between virus isolation rates from vaccinates and controls. The virus neutralization titers of post-challenge serums and respiratory symptoms and temperatures from all animals shall be considered in the evaluation of the test validity.

(7) Designated animal alternates for test animals showing anamnestic antibody responses (titers 1:32 or greater) on day 6 serums may be included in the study under the following provisions:

(i) No more than five alternates shall be allowed for the vaccinates and no more than two for the controls.

(ii) Alternates shall be subject to all requirements outlined for the animals for which they are alternates.

(iii) Antibody values from alternate animals may be used only to replace values from up to and including five vaccinates which develop antibody of 1:32 or greater by day 6 ±2 days post-vaccination or up to and including two controls which develop antibody titers of 1:32 or greater by day 6 ±2 days post-challenge.

(8) A sequential test procedure may be used in lieu of the 20 calf requirement. A beta value of .05 and a tolerance level of .78 shall be required.

(9) An Outline of Production change shall be made before authority for use of a new lot of Master Seed Virus shall be granted by Animal and Plant Health Inspection Service.

(d) Test requirements for release: Each serial and subserial shall meet the applicable general requirements prescribed in § 113.300 and the requirements in this paragraph. Final container samples of completed product shall be tested except as prescribed in paragraph (d)(1) of this section. Any serial or subserial found unsatisfactory by a prescribed test shall not be released.

(1) *Purity test.* The test for Brucella contamination prescribed in § 113.32 shall be conducted on each batch of primary cells intended for production use.

(2) *Safety test.* The mouse safety test prescribed in § 113.33(a) and the calf safety test prescribed in § 113.41 shall be conducted.

(3) *Virus titer requirements.* Final container samples of completed product shall be tested for virus titer using the titration method used in paragraph (c)(2) of this section. To be eligible for release, each serial and each subserial shall have a virus titer per dose sufficiently greater than the titer of vaccine virus used in the immunogenicity test prescribed in paragraph (c) of this section to assure that when tested at any time within the expiration period, each serial and subserial shall have a virus titer of $10^{0.7}$ greater than that used in the immunogenicity test but not less than $10^{2.5}$ $TCID_{50}$ per dose.

[39 FR 44719, Dec. 27, 1974, as amended at 40 FR 41089, Sept. 5, 1975; 43 FR 49529, Oct. 24, 1978; 48 FR 33472, July 22, 1983. Redesignated at 55 FR 35562, Aug. 31, 1990, as amended at 56 FR 66784, 66786, Dec. 26, 1991; 60 FR 14357, Mar. 17, 1995; 72 FR 72564, Dec. 21, 2007]

§ 113.310 Bovine Rhinotracheitis Vaccine.

Bovine Rhinotracheitis Vaccine shall be prepared from virus-bearing cell culture fluids. Only Master Seed Virus which has been established as pure, safe, and immunogenic shall be used for preparing the production seed virus for vaccine production. All serials of vaccine shall be prepared from the first through the tenth passage from the Master Seed Virus.

(a) The Master Seed Virus shall meet the applicable general requirements prescribed in § 113.300.

(b) Each lot of Master Seed Virus shall meet the special requirements prescribed in this section.

(c) Each lot of Master Seed Virus used for vaccine production shall be tested for immunogenicity. The selected virus dose from the lot of Master Seed Virus shall be established as follows:

(1) Twenty-five infectious bovine rhinotracheitis susceptible calves shall be used as test animals (20 vaccinates and five controls). Blood samples shall be drawn from these animals and individual serums tested. The calves shall be considered susceptible if the results are negative at a 1:2 final serum dilution by the virus plaque reduction method.

(2) A geometric mean titer of the dried vaccine produced from the highest passage of the Master Seed Virus shall be established before the immunogenicity test is conducted. The 20 calves to be used as vaccinates shall be injected with a predetermined quantity of vaccine virus and the remaining five calves held as uninjected controls. To confirm the dosage calculations, five replicate virus titrations shall be conducted on a sample of the vaccine virus dilution used.

(3) At least once during a period of 14 to 28 days post-vaccination, individual serum samples shall be collected for virus-neutralization tests from each of the vaccinates. The test virus shall be 100 to 500 $TCID_{50}$ bovine rhinotracheitis virus. Results shall be used in making a determination as prescribed in paragraph (c)(6) of this section.

(4) The vaccinates and the controls shall each be challenged with virulent infectious bovine rhinotracheitis virus and observed for 14 days. The rectal temperature of each animal shall be taken and the presence or absence of respiratory or other clinical signs of bovine rhinotracheitis noted and recorded on each of the 14 consecutive days.

(5) If at least four of the five controls do not show clinical signs of infectious bovine rhinotracheitis and a marked temperature rise to 104.5 °F. or higher post-challenge, the test shall be considered a No Test and may be repeated.

(6) If less than 19 of the post-injection serum samples tested as prescribed in paragraph (c)(3) of this section show neutralization in all tubes of the 1:2 final serum dilution, or if more than one of the vaccinates show a temperature of 103.5 °F. or higher for 2 or more

days, or if more than one of the vaccinates exhibit respiratory or other clinical signs of infectious bovine rhinotracheitis, or both, the Master Seed Virus is unsatisfactory.

(7) A sequential test procedure may be used in lieu of the 20 calf requirement. A beta value of .05 and a tolerance level of .78 shall be required.

(8) An outline of Production change shall be made before authority for use of a new lot of Master Seed Virus shall be granted by Animal and Plant Health Inspection Service.

(d) Test requirements for release: Each serial and subserial shall meet the applicable general requirements prescribed in § 113.300 and the requirements in this paragraph. Final container samples of completed product shall be tested except as prescribed in paragraph (d)(1) of this section. Any serial or subserial found unsatisfactory by a prescribed test shall not be released.

(1) *Purity test.* The test for Brucella contamination prescribed in § 113.32 shall be conducted on each batch of primary cells intended for production use.

(2) *Safety test.* The mouse safety test prescribed in § 113.33(a) and the calf safety test prescribed in § 113.41 shall be conducted.

(3) *Virus titer requirements.* Final container samples of completed product shall be tested for virus titer using the titration method used in paragraph (c)(2) of this section. To be eligible for release, each serial and each subserial shall have a virus titer per dose sufficiently greater than the titer of vaccine virus used in the immunogenicity test prescribed in paragraph (c) of this section to assure that when tested at any time within the expiration period, each serial and subserial shall have a virus titer of $10^{0.7}$ greater than that used in the immunogenicity test but not less than $10^{2.5}$ $TCID_{50}$ per dose.

[39 FR 44720, Dec. 27, 1974, as amended at 40 FR 20067, May 8, 1975; 40 FR 23989, June 4, 1975; 40 FR 41089, Sept. 5, 1975; 43 FR 49529, Oct. 24, 1978; 48 FR 33472, July 22, 1983. Redesignated at 55 FR 35562, Aug. 31, 1990, as amended at 56 FR 66784, 66786, Dec. 26, 1991; 72 FR 72564, Dec. 21, 2007]

§ 113.311 Bovine Virus Diarrhea Vaccine.

Bovine Virus Diarrhea Vaccine shall be prepared from virus-bearing cell culture fluids. Only Master Seed Virus which has been established as pure, safe, and immunogenic shall be used for preparing the production seed virus for vaccine production. All serials of vaccine shall be prepared from the first through the tenth passage from the Master Seed Virus.

(a) The Master Seed Virus shall meet the applicable general requirements prescribed in § 113.300.

(b) Each lot of Master Seed Virus shall meet the special requirements prescribed in this section.

(c) Each lot of Master Seed Virus used for vaccine production shall be tested for immunogenicity. The selected virus dose from the lot of Master Seed Virus shall be established as follows:

(1) Twenty-five bovine virus diarrhea susceptible calves shall be used as test animals (20 vaccinates and five controls). Blood samples shall be drawn from these animals and individuals serum samples tested. The calves shall be considered susceptible to bovine virus diarrhea virus infection if the results are negative at a 1:2 final serum dilution in a varying serum-constant virus neutralization test with less than 500 $TCID_{50}$ of bovine virus diarrhea virus.

(2) A geometric mean titer of the dried vaccine produced from the highest passage of the Master Seed Virus shall be established before the immunogenicity test is conducted. The 20 calves to be used as vaccinates shall be injected with a predetermined quantity of vaccine virus and the remaining five calves held as uninjected controls. To confirm the dosage calculations, five replicate virus titrations shall be conducted on a sample of the vaccine virus dilution used.

(3) At least once during a period 14 to 28 days post-vaccination, individual serum samples shall be collected for virus-neutralization tests from each of the vaccinates. The test virus shall be less than 500 $TCID_{50}$ of bovine virus diarrhea virus. The white cell count for all vaccinates and controls shall be established at least 3 days just before

challenge. Results shall be used in making a determination as prescribed in paragraph (c)(5) of this section.

(4) The vaccinates and the controls shall each be challenged with virulent bovine virus diarrhea virus and observed for 14 consecutive days. The white cell count shall be determined daily on each animal from the second through the eighth day post-challenge. If leukopenia does not develop in at least four of the five controls as compared with the vaccinates, the test shall be considered a No Test and may be repeated.

(5) If less than 19 of the post-injection serum samples, tested as prescribed in paragraph (c)(3) of this section, show neutralization in all tubes of the 1:8 dilution; or if more than one of the vaccinates exhibits respiratory or other clinical signs of bovine virus diarrhea post-challenge; or both, the Master Seed Virus is unsatisfactory.

(6) A sequential test procedure may be used in lieu of the 20 calf requirement. A beta value of .05 and a tolerance level of .78 shall be required.

(7) An Outline of Production change shall be made before authority for use of a new lot of Master Seed Virus shall be granted by Animal and Plant Health Inspection Service.

(d) Test requirements for release: Each serial and subserial shall meet the applicable general requirements prescribed in § 113.300 and the requirements in this paragraph. Final container samples of completed product shall be tested except as prescribed in paragraph (d)(1) of this section. Any serial or subserial found unsatisfactory by a prescribed test shall not be released.

(1) *Purity test.* The test for Brucella contamination prescribed in § 113.32 shall be conducted on each batch of primary cells intended for production use.

(2) *Safety test.* The mouse safety test prescribed in § 113.33(a) and the calf safety test prescribed in § 113.41 shall be conducted.

(3) *Virus titer requirements.* Final container samples of completed product shall be tested for virus titer using the titration method used in paragraph (c)(2) of this section. To be eligible for release, each serial and each subserial shall have a virus titer per dose sufficiently greater than the titer of vaccine virus used in the immunogenicity test prescribed in paragraph (c) of this section to assure that when tested at any time within the expiration period, each serial and subserial shall have virus titer of $10^{0.7}$ greater than that used in the immunogenicity test but not less than $10^{2.5}$ $TCID_{50}$ per dose.

[39 FR 44721, Dec. 27, 1974, as amended at 40 FR 20067, May 8, 1975; 40 FR 41089, Sept. 5, 1975; 43 FR 49529, Oct. 24, 1978; 48 FR 33472, July 22, 1983. Redesignated at 55 FR 35562, Aug. 31, 1990, as amended at 56 FR 66784, 66786, Dec. 26, 1991; 72 FR 72564, Dec. 21, 2007]

§ 113.312 Rabies Vaccine, Live Virus.

Rabies Vaccine shall be prepared from virus-bearing cell cultures or embryonated chicken eggs. Only Master Seed Virus which has been established as pure, safe and immunogenic shall be used for preparing the production seed virus for vaccine production. All serials of vaccine shall be prepared from the first through the fifth passage from the Master Seed Virus.

(a) The Master Seed Virus shall meet the applicable general requirements prescribed in § 113.300.

(1) Each lot of Master Seed Virus shall meet the special requirements prescribed in this section.

(2) Each lot of Master Seed Virus propagated in tissues or cells of avian origin shall be tested for pathogens by procedures prescribed in § 113.37.

(3) Each lot of Master Seed Virus propagated in primary cell cultures of mouse or hamster origin or brain tissues of mouse origin shall be tested for lymphocytic choriomeningitis (LCM) virus by the procedure prescribed in § 113.42. If LCM virus is detected, the Master Seed Virus is unsatisfactory.

(4) The Master Seed Virus shall be studied in each species of carnivore or domesticated wild animal for which the vaccine is specifically recommended to attempt to determine the fate of the vaccine virus. Results shall be considered in evaluating safety of vaccine virus.

(i) Obtain at least 10 unvaccinated animals, negative at 1:2 final serum dilution, of each species in which tests will be conducted. Divide each species into two groups of five animals.

(ii) For each species of animal, inject one group of five animals intramuscularly. Infiltrate a major nerve and the surrounding tissue in each of the five animals in the other group. Use 1.0 ml of high titer virus for each method of administration.

(iii) Observe all animals for signs of rabies until scheduled time to sacrifice. If animals show definite symptoms, sacrifice and check regional lymph nodes, brain, salivary glands, and kidney for rabies virus by injection of suckling mice (not more than 7 days of age). Tissues may be held frozen at −70 °C. until suckling mice are available. Inject each mouse in one litter intracerebrally with 0.02 ml of a ground tissue suspension from each organ. Observe mice each day for 21 days. If any mice die, determine if the deaths were due to rabies virus in the brain by a fluorescent antibody test.

(iv) Sacrifice animals that do not show signs of rabies according to the following schedule and check regional lymph nodes, brain, salivary glands, and kidney in suckling mice.

Route of injection	Days after injection	Number of animals
Intramuscularly	15, 20, 25, 30, 35	1 each day.
Intraneurally	3, 6, 9, 15, 30	1 each day.

(5) Each lot of Master Seed Virus shall be tested for safety in at least 10 unvaccinated serologically negative animals of each domestic species for which the vaccine is recommended.

(i) Each group of 10 animals shall be divided into 2 groups of 5 animals. For each species, inject one group intramuscularly with 10 doses of high titer virus.

(ii) Infiltrate a major nerve of each of the animals in the other group of 5 with 10 doses of the same high titer virus. For all species except dogs and cats, multiple injections along the cervical spine in the proximity to the nerve trunks emerging from the spinal cord may be used: *Provided*, That a 1-dose volume shall be injected into each of four or more sites bilaterally.

(iii) Observe all animals each day for 90 days.

(iv) If any animals show clinical signs of rabies, sacrifice the animal and check appropriate brain tissue for rabies virus by the fluorescent antibody test and by mouse injection.

(v) If rabies is confirmed, the lot of Master Seed Virus is unsatisfactory.

(b) The immunogenicity of vaccine prepared with virus at the highest passage of the Master Seed shall be established in each species for which the vaccine is recommended. Tests shall be conducted in accordance with a protocol filed with Animal and Plant Health Inspection Service before initiation of the tests. The vaccine shall be prepared using methods prescribed in the Outline of Production. If Rabies Vaccine is to be in combination with other fractions, the product tested shall include all fractions to be recommended.

(1) A geometric mean virus titer of the dried vaccine produced from the highest passage of the Master Seed Virus shall be established before the immunogenicity test is conducted. To confirm the dosage calculations, five replicate virus titrations shall be conducted on a sample of the vaccine virus dilution used.

(2) The dose of vaccine to be used in the immunogenicity test shall be no more than the amount of rehydrated vaccine which, on the basis of previous titrations, has been diluted to the proposed minimum acceptable virus titer.

(3) Test animals shall be uniform and have no neutralizing antibodies to rabies as determined by serum-neutralization (SN) tests.

(i) Twenty-five or more animals shall be used as vaccinates. Each shall be injected intramuscularly at one site in the thigh with a dose of vaccine at the proposed minimum virus titer as specified in the filed Outline of Production.

(ii) Ten or more additional animals shall be held as controls.

(iii) On or about days 30, 90, 180, 270, and 365 postvaccination, all animals shall be bled and individual serums tested for neutralizing antibodies to rabies virus.

(iv) All surviving test animals of each species shall be challenged intramuscularly with virulent rabies virus furnished or approved by Animal and Plant Health Inspection Service 1 year after vaccination, except as provided in paragraphs (b)(4), (b)(5), and (b)(6) of this section. The challenged animals shall be observed each day for 90 days as prescribed in § 113.5(b). The brain of each test animal that dies following challenge shall be examined for rabies by the fluorescent antibody test or other method acceptable to Animal and Plant Health Inspection Service.

(v) Requirements for acceptance in challenge tests shall be death due to rabies in at least 80 percent of controls while at least 22 of 25 or 26 of 30 or a statistically equivalent number of the vaccinates remain well for a period of 90 days.

(4) An alternative to challenging all surviving test animals in accordance with paragraph (b)(3)(iv) of this section may be used when the test animals are of species other than carnivores. Vaccinates shall be challenged at 1 year postvaccination. These shall include five vaccinates with the lowest SN titers at the 270th-day bleeding, five vaccinates with the lowest SN titers at the 365th-day bleeding, and all vaccinates with SN titers below 1:10 by the mouse SN test or below 1:16 by the rapid-fluorescent-focus-inhibition test at any bleeding. At least five SN-negative controls of each species shall be challenged at the same time as the vaccinates. All SN titers shall be iterated to an endpoint. All of the challenged vaccinates must remain well for a period of 90 days, and at least 80 percent of the controls must die of rabies for a satisfactory test without further challenge. If one or more of the vaccinates die from rabies, all the remaining vaccinates, regardless of titer, along with the five controls shall be challenged. The cumulative results from the two challenges shall be evaluated for acceptance as specified in paragraph (b)(3)(v) of this section.

(5) An outline of Production change shall be made before authority for use of a new lot of Master Virus shall be granted by Animal and Plant Health Inspection Service.

(c) If more than 1 year duration of immunity is to be claimed, a duration of immunity test for the additional time shall be conducted and interpreted as prescribed in paragraph (b) of this section for the 1 year test. The test animals shall be monitored serologically at least every 180 days. The time of challenge may be adjusted accordingly.

(d) Test requirements for release: Each serial and each subserial shall meet the general requirements prescribed in § 113.300 and special requirements in this paragraph.

(1) *Purity and safety tests.* Final container samples of completed product from each serial or one subserial shall be tested.

(i) The test for pathogens, prescribed in § 113.37 shall be conducted on each serial or one subserial of avian origin. If necessary, neutralize the rabies virus with specific rabies antiserum.

(ii) A test for safety in three young seronegative animals of the most susceptible species for which the vaccine is recommended shall be conducted. Each shall be injected intramuscularly with 10 recommended doses of vaccine. If unfavorable reactions attributable to the product occur during a 28 day observation period, the serial is unsatisfactory.

(iii) If primary cell cultures of hamster origin or of mouse origin are used vaccine production, they shall be tested for LCM virus as prescribed in § 113.42. The cells shall be disrupted and undiluted cell fluids from each lot shall be tested.

(2) *Virus titrations.* Final container samples of completed product shall be tested for virus titer using the titration method used in paragraph (b)(1) of this section. To be eligible for release, each serial and each subserial shall have a virus titer sufficiently higher than the titer of the vaccine virus used in paragraph (b) of this section to assure that, when tested at any time within the expiration period, each serial and subserial shall have a virus titer equal to or greater than that used in the immunogenicity test.

(3) Young adult mice, each weighing 14 to 16 grams, shall be used as test animals when the virus in vaccine prepared with a low egg passage Flury Strain or high cell passage Street Alabama Dufferin Strain (HCP SAD) of rabies virus is titrated. At least 10 mice for each dilution shall be used.

(i) At least 10 mice shall be used for each dilution. Each shall be injected intracerebrally with 0.03 ml.

(ii) The injected young adult mice shall be observed each day for 14 days except when testing vaccines made with HCP SAD strain of rabies virus, in which case, the mice shall be observed each day for 21 days. Deaths and paralysis occurring subsequent to the fourth day post-injection shall be noted and the LD_{50} titer calculated by the Reed and Muench Method.

(iii) Virus titer requirements for release and at expiration date shall be determined for each vaccine on the basis of data available: *Provided*, That, the lowest titer permitted at expiration date when determined by this test shall be $10^{3.0}$ LD_{50} per 0.03 ml.

(4) Suckling mice, 6 days of age or younger, shall be used as test animals when virus in vaccine prepared with a high egg passage Flury Strain of rabies virus is titrated.

(i) Six to twelve mice shall be used for each dilution. Each shall be injected intracerebrally with 0.02 ml.

(ii) The injected suckling mice shall be observed each day for 21 days. Deaths and paralysis occurring subsequent to the fourth day post-injection shall be noted and the LD_{50} titer calculated by the Reed and Muench Method; and

(iii) Virus titer requirements for release and at expiration date shall be determined for each vaccine on the basis of data available: *Provided*, That, the lowest titer permitted at expiration date when determined by this test shall be $10^{3.0}$ LD_{50} per 0.02 ml.

[39 FR 44721, Dec. 27, 1974, as amended at 40 FR 20067, May 8, 1975; 42 FR 6795, Feb. 4, 1977; 43 FR 49529, Oct. 24, 1978; 50 FR 20090, May 14, 1985; 50 FR 23797, June 6, 1985. Redesignated at 55 FR 35562, Aug. 31, 1990, as amended at 56 FR 66784, 66786, Dec. 26, 1991; 61 FR 31823, June 21, 1996; 72 FR 72564, Dec. 21, 2007]

§ 113.313 Measles Vaccine.

Measles Vaccine shall be prepared from virus-bearing cell culture fluids. Only Master Seed Virus which has been established as pure, safe, and immunogenic shall be used for preparing the production seed virus for vaccine production. All serials of vaccine shall be prepared from the first through the fifth passage from the Master Seed Virus.

(a) The Master Seed Virus shall meet the applicable general requirements prescribed in § 113.300. Each lot of Master Seed Virus shall meet the special requirements prescribed in this section.

(b) To detect virulent canine distemper virus, each of two canine distemper susceptible ferrets shall be injected with a sample of the Master Seed Virus equivalent to the amount of virus to be used in one dog dose and observed each day for 21 days. If undesirable reactions occur in either ferret, the lot of Master Seed Virus is unsatisfactory.

(c) Each lot of Master Seed Virus used for vaccine production shall be tested for immunogenicity. The selected virus dose from the lot of Master Seed Virus shall be established as follows:

(1) Twenty-five dogs, less than 12 weeks of age and free of measles antibody, shall be used as test animals (20 vaccinates and five controls). Blood samples shall be drawn from these animals and individual serum samples tested. The dogs shall be considered susceptible if the results are negative at a 1:2 final serum dilution in a varying serum-constant virus neutralization test with less than 500 ID_{50} of measles virus.

(2) A geometric mean titer of the dried vaccine produced from the highest passage of the Master Seed Virus shall be established before the immunogenicity test is conducted. Twenty dogs shall be vaccinated with a predetermined quantity of vaccine virus and the remaining five dogs held as unvaccinated controls. To confirm the dosage calculations, five replicate virus titrations shall be conducted on a sample of the vaccine virus dilution used.

(3) On the day of challenge, serum samples shall be obtained from each vaccinate and individually tested for antibody against canine distemper virus. For a valid test, each vaccinate shall be negative at a 1:4 final serum dilution in varying serum-constant virus neutralization test using less than 500 ID_{50} of canine distemper virus.

(4) At least 21 days postinoculation, the immunity of the vaccinates and

controls shall be challenged by exposure to a uniform dose of aerosolized virulent canine distemper virus. All test dogs shall be observed daily for 21 days postchallenge.

(i) If at least 4 of the 5 controls do not die or show signs of distemper, including a temperature of 104.0 °F. or higher and at least 15 percent weight loss, the test is a No Test and may be repeated.

(ii) If at least 19 of the 20 vaccinates do not survive without showing a temperature of 104.0 °F. or higher and a weight loss exceeding 15 percent after day 8 postchallenge, the Master Seed Virus is unsatisfactory.

(5) When approved in advance by Animal and Plant Health Inspection Service, a sequential test procedure may be used in lieu of the 20 dog requirement. A beta value of 0.05 and a tolerance level of 0.78 shall be required.

(6) An Outline of Production change shall be made before authority for use of a new lot of Master Seed Virus shall be granted by Animal and Plant Health Inspection Service.

(d) Test requirements for release: Each serial and subserial shall meet the general requirements prescribed in § 113.300 and the requirements in this paragraph. Final container samples of completed product shall be tested. Any serial or subserial found unsatisfactory by a prescribed test shall not be released.

(1) *Safety tests.* The dog safety test prescribed in § 113.40 and the mouse safety test prescribed in § 113.33(a) shall be conducted.

(2) *Virus titer requirements.* Final container samples of completed product shall be tested for virus titer using the titration method used in paragraph (c)(2) of this section. To be eligible for release, each serial and each subserial shall have a virus titer sufficiently greater than the titer of the vaccine virus used in the immunogenicity test prescribed in paragraph (c) of this section to assure that when tested at any time within the expiration period, each serial and subserial shall have a virus titer of $10^{0.7}$ greater than that used in the immunogenicity test but not less than $10^{2.5}$ ID_{50} per dose.

[40 FR 53001, Nov. 14, 1975, as amended at 43 FR 49529, Oct. 24, 1978; 48 FR 33472, July 22, 1983. Redesignated at 55 FR 35562, Aug. 31, 1990, as amended at 56 FR 66784, 66786, Dec. 26, 1991; 72 FR 72564, Dec. 21, 2007]

§ 113.314 Feline Calicivirus Vaccine.

Feline Calicivirus Vaccine shall be prepared from virus-bearing cell culture fluids. Only Master Seed Virus which has been established as pure, safe, and immunogenic shall be used for preparing the production seed virus for vaccine production. All serials of vaccine shall be prepared from the first through the fifth passage from the Master Seed Virus.

(a) The Master Seed Virus shall meet the applicable general requirements prescribed in § 113.300.

(b) The Master Seed Virus shall be tested for chlamydial agents as prescribed in § 113.43.

(c) Each lot of Master Seed Virus used for vaccine production shall be tested for immunogenicity. The selected virus dose from the lot of Master Seed Virus shall be established as follows:

(1) Thirty feline calicivirus susceptible cats shall be used as test animals (20 vaccinates and 10 controls). Throat swabs shall be collected from each cat and individually tested on susceptible cell cultures for the presence of feline calicivirus. Blood samples shall be drawn and individual serum samples tested. The cats shall be considered suitable for use if all swabs are negative for virus isolation and if all serums are negative for calicivirus antibody at the 1:2 final dilution in a 50 percent plaque reduction test or other SN test of equal sensitivity.

(2) A geometric mean titer of the dried vaccine produced from the highest passage of the Master Seed Virus shall be established before the immunogenicity test is conducted. The 20 cats used as vaccinates shall be administered a predetermined quantity of vaccine virus by the method to be recommended on the label and the remaining 10 cats shall be held as controls. To confirm the dosage calculations, five replicate virus titrations shall be conducted on a sample of the

vaccine virus dilution used. If two doses are used, five replicate confirming titrations shall be conducted on each dose.

(3) Twenty-one or more days after the final dose of vaccine, the vaccinates and controls shall each be challenged intranasally with a minimum of 100,000 $TCID_{50}$ or plaque forming units of virulent feline calicivirus furnished or approved by Animal and Plant Health Inspection Service and observed each day for 14 days postchallenge. The rectal temperature of each animal shall be taken and the presence or absence of clinical signs, particularly lesions on the oral mucosa, noted and recorded each day.

(i) If less than 8 of 10 controls show clinical signs of feline calicivirus infection other than fever, the test is a No Test and may be repeated.

(ii) If a significant difference in clinical signs cannot be demonstrated between vaccinates and controls using a scoring system approved by Animal and Plant Health Inspection Service and prescribed in the Outline of Production, the Master Seed Virus is unsatisfactory.

(4) An Outline of Production change shall be made before authority for use of a new lot of Master Seed Virus shall be granted by Animal and Plant Health Inspection Service.

(d) *Test requirements for release.* Each serial and subserial shall meet the requirements prescribed in §113.300 and in this paragraph. Final container samples of completed product shall be tested. Any serial or subserial found unsatisfactory by a prescribed test shall not be released.

(1) *Safety test.* The mouse safety test prescribed in §113.33(a) and the cat safety test prescribed in §113.39(b) shall be conducted.

(2) *Virus titer requirements.* Final container samples of completed product shall be tested for virus titer using the titration method used in paragraph (c)(2) of this section. To be eligible for release, each serial and each subserial shall have a virus titer sufficiently greater than the titer of vaccine virus used in the immunogenicity test prescribed in paragraph (c) of this section to assure that when tested at any time within the expiration period, each serial and subserial shall have a virus titer of $10^{0.7}$ greater than that used in the immunogenicity test but not less than $10^{2.5}$ $TCID_{50}$ or plaque forming units per dose.

[44 FR 58899, Oct. 12, 1979; 44 FR 63083, Nov. 2, 1979, as amended at 48 FR 33472, July 22, 1983. Redesignated at 55 FR 35562, Aug. 31, 1990, as amended at 56 FR 66784, 66786, Dec. 26, 1991; 72 FR 72564, Dec. 21, 2007]

§ 113.315 Feline Rhinotracheitis Vaccine.

Feline Rhinotracheitis Vaccine shall be prepared from virus-bearing cell culture fluids. Only Master Seed Virus which has been established as pure, safe, and immunogenic shall be used for preparing the production seed virus for vaccine production. All serials of vaccine shall be prepared from the first through the fifth passage from the Master Seed Virus.

(a) The Master Seed Virus shall meet the applicable general requirements prescribed in §113.300.

(b) The Master Seed Virus shall be tested for chlamydial agents as prescribed in §113.43.

(c) Each lot of Master Seed Virus used for vaccine production shall be tested for immunogenicity. The selected virus dose from the lot of Master Seed Virus shall be established as follows:

(1) Thirty feline rhinotracheitis susceptible cats shall be used as test animals (20 vaccinates and 10 controls). Throat swabs shall be collected from each cat and individually tested on susceptible cell cultures for the presence of feline rhinotracheitis virus. Blood samples shall be drawn and individual serum samples tested. The cats shall be considered suitable for use if all swabs are negative for virus isolation and if all serums are negative for feline rhinotracheitis virus antibody at the 1:2 final dilution in a 50 percent plaque reduction test or other SN test of equal sensitivity.

(2) A geometric mean titer of the dried vaccine produced from the highest passage of the Master Seed Virus shall be established before the immunogenicity test is conducted. The 20 cats used as vaccinates shall be administered a predetermined quantity of

vaccine virus by the method to be recommended on the label and the remaining 10 cats shall be held as controls. To confirm the dosage calculations, five replicate virus titrations shall be conducted on a sample of the vaccine virus dilution used. If two doses are used, five replicate confirming titrations shall be conducted on each dose.

(3) Twenty-one or more days after the final dose of vaccine, the vaccinates and controls shall each be challenged intranasally with a minimum of 100,000 $TCID_{50}$ or plaque forming units of virulent feline rhinotracheitis virus furnished or approved by Animal and Plant Health Inspection Service and observed each day for 14 days postchallenge. The rectal temperature of each animal shall be taken and the presence of respiratory or other clinical signs of feline rhinotracheitis noted and recorded each day.

(i) If less than 8 of 10 controls show clinical signs of feline rhinotracheitis infection other than fever, the test is a No Test and may be repeated.

(ii) If a significant difference in clinical signs cannot be demonstrated between vaccinates and controls using a scoring system approved by Veterinary Services and prescribed in the Outline of Production, the Master Seed Virus is unsatisfactory.

(4) An Outline of Production change shall be made before authority for use of a new lot of Master Seed Virus shall be granted by Animal and Plant Health Inspection Service.

(d) *Test requirements for release.* Each serial and subserial shall meet the requirements prescribed in § 113.300 and in this paragraph. Final container samples of completed product shall be tested. Any serial or subserial found unsatisfactory by a prescribed test shall not be released.

(1) *Safety test.* The mouse safety test prescribed in § 113.33(a) and the cat safety test prescribed in § 113.39(b) shall be conducted.

(2) *Virus titer requirements.* Final container samples of completed product shall be tested for virus titer using the titration method used in paragraph (c)(2) of this section. To be eligible for release, each serial and each subserial shall have a virus titer sufficiently greater than the titer of vaccine virus used in the immunogenicity test prescribed in paragraph (c) of this section to assure that when tested at any time within the expiration period, each serial and subserial shall have a virus titer of $10^{0.7}$ greater than that used in the immunogenicity test but not less than $10^{2.5}$ $TCID_{50}$ or plaque forming units per dose.

[44 FR 58899, Oct. 12, 1979, as amended at 48 FR 33472, July 22, 1983. Redesignated at 55 FR 35562, Aug. 31, 1990, as amended at 56 FR 66784, 66786, Dec. 26, 1991; 72 FR 72564, Dec. 21, 2007]

§ 113.316 Canine Parainfluenza Vaccine.

Canine Parainfluenza Vaccine shall be prepared from virus-bearing cell culture fluids. Only Master Seed which has been established as pure, safe, and immunogenic shall be used for preparing seeds for vaccine production. All serials of vaccine shall be prepared from the first through the fifth passage from the Master Seed.

(a) The Master Seed shall meet the applicable general requirements prescribed in § 113.300 and the requirements in this section.

(b) Each lot of Master Seed shall be tested for immunogenicity. The selected virus dose shall be established as follows:

(1) Twenty-five canine parainfluenza susceptible dogs (20 vaccinates and 5 controls) shall be used as test animals. Nasal swabs shall be collected from each dog on the day the first dose of vaccine is administered and individually tested on susceptible cell cultures for the presence of canine parainfluenza virus. Blood samples shall also be drawn and individual serum samples tested for neutralizing antibody. Dogs shall be considered susceptible if all swabs are negative for virus isolation and if all serums are negative for canine parainfluenza antibody at a 1:2 final dilution in a constant virus-varying serum neutralization test using 50 to 300 $TCID_{50}$ of canine parainfluenza virus.

(2) A geometric mean titer of vaccine produced at the highest passage from the Master Seed shall be established before the immunogenicity test is conducted. The 20 dogs used as vaccinates

shall be administered a predetermined quantity of vaccine virus. Five replicate virus titrations shall be conducted on a sample of the vaccine virus dilution used to confirm the dosage administered. If two doses are used, five replicate confirming titrations shall be conducted on each dose.

(3) Three to 4 weeks after the final dose of vaccine, all dogs shall be bled for serum antibodies and nasal swabs shall be collected for canine parainfluenza virus isolation. On the same day, all vaccinates and controls shall be challenged with canine parainfluenza virus furnished or approved by Animal and Plant Health Inspection Service.

(4) The rectal temperature of each dog shall be taken and the presence of respiratory or other clinical signs of canine parainfluenza virus infection noted and recorded each day for 14 consecutive days postchallenge. Nasal swabs shall be collected from each dog each day for at least 10 consecutive days postchallenge. Individual swabs shall be tested for virus isolation by culture in canine parainfluenza virus susceptible cells for at least 7 days. Results shall be evaluated according to the following criteria:

(i) If five of five controls have not remained seronegative at a final serum dilution of 1:2 during the prechallenge period, the test is a No Test and may be repeated.

(ii) If more than one vaccinate shows febrile response, respiratory or other clinical signs of canine parainfluenza virus infection; or, if less than 19 of 20 vaccinates show serum neutralization titers of 1:4 or greater; or, if there is not a significant reduction in virus isolation rate in vaccinates when compared with controls, the Master Seed is unsatisfactory.

(5) An Outline of Production change shall be made before authority for use of a new lot of Master Seed shall be granted by Animal and Plant Health Inspection Service.

(c) *Test requirements for release.* Each serial and subserial shall meet the applicable general requirements prescribed in § 113.300 and the requirements in this paragraph. Any serial or subserial found unsatisfactory by a prescribed test shall not be released.

(1) *Virus titer requirements.* Final container samples of completed product shall be tested for virus titer using the titration method used in paragraph (b)(2) of this section. To be eligible for release, each serial and each subserial shall have a virus titer sufficiently greater than the titer of vaccine virus used in the immunogenicity test prescribed in paragraph (b) of this section to assure that, when tested at any time within the expiration period, each serial and subserial shall have a virus titer at least $10^{0.7}$ greater than that used in the immunogenicity test but not less than $10^{2.5}$ $TCID_{50}$ per dose.

(2) [Reserved]

[50 FR 436, Jan. 4, 1985. Redesignated at 55 FR 35562, Aug. 31, 1990, as amended at 56 FR 66784, 66786, Dec. 26, 1991; 72 FR 72564, Dec. 21, 2007]

§ 113.317 Parvovirus Vaccine (Canine).

Parvovirus Vaccine recommended for use in dogs shall be prepared from virus-bearing cell culture fluids. Only Master Seed which has been established as pure, safe, and immunogenic shall be used for preparing seeds for vaccine production. All serials of vaccine shall be prepared from the first through the fifth passage from the Master Seed.

(a) The Master Seed shall meet the applicable general requirements prescribed in § 113.300 and the requirements in this section.

(b) The Master Seed shall be tested for reversion to virulence in dogs using a method acceptable to Animal and Plant Health Inspection Service. If a significant increase in virulence is seen within five backpassages, the Master Seed is unsatisfactory.

(c) Each lot of Master Seed shall be tested for immunogenicity. The selected virus dose shall be established as follows:

(1) Twenty-five canine parvovirus susceptible dogs (20 vaccinates and 5 controls) shall be used as test animals. Blood samples drawn from each dog shall be individually tested for neutralizing antibody against canine parvovirus to determine susceptibility. Dogs shall be considered susceptible if there is no neutralization at a 1:2 final serum dilution in a constant virus-varying serum neutralization test in

cell culture using 50 to 300 $TCID_{50}$ of canine parvovirus.

(2) A geometric mean titer of the vaccine produced at the highest passage from the Master Seed shall be established before the immunogenicity test is conducted. The 20 dogs used as vaccinates shall be administered a predetermined quantity of vaccine virus by the method recommended on the label. To confirm the dosage calculations, five replicate virus titrations shall be conducted on a sample of the vaccine virus dilution used. If two doses are used, five replicate confirming titrations shall be conducted on each dose.

(3) Fourteen days or more after the final dose of vaccine the vaccinates and the controls shall be challenged with virulent canine parvovirus furnished or approved by Animal and Plant Health Inspection Service and the dogs observed each day for 14 days. Rectal temperature, blood lymphocyte count, and feces for viral detection shall be taken from each dog each day for at least 10 days postchallenge and the presence or absence of clinical signs noted and recorded each day.

(i) The immunogenicity of the Master Seed shall be evaluated on the following criteria of infection: temperature ≥103.4 °F; lymphopenia of ≥50 percent of prechallenge normal; clinical signs such as diarrhea, mucus in feces, or blood in feces; and viral hemagglutinins at a level of ≥1:64 in a 1:5 dilution of feces or a test of equal sensitivity. If at least 80 percent of the controls do not show at least three of the four criteria of infection during the observation period, the test is a No Test and may be repeated.

(ii) If at least 19 of the 20 vaccinates do not survive the observation period without showing more than one criterion of infection described in paragraph (c)(3)(i), of this section, the Master Seed is unsatisfactory.

(4) An Outline of Production change shall be made before authority for use of a new lot of Master Seed shall be granted by Animal and Plant Health Inspection Service.

(d) *Test requirements for release.* Each serial and subserial shall meet the applicable general requirements prescribed in § 113.300 and the requirements in this paragraph. Any serial or subserial found unsatisfactory by a prescribed test shall not be released.

(1) *Virus titer requirements.* Final container samples of completed product shall be tested for virus titer using the titration method used in paragraph (c)(2) of this section. To be eligible for release, each serial and each subserial shall have a virus titer sufficiently greater than the titer of vaccine used in the immunogenicity test in paragraph (c) of this section to assure that, when tested at any time within the expiration period, each serial and subserial shall have a virus titer of $10^{0.7}$ greater than that used in the immunogenicity test, but not less than $10^{2.5}$ ID_{50} per dose.

[50 FR 436, Jan. 4, 1985. Redesignated at 55 FR 35562, Aug. 31, 1990, as amended at 56 FR 66784, 66786, Dec. 26, 1991; 72 FR 72564, Dec. 21, 2007]

§ 113.318 Pseudorabies Vaccine.

Pseudorabies Vaccine shall be prepared from virus-bearing cell culture fluids. Only Master Seed which has been established as pure, safe, and immunogenic shall be used for preparing seeds for vaccine production. All serials of vaccine shall be prepared from the first through the fifth passage from the Master Seed.

(a) The Master Seed shall meet the applicable general requirements prescribed in § 113.300 and the requirements in this section.

(b) Each lot of Master Seed shall be tested for immunogenicity. The selected virus dose shall be established as follows:

(1) Twenty-five pseudorabies susceptible pigs (20 vaccinates and 5 controls) of the youngest age for which the vaccine is recommended, shall be used as test animals. Blood samples shall be taken from each pig and the serums inactivated and individually tested for neutralizing antibody against pseudorabies virus. Pigs shall be considered susceptible if there is no neutralization at a 1:2 final serum dilution in a constant virus-varying serum neutralization test using 50 to 300 $TCID_{50}$ pseudorabies virus.

(2) A geometric mean titer of the vaccine produced at the highest passage

from the Master Seed shall be established before the immunogenicity test is conducted. The 20 pigs used as vaccinates shall be administered a predetermined quantity of vaccine virus by the method recommended on the label. To confirm the dosage administered, five replicate virus titrations shall be conducted on a sample of the vaccine virus dilution used.

(3) Fourteen to 28 days postvaccination, the vaccinates and controls shall be challenged with virulent pseudorabies virus furnished or approved by Animal and Plant Health Inspection Service and observed each day for 14 days.

(i) If at least four of the five controls do not develop severe central nervous system signs or die, the test is a No Test and may be repeated.

(ii) If at least 19 of the 20 vaccinates in a valid test do not remain free of signs of pseudorabies, the Master Seed is unsatisfactory.

(4) An Outline of Production change shall be made before authority for use of a new lot of Master Seed shall be granted by Animal and Plant Health Inspection Service.

(c) *Test requirements for release.* Each serial and subserial shall meet the applicable general requirements prescribed in §113.300 and the requirements in this paragraph.

(2) *Virus titer requirements.* Final container samples of completed product shall be titrated by the method used in paragraph (b)(2) of this section. To be eligible for release, each serial and subserial shall have a virus titer sufficiently greater than the titer of the vaccine used in the immunogenicity test prescribed in paragraph (b) of this section to assure that, when tested at any time within the expiration period, each serial and subserial shall have a virus titer at least $10.^{0.7}$ greater than that used in the immunogenicity test, but not less than $10^{2.5}$ $TCID_{50}$ per dose.

[50 FR 437, Jan. 4, 1985. Redesignated at 55 FR 35562, Aug. 31, 1990, as amended at 56 FR 66784, 66786, Dec. 26, 1991; 72 FR 72564, Dec. 21, 2007]

§§ 113.319–113.324 [Reserved]

§ 113.325 Avian Encephalomyelitis Vaccine.

Avian Encephalomyelitis Vaccine shall be prepared from virus-bearing tissues or fluids from embryonated chicken eggs. Only Master Seed Virus which has been established as pure, safe, and immunogenic in accordance with the requirements in paragraphs (a), (b), and (c) of this section shall be used for preparing the production seed virus for vaccine production. All serials shall be prepared from the first through the fifth passage from the Master Seed Virus.

(a) The Master Seed Virus shall meet the applicable requirements prescribed in §113.300 and the requirements prescribed in this section.

(b) Each lot of Master Seed Virus shall be tested for pathogens by the chicken embryo inoculation test prescribed in §113.37, except that, if the test is a No Test because of a vaccine virus override, the test may be repeated and if the repeat test is inconclusive for the same reason, the chicken inoculation test prescribed in §113.36 may be conducted and the virus judged accordingly.

(c) Each lot of Master Seed Virus shall be tested for immunogenicity and the selected virus dose to be used shall be established as follows:

(1) Avian encephalomyelitis susceptible chickens, all of the same age (eight weeks or older) and from the same source, shall be used. Twenty or more chickens shall be used as vaccinates for each method of administration recommended on the label. Ten additional chickens of the same age and from the same source shall be held as unvaccinated controls.

(2) A geometric mean titer of the vaccine produced from the highest passage of the Master Seed Virus shall be established before the immunogenicity test is conducted. Each vaccinate shall receive a predetermined quantity of vaccine virus. Five replicate virus titrations shall be conducted on an aliquot of the vaccine virus to confirm the amount of virus administered to each chicken used in the test. At least

three appropriate (not to exceed tenfold) dilutions shall be used and the test conducted as follows:

(i) For each dilution, inoculate at least 10 embryos, 5 or 6 days old, in the yolk sac with 0.2 ml each. Twenty similar embryos obtained from the same source shall be kept as uninoculated negative controls. Disregard all deaths during the first 48 hours post-inoculation.

(ii) Eggs for each dilution shall be kept in separate containers and allowed to hatch. Sufficient precaution shall be taken to assure that chickens from each dilution remain separated. To be a valid test, at least 75 percent of the uninoculated eggs shall hatch.

(iii) On the third day after normal hatching time, count all unhatched eggs and all dead, paralyzed and ataxic chickens as positive evidence of viral infection.

(iv) A satisfactory titration shall have at least one dilution with between 50 and 100 percent positives and at least one dilution with between 50 and 0 percent positives.

(v) Calculate the EID_{50} by the Spearman-Karber or Reed-Muench method.

(3) At least 21 days post-vaccination, the vaccinates and the controls shall be challenged intracerebrally with a virulent avian encephalomyelitis virus and observed each day for 21 days.

(4) If at least 80 percent of the controls do not show signs of avian encephalomyelitis or die, the test is a No Test and may be repeated. If at least 19 of 20, or 27 of 30, or 36 of 40 of the vaccinates in each group do not remain free from clinical signs of avian encephalomyelitis during the observation period, the Master Seed Virus is unsatisfactory.

(5) An Outline of Production change shall be made before authority for use of a new lot of Master Seed Virus shall be granted by Animal and Plant Health Inspection Service.

(d) After a lot of Master Seed Virus has been established as prescribed in paragraphs (a), (b), and (c) of this section, each serial and subserial shall meet the applicable requirements in § 113.300 and the requirements prescribed in this paragraph.

(1) Final container samples from each serial shall be tested for pathogens by the chicken embryo inoculation test prescribed in § 113.37, except that, if the test is a No Test because of a vaccine virus override, the chicken inoculation test prescribed in § 113.36 may be conducted and the vaccine judged accordingly.

(2) *Safety test.* Final container samples of completed product shall be tested for safety as follows:

(i) At least 25 AE susceptible birds (6 to 10 weeks of age) shall be vaccinated with the equivalent of 10 doses by each of all routes recommended on the label and be observed each day for 21 days.

(ii) If unfavorable reactions attributable to the biological product occur during the observation period, the serial is unsatisfactory. If unfavorable reactions occur which are not attributable to the product, the test shall be declared a No Test and repeated, except that, if the test is not repeated, the serial shall be unsatisfactory.

(3) *Virus titer requirements.* Final container samples of completed product shall be tested for virus titer using the titration method used in paragraph (c)(2) of this section. To be eligible for release, each serial and each subserial shall have a virus titer sufficiently greater than the titer of vaccine virus used in the immunogenicity test prescribed in paragraph (c) of this section to assure that when tested at any time within the expiration period, each serial and subserial shall have a virus titer of $10^{0.7}$ greater than that used in such immunogenicity test but not less than $10^{.5}$ EID_{50} per dose.

[39 FR 44723, Dec. 27, 1974, as amended at 40 FR 18405, Apr. 28, 1975; 40 FR 41089, Sept. 5, 1975; 42 FR 43617, Aug. 30, 1977; 48 FR 33473, July 22, 1983. Redesignated at 55 FR 35562, Aug. 31, 1990, as amended at 56 FR 66784, 66786, Dec. 26, 1991; 72 FR 72564, Dec. 21, 2007; 79 FR 55969, Sept. 18, 2014]

§ 113.326 Avian Pox Vaccine.

Fowl Pox Vaccine and Pigeon Pox Vaccine shall be prepared from virus-bearing cell culture fluids or embryonated chicken eggs. Only Master Seed Virus which has been established as pure, safe, and immunogenic in accordance with the requirements in paragraphs (a), (b), and (c) of this section shall be used for preparing the production seed virus for vaccine production. All serials shall be prepared from the first through the fifth passage from the Master Seed Virus.

(a) The Master Seed Virus shall meet the applicable requirements prescribed in § 113.300 except paragraph (c) of this section and shall meet the requirements prescribed in this section.

(b) Each lot of Master Seed Virus shall be tested for pathogens by the chicken inoculation test prescribed in § 113.36.

(c) Each lot of Master Seed Virus shall be tested for immunogenicity and the selected virus dose to be used shall be established as follows:

(1) Fowl pox susceptible birds all of the same age and from the same source, shall be used as test birds. Twenty or more birds shall be used as vaccinates for each method of administration recommended on the label. Ten additional birds of the same age and from the same source as the vaccinates shall be held as unvaccinated controls.

(2) A geometric mean titer of the dried vaccine produced from the highest passage of the Master Seed Virus shall be established before the immunogenicity test is conducted. Each vaccinate shall receive a predetermined quantity of vaccine virus. Five replicate virus titrations shall be conducted on an aliquot of the vaccine virus to confirm the amount of virus administered to each bird used in the test. At least three appropriate (not to exceed tenfold) dilutions shall be used and the test conducted as follows:

(i) For each dilution, inoculate at least five embryos, 9 to 11 days old, on the chorioallantoic membrane with at least 0.2 ml each. Disregard all deaths during the first 24 hours post-inoculation. To be a valid test, at least four embryos in each dilution shall remain viable beyond 24 hours.

(ii) Examine the surviving embryos for evidence of infection 5 to 7 days post-inoculation.

(iii) A satisfactory titration shall have at least one dilution with between 50 and 100 percent positives and at least one dilution with between 50 and 0 percent positives.

(iv) Calculate the EID_{50} by the Spearman-Karber or Reed-Muench method.

(3) Fourteen to twenty-one days post-vaccination, all vaccinates and controls shall be challenged by the wing web method and observed each day for 10 days. If the wing web method was used for vaccination, the opposite wing shall be used for challenge. Challenge virus shall be provided or approved by Animal and Plant Health Inspection Service.

(4) If at least 90 percent of the controls do not develop fowl pox during the observation period, the test is a No Test and may be repeated. If at least 19 of 20, or 27 of 30, or 36 of 40 of the vaccinates in each group do not remain free from clinical signs of fowl pox during the observation period, the Master Seed Virus is unsatisfactory.

(5) An Outline of Production change shall be made before authority for use of a new lot of Master Seed Virus shall be granted by Animal and Plant Health Inspection Service.

(d) After a lot of Master Seed Virus has been established as prescribed in paragraphs (a), (b), and (c) of this section, each serial and subserial shall meet the requirements in § 113.36, in § 113.300 except paragraph (c), and in this paragraph.

(1) *Safety test.* Final container samples of completed product from each serial shall be tested. Vaccines recommended for use in birds 10 days of age or younger shall be tested in accordance with paragraphs (d)(1)(i), (ii), and (iii) of this section.

(i) Each of 25 susceptible birds 5 days of age or younger, properly identified and obtained from the same source and hatch, shall be vaccinated with the equivalent of 10 doses of vaccine by each of all routes recommended on the label and observed each day for 14 days. Severe clinical signs or death shall be counted as failures. Two-stage sequential testing may be conducted if the first test (which then becomes stage one) has three failures.

(ii) The results shall be evaluated according to the following table:

CUMULATIVE TOTALS

Stage	Number of birds	Failures for satisfactory serials	Failures for unsatisfactory serials
1	25	2 or less	4 or more.
2	50	5 or less	6 or more.

(iii) If unfavorable reactions occur which are not attributable to the product, the test shall be declared a No Test and may be repeated or, in lieu thereof, the serial declared unsatisfactory.

(iv) Vaccines not recommended for use in birds 10 days of age or younger shall be tested for safety as follows: Each of twenty-five 3- to 5-week-old, fowl-pox susceptible birds shall be vaccinated with the equivalent of 10 doses of vaccine by each of all routes recommended on the label and observed each day for 14 days. If any of the birds show severe clinical signs of disease or death during the observation period due to causes attributable to the product, the serial is unsatisfactory. If unfavorable reactions occur which are not attributable to the product, the test shall be declared a No Test and may be repeated or, in lieu thereof, the serial declared unsatisfactory.

(2) *Virus titer requirements.* Final container samples of completed product shall be tested for virus titer using the titration method used in paragraph (c)(2) of this section. To be eligible for release, each serial and each subserial shall have a virus titer sufficiently greater than the titer of vaccine virus used in the immunogenicity test prescribed in paragraph (c) of this section to assure that when tested at any time within the expiration period, each serial and subserial shall have a virus titer of $10^{0.7}$ greater than that used in such immunogenicity test but not less than $10^{2.0}$ EID_{50} per dose.

[39 FR 44724, Dec. 27, 1974, as amended at 40 FR 18406, Apr. 28, 1975; 40 FR 41089, Sept. 5, 1975; 44 FR 33051, June 8, 1979; 48 FR 33473, July 22, 1983. Redesignated at 55 FR 35562, Aug. 31, 1990, as amended at 56 FR 66784, 66786, Dec. 26, 1991; 72 FR 72564, Dec. 21, 2007]

§ 113.327 Bronchitis Vaccine.

Bronchitis Vaccine shall be prepared from virus-bearing cell culture fluids or embryonated chicken eggs. Only Master Seed Virus which has been established as pure, safe, and immunogenic in accordance with the requirements in paragraphs (a), (b), and (c) of this section shall be used for preparing the production seed virus for vaccine production. All serials shall be prepared from the first through the fifth passage from the Master Seed Virus.

(a) The Master Seed Virus shall meet the applicable requirements prescribed in § 113.300 and the requirements prescribed in this section.

(b) Each lot of Master Seed Virus shall be tested for pathogens by the chicken embryo inoculation test prescribed in § 113.37, except that, if the test is a No Test because of a vaccine virus override, the test may be repeated and if the repeat test is a No Test for the same reason, the chicken inoculation test prescribed in § 113.36 may be conducted and the virus judged accordingly.

(c) Each lot of Master Seed Virus used for vaccine production shall be tested for immunogenicity and the selected virus dose to be used shall be established as follows:

(1) Bronchitis susceptible chickens, all of the same age and from the same source, shall be used in the virus-recovery test. For each method of administration recommended on the label for each serotype against which protection is claimed, twenty or more chickens shall be used as vaccinates. Ten additional chickens for each serotype against which protection is claimed shall be held as unvaccinated controls.

(2) A geometric mean titer of the dried vaccine produced from the highest passage of the Master Seed Virus shall be established before the immunogenicity tests are conducted. Each vaccinate shall receive a predetermined quantity of vaccine virus. Five replicate virus titrations shall be conducted on an aliquot of the vaccine virus to confirm the amount of virus administered to each chicken used in such tests. At least three approved (not to exceed tenfold) dilutions shall be used and the test conducted as follows;

(i) For each dilution, inject at least five embryos, 9 to 11 days old, in the allantoic cavity with 0.1 ml each. Deaths occurring during the first 24 hours shall be disregarded, but at least four viable embyros in each dilution shall survive beyond 24 hours of a valid test. After 5 to 8 days incubation, examine the surviving embryos for evidence of infection.

(ii) A satisfactory titration shall have at least one dilution with between 50 and 100 percent positives and at least one dilution with between 50 and 0 percent positives.

(iii) Calculate the EID_{50} by the Spearman-Karber or Reed-Muench method.

(3) Twenty-one to twenty-eight days post-vaccination, all vaccinates and controls shall be challenged by eye-drop with virulent bronchitis virus. A separate set of vaccinates and controls shall be used for each serotype against which protection is claimed. Each challenge virus shall be approved or provided by Animal and Plant Health Inspection Service and shall titer at least $10^{4.0}$ EID_{50} per ml.

(i) Tracheal swabs shall be taken once, 5 days post-challenge, from each control and vaccinate. Each swab shall be placed in a test tube containing 3 ml of tryptose phosphate broth and antibiotics. The tube and swab shall be swirled thoroughly and if they are to be stored, be immediately frozen and be stored at below −40 °C. pending egg evaluation. For each chicken swab, at least five chicken embryos 9 to 11 days old shall be inoculated in the allantoic cavity with 0.2 ml each of broth from each tube.

(ii) All embryos surviving the third day post-inoculation shall be used in the evaluation, except that, if a swab is not represented by at least four embryos, the test of that swab is invalid and the results a No Test. A tracheal swab shall be positive for virus recovery when any of the embryos in a valid test show typical infectious bronchitis virus lesions, such as but not limited to, stunting, curling, kidney urates, clubbed down, or death during the 4 to 7 day post-inoculation period. If less than 20 percent of the embryos which survive the third day post-inoculation die during the 4 to 7 day post-inoculation period and show no gross lesions typical of infectious bronchitis, they may be disregarded.

(iii) If less than 90 percent of the controls are positive for virus recovery, the test is a No Test and may be repeated.

(iv) If less than 90 percent of the vaccinates are negative for virus recovery, the Master Seed Virus is unsatisfactory.

(4) An Outline of Production change shall be made before authority for use of a new lot of Master Seed Virus shall be granted by Animal and Plant Health Inspection Service.

(d) After a lot of Master Seed Virus has been established as prescribed in paragraphs (a), (b), and (c) of this section, each serial and subserial shall meet the applicable requirements in §113.300 and the requirements prescribed in this paragraph, except that, if the vaccine contains more than one virus type, bulk samples taken from each type prior to mixing shall be used in the virus identity tests prescribed in §113.300(c). The additional requirements in this paragraph shall also be met.

(1) Final container samples from each serial shall be tested for pathogens by the chicken embryo inoculation test prescribed in §113.37, except that, if the test is a No Test because of a vaccine virus override, the chicken inoculation test prescribed in §113.36 may be conducted and the vaccine judged accordingly.

(2) *Safety test.* Final container samples of completed product shall be tested to determine safety for use in bronchitis susceptible young chickens.

(i) Twenty-five susceptible chickens, 5 days of age or younger, properly identified and obtained from the same source and hatch, shall be vaccinated by the eye-drop method with the equivalent of 10 doses of vaccine and observed each day for 21 days post-vaccination. Severe respiratory signs or death shall be counted as failures. Two-stage sequential testing may be conducted if the first test (which then becomes stage one) has three failures.

(ii) The results shall be evaluated according to the following table:

CUMULATIVE TOTALS

Stage	Number of chickens	Failures for satisfactory serials	Failures for unsatisfactory serials
1	25	2 or less	4 or more.
2	50	5 or less	6 or more.

If unfavorable reactions occur which are not attributable to the product, the test shall be declared a No Test and repeated or, in lieu thereof, the serial declared unsatisfactory.

(3) *Virus titer requirements.* Final container samples of completed product shall be tested for virus titer using the procedure prescribed in paragraph (c)(2) of this section and in this paragraph.

(i) The Newcastle disease virus fraction of combined Newcastle-Bronchitis Vaccines shall be neutralized prior to titration of the bronchitis virus fraction. Equal parts of heat-inactivated Newcastle disease antiserum shall be mixed with each appropriate serial tenfold dilution of the vaccine. After inactivation, embryos shall be injected with 0.2 ml each and results calculated as a 0.1 ml dose to allow for serum dilution of the vaccine. The allantoic fluids, tested as prescribed in § 113.34 shall not show hemagglutinating activity in the lowest dilution used in the titration.

(ii) Each bronchitis virus type shall be harvested separately and a sample of bulk harvested material shall be collected prior to mixing with the other virus type(s). Each sample shall contain not less than the minimum virus titer stated in the filed Outline of Production.

(iii) To be eligible for release, each serial and each subserial shall have a virus titer sufficiently greater than the titer of vaccine virus used in the immunogenicity test prescribed in paragraph (c) of this section to assure that when tested at any time within the expiration period, each serial and subserial shall have a virus titer of $10^{0.7}$ greater than that used in such immunogenicity test but not less than $10^{2.0}$ EID_{50} per dose.

[39 FR 44724, Dec. 27, 1974, as amended at 40 FR 18406, Apr. 28, 1975; 40 FR 41089, Sept. 5, 1975; 42 FR 43617, Aug. 30, 1977; 48 FR 33473, July 22, 1983. Redesignated at 55 FR 35562, Aug. 31, 1990, as amended at 56 FR 66784, 66786, Dec. 26, 1991; 64 FR 43045, Aug. 9, 1999; 72 FR 72564, Dec. 21, 2007]

§ 113.328 Fowl Laryngotracheitis Vaccine.

Fowl Laryngotracheitis Vaccine shall be prepared from virus-bearing cell culture fluids or embryonated chicken eggs. Only Master Seed Virus which has been established as pure, safe, and immunogenic in accordance with the requirements in paragraphs (a), (b), and (c) of this section shall be used for preparing the production seed virus for vaccine production. All serials shall be prepared from the first through the fifth passage from the Master Seed Virus.

(a) The Master Seed Virus shall meet the applicable requirements prescribed in § 113.300 and the requirements prescribed in this section.

(b) Each lot of Master Seed Virus shall be tested for pathogens by the chicken embryo inoculation test prescribed in § 113.37, except that, if the test is a No Test because of vaccine virus override, the test may be repeated and if the repeat test is a No Test for the same reason, the chicken inoculation test prescribed in § 113.36 may be conducted and the virus judged accordingly. Each lot shall also be tested for safety as follows:

(1) Each of at least ten 3 to 4 week old susceptible chickens obtained from the same source and hatch as those used in the immunogenicity test prescribed in paragraph (c) of this section shall be injected intratracheally with 0.2 ml of the virus as used in the vaccine and the chickens observed each day for 14 days.

(2) If more than 20 percent of the chickens die during the observation period, the virus is unsatisfactory.

(c) Each lot of Master Seed Virus used for vaccine production shall be tested for immunogenicity and the selected virus dose to be used shall be established as follows:

(1) Fowl laryngotracheitis susceptible chickens all of the same age and from the same source shall be used. Twenty or more chickens shall be used as vaccinates for each method of administration recommended on the label. Ten additional chickens of the same age and from the same source shall be held as unvaccinated controls.

(2) A geometric mean titer of the dried vaccine produced from the highest passage of the Master Seed Virus shall be established before the immunogenicity test is conducted.

Each vaccinate shall receive a predetermined quantity of vaccine virus. Five replicate virus titrations shall be conducted on an aliquot of the vaccine virus to confirm the amount of virus administered to each chicken used in the test. At least three appropriate (not to exceed tenfold) dilutions shall be used for vaccine of chicken embryo origin and the test conducted as follows:

(i) For each dilution, inject at least five embryos, 9 to 11 days old, on the chorioallantoic membrane with 0.2 ml each. Disregard all deaths during the first 24 hours post-injection. To be a valid test, at least four embryos in each dilution shall remain viable beyond 24 hours.

(ii) Examine the surviving embryos for evidence of infection 5 to 8 days post-injection.

(iii) A satisfactory titration shall have at least one dilution with between 50 and 100 percent positives and at least one dilution with between 50 and 0 percent positives.

(iv) Calculate the EID_{50} by the Spearman-Karber or Reed-Muench method.

(3) Tissue culture origin vaccine may be titrated by a tissue culture method approved by Animal and Plant Health Inspection Service and written into the filed Outline of Productions.

(4) Ten to fourteen days post-vaccination, all vaccinates and controls shall be challenged intratracheally or in the orbital sinus with infectious fowl laryngotracheitis virus and observed each day for 10 days. Challenge virus shall be provided or approved by Animal and Plant Health Inspection Service.

(5) If at least 80 percent of the controls do not die or show clinical signs of fowl laryngotracheitis during the observation period, the test is a No Test and may be repeated. If at least 19 of 20, 27 of 30, or 36 of 40 of the vaccinates in each group do not remain free of clinical signs of fowl laryngotracheitis during the observation period, the Master Seed Virus is unsatisfactory.

(6) An Outline of Production change shall be made before authority for use of a new lot of Master Seed Virus shall be granted by Animal and Plant Health Inspection Service.

(d) After a lot of Master Seed Virus has been established as prescribed in paragraphs (a), (b), and (c) of this section, each serial and subserial shall meet the applicable requirements in § 113.300 and the requirements prescribed in this paragraph.

(1) Final container samples from each serial shall be tested for pathogens by the chicken embryo inoculation test prescribed in § 113.37, except that, if the test is a No Test because of a vaccine virus override, the chicken inoculation test prescribed in § 113.36 may be conducted and the vaccine judged accordingly.

(2) *Safety test.* Final container samples of completed product from each serial of modified live virus vaccine shall be tested for safety as provided in this paragraph. Live virus vaccine not prepared with modified live virus shall be tested for safety as provided in the filed Outline of Production.

(i) Twenty-five 3 to 4 week old laryngotracheitis susceptible chickens shall be injected intratracheally with 0.2 ml of vaccine rehydrated at the rate of 30 ml for 1,000 doses. Chickens shall be observed each day for 14 days. Deaths shall be counted as failures. Two-stage sequential testing may be conducted if the first test (which then becomes stage one) has five, six, or seven failures.

(ii) The results shall be evaluated according to the following table:

CUMULATIVE TOTALS

Stage	Number of chickens	Failures for satisfactory serials	Failures for unsatisfactory serials
1	25	4 or less	8 or more.
2	50	10 or less	11 or more.

(iii) If unfavorable reactions occur which are not attributable to the product, the test shall be declared a No Test and repeated or in lieu thereof, the serial declared unsatisfactory.

(3) *Virus titer requirements.* Final container samples of completed product shall be tested for virus titer using the titration method provided in paragraphs (c)(2) or (3) of this section. To be eligible for release, each serial and each subserial shall have a virus titer sufficiently greater than the titer of vaccine virus used in the

immunogenicity test prescribed in paragraph (c) of this section to assure that when tested at any time within the expiration period, each serial and subserial shall have a virus titer of $10^{0.7}$ greater than that used in such immunogenicity test but not less than $10^{2.5}$ EID_{50} per dose for chicken embryo origin vaccine and $10^{2.0}$ EID_{50} or $10^{2.5}$ $TCID_{50}$ per dose for tissue culture origin vaccine.

[39 FR 44726, Dec. 27, 1974, as amended at 40 FR 18407, Apr. 28, 1975; 40 FR 41089, Sept. 5, 1975; 41 FR 44359, Oct. 8, 1976; 42 FR 43617, Aug. 30, 1977; 48 FR 33473, July 22, 1983. Redesignated at 55 FR 35562, Aug. 31, 1990, as amended at 56 FR 66784, 66786, Dec. 26, 1991; 72 FR 72564, Dec. 21, 2007]

§ 113.329 Newcastle Disease Vaccine.

Newcastle Disease Vaccine shall be prepared from virus-bearing cell culture fluids or embryonated chicken eggs. Only Master Seed Virus which has been established as pure, safe, and immunogenic in accordance with the requirements in paragraphs (a), (b), and (c) of this section shall be used for preparing the production seed virus for vaccine production. All serials shall be prepared from the first through the fifth passage from the Master Seed Virus.

(a) The Master Seed Virus shall meet the applicable requirements prescribed in § 113.300, except § 113.34, and the requirements prescribed in this section.

(b) Each lot of Master Seed Virus shall be tested for pathogens by the chicken embryo inoculation test prescribed in § 113.37, except that, if the test is a No Test because of a vaccine virus override, the test may be repeated and if the repeat test is a No Test for the same reason, the chicken inoculation test prescribed in § 113.36 may be conducted and the virus judged accordingly.

(c) Each lot of Master Seed Virus used for vaccine production shall be tested for immunogenicity and the selected virus dose to be used shall be established as follows:

(1) Newcastle Disease susceptible chickens, all of the same age and from the same source, shall be used. Twenty or more chickens shall be used as vaccinates for each method of administration recommended on the label. Ten additional chickens of the same age and from the same source shall be held as unvaccinated controls.

(2) A geometric mean titer of the dried vaccine produced from the highest passage of the Master Seed Virus shall be established before the immunogenicity test is conducted. Each vaccinate shall receive a predetermined quantity of vaccine virus. Five replicate virus titrations shall be conducted on an aliquot of the vaccine virus to confirm the amount of virus administered to each chicken used in the test. At least three appropriate (not to exceed tenfold) dilutions shall be used and the test conducted as follows:

(i) For each dilution, inject at least five embryos, 9 to 11 days old, in the allantoic cavity with at least 0.1 ml each. Disregard all deaths during the first 24 hours post-injection. To be a valid test, at least four embryos in each dilution shall remain viable beyond 24 hours.

(ii) Examine the surviving embryos for evidence of infection 5 to 7 days post-injection.

(iii) A satisfactory titration shall have at least one dilution with between 50 and 100 percent positives and at least one dilution with between 50 and 0 percent positives.

(iv) Calculate the EID_{50} by the Spearman-Karber or Reed-Muench method.

(3) Twenty to twenty-eight days postvaccination, all vaccinates and controls shall be challenged intramuscularly with at least $10^{4.0}$ EID_{50} of virus per chicken and observed each day for 14 days. Challenge virus shall be provided or approved by Animal and Plant Health Inspection Service.

(4) If at least 90 percent of the controls do not develop clinical signs of Newcastle disease during the observation period, the test is a No Test and may be repeated. If at least 19 of 20, or 27 of 30, or 36 of 40 of the vaccinates in each group do not remain free from clinical signs of Newcastle disease during the observation period, the Master Seed Virus is unsatisfactory.

(5) A strain identity test acceptable to Animal and Plant Health Inspection Service shall be conducted.

(6) An Outline of Production change shall be made before authority for use of a new lot of Master Seed Virus shall be granted by Animal and Plant Health Inspection Service.

(d) After a lot of Master Seed Virus has been established as prescribed in paragraphs (a), (b), and (c) of this section, each serial and subserial shall meet the applicable requirements in § 113.300, except § 113.34, and the requirements prescribed in this paragraph.

(1) Final container samples from each serial shall be tested for pathogens by the chicken embryo inoculation test prescribed in § 113.37, except that, if the test is a No Test because of a vaccine virus override, the chicken inoculation test prescribed in § 113.36 may be conducted and the vaccine judged accordingly.

(2) Safety test: Final container samples of completed product from each serial shall be tested to determine whether the vaccine is safe for use in susceptible young chickens. Vaccines recommended for use in chickens 10 days of age or younger shall be tested in accordance with paragraphs (d)(2)(i), (ii), and (iii) of this section.

(i) Twenty-five susceptible chickens, 5 days of age or younger, properly identified and obtained from the same source and hatch, shall be vaccinated by the eye drop method with the equivalent of 10 doses of vaccine and the chickens observed each day for 21 days. Severe respiratory signs or death shall be counted as failures. Two-stage sequential testing may be conducted if the first test (which then becomes stage one) has 3 failures.

(ii) The results shall be evaluated according to the following table:

CUMULATIVE TOTALS

Stage	Number of chickens	Failures for satisfactory serials	Failures for unsatisfactory serials
1	25	2 or less	4 or more.
2	50	5 or less	6 or more.

(iii) If unfavorable reactions occur which are not attributable to the product, the test shall be declared a No Test and may be repeated.

(iv) Vaccines not recommended for use in chickens 10 days of age or younger shall be tested for safety as follows:

Each of twenty-five 3 to 5 week old Newcastle disease susceptible chickens shall be vaccinated as recommended on the label with the equivalent of ten doses and observed each day for 21 days. If any of the birds show severe clinical signs of disease or death during the observation period due to causes attributable to the product, the serial is unsatisfactory.

(3) *Virus titer requirements.* Final container samples of completed product shall be tested for virus titer using the titration method used in paragraph (c)(2) of this section. To be eligible for release, each serial and each subserial shall have a virus titer per dose sufficiently greater than the titer of vaccine virus used in the immunogenicity test prescribed in paragraph (c) of this section to assure that when tested at any time within the expiration period, each serial and subserial shall have a virus titer of $10^{0.7}$ greater than that used in the immunogenicity test but not less than $10^{5.5}$ EID_{50} per dose.

[39 FR 44727, Dec. 27, 1974, as amended at 40 FR 18407, Apr. 28, 1975; 40 FR 23721, June 2, 1975; 40 FR 41090, Sept. 5, 1975; 42 FR 43618, Aug. 30, 1977; 48 FR 33473, July 22, 1983. Redesignated at 55 FR 35562, Aug. 31, 1990, as amended at 56 FR 66784, 66786, Dec. 26, 1991; 72 FR 72564, Dec. 21, 2007]

§ 113.330 Marek's Disease Vaccines.

Marek's disease vaccine shall be prepared from virus-bearing tissue culture cells. Only Master Seed Virus which has been established as pure, safe, and immunogenic shall be used for preparing the production seed virus for vaccine production.

(a) The Master Seed Virus shall meet the applicable requirements prescribed in § 113.300, and the requirements prescribed in this section. The identity test required in § 113.300(c) shall be conducted in a serotype-specific manner by a method acceptable to APHIS. Each lot of Master Seed Virus shall also be tested for pathogens by the chicken embryo inoculation test prescribed in § 113.37, except that, if the test is a No Test because of a vaccine virus override, the chicken inoculation test prescribed in § 113.36 may be conducted and the virus judged accordingly.

(b) *Safety test.* The Master Seed Virus shall be nonpathogenic for chickens as determined by the following procedure:

(1) Specific pathogen free chickens or embryos, negative for Marek's disease virus antibodies, and from the same source, shall be isolated into the following groups:

(i) *Group 1.* At least 50 test subjects shall be inoculated with 10 times as much viable virus as will be contained in one dose of vaccine, by the route recommended for vaccination.

(ii) *Group 2.* At least 50 test subjects shall be injected with a very virulent Marek's disease virus provided or approved by APHIS, at a dosage level that will cause gross lesions of Marek's disease in at least 80 per cent of the chickens within 50 days.

(iii) *Group 3.* Fifty uninoculated controls. For *in ovo* studies, this group should receive a sham inoculation of diluent.

(iv) *Group 4.* For studies evaluating Serotype 1 Master Seed Viruses, a group of 50 uninoculated control chickens shall be housed in contact with the group 1 vaccinated chickens.

(2) At least 40 chickens in each group shall survive to 5 days of age. All chickens that die shall be necropsied and examined for lesions of Marek's disease and cause of death. The test shall be judged according to the following criteria:

(i) At 50 days of age, the remaining chickens in group 2 shall be killed and examined for gross lesions of Marek's disease. If at least 80 percent of this group do not develop Marek's disease, the test is a No Test and may be repeated.

(ii) At 120 days of age, the remaining chickens in groups 1, 3, and 4 shall be weighed, killed, and necropsied. If less than 30 of the chickens in group 3 survive the 120 day period, or if any of the chickens in group 3 have gross lesions of Marek's disease at necropsy, the test is declared a No Test. If less than 30 chickens in groups 1 and 4 survive the 120 day period; or if any of the chickens in groups 1 and 4 have gross lesions of Marek's disease at necropsy; or if the average body weight of the chickens in groups 1 or 4 is significantly (statistically) different from the average in group 3 at the end of the 120 days, the lot of Master Seed Virus is unsatisfactory.

(3) For tests involving *in ovo* inoculation, hatchability results shall also be reported for each group.

(c) *Immunogenicity.* Each lot of Master Seed Virus used for vaccine production shall be tested for immunogenicity at the highest passage level allowed for the product, and the virus dose to be used shall be established as follows:

(1) Specific pathogen free chickens or embryos, negative for Marek's disease antibodies, and from the same source, shall be isolated into the following groups:

(i) *Group 1.* A minimum of 35 test subjects shall be inoculated with the vaccine, using the recommended route, at 1 day of age for chicks or 18 days of embryonation for embryos. The dose used shall be established by 5 replicate virus titrations conducted by a cell culture system or other titration method acceptable to APHIS.

(ii) *Group 2.* A minimum of 35 nonvaccinated test subjects shall be held as challenge controls.

(iii) *Group 3.* A minimum of 25 nonvaccinated test subjects shall be held as nonchallenge controls.

(iv) *Group 4.* Except for studies evaluating vaccines which contain only a Serotype 3 virus as the Marek's disease fraction, a minimum of 35 chicks shall be vaccinated at 1 day of age with a licensed Serotype 3 vaccine, in order to document the severity of the very virulent challenge.

(2) At least 30 chickens in groups 1, 2, and 4, and at least 20 chickens in group 3, shall survive to 5 days of age. All chickens in groups 1, 2, and 4 shall be challenged at 5 days of age in the following manner:

(i) For studies evaluating vaccines which contain only a Serotype 3 virus as the Marek's disease fraction, groups 1 and 2 shall be inoculated with a standard virulent challenge virus provided or approved by APHIS.

(ii) For all other Marek's disease vaccines, groups 1, 2, and 4 shall be inoculated with a very virulent challenge virus provided or approved by APHIS.

(3) All chickens shall be observed until 7 weeks of age, necropsied, and examined for grossly observable lesions consistent with Marek's disease. All chickens dying before the end of the 7 week observation period shall be necropsied and evaluated for gross lesions of Marek's disease. Any chickens not so examined shall be scored as positive for Marek's disease.

(4) For a valid test, at least 80 percent of the chickens in group 2 must develop grossly observable lesions, none of the chickens in group 3 shall develop grossly observable lesions, and (when included) greater than 20 percent of the chickens in group 4 must develop grossly observable lesions.

(5) For a valid test to be considered satisfactory, at least 80 percent of the chickens in group 1 must remain free of grossly observable lesions. The appropriate product claim resulting from a satisfactory test would be to aid in the prevention of Marek's disease, for vaccines containing only a Serotype 3 virus as the Marek's disease fraction, or to aid in the prevention of very virulent Marek's disease, for all other vaccines.

(d) *Test requirements for release.* Each serial and subserial shall meet the applicable requirements prescribed in § 113.300. The identity test required in § 113.300(c) shall be conducted in a serotype-specific manner by a method acceptable to APHIS. Final container samples of completed product shall also meet the requirements in paragraphs (d) (1), (2), and (3) of this section. Any serial or subserial found unsatisfactory by a prescribed test shall not be released.

(1) *Purity test.* The chicken embryo inoculation test prescribed in § 113.37 shall be conducted, except that, if the test is a No Test because of a vaccine virus override, the chicken inoculation test prescribed in § 113.36 may be conducted and the virus judged accordingly.

(2) *Safety test.* At least 25 one-day-old, specific pathogen free chickens shall be injected, by the subcutaneous route, with the equivalent of 10 chicken doses of virus (vaccine concentrated 10X). The chickens shall be observed each day for 21 days. Chickens dying during the period shall be examined, cause of death determined, and the results recorded.

(i) If at least 20 chickens do not survive the observation period, the test is a No Test.

(ii) If lesions of any disease or cause of death are directly attributable to the vaccine, the serial is unsatisfactory.

(iii) If less than 20 chicks survive the observation period and there are no deaths or lesions attributable to the vaccine, the test may be repeated one time, *Provided,* that if the test is not repeated, the serial shall be declared unsatisfactory.

(3) *Potency test.* The samples shall be titrated using a cell culture system or other titration method acceptable to APHIS. For vaccines composed of more than one Marek's disease virus serotype, each fraction shall be titrated in a serotype-specific manner.

(i) Samples of desiccated vaccine shall be incubated at 37 °C for 3 days before preparation for use in the potency test. Samples of desiccated or frozen vaccine shall be reconstituted in diluent according to the label recommendations, and held in an ice bath at 0 °C to 4 °C for 2 hours prior to use in the potency test.

(ii) For a serial or subserial to be eligible for release, each serotype contained in the vaccine shall have a virus titer per dose which is at least 3 times greater than the number of plaque forming units (pfu) used in the immunogenicity test prescribed in paragraph (c) of this section, but not less than 1000 pfu per dose.

(iii) When tested (without the pretest incubation of desiccated products) at any time within the expiration period, each serotype contained in the vaccine shall have a virus titer per dose which is at least 2 times the number of pfu used in the immunogenicity test, but not less than 750 pfu per dose.

[61 FR 33841, July 1, 1996]

§ 113.331 Bursal Disease Vaccine.

Bursal Disease Vaccine shall be prepared from virus-bearing cell culture fluids or embryonated chicken eggs. Only Master Seed Virus which has been established as pure, safe, and immunogenic in accordance with the requirements in paragraphs (a), (b), and

(c) of this section shall be used for preparing the production seed virus for vaccine production. All serials shall be prepared from the first through the fifth passage from the Master Seed Virus.

(a) The Master Seed Virus shall meet the applicable requirements prescribed in § 113.300 and the requirements prescribed in this section.

(b) Each lot of Master Seed Virus shall be tested for pathogens by the chicken embryo inoculation test prescribed in § 113.37, except that, if the test is a No Test because of a vaccine virus override, the chicken inoculation test prescribed in § 113.36 may be conducted and the virus judged accordingly. Each lot of Master Seed Virus used in the preparation of modified live virus vaccines shall also be nonpathogenic to chickens as determined by the following procedures:

(1) Each of twenty-five 1-day-old bursal disease susceptible chickens (vaccinates) shall be injected subcutaneously with 10 times the recommended dose of vaccine virus and observed for 21 days. Fifteen chickens of the same source and hatch shall be kept isolated as controls.

(i) Seventeen days postvaccination, each of five controls shall be administered at least $10^{2.0}$ EID_{50} of a virulent bursal disease virus by eye-drop, isolated, and used as positive controls. The remaining controls shall be used as negative controls.

(ii) If the vaccinates do not remain free of clinical signs of bursal disease, the Master Seed Virus is unsatisfactory. If unfavorable reactions which are not attributable to the Master Seed Virus occur in more than two of the vaccinates, the test shall be declared a No Test and may be repeated.

(iii) Twenty-one days postvaccination, the vaccinates and the controls shall be necropsied and examined for gross lesions of bursal disease. If more than two of the vaccinates have such lesions, the Master Seed Virus is unsatisfactory, except that, if any of the negative controls or less than four of the positive controls have such lesions, the test is a No Test and may be repeated. For purposes of this test, gross lesions shall include obvious pathological processes and/or obvious reduction in size of the bursa from normal.

(2) Each of thirty-five 3- to 4-week-old bursal disease susceptible chickens (vaccinates) shall be vaccinated with approximately one minimum protective dose of vaccine virus as determined in paragraph (c) of this section. Each of 10 chickens of the same source and hatch shall be administered at least $10^{2.0}$ EID_{50} of a virulent bursal disease virus by eye-drop, isolated, and used as positive controls. Also, each of 20 additional chickens of the same source and hatch shall be isolated and held as negative controls.

(i) Three or four days postvaccination, 10 of the vaccinates, the 10 positive controls, and 10 of the negative controls shall be necropsied and examined for gross lesions of bursal disease. If any of the vaccinates have such lesions, the Master Seed Virus is unsatisfactory, except that, if any of the negative controls or less than 8 of the positive controls have such lesions, the test is a No Test and may be repeated. For purposes of this test, gross lesions shall include peribursal edema and/or edema and/or macroscopic hemorrhage in the bursal tissue.

(ii) Fourteen days post-vaccination, the remaining vaccinates and negative controls shall be necropsied and examined for obvious bursal atrophy. If any of the vaccinates have such atrophy, the Master Seed Virus is unsatisfactory, except that, if any of the negative controls have such atrophy, the test is a No Test and may be repeated.

(c) Each lot of Master Seed Virus shall be tested for immunogenicity and the selected virus dose to be used shall be established as follows:

(1) Bursal Disease susceptible chickens, all of the same age (3 weeks or younger) and from the same source, shall be used. Twenty or more chickens shall be used as vaccinates for each method of administration recommended on the label. Ten additional chickens of the same age and from the same source shall be held as unvaccinated controls.

(2) A geometric mean titer of the vaccine produced from the highest passage of the Master Seed Virus shall be established before the immunogenicity

test is conducted. Each vaccinate shall receive a predetermined quantity of vaccine virus. Five replicate virus titrations shall be conducted on an aliquot of the vaccine virus to confirm the amount of virus administered to each chicken used in the test. At least three appropriate (not to exceed tenfold) dilutions shall be used to conduct the titrations by a method acceptable to Animal and Plant Health Inspection Service.

(3) When the test chickens are 28 to 35 days of age but not less than 14 days postvaccination, each vaccinate and each control shall be challenged by eye-drop with a virulent bursal disease virus provided or approved by Animal and Plant Health Inspection Service.

(i) Three to five days postchallenge, all vaccinates and controls shall be necropsied and examined for gross lesions of bursal disease as described in paragraph (b)(2)(i) of this section.

(ii) If at least 19 of 20, or 27 of 30, or 36 of 40 vaccinates in each group are not free from such lesions, the Master Seed Virus is unsatisfactory, except that, if less than 90 percent of the controls have such lesions, the test is a No Test and may be repeated.

(4) An Outline of Production change shall be made before authority for use of a new lot of Master Seed Virus shall be granted by Animal and Plant Health Inspection Service.

(d) After a lot of Master Seed Virus has been established as prescribed in paragraphs (a), (b), and (c) of this section, each serial and subserial shall meet the applicable requirements in §113.300 and the requirements prescribed in this paragraph.

(1) *Tests for pathogens.* Final container samples from each serial shall be tested for pathogens by the chicken embryo inoculation test prescribed in §113.37, except that, if the test is a No Test because of a vaccine virus override, the chicken inoculation test prescribed in §113.36 may be conducted and the serial judged accordingly.

(2) *Safety tests.* (i) Final container samples of completed product from each serial shall be tested to determine whether the vaccine is safe as follows:

(A) For vaccines intended for parenteral administration, each of twenty-five 1-day-old bursal disease susceptible chickens shall be vaccinated with the equivalent of 10 doses by subcutaneous injection.

(B) For vaccines intended for drinking water administration, each of twenty-five 4- to 5-week-old bursal disease susceptible chickens shall be vaccinated orally with the equivalent of 10 doses.

(C) Ten chickens of the same source and hatch shall be maintained in isolation as negative controls. The vaccinates and controls shall be observed each day for 21 days.

(ii) If unfavorable reactions which are attributable to the biological product occur during the observation period, the serial is unsatisfactory. If unfavorable reactions occur in more than one of the controls or if unfavorable reactions which are not attributable to the biological product occur in more than two of the vaccinates, the test shall be declared a No Test and repeated, except that, if the test is not repeated, the serial shall be unsatisfactory.

(3) *Virus titer requirements.* Final container samples of completed product shall be tested for virus titer using the titration method used in paragraph (c)(2) of this section. To be eligible for release, each serial and each subserial shall have a virus titer sufficiently greater than the titer of vaccine virus used in the immunogenicity test prescribed in paragraph (c) of this section to assure that when tested at any time within the expiration period, each serial and subserial shall have a virus titer of $10^{0.7}$ times greater than that used in such immunogenicity test, but not less than $10^{2.0}$ titration units (PFU or ID_{50}'s) per dose.

[44 FR 60263, Oct. 19, 1979, as amended at 44 FR 67087, Nov. 23, 1979; 48 FR 33473, July 22, 1983. Redesignated at 55 FR 35562, Aug. 31, 1990, as amended at 56 FR 66784, 66786, Dec. 26, 1991; 64 FR 43045, Aug. 9, 1999; 72 FR 72564, Dec. 21, 2007]

§ 113.332 Tenosynovitis Vaccine.

Tenosynovitis Vaccine shall be prepared from virus-bearing cell culture fluids or embryonated chicken eggs.

Only Master Seed which has been established as pure, safe, and immunogenic shall be used for preparing seeds for vaccine production. All serials of vaccine shall be prepared from the first through the fifth passage from the Master Seed.

(a) The Master Seed shall meet the applicable general requirements prescribed in § 113.300, except (a)(3)(ii) and (c), and the special requirements in this section.

(b) Each lot of Master Seed shall be tested for:

(1) Pathogens by the chicken inoculation test prescribed in § 113.36.

(2) Lymphoid leukosis virus contamination as follows:

(i) Each of at least 10 3-week-old or older lymphoid leukosis free chickens from the same source and hatch shall be injected intra-muscularly with an amount of Master Seed equal to 100 label doses of vaccine. At least 15 chickens of the same source and hatch shall be used as controls; 5 or more shall be unvaccinated and serve as negative controls; 5 or more shall be injected with subgroup A lymphoid leukosis virus; and 5 or more with subgroup B lymphoid leukosis virus. Each group of control chickens shall be held isolated from each other and from the vaccinates.

(ii) Twenty-one to 28 days postinoculation, blood samples shall be taken from each chicken and the serum separated using a technique conducive to virus preservation. These serums shall be used as inocula in the complement fixation for avian lymphoid leukosis (COFAL) test prescribed in § 113.31.

(iii) Serums from the vaccinates shall be tested separately, but serums within each control group may be pooled. A valid test shall have positive COFAL reactions from each virus inoculated group and negative reactions from the uninoculated controls. If any of the chickens injected with the Master Seed have positive COFAL test reactions in a valid test, the Master Seed is unsatisfactory.

(3) Identity using the following agar gel immunodiffusion test. The undiluted Master Seed may be used as test antigen or the Master Seed may be inoculated onto the chorioallantoic membrane (CAM) of fully susceptible chicken embryos and the infected CAMs ground and used as antigen. A known tenosynovitis antiserum and a known tenosynovitis antigen shall be used in the test. A precipitin line shall form between the test antigen and the known antiserum in the center well which shows identity with the line formed between the antiserum and the known antigen, or the Master Seed is unsatisfactory.

(4) Safety using the following chicken test:

(i) For vaccines intended for use in chickens less than 14 days of age, Master Seed equal to 10 label doses shall be administered subcutaneously to each of 25 1-day-old tenosynovitis susceptible chickens.

(ii) For vaccines intended for use only in chickens 14 days of age or older, Master Seed equal to 10 label doses shall be administered subcutaneously to each of 25 4-week-old or older tenosynovitis susceptible chickens.

(iii) The vaccinates shall be observed each day for 21 days. If unfavorable reactions occur which are attributable to the vaccine, the Master Seed is unsatisfactory. If unfavorable reactions occur which are not attributable to the vaccine, the test is a No Test and may be repeated.

(c) Each lot of Master Seed shall be tested for immunogenicity. The selected virus dose shall be established as follows:

(1) Tenosynovitis susceptible chickens, of the same age and from the same source shall be used as test birds. Vaccines intended for use in very young chickens shall be administered to chickens of the youngest age for which the vaccine is recommended. Vaccines intended for use in older chickens shall be administered to 4-week-old or older chickens. Twenty or more vaccinates shall be used for each method of administration recommended on the label. Ten or more chickens shall be held as unvaccinated controls.

(2) A geometric mean titer of the vaccine produced at the highest passage from the Master Seed shall be established using a method acceptable to Animal and Plant Health Inspection Service before the immunogenicity test is conducted. A predetermined

quantity of vaccine virus shall be administered to each vaccinate. Five replicate virus titrations shall be conducted on an aliquot of the vaccine virus to confirm the dose.

(3) Twenty-one to 28 days postvaccination, each vaccinate and control shall be challenged by injecting virulent virus furnished or approved by Animal and Plant Health Inspection Service into one foot pad. The vaccinates and controls shall be observed each day for 14 days. If at least 90 percent of the controls do not develop swelling and discoloration in the phalangeal joint area of the injected foot pad typical of infection with tenosynovitis virus, the test is a No Test and may be repeated. If at least 19 of 20, 27 of 30, or 36 of 40 vaccinates do not remain free from these signs, disregarding transient swelling which subsides within 5 days postchallenge, the Master Seed is unsatisfactory.

(4) An Outline of Production change shall be made before authority for use of a new lot of Master Seed shall be granted by Animal and Plant Health Inspection Service.

(d) *Test requirements for release.* Each serial and subserial shall meet the applicable general requirements prescribed in § 113.300, except (c), and the requirements in this paragraph.

(1) *Purity.* Final container samples of completed product from each serial shall be tested for pathogens by the chicken inoculation test prescribed in § 113.36.

(2) *Safety.* (i) Final container samples of completed product from each serial shall be safety tested as follows:

(A) For vaccines intended for use in very young chickens, each of 25 1-day-old tenosynovitis susceptible chickens shall be vaccinated with the equivalent of 10 doses by one method recommended on the label.

(B) For vaccines intended for use in older chickens, each of 25 4-week-old or older tenosynovitis susceptible chickens shall be vaccinated with the equivalent of 10 doses by one method recommended on the label.

(ii) The vaccinates shall be observed each day for 21 days. If unfavorable reactions occur which are attributable to the product, the serial is unsatisfactory. If unfavorable reactions occur in more than two vaccinates which are not attributable to the product, the test is a No Test and may be repeated. If the test is not repeated, the serial is unsatisfactory.

(3) *Virus titer requirements.* Final container samples of completed product shall be titrated by the method used in paragraph (c)(2) of this section. To be eligible for release, each serial and subserial shall have a virus titer sufficiently greater than the titer of the vaccine virus used in the immunogenicity test prescribed in paragraph (c) of this section to assure that, when tested at any time within the expiration period, each serial and subserial shall have a virus titer $10^{0.7}$ times greater than that used in the immunogenicity test, but not less than $10^{2.0}$ titration units (PFU or ID_{50}) per dose.

(4) *Identity.* Bulk or final container samples of completed product from each serial shall be tested for identity as prescribed in paragraph (b)(3) of this section and shall meet the criteria stated therein.

[50 FR 438, Jan. 4, 1985. Redesignated at 55 FR 35562, Aug. 31, 1990, as amended at 56 FR 66784, 66786, Dec. 26, 1991; 64 FR 43045, Aug. 9, 1999; 72 FR 72564, Dec. 21, 2007]

DIAGNOSTICS AND REAGENTS

§§ 113.400–113.405 [Reserved]

§ 113.406 Tuberculin, Intradermic.

Tuberculin, Intradermic, is a filtrate produced from cultures of Pn, C, and Dt strains of *Mycobacterium tuberculosis* (supplied by Animal and Plant Health Inspection Service) which has been inactivated and is non-toxic. Each serial shall be tested for purity, safety, potency, and special chemical tests in accordance with the conditions prescribed for each test. A serial found unsatisfactory by any prescribed test shall not be released.

(a) *Purity test.* Each serial shall be tested for purity as provided in this paragraph.

(1) Final container samples of completed product shall be tested for viable bacteria and fungi as prescribed in § 113.26.

(2) A 20 ml sample shall be centrifuged and the sediment examined

microscopically for the presence of acidfast (Ziehl-Nielsen stain) or other microorganisms (Gram stain). A serial which contains microorganisms is unsatisfactory for release.

(b) *Safety test.* Final container samples of completed product from each serial shall be tested for safety. Two mature guinea pigs shall be injected subcutaneously with 1 ml and observed for 10 days. If unfavorable reactions attributable to the product occur during the observation period, the serial is unsatisfactory. If unfavorable reactions occur which are not attributable to the product, the test shall be declared a No Test and repeated: *Provided,* That if the test is not repeated, the serial shall be declared unsatisfactory.

(c) *Potency test.* Bulk or final container samples of completed product from each serial shall be subjected to a comparison test using a Reference Tuberculin supplied by Animal and Plant Health Inspection Service. Test animals shall be 10 sensitized white female guinea pigs from one source which weigh 500–700 grams at the beginning of the test and which have not been used in a previous test. The comparison test shall be conducted in accordance with the procedures prescribed in paragraphs (c)(1), (2), (3), (4), (5), (6), (7), and (8) of this section.

(1) The guinea pigs shall be sensitized with a sterile heat-killed suspension of equal amounts of strains Pn, C, and Dt of *Mycobacterium tuberculosis.* The heat-killed sensitizing agent shall be injected in a volume of 0.5 ml per guinea pig. The guinea pigs shall be considered sensitized for testing not less than 30 days nor more than 120 days post-injection.

(2) The guinea pigs shall be prepared for sensitivity testing at least 4 hours prior to the injection of tuberculin. The entire abdominal and flank areas shall be clipped, a depilatory agent applied for 5–10 minutes, the area rinsed with warm water, and dried.

(3) Dilutions of 1:100, 1:200, and 1:400 shall be prepared with the Reference Tuberculin and the unknown tuberculin. Three test sites on each side of and equidistant from the abdominal midline shall be chosen on each guinea pig. Using a tuberculin syringe and needle, 0.05 ml of each dilution shall be injected intradermally at one of the test sites which has been randomly selected for the dilution.

(4) The sensitivity of the tuberculins shall be determined 24 hours after injected by measuring the area of erythema. Measurements in millimeters shall be made anterior of the greatest diameter and perpendicular to the first measurement. The square millimeter shall be calculated by multiplying the two measurements.

(5) The total area of response for each tuberculin tested shall be determined by adding the areas of erythema for each dilution of each of the test animals in a group. The sums of the areas of erythema for all three dilutions of each tuberculin shall be added to give the total area of tuberculin response.

(6) The total tuberculin response area of the serial being tested shall be expressed as a percentage of the total tuberculin response area of the Reference Tuberculin. (The total response area of the serial divided by the total response area of the Reference Tuberculin times 100.)

(7) If the total tuberculin response area of the serial being tested does not fall between 75 percent and 125 percent of the total tuberculin response area of the Reference Tuberculin, the serial is unsatisfactory.

(8) Two unsensitized guinea pigs are given 0.05 ml intradermal injections of 1:4 and 1:10 dilutions of both the serial being tested and the Reference Tuberculin as a control for nonspecific positive reactions. If positive reactions are observed with the Reference Tuberculin, the test is considered a "No Test" and repeated. If positive reactions are observed with the serial being tested only, the serial is unsatisfactory.

(d) *Special chemical tests and requirements.* Final container samples of completed product from each serial shall be tested as follows:

(1) *Hydrogen ion concentration.* The hydrogen ion concentration shall be determined with a pH meter which has been standardized with a pH 7.0 buffer just prior to use. The pH of the product shall be 7.0 ±0.3.

(2) *Total nitrogen determination.* The nitrogen content shall be determined by the Kjeldahl method on duplicate 15

ml samples consisting of 5 ml from each of three vials. The total nitrogen content of the product shall be 0.18 percent ±0.06 percent.

(3) *Trichloroacetic acid precipitable nitrogen.* The determination of precipitable nitrogen by a final concentration of 4 percent trichloroacetic acid shall be made by the Kjeldahl method on duplicate 15 ml samples, consisting of 5 ml from each of three vials. The trichloroacetic acid precipitable nitrogen content shall be 0.047 percent ±0.01 percent.

(4) *Phenol determination.* The phenol content shall be determined by direct titration with a standardized bromide-bromate solution. (A correction factor of 0.04 should be subtracted from the final value in the determination of phenol in tuberculin.) The phenol content shall be 0.54 percent ±0.04 percent.

(5) *Clarity.* The product shall be optically clear and free from any extraneous particles.

[39 FR 16857, May 10, 1974. Redesignated at 39 FR 25463, July 11, 1974. Redesignated at 55 FR 35561, Aug. 31, 1990, as amended at 56 FR 66784, Dec. 26, 1991]

§ 113.407 Pullorum antigen.

Pullorum Antigen shall be produced from a culture of representative strains of *Salmonella pullorum* which are of known antigenic composition, high agglutinability, but are not sensitive to negative and nonspecific serum. Each serial shall be tested for purity, density, preservative content, sensitivity, homogeneity, and hydrogen ion concentration. A serial found unsatisfactory by any prescribed test shall not be released.

(a) *Purity test.* Final container samples of completed product shall be tested for viable bacteria and fungi as prescribed in §113.26. In addition, each serial shall be free from extraneous organisms as determined by Gram staining and microscopic examination.

(b) *Nephelometric determination of bacterial density.* The bacterial density shall be 80 ±15 times McFarland No. 1 standard for stained antigen K's and 50 ±10 times McFarland No. 1 standard for tube antigen.

(c) *Preservative requirements.* (1) The formalin content of Pullorum Stained Antigen K shall be 1.0 ±0.2 percent as determined by a colorimetric method.

(2) The phenol content for Pullorum Tube Antigen shall be 0.55 ±0.05 percent as determined by direct titration with a standardized bromide-bromate solution.

(d) *Sensitivity requirements.* (1) Each serial of antigen shall be compared with a reference antigen of known sensitivity using positive and negative chicken serum. The manufacturers' recommendations for use on the accompanying label or package insert shall be followed. The recommended time limit specified for each antigen shall be carefully observed in the test.

(2) A total of at least 12 serums shall be used. This shall include at least three definitely positive, at least three weakly positive, and at least six negative serums. At least three positive chicken serums diluted with negative chicken serum shall be used to further assay comparative sensitivity between test and reference plate antigens. All test antigens shall agree closely with the reference antigen. Tests in which variation of readings between the reference and test antigen would result in a different National Poultry Improvement Plan classification shall be regarded as unsatisfactory. No unsatisfactory tests among the six or more negative serums and not more than one unsatisfactory test among the six or more positive serums shall be permitted. All tests performed shall be included for evaluation of the sensitivity assay. In the event of an unsatisfactory test using positive serums, at least three additional definitely positive and three additional weakly positive serums shall be tested. If not more than one unsatisfactory test is obtained with the additional serums, the antigen shall be acceptable.

(e) *Homogeneity requirement.* Antigens shall show no evidence of autoagglutination or unusual appearance such as the presence of flakes, specks, or a preponderance of filament forms. Microscopic examination shall be made in this determination.

(f) *Hydrogen ion concentration.* The hydrogen ion concentration shall be determined with a pH meter which has been standardized with a pH 4.0 buffer just prior to use. The pH of Pullorum

Stained Antigen K shall be 4.6 ±0.4. No pH level is specified for Pullorum Tube Antigen but after dilution as recommended for use, it shall have a pH of 8.2 to 8.5.

[39 FR 16857, May 10, 1974. Redesignated at 39 FR 25463, July 11, 1974, and amended at 40 FR 760, Jan. 3, 1975. Redesignated at 55 FR 35561, Aug. 31, 1990]

§ 113.408 Avian mycoplasma antigen.

Mycoplasma antigens shall be prepared from organisms, grown in broth cultures, that are inactivated and standardized. Plate antigens shall be stained with a dye acceptable to Animal and Plant Health Inspection Service (APHIS). Final container samples of completed product from each serial shall be tested for density, preservative content, homogeneity, hydrogen ion concentration, purity, sensitivity, and specificity in accordance with the conditions prescribed for each test. A serial found unsatisfactory by any prescribed test shall not be released.

(a) *Density requirements.* A 2.5 ml sample of completed antigen shall be diluted with 2.5 ml of buffer solution formulated in the same manner as the vehicle of the antigen being tested in a modified Hopkins tube and then sedimented at 1,000 × g in a refrigerated centrifuge at 20 °C for 90 minutes. If the packed cell volume of the completed antigen is not 1.2 percent (±0.4 percent), the serial is unsatisfactory.

(b) *Preservative requirements.* Preservatives shall be as specified in the Outline of Production filed with APHIS in accordance with 9 CFR 114.8. If phenol is used, a direct titration with a standardized bromide-bromate solution shall be made. If the final concentration of phenol is not 0.25 percent (±0.05 percent), the serial is unsatisfactory.

(c) *Homogeneity requirements.* (1) Plate antigen shall be checked on a plate for homogeneity and autoagglutination. If plate antigen is not homogeneous and free of large visible particles (strands or clumps) or if it autoagglutinates, the serial is unsatisfactory.

(2) Stereo-microscopic examination shall be used when necessary to evaluate a granular appearing antigen.

(d) *Hydrogen ion concentration.* The hydrogen ion concentration shall be determined with a pH meter which has been standardized with a pH buffer just prior to use. The pH of Mycoplasma Gallisepticum Antigen shall be 6.0±0.2. The pH of Mycoplasma Synoviae Antigen and Mycoplasma Meleagridis Antigen shall be 7.0±0.2.

(e) *Purity requirements.* The antigen shall be tested for viable bacteria and fungi as prescribed in § 113.26.

(f) *Sensitivity requirements.* The reactivity of each antigen shall be tested by comparing the agglutination reactions of each serial of antigen with the agglutination reactions of a standard reference antigen which is supplied by or acceptable to APHIS. A set consisting of five known positive and five known negative serums shall be used. The negative serums shall be tested against the antigens undiluted and the positive serums shall be tested against the antigens diluted 1:4 in buffer solution formulated in the same manner as the vehicle of the antigen being tested. If negative serums do not have negative reactions in this test, the serial is unsatisfactory. If the test antigen and the reference antigen do not have the same agglutination reactions with at least four of the five positive serums used, the serial is unsatisfactory.

(1) The sensitivity of Mycoplasma Gallisepticum Antigen shall be tested using a set of chicken and a set of turkey serums (the positive serums shall have varying degrees of reactivity from weakly positive to strongly positive).

(2) The sensitivity of Mycoplasma Synoviae Antigen shall be tested using chicken serums.

(3) The sensitivity of Mycoplasma Meleagridis Antigen shall be tested using turkey serums.

(g) *Specificity requirements.* Mycoplasma Synoviae Antigen shall be examined for cross-agglutination with five *Mycoplasma gallisepticum* antiserums (chicken origin); Mycoplasma Meleagridis Antigen shall be examined for cross-agglutination with five *Mycoplasma gallisepticum* antiserums (turkey origin) and five *Mycoplasma synoviae* antiserums (turkey origin). Tests shall be conducted with undiluted antigen. If cross-agglutination occurs, the serial is unsatisfactory.

[48 FR 33474, July 22, 1983. Redesignated at 55 FR 35561, Aug. 31, 1990, as amended at 56 FR 66784, Dec. 26, 1991]

§ 113.409 Tuberculin—PPD Bovis, Intradermic.

Tuberculin—PPD Bovis, Intradermic is a purified protein derivative produced from cultures of *Mycobacterium bovis* Strain AN–5 (supplied by Animal and Plant Health Inspection Service), which has been inactivated and is nontoxic. Each serial shall be tested for purity, safety, potency, and special chemical characteristics in accordance with the conditions prescribed for each test. A serial found unsatisfactory by any prescribed test shall not be released.

(a) *Purity test.* Each serial shall be tested for viable bacteria and fungi as prescribed in § 113.26.

(b) *Safety test.* Final container samples of completed product from each serial shall be tested for safety as prescribed in § 113.38.

(c) *Potency test.* Bulk or final container samples of completed product from each serial shall be subjected to a comparison specificity test using a Reference PPD Tuberculin supplied by Animal and Plant Health Inspection Service.

(1) *Test animals.* White female guinea pigs from one source, which weigh 500 to 700 grams at the beginning of the test, and which have not been used in a previous test, shall be used in the specificity test. Twenty-three guinea pigs (10 sensitized with *M. bovis*, 10 sensitized with *M. avium* and three unsensitized) shall be required for each serial being tested, and 20 guinea pigs (10 sensitized with *M. bovis* and 10 sensitized with *M. avium*) shall be required for the Reference PPD Tuberculin. Allowance should be made for deaths during the sensitization period.

(2) *Sensitization of guinea pigs.* (i) Sensitize one group of guinea pigs to *M. bovis.* Inject each animal intramuscularly with 0.5 ml of a sterile heat-killed suspension of *M. bovis* Strain AN–5 supplied by Animal and Plant Health Inspection Service.

(ii) Sensitize one group of guinea pigs to *M. avium.* Inject each animal intramuscularly with 0.5 ml of a sterile heat-killed suspension of *M. avium* Strain D–4 supplied by Animal and Plant Health Inspection Service.

(iii) Maintain an unsensitized group as control animals.

(3) Thirty-five days post-injection, the guinea pigs shall be used for tuberculin testing.

(4) The sensitized animals and controls shall be prepared at least 4 hours prior to injection of PPD tuberculin by clipping the hair from the entire abdominal and flank areas, applying a depilatory agent for 5 to 10 minutes, then rinsing with warm water and drying.

(i) Select four sites on each guinea pig for injection of PPD tuberculin. Two sites shall be on each side of the midline and spaced a sufficient distance from each other to avoid overlapping of skin reactions.

(ii) Prepare four dilutions of the Reference PPD Tuberculin and each serial of PPD tuberculin being tested so as to contain 0.6, 1.2, 2.4, and 4.8 micrograms of protein per 0.1 ml dose. Each of the four dilutions of the same tuberculin shall be randomly assigned a site on a guinea pig.

(iii) Inject one dose of each dilution at the assigned site using a tuberculin syringe.

(5) *Measurement of skin reactions.* Measure the area of erythema produced at each site on each guinea pig 24 hours following injection of PPD tuberculin. Measurements in millimeters shall be made anterior to posterior across the greatest diameter and perpendicular to the first measurement. Calculate the area of erythema in square millimeters at each site by multiplying the two measurements.

(6) *Calculation of average response per guinea pig.* Obtain the total area of erythema for each guinea pig by adding the areas of the four test sites. Add these composite areas of erythema from all guinea pigs with the same sensitization and the same PPD tuberculin injection, then divide by the number of animals in the group. The number obtained is the average response per guinea pig to the PPD tuberculin for the given type of sensitization.

(7) *Determination of specificity index.* The specificity index of a PPD tuberculin is determined by subtracting the average response obtained on *M. avium* sensitized guinea pigs from the average response obtained on *M. bovis* sensitized guinea pigs.

(8) *Validity of bioassay.* The bioassay test results obtained on serials tested concurrently in a single test series are valid if the specificity index of the reference PPD tuberculin is at least 400 square millimeters. If the results are not valid, the bioassay test series must be repeated with a different set of sensitized guinea pigs.

(9) *Reactions in unsensitized guinea pigs.* If a positive reaction (erythema) is observed in one or more of the 3 unsensitized guinea pigs, the serial is unsatisfactory.

(10) *Interpretation of specificity index.* When a bioassay is valid and reactions are not observed in unsensitized guinea pigs, the following interpretation of the specificity index will be used for classifying each serial of PPD tuberculin:

Specificity index	Classification
440 mm^2 or greater	Satisfactory.
Between 360 mm^2 and 440 mm^2	Inconclusive.
Less than 360 mm^2	Unsatisfactory.

(11) *Second stage test.* If a serial is classified as inconclusive, it can be declared unsatisfactory or undergo a second stage test. The second stage shall be conducted in a manner identical to the first stage, except that unsensitized guinea pig controls are not necessary. The results are evaluated by combining the results obtained on all guinea pigs tested in stages one and two. Calculate the average response on the 20 *M. bovis* sensitized animals and on the 20 *M. avium* sensitized animals and determine the specificity index. An inconclusive serial is satisfactory after the second stage test, if its specificity index is 400 square millimeters or more, and unsatisfactory if its specificity index is less than 400 square millimeters.

(d) *Special chemical tests and requirements.* Final container samples of completed product from each serial shall be tested as follows:

(1) *Protein concentration.* The final product shall contain a protein concentration of 1.0 ±0.1 mg/ml. The Micro-kjeldahl Test for Nitrogen shall be used.

(2) *Phenol content.* Phenol content of the final product shall be 0.50 percent plus or minus 0.04 percent. A direct titration with a standardized bromide-bromate solution shall be conducted.

[41 FR 8471, Feb. 27, 1976, as amended at 41 FR 21760, May 28, 1976; 41 FR 32883, Aug. 6, 1976. Redesignated at 55 FR 35561, Aug. 31, 1990, as amended at 56 FR 66784, Dec. 26, 1991]

ANTIBODY PRODUCTS

§ 113.450 General requirements for antibody products.

Unless otherwise prescribed in a Standard Requirement or in a filed Outline of Production, all antibody products shall meet the applicable requirements of this section.

(a) *Terminology.* The following terms in the regulations and standards concerning antibody products shall mean:

Antibody. An immunoglobulin molecule, having a precise glycoprotein structure, produced by certain cells of the B lymphocyte lineage in response to antigenic stimulation, and functioning to specifically bind and influence the antigens that induced its synthesis.

IgG (Immunoglobulin G). One of the several recognized classes of structurally related glycoproteins whose representatives include all known antibodies.

Monoclonal. Produced by, or derived from, the offspring of a single common progenitor cell.

Failure of passive transfer. A condition of neonates characterized by an abnormally low concentration of circulating maternal IgG.

(b) *Nomenclature.* Antibody products shall be named as follows:

(1) *Virus-specific products.* The true name of a virus-specific product shall: include the term "antibody," specify the disease for which the product is intended, and indicate the type of animal that supplied the component antibodies. If the antibodies are monoclonal, the term "monoclonal" shall be used. Example: "Duck Virus Hepatitis Antibody, Duck Origin."

(2) *Bacterium-specific products.* The true name of a bacterium-specific product shall: include the term "antibody" if the component antibodies are directed against a nontoxin antigen or the term "antitoxin" if the component antibodies are directed against toxin, specify the organism against which the product is intended, and indicate the type of animal that supplied the component antibodies. If the antibodies are monoclonal, the term "monoclonal" shall be used. Example: "Escherichia Coli Monoclonal Antibody, Murine Origin."

(3) *Failure of passive transfer products.* The true name of a product for treatment of failure of passive transfer shall include the term "IgG" and indicate the type of animal that supplied the component IgG. Example: "Bovine IgG."

(4) *Combination products.* The true name of a product for treatment of failure of passive transfer as well as for the prevention and/or alleviation of a specific viral or bacterial disease shall be named according to the nomenclature prescribed above for virus-specific or bacterium-specific products.

(c) *Animals.* All animals used in the production of antibody products shall be healthy. Their health status shall be determined by physical examination by, or under the direct supervision of, a licensed veterinarian and by tests for infectious diseases. Such animals shall be maintained at licensed establishments: *Provided,* That cows maintained at Grade A dairies (or the equivalent) that are not injected with antigens for the purpose of stimulating the production of specific antibodies and that are used only for the purpose of supplying lacteal secretions are exempt from being maintained at a licensed establishment.

(1) No animal shall be used while showing clinical signs of disease. The presence of minor localized injuries or lesions (contusions, lacerations, burns, etc.) without body temperature elevation and without significant pain and distress shall not be construed as clinical evidence of disease.

(2) Before first use and on a regular basis, all animals used in the manufacture of antibody products shall be individually subjected to applicable tests for infectious diseases. Records of all test results shall be maintained. An animal which tests positive for an infectious disease shall not be used in the manufacture of antibody products. Retests shall be conducted as deemed necessary by the Administrator.

(i) Before first use, horses shall be tested as follows for:

(A) Equine infectious anemia (EIA) at a laboratory approved by APHIS.

(B) Piroplasmosis, dourine, and glanders at the National Veterinary Services Laboratories.

(C) Brucellosis at a laboratory approved by APHIS. Horses with standard agglutination titers of 1:50 or less can be used for production. Horses with standard agglutination titers equal to or greater than 1:100 may be tested by the Rivanol or card tests. Reactors to these supplemental tests shall not be used for production. Nonreactors to the supplemental tests shall be retested after 30 days. If the supplemental tests are negative and the agglutination titer has not increased, the animal may be used for production. Otherwise, the animal is unsatisfactory for this purpose.

(ii) Horses shall be retested annually for EIA and, if housed or pastured with any other species, shall be retested annually for brucellosis.

(iii) Before first use, cattle shall be tested as follows for:

(A) Tuberculosis by an accredited veterinarian: *Provided,* That cattle at Grade A dairies supplying only lacteal secretions need only be tested for tuberculosis in accordance with applicable Milk Ordinances or similar laws or regulations.

(B) Brucellosis at a laboratory approved by APHIS. Cattle with standard agglutination titers of 1:50 or less can be used for production. Cattle with standard agglutination titers equal to or greater than 1:100 may be tested by the Rivanol or card tests. Reactors to these supplemental tests shall not be used for production. Nonreactors to the supplemental tests shall be retested after 30 days. If the supplemental tests are negative and the agglutination titer has not increased, the animal may be used for production; otherwise, the animal is unsatisfactory for this purpose. Cattle at Grade A dairies supplying only lacteal secretions need not be tested individually for brucellosis if a portion of their secretions contribute to the herd milk pool tested as required by the brucellosis ring test. An animal of a herd testing positive by this test shall not be used in production.

(iv) Cattle shall be retested annually for both tuberculosis and brucellosis. Cattle at Grade A dairies supplying only lacteal secretions need only be tested for tuberculosis in accordance with applicable Milk Ordinances or similar laws or regulations. Cattle at Grade A dairies supplying only lacteal secretions need not be tested individually for brucellosis if a portion of their secretions contribute to the herd milk pool tested as required by the brucellosis ring test. An animal of a herd testing positive by this test shall not be used in production.

(v) For other species, appropriate tests and the frequency with which they are applied shall be specified in the filed Outline of Production for the product.

(vi) If a positive result is obtained on any prescribed test, the positive animal(s) shall be removed from the herd and the remaining animals retested. Production shall not be renewed until a negative herd test is obtained not less than 28 days following removal of the positive animal(s).

(vii) Negative animals shall be maintained separate and apart from untested or positive animals of any species. Production animals shall not be used for any other purpose, such as testing, work, or recreation.

(d) *Collection procedures.* Blood, lacteal secretions, and egg material shall be collected as described in the filed Outline of Production for the product.

(e) *Ingredient handling and processing.* Blood derivatives (serum, plasma, etc.), lacteal secretions, and egg material used in the production of antibody products shall be subjected to an appropriate procedure for the inactivation of potential contaminating microorganisms. The procedure shall be one of those described below and specified in the filed Outline of Production for the product: *Provided,* That another procedure may be substituted if demonstrated to be at least as effective by data acceptable to APHIS and specified in the filed Outline of Production for the product. These data are expected to come from a study comparing the effectiveness of the established and substitute procedures against a satisfactory battery of potential contaminating microorganisms.

(1) Blood derivatives of equine origin shall be heated at 58.0–59.0 °C for 60 minutes, and blood derivatives of bovine, porcine, or other origin shall be heated at 58.0–59.0 °C for 30 minutes. In lieu of heat treatment, blood derivatives of any origin may be treated with at least 2.5 megarads of ionizing radiation, with a maximum radiation dosage specified in the filed Outline of Production for the product.

(2) Lacteal secretions shall be heated as described in paragraph (e)(1) of this section, or shall be pasteurized at either 72 °C for 15 seconds or 89 °C for 1 second using appropriate equipment. In lieu of the heat treatment regimens prescribed, lacteal secretions may be treated with at least 2.5 megarads of ionizing radiation, with a maximum radiation dosage specified in the Outline of Production for the product.

(3) Egg material shall be heated at 58.0–59.0 °C for 30 minutes, or treated with at least 2.5 megarads of ionizing radiation, with a maximum radiation dosage specified in the filed Outline of Production for the product.

(4) Blood derivatives, lacteal secretions, and egg material shall not contain preservatives at the time of heat treatment, and immediately after heat treatment shall be cooled to 7 °C or lower.

(5) Licensees shall keep detailed records as to each batch treated and each serial of product prepared for marketing. Recording charts shall bear full information concerning the material treated and tests made of the equipment used for treatment.

(f) *Preservatives.* Liquid antibody products, except those immediately frozen following preparation and maintained in a frozen state until time of use, shall contain at least one preservative from the following list, within the range of concentration set forth:

(1) Phenol 0.25 to 0.55 percent, or

(2) Cresol 0.10 to 0.30 percent, and/or

(3) Thimerosal 0.01 to 0.03 percent, or

(4) Other preservative(s) specified in the filed Outline of Production for the product.

(g) *Antigens for hyperimmunization.* If animals are hyperimmunized to generate antibodies for a product for the prevention and/or alleviation of a specific infectious disease, and a USDA-licensed veterinary biological product is not employed for this purpose, the following shall apply:

(1) For each antigen, a Master Seed shall be established.

(i) Bacterial Master Seeds shall be tested for purity and identity as prescribed for live bacterial vaccines in § 113.64.

(ii) Viral Master Seeds shall be tested for purity and identity as prescribed for live virus vaccines in § 113.300.

(2) The maximum allowable passage level of the hyperimmunizing antigen shall be the passage level of the antigen used to generate product shown to be efficacious and shall not exceed 10 passages from the Master Seed.

(h) *Purity tests.* Final container samples of each serial and each subserial shall be tested for viable bacteria and fungi as follows:

(1) Dried products for parenteral administration and liquid products shall be tested as prescribed in § 113.26.

(2) For dried products for oral administration, 10 final container samples shall be reconstituted with sterile water at the volume recommended on the label and tested for the following contaminants:

(i) *Coliforms.* One milliliter of each rehydrated sample shall be pipetted into a 100 × 15 mm petri dish and 10–15 ml of violet red bile agar at 45–50 °C added. The plate shall be manipulated to coat its entirety with the agar-sample mixture and allowed to stand until the mixture solidifies. The plate shall then be incubated at 35 °C for 24 hours. A positive control plate and a negative control plate shall be prepared at the same time and in the same manner as the plates containing samples of the serial. All plates shall be examined at the end of the incubation period. If characteristic growth is observed on the negative control plate, or no characteristic growth is observed on the positive control plate, the test shall be considered a No Test and may be repeated. If characteristic growth is observed on any of the 10 plates containing samples of the serial, one retest to rule out faulty technique may be conducted on samples from 20 final containers. If characteristic growth is observed on any of the retest plates, or if a retest is not initiated within 21 days of the completion of the original test, the serial or subserial is unsatisfactory.

(ii) *Salmonellae.* One milliliter of each rehydrated sample shall be pipetted into a 100 × 15 mm petri dish and 10–15 ml of brilliant green agar at 45–50 °C added. The dish shall be manipulated to coat its entirety with the agar-sample mixture and allowed to stand until the mixture solidifies. The plate shall then be incubated at 35 °C for 24 hours. A positive control plate and a negative control plate shall be prepared at the same time and in the same manner as the plates containing samples of the serial. All plates shall be examined at the end of the incubation period. If characteristic growth is observed on the negative control plate, or no characteristic growth is observed on the positive control plate, the test shall be considered a No Test and may be repeated. If characteristic growth is observed on any of the 10 plates containing samples of the serial, one retest to rule out faulty technique may be conducted on samples from 20 final containers. If characteristic growth is observed on any of the retest plates, or if a retest is not initiated within 21 days of the completion of the original test, the serial or subserial is unsatisfactory.

(iii) *Fungi.* One milliliter of each rehydrated sample shall be pipetted into a 100 × 15 mm petri dish and 10–15 ml of appropriately acidified potato dextrose agar at 45–50 °C added. The plate shall be manipulated to coat its entirety with the agar-sample mixture and allowed to stand until the mixture solidifies. The plate shall then be incubated at 20–25 °C for 5 days. A positive control plate and a negative control plate shall be prepared at the same time and in the same manner as the plates containing samples of the serial. All plates shall be examined at the end of the incubation period. If growth is observed on the negative control plate, or no growth is observed on the positive control plate, the test shall be considered a No Test and may be repeated. If growth is observed on any of the 10 plates containing samples of the serial, one retest to rule out faulty technique may be conducted on samples from 20 final containers. If growth is observed on any of the retest plates, or if a retest is not initiated within 21 days of the completion of the original test, the serial or subserial is unsatisfactory.

(iv) *Total bacterial count.* One milliliter of each rehydrated sample, undiluted or diluted as prescribed in the Outline of Production, shall be pipetted into a 100 × 15 mm petri dish and 10–15 ml of tryptone glucose extract agar at 45–50 °C added. The plate shall be manipulated to coat its entirety with the agar-sample mixture and allowed to stand until the mixture solidifies. The plate shall then be incubated at 35 °C for 48 hours. A positive control plate and a negative control plate shall be prepared at the same time and in the same manner as the plates containing samples of the serial. All plates shall be examined at the end of the incubation period. If growth is observed on the negative control plate, or no growth is observed on the positive control plate, the test shall be considered a No Test and may be repeated. If the average number of bacterial colonies on the 10 plates containing samples of the serial exceeds that specified in the filed Outline of Production for the product, one retest to rule out faulty technique may be conducted on samples from 20 final containers. If the average number of bacterial colonies on the retest plates exceeds that specified in the filed Outline of Production for the product, or if a retest is not initiated within 21 days of the completion of the original test, the serial or subserial is unsatisfactory.

(i) *Safety tests.* Bulk or final container samples of each serial shall be tested as prescribed in § 113.33(b). Dried product shall be reconstituted as indicated on the label and 0.5 ml injected per mouse.

[61 FR 51774, Oct. 4, 1996]

§ 113.451 Tetanus Antitoxin.

Tetanus Antitoxin is a specific antibody product containing antibodies directed against the toxin of *Clostridium tetani*. Each serial shall meet the applicable general requirements provided in § 113.450 and paragraph (a) of this section, and be tested for potency as provided in paragraph (b) of this section. Any serial found unsatisfactory by a prescribed test shall not be released.

(a) *General requirements.* The amount of antitoxin in a final container shall be the amount which is delivered from such container when opened and inverted until the flow stops. A graduated volumetric cylinder which conforms to the National Institute of Standards and Technology requirements shall be used. The reading shall be made at the bottom of the meniscus. Volumes of 10 ml or less shall be recorded to the nearest 0.1 and volumes over 10 ml shall be recorded to the nearest ml.

(1) All final containers of Tetanus Antitoxin shall yield not less than the labeled unitage of antitoxin throughout the dating period. The minimum package size permitted for marketing in the United States shall be a 1,500 unit vial.

(2) The expiration date of Tetanus Antitoxin shall be not more than 3 years after the date of a potency test which demonstrates that the recoverable antitoxin from the final container provides at least 20 percent excess over the number of units claimed on the label or not more than 1 year after the date of a potency test which demonstrates that the recoverable antitoxin from the final container provides 10 to 19 percent excess over the number of units claimed on the label.

(b) *Potency test.* Bulk or final container samples of completed product from each serial shall be assayed to calculate the units of Tetanus Antitoxin in each final container. A comparative toxin-antitoxin neutralization test shall be conducted using a standard antitoxin and a standard toxin. All dilutions shall be made in M/15 phosphate buffered (pH) 7.4 physiological saline with 0.2 percent gelatin.

(1) One ml of the Standard Antitoxin shall be diluted before use so the final volume contains 0.1 unit per ml. The

dilution shall be held at 20° to 25 °C for 30 minutes prior to combination with a test does of toxin.

(2) The Standard Toxin test dose is that amount which when mixed with 0.1 unit of Standard Antitoxin, incubated at 20° to 25 °C for 1 hour, and injected subcutaneously into a 340 to 380 gram guinea pig, results in death of that guinea pig within 60 to 120 hours with clinical signs of tetanus. The toxin shall be diluted so the test dose shall be in 2.0 ml.

(3) A mixture of diluted Standard Toxin and diluted Standard Antitoxin shall be made so that 0.1 unit of antitoxin in 1 ml is combined with a test dose of toxin. This Standard Toxin-Antitoxin mixture shall be held at 20° to 25 °C for 1 hour before injections of guinea pigs are made.

(4) A sample from each serial of antitoxin shall be prepared as was the Standard Toxin-Antitoxin mixture; except the amount of antitoxin shall be based on an estimation of the expected potency. When testing is done on bulk material, the final container fill shall reflect the endpoint value plus 10 percent overage for 1 year dating and 20 percent overage for 3 year dating.

(5) Normal guinea pigs weighing within a range of 340 to 380 grams shall be used. Pregnant guinea pigs must not be used.

(i) Each of two guinea pigs (controls) shall be injected subcutaneously with a 3 ml dose of the Standard Toxin-Antitoxin mixture. Injections shall be made in the same order that toxin is added to the dilutions of antitoxins. These shall be observed parallel with the titration of one or more unknown antitoxins.

(ii) Two guinea pigs shall be used as test animals for each dilution of the unknown antitoxin. A 3.0 ml dose shall be injected subcutaneously into each animal.

(6) Controls shall be observed until they are down and are unable to rise or stand under their own power. At this time they are euthanized and the time of death is recorded in hours. For a satisfactory test, the controls must reach this point with clinical signs of tetanus within 24 hours of each other and within an overall time of 60 to 120 hours. The clinical signs to be observed are increased muscle tonus, curvature of the spine, asymmetry of the body outline when the resting animal is viewed from above, generalized spastic paralysis, particularly of the extensor muscles, inability to rise from a smooth surface when the animal is placed on its side, or any combination of these signs. If the control guinea pigs do not respond in this manner, the entire test shall be repeated.

(7) Potency of an unknown antitoxin is determined by finding the mixture which will protect the test animal the same as the Standard Toxin-Antitoxin mixture. Test animals dying sooner than the controls indicate the unit value selected in that dilution was not present, whereas those living longer indicate a greater unit value.

[39 FR 16859, May 10, 1974. Redesignated at 39 FR 25463, July 11, 1974, and amended at 40 FR 760, Jan. 3, 1975; 40 FR 41996, Sept. 10, 1975; 43 FR 1479, Jan. 10, 1978; 50 FR 24905, June 14, 1985. Redesignated at 55 FR 35561, Aug. 31, 1990; 61 FR 51776, Oct. 4, 1996; 64 FR 43045, Aug. 9, 1999]

§ 113.452 Erysipelothrix Rhusiopathiae Antibody.

Erysipelothrix Rhusiopathiae Antibody is a specific antibody product containing antibodies directed against one or more somatic antigens of *Erysipelothrix rhusiopathiae*. Each serial shall be tested as provided in this section. Any serial found unsatisfactory by a prescribed test shall not be released.

(a) Each serial shall meet the applicable general requirements provided in § 113.450.

(b) *Potency test*. Bulk or final container samples of completed product from each serial shall be tested using the two-stage test provided in this section.

(1) In the first stage, each of 40 Swiss mice, each weighing 16 to 20 grams, shall be injected subcutaneously with 0.1 ml of product (dried product shall be rehydrated according to label directions). Twenty-four hours postinjection, the injected mice and 10 additional mice designated controls shall be challenged subcutaneously with the same culture of *Erysipelothrix rhusiopathiae*.

(2) If less than eight of the 10 controls die from erysipelas within 7 days post-challenge, the test is invalid. All dead mice shall be examined to determine if the cause of death was *Erysipelothrix rhusiopathiae* infection.

(3) The mice injected with product shall be observed for 10 days postchallenge and all deaths recorded. The second stage shall be required when 7–10 of the mice injected with product die in the first stage. The second stage shall be conducted in a manner identical to the first stage.

(4) The results of the test shall be evaluated according to the following table:

Stage	Number of vaccinates	Cumulative number of vaccinates	Cumulative total number of deaths for a satisfactory test	Cumulative total number of deaths for an unsatisfactory test
1	40	40	6 or less	11 or more.
2	40	80	12 or less	13 or more.

[39 FR 16859, May 10, 1974. Redesignated at 39 FR 25463, July 11, 1974, as amended at 40 FR 20067, May 8, 1975; 40 FR 23989, June 4, 1975. Redesignated at 55 FR 35561, Aug. 31, 1990; 61 FR 51776, Oct. 4, 1996; 64 FR 43045, Aug. 9, 1999]

§ 113.453 [Reserved]

§ 113.454 Clostridium Perfringens Type C Antitoxin.

Clostridium Perfringens Type C Antitoxin is a specific antibody product containing antibodies directed against the toxin of *Clostridium perfringens* Type C. Each serial shall be tested as provided in this section. Any serial found unsatisfactory by a prescribed test shall not be released.

(a) Each serial shall meet the applicable general requirements provided in § 113.450.

(b) *Potency test.* Bulk or final container samples of completed product from each serial shall be tested using the toxin-neutralization test for Beta Antitoxin provided in this section. Dried products shall be rehydrated according to label directions.

(1) When used in this test, the following words and terms shall mean:

(i) *International antitoxin unit.* (I.U.) That quantity of Beta Antitoxin which reacts with L_0 and L_+ doses of Standard Toxin according to their definitions.

(ii) *L_0dose.* The largest quantity of toxin which can be mixed with one unit of Standard Antitoxin and not cause sickness or death in injected mice.

(iii) *L_+dose.* The smallest quantity of toxin which can be mixed with one unit of Standard Antitoxin and cause death in at least 80 percent of injected mice.

(iv) *Standard antitoxin.* The Beta Antitoxin preparation which has been standardized as to antitoxin unitage on the basis of the International *Clostridium perfringens* Beta Antitoxin Standard and which is either supplied by or acceptable to Animal and Plant Health Inspection Service. The antitoxin unit value shall be stated on the label.

(v) *Standard toxin.* The Beta toxin preparation which is supplied by or is acceptable to Animal and Plant Health Inspection Service.

(vi) *Diluent.* The solution used to make proper dilutions prescribed in this test. Such solution shall be made by dissolving 1 gram of peptone and 0.25 gram of sodium chloride in each 100 ml of distilled water; adjusting the pH to 7.2; autoclaving at 250 °F. for 25 minutes; and storing at 4 °C. until used.

(2) The antitoxin content of the test sample shall be determined as follows:

(i) Make a dilution of Standard Antitoxin to contain 10 International Units of antitoxin per ml.

(ii) Make one dilution of Standard Toxin to contain 10 L_0 doses per ml and make a second dilution of Standard Toxin to contain 10 L_+ doses per ml.

(iii) Dilute 1 ml of the test sample with 49 ml of diluent and combine 1 ml of this dilution with 1 ml of the Standard Toxin diluted to contain 10 L_0 doses.

(iv) Combine 10 International Units of Standard Antitoxin with 10 L_0 doses of diluted Standard Toxin and combine 10 International Units of Standard Antitoxin with 10 L_+ doses of diluted Standard Toxin.

(v) Neutralize all toxin-antitoxin mixtures at room temperature for 1 hour and hold in ice water until injections of mice can be made.

(vi) Five Swiss white mice, each weighing 16–20 grams, shall be used for each toxin-antitoxin mixture. A dose of 0.2 ml shall be injected intravenously into each mouse. Conclude the test 24 hours post-injection and record all deaths.

(3) *Test Interpretation.* (i) If any mice inoculated with the mixture of 10 International Units of Standard Antitoxin and 10 L_0 doses of Standard Toxin die, the results of the test are a No Test and shall be repeated: *Provided,* That, if the test is not repeated, the serial shall be declared unsatisfactory.

(ii) If less than 80 percent of the mice inoculated with the mixture of 10 International Units of Standard Antitoxin and 10 L_+ doses of Standard Toxin die, the results of the test are a No Test and shall be repeated: *Provided,* That, if the test is not repeated, the serial shall be declared unsatisfactory.

(iii) If any mice inoculated with the mixture of Clostridium Perfringens Type C Antitoxin diluted 1:50 and 10 L_0 doses of Standard Toxin die, the antitoxin is considered to contain less than 500 International Unit per ml and the serial is unsatisfactory.

[39 FR 16859, May 10, 1974. Redesignated at 39 FR 25463, July 11, 1974. Redesignated at 55 FR 35561, Aug. 31, 1990, as amended at 56 FR 66784, Dec. 26, 1991; 61 FR 51777, Oct. 4, 1996]

§ 113.455 Clostridium Perfringens Type D Antitoxin.

Clostridium Perfringens Type D Antitoxin is a specific antibody product containing antibodies directed against the toxin of *Clostridium perfringens* Type D. Each serial shall be tested as provided in this section. Any serial found unsatisfactory by a prescribed test shall not be released.

(a) Each serial shall meet the applicable general requirements provided in § 113.450.

(b) *Potency test.* Bulk or final container samples of completed product from each serial shall be tested using the toxin-neutralization test for Epsilon Antitoxin provided in this section. Dried products shall be rehydrated according to label directions.

(1) When used in this test, the following words and terms shall mean:

(i) *International antitoxin unit.* (I.U.) That quantity of Epsilon Antitoxin which reacts with L_0 and L_+ doses of Standard Toxin according to their definitions.

(ii) *L_0dose.* The largest quantity of toxin which can be mixed with one-tenth unit of Standard Antitoxin and not cause sickness or death in injected mice.

(iii) *L_+dose.* The smallest quantity of toxin which can be mixed with one-tenth unit of Standard Antitoxin and cause death in at least 80 percent of injected mice.

(iv) *Standard antitoxin.* The Epsilon Antitoxin preparation which has been standardized as to antitoxin unitage on the basis of the International *Clostridium perfringens* Epsilon Antitoxin Standard and which is either supplied by or acceptable to Animal and Plant Health Inspection Service. The antitoxin unit value shall be stated on the label.

(v) *Standard toxin.* The Epsilon toxin preparation which is supplied by or is acceptable to Animal and Plant Health Inspection Service.

(vi) *Diluent.* The solution used to make proper dilutions prescribed in this test. Such solution shall be made by dissolving 1 gram of peptone and 0.25 gram of sodium chloride in each 100 ml of distilled water; adjusting the pH to 7.2; autoclaving at 250 °F. for 25 minutes; and storing at 4 °C. until used.

(2) The antitoxin content of the test sample shall be determined as follows:

(i) Make a dilution of Standard Antitoxin to contain 1 International Unit of antitoxin per ml.

(ii) Make one dilution of Standard Toxin to contain 10 L_0 doses per ml and make a second dilution of Standard Toxin to contain 10 L_+ doses per ml.

(iii) Dilute 1 ml of the test sample with 33 ml of diluent and combine 1 ml of this dilution with 1 ml of the Standard Toxin diluted to contain 10 L_0 doses.

(iv) Combine 1 International Unit of Standard Antitoxin with 10 L_0 doses of Standard Toxin and combine 1 International Unit of Standard Antitoxin with 10 L_+ doses of Standard Toxin.

(v) Neutralize all toxin-antitoxin mixtures at room temperature for 1 hour, and hold in ice water until injections of mice can be made.

(vi) Five Swiss white mice, each weighing 16–20 grams, shall be used for each toxin-antitoxin mixture. A dose of 0.2 ml shall be injected intravenously into each mouse. Conclude the test 24 hours post-injection and record all deaths.

(3) Test Interpretation. (i) If any mice inoculated with the mixture of 1 International Unit of Standard Antitoxin and 10 L_0 doses of Standard Toxin die, the results of the test are a No Test and shall be repeated: *Provided*, That, if the test is not repeated, the serial shall be declared unsatisfactory.

(ii) If less than 80 percent of the mice inoculated with mixture of 1 International Unit of Standard Antitoxin and 10 L_+ doses of Standard Toxin die, the results of the test are a No Test and shall be repeated: *Provided*, That, if the test is not repeated, the serial shall be declared unsatisfactory.

(iii) If any mice inoculated with the mixture of Clostridium Perfringens Type D Antitoxin diluted 1:34 and 10 L_0 doses of Standard Toxin die, the antitoxin is considered to contain less than 34 International Units per ml and the serial is unsatisfactory.

[39 FR 16859, May 10, 1974. Redesignated at 39 FR 25463, July 11, 1974, as amended at 40 FR 760, Jan. 3, 1975. Redesignated at 55 FR 35561, Aug. 31, 1990, as amended at 56 FR 66784, Dec. 26, 1991; 61 FR 51777, Oct. 4, 1996]

§§ 113.456–113.498 [Reserved]

§ 113.499 Products for treatment of failure of passive transfer.

A product for the treatment of failure of passive transfer (FPT) shall contain a specified minimum quantity of IgG per dose and shall be recommended for use only in neonates of the same species as that of antibody origin. A product for oral administration shall not be recommended for use in animals more than 24 hours of age, while one for parenteral administration shall only be recommended for use in neonatal animals. Each serial shall meet the applicable general requirements provided in § 113.450 and be tested for potency as provided in this section. Any serial found unsatisfactory by a prescribed test shall not be released.

(a) *Qualification of an IgG Reference Product*. An IgG Reference Product (reference) shall be a serial of product that is manufactured according to the filed Outline of Production, properly qualified, and used to assess the potency of subsequent product serials, as described in paragraph (c) below. The reference shall be qualified as follows:

(1) At least 20 newborn, colostrum-deprived animals of the species for which the product is recommended shall be randomly selected.

(2) Blood samples shall be taken from each animal.

(3) Each animal shall be administered one dose of reference by the recommended route and shall be observed for 24 hours.

(i) Any adverse reactions shall be recorded.

(ii) The dosage of reference administered to each animal shall be in accordance with label directions. Label directions may indicate a single dosage regardless of weight, in which case the animals in the study shall be at or near the maximum weight for neonates of the species.

(4) After 24 hours, blood samples shall be taken from each animal.

(5) Pretreatment and post treatment serum IgG concentrations shall be concurrently determined for each animal using a radial immunodiffusion (RID) method acceptable to APHIS and described in the filed Outline of Production for the product.

(6) Concurrently, using the same method, five IgG measurements shall be made on an IgG Species Standard supplied or approved by APHIS. The IgG Species Standard shall be a preparation that contains IgG specific for the species in question at a concentration acceptable to APHIS.

(7) For an IgG Reference Product to be satisfactory, all animals used to qualify the reference must remain free of unfavorable product-related reactions and at least 90 percent of the paired serum samples must reflect an increase in IgG concentration (posttreatment minus pretreatment concentration) equal to or greater than the IgG concentration of the IgG Species Standard.

(b) *Antibody functionality*. Prior to licensure, the prospective licensee shall perform a neutralization study, or another type of study acceptable to APHIS, to demonstrate functionality of product antibody.

(c) *Potency.* Bulk or final container samples of completed product from each serial shall be tested for IgG content as provided in this paragraph. Samples of the test serial and of an IgG Reference Product established in accordance with paragraph (a) of this section shall be concurrently tested for IgG content by the RID method referred to in paragraph (a)(5) of this section. Five IgG measurements shall be made on each. If the IgG level per dose of the test serial does not meet or exceed that of the reference, one complete retest, involving five IgG measurements on both the reference and two samples of the test serial, may be conducted. If, upon retest, the average IgG level per dose of the two samples of the test serial does not meet or exceed that of the reference, or if a retest is not conducted, the serial is unsatisfactory.

[61 FR 51777, Oct. 4, 1996]

PART 114—PRODUCTION REQUIREMENTS FOR BIOLOGICAL PRODUCTS

Sec.

AUTHORITY: 21 U.S.C. 151–159; 7 CFR 2.22, 2.80, and 371.4.

SOURCE: 39 FR 16869, May 10, 1974, unless otherwise noted.

§ 114.1 Applicability.

Unless exempted by regulation or otherwise authorized by the Administrator, all biological products prepared, sold, bartered or exchanged, shipped or delivered for shipment in or from the United States, the District of Columbia, any Territory of the United States, or any place under the jurisdiction of the United States shall be prepared in accordance with the regulations in this part. The licensee or permittee shall adopt and enforce all necessary measures and shall comply with all directions the Administrator prescribes for carrying out such regulations.

[52 FR 11026, Apr. 7, 1987, as amended at 56 FR 66784, Dec. 26, 1991]

§ 114.2 Products not prepared under license.

(a) When an establishment license is issued, if biological products which were not prepared in compliance with the regulations are in the establishment, such products shall not be shipped or delivered for shipment or otherwise dealt with as having been prepared under such regulations.

(b) Except as provided in 9 CFR part 103, a biological product shall not be prepared in a licensed establishment unless the person to whom the establishment license is issued holds an unexpired, unsuspended, and unrevoked product license issued by the Administrator to prepare such biological product, or unless the products prepared are subject to the provisions of § 107.2 of this subchapter.

(c) A biological product produced in a USDA-licensed establishment shall be produced under a U.S. Veterinary Biological Product License or a license granted by a State under § 107.2 (referred to as a State biological product license and the products prepared pursuant thereto as State-licensed biological products, including autogenous biologics), but not under both a U.S. Veterinary Biological Product License and a State biological product license. Before a U.S. Veterinary Biological Product License (including a conditional license) is issued, the licensee shall relinquish its State license for that product: *Provided*, That autogenous biologics shall not be subject to this provision when they are prepared in accordance with the provisions of paragraph (c)(5) of this section.

(1) State-licensed biological products (including autogenous biologics) shall only be distributed or shipped intrastate, must not bear a U.S. Veterinary Biologics Establishment License Number, and must not otherwise be represented in any manner as having met the requirements for a U.S. Veterinary Biological Product license. Labeling of State- and USDA-licensed biological products produced in the same establishment must be distinctly different in color and design.

(2) All biological products in USDA-licensed establishments, whether licensed by USDA or by the State, shall be prepared only in locations indicated in legends filed in accordance with 9 CFR part 108. A description of each State-licensed product must be filed with the Animal and Plant Health Inspection Service as part of the blueprint legends and must be sufficient for Animal and Plant Health Inspection Service to determine any risk to the production of other products in the licensed establishment and to determine that adequate procedures are followed to prevent contamination during production.

(3) Records in such establishments must be maintained in accordance with §§ 116.1 and 116.2 of this subchapter and shall include all products licensed by the State or USDA.

(4) Reports prescribed in § 116.5 of this subchapter for USDA-licensed establishments shall be submitted for all veterinary biological products in the establishment.

(5) Under the following conditions, an autogenous biologic may be produced in a USDA-licensed establishment under either a State or U.S. Veterinary Biological Product License:

(i) When a culture of microorganisms, isolated from a herd in a State, is received at a USDA-licensed establishment that is in the same State but that holds both a State and a U.S. Veterinary Biological Products License for autogenous biologics, the isolate shall be designated by the licensee for use in the production of an autogenous biological product under either the State product license, or the U.S. Veterinary Biological Product License: *Provided*, That the isolate meets the requirements of the respective regulatory authority for an autogenous biologic. If, after producing the product pursuant to one license, the licensee elects to produce an autogenous biologic from the same isolate under provisions of the other license, the licensee may do so only with the approval of the other licensing authority.

(ii) The true name of a State-licensed autogenous biologic shall specify the State of licensure: e.g.

"_________ Autogenous Bacterin"
(State)

or _________ Autogenous Vaccine".
(State)

[39 FR 16869, May 10, 1974, as amended at 60 FR 48021, Sept. 21, 1995]

§ 114.3 Separation of establishments.

(a) Each licensed establishment shall be separate and distinct from any other establishment in which a biological product is prepared.

(b) No biological products authorized to be prepared in a licensed establishment shall be prepared in whole or in part by another licensed establishment except as provided in paragraphs (c) and (d) of this section.

(c) When a partially prepared biological product cannot be completed at a licensed establishment due to failure of essential equipment, the Administrator may authorize the use of similar equipment at another licensed establishment: *Provided*, That, such authorization shall be limited to the duration of the emergency and to the phase of production affected by the equipment failure.

(d) Partially prepared products or serials of completed products for further manufacture may be moved from one licensed establishment to another licensed establishment, imported under the provisions of § 104.5, or moved from a licensed establishment for purpose of being exported under conditions prescribed in an Outline of Production filed with Animal and Plant Health Inspection Service. Licensed products or products imported for distribution and sale may be prepared and recommended for final use, for further manufacturing purposes, or both. All serials shall be subject to the requirements for testing and release specified in §113.5 or §113.10 and to the requirements for identification specified in §114.4.

[39 FR 16869, May 10, 1974, as amended at 40 FR 46093, Oct. 6, 1975; 49 FR 45846, Nov. 21, 1984; 56 FR 66784, Dec. 26, 1991]

§114.4 Identification of biological products.

Suitable tags or labels of a distinct design shall be used for identifying all ingredients used in the preparation of biological products, all component parts to be combined to form a biological product, all biological products while in the course of preparation and all completed biological products held in storage at licensed establishments: *Provided*, That, if such ingredients, components, or biological products are not so identified, they shall be disposed of as provided in §114.15.

§114.5 Micro-organisms used as seed.

Micro-organisms used in the preparation of biological products at licensed establishments shall be free from the causative agents of other diseases or conditions. A complete record of such micro-organisms shall be kept currently correct and a list submitted to Animal and Plant Health Inspection Service upon request of the Administrator.

(Approved by the Office of Management and Budget under control number 0579–0059)

[39 FR 16869, May 10, 1974, as amended at 48 FR 57473, Dec. 30, 1983; 56 FR 66784, Dec. 26, 1991]

§114.6 Mixing biological products.

Each biological product, when in liquid form, shall be mixed thoroughly in a single container. During bottling operations, the product shall be constantly mixed sufficient to maintain physical uniformity of the entire fill. A serial number, with any other markings that may be necessary for ready identification of the serial, shall be applied to identify it with the records of preparation and labeling.

§114.7 Personnel at licensed establishments.

(a) Each licensee shall designate a person(s) to make all official contacts with Animal and Plant Health Inspection Service on matters pertaining to the preparation of biological products under the Virus-Serum-Toxin Act. The licensee shall file three copies of biographical summary with Animal and Plant Health Inspection Service for such designated person and for each person responsible for any phase of preparation of a biological product.

(b) All personnel employed in the preparation of biological products at a licensed establishment shall be competent in good laboratory techniques through education or training, or both, so as to consistently prepare high quality products.

(c) All biological products prepared at licensed establishments shall be prepared and handled with due sanitary precautions. Good sanitary measures shall be practiced at all times by all personnel involved in such preparation and handling of biological products.

(1) The clothing worn by persons while preparing biological products shall be clean. All persons, immediately before entering laboratory rooms of a licensed establishment, shall change their outer clothing or effectively cover the same with gowns or other satisfactory clean garments.

(2) Unsanitary practices such as, but not limited to, eating, smoking, or expectorating on the floors or otherwise creating a nuisance in any room, compartment, or place in which biological products are prepared, handled, or stored at licensed establishments are prohibited.

(Approved by the Office of Management and Budget under control number 0579–0013)

[39 FR 16869, May 10, 1974, as amended at 48 FR 57473, Dec. 30, 1983; 56 FR 66784, Dec. 26, 1991]

§114.8 Outline of Production required.

An Outline of Production shall be on file with Animal and Plant Health Inspection Service for each licensed biological product or for each biological product authorized to be imported into the United States for Distribution and Sale. Preparation of a biological product in a licensed establishment shall be in accordance with the Outline of Production for such product filed with Animal and Plant Health Inspection Service as provided in this section, but subject to changes as may be required under § 114.8(f).

(a) The Outline of Production shall be prepared as prescribed in § 114.9 and submitted to Animal and Plant Health Inspection Service for filing. When objectionable features, if any, are corrected and no further exceptions are taken by Animal and Plant Health Inspection Service to an Outline of Production for a biological product, such Outline of Production shall be approved for filing.

(b) Each page shall be stamped as filed on the date such action was taken in the bottom right hand corner. Although the filed outline may be referred to as an approved outline, approval for filing constitutes no endorsement by Animal and Plant Health Inspection Service of such biological product or the methods and procedures used to prepare such biological product.

(c) One copy of the Outline of Production shall be retained by the Animal and Plant Health Inspection Service and one copy returned to the licensee or permittee.

(d) Each licensee shall review each Outline of Production for accuracy and sufficiency not less frequently than once a year. Revisions necessary to bring an Outline of Production into compliance with the regulations shall be submitted to Animal and Plant Health Inspection Service.

(e) When a list of licensed products to be continued in production at a licensed establishment is requested by the Administrator in accordance with § 102.5(d) of this subchapter, the licensee shall supplement the list with information for each product as follows:

(1) The Outline of Production currently being used shall be identified as to the date when last revised and filed with Animal and Plant Health Inspection Service and the date of the last review made by the licensee.

(2) The Outline of Production to be kept in the active file shall be designated. If more than one has been filed for a product, only the Outline of Production currently being used shall be included.

(f) The Administrator may, upon the basis of information not available to him at the time the current Outline of Production for a biological product was filed, object to the methods or procedures being used in the preparation of such biological product and notify the licensee to modify the filed Outline of Production to eliminate such objections. If the licensee does not comply with the notice, the Administrator may, after affording opportunity for a hearing to the licensee, suspend the product license for the biological product involved; in which case, the licensee shall not prepare such product until subsequent notice of withdrawal of the suspension is given to the licensee.

(Approved by the Office of Management and Budget under control number 0579–0013)

[39 FR 16869, May 10, 1974, as amended at 48 FR 57473, Dec. 30, 1983; 56 FR 66784, Dec. 26, 1991; 75 FR 20773, Apr. 21, 2010]

§ 114.9 Outline of Production guidelines.

Each Outline of Production shall be prepared in accordance with the applicable directions provided in this section.

(a) *General requirements.* (1) All copies of each Outline of Production or special outline or revised pages of either shall be prepared on heavy paper (8.5″ × 11″) of a type receptive to permanent stamp ink.

(2) The name of the biological product (or component), the establishment license number, and the date prepared shall appear on a front cover page and each page of the Outline of Production or special outline. The name of the licensee (or foreign manufacturer) shall appear on the front cover page.

(3) The pages shall be numbered in the upper center. At least 1½ inch margin shall be left at the top of the first page and a 2 inch margin at the bottom of each page for the Animal and Plant Health Inspection Service stamp.

(4) Amended pages shall be numbered the same as those being superseded.

They shall bear the date prepared and refer to the date on the pages being superseded. If one replacement page supersedes more than one page, the new page shall indicate same, but if several replacement pages are added to supersede one page, the page number followed by letters shall be used.

(5) The last page of both copies of either a new or a completely rewritten Outline of Production and each page revised separately shall be signed in the lower left corner by the authorized representative of the licensee (or foreign producer). Stamped or facsimile signatures are not acceptable.

(6) A summary of changes shall appear on an attached page and refer to each page, paragraph, or subparagraph being changed.

(7) Transmittal forms shall be used for the original and subsequent revisions. Transmittal forms are available on the Internet at (*http://www.aphis.usda.gov/animal_health/vet_biologics/vb_forms.shtml*).

(b) *Special outline*. An outline describing the preparation of a component of a biological product or an operation performed in the preparation of a biological product may be required if such special outline could be referred to in Outlines of Production to eliminate repetition. Each special outline shall be identified by number and shall not be used until accepted and filed by Animal and Plant Health Inspection Service.

(c) Outline of Production for antiserum, antitoxin, and normal serum shall be written according to the following:

OUTLINE GUIDE FOR PRODUCTION OF ANTISERUM AND ANTITOXIN AND NORMAL SERUM

License No. Name of Product Date

I. *Serum animals*. A. Species, conditions, age, and general health.

B. Examination, preparation, care, quarantine, tests, and treatment of animals before injections are started.

C. Holding, handling, exercising, and monitoring the condition of animals after injections are started.

II. *Antigens*. A. Composition and character of the antigen.

1. Micro-organisms.
2. Source and date of accession of each micro-organism.
3. Strains.
4. Proportions of each micro-organism and strain.

B. Identification methods used for each micro-organism and frequency with which these methods are applied.

C. Virulence and purity of cultures or antigen and the determination and maintenance thereof. Range of subcultures or passages to be used in production.

D. Attenuation, if any, before use for production purposes.

E. Character, size, and shape of containers used for growing micro-organisms.

F. Media used for stock, seed, and antigen cultures (composition and reaction of). May refer to a special outline by number.

G. Preparation of the antigen or toxin and toxoid. Complete and full description of each step and its manner of accomplishment and number these steps in sequence. Include all tests for each antigen, and the specifications for character, identity, virulence, concentration, and standardization.

III. *Immunization of animals*. A. Outline fully with special attention given to the following:

1. Character and dose of the antigen.
2. Method and frequency of injections.
3. Time required for immunization or hyperimmunization.
4. Preliminary bleedings and tests, if any, to ascertain quality of serum.
5. All other similar matters, including treatments between bleedings.

B. Period of time elapsing between last injection and first bleeding; and between bleedings.

C. Technique of bleeding operations; volume of blood collected at each bleeding; and period of rest.

IV. *Preparation of the biological product*. A. Describe fully and show each step of preparation from the first bleeding to the completion of the preserved product in bulk containers prior to filling of final containers.

B. Composition of the preservative and proportions used. Indicate at which step of production, and the method used in adding the preservative.

C. Agglutination and complement-fixation titers and the methods of their determinations.

D. Disposition of unsatisfactory biological products and infective materials not used in production.

E. Assembly of units to make a serial; volume of the average serial; and the volume of the maximum serial.

V. *Testing*. Indicate the stages in the preparation of the biological product at which samples are collected. Refer to all applicable Standard Requirements. Outline all additional tests in detail and state minimum requirements for each satisfactory test.

A. Purity.
B. Safety.
C. Potency.

D. Other tests.

VI. *Post preparatory steps.*

A. Form and size of final containers in which the product is to be distributed.

B. Methods and techniques of filling final containers. Volume of fill for each size final container.

C. Collection, storage, and submission of representative samples. Indicate at which steps in the production these samples are taken.

D. Expiration date based on the earliest date of harvest and the date of the last satisfactory potency test.

E. Use, dosage, and route of administration for each animal species for which it is recommended.

F. Include any additional pertinent information.

(d) Outline of Production for *vaccines, bacterins, antigens,* and *toxoids* shall be written according to the following:

OUTLINE GUIDE FOR VACCINES, BACTERINS, ANTIGENS, AND TOXOIDS

License No. Name of Product Date

I. *Composition, etc., of the product.* A. Micro-organisms used. Give the isolation and passage history.

B. Source and date of accession of each micro-organism.

C. Strains.

D. Proportions of each strain.

II. *Cultures.* A. Brief description of methods of identifying each micro-organism and the frequency with which these methods are applied.

B. Virulence and purity of cultures and the determination and maintenance thereof. Range of subcultures or passages to be used in production.

C. Composition and reaction of media used for seed and production cultures. Include the source of eggs, tissue, or cell cultures, and the tests to determine that eggs, tissues, and cells are free of contamination.

D. Character, size, and shape of containers used for growing cultures.

E. Storage conditions of seed cultures.

F. Methods of preparing suspensions for seeding or inoculation.

G. Technique of inoculating (1) seed media; (2) production media. Titer or concentration of inoculum, and the volume of medium for each size and type of culture container.

H. Period of time and conditions for incubation and degree of temperature used for each micro-organism or group of micro-organisms.

I. Character and amount of growth; observation as to contamination of growth.

J. Method of attenuation, if any, before used for production purposes.

III. *Harvest.* A. Handling and preparation of cultures and media (including eggs) before removal of micro-organisms or tissues for production purposes.

B. Minimum and maximum period of time elapsing from time of inoculation until harvest.

C. Technique of harvesting micro-organisms or tissues (specify) for production purposes.

D. Specifications for acceptable harvest material.

E. Handling of discarded material not used in production.

F. Include any additional pertinent information.

IV. *Preparation of the product.* Describe fully and show each step of preparation from harvest of antigen containing tissues or production cultures to the completion of the finished product in final containers. In describing the preparation of the product, emphasize the following:

A. Method of inactivation, attenuation, or detoxification.

B. Composition of preservative, adjuvant or stabilizer, and proportions used stated in such a manner that the concentration can be calculated; stage and method of addition.

C. Method and degree of concentration.

D. If product is standardized to give concentration of antigen, show procedures and calculations.

E. 1. Assembly of units to make a serial (illustrate by example).

2. Volume of average serial.

3. Volume of maximum serial.

4. Any other pertinent information.

F. Volume of fill for each size vial. Type of vial if unusual.

G. Method and technique of filling and sealing of final containers.

H. Desiccation, including moisture control. Give maximum percent moisture.

I. Amount of antigenic material per dose or doses in final container.

V. *Testing.* Indicate the stages in the preparation of the biological product at which the samples are collected. Refer to all applicable Standard Requirements. Outline all additional tests in detail and state the minimum requirement for each satisfactory test.

A. Purity.

B. Safety.

C. Potency.

D. Moisture, if desiccated.

E. Any other tests.

VI. *Post preparatory steps.* A. Form and size of final containers in which the product is to be distributed.

B. Collection, storage, and submission of representative samples. Indicate at which steps in the production these samples are taken.

C. Expiration date based on the earliest date of harvest and the date of the last satisfactory potency test. If applicable, give the date of lyophilization.

D. Use, dosage, and route of administration for each animal species for which the biological product is recommended.

(e) Outlines of Production for allergenic extracts shall be written according to the following:

OUTLINE GUIDE FOR ALLERGENIC EXTRACTS

License No. Name of Product Date

I. *Composition of the product.* A. Source and type of raw material.

B. Weight/volume concentration.

II. *Preparation of the product.* A. Describe fully and show each step of preparation to the completion of the finished product in true containers. In describing the preparation of the product, emphasize the following:

1. Method of extraction.

2. Composition of preservative, adjuvant or stabilizer, and proportions used; stage and method of addition.

3. Method and degree of concentration.

4. Standardization of the product.

5. (a) Assembly of units to make a serial.

(b) Volume of average serial.

(c) Maximum serial.

6. Volume of fill for each size vial.

7. Method and technique of filling and sealing of final containers.

8. Amount material per dose or doses in final container.

III. *Testing.* Indicate the stages in the preparation of the biological product at which the samples are collected. Refer to all applicable Standard Requirements. Outline all additional tests in detail and state the minimum requirement for each satisfactory test.

A. Purity.

B. Safety.

C. Potency.

D. Any other tests.

E. Include any additional pertinent information.

IV. *Post preparatory steps.* A. Form and size of final containers in which the product is to be distributed.

B. Collection, storage, and submission of representative samples. Indicate at which steps in the production these samples are taken.

C. Expiration date based on the earliest date of harvest and the date of the last satisfactory potency test.

D. Use, dosage, and route of administration for each animal species for which the biological product is recommended.

(f) Outlines of Production for diagnostic test kits based on antigen-antibody reactions, and other diagnostics whose production methods are amenable to description as described herein shall be written according to the following requirements:

OUTLINE GUIDE FOR DIAGNOSTIC TEST KITS

License No. Name of product Date

Introduction

Provide a brief description of the kit as follows:

1. Principle of the test (ELISA, latex agglutination, etc.).

2. Antigen or antibody detection test.

3. Sample(s) used for testing (serum, whole blood, tears, etc.).

4. List reagents, references, and equipment included.

5. Identify materials obtained under split manufacturing agreements.

6. General description of test interpretations and their limitations, including followup tests.

I. *Antibody Components*

A. Production of polyclonal antibody components.

1. If purchased, list suppliers, criteria for acceptability, and describe all tests performed after receipt to determine that specifications have been met.

2. If produced in-house, describe the species, age, weight, conditions, and general health of all animals used in antiserum production.

a. Preinjection considerations:

Describe the examination, preparation, care, quarantine procedures, and treatments administered before immunization(s). Describe all tests used to determine suitability for use. Describe the preparation of any standard negative serum(s) collected prior to immunization.

b. Immunization of animals.

i. Describe the character and dose of the antigen; if adjuvant is used provide details on its preparation. If commercial product is used include its true name as shown on the label, the manufacturer, serial number, and expiration date.

ii. Describe the method and schedule for immunizations.

iii. Describe the method for harvesting and evaluating the immunization product, including tests for acceptability.

iv. Provide number and intervals between harvests, volume obtained, and any other pertinent information.

B. Production of Monoclonal Antibody Components.

1. Hybridoma components:

a. If hybridoma components are purchased, list suppliers and criteria for acceptability; if tests are performed after receipt, describe fully.

b. If hybridomas are prepared inhouse, identify the antigen(s) used, describe the immunization scheme, and the species of animal used.

c. Identify the tissue of origin, and the procedures for harvesting, isolating, and identifying the immune cells.

d. Describe the source, identity, and the product secreted (light or heavy chain) by the parent Myeloma Cell Line.

e. Summarize cloning and recloning procedures, including clone characterization and propagation, if appropriate.

f. If appropriate, describe procedures for establishing and maintaining seed lots.

g. Describe any other pertinent tests or procedures performed on the hybridoma cell line.

2. Antibody production:

a. Describe the production method. If produced in cell culture, animal serum additives must conform to 9 CFR 113.53. If produced in animals, describe fully including husbandry practices and passage procedures.

b. Provide the criteria for acceptable monoclonal antibody, including tests for purity.

c. Describe all tests or other methods used to ensure uniformity between production lots of monoclonal antibody. Include all reaction conditions, equipment used, and reactivity of the component.

d. Describe all characterization procedures and include the expected reactivity of all reference monoclonal antibodies.

II. *Antigen Preparation*

A. Identify the microorganism(s) or antigen being used. If previously approved Master Seed virus, bacteria, or antigen derived therefrom is used, provide pertinent information on the testing performed, and details of dates of United States Department of Agriculture confirmatory tests and approval, as appropriate.

B. Describe all propagation steps, including identification of cell cultures, media ingredients, cell culture conditions, and harvest methods. For antigen produced in eggs, give the egg source, age, and route of inoculation. If cell lines are being used, give dates of testing and approval as specified in 9 CFR 113.52.

C. Describe procedures used for extracting and characterizing the antigen.

D. Describe the method used to standardize the antigen.

E. If the antigen is purchased, identify the supplier and describe the criteria for acceptable material, including all tests performed by the producer and/or the recipient to determine acceptability.

III. *Preparation of Standard Reagents*

A. Describe the positive and negative controls included in the kit. If purchased, list suppliers and criteria for acceptance.

B. Describe the preparation and standardization of the conjugate(s). If purchased, list suppliers and criteria for acceptance.

C. Describe the preparation and standardization of the substrate(s). If purchased, list suppliers and criteria for acceptance.

D. Identify buffers, diluents, and other reagents included in the kit. The preparation of these components may be described in this section or in filed Special Outlines.

IV. *Preparation of the Product*

Fully describe methods used to standardize antigens, reference standards, positive control serum, negative control serum, and standard reagents from production/purchase to completion of finished product in final containers, including the following:

1. Composition and quantity of preservative in each.

2. Method of filling, plating, or attaching the antigen or antibody component to a solid phase.

3. Minimum and maximum acceptable fill volumes for each final container of reagent included in the kit.

4. The disposition of unsatisfactory material.

V. *Testing*

Refer to all applicable standard requirements.

A. Purity.

Describe all tests of the kit for purity or specify the exemption as provided in 9 CFR 113.4.

B. Safety.

In vitro products are exempt from safety tests.

C. Potency.

Provide details of tests used to determine the relative reactivity of the kit including minimum requirements for a satisfactory test. Reference standards and control serum used for this purpose should be identified by unique codes or lot numbers.

VI. *Postpreparatory Steps*

A. Describe the form and size of final containers of each reagent/component included in the kit.

B. Describe the collection, storage, and submission of representative samples. Refer to 9 CFR 113.3(b)(7).

C. Specify the expiration date. Refer to 9 CFR 114.13.

D. Provide details of recommendations for use, including all limitations, qualifications, and interpretation of results.

E. Submit confidentiality statement identifying specific parts of the outline containing information, the release of which would cause harm to the submitter.

(Approved by the Office of Management and Budget under control number 0579–0013)

[39 FR 16869, May 10, 1974, as amended at 48 FR 57473, Dec. 30, 1983; 56 FR 20124, May 2, 1991; 56 FR 66784, Dec. 26, 1991; 75 FR 20773, Apr. 21, 2010]

§ 114.10 Antibiotics as preservatives.

Antibiotics are authorized for use as preservatives for biological products if used within the limitations as to kinds and amounts prescribed in this section.

(a) When an antibiotic or combination of antibiotics, with or without a fungistat is to be used in the preparation of a biological product, the kind(s) and amount(s) of each shall be specified in the outline for such product in such a way that the concentration in the final product may be calculated. Except as may be approved by the Administrator, only those individual antibiotics or combinations of antibiotics listed in paragraphs (b) and (c) of this section shall be used.

(b) Permitted individual antibiotics:

(1) The antibiotic level of a specified individual antibiotic in one ml. of a biological product, when prepared as recommended for use, shall not exceed the amounts listed in this paragraph: *Provided*, That in the case a desiccated biological product is to be used with an indefinite quantity of water or other menstruum, the determination shall be based on 30 ml. per 1,000 dose vial or equivalent.

(2) Except as prescribed in paragraph (c) of this section, only one antibiotic shall be used as a preservative in a biological product. The kind and maximum amount per ml. of such antibiotic shall be restricted to:

Amphotericin B	2.5 mcg.
Nystatin (Mycostatin)	30.0 units
Tetracyclines	30.0 mcg.
Penicillin	30.0 units
Streptomycin	30.0 mcg.
Polymyxin B	30.0 mcg.
Neomycin	30.0 mcg.
Gentamicin	30.0 mcg.

(c) Permitted combinations:

(1) Penicillin and streptomycin.

(2) Either amphotericin B or nystatin, but not both, may be used with one of the other antibiotics listed in paragraph (b) of this section, or with a combination of penicillin and streptomycin, or with a combination of polymyxin B and neomycin.

(3) The maximum amount of each antibiotic in a combination shall be the amount prescribed for such antibiotic in paragraph (b) of this section.

(d) Antibiotics used in virus seed stock purification are not restricted as to kind or amounts provided carryover into the final product is controlled and specified in outlines of production.

[39 FR 16869, May 10, 1974, as amended at 56 FR 66784, Dec. 26, 1991]

§ 114.11 Storage and handling.

Biological products at licensed establishments must be protected at all times against improper storage and handling. Completed product must be kept under refrigeration at 35 to 46 °F (2 to 8 °C), unless the inherent nature of the product makes storage at different temperatures advisable, in which case, the proper storage temperature must be specified in the filed Outline of Production. All biological products to be shipped or delivered must be securely packed.

[81 FR 59436, Aug. 30, 2016]

§ 114.12 Expiration date required.

Each serial or subserial of biological product prepared in a licensed establishment shall be given an expiration date determined in accordance with the requirements provided in § 114.13 or § 114.14. A licensed biological product shall be considered worthless under the Virus-Serum-Toxin Act subsequent to the expiration date appearing on the label.

[41 FR 44687, Oct. 12, 1976]

§ 114.13 Expiration date determination.

Unless otherwise provided for in a Standard Requirement of filed Outline of Production, the expiration date for each product shall be computed from the date of the initiation of the potency test. Prior to licensure, stability of each fraction shall be determined by methods acceptable to Animal and Plant Health Inspection Service. Expiration dates based on this stability data shall be confirmed as follows:

(a) *Products consisting of viable organisms.* Each serial shall be tested for potency at release and at the approximate expiration date until a statistically valid stability record has been established.

(b) *Nonviable biological products.* Each serial presented in support of licensure shall be tested for potency at release and at or after the dating requested.

(c) Subsequent changes in the dating period for a product may be granted, based on statistically valid data submitted to support a revision of the Outline of Production.

[50 FR 24903, June 14, 1985, as amended at 56 FR 66784, Dec. 26, 1991]

§ 114.14 Extension of expiration date for a serial or subserial.

(a) Unless otherwise provided for in a filed Outline of Production for the product, the expiration date shall not be extended:

(1) If all fractions of the product are not evaluated for potency by tests designated in the filed Outline of Production for such product in accordance with § 113.4(b) of this subchapter.

(2) For any serial or portion of any serial which has left licensed premises: *Provided,* That product which has been shipped from one licensed premises to another licensed premises shall be exempt from this requirement.

(3) For a serial or portion of a serial if the expiration date has been extended previously, unless otherwise authorized in accordance with § 114.1.

(b) An extension of the expiration date may be granted by Animal and Plant Health Inspection Service if a request from the licensee is substantiated by valid test data which demonstrate the potency of the product meets or exceeds the requirements for release. The new expiration date shall be calculated from the date the latest satisfactory potency test was initiated. The extension of the expiration date shall not exceed the maximum dating allowed in the filed Outline of Production.

(1) Serials are approved for redating under the condition that Animal and Plant Health Inspection Service may require the firm to retest the redated serial for potency during the extended dating period and if found unsatisfactory require it be removed from the market by the licensee.

(2) [Reserved]

[50 FR 24903, June 14, 1985, as amended at 56 FR 66784, Dec. 26, 1991]

§ 114.15 Disposal of unsatisfactory products and byproducts.

All biological products found to be unsatisfactory for marketing, all biological products which have become worthless subsequent to the expiration date, all refuse, other materials deemed unsatisfactory for production purposes, all carcasses (part or whole) of production or test animals, and any undesirable byproducts of manufacture shall be disposed of as may be required by the Administrator.

[41 FR 44687, Oct. 12, 1976, as amended at 56 FR 66784, Dec. 26, 1991]

§ 114.16 Producing subsidiaries.

A serial or subserial of a biological product may be produced jointly by a licensee and one or more subsidiaries, or by two or more subsidiaries. The exact amount of each serial or subserial credited to each participating producer shall be determined at the time of labeling and packaging and shall be noted in the records for such serial or subserial.

[40 FR 46093, Oct. 6, 1975]

§ 114.17 Rebottling of biological products.

The Administrator may authorize the rebottling of a completed product in liquid form subject to the conditions prescribed in this section.

(a) All or part of a serial which has not left the licensed establishment may be aseptically returned to the mixing tank, thoroughly mixed, and rebottled in new final containers.

(b) The rebottled product shall be adequately identified by serial number or subserial number, as the case may be.

(c) Required purity tests for final container samples of the product shall be conducted on new samples selected from the rebottled product (serial or subserials). Rebottled product found to be unsatisfactory by such tests shall not be released.

(d) New test samples from each serial or subserial and copies of test reports of all tests conducted on the rebottled product shall be submitted to Animal and Plant Health Inspection Service.

(e) The licensee shall not release the rebottled product unless notified by Animal and Plant Health Inspection Service that such product is eligible for release. Production records shall show the results of all tests conducted and shall accurately reflect the actions taken.

[39 FR 16869, May 10, 1974, as amended at 56 FR 66784, Dec. 26, 1991]

§114.18 Reprocessing of biological products.

The Administrator may authorize a licensee to reprocess a serial of completed product subject to the conditions prescribed in this section.

(a) Reprocessing shall not include any method or procedure which would be deleterious to the product.

(b) All appropriate tests for purity, safety, potency, and efficacy for the product shall be conducted on the reprocessed product. A serial found unsatisfactory by a required test shall not be released.

(c) The reprocessed serial shall be identified by a new serial number and the records for the serial shall accurately reflect the action taken.

(d) Test samples of the reprocessed serial and test reports for all tests conducted shall be submitted to Animal and Plant Health Inspection Service. The licensee shall not release the serial until notified by Animal and Plant Health Inspection Service that the serial is eligible for release.

[50 FR 24904, June 15, 1985, as amended at 56 FR 66784, Dec. 26, 1991]

PART 115—INSPECTIONS

Sec.

AUTHORITY: 21 U.S.C. 151–159; 7 CFR 2.22, 2.80, and 371.4.

§115.1 Inspections of establishments.

(a) Any inspector shall be permitted to enter any establishment where any biological product is prepared, at any hour during the day or night, and shall be permitted to inspect, without previous notification, the entire premises of the establishment, including all buildings, compartments, and other places, all biological products, and organisms and vectors in the establishment, and all materials and equipment, such as chemicals, instruments, apparatus, and the like, and the methods used in the manufacture of, and all records maintained relative to, biological products produced at such establishment.

(b) Each inspector will have in his or her possession a numbered USDA badge or identification card. Either shall be sufficient identification to entitle him/her to admittance at all regular entrances and to all parts of such establishment and premises and to any place at any time for the purpose of making an inspection pursuant to paragraph (a) of this section.

[52 FR 30134, Aug. 13, 1987]

§115.2 Inspections of biological products.

(a) Any biological product, the container of which bears a United States veterinary license number or a United States veterinary permit number or other mark required by these regulations, may be inspected at any time or place. If, as a result of such inspection, it appears that any such product is worthless, contaminated, dangerous, or harmful, the Secretary shall give notice to stop distribution and sale to the manufacturer (licensee) or importer (permittee) and may proceed against such product pursuant to the provisions of part 118 of this subchapter.

(b) When notified to stop distribution and sale of a serial or subserial of a veterinary biological product by the Secretary, veterinary biologics licensees or permittees shall:

(1) Stop the preparation, distribution, sale, barter, exchange, shipment, or importation of the affected serial(s) or subserial(s) of any such veterinary biological product pending further instructions from APHIS.

(2) Immediately, but no later than 2 days, send stop distribution and sale notifications to any jobbers, wholesalers, dealers, foreign consignees, or other persons known to have any such

veterinary biological product in their possession, which instruct them to stop the preparation, distribution, sale, barter, exchange, shipment, or importation of any such veterinary biological product. All notifications shall be documented in writing by the licensee or permittee.

(3) Account for the remaining quantity of each serial(s) or subserial(s) of any such veterinary biological product at each location in the distribution channel known to the manufacturer (licensee) or importer (permittee).

(4) When required by the Administrator, submit complete and accurate reports of all notifications concerning stop distribution and sale actions to the Animal and Plant Health Inspection Service pursuant to §116.5 of this subchapter.

(c) Unless and until the Secretary shall otherwise direct, no persons so notified shall thereafter sell, barter, or exchange any such product in any place under the jurisdiction of the United States or ship or deliver for shipment any such product in or from any State, Territory, or the District of Columbia. However, failure to receive such notice shall not excuse any person from compliance with the Virus-Serum-Toxin Act.

(Approved by the Office of Management and Budget under control number 0579–0318)

[72 FR 17798, Apr. 10, 2007]

PART 116—RECORDS AND REPORTS

Sec.

AUTHORITY: 21 U.S.C. 151–159; 7 CFR 2.22, 2.80, and 371.4.

§116.1 Applicability and general considerations.

(a) Each licensee, permittee, and foreign manufacturer of biological products imported into the United States shall maintain, at the licensed or foreign establishment in which the products are prepared, detailed records of information necessary to give a complete accounting of all the activities within each establishment. Such records shall include, but shall not be limited to, the items enumerated in this part.

(1) Records shall be made concurrently with the performance of successive steps in the development and preparation of biological products, including new products under development. Such records shall include the date and where critical, the time that each essential step was taken, the identity and quantity of ingredients added or removed at each step, and any gain or loss of product from the beginning to the end of product preparation.

(2) Records shall be legible and indelible; shall be as detailed as necessary for a clear understanding of each step by one experienced in the preparation of biological products; and shall be verified by initials or signature of the person immediately responsible for the action taken.

(3) Records (other than disposition records) required by this part shall be completed by the licensee or the foreign manufacturer, as the case may be, before any portion of a serial of any product shall be marketed in the United States or exported.

(b) In the case of imported products, each permittee shall maintain at the permittee's place of business detailed and accurate records that are relevant to each imported product and that include, but are not limited to, importation documents, sampling records, test summaries, shipping records, and inventory and disposition records as required in §116.2.

(c) When authorized by the Administrator, the licensee, permittee, or foreign manufacturer may maintain and retain records required under this part at an alternative location. Such authorization shall be confirmed by the filing of an addendum to the plot plan legend. The addendum shall list the location of the records and the condition of their storage and shall permit the inspection of the records by APHIS inspectors, or foreign inspectors acting on behalf of APHIS.

(Approved by the Office of Management and Budget under control number 0579–0013)

[39 FR 16872, May 10, 1974, as amended at 48 FR 57473, Dec. 30, 1983; 61 FR 52874, Oct. 9, 1996; 66 FR 21064, Apr. 27, 2001]

§ 116.2 Inventory and disposition records.

(a) Records shall show the quantity and location of each biological product being prepared, in storage, and in distribution channels.

(b) Detailed disposition records, in a form satisfactory to the Administrator, shall be maintained by each licensee, each distributor, and each permittee showing the sale, shipment, or other disposition made of the biological products handled by such person.

(Approved by the Office of Management and Budget under control number 0579–0013)

[39 FR 16872, May 10, 1974, as amended at 48 FR 57473, Dec. 30, 1983; 56 FR 66784, Dec. 26, 1991; 61 FR 52874, Oct. 9, 1996; 66 FR 21064, Apr. 27, 2001]

§ 116.3 Label records.

(a) Each licensee and permittee shall maintain a list of all approved labels currently being used. Each label shall be identified as to:

(1) Name and product code number as it appears on the product license or permit for the product;

(2) Where applicable, the size of the package (doses, ml, cc, or units) on which the label shall be used;

(3) Label number and date assigned; and

(4) Name of licensee or subsidiary appearing on the label as the producer.

(b) All labels printed shall be accounted for and an inventory maintained.

Records shall include the disposition of such labels including those not used in labeling a product.

(Approved by the Office of Management and Budget under control number 0579–0013)

[39 FR 16872, May 10, 1974, as amended at 48 FR 57473, Dec. 30, 1983; 61 FR 52874, Oct. 9, 1996; 66 FR 21064, Apr. 27, 2001]

§ 116.4 Sterilization and pasteurization records.

Records shall be made by means of automatic recording devices or an equivalent accurate and reliable system. Such records shall be identified with the ingredients, equipment, or biological product subjected to sterilization or pasteurization.

(Approved by the Office of Management and Budget under control number 0579–0013)

[39 FR 16872, May 10, 1974, as amended at 48 FR 57473, Dec. 30, 1983; 61 FR 52874, Oct. 9, 1996; 66 FR 21064, Apr. 27, 2001]

§ 116.5 Reports.

(a) When required by the Administrator, reports containing accurate and complete information concerning biological products, including but not limited to, product development and preparation, and market suspensions and recalls, shall be prepared and submitted to the Animal and Plant Health Inspection Service by the licensee, permittee, or foreign manufacturer (whose products are being imported or offered for importation). Unless otherwise authorized by the Administrator, records necessary to make such reports shall be maintained in each establishment.

(b) If, at any time, there are indications that raise questions regarding the purity, safety, potency, or efficacy of a product, or if it appears that there may be a problem regarding the preparation, testing, or distribution of a product, the licensee, permittee, or foreign manufacturer must immediately notify the Animal and Plant Health Inspection Service concerning the circumstances and the action taken, if any. Notification may be made by mail to Director, Center for Veterinary Biologics, Inspection and Compliance, 1920 Dayton Avenue, P.O. Box 844, Ames, IA 50010; by electronic mail to (*cvb@aphis.usda.gov*); by fax to (515) 337-6120; or by telephone to (515) 337-6100.

(Approved by the Office of Management and Budget under control number 0579–0013)

[61 FR 52874, Oct. 9, 1996, as amended at 64 FR 43045, Aug. 9, 1999; 75 FR 20773, Apr. 21, 2010]

§ 116.6 Animal records.

Complete records shall be kept for all animals at a licensed establishment. Results of tests performed, antigens or treatment administered, maintenance and production records, disposition records, necropsy records, if any, and all other pertinent records shall be included.

(Approved by the Office of Management and Budget under control number 0579–0013)

[39 FR 16872, May 10, 1974, as amended at 48 FR 57473, Dec. 30, 1983; 61 FR 52874, Oct. 9, 1996; 66 FR 21064, Apr. 27, 2001]

§ 116.7 Test records.

Detailed records of all tests conducted on each serial and each subserial shall be maintained by the licensee. Summaries of such tests shall be prepared from such records and submitted to the Animal and Plant Health Inspection Service using APHIS Form 2008 or an acceptable equivalent form prior to release of the serial or subserial. Blank forms for such summaries shall be available from Animal and Plant Health Inspection Service upon request.

(Approved by the Office of Management and Budget under control number 0579–0013)

[39 FR 16872, May 10, 1974, as amended at 48 FR 57473, Dec. 30, 1983; 56 FR 66784, Dec. 26, 1991; 61 FR 52874, Oct. 9, 1996]

§ 116.8 Completion and retention of records.

All records (other than disposition records) required by this part shall be completed by the licensee, permittee, or foreign manufacturer before any portion of a serial of any product may be marketed in the United States or exported. All records shall be retained at the licensed or foreign establishment or permittee's place of business for a period of two years after the expiration date of a product, or for such longer period as may be required by the Administrator.

(Approved by the Office of Management and Budget under control number 0579–0013)

[61 FR 52874, Oct. 9, 1996]

PART 117—ANIMALS AT LICENSED ESTABLISHMENTS

Sec.

AUTHORITY: 21 U.S.C. 151–159; 7 CFR 2.22, 2.80, and 371.4.

SOURCE: 38 FR 15499, June 13, 1973, unless otherwise noted.

§ 117.1 Applicability.

(a) All animals used in licensed establishments in the preparation or testing of biological products shall meet the regulations in this subchapter and special requirements as may be prescribed by the Administrator to prevent the preparation, sale, and distribution of worthless, contaminated, dangerous, or harmful biological products.

(b) Unless otherwise authorized or directed by the Administrator, animals used in the preparation or testing of biological products shall be admitted to and maintained at the licensed establishment and ultimately disposed of in accordance with the regulations in this part, and with the Act of August 24, 1966 (Pub. L. 89–544) as amended by the Animal Welfare Act of 1970 (Pub. L. 91–579) and the regulations in parts 1, 2, and 3 of this chapter. Personnel who supervise the care and welfare of such animals shall be qualified by education, training, and experience to carry out the regulations in this part.

[38 FR 15499, June 13, 1973, as amended at 56 FR 66784, Dec. 26, 1991]

§ 117.2 Animal facilities.

Animal facilities shall comply with the requirements provided in part 108 of this chapter.

§ 117.3 Admittance of animals.

(a) No animal which shows clinical signs or other evidence of disease shall be admitted to the premises of licensed establishments, except as provided in paragraphs (d) and (e) of this section. The health status of all animals offered for admission shall be determined by or under the direction of a veterinarian prior to admission. If the determination cannot be made prior to admission, the animals shall be kept separate from animals already on the premises and in a quarantine area to be provided by the licensee for this purpose until the animal's health status is determined.

(b) If special test requirements for admittance of the animals are specified in the Outline of Production for the product to be produced, the animals shall remain in the quarantine area until such tests have been performed and the results obtained. Animals which do not meet the requirements shall not be admitted to the production area or allowed to contact production animals.

(c) All animals admitted to the premises of a licensed establishment shall be permanently identified either collectively or individually by the licensee with tags, marks, or other means acceptable to the Administrator.

(d) When an animal which has a disease is to be used to prepare a biological product for control of such disease, the animal shall be admitted directly to the processing facilities in which the product is to be prepared but shall not be permitted contact with other animals on the premises.

(e) The Administrator may authorize the maintenance of diagnostic facilities at the licensed establishment: *Provided,* That safeguards proposed by the licensee are adequate to prevent diseased or dead animals brought into such facilities from being a threat to biological products prepared in such establishment or to other animals on the premises used in the preparation of biological products.

[38 FR 15499, June 13, 1973, as amended at 56 FR 66784, Dec. 26, 1991]

§ 117.4 Test animals.

(a) All test animals shall be examined for clinical signs of illness, injury, or abnormal behavior prior to the start of a test and throughout the observation period specified in the test protocol.

(b) All animals used for test purposes shall be identified either collectively or individually in a manner conducive to an accurate interpretation of the results of the test.

(c) No test animals shall be given a biological product during the preconditioning period which would affect its eligibility according to the test requirements. No treatment, with a biological product or otherwise, shall be administered to a test animal during a test period which could interfere with a true evaluation of the biological product being tested.

(d) During the course of a test, animals that are injured or show clinical signs of illness or unfavorable reactions that are not due to the test may be removed from the test and treated or humanely destroyed. If sufficient animals do not remain for the test to be evaluated, the test shall be declared inconclusive and may be repeated.

(e) Test animals that show clinical signs of illness that are due to the test may be treated or humanely destroyed if the illness has progressed to a point (defined in the filed Outline of Production) when death is certain to occur without therapeutic intervention. When interpreting the results of the test, the animals that were treated or humanely destroyed because of illness due to the test and the animals that have died from illness due to the test prior to being humanely destroyed shall be combined into a common statistic of mortality due to the test.

[38 FR 15499, June 13, 1973, as amended at 60 FR 43356, Aug. 21, 1995]

§ 117.5 Segregation of animals.

Animals which have been infected with or exposed to a dangerous, infectious, contagious, or communicable disease shall be kept effectively segregated at a licensed establishment until such time as they are humanely destroyed or successfully treated and removed as healthy animals.

§ 117.6 Removal of animals.

Production animals or ex-test animals which are no longer useful at the licensed establishment may be removed from the premises of the licensed establishment; provided, such removal is accomplished in a manner as shall preclude the dissemination of disease and in accordance with the following conditions:

(a) Meat-producing animals which received a biological product containing inactivated microorganisms and adjuvants within 21 days shall not be removed; or

(b) Animals which received virulent microorganisms within 30 days shall not be removed; or

(c) Only animals that are in a healthy condition as determined by a veterinarian shall be removed, except as provided in paragraph (d) of this section.

(d) Other animals that are injured or otherwise unhealthy, except when affected with a communicable disease, may be removed for immediate slaughter to an abattoir operated in accordance with the Federal Meat Inspection Act of March 4, 1907, 34 Stat. 1260, as amended by the Wholesome Meat Act of 1967, 81 Stat. 585 (21 U.S.C. sec. 601 *et seq.*): *Provided,* That such animals shall be properly marked for identification and the inspector in charge of slaughter operations is given due notice in advance.

(e) All animals on the premises shall be disposed of in accordance with the provisions of the regulations in this part and where specific provision is not made therefor shall be disposed of as required by the Administrator.

[38 FR 15499, June 13, 1973, as amended at 56 FR 66784, Dec. 26, 1991]

PART 118—DETENTION; SEIZURE AND CONDEMNATION

Sec.

AUTHORITY: 21 U.S.C. 151–159; 7 CFR 2.22, 2.80, and 371.4.

SOURCE: 52 FR 30135, Aug. 13, 1987, unless otherwise noted.

§ 118.1 Administrative detention.

Whenever any biological product which is prepared, sold, bartered, exchanged, or shipped in violation of the Act or regulations is found by any authorized representative of the Administrator upon any premises, it may be detained by such representative for a period not to exceed 20 days, pending action under § 118.4, and shall not be moved by any person from the place at which it is located when so detained, until released by such representative.

[52 FR 30135, Aug. 13, 1987, as amended at 56 FR 66784, Dec. 26, 1991]

§ 118.2 Method of detention; Notifications.

An authorized representative of the Administrator shall detain any biological product subject to detention under this part by:

(a) Giving oral notification to the owner of the biological product if such owner can be ascertained, and, if not, to the agent representing the owner or to the immediate custodian of the biological product; and

(b) Promptly furnishing the person so notified with a preliminary notice of detention which shall include identity and quantity of the product detained, the location where detained, the reason for the detention, and the name of the authorized representative of the Administrator.

(c) Within 48 hours after the detention of any biological product, an authorized representative of the Administrator shall, if the detention is to continue, give written notification to the owner of the biological product detained by furnishing a written statement which shall include the identity and quantity of the product detained, the location where detained, specific description of the alleged noncompliance including reference to the provisions in the Act or the regulations which have resulted in the detention, and the identity of the authorized representative of the Administrator; or, if such owner cannot be ascertained and notified within such period of time, furnish such notice to the agent representing such owner, or the carrier or other person having custody of the biological product detained. The notification, with a copy of the preliminary notice of detention shall be served by either delivering the notification to the owner or to the agent or to such other person, or by certifying and mailing the notification, addressed to such owner, agent, or other person, at the last known residence or principal office or place of business.

[52 FR 30135, Aug. 13, 1987, as amended at 56 FR 66784, Dec. 26, 1991]

§ 118.3 Movement of detained biological products; Termination of detention.

Except as provided in paragraphs (a) and (b) of this section, no biological product detained in accordance with the provisions in this part shall be moved by any person from the place at which such product is located when it is detained.

(a) A detained biological product may be moved from the place at which it is located when so detained for the purpose of providing proper storage conditions if such movement has been approved by an authorized representative of the Administrator; *Provided*, That, the biological product so moved shall be detained by an authorized representative of the Administrator after such movement.

(b) A detained biological product may be moved from the place at which it is detained on written notification by an authorized representative of the Administrator that the detention is terminated; *Provided*, That, the conditions under which the detained biological product may be moved will be specified in the written notification of the termination. The notification of termination shall be served by either personally delivering the notification, or by certifying and mailing the notification addressed to such person at the last known residence or principal office or place of business of the owner, agent, or other person having custody of the biological product.

[52 FR 30135, Aug. 13, 1987, as amended at 56 FR 66784, Dec. 26, 1991]

§ 118.4 Seizure and condemnation.

Any biological product which is prepared, sold, bartered, exchanged, or shipped in violation of the Act or regulations shall be liable to be proceeded against and seized and condemned, at any time, on a libel of information in any United States district court or other proper court within the jurisdiction of which the product is found. If the product is condemned, it shall, after entry of the decree, be disposed of by destruction or sale as the court may direct, and the proceeds, if sold, less the court costs and fees, and storage and other proper expenses, shall be paid into the Treasury of the United States, but the product shall not be sold contrary to the provisions of the Act or the laws of the jurisdiction in which it is sold; *Provided*, That, upon the execution and delivery of a good and sufficient bond conditioned that the product shall not be sold or otherwise disposed of contrary to the provisions of the Act or the laws or jurisdiction in which disposal is made, the court may direct that such product be delivered to the owner thereof subject to such supervision by authorized representatives of the Administrator as is necessary to ensure compliance with the applicable laws. When a decree of condemnation is entered against the product and it is released under bond, or destroyed, court costs and fees, and storage and other proper expenses shall be awarded against the person, if any, intervening as claimant of the product. The proceedings in such libel cases shall conform, as nearly as may be practicable, to the proceedings in admiralty, except that either party may demand trial by jury of any issue of fact joined in any case, and all such proceedings shall be at the suit of and in the name of the United States.

[52 FR 30135, Aug. 13, 1987, as amended at 56 FR 66784, Dec. 26, 1991]

PART 121—POSSESSION, USE, AND TRANSFER OF SELECT AGENTS AND TOXINS

Sec.

AUTHORITY: 7 U.S.C. 8401; 7 CFR 2.22, 2.80, and 371.4.

SOURCE: 70 FR 13284, Mar. 18, 2005, unless otherwise noted.

§ 121.1 Definitions.

Administrator. The Administrator, Animal and Plant Health Inspection Service, or any person authorized to act for the Administrator.

Animal and Plant Health Inspection Service (APHIS). The Animal and Plant Health Inspection Service of the U.S. Department of Agriculture.

Attorney General. The Attorney General of the United States or any person authorized to act for the Attorney General.

Biological agent. Any microorganism (including, but not limited to, bacteria, viruses, fungi, or protozoa), or infectious substance, or any naturally occurring, bioengineered, or synthesized component of any such microorganism or infectious substance, capable of causing:

(1) Death, disease, or other biological malfunction in a human, an animal, a plant, or another living organism;

(2) Deterioration of food, water, equipment, supplies, or material of any kind; or

(3) Deleterious alteration of the environment.

Centers for Disease Control and Prevention (CDC). The Centers for Disease Control and Prevention of the U.S. Department of Health and Human Services.

Diagnosis. The analysis of specimens for the purpose of identifying or confirming the presence or characteristics of a select agent or toxin, provided that such analysis is directly related to protecting the public health or safety, animal health or animal products, or plant health or plant products.

Entity. Any government agency (Federal, State, or local), academic institution, corporation, company, partnership, society, association, firm, sole proprietorship, or other legal entity.

HHS Secretary. The Secretary of the Department of Health and Human Services or his or her designee, unless otherwise specified.

HHS select agent and/or toxin. A biological agent or toxin listed in 42 CFR 73.3.

Import. To move into, or the act of movement into, the territorial limits of the United States.

Information security. Protecting information and information systems from unauthorized access, use, disclosure, disruption, modification, or destruction in order to provide:

(1) *Integrity,* which means guarding against improper information modification or destruction, and includes ensuring information authenticity;

(2) *Confidentiality,* which means preserving authorized restrictions on access and disclosure, including means for protecting personal privacy and proprietary information; and

(3) *Availability,* which means ensuring timely and reliable access to and use of information.

Interstate. From one State into or through any other State, or within the District of Columbia, Guam, the Virgin Islands of the United States, or any other territory or possession of the United States.

Occupational exposure. Any reasonably anticipated skin, eye, mucous membrane, parenteral contact, or respiratory aerosol exposure to select agents or toxins that may result from the performance of an employee's duties.

Overlap select agent and/or toxin. A biological agent or toxin that is listed in § 121.4 and 42 CFR 73.4.

Permit. A written authorization by the Administrator to import or move interstate select agents or toxins, under conditions prescribed by the Administrator.

Principal investigator. The one individual who is designated by the entity to direct a project or program and who is responsible to the entity for the scientific and technical direction of that project or program.

Proficiency testing. The process of determining the competency of an individual or laboratory to perform a specified test or procedure.

Recombinant nucleic acids. (1) Molecules that are constructed by joining nucleic acid molecules and that can replicate in a living cell; or

(2) Molecules that result from the replication of those described in paragraph (1) of this definition.

Responsible official. The individual designated by an entity with the authority and control to ensure compliance with the regulations in this part.

Security barrier. A physical structure that is designed to prevent entry by unauthorized persons.

Select agent and/or toxin. Unless otherwise specified, all of the biological agents or toxins listed in §§ 121.3 and 121.4.

Specimen. Samples of material from humans, animals, plants, or the environment, or isolates or cultures from such samples, for diagnosis, verification, or proficiency testing.

State. Any of the several States of the United States, the Commonwealth of the Northern Mariana Islands, the Commonwealth of Puerto Rico, the District of Columbia, Guam, the Virgin Islands of the United States, or any other territory or possession of the United States.

Synthetic nucleic acids. (1) Molecules that are chemically or by other means synthesized or amplified, including those that are chemically or otherwise modified but can base pair with naturally occurring nucleic acid molecules (*i.e.*, synthetic nucleic acids); or

(2) Molecules that result from the replication of those described in paragraph (1) of this definition.

Toxin. The toxic material or product of plants, animals, microorganisms (including, but not limited to, bacteria, viruses, fungi, or protozoa), or infectious substances, or a recombinant or synthesized molecule, whatever their origin and method of production, and includes:

(1) Any poisonous substance or biological product that may be engineered as a result of biotechnology produced by a living organism; or

(2) Any poisonous isomer or biological product, homolog, or derivative of such a substance.

United States. All of the States.

USDA. The U.S. Department of Agriculture.

Validated inactivation procedure. A procedure, whose efficacy is confirmed by data generated from a viability testing protocol, to render a select agent non-viable but allows the select agent to retain characteristics of interest for future use; or to render any nucleic acids that can produce infectious forms of any select agent virus non-infectious for future use.

Verification. The demonstration of obtaining established performance (e.g., accuracy, precision, and the analytical sensitivity and specificity) specifications for any procedure used for diagnosis.

Viability testing protocol. A protocol to confirm the validated inactivation procedure by demonstrating the material is free of all viable select agent.

VS. The Veterinary Services Programs of the Animal and Plant Health Inspection Service.

VS select agent and/or toxin. A biological agent or toxin listed in § 121.3.

[70 FR 13284, Mar. 18, 2005, as amended at 77 FR 61077, Oct. 5, 2012; 82 FR 6206, Jan. 19, 2017]

§ 121.2 Purpose and scope.

This part implements the provisions of the Agricultural Bioterrorism Protection Act of 2002 setting forth the requirements for possession, use, and transfer of select agents and toxins. The biological agents and toxins listed in this part have the potential to pose a severe threat to public health and safety, to animal health, or to animal products. Overlap select agents and toxins are subject to regulation by both APHIS and CDC.

§ 121.3 VS select agents and toxins.

(a) Except as provided in paragraphs (d) and (e) of this section, the Administrator has determined that the biological agents and toxins listed in this section have the potential to pose a severe threat to animal health or to animal products. The select agents and toxins marked with an asterisk (*) are designated as Tier 1 select agents and toxins and are subject to additional requirements as listed in this part.

(b) VS select agents and toxins: African horse sickness virus; African swine fever virus; Avian influenza virus; Classical swine fever virus; *Foot-and-mouth disease virus; Goat pox virus; Lumpy skin disease virus; *Mycoplasma* *capricolum*; *Mycoplasma mycoides*; Newcastle disease virus;[1] Peste des petits ruminants virus; *Rinderpest virus; Sheep pox virus; Swine vesicular disease virus.

(c) Genetic elements, recombinant and/or synthetic nucleic acids, and recombinant and/or synthetic organisms:

(1) Nucleic acids that can produce infectious forms of any of the select agent viruses listed in paragraph (b) of this section.[2]

(2) Recombinant and/or synthetic nucleic acids that encode for the functional forms of any toxin listed in paragraph (b) of this section if the nucleic acids:

(i) Can be expressed *in vivo* or *in vitro;* or

(ii) Are in a vector or recombinant host genome and can be expressed *in vivo* or *in vitro*.

(3) VS select agents and toxins listed in paragraph (b) of this section that have been genetically modified.

(d) VS select agents or toxins that meet any of the following criteria are excluded from the requirements of this part:

(1) Any VS select agent or toxin that is in its naturally occurring environment, provided that the agent or toxin has not been intentionally introduced, cultivated, collected, or otherwise extracted from its natural source.

(2) Nonviable VS select agents or nontoxic VS toxins.[3]

(3) A select agent or toxin that has been subjected to decontamination or a destruction procedure when intended for waste disposal.

(4) A select agent or regulated nucleic acids that can produce infectious forms of any select agent virus that has been subjected to a validated inactivation procedure that is confirmed through a viability testing protocol. Surrogate strains that are known to possess equivalent properties with respect to inactivation can be used to validate an inactivation procedure; however, if there are known strain-to-strain variations in the resistance of a select agent to an inactivation procedure, then an inactivation procedure validated on a lesser resistant strain must also be validated on the more resistant strains.

(5) Material containing a select agent that is subjected to a procedure that removes all viable select agent cells, spores, or virus particles if the material is subjected to a viability testing protocol to ensure that the removal method has rendered the material free of all viable select agent.

(6) A select agent or regulated nucleic acids that can produce infectious forms of any select agent virus not subjected to a validated inactivation procedure or material containing a select agent not subjected to a procedure that removes all viable select agent cells, spores, or virus particles if the material is determined by the Administrator to be effectively inactivated or effectively removed. To apply for a determination an individual or entity must submit a written request and supporting scientific information to APHIS. A written decision granting or denying the request will be issued.

(7) A VS select toxin identified in an original food sample or clinical sample.

(8) Waste generated during the delivery of patient care by health care professionals from a patient diagnosed with an illness or condition associated with a select agent, where that waste is decontaminated or transferred for destruction by complying with State and Federal regulations within 7 calendar days of the conclusion of patient care.

(9) Any low pathogenic strains of avian influenza virus, avian paramyxovirus serotype-1 (APMV–1) viruses which do not meet the criteria

[1] A virulent Newcastle disease virus (avian paramyxovirus serotype 1) has an intracerebral pathogenicity index in day-old chicks (*Gallus gallus*) of 0.7 or greater or has an amino acid sequence at the fusion (F) protein cleavage site that is consistent with virulent strains of Newcastle disease virus. A failure to detect a cleavage site that is consistent with virulent strains does not confirm the absence of a virulent virus.

[2] The importation and interstate movement of VS select agents or toxins listed in paragraphs (c)(1) through (c)(3) of this section may be subject to the permit requirements under part 122 of this subchapter.

[3] However, the importation and interstate movement of these nonviable select agents may be subject to the permit requirements under part 122 of this subchapter.

for Newcastle disease virus,[4] including those identified as pigeon paramyxovirus-12[5] isolated from a non-poultry species, all subspecies *Mycoplasma capricolum* except subspecies *capripneumoniae* (contagious caprine pleuropneumonia), and all subspecies *Mycoplasma mycoides* except subspecies *mycoides* small colony (*Mmm* SC) (contagious bovine pleuropneumonia), provided that the individual or entity can identify that the agent is within the exclusion category.

(e) An attenuated strain of a select agent or a select toxin modified to be less potent or toxic may be excluded from the requirements of this part based upon a determination by the Administrator that the attenuated strain or modified toxin does not pose a severe threat to animal health or animal products.

(1) To apply for exclusion, an individual or entity must submit a written request and supporting scientific information. A written decision granting or denying the request will be issued. An exclusion will be effective upon notification to the applicant. Exclusions will be listed on the National Select Agent Registry Web site at *http://www.selectagents.gov/*.

(2) If an excluded attenuated strain or modified toxin is subjected to any manipulation that restores or enhances its virulence or toxic activity, the resulting select agent or toxin will be subject to the requirements of this part.

(3) An individual or entity may make a written request to the Administrator for reconsideration of a decision denying an application for the exclusion of an attenuated strain of a select agent or a select toxin modified to be less potent or toxic. The written request for reconsideration must state the facts and reasoning upon which the individual or entity relies to show the decision was incorrect. The Administrator will grant or deny the request for reconsideration as promptly as circumstances allow and will state, in writing, the reasons for the decision.

(f) Any VS select agent or toxin seized by a Federal law enforcement agency will be excluded from the requirements of this part during the period between seizure of the agent or toxin and the transfer or destruction of such agent or toxin provided that:

(1) As soon as practicable, the Federal law enforcement agency transfers the seized agent or toxin to an entity eligible to receive such agent or toxin or destroys the agent or toxin by a recognized sterilization or inactivation process.

(2) The Federal law enforcement agency safeguards and secures the seized agent or toxin against theft, loss, or release, and reports any theft, loss, or release of such agent or toxin.

(3) The Federal law enforcement agency reports the seizure of the select agent or toxin to APHIS or CDC.

(i) The seizure of any of the following VS select agents and toxins must be reported within 24 hours by telephone, facsimile, or e-mail: African horse sickness virus, African swine fever virus, avian influenza virus (highly pathogenic), bovine spongiform encephalopathy agent, classical swine fever virus, foot-and-mouth disease virus, virulent Newcastle disease virus, rinderpest virus, and swine vesicular disease virus. This report must be followed by submission of APHIS/CDC Form 4 within 7 calendar days after seizure of the select agent or toxin.

(ii) For all other VS select agents or toxins, APHIS/CDC Form 4 must be submitted within 7 calendar days after seizure of the agent or toxin.

(iii) A copy of APHIS/CDC Form 4 must be maintained for 3 years.

(4) The Federal law enforcement agency reports the final disposition of the select agent or toxin by submission of APHIS/CDC Form 4. A copy of the

---

[4] An APMV–1 virus isolated from poultry which has an intracerebral pathogenicity index in day-old chicks (*Gallus gallus*) of 0.7 or greater or has an amino acid sequence at the fusion (F) protein cleavage site that is consistent with virulent strains of Newcastle disease virus. A failure to detect a cleavage site that is consistent with virulent strains does not confirm the absence of a virulent virus.

[5] Pigeon paramyxovirus (PPMV–1) is a species-adapted APMV–1 virus which is endemic in pigeons and doves in the United States and can be identified through monoclonal antibody testing and demonstration of their characteristic amino acid signature at the fusion gene cleavage site.

completed form must be maintained for 3 years.

[70 FR 13284, Mar. 18, 2005, as amended at 73 FR 61331, Oct. 16, 2008; 77 FR 61077, Oct. 5, 2012; 79 FR 26830, May 12, 2014; 82 FR 6207, Jan. 19, 2017]

§ 121.4 Overlap select agents and toxins.

(a) Except as provided in paragraphs (d) and (e) of this section, the Administrator has determined that the biological agents and toxins listed in this section have the potential to pose a severe threat to public health and safety, to animal health, or to animal products. The select agents and toxins marked with an asterisk (*) are designated as Tier 1 select agents and toxins and are subject to additional requirements as listed in this part.

(b) Overlap select agents and toxins: **Bacillus anthracis; Bacillus anthracis* (Pasteur strain); *Brucella abortus; Brucella melitensis; Brucella suis;* **Burkholderia mallei;* **Burkholderia pseudomallei;* Hendra virus; Nipah virus; Rift Valley fever virus; Venezuelan equine encephalitis virus.

(c) Genetic elements, recombinant and/or synthetic nucleic acids, and recombinant and/or synthetic organisms:

(1) Nucleic acids that can produce infectious forms of any of the overlap select agent viruses listed in paragraph (b) of this section.[6]

(2) Recombinant and/or synthetic nucleic acids that encode for the toxic forms of any overlap toxin listed in paragraph (b) of this section if the nucleic acids:

(i) Can be expressed *in vivo* or *in vitro;* or

(ii) Are in a vector or recombinant host genome and can be expressed *in vivo* or *in vitro.*

(3) Overlap select agents and toxins listed in paragraph (b) of this section that have been genetically modified.

(d) Overlap select agents or toxins that meet any of the following criteria are excluded from the requirements of this part:

(1) Any overlap select agent or toxin that is in its naturally occurring environment, provided that the agent or toxin has not been intentionally introduced, cultivated, collected, or otherwise extracted from its natural source.

(2) Nonviable overlap select agents or nontoxic overlap toxins.[7]

(3) A select agent or toxin that has been subjected to decontamination or a destruction procedure when intended for waste disposal.

(4) A select agent or regulated nucleic acids that can produce infectious forms of any select agent virus that has been subjected to a validated inactivation procedure that is confirmed through a viability testing protocol. Surrogate strains that are known to possess equivalent properties with respect to inactivation can be used to validate an inactivation procedure; however, if there are known strain-to-strain variations in the resistance of a select agent to an inactivation procedure, then an inactivation procedure validated on a lesser resistant strain must also be validated on the more resistant strains.

(5) Material containing a select agent that is subjected to a procedure that removes all viable select agent cells, spores, or virus particles if the material is subjected to a viability testing protocol to ensure that the removal method has rendered the material free of all viable select agent.

(6) A select agent or regulated nucleic acids that can produce infectious forms of any select agent virus not subjected to a validated inactivation procedure or material containing a select agent not subjected to a procedure that removes all viable select agent cells, spores, or virus particles if the material is determined by the Administrator or HHS Secretary to be effectively inactivated or effectively removed. To apply for a determination an individual or entity must submit a written request and supporting scientific information to APHIS or CDC. A written decision granting or denying the request will be issued.

[6] The importation and interstate movement of overlap select agents or toxins listed in paragraphs (c)(1) through (c)(3) of this section may be subject to the permit requirements under part 122 of this subchapter.

[7] However, the importation and interstate movement of these nonviable overlap select agents may be subject to the permit requirements under part 122 of this subchapter.

(7) An overlap select toxin identified in an original food sample or clinical sample.

(8) Waste generated during the delivery of patient care by health care professionals from a patient diagnosed with an illness or condition associated with a select agent, where that waste is decontaminated or transferred for destruction by complying with State and Federal regulations within 7 calendar days of the conclusion of patient care.

(9) Any subtypes of Venezuelan equine encephalitis virus except for Subtypes IAB or IC, provided that the individual or entity can identify that the agent is within the exclusion category.

(e) An attenuated strain of a select agent or a select toxin modified to be less potent or toxic may be excluded from the requirements of this part based upon a determination by the Administrator that the attenuated strain or modified toxin does not pose a severe threat to public health and safety, animal health, or animal products.

(1) To apply for exclusion, an individual or entity must submit a written request and supporting scientific information. A written decision granting or denying the request will be issued. An exclusion will be effective upon notification to the applicant. Exclusions will be listed on the National Select Agent Registry Web site at *http://www.selectagents.gov/*.

(2) If an excluded attenuated strain or modified toxin is subjected to any manipulation that restores or enhances its virulence or toxic activity, the resulting select agent or toxin will be subject to the requirements of this part.

(3) An individual or entity may make a written request to the Administrator or HHS Secretary for reconsideration of a decision denying an application for the exclusion of an attenuated strain of a select agent or a select toxin modified to be less potent or toxic. The written request for reconsideration must state the facts and reasoning upon which the individual or entity relies to show the decision was incorrect. The Administrator or HHS Secretary will grant or deny the request for reconsideration as promptly as circumstances allow and will state, in writing, the reasons for the decision.

(f) Any overlap select agent or toxin seized by a Federal law enforcement agency will be excluded from the requirements of this part during the period between seizure of the agent or toxin and the transfer or destruction of such agent or toxin provided that:

(1) As soon as practicable, the Federal law enforcement agency transfers the seized agent or toxin to an entity eligible to receive such agent or toxin or destroys the agent or toxin by a recognized sterilization or inactivation process.

(2) The Federal law enforcement agency safeguards and secures the seized agent or toxin against theft, loss, or release, and reports any theft, loss, or release of such agent or toxin.

(3) The Federal law enforcement agency reports the seizure of the overlap select agent or toxin to APHIS or CDC.

(i) The seizure of any of the following overlap select agents and toxins must be reported within 24 hours by telephone, facsimile, or e-mail: *Bacillus anthracis*, *Burkholderia mallei*, or *Burkholderia pseudomallei*. This report must be followed by submission of APHIS/CDC Form 4 within 7 calendar days after seizure of the overlap select agent or toxin.

(ii) For all other overlap select agents or toxins, APHIS/CDC Form 4 must be submitted within 7 calendar days after seizure of the agent or toxin.

(iii) A copy of APHIS/CDC Form 4 must be maintained for 3 years.

(4) The Federal law enforcement agency reports the final disposition of the overlap select agent or toxin by submission of APHIS/CDC Form 4. A copy of the completed form must be maintained for 3 years.

[70 FR 13284, Mar. 18, 2005, as amended at 73 FR 61331, Oct. 16, 2008; 77 FR 61078, Oct. 5, 2012; 79 FR 26830, May 12, 2014; 82 FR 6207, Jan. 19, 2017]

§ 121.5 Exemptions for VS select agents and toxins.

(a) Diagnostic laboratories and other entities that possess, use, or transfer a VS select agent or toxin that is contained in a specimen presented for diagnosis or verification will be exempt from the requirements of this part for such agent or toxin contained in the specimen, provided that:

(1) Unless directed otherwise by the Administrator, within 7 calendar days after identification of the select agent or toxin, the select agent or toxin is transferred in accordance with § 121.16 or destroyed on-site by a recognized sterilization or inactivation process;

(2) The agent or toxin is secured against theft, loss, or release during the period between identification of the agent or toxin and transfer or destruction of such agent or toxin, and any theft, loss, or release of such agent or toxin is reported;

(3) Unless otherwise directed by the Administrator, the clinical or diagnostic specimens collected from a patient infected with a select agent are transferred in accordance with § 121.16 or destroyed on-site by a recognized sterilization or inactivation process within 7 calendar days after delivery of patient care by heath care professionals has concluded; and

(4) The identification of the agent or toxin is reported to APHIS or CDC, the specimen provider, and to other appropriate authorities when required by Federal, State, or local law by telephone, facsimile, or email. This report must be followed by submission of APHIS/CDC Form 4 to APHIS or CDC within 7 calendar days after identification.

(b) Diagnostic laboratories and other entities that possess, use, or transfer a VS select agent or toxin that is contained in a specimen presented for proficiency testing will be exempt from the requirements of this part for such agent or toxin contained in the specimen, provided that:

(1) Unless directed otherwise by the Administrator, within 90 calendar days of receipt, the agent or toxin is transferred in accordance with § 121.16 or destroyed on-site by a recognized sterilization or inactivation process;

(2) The agent or toxin is secured against theft, loss, or release during the period between identification of the agent or toxin and transfer or destruction of such agent or toxin, and any theft, loss, or release of such agent or toxin is reported; and

(3) The identification of the agent or toxin, and its derivative, is reported to APHIS or CDC. To report the identification of a select agent or toxin, APHIS/CDC Form 4 must be submitted within 90 days of receipt of the agent or toxin. A copy of the completed form must be maintained for 3 years.

(c) Diagnostic reagents and vaccines that are, bear, or contain VS select agents or toxins that are produced at USDA diagnostic facilities will be exempt from the requirements of this part.

(d) Unless the Administrator by order determines that additional regulation is necessary to protect animal health or animal products, products that are, bear, or contain VS select agents or toxins will be exempt from the requirements of this part if the products have been cleared, approved, licensed, or registered pursuant to:

(1) The Federal Food, Drug, and Cosmetic Act (21 U.S.C. 301 *et seq.*);

(2) Section 351 of Public Health Service Act (42 U.S.C. 262);

(3) The Virus-Serum-Toxin Act (21 U.S.C. 151–159); or

(4) The Federal Insecticide, Fungicide, and Rodenticide Act (7 U.S.C. 131 *et seq.*).

(e) The Administrator may exempt from the requirements of this part an experimental product that is, bears, or contains a VS select agent or toxin if such product is being used in an investigation authorized by any Federal law and the Administrator determines that additional regulation under this part is not necessary to protect animal health or animal products. To apply for an exemption, an individual or entity must submit APHIS/CDC Form 5. A written decision granting or denying the exemption will be issued. The applicant must notify APHIS when an authorization for an investigation no longer exists. This exemption automatically terminates when such authorization is no longer in effect.

(f) In addition to the exemptions provided in paragraphs (a) through (e) of this section, the Administrator may grant a specific exemption upon a showing of good cause and upon his or her determination that such exemption is consistent with protecting animal health or animal products. An individual or entity may request in writing an exemption from the requirements of this part. If granted, such exemptions are valid for a maximum of 3 years; thereafter, an individual or entity must request a new exemption. If a request for exemption is denied, an individual or entity may request reconsideration in writing to the Administrator. The request for reconsideration must state all of the facts and reasons upon which the individual or entity relies to show that the exemption was wrongfully denied. The Administrator will grant or deny the request for reconsideration as promptly as circumstances allow and will state, in writing, the reasons for the decision.

[70 FR 13284, Mar. 18, 2005, as amended at 73 FR 61331, Oct. 16, 2008; 77 FR 61078, Oct. 5, 2012; 79 FR 26831, May 12, 2014; 82 FR 6208, Jan. 19, 2017]

§ 121.6 Exemptions for overlap select agents and toxins.

(a) Clinical or diagnostic laboratories and other entities that possess, use, or transfer an overlap select agent or toxin that is contained in a specimen presented for diagnosis or verification will be exempt from the requirements of this part for such agent or toxin contained in the specimen, provided that:

(1) Unless directed otherwise by the Administrator, within 7 calendar days after identification of the select agent or toxin, the select agent or toxin is transferred in accordance with § 121.16 or destroyed on-site by a recognized sterilization or inactivation process;

(2) The agent or toxin is secured against theft, loss, or release during the period between identification of the agent or toxin and transfer or destruction of such agent or toxin, and any theft, loss, or release of such agent or toxin is reported;

(3) Unless otherwise directed by the Administrator or HHS Secretary, the clinical or diagnostic specimens collected from a patient infected with a select agent are transferred in accordance with § 121.16 or destroyed on-site by a recognized sterilization or inactivation process within 7 calendar days after delivery of patient care by heath care professionals has concluded; and

(4) The identification of the agent or toxin is reported to APHIS or CDC, the specimen provider, and to other appropriate authorities when required by Federal, State, or local law by telephone, facsimile, or email. This report must be followed by submission of APHIS/CDC Form 4 to APHIS or CDC within 7 calendar days after identification.

(b) Clinical or diagnostic laboratories and other entities that possess, use, or transfer an overlap select agent or toxin that is contained in a specimen presented for proficiency testing will be exempt from the requirements of this part for such agent or toxin contained in the specimen, provided that:

(1) Unless directed otherwise by the Administrator or the HHS Secretary, within 90 days of receipt, the agent or toxin is transferred in accordance with § 121.16 or 42 CFR 73.16 or destroyed on-site by a recognized sterilization or inactivation process;

(2) The agent or toxin is secured against theft, loss, or release during the period between identification of the agent or toxin and transfer or destruction of such agent or toxin, and any theft, loss, or release of such agent or toxin is reported; and

(3) The identification of the agent or toxin, and its derivative, is reported to APHIS or CDC. To report the identification of an overlap select agent or toxin, APHIS/CDC Form 4 must be submitted within 90 calendar days of receipt of the agent or toxin. A copy of the completed form must be maintained for 3 years.

(c) Unless the Administrator by order determines that additional regulation of a specific product is necessary to protect animal health or animal products, products that are, bear, or contain overlap select agents or toxins will be exempt from the requirements of this part if the products have been cleared, approved, licensed, or registered pursuant to:

(1) The Federal Food, Drug, and Cosmetic Act (21 U.S.C. 301 *et seq.*);

(2) Section 351 of Public Health Service Act (42 U.S.C. 262);

(3) The Virus-Serum-Toxin Act (21 U.S.C. 151–159); or

(4) The Federal Insecticide, Fungicide, and Rodenticide Act (7 U.S.C. 131 *et seq.*).

(d) After consultation with the HHS Secretary, the Administrator may exempt from the requirements of this part an investigational product that is, bears, or contains an overlap select agent or toxin if such product is being used in an investigation authorized by any Federal law and the Administrator determines that additional regulation under this part is not necessary to protect animal health or animal products.

(1) To apply for an exemption, an individual or entity must submit APHIS/CDC Form 5.

(2) The Administrator will make a determination regarding an exemption within 14 calendar days after receipt of the application and notification that the investigation has been authorized under a Federal law. A written decision granting or denying the exemption will be issued.

(3) The applicant must notify APHIS or CDC when an authorization for an investigation no longer exists. This exemption automatically terminates when such authorization is no longer in effect.

(e) If it is necessary to respond to a domestic or foreign agricultural emergency involving an overlap select agent or toxin, the Administrator may exempt an individual or entity from the requirements, in whole or in part, of this part for up to 30 calendar days. The Administrator may extend the exemption once for an additional 30 days.

(f) Upon request of the Secretary of Health and Human Services, the Administrator may exempt an individual or entity from the requirements, in whole or in part, of this part for up to 30 calendar days if the Secretary of Health and Human Services has granted an exemption for a public health emergency involving an overlap select agent or toxin. The Administrator may extend the exemption once for an additional 30 days.

[70 FR 13284, Mar. 18, 2005, as amended at 73 FR 61331, Oct. 16, 2008; 77 FR 61078, Oct. 5, 2012; 79 FR 26831, May 12, 2014; 82 FR 6208, Jan. 19, 2017]

§ 121.7 Registration and related security risk assessments.

(a) Unless exempted under § 121.5, an individual or entity shall not possess, use, or transfer any VS select agent or toxin without a certificate of registration issued by the Administrator. Unless exempted under § 121.6 or 42 CFR 73.6, an individual or entity shall not possess, use, or transfer any overlap select agent or toxin without a certificate of registration issued by the Administrator and the HHS Secretary.

(b) As a condition of registration, each entity is required to be in compliance with the requirements of this part for select agents and toxins listed on the registration regardless of whether the entity is in actual possession of the select agent or toxin. With regard to toxins, the entity registered for possession, use, or transfer of a toxin must be in compliance with the requirements of this part regardless of the amount of toxins currently in its possession.

(c) As a condition of registration, each entity must designate an individual to be its responsible official. While most registrants are likely to be entities, in the event that an individual applies for and is granted a certificate of registration, the individual will be considered the responsible official.

(d)(1) As a condition of registration, the following must be approved by the Administrator or the HHS Secretary based on a security risk assessment by the Attorney General:

(i) The individual or entity;

(ii) The responsible official; and

(iii) Unless otherwise exempted under this section, any individual who owns or controls the entity.

(2) Federal, State, or local governmental agencies, including public accredited academic institutions, are exempt from the security risk assessments for the entity and the individual who owns or controls such entity.

(3) An individual will be deemed to own or control an entity under the following conditions: [8]

(i) For a private institution of higher education, an individual will be deemed

[8] These conditions may apply to more than one individual.

to own or control the entity if the individual is in a managerial or executive capacity with regard to the entity's select agents or toxins or with regard to the individuals with access to the select agents or toxins possessed, used, or transferred by the entity.

(ii) For entities other than institutions of higher education, an individual will be deemed to own or control the entity if the individual:

(A) Owns 50 percent or more of the entity, or is a holder or owner of 50 percent or more of its voting stock; or

(B) Is in a managerial or executive capacity with regard to the entity's select agents or toxins or with regard to the individuals with access to the select agents or toxins possessed, used, or transferred by the entity.

(4) An entity will be considered to be an institution of higher education if it is an institution of higher education as defined in section 101(a) of the Higher Education Act of 1965 (20 U.S.C. 1001(a)), or is an organization described in 501(c)(3) of the Internal Revenue Code of 1986, as amended (26 U.S.C. 501(c)(3)).

(5) To obtain a security risk assessment, an individual or entity must submit the information necessary to conduct a security risk assessment to the Attorney General.

(e) To apply for a certificate of registration for only VS select agents or toxins, or for VS and PPQ select agents or toxins, an individual or entity must submit the information requested in the registration application package (APHIS/CDC Form 1) to APHIS. To apply for a certificate of registration for overlap select agents or toxins, overlap select agents or toxins and any combination of PPQ or VS select agents or toxins, or HHS select agents or toxins and any combination of PPQ or VS select agents or toxins, an individual or entity must submit the information requested in the registration application package (APHIS/CDC Form 1) to APHIS or CDC, but not both.

(f) Prior to the issuance of a certificate of registration, the responsible official must promptly provide notification of any changes to the application for registration by submitting the relevant page(s) of the registration application.

(g) The issuance of a certificate of registration may be contingent upon inspection or submission of additional information, such as the security plan, biosafety plan, incident response plan, or any other documents required to be prepared under this part.

(h) A certificate of registration will be valid for one physical location (a room, a building, or a group of buildings) where the responsible official will be able to perform the responsibilities required in this part, for specific select agents or toxins, and for specific activities.

(i) A certificate of registration may be amended to reflect changes in circumstances (e.g., replacement of the responsible official or other personnel changes, changes in ownership or control of the entity, changes in the activities involving any select agents or toxins, or the addition or removal of select agents or toxins).

(1) Prior to any change, the responsible official must apply for an amendment to a certificate of registration by submitting the relevant page(s) of the registration application.[9]

(2) The responsible official will be notified in writing if an application to amend a certificate of registration has been approved. Approval of an amendment may be contingent upon an inspection or submission of additional information, such as the security plan, biosafety plan, incident response plan, or any other documents required to be prepared under this part.

(3) No change may be made without such approval.

(j) An entity must immediately notify APHIS or CDC if it loses the services of its responsible official. In the event that an entity loses the services of its responsible official, an entity may continue to possess or use select agents or toxins only if it appoints as the responsible official another individual who has been approved by the Administrator or the HHS Secretary following a security risk assessment by

[9] Depending on the change, a security risk assessment by the Attorney General may also be required (e.g., replacement of the responsible official, changes in ownership or control of the entity, new researchers or graduate students, etc.)

the Attorney General and who meets the requirements of this part.

(k) A certificate of registration will be terminated upon the written request of the entity if the entity no longer possesses or uses any select agents or toxins and no longer wishes to be registered.

(l) A certificate of registration will be valid for a maximum of 3 years.

[70 FR 13284, Mar. 18, 2005, as amended at 73 FR 61331, Oct. 16, 2008; 82 FR 6208, Jan. 19, 2017]

§ 121.8 Denial, revocation, or suspension of registration.

(a) An application may be denied or a certificate of registration revoked or suspended if:

(1) The individual or entity, the responsible official, or an individual who owns or controls the entity is within any of the categories described in 18 U.S.C. 175b;

(2) The individual or entity, the responsible official, or an individual who owns or controls the entity is reasonably suspected by any Federal law enforcement or intelligence agency of:

(i) Committing a crime set forth in 18 U.S.C. 2332b(g)(5); or

(ii) Knowing involvement with an organization that engages in domestic or international terrorism (as defined in 18 U.S.C. 2331) or with any other organization that engages in intentional crimes of violence; or

(iii) Being an agent of a foreign power as defined in 50 U.S.C. 1801;

(3) The individual or entity does not meet the requirements of this part;[10] or

(4) It is determined that such action is necessary to protect animal health or animal products.

(b) Upon revocation or suspension of a certificate of registration, the individual or entity must:

(1) Immediately stop all use of each select agent or toxin covered by the revocation or suspension order;

(2) Immediately safeguard and secure each select agent or toxin covered by the revocation or suspension order from theft, loss, or release; and

(3) Comply with all disposition instructions issued by the Administrator for each select agent or toxin covered by the revocation or suspension.

(c) Denial of an application for registration and revocation of registration may be appealed under § 121.20. However, any denial of an application for registration or revocation of a certificate of registration will remain in effect until a final agency decision has been rendered.

[70 FR 13284, Mar. 18, 2005, as amended at 73 FR 61331, Oct. 16, 2008; 82 FR 6208, Jan. 19, 2017]

§ 121.9 Responsible official.

(a) An individual or entity required to register under this part must designate an individual to be the responsible official. The responsible official must.

(1) Be approved by the Administrator or the HHS Secretary following a security risk assessment by the Attorney General.

(2) Be familiar with the requirements of this part.

(3) Have authority and responsibility to act on behalf of the entity.

(4) Ensure compliance with the requirements of this part.

(5) Have a physical (and not merely a telephonic or audio/visual) presence at the registered entity to ensure that the entity is in compliance with the select agent regulations and be able to respond in a timely manner to onsite incidents involving select agents and toxins in accordance with the entity's incident response plan.

(6) Ensure that annual inspections are conducted for each registered space where select agents or toxins are stored or used in order to determine compliance with the requirements of this part. The results of each inspection must be documented, and any deficiencies identified during an inspection must be corrected and the corrections documented.

(7) Ensure that individuals are provided the contact information for the USDA Office of Inspector General Hotline and the HHS Office of Inspector General Hotline so that they may anonymously report any biosafety/biocontainment or security concerns related to select agents and toxins.

[10] If registration is denied for this reason, we may provide technical assistance and guidance.

(8) Investigate to determine the reason for any failure of a validated inactivation procedure or any failure to remove viable select agent from material. If the responsible official is unable to determine the cause of a deviation from a validated inactivation procedure or a viable select agent removal method; or receives any report of any inactivation failure after the movement of material to another location, the responsible official must report immediately by telephone or email the inactivation or viable agent removal method failure to APHIS or CDC.

(9) Review, and revise as necessary, each of the entity's validated inactivation procedures or viable select agent removal methods. The review must be conducted annually or after any change in principal investigator, change in the validated inactivation procedure or viable select agent removal method, or failure of the validated inactivation procedure or viable select agent removal method. The review must be documented and training must be conducted if there are any changes to the validated inactivation procedure, viable select agent removal method, or viability testing protocol.

(b) An entity may designate one or more individuals to serve as an alternate responsible official who acts for the responsible official in his/her absence. These individuals must have the authority and control to ensure compliance with the regulations when acting as the responsible official.

(c) The responsible official must report the identification and final disposition of any select agent or toxin contained in a specimen presented for diagnosis or verification.

(1) The identification of any of the following select agents or toxins must be immediately reported by telephone, facsimile, or email: African horse sickness virus, African swine fever virus, avian influenza virus (highly pathogenic), *Bacillus anthracis*, *Burkholderia mallei*, *Burkholderia pseudomallei*, classical swine fever virus, foot-and-mouth disease virus, virulent Newcastle disease virus, rinderpest virus, or swine vesicular disease virus. The final disposition of the agent or toxin must be reported by submission of APHIS/CDC Form 4 within 7 calendar days after identification. A copy of the completed form must be maintained for 3 years.

(2) To report the identification and final disposition of any other select agent or toxin, APHIS/CDC Form 4 must be submitted within 7 calendar days after identification. A copy of the completed form must be maintained for 3 years.

(3) Less stringent reporting may be required during agricultural emergencies or outbreaks, or in endemic areas.

(d) The responsible official must report the identification and final disposition of any select agent or toxin contained in a specimen presented for proficiency testing. To report the identification and final disposition of a select agent or toxin, APHIS/CDC Form 4 must be submitted within 90 calendar days of receipt of the agent or toxin. A copy of the completed form must be maintained for 3 years.

[70 FR 13284, Mar. 18, 2005, as amended at 73 FR 61332, Oct. 16, 2008; 77 FR 61078, Oct. 5, 2012; 79 FR 26831, May 12, 2014; 82 FR 6208, Jan. 19, 2017]

§ 121.10 Restricting access to select agents and toxins; security risk assessments.

(a) An individual or entity required to register under this part may not provide an individual access to a select agent or toxin, and an individual may not access a select agent or toxin, unless the individual is approved by the Administrator or the HHS Secretary following a security risk assessment by the Attorney General.

(b) An individual will be deemed to have access at any point in time if the individual has possession of a select agent or toxin (e.g., carries, uses, or manipulates) or the ability to gain possession of a select agent or toxin.

(c) Each individual with access to select agents or toxins must have the appropriate education, training, and/or experience to handle or use such agents or toxins.

(d) To apply for access approval, each individual must submit the information necessary to conduct a security risk assessment to the Attorney General.

(e) A person with valid approval from the HHS Secretary or Administrator to have access to select agents or toxins may request, through his or her Responsible Official, that the HHS Secretary or Administrator provide their approved access status to another registered individual or entity for a specified period of time. A responsible official must immediately notify the responsible official of the visited entity if the person's access to select agents and toxins has been terminated.

(f) An individual's security risk assessment may be expedited upon written request by the responsible official and a showing of good cause (e.g., public health or agricultural emergencies, national security, or a short-term visit by a prominent researcher). A written decision granting or denying the request will be issued.

(g) An individual's access approval for VS select agents or toxins may be denied, limited, or revoked if:

(1) The individual is within any of the categories described in 18 U.S.C. 175b;

(2) The individual is reasonably suspected by any Federal law enforcement or intelligence agency of committing a crime set forth in 18 U.S.C. 2332b(g)(5); knowing involvement with an organization that engages in domestic or international terrorism (as defined in 18 U.S.C. 2331) or with any other organization that engages in intentional crimes of violence; or being an agent of a foreign power as defined in 50 U.S.C. 1801; or

(3) It is determined that such action is necessary to protect animal health or animal products.

(h) For overlap select agents or toxins, an individual's access approval will be denied or revoked if the individual is within any of the categories described in 18 U.S.C. 175b. An individual's access approval may be denied, limited, or revoked for the reasons set forth in paragraphs (f)(2) through (f)(3) of this section.

(i) An individual may appeal the Administrator's decision to deny, limit, or revoke access approval under § 121.20.

(j) Access approval is valid for a maximum of 3 years.

(k) The responsible official must immediately notify APHIS or CDC when an individual's access to select agents or toxins is terminated by the entity and the reasons therefore.

[70 FR 13284, Mar. 18, 2005, as amended at 77 FR 61079, Oct. 5, 2012; 82 FR 6209, Jan. 19, 2017]

§ 121.11 Security.

(a) An individual or entity required to register under this part must develop and implement a written security plan. The security plan must be sufficient to safeguard the select agent or toxin against unauthorized access, theft, loss, or release.

(b) The security plan must be designed according to a site-specific risk assessment and must provide graded protection in accordance with the risk of the select agent or toxin, given its intended use. A current security plan must be submitted for initial registration, renewal of registration, or when requested.

(c) The security plan must:

(1) Describe procedures for physical security, inventory control, and information systems control;

(2) Contain provisions for the control of access to select agents and toxins, including the safeguarding of animals (including arthropods) or plants intentionally or accidentally exposed to or infected with a select agent, against unauthorized access, theft, loss or release.

(3) Contain provisions for routine cleaning, maintenance, and repairs;

(4) Establish procedures for removing unauthorized or suspicious persons;

(5) Describe procedures for addressing loss or compromise of keys, keycards, passwords, combinations, etc. and protocols for changing access permissions or locks following staff changes;

(6) Contain procedures for reporting unauthorized or suspicious persons or activities, loss or theft of select agents or toxins, release of select agents or toxins, or alteration of inventory records;

(7) Contain provisions for ensuring that all individuals with access approval from the Administrator or the HHS Secretary understand and comply with the security procedures.

(8) Describe procedures for how the responsible official will be informed of suspicious activity that may be criminal in nature and related to the entity,

its personnel, or its select agents or toxins; and describe procedures for how the entity will notify the appropriate Federal, State, or local law enforcement agencies of such activity.

(9) Contain provisions for information security that:

(i) Ensure that all external connections to systems which manage security for the registered space are isolated or have controls that permit only authorized and authenticated users;

(ii) Ensure that authorized and authenticated users are only granted access to select agent and toxin related information, files, equipment (e.g., servers or mass storage devices), and applications as necessary to fulfill their roles and responsibilities, and that access is modified when the user's roles and responsibilities change or when their access to select agents and toxins is suspended or revoked;

(iii) Ensure that controls are in place that are designed to prevent malicious code (such as, but not limited to, computer viruses, worms, spyware) from compromising the confidentiality, integrity, or availability of information systems which manage access to spaces registered under this part or records as specified in § 121.17;

(iv) Establish a robust configuration management practice for information systems to include regular patching and updates made to operating systems and individual applications; and

(v) Establish procedures that provide backup security measures in the event that access control systems, surveillance devices, and/or systems that manage the requirements of § 121.17 are rendered inoperable.

(10) Contain provisions and policies for shipping, receiving, and storage of select agents and toxins, including documented procedures for receiving, monitoring, and shipping of all select agents and toxins. These provisions must provide that an entity will properly secure containers on site and have a written contingency plan for unexpected shipments.

(d) An individual or entity must adhere to the following security requirements or implement measures to achieve an equivalent or greater level of security:

(1) Allow access only to individuals with access approval from the Administrator or the HHS Secretary;

(2) Allow individuals not approved for access by the Administrator or the HHS Secretary to conduct routine cleaning, maintenance, repairs, and other activities not related to select agents or toxins only when continuously escorted by an approved individual if the potential to access to select agents or toxins exists;

(3) Provide for the control of select agents and toxins by requiring freezers, refrigerators, cabinets, and other containers where select agents or toxins are stored to be secured against unauthorized access (e.g., card access system, lock boxes);

(4) Inspect all suspicious packages before they are brought into or removed from an area where select agents or toxins are used or stored;

(5) Establish a protocol for intra-entity transfers under the supervision of an individual with access approval from the Administrator or the HHS Secretary, including chain-of-custody documents and provisions for safeguarding against theft, loss, or release; and

(6) Require that individuals with access approval from the Administrator or the HHS Secretary refrain from sharing with any other person their unique means of accessing a select agent or toxin (e.g., keycards or passwords);

(7) Require that individuals with access approval from the Administrator or the HHS Secretary immediately report any of the following to the responsible official:

(i) Any loss or compromise of keys, passwords, combinations, etc.;

(ii) Any suspicious persons or activities;

(iii) Any loss or theft of select agents or toxins;

(iv) Any release of a select agent or toxin;

(v) Any sign that inventory or use records for select agents or toxins have been altered or otherwise compromised; and

(vi) Any loss of computer, hard drive or other data storage device containing information that could be used to gain access to select agents or toxins; and

(8) Separate areas where select agents and toxins are stored or used from the public areas of the building.

(e) Entities must conduct complete inventory audits of all affected select agents and toxins in long-term storage when any of the following occur:

(1) Upon the physical relocation of a collection or inventory of select agents or toxins for those select agents or toxins in the collection or inventory;

(2) Upon the departure or arrival of a principal investigator for those select agents and toxins under the control of that principal investigator; or

(3) In the event of a theft or loss of a select agent or toxin, all select agents and toxins under the control of that principal investigator.

(f) In addition to the requirements contained in paragraphs (c) and (d) of this section, the security plan for an individual or entity possessing a Tier 1 select agent or toxin must also:

(1) Describe procedures for conducting a pre-access suitability assessment of persons who will have access to a Tier 1 select agent or toxin;

(2) Describe procedures for how an entity's responsible official will coordinate their efforts with the entity's safety and security professionals to ensure security of Tier 1 select agents and toxins and share, as appropriate, relevant information; and

(3) Describe procedures for the ongoing assessment of the suitability of personnel with access to a Tier 1 select agent or toxin. The procedures must include:

(i) Self- and peer-reporting of incidents or conditions that could affect an individual's ability to safely have access to or work with select agents and toxins, or to safeguard select agents and toxins from theft, loss, or release;

(ii) The training of employees with access to Tier 1 select agents and toxins on entity policies and procedures for reporting, evaluation, and corrective actions concerning the assessment of personnel suitability; and

(iii) The ongoing suitability monitoring of individuals with access to Tier 1 select agents and toxins.

(4) Entities with Tier 1 select agents and toxins must prescribe the following security enhancements:

(i) Procedures that will limit access to a Tier 1 select agent or toxin to only those individuals who are approved by the HHS Secretary or Administrator following a security risk assessment by the Attorney General, have had an entity-conducted pre-access suitability assessment, and are subject to the entity's procedures for ongoing suitability assessment;

(ii) Procedures that limit access to laboratory and storage facilities outside of normal business hours to only those specifically approved by the responsible official or designee;

(iii) Procedures for allowing visitors, their property, and vehicles at the entry and exit points to the registered space, or at other designated points of entry to the building, facility, or compound that are based on the entity's site-specific risk assessment;

(iv) A minimum of three security barriers where each security barrier adds to the delay in reaching secured areas where select agents and toxins are used or stored. One of the security barriers must be monitored in such a way as to detect intentional and unintentional circumventing of established access control measures under all conditions (day/night, severe weather, etc.) The final barrier must limit access to the select agent or toxin to personnel approved by the HHS Secretary or Administrator, following a security risk assessment by the Attorney General.

(v) All registered space or areas that reasonably afford access to the registered space must be protected by an intrusion detection system (IDS) unless physically occupied;

(vi) Personnel monitoring the IDS must be capable of evaluating and interpreting the alarm and alerting the designated security response force or law enforcement;

(vii) For powered access control systems, describe procedures to ensure that security is maintained in the event of the failure of access control systems due to power disruption affecting registered space;

(viii) The entity must:

(A) Determine that the response time for security forces or local police will not exceed 15 minutes where the response time is measured from the time of an intrusion alarm, or report of a security incident, to the arrival of the responders at the first security barrier or;

(B) Provide security barriers that are sufficient to delay unauthorized access until the response force arrives in order to safeguard the select agents and toxins from theft, intentional release, or unauthorized access. The response time is measured from the time of an intrusion alarm, or report of a security incident, to the arrival of the responders at the first security barrier.

(5) Entities that possess foot-and-mouth disease virus and rinderpest virus must have the following additional security requirements:

(i) A minimum of four barriers, one of which must be a perimeter security fence or equivalent which is monitored 24 hours a day, 7 days a week (24/7) to detect the presence of unauthorized persons, vehicles, materials, or unauthorized activities;

(ii) Onsite 24/7 armed security response force with roving patrol. Response time must not exceed 5 minutes from the time of an intrusion alarm or report of a security incident;

(iii) CCTV surveillance with 24/7 monitoring and recording; and

(iv) Transport vehicle with GPS tracking designed to serve as a containment vehicle.

(g) In developing a security plan, an individual or entity should consider the document entitled, "Security Guidance for Select Agent or Toxin Facilities." This document is available on the National Select Agent Registry at *http://www.selectagents.gov/*.

(h) The plan must be reviewed annually and revised as necessary. Drills or exercises must be conducted at least annually to test and evaluate the effectiveness of the plan. The plan must be reviewed and revised, as necessary, after any drill or exercise and after any incident. Drills or exercises must be documented to include how the drill or exercise tested and evaluated the plan, any problems that were identified and corrective action(s) taken, and the names of registered entity personal participants.

[70 FR 13284, Mar. 18, 2005, as amended at 77 FR 61079, Oct. 5, 2012; 79 FR 26831, May 12, 2014; 82 FR 6209, Jan. 19, 2017]

§ 121.12 Biosafety.

(a) An individual or entity required to register under this part must develop and implement a written biosafety plan that is commensurate with the risk of the select agent or toxin, given its intended use.[11] The biosafety plan must contain sufficient information and documentation to describe the biosafety and containment procedures for the select agent or toxin, including any animals (including arthropods) or plants intentionally or accidentally exposed to or infected with a select agent. The current biosafety plan must be submitted for initial registration, renewal of registration, or when requested. The biosafety plan must include the following provisions:

(1) The hazardous characteristics of each agent or toxin listed on the entity's registration and the biosafety risk associated with laboratory procedures related to the select agent or toxin;

(2) Safeguards in place with associated work practices to protect entity personnel, the public, and the environment from exposure to the select agent or toxin including, but not limited to: Personal protective equipment and other safety equipment; containment equipment including, but not limited to, biological safety cabinets, animal caging systems, and centrifuge safety containers; and engineering controls and other facility safeguards;

(3) Written procedures for each validated method used for disinfection, decontamination, or destruction, as appropriate, of all contaminated or presumptively contaminated materials including, but not limited to: Cultures and other materials related to the propagation of select agents or toxins, items related to the analysis of select agents and toxins, personal protective equipment, animal caging systems and bedding (if applicable), animal carcasses or extracted tissues and fluids (if applicable), laboratory surfaces and equipment, and effluent material; and

(4) Procedures for the handling of select agents and toxins in the same spaces with non-select agents and toxins to prevent unintentional contamination.

[11] Technical assistance and guidance may be obtained by contacting APHIS.

(b) The biosafety and containment procedures must be sufficient to contain the select agent or toxin (e.g., physical structure and features of the entity, and operational and procedural safeguards).

(c) In developing a biosafety plan, an individual or entity should consider the following:

(1) The CDC/NIH publication, "Biosafety in Microbiological and Biomedical Laboratories." This document is available on the National Select Agent Registry at *http://www.selectagents.gov/*.

(2) The "NIH Guidelines for Research Involving Recombinant or Synthetic Nucleic Acid Molecules." This document is available on the Internet at *http://www.selectagents.gov/*.

(d) The biosafety plan must include an occupational health program for individuals with access to Tier 1 select agents and toxins, and those individuals must be enrolled in the occupational health program.

(e) The plan must be reviewed annually and revised as necessary. Drills or exercises must be conducted at least annually to test and evaluate the effectiveness of the plan. The plan must be reviewed and revised, as necessary, after any drill or exercise and after any incident. Drills or exercises must be documented to include how the drill or exercise tested and evaluated the plan, any problems that were identified and corrective action(s) taken, and the names of registered entity personnel participants.

[70 FR 13284, Mar. 18, 2005, as amended at 73 FR 61331, Oct. 16, 2008; 77 FR 61080, Oct. 5, 2012; 82 FR 6209, Jan. 19, 2017]

§ 121.13 Restricted experiments.

(a) An individual or entity may not conduct, or possess products resulting from, the following experiments unless approved by and conducted in accordance with the conditions prescribed by the Administrator:

(1) Experiments that involve the deliberate transfer of, or selection for, a drug resistance trait to select agents that are not known to acquire the trait naturally, if such acquisition could compromise the control of disease agents in humans, veterinary medicine, or agriculture.

(2) Experiments involving the deliberate formation of synthetic or recombinant DNA containing genes for the biosynthesis of select toxins lethal for vertebrates at an LD[50] <100 ng/kg body weight.

(b) The Administrator may revoke approval to conduct any of the experiments in paragraph (a) of this section, or revoke or suspend a certificate of registration, if the individual or entity fails to comply with the requirements of this part.

(c) To apply for approval to conduct any of the experiments in paragraph (a) of this section, an individual or entity must submit a written request and supporting scientific information. A written decision granting or denying the request will be issued.

[70 FR 13284, Mar. 18, 2005, as amended at 73 FR 61331, Oct. 16, 2008; 77 FR 61080, Oct. 5, 2012; 79 FR 26831, May 12, 2014]

§ 121.14 Incident response.[12]

(a) An individual or entity required to register under this part must develop and implement a written incident response plan[13] based upon a site specific risk assessment. The incident response plan must be coordinated with any entity-wide plans, kept in the workplace, and available to employees for review. The current incident response plan must be submitted for initial registration, renewal of registration, or when requested.

(b) The incident response plan must fully describe the entity's response procedures for the theft, loss, or release of a select agent or toxin; inventory discrepancies; security breaches (including information systems); severe weather and other natural disasters; workplace violence; bomb threats and suspicious packages; and emergencies such as fire, gas leak, explosion, power outage, and other natural and man-made events.

(c) The response procedures must account for hazards associated with the select agent or toxin and appropriate

[12] Nothing in this section is meant to supersede or preempt incident response requirements imposed by other statutes or regulations.

[13] Technical assistance and guidance may be obtained by contacting APHIS.

actions to contain such select agent or toxin, including any animals (including arthropods) or plants intentionally or accidentally exposed to or infected with a select agent.

(d) The incident response plan must also contain the following information:

(1) The name and contact information (e.g., home and work) for the individual or entity (e.g., responsible official, alternate responsible official(s), biosafety officer, etc.);

(2) The name and contact information for the building owner and/or manager, where applicable;

(3) The name and contact information for tenant offices, where applicable;

(4) The name and contact information for the physical security official for the building, where applicable;

(5) Personnel roles and lines of authority and communication;

(6) Planning and coordination with local emergency responders;

(7) Procedures to be followed by employees performing rescue or medical duties;

(8) Emergency medical treatment and first aid;

(9) A list of personal protective and emergency equipment, and their locations;

(10) Site security and control;

(11) Procedures for emergency evacuation, including type of evacuation, exit route assignments, safe distances, and places of refuge; and

(12) Decontamination procedures.

(e) Entities with Tier 1 select agents and toxins must have the following additional incident response policies or procedures:

(1) The incident response plan must fully describe the entity's response procedures for failure of intrusion detection or alarm system; and

(2) The incident response plan must describe procedures for how the entity will notify the appropriate Federal, State, or local law enforcement agencies of suspicious activity that may be criminal in nature and related to the entity, its personnel, or its select agents or toxins.

(f) The plan must be reviewed annually and revised as necessary. Drills or exercises must be conducted at least annually to test and evaluate the effectiveness of the plan. The plan must be reviewed and revised, as necessary, after any drill or exercise and after any incident. Drills or exercises must be documented to include how the drill or exercise tested and evaluated the plan, any problems that were identified and corrective action(s) taken, and the names of registered entity personnel participants.

[70 FR 13284, Mar. 18, 2005, as amended at 73 FR 61331, Oct. 16, 2008; 77 FR 61080, Oct. 5, 2012; 82 FR 6209, Jan. 19, 2017]

§ 121.15 Training.

(a) An individual or entity required to register under this part must provide information and training on biocontainment, biosafety, security (including security awareness), and incident response to:

(1) Each individual with access approval from the Administrator or HHS Secretary. The training must address the particular needs of the individual, the work they will do, and the risks posed by the select agents or toxins. The training must be accomplished prior to the individual's entry into an area where a select agent is handled or stored, or within 12 months of the date the individual was approved by the Administrator or the HHS Secretary for access, whichever is earlier.

(2) Each individual not approved for access to select agents and toxins by the Administrator or HHS Secretary before that individual enters areas under escort where select agents or toxins are handled or stored (*e.g.*, laboratories, growth chambers, animal rooms, greenhouses, storage areas, shipping/receiving areas, production facilities, etc.). Training for escorted personnel must be based on the risk associated with accessing areas where select agents and toxins are used and/or stored. The training must be accomplished prior to the individual's entry into where select agents or toxins are handled or stored (*e.g.*, laboratories, growth chambers, animal rooms, greenhouses, storage areas, shipping/receiving areas, production facilities, etc.).

(b) Entities with Tier 1 select agents and toxins must conduct annual insider threat awareness briefings on how to identify and report suspicious behaviors.

(c) Refresher training must be provided annually for individuals with access approval from the HHS Secretary or Administrator or at such time as the registered individual or entity significantly amends its security, incident response, or biosafety plans.

(d) The responsible official must ensure a record of the training provided to each individual with access to select agents and toxins and each escorted individual (e.g., laboratory workers, visitors, etc.) is maintained. The record must include the name of the individual, the date of the training, a description of the training provided, and the means used to verify that the employee understood the training.

(e) The responsible official must ensure and document that individuals are provided the contact information of the USDA Office of Inspector General Hotline and the HHS Office of Inspector General Hotline so that they may anonymously report any safety or security concerns related to select agents and toxins.

[77 FR 61081, Oct. 5, 2012, as amended at 82 FR 6209, Jan. 19, 2017]

§ 121.16 Transfers.

(a) Except as provided in paragraphs (c) and (d) of this section, a select agent or toxin may only be transferred to individuals or entities registered to possess, use, or transfer that agent or toxin. A select agent or toxin may only be transferred under the conditions of this section and must be authorized by APHIS or CDC prior to the transfer.[14]

(b) A transfer may be authorized if:

(1) The sender:

(i) Has at the time of transfer a certificate of registration that covers the particular select agent or toxin to be transferred and meets all the requirements of this part;

(ii) Meets the exemption requirements for the particular select agent or toxin to be transferred; or

(iii) Is transferring the select agent or toxin from outside of the United States and meets all import requirements.

(2) At the time of transfer, the recipient has a certificate of registration that includes the particular select agent or toxin to be transferred and meets all of the requirements of this part.

(c) A select agent or toxin that is contained in a specimen for proficiency testing may be transferred without prior authorization from APHIS or CDC provided that, at least 7 calendar days prior to the transfer, the sender reports to APHIS or CDC the select agent or toxin to be transferred and the name and address of the recipient.

(d) On a case-by-case basis, the Administrator may authorize a transfer of a select agent or toxin not otherwise eligible for transfer under this part under conditions prescribed by the Administrator.

(e) To obtain authorization for a transfer, APHIS/CDC Form 2 must be submitted.

(f) After authorization is provided by APHIS or CDC, the packaging of the select agent(s) and toxin(s) is performed by an individual approved by the HHS Secretary or Administrator to have access to select agents and toxins and is in compliance with all applicable laws concerning packaging.

(g) The sender must comply with all applicable laws governing shipping.

(h) Transportation in commerce starts when the select agent(s) or toxin(s) are packaged for shipment and ready for receipt by a courier transporting select agent(s) or toxin(s) and ends when the package is received by the intended recipient who is an individual approved by the HHS Secretary or Administrator to have access to select agents and toxins, following a security risk assessment by the Attorney General.

(i) The recipient must submit a completed APHIS/CDC Form 2 within 2 business days of receipt of a select agent or toxin.

(j) The recipient must immediately notify APHIS or CDC if the select agent or toxin has not been received within 48 hours after the expected delivery time or if the package containing the select agent or toxin has been damaged to the extent that a release of the select agent or toxin may have occurred.

[14] The requirements of this section do not apply to transfers within a registered entity (*i.e.*, the sender and the recipient are covered by the same certificate of registration).

(k) An authorization for a transfer shall be valid only for 30 calendar days after issuance, except that such an authorization becomes immediately null and void if any facts supporting the authorization change (e.g., change in the certificate of registration for the sender or recipient, change in the application for transfer).

(l) Transfer the amounts only after the transferor uses due diligence and documents that the recipient has a legitimate need (*e.g.*, prophylactic, protective, bona fide research, or other peaceful purpose) to handle or use such toxins. Information to be documented includes, but is not limited, to the recipient information, toxin and amount transferred, and declaration that the recipient has legitimate purpose to store and use such toxins.

[70 FR 13284, Mar. 18, 2005, as amended at 73 FR 61331, Oct. 16, 2008; 77 FR 61081, Oct. 5, 2012; 82 FR 6210, Jan. 19, 2017]

§ 121.17 Records.

(a) An individual or entity required to register under this part must maintain complete records relating to the activities covered by this part. Such records must include:

(1) An accurate, current inventory for each select agent (including viral genetic elements, recombinant and/or synthetic nucleic acids, and organisms containing recombinant and/or synthetic nucleic acids) held in long-term storage (placement in a system designed to ensure viability for future use, such as in a freezer or lyophilized materials), including:

(i) The name and characteristics (e.g., strain designation, GenBank Accession number, etc.);

(ii) The quantity acquired from another individual or entity (e.g., containers, vials, tubes, etc.), date of acquisition, and the source;

(iii) Where stored (e.g., building, room, and freezer or other storage container);

(iv) When moved from storage and by whom and when returned to storage and by whom;

(v) The select agent used, purpose of use, and, when applicable, final disposition;

(vi) Records created under § 121.16 or 42 CFR 73.16 (Transfers);

(vii) For intra-entity transfers (sender and the recipient are covered by the same certificate of registration), the select agent, the quantity transferred, the date of transfer, the sender, and the recipient; and

(viii) Records created under § 121.19 or 42 CFR 73.19 (Notification of theft, loss, or release);

(2) An accurate, current accounting of any animals or plants intentionally or accidentally exposed to or infected with a select agent (including number and species, location, and appropriate disposition);

(3) An accurate, current inventory for each toxin held, including:

(i) The name and characteristics;

(ii) The quantity acquired from another individual or entity (e.g., containers, vials, tubes, etc.), date of acquisition, and the source;

(iii) The initial and current quantity amount (e.g., milligrams, milliliters, grams, etc.);

(iv) The toxin used and purpose of use, quantity, date(s) of the use and by whom;

(v) Where stored (e.g., building, room, and freezer or other storage container);

(vi) When moved from storage and by whom and when returned to storage and by whom, including quantity amount;

(vii) Records created under § 121.16 or 42 CFR 73.16 (Transfers);

(viii) For intra-entity transfers (sender and the recipient are covered by the same certificate of registration), the toxin, the quantity transferred, the date of transfer, the sender, and the recipient;

(ix) Records created under § 121.19 or 42 CFR 73.19 (Notification of theft, loss, or release);

(x) If destroyed, the quantity of toxin destroyed, the date of such action, and by whom.

(4) A current list of all individuals that have been granted access approval by the Administrator or the HHS Secretary;

(5) Information about all entries into areas containing select agents or toxins, including the name of the individual, name of the escort (if applicable), and the date and time of entry;

(6) Accurate, current records created under § 121.9 or 42 CFR 73.9 (Responsible

official), § 121.11 or 42 CFR 73.11 (Security), § 121.12 or 42 CFR 73.12 (Biosafety), § 121.14 or 42 CFR 73.14 (Incident response), and § 121.15 or 42 CFR 73.15 (Training);

(7) A written explanation of any discrepancies; and

(8) For select agents or material containing select agents or regulated nucleic acids that can produce infectious forms of any select agent virus that have been subjected to a validated inactivation procedure or a procedure for removal of viable select agent:

(i) A written description of the validated inactivation procedure or viable select agent removal method used, including validation data;

(ii) A written description of the viability testing protocol used;

(iii) A written description of the investigation conducted by the entity responsible official involving an inactivation or viable select agent removal failure and the corrective actions taken;

(iv) The name of each individual performing the validated inactivation or viable select agent removal method;

(v) The date(s) the validated inactivation or viable select agent removal method was completed;

(vi) The location where the validated inactivation or viable select agent removal method was performed; and

(vii) A certificate, signed by the principal investigator, that includes the date of inactivation or viable select agent removal, the validated inactivation or viable select agent removal method used, and the name of the principal investigator. A copy of the certificate must accompany any transfer of inactivated or select agent removed material.

(b) The individual or entity must implement a system to ensure that all records and databases created under this part are accurate and legible, have controlled access, and that their authenticity may be verified.

(c) The individual or entity must promptly produce upon request any information that is related to the requirements of this part but is not otherwise contained in a record required to be kept by this section. The location of such information may include, but is not limited to, biocontainment certifications, laboratory notebooks, institutional biosafety and/or animal use committee minutes and approved protocols, and records associated with occupational health and suitability programs. All records created under this part must be maintained for 3 years.

[70 FR 13284, Mar. 18, 2005, as amended at 77 FR 61081, Oct. 5, 2012; 82 FR 6210, Jan. 19, 2017]

§ 121.18 Inspections.

(a) Without prior notification, APHIS must be allowed to inspect any site at which activities regulated under this part are conducted and must be allowed to inspect and copy any records relating to the activities covered by this part.

(b) Prior to issuing a certificate of registration to an individual or entity, APHIS may inspect and evaluate the premises and records to ensure compliance with this part.

§ 121.19 Notification of theft, loss, or release.

(a) An individual or entity must immediately notify APHIS or CDC upon discovery of the theft or loss of a select agent or toxin. Thefts or losses must be reported even if the select agent or toxin is subsequently recovered or the responsible parties are identified.

(1) The theft or loss of a select agent or toxin must be reported by telephone, facsimile, or e-mail. The following information must be provided:

(i) The name of the select agent or toxin and any identifying information (e.g., strain or other characterization information);

(ii) An estimate of the quantity stolen or lost;

(iii) An estimate of the time during which the theft or loss occurred;

(iv) The location (building, room) from which the theft or loss occurred; and

(v) The list of Federal, State, or local law enforcement agencies to which the individual or entity reported, or intends to report, the theft or loss.

(2) A completed APHIS/CDC Form 3 must be submitted within 7 calendar days.

(b) An individual or entity must immediately notify APHIS or CDC upon discovery of a release of a select agent or toxin causing occupational exposure or a release of a select agent or toxin outside of the primary barriers of the biocontainment area.

(1) The release of a select agent or toxin must be reported by telephone, facsimile, or e-mail. The following information must be provided:

(i) The name of the select agent or toxin and any identifying information (e.g., strain or other characterization information);

(ii) An estimate of the quantity released;

(iii) The time and duration of the release;

(iv) The environment into which the release occurred (e.g., in building or outside of building, waste system);

(v) The location (building, room) from which the release occurred; and

(vi) The number of individuals potentially exposed at the entity;

(vii) Actions taken to respond to the release; and

(viii) Hazards posed by the release.

(2) A completed APHIS/CDC Form 3 must be submitted within 7 calendar days.

§ 121.20 Administrative review.

(a) An individual or entity may appeal a denial, revocation, or suspension of registration under this part. The appeal must be in writing, state the factual basis for the appeal, and be submitted to the Administrator within 30 calendar days of the decision.

(b) An individual may appeal a denial, limitation, or revocation of access approval under this part. The appeal must be in writing, state the factual basis for the appeal, and be submitted to the Administrator within 180 calendar days of the decision.

(c) The Administrator's decision constitutes final agency action.

[77 FR 61081, Oct. 5, 2012]

PART 122—ORGANISMS AND VECTORS

Sec.

AUTHORITY: 7 U.S.C. 8301–8317; 21 U.S.C. 151–158; 7 CFR 2.22, 2.80, and 371.4.

§ 122.1 Definitions.

The following words, when used in the regulations in this part 122, shall be construed, respectively, to mean:

(a) *Department.* The U.S. Department of Agriculture.

(b) *Secretary.* "Secretary" means the Secretary of Agriculture of the United States, or any officer or employee of the Department to whom authority has heretofore been delegated, or to whom authority may hereafter be delegated, to act in his stead.

(c) *Administrator.* The Administrator, Animal and Plant Health Inspection Service, United States Department of Agriculture, or any person authorized to act for the Administrator.

(d) *Organisms.* All cultures or collections of organisms or their derivatives, which may introduce or disseminate any contagious or infectious disease of animals (including poultry).

(e) *Vectors.* All animals (including poultry) such as mice, pigeons, guinea pigs, rats, ferrets, rabbits, chickens, dogs, and the like, which have been treated or inoculated with organisms, or which are diseased or infected with any contagious, infectious, or communicable disease of animals or poultry or which have been exposed to any such disease.

(f) *Permittee.* A person who resides in the United States or operates a business establishment within the United States, to whom a permit to import or transport organisms or vectors has been issued under the regulations.

(g) *Person.* Any individual, firm, partnership, corporation, company, society, association, or other organized group of any of the foregoing, or any agent, officer, or employee of any thereof.

[31 FR 81, Jan. 5, 1966, as amended at 57 FR 30899, July 13, 1992]

§ 122.2 Permits required.

No organisms or vectors shall be imported into the United States or transported from one State or Territory or the District of Columbia to another State or Territory or the District of Columbia without a permit issued by the Secretary and in compliance with the terms thereof: *Provided,* That no permit shall be required under this section for importation of organisms for which an import permit has been issued pursuant to part 102 of this subchapter or for transportation of organisms produced at establishments licensed under part 102 of this subchapter. As a condition of issuance of permits under this section, the permittee shall agree in writing to observe the safeguards prescribed by the Administrator for public protection with respect to the particular importation or transportation.

(Approved by the Office of Management and Budget under control number 0579–0015)

[28 FR 7896, Aug. 2, 1963. Redesignated at 31 FR 81, Jan. 5, 1966 and amended at 48 FR 57473, Dec. 30, 1983; 57 FR 30899, July 13, 1992; 59 FR 67134, Dec. 29, 1994]

§ 122.3 Application for permits.

The Secretary may issue, at his discretion, a permit as specified in § 122.2 when proper safeguards are set up as provided in § 122.2 to protect the public. Application for such a permit shall be made in advance of shipment, and each permit shall specify the name and address of the consignee, the true name and character of each of the organisms or vectors involved, and the use to which each will be put.

(Approved by the Office of Management and Budget under control number 0579–0015)

[23 FR 10065, Dec. 23, 1958. Redesignated at 31 FR 81, Jan. 5, 1966 and amended at 48 FR 57473, Dec. 30, 1983; 59 FR 67134, Dec. 29, 1994]

§ 122.4 Suspension or revocation of permits.

(a) Any permit for the importation or transportation of organisms or vectors issued under this part may be formally suspended or revoked after opportunity for hearing has been accorded the permittee, as provided in part 123 of this subchapter, if the Secretary finds that the permittee has failed to observe the safeguards and instructions prescribed by the Administrator with respect to the particular importation or transportation or that such importation or transportation for any other reason may result in the introduction or dissemination from a foreign country into the United States, or from one State, Territory or the District of Columbia to another, of the contagion of any contagious, infectious or communicable disease of animals (including poultry).

(b) In cases of wilfulness or where the public health, interest or safety so requires, however, the Secretary may without hearing informally suspend such a permit upon the grounds set forth in paragraph (a) of this section, pending determination of formal proceedings under part 123 of this subchapter for suspension or revocation of the permit.

[23 FR 10065, Dec. 23, 1958. Redesignated at 31 FR 81, Jan. 5, 1966, and amended at 57 FR 30899, July 13, 1992]

PART 123—RULES OF PRACTICE GOVERNING PROCEEDINGS UNDER THE VIRUS-SERUM-TOXIN ACT

AUTHORITY: 7 U.S.C. 8301–8317; 21 U.S.C. 151–159; 7 CFR 2.22, 2.80, and 371.4.

§ 123.1 Scope and applicability of rules of practice.

The Uniform Rules of Practice for the Department of Agriculture promulgated in subpart H of part 1, subtitle A, title 7, Code of Federal Regulations, are the Rules of Practice applicable to adjudicatory, administrative proceedings under the Virus-Serum-Toxin Act.

[42 FR 10960, Feb. 25, 1977]

PART 124—PATENT TERM RESTORATION

Subpart A—General Provisions

Sec.

Subpart B—Eligibility Assistance

Subpart C—Regulatory Review Period

AUTHORITY: 35 U.S.C. 156; 7 CFR 2.22, 2.80, and 371.4.

SOURCE: 58 FR 11369, Feb. 25, 1993, unless otherwise noted.

Subpart A—General Provisions

§ 124.1 Scope.

(a) This parts sets forth procedures and requirements for APHIS review of applications for the extension of the term of certain patents for veterinary biological products pursuant to 35 U.S.C. 156—Extension of patent term. Responsibilities of APHIS include:

(1) Assisting PTO in determining eligibility for patent term restoration;

(2) Determining the length of a product's regulatory review period;

(3) If petitioned, reviewing and ruling on due diligence challenges to APHIS's regulatory review period determinations; and

(4) Conducting hearings to review initial APHIS findings on due diligence challenges.

(b) The regulations in this part are designed to be used in conjunction with regulations issued by PTO concerning patent term extension which may be found at 37 CFR 1.710 through 1.791.

[58 FR 11369, Feb. 25, 1993, as amended at 64 FR 43045, Aug. 9, 1999]

§ 124.2 Definitions.

Animal and Plant Health Inspection Service (APHIS). The agency in the Department of Agriculture responsible for licensing veterinary biological products under the Virus-Serum-Toxin Act.

Applicant. Any person who submits an application or an amendment or supplement to an application under 35 U.S.C. 156 seeking extension of the term of a patent.

Due diligence petition. A petition submitted under § 124.30 of this part.

Informal hearing. A hearing that is not subject to the provisions of 5 U.S.C. 554, 556, and 557 and that is conducted as provided in 21 U.S.C. 321(x).

License applicant. Any person who, in accordance with part 102 of this chapter, submits an application to the Animal and Plant Health Inspection Service of the U.S. Department of Agriculture for a U.S. Veterinary Biological Product License.

Patent. A patent issued by the Patent and Trademark Office of the United States Department of Commerce.

Person. Any individual, firm, partnership, corporation, company, association, educational institution, State or local government agency, or other organized group of any of the foregoing, or any agent, officer, or employee of any thereof.

PTO. The Patent and Trademark Office of the United States Department of Commerce.

[58 FR 11369, Feb. 25, 1993, as amended at 68 FR 6346, Feb. 7, 2003]

Subpart B—Eligibility Assistance

§ 124.10 APHIS liaison with PTO.

Upon receipt of a copy of an application for extension of the term of a veterinary biologic patent from PTO, APHIS will assist PTO in determining whether a patent related to a biological product is eligible for patent term extension by:

(a)(1) Verifying whether the product was subject to a regulatory review period before its commercial marketing or use;

(2) Determining whether the permission for commercial marketing or use of the product after the regulatory review period was the first permitted commercial marketing or use of the product under the provision of law under which such regulatory review period occurred, and, if so, whether it was the first permitted commercial marketing or use of the veterinary biological product for administration to a food-producing animal;

(3) Ascertaining whether the patent term restoration application was submitted within 60 days after the product was approved for marketing or use; and

(4) Providing such other information as may be necessary and relevant to PTO's determination of whether a patent related to a product is eligible for patent term restoration.

(b) APHIS will notify PTO of its findings in writing, send a copy of this notification to the applicant, and make a copy available for public inspection in room 1141, South Building, 14th Street and Independence Avenue SW., Washington, DC, between 8 a.m. and 4:30 p.m., Monday through Friday, except holidays.

Subpart C—Regulatory Review Period

§ 124.20 Patent term extension calculation.

(a) As provided in 37 CFR 1.779 of PTO's regulations, in order to determine a product's regulatory review period, APHIS will review the information in each application to determine the lengths of the following phases of the review period, and will then find their sum:

(1) The number of days in the period beginning on the date authorization to prepare an experimental biological product under the Virus-Serum-Toxin Act became effective and ending on the date an application for a license was initially submitted under the Virus-Serum-Toxin Act; and

(2) The number of days in the period beginning on the date an application for a license was initially submitted for approval under the Virus-Serum-Toxin Act and ending on the date such license was issued.

(b) A license application is "initially submitted" on the date it contains sufficient information to allow APHIS to commence review of the application. A product license is issued on the date of the APHIS letter informing the applicant of the issuance. The issuance of a license releases the product for commercial marketing or use.

§ 124.21 Regulatory review period determination.

(a) Not later than 30 days after the receipt of an application from PTO, APHIS shall determine the regulatory review period. Once the regulatory review period for a product has been determined, APHIS will notify PTO in writing of the determination, send a copy of the determination to the applicant, and make a copy available for public inspection in room 1141, South Building, 14th Street and Independence Avenue SW., Washington, DC, between 8 a.m. and 4:30 p.m., Monday through Friday, except holidays.

(b) APHIS will also publish a notice of the regulatory review period determination in the FEDERAL REGISTER. The notice will include the following:

(1) The name of the applicant;

(2) The trade name and true name of the product;

(3) The number of the patent for which an extension of the term is sought;

(4) The approved indications or uses for the product;

(5) The regulatory review period determination, including a statement of the length of each phase of the review period and the dates used in calculating each phase.

§ 124.22 Revision of regulatory review period determination.

(a) Any interested person may request a revision of the regulatory review period determination within the 30 day period beginning on its publication in the FEDERAL REGISTER. The request must be sent to the Director, Center for Veterinary Biologics, Policy, Evaluation, and Licensing, 1920 Dayton Avenue, P.O. Box 844, Ames, IA 50010. The request must specify the following:

(1) The identity of the product;

(2) The identity of the applicant for patent term restoration;

(3) The docket number of the FEDERAL REGISTER notice announcing the regulatory review period determination; and

(4) The basis for the request for revision, including any documentary evidence.

(b) If APHIS decides to revise its prior determination, APHIS will notify PTO of the decision, and will send a copy of notification to the applicant and the person requesting the revision (if different from the applicant) with a request for comments within 10 days of notification. If no comment on the proposed revision is received, APHIS will publish the revision in the FEDERAL REGISTER, and include a statement giving the reasons for the revision. If comment is received, APHIS will make a final determination regarding the revision based on such comment and will then publish the revision in the FEDERAL REGISTER, giving reasons for its determination.

[59 FR 11369, Feb. 25, 1993, as amended at 59 FR 67617, Dec. 30, 1994; 64 FR 43045, Aug. 9, 1999; 75 FR 20773, Apr. 21, 2010]

§ 124.23 Final action on regulatory review period determination.

APHIS will consider its regulatory review period determination to be final upon expiration of the 180-day period for filing a due diligence petition under § 124.30 unless it receives:

(a) New information from PTO records, or APHIS records, that affects the regulatory review period determination;

(b) A request under § 124.22 for revision of the regulatory review period determination;

(c) A due diligence petition filed under § 124.30; or

(d) A request for a hearing filed under § 124.40.

[58 FR 11369, Feb. 25, 1993; 58 FR 29028, May 18, 1993]

Subpart D—Due Diligence Petitions

§ 124.30 Filing, format, and content of petitions.

(a) Any interested person may file a petition with APHIS, no later than 180 days after the publication of a regulatory review period determination under § 124.21, alleging that a license applicant did not act with due diligence in seeking APHIS approval of the product during the regulatory review period.

(b) The petition must be filed with APHIS under the docket number of the FEDERAL REGISTER notice of the agency's regulatory review period determination. The petition must contain any additional information required by this subpart.

(c) The petition must allege that the applicant failed to act with due diligence sometime during the regulatory review period and must set forth sufficient facts to merit an investigation by APHIS of whether the applicant acted with due diligence.

(d) The petition must contain a certification that the petitioner has served a true and complete copy of the petition on interested parties by certified or registered mail (return receipt requested) or by personal delivery.

§ 124.31 Applicant response to petition.

(a) The applicant may file with APHIS a written response to the petition no later than 20 days after the applicant's receipt of a copy of the petition.

(b) The applicant's response may present additional facts and circumstances to address the assertions in the petition, but shall be limited to the issue of whether the applicant acted with due diligence during the regulatory review period. The applicant's response may include documents that were not in the original patent term extension application.

(c) If the applicant does not respond to the petition, APHIS will decide the matter on the basis of the information submitted in the patent term restoration application, the due diligence petition, and APHIS records.

§ 124.32 APHIS action on petition.

(a) Within 90 days after APHIS receives a petition filed under § 124.30, the Under Secretary for Marketing and Regulatory Programs shall make a determination under paragraphs (b) or (c) of this section or under § 124.33 whether the applicant acted with due diligence during the regulatory review period. APHIS will publish its determination in the FEDERAL REGISTER together with factual and legal basis for the determination, notify PTO of the determination in writing, and send copies of the determination to PTO, the applicant, and the petitioner.

(b) APHIS may deny a due diligence petition without considering the merits of the petition if:

(1) The petition is not filed in accordance with § 124.30;

(2) The petition does not contain information or allegations upon which APHIS may reasonably determine that

the applicant did not act with due diligence during the applicable regulatory review period; or

(3) The petition fails to allege a sufficient total amount of time during which the applicant did not exercise due diligence so that, even if the petition were granted, the petition would not affect the maximum patent term extension which the applicant is entitled to under 35 U.S.C. 156.

[59 FR 11369, Feb. 25, 1993, as amended at 64 FR 43045, Aug. 9, 1999]

§ 124.33 Standard of due diligence.

(a) In determining the due diligence of an applicant, APHIS will examine the facts and circumstances of the applicant's actions during the regulatory review period to determine whether the applicant exhibited the degree of attention, continuous directed effort, and timeliness as may reasonably be expected from, and are ordinarily exercised by, a person during a regulatory review period. APHIS will take into consideration all relevant factors, such as the amount of time between the approval of an experimental use permit and licensure of the veterinary biological product.

(b) For purposes of this Part, the actions of the marketing applicant shall be imputed to the applicant for patent term restoration. The actions of an agent, attorney, contractor, employee, licensee, or predecessor in interest of the marketing applicant shall be imputed to the applicant for patent term restoration.

Subpart E—Due Diligence Hearing

§ 124.40 Request for hearing.

(a) Any interested person may request, within 60 days beginning on the date of publication of a due diligence determination by APHIS in accordance with § 124.32, that APHIS conduct an informal hearing on the due diligence determination.

(b) The request for a hearing must:

(1) Be in writing;

(2) Contain the docket number of the FEDERAL REGISTER notice of APHIS's regulatory review period determination;

(3) Be delivered to the Director, Center for Veterinary Biologics, Policy, Evaluation, and Licensing, 1920 Dayton Avenue, P.O. Box 844, Ames, IA 50010.

(4) Contain a full statement of facts upon which the request for hearing is based;

(5) Contain the name, the address, and the principal place of business of the person requesting the hearing; and

(6) Contain a certification that the person requesting the hearing has served a true and complete copy of the request upon the petitioner of the due diligence determination and the applicant for patent term extension by certified or registered mail (return receipt requested) or by personal service.

(c) The request must state whether the requesting party seeks a hearing not later than 30 days after the date APHIS receives the request, or, at the request of the person making the request, not later than 60 days after such date.

[58 FR 11369, Feb. 25, 1993, as amended at 59 FR 67617, Dec. 30, 1994; 64 FR 43045, Aug. 9, 1999; 75 FR 20773, Apr. 21, 2010]

§ 124.41 Notice of hearing.

No later than ten days before the hearing, APHIS will notify the requesting party, the applicant, the petitioner, and any other interested person of the date, time, and location of the hearing.

§ 124.42 Hearing procedure.

(a) The presiding officer shall be appointed by the Administrator of APHIS from officers and employees of the Department who have not participated in any action of the Secretary which is the subject of the hearing and who are not directly responsible to an officer or employee of the Department who has participated in any such action.

(b) Each party to the hearing shall have the right at all times to be advised and accompanied by an attorney.

(c) Before the hearing, each party to the hearing shall be given reasonable notice of the matters to be considered at the hearing, including a comprehensive statement of the basis for the action taken or proposed by the Secretary which is the subject of the hearing and any general summary of the information which will be presented at the hearing in support of such action.

(d) At the hearing the parties to the hearing shall have the right to hear a full and complete statement of the action which is the subject of the hearing together with the information and reasons supporting such action, to conduct reasonable questioning, and to present any oral and written information relevant to such action.

(e) The presiding officer in such hearing shall prepare a written report of the hearing to which shall be attached all written material presented at the hearing. The participants in the hearing shall be given the opportunity to review and correct or supplement the presiding officer's report of the hearing.

(f) The Secretary may require the hearing to be transcribed. A party to the hearing shall have the right to have the hearing transcribed at his expense. Any transcription of a hearing shall be included in the presiding officer's report of the hearing.

(g) The due diligence hearing will be conducted in accordance with rules of practice adopted for the proceeding. APHIS will provide the requesting party, the applicant, and the petitioner with an opportunity to participate as a party in the hearing. The standard of due diligence set forth in § 124.33 will apply at the hearing. The party requesting the due diligence hearing will have the burden of proof at the hearing.

§ 124.43 Administrative decision.

Within 30 days after completion of the due diligence hearing, the Under Secretary for Marketing and Regulatory Programs, taking into consideration the recommendation of the Administrator, will affirm or revise the determination made under § 124.32. APHIS will publish the due diligence redetermination in the FEDERAL REGISTER, notify PTO of the redetermination, and send copies of the notice to PTO and the requesting party, the applicant, and the petitioner.

[59 FR 11369, Feb. 25, 1993, as amended at 64 FR 43045, Aug. 9, 1999]

SUBCHAPTER F—USER FEES

PART 130—USER FEES

AUTHORITY: 5 U.S.C. 5542; 7 U.S.C. 1622 and 8301–8317; 21 U.S.C. 136 and 136a; 31 U.S.C. 3701, 3716, 3717, 3719, and 3720A; 7 CFR 2.22, 2.80, and 371.4.

SOURCE: 57 FR 771, Jan. 9, 1992, unless otherwise noted.

§ 130.1 Definitions.

As used in this part, the following terms shall have the meaning set forth in this section.

Administrator. The Administrator of the Animal and Plant Health Inspection Service, or any person authorized to act for the Administrator.

Animal. All animals except birds, but including poultry.

Animal and Plant Health Inspection Service (APHIS). The Animal and Plant Health Inspection Service of the United States Department of Agriculture.

Animal Import Center. Quarantine facilities operated by APHIS in Newburgh, New York, and Miami, Florida.[1]

APHIS representative. An individual, including, but not limited to, an animal health technician or veterinarian, authorized by the Administrator to perform the services for which the user fees in this part are charged.

Approved establishment. An establishment approved by the Animal and Plant Health Inspection Service for the receipt and handling of restricted import animal products or byproducts under 9 CFR chapter I, subchapter D.

Biosecurity level three laboratory. A laboratory or production facility that works with foreign or domestic animal disease agents, organisms, or vectors that spread by aerosol route and that have serious or lethal effects, therefore requiring special biocontainment measures.

Bird. Any member of the class aves, other than poultry.

Breeding animal. Any animal imported into the United States for breeding purposes.

Diagnostic reagent. Substances used in diagnostic tests to detect disease

[1] The addresses of Animal Import Centers may be obtained from the Animal and Plant Health Inspection Service, Veterinary Services, National Center for Import-Export, 4700 River Road, Unit 38, Riverdale, Maryland 20737–1231.

agents or antibodies by causing an identifiable reaction.

Domestic animal. Any animal imported into the United States for any purpose other than exhibition in a zoo, park or other place maintained for the exhibition of live animals for recreational or educational purposes.

Equine. Any horse, ass, mule, or zebra.

Export health certificate. An official document that, as required by the importing country, is endorsed by an APHIS representative and states that animals, animal products, organisms, vectors, or birds to be exported from the United States were found to be healthy and free from evidence of communicable diseases and pests.

Feeder animal. Any animal imported into the United States under 9 CFR part 93 for feeding.

Game cock. Any chicken bred, trained, or imported for cock fighting.

Germ plasm. Semen, embryos, or ova.

Grade animal. Any unregistered animal.

Import compliance assistance. Import compliance assistance includes services provided to an importer whose shipment arrives at a port of entry without the necessary paperwork or with incomplete paperwork and who requires assistance to meet the requirements for entry into the United States. Fees for import compliance assistance are charged in addition to the flat rate user fees.

In-bond animal. Any animal imported into the United States under a United States Customs Service bond, as described in 19 CFR part 113.

Load. Those animals, birds, or animal germ plasm, presented for importation into the United States in a single shipment, that originate from one address, are destined for one address, and require one entry permit or authorization.

Miniature horse. Any horse which at maturity measures 34 inches high or less from the ground to the base of the last hair of the mane at the withers.

National Veterinary Services Laboratories (NVSL). The National Veterinary Services Laboratories of the Animal and Plant Health Inspection Service, located in Ames, Iowa.

National Veterinary Services Laboratories, Foreign Animal Disease Diagnostic Laboratory (FADDL). The National Veterinary Services Laboratories, Foreign Animal Disease Diagnostic Laboratory, located in Greenport, New York.

Nonstandard care and handling. Nonstandard care and handling includes hand-feeding, more than one feeding per day, frequent observation, and any handling or observation that requires personnel to attend to the birds or poultry outside of normal business hours.[2]

Nonstandard housing. Nonstandard housing is individual housing not normally available at an APHIS animal import center, any housing constructed or purchased at the request of the importer, any housing with blinds, dense foliage, or plants, and any housing where the temperature can be adjusted.

Person. An individual, corporation, partnership, trust, association, or any other public or private entity, or any officer, employee, or agent thereof.

Pet birds. Birds, except hatching eggs and ratites, that are imported or exported for the personal pleasure of their individual owners and are not intended for resale.

Poultry. Chickens, doves, ducks, geese, grouse, guinea fowl, partridges, pea fowl, pheasants, pigeons, quail, swans, and turkeys.

Privately operated permanent import-quarantine facility. Any permanent facility approved under 9 CFR part 93 to quarantine animals or birds, except facilities operated by APHIS.

Registered animal. Any animal recorded in the book of record of an animal registry association which issues certificates concerning the pedigree of animals.

Slaughter animal. Any animal moving directly to slaughter.

Standard feed. Seed, or dry feeds such as dog food or monkey biscuits, whether soaked in water or not.

State animal health official. The State official responsible for livestock and poultry disease control and eradication programs.

[2] Normal business hours at the APHIS Animal Import Centers are: 7 a.m. to 3:30 p.m., Miami, FL; and 8 a.m. to 4:30 p.m., Newburgh, NY.

Test. A single analysis performed on a single specimen from an animal, animal product, commercial product, or animal feed.

United States. The several States of the United States, the District of Columbia, Guam, the Commonwealth of the Northern Mariana Islands, the Commonwealth of Puerto Rico, the Virgin Islands of the United States, and all other territories and possessions of the United States.

Zoo animal. Any animal, including poultry, intended for exhibition in a zoo, park or other place maintained for the exhibition of live animals for recreational or educational purposes.[3]

Zoo bird. Any bird intended for exhibition in a zoo, park or other place maintained for the exhibition of live animals or birds for recreational or educational purposes.

Zoo equine. Any equine intended for exhibition in a zoo, park or other place maintained for the exhibition of live animals for recreational or educational purposes.

[57 FR 771, Jan. 9, 1992, as amended at 58 FR 38957, July 21, 1993; 58 FR 67654, Dec. 22, 1993; 59 FR 67617, Dec. 30, 1994; 61 FR 20432, May 7, 1996; 62 FR 56026, Oct. 28, 1997; 63 FR 53788, Oct. 7, 1998; 63 FR 64175, Nov. 19, 1998; 64 FR 67698, Dec. 3, 1999; 65 FR 38178, 38180, June 20, 2000; 68 FR 64507, Nov. 14, 2003; 74 FR 14001, Mar. 30, 2009]

§ 130.2 User fees for individual animals and certain birds quarantined in the APHIS-owned or -operated quarantine facilities, including APHIS Animal Import Centers.

(a) *Standard requirements.* User fees for any service rendered by an APHIS representative for each animal or bird receiving standard housing, care, feed, and handling while quarantined in an APHIS owned or operated animal import center or quarantine facility are listed in the following table. Each user fee listed in the table is assessed per animal or bird quarantined by APHIS. The person for whom the service is provided and the person requesting the service are jointly and severally liable for payment of these user fees in accordance with §§ 130.50 and 130.51.

Animal or bird	Daily user fee				
	Apr. 29, 2009–Sept. 30, 2009	Oct. 1, 2009–Sept. 30, 2010	Oct. 1, 2010–Sept. 30, 2011	Oct. 1, 2011–Sept. 30, 2012	Beginning Oct. 1, 2012
Birds (excluding ratites and pet birds imported in accordance with part 93 of this subchapter):					
0–250 grams	$2.50	$2.75	$2.75	$2.75	$3.00
251–1,000 grams	8.25	8.50	8.75	9.00	9.25
Over 1,000 grams	18.00	19.00	19.00	20.00	21.00
Domestic or zoo animals (except equines, birds, and poultry):					
Bison, bulls, camels, cattle, or zoo animals	144.00	149.00	153.00	158.00	162.00
All others, including, but not limited to, alpacas, llamas, goats, sheep, and swine	38.00	39.00	40.00	42.00	43.00
Equines (including zoo equines, but excluding miniature horses):					
1st through 3rd day (fee per day)	382.00	393.00	405.00	417.00	429.00
4th through 7th day (fee per day)	276.00	284.00	292.00	301.00	310.00
8th and subsequent days (fee per day)	235.00	242.00	249.00	256.00	264.00
Miniature horses	86.00	89.00	91.00	94.00	97.00
Poultry (including zoo poultry):					
Doves, pigeons, quail	5.00	5.25	5.50	5.50	5.75
Chickens, ducks, grouse, guinea fowl, partridge, pea fowl, pheasants	9.00	9.25	9.50	9.75	10.00

[3] Regulations concerning approval of zoos and requirements for importing wild animals are found in part 93 of this chapter.

Animal or bird	Daily user fee				
	Apr. 29, 2009–Sept. 30, 2009	Oct. 1, 2009–Sept. 30, 2010	Oct. 1, 2010–Sept. 30, 2011	Oct. 1, 2011–Sept. 30, 2012	Beginning Oct. 1, 2012
Large poultry and large waterfowl, including, but not limited to, gamecocks, geese, swans, and turkeys	21.00	22.00	22.00	23.00	24.00
Ratites:					
Chicks (less than 3 months old)	13.00	13.00	14.00	14.00	15.00
Juveniles (3 months through 10 months old)	20.00	20.00	21.00	22.00	22.00
Adults (11 months old or older)	38.00	39.00	40.00	42.00	43.00

(b) *Special requirements.* User fees for birds or poultry, including zoo birds or poultry, receiving nonstandard housing, care, or handling to meet special requirements while quarantined in an APHIS owned or operated Animal Import Center or quarantine facility are listed in the following table. The user fees listed in the table are assessed for each bird or poultry quarantined by APHIS. Special requirements may be requested by the importer or required by an APHIS representative. Certain conditions or traits, such as pregnancy or aggression, may necessitate special requirements for certain birds or poultry. The person for whom the service is provided and the person requesting the service are jointly and severally liable for payment of these user fees in accordance with §§ 130.50 and 130.51.

Bird or poultry (nonstandard housing, care, or handling)	Daily user fee				
	Apr. 29, 2009–Sept. 30, 2009	Oct. 1, 2009–Sept. 30, 2010	Oct. 1, 2010–Sept. 30, 2011	Oct. 1, 2011–Sept. 30, 2012	Beginning Oct. 1, 2012
Birds 0–250 grams and doves, pigeons and quail	$8.25	$8.50	$8.75	$9.00	$9.25
Birds 251–1,000 grams and poultry such as chickens, ducks, grouse, guinea fowl, partridge, pea fowl, and pheasants	18.00	19.00	19.00	20.00	21.00
Birds over 1,000 grams and large poultry and large waterfowl, including, but not limited to gamecocks, geese, swans, and turkeys	35.00	36.00	37.00	39.00	40.00

(c) *Feed.* The importer must either provide feed or pay for it on an actual cost basis, including the cost of delivery to the APHIS owned or operated Animal Import Center or quarantine facility, for any animal or bird that requires a diet other than standard feed, including but not limited to diets of fruit, insects, nectar, or fish.

(Approved by the Office of Management and Budget under control number 0579–0094)

[63 FR 53788, Oct. 7, 1998, as amended at 65 FR 52005, Aug. 28, 2000; 68 FR 51883, Aug. 29, 2003; 68 FR 62227, Nov. 3, 2003; 72 FR 70765, Dec. 13, 2007; 74 FR 14001, Mar. 30, 2009]

§ 130.3 User fees for exclusive use of space at APHIS Animal Import Centers.

(a)(1) An importer may request to exclusively occupy a space at an APHIS animal import center. The user fees for spaces at APHIS animal import centers are listed in the following table. The person for whom the service is provided and the person requesting the service are jointly and severally liable for payment of these user fees in accordance with §§ 130.50 and 130.51.

Animal import center	Monthly user fee				
	Apr. 29, 2009–Sept. 30, 2009	Oct. 1, 2009–Sept. 30, 2010	Oct. 1, 2010–Sept. 30, 2011	Oct. 1, 2011–Sept. 30, 2012	Beginning October 1, 2012
Newburgh, NY:					

Animal import center	Monthly user fee				
	Apr. 29, 2009–Sept. 30, 2009	Oct. 1, 2009–Sept. 30, 2010	Oct. 1, 2010–Sept. 30, 2011	Oct. 1, 2011–Sept. 30, 2012	Beginning October 1, 2012
Space A 5,396 sq. ft. (503.1 sq. m.)	$83,756.00	$86,268.00	$88,856.00	$91, 513.00	$94,249.00
Space B 8,903 sq. ft. (827.1 sq. m.)	138,190.00	142,335.00	146,605.00	150,989.00	155,504.00
Space C 905 sq. ft. (84.1 sq. m.)	14,047.00	14,469.00	14,903.00	15,348.00	15,807.00

(2) Any importer who occupies space for more than 30 days must pay 1/30th of the 30-day fee for each additional day or part of a day. The person for whom the service is provided and the person requesting the service are jointly and severally liable for any additional charges.

(3) Unless the importer cancels the reservation for exclusive use of space in time to receive a refund of the reservation fee in accordance with 9 CFR 93.103, 93.204, 93.304, 93.404, or 93.504, as appropriate, the 30-day user fee will be effective as of the first day for which the importer has reserved the space, regardless of whether the user occupies the space on that date or not.

(b) Users must provide APHIS personnel at the Animal Import Center, at the time they make a reservation for quarantine space, with the following information:

(1) Species of animals and birds to be quarantined;

(2) Ages of animals and birds to be quarantined; and

(3) Sizes of animals and birds to be quarantined.

(c)(1) APHIS personnel at the Animal Importer Center will determine, based on the information provided by the importer under paragraph (b) of this section, and on routine husbandry needs, the maximum number of animals and birds permitted in the requested building.

(2) If the number of animals and birds requested by the importer can be housed in the space requested, as determined by APHIS personnel at the Animal Import Center, but two animal health technicians cannot fulfill the routine husbandry needs of the number of animals or birds proposed by the importer, then the importer must pay for additional services on an hourly basis, or reduce the number of animals or birds to be quarantined to a number which APHIS personnel at the Animal Import Center determine can be handled by two animal health technicians.

(3) If the importer requests additional services, then the user fees for any service rendered by an APHIS representative will be calculated at the hourly rate user fee listed in § 130.30, for each employee required to perform the service.

(d) The importer must provide feed, or pay for it on an actual cost basis, including cost of delivery to the Animal Import Center.

(Approved by the Office of Management and Budget under control numbers 0579–0040 and 0579–0094)

[57 FR 771, Jan. 9, 1992, as amended at 58 FR 67654, Dec. 22, 1993; 61 FR 20432, May 7, 1996; 62 FR 56026, Oct. 28, 1997; 63 FR 53789, Oct. 7, 1998; 65 FR 52006, Aug. 28, 2000; 68 FR 51883, Aug. 29, 2003; 72 FR 70765, Dec. 13, 2007; 74 FR 14002, Mar. 30, 2009; 74 FR 18115, Apr. 21, 2009]

§ 130.4 User fees for processing import permit applications.

User fees for any service rendered by an APHIS representative for processing applications for permits to import certain animals and animal products (using VS forms 16–3 and 17–129) are listed in the table in this section. The person for whom the service is provided and the person requesting the service are jointly and severally liable for payment of these user fees in accordance with §§ 130.50 and 130.51. These fees are nonrefundable. The table follows:

Service	Unit	User fee				
		Apr. 29, 2009–Sept. 30, 2009	Oct. 1, 2009–Sept. 30, 2010	Oct. 1, 2010–Sept. 30, 2011	Oct. 1, 2011–Sept. 30, 2012	Beginning Oct. 1, 2012
Import compliance assistance:						
Simple (4 hours or less) ..	Per shipment ..	$99.00	$102.00	$105.00	$108.00	$111.00
Complicated (more than 4 hours).	Per shipment ..	514.00	514.00	531.00	548.00	565.00
Processing an application for a permit to import live animals, animal products or by products, organisms, vectors, or germ plasm (embryos or semen) or to transport organisms or vectors [1]						
Initial permit	Per application	133.00	137.00	141.00	145.00	150.00
Amended permit	Per amended application.	66.00	68.00	70.00	73.00	75.00
Renewed permit [2]	Per application	86.00	89.00	91.00	94.00	97.00
Processing an application for a permit to import fetal bovine serum when facility inspection is required.	Per application	455.00	469.00	483.00	497.00	512.00

[1] Using Veterinary Services Form 16–3, "Application for Permit to Import or Transport Controlled Material or Organisms or Vectors," or Form 17–129, "Application for Import or In Transit Permit (Animals, Animal Semen, Animal Embryos, Birds, Poultry, or Hatching Eggs)."

[2] Permits to import germ plasm and live animals are not renewable.

[66 FR 39631, Aug. 1, 2001, as amended at 68 FR 51883, Aug. 29, 2003; 72 FR 70766, Dec. 13, 2007; 74 FR 14002, Mar. 30, 2009]

§ 130.5 User fees for services at privately owned permanent and temporary import quarantine facilities.

(a) User fees for any service rendered by an APHIS representative for each animal quarantined in a privately operated permanent or temporary import quarantine facility will be calculated at the hourly user fee rate listed in § 130.30, for each employee required to perform the service. The person for whom the service is provided and the person requesting the service are jointly and severally liable for payment of these user fees in accordance with §§ 130.50 and 130.51.

(b) [Reserved]

(Approved by the Office of Management and Budget under control number 0579–0094)

[65 FR 52006, Aug. 28, 2000, as amended at 72 FR 70766, Dec. 13, 2007]

§ 130.6 User fees for inspection of live animals at land border ports along the United States-Mexico border.

(a) User fees for any service rendered by an APHIS representative for live animals presented for importation into or entry into the United States through a land border port along the United States-Mexico border are listed in the following table. The minimum user fee for this service is listed in § 130.30. The person for whom the service is provided and the person requesting the service are jointly and severally liable for payment of these user fees in accordance with §§ 130.50 and 130.51.

Type of live animal	Per head user fee				
	April 29, 2009–Sept. 30, 2009	Oct. 1, 2009–Sept. 30, 2010	Oct. 1, 2010–Sept. 30, 2011	Oct. 1, 2011–Sept. 30, 2012	Beginning Oct. 1, 2012
Any ruminants (including breeder ruminants) not covered below	$13.00	$13.00	$14.00	$14.00	$14.00
Feeder	3.75	3.75	4.00	4.00	4.00
Horses, other than slaughter	62.00	64.00	66.00	68.00	70.00
In-bond or in-transit	8.25	8.50	8.75	9.00	9.25

Type of live animal	Per head user fee				
	April 29, 2009–Sept. 30, 2009	Oct. 1, 2009–Sept. 30, 2010	Oct. 1, 2010–Sept. 30, 2011	Oct. 1, 2011–Sept. 30, 2012	Beginning Oct. 1, 2012
Slaughter	5.50	5.50	5.75	6.00	6.00

(b) [Reserved]

(Approved by the Office of Management and Budget under control numbers 0579–0055 and 0579–0094)

[65 FR 52006, Aug. 28, 2000, as amended at 68 FR 51884, Aug. 29, 2003; 72 FR 70766, Dec. 13, 2007; 74 FR 14003, Mar. 30, 2009]

§ 130.7 User fees for import or entry services for live animals at land border ports along the United States-Canada border.

(a) User fees for any service rendered by an APHIS representative for live animals presented for importation into or entry into the United States through a land border port along the United States-Canada border are listed in the following table. The minimum user fee for this service is listed in § 130.30. The person for whom the service is provided and the person requesting the service are jointly and severally liable for payment of these user fees in accordance with §§ 130.50 and 130.51.

Type of live animal	Unit	User fee				
		Apr. 29, 2009–Sept. 30, 2009	Oct. 1, 2009–Sept. 30, 2010	Oct. 1, 2010–Sept. 30, 2011	Oct. 1, 2011–Sept. 30, 2012	Beginning Oct. 1, 2012
Animals being imported into the United States: Breeding animals (Grade animals, except horses):						
Sheep and goats	Per head	$0.75	$0.75	$0.75	$1.00	$1.00
Swine	Per head	1.25	1.25	1.25	1.25	1.25
All others	Per head	4.75	4.75	5.00	5.25	5.25
Feeder animals:						
Cattle (not including calves).	Per head	2.25	2.25	2.50	2.50	2.50
Sheep and calves	Per head	0.75	0.75	1.00	1.00	1.00
Swine	Per head	0.50	0.50	0.50	0.50	0.50
Horses (including registered horses) other than slaughter and in-transit.	Per head	41.00	42.00	43.00	45.00	46.00
Poultry (including eggs), imported for any purpose.	Per load	71.00	73.00	75.00	77.00	80.00
Registered animals, all types (except horses).	Per head	8.50	8.75	9.25	9.50	9.75
Slaughter animals, all types (except poultry).	Per load	35.00	36.00	37.00	39.00	40.00
Animals transiting [1] the United States:						
Cattle	Per head	2.25	2.25	2.50	2.50	2.50
Sheep and goats	Per head	0.50	0.50	0.50	0.50	0.50
Swine	Per head	0.50	0.50	0.50	0.50	0.50
Horses and all other animals.	Per head	9.75	10.00	10.00	10.00	11.00

[1] The user fee in this section will be charged for in-transit authorizations at the port where the authorization services are performed. For additional services provided by APHIS, at any port, the hourly user fee in § 130.30 will apply.

(b) If a service must be conducted on a Sunday or holiday or at any other time outside the normal tour of duty of the employee, then reimbursable overtime, as provided for in part 97 of this chapter, must be paid for each service, in addition to the user fee listed in this section.

(Approved by the Office of Management and Budget under control numbers 0579–0055 and 0579–0094)

[65 FR 52007, Aug. 28, 2000, as amended at 67 FR 48524, July 25, 2002; 68 FR 51884, Aug. 29, 2003; 72 FR 70766, Dec. 13, 2007; 74 FR 14003, Mar. 30, 2009]

§ 130.8 User fees for other services.

(a) User fees for any service rendered by an APHIS representative for other services that are not specifically addressed elsewhere in part 130 are listed in the following table. The person for whom the service is provided and the person requesting the service are jointly and severally liable for payment of these user fees in accordance with §§ 130.50 and 130.51.

Service	Unit	User fee				
		Apr. 29, 2009–Sept. 30, 2009	Oct. 1, 2009–Sept. 30, 2010	Oct. 1, 2010–Sept. 30, 2011	Oct. 1, 2011–Sept. 30, 2012	Beginning Oct. 1, 2012
Germ plasm being exported: [1]						
Embryo:						
Up to 5 donor pairs	Per certificate	$117.00	$121.00	$124.00	$128.00	$132.00
Each additional group of donor pairs, up to 5 pairs per group on the same certificate.	Per group of donor pairs.	52.00	54.00	55.00	57.00	59.00
Semen	Per certificate	72.00	74.00	76.00	79.00	81.00
Release from export agricultural hold:						
Simple (2 hours or less)	Per release	99.00	102.00	105.00	108.00	111.00
Complicated (more than 2 hours).	Per release	254.00	262.00	270.00	278.00	286.00

[1] This user fee includes a single inspection and resealing of the container at the APHIS employee's regular tour of duty station or at a limited port. For each subsequent inspection and resealing required, the hourly user fee in § 130.3 will apply.

(b) [Reserved]

(Approved by the Office of Management and Budget under control numbers 0579–0015, 0579–0040, 0579–0055 and 0579–0094)

[65 FR 52007, Aug. 28, 2000, as amended at 66 FR 39632, Aug. 1, 2001; 68 FR 51884, Aug. 29, 2003; 72 FR 70766, Dec. 13, 2007; 74 FR 14004, Mar. 30, 2009]

§ 130.9 [Reserved]

§ 130.10 User fees for pet birds.

(a) User fees for pet birds of U.S. origin returning to the United States, except pet birds of U.S. origin returning from Canada, are as follows:

Service	Per lot user fee				
	Apr. 29, 2009–Sept. 30, 2009	Oct. 1, 2009–Sept. 30, 2010	Oct. 1, 2010–Sept. 30, 2011	Oct. 1, 2011–Sept. 30, 2012	Beginning Oct. 1, 2012
(1) Which have been out of the United States 60 days or less	$153.00	$157.00	$162.00	$167.00	$172.00
(2) Which have been out of the United States more than 60 days	363.00	374.00	385.00	397.00	409.00

(b) User fees for each pet bird quarantined in an animal import center or other APHIS-owned or supervised quarantine facility are listed in the following table. These user fees include standard care, feed, and handling. The person for whom the service is provided and the person requesting the service are jointly and severally liable for payment of these user fees in accordance with §§ 130.50 and 130.51.

Number of birds in isolette	Daily user fee				
	Apr. 29, 2009–Sept. 30, 2009	Oct. 1, 2009–Sept. 30, 2010	Oct. 1, 2010–Sept. 30, 2011	Oct. 1, 2011–Sept. 30, 2012	Beginning Oct. 1, 2012
1	$13.00	$13.00	$14.00	$14.00	$15.00
2	16.00	16.00	17.00	17.00	18.00
3	18.00	19.00	19.00	20.00	21.00
4	21.00	22.00	22.00	23.00	24.00
5 or more	25.00	26.00	27.00	28.00	29.00

(c) Based on the information provided to APHIS personnel, APHIS personnel at the Animal Import Center or other APHIS owned or supervised quarantine facility will determine the appropriate number of birds that should be housed per isolette.

(d) If the importer requests additional services, then the user fees for those services will be calculated at the hourly rate user fee listed in § 130.30, for each employee required to perform the service.

(Approved by the Office of Management and Budget under control number 0579–0094)

[61 FR 20434, May 7, 1996; 61 FR 25513, May 21, 1996, as amended at 62 FR 56026, Oct. 28, 1997; 63 FR 53791, Oct. 7, 1998; 64 FR 67700, Dec. 3, 1999; 65 FR 52008, Aug. 28, 2000; 68 FR 51885, Aug. 29, 2003; 74 FR 14004, Mar. 30, 2009]

§ 130.11 User fees for inspecting and approving import/export facilities and establishments.

(a) User fees for the inspection of various import and export facilities and establishments are listed in the following table. The person for whom the service is provided and the person requesting the service are jointly and severally liable for payment of these user fees in accordance with §§ 130.50 and 130.51. These user fees do not apply to inspection activities covered in § 130.30(a)(2).

Service	Unit	User fee				
		Apr. 29, 2009–Sept. 30, 2009	Oct. 1, 2009–Sept. 30, 2010	Oct. 1, 2010–Sept. 30, 2011	Oct. 1, 2011–Sept. 30, 2012	Beginning Oct. 1, 2012
Embryo collection center inspection and approval (all inspections required during the year for facility approval).	Per year	$537.00	$553.00	$570.00	$587.00	$604.00
Inspection for approval of biosecurity level three labs (all inspections related to approving the laboratory for handling one defined set of organisms or vectors) [1].	Per inspection	1,381.00	1,422.00	1,465.00	1,509.00	1,554.00
Inspection for approval of slaughter establishment:						
Initial approval (all inspections).	Per year	527.00	543.00	559.00	576.00	593.00
Renewal (all inspections)	Per year	457.00	470.00	484.00	499.00	514.00
Inspection of approved establishments, warehouses, and facilities under 9 CFR parts 94 through 96:						
Approval (compliance agreement) (all inspections for first year of 3-year approval).	Per year	563.00	579.00	597.00	615.00	633.00
Renewal (all inspections for second and third years of 3-year approval).	Per year	325.00	335.00	345.00	355.00	366.00

[1] The hourly user fee rate in § 130.30(2) applies to biosecurity level two laboratories.

(b) [Reserved]

[65 FR 52008, Aug. 28, 2000, as amended at 68 FR 51885, Aug. 29, 2003; 68 FR 64507, Nov. 14, 2003; 72 FR 70766, Dec. 13, 2007; 74 FR 14004, Mar. 30, 2009]

§§ 130.12–130.13 [Reserved]

§ 130.14 User fees for FADDL veterinary diagnostics.

(a) Diagnostic reagents. User fees for diagnostic reagents[4] provided by FADDL are listed in the following table. The person for whom the service is provided and the person requesting the service are jointly and severally liable for payment of these user fees in accordance with §§ 130.50 and 130.51.

Reagent	Unit	User fee			
		June 7, 2004–Sept. 30, 2004	Oct. 1, 2004–Sept. 30, 2005	Oct. 1, 2005–Sept. 30, 2006	Beginning Oct. 1, 2006
Bovine antiserum, any agent	1 mL	$150.00	$155.00	$160.00	$165.00
Caprine antiserum, any agent	1 mL	184.00	189.00	195.00	202.00
Cell culture antigen/microorganism	1 mL	103.00	106.00	109.00	111.00
Equine antiserum, any agent	1 mL	186.00	192.00	198.00	204.00
Fluorescent antibody conjugate	1 mL	169.00	172.00	176.00	179.00
Guinea pig antiserum, any agent	1 mL	184.00	189.00	194.00	200.00
Monoclonal antibody	1 mL	222.00	229.00	235.00	243.00
Ovine antiserum, any agent	1 mL	176.00	181.00	187.00	193.00
Porcine antiserum, any agent	1 mL	152.00	157.00	162.00	167.00
Rabbit antiserum, any agent	1 mL	179.00	185.00	190.00	196.00

(b) *Veterinary diagnostics tests*. User fees for veterinary diagnostic tests performed at FADDL are listed in the following table. The person for whom the service is provided and the person requesting the service are jointly and severally liable for payment of these user fees in accordance with §§ 130.50 and 130.51.

Test	Unit	User fee			
		June 7, 2004–Sept. 30, 2004	Oct. 1, 2004–Sept. 30, 2005	Oct. 1, 2005–Sept. 30, 2006	Beginning Oct. 1, 2006
Agar gel immunodiffusion	Test	$30.00	$31.00	$32.00	$33.00
Card	Test	17.00	17.00	18.00	18.00
Complement fixation	Test	36.00	37.00	38.00	40.00
Direct immunofluorescent antibody	Test	22.00	23.00	24.00	25.00
Enzyme linked immunosorbent assay	Test	26.00	27.00	28.00	29.00
Fluorescent antibody neutralization (classical swine fever).	Test	194.00	201.00	208.00	215.00
Hemagglutination inhibition	Test	57.00	59.00	61.00	63.00
Immunoperoxidase	Test	29.00	30.00	31.00	32.00
Indirect fluorescent antibody	Test	35.00	36.00	37.00	39.00
In-vitro safety	Test	570.00	589.00	609.00	630.00
In-vivo safety	Test	5,329.00	5,387.00	5,447.00	5,509.00
Latex agglutination	Test	23.00	24.00	25.00	26.00
Tube agglutination	Test	28.00	28.00	29.00	30.00
Virus isolation (oesophageal/pharyngeal).	Test	180.00	186.00	192.00	199.00
Virus isolation in embryonated eggs	Test	346.00	358.00	370.00	383.00
Virus isolation, other	Test	155.00	160.00	166.00	171.00
Virus neutralization	Test	52.00	54.00	56.00	58.00

[4] Reagents provided by FADDL are for the diagnosis of animal diseases foreign to the United States. These reagents may be available to customers on the mainland after safety testing with permission from the Administrator. The customer may have to pay the cost for the safety test in addition to the reagent user fee. For more information on the specific reagents contact: Laboratory Chief, USDA, APHIS, VS, FADDL, Greenport, NY 11344; phone (516) 323–2500, FAX (516) 323–2798.

(c) *Other veterinary diagnostic services.* User fees for other veterinary diagnostic services performed at FADDL are listed in the following table. The person for whom the service is provided and the person requesting the service are jointly and severally liable for payment of these user fees in accordance with §§ 130.50 and 130.51.

Veterinary diagnostic service	Unit	User fee			
		June 7, 2004–Sept. 30, 2004	Oct. 1, 2004–Sept. 30, 2005	Oct. 1, 2005–Sept. 30, 2006	Beginning Oct. 1, 2006
Bacterial isolation	Test	$112.00	$115.00	$119.00	$123.00
Hourly user fee services [1]	Hour	445.00	460.00	476.00	492.00
Hourly user fee services—Quarter hour	Quarter hour	111.00	115.00	119.00	123.00
Infected cells on chamber slides or plates.	Slide	49.00	50.00	51.00	53.00
Reference animal tissues for immunohistochemistry.	Set	171.00	177.00	182.00	187.00
Sterilization by gamma radiation	Can	1,740.00	1,799.00	1,860.00	1,923.00
Training (school or technical assistance)	Per person per day.	910.00	941.00	973.00	1,006.00
Virus titration	Test	112.00	115.00	119.00	123.00

[1] For all veterinary diagnostic services for which there is no flat rate user fee, the hourly rate user fee will be calculated for the actual time required to provide the service.

(Approved by the Office of Management and Budget under control numbers 0579–0055 and 0579–0094)

[63 FR 53791, Oct. 7, 1998, as amended at 64 FR 67700, Dec. 3, 1999; 68 FR 16940, Apr. 7, 2003; 69 FR 25307, May 6, 2004]

§ 130.15 User fees for veterinary diagnostic isolation and identification tests performed at NVSL (excluding FADDL) or other authorized site.

(a) *Bacteriology isolation and identification tests.* User fees for bacteriology isolation and identification tests performed at NVSL (excluding FADDL) or other authorized sites are listed in the following table. The person for whom the service is provided and the person requesting the service are jointly and severally liable for payment of these user fees in accordance with §§ 130.50 and 130.51.

Test	Unit	User fee				
		Jan. 18, 2008–Sept. 30, 2008	Oct. 1, 2008–Sept. 30, 2009	Oct. 1, 2009–Sept. 30, 2010	Oct. 1, 2010–Sept. 30, 2011	Beginning Oct. 1, 2011
Bacterial identification, automated	Isolate	$53.00	$54.00	$55.00	$57.00	$58.00
Bacterial identification, non-automated.	Isolate	90.00	92.00	94.00	96.00	98.00
Bacterial isolation	Sample	36.00	37.00	38.00	39.00	40.00
Bacterial serotyping, all other	Isolate	55.00	56.00	56.00	57.00	58.00
Bacterial serotyping, Pasteurella multocida.	Isolate	18.00	19.00	19.00	19.00	20.00
Bacterial serotyping, Salmonella	Isolate	36.00	37.00	38.00	39.00	40.00
Bacterial toxin typing	Isolate	120.00	123.00	126.00	128.00	131.00
Bacteriology requiring special characterization.	Test	92.00	94.00	96.00	98.00	101.00
DNA fingerprinting	Test	59.00	61.00	62.00	63.00	64.00
DNA probe	Test	83.00	85.00	86.00	88.00	89.00
Fluorescent antibody	Test	19.00	19.00	20.00	20.00	20.00
Mycobacterium identification (biochemical).	Isolate	115.00	117.00	120.00	122.00	125.00
Mycobacterium identification (gas chromatography).	Procedure	96.00	99.00	101.00	103.00	105.00
Mycobacterium isolation, animal inoculations.	Submission	844.00	852.00	868.00	884.00	900.00
Mycobacterium isolation, all other	Submission	151.00	154.00	158.00	161.00	165.00
Mycobacterium paratuberculosis isolation.	Submission	72.00	74.00	75.00	77.00	79.00
Phage typing, all other	Isolate	42.00	43.00	44.00	45.00	46.00

Test	Unit	User fee				
		Jan. 18, 2008–Sept. 30, 2008	Oct. 1, 2008–Sept. 30, 2009	Oct. 1, 2009–Sept. 30, 2010	Oct. 1, 2010–Sept. 30, 2011	Beginning Oct. 1, 2011
Phage typing, Salmonella enteritidis.	Isolate	24.00	24.00	25.00	25.00	26.00

(b) *Virology identification tests.* User fees for virology identification tests performed at NVSL (excluding FADDL) or other authorized sites are listed in the following table. The person for whom the service is provided and the person requesting the service are jointly and severally liable for payment of these user fees in accordance with §§ 130.50 and 130.51.

Test	Unit	User fee				
		Jan. 18, 2008–Sept. 30, 2008	Oct. 1, 2008–Sept. 30, 2009	Oct. 1, 2009–Sept. 30, 2010	Oct. 1, 2010–Sept. 30, 2011	Beginning Oct. 1, 2011
Fluorescent antibody tissue section.	Test	$29.00	$30.00	$30.00	$31.00	$31.00
Virus isolation	Test	48.00	49.00	50.00	51.00	52.00

(Approved by the Office of Management and Budget under control numbers 0579–0055 and 0579–0094)

[63 FR 53792, Oct. 7, 1998, as amended at 69 FR 25308, May 6, 2004; 72 FR 71746, Dec. 19, 2007]

§ 130.16 User fees for veterinary diagnostic serology tests performed at NVSL (excluding FADDL) or at authorized sites.

(a) *Bacteriology serology tests.* User fees for bacteriology serology tests performed at NVSL (excluding FADDL) or other authorized sites are listed in the following table. The person for whom the service is provided and the person requesting the service are jointly and severally liable for payment of these user fees in accordance with §§ 130.50 and 130.51.

Test	Unit	User fee				
		Jan. 18, 2008–Sept. 30, 2008	Oct. 1, 2008–Sept. 30, 2009	Oct. 1, 2009–Sept. 30, 2010	Oct. 1, 2010–Sept. 30, 2011	Beginning Oct. 1, 2011
Brucella ring (BRT)	Test	$36.00	$37.00	$38.00	$39.00	$40.00
Brucella ring, heat inactivated (HIRT).	Test	36.00	37.00	38.00	39.00	40.00
Brucella ring, serial (Serial BRT)	Test	54.00	56.00	57.00	58.00	59.00
Buffered acidified plate antigen presumptive.	Test	7.00	7.25	7.50	7.50	8.00
Card	Test	4.00	4.00	4.25	4.25	4.50
Complement fixation	Test	16.00	17.00	17.00	18.00	18.00
Enzyme linked immunosorbent assay.	Test	16.00	17.00	17.00	18.00	18.00
Indirect fluorescent antibody	Test	14.00	15.00	15.00	15.00	16.00
Microscopic agglutination—includes up to 5 serovars.	Sample	24.00	24.00	25.00	25.00	26.00
Microscopic agglutination—each serovar in excess of 5 serovars.	Sample	4.25	4.50	4.50	4.50	4.75
Particle concentration fluorescent immunoassay (PCFIA).	Test	36.00	37.00	38.00	38.00	39.00
Plate	Test	7.00	7.25	7.50	7.50	7.75
Rapid automated presumptive	Test	7.00	7.00	7.25	7.25	7.25
Rivanol	Test	7.00	7.25	7.50	7.50	7.75
Tube agglutination	Test	7.00	7.25	7.50	7.50	7.75

(b) *Virology serology tests.* User fees for virology serology tests performed at NVSL (excluding FADDL) or at authorized sites are listed in the following table. The person for whom the service is provided and the person requesting the service are jointly and severally liable for payment of these user fees in accordance with §§ 130.50 and 130.51.

Test	Unit	User fee				
		Jan. 18, 2008–Sept. 30, 2008	Oct. 1, 2008–Sept. 30, 2009	Oct. 1, 2009–Sept. 30, 2010	Oct. 1, 2010–Sept. 30, 2011	Beginning Oct. 1, 2011
Agar gel immunodiffusion	Test	$16.00	$17.00	$17.00	$17.00	$18.00
Complement fixation	Test	16.00	17.00	17.00	18.00	18.00
Enzyme linked immunosorbent assay.	Test	16.00	17.00	17.00	18.00	18.00
Hemagglutination inhibition	Test	14.00	15.00	15.00	15.00	16.00
Indirect fluorescent antibody	Test	14.00	15.00	15.00	15.00	16.00
Latex agglutination	Test	16.00	17.00	17.00	17.00	18.00
Peroxidase linked antibody	Test	15.00	16.00	16.00	16.00	17.00
Plaque reduction neutralization	Test	18.00	18.00	19.00	19.00	19.00
Rabies fluorescent antibody neutralization.	Test	45.00	46.00	47.00	49.00	50.00
Virus neutralization	Test	13.00	13.00	14.00	14.00	14.00

(Approved by the Office of Management and Budget under control numbers 0579–0055 and 0579–0094)

[63 FR 53793, Oct. 7, 1998, as amended at 69 FR 25309, May 6, 2004; 72 FR 71746, Dec. 19, 2007]

§ 130.17 User fees for other veterinary diagnostic laboratory tests performed at NVSL (excluding FADDL) or at authorized sites.

(a) User fees for veterinary diagnostics tests performed at the Pathobiology Laboratory at NVSL (excluding FADDL) or at authorized sites are listed in the following table. The person for whom the service is provided and the person requesting the service are jointly and severally liable for payment of these user fees in accordance with §§ 130.50 and 130.51.

Test	Unit	User fee				
		Jan. 18, 2008–Sept. 30, 2008	Oct. 1, 2008–Sept. 30, 2009	Oct. 1, 2009–Sept. 30, 2010	Oct. 1, 2010–Sept. 30, 2011	Beginning Oct. 1, 2011
Aflatoxin quantitation	Test	$30.00	$31.00	$32.00	$32.00	$33.00
Aflatoxin screen	Test	29.00	29.00	30.00	30.00	31.00
Agar gel immunodiffusion spp. identification.	Test	13.00	13.00	13.00	14.00	14.00
Antibiotic (bioautography) quantitation.	Test	66.00	67.00	68.00	70.00	72.00
Antibiotic (bioautography) screen	Test	119.00	122.00	125.00	128.00	130.00
Antibiotic inhibition	Test	66.00	67.00	68.00	70.00	72.00
Arsenic	Test	17.00	18.00	18.00	19.00	19.00
Ergot alkaloid screen	Test	66.00	67.00	68.00	70.00	72.00
Ergot alkaloid confirmation	Test	86.00	88.00	89.00	91.00	94.00
Feed microscopy	Test	66.00	67.00	68.00	70.00	72.00
Fumonisin only	Test	37.00	38.00	39.00	40.00	40.00
Gossypol	Test	98.00	100.00	103.00	105.00	107.00
Mercury	Test	145.00	148.00	151.00	155.00	158.00
Metals screen	Test	44.00	45.00	46.00	47.00	48.00
Metals single element confirmation.	Test	13.00	13.00	13.00	14.00	14.00
Mycotoxin: aflatoxin-liver	Test	119.00	122.00	125.00	128.00	130.00
Mycotoxin screen	Test	48.00	49.00	50.00	51.00	52.00
Nitrate/nitrite	Test	66.00	67.00	68.00	70.00	72.00
Organic compound confirmation	Test	88.00	90.00	92.00	94.00	96.00
Organic compound screen	Test	151.00	155.00	158.00	161.00	165.00
Parasitology	Test	29.00	29.00	30.00	30.00	31.00
Pesticide quantitation	Test	132.00	135.00	138.00	141.00	144.00
Pesticide screen	Test	60.00	62.00	63.00	64.00	66.00
pH	Test	26.00	27.00	28.00	28.00	29.00
Plate cylinder	Test	98.00	100.00	103.00	105.00	107.00

Test	Unit	User fee				
		Jan. 18, 2008–Sept. 30, 2008	Oct. 1, 2008–Sept. 30, 2009	Oct. 1, 2009–Sept. 30, 2010	Oct. 1, 2010–Sept. 30, 2011	Beginning Oct. 1, 2011
Selenium	Test	44.00	45.00	46.00	47.00	48.00
Silicate/carbonate disinfectant	Test	66.00	67.00	68.00	70.00	72.00
Temperature disks	Test	130.00	133.00	136.00	139.00	142.00
Toxicant quantitation, other	Test	110.00	112.00	115.00	117.00	120.00
Toxicant screen, other	Test	33.00	33.00	34.00	35.00	36.00
Vomitoxin only	Test	53.00	54.00	55.00	56.00	58.00
Water activity	Test	33.00	33.00	34.00	35.00	36.00
Zearaleone quantitation	Test	53.00	54.00	55.00	56.00	58.00
Zearaleone screen	Test	29.00	29.00	30.00	30.00	31.00

(b) [Reserved]

(Approved by the Office of Management and Budget under control numbers 0579–0055 and 0579–0094)

[63 FR 53793, Oct. 7, 1998, as amended at 69 FR 25309, May 6, 2004; 72 FR 71747, Dec. 19, 2007]

§ 130.18 User fees for veterinary diagnostic reagents produced at NVSL or other authorized site (excluding FADDL).

(a) *Bacteriology reagents.* User fees for bacteriology reagents produced by the Diagnostic Bacteriology Laboratory at NVSL (excluding FADDL) or other authorized site are listed in the following table. The person for whom the service is provided and the person requesting the service are jointly and severally liable for payment of these user fees in accordance with §§ 130.50 and 130.51.

Reagent	Unit	User fee				
		Jan. 18, 2008–Sept. 30, 2008	Oct. 1, 2008–Sept. 30, 2009	Oct. 1, 2009–Sept. 30, 2010	Oct. 1, 2010–Sept. 30, 2011	Beginning Oct. 1, 2011
Anaplasma card test antigen	2 mL	$95.00	$97.00	$99.00	$101.00	$103.00
Anaplasma card test kit without antigen.	Kit	127.00	130.00	133.00	136.00	139.00
Anaplasma CF antigen	2 mL	46.00	46.00	46.00	47.00	47.00
Anaplasma stabilate	4.5 mL	175.00	178.00	181.00	185.00	188.00
Avian origin bacterial antiserums	1 mL	48.00	49.00	50.00	51.00	52.00
Bacterial agglutinating antigens other than brucella and salmonella pullorum.	5 mL	54.00	55.00	57.00	58.00	59.00
Bacterial conjugates	1 mL	96.00	99.00	101.00	103.00	105.00
Bacterial disease CF antigens, all other.	1 mL	29.00	30.00	30.00	31.00	32.00
Bacterial ELISA antigens	1 mL	29.00	30.00	31.00	31.00	32.00
Bacterial or protozoal antiserums, all other.	1 mL	60.00	61.00	63.00	64.00	66.00
Bacterial reagent culture [1]	Culture	73.00	74.00	76.00	78.00	79.00
Bacterial reference culture [2]	Culture	228.00	233.00	239.00	244.00	249.00
Bacteriophage reference culture	Culture	172.00	176.00	180.00	183.00	188.00
Bovine serum factor	1 mL	18.00	18.00	19.00	19.00	19.00
Brucella abortus CF antigen	60 mL	151.00	154.00	158.00	161.00	165.00
Brucella agglutination antigens, all other.	60 mL	151.00	154.00	158.00	161.00	165.00
Brucella buffered plate antigen	60 mL	172.00	176.00	180.00	183.00	188.00
Brucella canis tube antigen	25 mL	114.00	116.00	119.00	121.00	124.00
Brucella card test antigen (packaged).	Package	90.00	92.00	94.00	96.00	98.00
Brucella card test kit without antigen.	Kit	113.00	114.00	116.00	117.00	119.00
Brucella cells	Gram	19.00	19.00	19.00	20.00	20.00
Brucella cells, dried	Pellet	6.00	6.00	6.25	6.25	6.25
Brucella ring test antigen	60 mL	241.00	246.00	252.00	257.00	263.00
Brucella rivanol solution	60 mL	29.00	30.00	31.00	31.00	32.00
Dourine CF antigen	1 mL	89.00	91.00	93.00	95.00	97.00
Dourine stabilate	4.5 mL	109.00	111.00	112.00	114.00	116.00

Reagent	Unit	User fee				
		Jan. 18, 2008–Sept. 30, 2008	Oct. 1, 2008–Sept. 30, 2009	Oct. 1, 2009–Sept. 30, 2010	Oct. 1, 2010–Sept. 30, 2011	Beginning Oct. 1, 2011
Equine and bovine origin babesia species antiserums.	1 mL	127.00	130.00	133.00	136.00	139.00
Equine negative control CF antigen.	1 mL	282.00	283.00	286.00	290.00	293.00
Flazo-orange	3 mL	13.00	13.00	13.00	13.00	14.00
Glanders CF antigen	1 mL	77.00	79.00	81.00	82.00	84.00
Hemoparasitic disease CF antigens, all other.	1 mL	541.00	553.00	565.00	577.00	590.00
Leptospira transport medium	10 mL	4.25	4.50	4.50	4.50	4.75
Monoclonal antibody	1 mL	95.00	97.00	99.00	101.00	103.00
Mycobacterium spp. old tuberculin	1 mL	24.00	24.00	25.00	25.00	26.00
Mycobacterium spp. PPD	1 mL	18.00	19.00	19.00	19.00	20.00
Mycoplasma hemagglutination antigens.	5 mL	180.00	184.00	188.00	192.00	197.00
Negative control serums	1 mL	18.00	19.00	19.00	19.00	20.00
Rabbit origin bacterial antiserum	1 mL	52.00	53.00	54.00	55.00	56.00
Salmonella pullorum microagglutination antigen.	5 mL	15.00	16.00	16.00	16.00	17.00
Stabilates, all other	4.5 mL	684.00	690.00	703.00	716.00	730.00

[1] A reagent culture is a bacterial culture that has been subcultured one or more times after being tested for purity and identity. It is intended for use as a reagent with a diagnostic test such as the leptospiral agglutination test.

[2] A reference culture is a bacterial culture that has been thoroughly tested for purity and identity. It should be suitable as a master seed for future cultures.

(b) *Virology reagents*. User fees for virology reagents produced by the Diagnostic Virology Laboratory at NVSL (excluding FADDL) or at authorized sites are listed in the following table. The person for whom the service is provided and the person requesting the service are jointly and severally liable for payment of these user fees in accordance with §§ 130.50 and 130.51.

Reagent	Unit	User fee				
		Jan. 18, 2008–Sept. 30, 2008	Oct. 1, 2008–Sept. 30, 2009	Oct. 1, 2009–Sept. 30, 2010	Oct. 1, 2010–Sept. 30, 2011	Beginning Oct. 1, 2011
Antigen, except avian influenza and chlamydia psittaci antigens, any.	2 mL	$61.00	$62.00	$64.00	$65.00	$67.00
Avian antiserum except avian influenza antiserum, any.	2 mL	48.00	49.00	51.00	52.00	53.00
Avian influenza antigen, any	2 mL	33.00	34.00	35.00	36.00	36.00
Avian influenza antiserum, any	6 mL	103.00	105.00	108.00	110.00	113.00
Bovine or ovine serum, any	2 mL	127.00	130.00	133.00	136.00	139.00
Cell culture	Flask	151.00	154.00	158.00	161.00	165.00
Chlamydia psittaci spp. of origin monoclonal antibody panel.	Panel	95.00	96.00	98.00	99.00	101.00
Conjugate, any	1 mL	73.00	75.00	76.00	78.00	80.00
Diluted positive control serum, any.	2 mL	24.00	25.00	25.00	26.00	27.00
Equine antiserum, any	2 mL	45.00	46.00	47.00	48.00	49.00
Monoclonal antibody	1 mL	102.00	104.00	106.00	108.00	110.00
Other spp. antiserum, any	1 mL	52.00	52.00	52.00	53.00	53.00
Porcine antiserum, any	2 mL	105.00	108.00	110.00	113.00	115.00
Porcine tissue sets	Tissue set	157.00	157.00	158.00	159.00	161.00
Positive control tissues, all	2 cm^2 section	60.00	62.00	63.00	65.00	66.00
Rabbit origin antiserum	1 mL	52.00	53.00	54.00	55.00	56.00
Reference virus, any	0.6 mL	180.00	184.00	188.00	193.00	197.00
Viruses (except reference viruses), chlamydia psittaci agent or chlamydia psittaci antigen, any.	0.6 mL	30.00	31.00	32.00	32.00	33.00

(Approved by the Office of Management and Budget under control number 0579–0094)

[63 FR 53794, Oct. 7, 1998, as amended at 68 FR 16940, Apr. 7, 2003; 69 FR 25310, May 6, 2004; 72 FR 71748, Dec. 19, 2007]

§ 130.19 User fees for other veterinary diagnostic services or materials provided at NVSL (excluding FADDL).

(a) User fees for other veterinary diagnostic services or materials available from NVSL (excluding FADDL) are listed in the following table. The person for whom the service is provided and the person requesting the service are jointly and severally liable for payment of these user fees in accordance with §§ 130.50 and 130.51.

Service	Unit	User fee				
		Jan. 18, 2008–Sept. 30, 2008	Oct. 1, 2008–Sept. 30, 2009	Oct. 1, 2009–Sept. 30, 2010	Oct. 1, 2010–Sept. 30, 2011	Beginning Oct. 1, 2011
Antimicrobial susceptibility test	Isolate	$105.00	$107.00	$109.00	$112.00	$114.00
Avian safety test	Test	4,082.00	4,090.00	4,099.00	4,109.00	4,180.00
Check tests, culture	Kit [1]	176.00	179.00	182.00	185.00	189.00
Check tests, serology	Kit [1]	361.00	369.00	377.00	385.00	394.00
Fetal bovine serum safety test	Verification	1,119.00	1,122.00	1,134.00	1,147.00	1,160.00
Hourly user fees: [2]						
Hour	Hour	104.00	104.00	108.00	112.00	112.00
Quarter hour	Quarter Hour	26.00	26.00	27.00	28.00	28.00
Minimum	30.00	31.00	32.00	33.00	33.00	
Manual, brucellosis culture.	1 copy	115.00	117.00	120.00	122.00	125.00
Manual, tuberculosis Culture (English or Spanish).	1 copy	172.00	176.00	180.00	183.00	188.00
Manual, Veterinary mycology.	1 copy	172.00	176.00	180.00	183.00	188.00
Manuals or standard operating procedure (SOP), all other.	1 copy	34.00	35.00	36.00	37.00	37.00
Manuals or SOP, per page.	1 page	2.25	2.50	2.50	2.75	2.75
Training (school or technical assistance).	Per person per day.	332.00	339.00	346.00	354.00	362.00

[1] Any reagents required for the check test will be charged separately.

[2] For veterinary diagnostic services for which there is no flat user fee the Hourly rate user fee will be calculated for the actual time required to provide the service.

(b) [Reserved]

(Approved by the Office of Management and Budget under control number 0579–0094)

[63 FR 53795, Oct. 7, 1998, as amended at 69 FR 25311, May 6, 2004; 72 FR 71749, Dec. 19, 2007]

§ 130.20 User fees for endorsing export certificates.

(a) User fees for the endorsement of export health certificates that do not require the verification of tests or vaccinations are listed in the following table. The user fees apply to each export health certificate[5] endorsed for the following types of animals, birds, or animal products, regardless of the number of animals, birds, or animal products covered by the certificate. The person for whom the service is provided and the person requesting the service are jointly and severally liable for payment of these user fees in accordance with §§ 130.50 and 130.51.

Certificate categories	User fee				
	Apr. 29, 2009–Sept. 30, 2009	Oct. 1, 2009–Sept. 30, 2010	Oct. 1, 2010–Sept. 30, 2011	Oct. 1, 2011–Sept. 30, 2012	Beginning Oct. 1, 2012
Animal and nonanimal products	$45.00	$47.00	$48.00	$49.00	$51.00
Hatching eggs	42.00	44.00	45.00	46.00	48.00
Poultry, including slaughter poultry	42.00	44.00	45.00	46.00	48.00

[5] An export health certificate may need to be endorsed for an animal being exported from the United States if the country to which the animal is being shipped requires one. APHIS endorses export health certificates as a service.

Certificate categories	User fee				
	Apr. 29, 2009–Sept. 30, 2009	Oct. 1, 2009–Sept. 30, 2010	Oct. 1, 2010–Sept. 30, 2011	Oct. 1, 2011–Sept. 30, 2012	Beginning Oct. 1, 2012
Ruminants, except slaughter ruminants moving to Canada or Mexico	47.00	48.00	49.00	51.00	52.00
Slaughter animals (except poultry but including ruminants) moving to Canada or Mexico	49.00	51.00	52.00	54.00	56.00
Other endorsements or certifications	34.00	35.00	36.00	37.00	38.00

(b)(1) User fees for the endorsement of export health certificates that require the verification of tests or vaccinations are listed in the following table. The user fees apply to each export health certificate[5] endorsed for animals and birds depending on the number of animals or birds covered by the certificate and the number of tests or vaccinations required. However, there will be a maximum user fee of 12 times the hourly rate user fee listed in § 130.30(a) of this part for any single shipment. The person for whom the service is provided and the person requesting the service are jointly and severally liable for payment of these user fees in accordance with the provisions in §§ 130.50 and 130.51.

Number[1] of tests or vaccinations and number of animals or birds on the certificate	User fee				
	Apr. 29, 2009–Sept. 30, 2009	Oct. 1, 2009–Sept. 30, 2010	Oct. 1, 2010–Sept. 30, 2011	Oct. 1, 2011–Sept. 30, 2012	Beginning Oct. 1, 2012
1–2 tests or vaccinations					
Nonslaughter horses to Canada:					
First horse	$54.00	$55.00	$57.00	$59.00	$60.00
Each additional horse	6.25	6.25	6.50	6.75	7.00
Other animals or birds:					
First animal	107.00	111.00	114.00	117.00	121.00
Each additional animal	6.25	6.25	6.50	6.75	7.00
3–6 tests or vaccinations					
First animal	133.00	137.00	141.00	145.00	150.00
Each additional animal	10.00	11.00	11.00	11.00	12.00
7 or more tests or vaccinations					
First animal	154.00	159.00	163.00	168.00	173.00
Each additional animal	12.00	12.00	13.00	13.00	14.00

[1] Rabies vaccinations are not included in this number.

(2) If an export certificate covers more than one animal, but the number of tests required for different animals are not the same, the user fee for the certificate is the fee which would be due if all the animals on the certificate required the same number of tests as the animal which requires the greatest number of tests.

(c) The user fees prescribed in this section will not apply to an export health certificate if the export health certificate is prepared for endorsement completely at the site of the inspection by an APHIS veterinarian in the course of performing inspection or supervision services for the animals listed on the certificate, and an APHIS user fee is payable under § 130.30 of this part for the inspection or supervision services performed by the veterinarian.

(d) If a service must be conducted on a Sunday or holiday or at any other time outside the normal tour of duty of the employee, then reimbursable overtime, as provided for in part 97 of this chapter, must be paid for each service,

[5] An export health certificate may need to be endorsed for an animal being exported from the United States of the country to which the animal is being shipped requires one. APHIS endorses export health certificates as a service.

in addition to the user fee listed in this section.

(Approved by the Office of Management and Budget under control number 0579–0055)

[57 FR 771, Jan. 9, 1992. Redesignated at 58 FR 67655, Dec. 22, 1993]

EDITORIAL NOTE: For FEDERAL REGISTER citations affecting § 130.20, see the List of CFR Sections Affected, which appears in the Finding Aids section of the printed volume and at *www.fdsys.gov*.

§ 130.21 [Reserved]

§ 130.22 User fees for inspection services outside the United States.

(a) If inspection services (including inspection, testing, and supervision services) are performed outside the United States, in accordance with this title, and the regulations do not contain a provision for payment of the cost of the service, the person requesting the service must pay a user fee under this section.

(b) Any person who wants APHIS to provide inspection services outside the United States must contact the Animal and Plant Health Inspection Service, Veterinary Services, National Center for Import-Export, 4700 River Road, Unit 38, Riverdale, Maryland 20737–1231, to make an agreement.

(c) All agreements must include the following:

(1) Name, mailing address, and telephone number of either the person requesting the inspection services, or his or her agent;

(2) Explanation of inspection services to be provided, including the regulations in title 9, Code of Federal Regulations which provide for the services;

(3) Date(s) and time(s) the inspection services are to be provided;

(4) Location (including street address) where inspection services are to be provided;

(5) An estimate of the actual cost, as calculated by APHIS, to provide the described inspection services for 6 months;

(6) A statement that APHIS agrees to provide the inspection services;

(7) A statement that the person requesting the inspection services, or, if appropriate, his or her agent, agrees to pay, at the time the agreement is entered into, a user fee equal to the estimated cost of providing the described inspection services for 6 months; and

(8) A statement that the person requesting the inspection services, or, if appropriate, his or her agent, agrees to maintain a user fee payment account equal to the cost of providing the described inspection services for 6 months, as calculated monthly by APHIS.

(d) APHIS will enter into an agreement only if qualified personnel can be made available to provide the inspection services.

(e) An agreement can be terminated by either party on 30 days written notice.

(f) If, at the time an agreement is terminated, any unobligated funds remain in the user fee payment account, APHIS will refund the funds to the person who requested the inspection services, or his or her agent.

[57 FR 771, Jan. 9, 1992. Redesignated at 58 FR 67655, Dec. 22, 1993; 59 FR 67617, Dec. 30, 1994]

§§ 130.23–130.29 [Reserved]

§ 130.30 Hourly rate and minimum user fees.

(a) User fees for import- or export-related veterinary services listed in paragraphs (a)(1) through (a)(18) of this section, except those services covered by flat rate user fees elsewhere in this part, will be calculated at the hourly rate listed in the following table for each employee required to perform the service. The person for whom the service is provided and the person requesting the service are jointly and severally liable for payment of these user fees in accordance with §§ 130.50 and 130.51.

	User fee				
	Apr. 29, 2009–Sept. 30, 2009	Oct. 1, 2009–Sept. 30, 2010	Oct. 1, 2010–Sept. 30, 2011	Oct. 1, 2011–Sept. 30, 2012	Beginning Oct. 1, 2012
Hourly rate:					
Per hour	$120.00	$120.00	$124.00	$128.00	$132.00

	User fee				
	Apr. 29, 2009–Sept. 30, 2009	Oct. 1, 2009–Sept. 30, 2010	Oct. 1, 2010–Sept. 30, 2011	Oct. 1, 2011–Sept. 30, 2012	Beginning Oct. 1, 2012
Per quarter hour	30.00	30.00	31.00	32.00	33.00
Per service minimum fee	35.00	36.00	37.00	39.00	40.00

(1) Providing services to live animals for import or entry at airports, ocean ports, and rail ports.

(2) Conducting inspections, including inspections of laboratories and facilities (such as biosecurity level two facilities), required either to obtain import permits for animal products, aquaculture products, or organisms or vectors, or to maintain compliance with import permits. This hourly rate does not apply to inspection activities covered in § 130.11.

(3) Obtaining samples required to be tested, either to obtain import permits or to ensure compliance with import permits.

(4) Providing services for imported birds or ratites that are not subject to quarantine, such as monitoring birds—including but not limited to pet birds—between flights.

(5) Supervising the opening of in-bond shipments.

(6) Providing services for in-bond or in-transit animals to exit the United States.

(7) Inspecting an export isolation facility and the animals in it.

(8) Supervising animal or bird rest periods prior to export.

(9) Supervising loading and unloading of animals or birds for export shipment.

(10) Inspecting means of conveyance used to export animals or birds.

(11) Conducting inspections under part 156 of this chapter.

(12) Inspecting and approving an artificial insemination center or a semen collection center or the animals in it.

(13) Import or entry services for feeder animals including, but not limited to, feeder goats and feeder bison not covered by a flat rate user fee in § 130.7.

(14) Export-related bird banding for identification.

(15) Export-related inspection and approval of pet food facilities, including laboratories that perform pet food testing.

(16) Export-related services provided at animal auctions.

(17) Various export-related facility inspections, including, but not limited to, fertilizer plants that utilize poultry waste, rendering plants, and potential embarkation facilities.

(18) Providing other import-or export-related veterinary services for which there is no flat rate user fee specified elsewhere in this part.

(b) *When do I pay an additional amount for employee(s) working overtime?* You must pay an additional amount if you need an APHIS employee to work on a Sunday, on a holiday, or at any time outside the normal tour of duty of that employee. Instead of paying the hourly rate user fee, you pay the rate listed in the following table for each employee needed to get the work done.

Overtime rates (outside the employee's normal tour of duty)	Premium rate user fee				
	Apr. 29, 2009–Sept. 30, 2009	Oct. 1, 2009–Sept. 30, 2010	Oct. 1, 2010–Sept. 30, 2011	Oct. 1, 2011–Sept. 30, 2012	Beginning Oct. 1, 2012
Premium hourly rate Monday through Saturday and holidays:					
Per hour	$140.00	$144.00	$148.00	$152.00	$156.00
Per quarter hour	35.00	36.00	37.00	38.00	39.00
Premium hourly rate for Sundays:					
Per hour	160.00	164.00	168.00	172.00	$176.00
Per quarter hour	40.00	41.00	42.00	43.00	44.00

(Approved by the Office of Management and Budget under control numbers 0579–0055 and 0579–0094)

[65 FR 52009, Aug. 28, 2000, as amended at 68 FR 51886, Aug. 29, 2003; 72 FR 70766, Dec. 13, 2007; 74 FR 14006, Mar. 30, 2009]

§§ 130.31–130.48 [Reserved]

§ 130.49 Exemptions.

(a) *Veterinary diagnostics.* User fees for veterinary diagnostic services, including, but not limited to, tests and diagnostic reagents specified in §§ 130.14 through 130.19, are not charged under the following conditions:

(1) When veterinary diagnostic services are provided in connection with Federal programs to control or eradicate diseases or pests of livestock or poultry in the United States (program diseases);

(2) When veterinary diagnostic services are provided in support of zoonotic disease surveillance when the Administrator has determined that there is a significant threat to human health; and

(3) When veterinary diagnostic reagents are distributed within the United States for testing for foreign animal diseases.

(b) [Reserved]

[62 FR 61007, Nov. 14, 1997, as amended at 63 FR 53796, Oct. 7, 1998]

§ 130.50 Payment of user fees.

(a) *Who must pay APHIS user fees?* Any person for whom a service is provided related to the importation, entry, or exportation of an animal, article, or means of conveyance or related to veterinary diagnostics, and any person requesting such service, shall be jointly and severally liable for payment of fees assessed.

(b) *Associated charges*—(1) *Reservation fee.* Any reservation fee paid by an importer under part 93 of this chapter will be applied to the APHIS user fees specified in §§ 130.2 and 130.3 for animals or birds quarantined in an animal import center.

(2) *Special handling expenses.* The user fees in this part do not include any costs that may be incurred due to special mail handling, including, but not limited to, express, overnight, or foreign mailing. If any service requires special mail handling, the user must pay all costs incurred, in addition to the user fee for the service.

(3) *When do I pay an additional amount for employee(s) working overtime?* You must pay an additional amount if you need an APHIS employee to work on a Sunday, on a holiday, or at any time outside the normal tour of duty of that employee. You pay the amount specified in paragraphs (b)(3) (i), (ii), or (iii) as relevant, for each employee needed to get the work done.

(i) *What additional amount do I pay if I receive a flat rate user fee service?* In addition to the flat rate user fee(s), you pay the overtime rate listed in the following table for each employee needed to get the work done:

OVERTIME FOR FLAT RATE USER FEES [1] [2]

	Outside of the employee's normal tour of duty	Overtime rates (per hour)		
		Nov. 2, 2015–Sept. 30, 2016	Oct. 1, 2016–Sept. 30, 2017	Beginning Oct. 1, 2017
Rate for inspection, testing, certification or quarantine of animals, animal products or other commodities [3].	Monday–Saturday and holidays.	$75	$75	$75
	Sundays	99	99	100
Rate for commercial airline inspection services [4].	Monday–Saturday and holidays.	64	65	65
	Sundays	85	86	86

[1] Minimum charge of 2 hours, unless performed on the employee's regular workday and performed in direct continuation of the regular workday or begun within an hour of the regular workday.

[2] When the 2-hour minimum applies, you may need to pay commuted travel time. (See § 97.1(b) of this chapter for specific information about commuted travel time.)

[3] See § 97.1(a) of this chapter or 7 CFR 354.3 for details.

[4] See § 97.1(a)(3) of this chapter for details.

(ii) *What amount do I pay if I receive an hourly rate user fee service?* Instead of paying the normal hourly rate user fee under § 130.30(a), you pay the premium rate listed in § 130.30(b) for each employee needed to get the work done.

(iii) For information on rules pertaining to the charges associated with employees of U.S. Customs and Border Protection performing agricultural inspection services, please see 7 CFR 354.1 and 9 CFR 97.1.

(c) *When are APHIS user fees due?*—(1) *Animal and bird quarantine and related tests.* User fees specified in §§ 130.2, 130.3, 130.5, 130.10, and tests specified in §§ 130.14 through 130.19 for animals and birds in an Animal Import Center or privately operated permanent or temporary import quarantine facilities, including user fees for tests conducted on these animals or birds, must be paid prior to the release of those animals or birds from quarantine.

(2) *Supervision and inspection services for export animals, animal products.* User fees for supervision and inspection services specified in § 130.30 must be paid when billed, or, if covered by a compliance agreement signed in accordance with this chapter, must be paid when specified in the agreement.

(3) *Export health certificates.* User fees for export health certificates specified in § 130.20 must be paid prior to receipt of endorsed certificates unless APHIS determines that the user has established an acceptable credit history, at which time payment may, at the option of the user, be made when billed.

(4) *Veterinary diagnostics.* User fees specified in §§ 130.14 through 130.19 for veterinary diagnostic services, such as tests on samples submitted to NVSL or FADDL, diagnostic reagents, slide sets, tissue sets, and other veterinary diagnostic services, must be paid when the veterinary diagnostic service is requested, unless APHIS determines that the user has established an acceptable credit history, at which time payment may, at the option of the user, be made when billed.

(5) *Other user fee services.* User fees specified in §§ 130.6, 130.7, 130.8, and 130.30 must be paid when service is provided (for example when live animals are inspected when presented for importation at a port of entry), unless APHIS determines that the user has established an acceptable credit history, at which time payment may, at the option of the user, be made when billed.

(d) *What payment methods are acceptable?* Payment must be for the exact amount due and may be paid by:

(1) Cash, will be accepted only during normal business hours if payment is made at an APHIS office [7] or an Animal Import Center;

(2) All types of checks, including traveler's checks, drawn on a U.S. bank in U.S. dollars and made payable to the U.S. Department of Agriculture or USDA;

(3) Money orders, drawn on a U.S. bank in U.S. dollars and made payable to the U.S. Department of Agriculture or USDA; or

(4) Credit cards (VISA™ and MasterCard™) if payment is made at an Animal Import Center or an APHIS office that is equipped to process credit cards. [7]

[63 FR 53796, Oct. 7, 1998, as amended at 64 FR 67700, Dec. 3, 1999; 65 FR 52010, Aug. 28, 2000; 67 FR 48524, July 25, 2002; 68 FR 51887, Aug. 29, 2003; 80 FR 59567, Oct. 2, 2015]

§ 130.51 Penalties for nonpayment or late payment.

(a) *Unpaid debt.* If any person for whom the service is provided fails to pay when due any debt to APHIS, including any user fee due under 7 CFR chapter III or chapter I of this title, then:

(1) *Subsequent user fee payments.* Payment must be made for subsequent user fees before the service is provided if:

(i) For unbilled fees, the user fee is unpaid 60 days after the date the pertinent regulatory provision indicates payment is due;

(ii) For billed fees, the user fee is unpaid 60 days after date of bill;

(iii) The person for whom the service is provided or the person requesting the service has not paid the late payment penalty or interest on any delinquent APHIS user fee; or

(iv) Payment has been dishonored.

(2) *Resolution of difference between estimate and actual.* APHIS will estimate the user fee to be paid; any difference

[7] A list of APHIS offices and Animal Import Centers that accept cash or credit cards may be obtained from the Animal and Plant Health Inspection Service, Veterinary Services, National Center for Import and Export, 4700 River Road Unit 38, Riverdale, MD 20738–1231.

between the estimate and the actual amount owed to APHIS will be resolved as soon as reasonably possible following the delivery of the service, with APHIS returning any excess to the payor or billing the payor for the additional amount due.

(3) *Prepayment form.* The prepayment must be in guaranteed form, such as money order, certified check, or cash. Prepayment in guaranteed form will continue until the debtor pays the delinquent debt.

(4) *Denied service.* Service will be denied until the debt is paid if:

(i) For unbilled fees, the user fee is unpaid 90 days after date the pertinent regulatory provision indicates payment is due;

(ii) For billed fees, the user fee is unpaid 90 days after date of bill;

(iii) The person for whom the service is provided or the person requesting the service has not paid the late payment penalty or interest on any delinquent APHIS user fee; or

(iv) Payment has been dishonored.

(b) *Unpaid debt during service.* If APHIS is in the process of providing a service for which an APHIS user fee is due, and the user has not paid the fee within the time required, or if the payment offered by the user is inadequate or unacceptable, then APHIS will take the following action:

(1) *Animals or birds in quarantine.* If an APHIS user fee specified in §130.2 or §130.3 is due for animals or birds in quarantine at an animal import center or at a privately operated import quarantine facility, APHIS will not release them.

(2) *Export health certificate.* If an APHIS user fee specified in §130.20 is due for an export health certificate, APHIS will not release the certificate.

(3) *Veterinary diagnostics.* If an APHIS user fee specified in §§130.14 through 130.19 is due for a veterinary diagnostic test or service, APHIS will not release the test result, any endorsed certificate, or any other veterinary diagnostic service.

(c) *Late payment penalty.* If for unbilled user fees, the user fees are unpaid 30 days after the date the pertinent regulatory provisions indicates payment is due, or if billed, are unpaid 30 days after the date of the bill, APHIS will impose a late payment penalty and interest charges in accordance with 31 U.S.C. 3717.

(d) *Dishonored payment penalties.* User fees paid with dishonored forms of payment, such as a check returned for insufficient funds, will be subject to interest and penalty charges in accordance with 31 U.S.C. 3717. Administrative charges will be assessed at $20.00 per dishonored payment to be paid in addition to the original amount owed. Payment must be in guaranteed form, such as cash, money order, or certified check.

(e) *Debt collection management.* In accordance with the Debt Collection Improvement Act of 1996, the following provisions apply:

(1) *Taxpayer identification number.* APHIS will collect a taxpayer identification number from all persons, other than Federal agencies, who are liable for a user fee.

(2) *Administrative offset.* APHIS will notify the Department of Treasury of debts that are over 180 days delinquent for the purposes of administrative offset. Under administrative offset, the Department of Treasury will withhold funds payable by the United States to a person (*i.e.*, Federal income tax refunds) to satisfy the debt to APHIS.

(3) *Cross-servicing.* APHIS will transfer debts that are over 180 days delinquent to the Department of Treasury for cross-servicing. Under cross-servicing, the Department of Treasury will collect debts on behalf of APHIS. Exceptions will be made for debts that meet certain requirements, for example, debts that are already at a collection agency or in payment plan.

(4) *Report delinquent debt.* APHIS will report all unpaid debts to credit reporting bureaus.

(f) *Animals or birds abandoned after quarantine at an animal import center.* Animals or birds left in quarantine at an animal import center for more than 30 days after the end of the required quarantine period will be deemed to be abandoned.

(1) After APHIS releases the abandoned animals or birds from quarantine, APHIS may seize them and sell or otherwise dispose of them, as determined by the Administrator, provided that their sale is not contrary to any

Federal law or regulation, and may recover all expenses of handling the animals or birds from the proceeds of their sale or disposition.

(2) If animals or birds abandoned in quarantine at an animal import center cannot be released from quarantine, APHIS may seize and dispose of them, as determined by the Administrator, and may recover all expenses of handling the animals or birds from the proceeds of their disposition and from persons liable for user fees under § 130.50(a).

[63 FR 53797, Oct. 7, 1998, as amended at 68 FR 6346, Feb. 7, 2003]

SUBCHAPTER G—LIVESTOCK IMPROVEMENT

PART 145—NATIONAL POULTRY IMPROVEMENT PLAN FOR BREEDING POULTRY

AUTHORITY: 7 U.S.C. 8301–8317; 7 CFR 2.22, 2.80, and 371.4.

SOURCE: 36 FR 23112, Dec. 3, 1971, unless otherwise noted. Redesignated at 44 FR 61586, Oct. 26, 1979.

Subpart A—General Provisions

§ 145.1 Definitions.

Words used in this part in the singular form shall be deemed to import the plural, and vice versa, as the case may demand. Except where the context otherwise requires, for the purposes of this part the following terms shall be construed, respectively, to mean:

Administrator. The Administrator, Animal and Plant Health Inspection Service, or any person authorized to act for the Administrator.

Affiliated flockowner. A flockowner who is participating in the Plan through an agreement with a participating hatchery.

Animal and Plant Health Inspection Service. The Animal and Plant Health Inspection Service of the U.S. Department of Agriculture.

Authorized agent. Any person designated under § 145.11(a) to collect official samples for submission to an authorized laboratory in accordance with part 147 of this subchapter.

Authorized laboratory. An authorized laboratory is a laboratory that meets the requirements of § 147.52 and is thus qualified to perform assays in accordance with part 147 of this subchapter.

Authorized testing agent. Any person designated under § 145.11(a) to collect official samples for submission to an authorized laboratory in accordance with part 147 of this subchapter and to perform the stained antigen, rapid whole blood test for pullorum typhoid.

Avian influenza. An infection or disease of poultry caused by viruses in the family *Orthomyxoviridae*, genus *Influenzavirus* A.

Baby poultry. Newly hatched poultry (chicks, poults, ducklings, goslings, keets, etc.).

Colon bacilli. For the purpose of this chapter, those organisms which are gram negative, non spore-forming bacilli, which ferment lactose with gas formation, and serve as an index of fecal contamination.

Dealer. An individual or business that deals in commerce in hatching eggs, newly-hatched poultry, and started poultry obtained from breeding flocks and hatcheries. This does not include an individual or business that deals in commerce in buying and selling poultry for slaughter only.

Department. The U.S. Department of Agriculture.

Domesticated. Propagated and maintained under the control of a person.

Equivalent or equivalent requirements. Requirements which are equal to or exceed the program, conditions, criteria, or classifications with which they are compared, as determined by the Official State Agency and with the concurrence of the Service.

Exposed (Exposure). Contact with birds, equipment, personnel, supplies, or any article infected with, or contaminated by, communicable poultry disease organisms.

Flock—(1) *As applied to breeding.* All poultry of one kind of mating (breed and variety or combination of stocks) and of one classification on one farm;

(2) *As applied to disease control.* All of the poultry on one farm except that, at the discretion of the Official State Agency, any group of poultry which is segregated from another group and has been so segregated for a period of at least 21 days may be considered as a separate flock.

Fluff sample. Feathers, shell membrane, and other debris resulting from the hatching of poultry.

Fowl typhoid or typhoid. A disease of poultry caused by Salmonella gallinarum.

Franchise breeder. A breeder who normally sells products under a specific strain or trade name and who authorizes other hatcheries to produce and sell products under this same strain or trade name.

Franchise hatchery. A hatchery which has been authorized by a franchise breeder to produce and sell products under the breeder's strain or trade name.

H5/H7 low pathogenic avian influenza (LPAI). An infection of poultry caused by an influenza A virus of H5 or H7 subtype that has an intravenous pathogenicity index in 6-week-old chickens less than or equal to 1.2 or causes less than 75 percent mortality in 4- to 8-week-old chickens infected intravenously, or an infection with influenza A viruses of H5 or H7 subtype with a cleavage site that is not consistent with a previously identified highly pathogenic avian influenza virus.

Hatchery. Hatchery equipment on one premises operated or controlled by any person for the production of baby poultry.

Independent flock. A flock that produces hatching eggs and that has no ownership affiliation with a specific hatchery.

Infected flock. A flock in which an authorized laboratory has discovered one or more birds infected with a communicable poultry disease for which a program has been established under the Plan.

Midlay. Approximately 2–3 months after a flock begins to lay or after a molted flock is put back into production.

Multiplier breeding flock. A flock that is intended for the production of hatching eggs used for the purpose of producing progeny for commercial egg or meat production or for other nonbreeding purposes.

NPIP Program Standards. A document that contains tests and sanitation procedures approved by the Administrator in accordance with § 147.53 of this subchapter for use under this subchapter. This document may be obtained from the NPIP Web site at *http://www.aphis.usda.gov/animal_health/animal_dis_spec/poultry/* or by writing to the Service at National Poultry Improvement Plan, APHIS, USDA, 1506 Klondike Road, Suite 101, Conyers, GA 30094.

NPIP Technical Committee. A committee made up of technical experts on poultry health, biosecurity, surveillance, and diagnostics. The committee consists of representatives from the poultry and egg industries, universities, and State and Federal governments and is appointed by the Senior Coordinator and approved by the General Conference Committee.

Official State Agency. The State authority recognized by the Department to cooperate in the administration of the Plan.

Official supervision—(1) *As applied to Plan programs.* The direction, inspection, and critical evaluation by the Official State Agency of compliance with the provisions of the Plan;

(2) *As applied to non-Plan but equivalent State poultry improvement programs.* The direction, inspection, and critical evaluation by an officer or agency of a State government, of compliance with a publicly announced State poultry improvement program.

Person. A natural person, firm, or corporation.

Plan. The provisions of the National Poultry Improvement Plan contained in this part.

Poultry. Domesticated fowl, including chickens, turkeys, ostriches, emus, rheas, cassowaries, waterfowl, and game birds, except doves and pigeons, which are bred for the primary purpose of producing eggs or meat.

Primary breeding flock. A flock composed of one or more generations that is maintained for the purpose of establishing, continuing, or improving parent lines.

Products. Poultry breeding stock and hatching eggs, baby poultry, and started poultry.

Program. Management, sanitation, testing, and monitoring procedures which, if complied with, will qualify, and maintain qualification for, designation of a flock, products produced from the flock, or a state by an official Plan classification and illustrative design, as described in § 145.10 of this part.

Public exhibition. A public show of poultry.

Pullorum disease or pullorum. A disease of poultry caused by Salmonella pullorum.

Reactor. A bird that has a positive reaction to a test, required or recommended in this part or in accordance with part 147 of this subchapter, for any poultry disease for which a program has been established under the Plan.

Salmonella. Any bacteria belonging to the genus Salmonella, including the arizona group.

Sanitize. To treat with a product which is registered by the Environmental Protection Agency as germicidal, fungicidal, pseudomonocidal, or tuberculocidal, in accordance with the specifications for use as shown on the label of each product. The Official State Agency, with the concurrence of the Service, shall approve each product or procedure according to its specified usage.

Senior Coordinator. An employee of the Service whose duties may include, but will not necessarily be limited to:

(1) Serving as executive secretary of the General Conference Committee;

(2) Serving as chairperson of the Plan Conference described in § 147.47;

(3) Planning, organizing, and conducting the Plan Conference;

(4) Reviewing NPIP authorized laboratories as described in § 147.52;

(5) Coordinating the State administration of the NPIP through periodic reviews of the administrative procedures of the Official State Agencies, according to the applicable provisions of the Plan and the Memorandum of Understanding;

(6) Coordinating rulemaking to incorporate the proposed changes of the provisions approved at the Plan conference into the regulations in parts 145, 146, and 147 of this subchapter;

(7) Directing the production of official NPIP publications;

(8) Proposing an annual budget for plan activities and the General Conference Committee; and

(9) Providing overall administration of the NPIP.

Service. The Animal and Plant Health Inspection Service, Veterinary Services, of the Department.

Serial. The total quantity of completed product which has been thoroughly mixed in a single container and identified by a serial number.

Sexual maturity. The average age at which a species of poultry is biologically capable of reproduction.

Started poultry. Young poultry (chicks, pullets, cockerels, capons, poults, ducklings, goslings, keets, etc.) that have been fed and watered and are less than 6 months of age.

State. Any State, the District of Columbia, or Puerto Rico.

State Inspector. Any person employed or authorized under § 145.11(b) to perform functions under this part.

Stock. A term used to identify the progeny of a specific breeding combination within a species of poultry. These breeding combinations may include pure strains, strain crosses, breed crosses, or combinations thereof.

Strain. Poultry breeding stock bearing a given name produced by a breeder through at least five generations of closed flock breeding.

Succeeding flock. A flock brought onto a premises during the 12 months following removal of an infected flock.

Suspect flock. A flock shall be considered, for the purposes of the Plan, to be a suspect flock if any evidence exists that it has been exposed to a communicable poultry disease.

Trade name or number. A name or number compatible with State and Federal laws and regulations applied to a specified stock or product thereof.

[36 FR 23112, Dec. 3, 1971. Redesignated at 44 FR 61586, Oct. 26, 1979]

EDITORIAL NOTE: For FEDERAL REGISTER citations affecting § 145.1, see the List of CFR Sections Affected, which appears in the Finding Aids section of the printed volume and at *www.fdsys.gov*.

§ 145.2 Administration.

(a) The Department cooperates through a Memorandum of Understanding with Official State Agencies in the administration of the Plan. In the Memorandum of Understanding, the Official State Agency must designate a contact representative to serve as a liaison between the Service and the Official State Agency.

(b) The administrative procedures and decisions of the Official State Agency are subject to review by the Service. The Official State Agency shall carry out the administration of the Plan within the State according to the applicable provisions of the Plan and the Memorandum of Understanding.

(c) An Official State Agency may accept for participation an affiliated flock located in another State under a mutual understanding and agreement, in writing, between the two Official State Agencies regarding conditions of participation and supervision.

(d) The Official State Agency of any State may, except as limited by § 145.3(e), adopt regulations applicable to the administration of the Plan in such State further defining the provisions of the Plan or establishing higher standards compatible with the Plan.

(e) An authorized laboratory of the National Poultry Improvement Plan will conduct tests in accordance with part 147 of this subchapter when determining the status of a participating flock with respect to an official Plan classification.

(Approved by the Office of Management and Budget under control number 0579–0007)

[36 FR 23112, Dec. 3, 1971. Redesignated at 44 FR 61586, Oct. 26, 1979, and amended at 48 FR 57473, Dec. 30, 1983; 67 FR 8468, Feb. 25, 2002; 74 FR 14714, Apr. 1, 2009; 79 FR 38754, July 9, 2014; 81 FR 53249, Aug. 12, 2016]

§ 145.3 Participation.

(a) The National Poultry Improvement Plan is a cooperative Federal-State-Industry program through which new or existing diagnostic technology can be effectively applied to improve poultry and poultry products by controlling or eliminating specific poultry diseases. The Plan consists of programs that identify States, flocks, hatcheries, dealers, and slaughter plants that meet specific disease control standards specified in the Plan. Participants shall maintain records to demonstrate that they adhere to the disease control programs in which they participate.

(b) Any person producing or dealing in products may participate in the Plan when he has demonstrated, to the satisfaction of the Official State Agency, that his facilities, personnel, and practices are adequate for carrying out the applicable provisions of the Plan, and has signed an agreement with the Official State Agency to comply with the general and the applicable specific provisions of the Plan and any regulations of the Official State Agency under § 145.2. Affiliated flockowners may participate without signing an agreement with the Official State Agency.

(c) Each participant shall comply with the Plan throughout the operating year of the Official State Agency, or until released by such Agency.

(d) A participant in any State shall participate with all of his poultry hatching egg supply flocks and hatchery operations within such State. The participant shall report to the Official State Agency on VS Form 9–2 (formerly NPIP Form 3B) or through other appropriate means each breeding flock before the birds reach 24 weeks of age or, in the case of ostriches, emus, rheas, and cassowaries, before the birds reach 20 months of age. This report will include:

(1) Name and address of flockowner;

(2) Flock location and designation;

(3) Type: Primary or Multiplier;

(4) Breed, variety, strain, or trade name of stock;

(5) Source of males;

(6) Source of females;

(7) Number of birds in the flock; and

(8) Intended classification of flock.

(e) To ensure that Plan diseases are not spread, flocks must be qualified for their intended Plan classifications before being moved into breeder production facilities.

(f) No person shall be compelled by the Official State Agency to qualify products for any of the other classifications described in § 145.10 as a condition of qualification for the U.S. Pullorum-Typhoid Clean classification.

(g) Participation in the Plan shall entitle the participant to use the Plan emblem reproduced below:

NATIONAL POULTRY IMPROVEMENT PLAN

FIGURE 1.

(Approved by the Office of Management and Budget under control number 0579–0007)

[36 FR 23112, Dec. 3, 1971, as amended at 40 FR 1500, Jan. 8, 1975. Redesignated at 44 FR 61586, Oct. 26, 1979 and amended at 48 FR 57473, Dec. 30, 1983; 57 FR 57341, Dec. 4, 1992; 63 FR 40010, July 27, 1998; 65 FR 8016, Feb. 17, 2000; 79 FR 38754, July 9, 2014; 81 FR 53249, Aug. 12, 2016]

§ 145.4 General provisions for all participants.

(a) Records of purchases and sales and the identity of products handled shall be maintained in a manner satisfactory to the Official State Agency.

(b) Products, records of sales and purchase of products, and material used to advertise products shall be subject to inspection by the Official State Agency at any time.

(c) Advertising must be in accordance with the Plan, and applicable rules and regulations of the Official State Agency and the Federal Trade Commission. A participant advertising products as being of any official classification may include in his advertising reference to associated or franchised hatcheries only when such hatcheries produce the same kind of products of the same classification.

(d) Except as provided by this paragraph, participants in the Plan may not buy or receive products for any purpose from nonparticipants unless they are part of an equivalent program, as determined by the Official State Agency. Participants in the Plan may buy or receive products from flocks that are neither participants nor part of an equivalent program, for use in breeding flocks or for experimental purposes, under the following conditions only:

(1) With the permission of the Official State Agency and the concurrence of the Service; and

(2) By segregation of all birds before introduction into the breeding flock. Upon reaching sexual maturity, the segregated birds must be tested and found negative for pullorum-typhoid. The Official State Agency may require a second test at its discretion.

(e) Each participant shall be assigned a permanent approval number by the Service. This number, prefaced by the numerical code of the State, will be the official approval number of the participant and may be used on each certificate, invoice, shipping label, or other document used by the participant in the sale of his products. Each Official State Agency which requires an approval or permit number for out-of-State participants to ship into its State should honor this number. The approval number shall be withdrawn when the participant no longer qualifies for participation in the Plan.

(Approved by the Office of Management and Budget under control number 0579–0057)

[36 FR 23112, Dec. 3, 1971, as amended at 38 FR 13706, May 24, 1973; 41 FR 48723, Nov. 5, 1976. Redesignated at 44 FR 61586, Oct. 26, 1979, as amended at 47 FR 21991, May 20, 1982; 48 FR 57473, Dec. 30, 1983; 57 FR 57341, Dec. 4, 1992]

§ 145.5 Specific provisions for participating flocks.

(a) Poultry equipment, and poultry houses and the land in the immediate vicinity thereof, shall be kept in sanitary condition in accordance with part 147 of this subchapter. The participating flock, its eggs, and all equipment used in connection with the flock shall be separated from nonparticipating flocks, in a manner acceptable to the Official State Agency.

(b) All flocks shall consist of healthy, normal individuals characteristic of the breed, variety, cross, or other combination which they are stated to represent.

(c) A flock shall be deemed to be a participating flock at any time only if it has qualified for the U.S. Pullorum-Typhoid Clean classification, as prescribed in Subparts B, C, D, E, F, G, H, or I of this part.

(d) Each bird shall be identified with a sealed and numbered band obtained through or approved by the Official State Agency: *Provided*, That exception may be made at the discretion of the Official State Agency.

[36 FR 23112, Dec. 3, 1971, as amended at 38 FR 13706, May 24, 1973. Redesignated at 44 FR 61586, Oct. 26, 1979, as amended at 63 FR 40010, July 27, 1998; 79 FR 38754, July 9, 2014]

§ 145.6 Specific provisions for participating hatcheries.

(a) Hatcheries must be kept in sanitary condition, acceptable to the Official State Agency. The sanitary procedures outlined in the NPIP Program Standards, or other procedures approved by the Administrator in accordance with § 147.53(d), will be considered as a guide in determining compliance with this provision. The minimum requirements with respect to sanitation include the following:

(1) Egg room walls, ceilings, floors, air filters, drains, and humidifiers should be cleaned and disinfected at least two times per week. Cleaning and disinfection procedures should be in accordance with part 147 of this subchapter.

(2) Incubator room walls, ceilings, floors, doors, fan grills, vents, and ducts should be cleaned and disinfected after each set or transfer. Incubator rooms should not be used for storage. Plenums should be cleaned at least weekly. Egg trays and buggies should be cleaned and disinfected after each transfer. Cleaning and disinfection procedures should be in accordance with part 147 of this subchapter.

(3) Hatcher walls, ceilings, floors, doors, fans, vents, and ducts should be cleaned and disinfected after each hatch. Hatcher rooms should be cleaned and disinfected after each hatch and should not be used for storage. Plenums should be cleaned after each hatch. Cleaning and disinfection procedures should be in accordance with part 147 of this subchapter.

(4) Chick/poult processing equipment and rooms should be thoroughly cleaned and disinfected after each hatch. Chick/poult boxes should be cleaned and disinfected before being reused. Vaccination equipment should be cleaned and disinfected after each use. Cleaning and disinfection procedures should be in accordance with part 147 of this subchapter.

(5) Hatchery residue, such as chick/poult down, eggshells, infertile eggs, and dead germs, should be disposed of promptly and in a manner satisfactory to the Official State Agency.

(6) The entire hatchery should be kept in a neat, orderly condition and cleaned and disinfected after each hatch.

(7) Effective insect and rodent control programs should be implemented.

(b) A hatchery that keeps started poultry must keep such poultry separated from the incubator room in a manner satisfactory to the Official State Agency.

(c) All baby and started poultry offered for sale under Plan terminology should be normal and typical of the breed, variety, cross, or other combination represented.

(d) Eggs incubated should be sound in shell, typical for the breed, variety, strain, or cross thereof and reasonably uniform in shape. Hatching eggs should be trayed and the baby poultry boxed with a view to uniformity of size.

(e) Any nutritive material provided to baby poultry must be free of the avian pathogens that are officially represented in the Plan disease classifications listed in § 145.10.

(f) If a person is responsibly connected with more than one hatchery, all of such hatcheries must participate in the Plan if any of them participate. A person is deemed to be responsibly connected with a hatchery if he or she is a partner, officer, director, holder, owner of 10 percent or more of the voting stock, or an employee in a managerial or executive capacity.

[36 FR 23112, Dec. 3, 1971. Redesignated at 44 FR 61586, Oct. 26, 1979, and amended at 49 FR 19802, May 10, 1984; 65 FR 8016, Feb. 17, 2000; 67 FR 8468, Feb. 25, 2002; 79 FR 38754, July 9, 2014]

§ 145.7 Specific provisions for participating dealers.

Dealers in poultry breeding stock, hatching eggs, or baby or started poultry shall comply with all provisions in this part which apply to their operations.

§ 145.8 Terminology and classification; general.

(a) The official classification terms defined in §§ 145.9 and 145.10 and the various designs illustrative of the official classifications reproduced in § 145.10 may be used only by participants and to describe products that have met all the specific requirements of such classifications.

(b) Products produced under the Plan shall lose their identity under Plan terminology when they are purchased for resale by or consigned to nonparticipants.

(c) Participating flocks, their eggs, and the baby and started poultry produced from them may be designated by their strain or trade name. When a breeder's trade name or strain designation is used, the participant shall be able by records to substantiate that the products so designated are from flocks that are composed of either birds hatched from eggs produced under the direct supervision of the breeder of such strain, or stock multiplied by persons designated and so reported by the breeder to each Official State Agency concerned.

§ 145.9 Terminology and classification; hatcheries and dealers.

Participating hatcheries and dealers shall be designated as "National Plan Hatchery" and "National Plan Dealer", respectively. All Official State Agencies shall be notified by the Service of additions, withdrawals, and changes in classification.

[36 FR 23112, Dec. 3, 1971. Redesignated at 44 FR 61586, Oct. 26, 1979, and amended at 47 FR 21991, May 20, 1982]

§ 145.10 Terminology and classification; flocks, products, and States.

Participating flocks, products produced from them, and States that have met the requirements of a classification in this part may be designated by the corresponding illustrative design in this section.

(a) [Reserved]

(b) *U.S. Pullorum-Typhoid Clean.* (See § 145.23(b), § 145.33(b), § 145.43(b), §§ 145.53(b), 145.63(a), 145.73(b), 145.83(b), and 145.93(b).)

FIGURE 3

(c) *U.S. M. Gallisepticum Clean.* (See §§ 145.23(c), 145.23(f), 145.33(c), 145.33(f), 145.43(c), 145.53(c), 145.73(c), and 145.83(c).)

Figure 4

(d) *U.S. Sanitation Monitored.* (See § 145.33(d).)

FIGURE 5

(e) *U.S. M. Synoviae Clean.* (See § 145.23(e), § 145.23(g), § 145.33(e), § 145.33(g), § 145.43(e), and § 145.53(d)).

Figure 6

(f) *U.S. M. Meleagridis Clean*—(See § 145.43(d)).

Figure 7

(g) *U.S. Pullorum-Typhoid Clean State.* (See §§ 145.24(a), 145.34(a), 145.44(a), 145.54(a), and 145.94(a).)

Figure 8

(h) *U.S. Pullorum-Typhoid Clean State, Turkeys.* (See § 145.44(b).)

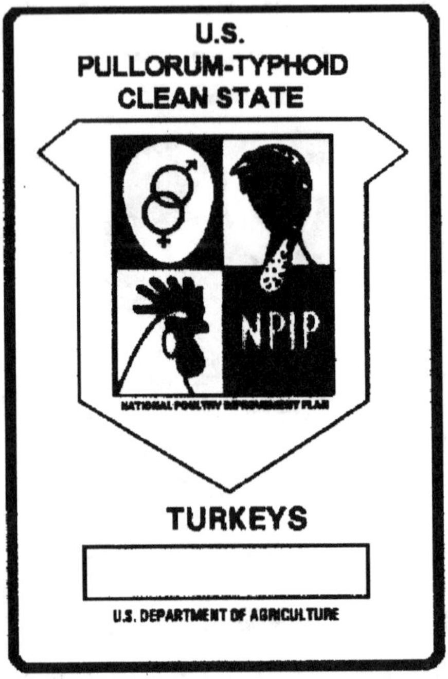

Figure 9

(i) *U.S.M. Gallisepticum Clean State, Turkeys.* (See § 145.44(c).)

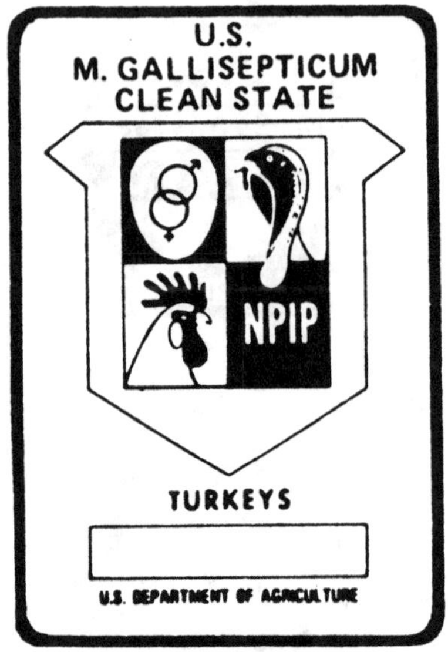

Figure 10

(j) *U.S. M. Gallisepticum Clean State, Meat-Type Chickens.* (See § 145.34(b).)

Figure 11

(k) *U.S. Sanitation Monitored, Turkeys.* (See § 145.43(f).)

FIGURE 12

(l) [Reserved]

(m) *U.S. S. Enteritidis Clean.* (See §§ 145.23(d), 145.73(d), and 145.83(e).)

Figure 14

(n) *U.S. M. Synoviae Clean State, Turkeys.* (See § 145.44(d).)

Figure 15

(o) *U.S. Salmonella Monitored.* (See §§ 145.53(f), 145.83(f), and 145.93(d).)

Figure 16

(p) *U.S. M. Gallisepticum Monitored.* (See § 145.33(j).)

Figure 17

(q) *U.S. M. Synoviae Monitored.* (See § 145.33(k).)

Figure 18

(r) *U.S. Avian Influenza Clean.* (See §§ 145.23(h), 145.33(l), 145.63(b), 145.73(f), and 145.83(g).)

FIGURE 19

(s) *U.S. M. Meleagridis Clean State, Turkeys.* (See § 145.44(e).)

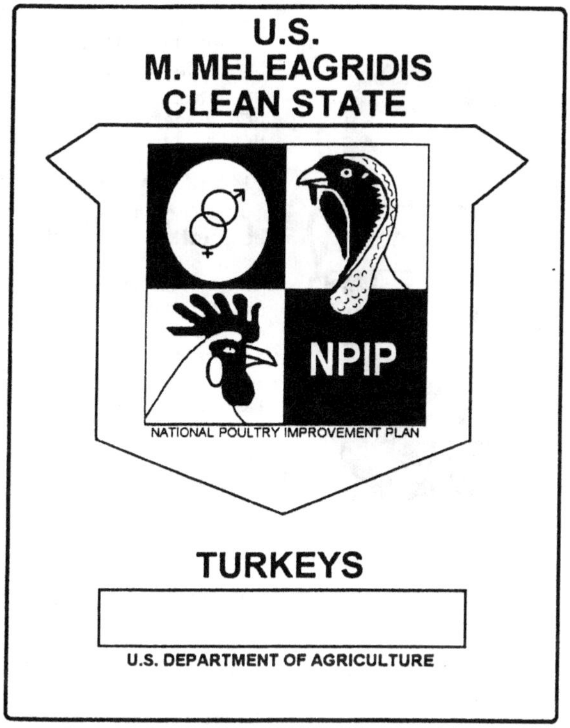
U.S.
M. MELEAGRIDIS
CLEAN STATE
NPIP
NATIONAL POULTRY IMPROVEMENT PLAN
TURKEYS
U.S. DEPARTMENT OF AGRICULTURE

FIGURE 20

(t) *U.S. H5/H7 Avian Influenza Clean.* (See §§ 145.43(g), 145.53(e), and 145.93(c).)

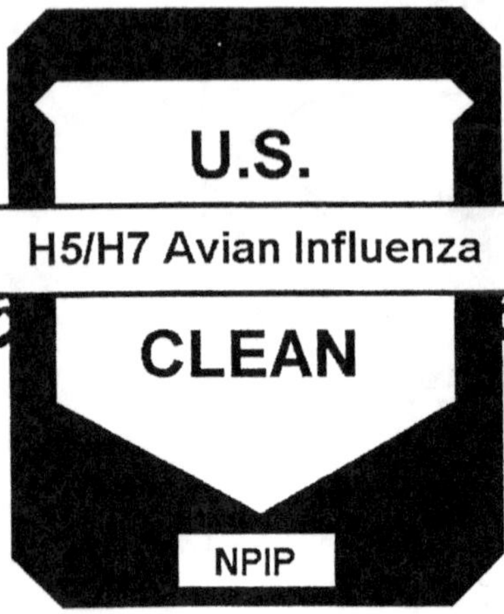

FIGURE 21

[38 FR 13706, May 24, 1973. Redesignated at 44 FR 61586, Oct. 26, 1979]

EDITORIAL NOTE: For FEDERAL REGISTER citations affecting § 145.10, see the List of CFR Sections Affected, which appears in the Finding Aids section of the printed volume and at *www.fdsys.gov.*

§ 145.11 Supervision.

(a) The Official State Agency may designate qualified persons as Authorized Agents to do the sample collecting provided for in § 145.14 and may designate qualified persons as Authorized Testing Agents to do the sample collecting and blood testing provided for in § 145.14.

(b) The Official State Agency shall employ or authorize qualified persons as State Inspectors to perform the qualification testing of participating flocks, and to perform the official inspections necessary to verify compliance with the requirements of the Plan.

(c) Authorities issued under the provisions of this section shall be subject to cancellation by the official State agency on the grounds of incompetence or failure to comply with the provisions of the Plan or regulations of the official State agency. Such actions shall not be taken until a thorough investigation has been made by the official State agency and the authorized person has been given notice of the proposed action and the basis therefor and an opportunity to present his views.

[36 FR 23112, Dec. 3, 1971, as amended at 38 FR 13706, May 24, 1973; 41 FR 48723, Nov. 5, 1976. Redesignated at 44 FR 61586, Oct. 26, 1979, as amended at 72 FR 1418, Jan. 12, 2007]

§ 145.12 Inspections.

(a) Each participating hatchery shall be audited at least one time annually or a sufficient number of times each year to satisfy the Official State Agency that the operations of the hatchery are in compliance with the provisions of the Plan.

(b) The records of all flocks maintained primarily for production of hatching eggs shall be made available to and examined annually by a State Inspector. Records shall include VS Form 9–2, "Flock Selecting and Testing Report"; VS Form 9–3, "Report of Sales of Hatching Eggs, Chicks, and Poults"; set and hatch records; egg receipts; and egg/chick orders or invoices. Records shall be maintained for 3 years. On-site inspections of flocks and premises will be conducted if the State Inspector determines that a breach of sanitation, blood testing, or other provisions has occurred for Plan programs for which the flocks have or are being qualified.

[36 FR 23112, Dec. 3, 1971, as amended at 40 FR 1501, Jan. 8, 1975. Redesignated at 44 FR 61586, Oct. 26, 1979, and amended at 54 FR 23955, June 5, 1989; 59 FR 12798, Mar. 18, 1994; 72 FR 1418, Jan. 12, 2007; 81 FR 53249, Aug. 12, 2016]

§ 145.13 Debarment from participation.

Participants in the Plan, who after investigation by the Official State Agency or its representative, are notified in writing of their apparent noncompliance with the Plan provisions or regulations of the Official State Agency, shall be afforded a reasonable time, as specified by the Official State Agency, within which to demonstrate or achieve compliance. If compliance is not demonstrated or achieved within the specified time, the Official State Agency may debar the participant from further participation in the Plan for such period, or indefinitely, as the Agency may deem appropriate. The debarred participant shall be afforded notice of the bases for the debarment and opportunity to present his views with respect to the debarment in accordance with procedures adopted by the Official State Agency. The Official State Agency shall thereupon decide whether the debarment order shall continue in effect. Such decision shall be final unless the debarred participant, within 30 days after the issuance of the debarment order, requests the Administrator to determine the eligibility of the debarred participant for participation in the Plan. In such event the Administrator shall determine the matter de novo in accordance with the rules of practice in 7 CFR part 50, which are hereby made applicable to proceedings before the Administrator under this section. The definitions in 7 CFR 50.10 and the following definitions shall apply with respect to terms used in such rules of practice:

(a) *Administrator* means the Administrator, Animal and Plant Health Inspection Service of the U.S. Department of Agriculture or any officer or employee to whom authority has heretofore been delegated or to whom authority may hereafter be delegated to act in his stead.

[36 FR 23112, Dec. 3, 1971, as amended at 38 FR 3038, Feb. 1, 1973. Redesignated at 44 FR 61586, Oct. 26, 1979, and amended at 47 FR 21991, May 20, 1982; 67 FR 8468, Feb. 25, 2002]

§ 145.14 Testing.

Poultry must be more than 4 months of age when tested for an official classification: *Provided,* That turkey candidates under subpart D of this part may be tested at more than 12 weeks of age; game bird candidates under subpart E of this part may be tested when more than 4 months of age or upon reaching sexual maturity, whichever comes first; and ostrich, emu, rhea, and cassowary candidates under subpart F of this part may be tested when more than 12 months of age. Samples for official tests shall be collected by an Authorized Agent, Authorized Testing Agent, or State Inspector and tested by an authorized laboratory, except that the stained antigen, rapid whole-blood test for pullorum-typhoid may be conducted by an Authorized Testing Agent or State Inspector. For Plan programs in which a representative sample may be tested in lieu of an entire flock, except the ostrich, emu, rhea, and cassowary program in § 145.63(a), the minimum number tested shall be 30 birds per house, with at least 1 bird taken from each pen and unit in the house. The ratio of male to female birds in representative samples of birds from meat-type chicken, waterfowl, exhibition poultry, and game bird flocks must be the same as the ratio of male to female birds in the flock. In houses containing fewer than 30 birds other than ostriches, emus, rheas, and cassowaries, all birds in the house must be tested.

(a) *For Pullorum-Typhoid.* (1) The official blood tests for pullorum-typhoid shall be the standard tube agglutination test, the microagglutination test, the enzyme-linked immunosorbent assay test (ELISA), or the rapid serum test for all poultry; and the stained antigen, rapid whole-blood test for all poultry except turkeys. Official blood tests must be conducted in accordance with part 147 of this subchapter or according to literature provided by the producer. Only antigens approved by the Department and of the polyvalent type shall be used for the rapid whole-blood and tube agglutination tests. Each serial of tube antigen shall be submitted by the antigen producer to the Department for approval upon manufacture and once a year thereafter as long as antigen from that serial continues to be made available for use. All microtest antigens and enzyme-linked immunosorbent assay reagents shall also be approved by the Department. [1]

(2) [Reserved]

(3) There shall be an interval of at least 21 days between any official blood test and any previous test with pullorum-typhoid antigen.

(4) [Reserved]

(5) The official blood test shall include the testing of a sample of blood from each bird in the flock: Provided, That under specified conditions (see

[1] The criteria and procedures for Department approval of antigens and reagents may be obtained from the Animal and Plant Health Inspection Service, Veterinary Services, Center for Veterinary Biologics, 510 South 17th Street, Suite 104, Ames, IA 50010–8197.

applicable provisions of §§ 145.23, 145.33, 145.43, 145.53, 145.63, 145.73, 145.83, and 145.93) the testing of a portion or sample of the birds may be used in lieu of testing each bird.

(6) Poultry from flocks undergoing qualification testing for participation in the Plan that have a positive reaction to an official blood test named in paragraph (a)(1) of this section shall be evaluated for pullorum-typhoid as follows:

(i) Serum samples that react on rapid serum test or enzyme-labeled immunosorbent assay test (ELISA), or blood from birds that react on the stained antigen, rapid whole-blood test for all birds except turkeys, shall be tested with either the standard tube agglutination test or the microagglutination test.

(ii) Reactors to the standard tube agglutination test (in dilutions of 1:50 or greater) or the microagglutination test (in dilutions of 1:40 or greater) shall be submitted to an authorized laboratory for bacteriological examination. If there are more than four reactors in a flock, a minimum of four reactors shall be submitted to the authorized laboratory; if the flock has four or fewer reactors, all of the reactors must be submitted. Bacteriological examination must be conducted in accordance with part 147 of this subchapter. When reactors are submitted to the authorized laboratory within 10 days of the date of reading an official blood test named in paragraph (a)(6)(i) of this section, and the bacteriological examination fails to demonstrate pullorum-typhoid infection, the Official State Agency shall presume that the flock has no pullorum-typhoid reactors.

(iii) If a flock owner does not wish to submit reactors for bacteriological examination, then the reactors shall be isolated and retested within 30 days using an official blood test named in paragraph (a)(1) of this section. If this retest is positive, additional examination of the reactors and flock will be performed in accordance with paragraph (a)(6)(ii) of this section. During this 30-day period, the flock must be maintained under a security system, specified or approved by the Official State Agency, that will prevent physical contact with other birds and assure that personnel, equipment, and supplies that could be a source of pullorum-typhoid spread are sanitized.

(7) When *S. pullorum* or *S. gallinarum* organisms are isolated by an authorized laboratory from baby poultry, or from fluff samples produced by hatching eggs, the infected flock shall qualify for participation in the Plan with two consecutive negative results to an official blood test named in paragraph (a)(1) of this section. A succeeding flock must be qualified for participation in the Plan's pullorum-typhoid program with a negative result to an official blood test named in paragraph (a)(1) of this section. Testing to qualify flocks for Plan participation must include the testing of all birds in infected flocks and succeeding flocks for a 12-month period, and shall be performed or physically supervised by a State Inspector; Provided, That at the discretion of the Official State Agency, a sample of at least 500 birds, rather than all birds in the flock, may be tested by the State Inspector if it is agreed upon by the Official State Agency, the flockowner, and the Administrator. If the State Inspector determines that a primary breeding flock has been exposed to *S. pullorum* or *S. gallinarum*,[2] the Official State Agency shall require:

(i) The taking of blood samples—performed by or in the presence of a State Inspector—from all birds on premises exposed to birds, equipment, supplies, or personnel from the primary breeding flock during the period when the State Inspector determined that exposure to *S. pullorum* or *S. gallinarum* occurred.[2]

(ii) The banding of all birds of these premises—performed or physically supervised by a State Inspector—in order to identify any bird that tests positive; and

(iii) The testing of blood samples at an authorized laboratory using an official blood test named in paragraph (a)(1) of this section.

---

[2] In making determinations of exposure, the State Inspector shall evaluate both evidence proving that exposure occurred and circumstances indicating a high probability of contacts with: infected wild birds; contaminated feed or waste; or birds, equipment, supplies, or persons from or exposed to flocks infected with *S. pullorum* or *S. gallinarum*.

(8) All domesticated fowl, except waterfowl, on the farm of the participant shall either be properly tested to meet the same standards as the participating flock or these birds and their eggs shall be separated from the participating flock and its eggs.

(9) All tests for pullorum-typhoid in flocks participating in or candidates for participation in the Plan shall be reported to the Official State Agency within 10 days following the completion of such tests. All reactors shall be considered in determining the classification of the flock.

(10) Any drug, for which there is scientific evidence of masking the test reaction or hindering the bacteriological recovery of Salmonella organisms, shall not be fed or administered to poultry within 3 weeks prior to a test or bacteriological examination upon which a Salmonella classification is based.

(11) When suitable evidence, as determined by the Official State Agency or the State Animal Disease Control Official, indicates that baby or started poultry produced by participating hatcheries are infected with organisms for which the parent flock received an official control classification and this evidence indicates that the infection was transmitted from the parent flock, the Official State Agency may, at its discretion, require additional testing of the flock involved. If infection is found in the parent flock, its classification shall be suspended until the flock is requalified under the requirements for the classification. Furthermore, the Official State Agency may require that the hatching eggs from such flocks be removed from the incubator and destroyed prior to hatching. When Salmonella organisms are isolated from a specimen which originated in a participating hatchery, the Official State Agency shall attempt to locate the source of the infection. The results of the investigation and the action taken to eliminate the infection shall be reported by the Official State Agency to the Service.

(b) *For Mycoplasma gallisepticum, M. meleagridis, and M. synoviae.* (1) The official tests for *M. gallisepticum, M. meleagridis,* and *M. synoviae* shall be the serum plate agglutination test, the hemagglutination inhibition (HI) test, the enzyme-linked immunosorbent assay (ELISA) test,[3] or a molecular based test. The HI test or molecular based test shall be used to confirm the positive results of other serological screening tests. HI titers of 1:40 or more may be interpreted as suspicious, and final judgment must be based on further samplings and/or culture of reactors. Tests must be conducted in accordance with this paragraph (b) and in accordance with part 147 of this subchapter.

(2) The serological tests shall be conducted using *M. gallisepticum, M. meleagridis,* or *M. synoviae* antigens approved by the Department or the Official State Agency and shall be performed in accordance with the recommendations of the producer of the antigen.

(3) When reactors to the test for which the flock was tested are submitted to a laboratory as prescribed by the Official State Agency, the final status of the flock will be determined in accordance with part 147 of this subchapter.

(4) Any drug, for which there is scientific evidence of masking the test reaction or hindering the bacteriological recovery of mycoplasma organisms, shall not be fed or administered to poultry within three weeks prior to a test or bacteriological examination upon which a Mycoplasma classification is based.

(5) The official molecular examination procedures for *M. gallisepticum* are

[3] Procedures for the enzyme-linked immunosorbent assay (ELISA) test are set forth in the following publications:

A.A. Ansari, R.F. Taylor, T.S. Chang, "Application of Enzyme-Linked Immunosorbent Assay for Detecting Antibody to Mycoplasma gallisepticum Infections in Poultry," *Avian Diseases,* Vol. 27, No. 1, pp. 21–35, January-March 1983; and

H.M. Opitz, J.B. Duplessis, and M.J. Cyr, "Indirect Micro-Enzyme-Linked Immunosorbent Assay for the Detection of Antibodies to Mycoplasma synoviae and M. gallisepticum," *Avian Diseases,* Vol. 27, No. 3, pp. 773–786, July-September 1983; and

H.B. Ortmayer and R. Yamamoto, "Mycoplasma Meleagridis Antibody Detection by Enzyme-Linked Immunosorbent Assay (ELISA)," *Proceedings, 30th Western Poultry Disease Conference,* pp. 63–66, March 1981.

the PCR test described in § 147.30 of this subchapter and the real-time PCR test described in § 147.31 of this subchapter. The official molecular examination procedure for *M. synoviae* is the PCR test described in § 147.30 of this subchapter.

(c) [Reserved]

(d) *For avian influenza.* The official tests for avian influenza are described in paragraphs (d)(1) and (d)(2) of this section.

(1) *Antibody detection tests*—(i) *Enzyme-linked immunosorbent assay (ELISA).* ELISA must be conducted using test kits approved by the Department and the Official State Agency and must be conducted in accordance with the recommendations of the producer or manufacturer.

(ii) *The agar gel immunodiffusion (AGID) test.* (A) The AGID test must be conducted on all ELISA-positive samples.

(B) The AGID test must be conducted using reagents approved by the Department and the Official State Agency.

(C) The AGID test for avian influenza must be conducted in accordance with part 147 of this subchapter. The test can be conducted on egg yolk or blood samples. The AGID test is not recommended for use in waterfowl.

(D) Positive tests for the AGID must be further tested by Federal Reference Laboratories using appropriate tests for confirmation. Final judgment may be based upon further sampling and appropriate tests for confirmation.

(2) *Agent detection tests.* Agent detection tests may be used to detect influenza A matrix gene or protein but not to determine hemagglutinin or neuraminidase subtypes. Samples for agent detection testing should be collected from naturally occurring flock mortality or clinically ill birds.

(i) *The real time reverse transcriptase/polymerase chain reaction (RRT–PCR) assay.* (A) The RRT–PCR tests must be conducted using reagents approved by the Department and the Official State Agency. The RRT–PCR must be conducted using the National Veterinary Services Laboratories (NVSL) official protocol for RRT–PCR and must be conducted by personnel who have passed an NVSL proficiency test.

(B) Positive results from the RRT–PCR must be further tested by Federal Reference Laboratories using appropriate tests for confirmation. Final judgment may be based upon further sampling and appropriate tests for confirmation.

(ii) *USDA-licensed type A influenza antigen capture immunoassay (ACIA).* (A) The USDA-licensed type A influenza ACIA must be conducted using test kits approved by the Department and the Official State Agency and must be conducted in accordance with the recommendations of the producer or manufacturer.

(B) Chicken and turkey flocks that test positive on the ACIA must be further tested using the RRT–PCR or virus isolation. Positive results from the RRT–PCR or virus isolation must be further tested by Federal Reference Laboratories using appropriate tests for confirmation. Final judgment may be based upon further sampling and appropriate tests for confirmation.

(3) The official determination of a flock as positive for the H5 or H7 subtypes of avian influenza may be made only by NVSL.

(Approved by the Office of Management and Budget under control number 0579–0007)

[36 FR 23112, Dec. 3, 1971]

EDITORIAL NOTE: For FEDERAL REGISTER citations affecting § 145.14, see the List of CFR Sections Affected, which appears in the Finding Aids section of the printed volume and at *www.fdsys.gov*.

§ 145.15 Diagnostic surveillance program for low pathogenic avian influenza.

(a) The Official State Agency must develop a diagnostic surveillance program for H5/H7 low pathogenic avian influenza for all poultry in the State. The exact provisions of the program are at the discretion of the States. The Service will use the standards in paragraph (b) of this section in assessing individual State plans for adequacy, including the specific provisions that the State developed. The standards should be used by States in developing those plans.

(b) Avian influenza must be a disease reportable to the responsible State authority (State veterinarian, etc.) by all licensed veterinarians. To accomplish this, all laboratories (private, State, and university laboratories) that perform diagnostic procedures on poultry must examine all submitted cases of unexplained respiratory disease, egg production drops, and mortality for avian influenza by both an approved serological test and an approved antigen detection test. Memoranda of understanding or other means must be used to establish testing and reporting criteria (including criteria that provide for reporting H5 and H7 low pathogenic avian influenza directly to the Service) and approved testing methods. In addition, States should conduct outreach to poultry producers, especially owners of smaller flocks, regarding the importance of prompt reporting of clinical symptoms consistent with avian influenza.

[74 FR 14715, Apr. 1, 2009]

Subpart B—Special Provisions for Multiplier Egg-Type Chicken Breeding Flocks and Products

§ 145.21 Definitions.

Except where the context otherwise requires, for the purposes of this subpart the following terms shall be construed, respectively, to mean:

Chicks. Newly hatched chickens.

Egg type chicken breeding flocks. Flocks that are composed of stock that has been developed for egg production and are maintained for the principal purpose of producing chicks for the ultimate production of eggs for human consumption.

Started chickens. Young chickens (chicks, pullets, cockerels, capons) which have been fed and watered and are less than 6 months of age.

[36 FR 23112, Dec. 3, 1971, as amended at 38 FR 13707, May 24, 1973; 41 FR 48723, Nov. 5, 1976. Redesignated at 44 FR 61586, Oct. 26, 1979, and amended at 59 FR 12798, Mar. 18, 1994; 65 FR 8017, Feb. 17, 2000]

§ 145.22 Participation.

Participating flocks of multiplier egg type chickens, and the eggs and chicks produced from them, shall comply with the applicable general provisions of subpart A of this part and the special provisions of this subpart B.

(a) Started chickens shall lose their identity under Plan terminology when not maintained by Plan participants under the conditions prescribed in § 145.5(a).

(b) Hatching eggs produced by multiplier breeding flocks should be nest clean. They may be fumigated in accordance with part 147 of this subchapter or otherwise sanitized.

(c) Any nutritive material provided to chicks must be free of the avian pathogens that are officially represented in the Plan disease classifications listed in § 145.10.

[36 FR 23112, Dec. 3, 1971, as amended at 40 FR 1501, Jan. 8, 1975. Redesignated at 44 FR 61586, Oct. 26, 1979, and amended at 49 FR 19802, May 10, 1984; 57 FR 57341, Dec. 4, 1992; 65 FR 8017, Feb. 17, 2000; 68 FR 64510, Nov. 14, 2003; 72 FR 1419, Jan. 12, 2007; 79 FR 38755, July 9, 2014]

§ 145.23 Terminology and classification; flocks and products.

Participating flocks, and the eggs and chicks produced from them, which have met the respective requirements specified in this section may be designated by the following terms and the corresponding designs illustrated in § 145.10:

(a) [Reserved]

(b) *U.S. Pullorum-Typhoid Clean.* A flock in which freedom from pullorum and typhoid has been demonstrated to the official State agency under the criteria in one of the following paragraphs (b)(1) through (4) of this section: *Provided,* That a flock qualifying by means of a blood test shall be tested within the past 12 months, except that the retesting of a participating flock which is retained for more than 12 months shall be conducted a minimum of 4 weeks after the induction of molt. (See § 145.14 relating to the official blood test where applicable.)

(1) It has been officially blood tested with no reactors.

(2) It is a multiplier breeding flock and meets the following specifications as determined by the Official State Agency and the Service:

(i) The flock is located in a State where all persons performing poultry disease diagnostic services within the State are required to report to the Official State Agency within 48 hours the source of all poultry specimens from which S. pullorum or S. gallinarum is isolated;

(ii) The flock is composed entirely of birds that originated from U.S. Pullorum-Typhoid Clean breeding flocks or from flocks that met equivalent requirements under official supervision; and

(iii) The flock is located on a premises where a flock not classified as U.S. Pullorum-Typhoid Clean was located the previous year; *Provided*, That an Authorized Testing Agent must blood test up to 300 birds per flock, as described in § 145.14, if the Official State Agency determines that the flock has been exposed to pullorum-typhoid. In making determinations of exposure and setting the number of birds to be blood tested, the Official State Agency shall evaluate the results of any blood tests, described in § 145.14(a)(1) that were performed on an unclassified flock located on the premises during the previous year; the origins of the unclassified flock; and the probability of contacts between the flock for which qualification is being sought and (a) infected wild birds, (b) contaminated feed or waste, or (c) birds, equipment, supplies, or personnel from flocks infected with pullorum-typhoid.

(3) It is a multiplier breeding flock that originated from U.S. Pullorum-Typhoid Clean breeding flocks or from flocks that met equivalent requirements under official supervision, and is located in a State in which it has been determined by the Service that:

(i) All hatcheries within the State are qualified as "National Plan Hatcheries" or have met equivalent requirements for pullorum-typhoid control under official supervision;

(ii) All hatchery supply flocks within the State, are qualified as U.S. Pullorum-Typhoid Clean or have met equivalent requirements for pullorum-typhoid control under official supervision: *Provided*, That if other domesticated fowl, except waterfowl, are maintained on the same premises as the participating flock, freedom from pullorum-typhoid infection shall be demonstrated by an official blood test of each of these fowl;

(iii) All shipments of products other than U.S. Pullorum-Typhoid Clean, or equivalent, into the State are prohibited;

(iv) All persons performing poultry disease diagnostic services within the State are required to report to the Official State Agency within 48 hours the source of all poultry specimens from which S. pullorum or S. gallinarum is isolated;

(v) All reports of any disease outbreak involving a disease covered under the Plan are promptly followed by an investigation by the Official State Agency to determine the origin of the infection; *Provided*, That if the origin of the infection involves another State, or if there is exposure to poultry in another State from the infected flock, then the National Poultry Improvement Plan will conduct an investigation;

(vi) All flocks found to be infected with pullorum or typhoid are quarantined until marketed or destroyed under the supervision of the Official State Agency, or until subsequently blood tested, following the procedure for reacting flocks as contained in § 145.14(a)(5), and all birds fail to demonstrate pullorum or typhoid infection;

(vii) All poultry, including exhibition, exotic, and game birds, but excluding waterfowl, going to public exhibition shall come from U.S. Pullorum-Typhoid Clean or equivalent flocks, or have had a negative pullorum-typhoid test within 90 days of going to public exhibition;

(viii) Discontinuation of any of the conditions or procedures described in paragraphs (b)(3)(i), (ii), (iii), (iv), (v), (vi), and (vii) of this section, or the occurrence of repeated outbreaks of pullorum or typhoid in poultry breeding flocks within or originating within the State shall be grounds for the Service to revoke its determination that such conditions and procedures have been met or complied with. Such action shall not be taken until a thorough investigation has been made by the Service and the Official State Agency has been given an opportunity to present its views.

(4) It is a multiplier breeding flock located in a State which has been determined by the Service to be in compliance with the provisions of (b)(3) of this section, and in which pullorum

disease or fowl typhoid is not known to exist nor to have existed in hatchery supply flocks within the State during the preceding 12 months.

(c) *U.S. M. Gallisepticum Clean.* (1) A flock maintained in accordance with part 147 of this subchapter with respect to Mycoplasma isolation, sanitation, and management and in which freedom from *M. gallisepticum* has been demonstrated under the criteria specified in paragraph (c)(1)(i) or (ii) of this section.

(i) [Reserved]

(ii) It is a multiplier breeding flock which originated as U.S. M. Gallisepticum Clean chicks from primary breeding flocks and from which a sample comprised of a minimum of 150 birds per flock has been tested for *M. gallisepticum* as provided in § 145.14(b) when more than 4 months of age: *Provided,* That to retain this classification, the flock shall be subjected to one of the following procedures:

(A) At intervals of not more than 90 days, 75 birds from the flock shall be tested, *Provided,* that fewer than 75 birds from the flock may be tested at any one time if all pens are equally represented and a total of at least 75 birds from the flock is tested within each 90-day period; or

(B) At intervals of not more than 30 days, a sample of 25 cull chicks produced from the flock shall be subjected to laboratory procedures acceptable to the Official State Agency and approved by the Service, for the detection and recovery of *M. gallisepticum*; or

(C) At intervals of not more than 30 days, egg yolk testing shall be conducted in accordance with part 147 of this subchapter.

(2) A participant handling U.S. M. Gallisepticum Clean products shall keep these products separate from other products in a manner satisfactory to the Official State Agency.

(3) U.S. M. Gallisepticum Clean chicks shall be boxed in clean boxes and delivered in trucks that have been cleaned and disinfected in accordance with part 147 of this subchapter.

(d) *U.S. S. Enteritidis Clean.* This classification is intended for egg-type breeders wishing to assure their customers that the hatching eggs and chicks produced are certified free of *Salmonella enteritidis.*

(1) A flock and the hatching eggs and chicks produced from it which have met the following requirements as determined by the Official State Agency:

(i) The flock originated from a U.S. *S. enteritidis* Clean flock, or meconium from the chick boxes and a sample of chicks that died within 7 days after hatching are examined bacteriologically for salmonella at an authorized laboratory. Cultures from positive samples shall be serotyped.

(ii) All feed fed to the flock shall meet the following requirements:

(A) Pelletized feed shall contain either no animal protein or only animal protein products produced under the Animal Protein Products Industry (APPI) *Salmonella* Education/Reduction Program. The protein products must have a minimum moisture content of 14.5 percent and must have been heated throughout to a minimum temperature of 190 °F., or above, or to a minimum temperature of 165 °F. for at least 20 minutes, or to a minimum temperature of 184 °F. under 70 lbs. pressure during the manufacturing process.

(B) Mash feed may contain no animal protein other than an APPI animal protein product supplement manufactured in pellet form and crumbled: *Provided,* that mash feed may contain nonpelleted APPI animal protein product supplements if the finished feed is treated with a salmonella control product approved by the Food and Drug Administration.

(iii) Feed shall be stored and transported in such a manner as to prevent possible contamination;

(iv) The flock is maintained in accordance with part 147 of this subchapter with respect to flock sanitation, cleaning and disinfection, and Salmonella isolation, sanitation, and management. Rodents and other pests should be effectively controlled;

(v) Environmental samples shall be collected from the flock by an Authorized Agent, in accordance with part 147 of this subchapter, when the flock is 2 to 4 weeks of age. The samples shall be examined bacteriologically for group D salmonella at an authorized laboratory. Cultures from positive samples shall be serotyped. The authorized agent shall also collect samples every 30 days after the first sample has been collected.

(vi) If a *Salmonella* vaccine is used that causes positive reactions with pullorum-typhoid antigen, one of the following options must be utilized:

(A) Administer the vaccine after the pullorum-typhoid testing is done as described in paragraph (d)(1)(vii) of this section.

(B) If an injectable bacterin or live vaccine that does not spread is used, keep a sample of 350 birds unvaccinated and banded for identification until the flock reaches at least 4 months of age. Following negative serological and bacteriological examinations as described in paragraph (d)(1)(vii) of this section, vaccinate the banded, non-vaccinated birds.

(vii) Blood samples from 300 non-vaccinated birds as described in paragraph (d)(1)(vi) of this section shall be tested with either pullorum antigen or by a federally licensed Salmonella enteritidis enzyme-linked immunosorbent assay (ELISA) test when the flock is more than 4 months of age. All birds with positive or inconclusive reactions, up to a maximum of 25 birds, shall be submitted to an authorized laboratory and examined for the presence of group D salmonella, in accordance with part 147 of this subchapter. Cultures from positive samples shall be serotyped.

(viii) Hatching eggs are collected as quickly as possible, and their sanitation is maintained in accordance with part 147 of this subchapter.

(ix) Hatching eggs produced by the flock are incubated in a hatchery whose sanitation is maintained in accordance with part 147 of this subchapter and sanitized either by a procedure approved by the Official State Agency or in accordance with part 147 of this subchapter.

(2) A flock shall not be eligible for this classification if *Salmonella enteritidis* ser *enteritidis* (SE) is isolated from a specimen taken from a bird in the flock. Isolation of SE from an environmental or other specimen, as described in paragraph (d)(1)(v) of this section, will require bacteriological examination for SE in an authorized laboratory, in accordance with part 147 of this subchapter, of a random sample of 60 live birds from a flock of 5,000 birds or more, or 30 live birds from a flock with fewer than 5,000 birds. If only one specimen is found positive for SE, the participant may request bacteriological examination of a second sample, equal in size to the first sample, from the flock. If no SE is recovered from any of the specimens in the second sample, the flock will be eligible for the classification.

(3) A non-vaccinated flock shall be eligible for this classification if *Salmonella enteritidis* (*S. enteritidis* ser Enteritidis) is isolated from an environmental sample collected from the flock in accordance with paragraph (d)(1)(v) of this section: *Provided*, That testing is conducted in accordance with paragraph (d)(1)(vii) of this section each 30 days and no positive samples are found.

(4) In order for a hatchery to sell products of this classification, all products handled shall meet the requirements of the classification.

(5) This classification may be revoked by the Official State Agency if the participant fails to follow recommended corrective measures.

(e) *U.S.M. Synoviae Clean.* (1) A flock maintained in accordance with part 147 of this subchapter with respect to Mycoplasma isolation, sanitation, and management and in which freedom from *M. synoviae* has been demonstrated under the criteria specified in paragraph (e)(1)(i) or (ii) of this section.

(i) [Reserved]

(ii) It is a multiplier breeding flock which originated as U.S. M. Synoviae Clean chicks from primary breeding flocks and from which a sample comprised of a minimum of 150 birds has been tested for *M. synoviae* as provided in §145.14(b) when more than 4 months of age: *Provided*, That to retain this classification, the flock shall be subjected to one of the following procedures:

(A) At intervals of not more than 90 days, 75 birds from the flock shall be tested: *Provided*, That fewer than 75 birds from the flock may be tested at any one time if all pens are equally represented and a total of at least 75 birds from the flock is tested within each 90-day period; or

(B) At intervals of not more than 30 days, egg yolk testing shall be conducted in accordance with part 147 of this subchapter.

(2) A participant handling U.S. M. Synoviae Clean products shall keep these products separate from other products in a manner satisfactory to the Official State Agency.

(3) U.S. M. Synoviae Clean chicks shall be boxed in clean boxes and delivered in trucks that have been cleaned and disinfected in accordance with part 147 of this subchapter.

(f) *U.S. M. Gallisepticum Clean Started Poultry.* (1) A flock which originated from U.S. M. Gallisepticum Clean breeding flocks and was hatched in a hatchery approved by the Official State Agency for the production of U.S. M. Gallisepticum Clean chicks.

(2) All other poultry on the premises of the candidate flock must originate from U.S. M. Gallisepticum Clean sources.

(3) The flock is maintained in accordance with part 147 of this subchapter with respect to Mycoplasma isolation, sanitation, and management.

(4) The flock's freedom from *M. Gallisepticum* is demonstrated by a negative blood test, as provided in §145.14(b), of a sample of 75 birds, with a minimum of 50 birds per poultry house, between 15–20 days prior to the flock being moved to laying quarters.

(5) Started poultry shall be delivered to and from the farm premises in crates and vehicles which have been cleaned and disinfected in accordance with part 147 of this subchapter.

(g) *U.S. M. Synoviae Clean Started Poultry.* (1) A flock which originated from U.S. M. Synoviae Clean breeding flocks and was hatched in a hatchery approved by the Official State Agency for production of U.S. M. Synoviae Clean chicks.

(2) All other poultry on the premises of the candidate flock must originate from U.S. M. Synoviae Clean sources.

(3) The flock is maintained in accordance with part 147 of this subchapter with respect to Mycoplasma isolation, sanitation, and management.

(4) The flocks's freedom from *M. synoviae* is demonstrated by a negative blood test, as provided in §145.14(b), of a sample of 75 birds, with a minimum of 50 birds per poultry house, between 15–20 days prior to the flock being moved to laying quarters.

(5) Started poultry shall be delivered to and from the farm premises in crates and vehicles which have been cleaned and disinfected in accordance with part 147 of this subchapter.

(h) *U.S. Avian Influenza Clean.* This program is intended to be the basis from which the breeding-hatchery industry may conduct a program for the prevention and control of avian influenza. It is intended to determine the presence of avian influenza in breeding chickens through routine surveillance of each participating breeding flock. A flock and the hatching eggs and chicks produced from it will qualify for this classification when the Official State Agency determines that they have met the following requirements:

(1) It is a multiplier breeding flock in which a minimum of 30 birds have been tested and found negative to avian influenza when more than 4 months of age. To retain this classification:

(i) A sample of at least 30 birds must be tested negative at intervals of 90 days; or

(ii) A sample of fewer than 30 birds may be tested, and found to be negative, at any one time if all pens are equally represented and a total of 30 birds is tested within each 90-day period; or

(iii) The flock is tested as provided in §145.14(d) at intervals of 30 days or less and found to be negative, and a total of 30 samples are collected and tested within each 90-day period; and

(2) A sample of at least 11 birds must be tested and found negative to avian influenza within 21 days prior to slaughter.

(Approved by the Office of Management and Budget under control number 0579–0007)

[36 FR 23112, Dec. 3, 1971]

EDITORIAL NOTE: For FEDERAL REGISTER citations affecting §145.23, see the List of CFR Sections Affected, which appears in the Finding Aids section of the printed volume and at *www.fdsys.gov*.

§ 145.24 Terminology and classification; States.

(a) *U.S. Pullorum-Typhoid Clean State.* (1) A State will be declared a U.S. Pullorum-Typhoid Clean State when it has been determined by the Service that:

(i) The State is in compliance with the provisions contained in § 145.23(b)(3)(i) through (vii), § 145.33(b)(3)(i) through (vii), § 145.43(b)(3)(i) through (vi), § 145.53(b)(3)(i) through (vii), § 145.73(b)(2)(i), § 145.83(b)(2)(i), and § 145.93(b)(3)(i) through (vii).

(ii) No pullorum disease or fowl typhoid is known to exist nor to have existed in hatchery supply flocks within the State during the preceding 12 months: *Provided,* That pullorum disease or fowl typhoid found within the preceding 24 months in waterfowl, exhibition poultry, and game bird breeding flocks will not prevent a State, which is otherwise eligible, from qualifying.

(2) Discontinuation of any of the conditions described in paragraph (a)(1)(i) of this section, or repeated outbreaks of pullorum or typhoid occur in hatchery supply flocks described in paragraph (a)(1)(ii) of this section, or if an infection spreads from the originating premises, the Service shall have grounds to revoke its determination that the State is entitled to this classification. Such action shall not be taken until a thorough investigation has been made by the Service and the Official State Agency has been given an opportunity for a hearing in accordance with rules of practice adopted by the Administrator.

(b) [Reserved]

[40 FR 1502, Jan. 8, 1975. Redesignated at 44 FR 61586, Oct. 26, 1979, and amended at 54 FR 23957, June 5, 1989; 67 FR 8469, Feb. 25, 2002; 72 FR 1419, Jan. 12, 2007; 76 FR 15793, Mar. 22, 2011]

Subpart C—Special Provisions for Multiplier Meat-Type Chicken Breeding Flocks and Products

§ 145.31 Definitions.

Except where the context otherwise requires, for the purposes of this subpart the following terms shall be construed, respectively, to mean:

Chicks. Newly hatched chickens.

Meat type chicken breeding flocks. Flocks that are composed of stock that has been developed for meat production and are maintained for the principal purpose of producing chicks for the ultimate production of meat.

Started chickens. Young chickens (chicks, pullets, cockerels, capons) which have been fed and watered and are less than 6 months of age.

[36 FR 23112, Dec. 3, 1971, as amended at 41 FR 48724, Nov. 5, 1976. Redesignated at 44 FR 61586, Oct. 26, 1979, and amended at 59 FR 12799, Mar. 18, 1994; 65 FR 8018, Feb. 17, 2000]

§ 145.32 Participation.

Participating flocks of multiplier meat type chickens, and the eggs and chicks produced from them, shall comply with the applicable general provisions of subpart A of this part and the special provisions of this subpart C.

(a) Started chickens shall lose their identity under Plan terminology when not maintained by Plan participants under the conditions prescribed in § 145.5(a).

(b) Hatching eggs produced by multiplier breeding flocks should be nest clean. They may be fumigated in accordance with part 147 of this subchapter or otherwise sanitized.

(c) Any nutritive material provided to chicks must be free of the avian pathogens that are officially represented in the Plan disease classifications listed in § 145.10.

[36 FR 23112, Dec. 3, 1971, as amended at 40 FR 1502, Jan. 8, 1975; 41 FR 48724, Nov. 5, 1976. Redesignated at 44 FR 61586, Oct. 26, 1979, and amended at 49 FR 19802, May 10, 1984; 57 FR 57341, Dec. 4, 1992; 65 FR 8018, Feb. 17, 2000; 68 FR 64510, Nov. 14, 2003; 72 FR 1419, Jan. 12, 2007; 79 FR 38756, July 9, 2014]

§ 145.33 Terminology and classification; flocks and products.

Participating flocks, and the eggs and chicks produced from them, which have met the respective requirements specified in this section may be designated by the following terms and the corresponding designs illustrated in § 145.10:

(a) [Reserved]

(b) *U.S. Pullorum-Typhoid Clean.* A flock in which freedom from pullorum and typhoid has been demonstrated to the official State agency under the criteria in one of paragraphs (b)(1) through (4) of this section: *Provided*, That a flock qualifying by means of a blood test shall be tested within the past 12 months, except that the retesting of a participating flock which is retained for more than 12 months shall be conducted a minimum of 4 weeks after the induction of molt. (See §145.14 relating to the official blood test where applicable.)

(1) It has been officially blood tested with no reactors.

(2) It is a multiplier breeding flock and meets the following specifications as determined by the Official State Agency and the Service:

(i) The flock is located in a State where all persons performing poultry disease diagnostic services within the State are required to report to the Official State Agency within 48 hours the source of all poultry specimens from which S. pullorum or S. gallinarum is isolated;

(ii) The flock is composed entirely of birds that originated from U.S. Pullorum-Typhoid Clean breeding flocks or from flocks that met equivalent requirements under official supervision; and

(iii) The flock is located on a premises where a flock not classified as U.S. Pullorum-Typhoid Clean was located the previous year; *Provided*, That an Authorized Testing Agent must blood test up to 300 birds per flock, as described in §145.14, if the Official State Agency determines that the flock has been exposed to pullorum-typhoid. In making determinations of exposure and setting the number of birds to be blood tested, the Official State Agency shall evaluate the results of any blood tests, described in §145.14(a)(1), that were performed on an unclassified flock located on the premises during the previous year; the origins of the unclassified flock; and the probability of contacts between the flock for which qualification is being sought and (a) infected wild birds, (b) contaminated feed or waste, or (c) birds, equipment, supplies, or personnel from flocks infected with pullorum-typhoid.

(3) It is a multiplier breeding flock that originated from U.S. Pullorum-Typhoid Clean breeding flocks or from flocks that met equivalent requirements under official supervision, and is located in a State in which it has been determined by the Service that:

(i) All hatcheries within the State are qualified as "National Plan Hatcheries" or have met equivalent requirements for pullorum-typhoid control under official supervision;

(ii) All hatchery supply flocks within the State, are qualified as U.S. Pullorum-Typhoid Clean or have met equivalent requirements for pullorum-typhoid control under official supervision: *Provided*, That if other domesticated fowl, except waterfowl, are maintained on the same premises as the participating flock, freedom from pullorum-typhoid infection shall be demonstrated by an official blood test of each of these fowl;

(iii) All shipments of products other than U.S. Pullorum-Typhoid Clean, or equivalent, into the State are prohibited;

(iv) All persons performing poultry disease diagnostic services within the State are required to report to the Official State Agency within 48 hours the source of all poultry specimens from which S. pullorum or S. gallinarum is isolated;

(v) All reports of any disease outbreak involving a disease covered under the Plan are promptly followed by an investigation by the Official State Agency to determine the origin of the infection; *Provided*, That if the origin of the infection involves another State, or if there is exposure to poultry in another State from the infected flock, then the National Poultry Improvement Plan will conduct an investigation;

(vi) All flocks found to be infected with pullorum or typhoid are quarantined until marketed or destroyed under the supervision of the Official State Agency, or until subsequently blood tested following the procedure for reacting flocks as contained in §145.14(a)(5), and all birds fail to demonstrate pullorum or typhoid infection;

(vii) All poultry, including exhibition, exotic, and game birds, but excluding waterfowl, going to public exhibition shall come from U.S. Pullorum-Typhoid Clean or equivalent flocks, or have had a negative pullorum-typhoid test within 90 days of going to public exhibition;

(viii) Discontinuation of any of the conditions or procedures described in paragraphs (b)(3)(i), (ii), (iii), (iv), (v), (vi), and (vii) of this section, or the occurrence of repeated outbreaks of pullorum or typhoid in poultry breeding flocks within or originating within the State shall be grounds for the Service to revoke its determination that such conditions and procedures have been met or complied with. Such action shall not be taken until a thorough investigation has been made by the Service and the Official State Agency has been given an opportunity to present its views.

(4) It is a multiplier breeding flock located in a State which has been determined by the Service to be in compliance with the provisions of paragraph (b)(3) of this section, and in which pullorum disease or fowl typhoid is not known to exist nor to have existed in hatchery supply flocks within the State during the preceding 12 months.

(c) *U.S. M. Gallisepticum Clean.* (1) A flock maintained in accordance with part 147 of this subchapter with respect to Mycoplasma isolation, sanitation, and management and in which freedom from *M. gallisepticum* has been demonstrated under the criteria specified in paragraph (c)(1)(i) or (ii) of this section.

(i) [Reserved]

(ii) It is a multiplier breeding flock which originated as U.S. M. Gallisepticum Clean chicks from primary breeding flocks and from which a sample comprised of a minimum of 150 birds per flock has been tested for *M. gallisepticum* as provided in §145.14(b) when more than 4 months of age: *Provided,* That to retain this classification, the flock shall be subjected to one of the following procedures:

(A) At intervals of not more than 90 days, 75 birds from the flock shall be tested, *Provided,* That fewer than 75 birds from the flock may be tested at any one time if all pens are equally represented and a total of at least 75 birds from the flock is tested within each 90-day period; or

(B) At intervals of not more than 30 days, a sample of 25 cull chicks produced from the flock shall be subjected to laboratory procedures acceptable to the Official State Agency and approved by the Service, for the detection and recovery of *M. gallisepticum*; or

(C) At intervals of not more than 30 days, egg yolk testing shall be conducted in accordance with part 147 of this subchapter.

(2) A participant handling U.S. M. Gallisepticum Clean products must keep these products separate from other products through the use of separate hatchers and incubators, separate hatch days, and proper hatchery sanitation and biosecurity in a manner satisfactory to the Official State Agency and in accordance with part 147 of this subchapter.

(3) U.S. M. Gallisepticum Clean chicks shall be boxed in clean boxes and delivered in trucks that have been cleaned and disinfected in accordance with part 147 of this subchapter.

(4) Before male breeding birds may be added to a participating multiplier breeding flock, a sample of at least 30 birds to be added, with a minimum of 10 birds per pen, shall be tested for *M. gallisepticum* as provided in §145.14(b), or by a polymerase chain reaction (PCR)-based procedure in accordance with part 147 of this subchapter. If fewer than 30 male breeding birds are being added, all the birds shall be tested as described above. The male birds shall be tested no more than 14 days prior to their intended introduction into the flock. If the serologic testing of the birds yields hemagglutination inhibition titers of 1:40 or higher as provided in §145.14(b), or if the PCR testing is positive for *M. gallisepticum,* the male birds may not be added to the flock and must be either retested or destroyed.

(d) *U.S. Sanitation Monitored.* This program is intended to be the basis from which the breeding-hatching industry may conduct a program for the prevention and control of Salmonellosis. It is intended to reduce the incidence of Salmonella organisms in hatching eggs and chicks through an effective and practical sanitation program at the breeder farm and in the hatchery. This will afford other segments of the poultry industry an opportunity to reduce the incidence of Salmonella in their products.

(1) A flock and the hatching eggs and chicks produced from it which have met the following requirements as determined by the Official State Agency:

(i) The flock shall originate from a source where sanitation and management practices, as outlined in § 145.33(d)(1) of this paragraph, are conducted;

(ii) The flock is maintained in accordance with part 147 of this subchapter with respect to flock sanitation, cleaning and disinfection, and Salmonella isolation, sanitation, and management;

(iii) If pelletized feed contains animal protein, the protein products shall be purchased from participants in the Animal Protein Products Industry (APPI) *Salmonella* Education/Reduction Program or the Fishmeal Inspection Program of the National Marine Fisheries Service. The protein products must have a minimum moisture content of 14.5 percent and must have been heated throughout to a minimum temperature of 190 °F. or above, or to a minimum temperature of 165 °F. for at least 20 minutes, or to a minimum temperature of 184 °F. under 70 lbs. pressure during the manufacturing process;

(iv) If mash feed contains animal protein, the protein products shall be purchased from participants in the Animal Protein Products Industry (APPI) *Salmonella* Education/Reduction Program or the Fishmeal Inspection Program of the National Marine Fisheries Service;

(v) Feed shall be stored and transported in such a manner as to prevent possible contamination;

(vi) Chicks shall be hatched in a hatchery whose sanitation is maintained in accordance with part 147 of this subchapter and sanitized or fumigated in accordance with part 147 of this subchapter;

(vii) An Authorized Agent shall take environmental samples, in accordance with part 147 of this subchapter, from each flock at 4 months of age and every 90 days thereafter. An authorized laboratory for *Salmonella* shall examine the environmental samples bacteriologically;

(viii) Owners of flocks found infected with a paratyphoid *Salmonella* may vaccinate these flocks with an autogenous bacterin with a potentiating agent.[4]

(2) The Official State Agency may monitor the effectiveness of the sanitation practices in accordance with part 147 of this subchapter.

(3) In order for a hatchery to sell products of this classification, all products handled shall meet the requirements of the classification.

(4) This classification may be revoked by the Official State Agency if the participant fails to follow recommended corrective measures.

(e) *U.S. M. Synoviae Clean.* (1) A flock maintained in accordance with part 147 of this subchapter with respect to Mycoplasma isolation, sanitation, and management and in which freedom from *M. synoviae* has been demonstrated under the criteria specified in paragraph (e)(1)(i) or (ii) of this section.

(i) [Reserved]

(ii) It is a multiplier breeding flock which originated as U.S. M. Synoviae Clean chicks from primary breeding flocks and from which a sample comprised of a minimum of 150 birds has been tested for *M. synoviae* as provided in § 145.14(b) when more than 4 months of age: *Provided,* That to retain this classification, the flock shall be subjected to one of the following procedures:

(A) At intervals of not more than 90 days, 75 birds from the flock shall be tested: *Provided,* That fewer than 75 birds from the flock may be tested at any one time if all pens are equally represented and a total of at least 75 birds from the flock is tested within each 90-day period; or

(B) At intervals of not more than 30 days, egg yolk testing shall be conducted in accordance with part 147 of this subchapter.

(2) A participant handling U.S. M. Synoviae Clean products shall keep these products separate from other products in a manner satisfactory to the official State Agency.

[4] Preparation and use of this type of vaccine may be regulated by State statutes.

(3) U.S. M. Synoviae Clean chicks shall be boxed in clean boxes and delivered in trucks that have been cleaned and disinfected in accordance with part 147 of this subchapter.

(4) Before male breeding birds may be added to a participating multiplier breeding flock, a sample of at least 30 birds to be added, with a minimum of 10 birds per pen, shall be tested for *M. synoviae* as provided in § 145.14(b) or by a polymerase chain reaction (PCR)-based procedure in accordance with part 147 of this subchapter. If fewer than 30 male breeding birds are being added, all the birds shall be tested as described above. The male birds shall be tested no more than 14 days prior to their intended introduction into the flock. If the serologic testing of the birds yields hemagglutination inhibition titers of 1:40 or higher as provided in § 145.14(b), or if the PCR testing is positive for *M. synoviae*, the male birds may not be added to the flock and must be either retested or destroyed.

(f) *U.S. M. Gallisepticum Clean Started Poultry.* (1) A flock which originated from U.S. M. Gallisepticum Clean breeding flocks and was hatched in a hatchery approved by the Official State Agency for the production of U.S. M. Gallisepticum Clean chicks.

(2) All other poultry on the premises of the candidate flock must originate from U.S. M. Gallisepticum Clean sources.

(3) The flock is maintained in accordance with part 147 of this subchapter with respect to Mycoplasma isolation, sanitation, and management.

(4) The flock's freedom from *M. gallisepticum* is demonstrated by a negative blood test, as provided in § 145.14(b), of a sample of 75 birds, with a minimum of 50 birds per poultry house, between 15–20 days prior to the flock being moved to laying quarters.

(5) Started poultry shall be delivered to and from the farm premises in crates and vehicles which have been cleaned and disinfected in accordance with part 147 of this subchapter.

(g) *U.S. M. Synoviae Clean Started Poultry.* (1) A flock which originated from U.S. M. Synoviae Clean breeding flocks and was hatched in a hatchery approved by the Official State Agency for the production of U.S. M. Synoviae Clean chicks.

(2) All other poultry on the premises of the candidate flock must originate from U.S. M. Synoviae Clean sources.

(3) The flock is maintained in accordance with part 147 of this subchapter with respect to Mycoplasma isolation, sanitation, and management.

(4) The flock's freedom from *M. synoviae* is demonstrated by a negative blood test, as provided in § 145.14(b), of a sample of 75 birds, with a minimum of 50 birds per poultry house, between 15–20 days prior to the flock being moved to laying quarters.

(5) Started poultry shall be delivered to and from the farm premises in crates and vehicles which have been cleaned and disinfected in accordance with part 147 of this subchapter.

(h)–(i) [Reserved]

(j) *U.S. M. Gallisepticum Monitored.* (1) A multiplier breeding flock in which all birds or a sample of at least 30 birds per house has been tested for *M. gallisepticum* as provided in § 145.14(b) when more than 4 months of age: *Provided,* That to retain this classification, a minimum of 30 birds per house shall be tested again at 36 to 38 weeks and at 48 to 50 weeks at a minimum: *And provided further,* That each 30-bird sample should come from 2 locations within the house (15 from the front half of the house and 15 from the back half of the house). A representative sample of males and females should be sampled. The samples shall be marked "male" or "female."

(2) A participant handling U.S. M. Gallisepticum Monitored products shall keep these products separate from other products in a manner satisfactory to the Official State Agency: *Provided,* That U.S. M. Gallisepticum Monitored chicks from multiplier breeding flocks shall be produced in incubators and hatchers in which only eggs from flocks qualified under paragraph (j)(1) of this section are set. Eggs from U.S. M. Gallisepticum Monitored multiplier breeding flocks shall not be set in hatchers or incubators in which eggs from U.S. M. Gallisepticum Clean primary breeding flocks qualified under § 145.83(c)(1)(i) are set.

(3) U.S. M. Gallisepticum Monitored chicks shall be boxed in clean boxes

and delivered in trucks that have been cleaned and disinfected in accordance with part 147 of this subchapter.

(k) *U.S. M. Synoviae Monitored.* (1) A multiplier breeding flock in which all birds or a sample of at least 30 birds per house has been tested for *M. synoviae* as provided in § 145.14(b) when more than 4 months of age: *Provided,* That to retain this classification, a minimum of 30 birds per house shall be tested again at 36 to 38 weeks and at 48 to 50 weeks at a minimum: *And provided further,* That each 30-bird sample should come from 2 locations within the house (15 from the front half of the house and 15 from the back half of the house). A representative sample of males and females should be sampled. The samples shall be marked "male" or "female."

(2) A participant handling U.S. M. Synoviae Monitored products shall keep these products separate from other products in a manner satisfactory to the Official State Agency: *Provided,* That U.S. M. Synoviae Monitored chicks from multiplier breeding flocks shall be produced in incubators and hatchers in which only eggs from flocks qualified under paragraph (k)(1) of this section are set. Eggs from U.S. M. Synoviae Monitored multiplier breeding flocks shall not be set in hatchers or incubators in which eggs from U.S. M. Synoviae Clean primary breeding flocks qualified under § 145.83(d)(1)(i) are set.

(3) U.S. M. Synoviae Monitored chicks shall be boxed in clean boxes and delivered in trucks that have been cleaned and disinfected in accordance with part 147 of this subchapter.

(l) *U.S. Avian Influenza Clean.* This program is intended to be the basis from which the breeding-hatchery industry may conduct a program for the prevention and control of avian influenza. It is intended to determine the presence of avian influenza in multiplier breeding chickens through routine surveillance of each participating breeding flock. A flock and the hatching eggs and chicks produced from it will qualify for this classification when the Official State Agency determines that they have met the following requirements:

(1) It is a multiplier breeding flock in which a minimum of 30 birds have been tested negative for antibodies to avian influenza using an approved test as described in § 145.14 when more than 4 months of age. To retain this classification:

(i) A sample of at least 15 birds must be tested negative at intervals of 90 days; or

(ii) A sample of fewer than 15 birds may be tested, and found to be negative, at any one time if all pens are equally represented and a total of 30 birds is tested within each 90-day period; or

(iii) The flock is tested as provided in § 145.14(d) at intervals of 30 days or less and found to be negative, and a total of 15 samples are collected and tested within each 90-day period; and

(2) During each 90-day period, all multiplier spent fowl, up to a maximum of 30, must be tested serologically and found negative for antibodies for avian influenza within 21 days prior to movement to slaughter.

(m) *U.S. Salmonella Enteritidis Monitored.* This classification is intended for multiplier meat-type breeders wishing to monitor their breeding flocks for *Salmonella enteritidis.*

(1) A flock and the hatching eggs and chicks produced from it shall be eligible for this classification if they meet the following requirements, as determined by the Official State Agency:

(i) The flock originated from a U.S. S. Enteritidis Clean primary meat-type breeding flock.

(ii) The flock is maintained in accordance with part 147 of this subchapter with respect to Salmonella isolation, sanitation, and management.

(iii) Environmental samples are collected from the flock in accordance with part 147 of this subchapter at 16–18 and 40–45 weeks of age. The samples shall be examined bacteriologically for group D Salmonella at an authorized laboratory, and cultures from group D positive samples shall be serotyped.

(2) The following actions must be taken with respect to the test results that are generated from this *S. enteritidis* monitoring program:

(i) If *S. enteritidis* is isolated from an environmental sample collected from the flock in accordance with paragraph (m)(1)(iii) of this section, a thorough evaluation of the practices and programs associated with the sampled flock shall be conducted with the goal of ascertaining the reason(s) for the positive finding.

(ii) The test results and the results of any evaluations performed in accordance with paragraph (m)(2)(i) of this section will be reported on a quarterly basis to the Official State Agency and the NPIP Senior Coordinator.

(iii) Participating broiler integrators shall combine their respective test results (and the results of any associated evaluations) to help guide their decisionmaking regarding programs and practices to implement or maintain to address *S. enteritidis*.

(iv) Aggregate data regarding the prevalence of *S. enteritidis* in participating U.S. meat-type parent breeding flocks shall be made available to the U.S. Poultry and Egg Association and the National Chicken Council.

(3) This classification may be revoked by the Official State Agency if the participant fails to comply with the requirements of this classification. The Official State Agency shall not revoke the participant's classification until the participant has been given an opportunity for a hearing in accordance with rules of practice adopted by the Official State Agency.

(Approved by the Office of Management and Budget under control number 0579–0007)

[36 FR 23112, Dec. 3, 1971]

EDITORIAL NOTE: For FEDERAL REGISTER citations affecting § 145.33, see the List of CFR Sections Affected, which appears in the Finding Aids section of the printed volume and at *www.fdsys.gov*.

§ 145.34 Terminology and classification; States.

(a) *U.S. Pullorum-Typhoid-Clean State.* (1) A State will be declared a U.S. Pullorum-Typhoid Clean State when it has been determined by the Service that:

(i) The State is in compliance with the provisions contained in § 145.23(b)(3)(i) through (vii), § 145.33(b)(3)(i) through (vii), § 145.43(b)(3)(i) through (vi), § 145.53(b)(3)(i) through (vii), § 145.73(b)(2)(i), § 145.83(b)(2)(i), and § 145.93(b)(3)(i) through (vii).

(ii) No pullorum disease or fowl typhoid is known to exist nor to have existed in hatchery supply flocks within the State during the preceding 12 months: *Provided*, That pullorum disease or fowl typhoid found within the preceding 24 months in waterfowl, exhibition poultry, and game bird breeding flocks will not prevent a State, which is otherwise eligible from qualifying.

(2) Discontinuation of any of the conditions described in paragraph (a)(1)(i) of this section, or repeated outbreaks of pullorum or typhoid occur in hatchery supply flocks described in paragraph (a)(1)(ii) of this section, or if an infection spreads from the originating premises, the Service shall have grounds to revoke its determination that the State is entitled to this classification. Such action shall not be taken until a thorough investigation has been made by the Service and the Official State Agency has been given an opportunity for a hearing in accordance with rules of practice adopted by the Administrator.

(b) *U.S. M. Gallisepticum Clean State, Meat-Type Chickens.* (1) A State will be declared a U.S. M. Gallisepticum Clean State, Meat-Type Chickens, when it has been determined by the Service that:

(i) No *M. gallisepticum* is known to exist nor to have existed in meat-type chicken breeding flocks in production within the State during the preceding 12 months;

(ii) All meat-type chicken breeding flocks in production are classified as U.S. M. Gallisepticum Clean in accordance with §§ 145.33(c) and 145.83(c) or have met equivalent requirements for *M. gallisepticum* control under official supervision;

(iii) All hatcheries within the State which handle products from meat-type chicken breeding flocks only handle products which are classified as U.S. M. Gallisepticum Clean or have met equivalent requirements for *M. gallisepticum* control under official supervision;

(iv) All shipments of products from meat-type chicken breeding flocks other than those classified as U.S. M. Gallisepticum Clean, or equivalent, into the State are prohibited;

(v) All persons performing poultry disease diagnostic services within the

State are required to report to the Official State Agency within 48 hours the source of all specimens from chickens from meat-type chicken breeding flocks that have been identified as being infected with *M. gallisepticum*;

(vi) All reports of *M. gallisepticum* infection in chickens from meat-type chicken breeding flocks are promptly followed by an investigation by the Official State Agency to determine the origin of the infection;

(vii) All chickens from meat-type chicken breeding flocks found to be infected with *M. gallisepticum* are quarantined until marketed under supervision of the Official State Agency.

(2) Discontinuation of any of the conditions described in paragraph (b)(1) of this section, or if repeated outbreaks of *M. gallisepticum* occur in meat-type chicken breeding flocks described in paragraph (b)(1)(ii) of this section, or if an infection spreads from the originating premises, the Service shall have grounds to revoke its determination that the State is entitled to this classification. Such action shall not be taken until a thorough investigation has been made by the Service and the Official State Agency has been given an opportunity for a hearing in accordance with rules of practice adopted by the Administrator.

[40 FR 1503, Jan. 8, 1975. Redesignated at 44 FR 61586, Oct. 26, 1979, and amended at 50 FR 19899, May 13, 1985; 54 FR 23957, June 5, 1989; 67 FR 8469, Feb. 25, 2002; 72 FR 1419, Jan. 12, 2007; 76 FR 15793, Mar. 22, 2011]

Subpart D—Special Provisions for Turkey Breeding Flocks and Products

§ 145.41 Definitions.

Except where the context otherwise requires, for the purposes of this subpart the following terms shall be construed, respectively, to mean:

Poults. Newly hatched turkeys.

[36 FR 23112, Dec. 3, 1971, as amended at 41 FR 48725, Nov. 5, 1976. Redesignated at 44 FR 61586, Oct. 26, 1979, and amended at 59 FR 12799, Mar. 18, 1994; 65 FR 8018, Feb. 17, 2000]

§ 145.42 Participation.

(a) Participating turkey flocks, and the eggs and poults produced from them, shall comply with the applicable general provisions of subpart A of this part and the special provisions of this subpart D.

(b) Hatching eggs should be nest clean. They may be fumigated in accordance with part 147 of this subchapter or otherwise sanitized.

(c) Any nutritive material provided to poults must be free of the avian pathogens that are officially represented in the Plan disease classifications listed in § 145.10.

[36 FR 23112, Dec. 3, 1971, as amended at 38 FR 13707, May 24, 1973; 40 FR 1503, Jan. 8, 1975. Redesignated at 44 FR 61586, Oct. 26, 1979, and amended at 49 FR 19802, May 10, 1984; 57 FR 57341, Dec. 4, 1992; 65 FR 8018, Feb. 17, 2000; 68 FR 64511, Nov. 14, 2003; 79 FR 38757, July 9, 2014; 81 FR 53249, Aug. 12, 2016]

§ 145.43 Terminology and classification; flocks and products.

Participating flocks, and the eggs and poults produced from them, which have met the respective requirements specified in this section may be designated by the following terms and the corresponding designs illustrated in § 145.10:

(a) [Reserved]

(b) *U.S. Pullorum-Typhoid Clean.* A flock in which freedom from pullorum and typhoid has been demonstrated to the official State agency under the criteria in one of the following paragraphs (b)(1) through (5) of this section: *Provided,* That a flock qualifying by means of a blood test shall be tested within the past 12 months, except that the retesting of a participating flock which is retained for more than 12 months shall be conducted a minimum of 4 weeks after the induction of molt. (See § 145.14 relating to the official blood test where applicable.)

(1) It has been officially blood tested with no reactors.

(2) It is a multiplier breeding flock, or a breeding flock composed of progeny of a primary breeding flock which is intended solely for the production of multiplier breeding flocks, and meets the following specifications as determined by the Official State Agency and the Service:

(i) The flock is located in a State where all persons performing poultry disease diagnostic services within the

State are required to report to the Official State Agency within 48 hours the source of all poultry specimens from which S. pullorum or S. gallinarum is isolated;

(ii) The flock is composed entirely of birds that originated from U.S. Pullorum-Typhoid Clean breeding flocks or from flocks that met equivalent requirements under official supervision; and

(iii) The flock is located on a premises where a flock not classified as U.S. Pullorum-Typhoid Clean was located the previous year; *Provided,* That an Authorized Testing Agent must blood test up to 300 birds per flock, as described in §145.14, if the Official State Agency determines that the flock has been exposed to pullorum-typhoid. In making determinations of exposure and setting the number of birds to be blood tested, the Official State Agency shall evaluate the results of any blood tests, described in §145.14(a)(1), that were performed on an unclassified flock located on the premises during the previous year; the origins of the unclassified flock; and the probability of contacts between the flock for which qualification is being sought and (a) infected wild birds, (b) contaminated feed or waste, or (c) birds, equipment, supplies, or personnel from flocks infected with pullorum-typhoid.

(3) It is a multiplier breeding flock, or a breeding flock composed of progeny of a primary breeding flock which is intended solely for the production of multiplier breeding flocks, that originated from U.S. Pullorum-Typhoid Clean breeding flocks or from flocks that met equivalent requirements under official supervision, and is located in a State in which it has been determined by the Service that:

(i) All turkey hatcheries within the State are qualified as "National Plan Hatcheries" or have met equivalent requirements for pullorum-typhoid control under official supervision;

(ii) All turkey hatchery supply flocks within the State are qualified as U.S. Pullorum-Typhoid Clean or have met equivalent requirements for pullorum-typhoid control under official supervision: *Provided,* That if other domesticated fowl, except waterfowl, are maintained on the same premises as the participating flock, freedom from pullorum-typhoid infection shall be demonstrated by an official blood test of each of these fowl;

(iii) All shipments of products other than U.S. Pullorum-Typhoid Clean, or equivalent, into the State are prohibited;

(iv) All persons performing poultry disease diagnostic services within the State are required to report to the Official State Agency within 48 hours the source of all poultry specimens from which S. pullorum or S. gallinarum is isolated;

(v) All reports of any disease outbreak involving a disease covered under the Plan are promptly followed by an investigation by the Official State Agency to determine the origin of the infection; *Provided,* That if the origin of the infection involves another State, or if there is exposure to poultry in another State from the infected flock, then the National Poultry Improvement Plan will conduct an investigation;

(vi) All flocks found to be infected with pullorum or typhoid are quarantined until marketed or destroyed under the supervision of the Official State Agency, or until subsequently blood tested, following the procedure for reacting flocks as contained in §145.14(a)(5), and all birds fail to demonstrate pullorum or typhoid infection;

(vii) [Reserved]

(viii) Discontinuation of any of the conditions or procedures described in paragraphs (b)(3)(i), (ii), (iii), (iv), (v), and (vi) of this section, or the occurrence of repeated outbreaks of pullorum or typhoid in turkey breeding flocks within or originating within the State shall be grounds for the Service to revoke its determination that such conditions and procedures have been met or complied with. Such action shall not be taken until a thorough investigation has been made by the Service and the Official State Agency has been given an opportunity to present its views.

(4) It is a multiplier breeding flock located in a State which has been determined by the Service to be in compliance with the provisions of paragraph (b)(3) of this section and in which pullorum disease or fowl typhoid is not

known to exist nor to have existed in turkey hatchery supply flocks within the State during the preceding 24 months.

(5) It is a primary breeding flock located in a State determined to be in compliance with the provisions of paragraph (b)(4), of this section and in which a sample of 300 birds from flocks of more than 300, and each bird in flocks of 300 or less, has been officially tested for pullorum-typhoid with no reactors: *Provided,* That a bacteriological examination monitoring program acceptable to the Official State Agency and approved by the Service may be used in lieu of blood testing.

(c) *U.S. M. Gallisepticum Clean.* (1) A flock maintained in accordance with part 147 of this subchapter with respect to Mycoplasma isolation, sanitation, and management, and in which no reactors are found when a random sample of at least 10 percent of the birds in the flock, or 300 birds in flocks of more than 300 and each bird in flocks of 300 or less, is tested when more than 12 weeks of age, in accordance with the procedures described in § 145.14(b): *Provided,* That to retain this classification, a minimum of 30 samples from male flocks and 60 samples from female flocks shall be retested at 28–30 weeks of age and at 4–6 week intervals thereafter.

(2) A flock qualified as U.S. M. Gallisepticum Clean may retain the classification through its first egg-laying cycle, provided it is maintained in isolation and no evidence of *M. gallisepticum* infection is revealed. A flock which is molted following completion of an egg-laying cycle and subsequently brought back into production, shall be retested within 2 weeks prior to production, as described in paragraph (c)(1) of this section. A State inspector shall visit with the owner or manager of each flock at least once during each laying cycle to discuss and ascertain whether the flock is being maintained in accordance with part 147 of this subchapter with respect to Mycoplasma isolation, sanitation, and management. If a flock proves to be infected with *M. gallisepticum,* it shall lose this classification.

(3) In order to sell hatching eggs or poults of this classification, all hatching eggs and poults handled by the participant must be of this classification.

(d) *U.S. M. Meleagridis Clean.* (1) A flock in which freedom from *M. meleagridis* has been demonstrated under the following criteria:

(i) A sample of 100 birds from each flock has been tested for *M. meleagridis* when more than 12 weeks of age: *Provided,* That to retain this classification, a minimum of 30 samples from male flocks and 60 samples from female flocks shall be retested at 28–30 weeks of age and at 4–6 week intervals thereafter.

(2)–(3) [Reserved]

(4) When reactors to the official test are found and can be identified, 10 tracheal swabs and/or vaginal or phallus swabs and their corresponding blood samples shall be submitted to a laboratory for serological and cultural examination. If reactors cannot be identified, at least 30 tracheal swabs and/or vaginal or phallus swabs and their corresponding blood samples shall be submitted. In a flock with a low reactor rate (less than 5 reactors) the reactors may be submitted to the laboratory within 10 days for serology, necropsy, and thorough bacteriological examination.

(5) If a mycoplasma is isolated, the organism must be serotyped. If *M. meleagridis* is isolated, the block shall be considered infected.

(e) *U.S. M. Synoviae Clean.* (1) All birds, or a sample of at least 100 birds from flocks of more than 100 and each bird in flocks of 100 or less, have been tested for *M. synoviae* when more than 12 weeks of age in accordance with the procedures in § 145.14(b): *Provided,* That to retain this classification a minimum of 30 samples from male flocks and 60 samples from female flocks shall be retested at 28–30 weeks of age and at 4–6 week intervals thereafter. It is recommended that any birds that are showing clinical signs of *M. synoviae* infection be included in samples taken.

(2) When reactors to the official test are found and can be identified, tracheal swabs and their corresponding blood samples from 10 (all if fewer than 10) reacting birds shall be submitted to an authorized laboratory for serological and cultural examination. If reactors cannot be identified, at least 30

tracheal swabs and their corresponding blood samples shall be submitted. In a flock with a low reactor rate (less than five reactors) the reactors may be submitted to the laboratory within 10 days for serology, necropsy, and thorough bacteriological examination. When reactors to the official test are found, the procedures outlined in part 147 of this subchapter will be used to determine the status of the flock.

(f) *U.S. Sanitation Monitored, Turkeys.* A flock or hatchery whose owner is controlling or reducing the level of salmonella through compliance with sanitation and management practices in accordance with part 147 of this subchapter, and where the following monitoring, testing, and management practices are conducted:

(1) Hatchery debris (dead germ hatching eggs, fluff, and meconium collected by sexors), swabs collected from hatch debris in hatcher trays, a sample of all the poults that died within 10 days after hatching up to 10 poults, or a combination of 2 or all 3 of the above, from each hatch or a candidate breeding flock produced by a primary breeder, are examined bacteriologically at an authorized laboratory for *Salmonella*.

(2) The poults for the candidate breeding flock are placed in a building that has been cleaned and disinfected. An Authorized Agent must collect environmental samples from the building and submit them to an authorized laboratory for a bacteriological examination for the presence of *Salmonella*, in accordance with part 147 of this subchapter.

(3) Feed for turkeys in the candidate and breeding flock should meet the following requirements:

(i) All feed manufactured in pellet form must have a maximum moisture content of 13.5 percent upon delivery to the farm. It should have been preconditioned to the minimum of one of the following parameters before pelleting:

(A) Feed is to reach a minimum temperature of 185 °F for a minimum of 6 minutes of retention in the conditioning chamber. The conditioned mash feed moisture must be a minimum of 16 percent during the conditioning process. This method utilizes time retention to allow permeation to the center core of each feed particle; or

(B) The feed is to be pressurized in order to expedite the transfer of the heat and moisture to the core of each feed particle. The feed should be conditioned to the parameters of a minimum of 16 percent moisture and 200 °F; or

(C) The feed should be submitted to pressurization to the extent that the initial feed temperature rises to 235 °F for 4 seconds; or

(D) The feed should be submitted to an equivalent thermal lethality treatment; or

(E) A Food and Drug Administration (FDA)-approved product for *Salmonella* control should be added to the finished pellets.

(ii) Mash feed should be treated with an FDA-approved *Salmonella* control product.

(iii) All feed is to be stored and transported in such a manner as to prevent possible contamination with pathogenic bacteria.

(iv) FDA-approved products for *Salmonella* control may be added to either unfinished or finished feed.

(4) Environmental samples shall be taken by an Authorized Agent, in accordance with part 147 of this subchapter, from each flock at 12–20 weeks of age and examined bacteriologically at an authorized laboratory for Salmonella.

(5) Owners of flocks found infected with a paratyphoid Salmonella may vaccinate these flocks with an autogenous bacterin with a potentiating agent.[5]

(6) Environmental samples shall be taken by an Authorized Agent, in accordance with part 147 of this subchapter, from each flock at 35–50 weeks of age and from each molted flock at midlay, and examined bacteriologically at an authorized laboratory for Salmonella.

(7) Hatchery debris (dead germ hatching eggs, fluff, and meconium collected by sexors), swabs collected from hatch debris in hatcher trays, a sample of all the poults that died within 10 days after hatching up to 10 poults, or a combination of 2 or all 3 of the above,

[5] Preparation and use of this type of vaccine may be regulated by state statutes.

shall be cultured as a means of evaluating the effectiveness of the control procedures.

(g) *U.S. H5/H7 Avian Influenza Clean.* This program is intended to be the basis from which the turkey breeding industry may conduct a program for the prevention and control of the H5/H7 subtypes of avian influenza. It is intended to determine the presence of the H5/H7 subtypes of avian influenza in breeding turkeys through routine surveillance of each participating breeding flock. A flock, and the hatching eggs and poults produced from it, will qualify for this classification when the Official State Agency determines that it has met one of the following requirements:

(1) It is a primary breeding flock in which a minimum of 30 birds have been tested negative to the H5/H7 subtypes of avian influenza as provided in §145.14(d) when more than 4 months of age and prior to the onset of egg production. To retain this classification:

(i) A sample of at least 30 birds must be tested negative at intervals of 90 days; or

(ii) A sample of fewer than 30 birds may be tested, and found to be negative, at any one time if all pens are equally represented and a total of 30 birds are tested within each 90-day period.

(2) It is a multiplier breeding flock in which a minimum of 30 birds have been tested negative for antibodies for avian influenza to the H5/H7 subtypes of avian influenza as provided in §145.14(d) when more than 4 months of age and prior to the onset of egg production. To retain this classification:

(i) A sample of at least 30 birds must be tested negative at intervals of 90 days; or

(ii) A sample of fewer than 30 birds may be tested, and found to be negative, at any one time if all pens are equally represented and a total of 30 birds are tested within each 90-day period.

(3) All spent fowl being marketed for meat from flocks that have been tested as required by this paragraph shall be tested at a rate of 6 birds per flock within 21 days prior to movement to slaughter.

(4) For both primary and multiplier breeding flocks, if a killed influenza vaccine against avian influenza subtypes other than H5 and H7 is used, then the hemagglutinin and the neuraminidase subtypes of the vaccine must be reported to the Official State Agency for laboratory and reporting purposes.

(Approved by the Office of Management and Budget under control number 0579–0007)

[36 FR 23112, Dec. 3, 1971]

EDITORIAL NOTE: For FEDERAL REGISTER citations affecting §145.43, see the List of CFR Sections Affected, which appears in the Finding Aids section of the printed volume and at *www.fdsys.gov*.

§ 145.44 Terminology and classification; States.

(a) *U.S. Pullorum-Typhoid Clean State.* (1) A State will be declared a U.S. Pullorum-Typhoid Clean State when it has been determined by the Service that:

(i) The State is in compliance with the provisions contained in §145.23(b)(3)(i) through (vii), §145.33(b)(3)(i) through (vii), §145.43(b)(3)(i) through (vi), §145.53(b)(3)(i) through (vii), §145.73(b)(2)(i), §145.83(b)(2)(i), and §145.93(b)(3)(i) through (vii).

(ii) No pullorum disease or fowl typhoid is known to exist nor to have existed in hatchery supply flocks within the State during the preceding 12 months: *Provided,* That pullorum disease or fowl typhoid found within the preceding 24 months in waterfowl, exhibition poultry, and game bird breeding flocks will not prevent a State, which is otherwise eligible, from qualifying.

(2) Discontinuation of any of the conditions described in paragraph (a)(1)(i) of this section, or repeated outbreaks of pullorum or typhoid occur in hatchery supply flocks described in paragraph (a)(1)(ii) of this section, or if an infection spreads from the originating premises, the Service shall have grounds to revoke its determination that the State is entitled to this classification. Such action shall not be taken until a thorough investigation has been made by the Service and the Official State Agency has been given an opportunity for a hearing in accordance with rules of practice adopted by the Administrator.

(b) *U.S. Pullorum-Typhoid Clean State, Turkeys.* (1) A State will be declared a U.S. Pullorum-Typhoid Clean State, Turkeys, when it has been determined by the Service that:

(i) The State is in compliance with the provisions contained in § 145.43(b)(3)(i) through (vi).

(ii) No pullorum disease or fowl typhoid is known to exist nor to have existed in turkey hatchery supply flocks within the State during the preceding 24 months.

(2) Discontinuation of any of the conditions described in paragraph (b)(1)(i) of this section, or repeated outbreaks of pullorum or typhoid occur in hatchery supply flocks described in paragraph (b)(1)(ii) of this section, or if an infection spreads from the originating premises, Service shall have grounds to revoke its determination that the State is entitled to this classification. Such action shall not be taken until a thorough investigation has been made by the Service and the Official State Agency has been given an opportunity for a hearing in accordance with rules of practice adopted by the Administrator.

(c) *U.S. M. Gallisepticum Clean State, Turkeys.* (1) A State will be declared a U.S. M. Gallisepticum Clean State, Turkeys when it has been determined by the Service that:

(i) No *M. gallisepticum* is known to exist nor to have existed in turkey breeding flocks in production within the State during the preceding 12 months.

(ii) All turkey breeding flocks in production are classified as U.S. M. Gallisepticum Clean or have met equivalent requirements for *M. gallisepticum* control under official supervision.

(iii) All turkey hatcheries within the State handle products which are classified as U.S. M. Gallisepticum Clean or have met equivalent requirements for *M. gallisepticum* control under official supervision.

(iv) All shipments of turkey products other than those classified as U.S. M. Gallisepticum Clean, or equivalent, into the State are prohibited.

(v) All persons performing poultry disease diagnostic services within the State are required to report to the Official State Agency within 48 hours the source of all turkey specimens that have been identified as being infected with *M. gallisepticum.*

(vi) All reports of *M. gallisepticum* infection in turkeys are promptly followed by an investigation by the Official State Agency to determine the origin of the infection.

(vii) All turkey flocks found to be infected with *M. gallisepticum* are quarantined until marketed under supervision of the Official State Agency.

(2) Discontinuation of any of the conditions described in paragraph (c)(1) of this section, or if repeated outbreaks of *M. gallisepticum* occur in turkey breeding flocks described in paragraph (c)(1)(ii) of this section, or if an infection spreads from the originating premises, the Service shall have grounds to revoke its determination that the State is entitled to this classification. Such action shall not be taken until a thorough investigation has been made by the Service and the Official State Agency has been given an opportunity for a hearing in accordance with rules of practice adopted by the Administrator.

(3) If a State retains this status for 2 or more years, individual breeding flocks in the State may qualify for an *M. gallisepticum* classification based on a negative test of a sample of 100 birds.

(d) *U.S. M. Synoviae Clean State, Turkeys.* (1) A State will be declared a U.S. M. Synoviae Clean State, Turkeys, if the Service determines that:

(i) No *Mycoplasma synoviae* is known to exist nor to have existed in turkey breeding flocks in production within the State during the preceding 12 months;

(ii) All turkey breeding flocks in production are tested and classified as U.S. M. Synoviae Clean or have met equivalent requirements for *M. synoviae* control under official supervision;

(iii) All turkey hatcheries within the State only handle products that are classified as U.S. M. Synoviae Clean or have met equivalent requirements for *M. synoviae* control under official supervision;

(iv) All shipments of products from turkey breeding flocks other than those classified as U.S. M. Synoviae

Clean, or equivalent, into the State are prohibited;

(v) All persons performing poultry disease diagnostic services within the State are required to report to the Official State Agency within 48 hours the source of all turkey specimens that have been identified as being infected with *M. synoviae;*

(vi) All reports of *M. synoviae* infection in turkeys are promptly followed by an investigation by the Official State Agency to determine the origin of the infection; and

(vii) All turkey breeding flocks found to be infected with *M. synoviae* are quarantined until marketed under supervision of the Official State Agency.

(2) The Service may revoke the State's classification as a U.S. M. Synoviae Clean State, Turkeys, if any of the conditions described in paragraph (d)(1) of this section are discontinued. The Service shall not revoke the State's classification as a U.S. M. Synoviae Clean State, Turkeys, until it has conducted an investigation and the Official State Agency has been given an opportunity for a hearing in accordance with rules of practice adopted by the Administrator of the Service.

(e) *U.S. M. Meleagridis Clean State, Turkeys.* (1) A State will be declared a U.S. M. Meleagridis Clean State, Turkeys, if the Service determines that:

(i) No *Mycoplasma meleagridis* is known to exist nor to have existed in turkey breeding flocks in production within the State during the preceding 12 months;

(ii) All turkey breeding flocks in production are tested and classified as U.S. M. Meleagridis Clean or have met equivalent requirements for *M. meleagridis* control under official supervision;

(iii) All turkey hatcheries within the State only handle products that are classified as U.S. M. Meleagridis Clean or have met equivalent requirements for *M. meleagridis* control under official supervision;

(iv) All shipments of products from turkey breeding flocks other than those classified as U.S. M. Meleagridis Clean, or equivalent, into the State are prohibited;

(v) All persons performing poultry disease diagnostic services within the State are required to report to the Official State Agency within 48 hours the source of all turkey specimens that have been identified as being infected with *M. meleagridis;*

(vi) All reports of *M. meleagridis* infection in turkeys are promptly followed by an investigation by the Official State Agency to determine the origin of the infection; and

(vii) All turkey breeding flocks found to be infected with *M. meleagridis* are quarantined until marketed under supervision of the Official State Agency.

(2) The Service may revoke the State's classification as a U.S. M. Meleagridis Clean State, Turkeys, if any of the conditions described in paragraph (d)(1) of this section are discontinued. The Service will not revoke the State's classification as a U.S. M. Meleagridis Clean State, Turkeys, until it has conducted an investigation and the Official State Agency has been given an opportunity for a hearing in accordance with rules of practice adopted by the Administrator.

(Approved by the Office of Management and Budget under control number 0579–0007)

[40 FR 1503, Jan. 8, 1975. Redesignated at 44 FR 61586, Oct. 26, 1979, and amended at 45 FR 10316, Feb. 15, 1980; 48 FR 57473, Dec. 30, 1983; 49 FR 19803, May 10, 1984; 54 FR 23957, June 5, 1989; 61 FR 11521, Mar. 21, 1996; 65 FR 8018, Feb. 17, 2000; 67 FR 8469, Feb. 25, 2002; 76 FR 15793, Mar. 22, 2011]

§ 145.45 Terminology and classification; compartments.

(a) *U.S. H5/H7 Avian Influenza Clean Compartment.* This program is intended to be the basis from which the primary turkey breeding-hatchery industry may demonstrate the existence and implementation of a program that has been approved by the Official State Agency and the Service to establish a compartment consisting of a primary breeding-hatchery company that is free of H5/H7 avian influenza (AI), also referred to as notifiable avian influenza (NAI). This compartment has the purpose of protecting the defined subpopulation and avoiding the introduction and spread of NAI within that subpopulation by prohibiting contact with other commercial poultry operations, other domestic and wild birds, and other intensive animal operations. The program shall consist of the following:

(1) *Definition of the compartment.* Based on the guidelines established by the World Organization for Animal Health (OIE) in the Terrestrial Animal Health Code and the guidelines in this paragraph (a), the primary breeder company will define the compartment with respect to NAI. Specifically, the company will use a comprehensive biosecurity program to define the compartment as a subpopulation of poultry with a health status for NAI that is separate from birds and poultry outside the compartment. The Official State Agency and the Service must approve all documentation submitted to substantiate the defined compartment as adequate to qualify for epidemiological separation from other potential sources of infection of NAI. Guidelines for the definition of the compartment include:

(i) *Definition and description of the subpopulation of birds and their health status.* All birds included in the compartment must be U.S. H5/H7 Avian Influenza Clean in accordance with § 145.43(g). The poultry must also be located in a State that has an initial State response and containment plan approved by APHIS under § 56.10 of this chapter and that participates in the diagnostic surveillance program for H5/H7 low pathogenicity AI as described in § 145.15. Within the compartment, all official tests for AI, as described in § 145.14(d), must be conducted in State or Federal laboratories or in NPIP authorized laboratories that meet the minimum standards described in § 147.52 of this subchapter. In addition, the company must provide to the Service upon request any relevant historical and current NAI-related data for reference regarding surveillance for the disease within the compartment. Upon request, the Official State Agency may provide such data for other commercial poultry populations located in the State.

(ii) *Description of animal identification and traceability processes.* The primary breeder company must also include a description of its animal identification and traceability records, including examples of Veterinary Services (VS) Form 9–5, "Report of Hatcheries, Dealers and Independent Flocks"; VS Form 9–2, "Flock Selection and Testing Report"; VS Form 9–3, "Report of Sales of Hatching Eggs, Chicks and Poults"; VS Form 9–9, " Hatchery Inspection Report"; set and hatch records; egg receipts; and egg/chick invoices for the subpopulation. Documentation must also include breed identification (NPIP stock code). The Service should ensure that an effective flock identification system and traceability system are in place.

(iii) *Definition and description of the physical components or establishments of the defined compartment.* The primary breeder company must provide documentation establishing that the defined compartment is epidemiologically separated from other poultry and bird populations. The documentation must be approved by the Official State Agency and the Service as indicating adequate epidemiological separation to maintain the compartment's separate health status with respect to NAI. The documentation should include descriptions of:

(A) The physical and spatial factors that separate the compartment from surrounding bird populations and affect the biosecurity status of the compartment.

(B) Relevant environmental factors that may affect exposure of the birds to AI.

(C) The functional boundary and fencing that are used to control access to the compartment.

(D) Facilities and procedures to prevent access by wild birds and to provide separation from other relevant hosts.

(E) The relevant infrastructural factors that may affect exposure to AI, including the construction and design of buildings or physical components, cleaning and disinfection of buildings and physical components between production groups with quality assurance verification, cleaning and disinfection of equipment, and introduction of equipment or material into the compartment.

(iv) *Definition and description of the functional relationships between components of the defined compartment.* Functional relationships between components of the compartment include traffic movement and flow at and among premises, personnel movement at and among premises, exposure to live bird populations, and any other factors that could affect biosecurity of the compartment. All physical components of the compartment must be maintained in compliance with hygiene and biosecurity procedures for poultry primary breeding flocks and hatcheries in accordance with part 147 of this subchapter. In addition, the company must provide a biosecurity plan for the compartment and all included components. The biosecurity plan should include:

(A) Requirements that company employees and contract growers limit their contact with live birds outside the compartment.

(B) An education and training program for company employees and contractors.

(C) Standard operating procedures for company employees, contractors, and outside maintenance personnel.

(D) Requirements for company employees and non-company personnel who visit any premises within the compartment.

(E) Company veterinary infrastructure to ensure flock monitoring and disease diagnosis and control measures.

(F) Policies for management of vehicles and equipment used within the compartment to connect the various premises.

(G) Farm site requirements (location, layout, and construction).

(H) Pest management program.

(I) Cleaning and disinfection process.

(J) Requirements for litter and dead bird removal and/or disposal.

(v) *Description of other factors important for maintaining the compartment.* The company veterinary infrastructure will assess sanitary measures, environmental risk factors, and management and husbandry practices that relate to the separation of the compartment and the health status of the birds contained within the compartment that may affect risk of exposure to NAI. This assessment must include a description of internal monitoring and auditing systems (e.g., quality assurance and quality control programs) to demonstrate the effectiveness of the compartment. Upon request, the Service will provide the company with information on the epidemiology of NAI and the associated risk pathways in which the components of the compartment are located.

(vi) *Approval or denial.* Based on this documentation provided under this paragraph (a)(1), as well as any other information the Service and the Official State Agency determine to be necessary, the Service and the Official State Agency will approve or deny the classification of the compartment as U.S. H5/H7 Avian Influenza Clean.

(2) *Company activities for maintenance of the compartment.* (i) The primary breeder company's management of biosecurity, surveillance, and disease control efforts must be uniform and equivalent among all components that are a part of the compartment. Oversight and inspection of these management practices must be conducted by the company's licensed, accredited veterinarians.

(ii) Veterinary staff from the Official State Agency and NPIP staff will work in partnership with licensed, accredited veterinarians to train and certify auditors through Service-approved workshops. The trained auditors will conduct biosecurity and operational audits at least once every 2 years to ensure the integrity of the compartment. These audits will include evaluation of the critical control points and standard operating practices within the compartment, verification of the health status of the flock(s) contained within the compartment, and examination of the biosecurity and management system of the integrated components of the compartment.

(iii) In addition, the company must demonstrate compliance with paragraph (a)(1) of this section for remaining in the U.S. H5/H7 Avian Influenza Clean classification, surveillance for NAI within the compartment, and conducting tests in State or Federal laboratories or in NPIP authorized laboratories. Accredited veterinarians are responsible for the enforcement of active and passive surveillance of NAI in primary breeder flocks. Baseline health status must be maintained for all flocks or subpopulations within the compartment, indicating the dates and negative results of all avian influenza surveillance and monitoring testing, the dates and history of last disease occurrence (if any), the number of outbreaks, and the methods of disease control that were applied.

(iv) Documentation will be maintained in the company's database and will be verified as required by the Service and/or the Official State Agency.

(3) *Service and Official State Agency activities for maintenance of the compartment.* The Service will work in cooperation with the Official State Agencies to ensure the continued integrity of any recognized compartments. Activities will include:

(i) Oversight of the establishment and management of compartments;

(ii) Establishment of effective partnerships between the Service, the Plan, and the primary breeder industry;

(iii) Approval or denial of classification of compartments as U.S. H5/H7 Avian Influenza Clean Compartments under paragraph (a)(1) of this section;

(iv) Official certification of the health status of the compartment, and commodities that may be traded from it through participation in the Plan for avian diseases, including the U.S. H5/H7 Avian Influenza Clean program as described in § 145.43(g) and diagnostic surveillance for H5/H7 low pathogenicity AI as described in § 145.15;

(v) Conducting audits of compartments at least once every 2 years to:

(A) Confirm that the primary breeding company's establishments are epidemiologically distinct and pathways for the introduction of disease into the compartment are closed through routine operational procedures; and

(B) Evaluate and assess the management and husbandry practices relating to biosecurity to determine whether they are in compliance with hygiene and biosecurity procedures for poultry primary breeding flocks and hatcheries in accordance with part 147 of this subchapter;

(vi) Providing, upon request, model plans for management and husbandry practices relating to biosecurity in accordance with part 147 of this subchapter, risk evaluations in conjunction with the primary breeder industry (including disease surveillance such as VS Form 9–4, "Summary of Breeding Flock Participation"), and diagnostic capability summaries and systems for initial State response and containment plans in accordance with § 56.10 of this chapter; and

(vii) Publicizing and sharing compartment information with international trading partners, upon request, to establish approval and recognition of the compartment, including timeliness and accuracy of disease reporting and surveillance measures as described in §§ 145.15 and 145.43(g).

(4) *Emergency response and notification.* In the case of a confirmed positive of NAI in the subpopulation of the compartment, the management of the compartment must notify the Service. The Service will immediately suspend the status of the compartment. A compartment will be eligible to resume trade with importing countries only after the compartment has adopted the necessary measures to reestablish the biosecurity level and confirm that NAI is not present in the compartment and the Service has reevaluated the management and biosecurity measures of the compartment and approved said compartment for trade.

(b) [Reserved]

[79 FR 38757, July 9, 2014]

Subpart E—Special Provisions for Hobbyist and Exhibition Waterfowl, Exhibition Poultry, and Game Bird Breeding Flocks and Products

§ 145.51 Definitions.

Except where the context otherwise requires, for the purposes of this subpart the following terms shall be construed, respectively, to mean:

Exhibition Poultry. Domesticated fowl which are bred for the combined purposes of meat or egg production and competitive showing.

Game birds. Domesticated fowl such as pheasants, partridge, quail, grouse, and guineas, but not doves and pigeons.

Waterfowl. Domesticated fowl that normally swim, such as ducks and geese.

[36 FR 23112, Dec. 3, 1971. Redesignated at 44 FR 61586, Oct. 26, 1979, and amended at 59 FR 12799, Mar. 18, 1994]

§ 145.52 Participation.

Participating flocks of hobbyist and exhibition waterfowl, exhibition poultry, and game birds, and the eggs and baby poultry produced from them shall comply with the applicable general provisions of subpart A of this part and the special provisions of this subpart E. The special provisions that apply to meat-type waterfowl flocks are found in subpart I of this part.

(a) Started poultry shall lose their identity under Plan terminology when not maintained by Plan participants under the conditions prescribed in § 145.5(a).

(b) Hatching eggs produced by primary breeding flocks shall be fumigated or otherwise sanitized in accordance with part 147 of this subchapter.

(c) It is recommended that waterfowl flocks and gallinaceous flocks in open-air facilities be kept separate.

(d) Subject to the approval of the Service and the Official State Agencies in the importing and exporting States, participating flocks may report poultry sales to importing States by using either VS Form 9–3, "Report of Sales of Hatching Eggs, Chicks, and Poults," or by using a hatchery invoice form (9–3I) approved by the Official State Agency and the Service to identify poultry sales to clients. If the selling hatchery uses the 9–3I form, the following information must be included on the form:

(1) The form number "9–3I", printed or stamped on the invoice;

(2) The hatchery name and address;

(3) The date of shipment;

(4) The hatchery invoice number;

(5) The purchaser name and address;

(6) The quantity of products sold;

(7) Identification of the products by bird variety or by NPIP stock code as listed in the NPIP APHIS 91–55–078 appendix; and

(8) The appropriate NPIP illustrative design in § 145.10. One of the designs in § 145.10(b) or (g) must be used. The following information must be provided in or near the NPIP design:

(i) The NPIP State number and NPIP hatchery approval number; and

(ii) The NPIP classification for which product is qualified (e.g., U.S. Pullorum-Typhoid Clean).

(e) Any nutritive material provided to baby poultry must be free of the avian pathogens that are officially represented in the Plan disease classifications listed in § 145.10.

[36 FR 23112, Dec. 3, 1971. Redesignated at 44 FR 61586, Oct. 26, 1979, and amended at 49 FR 19803, May 10, 1984; 57 FR 57341, Dec. 4, 1992; 61 FR 11521, Mar. 21, 1996; 65 FR 8019, Feb. 17, 2000; 74 FR 14715, Apr. 1, 2009; 76 FR 15793, Mar. 22, 2011; 79 FR 38759, July 9, 2014]

§ 145.53 Terminology and classification; flocks and products.

Participating flocks, and the eggs and baby poultry produced from them, which have met the respective requirements specified in this section may be designated by the following terms and the corresponding designs illustrated in § 145.10.

(a) [Reserved]

(b) *U.S. Pullorum-Typhoid Clean.* A flock in which freedom from pullorum and typhoid has been demonstrated to the Official State Agency under the criteria in one of the following paragraphs (b)(1) through (5) of this section (See § 145.14 relating to the official blood test where applicable.):

(1) It has been officially blood tested within the past 12 months with no reactors.

(2) It is a multiplier breeding flock, or a breeding flock composed of progeny of a primary breeding flock which is intended solely for the production of multiplier breeding flocks, and meets the following specifications as determined by the Official State Agency and the Service:

(i) The flock is located in a State where all persons performing poultry disease diagnostic services within the State are required to report to the Official State Agency within 48 hours the source of all poultry specimens from which S. pullorum or S. gallinarum is isolated;

(ii) The flock is composed entirely of birds that originated from U.S. Pullorum-Typhoid Clean breeding flocks or from flocks that met equivalent requirements under official supervision; and

(iii) The flock is located on a premises where a flock not classified as U.S. Pullorum-Typhoid Clean was located the previous year; *Provided,* That an Authorized Testing Agent must blood test up to 300 birds per flock, as described in § 145.14, if the Official State Agency determines that the flock has been exposed to pullorum-typhoid. In making determinations of exposure and setting the number of birds to be blood tested, the Official State Agency shall evaluate the results of any blood tests, described in § 145.14(a)(1), that were performed on an unclassified flock located on the premises during the previous year; the origins of the unclassified flock; and the probability of contacts between the flock for which qualification is being sought and (a) infected wild birds, (b) contaminated feed or waste, or (c) birds, equipment, supplies, or personnel from flocks infected with pullorum-typhoid.

(3) It is a multiplier breeding flock that originated from U.S. Pullorum-Typhoid Clean breeding flocks or from flocks that met equivalent requirements under official supervision, and is located in a State in which it has been determined by the Service that:

(i) All hatcheries within the State are qualified as "National Plan Hatcheries" or have met equivalent requirements for pullorum-typhoid control under official supervision;

(ii) All hatchery supply flocks within the State, are qualified as U.S. Pullorum-Typhoid Clean or have met equivalent requirements for pullorum-typhoid control under official supervision: *Provided,* That if other domesticated fowl, except waterfowl, are maintained on the same premises as the participating flock, freedom from pullorum-typhoid infection shall be demonstrated by an official blood test of each of these fowl;

(iii) All shipments of products other than U.S. Pullorum-Typhoid Clean, or equivalent, into the State are prohibited;

(iv) All persons performing poultry disease diagnostic services within the State are required to report to the Official State Agency within 48 hours the source of all poultry specimens from which S. pullorum or S. gallinarum is isolated;

(v) All reports of any disease outbreak involving a disease covered under the Plan are promptly followed by an investigation by the Official State Agency to determine the origin of the infection; *Provided,* That if the origin of the infection involves another State, or if there is exposure to poultry in another State from the infected flock, then the National Poultry Improvement Plan will conduct an investigation;

(vi) All flocks found to be infected with pullorum or typhoid are quarantined until marketed or destroyed under the supervision of the Official State Agency, or until subsequently blood tested, following the procedure for reacting flocks as contained in § 145.14(a)(5), and all birds fail to demonstrate pullorum or typhoid infection;

(vii) All poultry, including exhibition, exotic, and game birds, but excluding waterfowl, going to public exhibition shall come from U.S. Pullorum-Typhoid Clean or equivalent flocks, or have had a negative pullorum-typhoid test within 90 days of going to public exhibition;

(viii) Discontinuation of any of the conditions or procedures described in paragraphs (b)(3)(i), (ii), (iii), (iv), (v), (vi), and (vii) of this section, or the occurrence of repeated outbreaks of pullorum or typhoid in poultry breeding flocks within or originating within the State shall be grounds for the Service to revoke its determination that such conditions and procedures have been met or complied with. Such action shall not be taken until a thorough investigation has been made by the Service and the Official State Agency has been given an opportunity to present its views.

(4) It is a multiplier breeding flock located in a State which has been determined by the Service to be in compliance with the provisions of paragraph (b)(3) of this section, and in which pullorum disease or fowl typhoid is not known to exist nor to have existed in hatchery supply flocks within the State during the preceding 24 months.

(5) It is a primary breeding flock located in a State determined to be in compliance with the provisions of paragraph (b)(4) of this section, and in which a sample of 300 birds from flocks of more than 300, and each bird in flocks of 300 or less, has been officially tested for pullorum-typhoid within the past 12 months with no reactors: *Provided,* That a bacteriological examination monitoring program or serological examination monitoring program for game birds acceptable to the Official State Agency and approved by the Service may be used in lieu of annual blood testing: *And Provided further,* That when a flock is a hobbyist or exhibition waterfowl or exhibition poultry primary breeding flock located in a State which has been deemed to be a U.S. Pullorum-Typhoid Clean State for the past three years, and during which time no isolation of pullorum or typhoid has been made that can be traced to a source in that State, a bacteriological examination monitoring program or a serological examination monitoring program acceptable to the Official State Agency and approved by the Service may be used in lieu of annual blood testing.

(c) *U.S. M. Gallisepticum Clean.* (1) A flock maintained in accordance with part 147 of this subchapter with respect to Mycoplasma isolation, sanitation, and management and in which freedom from M. gallisepticum has been demonstrated under the criteria specified in paragraph (c)(1)(i) or (ii) of this section.

(i) It is a flock in which all birds or a sample of at least 300 birds has been tested for *M. gallisepticum* as provided in §145.14(b) when more than 4 months of age or upon reaching sexual maturity: *Provided,* That to retain this classification, a random sample of serum or egg yolk or a targeted bird sample of the choanal palatine cleft/fissure area using appropriate swabs from all the birds in the flock if the flock size is less than 30, but at least 30 birds, shall be tested at intervals of not more than 90 days: *And provided further,* That a sample comprised of less than 30 birds may be tested at any one time, with the approval of the Official State Agency and the concurrence of the Service, provided that a total of at least 30 birds, or all birds in the flock if flock size is less than 30, is tested within each 90-day period; or

(ii) It is a multiplier breeding flock which originated as U.S. M. Gallisepticum Clean baby poultry from primary breeding flocks and a random sample comprised of 50 percent of the birds in the flock, with a maximum of 200 birds and a minimum of 30 birds per flock or all birds in the flock if the flock size is less than 30 birds, has been tested for *M. gallisepticum* as provided in §145.14(b) when more than 4 months of age or upon reaching sexual maturity: Provided, That to retain this classification, the flock shall be subjected to one of the following procedures:

(A) At intervals of not more than 90 days, a random sample of serum or egg yolk or a targeted bird sample of the choanal palatine cleft/fissure area using appropriate swabs from all the birds in the flock if flock size is less than 30, but at least 30 birds, shall be tested; or

(B) At intervals of not more than 30 days, a sample of 25 cull baby poultry produced from the flock shall be subjected to laboratory procedures acceptable to the Official State Agency and approved by the Service, for the detection and recovery of M. gallisepticum.

(2) A participant handling U.S. M. Gallisepticum Clean products shall keep these products separate from other products in a manner satisfactory to the Official State Agency: *Provided,* That U.S. M. Gallisepticum Clean baby poultry from primary breeding flocks shall be produced in incubators and hatchers in which only eggs from flocks qualified under paragraph (c)(1)(i) of this section are set.

(3) U.S. M. Gallisepticum Clean baby poultry shall be boxed in clean boxes and delivered in trucks that have been cleaned and disinfected in accordance with part 147 of this subchapter.

(d) *U.S. M. Synoviae Clean.* (1) A flock maintained in accordance with part 147 of this subchapter with respect to Mycoplasma isolation, sanitation, and management and in which freedom from *Mycoplasma synoviae* has been demonstrated under the criteria specified in paragraph (d)(1)(i) or (d)(1)(ii) of this section.

(i) It is a flock in which all birds or a sample of at least 300 birds has been tested for *M. synoviae* as provided in § 145.14(b) when more than 4 months of age or upon reaching sexual maturity: *Provided,* That to retain this classification, a random sample of serum or egg yolk or a targeted bird sample of the choanal palatine cleft/fissure area using appropriate swabs (C.P. swabs) from all the birds in the flock if flock size is less than 30, but at least 30 birds, shall be tested at intervals of not more than 90 days: *And provided further,* That a sample comprised of less than 30 birds may be tested at any one time with the approval of the Official State Agency and the concurrence of the Service, provided that a total of at least 30 birds is tested within each 90-day period; or

(ii) It is a multiplier breeding flock that originated as U.S. M. Synoviae Clean chicks from primary breeding flocks and from which a random sample comprised of 50 percent of the birds in the flock, with a maximum of 200 birds and a minimum of 30 birds per flock or all birds in the flock if the flock is less than 30 birds, has been tested for *M. synoviae* as provided in § 145.14(b) when more than 4 months of age or upon reaching sexual maturity: *Provided,* That to retain this classification, the flock shall be subjected to one of the following procedures:

(A) At intervals of not more than 90 days, a random sample of serum or egg yolk or a targeted bird sample of the choanal palantine cleft/fissure area using appropriate swabs from all the birds in the flock if the flock size is less than 30, but at least 30 birds shall be tested: *Provided,* That a sample of fewer than 30 birds may be tested at any one time with the approval of the Official State Agency and the concurrence of the Service, provided that a total of at least 30 birds, or the entire flock if flock size is less than 30, is tested each time and a total of at least 30 birds is tested within each 90-day period; or

(B) At intervals of not more than 30 days, egg yolk testing shall be conducted in accordance with part 147 of this subchapter.

(2) A participant handling U.S. M. Synoviae Clean products shall keep those products separate from other products in a manner satisfactory to the Official State Agency: *Provided,* That U.S. M. Synoviae Clean chicks from primary breeding flocks shall be produced in incubators and hatchers in which only eggs from flocks qualified under paragraph (d)(1)(i) or (d)(1)(ii) of this section are set.

(3) U.S. M. Synoviae Clean chicks shall be boxed in clean boxes and delivered in trucks that have been cleaned and disinfected as described in in accordance with part 147 of this subchapter.

(e) *U.S. H5/H7 Avian Influenza Clean.* This program is intended to be the basis from which the breeding-hatchery industry may conduct a program for the prevention and control of the H5 and H7 subtypes of avian influenza. It is intended to determine the presence of the H5 and H7 subtypes of avian influenza in hobbyist or exhibition waterfowl, exhibition poultry, and game bird breeding flocks through routine surveillance of each participating breeding flock. A flock, and the hatching eggs and chicks produced from it, will qualify for this classification when the Official State Agency determines that it has met one of the following requirements:

(1) It is a primary breeding flock in which a minimum of 30 birds has been tested negative to the H5 and H7 subtypes of avian influenza as provided in § 145.14(d) when more than 4 months of age; *Provided,* that waterfowl flocks may test a minimum of 30 cloacal swabs for virus isolation. To retain this classification:

(i) A sample of at least 30 birds must be tested negative at intervals of 180 days; or

(ii) A sample of fewer than 30 birds may be tested, and found to be negative, at any one time if all pens are equally represented and a total of 30 birds are tested within each 180-day period.

(2) It is a multiplier breeding flock in which a minimum of 30 birds has been tested negative to the H5 and H7 subtypes of avian influenza as provided in § 145.14(d) when more than 4 months of age; *Provided,* that waterfowl flocks may test a minimum of 30 cloacal

swabs for virus isolation. To retain this classification:

(i) A sample of at least 30 birds must be tested negative at intervals of 180 days; or

(ii) A sample of fewer than 30 birds may be tested, and found to be negative, at any one time if all pens are equally represented and a total of 30 birds are tested within each 180-day period.

(3) A sample of at least 30 birds must be tested and found negative to H5/H7 avian influenza within 21 days prior to movement to slaughter.

(f) *U.S. Salmonella Monitored.* This program is intended to be the basis from which the hatching industry may conduct a program for the prevention and control of salmonellosis. It is intended to reduce the incidence of *Salmonella* organisms in day-old poultry through an effective and practical sanitation program in the hatchery. This will afford other segments of the poultry industry an opportunity to reduce the incidence of *Salmonella* in their products. The following requirements must be met for a flock to be of this classification:

(1) An Authorized Agent shall collect a minimum of five environmental samples, e.g., chick papers, hatching trays, and chick transfer devices, from the hatchery at least every 30 days. Testing must be performed at an authorized laboratory.

(2) To claim products are of this classification, all products shall be derived from a hatchery that meets the requirements of the classification.

(3) This classification may be revoked by the Official State Agency if the participant fails to follow recommended corrective measures.

(Approved by the Office of Management and Budget under control number 0579–0007)

[36 FR 23112, Dec. 3, 1971. Redesignated at 44 FR 61586, Oct. 26, 1979]

EDITORIAL NOTE: For FEDERAL REGISTER citations affecting § 145.53, see the List of CFR Sections Affected, which appears in the Finding Aids section of the printed volume and at *www.fdsys.gov*.

§ 145.54 Terminology and classification; States.

(a) *U.S. Pullorum-Typhoid Clean State.* (1) A State will be declared a U.S. Pullorum-Typhoid Clean State when it has been determined by the Service that:

(i) The State is in compliance with the provisions contained in § 145.23(b)(3)(i) through (vii), § 145.33(b)(3)(i) through (vii), § 145.43(b)(3)(i) through (vi), § 145.53(b)(3)(i) through (vii), § 145.73(b)(2)(i), § 145.83(b)(2)(i), and § 145.93(b)(3)(i) through (vii).

(ii) No pullorum disease or fowl typhoid is known to exist nor to have existed in hatchery supply flocks within the State during the preceding 12 months: *Provided,* That pullorum disease or fowl typhoid found within the preceding 24 months in waterfowl, exhibition poultry, and game bird breeding flocks will not prevent a State, which is otherwise eligible, from qualifying.

(2) Discontinuation of any of the conditions described in paragraph (a)(1)(i) of this section, or repeated outbreaks of pullorum or typhoid occur in hatchery supply flocks described in paragraph (a)(1)(ii) of this section, or if an infection spreads from the originating premises, the Service shall have grounds to revoke its determination that the State is entitled to this classification. Such action shall not be taken until a thorough investigation has been made by the Service and the Official State Agency has been given an opportunity for a hearing in accordance with rules of practice adopted by the Administrator.

[40 FR 1504, Jan. 8, 1975. Redesignated at 44 FR 61586, Oct. 26, 1979, and amended at 54 FR 23957, June 5, 1989; 67 FR 8469, Feb. 25, 2002; 76 FR 15794, Mar. 22, 2011]

Subpart F—Special Provisions for Ostrich, Emu, Rhea, and Cassowary Breeding Flocks and Products

SOURCE: 63 FR 40010, July 27, 1998, unless otherwise noted.

§ 145.61 Definitions.

Except where the context otherwise requires, for the purposes of this subpart the following terms shall be construed, respectively, to mean:

Chicks. Newly hatched ostriches, emus, rheas, or cassowaries.

Ostrich. Birds of the species *Struthio camelus*, including all subspecies and subspecies hybrids.

[63 FR 40010, July 27, 1998, as amended at 65 FR 8019, Feb. 17, 2000]

§ 145.62 Participation.

Participating flocks of ostriches, emus, rheas, and cassowaries, and the eggs and chicks produced from them, shall comply with the applicable general provisions of subpart A of this part and the special provisions of this subpart.

(a) Started poultry shall lose their identity under Plan terminology when not maintained by Plan participants under the conditions prescribed in § 145.5(a).

(b) Hatching eggs produced by primary breeding flocks shall be fumigated or otherwise sanitized in accordance with part 147 of this subchapter.

(c) Any nutritive material provided to chicks must be free of the avian pathogens that are officially represented in the Plan disease classifications listed in § 145.10.

[63 FR 40010, July 27, 1998, as amended at 65 FR 8019, Feb. 17, 2000; 79 FR 38759, July 9, 2014]

§ 145.63 Terminology and classification; flocks and products.

Participating flocks, and the eggs and baby poultry produced from them, that have met the respective requirements specified in this section may be designated by the following terms and their corresponding designs illustrated in § 145.10.

(a) *U.S. Pullorum-Typhoid Clean.* A flock in which freedom from pullorum and typhoid has been demonstrated to the Official State Agency under the criteria in paragraph (a)(1) or (a)(2) of this section. (See § 145.14(a) relating to the official blood test for pullorum-typhoid where applicable.)

(1) It has been officially blood tested within the past 12 months with no reactors.

(2) It is a breeding flock that meets one of the following criteria:

(i)(A) It is a multiplier or primary breeding flock of fewer than 300 birds in which a sample of 10 percent of the birds in a flock or at least 1 bird from each pen, whichever is more, has been officially tested for pullorum-typhoid within the past 12 months with no reactors; or

(B) It is a multiplier or primary breeding flock of 300 birds or more in which a sample of a minimum of 30 birds has been officially tested for pullorum-typhoid within the past 12 months with no reactors.

(ii) It is a flock that has already been designated U.S. Pullorum-Typhoid Clean and uses a subsequent bacteriological examination monitoring program of hatcher debris or eggs for ostriches, emus, rheas, or cassowaries acceptable to the Official State Agency and approved by the Service in lieu of annual blood testing.

(iii) It is a multiplier breeding flock located in a State that has been deemed to be a U.S. Pullorum-Typhoid Clean State for the past 3 years, and during which time no isolation of pullorum or typhoid has been made that can be traced to a source in that State, that uses a bacteriological examination monitoring program of hatcher debris or eggs or a serological examination monitoring program acceptable to the Official State Agency and approved by the Service in lieu of annual blood testing.

(b) *U.S. Avian Influenza Clean.* This program is intended to be the basis from which the breeding-hatchery industry may conduct a program for the prevention and control of avian influenza. It is intended to determine the presence of avian influenza in all ostrich, emu, rhea, and cassowary breeding flocks through routine serological surveillance of each participating breeding flock. Acceptable tests include antigen and antibody detection tests, as approved by the Official State Agency. A flock, and the hatching eggs and chicks produced from it, will qualify for this classification when the Official State Agency determines that it has met one of the following requirements:

(1) It is a primary breeding flock in which 10 percent of the flock, up to a maximum of 30 birds, has been tested negative for type A influenza virus with all pens represented equally and when the tested birds are more than 4 months of age. Positive samples shall

be further tested by an authorized laboratory. To retain this classification:

(i) A sample of at least 30 birds must be tested negative at intervals of 180 days, or

(ii) A sample of less than 10 percent of the birds, up to a maximum of 30 birds, may be tested and found to be negative at any one time if all pens are equally represented and a total of 30 birds are tested within each 180-day period.

(2) It is a multiplier breeding flock in which a minimum of 30 birds has been tested negative to type A influenza virus with all pens represented equally and when the tested birds are more than 4 months of age. Positive samples shall be further tested by an authorized laboratory. To retain this classification:

(i) A sample of at least 30 birds must be tested negative at intervals of 180 days, or

(ii) A sample of at least 10 percent of birds from each pen with all pens being represented must be tested negative at intervals of 180 days; or

(iii) A sample of less than 10 percent of the birds may be tested, and found to be negative, at any one time if all pens are equally represented and a total of 10 percent of the birds are tested within each 180-day period.

[63 FR 40010, July 27, 1998, as amended at 65 FR 8019, Feb. 17, 2000; 72 FR 1420, Jan. 12, 2007; 74 FR 14715, Apr. 1, 2009]

Subpart G—Special Provisions for Primary Egg-Type Chicken Breeding Flocks and Products

SOURCE: 72 FR 1420, Jan. 12, 2007, unless otherwise noted.

§ 145.71 Definitions.

Except where the context otherwise requires, for the purposes of this subpart the following terms shall be construed, respectively, to mean:

Chicks. Newly hatched chickens.

Primary egg-type chicken breeding flocks. Foundation flocks that are composed of pedigree, great-grandparent, and grandparent stock that has been developed for egg production and are maintained for the principal purpose of producing multiplier breeding chicks used to produce table egg layers.

Started chickens. Young chickens (chicks, pullets, cockerels, capons) which have been fed and watered and are less than 6 months of age.

§ 145.72 Participation.

Participating flocks of primary egg-type chickens, and the eggs and chicks produced from them, shall comply with the applicable general provisions of subpart A of this part and the special provisions of this subpart G.

(a) Started chickens shall lose their identity under Plan terminology when not maintained by Plan participants under the conditions prescribed in § 145.5(a).

(b) Hatching eggs produced by primary breeding flocks should be nest clean. They may be fumigated in accordance with part 147 of this subchapter or otherwise sanitized.

(c) Any nutritive material provided to chicks must be free of the avian pathogens that are officially represented in the Plan disease classifications listed in § 145.10.

[72 FR 1420, Jan. 12, 2007, as amended at 79 FR 38759, July 9, 2014]

§ 145.73 Terminology and classification; flocks and products.

Participating flocks, and the eggs and chicks produced from them, which have met the respective requirements specified in this section, may be designated by the following terms and the corresponding designs illustrated in § 145.10:

(a) [Reserved]

(b) *U.S. Pullorum-Typhoid Clean.* A flock in which freedom from pullorum and typhoid has been demonstrated to the Official State Agency under the criteria in paragraph (b)(1) or (b)(2) of this section: *Provided*, That a flock qualifying by means of a blood test shall be tested within the past 12 months, except that the retesting of a participating flock which is retained for more than 12 months shall be conducted a minimum of 4 weeks after the induction of molt. (See § 145.14 relating to the official blood test where applicable.)

(1) It has been officially blood tested with no reactors.

(2) It is a primary breeding flock that meets the following criteria:

(i) The primary breeding flock is located in a State in which pullorum disease or fowl typhoid is not known to exist nor to have existed in hatchery supply flocks during the preceding 12 months and in which it has been determined by the Service that:

(A) All hatcheries within the State are qualified as "National Plan Hatcheries" or have met equivalent requirements for pullorum-typhoid control under official supervision;

(B) All hatchery supply flocks within the State are qualified as U.S. Pullorum-Typhoid Clean or have met equivalent requirements for pullorum-typhoid control under official supervision: *Provided*, That if other domesticated fowl, except waterfowl, are maintained on the same premises as the participating flock, freedom from pullorum-typhoid infection shall be demonstrated by an official blood test of each of these fowl;

(C) All shipments of products other than U.S. Pullorum-Typhoid Clean, or equivalent, into the State are prohibited;

(D) All persons performing poultry disease diagnostic services within the State are required to report to the Official State Agency within 48 hours the source of all poultry specimens from which *S. pullorum* or *S. gallinarum* is isolated;

(E) All reports of any disease outbreak involving a disease covered under the Plan are promptly followed by an investigation by the Official State Agency to determine the origin of the infection; *Provided*, That if the origin of the infection involves another State, or if there is exposure to poultry in another State from the infected flock, then officials administering the National Poultry Improvement Plan will conduct an investigation;

(F) All flocks found to be infected with pullorum or typhoid are quarantined until marketed or destroyed under the supervision of the Official State Agency, or until subsequently blood tested following the procedure for reacting flocks as contained in §145.14(a)(5), and all birds fail to demonstrate pullorum or typhoid infection;

(G) All poultry, including exhibition, exotic, and game birds, but excluding waterfowl, going to public exhibition shall come from U.S. Pullorum-Typhoid Clean or equivalent flocks, or have had a negative pullorum-typhoid test within 90 days of going to public exhibition; and

(H) Discontinuation of any of the conditions or procedures described in paragraphs (b)(2)(i)(A) through (b)(2)(i)(G) of this section, or the occurrence of repeated outbreaks of pullorum or typhoid in poultry breeding flocks within or originating within the State shall be grounds for the Service to revoke its determination that such conditions and procedures have been met or complied with. Such action shall not be taken until a thorough investigation has been made by the Service and the Official State Agency has been given an opportunity to present its views; and

(ii) In the primary breeding flock, a sample of 300 birds from flocks of more than 300, and each bird in flocks of 300 or less, has been officially tested for pullorum-typhoid with no reactors: *Provided*, That a bacteriological examination monitoring program acceptable to the Official State Agency and approved by the Service may be used in lieu of blood testing.

(c) *U.S. M. Gallisepticum Clean.* (1) A flock maintained in accordance with part 147 of this subchapter with respect to Mycoplasma isolation, sanitation, and management and in which freedom from *M. gallisepticum* has been demonstrated under the criteria specified in paragraph (c)(1)(i) of this section.

(i) It is a flock in which all birds or a sample of at least 300 birds has been tested for *M. gallisepticum* as provided in §145.14(b) when more than 4 months of age: *Provided*, That to retain this classification, a minimum of 150 birds shall be tested at intervals of not more than 90 days: *And provided further*, That a sample comprised of fewer than 150 birds may be tested at any one time, if all pens are equally represented and a total of 150 birds is tested within each 90-day period.

(ii) [Reserved]

(2) A participant handling U.S. M. Gallisepticum Clean products shall

handle only products of equivalent status.

(3) U.S. M. Gallisepticum Clean chicks shall be boxed in clean boxes and delivered in trucks that have been cleaned and disinfected in accordance with part 147.

(d) *U.S. S. Enteritidis Clean*. This classification is intended for primary egg-type breeders wishing to assure their customers that the hatching eggs and multiplier chicks produced are certified free of *Salmonella enteritidis*.

(1) A flock and the hatching eggs and chicks produced from it which have met the following requirements as determined by the Official State Agency:

(i) The flock originated from a U.S. S. Enteritidis Clean flock, or meconium from the chick boxes and a sample of chicks that died within 7 days after hatching are examined bacteriologically for salmonella at an authorized laboratory. Cultures from positive samples shall be serotyped.

(ii) All feed fed to the flock shall meet the following requirements:

(A) Pelletized feed shall contain either no animal protein or only animal protein products produced under the Animal Protein Products Industry (APPI) *Salmonella* Education/Reduction Program. The protein products must have a minimum moisture content of 14.5 percent and must have been heated throughout to a minimum temperature of 190 °F, or above, or to a minimum temperature of 165 °F for at least 20 minutes, or to a minimum temperature of 184 °F under 70 lbs. pressure during the manufacturing process.

(B) Mash feed may contain no animal protein other than an APPI animal protein product supplement manufactured in pellet form and crumbled: *Provided*, That mash feed may contain nonpelleted APPI animal protein product supplements if the finished feed is treated with a salmonella control product approved by the U.S. Food and Drug Administration.

(iii) Feed shall be stored and transported in such a manner as to prevent possible contamination;

(iv) The flock is maintained in accordance with part 147 of this subchapter with respect to flock sanitation, cleaning and disinfection, and Salmonella isolation, sanitation, and management. Rodents and other pests should be effectively controlled;

(v) Environmental samples shall be collected from the flock by an Authorized Agent, in accordance with part 147 of this subchapter, when the flock is 2 to 4 weeks of age. The samples shall be examined bacteriologically for group D salmonella at an authorized laboratory. Cultures from positive samples shall be serotyped. The Authorized Agent shall also collect samples every 30 days after the first sample has been collected.

(vi) If a *Salmonella* vaccine is used that causes positive reactions with pullorum-typhoid antigen, one of the following options must be utilized.

(A) Administer the vaccine after the pullorum-typhoid testing is done as described in paragraph (d)(1)(vii) of this section.

(B) If an injectable bacterin or live vaccine that does not spread is used, keep a sample of 350 birds unvaccinated and banded for identification until the flock reaches at least 4 months of age. Following negative serological and bacteriological examinations as described in paragraph (d)(1)(vii) of this section, vaccinate the banded, non-vaccinated birds.

(vii) Blood samples from 300 non-vaccinated birds as described in paragraph (d)(1)(vi) of this section shall be tested with either pullorum antigen or by a federally licensed *Salmonella enteritidis* enzyme-linked immunosorbent assay (ELISA) test when the flock is more than 4 months of age. All birds with positive or inconclusive reactions, up to a maximum of 25 birds, shall be submitted to an authorized laboratory and examined for the presence of group D salmonella, in accordance with part 147 of this subchapter. Cultures from positive samples shall be serotyped.

(viii) Hatching eggs are collected as quickly as possible and are handled as described in §147.22 of this subchapter and are sanitized or fumigated (see §147.25 of this subchapter).

(ix) Hatching eggs produced by the flock are incubated in a hatchery whose sanitation is maintained in accordance with part 147 of this subchapter and sanitized either by a procedure approved by the Official State

Agency or in accordance with part 147 of this subchapter.

(2) A flock shall not be eligible for this classification if *Salmonella enteritidis* serotype *enteritidis* (SE) is isolated from a specimen taken from a bird in the flock. Isolation of SE from an environmental or other specimen, as described in paragraph (d)(1)(v) of this section, will require bacteriological examination for SE in an authorized laboratory, in accordance with part 147 of this subchapter, of a random sample of 60 live birds from a flock of 5,000 birds or more, or 30 live birds from a flock with fewer than 5,000 birds. If only one specimen is found positive for SE, the participant may request bacteriological examination of a second sample, equal in size to the first sample, from the flock. If no SE is recovered from any of the specimens in the second sample, the flock will be eligible for the classification.

(3) A non-vaccinated flock shall be eligible for this classification if SE is isolated from an environmental sample collected from the flock in accordance with paragraph (d)(1)(v) of this section: *Provided,* That testing is conducted in accordance with paragraph (d)(1)(vii) of this section each 30 days and no positive samples are found.

(4) In order for a hatchery to sell products of this classification, all products handled shall meet the requirements of the classification.

(5) This classification may be revoked by the Official State Agency if the participant fails to follow recommended corrective measures. The Official State Agency shall not revoke the participant's classification until the participant has been given an opportunity for a hearing in accordance with rules of practice adopted by the Official State Agency.

(e) *U.S. M. Synoviae Clean.* (1) A flock maintained in accordance with part 147 of this subchapter with respect to Mycoplasma isolation, sanitation, and management and in which freedom from *M. synoviae* has been demonstrated under the criteria specified in paragraph (e)(1)(i) of this section.

(i) It is a flock in which a minimum of 300 birds has been tested for *M. synoviae* as provided in §145.14(b) when more than 4 months of age: *Provided,* That to retain this classification, a sample of at least 150 birds shall be tested at intervals of not more than 90 days: *And provided further,* That a sample comprised of fewer than 150 birds may be tested at any one time if all pens are equally represented and a total of 150 birds is tested within each 90-day period.

(ii) [Reserved]

(2) A participant handling U.S. M. Synoviae Clean products shall handle only products of equivalent status.

(3) U.S. M. Synoviae Clean chicks shall be boxed in clean boxes and delivered in trucks that have been cleaned and disinfected in accordance with part 147 of this subchapter.

(f) *U.S. Avian Influenza Clean.* This program is intended to be the basis from which the breeding-hatchery industry may conduct a program for the prevention and control of avian influenza. It is intended to determine the presence of avian influenza in primary breeding chickens through routine surveillance of each participating breeding flock. A flock and the hatching eggs and chicks produced from it will qualify for this classification when the Official State Agency determines that they have met the following requirements:

(1) It is a primary breeding flock in which a minimum of 30 birds have been tested and found negative for avian influenza when more than 4 months of age. To retain this classification:

(i) A sample of at least 30 birds must be tested negative at intervals of 90 days; or

(ii) A sample of fewer than 30 birds may be tested, and found to be negative, at any one time if all pens are equally represented and a total of 30 birds is tested within each 90-day period; or

(iii) The flock is tested as provided in §145.14(d) at intervals of 30 days or less and found to be negative, and a total of 30 samples are collected and tested within each 90-day period; and

(2) A sample of at least 11 birds must be tested and found negative for avian influenza within 21 days prior to movement to slaughter.

[72 FR 1420, Jan. 12, 2007, as amended at 76 FR 15794, Mar. 22, 2011; 79 FR 38759, July 9, 2014]

§ 145.74 Terminology and classification; compartments.

(a) *U.S. Avian Influenza Clean Compartment.* This program is intended to be the basis from which the primary egg-type chicken breeding-hatchery industry may demonstrate the existence and implementation of a program that has been approved by the Official State Agency and the Service to establish a compartment consisting of a primary breeding-hatchery company that is free of H5/H7 avian influenza (AI), also referred to as notifiable avian influenza (NAI). This compartment has the purpose of protecting the defined subpopulation and avoiding the introduction and spread of NAI within that subpopulation by prohibiting contact with other commercial poultry operations, other domestic and wild birds, and other intensive animal operations. The program shall consist of the following:

(1) *Definition of the compartment.* Based on the guidelines established by the World Organization for Animal Health (OIE) in the Terrestrial Animal Health Code and the guidelines in this paragraph (a), the primary breeder company will define the compartment with respect to NAI. Specifically, the company will use a comprehensive biosecurity program to define the compartment as a subpopulation of poultry with a health status for NAI that is separate from birds and poultry outside the compartment. The Official State Agency and the Service must first approve all documentation submitted by the company to substantiate the defined compartment as adequate to qualify for epidemiological separation from other potential sources of infection of NAI. Guidelines for the definition of the compartment include:

(i) *Definition and description of the subpopulation of birds and their health status.* All birds included in the compartment must be U.S. Avian Influenza Clean in accordance with § 145.73(f). The poultry must also be located in a State that has an initial State response and containment plan approved by APHIS under § 56.10 of this chapter and that participates in the diagnostic surveillance program for H5/H7 low pathogenicity AI as described in § 145.15. Within the compartment, all official tests for AI, as described in § 145.14(d), must be conducted in State or Federal laboratories or in NPIP authorized laboratories that meet the minimum standards described in § 147.52 of this subchapter. In addition, the company must provide to the Service upon request any relevant historical and current NAI-related data for reference regarding surveillance for the disease within the compartment. Upon request, the Official State Agency may provide such data for other commercial poultry populations located in the State.

(ii) *Description of animal identification and traceability processes.* The primary breeder company must also include a description of its animal identification and traceability records, including examples of Veterinary Services (VS) Form 9–5, "Report of Hatcheries, Dealers and Independent Flocks"; VS Form 9–2, "Flock Selection and Testing Report"; VS Form 9–3, "Report of Sales of Hatching Eggs, Chicks and Poults"; VS Form 9–9, " Hatchery Inspection Report"; set and hatch records; egg receipts; and egg/chick invoices for the subpopulation. Documentation must also include breed identification (NPIP stock code). The Service should ensure that an effective flock identification system and traceability system are in place.

(iii) *Definition and description of the physical components or establishments of the defined compartment.* The primary breeder company must provide documentation establishing that the defined compartment is epidemiologically separated from other poultry and bird populations. The documentation must be approved by the Official State Agency and the Service as indicating adequate epidemiological separation to maintain the compartment's separate health status with respect to NAI. The documentation should include descriptions of:

(A) The physical and spatial factors that separate the compartment from surrounding bird populations and affect the biosecurity status of the compartment.

(B) Relevant environmental factors that may affect exposure of the birds to AI.

(C) The functional boundary and fencing that are used to control access to the compartment.

(D) Facilities and procedures to prevent access by wild birds and to provide separation from other relevant hosts.

(E) The relevant infrastructural factors that may affect exposure to AI, including the construction and design of buildings or physical components, cleaning and disinfection of buildings and physical components between production groups with quality assurance verification, cleaning and disinfection of equipment, and introduction of equipment or material into the compartment.

(iv) *Definition and description of the functional relationships between components of the defined compartment.* Functional relationships between components of the compartment include traffic movement and flow at and among premises, personnel movement at and among premises, exposure to live bird populations, and any other factors that could affect biosecurity of the compartment. All physical components of the compartment must be maintained in compliance with hygiene and biosecurity procedures for poultry primary breeding flocks and hatcheries in accordance with part 147 of this subchapter. In addition, the company must provide a biosecurity plan for the compartment and all included components. The biosecurity plan should include but not be limited to:

(A) Requirements that company employees and contract growers limit their contact with live birds outside the compartment.

(B) An education and training program for company employees and contractors.

(C) Standard operating procedures for company employees, contractors, and outside maintenance personnel.

(D) Requirements for company employees and non-company personnel who visit any premises within the compartment.

(E) Company veterinary infrastructure to ensure flock monitoring and disease diagnosis and control measures.

(F) Policies for management of vehicles and equipment used within the compartment to connect the various premises.

(G) Farm site requirements (location, layout, and construction).

(H) Pest management program.

(I) Cleaning and disinfection process.

(J) Requirements for litter and dead bird removal and/or disposal.

(v) *Description of other factors important for maintaining the compartment.* The company veterinary infrastructure will assess sanitary measures, environmental risk factors, and management and husbandry practices that relate to the separation of the compartment and the health status of the birds contained within the compartment that may affect risk of exposure to NAI. This assessment must include a description of internal monitoring and auditing systems (e.g., quality assurance and quality control programs) to demonstrate the effectiveness of the compartment. Upon request, the Service will provide the company with information on the epidemiology of NAI and the associated risk pathways in which the components of the compartment are located.

(vi) *Approval or denial.* Based on the documentation provided under this paragraph (a)(1), as well as any other information the Service and the Official State Agency determine to be necessary, the Service and the Official State Agency will approve or deny the classification of the compartment as U.S. Avian Influenza Clean.

(2) *Company activities for maintenance of the compartment.* (i) The primary breeder company's management of biosecurity, surveillance, and disease control efforts must be uniform and equivalent among all components that are a part of the compartment. Oversight and inspection of these management practices must be conducted by the company's licensed, accredited veterinarians.

(ii) Veterinary staff from the Official State Agency and NPIP staff will work in partnership with licensed, accredited veterinarians to train and certify auditors through Service-approved workshops. The trained auditors will conduct biosecurity and operational audits at least once every 2 years to ensure the integrity of the compartment. These audits will include evaluation of the critical control points and standard operating practices within the compartment, verification of the health status of the flock(s) contained within the compartment, and examination of the biosecurity and management system of the integrated components of the compartment.

(iii) In addition, the company must demonstrate compliance with paragraph (a)(1) of this section for remaining in the U.S. Avian Influenza Clean classification, surveillance for NAI within the compartment, and conducting tests in State or Federal laboratories or in NPIP authorized laboratories. Accredited veterinarians are responsible for the enforcement of active and passive surveillance of NAI in primary breeder flocks. Baseline health status must be maintained for all flocks or subpopulations within the compartment, indicating the dates and negative results of all avian influenza surveillance and monitoring testing, the dates and history of last disease occurrence (if any), the number of outbreaks, and the methods of disease control that were applied.

(iv) Documentation will be maintained in the company's database and will be verified as required by the Service and/or the Official State Agency.

(3) *Service and Official State Agency activities for maintenance of the compartment.* The Service will work in cooperation with the Official State Agencies to ensure the continued integrity of any recognized compartments. Activities include:

(i) Oversight of the establishment and management of compartments;

(ii) Establishment of effective partnerships between the Service, the Plan, and the primary breeder industry;

(iii) Approval or denial of classification of compartments as U.S. Avian Influenza Clean Compartments under paragraph (a)(1) of this section;

(iv) Official certification of the health status of the compartment, and commodities that may be traded from it through participation in the Plan for avian diseases, including the U.S. Avian Influenza Clean program as described in § 145.73(f) and diagnostic surveillance for H5/H7 low pathogenicity AI as described in § 145.15;

(v) Conducting audits of compartments at least once every 2 years to:

(A) Confirm that the primary breeding company's establishments are epidemiologically distinct and pathways for the introduction of disease into the compartment are closed through routine operational procedures; and

(B) Evaluate and assess the management and husbandry practices relating to biosecurity to determine whether they are in compliance with hygiene and biosecurity procedures for poultry primary breeding flocks and hatcheries in accordance with part 147 of this subchapter;

(vi) Providing, upon request, model plans for management and husbandry practices relating to biosecurity in accordance with part 147 of this subchapter, risk evaluations in conjunction with the primary breeder industry (including disease surveillance such as VS Form 9–4, "Summary of Breeding Flock Participation"), and diagnostic capability summaries and systems for initial State response and containment plans in accordance with § 56.10 of this chapter; and

(vii) Publicizing and sharing compartment information with international trading partners, upon request, to establish approval and recognition of the compartment, including timeliness and accuracy of disease reporting and surveillance measures as described in §§ 145.15 and 145.73(f).

(4) *Emergency response and notification.* In the case of a confirmed positive of NAI in the subpopulation of the compartment, the management of the compartment must notify the Service. The Service will immediately suspend the status of the compartment. A compartment will be eligible to resume trade with importing countries only after the compartment has adopted the necessary measures to reestablish the biosecurity level and confirm that NAI is not present in the compartment and the Service has reevaluated the management and biosecurity measures of the compartment and approved said compartment for trade.

(b) [Reserved]

[79 FR 38760, July 9, 2014]

Subpart H—Special Provisions for Primary Meat-Type Chicken Breeding Flocks and Products

SOURCE: 72 FR 1422, Jan. 12, 2007, unless otherwise noted.

§ 145.81 Definitions.

Except where the context otherwise requires, for the purposes of this subpart the following terms shall be construed, respectively, to mean:

Chicks. Newly hatched chickens.

Primary meat-type chicken breeding flocks. Foundation flocks that are composed of pedigree, great-grandparent, and grandparent stock that has been developed for meat production and are maintained for the principal purpose of producing multiplier breeding chicks used to produce commercial broilers.

Started chickens. Young chickens (chicks, pullets, cockerels, capons) which have been fed and watered and are less than 6 months of age.

§ 145.82 Participation.

Participating flocks of primary meat-type chickens, and the eggs and chicks produced from them, shall comply with the applicable general provisions of subpart A of this part and the special provisions of this subpart H.

(a) Started chickens shall lose their identity under Plan terminology when not maintained by Plan participants under the conditions prescribed in § 145.5(a).

(b) Hatching eggs produced by primary breeding flocks should be nest clean. They may be fumigated in accordance with part 147 of this subchapter or otherwise sanitized.

(c) Any nutritive material provided to chicks must be free of the avian pathogens that are officially represented in the Plan disease classifications listed in § 145.10.

[72 FR 1422, Jan. 12, 2007, as amended at 79 FR 38762, July 9, 2014]

§ 145.83 Terminology and classification; flocks and products.

Participating flocks, and the eggs and chicks produced from them, which have met the respective requirements specified in this section, may be designated by the following terms and the corresponding designs illustrated in § 145.10:

(a) [Reserved]

(b) *U.S. Pullorum-Typhoid Clean.* A flock in which freedom from pullorum and typhoid has been demonstrated to the Official State Agency under the criteria in paragraph (b)(1) or (b)(2) of this section: *Provided,* That a flock qualifying by means of a blood test shall be tested within the past 12 months, except that the retesting of a participating flock which is retained for more than 12 months shall be conducted a minimum of 4 weeks after the induction of molt. (See § 145.14 relating to the official blood test where applicable.)

(1) It has been officially blood tested with no reactors.

(2) It is a primary breeding flock that meets the following criteria:

(i) The primary breeding flock is located in a State in which pullorum disease or fowl typhoid is not known to exist nor to have existed in hatchery supply flocks within the State during the preceding 12 months and in which it has been determined by the Service that:

(A) All hatcheries within the State are qualified as "National Plan Hatcheries" or have met equivalent requirements for pullorum-typhoid control under official supervision;

(B) All hatchery supply flocks within the State are qualified as U.S. Pullorum-Typhoid Clean or have met equivalent requirements for pullorum-typhoid control under official supervision: *Provided,* That if other domesticated fowl, except waterfowl, are maintained on the same premises as the participating flock, freedom from pullorum-typhoid infection shall be demonstrated by an official blood test of each of these fowl;

(C) All shipments of products other than U.S. Pullorum-Typhoid Clean, or equivalent, into the State are prohibited;

(D) All persons performing poultry disease diagnostic services within the State are required to report to the Official State Agency within 48 hours the source of all poultry specimens from which *S. pullorum* or *S. gallinarum* is isolated;

(E) All reports of any disease outbreak involving a disease covered under the Plan are promptly followed by an investigation by the Official State Agency to determine the origin of the infection; *Provided*, That if the origin of the infection involves another State, or if there is exposure to poultry in another State from the infected flock, then officials administering the National Poultry Improvement Plan will conduct an investigation;

(F) All flocks found to be infected with pullorum or typhoid are quarantined until marketed or destroyed under the supervision of the Official State Agency, or until subsequently blood tested following the procedure for reacting flocks as contained in §145.14(a)(5) of this subchapter, and all birds fail to demonstrate pullorum or typhoid infection;

(G) All poultry, including exhibition, exotic, and game birds, but excluding waterfowl, going to public exhibition shall come from U.S. Pullorum-Typhoid Clean or equivalent flocks, or have had a negative pullorum-typhoid test within 90 days of going to public exhibition; and

(H) Discontinuation of any of the conditions or procedures described in paragraphs (b)(2)(i)(A) through (b)(2)(i)(G) of this section, or the occurrence of repeated outbreaks of pullorum or typhoid in poultry breeding flocks within or originating within the State shall be grounds for the Service to revoke its determination that such conditions and procedures have been met or complied with. Such action shall not be taken until a thorough investigation has been made by the Service and the Official State Agency has been given an opportunity to present its views; and

(ii) In the primary breeding flock, a sample of 300 birds from flocks of more than 300, and each bird in flocks of 300 or less, has been officially tested for pullorum-typhoid with no reactors: *Provided*, That a bacteriological examination monitoring program acceptable to the Official State Agency and approved by the Service may be used in lieu of blood testing.

(c) *U.S. M. Gallisepticum Clean*. (1) A flock maintained in accordance with part 147 of this subchapter with respect to Mycoplasma isolation, sanitation, and management and in which freedom from *M. gallisepticum* has been demonstrated under the criteria specified in paragraph (c)(1)(i) of this section.

(i) It is a flock in which all birds or a sample of at least 300 birds has been tested for *M. gallisepticum* as provided in §145.14(b) of this subchapter when more than 4 months of age: *Provided*, That to retain this classification, a minimum of 40 birds shall be tested at intervals of not more than 28 days, and a total of at least 150 birds shall be tested within each 90-day period.

(ii) [Reserved]

(2) A participant handling U.S. M. Gallisepticum Clean products must handle only products of equivalent status.

(3) U.S. M. Gallisepticum Clean chicks shall be boxed in clean boxes and delivered in trucks that have been cleaned and disinfected in accordance with part 147 of this subchapter.

(d) *U.S. M. Synoviae Clean*. (1) A flock maintained in accordance with part 147 of this subchapter with respect to Mycoplasma isolation, sanitation, and management and in which freedom from *M. synoviae* has been demonstrated under the criteria specified in paragraph (d)(1)(i) of this section.

(i) It is a flock in which all birds or a sample of at least 300 birds has been tested for *M. synoviae* as provided in §145.14(b) of this subchapter when more than 4 months of age: *Provided*, That to retain this classification, a sample of at least 40 birds shall be tested at intervals of not more than 28 days, and a total of at least 150 birds shall be tested within each 90-day period.

(ii) [Reserved]

(2) A participant handling U.S. M. Synoviae Clean products shall handle only products of equivalent status.

(3) U.S. M. Synoviae Clean chicks shall be boxed in clean boxes and delivered in trucks that have been cleaned and disinfected in accordance with part 147 of this subchapter.

(e) *U.S. S. Enteritidis Clean*. This classification is intended for primary meat-type breeders wishing to assure their customers that the chicks produced are certified free of *Salmonella enteritidis*.

(1) A flock and the hatching eggs and chicks produced from it shall be eligible for this classification if they meet the following requirements, as determined by the Official State Agency:

(i) The flock originated from a U.S. S. Enteritidis Clean flock, or one of the following samples has been examined bacteriologically for *S. enteritidis* at an authorized laboratory in accordance with part 147 of this subchapter and any group D Salmonella samples have been serotyped:

(A) A sample of chick papers, hatcher tray swabs, or fluff collected and cultured in accordance with part 147 of this subchapter; and

(B) Samples of intestinal and liver or spleen tissues from a minimum of 30 chicks that died within 7 days after hatching and have been preserved daily by freezing prior to shipment to an authorized laboratory.

(ii) The flock is maintained in compliance with isolation, sanitation, and management procedures for Salmonella in accordance with part 147 of this subchapter.

(iii) Environmental samples are collected from the flock by or under the supervision of an Authorized Agent, in accordance with part 147 of this subchapter, when the flock reaches 4 months of age and every 30 days thereafter. Once the flock is in egg production and chicks are hatching from it, the samples must include at least 4 individual test assay results every 30 days in flocks of more than 500 birds or 2 individual assays per month in flocks of 500 birds or fewer. One of these results must come from samples collected from hatched chicks at a participating hatchery derived from said flock. These individual test assays may be derived from pooled samples from the farm or hatchery in accordance with part 147 of this subchapter, but must be run as separate test assays in the laboratory. The environmental samples shall be examined bacteriologically for group D Salmonella at an authorized laboratory, and cultures from group D positive samples shall be serotyped.

(iv) Blood samples from 300 birds from the flock are officially tested with pullorum antigen when the flock is at least 4 months of age. All birds with positive or inconclusive reactions, up to a maximum of 25 birds, shall be submitted to an authorized laboratory and examined for the presence of group D Salmonella in accordance with part 147 of this subchapter. Cultures from group D positive samples shall be serotyped.

(v) Hatching eggs produced by the flock are collected as quickly as possible and their sanitation is maintained in accordance with part 147 of this subchapter.

(vi) Hatching eggs produced by the flock are incubated in a hatchery whose sanitation is maintained in accordance with part 147 of this subchapter, and the hatchery must have been sanitized either by a procedure approved by the Official State Agency or by fumigation in accordance with part 147 of this subchapter.

(2) If *Salmonella enteritidis* serotype *enteritidis* (SE) is isolated from a specimen taken from a bird in the flock, except as provided in paragraph (e)(3) of this section, the flock shall not be eligible for this classification.

(3) If SE is isolated from an environmental sample collected from the flock in accordance with paragraph (e)(1)(iii) of this section, an additional environmental sampling and 25 live cull birds or fresh dead birds (if present), or other randomly selected live birds if fewer than 25 culls can be found in the flock, must be bacteriologically examined for SE in accordance with part 147 of this subchapter. If only 1 bird from the 25-bird sample is found positive for SE., the participant may request bacteriological examination of a second 25-bird sample from the flock. In addition, if the flock with the SE isolation is in egg production and eggs are under incubation, the next four consecutive hatches shall be examined bacteriologically in accordance with part 147 of this subchapter. Samples shall be collected from all of the hatching unit's chick trays and basket trays of hatching eggs, or from all chick box papers from the flock, and tested, pooling the samples into a minimum of 10 separate assays. Any followup hatchery-positive SE isolations shall result in discontinuation of subsequent hatches until the flock status is determined by

bird culture. The flock will be disqualified for the U.S. S. Enteritidis Clean classification if a bird or subsequent flock environmental assay results in isolation of SE.

(4) In order for a hatchery to sell products of this classification, all products handled by the hatchery must meet the requirements of this paragraph.

(5) This classification may be revoked by the Official State Agency if the participant fails to follow recommended corrective measures. The Official State Agency shall not revoke the participant's classification until the participant has been given an opportunity for a hearing in accordance with rules of practice adopted by the Official State Agency.

(6) A pedigree, experimental, great-grandparent, or grandparent flock that is removed from the U.S. S. Enteritidis Clean program may be reinstated whenever the following conditions are met:

(i) The owner attests that corrective measures have been implemented, which may include one or more of the following:

(A) Test and slaughter infected birds based on blood tests of every bird in the flock, with either pullorum antigen or by a federally licensed *Salmonella enteritidis* enzyme-linked immunosorbent assay (ELISA) test when the flock is more than 4 months of age.

(B) Perform other corrective actions including, but not limited to, vaccination, medication, cleaning and disinfection of houses, rodent control, and movement of uninfected birds to premises that have been determined to be environmentally negative for *S. enteritidis* in accordance with par 147 of this subchapter.

(C) One hundred percent of blood samples from the birds moved to the clean premises are tested negative for *Salmonella pullorum* and group D *Salmonella*. All birds with positive or inconclusive reactions, up to a maximum of 25 birds, shall be submitted to an authorized laboratory and examined for the presence of group D *Salmonella*, in accordance with part 147 of this subchapter. Cultures from positive samples shall be serotyped.

(D) Two consecutive environmental drag swabs taken at the clean premises collected in accordance with part 147 of this subchapter 4 weeks apart are negative for *S. enteritidis*.

(E) Other corrective measures at the discretion of the Official State Agency.

(ii) Following reinstatement, a flock will remain eligible for this classification if the flock is tested in accordance with paragraph (e)(1)(v) of this section every 30 days and no positive samples are found and the flock meets the requirements set forth in § 145.83(e).

(f) *U.S. Salmonella Monitored.* This program is intended to be the basis from which the breeding-hatching industry may conduct a program for the prevention and control of salmonellosis. It is intended to reduce the incidence of *Salmonella* organisms in hatching eggs and chicks through an effective and practical sanitation program at the breeder farm and in the hatchery. This will afford other segments of the poultry industry an opportunity to reduce the incidence of *Salmonella* in their products.

(1) A flock and the hatching eggs and chicks produced from it that have met the following requirements, as determined by the Official State Agency.

(i) Measures shall be implemented to control *Salmonella* challenge through feed, feed storage, and feed transport.

(ii) Chicks shall be hatched in a hatchery whose sanitation is maintained in accordance with part 147 of this subchapter and sanitized or fumigated in accordance with part 147 of this subchapter.

(iii) An Authorized Agent shall take environmental samples from the hatchery every 30 days; *i.e.*, meconium or chick papers. An authorized laboratory for *Salmonella* shall examine the samples bacteriologically;

(iv) An Authorized Agent shall take environmental samples in accordance with part 147 of this subchapter from each flock at 4 months of age and every 30 days thereafter. An authorized laboratory for *Salmonella* shall examine the environmental samples bacteriologically. All *Salmonella* isolates from a flock shall be serogrouped and shall be reported to the Official State Agency on a monthly basis;

(v) Owners of flocks may vaccinate with a paratyphoid vaccine: *Provided*, That a sample of 350 birds, which will be banded for identification, shall remain unvaccinated until the flock reaches at least 4 months of age to allow for the serological testing required under paragraph (f)(1)(iv) of this section.

(vi) Any flock entering the production period that is in compliance with all the requirements of § 145.83(f) with no history of *Salmonella* isolations shall be considered "*Salmonella* negative" and may retain this definition as long as no environmental or bird *Salmonella* isolations are identified and confirmed from the flock or flock environment by sampling on 4 separate collection dates over a minimum of a 2-week period. Sampling and testing must be performed as described in paragraph (f)(1)(iv) of this section. An unconfirmed environmental *Salmonella* isolation shall not change this *Salmonella* negative status.

(2) The Official State Agency may monitor the effectiveness of the sanitation practices in accordance with part 147 of this subchapter.

(3) In order for a hatchery to sell products of paragraphs (f)(1)(i) through (f)(1)(vi) of this section, all products handled shall meet the requirements of the classification.

(4) This classification may be revoked by the Official State Agency if the participant fails to follow recommended corrective measures.

(g) *U.S. Avian Influenza Clean*. This program is intended to be the basis from which the breeding-hatchery industry may conduct a program for the prevention and control of avian influenza. It is intended to determine the presence of avian influenza in primary breeding chickens through routine surveillance of each participating breeding flock. A flock and the hatching eggs and chicks produced from it will qualify for this classification when the Official State Agency determines that they have met the following requirements:

(1) It is a primary breeding flock in which a minimum of 30 birds have been tested negative for antibodies to avian influenza using an approved test as described in § 145.14 when more than 4 months of age. To retain this classification:

(i) A sample of at least 30 birds must be tested negative at intervals of 90 days; or

(ii) A sample of fewer than 30 birds may be tested, and found to be negative, at any one time if all pens are equally represented and a total of 30 birds is tested within each 90-day period; or

(iii) The flock is tested as provided in § 145.14(d) at intervals of 30 days or less and found to be negative, and a total of 30 samples are collected and tested within each 90-day period; and

(2) During each 90-day period, all primary spent fowl, up to a maximum of 30, must be tested serologically and found negative for antibodies for avian influenza within 21 days prior to movement to slaughter.

[72 FR 1422, Jan. 12, 2007, as amended at 76 FR 15794, Mar. 22, 2011; 79 FR 38762, July 9, 2014; 79 FR 71624, Dec. 3, 2014; 81 FR 53250, Aug. 12, 2016]

§ 145.84 Terminology and classification; compartments.

(a) *U.S. Avian Influenza Clean Compartment*. This program is intended to be the basis from which the primary meat-type chicken breeding-hatchery industry may demonstrate the existence and implementation of a program that has been approved by the Official State Agency and the Service to establish a compartment consisting of a primary breeding-hatchery company that is free of H5/H7 avian influenza (AI), also referred to as notifiable avian influenza (NAI). This compartment has the purpose of protecting the defined subpopulation and avoiding the introduction and spread of NAI within that subpopulation by prohibiting contact with other commercial poultry operations, other domestic and wild birds, and other intensive animal operations. The program shall consist of the following:

(1) *Definition of the compartment*. Based on the guidelines established by the World Organization for Animal Health (OIE) in the Terrestrial Animal Health Code and the guidelines in this paragraph (a), the primary breeder company will define the compartment with respect to NAI. Specifically, the

company will use a comprehensive biosecurity program to define the compartment as a subpopulation of poultry with a health status for NAI that is separate from birds and poultry outside the compartment. The Official State Agency and the Service must first approve all documentation submitted by the company to substantiate the defined compartment as adequate to qualify for epidemiological separation from other potential sources of infection of NAI. Guidelines for the definition of the compartment include:

(i) *Definition and description of the subpopulation of birds and their health status.* All birds included in the compartment must be U.S. Avian Influenza Clean in accordance with §145.83(g). The poultry must also be located in a State that has an initial State response and containment plan approved by APHIS under §56.10 of this chapter and that participates in the diagnostic surveillance program for H5/H7 low pathogenicity AI as described in §145.15. Within the compartment, all official tests for AI, as described in §145.14(d), must be conducted in State or Federal laboratories or in NPIP authorized laboratories that meet the minimum standards described in §147.52 of this subchapter. In addition, the company must provide to the Service upon request any relevant historical and current NAI-related data for reference regarding surveillance for the disease and the health status of the compartment. Upon request, the Official State Agency may provide such data for other commercial poultry populations located in the State.

(ii) *Description of animal identification and traceability processes.* The primary breeder company must also include a description of its animal identification and traceability records, including examples of Veterinary Services (VS) Form 9–5, "Report of Hatcheries, Dealers and Independent Flocks"; VS Form 9–2, "Flock Selection and Testing Report"; VS Form 9–3, "Report of Sales of Hatching Eggs, Chicks and Poults"; VS Form 9–9, " Hatchery Inspection Report"; set and hatch records; egg receipts; and egg/chick invoices for the subpopulation. Documentation must also include breed identification (NPIP stock code). The Service should ensure that an effective flock identification system and traceability system are in place.

(iii) *Definition and description of the physical components or establishments of the defined compartment.* The primary breeder company must provide documentation establishing that the defined compartment is epidemiologically separated from other poultry and bird populations. The documentation must be approved by the Official State Agency and the Service as indicating adequate epidemiological separation to maintain the compartment's separate health status with respect to NAI. The documentation should include descriptions of:

(A) The physical and spatial factors that separate the compartment from surrounding bird populations and affect the biosecurity status of the compartment.

(B) Relevant environmental factors that may affect exposure of the birds to AI.

(C) The functional boundary and fencing that are used to control access to the compartment.

(D) Facilities and procedures to prevent access by wild birds and to provide separation from other relevant hosts.

(E) The relevant infrastructural factors that may affect exposure to AI, including the construction and design of buildings or physical components, cleaning and disinfection of buildings and physical components between production groups with quality assurance verification, cleaning and disinfection of equipment, and introduction of equipment or material into the compartment.

(iv) *Definition and description of the functional relationships between components of the defined compartment.* Functional relationships between components of the compartment include traffic movement and flow at and among premises, personnel movement at and among premises, exposure to live bird populations, and any other factors that could affect biosecurity of the compartment. All physical components of the compartment must be maintained in compliance with hygiene and biosecurity procedures for poultry primary breeding flocks and hatcheries in accordance with part 147 of this subchapter. In addition, the company must provide a biosecurity plan for the compartment and all included components. The biosecurity plan should include but not be limited to:

(A) Requirements that company employees and contract growers limit their contact with live birds outside the compartment.

(B) An education and training program for company employees and contractors.

(C) Standard operating procedures for company employees, contractors, and outside maintenance personnel.

(D) Requirements for company employees and non-company personnel who visit any premises within the compartment.

(E) Company veterinary infrastructure to ensure flock monitoring and disease diagnosis and control measures.

(F) Policies for management of vehicles and equipment used within the compartment to connect the various premises.

(G) Farm site requirements (location, layout, and construction).

(H) Pest management program.

(I) Cleaning and disinfection process.

(J) Requirements for litter and dead bird removal and/or disposal.

(v) *Description of other factors important for maintaining the compartment.* The company veterinary infrastructure will assess sanitary measures, environmental risk factors, and management and husbandry practices that relate to the separation of the compartment and the health status of the birds contained within the compartment that may affect risk of exposure to NAI. This assessment must include a description of internal monitoring and auditing systems (e.g., quality assurance and quality control programs) to demonstrate the effectiveness of the compartment. Upon request, the Service will provide the company with information on the epidemiology of NAI and the associated risk pathways in which the components of the compartment are located.

(vi) *Approval or denial.* Based on the documentation provided under this paragraph (a)(1), as well as any other information the Service and the Official State Agency determine to be necessary, the Service and the Official State Agency will approve or deny the classification of the compartment as U.S. Avian Influenza Clean.

(2) *Company activities for maintenance of the compartment.* (i) The primary breeder company's management of biosecurity, surveillance, and disease control efforts must be uniform and equivalent among all components that are a part of the compartment. Oversight and inspection of these management practices must be conducted by the company's licensed, accredited veterinarians.

(ii) Veterinary staff from the Official State Agency and NPIP staff will work in partnership with licensed, accredited veterinarians to train and certify auditors through Service-approved workshops. The trained auditors will conduct biosecurity and operational audits at least once every 2 years to ensure the integrity of the compartment. These audits will include evaluation of the critical control points and standard operating practices within the compartment, verification of the health status of the flock(s) contained within the compartment, and examination of the biosecurity and management system of the integrated components of the compartment.

(iii) In addition, the company must demonstrate compliance with paragraph (a)(1) of this section for remaining in the U.S. Avian Influenza Clean classification, surveillance for NAI within the compartment, and conducting tests in State or Federal laboratories or in NPIP authorized laboratories. Accredited veterinarians are responsible for the enforcement of active and passive surveillance of NAI in primary breeder flocks. Baseline health status must be maintained for all flocks or subpopulations within the compartment, indicating the dates and negative results of all avian influenza surveillance and monitoring testing, the dates and history of last disease occurrence (if any), the number of outbreaks, and the methods of disease control that were applied.

(iv) Documentation will be maintained in the company's database and will be verified as required by the Service and/or the Official State Agency.

(3) *Service and Official State Agency activities for maintenance of the compartment.* The Service will work in cooperation with the Official State Agencies to ensure the continued integrity of any recognized compartments. Activities include:

(i) Oversight of the establishment and management of compartments;

(ii) Establishment of effective partnerships between the Service, the Plan, and the primary breeder industry;

(iii) Approval or denial of classification of compartments as U.S. Avian Influenza Clean Compartments under paragraph (a)(1) of this section;

(iv) Official certification of the health status of the compartment, and commodities that may be traded from it through participation in the Plan for avian diseases, including the U.S. Avian Influenza Clean program as described in § 145.83(g) and diagnostic surveillance for H5/H7 low pathogenicity AI as described in § 145.15;

(v) Conducting audits of compartments at least once every 2 years to:

(A) Confirm that the primary breeding company's establishments are epidemiologically distinct and pathways for the introduction of disease into the compartment are closed through routine operational procedures; and

(B) Evaluate and assess the management and husbandry practices relating to biosecurity to determine whether they are in compliance with hygiene and biosecurity procedures for poultry primary breeding flocks and hatcheries in accordance with part 147 of this subchapter;

(vi) Providing, upon request, model plans for management and husbandry practices relating to biosecurity in accordance with part 147 of this subchapter, risk evaluations in conjunction with the primary breeder industry (including disease surveillance such as VS Form 9-4, "Summary of Breeding Flock Participation"), and diagnostic capability summaries and systems for initial State response and containment plans in accordance with § 56.10 of this chapter; and

(vii) Publicizing and sharing compartment information with international trading partners, upon request, to establish approval and recognition of the compartment, including timeliness and accuracy of disease reporting and surveillance measures as described in §§ 145.15 and 145.83(g).

(4) *Emergency response and notification.* In the case of a confirmed positive of NAI in the subpopulation of the compartment, the management of the compartment must notify the Service. The Service will immediately suspend the status of the compartment. A compartment would be eligible to resume trade with importing countries only after the compartment has adopted the necessary measures to reestablish the biosecurity level and confirm that NAI is not present in the compartment and the Service has reevaluated the management and biosecurity measures of the compartment and approved said compartment for trade.

(b) [Reserved]

[79 FR 38763, July 9, 2014]

Subpart I—Special Provisions for Meat-Type Waterfowl Breeding Flocks and Products

SOURCE: 76 FR 15794, Mar. 22, 2011, unless otherwise noted.

§ 145.91 Definitions.

Except where the context otherwise requires, for the purposes of this subpart the following term shall be construed to mean:

Meat-type waterfowl breeding flocks. Flocks of domesticated duck or goose that are composed of stock that has been developed and is maintained for the primary purpose of producing baby poultry that will be raised under confinement for the primary purpose of producing meat for human consumption.

§ 145.92 Participation.

Participating flocks of meat-type waterfowl and the eggs and baby poultry produced from them shall comply with the applicable general provisions of subpart A of this part and the special provisions of this subpart I.

(a) Started poultry shall lose their identity under Plan terminology when not maintained by Plan participants under the conditions prescribed in § 145.5(a).

(b) Hatching eggs produced by primary and multiplier breeding flocks should be nest clean. They may be fumigated in accordance with part 147 of this subchapter or otherwise sanitized.

(c) Any nutritive material provided to baby poultry must be free of the avian pathogens that are officially represented in the Plan disease classifications listed in § 145.10.

[76 FR 15794, Mar. 22, 2011, as amended at 79 FR 38764, July 9, 2014; 81 FR 53250, Aug. 12, 2016]

§ 145.93 Terminology and classification; flocks and products.

Participating flocks, and the eggs and baby poultry produced from them, that have met the respective requirements specified in this section may be designated by the following terms and the corresponding designs illustrated in § 145.10.

(a) [Reserved]

(b) *U.S. Pullorum-Typhoid Clean.* A flock in which freedom from pullorum and typhoid has been demonstrated to the Official State Agency under the criteria in one of the following paragraphs (b)(1) through (b)(5) of this section (*See* § 145.14 relating to the official blood test where applicable.):

(1) It has been officially blood tested within the past 12 months with no reactors.

(2) It is a multiplier breeding flock, or a breeding flock composed of progeny of a primary breeding flock which is intended solely for the production of multiplier breeding flocks, and meets the following specifications as determined by the Official State Agency and the Service:

(i) The flock is located in a State where all persons performing poultry disease diagnostic services within the State are required to report to the Official State Agency within 48 hours the source of all poultry specimens from which *S. pullorum* or *S. gallinarum* is isolated;

(ii) The flock is composed entirely of birds that originated from U.S. Pullorum-Typhoid Clean breeding flocks or from flocks that met equivalent requirements under official supervision; and

(iii) The flock is located on a premises where a flock not classified as U.S. Pullorum-Typhoid Clean was located the previous year; *Provided*, that an Authorized Testing Agent must blood test up to 300 birds per flock, as described in § 145.14, if the Official State Agency determines that the flock has been exposed to pullorum-typhoid. In making determinations of exposure and setting the number of birds to be blood tested, the Official State Agency shall evaluate the results of any blood tests, described in § 145.14(a)(1), that were performed on an unclassified flock located on the premises during the previous year; the origins of the unclassified flock; and the probability of contacts between the flock for which qualification is being sought and infected wild birds, contaminated feed or waste, or birds, equipment, supplies, or personnel from flocks infected with pullorum-typhoid.

(3) It is a multiplier breeding flock that originated from U.S. Pullorum-Typhoid Clean breeding flocks or from flocks that met equivalent requirements under official supervision, and is located in a State in which it has been determined by the Service that:

(i) All hatcheries within the State are qualified as "National Plan Hatcheries" or have met equivalent requirements for pullorum-typhoid control under official supervision;

(ii) All hatchery supply flocks within the State are qualified as U.S. Pullorum-Typhoid Clean or have met equivalent requirements for pullorum-typhoid control under official supervision: *Provided*, That if other domesticated fowl are maintained on the same premises as the participating flock, freedom from pullorum-typhoid infection shall be demonstrated by an official blood test of each of these fowl;

(iii) All shipments of products other than U.S. Pullorum-Typhoid Clean, or equivalent, into the State are prohibited;

(iv) All persons performing poultry disease diagnostic services within the State are required to report to the Official State Agency within 48 hours the source of all poultry specimens from which *S. pullorum* or *S. gallinarum* is isolated;

(v) All reports of any disease outbreak involving a disease covered under the Plan are promptly followed by an investigation by the Official State Agency to determine the origin of the infection; *Provided,* That if the origin of the infection involves another State, or if there is exposure to poultry in another State from the infected flock, then the National Poultry Improvement Plan will conduct an investigation;

(vi) All flocks found to be infected with pullorum or typhoid are quarantined until marketed or destroyed under the supervision of the Official State Agency, or until subsequently blood tested, following the procedure for reacting flocks as contained in §145.14(a)(5), and all birds fail to demonstrate pullorum or typhoid infection;

(vii) All poultry, including exhibition, exotic, and game birds, but excluding waterfowl, going to public exhibition shall come from U.S. Pullorum-Typhoid Clean or equivalent flocks, or have had a negative pullorum-typhoid test within 90 days of going to public exhibition;

(viii) Discontinuation of any of the conditions or procedures described in paragraphs (a)(3)(i), (ii), (iii), (iv), (v), (vi), and (vii) of this section, or the occurrence of repeated outbreaks of pullorum or typhoid in poultry breeding flocks within or originating within the State shall be grounds for the Service to revoke its determination that such conditions and procedures have been met or complied with. Such action shall not be taken until a thorough investigation has been made by the Service and the Official State Agency has been given an opportunity to present its views.

(4) It is a multiplier breeding flock located in a State which has been determined by the Service to be in compliance with the provisions of paragraph (a)(3) of this section, and in which pullorum disease or fowl typhoid is not known to exist nor to have existed in hatchery supply flocks within the State during the preceding 24 months.

(5) It is a primary breeding flock located in a State determined to be in compliance with the provisions of paragraph (a)(4) of this section, and in which a sample of 300 birds from flocks of more than 300, and each bird in flocks of 300 or less, has been officially tested for pullorum-typhoid within the past 12 months with no reactors: *Provided,* That when a flock is a primary breeding flock located in a State which has been deemed to be a U.S. Pullorum-Typhoid Clean State for the past 3 years, and during which time no isolation of pullorum or typhoid has been made that can be traced to a source in that State, a bacteriological examination monitoring program or a serological examination monitoring program acceptable to the Official State Agency and approved by the Service may be used in lieu of annual blood testing.

(c) *U.S. H5/H7 Avian Influenza Clean.* This program is intended to be the basis from which the breeding-hatchery industry may conduct a program for the prevention and control of the H5/H7 subtypes of avian influenza. It is intended to determine the presence of the H5/H7 subtypes of avian influenza in meat-type waterfowl breeding flocks through routine surveillance of each participating breeding flock. A flock, and the hatching eggs and baby poultry produced from it, will qualify for this classification when the Official State Agency determines that it has met one of the following requirements:

(1) It is a primary breeding flock in which a minimum of 30 birds have been tested negative to the H5/H7 subtypes of avian influenza as provided in §145.14(d) when more than 4 months of age. To retain this classification:

(i) A sample of at least 30 birds must be tested and found to be negative at intervals of 90 days; or

(ii) A sample of fewer than 30 birds may be tested, and found to be negative, at any one time if all pens are equally represented and a total of 30 birds are tested within each 90-day period.

(2) It is a multiplier breeding flock in which a minimum of 30 birds have been tested negative to the H5/H7 subtypes of avian influenza as provided in §145.14(d) when more than 4 months of age. To retain this classification:

(i) A sample of at least 30 birds must be tested negative at intervals of 180 days; or

(ii) A sample of fewer than 30 birds may be tested, and found to be negative, at any one time if all pens are equally represented and a total of 30 birds are tested within each 180-day period.

(3) A sample of at least 11 birds must be tested and found negative to H5/H7 avian influenza within 21 days prior to movement to slaughter.

(d) *U.S. Salmonella Monitored.* This program is intended to be the basis from which the breeding-hatching industry may conduct a program for the prevention and control of salmonellosis. It is intended to reduce the incidence of *Salmonella* organisms in hatching eggs and day-old waterfowl through an effective and practical sanitation program at the breeder farm and in the hatchery. This will afford other segments of the poultry industry an opportunity to reduce the incidence of Salmonella in their products.

(1) A flock and the hatching eggs and day-old waterfowl produced from it must meet the following requirements, as determined by the Official State Agency, to be eligible for this classification:

(i) The flock is maintained in compliance with isolation, sanitation, and management procedures for Salmonella in accordance with part 147 of this subchapter.

(ii) If feed contains animal protein, the protein products must have been heated throughout to a minimum temperature of 190 °F or above, or to a minimum temperature of 165 °F for at least 20 minutes, or to a minimum temperature of 184 °F under 70 lbs. pressure during the manufacturing process.

(iii) Feed shall be stored and transported in a manner that prevents contamination.

(iv) Waterfowl shall be hatched in a hatchery whose sanitation is maintained in accordance with part 147 of this subchapter and sanitized or fumigated in accordance with part 147 of this subchapter.

(v) An Authorized Agent shall take environmental samples from the hatchery every 30 days, i.e., meconium or box liner paper. An authorized laboratory for Salmonella shall examine the samples bacteriologically.

(vi) An Authorized Agent shall take environmental samples in accordance with part 147 of this subchapter from each flock at 4 months of age and every 30 days thereafter. An authorized laboratory for Salmonella shall examine the environmental samples bacteriologically.

(vii) Flocks may be vaccinated with a paratyphoid vaccine: *Provided,* that a sample of at least 100 birds will be segregated and shall remain unvaccinated until the flock reaches at least 4 months of age.

(2) The Official State Agency may monitor the effectiveness of the egg sanitation practices in accordance with part 147 of this subchapter.

(3) To claim products are of this classification, all products shall be derived from a hatchery and flock that meet the requirements of the classification.

(4) This classification may be revoked by the Official State Agency if the participant fails to follow recommended corrective measures.

[76 FR 15794, Mar. 22, 2011, as amended at 79 FR 38764, July 9, 2014; 81 FR 53250, Aug. 12, 2016]

§ 145.94 Terminology and classification; States.

(a) *U.S. Pullorum-Typhoid Clean State.* (1) A State will be declared a U.S. Pullorum-Typhoid Clean State when it has been determined by the Service that:

(i) The State is in compliance with the provisions contained in §§ 145.23(b)(3)(i) through (vii), 145.33(b)(3)(i) through (vii), 145.43(b)(3)(i) through (vi), 145.53(b)(3)(i) through (vii), 145.73(b)(2)(i), 145.83(b)(2)(i), and 145.93(b)(3)(i) through (vii).

(ii) No pullorum disease or fowl typhoid is known to exist nor to have existed in hatchery supply flocks within the State during the preceding 12 months: *Provided,* That pullorum disease or fowl typhoid found within the preceding 24 months in waterfowl, exhibition poultry, and game bird breeding flocks will not prevent a State that is otherwise eligible from qualifying.

(2) Discontinuation of any of the conditions described in paragraph (a)(1)(i) of this section, or repeated outbreaks of pullorum or typhoid occur in hatchery supply flocks described in paragraph (a)(1)(ii) of this section, or if an infection spreads from the originating premises, the Service shall have grounds to revoke its determination

that the State is entitled to this classification. Such action shall not be taken until a thorough investigation has been made by the Service and the Official State Agency has been given an opportunity for a hearing in accordance with rules of practice adopted by the Administrator.

(b) [Reserved]

PART 146—NATIONAL POULTRY IMPROVEMENT PLAN FOR COMMERCIAL POULTRY

Subpart A—General Provisions

Subpart B—Special Provisions for Commercial Table-Egg Layer Flocks

Subpart C—Special Provisions for Meat-Type Chicken Slaughter Plants

Subpart D—Special Provisions for Meat-Type Turkey Slaughter Plants

Subpart E—Special Provisions for Commercial Upland Game Birds, Commercial Waterfowl, Raised-for-Release Upland Game Birds, and Raised-for-Release Waterfowl

AUTHORITY: 7 U.S.C. 8301–8317; 7 CFR 2.22, 2.80, and 371.4.

SOURCE: 71 FR 56328, Sept. 26, 2006, unless otherwise noted.

Subpart A—General Provisions

§ 146.1 Definitions.

Except where the context otherwise requires, for the purposes of this subpart the following terms shall be construed, respectively, to mean:

Administrator. The Administrator, Animal and Plant Health Inspection Service, or any person authorized to act for the Administrator.

Affiliated flock. A meat-type flock that is owned by or has an agreement to participate in the Plan with a slaughter plant and that participates in the Plan through that slaughter plant.

Animal and Plant Health Inspection Service (APHIS). The Animal and Plant Health Inspection Service of the U.S. Department of Agriculture.

Authorized Agent. Any person designated under § 146.10(a) to perform functions under this part.

Authorized laboratory. An authorized laboratory is a laboratory that meets the requirements of § 147.52 and is thus qualified to perform the assays in accordance with part 147 of this subchapter.

Classification. A designation earned by participation in a Plan program.

Commercial meat-type flock. All of the meat-type chickens, spent fowl, meat-type turkeys, commercial upland game birds, or commercial waterfowl on one farm. However, at the discretion of the Official State Agency, any group of poultry which is segregated from another group in a manner sufficient to prevent the transmission of H5/H7 LPAI and has been so segregated for a period of at least 21 days may be considered as a separate flock.

Commercial table-egg layer flock. All table-egg layers of common age or pullet source on one premises.

Commercial table-egg layer premises. A farm containing contiguous flocks of commercial table-egg layers under common ownership.

Commercial table-egg layer pullet flock. A table-egg layer flock prior to the onset of egg production.

Cooperating State Agency. Any State authority recognized by the Department to cooperate in the administration of the provisions of part 56 of this chapter. This may include the State animal health authority or the Official State Agency.

Department. The U.S. Department of Agriculture.

Domesticated. Propagated and maintained under the control of a person.

Equivalent. Requirements which are equal to or exceed the program, conditions, criteria, or classifications with which they are compared, as determined by the Official State Agency and with the concurrence of the Service.

H5/H7 low pathogenic avian influenza (LPAI). An infection of poultry caused by an influenza A virus of H5 or H7 subtype that has an intravenous pathogenicity index in 6-week-old chickens less than or equal to 1.2 or causes less than 75 percent mortality in 4- to 8-week-old chickens infected intravenously, or an infection with influenza A viruses of H5 or H7 subtype with a cleavage site that is not consistent with a previously identified highly pathogenic avian influenza virus.

H5/H7 LPAI virus infection (infected). (1) Poultry will be considered to be infected with H5/H7 LPAI for the purposes of this part if:

(i) H5/H7 LPAI virus has been isolated and identified as such from poultry; or

(ii) Viral antigen or viral RNA specific to the H5 or H7 subtype of AI virus has been detected in poultry; or

(iii) Antibodies to the H5 or H7 subtype of the AI virus that are not a consequence of vaccination have been detected in poultry. If vaccine is used, methods should be used to distinguish vaccinated birds from birds that are both vaccinated and infected. In the case of isolated serological positive results, H5/H7 LPAI infection may be ruled out on the basis of a thorough epidemiological investigation that does not demonstrate further evidence of H5/H7 LPAI infection, as determined by the Cooperating State Agency, the Official State Agency, and APHIS.

(2) The official determination that H5/H7 LPAI virus has been isolated and identified, viral antigen or viral RNA specific to the H5 or H7 subtype of AI virus has been detected, or antibodies to the H5 or H7 subtype of AI virus have been detected may only be made by the National Veterinary Services Laboratories.

Official State Agency. The State authority recognized by the Department to cooperate in the administration of the Plan.

Person. A natural person, firm, or corporation.

Plan. The provisions of the National Poultry Improvement Plan contained in this part.

Poultry. Domesticated fowl, including chickens, turkeys, waterfowl, and game birds, except doves and pigeons, that are bred for the primary purpose of producing eggs or meat.

Program. Management, sanitation, testing, and monitoring procedures which, if complied with, will qualify, and maintain qualification for, designation of a flock, a slaughter plant, or a State by an official Plan classification and illustrative design, as described in § 146.9 of this part.

Service. The Animal and Plant Health Inspection Service of the U.S. Department of Agriculture.

State. Any of the States, the District of Columbia, the Commonwealth of Puerto Rico, Guam, the Commonwealth of the Northern Mariana Islands, the Virgin Islands of the United States, or any territory or possession of the United States.

State Inspector. Any person employed or authorized under § 146.10(b) to perform functions under this part.

United States. All of the States.

[71 FR 56328, Sept. 26, 2006, as amended at 74 FR 14715, Apr. 1, 2009; 75 FR 10658, Mar. 9, 2010; 76 FR 15796, Mar. 22, 2011; 79 FR 38765, July 9, 2014; 81 FR 53250, Aug. 12, 2016]

§ 146.2 Administration.

(a) The Department cooperates through a Memorandum of Understanding with the Official State Agency in the administration of the Plan. In the Memorandum of Understanding, the Official State Agency must designate a contact representative to serve as a liaison between the Service and the Official State Agency.

(b) The administrative procedures and decisions of the Official State Agency are subject to review by the Service. The Official State Agency shall carry out the administration of the Plan within the State according to the applicable provisions of the Plan and the Memorandum of Understanding.

(c)(1) An Official State Agency may accept for participation a commercial table-egg layer pullet flock, commercial table-egg layer flock, or a commercial meat-type flock (including an affiliated flock) located in another participating State under a mutual understanding and agreement, in writing, between the two Official State Agencies regarding conditions of participation and supervision.

(2) An Official State Agency may accept for participation a commercial table-egg layer pullet flock, commercial table-egg layer flock, or a commercial meat-type flock (including an affiliated flock) located in a State that does not participate in the Plan under a mutual understanding and agreement, in writing, between the owner of the flock and the Official State Agency regarding conditions of participation and supervision.

(d) The Official State Agency of any State may adopt regulations applicable to the administration of the Plan in such State further defining the provisions of the Plan or establishing higher standards, compatible with the Plan.

(e) An authorized laboratory will conduct tests in accordance with part 147 of this subchapter when determining the status of a participating flock with respect to an official Plan classification.

(f) Cooperating State Agencies will be responsible for making the determination to request Federal assistance under part 56 of this chapter in the event of an outbreak of H5/H7 LPAI.

[71 FR 56328, Sept. 26, 2006, as amended at 74 FR 14716, Apr. 1, 2009; 75 FR 10658, Mar. 9, 2010; 79 FR 38765, July 9, 2014; 81 FR 53250, Aug. 12, 2016]

§ 146.3 Participation.

(a) Any commercial table-egg layer pullet flock, table-egg producer, raised-for-release upland game bird premises, and raised-for-release waterfowl premises and any commercial upland game bird, commercial waterfowl, meat-type chicken or meat-type turkey slaughter plant, including its affiliated flocks, may participate in the Plan when the producer or plant has demonstrated, to the satisfaction of the Official State Agency, that its facilities, personnel, and practices are adequate for carrying out the relevant special provisions of this part and has signed an agreement with the Official State Agency to comply with the relevant special provisions of this part.

(b) Each participant shall comply with the Plan throughout the operating year, or until released by the Official State Agency.

(c) A participating slaughter plant shall participate with all of the commercial upland game bird, commercial waterfowl, meat-type chicken, spent fowl, and/or meat-type turkey flocks that are processed at the facility, including affiliated flocks. Affiliated flocks must participate through a written agreement with a participating slaughter plant that is approved by the Official State Agency.

(d) Participation in the Plan shall entitle the participant to use the Plan emblem reproduced as follows:

FIGURE 1.

[71 FR 56328, Sept. 26, 2006, as amended at 74 FR 14716, Apr. 1, 2009; 79 FR 38765, July 9, 2014; 81 FR 53250, Aug. 12, 2016]

§ 146.4 General provisions for all participating flocks and slaughter plants.

(a) Records that establish the identity of products handled shall be maintained in a manner satisfactory to the Official State Agency.

(b) Material that is used to advertise products shall be subject to inspection by the Official State Agency at any time.

(c) Advertising must be in accordance with the Plan, and applicable rules and regulations of the Official State Agency and the Federal Trade Commission. A participant advertising products as being of any official classification may include in their advertising reference to associated or franchised slaughter or production facilities only when such facilities produce products of the same classification.

(d) Each participant shall be assigned a permanent approval number by the Service. This number, prefaced by the numerical code of the State, will be the official approval number of the participant and may be used on each certificate, invoice, shipping label, or other document used by the participant in the sale of the participant's products. Each Official State Agency which requires an approval number for out-of-State participants to ship into its State shall honor this number.

(Approved by the Office of Management and Budget under control number 0579–0007)

[71 FR 56328, Sept. 26, 2006, as amended at 75 FR 10658, Mar. 9, 2010]

§ 146.5 Specific provisions for all participating flocks.

(a) Participating flocks, and all equipment used in connection with the flocks, shall be separated from nonparticipating flocks in a manner acceptable to the Official State Agency.

(b) Poultry equipment, and poultry houses and the land in the immediate vicinity thereof, shall be kept in sanitary condition in accordance with part 147 of this subchapter.

[71 FR 56328, Sept. 26, 2006, as amended at 79 FR 38765, July 9, 2014]

§ 146.6 Specific provisions for participating slaughter plants.

(a) Only commercial upland game bird, commercial waterfowl, meat-type chicken, and meat-type turkey slaughter plants that are under continuous inspection by the Food Safety and Inspection Service of the Department or under State inspection that the Food Safety and Inspection Service has recognized as equivalent to Federal inspection may participate in the Plan.

(b) To participate in the Plan, meat-type chicken, meat-type turkey, and commercial upland game bird and commercial waterfowl slaughter plants must follow the relevant special provisions in §§ 146.33(a), 146.43(a), and 146.53(a), respectively, for sample collection and flock monitoring, unless they are exempted from the special provisions under §§ 146.32(b), 146.42(b), or 146.52(b), respectively.

[74 FR 14716, Apr. 1, 2009]

§ 146.7 Terminology and classification; general.

The official classification terms defined in §§ 146.8 and 146.9 and the various designs illustrative of the official classifications reproduced in § 146.9 may be used only by participants and to describe products that have met all of the specific requirements of such classifications.

§ 146.8 Terminology and classification; slaughter plants.

Participating slaughter plants shall be designated as "U.S. H5/H7 Avian Influenza Monitored." All Official State Agencies shall be notified by the Service of additions, withdrawals, and changes in classification.

§ 146.9 Terminology and classification; flocks, products, and States.

Participating flocks, products produced from them, and States that have met the requirements of a classification in this part may be designated by the corresponding illustrative design in this section.

(a) *U.S. H5/H7 Avian Influenza Monitored.* (See §§ 146.23(a), 146.33(a), 146.43(a), and 146.53(a) and (b).)

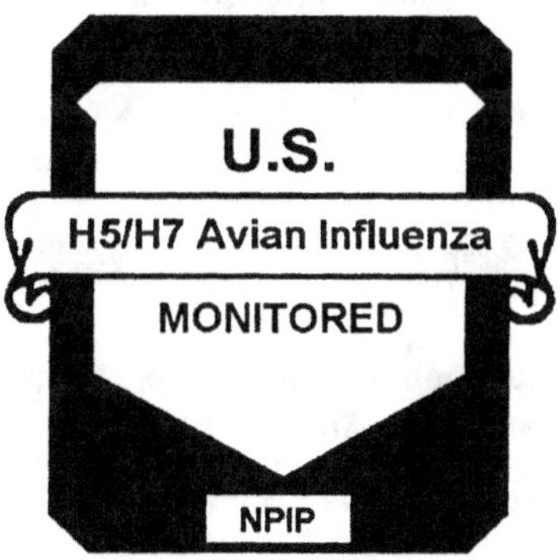

Figure 2.

(b) *U.S. H5/H7 Avian Influenza Monitored State, Layers.* (See § 146.24.)

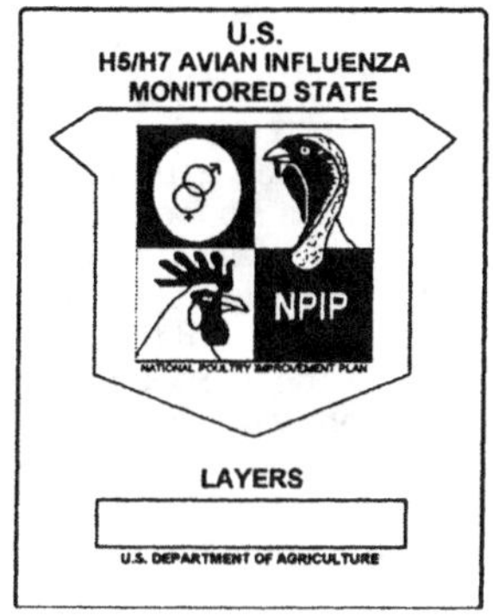

Figure 3.

(c) *U.S. H5/H7 Avian Influenza Monitored State, Turkeys.* (See § 146.44.)

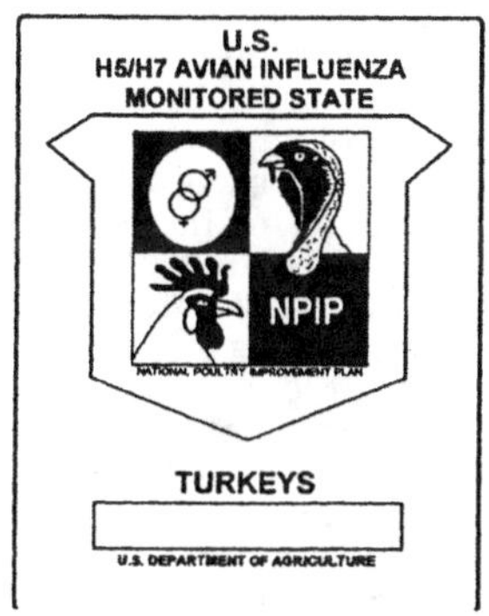

Figure 4.

[71 FR 56328, Sept. 26, 2006, as amended at 74 FR 14716, Apr. 1, 2009; 76 FR 15796, Mar. 22, 2011]

§ 146.10 Supervision.

(a) The Official State Agency may designate qualified persons as Authorized Agents to do the sample collecting provided for in § 146.13 of this part.

(b) The Official State Agency shall employ or authorize qualified persons as State Inspectors to perform the selecting and testing of participating flocks and to perform the official inspections necessary to verify compliance with the requirements of the Plan.

(c) Authorities issued to Authorized Agents or State Inspectors under the provisions of this section shall be subject to cancellation by the Official State Agency on the grounds of incompetence or failure to comply with the provisions of the Plan or regulations of the Official State Agency. Such actions shall not be taken until thorough investigation has been made by the Official State Agency and the authorized person has been given notice of the proposed action and the basis thereof and an opportunity to present his or her views.

§ 146.11 Inspections.

(a) Each participating slaughter plant shall be audited at least once annually or a sufficient number of times each year to satisfy the Official State Agency that the participating slaughter plant is in compliance with the provisions of this part. The yearly audit will consist of an evaluation of 2 weeks' worth of records, selected at random, of the following data:

(1) The actual flock slaughter date for each flock. This information must come from a verifiable source. Verifiable sources include electronic record systems that have oversight from the Department's Grain Inspectors, Packers and Stockyards Administration or Food Safety and Inspection Service (FSIS) documents such as FSIS Form 9061–2.

(2) Laboratory test results for each flock slaughtered with the sample collection date and test result. The test must be NPIP-approved and performed in an authorized laboratory of the NPIP.

(b) A flock will be considered to be conforming to protocol if it meets the requirements as described in § 146.33(a), § 146.43(a), or § 146.53(a).

(c) Two or more flocks that are found to be not conforming to protocol in the yearly audit for a slaughter plant shall be cause for a deficiency rating for that plant. However, if the root cause for the deficiency was identified, corrected, and documented, the plant will be eligible for an immediate reevaluation of 2 additional weeks' worth of records, again selected at random. If no more than one missed flock is identified in this reevaluation, the plant will be considered in compliance and no further action will be required. Plants found to be deficient must provide a written corrective action plan to the auditor within 2 weeks of receipt of the deficiency rating. A followup audit on the information in paragraphs (a)(1) and (a)(2) of this section will occur within 90 days from the receipt of the corrective action plan. Slaughter plants will retain their classification and may continue to use the Plan emblem in § 146.9(a) during this process. A failure on the followup audit may result in disbarment from participation according to the procedures in § 146.12.

(d) On-site inspections of any participating flocks and premises will be conducted if a State Inspector determines that a breach of testing has occurred for the Plan programs for which the flocks are certified.

(e) The official H5/H7 LPAI testing records of all participating flocks and slaughter plants shall be examined annually by a State Inspector. Official H5/H7 LPAI testing records shall be maintained for 3 years.

(Approved by the Office of Management and Budget under control number 0579–0007)

[71 FR 56328, Sept. 26, 2006, as amended at 74 FR 14716, Apr. 1, 2009; 75 FR 10658, Mar. 9, 2010; 81 FR 53250, Aug. 12, 2016]

§ 146.12 Debarment from participation.

Participants in the Plan who, after investigation by the Official State Agency or its representative, are notified in writing of their apparent noncompliance with the Plan provisions or regulations of the Official State Agency shall be afforded a reasonable time, as specified by the Official State Agency, within which to demonstrate or achieve compliance. If compliance is not demonstrated or achieved within the specified time, the Official State Agency may debar the participant from further participation in the Plan for such period, or indefinitely, as the Official State Agency may deem appropriate. The debarred participant shall be afforded notice of the bases for the debarment and opportunity to present his or her views with respect to the debarment in accordance with procedures adopted by the Official State Agency. The Official State Agency shall thereupon decide whether the debarment order shall continue in effect. Such decision shall be final unless the debarred participant, within 30 days after the issuance of the debarment order, requests the Administrator to determine the eligibility of the debarred participant for participation in the Plan. In such an event, the Administrator shall determine the matter de novo in accordance with the rules of practice in 7 CFR part 50, which are hereby made applicable to proceedings before the Administrator under this section. The definitions in 7 CFR 50.10 and the following definitions shall apply with respect to terms used in such rules of practice:

(a) *Administrator* means the Administrator, Animal and Plant Health Inspection Service of the U.S. Department of Agriculture, or any officer or employee to whom authority has heretofore been delegated or to who authority may hereafter be delegated to act in his or her stead.

(b) [Reserved]

§ 146.13 Testing.

(a) *Samples.* Either egg or blood samples may be used for testing. Samples must be collected in accordance with the following requirements:

(1) *Egg samples.* Egg samples must be collected and prepared in accordance with part 147 of this subchapter.

(2) *Blood samples.* Blood samples obtained in the slaughter plant should be collected after the kill cut with birds remaining on the kill line. Hold an open 1.5 mL snap cap micro-centrifuge tube under the neck of the bird directly after the kill cut and collect drips of blood until the tube is half full. Keep the blood tubes at room temperature for the clot to form, which should require a minimum of 4 hours and a maximum of 12 hours. Refrigerate the tube after the clot has formed. Put tubes in a container and label it with plant name, date, shift (A.M. or Day, P.M. or Night), and flock number. After the clot is formed, the clot should be removed by the Authorized Agent in order to ensure good-quality sera. Prepare a laboratory submission form and ship samples with submission forms to the laboratory in a polystyrene foam cooler with frozen ice packs. Submission forms and the manner of submission must be approved by the Official State Agency and the authorized laboratory to ensure that there is sufficient information to identify the samples and that the samples are received in an acceptable condition for further tests to be reliably performed. Blood samples should be shipped routinely to the laboratory. Special arrangements should be developed for samples held over the weekend to ensure that the samples can be reliably tested. Blood samples for official tests shall be drawn by an Authorized Agent or State Inspector.

(b) *Avian influenza.* The official tests for avian influenza are described in paragraphs (b)(1) and (b)(2) of this section:

(1) *Antibody detection tests*—(i) *Enzyme-linked immunosorbent assay (ELISA).* ELISA must be conducted using test kits approved by the Department and the Official State Agency and must be conducted in accordance with the recommendations of the producer or manufacturer.

(ii) *The agar gel immunodiffusion (AGID) test.* (A) The AGID test must be conducted on all ELISA-positive samples.

(B) The AGID test must be conducted using reagents approved by the Department and the Official State Agency.

(C) The AGID test for avian influenza must be conducted in accordance with part 147 of this subchapter. The test can be conducted on egg yolk or blood samples. The AGID test is not recommended for use in waterfowl.

(D) Positive tests for the AGID must be further tested by Federal Reference Laboratories using appropriate tests for confirmation. Final judgment may be based upon further sampling and appropriate tests for confirmation.

(2) *Agent detection tests.* Agent detection tests may be used to detect influenza A matrix gene or protein but not to determine hemagglutinin or neuraminidase subtypes. Samples for this testing should be collected from naturally occurring flock mortality or clinically ill birds.

(i) *The real time reverse transcriptase/polymerase chain reaction (RRT–PCR) assay.* (A) The RRT–PCR tests must be conducted using reagents approved by the Department and the Official State

Agency. The RRT–PCR must be conducted using the National Veterinary Services Laboratories (NVSL) official protocol for RRT–PCR and must be conducted by personnel who have passed an NVSL proficiency test.

(B) Positive results from the RRT–PCR must be further tested by Federal Reference Laboratories using appropriate tests for confirmation. Final judgment may be based upon further sampling and appropriate tests for confirmation.

(ii) *USDA-licensed type A influenza antigen capture immunoassay (ACIA).* (A) The USDA-licensed type A influenza ACIA must be conducted using test kits approved by the Department and the Official State Agency and must be conducted in accordance with the recommendations of the producer or manufacturer.

(B) Chicken and turkey flocks that test positive on the ACIA must be retested using the RRT–PCR or virus isolation. Positive results from the RRT–PCR or virus isolation must be further tested by Federal Reference Laboratories using appropriate tests for confirmation. Final judgment may be based upon further sampling and appropriate tests for confirmation.

(3) The official determination of a flock as positive for the H5 or H7 subtypes avian influenza may be made only by NVSL.

(Approved by the Office of Management and Budget under control number 0579–0007)

[71 FR 56328, Sept. 26, 2006, as amended at 74 FR 14716, Apr. 1, 2009; 75 FR 10658, Mar. 9, 2010; 79 FR 38765, July 9, 2014]

§ 146.14 Diagnostic surveillance program for H5/H7 low pathogenic avian influenza.

(a) The Official State Agency must develop a diagnostic surveillance program for H5/H7 low pathogenic avian influenza for all poultry in the State. The exact provisions of the program are at the discretion of the States. The Service will use the standards in paragraph (b) of this section in assessing individual State plans for adequacy, including the specific provisions that the State developed. The standards should be used by States in developing those plans.

(b) Avian influenza must be a disease reportable to the responsible State authority (State veterinarian, etc.) by all licensed veterinarians. To accomplish this, all laboratories (private, State, and university laboratories) that perform diagnostic procedures on poultry must examine all submitted cases of unexplained respiratory disease, egg production drops, and mortality for avian influenza by both an approved serological test and an approved antigen detection test. Memoranda of understanding or other means must be used to establish testing and reporting criteria (including criteria that provide for reporting H5 and H7 low pathogenic avian influenza directly to the Service) and approved testing methods. In addition, States should conduct outreach to poultry producers, especially owners of smaller flocks, regarding the importance of prompt reporting of clinical symptoms consistent with avian influenza.

(Approved by the Office of Management and Budget under control number 0579–0007)

[71 FR 56328, Sept. 26, 2006, as amended at 75 FR 10658, Mar. 9, 2010]

Subpart B—Special Provisions for Commercial Table-Egg Layer Flocks

§ 146.21 Definitions.

Table-egg layer. A domesticated chicken grown for the primary purpose of producing eggs for human consumption.

Table-egg layer pullet. A sexually immature domesticated chicken grown for the primary purpose of producing eggs for human consumption.

[71 FR 56328, Sept. 26, 2006, as amended at 76 FR 15796, Mar. 22, 2011]

§ 146.22 Participation.

(a) Participating commercial table-egg layer flocks shall comply with the applicable general provisions of subpart A of this part and the special provisions of subpart B of this part.

(b) Commercial table-egg laying premises with fewer than 75,000 birds are exempt from the special provisions of subpart B of this part.

§ 146.23 Terminology and classification; flocks and products.

Participating flocks which have met the respective requirements specified in this section may be designated by the following terms and the corresponding designs illustrated in § 146.9 of this part:

(a) *U.S. H5/H7 Avian Influenza Monitored*—(1) *Table-egg layer pullet flocks.* This program is intended to be the basis from which the table-egg layer industry may conduct a program to monitor for the H5/H7 subtypes of avian influenza. It is intended to determine the presence of the H5/H7 subtypes of avian influenza in table-egg layer pullets through routine surveillance of each participating commercial table-egg layer pullet flock. A flock will qualify for this classification when the Official State Agency determines that it has met one of the following requirements:

(i) It is a commercial table-egg layer pullet flock in which a minimum of 11 birds have been tested negative to the H5/H7 subtypes of avian influenza as provided in § 146.13(b) within 30 days prior to movement; or

(ii) It is a commercial table-egg layer pullet flock that has an ongoing active and diagnostic surveillance program for the H5/H7 subtypes of avian influenza in which the number of birds tested is equivalent to the number required in paragraph (a)(1)(i) of this section and that is approved by the Official State Agency and the Service.

(2) *Table-egg layer flocks.* This program is intended to be the basis from which the table-egg layer industry may conduct a program to monitor for the H5/H7 subtypes of avian influenza. It is intended to determine the presence of the H5/H7 subtypes of avian influenza in table-egg layer through routine surveillance of each participating commercial table-egg layer flock. A flock will qualify for this classification when the Official State Agency determines that it has met the following requirements:

(i) It is a commercial table-egg layer flock in which a minimum of 11 birds have been tested negative to the H5/H7 subtypes of avian influenza as provided in § 146.13(b) within 30 days prior to disposal; and either

(ii) It is a commercial table-egg layer flock in which a minimum of 11 birds have been tested negative for the H5/H7 subtypes of avian influenza as provided in § 146.13(b) within a 12-month period; or

(iii) It is a commercial table-egg layer flock that has an ongoing active and diagnostic surveillance program for the H5/H7 subtypes of avian influenza in which the number of birds tested is equivalent to the number required in paragraph (a)(2)(i) or paragraph (a)(2)(ii) of this section and that is approved by the Official State Agency and the Service.

(b) [Reserved]

[71 FR 56328, Sept. 26, 2006, as amended at 76 FR 15796, Mar. 22, 2011; 79 FR 38765, July 9, 2014; 79 FR 71624, Dec. 3, 2014]

§ 146.24 Terminology and classification; States.

(a) *U.S. H5/H7 Avian Influenza Monitored State, Layers.* (1) A State will be declared a U.S. H5/H7 Avian Influenza Monitored State, Layers when it has been determined by the Service that:

(i) All commercial table-egg layer flocks and all commercial table-egg layer pullet flocks that supply those flocks in production within the State that are not exempt from the special provisions of this subpart B under § 146.22 are classified as U.S. H5/H7 Avian Influenza Monitored under § 146.23(a) of this part;

(ii) All egg-type chicken breeding flocks in production within the State are classified as U.S. Avian Influenza Clean under § 145.23(h) of this subchapter;

(iii) All persons performing poultry disease diagnostic services within the State are required to report to the Official State Agency, within 24 hours, the source of all table-egg layer and table-egg layer pullet specimens that were deemed positive on an official test for avian influenza, as designated in § 146.13(a) of this chapter;

(iv) All table-egg layer and table-egg layer pullet specimens that were deemed positive on an official test for avian influenza, as designated in § 146.13(a) of this chapter, are sent to an authorized laboratory for subtyping; and

(v) All table-egg layer and table-egg layer pullet flocks within the State that are found to be infected with the H5/H7 subtypes of avian influenza are quarantined, in accordance with an initial State response and containment plan as described in part 56 of this chapter and under the supervision of the Official State Agency.

(2) If there is a discontinuation of any of the conditions described in paragraph (a)(1) of this section, or if repeated outbreaks of the H5/H7 subtypes of avian influenza occur in commercial table-egg layer flocks as described in paragraph (a)(1)(i) of this section, or if an infection spreads from the originating premises, the Service shall have grounds to revoke its determination that the State is entitled to this classification. Such action shall not be taken until a thorough investigation has been made by the Service and the Official State Agency has been given an opportunity for a hearing in accordance with rules of practice adopted by the Administrator.

(b) [Reserved]

(Approved by the Office of Management and Budget under control number 0579–0007)

[71 FR 56328, Sept. 26, 2006, as amended at 75 FR 10658, Mar. 9, 2010; 76 FR 15797, Mar. 22, 2011]

Subpart C—Special Provisions for Meat-Type Chicken Slaughter Plants

§ 146.31 Definitions.

Meat-type chicken. A domesticated chicken grown for the primary purpose of producing meat, including but not limited to broilers, roasters, fryers, and cornish.

Meat-type chicken slaughter plant. A meat-type chicken slaughter plant that is federally inspected or under State inspection that the Food Safety Inspection Service has recognized as equivalent to federal inspection.

Shift. The working period of a group of employees who are on duty at the same time.

Spent fowl. Domesticated poultry that were in production of hatching eggs or commercial table eggs and have been removed from such production.

[71 FR 56328, Sept. 26, 2006, as amended at 79 FR 38766, July 9, 2014]

§ 146.32 Participation.

(a) Participating meat-type chicken slaughter plants shall comply with applicable general provisions of subpart A of this part and the special provisions of this subpart C.

(b) Meat-type chicken slaughter plants that slaughter fewer than 200,000 meat-type chickens in an operating week are exempt from the special provisions of this subpart C.

(c) If spent fowl are slaughtered at meat-type chicken slaughter plants that participate in the Plan, they may participate in the Plan through the provisions of this subpart C.

[71 FR 56328, Sept. 26, 2006, as amended at 79 FR 38766, July 9, 2014]

§ 146.33 Terminology and classification; meat-type chicken slaughter plants.

Participating meat-type chicken slaughter plants that have met the respective requirements specified in this section may be designated by the following terms and the corresponding designs illustrated in § 146.9 of this part:

(a) *U.S. H5/H7 Avian Influenza Monitored.* This program is intended to be the basis from which the meat-type chicken industry may conduct a program to monitor for the H5/H7 subtypes of avian influenza. It is intended to determine the presence of the H5/H7 subtypes of avian influenza in meat-type chickens through routine surveillance of each participating meat-type chicken slaughter plant. A meat-type chicken slaughter plant will qualify for this classification when the Official State Agency determines that it has met one of the following requirements:

(1) It is a meat-type chicken slaughter plant where a minimum of 11 birds per shift are tested negative for the H5/H7 subtypes of avian influenza, as provided in § 146.13(b), at slaughter; *Provided*, that with the approval of the Official State Agency, fewer than 11 birds per shift may be tested on any given shift if the total number of birds tested during the operating month is equivalent to testing 11 birds per shift; or

(2) It is a meat-type chicken slaughter plant which accepts only meat-type chickens from flocks where a minimum of 11 birds have been tested negative for antibodies to the H5/H7 subtypes of avian influenza, as provided in § 146.13(b), no more than 21 days prior to slaughter; or

(3) It is a meat-type chicken slaughter plant that has an ongoing active and diagnostic surveillance program for the H5/H7 subtypes of avian influenza in which the number of birds tested is equivalent to the number required in paragraph (a)(1) or (a)(2) and that is approved by the Official State Agency and the Service.

(b) [Reserved]

[71 FR 56328, Sept. 26, 2006, as amended at 76 FR 15797, Mar. 22, 2011; 79 FR 38766, July 9, 2014]

Subpart D—Special Provisions for Meat-Type Turkey Slaughter Plants

§ 146.41 Definitions.

Meat-type turkey. A domesticated turkey grown for the primary purpose of producing meat.

Meat-type turkey slaughter plant. A meat-type turkey slaughter plant that is federally inspected or under State inspection that the Food Safety Inspection Service has recognized as equivalent to federal inspection.

§ 146.42 Participation.

(a) Participating meat-type turkey slaughter plants shall comply with applicable general provisions of subpart A of this part and the special provisions of this subpart D.

(b) Meat-type turkey slaughter plants that slaughter fewer than 2 million meat-type turkeys in a 12-month period are exempt from the special provisions of this subpart D.

§ 146.43 Terminology and classification; meat-type turkey slaughter plants.

Participating meat-type turkey slaughter plants which have met the respective requirements specified in this section may be designated by the following terms and the corresponding designs illustrated in § 146.9 of this part:

(a) *U.S. H5/H7 Avian Influenza Monitored.* This program is intended to be the basis from which the meat-type turkey industry may conduct a program to monitor for the H5/H7 subtypes of avian influenza. It is intended to determine the presence of avian influenza in meat-type turkeys through routine surveillance of each participating meat-type turkey slaughter plant. A participating meat-type turkey slaughter plant will qualify for this classification when the Official State Agency determines that it has met one of the following requirements:

(1) It is a meat-type turkey slaughter plant that accepts only meat-type turkeys from flocks where a minimum of 6 samples per flock have been collected no more than 21 days prior to movement to slaughter and tested negative with an approved test for type A avian influenza, as provided in § 146.13(b). It is recommended that samples be collected from flocks over 10 weeks of age with respiratory signs such as coughing, sneezing, snicking, sinusitis, or rales; depression; or decreases in food or water intake.

(2) It is a meat-type turkey slaughter plant that has an ongoing active and diagnostic surveillance program for the H5/H7 subtypes of avian influenza in which the number of birds tested is equivalent to the number required in paragraph (a)(1) and that is approved by the Official State Agency and the Service.

(b) [Reserved]

[71 FR 56328, Sept. 26, 2006, as amended at 74 FR 14717, Apr. 1, 2009; 76 FR 15797, Mar. 22, 2011; 79 FR 38766, July 9, 2014]

§ 146.44 Terminology and classification; States.

(a) *U.S. H5/H7 Avian Influenza Monitored State, Turkeys.* (1) A State will be declared a U.S. H5/H7 Avian Influenza Monitored State, Turkeys when it has been determined by the Service that:

(i) All meat-type turkey slaughter plants within the State that are not exempt from the special provisions of this subpart D under § 146.42 are classified as U.S. H5/H7 Avian Influenza Monitored under § 146.43(a) of this part;

(ii) All turkey breeding flocks in production within the State are classified as U.S. H5/H7 Avian Influenza Clean under § 145.43(g) of this subchapter;

(iii) All persons performing poultry disease diagnostic services within the State are required to report to the Official State Agency, within 24 hours, the source of all meat-type turkey specimens that were deemed positive on an official test for avian influenza, as designated in § 146.13(a) of this chapter;

(iv) All meat-type turkey specimens that were deemed positive on an official test for avian influenza, as designated in § 146.13(a) of this chapter, are sent to an authorized laboratory for subtyping; and

(v) All meat-type turkey flocks within the State that are found to be infected with the H5/H7 subtypes of avian influenza are quarantined, in accordance with an initial State response and containment plan as described in part 56 of this chapter, and under the supervision of the Official State Agency.

(2) If there is a discontinuation of any of the conditions described in paragraph (a)(1) of this section, or if repeated outbreaks of the H5/H7 subtypes of avian influenza occur in meat-type turkey flocks as described in paragraph (a)(1)(i) of this section, or if an infection spreads from the originating premises, the Service shall have grounds to revoke its determination that the State is entitled to this classification. Such action shall not be taken until a thorough investigation has been made by the Service and the Official State Agency has been given an opportunity for a hearing in accordance with rules of practice adopted by the Administrator.

(Approved by the Office of Management and Budget under control number 0579–0007)

[71 FR 56328, Sept. 26, 2006, as amended at 75 FR 10658, Mar. 9, 2010]

Subpart E—Special Provisions for Commercial Upland Game Birds, Commercial Waterfowl, Raised-for-Release Upland Game Birds, and Raised-for-Release Waterfowl

SOURCE: 74 FR 14717, Apr. 1, 2009, unless otherwise noted.

§ 146.51 Definitions.

Commercial upland game bird slaughter plant. A commercial upland game bird slaughter plant that is federally inspected or under State inspection that the U.S. Department of Agriculture's Food Safety and Inspection Service has recognized as equivalent to Federal inspection.

Commercial upland game birds. Upland game bird pheasants, quail, or partridges grown under confinement for the primary purposes of producing eggs and/or meat for human consumption.

Commercial waterfowl. Domesticated ducks or geese grown under confinement for the primary purposes of producing eggs and/or meat for human consumption.

Commercial waterfowl slaughter plant. A commercial waterfowl slaughter plant that is federally inspected or under State inspection that the U.S. Department of Agriculture's Food Safety and Inspection Service has recognized as equivalent to Federal inspection.

Raised-for-release upland game birds. Pheasants, quail, and partridge that are raised under confinement for release in game preserves and are not breeding stock.

Raised-for-release waterfowl. Waterfowl that are raised under confinement for release in game preserves and are not breeding stock.

Shift. The working period of a group of employees who are on duty at the same time.

[74 FR 14717, Apr. 1, 2009, as amended at 81 FR 53250, Aug. 12, 2016]

§ 146.52 Participation.

(a) Participating commercial upland game bird slaughter plants, commercial waterfowl slaughter plants, raised-for-release upland game bird premises, raised-for-release waterfowl premises, and commercial upland game bird and commercial waterfowl producing eggs for human consumption premises shall comply with the applicable general provisions of subpart A of this part and the special provisions of this subpart E.

(b) Commercial waterfowl and commercial upland game bird slaughter plants that slaughter fewer than 50,000 birds annually are exempt from the special provisions of this subpart E.

(c) Raised-for-release upland game bird premises, raised-for-release waterfowl premises, and commercial upland game bird and commercial waterfowl producing eggs for human consumption premises that raise fewer than 25,000 birds annually are exempt from the special provisions of this subpart E.

[74 FR 14717, Apr. 1, 2009, as amended at 81 FR 53250, Aug. 12, 2016]

§ 146.53 Terminology and classification; slaughter plants and premises.

Participating flocks which have met the respective requirements specified in this section may be designated by the following terms and the corresponding designs illustrated in § 146.9 of this part:

(a) *U.S. H5/H7 Avian Influenza Monitored.* This program is intended to be the basis from which the commercial waterfowl and commercial upland game bird industry may conduct a program to monitor for the H5/H7 subtypes of avian influenza. It is intended to determine the presence of the H5/H7 subtypes of avian influenza in commercial waterfowl and commercial upland game birds through routine surveillance of each participating slaughter plant or, in the case of egg-producing flocks, the regular surveillance of these flocks. A slaughter plant will qualify for this classification when the Official State Agency determines that it has met one of the following requirements:

(1) It is a commercial upland game bird slaughter plant or commercial waterfowl slaughter plant where a minimum of 11 birds per shift are tested negative for the H5/H7 subtypes of avian influenza, as provided in § 146.13(b), at slaughter;

(2) It is a commercial upland game bird slaughter plant or commercial waterfowl slaughter plant that only accepts commercial upland game birds or commercial waterfowl from flocks where a minimum of 11 birds per flock have been tested negative for the H5/H7 subtypes of avian influenza, as provided in § 146.13(b), no more than 21 days prior to slaughter; or

(3) It is a commercial upland game bird slaughter plant or commercial waterfowl slaughter plant that has an ongoing active and passive surveillance program for H5/H7 subtypes of avian influenza that is approved by the Official State Agency and the Service.

(4) It is a commercial upland game bird or waterfowl flock that produces eggs for human consumption where a minimum of 11 birds per flock have been tested negative to the H5/H7 subtypes of avian influenza as provided in § 146.13(b) within 30 days of disposal or within a 12 month period.

(5) It is a commercial upland game bird or waterfowl flock that has an ongoing active and passive surveillance program for H5/H7 subtypes of avian influenza that is approved by the Official State Agency and the Service.

(b) *U.S. H5/H7 Avian Influenza Monitored.* This program is intended to be the basis from which the raised-for-release upland game bird and raised-for-release waterfowl industries may conduct a program to monitor for the H5/H7 subtypes of avian influenza. It is intended to determine the presence of the H5/H7 subtypes of avian influenza through routine surveillance of each participating premises. A premises will qualify for the classification when the Official State Agency determines that a representative sample of 30 birds from the participating premises has been tested with negative results for the H5/H7 subtypes of avian influenza, as provided in § 146.13(b), every 90 days.

[74 FR 14717, Apr. 1, 2009, as amended at 76 FR 15797, Mar. 22, 2011; 81 FR 53250, Aug. 12, 2016]

PART 147—AUXILIARY PROVISIONS ON NATIONAL POULTRY IMPROVEMENT PLAN

Subpart A—Blood Testing Procedures

Sec.

Subpart B—Bacteriological Examination Procedure

Subpart C—Sanitation Procedures

Subpart D—Molecular Examination Procedures

Subpart E—Procedure for Changing National Poultry Improvement Plan

Subpart F—Authorized Laboratories and Approved Tests and Sanitation Procedures

AUTHORITY: 7 U.S.C. 8301–8317; 7 CFR 2.22, 2.80, and 371.4.

SOURCE: 36 FR 23121, Dec. 3, 1971, unless otherwise noted. Redesignated at 44 FR 61586, Oct. 26, 1979.

Subpart A—Blood Testing Procedures

§ 147.1 Blood testing procedures.

Blood testing must be conducted in a manner approved by the Administrator. Approved blood testing procedures are listed in the NPIP Program Standards, as defined in § 147.51. Blood testing procedures may also be approved by the Administrator in accordance with § 147.53(d)(1).

(Approved by the Office of Management and Budget under control number 0579–0007)

[79 FR 38766, July 9, 2014]

§§ 147.2–147.9 [Reserved]

Subpart B—Bacteriological Examination Procedure

§ 147.10 Bacteriological examination procedures.

Bacteriological examination must be conducted in a manner approved by the Administrator. Approved bacteriological examination procedures are listed in the NPIP Program Standards, as defined in § 147.51. Bacteriological examination procedures may also be approved by the Administrator in accordance with § 147.53(d)(1).

[79 FR 38766, July 9, 2014]

§§ 147.11–147.17 [Reserved]

Subpart C—Sanitation Procedures

§ 147.21 Sanitation procedures.

Sanitation must be maintained in a manner approved by the Administrator. Approved procedures for maintaining sanitation are listed in the NPIP Program Standards, as defined in § 147.51. Sanitation procedures may also be approved by the Administrator in accordance with § 147.53(d)(2).

(Approved by the Office of Management and Budget under control number 0579–0007)

[79 FR 38766, July 9, 2014; 79 FR 44263, July 31, 2014]

§§ 147.22–147.27 [Reserved]

Subpart D—Molecular Examination Procedures

SOURCE: 72 FR 1425, Jan. 12, 2007, unless otherwise noted.

§ 147.30 Molecular examination procedures.

Molecular examination must be conducted in a manner approved by the Administrator. Approved molecular examination procedures are listed in the NPIP Program Standards, as defined in § 147.51. Molecular examination procedures may also be approved by the Administrator in accordance with § 147.53(d)(1).

[79 FR 38766, July 9, 2014]

§ 147.31 [Reserved]

Subpart E—Procedure for Changing National Poultry Improvement Plan

§ 147.41 Definitions.

Except where the context otherwise requires, for the purposes of this subpart the following terms shall be construed, respectively, to mean:

Department. The U.S. Department of Agriculture.

Egg type chickens. Chickens bred for the primary purpose of producing eggs for human consumption.

Exhibition Poultry. Domesticated fowl which are bred for the combined purposes of meat or egg production and competitive showing.

Game birds. Domesticated fowl, such as pheasants, partridge, quail, grouse, and guineas, but not doves and pigeons.

Meat type chickens. Chickens bred for the primary purpose of producing meat.

NPIP Technical Committee. A committee made up of technical experts on poultry health, biosecurity, surveillance, and diagnostics. The committee consists of representatives from the poultry and egg industries, universities, and State and Federal governments and is appointed by the Senior Coordinator and approved by the General Conference Committee.

Plan Conference. A meeting convened for the purpose of recommending changes in the provisions of the Plan.

Plan or NPIP. The National Poultry Improvement Plan.

Service. The Animal and Plant Health Inspection Service, Veterinary Services, of the Department.

State. Any State, the District of Columbia, or Puerto Rico.

Waterfowl. Domesticated fowl that normally swim, such as ducks and geese.

[36 FR 23121, Dec. 3, 1971, as amended at 38 FR 3038, Feb. 1, 1973. Redesignated at 44 FR 61586, Oct. 26, 1979; 59 FR 12805, Mar. 18, 1994, as amended at 79 FR 38766, July 9, 2014]

§ 147.42 General.

Changes in this subchapter shall be made in accordance with the procedure described in this subpart: *Provided,* That the Department reserves the right to make changes in this subchapter without observance of such procedure when such action is deemed necessary in the public interest.

§ 147.43 General Conference Committee.

(a) The General Conference Committee Chairperson and the Vice Chairperson shall be elected by the members of the General Conference Committee. A representative of the Animal and Plant Health Inspection Service will serve as Executive Secretary and will provide the necessary staff support for the General Conference Committee. The General Conference Committee shall consist of one member-at-large who is a participant in the National Poultry Improvement Plan and one member to be elected, as provided in paragraph (b) of this section, from each of the following regions:

(1) North Atlantic: Maine, New Hampshire, Vermont, Massachusetts, Rhode Island, Connecticut, New York, New Jersey, and Pennsylvania.

(2) East North Central: Ohio, Indiana, Illinois, Michigan, and Wisconsin.

(3) West North Central: Minnesota, Iowa, Missouri, North Dakota, South Dakota, Nebraska, and Kansas.

(4) South Atlantic: Delaware, District of Columbia, Maryland, Virginia, West Virginia, North Carolina, South Carolina, Georgia, Florida, and Puerto Rico.

(5) South Central: Kentucky, Tennessee, Alabama, Mississippi, Arkansas, Louisiana, Oklahoma, and Texas.

(6) Western: Montana, Idaho, Wyoming, Colorado, New Mexico, Arizona, Utah, Nevada, Washington, Oregon, California, Alaska, and Hawaii.

(b) The regional committee members and their alternates will be elected by the official delegates of their respective regions, and the member-at-large will be elected by all official delegates. There must be at least two nominees for each position, the voting will be by secret ballot, and the results will be recorded. At least one nominee from each region must be from an underrepresented group (minorities, women, or persons with disabilities). The process for soliciting nominations for regional committee members will include, but not be limited to: Advertisements in at least two industry journals, such as the newsletters of the American Association of Avian Pathologists, the National Chicken Council, the United Egg Producers, and the National Turkey Federation; a FEDERAL REGISTER announcement; and special inquiries for nominations from universities or colleges with minority/disability enrollments and faculty members in poultry science or veterinary science.

(c) Three regional members shall be elected at each Plan Conference. All members shall serve for a period of 4 years, subject to the continuation of the Committee by the Secretary of Agriculture, and may not succeed themselves: *Provided*, That an alternate member who assumed a Committee member vacancy following mid-term would be eligible for re-election to a full term. When there is a vacancy for the member-at-large position, the General Conference Committee shall make an interim appointment and the appointee shall serve until the next Plan Conference at which time an election will be held. If a vacancy occurs due to both a regional member and alternate being unable to serve, the vacant position will be filled by an election at the earliest regularly scheduled national or regional Plan Conference, where members of the affected region have assembled.

(d) The duties and functions of the General Conference Committee shall be as follows:

(1) Advise and make recommendations to the Department on the relative importance of maintaining, at all times, adequate departmental funding for the NPIP to enable the Senior Coordinator and staff to fully administer the provisions of the Plan.

(2) Advise and make yearly recommendations to the Department with respect to the NPIP budget well in advance of the start of the budgetary process.

(3) Assist the Department in planning, organizing, and conducting the biennial National Poultry Improvement Plan Conference.

(4) Consider each proposal submitted as provided in §147.44 and make recommendations to subpart Committees and the Conference. Meet jointly with the NPIP Technical Committee and consider the technical aspects and accuracy of each proposal. Recommend whether new proposals (*i.e.*, proposals that have not been submitted as provided in §147.44) should be considered by the delegates to the Plan Conference.

(5) During the interim between Plan Conferences, represent the cooperating States in:

(i) Advising the Department with respect to administrative procedures and interpretations of the Plan provisions as contained in 9 CFR.

(ii) Assisting the Department in evaluating comments received from interested persons concerning proposed amendments to the Plan provisions.

(iii) Recommending to the Secretary of Agriculture any changes in the provisions of the Plan as may be necessitated by unforeseen conditions when postponement until the next Plan Conference would seriously impair the operation of the program. Such recommendations shall remain in effect only until confirmed or rejected by the next Plan Conference, or until rescinded by the committee.

(6) Serve as an official advisory committee for the study of problems relating to poultry health and as the need arises, to make specific recommendations to the Secretary of Agriculture concerning ways in which the Department may assist the industry in solving these problems.

(7) Serve as a direct liaison between the NPIP and the United States Animal Health Association.

(8) Advise and make recommendations to the Department regarding NPIP involvement or representation at poultry industry functions and activities as deemed necessary or advisable for the purposes of the NPIP.

[36 FR 23121, Dec. 3, 1971, as amended at 40 FR 1505, Jan. 8, 1975. Redesignated at 44 FR 61586, Oct. 26, 1979, and amended at 45 FR 10316, Feb. 15, 1980; 47 FR 21996, May 20, 1982; 50 FR 19900, May 13, 1985; 59 FR 12805, Mar. 18, 1994; 61 FR 11525, Mar. 21, 1996; 65 FR 8023, Feb. 17, 2000; 67 FR 8475, Feb. 25, 2002; 74 FR 14718, Apr. 1, 2009]

§ 147.44 Submitting, compiling, and distributing proposed changes.

(a) Changes in this subchapter may be proposed by any participant, Official

State Agency, the Department, or other interested person or industry organization.

(b) Except as provided in § 147.43(d)(4), proposed changes shall be submitted in writing so as to reach the Service not later than 150 days prior to the opening date of the Plan Conference, and participants in the Plan shall submit their proposed changes through their Official State Agency.

(c) The name of the proponent shall be indicated on each proposed change when submitted. Each proposal should be accompanied by a brief supporting statement.

(d) The Service will notify all persons on the NPIP mailing lists concerning the dates and general procedure of the conference. Hatchery and dealer participants will be reminded of their privilege to submit proposed changes and to request copies of all the published proposed changes.

(e) The proposed changes, together with the names of the proponents and supporting statements, will be compiled by the Service and issued in processed form. When two or more similar changes are submitted, the Service will endeavor to unify them into one proposal acceptable to each proponent. Copies will be distributed to officials of the Official State Agencies cooperating in the NPIP. Additional copies will be made available for meeting individual requests.

[36 FR 23121, Dec. 3, 1971. Redesignated at 44 FR 61586, Oct. 26, 1979, and amended at 49 FR 19807, May 10, 1984; 79 FR 38766, July 9, 2014]

§ 147.45 Official delegates.

Each cooperating State shall be entitled to one official delegate for each of the programs prescribed in parts 145 and 146 of this chapter in which it has one or more participants at the time of the Conference. The official delegates shall be elected by a representative group of participating industry members and be certified by the Official State Agency. It is recommended but not required that the official delegates be Plan participants. Each official delegate shall endeavor to obtain, prior to the Conference, the recommendations of industry members of his State with respect to each proposed change.

[41 FR 48727, Nov. 5, 1976. Redesignated at 44 FR 61586, Oct. 26, 1979, and amended at 45 FR 10317, Feb. 15, 1980; 65 FR 8023, Feb. 17, 2000; 71 FR 56333, Sept. 26, 2006; 74 FR 14718, Apr. 1, 2009; 76 FR 15797, Mar. 22, 2011]

§ 147.46 Committee consideration of proposed changes.

(a) The following committees shall be established to give preliminary consideration to the proposed changes falling in their respective fields:

(1) Egg-type breeding chickens.

(2) Meat-type breeding chickens.

(3) Breeding turkeys.

(4) Breeding waterfowl, exhibition poultry, and game birds.

(5) Breeding ostriches, emus, rheas, and cassowaries.

(6) Egg-type commercial chickens.

(7) Meat-type commercial chickens.

(8) Meat-type commercial turkeys.

(9) Commercial upland game birds and waterfowl and raised-for-release upland game birds and waterfowl.

(b) Each official delegate shall be appointed a voting member in one of the committees specified in paragraph (a) of this section.

(c) Since several of the proposals may be interrelated, the committees shall consider them as they may relate to others, and feel free to discuss related proposals with other committees.

(d) The committees shall make recommendations to the conference as a whole concerning each proposal. The committee report shall show any proposed change in wording and the record of the vote on each proposal, and suggest an effective date for each proposal recommended for adoption. The individual committee reports shall be submitted to the chairman of the conference, who will combine them into one report showing, in numerical sequence, the committee recommendations on each proposal.

(e) The committee meetings shall be open to any interested person. Advocates for or against any proposal should feel free to appear before the appropriate committee and present their views.

[36 FR 23121, Dec. 3, 1971, as amended at 41 FR 48727, Nov. 5, 1976. Redesignated at 44 FR 61586, Oct. 26, 1979, as amended at 65 FR 8023, Feb. 17, 2000; 71 FR 56333, Sept. 26, 2006; 74 FR 14718, Apr. 1, 2009]

§ 147.47 Conference consideration of proposed changes.

(a) The chairman of the conference shall be a representative of the Department.

(b) At the time designated for voting on proposed changes by the official delegates, the chairman of the General Conference Committee and the four committee chairmen shall sit at the speaker's table and assist the chairman of the conference.

(c) Each committee chairman shall present the proposals which his committee approves or recommends for adoption as follows: "Mr. Chairman. The committee for Egg-type chickens recommends the adoption of Proposal No. ______, for the following reasons (stating the reasons): I move the adoption of Proposal No. ______." A second will then be called for. If the recommendation is seconded, discussion and a formal vote will follow.

(d) Each committee chairman shall present the proposals which his committee does not approve as follows: "Mr. Chairman. The Committee for Egg-type chickens does not approve Proposal No. ______." The chairman will then ask if any official delegate wishes to move for the adoption of the proposal. If moved and seconded, the proposal is subject to discussion and voted. If there is no motion for approval, or if moved but not seconded, there can be no discussion or vote.

(e) Discussion on any motion must be withheld until the motion has been properly seconded, except that the delegate making the motion is privileged, if he desires, to give reasons for his motion at the time of making it. To gain the floor for a motion or for discussion on a motion, the official delegate in the case of a motion, or anyone in case of discussion on a motion, shall rise, address the chair, give his name and State, and be recognized by the chair before proceeding further. While it is proper to accept motions only from official delegates and to limit voting only to such delegates, it is, however, equally proper to accept discussion from anyone interested. To conserve time, discussion should be pointed and limited to the pertinent features of the motion.

(f) Proposals that have not been submitted in accordance with § 147.44 will be considered by the conference only with the unanimous consent of the General Conference Committee. Any such proposals must be referred to the appropriate committee for consideration before being presented for action by the conference.

(g) Voting will be by States, and each official delegate, as determined by § 147.45, will be allowed one vote on each proposal pertaining to the program prescribed by the subpart which he represents.

(h) A roll call of States for a recorded vote will be used when requested by a delegate or at the discretion of the chairman.

(i) All motions on proposed changes shall be for adoption.

(j) Proposed changes shall be adopted by a majority vote of the official delegates present and voting.

(k) The conference shall be open to any interested person.

[36 FR 23121, Dec. 3, 1971, as amended at 41 FR 48727, Nov. 5, 1976. Redesignated at 44 FR 61586, Oct. 26, 1979]

§ 147.48 Approval of conference recommendations by the Department.

Proposals adopted by the official delegates will be recommended to the Department for incorporation into the provisions of the NPIP. The Department reserves the right to approve or disapprove the recommendations of the conference as an integral part of its sponsorship of the National Poultry Improvement Plan.

Subpart F—Authorized Laboratories and Approved Tests and Sanitation Procedures

SOURCE: 79 FR 38766, July 9, 2014, unless otherwise noted.

§ 147.51 Definitions.

The following definitions apply in this subpart:

Administrator. The Administrator, Animal and Plant Health Inspection Service, or any other employee of the Animal and Plant Health Inspection Service delegated to act in the Administrator's stead.

Animal and Plant Health Inspection Service (APHIS, the Service). The Animal and Plant Health Inspection Service of the U.S. Department of Agriculture.

NPIP or Plan. The National Poultry Improvement Plan.

NPIP Program Standards. A document that contains tests and sanitation procedures approved by the Administrator under § 147.53 for use under this subchapter. This document may be obtained from the NPIP Web site at *http://www.poultryimprovement.org/* or by writing to the Service at National Poultry Improvement Plan, APHIS, USDA, 1506 Klondike Road, Suite 101, Conyers, GA 30094.

NPIP Technical Committee. A committee made up of technical experts on poultry health, biosecurity, surveillance, and diagnostics. The committee consists of representatives from the poultry and egg industries, universities, and State and Federal governments and is appointed by the Senior Coordinator and approved by the General Conference Committee.

§ 147.52 Authorized laboratories.

These minimum requirements are intended to be the basis on which an authorized laboratory of the Plan can be evaluated to ensure that official Plan assays are performed in accordance with the NPIP Program Standards or other procedures approved by the Administrator in accordance with § 147.53(d)(1) and reported as described in paragraph (f) of this section. A satisfactory evaluation will result in the laboratory being recognized by the NPIP office of the Service as an authorized laboratory qualified to perform the assays provided for in this part.

(a) *Check-test proficiency.* The NPIP will serve as the lead agency for the coordination of available check tests from the National Veterinary Services Laboratories. The authorized laboratory must use a regularly scheduled check test for each assay that it performs.

(b) *Trained technicians.* The testing procedures at the laboratory must be run or overseen by a laboratory technician who has attended and satisfactorily completed Service-approved laboratory workshops for Plan-specific diseases within the past 4 years.

(c) *Laboratory protocol.* Official Plan assays must be performed and reported as described in the NPIP Program Standards or in accordance with other procedures approved by the Administrator in accordance with § 147.53(d)(1). Assays must be performed using control reagents approved by the Plan or the reagent manufacturer.

(d) *State site visit.* The Official State Agency will conduct a site visit and recordkeeping audit at least once every 2 years. This will include, but may not be limited to, review of technician training records, check test proficiency, and test results. The information from the site visit and recordkeeping audit will be made available to the NPIP upon request.

(e) *Service review.* Authorized laboratories will be reviewed by the Service (NPIP staff) every 3 years. The Service's review may include, but will not necessarily be limited to, checking records, laboratory protocol, check-test proficiency, technician training, and peer review.

(f) *Reporting.* (1) A memorandum of understanding or other means shall be used to establish testing and reporting criteria to the Official State Agency, including criteria that provide for reporting H5 and H7 low pathogenic avian influenza directly to the Service.

(2) *Salmonella pullorum* and *Mycoplasma* Plan disease reactors must be reported to the Official State Agency within 48 hours.

(g) *Verification.* Random samples may also be required to be submitted for verification as specified by the Official State Agency.

[79 FR 38766, July 9, 2014, as amended at 81 FR 53251, Aug. 12, 2016]]

§ 147.53 Approved tests and sanitation procedures.

(a)(1) All tests that are used to qualify flocks for NPIP classifications must be approved by the Administrator as effective and accurate at determining whether a disease is present in a poultry flock or in the environment.

(2) All sanitation procedures performed as part of qualifying for an NPIP classification must be approved by the Administrator as effective at reducing the risk of incidence of disease in a poultry flock or hatchery.

(b) Tests and sanitation procedures that have been approved by the Administrator may be found in the NPIP Program Standards. In addition, all tests that use veterinary biologics (e.g., antiserum and other products of biological origin) that are licensed or produced by the Service and used as described in the NPIP Program Standards are approved for use in the NPIP.

(c) New tests and sanitation procedures, or changes to existing tests and sanitation procedures, that have been approved by the NPIP in accordance with the process described in subpart E of this part are subject to approval by the Administrator. NPIP participants may submit new tests and sanitation procedures, or changes to current tests and sanitation procedures, through that process.

(d)(1) Persons who wish to have a test approved by the Administrator as effective and accurate at determining whether a disease is present in a flock or in the environment may apply for approval by submitting the test, along with any supporting information and data, to the National Poultry Improvement Plan, APHIS, USDA, 1506 Klondike Road, Suite 101, Conyers, GA 30094. Upon receipt of such an application, the NPIP Technical Committee will review the test and any supporting information and data supplied with the application. If the NPIP Technical Committee determines the test to be of potential general use, the test will be submitted for consideration by the General Conference Committee of the NPIP in accordance with subpart E of this part, and the Administrator will respond with approval or denial of the test.

(2) Persons who wish to have a sanitation procedure approved by the Administrator as effective at reducing the risk of incidence of disease in a poultry flock or hatchery may apply for approval by submitting the sanitation procedure, along with any supporting information and data, to the National Poultry Improvement Plan, APHIS, USDA, 1506 Klondike Road, Suite 101, Conyers, GA 30094. Upon receipt of such an application, the NPIP Technical Committee will review the sanitation procedure and any supporting information and data supplied with the application. If the NPIP Technical Committee determines the sanitation procedure to be of potential general use, the sanitation procedure will be submitted for consideration by the General Conference Committee of the NPIP in accordance with subpart E of this part, and the Administrator will respond with approval or denial of the test.

(e)(1) When the Administrator approves a new test or sanitation procedure or a change to an existing test or sanitation procedure, APHIS will publish a notice in the FEDERAL REGISTER making available the test or sanitation procedure. The notice will also provide for a public comment period.

(2)(i) After the close of the public comment period, APHIS will publish a notice in the FEDERAL REGISTER indicating that the test or sanitation procedure will be added to the NPIP Program Standards, or that the NPIP Program Standards will be updated to reflect changes to an existing test or sanitation procedure, if:

(A) No comments were received on the notice;

(B) The comments on the notice supported the action described in the notice; or

(C) The comments on the notice were evaluated but did not change the Administrator's determination that approval of the test or sanitation procedure is appropriate based on the standards in paragraph (a) of this section.

(ii) If comments indicate that changes should be made to the test or sanitation procedure as it was made available in the initial notice, APHIS will publish a notice in the FEDERAL REGISTER indicating that changes were made to the initial test or sanitation procedure.

(iii) Whenever APHIS adds or makes changes to tests or sanitation procedures, APHIS will make available a new version of the NPIP Program Standards that reflects the additions or changes.

(iv) If comments present information that causes the Administrator to determine that approval of the test or sanitation procedure would not be appropriate, APHIS will publish a notice informing the public of this determination after the close of the comment period.

§ 147.54 Approval of diagnostic test kits not licensed by the Service.

(a) Diagnostic test kits that are not licensed by the Service (e.g., bacteriological culturing kits) may be approved through the following procedure:

(1) The sensitivity of the kit will be evaluated in at least three NPIP authorized laboratories by testing known positive samples, as determined by the official NPIP procedures found in the NPIP Program Standards or through other procedures approved by the Administrator. Field samples for which the presence or absence of the target organism or analyte has been determined by the current NPIP test should be used, not spiked samples or pure cultures. Samples from a variety of field cases representing a range of low, medium, and high analyte concentrations should be used. In some cases it may be necessary to utilize samples from experimentally infected animals. Spiked samples (clinical sample matrix with a known amount of pure culture added) should only be used in the event that no other sample types are available. Pure cultures should never be used. Additionally, laboratories should be selected for their experience with testing for the target organism or analyte with the current NPIP approved test. If certain conditions or interfering substances are known to affect the performance of the kit, appropriate samples will be included so that the magnitude and significance of the effect(s) can be evaluated.

(2) The specificity of the kit will be evaluated in at least three NPIP authorized laboratories by testing known negative samples, as determined by tests conducted in accordance with the NPIP Program Standards or other procedures approved by the Administrator in accordance with § 147.53(d)(1). If certain conditions or interfering substances are known to affect the performance of the kit, appropriate samples will be included so that the magnitude and significance of the effect(s) can be evaluated.

(3) The kit will be provided to the cooperating laboratories in its final form and include the instructions for use. The cooperating laboratories must perform the assay exactly as stated in the supplied instructions. Each laboratory must test a panel of at least 25 known positive samples. In addition, each laboratory will be asked to test at least 50 known negative samples obtained from several sources, to provide a representative sampling of the general population. The cooperating laboratories must perform a current NPIP procedure or NPIP approved test on the samples alongside the test kit for comparison.

(4) Cooperating laboratories will submit to the kit manufacturer all raw data regarding the assay response. Each sample tested will be reported as positive or negative, and the official NPIP procedure used to classify the sample must be submitted in addition to the assay response value. A completed worksheet for diagnostic test evaluation is required to be submitted with the raw data and may be obtained by contacting the NPIP Senior Coordinator. Raw data and the completed worksheet for diagnostic test evaluation must be submitted to the NPIP Senior Coordinator 4 months prior to the next scheduled General Conference Committee meeting, which is when approval will be sought.

(5) The findings of the cooperating laboratories will be evaluated by the NPIP Technical Committee, and the Technical Committee will make a majority recommendation whether to approve the test kit to the General Conference Committee at the next scheduled General Conference Committee meeting. If the Technical Committee recommends approval, the final approval will be granted in accordance with the procedures described in §§ 147.46, 147.47, and 147.48.

(6) Diagnostic test kits that are not licensed by the Service (e.g., bacteriological culturing kits) and that have been approved for use in the NPIP in

accordance with this section are listed in the NPIP Program Standards.

(b) *Approved tests modification and removal.* (1) The specific data required for modifications of previously approved tests will be taken on a case-by-case basis by the technical committee.

(2) If the Technical Committee determines that only additional field data is needed at the time of submission for a modification of a previously approved test, allow for a conditional approval for 60 days for data collection side-by-side with a current test. The submitting party must provide complete protocol and study design, including criteria for pass/fail to the Technical Committee. The Technical Committee must review the data prior to final approval. This would only apply to the specific situation where a modified test needs additional field data with poultry to be approved.

(3) Approved diagnostic tests may be removed from the Plan by submission of a proposed change from a participant, Official State Agency, the Department, or other interested person or industry organization. The data in support of removing an approved test will be compiled and evaluated by the NPIP Technical Committee, and the Technical Committee will make a majority recommendation whether to remove the test kit to the General Conference Committee at the next scheduled General Conference Committee meeting. If the Technical Committee recommends removal, the final decision to remove the test will be granted in accordance with the procedures described in §§147.46, 147.47, and 147.48.

[81 FR 53251, Aug. 12, 2016]

PART 149—VOLUNTARY TRICHINAE CERTIFICATION PROGRAM

Sec.

AUTHORITY: 7 U.S.C. 1622 and 8301–8317; 21 U.S.C. 136a; 7 CFR 2.22, 2.80, and 371.4.

SOURCE: 73 FR 60479, Oct. 10, 2008, unless otherwise noted.

§ 149.0 Purpose and scope.

The Trichinae Certification Program described in this part is intended to enhance the ability of swine producers, as well as slaughter facilities and other persons that handle or process swine from pork production sites that have been certified under the program, to export fresh pork and pork products to foreign markets.

§ 149.1 Definitions.

Accredited veterinarian. A veterinarian approved by the APHIS Administrator in accordance with part 161 of this chapter to perform functions specified in subchapters B, C, D, and G of this chapter.

Agricultural Marketing Service (AMS). The Agricultural Marketing Service of the United States Department of Agriculture.

AMS Administrator. The Administrator, Agricultural Marketing Service, or any person authorized to act for the AMS Administrator.

AMS representative. Any individual employed by or acting as an agent on behalf of the Agricultural Marketing Service who is authorized by the AMS Administrator to perform services required by this part.

Animal and Plant Health Inspection Service (APHIS). The Animal and Plant Health Inspection Service of the United States Department of Agriculture.

Animal disposal plan. A written document that describes methods for the removal and disposal of dead swine or swine remains from a pork production site.

Animal movement record. A written record of the movement of swine into or from a pork production site.

APHIS Administrator. The Administrator, Animal and Plant Health Inspection Service, or any person authorized to act for the APHIS Administrator.

APHIS representative. Any individual employed by or acting as an agent on behalf of the Animal and Plant Health Inspection Service who is authorized by the APHIS Administrator to perform the services required by this part.

Approved laboratory. A non-Federal laboratory approved by the Agricultural Marketing Service and recognized by the APHIS Administrator or FSIS Administrator for performing validated tests to determine the presence of trichinae infection in reference to the Trichinae Certification Program.

Audit. An inspection process, as provided in this part, that generates a written record documenting a pork production site's adherence to the required good production practices.

Auditor. A qualified accredited veterinarian (QAV) or a qualified veterinary medical officer (QVMO) who is trained and authorized by APHIS to perform auditing activities under the Trichinae Certification Program.

Certification (certified). A designation given by the APHIS Administrator to a pork production site for compliance with good production practices and other program requirements of the Trichinae Certification Program as provided in this part.

Certified pork. Pork products originating from certified swine from a certified production site with identity of such animals or carcasses maintained throughout receiving, handling, and processing.[1]

Certified production site. A pork production site that has attained a program status of Stage II or higher, based on adherence to good production practices and other program requirements as provided in this part.

Certified swine. Swine produced under the Trichinae Certification Program on a certified production site.

Confinement unit. A structure on a pork production site in which swine are housed and fed that is totally roofed and that is constructed in such a manner as to prevent swine from being exposed to free-flying birds and other wildlife, and from coming into contact with the carrion of free-flying birds or other wildlife.

Decertification (decertified). Removal of the certified status of a production site by the APHIS Administrator when it has been determined that the criteria of the Trichinae Certification Program are not being met or maintained.

Enzyme-linked immunosorbent assay (ELISA). A method of testing swine for the presence of trichinae infection by looking for antibodies to *Trichinella* spp. in the sera, plasma, whole blood, tissue fluid, or meat juice of swine.

EPA. The United States Environmental Protection Agency.

Feed mill quality assurance affidavit. A written statement signed by the feed mill representative and the producer that documents the quality and safety of feed or feed ingredients delivered from the feed mill to the pork production site.

Food Safety and Inspection Service (FSIS). The Food Safety and Inspection Service of the United States Department of Agriculture.

FSIS Administrator. The Administrator, Food Safety and Inspection Service, or any person authorized to act for the Administrator.

FSIS program employee. Any individual employed by or acting as an agent on behalf of the Food Safety and Inspection Service who is authorized by the FSIS Administrator to perform the services required by this part.

Good manufacturing practices. Feed manufacturing practices that reduce, eliminate, or avoid the risk of exposure of swine to *Trichinella* spp.

Good production practices. Pork production management practices that reduce, eliminate, or avoid the risk of exposure of swine to *Trichinella* spp.

Harborage. Any object, debris, clutter, or area that could serve as shelter or refuge for rodents or wildlife.

Laboratory approval audit. An audit performed by AMS representatives to determine if a laboratory meets minimum requirements for approval, as established by AMS, for performing validated tests under this part.

National Trichinae Certified Herd. All swine raised on certified production sites in the United States.

Person. Any individual, corporation, company, association, firm, partnership, society, joint stock company, or other legal entity.

[1] The labeling of all certified pork or pork products leaving a slaughter or processing facility must comply with 9 CFR 317.4 and all other applicable FSIS labeling regulations.

Pest control operator. A person trained and State-licensed in the control of pests and vermin (particularly rodents).

Pooled sample digestion method (digestion method). A method of testing swine for trichinae infection by identifying the presence of *Trichinella* spp. from a sample of the animal's muscle tissue.

Pork production site (site). A geographically definable area that includes pork production facilities and ancillary structures under common ownership or management systems and the surrounding space within a 100-foot perimeter of the confinement unit.

Positive test result. Outcome of a validated test indicating the presence of *Trichinella* spp.

Premises Identification Number (PIN). A number assigned to a pork production site by the APHIS Administrator.

Process-verification testing. Testing of a statistically valid sample of swine belonging to the National Trichinae Certified Herd at the time of slaughter using a validated test to verify that the adherence to good manufacturing practices and good production practices is resulting in the absence of *Trichinella* spp. infection in swine from that herd.

Producer. An individual or entity that owns or controls the production or management of swine.

Qualified accredited veterinarian (QAV). An accredited veterinarian who has been granted a program certification by the APHIS Administrator pursuant to § 161.5 of this chapter based on completion of an APHIS-approved training program in good production practices in swine management, and who is authorized by the APHIS Administrator to perform site audits and other specified program services required by this part. [2]

Qualified veterinary medical officer (QVMO). A VMO of the State or Federal Government who is trained in good production practices and is authorized by the APHIS Administrator to perform site audits, spot audits, and other specified program services required by this part.

Rodent control logbook. A written record that documents a rodent control program for a pork production site.

Site audit. An audit, performed by a QAV or a QVMO, to determine the trichinae risk factor status of a pork production site based on the site's adherence to all of the required good production practices that reduce, eliminate, or avoid the risk of exposure of swine to *Trichinella* spp.

Slaughter facility. A slaughtering establishment operating under the Federal Meat Inspection Act (21 U.S.C. 601 *et seq.*) or a State meat inspection act that receives certified swine under the Trichinae Certification Program.

Slaughter facility representative. Any individual employed by, or acting as an agent on behalf of, a slaughter facility who is authorized by the slaughter facility to perform the specified program services required by this part.

Spot audit. An audit of a certified pork production site performed by a QVMO to ensure program integrity and consistency.

Stage I enrolled. Preliminary program status of a pork production site attained when the APHIS Administrator approves the outcome of an initial site audit.

Stage II certified. Program status attained upon APHIS approval of a site audit of a Stage I enrolled site.

Stage III certified. Program status attained upon APHIS approval of a site audit of a Stage II certified site and maintained upon APHIS approval of subsequent site audits for renewal of Stage III certified status.

Sterile zone. An open area immediately adjacent to and surrounding the confinement unit that serves as both a buffer and detection zone for rodent and wildlife activity.

Temporary withdrawal. The voluntary withdrawal of a certified production site from the Trichinae Certification Program at the request of the producer for a period not to exceed 180 days.

Trichinae. A generic term that refers to *Trichinella* spp.

Trichinae Certification Program (program). A voluntary pre-harvest pork

[2] Accredited veterinarians interested in obtaining program certification related to the Trichinae Certification Program should contact APHIS' National Trichinae Coordinator at (515) 284–4122 or write to: USDA, APHIS, Veterinary Services, Trichinae Certification Program, 210 Walnut St., Room 891, Des Moines, IA 50309.

safety program in which APHIS certifies pork production sites that follow all of the required good production practices that reduce, eliminate, or avoid the risk of exposure of swine from their sites to *Trichinella* spp.

Trichinella spp. Parasitic nematodes (roundworms) capable of infecting many warm-blooded carnivores and omnivores, including swine.

USDA. The United States Department of Agriculture.

Validated test. An analytical method licensed by APHIS or accepted by AMS for the diagnosis of *Trichinella* spp. in swine.

Veterinary medical officer (VMO). A veterinarian employed by the State or Federal Government who is authorized to perform official animal health activities on their behalf.

[73 FR 60479, Oct. 10, 2008, as amended at 74 FR 65010, Dec. 9, 2009]

§ 149.2 Program participation.

A producer's initial enrollment and continued participation in the Trichinae Certification Program requires that the producer adhere to all of the good production practices, as confirmed by periodic site audits, and comply with other recordkeeping and program requirements provided in this part. Pork production sites accepted into the program by APHIS will participate under one of the following three program stages:

(a) *Stage I enrolled status.* (1) Stage I enrolled status signifies that the site has met good production practices and other recordkeeping and program requirements provided in this part.

(2) Swine from a Stage I enrolled site cannot be identified as products from a certified production site.

(3) A Stage I enrolled site must complete a site audit for Stage II certified status in accordance with § 149.3(d). Under § 149.3(d), the site audit must be performed no sooner than 150 days from the date the site was awarded Stage I enrolled status, and must be completed, with the audit form and payment submitted to APHIS, no later than 210 days from the date the site was awarded Stage I enrolled status.

(4) A Stage I enrolled site that is found not to be adhering to one or more good production practices as a result of a site audit or spot audit, or that fails to follow the prescribed timetable for completing a site audit and submitting the completed audit form and payment for consideration as a Stage II certified site, will be subject to a review by APHIS to consider the nature of the infraction(s), and may lose its status as a Stage I enrolled site.

(b) *Stage II certified status.* (1) Stage II certified status signifies that the site is adhering to all of the required good production practices and other recordkeeping and program requirements provided in this part.

(2) An APHIS-issued certificate or letter indicating the site's status as a Stage II certified site must be filed at the site and be readily available for inspection.

(3) Swine from a Stage II certified site may be identified as certified products from a certified production site.

(4) A Stage II certified site must complete a site audit for Stage III certified status in accordance with § 149.3(e). Under § 149.3(e), the site audit must be performed no sooner than 240 days from the date the site was awarded Stage II certified status, and must be completed, with the audit form and payment submitted to APHIS, no later than 300 days from the date the site was awarded Stage II certified status.

(5) A Stage II certified site that is found not to be adhering to one or more good production practices as a result of a site audit or spot audit, or that fails to meet the Stage III site audit requirements of § 149.3(e) within the prescribed timetable, will be subject to a review by APHIS to consider the nature of the infraction(s) and determine whether to decertify the site, as provided in paragraph (e)(1) of this section. During the time a site is decertified, swine from that site cannot be identified as certified products from a certified production site.

(c) *Stage III certified status.* (1) Stage III certified status signifies that the site is adhering to all of the required good production practices and other recordkeeping and program requirements provided in this part.

(2) An APHIS-issued certificate or letter indicating the site's status as a Stage III certified site must be filed at

the site and be readily available for inspection.

(3) Swine from a Stage III certified site may be identified as certified products from a certified production site.

(4) In order to maintain Stage III certified status, sites must arrange for site audits to renew such status according to the timetable set forth in § 149.3(f). Under § 149.3(f), the site audit must be performed no sooner than 14 months from the date the site was awarded Stage III certified status or the date that status was last renewed, and must be completed, with the audit form and payment submitted to APHIS, no later than 16 months from either the date the site was awarded Stage III certified status or the date that status was last renewed.

(5) A Stage III certified site that is found not to be adhering to one or more good production practices as a result of a site audit or spot audit, or that fails to follow the prescribed timetable for completing a site audit and submitting the completed audit form and payment to determine its continued participation as a Stage III certified site, will be subject to a review by APHIS to consider the nature of the infraction(s) and determine whether to decertify the site, as provided in paragraph (e)(1) of this section. During the time a site is decertified, swine from that site cannot be identified as certified products from a certified production site.

(d) *Change of ownership*—(1) *Stage I enrolled site.* If there is a change in ownership in a Stage I enrolled site, and the new ownership wishes to remain in the program, then the Stage I enrolled site will remain on the same timetable as under the previous ownership for purposes of completing a site audit for Stage II certified status. No additional site audit is necessary as a result of the change of ownership of the site.

(2) *Stage II or Stage III certified sites.* When a change of ownership occurs at a Stage II or Stage III certified site, the previous owner of the site must notify APHIS of this change as soon as the transaction is finalized. Within 60 days of this notification, a site audit must be performed in order for the site to maintain its certified status. It is the new ownership's responsibility that a site audit be performed within 60 days of this notification, otherwise the site may be subject to decertification, in accordance with paragraph (e)(1) of this section. If the site audit is satisfactory, then the Stage II or Stage III certified site will continue in the program, initially as a Stage II certified site. However, a new program anniversary date for that site will be established based on the date the site was audited to continue in the program as a Stage II certified site, and the producer of the site must arrange for a site audit to gain (or regain) Stage III certified status based on that new anniversary date and according to the timetable prescribed in § 149.3(e). If the results of the site audit do not meet program requirements, the Stage II or Stage III site will be subject to a review by APHIS to consider the nature of the infraction(s) and determine whether to decertify the site, as provided in paragraph (e)(1) of this section. Once a site is decertified by APHIS, either because the new ownership fails to arrange for a site audit to be performed within the allotted 60-day time period, or because the site is found not to meet program requirements, a producer wishing to participate in the program again must follow the procedures for requesting an initial audit for Stage I enrolled status. If a decertified site is reenrolled after a successful Stage I site audit, a new program anniversary date for that site will be established based on the date of reenrollment.

(e) *Site decertification and program withdrawal*—(1) *Decertification by APHIS.* (i) A Stage II or Stage III certified site that is found not to be adhering to one or more of the good production practices as a result of a site audit, or that fails to follow the prescribed timetable for completing a site audit and submitting the completed audit form and payment to continue participation in the program, will be subject to a review by APHIS to consider the nature of the infraction(s) and to determine whether the site should be decertified. Decertification will result from infraction(s) that APHIS determines to be substantive, prolonged, and/or repeated as a result of this review.

(ii) During the time a site is decertified, swine from such sites cannot be identified as certified products from a certified production site.

(iii) Once a site is decertified by APHIS, a producer wishing to participate in the program again must follow the procedures for requesting a site audit for Stage I enrolled status. If a decertified site is reenrolled after a successful Stage I site audit, a new program anniversary date for that site will be established based on the date of recertification. If a decertified site is recertified after a successful Stage II site audit, a new program anniversary date for that site will be established based on the date of recertification.

(2) *Temporary withdrawal by producer.* (i) A producer may request that one or more certified production sites be temporarily withdrawn. A producer's request must be made in writing and is subject to the APHIS Administrator's approval.

(ii) Each certified production site can be temporarily withdrawn no more than once every 2 years for a period not to exceed 180 days.

(iii) During the time a site is temporarily withdrawn:

(A) Swine from such sites cannot be identified as certified products from a certified production site; and

(B) The producer must continue to adhere to all good production practices and other recordkeeping and program requirements provided in this part, including documentation in the animal movement record of the arrival and departure of all swine from this site, as well as whether the swine arriving at the site are from certified or noncertified sources, unless a program requirement is specifically waived by the Administrator.

(iv) If granted a waiver by the Administrator, a producer may receive swine 5 weeks of age or older originating from a noncertified source during the period of withdrawal.

(v) Before being reinstated as a certified production site, the temporarily withdrawn site must pass a site audit to indicate that it is now adhering to all good production practices (including any practices waived by the Administrator at the beginning of the period of withdrawal) as follows:

(A) The site audit must be performed while the site is still under temporary withdrawal status. If swine 5 weeks of age or older originating from a noncertified source have been received at the site during the time of withdrawal, then the site audit for reinstatement must be performed within 30 days of the date the last swine from a noncertified source was removed from the site, but no later than 180 days from the date the site was granted temporary withdrawal status.

(B) If the results of the site audit are satisfactory and it is determined that the site is now adhering to good production practices and other program requirements provided in this part, then the withdrawn site will be reinstated as a Stage II certified site. The timetable for performing future site audits for attaining and renewing Stage III certified status will be based on the date the site was reinstated as a Stage II certified site.

(C) If the results of the site audit are not satisfactory, or, if the period of temporary withdrawal has exceeded 180 days, then the site will be subject to a review by APHIS to consider the nature of the infraction(s) and to determine whether to decertify the site, as provided in paragraph (e)(1) of this section. Once the site is decertified by APHIS, the producer must follow the procedures for requesting an initial site audit for Stage I enrolled status in order for the site to be reenrolled in the program. If a site is decertified by APHIS and then reenrolled after a successful Stage I site audit, a new program anniversary date for that site will be established based on the date of enrollment.

(3) *Program withdrawal.* (i) If a producer decides to withdraw one or more of pork production sites from the program, then it is the producer's responsibility to notify the APHIS Administrator in writing of this intent. When this is done, the site will be removed from the program.

(ii) If at a later date the producer requests that a site be reinstated in the program, then the producer must follow the procedures for requesting an initial audit for Stage I enrolled status. If a withdrawn site is reenrolled after a successful Stage I site audit, then a new program anniversary date for that site will be established based on the date of reenrollment.

(f) *Request for review.* If there is a conflict as to any material fact relating to the results of a site audit, spot audit, or other determination affecting a producer's program status or ability to participate in the program, the producer may submit a written request for review to the Administrator. The producer must include in the request the reasons, including any supporting documentation, why the audit result or other determination should be different than the result or determination made by the Administrator. The initial audit result or other determination will remain in force pending the completion of the Administrator's review. The decision by the Administrator upon reviewing the producer's written request will be final.

§ 149.3 Site audit.

(a) *General.* (1) The producer must contact a QAV or QVMO to request a site audit. A list of available QAVs may be obtained by accessing the Trichinae Certification Program Web site on the Internet at *http://www.aphis.usda.gov/vs/trichinae.* If a QAV is not available to perform a site audit, the producer must then contact the APHIS area office to request that a QVMO perform the site audit. The site audit is to be arranged at a mutually agreed-upon time.

(2) The producer or the producer's designated representative will accompany the auditor during the site audit.

(3) During the site audit, the auditor will record whether the producer is adhering to all of the required good production practices at the site, as provided in paragraph (b) of this section, in order to reduce, eliminate, or avoid the risk of exposure of swine to *Trichinella* spp.

(4) The auditor will use APHIS-approved audit forms in performing the site audit. After the auditor has completed all sections of the audit form, the producer or the producer's designated representative must sign the audit form attesting to the accuracy of the information obtained during the site audit and to evidence his or her intent to continue adhering to the good production practices and other program requirements, as provided in this part. The auditor also must sign the audit form at this time.

(5) If a QVMO performs the site audit, then the producer will pay the QVMO at the time the site audit is performed in accordance with the rate and other conditions set by the QVMO's governmental employer. If an APHIS-employed QVMO performs the site audit, then the producer will pay APHIS by certified check or U.S. money order for this service at a rate determined in accordance with § 149.8.

(6) In addition to the possible cost of the site audit, the producer is also responsible for paying a separate program fee in an amount specified in § 149.8 to cover APHIS' administrative costs in processing the audit and operating the program. This program fee, payable to APHIS by certified check or U.S. money order, must be remitted to the auditor at the time each site audit is performed.

(7) The auditor will submit the completed audit form, program fee, and payment for the services of an APHIS-employed QVMO, if applicable, to the nearest APHIS area office. If a QAV performs the site audit, the producer will be responsible for ensuring that the QAV submits the completed audit form and program fee to APHIS in a timely manner.

(8) Upon receipt of the completed audit form and payment, APHIS will determine the initial enrollment or certification status for the site based on an evaluation of the site audit. APHIS will provide the producer with written notification of the audit results. Pork production sites that meet all good production practices as provided in paragraph (b) of this section, as well as other program requirements provided in this part, will be issued program status at the appropriate program stage.

(9) If the site audit shows that the site does not substantively meet all good production practices or other program requirements, APHIS will provide the producer with written notification

that includes documentation of the deficiencies that prevented the site from being conferred program status.

(b) *Good production practices.* In a site audit, the auditor will determine whether all of the required good production practices are being carried out at the site to reduce, eliminate, or avoid the risk of exposure of swine to *Trichinella* spp. as follows:

(1) The movement of all non-breeding swine 5 weeks of age or older into or from the pork production site must be documented in an animal movement record, as provided in § 149.7, that ensures that all such swine moved into or from the site can be subsequently traced back to that site, or to any previous site (if applicable).

(2) All non-breeding swine entering a site must have originated from another certified production site, except that non-breeding swine less than 5 weeks of age may have originated from either a certified or noncertified production site. The animal movement record must include the PIN of the certified production site from which the swine originated. If the swine are less than 5 weeks of age and come from a noncertified site, then the animal movement record must provide the name and full address of the noncertified site where the swine originated.

(3) Feed or feed ingredients from off-site sources that are used at the site must meet good manufacturing practices or other quality assurance standards recognized by the feed industry. The adherence to good manufacturing practices or other quality assurance standards must be documented in a feed mill quality assurance affidavit, as provided in § 149.7.

(4) Swine at the site must be housed and fed in a confinement unit. The confinement unit, feed preparation and storage areas, and office areas and connecting hallways at the site must be inspected regularly and found free of signs of rodent and wildlife activity (evidence of rodent activity consists of fresh rodent droppings, fresh gnawing marks, new structural damage, rodent urine, rodent blood, rodent smear marks (body oil), rodent tracks, or recent burrowing or burrow use. Evidence of wildlife activity consists of wildlife feces, footprints, fur, or hair observed in or near the stored feed or feed ingredients, dead or live wildlife observed in or near the stored feed or feed ingredients, or wildlife burrows or nests observed in or near the stored feed or feed ingredients). Any movable harborage (exterior or interior) on the site that is not necessary to the day-to-day operation of the site must be removed. Harborage that cannot be removed or is movable but necessary to the day-to-day operation of the site (e.g., equipment) must be checked for signs of rodent or wildlife activity. In addition, domesticated animals, including pets such as dogs and cats, must be excluded from the confinement unit and feed preparation and storage areas at the site. Exterior rodent bait stations and/or traps must be placed around the perimeter of the confinement unit. Exterior rodent bait stations and/or traps also must be placed around areas of potential rodent entry into the confinement unit (*i.e.*, doorways, vent openings, loading chutes, cool cells, etc.). Interior rodent bait stations and/or traps must be placed near high-risk rodent zones such as entryways, hallways, office areas, swine load-out areas, vents, cool cells, storage areas, utility rooms, cabinets, locker rooms, bathrooms, and break rooms, and systematically maintained. Interior rodent bait stations and/or traps must be placed so that swine will not come in contact with the bait or trap. Rodent bait stations and/or traps also must be placed near exterior or interior harborage on the site that cannot be removed or that is movable but necessary to the day-to-day operation of the site. In all instances, rodent bait stations must be intact, systematically maintained, and contain fresh bait that consists of an EPA-registered rodenticide formulation that is applied according to its label. In addition, a sterile zone must be maintained around the perimeter of the confinement unit. The sterile zone must be devoid of any harborage or feed or water sources that could attract rodents or wildlife, but must contain rodent bait stations and/or rodent traps. The sterile zone also must be devoid of any vegetation unless it is decorative vegetation that is well maintained (*i.e.*, residential height

grass, flowers, shrubs, or trees). A sterile zone with decorative vegetation will require increased rodent control measures. The producer must provide documentation of rodent control practices by maintaining at the site an up-to-date rodent control logbook with a site diagram and other recordkeeping evidencing implementation of rodent control measures, which can include documents provided by a pest control operator, as provided in § 149.7.

(5) Feed or feed ingredients stored at the site must be prepared, maintained, and handled in a manner that protects the feed or feed ingredients from possible exposure to or contamination by rodents or wildlife. Any movable harborage in the immediate vicinity of feed production and feed storage areas that is not necessary to the day-to-day operation of the site must be removed. Harborage that cannot be removed or harborage that is movable but necessary to the day-to-day operation of the site (e.g., equipment, etc.) must be checked for signs of rodent or wildlife activity. Rodent bait stations and/or traps must be placed around (and in, if applicable) all feed preparation and storage areas, as well as near any harborage in the vicinity that cannot be removed or that is movable but necessary to the day-to-day operation of the site. Rodent bait stations must be intact, systematically maintained, and contain fresh bait that consists of an EPA-registered rodenticide formulation that is applied according to its label. In addition, feed or feed ingredients that are stored in paper bags must be elevated off the floor and be a sufficient distance away from the walls to allow for inspection, baiting, and/or trapping. The rodent control logbook, as provided in § 149.7, must document that adequate rodent control procedures have been implemented in the feed production and feed storage areas.

(6) Swine must not have access to dead or live wildlife at the site. Dead or live wildlife must not be intentionally fed to swine.

(7) Swine at the site must not be fed waste that contains meat.

(8) Procedures must be in place and carried out for the prompt removal and proper disposal of dead swine or swine remains found in pens in order to eliminate the opportunity for cannibalism, as well as to prevent the attraction of rodents or wildlife. Such procedures must be documented in the animal disposal plan, as provided in § 149.7.

(9) General hygiene and sanitation of the site must be maintained at all times to prevent the attraction of rodents and wildlife. Solid non-fecal waste (facility refuse) must be placed in covered receptacles and be regularly removed from the site. Spilled feed also must be regularly removed and properly disposed of.

(10) All records required under § 149.7 must be kept up to date and readily available for inspection at the site.

(c) *Initial site audit for Stage I enrolled status.* (1) Producers interested in participating in the program should request and review a pre-audit information packet prepared by APHIS that discusses the program, as well as the steps in preparing for and requesting an initial site audit.[3] When the producer and the producer's herd health personnel believe that a site meets program standards, the producer must arrange for an initial site audit, as provided in paragraph (a) of this section.

(2) Upon completion of the initial site audit and submission of the completed audit form and payment, APHIS will review the completed audit form and make a determination within 30 days as to enrollment of the site in the program. A pork production site that is found to meet all good production practices and other program requirements in this part will be awarded Stage I enrolled status.

(d) *Site audit for Stage II certified status.* (1) A producer of a Stage I enrolled site must arrange for another site audit for Stage II certified status. The site audit must be performed no sooner than 150 days (*i.e.*, approximately 5

[3] The pre-audit information packet may be obtained from a qualified accredited veterinarian (QAV), State or Federal animal health offices, or the National Pork Board, or by writing to: USDA, APHIS, Veterinary Services, Trichinae Certification Program, 210 Walnut St., Room 891, Des Moines, IA 50309. A pre-audit packet also may be requested electronically through the program Web site on the Internet at *http://www.aphis.usda.gov/vs/trichinae.*

months) from the date the site was awarded Stage I enrolled status, and must be completed, with the audit form and payment submitted to APHIS, no later than 210 days (*i.e.*, approximately 7 months) from the date the site was awarded Stage I enrolled status.

(2) APHIS will review the completed audit form and make a determination as to Stage II certified status within 7 days of receipt of the audit form and payment.

(i) A Stage I enrolled site that is found to meet all good production practices and other program requirements in this part will be awarded Stage II certified status.

(ii) A Stage I enrolled site that is found, during a site audit, not to be adhering to one or more good production practices, or that fails to follow the prescribed timetable for completing a site audit and submitting the completed audit form and payment, will be subject to a review by APHIS to consider the nature of the infraction(s), and may lose its status as a Stage I site.

(e) *Site audit for Stage III certified status.* (1) A producer of a Stage II enrolled site must arrange for another site audit for Stage III certified status. The site audit must be performed no sooner than 240 days (*i.e.*, approximately 8 months) from the date the site was awarded Stage II certified status, and must be completed, with the audit form and payment submitted to APHIS, no later than 300 days (*i.e.*, approximately 10 months) from the date the site was awarded Stage II certified status.

(2) APHIS will review the completed audit form and make a determination as to Stage III certified status within 30 days of receipt of the audit form and payment.

(i) A Stage II certified site that is found to meet all good production practices and other program requirements in this part will be awarded Stage III certified status.

(ii) A Stage II certified site that is found, during a site audit, not to be adhering to one or more good production practices, or that fails to follow the prescribed timetable for completing a site audit and submitting the completed audit form and payment, will be subject to a review by APHIS to consider the nature of the infraction(s) and determine whether to decertify the site, as provided in § 149.2(e)(1).

(f) *Site audit for renewal of Stage III certified status.* (1) A producer seeking to renew a site's Stage III certified status must arrange for another site audit. The site audit must be performed no sooner than 14 months from the date the site was awarded Stage III certified status or the date that status was last renewed, and must be completed, with the audit form and payment submitted to APHIS, no later than 16 months from either the date the site was awarded Stage III certified status or the date the that status was last renewed.

(2) APHIS will review the completed audit form and make a determination as to renewing the site's Stage III certified status within 30 days of receipt of the audit form and payment.

(i) A Stage III certified site that is found to meet all good production practices and other program requirements in this part will have its status as a Stage III certified site renewed.

(ii) A Stage III certified site that is found, during a site audit, not to be adhering to one or more good production practices, or that fails to follow the prescribed timetable for completing a site audit and submitting the completed audit form and payment, will be subject to a review by APHIS to consider the nature of the infraction(s) and determine whether to decertify the site, as provided in § 149.2(e)(1).

(Approved by the Office of Management and Budget under control number 0579–0323)

§ 149.4 Spot audit.

(a) In addition to regularly scheduled site audits, certified production sites will be subject to spot audits.

(1) *Random spot audit.* Certified production sites will be selected by the APHIS Administrator at random for a spot audit in order to:

(i) Ensure the integrity of the audit process;

(ii) Verify that the audit process is performed in a consistent manner across the program; and

(iii) Verify that all required good production practices are being maintained between regularly scheduled site audits.

(2) *Spot audit for cause.* A certified production site may be subject to a spot audit to trace back and investigate any positive test results as a result of testing of certified swine from that site at the slaughter facility.

(b) All spot audits will be performed by a QVMO. The producer of the certified production site subject to spot audit will not be charged for the spot audit. APHIS will provide the producer with written notification of the results of the spot audit, including documentation of any deficiencies noted during the audit. If the site is found not to be adhering to one or more of the required good production practices, then the site will be subject to a review by APHIS to consider the nature of the infraction and to determine whether to decertify the site, as provided in § 149.2(e)(1). Unless a spot audit results in decertification, it does not otherwise affect the timetables for the completion of site audits set forth in paragraphs (e) and (f) of § 149.3.

§ 149.5 Offsite identification and segregation of certified swine.

Certified swine moved from a certified production site to another location, whether to another certified production site, buying station, collection point, or slaughter facility, must remain segregated from noncertified swine at all times and otherwise maintain their identity as certified swine in such a way that they could be readily traced back to the certified production site from which they came. Information relating to the identification of the certified swine must be documented in the animal movement record maintained by the producer. Failure to properly segregate or maintain the identity of certified swine from noncertified swine after leaving the certified production site will result in the loss of certified status for that shipment of swine.

§ 149.6 Slaughter facilities.

Only slaughter facilities that are under continuous inspection by the Food Safety and Inspection Service or under State inspection that the Food Safety and Inspection Service has recognized as equivalent to Federal inspection may participate in the program. To participate in the program, slaughter facilities must follow the relevant provisions of this section relating to verification, segregation, testing, and recordkeeping. Participating slaughter facilities that fail to comply with any of the applicable requirements of this section will not be allowed to continue to participate in the Trichinae Certification Program and the pork or pork products prepared by the facility will not be eligible for a certificate of export that identifies the product as meeting the standards of the Trichinae Certification Program.

(a) *Verification of certification.* A slaughter facility receiving certified swine must verify the current certification status of the pork production site from which the animals came. The current certification status may be verified by maintaining dated certification documentation on file or by accessing the Trichinae Certification Program Web site on the Internet at *http://www.aphis.usda.gov/vs/trichinae.* If the slaughter facility is unable to verify a site's certification status through documentation on file or through the program Web site, the slaughter facility then should contact the APHIS area office in the State where the site is located.

(b) *Maintaining identity and segregation of certified swine and pork products.* For certified swine to be identified as certified pork, certified swine and edible pork products derived from certified swine must remain segregated from swine and edible pork products from noncertified sites throughout receiving, handling, and processing at the slaughter facility, as well as while awaiting shipment from the facility. The slaughter facility must maintain the identity of the certified swine or pork in a manner that allows the certified swine or pork to be traced back to the certified production site from which it came. A slaughter facility's failure to properly segregate or maintain the identity of certified swine and edible pork products derived from the certified swine will result in the loss of certified status for that shipment of swine, as well as the edible pork products derived from those animals.

(c) *Process-verification testing.* A slaughter facility processing certified swine is responsible for performing process-verification testing to determine the *Trichinella* spp. infection status of certified swine under its control as follows:

(1) *Validated tests.* Process-verification testing must be performed by using a validated test. When testing involves meat, the sample used for such testing must be at least 20 grams.[4]

(2) *Laboratory approval.* Process-verification testing must be performed in an approved laboratory that has been approved for trichinae testing by the Agricultural Marketing Service (AMS).[5] The approved laboratory may be maintained and operated by the slaughter facility or by another business entity either on the premises of the slaughter facility or at another location. Laboratory staff performing process-verification testing must be accredited by AMS to perform this program function. For purposes of quality assurance, all laboratory staff approved to perform process-verification testing will receive periodic proficiency test panels from AMS that must be analyzed correctly in order to maintain their approval status.

(3) *Testing sample size and frequency.* Process-verification testing must meet the following minimum requirements relating to sample size and frequency:

(i) Slaughter facility representatives shall determine the yearly processing capacity of the slaughter facility for the next 12 months. Officials may use the processing capacity over the previous 12 months if this period is representative of a typical processing year.

(ii) Slaughter facility representatives shall estimate the percentage of swine processed that are likely to come from certified production sites considering all swine expected to be processed at the slaughter facility during the selected 12-month period. Swine that come from certified production sites are considered the eligible population to be sampled.

(iii) Slaughter facility representatives shall use the Trichinae Certification Slaughter Facility Sample Size Determination Table on the Internet at *http://www.aphis.usda.gov/vs/trichinae* to find the number of samples to collect from the population of swine from certified production sites.[6] If the eligible population is not listed in that table, the next largest number will be used to determine the number of samples to collect. Select the number of samples to collect from the column on that table that reflects a 99 percent confidence level of detecting a positive carcass in a population with a prevalence rate of 0.013 percent. The number selected from the table will be the total number of samples that slaughter facility representatives must collect and test per year and per month during the selected 12-month period.

(iv) For each sample collected, slaughter facility representatives must maintain the identity of the sample using the PIN of the certified production site that was the source of the swine from which the sample was taken.

(v) FSIS program employees at the slaughter facility will review and verify that an adequate number of samples have been collected and that proper frequency of collection is maintained. FSIS will report this information to APHIS.

(vi) AMS representatives will verify through a laboratory approval audit that the laboratory performing process-verification testing is correctly following written procedures relating to the receipt, handling, identification,

[4] A copy of the testing methods and checklist for conducting validated tests may be obtained by contacting the AMS Trichinae Analyst and Laboratory Certification Program Manager, USDA, AMS, Science and Technology Programs, Technical Services Branch, 1400 Independence Ave., SW., Mail Stop 0272, Washington, DC 20250–0272. The manager may be contacted by phone at (202) 690–0621.

[5] A copy of the AMS Trichinae Accredited Laboratory Program Requirements may be obtained by contacting the AMS Trichinae Analyst and Laboratory Certification Program Manager (see footnote 4).

[6] More information regarding sampling sizes may be obtained by writing to USDA, APHIS, Veterinary Services, Trichinae Certification Program, 210 Walnut St., Room 891, Des Moines, IA 50309.

and testing of samples. These written procedures must be maintained by the laboratory in a quality assurance manual, as provided in paragraph (c)(6) of this section. In addition, a laboratory that performs process-verification testing at a location other than the slaughter facility must include a declaration of methodology used to test samples when providing test results.

(vii) The APHIS Administrator may, at APHIS' expense, periodically request that testing be performed on swine brought to the slaughter facility from specific certified production sites. Requests to test swine from specific certified production sites will count towards the slaughter facility's total monthly testing requirement.

(4) *Results of testing.* (i) The results of all process-verification testing relating to certified swine handled at the slaughter facility must be retained in a separate file or notebook as written records at the slaughter facility and must be readily available for inspection by FSIS program employees.

(ii) FSIS will report to APHIS the results of all process-verification testing.

(iii) In the event of a positive test result, the slaughter facility representative must notify the FSIS program employee designated by the FSIS Administrator immediately, who in turn will report the PIN of the certified production site that was the source of the swine from which the sample was taken and the test results of the affected sample to the respective APHIS area office. The following sequence of events must take place following a positive test result:

(A) If a test sample yields a positive test result based on the digestion method, the certified production site that was the source of the swine from which the sample was taken will be decertified.

(B) If a test sample yields a positive test result based on an ELISA method and is confirmed positive by further testing using the digestion method, the certified production site that was the source of the swine from which the sample was taken will be decertified.

(C) If a test sample yields a positive test result based on an ELISA method, but is not confirmed positive by further testing using the digestion method, then the certified production site that was the source of the swine from which the sample was taken will be investigated by APHIS.

(*1*) The investigation may include a spot audit of the affected site. Further testing of animals or carcasses from the affected site also may be performed as part of the investigation. This investigation would determine if the production facility has sufficient safeguards and is following good production practices.

(*2*) While the affected site is under investigation, its program status as a certified production site will be suspended. While the site is under suspension, the producer must continue to adhere to all of the required good production practices and other recordkeeping and program requirements provided in this part. During this suspension, swine at the site may be sent to slaughter; however, swine from the suspended site cannot be identified as product from a certified production site. The Administrator will determine the program status of the affected site within 30 days of the initiation of the suspension.

(*3*) A finding that risk factors are inadequately addressed in the site investigation or the finding of additional positive test results based on samples from animals or carcasses from the affected site will be grounds for APHIS decertification of the site.

(5) *Slaughter facility recordkeeping.* (i) All slaughter facilities that receive certified swine must maintain records relating to such animals, including the number of certified swine processed, the source of the certified swine, including the PIN of the certified production site from which the swine came from, and all test results relating to process-verification testing. Records relating to certified swine must be retained at the slaughter facility for a period of at least 3 years following the processing of such animals.

(ii) All slaughter facilities must have documented procedures on how certified swine under its control, and edible pork products derived from certified swine, will remain segregated from swine and edible pork products from noncertified sites throughout receiving, handling, and processing at the facility, as well as while awaiting shipment from the facility. The slaughter facility must also have documented procedures for maintaining the identity of the certified swine or pork with respect to the certified production site from which it came.

(iii) All such records and other documentation required to be maintained by slaughter facilities under this part must be readily available for inspection by FSIS program employees.

(6) *Approved laboratory recordkeeping.* Approved laboratories must have written procedures that specify standards for sample size, sample handling, sample identification, and sample test methods used in process-verification testing. All such written procedures must be maintained in a laboratory quality assurance manual specifically for this program, or as a separate section of an existing laboratory quality assurance manual, and must be retained at the approved laboratory throughout the time the approved laboratory is performing process-verification testing under this program. All such written procedures relating to process-verification testing must be readily available for inspection by FSIS program employees or AMS representatives.

(7) *Slaughter facility overall responsibility for process-verification testing.* The slaughter facility is responsible for obtaining testable samples and for ensuring that the correct number of testable samples are sent to the testing laboratory. Once the slaughtering facility receives the test results, it is responsible for reporting those results in its facility trichinae testing record. Moreover, the slaughter facility is responsible for ensuring that process-verification testing is carried out in accordance with this part, including the reporting of test results, regardless of whether it is performed at the slaughter facility or another location, and regardless of whether the testing is performed by slaughter facility personnel or other persons.

§ 149.7 Recordkeeping at site.

(a) Stage I enrolled sites, Stage II or Stage III certified sites, and any site that has been suspended or voluntarily decertified must maintain the following program records: Animal disposal plan, animal movement record, feed mill quality assurance affidavit (if applicable), and rodent control logbook. All such records must be readily available for inspection at the pork production site at the time of an audit by a QAV or QVMO, or by other APHIS representatives during normal business hours.

(1) *Animal disposal plan.* The animal disposal plan must meet the following minimum requirements:

(i) It must provide for the removal of all dead swine or swine remains from swine pens immediately upon detection. Inspections for purposes of detecting dead animals must occur at least once every 24 hours.

(ii) It must specify how often and at what intervals the swine pens are observed each day.

(iii) It must provide for the proper storage of dead swine or swine remains in accordance with local, State, and Federal laws and regulations. If the carcass storage facility or composting facility is located on the site, then the animal disposal plan must provide for a storage or composting facility that precludes rodent or wildlife contact with dead swine or swine remains being stored or composted.

(iv) It must provide for the disposal of swine and other mammals by rendering, incineration, composting, burial, or other means, as allowed by and in accordance with local, State, and Federal laws and regulations. For sites that use rendering services, the animal disposal plan also must include the name, address, and phone number of the renderer.

(v) It must be updated as animal disposal practices are changed at the site.

(vi) It must be signed and dated by the producer, as well as the caretaker of the site (if the caretaker is a different person than the producer).

(vii) It may be valid for a period no longer than 2 years after the date of signature by the producer and (if applicable) the site caretaker.

(2) *Animal movement record.* The animal movement record must meet the following minimum requirements:

(i) It must be filled out completely and properly, accounting for the movement of all non-breeding swine into and from the pork production site.

(ii) In the case of non-breeding swine coming into the site, it must include the date and number of arriving animals, as well as the PIN of the certified production site where the animals originated, or alternatively, if the swine are less than 5 weeks of age and originated from a noncertified site, the name and full address of the noncertified site where the animals originated. The animal movement record must clearly document that all non-breeding swine 5 weeks of age or older arriving at the site originated from another certified production site.

(iii) In the case of non-breeding swine leaving the site, it must include the date and number of departing animals, and their destination.

(iv) It must document the number of dead non-breeding swine that are removed from the site, as well as the number of dead non-breeding swine that are buried or composted at the site, if swine burial or composting is permitted in that State or locality.

(v) All entries to the animal movement record must be signed or initialed and dated by the producer or other site caretaker making the entry.

(3) *Rodent control logbook.* The rodent control logbook, which may include records from a pest control operator, must meet the following minimum requirements:

(i) It must include a rodent control diagram for the site indicating the location of all rodent bait stations and rodent traps at the site. The diagram must be updated whenever bait stations are added, moved, or removed.

(ii) It must document the number of rodent traps set (if applicable), the number of new rodent bait stations set, and how often bait is refreshed.

(iii) It must document the disposal method for all unused bait that is replaced.

(iv) It must document the brand name and active ingredient of bait, which must be EPA-registered and applied according to its label, as well as the quantity of bait used (number of pounds).

(v) If possible, it should document the number of rodents caught or killed and indicate how many were rats.

(vi) If possible, it should document the number of rats sighted monthly.

(vii) All entries to the rodent control logbook must be signed or initialed, as well as dated by the producer or other site caretaker making the entry. It must be updated at least monthly.

(4) *Feed mill quality assurance affidavit.* The feed mill quality assurance affidavit, to be used in conjunction with feed or feed ingredients delivered to the pork production site, must meet the following minimum requirements:

(i) It must include the name of the producer and the identity of the site, including the PIN if it has been issued, and the site address, as well as the name and address of the feed mill and the name and title of the feed mill representative.

(ii) It must provide information that the feed mill is following good manufacturing practices, and further specify, as evidence of these good manufacturing practices, the following:

(A) That the feed mill has a rodent control system that is maintained by the feed mill itself or by a pest control firm (include name and address of pest control firm).

(B) The frequency with which such rodent control system is maintained (*i.e.*, on a weekly basis, etc.); and

(C) That the feed mill maintains records of pest management practices or has records generated by a pest control operator, which must be made available to the producer upon request.

(iii) It must be signed by the feed mill representative and by the producer or the producer's designated representative, to remain in effect for a period of 2 years.

(b) All such records and other documentation required under this section must be retained at the pork production site for a period of 2 years.

(c) All such records and other documentation required under this section must be readily available for inspection at the pork production site at the time of an audit by a QAV or QVMO, or by other APHIS representatives during normal business hours.

(Approved by the Office of Management and Budget under control number 0579–0323)

§ 149.8 Program fees and charges.

(a) *Site audit.* If a QVMO performs the site audit, then the producer will pay the QVMO at the time the site audit is performed in accordance with the rate and other conditions set by the QVMO's governmental employer. Further, if the QVMO who performs the site audit is employed by APHIS, then the producer will pay APHIS for this service at the hourly rate listed in table 1 for each employee required to perform the service. If the APHIS-employed QVMO performs the site audit on a Sunday, on a holiday, or at any time outside the normal tour of duty of that employee, then the producer will pay APHIS for this service at the hourly rate listed in table 2 for each employee required to perform the service. Payment to APHIS for the services of an APHIS-employed QVMO, by certified check or U.S. money order, must be remitted to the QVMO at the time the site audit is performed.

TABLE 1—RATES FOR SERVICES OF QVMO

Hourly rate:	
Per hour	$84.00
Per quarter hour	21.00
Per service minimum fee	25.00

TABLE 2—OVERTIME RATES FOR SERVICES OF QVMO (OUTSIDE THE EMPLOYEE'S NORMAL TOUR OF DUTY)

Premium hourly rate Monday through Saturday and holidays:	
Per hour	$100.00
Per quarter hour	25.00
Premium hourly rate for Sundays:	
Per hour	112.00
Per quarter hour	28.00

(b) *Program fee.* The producer must pay APHIS a program fee at the time of each site audit in the amount of $51 to cover APHIS' administrative costs in processing the audit and operating the program. This program fee, payable to APHIS by certified check or U.S. money order, is due at the time of submitting the completed site audit form for APHIS evaluation.

(c) A producer will not be charged for the cost of having a spot audit performed at the pork production site.

§ 149.9 Pilot program sites.

Pork production sites participating in an APHIS-approved trichinae pilot program at the time of implementation of the Trichinae Certification Program on November 10, 2008 will maintain their same program status as either a Stage I enrolled, Stage II certified, or Stage III certified site, as well as their same program anniversary date for purposes of completing a site audit and submitting the completed audit form and payment.

SUBCHAPTER H—ANIMAL BREEDS

PART 151—RECOGNITION OF BREEDS AND BOOKS OF RECORD OF PUREBRED ANIMALS

AUTHORITY: 19 U.S.C. 1202; 7 CFR 2.22, 2.80, and 371.4.

DEFINITIONS

§ 151.1 Definitions.

Words used in this part in the singular form shall be deemed to import the plural, and vice versa, as the case may demand. As used in this part, the following words, names, or terms shall have the meanings set forth in this section, unless otherwise clearly indicated by the context.

The Act. Item 100.01 in part 1, schedule 1, of title I of the Tariff Act of 1930, as amended (19 U.S.C. 1202, schedule 1, part 1, item 100.01).

Administrator. The Administrator, Animal and Plant Health Inspection Service, or any person authorized to act for the Administrator.

Agent. Custom broker or other person authorized to act as agent for the importer or owner of an animal.

Animal. Any purebred animal imported specially for breeding purposes except a black, silver, or platinum fox, or any fox which is a mutation or type developed therefrom.

Animal and Plant Health Inspection Service. The Animal and Plant Health Inspection Service of the United States Department of Agriculture (APHIS).

Book of record. A printed book or an approved microfilm record sponsored by a registry association and containing breeding data relative to a large number of registered purebred animals used as a basis for the issuance of pedigree certificates.

Certificates of pure breeding. A certificate issued by the Administrator, for Bureau of Customs use only, certifying that the animal to which the certificate refers is a purebred animal of a recognized breed and duly registered in a book of record recognized under the regulations in this part for that breed.

Department. The United States Department of Agriculture.

Inspector. An inspector of APHIS or of the Bureau of Customs of the United States Treasury Department authorized to perform functions under the regulations in this part.

Pedigree certificate. A document issued by a registry association giving the pedigree of an animal and certifying that it is registered in the book of record of the association issuing the document, and containing all pertinent information relating to the registered animal, such as color and natural and artificial markings, a record of the name and address of the breeder, and the name and address of each subsequent owner of the animal.

Port of entry. Any port designated under § 92.102 for birds, § 92.203 for poultry, § 92.303 for horses, § 92.403 for ruminants, or § 92.503 for swine of this chapter.

Purebred. A term applicable to animals which are the progeny of known and registered ancestors of the same recognized breed and for which at least three generations of ancestry can be traced: *Provided, however*, That in the case of sheep registered on the basis of flocks, the term is applicable to animals of a recognized breed which originate in a flock for which available breeding data, as shown in the registry association's records, establish that the flock has been in existence at least ten years.

[23 FR 10103, Dec. 23, 1958, as amended at 24 FR 2643, Apr. 7, 1959; 26 FR 6072, July 7, 1961; 36 FR 23356, Dec. 9, 1971; 54 FR 34969, 34970, Aug. 23, 1989; 55 FR 31562, Aug. 2, 1990]

CERTIFICATION OF PUREBRED ANIMALS

§ 151.2 Issuance of a certificate of pure breeding.

The Administrator will issue a certificate of pure breeding for an animal claimed to be entitled to free entry under the act provided the requirements of the regulations in this part are complied with. Such certificate will be presented to the owner, agent, or importer who in turn shall present it to the collector of customs at the port where customs entry is made.

[26 FR 6072, July 7, 1961, as amended at 54 FR 34969, Aug. 23, 1989]

§ 151.3 Application for certificate of pure breeding.

An application for a certificate of pure breeding executed by the owner, agent, or importer of an animal shall be made on ANH Form 17–338 (available from the collector of customs) before the animal will be examined as provided in § 151.7. Such application shall be made to the inspector at the port of entry for all animals: *Provided, however,* That the application for a certificate of pure breeding for dogs, other than those regulated under § 92.600 of this chapter, and cats may be made to the inspector either at the port of entry or at any other port where customs entry is made. An agent shall show the inspector written authorization from the owner or importer authorizing him to act for the owner or importer in connection with the application for a certificate of pure breeding.

(Approved by the Office of Management and Budget under control number 0579–0011)

[26 FR 6072, July 7, 1961, as amended at 36 FR 23356, Dec. 9, 1971; 48 FR 57473, Dec. 30, 1983; 55 FR 31562, Aug. 2, 1990]

§ 151.4 Pedigree certificate.

A pedigree certificate for an animal of a breed listed in § 151.9 issued by the custodian of the appropriate book of record listed in said section and on which there has been entered in accordance with the rules of entry of the registry association, a complete record of transfers of ownership from the breeder to and including the United States importer, or a complete record of transfers of ownership from the breeder to and including the person who owns the animal when it is imported into the United States and the name of the United States importer (for example, a lessee), shall be furnished by the owner, agent, or importer to the inspector at the time of the examination of the animal as provided in § 151.7. The inspector will return the document to the party who submitted it. A verbatim translation of the description relating to color and markings shall appear in English in the pedigree certificate for the animal or in a separate certificate appended to the pedigree certificate.

[26 FR 6072, July 7, 1961]

§ 151.5 Alteration of pedigree certificate.

No pedigree certificate which in the opinion of the Administrator has been substantially altered will be accepted.

[23 FR 10104, Dec. 23, 1958, as amended at 54 FR 34969, Aug. 23, 1989]

§ 151.6 Statement of owner, agent, or importer as to identity of animals.

The owner, agent, or importer who applies for a certificate of pure breeding for any animal offered for duty-free entry under this part, shall execute on ANH Form 17–338 a statement that the animal so offered for entry is the animal described in the pedigree certificate furnished to the inspector as prescribed in § 151.4. This form shall be presented to the inspector before the animal and pedigree certificate are examined as provided in § 151.7.

[36 FR 23357, Dec. 9, 1971]

§ 151.7 Examination of animal.

(a) For the purpose of determining identity, an examination shall be made by an inspector of each animal for which free entry is claimed under the act. All animals shall be examined at the port of entry: *Provided, however,* That dogs, other than those regulated under § 92.600 of this chapter, and cats may be examined either at the port of entry or at any other port where customs entry is made.

(b) The owner, agent, or importer shall provide adequate assistance and facilities for restraining and otherwise handling the animal and present it in such manner and under such conditions as in the opinion of the inspector will make a proper examination possible. Otherwise, the examination of the animal will be refused or postponed by the inspector until the owner, agent, or importer meets these requirements.

(c) A pedigree certificate, as required by § 151.4 shall be presented at the time of examination to the inspector making the examination in order that proper identification of the animal may be made. When upon such examination of any animal, the color, markings, or other identifying characteristics do not conform with the description given in the pedigree certificate and the owner, agent, or importer desires to pursue the matter further, the inspector shall issue ANH Form 17–419 to the owner, agent, or importer, and shall forward the pedigree certificate for this animal, together with ANH Form 17–419, to the Washington office of APHIS by certified mail. A determination will be made by such office as to the identity of the animal in question and the eligibility of the animal for certification under § 151.2. The pedigree certificate will be returned to the party who submitted it as soon as such determination is made. Removal of an animal from the port where examination is made prior to presentation of the pedigree certificate or other failure to comply with the requirements of this paragraph shall constitute a waiver of any further claim to certification under the regulations in this part.

[26 FR 6072, July 7, 1961, as amended at 54 FR 34970, Aug. 23, 1989; 55 FR 31562, Aug. 2, 1990]

§ 151.8 Eligibility of an animal for certification.

To be eligible for certification under the act, an animal must be purebred of a recognized breed and have been registered in good faith in a book of record listed in § 151.9 and must not have been registered on inspection without regard to purity of breeding.

[23 FR 10104, Dec. 23, 1958]

Recognition of Breeds and Books of Record

§ 151.9 Recognized breeds and books of record.

Breeds of animals and books of record listed in paragraphs (a) and (b) are hereby recognized. Recognition of such breeds and books of record will be continued, however, only if the books of record involved are kept by the custodians thereof in a form which is reasonably current and the book otherwise meets the requirements of this part, in the opinion of the Administrator. When a registry association which publishes a book of record that was recognized in printed form ceases to publish the book in such form and in lieu thereof publishes the book in microfilm form, the recognition of such book of record will be continued only if the book meets the requirements of this part. A copy of each printed volume and microfilm record of a book of record published after the book is recognized under this part shall be sent to APHIS immediately following such publication. All books of record sent to the Animal and Plant Health Inspection Service, United States Department of Agriculture, shall be submitted through the Veterinary Services, Operational Support, 4700 River Road, Unit 33, Riverdale, Maryland 20737–1231.

(a) *Breeds and books of record in countries other than Canada.* Books of the registry associations listed below are recognized for the following breeds: *Provided,* That no Belted Galloway cattle, horse of Criolla, Fjordhest (formerly known as Westland), Holstein, Shetland Pony or Welsh Pony and Cob breed, dog or cat registered in any of the books named shall be certified under the act as purebred unless a pedigree certificate showing three complete generations of known and recorded purebred ancestry of the particular breed involved, issued by the appropriate association listed below, is submitted for such animal.

CATTLE

Code	Name of breed	Book of record	By whom published
1101	Aberdeen-Angus	Aberdeen-Angus Herd Book	Aberdeen-Angus Cattle Society, Hugh R. Neilson, secretary, Pedigree House, 17 Bon-Accord Sq., Aberdeen, Scotland.
1112	......do	New Zealand Aberdeen-Angus Herd Book.	New Zealand Aberdeen-Angus Cattle Breeders' Association, Post Office Box 83, Hastings, New Zealand.
116	......do	Irish Angus Herd Book	Irish Angus Cattle Society Ltd., John L. Murphy, Secretary, Agriculture House, Kildare Street, Dublin 2, Ireland.
1102	Africander	Africander Cattle Herd Book	The Africander Cattle Breeders' Society, under the supervision and authority of the South African Stud Book Association, E.L. Househam, secretary, 40 Henry St., Bloemfontein, Union of South Africa.
1201	Alderney	Herd Book of the Bailiwick of Guernsey (Alderney Branch).	Royal Alderney Agricultural Society (The Alderney Branch of the Royal Guernsey A. and H. Society), P.D. Sumner, secretary, The Bungalow, Butes, Alderney, Channel Isles.
1202	Ayrshire	Ayrshire Herd Book	Ayrshire Cattle Herd Book Society of Great Britain and Ireland, John Graham, secretary, 1 Racecourse Rd., Ayr, Scotland.
1301	Devon	Davy's Devon Herd Book	Devon Cattle Breeders' Society, Cyril Ernest Berry, secretary, Court House, The Square, Wiveliscombe, Somerset, England.
1302	Dexter	Dexter Herd Book	Dexter Cattle Society, T. S. Pick, secretary, Manor Farm, Stubbs Lane, Lower Kingswood, Tadworth, Surrey, England.
1103	Belted Galloway	Belted Galloway Herd Book	Belted Galloway Cattle Society, J. Campbel Laing, secretary, Galloway Estate Office, Newton Stewart, Wigtownshire, Scotland.
1104	Galloway	Galloway Herd Book	Galloway Cattle Society of Great Britain and Ireland, Donald M. McQueen, secretary, Roughhills, Dalbeattie, Scotland.
1113	Gelbvieh	Herd Book of the Gelbvieh	American Gelbvieh Association, 10900 Dover Street, Westminster, CO 80021.
1203	Guernsey	English Guernsey Herd Book	English Guernsey Cattle Society, J. W. Barker, secretary, Mappin House, Winsley St., Oxford St., London, W. 1, England.
1204	......do	Herd Book of the Baliwick of Guernsey (Guernsey Branch).	Royal Guernsey Agricultural and Horticultural Society, H. C. Le Page, secretary, States Arcade Balcony, St. Peter Port, Guernsey, Channel Isles.
1105	Hereford	Herd Book of Hereford Cattle	Hereford Herd Book Society, R.J. Bentley, secretary, 3 Offa St., Hereford, England.
1106	Highland	Highland Herd Book	Highland Cattle Society of Scotland, Donald G. Noble, secretary, 17 York Pl., Perth, Scotland.
1205	Holstein-Friesian	Friesch Rundvee-Stamboek	Vereeniging: "Het Friesch Rundvee-Stamboek," Dr. J. M. Dijkstra, secretary, Zuiderplein 2–6, Leeuwarden, The Netherlands.
1206	......do	Nederlandsch Rundvee-Stamboek.	Vereeniging: "Het Nederlandsche Rundvee-Stamboek," H. W. J. Dekker, Chief Administrator, Stadhouders-plantsoen 24, 's-Gravenhage, The Netherlands.
1207	Jersey	Jersey Herd Book	Royal Jersey Agricultural and Horticultural Society, H. G. Shepard, secretary, 3 Mulcaster St., St. Helier, Jersey, Channel Isles.
1208	......do	Jersey Herd Book of United Kingdom.	Jersey Cattle Society of the United Kingdom, Edward Ashby, secretary, 19 Bloomsbury Sq., London, W. C. 1, England.
1303	Kerry	British Kerry Cattle Herd Book ...	British Kerry Cattle Society, R. O. Hubl, secretary, The Milestone, Stanmore Hill, Stanmore, Middlesex, England.
1304	......do	Kerry Cattle Herd Book	Royal Dublin Society, Horace H. Poole, registrar, Ball's Bridge, Dublin, Ireland.
1305	Lincoln Red	Lincoln Red Herd Book	Lincoln Red Cattle Society, W. Dunnaway secretary, Agriculture House, Park St., Lincoln, England.
1209	Red Danish	Stambog over Koer af Rod Dansk Malkerace. Stambog over Tyre af Rod Dansk Malkerace. Register-Stambog over Kvaeg af Rod Dansk Malkerace.	De Samvirkende Danske Landboforeninger, A. Wulff Pedersen, secretary, Vindegade 72, Odense, Denmark.
1306	Red Poll	Red Poll Herd Book	Red Poll Cattle Society of Great Britain and Ireland, Inc., A. C. Burton, secretary, 32 Princes St., Ipswich, Suffolk, England.
1307	Shorthorn	Coates's Herd Book	Shorthorn Society of Great Britain and Ireland, Arthur Greenhalgh, secretary, Victoria House, Southampton Row, London, W.C. 1, England.

CATTLE—Continued

Code	Name of breed	Book of record	By whom published
1107	South Devon	Herd Book of South Devon Cattle.	South Devon Herd Book Society, W. G. Turpitt, secretary, 16 Sherborne Rd., Newton Abbot, Devon, England.
1115	Simmental	Irish Simmental Cattle Society ...	Irish Simmental Cattle Society Ltd., Springhill Carrigtwohill, Co. Cork, Ireland.
1308	Sussex	Sussex Herd Book	Sussex Herd Book Society, A. G. Holland, secretary, 17 Devonshire St., London, W. 1, England.
1309	Welsh	Welsh Black Cattle Herd Book ...	Welsh Black Cattle Society, G. Williams Edwards, secretary, 13 Bangor St., Caernarvon, No. Wales.

HORSES

Code	Name of breed	Book of record	By whom published
2201	Arabian	Arab Horse Stud Book	The Arab Horse Society, Col. R. C. de V. Askin, secretary, Beechmead, Rowledge, Farnham, Surrey, England.
2202	......do	Polska Ksiega Stadna Koni, Arabskich Czystej Krwi.	Towarzystwo Hodowli Konia Arabskiego, Maria Brykczynska, secretary, Krako 1w, Sarego 2, Poland.
2203	......do	General Stud Book	Weatherby & Sons, 15 Cavendish Sq., London, W. 1, England.
2204	......do	Registro-Matricula de Caballos de Pura Sangre.	Jefatura de Cria Caballar y Remonta, Don Manuel Diaz Calderon, Secretario Stud-book, Ministerio del Ejercito, Madrid, Spain.
2205	......do	Stud Book Argentino	Ministerio de Hacienda de la Nacion, Loteria de Beneficencia Nacional y Casinos, Ricardo A. Maestri, Jefe, Av. Libertador General San Martin 4101, Capital Federal, Republica Argentina.
2206	......do	Stud Book Francais Registre des Chevaux de Pur Sang.	Commission du Studbook Francais de Pur Sang, M. Maze-Sencier, Inspecteur General, Chef, Service des Haras, Ministere de l'Agriculture, 78 rue de Varenne (7), Paris, France.
2207	......do	Stud Book de Venezuela	Instituto Nacional de Hipodromos, Jorge Coll Nunez, Jefe, Hipodromo "La Rinconada," Caracas, Venezuela.
2208	......do	The Arabian Stud Book. (Recognition of this book will be restricted to Arabian horses which originate for importation in Saudi Arabia, or trace to pure Arabian stock of that country.).	The Arabian Horse Club Registry of America, Inc., Henry B. Babson, secretary, 120 So. La Salle St., Chicago 3, Ill.
2304	......do	Russian Arabian Stud Book of Moscow, Union of Soviet Socialist Republics.	Ministry of Agriculture USSR, All-Union Research Institute of Horsebreeding.
2101	Belgian	Stud-Book des Chevaux de Trait Belges.	Societe 1 Royale "Le Cheval de Trait Belge," Edgard Bedoret, Secretaire general, 45a rue de l'Ecuyer, Brussels, Belgium.
2209	Cleveland Bay	Cleveland Bay Stud Book	Cleveland Bay Horse Society, Oswald Welford, secretary, The Angelus, Roxby, Staithes, Saltburn, Yorkshire, England.
2102	Clydesdale	Clydesdale Stud-Book	Clydesdale Horse Society of Great Britain & Ireland, Robert Jarvis, secretary, 19 Hillington Gardens, Glasgow, S.W. 2, Scotland.
2210	Criolla	"Registre Definitivo Seccion" de Registro Genealogico para la Raza Criolla.	Sociedad Rural Argentina, E. F. Garay, Gerente Tecnico, Florida 460, Buenos Aires, Argentina.
2301	Fjordhest (formerly known as Westland).	Stambok over Fjordhest	Statens Stambokkontor, Arne Hogstad, Statens Stambokforer, Munkedamsveien 35 VI, Oslo, Norway.
2211	Hackney	Hackney Stud Book	Hackney Horse Society, R. A. Brown, secretary, 16 Bedford Sq., London, W.C. 1, England.
2212	Holstein	Holsteinisches Gestutbuch	Verband der Zuchter des Holsteiner Pferdes e. V., Herr H. Horstmann, Geschaftsfuhrer, Klostersande 93, Elmshorn, Germany.
2112	Morab	Morab Stud Book	North American Morab Horse Association, Inc., W 3174 Fero Springs Road, Hilbert, WI 54129.
2103	Percheron	British Percheron Stud Book	British Percheron Horse Society, A. E. Vyse, secretary, Owen Webb House, Gresham Rd., Cambridge, England.
2104	......do	Stud-Book Percheron de France	Societe 1 Hippique Percheronne de France, E. Lemarie, secretaire general, 7 rue Villette-Gate 1. Nogent-le-Rotrou (E–&–L), France.
2302	Shetland Pony	Shetland Pony Stud-Book	Shetland Pony Stud-Book Society, Thomas H. F. Myles, secretary, 61 George St., Perth, Scotland.

HORSES—Continued

Code	Name of breed	Book of record	By whom published
2105	Shire	Shire Horse Stud Book	Shire Horse Society, A. G. Holland, secretary, 17 Devonshire St., London, W. 1, England.
2106	Suffolk	Suffolk Stud-Book	Suffolk Horse Society, Raymond Keer, secretary, 6 Church St., Woodbridge, Suffolk, England.
2213	Thoroughbred	Australian Stud Book	Australian Jockey Club and Victoria Racing Club, W. J. McFadden, Keeper of the Stud Book, 6 Bligh St., Sydney, N.S.W., Australia.
2214	......do	General Stud Book	Weatherby & Sons, 15 Cavendish Sq., London, W. 1, England.
2215	......do	Jamaica Stud-Book	The Jockey Club of Jamaica, Miss L. Pike, secretary, 10 Duke St., Kingston, Jamaica, B.W.I.
2216	......do	Stud Book de Chile	Club Hipico de Santiago, Alejandro Obolensky Dadian, Jefe de Stud-Book, Casilla 3674, Santiago, Chile.
2217	......do	Stud Book de Venezuela	Instituto Nacional de Hipodromos, Jorge Coll Nunez, Jefe, Hipodromo "La Rinconada," Caracas, Venezuela.
2218	......do	New Zealand Stud Book	New Zealand Racing Conference, A. M. McBeath, secretary, P.O. Box 1430, Wellington, C. 1, New Zealand.
2219	......do	Registro-Matricula de Caballos de Pura Sangre.	Jefatura de Cria Caballar y Remonta, Don Manuel Diaz Calderon, Secretario Stud-book, Ministerio del Ejercito, Madrid, Spain.
2220	......do	Stud Book Francais Registre des Chevaux de Pur Sang.	Commission du Studbook Francais de Pur Sang, M. Maze-Sencier, Inspecteur General, Chef, Service des Haras, Ministere de l'Agriculture, 78 rue de Varenne (7), Paris, France.
2221	......do	Libro Genealogico dei Cavalli di Puro Sangue.	Jockey Club Italiano, Gen. Federico Garofoli, segretario, Corso Vittorio Emanuele 87, Rome, Italy.
2222	......do	Registre des Chevaux de Pur Sang.	Jockey-Club de Belgique, Lt. Col. Baron Jacques van Zuylen van Nyevelt, Secretaire general, 1 rue Guimard, Brussels 4, Belgium.
2223	......do	Stud Book Brasileiro	Jockey Club Brasileiro, Ricardo Xavier da Silveira, Diretor do Stud Book, Av., Rio Branco 197, Rio de Janeiro, Brazil.
2224	......do	Stud Book Peruano	Jockey Club del Pera, Alberto Alvarez Calderon, Gerente, Union 1066, Lima, Peru.
2225	......do	Stud Book Argentino	Ministerio de Hacienda de la Nacion, Loteria de Beneficencia Nacional y Casinos, Ricardo A. Maestri, Jefe, Av. Libertador General San Martin 4101, Capital Federal, Republica Argentina.
2226	......do	American Stud Book. (Recognition of this book will be restricted to Thoroughbreds imported as follows: (a) Horses bred or born in the United States, shipped to a foreign country and returned to this country; (b) horses bred or born in Great Britain, Northern Ireland, Eire, or France, whose pedigrees trace wholly, or in part, to horses bred or born in the United States; (c) horses from countries where a book of purebred registration for Thoroughbreds does not exist; or (d) horses previously certified for entry under the act and for which Certificates of Foreign Registration were issued by The Jockey Club of New York, and which were subsequently exported to any country and returned to the United States with such certificates.).	The Jockey Club, Mrs. L. Brennan, Registrar, 300 Park Ave., New York 22, N.Y.
2233	......do	Allgemeines deutsches Gestubuch fur Vollblut.	Direktorium fur Vollblutzucht und Rennen, 6 Cologne Weidenpesch, Rennbahnstrasse 100, Postfach 180, Republic of Germany.
2234	......do	Stud Book Uruguayo	Jefe del Stud Book Uruguayo, Jose C. Frigerio, Head, Uruguayan Jockey Club, Montevideo, Uruguay.
2235	......do	The General Stud Book of South Africa.	The Jockey Club of South Africa, Box 3409, Johannesburg, Union of South Africa.

HORSES—Continued

Code	Name of breed	Book of record	By whom published
2113	Trakehner	Trakehner Stud Book	American Trakehner Association, 2305 November Lane, Reston, VA 22091.
2303	Welsh Pony and Cob	Welsh Stud Book	Welsh Pony & Cob Society, J. A. George, secretary, Offices of the Royal Welsh Agricultural Society, Queen's Rd., Aberystwyth, Cardiganlshire, Wales.
2240	Wielkopolskich	Ksiega Stadna Koni Wielkopolskich.	Warm Blood & Full Blood Breeders of the Great Polish Horses, Pulewski 14, 02–152 Warsaw, Poland.

ASSES

Code	Name of breed	Book of record	By whom published
3001	Poitou	Jack and Jennet Section of Stud-Book ou Livre Genealogique des Animaux Mulassiers due Poitou.	Societe Centrale d'Agriculture des Deux-Sevres R. Martinet, Secretaire, Cite Administrative, rue Duguesclin, Niort (Deux-Sevres), France.

SHEEP

Code	Name of breed	Book of record	By whom published
4101	Border Leicester	Border Leicester Flock Book	Society of Border Leicester Sheep Breeders, Robert Jarvis, secretary, Room 273, 93 Hope St., Glasgow, C. 2, Scotland.
4102	Cheviot	Cheviot Sheep Flock Book	Cheviot Sheep Society, Guy H. Armstrong, secretary, Commercial Bank Bldgs., Hawick, Scotland.
4103	Corriedale	Flock Book for Corriedale Sheep in Australia.	The Australian Corriedale Association, H.T.C. Woodfull, secretary, Royal Showgrounds, Epsom Road, Ascot Vale, W. 2, Victoria, Australia.
4104	......do	Corriedale Flock Book (New Zealand).	The Corriedale Sheep Society, Inc., C. H. Lawrence, secretary, 154 Hereford St., Christchurch, New Zealand.
4201	Dorset Horn	Dorset Horn Flock Book	Dorset Horn Sheep Breeders' Association, E. F. B. Lucas, secretary, Bank Chambers, Dorchester, Dorset, England.
4202	Hampshire Down	Hampshire Down Flock Book	Hampshire Down Sheep Breeders' Association, Miss Doris M. Stanbury, secretary, 38 Endless St., Salisbury, Wilts., England.
4105	Kent or Romney Marsh.	Kent or Romney Marsh Flock Book.	Kent or Romney Marsh Sheep-Breeders' Association, G. W. Tuffrey, secretary, Station Rd., Ashford, Kent, England.
4203	Kerry Hill	Kerry Hill Flock Book	Kerry Hill (Wales) Flock Society, Ralph P. Evans, secretary, c/o The Radnorshire Co., Ltd., Knighton, Radnorshire, Wales.
4106	Leicester	Leicester Flock Book	Leicester Sheep Breeders' Association, P. S. Atkinson, secretary, The Exchange, Exchange St., Driffield, E. Yorks., England.
4107	Lincoln	Flock Book of Lincoln Longwool Sheep.	Lincoln Longwool Sheep Breeders' Association, Brian Shelley, secretary, Westminster Bank Chambers, 8 Guildhall St., Lincoln, England.
4204	Oxford Down	Flock Book of Oxford Down Sheep.	Oxford Down Sheep Breeders' Association, Mrs. L. I. Deacon, secretary, Thornyfields, Billing Rd., Brafield-on-the-Green, Northampton, England.
4108	Romney Marsh	New Zealand Romney Marsh Flock Book.	New Zealand Romney Marsh Sheep Breeders' Association, Inc., R. J. J. Campbell, secretary, 117 Kimbolton Rd., Feilding, New Zealand.
4205	Ryeland	Ryeland Flock Book	Ryeland Flock Book Society, Ltd., P. J. Hoskins, secretary, 20 King St., Hereford, England.
4206	Shropshire	Shropshire Flock Book	Shropshire Sheep Breeders' Association and Flock Book Society, Ivor Guy Mansell, secretary, College Hill, Shrewsbury, Shropshire, England.
4207	Southdown	Southdown Flock Book	Southdown Sheep Society, Inc., R. G. Noakes, secretary, Westways, Barming Woods, Maidstone, Kent, England.
4218	......do	Southdown Sheep Society of New Zealand (Inc.).	The Southdown Sheep Society of New Zealand (Inc.), S. I. McKenzie, secretary, A.M.P., Chambers, 14 Broadway, Palmerston North, New Zealand.
4208	Suffolk	Suffolk Flock Book	Suffolk Sheep Society, Harry A. Byford, secretary, 30 Museum St., Ipswich, Suffolk, England.
4109	Wensleydale	Wensleydale Longwool Sheep Flock Book.	The Wensleydale Longwool Sheep Breeders' Association, W. Dickinson, secretary, "Cartmel," Church Walk, Ulverston, Lancashire, England.

SHEEP—Continued

Code	Name of breed	Book of record	By whom published
4001	Various recognized breeds.	Flock Book for British Breeds of Sheep in Australia.	Australian Society of Breeders of British Sheep, H.T.C. Woodfull, secretary, Royal Show Grounds, Epsom Rd., Ascot Vale, W. 2, Victoria, Australia.
4002	......do	New Zealand Flock Book	New Zealand Sheep Breeders' Association, H.M. Studholme, secretary, P.O. Box 9002, Addington, Christchurch, New Zealand.

GOATS

Code	Name of breed	Book of record	By whom published
5001	Saanen and Toggenburg.	British Goat Society Herd Book (Saanen and Toggenburg Sections).	British Goat Society, Miss M.F. Rigg, secretary, Diss, Norfolk, England.

SWINE

Code	Name of breed	Book of record	By whom published
6001	Irish Large White	Herd Book of Irish Large White Pigs.	Royal Dublin Society, Horace H. Poole, registrar, Ball's Bridge, Dublin, Ireland.
	Berkshire.		
	Gloucestershire Old. Spots..		
	Large Black.		
6002	Large White	Herd Book of the National Pig Breeders' Association.	National Pig Breeders' Association, E.G. Wake, secretary, 69 Clarendon Rd., Watford, Herts, England
	Middle White		
	Tamworth.		
	British Saddleback.		

DOGS

Code	Name of breed	Book of record	By whom published
7306	Australian Kelpie	The Working Kelpie Council National Stud Book.	The Working Kelpie Council, P.O. Box E31 St. James, Sidney 2000, Australia.
7301	Boxer	Boxer-Zuchtbuch	Boxer-Klub e. V. Sitz Munchen, Bernhard Schmitz, Prasident, 38 Otkerstrasse, Munchen 9, Germany.
7201	Dachshund	Teckel-Stammbuch	Deutscher Teckelklub e. V., Josef Chateau, Stammbuchfuhrer, Vallendar/Rhein, Haus Rheinnieder, Germany.
7202	Foxhound	Foxhound Kennel Stud Book	Masters of Foxhounds Association, Lt. Col. J. E. S. Chamberlayne, Hon. secretary, 51 Victoria St., London, S. W. 1, England.
7203	......do	Welsh Hound Stud Book	Welsh Hound Association, Islwyn E. E. Davies, Hon. secretary, Berthddu, Llandinam, Montgomeryshire, East Wales.
7302	German Shepherd	Zuchtbuch fur deutsche Schaferhunde (SZ).	Verein fur deutsche Schaferhunde (SV), Hann Kremhelmer, Hauptgeschaftsfuhrer, Beim Schnarrbrunnen 4, Augsburg 5, Germany.
7303	Great Dane	Zuchtbuch fur Deutsche Doggen	Deutscher Doggen-Club, Richard Staadt, Prasident, Ellerstrasse 25, Solingen-Ohligs, Germany.
7204	Greyhound	Australian Greyhound Stud Book	The Australian and New Zealand Greyhound Association, Robert John Maidment, secretary, 349 Collins St., Melbourne, C. 1, Australia.
7205	......do	Greyhound Stud Book	National Coursing Club, Sydney H. Dalton, secretary, College Hill Chambers, London, E.C. 4. England.
7206	......do	Irish Greyhound Stud Book	Irish Coursing Club, Miss K. Butler, secretary, Davis Rd., Clonmel, Co. Tipperary, Ireland.
7207	Harrier and Beagle	Harrier and Beagle Stud Book	Association of Masters of Harriers and Beagles, J. J. Kirkpatrick, Hon. secretary, East Wing, Kirtlington Park, Oxford, England.
7304	Rottweiler	Zucht- und Korbuch	Allgemeiner Deutscher Rottweiler-Klub, Mrs. Josephine Rieble, Sekretarin, Vorsteigstrasse 5, Stuttgart-West, Germany.
7305	St. Bernard	Bernhardiner-Zuchtbuch	St. Bernhardsklub e. V., Franz Hrachowina, Zuchtbuchfuhrer, Bergmannstrasse 35, Munchen 12, Germany.

DOGS—Continued

Code	Name of breed	Book of record	By whom published
7001	Various recognized breeds.	Irish Kennel Club Stud Book	Irish Kennel Club, Miss Maud C. Fox, secretary, 23 Eden Quay, Dublin, C. 8, Ireland.
7002	......do	Kennel Club Stud Book	English Kennel Club, E. Holland Buckley, secretary, 1–4 Clarges St., Piccadilly, London, W. 1, England.
7003	......do	Livre des Origines Francais	Societe 1 Centrale Canine pour l'Amelioration des Races de Chiens en France, Col. Raoul Nicole, Directeur Administrateur, 3 Rue de Choiseul, Paris 2, France.
7004	......do	Livre des Origines de la Societe 1 Royale Saint-Hubert.	Societe 1 Royale Saint-Hubert, R. Willocq, Secretaire 1, 391 Chaussee Saint-Pierre, Brussels 4, Belgium.
7005	......do	Norsk Kennelklubs Stambok	Norsk Kennel Klub, Olaf A. Roig, secretary, Bjorn Farmannsgate 16, Oslo, Norway.
7006	......do	Zuchtbuch des Klub fur Terrier e. V.	Klub fur Terrier e.V., Wilhelm Vahle, Sekretar, Schone Aussicht 9, Kelsterbach b. Frankfurt/Main, Germany.
7007	......do	Schweizerisches Hunde-Stammbuch.	Schweizerische Kynologischen Gesellschaft, Carl Wittwer, secretary, Seestrasse 64, Kilchberg/Zurich, Switzerland.
7008	......do	Svenska Kennelklubbens Register.	Svenska Kennelklubben, Ivan Swedrup, secretary, Linnegatan 25, Stockholm O 4, Sweden.

CATS

Code	Name of breed	Book of record	By whom published
8001	Long-haired and short-haired.	The Governing Council of the Cat Fancy Stud Book.	The Governing Council of the Cat Fancy, W.A. Hazeldine, secretary, 1 Roundwood Way, Banstead, Surrey, England.

(b) *Breeds and books of record in Canada*—(1) *Animals generally.* The books of record of the Canadian National Live Stock Records, Ottawa, Canada, of which F. G. Clark is Director, are recognized for the following breeds: *Provided,* That no animals registered in the Canadian National Live Stock Records shall be certified under the act as purebred unless such animals trace only to animals which are proved to the satisfaction of Veterinary Services to be of the same breed: *Provided further,* That no Dexter cattle, Karakul sheep, Alpine goat, Nubian goat, or horse of the American Saddle Horse, Arabian, Canadian, Morgan, Shetland Pony or Welsh Pony and Cob breed in Canada shall be certified under the act as purebred unless a pedigree certificate showing three complete generations of known and recorded purebred ancestry of the particular breed involved, issued by the Canadian National Live Stock Records, is submitted for such animal.

Code	Name of breed	Code	Name of breed
	CATTLE		
1108	Aberdeen, Angus.		
1210	Ayrshire.	1111	Highland.
1110	Belgian Blue		
1211	Brown Swiss.	1214	Jersey.
1212	Canadian.	1311	Lincoln Red.
1310	Dexter.	1312	Red Poll.
1109	Galloway.	1313	Shorthorn.
1114	Gelbvieh		
1213	Guernsey.		
	HORSES		
2227	American Saddle Horse.	2109	Percheron.
2228	Arabian.	2304	Shetland Pony.
2107	Belgian Draft.	2110	Shire Suffolk.
2229	Canadian.	2111	Thoroughbred.
2108	Clydesdale.	2232	Welsh Pony.
2230	Hackney.	2305	and Cob.
2236	Morgan.		
	SHEEP		
4110	Blackface.	4115	Lincoln.
4111	Cheviot.	4116	Merino.
4112	Corriedale.	4213	Oxford Down.
4113	Cotswold.	4117	Rambouillet.
4209	Dorset Horn.	4214	Ryeland.
4210	Hampshire.	4215	Shropshire.
4211	Karakul.	4216	Southdown.
4212	Kerry Hill.	4217	Suffolk.
4114	Leicester.		
	GOATS		
5002	Alpine. Angora. Nubian. Saanen. Toggenburg.		

Code	Name of breed	Code	Name of breed
	SWINE		
6003	Berkshire. Chester White. Duroc-Jersey. Hampshire. Lacombe. Landrace. Large Black. Poland China. Tamworth. British Saddleback. Yorkshire.		

(2) *Holstein-Friesian cattle in Canada* (*Code 1215*). The Holstein-Friesian Association of Canada, Brantford, Ontario, Canada, of which G. M. Clemons is secretary and editor, is recognized for the Holstein-Friesian breed registered in the Holstein-Friesian Herd Book of that Association.

(3) *Dogs in Canada* (*Code 7009*). The Stud Book of the Canadian Kennel Club, Incorporated (Canadian National Live Stock Records) is recognized for all the breeds of dogs registered therein: *Provided*, That no dog so registered shall be certified under the act as purebred unless a pedigree certificate showing three complete generations of known and recorded purebred ancestry of the particular breed involved, issued by the Canadian Kennel Club, Incorporated, is submitted for such dog.

(4) *Standardbred horses in Canada* (*Code 2231*). The Canadian Standard Bred Stud Book kept by the Canadian Standard Bred Horse Society, 122 Brown's Line, Toronto 14, Ontario, Canada, is recognized for all Standardbred horses registered therein: *Provided*, That no Standard bred so registered shall be certified under the act as purebred unless a pedigree certificate showing three complete generations of known and recorded purebred Standardbred ancestry, issued by the Canadian Standard Bred Horse Society, is submitted for each such horse.

(5) *Charolais cattle in canada (Code 1112)*. The full French book of record of the Canadian Charolais Association, Calgary, Alberta, Canada, is recognized for the Charolais breed registered therein.

(6) *Maine-Anjou cattle in Canada (Code 1113*). The full French book of record of the Canadian Maine-Anjou Association, which is maintained by the Canadian National Live Stock Records, is recognized for the Maine-Anjou breed registered in the Canadian Maine-Anjou Herd Book: *Provided*, That no Maine-Anjou cattle so registered shall be certified under the act as purebred unless a pedigree certificate showing at least three generations of known and recorded purebred ancestry of the breed involved, issued by the Canadian National Live Stock Records, is submitted for each such animal.

(7) *Simmental cattle in Canada* (*Code 1114*). The Canadian Simmental Association, Calgary, Alberta, Canada, of which Mr. John Kish is Executive Secretary, is recognized for the Simmental breed registered in the Canadian Simmental Association Full Blood Herd Book: *Provided*, That no simmental cattle so registered shall be certified under the act as purebred unless a pedigree certificate showing at least three generations of known and recorded purebred ancestry of the breed involved, issued by the Canadian Simmental Association is submitted for each such animal.

(8) *Hereford cattle in Canada (Code 1110)*. The Canadian Hereford Herd Book of The Canadian Hereford Association, 5160 Skyline Way NE., Calgary, Alberta, Canada, of which Dr. Duncan J. Porteous is General-Manager, is recognized for the Hereford breed registered therein.

[23 FR 10104, Dec. 23, 1958]

EDITORIAL NOTE: For FEDERAL REGISTER citations affecting § 151.9, see the List of CFR Sections Affected, which appears in the Finding Aids section of the printed volume and at *www.fdsys.gov*.

§ 151.10 Recognition of additional breeds and books of record.

Before a breed or a book of record shall be added to those listed in this part, the custodian of the book of record involved shall submit to APHIS a complete copy of the book of record, consisting of any published printed volumes and any microfilm records issued by the registry association up to date of application, together with a copy of all rules and forms in force on said date affecting the registration of animals in said book.

[24 FR 2644, Apr. 7, 1959, as amended at 54 FR 34970, Aug. 23, 1989]

§ 151.11 Form of books of record.

(a) If a registry association has not published its book of record in printed form, a record in approved microfilm form which the Administrator finds provides a system for determining the recorded ancestry of the animals identified therein will be acceptable. When a registry association which has published its book of record in printed form ceases such publication and in lieu thereof publishes a microfilm record, the microfilm record shall commence with the first pedigree recorded by the association which is not in the printed volumes and shall otherwise be in approved form.

(b) A microfilm record will be approved under this part only if it is 16 mm. non-perforated safety film exposed at a reduction ratio not to exceed 24 diameters. All information on the original document shall be reproduced onto the microfilm so that it is clearly readable. The microfilm carton shall be indexed to state the numbers of the pedigree certificates on the roll of film it contains.

[24 FR 2644, Apr. 7, 1959, as amended at 54 FR 34969, Aug. 23, 1989]

SUBCHAPTER I—VOLUNTARY INSPECTION AND CERTIFICATION SERVICE

PART 156—VOLUNTARY INSPECTION AND CERTIFICATION SERVICE

AUTHORITY: 7 U.S.C. 1622 and 1624; 21 U.S.C. 136a; 7 CFR 2.22, 2.80, and 371.4.

SOURCE: 23 FR 10111, Dec. 23, 1958, unless otherwise noted.

§ 156.1 Meaning of words.

Words used in this part in the singular form shall import the plural, and vice versa, as the case may demand.

§ 156.2 Definitions.

For the purposes of this part, unless the context otherwise requires, the following terms shall be construed, respectively, to mean:

Administrator. The Administrator, Animal and Plant Health Inspection Service, or any person authorized to act for the Administrator.

Animal product. Anything made of, derived from, or containing any material of animal origin.

Applicant. Any person who requests service under this part.

Department. The United States Department of Agriculture.

Inspector. Any officer or employee of the Department of cooperating agency authorized to perform any duties at any plant furnished service under this part.

Inspector in charge. An inspector of the Department assigned by the Administrator to supervise, review, and perform official work pertaining to a plant furnished service under this part.

Person. Any individual, corporation, company, association, firm, partnership, society, joint stock company, or other form of organization.

[23 FR 10111, Dec. 23, 1958, as amended at 57 FR 30899, July 13, 1992; 62 FR 19040, Apr. 18, 1997; 72 FR 70766, Dec. 13, 2007]

§ 156.3 Kind of service; records.

Laws, regulations or other requirements of foreign countries and specifications of contracts for the purchase and sale of animal products, on occasion require vendors of such products to furnish official certificates concerning the class, quality, quantity, or condition of such products to be imported into such countries or to be delivered under the contracts. The service under this part, shall consist of the inspection of the processing, handling, and storage of the products at any plant at which service is furnished and the certification, on the basis of such requirements of foreign countries or such contract specifications, of the class, quality, quantity, or condition of such of the products as are found to conform to such requirements or specifications as the case may be. Processing procedures will be actually supervised. The operator of the plant shall fully inform the inspector with respect to, and the inspector shall actually observe, the processing procedures, handling, and storage of the products intended for certification. The inspector shall keep such records of the temperatures reached, the duration of time the temperatures are maintained, and the pounds of pressure under which the products are cooked in the course of processing, and such other information, as are needed to justify the issuance of the certificates required.

[23 FR 10111, Dec. 23, 1958, as amended at 62 FR 19040, Apr. 18, 1997]

§ 156.4 Application for service.

Any person who is eligible to receive service under this part may apply therefor to the Administrator, upon an application form which will be furnished by the Administrator upon request. The application form shall require the applicant to state, among other things, the forms of certificates desired.

(Approved by the Office of Management and Budget under control number 0579–0008)

[23 FR 10111, Dec. 23, 1958, as amended at 48 FR 57473, Dec. 30, 1983; 57 FR 30899, July 13, 1992; 72 FR 70766, Dec. 13, 2007]

§ 156.5 Availability of service.

Subject to § 156.8, service under this part will be furnished, upon application, within the limits of available Department personnel and facilities, at any plant the operator of which applies for or endorses the application for the service if the Administrator finds that: the forms of certificates desired by the applicant require the certification of class, quality, quantity, or condition; the plant and its methods of processing, handling and storage of the products intended for certification are adequate to warrant the issuance of the desired certificates; the requirements of part 130 of this title are met; and the requirements of § 156.7 are met.

[23 FR 10111, Dec. 23, 1958, as amended at 57 FR 30899, July 13, 1992; 62 FR 19040, Apr. 18, 1997; 72 FR 70766, Dec. 13, 2007]

§ 156.6 Certificates.

The inspector shall sign and issue certificates in forms approved by the Administrator for animal products, if the inspector finds that the requirements as stated in the certification have been met. The original and one copy of each certificate shall be furnished to the applicant, and one copy of each certificate shall be retained by the Department until disposal is authorized in accordance with law. Additional copies may be furnished the applicant at his request upon payment of the fees prescribed in § 156.7. Copies of the certificates may be furnished without charge to other properly interested Federal agencies or under compulsory process.

[23 FR 10111, Dec. 23, 1958, as amended at 57 FR 30899, July 13, 1992; 62 FR 19040, Apr. 18, 1997]

§ 156.7 User fees under 9 CFR part 130.

User fees under part 130 of this chapter for service (including travel and other expenses incurred in connection with the furnishing of service) under this part shall be paid by the applicant. If required by the Administrator, the user fees under part 130 of this chapter shall be paid in advance. Since the user fees under part 130 of this chapter are for the purpose of reimbursing the Department for all costs incurred in connection with the furnishing of service under this part, the appropriate user fees under part 130 of this chapter to cover any such costs shall be paid even if service is withheld pursuant to § 156.8.

[72 FR 70766, Dec. 13, 2007]

§ 156.8 Refusal of service; denial or withdrawal of service.

(a) Service under this part will be refused if the conditions stated in §§ 156.5 and 156.6 are not met.

(b) Service under this part may be withdrawn from, or denied to, any applicant by the Administrator, for such period as the Administrator may prescribe, when the Administrator is satisfied, after opportunity for hearing before a proper official has been accorded the applicant, that the applicant or other operator of the plant where service has been or would be furnished under the application, or the agent or employee of such applicant or operator within the scope of his employment, has persistently failed to give the inspector full and correct information with respect to the processing procedures, handling, and storage of animal products intended for certification or certified; or has given to any employee of the Department false information in connection with service under this part; or has altered or imitated any certificate, mark, or device provided for under this part; or has used any such certificate, mark, or device without authority from the Administrator, or any imitation of any such certificate, mark, or device, on or with respect to any animal products; or has knowingly and without promptly notifying the Administrator retained possession of any such device or imitation thereof or altered or imitation certificate or of any animal products marked with any such device without authority from the Administrator or marked with any imitation of such device; or has given or attempted to give, for any purpose whatsoever, any money, favor, or other thing of value, to any employee of the Department authorized to perform any function under this part; or has interfered with or obstructed, or attempted to interfere with or to obstruct, any employee of the Department in or with respect to the performance of his duties under this part by intimidation, threats, assaults, or any other improper means. The inspector assigned to any plant may suspend service at such plant for any of the reasons set forth in this paragraph, without hearing, and in that event shall report his actions to the Administrator, and the Administrator may continue such suspension or otherwise deny or suspend service at any plant for any of such reasons, without hearing, pending final disposal of the matter under this paragraph.

(c) All final orders in any proceeding to deny or withdraw the service for any of the reasons set forth in paragraph (b) of this section (except orders required for good cause to be held confidential and not cited as precedents) shall be filed with the Hearing Clerk of the Department and be available to public inspection.

[23 FR 10111, Dec. 23, 1958, as amended at 57 FR 30899, July 13, 1992; 62 FR 19040, Apr. 18, 1997]

SUBCHAPTER J—ACCREDITATION OF VETERINARIANS AND SUSPENSION OR REVOCATION OF SUCH ACCREDITATION

PART 160—DEFINITION OF TERMS

AUTHORITY: 7 U.S.C. 8301–8317; 15 U.S.C. 1828; 7 CFR 2.22, 2.80, and 371.4.

§ 160.1 Definitions.

For the purposes of this subchapter the following words, phrases, names and terms shall be construed, respectively, to mean:

Accredited veterinarian. A veterinarian approved by the Administrator in accordance with the provisions of part 161 of this subchapter to perform functions specified in subchapters B, C, and D of this chapter.

Administrator. The Administrator of the Animal and Plant Health Inspection Service or any individual authorized to act for the Administrator.

Animal, animals. All animals except humans, including but not limited to cattle, sheep, goats, other ruminants, swine, horses, asses, mules, zebras, birds, and poultry.

Animal and Plant Health Inspection Service. The Animal and Plant Health Inspection Service, United States Department of Agriculture.

APHIS. The Animal and Plant Health Inspection Service.

Approved digital signature. Digital signatures approved by the Administrator for electronic transmission, for example, via a computer. To be approved, a digital signature must be able to verify the identity of the accredited veterinarian signing the document and indicate if the integrity of the data in the signed document was compromised.

Category I animals. Any animals other than Category II animals, e.g., cats and dogs.

Category II animals. Food and fiber animal species; horses; birds; farm-raised aquatic animals; all other livestock species; and zoo animals that can transmit exotic animal diseases to livestock.

Examine, examination. Physical study of an individual animal that enables an accredited veterinarian to determine if any abnormality in physical condition or bodily function is suggestive of clinical signs of communicable disease.

Herd or flock health plan. A written herd or flock health management plan, which may include an agreement signed by the owner of a herd or flock, the accredited veterinarian, and a State or APHIS representative, in which each participant agrees to undertake actions specified in the agreement to maintain the health of the animals and detect signs of communicable disease.

Inspect, inspection. Visual study of the physical appearance, physical condition, and behavior of animals (singly or in groups) that enables an accredited veterinarian to determine whether any abnormality in physical condition or bodily function is evident.

Issue. The distribution, including electronic transmission, of an official animal health document that has been signed.

Official certificate, form, record, report, tag, band, or other identification. Means any certificate, form, record, report, tag, band, or other identification, prescribed by statute or by regulations issued by the Administrator, for use by an accredited veterinarian performing official functions under this subchapter.

Qualified accredited veterinarian (QAV). An accredited veterinarian who has been granted a program certification by the Administrator pursuant to § 161.5 of this subchapter based on completion of an APHIS-approved orientation or training program.

Regular health maintenance program. An arrangement between an accredited veterinarian and a livestock producer whereby the veterinarian inspects every animal on the premises of the producer at least once every 30 days.

Sign, (Signed). For an accredited veterinarian to put his or her signature in his or her own hand, or by means of an approved digital signature, on a certificate, form, record, or report. No certificate, form, record, or report is signed if:

(1) Someone other than the accredited veterinarian has signed it on behalf of or in the name of the accredited veterinarian, regardless of the authority granted them by the accredited veterinarian; or

(2) If any mechanical device, other than an approved digital signature, has been used to affix the signature.

State. Any State, the District of Columbia, Puerto Rico, Guam, the Northern Mariana Islands, the Virgin Islands of the United States, and any other territory or possession of the United States.

State Animal Health Official. The State animal health official who is responsible for the livestock and poultry disease control and eradication programs of a State.

Veterinarian-in-Charge. The veterinary official of APHIS who is assigned by the Administrator to supervise and perform the official work of APHIS in a State or group of States.

[57 FR 54912, Nov. 23, 1992, as amended at 59 FR 40797, Aug. 10, 1994; 60 FR 39842, Aug. 4, 1995; 62 FR 25445, May 9, 1997; 73 FR 60488, Oct. 10, 2008; 74 FR 65010, Dec. 9, 2009]

PART 161—REQUIREMENTS AND STANDARDS FOR ACCREDITED VETERINARIANS AND SUSPENSION OR REVOCATION OF SUCH ACCREDITATION

Sec.

AUTHORITY: 7 U.S.C. 8301–8317; 15 U.S.C. 1828; 7 CFR 2.22, 2.80, and 371.4.

SOURCE: 57 FR 54912, Nov. 23, 1992, unless otherwise noted.

§161.1 Statement of purpose; requirements and application procedures for accreditation.

(a) This subchapter concerns a program administered by APHIS to accredit veterinarians and thereby authorize them to perform, on behalf of APHIS, certain activities specified in this chapter. This program is intended to ensure that an adequate number of qualified veterinarians are available in the United States to perform such activities.

(b) *Categories of accreditation.* A veterinarian may be accredited as a Category I veterinarian or a Category II veterinarian. A veterinarian who is accredited under Category I is only authorized to perform accredited duties on Category I animals, as defined in §160.1. A veterinarian who is accredited under Category II is authorized to perform accredited duties on both Category I animals and Category II animals.

(c) *Application for initial accreditation.* A veterinarian may apply for accreditation by completing an application for accreditation and submitting it to APHIS. In completing the application, the veterinarian will choose one of the accreditation activity categories, either Category I or Category II, as discussed in paragraph (b) of this section. Applications for Category I accreditation must include certification that the applicant is able to perform the tasks listed in paragraph (g)(1) of this section. Applications for Category II accreditation must include certification that the applicant is able to perform the tasks listed in paragraph (g)(2) of this section. An accredited veterinarian must not perform duties requiring a program certification unless he or she is accredited under Category II and qualified to perform such duties in accordance with §161.5 of this part.

(d) *Review of application.* Applications for accreditation received by APHIS shall be forwarded to the State Animal Health Official for the State in which the veterinarian wishes to perform accredited duties for approval. Within 14 days after receiving an application, a State Animal Health Official shall either endorse the application or send a written statement to the Administrator explaining why it was not endorsed; but if the State Animal Health Official fails to take one of these actions within 14 days, APHIS shall proceed to review the application. The Administrator will review the application and the written statement, if any, and determine whether the applicant meets the requirements for accreditation contained in this part.

(e) *Accreditation requirements.* The Administrator is hereby authorized to accredit a veterinarian when he or she determines that:

(1) The veterinarian is a graduate with a Doctorate of Veterinary Medicine or an equivalent degree (any degree that qualifies the holder to be licensed by a State to practice veterinary medicine) from a college of veterinary medicine;

(2) The veterinarian is licensed or legally able to practice veterinary medicine in the State in which the veterinarian wishes to perform accredited duties. APHIS will confirm the licensing status of the applicant by contacting the State board of veterinary medical examiners or any similar State organization that maintains records of veterinarians licensed in a State;

(3) The veterinarian has completed initial accreditation training, using content provided by APHIS; and

(4) The veterinarian has completed an orientation program approved by the Veterinarian-in-Charge for the State in which the veterinarian wishes to perform accredited duties, and upon completion of the orientation, has signed a written statement listing the date and place of orientation, the subjects covered in the orientation, and any written materials provided to the veterinarian at the orientation. The Veterinarian-in-Charge shall also give the State Animal Health Official an opportunity to review the contents of the orientation, and invite him or her to participate in developing orientation materials and conducting the orientation. The veterinarian applying for accreditation must have completed the orientation program within 3 years prior to submitting the application for accreditation. The core orientation program shall include the following topics:

(i) Federal animal health laws, regulations, and rules;

(ii) Interstate movement requirements for animals;

(iii) Import and export requirements for animals;

(iv) USDA animal disease eradication and control programs;

(v) Laboratory support in confirming disease diagnoses;

(vi) Ethical and professional responsibilities of an accredited veterinarian;

(vii) Foreign animal disease awareness;

(viii) Animal health emergency management; and

(ix) Animal health procedures, issues, and information resources relevant to the State in which the veterinarian wishes to perform accredited duties.

(f) *Change in accreditation category*—(1) *Category I to Category II.* A veterinarian who is accredited under Category I may become accredited under Category II if the veterinarian applies for accreditation under Category II by completing an application for accreditation, including certification that the applicant is able to perform the tasks listed in paragraph (g)(2) of this section, and submitting it to APHIS. The veterinarian must also have fulfilled the training requirements in § 161.3(b) that are associated with renewal of accreditation under Category II.

(2) *Category II to Category I.* A veterinarian who is accredited under Category II may become accredited under Category I if the veterinarian applies for accreditation under Category I by completing an application for accreditation, including certification that the applicant is able to perform the tasks listed in paragraph (g)(1) of this section, and submitting it to APHIS. The veterinarian must also have fulfilled the training requirements in § 161.3(b) that are associated with renewal of accreditation under Category I.

(g) *Tasks that applicants for accredited status must be able to perform.* Applicants for accredited status must be able to:

(1) *Category I.* (i) Perform physical examination of individual Category I animals to determine whether they are

free from any clinical signs suggestive of communicable disease.

(ii) Recognize the common breeds of Category I animals and accurately record breed information on official documents.

(iii) Apply common animal identification for Category I animals.

(iv) Properly complete certificates for domestic and international movement of Category I animals.

(v) Perform necropsies on Category I animals.

(vi) Recognize and report clinical signs and lesions of exotic animal diseases that occur in Category I animals.

(vii) Vaccinate Category I animals and accurately complete the vaccination certificates.

(viii) Properly collect and ship specimen samples to the appropriate laboratory for testing with complete and accurate paperwork.

(ix) Develop appropriate biosecurity protocols, as well as cleaning and disinfection protocols, to control communicable disease spread in Category I animals.

(2) *Category II.* (i) Perform physical examination of individual animals and visually inspect herds or flocks to determine whether the animals are free from any clinical signs suggestive of communicable disease.

(ii) Recognize the common breeds of Category I and Category II animals, including the types of poultry as defined by the National Poultry Improvement Plan in subchapter G of this chapter and the common breeds of livestock, and be able to accurately record breed information on official documents.

(iii) Recognize all USDA animal identification systems.

(iv) Estimate the age of livestock using a dental formula.

(v) Apply USDA-recognized identification (e.g., eartag, microchip, tattoo) for the USDA animal identification system.

(vi) Certify the health status of an avian flock regarding diseases of domestic or international regulatory concern, and evaluate records pertaining to poultry flock testing and participation in Federal and State poultry health programs and classifications.

(vii) Properly complete certificates for domestic and international movement of animals.

(viii) Apply and remove official seals.

(ix) Perform necropsies on animals.

(x) Recognize and report clinical signs and lesions of exotic animal diseases.

(xi) Develop a herd or flock health plan consistent with requirements in subchapters B, C, and D of this chapter.

(xii) Vaccinate for USDA program diseases and accurately complete the vaccination certificate.

(xiii) Properly collect and ship sample specimens to an appropriate laboratory for testing with complete and accurate paperwork.

(xiv) Properly perform testing for tuberculosis (e.g., caudal fold test).

(xv) Develop appropriate biosecurity protocols, as well as cleaning and disinfection protocols, to control communicable disease spread.

(xvi) Explain basic principles for control of diseases for which APHIS or APHIS-State cooperative programs presently exist.

(h) *Authorization to perform duties.* An accredited veterinarian may not perform accredited duties in a State until after receiving written authorization from APHIS. If a Category I accredited veterinarian completes the necessary training requirements and becomes a Category II accredited veterinarian, the veterinarian may not perform Category II accredited duties in a State until after receiving written authorization from APHIS.

(Approved by the Office of Management and Budget under control number 0579–0297)

[57 FR 54912, Nov. 23, 1992, as amended at 74 FR 65010, Dec. 9, 2009]

§ 161.2 Performance of accredited duties in different States.

(a) If an accredited veterinarian wishes to perform accredited duties in a State other than the State in which the veterinarian was initially accredited in accordance with § 161.1(e), the accredited veterinarian must complete an application to request authorization to perform accredited duties in the new State from the Veterinarian-in-Charge of that State. The Veterinarian-in-Charge of the new State may require the accredited veterinarian to complete, prior to performing any accredited duties in the new State, an orientation in animal health procedures and issues relevant to the new State. The Veterinarian-in-Charge shall review the content of each such orientation and shall approve its use after determining that it includes adequate information about animal health agencies, regulatory requirements, administrative procedures, and animal disease issues in the new State, to prepare an accredited veterinarian from another State to perform accredited duties in the new State. The Veterinarian-in-Charge shall also give the State Animal Health Official of the new State an opportunity to review the contents of the orientation, and invite him or her to participate in developing orientation materials and conducting the orientation.

(b) An accredited veterinarian may not perform accredited duties in a State in which the accredited veterinarian is not licensed or legally able to practice veterinary medicine.

(c) An accredited veterinarian may not perform accredited duties in a State other than the one in which the veterinarian was initially accredited until the veterinarian receives written authorization from APHIS to perform accredited duties in the new State.

(Approved by the Office of Management and Budget under control numbers 0579–0032 and 0579–0297)

[74 FR 65011, Dec. 9, 2009]

§ 161.3 Renewal of accreditation.

(a) Accredited veterinarians who wish to continue participating in the National Veterinary Accreditation Program must renew their accreditation every 3 years by completing an application for accreditation renewal and submitting it to APHIS. Newly accredited veterinarians must renew their accreditation within 3 years of completing the orientation program described in § 161.1(e)(4) of this part, regardless of when their accreditation was granted. Other veterinarians must renew their accreditation within 3 years of the previous renewal.

(b) Accredited veterinarians who wish to renew their accreditation under Category I must complete 3 supplemental training units approved by APHIS by the end of their 3-year tenure as an accredited veterinarian. Accredited veterinarians who wish to renew their accreditation under Category II must complete 6 supplemental training units approved by APHIS by the end of their 3-year tenure as an accredited veterinarian. Accredited veterinarians who wish to change the category in which they are accredited, rather than renew accreditation in their current accreditation category, should follow the procedure in § 161.1(f) of this part.

(c) Accredited veterinarians who do not complete the required training within 3 years as specified in paragraph (a) of this section will have their accredited status expire. Veterinarians whose accreditation has expired will not be allowed to perform accredited duties until they receive notification of their reinstatement from APHIS. Veterinarians who perform duties that only accredited veterinarians are authorized to perform while their accredited status has expired will be subject to such criminal and civil penalties as are provided by the Animal Health Protection Act (7 U.S.C. 8301 *et seq.*) or other applicable Federal statutes or regulations. To be reinstated, the veterinarian must complete the necessary supplemental training units for the appropriate category and submit an application for renewal of veterinary accreditation to APHIS. A veterinarian who allows his or her accredited status to expire must have completed the required number of supplemental training units within 3 years of his or her application for renewal in order to be approved for renewal. Supplemental training units completed since the veterinarian's last renewal but more than 3 years before the veterinarian's application for renewal will not count towards fulfilling his or her training requirement.

(d) Veterinarians who are accredited as of February 1, 2010, may continue to perform accredited duties between February 1, 2010, and the date of their first renewal. APHIS will provide notice for 3 months to accredited veterinarians who are accredited as of February 1, 2010, to notify them that they must elect to participate in the NVAP as a

Category I or Category II veterinarian. Veterinarians must elect to continue to participate by October 1, 2011, or their accredited status will expire. When APHIS receives notice from an accredited veterinarian that he or she elects to participate, APHIS will notify the accredited veterinarian of his or her date for first renewal. The accredited veterinarian must then complete all the training requirements for renewal, as described in this section, by his or her first renewal date.

(Approved by the Office of Management and Budget under control number 0579–0297)

[74 FR 65011, Dec. 9, 2009, as amended at 76 FR 52549, Aug. 23, 2011]

§ 161.4 Standards for accredited veterinarian duties.

An accredited veterinarian shall perform the functions of an accredited veterinarian only in a State in which the accredited veterinarian is licensed or legally able to practice veterinary medicine. An accredited veterinarian shall perform the functions of an accredited veterinarian and carry out all responsibilities under applicable Federal programs and cooperative programs subject to direction provided by the Veterinarian-in-Charge and in accordance with any regulations and instructions issued to the accredited veterinarian by the Veterinarian-in-Charge, and shall observe the following specific standards:

(a) An accredited veterinarian shall not issue a certificate, form, record or report which reflects the results of any inspection, test, vaccination or treatment performed by him or her with respect to any animal, other than those in regular health maintenance programs, unless he or she has personally inspected that animal within 10 days prior to issuance. Inspections under this paragraph must be conducted in a location that allows the accredited veterinarian sufficient space to observe the animal in such a manner as to detect abnormalities related to areas such as, but not limited to, locomotion, body excretion, respiration, and skin conditions. An accredited veterinarian shall examine such an animal showing abnormalities, in order to determine whether or not there is clinical evidence compatible with the presence or absence of a communicable disease.

(1) Following the first two inspections of a herd or flock as part of a regular health maintenance program, an accredited veterinarian shall not issue a certificate, form, record or report which reflects the results of any inspection, test, vaccination or treatment performed by him or her with respect to any animal in that program, unless he or she has personally inspected that animal within 10 days prior to issuance.

(2) Following the third and subsequent inspections of a herd or flock in a regular health maintenance program, an accredited veterinarian shall not issue a certificate, form, record or report which reflects the results of any inspection, test, vaccination or treatment performed by him or her with respect to any animal in that program, unless he or she has personally inspected that animal within 30 days prior to issuance.

(b) An accredited veterinarian shall not issue, or allow to be used, any certificate, form, record or report, until, and unless, it has been accurately and fully completed, clearly identifying the animals to which it applies, and showing the dates and results of any inspection, test, vaccination, or treatment the accredited veterinarian has conducted, except as provided in paragraph (c) of this section, and the dates of issuance and expiration of the document. Certificates, forms, records, and reports shall be valid for 30 days following the date of inspection of the animal identified on the document, except that origin health certificates may be valid for a longer period of time as provided in § 91.3(a) of this chapter. The accredited veterinarian must distribute copies of certificates, forms, records, and reports according to instructions issued to him or her by the Veterinarian-in-Charge.

(c) An accredited veterinarian shall not issue any certificate, form, record, or report which reflects the results of any inspection, test, vaccination, or treatment performed by another accredited veterinarian, unless:

(1) The signing accredited veterinarian has exercised reasonable care,

that is, a standard of care that a reasonably prudent person would use under the circumstances in the course of performing professional duties, to determine that the certificate, form, or report is accurate;

(2) The certificate, form, or report indicates that the inspection, test, vaccination, or treatment was performed by the other accredited veterinarian; identifies the other accredited veterinarian by name; and includes the date and the place where such inspection, test, or vaccination was performed; and,

(3) For a certificate, form, or report indicating results of a laboratory test, the signing accredited veterinarian shall keep a copy of the certificate, form, or report and shall attach to it either a copy of the test results issued by the laboratory, or a written record (including date and participants' names) of a conversation between the signing accredited veterinarian and the laboratory confirming the test results.

(d) An accredited veterinarian shall perform official tests, inspections, treatments, and vaccinations and shall submit specimens to designated laboratories in accordance with Federal and State regulations and instructions issued to the accredited veterinarian by the Veterinarian-in-Charge.

(e) An accredited veterinarian shall identify or be physically present to supervise the identification of reactor animals by tagging or such other method as may be prescribed in instructions issued to him or her by the Veterinarian-in-Charge or by a State Animal Health Official through the Veterinarian-in-Charge.

(f) An accredited veterinarian shall immediately report to the Veterinarian-in-Charge and the State Animal Health Official all diagnosed or suspected cases of a communicable animal disease for which a APHIS has a control or eradication program in 9 CFR chapter I, and all diagnosed or suspected cases of any animal disease not known to exist in the United States as provided by § 71.3(b) of this chapter.

(g) While performing accredited work, an accredited veterinarian shall take such measures of sanitation as are necessary to prevent the spread of communicable diseases of animals by the accredited veterinarian.

(h) An accredited veterinarian shall keep himself or herself currently informed on Federal and State regulations that are provided to him or her by the Veterinarian-in-Charge, or by a State official through the Veterinarian-in-Charge, governing the movement of animals, and on procedures applicable to disease control and eradication programs, including emergency programs.

(i) An accredited veterinarian shall not use or dispense in any manner, any pharmaceutical, chemical, vaccine or serum, or other biological product authorized for use under any Federal regulation or cooperative disease eradication program, in contravention of applicable Federal or State statutes, regulations, and policies.

(j) An accredited veterinarian shall be responsible for the security and proper use of all official certificates, forms, records, and reports; tags, bands, or other identification devices; and approved digital signature capabilities used in his or her work as an accredited veterinarian and shall take reasonable care to prevent the misuse thereof. An accredited veterinarian shall immediately report to the Veterinarian-in-Charge the loss, theft, or deliberate or accidental misuse of any such certificate, form, record, or report; tag, band, or other identification device; or approved digital signature capability.

(k) An accredited veterinarian may issue an origin health certificate for export use pursuant to part 91 of this chapter without including test results from a laboratory, if the Veterinarian-in-Charge has determined that such action is necessary to save time in order to meet an exportation schedule and agrees to add the test results to the certificate at a later time. In such cases, the accredited veterinarian shall state on a removable attachment to the certificate that such test results are to be added by the Veterinarian-in-Charge.

[57 FR 54912, Nov. 23, 1992; 58 FR 8820, Feb. 17, 1993; 60 FR 39842, Aug. 4, 1995; 60 FR 55443, Nov. 1, 1995; 62 FR 25445, May 9, 1997; 67 FR 11561, Mar. 15, 2002. Redesignated at 74 FR 65011, Dec. 9, 2009]

§ 161.5 Program certifications.

A program certification recognized by the Administrator may be granted to an accredited veterinarian in Category II upon completion of an additional orientation or training program approved by APHIS that focuses on the specific area for which the veterinarian is seeking program certification. Veterinarians accredited under Category I are not eligible to earn program certifications. Accredited veterinarians may elect to participate in a program certification on a voluntary basis. Participants in these program certifications will be qualified in a particular area or specialty. In addition to Category II training, qualification for a program certification will include additional specialized training, which may include periodic training updates. For certain program certifications, the cost of orientation or training may be borne by the accredited veterinarian. An accredited veterinarian granted a program certification will be referred to as a qualified accredited veterinarian or QAV. A QAV will be authorized to perform those accredited duties related to the program certification he or she has earned; accredited veterinarians not granted program certifications will not be permitted to perform accredited duties related to that particular program certification. If a QAV allows his or her Category II accreditation to expire, the QAV's program certification expires as well, and the QAV must be qualified for the program certification again in accordance with this section.

[74 FR 65012, Dec. 9, 2009]

§ 161.6 Suspension or revocation of veterinary accreditation and reaccreditation; criminal and civil penalties.

(a) The Administrator is authorized to suspend for a given period of time, or to revoke, the accreditation of a veterinarian when he or she determines that the accredited veterinarian has not complied with the "Standards for Accredited Veterinarian Duties" as set forth in § 161.4 of this part or with any of the other regulations in this subchapter, or is otherwise found to be unfit to be accredited. Veterinarians who perform duties that only accredited veterinarians are authorized to perform while their accredited status is suspended or revoked will be subject to such criminal and civil penalties as are provided by the Animal Health Protection Act (7 U.S.C. 8301 *et seq.*) or other applicable Federal statutes or regulations. Performing accredited duties while accreditation status is suspended or revoked will be considered grounds for the Administrator to suspend accreditation, revoke accreditation, or deny application for reaccreditation, as circumstances warrant. A veterinarian whose accreditation has been suspended or revoked or whose application for reaccreditation has been denied may request a hearing under § 162.13 to challenge the Administrator's decision.

(b) *Reinstatement after suspension.* A veterinarian whose accreditation has been suspended for less than 6 months (other than a summary suspension that is changed to a revocation as a result of an adjudicatory proceeding) will be automatically reinstated as an accredited veterinarian upon completion of the suspension. A veterinarian whose accreditation has been suspended for 6 months or more must complete a reaccreditation orientation program in accordance with paragraph (c)(2)(ii) of this section before accreditation will be reinstated.

(c) *Reaccreditation after revocation.* A veterinarian whose accreditation has been revoked may apply for reaccreditation by completing an application for reaccreditation and submitting it to the Veterinarian-in-Charge of the State or area where he or she wishes to perform accredited work. The application may be submitted when the revocation has been in effect for not less than 2 years, unless the revocation order specifies that the veterinarian whose accreditation has been revoked may not submit an application for reaccreditation until the revocation has been in effect for a period of time longer than 2 years.

(1) Completed applications for reaccreditation received by a Veterinarian-in-Charge shall be reviewed by the State Animal Health Official for the State in which the veterinarian wishes to perform accredited duties.

Within 14 days after receiving an application, the State Animal Health Official shall either endorse the application or send a written statement to the Administrator explaining why it was not endorsed; but if the State Animal Health Official fails to take one of these actions within 14 days, the Veterinarian-in-Charge shall proceed to review the application. The Administrator will review the application and the written statement, if any, and determine whether the applicant meets the requirements for reaccreditation contained in this part.

(2) Once a veterinarian whose accreditation has been revoked has correctly applied for reaccreditation in accordance with the requirements of paragraph (c) of this section, the Administrator will determine whether to reaccredit or to deny reaccreditation. This determination will be based on whether the veterinarian has fulfilled the following conditions:

(i) The veterinarian is licensed or legally able to practice veterinary medicine in the State in which the veterinarian wishes to perform accredited duties;

(ii) The veterinarian has completed a reaccreditation orientation program approved by the Veterinarian-in-Charge for the State in which the veterinarian wishes to perform accredited work, and upon completion of the orientation, has signed a written statement listing the date and place of orientation, the subjects covered in the orientation, and any written materials provided to the veterinarian at the orientation. The Veterinarian-in-Charge shall also give the State Animal Health Official an opportunity to review the contents of the reaccreditation orientation, and invite him or her to participate in developing orientation materials and conducting the orientation. The orientation program shall include topics addressing the subject areas which led to loss of accreditation for the applicant, and subject areas which have changed since the applicant lost accreditation; and

(iii) The professional integrity and reputation of the applicant support a conclusion that the applicant will faithfully fulfill the duties of an accredited veterinarian in the future. In making this conclusion, the Administrator shall review all available information about the applicant, including recommendations of the State Animal Health Official, and shall consider:

(A) Any criminal conviction records indicating that the applicant may lack the honesty, integrity, and reliability to appropriately and effectively perform accredited duties and to uphold the integrity of the National Veterinary Accreditation Program;

(B) Official records of the applicant's actions participating in Federal, State, or local veterinary programs;

(C) Judicial determinations in civil litigation adversely reflecting on the honesty, integrity, and reliability of the applicant; and

(D) Any other evidence reflecting on the honesty, professional integrity, reliability and reputation of the applicant.

(3)(i) If a veterinarian is reaccredited under paragraph (c)(2) of this section, the veterinarian may begin performing accredited duties again upon receipt of notification from the Administrator that he or she is eligible to do so.

(ii) If an application for reaccreditation is denied under paragraph (c)(2) of this section, the veterinarian may apply for reaccreditation in accordance with this paragraph (c) not less than 2 years after the application was last denied, unless the decision specifies that the veterinarian may not reapply for reaccreditation until a period of time longer than 2 years has passed.

(d) Accreditation shall be automatically terminated when an accredited veterinarian is not licensed or legally able to practice veterinary medicine in at least one State.

(e) Accreditation shall be automatically revoked when an accredited veterinarian is convicted of a crime in either State or Federal court, if such conviction is based on the performance or nonperformance of any act required of the veterinarian in his or her capacity as an accredited veterinarian.

(f) Any accredited veterinarian who knowingly issues or signs a false, incorrect, or mislabeled animal health or inspection certificate, blood sample, official brucellosis vaccination certificate, or official tuberculin test certificate in accordance with this chapter, shall be subject to such civil penalties and such criminal liabilities as are provided by 7 U.S.C. 8313, 18 U.S.C. 1001, or other applicable Federal statutes. Such action may be in addition to, or in lieu of, suspension or revocation of accredited veterinarian status in accordance with this section.

(g) *Notice of warning.* In lieu of suspension or revocation, the Administrator is authorized to issue a written notice of warning to an accredited veterinarian when the Administrator determines a notice of warning will be adequate to attain compliance with the Standards for Accredited Veterinarian Duties in § 161.4 of this part.

[57 FR 54912, Nov. 23, 1992, as amended at 68 FR 6346, Feb. 7, 2003. Redesignated and amended at 74 FR 65011, 65012, Dec. 9, 2009]

§ 161.7 Activities performed by non-accredited veterinarians.

(a) Full-time Federal (including military) and State employed veterinarians are authorized to perform functions specified in subchapters B, C, and D of this chapter, pursuant to delegation of authority by the Administrator or cooperative agreements, without specific accreditation under the provisions of this subchapter.

(b) Except as provided by paragraph (a) of this section, anyone who performs accredited veterinarian duties that he or she is not authorized to perform will be subject to such criminal and civil penalties as are provided by the Animal Health Protection Act (7 U.S.C. 8301 *et seq.*) or other applicable Federal statutes or regulations. Performing accredited duties without having been accredited will be considered grounds for the Administrator to deny an application for accreditation.

[74 FR 65013, Dec. 9, 2009]

PART 162—RULES OF PRACTICE GOVERNING REVOCATION OR SUSPENSION OF VETERINARIANS' ACCREDITATION

Subpart A—General

Subpart B—Supplemental Rules of Practice

AUTHORITY: 7 U.S.C. 8301–8317; 15 U.S.C. 1828; 7 CFR 2.22, 2.80, and 371.4.

SOURCE: 57 FR 54915, Nov. 23, 1992, unless otherwise noted.

Subpart A—General

§ 162.1 Scope and applicability of rules of practice.

The Uniform Rules of Practice for the Department of Agriculture promulgated in subpart H of part 1, subtitle A, title 7, Code of Federal Regulations, are the Rules of Practice applicable to adjudicatory, administrative proceedings for the revocation or suspension of accreditation of veterinarians (9 CFR parts 160 and 161). In addition, the Supplemental Rules of Practice set forth in subpart B of this part shall be applicable to such proceedings.

Subpart B—Supplemental Rules of Practice

§ 162.10 Summary suspension or revocation of accreditation of veterinarians.

In any situation where the Administrator has reason to believe that any veterinarian accredited under the provisions of parts 160 and 161 of this subchapter has knowingly violated the Animal Health Protection Act (7 U.S.C. 8301 *et seq.*), the Administrator may summarily suspend the accreditation of such veterinarian pending final determination in either a suspension or revocation proceeding, effective upon oral or written notification, whichever is earlier. In the event of oral notification, a written confirmation thereof shall be given to such veterinarian as promptly as circumstances permit.

[74 FR 65013, Dec. 9, 2009]

§ 162.11 Notification.

The Veterinarian-in-Charge shall notify an accredited veterinarian when there is reason to believe that the accredited veterinarian has not complied with the "Standards for Accredited

Veterinarian Duties'' as contained in § 161.4 of this subchapter. The notification shall be in writing, with a copy to the State Animal Health Official, and shall include a statement of the basis for the belief that the accredited veterinarian has failed to comply with the Standards and shall notify the accredited veterinarian if the Veterinarian-in-Charge has arranged to hold an informal conference to discuss the matter.

[57 FR 54915, Nov. 23, 1992, as amended at 75 FR 57658, Sept. 22, 2010]

§ 162.12 Informal conference.

(a) The Veterinarian-in-Charge, in consultation with the State Animal Health Official and the accredited veterinarian, shall designate the time and place for the holding of an informal conference to review the matter, unless the Veterinarian-in-Charge determines that an informal conference is inappropriate. An informal conference is inappropriate only if the Veterinarian-in-Charge decides to dismiss the case based on available facts, or if civil or criminal charges based on the actions or inactions believed to be in violation of the ''Standards for Accredited Veterinarian Duties'' contained in § 161.4 of this subchapter are pending against the accredited veterinarian. An informal conference shall include the Veterinarian-in-Charge or his or her representative, the accredited veterinarian, and any other persons the Veterinarian-in-Charge requests to attend due to their involvement in or knowledge of the possible violation. The State Animal Health Official will be invited to attend each informal conference held regarding activities in his or her State.

(b) If prior to, during, or after the informal conference, but prior to the issuance of a formal complaint, the accredited veterinarian is found not to have violated the regulations, the Veterinarian-in-Charge will issue a letter dismissing the case, and provide a copy of the letter to the accredited veterinarian and to the State Animal Health Official. Prior to, during, or after the informal conference, the Veterinarian-in-Charge may issue a letter identifying actions of the accredited veterinarian that were minor violations of the Standards, instructing the accredited veterinarian in proper procedures, and admonishing the accredited veterinarian to use greater care in performing these procedures in the future.

(c) Prior to, during, or at the conclusion of the informal conference, the Veterinarian-in-Charge may issue a written warning to the accredited veterinarian without further procedure after determining that a warning with appropriate instructions will be adequate to attain compliance with the Standards.

(d) If prior to, during, or at the conclusion of, the informal conference, the accredited veterinarian consents, in writing, to the issuance of an order revoking or suspending his or her accreditation for a specified period of time, in lieu of further procedure, the Veterinarian-in-Charge may issue such a consent order without further procedure.

[57 FR 54915, Nov. 23, 1992; 57 FR 60086, Dec. 18, 1992, as amended at 74 FR 65013, Dec. 9, 2009; 75 FR 57659, Sept. 22, 2010]

§ 162.13 Formal complaint.

If a consent order has not been issued, or if, after an informal conference, the Veterinarian-in-Charge has not issued a letter of dismissal or letter of warning to the accredited veterinarian, a formal complaint may be issued by the Administrator in accordance with § 1.135 of the Uniform Rules of Practice (7 CFR 1.135).

SUBCHAPTER K—PUBLIC INFORMATION

PART 165—AVAILABILITY OF INFORMATION

§ 165.1 Availability of information.

The Animal and Plant Health Inspection Service regulations relating to availability of information to the public and disclosure of records under 5 U.S.C. 552, which are set forth in 7 CFR part 370, are incorporated into this subchapter.

(5 U.S.C. 552, 559)

[32 FR 10915, July 26, 1967, as amended at 36 FR 24928, Dec. 24, 1971]

SUBCHAPTER L—SWINE HEALTH PROTECTION

PART 166—SWINE HEALTH PROTECTION

AUTHORITY: 7 U.S.C. 3801–3813; 7 CFR 2.22, 2.8, and 371.4

SOURCE: 47 FR 49945, Nov. 3, 1982, unless otherwise noted.

GENERAL PROVISIONS

§ 166.1 Definitions in alphabetical order.

For the purposes of this part, the following terms shall have the meanings assigned them in this section. Unless otherwise required by the context, the singular form shall also import the plural and the masculine form shall also import the feminine, and vice versa. Words undefined in the following paragraphs shall have the meaning attributed to them in general usage as reflected by definitions in a standard dictionary.

Act. The Swine Health Protection Act (Pub. L. 96–468) as amended by the Farm Credit Act Amendments of 1980 (Pub. L. 96–592).

Administrator. The Administrator, Animal and Plant Health Inspection Service, or any person authorized to act for the Administrator.

Animal and Plant Health Inspection Service (APHIS). The Animal and Plant Health Inspection Service of the United States Department of Agriculture.

Animals. All domesticated and wild mammalian, poultry, and fish species, and wild and domesticated animals, including pets such as dogs and cats.

Area Veterinarian in Charge. The veterinarian of APHIS who is assigned by the Administrator to supervise and perform the official work of APHIS in a State or States or any other official to whom authority has heretofore been delegated or to whom authority may hereafter be delegated to act in his stead.

Facility. The site and all objects at this site including equipment and structures where garbage is accumulated, stored, handled, and cooked as a food for swine and which are fenced in or otherwise constructed so that swine are unable to have access to untreated garbage.

Garbage. All waste material derived in whole or in part from the meat of any animal (including fish and poultry) or other animal material, and other refuse of any character whatsoever that has been associated with any such material, resulting from the handling, preparation, cooking or consumption of food, except that such term shall not include waste from ordinary household operations which is fed directly to swine on the same premises where such household is located.

Inspector. Any individual employed by the United States Department of Agriculture or by a State for the purposes of enforcing the Act and this part.

License. A permit issued to a person for the purpose of allowing such person to operate a facility to treat garbage that is to be fed to swine.

Licensee. Any person licensed pursuant to the Act and regulations.

Person. Any individual, corporation, company, association, firm, partnership, society or joint stock company or other legal entity.

Premises. The location of a garbage treatment facility, as defined in this part, and any areas owned or controlled by the operator of the facility where swine are kept or fed by the operator.

Processed product. Material derived in whole or in part from the meat of any animal (including fish and poultry) or other animal material, and other refuse of any character whatsoever that has been associated with any such material, that has undergone an industrial manufacturing procedure to prevent spoilage or add shelf stability, and that has, at a minimum, been cooked to a temperature of 167 °F (75 °C) for at least 30 minutes or has been subjected to an industrial process demonstrated to provide an equivalent level of inactivation of disease organisms, as approved by the Administrator.

Rendered product. Waste material derived in whole or in part from the meat of any animal (including fish and poultry) or other animal material, and other refuse of any character whatsoever that has been associated with any such material, resulting from the handling, preparation, cooking or consumption of food that has been ground and heated to a minimum temperature of 230 °F. to make products such as, but not limited to, animal, poultry, or fish protein meal, grease or tallow.

State. The fifty States, the District of Columbia, Guam, Puerto Rico, the Virgin Islands of the United States, American Samoa, the Commonwealth of the Northern Mariana Islands, and the territories and possessions of the United States.

State animal health official. The individual employed by a State who is responsible for livestock and poultry disease control and eradication programs or any other official to whom authority is delegated to act for the State animal health official.

Treated garbage. Edible waste for animal consumption derived from garbage (as defined in this section) that has been heated throughout at boiling or equivalent temperature (212 °F. or 100 °C. at sea level) for 30 (thirty) minutes under the supervision of a licensee.

Treatment. The heating of garbage to specifications as set forth in this part.

Untreated garbage. Garbage that has not been treated in accordance with the Act and these regulations.

[47 FR 49945, Nov. 3, 1982, as amended at 48 FR 22290, May 18, 1983; 52 FR 4890, Feb. 18, 1987; 56 FR 26899, June 12, 1991; 66 FR 21064, Apr. 27, 2001; 74 FR 15218, Apr. 3, 2009]

§166.2 General restrictions.

(a) No person shall feed or permit the feeding of garbage to swine unless the garbage is treated to kill disease organisms, pursuant to this part, at a facility operated by a person holding a valid license for the treatment of garbage; except that the treatment and license requirements shall not apply to the feeding or the permitting of the feeding to swine of garbage only because the garbage consists of any of the following: Processed products; rendered products; bakery waste; candy waste; eggs; domestic dairy products (including milk); fish from the Atlantic Ocean within 200 miles of the continental United States or Canada; or fish from inland waters of the United States or Canada which do not flow into the Pacific Ocean.

(b) No person operating such a facility may be licensed to treat garbage unless he or she meets the requirements of this part designed to prevent the introduction or dissemination of any infectious or communicable disease of animals and unless the facility is so constructed that swine are unable to have access to untreated garbage or equipment and material coming in contact with untreated garbage.

(c) The regulations of this part shall not be construed to repeal or supersede State laws that prohibit feeding of garbage to swine or to prohibit any State from enforcing requirements relating to the treatment of garbage that is to be fed to swine or the feeding thereof which are more stringent than the requirements contained in this part. In a State which prohibits the feeding of garbage to swine, a license under the Act will not be issued to any applicant.

[47 FR 49945, Nov. 3, 1982, as amended at 49 FR 14497, Apr. 12, 1984; 52 FR 4890, Feb. 18, 1987; 66 FR 21064, Apr. 27, 2001; 74 FR 15218, Apr. 3, 2009]

§166.3 Separation of swine from the garbage handling and treatment areas.

(a) Access by swine to garbage handling and treatment areas shall be prevented by construction of facilities to exclude all ages and sizes of swine.

(b) All areas and drainage therefrom, used for the handling and treatment of untreated garbage shall be inaccessible to swine on the premises. This shall include the roads and areas used to transport and handle untreated garbage on the premises.

§ 166.4 Storage of garbage.

(a) Untreated garbage at a treatment facility shall be stored in covered and leakproof containers until treated.

(b) Treated garbage shall be transported to a feeding area from the treatment facility only in (1) containers used only for such treated garbage; (2) containers previously used for garbage which have been cleaned and disinfected in accordance with § 166.14 of this part; or (3) containers in which the garbage was treated.

[47 FR 49945, Nov. 3, 1982, as amended at 52 FR 4890, Feb. 18, 1987]

§ 166.5 Licensed garbage-treatment facility standards.

Garbage-treatment facilities shall be maintained as set forth in this section.

(a) Insects and animals shall be controlled. Accumulation of any material at the facility where insects and rodents may breed is prohibited.

(b) Equipment used for handling untreated garbage, except for the containers in which the garbage has been treated, may not be subsequently used in the feeding of swine unless first cleaned and disinfected as set forth in § 166.14(b).

(c) Untreated garbage that is not to be fed to swine and materials in association with such garbage shall be disposed of in a manner consistent with all applicable governmental environmental regulations and in an area inaccessible to swine.

[47 FR 49945, Nov. 3, 1982, as amended at 52 FR 4890, Feb. 18, 1987]

§ 166.6 Swine feeding area standards.

Untreated garbage shall not be allowed into swine feeding areas. Any equipment or material associated with untreated garbage, except for containers holding treated garbage which was treated in such containers, shall not be allowed into swine feeding areas at treatment premises until properly cleaned and disinfected as set forth in § 166.14(b) of this part.

[47 FR 49945, Nov. 3, 1982, as amended at 52 FR 4890, Feb. 18, 1987]

§ 166.7 Cooking standards.

(a) Garbage shall be heated throughout at boiling (212 °F. or 100 °C. at sea level) for 30 (thirty) minutes.

(b) Garbage shall be agitated during cooking, except in steam cooking equipment, to ensure that the prescribed cooking temperature is maintained throughout the cooking container for the prescribed length of time.

§ 166.8 Vehicles used to transport garbage.

Vehicles used by a licensee to transport untreated garbage, except those that have also been used to treat the garbage so moved, shall not be used for hauling animals or treated garbage until cleaned and disinfected as set forth in § 166.14(c) of this part.

[47 FR 49945, Nov. 3, 1982, as amended at 52 FR 4890, Feb. 18, 1987]

§ 166.9 Recordkeeping.

(a) Each licensee shall record the destination and date of removal of all treated or untreated garbage removed from the licensee's premises.

(b) Such records shall be legible and indelible.

(c) Each entry in a record shall be certified as correct by initials or signature of the licensee or an authorized agent or employee of the licensee.

(d) Such records shall be maintained by the licensee for a period of 1 year from the date made and shall be made available to inspectors upon request during normal business hours at that treatment facility.

(Approved by the Office of Management and Budget under control number 0579–0066)

[47 FR 49945, Nov. 3, 1982, as amended at 48 FR 57474, Dec. 30, 1983; 52 FR 4890, Feb. 18, 1987]

§ 166.10 Licensing.

(a) *Application.* Any person operating or desiring to operate a treatment facility for garbage that is to be treated and fed to swine shall apply for a license on a form which will be furnished, upon request, by the Area Veterinarian in Charge or, in States with primary enforcement responsibility, by the State animal health official in the State in which the person operates or intends to operate. When a person operates more than one treatment facility, a separate application to be licensed shall be made for each facility. Exemptions to the requirements of this paragraph may be granted in States other than those with primary enforcement responsibility by the Administrator, if he finds that there would not be a risk to the swine industry in the United States. Any person operating or desiring to operate a facility to treat garbage to be fed to swine who would otherwise be required under this part to obtain a license to treat garbage only because it contains one or more of the items allowed to be fed to swine under §166.2(a) of this part is exempted from the requirements of this paragraph.

(b) *Acknowledgement of Act and regulations.* A copy of the Act and regulations shall be supplied to the applicant at the time the applicant is given a license application. The applicant shall sign a receipt at the time of the prelicensing inspection acknowledging that the applicant has received a copy of the Act and regulations, that the applicant understands them, and agrees to comply with the Act and regulations.

(c) *Demonstration of compliance with the regulations.* (1) Prior to licensing, each applicant shall demonstrate during an inspection of the premises, facilities, and equipment that the facilities and equipment to be used in the treatment of garbage comply with these regulations. If the applicant's facilities and equipment do not meet the standards established by the regulations, the applicant shall not be licensed and shall be advised of the deficiencies and the measures that must be taken to comply with the regulations.

(2) The licensee shall make the premises, facilities, and equipment available during normal business hours for inspections by an inspector to determine continuing compliance with the Act and regulations.

(3) The facilities and equipment of an applicant for a license shall be in compliance with all applicable governmental environmental regulations before the applicant will be licensed.

(d) *Issuance of license.* A license will be issued to an applicant when the requirements of paragraphs (a), (b), and (c) of this section have been met, provided that such facility is not located in a State which prohibits the feeding of garbage to swine; and further, that if the Administrator has reason to believe that the applicant for a license is unfit to engage in the activity for which application has been made by reason of the fact that the applicant is engaging in or has, in the past, engaged in any activity in apparent violation of the Act or the regulations which has not been the subject of an administrative proceeding under the Act, an administrative proceeding shall be promptly instituted in which the applicant will be afforded an opportunity for a hearing in accordance with the rules of practice under the Act, for the purpose of giving the applicant an opportunity to show cause why the application for license should not be denied. In the event it is determined that the application should be denied, the applicant shall be precluded from reapplying for a license for 1 year from the date of the order denying the application.

(Approved by the Office of Management and Budget under control number 0579–0065)

[47 FR 49945, Nov. 3, 1982, as amended at 48 FR 57474, Dec. 30, 1983; 49 FR 14497, Apr. 12, 1984; 52 FR 4890, Feb. 18, 1987; 56 FR 26899, June 12, 1991; 66 FR 21064, Apr. 27, 2001]

§166.11 Suspension and revocation of licenses.

(a) *Suspension or revocation after notice.* In addition to the imposition of civil penalties and the issuance of cease and desist orders under the Act, the license of any facility may be suspended or revoked for any violation of the Act or the regulations in this part. Before such action is taken, the licensee of the facility will be informed in writing of the reasons for the proposed action and, upon request, shall be afforded an opportunity for a hearing with respect to the merits or validity of such action, in accordance with rules of practice which shall be adopted for the proceeding.

(b) *Summary suspension.* If the Administrator has reason to believe that any licensee has not complied or is not complying with any provisions of the Act or regulations in this part and the Administrator deems such action necessary in order to protect the public health, interest, or safety, the Administrator may summarily suspend the license of such persons pending a final determination in formal proceedings and any judicial review thereof, effective upon verbal or written notice of such suspension and the reasons therefor. In the event of verbal notification, written confirmation shall follow as soon as circumstances permit. This summary suspension shall continue in effect pending the completion of the proceeding and any judicial review thereof, unless otherwise ordered by the Administrator.

(c) The license of a person shall be automatically revoked, without action of the Administrator, upon the final effective date of the second criminal conviction of such person, as is stated in section 5(c) of the Act. The licensee will be notified in writing of such revocation by the Area Veterinarian in Charge or, in States having primary enforcement responsibility, by the State animal health official.

(d) Any person whose license has been suspended or revoked for any reason shall not be licensed in such person's own name or in any other manner, nor shall any of such person's employees be licensed for the purpose of operating the facility owned or operated by said licensee while the order of suspension or revocation is in effect. Any person whose license has been revoked shall not be eligible to apply for a new license for a period of 1 year from the effective date of such revocation. Any person who desires the reinstatement of a license that has been revoked must follow the procedure for new licensees set forth in § 166.10 of this part.

[47 FR 49945, Nov. 3, 1982, as amended at 52 FR 4890, Feb. 18, 1987; 56 FR 26899, June 12, 1991]

§ 166.12 Cancellation of licenses.

(a) The Area Veterinarian in Charge or, in States listed in § 166.15(d) of this part, the State animal health official shall cancel the license of a licensee when the Area Veterinarian in Charge or, in States listed in § 166.15(d) of this part, the State animal health official finds that no garbage has been treated for a period of 4 consecutive months at the facility operated by the licensee. Before such action is taken, the licensee of the facility will be informed in writing of the reasons for the proposed action and be given an opportunity to respond in writing. In those instances where there is a conflict as to the facts, the licensee shall, upon request, be afforded a hearing in accordance with rules of practice which shall be adopted for the proceeding.

(b) Any licensee may voluntarily have his or her license canceled by requesting such cancellation in writing and sending such request to the Area Veterinarian in Charge,[1] or, in States listed in § 166.15(d) of this part, to the State animal health official. The Area Veterinarian in Charge or, in States listed in § 166.15(d) of this part, the State animal health official shall cancel such license and shall notify the licensee of the cancellation in writing.

(c) Any person whose license is canceled in accordance with paragraph (a) or (b) of this section may apply for a new license at any time by following the procedure for obtaining a license set forth in § 166.10 of this part.

[52 FR 4891, Feb. 18, 1987, as amended at 56 FR 26899, June 12, 1991; 59 FR 67618, Dec. 30, 1994]

§ 166.13 Licensee responsibilities.

(a) A licensed facility shall be subject to inspections. Each inspector will be furnished with an official badge or identification card, either of which shall be sufficient identification to entitle access during normal business hours to the facility for the purposes of inspection. At such time the inspector is duly authorized to:

[1] The name and address of the Area Veterinarian in Charge may be obtained from the Veterinary Services, Operational Support, 4700 River Road, Unit 33, Riverdale, Maryland 20737–1231.

(1) Inspect the facility, including cooker function;

(2) Take samples of garbage;

(3) Observe and physically inspect the health status of all species of animals on the premises;

(4) Review records and make copies of such records; and

(5) Take photographs. A copy of each photograph will be provided to the licensee within 14 days.

(b) A licensee shall notify an inspector immediately upon detection of illness or death not normally associated with the licensee's operation in any animal species on the licensee's premises.

(c) A licensee shall notify an inspector or the State animal health official or the Area Veterinarian in Charge, as appropriate, of any change in the name, address, management or substantial control or ownership of his business or operation within 30 days after making such change.

(d) A licensee shall supply, upon request by an inspector, information concerning sources of garbage. Such information shall include the dates of supply and the names and addresses of the person and/or organization from which the garbage was received.

(Approved by the Office of Management and Budget under control number 0579–0065)

[47 FR 49945, Nov. 3, 1982, as amended at 48 FR 57474, Dec. 30, 1983; 52 FR 4890, Feb. 18, 1987. Redesignated at 52 FR 4891, Feb. 18, 1987]

§ 166.14 Cleaning and disinfecting.

(a) *Disinfectants to be used.* Disinfection required under the regulations in this Part shall be performed with one of the following:

(1) A permitted brand of sodium orthophenylphenate that is used in accordance with directions on the Environmental Protection Agency (EPA) approved label.

(2) A permitted cresylic disinfectant that is used in accordance with directions on the EPA-approved label, provided such disinfectant also meets the requirements set forth in §§ 71.10(b) and 71.11 of this chapter.

(3) Distinfectants which are registered under the Federal Insecticide, Fungicide, and Rodenticide Act (7 U.S.C. 136 *et seq.*), with tuberculocidal claims and labeled as efficacious against any species within the viral genus *Herpes*, that are used for purposes of this Part in accordance with directions on the EPA-approved label.

(b) All premises at which garbage has been fed to swine in violation of the Act or regulations in this part shall, prior to continued use for swine feeding purposes, be cleaned and disinfected under the supervision of an inspector or an accredited veterinarian as defined in Part 160 of this chapter as follows: Empty all troughs and other feeding and watering appliances, remove all litter, garbage, manure, and other organic material from the floors, posts, or other parts of such equipment, and handle such litter, garbage, manure, and other organic material in such manner as not to allow animal contact with such material; clean all surfaces with water and detergent and saturate the entire surface of the equipment, fencing, troughs, chutes, floors, walls, and all other parts of the facilities, with a disinfectant prescribed in paragraph (a) of this section. An exemption to the requirements of this paragraph may be given by the Administrator or, in States with primary enforcement responsibility, by the State animal health official, when it is determined that a threat to the swine industry does not exist.

(c) Any vehicle or other means of conveyance and its associated equipment which has been used by the licensee to move garbage, except any vehicle or other means of conveyance which also has been used to treat the garbage so moved, shall, prior to use for livestock-related or treated garbage hauling purposes, be cleaned and disinfected as follows: Remove all litter, garbage, manure, and other organic material from all portions of each means of conveyance, including all ledges and framework inside and outside, and handle such litter, garbage, manure, and other organic material in such manner as not to allow animal contact with such material; clean the interior and the exterior of such vehicle or other means of conveyance and its associated equipment with water and detergent; and saturate the entire interior surface, including all doors, endgates, portable chutes, and similar equipment with a disinfectant prescribed in paragraph (a) of this section.

(d) The owner of such facilities and vehicles shall be responsible for cleaning and disinfecting as required under this section, and the cleaning and disinfecting shall be done without expense to the United States Department of Agriculture.

[47 FR 49945, Nov. 3, 1982. Redesignated and amended at 52 FR 4891, Feb. 18, 1987; 56 FR 26899, June 12, 1991; 68 FR 6346, Feb. 7, 2003]

§ 166.15 State status.

(a) The following States prohibit the feeding of garbage to swine: Alabama, Delaware, Georgia, Idaho, Illinois, Indiana, Iowa, Kansas, Kentucky, Louisiana, Mississippi, Nebraska, New York, North Dakota, Oregon, South Carolina, South Dakota, Tennessee, Virginia, and Wisconsin.

(b) The following States and Puerto Rico permit the feeding of treated garbage to swine: Alaska, Arizona, Arkansas, California, Colorado, Connecticut, Florida, Hawaii, Maine, Maryland, Massachusetts, Michigan, Minnesota, Missouri, Montana, Nevada, New Hampshire, New Jersey, New Mexico, North Carolina, Ohio, Oklahoma, Pennsylvania, Puerto Rico, Rhode Island, Texas, Utah, Vermont, Washington, West Virginia, and Wyoming.

(c) The following States have primary enforcement responsibility under the Act: Alabama, Arizona, California, Colorado, Florida, Georgia, Hawaii, Idaho, Illinois, Indiana, Iowa, Michigan, Minnesota, Mississippi, Missouri, Montana, Nebraska, Nevada, New Jersey, New York, North Dakota, Ohio, Pennsylvania, South Carolina, South Dakota, Tennessee, Utah, Virginia, West Virginia, and Wisconsin.

(d) The following States issue licenses under cooperative agreements with the Animal and Plant Health Inspection Service, but do not have primary enforcement responsibility under the Act: Maryland, Puerto Rico, Texas, and Washington.

(e) The public may contact the Area Veterinarian in Charge, Animal and Plant Health Inspection Service, United States Department of Agiculture or State animal health official, or the Animal and Plant Health Inspection Service, Veterinary Services, Swine Health, 4700 River Road, Unit 37, Riverdale, Maryland 20737–1231, concerning the feeding of garbage to swine.

[47 FR 49945, Nov. 3, 1982. Redesignated at 52 FR 4891, Feb. 18, 1987]

EDITORIAL NOTE: For FEDERAL REGISTER citations affecting § 166.15, see the List of CFR Sections Affected, which appears in the Finding Aids section of the printed volume and at *www.fdsys.gov*.

PART 167—RULES OF PRACTICE GOVERNING PROCEEDINGS UNDER THE SWINE HEALTH PROTECTION ACT

Subpart A—General

Subpart B—Supplemental Rules of Practice

AUTHORITY: 7 U.S.C. 3804, 3805, and 3811; 7 CFR 2.22, 2.80, and 371.4.

SOURCE: 48 FR 30095, June 30, 1983, unless otherwise noted.

Subpart A—General

§ 167.1 Scope and applicability of rules of practice.

The Uniform Rules of Practice for the Department of Agriculture promulgated in subpart H of part 1, subtitle A, title 7, Code of Federal Regulations, are the Rules of Practice applicable to adjudicatory, administrative proceedings under sections 5 and 6 of the Swine Health Protection Act (7 U.S.C. 3804, 3805). In addition, the Supplemental Rules of Practice set forth in subpart B of this part shall be applicable to such proceedings.

Subpart B—Supplemental Rules of Practice

§ 167.10 Stipulations.

(a) At any time prior to the issuance of a complaint seeking a civil penalty under the Act, the Administrator, in his discretion, may enter into a stipulation with any person in which:

(1) The Administrator or the Administrator's delegate gives notice of an

apparent violation of the Act, or the regulations issued thereunder, by such person and affords such person an opportunity for a hearing regarding the matter as provided by the Act;

(2) Such person expressly waives hearing and agrees to a specified order which may include an agreement to pay a specified penalty within a designated time; and

(3) The Administrator agrees to accept the order in settlement of the particular matter conditioned upon timely payment of the penalty if the order includes an agreement to pay a penalty.

(b) If the order includes an agreement to pay a penalty and the penalty is not paid within the time designated in such a stipulation, the amount of the penalty shall not be relevant in any respect to the penalty which may be assessed after issuance of a complaint.

PARTS 168–199 [RESERVED]

FINDING AIDS

A list of CFR titles, subtitles, chapters, subchapters and parts and an alphabetical list of agencies publishing in the CFR are included in the CFR Index and Finding Aids volume of the Code of Federal Regulations which is published separately and revised annually.

Table of CFR Titles and Chapters

(Revised as of January 1, 2018)

Title 1—General Provisions

I	Administrative Committee of the Federal Register (Parts 1—49)
II	Office of the Federal Register (Parts 50—299)
III	Administrative Conference of the United States (Parts 300—399)
IV	Miscellaneous Agencies (Parts 400—599)
VI	National Capital Planning Commission (Parts 600—699)

Title 2—Grants and Agreements

	SUBTITLE A—OFFICE OF MANAGEMENT AND BUDGET GUIDANCE FOR GRANTS AND AGREEMENTS
I	Office of Management and Budget Governmentwide Guidance for Grants and Agreements (Parts 2—199)
II	Office of Management and Budget Guidance (Parts 200—299)
	SUBTITLE B—FEDERAL AGENCY REGULATIONS FOR GRANTS AND AGREEMENTS
III	Department of Health and Human Services (Parts 300—399)
IV	Department of Agriculture (Parts 400—499)
VI	Department of State (Parts 600—699)
VII	Agency for International Development (Parts 700—799)
VIII	Department of Veterans Affairs (Parts 800—899)
IX	Department of Energy (Parts 900—999)
X	Department of the Treasury (Parts 1000—1099)
XI	Department of Defense (Parts 1100—1199)
XII	Department of Transportation (Parts 1200—1299)
XIII	Department of Commerce (Parts 1300—1399)
XIV	Department of the Interior (Parts 1400—1499)
XV	Environmental Protection Agency (Parts 1500—1599)
XVIII	National Aeronautics and Space Administration (Parts 1800—1899)
XX	United States Nuclear Regulatory Commission (Parts 2000—2099)
XXII	Corporation for National and Community Service (Parts 2200—2299)
XXIII	Social Security Administration (Parts 2300—2399)
XXIV	Housing and Urban Development (Parts 2400—2499)
XXV	National Science Foundation (Parts 2500—2599)
XXVI	National Archives and Records Administration (Parts 2600—2699)

Title 2—Grants and Agreements—Continued

Chap.

XXVII	Small Business Administration (Parts 2700—2799)
XXVIII	Department of Justice (Parts 2800—2899)
XXIX	Department of Labor (Parts 2900—2999)
XXX	Department of Homeland Security (Parts 3000—3099)
XXXI	Institute of Museum and Library Services (Parts 3100—3199)
XXXII	National Endowment for the Arts (Parts 3200—3299)
XXXIII	National Endowment for the Humanities (Parts 3300—3399)
XXXIV	Department of Education (Parts 3400—3499)
XXXV	Export-Import Bank of the United States (Parts 3500—3599)
XXXVI	Office of National Drug Control Policy, Executive Office of the President (Parts 3600—3699)
XXXVII	Peace Corps (Parts 3700—3799)
LVIII	Election Assistance Commission (Parts 5800—5899)
LIX	Gulf Coast Ecosystem Restoration Council (Parts 5900—5999)

Title 3—The President

I	Executive Office of the President (Parts 100—199)

Title 4—Accounts

I	Government Accountability Office (Parts 1—199)

Title 5—Administrative Personnel

I	Office of Personnel Management (Parts 1—1199)
II	Merit Systems Protection Board (Parts 1200—1299)
III	Office of Management and Budget (Parts 1300—1399)
IV	Office of Personnel Management and Office of the Director of National Intelligence (Parts 1400—1499)
V	The International Organizations Employees Loyalty Board (Parts 1500—1599)
VI	Federal Retirement Thrift Investment Board (Parts 1600—1699)
VIII	Office of Special Counsel (Parts 1800—1899)
IX	Appalachian Regional Commission (Parts 1900—1999)
XI	Armed Forces Retirement Home (Parts 2100—2199)
XIV	Federal Labor Relations Authority, General Counsel of the Federal Labor Relations Authority and Federal Service Impasses Panel (Parts 2400—2499)
XVI	Office of Government Ethics (Parts 2600—2699)
XXI	Department of the Treasury (Parts 3100—3199)
XXII	Federal Deposit Insurance Corporation (Parts 3200—3299)
XXIII	Department of Energy (Parts 3300—3399)
XXIV	Federal Energy Regulatory Commission (Parts 3400—3499)
XXV	Department of the Interior (Parts 3500—3599)
XXVI	Department of Defense (Parts 3600—3699)

Title 5—Administrative Personnel—Continued

Title 5—Administrative Personnel—Continued

Chap.	
LXXIV	Federal Mine Safety and Health Review Commission (Parts 8400—8499)
LXXVI	Federal Retirement Thrift Investment Board (Parts 8600—8699)
LXXVII	Office of Management and Budget (Parts 8700—8799)
LXXX	Federal Housing Finance Agency (Parts 9000—9099)
LXXXIII	Special Inspector General for Afghanistan Reconstruction (Parts 9300—9399)
LXXXIV	Bureau of Consumer Financial Protection (Parts 9400—9499)
LXXXVI	National Credit Union Administration (Parts 9600—9699)
XCVII	Department of Homeland Security Human Resources Management System (Department of Homeland Security—Office of Personnel Management) (Parts 9700—9799)
XCVIII	Council of the Inspectors General on Integrity and Efficiency (Parts 9800—9899)
XCIX	Military Compensation and Retirement Modernization Commission (Parts 9900—9999)
C	National Council on Disability (Parts 10000—10049)

Title 6—Domestic Security

I	Department of Homeland Security, Office of the Secretary (Parts 1—199)
X	Privacy and Civil Liberties Oversight Board (Parts 1000—1099)

Title 7—Agriculture

SUBTITLE A—OFFICE OF THE SECRETARY OF AGRICULTURE (PARTS 0—26)

SUBTITLE B—REGULATIONS OF THE DEPARTMENT OF AGRICULTURE

I	Agricultural Marketing Service (Standards, Inspections, Marketing Practices), Department of Agriculture (Parts 27—209)
II	Food and Nutrition Service, Department of Agriculture (Parts 210—299)
III	Animal and Plant Health Inspection Service, Department of Agriculture (Parts 300—399)
IV	Federal Crop Insurance Corporation, Department of Agriculture (Parts 400—499)
V	Agricultural Research Service, Department of Agriculture (Parts 500—599)
VI	Natural Resources Conservation Service, Department of Agriculture (Parts 600—699)
VII	Farm Service Agency, Department of Agriculture (Parts 700—799)
VIII	Grain Inspection, Packers and Stockyards Administration (Federal Grain Inspection Service), Department of Agriculture (Parts 800—899)
IX	Agricultural Marketing Service (Marketing Agreements and Orders; Fruits, Vegetables, Nuts), Department of Agriculture (Parts 900—999)

Title 7—Agriculture—Continued

Chap.

Chap.	
X	Agricultural Marketing Service (Marketing Agreements and Orders; Milk), Department of Agriculture (Parts 1000—1199)
XI	Agricultural Marketing Service (Marketing Agreements and Orders; Miscellaneous Commodities), Department of Agriculture (Parts 1200—1299)
XIV	Commodity Credit Corporation, Department of Agriculture (Parts 1400—1499)
XV	Foreign Agricultural Service, Department of Agriculture (Parts 1500—1599)
XVI	Rural Telephone Bank, Department of Agriculture (Parts 1600—1699)
XVII	Rural Utilities Service, Department of Agriculture (Parts 1700—1799)
XVIII	Rural Housing Service, Rural Business-Cooperative Service, Rural Utilities Service, and Farm Service Agency, Department of Agriculture (Parts 1800—2099)
XX	Local Television Loan Guarantee Board (Parts 2200—2299)
XXV	Office of Advocacy and Outreach, Department of Agriculture (Parts 2500—2599)
XXVI	Office of Inspector General, Department of Agriculture (Parts 2600—2699)
XXVII	Office of Information Resources Management, Department of Agriculture (Parts 2700—2799)
XXVIII	Office of Operations, Department of Agriculture (Parts 2800—2899)
XXIX	Office of Energy Policy and New Uses, Department of Agriculture (Parts 2900—2999)
XXX	Office of the Chief Financial Officer, Department of Agriculture (Parts 3000—3099)
XXXI	Office of Environmental Quality, Department of Agriculture (Parts 3100—3199)
XXXII	Office of Procurement and Property Management, Department of Agriculture (Parts 3200—3299)
XXXIII	Office of Transportation, Department of Agriculture (Parts 3300—3399)
XXXIV	National Institute of Food and Agriculture (Parts 3400—3499)
XXXV	Rural Housing Service, Department of Agriculture (Parts 3500—3599)
XXXVI	National Agricultural Statistics Service, Department of Agriculture (Parts 3600—3699)
XXXVII	Economic Research Service, Department of Agriculture (Parts 3700—3799)
XXXVIII	World Agricultural Outlook Board, Department of Agriculture (Parts 3800—3899)
XLI	[Reserved]
XLII	Rural Business-Cooperative Service and Rural Utilities Service, Department of Agriculture (Parts 4200—4299)

Title 8—Aliens and Nationality

Chap.

I Department of Homeland Security (Immigration and Naturalization) (Parts 1—499)

V Executive Office for Immigration Review, Department of Justice (Parts 1000—1399)

Title 9—Animals and Animal Products

I Animal and Plant Health Inspection Service, Department of Agriculture (Parts 1—199)

II Grain Inspection, Packers and Stockyards Administration (Packers and Stockyards Programs), Department of Agriculture (Parts 200—299)

III Food Safety and Inspection Service, Department of Agriculture (Parts 300—599)

Title 10—Energy

I Nuclear Regulatory Commission (Parts 0—199)

II Department of Energy (Parts 200—699)

III Department of Energy (Parts 700—999)

X Department of Energy (General Provisions) (Parts 1000—1099)

XIII Nuclear Waste Technical Review Board (Parts 1300—1399)

XVII Defense Nuclear Facilities Safety Board (Parts 1700—1799)

XVIII Northeast Interstate Low-Level Radioactive Waste Commission (Parts 1800—1899)

Title 11—Federal Elections

I Federal Election Commission (Parts 1—9099)

II Election Assistance Commission (Parts 9400—9499)

Title 12—Banks and Banking

I Comptroller of the Currency, Department of the Treasury (Parts 1—199)

II Federal Reserve System (Parts 200—299)

III Federal Deposit Insurance Corporation (Parts 300—399)

IV Export-Import Bank of the United States (Parts 400—499)

V Office of Thrift Supervision, Department of the Treasury (Parts 500—599)

VI Farm Credit Administration (Parts 600—699)

VII National Credit Union Administration (Parts 700—799)

VIII Federal Financing Bank (Parts 800—899)

IX Federal Housing Finance Board (Parts 900—999)

X Bureau of Consumer Financial Protection (Parts 1000—1099)

XI Federal Financial Institutions Examination Council (Parts 1100—1199)

XII Federal Housing Finance Agency (Parts 1200—1299)

Title 12—Banks and Banking—Continued

Chap.

XIII Financial Stability Oversight Council (Parts 1300—1399)

XIV Farm Credit System Insurance Corporation (Parts 1400—1499)

XV Department of the Treasury (Parts 1500—1599)

XVI Office of Financial Research (Parts 1600—1699)

XVII Office of Federal Housing Enterprise Oversight, Department of Housing and Urban Development (Parts 1700—1799)

XVIII Community Development Financial Institutions Fund, Department of the Treasury (Parts 1800—1899)

Title 13—Business Credit and Assistance

I Small Business Administration (Parts 1—199)

III Economic Development Administration, Department of Commerce (Parts 300—399)

IV Emergency Steel Guarantee Loan Board (Parts 400—499)

V Emergency Oil and Gas Guaranteed Loan Board (Parts 500—599)

Title 14—Aeronautics and Space

I Federal Aviation Administration, Department of Transportation (Parts 1—199)

II Office of the Secretary, Department of Transportation (Aviation Proceedings) (Parts 200—399)

III Commercial Space Transportation, Federal Aviation Administration, Department of Transportation (Parts 400—1199)

V National Aeronautics and Space Administration (Parts 1200—1299)

VI Air Transportation System Stabilization (Parts 1300—1399)

Title 15—Commerce and Foreign Trade

SUBTITLE A—OFFICE OF THE SECRETARY OF COMMERCE (PARTS 0—29)

SUBTITLE B—REGULATIONS RELATING TO COMMERCE AND FOREIGN TRADE

I Bureau of the Census, Department of Commerce (Parts 30—199)

II National Institute of Standards and Technology, Department of Commerce (Parts 200—299)

III International Trade Administration, Department of Commerce (Parts 300—399)

IV Foreign-Trade Zones Board, Department of Commerce (Parts 400—499)

VII Bureau of Industry and Security, Department of Commerce (Parts 700—799)

VIII Bureau of Economic Analysis, Department of Commerce (Parts 800—899)

IX National Oceanic and Atmospheric Administration, Department of Commerce (Parts 900—999)

Title 15—Commerce and Foreign Trade—Continued

Chap.

XI National Technical Information Service, Department of Commerce (Parts 1100—1199)

XIII East-West Foreign Trade Board (Parts 1300—1399)

XIV Minority Business Development Agency (Parts 1400—1499)

SUBTITLE C—REGULATIONS RELATING TO FOREIGN TRADE AGREEMENTS

XX Office of the United States Trade Representative (Parts 2000—2099)

SUBTITLE D—REGULATIONS RELATING TO TELECOMMUNICATIONS AND INFORMATION

XXIII National Telecommunications and Information Administration, Department of Commerce (Parts 2300—2399) [Reserved]

Title 16—Commercial Practices

I Federal Trade Commission (Parts 0—999)

II Consumer Product Safety Commission (Parts 1000—1799)

Title 17—Commodity and Securities Exchanges

I Commodity Futures Trading Commission (Parts 1—199)

II Securities and Exchange Commission (Parts 200—399)

IV Department of the Treasury (Parts 400—499)

Title 18—Conservation of Power and Water Resources

I Federal Energy Regulatory Commission, Department of Energy (Parts 1—399)

III Delaware River Basin Commission (Parts 400—499)

VI Water Resources Council (Parts 700—799)

VIII Susquehanna River Basin Commission (Parts 800—899)

XIII Tennessee Valley Authority (Parts 1300—1399)

Title 19—Customs Duties

I U.S. Customs and Border Protection, Department of Homeland Security; Department of the Treasury (Parts 0—199)

II United States International Trade Commission (Parts 200—299)

III International Trade Administration, Department of Commerce (Parts 300—399)

IV U.S. Immigration and Customs Enforcement, Department of Homeland Security (Parts 400—599) [Reserved]

Title 20—Employees' Benefits

I Office of Workers' Compensation Programs, Department of Labor (Parts 1—199)

II Railroad Retirement Board (Parts 200—399)

Title 20—Employees' Benefits—Continued

Title 21—Food and Drugs

Title 22—Foreign Relations

Title 23—Highways

Title 23—Highways—Continued

Chap.

Chap.	
II	National Highway Traffic Safety Administration and Federal Highway Administration, Department of Transportation (Parts 1200—1299)
III	National Highway Traffic Safety Administration, Department of Transportation (Parts 1300—1399)

Title 24—Housing and Urban Development

SUBTITLE A—OFFICE OF THE SECRETARY, DEPARTMENT OF HOUSING AND URBAN DEVELOPMENT (PARTS 0—99)

SUBTITLE B—REGULATIONS RELATING TO HOUSING AND URBAN DEVELOPMENT

Chap.	
I	Office of Assistant Secretary for Equal Opportunity, Department of Housing and Urban Development (Parts 100—199)
II	Office of Assistant Secretary for Housing-Federal Housing Commissioner, Department of Housing and Urban Development (Parts 200—299)
III	Government National Mortgage Association, Department of Housing and Urban Development (Parts 300—399)
IV	Office of Housing and Office of Multifamily Housing Assistance Restructuring, Department of Housing and Urban Development (Parts 400—499)
V	Office of Assistant Secretary for Community Planning and Development, Department of Housing and Urban Development (Parts 500—599)
VI	Office of Assistant Secretary for Community Planning and Development, Department of Housing and Urban Development (Parts 600—699) [Reserved]
VII	Office of the Secretary, Department of Housing and Urban Development (Housing Assistance Programs and Public and Indian Housing Programs) (Parts 700—799)
VIII	Office of the Assistant Secretary for Housing—Federal Housing Commissioner, Department of Housing and Urban Development (Section 8 Housing Assistance Programs, Section 202 Direct Loan Program, Section 202 Supportive Housing for the Elderly Program and Section 811 Supportive Housing for Persons With Disabilities Program) (Parts 800—899)
IX	Office of Assistant Secretary for Public and Indian Housing, Department of Housing and Urban Development (Parts 900—1699)
X	Office of Assistant Secretary for Housing—Federal Housing Commissioner, Department of Housing and Urban Development (Interstate Land Sales Registration Program) (Parts 1700—1799)
XII	Office of Inspector General, Department of Housing and Urban Development (Parts 2000—2099)
XV	Emergency Mortgage Insurance and Loan Programs, Department of Housing and Urban Development (Parts 2700—2799) [Reserved]
XX	Office of Assistant Secretary for Housing—Federal Housing Commissioner, Department of Housing and Urban Development (Parts 3200—3899)

Chap.

XXIV Board of Directors of the HOPE for Homeowners Program (Parts 4000—4099) [Reserved]

XXV Neighborhood Reinvestment Corporation (Parts 4100—4199)

Title 25—Indians

I Bureau of Indian Affairs, Department of the Interior (Parts 1—299)

II Indian Arts and Crafts Board, Department of the Interior (Parts 300—399)

III National Indian Gaming Commission, Department of the Interior (Parts 500—599)

IV Office of Navajo and Hopi Indian Relocation (Parts 700—899)

V Bureau of Indian Affairs, Department of the Interior, and Indian Health Service, Department of Health and Human Services (Part 900)

VI Office of the Assistant Secretary, Indian Affairs, Department of the Interior (Parts 1000—1199)

VII Office of the Special Trustee for American Indians, Department of the Interior (Parts 1200—1299)

Title 26—Internal Revenue

I Internal Revenue Service, Department of the Treasury (Parts 1—End)

Title 27—Alcohol, Tobacco Products and Firearms

I Alcohol and Tobacco Tax and Trade Bureau, Department of the Treasury (Parts 1—399)

II Bureau of Alcohol, Tobacco, Firearms, and Explosives, Department of Justice (Parts 400—699)

Title 28—Judicial Administration

I Department of Justice (Parts 0—299)

III Federal Prison Industries, Inc., Department of Justice (Parts 300—399)

V Bureau of Prisons, Department of Justice (Parts 500—599)

VI Offices of Independent Counsel, Department of Justice (Parts 600—699)

VII Office of Independent Counsel (Parts 700—799)

VIII Court Services and Offender Supervision Agency for the District of Columbia (Parts 800—899)

IX National Crime Prevention and Privacy Compact Council (Parts 900—999)

XI Department of Justice and Department of State (Parts 1100—1199)

Title 29—Labor

Chap.

SUBTITLE A—OFFICE OF THE SECRETARY OF LABOR (PARTS 0—99)

SUBTITLE B—REGULATIONS RELATING TO LABOR

I National Labor Relations Board (Parts 100—199)

II Office of Labor-Management Standards, Department of Labor (Parts 200—299)

III National Railroad Adjustment Board (Parts 300—399)

IV Office of Labor-Management Standards, Department of Labor (Parts 400—499)

V Wage and Hour Division, Department of Labor (Parts 500—899)

IX Construction Industry Collective Bargaining Commission (Parts 900—999)

X National Mediation Board (Parts 1200—1299)

XII Federal Mediation and Conciliation Service (Parts 1400—1499)

XIV Equal Employment Opportunity Commission (Parts 1600—1699)

XVII Occupational Safety and Health Administration, Department of Labor (Parts 1900—1999)

XX Occupational Safety and Health Review Commission (Parts 2200—2499)

XXV Employee Benefits Security Administration, Department of Labor (Parts 2500—2599)

XXVII Federal Mine Safety and Health Review Commission (Parts 2700—2799)

XL Pension Benefit Guaranty Corporation (Parts 4000—4999)

Title 30—Mineral Resources

I Mine Safety and Health Administration, Department of Labor (Parts 1—199)

II Bureau of Safety and Environmental Enforcement, Department of the Interior (Parts 200—299)

IV Geological Survey, Department of the Interior (Parts 400—499)

V Bureau of Ocean Energy Management, Department of the Interior (Parts 500—599)

VII Office of Surface Mining Reclamation and Enforcement, Department of the Interior (Parts 700—999)

XII Office of Natural Resources Revenue, Department of the Interior (Parts 1200—1299)

Title 31—Money and Finance: Treasury

SUBTITLE A—OFFICE OF THE SECRETARY OF THE TREASURY (PARTS 0—50)

SUBTITLE B—REGULATIONS RELATING TO MONEY AND FINANCE

I Monetary Offices, Department of the Treasury (Parts 51—199)

II Fiscal Service, Department of the Treasury (Parts 200—399)

IV Secret Service, Department of the Treasury (Parts 400—499)

V Office of Foreign Assets Control, Department of the Treasury (Parts 500—599)

Title 31—Money and Finance: Treasury—Continued

Chap.

VI Bureau of Engraving and Printing, Department of the Treasury (Parts 600—699)

VII Federal Law Enforcement Training Center, Department of the Treasury (Parts 700—799)

VIII Office of Investment Security, Department of the Treasury (Parts 800—899)

IX Federal Claims Collection Standards (Department of the Treasury—Department of Justice) (Parts 900—999)

X Financial Crimes Enforcement Network, Department of the Treasury (Parts 1000—1099)

Title 32—National Defense

SUBTITLE A—DEPARTMENT OF DEFENSE

I Office of the Secretary of Defense (Parts 1—399)

V Department of the Army (Parts 400—699)

VI Department of the Navy (Parts 700—799)

VII Department of the Air Force (Parts 800—1099)

SUBTITLE B—OTHER REGULATIONS RELATING TO NATIONAL DEFENSE

XII Defense Logistics Agency (Parts 1200—1299)

XVI Selective Service System (Parts 1600—1699)

XVII Office of the Director of National Intelligence (Parts 1700—1799)

XVIII National Counterintelligence Center (Parts 1800—1899)

XIX Central Intelligence Agency (Parts 1900—1999)

XX Information Security Oversight Office, National Archives and Records Administration (Parts 2000—2099)

XXI National Security Council (Parts 2100—2199)

XXIV Office of Science and Technology Policy (Parts 2400—2499)

XXVII Office for Micronesian Status Negotiations (Parts 2700—2799)

XXVIII Office of the Vice President of the United States (Parts 2800—2899)

Title 33—Navigation and Navigable Waters

I Coast Guard, Department of Homeland Security (Parts 1—199)

II Corps of Engineers, Department of the Army, Department of Defense (Parts 200—399)

IV Saint Lawrence Seaway Development Corporation, Department of Transportation (Parts 400—499)

Title 34—Education

SUBTITLE A—OFFICE OF THE SECRETARY, DEPARTMENT OF EDUCATION (PARTS 1—99)

SUBTITLE B—REGULATIONS OF THE OFFICES OF THE DEPARTMENT OF EDUCATION

I Office for Civil Rights, Department of Education (Parts 100—199)

Title 34—Education—Continued

Chap.	
II	Office of Elementary and Secondary Education, Department of Education (Parts 200—299)
III	Office of Special Education and Rehabilitative Services, Department of Education (Parts 300—399)
IV	Office of Career, Technical and Adult Education, Department of Education (Parts 400—499)
V	Office of Bilingual Education and Minority Languages Affairs, Department of Education (Parts 500—599) [Reserved]
VI	Office of Postsecondary Education, Department of Education (Parts 600—699)
VII	Office of Educational Research and Improvement, Department of Education (Parts 700—799) [Reserved]
	SUBTITLE C—REGULATIONS RELATING TO EDUCATION
XI	(Parts 1100—1199) [Reserved]
XII	National Council on Disability (Parts 1200—1299)

Title 35 [Reserved]

Title 36—Parks, Forests, and Public Property

I	National Park Service, Department of the Interior (Parts 1—199)
II	Forest Service, Department of Agriculture (Parts 200—299)
III	Corps of Engineers, Department of the Army (Parts 300—399)
IV	American Battle Monuments Commission (Parts 400—499)
V	Smithsonian Institution (Parts 500—599)
VI	[Reserved]
VII	Library of Congress (Parts 700—799)
VIII	Advisory Council on Historic Preservation (Parts 800—899)
IX	Pennsylvania Avenue Development Corporation (Parts 900—999)
X	Presidio Trust (Parts 1000—1099)
XI	Architectural and Transportation Barriers Compliance Board (Parts 1100—1199)
XII	National Archives and Records Administration (Parts 1200—1299)
XV	Oklahoma City National Memorial Trust (Parts 1500—1599)
XVI	Morris K. Udall Scholarship and Excellence in National Environmental Policy Foundation (Parts 1600—1699)

Title 37—Patents, Trademarks, and Copyrights

I	United States Patent and Trademark Office, Department of Commerce (Parts 1—199)
II	U.S. Copyright Office, Library of Congress (Parts 200—299)
III	Copyright Royalty Board, Library of Congress (Parts 300—399)
IV	National Institute of Standards and Technology, Department of Commerce (Parts 400—599)

Title 38—Pensions, Bonuses, and Veterans' Relief

Chap.

I Department of Veterans Affairs (Parts 0—199)

II Armed Forces Retirement Home (Parts 200—299)

Title 39—Postal Service

I United States Postal Service (Parts 1—999)

III Postal Regulatory Commission (Parts 3000—3099)

Title 40—Protection of Environment

I Environmental Protection Agency (Parts 1—1099)

IV Environmental Protection Agency and Department of Justice (Parts 1400—1499)

V Council on Environmental Quality (Parts 1500—1599)

VI Chemical Safety and Hazard Investigation Board (Parts 1600—1699)

VII Environmental Protection Agency and Department of Defense; Uniform National Discharge Standards for Vessels of the Armed Forces (Parts 1700—1799)

VIII Gulf Coast Ecosystem Restoration Council (Parts 1800—1899)

Title 41—Public Contracts and Property Management

SUBTITLE A—FEDERAL PROCUREMENT REGULATIONS SYSTEM [NOTE]

SUBTITLE B—OTHER PROVISIONS RELATING TO PUBLIC CONTRACTS

50 Public Contracts, Department of Labor (Parts 50–1—50–999)

51 Committee for Purchase From People Who Are Blind or Severely Disabled (Parts 51–1—51–99)

60 Office of Federal Contract Compliance Programs, Equal Employment Opportunity, Department of Labor (Parts 60–1—60–999)

61 Office of the Assistant Secretary for Veterans' Employment and Training Service, Department of Labor (Parts 61–1—61–999)

62—100 [Reserved]

SUBTITLE C—FEDERAL PROPERTY MANAGEMENT REGULATIONS SYSTEM

101 Federal Property Management Regulations (Parts 101–1—101–99)

102 Federal Management Regulation (Parts 102–1—102–299)

103—104 [Reserved]

105 General Services Administration (Parts 105–1—105–999)

109 Department of Energy Property Management Regulations (Parts 109–1—109–99)

114 Department of the Interior (Parts 114–1—114–99)

115 Environmental Protection Agency (Parts 115–1—115–99)

128 Department of Justice (Parts 128–1—128–99)

129—200 [Reserved]

SUBTITLE D—OTHER PROVISIONS RELATING TO PROPERTY MANAGEMENT [RESERVED]

Title 42—Public Health

Title 43—Public Lands: Interior

Title 44—Emergency Management and Assistance

Title 45—Public Welfare

Title 45—Public Welfare—Continued

Chap.

III	Office of Child Support Enforcement (Child Support Enforcement Program), Administration for Children and Families, Department of Health and Human Services (Parts 300—399)
IV	Office of Refugee Resettlement, Administration for Children and Families, Department of Health and Human Services (Parts 400—499)
V	Foreign Claims Settlement Commission of the United States, Department of Justice (Parts 500—599)
VI	National Science Foundation (Parts 600—699)
VII	Commission on Civil Rights (Parts 700—799)
VIII	Office of Personnel Management (Parts 800—899)
IX	Denali Commission (Parts 900—999)
X	Office of Community Services, Administration for Children and Families, Department of Health and Human Services (Parts 1000—1099)
XI	National Foundation on the Arts and the Humanities (Parts 1100—1199)
XII	Corporation for National and Community Service (Parts 1200—1299)
XIII	Administration for Children and Families, Department of Health and Human Services (Parts 1300—1399)
XVI	Legal Services Corporation (Parts 1600—1699)
XVII	National Commission on Libraries and Information Science (Parts 1700—1799)
XVIII	Harry S. Truman Scholarship Foundation (Parts 1800—1899)
XXI	Commission of Fine Arts (Parts 2100—2199)
XXIII	Arctic Research Commission (Part 2301)
XXIV	James Madison Memorial Fellowship Foundation (Parts 2400—2499)
XXV	Corporation for National and Community Service (Parts 2500—2599)

Title 46—Shipping

I	Coast Guard, Department of Homeland Security (Parts 1—199)
II	Maritime Administration, Department of Transportation (Parts 200—399)
III	Coast Guard (Great Lakes Pilotage), Department of Homeland Security (Parts 400—499)
IV	Federal Maritime Commission (Parts 500—599)

Title 47—Telecommunication

I	Federal Communications Commission (Parts 0—199)
II	Office of Science and Technology Policy and National Security Council (Parts 200—299)
III	National Telecommunications and Information Administration, Department of Commerce (Parts 300—399)

Title 47—Telecommunication—Continued

Title 48—Federal Acquisition Regulations System

Title 48—Federal Acquisition Regulations System—Continued

Chap.

54 Defense Logistics Agency, Department of Defense (Parts 5400—5499)

57 African Development Foundation (Parts 5700—5799)

61 Civilian Board of Contract Appeals, General Services Administration (Parts 6100—6199)

99 Cost Accounting Standards Board, Office of Federal Procurement Policy, Office of Management and Budget (Parts 9900—9999)

Title 49—Transportation

SUBTITLE A—OFFICE OF THE SECRETARY OF TRANSPORTATION (PARTS 1—99)

SUBTITLE B—OTHER REGULATIONS RELATING TO TRANSPORTATION

I Pipeline and Hazardous Materials Safety Administration, Department of Transportation (Parts 100—199)

II Federal Railroad Administration, Department of Transportation (Parts 200—299)

III Federal Motor Carrier Safety Administration, Department of Transportation (Parts 300—399)

IV Coast Guard, Department of Homeland Security (Parts 400—499)

V National Highway Traffic Safety Administration, Department of Transportation (Parts 500—599)

VI Federal Transit Administration, Department of Transportation (Parts 600—699)

VII National Railroad Passenger Corporation (AMTRAK) (Parts 700—799)

VIII National Transportation Safety Board (Parts 800—999)

X Surface Transportation Board (Parts 1000—1399)

XI Research and Innovative Technology Administration, Department of Transportation (Parts 1400—1499) [Reserved]

XII Transportation Security Administration, Department of Homeland Security (Parts 1500—1699)

Title 50—Wildlife and Fisheries

I United States Fish and Wildlife Service, Department of the Interior (Parts 1—199)

II National Marine Fisheries Service, National Oceanic and Atmospheric Administration, Department of Commerce (Parts 200—299)

III International Fishing and Related Activities (Parts 300—399)

IV Joint Regulations (United States Fish and Wildlife Service, Department of the Interior and National Marine Fisheries Service, National Oceanic and Atmospheric Administration, Department of Commerce); Endangered Species Committee Regulations (Parts 400—499)

V Marine Mammal Commission (Parts 500—599)

Alphabetical List of Agencies Appearing in the CFR

(Revised as of January 1, 2018)

Agency	CFR Title, Subtitle or Chapter
Administrative Committee of the Federal Register	1, I
Administrative Conference of the United States	1, III
Advisory Council on Historic Preservation	36, VIII
Advocacy and Outreach, Office of	7, XXV
Afghanistan Reconstruction, Special Inspector General for	5, LXXXIII
African Development Foundation	22, XV
Federal Acquisition Regulation	48, 57
Agency for International Development	2, VII; 22, II
Federal Acquisition Regulation	48, 7
Agricultural Marketing Service	7, I, IX, X, XI
Agricultural Research Service	7, V
Agriculture Department	2, IV; 5, LXXIII
Advocacy and Outreach, Office of	7, XXV
Agricultural Marketing Service	7, I, IX, X, XI
Agricultural Research Service	7, V
Animal and Plant Health Inspection Service	7, III; 9, I
Chief Financial Officer, Office of	7, XXX
Commodity Credit Corporation	7, XIV
Economic Research Service	7, XXXVII
Energy Policy and New Uses, Office of	2, IX; 7, XXIX
Environmental Quality, Office of	7, XXXI
Farm Service Agency	7, VII, XVIII
Federal Acquisition Regulation	48, 4
Federal Crop Insurance Corporation	7, IV
Food and Nutrition Service	7, II
Food Safety and Inspection Service	9, III
Foreign Agricultural Service	7, XV
Forest Service	36, II
Grain Inspection, Packers and Stockyards Administration	7, VIII; 9, II
Information Resources Management, Office of	7, XXVII
Inspector General, Office of	7, XXVI
National Agricultural Library	7, XLI
National Agricultural Statistics Service	7, XXXVI
National Institute of Food and Agriculture	7, XXXIV
Natural Resources Conservation Service	7, VI
Operations, Office of	7, XXVIII
Procurement and Property Management, Office of	7, XXXII
Rural Business-Cooperative Service	7, XVIII, XLII
Rural Development Administration	7, XLII
Rural Housing Service	7, XVIII, XXXV
Rural Telephone Bank	7, XVI
Rural Utilities Service	7, XVII, XVIII, XLII
Secretary of Agriculture, Office of	7, Subtitle A
Transportation, Office of	7, XXXIII
World Agricultural Outlook Board	7, XXXVIII
Air Force Department	32, VII
Federal Acquisition Regulation Supplement	48, 53
Air Transportation Stabilization Board	14, VI
Alcohol and Tobacco Tax and Trade Bureau	27, I
Alcohol, Tobacco, Firearms, and Explosives, Bureau of	27, II
AMTRAK	49, VII
American Battle Monuments Commission	36, IV
American Indians, Office of the Special Trustee	25, VII

Agency	CFR Title, Subtitle or Chapter
Air Force Department	32, VII
Army Department	32, V; 33, II; 36, III; 48, 51
Defense Acquisition Regulations System	48, 2
Defense Intelligence Agency	32, I
Defense Logistics Agency	32, I, XII; 48, 54
Engineers, Corps of	33, II; 36, III
National Imagery and Mapping Agency	32, I
Navy Department	32, VI; 48, 52
Secretary of Defense, Office of	2, XI; 32, I
Defense Contract Audit Agency	32, I
Defense Intelligence Agency	32, I
Defense Logistics Agency	32, XII; 48, 54
Defense Nuclear Facilities Safety Board	10, XVII
Delaware River Basin Commission	18, III
Denali Commission	45, IX
District of Columbia, Court Services and Offender Supervision Agency for the	5, LXX; 28, VIII
Drug Enforcement Administration	21, II
East-West Foreign Trade Board	15, XIII
Economic Analysis, Bureau of	15, VIII
Economic Development Administration	13, III
Economic Research Service	7, XXXVII
Education, Department of	2, XXXIV; 5, LIII
Bilingual Education and Minority Languages Affairs, Office of	34, V
Career, Technical and Adult Education, Office of	34, IV
Civil Rights, Office for	34, I
Educational Research and Improvement, Office of	34, VII
Elementary and Secondary Education, Office of	34, II
Federal Acquisition Regulation	48, 34
Postsecondary Education, Office of	34, VI
Secretary of Education, Office of	34, Subtitle A
Special Education and Rehabilitative Services, Office of	34, III
Career, Technical, and Adult Education, Office of	34, IV
Educational Research and Improvement, Office of	34, VII
Election Assistance Commission	2, LVIII; 11, II
Elementary and Secondary Education, Office of	34, II
Emergency Oil and Gas Guaranteed Loan Board	13, V
Emergency Steel Guarantee Loan Board	13, IV
Employee Benefits Security Administration	29, XXV
Employees' Compensation Appeals Board	20, IV
Employees Loyalty Board	5, V
Employment and Training Administration	20, V
Employment Standards Administration	20, VI
Endangered Species Committee	50, IV
Energy, Department of	2, IX; 5, XXIII; 10, II, III, X
Federal Acquisition Regulation	48, 9
Federal Energy Regulatory Commission	5, XXIV; 18, I
Property Management Regulations	41, 109
Energy, Office of	7, XXIX
Engineers, Corps of	33, II; 36, III
Engraving and Printing, Bureau of	31, VI
Environmental Protection Agency	2, XV; 5, LIV; 40, I, IV, VII
Federal Acquisition Regulation	48, 15
Property Management Regulations	41, 115
Environmental Quality, Office of	7, XXXI
Equal Employment Opportunity Commission	5, LXII; 29, XIV
Equal Opportunity, Office of Assistant Secretary for	24, I
Executive Office of the President	3, I
Environmental Quality, Council on	40, V
Management and Budget, Office of	2, Subtitle A; 5, III, LXXVII; 14, VI; 48, 99
National Drug Control Policy, Office of	2, XXXVI; 21, III
National Security Council	32, XXI; 47, 2

Agency	CFR Title, Subtitle or Chapter
Contract Appeals, Board of	48, 61
Federal Acquisition Regulation	48, 5
Federal Management Regulation	41, 102
Federal Property Management Regulations	41, 101
Federal Travel Regulation System	41, Subtitle F
General	41, 300
Payment From a Non-Federal Source for Travel Expenses	41, 304
Payment of Expenses Connected With the Death of Certain Employees	41, 303
Relocation Allowances	41, 302
Temporary Duty (TDY) Travel Allowances	41, 301
Geological Survey	30, IV
Government Accountability Office	4, I
Government Ethics, Office of	5, XVI
Government National Mortgage Association	24, III
Grain Inspection, Packers and Stockyards Administration	7, VIII; 9, II
Gulf Coast Ecosystem Restoration Council	2, LIX; 40, VIII
Harry S. Truman Scholarship Foundation	45, XVIII
Health and Human Services, Department of	2, III; 5, XLV; 45, Subtitle A
Centers for Medicare & Medicaid Services	42, IV
Child Support Enforcement, Office of	45, III
Children and Families, Administration for	45, II, III, IV, X, XIII
Community Services, Office of	45, X
Family Assistance, Office of	45, II
Federal Acquisition Regulation	48, 3
Food and Drug Administration	21, I
Indian Health Service	25, V
Inspector General (Health Care), Office of	42, V
Public Health Service	42, I
Refugee Resettlement, Office of	45, IV
Homeland Security, Department of	2, XXX; 5, XXXVI; 6, I; 8, I
Coast Guard	33, I; 46, I; 49, IV
Coast Guard (Great Lakes Pilotage)	46, III
Customs and Border Protection	19, I
Federal Emergency Management Agency	44, I
Human Resources Management and Labor Relations Systems	5, XCVII
Immigration and Customs Enforcement Bureau	19, IV
Transportation Security Administration	49, XII
HOPE for Homeowners Program, Board of Directors of	24, XXIV
Housing and Urban Development, Department of	2, XXIV; 5, LXV; 24, Subtitle B
Community Planning and Development, Office of Assistant Secretary for	24, V, VI
Equal Opportunity, Office of Assistant Secretary for	24, I
Federal Acquisition Regulation	48, 24
Federal Housing Enterprise Oversight, Office of	12, XVII
Government National Mortgage Association	24, III
Housing—Federal Housing Commissioner, Office of Assistant Secretary for	24, II, VIII, X, XX
Housing, Office of, and Multifamily Housing Assistance Restructuring, Office of	24, IV
Inspector General, Office of	24, XII
Public and Indian Housing, Office of Assistant Secretary for	24, IX
Secretary, Office of	24, Subtitle A, VII
Housing—Federal Housing Commissioner, Office of Assistant Secretary for	24, II, VIII, X, XX
Housing, Office of, and Multifamily Housing Assistance Restructuring, Office of	24, IV
Immigration and Customs Enforcement Bureau	19, IV
Immigration Review, Executive Office for	8, V
Independent Counsel, Office of	28, VII
Independent Counsel, Offices of	28, VI
Indian Affairs, Bureau of	25, I, V
Indian Affairs, Office of the Assistant Secretary	25, VI

Agency	CFR Title, Subtitle or Chapter
Indian Arts and Crafts Board	25, II
Indian Health Service	25, V
Industry and Security, Bureau of	15, VII
Information Resources Management, Office of	7, XXVII
Information Security Oversight Office, National Archives and Records Administration	32, XX
Inspector General	
Agriculture Department	7, XXVI
Health and Human Services Department	42, V
Housing and Urban Development Department	24, XII, XV
Institute of Peace, United States	22, XVII
Inter-American Foundation	5, LXIII; 22, X
Interior Department	2, XIV
American Indians, Office of the Special Trustee	25, VII
Endangered Species Committee	50, IV
Federal Acquisition Regulation	48, 14
Federal Property Management Regulations System	41, 114
Fish and Wildlife Service, United States	50, I, IV
Geological Survey	30, IV
Indian Affairs, Bureau of	25, I, V
Indian Affairs, Office of the Assistant Secretary	25, VI
Indian Arts and Crafts Board	25, II
Land Management, Bureau of	43, II
National Indian Gaming Commission	25, III
National Park Service	36, I
Natural Resource Revenue, Office of	30, XII
Ocean Energy Management, Bureau of	30, V
Reclamation, Bureau of	43, I
Safety and Enforcement Bureau, Bureau of	30, II
Secretary of the Interior, Office of	2, XIV; 43, Subtitle A
Surface Mining Reclamation and Enforcement, Office of	30, VII
Internal Revenue Service	26, I
International Boundary and Water Commission, United States and Mexico, United States Section	22, XI
International Development, United States Agency for	22, II
Federal Acquisition Regulation	48, 7
International Development Cooperation Agency, United States	22, XII
International Joint Commission, United States and Canada	22, IV
International Organizations Employees Loyalty Board	5, V
International Trade Administration	15, III; 19, III
International Trade Commission, United States	19, II
Interstate Commerce Commission	5, XL
Investment Security, Office of	31, VIII
James Madison Memorial Fellowship Foundation	45, XXIV
Japan–United States Friendship Commission	22, XVI
Joint Board for the Enrollment of Actuaries	20, VIII
Justice Department	2, XXVIII; 5, XXVIII; 28, I, XI; 40, IV
Alcohol, Tobacco, Firearms, and Explosives, Bureau of	27, II
Drug Enforcement Administration	21, II
Federal Acquisition Regulation	48, 28
Federal Claims Collection Standards	31, IX
Federal Prison Industries, Inc.	28, III
Foreign Claims Settlement Commission of the United States	45, V
Immigration Review, Executive Office for	8, V
Independent Counsel, Offices of	28, VI
Prisons, Bureau of	28, V
Property Management Regulations	41, 128
Labor Department	2, XXIX; 5, XLII
Employee Benefits Security Administration	29, XXV
Employees' Compensation Appeals Board	20, IV
Employment and Training Administration	20, V
Employment Standards Administration	20, VI
Federal Acquisition Regulation	48, 29
Federal Contract Compliance Programs, Office of	41, 60

Agency	CFR Title, Subtitle or Chapter
Federal Acquisition Regulation	48, 25
National Security Council	32, XXI
National Security Council and Office of Science and Technology Policy	47, II
National Telecommunications and Information Administration	15, XXIII; 47, III, IV, V
National Transportation Safety Board	49, VIII
Natural Resources Conservation Service	7, VI
Natural Resource Revenue, Office of	30, XII
Navajo and Hopi Indian Relocation, Office of	25, IV
Navy Department	32, VI
Federal Acquisition Regulation	48, 52
Neighborhood Reinvestment Corporation	24, XXV
Northeast Interstate Low-Level Radioactive Waste Commission	10, XVIII
Nuclear Regulatory Commission	2, XX; 5, XLVIII; 10, I
Federal Acquisition Regulation	48, 20
Occupational Safety and Health Administration	29, XVII
Occupational Safety and Health Review Commission	29, XX
Ocean Energy Management, Bureau of	30, V
Oklahoma City National Memorial Trust	36, XV
Operations Office	7, XXVIII
Overseas Private Investment Corporation	5, XXXIII; 22, VII
Patent and Trademark Office, United States	37, I
Payment From a Non-Federal Source for Travel Expenses	41, 304
Payment of Expenses Connected With the Death of Certain Employees	41, 303
Peace Corps	2, XXXVII; 22, III
Pennsylvania Avenue Development Corporation	36, IX
Pension Benefit Guaranty Corporation	29, XL
Personnel Management, Office of	5, I, XXXV; 5, IV; 45, VIII
Human Resources Management and Labor Relations Systems, Department of Homeland Security	5, XCVII
Federal Acquisition Regulation	48, 17
Federal Employees Group Life Insurance Federal Acquisition Regulation	48, 21
Federal Employees Health Benefits Acquisition Regulation	48, 16
Pipeline and Hazardous Materials Safety Administration	49, I
Postal Regulatory Commission	5, XLVI; 39, III
Postal Service, United States	5, LX; 39, I
Postsecondary Education, Office of	34, VI
President's Commission on White House Fellowships	1, IV
Presidential Documents	3
Presidio Trust	36, X
Prisons, Bureau of	28, V
Privacy and Civil Liberties Oversight Board	6, X
Procurement and Property Management, Office of	7, XXXII
Public Contracts, Department of Labor	41, 50
Public and Indian Housing, Office of Assistant Secretary for	24, IX
Public Health Service	42, I
Railroad Retirement Board	20, II
Reclamation, Bureau of	43, I
Refugee Resettlement, Office of	45, IV
Relocation Allowances	41, 302
Research and Innovative Technology Administration	49, XI
Rural Business-Cooperative Service	7, XVIII, XLII
Rural Development Administration	7, XLII
Rural Housing Service	7, XVIII, XXXV
Rural Telephone Bank	7, XVI
Rural Utilities Service	7, XVII, XVIII, XLII
Safety and Environmental Enforcement, Bureau of	30, II
Saint Lawrence Seaway Development Corporation	33, IV
Science and Technology Policy, Office of	32, XXIV
Science and Technology Policy, Office of, and National Security Council	47, II
Secret Service	31, IV

Agency	CFR Title, Subtitle or Chapter
Workers' Compensation Programs, Office of	20, I, VII
World Agricultural Outlook Board	7, XXXVIII

List of CFR Sections Affected

All changes in this volume of the Code of Federal Regulations (CFR) that were made by documents published in the FEDERAL REGISTER since January 1, 2013 are enumerated in the following list. Entries indicate the nature of the changes effected. Page numbers refer to FEDERAL REGISTER pages. The user should consult the entries for chapters, parts and subparts as well as sections for revisions.

For changes to this volume of the CFR prior to this listing, consult the annual edition of the monthly List of CFR Sections Affected (LSA). The LSA is available at *www.fdsys.gov*. For changes to this volume of the CFR prior to 2001, see the "List of CFR Sections Affected, 1949–1963, 1964–1972, 1973–1985, and 1986–2000" published in 11 separate volumes. The "List of CFR Sections Affected 1986–2000" is available at *www.fdsys.gov*.

2013

9 CFR

78 FR Page

Chapter I

1.1 Amended 57249
2.1 (a)(3)(i), (iii) and (vii) revised; (a)(3)(ii) amended (OMB numbers) 57249
2.38 (l) stayed indefinately 46255
2.134 Stayed indefinately 46255
11.21 (d) correctly amended 27001
53.1 Amended 19082
53.2 (b) amended 19082
71.1 Amended 2063
71.3 (b) amended 19083
71.18 Removed 2064
71.19 (b)(2) and (d) introductory text amended 2064
71.20 (a)(7) revised; (a)(8) amended (OMB number) 26489
71.21 (a)(1), (2) and (3) redesignated as (a)(2), (3) and (4); new (a)(1) and (5) added (OMB number) 26489
71.22 Removed 2064
72 Heading revised 8960
72.1 Revised 8960
72.2 Heading revised; amended 8960
72.13 (b) introductory text amended; (b)(1), (3) and (4) removed; (b)(2) redesignated as (b)(1) 8961
77.2 Amended 2064
77.5 Amended 2065
77.8 Revised 2065
77.10 Revised 2065

9 CFR—Continued

78 FR Page

Chapter I—Continued

77.12 Revised 2066
77.14 Revised 2066
77.16 Amended 2066
77.17 (a) introductory text, (4), (b) introductory text and (c) amended 2066
77.20 Amended; interim 1721
77.23 Revised 2066
77.25 Revised 2066
77.27 Revised 2066
77.29 Revised 2067
77.31 Amended 2067
77.32 (a) and (c) amended 2067
77.33 (a) introductory text and (1) amended; (a)(2), (d)(2), (e)(3) and (4) added; interim 1722
77.34 Revised; interim 1722
77.35 (b) revised 2067
77.36 (b)(2), (3) and (4) revised 2067
77.37 (b)(2) and (3) revised 2067
77.39 (a)(1)(iii) and (iv) added; (a)(2) and (f)(2) amended; (e) introductory text, (3) and (f)(1) revised; interim 1723
77.40 (a)(3) amended 2068
78.1 Amended 2068
78.2 Revised 2069
78.5 Revised 2069
78.6 Revised 2069

9 CFR—Continued

9 CFR—Continued

9 CFR—Continued

9 CFR—Continued

2014

9 CFR

79 FR Page

Chapter I

2.150—2.153 (Subpart J) Added....... 48659
11.25 (c)(6) correctly revised 3071
55 Regulation at 77 FR 35565 confirmed 23891
55.1 Regulation at 77 FR 35565 confirmed; amended 23891
55.21—55.25 (Subpart B) Regulation at 77 FR 35566 confirmed 23891
56.1 Amended................................ 38753
56.4 (d) added 38753
56.5 (c)(1)(i), (d)(1)(i) and (iii) revised; (c)(1)(iii) and (iv) added; (d)(1)(iv) removed; (d)(2)(i) and (3) amended 38753
77.2 Amended; interim 43926
77.7 (b)(1) amended; interim 53608
77.9 (b) revised; interim................. 53608
77.20 Amended; interim 43926
77.33 (a)(2) amended; (d)(2) and (e)(3) revised; (e)(4) removed; OMB number; interim.............. 43926
77.34 (a)(1) and (b)(1) amended; (a)(2) and (b)(2) revised; interim 43926
77.39 (a)(1)(iii) removed; (a)(1)(iv) redesignated as new (a)(1)(iii); (b)(2)(iv), (c), (e) introductory text, (2), (3), (f)(1) and (2) amended; interim 43926
78.1 Amended................................ 66507
81 Regulation at 77 FR 35569 confirmed 23891
81.1 Amended................................ 23891
93.100 Amended............................ 71004
93.101 Regulation at 76 FR 4053 confirmed; (a), (c)(4)(i), (g)(2), (3) and (4) amended; footnote 7 revised 71004
93.104 Regulation at 76 FR 4053 confirmed................................ 71004
(b)(2), (3), (5), (6), (7), (c)(3), (4), (6), (7), (11), (d)(3), (4), (5) and (7) amended; (b)(4) revised............. 71005
93.106 (b)(3), (c)(3)(ii)(E), (5)(iii)(A)(*14*), (*17*), (B)(*4*) and (*5*) amended.................................. 71005
93.200 Amended............................ 71005
93.201 Regulation at 76 FR 4053 confirmed................................ 71004
(a) amended; (e) added 71005
93.205 Regulation at 76 FR 4053 confirmed................................ 71004
(a) and (b) revised 71006

9 CFR—Continued

79 FR Page

Chapter I—Continued

93.209 Regulation at 76 FR 4054 confirmed................................ 71004
94.0 Amended................................ 71006
94.6 Regulation at 76 FR 4054 confirmed 71004
(a)(1)(i) revised; (a)(1)(ii), (b)(2), (c) heading, introductory text, (1)(ix) introductory text, (A), (B), (C), (2), (3) and (4) amended 71006
94.8 Regulation at 76 FR 4054 confirmed 71004
94.9 Regulation at 76 FR 4054 and 4055 confirmed 71004
94.12 Regulation at 76 FR 4054 and 4055 confirmed 71004
94.16 Regulation at 76 FR 4054 confirmed 71004
94.17 Regulation at 76 FR 4054 and 4055 confirmed 71004
94.18 Regulation at 76 FR 4054 confirmed 71004
94.24 Regulation at 76 FR 4054 confirmed 71004
94.26 Regulation at 76 FR 4055 confirmed 71004
94.28 (a)(1) introductory text revised; (a)(3) and (b)(3) removed; (a)(4), (5), (b)(4) and (5) redesignated as new (a)(3), (4), (b)(3) and (4); new (a)(4) and new (b)(4) amended 7568
Regulation at 78 FR 73001 withdrawn...7568
95.1 Amended................................ 71007
95.3 Amended................................ 71007
95.16 Introductory text and footnote 1 amended 71007
95.17 (c) amended 71007
95.23 (c) amended 71007
95.30 Regulation at 76 FR 4055 confirmed 71004
95.41 Removed 71007
101.5 (l) revised 55969
113.5 (d) revised............................ 55969
113.8 (c) footnote 1 removed........... 31021
113.33 Amended............................ 55969
113.36 Amended............................ 55969
113.38 Amended............................ 55969
113.39 Amended............................ 55969
113.40 Amended............................ 55969
113.41 Amended............................ 55969
113.44 Amended............................ 55969
113.45 Amended............................ 55969
113.47 Amended............................ 55969
113.67 Amended............................ 55969

9 CFR—Continued

79 FR Page

9 CFR—Continued

79 FR Page

9 CFR—Continued

79 FR Page

Chapter I—Continued

145.45 Added 38757
145.52 (b) amended; (c) and (d) redesignated as (d) and (e); new (c) added 38759
145.53 (c)(1) introductory text, (3), (d)(1) introductory text, (ii)(B), (3), (e)(1)(i) and (ii) amended; (e)(1) introductory text, (2) introductory text and (3) revised; (f) added 38759
145.62 (b) amended 38759
145.72 (b) revised 38759
145.73 (c)(1) introductory text, (3), (d)(1)(iv), (v), (vii), (2), (e)(1) introductory text, (3) and (f)(1) introductory text amended; (d)(1)(ix) and (f)(2) revised 38759
145.74 Added 38759
145.82 (b) revised 38762
145.83 (c)(1) introductory text, (3), (d)(1) introductory text, (3), (e)(6) introductory text, (i)(B), (C), (D), (f)(1)(i), (vi) and (g)(1) introductory text amended; (e)(1), (3), (f)(1)(iv) and (2) revised 38762
(g)(2) amended 71624
145.84 Added 38763
145.92 (b) amended 38764
145.93 (c)(3) revised; (d) added 38764
146.1 Amended 38765
146.2 (e) amended 38765
146.3 (c) amended; (e) removed 38765
146.5 (b) amended 38765
146.13 (a)(1) and (b)(2)(i) amended; (b)(1)(ii)(C) and (2)(ii)(B) revised 38765
146.23 (a) heading, (1) introductory text and (2) introductory text revised; (a) introductory text removed 38765
(a)(2) introductory text and (i) amended 71624
146.31 Amended 38766
146.32 (c) added 38766
146.33 (a)(1) amended 38766
146.43 (a)(1) revised 38766
147.1 Revised 38766
147.2 Removed 38766
147.3 Removed 38766
147.4 Removed 38766
147.5 Removed 38766
147.6 Removed 38766
147.7 Removed 38766
147.8 Removed 38766
147.9 Removed 38766

9 CFR—Continued

79 FR Page

Chapter I—Continued

147.10 Revised 38766
147.11 Removed 38766
147.12 Removed 38766
147.13 Removed 38766
147.14 Removed 38766
147.15 Removed 38766
147.16 Removed 38766
147.17 Removed 38766
147.21 Revised 38766
Corrected 44263
147.22 Removed 38766
147.23 Removed 38766
147.24 Removed 38766
147.25 Removed 38766
147.26 Removed 38766
147.27 Removed 38766
147.30 Revised 38766
147.31 Removed 38766
147.41 Amended 38766
147.44 (b) amended 38766
147.51—147.54 (Subpart F) Revised 38766

2015

9 CFR

80 FR Page

Chapter I

2.132 (d) amended 3463
71.3 Regulation at 73 FR 52184 withdrawn 2285
78.1 Amended 5665
83 Regulation at 73 FR 52184 withdrawn 2285
93.400 Amended 10324
93.423 (c) amended 10324
93.427 (b) revised; OMB number 10324
93.900 Regulation at 73 FR 52186 withdrawn 2285
93.901—93.906 Regulation at 73 FR 52186 withdrawn 2285
93.910 Regulation at 73 FR 52186 withdrawn 2285
93.911 Regulation at 73 FR 52186 withdrawn 2285
93.912 Regulation at 73 FR 52186 withdrawn 2285
93.913 Regulation at 73 FR 52186 withdrawn 2285
93.914 Regulation at 73 FR 52186 withdrawn 2285
93.915 Regulation at 73 FR 52186 withdrawn 2285
93.916 Regulation at 73 FR 52186 withdrawn 2285
94.6 (c)(4) amended 10576

9 CFR—Continued

80 FR Page

Chapter I—Continued

97.1 (a) introductory text and (3) table revised; (a)(1), (b), (d)(1) through (4), (e)(1), (2), (4) and (f) amended; (a)(4) added 59566

97.2 Table correctly amended 5666

107.1 Introductory text and (a)(1) introductory text amended; (a)(2) redesignated as (a)(3); new (a)(2) added 26821

112.2 (a)(5) amended; (a)(9)(v) added 39674

112.5 (b) through (g) redesignated as (c) through (h); new (b) added; introductory text, (a), new (d)(1), new (e)(1)(ii), (iii), (iv) and new (h) amended 39675

130.50 (b)(3) introductory text amended; (b)(3)(i) table revised; (b)(3)(iii) added 59567

2016

9 CFR

81 FR Page

Chapter I

53.2 (b) revised; interim 6750

53.3 Heading revised; (a) amended; (e) added; interim 6750

53.4 Heading revised; (b) added; interim 6750

53.9 Heading revised; amended; interim 6750

53.10 (c) and (d) amended; (g) added; interim.............................. 6750

53.11 Added; interim 6750

56.1 Amended................................ 53249

77.7 (a) amended; interim 52326

77.9 (a) amended; interim 52326

91 Revised 2980

91.3 (a)(2) revised 74279

93.101 (d) introductory text footnote 4 and (f)(2)(iii)(B) introductory text amended 40151

93.103 (a)(1) introductory text footnote 8 amended 40151

93.206 (c) added.............................. 40151

93.215 (a)(2) amended 40151

93.305 (c) added.............................. 40151

93.407 (c) added.............................. 40151

93.421 (a)(2) amended...................... 40151

93.506 (c) added.............................. 40151

93.519 (a)(2) amended...................... 40151

93.704 (b) revised 40151

93.802 (b) revised 40151

93.804 Introductory text amended 40151

93.905 (b) added 40152

9 CFR—Continued

81 FR Page

Chapter I—Continued

94.6 (d) amended........................... 40152

94.15 (b)(1) and (c)(1) amended 40152

94.24 (b)(2) revised 40152

94.27 (b) introductory text amended.................................. 40152

101.3 (q) added 59433

103.3 (d) revised.............................. 59433

112.2 (a)(1) through (5), (7), (10), (d)(3), (e) and (f) revised; (a)(6) and (9)(iv) amended 59433

(a)(12) added 78500

112.3 (f)(2) revised 59434

112.5 (a) correctly amended 47005

(a) and (d)(2)(vi) amended; (d)(2)(ii), (v), (e)(1)(iii), (iv), (4) and (f)(1) revised; (d)(2)(vii) through (x) added; (f)(2) removed; (f)(3) redesignated as new (f)(2) 59435

112.6 (a) revised............................ 59435

112.7 (e), (f), (i) and (l) revised; (n) added....................................... 59435

113.206 (d)(2) amended 59436

114.11 Revised 59436

145.2 (d) amended 53249

145.3 (a) through (f) redesignated as (b) through (g); new (a) added... 53249

145.12 (b) amended 53249

145.14 (a)(5) and (b)(1) revised......... 53249

145.42 (b) revised 53249

145.53 (c)(1)(i), (ii) introductory text, (A), (d)(1)(i), (ii) introductory text and (A) revised 53249

145.83 (f)(1)(i) and (3) revised; (f)(1)(ii) and (iii) removed; (f)(1)(iv) through (viii) redesignated as new (f)(1)(ii) through (vi); new (f)(1)(v) and (vi) amended.................................. 53250

145.92 (b) revised 53250

145.93 (c)(3) amended..................... 53250

146.1 Amended 53250

146.2 (c) revised 53250

146.3 (a) amended 53250

146.11 (b) revised 53250

146.51 Amended............................ 53250

146.52 (a) and (c) revised 53250

146.53 (a) introductory text amended; (a)(4) and (5) added... 53250

147.52 (d) revised 53251

147.54 Revised.............................. 53251

2017

9 CFR

9 CFR—Continued

○

www.ingramcontent.com/pod-product-compliance
Lightning Source LLC
LaVergne TN
LVHW052201200926
848481LV00001B/6
* 9 7 8 1 6 4 0 2 4 2 6 8 5 *